ST. JAMES ENCYCLOPEDIA OF
POPULARCULTURE

ST. JAMES ENCYCLOPEDIA OF
POPULARCULTURE

VOLUME 1: A-D

EDITORS: Tom Pendergast   Sara Pendergast

with an introduction by Jim Cullen

ST. JAMES PRESS

AN IMPRINT OF THE GALE GROUP

DETROIT • SAN FRANCISCO • LONDON
BOSTON • WOODBRIDGE, CT

Tom Pendergast, Sara Pendergast, *Editors*

Michael J. Tyrkus, *Project Coordinator*

Laura Standley Berger, Joann Cerrito, Dave Collins,
Steve Cusack, Nicolet V. Elert, Miranda Ferrara, Jamie FitzGerald,
Kristin Hart, Laura S. Kryhoski, Margaret Mazurkiewicz
St. James Press Staff

Peter M. Gareffa, *Managing Editor, St. James Press*

Maria Franklin, *Permissions Manager*
Kimberly F. Smilay, *Permissions Specialist*
Kelly A. Quin, *Permissions Associate*
Erin Bealmear, Sandy Gore, *Permissions Assistants*
Mary Grimes, Leitha Etheridge-Sims, *Image Catalogers*

Mary Beth Trimper, *Composition Manager*
Dorothy Maki, *Manufacturing Manager*
Wendy Blurton, *Senior Buyer*

Cynthia Baldwin, *Product Design Manager*
Martha Schiebold, *Graphic Artist*

Randy Bassett, *Image Database Supervisor*
Robert Duncan, Michael Logusz, *Imaging Specialists*
Pamela A. Reed, *Imaging Coordinator*

Library of Congress Cataloging-in-Publication Data
St. James Encyclopedia of Popular Culture / with an introduction by Jim Cullen; editors,
Tom Pendergast and Sara Pendergast.
        p. cm.
    Includes bibliographical references and index.
    ISBN 1-558-62400-7 (set) — ISBN 1-558-62401-5 (v.1) — ISBN 1-558-62402-3 (v.2) —
    ISBN 1-558-62403-1 (v.3) — ISBN 1-558-62404-x (v.4) — ISBN 1-558-62405-8 (v. 5)
    1. United States—Civilization—20th century—Encyclopedias. 2. Popular culture—United
States—History—20th century—Encyclopedias. I. Pendergast, Tom. II. Pendergast, Sara.
E169.1.S764 1999
973.9 21—dc21   99-046540

Printed in the United States of America

St. James Press is an imprint of Gale Group
Gale Group and Design is a trademark used herein under license

10 9 8 7 6 5 4 3 2 1

CONTENTS

EDITOR'S NOTE

Thirty some years ago Ray Browne and several of his colleagues provided a forum for the academic study of popular culture by forming first the *Journal of Popular Culture* and later the Popular Culture Association and the Center for the Study of Popular Culture at Bowling Green State University. Twenty some years ago Thomas Inge thought the field of popular culture studies well enough established to put together the first edition of his *Handbook of Popular Culture*. In the years since, scholars and educators from many disciplines have published enough books, gathered enough conferences, and gained enough institutional clout to make popular culture studies one of the richest fields of academic study at the close of the twentieth century. Thirty, twenty, in some places even ten years ago, to study popular culture was to be something of a pariah; today, the study of popular culture is accepted and even respected in departments of history, literature, communications, sociology, film studies, etc. throughout the United States and throughout the world, and not only in universities, but in increasing numbers of high schools. Thomas Inge wrote in the introduction to the second edition of his *Handbook*: "The serious and systematic study of popular culture may be the most significant and potentially useful of the trends in academic research and teaching in the last half of this century in the United States."[2] It is to this thriving field of study that we hope to contribute with the *St. James Encyclopedia of Popular Culture*.

The *St. James Encyclopedia of Popular Culture* includes over 2,700 essays on all elements of popular culture in the United States in the twentieth century. But what is "popular culture?" Academics have offered a number of answers over the years. Historians Norman F. Cantor and Michael S. Werthman suggested that "popular culture may be seen as all those things man does and all those artifacts he creates for their own sake, all that diverts his mind and body from the sad business of life."[1] Michael Bell argues that:

> At its simplest popular culture is the culture of mass appeal. A creation is popular when it is created to respond to the experiences and values of the majority, when it is produced in such a way that the majority have easy access to it, and when it can be understood and interpreted by that majority without the aid of special knowledge or experience.[3]

While tremendously useful, both of these definitions tend to exclude more than they embrace. Was the hot dog created for its own sake, as a diversion? Probably not, but we've included an essay on it in this collection. Were the works of Sigmund Freud in any way shaped for the majority? No, but Freud's ideas—borrowed, twisted, and reinterpreted—have shaped novels, films, and common speech in ways too diffuse to ignore. Thus we have included an essay on Freud's impact on popular culture. Our desire to bring together the greatest number of cultural phenomena impacting American culture in this century has led us to prefer Ray Browne's rather broader early definition of popular culture as "all the experiences in life shared by people in common, generally though not necessarily disseminated by the mass media."[4]

Coverage

In order to amass a list of those cultural phenomena that were widely disseminated and experienced by people in relatively unmediated form we asked a number of scholars, teachers, librarians, and archivists to serve as advisors. Each of our 20 advisors provided us with a list of over 200 topics from their field of specialty that they considered important enough to merit an essay; several of our advisors provided us with lists much longer than that. Their collective lists numbered nearly 4,000 potential essay topics, and we winnowed this list down to the number that is now gathered in this collection. We sought balance (but not equal coverage) between the major areas of popular culture: film; music; print culture; social life; sports; television and radio; and art and perfomance (which includes theatre, dance, stand-up comedy, and other live performance). For those interested, the breakdown of coverage is as follows: social life, 23 percent (a category which covers everything from foodways to fashion, holidays to hairstyles); music, 16 percent; print culture, 16 percent; film, 15 percent; television and radio, 14 percent; sports, 10 percent; and art and performance, 6 percent. A variety of considerations led us to skew the coverage of the book in favor of the second half of the century. The massive popularity of television and recorded music, the mass-marketing of popular fiction, and the national attention given to professional sports are historical factors contributing to the emphasis on post-World War II culture, but we have also considered the needs of high school and undergraduate users in distributing entries in this way.

The Entries

The entries in this volume vary in length from brief (75 to 150-word) introductions to the topic to in-depth 3,000-word explorations. No matter the length, we have asked our contributors to do two things in each entry: to describe the topic and to analyze its significance in and relevance to American popular culture. While we hope that users will find the basic factual information they need concerning the topic in an entry, it was even more important to us that each user gain some perspective on the cultural context in which the topic has importance. Thus the entry on MTV, for example, chronicles the channel's rise to world popularity, but also analyzes the relationship between MTV, youth culture, and consumerism. The entry on John Ford, while tracing the outlines of the film director's long career, assesses the impact Ford's films have had on the film Western and on Americans' very perceptions of the West. Given the brevity of the entries, we chose to emphasize analysis of a topic's contribution to popular culture over a full presentation of biographical/historical information. The entry on World War I, for example, offers an analysis of how the war was understood in popular film, print culture, and propaganda rather than a blow-by-blow description of the actual military conflict.

Entries are accompanied by a list of further readings. These readings are meant to provide the user with readily accessible sources that provide more information on the specific topic. As befits a multimedia age, these "further readings" come not just from books and magazines, but also from albums, liner notes, films, videos, and web sites. Users of the Internet know well the perils of trusting the information found on the World Wide Web; there are as yet few filters to help browsers sift the useful from the absurd. We cited web sites when they provided information that was unavailable in any other known form and when our reasonable efforts to determine the veracity of the information led us to believe that the information provided was valid and useful. We have occasionally provided links to "official" web sites of performers or organizations, for the same reason that we provide citations to autobiographies. All web links cited were accurate as of the date indicated in the citation.

Organization and Indexing

Entries are arranged alphabetically by the name under which the topic is best known. For topics which might reasonably be sought out under differing names, we have provided in-text cross references. For example, a user seeking an entry on Huddie Ledbetter will be referred to the entry on Leadbelly, and a user seeking an entry on Larry Flynt will be referred to the entry on *Hustler* magazine. Far more powerful than the cross references, however, are the indexes provided in the fifth volume of the collection. The general index is by far the most powerful, for it leads the user searching for information on Humphrey Bogart, for example, to the entries on Lauren Bacall, *Casablanca, The Maltese Falcon, The African Queen,* and several other entries that contain substantive information about Bogie. Equally powerful is the subject index, a list of categories under which we listed all pertinent entries. Consulting the subject index listing for Sex Symbols, for example, will lead the user to entries on Marilyn Monroe, the Varga Girl, *Playboy* magazine, David Cassidy, Mae West, and a long entry on the Sex Symbol, among others. Finally, a time index, organized by decades, provides a list of the entries that concern each decade of the twentieth century. Those entries that concern nineteenth-century topics are indexed by the first decade of the twentieth century.

We encourage readers to use the indexes to discover the fascinating intertwinings that have made the development of popular culture in the twentieth century such a vital field of study. Using the indexes, it is possible to uncover the story of how the American humor that was first made popular on the vaudeville stage evolved into first the radio comedies that entertained so many Americans during the Depression and War years and later the sitcoms that have kept Americans glued to their television screens for the last 50 years. That story is here, in the entries on Vaudeville, the Sitcom, *Amos 'n' Andy,* and the many other programs and comedians that have defined this tradition. A teacher who wishes students to uncover the similarities between sitcoms of the 1950s, 1960s, 1970s, 1980s, and 1990s might well ask the students to use this collection to begin their research into such comedies. Similarly, a teacher who asks students to explore the cross-pollination between musical genres will find that the indexes reveal the mixing of "race music," rhythm and blues, gospel, soul, and rock 'n' roll. It is hoped that this collection will be of particular use to those instructors of high school and undergraduate courses who challenge their students to discover the real cultural complexity of the music, films, magazines, and television shows that they take for granted. This collection should also be of use to those more advanced scholars who are beginning new research into an area of popular culture or who are looking for some context in which to place their existing research.

Acknowledgments

The *St. James Encyclopedia of Popular Culture* represents the work of hundreds of people, and we owe our thanks to all of them. We have had the privilege of working with 20 advisors whose experience, knowledge, and wisdom have truly helped shape the contents of this collection. Each of our advisors helped us to discover hidden corners of popular culture that we would not have considered on our own, and the breadth of coverage in this collection is a tribute to their collective knowledge. Several of our advisors deserve special thanks: Paul Buhle, George Carney, B. Lee Cooper, Jerome Klinkowitz, and Ron Simon all showed an extraordinary level of commitment and helpfulness.

It has been a pleasure to work with the nearly 450 contributors to this collection; we've appreciated their expertise, their professionalism, and their good humor. Several of our contributors deserve special mention for the quality of their contributions to this collection: Jacob Appel, Tim Berg, Pat Broeske, Richard Digby-Junger, Jeffrey Escoffier, Bryan Garman, Tina Gianoulis, Milton Goldin, Ian Gordon, Ron Goulart, Justin Gustainis, Preston Jones, Robyn Karney, Deborah Mix, Leonard Moore, Edward Moran, Victoria Price, Bob Schnakenberg, Steven Schneider, Charles Shindo, Robert Sickels, Wendy Woloson, and Brad Wright. Our team of copyeditors helped us bring a uniformity of presentation to the writings of this mass of contributors, and spotted and corrected innumerable small errors. Heidi Hagen, Robyn Karney, Edward Moran, and Tim Seul deserve special thanks for the quality and quantity of their work; we truly couldn't have done it without them. The contributors and copyeditors provided us with the material to build this collection, but it has been the editors' responsibility to ensure its accuracy and reliability. We welcome any corrections and comments; please write to: The Editors, *St. James Encyclopedia of Popular Culture,* St. James Press, 27500 Drake Road, Farmington Hills, MI 48331-3535.

Gathering the photos for this collection was an enormous task, and we were helped immeasurably by the knowledgeable and efficient staff at several photo agencies. We'd like to thank Marcia Schiff at AP/Wide World Photos; Eric Young at Archive Photos; and Kevin Rettig at Corbis Images. Lisa Hartjens of ImageFinders, Inc. also helped us acquire a number of photos.

We would like to thank Shelly Andrews, Anne Boyd, Melissa Doig, Tina Gianoulis, Heidi Hagen, Robyn Karney, Edward Moran, Victoria Price, Rebecca Saulsbury, Tim Seul, and Mark Swartz for their careful copyediting of the entries.

At the St. James Press, we'd like to thank Mike Tyrkus for his good humor and efficiency in helping us see this project to completion; Peter Gareffa for his usual wise and benevolent leadership; Janice Jorgensen for helping us shape this project at the beginning; the permissions department for smiling as we piled the photos on; and the staff at the St. James Press for their careful proofreading and for all their work in turning so many computer files into the volumes you see today.

Finally, we'd like to thank Lee Van Wormer for his sage management advice and our children, Conrad and Louisa, for their warm morning cuddles and for the delightful artwork that adorns our office walls.

—Tom Pendergast and Sara Pendergast,
Editors

NOTES
1. Cantor, Norman F. and Michael S. Werthman. *The History of Popular Culture to 1815.* New York, Macmillan, 1968, xxiv.
2. Inge, M. Thomas, editor. *Handbook of American Popular Culture.* 2nd edition. Westport, Connecticut, Greenwood Press, 1989, xxiii.
3. Bell, Michael. "The Study of Popular Culture," in *Concise Histories of American Popular Culture,* ed. Inge, M. Thomas. Westport, Connecticut, Greenwood Press, 1982, 443.
4. Browne, Ray B. *Popular Culture and the Expanding Consciousness.* New York, Wiley, 1973, 6.

INTRODUCTION

The Art of Everyday Life

Sometimes, when I'm wandering in an art museum looking at the relics of an ancient civilization, I find myself wondering how a future society would represent a defunct American culture. What objects would be chosen—or would survive—to be placed on display? Would I agree with a curator's choices? Were I to choose the items that some future American Museum of Art should exhibit to represent twentieth-century American culture, here are some I would name: an Elvis Presley record; a Currier & Ives print; a movie still from *Casablanca*. To put it a different way, my priority would *not* be to exhibit fragments of an urban cathedral, a painted landscape, or a formal costume. I wouldn't deny such objects could be important artifacts of American culture, or that they belong in a gallery. But in my avowedly biased opinion, the most vivid documents of American life—the documents that embody its possibilities and limits—are typically found in its popular culture.

Popular culture, of course, is not an American invention, and it has a vibrant life in many contemporary societies. But in few, if any, of those societies has it been as central to a notion of national character at home as well as abroad. For better or worse, it is through icons like McDonald's (the quintessential American cuisine), the Western (a uniquely American narrative genre), and Oprah Winfrey (a classic late-twentieth century embodiment of the American Dream) that this society is known—and is likely to be remembered.

It has sometimes been remarked that unlike nations whose identities are rooted in geography, religion, language, blood, or history, the United States was founded on a democratic ideal—a notion of life, liberty, and the pursuit of happiness elaborated in the Declaration of Independence. That ideal has been notoriously difficult to realize, and one need only take a cursory look at many aspects of American life—its justice system, electoral politics, residential patterns, labor force, et. al.—to see how far short it has fallen.

American popular culture is a special case. To be sure, it evinces plenty of the defects apparent in other areas of our national life, among them blatant racism and crass commercialism. If nothing else, such flaws can be taken as evidence of just how truly representative it is. There is nevertheless an openness and vitality about pop culture—its appeal across demographic lines; its interplay of individual voices and shared communal experience; the relatively low access barriers for people otherwise marginalized in U.S. society—that give it real legitimacy as the art of democracy. Like it or hate it, few dispute its centrality.

This sense of openness and inclusion—as well as the affection and scorn it generated—has been apparent from the very beginning. In the prologue of the 1787 play *The Contrast* (whose title referred to the disparity between sturdy republican ideals and effete monarchical dissipation), American playwright Royall Tyler invoked a cultural sensibility where "proud titles of 'My Lord! Your Grace/To the humble 'Mr.' and plain 'Sir' give place." Tyler, a Harvard graduate, Revolutionary War officer, and Chief Justice of the Vermont Supreme Court, was in some sense an unlikely prophet of popular culture. But the sensibility he voiced—notably in his beloved character Jonathon, a prototype for characters from Davy Crockett to John Wayne—proved durable for centuries to come.

For much of early American history, however, artists and critics continued to define aesthetic success on European terms, typically invoking elite ideals of order, balance, and civilization. It was largely taken for granted that the most talented practitioners of fine arts, such as painters Benjamin West and John Singleton Copley, would have to go abroad to train, produce, and exhibit their most important work. To the extent that newer cultural forms—like the novel, whose very name suggests its place in late eighteenth- and early nineteenth-century western civilization—were noted at all, it was usually in disparaging terms. This was especially true of novels written and read by women, such as Susanna Rowson's widely read *Charlotte Temple* (1791). Sermons against novels were common; Harvard devoted its principal commencement address in 1803 to the dangers of fiction.

The industrialization of the United States has long been considered a watershed development in many realms of American life, and popular culture is no exception. Indeed, its importance is suggested in the very definition of popular culture coined by cultural historian Lawrence Levine: "the folklore of industrial society." Industrialization allowed the mass-reproduction and dissemination of formerly local traditions, stories, and art forms across the continent, greatly intensifying the spread—and development—of culture by, for, and of the people. At a time when North America remained geographically and politically fragmented, magazines, sheet music, dime novels, lithographs, and other print media stitched it together.

This culture had a characteristic pattern. Alexis de Tocqueville devoted 11 chapters of his classic 1835-40 masterpiece *Democracy in America* to the art, literature, and language of the United States, arguing that they reflected a democratic ethos that required new standards of evaluation. "The inhabitants of the United States have, at present, properly speaking, no literature," he wrote. This judgment, he made clear, arose from a definition of literature that came from aristocratic societies like his own. In its stead, he explained, Americans sought books "which may be easily procured, quickly read, and which require no learned researches to be understood. They ask for beauties self-proffered and easily enjoyed; above all they must have what is unexpected and new." As in so many other ways, this description of American literature, which paralleled what Tocqueville saw in other arts, proved not only vivid but prophetic.

The paradox of American democracy, of course, is that the freedom Euro-Americans endlessly celebrated co-existed with—some might say depended on—the enslavement of African Americans. It is therefore one of the great ironies of popular culture that the contributions of black culture (a term here meant to encompass African, American, and amalgamations between the two) proved so decisive. In another sense, however, it seems entirely appropriate that popular culture, which has always skewed its orientation toward the lower end of a demographic spectrum, would draw on the most marginalized groups in American society. It is, in any event, difficult to imagine that U.S. popular culture would have had anywhere near the vitality and influence it has without slave stories, song, and dance. To cite merely one example: every American musical idiom from country music to rap has drawn on, if not actually *rested* upon, African-American cultural foundations, whether in its use of the banjo (originally an African instrument) or its emphasis on the beat (drumming was an important form of slave communication). This heritage has often been overlooked, disparaged, and even satirized. The most notable example of such racism was the minstrel show, a wildly popular nineteenth century form of theater in which white actors blackened their faces with burnt cork and mocked slave life. Yet even the most savage parodies could not help but reveal an engagement with, and even a secret admiration for, the cultural world the African Americans made in conditions of severe adversity, whether on plantations, tenant farms, or in ghettoes.

Meanwhile, the accelerating pace of technological innovation began having a dramatic impact on the form as well as the content of popular culture. The first major landmark was the development of photography in the mid-nineteenth century. At first a mechanically complex and thus inaccessible medium, it quickly captured American imaginations, particularly by capturing the drama and horror of the Civil War. The subsequent proliferation of family portraits, postcards, and pictures in metropolitan newspapers began a process of orienting popular culture around visual imagery that continues unabated to this day.

In the closing decades of the nineteenth century, sound recording, radio transmission, and motion pictures were all developed in rapid succession. But it would not be until well after 1900 that their potential as popular cultural media would be fully exploited and recognizable in a modern sense (radio, for example, was originally developed and valued for its nautical and military applications). Still, even if it was not entirely clear how, many people at the time believed these new media would have a tremendous impact on American life, and they were embraced with unusual ardor by those Americans, particularly immigrants, who were able to appreciate the pleasures and possibilities afforded by movies, records, and radio.

Many of the patterns established during the advent of these media repeated themselves as new ones evolved. The Internet, for example, was also first developed for its military applications, and for all the rapidity of its development in the 1990s, it remains unclear just how its use will be structured. Though the World Wide Web has shown tremendous promise as a commercial enterprise, it still lacks the kind of programming—like *Amos 'n' Andy* in radio, or *I Love Lucy* in television—that transformed both into truly mass media of art and entertainment. Television, for its part, has long been the medium of a rising middle class of immigrants and their children, in terms of the figures who have exploited its possibilities (from RCA executive David Sarnoff to stars like Jackie Gleason); the new genres it created (from the miniseries to the situation-comedy); and the audiences (from urban Jews to suburban Irish Catholics) who adopted them with enthusiasm.

For much of this century, the mass appeal of popular culture has been viewed as a problem. "What is the jass [*sic*] music, and therefore the jass band?" asked an irritated New Orleans writer in 1918. "As well as ask why the dime novel or the grease-dripping doughnut. All are manifestations of a low stream in man's taste that has not come out in civilization's wash." However one may feel about this contemptuous dismissal of jazz, now viewed as one of the great achievements of American civilization, this writer was clearly correct to suggest the demographic, technological, and cultural links between the "lower" sorts of people in American life, the media they used, and forms of expression that were often presumed guilty until proven innocent.

Indeed, because education and research have traditionally been considered the province of the "higher" sorts of people in American life, popular culture was not considered a subject that should even be discussed, much less studied. Nevertheless, there have always been those willing to continue what might be termed the "Tocquevillian" tradition of treating popular culture with intellectual seriousness and respect (if not always approval). In his 1924 book *The Seven Lively Arts* and in much of his journalism, critic Gilbert Seldes found in silent movies, cartoons, and pop music themes and motifs fully worthy of sustained exploration. Amid the worldwide crisis of the 1930s and 1940s, folklorist Constance Rourke limned the origins of an indigenous popular culture in books like *American Humor* (1931) and *The Roots of American Culture* (1942). And with the rise of the Cold War underlining the differences between democratic and totalitarian societies, sociologists David Riesman and Reuel Denny evaluated the social currents animating popular culture in Denny's *The Astonished Muse* (1957), for which Riesman, who showed a particular interest in popular music, wrote the introduction.

European scholars were also pivotal in shaping the field. Johan Huizinga's *Homo Ludens* (1938), Roland Barthes's *Mythologies* (1957), and Antonio Gramsci's prison letters (written in the 1920s and 1930s but not published until the 1970s) have proved among the most influential works in defining the boundaries, strategies, and meanings of popular culture. While none of these works focused on American popular culture specifically, their focus on the jetsam and flotsam of daily life since the medieval period proved enormously suggestive in an American context.

It has only been at the end of the twentieth century, however, that the study of popular culture has come into its own in its own right. To a great extent, this development is a legacy of the 1960s. The end of a formal system of racial segregation; the impact of affirmative action and government-funded financial aid; and the end of single-sex education at many long-established universities dramatically transformed the composition of student bodies and faculties. These developments in turn, began having an impact on the nature and parameters of academic study. While one should not exaggerate the impact of these developments—either in terms of their numbers or their effect on an academy that in some ways has simply replaced older forms of insularity and complacency with new ones—it nevertheless seems fair to say that a bona fide democratization of higher education occurred in the last third of the twentieth century, paving the way for the creation of a formal scholarly infrastructure for popular culture.

Once again, it was foreign scholars who were pivotal in the elaboration of this infrastructure. The work of Raymond Williams, Stuart Hall, and others at Britain's Centre for Contemporary Cultural Studies in the 1950s and 1960s drew on Marxist and psychoanalytic ideas to explain, and in many cases justify, the importance of popular culture. Though not always specifically concerned with popular culture, a panoply of French theorists—particularly Jacques Derrida, Louis Althusser, and Michel Foucault—also proved highly influential. At its best, this scholarship illuminated unexamined assumptions and highly revealing (and in many cases, damning) patterns in the most seemingly ordinary documents. At its worst, it lapsed into an arcane jargon that belied the directness of popular culture and suggested an elitist disdain toward the audiences it presumably sought to understand.

Like their European counterparts, American scholars of popular culture have come from a variety of disciplines. Many were trained in literature, among them Henry Nash Smith, whose *Virgin Land* (1950) pioneered the study of the Western, and Leslie Fiedler, who applied critical talents first developed to study classic American literature to popular fiction like *Gone with the Wind*. But much important work in the field has also been done by historians, particularly social historians who began their careers by focusing on labor history but became increasingly interested in the ways American workers spent their free time. Following the tradition of the great British historian E. P. Thompson, scholars such as Herbert Gutman and Lawrence Levine have uncovered and described the art and leisure practices of African Americans in particular with flair and insight. Feminist scholars of a variety of stripes (and sexual orientations) have supplied a great deal of the intellectual energy in the study of popular culture, among them Ann Douglas, Carroll Smith-Rosenberg, and Jane Tompkins. Indeed, the strongly interdisciplinary flavor of popular culture scholarship—along with the rise of institutions like the Popular Press and the Popular Culture Association, both based at Bowling Green University—suggests the way the field has been at the forefront of an ongoing process of redrawing disciplinary boundaries in the humanities.

By the 1980s, the stream of scholarship on popular culture had become a flood. In the 1990s, the field became less of a quixotic enterprise than a growing presence in the educational curriculum as a whole. Courses devoted to the subject, whether housed in communications programs or in traditional academic departments, have become increasingly common in colleges and universities—and, perhaps more importantly, have become integrated into the fabric of basic surveys of history, literature, and other fields. Political scientists, librarians, and curators have begun to consider it part of their domain.

For most of us, though, popular culture is not something we have to self-consciously seek out or think about. Indeed, its very omnipresence makes it easy to take for granted as transparent (and permanent). That's why trips to museums—or encyclopedias like this one—are so useful and important. In pausing to think about the art of everyday life, we can begin to see just how unusual, and valuable, it really is.

—Jim Cullen

FURTHER READING:

Barthes, Roland. *Mythologies.* Translated by Annette Lavers. 1957. Reprint, New York, The Noonday Press, 1972.

Cullen, Jim. *The Art of Democracy: A Concise History of Popular Culture in the United States.* New York, Monthly Review Press, 1996.

Fiske, John. *Understanding Popular Culture.* Boston, Unwin/Hyman, 1989.

Levine, Lawrence. *The Unpredictable Past: Explorations in American Cultural History.* New York, Oxford University Press, 1993.

Storey, John. *An Introductory Guide to Cultural Theory and Popular Culture.* Athens, University of Georgia Press, 1993.

Susman, Warren. *Culture as History: The Transformation of American Society in the Twentieth Century.* New York, Pantheon, 1984.

ADVISORS

Frances R. Aparicio
University of Michigan

Paul Buhle
Brown University

George O. Carney
Oklahoma State University

B. Lee Cooper
University of Great Falls

Corey K. Creekmur
University of Iowa

Joshua Gamson
Yale University

Jerome Klinkowitz
University of Northern Iowa

Richard Martin
Metropolitan Museum of Art
Columbia University
New York University

Lawrence E. Mintz
University of Maryland
Art Gliner Center for Humor Studies

Troy Paino
Winona State University

Grace Palladino
University of Maryland

Lauren Rabinovitz
University of Iowa

T. V. Reed
Washington State University

William L. Schurk
Bowling Green State University

Alison M. Scott
Bowling Green State University

Randall W. Scott
Michigan State University Libraries

Ron Simon
Museum of Television & Radio
Columbia University

Erin Smith
University of Texas at Dallas

June Sochen
Northeastern Illinois University

Colby Vargas
New Trier High School

CONTRIBUTORS

Nathan Abrams
Frederick Luis Aldama
Roberto Alvarez
Byron Anderson
Carly Andrews
Jacob M. Appel
Tim Arnold
Paul Ashdown
Bernardo Alexander Attias
Frederick J. Augustyn, Jr.

Beatriz Badikian
Michael Baers
Neal Baker
S. K. Bane
Samantha Barbas
Allen Barksdale
Pauline Bartel
Bob Batchelor
Vance Bell
Samuel I. Bellman
James R. Belpedio
Courtney Bennett
Timothy Berg
Lisa Bergeron-Duncan
Daniel Bernardi
R. Thomas Berner
Charlie Bevis
Lara Bickell
Sam Binkley
Brian Black
Liza Black
Bethany Blankenship
Rebecca Blustein
Aniko Bodroghkozy
Gregory Bond
Martyn Bone
Austin Booth
Gerry Bowler
Anne Boyd
Marlena E. Bremseth
Carol Brennan
Tony Brewer
Deborah Broderson
Michael Brody
Pat H. Broeske
Robert J. Brown
Sharon Brown
Craig Bunch
Stephen Burnett
Gary Burns
Margaret Burns

Manuel V. Cabrera, Jr.
Ross B. Care

Gerald Carpenter
Anthony Cast
Rafaela Castro
Jason Chambers
Chris Chandler
Michael K. Chapman
Roger Chapman
Lloyd Chiasson, Jr.
Ann M. Ciasullo
Dylan Clark
Frank Clark
Randy Clark
Craig T. Cobane
Dan Coffey
Adam Max Cohen
Toby I. Cohen
Susann Cokal
Jeffrey W. Coker
Charles A. Coletta, Jr.
Michael R. Collings
Willie Collins
Mia L. Consalvo
Douglas Cooke
ViBrina Coronado
Robert C. Cottrell
Corey K. Creekmur
Richard C. Crepeau
Jim Cullen
Susan Curtis

Glyn Davis
Janet M. Davis
Pamala S. Deane
S. Renee Dechert
John Deitrick
Gordon Neal Diem, D.A.
Richard Digby-Junger
Laurie DiMauro
John J. Doherty
Thurston Domina
Jon Griffin Donlon
Simon Donner
Randy Duncan
Stephen Duncombe
Eugenia Griffith DuPell
Stephanie Dyer

Rob Edelman
Geoff Edgers
Jessie L. Embry
Jeffrey Escoffier
Cindy Peters Evans
Sean Evans
William A. Everett

Alyssa Falwell
Richard Feinberg
G. Allen Finchum
S. Naomi Finkelstein
Dennis Fischer
Bill Freind
Bianca Freire-Medeiros
Shaun Frentner
James Friedman
Adrienne Furness

Paul Gaffney
Milton Gaither
Joan Gajadhar
Catherine C. Galley
Caitlin L. Gannon
Sandra Garcia-Myers
Bryan Garman
Eva Marie Garroutte
Frances Gateward
Jason George
Tina Gianoulis
James R. Giles
Milton Goldin
Ilene Goldman
Matthew Mulligan Goldstein
Dave Goldweber
Ian Gordon
W. Terrence Gordon
Ron Goulart
Paul Grainge
Brian Granger
Anna Hunt Graves
Steve Graves
Jill A. Gregg
Benjamin Griffith
Perry Grossman
Justin Gustainis
Dale Allen Gyure

Kristine J. Ha
Elizabeth Haas
Ray Haberski, Jr.
Jeanne Lynn Hall
Steve Hanson
Jacqueline Anne Hatton
Chris Haven
Ethan Hay
Jeet Heer
Andrew R. Heinze
Mary Hess
Joshua Hirsch
David L. Hixson
Scott W. Hoffman
Briavel Holcomb

Peter C. Holloran
David Holloway
Karen Hovde
Kevin Howley
Nick Humez

Judy L. Isaksen

Jennifer Jankauskas
E. V. Johanningmeier
Patrick Jones
Patrick Jones
Preston Neal Jones
Mark Joseph
Thomas Judd

Peter Kalliney
Nicolás Kanellos
Robyn Karney
Stephen Keane
James D. Keeline
Max Kellerman
Ken Kempcke
Stephen C. Kenny
Stephen Kercher
Matt Kerr
M. Alison Kibler
Kimberley H. Kidd
Matthew A. Killmeier
Jason King
Jon Klinkowitz
Leah Konicki
Steven Kotok
Robert Kuhlken
Andrew J. Kunka
Audrey Kupferberg
Petra Kuppers

Emma Lambert
Christina Lane
Kevin Lause
Nadine-Rae Leavell
Christopher A. Lee
Michele Lellouche
Robin Lent
Joan Leotta
Richard Levine
Drew Limsky
Daniel Lindley
Joyce Linehan
Margaret Litton
James H. Lloyd
David Lonergan
Eric Longley
Rick Lott
Bennett Lovett-Graff
Denise Lowe

Debra M. Lucas
Karen Lurie
Michael A. Lutes
James Lyons
John F. Lyons

Steve Macek
Alison Macor
David Marc
Robin Markowitz
Tilney L. Marsh
Richard Martin
Sara Martin
Linda A. Martindale
Kevin Mattson
Randall McClure
Allison McCracken
Jennifer Davis McDaid
Jason McEntee
Cheryl S. McGrath
Daryna McKeand
Jacquelyn Y. McLendon
Kembrew McLeod
Josephine A. McQuail
Alex Medeiros
Brad Melton
Myra Mendible
Jeff Merron
Thomas J. Mertz
Nathan R. Meyer
Jonathan Middlebrook
Andre Millard
Jeffrey S. Miller
Karen Miller
P. Andrew Miller
Dorothy Jane Mills
Andrew Milner
Deborah M. Mix
Nickianne Moody
Richard L. Moody
Charles F. Moore
Leonard N. Moore
Dan Moos
Robert A. Morace
Edward Moran
Barry Morris
Michael J. Murphy
Jennifer A. Murray
Susan Murray
Pierre-Damien Mvuyekure

Michael Najjar
Ilana Nash
Mary Lou Nemanic
Scott Newman
Joan Nicks
Martin F. Norden
Justin Nordstrom
Anna Notaro

William F. O'Connor
Paul O'Hara
Angela O'Neal
Christopher D. O'Shea
Lolly Ockerstrom
Kerry Owens
Marc Oxoby

D. Byron Painter
Henri-Dominique Paratte
Leslie Paris
Jay Parrent
Felicity Paxton
Sara Pendergast
Tom Pendergast
Jana Pendragon
Geoff Peterson
Kurt W. Peterson
Emily Pettigrew
Daniel J. Philippon
S. J. Philo
Allene Phy-Olsen
Ed Piacentino
Jürgen Pieters
Paul F. P. Pogue
Mark B. Pohlad
Fernando Porta
Michael L. Posner
John A. Price
Victoria Price
Luca Prono
Elizabeth Purdy
Christian L. Pyle

Jessy Randall
Taly Ravid
Belinda S. Ray
Ivan Raykoff
Wendy Wick Reaves
James E. Reibman
Yolanda Retter
Tracy J. Revels
Wylene Rholetter
Tad Richards
Robert B. Ridinger
Jeff Ritter
Thomas Robertson
Arthur Robinson
Todd Anthony Rosa
Ava Rose
Chris Routledge
Abhijit Roy
Adrienne Russell
Dennis Russell

Lisa Jo Sagolla
Frank A. Salamone
Joe Sutliff Sanders

Andrew Sargent
Julie Scelfo
Elizabeth D. Schafer
Louis Scheeder
James Schiff
Robert E. Schnakenberg
Steven Schneider
Kelly Schrum
Christine Scodari
Ann Sears
E. M. I. Sefcovic
Eric J. Segal
Carol A. Senf
Tim Seul
Alexander Shashko
Michele S. Shauf
Taylor Shaw
Anne Sheehan
Steven T. Sheehan
Pamela Shelton
Sandra Sherman
Charles J. Shindo
Mike Shupp
Robert C. Sickels
C. Kenyon Silvey
Ron Simon
Philip Simpson
Rosemarie Skaine
Ryan R. Sloane
Jeannette Sloniowski
Cheryl A. Smith

Kyle Smith
John Smolenski
Irvin D. Solomon
Geri Speace
Andrew Spieldenner
tova stabin
Scott Stabler
Jon Sterngrass
Roger W. Stump
Bob Sullivan
Lauren Ann Supance
Marc R. Sykes

Midori Takagi
Candida Taylor
Scott Thill
Robert Thompson
Stephen L. Thompson
Rosemarie Garland Thomson
Jan Todd
Terry Todd
John Tomasic
Warren Tormey
Grant Tracey
David Trevino
Marcella Bush Trevino
Scott Tribble
Tom Trinchera
Nicholas A. Turse

Anthony Ubelhor
Daryl Umberger

Rob Van Kranenburg
Robert VanWynsberghe
Colby Vargas

Sue Walker
Lori C. Walters
Nancy Lan-Jy Wang
Adam Wathen
Laural Weintraub
Jon Weisberger
David B. Welky
Christopher W. Wells
Celia White
Christopher S. Wilson
David B. Wilson
Kristi M. Wilson
Jeff Wiltse
Wendy Woloson
David E. Woodward
Bradford W. Wright

Sharon Yablon
Daniel Francis Yezbick
Stephen D. Youngkin

Kristal Brent Zook

LIST OF ENTRIES

Brown, Paul
Browne, Jackson
Brownie Cameras
Brubeck, Dave
Bruce, Lenny
Bryant, Paul "Bear"
Brynner, Yul
Bubblegum Rock
Buck, Pearl S.
Buck Rogers
Buckley, William F., Jr.
Buckwheat Zydeco
Budweiser
Buffalo Springfield
Buffett, Jimmy
Bugs Bunny
Bumper Stickers
Bundy, Ted
Bungalow
Burger King
Burlesque
Burma-Shave
Burnett, Carol
Burns, George, and Gracie
    Allen
Burns, Ken
Burr, Raymond
Burroughs, Edgar Rice
Burroughs, William S.
Buster Brown
*Butch Cassidy and the
    Sundance Kid*
Butkus, Dick
Butler, Octavia E.
Butterbeans and Susie
Buttons, Red
Byrds, The

Cabbage Patch Kids
Cable TV
Cadillac
Caesar, Sid
Cagney and Lacey
Cagney, James
Cahan, Abraham
Cakewalks
Caldwell, Erskine
Calloway, Cab
Calvin and Hobbes
Camacho, Héctor "Macho"
Camelot
Camp
Campbell, Glen
Campbell, Naomi
Camping
Cancer
Candid Camera
Caniff, Milton
Canova, Judy
Canseco, Jose

Cantor, Eddie
Capital Punishment
Capone, Al
Capote, Truman
Capra, Frank
Captain America
Captain Kangaroo
Captain Marvel
Car 54, Where Are You?
Car Coats
Caray, Harry
Carey, Mariah
Carlin, George
Carlton, Steve
Carmichael, Hoagy
Carnegie, Dale
Carnegie Hall
Carpenters, The
Carr, John Dickson
Cars, The
Carson, Johnny
Carter Family, The
Caruso, Enrico
Carver, Raymond
Casablanca
Cash, Johnny
Caspar Milquetoast
Cassette Tape
Cassidy, David
Castaneda, Carlos
Castle, Vernon and Irene
Castro, The
Casual Friday
Catalog Houses
Catch-22
Catcher in the Rye, The
Cather, Willa
Cathy
Cats
Cavett, Dick
CB Radio
*CBS Radio Mystery
    Theater, The*
Celebrity
Celebrity Caricature
Cemeteries
Central Park
Century 21 Exposition
    (Seattle, 1962)
Century of Progress
    (Chicago, 1933)
Challenger Disaster
Chamberlain, Wilt
Chandler, Raymond
Chandu the Magician
Chanel, Coco
Chaplin, Charlie
Charles, Ray
Charlie Chan
Charlie McCarthy

Charlie's Angels
Charm Bracelets
Chase, Chevy
Chautauqua Institution
Chavez, Cesar
Chavis, Boozoo
Chayefsky, Paddy
Checker, Chubby
Cheech and Chong
Cheerleading
Cheers
Chemise
Chenier, Clifton
Cherry Ames
Chessman, Caryl
Chicago Bears, The
Chicago Bulls, The
Chicago Cubs, The
Chicago Jazz
Chicago Seven, The
Child, Julia
Child Stars
China Syndrome, The
Chinatown
Chipmunks, The
Choose-Your-Own-Ending
    Books
Christie, Agatha
Christmas
Christo
Chrysler Building
Chuck D
Chun King
Church Socials
Cigarettes
Circus
Cisneros, Sandra
Citizen Kane
City Lights
City of Angels, The
Civil Disobedience
Civil Rights Movement
Civil War Reenactors
Claiborne, Liz
Clairol Hair Coloring
Clancy, Tom
Clapton, Eric
Clark, Dick
Clarke, Arthur C.
Clemente, Roberto
Cleopatra
Clift, Montgomery
Cline, Patsy
Clinton, George
Clockwork Orange, A
Clooney, Rosemary
*Close Encounters of the
    Third Kind*
Closet, The
CNN

Martin, Steve
Martini
Marvel Comics
Marx Brothers, The
Marx, Groucho
Mary Hartman, Mary Hartman
Mary Kay Cosmetics
Mary Poppins
Mary Tyler Moore Show, The
Mary Worth
*M*A*S*H*
Mason, Jackie
Mass Market Magazine
    Revolution
Masses, The
Masterpiece Theatre
Masters and Johnson
Masters Golf Tournament
Mathis, Johnny
Mattingly, Don
Maude
Maupin, Armistead
Maus
Max, Peter
Mayer, Louis B.
Mayfield, Curtis
Mayfield, Percy
Mays, Willie
McBain, Ed
McCaffrey, Anne
McCall's Magazine
McCarthyism
McCartney, Paul
McCay, Winsor
McClure's
McCoy, Horace
McCrea, Joel
McDaniel, Hattie
McDonald's
McEnroe, John
McEntire, Reba
McGwire, Mark
McHale's Navy
McKay, Claude
McKuen, Rod
McLish, Rachel
McLuhan, Marshall
McMurtry, Larry
McPherson, Aimee Semple
McQueen, Butterfly
McQueen, Steve
Me Decade
Meadows, Audrey
Mean Streets
Media Feeding Frenzies
Medicine Shows
Meet Me in St. Louis
Mellencamp, John
Mencken, H. L.
Mendoza, Lydia

Men's Movement
Merton, Thomas
Metalious, Grace
Metropolis
Metropolitan Museum of Art
MGM (Metro-Goldwyn-Mayer)
Miami Vice
Michener, James
Mickey Mouse Club, The
Microsoft
Middletown
Midler, Bette
Midnight Cowboy
Mildred Pierce
Militias
Milk, Harvey
Millay, Edna St. Vincent
Miller, Arthur
Miller Beer
Miller, Glenn
Miller, Henry
Miller, Roger
Milli Vanilli
Million Man March
Milton Bradley
Minimalism
Minivans
Minnelli, Vincente
Minoso, Minnie
Minstrel Shows
Miranda, Carmen
Miranda Warning
Miss America Pageant
Mission: Impossible
Mister Ed
Mister Rogers' Neighborhood
Mitchell, Joni
Mitchell, Margaret
Mitchum, Robert
Mix, Tom
Mod
Mod Squad, The
Model T
Modern Dance
Modern Maturity
Modern Times
Modernism
Momaday, N. Scott
Monday Night Football
Monkees, The
Monopoly
Monroe, Bill
Monroe, Earl ''The Pearl''
Monroe, Marilyn
Montalban, Ricardo
Montana, Joe
Montana, Patsy
Monty Python's Flying Circus
Moonies/Reverend Sun
    Myung Moon

Moonlighting
Moore, Demi
Moore, Michael
Moral Majority
Moreno, Rita
Mork & Mindy
Morris, Mark
Morrissette, Alanis
Morrison, Toni
Morrison, Van
Morse, Carlton E.
Morton, Jelly Roll
Mosley, Walter
Moss, Kate
Mother's Day
Mötley Crüe
Motley, Willard
Motown
Mount Rushmore
Mountain Biking
Mouseketeers, The
Movie Palaces
Movie Stars
Mr. Dooley
Mr. Smith Goes to Washington
Mr. Wizard
Ms.
MTV
Muckraking
Multiculturalism
Mummy, The
Muni, Paul
Munsey's Magazine
Muppets, The
Murder, She Wrote
Murphy Brown
Murphy, Eddie
Murray, Anne
Murray, Arthur
Murray, Bill
Murray, Lenda
Murrow, Edward R.
Muscle Beach
Muscle Cars
Muscular Christianity
Musical, The
Mutiny on the Bounty
Mutt & Jeff
Muzak
My Darling Clementine
My Fair Lady
My Family/Mi familia
My Lai Massacre
My So Called Life
My Three Sons

Nader, Ralph
Nagel, Patrick
Naismith, James
Namath, Joe

Roller Derby
Rolling Stone
Rolling Stones, The
Romance Novels
Romero, Cesar
Roots
Rose Bowl
Rose, Pete
Roseanne
Rosemary's Baby
Rosenberg, Julius and Ethel
Ross, Diana, and the Supremes
Roswell Incident
Roundtree, Richard
Rouse Company
Route 66
Royko, Mike
Rubik's Cube
Rudolph the Red-Nosed Reindeer
Run-DMC
Runyon, Damon
RuPaul
Rupp, Adolph
Russell, Bill
Russell, Jane
Russell, Nipsey
Russell, Rosalind
Ruth, Babe
RV
Ryan, Meg
Ryan, Nolan
Rydell, Bobby
Ryder, Winona

Safe Sex
Sagan, Carl
Sahl, Mort
Saks Fifth Avenue
Sales, Soupy
Salsa Music
Salt-n-Pepa
Sam and Dave
Sandburg, Carl
Sanders, Barry
Sandman
Sandow, Eugen
Sanford and Son
Santana
Sarandon, Susan
Saratoga Springs
Sarnoff, David
Sarong
Sassoon, Vidal
Sassy
Satellites
Saturday Evening Post, The
Saturday Morning Cartoons
Saturday Night Fever
Saturday Night Live

Savage, Randy ''Macho Man''
Savoy Ballroom
Schindler's List
Schlatter, George
Schlessinger, Dr. Laura
Schnabel, Julian
Schoolhouse Rock
Schwarzenegger, Arnold
Science Fiction Publishing
Scientific American
Scopes Monkey Trial
Scorsese, Martin
Scott, George C.
Scott, Randolph
Scream
Screwball Comedies
Scribner's
Scruggs, Earl
Sculley, Vin
Sea World
Seals, Son
Search for Tomorrow
Searchers, The
Sears Roebuck Catalogue
Sears Tower
Second City
Sedona, Arizona
Seduction of the Innocent
Seeger, Pete
Seinfeld
Selena
Seles, Monica
Sellers, Peter
Selznick, David O.
Sennett, Mack
Serial Killers
Serling, Rod
Sesame Street
Seven Days in May
Seven Year Itch, The
Seventeen
Sex and the Single Girl
Sex Scandals
Sex Symbol
Sexual Harassment
Sexual Revolution
Shadow, The
Shaft
Shakur, Tupac
Shane
Shaw, Artie
Shawn, Ted
She Wore a Yellow Ribbon
Sheldon, Sidney
Shepard, Sam
Sherman, Cindy
Shirelles, The
Shirer, William L.
Shock Radio
Shore, Dinah

Shorter, Frank
Show Boat
Shula, Don
Shulman, Max
SIDS (Sudden Infant Death Syndrome)
Siegel, Bugsy
Silence of the Lambs, The
Silent Movies
Silver Surfer, The
Simon and Garfunkel
Simon, Neil
Simon, Paul
Simpson, O. J.
Simpson Trial
Simpsons, The
Sinatra, Frank
Sinbad
Sinclair, Upton
Singer, Isaac Bashevis
Singin' in the Rain
Singles Bars
Sirk, Douglas
Siskel and Ebert
Sister Souljah
Sitcom
Six Million Dollar Man, The
60 Minutes
$64,000 Question, The
Skaggs, Ricky
Skateboarding
Skating
Skelton, Red
Skyscrapers
Slaney, Mary Decker
Slang
Slasher Movies
Slinky
Sly and the Family Stone
Smith, Bessie
Smith, Dean
Smith, Kate
Smith, Patti
Smithsonian Institution
Smits, Jimmy
Smothers Brothers, The
Snoop Doggy Dogg
Snow White and the Seven Dwarfs
Soap Operas
Soccer
Social Dancing
Soda Fountains
Soldier Field
Some Like It Hot
Sondheim, Stephen
Sonny and Cher
Sosa, Sammy
Soul Music
Soul Train

A

A&R Men/Women

Artist and Repertoire (A&R) representatives count among the great, unseen heroes of the recording industry. During the early decades of the recording industry, A&R men (there were very few women) were responsible for many stages in the production of recorded music. Since the 1960s though, A&R has become increasingly synonymous with "talent scouting." A&R is one of the most coveted positions in the recording industry, but it may also be the most difficult. The ability to recognize which acts will be successful is critical to the survival of all record companies, but it is a rare talent. Those with "good ears" are likely to be promoted to a leadership position in the industry. Several notable record company executives, especially Sun's Sam Phillips and Atlantic's Ahmet Ertegun, established their professional reputations as A&R men. A few of the more legendary A&R men have become famous in their own right, joining the ranks of rock n' roll's most exclusive social cliques.

The great A&R men of the pre-rock era were multitalented. First, the A&R man would scout the clubs, bars, and juke joints of the country to find new talent for his record company. After signing acts to contracts, A&R men accompanied musicians into the studio, helping them to craft a record. A&R men also occasionally functioned as promoters, helping with the "grooming" of acts for the stage or broadcast performances.

Some of the most astounding A&R work was done before World War II. A significant early figure in the history of A&R was Ralph Peer. Peer was the first record company man to recognize, albeit by sheer luck, the economic value of Southern and Appalachian music. While looking to make field recordings of gospel in the South, Peer reluctantly recorded "Fiddlin'" John Carson, whose record yielded a surprise hit in 1927. Subsequent field recording expeditions into the South were immediately organized and among the artists soon signed to Peer's Southern Music Company were Jimmie Rodgers and the Carter Family, the twin foundational pillars of country music. Peer's A&R strategies were emulated by other A&R men like Frank Walker and Art Satherly, both of whom would eventually play significant roles in the development of country and western music. John Hammond, who worked many years for Columbia Records, likewise had an impressive string of successes. He is credited with crafting the early careers of Billie Holiday, Benny Goodman, and Count Basie in the 1930s. In the post war years, Hammond discovered among others Aretha Franklin, Bob Dylan, Bruce Springsteen, and Stevie Ray Vaughn.

In the 1950s, many new record companies emerged with aggressive and visionary A&R strategies. Until the early 1960s, top executives at record companies substantially controlled day-to-day A&R functions. In most instances, the chief executives' personal biases and tastes conditioned company A&R strategies. These biases, which often hinged on old-fashioned notions of race, class, and region, permitted upstart companies to exploit the growing teen market for R&B and rock n' roll. Several of the noteworthy independent record companies of the 1950s were headed by astute A&R men, like Ahmet Ertegun (Atlantic); Leonard Chess (Chess); and Sam Phillips (Sun), who eagerly sought talent among blacks and the Southern whites. Phillips' discoveries alone read like a "who's who" list of early R&B and rock. Among the legends he found are B.B. King, Howlin' Wolf, Elvis Presley, Johnny Cash, and Jerry Lee Lewis. Major labels eventually realized that their conservative A&R practices were eroding their market share. Major labels began using the independent labels to do A&R work, purchasing artist contracts from small labels (e.g., RCA's purchase of Presley's contract from Sun). The payola scandal of the late 1950s was in many ways a means of compensating for A&R deficiencies at the majors.

In the early 1960s, the major labels continued to display conservative tendencies in their A&R practices. Several famous A&R gaffes were made during this era. Columbia Record's head, Mitch Miller, refused to recognize the staying power of rock n' roll, and tried to promote folk revival acts instead. Dick Rowe, head of A&R at Decca, became the infamous goat who rejected the Beatles. Four other labels passed on the Beatles before London picked them up. When the Beatles became a sensation, A&R representatives flocked to Liverpool in hopes of finding the "next Beatles." In the later 1960s, adjustments were made to overcome the scouting deficiencies displayed by the majors. Major labels increasingly turned to free-lance A&R persons, called "independent producers," who specialized in studio production, but who were also responsible for discovering new talent. Phil Spector and his "wall of sound" emerged as the most famous of all the independent producers in the 1960s.

In the later 1960s, younger and more "street savvy" music executives began replacing older executives at the major labels. Several stunning successes were recorded. Capitol's A&R machine brought them the Beach Boys. At Columbia, Mitch Miller was replaced by Clive Davis, who along with several other major label executives in attendance at the Monterrey Pop festival signed several popular San Francisco-based psychedelic acts. In an effort to increase both their street credibility and their street savvy, some labels even resorted to hiring "house hippies," longhaired youths who acted as A&R representatives. Still the major labels' scouting machines overlooked L.A.'s folk rock scene and London's blues revival subculture. The ever-vigilant Ahmet Ertegun at Atlantic led a scouting expedition to England that won them both Cream and Led Zeppelin. In the 1970s and 1980s, major label A&R departments became larger and more sophisticated, which helped them beat back the challenge posed by independent label A&R. Some labels even tried hiring rock critics as A&R representatives.

A&R remains a challenging job. The "copy-catting" behavior displayed in Liverpool in the mid 1960s repeats itself on a regular basis. The grunge rock craze of the early 1990s revealed that a herding mentality still conditions A&R strategies. Visionary A&R representatives still stand to benefit greatly. Shortly after Gary Gersh brought Nirvana to Geffen Records he was named head of Capitol Records. Few A&R persons maintain a consistent record of finding marketable talent and consequently few people remain in A&R long. Those who do consistently bring top talent to their bosses, wield enormous power within the corporate structure and are likely to be promoted.

—Steve Graves

FURTHER READING:

Chapple, Steve, and Reebee Garofalo. *Rock and Roll Is Here to Pay.* Chicago, Nelson Hall, 1977.

Dannen, Fredric. *Hit Men.* New York, Times Books, 1990.

Denisoff, R. Serge. *Solid Gold: The Popular Record Industry.* New Brunswick, New Jersey, Transaction Books, 1975.

Escott, Colin, and Martin Haskins. *Good Rockin' Tonight: Sun Records and the Birth of Rock n' Roll.* New York, St. Martin's Press, 1991.

Farr, Jory. *Moguls and Madmen: The Pursuit of Power in Popular Music.* New York, Simon and Schuster, 1994.

Aaron, Hank (1934—)

Atlanta Braves outfielder Hank Aaron was thrust onto the national stage in 1973 and 1974 when he threatened and then broke Babe Ruth's record of 714 home runs, one of the most hallowed records in all of American sports. In the mid-1970s, Ruth's legend was as powerful as it had been during his playing days five decades earlier and his epic home runs and colorful antics lived on in the American imagination. As Roger Maris had discovered when he broke Ruth's single season home run record in 1961, any player attempting to unseat the beloved Ruth from the record books battled, not only opposing pitchers, but also a hostile American public. When

Hank Aaron

a black man strove to eclipse the Babe's record, however, his pursuit revealed a lingering intolerance and an unseemly racial animosity in American society.

Henry Louis Aaron was born in Mobile, Alabama, in the depths of the Great Depression in 1934. One of eight children, Aaron and his family lived a tough existence like many other Southern black families of the time, scraping by on his father's salary as a dock worker. As a teenager, Aaron passed much of his time playing baseball in the neighborhood sandlots, and after short trials with two all-black teams Aaron attracted the attention of the Boston Braves, who purchased his contract in May of 1952.

Although Aaron faced several challenges in his introduction to organized baseball, he quickly rose through the Braves system. He was first assigned to the Braves affiliate in Eau Claire, Wisconsin, and he later wrote that "the middle of Wisconsin felt like a foreign country to [this] eighteen-year-old black kid from Mobile." After a successful season in Eau Claire, however, Aaron was moved up to the Braves farm team in Jacksonville, Florida, for the 1953 season, where, along with three other African-American players, he was faced with the unenviable task of integrating the South Atlantic League. Throughout the season, Aaron endured death threats, racial epithets from players and fans, and Jim Crow accommodations, yet he rose above the distractions and was named the SALLY League's Most Valuable Player.

By 1954, only two years removed from the sandlots of Mobile, Aaron was named to the opening day roster of the, now, Milwaukee Braves as a part-time player. The next year he won a starting position in the Braves outfield and stayed there for the next 19 years in Milwaukee and then in Atlanta as the franchise moved again. From 1955 until 1973, when he stopped playing full time, Aaron averaged nearly 37 home runs per year and hit over .300 in 14 different seasons.

As the years went by conditions began to improve for African-American players: by 1959 all major league teams had been integrated; gradually hotels and restaurants began to serve both black and white players; by the mid-1960s spring training sites throughout the South had been integrated; and racial epithets directed at black ball players from both the field and the grandstand began to diminish in number. Throughout the 1960s Americans, black and white, north and south, struggled with the civil rights movement and dealt with these same issues of desegregation and integration in their every day life. By the mid-1970s, however, African-Americans had achieved full legal equality, and the turbulence and violence of the sixties seemed to be only a memory for many Americans.

It was in this atmosphere that Hank Aaron approached Babe Ruth's all-time career home run record. By the end of the 1973 season, Aaron had hit 712 career home runs, only two shy of the Babe's record. With six months to wait for the opening of the 1974 season, Aaron had time to pour over the reams of mail he had begun to receive during his pursuit of Ruth's record. "The overwhelming majority of letters were supportive," wrote Aaron in his autobiography. Fans of all stripes wrote their encouragements to the star. A young African-American fan, for instance, wrote to say that "your race is proud." Similarly, another fan wrote, "Mazel Tov from the white population, [we've] been with you all the way. We love you and are thrilled."

Hidden in these piles of letters, however, were a distinct minority of missives with a more sinister tone. For the first time since integrating the South Atlantic League in 1953, Aaron was confronted with a steady stream of degrading words and racial epithets. "Listen Black Boy," one person wrote, "We don't want no nigger Babe

Ruth.'' Many ''fans'' of the game just could not accept an African-American as the new home run champion. ''I hope you don't break the Babe's record,'' one letter read. ''How do I tell my kids that a nigger did it?'' Even more disturbingly, Aaron received thousands of letters which threatened the lives of both himself and his family. In response, the Atlanta slugger received constant protection from the police and the FBI throughout his record chase.

As sportswriters began to write about the virulent hate mail that Aaron was receiving, his supporters redoubled their efforts to let him know how they felt. One young fan spoke eloquently for many Americans when he wrote, ''Dear Mr. Aaron, I am twelve years old, and I wanted to tell you that I have read many articles about the prejudice against you. I really think it is bad. I don't care what color you are.''

Hank Aaron would eventually break Babe Ruth's all-time record early in the 1974 season, and he would finish his career with a new record of 755 home runs. In 1982 he received the game's highest honor when he was voted into the Baseball Hall of Fame. Aaron's lifetime struggle against racism and discrimination served as an example for many Americans, both white and black, and he continued his public struggle against inequality after retiring from baseball.

Hank Aaron's relentless pursuit of the all-time home run record in 1973 and 1974 forced America to realize that the civil rights movement of the 1960s had not miraculously solved the long-standing problem of racial animosity in the United States. The prejudice and racism that had been pushed underground by the successes of the 1960s were starkly revealed once again when a black man attempted to surpass the record of a white American icon.

—Gregory Bond

FURTHER READING:

Aaron, Henry. *I Had a Hammer*. New York, Harper Collins, 1991.

Baldwin, Stan, and Jerry Jenkins. *Bad Henry*. Radnor, Pennsylvania, Chilton, 1974.

Thorn, John, et al. *Total Baseball*. New York, Viking Penguin, 1997.

AARP (American Association for Retired Persons)

The American Association for Retired Persons (AARP) is the premier special interest organization for Americans over age 50. AARP evolved from the National Retired Teachers Association, founded in 1947 and now an affiliated organization. Begun by Dr. Ethel Andrus, a pioneer in the field of gerontology and the first woman high-school principal in the state of California, AARP was created in large part to answer the need for affordable health insurance for seniors and to address the significant problem of age discrimination in society. By the end of the twentieth century AARP was commanding a membership of 31.5 million and, as critic Charles R. Morris points out, it had become known as the ''800 lb. gorilla of American politics.'' The organization states that ''AARP is a non-profit, non-partisan, membership organization, dedicated to addressing the needs and interests of people 50 and older. We seek through education, advocacy and service to enhance the quality of life for all by promoting independence, dignity and purpose.'' The motto of the organization is ''To Serve, Not to Be Served.''

Known for its intensive lobbying efforts to preserve Medicare and Social Security, AARP has a wide range of programs that serve its members, notably the ''55 ALIVE '' driving course (a special refresher class for older drivers linked to auto insurance discounts); AARP Connections for Independent Living (a volunteer organization to assist seniors to live on their own), and the Widowed Persons Service, which helps recently widowed people with their bereavement. The AARP's own publications range widely, but the best known is *Modern Maturity*, a glossy lifestyle magazine found in homes and doctors' offices across America, offering informational articles on travel, profiles of active senior Americans, and targeted advertising for Americans over 50. The AARP also funds research through its AARP Andrus Foundation, primarily in the field of gerontology, which exhibited rapid growth resulting from the aging of the enormous postwar ''Baby Boomer'' generation.

Probably the most visible program—and one that is a key part of its success in Washington politics—is ''AARP/VOTE.'' This has informed and organized voters to support AARP's legislative agenda, particularly in its ongoing campaign to protect entitlements in the late 1980s and 1990s. Social Security was once the ''sacred cow'' of American politics: former House Speaker Tip O' Neill dubbed Social Security ''the third rail of American politics—touch it and you die.'' AARP maintains that Social Security is a lifeline for many seniors, and has resisted any attempt to limit the program. It has also successfully weathered a challenge, based on a belief that Social Security is insolvent and is forcing young workers to pay for seniors with no hope of receiving future benefits themselves. The AARP was termed ''greedy geezers'' by the media, and its support of the ill-fated Medicare Catastrophic Care Act (since repealed) during the 1980s was an image disaster. The organization regained the high ground when Speaker of the House Newt Gingrich led a fight to slash entitlements as part of his ''Contract with America'' pledge, a centerpiece of the 1994 midterm elections. The AARP skillfully deflected the conservative assault on Social Security by utilizing its fabled public relations machine: member phone trees, press releases, and media pressure on Gingrich, who was singled out as ''picking on the elderly.''

The AARP has long been a controversial organization, subject to investigation by *Consumer Reports* magazine and the television show *60 Minutes* in 1978 for its too-cozy association with the insurance company Colonial Penn and its founder Leonard Davis. That association subsequently ended, and Davis' image and influence was banished from the organization's headquarters and promotional literature. In the 1990s, the AARP was attacked in Congress by long-time foe Senator Alan Simpson of Wyoming, who relentlessly investigated their nonprofit status. The AARP frequently testifies before Congress, but no longer functions as a lobbying organization because of Simpson's efforts. Yet it has continued to grow in numbers and influence, due in large part to a savvy marketing scheme that grants members attractive discounts on insurance, travel, and other services for the price of an eight-dollar membership fee. In return, the AARP can boast of a large membership in its legislative efforts and can deliver a highly desirable mailing list to its corporate partners.

The AARP has made a significant effort to define itself as an advocacy organization which is changing the way Americans view aging, yet this has been a difficult message to sell to Baby Boomers in particular, many of whom are more interested in preserving a youthful appearance and attitude than in considering retirement. It has been attacked from the left and the right of the political spectrum: in a May 25, 1995 editorial, the *Wall Street Journal* opined: ''AARP's own studies show that only 14% of its members join it to support its lobbying efforts. Its largely liberal staff has often felt free to go against the interest of its members. . . . AARP is the field artillery in a liberal army dedicated to defending the welfare state.'' At the same time, the AARP is viewed with suspicion by many on the left who deplore its size and moderate politics.

—Mary Hess

FURTHER READING:

Hess, John L. ''A Warm and Fuzzy Gorilla.'' *The Nation.* August 26-September 2, 1996.

Lieberman, Trudy. ''Social Insecurity: The Campaign to Take the System Private.'' *The Nation.* January 1, 1997.

Morris, Charles R. *The AARP: America's Most Powerful Lobby and the Clash of Generations.* New York, Times Books/Random House, 1996.

Peterson, Peter G. *Will America Grow Up Before It Grows Old? How the Coming Social Security Crisis Threatens You, Your Family, and Your Country.* New York, Random House, 1996.

Rosensteil, Thomas. ''Buying Off the Elderly: As the Revolution Gets Serious, Gingrich Muzzles the AARP.'' *Newsweek.* October 2, 1995.

ABBA

Associated with the disco scene of the 1970s, the Swedish quartet ABBA generated high charting hits for an entire decade, and for years trailed only the Volvo motor company as Sweden's biggest export. Comprised of two romantic couples—Bjorn Ulvaeus and Agnetha Faltskog, and Benny Andersson and Frida Lyngstad—ABBA formed in the early 1970s under the tutelage of songwriter Stig Anderson and scored their first success with ''Waterloo'' in 1974. From that point on, ABBA blazed a trail in pop sales history with ''Dancing Queen,'' ''Voulez Vous,'' ''Take a Chance on Me,'' and many other infectious singles, spending more time at the top of United Kingdom charts than any act except the Beatles. Although the group (as well as the Andersson-Lyngstad marriage) dissolved in the early 1980s, ABBA's legion of fans only grew into a new generation. Notably, ABBA was embraced by many gay male fans. Songs like ''Dancing Queen'' practically attained the status of gay anthems.

—Shaun Frentner

FURTHER READING:

Snaith, Paul. *The Music Still Goes On.* N.p. Castle Communications, 1994.

Tobler, John. *ABBA Gold: The Complete Story.* New York, St. Martin's Press, 1993.

Abbey, Edward (1927-1989)

Edward Abbey's essays and novels secured his position as a leading American environmentalist during the late 1960s through the 1980s. His nonconformist views, radical lifestyle, and revolutionary language created a cult following of fans whose philosophical outlooks developed from Abbey's books. He is the author of 21 full-length works, numerous periodical articles, and several introductions to others' books. With the exception of his first novel, all of Abbey's works have remained in print to the end of the twentieth century, a fact that attests to his continuing popularity. His writing has inspired readers to support ecological causes throughout America.

Abbey's father, a farmer, and his mother, a teacher, raised him on a small Appalachian farm in Home, Pennsylvania. When he was 18, Abbey served in the United States Army, and then in 1946 he hitchhiked west where he fell in love with the expansive nature of Arizona, New Mexico, and Utah. He studied philosophy and English at the University of New Mexico and the University of Edinburgh, earning a Master's Degree and pursuing his career as a writer. His first novel was poorly received, but in 1962 Abbey's second book, *The Brave Cowboy* (1958), was turned into a screenplay and released as a feature film, *Lonely Are the Brave.* From 1956 to 1971, to support himself and to enjoy the serenity of nature, Abbey worked for the Forest Service and the National Park Service. These early experiences provided subject matter for *Desert Solitaire* (1968), the book that catapulted him to the limelight of the growing environmental movement.

Desert Solitaire, and most of Abbey's subsequent works, assaulted the American government for its environmental policies while exalting the natural beauty of America's Southwest. Abbey became know as the ''angry young man'' of the environmental movement, a radical Thoreauvian figure whose adventures demonstrated the fulfillment that an individual might gain from nature if a commitment to protecting it exists. In 1975, Abbey published *The Monkey Wrench Gang,* a novel about environmental terrorists whose revolutionary plots to restore original ecology include blowing up the Glen Canyon Dam on the Colorado River. Even though its publisher did not promote it, the book became a best seller, an underground classic that inspired the formation of the radical environmentalist group ''Earth First!,'' whose policies reflect Abbey's ecological philosophy. The tactics Earth First! employs to prevent the development and deforestation of natural areas include sabotaging developers' chain saws and bulldozers, a practice that the group refers to as ''monkeywrenching.''

Abbey is the subject of a one-hour video documentary, *Edward Abbey: A Voice in the Wilderness* (1993), by Eric Temple which augments the continuing popularity of Abbey's writing. Abbey's novel, *Fire on the Mountain* (1962), was made into a motion picture in 1981. Quotations from his works have been imprinted on calendars throughout the 1990s. Devoted fans have created web pages to tell how Abbey's philosophy has influenced their lives. Even Abbey's death in 1989 has added to his legend; he is reportedly buried at a secret location in the Southwestern desert land that he praised. Though Abbey scoffed at the idea that his literature had the makings of American classics, his works and the personality they immortalized have remained a popular force in the environmental segment of American culture.

—Sharon Brown

FURTHER READING:

Abbey, Edward. *One Life at a Time, Please.* New York, H. Holt, 1988.

Bishop, James, Jr. *Epitaph for a Desert Anarchist: The Life and Legacy of Edward Abbey.* New York, Antheneum, 1994.

Edward Abbey

Foreman, Dave. *Confessions of an Eco-Warrior.* New York, Harmony Books, 1991.

McClintock, James. *Nature's Kindred Spirits: Aldo Leopold, Joseph Wood Krutch, Edward Abbey, Annie Dillard, and Gary Snyder.* Madison, University of Wisconsin Press, 1994.

Ronald, Ann. *The New West of Edward Abbey.* Albuquerque, University of New Mexico Press, 1982.

Abbott and Costello

One of the most popular comedy teams in movie history, Bud Abbott (1895-1974) and Lou Costello (1906-1959) began in burlesque and ended on television. Along the way, they sold millions of tickets (and war bonds), almost single-handedly saved Universal Pictures from bankruptcy, and made a legendary catch-phrase out of three little words: "Who's on first?" Straight man Abbott was the tall, slim, sometimes acerbic con artist; Costello was the short, pudgy, childlike patsy. Their unpretentious brand of knockabout comedy was the perfect tonic for a war-weary home front in the early 1940s. Though carefully crafted and perfected on the stage, their precision-timed patter routines allowed room for inspired bits of improvisation. Thanks to Abbott and Costello's films and TV shows, a wealth of classic burlesque sketches and slapstick tomfoolery has been preserved, delighting audiences of all ages and influencing new generations of comedians.

As it happens, both men hailed from New Jersey. William "Bud" Abbott was born October 2, 1895, in Asbury Park, but he grew up in Coney Island. Bored by school, and perhaps inspired by the hurly burly atmosphere of his home town, fourteen-year-old Abbott left home to seek a life in show business. The young man's adventures included working carnivals and being shanghaied onto a Norwegian freighter. Eventually landing a job in the box office of a Washington, D.C. theater, Abbott met and married dancer Betty Smith in 1918. He persisted for years in the lower rungs of show business, acting as straight man to many comics whose skills were not up to Abbott's high level. Louis Francis Cristillo was born in

Bud Abbott (left) and Lou Costello

Paterson, New Jersey, on March 6, 1906. As a child, he idolized Charlie Chaplin, and grew into a skillful basketball shooter. In 1927, he tried his luck in Hollywood, working his way at MGM from carpenter to stunt man, a job at which he excelled, until an injury forced him to quit the profession and leave California. Heading back east, he got as far as Missouri, where he talked his way into burlesque as a comedian. While the rest of the country suffered through the Depression, Lou Costello flourished in burlesque. In New York in 1934, he also married a dancer, Ann Battler.

When Abbott finally met Costello in the thirties, it was quickly apparent in their vaudeville act that each man had found in the other that ineffable quality every showbiz team needs: chemistry. Budding agent Eddie Sherman caught their act at Minsky's, then booked them into the Steel Pier at Atlantic City. (Sherman would remain their agent as long as they were a team.) The next big move for Abbott and Costello was an appearance on Kate Smith's radio program, for which they decided to perform a tried-and-true patter routine about Costello's frustration trying to understand Abbott's explanation of the nicknames used by the players on a baseball team.

Abbott: You know, they give ball-players funny names nowadays. On this team, Who's on first, What's on second, I Don't Know is on third.
Costello: That's what I want to find out. Who's on first?
Abbott: Yes.
Costello: I mean the fellow's name on first base.
Abbott: Who.

The boys and their baseball routine were such a sensation that they were hired to be on the show every week—and repeat "Who's on First?" once a month. When Bud and Lou realized that they would eventually run out of material, they hired writer John Grant to come up with fresh routines. Grant's feel for the special Abbott and Costello formula was so on target that, like Eddie Sherman, he also remained in their employ throughout their career. And what a career it was starting to become. After stealing the show from comedy legend Bobby Clark in *The Streets of Paris* on Broadway, Abbott and Costello graduated to their own radio program. There, they continued to contribute to the language they had already enriched with "Who's on first" by adding the catch phrases, "Hey-y-y-y-y, Ab-bott!" and "Oh—I'm a ba-a-a-d boy!" (For radio, Costello had adopted a childlike falsetto to distinguish his voice from Abbott's.)

Inevitably, Hollywood called, Abbott and Costello answered, and the result was 1940's *One Night in the Tropics*—"An indiscretion better overlooked," as Costello later called it. The comedy team was mere window dressing in this Jerome Kern operetta, but their next film put the boys center stage. 1941's *Buck Privates* had a bit of a boy-meets-girl plot, and a few songs from the Andrews Sisters, but this time the emphasis was clearly on Bud and Lou—and it was the surprise hit of the year. The boys naturally sparkled in their patented verbal routines, such as the "Clubhouse" dice game, while an army drill-training routine demonstrated Lou's gifts for slapstick and improvisation. Lou was overjoyed when his idol, Chaplin, praised him as the best clown since the silents. As for Universal, all they cared about was the box-office, and they were overjoyed, too. The studio rushed their new sensational comedy team into film after film (sometimes as many as four a year), and the public flocked to all of them: *In the Navy, Hold That Ghost, Ride'Em, Cowboy*, etc., etc. . . .

Compared to Laurel and Hardy, there was something rough and tumble about Abbott and Costello. It was like the difference between a symphony orchestra and a brass band. But clearly, Bud and Lou were playing the music the public wanted to hear. Once the war broke out, the government took advantage of the team's popularity to mount a successful war bond drive which toured the country and took in millions for defense.

As fast as Bud and Lou could earn their own money, they couldn't wait to spend it on lavish homes and dressing-room poker games. Amid the gags, high spirits, and big spending, there were also difficult times for the duo. They had a genuine affection for each other, despite the occasional arguments, which were quick to flare up, quick to be forgotten. But Lou inflicted a wound which Bud had a hard time healing when the comic insisted, at the height of their success, that their 50-50 split of the paycheck be switched to 60 percent for Costello and 40 percent for Abbott. Bud already had private difficulties of which the public was unaware; he was epileptic, and he had a drinking problem. As for Lou, he had a near-fatal bout of rheumatic fever which kept him out of action for many months. His greatest heartache, however, came on the day in 1943 when his infant son, Lou "Butch," Jr., drowned in the family swimming pool. When the tragedy struck, Lou insisted on going on with the team's radio show that night. He performed the entire show, then went offstage and collapsed. Costello subsequently started a charity in his son's name, but a certain sadness never left him.

On screen, Abbott and Costello were still riding high. No other actor, with the possible exception of Deanna Durbin, did as much to keep Universal Pictures solvent as Abbott and Costello. Eventually, however, the team suffered from overexposure, and when the war was over and the country's mood was shifting, the Abbott and Costello box office began to slip. Experimental films such as *The Time of Their Lives*, which presented Bud and Lou more as comic actors than as a comedy team per se, failed to halt the decline. But in the late forties, they burst back into the top money-making ranks with *Abbott and Costello Meet Frankenstein*, a film pairing the boys with such Universal horror stalwarts as Bela Lugosi's Dracula and Lon Chaney, Jr.'s Wolf Man. The idea proved inspired, the execution delightful; to this day, *Meet Frankenstein* is regarded as perhaps the best horror-spoof ever, with all due respect to *Ghostbusters* and *Young Frankenstein*. Abbott and Costello went on to *Meet the Mummy* and *Meet the Invisible Man*, and, when the team started running out of gas

again, they pitched their tent in front of the television cameras on *The Colgate Comedy Hour*. These successful appearances led to two seasons of *The Abbott and Costello Show*, a pull-out-the-stops sitcom which positively bordered on the surrealistic in its madcap careening from one old burlesque or vaudeville routine to another. On the show, Bud and Lou had a different job every week, and they were so unsuccessful at all of them that they were constantly trying to avoid their landlord, played by veteran trouper Sid Fields (who contributed to writing the show, in addition to playing assorted other characters). Thanks to the program, a new generation of children was exposed to such old chestnuts as the "Slowly I Turned. . ." sketch and the "hide the lemon" routine. One of those baby-boomers was Jerry Seinfeld, who grew up to credit *The Abbott and Costello Show* as the inspiration for his own NBC series, one of the phenomena of 1990s show business.

By the mid 1950s, however, the team finally broke up. It would be nice to be able to report that their last years were happy ones, but such was not the case. Both men were hounded by the IRS for back taxes, which devastated their finances. Lou starred in a lackluster solo comedy film, made some variety show guest appearances, and did a sensitive acting turn on an episode of TV's *Wagon Train* series, but in 1959 he suddenly died of a heart attack. Abbott lived for fifteen more years, trying out a new comedy act with Candy Candido, contributing his voice to an Abbott and Costello TV animation series, doing his own "straight acting" bit on an episode of *G.E. Theater*. Before he died of cancer in 1974, Abbott had the satisfaction of receiving many letters from fans thanking him for the joy he and his partner had brought to their lives.

In the 1940s, long before the animated TV show based on Bud and Lou, the Warner Bros. Looney Toons people had caricatured the boys as two cats out to devour Tweetie Bird. Already they had become familiar signposts in the popular culture. The number of comedians and other performers who have over the years paid homage to Abbott and Costello's most famous routine is impossible to calculate. In the fifties, a recording of Abbott and Costello performing "Who's on First" was placed in the Baseball Hall of Fame. This was a singular achievement, over and above the immortality guaranteed by the films in which they starred. How many other performers can claim to have made history in three fields—not only show business, but also sports and linguistics?

—Preston Neal Jones

FURTHER READING:

Costello, Chris. *Lou's on First.* New York, St. Martin's Press, 1981.

Cox, Stephen, and John Lofflin. *The Official Abbott and Costello Scrapbook.* Chicago, Contemporary Books, 1990.

Furmanek, Bob, and Ron Palumbo. *Abbott and Costello in Hollywood.* New York, Perigree Books, 1991.

Mulholland, Jim. *The Abbott and Costello Book.* New York, Popular Library, 1975.

Thomas, Bob. *Bud and Lou.* Philadelphia and New York, Lippincott, 1977.

Abdul-Jabbar, Kareem (1947—)

With an intensity that disguised his shyness and a dancing jump shot nicknamed the "sky hook," Kareem Abdul-Jabbar dominated

The Celtics' Greg Kite guards the Lakers' Kareem Abdul-Jabbar.

the National Basketball Association during the 1970s and 1980s. The seven-foot-two-inch center won three national collegiate championships at the University of California at Los Angeles (UCLA) and six professional championships with the Milwaukee Bucks and Los Angeles Lakers. He is the NBA's all-time leading scorer and was named the league's most valuable player a record six times. Beyond his athletic accomplishments, Jabbar also introduced a new level of racial awareness to basketball by boycotting the 1968 Olympic team, converting to Islam, and changing his name.

Abdul-Jabbar was born Ferdinand Lewis Alcindor in Harlem, New York, on April 16, 1947. His parents were both over six feet tall and Abdul-Jabbar reached six feet before the sixth grade. He attended a Catholic school in Inwood, a mixed middle-class section of Manhattan, and did not become aware of race until the third grade. Holding a black-and-white class photograph in his hand, he thought, "Damn I'm dark and everybody else is light." Able to dunk the basketball by the eighth grade, Abdul-Jabbar was highly recruited and attended Power Memorial Academy in New York. During Abdul-Jabbar's final three years of high school, Power lost only one game and won three straight Catholic league championships. He was named high school All-American three times and was the most publicized high school basketball player in the United States. The 1964 Harlem race riot was a pivotal event in Abdul-Jabbar's life, occurring the summer before his senior year. "Right then and there I knew who I was and who I was going to be," he wrote in *Kareem*. "I was going to be black rage personified, black power in the flesh."

Abdul-Jabbar accepted a scholarship from UCLA in 1965. Majoring in English, he studied in the newly emerging field of black

literature. As a freshman, Abdul-Jabbar worked on his basketball skills to overcome his awkwardness. He led the freshman squad to an undefeated season and a 75-60 victory over the varsity, which had won the national championship in two of the previous three years. In his second year, Abdul-Jabbar worked with coaching legend John Wooden, who emphasized strategy and conditioning in basketball. Abdul-Jabbar dominated the college game, averaging 29 points a game and leading the Bruins to an undefeated season. UCLA won the National Collegiate Athletic Association (NCAA) championship, defeating the University of Dayton. As a junior, Abdul-Jabbar developed jump and hook shots, averaging 26.2 points a game. He shut down University of Houston star Elvin Hayes in the NCAA semifinals before leading the Bruins to a victory over North Carolina. UCLA won a third consecutive national title during Adbul-Jabbar's senior year, and the young star was honored as the tournament's outstanding player for the third year in a row. "Alcindor has completely changed the aspect of the game. I saw great players actually afraid to shoot," said St. John's University coach Lou Carnesecca.

Abdul-Jabbar was the first pick in the professional draft of 1969 and went to the last-place Milwaukee Bucks. Averaging 28.8 points a game during his rookie season, Abdul-Jabbar led the Bucks to a 56-26 record, losing to the New York Knicks in the playoffs. Milwaukee play-by-play announcer Eddie Doucette coined the term "sky hook" for Abdul-Jabbar's trademark hook shot. During the off season, the Bucks obtained veteran Cincinnati Royals point guard Oscar Robertson, and the pair teamed up to help Milwaukee defeat the Baltimore Bullets for the 1971 NBA championship. Abdul-Jabbar was named the NBA's most valuable player and the playoff MVP. The Bucks returned to the finals in the 1973-74 season, but lost to the Boston Celtics. Robertson retired the following year and Abdul-Jabbar broke his hand on a backboard support. Milwaukee failed to make the playoffs.

Abdul-Jabbar made good on his promise to personify "black rage." Instead of starring in the 1968 Olympics, as he surely would have, he studied Islam with Hamaas Abdul-Khaalis. Abdul-Jabbar converted to the religion popular with many African Americans and changed his name to mean "generous powerful servant of Allah." Abdul-Khaalis arranged a marriage for Abdul-Jabbar in 1971 but the couple separated after the birth of a daughter two years later. Meanwhile, Abdul-Khaalis had been trying to convert black Muslims to traditional Islam. On January 18, 1973, a group of black Muslim extremists retaliated by invading a New York City townhouse owned by Abdul-Jabbar and killing Abdul-Khaalis' wife and children. Four years later, Abdul-Khaalis and some followers staged a protest in Washington, D.C. and a reporter was killed in the resulting disturbance. Abdul-Khaalis was sentenced to 40 years in prison with Abdul-Jabbar paying his legal expenses.

Feeling unfulfilled and conspicuous in the largely white, small-market city of Milwaukee, Abdul-Jabbar asked for a trade in 1975. He was sent to Los Angeles for four first-team players. Through the remainder of the 1970s, Abdul-Jabbar made the Lakers one of the NBA's top teams but even he wasn't enough to take the team to a championship alone. Angered by years of what he considered bullying by NBA opponents, Abdul-Jabbar was fined $5,000 in 1977 for punching Bucks center Kent Benson. In 1979, the Lakers drafted Earvin "Magic" Johnson, and the point guard gave Los Angeles the edge it needed. The Lakers won the NBA title over Philadelphia in 1980. Abdul-Jabbar broke his foot in the fifth game, was taped and returned to score 40 points, but watched the rest of the series on television. The Lakers won again in 1982, 1985, 1987, and 1988.

Abdul-Jabbar surpassed Wilt Chamberlain's all-time scoring record in 1984, eventually setting records for most points (38,387), seasons (20), minutes played (57,446), field goals made (15,837), field goals attempted (28,307), and blocked shots (3,189); he averaged 24.6 points a game before he retired at the age of 42 following the 1988-89 season. He held the record for most playoff points until surpassed by Michael Jordan in 1998. He was elected unanimously into the Basketball Hall of Fame in his first year of eligibility on May 15, 1995, and was named one of the 50 greatest basketball players in history to coincide with the NBA's 50th anniversary in 1996.

Abdul-Jabbar's personal life remained unsettled during and after his Los Angeles playing years. He was always uncomfortable with reporters, describing them as "scurrying around like cockroaches after crumbs." Fans, especially white, found it difficult to understand his conversion to Islam; his attitudes towards race; and his shy, introverted personality. Abdul-Jabbar's Islamic faith also estranged him from his parents, although they eventually reconciled. His Bel Air house was destroyed by fire on January 31, 1983, and the fire contributed to bankruptcy for the former NBA star four years later. Abdul-Jabbar wrote two autobiographical accounts, *Giant Steps* in 1983 and *Kareem* in 1990, and a children's collection, *Black Profiles in Courage: A Legacy of African-American Achievement,* in 1996. He acted in motion pictures and television including *Mannix*, *21 Jump Street*, *Airplane*, *Fletch*, and a 1994 Stephen King mini-series, *The Stand*. He was the executive producer of a made-for-television movie about civil rights pioneer Vernon Johns. He was arrested in 1997 for battery and false imprisonment following a traffic dispute and underwent anger-management counseling. He paid a $500 fine after drug-sniffing dogs detected marijuana in his possession at the Toronto airport the same year. He settled out of court with a professional football player in 1998 over a dispute involving the commercial use of his name.

Since his retirement, Abdul-Jabbar has made most of his living as a motivational speaker and doing product endorsements. He spends time with his five children, including his six-foot-six-inch namesake son who is a college basketball player. In the wake of former Boston Celtic Larry Bird's success as a head coach with the Indiana Pacers, Abdul-Jabbar embarked on an effort to return to the NBA by coaching high school boys on an Apache Reservation in Whiteriver, Arizona, learning to speak their language and writing another book in the process. The team's six-foot-six center remarked, "For the first time since I was little, I actually felt kind of small." "It's really a no-brainer for me," Abdul-Jabbar said. "Basketball is a simple game. My job [is to get] the guys ready to play."

—Richard Digby Junger

FURTHER READING:

Abdul-Jabbar, Kareem, and Peter Knobler. *Giant Steps: An Autobiography of Kareem Abdul-Jabbar.* New York, Bantam Books, 1983.

———, with Mignon McCarthy. *Kareem.* New York, Random House, 1990.

Bradley, John E. "Buffalo Soldier: In His Quest to Become an NBA Coach, Former Superstar Kareem Abdul-Jabbar Will Go Anywhere to Gain Experience." *Sports Illustrated.* November 30, 1998, 72.

Cart, Julie. "A Big Man, an Even Bigger Job: Friendship with a Tribal Elder Brought Kareem Abdul-Jabbar to the Fort Apache Reservation." *Los Angeles Times.* February 2, 1999, A1.

Gregory, Deborah. "Word Star: Kareem Abdul-Jabbar from Hoops to History." *Essence.* November 1996, 68.

Newman, Bruce. "Kareem Adbul-Jabbar's *Giant Steps* Is a Big Step into the Oven for Him." *Sports Illustrated.* December 26, 1983.

Wankoff, Jordan. "Kareem Abdul-Jabbar." *Contemporary Black Biography.* Vol. 8. Detroit, Gale Research, 1995.

Abortion

Abortion, or induced miscarriage, was one of the most controversial topics in the post-Civil War United States. Indeed, the rights an individual woman holds over her uterus seem to have been debated ever since the inception of such social institutions as religion and law. While some cultures have permitted or even encouraged selective termination of pregnancy—if, for example, the fetus turned out to be female when a family already had an ample supply of daughters; or if a woman was ill or not financially able to raise a child—in Western civilization, church and state traditionally forbade abortion and even contraceptive measures. If a woman was to be sexual, it seemed, she had to accept pregnancy and childbirth. Those opposed to abortion focused on the fetus and maintained that expelling it constituted the murder of a human being; the pro-abortion faction argued from the pregnant woman's perspective, saying that any woman had the right to choose elimination in case of risks to health or psyche, or if she simply did not feel ready to be a mother. Whatever opinions individuals might have held, by the end of the twentieth century the governments of almost all industrialized nations had stepped out of the debate; only in the United States did the availability of legal abortion remain the subject of political controversy, sparking demonstrations from both factions and even the bombing of abortion clinics and assassination of doctors.

Women seem to have had some knowledge of miscarriage-inducing herbs since prehistoric times, but that knowledge virtually disappeared during the medieval and Renaissance Inquisitions, when many midwives were accused of witchcraft and herbal lore was discredited. Thereafter, women of Western nations had to rely on furtive procedures by renegade doctors or self-accredited practitioners in back-street offices. Though exact statistics are difficult to calculate, in January 1942 the *New York Times* estimated that 100,000 to 250,000 illegal abortions were performed in the city every year. Pro-abortion doctors might use the latest medical equipment, but referrals were hard to get and appointments difficult to make; many women had to turn to the illegal practitioners, who might employ rusty coat hangers, Lysol, and other questionable implements to produce the desired results. The mortality and sterility rates among women who sought illegal abortions were high. Appalled by these dangerous conditions, activists such as Margaret Sanger (1883-1966) founded birth control clinics, fought for women's sexual health, and were often jailed for their trouble. Slowly evolving into organizations such as Planned Parenthood as they won government approval, however, such activists began distributing birth control and (in the

Anti-abortionists march in front of the United States Supreme Court on the 23rd anniversary of Roe v. Wade, 1996.

1970s) providing surgical abortions, which involved the dilation of the cervix and scraping or aspiration of the uterus. The mid-1990s saw the introduction of pharmaceutical terminations for early-term pregnancies; such remedies included a combination of methotrexate and misoprostol, or the single drug RU-486. At the end of the century, legal abortion was a safe minor procedure, considered much less taxing to a woman's body than childbirth.

Both parties in the abortion debate considered themselves to occupy a *pro* position—pro-life or pro-choice. Led by organizations such as Operation Rescue (founded 1988), the most extreme pro-lifers maintained that life begins at the moment of conception, that the smallest blastocyst has a soul, and that to willingly expel a fetus at any stage (even if the pregnancy is the result of rape or incest) is murder. Some argued that women considering abortion were mentally as well as morally deficient and should be taken in hand until their babies were born, at which time those infants could be adopted by deserving couples. The pro-choice faction, pointing out that many pro-lifers were also pro-death penalty, insisted that every woman had a right to decide what would happen to her own body. Extreme proponents

considered the fetus to be part of the mother until birth—thus asserted that aborting at any stage of pregnancy should be acceptable and legal.

Most people came down somewhere between the two extremes, and this moderate gray area was the breeding-ground for intense controversy. Arguments centered on one question: At what point did individual life begin? At conception, when the fetus started kicking, when the fetus could survive on its own, or at the moment of birth itself? The Catholic Church long argued for ensoulment at conception, while (in the landmark decision *Roe v. Wade*) the U.S. Supreme Court determined that for over a thousand years English common law had given women the right to abort a fetus before movement began. Even many pro-choicers separated abortion from the idea of or right to sexual freedom and pleasure; they felt abortion was to be used, as one scholar puts it, "eugenically," for the selective betterment of the race. Twentieth-century feminists, however, asserted a woman's right to choose sexual pleasure, motherhood, or any combination of the two; British activist Stella Browne gave the feminists their credo when, in 1935, she said, "Abortion must be the key to a new world for women, not a bulwark for things as they are, economically nor biologically. . . . It should be available for any woman without insolent inquisitions, nor ruinous financial charges, nor tangles of red tape. For our bodies are our own.'' Nonetheless, women who sought and underwent abortions in this era kept their experiences a secret, as tremendous shame attached to the procedure; a woman known to have had an abortion was often ostracized from polite society.

From December 13, 1971, to January 22, 1973, the U.S. Supreme Court considered a legal case that was to change the course of American culture. *Roe v. Wade,* the suit whose name is known to virtually every adult American, took the argument back to the Constitution; lawyers for Norma McCorvey (given the pseudonym Jane Roe) argued that Texan anti-abortion laws had violated her right to privacy as guaranteed in the First, Fourth, Fifth, Ninth, and Fourteenth Amendments. Texas district attorney Henry Wade insisted on the rights of the unborn ''person'' in utero. In its final decision, the Court announced it had ''inquired into . . . medical and medical-legal history and what that history reveals about man's attitudes toward the abortion procedure over the centuries''; religion, culturally imposed morals, and the ''raw edges of human existence'' were all factors. In the end, the Court astonished America by finding it ''doubtful that abortion was ever firmly established as a common-law crime even with respect to the destruction of a quick [moving] fetus.'' By a vote of seven to two, the justices eliminated nearly all state anti-abortion laws, and groups such as the National Abortion Rights Action League made sure the repeals were observed on a local level.

Right-to-lifers were incensed and renewed their social and political agitation. The Catholic Church donated millions of dollars to groups such as the National Right to Life Committee, and in 1979 Baptist minister Jerry Falwell established the Moral Majority, a ''pro-life, pro-family, pro-moral, and pro-American'' organization. Pressure from what came to be known as the New Right achieved a ban against Medicaid funding for abortions. Pro-lifers picketed clinics assiduously, shouting slogans such as ''Murderer—you are killing your baby!'', and sometimes eliminating abortionists before those workers could eliminate a fetus. There were 30 cases of anti-abortion bombing and arson in 1984, for example, and five U.S. abortion clinic workers were murdered between 1993 and 1994. U.S. President Ronald Reagan (in office 1981-1989) also got involved, saying abortion ''debases the underpinnings of our country''; in 1984 he wrote a book called *Abortion and the Conscience of the Nation.* Under President George Bush (in office 1989-1993), the Supreme Court found that a Missouri law prohibiting abortion in public institutions did not conflict with *Roe v. Wade*; consequently, some states renewed nineteenth-century anti-abortion laws.

During this agitation, proponents of choice noted that many pro-life politicians were also cutting welfare benefits—although many women (an estimated 20,000 in 1978) would not have been on the public rolls if they had been allowed access to low-cost abortions. These activists estimated that for every one dollar that might have been spent on a Medicaid-funded abortion, four dollars had to go to caring for mother and child in the first two years. They concluded that favoring capital punishment and welfare cuts, while forbidding women to terminate their own pregnancies, was both hypocritical and inconsistent—especially as many of the New Right refused to condemn the clinic bombings and doctor assassinations.

In the final decade of the century, the controversy still raged, though many politicians were trying to avoid the issue—a move that some pro-choicers saw as positive, expressing an uneasiness with traditional condemnations. Such politicians often said they would leave the decision up to individual doctors or law courts. Operation

Rescue workers claimed to have scored a major coup in 1995, when they managed to convert McCorvey herself (then working in a women's health clinic) to born-again Christianity; in a statement to the media, she said, ''I think I've always been pro-life, I just didn't know it.'' Less attention was granted to her more moderate assertion that she still approved of first-trimester abortion. Meanwhile activists from both sides tried to make abortion a personal issue for every American; bumper stickers, newspaper advertisements, billboards, and media-directed demonstrations became part of the daily landscape. Crying, ''If you don't trust me with a choice, how can you trust me with a child?'', pro-choicers organized boycotts against the purveyors of pizza and juice drinks who had donated money to Operation Rescue and other pro-life organizations; these boycotts were mentioned in mainstream movies such as 1994's *Reality Bites.* Eventually movie stars and other female celebrities also came out and discussed their own experiences with abortions both legal and illegal, hoping to ensure women's access to safe terminations. Thus abortion, once a subject to be discussed only in panicked whispers—and a procedure to be performed only in hidden rooms—had stepped into the light and become a part of popular culture.

—Susann Cokal

FURTHER READING:

Ciba Foundation Sympsium. *Abortion: Medical Progress and Social Implications.* London, Pitman, 1985.

Cook, Kimberly J. *Divided Passions: Public Opinions on Abortion and the Death Penalty.* Boston, Northeastern University Press, 1998.

Hadley, Janet. *Abortion: Between Freedom and Necessity.* Philadelphia, Temple University Press, 1996.

O'Connor, Karen. *No Neutral Ground?: Abortion Politics in an Age of Absolutes.* New York, Westview Press, 1996.

Riddle, John M. *Eve's Herbs: A History of Contraception and Abortion in the West.* Cambridge, Massachusetts, Harvard University Press, 1997.

Rudy, Kathy. *Beyond Pro-Life and Pro-Choice: Moral Diversity in the Abortion Debate.* Boston, Beacon Press, 1996.

Abstract Expressionism

The emergence of Abstract Expressionism in New York City during the late 1930s both shocked and titillated the cultural elite of the international art scene. Abstraction itself was nothing new—modernist painters had been regulating the viewer's eye to obscured images and distorted objects for quite some time. In fact, the bright, abstracted canvases and conceptual ideals of high modernist painters such as Joan Miro and Wassily Kandinsky tremendously influenced the Abstract Expressionists. What distinguished the movement from its contemporaries, and what effectively altered the acceptable standards of art, was the artists' absolute disregard for some kind of ''objective correlative'' that a viewer could grasp in attempt to understand the work. The central figures of Abstract Expressionism—Jackson Pollock, Mark Rothko, Willem de Kooning, Robert Motherwell, and Clyfford Still, among others—completely rejected any kind of traditional thematic narrative or naturalistic representation of objects as valid artistic methods. Rather, they focused on the stroke and movement of the brush and on the application of color to the canvas; the act of painting itself became a vehicle for the spontaneous and spiritual expression of the artist's unconscious mind. Pollock's method of "drip painting," or "all over painting" as some critics call it, involved spontaneous and uncalculated sweeping motions of his arm. He would set his large canvas on the floor and, using sticks and caked paintbrushes, would rhythmically fling paint at it. The act of painting became an art form in itself, like a dance. Under the rubric of Abstract Expressionism, colorfield painters like Rothko would layer one single color plane above another on a large surface, achieving a subtly glowing field of color that seems to vibrate or dance on the one dimensional canvas. The artists hoped that, independent of the formal language of traditional art, they would convey some kind of sublime, essential truth about humanity.

Interestingly, as a result of the highly subjective nature of the work, Abstract Expressionist painters actually negated "the subject matter of common experience." Rather, the artist turned to "the medium of his own craft," to the singular, aesthetic experience of painting itself. As art critic Clement Greenberg wrote in the seminal essay "Avant-garde and Kitsch," the very "expression" of the artist became more important than what was expressed. *The Partisan Review* published Greenberg's "Avant-garde and Kitsch" in 1939, and it was quickly adopted as a kind of manifesto for Abstract Expressionism. In the essay, Greenberg unapologetically distinguishes between an elite ruling class that supports and appreciates the avant-garde, and the Philistine masses, an unfortunate majority that has always been "more or less indifferent to culture," and has become conditioned to kitsch. Greenberg defines kitsch as a synthetic art that merely imitates life, while the avant-garde seeks "to imitate God by creating something valid in its own terms, in the way that nature itself is valid . . . independent of meanings, similars or originals." The Abstract Expressionist work, with a content that cannot be extracted from its form, answers Greenberg's call for an avant-garde "expression" in and of itself. The transcendentalist nature of an Abstract Expressionist painting, with neither object nor subject other than that implicit in its color and texture, reinforces Greenberg's assertion that the avant-garde *is* and *should be* difficult. Its inaccessibility serves as a barrier between the masses who will dismiss the work, and the cultured elite who will embrace it.

However valid or invalid Greenberg's claims in "Avant-garde and Kitsch" may be, inherent in the essay is a mechanism ensuring the allure of Abstract Expressionism. In the same way that the emperor's fabled new clothes won the admiration of a kingdom afraid to *not* see them, Abstract Expressionism quickly found favor with critics, dealers, collectors, and other connoisseurs of cultural capital, who did not wish to exclude themselves from the kind of elite class that would appreciate such a difficult movement. When *New York Times* art critic John Canaday published an article in 1961 opposed not only to Abstract Expressionism, but also to the critical reverence it had won, the newspaper was bombarded with over 600 responses from the artistic community, the majority of which bitterly attacked Canaday's judgement, even his sanity. Most art magazines and academic publications simply did not print material that questioned the validity or quality of a movement that the art world so fervently defended. By 1948, even *Life* magazine, ironically the most "popular" publication in the nation at the time, jumped on the bandwagon and ran a lengthy, illustrated piece on Abstract Expressionism.

While the enormous, vibrant canvases of Pollock, Rothko, and others certainly warranted the frenzy of approval and popularity they received, their success may also have been due to post-war U.S. patriotism, as well as to the brewing McCarthy Era of the 1950s. New

York City became a kind of nucleic haven for post-war exiles and émigrés from Europe, a melange of celebrities from the European art world among them. Surrealists Andre Breton and Salvador Dali, for example, arrived in New York and dramatically affected the young Abstract Expressionists, influencing their work with psychoanalysis. The immigration of such men, however, not only impacted the artistic circles, but also changed the cultural climate of the entire city. The birth of Abstract Expressionism in New York announced to the world that the United States was no longer a cultural wasteland and empire of kitsch, whose artists and writers would expatriate in order to mature and develop in their work. Thus the art world marketed and exploited Abstract Expressionism as *the* movement that single-handedly transformed America's reputation for cultural bankruptcy and defined the United States as a cultural as well as a political leader. Furthermore, as critic Robert Hughes writes, by the end of the 1950s Abstract Expressionism was encouraged by the "American government as a symbol of American cultural freedom, in contrast to the state-repressed artistic speech of Soviet Russia." What could be a better representation of democracy and capitalism than a formally and conceptually innovative art form that stretches all boundaries of art, and meets with global acclaim and unprecedented financial rewards?

Politics aside, of paramount importance in the discussion of this art movement is the realization that, more than any other art movement that preceded it, Abstract Expressionism changed the modern perception of and standards for art. As colorfield painter Alfred Gottleib wrote in a letter to a friend after Jackson Pollock's death in 1956: "neither Cubism nor Surrealism could absorb someone like myself; we felt like derelicts. . . . Therefore one had to dig inside one's self, excavate what one could, and if what came out did not seem to be art by accepted standards, so much the worse for those standards."

—Taly Ravid

FURTHER READING:

Chilvers, Ian, editor. *The Concise Oxford Dictionary of Art and Artists, Second Edition.* Oxford and New York, Oxford University Press, 1996.

Craven, Wayne. *American Art: History and Culture.* New York, Brown and Benchmark Publishers, 1994.

Hughes, Robert. *American Visions: The Epic History of Art in America.* New York, Alfred A. Knopf, 1997.

———. *The Shock of the New.* New York, Alfred A. Knopf, 1991.

Shapiro, Cecile, and David Shapiro. *Abstract Expressionism: A Critical Record.* Cambridge and New York, Cambridge University Press, 1990.

Academy Awards

Hollywood's biggest party—the Academy Awards—is alternately viewed as shameless self-promotion on the part of the movie industry and as glamour incarnate. Sponsored by the Academy of Motion Picture Arts and Sciences, the Academy Awards annually honor excellence in film. Although it has been said that the ceremony is merely a popularity contest, winning an Oscar still represents a significant change in status for the recipient. After more than 70 years

Kevin Costner at the Academy Awards ceremony in 1991.

of Academy Awards ceremonies, the event has been criticized as having become a self-congratulatory affair that gives Hollywood a yearly excuse to show off to a global televised audience of millions. But no one can deny that when Hollywood's stars don designer clothes and jewelry, the world turns up to watch, proving that star power and glamour are still the essence of American popular culture.

The Academy of Motion Picture Arts and Sciences (AMPAS) was the brainchild of Metro Golwyn Mayer (MGM) mogul Louis B. Mayer. In the late 1920s the motion picture industry was in a state of flux. Experiments being conducted with sound threatened the demise of silent pictures, even as the scandals which had rocked the industry in the early 1920s brought cries for government censorship. Additionally, Hollywood was seeking to unionize and, in 1926, the Studio Basic Agreement was signed, unionizing stagehands, musicians, electricians, carpenters, and painters. The major talent, however, still remained without bargaining power.

In this restive atmosphere, Louis B. Mayer proposed to create an organization that would bring together representatives from all the major branches of the movie industry in an effort to promote both progress and harmony. Thirty-six people attended the first meeting in January, 1928, including actress Mary Pickford, designer Cedric Gibbons, director John Stahl, producers Joseph Schenck and Louis B. Mayer, and actor Douglas Fairbanks, who became the first president of AMPAS. Six months later, an organizational banquet was held at the Biltmore Hotel, where 231 new members joined. During the next year, the new organization formed various committees, one of which sought to create an award that would honor excellence in the motion picture industry.

The first Academy Awards ceremony was held at the Hollywood Roosevelt Hotel on May 16, 1929. It took Academy president Douglas Fairbanks five minutes to hand out all the awards. Janet Gaynor and Emil Jannings were named Best Actress and Best Actor while *Wings* won Best Picture. The ceremony was brief and unspectacular. Janet Gaynor professed to have been equally thrilled to receive the award as to have met Douglas Fairbanks. The local and national media ignored the event completely.

Each winner received a small, gold-plated statuette of a knight holding a crusader's sword, standing on a reel of film whose five spokes represented the five branches of the Academy. The statuette quickly earned the nickname Oscar, although the source of the nickname has never been pinpointed; some say that Mary Pickford thought it looked like her Uncle Oscar, while others credit Bette Davis, columnist Sidney Skolsky, or Academy librarian and later executive director Margaret Herrick with the remark. Whatever the source, the award has since been known as an Oscar.

By 1930, the motion picture industry had converted to talkies, and the Academy Awards reflected the change in its honorees, signifying the motion picture industry's acceptance of the new medium. Silent stars such as Great Garbo, Gloria Swanson, and Ronald Coleman, who had successfully made the transition to talkies, were honored with Oscar nominations.

It was also during the 1930s that the Academy Awards began to receive press coverage. Once a year, an eager nation awaited the morning paper to discover the big Oscar winners. The decade saw the first repeat Oscar winner in actress Luise Rainer; the first film to win eight awards in *Gone with the Wind*; the first African-American recipient in Hattie McDaniel as best supporting actress for *Gone with the Wind*; and the first honorary statuettes awarded to child stars Judy Garland, Deanna Durbin, and Mickey Rooney.

In the 1940s, the Academy Awards were broadcast by radio for the first time, and Masters of Ceremonies included popular comedians and humorists such as Bob Hope, Danny Kaye, and Will Rogers. With a national audience, the Oscar ceremony, which had alternated annually between the banquet rooms of the Biltmore and Ambassador Hotels, moved to legitimate theaters such as the Pantages, the Santa Monica Civic Auditorium, and later the Shrine and the Dorothy Chandler Pavilion. No longer a banquet, the Oscars became a show— in 1936, AMPAS had hired the accounting firm of Price Waterhouse to tabulate votes, thus ensuring secrecy; in 1940, sealed envelopes were introduced to heighten the drama.

In 1945, the Oscars were broadcast around the world on ABC and Armed Forces radio, becoming an international event. With each passing year, the stars, who had first attended the banquets in suits and simple dresses, became more glamorous. The women now wore designer gowns and the men tuxedos. Additionally, each year the Oscars featured new hype. In 1942, sisters Joan Fontaine and Olivia de Havilland were both nominated for best actress. Fontaine won that year, but when the same thing happened four years later de Havilland had her turn and publicly spurned her sister at the ceremony. The press gleefully reported the feud between the two sisters, who never appeared together in public again. Rivalries were often played up between nominees, whether they were real or not. In 1955, for example, it was the veteran Judy Garland versus the new golden girl, Grace Kelly.

In 1953, the Oscars were televised for the first time. As the audience grew each year, the Oscar ceremony became a very public platform for the playing out of Hollywood dramas. In 1957, audiences eagerly awaited Ingrid Bergman's return from her exile to Europe. In

1972, Hollywood publicly welcomed back one of their most legendary performers, a man whom they had forced into exile during the McCarthy era, when Charlie Chaplin was awarded an honorary Oscar. And since the establishment of special awards such as the Irving G. Thalberg Memorial Award, considered the highest honor a producer can receive, and the Jean Hersholt Humanitarian Award, each year the Oscars honor lifetime achievement in a moving ceremony. Recipients of these special awards, often Hollywood veterans and audience favorites such as Henry Fonda and Jimmy Stewart, generally evoke tears and standing ovations.

Although the Academy Awards purport to be non-partisan, politics have always crept into the ceremony. In 1964, Sidney Poitier was the first African-American recipient of a major award, winning Best Actor for *Lilies of the Field.* In a country divided by the events of the civil rights movement, Hollywood showed the world where it stood. In 1972, Marlon Brando refused to accept his Oscar for Best Actor for *The Godfather,* instead sending Sacheen Littlefeather to make a proclamation about rights for Native Americans. When it was revealed that Miss Littlefeather was in fact Maria Cruz, the former Miss Vampire USA, the stunt backfired. In 1977, Vanessa Redgrave ruffled feathers around the world when she used her acceptance speech for best supporting actress in *Julia* to make an anti-Zionist statement. That, however, has not stopped actors such as Richard Gere and Alec Baldwin from speaking out against the Chinese occupation of Tibet in the 1990s.

Every March, hundreds of millions of viewers tune in from around the world to watch the Academy Awards. The tradition of having a comedic Master of Ceremonies has continued with Johnny Carson, David Letterman, Whoopi Goldberg, and Billy Crystal. Each year the ceremony seems more extravagant, as Hollywood televises its image around the globe. Academy president and two-time Oscar winner Bette Davis once wrote that ''An Oscar is the highest and most cherished of honors in a world where many honors are bestowed annually. The fact that a person is recognized and singled out by those who are in the same profession makes an Oscar the most coveted award for all of us.'' Although popular culture is now riddled with awards shows, the excitement of watching the world's most glamorous people honor their own has made the Academy Awards the Grande Dame of awards ceremonies and a perennial audience favorite.

—Victoria Price

FURTHER READING:

Academy of Motion Picture Arts and Sciences. ''Academy Awards: Academy of Motion Picture Arts and Sciences.'' http://www.oscars.org/awards/indexawards.html. September 11, 1998.

Osborne, Robert. *The Years with Oscar at the Academy Awards.* California: ESE, 1973.

Shale, Richard, editor. *Academy Awards: An Ungar Reference Index.* New York, Frederick Ungar Publishing, 1982.

AC/DC

The Australian rock group AC/DC appeared on the international music scene in 1975 with their first U.S. release, *High Voltage.* Their songs were deeply rooted in the blues and all about sexual adventure. By the end of the decade, they had a solid reputation in the United

Angus Young of AC/DC.

States and Europe as one of the best hard rock concert bands in the world. *Back in Black* marked their breakthrough release, the number two album in the United States in 1980, and the beginning of a decade of largely uninterrupted success.

Throughout their career, AC/DC lived up to their credo of living hard, fast, and simple. This lifestyle is typified in the song ''Rocker'': ''I'm a rocker, I'm a roller, I'm a right out of controller/ I'm a wheeler, I'm a dealer, I'm a wicked woman stealer/ I'm a bruiser, I'm a cruiser, I'm a rockin' rollin' man.'' The brothers Angus and Malcolm Young, Australians of Scottish descent, began AC/DC in the early 1970s. Discovered by American promoters, they first made a name for themselves opening for hard rock legends, Black Sabbath and Kiss.

Their music and stage show was built around the virtuoso solos and the schoolboy looks of Angus Young. He pranced, sweated profusely, rolled on the stage, and even mooned audiences mid-chord. AC/DC backed up their hedonistic tales in their lives off-stage. In 1979, Bon Scott, their first singer, was found dead in the backseat of a friend's car after drinking too much and choking on his own vomit. His death came soon after the release of the band's best-selling album at the time, *Highway to Hell* (1979). Whether they appreciated the irony of the album or not, fans began to believe in AC/DC's self-proclaimed role as rock n' roll purists. They also bought *Back in Black,* the first album to feature Scott's replacement, Brian Johnson, at a feverish pace. The title track and ''You Shook Me All Night Long'' would become college party standards. Johnson's voice was abrasive, his look blue-collar, and the band took off with Johnson and Angus at the helm. *Back in Black* also benefitted from the slick influence of young producer Mutt Lange, who would go on to produce many Heavy Metal bands in the 1980s and 1990s. AC/DC followed up *Back in Black* with *Dirty Deeds Done Dirt Cheap,* a collection of unreleased Bon Scott pieces that also proved successful. The band spent the next ten years selling almost anything they released, and heading many of the "Monsters of Rock" summer tours popular at the time.

However, AC/DC did experience their share of problems along the way. When serial killer Richard Ramirez, the Los Angeles Nightstalker, was convicted in 1989, it was quickly publicized that he was a fanatic follower of AC/DC. In 1991, three fans were crushed at an AC/DC concert in Salt Lake City. AC/DC managed to weather the controversy quietly, continuing to produce loud blues-rock and play a demanding concert schedule throughout the 1990s. While often regarded as part of the 1980s heavy metal genre, AC/DC never resorted to the outlandish spike-and-leather costumes or science-fiction themes of many of their contemporaries, and may have had a more lasting impact on popular music as a result. AC/DC reinforced the blues roots of all rock genres, keeping bass and drum lines simple and allowing for endless free-form solos from Angus Young. Young carried the torch of the guitar hero for another generation—his antics and youthful charisma made him more accessible than many of his somber guitar-playing colleagues.

With songs such as "Love at First Feel" and "Big Balls," and lyrics like "knocking me out with those American thighs," and "I knew you weren't legal tender/ But I spent you just the same," AC/DC reaffirmed the eternal role of rock n' roll: titillating adolescents while frightening their parents. AC/DC refused all attempts to analyze and categorize their music, claiming over and over that "Rock n' Roll ain't no pollution/ Rock n' Roll is just Rock n' Roll." Longer hair and more explicit language notwithstanding, these Australian rockers were really just singing about the same passions that had consumed Jerry Lee Lewis, Little Richard, and their screaming teenage fans.

—Colby Vargas

FURTHER READING:

Done, Malcolm. *AC/DC: The Kerrang! Files!: The Definitive History.* New York, Virgin Publishing, 1995.

Putterford, Mark. *AC/DC; Shock to the System, the Illustrated Biography.* New York, Omnibus, 1992.

Ace, Johnny (1929-1954)

On Christmas day, 1954, backstage at the Civic Auditorium in Houston, Texas, blues balladeer, songwriter, and pianist Johnny Ace flirted with death and lost, shooting himself in the head while playing Russian roulette. Ace was at the peak of his brief musical career. In two years, he had scored six hits, two of them reaching number one on the *Billboard* R&B chart, and *Cash Box* magazine had named him the "Top Rhythm and Blues Singer of 1953." Shocked by his violent death, Ace's fans and his colleagues in the music industry searched for an explanation. The musician had everything to live for, yet made his demise his legacy. While no one will ever know why he committed suicide, his plaintive melodies and vocal delivery conjure associations filled with pathos.

Ace's musical style, like that of many other Rhythm and Blues artists, was eclectic, drawing from both church and secular contexts and embracing blues, jazz, gospel, hymns, and popular songs. He was, however, first and foremost a blues balladeer whose effectively sorrowful baritone earned the description of "the guy with a tear in his voice." His piano technique was limited, but his strength lay in his abilities as a songwriter and vocalist, and his compositions were memorable. He generally used a repeated pattern of simple motifs that made retention easy for his listening audience, many of whom were teenagers. Ace's hits were sad, beautiful, touching songs that held his listeners and caused them to ponder life. While he could sing the straight 12-bar blues, this was not his forte. He was a convincing blues balladeer, and it was this genre that clearly established his popularity and his reputation. Ace's blues ballads borrowed the 32-bar popular song form, and were sung in an imploring but softly colloquial style in the tradition of California-based blues singer and pianist Charles Brown.

John Marshall Alexander was born on June 9, 1929 in Memphis, Tennessee. The son of the Rev. and Mrs. John Alexander Sr., Johnny Ace sang in his father's church as a child. He entered the navy in World War II, and after returning to Memphis began to study the piano and guitar. By 1949, he had joined the Beale Streeters, a group led by blues vocalist and guitarist B. B. King and which, at various times, included Bobby Bland, Roscoe Gordon, and Earl Forest. The Beale Streeters gained considerable experience touring Tennessee and neighboring states, and when King left the group, he charged young Ace as leader. John Mattis, a DJ at radio station WDIA in Memphis who is credited with discovering Ace, arranged a recording session at which Ace sang, substituting for Bobby "Blue" Bland, who allegedly couldn't remember the lyrics to the planned song. Ace and Mattis hurriedly wrote a composition called "My Song," and recorded it. While it was a technically poor recording with an out-of-tune piano, "My Song" was an artistic and commercial success, quickly becoming a number one hit and remaining on the R&B chart for 20 weeks. The song employed the popular 32-bar form that remained the formula for a number of Ace's later compositions.

Ace signed with Duke Records, which was one of the first black-owned independent record companies to expose and promote gospel and rhythm and blues to a wider black audience. They released Ace's second record, "Cross My Heart," which featured him playing the organ in a gospel style, with Johnny Otis's vibra-harp lending a sweet, blues-inspired counter melody to Ace's voice. Again, this was a recording of poor technical quality, but it was well received, and climbed to number three on the R&B chart. The musician toured as featured vocalist with his band throughout the United States, doing one nighters and performing with Willie Mae "Big Mama" Thornton, Charles Brown, and Bobby Bland, among others. Ace made several other hit records, such as the chart-topping "The Clock"—on which he accompanied himself on piano with a wistful melodic motif in response to his slow-tempo vocal—and the commercially successful "Saving My Love," "Please Forgive Me," and "Never Let Me Go." This last, given a memorable arrangement and superb accompaniment from Otis's vibes, was the most jazz-influenced and musically significant of Ace's songs, recalling the work of Billy Eckstine.

Two further recordings, "Pledging My Love" and "Anymore" (the latter featured in the 1998 film *Eve's Bayou*), were Ace's posthumous hits. Ironically, "Pledging My Love" became his biggest crossover success, reaching number 17 on the pop chart. The Late, Great Johnny Ace, who influenced California blues man Johnny Fuller and the Louisiana "swamp rock" sound, made largely poignant music which came to reflect his fate—that of a sad and lonely man, whose gentle songs were unable to quell his inner tension or prevent his tragic end.

—Willie Collins

FURTHER READING:

Hildebrand, Lee. *Stars of Soul and Rhythm and Blues: Top Recording Artists and Showstopping Performers from Memphis to Motown to Now.* New York, BillBoard Books, 1994.

Tosches, Nick. *Unsung Heroes of Rock 'n' Roll: The Birth of Rock in the Wild Years before Elvis.* New York, Harmony Books, 1991.

Salem, James M. *The Late, Great Johnny Ace and the Transition from R & B to Rock 'n' Roll.* Urbana, University of Illinois Press, 1999.

Acker, Kathy (1948-1997)

In a process she described as "piracy," Kathy Acker appropriated the plots and titles of works such as *Treasure Island, Great Expectations,* and *Don Quixote* and rewrote them in her own novels to reflect a variety of feminist, political, and erotic concerns. Critics and readers praised these techniques, but after she took a sex scene from a Harold Robbins novel and reworked it into a political satire, Robbins threatened to sue her publisher. When her publisher refused to support her, Acker was forced to make a humiliating public apology. Although her work is marked by an insistence that individual identity is both socially constructed and inherently fragmented, Acker herself became perhaps the most recognizable member of the literary avant-garde since William S. Burroughs, whose work she deeply admired.

—Bill Freind

FURTHER READING:

Friedman, Ellen G. "A Conversation with Kathy Acker." *Review of Contemporary Fiction,* Vol. 9, No. 3, 1989, 12-22.

Acupuncture

While acupuncture has been a successful Chinese medical treatment for over 5,000 years, it was not well known to the general U.S. public until the early 1970s, when President Nixon reopened relationships with China. Acupuncture was first met with skepticism, both by the U.S. public at large and the conventional American Medical Association. Slowly, Americans and other western countries began to conduct studies, sometimes in conjunction with the Chinese, about the efficacy of acupuncture. Certain types of acupuncture, particularly for pain management and drug related addictions, were easily translated into western medical theory and could be easily learned and used by western doctors. Thus, the idea of using some acupuncture gained mainstream acceptance. As this acceptance grew, so did the use of acupuncture and Chinese medical theories and methods, at least amongst the numbers of people open to "alternative" medicine. By the 1990s, despite initial scientific skepticism,

acupuncture became one of the most accepted "alternative" medicines in the United States, used to varying degrees by AMA physicians and licensed Chinese doctors, and accepted on some levels by health and government institutions.

Acupuncture theory purports that the body has an energy force called Qi ("chee") that runs through pathways, called meridians. Qi involves not only the physical, but also spiritual, intellectual, and emotional aspects of people. When the flow of Qi is disrupted for any reason, ill-health ensues. To get the Qi flowing smoothly and health restored, points along the meridians are stimulated either by acupuncture (very fine needles), moxibustion (burning herbs over the points), or acupressure (using massage on the points). Often, these three methods are used together. The concept of Qi is also used in other medical and spiritual philosophies, and was broadly used in the "New Age" theories of the 1980s and 1990s, which helped popularize acupuncture and vice versa.

Acupuncture began to be used in the United States primarily for pain relief and prevention for ailments including backaches, headaches, arthritic conditions, fibromylgia, and asthmatic conditions. Because the type of acupuncture used for these ailments was easy to learn and adapt to western medicine, it was more quickly accepted. The introduction of acupuncture in the United States sparked interest by western medical researchers to gain a more complete understanding of traditional Chinese medicine and to learn why, in western terms, acupuncture "works." Theories soon abounded and those couched in western terms further popularized acupuncture. A study by Canadian Dr. Richard Chen, for instance, found that acupuncture produces a large amount of cortisol, the body's "natural" cortisone, a pain killer. In 1977, Dr. Melzach, a noted physician in the field of pain, found that western medicine's trigger points, used to relieve pain, correspond with acupuncture points.

Methods of acupuncture that became common in western culture were ones that seemed "high-tech," were (partially or mostly) developed within western culture, or developed in contemporary times, such as Electro-acupuncture and Auricular acupuncture. Electro-acupuncture, often used for pain relief or prevention, administers a small amount of electric power with various frequencies to send small electrical impulses through an acupuncture needle. Electro-acupuncture was first reported successfully used as an anesthesia for a tonsillectomy in China in 1958, and the Chinese thereafter have used it as a common surgical anesthesia. Doctors at Albert Einstein Medical Center and Northville State Hospital successfully conducted surgeries using Electro-acupuncture as an anesthesia between 1971 and 1972. Contemporary Auricular acupuncture, or ear acupuncture, developed largely outside China in France in the 1950s. It started becoming popular in the United States mostly for treating addictions like cigarette smoking, alcoholism, and drug addiction.

By the 1980s, the popularity of acupuncture supported the establishment of many U.S. schools teaching acupuncture within a "Traditional Chinese Medicine" degree. Approximately sixty such schools existed by the late 1990s. A quasi-governmental peer review group recognized by the U.S. Department of Education and by the Commission on Recognition of Postsecondary Accreditation, called ACAOM (Accreditation Commission for Acupuncture and Oriental Medicine) was devoted specifically to accrediting schools of Traditional Chinese Medicine. Many states licensed acupuncturists and doctors of Traditional Chinese Medicine, while some states would allow only American Medical Association physicians to practice acupuncture.

Acupuncture also gained broader acceptance by the government and health institutions in the 1990s. The World Health Organization (WHO) estimated that there were approximately 10,000 acupuncture specialists in the United States and approximately 3,000 practicing acupuncturists who were physicians. In 1993 the Food and Drug Administration (FDA) reported that Americans were spending $500 million per year and making approximately 9 to 12 million patient visits for acupuncture treatments. A few years later, the FDA lifted their ban of acupuncture needles being considered ''investigational devices.'' In late 1997, the National Institute of Health announced that ''. . . there is clear evidence that needle acupuncture treatment is effective for postoperative and chemotherapy nausea and vomiting, nausea of pregnancy, and postoperative dental pain . . . there are a number of other pain-related conditions for which acupuncture may be effective as an adjunct therapy, an acceptable alternative, or as part of a comprehensive treatment program.'' In late 1998, the prestigious and often conservative Journal of the American Medical Association published an article agreeing that acupuncture, as well as other alternative therapies, can be effective for certain disease management. This admission from the AMA was a sign of how far acupuncture and Chinese medicine had been accepted in ''popular culture''— if the AMA had accepted acupuncture under certain conditions, then the general public certainly had accepted it to a much greater extent.

—tova stabin

FURTHER READING:

Bischko, Johannes. *An Introduction to Acupuncture.* 2nd ed. Heidelberg, Germany, Karl F. Haug, 1985.

Butler, Kurt. *A Consumer's Guide to ''Alternative Medicine'': A Close Look at Homeopathy, Acupuncture, Faith-healing, and Other Unconventional Treatments.* Buffalo, New York, Prometheus Books, 1992.

Cargill, Marie. *Acupuncture: A Viable Medical Alternative.* Westport, Connecticut, Praeger, 1994.

Cunningham, M. J. *East & West: Acupuncture, An Alternative to Suffering.* Huntington, West Virginia, University Editions, 1993.

Dale, Ralph Alan. *Dictionary of Acupuncture: Terms, Concepts and Points.* North Miami Beach, Florida, Dialectic Publishing, 1993.

Firebrace, Peter, and Sandra Hill. *Acupuncture: How It Works, How It Cures.* New Canaan, Connecticut, Keats, 1994.

Mann, Felix. *Acupuncture: The Ancient Chinese Art of Healing and How It Works Scientifically.* New York, Vintage Books, 1973.

Tinterow, Maurice M. *Hypnosis, Acupuncture and Pain: Alternative Methods for Treatment.* Wichita, Kansas, Bio-Communications Press, 1989.

Tung, Ching-chang; translation and commentary by Miriam Lee. *Tung shih chen chiu cheng ching chi hsüeh hsüeh/Master Tong's Acupuncture: An Ancient Alternative Style in Modern Clinical Practice.* Boulder, Colorado, Blue Poppy Press, 1992.

Adams, Ansel (1902-1984)

Photographer and environmentalist Ansel Adams is legendary for his landscapes of the American Southwest, and primarily Yosemite State Park. For his images, he developed the zone system of photography, a way to calculate the proper exposure of a photograph by rendering the representation into a range of ten specific gray tones. The resulting clarity and depth were characteristic of the photographs produced by the group f/64, an association founded by Adams and fellow photographers Edward Weston and Imogen Cunningham. Adams' other important contribution in the development of photography as an artform was his key role in the founding of the Museum of Modern Art's department of photography with curator Beaumont Newhall. Adams' timeless photographs are endlessly in reproduction for calendars and posters, making his images instantaneously recognizable. Ansel Adams has become one of the most popular and familiar of photographers.

—Jennifer Jankauskas

FURTHER READING:

Adams, Ansel, with Mary Street Alinder. *Ansel Adams: An Autobiography.* Boston, Little, Brown, 1985.

Read, Michael, editor. *Ansel Adams, New Light: Essays on His Legacy and Legend.* San Francisco, The Friends of Photography, 1993.

Adams, Scott

See Dilbert

Addams, Jane (1860-1935)

Born in Illinois, Jane Addams is remembered as an influential social activist and feminist icon; she was the most prominent member of a notable group of female social reformers who were active during the first half of the twentieth century. Foremost among her many accomplishments was the creation of Hull House in Chicago. Staff from this settlement provided social services to the urban poor and successfully advocated for a number of social and industrial reforms. An ardent pacifist, Addams was Chair of The Woman's Peace Party and President of the International Congress of Women; she was also the first woman to receive the Nobel Peace Prize (1931). Addams supported women's suffrage, Prohibition, and was a founding member of the ACLU (American Civil Liberties Union). Her writings include the widely read, autobiographical *Twenty Years at Hull House.* Unmarried, Addams had romantic friendships with several women. She is the ''patron'' saint of social workers and a symbol of indefatigable social activism on the part of women.

—Yolanda Retter

FURTHER READING:

Diliberto, Gioia. *A Useful Woman: The Early Life of Jane Addams.* New York, Scribner, 1999.

Hovde, Jane. *Jane Addams.* New York, Facts on File, 1989.

Linn, James Weber. *Jane Addams: A Biography.* New York, Appleton-Century, 1936.

Jane Addams holding a peace flag, and Mary McDowell holding an American flag.

The Addams Family

For years, beginning in the 1930s, cartoonist Charles Addams delighted readers of the *New Yorker* with his macabre graphic fantasies. Among his most memorable creations was a ghoulish brood known as the Addams Family. On television and film, the creepy, kooky clan has seemed determined to live on in popular culture long after its patriarch departed the earthly plane in 1988.

Like all of Addams's work, the Addams Family feature played off the identification the audience made with the characters. In many ways, the Addams clan—father, mother, two children, and assorted relatives (all unnamed)—were like a typical American family. But their delight in their own fiendishness tickled the inner ghoul in everyone. In one of Addams's most famous cartoons, the family gleefully prepared to pour a vat of boiling liquid from the roof of their Gothic mansion onto Christmas carolers singing below. No doubt millions of harried *New Yorker* readers harbored secret desires to follow suit.

To the surprise of many, the "sick humor" of the Addams Family found life beyond the printed page. In September 1964, a situation comedy based on the cartoons debuted on ABC. Producers initially sought input from Addams (who suggested that the husband

be called Repelli and the son Pubert) but eventually opted for a more conventional sitcom approach. The show was marred by a hyperactive laugh track but otherwise managed to adapt Addams's twisted sense of humor for mainstream consumption.

Veteran character actor John Astin played the man of the house, now dubbed Gomez. Carolyn Jones lent a touch of Hollywood glamour to the role of his wife, Morticia. Ted Cassidy, a heavy-lidded giant of a man, was perfectly cast as Lurch, the butler. The scene-stealing role of Uncle Fester went to Jackie Coogan, a child star of silent films now reincarnated as a keening, bald grotesquerie. Blossom Rock played the haggard Grandmama, with little person Felix Silla as the hirsute Cousin Itt. Lisa Loring and Ken Weatherwax rounded out the cast as deceptively innocent-looking children Wednesday and Pugsley, respectively.

The Addams Family lasted just two seasons on the network. Often compared to the contemporaneous horror comedy *The Munsters, The Addams Family* was by far the more sophisticated and well-written show. Plots were sometimes taken directly from the cartoons, though few seemed to notice. Whatever zeitgeist network executives thought they were tapping into when they programmed two supernatural sitcoms at the same time fizzled out quickly. *The Addams Family* was canceled in 1966 and languished in reruns for eleven years, at which point a Halloween TV movie was produced featuring most of the original cast. Loring did manage to capture a few headlines when she married porno actor Paul Siedermann. But the series was all but forgotten until the 1990s, when it was introduced to a new generation via the Nick at Nite cable channel.

The mid-1990s saw a craze for adapting old-school sitcom chestnuts into feature-length movies. On the leading edge of this trend was a movie version of *The Addams Family* released in 1991. Directed by Barry Sonnenfeld, the film boasted a top-rate cast, with Raul Julia as Gomez, Anjelica Huston as Morticia, and Christopher Lloyd as Uncle Fester. It was widely hailed as closer to Addams's original vision than the television series but derided for its woefully thin plot. A sequel, *Addams Family Values,* followed in 1993. In 1999, there was talk of yet another feature adaptation of Addams's clan of ghouls, this time with an entirely new cast.

—Robert E. Schnakenberg

FURTHER READING:

Cox, Stephen, and John Astin. *The Addams Chronicles: An Altogether Ooky Look at the Addams Family.* New York, Cumberland House, 1998.

Adderley, Cannonball (1928-1975)

Alto saxophonist, bandleader, educator, and leader of his own quintet, Cannonball Adderley was one of the preeminent jazz players of the 1950s and 1960s. Adderley's style combined hard-bop and soul jazz impregnated with blues and gospel. The first quintet he formed with his brother Nat Adderley disbanded because of financial difficulties. The second quintet, formed in 1959, successfully paved the way for the acceptance of soul jazz, achieved commercial viability, and remained intact until Adderley's untimely death on August 8, 1975. The group at various times consisted of Bobby Timmons, George Duke, Joe Zawinul, Victor Feldman, Roy McCurdy, and Louis

Anjelica Huston (left) with Raul Julia in the film *Addams Family Values*.

Hayes, among others. Occasionally, a second saxophonist was added to make a sextet.

The son of a jazz cornetist, Julian Edwin Adderley was born September 15, 1928 in Tampa, Florida. ''Cannonball'' was a corruption of cannibal, an appellation he earned during childhood for his rapacious appetite. His first professional musical experience was as a bandleader. He was band director at Dillard High School in Fort Lauderdale, Florida, while also leading a south Florida jazz group (1942-48); he later directed another high school band (1948-50) and the U.S. 36th Army Dance Band (1950-52).

Adderley captivated listeners when he moved to New York in the summer of 1955 and jammed with Oscar Pettiford at the Bohemia. This chance session landed him a job with Pettiford and a recording contract, causing him to abandon his plans for pursuing graduate studies at New York University. Adderley was labeled ''the new Bird,'' since his improvisations echoed those of Charlie ''Yardbird'' Parker, who died shortly before the younger man's discovery in New York. The comparison was only partly accurate. To be sure, Adderley's improvisations, like those of so many other saxophonists, imitated Parker; however, his style owed as much to Benny Carter as to blues and gospel. His quintet's hard-bop style was largely a reaction against the third-stream jazz style of the 1950s: the fusion of jazz and art music led by Gunther Schuller. As a kind of backlash, Adderley

joined other black jazz musicians such as Art Blakey in a sometimes pretentious attempt to restore jazz to its African-American roots by making use of black vernacular speech, blues, gospel, call-and-response, and handclap-eliciting rhythms. Adderley maintained that ''good'' jazz was anything the people liked and that music should communicate with the people.

The Cannonball Adderley Quintet became popular after the release of the Bobby Timmons composition ''This Here.'' Several hits followed, all in the hard-bop gospel-oriented call-and-response style, such as Nat Adderley's ''Work Song'' and ''Jive Samba''; Joe Zawinul's ''Mercy, Mercy, Mercy''; and Cannonball Adderley's ''Sack O' Woe.'' As an educator and bandleader, Adderley introduced the compositions and contextualized them for audiences. In the late 1960s and early 1970s, Adderley led quintet workshops for colleges and universities.

Adderley's musical legacy is assured due to his stellar improvisations and fluency on the alto saxophone. His style was not confined to hard-bop since he was equally adept at playing ballads, bebop, and funk. Adderley joined the Miles Davis Quintet in 1957, replacing Sonny Rollins, and remained through 1959, participating in the classic recording of the album *Kind of Blue,* one of the three most celebrated albums in jazz history. He also appeared on the albums *Porgy and Bess, Milestones, Miles and Coltrane,* and *58 Miles.* Davis

Cannonball Adderley

and Coltrane's modal style of jazz playing on *Kind of Blue* influenced Adderley. Musical characteristics such as a full-bodied tone, well-balanced phrases, sustained notes versus rapid flurries, and a hard-driving swinging delivery were the marks that distinguished Adderley's style.

Adderley recorded for a number of labels including Original Jazz Classics, Blue Note, Landmark, Riverside, and Capitol. Outstanding albums representing his work include *Somethin' Else* (1958) on Blue Note, *Cannonball and Coltrane* (1959) on Emarcy, *African Waltz* (1961; big band format), and *Nancy Wilson and Cannonball Adderley* (1961) on Capitol. The composition "Country Preacher," which appeared on the album *The Best of Cannonball Adderley* (1962), shows off Adderley's skillful soprano sax playing.

Cannonball Adderley's life and career are documented in a collection of materials held at Florida A&M University in Tallahassee. A memorial scholarship fund was established at UCLA by the Center for Afro-American Studies in 1976 to honor his memory with scholarships for UCLA students.

—Willie Collins

FURTHER READING:

Adderley, Cannonball. *The Best of Cannonball Adderley: The Capitol Years.* Capitol compact disc CDP 7954822.

Adidas

In an era before athletic-performance gear with distinctive logos existed as a market commodity, Adidas footwear were the designer sneakers of their day. For several decades, Adidas shoes were worn by professional and Olympic athletes, and the company's distinctive

three-stripe logo quietly sunk into the public consciousness through years of television cameras trained on Adidas-wearing athletes. The company and its clothing—especially the trefoil logo T-shirt—became indelibly linked with 1970s fashion, and during the early years of rap music's ascendancy, Adidas became the first fashion brand name to find itself connected with hip-hop cool.

Like a Mercedes-Benz, Adidas shoes were considered both well designed and well made—and much of this was due to the product's German origins. The company began in the early 1920s as slipper makers Gebruder Dassler Schuhfabrik, in Herzogenaurach, Germany, near Nuremberg. One day in 1925 Adolf (Adi) Dassler designed a pair of sports shoes; thereafter he began to study the science behind kinetics and footwear. By 1931 he and his brother Rudolph were selling special shoes for tennis players, and they soon began to design specific shoes for the needs of specific sports. They devised many technical innovations that made their footwear popular with athletes, not the least of which was the first arch support. The brothers were also quick to realize that athletes themselves were the best advertisement for their shoes. Initiating a long and controversial history of sports marketing, in 1928 the company gave away their first pairs of free shoes to the athletes of the Olympic Games in Amsterdam. Eight years later, American sprinter Jesse Owens was wearing Adidas when he won a gold medal in track at the Berlin Olympic Games.

In 1948 the Dassler brothers had a falling-out and never spoke again. The origins of their split, which dissolved their original firm, remain somewhat of a mystery, but probably revolve around their shifting alliances before, during, and after Hitler, the Nazi Party, and World War II. Rudi was drafted and was later captured by Allied forces, while Adi stayed home to run the factory that made boots for Wehrmacht soldiers during the war. After the war, Rudi Dassler moved to the other side of Herzogenaurach and founded his own line of athletic footwear, Puma. Adolf Dassler took his nickname, Adi, and combined it with the first syllable of his last name to get "Adidas," with the accent on the last syllable. Cutthroat competition between the two brands for hegemony at major sporting events, as well as formal legal battles, would characterize the next three decades of both Adidas and Puma corporate history.

At Olympic and soccer events, however, Adidas had the advantage, especially when television cameras began broadcasting such games to a much wider audience: Adi Dassler had devised a distinctive three-stripe logo back in 1941 (and registered it as a trademark for Adidas after the split) that was easily recognizable from afar. The company did not begin selling its shoes in the United States until 1968, but within the span of a few short years Adidas dominated the American market to such an extent that two American competitors, Wilson and MacGregor, quit making sports shoes altogether. In 1971 both Muhammad Ali and Joe Frazier wore Adidas in their much-publicized showdown. At the 1972 Olympic Games in Munich, every official wore Adidas, and so did 1,164 of the 1,490 international athletes. Adidas also made hip togs for tennis, a sport then enjoying a wave of popularity, and by 1976 the Adidas trefoil-logo T-shirt had become a status-symbol item and one of the first brand-name "must-haves" for teenagers.

The Adidas craze dovetailed perfectly with the growing number of Americans interested in physical fitness as a leisure activity. By 1979, 25 million Americans were running or jogging, and the end of the 1970s marked the high point of Adidas's domination of the market. When Adi Dassler died in 1978, his son Horst took over the company, but both men failed to recognize the threat posed by a small Oregon company named Nike. Founded in 1972, Nike offered more distinctive colors and styles than Adidas, while also patenting the technical innovations underneath and inside them. Adidas soon sunk far behind in sales. The company was overtaken by Nike in the 1980s and even damaged by the ubiquitousness of the Reebok brand, which made shoes that were considered anything but high-performance. When Horst Dassler died in 1987, Adidas spun further into financial misfortune, and would be bought and resold a number of times over the next few years.

Adidas's only high point of the decade came in 1986, when the New York rap group Run D.M.C.—the first of the genre to reach platinum sales—had a hit with "My Adidas," a break-beat homage to the footwear. The rappers wore theirs without laces, a style imitated by legions of fans. Adidas signed them to an endorsement deal. But by the 1990s, Adidas was holding on to just a two to three percent share of the U.S. market and seemed doomed as a viable company. A revival of 1970s fashions, however—instigated in part by dance-club-culture hipsters in England—suddenly vaulted the shoes back to designer status. Among American skateboarders, Adidas sneakers became de rigeur, since the company's older flat-bottomed styles from the 1970s turned out to be excellent for the particular demands of the sport.

In the United States, part of the brand's resurgence was the common marketing credo that teens will usually shun whatever their parents wear, and their parents wore Nike and Reebok. Twenty-year-old Adidas designs suddenly became vintage collectibles, and the company even began re-manufacturing some of the more popular styles of yore, especially the suede numbers. Arbiters of style from Elle MacPherson to Liam Gallagher sported Adidas gear, but a company executive told *Tennis* magazine that when Madonna was photographed in a vintage pair of suede Gazelles, "almost overnight they were *the* hot fashion item." In 1997 Adidas sales had climbed over fifty percent from the previous year, signaling the comeback of one of the twentieth century's most distinctive footwear brands.

—Carol Brennan

FURTHER READING:

Aletti, Vince. "Crossover Dreams." *Village Voice*. 27 May 1986, 73.

Bodo, Peter. "The Three Stripes Are Back in the Game." *Tennis*. July 1996, 20-21.

Jorgensen, Janice, editor. *Encyclopedia of Consumer Brands, Volume 3: Durable Goods*. Detroit, St. James Press, 1994.

Katz, Donald. *Just Do It: The Nike Spirit in the Corporate World*. New York, Random House, 1994.

Rigby, Rhymer. "The Spat That Begat Two Empires." *Management Today*. July 1998, 90.

Strasser, J. B., and Laurie Becklund. *Swoosh: The Unauthorized Story of Nike and the Men Who Played There*. New York, Harcourt, 1991.

Sullivan, Robert. "Sneaker Wars." *Vogue*. July, 1996, 138-141, 173.

Tagliabue, John. "Adidas, the Sport Shoe Giant, Is Adapting to New Demands." *New York Times*. 3 September 1984, sec. I, 33.

Adkins, David

See Sinbad

Adler, Renata (1938—)

Renata Adler achieved a controversial success and notoriety in the New York literary scene. Her film reviews for the *New York Times* (collected in *A Year in the Dark*, 1969) appeared refreshingly honest, insightful, and iconoclastic to some, opinionated and uninformed to others. But her essay collection *Towards a Radical Middle* (1970), a highly critical as well as high-profile review of the *New Yorker*'s venerable film critic Pauline Kael, and a 1986 exposé of the media's "reckless disregard" for "truth and accuracy" confirmed her role as gadfly. Adler's two novels, *Speedboat* (1976) and *Pitch Dark* (1983), defined her as a decidedly New York author with her distinctive, detached, anonymous voice; shallow characters; minimalist plot; and sparse, cinematic style. Her style garnered criticism from some but resonated with others, especially women of Adler's (and Joan Didion's) pre-feminist generation and class, similarly caught between romantic yearning and postmodern irony.

—Robert A. Morace

FURTHER READING:

Epstein, Joseph. "The Sunshine Girls." *Commentary*. June 1984, 62-67.

Kornbluth, Jesse. "The Quirky Brilliance of Renata Adler." *New York*. December 12, 1983, 34-40.

The Adventures of Ozzie and Harriet

As television's longest running situation comedy, airing from 1952 to 1966 on the ABC network, *The Adventures of Ozzie and Harriet* provides a window into that era's perception of the idealized American family. The program portrayed the real-life Nelson family as they faced the minor trials and tribulations of suburban life: husband Ozzie (1906-1975), wife Harriet (1909-1994), and their two sons, David (1936-) and Ricky (1940-1985). Its gentle humor was enhanced by viewers' ability to see the boys grow up before their eyes from adolescents to young adulthood. Although Ozzie had no apparent source of income, the family thrived in a middle-class white suburban setting where kids were basically good, fathers provided sage advice, and mothers were always ready to bake a batch of homemade brownies. Critic Cleveland Amory, in a 1964 review for *TV Guide*, considered the wholesome program a mirage of the "American Way of Life." Behind the scenes, however, the Nelsons worked hard to evoke their image of perfection.

The televised Ozzie, who is remembered, with Jim Anderson and Ward Cleaver, as the definitive 1950s TV dad—a bit bumbling but always available to solve domestic mishaps—stands in stark contrast to Ozzie Nelson, his driven, workaholic, off-screen counterpart. The New Jersey native was a youthful overachiever who had been the nation's youngest Eagle Scout, an honor student, and star quarterback at Rutgers. Upon graduating from law school he became a nationally known bandleader while still in his twenties. In 1935, he married the young starlet and singer Harriet Hilliard. The couple debuted on radio in 1944 with *The Adventures of Ozzie and Harriet*, a fictionalized version of their own lives as young entertainers raising two small boys. The children were originally portrayed by child

The cast of *The Adventures of Ozzie and Harriet* celebrate the show's 12th anniversary: (from left) Ricky, Harriet, Ozzie, and David.

actors, until the real-life Nelson kids took over the roles of "David" and "Ricky" in 1949. Eager to translate their radio success to television, Ozzie negotiated a deal with ABC and wrote a film script titled *Here Come the Nelsons*. The 1952 movie, in which the radio show's Hollywood setting was transformed into an anonymous suburbia, served as the pilot for the durable television program.

Ozzie's agreement with the ABC network gave him complete creative control over the series. Throughout its fourteen-year run on the television airwaves, he served as the program's star, producer, director, story editor, and head writer. He determined his show would be less frenetic than other sitcoms, like *I Love Lucy* or *The Honeymooners,* where zany characters were continually involved in outlandish antics. Rather, his series would feature gentle misunderstandings over mundane mishaps, such as forgotten anniversaries and misdelivered furniture. The Nelsons never became hysterical, but straightened out their dilemmas by each episode's end with mild good humor. The focus was strictly on the Nelsons themselves and only rarely were secondary characters like neighbors "Thorny" Thornberry and Wally Dipple allowed to participate in the main action. This

situation changed radically only late in the series after the Nelson boys married and their real-life wives joined the show to play themselves.

As the years went on, the show's focus shifted away from the parents and toward David and Ricky's teen experiences. David was portrayed as the reliable older brother, while Ricky was seen as more rambunctious and inclined to challenge his parents' authority. The younger brother's presence on the program was greatly expanded in 1957 with the broadcast of the episode "Ricky the Drummer." In real life, Ricky was interested in music and asked his father if he could sing on the show to impress a girl. Ozzie, who often based his scripts on the family's true experiences, agreed and allowed the boy to sing the Fats Domino hit "I'm Walkin'" in a party scene. Within days Ricky Nelson became a teen idol. His first record sold 700,000 copies as fan clubs formed across the nation. In 1958 he was the top-selling rock and roll artist in the country. To capitalize on the teen's popularity, Ozzie increasingly incorporated opportunities for Ricky to sing on the show. Filmed segments of Ricky performing such hits as "Travelin' Man" and "A Teenager's Romance" were placed in the final segment of many episodes. Often the songs were unconnected to that week's plot. The self-contained performance clips reveal Ozzie as a pioneer in the development of rock videos.

The TV world inhabited by the fictionalized Nelsons was a much different place than that occupied by the real-life family. Ozzie was an often distant and authoritarian father who demanded his boys live up to their squeaky-clean images. Family friend Jimmie Haskell commented that Ricky ''had been raised to know that there were certain rules that applied to his family. They were on television. They represented the wonderful, sweet, kind, good family that lived next door, and that Ricky could not do anything that would upset that image.'' Critics have charged that Ozzie exploited his family's most personal moments for commercial profit. The minor events of their daily lives were broadcast nationwide as the family unit became the foundation of a corporate empire. Tensions grew as Ricky began to assert himself and create an identity beyond his father's control. Their arguments over the teen's hair length, bad attitude, and undesirable friends foreshadowed disagreements that would take place in homes around America in the 1960s. It is ironic that Ricky's triumph as a rock singer revitalized his parents' show and allowed Ozzie to assert his control for several more years.

The Adventures of Ozzie and Harriet is not remembered as a particularly funny or well-written comedy. In many respects, it is a cross between a sitcom and soap opera. The incidents of individual episodes are enjoyable, but even more so is the recognition of the real-life developments of the Nelsons that were placed into an entertainment format. In the words of authors Harry Castleman and Walter Podrazik, '' [The Nelsons] are an aggravatingly nice family, but they interact the way only a real family can . . . This sense of down to earth normality is what kept audiences coming back week after week.'' Perhaps the greatest legacy of Ozzie, Harriet, David, and Ricky is their continuing effect upon the American people. They and similar shows, such as *Father Knows Best, Leave It to Beaver,* and *The Donna Reed Show* display an idealized version of 1950s American life free from economic problems, racial tensions, and violence more severe than a dented fender. Ozzie and his imitators perpetuated an idyllic world where all problems were easily resolved and all people were tolerant, attractive, humorous, inoffensive, and white. David Halberstam, author of *The Fifties,* cites such shows as creating a nostalgia for a past that never really existed. *The New Yorker* captured this sentiment when it published a cartoon of a couple watching TV, in which the wife says to her husband, ''I'll make a deal with you. I'll try to be more like Harriet if you'll try to be more like Ozzie.'' The senior Nelsons returned to television in the short-lived 1973 sitcom *Ozzie's Girls.* The plot revolved around the couple taking in two female boarders—one black and one white. The attempt to add ''relevance'' to the Ozzie and Harriet formula proved a failure. Audiences preferred to remember them as icons of a simpler past and not facing an uncertain present.

—Charles Coletta

FURTHER READING:

Castleman, Harry and Walter Podrazik. *Harry and Walter's Favorite TV Shows.* New York, Prentice Hall Press, 1989.

Halberstam, David. *The Fifties.* New York, Villard Books, 1993.

Mitz, Rick. *The Great TV Sitcom Book.* New York, Perigee Books, 1983.

Nelson, Ozzie. *Ozzie.* Englewood Cliffs, Prentice Hall, 1973.

Advertising

Advertising, the promotion of goods or services through the use of slogans, images, and other attention-getting devices, has existed for thousands of years, but by the late 1990s in the United States it had become ubiquitous, permeating almost every aspect of American life. Indeed, the most omnipresent trend was the placement of advertisements and logos on virtually any medium that could accommodate them. Advertising and brand logos appeared regularly on T-shirts, baseball caps, key chains, clothing, plastic cups and mugs, garbage cans, bicycle racks, parking meters, the bottom of golf cups, in public restrooms, on mousepads, in public school hallways, and, for schools fortunate enough to be located near major airports, on school rooftops. The quest for new advertising venues never stopped—advertising has been placed on cows grazing near a highway (in Canada), and on the edible skins of hot dogs.

Television screens became commonplace in many places where the audience was captive—doctor's offices, which were fed specialized health-related programs interspersed with commercials for health-related products, airports (fed by CNN's Airport Network), and supermarket checkout counters. Indeed, by 1998 place-based advertising, defined by advertising scholar Matthew P. McAllister in *The Commercialization of American Culture* as ''the systematic creation of advertising-supported media in different social locations'' had reached almost any space where people are ''captive'' and have little to distract them from the corporate plugs. Advertising had invaded even what was once regarded as private space—the home office, via the personal computer, where advertisements on Microsoft Windows ''desktop'' were sold for millions of dollars.

By 1998, almost all sporting events, from the high school to professional levels, had become advertising vehicles, and the link between sports and corporations had become explicit. Stadiums (San Francisco's 3Com stadium, formerly Candlestick Park), events (The Nokia Sugar Bowl, the Jeep Aloha Bowl), teams (the Reebok Aggie Running Club), awards (the Dr. Pepper Georgia High School Football Team of the Week, the Rolaids Relief Man award, for Major League Baseball's best relief pitcher), and even individual players had become, first and foremost, brand advertising carriers. Sports shoe manufacturers spent millions of dollars and competed intensely to have both teams and star players, at all levels of competitive sports, wear their shoes—as a basketball player wearing Nike shoes provided essentially a two-hour advertisement for the corporation each time the player appeared on television or in an arena.

It was not until the late 1800s that advertising became a major element of American life. Advertising had been a mainstay of U.S. newspapers beginning in 1704, when the first newspaper advertisement appeared. In the 1830s, new printing technologies led to the emergence of the ''penny press,'' inexpensive city newspapers that were largely supported by advertising, rather than subscriptions. Until the late 1800s, however, most advertisements were little more than announcements of what merchant was offering what goods at what price. But in the late 1800s, the confluence of mass production, the trans-continental railway, and the telegraph necessitated what had before been unthinkable—a national market for products that could be promoted through national publications. Advertising promoted and branded products that had, until around 1910, been seen as generic commodities, such as textiles, produce, and coal.

Calvin Klein Jeans

Brooke Shields in an ad for Calvin Klein jeans.

At the same time, printing technology also advanced to a stage where it became possible to create visually appealing ads. Still, before the 1920s, advertising was, by current standards, fairly crude. Patent medicines were advertised heavily during the late 1800s, and the dubious claims made by advertisers on behalf of these products tainted the advertising profession. But, by the turn of the century, the new "science" of psychology was melded with advertising techniques, and within ten years advertising agencies—which had emerged in the late 1800s—and the men who worked for them began to gain some respectability as professionals who practiced the "science" of advertising and who were committed to the truth. After the successful application of some of these psychological principles during the U.S. Government's "Creel Committee" World War I propaganda campaigns, advertising became "modern," and advertising leaders strove to associate themselves with the best in American business and culture. Advertising men, noted advertising historian Roland Marchand in *Advertising the American Dream,* viewed themselves as "modernity's 'town criers.' They brought good news about progress." The creators of advertisements believed that they played a critical role in tying together producers and consumers in a vast, impersonal marketplace, in part by propagating the idea that modern products and ideas were, by their very newness, good. Advertising men, wrote Marchand, believed that "Inventions and their technological applications made a

dynamic impact only when the great mass of people learned of their benefits, integrated them into their lives, and came to lust for more new products."

From the 1920s to the 1950s, advertisers and advertising dominated the major national media, both old (newspapers and magazines) and new (radio and television). The first radio advertisement was sent through the airwaves in 1922, and by the 1930s radio and its national networks—the Columbia Broadcasting System (CBS) and the National Broadcasting Corporation (NBC) were a firmly entrenched part of American life.

In the 1950s, television quickly became the medium of choice for national advertisers, and about 90 percent of all U.S. households had sets by 1960. After that, audiences became increasingly fragmented for all media and advertising soon became targeted to particular markets. Magazines and radio led the way in niche marketing. In the 1950s, these media were immediately threatened by television's mass appeal. Radio, whose programming moved to television, began offering talk shows and music targeted at specific audiences in the 1950s, and with the targeted programs came targeted advertising, including acne medicine ads for teens on rock 'n' roll stations and hemorrhoid ointment commercials for older people listening to classical music. By the late 1960s and early 1970s, magazines became increasingly specialized; such general-interest, mass-circulation magazines as *Life, Look,* and the *Saturday Evening Post* first lost advertising support and circulation, and in the case of the first two, went out of business. Meanwhile, the number of special-interest magazines increased from 759 in 1960 to 2,318 in the early 1990s. These magazines appealed to smaller audiences that shared common interests—hobbies, sports, fashion, and music. By the 1970s sleeping bags could be advertised in *Outside* magazine, rock albums in *Creem,* and gardening implements in *Herb Quarterly.*

Up until the 1990s, advertisers still had a relatively well-defined task: to determine where money would best be spent based on four primary criteria: reach, or how many people could possibly receive the message; frequency, or how often the message could be received; selectivity, or whether the advertisement would reach the desired potential customers; and efficiency, or the cost (usually expressed in cost per thousand people). However, during the 1980s, changes in society (government deregulation during the Reagan era) and technological changes (the broad acceptance of VCRs, cable television, and remote controls) forced advertisers to seek out new venues and to embrace new techniques. As the media became increasingly more complex and fragmented, corporations footing the bill for advertising also demanded more specific data than ever before, to the point where, in the late 1990s, there were serious—and increasingly effective—attempts to measure whether a specific ad led to a specific purchase or action by a consumer.

Advertisers in the late 1990s sought to regain some of the control they lost in targeting ads on television. Before the 1980s, most major markets had half a dozen or so outlets—CBS, NBC, ABC, PBS, and one or two independent stations. In addition, remote controls and VCRs were uncommon. Viewers' choices were limited, changing the channel was difficult, and it was difficult to "zap" commercials either by channel "surfing" (changing channels quickly with a remote control) or by recording a program and fast-forwarding over ads. "Advertisers are increasingly nervous about this recent, if superficial, level of power audiences have over their electronic media viewing," wrote McAllister. "New viewing technologies have been introduced into the marketplace and have become ubiquitous in most households. These technologies are, in some ways, anti-advertising devices."

Cable television had also, by the late 1980s, become troublesome for advertisers, because some stations, like MTV and CNN Headline News, had broken up programs into increasingly short segments that offered more opportunities to skip advertising. Sports programming, an increasing mainstay of cable, also puzzled advertisers, because commercials were not regularly scheduled—viewers could switch between games and never had to view a commercial. Attempts to subvert viewer control by integrating plugs directly into the broadcast had some success—and one advertiser might sponsor an ever-present running score in one corner of the screen, while another would sponsor instant replays and a third remote reports from other games. These techniques were necessary, as at least one study conducted in the 1980s indicated that when commercials came on, viewership dropped by 8 percent on network TV and 14 percent on cable stations.

Cable television, which had existed since the 1950s as a means of delivering signals to remote communities, blossomed in the 1970s. Home Box Office (HBO), became, in 1972, the first national cable network. By 1980, 28 percent of U.S. households had cable television, and by 1993 this figure reached 65 percent. Cable, with the ability to provide up to 100 channels in most areas by the late 1990s,

provided the means for niche marketing on television, and by the mid-1980s, advertisers took for granted that they could target television commercials at women via the Lifetime Network, teenagers through MTV, middle-class men through ESPN, blacks through BET, the highly educated through the Arts and Entertainment Network, and so on. Many advertisers found the opportunity to target specific audiences to be more cost-efficient than broadcasting to large, less well-defined audiences, because in the latter group, many viewers would simply have no interest in the product, service, or brand being pitched.

Advertising, in short, had a direct impact on television content. By the early 1990s, many individual programs had well-defined audiences, and could become "hits" even if they reached only a small portion of the potential general audience. For example, the WB network's *Dawson's Creek*, which debuted in 1998, only attracted nine percent of all viewers watching at the time it was broadcast, but it was considered a hit because it delivered a large teen audience to advertisers. Similarly, Fox's *Ally McBeal* achieved hit status by attracting only a 15 percent share of all viewers, because it appealed to a vast number of young women. These numbers would have been considered unimpressively small until the 1990s, but by then the demographics of the audience, rather than the size, had become all important to network marketers. In 1998, advertisers were paying between $75,000 and $450,000 for a 30-second commercial (depending on the show and the day and time it was broadcast), and demanded to know exactly who was watching. In the 1980s and 1990s, three new networks—Fox, UPN, and WB—had emerged to compete with the well-established CBS, NBC, and ABC, and succeeded by targeting younger viewers who were attractive to certain advertisers.

Despite strong responses to the many challenges advertisers faced, some groups remained elusive into the 1990s. People with active lifestyles were often those most desired by advertisers and could be the most difficult to reach. Non-advertising supported entertainment—pay cable (HBO, Showtime), pay-per-view, videos, CDs, laser disks, CD-ROMS, video games, the Internet, etc.—was readily available to consumers with the most disposable income. As opportunities to escape advertising increased, it paradoxically became more difficult to do so, as corporate and product logos found their way to the most remote places on earth. For example, outdoor gear manufacturer North Face provided tents for Mount Everest expeditions; these tents were featured in the popular IMAX film "Everest"; corporate logos like the Nike "swoosh" were embedded on every article of clothing sold by the company, making even the most reluctant individuals walking billboards who both carried and were exposed to advertising even in the wilderness.

As advertising proliferated in the 1980s and 1990s, so did its guises. Movie and television producers began to charge for including products (product placement) in films and programs. In exchange for money and tie-ins that plugged both the film and product, producers displayed brands as props in films, excluding competing brands. One of the most successful product placements was the use of Reese's Pieces in the movie *E.T.* (1982), which resulted in a sales increase of 85 percent. In *Rocky III*, the moviegoer saw plugs for Coca-Cola, Sanyo, Nike, Wheaties, TWA, Marantz, and Wurlitzer. Critics viewed such advertising as subliminal and objected to its influence on the creative process. The Center for the Study of Commercialism described product placement as "one of the most deceitful forms of advertising." Product placement, however, was a way of rising above clutter, a way to ensure that a message would not be "zapped."

Identifying targets for ads continued, through the late 1990s, to become increasingly scientific, with VALS research (Values and

Lifestyles) dividing audiences into categories such as ''actualizers,'' ''achievers,'' strivers,'' and ''strugglers.'' Even one of the most traditional advertising methods, the highway billboard, had, in the 1990s, adapted sophisticated audience-identification techniques. One research firm photographed license plate numbers as cars drove by billboards, then matched the number with the car owner's address, which gave the advertisers an indication of income and class by neighborhood. Billboard advertisers also successfully identified geographic areas with high numbers of people matching the characteristics of a company's or product's best customers. For example, Altoids, a strong mint, had, in the late 1990s, a strong customer base among young, urban, and socially active adults, who were best reached by billboards. Altoids' advertising agency, Leo Burnett, identified 54 demographic and lifestyle characteristics of Altoids customers and suggested placing ads in neighborhoods where people with those characteristics lived, worked, and played. This was a wildly successful strategy, resulting in sales increases of 50 percent in the target markets.

By 1998, many businesses were having increasing success marketing to individuals rather than consumer segments. Combinations of computers, telephones, and cable television systems had created literally thousands of market niches while other new technologies facilitated and increased the number of ways to reach these specialized groups.

The most promising medium for individually tailored advertising was the Internet. Online advertising developed quickly; within five years of the invention of the graphical web browser in 1994, the Direct Marketing Association merged with the Association for Interactive Media, combining the largest trade association for direct marketers with the largest trade association for internet marketers. Advertisers tracked world wide web ''page views'' and measured how often Web surfers ''clicked through'' the common banner advertisements that usually led directly to the marketing or sales site of the advertiser. Many companies embraced the even more common medium of e-mail to successfully market to customers. For example, Iomega, a disk drive manufacturer, sent e-mail to registered customers about new products and received favorable responses. Online retailers such as bookseller Amazon.com touted e-mail announcements of products that customers had expressed interest in as a customer service benefit. Although internet advertising was still largely experimental in the late 1990s, many manufacturers, wholesalers, and retailers recognized that web advertising was a necessary part of an overall marketing plan. Companies that provided audience statistics to the media and advertising industries struggled to develop trustworthy, objective internet audience measurement techniques.

—Jeff Merron

FURTHER READING:

Ewan, Stuart. *Captains of Consciousness: Advertising and the Social Roots of the Consumer Culture.* New York, McGraw-Hill, 1976.

Fox, Stephen. *The Mirror Makers: A History of American Advertising and Its Creators.* New York, William Morrow, 1984.

Marchand, Roland. *Advertising the American Dream: Making Way for Modernity, 1920—1940.* Berkeley and Los Angeles, University of California Press, 1985.

———. *Creating the Corporate Soul: The Rise of Public Relations and Corporate Imagery in American Big Business.* Berkeley and Los Angeles, University of California Press, 1998.

McAllister, Matthew P. *The Commercialization of American Culture: New Advertising, Control and Democracy.* Thousand Oaks, California, Sage Publications, 1996.

Pope, Daniel. *The Making of Modern Advertising.* New York, Basic Books, 1983.

Savan, Leslie. *The Sponsored Life: Ads, TV, and American Culture.* Philadelphia, Temple University Press, 1994.

Schudson, Michael. *Advertising: The Uneasy Persuasion.* New York, Basic Books, 1984.

Advice Columns

An often maligned and much parodied journalistic genre—though a telling and accurate barometer of moral assumptions and shifting sexual attitudes—the advice column has been a staple of various venues of American journalism for over a century.

Ironically, the grandmother of all advice columnists, Dorothy Dix, never existed in the real world at all. In fact, none of the major columnists—from Dix and Beatrice Fairfax to today's Abigail ''Dear Abby'' Van Buren—were real people, as such. In keeping with a turn-of-the-century custom that persisted into the 1950s among advice columnists, pseudonyms were assumed by most women writing what was initially described as ''Advice to the Lovelorn'' or ''Lonelyhearts'' columns. In the pioneering days of women's rights, journalism was one of the few professions sympathetic to women. In the so-called

Ann Landers

''hen coop'' sections of papers, several progressive women used the conventional woman's section—including its soon standard ''Lonelyhearts'' column—as both a stepping stone to other journalistic pursuits (and sometimes wealth and fame) and as a pioneering and functional forum for early feminist doctrine.

While the name of Dorothy Dix remains synonymous with the advice genre, the real woman behind Dix was much more than an advisor to the lovelorn. Elizabeth Meriwether Gilmer (1861-1951) was the daughter of a well-connected Southern family who had come to Tennessee from Virginia. In her early childhood she experienced both the Civil War and the death of her mother. Largely self-educated, she married a struggling inventor in 1882. The problematic union ended with George Gilmer's death in a mental institution in 1929.

Gilmer suffered a breakdown in the early 1890s and was sent to the Mississippi Gulf Coast to recuperate, where she met Eliza Nicholson, publisher of the *New Orleans Picayune.* Nicholson offered Gilmer a job on her paper, and after a brief apprenticeship, Gilmer's weekly column appeared in 1895 under the pen name of Dorothy Dix. Gilmer's first columns were amusing, literate social satire, many geared to early women's issues. They were an instant success, and readers began writing to Dorothy Dix for advice. In 1901 William Randolph Hearst assigned Gilmer to cover Carrie Nation's hatchet-wielding temperance campaign in Kansas, which eventually led to a position on Hearst's *New York Journal.* There Gilmer became a well-known crime reporter while continuing the Dix column, which was now running five times a week with an increasing volume of mail. In 1917 a national syndicate picked up Dorothy Dix, and Gilmer returned to New Orleans to devote all her time to the column. By the 1930s she was receiving 400 to 500 letters a day, and by 1939 she had published seven books. Even after achieving wealth and fame, she answered each of her letters personally, and when she retired in 1949 her column was the longest running one ever written by a single author. Elizabeth Gilmer, still better known to the world as columnist Dorothy Dix, died in 1951 at the age of 90.

In real life, Beatrice Fairfax, another name inextricably linked to the lovelorn genre, was Marie Manning (1873?-1945), who originated her column in 1898. Born of English parents in Washington, D.C., Manning received a proper education, graduating from a Washington finishing school in 1890. Shunning a life in Washington society, Manning (who shared Elizabeth Gilmer's feminist leanings and desire for financial independence) was soon pursuing a journalistic career, first at Joseph Pulitzer's *New York World,* and later at Hearst's *Evening Journal.* It was in the *Journal*'s ''Hen Coop'' that Beatrice Fairfax, a name fused from Dante and the Manning's family home in Virginia, was born.

Both Dix and Fairfax initially responded to traditional romantic/social problems of the times, but soon dealt with more essential quandaries as well. In the late Victorian era, when females were expected to be submissive dependents and when social codes dictated that certain aspects of marriage and relationships were taboo subjects for public airing in print, Dix and Fairfax provided practical, often progressive advice—counseling women to seek education, and to independently prepare to fend for themselves in a man's world. Gilmer often spoke of her personal difficulties as the basis for her empathy for the problems of others. The financial vulnerability of women, which Gilmer herself experienced during the early years of her marriage, was also a persistent theme, as was her oft-stated observation that ''being a woman has always been the most arduous profession any human being could follow.'' Gilmer was also an active suffragist, publicly campaigning in the cause of votes for women.

Both the Dix and Fairfax columns quickly became national institutions, their mutual success also due to their appearance in an era when the depersonalization of urban life was weakening the handling of personal and emotional problems within the domestic environment. Help was now being sought outside the family via the printed word, and the Dix/Fairfax columns were an impartial source of advice for many women of the period. Both Gilmer and Manning were noted for a more practical approach than many of the subsequent so-called ''sob sister'' writers who began to proliferate with the popularity of Dix and Fairfax.

Manning left journalism for family life in 1905, but again took over the column after the stock market crash of 1929, noting that while her previous column had only rarely dealt with marriage, in the 1930s it had become women's primary concern. By then the name of Beatrice Fairfax had become so familiar that it had even been mentioned in a verse of one of George and Ira Gershwin's most popular songs, ''But Not For Me'': ''Beatrice Fairfax, don't you dare, try to tell me he will care.'' Along with writing fiction, an autobiography—*Ladies Now and Then*—and reporting on the Washington scene, Manning continued to write the Fairfax column until her death in 1945. But Manning's demise was not to be the end of the column. In 1945 it was taken over by Marion Clyde McCarroll (1891-1977), a reporter/editor active in New York journalism during the 1920s and 1930s. McCarroll established a new, more functional column, referring persons needing more intensive counseling to professional help, while her personal responses took on an even more realistic, down-to-earth tone. McCarroll's Fairfax column, which she wrote until her retirement in 1966, is said to have established the precedent for most subsequent advice columns.

Gilmer had also noted a shift in public attitude when she commented that, in the 1890s, readers questioned the propriety of receiving gentlemen callers without a chaperone, while by the 1940s girls were wondering if it was acceptable to take a vacation with their boyfriends. Picking up the rapidly changing thread of public morality in the 1950s were a pair of advice columnists who together cornered a national market that they still dominated into the 1990s.

The identical Friedman twins, Esther Pauline ''Eppie'' (who became columnist Ann Landers), and Pauline Esther ''Popo'' (who became ''Dear Abby'' Abigail Van Buren) were born in Iowa in 1918. They were inseparable; when Pauline dropped out of college, Esther did the same, and after a double wedding in 1939 they shared a double honeymoon. By 1955 they were living separately in Chicago and Los Angeles. Esther, who was once elected a Democratic Party chairperson in Wisconsin, was active in politics, while Pauline busied herself with Los Angeles charity work.

Though conflicting stories have been published as to exactly how it happened, with the sudden death of Ruth Crowley, who had originated the *Chicago Sun-Times* advice column, Esther (now Lederer) became ''Ann Landers'' in 1955. Her common sense responses and droll humor soon put Ann Landers into syndication across the country. In her first column on October 16, 1955, a one-liner response to a racetrack lothario—''Time wounds all heels, and you'll get yours''—became an instant classic. Lander's skill with snappy one-liners contributed to creating an instant and intimate rapport with her readers, as did the fact she was not above reproving letter writers who she felt had it coming. David I. Grossvogel writes: ''From the earliest, Ann came on as the tough cookie who called a spade a spade, and a stupid reader Stupid.'' But he also noted: ''One of Ann Landers's main gifts, and an underlying cause of her huge and nearly instant success, was this ability to foster an intimate dialogue between herself and her readers. The caring Jewish mother appeared very soon and regularly. From the start she was able to turn the huge apparatus of a syndicated column into an expression of concern for the dilemma or pain of a single individual.''

Ann/Esther launched sister Pauline's journalistic career when the popularity of ''Ann Landers'' instigated an overwhelming avalanche of letters that necessitated assistance. Ironically, Pauline's independent success as Abigail Van Buren, a name chosen for her admiration of the American president, precipitated an eight-year feud between the twins who, nonetheless, separately but similarly developed into two of the most well-known women in America. (They eventually made up at their twenty-fifth high school reunion).

In tandem, the collected responses of Ann Landers and Abigail Van Buren reflect the changing values and assumptions of the second half of twentieth-century America—one of most rapid periods of overall social/cultural change in human history. While the essential issues remained naggingly the same—romance, sex, marriage, divorce—new and troubling variations appeared and persisted. In 1955 Landers and Van Buren could still refer to a generally accepted social structure, but one which was even then shifting, as family structure weakened, children became more assertive, and divorce more common. Even Ann Landers, basing her early judgments on her overriding belief in the traditional family as the center of society, had a difficult time dealing with issues such as the women's liberation and feminism, and was not above airing her apprehensions in print. Landers's involvement with the changing American values, as well as a profusely documented overview of both her letters and responses, is detailed in *Dear Ann Landers,* David Grossvogel's 1987 biography.

Aside from the increasing complexity of the issues and the new public mindset with which she had to deal, Landers was not above facing up to her more misguided judgments on any subject. She herself has said: ''When I make a mistake, I admit it. I don't believe admitting a mistake damages a person's credibility—in fact I think it enhances it.'' And well into the 1990s, when readers overwhelmingly call either Ann and Abby on faulty judgments, neither is afraid to offer retractions in print, and controversial issues often lead to a kind of open forum. Evolving post-1950s columns introduced such previously taboo subjects as explicit sexual matters (including disease), alcoholism, and drug use. In the 1990s recurring subjects have included homosexuality, including the issues of same-sex marriage, and the less controversial but delicate issue of family etiquette in dealing with same-sex couples. A new and particularly hot issue circa 1998 was sexual obsession and contacts via the Internet.

The popularity of advice columns inspired an unusual spin-off, the celebrity advice column. In the 1950s Eleanor Roosevelt wrote ''If You Ask Me'' for the popular woman's magazine, *McCall's*. While eschewing the more mundane lovelorn complaints, Roosevelt still responded to many deeper personal issues, such as religion and death, as well as to a broad spectrum of requests for personal opinions on subjects ranging from Unitarianism and Red China, to comic strips and rock and roll. (Mrs. Roosevelt responded that she had never read a comic strip, and that rock and roll was a fad that ''will probably pass.'') Nor was she above responding in a kindly but objective manner to such humble domestic concerns of young people such as hand-me-down clothes. In a similar serious vein, Norman Vincent Peale and Bishop Fulton Sheen also answered personal questions on faith and morality in some of the major magazines of the era.

On a more colorful level, movie magazines offered columns in which readers could solicit advice from famous stars. While no doubt ghostwritten, these columns are nonetheless also accurate barometers

of the popular moral climate and assumptions of the period, sometimes spiced up with a little Hollywood hoopla. In the early 1950s, Claudette Colbert provided the byline for a column entitled simply ''What Should I Do?'' in *Photoplay*. Around the same period *Movieland* was the home of ''Can I Help You?,'' a column by, of all people, Joan Crawford. (''Let glamorous Joan Crawford help you solve your problems. Your letter will receive her *personal* reply.'')

In the case of the *Photoplay* column, querying letters sometimes approached the complexity of a Hollywood melodrama. Colbert responded in kind with detailed and sometimes surprisingly frank comments, tinged with psychological spins popularized in 1940s Hollywood films such as *Spellbound*. To a detailed letter from ''Maureen A.'' which concluded with the terse but classic query, ''Do you think Bob is sincere?,'' Colbert responded: ''Please don't be hurt by my frankness, but I believe that stark honesty at this time may save you humiliation and heartbreak later. Your letter gives me the distinct impressions that you have been the aggressor in this romance, and that Bob is a considerate person, who perhaps really likes you and thinks he might come to love you. There are some men, usually the sons of dominant mothers, who go along the line of least resistance for long periods of time, but often these men rebel suddenly, with great fury. I also have the uncomfortable feeling that you were not so much thinking of Bob, as the fact you are twenty-seven and think you should be married.'' A typical (and less in-depth) Crawford column dealt with topics such as age differences in romance (''I am a young woman of twenty-six. I'm in love with a young man of twenty-one.''), blind dates, and marital flirting. Surprisingly, men were frequent writers to both columns.

At the approach of the millennium, the advice column remains a popular staple of both mass and alternative journalism, effortlessly adapting to the changing needs of both the times and the people. The cutting-edge alternative papers of the West Coast provide orientation-specific and often ''anything goes'' alternatives to Abby and Ann. *IN Los Angeles* offers ''advice from everyone's favorite fag hag'' in the regular column, ''Dear Hagatha.'' Readers are solicited to ''Send in your burning questions RIGHT NOW on any topic,'' and Hagatha's scathing and often X-rated responses are both a satire of, and an over-the-top comment on the venerable advice genre. Los Angeles's *Fab!* also offers ''Yo, Yolanda,'' by Yolanda Martinez, more earnest, but still biting advice to gays and lesbians. More serious aspects of gay mental and physical health are also addressed in many papers, among them *Edge*'s ''Out for Life'' column by psychotherapist Roger Winter, which frequently deals with issues such as sexual addiction, monogamy, depression, and AIDS.

A key and up-coming alternative advice column now featured in over sixty newspapers in the United States and Canada is Amy Alkon's ''Ask the Advice Goddess.'' While still dealing with the traditional romantic/sexual quandaries that are seemingly endemic to human society—although now as frequently (and desperately) voiced by men as by women—the Advice Goddess responds to both men and women with an aggressive, no nonsense, and distinctly feminist slant, albeit one remarkably free of the New Age vagaries that the title of her column might otherwise suggest. Alkon frequently (and ironically) reminds women of their sexual power in today's permissive, but still essentially patriarchal society: ''Worse yet for guys, when it comes to sex, women have all the power. (This remains a secret only to women.)'' Alkon started her advice-giving career on the streets of New York, as one of three women known as ''The Advice Ladies'' who dispensed free advice from a Soho street corner. The Advice Ladies co-authored a book, *Free Advice,* and Alkon also writes a column for the *New York Daily News,* and is developing a television talk show.

"Miss Lonelyhearts went home in a taxi. He lived by himself in a room as full of shadows as an old steel engraving." Nathanael West's 1933 novel, *Miss Lonelyhearts,* told a depressing story of that rare bird, the male advice columnist. They still exist, and are only slightly less rare today. In a highly publicized search, *Wall Street Journal* writer, Jeffery Zaslow, was chosen out of twelve thousand candidates to replace Ann Landers when she moved from the *Chicago Sun-Times* to the rival *Tribune* in 1987. Don Savage's "Savage Love" column offers witty male perspectives in the mode of the "Advice Goddess" to both gay and straight readers of Los Angeles's *New Times.* Many other male advice advocates have found voices among the alternative free presses of today.

In his biography of Ann Landers, David I. Grossvogel comments on the problems facing the contemporary advice sage: "At a time when many of the taboos that once induced letter-writing fears have dropped away, the comforting and socializing rituals afforded by those taboos have disappeared as well. The freedom resulting from the loss of taboos also creates a multitude of constituencies with a babel of voices across which it is proportionately difficult to speak with assurance." Grossvogel concludes that in the face of the increasingly depersonalization of modern society the "audibly human" voice of Ann Landers and others of her ilk "may well be the last form of help available at the end of advice."

The increasingly complex nature of contemporary life, compounded by the apparently never-ending story of humanity's depressingly changeless emotional, romantic, and sexual hang-ups, would seem to insure the enduring necessity of the advice column well into the next millennium. It remains the one element of the mass press still dedicated to the specific personal needs of one troubled, disgusted, hurting, frustrated, or bewildered human being, and thus to the needs of readers everywhere.

—Ross Care

FURTHER READING:

Culley, Margaret. "Sob-Sisterhood: Dorothy Dix and the Feminist Origins of the Advice Column." *Southern Studies.* Summer, 1977.

Green, Carol Hurd, and Barbara Sicherman, editors. *Notable American Women: The Modern Period. A Biographical Dictionary.* Cambridge, Massachusetts, The Belknap Press of Harvard University Press, 1980.

Grossvogel, David. I. *Dear Ann Landers: Our Intimate and Changing Dialogue with America's Best-Loved Confidante.* Chicago, New York, Contemporary Books, Inc., 1987.

West, Nathanael. *The Complete Works of Nathanael West.* New York, Farrar, Straus, and Giroux, 1957, 1975.

Zaslow, Jeffrey. *Tell Me All About It: A Personal Look at the Advice Business by "The Man Who Replaced Ann Landers."* New York, William Morrow, 1990.

The Advocate

The Advocate has garnered the reputation as the news magazine of national record for the gay and lesbian community. The first issue of *The Advocate* was published in the summer of 1967, and released under the September 1967 cover date. The magazine was an offspring of the Los Angeles Personal Rights in Defense and Education (PRIDE) newsletter. PRIDE members Richard Mitch, Bill Rau, and Sam Winston collaborated on the initial design of the news magazine. The inspiration for the magazine came from Richard Mitch's 1966 arrest in a police raid at a Los Angeles gay bar. The mission of *The Advocate* was clear and straightforward: It was to be a written record for the gay community of what was happening and impacting their world. The first copy, titled *The Los Angeles Advocate,* was 12 pages long and sold for 25 cents in gay bars and shops in the gay neighborhoods of Los Angeles. The first run of 500 copies was surreptitiously produced in the basement of ABC Television's Los Angeles office . . . late at night.

The following year Rau and Winston purchased the publishing rights for *The Advocate* from the PRIDE organization for one dollar. Gay activist and author Jim Kepner joined the staff and the goal was set to make the magazine the first nationally distributed publication of the gay liberation era. Within two years *The Advocate* had captured enough readership to move from a bimonthly to monthly publishing schedule. In April 1970, the title was shortened from *The Los Angeles Advocate* to *The Advocate,* mirroring its national focus. Five years later, David B. Goodstein purchased *The Advocate* and maintained control until his death in 1985. While Goodstein's wealth bolstered the stature of the magazine, he often proved to be a troublesome leader. When he moved the magazine's home base from Los Angeles to the gay mecca of San Francisco, the publication lost its political edge and adopted more of a commercial tabloid format. After noted gay author John Preston joined the staff as editor and Niles Merton assumed the role of publisher, however, *The Advocate* soon emerged as the "journal of record" for the gay community. Many other publications—gay and mainstream—began citing the news magazine as their source for information.

Near the end of Goodstein's tenure in 1984, *The Advocate* returned to its original home of Los Angeles where it met with some debate and rancor from loyal readers and staff when it was redesigned as a glossy news magazine. During the next ten year period the magazine would go through numerous editors, including Lenny Giteck, Stuart Kellogg, Richard Rouilard, and Jeff Yarborough. Each sought to bring a fresh spin to the publication which was being directly challenged by the burgeoning gay and lesbian magazine industry. When Sam Watters became the publisher of *The Advocate* in 1992, the magazine moved to a more mainstream glossy design, and spun off the sexually charged personal advertisements and classifieds into a separate publication.

Because it covered very few stories about lesbians and people of color in the 1970s, *The Advocate* has been criticized by gay and "straight" people alike. It has met with criticism that its stories focus predominately on urban gay white males. Indeed, it was not until 1990 that the word lesbian was added to the magazine's cover and more lesbian writers were included on the writing staff. The most grievous error *The Advocate* committed was its late response to the impending AIDS (Acquired Immune Deficiency Syndrome) crisis during the 1980s. Undoubtedly, when *The Advocate* moved from a hard edged political gay newspaper to a mainstream glossy news magazine, minus the infamous "pink pages" which made its so popular, many original readers lost interest.

In retrospect, no other news magazine has produced such a national chronicle of the growth and development of the gay community in the United States. *The Advocate* was a leader in the gay rights movement of the 1960s, and throughout its printing history has achieved notable reputation in the field of gay journalism, oft cited by those within and without the sphere of gay influence.

—Michael A. Lutes

FURTHER READING:

Ridinger, Robert B. Marks. *An Index to The Advocate: The National Gay Newsmagazine, 1967-1982.* Los Angeles, Liberation Publications, 1987.

Thompson, Mark, editor. *Long Road to Freedom: The Advocate History of the Gay and Lesbian Movement.* New York, St. Martin's Press, 1994.

Aerobics

Aerobics is a form of exercise based on cardiovascular activity that became a popular leisure-time activity for many Americans in the final quarter of the twentieth century. Dr. Kenneth H. Cooper, an Air Force surgeon, coined the term aerobics in a book of that title published in 1968. Cooper viewed aerobic activity as the cornerstone of physical fitness, and devised a cardiovascular fitness test based on one's ability to run a mile and a half in twelve minutes, a task that was used in military training. Cooper's work was endorsed by the medical community by the early 1970s, and contributed to the popularity of running during that period. By the end of the decade, aerobics had become synonymous with a particular form of cardiovascular exercise that combined traditional calisthenics with popular dance styles in a class-based format geared toward non-athletic people, primarily women. Jackie Sorenson, a former dancer turned fitness expert, takes credit for inventing aerobic dance in 1968 for Armed Forces Television after reading Cooper's book. Judi Sheppard Missett, creator of Jazzercise, another form of aerobic dance combining jazz dance and cardiovascular activity, began teaching her own classes in 1969. By 1972, aerobic dance had its own professional association for instructors, the International Dance Exercise Association (IDEA).

By 1980, aerobics was rapidly becoming a national trend as it moved out of the dance studios and into fast-growing chains of health clubs and gyms. The inclusion of aerobics classes into the regular mixture of workout machines and weights opened up the traditionally

A group of women participate in an exercise program at the YWCA in Portland, Maine, 1996.

male preserve of the gym to female customers and employees alike. In the process, it created a newly heterosexualized atmosphere in health clubs, which would make them popular social spots for singles. Simultaneously, aerobics marketing was moving beyond real-time classes and into media outlets. Aerobic workouts had appeared on records and in instructional books since the late 1970s, but it was the introduction of videotaped aerobic sessions in the early 1980s that brought the fitness craze to a broader market. Actress Jane Fonda pioneered the fitness video market with the release of her first exercise video in 1982, which appeared on the heels of her best-selling *Jane Fonda's Workout Book* (1981). Fitness instructors and celebrities would follow Fonda's lead into tape sales, which continued to be a strong component of the fitness market in the 1990s. Exercise shows on television experienced a resurgence during the aerobics craze of the 1980s, spawning new-style Jack La Lannes in the guise of Richard Simmons and Charlene Prickett (*It Figures*) among others.

Even more impressive than the ability of aerobics to move across media outlets was its seemingly unbounded capacity for synergistic marketing. Tie-ins such as clothing, shoes, music, books, magazines, and food products took off during the 1980s. Jane Fonda again demonstrated her leadership in the field, moving from books and videos into records and audiotapes, clothing, and even her own line of exercise studios. Spandex-based fitness clothing became enormously popular as they moved beyond traditional leotards into increasingly outrageous combinations. Recognizing the potentially lucrative female aerobics market, leading sports-footwear manufacturers began marketing shoes specifically designed for aerobic activity. Reebok was the first to score big in the aerobic footwear market with a line of high-top shoes in fashion colors, though its market dominance would be challenged by Nike and other competitors. By the 1990s, Reebok attempted to corner the aerobics market through tie-ins to fitness videos and by exploiting new trends in aerobics like the step and the slide. Fitness clothing designer Gilda Marx's Flexitard line introduced the exercise thong as an updated version of the leotard, which relaxed the taboos on such sexualized garb for the mainstream of physically-fit women. The aerobics craze among women spawned a new genre of women's mass-market fitness magazines, led by *Self,* a Condé-Nast title first published in 1982, which seamlessly blended articles on women's health and fitness with promotional advertisements for a wide variety of products.

During the 1980s, aerobics transcended the world of physical fitness activities to become a staple of popular culture. The aerobics craze helped facilitate the resurgent popularity of dance music in the 1980s following the backlash against disco music. A notable example was Olivia Newton-John's 1981 song "Let's Get Physical," which became a top-ten hit. Aerobics made it to the movies as well, as in the John Travolta-Jamie Lee Curtis vehicle *Perfect* (1982), a drama that purported to investigate the sordid world of physical fitness clubs and their aerobics instructors, and was also featured on television shows from *Dynasty* to *The Simpsons.*

Despite the enormous popularity of the exercise form among women, aerobics was often harshly criticized by sports experts and medical doctors who faulted instructors for unsafe moves and insufficient cardiovascular workouts, and the entire aerobics marketing industry for placing too much emphasis on celebrity and attractiveness. While these criticisms were certainly valid, they were often thinly veiled forms of ridicule directed against women's attempts to empower their bodies through an extraordinarily feminized form of physical exertion.

By the end of the 1980s, aerobics had become an international phenomenon attracting dedicated practitioners from Peru to the Soviet Union. Moreover, aerobics began attracting increasing numbers of male participants and instructors. Along with its growing international and inter-gender appeal, aerobics itself was becoming increasingly professionalized. IDEA, AFAA (the Aerobics and Fitness Association of America), and other fitness organizations developed rigorous instructor certification programs to insure better and safer instruction. The classes became more intense and hierarchical, spawning a hypercompetitive aerobics culture in which exercisers jockeyed for the best positions by the instructor; to execute the moves with the most precision; to wear the most stylish workout clothes; and to show off their well-toned bodies. This competitive aerobics culture even gave birth to professional aerobics competitions, such as the National Aerobics Championship, first held in 1984, and the World Aerobics Championship, first held in 1990. A movement to declare aerobics an Olympic sport has gained increasing popularity.

Beyond professionalization came a diversification of the field in the 1990s. Specialized aerobics classes danced to different beats, from low-impact to hip-hop to salsa. Simultaneously, aerobics instructors began to move beyond dance to explore different exercise regimens, such as circuit training, plyometrics, step aerobics, water aerobics, boxing, "sliding" (in which the participants mimic the moves of speed skaters on a frictionless surface), and "spinning" (in which the participants ride stationary bikes). Even IDEA recognized the changing fitness climate, adding "The Association of Fitness Professionals" to its name in order to extend its organizational reach. As the 1990s progressed, aerobics, as both a dance-based form of exercise and as a term used by fitness experts, increasingly fell out of favor. Nike ceased to use it in their advertising and promotions, preferring the terms "total body conditioning" and "group-based exercise" instead. By the mid-1990s, fitness professionals were reporting declining attendance in aerobics classes due to increasing levels of boredom among physically fit women. Women in the 1990s engage in diverse forms of exercise to stay in shape, from sports, to intensive physical conditioning through weightlifting and running, to less stressful forms of exercise exhibited by the resurgence of interest in yoga and tai chi.

—Stephanie Dyer

FURTHER READING:

"America's Fitness Binge." *U.S. News & World Report.* May 3, 1982.

Cooper, Kenneth H. *Aerobics.* New York, Bantam Books, 1968.

Eller, Daryn. "Is Aerobics Dead?" *Women's Sports and Fitness.* January/February 1996, 19.

Green, Harvey. *Fit for America: Health, Fitness, Sport, and American Society.* New York, Pantheon Books, 1986.

McCallum, Jack, and Armen Keteyian. "Everybody's Doin' It." *Sports Illustrated.* December 3, 1984.

Reed, J. D. "America Shapes Up." *Time.* November 2, 1981.

Aerosmith

Aerosmith's 1975 single "Sweet Emotion" cracked the Billboard Top 40 and effectively launched them from Boston phenomenons into the heart of a growing national hard rock scene. They would have significant impact on rock 'n' roll lifestyles and sounds for the next quarter of a century.

Vocalist Steven Tyler's leering bad-boy moves and androgynous charisma proved the perfect visual complement to lead guitarist Joe Perry's unstructured riffs and the band's bawdy subject matter. The band's most enduring single, ''Walk this Way,'' chronicles the sexual awakening of an adolescent male.

In 1985, just when it seemed Aerosmith had faded into the same obscurity as most 1970s bands, a drug-free Tyler and Perry engineered a reunion. They collaborated in 1986 with rappers Run DMC on a hugely successful remake of ''Walk this Way,'' won the Grammy in 1991 for ''Jamie's Got a Gun,'' and showed no signs of slowing down approaching the turn of the century.

—Colby Vargas

FURTHER READING:

Aerosmith with Stephen Davis. *Walk this Way: The Autobiography of Aerosmith.* New York, Avon Books, 1997.

Huxley, Stephen. *Aerosmith: The Fall and Rise of Rock's Greatest Band.* New York, St. Martin's Press, 1995.

African American Press

''We wish to plead our cause. Too long have others spoken for us.'' This statement, written in 1827, was the lead sentence for an editorial in the first African American publication, *Freedom's Journal,* published in New York City. From that time until the present there have been more than 3,000 African American newspapers, magazines, and book presses. The African American press, also referred to as the black press, is strongly based on color, that is, on publications that are for black readers, by black staff members and owners, dealing largely with black issues and society. The black press has been largely made up of newspapers, a format that dominated the first 130 years. From the beginning, most newspapers have been driven by a mission—to improve the plight of African Americans. Through the Civil War, the mission was emancipation of slaves followed by later issues of citizenship and equality. Not only did the press serve as a protest organ, but also documented normal black life, especially as it existed under segregation and Jim Crow laws. In many cases, these papers provide the only extant record of African American life in forgotten and remote towns.

The purposes of the African American press often followed the beliefs of the publishers or editors, for example, Frederick Douglass, founder and editor of *The North Star* in 1847. Douglass believed that a successful paper managed by blacks ''would be a telling fact against the American doctrine of natural inferiority and the inveterate prejudice which so universally prevails in the community against the colored race.'' A number of African American editors were also noted leaders in black liberation and civil rights, for example, P.B.S. Pinchback, Ida B. Wells Barnett, W.E.B. DuBois, and Adam Clayton Powell, Jr. These individuals, and many more like them, challenged the status quo by questioning social objectives in schools, the legal system, political structures, and the rights extended to minorities.

The high point of African American newspaper distribution came in the 1940s and 1950s, when circulation rose to more than two

million weekly. The top circulating black newspaper during this period was the *Pittsburgh Courier.* Following World War II, African Americans began demanding a greater role in society. Because of a significant role in the war, black social goals were slowly starting to be realized, and acts of overt discrimination moved toward more sophisticated and subtle forms. The civil rights movement made it seem that many battles were being won, and that there was less need for the black press. From the 1960s on, circulation dropped. There were additional problems in keeping newspapers viable. Advertising revenues could not keep pace with rising costs. Established editors found it difficult to pass on their editorial responsibilities to a new generation of black journalists. Mainstream presses had partially depleted the pool of African American journalists by offering them employment and giving space to the discussion of black issues.

African American magazines began in 1900 with the *Colored American.* Failures in the black magazine industry were frequent until John H. Johnson started the *Negro Digest* in 1942. The Johnson Publishing Company went on to publish some of the country's most successful African American magazines, including *Ebony* (beginning in 1945), a general consumer magazine that has outlasted its competitors including *Life* and *Look,* and *Jet* (beginning in 1951), a convenient-sized magazine that summarized the week's black news in an easy-to-read format. Among specialty magazines, the most successful has been *Essence.* Founded in 1970, it is a magazine dedicated to addressing the concerns of black women. The popularity of *Ebony* and *Essence* expanded to traveling fashion shows and television tie-ins. Examples of other specialty magazines include *Black Enterprise,* founded in 1970 to address the concerns of black consumers, businesses, and entrepreneurs, and *The Black Collegian,* a magazine addressing black issues in higher education. There have been a number of magazines from black associations and organizations, foremost *The Crisis,* a publication of the National Association for the Advancement of Colored People started by W.E.B. DuBois in 1910. There have also been a number of black literary and cultural magazines. Examples include *Phylon: A Review of Race and Culture,* founded by W.E.B. DuBois, and *CLA Journal,* a publication of the College Language Association. These journals have provided an outlet for works of scholars and poets, and have represented a social as well as literary effort where the act of writing became synonymous with the act of justice.

African American book presses have primarily published African American and multicultural authors. Typically, black book presses have been small presses, generally issuing fewer than a dozen titles per year. Examples of book presses include Africa World Press, Third World Press, and two children's book publishers, Just Us Books and Lee and Low. Publishers at these presses have been unable to give large advances to authors, and therefore have found it difficult to compete with large publishing houses. Large publishing houses, on the other hand, have regularly published books by black authors, though many have been popular celebrities and sports figures who were assisted by ghostwriters. These books have done little to add to the development of black literary voices, and have left the illusion that black writers are published in greater numbers than has been the case.

Throughout its history, the African American press grew out of distrust; that is, blacks could not trust white editors to champion their causes. Too many majority publications have portrayed blacks in a one-dimensional way—if they were not committing a crime or leeching off of society, they were running, jumping, joking or singing. It has taken the black press to portray African American people in non-stereotypical ways and present stories of black achievement. When a black news story broke, these publications reported ''what really went on.'' In addition, much of what has been found in the black press was not reported elsewhere, for example, special dispatches from Africa oriented toward American readers.

Despite more than 170 years of publishing, most African American presses struggle to survive. While the oldest, continuously operating African American publication, the *Philadelphia Tribune*, dates back to 1884, virtually thousands of others have come and gone. Of the approximate 200 plus current newspapers, most are weekly, and none publish daily, though there have been a number of attempts at providing a daily. Those that do survive are generally in urban areas with large black populations. Examples include the *Atlanta Daily World*, the *Los Angeles Sentinel*, and the *New York Amsterdam News* (in New York City). These newspapers and others like them compete for scarce advertising revenue and struggle to keep up with the changes in printing technology.

The attempts at building circulation and revenue have philosophically divided African American newspapers. Throughout its history, black journalism has been faced with large questions of what balance should be struck between militancy and accommodation, and what balance between sensationalism and straight news. Focusing on the latter, in the early 1920s, Robert Sengstack, founder and editor of the *Chicago Defender*, abandoned the moral tone common to black newspapers and patterned the *Defender* after William Randolph Hearst's sensationalist tabloids by focusing on crime and scandal. The formula was commercially successful and many other black newspapers followed suit.

The struggle of the African American press for survival, and questions of purpose and direction will likely continue into the foreseeable future. However, as long as a duel society based on skin color exists, there will be a need for an African American press. Given the dominance of majority points of view in mainstream publications and the low number of black journalists, it is more important than ever for the African American press to provide a voice for the black community. If African Americans do not tell their story, no one will.

—Byron Anderson

FURTHER READING:

''Black Press and Broadcast Media.'' In *Reference Library of Black America*, edited and compiled by Harry A. Plosk and James Williams. Vol. 5. Detroit, Gale Research, 1990.

Daniel, Walter C. *Black Journals of the United States*. Westport, Connecticut, Greenwood Press, 1982.

Joyce, Donald Franklin. *Black Book Publishers in the United States: A Historical Dictionary of the Presses, 1817-1990*. Westport, Connecticut, Greenwood Press, 1991.

Pride, Armistead S., and Clint C. Wilson II. *A History of the Black Press*. Washington, D.C., Howard University Press, 1997.

Simmons, Charles A. *The African American Press: A History of News Coverage during National Crises, with Special Reference to Four Black Newspapers, 1827-1965*. Jefferson, North Carolina, McFarland, 1998.

Suggs, Henry Lewis, editor. *The Black Press in the Middle West, 1865-1985*. Westport, Connecticut, Greenwood Press, 1996.

————. *The Black Press in the South, 1865-1979*. Westport, Connecticut, Greenwood Press, 1983.

The African Queen

John Huston's *The African Queen* (1951) is one of the most popular films of all time. The film chronicles the adventures of an obstinate drunkard, Charlie Allnut (Humphrey Bogart), and a head-strong spinster, Rose Sayer (Katherine Hepburn), as they head down an African river towards a giant lake in which waits the ''Louisa,'' a large German warship, which they ultimately sink. The film was shot nearly entirely on location in Africa. The on-set battles between the hard-living Huston and Bogart and the more reserved Hepburn have become part of Hollywood legend. Despite their difficulties, in the end all became friends and the results are remarkable. In addition to a great script and beautiful location scenery, the on-screen electricity between Hepburn and Bogart, two of the screen's most enduring stars, contributes to their equally spectacular performances. Hepburn was nominated as best actress, and Bogart won his only Academy Award for his role in *The African Queen*.

—Robert C. Sickels

FURTHER READING:

Brill, L. ''*The African Queen* and Huston, John, Filmmaking.'' *Cinema Journal*. Vol. 34, No. 2, 1995, 3-21.

Hepburn, Katherine. *The Making of The African Queen, or, How I Went to Africa With Bogart, Bacall, and Huston and Almost Lost My Mind*. New York, Knopf, 1987.

Meyers, J. ''Bogie in Africa (Bogart, Hepburn and the Filming of Huston's *The African Queen*).'' *American Scholar*. Vol. 66, No. 2, 1997, 237-250.

Agassi, Andre (1970—)

Tennis player Andre Agassi maintained the highest public profile of any tennis player in the 1990s—and he backed that profile up by playing some of the best tennis of the decade. Trained from a very early age to succeed in tennis by his father Mike, Agassi turned professional at age 16. By the end of his third year on tour in 1988 Agassi was ranked third in the world; by 1995 he was number one and, though he faltered thereafter, he remained among the top ten players in the world into the late 1990s. Through the end of 1998 Agassi had won three of the four major tournaments— Wimbledon, the Australian Open, and the U.S. Open, failing only at the French Open. Though his tennis game took Agassi to the top, it was his movie-star looks, his huge, high-profile endorsement deals—with Nike and Cannon, among others—and his marriage to model/actress Brooke Shields that made him one of sports' best-known celebrities.

—D. Byron Painter

FURTHER READING:

Bauman, Paul. *Agassi and Ecstasy: The Turbulent Life of Andre Agassi*. New York, Bonus Books, 1997.

Dieffenbach, Dan. ''Redefining Andre Agassi.'' *Sport*. August 1995, 86-88.

Sherrill, Martha. ''Educating Andre.'' *Esquire*. May 1995, 88-96.

Agents

Talent agents began the twentieth century as vaudeville "flesh-peddlers" selling the services of their stable of comedians, actors, singers, animal acts, and freaks to theaters and burlesque houses for a percentage of these performers' compensation. With the rise of radio, television, and the movies—and their accompanying star system—the balance of power shifted to the agents. With the influence to put together productions and dictate deals in the very visible business of media, these "superagents" themselves became powerful celebrities by the end of the century.

The emerging film industry of the 1910s and 1920s found that prominently featuring the lead actors and actresses of its movies— the "stars"—in advertisements was the most effective way to sell tickets. This gave the stars leverage to demand larger salaries and increased the importance of an agent to field their scripts and negotiate their salaries.

During this time, agents were often despised by the talent and the industry alike, called "leeches," "bloodsuckers," and "flesh-peddlers" because of their ruthless negotiating and the notion that they profited from the work of others, driving up film costs. In the 1930s, the Hollywood film industry began colluding to drive down star salaries and some studios banned agents from their premises. "Fadeout for Agents" read a 1932 headline in the film industry publication *Variety*. But in 1933, the Screen Actors Guild was formed to fight the collusion among studios and President Franklin Roosevelt signed a code of fair practices guaranteeing actors the freedom to offer their services to the highest bidder, making a good agent indispensable for most stars.

While it struggled during the days of vaudeville, the William Morris Agency, founded in 1898, came into its own with the advent of mass media and the star system. The agency recognized that it could make more money representing star talent than by representing the vaudeville houses in which the talent played. The newly codified freedoms agents and stars won in the 1930s helped William Morris grow from $500,000 in billings in 1930 to $15 million dollars in 1938, with a third of the revenue derived from each vaudeville, radio, and film. The agency also popularized the "back-end deal" in which stars received a percentage of the gross ticket sales from a production, elevating some actors' status from that of mere employees to partners.

Another agency, the Music Corporation of America (MCA), was founded in 1930 and quickly rose to become the top agency in the country for the booking of big bands. MCA began to put together, or "package," entire radio shows from its roster of clients, selling them to broadcasters and charging a special commission. By the mid-1950s, MCA was earning more from packaging radio and television shows than from its traditional talent agency business. Like the back-end deal, packaging effected a shift in power from the studio to the agent, enabling agents to put together entire productions. Studios could not always substitute one star for another and were forced to accept or reject packages as a whole.

In 1959, *TV Guide* published an editorial—titled "NOW is the Time for Action"—attacking the power and influence that MCA and William Morris had over television programming. In 1960, the Eisenhower administration held hearings on network programming and the practice of packaging. *Fortune* published an article in 1961 on MCA's controversial practice of earning—from the same television show—talent commissions, broadcast fees, and production revenue. When it moved to purchase a music and film production company in 1962, the Justice Department forced MCA to divest its agency business. In practice, and in the public consciousness, agents had evolved from cheap hustlers of talent to powerful media players.

In 1975, after a merger formed International Creative Management (ICM), the Hollywood agency business was largely a two-company affair. ICM and William Morris each earned about $20 million that year, primarily from commissions on actors they placed in television and film roles. That same year, five agents left William Morris to found Creative Artists Agency (CAA). Michael Ovitz emerged as CAA's president, leading it to the number one spot in the business. CAA employed a more strategic approach than other agencies and took packaging beyond television and into movies, forcing studios to accept multiple CAA stars along with a CAA director and screenwriter in the same film.

This was a time when agents were moving beyond traditional film and television deals and into a new, expanded sphere of entertainment. In 1976 the William Morris Agency negotiated a $1 million dollar salary for Barbara Walters as new co-anchor of the *ABC Nightly News*. This was double the amount anchors of other nightly news programs earned and reflected the expansion of the star and celebrity system to other realms. Another example of this phenomenon was the agency's representation of former President Gerald Ford in 1977.

This trend continued into the 1980s and 1990s. Ovitz brokered the purchase of Columbia Pictures by Sony in 1989, and in 1992 CAA was contracted to develop worldwide advertising concepts for Coca-Cola. With CAA's dominance and these high-profile deals, Ovitz himself became a celebrity. His immense power, combined with his policy of never speaking to the press and his interest in Asian culture, generated a mystique around him. A subject of profile pieces in major newspapers and magazines and the subject of two full-length biographies, he was labeled a "superagent." It was major news when, in 1995, the Disney Corporation tapped Ovitz to become its number two executive and heir apparent; and it was bigger news when Ovitz resigned as president of Disney 14 months later.

The 1980s and 1990s were also a period of the "celebritization" of sports stars and their agents. Lucrative endorsement fees—such as the tens of millions of dollars paid to Michael Jordan by Nike—were the result of the reconception of sports as popular entertainment. The proliferation of million-dollar marketing and endorsement deals created a new breed of sports superagent. The movie *Jerry Maguire* and the television show *Arli$$* played up the image of most sports agents as big-money operators. When sports superagent Leigh Steinberg was arrested for drunk driving, he apologized by admitting that he did "not conduct myself as a role model should." Agents were now public figures, caught in the spotlight like any other celebrity.

From their origins as mere brokers of talent, agents used the emerging star system to expand their reach, and in the process, helped build a culture of celebrity that fed on stars, enabling agents to win increasingly larger paydays for them. It was this culture that propelled agents to become celebrities themselves. While in practice "superagents" ranged from the flashy and aggrandizing to the low-key and secretive, their public image reflected their great power, wealth, and influence over the mechanisms of celebrity.

—Steven Kotok

FURTHER READING:

Rose, Frank. *The Agency: William Morris and the Hidden History of Show Business.* New York, HarperBusiness, 1995.

Singular, Stephen. *Power to Burn: Michael Ovitz and the New Business of Show Business.* Seacaucus, New Jersey, Birch Lane Press, 1996.

Slater, Robert. *Ovitz: The Inside Story of Hollywood's Most Controversial Power Broker.* New York, McGraw-Hill, 1997.

AIDS

Medically, AIDS is the acronym for "acquired immunodeficiency syndrome," a medical condition which enables a massive suppression of the human immune system, allowing the body to be debilitated by a wide variety of infectious and opportunistic diseases. Culturally, AIDS is the modern equivalent of the plague, a deadly disease whose method of transmission meshed with gay sexual lifestyles to attack inordinate numbers of gay men—to the barbaric glee of those eager to vilify gay lifestyles. The syndrome is characterized by more than two dozen different illnesses and symptoms. AIDS was officially named on July 27, 1982. In industrialized nations and Latin America AIDS has occurred most frequently in gay men and intravenous drug users, whereas on the African continent it has primarily afflicted the heterosexual population. From 1985 to 1995 there were 530,397 cases of AIDS reported in the United States. By 1996 it was the eighth leading cause of death (according to U.S. National Center for Health Statistics.) The AIDS epidemic transcended the human toll, having a devastating effect on the arts, literature, and sciences in the United States.

The first instance of this disease was noted in a Centers for Disease Control (CDC) report issued in June 1981. The article discussed five puzzling cases from the state of California where the disease exhibited itself in gay men. Following reports of pneumocystis carinii pneumonia, Karposi's sarcoma, and related opportunistic infections in gay men in San Francisco, New York, and Los Angeles, the U.S. Centers for Disease Control began surveillance for a newly recognized array of diseases, later known as AIDS. Because the homosexual community was the first group afflicted by the syndrome, the malady was given the initial title of GRID (Gay Related Immunodeficiency). In the first years of the AIDS outbreak, the number of cases doubled annually, and half of those previously infected died yearly. The caseload during the 1990s has reached a

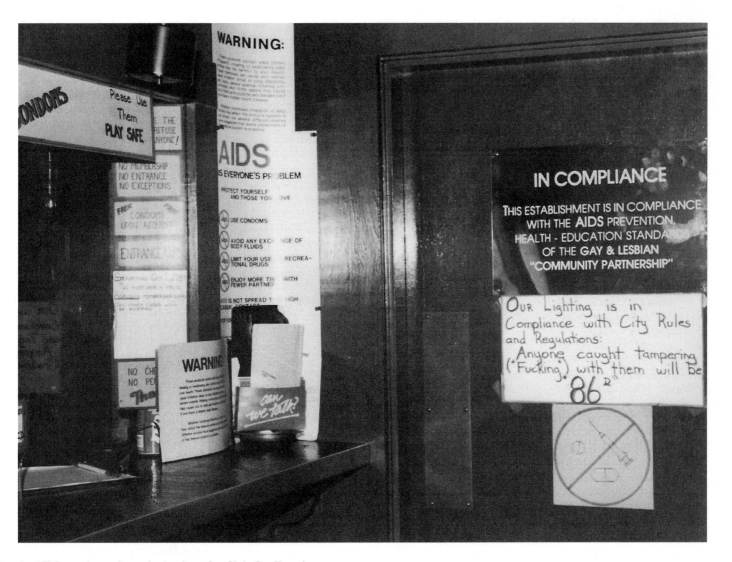

An AIDS warning notice at the Academy Sex Club, San Francisco.

plateau and with new medications on the market the death rate has started to decline. Discussions now focus on AIDS as a chronic manageable disease, rather than a fatal illness.

During the early years of the AIDS epidemic there was much fear of the disease, misinformation about its transmission, and lack of education covering prevention techniques. The United States closed its borders to HIV positive individuals. Members of the gay community became targets of homophobic attacks. The scientific community both nationally and worldwide took the lead in devoting time and research funds to unraveling the AIDS mystery, treatments for the disease, and possible future vaccines. Unfortunately many of the efforts have been dramatically underfunded, with university medical schools and major pharmaceutical corporations performing the majority of the research.

The vast majority of scientists believe AIDS originates from the human immunodeficiency virus (HIV). A number of forms of HIV have been identified, but those most prevalent to the AIDS epidemic are HIV1, globally disbursed, and HIV2, African in origin. HIV is classified as a retrovirus which, opposite to normal function, converts the RNA held in the virus core into DNA. Besides being a retrovirus, HIV is also a lentivirus. While most viruses cause acute infections and are cleared by the immune system, producing lifelong immunity, lentiviruses are never completely removed from the immune system. HIV's primary function is to replicate itself, with the unintended side effect of opportunistic infections in infected humans.

Scientists theorize that HIV originated from a virus which already existed and was now appearing for the first time in humans. Over the last decade there has been much contentious debate concerning the relationship of the West African simian immunodeficiency viruses (SIV) and a connection to HIV. A widely accepted theory is that the syndrome was transmitted to humans by monkeys with a different strain of the virus. Studies on the simian origin of HIV have made some progress beyond genetic comparison showing a close geographic relationship of HIV2 and SIV. Early in 1999 international AIDS researchers confirmed the virus originated with a subspecies of chimpanzee in West and Central Africa. This version was closely related to HIV1. Exposure probably resulted from chimp bites and exposure to chimp blood, but further research is still needed.

The rise of AIDS as a public health issue coincided with the ascension of a conservative national government. President Ronald Reagan established a political agenda based on decreased federal responsibility for social needs. Thus at the onset of the AIDS epidemic the issue was widely ignored by the federal government. Ever since, policy makers on the national, state, and local levels have been criticized for focusing upon prevention programs rather than the need for health care. Only after political pressure was exerted by gay activists, health care providers, and other concerned organizations was more money and effort directed toward funding medical care and research.

The AIDS epidemic has had a profound impact on gay and lesbian identity, politics, social life, sexual practices, and cultural expression. Many of those with AIDS were denied medical coverage by insurance companies, harassed in the workplace, and not given adequate treatment by medical practitioners. Meanwhile, there was a call by some right wing politicians and religious clergy for the quarantine or drastic treatment of AIDS patients. Gay-organized self help groups quickly developed around the country. By the 1990s over six hundred AIDS-related organizations were created nationwide. One of the first organizations was the Gay Men's Health Crisis in New York City; they were later joined by the Karposi's Sarcoma

Foundation (San Francisco), AIDS Project Los Angeles, Shanti Foundation, and countless others. Many people responded, especially those who had previously avoided gay movement work.

On the political front gay and lesbian activists waged a vigorous campaign to obtain adequate funding to halt the AIDS epidemic. Primarily through the media, activists waged a bitter campaign against the United States government and drug manufacturers, urging allocation of money and directing research for AIDS. The gay community has charged the federal government with negligence and inaction in response to the outbreak of AIDS. In the government's defense, it was the first time in years that industrialized nations had to come to terms with a previously unknown disease that was reaching epidemic proportions. Advancements in the analysis and treatment of the syndrome were impeded by institutional jealousies and red tape, and notable progress in the field did not start until the mid-1980s.

An unforeseen result of the epidemic was a renewed sense of cooperation between lesbians and gay men. Lesbians were quick to heed the call of gay men with AIDS in both the social service and political arenas of the crisis. Among gay men AIDS helped to bring together the community, but also encouraged the development of two classes of gay men, HIV "positive" and "negative." The sexually charged climate of the 1970s, with its sexual experimentation and unlimited abandon, gave way to a new sense of caution during the 1980s. Private and public programs were put into place urging the use of safer sexual practices, and a move toward long term monogamous relationships. The onslaught of AIDS made committed monogamous relationships highly attractive.

The collective effects of AIDS can be observed in the performing arts, visual arts, literature, and the media. The decimation of a generation of gay men from AIDS led to an outpouring of sentiment displayed in many spheres. The theater made strong statements concerning AIDS early on, and has continued ever since. Many AIDS-related plays have been staged on Off-Broadway, Off-Off-Broadway, and smaller regional theaters. Jeffrey Hagedorn's one-man play, *One,* which premiered in Chicago during August 1983, was the first theatrical work to touch upon the disease. Other plays such as William Hoffman's *As Is* (1985) and Larry Kramer's *The Normal Heart* (1985) were successfully presented onstage to countless audiences. Probably the most successful drama was Tony Kushner's *Angels in America* (1992).

Hollywood was a latecomer in the depiction of AIDS on the big screen. Most of the initial film productions were from independent filmmakers. Before *Philadelphia* (1993), the few other movies which dealt openly with AIDS as theme were Arthur Bressan Jr.'s *Buddies* (1985); Bill Sherwood's *Parting Glances* (1986); and Norman Rene and Craig Lucas's *Longtime Companion* (1990). Lucas's production was rejected by every major studio and was eventually funded by PBS's American Playhouse. Many of those afflicted with AIDS in the movie industry were treated as untouchables. Many times when AIDS was depicted in a film it was exhibited as a gay, white middle class disease. Meanwhile, photo documentaries produced outside Hollywood validated the lives of individuals with AIDS, revealing the gravity and reality of the disease and helping to raise funds for AIDS service organizations.

When the AIDS epidemic was first identified, the disease was not considered newsworthy by national television networks. The first mention of AIDS occurred on ABC's *Good Morning America* during an interview with the CDC's James Curran. Since the inception of CNN in 1980, the news network has provided continuous coverage of AIDS. Broadcast and cable television stations could have been used to calm fears about AIDS by educating viewers about how the disease was transmitted, realistically depicting people with AIDS, and fostering understanding towards those affected. However, HIV/AIDS proved to be too controversial for most mainstream media. Even public service announcements and advertisements depicting contraceptives or safe sex practices came under fire. However, as more people became aware of HIV/AIDS the major media sources began to air more information about the disease. In 1985 NBC Television presented one of the first dramas on the small screen, *An Early Frost.* Regular television programming covering HIV/AIDS has paralleled the disease. Countless made for television movies, dramas, and documentaries have been produced on the networks and cable television stations.

National Public Radio has been a leader in providing information and coverage of HIV/AIDS. NPR has since 1981 worked at interpreting issues surrounding the epidemic, with its broadcast reaching not only urban areas but also into the hinterlands. It has helped to dispel much misinformation and created a knowledge base on a national scale.

The literary response to AIDS has matched its history and growth. As the disease spread so did the written word covering it. Literature has served as socio-historical record of the onset and impact of the disease. Nearly every genre is represented, ranging from poetry, personal stories, histories, self-help books, fiction, and non-fiction. Literature has provided some of the more honest depictions of AIDS.

The most visible symbol of the disease is the AIDS Memorial Quilt. The quilt was started in early 1987 to commemorate the passing of loved ones to AIDS. Each person was given a rectangular piece of cloth three feet by six feet, the size of a human grave, to decorate with mementoes or special items significant to the life of the person who lost their battle with AIDS. At the close of 1998 there were over 42,000 panels in the Names Quilt, signifying the passing of more than 80,000 individuals. The entire quilt covers eighteen acres, and weighs over 50 tons. Still, only 21 percent of AIDS related deaths are depicted by the quilt.

The last two decades of the twentieth century have witnessed an immense human tragedy not seen in the United States for many years. A large portion of the gay population between the ages of twenty and fifty were lost to the disease. Along with them went their talents in the visual arts, performing arts, and literature. Many cultural artifacts from the end of the century stand as mute witness to their lives and passing, foreshadowing the symbolism provided by the AIDS Memorial Quilt.

—Michael A. Lutes

FURTHER READING:

Corless, Inge, and Mary Pittman. *AIDS: Principles, Practices, and Politics.* New York, Hemisphere Publishing, 1989.

Kinsella, James. *Covering the Plague: AIDS and the American Media.* New Brunswick, New Jersey, Rutgers University Press, 1989.

Kwitny, Jonathan. *Acceptable Risks.* New York, Poseidon Press, 1992.

McKenzie, Nancy. *The AIDS Reader: Social, Ethical, Political Issues.* New York, Meridian, 1991.

Shilts, Randy. *And the Band Played On: Politics, People, and the AIDS Epidemic.* New York, St. Martin's Press, 1987.

Smith, Raymond. *Encyclopedia of AIDS: A Social, Political, Cultural, and Scientific Record of the HIV Epidemic.* Chicago, Fitzroy Dearborn, 1998.

Ailey, Alvin (1931-1989)

Choreographer and dancer Alvin Ailey transformed the U.S. dance scene in the 1960s with his work *Revelations,* a powerful and moving dance which expresses Black experiences set to gospel music. By the 1980s this dance had been performed more often than *Swan Lake.* As the founder of the interracial Alvin Ailey American Dance Theatre in 1958, Ailey was an important and beloved figure in the establishment of Black artists in the American mainstream. His company was one of the first integrated American dance companies to gain international fame.

Other artists did not always share his vision of Black dance and accused his creations of commercialism. After early success and a stressful career, Ailey's creativity waned in the late 1970s. Manic depression and arthritis undermined his health. He tried to find refuge

Alvin Ailey

in drugs, alcohol, and gay bars, and died of an AIDS related disease in 1989. His company continues under the direction of Judith Jamison, a dancer who inspired Ailey's 1971 creation of a dance to honor Black women called *Cry*.

—Petra Kuppers

FURTHER READING:

Dunning, Jennifer. *Alvin Ailey. A Life in Dance*. New York, Da Capo Press, 1998.

Air Travel

For centuries people have been enthralled with the possibility of human flight. Early inventors imitated birds' wings and envisioned other devices that they hoped would enable them to conquer the sky. Not until the beginning of the twentieth century, however, did technology catch up with the dreams. Yet even after Orville and Wilbur Wright first flew at Kitty Hawk in 1902, most Americans did not view air travel as a realistic possibility.

Air shows during the first two decades of the twentieth century convinced Americans that flight was possible. Crowds thrilled as aviators flew higher and faster, and performed tricks with their small planes. Some tried to imagine the practical applications of flight, but at that point it was still a very dangerous endeavor. The early monoplanes and biplanes were fragile; wind and storms tossed them around and they frequently crashed. So when Americans went to air shows to see the "wonderful men in their flying machines," they also observed accidents and even death. Newspaper editorials, feature stories, and comics showed the positive and negative potential of flight.

World War I served as an impetus to the development of air travel in several ways. Initially, planes were viewed only as a means of observing enemy movements, but pilots soon began to understand their potential for offensive maneuvers such as strafing and bombardment. The use of planes in battle necessitated improvements in the strength, speed, and durability of planes. At the same time, as stories of the heroic exploits of such figures as Eddie Rickenbacker were reported in the press, the view of the pilot as romantic hero entered the popular imagination. Following their service in the war, trained pilots returned to participate in air shows, thrilling viewers with their expert flying and death-defying aerial tricks, known as "barnstorming," and offering plane rides.

During the 1920s and 1930s, far-sighted individuals began to seriously examine the possiblity of flight as a primary means of transportation in the United States. Entrepreneurs like William Randolph Hearst and Raymond Orteig offered cash awards for crossing the United States and the Atlantic Ocean. Aviators like Calbraith P. Rodger, who came close to meeting Hearst's requirement to cross the continent in thirty days in 1911, and Charles A. Lindbergh, who successfully traveled from New York to Paris in 1927, responded. Lindbergh became an overnight hero and flew throughout the United States promoting air travel.

As with railroad and highway transportation, it took the power and resources of the federal government to develop aviation. The United States Postal Service established the first airmail service as early as 1918, and airline companies formed to carry the mail and passengers. Federal and state governments established agencies and passed laws setting safety requirements. Then, in the 1930s, communities began to receive federal financial assistance to build airports as part of the 1930s New Deal. During World War II, the Allies and the Axis powers showed the destructive power of aviation, but the war also showed air travel was a pragmatic way to transport people and supplies.

By the end of World War II, most Americans viewed flying as a safe and efficient form of travel, and the air travel industry began to grow by leaps and bounds. Airlines emphasized comfort by hiring stewardesses and advertising "friendly skies," as federal agencies established flight routes and promoted safety. Aircraft manufacturers made bigger and better planes, and airports were expanded from mere shelters to dramatic and exciting structures, best exemplified by architect Eero Saarinen's TWA terminal in New York and his Dulles International Airport in Washington, D.C. With improved aircraft and reduced fares, flying became the way to go short or long distances, and even those who could not afford to fly would gather in or near airports to watch planes take off and land.

Within two decades, air travel had become central to the lives of increasingly mobile Americans, and the airline industry became one of the pillars of the American economy. Flying became as routine as making a phone call, and while dramatic airline disasters periodically reminded travelers of the risks involved, most agreed with the airlines that air travel was one of the safest means of transportation.

—Jessie L. Embry

FURTHER READING:

Corn, Joseph J. *The Winged Gospel: America's Romance with Aviation, 1900-1950*. New York, Oxford University Press, 1983.

Gibbs-Smith, Charles Harvard. *Aviation: An Historical Survey from Its Origins to the End of World War II*. London, Her Majesty's Stationery Office, 1985.

Ward, John W. "The Meaning of Lindbergh's Flight." *American Quarterly*. Vol. X, No. 1, 3-16.

Airplane!

The 1980 film *Airplane!* poked fun at an entire decade of American movie-making and showed movie producers that slapstick films could still be extremely successful at the box office. The movie appeared at the end of a decade that should well have left moviegoers a bit anxious. Disaster and horror films like *The Poseidon Adventure* (1972), *The Towering Inferno* (1974), *Earthquake* (1974), and *Jaws* (1975) schooled viewers in the menaces that lurked in and on the water, high in skyscrapers, and under the earth; and a whole series of *Airport* movies (beginning with *Airport* [1970], followed by sequels *Airport 1975, 1977,* and *1979*) exploited peoples' fears of being trapped in a metal tube flying high above the earth. *Airplane!* took the fears these movies preyed upon—and the filmmaking gimmicks they employed—and turned them on their head. The result was a movie (and a sequel) rich in humor and dead-on in skewering the pretensions of the serious disaster movie.

The familiar details of air travel in the *Airport* movies became the backdrop for an endless series of spoofs. The actual plot was fairly thin: a plane's pilots become sick and the lone doctor aboard must convince a neurotic ex-fighter pilot to help land the plane. The jokes, however, were multi-layered (which has led to the movie's attaining a kind of cult status, as fans view the film repeatedly in search of jokes they missed in previous viewings). In one scene, basketball star Kareem Abdul-Jabbar, who plays co-pilot Roger Murdoch, folds himself into the cramped cockpit and tries to ward off the skepticism of a visiting kid who insists that he is a basketball star, while the pilot, Captain Oveur (played with a straight face by Peter Graves), plies the boy with a series of increasingly obscene questions. When the tension created by the plane plummeting toward the earth is at its most intense, writer/directors David Zucker and Jim Abrahams have a nude woman jump in front of the camera. While he prepares to land the plane, Ted Striker (played by Robert Hays), who has been pressed into reluctant duty, confronts his fears and memories of previous flying experiences. Just when his flashbacks become serious, we return to a shot of Hays with fake sweat literally pouring down his face and drenching his clothing. While there is broad physical humor aplenty, some of the films funniest moments come from the verbal comedy. The dialogue between the crew is filled with word-play—"What's your vector, Victor?" "Over, Oveur," and "Roger, Roger"; every question that can be misunderstood is; and the disembodied voices over the airport loudspeakers begin by offering businesslike advice but soon engage in direct, romantic conversation while the airport business proceeds, unaffected. The latter is a fascinating statement about the ability of Americans to tune out such meaningless, background noise.

Earlier slapstick films had focused on the antics of specific characters such as Jerry Lewis or Charlie Chaplin, but *Airplane!* was different. It was a movie lover's movie, for its humor came from its spoofing of a wide range of movies and its skewering of the disaster film genre. It also featured an ensemble cast, which included Leslie Nielsen, Lloyd Bridges, Robert Hays, Julie Hagerty, and Peter Graves, many of whom were not previously known for comedic work. The two *Airplane!* films heralded a revival of the slapstick form, which has included several *Naked Gun* movies, and launched the comedic career of Leslie Nielsen.

—Brian Black

FURTHER READING:

Sklar, Robert. *Movie-made America.* New York, Vintage Books, 1994.

Alabama

Country music group Alabama's contribution to country music in the 1980s was one of the most significant milestones on the road to country music's extraordinary rise to prominence in the pop music scene of the 1990s. While various threads of artistic influence ran through country in the 1980s, the most important commercial innovations were the ones that brought it closer to rock and roll—following three decades in which country had often positioned itself as the antithesis of rock and roll, either by holding to traditional instrumentation (fiddles and banjoes, de-emphasis on drums) or by moving toward night-club, Las Vegas-style pop music (the Muzak-smooth Nashville sound, the Urban Cowboy fad). Alabama was one of the first major country acts to get its start playing for a college crowd. Most significantly, Alabama was the first pop-styled country "group": the first self-contained unit of singers/musicians/songwriters—along

Randy Owen, the lead singer of Alabama, performs at the 31st Annual Academy of Country Music Awards.

the lines of the Beatles, Rolling Stones, or Beach Boys—to succeed in country music.

Considering that the self-contained group had dominated pop music since the early 1960s, country was late to the table, and it was no accident. Country labels had quite deliberately avoided signing groups, believing that the image of a bunch of young men touring together, smoking marijuana, and smashing up motel rooms would be anathema to the core country audience and the upscale audience that country was trying to cultivate. As Alabama member Jeff Cook put it to Tom Roland, author of *The Billboard Book of Number One Country Hits,* the Nashville establishment felt that "if you were a band, you would have a hit record and then have internal problems and break up."

Alabama natives Randy Owen (1949—), Teddy Gentry (1952—), Jeff Cook (1949—), and drummer Bennett Vartanian formed the band's precursor, a group called Wild Country, in the early 1970s. They moved to the resort community of Myrtle Beach, South Carolina, where an engagement at a local club, the Bowery, extended for eight years. They were a party band, playing marathon sets that sometimes went round the clock. Vartanian left the group in 1976, and the group went through several drummers before settling on transplanted New Englander Mark Herndon (1955—), who had developed a reputation with rock bands around Myrtle Beach.

As the Alabama Band, the group cut some records for small independent labels. A few major labels approached lead singer Owen about signing as a solo act, but he refused to break up the band. Finally, RCA Victor took the chance and signed the group in 1980.

The band's first release, "Tennessee River," hit number one on the country charts, and was followed with two dozen number one hits. During one stretch, Alabama saw twenty-one consecutive releases go to number one, a record that no other act has come close to matching. Alabama won two Grammys and was named Entertainers of the Year three times by the Country Music Association and five times by the Academy of Country Music. In the *People* magazine readers' poll, Alabama three times was named favorite group, any musical style. In 1989, the Academy of Country Music named Alabama Entertainers of the Decade.

Following Alabama's success, pop groups like Exile crossed over to country music, and the self-contained group, from Sawyer Brown to the Kentucky Headhunters to the Mavericks, became a staple of new country.

—Tad Richards

Alaska-Yukon Exposition (Seattle, 1909)

Held in the University District of Seattle between June 1 and October 16 of 1909, the Alaska-Yukon Exposition attracted more than four million visitors. Housed in a collection of temporary (and a scattering of permanent) structures, the exposition promoted the achievements of American industry and commerce, and comprised a range of displays highlighting agriculture, manufacturing, forestry, and a wide range of other United States businesses. The exposition's principal legacy was its contribution to the development of the University of Washington, adding four permanent buildings and a landscaped campus to an institution which, prior to 1909, had comprised a mere three buildings.

—David Holloway

FURTHER READING:

Sale, Roger. *Seattle Past to Present.* Seattle, University of Washington Press, 1978.

Albert, Marv (1941—)

One of the most distinctive voices in sports broadcasting, Marv Albert prided himself on keeping his own personality subservient to the events he was covering. For most of his three decade career, the dry, sardonic New Yorker managed to hew to that credo. But when a personal scandal rocked his life off its moorings in 1997, the self-effacing Albert found himself the center of attention for all the wrong reasons.

Born Marvin Aufrichtig, Albert attended Syracuse University's highly-regarded broadcasting school. He mentored under legendary New York City sports announcer Marty Glickman and made his initial splash as a radio play-by-play man for the New York Knicks. A generation of New York basketball fans fondly recalls Albert's call of Game Seven of the 1970 NBA (National Basketball Association) Finals, in which an ailing Knick captain Willis Reed valiantly limped onto the court to lead his team to the championship. "Yesssss!"

Albert would bellow whenever a Knicks player sunk an important shot. "And it counts!" he would tack on when a made shot was accompanied by a defensive foul. These calls eventually became his trademarks, prompting a host of copycat signatures from the basketball voices who came after him.

Under Glickman's influence, Albert quickly developed a personal game-calling style that drew upon his New York cynicism. In a deep baritone deadpan, Albert teased and taunted a succession of wacky color commentators. Occasionally he would turn his mockery on himself, in particular for his frenetic work schedule and supposed lack of free time. Albert worked hard to manufacture this image, even titling his autobiography *I'd Love To, But I Have a Game.* This self-made caricature would later come back to haunt Albert when a sex scandal revealed that there was more going on away from the court than anyone could have possibly realized.

In 1979, Albert moved up to the national stage, joining the NBC (National Broadcasting Corporation) network as host of its weekly baseball pre-game show. The announcer's "Albert Achievement Awards," a clip package of wacky sports bloopers that he initially unveiled on local New York newscasts, soon became a periodic feature on NBC's *Late Night With David Letterman.* Like Letterman, Albert occasionally stepped over the line from humorous to nasty. When former Yale University President A. Bartlett Giamatti was named commissioner of major league baseball, Albert japed to St. Louis Cardinal manager Whitey Herzog that there now would be "an opening for you at Yale." "I don't think that's funny, Marv," the dyspeptic Herzog retorted.

Nevertheless, Albert was an enormously well-liked figure within the sports broadcasting community. He appeared comfortable on camera but was known to be painfully shy around people. Sensitive about his ludicrous toupee, Albert once cracked, "As a kid, I made a deal with God. He said, 'Would you like an exciting sports voice or good hair?' And I chose good hair." Bad hair or not, Albert found little standing in his way from a rapid ascent at NBC. He became the network's number two football announcer, and, when the network secured rights to televise the NBA in 1991, the lead voice for its basketball telecasts.

The genial Albert seemed to be on the top of his game. Then, in the spring of 1997, a bombshell erupted. A Virginia woman, Vanessa Perhach, filed charges against Albert for assault and forcible sodomy. She claimed that he had bitten and abused her during a sexual encounter in a Washington-area hotel room. The case went to trial in late summer, with accusations of cross-dressing and bizarre sexual practices serving to sully the sportscaster's spotless reputation. While Perhach's own credibility was destroyed when it came out that she had offered to bribe a potential witness, the public relations damage was done. In order to avoid any more embarrassing revelations, Albert eventually pled guilty to a misdemeanor charge, and received a suspended sentence.

Albert's career appeared to be finished. NBC fired him immediately, and he resigned from his position as New York Knicks play-by-play man rather than face the axe there. Many sports fans declared their unwillingness to watch any telecast of which Marv Albert was a part. Most painful of all, the reclusive Albert became the butt of nightly jokes by a ravenous *Tonight Show* host Jay Leno.

Slowly but surely, however, the humbled broadcaster began to put his life back together. As part of his plea agreement, he agreed to seek professional counseling for his psychosexual problems. He married his fiancee, television sports producer Heather Faulkner, in 1998. By September of that year, Albert was back on the air in New

Marv Albert

York, as host of a nightly cable sports highlight show. The MSG Network also announced that Albert would be returning to the airwaves as the radio voice of the Knicks for the 1998-1999 season.

Albert's professional life, it seemed, had come full circle. He appeared nervous and chastened upon his return to the airwaves, but expressed relief that his career had not been stripped from him along with his dignity. To the question of whether a man can face a maelstrom of criminal charges and humiliating sexual rumors and reclaim a position of prominence, Albert's answer would appear to be ''Yessssss!''

—Robert E. Schnakenberg

FURTHER READING:

''Second Effort.'' *People Weekly.* October 5, 1998.

Taafe, William. ''Warming Up the Airwaves? Yesssssss!'' *Sports Illustrated.* September 8, 1986.

Wulf, Steve. ''Oh, No! For the Yes Man.'' *Time.* October 6, 1997.

Album-Oriented Rock

Radio stations that specialized in rock music recorded during the later 1960s, 1970s, and 1980s were generally labeled Album-Oriented Rock (AOR) stations. The symbiosis between AOR stations and bands such as Deep Purple, Led Zeppelin, and Aerosmith has led many to refer to virtually all 1970s era hard rock bands as AOR as well. When it was first introduced in the late 1960s, the AOR format was only marginally commercial, but by the mid-1970s AOR stations were taking on many of the characteristics of top-40 stations. As the popularity of AOR stations grew, major label record companies exerted increasing influence over AOR playlists around the country, in the process squeezing out competition from independent label competitors. A by-product of this influence peddling was a creeping homogenization of rock music available on radio stations.

The AOR format was happened upon after the Federal Communication Commission (FCC) mandated a change in the way radio stations did their business in 1965. The FCC prohibited stations from offering the same programming on both AM and FM sides of the dial. This ruling opened the less popular FM side of the dial to a variety of less commercial formats, including jazz and classical. Coincidental with this change in radio programming law was the emergence of the so-called "concept album" among British art rock bands, the Beatles, and Bay Area psychedelic bands. Some of these albums featured songs substantially longer than the three minute time limit traditionally observed by radio station programmers. In areas with massive collegiate populations, especially San Francisco, a few FM stations began playing entire album sides. This approach to radio programming departed significantly from the singles-only AM pop rock format.

In the 1970s, rock album sales accounted for an increasing proportion of record company profits, but the AOR format remained somewhat experimental until technological improvements brought stereophonic capabilities to FM radio. This change attracted top 40 formats to FM and made it far more competitive. As FM rock radio matured, its audience widened and it became apparent to record labels that AOR stations, especially those in large market cities, were effective if not critical marketing media for their products. The growing importance of AOR radio, both to station owners and record companies, worked to narrow the weekly playlists. Station owners, hoping to maintain ratings, copied many top-40 programming strategies and curtailed the number of songs in heavy rotation, keeping many of the obscure bands and esoteric album cuts from ever getting air time.

Record companies sought to boost album sales by manipulating AOR stations' playlist. In order to avoid the recurrence of a 1950s style "payola" scandal, record companies subcontracted the promotion of their records to radio stations via "independent promoters." Through independent promotion, record companies could maintain a facade of legality, even though the means independent promoters employed to secure air time for the labels was clearly outside the bounds of fair access to public airwaves. Not only were station programmers frequently bribed with drugs and money, they were occasionally threatened with bodily harm if they did not comply with the demands of the independent promoters. According to Frederick Dannen, author of *Hit Men,* the secrecy, illegality, and lucrative nature of independent promotion eventually invited the involvement of organized crime syndicates, and the development of a cartel among the leading independent promoters.

In the 1980s, record companies hard hit by the disco crash lost all control over independent promoters. Not only had the costs of independent promotion become an overwhelming burden on the record companies' budgets, they had developed into an inextricable trap. Record companies who refused to pay the exorbitant fees required by members of the promotion cartel were subject to a crippling boycott of their product by stations under the influence of powerful independent promoters.

The effect of independent promotion on AOR formats and the rock music scene in general was a steady narrowing of FM rock fare. Bands on smaller record labels or those with experimental sounds had little chance of ever getting heard on commercial radio. Without some measure of public exposure, rock acts struggled to build audiences. Millions of dollars spent on independent promotion could not ensure increased album sales. There are dozens of examples of records that received heavy air play on FM radio, but failed to sell well at retail, a distinction that earns such records the title of "turntable hit." In the mid-1980s record companies banded together and took steps to reduce their debilitating reliance upon independent promotion.

For better or worse, the AOR format did allow musicians to expand well beyond the strict confines imposed by AM radio. Several important rock anthems of the 1970s, such as Led Zeppelin's "Stairway to Heaven" and Lynyrd Skynyrd's "Freebird," may have had far less success without AOR stations. The influence of AOR programming was not as absolute as it is frequently presupposed. Cynics often fail to recall that several bands, such as the Grateful Dead, Kiss, and later Metallica, managed to build massive audiences and enduring careers without the help of FM radio or independent promotion. The perception that rock music was hopelessly contaminated by crass commercialism drove many fans and musicians to spurn FM rock. This rejection invigorated punk rock and its various offspring, and also encouraged the development of alternative rock programming, especially college radio, which in turn helped propel the careers of bands like R.E.M., Hüsker Dü, and Soundgarden.

—Steve Graves

FURTHER READING:

Chapple, Steve, and Reebee Garofalo. *Rock and Roll Is Here to Pay.* Chicago, Nelson Hall, 1977.

Dannen, Fredric. *Hit Men.* New York, Times Books, 1990.

Sklar, Rick. *Rocking America: An Insider's Story: How the All-Hit Radio Stations Took Over.* New York, St. Martin's Press, 1987.

Alda, Alan (1936—)

Although his prolific and extremely successful career evolved from acting on stage to writing, directing, and acting in his own films, Alan Alda will forever be best remembered for his inimitable portrayal of Captain Benjamin Franklin "Hawkeye" Pierce in the award-winning TV comedy series *M*A*S*H,* which ran from 1972 to 1983. The most popular pre-*Seinfeld* series in television history, *M*A*S*H* concerned a Korean War medical unit struggling to maintain their humanity—indeed, their very *sanity*—throughout the duration of the war, by relying on humor in the form of constant wisecracking and elaborate practical jokes. Featuring humor that was often more black than conventional, the show proved an intriguingly anachronistic hit during the optimistic 1980s. Alda's Pierce was its jaded Everyman; a compassionate surgeon known for his skills with a knife and the razor sharp wit of his tongue, Hawkeye Pierce—frequently given to intellectual musings on the dehumanizing nature of war—had only disdain for the simplistic and often empty-headed military rules.

Born Alphonso Joseph D'Abruzzo—the son of popular film actor Robert Alda (*Rhapsody in Blue*)—Alan Alda made his stage debut in summer stock at 16. He attended New York's Fordham University, performed in community theater, appeared both off and on Broadway, and did improvisational work with the Second City troupe in New York. This eventually led to his involvement in television's *That Was the Week that Was.* His performance in the play *Purlie Victorious* led to his film acting debut in the screen adaptation *Gone are the Days* in 1963. Then followed a succession of notable film roles such as *Paper Lion* (1968) and Mike Nichols' *Catch-22* (1970).

Though his fledgling film career was sidelined by *M*A*S*H,* during the course of the show's increasingly successful eleven-year run Alda's popularity resulted in a succession of acting awards,

(From left) Alan Alda with David Ogden Stiers and Jamie Farr in a scene from *M*A*S*H*.

including three Emmy awards, six Golden Globes, and five People's Choice Awards as "Favorite Male Television Performer." Simultaneously, his increasing involvement behind the scenes in the creation of the show led to Alda writing and directing episodes, and, in turn, to receiving awards for these efforts as well. Ultimately, Alan Alda became the only person to be honored with Emmys as an actor, writer and director, totaling 28 nominations in all. He has also won two Writer's Guild of America Awards, three Director's Guild Awards, and six Golden Globes from the Hollywood Foreign Press Association.

While on hiatus from the show, Alda also began leveraging his TV popularity into rejuvenating his film career, appearing in the comedies *Same Time Next Year* (1978, for which he received a Golden Globe nomination) and Neil Simon's *California Suite* (1979). Alda also wrote and starred in the well-received *Seduction of Joe Tynan* (1979) about a senator's corruption by the lure of increasing power, and by the wiles of luminous lawyer Meryl Streep. In 1981, Alda expanded his talents—writing, directing, and starring in *Four Seasons*, which proved a critical and financial hit for the middle-aged set, and spawned a short-lived television series. His three subsequent and post-*M*A*S*H* films as writer/director/star—*Sweet Liberty* (1986), *A New Life* (1988), and *Betsy's Wedding* (1990)—have met with mediocre success, leading Alda to continue accepting acting roles. He has frequently worked for Woody Allen—appearing in *Crimes and*

Misdemeanors for which he won the New York Film Critic's Award for best supporting actor, *Manhattan Murder Mystery,* and *Everyone Says I Love You.* Alda even good-naturedly accepted the Razzie Award for "Worst Supporting Actor" for his work in the bomb *Whispers in the Dark* (1992). Alda has also continued to make television and stage appearances; his role in Neil Simon's *Jake's Women* led to a Tony Nomination (and the starring role in the subsequent television adaptation), and the recent *Art,* in which Alda starred on Broadway, won the Tony for Best New Play in 1998.

However, in the late 1990s, Alda also made a transition into unexpected territory as host of the PBS series, *Scientific American Frontiers,* which afforded him the opportunity both to travel the world and to indulge his obsession with the sciences, as he interviews world-renowned scientists from various fields.

An ardent and long-married (to photographer Arlene Weiss) family man, Alda has also been a staunch supporter of feminist causes, campaigning extensively for the passage of the Equal Rights Amendment, which led to his 1976 appointment by Gerald Ford to the National Commission for the Observance of International Women's Year. It was critic Janet Maslin, in her 1988 *New York Times* review of Alda's *A New Life,* who seemed to best summarize Alda's appeal to society: "Alan Alda is an actor, a film maker, and a person, of course, but he's also a state of mind. He's the urge, when one is riding in a gondola, to get up and start singing with the gondolier. He's the impulse to talk over an important personal problem with an entire roomful of concerned friends. He's the determination to keep looking up, no matter how many pigeons may be flying overhead.''

—Rick Moody

FURTHER READING:

Kalter, Suzy. *The Complete Book of M*A*S*H.* New York, H.N. Abrams, 1984.

Reiss, David S. *M*A*S*H: The Exclusive, Inside Story of TV's Most Popular Show.* Indianapolis, Bobbs-Merrill, 1980.

Strait, Raymond. *Alan Alda: A Biography.* New York, St. Martin's Press, 1983.

Ali, Muhammad (1942—)

In every generation there emerges a public figure who manages to dramatize the tensions, the aspirations, even the spirit of the epoch, and by so doing, define that era for posterity. Thus F. Scott Fitzgerald, the personification of the heady mixture of genius and new social possibilities played out in a very public manner, defined the Roaring Twenties. It is difficult to define how this process occurs, but when it happens it becomes obvious how ineluctably right the person is, how fated they are to play out the drama of their age; it appears that their ascendance is fated, so necessary that were the figure not existing, he or she would have to be created. Such was the impact of Muhammad Ali. Ali was a new kind of athlete, utterly divorced from the rags-to-riches saga of previous black boxers. By the close of the 1960s, Ali had become one of the most celebrated men on the planet, a hero in Africa, the third world, and in the ghettoes of black America. Placing his convictions before his career, Ali became the heavyweight boxing champion of the world, all the while acting as an ambassador for the emerging black power movement. Gifted, idiosyncratic, anomalous—we may never see the likes of him again.

Unlike previous black champions—Joe Louis, Floyd Patterson, Sonny Liston—Ali was anomalous in that he was not a product of poverty and had no dreadful past from which he sought to escape. Born Cassius Clay, in the border South city of Louisville, Kentucky, he was a child of the black middle class. His father, Cassius Clay, Sr., a loquacious man with a propensity for Marcus Garvey-inspired rhetoric, was a frustrated artist who painted signs for a living. For a black man of the time, he was one step removed from the smattering of black professionals who occupied the upper strata of black society. Although Louisville was a segregated city, and young Cassius suffered the slights of Jim Crow, Louisville was not the deep South. Still, the presence of inequity gnawed at the young boy. Behind his personal drive there would always exist the conviction that whatever status he attained would be used to uplift his race.

If it wasn't for the fact that it is true, the story of Ali's introduction to boxing would seem apocryphal. At the tender age of twelve, Clay was the victim of a petty crime: the theft of his new Schwinn bicycle from outside of a convention center. Furious at the loss, Cassius was directed to the basement of the building where he was told a police officer, one Joe Martin, could be found. Martin, a lesser figure in the annals of gym-philosophers, ran a boxing program for the young, and in his spare time produced a show, *Tomorrow's*

Champions, for a local TV station. Martin waited out Clay's threats of what he would do when he found the thief, suggesting the best way to prepare for the impending showdown was to come back to the gym. Clay returned the very next day, and soon the sport became an obsession. While still in his teens he trained like a professional athlete. Even at this tender age Clay possessed a considerable ego, and the mouth to broadcast his convictions. Exulting after his first amateur bout, won in a three round decision, he ecstatically danced around the ring, berating the crowd with claims to his superiority.

From the beginning Martin could see Clay's potential. He was quick on his feet with eyes that never left his opponent, always appraising, searching for an opening. And he was cool under pressure, never letting his emotions carry him away. Never a particularly apt student (he would always have difficulty reading), Clay nonetheless possessed an intuitive genius that expressed itself in his unique boxing style and a flair for promotion. He was already composing the poems that were to become his trademark, celebrating his imminent victory and predicting the round in which his opponent would fall in rhyming couplets. And even at this stage he was attracting vociferous crowds eager to see his notorious lip get buttoned. Clay did not care. Intuitively, he had grasped the essential component of boxing showmanship: *schadenfreude.* After turning pro, Clay would pay a visit to professional wrestler Gorgeous George, a former football player with long, blond tresses and a knack for narcissistic posturing. ''A lot of people will pay to see someone shut your mouth,'' George explained to the young boxer. In the ensuing years, Clay would use parts of George's schtick verbatim, but it was mere refinement to a well-developed sensibility.

Moving up the ranks of amateur boxing, Clay triumphed at the 1960 Rome Olympics, besting his opponents with ease and winning the gold medal in a bout against a Polish coffeehouse manager. Of his Olympic performance A.J. Liebling, boxing aficionado and *New Yorker* magazine scribe, wrote he had ''a skittering style, like a pebble scaled over water.'' Liebling found the agile boxer's style ''attractive, but not probative.'' He could not fathom a fighter who depended so completely on his legs, on his speed and quickness; one who presumed that taking a punch was not a prerequisite to the sport. Other writers, too, took umbrage with Clay's idiosyncratic style, accustomed to heavyweights who waded into their opponents and kept punching until they had reduced their opponents to jelly. But if there was a common denominator in the coverage of Clay's early career, it was a uniform underestimation of his tactical skills. The common assumption was that any fighter with such a big mouth had to be hiding something. ''Clay, in fact, was the latest showman in the great American tradition of narcissistic self-promotion,'' writes David Remnick in his chronicle of Ali's early career, *King of the World.* ''A descendant of Davy Crockett and Buffalo Bill by way of the dozens.'' By the time he had positioned himself for a shot at the title against Sonny Liston, a powerful slugger, and in many ways Clay's antithesis, Clay had refined his provocations to the level of psychological warfare.

Sonny Liston was a street-brawler, a convicted felon with mob affiliations both in and out of the ring (even after beginning his professional career, Liston would work as a strong-arm man on occasion). In his first title fight against Floyd Patterson, Liston had found himself reluctantly playing the role of the heavy, the jungle beast to Patterson's civil rights Negro (the black white hope, as he was called). He beat Patterson like a gong, twice, ending both fights in the second round, and causing much distress to the arbiters of public morality. After winning the championship, Liston had tried to reform

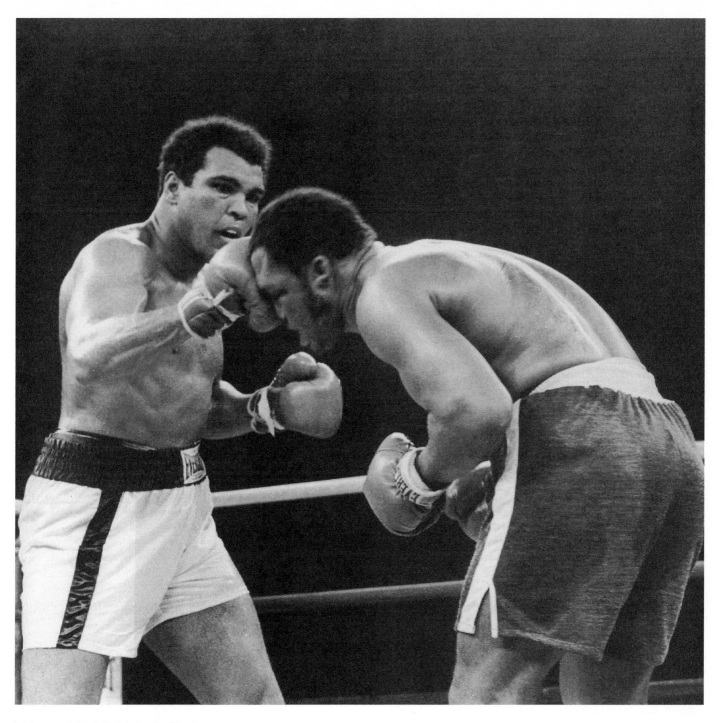

Muhammad Ali (left) fighting Joe Frazier.

his tarnished image, found the media unsympathetic, and subsided into a life of boozing and seedy amusement interrupted occasionally by a challenge to his title.

It was against this backdrop of racial posturing that Clay fought his first championship bout against Liston in 1964. A seven-to-one underdog, no one expected much of the brash, young fighter who had done little to engender sympathy with the sporting press (not especially cordial to begin with, the more conservative among them were already miffed by the presence of Malcolm X in Clay's entourage). His Louisville backers merely hoped their investment would exit the

ring without permanent damage. To unsettle his opponent and heighten interest in the bout, Clay launched a program of psychological warfare. Clay and his entourage appeared at Liston's Denver home early one morning, making a scene on his front lawn until the police escorted them from the premises. When Liston arrived in Miami to begin training, Clay met him airport, where he tried to pick a fight. He would periodically show up at Liston's rented home and hold court on his front lawn. Clay saved his most outrageous performance for the weigh-in, bugging his eyes out and shouting imprecations. ''Years later, when this sort of hysteria was understood as a standing joke, the writers merely rolled their eyes,'' writes Remnick, ''but no one had ever seen anything like this before. . . . Traditionally, anything but the most stoic behavior meant that a fighter was terrified, which was precisely what Clay wanted Liston to believe.''

An astute judge of character, Clay suspected Liston would train lightly, so sure was he of Clay's unbalanced condition, but Clay himself was in top shape. His game-plan was to tire out Liston in the first rounds, keeping him moving and avoiding his fearsome left until he could dispatch him. ''Round eight to prove I'm great!'' he shouted at the weigh-in. At the sparsely attended match, Liston called it quits after the sixth round. Incapable or unwilling to take more abuse, he ended the fight from his stool. ''Eat your words!'' Clay shouted to the assembled press, and a new era in boxing had begun.

If Clay's white backers, the cream of Louisville society who had bankrolled him for four years—and it should be mentioned, saved him from a career of servitude to organized crime—thought Clay, having gained the championship, would then settle into the traditional champion's role—public appearances at shopping malls, charity events, and so forth—they were sorely mistaken. Immediately following the fight, Clay publicly proclaimed his allegiance to Elijah Muhammad's Nation of Islam, a sect that had caused controversy for its segregationist beliefs and bizarre theology. In a break with the sect's normative habit of substituting X for their ''slave'' surname, the religious leader summarily bestowed upon Clay the name Muhammad Ali; loosely translated as meaning a cousin of the prophet who is deserving of great praise. Now his backers not only had a fighter who preferred visiting in the ghetto to meeting celebrities, but also one with a controversial religious affiliation.

In the press, the backlash was immediate and vindictive. True, writers such as Norman Mailer, Gay Talese, and Tom Wolfe were sympathetic, but the majority scorned him, disparaged him, taking his very existence as an affront. For Ali, the championship was a bully pulpit to launch a spirited attack against ''the white power structure.'' In time, he would drop the more arcane elements of Black Muslim belief (like the African mother-ship circling the earth waiting for the final confrontation between the races), but he would never lose his Muslim faith, merely temper it with his customary humor and lassitude. In the 1960s, he might ape Muhammad's racist screeds to reporters, but his orthodoxy was such that it allowed Ali to retain the white men in his corner, or his Jewish accountant, who Ali jokingly referred to as ''my Jewish brain.''

No one reacted so vehemently to Ali's public radicalism as Floyd Patterson. After Ali destroyed Liston in the first round of their rematch, Patterson took it as his personal mission to vanquish Ali, to return the crown to the fold of the NAACP, celebrity-endorsed, good Negroes of America and out of the hateful clutches of this Black Muslim upstart. He inveighed against Ali at every opportunity, attacking him in print in a series of articles in *Sports Illustrated* in which he staked his claim to the moral high ground. Ali called Patterson an Uncle Tom, and visited his training camp with a bag of carrots for ''The Rabbit.'' The fight, already something of a grudge match, assumed all the solemnity of a theological debate.

For Patterson, the match itself was a humiliation. Ali was not content to defeat Patterson: he was determined to humiliate him utterly, and in so doing, his temperate integrationist stance. Ali danced in circles around Patterson, taunting him unmercifully, and then he drew out the match, keeping Patterson on his feet for twelve rounds before the referee finally intervened.

Three months after the Patterson fight, Ali took on an opponent not so easily disposed of: the Federal Government. It began with a draft notice, eliciting from Ali the oft quoted remark: ''I ain't got no quarrel with them Vietcong.'' When he scored miserably on an aptitude test—twice and to his great embarrassment; he told reporters: ''I said I was the greatest, not the smartest''—Washington changed the law, so Ali alleged, solely in order to draft him. He refused the draft as a conscientious objector, and was summarily stripped of his title and banished from the ring. Many writers speak of this period—from 1967 to 1970—as Ali's period of exile. It was an exodus from the ring, true, but Ali was hardly out of sight; instead, he was touring the country to speak at Nation of Islam rallies and college campuses and, always, in the black neighborhoods. Ali's refusal of the draft polarized the country. Scorn was his due in the press, hate-mail filled his mail box, but on the streets and in the colleges he became a hero.

Three years later, in 1970, a Supreme Court decision overturned the adjudication of his draft status, heralding Ali's return to boxing. But he had lost a valuable three years, possibly the prime of his boxing career. His detractors, sure that age had diminished Ali's blinding speed, were quick to write him off, but once again they had underestimated his talent. It was true that three years of more or less enforced indolence had slowed Ali down, but his tactical brilliance was unimpaired. And he had learned something that would ultimately prove disastrous to his health: he could take a punch. While his great fights of the 1970s lacked the ideological drama of the bouts of the previous decade, they were in some ways a far greater testament to Ali the boxer, who, divested of his youth, had to resort to winning fights by strategy and cunning.

Though Ali lost his first post-exile fight to Joe Frazier (who had attained the championship in Ali's absence), many considered it to be the finest fight of his career, and the first in which he truly showed ''heart.'' Frazier was a good fighter, perhaps the best Ali had yet to fight, and Ali boxed gamely for fifteen rounds, losing in the fifteenth round when a vicious hook felled him (though he recovered sufficiently to end the fight on his feet). In the rematch, Ali beat Frazier in a fight that left the former champion (who had since lost his title to George Foreman) incapacitated after fourteen punishing rounds.

The victory cleared the way for a championship bout with Foreman, a massive boxer who, like Liston, possessed a sullen mien and a prison record. The 1974 fight, dubbed the ''Rumble in the Jungle'' after its location in Kinshasha, capitol city of Zaire, would prove his most dramatic, memorialized in an Academy Award-winning documentary, *When We Were Kings* (1996). What sort of physical alchemy could Ali, now 32, resort to to overcome Foreman, a boxer six years his junior? True, Foreman was a bruiser, a street-fighter like Liston. True, Ali knew how to handle such a man, but in terms of power and endurance he was outclassed. To compensate, he initiated the sort of verbal taunting used to such great affect on Liston while devising a plan to neutralize his young opponent's physical advantages: the much-vaunted rope-a-dope defense, which he would later claim was a spur-of-the-moment tactic. For the first rounds of the fight, Ali literally let Forman punch himself to exhaustion, leaning far back in the ropes to deprive Foreman of the opportunity to sneak through his defenses. By the sixth round, Foreman was visibly slowing: in the eighth he was felled with a stunning combination. Ali had once again proved his mastery, and while Foreman slunk back to America, the next morning found Ali in the streets of Kinshasha, glad-handing with the fascinated populace.

Ali would go on to fight some brilliant bouts; a rematch with Frazier which he lost, and at the age of 36, a return to win the championship for the third time from the gangly light-heavyweight, Leon Spinks. But he had continued to fight long after it was prudent to do so, firing his long-time physician, Ferdie Pacheco, after Pacheco had urged him to retire. The result: a career ending in ignominy, as he was unmercifully dissected by Larry Holmes in 1980, and by Trevor Berbick the following year in what would be his last professional bout. The aftermath was a slow slide into debilitating ''Parkinsonianism,'' which robbed Ali of the things he had treasured most: his fluid, bewitching patter and his expressiveness, replaced by tortured speech and a face with all the expressive possibilities of a mask.

It is a measure of the man—as well as the symbiotic relationship Ali had established between himself and his public—that his infirmities did not lead to retirement from public life. A born extrovert, Ali had always been the most public of public figures, popping up unexpectedly in the worst urban blight, effusing about what he would do to improve his people's lot. This one appetite has not been diminished by age. In the late 1980s and 1990s, Ali roamed the world, making paid appearances. Though the accumulated wealth of his career was largely eaten up, it is clear that Ali has not continued his public life out of sheer economic need. Much of the money he makes by signing autographed photos he donates to charity, and those who know him best claim Ali suffers when out of the spotlight.

Ali was always like catnip to writers. Writing about him was no mere exercise in superlatives, it provided an opportunity to grapple with the *zeitgeist*. Whether fully cognizant of the fact or not, Ali was like a metal house bringing down the lightning. He embodied the tumult and excitement of the 1960s, and there is no more fitting symbol for the era than this man who broke all the rules, refusing to be cowed or silenced, and did it all with style. His detractors always thought him a fraud, a peripatetic grandstander devoid of reason, if not rhyme. But they failed to understand Ali's appeal. For what his fans sensed early on was that even at the height of his buffoonery, his egotistical boasting, and his strident radicalism, the man was more than the measure of his talents, he was *genuine*. His love of his people was never a passing fad, and while the years stole his health, his ease of movement, and the banter he had used to such great effect, forcing him to resort to prestidigitation to compensate for the silencing of his marvelous mouth, his integrity remained beyond reproach. In the final judgment, Ali needed the crowds as much as they at one time needed him, not for mere validation, but because they each saw in the other the best in themselves.

—Michael Baers

FURTHER READING:

Ali, Muhammad, with Durham, Richard. *The Greatest*. New York, Random House, 1975.

Early, Gerald, editor. *The Muhammad Ali Reader*. Hopewell, New Jersey, The Ecco Press, 1998.

Gast, Leon, and Taylor Hackford. *When We Were Kings* (video). Los Angeles, David Sonenberg Productions, 1996.

Hauser, Thomas. *Muhammad Ali: His Life and Times*. New York, Simon and Schuster, 1991.

Mailer, Norman. *The Fight*. Boston, Little, Brown, 1975.

Oates, Joyce Carol. *On Boxing*. Hopewell, New Jersey, The Ecco Press, 1994.

Remnick, David. *King of the World*. New York, Random House, 1998.

Alice

Sitcom television in the 1970s featured a disproportionate number of liberated women, divorced or widowed, with or without children, making it on their own. CBS' blue (and pink) collar *Alice* was no exception, but for the fact of its tremendous success. *Alice* was one of the top 10 shows in most of its nine years on the air.

Alice was based on the 1975 film *Alice Doesn't Live Here Anymore*, which starred Academy Award winner Ellen Burstyn in the title role. The next year, CBS aired *Alice*, starring Linda Lavin as Alice Hyatt, the recent widow and aspiring singer from New Jersey who moves to Phoenix with her precocious 12-year-old son Tommy (Philip McKeon) to start a new life. While looking for singing work, Alice takes a ''temporary'' job (which lasted from 1976 to 1985) as a waitress at Mel's Diner, the local truck stop owned and operated by Mel Sharples (Vic Tayback, reprising his role from the movie). Mel was gruff, stingy, and famous for his chili. The other waitresses at the diner, at least at first, were Flo (Polly Holliday) and Vera (Beth Howland). Flo was experienced, slightly crude, outspoken and lusty, and became famous for her retort ''Kiss my grits!,'' which could be found on t-shirts throughout the late 1970s. Vera was flighty and none-too-bright; Mel liked to call her ''Dingie.'' The truck stop drew a fraternity of regulars, including Dave ''Reuben Kinkaid'' Madden.

Diane Ladd had played Flo in the movie, and when Holliday's Flo was spun off in 1980 (in the unsuccessful *Flo*, wherein the titular waitress moves to Houston to open her own restaurant), Ladd joined the sitcom's cast as Belle, a Mississippian who wrote country-western songs and lived near Alice and Tommy in the Phoenix Palms apartment complex. Belle was sort of a Flo clone; in fact, the only difference was the accent and the lack of catch phrase. Belle left after one year, and was replaced by Jolene (Celia Weston), yet another Southern waitress. In 1982, Mel's pushy mother Carrie (Martha ''Bigmouth'' Raye) joined and almost took over the diner. The fall of 1983 brought love to the hapless Vera, who, after a whirlwind courtship, married cop Elliot Novak (Charles Levin). The following fall Alice got a steady boyfriend, Nicholas Stone (Michael Durrell). Toward the end, things did get a little wacky, as is common for long-lasting shows; in one late episode, Mel purchases a robot to replace the waitresses.

In the last original episode of the series, Mel sold the diner, and despite his reputation for cheapness, gave each of his waitresses a $5000 bonus. Jolene was planning to quit and open a beauty shop anyway, Vera was pregnant, and Alice was moving to Nashville to sing with a band, finally. But viewers did get to hear Lavin sing every week. She over-enunciated the theme song to *Alice*, ''There's a New Girl in Town,'' written by Alan and Marilyn Bergman and David Shire.

Alice Hyatt was a no-nonsense, tough survivor, and her portrayer spoke out for equal opportunity for women. Lavin won Golden Globes in 1979 and 1980 and was one of the highest paid women on television, making $85,000 an episode and sending a palpable message to women. The National Commission on Working Women cited

Linda Lavin (left) and Polly Holliday in a scene from the television show *Alice*.

Alice as ''the ultimate working woman''; its annual award is now called the ''Alice.''

—Karen Lurie

FURTHER READING:

Brooks, Tim, and Earle Marsh. *The Complete Directory to Prime Time Network and Cable TV Shows, 1946-present.* New York, Ballantine Books, 1995.

Eftimiades, Maria. ''Alice Moves On.'' *People Magazine,* April 27, 1992, 67.

McNeil, Alex. *Total Television.* New York, Penguin, 1996.

Alien

Despite the success of Stanley Kubrick's *2001: A Space Odyssey* in 1968, science fiction films were often viewed as juvenile and escapist. Much of that changed in the late 1970s and the 1980s thanks to a new wave of films which challenged the notions of science fiction film, led by *Alien,* directed by Ridley Scott in 1979. The film was a critical and commercial success, garnering several awards including an Academy award nomination for Best Art Direction, an Oscar for Best Visual Effects, a Saturn Award from the Academy of Science Fiction, Horror, and Fantasy Films for Best Science Fiction Film, a Golden Globe nomination for Best Original Score, and a prestigious Hugo Award for Best Dramatic Presentation. Its adult sensibilities were enhanced by a stellar cast which included Tom Skerrit, Sigourney Weaver, Yaphet Kotto, John Hurt, Veronica Cartwright, and Harry Dean Stanton.

Inspired by *It, The Terror From Beyond Space, Alien* deftly combined the genres of horror and science fiction to create a thoroughly chilling and suspenseful drama. The slogan used to market the film aptly describes the film's effect: ''In space, no one can hear you scream.'' The storyline involved the crew of the Nostromo, an interplanetary cargo ship. They answer the distress call of an alien vessel, only to discover a derelict ship with no life forms. At least that is what they think, until further investigation reveals a number of large eggs. One "hatches" and the emergent life form attaches itself to a crew member. In an effort to save the man's life, they bring him back aboard their ship, where the creature escapes, grows at an accelerated rate, and continues through the rest of the film hunting the humans one by one. The film is often noted for its progressive politics. The film presented a racially mixed crew, with well-drawn class distinctions. The members of the upper echelon, represented by the science officer Ash, are cold and literally not-human (he is an artificial life form). It is later revealed in the story that the crew is put at risk purposely for the benefit of "the company," who wants to secure the alien life form for profit ventures. One of the most discussed aspects of the film was the prominence of the female characters, notably that of Ripley, played by Weaver. The film reflects changing gender roles in the culture for it posits Ripley as the hero of the film. She is intelligent, resourceful, and courageous, managing to save herself and destroy the creature.

The success of the film spawned three sequels, which as Thomas Doherty describes, were not so much sequels as extensions, for they continued the original storyline, concentrating on its aftermath. James Cameron, straight off the success of the box-office action film *The Terminator,* directed the second installment, *Aliens,* released in 1986. He continued the Alien tradition of genre blending by adding to the horror and science fiction elements that of the war film and action adventure. Unlike the first film which utilized a slow, creeping pace to enhance suspense, *Aliens* makes use of fast pacing and jumpcuts to enhance tension. Here, Ripley, the only expert on the alien species, volunteers to assist a marine unit assigned to rescue colonists from a planet overrun by the creatures. Again, she proves herself, eventually resting command from the incompetent lieutenant who leads them. She survives the second installment to return in *Alien 3,* directed by David Fincher in 1992. *Alien Resurrection (Alien 4),* directed by Jean-Pierre Juenet, was released in 1997.

—Frances Gateward

FURTHER READING:

Creed, Barbara. "Horror and the Monstrous Feminine." In *The Dread of Difference.* Edited by Barry Keith Grant. Austin, University of Texas Press, 1996, pp. 35-65.

Doherty, Thomas. "Gender, Genre, and the Aliens Trilogy." In *The Dread of Difference.* Austin, University of Texas Press, 1996, pp. 181-199.

Alka Seltzer

Alka Seltzer, which bubbles when placed in water, is an over the counter medication containing aspirin, heat-treated sodium bi carbonate, and sodium citrate. Originally created in 1931, it was mistakenly and popularly used to treat hangovers. The product has had a variety of well-known commercial advertisements. The first one introduced the character "Speedy" Alka Seltzer, who was used in 200 commercials between 1954-1964. The other two well received advertisements include a jingle, "Plop, Plop, Fizz, Fizz," and a slogan, "I can't believe I ate the whole thing"; both were used in the 1970s and 1980s. By the late 1990s, the medicine was still popular enough to be found on the shelves of various retail stores.

—S. Naomi Finkelstein

FURTHER READING:

McGrath, Molly. *Top Sellers USA: Success Stories Behind America's Best Selling Products from Alka Seltzer to Zippo.* New York, Morrow, 1983.

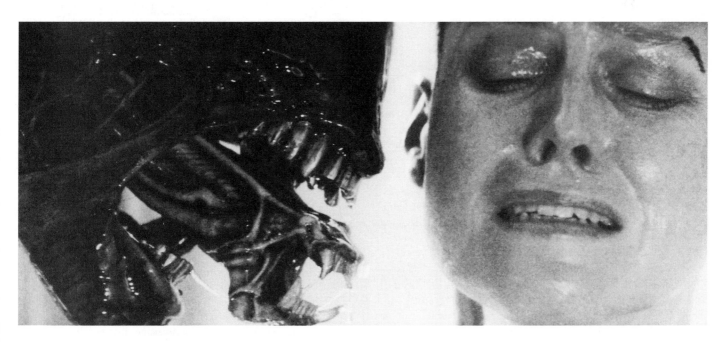

Sigourney Weaver and the "Alien" in *Alien 3.*

All About Eve

A brilliantly cynical backstage look at life in the theatre, *All About Eve* is a sophisticated movie gem that has become a cult classic since its debut in 1950. With a sparklingly witty script written and directed by Joseph Mankiewicz, *All About Eve* hinges on a consummate Bette Davis performance. Playing aging Broadway star Margo Channing, Davis is perfect as the vain, vulnerable, and vicious older actress, while delivering such oft-quoted epigrams as "Fasten your seat belts, it's going to be a bumpy night." When aspiring young actress Eve Harrington, played by Anne Baxter, conspires to take over both Margo Channing's part and her man, an all-out battle ensues between the two women. Co-starring George Sanders, Celeste Holm, Thelma Ritter, and featuring a very young Marilyn Monroe, *All About Eve* won six Oscars, including Best Picture and Best Director. *All About Eve* is the cinematic epitome of Hollywood wit and sophistication.

—Victoria Price

FURTHER READING:

Kael, Pauline. *5001 Nights at the Movies.* New York, Henry Holt, 1991

Microsoft Corporation, *Cinemania 96: The Best-Selling Interactive Guide to Movies and the Moviemakers.*

Monaco, James and the Editors of Baseline. *Encyclopedia of Film.* New York, Perigee, 1991.

All in the Family

All in the Family, with fellow CBS series *The Mary Tyler Moore Show* and *M*A*S*H,* redefined the American situation comedy in the early 1970s. Based on the hit British show *Till Death Us Do Part, All in the Family* introduced social realism and controversy, conveyed in frank language, to the American sitcom while retaining the genre's core domestic family and revisiting its early blue-collar milieu. That generic reconstruction proved to be as popular as it was innovative: It was number one in the Nielsen ratings for its first five full years on the air and ranked out of the Top 20 only once in its 12-year broadcast life. At the same time, it created a long and occasionally vituperative discussion over the propriety of racism, sexism, religious bias, and politics as the situation of a half-hour comedy.

All in the Family was the creation of writer/producer Norman Lear, who purchased the rights to *Till Death Us Do Part* in 1968 after reading of the turmoil the show had provoked in its homeland. Citing the British comedy's attention to major social issues such as class and race and to internal "generation gap" family conflicts, Lear and his Tandem production company developed two pilot remakes, *Justice for All* and *Those Were the Days,* in 1968-69 for ABC. Concerned about audience tests showing a negative reaction to protagonist Archie Justice, ABC rejected both pilots. Lear's agents shipped the second pilot to CBS, which was about to reconfigure its schedule to appeal to a younger, more urban demographic. Though sharing

ABC's concerns about the coarseness of renamed paterfamilias Archie Bunker, CBS programmers were enthusiastic about Lear's show, now called *All in the Family,* and scheduled its debut for January 12, 1971.

The first episode of *All in the Family* introduced audiences to loudmouth loading-dock worker Archie Bunker (played by Carroll O'Connor), his sweetly dim wife Edith (Jean Stapleton), their rebellious daughter Gloria (Sally Struthers), and her scruffy radical husband Michael Stivic (Rob Reiner), all of whom shared the Bunker domicile at 704 Hauser Street in Queens. After an opening that suggested a sexual interlude between Michael and Gloria far in excess of what sitcoms had previously offered, the audience heard Archie's rants about race ("If your spics and your spades want their rightful piece of the American dream, let them get out there and work for it!"), religion ("Feinstein, Feinberg—it all comes to the same thing and I know that tribe!"), ethnicity ("What do you know about it, you dumb Polack?") and the children's politics ("I knew we had a couple of pinkos in this house, but I didn't know we had atheists!"). Michael gave back as good as he got, Gloria supported her husband, and Edith forebore the tirades from both sides with a good heart and a calm, if occasionally stupefied, demeanor in what quickly came to be the show's weekly formula of comedic conflict.

Immediate critical reaction to all of this ranged from wild praise to apocalyptic denunciation, with little in between. Popular reaction, however, was noncommittal at first. The show's initial ratings were low, and CBS withheld its verdict until late in the season, when slowly rising Nielsen numbers convinced the network to renew it. Summer reruns of the series, along with two Emmys, exponentially increased viewership; by the beginning of the 1971-72 season, *All in the Family* was the most popular show in America. In addition to his "pinko" daughter and son-in-law, Archie's equally opinionated black neighbor George Jefferson, his wife's leftist family, his ethnically diverse workplace and his all-too-liberal church became fodder for his conservative cannon. Household saint Edith was herself frequently in the line of Archie's fire, with his repeated imprecation "Stifle yourself, you dingbat!" becoming a national catch phrase. The social worth of the Bunkers' battles became the focus of discussions and commentary in forums ranging from *TV Guide* to *The New Yorker* to *Ebony,* where Archie Bunker was the first white man to occupy the cover. Social scientists and communication scholars joined the debate with empirical studies that alternately proved and disproved that *All in the Family*'s treatment of race, class, and bigotry had a malign effect on the show's viewers and American society.

As the controversy over *All in the Family* raged throughout the 1970s, the series itself went through numerous changes. Michael and Gloria had a son and moved out, first to the Jeffersons' vacated house next door and then to California. Archie, after a long layoff, left his job on the loading dock and purchased his longtime neighborhood watering hole. And Edith, whose menopause, phlebitis, and attempted rape had been the subjects of various episodes, died of a stroke. With her passing, *All in the Family* in the fall of 1979 took on the new title, *Archie Bunker's Place.* Edith's niece Stephanie (Danielle Brisebois), who had moved in with the Bunkers after the Stivics left Queens, kept a modicum of "family" in the show; with Archie's bar and his cronies there now the focus, however, *Archie Bunker's Place,* which ran through 1983 under that title, addressed character much more than the social issues and generational bickering that had defined the original.

(From left) Sally Struthers, Rob Reiner, Jean Stapleton, and Carroll O'Connor in a scene from *All in the Family.*

Time has been less kind to *All in the Family* than to its fellow 1970s CBS sitcom originals. Its social realism, like that of Depression-era dramas, is so rooted in its age and presented so broadly that it translates to other places and eras far less successfully than the character-driven *MTM* and the early *M*A*S*H*. Its most lasting breakthrough in content was not a greater concern with political and social issues but a growing obsession with sex as a verbal and visual source of humor. Even Lear's resurrection of three-camera live videotaping, a standard of early television variety shows, which added speed and intensity to the bristling wit of the early episodes, looked cheap and tired by the end of the series. Nonetheless, at its best, *All in the Family* used sharp writing and strong acting to bring a "real" world the genre had never before countenanced into the American situation comedy. If its own legacy is disappointing, the disappointment may speak as much to the world it represented as it does the show itself.

—Jeffrey S. Miller

FURTHER READING:

Adler, Richard P. *All in the Family: A Critical Appraisal.* New York, Praeger, 1979.

Marc, David. *Comic Visions: Television Comedy and American Culture.* Boston, Unwin Hyman, 1989.

McCrohan, Donna. *Archie & Edith, Mike & Gloria.* New York, Workman, 1987.

Miller, Jeffrey S. *Something Completely Different: British Television and American Culture, 1960-1980.* Minneapolis, University of Minnesota Press, 1999.

All My Children

From its January 5, 1970, debut, soap opera *All My Children*, with its emphasis on young love and such topical issues as abortion, the Vietnam War, and the environment, attracted college students in unusually high numbers, suddenly expanding the traditional market and changing the focus of the genre forever. The structure of the program has been the traditional battling families concept with the wealthy, dysfunctional Tyler family of Pine Valley pitted against the morally upright but decidedly middle-class Martins. While the stories are mainly romantic and triangular, what makes the show unique is its outright celebration of young lovers and their loves.

Chuck Tyler and Phil Brent were teenagers when their rivalry for the affections of Tara Martin split apart their friendship and pitted the Martins against the Tylers. This conflict drove the series for many years until it was supplanted in 1980 by a romance between Greg Nelson and Jenny Gardner, which was beset by interference from his controlling mother; a devious young flame, Liza; and ultimately Greg's own paralysis. This was followed in succeeding years by a parade of almost unbelievable characters who, in their flamboyance and eccentricity, overcame some rather formulaic and often saccharine story lines. Among them was the matriarch Phoebe Tyler who, in her obsession with social propriety, bullied her family into almost hypocritical submission as they sought to achieve their fantasies out of sight of her all-observing eyes. Another was the gum-chewing Opal Gardner, Jenny's meddling mother. Despite being little more than caricatures rather than characters, they provided the audience with welcome comic relief from the earnestness of the show's young lovers and the stability of its tent-pole characters.

The show's most famous character is the beautiful, spoiled, and vindictive Erica Kane, played with an almost vampy flourish by soap queen Susan Lucci (perennially nominated for an Emmy but, as of the late 1990s, holding the record for most nominations without a win). Erica represents the little, lost, daddy's girl who wants nothing more than her father's love and will stop at nothing to achieve at least some facsimile of it. Although she steamrolls men in her quest for love, she has remained sympathetic even as she wooed and divorced three husbands and a succession of lovers in a reckless attempt to fill the void left by her father's absence and neglect. Much of this is due to Lucci's remarkable portrayal of Erica's inherent vulnerability and story lines that have dealt with rape, abortion, substance abuse, and motherhood. Yet, despite her increasing maturity as a character, Erica has remained compulsively destructive over the years, not only destroying her own happiness but the lives of all of those who come in contact with her.

Much of *All My Children*'s success can be attributed to its consistently entertaining and intelligent characterizations and its penchant for presenting a mix of styles with something calculated to please almost everyone. Although this may be somewhat emotionally unsettling within the context of its mingled story lines, it does reflect life as it is, which is anything but neat and tidy. Much of the credit for the show's remarkable constancy over its three-decade run is the fact that it has been almost entirely written by only two head writers— Agnes Nixon and Wisner Washam—and kept many of its original actors, including Lucci, Ruth Warrick (Phoebe), Mary Fickett (Ruth Brent) and Ray MacDonnell (Dr. Joseph Martin).

—Sandra Garcia-Myers

FURTHER READING:

Allen, Robert C. *Speaking of Soap Operas.* Chapel Hill, University of North Carolina Press, 1985.

Groves, Seli. *The Ultimate Soap Opera Guide.* Detroit, Visible Ink Press, 1985.

LaGuardia, Robert. *Soap World.* New York, Arbor House, 1983.

Schemering, Christopher. *The Soap Opera Encyclopedia.* New York, Ballantine Books, 1985.

Warner, Gary. *All My Children: The Complete Family Scrapbook.* Los Angeles, General Publishing Group, 1994.

All Quiet on the Western Front

One of the greatest pacifist statements ever to reach the screen, *All Quiet on the Western Front* follows a group of German youths from their patriotic fervor at the start of World War I in 1914, to the death of the last of their number in 1918. Based on Erich Maria Remarque's like-titled novel, *All Quiet* downplays the political issues that led to World War I and dwells instead on the folly and horror of war in general. Filmed at a cost of $1.2 million and populated with 2,000 extras, many of them war veterans, *All Quiet* garnered widespread critical acclaim and Academy Awards for Best Picture and Best Director (Lewis Milestone). It also made a star of Lew Ayres, a previously unknown 20 year-old who played Remarque's autobiographical figure of Paul Baumer. A 1990 addition to the National Film Registry, *All Quiet* remains a timely and powerful indictment of war.

—Martin F. Norden

FURTHER READING:

Millichap, Joseph R. *Lewis Milestone.* Boston, Twayne, 1981.

Norden, Martin F. *The Cinema of Isolation: A History of Physical Disability in the Movies.* New Brunswick, Rutgers University Press, 1994.

Allen, Steve (1921—)

As an actor, talk show host, game show panelist, musician, composer, author, and social commentator, Steve Allen helped define the role of television personality in the early days of the medium. No less a personage than Noel Coward dubbed Allen ''the most talented man in America.'' An encyclopedic knowledge of a variety of subjects combined with a remarkable ability to ad-lib has made him a distinctive presence on American TV sets since the 1950s.

Stephen Valentine Patrick William Allen was born in New York City on December 26, 1921 to vaudeville performers Billy Allen and Belle Montrose. Allen grew up on the vaudeville circuit, attending over a dozen schools in his childhood even as he learned the essence of performing virtually through osmosis. He began his professional career as a disk jockey in 1942 while attending the University of Arizona, and worked in West Coast radio throughout the decade. His first regular TV work was as host of *Songs for Sale* on NBC, beginning in 1951.

In September 1954, Allen was chosen to host NBC's *The Tonight Show*. The brainchild of NBC executive Pat Weaver, *The Tonight Show* was developed as a late-night version of the network's *Today Show*, a morning news and information series. Allen confidently took television to new vistas—outside, for example, where a

Steve Allen

uniformed Allen would randomly stop cars on Manhattan highways. Allen would frequently make elaborate prank phone calls on the air, or read the nonsensical rock lyrics of the era (''Sh-Boom,'' ''Tutti Frutti'') in a dramatic setting. Allen's potpourri of guests ranged from Lincoln biographer Carl Sandburg to beat comic Lenny Bruce. Allen even devoted broadcasts to discussions of serious subjects, including organized crime.

After two years on late night television, Allen shifted to a Sunday night variety series on NBC, opposite the then-reigning *Ed Sullivan Show* on CBS. Allen and Sullivan fiercely competed to land top guests. In his most memorable coup, Allen brought Elvis Presley on his show first, where the 21-year-old rock star sang ''Hound Dog'' to an actual basset hound. Allen's NBC show lasted until 1960.

The group of comedic sidekicks Allen introduced to a national audience included Tom Poston, Don Knotts, Louis Nye (whose confident greeting, ''Hi-ho, Steverino,'' became Allen's nickname), Don Adams, Bill Dana, and Pat Harrington, Jr. His *Tonight Show* announcer, Gene Rayburn, became a popular game show host in the 1970s. Allan Sherman, who would later achieve Top Ten status with such song parodies as ''Hello Muddah, Hello Faddah,'' originally produced Allen's 1960s syndicated talk show.

In public and private, Allen exhibited one of the quickest wits in show business. When told that politician Barry Goldwater was half-Jewish, Allen replied, ''Too bad it's not the top half.'' Addressing a drug rehabilitation clinic, Allen said he hoped his presence would give ''a real shot in the arm'' to the organization. As a panelist on the *What's My Line?* game show, Allen's question (used to identify a

product manufactured or used by the contestant), ''Is it bigger than a breadbox?'' entered the national language.

Allen's irreverent demeanor was a direct influence upon David Letterman; Letterman acknowledged watching Allen's 1960s television work while a teenager, and many of Allen's on-air stunts (wearing a suit made of tea bags, and being dunked in a giant cup) found their way onto Letterman's 1980s series (Letterman once wore a suit of nacho chips, and was lowered into a vat of guacamole).

Allen's ambitious *Meeting of Minds* series, which he had developed for over 20 years, debuted on PBS in 1977. Actors portraying world and philosophical leaders throughout history—on one panel, for example, Ulysses S. Grant, Karl Marx, Christopher Columbus, and Marie Antoinette—would come together in a forum (hosted by Allen) to discuss great ideas. The innovative series was among the most critically acclaimed in television history, winning numerous awards during its five-year span.

Allen has written over 4,000 songs, more than double Irving Berlin's output. His best known composition is ''The Start of Something Big,'' introduced by Steve Lawrence and Eydie Gorme, who were themselves introduced to one another by Allen. Allen also composed several Broadway musical comedy scores, including the 1963 show *Sophie*. His more than 40 books run the gamut from mystery novels to analyses of contemporary comedy and discussions on morality and religion. The sardonic Oscar Levant once remarked, ''When I can't sleep, I read a book by Steve Allen.''

Allen's best-known movie performance was the title role in the 1956 hit *The Benny Goodman Story*, and he has made cameo appearances in *The Sunshine Boys* (1975) and *The Player* (1992). He also played himself on two episodes of *The Simpsons*, including one in which Bart Simpson's voice was altered by computer to sound like Allen's.

While attaining the status of Hollywood elder statesman, he remained an outspoken social and political commentator through the 1990s, and lent his name to anti-smoking and pro-family values crusades. After Bob Hope called Allen ''the Adlai Stevenson of comedy,'' Allen said he preferred to describe himself as ''the Henny Youngman of politics.''

—Andrew Milner

FURTHER READING:

Allen, Steve. *Beloved Son: A Story of the Jesus Cults.* New York, Bobbs-Merrill, 1982.

———. *Funny People.* New York, Stein and Day, 1982.

———. *Hi-Ho, Steverino!: My Adventures in the Wonderful Wacky World of TV.* New York, Barricade, 1992.

Current Biography Yearbook 1982. Detroit, Gale Research, 1982.

Allen, Woody (1935—)

Woody Allen is as close to an auteur as contemporary popular culture permits. While his style has changed dramatically since the

Woody Allen

release of *Take the Money and Run* (1969), his work has always been distinctively his. Over the last thirty years, he has epitomized the ideal of complete artistic control. His reputation for eclectic casting, neurotic privacy, and the intertwining of his personal and professional lives has made him a recognizable public phenomenon even among people who have never seen one of his films.

Born Allan Stewart Konigsberg, Allen broke into show business while he was still in high school by writing jokes for newspaper columnists. As depicted in *Annie Hall* (1977), Allen grew tired of hearing other comedians do less than justice to his material and took to the Manhattan nightclub circuit. He also appeared as an actor on *Candid Camera, That Was the Week That Was,* and *The Tonight Show.*

In 1969, Allen was contracted to write a vehicle for Warren Beatty called *What's New Pussycat?* Though Beatty dropped out of the project, Peter O'Toole replaced him and the film was a moderate financial success. The experience (and the profit) provided Allen with the entrée to his own directorial debut, *Take the Money and Run* (1969). His early films—*Take the Money and Run* and *Bananas*—were retreads of his stand-up routines. They starred Allen and various members of improvisational groups of which he had been a part and were made on very low budgets. In 1972, he made a screen adaptation of his successful play *Play It Again Sam.* The film starred Allen and featured Tony Roberts and Diane Keaton, actors who would come to be known as among the most productive of Allen's stable of regular talent. *Play It Again Sam* was followed by a string of commercially viable, if not blockbuster, slapstick comedies—*Everything You Always Wanted to Know About Sex But Were Afraid to Ask* (1972),

Sleeper (1973), and *Love and Death* (1975)—which established Allen's hapless nebbish as the ideal anti-hero of the 1970s. Interestingly, while Allen is primarily identified as the personification of quasi-intellectual Manhattan, it bears mentioning that of these early features only *Bananas* was situationally linked to New York. In fact, the movie version of *Play It Again Sam* was moved from New York to San Francisco.

In 1977, Allen wrote, directed, and starred (with Keaton and Roberts) in *Annie Hall.* The film was a critical and commercial triumph. It won Oscars for itself, Allen, and Keaton. It was *Annie Hall*—a paean to Manhattan and a thinly veiled autobiography—that cemented Allen in the public mind as the penultimate modern New Yorker. It also established the tone and general themes of most of his later work. In 1978, he directed the dark and overly moody *Interiors,* which was met with mixed reviews and commercial rejection. In 1979, he rebounded with *Manhattan,* shot in black and white and featuring then little known actress Meryl Streep. *Manhattan* was nominated for a Golden Globe Award and three Oscars. It won awards from the National Society of Film Critics and the New York Film Critics' Circle. While it was not as popular with the public as *Annie Hall,* most critics agree that it was a substantially better film.

Refusing to be comfortable with an established style or intimidated by the public rejection of *Interiors,* Allen entered a period of experimentation: *Stardust Memories* (1980) a sarcastic analysis of his relationship to his fans; the technical tour-de-force *Zelig* (1983); *The Purple Rose of Cairo,* a Depression-era serio-comedy in which a character (Jeff Daniels) comes out of the movie screen and romances one of his fans (Mia Farrow); and others. All appealed to Allen's cadre of loyal fans, but none even nearly approached the commercial or critical success of *Annie Hall* or *Manhattan* until the release of *Hannah and Her Sisters* in 1986.

Since then, Allen has produced a steady stream of city-scapes, some provocative like *Another Woman* (1988) and *Deconstructing Harry* (1998), and others that were simply entertaining such as *Manhattan Murder Mystery* (1993) and *Mighty Aphrodite* (1995). All, however, have been sufficiently successful to sustain his reputation as one of the most creative and productive film makers in American history.

—Barry Morris

FURTHER READING:

Brode, Douglas. *Woody Allen: His Films and Career.* Secaucus, Citadel Press, 1985.

Girgus, Sam B. *The Films of Woody Allen.* Boston, Cambridge University Press, 1993.

Lax, Eric. *Woody Allen: A Biography.* New York, Vintage Books, 1992.

Allison, Luther (1939-1997)

Luther Allison was one of the most popular and critically-acclaimed blues guitar players of the 1990s, combining classic west

Luther Allison

side Chicago guitar with rock and soul in a unique style that appealed to the mostly white blues festival audiences. Record company disputes, false starts, and a prolonged residency in Europe kept him from attaining a large popularity in America until late in life, and his untimely death from cancer cut that success short.

Allison built a world-wide reputation with his intensity and stamina, often playing three or four hours at a stretch and leaving audiences decimated. "His urgency and intensity was amazing," long-time band leader James Solberg said in *Living Blues* magazine's tribute to Allison after his death. "I mean, to stand next to a guy that was 57 years old and watch him go for four and a half hours and not stop . . . I've seen teenagers that couldn't keep up with him . . . He just had to get them blues out no matter what."

Allison was born the fourteenth of 15 children on August 17, 1939 in Widener, Arkansas to a family of sharecroppers. His family moved to Chicago in 1951 where his older brother, Ollie, began playing guitar. Allison eventually joined his brother's outfit, the Rolling Stones, as a bass player. By 1957 he had switched to guitar and was fronting his own band in clubs around the west side.

Allison's early years as a front man were heavily influenced by Freddie King, Buddy Guy, Otis Rush, and Magic Sam. Although close in age to Allison, those guitar players had started their careers earlier and served as mentors. He also listened to B.B. King at an early age, and King's influence is perhaps the most prominent in Allison's style. In fact, Allison was perhaps one of the best at emulating King's fluttering vibrato.

Allison's first break came in 1969 when he performed at the Ann Arbor Blues Festival to an audience of mostly white middle-class college students and folk listeners. That performance built Allison's reputation as a fiery, indefatigable performer and one of the hottest new stars in Blues. Allison also released his first album, *Love Me Mama,* on Chicago's Delmark label that same year. Although the album suffered from a lack of original material, it was the best-selling release on Delmark by an artist not already established with a rhythm and blues single.

Partly because of his performance at Ann Arbor, Motown Records signed him to a contract that would produce three albums on the company's Gordy label. *Bad News Is Coming* (1972) and *Luther's Blues* (1974) were excellent blues albums, but the third album *Night Life* (1976) was a critical failure. The album was Allison's first attempt to blend soul and rhythm and blues with blues, but it left his guitar and vocal buried under layers of horns and backup singers.

As the only blues artist signed to Motown, Allison became more and more frustrated with the label's lack of interest and knowledge about how to promote and record him. During this period, however, Allison toured relentlessly around the Midwest, building a base of fans among the region's college towns and continuing to play his unrestrained high-energy brand of blues. After leaving Motown, Allison recorded *Gonna Be a Live One in Here Tonight!* for tiny Rumble Records in 1979. Perfectly capturing his live show at the time, the rare album quickly became a collector's item. Allison eventually became frustrated with the American music business, and spent more and more time touring Europe where he found a warm reception. By 1984, he was living full-time in Paris, France.

According to Solberg, Allison's arrival in Europe was monumental. "They had seen Mississippi Fred McDowell and Mance Lipscomb and all those cats, but a lot of them had never seen electric blues," he said. "I mean, to stick Luther in front of folks who had only seen an acoustic blues guy was pretty amazing, both good and bad at first. But ultimately I saw Luther turn blues aficionados' dismay into amazement and excitement. On a blues version, it was like when the Beatles hit the United States. It was like rock stardom in a blues sense." Allison's son, Bernard, also became a hit blues guitarist in Europe, often touring with his father and releasing albums under his own name.

Allison recorded nearly a dozen albums on various European labels, blending blues, rock, and soul with varying degrees of success, but he still yearned for success in the United States. By the early 1990s, Allison and his European agent Thomas Ruf returned to America and sought out Memphis producer Jim Gaines, who had previously recorded Carlos Santana and Stevie Ray Vaughan. The album *Soul Fixin' Man* was the result. Allison and Ruf formed their own label, Ruf Records, and released the record in Europe. Chicago's Alligator Records bought the album for release in the United States in 1994.

Allison had finally found the right formula, and the success of that album led to two more: *Blue Streak* (1995) and *Reckless* (1997). He won the W.C. Handy Award for Entertainer of the Year in 1996, 1997, and 1998 and collected 11 additional Handy Awards during those years.

Having conquered the blues world, Allison may have been on the verge of a cross-over breakthrough to mainstream rock similar to Stevie Ray Vaughan or Buddy Guy. But he was cut down at the height of his powers. While touring the midwest, he was diagnosed with lung cancer and metastatic brain tumors on July 10, 1997. He died while undergoing treatment in Madison, Wisconsin.

—Jon Klinkowitz

FURTHER READING:

Baldwin-Beneich, Sarah. "From Blues to Bleus." *Chicago Tribune Magazine.* March 31, 1991, pp. 19-20.

Bessman, Jim. "Alligator's Luther Allison Has a Mean 'Blue Streak.'" *Billboard.* July 29, 1995, pp. 11, 36.

Bonner, Brett J. "A Tribute to Luther Allison." *Living Blues.* November/December, 1997, pp. 44-47.

Freund, Steve. "Luther Allison." *Living Blues.* January/February, 1996, pp. 8-21.

The Allman Brothers Band

The Allman Brothers Band was America's answer to the British Invasion of the 1960s. The band's improvisational sound served as the basis of country rock through the 1970s and epitomized the cultural awakening of the New South which culminated in Jimmy Carter's presidency in 1976. The Allman Brothers were the first band to successfully combine twin lead guitars and drummers.

Guitarists Duane Allman and Dickey Betts, bass player Berry Oakley and drummers Jaimoe and Butch Trucks joined Duane's younger brother, organ player, vocalist, and songwriter Gregg in 1969. Duane, one of the greatest slide guitarists in rock history, was killed in a motorcycle accident in October, 1971 and Oakley died in a similar accident a year later. Betts assumed a dominant position in the band, writing and singing the band's biggest hit, "Ramblin' Man" in 1973. Surviving breakups and personnel changes, the band continued into the 1990s, building a devoted following much like The Grateful Dead.

—Jon Klinkowitz

FURTHER READING:

Freeman, Scott. *Midnight Riders: The Story of the Allman Brothers Band.* Boston, Little Brown, 1995.

Nolan, Tom. *The Allman Brothers Band: A Biography in Words and Pictures.* New York, Chappell Music Company, 1976.

Ally McBeal

The Fox Television series *Ally McBeal,* concerning the lives of employees at a contemporary law firm in Boston, struck a chord with viewers soon after its premier in September of 1997. Focusing on the life of the title character, played by Calista Flockhart, the show provoked a cultural dialogue about its portrayal of young, single career women. Fans enjoyed the updated take on working women as real human beings struggling with insecurities; the character of Ally was called a modern version of 1970s television heroine Mary Tyler Moore. Critics, however, derided the miniskirted characters in *Ally McBeal* as female stereotypes obsessed with getting married and having children. The show also gained notice for its frequent use of computer-enhanced effects, such as exaggerated facial expressions and the dancing baby that haunted Ally as a symbol of her desire for motherhood.

—Geri Speace

FURTHER READING:

Heywood, Leslie. "Hitting a Cultural Nerve: Another Season of 'Ally McBeal.'" *Chronicle of Higher Education.* September 4, 1998, B9.

Kingston, Philip. "You Will Love Her or Loathe Her—or Both." *The Sunday Telegraph.* February 8, 1998, 7.

Kloer, Phil. "The Secret Life of 'Ally McBeal': 'Seinfeld' Successor?" *The Atlanta Journal and Constitution.* February 2, 1998, B1.

Vorobil, Mary. "What's the Deal with 'Ally McBeal?'" *Newsday.* February 9, 1998, B6.

Herb Alpert and the Tijuana Brass

Though a life in music was not Herb Alpert's first choice—he initially attempted an acting career—he eventually became one of the most influential figures in the history of pop music. Throughout the 1960s, the Tijuana Brass, led by Alpert's trumpet playing, dominated the pop charts with singles including "The Lonely Bull," "A Taste of Honey," and "This Guy's in Love With You." Their unique Latin-influenced sound came to be dubbed "Ameriachi."

Alpert (1935—) was not only one of pop's most successful performers, but also one of its most gifted businessmen. With Jerry Moss he co-founded A&M Records, which later became one of the most prosperous record companies in the world; its successes included the Carpenters, Joe Cocker, and many others. After selling A&M to PolyGram in 1990 for over $500 million, Alpert and Moss founded a new label, Almo Sounds, whose artists included the punk band Garbage.

—Marc R. Sykes

FURTHER READING:

Alpert, Herb. *The DeLuxe Herb Alpert & the Tijuana Brass.* New York, Music Mates, 1965.

Altamont

Stung by accusations of profiteering during their 1969 United States tour, the Rolling Stones announced plans for a free concert in San Francisco at its conclusion. It would be a thank you to their adoring public, and a means to assuage their guilt. Unfortunately, the December 6 concert at Altamont Speedway near Livermore, California, ended in chaos and death. By day's end there would be four dead, four born, and 300,000 bummed-out. Although inadequate preparation was at fault, the Hell's Angels Motorcycle Club, contracted as a security force for 500 dollars worth of beer, rightfully received the lion's share of the blame—there was a film crew at hand to document their abuses from beginning to end. Over time, Altamont has achieved a kind of mythic significance. It epitomized the potential for violence in the counterculture . . . the ugliness lurking behind the bangles and beads. Altamont hailed both the real and metaphorical end to 1960s counterculture.

From its very inception, portents of doom and disaster hung in the air. It was a bad day for a concert, proclaimed astrologists. The Sun, Venus, and Mercury were in Sagittarius; the moon, on the cusp of Libra and Scorpio—very bad omens indeed. Events would soon bear them out. Almost from its inception the free concert was hampered by persistent bad luck. Initially to be held in Golden Gate Park, the San Francisco City Council turned down the permit application at the very last minute. With four days to go, an alternate site was secured; the Sears Point Speedway outside San Francisco. But even as scaffolding, generators, and sound equipment were assembled there, the owners hedged, insisting on an exorbitant bond. The deal quickly fell through. With scarcely 48 hours to go before the already announced concert date, Altamont Speedway owner, Dick Carter, volunteered the use of his property for free, anticipating a raft of favorable publicity for the race track in return. The Rolling Stones were not to be denied their magnanimous gesture.

Four members of the Hell's Angels security at the 1969 Altamont Concert.

A crew of more than 200 volunteers worked through the night to relocate and erect the massive sound and light system. As concert time approached, the organizers were hopeful the day would prove a success. With so little time to prepare, short shrift had been made with food, water, parking, and bathroom facilities, but the organizers hoped that the spirit of togetherness so apparent at Woodstock would manifest itself equally for Altamont. Daybreak arose upon a scene of chaos. Throughout the night, people had been arriving at the site. By morning automobiles ranged along the access road for ten miles; people were forced to stand in line for more than half an hour to make use of the portable toilets and queues some 300 yards long stretched from the water faucets.

As the show began in earnest, hostilities broke out almost immediately. Throughout the first set by Santana, Angels provoked fights, beat the enthusiastic, inebriated audience with pool cues when they ventured too close to the stage, and drove their motorcycles through the crowd with reckless abandon. As Jefferson Airplane began their set, Hell's Angels arranged themselves about the stage, jumping into the crowd to drub perceived trouble-makers, and finally turned on the band itself, knocking out singer Marty Balin when he made efforts to intervene in a particularly brutal melee.

The Angels calmed down briefly under the influence of the mellow country-rock of the Flying Burrito Brothers, but tempers flared once again as Crosby, Stills, Nash, and Young played. As night fell and the temperature dropped, the chilled crowd and the thoroughly soused Angels prepared for the final act.

One and a half hours later, the Stones threaded their way through the backstage crush and took the stage. Mick Jagger, dressed in a satin bat-winged shirt, half red and half black, pranced about like a Satanic jester, capering and dancing through the first number, ''Jumpin' Jack Flash,'' but as the Angels' violent assault on the audience continued,

he was soon reduced to nervously pacing the stage, a worried expression on his face as he implored the combatants to cool down.

At will, the Angels continued their violent forays into the stunned crowd. ''Sympathy for the Devil'' was interrupted several times by violence, while Jagger and Keith Richards vainly beseeched the Angels. In response, an Angel seized the microphone, yelling at the crowd: ''Hey, if you don't cool it, you ain't gonna hear no more music!'' Wrote Stanley Booth, a reporter at the concert: ''It was like blaming the pigs in a slaughterhouse for bleeding on the floor.''

In fits and starts the band continued to play. They were nearing the end of ''Under My Thumb'' when a whirl of motion erupted at stage left. ''Someone is shooting at the stage,'' an Angel cried. In fact, the gun had been pulled in self-defense by one Meredith Hunter, an 18-year-old black man, who had caught the Angels attention both because of his color and the fact that accompanying him was a pretty blond girl. As Hunter attempted to get closer to the stage, the Angels had chased him back into the crowd, and as they fell on him—with knife and boot and fist—he drew a gun in self defense. He was attacked with a savage fury and once the assault was completed, Angels guarded the body as the boy slowly bled to death, allowing onlookers to carry him away after they were certain he was beyond help. The Stones carried on. Unaware of what had happened—there had already been so much pandemonium—they finished their brief set then fled to a waiting helicopter.

They could not, however, escape the outrage to follow. The recriminations flew thick and fast in the press. *Rolling Stone Magazine* described Altamont as ''the product of diabolical egotism, hype, ineptitude, money manipulation, and, at base a fundamental lack of concern for humanity,'' while Angel president Sonny Barger insisted the Stones had used them as dupes, telling KSAN radio, ''I didn't go there to police nothing, when they started messing over our bikes, they started it. Ain't nobody gonna kick my motorcycle!'' Attacked from every direction, Mick Jagger initiated a ten million dollar suit against the owners of Sears Point Speedway in an effort at damage control, alleging breach of contract and fraud. No amount of litigation, however, could mitigate the simple fact that the Stones had presided over a fiasco of such magnitude that had dealt a fatal blow to the peaceful image of the hippie. Remembered as one of the most negative events of the 1960s counterculture, Altamont was, if not the final, the most memorable swan song in its prolonged death throes.

—Michael J. Baers

FURTHER READING:

Bangs, Lester, et al. ''Let It Bleed.'' *Rolling Stone Magazine.* January 21, 1970.

Booth, Stanley. *The True Adventures of the Rolling Stones.* New York, Vintage Books, 1985.

Burks, John. ''In the Aftermath of Altamont.'' *Rolling Stone Magazine.* February 7, 1970.

Eisner, Jonathan. *Altamont.* New York, Avon Books, 1970.

Hotchner, A.E. *Blown Away, the Rolling Stones and the Death of the '60s.* New York, Simon and Schuster, 1990.

Maysles, David and Albert. *Gimme Shelter.* New York, ABCO Pictures, 1970

Sanchez, Tony. *Up and Down With the Rolling Stones.* New York, William Morrow, 1979.

Sander, Ellen. *Trips: Rock Life in the '60s.* New York, Charles Scribners and Sons, 1970.

Alternative Country Music

Alternative country, also referred to as ''Americana,'' ''Cowpunk,'' ''Y'alternative,'' ''No Depression,'' and ''Insurgent Country,'' is a catch-all term describing a diverse musical genre that combines forms of traditional country music, such as twang, swing, rockabilly, and bluegrass, with the ethos and sound of punk rock. While a definition of ''alt.country'' may be difficult to pin down, what it is not remains clear: it is not the ''Hot Country'' music of commercial Nashville, which is seen as homogenous and lacking a sense of tradition. Gram Parsons, generally considered the godfather of alt.country, noted in 1972 to Frank Murphy, ''Yeah, my music is still country—but my feeling is there is no boundary between 'types' of music.'' His words forecast the diversity of a genre that would follow the trail he had blazed.

As with any genre, the exact origin of alt.country is open to debate. Ben Fong-Torres, Parsons' biographer, has noted, ''Parsons wasn't the first to conceive country-rock, but he was perhaps the most passionate about bringing country music into the increasingly rock 'n' roll world of the 1960s.'' His brief collaboration with the Byrds led to the seminal country-rock album *Sweetheart of the Rodeo* (1968),

which brought together the sounds and attitudes of rock and country. Prophetically, when the Byrds played at the Grand Ole Opry, Parsons substituted his own material for the traditional songs the band had planned to play, angering his band-mates, especially Roger McGuinn. Such an act foreshadows what would become the attitude of alt.country.

Later, Parsons extended his country-rock sound, first with the Flying Burrito Brothers and then as a solo artist on *GP* (1973) and *Grievous Angel* (1974), with then unheard of singer Emmylou Harris providing perfect harmonies. After Parsons' death in 1973, Harris went on to forge her own successful career, keeping his musical memory alive while experimenting in the tradition of her mentor with albums from the bluegrass *Roses in the Snow* to the alternative-influenced *Wrecking Ball.* Harris herself has noted, ''I always tried to fight against categories.''

The 1970s saw other bands exploring the possibilities of country-rock. The Flatlanders, the Nitty Gritty Dirt Band, New Riders of the Purple Sage, the Grateful Dead, and Asleep at the Wheel all revised traditional country music, while the Eagles and Poco generated a radio-friendly sound that proved commercially successful. Another important voice of the 1970s was that of the Outlaws, a group whose members included Willie Nelson, Waylon Jennings, Kris Kristofferson, and Johnny Cash. These artists left the constrictions of Nashville's ''progressive country'' to explore music on their own terms.

In the late 1970s and early 1980s, a change in the country-rock aesthetic took place with the arrival of ''cow-punk'' bands like Jason and the Scorchers, the Long Ryders, Rank and File, and the Mekons. Musicians such as these took Parsons' hybrid one step further by bringing the punk attitude of bands like Hüsker Dü, X, and the Replacements into the mix. Although the melding of these genres had initially seemed impossible, they actually blended beautifully, effectively re-invigorating both, as seen on the Scorchers' debut *Reckless Country Soul* (1982) and on albums like the Mekons' *Fear and Whiskey* (1985), which features punk music played with traditional country and bluegrass instruments. Meanwhile, musicians like Joe Ely and Lone Justice, while not punk per say, furthered Parsons' country-rock vision.

The late 1980s and early 1990s saw country-rock becoming increasingly experimental as artists like Steve Earle, Lucinda Williams, Lyle Lovett, k.d. lang, and the Jayhawks emerged. While marginally successful commercially, musicians such as these received critical acclaim and continued to explore the possibilities of country music, each focusing on a different feature of country-rock. From Earle's traditionalism to lang's gender explorations and Lovett's parody, each performer paid tribute to the genre while showing its diversity.

But 1987 marked a watershed year with the emergence of alt.country icons Uncle Tupelo whose debut, *No Depression* (1990), signaled a new era in the genre. Fronted by Jay Farrar and Jeff Tweedy, who loved punk as well as traditional country, the band played Carter Family songs as well as their own rock material. Although the band broke up in 1994, with Farrar and Tweedy pursuing their differing musical tastes, in Son Volt and Wilco, respectively, their mark has been a lasting one.

Since Uncle Tupelo, alt.country has continued to grow and explore new areas. *Billboard*'s Chet Flippo suggests four categories that are helpful in classifying this disparate genre, though it is important to bear in mind that such categories are subjective and that few of these artists confine themselves to one type of music. First are the ''Hot-eyed Rockers'' who are grounded in punk but respect country's emotion and musicianship as well as its history. While Flippo places Son Volt and Wilco in this category, bands such as Whiskeytown, the Backsliders, the Bad Livers, and the Bottle Rockets work under a similar ethos. Second are the ''Purist/Traditionalists.'' BR5-49 fits into this category as do Kelly Willis, Jack Ingram, Robert Earl Keen, the Derailers, Freakwater, Junior Brown, and any number of progressive bluegrass musicians like Laurie Lewis or Béla Fleck. Next are the ''Traditionalists,'' those who have been in country music for years but whose talents and contributions tend to be ignored by ''Hot Country.'' This includes artists like Johnny Cash, Waylon Jennings, Willie Nelson, Loretta Lynn, Guy Clark, Merle Haggard, and Don Walser. Many bluegrass performers, for instance Del McCoury and Peter Rowan, also fall into this category. The last of Flippo's classifications is the ''Folkies,'' those drawn to the songs of alt.country. Examples here are Townes Van Zandt, Nanci Griffith, Patti Griffin, James McMurtry, Richard Buckner, Gillian Welch, and Rosie Flores.

Alt.country continues to gain momentum. In 1995, Peter Blackstock and Grant Alden began publishing *No Depression: The Alternative Country (Whatever That Is) Bi-Monthly,* named for an Uncle Tupelo cover of a Carter Family original, which serves as the ex-officio magazine of alt.country. Moreover, a number of independent record labels are devoted primarily to alt.country artists; Bloodshot, Watermelon, and Black Dog along with Steve Earle's E-Squared make the material of lesser-known alt.country artists available.

While alt.country has strong fan bases in Chicago, Raleigh, and Austin in addition to regular music festivals, the Internet has played a tremendous role in its growth. America On-line's ''No Depression'' folder generates substantial material and led to the establishment of two central alt.country electronic mailing lists: Postcard and Postcard II. Postcard discusses primarily the work of Uncle Tupelo and its offspring bands, while its companion, Postcard II, was designed to cover other alt.country bands. Both listservs provide a network of support for alt.country music and artists. Clearly, Gram Parsons' vision continues to be realized.

—S. Renee Dechert

FURTHER READING:

Alden, Grant, and Peter Blackstock, editors. *No Depression: An Introduction to Alternative Country Music. Whatever That Is.* Nashville, Dowling, 1998.

Flippo, Chet. ''The Genre-Bustin' Rise of Insurgent Country.'' *Billboard.* December 28, 1996, 5-9.

Fong-Torres, Ben. *Hickory Wind: The Life and Times of Gram Parsons.* New York, St. Martin's Griffin, 1991.

Goodman, David. *Modern Twang: An Alternative Country Music Guide and Directory.* 2nd edition. Nashville, Dowling, 1999.

Kingsbury, Paul, editor. *The Encyclopedia of Country Music: The Ultimate Guide to the Music.* New York, Oxford University Press, 1998.

Weisbard, Eric, and Craig Marks, editors. *Spin Alternative Record Guide.* New York, Vintage-Random, 1995.

Alternative Press

Notwithstanding legitimate rivals for the title, most Americans hearing the words ''Alternative Press'' would probably think of the brash, crude, anti-establishment periodicals of the Vietnam Era (1963-1975). Most often tabloid in format, printed on the cheapest stock available, written with intent to maim, edited like frontline dispatches, and illustrated with ''psychedelic,'' provocative graphics, these ''underground'' newspapers and magazines offered themselves as the organs of the national and regional ''counter-culture'' for which the period is famous—and, by and large, the counter-culture accepted the offer. The epithet ''underground,'' however, was largely self-assumed and unmerited, since use of the police power of the state to suppress their publication was seldom if ever threatened, let alone exerted. By the time the Viet Cong forces took possession of Saigon (April 30, 1975), the great majority of the underground papers had either ceased publication or transformed themselves—like *Rolling Stone*—into the raffish fringe of the Establishment: the subject matter had not changed, but they had shed the guerilla style of their youth and moved, like their readers, above ground.

Since one of the overreaching goals of the 1960s counter-culture was to cancel all debts to the past, the insider histories of the Alternative Press—most of which appeared in the early 1970s—make no mention of any predecessors older than the end of World War II. But they were certainly not the first journalists to print rude, funny diatribes (or cartoons) against the establishment: the authors of the ''Mazarinades'' in mid-seventeenth-century France were as outrageous and one-sided in the expression of their disapproval of Cardinal Mazarin as any editorial in the Berkeley *Barb* or *L. A. Free Press* was of President Lyndon Johnson or Draft Board chief General Louis B. Hershey. More directly antecedent to the Alternative Press of the 1960s, the English Puritan pamphleteers of the 1640s were every bit as self-righteously insulting to the Anglican conformists—calling them the ''agents of Rome''—as any underground paper of the 1960s calling a Fire Marshal a ''fascist'' (which is not to say, in either case, that the accusers were always, or even usually, mistaken). The eighteenth and nineteenth centuries abound with similar serials expressing the perspectives and prejudices of a self-conscious, ambitious minority, on its way either to becoming a majority or to disappearing.

In the late nineteenth century, however, the exponential growth of literacy provided the demographic base in Europe and America for the first truly popular press, and men like Lord Northcliffe in England became rich and powerful ''press lords'' by giving these newly-literate people news on subjects which interested them: sporting events, disasters, success stories, and scandals. In much the same way, those representatives of the Alternative Press of the 1960s who survived and prospered did not do so on the basis of their political reporting or ideological preaching, but on their coverage of matters of what came to be known as ''life-style.'' The success of such entrepreneurs as Lord Northcliffe and William Randolph Hearst is a perfect paradigm for what happens when the ''established'' press becomes too narrowly identified with an elite as a new technology becomes available to an emerging majority.

Like so many phenomena identified with the 1960s, the Alternative Press got started during the 1950s—an era now remembered as a time of up-tight conformism and anti-Communist hysteria—when one puff on a reefer led immediately to more damaging addictions, one artistic impulse signaled infinite secret perversions, and any expressed support for the Bill of Rights was an admission of Communist sympathies. As far as the first waves of the Postwar "Baby Boom" were taught, at home or school, to be exposed as a drug addict, homosexual, or Communist was to be immediately cast into outer darkness, your name never to be spoken again in decent society, your family disgraced and forced to move to another town. All true pleasures were furtive.

Yet the 1950s was also the decade which saw the publication of Alan Ginsberg's *Howl* (1956), Jack Kerouac's *On the Road* (1957)—which became a bestseller—and William Burroughs' *Naked Lunch* (1957); when Chuck Berry, Elvis Presley, Buddy Holly, and the Everly Brothers established rock 'n' roll as THE American popular music; when the image of the rebel and misfit—Paul Newman in *The Left-Handed Gun,* Marlon Brando in *The Wild One,* James Dean in *Rebel Without a Cause*—gave attractive physical form to the restless dissatisfaction of middle class American teenagers; and when Aldous Huxley published the results of his experiments with hallucinogenic drugs in *Heaven and Hell* (1954) and *The Doors of Perception* (1956). Moreover, the 1950s witnessed the first significant gains of the Civil Rights movement—the model for all future liberation movements—and the first, largely unnoticed, involvement of the United States in the anti-colonial upheavals in French Indochina.

October 26, 1955 marked the publication of the first issue of the *Village Voice,* written and produced by a group of bohemian intellectuals (Michael Harrington, Norman Mailer, Katherine Anne Porter, Allen Ginsberg, Nat Hentoff, Anaïs Nin, and others) living in the Greenwich Village district of Manhattan—founded, it must be noted, not as an alternative to the *New York Times,* but in reaction to a tame neighborhood paper called *The Villager.* Among the many innovations of the early *Village Voice,* many of which were too mannered to endure, the most important was the total absence of any restrictions on language, either in the use of profanity or in the graphic treatment of taboo subjects. This latter characteristic made a quantum leap in June of 1958, when Paul Krassner—a 26-year-old writer from *Mad Magazine* (itself one of the major influences on the future Alternative Press)—brought out the first issue of *The Realist.* It instantly became the gold standard of satire, sneering irreverence, and the blurring of the line between fact and fiction which would characterize all utterances of the still-embryonic counter-culture.

Thus, by the time John F. Kennedy was elected president in November of 1960, the entire agenda of the Alternative Press had been set, as well as most of its attitude, style, and format. All that was needed to set things in motion was a spark to ignite the passions, and enlist the support, of the enormous Class of 1964. This was not long in coming: the assassination of President Kennedy, the advent of Bob Dylan and the Beatles, the publication of *The Feminine Mystique,* the Stonewall riots, the Gulf of Tonkin Resolution, the hide-bound conservatism of the educational establishment, the first experience with marijuana or LSD, or any combination of the above. Some grain of discontent worked its way inside the shell of middle class complacency, and a pearl of counter-culture began to form. In every large metropolitan area in the United States, these pearls of disaffection strung themselves into communities, usually near colleges or universities. The "Free Speech Movement" in Berkeley, site of Campus

One of the University of California, produced one of the first of the new style of radical communities, which in turn produced one of the first examples of the Alternative Press, the Berkeley *Barb* (first published October 13, 1965), although, in fact, the *L.A. Free Press*—modeled on the *Village Voice*—beat them into print by more than a year (May 25, 1964). On the opposite coast, a dissident group of writers of the *Village Voice* split from that publication to found the *East Village Other* (October 1965).

As the counter-culture began to subdivide into one-issue lobbies—drugs, communal living, sexual preference, racial separatism, radical politics, etc.—each subdivision felt the need for its own periodical soapbox. The *San Francisco Oracle,* founded in 1966, promoted the transformation of society through the use of hallucinogenic drugs; the *Advocate* started to speak on behalf of America's homosexuals in 1967, though its tame assimilationist line soon provoked more aggressive papers like *Come Out!* (November 1969) and *Free Particle* (September 1969); the *Black Panther* fired its first salvo against the white police state in June of 1967; *Screw* sought to unshackle the American (male) libido, and to challenge the censorship laws, beginning November 29, 1968; and in that same fall of 1968, the ecological-communitarian movement found its voice with the first, massive issue of the *Whole Earth Catalog.* Only *Rolling Stone* moved against the tide of special interest splintering: begun in November of 1967 to address the community formed by the revolution in rock 'n' roll, the paper has evolved steadily towards a more "general interest" publication—if the *Village Voice* is the *Christian Science Monitor* of the Alternative Press, *Rolling Stone* is its *Saturday Evening Post.* At some point—one might, for convenience, choose the year 1970—it was no longer valid to speak of "the" counter-culture as if it were one unified social structure; consequently, it became less and less meaningful to speak of "the" Alternative Press.

Technically a part of the Alternative Press, and definitely one of the purest expressions of the counter-culture Zeitgeist, the underground comic book is actually a separate phenomenon. The so-called Underground Press is a spent bullet, but the comic book, old and new, continues to thrive. While university libraries collect and catalogue back issues of the Berkeley *Barb* and the Seattle *Helix,* prosperous establishments all over the United States do a brisk trade in old copies of *Zap* and *Despair* along with the new graphic novels and standard classics of Marvel. And in the almost total absence of representative long prose fictions from the 1960s, R. Crumb's stories about "Mr. Natural," "Flakey Foont," "Projunior," and "Honeybunch Kaminsky"—not to mention Gilbert Sheldon's "Fabulous, Furry Freak Brothers" and S. Clay Wilson's Tales of "The Checkered Demon" and "Captain Pissgums"—remain the most reliable narratives of the period.

Something called an Alternative Press still exists in the late 1990s. They have annual meetings, publish newsletters, and give each other journalism awards. Many of the newspapers so defined still espouse progressive politics, support environmental causes, and celebrate the current popular music scene. But the counter-culture which they were founded to serve—the Woodstock Nation of love-ins, anti-war marches, LSD trips, and hippie communes—have gone the way of the Popular Front and the Dreyfussards to become a discrete historical episode. It remains to be seen whether the most lasting legacy of the Alternative Press, the disabling of any governing system of courtesy or restraint in public discourse, will turn out to have hastened the end of a nightmare or the beginning of one.

—Gerald Carpenter

FURTHER READING:

Glessing, Robert J. *The Underground Press in America.* Bloomington, Indiana University Press, 1970.

Kessler, Lauren. *The Dissident Press: Alternative Journalism in American History.* Beverly Hills, Sage Publications, 1984.

Leamer, Laurence. *The Paper Revolutionaries: The Rise of the Underground Press.* New York, Simon and Schuster, 1972.

Lewis, Roger. *Outlaws of America: The Underground Press and Its Context.* London, Penguin Books, Ltd., 1972.

Peattie, Noel. *The Living Z: A Guide to the Literature of the Counterculture, the Alternative Press, and Little Magazines.* New York, Margins, 1975.

Shore, Elliot, et al., editors. *Alternative Papers: Selections from the Alternative Press, 1979-1980.* Philadelphia, Temple University Press, 1982.

Smith, Mike P. *The Underground and Education: a Guide to the Alternative Press.* London, Methuen, 1977.

Alternative Rock

The popular musical genre called "alternative rock," immensely popular during the 1980s and 1990s, drew upon the conventions of rock music even while it attempted to distance itself from traditional or "classic" rock. Alternative rockers differentiated themselves from their traditional rock predecessors in part with their call for greater diversity and experimentation in music, and in part with their critique of mainstream society and of major record labels in favor of small independent companies. While alternative rockers produced catchy music geared for mass consumption, their music—with its emphasis on distorted guitars and ambiguous lyrics—wasn't suited to conventional tastes. Furthermore, alternative rock lyrics were often critical or skeptical of mainstream values.

Alternative rock—which is also referred to as "indie rock," "college rock," "post-punk," "new music," "power-pop," and more recently, "grunge"—traces its roots to the 1970s, when new wave and early punk bands experimented with diverse styles in music, dress, and ideology. Alternative rock was also influenced by "alternative music" more generally, which includes such genres as industrial, avant-garde, and experimental music, as well as gothic rock, ska, reggae, and alternative hip-hop. While influenced by these many styles, alternative rock is best understood as residing somewhere between rock and punk rock, and is ambivalent about its desire for mainstream appeal and its rejection of mainstream values.

New wave bands like Blondie, The Talking Heads, Devo, and Adam and the Ants as well as early punk rock bands like Iggy and the Stooges, The Ramones, The Sex Pistols, and The Clash had a major influence on alternative rock. Punk was particularly influential for its radical critique of society and its call for the destruction of conventional musical sensibilities. Alternative rock, however, blended punk attitude and aggression with rock melodies and song structure. The Police, U2, and R.E.M. became immensely popular during the 1980s

with catchy and energetic songs and had a major influence on the development of alternative rock. Indeed, the popularity of such bands as The Police, U2, R.E.M., The GoGos, The B-52s, and Midnight Oil can in some part be explained by their songs, which at 3-4 minutes long, with catchy riffs and steady beats, are well suited for radio play. In contrast, some of the longer and more complicated rock songs of such performers as Eric Clapton and The Who were less accessible and came to be seen as stagnant and old fashioned. Alternative rock bands aimed to reach out to a new generation of youth with high energy, melodic music which spoke to contemporary social issues.

Alternative rock shared much of the punk ideology of nonconformity and the questioning of mainstream values. Yet while punk was notable for its explicit anger, alternative rock offered more subdued critiques and covered a greater range of topics and emotions. Bands like The Jam, The Pixies, and The Lemonheads sang about political issues but also about love and other social relations. Isolation and loneliness were common themes which indicated an ambivalence about modern society. The Smiths, in particular, were known for their overwhelming sense of melancholy. The Replacements, an influential alternative rock band, blended energetic outbursts with subdued elements of folk-rock or jazz. Singing about comical aspects of social life as well as more sincere emotional concerns, lead singer Paul Westerberg was especially known for his self-deprecating sense of humor. As he asked in "I Will Dare," "How smart are you? How dumb am I?" Another Minneapolis band, Soul Asylum, known for their energetic music and powerful guitar work, was also self-mocking while singing about a variety of social concerns and emotional issues. Sonic Youth and Dinosaur Jr. were particularly important for their noisy guitar work and punk influences. These bands gave rise to what, in the 1990s, would come to be known as "grunge," which developed most visibly in Seattle with bands like Mudhoney, Nirvana, Soundgarden, and Pearl Jam. Grunge was characterized by a heavy guitar sound which harkened back to the classic rock of Deep Purple, Led Zeppelin, and other bands. Grunge became a major phenomenon in the 1990s as Nirvana, Pearl Jam, and others sold millions of records.

The musicians and fans of alternative rock tended to dress in a manner which was influenced by both punk and mainstream attire. Alternative clothing tended to be less extreme than punk and was not worn to explicitly shock people but was often slovenly and promoted an image of apathy toward conventional dress styles. However, because alternative dress was less radical, it allowed the wearer greater acceptance in mainstream culture, particularly in family, work, and school.

Alternative rock espoused a critical stance toward the music industry and capitalist society in general and shared with punk a "Do It Yourself" emphasis which is critical of major record labels. Many alternative bands, however, began on independent labels and later moved to major labels. Alternative rock bands faced the dilemma of trying to maintain the critical stance of punk while accepting many aspects of mainstream society. Thus, while criticizing conventional society and the rock industry, alternative bands frequently ended up becoming a part of it.

Despite its mass appeal, alternative rock has been critiqued on several grounds. Punks argued that alternative bands "sold out." Others argued that it alternative was a largely white and male-dominated enterprise. As Eric Weisbard states in the *Spin Alternative*

Record Guide, ''[alternative rock] is too indebted to a white American vocalist screaming about his betrayed entitlements over an exquisitely layered squall of guitars, bass and drums.'' In this sense, alternative rock, while espousing diversity and originality, became somewhat conventional. Many suggested that the term ''alternative'' may have outlived its usefulness. Alternative rock gained such popularity in the 1980s and 1990s that its music, style, and ideology were in many ways incorporated into the mainstream.

—Perry Grossman

FURTHER READING:

Arnold, Gina. *Route 666: On the Road to Nirvana.* New York, St. Martin's Press, 1993.

Frith, Simon, and Andrew Goodwin, editors. *On Record: Rock, Pop, and the Written Word.* New York, Pantheon, 1990.

Negus, Keith. *Producing Pop: Culture and Conflict in the Popular Music Industry.* New York, Routledge, 1992.

Weisbard, Eric. ''Introduction.'' *Spin Alternative Record Guide.* New York, Vintage Books, 1995.

Altman, Robert (1925—)

Considered to be the most prolific, if not the most influential film maker of the New Hollywood Cinema of the early 1970s, writer/producer/director Robert Altman made 13 films throughout the decade, including the Oscar-nominated hits *M*A*S*H* in 1970 and *Nashville* in 1975. His challenging and often idiosyncratic work dealt with genre, women's issues, male bonding, and institutions, and his movies always met with mixed critical and popular response. As critic Michael Wilmington observed, ''In the opinion of some, Altman is one of America's greatest moviemakers, a fountain of creativity and iconoclasm. For others, he is a troublemaker and a guy who won't get with the program: defiant, rebellious and unpleasantly unpredictable.''

This reputation—which has often alienated studios and irritated the public—is largely the result of Altman's unusual style, which he refers to as ''controlled chaos.'' The epitome of a maverick filmmaker, Altman essentially uses his script as a blueprint from which he freely improvises, tending to value moments of insight, mood, and character revelation over action and plot. Form then follows content, resulting in his trademark tendency to record his improvisations in wide angle shots with casual tracking movements and zooms—sometimes from the perspective of multiple cameras—to capture spontaneous moments. He also has consistently favored the usage of overlapping and often improvised dialogue (which grew more controlled once his Lions Gate studio developed an eight-track sound system that revolutionized film sound). Such treatment results in long and rambling narratives, which connect and communicate only over time through the interweaving of fragments of character—somewhat like a jigsaw puzzle or jazz riffs. As critic Henri Bohar observed of Altman's *Kansas City* (1996), ''Altman weaves several stories, and several moods, fleshing out a film script as if it were a score and the actors

Robert Altman

instruments.'' While such a style has proven challenging to impatient, narrative-driven audiences, Altman contends, ''We are trying to educate and develop our audiences.''

Far older than most of the rising film school-trained directors of the early 1970s, Altman began his film career upon his discharge from the military, making industrials for an independent company in the 1950s. Altman left when Alfred Hitchcock offered him the chance to direct his weekly television show, *Alfred Hitchcock Presents.* Work in series television and the occasional low budget feature (*The Delinquents* in 1957, starring Tom Laughlin, and later the famed *Billy Jack*) continued until he was asked to direct a script turned down by most of Hollywood. It was not only the extensive black humor and anti-war sentiments in *M*A*S*H* that attracted him; Altman knew that this was his opportunity to break into commercial filmmaking. The loosely woven story about Korean War doctors struggling to stay sane through a series of games and practical jokes was both a critical and commercial success— receiving the Grand Prize at Cannes, and Oscar nominations for Best Picture and Best Director—appealing to the more cynical and jaded audiences, who could identify with these characters worn down by years of war and political assassination.

But it was his next film, *Nashville* (1975), that came to be considered Altman's masterpiece. Dubbed a ''spiritual disaster movie'' by influential critic Robin Wood, this tapestry of 1970s culture interweaves the institutions of politics and country music as it focuses on the lives of 24 characters seeking celebrity status during a five-day period prior to a presidential rally. *Nashville* was lauded as Best Film by the National Society of Film Critics, the New York Film Critics Circle, and the National Board of Review. Of this work, historian David Cook concluded, Altman ''has seen us with our raw nerves exposed at a time in American history when the conflicting demands of community and individual freedom have never been more extreme, and he has become an epic poet of that conflict.''

However, as the 1970s wore on, in the aftermath of the Watergate scandal and the Vietnam War, cynicism gave way to the new optimism of the Bicentennial years, and Altman's later explorations of bizarre characters who are driven by American values only to suffer confusion, disillusionment, and often complete breakdowns grated on audiences seeking the upbeat in films such as *Rocky* and *Star Wars*. In the wake of the steadily decreasing box office draw of such flops as *Quintet* and *A Perfect Couple* (both 1979), critic Pauline Kael wryly observed, ''Altman has reached the point of wearing his failures like medals. He's creating a mystique of heroism out of emptied theaters.''

However, it was the mediocre box office returns of the big budget live-action cartoon *Popeye* (1980) that finally signaled Altman's inability to finance future products. He diverted himself by producing opera and stage productions in Europe that were transferred to video (*Come Back to the Five and Dime, Jimmy Dean, Jimmy Dean,* 1982, and *Streamers,* 1984), as well as working in television (*The Dumb Waiter,* 1987; *Tanner 88,* 1988). But in the early 1990s, he returned to form with *The Player.* This critical and financial success was ironically a scathing satirical indictment of the struggles Altman had undergone while working in Hollywood. This led to another well-received tapestry film, *Short Cuts* (1993) based on the short stories of Raymond Carver. Both films won major awards at Cannes and netted Altman Academy Award Nominations for Best Director, and *Short Cuts* also won Best Adapted Screenplay.

In the late 1990s, Altman divided his time between occasional television work (the anthology series *Gun*) and film projects, but continued to struggle with studio anxiety over his unconventional methods.

—Rick Moody

FURTHER READING:

Keyssar, Helen. *Robert Altman's America.* New York, Oxford University Press, 1991

Kolker, Robert Phillip. *A Cinema of Loneliness: Penn, Kubrick, Scorsese, Spielberg, Altman.* New York, Oxford University Press, 1988.

McGilligan, Patrick. *Robert Altman Jumping Off the Cliff.* New York, St. Martin's, 1989.

O'Brien, Daniel. *Robert Altman: Hollywood Survivor.* New York, Continuum, 1995.

Amazing Stories

Hugo Gernsback's pulp *Amazing Stories* virtually established the genre of the science fiction magazine when it was launched in 1926 and, despite frequent ownership and editorial policy changes, the magazine has maintained its position as one of the most prominent purveyors of science fiction throughout the century. *Amazing Stories* either launched or boosted the careers of dozens of sci-fi writers, and it helped create the intimate culture of sci-fi magazines by publishing letter columns, supervising competitions, and encouraging a relationship between readers, writers, and publishers. Still accepting science fiction, fantasy, and horror stories in the late 1990s, *Amazing Stories* was the oldest science fiction magazine in the nation.

Publisher Gernsback emigrated to America from Luxembourg in 1904, and quickly established a business selling dry cell batteries and home radio sets. In order to promote sales he issued a catalogue and then the first radio magazine, *Modern Electrics,* in 1908. In 1911 an issue of that magazine included the first episode of Gernsback's fiction series ''Ralph 124C 41+.'' Science fiction became a regular part of Gernsback's publication, indicating his preference for technological extrapolations of scientific articles. In August 1923, Gernsback experimented with a ''scientific fiction'' special issue of *Science and Invention,* which carried six stories and speculative articles. In April 1926, he published the first issue of *Amazing Stories,* a magazine of ''scientifiction.''

Gernsback defined ''scientifiction'' and established the character of the magazine through reprints of stories by H. G. Wells, Jules Verne, and Edgar Allan Poe. In his editorials, Gernsback stressed that he felt his readers could be educated by such romances ''intermingled with scientific fact and prophetic vision.'' Gernsback solicited the participation of fans through the letters column, ''Discussions,'' which encouraged reviews of fiction. The column published the full names and addresses of the writers, allowing for direct correspondence between readers and the circulation of amateur publications. He also initiated writing competitions, such as a contest that asked readers to supply a story to accompany the December 1926 Frank R. Paul cover illustration.

Amazing Stories and its associate publications, *Amazing Stories Annual* and *Amazing Stories Quarterly,* published work by Edgar Rice Burroughs, Ray Cummings, Abraham Merrit, and Murray Leinster with interplanetary settings. E. E. ''Doc'' Smith's serial ''The Skylark of Space'' began in August of 1928; that same issue featured the first Buck Rogers story, ''Armageddon 2419AD,'' written by Philip Francis Nowlan. Both Nowlan and Smith were major contributors to the popularity of science fiction through the wide appeal of space opera. Alongside this type of science fiction Gernsback also published the work of David Keller, who was interested in the social implications of scientific extrapolation. *Amazing Stories* also published fantasy, horror, and thriller storylines, including works by H. P. Lovecraft.

Despite the commercial success of *Amazing Stories,* Gernsback's company, Experimenter Publishing Co., was forced into bankruptcy in 1929. The title to the magazine was sold and continued under the editorship of Gernsback's assistant, T. O'Connor Sloan. He maintained a strict adherence to scientific fidelity, which included the space opera-serials of J.W. Campbell (before he became the editor of rival *Astounding Science Fiction*), Smith, Edmond Hamilton, and Jack Williamson; Sloan sustained the magazine until it was sold again in 1939. Under the editorship of Ray Palmer the publication policy was relaxed and the magazine accepted a wider range of stories. The magazine was briefly edited by Paul Fairman, but was then taken over by assistant editor Cele Goldsmith in 1958.

Goldsmith re-established the reputation of the magazine by encouraging new writers and creative experimentation. She was particularly interested in fantasy and published Marion Zimmer Bradley's first "Darkover" series. The magazine still included scientific articles, but the fiction became oriented toward the "soft sciences" and the writers Goldsmith discovered include Harlan Ellison, Thomas M. Disch, Roger Zelazny, and Ursula K. Le Guin. These writers later made their reputations in fantasy writing and in the new wave of critical and literary science fiction writing in the 1970s. *Amazing Stories* went into a period of decline after Goldsmith's departure in 1965, producing reprints under a series of writer/editors, until Ted White took over as editor beginning in 1970.

Despite the relative impoverishment of the magazine, White published original fiction and returned the magazine to its original interest in fan culture through a very outspoken editorial column. The magazine's fortunes again declined after White left in 1979, but *Amazing Stories* was reinvigorated in 1987 when it was purchased by TSR Inc., the company that produced the popular game "Dungeons and Dragons." Under TSR and, later, under owner Wizards of the Coast Inc. (another game manufacturer), *Amazing Stories* maintained its hard science fiction outlook, eschewing "sword and sorcery" in favor of science fiction stories from young writers.

—Nickianne Moody

FURTHER READING:

Aldiss, Brian W., with David Wingrove. *Trillion Year Spree: The History of Science Fiction.* New York, Atheneum, 1986.

Ashley, Michael, editor. *A History of the Science Fiction Magazine.* London, New English Library, 1974.

Ashley, Michael, and Robert A. W. Lowndes. *The Gernsback Days: The Evolution of Modern Science Fiction, from 1911-1936.* San Bernardino, California, Borgo Press, 1995.

Siegel, Mark Richard. *Hugo Gernsback: Father of Modern Science Fiction.* San Bernardino, California, Borgo Press, 1988.

Tymn, Marshall, and Mike Ashley, editors. *Science Fiction, Fantasy, and Weird Fiction Magazines.* Westport, Connecticut, Greenwood Press, 1985.

American Bandstand

American Bandstand became a powerful symbol of American teenage culture with its nearly four-decade look at the ever-changing tastes of the country's youth. Featuring guest artists who lip-synced to their latest tunes, and a teenage audience whose members danced for the cameras, the show launched a conga line of dance crazes, fashion and hair trends, and sent the latest teen slang expressions echoing from coast to coast.

From its beginning as a local Philadelphia telecast called, simply, *Bandstand* in 1952, to its 1957 national debut as *American Bandstand,* and on throughout its run, the show was known for treating teenagers with deference. Congenial host Dick Clark did not pontificate or preach; he instead let the kids and the music do the communicating. The antithesis of courageous rock 'n' roll proponents like fiery Alan Freed, Clark has been accused of homogenizing rock 'n' roll. Music historians have pointed out that he had a financial interest in some of the show's acts, but Clark has countered that the show reflected popular taste. Indeed, *American Bandstand* enjoys a reputation not only as a musical and cultural timeline, but as a fondly remembered part of adolescence for many if not most Americans.

Though Clark's name is synonymous with that of *American Bandstand,* the show originated with Philadelphia disc jockey Bob Horn, and the radio show *Bob Horn's Bandstand.* It was in October of 1952 that Horn and his *Bandstand* moved to Philadelphia's WFIL-TV as a live afternoon series. Against a painted canvas backdrop of a record store, the studio audience clustered on pine bleachers to watch lip-syncing artists such as pop singers Joni James and Frankie Laine. The show also featured dance and record-rating segments.

Because the TV studio was in the vicinity of three local high schools, *Bandstand* had no trouble finding an in-house audience. Within three months of its debut, some 5,000 students had applied for "membership" cards. Those who were given cards had to be between the ages of fourteen and eighteen. Gum chewing was prohibited, and there was a dress code. Males could not wear jeans or opened shirts, and were required to have a jacket or sweater with tie; females had to wear dresses or skirts—but not tight skirts. "When you dressed right, you behaved right," believed producer Tony Mammarella.

In retrospect, the show has been criticized for sanitizing its audience. And not just in regard to fashion. Though Philadelphia had a large African American population, it would take years for the show to reflect that segment of the population. Like many programs of the day, *Bandstand* did not officially ban African Americans from the audience; but neither did it issue them membership cards. And though the show became known for featuring the hottest African American artists of the 1950s, many of these artists did pop-style tunes. Additionally, there were early efforts to acquiesce to sponsors, who wanted white cover singers.

It was image-consciousness that led to the dismissal of original host Bob Horn. The *Philadelphia Inquirer,* which owned WFIL, was in the midst of an anti-drunk driving campaign when Horn made headlines with a 1956 drunk driving arrest. As a result, WFIL sought a new host. Enter twenty-six-year-old Dick Clark.

Voted the "Man Most Likely to Sell the Brooklyn Bridge" by his high school classmates, Clark was born November 30, 1929, in Bronxville, New York. He was in his early teens when he realized he wanted a career in radio. While still in high school he worked in the mailroom at a Utica, New York, station where his father was the promotional manager. At Syracuse University he majored in advertising and minored in radio, and was a disc jockey and newscaster for the campus station. Following graduation, he worked at a series of stations including the Syracuse, New York, station, WOLF-AM, where he hosted the country music show, *The WOLF Buckaroos.* After moving into television at Utica's WKTV, he became "Cactus Dick" of the station's country-western show, *Cactus Dick and the Santa Fe Riders.*

He relocated to Philadelphia in 1952 to host WFIL radio's daily easy listening show, *Dick Clark's Caravan of Music.* He also did commercials for WFIL-TV, and watched from the sidelines as

Dick Clark (holding microphone) with Bobby Rydell on *American Bandstand*.

Bandstand became a local hit. Though he was a novice in regard to rock 'n' roll, Clark was a marketing genius who intuitively understood the potential of both the show and the music. As the country's fourth-largest metropolitan city, Philadelphia was a break-out market for performers and their records.

It was on August 5, 1957 that ABC took *Bandstand* national. Debuting on 67 stations across the country, the live daily afternoon show was an instantaneous success. Just weeks into its run, *American Bandstand* was drawing 15,000 letters a week, topping the fan mail for the network's most popular show, *Wyatt Earp.* The success led to a Saturday night spin-off, *The Dick Clark Show,* which ran for two-and-a-half years.

As network television's first show devoted to rock 'n' roll, it became requisite for both established and upcoming performers to put in *American Bandstand* guest appearances. Of the leading rock 'n' roll stars of the 1950s and 1960s, only Elvis Presley and Ricky Nelson did not appear. Those artists who made their national debut on the program included Buddy Holly and the Crickets, Jerry Lee Lewis, Gene Vincent, the Everly Brothers, Jackie Wilson, Johnny Mathis,

Chuck Berry, and the duo of Tom and Jerry—later to be known as Simon and Garfunkel. As an integral force in the rise of the teen idol, *American Bandstand* also propelled Fabian, Frankie Avalon, Bobby Rydell, and other pin-up boys, to prominence.

Singer Gene Pitney once estimated that a single *American Bandstand* appearance could lead to next-day sales of 20,000 to 40,000 records. After nearly giving up on her career, Connie Francis had her first number one hit when Clark touted "Who's Sorry Now?" When Jerry Lee Lewis appeared on the show in April 1958 to perform "Breathless," viewers learned they could own the record by mailing in fifty cents and five wrappers from Beechnut gum, a leading sponsor. Within three days, tens of thousands of gum wrappers were mailed in.

Clark himself was the force behind the 1958 number-one hit "At the Hop." Danny and the Juniors had originally recorded a demo called "Do the Bop," which referred to one of the show's dance fads. Clark suggested that lyrics be changed to "At the Hop." It was also Clark who triggered Chubby Checker's enormous 1960 hit, "The Twist." Credited with revolutionizing popular dance, "The Twist" was written and first recorded by the raucous rhythm and blues group Hank Ballard and the Midnighters as the flip side to their 1958 tune "Teardrops on Your Letter." After seeing the dance performed on his show in the summer of 1960, Clark approached the local Cameo Records and suggested a new recording.

The Twist was but one of many dance fads popularized by *American Bandstand*. Others included the Strand, the Stroll, the Duck, the Calypso, the Fly, the Loco-Motion, the Watusi, the Limbo, the Bristol Stomp, the Mashed Potato, the Hully Gully, the Bird, and the Smurf. It wasn't just the dances that garnered the spotlight; some of the dancing "regulars" became celebrities in their own right, complete with fan mail, their own fan clubs, and coverage in the teen fan magazines. The show's most popular dance team of Bob Clayton and Justine Carrelli even cut their own record.

The show's reputation, as well as Clark's, was briefly jeopardized when the payola scandal broke in November of 1959. By this time, Clark was involved in music publishing, talent management, record pressing, label making, distribution, and more. But, he insisted to a Washington subcommittee that he had never accepted payola for playing or not playing a particular record. He survived the scandal, but ABC made him divest his music-related interests.

During the 1960s, *American Bandstand*'s influence was undermined by societal changes, as well as changes in the music world. Los Angeles, home of surf and car-culture music, had become the new heartbeat of the industry. And so, in February 1964 the Philadelphia fixture relocated to Southern California. No longer live, the show was taped; having lost its daily time slot, it aired on Saturday afternoons.

Oddly, the series failed to capitalize on the British invasion. Meanwhile, as FM radio grew in popularity, the diversity of music types created a conundrum. On a purely practical level, psychedelic songs were not danceable. To enliven the dance floor, *American Bandstand* cranked up the soul music—an irony, considering that it was 1965 before the series had a regular African American dance couple.

In the 1970s, *American Bandstand* exploited a new roll call of teen idols, including Bobby Sherman, David Cassidy, and John Travolta. The series also reached into its vaults for a highly rated twentieth-anniversary late night special. Still later in the decade, the show's dance floor was revitalized by disco. The following decade saw the abandonment of the dress code. But spandex and plunging necklines, and guests as disparate as Madonna, Jon Bon Jovi, Prince, and the Stray Cats, could not offset changing technology. MTV debuted on August 1, 1981; four years later, it spawned the sister network, VH-1, which was aimed at viewers ages twenty-five to forty-nine, a demographic group who had left *American Bandstand* behind. There was also competition from music-video oriented series, such as NBC's *Friday Night Videos*. Finally, after thirty-seven years of catering to and reflecting teenage taste, *American Bandstand* came to an end in October 1987. Through syndication, *The New American Bandstand* ran through September 1989.

But the beat goes on. Dick Clark Productions continues to exploit the *American Bandstand* moniker with tie-ins including a chain of theme restaurants. And the show continues in reruns. In fact, VH-1, which contributed to the original show's demise, has been an outlet for *The Best of American Bandstand*. Befitting a symbol of Americana, the show's podium, over which Clark used to preside, is on display in the Smithsonian Institution; the show itself was entered into the *Guinness Book of World Records* as TV's longest-running

variety program. Meanwhile, the theme song, "Bandstand Boogie," enjoys instant recognition. As does Clark, whose ever-youthful appearance, and association with the series, have won him the appellation, "the world's oldest living teenager."

—Pat H. Broeske

FURTHER READING:

Clark, Dick, and Richard Robinson. *Rock, Roll & Remember.* New York, Thomas Y. Crowell Co., 1976.

Dawson, Jim. *The Twist: The Story of the Song and Dance That Changed the World.* Boston, Faber & Faber, 1995.

Jackson, John A. *American Bandstand: Dick Clark and the Making of a Rock 'n' Roll Empire.* New York, Oxford University Press, 1997.

Shore, Michael, with Dick Clark. *The History of American Bandstand.* New York, Ballantine Books, 1985.

Uslan, Michael, and Bruce Solomon. *Dick Clark's The First 25 Years of Rock & Roll.* New York, Delacorte Press, 1981.

American Bandstand
See also Clark, Dick

American Girls Series

"We give girls chocolate cake with vitamins" explains Pleasant T. Rowland, the creator of the *American Girls* books, summing up the philosophy behind the bestselling historical fiction series. The 1980s and 1990s have seen a proliferation of series books for girls—the *Sweet Valley High* series, the *Baby-Sitters Club* series, the *American Girls* series—which have sold millions of copies. Pleasant Company's *American Girls Collection,* a set of 36 books about six girls from different eras in American history, is among the leaders in this popular and profitable field. Preadolescent girls are a powerful demographic in 1990s publishing; girl power, it seems, represents a significant buying power. Series books for girls have frequently been dismissed both because they are popular reading and children's literature and because they are series books, which have historically been disdained by critics. Such books, however, have been an important and influential (as well as lucrative) genre of children's literature since the middle of the nineteenth century, with the publication of *Little Women* (1868). Recently, there has been more critical attention paid to girls' culture as an area for scholarly inquiry and there is no reason that this inquiry should not be extended to girls' reading habits.

Founded as an alternative to mass market books and toys, The Pleasant Company was launched in 1985 by Pleasant Rowland, a former teacher and textbook author. The company's stated mission is "to celebrate all that is special about American girls—past and present—and in doing so, to create a community of American girls.'' The company has annual revenues in excess of 300 million dollars from the sale of books, dolls, clothing, accessories, and activity kits from both the *American Girls* historical collection and the American Girl contemporary products. Since 1986, Pleasant Company has sold 48 million *American Girl* books, and plans to release an additional 42 titles in 1999. Rowland got the idea for the *American Girls* books after she went shopping for dolls for her two nieces. All she found were ''Barbies that wore spiked heels, drove pink Corvettes, and looked as if they belonged in stripjoints.'' Rowland wanted to give girls dolls that could teach ''American history, family values, and self-reliance.'' Ironically, in 1998, Rowland sold Pleasant Company to Mattel, the makers of Barbie.

The *American Girls* book collection is based on the fictional lives of six ethnically diverse nine-year-old girls from different eras in American history: Felicity Merriman, a Williamsburg girl whose life is changed dramatically by the outbreak of the American Revolution; Josephina Montoya, a New Mexican girl of the early 1820s (whose books include a glossary of Spanish words used in the text); Kirsten Larson, an immigrant to the Minnesota frontier in the 1850s; Addy Walker, an African American girl who escapes from slavery in 1864; Samantha Parkington, an orphan who lives with her aunt and uncle in turn-of-the-century New York city; and Molly McIntire, a twentieth century girl whose father serves in England during World War II. Six books have been written about each girl's experiences, including volumes on family and friends, school, birthdays, Christmases, and summer and winter adventures. Each volume includes a ''Peek into the Past'' section in which photos, illustrations, and narratives are provided for historical background and context. The entire collection consists of the novel series, dolls and dolls' clothing, historically accurate replicas of furniture, girls' clothes, and memorabilia, and craft projects including (for each of the six characters) a cookbook, crafts book, theater kit, and paper dolls and accessories. The 18-inch dolls cost over $80 each. With all the accessories, including $80 dresses for actual girls, each collection costs approximately $1,000.

In 1992 the company launched the *American Girl* magazine, a bimonthly magazine free of advertisements that treats both historical and contemporary issues, which by 1995 had over 500,000 subscribers. The magazine is phenomenally popular—for each issue, the magazine receives over 10,000 pieces of mail, most asking for advice or directed at the help column. The magazine, aimed at 7-12 year old girls, features fiction and nonfiction articles on arts, sports, entertainment, history snippets about girlhood during various periods of American history, original short fiction, and a regular section called ''Grandmother, Mother, and Me'' which contains paper dolls and cut-out clothes from both past and present. Pleasant Company also began publishing the *American Girl Library,* which emerged from the most popular features of *American Girl* magazine and is completely contemporary. *The American Girl Library* serves as a counterpart to the *American Girls* collection, and includes activity books, fiction, biography, and (most significantly) advice books, such as the bestselling *Help!: An Absolutely Indispensable Guide to Life for Girls.* In recent years, Pleasant Company has also created special events and programs for fans of the series, including The American Girls Fashion Show, Samantha's Ice Cream Social, and Felicity in Williamsburg: An American Girls Experience.

Like most series books for girls, the plots of the *American Girls* books are somewhat formulaic: the books typically center on moral quandaries, and the heroine is always exceptionally capable and plucky, helpful and brave. Addy Walker's story is the most poignant, and it is her books which have received the most attention. The Addy books are historically accurate, which makes for some painful reading: before her family can flee slavery, for example, Addy's master sells some of her family, and her family is forced to leave her young sister, Esther, in the care of fellow slaves. Addy's parents' experience of prejudice in the north, where they are free, also clearly demonstrates to readers that the social effects of racism go beyond legal statutes.

What explains the long-lasting popularity of girls series books? What social values do the books promote? While the messages such books send can offer their readers newfound self respect, the books can also help to perpetuate stereotypes. The *American Girls* books do not hide the fact that they emphasize ''traditional values,'' and yet ''traditional values'' are reduced to a rather simplistic vision of the American past as a time when families were better off—when they were more closely-knit, more functional, safer, and most importantly, more likely a place where mothers and daughters spent time together. According to the Pleasant Company catalog, the *American Girls* books and programs have ''nurtured a sense of community among thousands of girls around the country, and in a fast-paced, over-scheduled world have provided a memorable experience that mothers and daughters can share.'' In fact, the *American Girls Collection* does what much of the genre of historical fiction (especially for children) does . . . it satisfies our need for formula and reaffirms simplistic notions about the past. The popularity of historical fiction has never been based, after all, on the degree to which it reflects an accurate picture of historical eras or events, but is based rather on the degree to which it reaffirms cultural myths. The *American Girls* books, nevertheless, combine education and entertainment. While we may wish for fiction that would complicate, rather than simply corroborate, our understanding of history, these novels serve as an informal, informative introduction to history, which may be more accessible to its readers than more formal or complex treatments of the same historical periods.

Problems in the *American Girls* books are often surmounted too easily, almost as if having a loving family guarantees a good outcome: Samantha's aunt and uncle decide to keep all of her orphan friends, for example, while Addy's family is successfully reunited. In addition, several of the novels contain messages of self-effacement. Kristin and Molly, for example, both learn that their concerns are trivial compared to those of other family members. Despite their memorialization of the past, and their cliched moral messages, the *American Girls* books do offer their readers greater independence and a sense of their own potential power by presenting images of independent, resourceful young girls. Simply reading historical fiction featuring girls can give girl readers a sense of pride and self-awareness that they might not acquire from historical fiction featuring boys. As Rowland says, ''I believe very strongly in the importance of gender-specific publishing. And, especially after recent reports that girls are given less attention than boys in the classroom, it is crucial that girls see themselves as significant characters in books—and in history. And it is also important for boys to recognize this, too.'' Perhaps most importantly, the *American Girls* books present exceptionally gutsy and articulate girls of different classes, races, and cultural backgrounds. Taken as a whole, the series says that what it means to be an American girl is significantly different than the white upper-middle class Victorian girl we are all familiar with from children's literature.

—Austin Booth

American Gothic

This painting of a stern-visaged, tight-lipped, nineteenth-century country couple posed in front of their pristine farmhouse has become not only one of the most reproduced images in American popular culture, it has also virtually become emblematic of the moral fiber and simple virtues for which America is said to stand. Painted by Grant Wood in 1930, *American Gothic* has been interpreted both as homage to the artist's Midwestern roots and as slyly witty commentary on American "family values." After winning an important prize in 1930, *American Gothic* quickly became, as Robert Hughes notes, "Along with the Mona Lisa and Whistler's Mother . . . one of the three paintings that every American knows. . . . One index of its fame is the number of variations run on it by cartoonists, illustrators, and advertisers. . . . The couple in front of the house have become preppies, yuppies, hippies, Weathermen, pot growers, Ku Klux Klaners, jocks, operagoers, the Johnsons, the Reagans, the Carters, the Fords, the Nixons, the Clintons, and George Wallace with an elderly black lady." In the visual culture of the millennium, *American Gothic* remains the most potent and pervasive symbol of America's heartland mythology, as witnessed by its perpetual permeation into all areas of popular culture.

—Victoria Price

FURTHER READING:

Hughes, Robert. *American Visions: The Epic History of Art in America.* New York, Alfred A. Knopf, 1997.

American Graffiti

The 1973 box office and critical smash *American Graffiti* epitomized the 1950s nostalgia craze, established the device of interweaving multiple stories, inspired such television series as *Happy Days* and *Laverne and Shirley,* and boosted the careers of Richard Dreyfuss, Cindy Williams, Candy Clark and, most notably, the film's co-writer and director, George Lucas. The story takes place in 1962—the proper if not the chronological end of the 1950s—when both the kids and the country were innocent. The evening depicted was a month before the Cuban missile crisis, a year before the assassination of John F. Kennedy, and years before the Vietnam War controversy, hippies, radicals, pot, free love, Nixon, and AIDS (Acquired Immune Deficiency Syndrome). But what makes the film universal is the way Lucas captures the innocence of youth, that

American Gothic **by Grant Wood.**

ephemeral moment when all options are still open, before irrevocable choices must be made. Everything is still possible, and the sky is the limit.

It is a bit surprising that such a popular and influential film almost did not get made. Lucas' first film, *THX 1138,* was a financial failure, and United Artists rejected the script for *American Graffiti* that Lucas had written with Gloria Katz and Willard Huyck. But Lucas' friend, Francis Ford Coppola, convinced Universal to back the film, on condition Coppola serve as producer and adviser, and with a $700,000 budget, Universal figured the risk was not great. The movie was shot on location in 28 nights, and the filming was plagued with problems from the outset. On the second night, the entire crew was evicted from the town in which they were shooting, and the assistant cameraman was hospitalized after falling off the camera car and being run over by a trailer. The film came in on time and, after editing, Lucas handed the completed film over to Universal, which was less than thrilled with the finished product. Studio executives were particularly put off by the presence of four central characters whose stories were intertwined. Lucas was furious when the studio cut five minutes from the film before releasing it. But Lucas' vision was vindicated when the film grossed over $100 million domestically, received five Academy Award nominations, and won the Golden Globe and New York Film Critics' Award. Stephen Farber in *The New York Times* called it "the most important American movie since *Five Easy Pieces*—maybe since *Bonnie and Clyde.*"

The story, based on Lucas' own youth in Modesto, California, begins when four friends meet up in the parking lot of Mel's Drive-In,

Ron Howard and Cindy Williams in a scene from the film *American Graffiti*.

a restaurant with roller-skating carhops. The friends are the teenage intellectual Curt (Dreyfuss), the class president Steve (Ron Howard), the nerd Terry "the Toad" (Charles Martin Smith), and the 22-year-old hot rodder John (Paul Le Mat). Three of these characters were based on Lucas himself who began as a nerd, was considered much cooler after winning several racing trophies, and was forced to exercise his intellect after a near-fatal car crash crushed his lungs and ended his racing career; only the class president, Steve, was pure fiction, and the major reason Lucas needed two co-writers. The year of the story may be 1962, but the cars and songs are solidly 1950s, as customized cars driven by ponytailed girls and ducktailed boys tool along the main drag in a mating ritual, with disc jockey Wolfman Jack supplying the tunes. Curt and Steve are due to fly east to college the next morning, but Curt's second thoughts about leaving the safety of his hometown provide the film's backbone. Steve is dating Curt's sister, Laurie (Williams), and she is upset about Steve leaving her behind. When Curt spots a beautiful blonde (Suzanne Somers) in a classic white 1956 T-bird and she mouths the words "I love you," he wants to follow her. Unfortunately, he is in the back seat of his sister's

1958 Edsel and cannot convince her to follow the T-bird, and spends the rest of the movie trying to track this vision down. Meanwhile, Steve and Laurie argue about his leaving, Toad can not believe his luck when he picks up a beautiful blonde (Clark), and John's cruising style is hampered by the presence of the 13-year-old Carol (Mackenzie Phillips) while his hot-rodding reputation is being challenged by Bob Falfa (Harrison Ford). Curt finally visits Wolfman Jack for advice, and the Wolfman convinces him that "this place ain't exactly the hub of the universe." When morning comes, Laurie has convinced Steve to stay in town, and they, the Toad, John, and Curt's parents say goodbye to Curt at the airport. As his plane wings its way eastward, he glances down and notices a lone car also leaving town and also headed east: a classic white 1956 T-bird.

The film may be nostalgic, but it is never sentimental. While films such as *Summer of '42* specialized in a soft-focus romanticism, Lucas bent over backwards to make sure the film was never pretty. One of the world's greatest cinematographers, Haskell Wexler, served as supervising cameraman, to capture Lucas' vision, and the film was shot in grainy Techniscope, in what Lucas called "a sort of jukebox lighting''—or what film co-editor Marcia Lucas termed ''ugly.'' Subsequent films and television shows have tried for this hard-edged nostalgia, but even more influential was the device of interweaving story lines, which has become a television staple, used on shows ranging from *Hill Street Blues* to *Northern Exposure* and *ER.* Significantly, Lucas used part of the profits from the film to help finance his next project: *Star Wars.*

—Bob Sullivan

FURTHER READING:

Champlin, Charles. *George Lucas: The Creative Impulse.* New York, Harry N. Abrams, Inc., 1992.

Farber, Stephen. '''Graffiti' Ranks With 'Bonnie and Clyde.''' *The New York Times.* August 5, 1973, sec. 2, p. 1.

Lucas, George, et al. *American Graffiti.* New York, Ballantine Books, Inc., 1973.

Pollock, Dale. *Skywalking: The Life and Films of George Lucas.* New York, Ballantine Books, Inc., 1984.

American International Pictures

For three decades, from the 1950s to the 1970s, American International Pictures (AIP) supplied America's drive-ins and movie theatres with cult favorites such as *It Conquered the World, I Was a Teenage Werewolf, Beach Blanket Bingo,* and *The Pit and the Pendulum.* The studio not only made the movies that the younger generation wanted to see, but it also helped to create the stars of the future. AIP gave directors such as Francis Ford Coppola, Woody Allen, and Martin Scorcese their first jobs, and cast actors such as Jack Nicholson, Robert De Niro, and Peter Fonda in their first movies. Hollywood had always made ''B'' movies, but no one made them as fast or with as much enthusiastic abandon as AIP. With miniscule budgets, ten or fifteen-day shooting schedules, recycled sets, and churned-out screenplays, AIP changed the way movies were made by creating a demand for a brand new kind of low-budget entertainment; Hollywood would never be the same again.

American International Pictures founder Samuel Z. Arkoff had wanted to be a part of the motion picture industry since boyhood. It took him almost twenty years to fulfill his dream. After serving in World War II, he moved to Los Angeles, where he attended law school on the G.I. Bill. For five years, Arkoff made a living as a minor television and film lawyer. When he met former theatre chain owner, James Nicholson, the two hatched an idea for a production company whose time, they felt, had come.

By the early 1950s, the Golden Age of Hollywood was at an end. During the previous decade, the U.S. Congress had filed an anti-trust suit against the eight major studios. The government's goal was to check the studios' monopolistic abuse of power by forcing them to close down their distribution arms, that is, to prevent studios from owning theaters. The case dragged on, but by the end of the 1940s, a consent decree was passed, forcing the studios to divest control of

their theaters. By 1954, the eight major studios no longer owned theaters and the studio system that had sustained Hollywood was gone.

But this was not the only major change to hit Hollywood. Television was wooing viewers away from the big screen. The neighborhood movie houses began shutting down as viewers flocked to the stores to buy television sets. In response, the major studios stopped making ''B'' pictures, concentrating their efforts instead on mega-productions, musicals, new gimmicks such as 3-D, and wide-angle processes such as CinemaScope and VistaVision, transforming movies into big screen special events that they hoped would lure viewers away from their televisions.

It was at this time that Arkoff and Nicholson spotted a hole in the movie market. They realized that the second-run movie houses and drive-ins were unable to afford these first-run Hollywood extravaganzas, and so were losing their audiences. Arkoff and Nicholson knew that if they could find a way to make first-run movies inexpensively and then supply them to exhibitors at a much lower cost, they would make a huge profit.

In 1954, Arkoff and Nicholson met a young filmmaker named Roger Corman who was looking for a distributor for a low-budget film he was producing. *The Fast and the Furious,* a race car movie starring John Ireland and Dorothy Malone, was just what Arkoff and Nicholson had in mind. They bought the film as part of a four-picture deal with Corman and AIP was born. With Corman as one of their main directors and teenagers their target audience, AIP turned out Westerns, action flicks, prison movies, sci-fi thrillers, and horror films, shamelessly jumping on every cinematic trend. By the late 1950s, with films such as *Invasion of the Saucer-Men, Sorority Girl,* and *Machine Gun Kelly,* the company was turning a steady profit.

By the early 1960s, AIP had found their formula and they felt they could start to take a few risks. When Roger Corman approached Arkoff and Nicholson about filming Edgar Allen Poe's *The Fall of the House of Usher,* the studio signed veteran star Vincent Price to a multi-picture contract, and the critically and financially successful Corman-Price-Poe cycle was born. Realizing that horror movies were in demand, they hired stars from the Golden Age of Horror such as Basil Rathbone, Peter Lorre, and Boris Karloff to appear in their films, fueling a horror renaissance that lasted well into the next decade.

During the 1960s, it seemed as if AIP could do no wrong. When the studio signed Annette Funicello and Frankie Avalon to frolic in the sand in *Beach Party,* they initiated a huge wave of successful beach movies. Hot young stars such as Funicello, Avalon, Jack Nicholson, Peter Fonda, and Nancy Sinatra were brought up in the AIP ranks, and by the early 1970s cutting-edge young directors began flocking to the studio to have their films made. Among these were Martin Scorcese, who directed *Boxcar Bertha*; Brian De Palma, who made *Sisters*; Ivan Reitman, who filmed *Cannibal Girls*; and Oliver Stone, who directed *Seizure.* Even Woody Allen got his first break at AIP, when the studio hired the young stand-up comedian to dub over a Japanese spy film. His *What's Up, Tiger Lily?* became an instant cult classic.

During the 1970s, AIP branched out into bigger productions with horror classic *The Abominable Dr. Phibes,* blaxploitation film *Foxy Brown,* futuristic thriller *Mad Max* with Mel Gibson, and Brian De Palma's *Dressed To Kill.* By the time the studio merged with Filmways in 1980, American International Pictures had become an integral part of moviemaking history.

In 1979, the Museum of Modern Art staged a retrospective of AIP's films, an honor about which Arkoff mused, ''In the early days of AIP, if anyone had told me that our pictures would be shown in the Museum of Modern Art, I would have been startled. That was the furthest thing from my mind. We did not deliberately make art. We were making economical pictures for our youthful market, but at the same time, I guess we were also doing something unique and evolutionary.'' Indeed, this unique and evolutionary approach to making movies changed not only the face of American cinema, but also helped to transform American popular culture. As the curators of the film department at MOMA noted, ''Not only are [American International's] films rich in their depiction of our culture, but indeed they have played a not insignificant part in it.''

—Victoria Price

FURTHER READING:

Arkoff, Sam, with Trubo, Richard. *Flying Through Hollywood By the Seat of My Pants.* New York, Birch Lane Press, 1992.

Sklar, Robert. *Movie-Made America: A Cultural History of American Movies.* New York, Vintage Books, 1994.

American Mercury

For about a decade the *American Mercury* magazine served as an irreverent cultural critic. The magazine's distinctive style came from the iconoclastic nature of its editor, Henry Louis (H. L.) Mencken. Under his leadership, the *Mercury*'s vitriolic attacks on mainstream American culture attracted a following among the intelligentsia and provoked controversy as well (censors tried to ban the April, 1926 issue).

The brainchild of publisher Alfred A. Knopf and journalist/social critic H. L. Mencken, the *Mercury* first appeared in 1924, and Mencken soon became the sole editor. The *Mercury* printed work by Charles Beard, W. J. Cash, Clarence Darrow, W. E. B. Du Bois, Emma Goldman, Langston Hughes, Eugene O'Neill, and Upton Sinclair, among others. In 1933, with readership falling off and his own interest in the magazine waning, Mencken relinquished the editorship. By the 1950s, after passing through a succession of owners and editors, the *Mercury* had degenerated into a racist, anti-semitic fringe publication. The magazine folded in 1980.

—Eric Longley

FURTHER READING:

Angoff, Charles. *H. L. Mencken: A Portrait from Memory.* New York, Thomas Yoseloff, 1956.

Hobson, Fred. *Mencken: A Life.* New York, Random House, 1994.

Mencken, H. L. *My Life as Author and Editor.* New York, Alfred A. Knopf, 1993.

Singleton, M. K. *H. L. Mencken and the American Mercury Adventure.* Durham, North Carolina, Duke University Press, 1962.

American Museum of Natural History

New York City's American Museum of Natural History—with its giant dinosaur skeletons and detailed dioramas—is both a primary repository for the scientific discoveries relating to the natural world and a major tourist attraction. Opened in 1869 when the Upper West Side of Manhattan was still on the edge of civilization, the fortress-like Museum later added wings reaching Central Park West and a major planetarium wholly updated in the 1990s. From a few hundred mounted birds and mammals, the museum's collection has grown to include more fossils, mammals, and dinosaurs than any other museum in the world. Critics have charged the museum with being an agent of colonialism and exploitation and have found the statue of President Theodore Roosevelt on horseback flanked by a walking Black and American Indian in front of the principal entrance an apt symbol of their charge. Such criticisms have not minimized the pleasures of the millions of people who visit the museum annually. In *The Catcher in the Rye* J. D. Salinger captured the delight of many visitors when his character Holden Caulfield fondly remembered his regular school visits to the museum, saying ''I get very happy when I think about it.''

—Richard Martin

FURTHER READING:

Oliver, James A. ''American Museum of Natural History at 100.'' *Nature* March 28, 1970.

Osborn, Henry Fairfield. *American Museum of Natural History: It's Origins, It's History, the Growth of It's Departments to December 31, 1909.* New York, Irving Press, 1911.

Titcomb, Mary. *American Museum of Natural History.* Austin, Texas, Booklab, 1991.

The Amos 'n' Andy Show

During the Great Depression *The Amos 'n' Andy Show* provided comic relief to a nation reeling from rapid deflation and skyrocketing unemployment. The day after the stock market crash of October 29, 1929, the following exchange took place on the Amos 'n' Andy radio show—Andy: ''Is you been keepin' yo' eye on de stock market?'' Lightnin': ''Nosah, I ain't never seed it.'' Andy: ''Well, de stock market crashed!'' Lightnin': ''Anybody git hurt?'' Andy: ''Well, 'course, Lightnin', when de stock market crashes, it hurts bizness men. Dat's whut puts de repression on things.'' Clearly, the show gave down-on-their-luck Americans a cast of characters at whom they could laugh and with whom they could identify. But there was more at stake on the show than economic satire. In its television incarnation in the 1950s and 1960s, the show became a window on changing race relations in America. From 1925 until 1966 *The Amos 'n' Andy Show* dominated several forms of media in America. It was the nation's most popular radio show, the subject of two films, a popular comic strip, and finally a television sitcom with an all-black cast. The show

The cast of the *Amos 'n' Andy* television show: (from left) Spencer Williams, Tim Moore, and Alvin Childress.

perpetuated the stereotypes of blackface minstrelsy, portraying clownish "Coons," docile and devout "Uncle Toms," shrewish "Mammies," and other stock black characters. As a television show it divided the black community. Some blacks thought it was a funny show which provided an excellent opportunity for blacks to work in the entertainment industry, while others—especially the National Association for the Advancement of Colored People (NAACP)—viewed it as an abominable racist burlesque which led all Americans to believe that blacks were unemployable, oafish fools.

The Amos 'n' Andy Show was the brainchild of Freeman Gosden and Charles Correll, two white performers with Southern roots. Gosden's father fought for the confederacy in the Civil War, and Correll was a distant relative of Jefferson Davis. Gosden and Correll met in North Carolina in 1919, and when their radio show, *Sam 'n' Henry,* debuted in Chicago in 1925 they were paid in food instead of cash. The title characters of the show were bumptious Southern blacks who had moved from Alabama to Chicago hoping for a better life. The humor on the show was part malapropistic (black characters creating unintended puns by mispronouncing words) and part derivative from the dim-witted characters' naivete. The show was historically significant because it was the first serialized radio program ever—in other words, it was the first show to have a continuous storyline woven through nightly episodes. As such, it was the pioneer of the soap opera and the television situation comedy.

In 1926 the *Chicago Tribune,* owner of Chicago radio station WGN, signed Gosden and Correll to a two year radio contract. When

that contract ended the duo moved to another station but had to change the names of the title characters because WGN owned the rights to *Sam 'n' Henry.* Gosden and Correll initially considered Jim 'n' Charlie for their new characters' names, but decided on Amos 'n' Andy instead because they thought that "Amos" was a "trusting, simple, and naive" Biblical name while Andy sounded "lazy" and "domineering." In show number 23 Gosden and Correll came up with the show's trademark, the "Fresh Air Taxicab of America Incorpulated." In 1929 NBC picked up the show and broadcast it to a national radio audience. The show was an instant sensation. It was so popular that it had to be recorded live twice each night so that it could be heard on the West Coast and the East Coast in prime time. It represented a unique approach to comedy because it was not based on one-liners like other comedy shows of the period. Gosden and Correll thought that if they created likeable, interesting characters, their listeners would tune in. The other stars of *The Amos 'n' Andy Show* were Kingfish, a boisterous schemer, Lightnin' a dimwitted foot-shuffling janitor, Calhoun, a bombastic lawyer, Kingfish's shrewish wife Sapphire, and Sapphire's ogreish mother.

The 1930s belonged to *The Amos 'n Andy Show.* In 1930 they made their first of two feature films, *Check and Double Check,* in which they appeared in blackface. Another film would follow in 1936. In 1931 40 million listeners tuned in each night to their radio show, representing 74 percent of the potential listening audience. The show was so popular that President Calvin Coolidge regularly excused himself from state dinners to listen to the 15 minute nightly broadcast, department stores broadcast the show over their public address systems so that their shoppers could listen to the show as they browsed, and movie theaters actually interrupted feature films in progress so that they could broadcast the radio program live to their audiences. Telephone activity also declined nationally during the 15 minutes during which the show was broadcast, and the sewers in many cities ran dry between 7:00 and 7:15 because listeners did not want to miss a moment of the show. Although the show was very popular among blacks and whites, the 1930s brought the first public protests against it by the NAACP.

In 1943 the NBC radio program was increased from 15 minutes to 30 minutes, but a ratings drop caused Gosden and Correll to revamp the show. When it returned after an eight month hiatus, it was a once-weekly show instead of a nightly show. It had a live audience, an orchestra instead of an organist, and a team of writers to co-write the show with Gosden and Correll. In 1948 CBS lured Gosden and Correll away from NBC by offering them the astounding sum of $2.5 million.

When the television version of *The Amos 'n' Andy Show* premiered with an all-black cast on June 28, 1951, it was immediately at the center of a firestorm of controversy. The NAACP strongly objected to the show, claiming that it "depicted Negroes in a stereotyped and derogatory manner." They soon filed a formal law suit against CBS which asserted that the show "strengthened the conclusion among uninformed and prejudiced people that Negroes are inferior, lazy, dumb, and dishonest." The suit claimed that the show presented every black character as "a clown or a crook," and argued that it led viewers to believe that all blacks were like the characters on the show. This was a minority position within the black community at large and within the black entertainment community in particular. The few blacks who had made it into show business saw the show as a positive step because it employed dozens of African Americans in an industry which had been all but off limits to black performers. Several of the show's cast members defended it against the barrage of criticism from the NAACP and the National Urban League.

The star of the short-lived television show was neither Amos nor Andy but George "Kingfish" Stevens, played by Tim Moore. Some have suggested that instead of *The Amos 'n' Andy Show,* the show should have been called "The Adventures of Kingfish." Moore created in Kingfish a complex character—a sympathetic, mischievous protagonist. Amos, played by Alvin Childress, made cameo appearances in most episodes, but had a very minor role. Andy, played by Spencer Williams, Jr., had a more prominent role, but still served primarily as Kingfish's foil. Horace Stewart played the ironically named Lightnin', Ernestine Wade played Sapphire, and Jonny Lee played the preachy lawyer Calhoun. Blatz Brewing Co., the sponsor of the television show, pulled out in 1953 under pressure from the NAACP, and later that year the network canceled the show despite its high ratings. It was the first television show ever shown as a rerun (during the summer of 1952), and it ran in syndication until 1966.

Black entertainers and civil rights leaders of the 1960s through the 1990s have disagreed over how the show should be remembered. Comedians Flip Wilson and Redd Foxx watched the show, enjoyed it, and thought it was a harmless comedy. Other black entertainers disagreed. Richard Pryor called the show an "outrage" and Bill Cosby claimed it was "not at all funny." Civil Rights leader and presidential candidate Jesse Jackson has offered one of the most insightful commentaries on the show. He said, "I think the record must show that *[The Amos 'n' Andy Show]* paid the dues that made it possible for those who now play roles with much more dignity." He added that the show "proved that blacks could act" and "proved that blacks could entertain." As demeaning as the television show was in terms of its stereotypical presentations of African Americans, it did give them unprecedented access to the highly segregated world of show business.

—Adam Max Cohen

FURTHER READING:

Andrews, Bart and Ahrgus Juilliard. *Holy Mackerel: The Amos 'n' Andy Story.* New York, E. P. Dutton, 1986.

Ely, Melvin Patrick. *The Adventures of Amos 'n' Andy: A Social History of an American Phenomenon.* New York, Free Press, 1991.

Leonard, William Torbert. *Masquerade in Black.* Metuchen, New Jersey, Scarecrow Press, 1986.

Amsterdam, Morey (1908-1996)

Morey Amsterdam brought a vaudeville sensibility into the electronic age. Best known for his role as Buddy Sorrell on *The Dick Van Dyke Show,* Amsterdam was a popular show business veteran before he was cast in the series. He made his mark in acting,

Morey Amsterdam

songwriting, film, and nightclub comedy—where he earned the nickname "The Human Joke Machine" for his ability to come up with a joke on any subject on demand. He wrote gags for presidents and performers, and his admirers included Pope John XXIII and Chicago mob boss Al Capone.

Morey Amsterdam was born in Chicago, Illinois, on December 14, 1908. From the beginning, the arts touched his life. His father was a concert violinist who played for the Chicago Opera and, later, the San Francisco Symphony. Like many vaudeville veterans, Amsterdam began his performing career as a child. His first public performance took place in 1922 when Morey sang as a tenor on a San Francisco radio program. The teenager then joined his piano-playing brother in his vaudeville act. He started out as a cellist, but soon the instrument merely became a prop for his comedy. When his brother left show business, Morey continued on his own. At age 16, he was hired as a regular performer by a nightclub owner named Al "Brown," who had been impressed with Amsterdam's stage act. Brown's real name was Al Capone. A shootout on the club premises inspired Amsterdam to seek greener, and safer, pastures in California.

Amsterdam attended the University of California at Berkeley for a time, but by 1930 he was in New York City, working as a comedy writer for radio stars Will Rogers and Fanny Brice. He soon realized that he felt at home on the air, where his quick wit and rapid-fire joke delivery, honed in front of live audiences, quickly won over listeners. In 1932 he started writing for *The Al Pierce Gang* radio program. It was on this show he met lifelong friend and future *Dick Van Dyke Show* costar, Rose Marie. He also found time to write jokes for another well-known client—President Franklin D. Roosevelt.

In the late 1930s, Morey Amsterdam continued to expand his creative horizons, serving as lyricist on the films *With Love and Kisses* (1937) and *Career Girl* (1943). His songwriting talents also yielded a number of popular compositions, including "Why Oh Why Did I Ever Leave Wyoming?" and The Andrews Sisters' "Rum and Coca-Cola." He wrote the films *The Ghost and the Guest* (1943) and *Bowery Champs* (1944) and provided additional dialogue for *Kid Dynamite* (1943).

In the midst of post-World War II prosperity, television came to America. As with radio, Morey Amsterdam wasted no time taking his place among the pioneers of the new medium. On December 17, 1948, CBS first telecast *The Morey Amsterdam Show* (a radio version, which had premiered six months earlier, continued during the TV series' run). Morey essentially played himself: His character, a nightclub owner, was a joke-telling cello player. CBS canceled the series after three months. In only one month it was back, this time on the Dumont network, where it remained until its final airing in October of 1950.

Throughout the 1950s, Morey Amsterdam remained visible to TV audiences in a variety of series and guest appearances. He appeared as a panelist on NBC's *Tag the Gag* in 1951 and *Who Said That?* (on which he had made his first TV appearance in 1948) in 1954. He hosted Dumont's intergenerational game, *Battle of the Ages,* from September to November of 1952. While his own show was still on CBS, he hosted NBC's *Broadway Open House* (1950), a precursor to *The Tonight Show,* on Monday and Wednesday nights.

It was Rose Marie who, in 1961, recommended Amsterdam for what would become his most memorable role. She was cast as comedy writer Sally Rogers on *The Dick Van Dyke Show.* The role of co-worker Buddy Sorrel was not yet cast. Rose Marie suggested that series creator Carl Reiner get in touch with her old friend Morey Amsterdam. Knowing Amsterdam's reputation, Reiner agreed. Amsterdam accepted the offer to audition without hesitation—happy for the opportunity to move from New York City to California, where the show was to be filmed. He quickly landed the role.

The Dick Van Dyke Show broke new ground in the television situation comedy genre. Viewers not only learned what Rob Petrie (Van Dyke) did at the office, they also got to know the people with whom he spent his workdays. These co-workers were fully formed characters, as richly drawn as Rob and his wife Laura (Mary Tyler Moore). The series pioneered the depiction of a "workplace family," a concept Moore would put to use in her own series in the next decade. Buddy was also one of the first TV characters to openly state a personal fact seldom mentioned on TV at the time: He was Jewish.

The series' casting and writing were works of genius. As the writers of the fictional "Alan Brady Show," Van Dyke, Amsterdam, and Rose Marie played off each other perfectly. Amsterdam's banter with Rose Marie and his fast-paced quips directed at "Brady" producer Mel Cooley (Richard Deacon) quickly became highlights of the show. Buddy Sorell was an ideal role for him: both were show

business veterans with sharp wits and an arsenal of jokes for any occasion. Amsterdam later declared, "I am Buddy. [He] is not only a comic, but an experienced writer, a fellow who knows timing and funny situations." In the final episode, the cast learns that Rob's life is to be adapted for a TV situation comedy that will be scripted by Rob, Buddy, and Sally. The fictional Buddy thus becomes a "real" person adapted into a television character. Just as Morey Amsterdam is Buddy, Buddy becomes, in a sense, Morey Amsterdam.

Amsterdam continued to work throughout the rest of his life, performing in clubs and guest starring on series from *The Partridge Family* (1970, as a comedy writer) to *Caroline in the City* (1996, with Rose Marie). He had just returned from a cabaret tour when he died of a heart attack on October 27, 1996. As Dick Van Dyke remarked, "Probably a hundred thousand jokes in his head went with him."

—David L. Hixson

FURTHER READING:

Amsterdam, Morey. *The Betty Cooker Crockbook for Drinkers.* New York, Regnery, 1977.

Hill, Tom, and Dick Van Dyke. *Nick At Nite's Classic TV Companion: The All Night, Every Night Guide to Better Living Through Television.* New York, Fireside, 1991.

Waldron, Vince, and Dick Van Dyke. *The Official Dick Van Dyke Show Book: The Definitive History and Ultimate Viewer's Guide to Television's Most Enduring Comedy.* New York, Hyperion, 1994.

Weisman, Ginny, and Coyne Steven Sanders. *The Dick Van Dyke Show.* New York, St. Martin's Press, 1983.

Amtrak

Amtrak was created in the early 1970s to rescue America's failing passenger rail system by bringing it under the control of a single quasi-governmental authority. Trains had been the primary means of intercity travel up to World War II, during which gasoline rationing filled many trains to standing-room-only. But passenger volume rapidly fell once the war was over, the automobile assuming primacy as a symbol of prosperity and mobility, a necessity for commuters in brand-new suburbs inaccessible by rail, and a commodity whose manufacture was central to the postwar industrial boom.

Nevertheless, a number of railroads continued to run passenger trains at a loss so long as they had a robust freight traffic to subsidize them. But by the end of the 1960s competition from truck freight, combined with inept management, spawned numerous bankruptcies (such as the New York Central and Pennsylvania Railroads, which merged to form the Penn Central in a last ditch but unsuccessful effort to avoid insolvency). In 1970, when President Nixon signed the Rail Passenger Service Act creating Amtrak, fewer than 10 percent of intercity travelers were riding the rails, on a total of only 450 scheduled trains a year—and three-quarters of the scheduled trains had discontinuance petitions pending before the Interstate Commerce Commission.

Passengers boarding an Amtrak train.

Many government officials in Washington were skeptical of Amtrak because they saw the new agency as an instance of throwing good money after bad, but the relatively modest appropriation passed by Congress included $40 million from the federal government plus another $100 million in guaranteed loans. A number of unprofitable routes were to be eliminated immediately, in return for which private railroads buying into the system would ultimately contribute $192 million in monthly installments over three years.

On May 1, 1971, Amtrak ran its first trains. At first, these were the same as before, but now run by the original railroads under contract (as some cities' commuter-rail systems, notably Boston's, would continue to be into the 1990s); later, the trains were motley assemblages of aging steam-heated cars in a rainbow of different companies' colors behind engines newly painted with Amtrak's red-white-and-blue arrow logo. An immediate and visible change, however, was in advertising. With such imagery as a frustrated Paul Revere on horseback surrounded by stalled bumper-to-bumper car traffic, and a one-way Boston-New York fare of $9.90 (and a round trip for just a dime more), Amtrak appealed both to the mind and the wallet.

And to a great extent the strategy worked. Students and young adults on tight budgets found the cheap fares irresistibly attractive, and enjoyed the camaraderie and adventure of train travel, even on antiquated equipment prone to failure (although, to its credit, Amtrak shops in Boston, Wilmington, Delaware, and elsewhere were reconditioning the old equipment as fast as they could) and with only a modest likelihood of on-time arrival. Thanks in large part to rebounding ridership, profitability was soon restored to the Washington-to-Boston corridor, most of which was bought outright from the bankrupt Penn Central in 1976.

Although the mingling of train travelers was arguably a social force for democratization, a second factor in the recovery of the Northeast Corridor was its first-class service. Although parlor cars were nothing new (complete with spacious seats and obliging service staff—mostly black, a holdover from the heyday of the Pullman sleepers), Amtrak sought to attract more affluent customers by introducing its priority Metroliner trains, which cut three-quarters of an hour off the Washington-New York run and whose interiors, reminiscent of airplane cabins, featured headrest-backed seats equipped with folding tray-tables, high-tech stainless-steel chemical toilets, and even on-board telephones. A fleet for ordinary coach service, with similar styling but no telephones, was gradually introduced to replace the rebuilt "Heritage" cars as well. As the quality of service improved, so did ridership among older citizens, many of whom were attracted both by the nostalgia of train travel and by affordable excursion and senior fares.

Amtrak's first decade saw a race of capital improvements against deteriorating infrastructure, for the earlier railroads had spent little on upkeep as they sank deeper into debt. In the Northeast Corridor, several hundred miles of worn track on deteriorating wooden ties were replaced by long sections of continuous-welded rail bolted to concrete, and roadbeds were regraded to allow higher operating speeds. A daily trip by a prototype turbo-train, the "Yankee Clipper"—the name borrowed from a former Boston and Maine train to Bangor, discontinued in the mid-1950s—was introduced on an experimental basis between Boston and New York for several months in 1975. (However, the turbo trimmed only a half hour off the time of the fastest conventional express run, the "Merchants' Limited," and wobbled alarmingly at its top speed of 90 miles per hour. It was quietly withdrawn from service several months later.)

Meanwhile, Congress was becoming increasingly uneasy about its allocations to Amtrak's budget, since it could not see the analogy between such subsidies and the less visible public underwriting of the competition—the highways and airports—through such self-perpetuating taxation schemes as the Highway Trust Fund. Amtrak managed to beat back challenges to its funding by pledging to become a break-even business by the turn of the century, a deadline subsequently extended to the year 2002.

In 1981, Amtrak declared that its policy would be to set fares "at a level designed to produce the highest possible revenue." Ceasing to try to compete with intercity bus prices, the company eliminated most excursion fares. By 1998, a round trip by train between Boston and New York cost more than twice the fare charged by the principal bus carrier, Greyhound; not surprisingly, many students and the urban poor now shunned the train as prohibitively expensive, so that even as Amtrak crossed the $1 billion mark in its annual revenues, it had for all practical purposes ceased to be passenger rail for all the people, and was now affordable only by the middle and upper classes.

—Nick Humez

FURTHER READING:

Dorin, Patrick C. *Amtrak Trains and Travel.* Seattle, Superior Publishing Company, 1979.

Edmonson, Harold A., editor. *Journey to Amtrak: The Year History Rode the Passenger Train.* Milwaukee, Kalmbach Publishing Company, 1972.

Gärtner, Michael. *Riding the Pennsy to Ruin: A Wall Street Journal Chronicle of the Penn Central Debacle.* Princeton, Dow Jones Books, 1971.

Hilton, George Woodman. *AMTRAK: The National Railroad Passenger Corporation.* Washington, American Enterprise Institute for Public Policy Research, 1980.

Miller, Henry W. *Trains of the Broadway Limited Route, 1922-1977.* Washington, Railways of the Americas, 1977.

National Railroad Passenger Corporation (Amtrak). *Amtrak 20th Anniversary Source Book.* National Railroad Passenger Corporation, 1990.

National Railroad Passenger Corporation (Amtrak). *1997 Annual Report.* Washington, National Railroad Passenger Corporation, 1997.

Pindell, Terry. *Making Tracks: An American Rail Odyssey.* New York, Grove Weidenfeld, 1990.

United States: Task Force Steering Committee, Executive Office of the President. *Transportation in the Northeastern Megalopolitan Corridor.* Washington, Executive Office of the President, 1962.

Amusement Parks

Spatial and temporal enclaves remote from everyday life, amusement parks are among the favorite recreational places of Americans, who imported the concept from Europe, developed it into a major artifact of American popular culture and have successfully re-exported it throughout the world since the 1980s. Amusement parks not only provide an abundance of entertainment to visitors by featuring roller coasters, Ferris wheels, carousels, games, food, and shows, but also have promoted very contested models of ideal future societies and utopian communities, especially since the creation of Disneyland in 1955.

Contemporary amusement parks are the descendants of medieval trade fairs and European pleasure gardens of the late seventeenth and eighteenth centuries. Originally expressing an idyllic Arcadian life within increasingly industrialized urban landscapes, later pleasure gardens displayed additional features such as live entertainment, exotic architecture, impressive lighting, fireworks, dancing, games, and even primitive amusement rides. However, as their popularity grew, they also attracted undesirable guests such as prostitutes, rakes, smugglers, and thieves, and the development of criminal activities caused many of these gardens to close.

At the end of the nineteenth century, the growth of the amusement park industry shifted to the United States, benefiting greatly from the Chicago's Columbian Exposition of 1893, which introduced the key elements of modern amusement parks. The World's Fair unveiled the first Ferris wheel and the exotic enticements of the Midway Plaisance but, more significantly, it pioneered the model of an enclosed, illusory, and temporary utopian world produced by architects, engineers, and planners. Disconnected from its urban and social environment, the White City allowed its visitors to temporarily escape from reality and experience the magic dream of a perfect future relying on technological progress. Following this example, Captain Paul Boynton opened Chutes Park in Chicago in 1894, the first enclosed amusement park charging an admission fee; a solution that allowed for the exclusion of criminal elements. One year later, he opened Sea Lion Park at Coney Island, Brooklyn, New York, which inspired numerous amusement parks in the United States, including the three Great Coney Island parks.

Coney Island embodied the American amusement park tradition from the 1890s until the mid-1950s. In 1875, the completion of the Andrew Culver's Prospect Park and Coney Island Trailway had transformed Coney Island from a traditional seaside resort into a popular playground. Steeplechase Park (1897-1964), Luna Park (1903-1947), and Dreamland (1904-1911) attracted millions of working-class New Yorkers who enjoyed the intense thrills provided by the roller coaster and other mechanical devices, and the fabulous atmosphere of fantasy, sensuality, and chaos created by the extravagant

A typical American amusement park.

architecture, incredible illuminations, and disorienting attractions. Coney Island offered an escape from a mundane existence and a sense of release from the responsibilities of adulthood.

Increasing leisure time and disposable personal income, as well as the development of electric trolley lines in major American cities, initiated a tremendous growth of the amusement park industry over the next three decades. By building amusement parks at the end of trolley lines, trolley magnates stimulated weekend ridership, thus generating additional revenues and maximizing the flat monthly rate charged by the electric light and power companies. The first "trolley

parks" consisted of picnic groves located in a pastoral landscape, but quickly, dance halls, restaurants, games, and a few amusement rides were added for the pleasure and entertainment of the patrons. These amusement parks became immediately successful among all social classes and, by 1920, over 1,800 operated in the United States. Unfortunately, the golden age did not last. In 1998, only twelve trolley parks remained.

The beginning of the 1920s marked the beginning of the dramatic decline of traditional amusement parks. With the new mobility provided by automobiles and the lack of parking facilities at the urban parks, visitors turned to new activities and attractions such as motion pictures or more independent leisure travel. In addition, Prohibition (of alcohol), some years of bad summer weather, the acquisition of parks by private individuals, the Stock Market Crash of 1929 and the Great Depression caused the closing of numerous parks. By 1939, only 245 amusement parks still remained, struggling to survive. World War II further hurt the industry, but the postwar baby boom and the creation of "kiddielands" allowed for a short resurgence of prosperity. Nevertheless, the radical cultural changes occurring in the 1950s made amusement parks obsolete. The industry could not face the competition from shopping centers and television entertainment, suburbanization of the middle class, intensifying racial tensions, gang conflicts, and urban decay. Most of the traditional amusement parks closed. The modern amusement park would soon appear. The new concept was a fantastic dream of Walt Disney, which cost $17 million to build.

On July 17, 1955, "Walt Disney's Magic Kingdom," more commonly referred to as Disneyland, opened in Anaheim, California. The nation's first modern theme park was born and would dramatically alter the future of the amusement park industry, despite the skepticism it faced at its beginning. Featuring five separate fantasy worlds—Main Street, U.S.A., Fantasyland, Adventureland, Frontierland, and Tomorrowland—Disneyland attracted nearly four million visitors in 1956 and has maintained its exceptional popularity ever since. Isolated and protected from the intrusion of the real world, Disneyland offers to its visitors the experience of a spotless and idyllic universe without sex, violence, or social problems. The attractions transport them into a romanticized past and future, providing maximum thrill and illusion of danger in a perfectly safe environment. Impeccably planned and engineered down to the smallest detail, the park is a realm of permanent optimism and artificiality, celebrating the American Dream of progress through high technology within a carefully designed and bucolic landscape.

After many failures to copy Disneyland's successful formula, Six Flags over Texas opened in 1961 and became the first prosperous regional theme park, followed in 1967 by Six Flags over Georgia. Throughout the late 1960s and 1970s, while traditional urban amusement parks continued to close, suffering from decaying urban conditions, large corporations such as Anheuser-Busch, Harcourt Brace Jovanovich, Marriott Corporation, MCA, Inc., and Taft Broadcasting invested in theme parks well connected to the interstate highway system. In 1971, the opening of what would become the world's biggest tourist attraction, Walt Disney World, opened on 27,500 acres in central Florida. Costing $250 million, it was the most expensive amusement park of that time. Less than ten years later, in 1982, EPCOT Center opened at Walt Disney World and the permanent world's fair surpassed $1 billion. After the fast development of theme parks in the 1970s, the United States faced domestic market saturation and the industry began its international expansion. With the opening of Wonderland in Canada (1981) and Tokyo Disneyland in Japan (1983), theme parks started to successfully conquer the world. Meanwhile, a renewed interest for the older parks permitted some of the traditional amusement parks to survive and expand. In 1987, Kennywood, in Pittsburgh, Pennsylvania, and Playland, in Rye, New York, became the first operating amusement parks to be listed on the National Register of Historic Places.

In 1992 Euro Disneyland, which cost $4 billion to build, opened near Paris. Jean Cau, cited by Alan Riding, described it as "a horror made of cardboard, plastic, and appalling colors, a construction of hardened chewing gum and idiotic folklore taken straight out of comic books written for obese Americans." Though dismissed by French intellectuals and suffering financial losses for the first three years, by 1995 the park showed profits and has become among the most visited attractions in Europe.

In 1993 the Disney Company announced plans for an American history theme park near a Civil War battlefield site in Virginia. Although welcomed by some for the jobs and tax revenues it would create, the plans engendered much criticism. Disney was called a "cultural strip miner" and the project labeled a "Trojan mouse." Leading historians took out large advertisements in national newspapers asking, "Should Disney pave over our real past to promote a commercial fantasy?" Ultimately, the plan was abandoned.

The intellectual community has endlessly criticized theme parks and particularly the Disney versions. In 1958, novelist Julian Halévy noted about Disneyland: "As in Disney movies, the whole world, the universe, and all man's striving for dominion over self and nature, have been reduced to a sickening blend of cheap formulas packaged to sell. Romance, Adventure, Fantasy, Science are ballyhooed and marketed: life is bright colored, clean, cute, titillating, safe, mediocre, inoffensive to the lowest common denominator, and somehow poignantly inhuman." Most criticisms emphasize the inauthentic, controlled and sanitized experience provided by the Disney parks. Totally disconnected from reality, the parks offer a decontextualized, selective, and distorted history, denying any components that could potentially challenge the perfect carefree world they exemplify. Ignoring environmental, political, and social issues, these ersatz of paradise are said to promote an unquestioned belief in consumerism, control through managerial hierarchy, and technologies to solve all the world's problems, and to supply permanent entertainment to millions of passive visitors pampered by a perpetually smiling and well-mannered staff.

A more critical aspect of theme parks is their heavy reliance on the automobile and airplane as means of access. While mass-transit connection to the urban centers allowed millions of laborers to enjoy the trolley parks, its absence creates a spatially and socially segregated promised land excluding the poor and the lower classes of the population. The customers tend to belong mainly to the middle- and upper-middle classes. Since many visitors are well-educated, it seems difficult to support fully the previous criticisms. Theme park visitors are certainly not completely fooled by the content of the fictitious utopias that they experience, but, for a few hours or days, they can safely forget their age, social status, and duties without feeling silly or guilty. The success of American amusement parks lies in their ability to allow their visitors to temporarily lapse into a second childhood and escape from the stress and responsibilities of the world.

—Catherine C. Galley and Briavel Holcomb

FURTHER READING:

Adams, Judith A. *The Amusement Park Industry: A History of Technology and Thrills.* Boston, Twayne, 1991.

Bright, Randy. *Disneyland: Inside Story.* New York, H.N. Abrams, 1987.

Cartmell, Robert. *The Incredible Scream Machine: A History of the Roller Coaster.* Bowling Green, Bowling Green State University Press, 1987.

Halévy, Julian. "Disneyland and Las Vegas." *Nation.* June 7, 1958, 510-13.

Mangels, William F. *The Outdoor Amusement Industry from Earliest Times to Present.* New York, Vantage Press, 1952.

Marling, Karal A. *Designing Disney's Theme Parks: The Architecture of Reassurance.* Paris, Flammarion, 1997.

Riding, Alan. ''Only the French Elite Scorn Mickey's Debut.'' *New York Times.* April 15, 1992, A1.

Snow, Richard. *Coney Island: A Postcard Journey to the City of Fire.* New York, Brightwaters Press, 1984.

Sorkin, Michael, editor. *Variations on a Theme Park: The New American City and the End of Public Space.* New York, Hill and Wang, 1992.

Throgmorton, Todd H. *Roller Coasters: An Illustrated Guide to the Rides in the United States and Canada, with a History.* Jefferson, McFarland & Co., 1993.

Amway

The Amway Corporation has grown from a two-man company selling all-purpose cleaner to become the largest and best known multi-level or network marketer in the world. Its diverse product line, ranging from personal care items to major appliances, generated sales of over seven billion dollars in 1998 and was sold by nearly one million distributors in 80 countries and territories. In the process, founders Richard M. DeVos and Jay Van Andel have made millionaires of some of their adherents and *Fortune* 400 billionaires of themselves. With the growth of home businesses in late twentieth-century America, Amway has inspired a slew of imitating companies, selling everything from soap to long distance telephone service. Amway, or the American Way Association as it was first called, has also revived interest in the American success story; rags-to-riches financial success based on hard work, individualism, positive thinking, free enterprise, and faith in God and country.

The prosperous years following World War II inspired people to search for their own piece of the American dream. A variant of the 1930s chain-letter craze, pyramid friendship clubs swept the United States in 1949. The clubs encouraged people to make new friends by requiring them to pay one or two dollars to join and then recruit at least two other paying members. The individual at the top of the pyramid hosted a party and received all of the proceeds before dropping out. This ''new mass hysteria,'' as *Life* magazine called it, was popular mostly among the lower middle class but attracted adherents even from the upper class. The pyramid aspect was illegal—a form of gambling—but authorities risked huge public protest if they intervened. Hundreds of irate readers even threatened to cancel their subscriptions to the *Detroit News* when the paper published stories condemning the clubs. That, however, did not stop magazines and movie newsreels from showing images of lucky participants waving fistfuls of cash at pyramid parties. But most of the schemers got nothing more than dreams of instant riches.

Amway co-founders Jay Van Andel (1924—) and Richard DeVos (1926—) met as students at Grand Rapids, Michigan, Christian High School in 1940. An oft-told business deal brought the high school buddies together; DeVos paid Van Andel a quarter each week for rides to and from school in Van Andel's old Ford Model A. The Dutch American DeVos and Van Andel shared the same church, the conservative Christian Reformed, and similar backgrounds, values, and interests. Their families encouraged hard work and both young

men were instructed to develop their own businesses as a means of assuring their financial future. World War II intervened, but the pair reunited after the war and founded their first businesses, a flight school and the first drive-in restaurant in Grand Rapids.

Following an adventure-filled trip to South America by air, sea, and land, the two men searched for a new business opportunity in 1949. The answer appeared—at the height of the pyramid craze—in the form of Nutrilite vitamins and food supplements. Nutrilite had been founded by Carl Rehnborg, a survivor of a Chinese prison camp. Rehnborg returned to the United States convinced of the health benefits of vitamins and nutritional supplements. His company used a different sales technique, multi-level or network marketing, that was similar to but not exactly the same as pyramiding. New distributors paid $49 for a sales kit, not as a membership fee but for the cost of the kit, and did not have to recruit new distributors or meet sales quotas unless desired. Nutrilite distributors simulated aspects of pyramid friendship clubs. They sold their products door-to-door and person-to-person and were encouraged to follow up sales to make sure customers were using the purchases properly or to ask if they needed more. Satisfied customers often became new distributors of Nutrilite and original distributors received a percentage of new distributors' sales, even if they left the business.

DeVos and Van Andel excelled at network marketing, making $82,000 their first year and more than $300,000 in 1950, working out of basement offices in their homes. Over the next ten years, they built one of the most successful Nutrilite distributorships in America. In 1958, a conflict within Nutrilite's management prompted the pair to develop their own organization and product line. The American Way Association was established with the name changed to Amway Corporation the following year. DeVos and Van Andel built their company around another product, a concentrated all-purpose cleaner known as L. O. C., or liquid organic cleaner. Ownership of the company had one additional benefit beyond being a distributor. DeVos and Van Andel now made money on every sale, not just those they or their distributors made.

The new enterprise ''took on a life of its own, quickly outgrowing its tiny quarters and outpacing the most optimistic sales expectations of its founders,'' according to a corporate biography. Operation was moved to a building on the corporation's current site in a suburb of Grand Rapids—Ada, Michigan—in 1960. In 1962, Amway became an international company, opening its first affiliate in Canada. By 1963, sales were 12 times the first-year sales. In its first seven years, Amway had to complete 45 plant expansions just to keep pace with sales growth. By 1965, the company that started with a dozen workers employed 500 and its distributor force had multiplied to 65,000. The original L. O. C. was joined by several distinct product lines with dozens of offerings each. Most of the products were ''knock-offs,'' chemically similar to name brands but sold under the Amway name. A fire in the company's aerosol plant in Ada in 1969 failed to slow growth.

The 1970s were an important decade for the company. Pyramid schemes attracted renewed public attention in 1972 when a South Carolina pitchman named Glenn Turner was convicted of swindling thousands through fraudulent cosmetic and motivational pyramid schemes. The Federal Trade Commission (FTC) accused Amway of similar pyramid tactics in 1975. ''They're not in a business, but some sort of quasi-religious, socio-political organization,'' a FTC lawyer said. The FTC alleged the company failed to disclose its distributor drop-out rate, well over 50 percent, as well. But an administrative law judge disagreed in 1978, arguing that Amway was a ''genuine business opportunity.'' The company began a vigorous public relations campaign against pyramid schemes, which was to continue on its corporate web-page through the late 1990s.

Amway expanded its international operations in earnest during the 1970s, adding countries in Europe and Asia. In 1972, Amway purchased Nutrilite Products, the firm that had started Van Andel and DeVos. The firm's first billion dollar year came in 1980. Amway World Headquarters continued to expand as a new cosmetics plant was opened in Ada. By the end of the 1980s, Amway distributors were operating in 19 countries on five continents, marketing hundreds of Amway-made products in addition to other name brand products sold through a catalog.

Personal computers and corporate downsizing aided to the rise in home businesses during the 1980s and 1990s, benefitting network marketing companies like Amway. Although less than five percent earned more than $40,000 a year, The Direct Selling Association estimated that 30,000 people became new direct marketing distributors each week in 1997. In an era of increasingly impersonal retailing, customers enjoyed a return to personal salesmanship. ''You buy a product at the store and the manager doesn't call to say, 'Hey, are you doing OK?','' one multi-level distributor told the Associated Press in 1997. Amway sales presentations stressed customer service but were blended with testimonials from successful distributors, healthy doses of positive thinking, and pitches to God and patriotism. The company's literature, including books, videos, and an internet site, was replete with rags-to-riches success stories, much like a Horatio Alger, Jr. novel of a century before. Not everyone, however, succeeded with the company. ''I saw a lot of other people making money, [but] things just didn't click for us,'' one former distributor told the Associated Press. Still, the *Wall Street Journal* reported in 1998 that an increasing number of doctors were recruiting patients and other doctors to sell Amway as a means of making up for lost income due to managed health care.

A second generation assumed senior management positions at the privately-held Amway Corporation during the 1990s. A board of directors comprised of DeVos, Van Andel, and eight family members was formed in 1992. Steve A. Van Andel (1955—) and Richard M. DeVos, Jr. (1955—) succeeded their fathers as chairman and president. Meanwhile, in 1998 the elder DeVos and Van Andel had personal fortunes estimated at $1.5 and $1.4 billion dollars respectively, and they have used their money to support educational and Christian philanthropy. But, Amway faced new legal problems as well. Beginning in 1982, Procter & Gamble sued various Amway distributors for telling customers that the company encouraged satanism. In 1998, Amway responded by suing Procter & Gamble for distributing ''vulgar and misleading statements'' about Amway and its executives. The litigation revealed the extent of Procter & Gamble's concern over Amway's competition.

The DeVos family attracted media attention toward the end of the twentieth century for their support of the Republican Party and other conservative political causes. Richard M. DeVos, Sr. and his wife gave the most money to Republicans, $1 million, during the 1996 presidential campaign while encouraging their Amway distributors to donate thousands of additional dollars. Amway put up $1.3 million to help the party provide its own coverage of the 1996 national convention on conservative evangelist Pat Robertson's cable television channel—''a public service,'' as Richard M. DeVos, Jr. explained. ''I have decided . . . to stop taking offense at the suggestion that we are buying influence. Now I simply concede the point. They are right. We do expect some things in return,'' DeVos' wife Betsy wrote in an

article for *Roll Call.* Regardless, or perhaps because of its politics, the ''easy money'' allure of Amway continued to attract new distributors to the firm. ''Amway wasn't just a soap business,'' one ex-school teacher couple related on the company's web-page in 1999. ''People's lives were changed by it. Now we are living our dream of building an Amway business as a family.''

—Richard Digby-Junger

FURTHER READING:

Cohn, Charles Paul. *The Possible Dream: A Candid Look at Amway.* Old Tappan, New Jersey, Fleming H. Revell Co., 1977.

———. *Promises to Keep: The Amway Phenomenon and How It Works.* New York, G. P. Putnam's Sons, 1985.

''Explore the Amway Opportunity.'' www.amway.com. April 1999.

Furtrelle, David. ''Soap-pushing Doctors.'' *In These Times.* July 28, 1997, 7.

''Pyramid Club Craze Sweeps Nation.'' *Life.* March 7, 1949, 27-29.

''Pyramiding Pyramids.'' *Newsweek.* February 28, 1949, 19-20.

Salter, Jim. ''Multi-level Marketing Goes Mainstream.'' *Marketing News.* September 1, 1997, 1.

''Soft Soap and Hard Sell.'' *Forbes.* September 15, 1975, 72.

Van Andel, Jay. *An Enterprising Life: An Autobiography.* New York, HarperBusiness, 1998.

Vlasic, Bill, Douglas Harbrecht, and Mary Beth Regan. ''The GOP Way is the Amway Way.'' *Business Week.* August 12, 1996, 28.

Zebrowski, John, and Jenna Ziman. ''The Power Couple Who Gives Political Marching Orders to Amway's Army Wields Influence Both Obvious and Subtle.'' *Mother Jones.* November, 1998, 56.

Analog

See Astounding Science Fiction

Anderson, Marian (1897-1977)

Although her magnificent contralto voice and extraordinary musical abilities were recognized early on, Marian Anderson's American career did not soar until 1939, when she performed on the steps of the Lincoln Memorial in Washington, D.C. At that juncture, her life mission was as much sociological as musical. Not only did she win acceptance for herself and all black performers to appear before unsegregated audiences but she helped initiate the civil rights movement that would flower in the 1960s.

Anderson had no singing instruction until she was seventeen. In 1925, she won a vocal competition in which 300 entrants sought an appearance with the New York Philharmonic in Lewisohn Stadium. Arturo Toscanini heard her in Salzburg, Austria, and declared, ''a voice like hers is heard only once in a hundred years.''

Popular belief is that her career nearly foundered again and again because she was black, but that is not true. By early 1939 she earned up to $2000 a concert and was in great demand. The problems she faced were the segregation of audiences in halls and the insult of sometimes not being able to find decent hotel accommodations

Marian Anderson, singing at the Lincoln Memorial.

because of her color. Her first manager, Arthur Judson, who could not deliver many high-paying dates he promised, suggested that she become a soprano. But she grasped that this was not a viable solution, not only because it evaded the real issue but because such a change could, possibly, seriously affect her vocal cords.

Not at loose ends, but discouraged, Anderson returned to Europe, where she had toured earlier. Between 1930 and 1937, she would appear throughout Western Europe, Eastern Europe (including the Soviet Union), Scandinavia, and Central Europe. After breaking with Judson, Anderson acquired a new manager. Her accompanist, Billy Taylor, bombarded impresario Sol Hurok with letters and copies of her reviews, in the hope that he would become interested in her work. Hurok had built his reputation on publicity feats for his clients. (Some stunts were outrageous, but nearly all of his clients were superb performers.) He had undoubtedly heard about Anderson before Taylor's missives, so his later story about stumbling across a concert she gave in Paris, in 1935, can be dismissed.

What is true is that the concert made a great impression on him, and both he and Anderson agreed to a business relationship that would last until she retired from the stage. When she returned to America in December 1935, Hurok billed her as the "American Colored Contralto," which evidently did not offend her. Under his management, she appeared frequently but still endured the sting of racism even in New

York, where she had to use the servants' entrance when she visited her dentist in Central Park South's exclusive Essex House.

Characteristically, Hurok would claim credit for the event that came to highlight the discrimination toward Anderson and other black artists. He had thought to present her in Washington's Constitution Hall, owned by the ultra-conservative Daughters of the American Revolution (DAR). As he expected, the hall's management duly notified him that Anderson could not appear there because of a "Whites Only" clause in artists' contracts.

Hurok thereupon notified the press about this terrible example of prejudice. After learning the news, a distinguished group of citizens of all races and religions, headed by Mrs. Franklin Delano Roosevelt, agreed to act as sponsors of a free concert Anderson would give on the steps of the Lincoln Memorial, on Easter Sunday, April 9, 1939. Mrs. Roosevelt's husband was in his second term in the White House, and to further emphasize the importance she assigned the event, Mrs. Roosevelt resigned her DAR membership.

An estimated 75,000 people, including Cabinet members and Members of Congress, and about half of whom were black, heard Anderson open the program with "America," continue with an aria from Donizetti's "La Favorita," and, after a few other selections, received an ovation. The crowd, in attempting to congratulate Anderson, threatened to mob her. Police rushed her back inside the

Memorial, where Walter White of the American Association for the Advancement of Colored People had to step to a microphone and make an appeal for calm.

The publicity generated by the event firmly established Anderson's career, not only at home but throughout the world. Racial discrimination in concert halls did not end, but its proponents had been dealt a mighty blow. Beginning after World War II and through the 1950s, Hurok managed tours for Anderson that were even more successful than those of pre-war years. She performed at the inaugurations of Dwight D. Eisenhower and John F. Kennedy and at the White House during their presidencies, as well as before Lyndon B. Johnson. Eventually she performed in over 600 American cities to over six million listeners in more than 1500 auditoriums.

In 1955, at the advanced age of fifty-eight, Anderson was the first black engaged as a permanent member of the Metropolitan Opera. Not only did this pave the way for other black artists to perform with the Met but it marked yet another major step forward in the struggle against racial discrimination.

In addition to opening up opportunities for black artists, Anderson made spirituals an almost mandatory part of the repertories of all vocalists, black *and* white. It was impossible to hear her rendition of *Sometimes I Feel Like a Motherless Child* and not be deeply moved. Audiences wept openly. Requests to hear more such music followed, wherever she performed.

Although Anderson made many recordings, she far preferred to appear before live audiences. "I have never been able to analyze the qualities that the audience contributes to a performance," she said. "The most important, I think, are sympathy, open-mindedness, expectancy, faith, and a certain support to your effort. I know that my career could not have been what it is without all these things, which have come from many people. The knowledge of the feelings other people have expended on me has kept me going when times were hard."

—Milton Goldin

FURTHER READING:

Anderson, Marian. *My Lord, What a Morning.* New York, Viking, 1956.

Hurok, Sol (in collaboration with Ruth Goode). *Impresario: A Memoir.* New York, Random House, 1946.

Roosevelt, Eleanor. *Eleanor Roosevelt's "My Day:" Her Acclaimed Columns 1936-1945.* Rochelle Chadakoff, editor. New York, Pharos Books, 1989.

Anderson, Sherwood (1876-1941)

Although Sherwood Anderson had a relatively brief literary career, publishing his first novel when he was forty years old, he has left an indelible mark on American literature. His critique of modern society and avant-garde prose served as a model for younger writers of the so-called "Lost Generation," who for a time venerated Anderson for his rather dramatic departure from mainstream family and corporate life for one of nonconformity and cultural rebellion. He is considered today one of the most important figures in twentieth century American fiction—one who combined turn-of-the-century realism with an almost poetic introspection into the frailties and uncertainties of modern man.

Such a career seemed unlikely for Anderson initially. Born in Camden, Ohio, in 1876, he came of age in the small Ohio town of Clyde before attending Wittenberg Academy in Springfield, Ohio. As a boy, Anderson was known around town for his dreams of someday shedding his modest surroundings to make a fortune in the business world—not unusual for a boy growing up in the late nineteenth century—but in his case such entrepreneurial spirit earned him the nickname "jobby" among his peers for his willingness to take on any and all types of employment to earn a dollar. In 1900, he put his plans into action by moving to Chicago and taking a job in advertising. He married, began a family, then moved to Elyria, Ohio, to become president of a company specializing in roofing materials.

Yet while Anderson pursued his fortune, his desire to write began to conflict with his career. He had developed an appreciation for letters while in college and considered himself talented enough to become a successful author, but had decided that his business plans were more important. In Chicago, he had in some ways enjoyed the best of both worlds—his work in advertising had allowed him to combine artistic creativity and business acumen; life in Ohio seemed stultifying and colorless in comparison. Over time, his frustration became more than he could bear, and in 1912, at the age of thirty-six, Anderson experienced a mental breakdown which left him wandering the streets of Cleveland in a disoriented state for days. Following this crisis, he left his wife and three children and moved back to Chicago to begin a new life as a writer. With a few manuscripts in hand, he made contact with publisher Floyd Dell, who saw potential in Anderson's writing and introduced him to members of Chicago's literary crowd such as Carl Sandburg and Margaret Anderson.

Dell also gave Anderson his first opportunity to see his writing in print, initially in the literary journal *Little Review* and later in the *Masses,* a radical magazine of which Dell served as an editor. Soon he was publishing short stories and poems in the noted journal *Seven Arts,* published by Waldo Frank, Frank Oppenheim, and Van Wyck Brooks. His first book, *Windy McPherson's Son* (1916), was a autobiographical account of a young man who escapes his empty life in a small Iowa town by moving to the city, makes a fortune as a robber baron, yet continues to yearn for fulfillment in what he views as a sterile and emotionally barren existence. Critics applauded the book for its critical examination of mainstream, corporate America; it was also a precursor to other works of the genre such as Sinclair Lewis's *Main Street.*

With the publication of his first book, Anderson established himself firmly in Chicago's literary scene. However, it was his third book, *Winesburg, Ohio* (1919), that catapulted him into national notoriety. A series of character sketches, most of which appeared in the *Masses* and *Seven Arts, Winesburg, Ohio* describes the experiences of individuals in a small midwestern town—"grotesques," as he called them, who base their lives on the existence of exclusive truth yet who live in a world devoid of such. To exacerbate the frustrated lives of his characters, he gave each one a physical or emotional deformity, preventing any of them from having positive relations with the outside world, and making the book both a critique of small town life and the modern age generally. Attracted to writers such as Gertrude Stein, who experimented with unconventional structure and style, Anderson used a disoriented prose to illustrate the precarious lives of his characters.

Critics and writers alike hailed *Winesburg, Ohio* as a pioneering work of American literature, and the book influenced a generation of writers attracted both to Anderson's style and his themes. The novel was the first of several works of fiction which stressed the theme of society as a ''wasteland,'' such as works by T. S. Eliot, F. Scott Fitzgerald, and Ernest Hemingway. Fitzgerald and Hemingway, along with William Faulkner, also sought to emulate Anderson's avant-garde style in their own works. For a short time, a number of young writers looked up to Anderson, whose age and experience, along with his unconventional lifestyle, served as a model for anyone who sought to critique and rebel against the norms of modern society.

Anderson's popularity proved fleeting, however. He published a few other novels, including *Poor White* (1920) and *The Triumph of the Egg: A Book of Impressions from American Life in Tales and Poems* (1921), but none enjoyed the success of his earlier works. Critics have paid considerable attention to his numerous autobiographical works, most notably *Tar: A Midwest Childhood* (1926) and *A Story Teller's Story* (1924), for their unconventional methodology. Believing that an individual's vision of himself, even if rooted in imagination, is more important than verifiable facts, he warned readers that at times he intentionally sacrificed factual accuracy for psychological disclosure, a device which has contributed to considerable confusion regarding his early life. Despite his rather rapid decline in popularity, and also despite the numerous critiques of his works appearing in later years which show that at times his talents were perhaps overrated, Anderson's influence on younger writers of his time establishes him as a central figure in twentieth-century fiction.

—Jeffrey W. Coker

FURTHER READING:

Anderson, Sherwood. *A Story Teller's Story: The Tale of an American Writer's Journey through his Own Imaginative World and through the World of Facts.* New York, B. W. Huebsch, 1924.

———. *Tar: A Midwest Childhood.* New York, Boni and Liveright, 1926.

Howe, Irving. *Sherwood Anderson.* New York, William Sloan, 1951.

Kazin, Alfred. *On Native Grounds: An Interpretation of Modern Prose Fiction,* fortieth anniversary edition. New York, Harcourt, Brace, Jovanovich, 1982.

Sutton, William A. *The Road to Winesburg.* Metuchen, New Jersey, Scarecrow Press, 1972.

Townsend, Kim. *Sherwood Anderson.* Boston, Houghton Mifflin, 1987.

Andretti, Mario (1940—)

Mario Andretti is one of the most outstanding and exciting race car drivers of all time. During a career that began in the late 1950s, Andretti won four National Indy Car Championships, logged more than one hundred career victories, and captured more pole positions than any other driver in history.

Andretti was born in Montona, Italy, on February 28, 1940. His parents were farmers in northern Italy, but were in a displaced persons camp following the Second World War. Shortly before his family immigrated to the United States in 1955, Andretti attended his first auto race, the famous Mille Miglia, a thousand-mile road race through central and southern Italy. The teenager was enthralled by the driving skill of Alberto Ascari, who profoundly impacted his life.

His family settled in Nazareth, Pennsylvania, and Andretti quickly set to work modifying stock cars. He won his first race in 1958 driving a Hudson Hornet. His racing career embraced dirt cars, midgets, sprint cars, sports cars, Indy cars, Formula One racers, and even dragsters. His versatility is seen in the fact that until 1989, Andretti was the only driver to win both a Formula One World Championship and an Indy Car National Title.

Andretti raced in his first Indianapolis 500 in 1965, and he had so much potential that he was selected ''Rookie of the Year.'' He won the Indianapolis 500 in 1969. Even though everyone believed this would be the first of many victories at ''The Greatest Spectacle in Racing,'' Andretti seemed jinxed at Indianapolis. In spite of the fact that he often had the fastest car and was the favorite to win, on race day his car would break down or he would be involved in a wreck that would steal the win from his grasp. In 1981 Andretti lost the race after a controversial ruling. Although he was initially declared the winner of the race, several months later a panel took his victory away because of alleged passing violations. Bobby Unser was declared the victor.

Andretti was more successful at other events. He won the Daytona 500, multiple Sebring 12-hour events, and 12 Formula One Grand Prix races. He was USAC's Dirt Track champion in 1974 and five years later captured the title of the International Race of Champions. He was recognized as the Driver of the Year in 1967, 1978, and 1984, and even the Driver of the Quarter Century in 1992. He won the Formula One world championship in 1978, and was hailed as Indy Car champion four different years (1965, 1966, 1969, and 1984).

Drivers of his generation evaluated the success of their career by their accomplishments at the Indianapolis 500. Andretti's name is in the record books at Indianapolis for two accomplishments. He is tied for the distinction of winning the most consecutive pole positions (2) and setting the most one-lap track records (5).

Andretti has two sons, Michael and Jeffry, who have been successful race car drivers. Mario and Michael were, in fact, the first father-son team at the Indianapolis 500. Andretti's popularity has resulted in the marketing of various collectibles including trading card sets, model cars, toy racers, and electronic games.

—James H. Lloyd

FURTHER READING:

Andretti, Mario. *Andretti.* San Francisco, Collins, 1994.

Engel, Lyle Kenyon. *Mario Andretti: The Man Who Can Win Any Race.* New York, Arco, 1972.

———. *Mario Andretti: World Driving Champion.* New York, Arco, 1979.

Prentzas, G. S. *Mario Andretti.* Broomall, Pennsylvania, Chelsea House, 1996.

The Andrews Sisters

The Andrews Sisters were the most popular music trio of the 1930s and 1940s. Their public image became synonymous with World War II, due to the popularity of their songs during the war years and because of their tireless devotion to entertaining American troops. Patty, LaVerne, and Maxene Andrews began singing professionally in 1932. They perfected their own style—a strong, clean vocal delivery with lush harmonic blends—but also recorded scores of songs in a wide array of other styles. More popular tunes like ''Bei Mir Bist Du Schöen,'' ''Beer Barrel Polka,'' and ''Boogie Woogie Bugle Boy of Company B'' sold millions of records and made them

Mario Andretti

national stars. Their songs were happy in tone, aimed at boosting the morale of the American public. The sisters appeared in a number of wartime movies, and earned a devoted audience in the millions of civilians and soldiers who heard their songs.

—Brian Granger

FURTHER READING:

Andrews, Maxene, and Bill Gilbert. *Over Here, Over There: The Andrews Sisters and the USO Stars in World War II*. New York, Zebra Books, 1993.

Androgyny

The blurring of the sexes has been a mainstay throughout the history of representational art, and popular art of the twentieth century has not broken with this tendency. Whether through consciously manipulated personae or otherwise, countless stars of film, television, and pop music have displayed again and again that the division between masculine and feminine is often a frail one, and in many cases have served to help reverse "natural" standards altogether.

Furthermore, while a number of androgynous figures in the media have sometimes become icons of gay and lesbian fans, many others have traversed the fantasy realms of heterosexual markets, challenging at yet another level the supposedly discrete categories of personal identity.

Of all of its many forms, the most obvious mode of gender-bending in popular culture has been drag. Male and female cross-dressing, however, has often been given unequal weight and meaning. On the one hand, men in women's clothes have most often been utilized for comic effect, from television comedian Milton Berle in the 1950s, to cartoon rabbit Bugs Bunny, and on to numerous characters on the *In Living Color* program in the 1990s. Females in drag, on the other hand, are rarely used in the same way, and to many connote a coded lesbianism rather than obvious slapstick comedy. German film diva Marlene Dietrich, for example, with the help of photographer Josef von Sternberg, created a seductive self-image wearing men's suits during the 1930s, gaining immense popularity among lesbian audiences—and shocking some conservative straight viewers. While this discrepancy in drag is probably the result of cultural factors, critics have suggested that popular standards of femininity are often already the result of a kind of everyday "costume," whereas masculinity is perceived as somehow more "natural" and unaffected. Reversing these roles, then, has markedly different effects.

If self-conscious drag such as Dietrich's can expose common assumptions of the opposition between masculine and feminine in a bold reversal, many other performers have embraced androgyny in the strictest sense by meeting conceptions of both genders in the middle, often with greater cultural reverberations. When American actress Jean Seberg appeared in the 1959 French film *Breathless,* for example, her closely cropped hair and boyish frame stood as a challenge to a culture that measured femininity in long tresses of hair and dramatic body curves. Nevertheless, Seberg became a major influence throughout the 1960s and beyond, ushering in a new type of waifish woman into the popular imagination—for example, actress Mia Farrow and models like Twiggy.

Popular male figures have equally relied upon similar gender play, perhaps most visibly within rock music. Beginning in the late 1960s, for example, much of American and British popular music often seemed to be an unequivocal celebration of androgyny. The "glam" scene, represented by acts like Marc Bolan and T-Rex, Bryan Ferry and Roxy Music, Elton John, and Lou Reed pushed costumed excess to new limits with vinyl pants, feather boas, and makeup of all sorts—to the approval of men and women of multiple orientations. Arguably, the most crucial single glam figure was British singer David Bowie, who adopted an ever changing series of ambiguous stage characters, including Aladdin Sane and Ziggy Stardust, highlighting the theatrical nature of all personae, sexual or otherwise. In the wake of glam came the punk and New Romantic movements in the late 1970s and 1980s, exemplified by groups like the Damned, the Cure, and Siouxsie and the Banshees. Although these two strains were often at odds musically, both were often allied in a project of shocking popular middle-class notions of rugged masculinity. Such shock, however, soon elided into popular faddism, and by the early 1980s a number of musical gender "subversives" such as Adam Ant, Prince, and Boy George nestled in Top 40 charts alongside traditional figures of masculinity.

At the same time that self-consciously androgynous entertainers have often "passed" into the acceptance of mainstream audiences, it has also been common for gender bending to appear to be quite unintentional. A strong example of this can be found in the phenomenon of the so-called "haircut" American heavy metal bands of the 1980s such as Poison, Motley Crue, and Winger. While these acts often espoused lyrics of the most extreme machismo, they often bedecked themselves with "feminine" makeup, heavily hairsprayed coifs, and tight spandex pants—in short, in a style similar to the glam rockers of a decade before. Perhaps even more than a conscious artist like Bowie, such ironies demonstrated in a symptomatic way how the signs of gender identification are anything but obvious or natural. Whether fully intended or not, however, images of androgyny continued to thrive into the 1990s and its musicians, actors, and supermodels, as America questioned the divisions of gender and sexuality more than ever.

—Shaun Frentner

FURTHER READING:

Bell-Metereau, Rebecca. *Hollywood Androgyny.* New York, Columbia University Press, 1993.

Geyrhalter, Thomas. "Effeminacy, Camp, and Sexual Subversion in Rock: The Cure and Suede." *Popular Music.* Vol. 15, No. 2, May 1996, 217-224.

Piggford, George. "'Who's That Girl?': Annie Lennox, Woolf's Orlando, and Female CampAndrogyny." *Mosaic.* Vol. 30, No.3, September 1997, 39-58.

Simels, Steven. *Gender Chameleons: Androgyny in Rock 'n' Roll.* New York, Arbor House, 1985.

The Andy Griffith Show

When Danny Thomas, the well-loved entertainer and benefactor of St. Jude's hospital for children, cast Andy Griffith as the affable slow-talking sheriff in an episode of *The Danny Thomas Show* (1953-65), he had no way of knowing that he was launching a phenomenon that would assume mythical proportions. In that episode, Thomas was given a ticket while traveling through the small town of Mayberry, North Carolina. Sheriff Andy Taylor, who also happened to be the justice of the peace, convinced the big city entertainer that Mayberry was a place to be reckoned with. Almost 40 years later, it still is. The show ran from 1960 to 1968, but by the end of the 1990s, more than five million people a day continued to watch *The Andy Griffith Show* in reruns on 120 television stations.

The genius of *The Andy Griffith Show* evolved from its characters. Each role seemed to be tailor-made for the actor who brought it to life. Mayberry was peopled by characters who were known and liked. The characters did ordinary things, such as making jelly, going to the

Don Knotts (left) and Andy Griffith in a scene from the television program *The Andy Griffith Show.*

movies, singing in the choir, and sitting on the porch on a summer night. No one accused Andy and Barney of commitment phobia even though they left Helen and Thelma hanging for years before marrying them. In point of fact, it took a reunion movie to bring Barney and Thelma Lou to the altar. It was simply accepted that people in small Southern towns behaved this way.

Five-time Emmy winner Don Knotts, as Barney Fife, became one of the most popular characters of all time. His slack jaw and pop-eyed look led to starring roles in several feature films, among them *The Ghost and Mr. Chicken* (1965), *The Incredible Mr. Limpet* (1964), and *The Reluctant Astronaut* (1967). Knotts' comedic timing is without parallel. Little Ronny Howard played Taylor's son, Opie; he grew up to be Ron Howard, played freckle-faced teenager Richie Cunningham (1974-80) on *Happy Days* (1974-84) and later forged a successful career as a director (*Apollo 13* (1995) and *Cocoon* (1985)). Jim Nabors played goofy neighborhood friend and gas station attendant, Gomer Pyle. The success of the Pyle character led to *Gomer Pyle, USMC* (1964-70) in which Pyle joins the Marines and becomes the bane of Sergeant Carter's life. After the demise of *Gomer Pyle, USMC,* Nabors hosted his own variety and talk shows and continued to perform in concerts and clubs. George Lindsey (Goober) became a regular on *Hee Haw* (1969-86) a hillbilly version of *Laugh-In.* However, it was Andy Griffith who provided the anchor for the show and who proved the glue that held its bumbling but well-meaning characters together. Without Andy, the characters might have been perceived as caricatures. After leaving the show, Griffith launched a second successful television series with *Matlock* (1986-95) playing a shrewd but amiable southern lawyer. He also returned to an old love and recorded two successful gospel albums.

The premise of the show was simple. Episodes would follow the life of Andy Taylor, a sheriff who provided law and order in a small southern town and who was raising his small son with the help of his Aunt Bee and various friends and neighbors. The plots were never complex; they involved the consequences of Opie killing a bird with his B-B gun, or Barney not being allowed to have bullets in his gun, or neighborhood friend Gomer making a "citizen's arrest," or Andy's fighting off the attentions of a mountain girl. The success of the show in the 1960s was understandable, for it poked fun at realistic human foibles. On the other hand, its continued success has been phenomenal. In the 1990s, fans all over the country band together in Andy Griffith Show Rerun Watchers Clubs. On the Internet, a number of web pages have been devoted to the show and its stars. These sites include a virtual Mayberry community. Most surprising of all is the devotion of the Church of Christ in Huntsville, Alabama, who plan their Wednesday night services around watching old episodes of the show and applying its moral lessons to their religious beliefs.

Almost 40 years after its 1960 launching, the stars of *The Andy Griffith Show* have grown up and older. Some of them, including Aunt Bee (Frances Bavier), have died. Yet in the minds of many nostalgic Americans, the town of Mayberry will forever be populated: Andy Taylor will be the sheriff, and his deputy will be Barney Fife. Aunt Bee and her friend Clara will wrangle over who is the best cook. Gomer and Goober Pyle will continue to run the gas station. Floyd will cut hair on Main Street. Howard Sprague will work at City Hall. Otis will lock himself up after a drunk. Helen and Thelma Lou will wait for Andy and Barney. The Darlings will live in the North Carolina mountains. Whatever the underlying cause of its continued success, the town of Mayberry and its inhabitants have become part of the American psyche, reminding a jaded public of gentler, friendlier times. It may be true that you cannot go home again, but you can go back to Mayberry again and again.

—Elizabeth Purdy

FURTHER READING:

Beck, Ken, and Jim Clark. *The Andy Griffith Show Book, From Miracle Salve to Kerosene Cucumbers: The Complete Guide to One of Television's Best Loved Shows.* New York, St. Martin's Press, 1985.

White, Yvonne. "The Moral Lessons of Mayberry; Alabama Bible Class Focuses on TV's Andy Griffith." *The Washington Post,* 29 August 1998, B-9.

Andy Hardy

Once one of the most popular boys in America, the Andy Hardy character flourished in a series of MGM family comedies from the late 1930s to the middle 1940s. Mickey Rooney's dynamic portrayal of the character was an important factor in the great success of the movies. The Hardy Family lived in Carvel, the sort of idealized small town that existed only on studio backlots. In addition to Andy, the household consisted of his father, Judge Hardy, his mother, his sister, and his maiden aunt. Millions of movie fans followed Andy from adolescence to young manhood in the years just before and during World War II.

The initial B-movie in the series was titled *A Family Affair.* Released in 1937, it was based on a play by a writer named Aurania Rouverol. Lionel Barrymore was Judge Hardy; Spring Byington played Andy's mother. The film was profitable enough to prompt MGM to produce a sequel. For *You're Only Young Once,* which came out early in 1938, Lewis Stone permanently took over as the judge and Fay Holden assumed the role of Andy's mom. Ann Rutherford joined the company as Andy's girlfriend Polly, a part she'd play in a full dozen of the Hardy films. Three more movies followed in 1938 and in the fourth in the series, *Love Finds Andy Hardy,* Andy's name appeared in a title for the first time. Extremely popular, the Hardy Family pictures were now reportedly grossing three to four times what they'd cost to make. The public liked the Hardys and they especially liked Mickey Rooney. By 1939 he was the number one box office star in the country. In addition to the Hardy films, he'd been appearing in such hits as *Captains Courageous, Boys' Town,* and *Babes In Arms.* In the years just before American entry into World War II, the brash, exuberant yet basically decent young man he played on the screen had enormous appeal to audiences.

The movies increasingly concentrated on the problems and perplexities that Andy faced in growing up. Schoolwork, crushes, financing such things as a car of one's own. While Polly remained Andy's one true love, MGM showcased quite a few of its young actresses in the series by having Andy develop a temporary crush. Among those so featured were Judy Garland, Lana Turner, Esther Williams, Kathryn Grayson, and Donna Reed. Early on Andy began

(Counterclockwise from right) Lana Turner, Ann Rutherford, Judy Garland, and Mickey Rooney in a scene from the film *Love Finds Andy Hardy*.

having heart-to-heart talks with his father about whatever happened to be bothering him. These father-and-son chats became an essential set piece in the series and no film was without one. Part judge, part therapist, the senior Hardy was also a good listener and his advice to his son, if sometimes a bit stiff and starchy, was always sound. For all his bounce, impatience, and aggressiveness, Andy was pretty much a traditional, middle-of-the-road kid at heart. He usually followed Judge Hardy's suggestions and, by the end of the movie if not before, came to see the wisdom of them. The whole family was a warm, loving one and the Hardy comedies became a template for many a family sitcom to come.

The fifteenth film in the series, *Love Laughs at Andy Hardy*, came out in 1946. Rooney, then in his middle twenties and just out of the service, was unable to recapture the audience he'd had earlier. The final, and unsuccessful, film was *Andy Hardy Comes Home* in 1958.

—Ron Goulart

FURTHER READING:

Balio, Tino. *Grand Design: Hollywood as a Modern Business Enterprise, 1930-1939*. Berkeley, University of California Press, 1993.

Parrish, James Robert and Ronald L. Bowers. *The MGM Stock Company*. New Rochelle, Arlington House, 1973.

Angell, Roger (1920—)

Writer, parodist, and magazine editor Roger Angell is most notable as an analyst of the philosophy and intricacies of professional baseball and its hidden meanings, what it reveals of the American psyche. Several of the titles of Angell's books, which are compilations of his baseball sketches, hint at his involvement with the metaphysical aspects of the game. These include *The Summer Game* (1972); *Five Seasons* (1977); *Late Innings* (1982); *Season Ticket* (1988); *Baseball* (1988); and *Once More around the Park* (1991).

Born and bred in New York City, Angell received a B.A. from Harvard in 1942, spent four years in the U.S. Army Air Force, and became a writer for Curtis Publications in 1946. Angell was senior editor of *Holiday* travel magazine from 1947 to 1958. In 1948, Angell became an editor and general contributor to the *New Yorker*, quite appropriate as his connection to that magazine was almost congenital. His mother, Katharine White, had joined the magazine in 1925, the year it was founded; his stepfather was E. B. White, long associated with that publication. Angell served as the magazine's senior fiction editor and shepherded the works of cultural figures John Updike, Garrison Keillor, and V. S. Pritchett. He also composed parodies, "Talk of the Town" pieces, and, from 1976, the annual rhymed Christmas verse "Greetings, Friends."

Since 1962, Angell's baseball articles have appeared in "The Sporting Scene" column of the *New Yorker*. Others have been published in the *New York Times*. In his quintessential article, "The Interior Stadium," the concluding essay in *The Summer Game,* Angell disclosed many of his conclusions about baseball. Consciously paraphrasing poet William Wordsworth in the opening line— "Sports are too much with us. Late and soon . . ."—like Wordsworth's "spots of time," Angell recalls not just events in the game, but emotions he feels when the events take place on the ballfield. The arrested moments that Angell recalls at will in the inner stadium of his mind focus on individual players and their challenges. Baseball, in his opinion, is so intensely remembered because it is so intensely watched (or listened to) and made personal by the observers.

It is one of Angell's hallmarks that he regards baseball as a test of the character found in solitary men rather than in team dynamics. He also waxes rhapsodic, as do George Will and other baseball literati, over the game's presumed liberation from the constraints of normal time. In baseball, in Angell's estimation, time is measured by outs rather than by clocks.

Angell dwells on the bond between spectator and player, a reciprocal but perhaps not equal relationship. Only baseball with its statistics and fragments of time arguably allows precise reconstruction of events. With such a lofty vision of what essentially is a popular way to spend leisure time, it is not surprising that Angell wrote the introduction to the companion volume to Ken Burns's video paean to the higher nature of the game.

—Frederick J. Augustyn, Jr.

FURTHER READING:

Angell, Roger. *A Day in the Life of Roger Angell: Parodies and Other Pleasures.* New York, Penguin Books, 1990.

Memmott, A. James. "Wordsworth in the Bleachers: The Baseball Essays of Roger Angell." *Sport Inside Out: Readings in Literature and Philosophy.* Edited by David L. Vanderwerken and Spencer K. Wertz. Fort Worth, Texas Christian University, 1985.

Porter, David L., ed. *Biographical Dictionary of American Sports: 1989-1992 Supplement for Baseball, Football, Basketball, and Other Sports.* Westport, Connecticut, Greenwood Press, 1992.

Vanderzwaag, Harold J. "The Interior Stadium: Enhancing the Illusion." *Sport Inside Out: Readings in Literature and Philosophy.* Edited by David L. Vanderwerken and Spencer K. Wertz. Forth Worth, Texas Christian University, 1985.

Ward, Geoffrey C., and Ken Burns. *Baseball: An Illustrated History.* Introduction by Roger Angell. New York, Alfred A. Knopf, 1994.

Will, George F. *Men at Work: The Craft of Baseball.* New York, Macmillan Publishing Company, 1990.

Angelou, Maya (1928—)

American author Maya Angelou is known for her poetry, autobiography, and novels that lyrically articulate the experience of Africans Americans and give a voice to black pride and heritage. Angelou's works, however, have appealed to all races with their strong messages of hope and strength. She served as a coordinator for the Southern Christian Leadership Conference in the 1960s and published the first volume of her autobiography, the acclaimed *I Know Why the Caged Bird Sings,* in 1970. Despite her distinguished career, she did not become a major public figure until after her moving delivery of a poem at President Bill Clinton's 1992 inauguration. A performer before her career in letters, Angelou has also written, directed, and starred in a number of television programs and movies.

—Geri Speace

FURTHER READING:

Angelou, Maya. *I Know Why the Caged Bird Sings.* New York, Random House, 1970.

Bloom, Lynn Z. "Maya Angelou." *Dictionary of Literary Biography, Volume 38: Afro-American Writers after 1955: Dramatists and Prose Writers.* Thadious M. Davis and Trudier Harris, editors. Detroit, Gale Research, 1985.

Animal House

Critics considered *National Lampoon's Animal House* to be cheap, terribly plotted, and in bad taste upon its release in the summer of 1978. Nevertheless, the comedy struck a chord with its public and grossed more than $90 million in its first year. The movie's success inspired an entirely new genre of teenage "animal comedy" movies and three television network series and started a craze of toga parties on college campuses nationwide. It also launched the movie career of comedian John Belushi.

Despite the lasting influence of the film, many movie studios agreed with the initial critics and passed on the script. John Landis remembers thinking that he was the last person asked to direct, and only then because everyone else had turned it down. As it was, the studio gave him less than $3 million to make the movie, which afforded him a cast of largely unknown actors and a set that is in real life the University of Oregon campus in Eugene, Oregon.

Based in part on co-writer Chris Miller's college experiences in the 1960s, *Animal House* begins innocently enough with two freshmen seeking to pledge to a fraternity. Set in the early 1960s at fictional Faber College (Miller was quoted as saying that this was the last class to graduate before the Kennedy assassination), the two freshmen discover that they are either too "dweebie" or fat for most of the fraternities except Delta House.

The Delta House fraternity is an image that most college Greek societies have been trying to forget since 1978. Simply put, it is a collection of politically incorrect and incorrigible students whose most intelligent member is averaging less than a 2.0 grade point average. The strait-laced Dean of the school is determined to see Delta evicted from campus and its members expelled. In what is questionably called a plot, the remainder of the movie is a series of skits about the run-ins between the Dean and Delta House. Among these skits are the food fight between Delta and the Dean's cohorts, Belushi's imitation of a zit, and the toga party.

It was Belushi's portrayal of Bluto Blutarsky that was one of the movies most enduring images, virtually typecasting the manic *Saturday Night Live* alumnus as a gross, excessive, drinking party animal on-screen and off. For most of the movie Bluto speaks in unintelligible grunts, his big monologue coming near the end when he encourages a demoralized Delta House to take its revenge on the Dean. Thus, *Animal House* ends with a Delta-inspired riot at the college's Homecoming Parade. The characters then all head off into the sunset, with captions revealing their eventual fates (Bluto's was to become a Senator).

Teenagers and college students were instantly struck by the movie's anti-establishment message. Of all the figures in the movie, Bluto was the one least cut out to be a Senator. Also, the only role model the students seem to look up to is the English professor who is seen smoking dope. Soon, the antics of Delta House were to be rehashed in such movies as *Police Academy, Porky's* and other "animal comedy." Studios sought to reinvent the success of the movie, as well as it's financial profits—virtually all of the following movies were made on shoestring budgets but returned large box office receipts. Jeff Kanew, director of *Revenge of the Nerds,* remembers that his studio told him to "Give us an *Animal House,*" and he directed a movie complete with food fights and beer-drinking contests.

Over time, however, the teenagers moved on to different fare, and *Animal House* could only be found on cable channels in the 1990s. Greek societies have tried to change the image of the "animal house," though it still comes back to haunt them every time there is a binge drinking related tragedy on a college campus. The stereotypical image of strange, ham-handed initiation rites, sex groupies, and excessive toga parties is still as fresh as in July 1978. The legacy of *Animal House* is best summed up in the names of the Bluto clones that appeared in the television series created to cash in on the movie: Blotto, Gobo, and Zipper.

—John J. Doherty

FURTHER READING:

Clarke, Gerald. "And 'Animal House' Begat. . . ." *Time.* April 15, 1985, 103.

Meyers, Kate. "'Animal House' Opens." *Entertainment Weekly.* July 25, 1997, 86.

Animated Films

Animated feature-length films have carved a niche in American culture as a viable and enduring art form. Whether the story concerned the X-rated adventures of Fritz the Cat or the G-rated fairy tales offered up over the course of 60 years by Disney animation, animated films have offered a glimpse into another world that often could not be shown by any other filmmaking means.

Animated feature films comprise what is perhaps the most flexible twentieth-century entertainment medium. From its very beginnings, animation offered possibilities undreamt of with conventional film. Ink and paint on paper (and later cels, for transfer to film) offered a much wider palette than the strict physical realism imposed by the motion picture camera. Animators could create other worlds, superhuman abilities, bizarre creatures, and impossible effects with the stroke of a pen. All of this was possible with televised animation or animated shorts, but the feature film format opens wide the doors of possibility. Film animators have much more time and money to fully

realize their vision, and movie screens provide a vast canvas on which to present their work.

Any serious discussion of popular animated film centers on one name: Walt Disney. Disney's prolific imagination and managerial skills helped shape the company that would completely dominate animation for decades to come. Disney's studio started out with a staff of talented animators who turned out animated shorts featuring soon-to-be-popular characters such as Oswald the Rabbit and Mickey Mouse. Perhaps the most important of Disney's partners was the prolific Ub Iwerks, who was with Disney from the beginning and designed many of the technical innovations that propelled animation ahead (most notably the multiplane camera.)

The first fully animated film was Disney's *Snow White and the Seven Dwarfs.* To be sure, *Snow White* was not an entirely groundbreaking project. Full-length films in a quasi-animated format, usually involving shadow puppets or actual animated puppets, had already been produced with limited success. Prior to *Snow White,* Disney and his stable of animators had many years of success with a wide variety of characters, most notably Mickey Mouse, but never before had a studio gambled on a full-length animated feature. Their risky play was rewarded with critical and financial success; *Snow White,* released at the end of 1937, became the most successful film of 1938, with $8 million in ticket sales.

Snow White allowed Disney and company to experiment with animation in many new ways, including a larger cast, more character development, comic relief, and high drama; in short, they placed into their animated film all the elements normally associated with a live-action feature film. They also paved the way for the format followed by dozens of future animated films, with such enduring elements as musical interludes, sneering villains, and wacky sidekicks for comic relief.

Snow White also featured a number of technical advances that allowed the animated feature to move beyond the limits that had been imposed by the short format. Animators studied at length the films of live actors going through the motions of the characters in order to best capture realistic human motion. The multiplane camera invented by Iwerks allowed the illusion of depth, and a new effects department added realism to images impossible to accurately draw by hand, such as violent weather and effective shadows.

One gimmick that punctuated animated film from the very beginning was a fascination animators had with combining animation with live action. A decade prior to *Snow White,* Disney's studio had produced 52 "Alice comedies," one-reelers that followed the adventures of a child actress interacting with animated characters. From time to time thereafter, animators made further attempts to combine the two forms, each time pushing the technology further. Disney released *Song of the South* in 1946, featuring life on a southern plantation illustrated by animated stories told by Uncle Remus. The live action/animation marriage reached its zenith in 1988, with the release of *Who Framed Roger Rabbit?* This 1940s-style cartoon noir featured the most realistic combination of live actors with animation seen before or since. No small amount of credit was due to director Robert Zemeckis and animation director Richard Williams, who managed technical feats long thought impossible in human-cartoon interaction.

The Disney studio's place as a dominant force in animation was sealed by the enormous success of its early movies, as was the place of animation in the annals of popular culture. Films such as *Fantasia* (1940), *Pinocchio* (1940), and *Bambi* (1942) further expanded the financial and artistic horizons Disney had set. Disney went through a variety of phases as the decades progressed. The ethereal, fairy-tale look of *Sleeping Beauty* (1959) gave way to stylized, intentionally exaggerated work in such films as *101 Dalmatians* (1961) and *The Rescuers* (1977). But there was one other very important effect of *Snow White* and those movies that followed: Although there would be many variants and offshoots, feature-length animation was irrevocably cast in the public mind as a medium for children's stories. And as children's stories, animated films for years were perceived as a kind of second-class genre.

After many disappointing years, animated film experienced a tremendous resurgence in 1989, when Disney released the hit *The Little Mermaid*. This adaptation of the Hans Christian Andersen tale kick-started an animation renaissance which was still well underway in the late 1990s. *The Little Mermaid* was an enormous hit, and it provided enough memorable characters and catchy tunes to sell stuffed toys, soundtrack albums, and sing-along videos for years to come. Disney's follow-up to *The Little Mermaid*, 1991's *Beauty and the Beast*, sealed the popular resurgence of animated film. It also earned for animated film the respect of both critics and the public. *Beauty and the Beast* was both a financial and critical success, and was the only animated film to be honored with an Academy Award nomination for Best Picture.

Disney followed this success with 1992's *Aladdin* and the most successful animated film of all time, *The Lion King*, in 1994. With over $350 million in domestic box office sales and tremendously profitable toys, tie-ins, and various other merchandising efforts, *The Lion King* re-established animation as a force to be reckoned with; putting it on the same level as even the most expensive or lucrative live-action franchises. With 1995's *Toy Story*, the first full-length movie animated completely on computer, Disney positioned itself once again at the top of the technological game. No longer were cartoons limited to what could be done with paint and pen.

Disney's animated films in the 1990s established a format that became nearly universal to films that hoped to emulate the success of Disney's releases. The so-called "Disney formula" included several basic elements: several show-stopping tunes, lovable sidekicks to add comic relief, and a cast of recognizable voice actors. A general theme of all post-*Little Mermaid* Disney animated features—that one's true worth is measured by what's inside rather than what is outside—is also often associated with this formula.

However, Disney was far from a monopoly in the crowded field for motion-picture success, especially in the wake of the enormous profit of *The Lion King*. Over the course of the 1980s and 1990s, one of the most consistent challenges to Disney's dominance came from Don Bluth and Gary Goldman. Bluth, a veteran Disney animator whose work stretched as far back as *Sleeping Beauty*, and Goldman both felt that the Disney studio had strayed from the ideals Walt Disney had exemplified and led a mass exodus of animators from the Disney stables in the early 1980s.

Bluth and Goldman went on to produce a number of successful animated projects, including *The Secret of NIMH* (1982), *An American Tail* (1986), *The Land Before Time* (1988), and the fully-animated video games *Dragon's Lair* and *Space Ace*. Their work met with acclaim and respectable box office—in fact, *The Secret of NIMH* was the most successful non-Disney animated film up until that time, and its $45-million take outgrossed many contemporary Disney films as well. However, while Bluth and Goldman's work was able to stand on its own and make a profit, Disney's box office dominance was still secure.

But, the rise of Bluth had a galvanizing effect on the animation industry. The success of Bluth's films showed that, even though knocking Disney from its position at the top was unlikely, there was still commercial viability in animated film. Furthermore, Bluth himself stated that he hoped his work would make Disney's improve as well, since competition tends to bring out the best in all parties involved. There might well be truth in his statement, since the success of *The Little Mermaid* and Disney's own renaissance soon followed.

In 1997 and 1998 the playing field for animation was reshuffled. Disney appeared vulnerable to competitors, as recent efforts such as *Pocahontas* (1995) and *Hercules* (1997) had done respectably at the box office, but had not achieved the smash hit status of *The Lion King*. Sensing an opportunity, other studios moved in to claim their piece of the animation pie. Bluth and Goldman signed on with 20th Century Fox to produce animated movies, starting with 1997's *Anastasia*. Several other animated efforts from rival studios, such as *Quest for Camelot* (1998), were released in the late 1990s during what might be accurately titled an animation binge.

Bluth was not the only former Disney man to challenge the giant. Jeffrey Katzenberg, formerly the head of Disney's animation division and the man credited by many with spearheading Disney's renaissance, split with Disney in 1994 to co-found DreamWorks SKG and head up that studio's animation efforts. By 1998, DreamWorks upped the animation ante by releasing two highly acclaimed challengers to Disney's throne: the computer-generated *Antz* (1998) and *The Prince of Egypt* (1998). Katzenberg's gamble paid off; *The Prince of Egypt*, as of early 1999, stands as the most successful non-Disney animated film of all time, with a total domestic take of nearly $100 million.

Feature-film animation has come a long way since the completely hand-drawn cels of *Snow White*. Even in traditionally animated films, computers are used extensively to enhance color, add depth, and create special effects, often in subtle ways. The brilliantly colored flying carpet in *Aladdin* and the stampede in *The Lion King* would both have been impossible or considerably more difficult without the aid of computers. Completely computer-generated fare such as *Toy Story* (1995) and *Antz* pushed the envelope even further, proving that photo-realistic detail and shading are possible without using a single cel of hand-drawn art.

Creating an animated film is an enormously time-consuming process. Several years of work by hundreds, if not thousands, of staffers goes into producing the hundreds of thousands of frames that make up one ninety-minute animated film. Special effects are even more time-consuming. DreamWorks estimated that 318,000 hours of labor went into creating the parting of the Red Sea in *The Prince of Egypt*.

Animated film's most important place in popular culture is the manner in which it has completely penetrated American society. Feature-length cartoons are considered by parents as one of the last bastions of wholesome family entertainment left in a world that feeds a constant diet of violence, disrespect, and vulgarity to their children. No matter how worried one might be about the general mental health of their children, so the conventional wisdom goes, one can't go wrong by taking them to a cartoon. The stars of animated films quite often become children's role models, favorite characters and imaginary playmates.

In addition, animated films tend to seep into popular culture and become the "official" versions of those stories, often overshadowing the originals. Disney's fairy tales are the best example. For children everywhere (and adults, for that matter), the images of Snow White and the Seven Dwarfs, Cinderella, Aladdin, and the Little Mermaid that they see on the big screen or television are the immutable canon. This same influence tends to frustrate teachers, parents and scholars when animated films veer too far away from the established story or, especially, historical fact. In 1995, Disney released *Pocahontas,* the animated story of the Indian princess who saved explorer John Smith when he encountered the Indians in the seventeenth century. Disney's version ran far afield of history in many ways, and teachers in many elementary schools prepared ''Pocahontas curriculums'' that were meant to counteract whatever false ideas about history their impressionable students got after seeing the film.

Disney was not above completely rewriting literature when crafting an animated feature from an established tale. In one famous anecdote, Disney gave one of the story men on *The Jungle Book* (1967) a copy of Rudyard Kipling's original novel and said, ''The first thing I want you to do is not to read it.'' In a similar vein, many Victor Hugo scholars expressed dismay when 1996's *The Hunchback of Notre Dame* strayed wildly from the novel, particularly in its ending.

The economic and cultural impact of animated film extends far beyond what appears on screen. Marketing, merchandising, and other promotional tie-ins are extremely lucrative side deals that go hand-in-hand with feature film animation. At times, the tie-ins can be more profitable than the movies themselves. By the 1990s, when movie marketing had become an irreversible force, animated film characters seemed to be everywhere. During a major marketing push for one animated film or another, it sometimes seemed impossible to walk down the street without being bombarded with one reference or another to the film in question. Toothbrushes, toys, lunchboxes, clothes, pencils, sheets, underwear, books, Broadway plays, and made-for-video sequels all bear the image of whomever happens to be the hot animated character of the moment. Fast food restaurants became part of the act, offering small toys and trinkets as part of value meals to promote the film.

If parents tend to put their complete trust in animated fare to provide wholesome entertainment for their children, then that trust is balanced by the susceptibility of those movies to backlash. It takes very little to set off severe criticism of real or perceived offensiveness in animated films aimed at children. Parents take such subjects very seriously. For example, Disney has been the subject of numerous boycotts and protests for the content of their work. Arab groups strongly protested a lyric in *Aladdin* that read, ''where they cut off your hand if they don't like your face/It's barbaric, but hey, it's a home!'' That line was excised in video copies of *Aladdin.* At other times Disney has had to fend off allegations of subliminal messages. Rumors at various times accused Disney of inserting the whispered line ''all good kids take off your clothes'' into *Aladdin* and the word ''sex'' into several frames of *The Lion King.*

If animated film is usually geared to appeal to the youngest members of society, it is also sometimes intended to appeal to the mature. Ralph Bakshi's *Fritz the Cat* (1972), based on the Robert Crumb comic strip, was the first X-rated animated movie, due to its numerous graphic sex scenes. On a somewhat less excessive level, *Heavy Metal* (1981), based on stories from the erotic science-fiction magazine of the same name, featured fantastic violence and sex to an extent rarely seen in animated film.

Whatever the subject matter, animated film also offered animators the opportunity to make creative statements that were impossible in any other medium. *Heavy Metal,* for example, displayed the vision of that magazine's creators in a far different manner than the limits

allowed by the magazine format. Music and animated films have gone hand-in-hand in a curious marriage for some years now. On occasion, popular musicians have used animated film to illustrate their work with varying success. The late-1960s psychedelic stylings of the Beatles found their perfect niche in the swirling, psychedelic *Yellow Submarine* (1968). On a much different point of the musical compass, *Pink Floyd The Wall* (19) featured numerous animated interludes that illustrated the main character's descent into madness in a way that conventional live-action film couldn't quite capture.

Television animation, an offshoot of the popularity of feature film animation, proved a profitable medium for broadcasters and producers, so it comes as no surprise that a number of successful television animation franchises have made the leap to the big screen, with varying levels of success. 1980s characters such as the Transformers, Go-Bots, and He-Man found modest success in theatrical releases. In the 1990s, *Beavis and Butt-Head Do America* (1996) and *The Rugrats Movie* (1998) proved to be tremendous moneymakers for their producers, ensuring that television would provide fodder for animated film for some time to come.

Animated films have been produced all around the world, although like much foreign film, most of them have not quite made their way into the lexicon of American popular culture. One exception to this is the distinctive look of Japanese animation—''anime.'' Slick, stylized visions such as the futuristic *Akira* (1988) appealed to animation fans who appreciated the detail found in Disney work but wanted more mature fare.

Animated films have been integral parts of popular culture for over six decades. Many of the classics are still popular with children and adults, and more are being pushed into production every month. With the advent of computer effects and completely computer-generated cartoons spearheading an entirely new kind of animation and freeing up the creative minds of animators to soar to greater heights, the art of animated film is set to launch into another sixty years of success.

—Paul F.P. Pogue

FURTHER READING:

Cawley, John, and Jim Korkis. *How to Create Animation.* Las Vegas, Pioneer, 1990.

Cohen, Karl F. *Forbidden Animation: Censored Cartoons and Blacklisted Animators in America.* Jefferson, North Carolina, McFarland, 1997.

Edera, Bruno, and John Halas, editors. *Full Length Animated Feature Films.* New York, Hastings House, 1977.

Kanfer, Stefan. *Serious Business: The Art and Commerce of Animation in America from Betty Boop to Toy Story.* New York, Scribner, 1997.

Rubin, Susan. *Animation: The Art and the Industry.* Englewood Cliffs, New Jersey, Prentice-Hall, 1984.

Schickel, Richard. *The Disney Version.* New York, Simon and Schuster, 1985.

Thomas, Bob. *Disney's Art of Animation: From Mickey Mouse to Hercules.* New York, Hyperion Press, 1997.

Thomas, Frank, and Ollie Johnston. *The Illusion of Life: Disney Animation.* New York, Hyperion Press, 1981.

Wells, Paul. *Understanding Animation.* New York, Routledge, 1998.

Anita Hill-Clarence Thomas Senate Hearings

In the fall of 1991, the nomination of Clarence Thomas as an associate justice of the Supreme Court became the most controversial nomination in all of American judicial history. During the background probe, information surfaced that Anita Hill, a law professor at the University of Oklahoma, had told someone that Thomas had sexually harassed her when she worked as his assistant at the Department of Education in 1981. Joseph Biden, Chair of the Senate Judiciary Committee, which conducts hearings on presidential nominations, chose not to interview Hill and refrained from repeating the allegations to some committee members. When the story became public knowledge, women's groups began to protest, and seven women from the House of Representatives marched to the Senate, demanding entrance to the Senate Chambers and insisting that a hearing into Hill's allegations be conducted. Biden, with what would later prove a serious lapse in judgment, chose to make the hearings public. Americans were, therefore, glued to their television sets for one long weekend, beginning Friday morning, October 11 and ending late Sunday night, October 13, 1991, watching and listening to accusations, denials, and character assassinations. The lives of both Anita Hill and Clarence Thomas would be changed forever. Of even more lasting consequence were the battles that were simultaneously conducted between men and women, and between Democrats and Republicans, which led to an altered political landscape in the United States.

Anita Hill, being sworn in.

From the beginning, President George Bush had been faced with a formidable task in choosing a replacement for Thurgood Marshall, associate justice of the Supreme Court since 1967 and the first African American ever to serve on the Supreme Court, who announced his retirement due to ill health. Marshall had been a pioneer of the Civil Rights movement, arguing such cases as *Brown v. Board of Education of Topeka, Kansas* (1954) before the Supreme Court when he was a young lawyer with the National Association for the Advancement of Colored People's (N.A.A.C.P.) Legal Defense Fund. This case essentially ended segregation in public schools and paved the way for integration in all walks of American life. Appointed by Democratic president Lyndon B. Johnson, Marshall had become one of the most revered Supreme Court Justices in American history. Because Bush was a Republican, his choice of a nominee to replace Marshall was certain to be a Republican; and because of the political climate of the 1980s and early 1990s, Bush's nominee had to be a conservative opposed to abortion rights.

The issue was further complicated by an earlier nomination made by President Ronald Reagan. Robert Bork was a conservative with a long record of judicial decisions, and writings that documented his opinions on almost every issue of concern to both Democrats and Republicans in the Senate; as a result, he was withdrawn as a nominee. Bush's advisors warned him that it would be better to nominate someone with less widely disseminated opinions in order to get the nomination past the Democrat-controlled Senate. Taking all of these things into consideration, Bush chose a little known Republican judge from Savannah, Georgia, to replace Marshall. At the time of his nomination, Clarence Thomas had been a federal judge for only 18 months. Despite his lack of judicial experience, he had served the Republican Party well in the Department of Education and in the Equal Employment Opportunity Commission.

It was this adherence to strict Republican ideology that created a lot of the early controversy surrounding the Thomas nomination. Since the campaign that elected John F. Kennedy president in 1963, black voters have been closely aligned with the Democratic Party. Many black leaders felt that nominating the conservative Thomas was a betrayal of the heritage of Thurgood Marshall. Women's groups were also opposed to Thomas' nomination because of his disdain for programs such as affirmative action, while legal scholars were opposed to Thomas' lack of experience as a judge. Although opposition was substantial, the chances that any of these groups could derail the nomination were slim. However, when it was learned that a black law professor had accused Thomas of sexual harassment, his opponents had a new focal point for protest.

Anita Hill was young, intelligent, attractive, and articulate. Moreover, she was credible when she presented her damaging testimony. She described in painstaking detail how Clarence Thomas had harassed her, repeatedly asking her for dates and frequently bringing graphic details about sexual encounters into the conversation. She stated that he described pornographic movies that he had seen. At a later point in the hearings, Hill's claims were corroborated by her friend, John William Carr, who testified that Hill had told him what was happening during a 1981 telephone conversation. Also waiting in the wings were other women who insisted that Thomas had sexually harassed them or who claimed to have known about the harassment of Hill when it occurred. None of these women were allowed to testify. In a thorough investigation conducted after the hearings were over, Jayne Mayer and Jill Abramson concluded that the preponderance of available evidence suggested that Clarence Thomas lied under oath when he denied harassing Anita Hill.

Clarence Thomas, however, was not without his supporters, either during the hearings or afterward. The Bush White House concocted the strategy that Thomas should claim that opposition to his nomination was racially motivated. Thus, the cries of a "high-tech lynching" were born. The strategy proved successful. Thomas went on to win the vote of the entire Senate by a vote of 52-48, though George Bush was so apprehensive about the nomination that he placed the then vice-president Dan Quayle at the ready to break the tie vote if it became necessary. The Bush strategy was particularly productive among Southern senators, unable to live down their heritage of racial discrimination. Of all Southern senators, only Hal Heflin, a Democrat from Alabama and a member of the Senate Judiciary Committee, voted against the Thomas nomination. Conservative author David Brock conducted his own investigation, concluding that there was no evidence that Hill had told the truth and announcing his support for Thomas.

That two books written about the hearings should draw such opposing conclusions is indicative of the overall reaction to the debacle that was the Clarence Thomas nomination. Generally, women tended to believe Hill and men tended to believe Thomas, and further divisions broke along party lines. Despite the fact that the authors of both books claim objectivity, it is evident that they approached the hearings from opposing contexts. Much of the blame for the ensuing battle of the sexes should be placed on Joseph Biden and the Senate Judiciary Committee. When American women were faced with an all-white, all-male committee conducting hearings into the sexual harassment of women, they were furious that Hill's charges were never placed in the overall context of how sexual harassment occurs and the subsequent feelings of helplessness and degradation that are common among victims of such harassment.

Furthermore, most scholars agree that the hearings should never have been made public. It was never the intention of the Judiciary Committee to discover the truth of the allegations. Republican members of the committee, such as Orrin Hatch and Alan Simpson, were allowed to grandstand and throw out suggestions that Hill's character was questionable without ever giving her a chance to answer specific charges. Perhaps the most questionable of the witnesses against Hill was John Doggett, who came on in the early hours of Monday morning, October 14, claiming that Hill was irrational and neurotic on the grounds that she had once asked him why he did not call her after they had gone out on a date.

No one knows whether it was Clarence Thomas or Anita Hill who told the truth in 1991. Most people continue to have their own opinions on the matter, but neither Hill, Thomas, nor the American people were well served by the way that the hearing was conducted. After the hearings, women continued to claim that men just "didn't get it." The Year of the Woman was declared in 1992, and a record-breaking number of women entered the two houses of Congress. Public recognition of sexual harassment become prominent, and new ways of dealing with the opposite sex within the workplace began to be mandated by legislatures at all levels. In a landmark decision, the Supreme Court upheld the requirement that employers provide a "non-hostile" working environment for their employees in *Harris v. Forklift Systems* (1993). The year after the Thomas hearings, the number of sexual harassment lawsuits in the United States jumped by 50 percent. Heightened awareness of sexual harassment has been one of the positive byproducts of the hearings, but the bitterness about the hearings did not disappear.

Anita Hill broke her silence about the hearings in her 1997 book *Speaking Truth to Power*. She writes that her life has never been the same since the hearings, and spoke of intimidation that she suffered at the hands of Thomas supporters. By the end of the 1990s, she was no longer teaching at the University of Oklahoma, a job she reportedly loved. A former friend and classmate of Clarence Thomas corroborated Hill's view of Thomas's character in a television interview, as did others who knew him. However, the support for Hill was essentially irrelevant once Thomas was confirmed as an associate justice of the Supreme Court.

Juan Williams, author of *The Eyes on the Prize,* said of Thomas that he was a sad, lonely, troubled, and deeply pessimistic public servant. To Williams' description of Thomas, it should be added that he grew bitter and angry at a system that allowed him to become the butt of jokes and the target of frequent attacks from opponents. His votes on Supreme Court decisions have placed him as a solidly conservative justice, who most often mirrors the decision making of Antonin Scalia, considered by judicial scholars to be the most conservative member of the Supreme Court. His voting record has continued to alienate Thomas from most of the African-American community and has frequently led to protest when he has been invited to lecture around the country. Richard Lacayo of *Time* reported that Thomas told someone in a 1994 interview that he intended to be on the Court for the next 40 years and those who did not like it should simply "get over it." Lacayo responded that it was not likely that Americans would get over it. The Hill-Thomas hearings have not slid gently into history. On the contrary, the memory of those hearings continues to elicit strong feelings of rage, bafflement, and bitterness. The Senate Judiciary Committee now holds closed hearings, and women now serve on the august body. What constitutes sexual harassment is now public knowledge, but the mistakes made in the fall of 1991 will forever haunt those who remember it.

—Elizabeth Purdy

FURTHER READING:

Brock, David. *The Real Anita Hill: The Untold Story.* New York, The Free Press, 1993.

Hill, Anita. *Speaking Truth to Power.* New York, Doubleday, 1997.

Hill, Anita, and Emma Coleman, editors. *Race, Gender, and Power in America: The Legacy of the Hill-Thomas Hearings.* Oxford, Oxford University Press, 1995.

Lacayo, Richard. "The Unheard Witnesses." *Time.* 14 November, 1994.

Mayer, Jayne, and Jill Abramson. *Strange Justice: The Selling of Clarence Thomas.* New York, Houghton Mifflin, 1994.

Morrison, Toni, editor. *Race-ing Justice, En-Gendering Power: Essays on Anita Hill, Clarence Thomas, and the Constructing of the Social Reality.* Berkeley and New York, Pantheon, 1992.

Phelps, Timothy M., and Helen Winternitz. *Capitol Games: Clarence Thomas, Anita Hill, and the Story of A Supreme Court Nomination.* New York, Hyperion, 1992.

Totenberg, Nina, and Anita Miller, editors. *The Complete Transcript of the Clarence Thomas-Anita Hill Hearings: October 11, 12, 13, 1991.* Chicago, Academy-Chicago Pub., 1994.

Anka, Paul (1941—)

With his 1957 number one hit record, ''Diana,'' about a teenage boy's unrequited crush on an older girl, 16-year-old singer-songwriter Paul Anka tapped into a collective angst. Catapulted into the ranks of the 1950s post-Elvis Presley teen idols, the Canadian-born Anka was a pervasive presence on the airwaves with songs including ''Lonely Boy,'' ''Put Your Head on My Shoulder,'' and ''Puppy Love,'' the latter about his romance with former Mousketeer, Annette Funicello. With his adenoidal sound, and a self-confidence that belied his years, he was more at home with ballads than rock 'n' roll. As a result, he weathered changing tastes to reinvent himself as an in-demand cocktail circuit headliner. His sophistication as a songwriter also grew. Along with hits for Barbra Streisand and Tom Jones, Anka wrote Frank Sinatra's signature song, ''My Way,'' and the theme to *The Tonight Show Starring Johnny Carson.*

—Pat H. Broeske

FURTHER READING:

Bronson, Fred. *The Billboard Book of Number One Hits.* New York, Billboard Publications, 1988.

Nolan, Tom. ''Paul Anka: The Lonely Boy Grows Up.'' *Rolling Stone.* October 24, 1974, pp. 9, 20.

Time. ''Anka's Aweigh.'' December 8, 1975, p. 61.

Anne Frank: The Diary of a Young Girl

No single individual has come to represent the six million Jewish victims of the Holocaust more than the Dutch schoolgirl Anne Frank. Through the postwar publication of her diary *Het Achterhuis (Anne Frank: The Diary of a Young Girl),* millions of readers around the world came to know one of Hitler's victims personally and a face was put on an otherwise unfathomable and anonymous horror. Chronicling her life in hiding in Amsterdam from the summer of 1942 to the arrest of her family in August 1944, the diary is considered among the most powerful anti-war documents of the era and has been adapted for both stage and screen. Translated into more than 50 languages, the Diary ranks among the best-selling literary works of the twentieth century and has been praised by ordinary readers, literary critics, and political and humanitarian leaders throughout the world. Discussing its poignancy in the foreword to the first Russian edition of the book, the novelist and poet Ilya Ehrenburg wrote, ''One voice speaks for six million—the voice not of a sage or a poet but of an ordinary little girl.''

Anne Frank was born June 12, 1929 to a wealthy Jewish family in Frankfurt, Germany. With the rise to power of Adolf Hitler and the National Socialists in 1933, the Frank family relocated to Amsterdam, where Frank's father, Otto, a former officer in the German army, established a food preservative business with a combined office and warehouse in a building on the Prinsengracht Canal. Anne Frank attended Montessori school and enjoyed a comfortable life absorbed in the average pursuits of childhood. Following the Nazi occupation of Holland in 1940, a number of restrictions were placed on Jews, and Anne was required to transfer to a Jewish school. Among her friends and classmates she was popular and outgoing and was known as ''Miss Chatterbox'' because of her incessant talking. On the occasion of her thirteenth birthday in June 1942, Anne was given a cloth-covered diary and began recording her activities in the form of letters to an imagined friend whom she addressed as ''Kitty.'' Soon afterward, Anne's 16 year-old sister, Margot, was summoned to report for transportation to the Westerbork concentration camp, and the family quickly went into hiding, installing themselves in makeshift living quarters arranged by Otto Frank in a ''secret annex'' at his company headquarters. The Franks were joined by Mr. and Mrs. Van Pelz and their 15 year-old son, Peter. Several months later, Albert Dussel, a dentist, also sought refuge with the group. For more than two years the group lived in the cramped quarters of the secret annex, unable to move around during the day or use bathroom facilities for fear of being discovered by workers in the offices below. Through a small group of protectors they received food and supplies, and at night they listened to war reports on the radio.

Anne and Margot continued their education under the guidance of their father, and Anne documented every facet of their restricted life in her diary, including the strained relations and petty bickering that often characterized interaction among the group. An unknown betrayer alerted police to the Franks' hiding place, and the secret annex was raided on August 4, 1944. The group was first sent to Westerbork and then was shipped by cattle-car to Auschwitz. Anne Frank died of typhoid fever in Bergen-Belsen concentration camp in March 1945, only two months before the surrender of Germany. She was 15 years old.

After the war, Otto Frank circulated typescript copies of Anne's Diary, which had been discovered in the aftermath of the police raid on the secret annex in 1944. The book was formally published in 1947 and was translated into English in 1952. While Anne herself wondered in the diary whether anyone would ever be interested in ''the unbosomings of a thirteen-year-old schoolgirl,'' the Diary quickly became an international sensation, drawing praise for its documentary value as an account of Jewish life in hiding during World War II, but to a greater degree for its lively and perceptive self-portrait of an intelligent and talented writer maturing from child to adult. Its compelling setting offers a consideration of ordinary people facing death in extraordinary circumstances, while revealing Anne's understanding of universal moral issues and her interest in typical concerns of adolescence, including the difficult relationships of mother and daughter and the teenage yearning for love. After reading the diary many young readers felt compelled to write to Otto Frank and until his death in 1980 he corresponded with young people throughout the world. The immense interest in Anne Frank led to the establishment of several humanitarian foundations and educational centers, including a foundation in Amsterdam that also maintains the secret annex as a historic site open to the public. Summarizing the broad appeal of the Diary, theatrical director Garson Kanin concluded in 1979 that ''Among other things, the vision of Anne Frank reminds us that the length of a life does not necessarily reflect its quality . . . [She] remains for us ever a shining star, a radiant presence, who, during her time of terror and humiliation and imprisonment, was able to find it within herself to write in her immortal diary, 'In spite of everything, I still believe that people are good at heart'.''

—Laurie DiMauro

FURTHER READING:

Ehrenburg, Ilya. *Anne Frank Diary: Chekhov, Stendahl, and Other Essays.* Trans. Tatiana Shebunia and Yvonne Kapp. New York, Alfred A. Knopf, 1963.

Frank, Otto H., and Mirjam Pressler, editors. *The Diary of a Young Girl: The Definitive Edition.* Trans.Susan Massotty. New York, Doubleday, 1995.

Kanin, Garson. ''Anne Frank at 50.'' *Newsweek.* June 25, 1979, pp. 14-15.

Steenmeijer, Anna G., editor. *A Tribute to Anne Frank.* Garden City, New York, Doubleday, 1971.

Annie

Loosely adapted from Harold Gray's comic strip *Little Orphan Annie*, the musical *Annie* opened on Broadway on April 21, 1977, eventually earning more than $100 million from its initial run of 2,377 performances and numerous revivals. Director and lyricist Martin Charnin was the guiding force behind this hit, with considerable assistance from composer Charles Strouse and scriptwriter Thomas Meehan. *Annie* also attracted a larger, more diverse crowd beyond Broadway: The cast album sold more than a million copies, the show was adapted into a Hollywood movie in 1982, and merchandise spinoffs included dolls and a line of fashion clothing for girls. Through countless local productions in schools and summer camps, the musical has become part of the fabric of American childhood, with Annie's signature song ''Tomorrow'' having become a standard.

Annie became a cultural icon through the adroit combination of strands that appealed to different audiences. For the elderly and nostalgic, the musical evoked not just the comic strip but also the simple and pure pre-World War II America of Shirley Temple movies. After the disillusioning eras of Vietnam and Watergate, Americans in the 1970s looked back with fondness to the past—a nostalgia that also fueled the success of *The Sting* (1974) and *Grease* (1972). As columnist Meg Greenfield noted in *Newsweek,* ''*Annie* gangs up on you, and you experience the most unexpected sentiments: reassurance, a feeling of well-being, and an agreeable connection with a long-gone world—a life built on assumptions and simplicities you had forgotten about.''

For the youngsters in the audience, especially girls, the main attraction was the spunky heroine, a two-fisted orphan who could more than hold her own in a rough world. As film critic Pauline Kael noted, *Annie* was ideal for children ''from about four to about eleven . . . how often do they get to see a musical that features a little girl conquering all?'' Appealing to the young and old alike, *Annie* became a Broadway success for all ages.

The plot of *Annie* has a folkloric simplicity. The Cinderella-like tale follows Annie, a frizzle-haired and freckled orphan, as she battles the cruel Miss Hannigan, who runs a wretched orphanage right out of Dickens. Searching for her parents, Annie constantly runs away, only to end up back in the clutches of Miss Hannigan. Annie's luck takes a turn for the better when she is temporarily adopted by the billionaire Oliver Warbucks. Although she wins Warbucks' heart, Annie refuses his offer of permanent adoption because she still longs for her natural parents. Warbucks instigates a nationwide search with a hefty reward. Enter Miss Hannigan's low-life brother, Rooster Hannigan and his floozy girlfriend, Lily St. Regis. Working with Miss Hannigan, these two schemers impersonate Annie's parents. Of course, all ends well, and Annie is happily reunited with Warbucks.

The relationship between Annie and Warbucks forms the emotional core of the musical. In explaining the appeal of the show, director Martin Charnin said, ''I saw it as the story of two orphans.

One happened to be eleven, the other fifty-two. I wanted to know how they met and fell in love with one another.'' Annie and Warbucks form an interesting study in contrasts. Warbucks is rich, big, strong, and protective; Annie is poor, small, weak and in need of protection. But Warbucks is cold—he barely notices his attractive assistant Grace Farrell until Annie starts praising her. Annie's warmth and kindness helps humanize Warbucks, just as his strength and power help give stability to her life.

The musical wisely softened the harsh right-wing philosophy of the original strip, where the heroic Daddy Warbucks was a robber-baron munitions manufacturer who battled liberal do-gooders. In the musical, Warbucks is still conservative, but not rigidly so. Indeed, Annie is able to reconcile him to Franklin Roosevelt, helping to inspire the New Deal. This spirit of reconciliation played well in the early days of the Carter administration. Not surprisingly, a special preview performance was given at the White House in 1977.

Annie: The Movie fared less well than the theatrical production. Columbia Pictures paid $9.5 million for the rights—total costs were $40 million—and hired the legendary director John Huston, but the movie was an expensive disappointment. It did not make a profit, and earned lukewarm reviews despite a critically acclaimed hammy performance by Carol Burnett as Miss Hannigan. Aileen Quinn made a winning Annie, although she was nearly over-staged by the youngest orphan Molly, sweetly played by Toni Ann Gisondi. As a capitalist with a well-buried heart of gold, Albert Finney was a convincing Warbucks. The production team behind the musical has made a few stabs at a sequel, which have been tried out in regional theatres. *Annie II* (1989) was a flop. ''We went over like a wet doughnut,'' said Charnin. *Annie Warbucks* (1993) was more successful but by decade's end had not yet reached Broadway.

—Jeet Heer

FURTHER READING:

Kael, Pauline. *Taking it All In.* New York, Holt, Rinehart and Winston, 1984.

Sheward, David. *It's a Hit!* New York, Back Stage Books, 1994.

Smith, Bruce. *The History of Little Orphan Annie.* New York, Ballantine Books, 1982.

Annie Get Your Gun

Annie Get Your Gun, a popular musical comedy based loosely on the life of the legendary American crack shot and theatrical performer Annie Oakley (1860-1926), opened May 17, 1946 at the Imperial Theater in New York. The show helped complete the postwar transformation of the Broadway musical begun by *Oklahoma!* (1943) and *Carousel* (1945) from lavish and naughty revues to substantive stories with songs integrated into the plot. Although *Annie Get Your Gun* lacked the operatic aspirations and social commentary of the two Rodgers and Hammerstein works, the show boasted an Irving Berlin score that set a record for hit songs (nine). *Annie Get Your Gun* broke no new ground in theatrical tradition, but its color, humor, and enthusiasm have held an irresistible appeal for audiences through the end of the century.

Dorothy and (brother) Herbert Fields specifically wrote their romanticization of Oakley's life as a vehicle for musical comedy star

Ethel Merman performing in *Annie Get Your Gun*.

Ethel Merman (1909-84). The foul-mouthed Merman was no dainty romantic soprano but squarely in the tradition of great chest wallopers who had transfixed Broadway in the early 1900s. *Annie Get Your Gun* demanded that she act as well as sing, and Merman responded by turning in one of Broadway's monumental performances. Her health was as legendary as her arrogance and outspokenness, and when she eventually took a vacation after two years of performing, the show's receipts dropped precipitously, and it almost closed. For Merman, *Annie Get Your Gun* turned out to be an unquestioned personal triumph, consolidating her position as the greatest figure in American musical comedy.

The Fieldses took their idea to the legendary hit-making team of Richard Rodgers and Oscar Hammerstein, II, who agreed to produce it, and added the esteemed Jerome Kern to write the lyrics. When Kern suffered a cerebral hemorrhage and died in November 1945, the producers persuaded Irving Berlin (1888-1989) to replace him. Berlin was initially reluctant to enter the unknown territory of a musical with a plot; he hadn't written a Broadway show in four years, and the theatrical form with which he was most closely associated—the revue—was in terminal decline. Over a weekend in Atlantic City, Berlin tried to write some songs and came back with three to six hit songs (depending on the source). The deal was signed, and Dorothy Fields obligingly agreed to withdraw as lyricist. Berlin finished the bulk of the score within two months, astounding everyone with his extraordinary virtuosity and the speed with which he composed the new songs. To the roster of classics of the musical theater Berlin added ''There's No Business Like Show Business,'' ''Doin' What Comes Natur'lly,'' ''They Say It's Wonderful,'' ''You Can't Get a Man with a Gun,'' ''The Girl That I Marry,'' ''I Got the Sun in the Morning,'' ''Anything You Can Do,'' ''My Defenses Are Down,'' and ''Who Do You Love, I Hope.'' The show went into rehearsal in March, and Berlin later called it the easiest show he ever worked on.

In *Annie Get Your Gun,* Annie Oakley's (Merman) ability as a sharpshooter wins her a job in Buffalo Bill's (William O'Neal) Wild West show. Her brilliant shooting offends the masculinity of the show's erstwhile star marksman, handsome baritone Frank Butler (Ray Middleton), and makes a romance between the pair impossible. Butler takes his wounded vanity to a competing vaudeville show, but neither the main characters nor their businesses prosper. A merger is proposed, but the happy ending only arrives when wise old Sitting Bull (Harry Bellaver) gently demonstrates to the naive Oakley that she can easily win the insecure Butler by intentionally losing a shooting competition.

Although critics initially gave *Annie Get Your Gun* mixed reviews, the show was an instant hit, running for three years and 1,147 performances on Broadway, and quickly assuming a place in the pantheon of great post-World War II musicals such as *South Pacific, Brigadoon, Kiss Me Kate, Guys and Dolls,* and *The King and I.* The success of *Annie Get Your Gun* made Irving Berlin a wealthy man and demonstrated the immense potential profitability of postwar Broadway musicals. Berlin's thirty percent share of the proceeds brought him $2500 a week, his music company made $500,000 from selling sheet music of the score, his royalties from the original cast recording exceeded $100,000, and MGM eventually paid $650,000 to Berlin and the Fieldses for the movie rights, a record for a musical. *Annie Get Your Gun* profitably toured the United States with Mary Martin as the lead and also proved to be a vast international success.

Although *Annie Get Your Gun* does not lend itself to excessive analysis, the show does capture some of the post-World War II American confusion over gender relations. The war had caused millions of women to enter the work force to replace absent soldiers, and their contributions had undeniably helped the United States win the war. The plot of *Annie Get Your Gun* was charged with subliminal sexual implications, based upon a woman who used her phallic gun with complete mastery. Ultimately, Oakley discovers ''you can't get a man with a gun,'' and understands that she must deny her superior talent and throw the shooting match in order to assuage Frank's fragile ego and win her man. The ending struck a chord with a society which had greatly elevated women's role both in the world of work and in propaganda during the war, and now was desperately attempting to return to the status quo ante.

The film version (1950) had a troubled history (Judy Garland was fired from the lead role) but eventually earned more than $8 million. The show was revived on its twentieth anniversary in 1966, for which the seventy-eight-year-old Berlin wrote the fifty-eight-year-old Merman a new song, ''An Old Fashioned Wedding.'' This showstopper proved to be the last of Berlin's popular hits. Many of the show's tunes have fallen out of the popular repertoire, but ''There's No Business Like Show Business'' remains a virtual anthem of performers everywhere and has become one of the most recognizable tunes in American popular music.

—Jon Sterngass

FURTHER READING:

Bergreen, Laurence. *As Thousands Cheer: The Life of Irving Berlin.* New York, Penguin, 1990.

Kasper, Shirl. *Annie Oakley.* Norman, University of Oklahoma Press, 1992.

Thomas, Bob. *I Got Rhythm! The Ethel Merman Story.* New York, G. P. Putnam's Sons, 1985.

Annie Hall

Despite its status in many circles as writer/director/star Woody Allen's comedic masterpiece, *Annie Hall* nonetheless will remain to many the film that ''stole'' the Best Picture Oscar away from the (retrospectively) far more influential *Star Wars*. At the time of their release in 1977, however, although *Star Wars* initiated a new era of upbeat science fiction films, *Annie Hall* was the culmination of America's nearly decade-long struggle to come to terms with the aftermath of political and sexual revolution of the 1960s. The film seemed to give voice to the frustrations of a generation regarding their inability to maintain romance. Surprised by the overwhelming acceptance of the picture, Allen himself commented, ''I guess what everybody understood was the impossibility of sustaining relationships, because of entirely irrational elements. . . . Later in life, you don't really know what went wrong.''

Annie Hall also represented the peak of America's love affair with stand-up comic turned filmmaker and film star Woody Allen. While he had been performing in films since 1965's *What's New, Pussycat?,* his screen vehicles had consistently been outrageous

A poster for the film *Annie Hall*.

fantasies that displaced him in either time or space—though Allen played essentially the same character, a neurotic, intellectual nerdish Everyman struggling to get the girl and avoid violence. But *Annie Hall* changed everything. According to his longtime editor, Ralph Rosenblum, Allen had been struggling to make the transition into maturer, less clownish films about the urban angst regarding love, sex, and romance. Toward this end Allen had initially set out to make a murder mystery entitled *Anhedonia* (the chronic inability to feel pleasure) that would illuminate these problems and would co-star former lover and frequent leading lady Diane Keaton. However, once they began viewing the dailies and establishing some structure to the rambling two-hour-and-twenty-minute narrative, which included extensive flashbacks and comedic asides, Rosenblum finally convinced Allen that the film came to life in the scenes involving the romance with Annie, which were set in the present. The murder mystery plot was thus altered to focus on the romance, becoming, in Rosenblum's words, ''A light-headed, devil-may-care Midwestern girl who grew up in a Norman Rockwell painting meets urban Jewish comedian who has enough awareness for both of them and hang-ups to match.''

Annie Hall then became the story of their rocky romance, as Alvy Singer (Allen) tells the camera that he and Annie have broken up and that he is ''sifting the pieces o' the relationship through my mind and—and examining my life to figure out where did the screw-up come?'' The ensuing stream of consciousness exploration of memory and fantasy—somewhat reminiscent of Ingmar Bergman's *Wild Strawberries*—results in Alvy coming to the conclusion, ''Relationships . . . You know they're totally irrational and crazy and absurd . . . but uh, I guess we keep goin' through it because, uh, most of us need the eggs,'' i.e., the fleeting moments of happiness they can bring. But even after these ruminations, he is unable to discern the reasons for his separation from Annie, though filmmaker Allen illuminates very clearly that it is because of Alvy's neuroses and insecurities. As critic Douglas Brode concludes, Alvy presents his own persona as a lost, bewildered man, shell-shocked in the sexual battleground of the mid-1970s; thus, Woody turns *Annie Hall* into a warning against the dangers of the Culture of Narcissism.

Annie Hall was rendered even more compelling due to the extreme autobiographical associations between the characters and Allen's own life. Like Allen, Alvy Singer was born in Brooklyn and grew up during World War II. Professionally their progress is also the same: both began as gag writers, evolved into stand-up comedy, then became playwrights. In terms of relationships, Alvy Singer has been married and divorced twice when he becomes involved with Annie Hall and then breaks up with her. Likewise twice divorced, Allen had a long-term relationship with Diane Keaton—real name Hall—, which also ended. Though Allen maintains that his introduction to Keaton and other factual aspects of their relationship were completely different from Alvy and Annie's, he has acknowledged that the ''mildly misanthropic and socially discontent'' Alvy and his constant complaints about love and life parallel his own, once telling columnist Alfred Bester, ''Sure it's me—but greatly exaggerated . . . my most embarrassing moments.'' *Annie Hall* seemed to be an autobiographical compendium of all the issues that Allen had always been obsessed with—death, sex, intellect, art, and mostly, himself—but this time without the fantasy elements to distract the viewer from the nakedness of this self-absorption.

According to a *Variety* survey of the ten best movie lists proposed by thirty-two American film reviewers, *Annie Hall* was the most frequently selected film, named on thirty of the lists. Beyond the many awards and acclaim, the popularity of the film also affected fashion. Diane Keaton's casual ensembles for *Annie Hall,* which she explained were basically her style and were largely clothes from her own closet, established new fashion trends, which included the appropriation of men's slacks, shirts, and neckties in a loose, unstructured look that paralleled Annie's idiosyncratic look at the world.

—Rick Moody

FURTHER READING:

Brode, Douglas. *The Films of Woody Allen.* New York, Citadel Press, 1991.

Rosenblum, Ralph, and Robert Karen. *When the Shooting Stops . . . the Cutting Begins: A Film Editor's Story.* New York, The Viking Press, 1979.

Wernblad, Annette. *Brooklyn Is Not Expanding: Woody Allen's Comic Universe.* Madison, Fairleigh Dickinson University Press, 1992.

Another World

Co-conceived by the prolific Irna Phillips and William Bell, *Another World* premiered on NBC television in 1964, eventually becoming one of Procter & Gamble's (P&G's) most enduring soap operas. Initially envisioned as a spinoff of one of Phillips and P&G's other creations, CBS's *As the World Turns, Another World* abandoned this link when CBS opted against airing it.

The introductory narration, "we do not live in this world alone, but in a thousand other worlds," was the signature of *Another World's* early seasons. Set in Bay City, in a Midwestern state later tagged as Illinois, the program focused on the Randolph and Matthews families in the 1960s, as Phillips and Bell offered timely stories involving illegal abortion and LSD. These topics proved too bold for traditional viewers, however, and backstage adjustments led to the hiring of Agnes Nixon, future creator of *All My Children,* who devised "crossovers" in which characters from P&G's veteran soap on CBS, *Guiding Light,* were temporarily imported in the hopes that their fans would follow. The tactic, however, failed to boost *Another World's* numbers.

The 1970s began under the headwriting leadership of Harding Lemay, who would shepherd *Another World* into its heyday. Several characters were extracted to launch a spinoff—*Somerset.* Lemay then broke ranks by having patriarch John Randolph (Michael Ryan) commit adultery, sending wife Pat (Beverly Penberthy) into an alcoholic tailspin. This displeased Irna Phillips, who lamented the loss of a solid, "core" couple. Gradually, the Randolph family was phased out, the farm-grown Frame clan was introduced, and a defining element of class difference marked the show. A triangle involving heroine Alice Matthews (Jacqueline Courtney), husband Steve Frame (George Reinholt), and working-class homewrecker Rachel Davis (Robin Strasser, later Victoria Wyndham) made the show a ratings leader in 1977/1978. Before long, Rachel was redeemed in the love of upper-crusted Mackenzie "Mac" Cory (Douglass Watson), a publishing magnate 25 years her senior. Mac's self-absorbed daughter Iris (Beverlee McKinsey) threatened the union of her father and Rachel, who deepened a trend of inter-class romance and were to become bastions of the soap's pre-eminent "core"

family. Additionally, in 1975, the soap became the first to make 60 minutes, rather than 30, the industry standard. As the 1970s concluded, *Another World* was pressured to focus on its younger generation in order to compete with *General Hospital* and other soaps making inroads into the profitable baby boom audience and displacing it atop the ratings ladder. Lemay resisted these efforts and exited the show in 1979, later publicizing his bittersweet experiences in a memoir entitled *Eight Years in Another World.* The book also recounts Lemay's battles with executives, including one in which Lemay's proposal to introduce a gay character was vetoed.

A musical chairs game of writers penned *Another World* in the 1980s, which began with Iris departing Bay City to anchor yet another spinoff—*Texas*—and Rachel's payoff tryst with a blackmailer. The tale spawned a divorce and Rachel's third child. Mac soon forgave Rachel and adopted the boy, Matthew, who followed in his siblings' footsteps by succumbing to the genre's accelerated aging process and sprouting into a teen overnight. Efforts to replicate the "super couple" phenomenon so efficient in attracting baby boomers to rival soaps evolved. These were spearheaded by a thirty-something, inter-class duo, Donna Love (Anna Stuart) and Michael Hudson (Kale Browne), and another composed of their teenaged daughter Marley (Ellen Wheeler) and Jake McKinnon (Tom Eplin), the ex-beau of Marley's wily, prodigal twin Vicky (also Wheeler). Two nefarious miscreants, Donna's father Reginald Love (John Considine) and ex-husband Carl Hutchins (Charles Keating), and a vixen, Cecile de Poulignac (Susan Keith, later Nancy Frangione), were added, along with dapper attorney Cass Winthrop (Stephen Schnetzer) and flamboyant romance novelist Felicia Gallant (Linda Dano). The latter three established screwball comedy humor as a distinctive trait of the program, and Cass's effort to elude gangsters by cross-dressing as a floozie named Krystal Lake was a first. Similar gender-bending escapades involving Cass, other characters, and other soaps would later re-emerge as a comic convention. The 1980s also featured the "sin stalker" murder mystery to which several actors fell victim, and the first of myriad soap opera AIDS (Acquired Immune Deficiency Syndrome) stories. While influential, these innovations were to little avail, and the show settled near the ratings cellar and suffered another blow—the death of Douglass Watson (Mac)—as the 1990s loomed.

Lack of headwriting and producing consistency continued to plague the soap in the 1990s, as the aftermath of Jake's rape of estranged wife Marley drove the story. Jake's eventual shooting injury at the hands of Paulina (Cali Timmons, later Judi Evans), the daughter Mac Cory never knew he had, dovetailed into his controversial redemption and courtship of Paulina. Vicky, the wicked half of the good twin/evil twin duo now portrayed by future film star Anne Heche and, later, Jensen Buchanan, was blossoming as the "tentpole" heroine. Vicky was saved in the love of true-blue cop Ryan Harrison (Paul Michael Valley), despite the machinations of Ryan's evil half brother, Grant (Mark Pinter). Redemption was also the watchword in the widowed Rachel's reluctant, marriage-bound romance with former nemesis Carl Hutchins and the delightful, screwball comedic pursuit of jaded, forty-something divorcée Donna Love by Rachel's ardent, twenty-something son, Matthew (Matt Crane).

Attempts by NBC to coax *Another World* into imitating the postmodern, youth-orientation of its "demographically correct" cousin, *Days of Our Lives,* were afoot. Producing and headwriting notables Jill Farren Phelps and Michael Malone were fired when they resisted such alterations as restoring Carl's villainy. The violent death of working mother Frankie Frame (Alice Barrett) sparked a viewer revolt. Trend-setting tales, including the Matthew/Donna romance

Cast members from *Another World* in the mid-1960s.

which had laid the groundwork for a similar effort on *Guiding Light,* and a planned white woman/black man liaison involving Felicia, were scuttled. Later, several over-forty stars, including Charles Keating (Carl), were axed, angering Internet fans, who mobilized letter-writing protests. The screwball humor, social relevance, feisty women, and multi-generational focus which had distinguished *Another World* and proven so influential had fallen victim to commercial dictates. Unable to overcome the challenge, the show was cancelled, the final episode airing on June 25, 1999.

—Christine Scodari

FURTHER READING:

Lemay, Harding. *Eight Years in Another World.* New York, Atheneum, 1981.

Matelski, Marilyn. *The Soap Opera Evolution: America's Enduring Romance with Daytime Drama.* Jefferson, North Carolina, McFarland & Co., 1988.

Museum of Television and Radio. *Worlds without End: The Art and History of the Soap Opera.* New York, Harry N. Abrams, Inc., 1997.

Scodari, Christine. "'No Politics Here': Age and Gender in Soap Opera 'Cyberfandom.'" *Women's Studies in Communication.* Fall 1998, 168-87.

Waggett, Gerard. *Soap Opera Encyclopedia.* New York, Harper Paperbacks, 1997.

Anthony, Piers (1934—)

Piers Anthony Dillingham Jacobs began writing science fiction/fantasy as early as his student years at Goddard College, Vermont (B.A. 1956). In 1967, he published *Chthon,* followed in 1968 by *Omnivore, Sos the Rope,* and *The Ring* (with Robert E. Margroff). *Macroscope* (1969) established him as a master of complex characters and cosmic story lines. Since then, Anthony has often published at least three novels annually—one science fiction, one fantasy, and one experimental. In 1977, he published *Cluster* and *A Spell for Chameleon,* each initiating a series. The *Cluster* novels, the three *Planet of Tarot* novels, the *Blue Adept* series, the *Incarnations of*

Immortality sequence, and others allowed Anthony to explore multiple science fictional themes, while the Xanth novels (*A Spell for Chameleon* followed by *Castle Roogna* and *The Source of Magic,* and a continuing series of sequels) have consistently placed him on the bestsellers lists.

—Michael R. Collings

FURTHER READING:

Anthony, Piers. *Bio of an Ogre: The Autobiography of Piers Anthony to Age 50.* New York, Ace Books, 1988.

Collings, Michael R. *Piers Anthony.* Mercer Island, Washington, Starmont House, 1983.

Aparicio, Luis (1934—)

Venezuelan Luis Aparicio won more Gold Gloves than any other American League shortstop in the history of baseball. He won every year from 1958 to 1962 and then again in 1964, 1966, 1968 and 1970. He led the American League shortstops in fielding for eight consecutive seasons and broke a major league record by leading the American League in assists for six straight years.

In addition, Aparicio became the first Hispanic American in professional baseball in the United States to be named ''Rookie of the Year.'' During his rookie season for Baltimore, Aparicio drove in 56 runs, scored 69 runs, and led the leagues in stolen bases. Aparicio was one of the first Hispanic players to really demonstrate what talent existed south of the border and the potential it had for making big league ball exciting.

—Nicolás Kanellos

FURTHER READING:

Kanellos, Nicolás. *Hispanic American Almanac.* Detroit, Gale, 1997.

Tardiff, Joseph T., and L. Mpho Mabunda, editors. *Dictionary of Hispanic Biography.* Detroit, Gale, 1996.

Apocalypse Now

Speaking in retrospect about his 1979 film, director Francis Ford Coppola once said, *"Apocalypse Now* is not about Vietnam, it is

Marlon Brando (left) and Martin Sheen in a scene from the film *Apocalypse Now*.

Vietnam.'' Coppola was referring to the immense difficulty and hardship he experienced in making the film, but his words are true in another sense as well. *Apocalypse Now* is not an accurate film—it does not depict any actual events that took place during the long history of American involvement in the Vietnam War. It is, however, a true film—it clearly conveys the surreal, absurd, and brutal aspects of the war that were experienced by many who took part in it.

The broad outline of the script is adapted from Joseph Conrad's bleak 1902 novella *Heart of Darkness,* which concerns nineteenth-century European imperialism in Africa. Screenwriter John Milius transplants the latter two-thirds of Conrad's tale to Southeast Asia, and gives us the story of Captain Willard (Martin Sheen), United States Army assassin, and his final assignment in Vietnam. ''I wanted a mission,'' Willard says in voice-over narration, ''and, for my sins, they gave me one. When it was over, I'd never want another.''

Willard's mission is to journey up the Nung River into Cambodia, and there find and kill Colonel Walter Kurtz, a renegade Green Beret officer who has organized a force of Montagnard tribesmen into his own private army, which Kurtz has been using to wage war in his own way, on his own terms. Kurtz's methods of fighting the Viet Cong are unremittingly savage—according to the General who briefs Willard on his mission: ''He's out there operating without any decent restraint, totally beyond the pale of any acceptable human conduct.''

And so Willard begins his own journey into the heart of darkness, courtesy of a Navy patrol boat and its crew: Chief Phillips (Albert Hall); Clean (Larry Fishburne); Chef (Frederic Forrest); and Lance (Joseph Bottoms). Along the way, Willard and the sailors encounter people and situations that highlight the absurdity of the American approach to the war. This idea is brought in early when Willard remarks after accepting the mission to find and kill Kurtz: ''Charging people with murder in this place was like handing out speeding tickets at the Indy 500.''

The absurdity escalates when Willard meets Colonel Kilgore (Robert Duvall), who commands the Airmobile unit that is supposed to escort Willard's boat to the mouth of the Nung River. Kilgore is bored at the prospect, until he learns that the section of coast where he is supposed to deliver Willard offers excellent currents for surfing. At dawn the next day, Kilgore's helicopters assault the Viet Cong village that overlooks their objective, wiping out the inhabitants so that Kilgore and his troops can surf—and, incidentally, allowing Willard to continue his mission. The aftermath of the air strike that Kilgore calls in to finish off the village allows Duvall to deliver one of the film's more famous lines: ''I love the smell of napalm in the morning! It smells like . . . victory!''

Later, in a remote American outpost where the boat stops for supplies, Willard and the crew arrive just in time to see a gaudy United Service Organizations (USO) show, replete with a band and go-go dancing Playboy Playmates. This highlights another theme in the film—the Americans do not like the jungle, so they attempt to turn the jungle into America. In Willard's words: ''They tried to make it just like home.'' And that, the film seems to say, is why they would lose—you cannot win a jungle war by trying to make the jungle into America. As the boat departs the outpost and its go-go dancers, Willard's thoughts turn to the enemy: ''Charlie didn't get much USO. He was either dug in too deep or moving too fast. His idea of good R&R [rest and relaxation] was a handful of cold rice, or a little rat meat.'' Willard's parting thought on the spectacle he has just witnessed is: ''The war was being run by clowns, who were going to end up giving the whole circus away.''

That quotation evokes another of the film's themes: the distinction between ''clowns'' and ''warriors.'' Most of the United States military people whom Willard encounters can be considered clowns. They commit massive, mindless violence, which is inefficient as well as counterproductive to the stated goal of ''winning the hearts and minds of the Vietnamese people.'' A warrior, on the other hand, uses violence only when it is necessary, and then does so surgically. His response is precise, controlled, and lethal.

The scene greeting Willard when he arrives at Kurtz's stronghold is like something out of a nightmare. The bodies of dead Viet Cong are everywhere. A crashed airplane hangs half out of a tree. A pile of human skulls leers from the shore. The Montagnard warriors, their faces painted white, stand silent and ominous as ghosts as they watch Willard's boat pull in.

And then there is Kurtz himself (Marlon Brando). His ragtag troops clearly consider him a mystic warrior. Willard thinks Kurtz may be insane—but, if so, it is a form of insanity perfectly suited to the kind of war he is fighting. As Willard notes while reading Kurtz's dossier on the trip upriver, ''The Viet Cong knew his name now, and they were scared of him.'' Willard is frightened of Kurtz, too. But his fear does not stop him, several nights later, from sneaking into Kurtz's quarters and hacking him to death with a machete. Willard is able to do this because, he says, Kurtz wished to die: ''He wanted someone to take the pain away.''

Twelve years after the release of *Apocalypse Now* came the documentary *Hearts of Darkness* (1991), which chronicles the making of Coppola's opus. Combining video footage shot by Coppola's wife Eleanor in 1978, interviews with cast and crew, and scenes left out of the final version of *Apocalypse Now,* the documentary is a fascinating look at the making of a film under the most adverse of conditions.

—Justin Gustainis

FURTHER READING:

Auster, Albert, and Leonard Quart. *How the War Was Remembered: Hollywood & Vietnam.* New York, Praeger, 1988.

Gustainis, J. Justin. *American Rhetoric and the Vietnam War.* Wesport, Connecticut, Greenwood Press, 1993.

Lanning, Michael Lee. *Vietnam at the Movies.* New York, Fawcett Columbine, 1994.

Apollo Missions

Between July 1969 and December 1972, 12 American astronauts walked upon the lunar surface. Their 240,000 mile journey to the moon began centuries earlier as the first human gazed skyward into the heavens. As the closest celestial body to the Earth, the moon inspired dreams of exploration through masterworks of literature and art. While such visionary dreams became reality with the technological giant known as Project Apollo, the atmosphere of the Cold War precipitated the drive to the moon.

By 1961 the Soviet Union garnered many of the important ''firsts'' in space—the artificial satellite (Sputnik I), a living creature in space (Sputnik II), and an un-manned lunar landing (Luna II). Space was no longer a vast territory reserved for stargazers and

Neil Armstrong becomes the first man to walk on the moon.

writers of science fiction; it was now at the forefront of national prestige. The race for placing a human into orbit was the next ''first'' prize. The American public eagerly looked to Cape Canaveral to finally capture the gold, only to once again be outdone by the Soviets with the orbital flight of Yuri Gagarin.

President John F. Kennedy consulted with scientific advisors about what first the United States might secure. On May 25, 1961, the President made a bold proclamation to the world, ''I believe that this nation should commit itself of achieving the goal, before this decade is out, of landing a man on the moon and returning him safely to the Earth.'' With these words he captured the imagination of the nation and set forth on a project whose size rivaled the bid for an atomic bomb with the Manhattan Project. When Kennedy delivered his speech, the United States had a mere 15 minutes and 22 seconds of space flight under its belt. Such a complicated venture would require billions of dollars and years to develop the systems and machinery.

Apollo was set to debut in 1967 with the orbital flight of its first crew in Apollo 1. On January 27, however, an electrical spark ignited the capsule's pure oxygen atmosphere ending the lives of astronauts Gus Grissom, Edward White II, and Roger Chaffee. The tragedy showed the first chink in Apollo's armor. As the political climate had changed in the years since President Kennedy's pledge, some began to wonder if the billions of dollars needed to fund Apollo were worth it.

The flight of Apollo 8 in December of 1968 resurrected the program, proving the redesigned hardware could deliver the goods by 1969. Astronauts Frank Borman, James Lovell, and William Anders became the first humans to escape the Earth's gravitational pull and circumnavigate the moon. The desolate and forbidding surface of a lifeless moon made the ''blue marble'' of Earth seem like a ''grand oasis'' in the dark void of space. For the first time humans could see their fragile planet in its entirety. Television cameras transmitted the images back to Earth as the crew quoted Genesis on the eve of Christmas. Apollo 8 had been one of the few bright spots in a year filled with domestic political turmoil, riots, war, and assassination.

Apollo 11 was the news event of 1969. Nearly half of the world's citizens watched Neil Armstrong take his historic first lunar steps on July 20. The images of Armstrong, Buzz Aldrin, and Michael Collins turned into a marketing bonanza. Their likeness graced buttons, towels, glasses, plates, lunchboxes, posters, and charms. Apollo 11 made the cover of magazines ranging from *Time* and *National Geographic* to *TV Guide*.

With the success of Apollo 11, however, came an end to the anxiety within the public raised by Sputnik. The United States had unequivocally regained its national honor with the fulfillment of the lunar pledge. Many Americans now felt it was time to put space aside and concentrate on problems on Earth. Moreover, the necessity to finance a protracted war in Southeast Asia and the social programs of the Great Society led to reductions in NASA (National Aeronautics and Space Administration) budgets.

As big as Apollo 11 was, Apollo 12 was not. It became NASA's equivalent to a summer rerun on television. The next mission, Apollo 13, would have suffered a similar fate had it not been for its near disaster in space. The explosion of an oxygen tank brought with it the prospect of suffering a loss of life in space, and Apollo once again captured headlines. Apollo 14 had moments of interest for the public—it featured Alan Shepard hitting golf balls for ''miles and miles'' courtesy of the moon's reduced gravity. The crews of Apollo 15, 16, and 17, regardless of the scientific value of the missions, became anonymous figures in bulky white suits bouncing around on

the lunar surface. Their activities were relegated to a mere mention on the evening news broadcast.

No great conquest program would supplant Apollo; the political circumstances of the early 1960s no longer prevailed by the decade's end. Even the original plans for Apollo were trimmed as budgetary constraints forced NASA to cut three of the ten scheduled lunar landings. Ironically, the last flight of Apollo in 1975 was a joint Earth-orbit mission with the Soviet Union, the very menace whose space efforts had given birth to the United States lunar program.

Apollo is not simply a collection of wires, transistors, nuts, and bolts put together by an incredible gathering of scientific minds. Rather, it is a story of great adventure. The missions of Apollo went beyond the redemption of national pride with the planting of the United States flag on the moon. Project Apollo was a victory for all to share, not only Americans.

—Dr. Lori C. Walters

FURTHER READING:

Aldrin, Buzz, and Malcolm McConnell. *Men from Earth.* New York, Bantam Books, 1989.

Chaikin, Andrew. *A Man on the Moon: The Voyages of the Apollo Astronauts.* New York, Viking Penguin, 1998.

Kauffman, James L. *Selling Outer Space: Kennedy, the Media, and Funding for Project Apollo, 1961-1963.* Tuscaloosa, University of Alabama Press, 1994.

McDougall, Walter A. *The Heavens and the Earth: A Political History of the Space Age.* New York, Basic Books, 1985.

Murray, Charles, and Catherine Bly Cox. *Apollo: The Race to the Moon.* New York, Simon and Schuster, 1989.

Shepard, Alan, et al. *Moon Shot: The Inside Story of America's Race to the Moon.* Atlanta, Turner Publishing, Inc., 1994.

Apollo Theatre

From 1934 until the present, the Apollo Theatre has been the most important venue for black entertainment in the United States. Located on 125th Street in New York's black Harlem neighborhood, the Apollo is more than just a venue, it is a cultural institution, a place where African Americans have come-of-age professionally, socially, and politically. As Ahmet Ertegun, chairman of Atlantic Records, noted, ''[The Apollo] represented getting out of the limitations of being a black entertainer. If you're a black entertainer in Charlotte or Mississippi you have great constraints put upon you. But coming to Harlem and the Apollo—Harlem was an expression of the black spirit in America, it was a haven. The Apollo Theatre stood for the greatest—the castle that you reach when you finally make it.''

The changing face of the Apollo—originally built as an Irish music hall, and later the site of a burlesque theatre—in the early twentieth century aptly represented the shifting demographics of the Harlem community itself. Real estate developers, intending to build a suburban paradise for well-off whites, found themselves forced to rent to blacks when the boom cycle went bust in the 1910s. Black

125th Street and the Apollo Theatre, Harlem, New York.

movement within New York City, combined with mass migrations from the southern states, made Harlem the largest black community in America. For African Americans in the 1920s and 1930s, Harlem became the center of the earth, and although its heyday came toward the end of the "Harlem Renaissance," no cultural establishment was more in vogue than the Apollo.

Of the many shows and performers that have graced Apollo's stage, none have been as enduring, as popular, or as influential as Ralph Cooper and his Wednesday evening Amateur Nights. In the midst of the worst economic depression in American history, Cooper aimed to restore the vision of the "American dream" to the people of Harlem. As he said at the time, "We can make people a unique offer: With nothing but talent and a lot of heart, you can make it." Early shows were successful enough to merit live broadcast on WMCA, and radio exposure extended the Apollo's influence far beyond the boundaries of Harlem. As Cooper later recalled, "You could walk down any street in town and that's all you heard—and not just in Harlem, but all over New York and most of the country." The entire nation, in fact, gained its first exposure to such notable talents as

Lionel Hampton, Billie Holiday, Ella Fitzgerald, and more recently, Luther Vandross, Gladys Knight, and Michael Jackson, from the Apollo's Amateur Night.

Ironically, the breakthrough success that artists like Knight, Donna Summer, and other black entertainers found in the early 1970s spelled doom for "Harlem's High Spot." A surge in record royalties led to less touring for major artists, and the Apollo found itself priced out of the market, unable to compete with larger venues like Madison Square Garden and the Lincoln Center. Furthermore, a 1975 gunfight in the Apollo's upper balcony during a Smokey Robinson concert severely damaged the theatre's reputation as a safe haven in a dangerous neighborhood. Eventually, the Apollo's owners were forced to sell the ailing theatre to a church group. After church leaders declared bankruptcy a few years later, however, the theatre was taken over by the Harlem Urban Development Corporation in 1982. In 1983, the Apollo became a National Historic Landmark, securing its future as, arguably, America's most important theatre.

—Marc R. Sykes

FURTHER READING:

Cooper, Ralph, and Steve Dougherty. *Amateur Night at the Apollo: Ralph Cooper Presents Five Decades of Great Entertainment.* New York, HarperCollins, 1990.

Fox, Ted. *Showtime at the Apollo.* New York, Holt, Rinehart, & Winston, 1983.

Schiffman, Jack. *Harlem Heyday: A Pictorial History of Modern Black Show Business and the Apollo Theatre.* Buffalo, Prometheus Books, 1984.

Apple Computer

Apple Computer was originally founded by Steven Wozniak and Steven Jobs in 1976. Wozniak and Jobs had been friends in high school, and they shared an interest in electronics. They both eventually dropped out of college and worked for electronics companies, Wozniak at Hewlett-Packard and Jobs at Atari. Wozniak, who experimented in computer design, built the prototype for the Apple I in his garage in early 1976. Jobs saw the potential of the Apple I, and he insisted that he and Wozniak try to sell the machine.

The computer world did not take the Apple I very seriously, and it saw limited success. When the Apple II debuted in 1977, things changed dramatically. The first personal computer to include color graphics, the Apple II was an impressive machine. Orders for Apple machines grew rapidly, and with the introduction of the Apple Disk II, an inexpensive machine with an easy-to-use floppy drive, Apple sales further increased.

With the increase in sales came increased company size. By 1980, when the Apple III was released, Apple had several thousand employees. Apple had taken on a number of new investors who opted to take seats on the board of directors. Older, more conservative men, the new directors wanted Apple to become a more traditional corporation, much to the dismay of many of its original employees.

By 1981, a saturated personal computer market forced Apple to lay off employees. In addition, Wozniak was injured in a plane crash. He took a leave of absence from Apple and returned only briefly. Jobs became chairman of Apple computer in March. Although the personal computer market was growing by leaps and bounds, Apple continued to find itself falling behind the market-share curve. When IBM introduced its first PC in late 1981, Jobs realized Apple needed to change direction.

In 1984, Apple released the Macintosh. The Mac, which would become synonymous with Apple, marked a dramatic revolution in the

The Apple IIGS personal computer.

field of personal computing. Although the Mac was not the first computer to use the Graphical User Interface (GUI) system of icons rather than text-line commands, it was the first GUI-based machine mass-marketed to the general public. By allowing computer users to simply point-and-click rather than having to understand a complex and often unintuitive set of typed commands, the Macintosh made it possible for the average person to operate a personal computer.

The advertisement promoting the launch of the Macintosh was equally dramatic. The ad, which aired during halftime of the Super Bowl, depicted a woman with a large hammer attacking a gigantic video screen that broadcast the image of a suit-wearing Big Brother figure to the gathered masses. Marrying a David vs. Goliath theme to imagery from George Orwell's dystopic *1984*, the commercial suggested that the Macintosh was ready to challenge the evil dominance of corporate giant IBM.

In 1985, after a heated and contentious struggle within the board of directors, Steve Jobs left Apple Computer. For the next eight years, Apple appeared to be on a roller-coaster ride, going from Wall Street darling to has-been several times. Beset by internal struggles and several poorly-designed advertising campaigns, Apple watched its share of the computer market dwindle. Microsoft introduced the Windows software for Intel-based computers, which further eroded Apple's market share. Windows, which essentially copied the Macintosh GUI, proved phenomenally successful. With its ease-of-use trump card gone, Apple continued to slide, despite the fact that many believed that Apple offered a superior computer.

By 1996, it appeared Apple was headed for bankruptcy. Quarterly losses continued to pile up, and layoffs continued. To the surprise of most industry insiders, Steve Jobs returned to Apple in July of 1996, and by July of 1997 he was the de facto CEO. Jobs made major changes in the Apple line, focusing on consumer machines rather than high-end workstations. He introduced the G3 processor, which was vastly superior to previous models. In 1998, he brought out the iMac, which was specifically targeted for the average home computer user. Jobs return to Apple cut costs, introduced new technologies, and brought Apple back into the black. Although some of his decisions were controversial, Apple's continued health was the best indicator of his abilities.

Although Apple remains a fairly small player in the consumer computer market, the Macintosh's superior graphics and sound capabilities have given it a dominant position is several high-end markets, notably desktop publishing, high-end graphics work (such as movie special effects), and music production. The Macintosh slogan "Think Different" became a mantra for many Mac users. Macintosh consistently has one of the highest brand loyalty ratings, and hardcore Mac users (sometimes called MacEvangelists) constantly preach the superiority of the Macintosh over other computer platforms.

Although the marketing skills of Apple are often suspect, the innovative thinking at Apple is peerless in the computer industry. The Apple GUI became the standard by which all other operating systems are evaluated, and the similarities between the Apple GUI and Windows is unmistakable. Apple was the first company to offer plug-and-play expansion, allowing computer users to configure new hardware using software alone. Plug-and-play has since become an industry standard across all major operating systems. Although the handwriting recognition software of the original Apple Newton was poorly designed, it laid the groundwork for the multitude of hand-held Personal Digital Assistants (PDAs) such as the Palm Pilot. These

innovations, along with many others, will keep Apple at the forefront of personal computing for the foreseeable future.

—Geoff Peterson

FURTHER READING:

Amelio, Gil. *On the Firing Line: My 500 Days at Apple.* New York, Harper Business, 1998.

Carlton, Jim. *Apple: The Insider Story of Intrigue, Egomania, and Business Blunders.* New York, Times Books, 1997.

Levy, Steven. *Insanely Great: The Life and Times of Macintosh, the Computer that Changed Everything.* New York, Viking, 1994.

Moritz, Michael. *The Little Kingdom: The Private Story of Apple Computer.* New York, William Morrow, 1984.

Arbuckle, Fatty (1887-1933)

In the annals of film history, no celebrity better illustrates the fragility of stardom than Roscoe "Fatty" Arbuckle. In 1919, Arbuckle was one of the most successful comedians in silent film. Two years later, accused of the rape and murder of a young actress, Arbuckle instantly became a national symbol of sin. An outraged public boycotted Arbuckle films, tore down movie posters, and demanded his conviction. For Arbuckle, who was found innocent in 1922, the scandal meant the end of a career. For the movie industry, it meant the beginning of self-censorship. And for many Americans, it represented the loss of a dream: as disappointed fans quickly learned, stars were very different from the heroes they portrayed on screen.

In his movies, Arbuckle typically portrayed a bumbling yet well-meaning hero who saved the day by pie-throwing, back-flipping, and generally outwitting his opponent. In spite of his bulky, 250-pound frame, Arbuckle proved to be an able acrobat—a skill he had perfected during his days in vaudeville. Abandoned by his father at the age of 12, Arbuckle earned his living performing in small-town theaters and later, in the Pantages theater circuit. After nearly 15 years on stage, though, in 1913 Arbuckle found himself out of a job, the victim of declining public interest in vaudeville. Almost by chance, Arbuckle wandered into Mack Sennett's Keystone film studio, where he was given the nickname "Fatty" and put to work. During his three years at Keystone, Arbuckle starred in the popular *Fatty and Mabel* series with actress Mabel Normand, and gained a reputation as a slapstick comedian. By 1917, when Arbuckle left Keystone to run his own production company, Comique, under the supervision of Joseph Schenck, he had become a nationally-known star.

At Comique, Arbuckle directed some of his most acclaimed comedies: *Butcher Boy* (1917), *Out West* (1918), and *Back Stage* (1919), which starred friend and fellow comedian Buster Keaton. In 1919, lured by a million dollar a year contract, Arbuckle agreed to star in six feature films for Paramount and began an intense schedule of shooting and rehearsals. But Paramount ultimately proved to be a disappointment. Dismayed by his lack of creative control and his frenetic schedule, Arbuckle went to San Francisco for a vacation in September 1921. On September 5, Arbuckle hosted a party in his room at the St. Francis Hotel—a wild affair complete with jazz, Hollywood starlets, and bootleg gin. Four days later, one of the actresses who had been at the party, 27-year-old Virginia Rappe, died of acute peritonitis, an inflammation of the lining of the abdomen that

Fatty Arbuckle

was allegedly caused by "an extreme amount of external force." Suspicion fell on Arbuckle, who was accused of raping Virginia and causing her death. Arbuckle was charged with murder and detained in San Francisco.

Meanwhile, news of the Arbuckle scandal sent shockwaves throughout the country. Theater owners withdrew Arbuckle films, and preachers gave sermons on Arbuckle and the evils of Hollywood. Paramount suspended Arbuckle's contract, and Will Hays—the "czar" of the movie industry, who had been hired to clean up Hollywood's image in the wake of the scandal—forbade Arbuckle from acting in any films. In the eyes of the public, Arbuckle was guilty as charged. But Arbuckle's trials told a different story. After two mistrials, Arbuckle was declared innocent in March 1922. This decision, however, meant little to moviegoers, who continued to speak out against Arbuckle in spite of his acquittal. In December 1922, Hays lifted the ban on Arbuckle, but it was too late: Arbuckle's career as an actor had been ruined.

Even though strong public opinion prevented Arbuckle from appearing on screen, Arbuckle managed to find work behind the camera, and between 1925 to 1932 directed several comedies under the pseudonym William Goodrich ("Will B. Good"). By 1932, though, bitter memories of the scandal had faded, and several of Arbuckle's friends published an article in *Motion Picture* magazine

begging the public for forgiveness and demanding Arbuckle's return to the screen. Later that year, Jack Warner hired Arbuckle to star in six short films, but soon after the films were released, Arbuckle died on June 30, 1933, at the age of 46. Arbuckle, who had never recovered from the stress and shock of the scandal, spent his last years wrestling with alcoholism and depression. Although the official cause of Arbuckle's death was heart failure, Buster Keaton said that he died of a broken heart.

The Fatty Arbuckle scandal, though, was more than a personal tragedy. Motion pictures—and the concept of the movie "star"— were still new in the early 1920s, and the Arbuckle scandal gave movie fans a rude wake-up call. For the first time, Americans saw the dark side of stardom. Drunk with fame and wealth, actors could abuse their power and commit horrible crimes—indeed, as many social reformers had claimed, Hollywood might be a breeding ground for debauchery. In the face of this threat, the movie industry established a series of codes controlling the conduct of actors and the content of films, which culminated in the Production Code of the 1930s. The industry hoped to project an image of wholesomeness, but in the wake of the Arbuckle scandal, the public remained unconvinced. Although American audiences still continued to be entranced by the Hollywood "dream factory," they would never put their faith in movie stars in the way they had before 1921.

—Samantha Barbas

FURTHER READING:

Edmonds, Andy. *Frame Up!: The Untold Story of Roscoe "Fatty" Arbuckle*. New York, Morrow, 1991.

Oderman, Stuart. *Roscoe "Fatty" Arbuckle: A Biography of the Silent Film Comedian*. Jefferson, North Carolina, McFarland and Company, 1994.

Yallop, David. *The Day the Laughter Stopped: The True Story of Fatty Arbuckle*. New York, St. Martin's Press, 1976.

Young, Robert. *Roscoe "Fatty" Arbuckle: A Bio-bibliography*. Westport, Connecticut, Greenwood Press, 1994.

Archie Comics

Archie has been a highly successful teenager for close to 60 years. He began life humbly, created by cartoonist Bob Montana and writer Vic Bloom, as a backup feature for the MLJ company's *Pep Comics* #22 in the winter of 1941. At that point, *Pep Comics* was inhabited predominantly by serious heroes, such as the Shield, a superpatriot, and the Hangman, a vindictive costumed crime-fighter. The redheaded, freckled Archie Andrews, along with his two girlfriends, the blonde Betty and the brunette Veronica, and his pal Jughead, gradually became the stars of the comic book and within a few years ousted all of the heroes. MLJ, who had been publishing a string of comic books, changed its name to Archie Comics Publications early in 1946.

The public had discovered teenagers a few years earlier, and fictional youths were flourishing in all the media. There was Henry Aldrich on the radio, Andy Hardy in the movies, and Junior Miss on Broadway. The quintessential media teen of the 1940s, clean-cut and bumbling, Archie has remained true to that stereotype throughout his long run in the comics. He came upon the scene with the full requisite of essential props—two sympathetic but perplexed parents, a jalopy, a spinster school teacher in the person of Miss Grundy, and an easily exasperated principal named Mr. Weatherbee.

Archie Andrews pretty much ignored involvement with sex, drugs, and delinquency as several generations of kid readers read him and then outgrew him. His biggest appeal has probably always been not to teenagers themselves but to the millions of preteens who accept him as a valid representative of the adolescent world.

Archie quickly began to branch out. He and the gang from Riverdale High were added to the lineup of *Jackpot Comics* soon after his debut in *Pep Comics* and, in the winter of 1942, MLJ introduced *Archie Comics*. An *Archie* radio show took to the air in 1943, settling into a Saturday morning slot on NBC. The newspaper strip was started in 1946, first syndicated by McClure and then King Features. Bob Montana, returning from the service, drew the strip. In his absence, several other cartoonists had turned out the increasing amount of *Archie Comics* material. Among them were Harry Sahle, Bill Vigoda, and Al Fagaly.

Archie reached television in the late 1960s as an animated cartoon character. The first show was called simply *The Archie Show*, and that was followed by such variations as *Archie's Funhouse* and *Archie's TV Funnies*. Later attempts at a live action version of life in Riverdale did not prove successful.

Over the years there have been several dozen different comic book titles devoted exclusively to Archie and his gang. These include *Archie's Mad House, Archie's Girls, Betty and Veronica, Archie's Joke Book, Archie's Pal, Jughead, Little Archie, Archie's Christmas Stocking,* and *Archie's Double Digest.* The spin-offs have included *Josie and the Pussycats* and George Gladir's *Sabrina the Teenage Witch.* The chief Archie artist for many years was Dan DeCarlo and his associates have included Tom Moore, George Frese, and Bob Bolling.

—Ron Goulart

FURTHER READING:

Goulart, Ron. *The Comic Book Reader's Companion.* New York, HarperCollins, 1993.

Arden, Elizabeth (1878-1966)

Elizabeth Arden symbolizes exorbitance and luxury in the multibillion dollar beauty industry. Born Florence Nightingale Graham, Elizabeth Arden was a self-made woman of steely determination. She started her business on New York's Fifth Avenue in 1910. Responding to women's desires for both well-being and beauty, she offered cosmetics and treatments for home application as well as salon pamperings at her famous Red Door salons and her Maine Chance retreat. While Arden always respected the laboratory matrix of beauty treatments—offering a selection of more than 300 varieties of creams and cosmetics—Arden added essential grace notes to her products. She replaced medicinal aromas with floral scents; she created elegant, systematic packaging; and she opened luxurious and artistic treatment venues, which contrasted strongly with the hospital-like austerity of other beauty-culture clinics. In the 1960 presidential election, Jacqueline Kennedy, responding to allegations of her extravagance, retorted

that Pat Nixon shopped at Elizabeth Arden. Arden's business sold for $40 million after her death in 1966.

—Richard Martin

FURTHER READING:

Lewis, Alfred Allan, and Constance Woodworth. *Miss Elizabeth Arden: An Unretouched Portrait.* New York, Coward, McCann, and Geoghegan, 1972.

Argosy

Born as a struggling weekly for adolescents in 1882, *Argosy* became the first adult magazine to rely exclusively on fiction for its content and the first to be printed on rough, pulpwood paper. "The story is worth more than the paper it is printed on," it was once said of *Argosy,* and thus was born the "pulp magazine." Between 1896 and its demise in 1979, *Argosy* introduced or helped inspire pulp fiction writers such as Edgar Rice Burroughs, Jack London, Dashiell Hammett, H. P. Lovecraft, Raymond Chandler, E. E. "Doc" Smith, Mickey Spillane, Earl Stanley Gardner, Zane Grey, and Elmore Leonard, and helped familiarize millions of readers with the detective, science fiction, and western writing genres.

Publisher Frank Munsey arrived in New York from Maine in 1882 with $40 in his pocket. Ten months later, he helped found *Golden Argosy: Freighted with Treasures for Boys and Girls.* Among the publication's early offerings were stories by the popular self-success advocate Horatio Alger, Jr., but the diminutive weekly fared poorly in the face of overwhelming competition from like juvenile publications "of high moral tone." Munsey gradually shifted the content to more adult topics, dropping any reference to children in the magazine in 1886 and shortening the title to *Argosy* in 1888. A year later, Munsey started another publication, what would become the highly profitable *Munsey's Magazine,* and *Argosy* languished as a weak imitation.

Munsey made two critical changes to rescue *Argosy* in 1896. First, he switched to cheap, smelly, ragged-edged pulpwood paper, made from and often sporting recovered wood scraps, as a way to reduce costs. More importantly, he began publishing serial fiction exclusively, emphasizing adventure, action, mystery, and melodrama in exotic or dangerous locations. No love stories, no drawings or photographs for many years, just "hard-boiled" language and coarse, often gloomy settings that appealed to teenaged boys and men. Circulation doubled, peaking at around 500,000 in 1907.

Munsey paid only slightly more for his stories than his paper. One author recalled that $500 was the top price for serial fiction, a fraction of what authors could make at other publications. *Argosy* featured prolific serial fictionists such as Frederick Van Rensselaer Dey, the creator of the Nick Carter detective series, William MacLeod Raine, Albert Payson Terhune, Louis Joseph Vance, and Ellis Parker Butler. It also published the writings of younger, undiscovered authors such as James Branch Cabell, Charles G. D. Roberts, Susan Glaspell, Mary Roberts Rinehart, a young Upton Sinclair, and William Sydney Porter (before he became known as O. Henry). Beginning in 1910, Munsey began merging *Argosy* with a variety of weaker competitors, a practice Munsey called "cleaning up the field." The new combination featured stories by authors such as Frank Condon,

Courtney Ryley, Octavus Roy Cohen, P. G. Wodehouse, Luke Short, Van Wyck Mason, C. S. Forester, and Max Brand.

Munsey died in 1925 and ordered that his $20,000,000 magazine empire, including *Argosy,* be broken up and sold, but not before *Argosy* and the pulps had become a dominant force in American popular culture, making characters such as Tarzan, Zorro, the Shadow, Sam Spade, and the Phantom Detective household names. It was purchased by William T. Dewart, but the Depression and declining interest in pulp fiction reduced circulation to 40,000 by 1940. Renamed *New Argosy* in 1942, it was temporarily banned from the mails for "obscenity." Two months later it was sold to Popular Publications, Inc. Under the supervision of Henry Steeger, *Argosy* abandoned its all-fiction format and began featuring news and war articles. Influenced by the success of newly founded men's magazine *Esquire,* the renamed *Argosy—The Complete Men's Magazine* became a "slick," with four-color layouts, quality fiction, and adventure, sports, crime, science, and humor stories.

One of the most popular features was the "Court of Last Resort." Written by Erle Stanley Gardner, the creator of attorney Perry Mason, the "court" presented the cases of men considered unjustly convicted of crimes. The feature helped free, pardon, commute, or parole at least 15 persons. Gardner was assisted by a criminologist, lie detector expert, detective, prison psychologist, and one-time FBI investigator.

The reformulated *Argosy* succeeded for a time. As Steeger explained to *Newsweek* in 1954, "After the Second World War 15 million veterans were no longer content to accept the whimsy and phoniness of fiction." By 1953, it had a circulation of 1,250,000 and charged over $5,000 for a single full-color page advertisement. An *Argosy* editor described an average reader to *Writer* magazine in 1965 as "factory-bound, desk-bound, work-bound, forced by economics and society to abandon his innate maleness and individuality to become a cog in the corporate machine."

But more explicit competitors such as *Playboy* and *Penthouse,* a shifting sense of male identity, and the prevalence of television doomed men's magazines such as *Argosy.* Popular Publications, Inc. was dissolved in 1972 with the retirement of Henry Steeger. *Argosy* and other titles were purchased by Joel Frieman and Blazing Publications, Inc., but *Argosy* was forced to cease publication in the face of postal rate increases in 1979 even though it still had a circulation of over one million. The magazine's title resurfaced when Blazing Publications changed its name to Argosy Communications, Inc., in 1988, and Frieman has retained copyrights and republished the writings of authors such as Burroughs, John Carroll Daly, Gardner, Rex Stout, and Ray Bradbury. In addition, the spirit of pulp magazines like *Argosy* survives in the twentieth-century invention of the comic book, with fewer words and more images but still printed on cheap, pulpwood paper.

—Richard Digby-Junger

FURTHER READING:

Britt, George. *Forty Years—Forty Millions: The Career of Frank A. Munsey.* Port Washington, N.Y., Kennikat Press, 1935, 1972.

Cassiday, Bruce. "When *Argosy* Looks for Stories." *Writer.* August 1965, 25.

Moonan, Williard. "*Argosy.*" In *American Mass-Market Magazines,* edited by Alan and Barbara Nourie. Westport, Connecticut, Greenwood Press, 1990, 29-32.

Mott, Frank L. "*The Argosy.*" *A History of American Magazines.* Vol. 4. Cambridge, Harvard University Press, 1957, 417-23.

"New *Argosy* Crew." *Newsweek.* May 17, 1954, 62.

Peterson, Theodore. *Magazines in the Twentieth Century.* Urbana, University of Illinois Press, 314-16.

Popular Publications, Inc. Records, c. 1910-95. Center for the Humanities, Manuscripts and Archives Division, New York Public Library.

Server, Lee. *Danger Is My Business: An Illustrated History of the Fabulous Pulp Magazines, 1896-1953.* New York, Chronicle, 1993.

Arizona Highways

Recognized by its splashy color photographs displaying Arizona's scenic wonders, *Arizona Highways* is the best known and most widely circulated state-owned magazine. Founded in 1925 with a starting circulation of 1,000 issues, *Arizona Highways* evolved from a drab engineering pamphlet laced with ugly, black-and-white construction advertisements to a full-color, advertisement-free, photographic essay promoting Arizona. Today, with subscribers in all fifty states and 120 foreign countries, it is the state's visual ambassador and an international proselytizer of the romanticized Southwest.

Arizona Highways was one of twenty-three state-published magazines that began with the expressed purpose of promoting the construction of new and better roads. Arizona, like many Western states, saw tourism as an important economic resource, but did not have the roads necessary to take advantage of America's dependable new automobiles and increased leisure time. This good-roads movement, which swept the country during the late nineteenth and early twentieth centuries, wrested power from the railroads and helped to democratize travel. The movement reached its peak in Arizona during the 1930s when the federal government began funding large transportation projects as part of President Franklin Delano Roosevelt's larger plan to help steer the country out of the Great Depression. The New Deal brought *Arizona Highways* the road construction it requested and gave the magazine a new cause in tourism.

The Great Depression shrank advertisers' budgets, forcing several Arizona-based travel magazines to either cease publishing or transform their missions. *Arizona Highways,* which survived because it received a regular state subsidy, was then able to aggressively pursue the wide-open tourist market. In 1939, the magazine's sixth editor, Raymond Carlson, stopped selling advertising in order to improve the magazine's visual appeal and avoid competition for advertising dollars with other Arizona-based publications. Carlson, also the magazine's philosophical architect, edited the magazine from 1938 to 1971 and is given most of the credit for the magazine's success. His folksy demeanor, home-spun superlatives, and zealous use of scenic color photography transformed the magazine into Arizona's postcard to the world.

The invention of Kodachrome in 1936 significantly advanced color photography and allowed *Arizona Highways* to better exploit the state's scenic wonders. The magazine's photographically driven editorial content emphasizes the natural beauty of the Grand Canyon, saguaro cactus, desert flora, and the state's other readily recognized symbols like the monoliths of Monument Valley, made famous by many appearances in John Ford's Western films, and the Painted Desert. In December 1946, *Arizona Highways* led the nation in the use of color photography and published the first all-color issue of a nationally circulated consumer magazine. The all-color format became standard for all issues starting in January of 1986.

In the 1940s, continuing in the tradition of Charles Lummis's California-based *Land of Sunshine* magazine and the Santa Fe Railroad's turn-of-the-century advertising campaigns, *Arizona Highways* began portraying a romanticized view of Arizona's natural beauty, climate, open land, Native American cultures, and Old West history. The Anglo-American pioneers—cowboys, ranchers, miners, and military figures—were portrayed as strong and fiercely independent, Hispanics were descendants of gallant explorers and brave frontier settlers, and Native Americans represented nobility, simplicity, and freedom. In addition to these sympathetic and sentimental portrayals, the magazine included the masterpieces of Western artists Ted DeGrazia, Frederic Remington, and Lon Megargee; the writing of Joseph Wood Krutch, Frank Waters, and Tony Hillerman; the photography of Ansel Adams, Joseph and David Muench, and Barry Goldwater; the architecture of Frank Lloyd Wright, Mary Colter, and Paolo Soleri; and the creations of Native American artists Fred Kabotie, Harrison Begay, and Allan Houser.

Undoubtedly the magazine's romanticization of the Southwest also benefited from the popularity of Western films, television and radio network programs, and pulp fiction. In fact, the mass media's portrayal of the West blurred the distinction between the mythic West and the real West in the American mind. Carlson's agrarian philosophy worked well with this blurred West because it enabled the increasingly industrial nation to, in the words of historian Gerald Nash, "escape from this new civilization, even while partaking of its material and other benefits and comforts." Although many readers do visit Arizona, much of the magazine's appeal outside the state is the reassurance it gives readers that the West—a place of opportunity and open land—still exists. The magazine's cultural influence as a symbol of this American identity was so powerful in 1965, during the height of the Cold War, that *Arizona Highways* was labeled subversive literature by the Soviet Union and banned there because it was "clearly intended to conduct hostile propaganda among the Soviet people."

The magazine's circulation reached a high of over 600,000 in the 1970s, but increased subscription rates (brought on by higher labor, postage, and paper costs) and competition from other magazines caused the circulation to drop to nearly 400,000 by the late 1990s. Even so, *Arizona Highways* has become a self-supporting operation that no longer requires state appropriations. The magazine accomplished this by marketing related products—books, calendars, cards, maps, and clothing—through bi-annual catalogs which account for approximately 40 percent of total revenue. To remain competitive and increase circulation, *Arizona Highways* maintains a delicate balance between satisfying the editorial appetites of its current subscribers, most of whom are over sixty, while pursuing a new generation of younger readers through more active magazine departments and the internet.

—Brad Melton

FURTHER READING:

Farrell, Robert J. *Arizona Highways: The People Who Shaped a Southwestern Magazine, 1925 to 1990.* Master's thesis, Prescott, Arizona, Prescott College, 1997.

Nash, Gerald D. "The West as Utopia and Myth, 1890-1990." In *Creating the West: Historical Interpretations, 1890-1990.* Albuquerque, University of New Mexico Press, 1990, 197-257.

Pomeroy, Earl. *In Search of the Golden West: The Tourist in Western America.* New York, Knopf, 1957.

Topping, Gary. "Arizona Highways: A Half-Century of Southwestern Journalism." *Journal of the West.* April 1980, 71-80.

Arledge, Roone (1931—)

Visionary producer Roone Arledge was instrumental in transforming network-televised sports and news into profitable ventures. Joining *ABC Sports* in 1960, he revolutionized broadcasts with his use of instant replay and slow motion, and his humanistic production sense brought the shows *Wide World of Sports, Monday Night Football,* and announcer Howard Cosell to national consciousness. A widely acclaimed and award winning broadcast of the terrorized 1972 Munich Olympics stirred wider ambitions, and in 1976 Arledge became president of *ABC News.* He soon pioneered ratings-savvy breakthroughs such as *Nightline* (1980) and the first television news magazine, *20/20* (1978). News, however, soon moved from being merely profitable to being profit-driven. Arledge was swallowed by the corporate establishment. Ted Turner's 24-hour *Cable News Network (CNN)* became the standard for network news coverage, and soon ABC was bought by Capital Cities Inc., which also owns the successful 24-hour sports network *ESPN.* Arledge stepped down in 1998.

—C. Kenyon Silvey

FURTHER READING:

Gunther, Marc. *The House That Roone Built.* New York, Little, Brown, 1994.

Powers, Ron. *Supertube: The Rise Of Television Sports.* New York, Coward-McCann, 1984.

Armani, Giorgio (1934—)

Milanese fashion designer Giorgio Armani did for menswear in 1974 what Chanel did sixty years before for women's tailoring: he dramatically softened menswear tailoring, eliminating stuffing and rigidity. The power of Armani styling comes from a non-traditional masculinity of soft silhouettes and earth colors in slack elegance. His 1980s "power suit" (padded shoulders, dropped lapels, two buttons, wide trousers, and low closure) and its 1990s successor (natural shoulders, three buttons, high closure, narrow trousers, and extended jacket length) defined prestige menswear. Armani is the first fashion designer to focus primarily on menswear, though he has designed womenswear since 1975. In the 1990s, Armani remained chiefly identified with expensive suits but produced numerous lines. Armani's popularity in America can be traced to Richard Gere's wardrobe in *American Gigolo* (1980).

—Richard Martin

FURTHER READING:

Martin, Richard and Harold Koda. *Giorgio Armani: Images of Man.* New York, Rizzoli, 1990.

Armed Forces Radio Service

During World War II American radio made three key contributions to the war effort: news broadcasts supporting U.S. involvement in the war, propaganda beamed at Nazi-occupied Europe, and entertainment and news broadcasts to American troops around the world via the Armed Forces Radio Service (AFRS). Since 1930, the airwaves had been dominated by the entertainment-oriented programming of the three major American networks, CBS, ABC, and NBC. With the AFRS a new type of network emerged, one historian Erik Barnouw describes as "global and without precedent."

In the pre-television era radio was considered such an integral part of American life that a concentrated effort was made to continue providing it to American troops in both the European and the Pacific theatres. Thus the Armed Forces Radio Service was born and commenced broadcasting in the first years of America's intervention in World War II. At the beginning of 1943 AFRS had 21 outlets, but by the end of the same year that number had grown to over 300. It was heard in 47 countries, and every week each outlet received over 40 hours of recorded programming by plane from the United States; additional material (such as news, sports, and special events coverage) was relayed by short-wave. (The very first programs for troops had actually gone out direct by short-wave in 1942 when AFRS began broadcasting on a limited scale). First leasing time on foreign (and mostly government run) stations, AFRS programming moved into high gear with the creation of its own "American expeditionary stations," the first set-up in Casablanca in March of 1943, with stations in Oran, Tunis, Sicily, and Naples soon following. By 1945 over 800 outlets were getting the weekly shipments of AFRS programs.

The nerve center of Armed Forces Radio was at 6011 Santa Monica Boulevard in Los Angeles. Its uniformed staff included Army and Navy personnel as well as civilians. Its commandant, Colonel Thomas H. A. Lewis, had been vice-president of a Hollywood advertising agency, and was also married to actress Loretta Young, a combination which assured AFRS access to major Hollywood talent. Also on the staff were Sergeants Jerome Lawrence and Robert E. Lee, who would later co-write *Auntie Mame, Inherit the Wind,* and other Broadway successes.

Ultimately the AFRS produced forty-three programs (14 hours) itself, and aired another thirty-six hours of U.S. network radio shows with all commercials deleted. The exorcising of commercial advertising was a particular AFRS innovation. Historian Susan Smulyan writes in *Selling Radio*: "The radio industry had worked since the 1920s to make broadcast advertising seem natural and reassuringly 'American,' but the stark contrast between wartime realities and radio merchandising appeals revealed that advertising was neither wholly accepted yet nor considered particularly patriotic." While dependent on the major networks for its most popular programs, the AFRS nonetheless still deleted all commercial references and advertising from its broadcasts. Programs such as the "Camel Caravan" became "Comedy Caravan," and the "Chase and Sanborn Hour" became simply "Charlie McCarthy."

A technical innovation pioneered by the AFRS was pre-recorded programming. During its early history radio had prided itself on its live broadcasts and shied away from developing recorded shows. But the ability to pre-record had obvious advantages, among them the capacity to select the best performances and "takes," and to delete controversial and time-sensitive material. Recorded shows were also cheaper to produce and gave everyone involved a flexibility and control impossible in live broadcasting.

Because recording tape had not yet been developed, the process involved the manipulation of a series of vinyl and glass discs similar to very large 78 rpm records. The final vinylite discs (which were the copies of the shows then shipped around the world) were pressed from a master disc which in turn had been edited from two duplicate glass disc copies of shows recorded off of live network radio. As Barnouw comments: "The process involved new techniques" requiring considerable skill on the part of the engineer/editor since it necessitated "dropping a playing needle into the right spot on the right groove at the right moment. Editing-on-disc, scarcely tried before the war, became a highly developed specialty at AFRS."

The AFRS show "Command Performance" was the first to be pre-recorded, and it proved that the technology existed to edit programs and re-broadcast them from disc copies. Smulyan speculated that it may have been Bing Crosby's experience on "Command Performance" that motivated him to demand a transcription clause in his 1946 contact with ABC, enabling him to record his shows in Los Angeles and ship them to ABC in New York for later broadcasting. In the late 1940s and early 1950s the phrase "Brought to you by transcription" became a familiar tag line at the conclusion of many network radio shows, the by-then standard procedure having been developed and perfected by AFRS. To this day some of the large and unwieldy 16-inch vinylite transcription discs from the World War II Armed Forces Radio Service occasionally turn up in the flea markets of southern California.

Today called Armed Forces Radio and Television Service, the AFRS continued to air pre-recorded radio shows in years following World War II. But by the early 1960s conventional radio had changed with the times, and the AFRS changed as well, both now emphasing recorded popular music of the day aired by disc-jockey personalities. The story of one of the more off-beat army DJs, Adrian Cronauer, and his controversial AFRS programming in Southeast Asia during the Vietnam conflict is portrayed in the 1987 film *Good Morning Vietnam.*

—Ross Care

FURTHER READING:

Barnouw, Erik. *The Golden Web: A History of Broadcasting in the United States, 1933-1953.* New York, Oxford University Press, 1968.

Smulyan, Susan. *Selling Radio: The Commercialization of American Broadcasting, 1920-1934.* Washington, D.C., Smithsonian Institution Press, 1994.

Armory Show

In 1913, the International Exhibition of Modern Art of 1913, popularly known as the Armory Show, brought modern art to America. The most highly publicized American cultural event of all time,

ENCYCLOPEDIA OF POPULAR CULTURE

the exhibition changed the face of art in the United States. As the media rained scorn, derision, fear, praise, hope, and simple curiosity on the Armory Show, the American public looked on modernism for the first time and went home to think about what they had seen. America would never be the same.

In 1911, sixteen young New York artists who had studied in Europe formed the Association of American Painters and Sculptors (AAPS). Their goal was to challenge the stranglehold of such mainstream art organizations as the National Academy of Design, a conservative group who held the first and last word on American art and American taste. Having been exposed to the avant-garde art being produced in Europe by the Impressionists, the Post-Impressionists, the Fauves, the Expressionists, the Cubists, and the Futurists, the members of the AAPS were fed up with the stodginess of the American art world. They hoped to foment artistic revolution, and their means of accomplishing this was to show the New York art world what modern art was all about.

To this end, they conceived the idea of putting on an exhibit of modern art and decided to rent out the 69th Regimental Headquarters of the New York National Guard, an armory built in case of worker unrest. They brought in some 1,300 pieces of art, arranged chronologically, beginning with a miniature by Goya, two small drawings by Ingres, and a Delacroix. But these were sedate compared to the Cézannes, Van Goghs, Picassos, Matisses, and Duchamps, which would spark public outcry when the show opened.

Indeed, the show succeeded beyond the wildest dreams of its organizers. As Robert Hughes has written in *American Visions: The Epic History of Art in America,* "No single exhibition before or since has had such a traumatic, stimulating, and disorienting effect on American art and its public. It shook the bag, reshuffled the deck, and changed the visual culture in ways that its American organizers could not have been expected to predict."

When the Armory Show opened on February 17, 1913, four thousand people lined up to get in. There was a media frenzy in which the exhibit was both decried as "the harbinger of universal anarchy" as well as praised for turning the New York art world on its ear and drawing record crowds for a cultural event. The detractors focused mainly on Matisse and the Cubists. Marcel Duchamps' *Nude Descending a Staircase* drew particular umbrage. As Hughes has written, "It became the star freak of the Armory Show—its bearded lady, its dog-faced boy. People compared it to an explosion in a shingle factory, an earthquake on the subway. . . . As a picture, *Nude Descending a Staircase* is neither poor nor great. . . . Its fame today is the fossil of the huge notoriety it acquired as a puzzle picture in 1913. It is, quite literally, famous for being famous—an icon of a now desiccated scandal. It is lodged in history because it embodied the belief that the new work of art, the revolutionary work of art, has to be scorned and stoned like a prophet by the uncomprehending crowd."

The Armory Show shook the New York, and thus the American, art world to its very foundation. Some saw modern art as pathological and deranged and resolutely held out against change. But for many, particularly young artists and collectors who had not seen anything other than academic European art, it opened their eyes to the possibilities of the modern. Many cite the Armory Show as the beginning of the Modern Age in America. After a six-week run in New York, the show traveled to Chicago and Boston. In total, about three hundred thousand people bought tickets to the show, three hundred thousand

people who then slowly began to turn their sights toward Europe, toward modernism, and toward the inevitable change that would transform popular culture in America during the twentieth century.

—Victoria Price

FURTHER READING:

Brown, M.W. *The Story of the Armory Show.* New York, The Hirshhorn Foundation, 1963.

Hughes, Robert. *American Visions: The Epic History of Art in America.* New York, Alfred A. Knopf, 1997.

Armstrong, Henry (1912-1988)

One of the best boxers in the history of the ring, Henry Armstrong was the first fighter to hold world titles in three weight classes simultaneously. Born Henry Jackson in Columbus, Mississippi, Armstrong began fighting in 1929. Eight years later he won the world featherweight title from Petey Sarron. A year later he won the lightweight and welterweight titles. Also known as "Hammerin' Hank" because of his many knockouts, Armstrong was considered one of the best fighters in the world during this period. He successfully defended his welterweight title 19 times (still a record) and is fourth on the list for consecutive defenses of a title. After he retired in 1945

Henry Armstrong

he was inducted into the International Boxing Hall of Fame. His career included 150 wins (100 KOs), 21 losses, and 9 draws.

—Lloyd Chiasson, Jr.

FURTHER READING:

Andre, Sam, and Nat Fleischer. *A Pictorial History of Boxing.* New York, Random House, 1975.

Heller, Peter. *In This Corner: Former World Champions Tell Their Stories.* New York, Simon and Schuster, 1973.

Armstrong, Louis (1901-1971)

Daniel Louis Armstrong—trumpeter and singer—was one of the most important musicians in jazz and in twentieth-century music, achieving seemingly insurmountable odds given his humble origins. Armstrong proved himself as the first vital jazz soloist and one of jazz's most creative innovators, winning worldwide appeal and achieving commercial success. Armstrong helped to transform the traditional New Orleans jazz style—based on collective improvisation—to jazz featuring a star solo, thereby elevating jazz to a sophisticated form of music. Clearly a versatile musician, he was an active participant in a number of jazz styles, including the New Orleans style of the 1910s, the Chicago style of the 1920s, the New York style in the 1930s, and the jazz of the wider world in the 1950s. Armstrong was one of the first blacks seen in feature-length films; in total he appeared in nearly 50. In addition to a sponsored radio show, the United States State Department and private organizations sponsored international tours of his music and performances, earning him the nickname ''Ambassador Satch.''

For many years, July 4, 1900 was cited as Armstrong's birth date, but the discovery of his baptismal records confirm that his real birth date was August 4, 1901. His birthplace of New Orleans was a haven for all kinds of music, from French Opera to the blues. He grew up in the ''Back o' Town'' section near the red-light district, and therefore heard and absorbed the rags, marches, and blues that were the precursors to early jazz. Because his family was so impoverished—he barely had enough to eat and wore rags as a child—Armstrong often sang on the street as a kid. His father, a laborer, abandoned the family when he was young and his mother was, at best, an irresponsible single parent who left the young Armstrong and his sister in the care of relatives. In addition to singing on the streets, Armstrong sang in a Barbershop quartet, providing an excellent opportunity for him to train his ear.

Louis Armstrong

As a teenager, Armstrong found himself in trouble for general delinquency and had to spend more than two years at the Home for Colored Waifs. He eventually found an outlet in the school band, first taking up the tambourine and later the cornet under his teacher Peter Davis. Armstrong mastered the school's repertoire of marches and rags, and eventually became the leader of the Home's brass band that frequently played for picnics and parades. Upon his release, Armstrong decided that he wanted to become a musician. Not owning a horn did not deter him. He played his first job at a honky-tonk in Storyville's red-light district; he used a borrowed horn and performed blues and other songs from his limited repertoire. When not playing his regular job, Armstrong would frequent clubs and listen to various musicians playing the blues.

Cornetist and bandleader Joe "King" Oliver was impressed with Armstrong and took him under his wing. When Oliver left for Chicago in 1918, Armstrong took his place as cornetist in the band led by Kid Ory. In the same year, he married a prostitute, but the relationship soon ending in divorce. He continued to work in clubs with established bands, and on the side formed his own group. Pianist and bandleader Fate Marable then hired Armstrong to work on the riverboats, and the job provided him with the opportunity to improve his musicianship. During this period, a melophone player named David Jones taught Armstrong to read music. By 1922, he was invited to join King Oliver as second cornetist in Chicago at the Lincoln Gardens. The Oliver job showcased the young Armstrong's prowess as a virtuoso improvisor who would "swing" at the slightest provocation. In 1924, Armstrong married pianist Lil Hardin and, upon her insistence, moved to New York where he joined the Fletcher Henderson Orchestra. His solos and improvisation drew the attention of New York musicians, but by 1925 he returned to Chicago where he joined the Erskine Tate "symphonic jazz" Orchestra and, subsequently, Carroll Dickerson's Orchestra. He was now billed as "Louis Armstrong, world's greatest trumpet player." With his popularity soaring, in 1929 Armstrong joined the hit show *Hot Chocolates*, where he sang "Ain't Misbehavin'." Significantly, Armstrong had become a sensation appreciated by both black and white audiences. It was a pivotal point in his career.

Armstrong could have easily chosen to pursue a career leading a jazz group, but instead, he opted for broadening his commercial appeal by singing popular tunes and becoming a showman. His decision was, perhaps, influenced by his childhood, but managers Tommy Rockwell and Joe Glaser also played an important role in the direction of his career. Many critics assert that Armstrong's musical legacy stopped in the year 1936, when, as the noted jazz critic Leonard Feather observed: "The greater his impact on the public, the less important were his musical settings and the less durable his musical contributions."

In 1925, Armstrong began to record under the name Louis Armstrong and His Hot Five. These recordings, which can be placed into four categories, had a profound influence on jazz, and are regarded as one of the most momentous recordings in the music of the twentieth century. The first category of the Hot Five recordings are in the New Orleans style, but Armstrong's scatting on "Heebie Jeebies" set a precedent for the scat style of singing. The second category was recorded with the enlargement of the quintet to include a tuba and drums, issued under the name of Louis Armstrong and His Hot Seven; "Potato Head Blues" is considered stellar in this group. The third category consisted of the group returning to the original Hot Five band with the extraordinary "Struttin' with some Barbecue," and the highly regarded "Hotter than that." The fourth category

included Earl Hines as pianist. The recordings in this category are considered by many critics as Armstrong's greatest. Including gems such as "Weather Bird," "West End Blues," and "Don't Jive Me," they were made in 1928 and reflect Armstrong's break with the New Orleans style. Hines possessed a facile technique and an inventive mind, the result of which were improvisations where the right hand of the piano mimicked the trumpet in octaves; the trademark gave rise to the term "trumpet style" piano. Armstrong and Hines complimented each other, feeding, inspiring, and spurring one another to create sheer musical excellence.

Armstrong's big band group of recordings represent him as a bandleader, solo variety attraction, and jester. In this format, he largely abandoned the jazz repertoire in favor of popular songs vis à vis the blues and original compositions. A majority of the bands he fronted, including Luis Russell and Les Hite, fell short of his musical genius.

Armstrong signaled his return to the New Orleans style with the All Stars in 1947. The sextet made their debut in August 1947 after his appearance in the mediocre film *New Orleans*. The music was superb and seemed to placate the critics. The All Stars featured trombonist Jack Teagarden, clarinetist Barney Bigard, pianist Dick Cary, drummer Sid Catlett, and bassist Arvell Shaw, although the group's personnel continually changed. This smaller group was an instant success and became the permanent format that Armstrong guided until his death; together they recorded the highly acclaimed *Autobiography* sessions.

As early as 1932 Armstrong toured Europe, playing at the London Palladium. This was the first of many trips taken for concerts and television appearances. The transformation from musician to entertainer had taken full effect. "You Rascal You," among other novelty songs, were audience favorites. Ella Fitzgerald, Oscar Peterson, and the Dukes of Dixieland were among the diverse stylists who recorded with Armstrong.

The excruciating touring demands that began in the 1930s would eventually take their toll on Armstrong. He had already experienced intermittent problems with his health and shortly after playing a date with the All Stars at the Waldorf Astoria in New York, Armstrong suffered a heart attack. He remained in intensive care for more than a month and returned home, where he died in his sleep on May 6, 1971.

A musical legend, Armstrong's style was characterized by a terminal vibrato, an exceptional ability to swing playing notes around the beat, and an uncanny appreciation for pauses and stops which showcased his virtuoso technique. He used dramatic devices to capture the attention of audiences, including sliding or ripping into notes, either ending a phrase or tune on a high note. His ebullient personality showed through his music, and his style was dictated by a savoir faire that was embraced by his fans throughout the world.

—Willie Collins

FURTHER READING:

Armstrong, Louis; edited by Thomas Brothers. *Louis Armstrong, In His Own Words: Selected Writings*. New York, Oxford University Press, 1999.

———. *Satchmo: My Life in New Orleans*. New York, Prentice-Hall, 1954.

Berrett, Joshua, editor. *The Louis Armstrong Companion: Eight Decades of Commentary*. New York, Schirmer Books, 1999.

Boujut, Michel. *Louis Armstrong*. New York, Rizzoli, 1998.

Chilton, John, and Max Jones. *Louis: The Louis Armstrong Story 1900-1971.* Boston, Little, Brown and Company. 1971.

Giddins, Gary. *Satchmo.* New York, Anchor Books, 1992.

Army-McCarthy Hearings

In the 1950s Joseph McCarthy, a Republican senator from Appleton, Wisconsin, waged a years-long battle against subversive conduct in the United States and against the Communists whom he believed to be hiding in all walks of American life—particularly in government, Hollywood, and academia. McCarthy's unsubstantiated claims led to upheaval, the destruction of careers, and to a concentrated attack on the freedoms guaranteed to Americans in the First Amendment of the Constitution. Despite attempts by conservative scholars to reinstate McCarthy's tarnished reputation, no one has proved that he ever identified an actual subversive. Nowhere were his bullying tactics more obvious than when he accused the United States Army of harboring Communists. The hearings on these activities and McCarthy's belligerent behavior were broadcast on network television in 1957.

Specifically, McCarthy targeted an army dentist who was in the process of being voluntarily discharged due to the illness of his wife and daughter. Irving Peress, who had been drafted under the McCarthy-supported Doctors and Dentists Draft Act, had checked "Federal Constitutional Privilege" instead of "Yes" or "No" when he signed the required Loyalty Oath. This was all that McCarthy needed to launch an attack against the dentist and the United States Army.

In a broader sense, McCarthy was responding to information in a letter that was later proved to be false. The letter named 34 scientists, engineers, and technicians at Fort Monmouth as subversives. In his history of the hearings, John G. Adams, a major player in the debacle and lawyer for the army, maintains that McCarthy was mad at the army for refusing to give special treatment to David Schine, a wealthy member of McCarthy's staff who had been drafted. At any rate, 26 of the 34 accused subversives were cleared by a loyalty board, and the other eight convictions were ultimately overturned by the courts. The Loyalty Board, made up of high-ranking officers and well-respected civilians, quickly became the target of McCarthy's ire. He demanded the right to question them. The army, determined to protect the Board's identity and its own reputation, refused. While President Dwight Eisenhower had been elected on the wave of anti-Communism fueled by McCarthy, the two were poles apart ideologically. When McCarthy went after the army, Eisenhower refused to remain on the sidelines.

Backed by the White House, the army belatedly stood up to McCarthy and refused to offer their officers as lambs to McCarthy's slaughter. Robert T. Stevens, Secretary of the Army, issued a press release stating that he had advised Brigadier General Ralph W. Zwicker of Camp Kilmer not to appear before the senator's committee. As part of the attack on the army, McCarthy, with his typical outrageousness, had accused Zwicker of being unfit to wear the army uniform and of having the brains of a five year-old, and he demanded his immediate dismissal. McCarthy ignored the fact that it was Zwicker who reported the allegedly subversive Peress. When a transcript from the closed hearings was leaked to the press and published by the *New York Times,* McCarthy's supporters—including several prestigious newspapers—began to back away.

Eisenhower used the diary of army lawyer John G. Adams to illuminate the extent of McCarthy's out-of-control behavior, including the fact that Roy Cohn, McCarthy's committee counsel, was being subsidized by the wealthy Schine. Reporter Joseph Alsop, who had secretly seen the diary in its entirety before it was commandeered by the White House, joined his brother in releasing additional information indicating that McCarthy was very much under the influence of Cohn, who had promised to end the attack on the army if Schine were given the requested special treatment. McCarthy then counterattacked, providing additional information to challenge the integrity of the army.

McCarthy's nemesis proved to be Joseph Nye, Chief Counsel for the army. With admirable skill, Nye led McCarthy into exhibiting his true arrogance and vindictiveness. Beforehand, McCarthy had agreed not to attack Fred Fisher, a young lawyer who had withdrawn from working with Nye on the case because he had once belonged to a Communist-front group known as the "Lawyer's Guild." When McCarthy reneged, Nye counterattacked: "Little did I dream you could be so reckless and so cruel as to do an injury to that lad . . . Let us not assassinate this lad further, Senator. You have done enough. Have you no sense of decency, sir, at long last? Have you left no sense of decency?"

It was a fitting epitaph for the horror that was the political career of Senator Joseph McCarthy. His lack of decency was evident, and he was subsequently censured by the United States Senate. In 1998, Godfrey Sperling, a reporter who dogged McCarthy's footsteps during the 1950s, responded to the newly developed efforts to reinstate McCarthy's reputation: "The Joe McCarthy I covered was a man who, at best, had overreached his capacity, he simply wasn't all that bright. At worst, he was a shifty politician who didn't mind using lies or guesses to try to destroy others." While the individuals attacked by McCarthy were often weak, the institution of the United States Army was not—it survived his attacks. Yet the Army-McCarthy hearings demonstrated the dangers inherent in politicians with too much power, too few controls, and the ability to manipulate a gullible public.

—Elizabeth Purdy

FURTHER READING:

Adams, John G. *Without Precedent: The Story of the Death of McCarthyism.* New York and London, W.W. Norton and Company, 1983.

Merry, Robert W. "McCarthyism's Self-Destruction." *Congressional Quarterly.* Vol. 54, No. 11, 1995, 923-26.

Sperling, Godfrey. "It's Wrong to Rehabilitate McCarthy—Even if He Was Right." *Christian Science Monitor.* November 17, 1998, 9.

Wannal, Ray. "The Red Road to McCarthyism." *Human Events.* Vol. 52, No. 5, 1996, 5-7.

Arnaz, Desi (1917-1986)

A famed Afro-Cuban music band leader and minor movie star, Desi Arnaz rose from nightclub performer to television magnate during the golden years of black-and-white television. Born Desiderio Alberto Arnaz y de Acha III on March 2, 1917, in Santiago, Cuba, to a

Lucille Ball and Desi Arnaz.

wealthy family. Arnaz accompanied his father into political exile in Miami when the family's fortune was destroyed and his father became persona non grata under the Fulgencia Batista regime. At the age of seventeen, Arnaz's musical talent was discovered by renowned band leader Xavier Cugat, and by 1937 he was leading his own band in Miami Beach. Arnaz began to make a name for himself as a band leader, drummer, and singer in New York City and Miami Beach nightclubs when Afro-Cuban music was making its first and largest impact on American popular music of the late 1930s and early 1940s.

It was in 1940 that he married the love of his life, Lucille Ball, who would later be cast as his on-screen wife in *I Love Lucy.* Ball had served as his co-star in the movie *Too Many Girls,* which was Arnaz's screen debut; the movie was the screen version of the Lorenz Hart and Richard Rogers Broadway hit of the same name, in which Arnaz had made his stage acting debut. His skyrocketing career was temporarily delayed by service in the Army during World War II. When he returned to Hollywood after his discharge from the service, Arnaz found that his heavy accent and Hispanic looks not only limited his opportunities but kept him type cast.

It was Arnaz's particular genius that converted the typecasting into an asset, and he was able to construct a television persona based not only on a comic version of the Latin Lover, but also on his success as a singer and rumba band leader. Mass popularity was finally achieved when, in 1952, Arnaz became the first Hispanic star on television with his pioneering what became the longest running sitcom in history: *I Love Lucy.* Eventually lasting nine years, Arnaz and Lucille Ball modified the Latin Lover and Dumb Blonde stereotypes to capture the attention of television audiences, who were also engaged by the slightly titillating undercurrent of a mixed marriage between an Anglo and an Hispanic who played and sang Afro-Cuban music, while banging on an African-derived conga drum and backed up by musicians of mixed racial features. The formula of pairing a Wasp and a minority or outcast has since been duplicated repeatedly on television to this date through such programs as *Chico and the Man, Who's the Boss?,* and *The Nanny,* and others.

His business acumen had already been revealed when in 1948 he and Ball founded Desilu Productions to consolidate their various stage, screen, and radio activities. Under Arnaz's direction Desilu

Productions grew into a major television studio. In 1960, Arnaz and Ball divorced; their son and daughter followed in their parents' acting footsteps, but never achieved the success of their parents. Included among Desi Arnaz's films are *Too Many Girls* (1940), *Father Takes a Wife* (1941), *The Navy Comes Through* (1942), *Bataan* (1943), *Cuban Pete* (1946), *Holiday in Havana* (1949), *The Long Trailer* (1954), and *Forever Darling* (1956). *I Love Lucy* can still be seen in black-and-white re-runs in many parts of the United States. In 1976, Arnaz published his own rather picaresque and acerbic autobiography, *A Book,* detailing his rise to fame and riches and proclaiming his undying love for Lucille Ball. Arnaz died on December 2, 1986.

—Nicolás Kanellos

FURTHER READING:

Kanellos, Nicolás. *The Hispanic American Almanac.* Detroit, Gale Research, 1997.

Pérez-Firmat, Gustavo. *Life on the Hyphen: The Cuban American Way.* Austin, University of Texas Press, 1993.

Tardiff, Joseph T., and L. Mpho Mabunda, editors. *Dictionary of Hispanic Biography.* Detroit, Gale Research, 1996.

Arrow Collar Man

The advertising icon of the Cluett, Peabody & Company's line of Arrow shirts from 1905 to 1930 was the era's symbol for the ideal athletic, austere, confident American man. He was the somewhat eroticized male counterpart to Charles Dana Gibson's equally emblematic and elegant all-American woman. No less a cultural spokesman than Theodore Roosevelt considered him to be a superb portrait of "the common man," although admittedly an Anglo-Saxon version of it that suited the times. This Arrow Collar Man was the inspiration of J(oseph) C(hristian) Leyendecker (1874-1951), the foremost American magazine illustrator of the first four decades of the twentieth century.

Born in Germany but emigrating at age eight with his parents, Leyendecker was trained at the Art Institute of Chicago and in Paris. He worked on advertising campaigns for Kuppenheimer suits as well as other products and did cover art for *Collier's* and the *Saturday Evening Post.* In that last role, he was the direct predecessor and a major influence on a near-contemporary illustrator, Norman Rockwell, who idolized his work.

The Arrow Man ads sold more than 400 styles of detachable shirt collars with images of an insouciant, aquiline-nosed young man, often depicted in vigorous stances or with the jaunty prop of a pipe. Leyendecker's figures were characterized by their glistening, polished appearance, indicating a healthy athletic glow. After World War I, when soldiers learned the practicality of attached collars, Leyendecker switched to doing ads for Arrow's new line of shirts.

The generic Arrow Collar Man received more fan mail in the 1920s (sent to corporate headquarters) than Rudolph Valentino or any other male film star of the era. In 1920, approximately seventeen thousand love letters arrived a week, and there was a Broadway play about him as well as a surfeit of popular songs and poems.

Leyendecker sometimes used future film stars such as John Barrymore, Fredric March, Brian Donlevy, Jack Mulhall, and his good friend Neil Hamilton as models. A perfectionist in his craft, Leyendecker always preferred to work from live figures rather than

from photographs, as Rockwell and others sometimes did. But the illustrator's first, most important, and enduring muse for the Arrow ads was Charles Beach. After a meeting in 1901, Beach became Leyendecker's companion, housemate, and business manager for close to fifty years, a personal and professional relationship ended only by Leyendecker's death at his estate in New Rochelle, New York.

The Arrow contract, as well as those with other clothiers, ended soon after the onset of the Great Depression. The image of the ruddy-complexioned, sophisticated young man, however, did not soon fade in the popular mind. A teasing ad in the *Saturday Evening Post* on February 18, 1939, queried, "Whatever Became of the 'Arrow Collar Man'?. . . Though he passed from our advertising some years ago, he is still very much with us. . . . [Today's man dressed in an Arrow shirt] is just as much an embodiment of smartness as that gleaming Adonis was in his heyday."

Perhaps his era had passed, for the Arrow Man had reflected the education, position, breeding, and even ennui that figured so prominently in the novels of F. Scott Fitzgerald during the previous decade. Leyendecker continued with his magazine illustrations, but a change in the editorial board at the *Saturday Evening Post* in the late 1930s resulted in his gradual fall from grace. Leyendecker's last cover for that publication appeared on January 2, 1943. The mantle then rested permanently upon Norman Rockwell, who fittingly served as one of the pallbearers at Leyendecker's funeral fewer than ten years later.

—Frederick J. Augustyn, Jr.

FURTHER READING:

Rockwell, Norman. *Norman Rockwell: My Adventures as an Illustrator.* New York, Curtis Publishing, 1979.

Schau, Michael. *J. C. Leyendecker.* New York, Watson-Guptill Publications, 1974.

Arthur, Bea (1923—)

With her tall, rangy frame and distinctive, husky voice, actress Bea Arthur has never been anyone's idea of a starlet. However, using her dry humor and impeccable comic timing coupled with an exceptional comfort with her body, she has created some of the most memorable strong female characters on television, in film, and on the musical stage.

Arthur was born Bernice Frankel in New York City and grew up, the daughter of department store owners, in Cambridge, Massachusetts. Her first attempts on the stage as a torch singer failed when, as she said, "Audiences laughed when I sang about throwing myself in the river because my man got away." Her imposing height and deep voice suited her better for comedy, she decided, and she honed her skills doing sketch comedy at resorts in the Poconos. In 1954 she got her first big break when she landed a role off-Broadway playing opposite Lotte Lenya in *The Threepenny Opera.* Audiences loved her, and throughout her career she has looked back fondly on the role that started her successful career: "Of everything I've done, that was the most meaningful. Which is like the first time I felt, I'm here, I can do it."

Arthur continued to "do it," wowing audiences with her comedic skill as well as song and dance. She originated the role of Yente the matchmaker in *Fiddler on the Roof* on Broadway, and she won a

Bea Arthur

Tony playing Angela Lansbury's "bosom buddy" Vera Charles in *Mame.* She reprised the role in the film version (1974), this time opposite comedy legend Lucille Ball. Her other films include *Lovers and Other Strangers* (1970) and *The Floating Lightbulb.*

But it is on television that Arthur has created her most enduring characters. In the early 1970s, she guest-starred on Norman Lear's groundbreaking situation comedy *All in the Family,* playing Edith's abrasively opinionated cousin, Maude. Maude was so popular with viewers that she was spun off into her own Lear series. Finding a welcoming groove in the early years of women's liberation, *Maude* remained on the air for a six-year run, winning an Emmy for Arthur for her portrayal of a strong woman who took no guff from anyone. Tired of the "yes, dear" stereotype of sitcom wives, 1970s audiences welcomed a woman who spoke her mind, felt deeply, and did not look like a young model. In her fifties, Arthur, with her graying hair, big body, and gravelly voice, was the perfect embodiment for the no-nonsense, middle-aged woman, genuine and believable, as she dealt with the controversial issues the show brought up. Even hot potato issues were tackled head-on, such as when an unexpected midlife pregnancy forces Maude to have an abortion, a move that more modern situation comedies were too timid to repeat.

After *Maude,* Arthur made an unsuccessful sitcom attempt with the dismal *Amanda's,* which only lasted ten episodes, but in 1985, she struck another cultural nerve with the hit *Golden Girls.* An ensemble piece grouping Arthur with Estelle Getty, Rue McClanahan (a co-star from *Maude*), and Betty White, *Golden Girls* was an extremely successful situation comedy about the adventures of a household of older women. The show had a long first run and widely syndicated reruns. All of the stars won Emmys, including two for Arthur, who played Dorothy Sbornak, a divorcee who cares for her elderly mother (Getty).

Arthur, herself divorced in the 1970s after thirty years of marriage, has brought her own experiences to the characters that she has added to the American lexicon. In spite of her exceptional success, she is a deeply shy and serious person who avoids talk shows and personal interviews. Though she does not define herself as political or spiritual, she calls herself a humanitarian and is active in AIDS support work and animal rights. She once sent a single yellow rose to each of the 237 congresspeople who voted to end a $2 million subsidy to the mink industry. In perhaps the ultimate test of her humanitarian principles, she assisted in her elderly mother's suicide.

Arthur has become somewhat of a cult figure in the 1990s. The satirical attention is partially inspired by the movie *Airheads* (1994) in which screwball terrorists take over a radio station, demanding, among other outrageous requests, naked pictures of Bea Arthur. Bumper stickers with the catch phrase "Bea Arthur—Be Naked" and a cocktail called Bea Arthur's Underpants, a questionable combination of such ingredients as Mountain Dew, vodka, and beer, are some of the results of Arthur's cult status.

—Tina Gianoulis

FURTHER READING:

"Bea Arthur." http://www.jps.net/bobda/bea/index.html. March 1999.

Gold, Todd. "Golden Girls in Their Prime." *Saturday Evening Post.* Vol. 255, July-August 1986, 58.

Sherman, Eric. "Gabbing with the Golden Girls." *Ladies Home Journal.* Vol. 107, No. 2, February 1990, 44.

Arthurian Legend

The name of King Arthur resounds with images of knightly romance, courtly love, and mystical magic. Arthur, Lancelot, Guinevere, Galahad, and Merlin all carry meanings reflecting the enduring themes of adultery, saintliness, and mysterious wisdom from the Arthurian legend, which can truly be described as a living legend. The popularity of the tales of King Arthur, the Knights of the Round Table, Avalon, Camelot, and the Holy Grail is at a height unrivaled after more than 1,500 years of history. By the 1990s the legend had appeared as the theme of countless novels, short stories, films, television serials and programs, comics, and games.

Some recent writers have attempted to explain why there should be such a popular fascination with the reworkings of so familiar a story. Much of the enchantment of Arthur as hero has come from writers' ability to shift his shape in accordance with the mood of the age. C.S. Lewis noted this ability, and compared the legend to a cathedral that has taken many centuries and many builders to create:

> I am thinking of a great cathedral, where Saxon, Norman, Gothic, Renaissance, and Georgian elements all co-exist, and all grow together into something strange and admirable which none of its successive builders intended or foresaw.

In a general view of this "cathedral" as it has evolved into today, one can see several characteristics of the legend immediately: it focuses on King Arthur, a noble and heroic person about whom are gathered the greatest of knights and ladies; who has had a mysterious beginning and an even more mysterious ending; whose childhood mentor and foremost adviser in the early days of his reign is the enchanter Merlin; and who has a sister, son, wife, and friend that betray him in some fashion, leading to his eventual downfall at a great battle, the last of many he has fought during his life. Quests are also common, especially for the Grail, which (if it appears) is always the supreme quest.

Probably one of the most familiar and successful modern tales of King Arthur is Mark Twain's *A Connecticut Yankee in King Arthur's Court* (1889). At first poorly received, this novel has since established itself as one of the classics of American literature. Twain's characteristic combination of fantasy and fun, observation and satire, confronts the customs of chivalric Arthurian times with those of the New World. In it, Hank Morgan travels back in time and soon gains power through his advanced technology. In the end, Hank is revealed to be as ignorant and bestial as the society he finds himself in.

In recent times, however, the legend appears most frequently in mass market science fiction and fantasy novels, especially the latter. Since the publication of T.H. White's *The Sword in the Stone* (1938), it has appeared as the theme in some of the most popular novels, including Mary Stewart's *The Crystal Cave* (1970), Marion Zimmer Bradley's *The Mists of Avalon* (1982), and Stephen R. Lawhead's *Pendragon Cycle* (1987-1999). For the most part, the fantasy tales retell the story of Arthur and his knights as handed down through the centuries. They also build on the twist of magic that defines modern fantasy. Merlin, therefore, the enigmatic sorcerer, becomes the focus of most of the novels, particularly Stewart's and Lawhead's.

Due to Merlin's popularity, he has also appeared as the main character of some recent television serials, including the 1998 *Merlin.* Sam Neill is cast as Merlin, son of the evil Queen Mab. He tries to deny his heritage of magic, but is eventually forced to use it to destroy Mab and her world, making way for the modern world. This has been one of the most popular mini-series broadcasts on network television since *Roots* (1977) even though Arthur and his knights are barely seen in this story.

In the movies, however, Merlin fades into the background, with Hollywood focusing more on Arthur and the knights and ladies of his court. The first Arthurian film was the 1904 *Parsifal* from the Edison Company. It was soon followed by other silent features, including the first of twelve film and television adaptations of Twain's *Connecticut Yankee.* With the advent of talking pictures, the Arthurian tale was told in music as well as sound. After World War II and with the arrival of Cinemascope, the Arthurian tale was also told in full color. Most of the early movies (including the 1953 *The Knights of the Round Table, Prince Valiant,* and *The Black Knight*), however, were reminiscent of the western genre in vogue at that time.

In the 1960s two adaptations of T.H. White's tales, *Camelot* (1967) and Disney's *The Sword in the Stone* (1965), brought the legend to the attention of young and old alike. Disney's movie introduces Mad Madame Mim as Merlin's nemesis and spends a great deal of time focusing on their battles, while *Camelot,* an adaptation of the Lerner and Lowe Broadway musical, focuses on the love triangle between Arthur, Lancelot, and Guinevere. This was also the theme of the later movie, *First Knight* (1995). However, Britain's Monty Python comedy troupe made their first foray onto the movie screen with the spoof *Monty Python and the Holy Grail* (1975). This movie not only satirized all movie adaptations of the Arthurian tale, but took a swipe at virtually every medieval movie produced by Hollywood until that time.

It is Twain's novel, however, that has produced some of the best and worst of the movie adaptions. Fox's 1931 version, with Will Rogers and Myrna Loy, was so successful it was re-released in 1936. Paramount's 1949 version, with Bing Crosby, was the most faithful to Twain's novel, but was hampered by the fact that each scene seemed to be a build up to a song from Crosby. Disney entered the fray with its own unique live-action adaptations, including the 1979 *Unidentified Flying Oddball* and 1995's *A Kid in King Arthur's Court.* Bugs Bunny also got the opportunity to joust with the Black Knight in the short cartoon *A Connecticut Rabbit in King Arthur's Court* (1978), complete with the obligatory "What's up Doc?"

The traditional Arthurian legend has appeared as the main theme or as an integral part of the plot of some recent successful Hollywood movies, including 1981's *Excalibur,* 1989's *Indiana Jones and the Last Crusade,* 1991's *The Fisher King,* and 1998's animated feature *The Quest for Camelot.* While the Arthurian legend has not always been at the fore of these movies, merely being used as a convenient vehicle, its presence confirms the currency and popularity of Arthur and his knights.

The legend has not remained fixed to films and books. Other places where the legend appears include the New Orleans Arthurians' Ball held at Arthur's Winter Palace, where Merlin uses his magic wand to tap a lady in attendance as Arthur's new queen, and the Arthurian experience of Camelot in Las Vegas. Also, in the academic field, an International Arthurian Society was founded in 1949 and is currently made up of branches scattered all over the world. Its main focus is the scholarly dissemination of works on the Arthurian world, and the North American Branch now sponsors a highly respected academic journal, *Arthuriana*.

Throughout its long history the Arthurian legend has been at the fore of emerging technologies: Caxton's printing press (the first in England), for example, published the definitive Arthurian tale, Thomas Mallory's *Le Morte D'Arthur*. Today the new technology is the Internet and the World Wide Web. Arthurian scholars of all calibers have adapted to this new forum, producing some top web sites for the use of scholars and other interested parties alike. One site, for example, *The Camelot Project*, makes available a database of Arthurian texts, images, bibliographies, and basic information. The site can be found at: http://www.lib.rochester.edu/camelot/cphome.stm.

The legend has been a staple of the fantasy role playing games from the late 1970s onward. In higher level modules of the popular *Dungeons and Dragons* game, characters from the legend appear. Shari and Sam Lewis created the ''Pillars of Clinschor'' module (1983) for the game, where the adventurers had to seize a castle from Arthurian arch-villainess Morgan Le Fay. With the rise of computer games, the Arthurian game has entered a new dimension of role-playing and graphical user interfaces. The Monty Python troupe, for example, released their *Monty Python and the Holy Grail* multimedia game in the mid 1990s, where the player takes Arthur on his quest through scenes from the movie in search of the Grail and an out-take.

The legend's prominence in comic books cannot be underrated either, given that it forms the backdrop of *Prince Valiant*, one of the longest running comic strips in America (1937-). Creator Hal Foster brought the exiled Valiant to Arthur's court, where he eventually earned a place at the Round Table. *Prince Valiant* itself has engendered a movie (1953), games, and novels. Another major comic to deal with Arthur had him returning to Britain to save the country from invading space aliens (*Camelot 3000*, 1982-1985). The success of these comics have seen some imitations, most poorer than their originals, but in some instances even these comics have remained very faithful to the legend.

The popular fascination is not limited to the various fictionalizations of Arthur. Major works have been devoted to the search for the man that became the legend. People are curious as to who he really was, when he lived, and what battles he conclusively fought. Archaeological and historical chronicles of Britain have been subjected to as much scrutiny as the literary in search of the elusive historical Arthur. A recent examination notes that this interest in Arthur's historicity is as intense as the interest in his knightly accomplishments. Yet, the search for the historical Arthur has yet to yield an uncontroversial candidate; those that do make the short list appear in cable documentaries, biographies, and debatable scholarly studies.

Finally, the image of Camelot itself, a place of vibrant culture, was appropriated to describe the Kennedy years, inviting comparison between the once and future king and the premature end of the Kennedy Administration.

King Arthur and the Arthurian Legend are inextricably a part of popular culture and imagination. At the turn of a new millennium, the once and future king is alive and well, just as he was at the turn of the last, a living legend that will continue to amaze, thrill, and educate.

—John J. Doherty

FURTHER READING:

Doherty, John J. ''Arthurian Fantasy, 1980-1989: An Analytical and Bibliographical Survey.'' *Arthuriana*. Ed. Bonnie Wheeler. March 1997. Southern Methodist University. http://dc.smu.edu/Arthuriana/BIBLIO-PROJECT/DOHERTY/doherty.html. March 5, 1997.

Harty, Kevin J. ''Arthurian Film.'' *The Arthuriana/Camelot Project Bibliographies*. Ed. Alan Lupack. April 1997. University of Rochester. http://www.lib.rochester.edu/camelot/acpbibs/bibhome.stm. November 2, 1998.

Harty, Kevin J. *Cinema Arthuriana: Essays on Arthurian Film*. New York, Garland, 1991.

Lacy, Norris J., editor. *The New Arthurian Encyclopedia*. New York, Garland, 1996.

Lupack, Alan, and Barbara Tepa Lupack. *King Arthur in America*. Cambridge, D. S. Brewer, 1999.

Mancoff, Debra, editor. *King Arthur's Modern Return*. New York, Garland, 1998.

Stewart, H. Alan. ''King Arthur in the Comics.'' *Avalon to Camelot*, 2 (1986), 12-14.

Thompson, Raymond H. *The Return from Avalon: A Study of the Arthurian Legend in Modern Fiction*. Westport, Connecticut, Greenwood, 1985.

Artist Formerly Known as Prince, The
See Prince

As the World Turns

Four-and-a-half decades after its April 2, 1956, debut, top-rated daytime soap opera *As the World Turns* keeps spinning along. Created by Irna Phillips, whose other soaps include *The Guiding Light, Another World, Days of Our Lives* and *Love Is a Many-Splendored Thing, As the World Turns* debuted on CBS the same day as *The Edge of Night* (which played on CBS through 1975 before moving to ABC for nine years), and the two were television's first thirty-minute-long soap operas, up from the fifteen minutes of previous soaps.

The show is set in the generic Midwestern burg of Oakdale, a veritable Peyton Place whose inhabitants are forever immersed in sin and scandal, conquest and confession, deceit and desire. Originally, the plot lines spotlighted two dissimilar yet inexorably intertwined families: the middle-income Hughes and the ambitious Lowell clans, each consisting of married couples and offspring. One of the first plot threads involved law partners Jim Lowell and Chris Hughes, with Edith, the sister of Chris, becoming involved in an affair with married Jim. The Lowells eventually were written out of the show; however, a number of characters with the Hughes surname have lingered in the story lines. Over the years, the plots have been neck-deep in additional extramarital liaisons along with divorces, child custody cases, car crashes, blood diseases, and fatal falls down stairs—not to mention murders. The dilemmas facing characters in the late 1990s—''Will Emily confront her stalker?'' ''Is David the guilty party?'' ''Will Denise develop a passion for Ben?''—are variations on the same impasses and emotional crises facing characters decades earlier.

In some cases, five, seven, and nine actors have played the same *As the World Turns* characters. However, one performer has become synonymous with the show: soap opera queen Eileen Fulton, who has been a regular since 1960. Fulton's role is the conniving, oft-married Lisa. Beginning as simply ''Lisa Miller,'' over the years her name has been expanded to ''Lisa Miller Hughes Eldridge Shea Colman McColl Mitchell Grimaldi Chedwy.'' Don MacLaughlin, who played Chris Hughes, was the original cast member who remained longest on the show. He was an *As the World Turns* regular for just more than three decades until his death in 1986.

Of the endless actors who have had roles on *As the World Turns,* some already had won celebrity but had long been out of the prime-time spotlight. Gloria DeHaven appeared on the show in 1966 and 1967 as ''Sara Fuller.'' Margaret Hamilton was ''Miss Peterson'' in 1971. Zsa Zsa Gabor played ''Lydia Marlowe'' in 1981. Abe Vigoda was ''Joe Kravitz'' in 1985. Claire Bloom was ''Orlena Grimaldi'' from 1993 through 1995. Robert Vaughn appeared as ''Rick Hamlin'' in 1995. Valerie Perrine came on board as ''Dolores Pierce'' in 1998. Other regulars were movie stars/television stars/celebrities-to-be who were honing their acting skills while earning a paycheck. James Earl Jones played ''Dr. Jerry Turner'' in 1966. Richard Thomas was ''Tom Hughes'' in 1966 and 1967. Swoosie Kurtz played ''Ellie Bradley'' in 1971. Dana Delany was ''Hayley Wilson Hollister'' in 1981. Meg Ryan played ''Betsy Stewart Montgomery Andropoulos'' between 1982 and 1984. Marisa Tomei was ''Marcy Thompson Cushing'' from 1983 through 1988. Julianne Moore played ''Frannie/Sabrina Hughes'' from 1985 through 1988. Parker Posey was ''Tess Shelby'' in 1991 and 1992.

As the World Turns was the top-rated daytime soap from its inception through the 1960s. Its success even generated a brief nighttime spin-off, *Our Private World,* which aired on CBS between May and September 1965. In the early 1970s, however, the ratings began to decline. On December 1, 1975, the show expanded to one hour, with little increase in viewership, but the ratings never descended to the point where cancellation became an option—and the show was celebrated enough for Carol Burnett to toy with its title in her classic soap opera parody *As the Stomach Turns.* From the 1980s on, the *As the World Turns* audience remained steady and solid, with its ratings keeping it in daytime television's upper echelon. Over the years, the show has been nominated for various Writers Guild of America, *Soap Opera Digest,* and Emmy awards. In 1986-87, it garnered its first Emmy as ''Outstanding Drama Series.''

—Rob Edelman

FURTHER READING:

Fulton, Eileen, as told to Brett Bolton. *How My World Turns.* New York, Taplinger Publishing, 1970.

Fulton, Eileen, with Desmond Atholl and Michael Cherkinian. *As My World Still Turns: The Uncensored Memoirs of America's Soap Opera Queen.* Secaucus, N.J., Birch Lane Press, 1995.

Poll, Julie. *As the World Turns: The Complete Family Scrapbook.* Los Angeles, General Publishing Group, 1996.

Ashcan School

The Ashcan School was the first art movement of the new century in America, and its first specifically modern style. Active in the first two decades of the twentieth century, Ashcan artists opposed the formality of conservative American art by painting urban subjects in a gritty, realistic manner. They gave form to the tough, optimistic, socially conscious outlook associated with Theodore Roosevelt's time. The Ashcan School artists shared a similar muckraking spirit with contemporary social reformers. Their exuberant and romantic sense of democracy had earlier been expressed in the poetry of Walt Whitman.

At a time before the camera had not yet replaced the hand-drawn sketch, four Philadelphia artist-reporters—William Glackens, John Sloan, George Luks, and Everett Shinn—gathered around the artist Robert Henri (1865-1929), first in his Walnut Street studio, then later in New York. Henri painted portraits in heavy, dark brown brushstrokes in a manner reminiscent of the Dutch painter Frans Hals. He taught at the New York School of Art between 1902 and 1912 where some of his students included the Ashcan artists George Bellows, Stuart Davis, and Edward Hopper. The artists exhibited together only once, as ''The Eight''—a term now synonymous with the Ashcan School—at the Macbeth Gallery in New York City in 1908. They had formally banded together when the National Academy of Design refused to show their works.

Better thought of as New York Realists, the Ashcan artists were fascinated by the lifestyles of the inhabitants of the Lower East Side and Greenwich Village, and of New York and the urban experience in general. Conservative critics objected to their choice of subjects. Nightclubs, immigrants, sporting events, and alleys were not considered appropriate subjects for high art. It was in this spirit that the art critic and historian Holger Cahill first used the term ''Ashcan School'' . . . ashcan meaning garbage can . . . in a 1934 book about recent art.

John Sloan (1871-1951), the most renowned Ashcan artist, made images of city streets, Greenwich Village backyards, and somewhat voyeuristic views of women of the city. His most well known painting, but one which is not entirely typical of his art, is *The Wake of the Ferry II* (1907, The Phillips Collection, Washington, D.C.). The dull blues and greens of the ship's deck and the steely water introduced an element of melancholy in what millions of commuters experienced daily on the Staten Island Ferry. Sloan's art sometimes reflected his socialist leanings, but never at the expense of a warm humanity. Although he made etchings for the left wing periodical *The Masses,* he refused to inject his art with ''socialist propaganda,'' as he once said.

The reputation of George Luks (1867-1933) rests on the machismo and bluster of his art and of his own personality. ''Guts! Guts! Life! Life! That's my technique!'' he claimed. He had been an amateur actor—which undoubtedly helped him in his pose as a bohemian

An example from the Ashcan School: Reginald Marsh's *Bread Line*.

artist—and had drawn comic strips in the 1890s before meeting Henri at the Pennsylvania Academy of the Fine Arts. His *Hester Street* (1905, The Brooklyn Museum) shows Jewish immigrants on the Lower East Side in an earnest, unstereotypical manner.

George Bellows (1882-1925) was probably the most purely talented of the group, and made many of the most interesting Ashcan paintings of the urban environment. An athletic, outgoing personality, Bellows' most well known paintings involve boxing matches. Composed of fleshy brushstrokes, *Stag at Sharkey's* (1909, Cleveland Museum of Art) shows a barely legal ''club'' where drinkers watched amateur sluggers. Bellows was also an accomplished printmaker and made more than 200 lithographs during his career.

Much of the art of the Ashcan School has the quality of illustration. Their heroes included Rembrandt and Francisco Goya, as well as realists such as Honoré Daumier, Edouard Manet, and the American Winslow Homer. But not all the Ashcan artists drew their inspiration from city streets. The paintings of William Glackens (1870-1938) and Everett Shinn (1876-1953) often deal with the world of popular entertainment and fashionable nightlife. Glackens' elegant *Chez Mouquin* (1905, Art Institute of Chicago), shows one of the favorite haunts of the Ashcan artists. Maurice Prendergast (1859-1924) painted park visitors in a patchy, decorative style. Ernest Lawson (1873-1939) used a hazy, Impressionist technique to paint scenes of New York and the Harlem River. The traditional nude female figures of Arthur B. Davies (1862-1928) seem to owe little to Ashcan art.

The Ashcan School was not a coherent school nor did the artists ever paint ashcans. They expanded the range of subjects for American artists and brought a new vigor to the handling of paint. Their identity as tough observers of the city, unimpressed by contemporary French art, changed the way American artists thought of themselves. They demonstrated that artists who stood apart from the traditional art establishment could attain popular acceptance. Among their contributions was their promotion of jury-less shows which gave artists the right to exhibit with whomever they chose. This spirit of independence was felt in the famous 1913 Armory Show in which some of the organizers were Ashcan artists.

—Mark B. Pohlad

FURTHER READING:

Braider, Donald. *George Bellows and the Ashcan School of Painting.* Garden City, New York, Doubleday, 1971.

Glackens, Ira. *William Glackens and the Eight: the Artists who Freed American Art.* New York, Horizon Press, 1984.

Homer, William I. *Robert Henri and His Circle.* Ithaca and London, Cornell University Press, 1969.

Perlmann, Bennard P. *Painters of the Ashcan School: The Immortal Eight.* New York, Dover, 1988.

Zurrier, Rebecca, et al. *Metropolitan Lives: The Ashcan Artists and Their New York.* New York, Norton, 1995.

Ashe, Arthur (1943-1993)

Tennis great and social activist Arthur Ashe is memorialized on a famous avenue of his hometown of Richmond, Virginia, by a bronze statue that shows him wielding a tennis racquet in one hand and a book in the other. Children sit at his feet, looking up at him for inspiration. Though the statue represents a storm of controversy, with everyone from racist white Virginians to Ashe's own wife Jeanne calling it inappropriate, it also represents an effort to capture what it was that Arthur Ashe gave to the society in which he lived.

Born well before the days of integration in Richmond, the heart of the segregated south, Ashe learned first-hand the pain caused by racism. He was turned away from the Richmond City Tennis Tournament in 1955 because of his race, and by 1961 he left the south, seeking a wider range of opportunities. He found them at UCLA (University of California, Los Angeles), where he was the first African American on the Davis Cup team, and then proceeded to a series of "firsts." In 1968, he was the first (and only) African American man to win the United States Open; in 1975 he was the first (and only) African American man to win the men's singles title at Wimbleton. He won 46 other titles during his tennis career, paving the way for other people of color in a sport that still remains largely the domain of white players.

Ashe was a distinguished, if not brilliant tennis player, but it was his performance off the court that ensured his place in history. Like many African Americans raised before integration, Ashe felt that a calm and dignified refusal to give in to oppression was more effective than a radical fight. His moderate politics prompted fellow tennis professional, white woman Billie Jean King, to quip, "I'm blacker

than Arthur is." But Ashe felt his responsibility as a successful African American man keenly. He wrote a three volume *History of the American Black Athlete,* which included an analysis of racism in American sports, and he sponsored and mentored many disadvantaged young African American athletes himself. He also took his fight against racism out into the world. When he was refused entry to a tennis tournament in apartheid South Africa in 1970, Ashe fought hard to be allowed to enter that intensely segregated country. Once there he saw for himself the conditions of Blacks under apartheid, and the quiet moderate became a freedom fighter, even getting arrested at anti-apartheid demonstrations.

In 1979 Ashe was pushed down the path to his most unwilling contribution to his times. He had a heart attack, which ended his tennis career and eventually led, in 1983, to bypass surgery. During surgery, he received blood transfusions, and it is believed those transfusions passed the AIDS (Acquired Immune Deficiency Syndrome) virus into his blood. Even after he discovered he had AIDS, the intensely private Ashe had no intention of going public with the information. When the tabloid newspaper *USA Today* discovered the news, however, Ashe had little choice but to make the announcement himself. He was angry at being forced to make his personal life public, but, as he did in every

Arthur Ashe

aspect of his life, he turned his personal experience into public service. He became an activist in the fight against AIDS, which he said did not compare to racism as a challenge in his life. It is perhaps indicative of the stigma attached to the disease that Ashe's AIDS is never mentioned without the hastily added disclaimer that he probably contracted it through a blood transfusion. He was a widely respected public figure, however, and his presence in the public eye as a person with AIDS helped to de-stigmatize the disease.

Arthur Ashe died of AIDS-related pneumonia in 1993, but his legacy is durable and widespread. A tennis academy in Soweto, South Africa, bears his name, as does a stadium in Queens and a Junior Athlete of the Year program for elementary schools. He helped found the Association of Tennis Professionals, the first player's union. And, only a short time before his death, he was arrested at a demonstration, this time protesting the United States Haitian immigration policy. He was a role model at a time when African Americans desperately needed successful role models. He was a disciplined moderate who was not afraid to take a radical stand.

The statue of Ashe which stands on Monument Avenue in Richmond is, perhaps, a good symbol of the crossroads where Ashe stood in life. The fame of Monument Avenue comes from its long parade of statues of heroes of the Confederacy. Racist whites felt Ashe's statue did not belong there. Proud African Americans, the descendants of slavery, felt that Ashe's statue did not belong there. Ashe's wife Jeanne insists that Ashe himself would have preferred the statue to stand outside an African American Sports Hall of Fame he wished to found. But willingly or not, the statue, like the man, stands in a controversial place in history, in a very public place, where children look up at it.

—Tina Gianoulis

FURTHER READING:

Kallen, Stuart A. *Arthur Ashe: Champion of Dreams and Motion.* Edina, Minnesota, Abdu and Daughters, 1993.

Lazo, Caroline Evensen. *Arthur Ashe.* Minneapolis, Lerner Publications, 1999.

Martin, Marvin. *Arthur Ashe: Of Tennis and the Human Spirit.* New York, Franklin Watts, 1999.

Wright, David K. *Arthur Ashe: Breaking the Color Barrier in Tennis.* Springfield, New Jersey, Enslow Publishers, 1996.

Asimov, Isaac (1920-1992)

Scientist and science fiction writer Isaac Asimov made his reputation in both fields with his prolific writings and his interest in the popularization of science. Asimov published over three hundred books and a considerable number of short stories, essays, and columns. He is considered to be a founding figure in the field of science fiction in his rejection of the space-adventure formula in favor of a more directly scientific, social, and political aproach. He established several central conventions for the genre, including robotics and the idea of a galactic empire. Asimov was also extremely influential through his nonfiction writings, producing popular introductory texts and textbooks in biochemistry.

Isaac Asimov

Asimov was born in Petrovichi, Russia, on January 2, 1920, and moved to America with his family when he was three years old. He first discovered science fiction through the magazines sold in his father's candy store, and in 1938 he began writing for publication. He sold his story "Marooned Off Vesta" to *Amazing Stories* the following year, when he was an undergraduate at Columbia University. That same year, he sold his story "Trends" to John W. Campbell, Jr., editor of *Astounding Science Fiction*, and it was through his creative relationship with Campbell that Asimov developed an interest in the social aspects of science fiction.

Campbell's editorial policy allowed Asimov to pursue his interest in science fiction as a literature that could respond to problems arising in his contemporary period. In "Half-Breed" (1941), for example, he discussed racism, and in "The Martian Way," he voiced his opposition to McCarthyism. Asimov's marked ambivalence about the activities of the scientific community is a major characteristic of his writing. Later novels examined the issue of scientific responsibility and the power struggles within the scientific community. Asimov himself was a member of the Futurians, a New York science-fiction group which existed from 1938 to 1945 and was notable for its radical politics and belief that science fiction fans should be forward-looking and help shape the future with their positive and progressive ideas.

Asimov spent the Second World War years at the U.S. Naval Air Experimental Station as a research scientist in the company of fellow science-fiction writers L. Sprague de Camp and Robert Heinlein. He made a name for himself as a writer in 1941 with the publication of "Nightfall," which is frequently anthologized as an example of good science fiction and continues to top readers' polls as their favorite science fiction story. During this period, Asimov also started work on the series of stories that would be brought together as the ''Foundation Trilogy'' and published as the novels *Foundation* (1951), *Foundation and Empire* (1952), and *Second Foundation* (1953). Asimov has stated that their inception came from reading Gibbon's *Decline and Fall of the Roman Empire.*

Asimov's other significant series comprises his robot stories, collected in *I, Robot* (1950), *The Rest of the Robots* (1964), and further collections in the 1980s. Two novels—*The Caves of Steel* (1954) and *The Naked Sun* (1956)—bring together a detective and his robotic partner, fusing Asimov's interest in mystery with his interest in science fiction. He also wrote several stories about the science fiction detective Wendell Worth during the same period. It is the third story of the robot series, ''Liar!'' (1941), that introduced ''The Three Laws of Robotics,'' a formulation that has had a profound effect upon the genre.

In 1948 Asimov received his doctorate in biochemistry and a year later took up a position with the Boston University School of Medicine as an associate professor. He remained there until 1958 when he resigned the post in order to concentrate on his writing career. He remained influential in the sci-fi genre by contributing a monthly science column to *The Magazine of Science Fiction and Fantasy* for the next thirty years, but his aim during this period was to produce popular and accessible science writing. During the 1950s he had published juvenile fiction for the same purpose under the pseudonym of Paul French. In 1960 he published *The Intelligent Man's Guide to Science,* which has gone through several editions and is now known as *Asimov's New Guide to Science.* In the interest of popular science he also produced a novelization in 1966 of the film *Fantastic Voyage.* However, he also wrote in vastly different fields and published *Asimov's Guide to the Bible* in 1968 and *Asimov's Guide to Shakespeare* in 1970.

Asimov returned to science-fiction writing in 1972 with the publication of *The Gods Themselves,* a novel that was awarded both the Hugo and Nebula Awards. In this later stage of his career Asimov produced other novels connected with the ''Foundation'' and ''Robot'' series, but he also published novels with new planetary settings, such as *Nemesis* in 1989. His influence continued with his collections of Hugo Award winners and the launch of *Isaac Asimov Science Fiction Magazine* in 1977. Overall his contribution lies in his thought-provoking attitude to science and its place in human society. Asimov helped transform immediate postwar science fiction from the space formula of the 1930s into a more intellectually challenging and responsible fiction. He died of heart and kidney failure on April 6, 1992.

—Nickianne Moody

FURTHER READING:

Asimov, Isaac. *I, Asimov: A Memoir.* New York, Doubleday, 1994.

Gunn, James. *Isaac Asimov: The Foundations of Science Fiction.* Oxford, Oxford University Press, 1982; revised, Lanham, Maryland, Scarecrow Press, 1996.

Miller, Marjorie Mithoff. *Isaac Asimov: A Checklist of Works Published in the United States.* Kent, Ohio, Kent State University Press, 1972.

Olander, Joseph D., and Martin H. Greenberg, editors. *Isaac Asimov.* New York, Taplinger, 1977.

Slusser, George. *Isaac Asimov: The Foundations of His Science Fiction.* New York, Borgo Press, 1979.

Touponce, William F. *Isaac Asimov.* Boston, Twayne Publishers, 1991.

Asner, Ed (1929—)

Ed Asner is an award winning actor who holds the distinction of accomplishing one of the most extraordinary transitions in television programming history: he took his character Lou Grant—the gruff, hard drinking, but lovable boss of the newsroom at WJM TV Minneapolis on the *Mary Tyler Moore Show,* a half-hour situation comedy—to the city editorship of the *Los Angeles Tribune,* on the one hour drama *Lou Grant.* Lou Grant's 12-year career on two successful, but very different, television shows established Asner as a major presence in American popular culture.

Yitzak Edward Asner was born on November 15, 1929 in Kansas City, Kansas. After high school, he attended the University of Chicago, where he appeared in student dramatic productions and firmly decided upon a life in the theater. After graduation and two years in the army, he found work in Chicago as a member of the

Ed Asner

Playwrights' Theater Club. He then headed for New York to try his luck on Broadway.

His success on Broadway was middling at best. He appeared in *Face of a Hero* with Jack Lemmon, and in a number of off-Broadway productions, as well as several New York and American Shakespeare Festivals in the late 1950s. In 1961, he packed up his family and moved to Hollywood. His first film was the Elvis Presley vehicle *Kid Galahad,* a remake of the 1937 Edward G. Robinson/Bette Davis/ Humphrey Bogart film. Following this were featured roles in such films as *The Satan Bug* (1965), *El Dorado* (1965), and *Change of Habit* (1969), Elvis Presley's last film. He also performed guest appearances in numerous television series, and he had a continuing role as a crusading reporter on the short-lived Richard Crenna series, *Slattery's People.*

In early 1969, Moore and Dick Van Dyke, stars of television's *The Dick Van Dyke Show* (1961-1966), appeared in a reunion special on CBS that did so well in the ratings that the network offered Moore the opportunity to come up with a series. Together with her husband, Grant Tinker, and writers James L. Brooks and Allan Burns, she created *The Mary Tyler Moore Show,* one of the happiest and most successful marriages of writing and ensemble casting in the history of American television. The program was first telecast on September 19, 1970 and centered around Mary Richards, an unmarried, independent 30-year-old woman who was determined to succeed on her own. She became the assistant producer in the newsroom at fictional WJM-TV in Minneapolis. Asner was cast as Lou Grant, the gruff and abrupt but sentimental boss of the somewhat wacky newsroom crew and their inept news anchor, Ted Baxter, played by Ted Knight. Lou Grant constantly struggled to maintain a higher than mediocre level of standards in the newsroom, while he coped with his personal problems and the problems created by the interaction of the members of the newsroom crew. His blustery, realistic approach to the job, and his comedic resort to the ever-present bottle in his desk drawer to vent his frustration and mask his vulnerability, nicely balanced Mary Richards' more idealistic, openly vulnerable central character.

Asner was a perennial nominee for Emmy awards for the role, receiving the Best Supporting Actor awards in 1971, 1972, and 1975. When the show ended its spectacular run in 1977, Asner was given the opportunity to continue the role of Lou Grant in an hour-long drama series that MTM Productions, Moore and Tinker's production company, was working up. In the last episode of *The Mary Tyler Moore Show,* station WJM was sold and the entire newsroom crew was fired except, ironically, Ted Baxter. Lou Grant, out of a job, went to Los Angeles to look up an old Army buddy, Charlie Hume, who, it turned out, was managing editor of the *Los Angeles Tribune.* Lou was hired as city editor. The series was called simply *Lou Grant* and it presented weekly plots of current social and political issues torn from the headlines and presented with high production values. It emphasized the crusading zeal of the characters to stamp out evil, the conflicts and aspirations of the reporters, the infighting among the editors, and the relationship between Grant and the publisher Mrs. Pynchon, played by Nancy Marchand. The program succeeded because of Asner's steady and dominating portrayal of the show's central character, who represented a high standard of professional ethics and morals, and who was often in conflict with the stubborn and autocratic Mrs. Pynchon. Asner was again nominated for Emmy awards, winning the award in 1978 and 1980 as Best Actor in a Series.

In 1982, CBS suddenly canceled *Lou Grant,* ostensibly for declining ratings, but Asner and other commentators insist that the show was canceled for political reasons. He was a leading figure in the actor's strike of 1980 and was elected president of the Screen Actors' Guild in 1981, a post he held until 1985. He also was an outspoken advocate of liberal causes and a charter member of Medical Aid for El Salvador, an organization at odds with the Reagan Administration's policies in Central America. This created controversy and led to political pressure on CBS to rein in the *Lou Grant* show which, to many observers, was becoming an organ for Asner's liberal causes. "We were still a prestigious show. [The controversy] created demonstrations outside CBS and all that. It was 1982, the height of Reagan power," he would recall later in an interview on Canadian radio. "I think it was in the hands of William Paley to make the decision to cancel it."

Following *Lou Grant,* Asner has done roles in *Off the Rack* (1985) and *Thunder Alley* (1994-1995). With Bette Midler, he played a wonderfully subdued role as Papa in the made for television rendition of *Gypsy* (1993). In addition to the five Emmies noted above, he won Best Actor awards for the CBS miniseries *Rich Man, Poor Man* (1976) and *Roots* (1977), a total of seven Emmy awards on 15 nominations. In addition, he holds five Golden Globe Awards and two Critics Circle Awards.

—James R. Belpedio

FURTHER READING:

Brooks, Tim, and Earle Marsh. *The Complete Directory to Prime Time Network and Cable TV Shows, 1946-Present.* New York, Ballantine Books, 1995.

Brooks, Tim. *The Complete Directory to Prime Time TV Stars, 1946-Present.* New York, Ballantine, 1987.

CJAD Radio Montreal. *Interview with Ed Asner.* Transcript of an interview broadcast May 12, 1995, http://www.pubnix.net/~peterh/cjad09.htm.

Astaire, Fred (1899-1987), and Ginger Rogers (1911-1995)

Fred Astaire and Ginger Rogers were the greatest dance team in the history of American movies. In the course of developing their partnership and dancing before the movie camera they revolutionized the Hollywood musical comedy in the 1930s. Though their partnership only lasted for six years and nine films between 1933 and 1939, with a tenth film as an encore ten years later, they definitively set the standards by which dancing in the movies would be judged for a long time to come. Although they both had independent careers before and after their partnership, neither ever matched the popularity or the artistic success of their dancing partnership.

The dancing of Astaire and Rogers created a style that brought together dance movements from vaudeville, ballroom dancing, tap dancing, soft shoe, and even ballet. Ballroom dancing provided the basic framework—every film had at least one ballroom number. But tap dancing provided a consistent rhythmic base for Astaire and Rogers, while Astaire's ballet training helped to integrate the upper body and leaps into their dancing. Because Astaire was the more accomplished and experienced dancer—Rogers deferred to him and imitated him—they were able to achieve a flawless harmony. "He gives her class and she gives him sex," commented Katherine Hepburn. Astaire and Rogers developed their characters through the drive to dance that they exhibited and the obstacles, spatial distances, and social complications they had to surmount in order to dance. "Dancing isn't the euphemism for sex; in Astaire-Rogers films it is much better," wrote critic Leo Braudy. In their performances, Fred Astaire and Ginger Rogers suggested that dance is the perfect form of movement because it allows the self to achieve a harmonious balance between the greatest freedom and the most energy.

Astaire was born in Omaha, Nebraska in 1899. By the age of seven he was already touring the vaudeville circuit and made a successful transition to a dancing career on Broadway with his sister Adele in 1917. After Adele married and retired from the stage in 1932, Astaire's career seemed at a standstill. Despite the verdict on a screen test—"Can't act. Slightly bald. Can dance a little"—he made his first film appearance in *Dancing Lady* (1933) opposite Joan Crawford. Rogers, born in 1911 in Independence, Missouri, made her performing debut as a dancer in vaudeville—under the tutelage of her ambitious "stage" mother—at age 14. She first performed on Broadway in the musical *Top Speed* in 1929, and two years later headed out to Hollywood. She was under contract to RKO where she began her legendary partnership with Fred Astaire.

When sound came to film during the late 1920s, Hollywood studios rushed to make musicals. This created vast opportunities for musical comedy veterans like Astaire and Rogers. From the very beginning Astaire envisioned a new approach to filmed dancing and, together with Rogers, he exemplified a dramatic change in the cinematic possibilities of dance. Initially, the clumsiness of early cameras and sound equipment dictated straight-on shots of musical dance numbers from a single camera. These straight-on shots were broken by cutaways which would focus on someone watching the dance, then on the dancer's feet, next to someone watching, then back again to the dancer's face, concluding—finally—with another full-on shot. Thus, dances were never shown (or even filmed) in their entirety. Because of this, Busby Berkeley's big production numbers featured very little dancing and only large groups of dancers moving in precise geometric patterns.

Astaire's second movie, *Flying Down to Rio* (1933), was a glorious accident. It brought him together with Ginger Rogers. It also brought together two other members of the team that helped make Fred Astaire and Ginger Rogers the greatest dance partnership in American movies—Hermes Pan who became Astaire's steady choreographic assistant, and Hal Borne, Astaire's rehearsal pianist and musical arranger. Before *Flying Down to Rio,* no one had ever seen an entire dance number on the screen. Starting with the famous "Carioca" number, Astaire and Pan began insisting that numbers should be shot from beginning to end without cutaways. Pan later related that when the movie was previewed "something happened that had never happened before at a movie." After the "Carioca" number, the audience "applauded like crazy."

The success of *Flying Down to Rio* and the forging of Astaire and Rogers' partnership established a set of formulas which they thoroughly exhausted over the course of their partnership. In their first six films, as Arlene Croce has noted, they alternated between playing the lead romantic roles and the couple who are the sidekicks to the romantic leads. Their second film, *The Gay Divorcee* (1934), was based on Astaire's big Broadway hit before he decided to go to Hollywood. It provides the basic shape of those movies in which Astaire and Rogers are the romantic leads—boy wants to dance with girl, girl does not want to dance with boy, boy tricks girl into dancing with him, she loves it, but she needs to iron out the complications. They consummate their courtship with a dance. Most Astaire and Rogers movies also played around with social class—there is always a contrast between top hats, tails, and evening gowns, and even their vernacular dance forms aimed at a democratic egalitarianism. These films were made in the middle of the Great Depression when movies about glamorous upper class people often served as a form of escape. Dancing is shown both as entertainment and an activity that unites people from different classes.

The standard complaint about Astaire and Rogers movies are that they do not have enough dancing. Amazingly, most of their movies have only about ten minutes of dancing out of roughly 100 minutes of running time. There are usually four to seven musical numbers in each film, although not all of them are dance numbers. On the average, a single dance takes approximately three minutes. Certainly, no one would ever watch most of those movies if they were not vehicles for the dancing of Fred Astaire and Ginger Rogers. That these movies find viewers on the basis of no more than ten or 12 minutes of dancing suggests the deep and continuing pleasure that their performances give.

Each movie assembled several different types of dance numbers including romantic duets, big ballroom numbers, Broadway show spectacles, challenge dances, and comic and novelty numbers. In the best of the movies the song and dance numbers are integrated into the plot—*Top Hat* (1935), *Swing Time* (1936), *Shall We Dance* (1937). The centerpiece of most movies was the romantic duet. The incomparable "Night and Day" in *The Gay Divorcee* was the emotional turning point of the movie's plot. Other romantic duets like "Cheek to Cheek" in *Top Hat* and "Waltz" in *Swing Time,* are among the great romantic dance performances in movies. Some of the movies tried to

Fred Astaire and Ginger Rogers

replicate the success of the big ballroom number in *Rio* and the popularity of ''Carioca'' as a dance fad. Each movie also included an original variation on the different types of dances showcased in them. For example, ''Let's Call the Whole Thing Off'' in *Shall We Dance* included Astaire and Rogers dancing the entire routine on roller skates. ''Pick Yourself Up'' from *Swing Time* shows them using dance as an example of physical comedy: Astaire stumbles, falls, trips, and otherwise pretends he can not dance in order to flirt with Rogers, who teaches ballroom dancing. Another familiar genre is the ''challenge'' dance where Astaire does a step, Rogers imitates it, he does another, and then she tops it. Challenge dances usually played out Rogers' resistance to Astaire.

Shall We Dance (1937) has music and lyrics by George and Ira Gershwin including such well known songs as ''They All Laughed,'' ''Let's Call the Whole Thing Off,'' ''They Can't Take that Away From Me,'' and ''Shall We Dance.'' The movie stages an encounter between high art and popular forms of self-expression, ballet and tap dancing, and seriousness and fun. Astaire plays the Great Petrov, star of the Russian ballet, whose real name is Pete Peters, from Philadelphia. The film opens with Petrov's manager surprising him in the midst of tap dancing. The manager is horrified: ''The Great Petrov doesn't dance for fun,'' he exclaims. Ballet is a serious business to which the artist must devote his full time, the manager explains. *Shall We Dance* mocks ballet and European culture, and offers up instead popular American dance forms. The encounter is first staged when Astaire and Rogers dance to ''They All Laughed,'' another example of a challenge duet. Astaire begins with ballet-like steps while Rogers, feeling left out, stands still. She lightly snubs him by starting to tap. He responds with tap-like ballet, and then, at last, goes into straight tap dancing. Only then do they successfully dance together.

Fred Astaire and Ginger Rogers had long careers after they had ceased dancing together. Rogers went on to expand her range. She was an excellent comedienne, and in 1940 won an Oscar for her dramatic role in *Kitty Foyle*. Astaire appeared in over 40 movies, and unlike Rogers, he continued to dance. Among his later partners were Rita Hayworth, Eleanor Powell, and Cyd Charisse. No other partnership, however, produced work of the artistic quality that he was able to achieve with Rogers. The dancing partnership of Fred Astaire and Ginger Rogers promised a kind of happiness in which two individuals are able to successfully combine freedom and fun.

—Jeffrey Escoffier

FURTHER READING:

Croce, Arlene. *The Fred Astaire and Ginger Rogers Book*. New York, Galahad Books, 1972.

Morley, Sheridan. *Shall We Dance: A Biography of Ginger Rogers*. New York, St. Martin's Press, 1995.

Astounding Science Fiction

Spanning three incarnations since 1930, this is perhaps the most influential magazine in the history of the genre. Begun as *Astounding Stories* between 1930-1938, it published lurid pulp fare and launched E. E. Smith's *Lensmen* series. A name change to *Astounding Science Fiction* established a new direction for both the magazine and the genre under editor John W. Campbell, Jr. Between 1938-1960,

Campbell militated for plausible scientific extrapolation and straightforward prose. His editorship catalyzed the careers of Isaac Asimov and Robert Heinlein, among others. It also introduced the controversial dianetic theories of L. Ron Hubbard in May 1950. Emphasizing hardware-orientated stories that eschewed literary experimentation—what has come to be labeled ''hard science fiction''—the magazine became *Analog* and remained under Campbell's guidance until his death in 1971. Such classics as Frank Herbert's *Dune* and Anne McCaffrey's *Dragonflight* initially appeared in *Analog*. It remains a fixture of the genre today.

—Neal Baker

FURTHER READING:

Aldiss, Brian. *Trillion Year Spree: The History of Science Fiction*. New York, Atheneum, 1986.

Astrology

Astrology, the practice of predicting mundane events based upon the configuration and alignment of the planets and stars, has ancient origins. In the latter half of the twentieth century, however, the so-called ''oldest science'' has enjoyed renewed popularity due, in large part, to public fascination with ''New Age'' mysticism.

The origins of astrology lie with the ancient Babylonians, a nomadic people who readily accepted the idea that divine energy was manifested in the movements of the sun and planets. Gradually, this concept expanded and the relative positions of the planets—both in relation to each other and to fixed stars—became tied to the idea of omens; that is, if an event occurred while the planets were in a particular position, the recurrence of that position heralded a recurrence of the same sort of event. Soon, the planets became associated with almost every aspect of human life. They were linked to the emotions and to parts of the body, such that astrology played a significant part in medicine up to late medieval times. Not only was the position of the planet to be considered, but also the sign of the zodiac it was occupying, as it was believed possible to foretell the destiny of an individual by calculating which star was in the ascendant at the time of his or her birth.

Astrology later became popular with the Egyptians, Greeks, and Romans. Romans emperors, for instance, had court astrologers advise them on such matters as the timing of coronations and the prospects of possible heirs. The advent of Christianity, though, stifled the fledgling science—early Christians refused to tolerate the practice's alleged pagan mysticism. Astrology, as a result, became nearly extinct in the West between the sixth and twelfth centuries. It survived only in the Middle East, where Islamic scholars continued to practice the art. The Crusades brought astrology back to Europe, where it managed to co-exist with a more tolerant Christianity for nearly four centuries. Along with alchemy, astrology became an accepted science, and its doctrines pervaded some of the most popular writings of the time, including Chaucer's *Canterbury Tales*.

The massive growth of scientific astronomy paralleled an explosive decline in the fortunes of astrology in the sixteenth century. The discoveries by sixteenth-century astronomers Galieo Galilei and Nicolaus Copernicus sapped the foundations of astrology, as the idea of an earth-centered universe became completely untenable. In addition, in the Age of Empiricism the failure of astrologers to produce experimental evidence boded poorly for popular and intellectual support. By 1900, a French encyclopedia would accurately describe astrology as a vanishing cult with no young adherents. During the eighteenth century and much of the nineteenth century, a degraded astrology survived only in popular almanacs and amongst amateur and fraudulent practitioners.

In the late nineteenth and early twentieth centuries, however, astrology experienced a rebirth, in large part assisted by wider literacy and contemporary interest in popular psychology, Eastern thought, and the occult. Practitioners refined their art to focus on spiritual, therapeutic, and psychological goals, to the point that the emphasis on prediction almost entirely diminished amongst serious astrologers. Modern audiences, increasingly disillusioned with and distrustful of the order imposed by institutions and governments, found themselves drawn to astrology's promise to explain the self and the world. Modern astrology has come to represent a social support system of sorts, posited somewhere between religion and psychotherapy.

Astrology built its modern audience through daily horoscopes published in magazines and newspapers throughout the world. Horoscopes—charts of the heavens—show the relative positions of the sun, moon, and planets as well as the ascendant and mid-heaven signs of the zodiac at a specific moment in time. The first newspaper astrology columns appeared in the 1930s and focused on the lives of celebrities. Later, the columns directed their advice to the general public, enjoining readers to meet broad emotional goals such as "learning to compromise" and "controlling temper," all in accordance with the alignment of celestial bodies on a given day.

Astrology remained on the margins of society for much of the twentieth century, appealing to lower classes as well as to the uneducated segments of society. But the practice received a major boon when White House sources revealed that First Lady Nancy Reagan regularly consulted with an astrologer. According to reports, the First Lady altered her husband's schedules according to advice from Joan Quigley, a noted California astrologer. Quigley claimed, among other feats, to have convinced the First Lady and her husband to re-schedule the presidential debates with Jimmy Carter in 1980 to coincide with "Aquarius rising," a sign favorable to Reagan. Quigley also allegedly helped to maintain the president's popularity by arranging for executive decisions to coincide with astrologically propitious moments. "I was the Teflon in what came to be known as the 'Teflon Presidency,'" she later boasted. At the same time, famed philosopher and psychologist Carl Jung became an outspoken adherent of astrological doctrines. Jung became convinced in the validity of astrology after comparing the birth signs of happily married and divorced couples; he allegedly found that those most favorably matched in astrological terms were more likely to enjoy marital bliss. French mathematician Michael Gauquelin likewise converted to astrology's teachings after claiming to have discovered a discernible correspondence between certain astrological signs and the professions of a large number of Frenchmen whose birth-times had been accurately recorded.

The existence of such prominent believers brought astrology into the mainstream of American society. A 1992 study revealed that nearly 25 percent of Americans believed in astrology. For the first time, most believers came from middle income brackets and had some college education. By the late 1990s, more than 10,000 astrologers practiced their art in the United States, and more than 90 percent of newspapers published horoscopes in daily form. According to reports, Americans of the 1990s spent more than $200 million per annum consulting with astrologers. Moreover, infomercials hawking

the talents of various astrologers and diviners pervaded television networks, and the burgeoning market for astrology-related services and products resulted in the proliferation of astrology shops and stores throughout the country. Astrology also had entrenched itself in late twentieth century American vocabulary and popular culture. The question "What's your sign?" had become an accepted as well as quite widely used "pick-up" line by the end of the twentieth century.

Still, while astrology gained mainstream acceptance, it remained a discredited belief in scientific circles. Most scientists attacked the notion that the pattern of light from stars billions of miles away could influence the temperament of individuals on Earth. As a source of popular belief, scientists pointed to what they called the "Barnum effect," named after the hugely-successful nineteenth century entertainer and hoax perpetrator P.T. Barnum. Skeptics located the transcendent source of astrology's appeal in the tendency of men and women to accept imprecise and widely applicable statements as being specific to them. Barnum manipulated this tendency in the nineteenth century to make millions; scientists of the late twentieth century charged astrologers with doing the same to the masses of their time. American scientists also were vexed by, and perhaps a little jealous of, the popularity of the alleged pseudo-science. By the end of the twentieth century, there were ten times more astrologers in the United States than astronomers, and newspapers provided far more coverage of astrology-related matters than any of the breakthrough astronomical findings of the Hubble Space Telescope.

—Scott Tribble

FURTHER READING:

Gauquelin, Michael. *Dreams and Illusions of Astrology*. Buffalo, Prometheus Books, 1979.

Stewart, J.V. *Astrology: What's Really in the Stars*. Amherst, Prometheus Books, 1996.

Tester, Jim. *A History of Western Astrology*. Woodbridge, New Jersey, Boydell Press, 1987.

Zolar. *The History of Astrology*. New York, Arco, 1972.

AT&T

The American Telephone and Telegraph company—better known as AT&T—and the telephone are virtually synonymous. Both the company and invention which made it famous hold lofty positions in American history. AT&T was the largest corporation in the world for much of the twentieth century, employing over one million people. At the time of its court-mandated breakup 1984, the company's assets totaled $155 billion, more than General Motors, Mobil, and Exxon combined. The telephone's impact is harder to calculate, but it played a major role in the rise of the modern corporation, served as a symbol of American ingenuity and power, and continues to connect people worldwide.

The parent company of the Bell System, commonly referred to as "Ma Bell," AT&T was a government-regulated monopoly for much of its existence. Federal and state officials allowed AT&T to have monopolistic control over the nation's telephone industry because the corporation pledged to provide universal phone service at a reasonable cost. The regulated system worked, especially when comparing the telephone system in the United States to others around the world. It wasn't until the early 1980s that the dawn of a new information age, political maneuverings, and long-distance competition teamed to breakup the Bell System.

Alexander Graham Bell invented the telephone in 1876 and founded the Bell Telephone Company a year later, which would eventually become AT&T. In the early years, after waging patent battles and squeezing out its competition, the company symbolized corporate greed, poor quality, and terrible customer service. But in the early twentieth century, under the leadership of financier J.P. Morgan and Theodore Vail, AT&T became a model for the modern corporation.

Vail revitalized the phone giant, which had over 3 million telephones in service his first year. Within a decade, Vail turned a company with low morale, poor customer service, and a horrible reputation into a model of success. Vail increased AT&T's commitment to research and development, which ultimately led to the formation of Bell Labs in 1925, one of the world's foremost scientific laboratories. Vail also centralized management and rededicated the company to customer service. AT&T's management training program served as a breeding ground for quality leaders. People who left the company then spread the AT&T management philosophy to firms nationwide long before MBA programs were fashionable.

Through its Western Electric subsidiary, AT&T formed alliances with companies around the globe to manufacture telephone equipment. By 1914, AT&T had offices in Antwerp, London, Berlin, Milan, Paris, Tokyo, Buenos Aires, and many other cities. Thus, AT&T was an early leader in developing a global community. The company has always been a leader in opening foreign markets, noted by its recent move into China and long history in East Asia, South America, and Europe.

AT&T's scientific innovations, through Bell Labs (now the independent Lucent Technologies), provided an exhaustive list of inventions. In addition to the company's important work spreading phone service across the nation and then around the world, Bell Labs invented the transistor, which replaced vacuum tubes, in 1948. Widely regarded as one of the most important inventions of the twentieth century, the transistor won Bell Labs the Nobel Prize in 1956. AT&T's research and development lab was also instrumental in developing cellular wireless technology (1947), the computer modem (1957), communications satellites (1962), and commercial ISDN long-distance network services (1988). The electronic switching systems AT&T installed in 1965 after years of research permitted a vast increase in phone traffic and paved the way for the Information Age. These advances in switching technology allow the internet to exist today.

AT&T also played a role in the growth of the U.S. military-industrial complex, dating back to World War I when it expanded domestic military communications and installed telephone lines in France. Western Electric and Bell Labs completed projects for the military throughout World War II. AT&T made important advances in radar technology, which later became the chief means of transmitting long-distance phone calls and television signals after the war. In the 1950s and 1960s, AT&T worked on satellite communications and launched its first in 1962.

Culturally, AT&T's impact has been immense. By the early 1900s, the telephone was already considered an indispensable part of life for most individuals and businesses. The telephone connected rural and farm areas with growing cities and urban centers. AT&T also created the distinction between local and long-distance phone calls, which has become a staple of modern telecommunications. The separation between the two markets facilitated to the rise of the

regional Bell Companies, the "Baby Bells," and ultimately to the breakup of the parent company.

AT&T has also figured in the creation of several cultural icons. The Yellow Pages, more widely-read than the Bible, were developed to help customers use their phones more often and more effectively. AT&T began the use of the telephone as a service tool. Initially, the phone served as a means to get weather and time reports. Today, one can receive almost any information over the phone, from sports scores and soap opera updates to movie listings and bank information. The ubiquitous image of teenagers on the phone in movies and television mirrored the real life development in the 1950s when disposable income and a population explosion made phones readily available for teens to use.

AT&T continues to influence popular culture. The company spent a reported $1 billion in marketing and advertising in 1996 and $650 million in 1997. Although the company continues to reduce its marketing budget, the AT&T brand retains its strength. When asked if they would choose AT&T to be their local phone carrier, the majority say yes. The company's national campaigns are routinely treated as news stories. A more ominous connection the public makes with the AT&T name is corporate downsizing. Throughout the early 1990s, the phone giant seemed to announce layoffs of 10 to 20 thousand employees on a regular basis.

With over 2 million shareholders, AT&T is the most widely held stock in the world. Thus, the company's fortunes continue to have an impact on people everywhere. It is a corporate giant that produces major headlines with every significant action.

—Bob Batchelor

FURTHER READING:

Brooks, John. *Telephone: The First Hundred Years*. New York, Harper & Row, 1976.

Cohen, Jeffrey E. *The Politics of Telecommunications Regulation: The States and the Divestiture of AT&T*. Armonk, New York, M.E. Sharpe, 1992.

Cole, Barry G., editor. *After the Breakup: Assessing the New Post-AT&T Divestiture Era*. New York, Columbia University Press, 1991.

Coll, Steve. *The Deal of the Century: The Breakup of AT&T*. New York, Atheneum, 1986.

Garnet, Robert W. *The Telephone Enterprise: The Evolution of the Bell System's Horizontal Structure, 1876-1909*. Baltimore, The Johns Hopkins University Press, 1985.

Henck, Fred W., and Bernard Strassburg. *A Slippery Slope: The Long Road to the Breakup of AT&T*. New York, Greenwood Press, 1988.

Kleinfield, Sonny. *The Biggest Company on Earth: A Profile of AT&T*. New York, Holt, Rinehart, and Winston, 1981.

Lipartito, Kenneth. *The Bell System and Regional Business: The Telephone in the South, 1877-1920*. Baltimore, Johns Hopkins University Press, 1989.

Shooshan, III, Harry M., editor. *Disconnecting Bell: The Impact of the AT&T Divestiture*. New York, Pergamon Press, 1984.

Smith, George David. *The Anatomy of a Business Strategy: Bell, Western Electric, and the Origins of the American Telephone Industry*. Baltimore, Johns Hopkins University Press, 1985.

Stone, Alan. *Wrong Number: The Breakup of AT&T*. New York, Basic Books, 1989.

Temin, Peter, and Louis Galambos. *The Fall of the Bell System: A Study in Prices and Politics.* Cambridge, Massachusetts, Cambridge University Press, 1987.

Tunstall, W. Brooke. *Disconnecting Parties: Managing the Bell System Break-up: An Inside View.* New York, McGraw-Hill, 1985.

Wasserman, Neil H. *From Invention to Innovation: Long-distance Telephone Transmission at the Turn of the Century.* Baltimore, Johns Hopkins University Press, 1985.

The A-Team

The A-Team television series capitalized on the flamboyant personality of Mr. T, a well-known wrestler and bodyguard to the stars. A kind-hearted tough guy with a dramatic mohawk hairstyle and gaudy jewelry, Mr. T helped win the show a strong fan following and reversed NBC's ratings tailspin in 1983. *The A-Team* saved NBC from critic Tony Schwartz's earlier prediction that the network would ''die, or shrink severely, within the next decade.''

Veteran producer Stephen J. Cannell created this mid-season replacement series as an action adventure comedy. The members of the A-Team were soldiers of fortune running from the government. Cannell shaped the show around the real-life personality of Mr. T as the character Sergeant Bosco ''Bad Attitude'' Baracus. The show's four-year run produced the catch-phrase ''I love it when a plan comes together,'' uttered by George Peppard's character, Colonel John ''Hannibal'' Smith, at the end of an episode, as well as a change in the dress of some of Mr. T's fans.

—Margaret E. Burns

FURTHER READING:

Christensen, Mark, and Cameron Stauth. *The Sweeps: Behind the Scenes in Network TV.* New York, William Morrow, 1992.

Pellegrini, N.N., compiler. ''The A-Team Most FAQ.'' http://www.seas.upenn.edu/~pellegri/AFAQ.html. November 1998.

Athletic Model Guild

Bob Mizer (1922-1992) was the driving force behind the Athletic Model Guild (AMG), a photography studio founded in Los Angeles in 1944, and the magazine *Physique Pictorial,* which published AMG pictures. AMG produced images of nearly nude muscular men; their publication in *Physique Pictorial* was ostensibly for artists and ''physical culture enthusiasts,'' but attained currency primarily with gay men. Before the birth of gay rights, *Physique Pictorial* and the AMG enabled the dissemination of homoerotic images; the magazine also contained idealized, sexualized drawings of macho men by such artists as George Quaintance, Spartacus, and Tom of Finland. The influence of Mizer's presentation of the male body as a beautiful sexual object can be seen in the photography of Robert Mapplethorpe, Bruce Weber, and Herb Ritts.

—Glyn Davis

FURTHER READING:

The Complete Reprint of Physique Pictorial: 1951-1990. New York, Taschen, 1997.

Atkins, Chet (1924—)

Nashville's emergence as the center of country music recording in the late 1950s, and the development of the unique Nashville sound, helped to revive the industry at a time when country was losing ground to rock 'n' roll. Chet Atkins, who became a permanent fixture at the Grand Ole Opry as a talented and technically precise guitarist, was one of the pioneers of Nashville's new sound. He is also recognized as one of the more influential figures in the history of country music recording, having been responsible for both the discovery and development of many prominent country stars.

Atkins was born in 1924 in Luttrell, Tennessee, a small Appalachian town tucked away in the state's eastern corner. His half-brother Jim, a talented guitarist who played in the Les Paul Trio in the 1930s, served as a role model for Chet, who began playing the guitar at a young age. In the early stages of his career, Atkins worked as a guitarist for local radio stations in the region and played as a backup for several recording artists, including the Carter family. In the late 1940s, Steve Sholes, who worked for RCA in New York, noticed Atkins' talents and hired him to record his own songs. His first single, in which he was the featured vocalist, met with little success, but other early instrumental recordings, such as ''Canned Heat'' and ''Country Gentleman,'' found receptive audiences. His intricate style of play established Atkins as one of the more technically gifted guitarists in the industry.

Chet Atkins

Atkins the musician, however, soon gave way to Atkins the producer. His administrative skills equaled his musical ones, prompting Sholes to give Atkins increasing responsibilities in RCA's studios. By the late 1950s, he was head of operations for the Nashville offices. He soon discovered his first hit artist, Don Gibson, whose singles "Oh Lonesome Me" and "I Can't Stop Loving You," both of which Atkins produced, enjoyed immediate success. Atkins then began to bring in an assortment of artists, with diverse and innovative styles, into the studio, marking the beginnings of the Nashville sound. In the late 1950s he was named Vice President at RCA, and continued to produce recordings for some of Nashville's most popular stars. Hank Snow, Elvis Presley, Jim Reeves, Charlie Pride, and Jerry Reed are only a few of the many artists whose careers were enhanced by Atkins' production talents. Atkins has also released many of his own albums, and continues to appear regularly on Nashville's Grand Ole Opry.

Atkins' legacy is in some ways controversial, a fact that he himself has admitted. As an innovator, Atkins changed the face of country music considerably, bringing in new instrumentation such as strings and horns, giving country music a richer and more technically complicated style. As his own music was influenced by a variety of styles, including jazz, pop, and classical, Atkins brought such diversity to bear on the industry, giving rise to crossover artists who were comfortable in front of country, rock, or pop audiences. Such changes, while broadening the audience for country music, also set into motion changes which have caused some within the industry to bemoan the loss of country's proper roots. Regardless of the meanings behind country music's development over the past decades, Chet Atkins undoubtedly has had an enormous impact on both the music and the industry.

—Jeffrey W. Coker

FURTHER READING:

Carr, Patrick, editor. *The Illustrated History of Country Music.* Garden City, New York, Doubleday, 1979.

Malone, Bill C. *Country Music USA.* Austin, University of Texas Press, 1985.

Nash, Alanna. *Behind Closed Doors: Talking with the Legends of Country Music.* New York, Alfred A. Knopf, 1988.

Atlantic City

Called the "City by the Sea," the "Queen of Resorts," or "The World's Favorite Playground," Atlantic City, New Jersey, was the most celebrated family entertainment resort in the United States from the 1880s until World War II. Theodore Roosevelt once claimed that "A man would not be a good American citizen if he did not know of Atlantic City." After falling into decline for almost thirty years, since 1978 Atlantic City has become a center for legalized casino gambling and is once again one of America's most popular destinations, with over 37 million visitors in 1997. Famous for its Boardwalk, amusement piers, and street names, which were the basis of the original Monopoly board game, Atlantic City is also an important convention center and the home of the Miss America Pageant, which has been held there since its origin in 1921 and continues to be one of the most popular television spectaculars.

Located on Absecon Island along the New Jersey seashore, sixty miles southeast of Philadelphia, Atlantic City's development started in 1852 when civil engineer Richard Osborne and prominent local physician Dr. Jonathan Pitney persuaded some investors to bring the railroad to the island, thus forming the Camden-Atlantic Railroad Company. The first train to Atlantic City arrived on July 1, 1854, after a two-and-a-half-hour trip from Camden. Subsequently, flows of tourists followed, and the national aspirations already present in the street nomenclature established by Samuel Richards began to become reality. After the Civil War, the popularity of the wide avenues parallel to the ocean, named after the world's great bodies of water, and the perpendicular streets running east to west and named after the States, expanded and gained international fame, drawing guests from all over the world.

Between 1875 and 1910, Atlantic City boomed. Growing from around 250 inhabitants in 1855 and 2,000 in 1875, the population reached 27,000 residents by the census of 1900 and almost 50,000 in 1910. With inexpensive train access and, within a couple of years, a declining travelling time to Philadelphia from 90 to 50 minutes, daily round trips became very attractive to lower-middle-class urban dwellers. Consequently, hordes of transient visitors flocked to the resort, especially on sunny Sundays. As Atlantic City grew, massive and grandiose hotels like the United States, the Traymore, the glamorous Shellburne, or the fantastic Marlborough-Blenheim, as well as smaller boardinghouses sprang up all over the city. Atlantic City's hotels not only met the demand for accommodations, but they also provided popular entertainment such as dances, concerts, billiards, and roller-skating. By 1888, Atlantic City counted over five hundreds hotels and boardinghouses. They constituted the heart of the town.

In 1870, in order to allow tourists to enjoy walking along the ocean without the inconvenience of rugged nature, the City Council—encouraged by the railroad companies—built the nation's first boardwalk, an 8 foot wide wood structure, which, over the years, would become "the" place to be seen and the social and economic spine of the town. Enlarged successively to 14, 20, and 24 feet in 1880, 1884, and 1890, respectively, the fifth boardwalk of 1896 was a 40-foot wide steel-framed wooden esplanade extending about four miles long, packed with hotels, restaurants, and shops offering souvenirs, photographic portraits, refreshments, and saltwater taffy—a candy that was invented here in 1883. Tourists quickly discovered the pleasure of engaging in recreational shopping, a new phenomenon that would become an institutionalized feature of American culture.

The Boardwalk was an open stage upon which strollers could participate in a permanent great show. As its popularity increased, Colonel George W. Howard constructed the world's first ocean amusement pier in 1882, a 650-foot long structure located off the boardwalk, into the Atlantic Ocean. In the following years, many developers and advertisers re-used his brilliant idea and amusement piers started to spring up along the boardwalk. Some of the most well known and successful ones were Ocean Pier (1891), Steel Pier (1898) named also "The Show Place of the Nation," Million Dollar Pier (1906), Steeplechase Pier (1908) and the Garden Pier (1912). They provided plenty of varied attractions and almost continuous entertainment from band concerts, light operas and musicals, dance contests, vaudeville shows, spectacles led by performers like W.C. Fields, Frank Sinatra, or the escape artist Harry Houdini, to the high-diving horse at Steel Pier, the inauguration of the Miss America Pageant, Dr. Couney's premature infant exhibit, merry-go-rounds, Ferris wheels, roller coasters, sand "sculptures," and other amusements in endless variety to please everyone's taste.

In this pre-Disneyland era, Atlantic City had converted itself into an urban amusement park for visitors, a glamorous fairyland of grandiose display, and a kingdom of flashy architecture and perpetual pleasure. Atlantic City was a cultural symbol. A product of the lower-middle-class urban masses that constituted the largest part of its patrons and sources of revenues, the city reflected their tastes and aspirations. For many of its visitors, Atlantic City was a dream that had come true, a city from the tales of the Arabian nights, heaven on earth, or the eighth wonder of the world—all this despite its omnipresent commercial atmosphere, aggressive advertising campaigns, and strong emphasis on financial profits.

Until World War II, Atlantic City's future seemed bright, but the post-war development of commercial air travel ended its heyday. As tourists from the Northeast United States increasingly flew to Florida and the Caribbean for their vacation, the city declined and became a decaying shadow of its former self. The city's population fell from 64,000 in 1940 to 37,000 in 1990. In 1989, the median income of the city was $12,017 compared with a New Jersey statewide median of $18,870. With the passage of the casino gambling referendum in 1976 and since the opening of the first casino in May 1978, Atlantic City has struggled to revive its economy and undergo a renewal and a revitalization process. Twenty years later, the city boasts thirteen casinos offering 24-hour non-stop action and is now recognized worldwide as a gaming mecca. Nevertheless, even though the Boardwalk and the waterfront have been restored and made prosperous, many neighborhoods of Atlantic City continue to suffer from urban blight and the role of gambling in urban revitalization is still being debated.

—Catherine C. Galley and Briavel Holcomb

FURTHER READING:

Funnel, Charles E. *By the Beautiful Sea: The Rise and High Times of that Great American Resort, Atlantic City.* New Brunswick, New Jersey, Rutgers University Press, 1983.

Lencek, Lena, and Gideon Bosker. *The Beach: The History of Paradise on Earth.* Harmondsworth, Viking Penguin, 1998.

Mahon, Gigi. *The Company that Bought the Boardwalk: A Reporter's Story of How Resorts International Came to Atlantic City.* New York, Random House, 1980.

McMahon, William H. *So Young—So Gay! Story of the Boardwalk, 1870-1970.* Atlantic City, New Jersey, Atlantic City Press, 1970.

Sternlieb, George, and James W. Hughes. *The Atlantic City Gamble.* Cambridge, Harvard University Press, 1983.

Teski, Marea, et al. *A City Revitalized: The Elderly Lose at Monopoly.* London, University Press of America, 1983.

Atlantic Monthly

Despite its low circulation and budget, the *Atlantic Monthly* magazine has maintained a strong influence in American culture by publishing many of the most prominent authors and cultural authorities and maintaining its status as one of the nation's leading general-interest monthlies. It began the twentieth century as America's foremost elite literary magazine, and although it has embraced a wider readership and broadened its scope to focus on political and social issues, it is still known as a magazine for intellectual and highly cultivated readers. Throughout its history, the *Atlantic Monthly* has attempted to reconcile its distrust of the masses, or the "mob," to whom it has not wanted to pander, with its need to appeal to a broad spectrum of readers in order to stay financially afloat. It has made the compromise by positioning itself as the setter of standards and the interpreter of culture for well-informed readers aspiring to ascend to the ranks of the cultural elite.

When the *Atlantic Monthly* was founded in 1857, it quickly became known all over the country as the organ of America's burgeoning high literature. Although it was subtitled "A Magazine of Literature, Art and Politics," it was primarily as a literary magazine that it made its mark. In its first issue (November 1857), it declared itself to be "the exponent of . . . the American idea," but nineteenth century readers associated the magazine with New England and a select group of elite writers. Ralph Waldo Emerson, Henry Wadsworth Longfellow, Nathaniel Hawthorne, William Dean Howells, and Henry James were among its staple contributors. The magazine also published the works of America's leading female writers, such as Harriet Beecher Stowe and Sarah Orne Jewett, and prominent African American writers like Charles Chesnutt. But at the turn of the twentieth century, the *Atlantic Monthly* was instrumental in establishing the American literary canon, which consisted of only its foremost white male contributors. It therefore became associated with a selective, elite vision of American literature rather than a more democratic, diversified literature that had, for a while, seemed possible in its pages.

As the twentieth century dawned, the *Atlantic Monthly* was known as a conservative, even reactionary magazine that defensively tried to promote the values of a by-gone elitist literary and cultural tradition in the face of social upheavals like immigration and the birth of a consumer mass culture. Throughout its history, the *Atlantic Monthly* has attempted to maintain the cultural authority it achieved in the nineteenth century, but it has had a hard time doing so in competition with a widely-diversified literary market. Although its circulation was never large, reaching a height of 50,000 in the 1860s, it declined steadily through the rest of the century. In the early 1900s, while magazines like the popular *Saturday Evening Post* reached circulations of two million, the *Atlantic Monthly* dipped to 7,000. Drastic measures were needed. In an age when illustrations moved magazines, the *Atlantic Monthly* steadfastly refused to appeal to readers with pictures, fearing the blurring of boundaries between itself and the new cadre of mass-market magazines like the *Saturday Evening Post* and *Collier's*. So instead of illustrating it pages, it began to disentangle itself somewhat from its New England literary roots and broaden its appeal by fostering young, up-and-coming writers and by publishing more thought-provoking, general-interest essays.

The *Atlantic Monthly*'s strategy for maintaining its influence has been to lead the nation's discussions of politics, literature, and the arts, publishing the writings of leading thinkers and writers. It has prided itself on the discovery of new talents, publishing some of the first works by Ernest Hemingway, Philip Roth, Eudora Welty, Louise Erdrich, James Dickey, Joyce Carol Oates, and Bobbie Ann Mason. Because of its limited funds, editors have gone in search of unestablished writers, becoming the maker of many writers' careers. In addition to its strong fiction department, the *Atlantic Monthly* has been the mouthpiece of influential thinkers like Theodore Roosevelt, John Muir, Woodrow Wilson, W. E. B. DuBois, and Albert Einstein. It has also been a stage for some of the twentieth century's most prominent debates, publishing scathing analyses of the defects of Wall Street in

1928, a defense of Sacco and Vinzetti shortly before they were sentenced to death in 1927, critiques of the use of the atom bomb, and what would become Martin Luther King's ''Letter from a Birmingham Jail'' in 1963.

In the twentieth century, the *Atlantic Monthly* has steadily progressed from an elitist magazine in which, as its editor Bliss Perry argued in 1902, ''The ideal reading mood . . . is that of well-bred people listening to the after-dinner conversation in public,'' to a populist magazine that wishes to serve ''as the nation's dining-room table,'' in the words of its managing editor, Cullen Murphy, in 1994. As America has grown more democratic in its cultural life, the *Atlantic Monthly* has responded in order to survive. In 1947, for example, the *Atlantic Monthly* joined the rest of America's magazine in printing illustrations. In its attempt to stay afloat, the magazine has made a few compromises while maintaining its status as a cultural authority by helping to shape Americans' tastes and views. This formula for success has paid off in steadily increasing circulation. In 1994, the magazine's circulation topped 500,000, indicating that it is still a strong presence in the magazine market and in American culture. As Murphy defensively declares, ''One thing that the *Atlantic Monthly* is not is an antiquarian enterprise, a museum piece.''

—Anne Boyd

FURTHER READING:

Parker, Jean M. ''Atlantic Monthly.'' *American Mass-Market Magazines*. Ed. Alan and Barbara Nourie. New York, Greenwood Press, 1990, pp. 32-39.

Sedgwick, Ellery. *The Atlantic Monthly, 1857-1909: Yankee Humanism and High Tide and Ebb*. Amherst, University of Massachusetts Press, 1994.

Tebbel, John and Mary Ellen Zuckerman. *The Magazine in America, 1741-1990*. New York, Oxford University Press, 1991.

Atlantic Records

Founded in 1947 by Herb Abrahamson and Ahmet Ertegun, Atlantic Records went on to become one of the most successful independent record companies in the history of music by challenging the economic dominance and musical hegemony of the major record labels in the 1950s. Ertegun and Abrahamson were music lovers who wanted to record the blues and gospel music that was ignored by the major labels. Their taste in rhythm and blues music just happened to coincide with the growing appetite for these records by white teenagers and their parents. Atlantic signed many rhythm and blues artists (such as Big Joe Turner) who made important contributions to what was later called rock 'n' roll.

In the 1960s Atlantic broadened its base in African American music, especially soul music, and made it accessible to the larger white mainstream audience. Its leading record producer— Jerry Wexler—moved many sessions to Muscle Shoals, Alabama where he produced a string of hits for singers such as Aretha Franklin and Wilson Pickett. In 1967 Warner Brothers took over the label.

—Andre Millard

FURTHER READING:

Gillett, Charlie. *Making Tracks: The Story of Atlantic Records*. London, Souvenir, 1988.

Wexler, Jerry, and David Ritz. *Rhythm and the Blues: A Life in American Music*. New York, St Martins, 1994.

Atlas, Charles (1893-1972)

Born Angelo Siciliano in 1893, Charles Atlas went on to become one of the iconic cultural symbols of the twentieth century, influencing generations of men to embrace the ideal of muscular masculinity. Through his popular mail-order courses, advertised in comic books and boys' magazines, Atlas outlined his method to transform oneself from scrawny to brawny and, in doing so, become ''a real man.''

Shrouded in advertising lore, the biography of Charles Atlas must be viewed with a certain amount of skepticism. According to the muscleman's promotional literature, in 1903 the young Angelo Siciliano, newly arrived in the United States, was a puny, ninety-seven-pound weakling and a favorite target of neighborhood bullies and, on occasion, family members. Swearing ''never [to] allow any man on this earth to hurt me again,'' Siciliano set about building his body with a variety of training apparatuses. Despite his best efforts, however, Siciliano proved unable to increase his muscular size to the proportions he desired until a trip to Brooklyn's Prospect Park Zoo yielded an exercise epiphany which would change his life.

Charles Atlas

While at the zoo, Siciliano watched lions and tigers and marveled at their muscularity. It was at this time that he first theorized the principles of "Dynamic Tension." Noting that the animals had no exercise equipment with which to build muscles, Siciliano determined that they must be working "one muscle against the other." He began experimenting with the principles of what would later become known as isometric exercise and within a year had perfected his system of apparatus-free exercise and, allegedly, doubled his body weight.

With his very own muscle-building system, Siciliano adopted the name Charles Atlas to evoke a classical image of muscularity and began performing feats of strength. While showcasing his musculature on a Coney Island, New York, boardwalk, Atlas was discovered by a sculptor who introduced him to the art world. The young bodybuilder became renowned for his well-muscled physique and served as the body model for numerous sculptures including the statue of Alexander Hamilton in front of the United States Treasury building and that of George Washington on the Washington Square Arch in New York City.

In 1921, Atlas received the title of "World's Most Perfectly Developed Man," having triumphed at a prestigious bodybuilding competition hosted by physical culture advocate and publisher Bernarr MacFadden. To capitalize on his growing fame, Atlas co-wrote and sold a manual that explained his isometric principles and various sporting pursuits, and offered general nutritional and health information and "inspirational" passages such as, "Don't dilly dally!" and "Get Up!" Despite his best efforts, Atlas' mail-order business struggled until 1928, when he teamed-up with Charles Roman, a young graduate of New York University's business school. Roman's advertising acumen and flair for ad copy helped transform Atlas from a mere muscleman into an international star.

Roman concocted a simple but effective advertising campaign centered around a cartoon titled, "The Insult Which Made a Man Out of Mac." The short sketch featured a somewhat trite but highly effective sketch in which a bully kicks sand in the face of a scrawny youth (Mac) in front of the weakling's girlfriend. This action prompts the frail Mac to follow Atlas' course and vanquish the bully, thus winning the respect of his sweetheart. Soon spindly youths everywhere were seeking Atlas' remedy for the neighborhood ruffian. This basic appeal, which blended together violence and stereotypical masculinity, propelled the physical culturalist to great financial success and increased celebrity. Although his cartoon advertising yielded impressive results, Atlas refused to rest on his laurels and continued to engage in strength-related publicity stunts such as pulling train cars and bending iron bars for years to come. He retired to Florida, after selling Charles Atlas Ltd. to Roman, where he continued to showcase his still imposing, although markedly less chiseled, physique. In 1972, Atlas died of a heart attack at the age of 79.

After his death, Charles Atlas Ltd. continued to sell the original Dynamic Tension program using Atlas' trademark cartoons and black-and-white photographs of the muscleman in his prime. While still featured in traditional publications geared for boys and young men, Charles Atlas also took to cyberspace, where his courses and an expanded product line are sold via the Internet.

Atlas' trademark program, combining calisthenics and isometric exercises, once well ahead of its time in the field of exercise science, has long since fallen out of favor with the weightlifting and bodybuilding community. A full range of motion exercises involving freeweights or exercise machines have taken precedence over Atlas'

exercises. While considered somewhat archaic, Atlas' exercises often did, and still can, deliver muscular results designed to drive away bullies and stop sand from being kicked in one's face.

—Nicholas Turse

FURTHER READING:

Butler, George, and Charles Gaines. *The Life and Times of Charles Atlas.* Angus and Robertson, 1982.

"Charles Atlas: The World's Most Perfectly Developed Man." http://www.charlesatlas.com. June 1999.

Dutton, Kenneth. *The Perfectible Body: The Western Ideal of Male Physical Development.* New York, Continuum, 1995.

Gaines, Charles. *Yours in Perfect Manhood, Charles Atlas: The Most Effective Fitness Program Ever Devised.* New York, Simon and Schuster, 1982.

Green, Harvey. *Fit for America: Health, Fitness, Sport, and American Society.* New York, Pantheon, 1986.

Schwarzenegger, Arnold, and Bill Dobbins. *Encyclopedia of Modern Bodybuilding.* New York, Simon and Schuster, 1987.

Auerbach, Red (1917—)

Boston Celtics coach Arnold "Red" Auerbach led his team to nine National Basketball Association championships, including an unprecedented eight consecutive wins (1959-1966) during the Celtics' run of eleven championships in thirteen years (1957-1969)—compare that to the Chicago Bulls' six out of eight streak in the 1990s—and introduced coaching innovations that became widespread in the NBA. One of the most enduring images in NBA history is that of Auerbach lighting a victory cigar on the team's bench once another Celtics' victory was safely in hand.

The son of Russian immigrants who settled in Brooklyn, New York, Auerbach devoted himself at an early age to basketball. He excelled as a high school player, eventually being named Second Team, All-Brooklyn during his senior year at Eastern District High School. After attending Seth Low Junior College in New York for two years, Auerbach earned a basketball scholarship to George Washington University in Washington, D.C. As a junior college transfer, Auerbach was joining a highly successful team at George Washington and had to fight, sometimes literally, for playing time. As he recounts in *On and Off the Court,* he asked himself "How the hell was I supposed to break in? The answer was defense. I was all over them like a blanket, hounding them every step, shutting them off every chance I got. Naturally, they didn't like that, so one thing led to another and before you knew it, fists were flying."

Auerbach's service in the navy during World War II helped him gain his first professional coaching job. In 1946, the Basketball Association of America, a forerunner of today's NBA, was formed, consisting of eleven teams. According to Celtics historian Joe Fitzgerald in *That Championship Feeling,* because there was no provision for drafting players for the league's first season, each team had to come up with its own players. Auerbach, a "brash young kid" of twenty-nine, talked the owner of the Washington Capitols into hiring him as coach by convincing him that he could put together a team of former servicemen he knew.

In 1950, after brief stints coaching the BAA's Washington Capitols and the Tri-City Hawks, thirty-two-year-old Auerbach arrived in Boston, a team which had made the playoffs only once in its first four seasons and enjoyed little popularity in contrast to the city's beloved baseball Red Sox and hockey Bruins. At the same time, Boston acquired guard Bob Cousy, a local legend who had played college basketball at Holy Cross in Worcester, Massachusetts. Cousy, with Auerbach's encouragement, was known for his spectacular passing and "fast breaking" style. During Auerbach's first six seasons, due primarily to Cousy's efforts, the Celtics led the league in scoring every year but never won a championship.

It was the acquisition of center Bill Russell in 1956 which provided Auerbach's Celtics with what they had been missing: defense. Combining Russell's rebounding and shot-blocking with Cousy's offense, the Celtics won their first NBA championship in the 1956-1957 season, defeating the St. Louis Hawks in a decisive double overtime game to clinch the title. The Celtics failed to defend their championship the following season, losing in the finals to the same St. Louis team they had defeated the previous year, but began their eight-year, championship streak in 1959. Although Auerbach was just forty-seven years old in 1966, he decided to retire from coaching, as he felt worn out from the pressures of keeping his team at such a high level of performance over a long period of time.

As a coach, Auerbach made a number of innovations which were keys to the Celtics' immense success. Auerbach was one of the first to utilize so-called "role" players, meaning players who specialized in one or two aspects of the game, filling gaps which were essential to the team's success. Because of this philosophy, Auerbach put little stock in statistics, caring more about how well a player fit into his concept of what it took to ensure victory than about how many points he scored. Another of Auerbach's innovations was the use of the so-called "Sixth Man," which referred to a highly skilled reserve player who would come off the bench late in the first quarter of a game and provide a spark with instant scoring. The use of such players became so widespread that the NBA now offers an award to the player considered to be the best Sixth Man in the league. Finally, Auerbach had an uncanny ability to acquire players who were nearing the ends of their careers with other teams or had achieved bad reputations and use them to contribute to Boston championships. Cousy summed up Auerbach's coaching philosophy in *Cousy on the Celtic Mystique:* "With Red it was, What does it take to win? Find the talent, get them in shape, keep them motivated, and don't get fancy."

Auerbach's departure from coaching in 1966 did not, however, spell the end of his contribution to Boston's success. As the team's general manager, he made a number of farsighted deals which contributed to seven subsequent Boston championships between the late 1960s and mid-1980s. Perhaps his most celebrated move was his decision in 1978 to draft forward Larry Bird after his junior year in college, meaning that the Celtics had exclusive rights to the player after the completion of his senior season. Bird became one of the greatest players in NBA history, leading the Celtics to NBA championships in 1981, 1984, and 1986. Auerbach was elected to the Basketball Hall of Fame in 1968.

—Jason George

FURTHER READING:

Auerbach, Red, with Joe Fitzgerald. *On and Off the Court.* New York, MacMillan, 1985.

Cousy, Bob, and Bob Ryan. *Cousy on the Celtic Mystique.* New York, McGraw-Hill, 1988.

Fitzgerald, Joe T. *That Championship Feeling: The Story of the Boston Celtics.* New York, Charles Scribner's Sons, 1975.

Ryan, Bob. *The Boston Celtics: The History, Legends, and Images of America's Most Celebrated Team.* Reading, Mass., Addison-Wesley, 1989.

Aunt Jemima

The advertising image of Aunt Jemima was born at the 1893 World Columbian Exhibition in Chicago, Illinois, with ex-slave Nancy Green's promotion of inventor Charles Rutt's pancake mix. More than an American corporate icon, Aunt Jemima not only advertises the great American breakfast, but also conveys a stereotype of blackness and embodies the haunting legacy of the racial past. As a white construction of black identity, Aunt Jemima represents an easygoing, nostalgic and non-threatening domesticated character highly reminiscent of Mammy in *Gone with the Wind.* Despite a corporate image makeover in the early 1980s, which involved slimmer features and the loss of the servitude-signifying bandanna, the trademark "Aunt Jemima" continues to invoke memories of slavery and segregation and reminds us of the persistence of racial prejudice.

—Stephen C. Kenny

FURTHER READING:

Manring, M. M. *Slave in a Box: The Strange Career of Aunt Jemima.* Charlottesville, University Press of Virginia, 1998.

Pieterse, Jan Nederveen. *White on Black: Images of Africa and Blacks in Western Popular Culture.* New Haven and London, Yale University Press, 1992.

Automobile

The first inventors to build automobiles lived in Europe, but the United States rapidly coopted their inventions to become the world's preeminent car culture. Over the course of the twentieth century, Americans completely reorganized the country's built environment to accommodate a technological system of universal car ownership, an extensive network of high quality roads, and a well developed automobile service industry. By mid-century, automobiles had become the country's primary mode of transportation, replacing horses, railroads, and urban mass transit systems. At the same time, automobiles became objects of cultural disagreement, praise, humor, symbolism, status, and innumerable hopes and fears. More than providing a way to move around, over the course of the twentieth century automobiles became a central defining characteristic of American culture.

From the 1890s forward, designers of horseless carriages spent a great deal of time in their backyard workshops building the experimental prototypes that introduced the country to automobiles. Some produced high-quality electric, gasoline, and steam-powered vehicles; others struggled simply to make their machines work. While the

The advertising representation of "Aunt Jemima."

inventors tinkered, advocates raised their voices to promote the novel contraptions, employing the era's colorful rhetoric to hail the potential of the new machines. Design breakthroughs soon made cars more reliable, and a proliferating number of manufacturers—usually little more than parts assemblers—took advantage of the low start-up costs characterizing the early industry and opened their doors for business. Publicity stunts to popularize automobiles such as races, long-distance reliability tours, and auto shows became more and more common, and manufacturers found a ready and enthusiastic market among Americans who could afford the high price tags, most of whom were members of the urban elite.

Boosters in the 1890s were particularly enthusiastic about pointing out the many advantages automobiles offered compared to horses, the primary mode of quick local transportation for most of the nineteenth century. Automobiles did not bite, kick, or scare, a number of writers pointed out, while more sober commentators provided detailed cost comparisons between cars and horses, invariably concluding that car owners would enjoy long-term savings. Other pundits described the potential uses of the automobile in utopian terms. In rural areas, automobiles would eliminate the isolation that plagued farm life and draw cities and countryside closer together. In urban areas, cars would solve growing traffic problems, replacing a hodge-podge of horses, trolleys, pushcarts, and pedestrians with smaller individual conveyances. Since they were more mobile and easier to handle than trolleys or horse-drawn wagons, cars would decrease traffic fatalities. Since they could take advantage of back streets instead of following fixed rails, automobiles would free suburban homeowners from the trolley lines. Finally, by replacing horses, automobiles would eliminate the health and smell problems posed by the large quantities of manure and urine that coated city streets every day. According to boosters writing in the popular press, then, automobiles appeared to be a true Godsend.

Not everyone saw cars or the growing number of motorists in such a favorable light, especially since only urban elites and rural professionals such as doctors could afford automobiles for many years after they became commercially available. Farmers in particular complained about urban joyriders who scared their horses, tore up their roads, sprinkled their crops in dust, and picnicked in their fields. "Nothing has spread the socialist feeling in this country more than the automobile," Woodrow Wilson announced in 1906. "To the countryman they are a picture of the arrogance of wealth, with all its independence and carelessness."

Though Wilson was attuned to real rural- and class-based discontent about car use at the turn of the century, automobiles did not remain toys of the wealthy for long because a growing number of manufacturers began to produce cheap cars intended for a mass market. Ransom Olds produced the first widely popular and inexpensive model, his "curved dash" Oldsmobile, of which he made over 12,000 between 1901 and 1904. His small, lightweight, reliable runabout took such a hold of the public's imagination that a composer commemorated it in a popular song, "In My Merry Oldsmobile":

> Come away with me, Lucille,
> In my merry Oldsmobile,
> Over the road of life we'll fly,
> Autobubbling you and I,
> To the church we'll swiftly steal,
> And our wedding bells will peal,
> You can go as far as you like with me,
> In our merry Oldsmobile.

As much success as the Oldsmobile enjoyed, it took Henry Ford, a manufacturer from Dearborn, Michigan, to seize the idea of mass production and use it to change the face of the automobile industry. The Ford Model T—alternately dubbed the "Tin Lizzie" and the "flivver" by an enthusiastic public—first became available in 1908. The car coupled a simple, durable design and new manufacturing methods, which kept it relatively inexpensive at $850. After years of development, experimentation, and falling prices, the Ford Company launched the world's first fully automated assembly line in 1914. Between 1909 and 1926, the Model T averaged nearly forty-three percent of the automobile industry's total output. As a result of its assembly-line construction, the car's price dropped steadily to a low of $290 on the eve of its withdrawal from the market in 1927. The company also set new standards for the industry by announcing in 1914 that it would more than double its workers' minimum wages to an unprecedented five dollars per day. Over the course of the Model T's production run, the Ford Company combined assembly-line manufacturing, high wages, aggressive mass-marketing techniques, and an innovative branch assembly system to make and sell over fifteen million cars. As a result, Henry Ford became something of a folk hero, particularly in grass-roots America, while the car so well-suited to the poor roads of rural America became the subject of its own popular genre of jokes and stories. In 1929, the journalist Charles Merz called the Model T "the log cabin of the motor age." It was an apt description, for more first-time buyers bought Model T's than any other type, making it the car that ushered most Americans into the automobile era.

Between 1908 and 1920, as automobiles became affordable to a greater percentage of Americans, farmers quickly abandoned their prejudices against the newfangled machines and embraced them as utilitarian tools that expanded the possibilities of rural life. The diffusion of cars among rural residents had a significant effect on farm families, still forty percent of the United States population in 1920. Because automobiles increased the realistic distance one could travel in a day—and unlike horses did not get so tired after long trips that they were unable to work the next day—cars allowed farmers to make more frequent trips to see neighbors and visit town. In addition, rural Americans found a number of uses for the versatile, tough machines on farms themselves, hauling supplies, moving quickly around the farm, and using the engine to power other farm machinery.

As car sales soared before 1920, the movement for good roads gained momentum and became a priority for many state legislatures. Rural roads had fallen into a bad state of neglect since the advent of the railroads, but early "Good Roads" reformers nevertheless met stiff opposition to their proposed plans for improvement. Farmers argued that expensive road improvement programs would cost local citizens too much in taxes, and that good roads would benefit urban motorists much more than the rural residents footing the bill. Reformers had to wage fierce political battles to overcome rural opposition, and succeeded only after convincing state legislatures to finance improvements entirely with state funds, completely removing road maintenance from local control. Resistance was not limited to rural areas, however. Even within cities, many working-class neighborhoods opposed the attempts of Good Roads advocates to convert streets into arteries for traffic, preferring instead to protect the more traditional function of neighborhood streets as social spaces for public gatherings and recreation. In addition, special interest groups such as street-car monopolies and political machines fought to maintain their control over the streets. Only after the victory of other Progressive Era municipal reformers did road engineers succeed in bringing their values of efficiency and expertise to city street system management.

In the 1920s, car prices dropped, designs improved, roads became more drivable, and automobiles increasingly seemed to provide the key to innumerable advantages of modern life. To many people, cars embodied freedom, progress, and social status all at the same time. Not only could car owners enjoy the exhilaration of speeding down open roads, but they also had the power to choose their own travel routes, departure times, and passengers. Outdoor "autocamping" became a popular family pastime, and an entire tourist industry designed to feed, house, and entertain motorists sprang up almost overnight. Even advertising adapted to a public traveling thirty miles per hour, led by the innovative Burma Shave campaign that spread its jingles over consecutive roadside billboards. One set informed motorists that "IF YOU DON'T KNOW / WHOSE SIGNS / THESE ARE / YOU CAN'T HAVE / DRIVEN VERY FAR / BURMA SHAVE." In a variety of ways, then, automobile engines provided much of the roar of the Roaring Twenties, and stood next to the flapper, the flask, and the Charleston as a quintessential symbol of the time.

As an icon of the New Era, the automobile also symbolized the negative aspects of modern life to those who lamented the crumbling of Victorian standards of morality, family, and propriety. Ministers bewailed the institution of the "Sunday Drive," the growing tendency of their flocks to skip church on pretty days to motor across the countryside. Law enforcement officials and members of the press expressed frustration over the growing number of criminals who used getaway cars to flee from the police. Even social critics who tended to approve of the passing of Victorian values noted that the rapid diffusion of automobiles in the 1920s created a number of unanticipated problems. Rather than solving traffic problems, widespread car ownership increased the number of vehicles on the road—and lining the curbs—which made traffic worse than ever before. Parking problems became so acute in many cities that humorist Will Rogers joked in 1924 that "Politics ain't worrying this Country one tenth as much as Parking Space." Building expensive new roads to alleviate congestion paradoxically increased it by encouraging people to use them more frequently. Individual automobiles seemed to be a great idea, but people increasingly began to see that too many cars could frustrate their ability to realize the automobile's promises of freedom, mobility, and easy escape.

Despite these problems and a small group of naysayers, American popular culture adopted the automobile with alacrity. Tin Pan Alley artists published hundreds of automobile-related songs, with titles like "Get A Horse," "Otto, You Ought to Take Me in Your Auto," and "In Our Little Love Mobile." Broadway and vaudeville

An example of the early automobile assembly line.

shows both adopted cars as comic props, a tradition the Keystone Kops carried over into the movie industry. Gangster films in particular relied on cars for high-speed chases and shoot-outs, but even films without automobile-centered plots used cars as symbols of social hierarchy: Model T's immediately signaled humble origins, while limousines indicated wealth. In *Babbitt* (1922), Sinclair Lewis noted that "a family's motor indicated its social rank as precisely as the grades of the peerage determined the rank of an English family," and in the eyes of Nick Carraway, the narrator of F. Scott Fitzgerald's *The Great Gatsby* (1925), Gatsby's Rolls-Royce represented the "fresh, green breast of the new world." Parents worried that teenagers used automobiles as mobile bedrooms, a growing number of women declared their independence by taking the wheel, and sociologists Robert and Helen Lynd declared that automobiles had become "an accepted essential of normal living" during the 1920s.

After the stock market crashed in 1929, automobiles remained important cultural symbols. Throughout the Great Depression, cars reminded people of the prosperity that they had lost. On the other hand, widespread car ownership among people without homes or jobs

called attention to the country's comparatively high standard of living; in the United States, it seemed, poverty did not preclude automobile ownership. Countless families traveled around the country by car in search of work, rationing money to pay for gasoline even before buying food. Dorothea Lange's photography and John Steinbeck's *The Grapes of Wrath* (1939) immortalized these migrants, who became for many the symbolic essence of the decade's economic ills. Automobiles had become such a permanent fixture in American life when the Depression hit that even in its pit, when the automobile industry's production had fallen to below a quarter of its 1929 figures, car registrations remained at over ninety percent of their 1929 number. Even before the Depression began most Americans had thoroughly modified their lifestyles to take advantage of what automobiles had to offer, and they refused to let a weak economy deprive them of their cars. Tellingly, steady automobile use through the 1930s provided an uninterrupted flow of income from gasoline taxes, which the country used to build roads at an unprecedented rate.

The thousands of miles of paved highway built during the Depression hint at one of the most profound developments of the first half of the twentieth century: the extensive modification and rearrangement of the country's built environment to accommodate widespread automobile use. In urban areas, general car ownership undermined the centralizing influence of the railroads. Because businesses could unload railroad freight into motorized trucks instead of horse-drawn wagons, which significantly reduced their short-haul transportation costs, proximity to railroad depots became much less important. At the same time, growing traffic problems in urban cores along with a more mobile buying public made relocating to less congested areas with better parking for their customers an increasingly attractive option for small-volume businesses.

Although cities continued to expand, Americans used their cars to move in ever-growing numbers to the suburbs. As early as the 1920s suburban growth had begun to rival that of cities, but only after World War II did American suburbs come into their own. Beginning in the mid-1940s, huge real estate developers took advantage of new technology, federally insured home loans, and low energy costs to respond to the acute housing shortage that returning GIs, the baby boom, and pent-up demand from the Depression had created. Developers purchased large land holdings on the border of cities, bulldozed everything to facilitate new standardized construction techniques, and rebuilt the landscape from the ground up. Roads and cars, of course, were essential components of the suburban developers' visions. So were large yards (which provided the social spaces for suburbanites that streets had once supplied for urban residents) and convenient local shopping centers (with plenty of parking). Even the design of American houses changed to accommodate automobiles, with more and more architects including carports or integrated garages as standard features on new homes.

In rural America, the least direct but most far-reaching effects of widespread car ownership came as rural institutions underwent a spatial reorganization in response to the increased mobility and range of the rural population. In the first decade or so of the century, religious, educational, commercial, medical, and even mail services consolidated, enabling them to take advantage of centralized distribution and economies of scale. For most rural Americans, the centralization of institutions meant that by mid-century access to motorized transportation had become a prerequisite for taking advantage of many rural services.

At about the same time suburban growth exploded in the mid-1940s, road engineers began to focus on developing the potential of automobiles for long-distance travel. For the first several decades of the century, long-distance travelers by automobile had to rely on detailed maps and confusing road signs to navigate their courses. In the 1920s, limited-access roads without stop lights or intersections at grade became popular in some parts of the country, but most people judged these scenic, carefully landscaped "parkways" according to their recreational value rather than their ability to move large numbers of people quickly and efficiently. By 1939, however, designers like Norman Bel Geddes began to stress the need for more efficient road planning, as his "Futurama" exhibit at the New York World's Fair demonstrated. Over five million people saw his model city, the most popular display at the exhibition, which featured elevated freeways and high-speed traffic coursing through its center. Impressed, many states followed the lead of Pennsylvania, which in 1940 opened 360 miles of high-speed toll road with gentle grades and no traffic lights. By 1943, a variety of automobile-related interest groups joined together to form the American Road Builders Association, which began lobbying for a comprehensive national system of new super-highways. Then in 1954, President Dwight Eisenhower appointed a

committee to examine the issue of increasing federal road aid—headed by a member of the General Motors board of directors. Two years later, Eisenhower signed the Interstate Highway Act, committing the federal government to provide ninety percent of the cost of a 41,000-mile highway system, the largest peacetime construction project in history.

The new interstates transformed the ability of the nation's road system to accommodate high-speed long-distance travel. As a result, the heavy trucking industry's share of interstate deliveries rose from about fifteen percent of the national total in 1950 to almost twenty-five percent by the end of the decade, a trend which accelerated the decentralization of industry that had started before the war. Suburbs sprang up even farther away from city limits, and Americans soon began to travel more miles on interstates than any other type of road. The new highways also encouraged the development of roadside businesses that serviced highway travelers. A uniform highway culture of drive-in restaurants, gas stations, and huge regional shopping malls soon developed, all of it advertised on large roadside billboards. Industries designed to serve motorists expanded, with the motel industry in particular growing in lock-step with the interstates, taking advantage of the same increase in family vacations that caused visits to national parks to double over the course of the 1950s.

While car designers in the 1950s subordinated all other considerations to style and comfort, engineers focused on boosting acceleration and maximum speed. With eager enthusiasm, Americans embraced the large, gas-guzzling, chrome-detailed, tail-finned automobiles that Detroit produced. Teens in particular developed an entire subculture with automobiles at the center. Cruising the local strip, hanging out at drive-in restaurants, drag-racing, and attending drive-in movies all became standard nationwide pastimes.

Yet trouble brewed beneath the surface of the 1950s car culture, and in the 1960s and 1970s a number of emerging problems drove home several negative unanticipated consequences of universal car ownership. Safety concerns, for example, became increasingly important in the mid-1960s since annual automobile-related deaths had increased from roughly 30,000 to 50,000 between 1945 and 1965. Environmental damage, too, became an issue for many Americans, who focused on problems like air pollution, oil spills, the tendency of heavy automobile tourism to destroy scenic areas, and the damaging effects of new road construction on places ranging from urban neighborhoods to national wilderness preserves.

In both cases, concerned citizens turned to the government to regulate the automobile industry after less coercive attempts to address problems failed. In 1965, Ralph Nader's *Unsafe at Any Speed* galvanized popular concern over motor vehicle safety. Congress responded in 1966 with the National Traffic and Motor Vehicle Safety Act, which required a number of safety features on all models beginning in 1968, despite auto industry protests that regulations would be expensive and ineffective. Within two years of the implementation of the law, the ratio of deaths to miles driven had declined steeply, injuring Americans' trust in the good faith efforts of industry to respond to consumer concerns without active regulation. Similarly, since repeated requests to manufacturers throughout the 1950s to reduce emissions had failed, California required all new cars from 1966 on to have emissions-reducing technology. Other states followed suit, discounting the car industry's claims that once again solutions would be slow to develop, expensive, and difficult to implement.

The most significant example of cultural backlash against the problems of widespread dependence on automobiles came during and after the Arab oil embargo of 1973, when the price of crude oil increased over 130 percent in less than three months. Around the country, lines of cars snaked out of gas stations, where pump prices had doubled nearly overnight. Recriminations and accusations about why the country had become so dependent on foreign oil flew back and forth—but the major result was that American manufacturers steadily lost market share after 1973 to small foreign imports that provided greater fuel-efficiency, cheaper prices, and lower emissions than Detroit models. Domestic full- and mid-size automobiles, once the undisputed champions of the United States, lost a substantial portion of their market share through the 1970s. By 1980, small cars comprised over 60 percent of all sales within the country.

The widespread cultural discontent with dependence on cars lasted only as long as the high gasoline prices. Rather than making changes that would decrease reliance on automobiles, the country addressed new problems as they arose with complex technological and regulatory fixes. Oil prices eventually fell to pre-embargo lows in the 1980s, and by the late 1990s cheap fuel helped reverse the decades-long trend toward smaller cars. Large sport utility vehicles with lower fuel efficiency became increasingly popular, and somewhat ironically relied heavily on "back-to-nature" themes in their marketing strategies. Despite substantial advances in quality and responsiveness to consumers, American manufacturers never regained their dominance of the immediate postwar years. At the end of the twentieth century, however, the American car culture itself continued to be a central characteristic distinguishing the United States from most other countries around the world.

—Christopher W. Wells

FURTHER READING:

Berger, Michael. *The Devil Wagon in God's Country: The Automobile and Social Change in Rural America, 1893-1929.* Hamden, Connecticut, Archon Books, 1979.

Flink, James J. *America Adopts the Automobile, 1895-1910.* Cambridge, Massachusetts, MIT Press, 1970.

————. *The Car Culture.* Cambridge, Mass., MIT Press, 1975.

Jennings, Jan, editor. *Roadside America: The Automobile in Design and Culture.* Ames, Iowa, Iowa State University Press, 1990.

Lewis, David L., and Laurence Goldstein, editors. *The Automobile and American Culture.* Ann Arbor, University of Michigan Press, 1983.

Rae, John Bell. *The American Automobile: A Brief History.* Chicago, University of Chicago Press, 1965.

Rose, Mark H. *Interstate: Express Highway Politics, 1939-1989.* Knoxville, University of Tennessee Press, 1990.

Scharff, Virginia. *Taking the Wheel: Women and the Coming of the Motor Age.* New York, Free Press, 1991.

Sears, Stephen W. *The American Heritage History of the Automobile in America.* New York, American Heritage Publishing Company, 1977.

Wik, Reynold M. *Henry Ford and Grass-Roots America.* Ann Arbor, University of Michigan Press, 1972.

Autry, Gene (1907-1998)

Famous as the original "Singing Cowboy," Gene Autry rode the range in the tradition of Tom Mix—clean living, honest, and innocent. He established the singing cowboy stereotype (continued by Roy Rogers, who inherited Autry's sobriquet): that of the heroic horseman who could handle a guitar or a gun with equal aplomb. A star of film, radio, and television, Autry was probably best known for his trademark song, "Back in the Saddle Again," as well as for many more of the over 250 songs he wrote in his lifetime.

Born in Texas, Autry moved to Oklahoma as a teenager, and began working as a telegrapher for the railroad after high school. While with the railroad, he began composing and performing with Jimmy Scott, with whom he co-wrote his first hit, "That Silver-Haired Daddy of Mine," which sold half a million copies in 1929 (a record for the period). The same year, he auditioned for the Victor Recording Company in New York City but was told he needed more experience. He returned to Tulsa and began singing on a local radio program, earning the nickname "Oklahoma's Yodeling Cowboy." Columbia Records signed him to a contract in 1930 and sent him to Chicago to sing on various radio programs, including the *Farm and Home Hour* and the *National Barndance*. He recorded a variety of songs during the 1930s, such as "A Gangster's Warning," "My Old Pal of Yesterday," and even the labor song "The Death of Mother Jones."

In 1934, Autry began appearing in films as a "tuneful cowpuncher" and made numerous highly successful pictures with his

Gene Autry

horse, Champion, before he retired from the film industry in the 1950s. His debut film was *In Old Santa Fe*, in which he made only a brief singing appearance, but reaction to his performance was favorable and it got him a lead role in the 13-part serial *Phantom Empire*. His first starring role in a feature film followed with *Tumblin' Tumbleweeds* (1935), and he became not only Republic Pictures' reigning king of ''B'' Westerns, but the only Western star to be featured on the list of top ten Hollywood moneymakers between 1938 and 1942. Autry's pictures are notable for the smooth integration of the songs into the plots, helping to move the action along. Some of his films were even built around particular songs, among them *Tumblin' Tumbleweeds, The Singing Cowboy* (1937), *Melody Ranch* (1940) and *Back in the Saddle* (1941).

After serving as a technical sergeant in the Army Air Corps during World War II, Autry returned to Hollywood to make more films. From film, Autry made the transition into both radio and television programming. He hosted the *Melody Ranch* show on radio (and later on television), and he was involved with numerous successful television series, including *The Gene Autry Show* (1950-56) and *The Adventures of Champion* (1955-56). A masterful merchandiser, he developed a lucrative and hugely successful lines of clothes, comic books, children's books, and toys, while at the same time managing and touring with his own rodeo company. In addition to his country songs, Autry wrote numerous other popular songs, including ''Frosty the Snowman,'' ''Peter Cottontail,'' and, most famously, the enduring ''Rudolph the Red-Nosed Reindeer.'' Thanks to his financial success, Autry was able to buy the California Angels baseball team and served as a vice president of the American Baseball League for many years.

Like Tom Mix before him, Autry's public image stressed strong morals and honesty, and fueled the romantic image of the American cowboy. His ten-point ''Cowboy Code'' featured such sincere advice as ''The Cowboy must never shoot first, hit a smaller man, or take unfair advantage''; ''He must not advocate or possess racially or religiously intolerant ideas''; ''He must neither drink nor smoke''; and ''The Cowboy is a patriot.'' Gene Autry was elected to the Country Music Hall of Fame 1969, 29 years before his death at the age of 91.

—Deborah M. Mix

FURTHER READING:

Autry, Gene. *The Essential Gene Autry.* Columbia/Legacy Records, 1992.

Autry, Gene, with Mickey Herskowitz. *Back in the Saddle Again.* Garden City, New York, Doubleday, 1978.

Rothel, David. *The Gene Autry Book.* Madison, North Carolina, Empire Publishing, 1988.

Avalon, Frankie (1939—)

During the late 1950s, as record producers and promoters rushed to capitalize on the potent youth market, they aggressively sought out clean-cut young males to mold into singing stars. Seeking to fill a void that had been created in part by the absence of Elvis Presley, who was then a G.I. stationed in Germany, they purposely toned down the controversial aspects of the new musical form, rock 'n' roll. Unlike

Frankie Avalon and Annette Funicello

Presley, who emoted a powerful sexuality, the manufactured teen idols elicited a friendly, non-threatening demeanor. The engaging Frankie Avalon, whose skinniness prompted comparisons to an earlier generation's teen idol, Frank Sinatra, perfectly filled that bill. As he once explained, ''I was one of those guys who there was a possibility of dating . . . I had a certain innocence.''

A native of South Philadelphia, Francis Thomas Avallone was just eleven when he talked his father into buying him a thirty-five-dollar pawn shop trumpet (after seeing the 1950 Kirk Douglas movie, *Young Man with a Horn*). Avalon went on to appear in local talent shows, including the program *TV Teen Club.* The show's host, Paul Whiteman, christened him ''Frankie Avalon.''

A meeting with singer Al Martino led to an introduction to a New York talent scout, who in turn arranged an audition with Jackie Gleason. After appearing on Gleason's TV show, additional national shows followed, as did a contract with an RCA subsidiary label. For his first two records—the instrumentals ''Trumpet Sorrento'' and ''Trumpet Tarantella''—the performer was billed as ''11-year-old Frankie Avalon.'' He was twelve when he became the trumpet player for the South Philadelphia group, Rocco and the Saints, which also included Bobby Rydell on drums. As a member of the Saints, Avalon performed at local clubs, on local television, and even toured Atlantic City. The talented trumpeter also sometimes doubled as the group's singer. As a result of one such performance he caught the attention of Bob Marcucci and Peter De Angelis, owners of Chancellor Records. In 1958 Avalon signed a contract with their label, and went on to be managed by Marcucci, who also handled Fabian.

Though his first two Chancellor records were unsuccessful, Avalon enjoyed a hit with his third effort, "Dede Dinah," which he performed while pinching his nose for a nasal inflection. Though the record went gold, it was with the 1959 "Venus" that Avalon enjoyed his biggest success. Recorded after nine takes, and released three days later, it sold more than a million copies in less than one week.

Along with other heartthrobs of the day, Avalon became a frequent guest artist on *American Bandstand.* And like his teen idol brethren, including Philadelphia friends Fabian and Rydell, he headed to Hollywood where he was given co-starring roles alongside respected veterans. In *Guns of the Timberland* he shared the screen with Alan Ladd; in *The Alamo* he joined an all-star cast, led by John Wayne.

In the early 1960s, Avalon used his affable, clean-cut image to clever effect as the star and a producer of the *Beach Party* movies, in which he was sometimes romantically teamed with another former 1950s icon and close friend Annette Funicello. Made by the youth-oriented American International Pictures, the movies were filmed in less than two weeks, on shoestring budgets, and featured a melange of robust young performers, musical numbers, surfing, drag racing, and innocuous comedy. Despite the preponderance of bikini-clad starlets, the overall effect was one of wholesome, fun-loving youth. But in fact, the young people of the decade were on the verge of a counter-culture revolution. When it happened, Avalon, like many others who got their start in the 1950s, was passé.

He attempted to change his image by appearing in low-budget exploitation movies such as the 1970 *Horror House.* But despite his rebellion at what he once called "that damn teen idol thing," it was precisely that reputation that propelled his comeback. In the 1976 movie version of *Grease,* which celebrates the 1950s, Avalon seemingly emerges from heaven to dispense advice in the stand-out musical number, "Beauty School Dropout." Avalon's cameo appearance generated so much attention that he went on to record a disco-version of "Venus." He further capitalized on his early image with the 1987 movie, *Back to the Beach,* in which he was reunited with Funicello.

Avalon, who is the father of eight and a grandfather, has also capitalized on his still-youthful looks to market a line of beauty and health care products on the Home Shopping Nework. In addition, he performs in the concert tour "The Golden Boys of Rock 'n' Roll," in which he and Fabian and Rydell star.

—Pat H. Broeske

FURTHER READING:

Bronson, Fred. *The Billboard Book of Number One Hits.* New York, Billboard Publications, 1988.

Miller, Jim, editor. *The Rolling Stone Illustrated History of Rock & Roll.* New York, Random House, 1980.

Whitney, Dwight. "Easy Doesn't Do It—Starring Frankie Avalon." *TV Guide.* August 21, 1976, 14-17.

Avedon, Richard (1923—)

Richard Avedon added new depth to fashion photography beginning in 1945. His fashion photographs—in *Harper's Bazaar,* 1945-66, and in *Vogue,* 1966-90—were distinctive in expressing both motion and emotion. Avedon imparted the animation of streets, narrative, and energy to the garment. His most famous fashion image, *Dovima with Elephants* (1955), is an unabashed beauty-and-the-beast study in sexuality. By the 1950s, Avedon also made memorable non-fashion images, including a 1957 portrait of the Duke and Duchess of Windsor in vacant melancholy, 1960s heroic studies of Rudolf Nureyev dancing nude, and 1960s epics of the civil rights movement and mental patients at East Louisiana State Hospital. Although Avedon's photographs moved away from fashion toward the topical, social, and character-revealing, the common theme of all his photography has been emotion, always aggressive and frequently shocking.

—Richard Martin

FURTHER READING:

Avedon, Richard. *An Autobiography.* New York, Random House, 1993.

Evidence, 1944-1994 (exhibition catalogue). New York, Whitney Museum of American Art/Random House, 1994.

The Avengers

The Avengers (which appeared on ABC from 1961 to 1969) has the distinction of being the most popular British television series to run on an American commercial network, and was the first such series to do so in prime time. Sophisticated, tongue-in-cheek, but never camp or silly, *The Avengers* was also one of the first and best of the soon-to-be-popular television spy series, and varied in tone from crime melodrama to outright science fiction. Every episode starred John Steed (Patrick Macnee), an urbane British intelligence agent who heads a mysterious elite squad known as the Avengers, so named for their propensity to right wrongs.

The first four seasons of the show were not run in the United States, but were videotaped and aired only in Britain. The series began as a follow-up to *Police Surgeon* (1960), which starred Ian Hendry as a doctor who helped the police solve mysteries. Sydney Newman, the head of programming at ABC-TV in England, wanted to feature Hendry in a new series that would pair him as Dr. David Keel with a secret agent, John Steed, in a fight against crime.

Patrick Macnee had had a successful acting career in Canada and Hollywood, but when he returned to England, he was unable to find work as an actor. An old friend got him a position as an associate producer on *The Valiant Years* (1960-63) about Winston Churchill, and Macnee soon found himself producing the entire show. He planned on remaining a producer when he was asked to star in *The Avengers* (on which he initially received second billing) and asked for a ridiculously high salary, expecting the producers to reject it. When they didn't, Steed was born.

Though he initially used a gun, Macnee quickly altered the character, which he saw as a combination of the Scarlet Pimpernel, his father, Ralph Richardson, and his C.O. in the Navy. As the series went on, Steed appeared more and more as a well-dressed, upper crust fop with more than a soupçon of charm, dash, and derring-do. Apart from his fighting skills, with the third season his chief weapon became his umbrella, which he used variously as a camera, a gas projector, a sword case, and a tape recorder.

After two seasons, Hendry bowed out and Honor Blackman was hired to be Steed's first female sidekick, anthropologist Cathy Gale, whom Blackman modeled after *Life* magazine photographer Margaret Bourke-White with a dash of Margaret Mead. Initially, Gale was given a pistol which could be hidden in her make-up kit or under her skirt, but it was eventually decided this was too unwieldy. Miniature swords and daggers were briefly tried when Leonard White urged that Blackman take up judo seriously and arranged for her to be trained by Douglas Robinson.

The action-oriented series required that Blackman have at least one fight scene in every episode, and Blackman soon became adept at judo. White wanted Cathy to be pure, a woman who fought bad guys because she cared so much about right and justice, as a contrast to Steed's wicked, devilish, and saucy nature. Blackman added to the character by dressing her in leather simply because she needed clothes that would not rip during the fight scenes (at the beginning of the series, she once ripped her trousers in close-up). Because the only thing that went with leather pants were leather boots, she was given calf-length black boots and inadvertently started a kinky fashion trend. (In fact, Macnee and Blackman released a single celebrating ''Kinky Boots'' on Decca in 1964).

However, after two years, Blackman likewise decided to call it quits to concentrate on her movie career (she had just been cast as Pussy Galore in *Goldfinger* [1964]). The surprised producers searched frantically for a replacement, at first choosing Elizabeth Shepherd, but after filming one-and-a-half episodes she was replaced by Diana Rigg, who played Mrs. Emma Peel (named after the phrase ''M Appeal'' for ''Man Appeal,'' which was something the character was expected to have). Rigg and Macnee proved to have tremendous chemistry and charm together, with their sexual relationship largely left flirtatious and ambiguous. Rigg, like Blackman, played a tough, capable female fighter who possessed both high intelligence and tremendous sex appeal. Her outlandish costumes (designed by John Bates) for the episodes ''A Touch of Brimstone'' and ''Honey for the Prince'' were especially daring (and in fact, ABC refused to air these and three other episodes of the British series, considering them too racy, though they later appeared in syndication).

The two years with Diana Rigg are universally considered the best in the series, which ABC in the United States agreed to pick up provided the episodes were shot on film. Albert Fennell now produced the series and served as its guiding light, with writers Brian Clemens and Philip Levene writing the majority and the best of the episodes. These new shows became more science-fiction oriented, with plots about power-mad scientists bent on ruling the world, giant man-eating plants from outer space, cybermen, androids and robots, machines that created torrential rains, personalities switching bodies, people being miniaturized, and brainwashing. The fourth season and all subsequent episodes were filmed in color.

Commented Clemens about the series, ''We admitted to only one class—and that was the upper. Because we were a fantasy, we have not shown policemen or coloured men. And you have not seen anything as common as blood. We have no social conscience at all.'' Clemens also emphasized the Britishness of the series rather than trying to adapt it to American tastes, feeling that helped give the show a unique distinction.

Rigg called it quits after two seasons, and she also joined the Bond series, having the distinction of playing Mrs. James Bond in *On*

Her Majesty's Secret Service (1969). The series limped on for a final season with Steed's new partner Tara King (played by Linda Thorson), also known as Agent 69, who always carried a brick in her purse. The last season also introduced us to Mother (Patrick Newell), Steed's handicapped boss, and his Amazonian secretary Rhonda (Rhonda Parker). The running gag for the season was that Mother's office would continually turn up in the most unlikely of places and the plots were most often far-fetched, secret-agent style plots.

The series later spawned a stageplay, *The Avengers on Stage,* starring Simon Oates and Sue Lloyd in 1971, a South African radio series, a series of novel adventures, a spin-off series, *The New Avengers* (starring Macnee, Gareth Hunt, and Joanna Lumley) in 1976, and finally a 1998 big-budgeted theatrical version starring Ralph Fiennes as John Steed and Uma Thurman as Emma Peel. The latter was greeted with universally derisive reviews and was considered a debacle of the first order as it served to remind everyone how imitators had failed to capture the charm, wit, escapism, and appeal of the original series, which has long been regarded as a television classic.

—Dennis Fischer

FURTHER READING:

Javna, John. *Cult TV: A Viewer's Guide to the Shows America Can't Live Without!!* New York, St. Martin's Press, 1985.

Macnee, Patrick, and Marie Cameron. *Blind in One Ear: The Avenger Returns.* San Francisco, Mercury House, 1989.

Macnee, Patrick, with Dave Rogers. *The Avengers and Me.* New York, TV Books, 1998.

Rogers, Dave. *The Complete Avengers.* New York, St. Martin's Press, 1989.

Avery, Tex (1908-1980)

Tex Avery, one of the most important and influential American animators, produced dozens of cartoon masterpieces primarily for the Warner Brothers and Metro-Goldwyn-Meyer (MGM) studios from the 1930s to the 1950s. Frenetic action, perfect comedic timing, and a never-ending stream of sight gags characterize his short, animated films. He is credited with providing the most definitive characterization of Bugs Bunny and creating such classic cartoon figures as Droopy, Chilly Willy, Screwy Squirrel, and Red Hot Riding Hood. Avery was most intrigued by the limitless possibilities of animation and filled his work with chase sequences, comic violence, and unbelievable situations that could not be produced in any other medium. Avery's manic style was best described by author Joe Adamson when he stated, ''Avery's films will roll along harmlessly enough, with an interesting situation treated in a more or less funny way. Then, all of a sudden, one of the characters will lose a leg and hop all over the place trying to find it again.''

Born Frederick Bean Avery on February 26, 1908, in Taylor, Texas, a direct descendant of the infamous Judge Roy Bean, Avery hoped to turn his boyhood interest in illustration into a profession when he attended the Chicago Art Institute. After several failed attempts to launch a syndicated comic strip, he moved to California and took a job in Walter Lanz's animation studio. Avery's talent as an animator led him to join the Warner Brothers studio in 1935. There, he became a leading member of a unit including now legendary animators Chuck Jones and Bob Clampett. From their dilapidated headquarters on the studio lot, which they dubbed the Termite Terrace, the young artists set about creating a new cartoon sensibility which was more adult, absurd, and filled with slapstick. Avery and his crew's characters were more irreverent than those of their Disney competitors and the cartoons themselves were marked by direct addresses to the audience, split screen effects, and abrupt changes in pacing. Avery also insisted that their films acquire a more satiric tone so as to comment on contemporary popular culture. An early example of this satire is found in *I Love to Singa* (1936), which features "Owl Jolson" in a take-off of *The Jazz Singer*. Avery constantly reminded his viewers of the illusionary nature of animation. Unlike Disney, which was known for its spectacle, Avery's Warner Brothers films highlight their unreality. This abundant self-reflexivity is considered an early example of animated postmodernism.

Avery's talent also extended into the area of characterization. He, along with Jones and Clampett, refined an existing character named Porky Pig and transformed him into the first popular Looney Tunes character of the 1930s. In a 1937 cartoon called *Porky's Duck Hunt* he introduced Daffy Duck, who became so popular that he soon earned his own cartoon series. Avery's greatest contribution to animation, however, was his development of Bugs Bunny. A crazy rabbit character had appeared in several Warner cartoons beginning in 1938, but with few of the later Bugs personality traits. Animation historians regard Avery's 1940 cartoon *A Wild Hare* as the moment Bugs Bunny was introduced to America. Avery had eliminated the earlier rabbit's cuteness and craziness and, instead, fashioned an intelligent, streetwise, deliberate character. It was also in this cartoon that Avery bestowed upon Bugs a line from his Texas childhood— "What's up, doc?"—that would become the character's catchphrase. Avery's style became so important to the studio and imitated by his colleagues that he became known as the "Father of Warner Bros. Cartoons."

Despite all his success at Warner Brothers, Avery's most creative period is considered to be his time producing MGM cartoons from 1942 to 1954. In these films he dealt less with characterization and concentrated on zany gags. This fast-paced humor was developed to accommodate Avery's desire to fit as many comic moments as possible into his animated shorts. The MGM films feature nondescript cats and dogs in a surreal world where anything can, and does, happen. The 1947 cartoon *King-Size Canary* is regarded as Avery's masterpiece and reveals the lunacy of his later work. The film features a cat, mouse, dog, and canary each swallowing portions of "Jumbo-Gro." The animals chase each other and grow to enormous heights. Finally, the cat and mouse grow to twice the earth's size and are unable to continue the cartoon. They announce that the show is over and simply wave to the audience. Avery once again revealed the absurdities inherent to the cartoon universe.

In 1954, Avery left MGM and began a career in commercial animation. He directed cartoon advertisements for Kool-Aid, Pepsodent, and also produced the controversial Frito Bandito spots. Indeed, his animation has been enjoyed for more than half a century due to its unique blend of absurdity, quick humor, and fine characterization. He inspired his peers and generations of later animators to move their art form away from the saccharine style embodied by Disney. He revealed that animation is truly limitless. Because of his ability to create cartoons with an adult sophistication mixed with intelligent

and outlandish humor, he has often been characterized as a "Walt Disney who has read Kafka."

—Charles Coletta

FURTHER READING:

Adamson, Joe. *Tex Avery: King of Cartoons*. New York, De Capo Press, 1975.

Schneider, Steve. *That's All Folks!: The Art of Warner Bros. Animation*. New York, Henry Holt & Co., 1988.

Avon

American cosmetic and gift company Avon Products, Inc. is known for its eye-catching, digest-sized catalogs shimmering with fresh-faced models wearing reasonably priced makeup and advertising costume jewelry, colognes, and an array of other items. Their goods are backed by a satisfaction guarantee and delivered by a friendly face, usually female, who earns or supplements an income by the commission received. Avon's retail concept, symbolized by the direct-sales "Avon lady," is a cherished part of American culture, and now, a recognized addition to countries around the globe as well. In the 1990s, Avon was the world's top direct-sales cosmetics firm, with a total work force of 2.6 million in over 130 countries, producing sales of $4.8 billion ($1.7 billion in the United States alone). Ninety percent of American women have purchased Avon products in their lifetime, most likely because of the convenience, price, and quality, but perhaps also due to the history of female fraternity and empowerment that Avon promotes. The company's overwhelmingly female employee base and tradition of visiting customers in their homes allowed women control of their own earnings long before it was widely accepted.

Avon was founded in 1886, and Mrs. P.F.E. Albee of Winchester, New Hampshire, originated the idea of going door-to-door to push her wares. The company offered a money-back guarantee on their products and the salespeople nurtured relationships with customers, minimizing the need for advertising. The company prospered with their pleasant, neighborly image and low-cost, dependable products. However, in the 1970s and 1980s Avon's fortunes declined when a number of unsavvy business moves hurt sales and provoked an exodus of salespeople. At that time, the company also suffered from its outdated approach: Women were no longer waiting at home for the doorbell to ring; they were at work all day. In 1993, Avon began boosting morale and incentives for salespeople, then updated its image, and in 1998 launched a $30 million advertising campaign. The company recruited a bevy of new representatives who would sell in offices and other business settings, and they focused on a more desirable product line. In addition, Avon reached out overseas, prompting women in South American, Russia, Eastern Europe, and China to sign up as salespeople. In fact, the number of Avon representatives in Brazil—478,000—is more than twice that of Brazil's army, with 200,000 soldiers. Avon's strategies sharply increased profits and swelled its stock.

Though the cherished but politically incorrect term "Avon lady" is not quite accurate—two percent of the force is male—the company still primarily consists of women selling cosmetics to female friends, family members, neighbors, and coworkers, with 98 percent of its revenue coming from direct sales. Avon used the slogan

Dan Aykroyd (center) with Jane Curtin (left) and Laraine Newman (right) in the popular Conehead skit on *Saturday Night Live*.

"Avon calling!" accompanied by a "ding-dong" doorbell noise when it was known mainly for reaching clients at home before the rise of women in the work force. However, the company in 1996 sold about 50 percent of its goods in the workplace, and branched out to offer a more extensive line of gifts for time-constrained working women. Although Avon has traditionally carried skin care and other hygiene products as well as cologne and jewelry for women, men, and children, in the 1990s it expanded its selection greatly to become a convenient way to shop for knick-knacks, toys, clothing and lingerie, books, and videos.

Though management ranks were off-limits to women until roughly the 1980s, Avon has quickly risen to become known for its respected record in the area of female promotions. In 1997, however, some were rankled when Christina Gold, president of North American operations, was slighted for a promotion to CEO in favor of an outside male candidate. She later resigned. Despite this incident, *Working Woman* magazine still called Avon one of the top female-friendly firms in 1998 due to its largely female employee base and number of corporate women officers. Overall, only three percent of top executives at Fortune 500 companies in 1997 were women. At Avon, on the other hand, over 30 percent of corporate officers are women, and four of the eleven members of the board of directors are women. Avon also has a good record of promoting women, with more

women in management slots—86 percent—than any other Fortune 500 firm. The company is also heavily involved in supporting research for breast cancer.

—Geri Speace

FURTHER READING:

Morris, Betsy. "If Women Ran the World, It Would Look a Lot Like Avon." *Fortune.* July 21, 1997, 74.

Reynolds, Patricia. "Ding Dong! Avon Lady Is Still Calling." *Star Tribune.* September 9, 1996, 3E.

Stanley, Alessandra. "Makeover Takeover." *Star Tribune,* August 21, 1996, 1D.

Zajac, Jennifer. "Avon Finally Glowing Thanks to Global Sales—And New Lip-Shtick." *Money.* September 1997, 60.

Aykroyd, Dan (1952—)

Actor and writer Dan Aykroyd achieved stardom as a member of the original *Saturday Night Live* (SNL) "Not Ready for Prime Time Players." During his tenure on SNL, he created some of the show's classic skits and impersonations. He also memorably teamed up with SNL's John Belushi to perform as Elwood ''On a Mission from God'' Blues, one half of the ''The Blues Brothers'' band. Aykroyd is one of the busiest actors on screen. Since SNL, Aykroyd has appeared in more than twenty movies, including *Ghostbusters* (1984), which he also wrote, *Driving Miss Daisy* (1989), and two movies based on the SNL act, *The Blues Brothers* (1980) and *Blues Brothers 2000* (1998). He also stars, as an ex-biker priest, in the TV sitcom *Soul Man,* and fronts a successful syndicated series, *Psi Factors.* Additionally, he is also a highly productive writer, continuing to pen some of Hollywood's most successful comedies.

—John J. Doherty

FURTHER READING:

''Aykroyd, Dan.'' *Current Biography Yearbook.* New York, Wilson, 1992.

B

"B" Movies

A "B" movie, according to industry lore, is a movie in which the sets shake when an actor slams the door. Although it has come to mean any low-budget feature that appeals to the broadest possible audience, the term "B" movies was first applied to movies of the 1930s and 1940s that were made quickly, cheaply, in black-and-white, usually without notable stars, and usually with a running time between 60 and 80 minutes, in order to fill out the second half of a double feature. During the Great Depression, the movie business was one of the few businesses earning profits, and many distributors competed for the patronage of increasingly frugal moviegoers by offering them more for their money: two films for the price of one, plus cartoons, a newsreel, and several trailers. The practice began in 1932, and by the end of 1935, 85 percent of the theaters in the United States were playing double features. Some suggest the "B" stands for "bread and butter," others suggest "block-booking," but most likely "B" was chosen simply to distinguish these films from the main, or "A," features. At first only "Poverty Row" studios, such as Republic, Monogram, Majestic, and Mayfair,, produced "B" movies, but soon all the major studios were producing their own "B"s in order to fill the increased demand. In the 1940s, with moviegoers seeking escapism from a world at war, theater attendance reached an all-time high; of 120 million Americans, 90 million were attending a film every week, and many theaters changed their fare two or three times weekly. During this time, the business of "B" moviemaking reached its artistic and commercial apex, with Universal, Warner Brothers, Twentieth-Century Fox, Columbia, RKO, and Paramount all heavily involved in production. For the first half of the 1940s, Universal alone was producing a "B" movie a week. In 1942, a number of "B" units were set up at RKO, with Val Lewton assigned to head one of them. According to his contract, Lewton was limited to horror films with budgets not to exceed $150,000, to be shot in three weeks or less, with an average running time of 70 minutes—but within these confines, Lewton produced such classics as *Cat People, Curse of the Cat People, The Seventh Victim,* and *Isle of the Dead.* A common practice for "B" directors was to shoot their films on the abandoned sets of "A" films, and *Cat People* (which cost $134,000 and grossed over $3 million) was shot on the abandoned set of Orson Welles' second film, *The Magnificent Ambersons.*

What separates "A"s from "B"s has little to do with genre and everything to do with budget. Film noir, Westerns, straight detective stories, comedies, and other genres had their "A" and "B" versions—*The Maltese Falcon* was an "A" while *The House of Fear* was a "B." At the studios making both "A"s and "B"s, specific film units were budgeted certain limited amounts to quickly produce films generally too short to be feature films. But just because these films were being churned out doesn't mean that some of them weren't even better received by audiences than the big-budget, high-minded "A" features. Some are now considered classics. *Detour* (1945) has become a cult noir favorite, and *The Wolf Man* (1941) is one of the best horror films ever made. The award-winning *The Biscuit Eater* (1940) was distinguished by its location in Albany, Georgia, deep in the South's hunting country, with Disney producing its "A" version 32 years later. Successful "A"s often inspired sequels or spinoffs that might be "A"s or "B"s. *King Kong* and *Dead End* were "A" films, while *Son of Kong* and the series of Dead End Kids films spun off from *Dead End* were all "B"s. *Frankenstein* was an "A," but then so were *The Bride of Frankenstein* and *Son of Frankenstein.* It all boiled down to the film's budget, length, stars and, ultimately, whether audiences saw the film first or second during an evening out. Because the "B"s were not expected to draw people into theaters—that was the job of the "A"s—these films were able to experiment with subjects and themes deemed too much of a gamble for "A" films; *Thunderhoof* showed sympathetic Indians, *Bewitched* involved multiple personality disorder, and *The Seventh Victim* touched on Satan worship. Technicians were forced to improvise with lighting, sets, and camera angles in order to save money, and the more successful of these experiments carried over into "A" films.

Many "B"s were parts of series. More than simple sequels, these were more like the James Bond series or a television series of later decades. In the 1980s and 1990s, a successful film might have two or three sequels but a single old-time "B" movie series might include up to 30 or 40 films. Besides the Dead End Kids series (which begat the Bowery Boys and East Side Kids series), there were Sherlock Holmes, Dick Tracy, Charlie Chan, Mr. Moto, Mr. Wong, Boston Blackie, Michael Shayne, The Whistler, The Saint, The Falcon, The Lone Wolf, Tarzan, Jungle Jim, the Mexican Spitfire and Blondie, to name but a few. The Sherlock Holmes series produced a number of classic films, and many film buffs still consider Basil Rathbone and Nigel Bruce the definitive Holmes and Watson. The Holmes series took an odd turn after the start of World War II, with the turn-of-the-century supersleuth and his loyal assistant suddenly working for the Allies against the Nazis. A few of the series, such as the Crime Doctor films, were based on successful radio shows, while most came from books or were sequels or spinoffs from successful "A" films. For example, Ma and Pa Kettle first appeared as minor rustic characters in the "A" hit *The Egg and I* before being spun off into their own series.

Most of the studios used the "B"s as a farm team, where future actors, actresses, writers, and directors could get their start and hone their craft before moving up to the majors. Frequently, young actors who were on their way up worked with older actors, who, no longer finding roles in "A" movies, were on their way down. John Wayne, Susan Hayward, and Peter Lorre appeared in a number of "B" films. Director Robert Wise's first film was the aforementioned *Curse of the Cat People,* though he is better known for *The Day the Earth Stood Still, The Sand Pebbles, The Sound of Music,* and *West Side Story.* "B" director Fred Zinneman went on to direct *High Noon, From Here to Eternity,* and *A Man for All Seasons.* Other noted directors beginning in "B"s include Mark Robson (who later directed *Von Ryan's Express*), Edward Dmytryk (*The Caine Mutiny*) and Anthony Mann (*El Cid*).

In the mid-1940s, theater attendance started waning, and Universal was hit quite hard. In a November 1946 shake-up, the studio attempted to turn things around by shutting down all of its "B" film units and announcing that, henceforth, it would be making only prestige pictures. What ultimately put an end to the "B"s, however, was the Justice Department and the U.S. Supreme Court. On May 3, 1948, in *U.S. v. Paramount Pictures* (334 U.S. 131), the high court found that Paramount, Columbia, United Artists, Universal, Loew's, and others had violated antitrust laws by engaging in price-fixing conspiracies, block-booking and blindselling, and by owning many of the theater chains where the films were shown, thereby stifling competition. "It is clear, so far as the five major studios are concerned, that the aim of the conspiracy was exclusionary, i.e., that it was designed to strengthen their hold on the exhibition field," wrote Justice William O. Douglas. The studios agreed to sell off their total of 1,400 movie theaters, though it took them a few years to do so. With theater owners then acting independently and free to negotiate, an exhibitor could beat the competition by showing two "A"s, so the market for "B"s quickly dried up. The days of guaranteed distribution were over, though with television coming around the corner, it is doubtful the "B" industry would have lasted much longer in any case.

Once the "B" market dried up, there were still moviemakers with limited budgets who carried on the grand tradition of guerrilla filmmaking. Purists would not use the term "B" film to describe their output; in fact, most purists strenuously object when the term is used for anything other than the "second feature" short films of the 1930s and 1940s. These new low-budget films were usually exploitive of current social issues, from teenage rebellion (*The Wild Angels*) to drugs (*The Trip*) to sexual liberation (*The Supervixens*) to black power (*Shaft*). The name Roger Corman has become synonymous with this type of film. The book *The "B" Directors* refers to Corman as "probably the most important director of "B" films," yet Corman may be one of those purists who objects to the use of the term "B" movies being applied to his work. In a 1973 interview reprinted in *Kings of the Bs,* Corman said, "I'd say I don't make B movies and nobody makes B movies anymore. The changing patterns of distribution, and the cost of color film specifically, has just about eliminated the B movie. The amount of money paid for a second feature is so small that if you're paying for color-release prints, you can't get it back. You can't get your negative costs back distributing your film as a B or supporting feature." Corman said every film is made in an attempt to make it to the top half of the bill, with those that fail going to the bottom half. He admitted that the first one or two films he made were "B"s—though film historians who aren't purists still consider him the King of the "B"s. With the widespread popularity of drive-ins in the 1950s and 1960s, many of his films not only appeared as second features, but as third or fourth features.

Working as a writer/producer/director for American International Pictures, Allied Artists, and other studios in the 1950s and 1960s, Corman's output was phenomenal; between 1955 and 1970, he directed 48 features, including such classics as *The House of Usher, The Pit and the Pendulum, The Premature Burial, The Wild Angels,* and *The Trip.* Nearly all of these films were directed on minuscule budgets at breakneck speed; his *The Little Shop of Horrors* was completed in two and a half days. In 1970, he began his own company, New World Pictures, which not only produced "B" films and served as a training ground for younger filmmakers, but also distributed both "A" and "B" films. Corman produced one of Martin Scorsese's first films, *Boxcar Bertha,* one of Francis Ford Coppola's first films, *Dementia 13,* and Peter Bogdanovich's first film, *Targets.* Jack Nicholson appeared in *The Little Shop of Horrors* and scripted *The Trip,* and while filming *The Trip,* Corman allowed actors Peter Fonda and Dennis Hopper to direct some second unit sequences, just before they went off to make *Easy Rider,* another low-budget classic. James (*Titanic*) Cameron began his film career at New World, and Jonathan Demme's first two films were New World's

Caged Heat and *Crazy Mama.* Demme showed his appreciation to Corman by giving him acting roles in *Silence of the Lambs* and *Philadelphia,* just as Coppola gave Corman a role in *The Godfather: Part II.* According to Corman, after a couple of decades in Hollywood, a veteran filmmaker who is any good will have moved onto bigger budget films; if he is still working in "B"s, the best you can expect from him is a competent "B." "And what I've always looked for is the "B" picture, the exploitation picture, that is better than that, that has some spark that will lift it out of its bracket," Corman said, explaining why he liked employing younger filmmakers. When he allowed Ron Howard to direct his first feature, *Grand Theft Auto,* for New World, Corman told the young director, "If you do a good job for me on this picture, you will never work for me again." A 1973 *Los Angeles Times* article suggested that Corman was doing more for young filmmakers than the entire American Film Institute.

While it may be easy to dismiss the "B"s of the 1930s and 1940s or Roger Corman's films as popular trash, even trash itself has undergone a significant reappraisal in recent years. In her seminal essay "Trash, Art, and the Movies," film critic Pauline Kael said, "Because of the photographic nature of the medium and the cheap admission prices, movies took their impetus not from the desiccated imitation European high culture, but from the peep show, the Wild West show, the music hall, the comic strip—from what was coarse and common." She argued that, while many universities may view film as a respectable art form, "It's the feeling of freedom from respectability we have always enjoyed at the movies that is carried to an extreme by American International Pictures and the Clint Eastwood Italian Westerns; they are stripped of cultural values. Trash doesn't belong to the academic tradition, and that's part of the *fun* of trash— that you know (or *should* know) that you don't have to take it seriously, that it was never meant to be any more than frivolous and trifling and entertaining." While the "A" film units were busy making noble, message films based on uplifting stage successes or prize-winning novels, the "B" film units were cranking out films that were meant to be enjoyed—and what's wrong with enjoyment? Isn't enjoyment exactly why we started going to movies in the first place, not to be preached to but to get away from all the preaching, to enjoy the clever plot twist or intriguing character or thrilling car chase or scary monster? Over time, trash may develop in the moviegoer a taste for art, and taking pleasure in trash may be intellectually indefensible but, as Kael argues, "Why should pleasure need justification?" Acclaimed writer-director Quentin Tarantino had his biggest success with *Pulp Fiction,* the title of which refers to the literary equivalent of "B" movies: less respectable fiction printed on cheap paper, sold for a dime, and containing a heady mix of violence, black humor, criminals swept along by fate, familiar scenarios with unexpected twists, and postmodern irony. Most of the film covers the same ground as some of Corman's films, and as Tarantino has said of Corman, "He's the most. That's all there is to say. I've been a fan of his films since I was a kid."

Just as importantly, "B" movies, and particularly Corman, demonstrated to a whole new generation of filmmakers that films could be made quickly and cheaply. In fact, with so many studios being run by greedy corporations looking for the next mass-appeal blockbuster, the independent filmmaker may be one of the last refuges of true cinema art. Films like *Reservoir Dogs, Blood Simple,* and *El Mariachi* owe a lot to "B" films for their subject matter, but they owe perhaps even more to "B"s for proving that such films can be made. Other films, such as *sex, lies and videotape, In the Company* of Men, Pi, Ruby in Paradise, and Welcome to the Dollhouse, may address subjects that make them more ''arty'' than your typical potboiler, but perhaps they never would have been made if Corman and the other ''B'' moviemakers hadn't proven that guerrilla filmmaking was still alive and well in the waning years of the twentieth century.

—Bob Sullivan

FURTHER READING:

Corman, Roger. How I Made a Hundred Movies in Hollywood and Never Lost a Dime. New York, Da Capo Press, 1998.

Dixon, Wheeler W. The ''B'' Directors. Metuchen, New Jersey, Scarecrow Press, 1985.

Kael, Pauline. Going Steady. New York, Warner Books, 1979.

Koszarski, Richard. Hollywood Directors, 1941-76. New York, Oxford University Press, 1977.

McCarthy, Todd, and Charles Flynn, editors. Kings of the Bs. New York, Dutton, 1975.

McClelland, Doug. The Golden Age of ''B'' Movies. Nashville, Charter House, 1978.

Parish, James Robert, editor-in-chief. The Great Movie Series. New York, A.S. Barnes, 1971.

Sarris, Andrew. You Ain't Heard Nothin' Yet. New York, Oxford University Press, 1998.

Babar

Perhaps the best known elephant in the world, Babar was born in France in 1931. He was first seen in a children's book titled Histoire de Babar, written and illustrated by painter and first-time author Jean de Brunhoff. It told the story of a young elephant, orphaned when a hunter killed his mother, who traveled to Paris. Babar became a well-dressed gentleman and took to walking on his hind legs, wearing a green suit and a bowler hat. By the end of the book he had married Celeste and was king of an imaginary African country. Jean de Brunhoff died in 1937 and after the Second World War his eldest son, Laurent, resumed the series. He drew and wrote in a manner close to that of his father. In addition to Babar and his queen, the books feature the couple's four children as well as the Old Lady and Zephir the monkey. The books feature a solid family structure, strong female characters, and lessons on the choices children must make to become decent people.

Published in America as The Story of Babar, the story became a hit and served as a foundation for an impressive quantity of books, toys, and merchandise. Beginning in the 1980s, the creation of several Babar children's videos bolstered the character's popularity. The Canadian animation studio, Nelvana, produced a popular television cartoon show that continued to be popular into the 1990s. Kent State University in Ohio houses an large archive of Babar materials.

—Ron Goulart

FURTHER READING:

De Brunhoff, Jean and Laurent. Babar's Anniversary Album. New York, Random House, 1981.

Hildebrand, Ann Meinzen. Jean and Laurent de Brunhoff: The Legacy of Babar. New York, Twayne, 1991.

Baby Boomers

''For many a family, now that prosperity seems to be here, there's a baby just around the corner.'' This is how the April 2, 1941 issue of Business Week described the upcoming demographic phenomenon that would come to be known as the ''baby boom.'' Between the years of 1946 and 1964, 78 million babies were born in the United States alone, and other countries also experienced their own baby booms following World War II. The baby-boom generation was the largest generation yet born on the planet. Other generations had received nicknames, such as the ''lost generation'' of the 1920s, but it took the label-obsessed media of the late twentieth century combined with the sheer size of the post-World War II generation to give the name ''baby boomers'' its impact.

Since those born at the end of the baby boom (1964) could, in fact, be the children of those born at the beginning (1946), many consider the younger baby boomers part of a different generation. Some of those born after 1960 call themselves ''thirteeners'' instead, referring to the thirteenth generation since the founding of the United States.

Variously called the ''now generation,'' the ''love generation,'' and the ''me generation'' among other names, the baby boomers have molded and shaped society at every phase, simply by moving through it en masse. Demographers frequently describe the baby boomers' effect on society by comparing it to a python swallowing a pig. In the same way that peristalsis causes the huge lump to move down the body of the snake, the huge demographic lump of baby boomers has been squeezed through its societal phases. First it was the maternity wards in hospitals that were overcrowded, as mothers came in unprecedented numbers to give birth the ''scientific'' way. Then, in the 1950s, swollen school enrollment caused overcrowding, resulting in the construction of new schools. The 1950s and 1960s also saw the institutions of juvenile justice filled to capacity, as the term ''juvenile delinquent'' was coined for those who had a hard time fitting into the social mold. By the 1960s and 1970s, it was the colleges that were overfilled, with twice the number of students entering higher education as the previous generation. In the 1970s and 1980s, the job markets began to be glutted, as the young work force flooded out of colleges, and by the 1990s housing prices were pushed up as millions of baby boomers approaching middle age began to think of settling down and purchasing a house.

Giving a unified identity to any generational group is largely an over-simplified media construct, and, as with most American media constructs, the baby boomer stereotype refers almost exclusively to white middle-class members of the generation. Poor baby boomers and baby boomers of color will, in all likelihood, not recognize themselves in the media picture of the indulged suburban kid-turned college radical-turned spendthrift yuppie, but it is not only the white and the affluent who have shaped their generation. The revolutionary vision and radical politics that are most closely associated with young baby boomers have their roots in the civil rights movement and even in the street gangs of poor urban youth of the 1950s. In addition, the African American and Latino music that emerged during the boomer's formative years continued to influence pop music at the end of the century. Even though their lives may be vastly different, it cannot be denied that members of a generation share certain formative experiences. The baby boomers' shared experiences began with its parental generation.

Raised during the privation of the Great Depression of the 1930s, the parents of the baby boomers learned to be conservative and thrifty and to value security. Because parents were unwilling or unable to bring children into such economic uncertainty, U.S. birth rates had dropped during the depression from 22.4 births per thousand in 1924 to just 16.7 by 1936. Experts and media of the time, fearful of the consequences of an ever-decreasing birth rate, encouraged procreation by pointing out the evils of a child-poor society, some even blaming the rise of Hitler on the declining birth rate.

Beginning as early as 1941, with war on the horizon, the birth rates began to rise. The first four months of 1941 boasted 20,000 more births than the same four months of the previous year. The uncertainties of war prompted many young couples to seize the moment and attempt to create a future by marrying and having children quickly. Those who postponed children because of the war were quick to start families once the war was over. In 1942, 2,700,000 babies had been born, more than any year since 1921. By 1947 the number had leaped to 3,600,000 and it stayed high until 1965, when birth rates finally began to slow. The arrival of ''the Pill,'' a reliable oral contraceptive, plus changing attitudes about family size and population control combined to cause the mid-1960s decline in birth rates.

Following the enormous disruptions caused by World War II, the forces of government and business were anxious to get society back to ''normal.'' A campaign to remove women from the work force and send them back to the home was an integral part of this normalization. Women without husbands and poor women continued to work, but working women were widely stigmatized. During the war, working mothers received support, such as on-site daycare, but by the 1950s the idea of a working mother was unconventional to say the least. Sparked by the postwar prosperity, a building boom was underway. Acres of housing developments outside the cities went perfectly with the new American image of the family—Mom, Dad, and the kids, happily ensconced in their new house in the suburbs. Many white middle-class baby boomers grew up in the suburbs, leaving the inner cities to the poor and people of color.

Suburban life in the 1950s and early 1960s is almost always stereotyped as dull, conventional, and secure. In many ways, these stereotypes contain truth, and some of the roots of the baby boomers' later rebellion lay in both the secure predictability of suburban life and the hypocrisy of the myth of the perfect family. While baby boomers and their nuclear families gathered around the television to watch familial mythology such as *Father Knows Best,* quite another kind of dynamic might have been played out within the family itself. The suburban houses, separated from each other by neat, green lawns, contained families which were also isolated from each other by the privacy which was mandated by the mores of the time. Within many of these families physical, sexual, and emotional abuse occurred; mothers were stifled and angry; fathers were overworked and frustrated. Communication was not encouraged, especially with outsiders, so the baby boomers of the suburbs, prosperous and privileged, grew up with explosive secrets seething just beneath the surface of a shiny facade.

The peace and prosperity of the 1950s and early 1960s also contained another paradox. The atomic bombs that the United States dropped on the Japanese cities of Hiroshima and Nagasaki had opened the door to a new age—the possibility of nuclear annihilation. The baby boomers had inherited another first—they were the first generation to know that humankind possessed the power to destroy itself. Coupled with the simmering tension of the cold war between the United States and the Union of Soviet Socialist Republics, nuclear war seemed a very real threat to the children of the 1950s. Bomb shelters were built, and schools carried out atomic bomb drills where students learned to hide from nuclear attacks by crawling under their desks. It was not the security of the 1950s, but the juxtaposition of the facade of security with preparation for unimaginable destruction that sowed the seeds of the baby boomers' later revolt. It was a revolt against racism and war, a revolt against conventionality and safety. But most of all, perhaps, it was a revolt against hypocrisy.

While World War II had brought death to thousands of Americans in the military and prosperity to many on the homefront, it had also brought unprecedented opportunity to African Americans. Having worked next to whites in the defense industries, serving next to whites in the armed forces, and having gone abroad and experienced more open societies, American blacks found it difficult to return to their allotted place at the bottom of American society, especially in the segregated South. When the civil rights movement began in the 1950s and 1960s, it attracted young baby boomers, both black and white, to work for justice for African Americans. As the movement began to build, many young white college students came south to participate.

Almost simultaneously, another movement was beginning to build. Though the U.S. government had been sending military advisors and some troops since 1961 to preside over its interests in South Vietnam, it wasn't until 1964 that the war was escalated with bombings and large troop deployments. The war in Vietnam did not inspire the same overwhelming popular support as World War II. As the conflict escalated, and as the brutal realities of war were shown on the nightly television news, opposition to the war also escalated. In 1965, the first large march against the Vietnam war drew an estimated 25,000 protesters in New York City. Within two years, similar protests were drawing hundreds of thousands of people. Though there were war protesters of all ages, it was the baby boomers who were of draft age, and many did not want to go to a distant country few had heard of, to fight in an undeclared war over a vague principle. Draft cards were burned and draft offices were taken over to protest forced conscription. Students held demonstrations and took over buildings at their own colleges to draw attention to the unjustness of the war.

Soon, organizations like Students for a Democratic Society began to broaden the focus of protest. Radicals pointed to the Vietnam war as merely one example of a U.S. policy of racism and imperialism, and called for no less than a revolution as the solution. Militancy became a strong voice in the civil rights movement as well, as organizations like the Black Panthers replaced the call for ''equal rights'' with a cry of ''Black power!'' For a number of turbulent years, armed struggle in the United States appeared to be a real possibility.

The other side of militant protest was to be found in the hippie counterculture, who protested the war from a pacifist stand and whose battle cry was ''make love not war.'' Culminating in the ''summer of love'' and the Woodstock Music Festival of 1969, the hippies' espoused free love and the use of mind expanding drugs as the path to revolution. Many hippies, or ''freaks'' as they often called themselves, began to search for new forms of spiritual practice, rejecting the hypocrisy they found in traditional religions in favor or ''new age'' spirituality such as astrology and paganism. Some dropped out of mainstream society, moving to the country and creating communes where they attempted to transcend materialistic values and hierarchical power structures.

Impelled by the general spirit of questioning the oppressive status quo, women began to question their own second-class status in the greater society and even within progressive movements. As they joined together in consciousness raising groups to share previously unspoken grievances, they launched the women's liberation movement. At almost the same moment, homosexuals, tired of accepting the stigma surrounding their lifestyle, began to fight for gay liberation. Together, the black, women's, and gay liberation movements began to change the face of American society. The movements questioned gender roles, the form of the family, and the value priorities that had been handed down from the previous generation.

The music of the 1960s and 1970s is one of the baby boomers' most enduring contributions to American culture. Whether it is the earthy blues-influenced rock 'n' roll of the 1950s, the "Motown beat" soul music of the 1960s, or the rebellious folk-rock and drug-culture acid rock of the late 1960s, the music of the era is still considered *the* classic pop music. Though aging hippies and radicals may be horrified to hear the Beatles' "Revolution" or Janis Joplin's "Mercedes Benz" used as commercial jingles, the usage proves how thoroughly those rebellious years have been assimilated into American society.

If rock 'n' roll, soul, and protest music was the soundtrack of the baby-boom generation, television was its baby-sitter. From the idealized *Leave It to Beaver* families of the 1950s and early 1960s, to the in-your-face realism of the Norman Lear sitcoms of the late 1960s and 1970s, boomers spent much of their youth glued to the medium that was born almost when they were. Many of them would spend much of their adulthood trying to overcome the sense of inadequacy created when no family they would ever be a part of could live up to the fantasies they had watched on television as children. Later, shows like "thirtysomething" would make a realistic attempt to broach some of the issues facing baby boomers as they began the passage into middle age. Nostalgia for boomers' lost youth began almost before they had left it, and shows like *The Wonder Years* allowed boomers and their children to revisit a slightly less sanitized version of nuclear family life in the 1960s suburbs than the sitcoms of the time had offered.

Controversy and innovation came to television as it came to every aspect of American life in the late 1960s and 1970s. *The Smothers Brothers, All in the Family,* and the like fought constant battles with censors over political content as well as strong language. The fast-paced visual humor of *Laugh-In* pre-dated the rapid-fire video techniques of 1980s music videos.

Though not as much of a movie-addicted generation as either their pre-television parents or their VCR-oriented children, baby boomers did stand in long lines, when they were children, to watch the latest Walt Disney fantasies, and went as teenagers to the films of teenage rebellion like *Rebel without a Cause* and *West Side Story.* Nostalgia is also a mainstay of the movies made to appeal to grown up baby boomers. *The Big Chill* was a baby boomer favorite, with its bittersweet picture of young adults looking back on their glory days, and movies like *Back to the Future* and *Peggy Sue Got Married* played on every adult's fantasy of reliving the years of youth with the wisdom of hindsight. The fantastic success of the *Star Wars* trilogy, in the late 1970s and early 1980s, was due not only to the millions of children who flocked to see the films, but to their special appeal to baby boomers, combining as they did, new age spirituality with a childlike fantasy adventure.

Baby boomers are stereotyped as eternal Peter Pans, refusing to grow up. As time passed, and baby boomers passed out of youth into their thirties, they had to learn to assimilate the enormous upheaval that had accompanied their coming of age. Government crackdowns and a more savvy media, which learned to control which images were presented to the public, took much of the steam out of the radical movements. While many radicals remained on the left and continued to work for social change, other baby boomers slipped back into the more conventional societal roles that were waiting for them. The college-educated upper-middle-class boomers found lucrative jobs and an economic boom waiting. They were still affected by the revolution in social mores, which left a legacy of greater opportunity for women and an unprecedented acceptance of divorce. They developed an extravagant lifestyle, which many considered self-indulgent, and which prompted the press to dub them "yuppies," for "young, upwardly mobile professionals."

The yuppies were the perfect backlash to the gentle "flower children" hippies and the angry militants who preceded them as baby boomer stereotypes. Seeming to care for nothing except their own pleasure, the yuppies were portrayed in the press as brie-eating, Perrier-drinking, BMW-driving snobs, obsessed with their own inner processes. Again, wealthy young boomers were not acting much differently than wealthy young professionals had ever acted—their crime was that there were so *many* of them. Society feared the effect of so many hungry young job hunters, just as later it came to fear the effects of so many house hunters, and, as the economic boom went flat, many workers were laid off.

This fear continues to follow the baby boomers, as dire predictions precede their retirement. The press is full of articles recounting the anger of the younger generation, the so-called "baby busters," who fear they will be saddled with the care of the gigantic lump of boomers as they are squeezed through the tail end of the python. The "greedy geezers" as the press has dubbed them, are expected to cause a number of problems, including a stock market crash, as retiring boomers cash in their investments.

The aging of the baby boomers is sure to be well-documented by the boomers themselves. Spawned by a generation that kept silent on most personal matters, the baby boomers have broken that silence about almost everything. Following them through each stage of their lives have been consciousness raising groups, support groups, therapies, exposes, radio, television talk shows, and self-help books. Having grown up with the negative effects of secrecy, baby boomers want to share everything they experience. Beginning with childhood abuse and continuing through intimate relationships, childbearing, menopause, aging and death, the baby boomers' drive for introspection and communication has brought the light of open discussion to many previously taboo subjects. In literature as well, from Holden Caulfield's rants against "phoniness" in J.D. Salinger's *Catcher in the Rye*, to Sylvia Plath's "confessional" poetry, the trend has been toward exposure of the most inner self. It is perhaps the solidarity created by this communication about shared experiences that has enabled the many social changes that have occurred during the lives of the baby-boom generation.

Throughout their lives, baby boomers have refused to acquiesce to the say-so of authority figures, choosing instead to seek alternative choices, often looking back to pre-technological or non-western solutions. One example of this is the boomer exploration of medical care. Where their parents were much more likely to follow doctors' orders without question, baby boomers have sought more control over their health care, experimenting with treatments non-traditional for Americans, such as naturopathy, homeopathy and acupuncture. The boomer preference for herbal cures over prescription drugs has resulted in national marketing for herbs that once would have only been available in specialty stores, promising help with everything from memory loss to weight loss.

Though the media invented and popularized the term "baby boomer," the media itself has always had a love-hate relationship with the generation. While the entertainment industry has been forced by the law of supply and demand to pander to baby boomers in their prime spending years, there has never been a shortage of media pundits attempting to put the boomers in their place, whether with ridicule of their youthful principles or accusations of greed and self-absorption. In reality, all of society has been absorbed by the baby-boom generation's passage through it. Once the agents for tremendous social change, the boomers are now the establishment as the new millennium begins. The first baby boomer president, Bill Clinton, was elected in 1992. The generation that invented the catch phrase, "Don't trust anyone over thirty," will be well into its fifties by the year 2000. It may take many more generations before the real impact and contributions of the post-World War II baby boom will be understood and assimilated into American culture.

—Tina Gianoulis

FURTHER READING:

Evans, Susan. *The Women Who Changed All the Rules: Challenges, Choices and Triumphs of a Generation.* Naperville, Illinois, Sourcebooks. 1998.

Heflin, Jay S., and Richard D. Thau. *Generations Apart: Xers vs. Boomers vs. the Elderly.* Amherst, New York, Prometheus Books, 1997.

Lyons, Paul. *New Left, New Right and the Legacy of the '60's.* Philadelphia, Temple University Press, 1996.

May, Elaine Tyler. *Homeward Bound: American Families in the Cold War Era.* New York, Basic Books, 1988.

Owram, Doug. *Born at the Right Time: A History of the Baby Boom Generation.* Toronto, Buffalo, University of Toronto Press, 1996.

Babyface (1959—)

The significant position Rhythm and Blues (R&B) held in the mainstream pop charts of the late 1980s can be exemplified in the meteoric rise of singer/songwriter/producer Kenneth "Babyface" Edmonds. He is responsible for numerous gold- and platinum-selling artists, including Toni Braxton and TLC, and hit singles, such as Boyz II Men's two record-breaking songs "End of the Road" and "I'll Make Love to You." The winner of over 40 Billboard, BMI, Soul Train Music and Grammy awards, Babyface has become the master of heartbreak and love songs. He has pushed the visibility of music producers to new levels, illustrated by his phenomenally successful *Waiting to Exhale* soundtrack. His company, LaFace Records, moved Atlanta to the center of R&B music, and has expanded to multimedia productions, beginning with the film *Soul Food.* Babyface personifies the changing possibilities in masculinity for black men, the other side of rap's rage.

—Andrew Spieldenner

Bacall, Lauren (1924—)

Hollywood icon Lauren Bacall defined sex appeal with a single look and became an instant movie legend. As a starstruck New York teenager, Bacall was discovered by *Harper's Bazaar* editor Diana Vreeland and featured on the cover at nineteen. When she was brought out to Hollywood to star opposite Humphrey Bogart in *To Have and Have Not,* the twenty-year-old was so nervous while filming that she physically shook. She found that the only way to hold her head still was to tuck her chin down almost to her chest and then look up at her co-star. "The Look" became Bacall's trademark, and Bogie and Bacall became Hollywood's quintessential couple, both on and off the screen. The pair filmed two more classics, *Key Largo* and *The Big Sleep,* and also raised a family. After Bogart died of cancer in 1957, Bacall was linked with Frank Sinatra before marrying actor Jason Robards. In the 1960s and 1970s, Bacall returned to her Broadway roots, and won two Tony awards. The personification of Hollywood glamour and New York guts, Lauren Bacall remains a peerless pop culture heroine.

—Victoria Price

Lauren Bacall

FURTHER READING:

Bacall, Lauren. *Lauren Bacall: By Myself.* New York, Ballantine Books, 1978.

———. *Now.* New York, Del Rey, 1996.

Bogart, Stephen Humphrey. *Bogart: In Search of My Father.* New York, Plume, 1996.

Quirk, Lawrence J. *Lauren Bacall: Her Films and Career.* Secaucus, New Jersey, Citadel Press, 1990.

Bach, Richard (1936—)

Richard Bach, a pilot and aviation writer, achieved success as a new age author with the publication of *Jonathan Livingston Seagull,* a novel that Bach maintains was the result of two separate visionary experiences over a period of eight years. Bach's simple allegory with spiritual and philosophical overtones received little critical recognition but captured the mood of the 1970s, becoming popular with a wide range of readers, from members of the drug culture to mainstream Christian denominations.

Jonathan Livingston Seagull (1970) deals with the new age theme of transformation. It is the story of a spirited bird who by trial and error learns to fly for grace and speed, not merely for food and survival. When he returns to his flock with the message that they can become creatures of excellence, he is banished for his irresponsibility. He flies alone until he meets two radiant gulls who teach him to achieve perfect flight by transcending the limits of time and space. Jonathan returns to the flock, gathering disciples to spread the idea of perfection. With a small edition of only 7,500 copies and minimal promotion, the book's popularity spread by word of mouth, and within two years sold over one million copies, heading the New York Times Bestseller List for ten months. In 1973 a Paramount film version, with real seagulls trained by Ray Berwick and music by Neil Diamond, opened to mostly negative reviews.

Bach has been inundated with questions about the book's underlying metaphysical philosophy. Ray Bradbury called it "a great Rorschach test that you read your own mystical principles into." Buddhists felt that the story of the seagull, progressing through different stages of being in his quest for perfect flight, epitomized the spirit of Buddhism, while some Catholic priests interpreted the book as an example of the sin of pride. Many have turned to the novel for inspiration, and passages have been used for important occasions such as weddings, funerals, and graduations. Bach continues to insist that he merely recorded the book from his visions and is not the author. He emphasizes that his usual writing style is more descriptive and ornate and that he personally disapproves of Jonathan's decision to return to his flock.

A direct descendant of Johann Sebastian Bach, Richard David Bach was born in Oak Park, Illinois, to Roland Bach, a former United States Army Chaplain, and Ruth (Shaw) Bach. While attending Long Beach State College in California, he took flying lessons, igniting his lifelong passion for aviation. From 1956-1959 he served in the United States Air Force and earned his pilot wings. In the 1960s he directed the Antique Airplane Association and also worked as a charter pilot, flight instructor, and barnstormer in the Midwest, where he offered plane rides for three dollars a person. During this period, he worked as a free-lance writer, selling articles to *Flying, Soaring, Air Facts,* and other magazines. He also wrote three books about flying which were *Stranger to the Ground* (1963), *Biplane* (1966), and *Nothing by Chance* (1969).

Since *Jonathan Livingston Seagull,* he has continued to share his philosophies on life, relationships, and reincarnation in six different books. *Gift of Wings* (1974) is a collection of inspirational essays, most with some connection to flying. The 1977 book *Illusions: The Adventures of a Reluctant Messiah,* which received an American Book Award nomination in 1980, deals with Bach's encounter with Shimode, a self-proclaimed Messiah. *There's No Such Place as Far Away* (1979) tells the story of a child who learns about the meaning of life from an encounter with a hummingbird, owl, eagle, hawk, and seagull on the way to a birthday party. The autobiographical book *The Bridge Across Forever* (1984) discusses the need to find a soul mate and describes Bach's real-life relationship with actress Leslie Parrish, whom he married in 1977. *One* (1988) and *Running from Safety: An Adventure of the Spirit* (1995) use flashbacks to express Bach's philosophies. In *One,* Bach and his wife Leslie fly from Los Angeles to Santa Monica and find themselves traveling through time, discovering the effects of their past decisions both on themselves and others. In *Running from Safety,* Bach is transformed into a nine-year-old boy named Dickie, a representation of his inner child. In 1998, Bach opened a new channel of communication with his followers through his own internet web site where he shares his thoughts and answers questions.

—Eugenia Griffith DuPell

FURTHER READING:

Metzger, Linda, and Deborah Straub, editors. *Contemporary Authors.* New Revision Series. Vol 18. Detroit, Gale, 1986.

Mote, Dave, editor. *Contemporary Popular Writers.* Detroit, St. James, 1996.

Podolsky, J. D. "The Seagull Has Landed." *People Weekly.* April 27, 1992, 87-88.

Back to the Future

In the fast-paced comedy *Back to the Future,* Marty McFly (Michael J. Fox) is transported backwards in time to 1955 in a time machine invented by his friend Doc Brown (Christopher Lloyd). He accidentally interrupts the first meeting of his parents (Lea Thompson and Crispin Glover), creating a paradox that endangers his existence. The task of playing Cupid to his parents is complicated because his future mother develops a crush on him. Critics were impressed by this Oedipal theme, and audiences responded to the common fantasy of discovering what one's parents were like as teens. *Back to the Future* (1985) was followed by two sequels—*Back to the Future Part II* (1989) and *Back to the Future Part III* (1990)—and an animated TV series (1991-1993).

—Christian L. Pyle

The Bad News Bears

A fictional children's baseball team, the Bad News Bears, was the focus of three films and a CBS Television series between 1976 and

Michael J. Fox (left) and Christopher Lloyd in a scene from *Back to the Future*.

1979. The first of these films, *The Bad News Bears* (Paramount, 1976), struck an unexpected chord in both children and adults and became a hugely popular and profitable box-office hit. Although vulgar, raucous, and without intrinsic worth, *The Bad News Bears* became culturally significant in the 1970s, thanks to the unmistakable broadside it delivered against the values of American suburbia, and the connection it forged between adult and child audiences. In juxtaposing children and adults, slapstick comedy, and social commentary, the film demonstrated that it was possible to address adult themes through entertainment ostensibly designed for, and made with, children.

Directed by Michael Ritchie from a screenplay by Bill Lancaster (son of actor Burt), the plot of *The Bad News Bears* was simple enough. A local politician concerned with rehabilitating a junior baseball team composed of losers, misfits, and ethnic minorities, persuades beer-guzzling ex-pro Morris Buttermaker (Walter Matthau), now reduced to cleaning pools for a living, to take on the task of coaching the team. After a disastrous first game under Buttermaker's tenure, he recruits an ace pitcher—a girl named Amanda Whurlitzer—and a home-run hitting delinquent named Kelly Leak, whose combined skills carry the team to the championship game. During the game, Buttermaker realizes that he has come to embrace the win-at-all-costs philosophy that he had once despised in Little League coaches, and allows a group of substitute Bears to play the final inning. The team fails to win, but their efforts bring a worthwhile sense of achievement and self-affirmation to the players, which is celebrated at the film's ending.

Benefiting from the expertise of Matthau's Buttermaker, the star presence of Tatum O'Neal, and a string of good one-liners, the film emerged as one the top grossers of the year, although it was initially attacked in certain quarters for the use of bad language and risqué behavior of its juvenile protagonists. Little League president Peter McGovern wrote a letter to Paramount protesting the use of foul language as a misrepresentation of Little League baseball. However, most adults appreciated the kids' sarcastic wisdom in criticizing the adults' destructive obsession with winning a ball game, and applauded the movie and its message. Furthermore, the inclusion of Jewish, African American, Chicano, and female players on the Bears, and the team's exclusion from the elite WASP-dominated North Valley League, hinted at the racism and bigotry that lay beneath the surface of comfortable suburbia. For their part, children loved the Bears' incorrigible incompetence and their ability to lampoon adults through physical comedy and crude wit. Ultimately, the film and the team criticized an adult world willing to sacrifice ideals, fair play, and even the happiness of its own children to win a game.

Paramount—and the original idea—fell victim to the law of diminishing returns that afflicts most sequels when, hoping to cash in on the financial success of the first film, they hastily made and released two more Bears movies. *The Bad News Bears in Breaking Training* (1977) and *The Bad News Bears Go to Japan* (1978) offered increased doses of sentimentality in place of a message, dimwitted plots, and an unpalatable escalation of the cruder elements and bad language of the original. Without even the benefit of Matthau (*Breaking Training* offered William Devane, as a last-minute to-the-rescue coach; *Japan* Tony Curtis as a con-man promoter), the sequels degenerated into vacuous teen fare for the summer season, alienating the adult support won by the original. Vincent Canby of the *New York Times*, reviewing the third Bears film, summed up the problem in dismissing it as "a demonstration of the kind of desperation experienced by people trying to make something out of a voyage to nowhere."

By 1979, the Bad News Bears could no longer fill movie theaters but CBS nevertheless attempted to exploit the team's remaining popularity in a Saturday morning series called *The Bad News Bears*. Based on the first film but featuring a new cast, the show presented Morris Buttermaker as the reluctant coach of the Hoover Junior High Bears. Most episodes centered on Amanda Whurlitzer's attempts to reinvigorate a romantic relationship between Buttermaker and her mother. The series abandoned Buttermaker's use of alcohol, the Bears' swearing, and any attempt at social commentary, and failed to revitalize the team for future outings.

—Steven T. Sheehan

Baez, Joan (1941—)

Folk singer and icon of 1960s flower-children, Joan Baez sang anthems and ballads that gave voice to the frustrations and longing of the Vietnam War and Civil Rights years. Baez was seen as a Madonna with a guitar, a virginal mother of a new folk movement. As much a political activist as a musician, Baez founded the Institute for the Study of Nonviolence in Carmel Valley, California. Music and politics have gone hand-in-hand for Baez throughout her long career.

Joan Chandos Baez was born on January 9, 1941, in Staten Island, New York, to Scottish-American Joan Bridge Baez and

Walter Matthau (left) and Tatum O'Neal in a scene from *The Bad News Bears.*

Mexican-American Albert Baez. She was the second of three daughters in this multi-ethnic, politically liberal, Quaker family. Her father was a physicist who, on principle, turned down a well-paying military job to work as a professor. The family moved around a great deal, living in several towns in New York and California, and this nomadic childhood was hard for Joan. While at junior high in Redlands, California, she experienced racial prejudice because of her dark skin and Mexican heritage. Most of the other Mexicans in the area were migrant workers and were largely disdained by the rest of the population. This experience caused her to feel alone and scared, but also became one of the sources for her emerging artistic voice.

In 1958, she and her family moved to Boston, where her father took at teaching job at M.I.T. and Joan entered Boston University as a theater major. She hated school and eventually quit, but at about the same time discovered a love for the coffee-house scene. Her father had taken her to Tulla's Coffee Grinder, and from that first visit she knew she had found her niche. The folk music and intellectual atmosphere appealed to her, and she enjoyed its crowd as well. By the age of 19, after playing several Tuesday nights for $10 a show at Club

47 in Harvard Square, she was discovered by singer Bob Gibson and asked to play with him at the 1959 Newport Folk Festival.

Baez released her eponymous debut in 1960 on the Vanguard label and toured to support it. The following year Vanguard released *Joan Baez—Volume 2,* and in 1962, *Joan Baez in Concert.* All of these first three albums earned Gold Record status. She toured campuses, refusing to play at any segregated venues, and rapidly gained star status. As the civil rights movement and the Vietnam War took center stage in American politics, the views expressed in her music became more strident. Her increasing presence earned her a place on the cover of *Time* in November 1962. Between 1962 and 1964 she headlined festivals, concert tours, and rallies in Washington, D.C., notably Martin Luther King's ''March on Washington'' in 1963, where she sang ''We Shall Overcome.'' Baez was generally considered queen of the folk scene, with Bob Dylan as king.

Famous for her commitment to nonviolence, inspired both by her Quaker faith and her readings of Ghandi, Baez went to jail twice in 1968 for protesting the draft. That year, she also married antiwar activist David Harris. She played the Woodstock festival while

Joan Baez

pregnant with her only son, Gabriel, the following year. Divorced in 1972, the couple had spent most of their marriage apart from each other, either in jail, on concert tour, or protesting.

While her albums had sold well, Baez didn't have a top-ten hit on the singles chart until 1971, when she hit with a cover of The Band's ''The Night They Drove Old Dixie Down.'' Her interest in nonviolence never wavering, Baez visited Hanoi on a musical tour in 1972, and recorded her experience on 1973 album, *Where Are You Now, My Son?* A total of 18 of her albums were released in the 1970s. The bestseller among these was the 1975 album, *Diamonds and Rust.* The album contained some of the first songs penned by Baez, and more of a rock attitude as well.

In the 1980s, Baez continued her interest in social and political causes, including disarmament, anti-apartheid, prisoners of conscience, and hunger. Her appearance at Live Aid was said to have given the proceedings a certain authority and authenticity: her long career as a folk singer and activist was well-known and respected, even by younger generations. In the 1990s Baez continued to make music, releasing *Play Me Backwards* in 1992. The album featured Baez's performances of songs by Janis Ian and Mary-Chapin Carpenter. She performed a year later in war-torn Sarajevo. ''The only thing people have left is morale,'' Baez said of her audiences there.

Baez's influence continues, and can be heard in the melodies of contemporary singer-songwriter female performers like Tracy Chapman, Suzanne Vega, the Indigo Girls, and Jewel. In 1998, the Martin Guitar Company produced a limited edition Joan Baez guitar with a facsimile of a note scribbled on the inside soundboard of Joan's own guitar. The note, written by a repairman in the 1970s, read, ''Too bad

you are a Communist!'' Perhaps a more fitting quote would have been Baez's own comment: ''Action is the antidote to despair.''

—Emily Pettigrew

FURTHER READING:

Chonin, Neva. ''Joan Baez.'' *Rolling Stone.* November 13, 1997, 155.

Goldsmith, Barbara. ''Life on Struggle Mountain.'' *New York Times.* June 21, 1987.

Hendrickson, Paul. ''Baez; Looking Back on the Voice, the Life.'' *Washington Post.* July 5, 1987, 1.

''Joan Baez and David Harris: We're Just Non-violent Soldiers.'' *Look.* May 5, 1970, 58-61.

''Joan Baez, the First Lady of Folk.'' *New York Times.* November 29, 1992.

Loder, Kurt. ''Joan Baez.'' *Rolling Stone.* October 15, 1992, 105.

Bagels

Round, with a hole in the middle, the bagel is made with high gluten flour and is boiled before it is baked creating a crispy outer crust and a chewy inside. Brought to the United States by Jewish immigrants from Eastern Europe during the 1900s-1920s, the bagel has become a popular food. From 1960-1990, consumption of bagels has skyrocketed throughout the United States with the invention of mass marketed frozen bagels and the addition of flavors such as blueberry. Bagel purists, however, insist that they are best when eaten fresh and plain.

—S. Naomi Finkelstein

FURTHER READING:

Bagel, Marilyn. *The Bagel Bible: For Bagel Lovers, the Complete Guide to Great Noshing.* Old Saybrook, Connecticut, Globe Pequot, 1995.

Berman, Connie, and Suzanne Munshower. *Bagelmania: The ''Hole'' Story.* Tucson, Arizona, HP Books, 1987.

Baker, Josephine (1906-1975)

On stage, Josephine Baker epitomized the flamboyant and risqué entertainment of the Jazz Age. Her overtly erotic *danse sauvage,* her exotic costumes of feathers and bananas, and her ability to replicate the rhythms of jazz through contortions of her body made the young African American dancer one of the most original and controversial performers of the 1920s. From her Parisian debut in 1925, Baker rocked middle-class sensibilities and helped usher in a new era in popular culture. In the words of newspaperwoman and cultural critic Janet Flanner, Baker's ''magnificent dark body, a new model to the French, proved for the first time that black was beautiful.'' Off stage, Baker's decadent antics and uncanny ability to market herself helped to transform her into one of the first popular celebrities to build an international, mass appeal which cut across classes and cultures.

For a woman who would end her life with one of the most recognized faces in the world, Baker's beginnings were inauspicious. She was born Josephine Freda McDonald in the slums of St. Louis, Missouri, on June 3, 1906 and, according to her own accounts, grew up "sleeping in cardboard shelters and scavenging for food in garbage cans." She left home at the age of thirteen, married and divorced, and went to work as a waitress. By sixteen she had joined the Jones Family Band and was scraping out an income as part of a minor act in black vaudeville. Her ungainly appearance and dark skin made her a comic figure. Even after her New York debut as a chorus girl in *Shuffle Along,* a popular musical review, Baker's talents remained unrecognized. The young dancer's career changed dramatically when she accompanied La Revue Nègre to France in 1925. In New York, her ebony features had earned her the contempt of audiences partial to light-skinned blacks; in Paris, her self-styled "exotic" beauty made her an instant sensation. Her *danse sauvage,* sensual and frenetic, both shocked and charmed Parisian audiences. She grew increasingly daring when she earned lead billing at the Folies-Bergère and performed her exotic jazz dances seminude to popular acclaim. Her antics soon attracted the attention of such artistic luminaries as Pablo Picasso and Man Ray. In a Western Europe recovering from the disruptions of the First World War, Baker's untamed style came to embody for many observers the pure and primitive beauty of the non-Western world.

Baker thrived on the controversy surrounding her routine. She coveted the appreciation of her numerous fans and, in an effort to promote herself, adopted many of the mass-market tactics that soon became the hallmarks of most popular celebrities. She encouraged the dissemination of her image through such products as Josephine Baker dolls and hired a press agent to answer her fan mail. She also exposed her private life to the public, writing one of the first tell-all biographies; she invited reporters into her home to photograph her with her "pet" tiger and to admire her performing daily chores in her stage costumes. The line between Baker the performer and Baker the private individual soon blurred—increasing her popularity and creating an international Josephine Baker cult of appreciation. In the early 1930s, Baker embarked on a second career as a singer and actress. Her films, *Zou-Zou* and *Princess Tam-Tam,* proved mildly successful. Yet by 1935 the Josephine Baker craze in Europe had come to an end and the twenty-nine year old dancer returned to the United States to attempt to repeat in New York what she had done in Paris. She flopped miserably. Her *danse sauvage* found no place in depression-era America and white audiences proved to be overtly hostile to a black woman of Baker's sophistication and flamboyance. She returned to France, retired to the countryside, and exited public life. She became a French citizen in 1937.

The second half of Baker's life was defined both by personal misfortune and public service. She engaged in espionage work for the French Resistance during World War II, then entered the Civil Rights crusade, and finally devoted herself to the plight of impoverished children. She adopted twelve orphans of different ethnic backgrounds and gained some public attention in her later years as the matron of her "Rainbow Tribe." At the same time, Baker's personal intrigues continued to cloud her reputation. She exhausted four marriages and offered public praise for right-wing dictators Juan Perón and Benito Mussolini. What little support she had in the American media collapsed in 1951 after a public feud with columnist Walter Winchell. In 1973, financial difficulties forced her to return to the stage. She died in Paris on April 12, 1975.

Few performers can claim to be more "of an age" than Josephine Baker. Her star, rising so rapidly during the 1920s and then collapsing in the wake of World War II, paralleled the emergence of the wild, free-spirited culture of the Jazz Age. Her self-promotion tactics made her one of the first popular celebrities; these tactics were later copied by such international figures as Charles Lindbergh, Charlie Chaplin, and Marlene Dietrich. Yet it was Baker's ability to tap into the pulsing undercurrents of 1920s culture that made her a sensation. Picasso once said that Baker possessed "a smile to end all smiles"; it should be added, to her credit, that she knew how to use it.

—Jacob M. Appel

FURTHER READING:

Baker, Jean-Claude, and Chris Chase. *Josephine: The Hungry Heart.* New York, Random House, 1993.

Baker, Josephine, with Jo Bouillon. *Josephine.* Translated by Mariana Fitzpatrick. New York, Harper & Row, 1977.

Colin, Paul, with introduction by Henry Louis Gates, Jr., and Karen C. C. Dalton. *Josephine Baker and La Revue Nègre: Paul Colin's Lithographs of Le Tumulte Noir in Paris, 1927.* New York, H. N. Abrams, 1998.

Hammond, Bryan. *Josephine Baker.* London, Cape, 1988.

Haney, Lynn. *Naked at the Feast: A Biography of Josephine Baker.* New York, Dodd, Mead, 1981.

Rose, Phyllis. *Jazz Cleopatra: Josephine Baker in Her Time.* New York, Doubleday, 1989.

Baker, Ray Stannard (1870-1946)

Ray Stannard Baker became both a leading muckraking journalist of the Progressive era and an acclaimed writer of nonfiction books and pastoral prose. A native of Michigan, he worked as a reporter for the *Chicago Record* from 1892 to 1897 and joined the staff of the innovative and popular *McClure's* magazine in 1898. His influential articles, including "The Right to Work" (1903) and "The Railroads on Trial" (1905-1906), helped make the magazine the nation's foremost muckraking journal. Known for his fair-mindedness, Baker exposed both union and corporate malfeasance. In 1906 he helped form the *American Magazine,* also devoted to progressive causes, and co-edited it until 1916. From 1906 to 1942, under the pseudonym of David Grayson, Baker wrote an extremely popular series of novels celebrating the rural life. He was awarded a Pulitzer Prize in 1940 for his eight-volume biography of Woodrow Wilson.

—Daniel Lindley

FURTHER READING:

Baker, Ray Stannard. *Native American: The Book of My Youth.* New York, Charles Scribner's Sons, 1941.

———. *American Chronicle: The Autobiography of Ray Stannard Baker.* New York, Charles Scribner's Sons, 1945.

Bannister, Robert C., Jr. *Ray Stannard Baker: The Mind and Thought of a Progressive.* New Haven, Yale University Press, 1966.

Semonche, John E. *Ray Stannard Baker: A Quest for Democracy in Modern America, 1870-1918.* Chapel Hill, University of North Carolina Press, 1969.

Bakker, Jim (1940—), and Tammy Faye (1942—)

Husband and wife televangelist team Jim and Tammy Faye Bakker became a prominent part of American popular culture in the late 1980s when their vast PTL ministry was hit by scandal and accounts of fraud. The Bakker affair—and the activities of other TV preachers in the news at the time—inspired a popular reaction against TV preachers, and, fairly or unfairly, the Bakkers were seen as the embodiment of eighties materialist excess and Elmer Gantry-like religious hypocrisy. A country song by Ray Stevens summed up the popular feeling with the title "Would Jesus Wear a Rolex on His Television Show?"

Raised in Michigan, Jim Bakker received religious training at North Central Bible College in Minneapolis. There he met fellow student Tammy Faye LaValley, who, like Bakker, was raised in the Pentecostal tradition. The two were married and traveled the country as itinerant evangelists until 1965, when they went to work for Virginia television preacher (and 1988 presidential candidate) Pat Robertson, on whose station Jim Bakker established *The 700 Club.* (Robertson continued this show after Bakker left.)

After leaving Robertson's operation in 1972, the Bakkers started a new TV program, *The PTL Club,* on the Trinity Broadcasting Network in California. In 1974, after a quarrel with the network, the Bakkers moved to Charlotte, North Carolina, to broadcast the show on their own. Jim Bakker established a Christian theme park south of Charlotte called Heritage USA, which attracted fundamentalist Christians who came to pray and to enjoy themselves. There was a water slide as well as several shops selling Christian tapes, records, books, and action figures. *The PTL Club* was broadcast from Heritage USA to what became a large national audience.

"PTL" could stand for "Praise the Lord" or "People That Love": Bakker established many People That Love Centers where the poor could get free clothes, food, and furniture. To some of the Bakkers' detractors, however, "PTL" stood for "Pass the Loot," an allusion to the Bakkers' frequent and often lachrymose fund-raising appeals on the air and to their lavish lifestyle (including, it was later disclosed, an air-conditioned doghouse for their dog). Describing a visit he made in 1987, journalist P. J. O'Rourke said that being at

Jim and Tammy Faye Bakker

Heritage USA ''was like being in the First Church of Christ Hanging Out at the Mall.''

In 1979, the Federal Communications Commission began an investigation of PTL for questionable fund-raising tactics. In 1982, the FCC decided to take no further action in the case, provided that PTL sold its single TV station. This did not stop PTL from broadcasting on cable TV or from buying TV time on other stations, so the FCC action had no significant effect on PTL's operations. In 1986, the year before everything fell apart, PTL was raising $10 million a month, according to a subsequent audit.

A virtual tsunami of scandal hit the PTL ministry in 1987. Thanks in part to the efforts of an anti-Bakker preacher named Jimmy Swaggart and of the *Charlotte Observer* newspaper (which won a Pulitzer Prize for its coverage of the Bakker matter), a lurid scandal was uncovered at PTL. In 1980, Jim Bakker had a tryst with a church secretary named Jessica Hahn. PTL later gave money to Hahn in what looked like a payoff. In the wake of this revelation, Bakker turned PTL over to Jerry Falwell, a nationally known TV evangelist and political figure. Bakker later claimed that the handover was only meant to be temporary. Falwell denied this and took full control of PTL. PTL soon filed for bankruptcy; it ultimately was taken over by a group of Malaysian Christians.

This was only the beginning. The Pentecostal Assemblies of God, which had ordained Bakker, defrocked him. The IRS retroactively revoked PTL's tax exemption, ordering the payment of back taxes and penalties. In December of 1988, Jim Bakker was indicted by a federal grand jury on several counts of fraud and conspiracy. These charges centered around Bakker's promotion of an arrangement by which viewers who contributed a certain amount of money to PTL would be given ''partnerships'' entitling them to stay for free at Heritage USA. According to the prosecution, Bakker had lied to his TV viewers by understating the number of partnerships he had sold, that he had overbooked the hotels where the partners were supposed to stay during their visits, and that he had diverted partners' money into general PTL expenses (including the Hahn payoff) after promising that the money would be used to complete one of the hotels where the partners would stay. The jury convicted Bakker, who went to prison from 1989 to 1994. In a civil case brought by disgruntled partners, Bakker was found liable for common law fraud in 1990. Another civil jury, however, found in Bakker's favor in 1996 in a claim of securities fraud.

Meanwhile, Bakker foe Jimmy Swaggart was caught in a sex scandal, and evangelist Oral Roberts said that he would die unless his viewers sent him enough money.

While her husband was in prison, Tammy Faye tried to continue his ministry, but she finally divorced him and married Roe Messner, a contractor for church-building projects who had done much of the work at Heritage USA. She briefly had a talk show on the Fox network. Roe Messner was convicted of bankruptcy fraud in 1996.

—Eric Longley

FURTHER READING:

Albert, James A. *Jim Bakker: Miscarriage of Justice?* Chicago, Open Court, 1998.

Martz, Larry, and Ginny Carroll. *Ministry of Greed.* New York, Weidenfeld and Nicolson, 1988.

O'Rourke, P. J. ''Weekend Getaway: Heritage USA.'' *Holidays in Hell.* New York, Vintage Books, 1988, 91-98.

Shepard, Charles E. *Forgiven: The Rise and Fall of Jim Bakker and the PTL Ministry.* New York, Atlantic Monthly Press, 1989.

Balanchine, George (1904-1983)

The greatest choreographer of the twentieth century, George Balanchine transformed and modernized the classic tradition of Russian ballet. A graduate of the imperial St. Petersburg ballet academy, he left Russia in 1924 and soon became the resident choreographer for Diaghilev's Ballet Russes. Brought to the U.S. by the wealthy young impresario, Lincoln Kirstein, in 1933, together they founded the School of American Ballet and later, in 1948, the New York City Ballet. Until 1948 Ballanchine choreographed a number of successful Broadway musicals and Hollywood movies. Eschewing traditional ballet story lines, Balanchine created a series of unprecedented masterpieces, his ''black and white'' ballets—so called because the dancers wear only their practice clothes—*Apollo* (Stravinsky), *Agon* (Stravinsky), *Concerto Barocco* (Bach), *The Four Temperaments* (Hindemith), and *Symphony in Three Movements* (Stravinsky). They share the stage with rousing and colorful dances based on folk and popular music like *Stars and Stripes* (John Philip Sousa), *Western Symphony,* and *Who Cares?* (Gershwin).

—Jeffrey Escoffier

FURTHER READING:

New York City Ballet. *The Balanchine Celebration* (video). Parts I and II. The Balanchine Library, Nonesuch Video, 1993.

Taper, Bernard. *Balanchine: A Biography.* Berkeley, University of California Press, 1984.

Baldwin, James (1924-1987)

James Baldwin's impact on the American consciousness was twofold: as an author, his accounts of his experiences struck a cord with his readers; as an activist, his vision and abilities helped fuel the Civil Rights Movement. A gifted writer, he began his career immersed in artistic expression for the pleasure it offered. By the 1960s, however, he began to pen influential political essays, and by the end of his life he had evolved into one of the twentieth century's most politically charged writers decrying racism in all of its ugly forms.

Born in Harlem to a single mother who was a factory worker, James Baldwin was the first of nine children. Soon after his birth his mother married a clergyman, David Baldwin, who influenced the young James and encouraged him to read and write. He began his career as a storefront preacher while still in his adolescence. In 1942, after graduating from high school, he moved to New Jersey to begin working on the railroads. In *Notes of a Native Son* he described his experiences working as well as the deterioration and death of his stepfather, who was buried on the young Baldwin's nineteenth birthday. In 1944 he moved back to New York and settled in Greenwich Village where he met Richard Wright and began to work on his first novel, *In My Father's House.* In the late 1940s he wrote for *The Nation, The New Leader,* and *Partisan Review.* In 1948, disgusted with race relations in the United States, he moved to Paris where he

George Balanchine (center), working with a dancer.

lived, on and off, for the rest of his life. In 1953, he finished his most important novel, *Go Tell It on the Mountain*, a semi-autobiographical account of his youth. Baldwin received a Guggenheim Fellowship in 1954 and the following year published *Giovanni's Room*. He is also the author of several plays, including *The Amen Corner* and *Blues for Mr. Charlie*.

During the 1960s, Baldwin returned to the United States and became politically active in the Civil Rights Movement. In 1961, his essay collection *Nobody Knows My Name* won him numerous recognitions and awards. In 1963 he published *The Fire Next Time*, a book-length essay that lifted him into international fame and recognition. This work represents such a watershed event in his life that many scholars divide his career between ''before'' and ''after'' the publication of *The Fire Next Time*.

Before 1963, Baldwin had embraced an ''art for art's sake'' philosophy and was critical of writers like Richard Wright for their politically-charged works. He did not believe that writers needed to use their writing as a protest tool. After 1963 and the publication of his long essay, however, he became militant in his political activism and

as a gay-rights activist. He passionately criticized the Vietnam War, and accused Richard Nixon and J. Edgar Hoover of plotting the genocide of all people of color. Comparing the Civil Rights Movement to the independence movements in Africa and Asia, he drew the attention of the Kennedys. Robert Kennedy requested his advice on how to deal with the Birmingham, Alabama riots and tried to intimidate him by getting his dossier from Hoover.

In 1968, Baldwin published *Tell Me How Long the Train's Been Gone*, an account of American racism, bitter and incisive. *No Name in the Street* (1972) predicted the downfall of Euro-centrism and observed that only a revolution could solve the problem of American racism. In 1985, he published *The Evidence of Things Not Seen*, an analysis of the Atlanta child murders of 1979 and 1980.

During the last decade of his life Baldwin taught at the University of Massachusetts at Amherst and at Hampshire College, commuting between the United States and France. He died in 1987 at his home in St. Paul de Vence, France.

—Beatriz Badikian

FURTHER READING:

Metzger, Linda. *Black Writers.* Detroit, Gale Research, Inc., 1989.

Oliver, Clinton F. *Contemporary Black Drama.* New York, Charles Scribner's Sons, 1971.

Pratt, Louis H. *James Baldwin.* Boston, G. K. Hall and Company, 1978.

Ball, Lucille (1911-1989)

Almost fifty years after *I Love Lucy* first aired on television, the image of "Lucy" is still omnipresent in U.S. culture. In movies, on television, and emblazoned on various merchandise such as lunchboxes, dolls, piggybanks, and calendars, the zany redhead with the elastic face is an industrial and cultural institution. But beyond simply an image, Lucille Ball was, without a doubt, the first woman of television and the most adored American female comic of the twentieth century. However, the comedienne's struggling years as a model, dancer, and "B" movie actress are often forgotten in the light of her international fame that came at the age of 40.

As a 15-year-old Ball left her family in upstate New York to study acting in Manhattan. Although she acquired skills in acting, dancing, and modeling, she did not find any real success until she landed a job as a chorus girl in Eddie Cantor's 1933 film *Roman Scandals.* A talented and beautiful woman with a slim body and large blue eyes, Ball's star potential was recognized by a number of studios. Goldwyn was the first to sign her as a contract player after her turn in Cantor's film. Disappointed by the bit parts with little to no dialogue offered by Goldwyn, Ball soon left for RKO where her 1937 performance in *Stage Door* with Katherine Hepburn attracted the attention of studio heads. Consequently over the next few years, Ball won significant roles in films such as *Go Chase Yourself* (1938), *Too Many Girls* (1940), and *The Big Street* (1942), carving out a small career for herself in "B" pictures. She also found her future husband, Desi Arnaz, during her time in Hollywood when she starred alongside him in the film *Too Many Girls* (1940). Yet, by the mid-1940s, after switching studios once again (this time to MGM), it became apparent to both Ball and her studio that she did not fit the mold of a popular musical star or romantic leading lady. So, the platinum blonde glamour girl began the process of remaking herself into a feisty red-headed comedienne.

In 1948, Ball was cast as Liz Cooper, a high society housewife on CBS radio's situation comedy *My Favorite Husband*—a role that would help form the basis of her "Lucy" character. The show attracted a significant following and CBS offered Ball the opportunity to star in a television version of the program in 1950. But, concerned with what damage the new job might do to her already tenuous marriage, Ball insisted that Arnaz be cast as her on-screen husband. Network executives initially balked at the idea claiming that Arnaz lacked the talent and other qualities necessary to television stardom. However, after Ball rejected CBS's offer and took her and Arnaz's act on the vaudeville circuit to critical acclaim, the network finally backed down agreeing to sign the couple to play Lucy and Ricky Ricardo. But, Arnaz and Ball were able to finagle not only contracts as co-stars, but they also procured ownership of the programs after their initial airing. The unexpectedly large profits that came from the show's syndication, foreign rights, and re-runs enabled the couple to

James Baldwin

form their own production company, Desilu, which eventually produced such hit shows as *Our Miss Brooks, The Dick Van Dyke Show,* and *The Untouchables.*

On October 15, 1951 *I Love Lucy* was broadcast for the first time. The show focused primarily on the antics of Lucy, a frustrated housewife longing to break into show business and her husband Ricky, a moderately successful Cuban bandleader. Supported by co-stars William Frawley and Vivian Vance, playing the Ricardo's best friends and neighbors, along with the talents of *My Favorite Husband* writers Jess Oppenheimer, Carroll Carroll, and Madelyn Pugh, Ball and Arnaz's program quickly topped the ratings. Much of *I Love Lucy*'s success was credited to Ball's incredible timing and endlessly fascinating physical finesse. Able to project both the glamour of a former film star as well as the goofy incompetence of an ordinary (albeit zany) housewife, Ball proved that vaudeville routines could be incorporated into a domestic setting and that a female comedian could be both feminine and aggressively physical. She accomplished this, at least in part, by choreographing every move of her slapstick performances and accumulating a series of goofy facial expressions that were eventually cataloged by the writings staff under such cues as "light bulb," "puddling up," "small rabbit," and "foiled again."

Lucille Ball

In the spring of 1952, *I Love Lucy* set a rating record of 71.8 when Ball's real-life cesarean delivery of her and Arnaz's son occurred on the same day as the on-air birth of Lucy Ricardo's "little Ricky." Expertly exploiting the viewer's conflation of Ball and Arnaz's private life with that of the Ricardo's, the couple managed to achieve television super stardom through the event and appeared on the covers of *Time, Life,* and *Look* with their son and daughter (Lucille Arnaz was born in 1951) over the next year. But, not all the press attention was positive. Accused of being a communist in 1953, Ball was one of the only film or television stars to survive the machinations of the HUAC investigations. Explaining that she registered as a communist in 1936 in order to please her ailing socialist grandfather, she claimed that she was never actually a supporter of the communist party. Thousands of fans wrote to Ball giving her their support and the committee eventually backed down announcing that they had no real evidence of her affiliation with the party. The crisis passed quickly and Lucy remained the most popular comedienne of the 1950s.

After divorcing Arnaz in 1960 and buying out his share of Desilu, Ball became the first woman to control her own television production studio. During the 1960s she produced and starred in *The Lucy-Desi Comedy Hour, The Lucy Show,* and *Here's Lucy.* By the mid-1970s she had begun to appear in television specials and made-for-television movies, and by 1985 had garnered critical praise for her portrayal of a homeless woman in the drama *Stone Pillow.* But it was her brilliantly silly, mayhem-making Lucy character that lingered in the minds (and merchandise) of generations of television audiences even after her death in 1989.

—Sue Murray

FURTHER READING:

Andrews, Bart. *Lucy and Ricky and Fred and Ethel.* New York, Dutton, 1976.

Arnaz, Desi. *A Book by Desi Arnaz.* New York, Morrow, 1976.

Ball, Lucille with Betty Hannah Hoffman. *Love, Lucy.* New York, G.P. Putnam's Sons, 1996.

Brady, Kathleen. *Lucille: The Life of Lucille Ball.* New York, Hyperion, 1994.

Brochu, Jim. *Lucy in the Afternoon: An Intimate Memoir of Lucille Ball.* New York, William Morrow, 1990.

Oppenheimer, Jess with Gregg Oppenheimer. *Laughs, Luck . . . and Lucy: How I Came to Create the Most Popular Sitcom of All Time.* Syracuse, New York, Syracuse University Press, 1996.

Ballard, Hank (1936—)

Hank Ballard's distinctive tenor voice and knack for writing catchy, blues-flavored pop songs made him one of the living legends of rock 'n' roll, even as his notoriously earthy lyrics made him one of its most controversial figures. Born in Detroit on November 18, 1936, Ballard was orphaned at an early age. He was sent to Bessemer, Alabama, to live with relatives, and during these years he acquired his initial singing experience, performing gospel songs in church. This gospel edge would later characterize some of Ballard's best work, including the hit ballad "Teardrops on Your Letter."

Ballard returned to Detroit at age 15 to work on the Ford Motor Company assembly line. Inspired by rhythm and blues singers like the Dominoes' Clyde McPhatter, Ballard also joined a doo-wop outfit called the Royals. Although the Royals had already established themselves as a reasonably successful group, scoring a minor hit on Federal Records with their version of Johnny Otis' "Every Beat of My Heart," it was their acquisition of Ballard that would define their future style and sound. The group's next recording, a Ballard original entitled "Get It," was released in late 1953, and received as much attention for its "quite erotic" lyrics as it did for its musical qualities.

In early 1954, Federal Records acquired another, better known Rhythm and Blues group called the Five Royales, who had already produced a string of hits on the Apollo label. In an effort to avoid confusion, Federal president Syd Nathan changed the name of Ballard's group to the Midnighters (later Hank Ballard and the Midnighters). The newly-christened Midnighters subsequently produced their most important and influential song, "Work With Me Annie." With its raunchy, double-entendre lyrics, including lines like "Annie, please don't cheat/Give me all my meat," the hit single helped to fuel a firestorm of controversy over explicit lyrics (*Variety* magazine columnist Abel Green referred to them as "leer-ics" in a string of editorials). Enjoying their newfound popularity, the Midnighters, in the tradition established by country musicians, cut several "answers" to their hit, including "Annie Had a Baby" and later "Annie's Aunt Fannie." Other groups joined in the act, with the El Dorados producing "Annie's Answer" for the Vee Jay label, while the Platters mined similar terrain with "Maggie Doesn't Work Here Anymore." Eventually, the entire "Annie" series, along with two dozen other "erotic" Rhythm and Blues songs, was banned from radio airwaves virtually nationwide.

Hank Ballard

A few years later, Ballard matched new lyrics to a melody that he had first used on a Midnighters flop entitled "Is Your Love for Real?", and produced "The Twist." Dissatisfied with Federal's management of the group, Ballard took his new song to Vee-Jay Records, and later to King Records, which finally released it as the B-side of the ballad "Teardrops on Your Letter." American Bandstand host Dick Clark liked the tune enough to finance a rerecording by Ernest Evans (a.k.a Chubby Checker), who took the tune to the top of the pop charts not once but twice, in 1960 and 1962. Checker''s version emulated Ballard's to such a degree that Ballard, upon first hearing it, believed it was his own.

The Midnighters continued to experience chart action; at one point in 1960, they had three singles on the pop chart simultaneously. In 1961, however, Ballard elected to pursue a career as a solo act, and the Midnighters disbanded. Thereafter, Ballard found very little success, although he made the Rhythm and Blues charts in 1968 and 1972 with "How You Gonna Get Respect (If You Haven't Cut Your Process Yet)?" and "From the Love Side," respectively. After a long break from performing, Ballard formed a new "Midnighters" group in the mid-1980s and resumed his career. He also made special appearances with well known rock and blues artists, including guitarist Stevie Ray Vaughan, who in 1985 covered Ballard's "Look at Little Sister" on his critically-acclaimed album *Soul to Soul*. Ballard was among the first inductees into the Rock 'n' Roll Hall of Fame in 1990. In 1993, he released a "comeback" album entitled *Naked in the Rain*.

—Marc R. Sykes

FURTHER READING:

Martin, Linda, and Kerry Segrave. *Anti-Rock: The Opposition to Rock 'n' Roll*. Hamden, Connecticut, Archon Books, 1988.

Shaw, Arnold. *Honkers and Shouters: The Golden Years of Rhythm and Blues*. New York, Macmillan, 1978.

Ballet

Classical ballet is a form of theatrical entertainment that originated among the aristocracy of the sixteenth and seventeenth century royal court of France. In its original form it was performed by trained dancers as well as by members of the court themselves. The stories told in the ballet performances were usually based on mythical or allegorical themes. They contained no dialogue, but instead relied on pantomime to convey character, plot, and action. From its earliest days, ballets incorporated lavish costumes, scenery, and music. Although ballet dance performance often incorporated courtly ballroom dances, and even folk dances, it was organized around five basic dance positions—feet and arms rotated outward from the body with limbs extended. These positions maximize the visibility of the dancer's movements to the audience and thus serve as the grammar of ballet's language of communication.

The foundations of ballet were firmly established when King Louis XIV created a special dancing academy in order to train dancers for the court's ballets. That school continues to operate today as the school of the Paris Opera Ballet. During the nineteenth century French-trained ballet masters and dancers established vigorous dance companies and schools in Copenhagen and St. Petersburg. During this time Russia's Imperial ballet attracted several of the century's most talented ballet masters. The last of them, and the greatest, was Marius Petipa, who created the great classic works that define the Russian ballet tradition: *Le Cosaire, Don Quixote, La Bayadere, Swan Lake, Sleeping Beauty,* and *Raymonda.* All of these works are still in the repertory of ballet companies at the end of the twentieth-century, more than one hundred years later. Almost all of the great ballet companies of the late twentieth century are descended from the Imperial Russian ballet.

Serge Diaghilev's Ballets Russes, which employed many dancers and teachers trained at the Imperial Ballet and exiled by the Russian revolution, was absolutely key to the transformation of ballet from a court-sponsored elite entertainment into a commercially viable art form with a popular following. Diaghilev and his company forged a synthesis of modern art and music that revolutionized ballet in the twentieth century. Diaghilev mounted modernist spectacles using music and scenic design by the most important modern composers and artists: Igor Stravinsky, Claude Debussy, Maurice Ravel, Eric Satie, Serge Prokofiev, Pablo Picasso, Giorgio de Chirico, Joan Miro, Juan Gris, Georges Braque, and George Rouault. Among the company's brilliant dancers was Vaslav Nijinsky, probably one of greatest male dancers of century, but also an original choreographer. In ballets like *L'Apres-midi d'un faune* and *Jeux,* with music by Debussy, and *Le Sacre du Printemps,* with music by Stravinsky, Nijinsky created radical works that broke with the Russian tradition of Petipa and which relied upon an unorthodox movement vocabulary and a shallow stage space. The world famous 1912 premiere of Stravinsky's *Le Sacre du Printemps,* choreographed by Nijinsky, provoked a riot

Ballet stars Michael Shennon and Olga Suvorova perform a pas-de-deux from Corsair by A. Adan.

among its stuffy bourgeois audience and is considered one of the great events marking the arrival of modernist art.

The United States had no classic ballet tradition of its own. Instead, many strains of vernacular and ethnic dances flourished, such as square dances which were adapted from English folk dances. There were also many vigorous forms of social dancing, particularly the styles of dancing which emerged from jazz and black communities, such as jitterbug and swing. Popular theatrical entertainment and vaudeville also drew on vernacular forms like tap dancing. One new form of theatrical dance that emerged around the turn of the century was modern dance, inspired by Isadora Duncan and developed by dancers and choreographers Ruth Denis, Ted Shawn, and Martha Graham. It has remained a vital theatrical dance tradition up until the present with Paul Taylor, Twyla Tharp, and Mark Morris among its most noted contemporary practitioners.

The New York appearance in 1916 of Diaghilev's Ballets Russes marks the most important step towards the popularization of ballet in the United States. Two of the greatest dancers of the early twentieth century—Vaslav Nijinsky and Anna Pavlova—danced in the United States during those years. Nothing much of import occurred until 1933, when Lincoln Kirstein, a wealthy young admirer of ballet who was visiting Paris, invited George Balanchine to come to the United States and help establish ballet there. Balanchine accepted Kirstein's invitation only if they established "first, a school." Their School of American Ballet opened in 1934. Kirstein and Balanchine's School was an important link in the popularization of ballet in the United States. In 1913 Willa Cather had lamented that

"we have had no dancers because we had no schools." European dancers—among them some of the greatest of their era, such as Fanny Essler—had been coming to the United States since the early nineteenth century. Many of them settled down to privately teach young American girls, because ballet at the time was centered primarily on the ballerina. However no one had a greater influence than the great Russian ballerina, Anna Pavlova, and her partner, Mikhail Mordkin, who starting in 1910 spent 15 years performing and teaching ballet in almost every corner of the country. The appeal of ballet and its cultural prestige had been consolidated by New York's rapturous response in 1916 to Diaghilev's Ballet Russes. In 1933 the founding of the School of American Ballet with its network of scouts, scouring small-town and regional ballet classes, created the foundations for the development of native-born American dancers.

Beginning in 1935 Kirstein and Balanchine went on to form the first of the many unsuccessful companies that eventually solidified into a stable company in 1948 as the New York City Ballet. Meanwhile another group, led by Richard Pleasants and Lucia Chase, was also trying to establish a permanent ballet company; they succeeded in 1939 by setting up the American Ballet Theatre (ABT). Since the 1930s these two companies have dominated ballet in the United States. Both companies employed many of the Russian dancers, choreographers, and teachers displaced by revolution and world war. American Ballet Theater has a long tradition of performing the great romantic ballets—such as *Swan Lake, Giselle,* and *Sleeping Beauty*—created for the European audiences of the late nineteenth century. George Balanchine's New York City Ballet, on the other hand, was almost exclusively the showcase for his original work, which rejected the narrative conventions of romantic ballet for a modern approach that emphasized musicality, speed, and a deep stage space.

During the 1970s ballet and modern dance in the United States were the beneficiaries of a wave of popularity which resulted in many new dance companies being founded in cities and communities throughout the country. The same period was also marked by the increasing amount of crossover activity between modern dance and ballet on the part of choreographers and dancers. Although the dance boom (and the funding that supported it) has partially receded both ballet and modern dance remain a vital form of cultural activity and popular entertainment.

—Jeffrey Escoffier

FURTHER READING:

Amberg, George. *Ballet in America: The Emergence of an American Art.* New York, Duell, Sloan, and Pearce, 1949.

Coe, Robert. *Dance in America.* New York, Dutton, 1985.

Garafola, Lyn. *Diaghilev's Ballets Russes.* New York, Oxford University Press, 1989.

Greskovic, Robert. *Ballet 101.* New York, Hyperion, 1998.

Bambaataa, Afrika (1960—)

A Bronx, New York-based disc jockey (DJ) in the mid-1970s and the creator of a few popular hip-hop songs in the early 1980s, Afrika Bambaataa is one of the most important figures in the development of hip-hop music. Born April 10, 1960, Bambaataa developed a following in the mid-1970s by DJ-ing at events that led to the evolution of hip-hop music as it is known today. At these events, dancers developed a unique style of dancing called breakdancing, the rhythmic vocal style called rapping was cultivated, and DJs such as Bambaataa, Kool DJ Herc, and Grandmaster Flash demonstrated how turntables could be used as a musical instrument. In 1982, Bambaataa had a big hit in the *Billboard* Black charts with his single ''Planet Rock.''

—Kembrew McLeod

FURTHER READING:

Rose, Tricia. *Black Noise: Rap Music and Black Culture in Contemporary America.* Hanover, UP of New England, 1994.

Toop, David. *Rap Attack 2: African Rap to Global Hip-Hop.* New York, Serpent's Tail, 1991.

The Band

''They brought us in touch with the place where we all had to live,'' Greil Marcus wrote in *Mystery Train*. Thirty years after The Band's first appearance on the international music-scene toward the

The Band

end of the 1960s, Marcus' words still ring true. More than that of any other group, The Band's work represents America at its sincerest, the diversity of its musical heritage, the vividness of its culture, and the lasting attraction of its history. Marcus noted that ''against the instant America of the sixties they looked for the traditions that made new things not only possible, but valuable; against a flight from roots they set a sense of place. Against the pop scene, all flux and novelty, they set themselves: a band with years behind it, and meant to last.'' Last they certainly did.

Having started off as backing musicians (The Hawks) to rockabilly veteran Ronnie Hawkins, Rick Danko (1943—), Garth Hudson (1937—), Levon Helm (1942—), Richard Manuel (1944-1986), and Jaime 'Robbie' Robertson (1944—) played their first gigs in 1964 as an independent group called Levon and the Hawks. As this group they recorded a couple of singles that went largely unnoticed. Chance came their way though, when they met with Albert Grossman, Bob Dylan's manager at the time. Grossman felt that Levon and the Hawks might well be the backing group Dylan was on the look-out for after his legendary first electric appearance at the Newport Folk Festival in 1965. After having met and played with him, the group joined Dylan in 1966 for a tour that took them through the United States, and later to Australia and England.

Back in the States in the summer of 1966, they moved to the area around Woodstock—without Levon Helm, though, who had left the tour after two months. There, in Saugerties, New York, they rented a big pink house (appropriately named 'Big Pink'), in the basement of which they recorded well over a hundred songs with Dylan, who at the time was recovering from a serious motorcycle accident. Some twenty of these songs were later released on *The Basement Tapes* (1975). The sessions in the basement of 'Big Pink' must have made clear to Robertson, Danko, Hudson and Manuel that their musical talents and the originality of their sound were considerable enough to enable them to make it without Dylan. After Albert Grossman cut them a record deal with Capitol, Levon Helm returned to the group and together they recorded *Music from Big Pink,* still one of the all-time great debuts in the history of popular music. Upon the album's release in August 1968, both the critics and the public realized that something unique had come their way. *Music from Big Pink* confirmed the uniqueness of the group's sound—a highly individual blend of the most varied brands of American popular music: gospel, country, rhythm and blues, rockabilly, New Orleans jazz, etc. But it also set the themes which The Band (for this was what they had finally decided on as a name) would explore in albums to come.

Most of the songs on the album, three of which were written by Dylan, are set in the rural South. They belong to a tradition long gone, yet the revival of which the members of The Band considered to be beneficial to a country that yearned for a change but did not really know where to look for it. The songs of The Band should not be taken as nostalgic pleas for the past, for the simpler things in life or for values long lost and gone. The characters in the songs of *Music from Big Pink* and later albums are in no way successful romantic heroes who have truly found themselves. They are flesh-and-blood people, loners, burdened with guilt, and torn up by love and heartache.

Compared to most albums to come out of the wave of psychedelic rock at the end of the 1960s, the music of The Band was anything but typical of its era. It is a pleasant irony, therefore, that The Band's records have aged so easily, while those of contemporaries like Jefferson Airplane or Country Joe and the Fish already sounded dated a couple of years after their release. From the beginning, the music of

The Band—an idiosyncratic combination of several voices (Manuel, Danko, Helm), Robbie Robertson's guitar, the drums of Levon Helm, and the organ of musical wizard Garth Hudson—is full of seeming contradictions that somehow blend into a harmonious whole. The music is playful yet serious, soulful yet deliberate, traditional yet rebellious, harmonic yet syncopated.

The group's second album, *The Band* (1969), is generally rated as better than its predecessor, representing The Band at its best. The record shows that the group found their idiom, both lyrically and musically. From this album Robertson emerged as the most prominent member of the group; not only did he write most of the songs, but also he also looked after The Band's financial interests. There can be little doubt that at the time The Band was both at its artistic and commercial zenith. In 1970 they made it to the cover of *Time* magazine and gave their first public performances. The latter soon made clear, however, that the group was at its best in the recording studio.

The title-track of The Band's third album, *Stage Fright* (1970), may be taken as a comment on the problems some members of the group had with performing live. The record was a new artistic success, though, very much like its follow-up, *Cahoots* (1971) which featured both Van Morrison and Allen Toussaint. The latter was also present on *Rock of Ages,* a double album which contains live versions of the Band's greatest songs. The next two years, 1972 and 1973 were all in all lost years for The Band. Life on the road and world-wide success began to take their toll. They recorded *Moondog Matinee,* a collection of all-time favorites from the years when they were touring with Ronnie Hawkins. The record has mainly to be seen as an attempt to mask a collective lack of inspiration, partly brought on by an equally collective over-consumption of alcohol and drugs. Then followed a large tour with Dylan (1973-1974), the recording of *Northern Lights, Southern Cross* (1975)—which contains some of the best Band-songs in years—and their legendary farewell performance in the Winterland Arena, San Francisco, on Thanksgiving 1976. The event is known as *The Last Waltz*: it features friends and colleagues like Ronnie Hawkins, Muddy Waters, Neil Young, Van Morrison, Joni Mitchel and, of course, Dylan. (The film-version, by Martin Scorsese, remains one of the best rock-movies ever made.)

After *The Last Waltz,* the members of The Band went their separate ways: some of them made solo-records (Robertson most notably), others starred in movies (Helm). In 1983 The Band re-united, without Robertson however. Since the self-inflicted death of Richard Manuel in 1986, the three remaining members of the original Band have recorded two albums on which they were joined by two new musicians. While it is obvious that the magic of the early years is gone forever, we are lucky that the music of The Band is still with us.

—Jurgen Pieters

FURTHER READING:

Helm, Levon and Stephen Davis. *This Wheel's on Fire. Levon Helm and the Story of the Band.* New York, W. Morrow and Company, 1993.

Hoskins, Barney. *Across the Great Divide. The Band and America.* New York, Hyperion, 1993.

Marcus, Greil. "The Band: Pilgrim's Progress." *Mystery Train. Images of America in Rock 'n Roll Music,* revised third edition. New York, Dutton, 1990, 39-64.

Bara, Theda (1885?-1955)

Silent screen legend Theda Bara is synonymous with the term "vamp," a wicked woman of exotic sexual appeal who lures men into her web only to ruin them. Bara incarnated that type with her first film, *A Fool There Was* (1915), which attributed to her the famous line, "Kiss me, my fool." With that movie, her name changed from Theodosia to Theda, from Goodman to Bara (chosen as an anagram of Arab), and her star persona was launched. Considered the first movie star, Bara's biography and appearance were entirely manufactured by the studio. Publicized as having been born to a French actress beneath Egypt's Sphinx, the Cincinnati-native wore heavy eye make-up and risqué costumes, the most infamous, a snakeskin-coiled bra. She was the precursor to the femme fatale of 1940s film noir, and careers as diverse as those of Marilyn Monroe, Marlene Dietrich, and Madonna link back to Bara's.

—Elizabeth Haas

FURTHER READING:

Genini, Ronald. *Theda Bara, A Biography of the Silent Screen Vamp with a Filmography.* London, McFarland & Company, 1996.

Golden, Eve. *Vamp: The Rise and Fall of Theda Bara.* New York, Emprise, 1996.

Baraka, Amiri (1934—)

Writer Amiri Baraka founded the 1960s Black Arts Movement, transforming white, liberal aesthetics into black nationalist poetics and politics. In 1967, he converted to Islam and changed his name from Leroi Jones to Amiri Baraka. His career can be divided in three stages: beatnik/bohemian (1957-1964), black nationalism (1965-1974), and Marxist revolutionary (1974-present). In 1960 he travelled to Cuba with a group of black artists. As a result, he grew disillusioned with the bohemian/beatnik atmosphere of Greenwich Village and began seeing the necessity of art as a political tool. The play *Dutchman* (1964) brought him into the public limelight, a one-act play about Clay, a young, black, educated man who, while riding the New York subway, is murdered by a beautiful white woman symbolizing white society. No American writer has been more committed to social justice than Amiri Baraka. He is dedicated to bringing the voices of black America into the fiber of his writings.

—Beatriz Badikian

FURTHER READING:

Baraka, Amiri. *The Autobiography of LeRoi Jones.* Chicago, Lawrence Hill Books, 1997.

Harris, William, editor. *The LeRoi Jones/Amiri Baraka Reader.* New York, Thunder's Mouth Press, 1991.

Barbecue

Although the true source of barbecue is vague, its origin is most likely in the Southern region of the United States. A highly popular food and important community and family ritual, various regions and interests have attempted to lay claim to what has become an industry throughout the country. One theory states that the word ''barbecue'' is a derivative of the West Indian term ''barbacoa,'' which entails the slow-cooking of meat over hot coals. While most Americans view a ''barbecue'' as any type of outdoor cooking over flames, purists, as well as regional and ethnic food experts, agree that real barbecue is a particular style of cooking meat, usually outdoors, with some kind of wood or charcoal burning apparatus. While pork is the only acceptable barbecue meat in many areas of the south, beef, fish, and even lamb are used in many other areas of the United States. Needless to say, barbecue of some variety is found in almost every culture of the world that cooks meat.

Techniques for judging good barbecue include a highly defended personal taste and the particular tradition of an area. Common to most barbecue are flavorings which adhere to the meat, slowly seeping into it; at the same time, the heat breaks down the fatty substances that might make meat tough and reduces it to tender morsels filled with flavor. Different types of woods—hickory and mesquite among them—are frequently used by amateur barbecue enthusiasts as an addendum to charcoal. Wood chips, however, will not really contribute any specific flavor to meat prepared over charcoal flames. The true beauty of the barbecue is when slow cooking turns what were once cheap, tough cuts of meat—like the brisket and ribs—into a tender and succulent meal.

Barbecue began, and still remains, at the center of many family and social gatherings. From ''pig roasts'' and ''pig pulls'' to the backyard barbecue of the suburbs, people have long gathered around the cooking of meat outdoors. Additionally, church and political barbecues are still a vital tradition in many parts of the South. Unlike most food related gatherings that take place indoors, men have traditionally been at the center of the cooking activity. The ''pit men'' who tended the fires of outdoor barbecue pits evolved into the weekend suburban husband attempting to reach culinary perfection though the outdoor grilling of chicken, steak, hamburgers, and hot dogs.

Despite the disappearance of many locally owned restaurants throughout the country due to the popularity of chain stores and franchises, regional varieties of barbecue can still be found in the late 1990s; pork ribs, for example, are more likely to be found in the Southern states and beef ribs and brisket dominates in states like Missouri and Texas. The popularization of traditional regional foods in the United States has contributed to the widespread availability of many previously isolated foods. Just as bagels, muffins, and cappuccino have become widely available; ribs, brisket, smoked sausages, and other varieties of barbecue can be found in most urban areas throughout the United States. Barbecue has clearly become more popular through franchises and chain restaurants which attempt to serve versions of ribs, pork loin, and brisket. But finding an ''authentic'' barbecue shack—where a recipe and technique for smoking has been developed over generations and handed down from father to son—requires consulting a variety of local sources in a particular area, and asking around town for a place where the local ''flavor'' has not been co-opted by the mass market.

—Jeff Ritter

FURTHER READING:

Barich, David, and Thomas Ingalls. *The American Grill.* San Francisco, Chronicle Books, 1994.

Browne, Rick, and Jack Bettridge. *Barbecue America: A Pilgrimage in Search of America's Best Barbecue.* Alexandria, Virginia, Time-Life Books, 1999.

Elie, Lolis Eric. *Smokestack Lightning: Adventures in the Heart of Barbecue Country.* New York, Farrar, Straus, and Giroux, 1996.

Stern, Michael, and Jane Stern. *Roadfood and Goodfood: A Restaurant Guidebook.* New York, Harper Perennial 1992.

Trillen, Calvin. *The Tummy Trilogy: American Fried/Alice, Let's Eat/ Third Helpings.* New York, Farrar, Straus, and Giroux, 1994.

Barber, Red (1908-1992)

Walter Lanier ''Red'' Barber was a pioneer in sports broadcasting on both radio and television. In 1934 Barber was hired by Larry MacPhail of the Cincinnati Reds to be their first play-by-play announcer. He was also a pioneer in college and professional football broadcasting. In Cincinnati Barber broadcast the first major league night game, and in 1935 he broadcast his first World Series.

Barber followed MacPhail to Brooklyn, and there he pioneered baseball on radio in New York. He was at the microphone for the first televised major league baseball game in 1939, and he was with the Dodgers when Jackie Robinson came to Brooklyn in 1947. In 1954 Barber moved to Yankee Stadium where he remained until 1966. He made the radio call of Roger Maris's sixty-first home run.

Barber retired to Tallahassee, Florida, where he wrote seven books, and began a second career as commentator on National Public Radio's Morning Edition in 1981. His popular Friday morning conversations with host Bob Edwards covered a wide range of topics, from his garden, to sports, to the foibles of humanity.

—Richard C. Crepeau

FURTHER READING:

Barber, Red. *1947—When All Hell Broke Loose in Baseball.* Garden City, New York, Doubleday, 1982.

———. *The Broadcasters.* New York, The Dial Press, 1970.

Edwards, Bob. *Fridays with Red: A Radio Friendship.* New York, Simon and Schuster, 1993.

Barbershop Quartets

Barbershop quartets, a type of music group fashionable in early twentieth-century America, had a dramatic influence on American popular music styles. The sweet, close harmony of the quartets, the arrangement of voice parts, and their improvisational nature were all influences in the development of doo-wop (already heavily improvisational in form) as well as pre-rock group singing, close-harmony rock groups of the 1950s and 1960s like the Beach Boys and the teenaged ''girl groups,'' and in the later development of background groups and their vocal arrangements.

A barbershop quartet is any four-person vocal music group that performs a cappella, without instrumental accompaniment—the popular American music of the late nineteenth and early twentieth centuries. Each member of the quartet sings a particular voice part. One person in the group is considered the lead and sings the melody around which

A barbershop quartet, performing at the Buckeye Invitational in Ohio.

the other members base their harmonies. The tenor sings a harmony placed above the melody, while the bass sings the lowest harmony below the melody line. The baritone completes the chord structure by singing a harmony either below the melody but above the bass line, or above the melody but below the tenor line. The three voices singing in support of the lead traditionally sing one complete chord for every note in the melody, though there is, in this mode of singing, a wide array of styles and arrangement patterns.

The barbershop style of singing has its roots in an old American pastime known as "woodshedding," in which one person would lead a group in song by taking up the melody of a popular tune, and the rest of the group would then improvise harmonies to that melody. Before the appearance of television, barbershops were important meeting places for men in America. Unlike bars and taverns, barbershops were well respected in each community and provided a social forum for men of all ages. Grandfathers, married, and single men, as well as their little sons, could gather together and tell jokes or discuss everything from politics and war to sports, women, or religion. Most barbershops had a radio, and the term "barbershop singing" is said to have originally referred to the way in which customers would improvise or "woodshed" harmonies to whatever popular song might be playing on the radio as they waited their turns for a haircut or shave. The term is also said to refer to the barber himself, who—in earlier European culture—also had a musical role in the community. Musical training was not needed, and very often not present in the men who sang in this improvisational way. All that was required was a lead who had a memory for the words and melodies of the day, and at least the three supporting vocal parts, which were picked up or developed "off the ear" by listening to the lead.

During the 1920s and 1930s there was a major decline in the popularity of this kind of community singing. Much of the music in those decades was relegated either to the church or to the many clubs

and bars that had opened up since the end of Prohibition. In 1938, lawyer O. C. Cash of Tulsa, Oklahoma, and his friend banker Rupert Hall decided to create a social organization whose sole purpose was to maintain the tradition of barbershop singing as a unifying and fun recreation. From its inception, the Society for the Preservation and Encouragement of Barber Shop Quartet Singing in America, most commonly referred to by its initials SPEBSQSA, had a nostalgic function. Founders Cash and Hall felt the encouragement of barbershop quartets might bring back to American culture some sense of the "normalcy" that they felt America was losing in the mid-twentieth century. The image of sweet nostalgia is one that remained with the organization and with barbershop quartets through the end of the twentieth century.

SPEBSQSA, Inc., began as an informal quartet. Community support and renewed popularity led to the formation of more quartets, and eventually SPEBSQSA became a national, then international, organization, sponsoring competitions around the world. Printed sheet music was rarely used in the original groups but was later brought in as the organization expanded and became involved in activities that were more choral and not strictly focused on the traditional quartet. Many professional musicians looked down on barbershop because of its informality and emphasis on improvisation, yet that opinion began to change, too, as barbershop developed its own codified technique and the appearance of barbershop groups—both quartets and full choruses—increased. For much of its history, the barbershop quartet had been exclusively male. However, SPEBSQSA, Inc., began to include women, and in 1945 a barbershop group exclusively for women called the Sweet Adelines was formed. Like SPEBSQSA, the Sweet Adelines became international in scope, and by the 1950s both groups had spawned a number of branch organizations and related musical groups, with membership numbers in the tens of thousands. Collectively, these groups were responsible for achieving SPEBSQSA's founding goal, which was to preserve the music of the late nineteenth and early twentieth centuries. Because of their enthusiasm and pursuit of the craft, barbershop maintained its presence in American popular culture through decades of musical and social change, long outliving other popular entertainments of its age.

As a whole, barbershop quartets remained a hobby. Although some groups were able to make money, most could never make enough from performances to pursue it full-time or to consider it a career. A few groups were able to find national success and financial reward—the Buffalo Bills are perhaps the most famous of these professional groups. Their appearance in the 1962 movie musical *The Music Man* (which had been a successful Broadway stage musical four years earlier) gave them a permanent place in entertainment history but also led to a surge in barbershop popularity.

—Brian Granger

FURTHER READING:

Kaplan, Max, ed. *Barbershopping: Musical and Social Harmony.* New York, Associated University Presses, Inc., 1993.

Barbie

Barbie, the 11-½ inch, full-figured plastic doll from Mattel, Inc., is among the most popular toys ever invented; by 1998 Mattel estimated that the average American girl between the ages of 3 and 11 owned ten Barbie dolls. Precisely because it is so popular, the Barbie doll has become more than just a toy: it has become a central figure in American debates about women's relationship to fashion, their independence in the workplace, their dependence on men, and their body image. Satirized by musicians and comedians, criticized by feminist scholars, and embraced by young children throughout the world, the Barbie doll exists both as a physical toy and an image of femininity. The physical attributes of the doll—its shape and its beauty—along with the myriad costumes and props available to it have been tied to some of the most fundamental questions about what makes a woman successful and what are the appropriate roles for women in American society.

The Barbie doll's creator, Ruth Handler, was inspired when she noticed her daughter creating imaginative teenage or adult lives for her paper dolls. Handler investigated whether there was an opportunity to produce a doll in the likeness of an adult for the toy market. She was well positioned to do so, for she and her husband Elliot ran Mattel, Inc., which they had founded with Harold Matson in 1945 to manufacture plastic picture frames. By the end of World War II, Mattel had found its niche in toy manufacturing with the Ukedoodle, a plastic ukelele. When Handler introduced her idea, many of her colleagues were skeptical. She kept the idea in the back of her mind, however. During a trip to Switzerland, Ruth encountered the Lilli doll and realized that she had found the kind of toy she had hoped to produce at Mattel.

Created in 1952, the Lilli doll was based on a comic character from the German publication *Bild Zeitung* and was an 11½ inch, platinum-ponytailed, heavily made-up, full-figured doll, with high heels for feet. The Lilli doll had not been intended for children, but as an adult toy complete with tight sweaters and racy lingerie. Ruth Handler was not interested in the history of the doll's marketing, but rather in the doll's adult shape. Unable to produce a similar doll in the

United States cost effectively, Mattel soon discovered a manufacturing source in Japan.

The Barbie doll was introduced at a unique time in history: a time when the luxury of fashionable attire had become available to more women, when roles for women were beginning to change dramatically, when the term "teenager" had emerged as a definition of the distinct period between childhood and adult life, and when teenagers had been embraced by television and movie producers as a viable target market. Mattel capitalized on these trends in American culture when it introduced the Barbie doll in 1959 as a teenage fashion model.

As a fashion toy, the Barbie doll seemed especially well suited to the era in which it was introduced. When Christian Dior introduced his New Look in 1947, he changed women's fashion from the utilitarian style demanded by shortages during World War II to an extravagant style that celebrated the voluptuousness of the female form. With the dramatic change in styles, high fashion soon gained popular interest. By the early 1950s, designers had broadened their clientele by licensing designs to department stores. In addition, beauty and fashion were featured on the first nationally televised Miss America Pageant in 1954. The Barbie doll, with its fashionable accessories, was one of the first dolls to present young girls with an opportunity to participate in the emerging world of fashion. Meticulously crafted outfits that mimicked the most desirable fashions of the time could be purchased for the doll. By 1961, the Barbie doll had become the best-selling fashion doll of all time.

Just as the fashions for the Barbie doll were new to the toy market, so was the age of the doll. Mattel's decision to market the Barbie doll as a teenager in 1959 made sense when juxtaposed against themes resonating in popular culture. Teenagers were just emerging as a distinct and interesting social group, as evidenced by the attention directed toward them. At least eight movies with the word "teenage" in the title were released between 1956 and 1961, including *Teenage Rebel* (1956), *Teenage Bad Girl* (1957), *Teenagers from Outer Space* (1959), and *Teenage Millionaire* (1961). During these same years, the Little Miss America pageant debuted, *Teenbeat* magazine began publication for a teenage readership, and teen idols like Fabian and Frankie Avalon made youthful audiences swoon. The Barbie doll fit well into the emerging social scene made popular by such trends. Marketed without parents, the Barbie doll allowed children to imagine the teenage world as independent from the adult world of family. Though by 1961, Barbie did have a little sister in the Skipper doll, the role of a sibling did not impose any limiting family responsibilities on the Barbie doll. Early on, the Barbie doll could be a prom date for the Ken doll (introduced in 1961 after much consumer demand) or outfitted for a sock hop. Unlike real teenagers though, the Barbie doll possessed a fully developed figure.

Though the teenage identity for the Barbie doll has persisted in some of Mattel's marketing into the late 1990s, shortly after the doll's introduction Mattel also marketed the doll as a young adult capable of pursuing a career. Indeed, Handler had imagined a three-dimensional doll that children could use to imagine their grown-up lives. The Barbie doll did not portray traditional young adulthood, however. Introduced during a period when most women stayed home to raise families, Mattel offered extravagant wedding dresses for the Barbie doll, but never marketed the Ken doll as a spouse. Children were left to choose the marital status of the doll. With no set family responsibilities, the Barbie doll was the first doll to allow young girls to imagine an unrestricted, single adult life. Mattel soon marketed Barbie as a nurse, an airline stewardess, and a graduate. The career choices for the doll captured a developing trend in American culture:

The "Generation" dolls in the Barbie line, 1999.

the increase in female independence. As career opportunities for women broadened in the 1960s and 1970s, the Barbie doll fit well into the flux of American society. Within a decade of the doll's introduction, the career costumes available to the Barbie doll multiplied rapidly, faster at first than actual opportunities for women. The Barbie doll could be an astronaut (1965), a surgeon (1973), an Olympic athlete (1975), a veterinarian, a reporter, a doctor (1985), a UNICEF Ambassador (1989), a marine corps sergeant, presidential candidate (1992), a police officer (1993), and paleontologist (1997), to name a few.

As women embraced their new freedoms in the workplace, they also began to fear the effects of these freedoms on the family and femininity in general. Concerns about how a woman could balance the demands of a career and family became some of the most hotly debated topics in American society. Women's roles in popular television shows illustrated the debates. The stay-at-home mothers found in the characters of Harriet Nelson (*The Adventures of Ozzie and Harriet,* 1952-1966) and June Cleaver (*Leave It to Beaver,* 1957-1963) were replaced in the 1970s by the career women represented by Mary Tyler Moore and Rhoda. The 1980s featured the single mother

Murphy Brown, and the 1990s presented the successful lawyer Ally McBeal, a character who spent much of her time considering how difficult women's choices about career and family really are. Articles discussing the benefits of devoting oneself to a family or balancing a satisfying career with child rearing abounded in magazines like *Working Mother, Parenting,* and *Parents.*

In addition, as women grappled with their new roles in society, they began to question the role of physical beauty in their lives. In the 1950s, ''the commodification of one's look became the basis of success,'' according to author Wini Breines in *Young, White and Miserable: Growing Up Female in the Fifties.* But by the 1960s and early 1970s, the basis of success was no longer beauty. During these decades, women began to enter (and finish) college in greater numbers. As these educated women pursued careers outside the home and postponed marriage and childbirth they began to challenge the role of conventional beauty in a woman's life: some burned their bras, others discarded their makeup, others stopped shaving their legs, and others began to wear pants to work. With the triumph of feminism, America no longer had a set ideal of beauty.

The Barbie doll had become was the doll of choice for little girls to use to imagine their own lives as adults. Just as critics worried about whether toy guns or the violence in popular television shows would make children violent, they began to wonder if (and how) the now ubiquitous Barbie doll influenced children's ideas about womanhood. The doll's characteristics mirrored many aspects of the debates about modern womanhood—it could have any career a child imagined, it could remain single or marry, and it was conventionally beautiful.

Regarding the Barbie doll as a toy to envision an adult life, young mothers, struggling to balance careers and parenthood, wondered if the independent Barbie doll oversimplified the choices available to young women. Without family ties, the doll seemed to deny girls practice at the difficult balancing act their mothers attempted daily. But supporters of the Barbie doll reasoned that just as children could decide whether the Barbie doll would ''marry'' they could also decide whether the Barbie doll would ''have children.'' That Mattel did not define the doll as a mother or spouse was a gift of imaginative freedom for girls.

As women began to rethink the role of beauty in their lives some became conflicted about how a modern woman should shape or adorn herself to be attractive to the opposite sex and worried that if women obsessed over their looks they would neglect their minds. The Barbie doll, with its attractive face, silky hair, shapely body, and myriad beauty accessories, came under attack as promoting an obsession with ''good'' looks. Unlike the doll's family ties and career, children could not change the doll's physical attributes. Critics of the doll used the term ''Barbie'' to describe a beautiful but empty-headed woman. The former *Baywatch* actress Pamela Lee Anderson personified the struggle women had with regard to beauty and intellect. Anderson, who had dyed her hair blond and enhanced her breasts, resembled a living Barbie doll during her rise to fame. After achieving some success, she made news in 1999 when she removed her breast implants in order to be taken more seriously, according to some sources. Similarly, in the popular television show *Ally McBeal,* the character Georgia, with her shapely body and flowing blond hair, becomes so frustrated by people referring to her as ''Barbie'' that she cuts off her hair. Despite the negative connotation of the term ''Barbie,'' some women find the type of beauty represented by the Barbie doll a source of female power and advocate the use of female beauty as an essential tool for success. Some have gone to extremes; a woman named Cindy Jackson, for instance, has had more than 20 operations and has spent approximately $55,000 to mold herself into the image of the Barbie doll. Regardless of the critics' arguments or the extreme cases, however, the number of articles in women and teen's magazines dedicated to beauty issues attest to the continuing cultural obsession with physical beauty.

For many, beauty and fashion are indelibly linked. With regard to fashion, the Barbie doll has been consistently in style. From the first Barbie dolls, Mattel took care to dress them in detailed, fashionable attire. In the early years, Barbie doll fashions reflected French designs, but as fashion trends shifted to other areas, the attire for the Barbie doll mimicked the changes. In the early 1970s, for example, the Barbie doll wore Mod clothes akin to those popularized by fashion model Twiggy. And throughout the years, gowns and glamorous accessories for gala events have always been available to the Barbie doll. Some observers note that the fashions of the Barbie doll trace fashion trends perfectly since 1959. While critics complain about the use of waifish runway models who do not represent ''average'' female bodies, they also complain about the Barbie doll's size. Some have criticized the dimensions of the Barbie doll as portraying an unattainable ideal of the female shape. Various magazines have reported the dimensions the Barbie doll would have if she were life-sized (39-18-33) and have noted that a real woman with Barbie doll dimensions would be unable to menstruate. Charlotte Johnson, the Barbie doll's first dress designer, explained to M.G. Lord in *Forever Barbie* that the doll was not intended to reflect a female figure realistically, but rather to portray a flattering shape underneath fashionable clothes. According to Lord, Johnson ''understood scale: When you put human-scale fabric on an object that is one-sixth human size, a multi-layered cloth waistband is going to protrude like a truck tire around a human tummy. . . . Because fabric of a proportionally diminished gauge could not be woven on existing looms, something else had to be pared down—and that something was Barbie's figure.''

Despite the practical reasons for the dimensions of the Barbie doll, the unrealistic dimensions of the doll have brought the strongest criticism regarding the doll's encouragement of an obsession with weight and looks. In one instance, the Barbie doll's accessories supported the criticism. The 1965 ''Slumber Party'' outfit for the Barbie doll came complete with a bathroom scale set to 110 pounds and a book titled *How to Lose Weight* containing the advice: ''Don't Eat.'' The Ken doll accessories, on the other hand, included a pastry and a glass of milk. Convinced of the ill effects of playthings with negative images on children, Cathy Meredig of High Self Esteem Toys developed a more realistically proportioned doll in 1991. She believed that ''if we have enough children playing with a responsibly proportioned doll that we can raise a generation of girls that feels comfortable with the way they look,'' according to the *Washington Post.* Her ''Happy To Be Me'' doll, which looked frumpy and had uneven hair plugs, did not sell well, however. The Barbie doll was introduced with a modified figure in 1999.

Throughout the years, the Barbie doll has had several competitors, but none have been able to compete with the glamour or the comprehensiveness offered by the Barbie doll and its accessories. The Barbie doll offers children an imaginary world of individual success and, as witnessed by the pink aisle in most toy stores, an amazing array of props to fulfill children's fantasies. By the early 1980s, the Barbie doll also offered these ''opportunities'' to many diverse ethnicities, becoming available in a variety of ethnic and racial varieties. Although sometimes criticized for promoting excessive consumerism, the Barbie doll and its plethora of accessories offer more choices for children to play out their own fantasies than any other toy on the market.

While some wish to blame the Barbie doll for encouraging young girls to criticize their own physical attributes, to fashion themselves as ''Boy Toys,'' or to shop excessively, others see the doll as a blank slate on which children can create their own realities. For many the Barbie doll dramatizes the conflicting but abundant possibilities for women. And perhaps because there are so many possibilities for women at the end of the twentieth century, the Barbie doll—fueled by Mattel's ''Be Anything'' campaign—continues to be popular. By the end of the twentieth century, Mattel sold the doll in more than 150 countries and, according to the company, two Barbie dolls are sold worldwide every second.

—Sara Pendergast

FURTHER READING:

Boy, Billy. *Barbie: Her Life and Times*. New York, Crown, 1987.

Barbie Millicent Roberts. Preface by Valerie Steele. Photographs by David Levinthal. New York, Pantheon, 1998.

Breines, Wini. *Young, White and Miserable: Growing Up Female in the Fifties*. Boston, Beacon Press, 1992.

Handler, Ruth, with Jacqueline Shannon. *Dream Doll: The Ruth Handler Story*. Stamford, Longmeadow, 1994.

Kirkham, Pat, editor. *The Gendered Object*. Manchester, Manchester University Press, 1996.

Lawrence, Cynthia. *Barbie's New York Summer*. New York, Random House, 1962.

Lord, M.G. *Forever Barbie: The Unauthorized Biography of a Real Doll*. New York, William Morrow, 1994.

Riddick, Kristin. ''Barbie: The Image of Us All'' http://wsrv.clas.virginia.edu/~tsawyer/barbie/barb.html. May 1999.

Roberts, Roxanne. ''At Last a Hipper Doll: Barbie May Face Ample Competition.'' *Washington Post*. August 13, 1991, D01.

Tosa, Marco. *Barbie: Four Decades of Fashion, Fantasy, and Fun*. New York, Abrams, 1998.

Weiss, Michael J. ''Barbie: Life in Plastic, It's Fantastic . . . '' http://www.discovery.com/area/shoulda/shoulda970922/shoulda.html. May 1999.

Barker, Clive (1952—)

For much of the 1980s, it was impossible to pick up any of Clive Barker's books without encountering on the cover this blurb from fright-master Stephen King: ''I have seen the future of the horror genre, and his name is Clive Barker.'' Barker's more recent work, however, does not usually feature the King quotation, and this fact seems to represent his publisher's recognition that Barker has moved beyond the horror genre to become one of the modern masters of fantasy.

Clive Barker grew up in Liverpool, England,—not far from Penny Lane, celebrated in song by his fellow Liverpudlians, the Beatles. He studied literature and philosophy at the University of Liverpool and moved to London after graduation. Barker's first literary efforts took the form of plays which he wrote, directed, and produced, all on the shoestring budget that he was able to scrounge up for the small theater company he had formed. Several of his plays, with titles like *The History of the Devil* and *Frankenstein in Love*, display the fascination with fantasy and the macabre that would become hallmarks of his prose fiction.

While writing plays for public consumption, Barker was also crafting short stories and novellas that he circulated only among his friends. By the 1980s, however, he had concluded that some of his prose efforts might be marketable. He soon found a publisher for what would become known as the *Books of Blood*—six volumes of stories that were published in the United Kingdom during 1984-1985 and in the United States the following year. The collections sold poorly at first but gradually attracted a cult following among those who enjoy horror writing that does not flinch from the most gruesome of details. Barker is no hack writer who depends on mere shock value to sell books; even his early work shows a talent for imagery, characterization, and story construction. But it must also be acknowledged that Barker's writing from this period contains graphic depictions of sex, violence, and cruelty that are intense even by the standards of modern horror fiction.

Barker's next work was a novel, *The Damnation Game* (1985), in which an ex-convict is hired as a bodyguard for a reclusive millionaire, only to learn that his employer is not in fear for his life, but his immortal soul—and with good reason. The book reached the *New York Times* Bestseller List in its first week of American publication.

Barker's subsequent novels also enjoyed strong sales in both Europe and the United States. His next book—*Weaveworld* (1987)—began Barker's transition from horror to fantasy, although some graphic scenes were still present in the story. It concerns a man who falls into a magic carpet, only to discover that it contains an entire secret world populated by people with magical powers that are both wondrous and frightening. This was followed in 1989 by *The Great and Secret Show*, which features an epic struggle to control the ''Art,'' the greatest power in the Universe—the power of magic. Next was *Imajica* (1990), which reinterprets the Biblical story of creation in terms of a battle between four great powers for dominion over a fifth. Then came *The Thief of Always* (1992), a book for children about an enchanted house where a boy's every wish is granted, although the place turns out to be not quite as idyllic as it at first seemed.

Everville: The Second Book of the Art, which appeared in 1994, is a sequel to *The Great and Secret Show*. The book is essentially a quest story, with the action alternating between our world and a fantasy parallel universe. In *Sacrament* (1996), Barker's protagonist encounters a diabolical villain who can cause whole species to become extinct. The ideas of extinction, loss, and the inevitable passage of time combine like musical notes to form a melancholy chord that echoes throughout the book. The 1998 novel *Galilee: A Romance* represents Barker's greatest departure yet from the grand guignol style of his earlier work. The story involves a centuries-long feud between two formidable families, the Gearys and the Barbarossas. The advertised romance element is certainly present, although leavened by generous helpings of fantasy, conspiracy, and unconventional sexual escapades.

In addition to his work for the stage and the printed page, Barker has also manifested his abilities in other forms of media. He is a talented illustrator, heavily influenced by the work of the Spanish painter Goya. He has provided the cover art for several of his novels and has also published a book of his art entitled *Clive Barker: Illustrator*. In 1996, a collection of his paintings was the subject of a successful one-man exhibition at the Bess Culter Gallery in New York City. Barker has also written stories for several comic books, including the Marvel Comics series *Razorline*.

Barker's work is also well known to fans of horror movies. In the mid-1980s, he penned screenplays based on two of his stories, ''Underworld'' and ''Rawhead Rex,'' both of which were made into low-budget films. Barker was so dissatisfied with the final products that he was determined to have creative control over the next film based on his work. That turned out to be *Hellraiser*, derived from Barker's novella *The Hellbound Heart*. Barker served as both writer and director for this production, and the 1987 film quickly gained a reputation for depictions of violence and torture as graphic and unsettling as anything that Barker portrayed in the *Books of Blood*. The film spawned three sequels, although Barker's role in each was increasingly limited. He also directed two other films based on his stories: *Nightbreed* (1990) and *Lord of Illusions* (1995). Another Barker story, ''The Forbidden,'' was made into the 1992 film *Candyman,* directed by Bernard Ross, with Barker serving as Executive Producer. A sequel, *Candyman 2: Farewell to the Flesh,* was released in 1995, but Barker's involvement in the film was minimal.

Barker's company, Seraphim Productions, now coordinates all aspects of its founder's prodigious creative output—from novels to films, plays, CD-ROMs, comic books, and paintings. The term ''Renaissance man'' is much overused these days, but in Clive Barker's case it just might be an understatement.

—Justin Gustainis

FURTHER READING:

Badley, Linda. *Writing Horror and the Body: The Fiction of Stephen King, Clive Barker and Ann Rice.* Westport, Connecticut, Greenwood Press, 1996.

Barbieri, Suzanne J. *Clive Barker: Mythmaker for the Millennium.* Stockport, United Kingdom, British Fantasy Society, 1994.

Jones, Stephen, compiler. *Clive Barker's A-Z of Horror.* New York, HarperPrism, 1997.

Barkley, Charles (1963—)

Basketball player Charles Barkley was known for his outspoken and aggressive behavior on and off the court. In the early 1980s, he attracted national attention when he played for Auburn University. Dubbed the ''Round Mound of Rebound'' because he weighed almost 300 pounds and stood 6′4″, Barkley slimmed down for the 1984 NBA draft. Playing for the Philadelphia 76ers, Phoenix Suns, and Houston Rockets, Barkley was an Olympic gold medalist on the Dream Team in 1992 and 1996. A superstar player, he endorsed his line of shoes (while fighting Godzilla in one Nike advertisement) and hosted *Saturday Night Live* which featured him playing a mean game of one-on-one with PBS star Barney. He made cameo appearances in such movies as *Space Jam* (1996). The comic book series *Charles Barkley and the Referee Murders* depicted his antagonism toward officials. Known as Sir Charles, the entertaining and charismatic Barkley stressed he was not a role model. Egotistically stating, ''I'm the ninth wonder of the world,'' Barkley often provided controversial sound bites for the press because of his temperamental and opinionated outbursts.

—Elizabeth D. Schafer

FURTHER READING:

Barkley, Charles, with Rick Reilly. *Sir Charles: The Wit and Wisdom of Charles Barkley.* New York, Warner Books, 1994.

Barkley, Charles, with Roy S. Johnson. *Outrageous!: The Fine Life and Flagrant Good Times of Basketball's Irresistible Force.* New York, Simon and Schuster, 1992.

Casstevens, David. *''Somebody's Gotta Be Me'': The Wide, Wide World of the One and Only Charles Barkley.* Kansas City, Andrews and McMeel, 1994.

Barney and Friends

Barney, a huggable six-foot-four-inch talking purple dinosaur, starred in a daily half-hour children's television program that premiered April 6, 1992, on PBS. In 1988, the character's creator, Sheryl Leach, had grown dissatisfied with the selection of home videos on the market to amuse her young son. She wrote scripts for a children's video featuring a stuffed bear that came to life but changed the central character to a dinosaur, capitalizing on the renewed interest among children. Leach produced three ''Barney and the Backyard Gang'' videos and marketed them through day-care centers and video stores.

A PBS executive saw the videos and in 1991 secured a grant from the Corporation for Public Broadcasting to produce thirty episodes of the series. The PBS series was entitled *Barney and Friends* and featured Barney (played by David Joyner, voiced by Bob West), his younger dinosaur sidekick Baby Bop (Jeff Ayers, voiced by Carol Farabee), and a gaggle of children representing the country's major ethnic groups (Caucasian, African American, Asian-American, Native American, Indian, etc.). The young members of this politically correct sampling of American culture could make a small stuffed (and eminently marketable) dinosaur come to life as Barney. The group would dance, sing songs, and learn valuable lessons about getting along with each other in work and play. *Barney and Friends*' signature song, ''I Love You,'' took the tune of ''This Old Man'' and substituted lyrics remarkable for nothing if not their catchiness: children nationwide were soon singing ''I love you / you love me / we're a happy family'' and spreading Barney's feel-good message throughout the land.

Such popularity with the television-watching preschool demographic made *Barney and Friends* vulnerable to critical attacks that suggested the show was nothing but ''an infomercial for a stuffed animal.'' The four million Barney home videos and $300 million in other Barney merchandise that sold within one year after its PBS premiere confirmed that ''Barney'' was a media force to be reckoned with. On April 24, 1994, NBC aired Barney's first foray into commercial television, with a prime-time special entitled ''Bedtime with Barney: Imagination Island.''

The ubiquity of Barney, Barney's songs, and Barney-related paraphernalia caused a backlash on late-night television and radio talk shows, in stand-up comedy acts, and on world wide web sites. Speculations that Barney was Evil incarnate, for instance, or lists describing 101 ways to kill the fuzzy purple dinosaur were not uncommon. Thinly-disguised likenesses of Barney became targets of crude, sometimes physically violent attacks on stage and screen. But Barney's commercial success did not flag. Indeed, the critical backlash may have contributed to the high profile Barney maintained in American cultural (and fiscal) consciousness throughout the 1990s. *Forbes* magazine ranked Barney as the third richest Hollywood entertainer for the years 1993 and 1994, behind director Steven Spielberg and talk show host cum media phenom Oprah Winfrey. In 1998 Barney became a bonafide Hollywood fixture when he and his pals leapt onto the big screen in the feature-length *Barney's Great Adventure.*

—Tilney Marsh

FURTHER READING:

''Barney: Fill Their World with Love.'' http://barneyonline.com. February 1999.

Bianculli, David. *Dictionary of Teleliteracy: Television's 500 Biggest Hits, Misses, and Events.* New York, Continuum, 1996.

Dudko, Mary Ann, and Margie Larsen. *Watch, Play, and Learn.* Allen, Texas, Lyons Group, 1993.

Haff, Kevin. *Coping with the Purple Menace: A Barney Apathy Therapy Kit (A Parody).* Merced, California, Schone, 1993.

McNeil, Alex. *Total Television: A Comprehensive Guide to Programming from 1948 to the Present.* 4th ed. New York, Penguin, 1996.

Phillips, Phil. *Dinosaurs: The Bible, Barney, and Beyond.* Lancaster, Pennsylvania, Starburst, 1994.

Barney Miller

Through the 1970s and 1980s there were many police shows on television. Most were action shows full of car chases and shootouts, or shows dealing with the serious dramas of contemporary society. *Barney Miller* was different. From 1975 to 1982, this situation comedy presented the human stories of the detectives and officers of the 12th Precinct in New York (Greenwich Village Area) as well as the stories of the criminals and victims that they dealt with. Though it had its share of serious topics, it managed to let its characters develop and grow and let us laugh at the results. The main action was restricted to the detectives' office and the small connected office of Captain

Hal Linden (foreground) with the cast of *Barney Miller*.

Barney Miller on the upper floor of an old police building. The show's set was sparse, limited to the detectives' old desks, a holding cell, a coffee maker, and a restroom.

The 12th Precinct detectives' office was comprised of a diverse group of mostly men: Capt. Barney Miller (Hal Linden), Philip Fish (Abe Vigoda), Stan Wojciehowicz (Max Gail), Ron Harris (Ron Glass), Arthur Dietrich (Steve Landesberg), Chano Amengule (Gregory Sierra), Nick Yemana (Jack Soo), Inspector Frank Luger (James Gregory), and Officer Carl Levitt (Ron Carey). Several episodes included temporary women detectives (one played by Linda Lavin, who would soon move on to *Alice*), but the show focused predominantly on male police. The characters changed somewhat after the first few seasons, as the show focused exclusively on the office and away from any other storyline (originally the story was to be about the office and home life of the captain, but this aspect was phased out). Chano left, as did Fish, to be replaced by Dietrich. Jack Soo died during the series, and his character was not replaced.

Barney Miller was notable for other reasons as well. Critics Harry Castleman and Walter J. Podrazik explained that "Real-life police departments have praised *Barney Miller* as being one of the most realistic cop shows around. The detectives rarely draw their guns, and spend more time in conversation, paperwork, and resolving minor neighborhood squabbles than in blowing away some Mr. Big drug king." After the first season, *Barney Miller* rarely depicted anything outside of the squad room. Any action that did take place did so out of the audience's sight. For example, viewers learned about the crimes, the disagreements, and the ensuing action second-hand from the police detectives and other characters.

In contrast to other police shows of its time, *Barney Miller* showed viewers the more mundane aspects of its detectives' work lives, including their bad habits, passions, and their likes and dislikes, all with one of the finest ensemble casts of working people in television. Detective Harris developed and wrote a novel, "Blood on the Badge," over the years, and viewers learned about Fish's wife but almost never saw her. Viewers came to know about Wojo's personal life and Barney's divorce, but never saw them outside of the office.

For the most part, laughs came from the dialogue and watching the characters' responses to specific situations. Topical issues of the day, from women's rights, to gay rights, and nuclear weapons, were also addressed in humorous contexts. Many episodes dealt with the work life of the police, including questions from Internal Affairs, problems with promotions, and on-going troubles with an old building. Most stories, however, dealt with small crime and the day-to-day work of policing.

Barney Miller's lasting legacy might be the shows that developed following its gritty working ensemble mold (*Night Court,* for example), or the effect it had on future police shows, such as *Hill Street Blues, NYPD Blue,* and *Homicide.* In fact, NBC Chief Brandon Tartikoff presented his concept for *Hill Street Blues* to Steven Bochco as "*Barney Miller* outdoors." With 170 episodes to *Hill Street*'s 146, *Barney Miller* may have had a lasting impact all on its own.

—Frank E. Clark

FURTHER READING:

Brooks, Tim, and Earle Marsh. *The Complete Directory to Prime Time Network TV Shows.* 5th ed. New York, Ballantine, 1992.

Castleman, Harry, and Walter J. Podrazik. *Harry and Wally's Favorite TV Shows: A Fact-filled Opinionated Guide to the Best and Worst on TV.* New York, Prentice Hall, 1989.

Marc, David. *Comic Visions: Television Comedy and American Culture.* Boston, Unwin Hyman, 1989.

Marc, David, and Robert J. Thompson. *Prime Time, Prime Movers: From I Love Lucy to L.A. Law—America's Greatest TV Shows and the People Who Created Them.* Boston, Little Brown, 1992.

McNeil, Alex. *Total Television: A Comprehensive Guide to Programming from 1948 to the Present.* 3d ed. New York, Penguin Books, 1991.

Barr, Roseanne

See Roseanne

Barry, Dave (1947—)

Dave Barry, a bestselling author and a syndicated humor columnist based in Miami, is a significant player in the great American tradition of humor writing. Like Finley Peter Dunne, social satire is a mainstay of Barry's work—e.g., on the limitations of free speech: "[Y]ou can't shout 'FIRE!' in a crowded theater. Even if there *is* a fire, you can't shout it. A union worker has to shout it." Like Mark Twain, Barry explores the pomposities of life in the mid- to late twentieth century: describing the "grim" looks of a group of rich people in an ad, Barry remarks: "[It is] as if they have just received the tragic news that one of their key polo ponies had injured itself trampling a servant to death and would be unavailable for an important match." And like Will Rogers, Barry provides commentary on the issues of the day—Barry's description of Will Rogers in his book *Dave Barry Slept Here* reads: Rogers "used to do an act where he'd twirl a lasso and absolutely slay his audiences with such wry observations as 'The only thing I know is what I read in the papers.' Ha-ha! Get it? Neither do we. Must have been something he did with the lasso."

Barry grew up in Armonk, New York. He is self-consciously a member of the Baby Boom generation. In *Dave Barry Turns 40,* the author has this to say about his generation's musical tastes: "[W]e actually like to think we're still With It. Whereas in fact we are nowhere near It. The light leaving from It right now will not reach us for several years." Barry's father, David W. Barry, was a Presbyterian minister who worked in New York's inner city. In a serious column written after his father's death, Barry later wrote that "[t]hey were always asking [Barry's father] to be on those shows to talk about Harlem and the South Bronx, because back then he was the only white man they could find who seemed to know anything about it."

Barry graduated from New York's Pleasantville High School in 1965. In his yearbook photograph, according to Barry many years later, he looked like a "solemn little Junior Certified Public Accountant wearing glasses styled by Mister Bob's House of Soviet Eyewear." He then went on to Haverford College, where he earned a degree in English in 1969. Having been declared a conscientious war objector, Barry performed alternative service by working for the Episcopal Church in New York. Barry has remained fairly consistent in his antiwar views. In 1992, he declared himself a candidate for President on a platform which included an interesting method of conducting foreign policy without war. Foreign affairs "would be handled via [an] entity called The Department of A Couple of Guys Names Victor." Instead of invading Panama and causing "a whole lot of innocent people [to] get hurt," Barry would say to his foreign-affairs team, "'Victors, I have this feeling that something unfortunate might happen to Manuel Noriega, you know what I mean?' And, mysteriously, something would."

Barry got a job in 1971 writing for the *Daily Local News* in West Chester, Pennsylvania. After a stint with the Associated Press in Pennsylvania, in 1975 he went to work for the consulting firm Burger Associates teaching effective business writing ("This could be why we got so far behind Japan," he later speculated). During this time, he started a humor column in the *Daily Local News.* After his work became popular, he was hired by the *Miami Herald,* although he did not move to Miami until 1986. He also produced some spoofs on self-help books, such as *Homes and Other Black Holes.* These books were to be followed by collections of Barry's columns, as well as original works with titles like *Dave Barry Slept Here: A Sort of History of the United States,* and *Dave Barry's Guide to Guys.*

Barry was also honored with a television series, called *Dave's World* and based on two of his books, which ran from 1993 to 1997 on CBS before being canceled. The Barry character in the series was played by Harry Anderson, the judge on *Night Court.* "Lest you think I have 'sold out' as an artist," Barry reassured his readers while *Dave's World* was still on the air, "let me stress that I have retained total creative control over the show, in the sense that, when they send me a check, I can legally spend it however I want." The show's cancellation did not effect Barry's writing, and he continued to amuse his readers, offering refreshing views on American life.

—Eric Longley

FURTHER READING:

Achenbach, Joel. *Why Things Are: Answers to Every Essential Question in Life.* New York, Ballantine, 1991.

Barry, Dave. *Dave Barry Slept Here: A Sort of History of the United States.* New York, Random House, 1989.

———. *Dave Barry Turns 40.* New York, Fawcett Columbine, 1990.

———. *Dave Barry's Complete Guide to Guys.* New York, Random House, 1995.

———. *Homes and Other Black Holes.* New York, Fawcett Columbine, 1988.

Chepesiuk, Ron. "Class Clown: Dave Barry Laughs His Way to Fame, Fortune." *Quill.* January/February 1995, 18.

Garvin, Glenn. "All I Think Is That It's Stupid." *Reason.* December, 1994, 25-31.

Hiassen, Carl, et al. *Naked Came the Manatee.* New York, Putnam, 1997.

Marsh, Dave, editor. *Mid-life Confidential: The Rock Bottom Remainders Tour America with Three Chords and an Attitude.* New York, Viking, 1994.

Richmond, Peter. "Loon Over Miami: The On-Target Humor of Dave Barry." *The New York Times Magazine.* September 23, 1990, 44, 64-67, 95.

Winokur, Jon, editor. *The Portable Curmudgeon Redux.* New York, Penguin Books, 1992.

Barry, Lynda (1956—)

Lynda Barry was one of a new breed of artists and writers who brought underground comics to the light of day with her bitingly funny strip *Ernie Pook's Comeek,* first printed in 1980 in the *Chicago Reader* alternative newsweekly, and the acclaimed novel and play *The Good Times are Killing Me,* published in 1988. The crudely-drawn *Ernie Pook's Comeek* details the antics of a group of misfit adolescents, centering on the hapless Marlys Mullen, who gives a voice to sociocultural issues through the eyes of a young girl. It appeared in more than 60 newspapers in the 1990s. *The Good Times are Killing Me,* set in the 1960s, tackles race relations and other topics as understood by children. Barry's sharp wit and wry commentary is often compared to that of her college friend Matt Groening, creator of the *Life in Hell* comic and *The Simpsons* television show, who helped propel her career.

—Geri Speace

FURTHER READING:

Coburn, Marcia Froelke. "Her So-Called Life." *Chicago.* March 1997, 80.

Graham, Judith, editor. *Current Biography Yearbook.* New York, H.W. Wilson, 1994.

Barrymore, John (1882-1942)

John Barrymore, who appeared in over 40 plays, 60 films, and 100 radio shows during his forty-year career, was perhaps the most influential and idolized actor of his day. The best known of America's "Royal Family" of actors, the handsome and athletic Barrymore was renowned for his ability to flesh out underwritten roles with his charismatic charm and commanding presence. He reached new artistic heights with title-role performances in theatrical productions of *Richard III* (1920) and *Hamlet* (1922-25) before answering Hollywood's call to play romantic parts on screen. Though Barrymore brought these new figures to life with his customary ardor, his favorite roles were quite different: characters who required physical or psychological distortion, or both. Essentially a character actor trapped in a leading man's body, Barrymore wanted to prove to the world that he was much more than just "the Great Profile."

Born on February 14 or 15, 1882, in Philadelphia, Barrymore was the third of three children born to professional actors Maurice Barrymore and Georgiana Drew Barrymore. His parents, frequently on the road, shunted him off to numerous boarding schools, where he quickly developed a reputation for wildness. An early punishment—a detention in an empty classroom—happened to lead to what he believed would be his life's calling; he discovered a large book illustrated by Gustav Doré and was so enthralled by the images that he decided to become an artist himself.

Barrymore pursued art training in England during the late 1890s and then returned to America in 1900 to become a cartoonist for the *New York Evening Journal.* Family members had other ideas about his career, however; his father insisted that he accompany him in a vaudeville sketch in early 1901 and, later that year, his sister Ethel convinced him to appear as a last-minute replacement in one of her plays. Fired from the *Evening Journal* in 1902, he soon joined a theatrical company in Chicago headed by a distant relative.

Though Barrymore's stage work at this time was hardly memorable, several theater magnates could see comic potential in the young actor. Producer Charles Frohman cast Barrymore in his first Broadway play, the comedy *Glad of it,* in 1903. The following year, William Collier recruited Barrymore to appear in *The Dictator,* a gunboat-diplomacy farce. *The Dictator* became a major hit, with many reviewers citing Barrymore's all-too-believable performance as a drunken telegraph operator.

Other stage triumphs quickly followed. Barrymore played his first serious role, the dying Dr. Rank, in a Boston staging of *A Doll's House* in January 1907, and later that year he received fine reviews for his first leading role: Tony Allen in the hit comedy *The Boys of Company "B."* Barrymore scored a major success with *A Stubborn Cinderella* (1908-09) and peaked as a comic actor the next season in his longest running play, *The Fortune Hunter.*

Barrymore's ensuing stage work generated little enthusiasm among critics and audiences, but he scored with a series of slapstick movies produced from 1913 to 1916, beginning with *An American Citizen.* He longed to be regarded as a serious actor, however, and soon earned his credentials in a 1916 production of the John Galsworthy drama *Justice.* Other acclaimed performances followed: *Peter Ibbetson* in 1917, *Redemption* in 1918, and *The Jest* in 1919. Barrymore then raised his acting to another level by taking on two Shakespearean roles, Richard III and Hamlet, during the early 1920s. Critics and audiences were stunned by the power and passion of his work.

Aware of Barrymore's emerging marquee value, the Warner Bros. studio signed him to appear in *Beau Brummel* (1924), his first film made in California. After returning to *Hamlet* for a highly successful London run, Barrymore settled in Hollywood in 1926 for a long career in the movies. He appeared in nine more films for Warner Bros. (including *Don Juan* [1926], the first feature film with a synchronized soundtrack) before signing on with MGM for such movies as *Grand Hotel* (1932) opposite Greta Garbo and *Rasputin and the Empress* (1932) with his siblings Ethel and Lionel. He also offered memorable performances in David Selznick's *State's Attorney* (1932), *A Bill of Divorcement* (1932), and *Topaze* (1933) before returning to MGM for several more films. A journeyman actor from 1933, Barrymore turned in some of his finest film work ever in such vehicles as Universal's *Counsellor-at-Law* (1933) and Columbia's *Twentieth Century* (1934).

Despite these achievements, Barrymore found movie work increasingly elusive. His alcoholism and frequently failing memory were among the biggest open secrets in Hollywood, and the studios were now hesitant to work with him. MGM signed him back at a highly reduced salary to appear as Mercutio in *Romeo and Juliet* (1936), his only Shakespearean feature film, but few screen successes followed. He returned to the stage for one last fling—*My Dear Children,* a 1939 trifle about an aging ham and his daughters—and followed it up with several lamentable films. The worst was also his last: *Playmates* (1941), which featured him as an alcoholic, Shakespearean has-been named "John Barrymore."

Barrymore's radio broadcasts represented the few high points of his career from the mid-1930s onward. Building on a 1937 series of "Streamlined Shakespeare" radio plays, he appeared more than seventy times on Rudy Vallee's *Sealtest Show* beginning in October 1940. His comic and dramatic performances were well-received, and he remained associated with the Vallee program up to his death on May 29, 1942 in Los Angeles.

Theater critic Harold Clurman once suggested that John Barrymore "had everything an actor should ideally possess: physical beauty, a magnificent voice, intelligence, humor, sex appeal, grace and, to boot, a quotient of the demonic—truly the prince of players. There was unfortunately also a vein of self-destructiveness in him." In retrospect, the ignoble aspects of Barrymore's life—an extravagantly wasteful lifestyle, alcoholic binges, four failed marriages, numerous affairs, self-parodying performances—only contributed to his larger-than-life status. Though Barrymore the man passed on decades ago, Barrymore the myth has lost little of its power to captivate.

—Martin F. Norden

FURTHER READING:

Clurman, Harold. "The Barrymore Family." *Los Angeles Times.* May 1, 1977, C16.

Fowler, Gene. *Good Night, Sweet Prince: The Life and Times of John Barrymore.* New York, Viking, 1943.

Kobler, John. *Damned in Paradise: The Life of John Barrymore.* New York, Atheneum, 1977.

Norden, Martin F. *John Barrymore: A Bio-Bibliography.* Westport, Connecticut, Greenwood Press, 1995.

Peters, Margot. *The House of Barrymore.* New York, Knopf, 1990.

Barton, Bruce (1886-1967)

Advertizing man, religious writer, and United States Congressman, the name of Bruce Barton is synonymous with the advertising firm of Batten, Barton, Durstine, and Osborne, the agency Barton helped found in 1919. The firm's clients, including U.S. Steel, General Electric, General Motors, and Dunlop, were among the most powerful businesses of the American 1920s. Barton is best remembered for his bestselling book *The Man Nobody Knows* (1925), a conduct manual for American businessmen whose subtitle proclaimed itself "a discovery of the real Jesus."

The son of a prominent Congregational Minister, Barton was in the vanguard of the new advertising culture of the 1920s. In a period where the shift into a "mass" consumption economy had spawned a new service and leisure economy, advertising became an industry in its own right and led the way in reshaping the traditional Protestant morality of Victorian America into something more suited to the dictates of a modern consumer economy. Of those engaged in such work Barton was the most renowned. Orthodox Protestant values emphasized hard work, innate human sinfulness, and the evils of self-indulgence and idleness. These were not values that could be easily accommodated within a new commercial world which promoted the free play of conspicuous personal consumption and the selling of leisure. In a string of books and articles published across the decade Barton examined what he claimed were the New Testament origins of monopoly capitalism, arguing that the repression of desire, and the failure of the individual to pursue personal self-fulfillment (in private acts of consumption), were the greatest of all sins. His most famous book, *The Man Nobody Knows,* turned the life of Jesus into a template for the new commercial practices of the 1920s, citing the parables ("the most powerful advertisements of all time") alongside the insights of Henry Ford and J.P. Morgan. By making Jesus like a

Bruce Barton

businessman, Barton made businessmen like Jesus. This reassuring message sat easily with the colossal extension of the market into all areas of American life during the 1920s, and *The Man Nobody Knows* itself sold 750,000 copies in its first two years. A follow up, *The Book Nobody Knows* (1926), and two subsequent studies in the same idiom, *The Man of Galilee* (1928), and *On the Up and Up* (1929), failed to sell in the same quantities.

Barton's writing can also be considered alongside the popularizing of psychoanalysis which took place in the 1920s, an explosion of interest in "feel good," "self help" publishing which stressed the power of the individual mind over material circumstances. Again, this "feel good" message sold well in a time of rapid economic transformation and subsequent collapse in the 1930s, and the cultural historian Ann Douglas has numbered *The Man Nobody Knows* in a lineage which runs from Emile Coue's *Self-Mastery Through Conscious Auto-Suggestion* (1923), through Walter Pitkin's *Life Begins at Forty* (1932), to Dale Carnegie's *How to Win Friends and Influence People* (1936).

In the 1930s Barton launched a brief political career, running for Congress successfully in 1936, before returning to Batten, Barton, Durstine, and Osborne in 1940. He remained chairman of the firm until his retirement in 1961.

—David Holloway

FURTHER READING:

Barton, Bruce. *The Man Nobody Knows: A Discovery of the Real Jesus*. Indianapolis and New York, Bobbs-Merrill, 1925.

Douglas, Ann. *Terrible Honesty: Mongrel Manhattan in the 1920s*. London, Picador, 1996.

Ewen, Stuart. *Captains of Consciousness: Advertising and the Social Roots of the Consumer Culture*. New York, McGraw-Hill, 1977.

Leach, William. *Land of Desire: Merchants, Power, and the Rise of a New American Culture*. New York, Vintage, 1994.

Marchant, Roland. *Advertizing the American Dream: Making Way for Modernity, 1920-1940*. Berkeley, University of California Press, 1986.

Strasser, Susan. *Satisfaction Guaranteed: The Making of the American Mass Market*. New York, Smithsonian Institution Press, 1995.

Baryshnikov, Mikhail (1948—)

One of the greatest ballet dancers of the twentieth century, Baryshnikov overcame initial expectations that his stocky build, short height, and boyish demeanor precluded him from performing the romantic roles in ballets like *Giselle* and *Sleeping Beauty*. After leaving the Soviet Union in 1973, however, Baryshnikov joined the American Ballet Theater (ABT) and became its most celebrated performer. Throughout his career, Baryshnikov has striven to explore

Mikhail Baryshnikov

new choreography. One major achievement was the collaboration with choreographer Tywla Tharp, who created for him, among other works, the incredibly popular *Push Comes to Shove*. He left ABT to work with the great Russian-born choreographer George Balanchine at the New York City Ballet. Baryshnikov soon returned to ABT as its artistic director where he eliminated its over-reliance on internationally famous guest soloists, developed new repertory, and sought to promote soloists and lead dancers already a part of ABT. His charisma, spectacular dancing, and tempestuous love life contributed greatly to the popularity of ballet in the United States.

—Jeffrey Escoffier

FURTHER READING:

Joan Accocella. ''The Soloist.'' *New Yorker*. January 19, 1998.

Baseball

Originally an early nineteenth century variation of a venerable English game, baseball, by the late twentieth century, had developed into America's ''national pastime,'' a game so indelibly entwined with American culture and society that diplomat Jacques Barzun once remarked, ''Whoever wants to know the heart and mind of America had better learn baseball.''

Baseball lore places the origins of baseball in Cooperstown, a small town in upstate New York, where Abner Doubleday, a West Point cadet and Civil War hero, allegedly invented the bat-and-ball game in 1839. In reality, the sport was neither new nor indigenous. The game that ultimately developed into modern baseball was in fact a modified version of rounders, an English sport imported to the colonies prior to the American Revolution. Early forms of baseball were remarkably similar to rounders. Both games involved contending teams equipped with a ball as well as a bat with which to hit the ball. In addition, both baseball and rounders required the use of a level playing field with stations or bases to which the players advanced in their attempts to score.

Baseball quickly evolved from the sandlot play of children to the organized sport of adults. In 1845, a group of clerks, storekeepers, brokers, and assorted gentlemen of New York City, under the direction of bank clerk Alexander Joy Cartwright, founded the first baseball club in the United States—the New York Knickerbockers, which played its games at Elysian Fields in Hoboken, New Jersey. The club was more a social association than an athletic one, providing opportunities to play baseball, as well as hosting suppers, formal balls, and other festivities. Individuals could become members only through election. By the 1850s, a number of clubs patterned on the Knickerbocker model appeared throughout the Northeast and in some areas of the Midwest and Far West.

The need for codified orderly play had prompted clubs such as the Knickerbockers to draft rules for the fledgling sport. In 1857, a National Association of Baseball Players formed to unite the disparate styles of play throughout the country into a universal code of rules. Initially, the National Association attracted only New York clubs, and so the popular ''Knickerbocker'' style of baseball predominated. This version of the sport represented a decided evolution from rounders and resembled modern baseball in form. While no umpire as yet called balls or strikes in the Knickerbocker game, a

A baseball game between the New York Yankees and the Boston Red Sox.

batter was retired when he swung at and missed three pitches. The Knickerbocker rules limited a team at-bat to only three outs, and replaced "plugging," a painful practice by which a fielder could retire a base runner by hitting him with a thrown ball, with "tagging," simply touching a base runner with the ball. Within four years of its founding, the National Association came to include clubs in New Haven, Detroit, Philadelphia, Baltimore, and Washington, D.C. These clubs, for the most part, renounced their local variations on the sport and took up the "Knickerbocker" style of play.

After the Civil War, the "fraternal" club game took a decidedly commercial turn. Rather than relying exclusively on club membership to finance their teams, clubs began to earn money by charging admission to games. In order to maximize gate fees, clubs inclined away from friendly games played among club members, and turned more and more to external contests against clubs in other regions. At the same time, to guarantee fan interest, clubs felt increasing pressure to field the most highly skilled players. They began to recruit members based on talent, and, for the first time, offered financial remuneration to prospective players. In 1869, the Cincinnati Red

Stockings fielded an entire team of salaried players—the first professional baseball squad in American history.

As more clubs turned professional, a league structure emerged to organize competition. In 1871, ten teams formed the National Association of Professional Baseball Players, a loose confederation designed to provide a system for naming a national championship team. The National League, formed five years later, superseded this alliance, offering a circuit comprised of premier clubs based in Boston, Hartford, Philadelphia, New York, St. Louis, Chicago, Cincinnati, and Louisville. A host of competing leagues arose, among them the International League and the Northwestern League, but it was not until 1903 that the National League recognized the eight-team American League as its equal. Beginning that year, the two leagues concluded their schedules with the World Series, a post-season playoff between the two leagues.

Despite the game's increased commercialization, baseball, in the early years of the twentieth century, developed into the American national game. Players such as Ty Cobb and Walter Johnson as well as managers like Connie Mack and John McGraw approached the game in a scientific manner, utilizing various strategies and tactics to win ball games; in the process, they brought to the game a maturity and complexity that increased the sport's drama. The construction of great ballparks of concrete and steel and the game's continuing power to bind communities and neighborhoods together behind their team further solidified the coming of age of professional baseball. Baseball had achieved a new institutional prominence in American life. Boys grew up reading baseball fiction and dreaming of becoming diamond heroes themselves one day. The World Series itself became a sort of national holiday, and United States chief executives, beginning with William Howard Taft in 1910, ritualized the commencement of each new season with the ceremonial throwing of the first ball.

The appeal of the game had much to do with what many considered its uniquely American origins. "It's our game—that's the chief fact in connection with it: America's game," exclaimed poet Walt Whitman. Baseball, he wrote, "has the snap, go, fling of the American atmosphere—belongs as much to our institutions, fits into them as significantly, as our constitutions, laws: is just as important in the sum total of our historic life." To preserve this patriotic image, baseball administrators such as Albert Spalding and A.G. Mills vehemently dismissed any claims that baseball had evolved from rounders. In 1905, Mills headed a commission to investigate the origins of baseball. The group found that baseball was uniquely American and bore no traceable connection with rounders, "or any other foreign sport." Mills traced the game's genesis to Abner Doubleday in Cooperstown—a sketchy claim, to be sure, as Mills' only evidence rested on the recollections of a boyhood friend of Doubleday who ended his days in an institution for the criminally insane. Still, Doubleday was a war hero and a man of impeccable character, and so the commission canonized the late New Yorker as the founder of baseball, later consecrating ground in his native Cooperstown for the purpose of establishing the sport's Hall of Fame.

Baseball's revered image took a severe hit in 1920, when eight Chicago White Sox were found to have conspired with gamblers in fixing the 1919 World Series. The incident horrified fans of the sport and created distrust and disappointment with the behavior of ballplayers idolized throughout the nation. A young boy, perched outside the courtroom where the players' case was heard, summed up the feelings of a nation when he approached "Shoeless" Joe Jackson, one of the accused players, and said tearfully, "Say it ain't so, Joe." The eight players were later banned from the sport by baseball commissioner Kenesaw "Mountain" Landis, but the damage to the sport's reputation had already been done.

Baseball successfully weathered the storm created by the "Black Sox" scandal, as it came to be known, thanks in large part to the emergence of a new hero who brought the public focus back to the playing field, capturing the American imagination and generating excitement of mythic proportions. In the 1920s, George Herman "Babe" Ruth—aptly nicknames the "Sultan of Swat"—established himself as the colossal demigod of sports. With his landmark home runs and charismatic personality, Ruth triggered a renewed interest in baseball. While playing for the New York Yankees, Ruth established single-season as well as career records for home runs. Ruth's extravagant lifestyle and Paul Bunyan-like appearance made him a national curiosity, while his flair for drama, which included promising and delivering home runs for sick children in hospitals, elevated him to heroic proportions in the public eye. In mythologizing the sport, Ruth restored and even escalated the sanctity of the "national pastime" that had been diminished by the "Black Sox" scandal. Along with Ty Cobb, Honus Wagner, Christy Mathewson, and Walter Johnson, Ruth

gained immortality as a charter member of the Baseball Hall of Fame, opened in 1939.

By the 1940s, the heroes of the game came to represent an even more diverse body of the population. Substantial numbers of Italians, Poles, and Jews inhabited major league rosters, and a host of these Eastern Europeans became some of the game's biggest stars. Hank Greenberg and Joe DiMaggio, among many other children of immigrants, became national celebrities for their on-field exploits. In this respect, baseball served an important socializing function. As the *Sporting News* boasted, "The Mick, the Sheeney, the Wop, the Dutch and the Chink, the Cuban, the Indian, the Jap, or so the so-called Anglo-Saxon—his nationality is never a matter of moment if he can pitch, or hit, or field." During World War II, when teams were depleted by the war effort, even women became part of baseball history, as female leagues were established to satisfy the public's hunger for the sport. Still, the baseball-as-melting-pot image had one glaring omission. A "gentleman's agreement" dating back to the National Association excluded African Americans from playing alongside whites in professional baseball. Various so-called Negro Leagues had formed in the early twentieth century to satisfy the longings of African Americans to play the game, and a number of players such as Josh Gibson and Satchel Paige posted accomplishments that rivaled those of white major leaguers. Still, for all their talent, these players remained barred from major league baseball. In 1947, Brooklyn Dodgers general manager Brach Rickey signed Jackie Robinson to a major league contract, ostensibly to end segregation in baseball but also to capitalize on a burgeoning African American population newly migrated to the cities of the North. When Robinson played, blacks across the nation were glued to their radios, cheering him on as a symbol of their own hopes. Robinson was immensely unpopular with many white fans and players, but his performance on the field convinced other clubs of the correctness of Rickey's decision, and, by 1959, every team in baseball had been integrated.

The popularity of baseball reached an all-time high in the 1950s. A new generation of stars, among them Mickey Mantle, Ted Williams, and Willie Mays, joined Babe Ruth in the pantheon of American greats. Teams such as the Brooklyn Dodgers, affectionately known as "Dem Bums," won their way into the hearts of baseball fans with their play as well as with indelible personalities such as "Pee Wee" Reese, "Preacher" Roe, and Duke Snider. Baseball cards, small collectible photographs with player statistics on their flip sides, became a full-fledged industry, with companies such as Topps and Bowman capitalizing on boyhood idolatry of their favorite players. And Yogi Berra, catcher for the New York Yankees, single-handedly expanded baseball's already-sizable contribution to American speech with such head-scratching baseball idioms as "It ain't over 'til it's over." By the end of the twentieth century, Berra's witticisms had come to occupy an indelible place in the American lexicon.

The 1950s witnessed baseball at the height of its popularity and influence in American culture, but the decade also represented the end of an era in a sport relatively unchanged since its early days. Continuing financial success, buoyed especially by rising income from television and radio rights, led to club movement and league expansion. In 1953, the Boston Braves transferred its franchise to Milwaukee, and, five years, later, the New York Giants and Brooklyn Dodgers moved to California, becoming the San Francisco Giants and the Los Angeles Dodgers, respectively. Later, new franchises would emerge in Houston and Montreal. The location of the ballparks in areas geared toward suburban audiences destroyed many urban community ties to baseball forged over the course of a century.

Players also gained unprecedented power in the latter half of the twentieth century and, with it, astronomical salaries that did much to dampen public enthusiasm for their heroes. In 1976, pitchers Andy Messersmith and Dave McNally challenged the long-established reserve clause, which owners had, for more than a century, used to bind players to teams for the duration of their careers. Arbiter Peter Seitz effectively demolished the clause, ushering in the era of free agency. For the first time in baseball history, players could peddle their wares on the open market, and, as a result, salaries skyrocketed. In 1976, the Boston Red Sox made history by signing Bill Campbell, baseball's first free agent, to a four-year, $1 million dollar contract. The average annual salary rose from $41,000 in 1974 to $1,000,000 in 1992. In 1998, pitcher Kevin Brown signed the first $100 million contract in sport history, averaging over $13 million per annum. Free agency, by encouraging the constant movement of players from team to team, also did much to sever the long-term identification of players with particular teams and cities, thus further weakening community bonds with baseball.

Polls consistently revealed that fans resented the overpayment of players, but still they continued to attend big-league games en masse. Major league attendance records were broken six times in the 1985 through 1991 seasons. The players' strike of 1994 dramatically reversed this tide of goodwill. The players' rejection of a salary cap proposed by owners resulted in a 234-day labor stoppage during the 1994 season, with the cancellation of 921 regular-season games as well as the World Series. The strike, which ended early in the 1995 season, disrupted state and city economies and disappointed millions of fans. As a result, the 1995 season saw an unprecedented decline in attendance. The concurrent rise of basketball as a major spectator sport in the late 1990s also damaged the drawing power of baseball.

Stellar team performances as well as a number of stunning individual achievements in the latter half of the 1990s brought fans back to ballparks across the country in record numbers. The Atlanta Braves, with their remarkable seven divisional titles in the decade, reminded many of the glory days of baseball, when the New York Yankees and St. Louis Cardinals registered the word "dynasty" in the sport's lexicon. Similarly, the Yankees delivered one of the finest performances by a team in baseball history, logging 114 victories in 1998 and winning the World Series handily. On the players' end, Cal Ripken Jr., in eclipsing Lou Gehrig's mark of 2,130 consecutive games played, brought important positive press to baseball in the wake of its 1994 players' strike. Ripken's fortitude and passion for the game was a welcome relief to fans disillusioned by the image of selfish players concerned primarily with monetary returns. Similarly, Baltimore's Mark McGwire returned the focus of fans to the playing field with his assault on Roger Maris' single-season mark for home runs in 1998. McGwire's record-setting 70 round-trippers that season captured the nation's attention in a Ruth-ian fashion and did much to restore the mythos and romance of the sport, much as the Sultan of Swat's accomplishments had done in the 1920s.

Though professional baseball has had its moments of honor and of ignominy, perhaps the real legacy of the glory days of baseball is still to be found on community playing fields. Baseball is not only beloved as a spectator sport, but is still often the first team game played by both sexes in peewee and little leagues. While modern mothers may shudder to imagine their children imitating the tobacco-chewing ballplayers they see on television, there is an undeniable thrill at the little leaguer's first home run that harks back to the most truly electrifying quality of baseball—that moment when skill meets desire, enabling the ordinary person to perform magnificent feats.

—Scott Tribble

FURTHER READING:

Creamer, Robert. *Babe: The Legend Comes to Life.* New York, Simon and Schuster, 1974.

Goldstein, Warren. *Playing for Keeps: The History of Early Baseball.* Ithaca, Cornell University Press, 1989.

Rader, Benjamin. *Baseball: A History of America's Game.* Urbana, University of Illinois Press, 1992.

Seymour, Harold. *Baseball: The Early Years.* New York, Oxford University Press, 1960.

Voigt, David. *American Baseball.* Norman, University of Oklahoma Press, 1966.

Baseball Cards

Bought and traded by the youth of America who wanted to see their favorite players and exchange the cards with other young fans, baseball cards were a symbol of bubble gum hero worship and youthful innocence during the first three-quarters of the twentieth century. Serious collectibles only since about 1975, baseball card collecting has turned into a multimillion-dollar business, a transformation to commercial and financial enterprise.

The first baseball cards were a far cry from the high-tech, colorful prints of today. The Old Judge Company issued the first series of cards in 1887. They were distributed in cigarette packages and consisted of player photographs mounted on stiff cardboard. Those "Old Judges," produced until 1890, are treasured parts of many current collections. Included in those sets was one of the most valuable cards in the history of collecting—the Honus Wagner baseball card. According to legend, Wagner, a nonsmoker, was irate when he discovered his picture being used to promote smoking. As a result, he ordered his likeness removed from the set. Today, it appears there are no more than twenty-five Wagner cards in existence, each worth nearly one hundred thousand dollars.

By the 1920s, tobacco companies had given way to gum and confectionery enterprises as the prime distributors of baseball cards. Goudey Gum Company, a leading baseball card manufacturer, issued sets of baseball cards from 1933 to 1941. Goudey's attractive designs, with full-color line drawings on thick card stock, greatly influenced other cards issued during that era. Some of the most attractive and collectible cards were released in the two decades preceding World War II.

The war brought an abrupt end to the manufacture and collection of baseball cards because of the serious shortages of paper and rubber. Production was renewed in 1948 when the Bowman Gum Company issued a set of black-and-white prints with one card and one slab of gum in every penny pack. That same year, the Leaf Company of Chicago issued a set of colorized picture cards with bubble gum. Then in 1951, Topps Gum Company began issuing cards and became the undisputed leader in the manufacture of baseball cards, dominating

Dizzy Dean's 1934 baseball card.

the market for the next three decades. The Topps 1952 series set the standard for baseball cards by printing individual statistics, personal information, team logos, and large, clear, color pictures. There were continuing legal squabbles over who held the rights to players' pictures. With competition fierce during the 1950s, Topps finally bought out the Bowman Company.

It was not until the mid-1970s that the card collecting business began in earnest. One card collector stated that in 1972, there were only about ten card dealers in the New York area who would meet on Friday nights. No money ever changed hands—it was strictly trading. But several years later, the hobby began to grow. As more and more people began buying old cards, probably as a link to their youth, prices rose, and small trading meetings turned into major baseball card conventions at hotels and conference centers. By the end of the twentieth century, there are baseball card conventions, shows, and flea markets in nearly all major cities.

In the 1980s, various court decisions paved the way for other companies to challenge Topps's virtual monopoly. Fleer, Donruss, and Upper Deck issued attractive and colorful cards during the 1980s, although bubble gum was discarded as part of that package. In the 1990s, other companies followed: Leaf, Studio, Ultra, Stadium Club, Bowman, and Pinnacle. With competition fierce, these companies began offering ''inserts'' or special cards that would be issued as

limited editions in order to keep their prices high for collectors. However, these special sets began driving many single-player collectors out of the hobby. Average prices of cards were rising to unprecedented heights while the number of cards per pack was dropping.

—David E. Woodard

FURTHER READING:

Beckett, James. *The Official 1999 Price Guide to Baseball Cards.* 18th ed. New York, Ballantine Publishing, House of Collectibles, 1998.

Green, Paul. *The Complete Price Guide to Baseball Cards Worth Collecting.* Lincolnwood, Illinois, NTC/Contemporary Publishing, 1994.

Larsen, Mark. *Complete Guide to Baseball Memorabilia.* 3rd ed. Iola, Wisconsin, Krause Publications, 1996.

Lemke, Bob, and Robert Lemke, eds. *1999 Standard Catalogue of Baseball Cards.* 8th ed. Iola, Wisconsin, Krause Publishers, 1998.

Pearlman, Dan. *Collecting Baseball Cards: How to Buy Them, Store Them, Trade Them, and Keep Track of Their Value as Investments.* 3rd ed. Chicago, Bonus Books, 1991.

Thorn, John, and Pete Palmer, eds. *Total Baseball.* 2nd ed. New York, Warner Books, 1991.

Basie, Count (1904-1984)

One of the most imitated piano players, Count Basie brought a minimalist, subtle style to his powerful work at the keyboard and was the driving force behind a star-studded band that influenced the course of jazz during the big band era of the late 1930s and early 1940s. Its style of interspersing the Count's intricately timed piano chords with blasting ensemble passages and explosive solos made it one of the most admired of big bands for more than 30 years.

By sheer accident, Basie came under the influence of the Kansas City jazz style, the essence of which was ''relaxation.'' Franklin Driggs writes that the ''Southwestern style'' had ''intense drive and yet was relaxed.'' Notes might be played ''just before or just after'' the beat while the rhythm flowed on evenly. These are characteristics any listener to Basie's ''One O'Clock Jump'' would understand. At age 24, Basie was stranded in Kansas City when a vaudeville act he accompanied disbanded. Born William James Basie in Red Bank, New Jersey, he had become interested in jazz and ragtime in the New York area and had studied briefly with Fats Waller. Adrift in Kansas City, he played background to silent movies and then spent a year with Walter Page's Blue Devils, a band that included blues singer Jimmy Rushing, whose career would merge with the Count's.

The Blue Devils disbanded in 1929, and Basie and some of the other members joined bandleader Bennie Moten, who had recorded his Kansas City-style jazz on Okeh Records. After Moten died in 1935, Basie took the best of his jazzmen and started a band of his own. Basie gradually upgraded the quality of his personnel, and when jazz critic John Hammond happened to hear the band on a Kansas City radio station, he persuaded Basie to bring the band to New York in

Count Basie

1936. He recorded his first sides for Decca in January, 1937, and within a year the band's fame was becoming international.

There were a number of distinctive qualities about the Basie band other than the Count's unique piano style. The rhythm section—featuring Jo Jones, drums, Walter Page, bass, and Freddie Greene, guitar—was widely admired for its lightness, precision, and relaxed swing. Jimmy Rushing's alternatively virile and sensitive style of blues singing on such band numbers as "Sent for You Yesterday (Here You Come Today)" and "Goin' to Chicago" were longstanding hits. The Count recruited a bandstand-full of outstanding side men, whose solo improvisations took the band to ever higher plateaus. They included Lester Young and Herschel Evans on tenor sax, Earl Warren on alto, Buck Clayton and Harry Edison on trumpets, and Benny Morton and Dickie Wells on trombone. The band's chief arranger was Eddie Durham, but various members of the band made contributions to so-called "head" arrangements, which were informally worked out as a group and then memorized.

The soul of Count Basie's music was the blues, played in a style described by Stanley Dance as "slow and moody, rocking at an easy dancing pace, or jumping at passionate up-tempos." Most of the band's greatest successes have been blues based, including "One

O'Clock Jump" and numbers featuring the vocals of Jimmy Rushing. Woody Herman, whose first band was known as "The Band That Plays the Blues," was strongly influenced by the Basie sound.

In the 1950s, Basie and his band toured Europe frequently, with great success. During his second tour of Britain, in the fall of 1957, his became the first American band to play a command performance for the Queen. He set another precedent that fall by playing 13 weeks at the roof ballroom of the Waldorf-Astoria Hotel as the first African American jazz orchestra to play that prestigious venue.

During his long tenure at the head of a band that appealed to a wide variety of fans—both the jazz buffs and the uninitiated—swing music was becoming increasingly complex, rhythmically and harmonically, but Basie had no interest in the be-bop craze. George Simon writes that the Basie band "continued to blow and boom in the same sort of simple, swinging, straight-ahead groove in which it has slid out of Kansas City in the mid-1930s." He adds that the Count "displayed an uncanny sense of just how far to go in tempo, in volume, and in harmonic complexity."

Stanley Dance summed it up when he wrote in 1980 about the importance of Basie's "influence upon the whole course of jazz. By keeping it simple and sincere, and swinging at all times, his music provided a guiding light in the chaos of the past two decades.''

—Benjamin Griffith

FURTHER READING:

Basie, Count, as told to Albert Murray. *Good Morning Blues: The Autobiography of Count Basie.* New York, Random House, 1985.

Dance, Stanley. *The World of Count Basie.* New York, Scribner's, 1980.

Driggs, Franklin S. "Kansas City and the Southwest." *Jazz.* Edited by Nat Hentoff and Albert J. McCarthy. New York, Da Capo Press, 1974.

Simon, George T. *The Big Bands.* New York, MacMillan, 1974.

Basketball

The sport of basketball was invented at the close of the nineteenth century. By the end of the twentieth century, only soccer surpassed it as the world's most popular sport, as top basketball players from the United States were among the most recognized people on Earth.

Basketball was invented in late 1891 by Dr. James A. Naismith, physical education director at the Young Men's Christian Association (YMCA) in Springfield, Massachusetts. The YMCA students were tiring of standard calisthenics and demanded a new, team sport to be played indoors between the end of football season in autumn and the start of baseball season in the spring. Naismith hit upon the idea of two teams of players maneuvering a ball across a gymnasium towards a set target. He obtained a pair of peach baskets—he originally wanted to use boxes—and nailed them on beams on either end of the gym. The first game ever played resulted in a 1-0 score, with one William R. Chase scoring the lone point with a soccer ball; Naismith and his players quickly realized that the new sport had potential.

Naismith resisted efforts to name his invention "Naismith-ball," preferring "basket ball" instead. He wrote an article describing the sport in his YMCA's magazine in early 1892, and YMCAs across the country and around the world picked up on the sport during the 1890s. By 1895 Naismith had set up standard rules: five players on each team, with successful shots counting two points each. Eventually, players who were fouled by opponents would be able to make "free throws," counting one point each, shooting a short distance from the basket.

Within weeks of Naismith's first game, women athletes in Springfield were also playing basketball, and the first intercollegiate college basketball game, in fact, was between the Stanford women's team and the University of California women's squad in April 1895. Within a year the University of Chicago beat the University of Iowa, 15-12, in the first men's college basketball game. By the first decade of the twentieth century, many colleges were fielding men's and women's basketball teams. Men's college basketball exploded in popularity during the 1930s, with heavily promoted doubleheaders at New York's Madison Square Garden featuring the top teams in the country before packed audiences.

The first successful professional basketball team was the Original Celtics, which were formed in New York before World War I. The team of New Yorkers generally won 90 percent of their games against amateur and town teams, and had a record of 204 wins against only 11 defeats in the 1922-1923 season. In 1927, white promoter Abe Saperstein started the Harlem Globetrotters, a barnstorming basketball team made up of blacks (when most college and pro teams had no African American players). They became best known for their irreverent on-court antics and their theme song, the jazz standard "Sweet Georgia Brown."

The scores of basketball games prior to the 1940s seem shockingly low today, as teams rarely scored more than 40 points a game. It was customary in early basketball for players to shoot the ball with both hands. Once the one-hand jump shot, popularized by Stanford star Hank Lusietti, gained acceptance in 1940, players were more confident in taking shots, and scoring began to increase.

Professional basketball leagues began and folded many times in basketball's infancy. By the end of World War II, there were two leagues competing for top college prospects, the National Basketball League and the Basketball Association of America. The two leagues merged in 1949, forming the National Basketball Association (NBA). The NBA's first star was the first great basketball tall-man, George Mikan. Improbable as it seems now, players over six feet in height were once considered to make bad basketball players, seen as ungainly and uncoordinated. The 6' 10'' Mikan, who had starred as a collegian for DePaul University, erased this stereotype single-handedly, winning five NBA scoring titles as his Minneapolis (later Los Angeles) Lakers won four NBA championships. In a poll of sportswriters in 1950, Mikan was named "Mr. Basketball" for the first 50 years of the twentieth century.

As Mikan starred in the professional ranks, college basketball was shaken to the core by revelations of corruption. In 1951 the New York district attorney's office found that players at many of the top schools had agreed to play less than their best—to "shave points"—in exchange for gambler's money. The accused players frequently met gamblers during summers while working and playing basketball in New York's glamorous Catskills resort areas. Players from the City College of New York, which had won both the National Invitational Tournament and the NCAA (National Collegiate Athletic Association) basketball finals in 1951, were implicated, as were stars from Long Island University, coached by popular author Clair Bee. The image of top players testifying to grand juries would stain college basketball for the rest of the decade.

Basketball had been marked by stalling tactics, where one team would possess the ball for minutes at a time without shooting or scoring. In 1954, the NBA adopted a shot clock, requiring that a team shoot the ball within 24 seconds of gaining possession (College basketball would wait until 1985 before mandating a similar shot clock). This one rule resulted in an outburst of scoring, which helped push professional basketball attendance up in the 1950s. Fans of the era flocked to see the Boston Celtics. Led first by guard Bob Cousy, and later by center Bill Russell, the Celtics won eight straight NBA titles from 1959 through 1966. Their arch-nemesis was center Wilt Chamberlain of the Philadelphia Warriors and 76ers. The most dominant scorer in NBA history, Chamberlain averaged 50 points for the 1961-1962 season, including his memorable performance on March 2, 1962, where he scored 100 points. Chamberlain outperformed Bill Russell during Boston-Philadelphia matchups, but the Celtics almost inevitably won the titles.

As the Celtics were the NBA's dynasty in the 1960s, so were the UCLA (University of California, Los Angeles) Bruins college basketball's team to beat in the 1960s and 1970s. Coached by the soft-spoken, understated John Wooden, the UCLA Bruins won nine

NCAA tournament titles in one ten-year span, including seven straight from 1967 to 1973. Wooden's talent during this time included guards Walt Hazzard and Gail Goodrich, and centers Lew Alcindor (who would change his name to Kareem Abdul-Jabbar) and Bill Walton. During one stretch encompassing three seasons, UCLA won an improbable 88 consecutive games, an NCAA record.

The NBA found a new rival in 1967, with the creation of the American Basketball Association (ABA). The new league adopted a red, white, and blue basketball and established a line some 20 feet from the basket, beyond which a field goal counted for three points. The three-point line and the colored ball made the ABA something of a laughingstock to basketball traditionalists, and ABA attendance and media coverage indeed lagged behind the NBA's. But by the early 1970s, the ABA had successfully signed several top college picks from under the NBA's nose, and its top attraction was Julius Erving of the Virginia Squires and New York Nets. Erving, nicknamed "Dr. J," turned the slam-dunk into an art form, hanging in the air indefinitely, virtually at will. Erving was definitely the hottest young basketball talent in either league. In 1976 the NBA agreed to a merger, and four ABA teams joined the NBA. Erving signed a $6 million contract with Philadelphia. In the first All-Star game after the merger, five of the 10 NBA All-Star players had ABA roots.

The merger, however, was not enough to stem the NBA's declining attendance and fan interest. People were not only not following professional basketball in the 1970s, they seemed actively hostile to it. The perception of pro basketball as being dominated by black athletes, some felt, prevented the sport from commanding television revenue and advertising endorsements. According to one disputed report in the late 1970s, fully three-quarters of NBA players were addicted to drugs. Once again, the NBA found its salvation in the college ranks. In 1979 Michigan State, with star guard Earvin "Magic" Johnson, defeated Indiana State, and star forward Larry Bird, for the NCAA basketball title. The game drew a record television audience, and helped popularize the NCAA basketball tournament, later known as "March Madness." The tournament eventually included 64 teams each season, with underdog, "Cinderella" teams such as North Carolina State in 1983 and Villanova in 1985 emerging to win the championship. By the 1990s, the tournament spawned hundreds of millions of dollars in office pools and Vegas gambling, as cities vied to host the "Final Four," where the four remaining teams would compete in the semifinals and championship game. Even the official start of college basketball practice in the fall became a commercialized ritual, as schools hosted "Midnight Madness" events, inviting fans to count the minutes until midnight of the first sanctioned day college teams could practice.

In the fall of 1979 Bird had joined the Boston Celtics and Johnson the Los Angeles Lakers. Johnson led the Lakers to the 1980 NBA title, playing every position in the deciding championship game and scoring 42 points. Bird and Johnson would usher in a new era in the NBA—Bird, with his tactical defense and Johnson with his exuberant offense (the Lakers' offensive strategy would be called "Showtime"). The Celtics and Lakers won eight NBA titles in the 1980s, as Bird and Johnson reprised their 1979 NCAA performance by going head-to-head in three NBA finals.

The success of the NBA created by Bird and Johnson during the 1980s rose to an even greater level during the 1990s, due in no small measure to Michael Jordan. The guard joined the Chicago Bulls in 1984, having played three seasons at the University of North Carolina; as a collegian, Jordan had been on an NCAA championship team

and the 1984 gold medal United States Olympic squad. Jordan immediately established himself as a marquee NBA player in his first seasons, scoring a playoff record 63 points in one 1986 post-season game. His dunks surpassed even Erving's in their artistry, and Jordan developed a remarkable inside game to complement that. Slowly, a great Bulls team formed around him, and Jordan led the Bulls to three straight NBA titles in 1991-1993. Jordan then abruptly left basketball for 16 months to pursue a major league baseball career. A chagrined Jordan returned to the Bulls in February 1995, and in his final three complete seasons the Bulls won three more consecutive championships. The 1996 Bulls team went 72-10 in the regular season, and many experts consider this team, led by Jordan, Scottie Pippen, Dennis Rodman, and Toni Kukoc, to be the finest in NBA history. Jordan retired for good after the 1997-1998 season; his last shot in the NBA, in the closing seconds of the deciding championship game against Utah in June 1998, was the winning basket. Jordan's announcement of his retirement in January 1999 received media coverage usually reserved for presidential impeachments and state funerals.

Though the United States had been the birthplace of basketball, by the end of the twentieth century America had to recognize the emergence of international talent. The Summer Olympics introduced basketball as a medal sport in 1936, and the United States won gold medals in its first seven Olympics, winning 63 consecutive games before losing the 1972 Munich gold medal game, 50-49, to the Soviet Union on a controversial referee's call. After the United States lost in the 1988 Olympics, the International Olympic Committee changed its rules to allow the United States to assemble a team made up not of amateurs, but of NBA stars. The "Dream Team" for the 1992 Barcelona Games was, some insisted, the greatest all-star team ever, in any sport. The squad featured Larry Bird, Magic Johnson (who had retired from the NBA in 1991 after testing positive for the HIV virus), Michael Jordan, Charles Barkley, Patrick Ewing, Karl Malone, and David Robinson. The United States team crushed its opponents, frequently by margins of 50 points a game. Many of the Dream Team opponents eagerly waited, after being defeated, to get the American stars' autographs and pictures. The 1992 squad easily won a gold medal, as did a professional United States team in the 1996 Atlanta Olympics (whose stars included Grant Hill, Scottie Pippen, and Shaquille O'Neal).

The 1990s also saw an explosion of interest of women's basketball, on professional as well as collegiate levels. Many credit this popularity with the enforcement of Title IX, a 1971 federal statute requiring high schools and colleges to fund women's sports programs on an equal basis with men's. The top college team of the time was Tennessee, which won three straight women's NCAA titles in 1996-1998, narrowly missing a fourth in 1999. In 1996, a women's professional league, the American Basketball League (ABL) was inaugurated, followed a year later by the Women's National Basketball Association (WNBA), an offshoot of the NBA. The ABL folded in 1999, but the WNBA, which held its season during the summertime, showed genuine promise; its stars included Rebecca Lobo of the New York Liberty (she had starred at the University of Connecticut) and Cynthia Cooper of the Houston Comets, which won the first two WNBA championships. Women's basketball was characterized less by dunks and flamboyant moves, and more by fundamental offense and defense. John Wooden, for one, said he generally preferred watching women's basketball to men's. College and pro women's games were known, in fact, for having a strong male fan base, as well as entire families in attendance.

As the twentieth century closed, the NBA proved it was no longer immune to the pressures of American professional sports. As major league baseball and the National Football League had suffered through lengthy and devastating strikes during the 1980s and 1990s, the NBA had its first-ever work stoppage in the fall of 1998. NBA team owners locked players out in October, declaring the collective bargaining agreement with the player's union null and void. At issue was the league salary cap; each team had been previously allowed to exceed the cap for one player (in Chicago's case, for Michael Jordan), but the owners wanted to abolish this exception. The players steadfastly refused, and the first half of the 1998-1999 season was lost. Both sides reached an agreement in early 1999, and the regular season began three months late, on February 6. To the surprise of players and owners alike, the NBA lockout garnered little attention from the fans.

Basketball slowly entered other elements of American popular culture during the latter part of the twentieth century. "Rabbit" Angstrom, the middle-aged hero of four John Updike novels, had been a star basketball player in high school. Jason Miller's Pulitzer-Prize winning play *That Championship Season* (1972) reunited disillusioned, bitter ex-jocks on the anniversary of their state high school title victory. One of the most acclaimed documentaries of the 1990s, *Hoop Dreams* (1994), tracked two talented Chicago ghetto basketball players through their four years of high school, each with an eye towards a college scholarship and an NBA career. Novelist John Edgar Wideman, who had played basketball at the University of Pennsylvania during the 1960s, often used the game metaphorically in his award-winning fiction (his daughter Jamila was a star player at Stanford, and later the WNBA). Wideman's teammate at Oxford University while on a Rhodes Scholarship was Bill Bradley, who played for Princeton, and later had a Hall of Fame professional career with the Knicks. Bradley served three terms in the United States Senate, and wrote a bestselling book defining basketball's qualities (*Values of the Game*) as he prepared a presidential campaign for the year 2000.

—Andrew Milner

FURTHER READING:

Decourcy, Mike. *Inside Basketball: From the Playgrounds to the NBA.* New York, MetroBooks, 1996.

Dickey, Glenn. *The History of Professional Basketball since 1896.* New York, Stein and Day, 1982.

Douchant, Mike, editor. *Encyclopedia of College Basketball.* Detroit, Gale Research, 1995.

Fox, Stephen R. *Big Leagues: Professional Baseball, Football, and Basketball in National Memory.* New York, Morrow, 1994.

George, Nelson. *Elevating the Game: Black Men and Basketball.* New York, HarperCollins, 1992.

Koppett, Leonard. *The Essence of the Game Is Deception.* Boston, Little Brown & Company, 1973.

McCallum, John D. *College Basketball, U.S.A., since 1892.* New York, Stein and Day, 1978.

Peterson, Robert. *Cages to Jump Shots: Pro Basketball's Early Years.* New York, Oxford University Press, 1990.

Pluto, Terry. *Loose Balls.* New York, Fireside, 1991.

———. *Tall Tales.* New York, Fireside, 1994.

Sachare, Alex, editor. *The Official NBA Basketball Encyclopedia.* New York, Villard, 1994.

Bathhouses

In many cultures, bathing in communal bathhouses has been an important social and even religious ritual. In Japan it is the *sento,* among Yiddish-speaking Jews, the *shvitz,* and in the Arab world the *hammam,* all of them centers for socializing across class lines, providing relief from culturally imposed modesty, and a place to get luxuriously clean. By the early 1900s, New York City had built and maintained a network of public bathhouses—many of them resembling Roman temples—in immigrant neighborhoods. Because they are traditionally segregated by gender, bathhouses have also long been associated with same-sex eroticism. It is in this capacity that they have gained most of their notoriety in American culture. Though the increasing availability of indoor plumbing in private houses decreased the need for public baths, the bathhouse remained a mainstay of American gay male culture until the advent of the AIDS epidemic in the mid-1980s. One of the most prominent of these venues was the Club Baths chain, a nationwide members-only network that permitted access to facilities across the country. Most of the Club bathhouses offered clean but spartan accommodations (a cubicle with a mattress pad or locker for personal items, and a fresh towel) for about $10 for an eight-hour stay.

Even before the reconstruction of a "gay" identity from the 1960s, the baths had achieved some degree of fame as male-only enclaves: witness the depiction in films of businessmen, spies, or gangsters meeting in a Turkish bath, protected only by a towel around the waist. The Turkish baths of yore were part social club, part night club, and part sex club. They often had areas called "orgy rooms" where immediate and anonymous sex was available. The decade of the 1970s, after the beginning of gay liberation, was the "golden age" of the gay bathhouse. Gay male culture became chic, and these gathering places became celebrity "hot spots." The most famous of them was the Continental Baths on Manhattan's Upper West Side, where Bette Midler launched her career singing to an audience of towel-clad men. In the intoxicating years that followed the Stonewall riots of 1969, gay men reveled in their new visibility, with bathhouses emerging as carnal theme parks that became self-contained fantasy worlds for erotic play, though it is not clear how many of the patrons identified themselves as "gay," since the focus was on "men having sex with men," not on socially constructed identities. It was not uncommon for bathhouse patrons to include married "straight" men taking a break from domestic obligations in orgy rooms packed full of writhing bodies, or in private rooms for individual encounters. Gay or straight, customers hoped to find in the baths a passport to intense male pleasure in an environment that fairly throbbed with Dionysian energy. One large bathhouse in San Francisco boasted that it could serve up to eight hundred customers at a time. The St. Marks Baths in New York's East Village attracted customers from around the world with its sleek, modernistic facilities that were a far cry from the dumpy barracks of earlier decades, like the Everard Baths farther uptown, once the site of a church. The Beacon Baths in midtown Manhattan adjoined a cloistered convent, and it has long been rumored that the bathhouse once borrowed fresh towels from the nuns when its supply ran short.

The AIDS epidemic, which claimed gay men as some of its earliest victims, caused many public health officials and frightened patrons to recommend the bathhouses be closed, though others feared that such a move would only force sexual activity underground, beyond the reach of counseling, besides erasing the gains of gay liberation and leading to the repressive eradication of gay culture. The owners of the baths fought the closures, but most of them were shuttered by 1985. By the 1990s, gay baths had re-emerged in many large cities. Some have returned in the guise of the shadowy venues of pre-liberation days; others have re-opened as private sex clubs, taking great precautions to educate customers and enforce rules of safe sex by such means as installing video surveillance cameras and hiring ''lifeguards'' to monitor sexual activity.

—Tina Gianoulis

Further Reading:

Bayer, Ronald. ''AIDS and the Gay Community: Between the Specter and the Promise of Medicine.'' *Social Research.* December 1985.

Bolton, Ralph, John Zincke, and Rudolf Mak. ''Gay Baths Revisited: An Empirical Analysis.'' *GLQ.* Vol. 1, 1994.

Holleran, Andrew. ''Steam, Soap, and Sex.'' *The Advocate.* October 6, 1992.

Shilts, Randy. *And the Band Played On.* New York, Penguin, 1988.

Batman

Batman is one of the most popular and important characters created for comic books. In the entire pantheon of comic-book superheroes, only Superman and Spider-Man rival him in significance. Among the handful of comic-book characters who have transcended the market limitations of the comic-book medium, Batman has truly become an American cultural icon and an international marketing industry in and of himself.

Batman was born out of DC editor Vincent Sullivan's desire to create a costumed character to exploit the recent success of DC's first superhero, Superman. Taking inspiration from various Hollywood adventure, horror, and gangster movies, cartoonist Bob Kane prepared a design for a masked crime-fighter in the costume of a bat in 1939. He then consulted with writer Bill Finger, who contributed to the vigilante concept ideas derived from pulp magazines. The resulting character was thus visually and thematically a synthesis of the most lurid and bizarre representations of popular culture available to a 1930s mass audience. It was a concept seemingly destined for either the trashcan or comic-book immortality.

Like Superman, Batman wore a costume, maintained a secret identity, and battled the scourge of crime and injustice. But to anyone who read the comic books, the differences between the two leading superheroes were more striking than the similarities. Unlike Superman, Batman possessed no superhuman powers, relying instead upon his own wits, technical skills, and fighting prowess. Batman's motives were initially obscure, but after a half-dozen issues readers learned the disturbing origins of his crime-fighting crusade. As a child, Bruce Wayne had witnessed the brutal murder of his mother

Adam West as Batman.

and father. Traumatized but determined to avenge his parents' death, Wayne used the fortune inherited from his father to assemble an arsenal of crime-fighting gadgets while training his body and mind to the pinnacle of human perfection. One night when Wayne sits contemplating an appropriate persona that will strike fear into the heats of criminals, a bat flies through the window. He takes it as an omen and declares, ''I shall become a bat!''

Kane and Finger originally cast Batman as a vigilante pursued by the police even as he preyed upon criminals. Prowling the night, lurking in the shadows, and wearing a frightening costume with a hooded cowl and a flowing Dracula-like cape, Batman often looked more like a villain than a hero. In his earliest episodes, he even carried a gun and sometimes killed his opponents. The immediate popularity of his comic books testified to the recurring appeal of a crime-fighter who appropriates the tactics of criminals and operates free of legal constraints. As Batman himself once put it, ''If you can't beat [criminals] 'inside' the law, you must beat them 'outside' it—and that's where I come in!''

Batman's early adventures were among the most genuinely atmospheric in comic-book history. He waged a grim war against crime in a netherworld of gloomy castles, fog-bound wharves, and the dimly lit alleys of Gotham City—an urban landscape that seemed perpetually enshrouded in night. Bob Kane was one of the first comic-book artists to experiment—however crudely—with unusual angle shots, distorted perspectives, and heavy shadows to create a disturbing mood of claustrophobia and madness. These early classic issues also rank among the most graphically violent of their time. Murder, brutality, and bloodshed were commonplace therein until 1941, when

DC responded to public criticism by instituting a new code of standards to ''clean up'' its comic books. As a result Batman's adventures gradually moved out of the shadows and became more conventional superhero adventure stories.

The addition of Batman's teenage sidekick Robin also served to lighten the mood of the series. Kane and Finger introduced Robin, who, according to Kane, was named after Robin Hood, in the April 1940 issue of *Detective Comic*. They hoped that the character would open up more creative possibilities (by giving Batman someone to talk to) and provide a point of identification for young readers. Like Bruce Wayne, who adopts the orphaned youth and trains him in the ways of crime fighting, young Dick Grayson witnessed the murder of his parents.

Robin has been a figure of some controversy. Many believed that the brightly-colored costumed teenager was obnoxious and detracted too much from the premise of Batman as an obsessed and solitary avenger. Oftentimes it seemed that Robin's principle role was to be captured and await rescue by Batman. In his influential 1954 polemic against comic books, *Seduction of the Innocent*, Dr. Frederick Wertham even charged that the strange relationship between Batman and Robin was rife with homosexual implications. Nevertheless, the longevity and consistent commercial success of the Batman and Robin team from the 1940s to the 1960s suggested that the concept of the ''Dynamic Duo'' was popular with most readers.

Much of Batman's popularity over the decades must be attributed to his supporting cast of villains—arguably the cleverest and most memorable rogues gallery in comic books. Ludicrous caricatures based upon single motifs, villains like Cat Woman, Two-Face, the Penguin, and the Riddler were perfect adversaries for the equally ludicrous Batman. Without question, however, the most inspired and most popular of Batman's villains has always been the Joker. With his white face, green hair, purple suit, and perpetual leering grin, the homicidal Joker is the personification of sheer lunacy, at once delightful and horrifying. The laughing Joker was also the ideal archenemy for the stoic and rather humorless Batman, often upstaging the hero in his own comic book.

After years of strong sales, Batman's share of the comic-book market began to decline in the early 1960s. Facing stiff competition from the hip new antihero superheroes of Marvel Comics (Spider-Man, the Hulk, the Fantastic Four), Batman and his peers at DC epitomized the comic-book ''Establishment'' at a time when anti-establishment trends were predominating throughout youth culture.

In 1966, however, Batman's sales received a strong boost from a new source—television. That year the ABC television network launched the prime-time live-action series *Batman*. The campy program was part of a widespread trend whereby American popular culture made fun of itself. The *Batman* show ridiculed every aspect of the comic-book series from the impossible nobility of Batman and Robin (portrayed respectively by actors Adam West and Burt Ward, who both overacted—one would hope—deliberately) to the bewildering array of improbable gadgets (bat-shark repellent), to comic-book sound effects (Pow! Bam! Zowie!?). For a couple of years the show was a phenomenal hit. Film and television celebrities like César Romero (the Joker), Burgess Meredith (the Penguin), and Julie Newmar (Cat Woman) clamored to appear on the show, which sparked a boom in sales of toys, t-shirts, and other licensed bat-merchandise. Sales of Batman's comic book also increased dramatically for several years. But the show's lasting impact on the comic book was arguably a harmful one. For by making the entire Batman

concept out to be a big joke, the show's producers seemed to be making fun of the hero's many fans who took his adventures seriously. At a time when ambitious young comic-book creators were trying to tap into an older audience, the *Batman* show firmly reinforced the popular perception that comic books were strictly for children and morons.

New generations of writers and artists understood this dilemma and worked to rescue Batman from the perils of his own multi-media success. Writer Dennis O'Neil and artist Neal Adams produced a series of stylish and very serious stories that did much to restore Batman to his original conception as a nocturnal avenger. These efforts did not reverse Batman's declining sales throughout the 1970s—a bad time for comic-book sales generally—but they gave the comic book a grittier and more mature tone that subsequent creators would expand upon.

In the 1980s and 1990s writers have explored the darker implications of Batman as a vigilante seemingly on the brink of insanity. In a 1986 ''graphic novel'' (the trendy term given to ''serious'' comic books—with serious prices) titled *Bat Man: The Dark Knight Returns*, writer Frank Miller cast the hero as a slightly mad middle-aged fascist out to violently purge a dystopian future Gotham City gutted by moral decay. The success of *The Dark Knight Returns* sparked a major revival in the character's popularity. A series of graphic novels and comic-book limited-series, including *Batman: Year One* (1987), *Batman: the Killing Joke* (1988), and *Batman: Arkham Asylum* (1989), delved into the most gothic, violent, and disturbing qualities of the Batman mythos and proved especially popular with contemporary comic-book fans.

More importantly in terms of public exposure and profits were the much-hyped series of major motion picture releases produced by DC Comics' parent company Warner Brothers featuring characters from the Batman comic book. Director Tim Burton's *Batman* with Michael Keaton in the title role and Jack Nicholson as the Joker was the most successful both commercially and critically. But three sequels to date have all generated impressive box office receipts, video sales, and licensing revenue while introducing DC's superhero to new generations of comic-book readers. Also in the 1990s, a syndicated *Batman* animated series produced by the Fox network has managed the delicate task—never really achieved by the live-action films—of broadening the character's media exposure while remaining true to the qualities of the Batman comic books.

Batman is one of the few original comic-book characters to have generated more popular interest and revenue from exposure in media other than comic books. But Batman is first and foremost a product of comic books, and it is in this medium where he has been most influential. The whole multitude of costumed avengers driven to strike fear into the hearts of evil-doers owe much to Bob Kane and Bill Finger's Batman—the original comic-book caped crusader.

—Bradford Wright

FURTHER READING:

Daniels, Les. *DC Comics: Sixty Years of the World's Favorite Comic Book Heroes*. Boston, Little Brown, 1995.

The Greatest Batman Stories Ever Told. New York, Warner Books, 1988.

Kane, Bob, with Tom Andrae. *Batman and Me: An Autobiography of Bob Kane*. Forestville, California, Eclipse Books, 1989.

Pearson, Robert E., and William Uricchio, ed. *The Many Lives of the Batman: Critical Approaches to a Superhero and His Media.* New York, Routledge, 1991.

Vaz, Mark Cotta. *Tales of the Dark Knight: Batman's First Fifty Years, 1939-1989.* New York, Ballantine, 1989.

Baum, L. Frank (1856-1919)

With *The Wonderful Wizard of Oz* (1900), L. Frank Baum created a new kind of plain-language fairy tale, purely American, modern, industrial, and for the most part non-violent. He said in his introduction that the book ''was written solely to please children of today. It aspires to being a modernized fairy tale, in which the wonderment and joy are retained and the heart-aches and nightmares are left out.'' *The Wizard of Oz*—''Wonderful'' was dropped in later printings—became an institution for generations of children. Reinforced by the 1939 MGM film, the story and its messages quickly became a part of American culture. The belief that the power to fulfill your deepest desires lie within yourself, that good friends can help you get where you are going, and that not all Wizards are for real has offered many comfort through turbulent times.

The hero of the story—young Dorothy of Kansas, an orphan who lives with her Aunt Em and Uncle Henry—is a plucky and resourceful American girl. Yanked by a cyclone into Oz, she accidentally kills the Wicked Witch of the East and is given the witch's silver (changed to ruby in the 1939 movie) shoes. In hope of getting home again, Dorothy, with her little dog Toto, sets off down the Yellow Brick Road—to the Emerald City, of course—to ask the Wizard for help. Along the way, she meets the Scarecrow in search of a brain, the Tin Woodman who desires a heart, and the Cowardly Lion who is after courage. Following the storyline of most mythical quests, the friends encounter numerous adventures and must overcome great obstacles before realizing their destiny. The Wizard turns out to be a humbug, but after Dorothy destroys the Wicked Witch of the West by melting her with a bucket of water, he provides her friends with symbols of what they already have proven they possess. The book ends with Dorothy clicking her silver shoes together and being magically transported home, where her aunt and uncle have been awaiting her return.

In the *Wizard of Oz* series, Baum left out the dark, scary underbelly of the original Grimm fairy tales and created a world where people do not die and everyone is happy. He also incorporated twentieth-century technology into the books, and used recognizable characters and objects from American life such as axle grease, chinaware, scarecrows, and patchwork quilts. Although Baum poked gentle fun at some aspects of American life—such as the ''humbug'' nature of government—*The Wizard of Oz* goes directly to biting satire. Dorothy is a girl from the midwest (typical American) who meets up with a brainless scarecrow (farmers), a tin man with no heart (industry), a cowardly lion (politicians), and a flashy but ultimately powerless wizard (technology). It presents an American Utopia where no one dies, people work half the day and play half the day, and is a place where everyone is kind to one another. Ray Bradbury referred to the story as ''what we hope to be.''

Lyman Frank Baum was born on May 15, 1856 in Chittenango, New York. His childhood, by all accounts, was happy, marred only by

a minor heart condition. For his fourteenth birthday, his father gave him a printing press, with which young Frank published a neighborhood newspaper. His 1882 marriage to Maud Gage, daughter of women's rights leader Matilda Joslyn Gage, was also a happy one; Frank played the role of jovial optimist, and Maud was the disciplinarian of their four sons.

Baum worked as an actor, store owner, newspaper editor, reporter, and traveling salesman. In 1897, he found a publisher for his children's book *Mother Goose in Prose,* and from then on was a full-time writer. Baum teamed up with illustrator W. W. Denslow to produce *Father Goose, His Book* in 1899 and then *The Wonderful Wizard of Oz* in 1900. The book, splashed with color on almost every page, sold out its first edition of 10,000 copies in two weeks. Over four million copies were sold before 1956, when the copyright expired. Since then, millions more copies have been sold in regular, abridged, Golden, pop-up, and supermarket versions.

In 1902, Baum helped produce a hit musical version of his book, which ran until 1911, at which point the Baums moved to a new Hollywood home, ''Ozcot.'' In spite of failing health, he continued to write children's books, producing nearly 70 titles under his own name and seven pseudonyms including, as Edith Van Dyne, the popular *Aunt Jane's Nieces* series. Inundated with letters from children asking for more about Dorothy and Oz, Baum authored 14 Oz books altogether, each appearing annually in December. After Baum's death, the series was taken over by Ruth Plumly Thompson; others have since continued the series.

The books spawned a one-reel film version in 1910, a feature-length black and white film in 1925, a radio show in the 1930s sponsored by Jell-O, and, in 1939, the classic MGM movie starring Judy Garland, which guaranteed *The Wizard of Oz's* immortality. Beginning in 1956, the film was shown on television each year, bringing the story to generations of children and permanently ingraining it into American culture.

—Jessy Randall

FURTHER READING:

Baum, Frank Joslyn, and Russell P. Macfall. *To Please A Child: A Biography of L. Frank Baum, Royal Historian of Oz.* Chicago, Reilly & Lee, 1961.

Gardner, Martin, and Russel B. Nye. *The Wizard of Oz & Who He Was.* East Lansing, Michigan State University Press, 1957.

Hearn, Michael Patrick. *The Annotated Wizard of Oz.* New York, Clarkson Potter, 1973.

Leach, William. *Land of Desire: Merchants, Power, and the Rise of a New American Culture.* New York, Pantheon Books, 1993.

Riley, Michael O. *Oz and Beyond: The Fantasy World of L. Frank Baum.* Lawrence, Kansas, University Press of Kansas, 1997.

Bay, Mel (1913-1997)

Founder of Mel Bay Publications, Melbourne E. Bay was the most successful author and publisher of guitar method books in the late twentieth century. Born in Missouri, Bay became a popular self-taught guitarist and banjo player in the region. He established himself as a music teacher in St. Louis, and in 1947 began to write and publish guitar method materials; eventually he added instructions for playing other instruments, and by the 1990s his corporation also produced instructional videos.

Bay's books sold by the millions, and their quality earned Bay many awards and honors. Among others, Bay received the Lifetime Achievement Awards from the American Federation of Musicians and the Guitar Foundation of America, as well as a Certificate of Merit from the St. Louis Music Educators Association. St. Louis also celebrated Mel Bay Day on October 25, 1996. He died on May 14, 1997, at the age of 84.

—David Lonergan

FURTHER READING:

"Melbourne Bay." *American Music Teacher.* Vol. 47, No. 1, August 1997, 6.

"Passages: Melbourne E. Bay." *Clavier.* Vol. 36, No. 6, July 1997, 33.

Bay of Pigs Invasion

President John F. Kennedy's sanctioning of the Bay of Pigs operation had a significant impact on contemporary popular perceptions of his administration. For the majority, Kennedy's actions proved that he was willing to actively confront the perceived "communist threat" in Central and South America. However, his action also disillusioned student radicals who had supported Kennedy during his election campaign and accelerated the politicization of student protest in the United States.

In the early hours of April 17, 1961, a force consisting of 1400 Cuban exiles landed at the Bay of Pigs, Cuba, in an attempt to overthrow the revolutionary government headed by Fidel Castro. From the beginning, this "invasion" was marred by poor planning and poor execution. The force, which had been secretly trained and armed in Guatemala by the United States Central Intelligence Agency (CIA), was too large to engage in effective covert operations, yet too small to realistically challenge Castro in a military confrontation without additional support from the United States. Most significantly, the popular uprising upon which the invasion plan had been predicated did not occur. After three days of fighting, the insurgent force, which was running short of ammunition and other supplies, had been effectively subdued by Castro's forces. In a futile effort to avoid capture, the insurgents dispersed into the Zapata swamp and along the coast. Cuban forces quickly rounded up 1,189 prisoners, while a few escaped to waiting U.S. ships; 114 were killed.

Although the Bay of Pigs operation had initially been intended to be carried out in a manner that would allow America to deny involvement, it was readily apparent that the United States government was largely responsible for the invasion. Months before the Bay of Pigs operation commenced, American newspapers ran stories which revealed the supposedly covert training operations both in Miami and Guatemala. Consequently, when the invasion began, the official cover story that it was a spontaneous insurrection led by defecting Cuban forces was quickly discredited. Revelations concerning the United States' role in the attack served to weaken its

stature in Latin America and significantly undermined its foreign policy position. After the collapse of the operation, a *New York Times* columnist commented that the invasion made the United States look like "fools to our friends, rascals to our enemies, and incompetents to the rest." However, domestic political protest was allayed by President John F. Kennedy who, although he had been in office for less than one hundred days, assumed full responsibility for the fiasco. According to Kennedy biographer Theodore C. Sorensen, Kennedy's decisive action avoided uncontrolled leaks and eliminated the possibility of partisan investigations.

The operation which resulted in the Bay of Pigs disaster had initially been conceived in January 1960 under the Eisenhower Administration. Originally, this operation was envisioned as constituting the covert landing of a small, highly-trained force that would engage in guerrilla activities in order to facilitate a popular uprising. Over the ensuing fifteen months, the CIA systematically increased the scale of the proposed operation. According to both Sorensen and biographer Arthur M. Schlesinger, Kennedy, upon assuming office, had little choice but to approve the continuance of the operation. Its importance had been stressed by former president Dwight D. Eisenhower, it was supported by the Joint Chiefs of Staff, and by influential advisors such as John Foster Dulles. Further, as noted historian John L. Gaddis argued in *Now We Know: Rethinking Cold War History* (1997), Kennedy believed that "underlying historical forces gave Marxism-Leninism the advantage in the 'third world'" and viewed Cuba as a clear example of the threat that Communism posed in Latin America. As a result, Kennedy was predisposed to take action against Castro. Unfortunately, due to inaccurate and ineffective communication between planning and operational personnel, the significant changes that had been instituted within the operation were not sufficiently emphasized to Kennedy. Consequently, according to Sorensen, Kennedy "had in fact approved a plan bearing little resemblance to what he thought he had approved." Leaders of the Cuban exiles were given the impression that they would receive direct military support once they had established a beach head, and an underlying assumption of CIA planning was that the United States would inevitably intervene. However, Kennedy steadfastly refused to sanction overt military involvement.

The impact of the Bay of Pigs invasion on American public opinion was sharply divided. According to Thomas C. Reeves, Kennedy's public support of and sympathy for the Cuban exiles rallied the public in support of their "firm, courageous, self-critical, and compassionate chief executive." A poll conducted in early May indicated sixty-five percent support for Kennedy and his actions. Conversely, the Bay of Pigs invasion also served to spark student protests. Initially, students had been enchanted by Kennedy's vision of a transformed American society and by the idealism embodied by programs such as the Peace Corps. However, students, particularly those within the New Left, were disillusioned by Kennedy's involvement with the invasion. On the day of the landings, 1,000 students held a protest rally at Berkeley, and on April 22, 2,000 students demonstrated in San Francisco's Union Square. This disillusionment spawned a distrust of the Kennedy Administration and undoubtedly accelerated the political divisions that developed within American society during the 1960s.

Internationally, the Bay of Pigs invasion provided Castro with evidence of what he characterized as American imperialism, and this enabled him to consolidate his position within Cuba. Ultimately, the invasion drove Castro toward a closer alliance with the Soviet Union and significantly increased both regional and global political tensions. The failure of the invasion also convinced Soviet leader Nikita Khrushchev that Kennedy was weak and indecisive. This impression undoubtedly contributed to Khrushchev's decision to place nuclear missiles in Cuba and to the confrontation that developed during the Cuban Missile Crisis (1962). However, sympathetic biographers have argued that "failure in Cuba in 1961 contributed to success in Cuba in 1962," because the experience forced Kennedy to break with his military advisors and, consequently, enabled him to avoid a military clash with the Soviet Union.

—Christopher D. O'Shea

FURTHER READING:

Bates, Stephen, and Joshua L. Rosenbloom. *Kennedy and the Bay of Pigs.* Boston, John F. Kennedy School of Government, Harvard University, 1983.

Gaddis, John Lewis. *We Now Know: Rethinking Cold War History.* Oxford, Clarendon Press, 1997.

Higgins, Trumbull. *The Perfect Failure: Kennedy, Eisenhower, and the CIA at the Bay of Pigs.* New York, W.W. Norton, 1987.

Lader, Lawrence. *Power on the Left: American Radical Movements Since 1946.* New York, W.W. Norton, 1979.

Reeves, Thomas C. *A Question of Character: A Life of John F. Kennedy.* Rocklin, California, Prima Publishing, 1992.

Schlesinger, Arthur M. *A Thousand Days: John F. Kennedy in the White House.* Boston, Houghton Mifflin, 1965.

Sorensen, Theodore C. *Kennedy.* New York, Harper & Row, 1965.

Vickers, George R. *The Formation of the New Left: The Early Years.* Lexington, Lexington Books, 1975.

Wyden, Petre. *Bay of Pigs: The Untold Story.* London, Jonathan Cape, 1979.

Baywatch

Though dismissed by its critics with such disparagements as "Body watch" and "Babe watch," David Hasselhoff's *Baywatch* became the most popular television show in the world during the mid-1990s. Notorious for its risque bathing suits, the show depicted the Los Angeles County Beach Patrol as it braved dangerous surf and emotional riptides to save lives and loves. The show ran briefly on NBC during 1989-1990 before being canceled but became, in its new incarnation, one of the few shows in TV history not only to exonerate itself in a post-network afterlife but to actually become a mega-hit.

Baywatch began with David Hasselhoff as Mitch Buchannon, a veteran career lifeguard recently promoted to lieutenant; Parker Stevenson as Craig Pomeroy, a successful lawyer who continued to moonlight as a lifeguard; and a supporting cast of sun-bronzed characters who adopted life at the beach for reasons of their own. In its original incarnation, *Baywatch* finished in seventy-fourth place in the Neilsen ratings among 111 series to air on the three major networks. At the same time, it ranked as the number-one U.S. import in both Germany and Great Britain, where viewers perceived it to be a glimpse of what America was all about in a format that was at once wordless and instantly translatable to any culture in the world—beautiful people in a beautiful environment.

In 1990, after being canceled by the network, *Baywatch* star Hasselhoff and three of the show's other producers recognized its international potential and decided to invest their own money in the show. They cut production costs from $1.3 million per episode to $850,000, and marketed it to independent stations. In syndication, the show generated more than one billion viewers between 1994 and 1996 in more than one hundred countries around the world.

"We wanted to create a dramatic series that allows our lead characters to become involved with interesting and unusual people and situations," said executive producer Michael Berk. "Lifeguards are frequently involved in life and death situations and, as a part of their daily routine, come into contact with thousands of people from diverse walks of life." This format allows the lifeguards to interact with an amazing number of robbers, murderers, international drug runners, runaway teens, and rapists who seemingly stalk L.A.'s beaches between daring rescues, shark attacks, and boat sinkings. All of this is blended with the predictable love stories and plenty of exposed skin. Indeed, the show's opening, depicting the physically perfect male and female lifeguards running on the beach, has become one of the most satirized motifs on television.

Surprisingly, however, the soap-opera-type stories have allowed the characters to grow from episode to episode and have created some interesting dimensions for the show's regulars. Hasselhoff's character, Mitch, comes off a nasty divorce and custody battle for his son and begins to date again. "He's a guy about my age," says Hasselhoff (forty), "divorced, with a kid. With many years as a lifeguard under his belt, he's promoted to lieutenant and must take on a more supervisory role. But, he has mixed emotions. He is no longer one of the guys and must assume the role of an authority figure, while at home, as a newly divorced parent, he has to learn to cope with the responsibilities of a single father."

The other characters on the show have been significantly younger, with the average cast member being in his or her twenties. Each succeeding season has brought new cast members to the series as older characters drifted off, died in accidents, married, and otherwise moved on as the stars who played them became famous enough to move into other acting ventures. Pamela Anderson Lee, the former "Tool Time" girl" on *Home Improvement,* left *Baywatch* after becoming an international sex symbol and garnered a movie contract, only to be replaced by a succession of similarly endowed sun-drenched California blondes.

The reasons for the show's phenomenal success are varied. Many critics have argued that the sex appeal of the lifeguards in their scanty beach attire has been the primary reason for viewers (particularly young males) to tune in. *Baywatch* has, in fact, created its share of sex symbols with Hasselhoff, Lee, and, more recently, Yasmine Bleeth and Carmen Electra achieving international celebrity on tabloid covers and calendars. There is also the appeal of the beach itself and the California lifestyle—a sun-and-surf image that offers an escape from the grim reality of people's daily existence. Some say there is a more fundamental appeal that is as old as television itself: *Baywatch* is a family ensemble no less than *The Waltons, Little House on the Prairie* or *Dr. Quinn, Medicine Woman.* Hasselhoff's Mitch is the father figure for the group of lifeguards, while his female counterpart, Lt. Stephanie Holden (Alexandra Paul), serves as a surrogate mother for the beach people who wander in and out of each

The women of *Baywatch*.

episode (until the Holden character's death during the seventh season). The supporting cast of lifeguards are the quirky and quarreling siblings who ultimately must be rescued from their various escapades by Hasselhoff's character. Then there is Mitch's own son, Hobie, a thirteen-year-old who gets into his own adventures and who is just beginning to get to know his father. The two-part ending of the 1997-98 season featured Mitch's marriage to Neely Capshaw (Gena Lee Nolen).

In an effort to attract the whole family rather than its earlier self-professed teenager demographic, *Baywatch* gradually escalated the level of its story lines to include depictions of social ills, acceptance of aging and death, and a number of ethical and moral dilemmas. "What has happened," said Hasselhoff, "is that while people were making so many jokes about us, we became a real show."

—Steve Hanson

FURTHER READING:

Baber, Brendan, and Eric Spitznagel. *Planet Baywatch*. New York, St. Martin's Griffin, 1996.

Hollywood Reporter Baywatch Salute. January 17, 1995, 99.

McDougal, Dennis. "TV's Guilty Pleasures: *Baywatch*." *TV Guide*. August 13, 1994, 12.

Shapiro, Marc. *Baywatch: The Official Scrapbook*. New York, Boulevard Books, 1996.

Bazooka Joe

Gum manufacturers commonly used gimmicks, like sports trading cards, to help boost sales. Topps Chewing Gum, Inc., which began producing Bazooka bubble gum in 1947, included comics with its small chunk of pink bubble gum. The gum took its name from the unplayable musical instrument, which American comedian Bob Burns made from two gas pipes and a whiskey funnel, called a "bazooka."

The comic, featuring Joe, a blonde kid with an eye patch, and his gang, debuted in 1953. In the crowded chewing gum market of the 1950s, Topps used the comic to distinguish Bazooka from other brands. The jokes produced more groaning than laughter, and included a fortune. Collectors of the comics redeemed them for prizes, such as bracelets, harmonicas, and sunglasses. In the 1990s, Joe's popularity fell, and the strip was modernized in response to market studies in which kids said they wanted characters who were "more hip."

—Daryl Umberger

FURTHER READING:

Wardlaw, Lee. *Bubblemania: A Chewy History of Bubble Gum.* New York, Aladdin, 1997.

The Beach Boys

As long as bleach-blond beach bums ride the waves and lonely geeks fantasize of romance, the Beach Boys will blare from car radios into America's psyche. Emerging from Southern California in the early 1960s, the Beach Boys became the quintessential American teen band, their innocent songs of youthful longing, lust, and liberation coming to define the very essence of white, suburban teenage life. At the same time, they mythologized that life through the sun-kissed prism of Southern California's palm trees, beaches, and hot rods, much like the civic boosters and Hollywood moguls who preceded them. From 1962 to 1966, the Beach Boys joined Phil Spector and Berry Gordy as the most influential shapers of the American Top 40. But like the California myth itself, the Beach Boys' sunny dreams were tempered by an underlying darkness, born of their tempestuous personal and professional lives. That darkness sometimes fueled the group's greatest work. It also produced tragedy for the band's

members, especially resident genius Brian Wilson, and by the 1980s the band collapsed into self-parody.

The nucleus of the Beach Boys was the Wilson family, which lived in a simple bungalow in the Los Angeles suburb of Hawthorne. At home, brothers Brian (1942—), Dennis (1944-1983), and Carl (1946-1998) were introduced to music by their temperamental father, Murry Wilson, whose rare displays of affection were usually accompanied by the purchase of musical instruments, records, or lessons. Although each son adopted his father's love of music, it was the eldest, Brian Wilson, who embraced it with passion. His two earliest childhood memories were central to his musical evolution and future career. As a toddler, Brian remembered requesting George Gershwin's "Rhapsody in Blue" whenever he visited his grandmother's home. He also remembered his father slapping him at the age of three; he blamed the loss of hearing in his right ear in grade school on the incident. Brian was left unable to hear music in stereo for the rest of his life.

As the Wilsons entered high school, they absorbed the music and culture which would later fuel the Beach Boys. In addition to his classical training at school, Brian loved vocal groups (especially the close-harmony style of the Four Freshmen) and the complex ballads of Broadway and Tin Pan Alley. But the Wilsons—even the reclusive Brian—were also immersed in the teenage culture of suburban

The Beach Boys

America: hot rods, go-karts, drive-ins, and, most importantly, rock 'n' roll. They listened to Bill Haley and Elvis Presley and above all Chuck Berry, whom guitarist Carl Wilson idolized. By high school the boys were playing and writing songs together.

In 1961, the group expanded beyond Carl's improving guitar, Brian's accomplished bass, and Dennis' primitive drums. The Wilsons' cousin Mike Love (1941—), a star high school athlete with an excellent voice, joined on vocals. Brian's friend from school, Al Jardine (1942—), rounded out the band after aborting a folk-singing career. With that, America's most famous suburban garage band was born, at first hardly able to play but hungry for the money and fame that might follow a hit record.

Their sound came first, mixing the guitar of Chuck Berry and backbeat of rhythm and blues with Brian's beloved vocal harmonies. But they knew they lacked an angle, some theme to define the band's image. They found that angle one day when Dennis Wilson, sitting on the beach, got the idea to do a song about surfing. By the early 1960s, the surf craze in Southern California had already spawned the "surf music" of artists like Dick Dale and the Del-Tones, based around the crashing guitar sounds intended to mimic the sound of waves. Surf music, however, was just beginning to enter the national consciousness. With prodding, Dennis convinced Brian that there was lyrical and musical potential in the surf scene, and in September of 1961 they recorded "Surfin'" as the Pendeltones, a play on the name of Dale's band and in honor of the Pendleton shirts favored by beach bums. By December, the single had climbed the national charts, and the band renamed itself the Beach Boys.

In 1962 Capitol Records signed them, and over the next three years the Beach Boys became a hit machine, churning out nine Top 40 albums and 15 Top 40 singles, ten of which entered the top ten. In songs like "Surfin' U.S.A.," "Little Deuce Coupe," and "Fun, Fun, Fun" the group turned Southern California's youthful subculture into a teenage fantasy for the rest of America and the world. A baby boom generation hitting adolescence found exuberant symbols of their cultural independence from adults in the band's hot rods and surfboards. The songs, however, articulated a tempered rebellion in acts like driving too fast or staying out too late, while avoiding the stronger sexual and racial suggestiveness of predecessors like Presley or successors like the Rolling Stones. In their all-American slacks and short-sleeve striped shirts, the Beach Boys were equally welcome in teen hangouts and suburban America's living rooms.

By 1963, the Beach Boys emerged as international stars and established their place in America's cultural life. But tensions between the band's chief songwriter, Brian Wilson, and the band's fan-base emerged just as quickly. Wilson was uninterested in his audience, driven instead to compete obsessively for pop preeminence against his competitors, especially Phil Spector and later the Beatles. To make matters worse, Wilson was a shy introvert, more interested in songwriting and record production than the limelight and the stage. He retreated into the studio, abandoning the proven style of his earliest hits for Spector's wall-of-sound sophistication on songs like "Don't Worry Baby" and "I Get Around." At the same time, Wilson's personal melancholia increasingly entered his songwriting, most notably on the monumental ballad "In My Room." Together, these changes altered the Beach Boys' public persona. "I Get Around" was a number one single in 1964, but "Don't Worry Baby," arguably the most creative song Wilson had yet written, stalled ominously at number 24. And "In My Room," while unquestionably about teenagers, deserted innocent fun for painful longing. It also topped out at number 23. The Beach Boys were growing up, and

so was their audience. Unlike Wilson, however, the post-teen boomers already longed nostalgically for the past and struggled to engage the band's changes.

The audience was also turning elsewhere. The emergence of the Beatles in 1964 shook the foundations of the Beach Boys camp. Suddenly supplanted at the top of the pop charts, the rest of the band pushed Brian Wilson toward more recognizably "Beach Boys" songs, which he wisely rebuffed considering rock 'n' roll's rapid evolution during the mid-1960s. In addition, the entire band began living out the adolescent fantasies they had heretofore only sung about. Only now, as rich young adults, those fantasies meshed with the emerging counter-culture, mysticism, and heavy drug use of the late-1960s Southern Californian music scene. With the rest of the band tuning out, Wilson's Beatles obsession and drug abuse accelerated, Beach Boys albums grew more experimental, and Wilson suffered a nervous breakdown.

For two years after Wilson's breakdown, the Beach Boys' music miraculously remained as strong as ever. "Help Me, Rhonda" and "California Girls" (both 1965) were smash hits, and the live album *The Beach Boys Party!* proved the band retained some of its boyish charm. But no Beach Boys fan—or even the Beach Boys themselves—could have been prepared for Brian Wilson's unveiling of *Pet Sounds* (1966), a tremendous album with a legacy that far outshines its initial success. Completed by Brian Wilson and lyricist Tony Asher, with only vocal help from the other Beach Boys, *Pet Sounds* was Brian Wilson's most ambitious work, a dispiriting album about a young man facing adulthood and the pain of failed relationships. It also reflected the transformation of Southern California's youth culture from innocence to introspection—and excess—as the baby boomers got older. Moreover, *Pet Sounds'* lush pastiche pushed the boundaries of rock so far that no less than Paul McCartney hailed it as his favorite album ever and claimed it inspired the Beatles to produce *Sgt. Pepper's Lonely Hearts Club Band*. In subsequent decades, some critics would hail *Pet Sounds* as the greatest rock album ever made, and it cemented the Beach Boys' place in the pantheon of popular music. At the time, however, critics in the United States had already dismissed the band, and their fans, accustomed to beach-party ditties, failed to understand the album. Although two singles—"Sloop John B" and "Wouldn't It Be Nice"— entered the top ten, sales of the album fell below expectations.

Disappointed and increasingly disoriented, Wilson was determined to top himself again, and set to work on what would become the most famous still-born in rock history, *Smile* (1967). Intended to supplant *Pet Sounds* in grandeur, the *Smile* sessions instead collapsed as Wilson, fried on LSD, delusional, and abandoned by the rest of the group, was unable to finish the album. Fragments emerged over the years, on other albums and bootlegs, that suggested the germ of a great album. All that survived in completed form at the time, however, was one single, the brilliant number one hit "Good Vibrations," which *Smile* engineer Chuck Britz said took three months to produce and "was [Brian Wilson's] whole life's performance in one track."

If Britz was right then Wilson's timing could not have been better, for short on the heels of the failed *Smile* sessions came the release of *Sgt. Pepper*. As if he knew that his time had passed, Wilson, like his idol Spector, withdrew except for occasional Beach Boys collaborations, lost in a world of bad drugs and worse friends until the 1990s.

The Beach Boys carried on, occasionally producing decent albums like *Wild Honey* (1967), at least one more classic song,

Brian's 1971 "'Til I Die," but their days as a cultural and commercial powerhouse were behind them. In 1974, with the release of the greatest-hits package *Endless Summer*, the band finally succumbed to the wishes of its fans (and at least some of its members), who preferred celebrating their mythic land of teenage innocence the Beach Boys had so fabulously fabricated in their early years. The album shot to number one, spending 155 weeks on *Billboard's* Hot 100, and the quintessential American teen band now remade itself as the quintessential American oldies act. They traveled the country well into the 1990s with beach party-styled concerts, performing their standards thousands of times. In 1983, Interior Secretary James Watt denied them permission to play their annual July 4 concert in Washington, D.C. to maintain a more "family-oriented" show. Miraculously, they scored one more number one single with "Kokomo," a kitschy 1988 track intended to play on their nostalgic image. Along the way, they endured countless drug addictions, staff changes, inter-group lawsuits over song credits, and two deaths— Dennis Wilson in a 1981 drowning and Carl Wilson of cancer in 1998.

That some of the Beach Boys' early music perhaps sounds ordinary 30 years later owes something to the group's descent into self-parody. But it also reflects the degree to which their music infiltrated American culture. No artists better articulated California's mythic allure or adolescence's tortured energy. And when that allure and energy was lost, their music paved the road for the journeys later musicians—from the Doors to the Eagles and Hole—would take into the dark side of the Californian, and American, dream.

—Alexander Shashko

FURTHER READING:

Hoskyns, Barney. *Waiting for the Sun: Strange Days, Weird Scenes, and the Sound of Los Angeles.* New York, St. Martin's Press, 1996.

White, Timothy. *The Nearest Faraway Place: Brian Wilson, the Beach Boys, and the Southern California Experience.* New York, Henry Holt and Company, Inc., 1994.

Wilson, Brian, with Todd Gold. *Wouldn't It Be Nice: My Own Story.* New York, Bloomsbury Press, 1986.

Beach, Rex (1877-1949)

"Big hairy stories about big hairy men" is how one critic described the work of one of the early twentieth century's most prolific and successful popular writers, Rex Beach. He developed a devoted following among the reading public which remained loyal to his works into the mid-1930s. In addition, he led the way for later authors to reap greater profits by exploiting other media outlets for their works, thus defining what the twentieth-century author of popular literature became by mid-century—an independent entrepreneur.

Rex Ellingwood Beach was born in Atwater, Michigan, in 1877. At age twelve his family packed their belongings and sailed by raft down the Mississippi and across the Gulf of Mexico to Florida, where they took up residence on homesteaded land. Beach attended Rollins College at Winter Park but left shortly before graduation to move to Chicago. He read law in an older brother's law office and took one or

two law courses, but he never finished a law program. Afflicted with gold fever after reading of the vast gold discoveries in the far north, Beach headed for Alaska in 1897 to seek his fortune. He found little gold. Instead he discovered wealth of a different kind, a mine of stories and colorful characters and situations that he developed into best selling popular literature.

In the summer of 1900, Beach witnessed a bold attempt by North Dakota political boss Alexander McKenzie to steal gold from the placer mines at Nome, Alaska. When the scheme failed, McKenzie and his cronies were arrested. Beach transformed the events into a series of muckraking articles, "The Looting of Alaska," for *Appleton's Century* magazine in 1905. From this series came his first novel, *The Spoilers*. He added some fictional characters to the events at Nome, and the resulting novel, published in 1905, made the best-seller list in 1906. Later that year he transformed the novel into a play, which ran for two-week runs in Chicago and New York before it was sent out on the road for several years. In 1914 Beach contracted with the Selig Corporation to release the film version of *The Spoilers* for 25 percent of the gross profits, a unique arrangement for its time. On four subsequent occasions, in 1923, 1930, 1942, and 1955, Beach or his estate leased the rights to *The Spoilers* to film companies for the same financial arrangement. Beach published a total of twenty novels and seventy short stories and novelettes. He authorized thirty-two film adaptations of his work. In addition to *The Spoilers, The Barrier* was filmed three times; five of his novels were filmed twice; and fourteen of his novels and stories were each filmed once.

Writing in the school of realism, his novels and stories were works of romantic, frontier adventure aimed at young men. Plots involved ordinary hard-working citizens forced to confront the forces of nature and corruption. They overcame their adversaries by means of violence, loyalty to the cause and to each other, and heroic action. Rarely did these citizens rely on government agencies for assistance, in keeping with Beach's philosophy of rugged individualism.

From 1911 to 1918 Beach was president of the Author's League. In this capacity he constantly exhorted authors to put film clauses into their publishing contracts and to transform their writings into drama and screenplays. Most refused, believing that the cinema was a low art form that degraded their artistic endeavors. The only exception was Edna Ferber, who also demanded a percentage of the profits for filming her works. On the occasions that novels and short stories were adapted, the one-time payments that authors received to film their works were small, varying greatly from film company to film company. In frustration, Beach resigned the position in 1918 and concentrated on writing until the mid-1930s.

From his wandering search for gold and stories in Alaska to his unique film clause in his contract with Harper Brothers to his pioneering lease arrangement with film corporations, he established precedents that others would follow years later and that define popular authors after mid-century. He not only had an innate sense of what people would read, but also, ever alert to other potential media markets, he knew what people would pay to see as thrilling entertainment on stage and on film. Above all, Beach had a formidable passion for financial success. He viewed his mind as a creative factory producing a marketable product. Writing involved raw material, production, and sales. The end result was profit.

Not content with his literary and entertainment achievements, Beach used his profits to buy a seven-thousand-acre estate in Florida where he became a successful cattle rancher in the 1930s. He wrote articles about the nutritional value of growing crops in mineral-rich

Rex Beach

soils. He bought an additional two thousand acres at Avon Park and grew gladioli and Easter lilies at substantial profit. In the 1940s he developed and wrote more than forty episodes of an unproduced radio series based on his autobiography, *Personal Exposures.*

Beach sold everything he wrote, except for the radio series and an unfinished novel that he was writing at the time of his death. He and his wife, Edith Greta Crater, divided their time between a New York penthouse and their 250-acre estate in Sebring, Florida. His wife, whom he had met in Alaska and married in 1907, died in 1947 after a lengthy illness. On the morning of December 7, 1949, saddened by his wife's death, nearly blind, and devastated by the pain and other effects of throat cancer, Rex Beach ended his life with a pistol shot to the head. He was seventy-two.

—James R. Belpedio

FURTHER READING:

Beach, Rex. *Personal Exposures.* New York, Harper & Brothers, 1940.

————. *The Spoilers.* New York, Harper & Brothers, 1905.

Belpedio, James R. "Fact, Fiction, Film: Rex Beach and *The Spoilers.*" Ph.D. diss., University of North Dakota, 1995.

Beanie Babies

In 1993 Ty Corporation released Flash the Dolphin, Patti the Platypus, Splash the Orca, Spot the Dog, Legs the Frog, Squealer the Pig, Cubbie the Bear, Chocolate the Moose, and Pinchers the Lobster. These small plush beanbag toys called Beanie Babies retailed for about five dollars. By 1997, there were over 181 varieties of Beanie Babies, and most of the original nine were worth more than $50.

The interest Beanie Babies sparked in so many kids, parents, and collectors stems from their reflection of the consumer aesthetic of the 1990s. Ty Corporation built a cachet for each Beanie Baby by portraying itself as one of the "little guys" in the toy industry. It limited stores to only 36 of each Beanie Baby per month and initially refused to sell to chain or outlet toy stores. Ty Corporation guarded its strategy fiercely, cutting off future supplies to stores that sold the plush animals at a mark-up. The company's efforts kept Beanie Babies affordable to almost all, but increased their aftermarket value. The result of Ty's strategy strengthened Beanie Babies' celebration of the individual. Each baby is assigned a name, a birthday, and an accompanying poem, all found on the small heart-shaped Ty tag, the sign of an authentic Beanie Baby.

Some regard the market frenzy around Beanie Babies as ridiculous, but others see it as a benign introduction to capitalism for many young investors. The babies are portable, easily saved for investment purposes, and offer a chance for friendly competition between collectors. Judging a Beanie Baby's current value can be a hands-on lesson in supply and demand for the young collector. The value of Babies increases when varieties are "retired" or produced in limited numbers; and when custom Beanie Babies are released for sporting events, to commemorate the flags of certain countries, and to immortalize celebrities like Jerry Garcia (see Garcia bear) and Princess Diana (see Princess bear). In addition, Babies with defects or odd materials are highly sought-after. Because it is never clear how many of a new animal will be produced or when they might be retired, hobby collectors and Beanie Baby speculators periodically swarm stores reported to be "connected."

The market demand for Beanie Babies has grown without television advertising. Babies were listed as one of the most sought-after Christmas toys by several stores during the 1990s. Beanie Babies are traded, bought, and sold at hundreds of spots on the Internet, and those new to the hobby can buy guidebooks like the *1998 Beanie Baby Handbook,* which lists probable prices for the year 2008.

The *Handbook* speculates that Quacker, a yellow duck with no wings, may be worth as much as $6,000 by that time.

Beanie Babies have worked their way into the mainstream consciousness through a regular media diet of Beanie Baby hysteria and hoax stories. Many local news programs would feature a story about how to differentiate between a real Beanie Baby and a fake. By the end of the decade, almost every American would see the sign, "Beanie Babies Here!" appear in the window of a local card or flower shop. Established firmly in the same collectible tradition as Hot Wheels cars and Cabbage Patch dolls, Beanie Babies draw children into the world of capitalist competition, investment, and financial risk. Their simple, attainable nature has gained them a permanent place in the pantheon of American toys.

—Colby Vargas

FURTHER READING:

Fox, Les and Sue. *The Beanie Baby Handbook.* New York, Scholastic Press, 1998.

A McDonald's employee displays some of the Beanie Babies the restaurant sold in 1998.

Phillips, Beck, et al. *Beanie Mania: A Comprehensive Collector's Guide.* Binghamton, New York, Dinomates, 1997.

The Beastie Boys

In 1986 the Beastie Boys took the popular music world by storm with their debut album *License To Ill* and the single "Fight For Your Right (To Party)." The album was co-produced with fledgling hip-hop label Def Jam producer Rick Rubin. *License to Ill* became the fastest selling debut album in Columbia Records' history, going platinum within two months, and becoming the first rap album to reach number one on the charts.

Critics derided the Beastie Boys as one-hit wonder material, and as New York "white-boy rappers" who were leeching off African American street music forms known as "rap" and hip-hop, both of which were in their early stages of development. *Licensed To Ill* also relied heavily on a new technique called "sampling." Sampling is the act of lifting all or part of the music from another artist's song. This sample is then used to record a new song with the same music, often without credit or payment. Sampling, as it was originally practiced, was condemned as stealing by most critics and musicians. The technique was so new in the mid-1980s that there were no rules to regulate such "borrowing." Artist credit and payment terms for use of a sample, however, eventually became the record industry standard.

Michael Diamond ("Mike D"), bassist Adam Yauch ("MCA," also known as Nathanial Hornblower), guitarist John Berry, and drummer Kate Schellenbach formed the first version of The Beastie Boys in New York City in 1981. They were a hardcore punk style band and recorded the EP *Polywog Stew* on a local independent label. Eventually, Berry and Schellenbach quit. In 1983 Adam Horovitz ("Ad-Rock") joined Mike D and MCA to form the core of the Beastie Boys. Other musicians have been added to the onstage mix and toured with the Beastie Boys throughout their career, but it is this trio that is the creative and musical force behind the band.

It was at this time that Rick Rubin, a New York University student and Def Jam's record label entrepreneur, took notice of the Beastie Boys' rap inspired underground single hit "Cookie Puss." Rubin and the Boys then recorded "Rock Hard" for Def Jam in 1985. Later that year the Beastie Boys received enough attention from a

The Beastie Boys, from left: Adam Yauch (MCA), Adam Horovitz (King Ad-Rock), and Mike Diamond (Mike D) at the MTV video awards.

soundtrack cut, "She's On It," to earn an opening spot on Madonna's "Like A Virgin" tour, and then they went on tour with Run D.M.C.

In 1986 *License To Ill* was released, and despite their commercial success, the Beastie Boys were derided as sophomoric, sexist, and just plain dumb. After a long tour to promote *License To Ill,* the Beastie Boys left Def Jam for Capitol Records. The Beastie Boys moved to Los Angeles, took a break, and then began to examine their sound and style. They now had the task of following up their incredible success with a new album. They worked with a new production team known as the Dust Brothers, and in 1989 the Beastie Boys released *Paul's Boutique.* The album was critically acclaimed, but completely different from *License To Ill* and sold under a million copies.

After two more albums with Capitol Records, *Check Your Head* in 1992 and *Some Old Bullshit* in 1994, the Beastie Boys launched their own record label called Grand Royal. Their first Grand Royal release came in 1994. *Ill Communication* spawned the single "Sabotage," and the group toured with the yearly Lollapalooza alternative festival that summer.

Adam Yauch's conversion to Buddhism and his ties to the Dalai Lama then prompted the Beastie Boys to organize the Tibetan Freedom Festival in the summer of 1996. Popular artists continue to donate their performances in order to raise money for the Miarepa Fund, a charity that supports "universal compassion through music" and has been active in the fight for Tibetan independence.

In 1998 the Beastie Boys released *Hello Nasty.* In the midst of personal business and charity efforts, the Beastie Boys have continued to push the cutting edge of hip-hop and they have gained a respected place in the alternative music scene of the 1990s.

—Margaret E. Burns

FURTHER READING:

Batey, Angus. *The Beastie Boys.* New York, Music Sales Corporation, 1998.

Beat Generation

The Beat Generation, or "Beats," is a term used to describe the vanguard of a movement that swept through American culture after World War II as a counterweight to the suburban conformity and organization-man model that dominated the period, especially during the Eisenhower years (1953-1961), when Cold War tension was adding a unparalleled uptightness to American life. The term "Beat Generation" was apparently coined by Jack Kerouac, whose 1957 picaresque novel *On the Road* is considered a kind of manifesto for the movement. In 1952, John Clellon Holmes wrote in the *New York Times Magazine:* "It was John Kerouac . . . who several years ago . . . said 'You know, this is really a beat generation . . . More than the feeling of weariness, it implies the feeling of having been used, of being raw.'" Holmes used the term in his 1952 novel *Go,* with obvious references to New York's bohemian scene. The claim, advanced in some circles, that Kerouac intended "beat" to be related to "beatific" or "beatitude" is now considered spurious by etymologists, though *Beatitude* was the name of a San Francisco magazine published by poet Allen Ginsberg and others whose folding

in 1960 is regarded as the final chapter in that city's Beat movement (generally known as the San Francisco Renaissance).

Kerouac penned a dictionary definition of his own that characterized Beats as espousing "mystical detachment and relaxation of social and sexual tensions," terms that clearly include those at the literary epicenter of the Beat movement, such as Allen Ginsberg, Gregory Corso, John Clellon Holmes, William Burroughs, Neal Cassady, and Herbert Huncke, the latter an alienated denizen of Times Square who served as an important guide to the nascent movement. Each of these figures embodied creative brilliance with various combinations of psychotic episodes, unconventional sexuality, or antisocial traits. Later additions included Lawrence Ferlinghetti, Diane di Prima, and many others. They, along with the writers who were drawn to the experimental Black Mountain College in North Carolina—or, like the expatriate Burroughs, to drug-soaked residency in Tangiers—carried forward an essentially Blakean and Whitmanian vision that welcomed spontaneity, surrealism, and a certain degree of decadence in poetic expression and personal behavior. In the 1950s, this put them in opposition to the prevailing currents of literary modernism on the model of T. S. Eliot, Marianne Moore, and the middlebrow poetry of Robert Frost and Carl Sandburg. Poetry, like Ginsberg's "Howl" or Corso's Gasoline series, was the favored genre of expression and the "3-Ms"—marijuana, morphine, and mescaline—were the drugs of choice.

William Carlos Williams enthusiastically took on the role of unofficial mentor to the East-Coast Beat poets after meeting Allen Ginsberg, and Kenneth Rexroth has been described as the "godfather of the Beats" for acting as catalyst to the famous reading at the Six Gallery in San Francisco, where on October 13, 1955, Ginsberg offered his first highly dramatic performance-recital of "Howl." Nearby was Lawrence Ferlinghetti's City Lights Bookstore, which served as both shrine and paperback publisher for the literature of the Beat movement through its familiar black-and-white "Pocket Poet" series. Following the reading, Lawrence Ferlinghetti approached Ginsberg and convinced him to publish a chapbook of "Howl" through City Lights Press in San Francisco. In 1957, *Howl and Other Poems* was seized by customs officials, and Ferlinghetti was tried on charges of obscenity. The trial brought great notoriety and worldwide recognition to the message of Beat poetry, and the book's sales skyrocketed after the charges were dropped.

In general terms, the Beat poets were leftist in political orientation and committed to the preservation of the planet and the human species. Their literature speaks out against injustice, apathy, consumerism, and war. Despite such generalizations, however, at an individual level the poets are very difficult to classify. A highly diverse group, their political and spiritual views varied to extremes: Jack Kerouac and Gregory Corso, for example, supported the war in Vietnam; Allen Ginsberg was a Jewish radical and anarchist; and Philip Whalen was ordained a Zen priest. The difficulty of pinning down the essence of the Beat poets is part of their allure. The Beats earned their defiant image in part through the controversial themes in their work, which included celebration of the erotic, sexual freedom, exploration of Eastern thought, and the use of psychedelic substances. Fred McDarrah's *Time* magazine article offers evidence of how they were unkindly characterized in mainstream media: "The bearded, sandaled beat likes to be with his own kind, to riffle through his quarterlies, write craggy poetry, paint crusty pictures and pursue his never ending quest for the ultimate in sex and protest." Such condescending judgments only served to fuel the fascination with the Beat image among younger people.

Though the most well-known of the Beat poets are white males, the movement was not exclusively so. In contrast with many other literary movements, the Beats were tolerant of diversity and counted many women and poets of color among their ranks. Such poets as Ted Joans, Amiri Baraka (Leroi Jones), and Bob Kaufman were recognized by their peers for the importance of their work. The women of the Beat Generation, including Diane di Prima, Joanne Kyger, Anne Waldman, and many others, were as present if not as visible as the men. As Brenda Knight remarked, "the women of the Beat Generation, with rare exception, escaped the eye of the camera; they stayed underground, writing. They were instrumental in the literary legacy of the Beat Generation, however, and continue to be some of its most prolific writers."

Though many readers have been attracted to the work of the Beats by their cultural image, Anne Waldman contends that their durability stems from their varied and kaleidoscopic use of language. Beat poets abandoned traditional forms, syntax, and vocabulary in order to incorporate new rhythms, hip streetwise slang, and inventive imagery into their work. In her introduction to *The Beat Book,* Waldman describes this style as "candid American speech rhythms, jazz rhythms, boxcar rhythms, industrial rhythms, rhapsody, skillful cut-up juxtapositions, and an expansiveness that mirrors the primordial chaos. . . . This is writing that thumbs its nose at self-serving complacency." Though their style constituted a break from traditional forms, the Beats always acknowledged the contributions of their precursors. Poets of the early twentieth century such as William Carlos Williams and the imagists H.D. and Ezra Pound paved the way for them by loosening the constraints around poetic language.

When Kerouac and Holmes published articles in the 1950s using the term "Beat generation" to describe their cultural milieu, it was picked up by the mainstream media and solidified in popular culture. "Beat" in popular parlance meant being broke, exhausted, having no place to sleep, being streetwise, being hip. At a deeper level, as John Clellon Holmes wrote in his 1952 article, "beat . . . involves a sort of nakedness of mind, and, ultimately, of soul; a feeling of being reduced to the bedrock of consciousness." With increased usage of the term in the media, "Beat" came to signify the literary and political expression of the artists of the 1940s and 1950s.

The term "beatnik" has thus been rather generously applied to describe any devotee of the 1950s angst-ridden countercultural lifestyle, ranging from serious Beat intellectuals like Jack Kerouac, William Burroughs, and Allen Ginsberg to the more "cool cat" bongo-drumming pot-smoking denizens of coffee houses—males in beards and females in leotards—who "dug it" in such far flung bohemian outposts as New York's Greenwich Village and Venice, California. Strictly speaking, "beatnik" was a term invented by the popular press only toward the end of the decade, after the launch of the Russian Sputnik satellite in the fall of 1957 spawned a host of "-nik" words in popular lingo on the model of already existing Yiddish slang words like nudnik. Herb Caen, a columnist for the *San Francisco Chronicle,* coined the term "beatnik" in an article he wrote for the paper on April 2, 1958, though the Oxford English Dictionary records the first use of the word in a *Daily Express* article that July 23, describing San Francisco as "the home and the haunt of America's Beat generation . . . the Beatniks—or new barbarians."

Whatever its origins, it is clear that during 1958, the word "beatnik" suddenly began appearing in magazines and newspapers around the world as a catchall phrase to cover most forms of urban, intellectual eccentrics, sometimes used in tandem with the dismissive

"sicknik." It is also clear that few average Americans came into contact with self-avowing beatniks except by reading about them under the "Manners and Morals" heading in *Time* magazine or, more likely, through the rather stereotypical character of Maynard G. Krebs, who appeared on the CBS series *The Many Loves of Dobie Gillis* from 1959 to 1963. Krebs was described by Charles Panati in his 1991 book *Panati's Parade of Fads, Follies, and Manias* as a figure who "dressed shabbily, shunned work, and prefaced his every remark with the word like. " A decade earlier, however, a poetry-spouting proto-beatnik character named Waldo Benny had appeared regularly on *The Life of Riley* television sitcom, though he was never named as such.

Arguably the most definitive study of beatniks and the Beat Movement is Steven Watson's 1995 book *The Birth of the Beat Generation: Visionaries, Rebels, and Hipsters,* in which he describes the Beats as exemplifying "a pivotal paradigm in twentieth-century American literature, finding the highest spirituality among the marginal and the dispossessed, establishing the links between art and pathology, and seeking truth in visions, dreams, and other nonrational states." Watson and other cultural historians see the Beats as cultural antecedents to later countercultural groups that included Ken Kesey's Merry Pranksters and hippies in the 1960s and punks in the 1970s. Reflecting on his own earlier participation in the Beat Movement, Robert Creeley wrote in the afterword of the 1998 paperback version of Watson's book that being Beat was "a way of thinking the world, of opening into it, and it finally melds with all that cares about life, no matter it will seem at times to be bent on its own destruction," and closed with the lines by Walt Whitman used as the motto for "Howl": "Unscrew the locks from the doors!/Unscrew the doors themselves from their jambs!"

—Edward Moran and Caitlin L. Gannon

Further Reading:

Bartlett, Lee. *The Beats: Essays in Criticism.* Jefferson, N.C., London, McFarland, 1981.

Cassaday, Neal. *The First Third and Other Writings.* San Francisco, City Light Books, 1971, 1981.

Foster, Edward Halsey. *Understanding the Beats.* Columbia, S.C. University of South Carolina Press, 1992.

Ginsberg, Allen. *Howl and Other Poems.* San Francisco, City Light Books, 1956.

Huncke, Herbert. *Guilty of Everything.* New York, Paragon House, 1990.

Kerouac, Jack. *On the Road.* New York, Viking, 1957.

———. *Selected Letters, 1940-1956.* Edited by Ann Charters. New York, Viking, 1955.

Kherdian, David, editor. *Beat Voices: An Anthology of Beat Poetry.* New York, Henry Holt and Company, 1995.

Knight, Brenda. *Women of the Beat Generation: The Writers, Artists, and Muses at the Heart of a Revolution.* Berkeley, California, Conari Press, 1996.

Panati, Charles. *Panati's Parade of Fads, Follies, and Manias.* New York, HarperCollins, 1992.

Watson, Steven. *The Birth of the Beat Generation: Visionaries, Rebels, and Hipsters.* New York, Pantheon, 1995.

The Beatles

Emerging out of the Liverpool, England, rock scene of the 1950s, the Beatles became the most successful and best known band of the twentieth century. In 1956, a Liverpool local named John Lennon formed the Quarrymen. At one of their first performances, John met another guitarist, Paul McCartney. The two hit it off immediately: Paul was impressed by John's energetic performance, and John was impressed that Paul knew how to tune a guitar, knew more than three chords, and could memorize lyrics. John and Paul developed a close friendship based on their enthusiasm for rock'n'roll, their ambition to go ''to the toppermost of the poppermost,'' and a creative rivalry which drove them to constant improvement and experimentation. The pair soon recruited Paul's friend George Harrison to play lead guitar and nabbed a friend of John's, Stu Sutcliffe, to play the bass (though he did not know how). The Quarrymen, eventually renamed the Beatles, developed a local reputation for their rousing, exuberant performances and the appeal of their vocals. John and Paul were both excellent singers; Paul had a phenomenal range and versatility, while John had an uncanny ability to convey emotion through his voice. The sweetness and clarity of Paul's voice was ideal for tender love songs, while John specialized in larynx-wrenching rockers like ''Twist and Shout.'' Their voices complemented each other perfectly, both in unison and in harmony, and each enriched his own style by imitating the other. The inexplicable alchemy of their voices is one of the most appealing features of the Beatles' music.

In 1960 the band members recruited drummer Pete Best for a four-month engagement in Hamburg, Germany, where they perfected their stage act. In 1961, Sutcliffe quit the band, and Paul took up the bass, eager to distinguish himself from the other two guitarists. The Beatles procured a manager, Brian Epstein, who shared their conviction that they would become ''bigger than Elvis.'' After many attempts to get a recording contract, they secured an audition with producer George Martin in July, 1962. Martin, who liked their performance and was charmed by their humor and group chemistry, offered the Beatles a contract, but requested that they abandon Pete Best for studio work, whom he found musically unsuitable to the group chemistry. The Beatles gladly consented, and recruited Ringo Starr, whom they had befriended in Hamburg. Their first single—''Love Me Do'' (released October, 1962)—reached number 17 on the British charts. Their next single, ''Please Please Me'' (January, 1963), hit number one. Delighted with their success, they recorded their first album, *Please Please Me* (March, 1963), and it too reached the top of the charts.

In those days, rock albums were made to cash in on the success of a hit single, and were padded with filler material, usually covers of

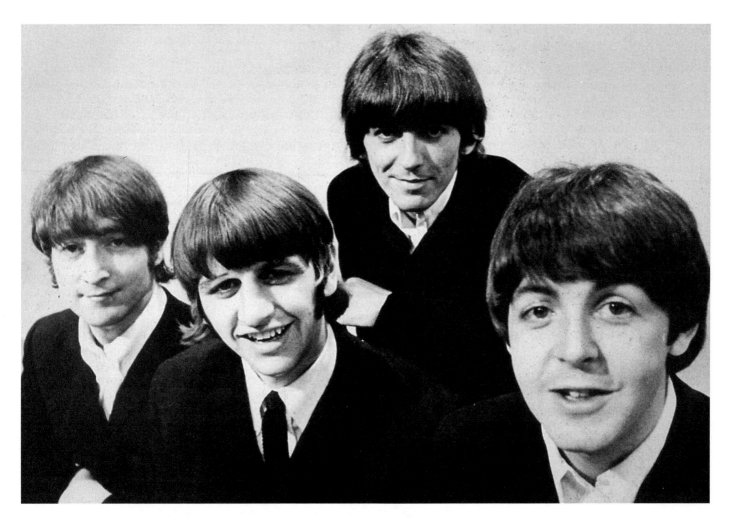

The Beatles, from left: John Lennon, Ringo Starr, George Harrison, and Paul McCartney.

other people's songs. If the artists had any more decent material, it was saved for the next single. However, the Beatles included eight Lennon-McCartney originals, along with six cover songs from their stage repertoire on their debut album. This generosity marked the beginning of the album as the primary forum of rock music, displacing the single, and setting a new standard of quality and originality. *Please Please Me* may sound less impressive today, but it was far superior to the average rock album of 1963. The opening track, ''I Saw Her Standing There,'' was a revelation, a rousing, energetic rocker teeming with hormonal energy. (Released in America as *Introducing the Beatles,* the album didn't sell well.)

Their third single, ''From Me To You'' (April, 1963), also hit number one in England, but it was their fourth, ''She Loves You'' (August, 1963), which brought ''Beatlemania''—the name given to the wild form of excitement which the Beatles elicited from their fans—to a fever pitch around the world. Most of the Beatles' lyrics during this period were inane—the ''yeah yeah yeah'' of ''She Loves You'' being perhaps the silliest—but when delivered with the Beatles' delirious enthusiasm, they worked. Real Beatlemania seems to have begun in late 1963 (the term was coined in a London paper's concert review in October). Their second album, *With the Beatles* (November, 1963), was similar to the first, with six cover songs and eight originals. The American release of ''She Loves You'' in January 1964 ignited Beatlemania there, and the group's first appearance on the *Ed Sullivan Show* on February 9, 1964, was viewed by an estimated 73 million people.

The phenomenon of Beatlemania wasn't just a matter of screaming girls; the madness took many forms. A music critic for the *London Times* declared the Beatles ''the greatest composers since Beethoven,'' and another detected ''Aeolian cadences'' in ''Not a Second Time,'' though none of the Beatles knew what these were. Beatlemania often seemed divorced from the music itself: everything from dolls to dinner trays bore the likeness of the Fab Four, who had by now become the most recognized faces in the world. Grown businessmen would wear Beatlesque ''moptop'' wigs to work on Wall Street. Soon the franchise led to film with *A Hard Day's Night,* a comedy which spotlighted the Beatles' charm and humor as much as their music. The soundtrack—released in July, 1964—was the best album of the Beatles' early phase. Side one contained the songs from the movie, and side two provided six more hits. It was their first album of all original material, an unheard of accomplishment in rock music. Unfortunately, Capitol Records ripped off American fans by including only the songs from the movie on their version of the soundtrack, and filled the rest of the album with instrumental versions of those same songs. The Beatles' popularity was so great at this point that American fans were willing to pay full price for albums that barely lasted a half hour. The first seven British albums were diluted into ten American albums by offering ten songs each instead of the usual thirteen or fourteen. (The situation was not rectified until the advent of the CD, when the British versions were finally released in America.)

The group's fourth album, *Beatles For Sale* (December, 1964), reverted to the earlier formula of originals songs mixed with covers. It was the weakest album of their career to date, but was still better than most pop albums of 1964, and hit number one. The album is important for John's improved lyrical efforts, beginning what he later called his ''Dylan period.'' The Beatles had met Bob Dylan earlier that year, and he had introduced them to marijuana. John was impressed by Dylan's lyrics and decided to improve his own. The first tentative effort was the introspective ''I'm a Loser.'' *Help!* (August 1965)— the soundtrack for their second movie—introduced the folkish ''You've

Got to Hide Your Love Away'' and Paul's acoustic ''I've Just Seen a Face.'' *Help!* was also important for its expanded instrumentation, including flute and electric piano.

As the Beatles grew as composers, they became more receptive to producer Martin's sophistication. Martin had studied music theory, composition, and orchestration, and encouraged the Beatles to ''think symphonically.'' A breakthrough in their collaboration with Martin came with ''Yesterday.'' Paul had written it two years before, but had held it back since the song was incongruous with the band's sound and image. By 1965, the Beatles and the world were ready, and Paul's lovely guitar/vocal composition, graced with Martin's string arrangement, dazzled both Beatlemaniacs and their parents with its beauty and sophistication, and became one of the most popular songs in the world.

Their craftsmanship and experimentation reached new heights on *Rubber Soul,* one of their greatest albums. They returned to the all-original format of *A Hard Day's Night* (henceforth all of their albums featured entirely original material, with the exception of *Let It Be,* which included the sailor's ditty, ''Maggie Mae''). John dabbled in social commentary with ''Nowhere Man,'' a critique of conformity reminiscent of Dylan's ''Ballad of a Thin Man.'' But John's song avoided Dylanesque superciliousness through his empathy with the character. John began to master understatement and poetic suggestion in the enigmatic ''Norwegian Wood.'' This was also the first song to feature George's sitar. George had discovered the sitar while filming *Help!* and had been turned on to Indian music by the Byrds. The Byrds contributed to the artistry of *Rubber Soul* by providing the Beatles with serious competition on their own debut album earlier that year. Hailed as the American Beatles, the Byrds were the only American band who attained a comparable level of craftsmanship and commercial appeal without simply imitating the Beatles. Before then, the Beatles' only serious competitors were the Rolling Stones. Soon competitors would rise all around the Beatles like rivals to the throne. But the Beatles kept ahead, constantly growing and expanding, experimenting with fuzz bass, harmonium, and various recording effects. The most impressive thing about *Rubber Soul* was that such innovation and sophistication were achieved without any loss of the exuberance and inspiration that electrified their earlier albums. It was an impressive union of pop enthusiasm and artistic perfection. Few would have guessed that the Beatles could surpass such a triumph— but they did.

Their next album, *Revolver* (August, 1966), is widely regarded as the Beatles' masterpiece, and some consider it the greatest album ever made, featuring fourteen flawless compositions. George's ''Taxman'' was the hardest rock song on the album, featuring a blistering, eastern-sounding guitar solo reminiscent of the Yardbirds' ''Heart Full of Soul'' and the Byrds' ''Eight Miles High.'' But George's masterpiece was ''Love You To.'' He had previously used the sitar to add an exotic coloring to songs, but here he built the entire composition around the sitar, and expressed his growing immersion in Eastern spirituality. John was even spacier in the acid-drenched ''She Said She Said'' and ''Tomorrow Never Knows,'' full of backwards-recorded guitar, tape loops, and countless studio effects to enhance the mind-boggling lyrics. John, George, and Ringo had experimented with LSD by this time, and John and George were tripping regularly and importing their visions into their music. (Paul did not sample LSD until February 1967). Paul's experiments were more conventional, but equally rewarding. He followed up the achievement of ''Yesterday'' with the beautiful ''Eleanor Rigby.'' The poignant lyrics marked the beginning of Paul's knack for creating vivid character portraits in a few deft verses. ''Here, There, and Everywhere'' was another beauty, containing the sweetest vocal of Paul's career, and the bright, bouncing melody of ''Good Day Sunshine'' showed Paul's increasing sophistication on the bass. *Revolver* set a new standard in rock music, and became the masterpiece against which all subsequent albums were measured.

The achievement of *Revolver* was due partially to the Beatles' decision to stop performing concerts after the current tour, which would free their music from the restrictions of live performability. They played their last concert on August 29, 1966, without playing any songs from the new album. Exhausted, they withdrew from public life, took a brief break, then began work on a new album. The silence between *Revolver* and *Sgt. Pepper's Lonely Hearts Club Band* lasted ten months—the longest interval between albums thus far, but ended with a stunning single, ''Strawberry Fields Forever''/''Penny Lane,'' which revealed the growing individuality of the composers' styles. John was visionary, introspective, and cryptic in ''Strawberry Fields Forever;'' while Paul was sentimental, suburban, and witty in ''Penny Lane.'' John was abstract, questioning his role in the human riddle; Paul was concrete, using odd little details to bring his characters to life. The two songs complemented each other perfectly, and hinted at the variegated brilliance of the album to come.

Sergeant Pepper's Lonely Heart's Club Band (June, 1967) has been hailed as the quintessential album of the sixties, and especially of the famous Summer of Love of 1967. It was the most esoteric and ambitious work ever attempted. To enumerate its charms, innovations, and influence would fill volumes, but special mention must be made of ''A Day in the Life,'' one of the last great Lennon-McCartney collaborations, and one of the most hauntingly beautiful songs of their careers. Weaving together the story of a wealthy heir who dies in a car crash, an estimate of potholes in Blackburn, Lancashire, and a vignette of a young man on his way to work, the song is an ironic montage of the quotidian and the universal, sleeping and waking, complacency and consciousness, establishment and counterculture, and an orgasmic union of high and low art, all rolled into one five-minute, three-second song.

Although ''A Day in the Life'' is the highlight of a bold, brilliant, stunning album, *Sgt. Pepper* is probably not the Beatles' greatest work, and has not aged as well as *Revolver*. If *Revolver* is a 14-course meal which delights, satisfies, and nourishes, *Sgt. Pepper* is an extravagant dessert for surfeited guests—overrich, decadent, fattening. Lavish and baroque, it did not maintain the energetic, youthful exuberance that shines through the complexities of *Revolver*. Many will agree with Martin's judgment that *Revolver* is the Beatles' best album, while *Sgt. Pepper* is their most significant work. It was also the last truly influential work by the Beatles. Although they continued to evolve and experiment, they would no longer monopolize centerstage, for 1967 saw a trend toward instrumental virtuosity and improvisation led by Cream and Jimi Hendrix.

The Beatles' next project, *Magical Mystery Tour* (December, 1967), coasted along on the plateau established by *Sgt. Pepper*. *Magical Mystery Tour* was a pointless film following the Beatles on a bus trip around England. Paul got the idea from the Merry Pranksters, a counterculture group traveling across America. The film was a flop, and the Beatles' first real failure. The soundtrack featured a mix of good and mediocre songs, but some recent singles gathered onto side two strengthened the album.

In 1968 the Beatles went to India to study meditation with Maharishi Mahesh Yogi, during which they learned of Epstein's death from an overdose of sleeping pills. Eventually disenchanted

with the Maharishi, the Beatles returned with a potpourri of songs. They proposed to release a double album to accommodate the abundance. Martin was unimpressed with the material however, and recommended releasing a potent single album like *Revolver*. But the rivalry among the band members was so intense that all four Beatles favored the double album to get their songs included. The result was one of the Beatles' strangest albums, *The Beatles* (November, 1968). The blank white cover and simple title reflected the minimalist nature of much of the material, which had been composed on acoustic guitars in India. Most of the 30 songs were individual efforts, often sung and played solo. McCartney played every instrument on some of his songs. The bewildering array of styles seemed like a history (or perhaps a parody) of western music.

Yellow Submarine was a cartoon made to fulfill the Beatles' film contract with United Artists (although *Let It Be* would actually fulfill this obligation a year later). The Beatles were not interested in the project, and contributed several older, unused songs to the soundtrack. The cartoon was entertaining, but the album *Yellow Submarine* (January, 1969) is the biggest ripoff of the Beatles' catalog, featuring only four original songs. Side two was padded with Martin's orchestral soundtrack. Still, Lennon's great rock song ''Hey Bulldog'' makes the album a must-have.

These odd albums of the late 1960s marked the beginning of the end of the Beatles. Musically, their individual styles were drifting apart, but the real sources of strife were more mundane. First, they had difficulty in agreeing on a manager to replace Epstein. Secondly, John had become smitten with avant-garde artist Yoko Ono, and insisted on bringing her into the Abbey Road Studios with him. Paul, too, had married and the creative core of the group began to feel the need to have a family life. This caused tension because as a band the Beatles had always been an inviolable unit, forbidding outsiders to intrude upon their creative process. But John had invited Yoko to recording sessions simply because he wanted to be constantly by her side. The tensions mounted so high that Ringo and George each briefly quit the band. These ill-feelings persisted on their next project, another McCartney-driven plan to film the Beatles, this time while at work in the studio. The documentary of their creative process (released the following year as *Let It Be*) was all the more awkward because of the tensions within the band. Martin became fed up with their bickering and quit, and the ''Get Back'' project was indefinitely canned.

Eventually Paul persuaded Martin to return, and the Beatles produced *Abbey Road* (September, 1969), one of their best-selling and all-time favorite albums. They once again aimed to ''get back'' to rock'n'roll, and recovered the enthusiasm and spontaneity of their pre-Pepper period, producing a solid performance that stood up to *Revolver*. George outdid himself with two of the greatest compositions of his career, ''Something'' and ''Here Comes the Sun.'' The main attraction of the album was the suite of interconnected songs on side two, culminating in the Beatles' only released jam session, a raunchy guitar stomp between Paul, George, and John. It was a brilliant ending to a brilliant album. Unfortunately, it was also the end of the Beatles as well, for the band broke up in June, 1970, due to insurmountable conflicts. Producer Phil Spector was summoned to salvage the ''Get Back'' project. He added lavish strings and horns to the patched-together recordings, and it was released as *Let It Be* (May, 1970) along with a film of the same name. Somewhat of an anticlimax after the perfection of *Abbey Road,* and marred by Spector's suffocating production, it was nevertheless a fine collection of songs, made all the more poignant by alternating moods of regret and resignation in Paul's songs, ''Two of Us'' and ''Let It Be.''

Her Majesty the Queen inducted the Beatles as Members of the British Order on October 26, 1965. This was not only the climax of Beatlemania, but a symbolic moment in history, bridging the realms of high and low culture. The other great honor of the Beatles' career was the invitation to appear on the world's first global broadcast, on June 25, 1967. The Beatles wrote ''All You Need Is Love'' for the occasion, and played it live for an estimated 350 million viewers. It is remarkable that they were allowed to represent England for the world when Paul had announced a week earlier that he had taken LSD, the BBC had recently banned radio play of ''A Day in the Life,'' and the whole world was scouring *Sgt. Pepper* for subversive messages. These two honors reveal the Beatles as unifiers, not dividers. One of their greatest achievements was to resonate across boundaries and appeal to multiple generations and classes, to represent the counter-culture while winning the respect of the establishment. Although they started as tough, leatherclad teddy boys, they achieved much more by working within the mainstream, creating rather than tearing down, combining meticulous skill with daring innovation. This was achieved by a blessed union: the reckless irreverence of John Lennon and the diplomacy, dedication, and craftsmanship of Paul McCartney.

—Douglas Cooke

FURTHER READING:

Hertsgaard, Mark. *A Day in the Life: The Music and Artistry of the Beatles.* New York, Delacorte Press, 1995.

MacDonald, Ian. *Revolution in the Head: The Beatles' Records and the Sixties.* New York, Henry Holt, 1994.

Martin, George, and Jeremy Hornsby. *All You Need Is Ears.* London, MacMillan, 1979.

Norman, Philip. *Shout! The Beatles in Their Generation.* New York, Warner Books, 1982.

Robertson, John, with Chris Charlesworth, editor. *The Complete Guide to the Music of the Beatles.* New York, Omnibus Press, 1994.

Warren Beatty

Beatty, Warren (1937—)

One of the most extraordinarily handsome screen actors of his generation, Warren Beatty proved remarkably sparing in exploiting his image. That image has tended to seem contradictory, often puzzling, to commentators and critics, but there is universal agreement that no subsequent disappointments in Beatty's work could obscure his achievement in portraying the impotent, crippled, trigger-happy Clyde Barrow, at once inept, ruthless, and curiously touching, in *Bonnie and Clyde* (1967).

Brilliantly directed and photographed, with meticulous attention paid to historical accuracy, *Bonnie and Clyde* was a watershed in the then thirty-year-old Beatty's career, for it was he who masterminded the entire project, from buying the script to hiring director Arthur Penn and choosing the cast. The superb production values and style of the film which, in its fearless and poetic use of bloodshed, made it both influential and highly controversial, stamped Warren Beatty as a producer of flair and intelligence, and his evident ambitions might account for the discomforting and enigmatic sense of detachment that has robbed several of his performances of conviction.

Born Henry Warren Beaty in Richmond, Virginia, Beatty is the younger brother of dancer and actress Shirley MacLaine. He acted in amateur productions staged by his mother, who was a drama coach, during childhood and later studied at Northwestern University and with Stella Adler. A slow progression via television in New York and a stock company took him to Broadway for the first and last time in William Inge's *A Loss of Roses,* where Beatty was seen by director Elia Kazan. Beatty made his Hollywood debut opposite Natalie Wood in Kazan's *Splendor in the Grass* (1961), a somber, archetypically 1960s examination of teenage sexual angst and confusion, in which the actor gave a suitably moody performance and mesmerized audiences with his brooding good looks.

For the next six years Beatty gave variable (but never bad) performances in a crop of films that ranged from the interesting through the inconsequential to the bad. Interesting were *The Roman Spring of Mrs. Stone* (1961), in which, despite a bizarre attempt at an Italian accent, he smoldered convincingly as the gigolo providing illusory comfort to Vivien Leigh; and Robert Rossen's *Lilith* (1964) with Beatty excellent as a therapist dangerously in love with a mental patient. The inconsequential included *Promise Her Anything* (1966), a romantic comedy set in Greenwich Village and costarring Leslie Caron. His reputation as a Don Juan was already in danger of outstripping his reputation as a star, and when Caron left her husband, the distinguished British theater director Peter Hall, he cited Beatty as co-respondent in the ensuing divorce.

Arthur Penn's *Mickey One* (1965), a pretentious failure, did nothing for Beatty, and neither did the comedy-thriller *Kaleidoscope* the same year. Next came *Bonnie and Clyde* followed by the first of several absences from the screen that punctuated his career over the next thirty-five years. His reappearance as a compulsive gambler in *The Only Game in Town* (1970), a film with no merit, was a severe disappointment and indicated a surprising lack of judgment, redeemed by his mature performance as another kind of gambler in the Old West in Robert Altman's imaginative evocation of frontier town life, *McCabe and Mrs. Miller* (1971). Julie Christie was his costar and his new headline-catching romance. In 1974 Beatty was perfectly cast as the lone investigative journalist at the center of Alan J. Pakula's compelling conspiracy thriller, *The Parallax View,* after which he turned producer again (and cowrote) for *Shampoo* (1975). A mildly satirical tale of a hairdresser who services more than his clients' coiffures, it was a good vehicle for Beatty's dazzling smile and sexual charisma, and it netted a fortune at the box office. After joining Jack Nicholson in *The Fortune*—awful—the same year, Beatty disappeared again.

He returned in 1978 with *Heaven Can Wait,* a surprisingly well-received and profitable remake of *Here Comes Mr. Jordan* (1941) that earned four Oscar nominations. Beatty coproduced, cowrote with Elaine May, and codirected (his first attempt) with Buck Henry, and won the Golden Globe for best actor in a comedy before another three-year absence. This time he came back with *Reds* (1981), the high-profile undertaking that brought him serious international recognition. A sprawling, ambitious epic running more than three-and-a-half hours, *Reds* recounted the political activities of American Marxist John Reed (Beatty) in Manhattan and Moscow, and Reed's love affair with Louise Bryant (Diane Keaton, the star's new off-screen love). The film, in which real-life characters appeared as themselves to bear witness to events, was better in its parts than in its sum, but there was no doubting Beatty's seriousness of purpose as producer, cowriter, director, and star. If his ambition had appeared to overreach itself, he was nonetheless rewarded with both the Golden Globe and Oscar for best director, Oscars for cinematographer Vittorio Storaro and supporting actress Maureen Stapleton, and an impressive number of other honors. He was thenceforth to be regarded as a heavyweight, and his future projects were eagerly anticipated.

These expectations remained unfulfilled for seventeen years, during which Beatty made only four films. The motive for making the $50 million catastrophe *Ishtar* (1987) has remained inexplicable, while *Dick Tracy* (1990), in which he directed himself as the comic-book hero, displayed an undiminished sense of style but failed to ignite. *Bugsy* (1991), about the notorious Bugsy Siegel, was slick and entertaining although both star and film lacked the necessary edge, but Beatty found true love at last with his costar Annette Bening and married her. It could only have been his desire to find a romantic vehicle for both of them that led him to such a failure of judgment as *Love Affair* (1994), a redundant and poor remake of a 1939 classic, already wonderfully remade by its creator, Leo McCarey, as *An Affair to Remember* (1957).

Four years later came *Bulworth* (1998), a striking political satire that reflected his own long-standing personal involvement with politics and a canny sense of commercialism in purveying a liberal message through a welter of bigotry. By then happily settled as a husband and father, Warren Beatty at last demonstrated that the faith of his admirers had not been misplaced.

—Robyn Karney

FURTHER READING:

Malcolm, David. "Warren Beatty." *The Movie Stars Story.* New York, Crescent Books, 1986.

Parker, John. *Warren Beatty: The Last Great Lover of Hollywood.* London, Headline, 1993.

Quirk, Lawrence J. *The Films of Warren Beatty.* New York, Citadel Press, 1990.

Beau Geste

Beau Geste, the best selling 1924 adventure novel by Percival Christopher Wren, has provided venerable screenplay fodder for successive generations of Hollywood filmmakers. First adapted in a silent version in 1926 with Ronald Colman in the title role, the property was most memorably executed by director William Wellman in 1939. Gary Cooper starred as Michael "Beau" Geste, one of three noble brothers who join the French Foreign Legion after being wrongly implicated in a jewel theft. An Academy Award nomination went to Brian Donlevy for his role as a villainous sergeant. A forgettable third version appeared in 1966.

—Robert E. Schnakenberg

FURTHER READING:

Wren, Percival Christopher. *Beau Geste (Gateway Movie Classics).* Washington, D.C., Regnery Publishing, 1991.

Beauty Queens

From America's Favorite Pre-Teen to Miss Nude World, America offers a plethora of beauty contests and competitions for females, and the occasional male, to be crowned a beauty queen. In *American Beauty,* Lois Banner suggests that beauty queens illustrate the American ideals of social mobility and democracy: anyone can be a pageant winner and better herself, since anyone can enter a contest. Additionally, there is always another chance to win because new queens are crowned every year.

Beauty queens are chosen for every conceivable reason. Their role is to represent pageant sponsors as an icon and a spokesperson. Queens represent commodities like Miss Cotton; products like Miss Hawaiian Tropic [suntan lotion]; ethnic identity such as Miss Polish America; festivals and fairs such as the Tournament of Roses queen; sports like Miss Rodeo America; and geographic regions such as Miss Palm Springs, Miss Camden County, Miss Utah-USA, Mrs. America, and Miss World, among others. While the best known contests are for young women, there are competitions for almost everyone from grandmothers to babies. Specialized contests include Ms. Senior, Miss Large Lovely Lady, and Miss Beautiful Back. Although not as numerous, men's contests garner entrants of different ages also. Males can choose from the conventional masculine contests like the International Prince Pageant or drag contests such as Miss Camp America.

Two beauty queens, c. 1959.

Early twentieth-century beauty queens were often referred to as bathing beauties. Their outdoor contests were held in Venice, California, Miami Beach, Florida, and Galveston, Texas, and other beach resorts as early as 1905. The contests were usually one of many competitions including comic contests for men dressed like women and contests for children. Early contenders were actresses and showgirls as well as amateurs in their teens. Without a hierarchy of lower contests, as there is today, to winnow down the number of participants (there could be over 300 entrants), sponsors regularly disqualified contestants for misrepresenting their marital status and the region they hailed from. Early contests in the United States invited foreign contestants, like Miss France, to vie for Queen of the Pageant or Beauty Queen of the Universe. Among these competitions is the most long-lived contest, the Miss America Pageant, which began in Atlantic City, New Jersey in 1921.

The presentation of ethnic queens began as early as Miss America, whose court included Miss Indian America (who did not compete). Early ethnic contests include the Nisei Week Japanese Festival, which started in Los Angeles in 1935, and Miss Sepia for African American women, which began as early as 1944.

Beauty pageants and beauty queens have not always been popular. Until the late 1940s, when Miss America gained respect because the winners sold war bonds and won college scholarships, beauty queens were not generally well thought of by the majority of Americans. One congressman around 1915 wanted to create a federal law banning beauty contests. At the time, women who exhibited their bodies or wore makeup were considered daring, if not suspect. Other early protesters were religious and women's groups who issued decrees about how contests exploited young women for the profit of the organizers who, in almost all cases, were men. By the 1950s beauty pageants had become status quo.

Since the 1960s protesters have become more theatrical in showing how the contests objectify women. The Women's Liberation Front crowned a sheep as Miss America as part of an all day demonstration in 1968. Students elected a cow as homecoming queen at one college in the 1970s. In the 1980s protesters at a Miss California contest wore costumes of baloney, skirt steak, and hot dogs.

As beauty competitions gained respect, the ideal American girl became engraved in the American psyche. By the 1950s, when the Miss Universe contest began, the beauty queen was at her pinnacle: a stereotypically pretty, talented, politically conservative, WASP young woman who was more focused on marriage than a career. The contests floated through the 1960s until the Women's Liberation Movement made contestants and sponsors reflect on their values. By the 1970s a career and self-fulfillment were added to the qualities of a beauty queen. Well-known contests like Miss America and Miss USA also were slowly being racially integrated. By the 1980s and 1990s many African American women had won national titles in mixed competitions. Contestants with disabilities that did not affect their appearance, such as hearing impairment, were also not uncommon. In fact, conquering an impediment such as diabetes or sexual abuse was seen as a competition asset.

A service industry has grown up around pageantry, the term used to describe the beauty contest phenomenon, supplying clothing, cosmetic surgery, photography, music, jewelry, awards, makeup, instructional books and videos, and personal trainers. While early models and actor contestants may have had an edge on the amateurs because of experience performing, almost all modern beauty contestants train intensely to win. They take lessons on speaking, walking, applying makeup and hairdressing, as well as studying current events.

The prizes beauty queens win have not changed much since the 1920s. Among these are public exposure, crowns, cash, savings bonds, fur coats, jewelry, complete wardrobes, cosmetics, automobiles, and opportunities to model or act for television and film. Scholarships, a relatively new prize, were introduced in the 1940s by the Miss America Pageant. Since then, national beauty queens have spent a year on the road—selling war bonds, appearing at shopping center and sport event openings, and speaking to government, educational, and civic organizations such as the National Parent Teacher Association or American Lung Association, among other duties. State, national, and international winners like Miss USA, Miss Universe, and Miss Arkansas make paid appearances for their pageant and sponsors. National and international winners can earn over $200,000 during their year.

—ViBrina Coronado

FURTHER READING:

Banner, Lois. *American Beauty*. New York, Knopf, 1982.

Burwell, Barbara Peterson, and Polly Peterson Bowles, with foreword by Bob Barker. *Becoming a Beauty Queen*. New York, Prentice Hall, 1987.

Cohen, Colleen Ballerino, Richard Wilk, and Beverly Stoeltje, editors. *Beauty Queens on the Global Stage: Gender, Contests, and Power*. New York, Routledge, 1996.

Deford, Frank. *There She Is—The Life and Times of Miss America*. New York, Viking, 1971.

Goldman, William. ''Part 3: The Miss America Contest or 'Do You Take Preparation H?''' *Hype and Glory.* New York, Villard Books, 1990, 189-298.

Morgan, Robin. ''Women vs. the Miss America Pageant (1968).'' *The Word of a Woman: Feminist Dispatches 1968-1992.* New York, W. W. Norton & Co., 1992, 21-29.

Prewitt, Cheryl, with Kathryn Slattery. *A Bright Shining Place.* Garden City, New York, Doubleday-Galilee, 1981.

Savage, Candace. *Beauty Queens: A Playful History.* New York, Abbeville Press, 1998.

Beavers, Louise (1902-1962)

Louise Beavers, whose first film role was as a slave in the silent version of *Uncle Tom's Cabin* (1927), was cast as the happily devoted black servant during most of her career. However, she broke out of that type of role in *Imitation of Life* (1934) in her moving portrayal of the heartsick Aunt Delilah, whose light-skinned daughter denied her mother to ''pass'' as white. Even after this critically praised performance, Beavers returned to the limited servant-type character roles available to black actors during this period.

Beavers later moved to television and replaced Ethel Waters as the star of *Beulah* (1950-1953), the managing maid to the inept Hendersons, during its final season. The series gave Beavers star billing. However, she tired of the pace and stereotypical role and left the series while it was still popular.

—Denise Lowe

FURTHER READING:

Hill, George. *Black Women in Television.* New York, Garland Publishing, 1990.

MacDonald, J. Fred. *Blacks and White TV.* Chicago, Nelson-Hall Publishers, 1992.

Beavis and Butthead

MTV's breakthrough hit of the 1990s, *Beavis and Butthead,* grew out of a series of animated shorts. Each half-hour episode chronicled the title characters' hormone-driven adventures while offering their commentary on popular music videos. Beavis and Butthead were almost universally-recognized pop icons by the time their run on MTV ended in 1997. They helped to usher in a new genre of irreverent television comedy and symbolized for many critics the decay of the American mind in the days of Generation X.

Those viewing ''Frog Baseball,'' Beavis and Butthead's premiere installment on MTV's animation showcase *Liquid TV,* might have judged the cartoon—in which the duo does indeed play our national pastime with a frog as the ball—nothing more than a demented teenage doodle. But creator Mike Judge's simplistically-rendered protagonists struck some chord with MTV's young audience, and more episodes were featured. Beavis and Butthead's appearance on the 1992 Video Music Awards marked a coming-out of sorts, and Judge and his creations were offered a weekly spot on the cable network in 1993. Including videos layered with the boys' comments from the couch was the network's idea. *The Beavis and Butthead Experience,* an album featuring the two heroes collaborating with several of their favorite artists, was released late in 1993. Beavis and Butthead were guests several times on *Late Night with David Letterman* and were a featured act at the 1994 Super Bowl halftime show. Judge's cartoon creations were becoming important Hollywood personalities in an age that demanded celebrities who could wield power in several media. The culmination of this process was the release of their 1996 movie, *Beavis and Butthead Do America,* in which they embark on a cross-country quest for their lost television.

Beavis and Butthead's rise to stardom was not without its wrinkles. The show was sued in late 1993, while their popularity surged, by an Ohio mother who claimed Beavis's repeated maniacal calls of ''Fire! Fire!'' had encouraged her son to set a fire in their trailer home that claimed the life of his older sister. As part of the settlement, all references to fire have been edited from old and new episodes of the show. Judge and MTV parted ways amicably in 1997, after 220 episodes. Judge continued creating animated shows for adults. Beavis and Butthead, despite their best efforts to do nothing, had irrevocably altered the fields of animation, comedy, and teen culture as a whole. Taboos had been broken. Crudity had soared to new heights.

On the surface, *Beavis and Butthead* is a celebration of the frustrated male adolescent sex drive. Butthead, the dominant member of the team, is described in his own *Beavis and Butthead Ensucklopedia* as '' . . . pretty cool. He hangs out a lot and watches TV. Or else he cruises for chicks . . . he just keeps changing the channels, and when a hot chick comes on he'll check out her thingies.'' Butthead's off-center whipping boy Beavis is, in comparison, '' . . . a poet, a storyteller, a wuss, a fartknocker, a dillweed, a doorstop and a paper weight.'' The show established and maintained its fan base with storylines about escape (from the law, social norms, or teenage boredom) and desire (for women, recognition, or some new stimulus). Judge's vignettes, peppered with Beavis' nerdy snicker and Butthead's brain dead ''Huh. Huh-huh,'' left no subject as sacred, from God and school to death itself. They destroyed public and private property, dodged responsibilities, let the world wash through the television and over them on their threadbare couch, and bragged about their fantasies of exploiting women. Critics and would-be censors were quick to point to the show as evidence of the current generation's desensitization to modern social issues and general dumbing-down. Beavis and Butthead, many said, were evidence enough that the current crop of kids were not ready to take over. ''I hate words,'' snorts Beavis while a music video flashes superimposed phrases on the screen. ''Words suck. If I wanted to read, I'd go to school.''

But Beavis and Butthead's innocent absorption of America's mass media and their simultaneous applause and ridicule of popular culture spoke to ''Gen X'' on some level. And deep in their observations were occasional gems of world-weary wisdom. ''The future sucks,'' insists Beavis in one episode, ''change it!'' Butthead replies, ''I'm pretty cool Beavis, but I cannot change the future.''

—Colby Vargas

FURTHER READING:

Judge, Mike, et al. *The Beavis and Butthead Ensucklopedia.* New York, MTV Pocket Books, 1994.

The Bee Gees

The Australian Brothers Gibb, Barry and twins Robin and Maurice (1949—), are one of the most successful, versatile, enduring recording groups in the world. Their trademark close harmonies, along with their remarkable songwriting abilities and talent for creating distinctive melodies, have earned them dozens of top 40 hits, including six consecutive number ones from 1977-79. Because of their involvement with the soundtrack to *Saturday Night Fever,* they are primarily artistically associated with late-1970s disco excesses. However, they released their first widely available record in 1967, and began a string of hits in several genres: pop, psychedelic, country, R&B, and soul. Though they still regularly top the charts in other parts of the world, they have not had major chart success in the United States since 1983. In 1997, the Bee Gees were inducted into the Rock 'n' Roll Hall of Fame.

—Joyce Linehan

FURTHER READING:

Bee Gees. *Bee Gees Anthology: Tales from the Brothers Gibb a History in Song 1967-1990.* Hal Leonard Publishing Corporation, 1991.

Beer

Given Americans' love of beer, one might be tempted to call it America's drink. In truth it is the world's drink. Originating in ancient Babylon, and passed on in various regional variations for thousands of years, beer is made in virtually every country in the world. Throughout Europe, but especially in Germany, Czechoslovakia, and the United Kingdom, the public house or alehouse serving locally-brewed beer has been an institution for hundreds of years. In Belgium, Trappist monks have been producing their distinctive beers since the eleventh century. But it wasn't until the twentieth century that beer was subjected to the peculiar modernizing effects of American mass culture. Mass-produced, packaged, and advertised everywhere, American lager beer in its various similar-tasting brands—Budweiser, Miller, Strohs, Coors, Pabst, etc.—became the drink of the masses. In 1995, American brewers produced 185 million barrels of beer, 176 million of which were consumed in the United States. The vast majority of the beer produced in the United States—over 95 percent—is produced by the major brewers, Anheuser-Busch, Miller, Strohs, Heileman, Coors, and Pabst. However, craft brewers have kept ancient brewing traditions alive and in the 1990s offer their microbrews to a growing number of beer drinkers looking for an alternative to mass-produced fare.

It is no exaggeration to say that beer came to America with the first colonists. Indeed, there is evidence that suggests that one of the main reasons the Mayflower stopped at Plymouth Rock in 1620 was that they were running out of beer. Had they made it to New Amsterdam they might have replenished their stock with ales made by the Dutch settlers who had been brewing beer there since 1612. The first commercial brewery opened in New Amsterdam in 1632 and as the colonies expanded many a small community boasted of a local brewer. But the failure of colonists to grow quality barley (a key ingredient in beer) and the easy availability of imported English beer

slowed the development of an indigenous brewing industry. As tensions between the colonies and England increased in the eighteenth century, beer became one of a number of British goods that were no longer wanted by colonists eager to declare their independence. By 1770, George Washington and Patrick Henry were among the many revolutionaries who called for a boycott of English beer and promoted the growth of domestic brewing. Some of the first legislation passed by the fledgling United States limited the taxes on beer to encourage such growth. Thomas Jefferson and Benjamin Franklin both supported a plan to create a state-supported national brewery (the plan came to naught.)

The nineteenth century saw a tremendous growth in brewing in America. Immigrants from the "beer belt" countries of Europe—Ireland, Germany, Poland, Czechoslovakia, and The Netherlands—brought their brewing knowledge and love of beer to many American communities, and by 1840 there were over 140 breweries operating in the United States. In that same year America was introduced to lager beer by a Bavarian brewer named Johann Wagner. Little did he know that he had introduced the future of American brewing. Prior to 1840, the beers produced in America were all ales, defined by their use of a top-fermenting yeast and aged and served at room temperature. Lagers—which used a bottom-fermenting yeast and required cold storage—tended to be mellower, smoother, and cleaner tasting, and they soon found an audience, especially when Bohemian brewers developed the Pilsner style, the lightest, clearest lager made. Milwaukee, Wisconsin—with its proximity to grain producers, its supply of fresh water, and its large German population—soon became the capital of American brewing. The Pabst, Schlitz, and Miller Brewing companies all trace their roots to nineteenth-century Milwaukee. In fact, Schlitz claimed for many years to the "beer that made Milwaukee famous."

Milwaukee was not alone in embracing beer, especially lager beer. By 1873 there were over 4,131 breweries operating in the United States and they produced nine million barrels of beer, according to Bill Yenne in *Beers of North America.* Most of the twentieth century's major brewers got their start in the late nineteenth-century boom in American brewing, including Anheuser-Busch (founded in 1852), the Miller Brewing Company (1850), the Stroh Brewery Company (1850), the G. Heileman Brewing Company (1858), the Adolph Coors Company (1873), and the Pabst Brewing Company (1844). Adolphus Busch, who some hail as the first genius in American brewing, dreamed of creating the first national beer, and by the 1870s the conditions were right to begin making his dream a reality. Backed by a huge brewery, refrigerated storehouses and rail cars, and a new process allowing the pasteurization of beer, Busch introduced his new beer, called Budweiser, in 1876. But the majority of the brewers were still small operations providing beer for local markets. It would take industrialization, Prohibition, and post-World War II consolidation to create the monolithic brewers that dominated the twentieth century.

At the dawn of the twentieth century several factors were reshaping the American brewing industry. First, large regional brands grew in size and productive capacity and began to squeeze competitors out of the market. New bottling technologies allowed these brewers to package and ship beer to ever-larger regions. Such brewers were aided by new legislation that prohibited the brewing and bottling of beer on the same premises, thus ending the tradition of the local brewhouse. "The shipping of bottled beer," notes Philip Van Munching in *Beer Blast: The Inside Story of the Brewing Industry's Bizarre Battles for Your Money,* "created the first real emphasis on brand identification, since shipping meant labeling, and labeling meant

A bartender pours a beer at the Copper Tank Brew Pub in Austin, Texas.

imagery.'' All these factors helped big brewers get bigger while small brewers left the industry. By 1910 the number of breweries had decreased to 1,568, though they produced 53 million barrels of beer a year. With fewer breweries producing more beer, the stage was set for the next century of American brewing. There was only one problem: numbers of Americans supported placing restrictions on alcohol consumption and they soon found the political clout to get their way.

For a number of years nativist Protestants, alarmed by the social disorder brought to the United States by the surge of immigrants from eastern and southern Europe, had been pressing for laws restricting the sale of alcohol, hoping that such laws would return social order to their communities. Fueled by anti-German (and thus anti-brewing) sentiment sparked by Germany's role in World War I, such groups as the National Prohibition Party, the Woman's Christian Temperance Union, and the Anti-Saloon League succeeded in pressing for legislation and a Constitutional Amendment banning the ''manufacture, sale, or transportation of intoxicating liquors.'' The Volstead Enforcement Act, which went into effect on January 18, 1920, made the brewing of beer punishable under the law. ''What had been a normal commercial activity one day,'' writes Penne, ''was a criminal act the next.'' Small and medium-sized breweries across the nation closed their doors, and the big brewers turned their vast productive capacity to producing near beer (with names like Vivo, Famo, Luxo, Hoppy,

Pablo, and Yip) and other non-alcoholic beverages. As a method of social control, Prohibition—as the period came to be known—failed miserably: American drinkers still drank, but now they got their booze from illicit ''speakeasies'' and ''bootleggers,'' which were overwhelmingly controlled by organized crime interests. Crime increased dramatically during Prohibition (or at least anti-Prohibition interests made it seem so) and the politicians who were against Prohibition, energized by the political realignment caused by the start of the Great Depression and the election of Franklin D. Roosevelt, repealed Prohibition by December of 1933.

The effects of Prohibition on the brewing industry were dramatic. Only 400 of the country's 1,568 breweries survived Prohibition, and half of these failed during the Depression that gripped the country throughout the 1930s. The big breweries survived, and in the years to come they would claim an ever-increasing dominance in the American beer market. Big brewers were aided in 1935 by the introduction of canned beer. Though brewers first put beer in tin or steel cans, Coors introduced the aluminum can in 1959 and it was quickly adopted by the entire brewing industry. More and more, beer was a mass-produced product that could be purchased in any grocery store, rather than a craft-brewed local product purchased at a local alehouse. But American brewing did not rebound immediately upon repeal of Prohibition. The economic troubles of the 1930s put a damper on production; in 1940, American brewers produced only 53 million barrels of beer, ''well below the pre-Prohibition peak of 66 million barrels,'' according to Yenne. It would take World War II and the post-war boom to spark a real resurgence in American brewing.

As World War II drew increasing numbers of American men off to foreign bases, military leaders wisely decided to permit the sale of beer on military bases. Brewers obliged by allocating 15 percent of their production for the troops and, according to Yenne, ''young men with long-standing loyalties to hometown brews were exposed to national brands,'' thus creating loyalty to these brands that they carried home. Brewers also took advantage of an expanding American economy to increase their output to 80 million barrels annually by 1945.

The story of post-War American brewing can be summed up in two words: nationalization and consolidation. Anheuser-Busch, Schlitz, and Pabst set out to make their beers national brands by building breweries in every region of the United States. In the years between 1946 and 1951, each of these brewers began to produce beer for the New York market—once dominated by Ballantine, Rheingold, and Schaefer—from newly-opened breweries. Soon they built breweries, giant breweries, on the West Coast and in the South. By 1976 Anheuser-Busch alone had opened 16 new breweries in locations throughout the United States. The other major brewers followed suit, but no one could keep up with Anheuser-Busch. By 1957 the company was selling more beer than any brewer in the United States, a position it has not relinquished since.

Nationalization was followed by consolidation, as the major brewers began acquiring smaller brewers at an astonishing pace and either marketing or burying their brands. According to Van Munching, ''In the sixties and seventies following the American beer business was like going to a ball game. To keep track of the players, you needed a scorecard.'' G. Heileman of Wisconsin purchased smaller regional brewers of beers like Old Style, Blatz, Rainier, and Lone Star; Washington brewer Olympia bought Hamms, but was in turn bought by Pabst. But the biggest buy came when tobacco giant Philip Morris purchased the Miller Brewing Company in 1970. Backed by Philip Morris's deep pockets, Miller suddenly joined the ranks of the country's major brewers. Van Munching claims that the purchase of Miller ''signaled the end of an era in the brewing industry: the end of skirmishes fought on a strictly regional scale, often with different contestants in each of the regions. Now, one battlefield was brought into sharp focus ... the whole U.S. of A.'' From 1970 on, the major national brewers battled fiercely for market share with a sophisticated arsenal of advertising, promotions, brand diffusion, and bluster.

In a market in which the major brands had little difference in taste, the biggest tool the brewers had to increase market share was advertising. The first brewer to turn its full attention to the promotion of its product on a national scale was Miller, which in the early 1970s began an unprecedented push into the sports marketplace. Miller advertised its brands on every televised sporting event it could get its hands on, from auto racing to football. While it pitched its flagship brand, Miller High Life, with the slogans ''If you've got the time, we've got the beer'' and the tag line ''Miller Time,'' Miller attracted the most attention with its ads for the relatively new Lite Beer from Miller that featured drinkers arguing whether the beer ''Tastes Great'' or was ''Less Filling.'' For a time, Miller dominated the available air time, purchasing nearly 70 percent of network television sports beer advertising. But Anheuser-Busch wasn't about to let

Miller outdo them, and they soon joined in the battle with Miller to dominate the airwaves, first purchasing local television air time and later outbidding Miller for national programs. With their classy Budweiser Clydesdales, ''This Bud's for You,'' and the ''Bud Man,'' Budweiser managed to retain their leading market share. Between them, Anheuser-Busch and Miller owned American television beer advertising, at least until the others could catch up.

Both Budweiser and Miller devoted significant resources to sponsoring sporting teams and events in an effort to get their name before as many beer drinkers as possible. Budweiser sponsored the Miss Budweiser hydroplane beginning in 1962, and beginning in the early 1980s regularly fielded racing teams on the NASCAR, NHRA, and CART racing circuits. Moreover, Budweiser sponsored major boxing events—including some of the classic championship fights of the 1980s—and in the late 1990s paired with a number of sportsmen's and conservation organizations, including Ducks Unlimited and the Nature Conservancy. For its part, Miller sponsored awards for National Football League players of the week and year, funded CART, NASCAR, and drag racing teams, and in the late 1990s started construction on a new baseball stadium, called Miller Park, for the aptly named Milwaukee Brewers. Miller has also put considerable resources into funding for the arts, both in Milwaukee, where it has sponsored annual ballet productions, and in other cities throughout the country. These brewers—and many others—also put their name on so many t-shirts, hats, banners, and gadgets that beer names sometimes seemed to be everywhere in American culture.

When American brewers couldn't expand their market share through advertising, they tried to do so by introducing new products. The first such ''new'' beer was light beer. The Rheingold brewery introduced the first low-calorie beer, Gablinger's, in 1967, but the taste was, according to Van Munching, so ''spectacularly awful'' that it never caught on. Miller acquired the rights to a beer called Meister Brau Lite in 1972 when it purchased the Meister Brau brewery in Chicago, and they soon renamed the beer and introduced it the same year as Lite Beer from Miller. Offered to drinkers worried about their protruding beer bellies, and to women who didn't want such a heavy beer, Lite Beer was an immediate success and eventually helped Miller overtake Schlitz as the number two brewer in the country. Not surprisingly, it spawned imitators. Anheuser-Busch soon marketed Natural Light and Bud Light; Coors offered Coors Light; Stroh's peddled Old Milwaukee Light. There was even an imported light beer, Amstel Light.

Light beer was an undoubted success: by 1990, the renamed Miller Lite led sales in the category with 19.9 million barrels, followed by Bud Light (11.8 million barrels) and Coors Light (11.6 million barrels). Following the success of light beer, beermakers looked for other similar line extensions to help boost sales. Anheuser-Busch introduced LA (which stood for ''low alcohol'') and others followed—with Schaefer LA, Blatz LA, Rainier LA, etc; the segment soon died. In 1985, Miller achieved some success with a cold-filtered, nonpasteurized beer they called Miller Genuine Draft, or MGD; Anheuser-Busch followed them into the market with several imitators, the most flagrant being Michelob Golden Draft (also MGD), with a similar bottle, label, and advertising campaign. Anheuser-Busch created the dry beer segment when it introduced Michelob Dry, followed shortly by Bud Dry. Their advertising slogan—''Why ask why? Try Bud Dry''—begged a real question: Why drink a dry beer? Consumers could think of no good reason, and the beers soon disappeared from the market. Perhaps, thought brewers, an ice beer would be better. Following Canadian brewer Molson Canada, Miller introduced Molson Ice in the United States in 1993; they were, once again, followed by many imitators and, once again, the category slowly fizzled after a brief period of popularity.

Though the attempts of American brewers to create new beer categories appeared to be a comedy of errors, there was reason behind their madness. Simply put, the market for their beers had grown stagnant and the same brewers were competing for a market that was no longer growing substantially. Many brewers sought to expand by peddling wine coolers or alternative beverages, such as Coors's Zima Clearmalt; most hastened their efforts to sell their beer in the international market. Anheuser-Busch, for example, began to market its beer in more than 60 countries worldwide. Still, the question was if American drinkers weren't drinking the "new" beers produced by the major brewers, what were they drinking? In the simplest terms, the answer was that more and more Americans were drinking "old" beers—carefully crafted ales and lagers with far more taste and body than anything brewed by the "big boys." Beginning in the late 1970s, the so-called "microbrew revolution" proved to be the energizing force in the American beer market.

American capitalism has proved extremely adept at producing and marketing vast numbers of mass-produced goods, and American brewers are quintessential capitalists. But with mass production comes a flattening of distinctions, a tendency to produce, in this case, beers that all taste the same. Beginning in the late 1970s and accelerating in the 1980s, American consumers began to express a real interest in products with distinction—in gourmet coffee (witness the birth of Starbucks and other gourmet coffee chains), in good cars (thus rising sales of BMW, Mercedes, and Japanese luxury brands Lexus and Acura), and in fine clothes (witness the rise of designers Ralph Lauren and Calvin Klein). The changing taste of American beer drinkers was first expressed as a preference for imported beers, which surged in sales in the late 1970s. But true beer connoisseurs soon turned to beer brewed closer to home. In 1977 the New Albion brewing company in Sonoma, California, offered the first American "microbrew," the name given to beer brewed in small batches. The first major microbrewer, the Sierra Nevada Brewing Company of Chico, California, opened in 1981, and was followed into the market by a succession of breweries first in the West and then throughout the country.

One of the first microbrewers to enter the national market was the contract-brewing Boston Beer Company, producers of the Samuel Adams Boston Lager and other beers, but for the most part the microbrew revolution was not about following the path of the big breweries into national marketing, but rather about producing high quality ales for the local market. In small- and medium-sized markets around the country, American beer drinkers were rediscovering the richness and variety of the brewer's art. In the microbrewing capital of the United States, the Pacific Northwest, alehouses can boast of carrying dozens of beers brewed within a day's drive. At places like Fred's Rivertown Alehouse in Snohomish, Washington, a group called the Cask Club even joined in the revival of one of the oldest brewing traditions—cask-conditioned or "real" ales.

Though the microbrew revolution wasn't big—craft-brewed beers only accounted for 2.1 percent of the domestic beer market in 1995—it exerted a great influence on the major brewers. Most of the big brewers responded to the challenge posed by microbrewers by marketing slightly richer, slightly better beers with "authentic" looking labels. Miller marketed beers under the label Plank Road Brewery and Michelob promoted its dark and amber beers. Miller

responded most ingeniously by claiming in advertisements that it was "time for a good old macrobrew," brewed in one of their "vats the size of Rhode Island." Meanwhile microbreweries, brewpubs, and regional specialty brewers kept opening; by 1995 there were 1,034 such breweries in the United States, heralding a return to the abundance of breweries that existed at the turn of the century, and a dramatic rise from the 60 breweries in existence in 1980.

It comes as no surprise that a drink as popular as beer should play a role in American entertainment. Beer could have been credited as a character on the long-running sitcom *Cheers* (1982-1993), which featured a group of men who felt most at home sitting in a Boston bar with a beer in their hands; the biggest beer drinker, Norm, perfected humorous ways of asking for his beer, and once called out "Give me a bucket of beer and a snorkel." Milwaukee's fictional Schotz Brewery employed the lead characters in the 1970s sitcom *Laverne and Shirley* (1976-1983). When Archie Bunker of *All in the Family* (1971-1979) left his union job he opened a bar—Archie's Place—that served beer to working class men. The characters on the *Drew Carey Show* (1995—) brewed and marketed a concoction they called Buzz Beer, and signed a professional wrestler to do celebrity endorsements. Homer Simpson, the father on the animated series *The Simpsons* (1989—) swore his allegiance to the locally-brewed Duff Beer. (The show's producer, Twentieth Century-Fox, sued the South Australian Brewing Company when it tried to market a beer under the same name). Movies have not provided so hospitable a home to beer, though the 1983 movie *Strange Brew* followed the exploits of beer drinking Canadians Bob and Doug McKenzie as they got a job at the Elsinore Brewery.

In the 1990s, with more beers than ever to choose from, Americans still turned with amazing frequency to the major brands Budweiser, Miller, and Coors. Such brands offered not only a familiar, uniform taste, but were accompanied by a corresponding set of images and icons produced by sophisticated marketing machines. Drinkers of the major brands found their beer on billboards, race cars, television ads, store displays, and t-shirts everywhere they looked; by drinking a Bud, for example, they joined a community unique to late-twentieth-century mass culture—a community of consumers. But for those who wished to tap into the age old tradition of brewing, an increasing number of brewers offered more authentic fare.

—Tom Pendergast

FURTHER READING:

Abel, Bob. *The Book of Beer*. Chicago, Henry Regnery Company, 1976.

Grant, Bert, with Robert Spector. *The Ale Master*. Seattle, Washington, Sasquatch Books, 1998.

Hernon, Peter, and Terry Ganey. *Under the Influence: The Unauthorized Story of the Anheuser-Busch Dynasty*. New York, Simon & Schuster, 1991.

Jackson, Michael. *Michael Jackson's Beer Companion*. Philadelphia, Running Press, 1993.

Nachel, Marty, with Steve Ettlinger. *Beer for Dummies*. Foster City, California, IDG Books Worldwide, 1996.

Plavchan, Ronald Jan. *A History of Anheuser-Busch, 1852-1933*. New York, Arno Press, 1976.

Porter, John. *All About Beer*. Garden City, New York, Doubleday, 1975.

Price, Steven D. *All the King's Horses: The Story of the Budweiser Clydesdales.* New York, Viking Penguin, 1983.

Rhodes, Christine P., editor. *The Encyclopedia of Beer.* New York, Henry Holt & Co., 1997.

Van Munching, Philip. *Beer Blast: The Inside Story of the Brewing Industry's Bizarre Battles for Your Money.* New York, Random House, 1997.

Yenne, Bill. *Beers of North America.* New York, Gallery Books, 1986.

Beiderbecke, Bix (1903-1931)

Leon Bismarck "Bix" Beiderbecke is one of the few white musicians to have influenced important black musicians. Considered one of the all-time great jazz artists, he was admired by Louis Armstrong, who always mentioned Beiderbecke as his favorite trumpet player. Beiderbecke actually played cornet, which was also Armstrong's first trumpet-like instrument.

Remarkably, Beiderbecke did not hear a jazz record until he was 14. The music of the Original Dixieland Jazz Band became his inspiration, and he copied the cornet solos verbatim. However, he resisted any formal musical instruction, and fingered the cornet in an unorthodox fashion that enabled him to solo with incredible speed. In common with many jazz musicians of his day, Beiderbicke never learned to read music very well, either. Rather, he relied upon his

Bix Beiderbecke

great ear for music. Despite his apparent talent, his parents sought to discourage his musical pursuits. They sent him to Wake Forest Academy, a military school near Chicago, in the hopes that its strict discipline would quell his interest in jazz.

Their ploy did not work. Beiderbecke managed to get himself expelled for cutting classes and soon turned to music full-time, coming to fame in the 1920s. In 1923, he joined the Wolverines and recorded with them in 1924. He soon left the Wolverines to join Jean Goldkette's Orchestra, but lost the job because of his inability to read music well. In 1926, he joined Frankie Trambauer's group and recorded his piano composition "In a Mist." In concert with his time, Beiderbecke lived the life of a "romantic" artist, drinking to excess and living for his art. Both made him a legend among his contemporaries. His tone on the cornet was gorgeous, very different from Armstrong's assertive brassy tone. It became a model for a number of later horn players, including Bunny Berrigan, Harry James, Fats Navarro, Clifford Brown, and Miles Davis, among others.

Beiderbecke recorded extensively with Eddie Lang, guitar, and Frankie Trambauer, C-Melody sax. He managed to improve his music reading enough to work with Jean Goldkette again, and later joined Paul Whiteman's Orchestra, the most popular group of his day. In 1929, Beiderbecke returned to Davenport, Iowa, to recuperate from the ill-effects of his hard drinking. Whiteman treated Beiderbecke well, paying him his full salary and offering to take him back when he was well. Beiderbecke never fully recovered. He made a few records with Hoagy Carmichael before his death in 1931 of lobar pneumonia and edema of the brain. Beiderbecke's romantic life and death inspired Dorothy Baker's book, *Young Man with a Horn,* as well as the movie of the same name. The Bix Beiderbecke Memorial Jazz Festival continues in Davenport, Iowa. It is billed as Iowa's Number One Attraction.

—Frank A. Salamone

FURTHER READING:

Berton, Ralph. *Remembering Bix.* New York, Harper & Row, 1974.

Burnett, James. *Bix Beiderbecke.* London, Cassell & Co., 1959.

Carmichael, Hoagy, and Stephen Longstreet. *Sometimes I Wonder.* New York, Hoagy, Farrar, Straus, and Giroux, 1965.

Sudhalter, Richard M., and Philip R. Evans. *Bix: Man And Legend.* Arlington House Publishers, 1974.

Belafonte, Harry (1927—)

Singer, actor, and activist Harry Belafonte with his "Jamaica Farewell" launched the calypso sound in American popular music and through his performances popularized folk songs of the world to American audiences. As an actor, Belafonte tore down walls of discrimination for other minority actors, and as an activist, profoundly influenced by the late Dr. Martin Luther King, Jr., he fought for the civil rights of Africans and African Americans for decades. A popular matinee idol since the 1950s, Belafonte achieved his greatest popularity as a singer. His "Banana Boat (Day-O)" shot to number five on

Harry Belafonte

the *Billboard* pop singles chart in 1957. His *Calypso* album released in 1956 was certified gold in 1963 and the 1959 album *Belafonte at Carnegie Hall* certified gold in 1961. Belafonte was the first African American television producer and the first African American to win an Emmy Award.

Born on March 1, 1927, in New York City, Harold George Belafonte, Jr. was the son of Caribbean immigrants. His mother, Melvine Love Belafonte, was from Jamaica and his father, Harold George Belafonte, Sr., was from Martinique. In 1935, after his father left the family, Belafonte and his mother moved to her native Jamaica where Belafonte spent five years attending school and assimilating the local music. In 1940, he returned to the public schools of New York but in 1944, at the age of seventeen, dropped out to enter the U.S. Navy for a two-year stint. In 1948, Belafonte married Julie Robinson, a dancer.

After seeing a production of the American Negro Theater, Belafonte knew he wanted to become an actor. He attended the Dramatic Workshop of the New School for Social Research, studying under the direction of Erwin Piscator. As a class project, he had to sing an original composition entitled "Recognition" and after his performance drew the attention of Monte Kay who later became his agent. Since few acting opportunities opened and Belafonte needed to support his family, Kay offered him a singing engagement at the Royal Roost, a jazz night club in New York. After attracting favorable reviews, Belafonte established himself as a creditable jazz and popular singer. But by 1950, feeling that he could not continue singing popular music with a sincere conviction, he abruptly switched

to folk songs and began independently studying, researching, and adapting folk songs to his repertoire. His folk singing debut in 1951 at the Village Vanguard in New York's Greenwich Village was a smashing success. Belafonte subsequently opened a restaurant catering to patrons who appreciated folk singing, but it closed in three years because it was not commercially viable.

Belafonte recorded for Jubilee Records in 1949 and signed with RCA Victor records in 1956 with his first hit, "Banana Boat (Day-O)," issued in 1957. He soon launched the calypso craze. While Belafonte was not a true calypsonian, i.e., one who had grown up absorbing the tradition, he was instead an innovator and took traditional calypso and other folk songs, dramatizing, adapting, and imitating the authentic prototypes, melding them into polished and consummate musical performances. He was called the "King of Calypso," and capitalized on the tastes of the American and European markets. His "Jamaica Farewell," "Matilda, Matilda," and "Banana Boat (Day-O)" are classics. Guitarist Millard Thomas became his accompanist. Belafonte also sang Negro spirituals and work songs, and European folk songs in addition to other folk songs of the world on recordings and in live concerts. While his hits had stopped by the 1970s, his attraction as a concert artist continued. He recorded with such well-known artists as Bob Dylan, Lena Horne, Miriam Makeba, and Odetta. Belafonte was responsible for bringing South African trumpeter and bandleader Hugh Masekela and other South African artists to the United States. In 1988, the acclaimed album *Paradise in Gazankulu* was banned in South Africa because of its depiction of the horrors of apartheid.

Belafonte took singing roles in the theatrical production *Almanac* in 1953 and opportunities for acting opened up. His first film was *The Bright Road* (1953) with Dorothy Dandridge. In 1954, he played the role of Joe in *Carmen Jones,* an adaptation of Bizet's *Carmen* that became one of the first all-black movie box-office successes. He starred in *Island in the Sun* in 1957 and *Odds Against Tomorrow* in 1959. In the 1970s, his film credits included *Buck and the Preacher* (1972) and *Uptown Saturday Night* (1974). Belafonte also appeared in numerous television specials and starred in videos and films documenting music, including *Don't Stop the Carnival* in 1991, *White Man's Burden* in 1995, and *Kansas City* in 1996.

As a student in Jamaica, Belafonte observed the effects of colonialism and the political oppression that Jamaicans suffered. He committed himself to a number of humanitarian causes including civil rights, world hunger, the arts, and children's rights. The ideas of W. E. B. DuBois, Paul Robeson, and Dr. Martin Luther King, Jr. exerted powerful influences on Belafonte. He participated in marches with Dr. King and in 1985 helped organize as well as perform on "We Are the World," a Grammy Award-winning recording project to raise money to alleviate hunger in Africa. Due to his civil rights work, he was selected as a board member of the Southern Christian Leadership Conference and also served as chair of the memorial fund named after Dr. King.

Belafonte continues to inspire audiences through his songs and his passion for racial justice has remained indomitable. He is one of the leading artists who has broken down barriers for people of color, made enormous contributions to black music as a singer and producer, and succeeded in achieving rights for oppressed people. His music, after more than forty years, still sounds fresh and engaging. Belafonte's genius lies in his ability to sway an audience to his point of view. His charisma, voice, and acting abilities enable him to make any song his own while at the same time keeping his audience spellbound. Selected songs from his repertoire will remain classics for generations to come.

—Willie Collins

FURTHER READING:

Fogelson, Genia. *Harry Belafonte: Singer and Actor.* Los Angeles, Melrose Square Publishing Company, 1980.

Shaw, Arnold. *Harry Belafonte: An Unauthorized Biography.* Philadelphia, Chilton Company, 1960.

The Bell Telephone Hour

Every Monday night for 18 years, from April 29, 1940, America was treated to *The Bell Telephone Hour,* a musical feast broadcast by NBC Radio. Featuring the 57-piece Bell Telephone Orchestra, directed by Donald Voorhees, who composed their theme, ''The Bell Waltz,'' the program brought the best in musical entertainment across a broad spectrum, in a format that made for easy and popular listening. Vocalists James Melton and Francia White performed with the orchestra until April 27, 1942, when the program initiated its ''Great Soloists'' tradition, showcasing individual artists of distinction. Among the many ''greats'' were opera stars Helen Traubel, Marion Anderson, and Ezio Pinza, concert pianists Jose Iturbi and Robert Casadesus, leading artists in jazz such as Benny Goodman, top Broadway stars such as Mary Martin, and popular crooners, including Bing Crosby.

NBC took *The Bell Telephone Hour* off the air in 1958, but revived it for television from October 9, 1959, with Donald Voorhees and the Orchestra still in place. Always stylish and elegant in presentation, the small-screen version ran for 10 years, offering the same eclectic mix as the radio original for eight of them. The visual medium allowed the inclusion of dance, and viewers were treated to appearances by ballet idol Rudolf Nureyev and veteran tap-dancer Ray Bolger, among others. On April 29, 1960, the program memorably brought Gilbert and Sullivan's operetta, *The Mikado,* to television with a cast led by soprano Helen Traubel as Katisha and comedian Groucho Marx as the Lord High Executioner.

In 1966, however, the show abandoned its established format in favor of documentary films. Subjects included such established performers as pianist Van Cliburn, conductor Zubin Mehta, and jazz man Duke Ellington, but the program lasted only two more years, ending a chapter in broadcasting history on April 26, 1968.

—James R. Belpedio

FURTHER READING:

Buxton, Frank, and Bill Owen. *The Big Broadcast.* New York, Viking Press, 1972.

Dunning, John. *Tune In Yesterday: The Ultimate Encyclopedia of Old Time Radio.* Englewood Cliffs, New Jersey, Prentice Hall, 1976.

Hickerson, Jay. *The New, Revised Ultimate History of Network Radio Programming and Guide to All Circulating Shows.* Hamden, Connecticut, Jay Hickerson, 1996.

Museum of Broadcasting. *The Telephone Hour: A Retrospective.* New York, Museum of Broadcasting, 1990.

Two women modeling bellbottoms.

Bellbottoms

Bellbottomed trousers, named for the bell-shaped cut of the cuffs, have been worn by sea-farers since the 17th century. While sailors prefer the cut because the wide bottoms of the trousers make them easy to roll up for deck-swabbing duty, young people bought the trousers from navy surplus stores in the 1960s because the fabric was cheap and durable. Bellbottoms flattered the slim, unisex figure in vogue during the late 1960s and 1970s, and soon designers were turning out high-price versions of the navy classic. In the 1990s, the revival of 1970s fashion has seen the return of bellbottoms, especially as jeans.

—Deborah Broderson

FURTHER READING:

Blue Jeans. London, Hamlyn, 1997.

Dustan, Keith. *Just Jeans: The Story 1970-1995.* Kew, Victoria, Australian Scholarly Press, 1995.

Belushi, John (1949-1982)

The name John Belushi conjures images of sword-wielding Samurai, cheeseburger-cooking Greek chefs, mashed-potato spewing human zits, and Ray Ban wearing ex-cons on a "mission from God." But his short life is also a popular metaphor for drug abuse and wild excess. His acting and comedy, undeniably energetic and highly creative, are overshadowed by his death, a tabloid cliché revisited every time another Hollywood star overdoses on drugs or alcohol.

In part, this sad legacy is influenced by Bob Woodward's clinical and unflattering biography, *Wired* (1984), in which Belushi is described as an insecure man who turns to cocaine and heroin to bolster his self-esteem. Woodward concluded that Belushi's extremes in personality were a representation of the 1970s and the drug-obsessed entertainment industry of the time. Yet this legacy is also inspired in part by Belushi's own stage, television, and movie personae, best exemplified in popular myth by his portrayal of the anti-establishment, hedonistic fraternity bum Bluto Blutarsky of *National Lampoon's Animal House* (1978). The dean's admonition that "fat, drunk, and stupid is no way to go through life" can be seen as an unbidden warning to Belushi.

Belushi first came to public notice as a member of Chicago's Second City comedy troupe. Led by Del Close, Second City used improvisational skits to entertain the audiences. While he later credited Close for teaching him how to be a part of an ensemble, Belushi's intense energy and raucous attitude soon began pushing the bounds of the troupe's comedy. In spite of Close's insistence that they were all a team, local reviews soon made it clear that Belushi was the "star" of the show. This soon earned him the notice of Tony Hendra, producer-director of the forthcoming *National Lampoon Magazine*'s musical satire *Lemmings*. Belushi fascinated Hendra, and he offered him the role of the manic emcee that instigates the mass suicide of the audience in *Lemmings*.

At that time, *National Lampoon Magazine* was at the forefront of alternative comedy, the borderline humor that mocked religion, sex, illness, and even death. *Lemmings* was envisioned as an off-Broadway send-up of the Woodstock concert that would showcase the magazine's brand of humor. For Belushi, it was a marriage made in heaven. The show got rave reviews, its original six-week run being extended for ten months. In reviews, Belushi was singled out for particular praise, his performance outshining the rest of the cast, including newcomer Chevy Chase. He tied himself more closely with National Lampoon by working as a writer, director, and actor of the *National Lampoon Radio Hour*.

In the spring of 1975 Lorne Michaels asked Belushi to join the regular cast of a new show he was preparing for NBC television. Envisioned as a show to appeal to the 18-to-34 audience, *Saturday Night Live* (SNL) was broadcast live from the NBC studios in New York. The live aspect gave these younger audiences a sense of adventure, of never knowing what was going to happen next. The cast, which also included Chevy Chase, Dan Aykroyd, and others, billed themselves as the "Not Ready for Prime Time Players," and set about redefining American television comedy in the irreverent image of Britain's *Monty Python's Flying Circus*.

Belushi was at first overshadowed by Chase, whose suave sophistication appealed to the viewers. He initially came to the audience's attention as a manic weatherman sitting next to Chase's deadpan "Weekly Update" anchorman, ending with his catchphrase "But nooooooooooooo!" When Chase departed for Hollywood at the end of the first season, Belushi became the viewers' new favorite. His most memorable SNL performances included the lunatic weatherman, a Samurai warrior with a short fuse and a long sword, the resentful leader of a band of killer bees, Joe Crocker, and a Greek chef

that would cook only cheeseburgers. He cultivated the image of "bad boy" both on and off screen: a picture of the third season SNL cast has a grim looking Belushi standing to one side, eyes covered with sun glasses, cigarette in hand, with Gilda Radner's arm draped over his shoulder. While some of the others tried to affect a similar look (especially Aykroyd), only Belushi seemed to truly exude attitude.

Like Chase, Belushi was also looking to advance his career in Hollywood. He began his movie career with a bit part in Jack Nicholson's poorly received comedy-western *Goin' South* (1978). Months before it was released, however, his second movie project was in the theaters and thrilling audiences. Returning to National Lampoon, he was cast as the gross undergraduate Bluto Blutarsky in John Landis' *National Lampoon's Animal House* (1978).

Based in part on co-writer Chris Miller's college experiences in the 1960s, *Animal House* begins innocently enough with two freshmen seeking to pledge to the Delta House fraternity, a collection of politically incorrect and incorrigible students whose most intelligent member is averaging less than a 2.0 grade point average. The strait-laced dean of the school is determined to see Delta evicted from campus and its members expelled. The remainder of the movie is a series of skits about the run-ins between the dean and Delta House. Among these skits is Belushi's potato-spewing imitation of a zit.

Bluto drank excessively, lived only to party, disrupted the campus, and urinated on the shoes of unsuspecting freshmen. It is Belushi's portrayal of Bluto that is one of the movie's most enduring images, virtually typecasting him as a gross, excessive, drinking party animal. For most of the movie his character speaks in grunts, his big monologue coming near the end when he encourages a demoralized Delta House to take its revenge on the dean: "What? Over? Did you say 'over'? Nothing is over until we decide it is! Was it over when the Germans [sic] bombed Pearl Harbor? Hell no!" The movie ends with a Delta-inspired riot at the college's Homecoming Parade. The characters then all head off into the sunset, with captions revealing their eventual fates (Bluto's was to become a senator).

John Belushi as the Samurai Warrior dry cleaner on *Saturday Night Live*.

The movie was vintage National Lampoon, and moviegoers loved it. It became the biggest earner of the year, critics attributing much of its success to Belushi. He wasn't so fortunate with his next movie, the romantic comedy *Old Boyfriends* (1979). To the public, Belushi was Bluto and the Samurai, and they had difficulty relating to him in a romantic role. As Wild Bill Kelso, in Steven Speilberg's flop *1941* (1979), Belushi played another character much like Bluto, this time in goggles and chewing on a stubby cigar.

During this time, Aykroyd and Belushi were cooperating on writing sketches for SNL, their partnership based on friendship and common interests. During a road trip they discovered a common love of blues music, and they returned to New York with an idea to develop a warm-up act for SNL, the Blues Brothers. Studio audiences were enthusiastic, and the actors convinced the producers to put the Blues Brothers on the telecast. The reaction was phenomenal. The Blues Brothers soon followed up their television success with a best-selling album (*Briefcase Full of Blues*), a hit single ("Soul Man") and a promotional tour. To Belushi, this was a dream come true: a rock band on tour with a best-selling record. The two stars decided it was time to quit television and concentrate on their movie and music careers.

Aykroyd, meanwhile, had teamed up with John Landis to bring the band to the big screen. The script they came up with began with Jake Blues (Belushi) being released from Joliet State Penitentiary and returning with his brother Elwood (Aykroyd) to the orphanage where they were raised. Learning it is to close unless they can get $5,000, the brothers decide to put their band back together. The first part of the movie concerns their attempts to find the rest of the band, while the second half involves the band's efforts to raise the money. Throughout, however, the brothers get involved in many car chases, destroying a mall in one scene and many of the Chicago Police Department's cars in another.

The Blues Brothers opened in 1980 to a mixed reception. The film was mainly criticized for the excess of car chases, but this is a part of the cult status *The Blues Brothers* achieved. The *Animal House* audience loved it, seeing the return of the Belushi they had missed in his other movies. While his character was not Bluto, it was the familiar back-flipping, blues-howling Joliet Jake from SNL. The opening scenes of the film further reinforced Belushi's bad-boy image, as his character is released from jail, promptly to go on the run from the police. Most critics, however, thought it was terrible, and one went so far as to criticize Landis for keeping Belushi's eyes covered for most of the movie with Jake's trademark Ray Bans.

Belushi had already moved on to his first dramatic role as reporter Ernie Souchak in *Continental Divide* (1981). He received good reviews, most of them expressing some surprise that he could do a dramatic role. The public, however, wanted still more of Bluto and Joliet Jake. *Continental Divide* barely broke even. He then returned to comedy, working on *Neighbors* (1981) with Aykroyd. The movie was a critical and box office disaster, in no small part due to the director's idea of having the partners switch roles, with Belushi playing the straight man to Aykroyd's quirky neighbor. The experience convinced Belushi that he needed more control of his movie projects, so he began working on a revision of the script for his next role in a movie called *Noble Rot*. He envisioned the role as a return to the Bluto character that his audience was demanding. However, by this time he was taking heroin. He died of a drug overdose before completing *Noble Rot*.

Sixteen years after his death (almost to the day) *National Enquirer* gave him the centerpiece of its story on unsolved Hollywood mysteries (March 3, 1998), rehashing conspiracy theories surrounding his death. His death had raised some questions, leading his widow, writer Judy Jacklin Belushi, to approach Woodward to investigate it. The result was *Wired,* more of an examination of Belushi's descent into drugs than a balanced portrait of the actor's life. Later, Belushi's family and friends were incensed when the book was made into a movie, which *Rolling Stone* called a "pathetic travesty" and an "insult" to his memory. In response to the book and the movie Jacklin published her own autobiography, *Samurai Widow* (1990), which Harold Ramis described as the perfect antidote to *Wired*. During the 1990s, a new generation discovered the actor and comedian that was John Belushi, while leaving his older fans wondering about what could have been. As one biography noted, Belushi helped to develop and make popular an energetic, creative form of improvisational comedy that continued to entertain audiences.

—John J. Doherty

FURTHER READING:

"Belushi, John." *Current Biography Yearbook.* 1980.

Jacklin Belushi, Judy. *Samurai Widow.* New York, Carroll and Graf, 1990.

John Belushi: Funny You Should Ask. Videocassette produced by Sue Nadell-Bailey. Weller/Grossman Productions, 1994.

Vickery-Bareford, Melissa. "Belushi, John." *American National Biography.* New York, Oxford University Press, 1999.

Woodward, Bob. *Wired: The Short Life and Fast Times of John Belushi.* New York, Simon and Schuster, 1984.

Ben Casey

The medical drama *Ben Casey* premiered in October 1961 and soon became the most popular program on ABC. It featured Vince Edwards as the intensely handsome young neurosurgeon at a large metropolitan hospital. The wise Dr. Zorba, who was played by veteran actor Sam Jaffe, mentored him in his efforts to combat disease and the medical establishment. The younger physician's brooding, almost grim, manner echoed the show's tensely realistic tone. The series often confronted controversial subjects and was praised for accurately presenting medical ethics and dilemmas. Each episode began with a voice intoning the words "Man. Woman. Birth. Death. Infinity" as the camera focused on a hand writing the symbols for the words, thus dramatically announcing the somber subject matter of the show. The series ended in 1966. Contemporary viewers have come to associate *Ben Casey* with other medical programs like *Dr. Kildare* and *Marcus Welby, M.D.* in that they all tended to project the image of the "perfect doctor."

—Charles Coletta

FURTHER READING:

Castleman, Harry, and Walter Podrazik. *Harry and Wally's Favorite TV Shows.* New York, Prentice Hall Press, 1989.

Harris, Jay. *TV Guide: The First 25 Years.* New York, New American Library, 1980.

Bench, Johnny (1947—)

Known as the popular catcher for the Cincinnati Reds during the 1970s, Johnny Bench set a standard of success as perhaps the finest at his position in modern Major League baseball. Bench first gained national attention by winning the National League MVP (Most Valuable Player) award in 1970 and 1972, recording ten straight Gold Gloves, and helping Cincinnati's "Big Red Machine" to World Series victories in 1975 and 1976. Bench revolutionized his position by popularizing a one-handed catching method that gave him greater mobility with his throwing arm. After retiring from baseball, Bench remained in the public spotlight through television appearances, golf outings, and broadcasting. He is President of Johnny Bench Enterprises and won an Emmy for a program called *The Baseball Bunch.* His success and popularity led to his induction into the Baseball Hall of Fame in 1989.

—Nathan R. Meyer

FURTHER READING:

Bench, Johnny, with William Brashler. *Catch You Later: The Autobiography of Johnny Bench.* New York, Harper and Row, 1979.

Benchley, Robert (1889-1945)

In his relatively short life Benchley managed to enjoy careers as a humorist, theater critic, newspaper columnist, screenwriter, radio performer and movie actor. His writing appeared in such magazines as the old *Life* and *The New Yorker* and his pieces were collected in several books with outlandish titles. Among the film directors he worked with were Alfred Hitchcock, Rene Clair, and Billy Wilder. Benchley won an Academy Award for one of the comedy shorts he wrote and starred in. Benchley was also a member in good standing of the Algonquin Circle in Manhattan and a longtime resident of the Garden of Allah in Hollywood. Talent runs in the Benchley family—his grandson wrote *Jaws,* and both his son, Nathaniel, and his grandson, Peter, became writers.

A genuinely funny man, it was his wit and humor that allowed Benchley to make his way through the world and assured him his assorted jobs. He was born in Worcester, Massachusetts and attended Harvard. His first humor was written for *The Lampoon.* Settling in New York, he got a staff job on *Vanity Fair* where his co-workers included Robert E. Sherwood and Dorothy Parker. Later in the 1920s he was hired by *Life,* which was a humor magazine in those days. He wrote a great many pieces and also did the theater column. He later said that one of the things he liked best in the world was "that 10 minutes at the theater before the curtain goes up, I always feel the way I did when I was a kid around Christmas time."

The 1920s was a busy decade on Broadway and Benchley was in attendance on the opening nights of such shows as *Funny Face, Show Boat, Dracula, Strange Interlude,* and *What Price Glory?* In May of 1922, *Abie's Irish Rose* opened and Benchley dismissed Anne Nichols' play as the worst in town, saying that its obvious Irish and Jewish jokes must have dated back to the 1890s. Much to his surprise, the play was a massive hit and ran for five years. Each week for *Life* he had to make up a Confidential Guide with a capsule review of every play then on Broadway. That meant he had to write something about

Abie's Irish Rose each and every week during its run of 2,327 performances. At first he would simply note "Something awful" or "Among the season's worst," but then he grew more inventive and said such things as "People laugh at this every night, which explains why democracy can never be a success," "Come on, now! A joke's a joke," and "No worse than a bad cold."

At the same time that he was reviewing plays, Benchley was also collecting his humor pieces in books. The gifted Gluyas Williams, an old school chum from Harvard, provided the illustrations. In addition to parodies, spoofs, and out and out nonsense pieces, some in the vein of his idol Stephen Leacock, he also wrote a great many small essays about himself, taking a left-handed and slightly baffled approach to life. Only on a shelf of books by Robert Benchley is it possible to find such titles as *My Ten Years in a Quandary and How They Grew, No Poems, or, Around the World Backwards and Sideways,* and *From Bed To Worse, or, Comforting Thoughts About the Bison.*

Benchley gradually drifted into the movies. He appeared in over two dozen feature length films, including *Foreign Correspondent* (for which he also wrote some of the dialogue), *I Married A Witch, The Major and the Minor* (where he delivered the line about "getting out of those wet clothes and into a dry martini"), *Take A Letter, Darling,* and *The Road to Utopia.* He also made nearly 50 short films. His first one, *The Treasurer's Report,* was done in 1928 for Fox. The shorts most often took the form of deadpan lectures, giving advice on such topics as how to read, how to take a vacation, and how to train a dog. *How To Sleep,* done for Metro-Goldwyn-Meyer in the mid-1930s, won him an Academy Award. Once in an ad in *Variety* he listed himself as specializing in "Society Drunk" roles.

When he was working in Hollywood, Benchley most often resided in a bungalow at the Garden of Allah, which was the favorite lodging place of visiting actors, writers, and "hangers-on." The Garden was torn down decades ago to make way for a bank. At one time the bank had a display of relics of the old hotel and among them was one of Benchley's liquor bills.

—Ron Goulart

FURTHER READING:

Benchley, Nathaniel. *Robert Benchley, A Biography.* New York, McGraw-Hill, 1955.

Trachtenberg, Stanley, editor. *American Humorists, 1800-1950.* Detroit, Gale Research Company, 1982.

Ben-Hur

As a novel, a play, two silent films, and a wide screen spectacular, Lew Wallace's *Ben-Hur: A Tale of the Christ* set the standard for the religious epic, inaugurating an amazing series of firsts in American popular culture. Published in 1880, the novel tells the story of Judah Ben-Hur, a young, aristocratic Jew, and his encounter with Jesus of Nazareth. The book begins with the Messiah's birth and then moves ahead 30 years to Ben-Hur's reunion with his boyhood friend, Messala, now a Roman officer. The latter's contempt for Jews, however, ends their friendship. When the Roman governor's life is threatened, Messala blames Ben-Hur, unjustly condemning him to the galleys and imprisoning Ben-Hur's mother and sister. As pirates attack Ben-Hur's ship, he manages to escape. Returning to Judea, he

Charlton Heston in the chariot race from the 1959 film *Ben-Hur*.

searches for his family and also raises a militia for the Messiah. Meeting Messala again, Ben-Hur beats him in a dramatic chariot race during which the Roman is crippled. Discovering that his mother and sister are now lepers, Ben-Hur searches for Jesus, hoping for a miraculous cure. They finally meet on the road to Calvary. Jesus refuses his offer of military assistance, but cures his family. Converted to Christianity, Ben-Hur resolves to help fellow Christians in Rome suffering persecution.

The book moved slowly at first, selling only some 2,800 copies in its first seven months. Eventually, word of mouth spread across America, particularly through schools and clubs. By 1889, 400,000 copies had been sold, outstripping *Uncle Tom's Cabin*, but falling just short of the Bible. Sales swelled to 1,000,000 by 1911, with translations appearing in German, French, Spanish, Swedish, Turkish, and Arabic, among other languages. A braille edition also was available. For many Americans, *Ben-Hur* was an example of edifying reading, the first work of fiction often allowed on their bookshelves. It was also the first book featured in the *Sears Catalogue.*

Wallace, a retired Union general from Indiana and one-time governor of the Territory of New Mexico, was quickly besieged with offers to dramatize his work. In 1899 he settled on a production adapted by William Young of Chicago, directed by Joseph Brooks, and featuring later cowboy film star William S. Hart as Messala. *Ben-Hur* ran on Broadway for 24 weeks and was, according to the *New*

York Clipper, a "triumphant success," generating "enormous business" and "record-breaking attendance." It continued to tour nationally and abroad for some 20 years, making it the first play seen by many Americans. *Ben-Hur* set precedents both for an author's control over rights to his/her work (rejecting one offer, Wallace declared, "The savages who sell things of civilized value for glass beads live further West than Indiana") and for control over the adaptation of material. Wallace insisted, for example, that no actor would portray Christ. Instead, the Messiah was represented by a 25,000-candle-power shaft of light. Similarly spectacular effects—such as a wave machine for the naval battle and, for the chariot race, actual horses and chariots running on a treadmill before a moving panorama of the arena—set the standard for later epic films.

A 1907 film version, produced two years after Wallace's death and without the copyright holders' authorization, set a different kind of precedent. The Wallace estate sued the film's producers for breach of copyright, receiving a $25,000 settlement. The case marked the first recognition of an author's rights in film adaptations.

In 1922, two years after the play's last tour, the Goldwyn company purchased the film rights to *Ben-Hur*. Shooting began in Italy in 1923, inaugurating two years of difficulties, accidents, and eventually—after the merger of Goldwyn into MGM (Metro-Goldwyn-Meyer)—a move back to Hollywood. Additional recastings (including Ramon Navarro as Ben-Hur) and a change of director helped skyrocket the production's budget to $4,000,000. With its trials and tribulations, then, this *Ben-Hur* helped set another pattern for later epic films. More positively, on the other hand, its thrilling chariot race changed the face of filmmaking. Following in the tracks of the stage play, its considerable expenditure of money and horses made this sequence a brilliant tour-de-force that established the lavish production values now associated with the Hollywood epic. Although audiences flocked to *Ben-Hur* after its premiere in 1925 and critics praised the film (more for its ''grandeur,'' however, than its story), MGM was unable to recoup its $4,000,000 investment. As a result, the studio imposed the block booking system on its other productions, another precedent. While not a financial success, however, the film still proved so popular that MGM was able to release it again in 1931, adding music and sound effects for the sound era.

In 1959, a decade that saw the resurgence of epic productions, MGM remade *Ben-Hur* for the wide screen, using state of the art Panavision techniques and stereophonic sound. Directed by William Wyler and starring Charlton Heston as Ben-Hur, this film again features a spectacular, thundering chariot race that took four months to rehearse and three months to produce. The sequence nearly overshadowed the rest of the movie, leading some to dub *Ben-Hur* ''Christ and a horse-race.'' The film was a box office and critical success, earning $40,000,000 in its first year and garnering 11 Academy Awards. Enjoying tremendous popularity and continuing *Ben-Hur's* tradition of establishing precedents, it was broadcast uncut on network television in 1971, earning the highest ratings at that time for any film. It has been rebroadcast and re-released in theaters several times since then.

Few works can claim to have made the same impact as has Wallace's *Ben-Hur*. As a novel and a play, it offered many people their first entry into the worlds of fiction and drama. In its various film adaptations, it elevated Hollywood's production values and defined the genre of the religious epic. It also established many legal precedents for stage and screen adaptations. The key to its enduring popularity, however, is that it provided audiences around the world with an exciting spectacle that combined piety and faith.

—Scott W. Hoffman

FURTHER READING:

Babington, Bruce, and Peter William Evans. *Biblical Epics: Sacred Narrative in the Hollywood Cinema.* Manchester, Manchester University Press, 1993.

Forshey, Gerald E. *American Religious and Biblical Spectaculars.* Westport, Connecticut, Praeger, 1992.

Searles, Baird. *Epic! History on the Big Screen.* New York, Harry N. Abrams, 1990.

Towne, Jackson E. "Lew Wallace's Ben-Hur." *New Mexico Historical Review.* Vol. 36, No. 1, December, 1961, 62-9.

Benneton

Italy-based clothier Benneton is best known for its ''shock'' advertising campaigns, many of which have sparked significant controversy in many regions of the globe. In their 1990s campaign, ''Sufferings of Our Earth,'' the fashion designer's ads showed among other things a dying AIDS victim, a dead Bosnian soldier, an oil smeared sea bird, and an overcrowded refugee ship. A series of ads in 1998 featured autistic and Down's syndrome kids modeling their clothing. The company operates some 7,000 stores in over 120 countries and had $2 billion in revenues in 1997. In addition to apparel, Benneton also markets a wide range of products from racing cars to sunglasses and condoms.

—Abhijit Roy

FURTHER READING:

''Benneton Enters Condom Market.'' *Marketing.* November 13, 1997.

Granatstein, Lisa. ''Benetton's Colors Dances with Mr.D.'' *Mediaweek.* February 23, 1998.

Rogers, Danny. ''Benetton Plans to Show Down's Syndrome Kids.'' *Marketing.* August 13, 1998.

Bennett, Tony (1926—)

Through perseverance, professionalism, and impeccable musical taste, Tony Bennett has emerged in the era of MTV as the senior statesman of the American popular song. Born Anthony Dominick

Tony Bennett

Benedetto in Queens, New York, Bennett joined the Italian-American *bel canto* tradition represented by such singers as Frank Sinatra and Vic Damone. In fact, Sinatra often publicly referred to Bennett as his favorite singer, a validation that undoubtedly means as much as a handful of gold records and Grammy awards combined.

Bennett's musical career started slowly. After serving in the armed forces in the final months of World War II, he studied vocal technique under the GI Bill and supported himself with a variety of jobs, including, according to some sources, a stint as a singing waiter. His first break occurred when he came in second to Rosemary Clooney on the network television show *Arthur Godfrey's Talent Scouts* in 1950. This exposure led to an introduction to Bob Hope, who helped Bennett to land an engagement in one of New York's premier clubs. Later that year, Mitch Miller signed Bennett as a recording artist for Columbia Records, and in 1951 he was named male vocalist of the year by *Cashbox* magazine.

Always attracted to jazz as well as pop styling, Bennett teamed up with some of the top musicians of the day, which gave him the freedom to choose songs that were more to his taste than the hit-oriented recording business normally allowed. Numerous records during the mid and late 1950s show Bennett at his best, singing jazz-inflected standards like ''These Foolish Things'' and ''Blues in the Night.''

Nevertheless, Bennett experienced a long hitless period in the early 1960s. It was during this time that the singer and his longtime arranger and accompanist Ralph Sharon played a gig at the Fairmont Hotel in San Francisco, where Bennett sang a new song by little-known writers George Cory and Douglass Cross for the first time. That song, ''I Left My Heart in San Francisco,'' changed the course of Bennett's career, earning him a sustained place on the charts in both the United States and Great Britain. It also brought Bennett two Grammy awards, for record of the year and best male vocal performance.

With his new public image, Bennett moved from supper clubs to the concert stage, giving a landmark recorded performance at Carnegie Hall. In the mid-1960s, he had hits with such singles as ''The Good Life,'' ''A Taste of Honey,'' and ''Fly Me to the Moon.'' Soon after that, however, Bennett, like other interpreters of American pop standards by Arlen, Gershwin, and Porter, began to suffer from the record companies' stubborn commitment to rock and roll. Bennett was not interested in singing songs he did not love, although he did compromise on a 1970 album titled *Tony Bennett Sings the Great Hits of Today,* which included such songs as ''MacArthur Park,'' ''Eleanor Rigby,'' and ''Little Green Apples.'' More to his taste were two albums made on the Improv label with the great jazz pianist Bill Evans in 1975 and 1977. Bennett also appeared with Evans at the Newport Jazz Festival and at Carnegie Hall.

In 1979, Bennett's son Danny, a former rock guitarist, took over his management, with a combination of shrewd marketing and musical acuity that helped his father bridge the gap between the old and new pop scene. It was this teaming that eventually led to the MTV video and album *Tony Bennett Unplugged* in 1994. In an era when smooth and mellow lounge music was reborn and martinis were once again the official cocktail, the album was a huge hit. Always generous to his younger colleagues—just as another generation of entertainers had been generous to him—Bennett gave high praise to k.d. lang, who joined him for a duet of ''Moonglow,'' and to Elvis Costello, who harmonized on ''They Can't Take That Away from Me.''

In addition to his singing career, Bennett is a serious painter in oils, watercolors, and pastels. His work has been exhibited widely,

and he claims David Hockney as a major influence. A graduate of New York's High School of Industrial Art, Bennett often paints familiar New York scenes, such as yellow cabs racing down a broad avenue and Sunday bicyclers in Central Park, capturing the milieu in which he lived, sang, and observed.

—Sue Russell

FURTHER READING:

Bennett, Tony, with Will Friedwald. *The Good Life.* New York, Simon & Schuster, 1998.

Hemming, Roy, and David Hajdu. *Discovering Great Singers of Classic Pop.* New York, Newmarket Press, 1991.

The Benny Hill Show

English comic Benny Hill became an international celebrity with his schoolboy brand of lecherous, burlesque humor. Bringing the tradition of the British vaudeville to television in 1955, the pudgy Hill hosted comedy series for the BBC and Thames Television over a period of thirty-four years. Featuring slapstick and sight gags, *The Benny Hill Show* always had a sexual energy, bursting with plenty of double-entendres and leggy starlets. The show was edited for world-wide syndication and became a cult phenomenon in the United States beginning in 1979. American audiences quickly identified Red Skelton as a main source of inspiration (Hill borrowed Skelton's closing line, ''Good night, God bless''); but there was little sentimentality in the ribaldry of Hill's characters. Hill was always criticized for his sexist obsessions, and his series in England was finally cancelled in 1989 because of complaints from the moral right and the politically correct left. Hill died three years later, and, although English audiences voted him ''Funniest Man in the World'' several times, he thought he never received the critical recognition he deserved. But to many, Hill was a genuine comic auteur, writing all his material and supervising every randy shot for his show that was enjoyed in over one hundred countries.

—Ron Simon

FURTHER READING:

Kingsley, Hilary, and Geoff Tibballs. *Box of Delights.* London, MacMillan, 1989.

Robinson, J. ''A Look at Benny Hill.'' *TV Guide.* December 10, 1983, 34-36.

Smith, John. *The Benny Hill Story.* New York, St. Martin's, 1989.

Benny, Jack (1894-1974)

Jack Benny is one of America's most venerated entertainers of the twentieth century. For over 50 years the nation identified with the

Jack Benny

persona that Benny created on the vaudeville circuit, sustained on radio, and successfully transferred to television. Few performers have lasted so long without any significant drop in popularity.

The character that Benny created exemplified the foibles of the American Everyman. Benny realized early on that "if you want the laughs you have to put something in a ridiculous light, even yourself." Benny was not a gifted clown or a sparkling wit, so he and his writers crafted a well-rounded persona with the weaknesses and imperfections of his audience. The Benny alter ego was penny-pinching, vain, anxious, and never willing to admit his true age (he was always 39 years old). Endless jokes were woven around these shortcomings, with Benny always the object of ridicule. Although the character had no identifiable ethnic or religious heritage, Americans had a deep affection for this insecure, sometimes petulant, creation.

The comedian was born Benjamin Kubelsky in Waukegan, Illinois on February 14, 1894, and began performing in vaudeville as a violinist. Still a teenager, he discovered the public responded to his jokes and wrong notes. Achieving moderate success on the New York stage, Benny first appeared on radio in 1929 and began a NBC radio series in 1932. Two years later, he was one of the medium's most popular entertainers. In 1935 he moved operations to Hollywood, and Jell-O became a trusted sponsor.

Benny found his character worked better as part of a group and helped to pioneer "gang" comedy. His wife, Sadie Marks, appeared as a sometimes girl friend, Mary Livingstone, and assumed the character's name as her own. Eddie Anderson portrayed Benny's personal valet, Rochester, and was hailed as radio's first black star.

Although there were stereotypical elements to Rochester's characterization, a genuine bond grew between Benny and his employee that transcended race. Don Wilson as the rotund announcer, Phil Harris as the boozy bandleader, and Dennis Day as the boy singer rounded out the stable of regulars "playing themselves."

Radio listeners delighted in Benny's recurring gags and show business feuds as well as such catchphrases as "Well!" and "Now cut that out!" Mel Blanc was popular as the voice of Carmichael, the bear that lived in the basement; the exasperated violin teacher, Professor LeBlanc; and the bellowing railroad announcer ("Anaheim, Azusa, and Cucamonga!"). Frank Nelson returned again and again as the unctuous clerk who harassed customers by squawking "Yeeeesss!" Benny is best remembered for his "Your money or your life?" routine, in which a burglar demands a difficult answer from the stingy comedian. After a long pause with the laughter building, Benny delivered his classic line, "I'm thinking it over." To Benny, timing was everything.

The cast frequently spoofed western serials with the skit "Buck Benny Rides Again." The parody was made into a movie in 1940. Benny made his first film appearance in the *Hollywood Revue of 1929,* but his radio stardom paved the way for substantial roles. Among his notable movie vehicles, Benny appeared as a vain actor in Ernst Lubitsch's classic, *To Be or Not to Be* (1942); a confirmed city-dweller in *George Washington Slept Here* (1942); and an avenging angel in Raoul Walsh's comedy, *The Horn Blows at Midnight* (1945).

In 1948 Benny took greater control of his career. He formed a production company to produce his radio series and generate more money for himself. William Paley also lured him to the CBS network. Although his vaudeville compatriots, Ed Wynn and Milton Berle, had become television stars in the late 1940s, Benny warmed slowly to the possibilities of the visual medium. Beginning with his first special, performed live in October 1950, Benny tried to approximate the radio series as closely as possible, retaining his cast and adapting appropriate scripts. Benny was also careful not to overexpose himself. Until 1953, *The Jack Benny Show* was a series of irregular specials on CBS; then, for seven years, it ran every other week on Sunday nights, his regular evening on radio. Beginning in 1960, the program aired every week, switching to Tuesday and Friday during its five year run.

Benny brought to television a defined, identifiable character forged during his stage and radio years. His persona was perfectly suited for the requirements of the small screen. Benny underlined his characterization with subtle gestures and facial expressions. The stare, which signaled Benny's pained exasperation, became his visual signature. Like the pause in radio, Benny's stare allowed the audience to participate in the joke.

The Benny program combined elements of the variety show and the situation comedy. As host, Benny, always in character, opened the proceedings with a monologue before the curtain. The bulk of each program was Benny performing with his regulars in a sketch that further played off his all-too-human frailties. Guest stars were also invited to play themselves in Benny's fictional world. Since the format was a known quantity, many movie stars made their television comedy debut on the Benny program, including Barbara Stanwyck, Marilyn Monroe, Gary Cooper, and James Stewart.

Throughout the 1950s and 1960s, Benny's writers kept his persona fresh and vital to a new generation of viewers. They crafted sketches around such television personalities as Dick Clark, Ernie

Kovacs, and Jack Webb. Benny also stayed eternally young by donning a wig and playing guitar on occasion. When his weekly series ended in 1965, he returned to comedy specials. Whether playing violin with Isaac Stern or impersonating a surfer in a routine with the Beach Boys, Jack Benny was able to bridge audiences of different ages and tastes.

Jack Benny was a comedian's comedian. His sense of understated style and exquisite delivery shaped a generation of entertainers from Johnny Carson to Kelsey Grammer. He was also a national institution. Although the public knew in reality that he was a kind and generous person, they wanted to believe the worst. Jack Benny held up a mirror to America's failings and pretensions. As his friend Bob Hope said in farewell after his death in 1974, "For Jack was more than an escape from life. He was life—a life that enriched his profession, his friends, his millions of fans, his family, his country."

—Ron Simon

FURTHER READING:

Benny, Jack and Joan. *Sunday Nights at Seven: The Jack Benny Story.* New York, Warner, 1990.

Fein, Irving. *Jack Benny: An Intimate Biography.* New York, Putnam, 1976.

Josefberg, Milt. *The Jack Benny Show.* New Rochelle, New York, Arlington House, 1977.

The Museum of Television & Radio. *Jack Benny: The Radio and Television Work* (published in conjunction with an exhibition of the same title). New York, Harper, 1971.

Candice Bergen

Bergen, Candice (1946—)

Candice Bergen may be the only female television star to be known and loved as a curmudgeon. Most noted curmudgeons are male, like Lou Grant of *The Mary Tyler Moore Show,* Archie Bunker of *All in the Family,* Homer Simpson from *The Simpsons,* and Oscar the Grouch from *Sesame Street.* Bergen's alter-ego, Murphy Brown, on the other hand, is the queen of curmudgeons. Despite her manly traits, Murphy has gone down in history as the only television curmudgeon to be criticized by the vice president of the United States and to be used as an argument in a national debate on family values. Her willingness to challenge traditional female roles and issues revolving around what is perceived as "decency," have, willingly or not, made her one of the twentieth century's most political actresses.

Murphy Brown, created by Diane English, was a female reporter who learned to operate in a man's world. She adopted what are generally considered male characteristics: intelligence, aggressiveness, ambitiousness, and perseverance. It has been suggested that reporter Linda Ellerbee was the specific role model for Bergen's character, but only Bergen herself could have made Murphy Brown so lovable through a decade of the weekly series of the same name, covering almost every political topic with satiric wit.

Candice Bergen grew up in an elite section of Beverly Hills playing with the children of Walt Disney, Judy Garland, Gloria Swanson, Jimmy Stewart, and other Hollywood notables. Her beauty was inherited from her mother, Frances Western, a former model who received national attention as the Ipana girl from a toothpaste advertisement. Her talent came from her father, ventriloquist Edgar Bergen. In her autobiography, *Knock Wood,* Bergen tells of being jealous of her father's famous sidekick, marionette Charlie McCarthy, and of spending years of her life trying to make her father proud.

Noted for her outstanding beauty, Candice Bergen was not always taken seriously as an individual. Nonetheless, by the time she accepted the role of Murphy Brown Bergen was well respected as an international photojournalist and as a writer. She had also starred in a number of high-profile films, most notably, Mary McCarthy's *The Group,* in which she played the distant and lovely lesbian Lakey. Bergen also received critical acclaim as the ex-wife of Burt Reynolds in the romantic comedy *Starting Over.*

At the age of 33 Bergen met the famed French director Louis Malle. Friends say they were destined to meet and to fall in love. The pair maintained a bi-continental marriage until his death in 1995, leaving Bergen to raise their daughter Chloe. After Malle's death, Bergen devoted her time exclusively to Chloe and to her television show. By all accounts, the cast of *Murphy Brown* was close and Bergen said in interviews that Faith Ford (who played Corky Sherwood) had been particularly comforting during her mourning over the death of her husband. This personal closeness gave the cast a professional camaraderie that was evident to audiences.

In 1988, *Murphy Brown* introduced the cast of *F.Y.I*, a fictional news show. Murphy Brown (Candice Bergen), Frank Fontana (Joe Regalbuto), Jim Dial (Charles Kimbrough), and Corky Sherwood (Faith Ford) shared anchor duties on air and traded wisecracks and friendship off the air. They were joined by producer Miles Silverberg (Grant Shaud), artist and handyman Eldin (Robert Pastorelli), and barkeeper Phil (Pat Corley). In 1996, Lily Tomlin replaced Shaud as the producer. Plot lines ranged from grocery shopping and consciousness raising, to romance, divorce, and the White House cat, Socks. The two most notable story lines involved unwed motherhood and breast cancer. During its tenure, *Murphy Brown* won 18 Emmys, five of them for its star. Bergen then withdrew her name from competition.

In 1992, Murphy Brown, a fictional character on a television show, became pregnant. After much soul searching, she decided to raise her baby without a father. In May of that election year, Vice President Dan Quayle stated in a speech (allegedly against the advise of his handlers): "It doesn't help matters when prime time television has Murphy Brown—a character who supposedly epitomizes today's intelligent, highly paid professional woman—mocking the importance of fathers by bearing a child alone and calling it just another 'lifestyle choice.'" The media was delighted, and the debate was on.

In the fall of 1992, Bergen and Diane English (who had offered to debate Quayle on the issue) had their say when Murphy responded to the vice president on *F.Y.I.* by gently reminding him that families come in all shapes and sizes. She then chided Quayle by agreeing that there were serious problems in American society and suggested that the vice president could blame the media, Congress, or an administration that had been in power for 12 years . . . or, he could blame her. The episode ended with the dumping of 1,000 pounds of potatoes in Quayle's driveway, a reference to an occasion when Quayle misspelled the word as a judge in an elementary speech contest. The episode won the Emmy for Best Comedy of 1992.

The final season of *Murphy Brown* (1997-1998) ended on a more solemn note. Murphy discovered that she had breast cancer. Throughout the season, real cancer survivors and medical advisors helped to deliver the message that cancer was serious business and that there was hope for recovery. An episode devoted to the medicinal use of marijuana demonstrated the strong bond among the cast and proved that the show could still arouse controversy. The final episode of the season was filled with emotional farewells and celebrated guest stars, including Bette Midler as the last in a long line of Murphy's secretaries, Julia Roberts, and George Clooney. God, in the person of Alan King, also made an appearance, as did Robert Pastorelli (Eldin) and Pat Corley (Phil), both of whom had left the series years before to pursue other interests.

Various media reports have indicated that Candice Bergen may become a commentator for *60 Minutes*. With her experience as a photojournalist and with her ten years on *F.Y.I.,* Bergen is imminently qualified to engage in a serious debate of national issues.

—Elizabeth Purdy

FURTHER READING:

Bergen, Candice. *Knock Wood*. Boston, G. K. Hall & Company, 1984.

Morrow, Lance. "But Seriously Folks." *Time*. June 1, 1992, 10-12.

Bergen, Edgar (1903-1978)

Chicago-born Edgar Bergen put himself through college as a part-time ventriloquist with a doll he had acquired while in high school. It was to his relationship with this doll, the cheeky, monocled toff Charlie McCarthy, that Edgar Bergen owed his fame and a special Oscar. Edgar and Charlie played the vaudeville circuit, then became popular radio performers in the medium's hey-day. They made several appearances in movies, beginning with *The Goldwyn Follies* (1938) and including *Charlie McCarthy Detective* (1939), while television further increased their visibility. They periodically had other puppets in tow, most famously Mortimer ("How did you get to be so dumb?") Snerd. The father of actress Candice Bergen, Edgar, sans Charlie, played a few minor roles in films, but it is for his influence on the art of puppetry that he is remembered. Muppet creator Jim Henson acknowledged his debt to Bergen's skills, and it was in *The Muppet Movie* (1979) that he made his last appearance. Bergen bequeathed Charlie McCarthy to the Smithsonian Institute.

—Robyn Karney

FURTHER READING:

Katz, Ephraim. *The International Film Encyclopedia*. New York, HarperCollins, 1994.

Press, Skip. *Candice & Edgar Bergen*. Persippany, New Jersey, Crestwood House, 1995.

Bergman, Ingmar (1918—)

Swedish director Ingmar Bergman's name is virtually synonymous with the sort of intellectual European films that most critics love to praise—but that many moviegoers love to hate. His complex explorations of sweeping topics like loneliness, spiritual faith, love, and death have been closely imitated, but also parodied for their overt reliance on symbol and metaphor, for their philosophical dialogue, and for their arguably opaque dreamlike qualities. Famous Bergman images reappear throughout the spectrum of popular culture, images like that of Death, scythe in hand, leading a line of dancing victims through an open field, the figures silhouetted against the sky. Bergman began his prolific career in Stockholm during the 1930s. He directed theater and eventually radio and television dramas. His catalogue of over fifty films includes classics like *The Seventh Seal* (1956), *Wild Strawberries* (1957), *Through a Glass Darkly* (1960), and *Fanny and Alexander* (1983).

—John Tomasic

FURTHER READING:

Bergman, Ingmar. *The Magic Lantern: An Autobiography*. New York, Viking, 1988.

Cohen, Hubert. *Ingmar Bergman: The Art of Confession.* New York, Twayne, 1993.

Steene, Birgitta. *Ingmar Bergman: A Guide to References and Resources.* Boston, G.K. Hall, 1987.

Bergman, Ingrid (1915-1982)

A star in Swedish, French, German, Italian, and British films before emigrating to the United States to star in *Intermezzo* in 1939, Ingrid Bergman, with her Nordic freshness and vitality, coupled with her beauty and intelligence, quickly became the ideal of American womanhood and one of Hollywood's most popular stars. A love affair with Italian director Roberto Rossellini during the filming of *Stromboli* in 1950 created a scandal that forced her to return to Europe, but she made a successful Hollywood comeback in 1956, winning her second Academy Award for the title role in *Anastasia.*

Born in Stockholm to a tragedy-prone family, she suffered at age two the death of her mother. Her father died when she was twelve, a few months before the spinster aunt who had raised her also died. She was sent to live with her uncle and later used her inheritance to study acting at the Royal Dramatic Theatre in Stockholm. With the encouragement of her friend Dr. Peter Lindstrom, who became her first husband in 1937, she turned to the cinema, playing a hotel maid in her

Ingrid Bergman

debut film *Monkbrogreven* (1934). The turning point in her career came in 1937, when the Swedish director Gustaf Molander chose her as the lead in the romantic drama *Intermezzo,* about a famous violinist who has an adulterous affair with a young pianist.

When David Selznick saw a print of Bergman in the Swedish film, he was unimpressed, but he was persuaded by Katharine Brown, his story-buyer, that the proposed American remake of *Intermezzo* would only be successful with Ingrid in the role of the pianist. He signed her to a contract for the one film, with an option for seven years. When *Intermezzo, A Love Story,* also starring Leslie Howard, was released in 1939, Hollywood saw an actress who was completely natural in style as well as lack of makeup. Film critic James Agee wrote that "Miss Bergman not only bears a startling resemblance to an imaginable human being; she really knows how to act, in a blend of poetic grace with quiet realism." Selznick exercised his option for the extended contract and recalled her from Sweden.

While waiting for Selznick to develop roles for her, Bergman played on Broadway in *Liliom* and was loaned out to MGM for two dramatic roles, as the governess in love with Warner Baxter in *Adam Had Four Sons* (1941) and as Robert Montgomery's ill-fated wife in *Dr. Jekyll and Mr. Hyde* (1941). MGM offered her the role of the ingenue in the latter film, but Bergman, always willing to take chances, begged for the role of the floozy and exchanged parts with Lana Turner. Theodore Strauss, writing in the *New York Times,* praised Bergman's "shining talent" in making something of a small part. He added that Turner and the rest of the cast moved "like well-behaved puppets."

In 1942 Warner Brothers, desperate for a continental heroine after being turned down by Hedy Lamarr, borrowed Bergman from Selznick to play opposite Humphrey Bogart in *Casablanca* (1942). The role made Bergman a surefire box-office star and led to her appearing opposite Gary Cooper the following year in Hemingway's *For Whom the Bell Tolls* (1943). Selznick's Swedish import was now in demand for major roles by several studios, and in 1944 MGM signed her for her Academy Award winning role as the manipulated wife in *Gaslight.* Her talent and popularity attracted Alfred Hitchcock, who gave her leads in two of his finest suspense thrillers, *Spellbound* (1945) and *Notorious* (1946). Then occurred a succession of ill-chosen parts, along with a shocking scandal, and the film *Notorious* became her last successful film for a decade.

Her affair with Roberto Rossellini, which erupted during the shooting of *Stromboli* on location in Italy in 1950, resulted in the birth of a daughter and a barrage of international criticism. Although she married Rossellini as soon as possible after her divorce, her fans, and particularly those in America, were unwilling to forgive her. *Stromboli* was boycotted by most of the movie-going public. Rossellini directed her in *Europa '51* in 1952, with the same dismal response.

In 1957 the Fox studios offered her $200,000 for the title role in *Anastasia.* She agreed to the terms, the film was shot in Britain, and it became a world-wide hit, earning Ingrid her second Oscar as well as the forgiveness of her fans. In 1958 two more films shot in Britain were released with great success: *Indiscreet,* with Cary Grant, and *The Inn of the Sixth Happiness,* based on the true story of a missionary in China. She continued to make films in Europe, but most of them received no bookings in the United States. Columbia lured her back to Hollywood for a two-picture deal, however, and she made the popular *Cactus Flower* (1969), co-starring Walter Matthau, and *A Walk in the*

Spring Rain (1970) with Anthony Quinn. Her last role was that of Golda Meir, the Israeli prime minister, in a drama made for television, *A Woman Called Golda* (1981). She made her home in France for the last 32 years of her life and died in London on August 29, 1982.

—Benjamin Griffith

FURTHER READING:

Bergman, Ingrid, and Alan Burgess. *Ingrid Bergman: My Story.* New York, Delacorte, 1980.

Leamer, Laurence. *As Time Goes By: The Life of Ingrid Bergman.* New York, Harper & Row, 1986.

Quirk, Lawrence J. *The Complete Films of Ingrid Bergman.* New York, Carol Communications, 1989.

Spoto, Donald. *Notorious: The Life of Ingrid Bergman.* New York, HarperCollins, 1997.

Taylor, John Russell. *Ingrid Bergman.* New York, St. Martin's Press, 1983.

Berkeley, Busby (1895-1976)

The premier dance director of 1930s Hollywood musicals, Busby Berkeley created outrageously fantastical production numbers

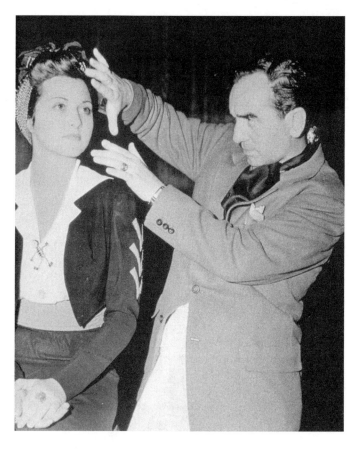

Busby Berkeley with actress Connie Russell.

featuring synchronized hordes of beautiful women moving in kaleidoscopic patterns that took audiences on surreal journeys away from the blues of their Depression-era realities. Berkeley took the spectacle traditions of popular American stage entertainments and the pulchritudinous aesthetic of the Ziegfeld Follies and extended them through cinematic techniques. His groundbreaking dance sequences revolutionized the way musicals were filmed by demonstrating how the camera could be used to liberate the directorial imagination from the constraints of theatrical realism. The distinctive look of his dancing screen geometries influenced the visual aesthetic of films, animation, television commercials, and music videos throughout the twentieth century. The term "busby berkeley" appears in the *American Thesaurus of Slang,* defined as "any elaborate dance number."

Born William Berkeley Enos on November 29, 1895, to a theatrical family in Los Angeles, Berkeley began choreographing while serving in the army. Stationed in France in 1917, Berkeley designed complex parade drills for his battalion, honing his abilities to move multitudes of bodies rhythmically through cunning configurations. After the war, Berkeley worked as an actor and, by 1921, had begun directing plays and musicals. Though he had no dance training, Berkeley soon became known for staging innovative, well-ordered movement sequences for Broadway revues and musicals, including the 1927 hit *A Connecticut Yankee.*

In 1930, Samuel Goldwyn brought Berkeley to Hollywood. Before embarking on his first assignment, directing the dance numbers for the film musical *Whoopee!,* Berkeley visited neighboring sets to learn how the camera was used. The pre-Berkeley approach to filming musicals was akin to documenting a theatrical production. Four stationary cameras were positioned to capture the performance from a variety of angles. The various shots were creatively combined during the editing process. Berkeley chose, instead, to use only one camera, which he moved around the set, thereby allowing his filming, rather than the editing, to dictate the flow of his numbers. Though a few attempts had been made earlier to film dance sequences from points of view other than that of a proscenium stage, it was Berkeley who fully and most inventively exploited the variety of possible camera placements and movements. Berkeley's work is characterized by plenty of panning and high overhead shots that sometimes necessitated cutting a hole in the studio ceiling and eventually resulted in his building a monorail for his camera's travels.

In 1932 Berkeley began a seven-year affiliation with Warner Bros. where he created the bulk of his most remarkable dance sequences for films such as *Gold Diggers of 1933* and *Dames* (1934). His first film there, *42nd Street* (1933), rescued the studio from bankruptcy and rejuvenated the film musical at a time when the genre's popularity had waned.

Berkeley's numbers had little to do with the text or story line of the films. His dances were often voyeuristic and contained undeniable sexual symbolism. Censors were hard-pressed to challenge their naughtiness, however, because the eroticism was in abstract forms—shapes that resembled giant zippers unzipping, long straight bodies diving into circles of women swimming below, or a row of huge rising bananas. No individual dancer ever did anything that could be interpreted as a sexual act.

In Berkeley's dance numbers there is very little actual dancing. It is the camera that executes the most interesting choreography. Berkeley was unconcerned with dance as physical expression and preferred to focus his creative efforts on cinematic tricks. The simple moves and tap dancing in Berkeley's routines were taught to the dancers by his assistants. Berkeley was not interested in the talents of solo dancers, but in how he could use numerous bodies to form magnificent designs.

In 1939, when Warner Bros. lost interest in producing big musicals, Berkeley went to MGM where he continued to create his signature-style dance sequences for films such as *Lady Be Good* (1941). He was also given the opportunity to both choreograph and direct three Mickey Rooney-Judy Garland vehicles, *Babes in Arms* (1939), *Strike Up the Band* (1940), and *Babes on Broadway* (1941). By the mid-1940s, Berkeley-esque movie musicals—those with flimsy plots interrupted by abstract movement sequences—were on their way out in favor of musicals in which the songs and dances were integrated with the drama. The demand for Berkeley's work gradually diminished. He retired in 1954 but returned to create numbers for the 1962 circus extravaganza, *Jumbo*.

By 1970, though the public had long tired of gigantic film musicals, there developed a resurgence of interest in Berkeley's work, seen as camp yet appreciated within the period's wave of 1930s nostalgia. Berkeley was interviewed extensively during this period, while his films were shown on late-night television and in numerous retrospectives. The 1971 revival of *No, No, Nanette* reintroduced Broadway audiences to old-style, large-scale, tap-dance routines reminiscent of Berkeley's heyday. Though he made no artistic contribution to this production, he was hired as an advisor, as it was thought Berkeley's name would boost ticket sales.

While Berkeley's work was light entertainment, his personality had a dark side, evidence of which can be found in aspects of his films as well as in his unsuccessful suicide attempts, his inability to maintain relationships (having been married six times), and his excessive drinking: in 1935 Berkeley was tried for the murders of three victims of his intoxicated driving. Some of Berkeley's dances indicate an obsession with the death of young women, including his favorite sequence—"Lullaby of Broadway" from *Gold Diggers of 1935*—which ends with a woman jumping to her death from atop a skyscraper.

On March 14, 1976, Berkeley died at his home in California. Though his oeuvre is an indelible part of the popular entertainment culture of the 1930s—as he so brilliantly satisfied Americans' escapist needs during one of the country's bleakest eras—his bewitching, dream-like realms peopled by abstract forms made of objectified women intrigue and influence each generation of spectators and visual artists that revisits his films.

—Lisa Jo Sagolla

FURTHER READING:

Delamater, Jerome. *Dance in the Hollywood Musical.* Ann Arbor, Michigan, UMI Research Press, 1981.

Pike, Bob, and Dave Martin. *The Genius of Busby Berkeley.* Reseda, California, Creative Film Society, 1973.

Rubin, Martin. *Showstoppers: Busby Berkeley and the Tradition of Spectacle.* New York, Columbia University Press, 1993.

Thomas, Tony, and Jim Terry with Busby Berkeley. *The Busby Berkeley Book.* Greenwich, Connecticut, New York Graphic Society, 1973.

Berle, Milton (1908—)

Milton Berle, a former vaudevillian, film actor, and radio comedian, was television's first real star. Credited with selling over a million television sets during his first years hosting the weekly Tuesday night NBC program *Texaco Star Theatre,* Berle became post war America's beloved "Uncle Miltie." Since *Texaco Star Theatre* first aired in 1948, only a year after the three major networks first began broadcasting programming on the new medium, much of Berle's urban audience was watching television in communal environs—in neighbors' homes, in taverns, and in community centers. A 1949 editorial in *Variety* magazine heralded the performer for his impact on the lives of city viewers: "When, single handedly, you can drive the taxis off the streets of New York between 8 and 9 on a Tuesday night; reconstruct neighborhood patterns so that stores shut down Tuesday nights instead of Wednesdays, and inject a showmanship in programming so that video could compete favorably with the more established show biz media—then you rate the accolade of 'Mr. Television.'"

Yet, the brash, aggressive, ethnic, and urban vaudeville style that made him such a incredible phenomenon during television's early years were, ironically, the very traits that lead to his professional decline in the mid-1950s. As television disseminated into suburban and rural areas, forever altering audience demographics, viewers turned away from Berle's broad and bawdy antics and towards the middle-class sensibilities of domestic sitcoms such as *I Love Lucy* and

Milton Berle

The Adventures of Ozzie and Harriet. Nevertheless, his infusion of vaudeville-style humor would impact the form and functions of television comedy for decades.

Born in Harlem in 1908, Berle (whose birth name was Mendel Berlinger) was the second youngest of Moses and Sarah (later changed to Sandra) Berlinger's five children. His father, a shopkeeper, was often sick and unable to work. His mother tried to bring in money working as a store detective, but it was a very young Milton who became the real breadwinner of the family. After winning a Charlie Chaplin imitation contest at the age of five, Sarah became convinced that her son had an innate comedic talent. As his manager, she got him work in Biograph-produced silent films, performing alongside the likes of Pearl White (in the famous *Perils of Pauline* serial), Mary Pickford, and Charlie Chaplin. He then performed in a number of traveling vaudeville "kid acts" and made his first appearance on Broadway in a 1920 production of *Floradora.* For four years Berle was teamed with Elizabeth Kennedy in a highly successful boy-girl comedy act on the Keith-Albee circuit. But, after Kennedy left to their act to get married, Berle, who was sixteen, found he had grown too tall to continue performing in kid acts. It was at this point that he developed his city-slicker, wise-cracking, physically frenetic, adult stage personality. His new act included a bit of soft-shoe, some pratfalls, one-liners, impersonations of comedians such as Eddie Cantor, and, occasionally, a drag performance. By the late 1920s, he had become a vaudeville headliner and master of ceremonies, often breaking attendance records at venues such as the famous Palace Theatre in Manhattan.

As Berle garnered praise for his comic timing and style many of his fellow comedians complained loudly and bitterly about his penchant for "stealing" material. Berle countered such accusations with his firm belief that jokes were public property and by incorporating his reputation as the "Thief of Bad Gags" into his on-stage persona. But ironically, just as the comedian's star was rising in the early 1930s, vaudeville entered a slump from which it would never recover. While performing in nightclubs and in Broadway shows, Berle tried his hand in radio. Yet, unlike other former vaudevillians such as Jack Benny and Eddie Cantor who found national stardom on the medium, Berle was never a success on radio—even though he starred in over six different programs. This was due, in large part, to Berle's reliance on physical humor and visual cues instead of scripted jokes and funny scenarios.

After failing in radio, Berle attempted to parlay his visual talents into a movie career. Beginning with RKO's *New Faces of 1937,* the comedian completed nine features in six years. Yet, most of them were "B" pictures and none of them attracted significant numbers at the box office. Although film allowed Berle to employ the essential physical cues of his humor, the medium proved too constricting for him as there was no audience interaction nor was there any room for ad-libbing or spontaneous pratfalls, elements essential to his performance style. Instead of seeing the ways in which his comedy was simply unsuited to the aesthetic characteristics of radio and film, the comedian (as well as many radio and Hollywood executives) began to question his appeal to a mass audience. So, Berle returned to what he knew best—working in front of a live audience in nightclubs and legitimate theaters.

In the spring of 1948, Berle was approached by Kudner, Texaco's advertising agency, to appear as a rotating host on their new television program. Although the agency had tried out other top comedy names such as Henny Youngman, Morey Amsterdam, and Jack Carter during their trial spring and summer, it was Berle that was chosen as the permanent host of the program for the following fall. It was the comedian, not the producers, who crafted the format and content on the show, as, at least for the first year on air, Berle was the program's sole writer and controlled every aspect of the production including lighting and choreography. His program and persona were an immediate hit with a primarily urban audience accustomed to the limited offerings of wrestling, roller derbys, news, and quiz programs. The vaudeville-inspired format of *Texaco Star Theatre,* although popular on radio, had not yet made it onto television, and Berle's innovative and flamboyant style proved irresistible. His aggressive emphasis on the physical aspects of comedy, slick vaudeville routines, ability to ad-lib, expressive gestures, and quick tongue made him an enormous success in an industry looking to highlight visuality and immediacy. What came to be known as the "Berle craze" not only brought major profits to NBC and Texaco, it also set off a proliferation of similar variety shows on television. Berle was rewarded for this with an unprecedented 30 year contract with NBC guaranteeing him $200,000 a year.

Berle became infamous with post war audiences for his drag routines, impersonations, and his constant joking references to his mother. Berle's relationship with Sarah was a key element in his on- and off-stage persona. Almost every article written about Berle during his years on television included at least one reference to the loving, but perhaps over-bearing, stage mother. Although reinforcing a long-standing cultural stereotype of the relationship between Jewish mothers and their sons, Berle's constant references to his mother helped domesticate his image. Often criticized for his inclusion of sexual innuendoes, ethnic jokes, and other material best suited to an adult nightclub audience, Berle, his sponsor, and NBC needed to ensure Texaco's appeal to a family audience. Although Sarah Berle helped remind the public of Berle's familial origins, his own troubled relationship with his first wife dancer Joyce Matthews threatened to taint his image as a wholesome family man. After adopting a child with Berle and then divorcing him twice, Matthews attempted suicide in the home of theatrical producer Billy Rose, her married lover. This scandal, along with rumors of Berle's own extramarital affairs, left him with a questionable reputation in an age when morality and duty to one's family was considered a man's utmost responsibility.

Just as his personal life was under scrutiny, so was his professional life. His popularity with audiences was beginning to wane in the early 1950s and a new style of comedy was on the horizon threatening to usurp his standing as television's most prominent face. In the fall of 1952, after the program's ratings began to drop and Berle was hospitalized for exhaustion, the producers of *Texaco* tried to revamp the program's format by placing Berle within a situational context and introducing a regular cast of characters. This move, however, did not save the show and Texaco dropped their sponsorship at the end of that season. Berle acquired a new sponsor and continued his program as *The Buick-Berle Show* for two more seasons until it to was taken off the air.

Although starring in *The Milton Berle Show* for one season in 1955 and appearing on various television programs and specials in the late 1950s and early 1960s, Berle never regained his once impenetrable hold on the American television audience. Eventually renegotiating his contract with NBC in 1965 to allow him to perform on other networks, Berle made quite a few guest appearances on both comedy and dramatic programs. In addition, he appeared in a number of films including *The Muppet Movie* in 1979 and Woody Allen's *Broadway Danny Rose* in 1984. Since then, he has been honored with numerous professional awards and in the late 1990s published his own magazine *Milton* with his third wife Lorna. Exploiting the nostalgia for the accouterments of a 1950s lifestyle, the magazine tried, with limited success, to revive Berle's persona for a new generation with the motto "we drink, we smoke, we gamble."

—Sue Murray

FURTHER READING:

Adair, Karen. *The Great Clowns of American Television.* New York, McFarland, 1988.

Berle, Milton. *B.S. I Love You.* New York, McGraw-Hill, 1987.

Berle, Milton with Haskel Frankel. *Milton Berle: An Autobiography.* New York, Delacourte, 1974.

"Highlights 48-49 Showmanagement Review: Television Awards." *Variety,* July 27, 1949, 35.

Rader, Dorothy. "The Hard Life, the Strong Loves of a Very Funny Man." *Parade* magazine, *The Boston Globe.* March 19, 1989, 6.

Wertheim, Frank. "The Rise and Fall of Milton Berle." *American History/American Television.* John O'Connor, editor. New York, Fredrick Ungar Publications, 1983, 55-77.

Berlin, Irving (1888-1989)

Irving Berlin's popular music served as a social barometer for much of the twentieth century: it marched to war with soldiers, offered hope and inspiration to a nation in bleak times, and rejoiced in the good things embodied in the American way of life. It also provided anthems for American culture in such standards as "White Christmas," "Easter Parade," "God Bless America," and "There's No Business Like Show Business."

Born Israel Baline on May 11, 1888, in Temun, Siberia, Berlin fled with his family to America to escape the Russian persecution of Jews. They arrived in New York in 1893, settling in Manhattan's Lower East Side. Compelled by poverty to work rather than attending school, Berlin made money by singing on streetcorners and later secured a job as a singing waiter at the Pelham Cafe. During this time, he also began writing songs of his own, and in 1907 he published "Marie from Sunny Italy," signing the work I. Berlin and thereby establishing the pseudonym under which he would become so well known.

Berlin continued his involvement in the burgeoning music industry as a young man, initially working at odd jobs in the neighborhood that was becoming known as Tin Pan Alley and eventually securing a job as a lyricist for the music-publishing firm of Waterson & Snyder. In 1911, his "Alexander's Ragtime Band" became a huge hit and immediately earned him the title "King of Tin Pan Alley." Entirely self-taught as a musician, Berlin developed a unique musical style by playing only on the black keys. Most of his early songs were therefore written in the key of F-sharp, but, by using a transposing keyboard, Berlin was able to compose in various keys.

By the 1920s, Berlin had become one of the most successful songwriters in the country, despite his lack of formal training.

Opening the Music Box Theater with Joseph N. Schenck and Sam Harris in 1921, Berlin began to stage his own revues and musical comedies. When the Great Depression hit in 1929, Berlin, like many others, lost his fortune. His misfortunes did not last long, and he returned to the theater with the show, *Face the Music* (1932). Berlin received his greatest accolades for the Broadway musical, *Annie Get Your Gun* (1946), starring Ethel Merman, which introduced the undeclared anthem of show business, "There's No Business Like Show Business."

Established on the Broadway stage, Berlin's took his musical talents to Hollywood, writing the scores for such hit musical films as *Top Hat* (1935) and *Holiday Inn* (1942). One song from *Holiday Inn,* "White Christmas," remains even today the best-selling song ever recorded. Written during World War II, the song's great appeal lay in part in its evocation of an earlier, happier time, enhanced greatly by Bing Crosby's mellow, wistful delivery.

Berlin's songs have also served as a rallying cry for the nation during two world wars. While serving in the army in World War I, Berlin wrote patriotic songs for the show *Yip, Yip Yaphank* (1918), and in 1942 he wrote *This Is the Army.* The proceeds from performances of the latter totalled over ten million dollars, and were donated to the Army Relief Fund. Berlin's most famous patriotic work remains the song, "God Bless America," written initially during World War I but sung in public for the first time by Kate Smith for an Armistice Day celebration in 1938.

Berlin also wrote some of the most popular love ballads of the century. "When I Lost You" was written in honor of his first wife, who died within the first year of their marriage, and some of his most poignant songs, including the hauntingly beautiful "What'll I Do," "Always," and "Remember" were written for his second wife, the heiress Ellin Mackay.

Berlin died on September 22, 1989 in New York City. His long, remarkable life seemed to illustrate that the American Dream was achievable for anyone who had a vision. He had received awards ranging from an Oscar to a Gold Medal ordered by President Dwight D. Eisenhower. He had become an icon of American popular music, rich and successful, and had helped shape the evolution of that genre through his use and adaptation of a variety of styles, despite a lack of education and formal training. Many of his songs had become an integral part of the tapestry of American life, accompanying representative scenes ranging from the idealized world of elegant dances by Fred Astaire and Ginger Rogers to the humble family fireside Christmas. It was his role as the spokesman of the American people as a collective whole—his ability to give voice to their fears, regrets, and hopes in a most compelling way—that constituted his great contribution to popular culture of the century.

—Linda Ann Martindale

FURTHER READING:

Bergreen, Laurence. *As Thousands Cheer: The Life of Irving Berlin.* New York, Viking Penguin, 1990.

Ewen, David. *Composers for the American Musical Theatre.* New York, Dodd, Mead, 1968.

———. *The Story of Irving Berlin.* New York, Henry Holt, 1950.

Freedland, Michael. *Irving Berlin.* New York, Stein and Day, 1974.

Green, Stanley. *The World of Musical Comedy.* New York, A. S. Barnes, 1976.

Irving Berlin

Bernhard, Sandra (1955—)

Sandra Bernhard's unique appeal derives, in part, from her resistance to categorization. This Flint, Michigan, native is a comedienne, pop singer, social satirist, and provocateur, often all at the same time. Her talents—wry humor, offbeat looks, earthy ease in front of an audience, and powerful singing voice—recall the cabaret and Broadway-nurtured divahood of Barbra Streisand and Bette Midler;

but while Bernhard has the magnetism of a superstar, she has found difficulty reaching that peak, insofar as a star is a commodity who can open a movie, carry a TV show, or sell millions of albums. She has fashioned a career from the occasional film (*Hudson Hawk,* 1991) or TV appearance (*Roseanne, Late Night with David Letterman*); humorous memoirs (*Confessions of a Pretty Lady*); a dance album (*I'm Your Woman*); and most notably, her acclaimed one-woman stage shows, *Without You I'm Nothing* (a film version followed in 1990) and 1998's *I'm Still Here . . . Damn It!* To her fans throughout the

Sandra Bernhard

1980s and 1990s, Bernhard has been both glamour-girl and truth-teller; her voice a magical siren's call from the surly fringes of mainstream success.

The King of Comedy (1989), the Martin Scorsese film which introduced Bernhard to the world, encapsulates the entertainer's contradictions and special allure. In this dark comedy, Robert DeNiro and Bernhard play a pair of star-struck eccentrics who hatch a bizarre plot to kidnap the object of their fantasies, a Johnny Carson-like talk-show host (Jerry Lewis). As Masha, Bernhard plays her deranged obsessive compellingly, triumphing as the one bright spot in this rather sour film, which is widely regarded as one of Scorsese's lesser efforts. In it she displays an outsize personality, hilarious comic delivery, and an undeniable presence, yet instead of offering her a career in films, Hollywood didn't seem to know what to make of Bernhard's strange gifts (in much the same way that Midler suffered a dry spell after her stunning debut in *The Rose* [1979]), and a mainstream movie career failed to materialize. In the 1990s Bernhard accepted roles in low-budget independent films such as *Inside Monkey Zetterland* (1993) and *Dallas Doll* (1995). Television gained her a wider audience, as with her 1992 HBO special *Sandra After Dark*.

The performer and the character share the same problem: both are unnerving in that they expose America's neurotic preoccupation with celebrity. As Justin Wyatt writes, "Bernhard's film debut as the maniacal Masha . . . offers a paradigm for the development of her subsequent career." Bernhard and Masha are not synonymous, yet they intersect at crucial points: having seized the spotlight by playing a gangling, fervent girl with stardust in her eyes, Bernhard has assumed a persona that rests on a love/hate relationship with fame. Having portrayed a fanatic who, in skimpy underwear, takes off down a Manhattan street after a star, in her later stage acts Bernhard's bid for stardom included facing down her audience in pasties or diaphanous get-ups. Finally, after putting her illustrious costar and director to shame in *The King of Comedy* as a novice actress, by the late 1990s Bernhard had become a skilled cult satirist accused of having greater talents than her world-famous targets.

Onstage, Bernhard is often physically revealed, yet protected emotionally within a cocoon of irony. Her humor relies on an exploration of the magical process of star-making, and her own thirst for this kind of success is just more fodder for her brand of satire. She both covets fame and mocks it. As *New Yorker* critic Nancy Franklin observes, "It has always been hard to tell where her sharp-tongued commentary on celebrity narcissism ends and her sharp-tongued narcissistic celebrity begins." Bernhard's references to figures in the entertainment world are trenchant but rarely hateful. When she sets her sights on various personalities, from Madonna to Courtney Love to Stevie Nicks, one finds it difficult to separate the envy from the disapproval, the derision from the adoration, as when she offers her doting audience the seemingly off-hand remark (in *I'm Still Here*): "Tonight, I have you and you and you. And I don't mean in a Diana Ross kind of way." She takes Mariah Carey to task for her using blackness as a commercial pose, and (in *Without You I'm Nothing*) gently mocks her idol Streisand, for singing the incongruous lyric to "Stoney End": "I was born from love and my poor mama worked the mines." Bernhard casts a doubtful look: "She worked in the mines? The diamond mines, maybe."

At times one finds it hard to identify her sly anecdotes as entirely fictional, or as liberal embellishments rooted in a kernel of truth. Even the seemingly genuine details about palling around with Liza Minnelli or sharing a domestic scene with Madonna and her baby are delivered in quotation marks, which is why Bernhard's art is camp in the truest sense; if "the essence of camp," according to Susan Sontag, "is its love of the unnatural: of artifice and exaggeration," then Bernhard must qualify as its high priestess. But there's a catch: she enjoys the facade almost as much as she enjoys stripping it away.

A few critics find this ambiguity trying, but many more applaud her ability to negotiate this tightrope successfully. Just as a female impersonator's act is comprised of both homage and parody (the artifice is simultaneously celebration and critique), Bernhard's take on fame carries a similarly ambivalent message, its pleasure deriving from its irresolution. For stardom, this absurdly artificial construct inspires in the performer deep affection as well as ridicule. She succeeds in transforming a caustic commentary on fame into a kind of fame itself, massaging a simulacrum of stardom into bona fide notoriety. The very tenuousness of her status functions as an asset—indeed, the basis—for what *New York Times* critic Peter Marks called her "mouth-watering after-dinner vitriol," as he recommended her show to anyone "who's fantasized about taking a trip to the dark side of *People* magazine."

—Drew Limsky

FURTHER READING:

Bernhard, Sandra. *Confessions of a Pretty Lady.* New York, Harper & Row, 1988.

Chua, Lawrence. "Guise and Dolls: Out and About with Sandra Bernhard." *Village Voice.* February 6, 1990, 6.

Franklin, Nancy. "Master of Her Domain." *New Yorker.* November 16, 1998, 112-113.

Marks, Peter. "Comedy Whose Barbs Just Won't Go Away." *The New York Times.* November 6, 1998, E3.

Sontag, Susan. "Notes on Camp." *Against Interpretation.* New York, Anchor, 1986, 275-292.

Wyatt, Justin. "Subversive Star-Making: Contemporary Stardom and the Case of Sandra Bernhard." *Studies in Popular Culture.* Vol. XIV, No. 1, 1991, 29-37.

Bernstein, Leonard (1918-1990)

After his sensational 1943 debut with the New York Philharmonic, conductor Leonard Bernstein overnight became an American folk hero with a mythic hold on audiences. His rags-to-riches story particularly appealed to a nation emerging from the Depression and learning about the Holocaust.

Raised in a Hasidic home, Bernstein attended Harvard and seemed the quintessential Jewish artist struggling against obscurity

Leonard Bernstein

and prejudice. His compositions for the musical theater, such as *West Side Story,* became classics, and his classical compositions became welcome additions to orchestral repertories. He was hailed by mass audiences for demonstrating that it was possible to treasure the old while welcoming the new.

Lenny, as Bernstein was popularly known, turned frequent television appearances into "Watch Mr. Wizard" episodes to explain classical music. College teachers claimed that he was not an original thinker and that many of his statements were oversweeping. Nonetheless, untold hundreds of thousands of admirers would continue to revere him, long after his death.

—Milton Goldin

FURTHER READING:

Secrest, Meryle. *Leonard Bernstein: A Life.* New York, Knopf, 1994.

Berra, Yogi (1925—)

Lawrence "Yogi" Berra is one of the most loved figures of the sporting world. The star catcher for the great New York Yankee baseball teams of the mid-twentieth century, he has built a legacy as a dispenser of basic wisdom worthy of his nickname.

Born to Italian immigrants in the "Dago Hill" neighborhood of St. Louis, Missouri, Berra acquired his moniker as childhood friends remarked that he walked like a "yogi" snake charmer they had seen in a movie. He grew up idolizing future Hall of Fame outfielder Joe "Ducky" Medwick of the St. Louis Cardinals, and as a teenager left school to play baseball with his friend Joe Garagiola. Cardinals General Manager Branch Rickey signed Garagiola for $500, but did not think Yogi was worth the money. A scout for the New York Yankees did, however, and Yogi started playing catcher in their farm system, until he turned 18 and the navy intervened.

After participating in D-Day and other landings, Berra returned to the United States and the Yankee farm club. He was noticed and promoted to the Yankees in 1946 after manager Mel Ott of the rival New York Giants offered to buy his contract for $50,000. At the time, Yankees general manager Larry McPhail said of Yogi's unique stature that he looked like "the bottom man on an unemployed acrobatic team." Jaded Yankee veterans and the New York press were soon amused to no end by his love for comic books, movies, and ice cream, and knack for making the classic comments that would come to be known as "Berra-isms" or "Yogi-isms." One of the first came in 1947 when a Yogi Berra Night was held in his honor. Berra took the microphone and stated, "I want to thank all those who made this night necessary."

Many more sayings were to follow over the years. He described his new house thusly: "It's got nothing but rooms." When asked why the Yankees lost the 1960 World Series to the Pittsburgh Pirates, Yogi answered, "We made too many wrong mistakes" (a quote later appropriated by George Bush in a televised debate). Asked what time it is, he replied, "Do you mean now?" Some sayings simply transcended context, zen-fashion: "You see a lot just by observing." "If the world was perfect, it wouldn't be." "When you get to a fork in the road, take it." After a time interviewers began making up their

Yogi Berra (right) blocking home plate.

own quotes and floating them as ''Yogi-isms.'' Stand-up comedians and late-night talk show hosts followed soon after.

A sensitive man, Yogi often seemed genuinely hurt by willful misquotes and jokes about his appearance and intelligence, but his serene nature triumphed in the end. He was also a determined competitor who could silence critics with clutch performances. In 1947, he would hit the first pinch-hit home run in World Series history as the Yankees beat the Brooklyn Dodgers. When Casey Stengel, a character in his own right, became the Yankee manager in 1949, Yogi gained a valuable ally and soon developed into the best catcher of the time, along with Dodger Roy Campanella. He would go on to set World Series records for games played and Series won, as well as leading in hits, doubles, and placing second behind Mickey Mantle in home runs and runs-batted-in (RBIs). Later, as a manager himself, he would lead the Yankees in 1964 and the New York Mets in 1973 to the World Series. Yogi was elected to the Baseball Hall of Fame in 1972.

Managing the Yankees again in 1985, he would be fired after standing up to tyrannical Yankee owner George Steinbrenner, an achievement some would liken to a World Series in itself. After not speaking for 14 years, a period during which Berra would not visit Yankee Stadium even when his plaque was erected in centerfield, the

pair would suddenly reconcile in early 1999. As Yogi had said about the 1973 Mets pennant drive, ''It ain't over 'til it's over.''

—C. Kenyon Silvey

FURTHER READING:

Berra, Yogi, with Tom Horton. *Yogi: It Ain't Over 'Til It's Over.* New York, McGraw-Hill, 1989.

Okrent, Daniel, and Steve Wulf. *Baseball Anecdotes.* New York, Harper & Row, 1989.

Berry, Chuck (1926—)

Singer, songwriter, and guitarist Charles Edward Anderson Berry, better known as Chuck Berry, epitomized 1950s rock 'n' roll through his songs, music, and dance. ''If you tried to give rock 'n' roll another name, you might call it 'Chuck Berry,''' commented John Lennon, one of the many artists influenced by Berry's groundbreaking works—others included the Rolling Stones and the Beach Boys. A consummate showman with an electrifying stage style, he originated such classic songs as ''School Days,'' in which he proclaimed ''hail, hail, rock and roll'' and ''long live rock and roll''; and ''Rock and Roll Music,'' in which he sang: ''It's gotta be rock and roll music, if you want to dance with me.'' Berry was the first black rock 'n' roll artist to cross the tracks and draw a significant white audience to his music. His career was sidetracked, however, with his arrest and imprisonment on morals charges in 1959.

Berry captured the exuberant teenage spirit of the 1950s in his music. In the early part of that decade, the precursors of white rock 'n' roll and the purveyors of black rhythm and blues lived on opposite sides of the tracks, with the music of each being played on small radio stations for their respective audiences. Berry combined black rhythm and blues, white country music, jazz, and boogie woogie into his style, and his music and lyrics became the catalyst for the music of the Rolling Stones, Beatles, and Beach Boys. His composition ''Nadine'' was a mirror of the later style of the Rolling Stones. Berry's ''Sweet Little Sixteen'' was adapted as ''Surfin' USA'' by the Beach Boys, becoming a million dollar single.

Berry was born on October 18, 1926 in St. Louis, Missouri. (Some sources attribute San Jose, California as his place of birth based on false information he originally gave his longtime secretary for a biographical sketch.) As a teenager, Berry was interested in photography and poetry, until he began performing. He came from a good home with a loving mother and father but strayed from his home training, first encountering the juvenile-justice system for a bungled armed robbery, serving two years in reform school. Upon his release in 1947, Berry returned home and began work at General Motors while taking up hair dressing and cosmetology. By 1950, he was married with two children and had formed a trio with pianist Johnny Johnson and drummer Ebby Harding. Their group played at the Cosmopolitan Club in East St. Louis, Illinois, gaining a considerable reputation in the surrounding area. He also studied and honed his guitar technique with a local jazz guitarist named Ira Harris. The trio played for a largely black audience, but with the drop of a cowboy hat, Berry could switch to country and hillbilly tunes.

Berry traveled to Chicago in 1955, visiting bands and inquiring about recording. Muddy Waters suggested that he contact Leonard Chess, president of Chess records. A week later, Berry was back in Chicago with a demo and subsequently recorded ''Maybellene'' (originally called ''Ida Mae'') which rose to the number one spot on the R&B chart and number five on the pop chart. Almost instantaneously, Berry had risen from relative regional obscurity to being a national celebrity with this crossover hit. From 1955 to 1960, Berry enjoyed a run of several R&B top-20 entries with several of the songs crossing over to the pop top-10. ''Thirty Days,'' ''Roll Over Beethoven,'' ''Too Much Monkey Business,'' ''School Days,'' ''Rock and Roll Music,'' ''Sweet Little Sixteen,'' ''Johnny B. Goode,'' and ''Almost Grown'' were not only commercial successes but well written, engaging songs that would stand the test of time and become classics.

Berry's musical influences were diverse. Latin rhythms are heard in ''Brown-Eyed Handsome Man'' and in ''Rock and Roll Music''; black folk-narrative styles in ''Too Much Monkey Business''; polka and the Italian vernacular in ''Anthony Boy''; the black folk-sermon and congregational singing style in ''You Can't Catch Me''; blues à la John Lee Hooker in ''Round and Round''; and country music in ''Thirty Days.'' Instrumentally, his slide and single string work was influenced by Carl Hogan, guitarist in Louis Jordan's

Chuck Berry

Tympany Five combo; and by jazz guitarist Charlie Christian and blues guitarist Aaron ''T-Bone'' Walker, whose penchant for repeating the same note for emphasis influenced Berry. Nat ''King'' Cole influenced Berry's early vocal style, and Charles Brown's influence is evident in ''Wee Wee Hours.'' Berry makes extensive use of the 12-bar blues form. He occasionally departs from the blues form with compositions such as ''Brown-Eyed Handsome Man,'' ''Thirty Days,'' ''Havana Moon,'' ''You Can't Catch Me,'' ''Too Pooped to Pop,'' and ''Sweet Little Sixteen.'' Berry makes extensive use of stop time as in ''Sweet Little Sixteen,'' creating a tension and release effect.

Berry was a featured performer on Alan Freed's radio programs and stage shows and appeared in the films *Go Johnny Go, Mister Rock and Roll, Rock, Rock, Rock,* and *Jazz on a Summer's Day.* He also appeared on Dick Clark's *American Bandstand.* Berry toured as a headliner on bills with artists such as Carl Perkins, Bill Haley and the Comets, and Little Richard, among others.

His recording success turned Berry into a wealthy businessman and club owner, and a developer of his own amusement park. His quick rise to fame and his robust appetite for women of all races caused resentment among some whites. In 1959 he allegedly transported a fourteen-year-old Spanish-speaking Apache prostitute across state lines to work as a hat checker in his night club outside of St. Louis. Berry fired her and she protested. A brazenly bigoted first trial ensued and was dismissed, but in the second trial, Berry was convicted and sent to prison, serving two years of a three-year sentence. This experience left him extremely embittered, with his marriage ruined. While he survived financially, he became inward, distrustful, and suspicious of people.

By the time Berry was released in 1964, the British Invasion with the Beatles and Rolling Stones was in full force; both groups included Berry's songs on their albums. He continued to tour, often with pick-up bands. In 1966, he left Chess Records to record for Mercury, an association that did not yield any best sellers. He returned to Chess in 1971 and had his first gold record with ''My Ding-a-Ling,'' a whimsical, double entendre-filled adaptation of Dave Bartholomew's ''Toy Bell.'' In 1972, Berry appeared as a featured attraction in Las Vegas hotels. By 1979, he had run afoul with the law again and was sentenced to four months and one thousand hours of community service for income tax evasion.

During his incarceration in Lompoc, California, he began work on *Chuck Berry: the Autobiography,* a book that made extensive use of wordplay, giving insight into his life, romances, comebacks, and context for his songs. For his sixtieth birthday celebration, in 1986, a concert was staged in conjunction with a documentary filming of *Chuck Berry: Hail, Hail, Rock and Roll* by producer Taylor Hackford. The film featured an all-star cast of rock and R&B artists, including Keith Richards of the Rolling Stones as musical director, plus Eric Clapton, Linda Ronstadt, Robert Cray, Etta James, and Julian Lennon.

In 1986, Berry was inducted into the Rock 'n' Roll Hall of Fame. His importance as a songwriter, guitarist, singer, innovator and ambassador of that genre remains unquestioned. To paraphrase one of his lines in ''Roll Over Beethoven,'' Berry's heart beats rhythm and his soul keeps on singin' the blues.

—Willie Collins

FURTHER READING:

Berry, Chuck. *Chuck Berry: The Autobiography.* New York, Harmony Books, 1987.

De Witt, Howard A. *Chuck Berry: Rock 'n' Roll Music.* Fremont, California, Horizon, 1981.

The Best Years of Our Lives

A 1946 film that perfectly captures the bittersweet sense of post-World War II American society, *The Best Years of Our Lives* examines three war veterans as they adjust to new stateside roles. Former sergeant Al Stephenson (Fredric March), disillusioned with his banking career, develops a drinking problem but learns to control it with the support of his wife Milly (Myrna Loy) and adult daughter Peggy (Teresa Wright). Fred Derry (Dana Andrews), one-time soda jerk and bombadier, finds that his wartime skills are now useless and eventually leaves his self-centered wife Marie (Virginia Mayo) for Peggy. Homer Parrish (Harold Russell), an ex-sailor who lost his hands in a shipboard accident, learns to deal with the rudeness of well-meaning civilians and shapes a new life with his fiancée Wilma (Cathy O'Donnell). A much-honored film (it won eight Oscars,

including Best Picture), *Best Years* is a beautiful, simple, and eloquent evocation of postwar America.

—Martin F. Norden

FURTHER READING:

Anderegg, Michael A. *William Wyler.* Boston, Twayne, 1979.

Gerber, David A. ''Heroes and Misfits: The Troubled Social Reintegration of Disabled Veterans in *The Best Years of Our Lives.*'' *American Quarterly.* Vol. 24, No. 4, 1994, 545-74.

Kern, Sharon. *William Wyler: A Guide to References and Resources.* Boston, G. K. Hall, 1984.

Norden, Martin F. *The Cinema of Isolation: A History of Physical Disability in the Movies.* New Brunswick, Rutgers University Press, 1994.

Bestsellers

As a group bestsellers conjure an image of lowbrow literature, of escapist fiction—bodice rippers, multi-generation epics, courtroom melodramas, and beach novels. Although books of all sorts, including nonfiction, cartoon anthologies, and genuine literature routinely make the bestseller lists in America, bestsellers have always been dismissed as popular reading. In *80 Years of Best Sellers* authors Alice Payne Hackett and James Henry Burke assert that, ''Bestselling books are not always the best in a critical sense, but they do offer what the reading public wants,'' and the truth is that bestseller status is more often associated with Danielle Steele than Sinclair Lewis, even though both have published best-selling novels.

Tracking and reporting the best-selling books in America officially began in 1895. Publishing of all sorts experienced a boom in the 1890s for a variety of reasons, including cheaper paper, substantial improvements in the printing press, a high literacy rate, better public education systems, and an increase in book stores and public libraries. Popular tastes were also shifting from educational books and other nonfiction to works of fiction; an 1893 survey of public libraries showed that the most frequently borrowed books were novels, which at that time were largely historical fiction with overtones of adventure, e.g. *The Last of the Mohicans, Lorna Doone, The House of the Seven Gables.* The first list of best-selling novels in America appeared in a literary magazine titled *The Bookman* in 1895. The best-selling novel that year was *Beside the Bonnie Brier Bush* by one Ian Maclaren. Although the phrase ''best seller'' was not used by *The Bookman* at this time; it seems to have been coined about a decade later by *Publishers Weekly* in an interview with a successful book dealer. Bookman referred to the novels on its first list as being sold ''in order of demand'' and started referring to ''Best Selling Books'' in 1897. *Publishers Weekly* began to run its own list of bestsellers in 1912, by which time the term was in general usage. The first several bestseller lists were dominated by European novels, with an average of only two or three American novels per year. While many European authors were undoubtedly popular with American readers and European settings were more glamorous, the primary reason that there were few highly successful American novelists was U.S. copyright law, which prior to 1891 had made it far less expensive to publish books written by Europeans than by Americans.

The existence of bestseller lists had an immediate effect on American publishers, who began to devise ways to promote their novels and ensure them bestseller status. The novel *The Honorable Peter Stirling,* written by Paul Leceister Ford and published in 1897, was selling very poorly until its publisher spread rumors that the book was based on President Grover Cleveland; the book saw a drastic increase in readership and 228,000 copies were sold that year. The 1904 novel *The Masquerade* was the first book to be published without an author credit; speculation as to who ''anonymous'' might be—it was novelist Katherine Cecil Thurston—increased public awareness of the novel and it was one of the top ten sellers of its year. The gimmick of publishing an anonymous book was used repeatedly throughout the century; the success of *Primary Colors* in 1996 indicates that it has remained an effective marketing device.

Two significant literary genres made their first appearances on the list in 1902. Owen Wister's *The Virginian*—which became a genuine publishing phenomenon over time, remaining continuously in print for over thirty years—was at the height of its success in 1902. Booksellers were ordering one thousand copies per day. *The Virginian* created a market for western novels; western fiction became a staple of the list when Zane Grey's *The Lone Star Ranger* was published in 1915 and the western audience has never truly disappeared. Arthur Conan Doyle's *The Hound of the Baskervilles* was not just the first Sherlock Holmes book to achieve bestseller status but was the first work of detective fiction to do so as well. The first American suspense novelist to reach the year's top ten list was Mary Roberts Rinehart in 1909. Not all turn of the century bestsellers were escapist fiction, Upton Sinclair's *The Jungle,* the famous muckraking exposé of the American meat packing industry, became a bestseller in 1906.

When *Publishers Weekly* began publishing its own list of bestsellers in 1912, it separated nonfiction from fiction. A third category, simply titled ''war books,'' was added for the duration of World War I. Books about the European conflict sold extremely well and appear to have created a larger market for nonfiction reading in general, since sales of nonfiction books increased in post-World War I America. A similar increase occurred after World War II, when self-help books began to appear regularly on the bestseller lists. Emily Post's *Etiquette,* first published in 1923, demonstrated that a nonfiction bestseller can be recognized as a definitive reference source and remain in print almost indefinitely

Since the 1910s, bestseller status has been determined in the same way. Several publications, most notably *Publishers Weekly* and more recently the *New York Times Book Review,* publish weekly lists of the ten best-selling fiction and nonfiction books in America. The lists originally referred only to cloth, or hardbound, books; separate lists for paperbacks were added in the 1960s. Information is gathered from book stores around the United States, so the list of bestsellers does refer to books sold, not just books distributed (as was the case with the record industry for decades). Because most books stay on the list for multiple weeks, approximately forty-five to fifty books reach either list per year. The method of determining which books are bestsellers has been criticized. The lists reflect what is selling well at any given week, so that a book that sold slowly but steadily, such as *The Betty Crocker Cookbook,* which is one of the highest selling books of all time, might never appear on a bestseller list. Likewise, it is possible for an author to sell millions of books during a career without ever having one be designated a bestseller. Most of the sales figures are gathered from larger book stores so that smaller stores, which frequently have more literary clientele, have little input into the lists. Substantial advance publicity from a publisher can almost certainly boost sales for a week or two, creating an artificial bestseller. Finally, book club editions are not taken into account when compiling the lists; the Book of the Month Club and the Literary Guild, founded in 1926 and 1928 respectively, have accounted for a large percentage of book sales each year, as have many other book clubs and mail order sources, all without being included in the bestseller statistics. Still, the bestseller lists remain a fairly accurate barometer of what America is reading at any given time.

Even by the 1920s, certain patterns were beginning to emerge on the lists. There was the phenomenon known as ''repeaters''—authors who could be counted on to produce one best-selling book after another. Edna Ferber in the 1930s, Mickey Spillane in the 1950s, Harold Robbins in the 1960s, and John Grisham in the 1990s were all repeaters whose publishers knew that practically anything they wrote would become a bestseller. John O'Hara took the concept of repeating to its extreme; not only did he write a bestseller every year or two for most of his career but his publisher, Random House, always released the book on the same date, Christmas Eve, to build a steady market. ''Repeaters'' are important to publishers, who need certain and dependable sales successes, so the practice of paying large advances to such authors is common and widespread. In contrast to the repeaters, some authors have only one or two bestsellers and never produce another. This phenomenon can be hard to explain. Some authors only produce one novel: Margaret Mitchell never wrote another after the enormous success of *Gone with the Wind*; Ross Lockridge committed suicide shortly after the publication of *Raintree County.* But others try to repeat their earlier successes and fail, so that while someone like Kathleen Winsor may write many books during her lifetime, only *Forever Amber* is successful. Bestsellers are very attuned to popular taste; an author has to be strongly in synch with national attitudes and concerns to produce a bestseller. After a few years have passed, author and society might not be so connected. Another phenomenon may affect both repeaters and authors of solitary bestsellers: fame for best-selling writers and their books can be remarkably short-lived. For every Daphne du Maurier, well remembered years after her death, there is a George Barr McCutcheon; for every *Peyton Place* there is a *Green Dolphin Street.* Decades ago Rex Beach and Fannie Hurst were household names, each with multiple bestsellers; someday Dean Koontz and Jackie Collins might have lapsed into obscurity. Again, this might be attributed to the popular nature of the bestseller; best-selling novels are frequently so topical and timely that they tend to become dated more rapidly than other fiction. They are rarely reprinted after the initial burst of popularity is over and slip easily from the public memory. Of course, on some occasions when the novel remains well known the author might not, so that everybody has heard of *Topper* but no one remembers Thorne Smith and everybody is familiar with *A Tree Grows in Brooklyn* while few recall it was written by Betty Smith.

Specific genres of books are more likely to become bestsellers and since the beginning of the bestseller lists, certain categories have dominated. Among the most common bestseller types are the historical novel, the *roman à clef,* the exposé novel, and the thriller.

The first best American bestsellers were long romantic novels that provided escapist reading to their audiences while appearing to be at least slightly educational; all were set in the past and most were set in Europe. Gradually American settings began to dominate, particularly the American frontier, but the historical novel has remained an extremely popular type of fiction and has changed relatively little since its earliest appearance. There is usually some romance at the core, with complications that keep it from being resolved for hundreds of pages. The novel is often built around a significant historical event; the Civil War has been an especially popular setting. Great attention is given to detail and many historical novelists spend years researching an era before writing about it. Some variations of the historical novel would include the multi-generational saga, which follows a family for several decades and generations, such as Edna Ferber's *Cimarron*; the religious epic, such as Charles Sheldon's *In His Steps*, a fictionalized life of Christ that introduced the phrase "What would Jesus do?"; and the historical adventure, as seen in much of Kenneth Roberts's many fictional accounts of westward expansion.

Literally "book with a key," the roman à clef is a work of fiction that is obviously based on real people; the "key" is determining who was the inspiration for the novel. Obviously, for the book to be successful it has to be easy for the reader to guess who it is supposed to be about; it takes no great deductive ability to realize, for example, that the presidential widow in Jacqueline Susann's *Dolores* is based on Jacqueline Onassis. Harold Robbins is the most successful author of the roman à clef, having written about Harold Hughes (*The Carpetbaggers*), Lana Turner (*Where Love Has Gone*), and Hugh Hefner (*Dreams Die First*), among others. More literary examples of the roman à clef include two genuine bestsellers, Sinclair Lewis's *Elmer Gantry*, based on Billy Sunday and Aimee Semple McPherson; and Robert Penn Warren's fictionalized account of Huey Long, *All the King's Men*.

The exposé novel examines a major American institution and purports to tell readers exactly how it works; of course, these novels always contain copious amounts of sex and intrigue no matter how dull their subject matter might appear. Arthur Hailey's *Airport*, for example, presents a romantic triangle between a pilot, his wife, and his pregnant mistress (one of his flight attendants); a bomb on board the plane; and an emergency landing in a snowstorm. Hailey is the recognized leader of the exposé novel, having also written *Wheels*, *Hotel*, and *The Moneychangers*, among others. Some exposé novels have the added attraction of being written by someone who actually worked within the industry, giving them an insider's view which they presumably pass along to their readers. Joseph Wambaugh, the police officer turned author is perhaps the best known of these. It has become fairly common to hire a celebrity to use their name on an exposé novel, which is then written in collaboration with a more professional author, as was done with Ilie Nastase's *The Net* and model Nina Blanchard's *The Look*.

Ever since *The Hound of the Baskervilles*, mysteries and suspense novels of some sort have been common on the list. It was not until the publication of John LeCarre's *The Spy Who Came in from the Cold* in 1964, however, that publishers recognized thrillers as a popular fiction form. Thrillers can be distinguished from mysteries by the fact that there is no puzzle to solve; the appeal of the novel lies in waiting to see what will happen to the characters. Crime novels like those of Elmore Leonard (*Get Shorty*) are frequently categorized as thrillers, but so are courtroom novels like John Grisham's *The Firm* and Scott Turow's *Above Suspicion*; technology based works like Tom Clancy's *The Hunt for Red October*; Lawrence Sanders's (*The First Deadly Kiss*) and Thomas Harris's (*Silence of the Lambs*) dissections of serial murder; and war novels like Len Deighton's *Bomber*.

Beginning in the 1970s there were fewer privately owned publishing houses; many have merged and some have been bought buy larger conglomerates. Bestsellers are now seen as part of a corporation's synergy; that is, a best-selling novel is part of a package that includes movie and/or television adaptations. Television in particular has proven an avid customer for adaptation rights; as fewer bestsellers are made into motion pictures, the television medium, which can provide longer running times that presumably allow more faithful adaptations, has produced hundreds of made for television movies and mini-series from best-selling novels. Television's interest in the bestseller can be traced to ABC's highly regarded production of Irwin Shaw's *Rich Man, Poor Man* in 1976. Given the variety of businesses that may now be contained under one corporate umbrella, it is not uncommon for one conglomerate to publish a book in hardcover, publish the paperback edition as well, and then produce the film or television adaptation. In fact, many publishing houses take such a possibility into consideration when reviewing manuscripts.

The most popular works within any society would not necessarily be its best; nevertheless, the reading habits of the American public say much about its culture. If Irving Wallace, Mario Puzo, Janet Daly, and Leon Uris are not the greatest authors of the twentieth century, they have still provided millions of readers with a great deal of pleasure. The best-selling novel might better be evaluated not as a work of literature but as a significant cultural byproduct, an artifact that reveals to subsequent generations the hopes and concerns of the past.

—Randall Clark

FURTHER READING:

Boca, Geoffrey. *Best Seller*. New York, Wyndham Books, 1981.

Hackett, Alice Payne and James Henry Burke. *80 Years of Best Sellers, 1895-1975*. New York, Bowker, 1977.

Hart, James D. *The Popular Book*. Berkely, University of California Press, 1961.

Sutherland, John. *Bestsellers*. London, Routledge and Keegan Paul, 1981.

Better Homes and Gardens

Taking on a snazzy new style, establishing its own website, and accentuating the acronym *BH&G* can not alter entirely the role that *Better Homes and Gardens* has played in constructing American ideals of domesticity, home life, and gender roles throughout the twentieth century. In 1913, Edwin T. Meredith introduced the idea of a new magazine within an advertisement contained in his magazine, *Successful Farming*. The small, discreet ad titled "Cash Prizes for Letters about Gardening" also made a simple request of readers: "Why not send fifty cents for a year's subscription to 'Garden, Fruit and Home' at the same time?" In truth no such magazine yet existed; nor would it be published until 1922. Meredith began publishing *Fruit, Garden and Home* before altering the name in 1924 to *Better Homes and Gardens*. By facilitating the dialogue that has constructed the ideal of housing, *Better Homes and Garden* helped to define exactly where home and life come together in the American experience.

The impermanence of American life, of course, befuddled many observers from the nation's outset. Alexis de Tocqueville wrote in the 1830s that "in the United States a man builds a house in which to spend his old age and he sells it before the roof is on. . . ." A great deal of interest and attention was paid by upper and upper-middle-class

Americans in the later 1800s to create traditions for civility, taste, and permanence—literally, to construct cultural ideals. One of the earliest ''taste makers,'' Andrew Jackson Downing, introduced many Americans to landscape architecture and gardening through his writings. The periodical that he edited, *The Horticulturalist,* helped to initiate an American tradition of popular magazines and journals helping to perfect designs of the prototypical American home.

Similarly, an entire genre of magazines would appeal directly to women of privilege, most of whom were not employed. From 1840 through the end of the nineteenth century, *Godey's Lady's Book* defined the habits, ideals, and aspirations of many Victorian women. Such general interest magazines helped to define the era, but had more to do with constructing femininity than with the American home. Magazines such as *Better Homes and Gardens* helped to merge the women's magazine with practical publications specifically concerned with home design. This bond, of course, would shape the role of the modern ''housewife'' into that of the domestic manager. The ideal that emerges from this union is referred to by many scholars as the ''Cult of Domesticity,'' which helps make *BH&G* one of the most popular magazines in America throughout the twentieth century.

BH&G helped define a national dialogue on home life through a combination of informative articles, basic cooking techniques, and contests that helped to rally the interest of readers. The first home plan design contest was first published in 1923 and, most importantly, the ''Cook's Round Table'' that began in 1926 would become the longest-running reader-driven contest in publishing history. This would later become part of *BH&G*'s test kitchen and what became known as ''Prize Tested Recipes.'' *BH&G* experimentation is attributed with introducing the American palate to tossed salad (1938) and barbecue cooking (1941) among many innovations. Published throughout World War II, the magazine even altered its recipes to cope with shortages of eggs, butter, and other foods.

These contests and recipes, however, were only a portion of the new domestic stress that *BH&G* fostered in the American public. The ideal of home ownership that can be found in the ideas of Thomas Jefferson and others began in the pages of the magazine in 1932 with the introduction of the *BH&G* building plan service. The marketing of building plans had taken place since the late 1800s; however, *BH&G*'s service grew out of new governmental initiatives. Following data that revealed that only 46 percent of Americans owned homes in the 1920s, Secretary of Commerce Herbert Hoover's ''Own Your Home'' campaign combined with efforts by the Bureau of Standards to stimulate home building while also modernizing American building practices. Better Homes in America, Inc. fulfilled Hoover's goal of voluntary cooperation between government and private enterprise for the public good. Formed in 1922, the organization soon had branches in over 500 communities.

Such groups worked with *BH&G* to permanently alter American ideas of domesticity. By 1930 there were 7,279 Better Homes committees across the country. During national Better Homes Week (usually the last week in April), each local committee sponsored home-improvement contests, prizes for the most convenient kitchen, demonstrations of construction and remodeling techniques, and lectures on how good homes build character. The demonstration house was the highlight of the week. Most communities built a single model residence, with donated materials and labor. Obviously, a national institution had been created and the private sector, through *Better Homes and Gardens,* would be responsible for perpetuating the jump start that the federal government had offered to systematizing and organizing American home design and construction.

BH&G and the Better Homes movement in general provided the essential conduit through which the dynamic changes in building could be channeled. While much of this movement was intended for the homeowner who was building his own house, the organization would also be instrumental in the evolving business organization of home development. Specifically, land developers who were constructing vast housing tracts would work with Better Homes to establish the guidelines that would form the standard suburban home. Each constituency had a stake in establishing ''Safe Guards Against Incongruity.'' At times the Better Homes forum would also be complicit in discussing the social organization of the evolving housing development, which would often restrict race and ethnicity through restrictive covenants and deed restrictions. *BH&G* would not be complicit in such restrictions, however, it would become active in the sales end of housing. After first considering a line of related restaurants, hotels, and insurance companies in 1965, Meredith launched Better Homes and Gardens Real Estate Service in 1975. It has grown to be one of the nation's largest real estate services.

In order to make certain of this continued popularity, the magazine's logo was lent to popular instructional books for many home improvement tasks as well as to cookbooks as early as 1930. This, however, was only the beginning of the better home informational empire: by the late 1990s a television network and many hours of programming and videos would offer techniques and pointers on home design, repair, as well as on cooking and personal relations. The magazine's involvement in homemaking reminds one of aggressive, corporate expansion that attempts to dominate every facet of an endeavor. In this case, homemaking truly has become an industry of such massive scale and scope. *BH&G* continued to influence American home life from finding a home, redecorating it, maintaining it, and, finally, to selling it at the end of the twentieth century.

—Brian Black

FURTHER READING:

Hayden, Dolores. *Redesigning the American Dream: The Future of Housing, Work, and Family Life.* New York, W.W. Norton, 1984.

Schuyler, David. *Apostle of Taste: Andrew Jackson Downing, 1815-1852.* Baltimore, Johns Hopkins University Press, 1996.

Wright, Gwendolyn. *Building the Dream: A Social History of Housing in America.* Cambridge, MIT Press, 1992.

Betty Boop

Betty Boop, the first major female animated screen star, epitomized the irresistible flapper in a series of more than one hundred highly successful cartoons in the 1930s. From her debut as a minor character in the 1930 *Talkartoons* short feature ''Dizzy Dishes,'' she quickly became the most popular character created for the Fleischer Studio, a serious animation rival to Walt Disney. Unlike Disney's *Silly Symphonies,* which emphasized fine, life-like drawings and innocent themes, the Fleischer films featuring Betty Boop were characterized by their loose, metamorphic style and more adult situations designed to appeal to the grown members of the movie-going audience. According to animation historian Charles Solomon, Betty Boop ''was the archetypal flapper, the speakeasy Girl Scout

Betty Boop's depiction in balloon form in the Macy's Thanksgiving Day Parade in New York City.

with a heart of gold—already something of an anachronism in 1930.'' Although her appearance rooted her to the Jazz Age, Betty Boop's popularity remained high throughout the decade of the Great Depression, as she was animation's first fully developed and liberated female character.

For a character that would come to personify overt female sexuality, the original version of Betty Boop created by animator Grim Natwick was a somewhat grotesque amalgamation of human and dog features. In her first screen appearance she was cast as a nightclub singer attempting to win the affection of then-Fleischer star, Bimbo, an anthropomorphized dog. Subsequent appearances reveal her gradual evolution into a fully human form. Her ''French doll'' figure was modeled after Mae West's, and she featured a distinctive spit curl hairdo and a singing style inspired by popular chanteuse Helen Kane (''the Boop Boop a-Doop Girl''). Miss Kane, however, was outraged by the animated character and claimed in a 1934 lawsuit that the Fleischers had limited her earning potential by stealing her distinctive singing style. Although Betty Boop certainly is a caricature of Kane, the singer lost in her claim against the Fleischers after it was proven that a black entertainer named Baby Esther had first popularized the phrase ''boop-oop-a-doop'' years earlier. Actress Mae Questel provided Betty's high-pitched New York twang for all of the character's screen appearances, beginning in 1931.

Betty's growing popularity prompted the Fleischers to promote their new female sensation to main character status and relegate the formerly top-billed Bimbo to the supporting role of Betty's constant admirer. Betty's femininity was repeatedly highlighted throughout her cartoon adventures, as her legs, busty frame, and frilly undies were displayed for the audience. Her personality was that of an innocent vamp who was not above lifting her skirt, standing in provocative poses, and batting her long eyelashes to achieve her goals. The series was also filled with humorous double entendres for adults that would generally pass over the heads of Betty's younger fans. For all the sexual antics, however, Betty often displayed proto-feminist qualities. She was generally portrayed as a career girl, who had to fight off the advances of lecherous male characters. The issue of sexual harassment in the workplace is most strongly presented in 1932's ''Boop-Oop-A-Doop,'' where she confronts a lewd ringmaster who demands her affection so that she may return to her job at a circus. By the cartoon's end she firmly proclaims, ''He couldn't take my boop-oop-a-doop away!'' The Fleischers even had Betty enter the male-dominated world of politics in *Betty Boop for President* (1932).

One of the most popular features of the Betty Boop cartoon series were her encounters with many of the most popular entertainment figures of the 1930s. At various times Cab Calloway, Lillian Roth, Ethel Merman, and Rudy Vallee all found themselves singing and dancing with the cartoon star. These appearances were designed to promote the recordings of the stars on the Paramount label, which also distributed the Betty Boop series. To further capitalize on the animated star's success, Betty Boop soon appeared on hundreds of products and toys. In 1935 King Features syndicated *Betty Boop* as a Sunday comic strip, which toned down the character's sexuality.

Betty Boop remained a popular character until the mid-1930s, when she fell victim to Will Hays and the Hollywood Production Code. The censor demanded Betty no longer be presented in her trademark short skirts and low tops. There were even claims that her ''romantic relationship'' with the dog Bimbo was immoral. The Fleischers responded by placing Betty in a more domestic setting and surrounding her with a more wholesome cast, including an eccentric inventor named Grampy and a little puppy called Pudgy. In several of these later cartoons Pudgy, not Betty, is the primary character. Ironically, a dog character reduced Betty's role in the same manner she had replaced Bimbo years earlier. The final Betty Boop cartoon, *Yip, Yip, Yippy!*, appeared in 1939. However, Betty's racy flapper persona had vanished sometime earlier and had been replaced by a long-skirted homemaker.

Betty Boop sat dormant until the mid-1970s when her cartoons began playing on television and in revival houses. Her increased visibility led to a resurgence of Betty merchandise in the 1980s and 1990s. In 1988, Betty made a brief appearance in the feature film *Who Framed Roger Rabbit?*, where she complained of her lack of acting jobs since cartoons went to color. Today, Betty Boop, remains a potent symbol of the Jazz Age and is considered a pioneer achievement in the development of female animated characters.

—Charles Coletta

FURTHER READING:

Callan, Kathleen. *Betty Boop: Queen of Cartoons.* New York, A&E Television Networks, 1995.

Solomon, Charles. *The History of Animation.* New York, Knopf, 1989.

Betty Crocker

Betty Crocker, an invented identity whose face adorns the packaging of more than 200 food products manufactured by General Mills, is one of the most recognized icons in American brand-name marketing. Together with the trademarked red spoon logo, the Betty Crocker brand name is found on many cake mixes and dessert products, main courses like Hamburger Helper and scalloped potatoes, and snacks like microwave popcorn and chewy fruit items. The Betty Crocker brand name accounts for over $1.5 billion each year, which is nearly thirty percent of annual sales for General Mills.

The name originated in 1921 when Washburn Crosby Company, as General Mills was then known, sponsored a jigsaw-puzzle contest and found that the entrants, mostly women, wanted more information about baking. The two most significant factors behind the creation of the Betty Crocker name, according to a General Mills document, "were the philosophy and doctrine of sincere, helpful, home service and the belief that the company's Home Service contract with homemakers should be personalized and feminized."

The choice of "Betty Crocker" as a name for General Mills Home Services Activities is attributable to then advertising manager, James A. Quint. "Betty" was considered a friendly nickname while "Crocker" was used as a tribute to retired company director and secretary, William Crocker. The name suggests a particular lifestyle involving a woman who is a traditional, suburban, all-American mother and who takes special care in her cooking and of her family. Although the face was altered slightly over the years from a more matronly to a younger image, the familiar face still reinforces a strong visual image over several generations. To many, Betty Crocker reminds them of childhood memories of Mom baking in the kitchen or an idealized childhood including that nurturing image.

Betty Crocker has over the years created a trustworthy reputation as the First Lady of Food. She receives millions of letters and phone calls and is listed as the author of several bestselling cook books. Her weekly advice column appears in more than 700 newspapers throughout the United States, and in the 1990s she acquired her own website, which includes recipes from ingredients provided by users as well as personalized weekly menu plans and household tips.

The Betty Crocker name has been affiliated with food products since 1947. Her pioneering cake mix was called Ginger Cake, which has now evolved into Gingerbread Cake and Cookie Mix. Since then, the name has been licensed to several types of food products as well as to a line of cooking utensils, small appliances, and kitchen clocks. In the 1990s, General Mills leveraged this brand in the cereal market by introducing Betty Crocker Cinnamon Streusel and Dutch Apple cereals, with packaging primarily designed to attract dessert lovers.

Even as Betty Crocker strides into the new millennium, she continues to leverage her past history by successfully practicing the art of retro-marketing. Betty's Baby Boomer constituents have lately inquired about "nostalgia foods" such as "Snickerdoodles," "Pink Azalea cake," and "Chicken A la King," to name a few. In 1998, General Mills published a facsimile edition of the original *Betty Crocker's Picture Cook Book,* first published in 1950.

—Abhijit Roy

FURTHER READING:

"Betty Crocker." http:www/betty-crocker.com. May 1999.

Salter, Susan. "Betty Crocker." In *Encyclopedia of Consumer Brands, Volume 1*. Detroit, St. James Press, 1998.

Shapiro, Laura. "Betty Goes Back to the Future." *Newsweek,* October 19, 1998.

Beulah

The first television network series to star an African American, *Beulah* ran on ABC from October 3, 1950 until September 22, 1953. The comic black maid had her beginnings on the 1940s radio series *Fibber McGee and Molly* where she was originally played by a white male actor. The African American Oscar winner, Hattie McDaniel, took over the role when Beulah was spun off onto her own radio show. The popular series then moved to the fledgling television medium with a new black actress playing Beulah, the noted singer, stage, and screen performer Ethel Waters. Waters left the series after two years and was briefly replaced by McDaniel. Illness forced her to leave the series, and another black actress famous for playing maids, Louise Beavers, took the role in the show's last season. The series followed the gently comic adventures of Beulah, her marriage-resistant male friend, Bill, the Henderson family whom Beulah served, and Beulah's feather-brained friend, also a black maid, Oriole (played first by Butterfly McQueen, then Ruby Dandridge). Debuting a year before the more famous black comedy *Amos 'n' Andy, Beulah* did not generate the other series' enormous controversy, despite the stereotyped representations of black servants whose lives revolve around their white superiors. In 1951, however, when the NAACP (National Association for the Advancement of Colored People) launched a highly publicized protest against the *Amos 'n' Andy* television show, the civil rights lobby group included *Beulah* in its condemnation. The series left the air the same time as *Amos 'n' Andy.*

—Aniko Bodroghkozy

The Beverly Hillbillies

One of the most durable television sitcoms and one of the most successful of the popular rural comedies at CBS during the 1960s, *The Beverly Hillbillies* (1962-71) has withstood critical disdain and become a favorite with viewers in reruns. *The Beverly Hillbillies* is the old story of city slicker versus country bumpkin, of education versus wisdom; and though the laughs are at the Hillbillies' expense, in the end they almost always come out on top despite their lack of sophistication. This simple account of simple country folk at odds with city folk hit a nerve in the country and was reflected in a number of other shows of the era, including fellow Paul Henning productions *Petticoat Junction* and *Green Acres. The Beverly Hillbillies* premiered to a critical blasting and yet within a few weeks was at the top of the ratings and remained popular for the length of its run.

In the theme song we learn the story of Jed Clampett (Buddy Ebsen), a mountain widower. One day, while hunting for food, Jed comes across some "bubbling crude" on his land: "Oil, that is, black gold, Texas tea." Jed sells the rights to his oil to the OK Oil Company

The Beverly Hillbillies (clockwise from bottom left): Buddy Ebsen, Donna Douglas, Irene Ryan, and Max Baer, Jr.

and becomes a millionaire. He is advised to move from the hills and go to California. Along with him he takes his mother-in-law, Granny (Irene Ryan); his daughter, Elly May (Donna Douglas); and his nephew, Jethro Bodine (Max Baer, Jr.). In California Jed's money is kept at the Commerce Bank, and along with the bank comes its president, Milburne Drysdale (Raymond Bailey), and his plain but smart assistant, Jane Hathaway (Nancy Kulp). Most of the interactions involve the Clampetts and the Drysdale/Hathaway team and occasionally Drysdale's snobby wife.

To keep a closer eye on his largest depositor, Drysdale arranges for the Clampetts to move into the mansion next to his house in Beverly Hills. Drysdale is obsessed with the fear that the family will move back to the hills along with their money, and he will do practically anything to assuage them and help them feel comfortable in their new home. This simple premise remains essentially unchanged through the bulk of the show's run. City life is not difficult for the rube man-child Jethro, who fancies himself a playboy or secret agent or movie producer and wants to keep his "hick" family from making him look bad. Elly May is the pretty tomboy who seems content to live in the city as long as she has her "critters." But crusty old Granny is not happy here, where she has lost her stature in society and she can no longer be the doctor, matchmaker, and keeper of wisdom. Most of the characters in *The Beverly Hillbillies* are caricatures and stereotypes of rich and poor. The only real exception is Jed Clampett, who alone seems to appreciate both sides.

The humor in this show comes from many sources. Initially, the jokes and obvious humor come at the expense of the Hillbillies. The

ragged clothes, the fascination with even the most ordinary aspects of everyday life (they assume the billiard table is for formal dining and that the cues are for reaching across the table), and odd customs and ideas about high society based on silent movies that reached their hometown. But just as funny are the city folk, like Mr. Drysdale and his transparent efforts to get them to stay, or Miss Jane and her proper and humorous look. *The Beverly Hillbillies* is at its best in showing how foolish modern-day life looks through the eyes of the transplanted country folk. Jed is the center and the speaker, pointing out those things that seem to not make sense, and upon reflection we can often agree. While this show is no work of high art or philosophy, and the story lines and situations are often ludicrous and sometimes downright foolish, it does an excellent job of entertaining with a basic backdrop and characters for thirty minutes. In the weeks following the assassination of President Kennedy, this show had four of its highest rated shows, and some of the highest rated shows of all time. It is likely not a coincidence that people would turn to a simple comedy in a time of crisis.

The Beverly Hillbillies was finally dropped in 1971 as part of the deruralification at CBS. Several members returned in the 1980s for a reunion television movie, and in the 1990s, this was one of many old television shows to be made into a theatrical movie with an all-new cast reprising the old familiar roles. Hipper, more urban, with less focus on caricature, we see an updating of the premise again in the early 1990s on the hit show *The Fresh Prince of Bel Air*—this time with a nephew from the ghetto streets of the east sent to live in the sun and opulence of Bel Air and again pointing out the foolishness of the so-called better life.

—Frank Clark

FURTHER READING:

Castleman, Harry, and Walter J. Podrazik. *Harry and Wally's Favorite Shows: A Fact-Filled Opinionated Guide to the Best and Worst on TV*. New York, Prentice Hall Press, 1989.

Ebsen, Buddy. *The Other Side of Oz*. Newport Beach, Calif., Donavan Publishing, 1993.

McNeal, Alex. *Total Television: A Comprehensive Guide to Programming from 1948 to the Present*. New York, Penguin Books, 1991.

Putterman, Barry. *On Television and Comedy: Essays on Style, Theme, Performer and Writer*. Jefferson, North Carolina, McFarland, 1995.

Beverly Hills 90210

Premiering in October 1990, television teen drama *Beverly Hills 90210* became a cultural phenomenon, both in the United States and abroad, and was the precursor to the deluge of teen-based dramas that were to dominate prime-time television in the late 1990s. The show helped to establish the new Fox Television Network, and was the first network to challenge the traditional big three—ABC, CBS, and NBC—for the youth audience.

The title of the program refers to the location of its setting, the posh city of Beverly Hills, California (zip code 90210). Produced by Aaron Spelling, the program focused on a group of high school students. The ensemble cast, featured Jason Priestly (twice nominated for a Golden Globe for Best Actor in a TV Series—Drama in 1993 and

The cast of *Beverly Hills 90210*.

1995), Shannon Doherty, Jennie Garth, Luke Perry, Tori Spelling, Ian Ziering, and Gabrielle Carteris. They were catapulted into the realm of teen idols (despite the fact that most were in their twenties), and their images graced publications and commercial products. Because of the setting, the program presented glamorous lifestyles and paid great attention to fashion, an aspect which was not lost on its audience, who followed clothing, music, and hairstyle trends.

Much of the show's appeal has been attributed to the story lines, which presented issues and concerns relevant to its teenage audience: parental divorce, eating disorders, learning disabilities, sexuality, substance abuse, and date rape. As the actors aged, so did their characters, and by the sixth season several were attending the fictitious California University, encountering more adult problems and issues. Although the show was praised for tackling such important, and often controversial, teen issues in a serious manner, many found the program problematic because it upheld narrowly defined concepts of physical beauty, presented a luxurious world of upper-class materialism, rarely included people of color, and constructed the problems presented in unrealistic terms.

—Frances Gateward

FURTHER READING:

McKinley, E. Graham. *Beverly Hills 90210: Television, Gender, and Identity.* Philadelphia, University of Pennsylvania, 1997.

Simonetti, Marie-Claire. "Teenage Truths and Tribulations across Cultures: Degrassi Junior High and Beverly Hills 90210." *Journal of Popular Film and Television.* Vol. 22, Spring 1994, 38-42.

Bewitched

In this innovative and immensely popular sitcom—it ranked in TV's top twenty-five all but two of its eight years on the air and was nominated for twenty-two Emmy awards—suburbia meets the supernatural in the guise of Samantha, television's most loveable witch. Played by the talented and genial Elizabeth Montgomery, Samantha is the all-American wife of Darrin Stephens, a hapless advertising executive who asks his wife to curb her witchery in the interest of having a normal life together. Originally broadcast from 1964 to 1972, on the surface *Bewitched* seemed like simply another suburban

The stars of *Bewitched*, (l-r) Elizabeth Montgomery, Dick Sargent, and Agnes Moorehead.

sitcom, but in fact it captured the mood of the nation in dealing with a "mixed marriage" between a witch and a mortal, as well as the difficulties faced by a strong woman forced to subdue her powers for the sake of her marriage. A quarter of a century later, *Bewitched* remains a pop culture favorite, a nostalgic take on the 1960s that has remained surprisingly hip.

Bewitched was borne of the marriage of actress Elizabeth Montgomery and award-winning television director William Asher. The couple met and fell in love in 1963, when Elizabeth starred in Asher's film, *Johnny Cool,* and they were married shortly thereafter. Suddenly, Montgomery—an Emmy nominee and a veteran of more than 200 television programs—began talking about retiring in order to raise a family. But Asher felt his wife was too talented to bow out of show business and suggested that they work together on a television series. When Elizabeth enthusiastically agreed, their search for the right property began.

Asher, an Emmy-award-winning director of *I Love Lucy,* forged an agreement with ABC, who forwarded him a script which had been written for Tammy Grimes. *The Witch of Westport* took as its premise a marriage between a witch and a mortal. Asher and Montgomery both liked the script and, with Grimes committed to a Broadway play, the couple worked to transform the series into a show suited to Montgomery's talents and sensibilities, by increasing the comedic

elements and losing a lot of what they felt was stereotypical witchery and hocus pocus.

The Ashers shot the pilot for their new series, which they called *Bewitched,* in November, 1963. But when ABC saw the show, the network feared that in airing a show about the supernatural they risked losing both their sponsors and their audiences in the Bible Belt. But after Asher personally flew to Detroit to secure Chevrolet's backing, ABC greenlighted *Bewitched* for their 1964 fall lineup.

From the start, *Bewitched* was a huge hit, climbing to number two in the ratings in its very first season. Much of the show's success was due to the superb ensemble cast of top-notch actors delivering superb comic acting. With Elizabeth Montgomery as Samantha, Dick York (later Dick Sargent) as Darrin, and veteran actress Agnes Moorehead as Samantha's meddling mother, Endora, at its core, the cast also featured David White as Darrin's troublesome boss, Larry Tate; George Tobias and Alice Pearce (later Sandra Gould) as the nosy-next-door-neighbor Kravitzes; the inimitable Paul Lynde as Uncle Arthur; the hysterical Marian Lorne as bumbling Aunt Clara; and the great English actor, Maurice Evans, as Samantha's father.

As Herbie J. Pilato writes in *The Bewitched Book,* "Each episode . . . is a new misadventure as Sam (as she's affectionately known to Darrin) tries to adapt her unique ways to the life of the average suburban woman. Learning to live with witchcraft is one thing, but Endora's petulant dislike of her son-in-law (due to his eagerness to succeed without witchcraft) is the story conflict that carried the sitcom through its extensive run. This dissension, coupled with the fact that Samantha and Darrin love each other in spite of their differences, is the core of the show's appeal.''

Unquestionably, the star of the show was Elizabeth Montgomery, a gifted actress whose dramatic and comedic acting abilities made her immensely attractive to TV audiences of both sexes and all ages. The daughter of movie star Robert Montgomery, Elizabeth had been a professional actress since her teens, with many credits to her name. But *Bewitched* made her both a television star and a pop culture icon. Capitalizing on his wife's unconscious habit of twitching her upper lip, William Asher created a magical nose twitch by which Samantha, with a mischievous glint in her eye, cast her spells. Though fans loved the show's magic, Samantha's supernatural powers were never overused. As Montgomery herself would later remark, ''If you have a weapon, be it a gun, witchcraft, or sharp-tongued wit, you recognize it as something you rely on. But your principles are such that you do not pull out the big guns unless you really have to. There's a certain dignity to Samantha's decision to hold back on her power. . . . It had to do with Samantha's promise to herself and to Darrin of not using witchcraft . . . her own self-expectations and living up to them.''

Audiences quickly came to adore Samantha and to eagerly await the use of her powers. And they identified with the character, seeing her as an outsider in mainstream society, trying to do her best to fit in. The appeal of Montgomery, as a beautiful and talented woman who wasn't afraid to be funny, carried the show, and Montgomery attracted a large and loyal fan following.

Although most episodes centered around the Stephens' household and Darrin's advertising office, among the most popular shows were those featuring magical incarnations in the form of animals or famous people from history, such as Leonardo da Vinci or Julius Caesar. Other popular episodes included Darrin and Samantha's baby daughter, Tabitha, a little witch played by twins Erin and Diane Murphy.

A television fixture throughout the Sixties, *Bewitched* finally dropped out of TV's top twenty-five in 1970 when Dick York left the show, forced into early retirement because of a chronic back injury. Although the chemistry between Montgomery and York's replacement, Dick Sargent, was superb, audiences didn't warm to the casting change. As more cutting-edge sitcoms like *All in the Family* hit the airwaves in the early 1970s, *Bewitched* no longer seemed so innovative, and Montgomery decided to call it quits.

Although *Bewitched* went off the air in 1972, it soon found its way into syndication, where it became a perennial favorite, until moving to the immensely popular Nick at Nite cable lineup, where it is a permanent feature of their prime-time lineup. Now, more than twenty-five years since the last episode was filmed, *Bewitched* continues to enchant audiences with its winning blend of award-winning sitcom humor and its wry look at suburban American culture.

—Victoria Price

FURTHER READING:

Pilato, Herbie J. *The Bewitched Book: The Cosmic Companion to TV's Most Magical Supernatural Situation Comedy.* New York, Delta, 1992.

BH&G

See Better Homes and Gardens

Bicycling

Although most Americans in the twentieth century associate bicycles and bicycling with children, Europeans, or fitness buffs, a bicycle craze among adults swept the United States in the late 1880s and 1890s that stimulated much excitement and new ways of thinking about transportation. Capitalists created a thriving and valuable bicycle manufacturing industry and a well-developed trade press, as leaders of substantial influence emerged and the industry made rapid advances in design and technology. Major pioneers in aviation (the Wright brothers) and the automobile industry (Henry Ford) got their start as bicycle designers and mechanics, applying their expertise to new motorized forms of transportation.

The early industry gained its footing in the late 1870s when Colonel Albert Pope, a successful Boston industrialist, converted an old sewing machine factory into a bicycle plant. Pope set about building an empire, hiring skilled machinists and die makers to craft interchangeable parts, enabling him to make his high-wheel bicycles for a mass market. Pope also founded the leading bicycle publication, *Outing,* in 1882. The industry became embroiled in a series of bitter legal battles over patent rights in the mid-1880s, but in 1886 everything changed with a major innovation in bicycle design from Europe: the ''safety'' bicycle. The new style introduced chain-driven gearing, allowing inventors to replace the dangerous high-wheel design with two equally sized wheels and the now-standard diamond frame. These changes significantly increased the safety of bicycles without sacrificing speed, thus creating a much larger market for bicycles. After 1886 prices fell, democratizing what had once been an elite sport. Bicycle clubs sprouted, and the nation developed bicycle fever. Sales soared as comfort and speed improved, reaching a peak in 1897 when about three thousand American manufacturers sold an estimated two million bicycles.

The popularity of bicycles in the 1890s engendered heated debates over the decency of the fashionable machines. Advocates catalogued their benefits: economic growth, the freedom of the open road, a push for improved roads, increased contact with the outdoors, and the leveling influence of providing cheap transportation for the workingman. Critics, however, attacked bicycles as dangerous (because they upset horses), detrimental to the nervous system (because riding required concentration), and antithetical to religion (because so many people rode on Sundays). In addition, many critics questioned the propriety of women riding bicycles. Particularly scandalous to the skeptics was the tendency of women cyclists to discard their corsets and don bloomers in place of long skirts, but censors also reprimanded courting couples for using bicycles to get away from parental supervision and criticized women's rights advocates for emphasizing the emancipatory qualities of their machines.

By the turn of the century the bicycle craze abated and, despite an urban indoor track racing subculture that persisted until World War II using European imports, bicycles survived for a number of decades primarily as children's toys. The quality of bicycles, which found their major retail outlets between 1900 and 1930 in department stores, deteriorated substantially. Then, in 1931, the Schwinn bicycle company sparked a minor revolution in the industry by introducing the balloon tire, an innovation from motorcycle technology that replaced one-piece inflatable tires with an outside tire coupled with a separate inner tube. The strength and comfort of these new tires could accommodate much heavier, sturdier frames, which could better withstand the use (and abuse) of children riders. Taking a cue from the 1933 Century of Progress Exposition in Chicago, a showcase for Art Deco styling, Schwinn inspired more than a decade of streamlined bicycles—and innumerable suburban childhood dreams of freedom and exhilaration—with its 1934 Aerocycle. Bicycle design changed again slightly in the mid-1940s when manufacturers began to capitalize on the baby boom market. Following the practice of the automobile industry, bicycle designers created their own version of planned obsolescence by styling bicycles differently to appeal to different age groups.

Beginning in the mid-1950s and early 1960s, bicycles again became popular among adults, this time as a healthy form of exercise and recreation. A turning point came in September of 1955, when President Dwight Eisenhower suffered a heart attack. His personal physician, Dr. Paul Dudley White, happened to be an avid cyclist who believed that bicycling provided significant cardiovascular benefits. When he prescribed an exercise regimen featuring a stationary bicycle for the president, the ensuing publicity generated a real, if small, increase in bicycling among adults. Small local racing clubs in California kept the idea of cycling as adult recreation alive through the 1950s, but not until the exercise chic of the 1960s spread from the West Coast to other parts of the country did adult bicycles become a significant proportion of all sales. Bicycle manufacturers responded by introducing European-style ten-speed gearing, focusing on racing, touring, and fitness in their marketing. The popularity of bicycling made modest gains through the 1970s and 1980s as racing and touring clubs gained membership and local bicycle competitions became more common around the country, including races called triathlons that mixed running, bicycling, and swimming.

Beginning in the early 1980s, a new breed of bicycles called "mountain bikes"—sturdy bicycles designed with fat, knobby tires and greater ground clearance for off-road riding—overtook the adult market with astonishing rapidity. The new breed of bicycles first reached a mass market in 1981, and by 1993 sales approached 8.5 million bicycles, capturing the large majority of the United States market. Earning substantial profits from booming sales, designers made rapid improvements in frame design and components that made new bicycles appreciably lighter and more reliable than older designs. Off-road races grew in number to rival the popularity of road racing, and professional races gained corporate sponsorship through the 1980s and 1990s. Somewhat ironically, however, only a small percentage of mountain bike owners take their bicycles off-road. Buyers seem to prefer their more comfortable, upright style compared to road racing machines, but use them almost exclusively on paved roads for exercise and eco-friendly short-distance transportation.

—Christopher W. Wells

FURTHER READING:

Pridmore, Jay, and Jim Hurd. *The American Bicycle*. Osceola, Wisconsin, Motorbooks International Publishers, 1995.

Smith, Robert A. *A Social History of the Bicycle: Its Early Life and Times in America*. New York, American Heritage Press, 1972.

The Big Apple

Among the great cities in the world—Paris, Chicago, or New Orleans, for example—none is better known by its nickname than New York City, "The Big Apple." Paris may be "The City of Lights," Chicago "The Windy City," and New Orleans "The Big Easy," but just mention "The Big Apple" and America's metropolis immediately comes to mind. New York is the nation's financial center, an entertainment, theater, and news capital, and the heart of the fashion and publishing industries. "The Big Apple," meaning the biggest, best, and brightest, seems to fit quite nicely.

A number of theories exist regarding the origin of New York's nickname. Some say it began as a term used in Harlem in the 1930s, meaning the biggest and best. Others have traced it to a dance craze called The Big Apple. The Museum of the City of New York found evidence in *The City in Slang*, a book published in 1995, of an earlier appearance. According to that book, a writer, Martin Wayfarer, used the term in 1909 as a metaphor to explain the vast wealth of New York compared to the rest of the nation. Wayfarer is cited as saying: "New York [was] merely one of the fruits of that great tree whose roots go down in the Mississippi Valley, and whose branches spread from one ocean to the other . . . [But] the big apple [New York City] gets a disproportionate share of the national sap."

The term gained popularity in the 1920s after John J. FitzGerald, a newspaperman who wrote about horse racing, heard stable hands at a New Orleans track refer to the big-time racetracks in New York state as the Big Apple. FitzGerald called his racing column "Around the Big Apple," which appeared in the *New York Morning Telegraph*. According to the Museum of the City of New York, FitzGerald's February 18, 1924 column began: "The Big Apple. The dream of every lad that ever threw a leg over a thoroughbred and the goal of all horsemen. There's only one Big Apple. That's New York."

Throughout the 1930s and 1940s, musicians used the term to make the point that when they played in New York, they were playing in the big time, not small-town musical dates. Later, the term fell somewhat out of favor. In the 1970s, however, when the city was suffering financial problems, in an act of boosterism the New York Convention and Visitor's Bureau revived the term. Charles Gillett, the president of the convention bureau, started a promotional campaign by getting comedians and sports stars to hand out little red "Big Apple" lapel pins. The symbol caught on and The Big Apple theme was established.

As for racing writer FitzGerald, his recognition for contributing to The Big Apple legend came in 1997 when New York City's Historic Landmarks Preservation Center placed a plaque on the corner where FitzGerald had lived, West 54th Street and Broadway. The plaque bore the name "Big Apple Corner."

—Michael L. Posner

FURTHER READING:

Allen, Irving Lewis. *The City in Slang: New York Life and Popular Speech*. New York, Oxford University Press, 1993.

Barie, Susan Paula. *The Bookworms's Big Apple: A Guide to Manhattan's Booksellers*. New York, Columbia University Press, 1994.

A view of the Big Apple from the New Jersey side of the Hudson River.

Big Bands

The Big Band Era (roughly 1935 to 1945) witnessed the emergence of jazz music into the American mainstream at a time, according to *Metronome* magazine in 1943, ''as important to American music as the time of Emerson and Thoreau and Whitman and Hawthorne and Melville was to American literature.'' Big band music evolved from the various forms of African American music—blues, ragtime, and dixieland jazz—performed by black and white musicians such as Bessie Smith, Buddy Bolden, Jelly Roll Morton, Scott Joplin, W.C. Handy, and the Original Dixieland Jazz Band (ODJB). The frenetic, chaotic, and spontaneous nature of 1920s jazz influenced the large orchestras, like Paul Whiteman's, that specialized in dance music. Four- and five-piece Dixieland bands became ten-piece bands such as Fletcher Henderson's, and eventually the twenty piece bands of Benny Goodman and Duke Ellington. The music not only marked a synthesis of rural African American music and European light classical music, but its widespread acceptance expressed the larger national search for a uniquely American culture during the Great Depression and World War II.

In the early decades of the twentieth century, popular music was dominated by theatrical music, minstrel shows, and vaudeville, produced primarily in New York City's Tin Pan Alley. The music followed typical European conventions of melody, harmony, tone, and rhythm, with melody receiving priority over all else. Even minstrel shows conformed to these conventions of western music despite their claims to represent African American culture. Emphasis on the melody was reinforced by the preferential status of lyrics in Tin Pan Alley music. Both elements lent themselves well to the fact that this music was primarily sold as sheet music for individual home use. Simple melodies and arrangements with clever and timely lyrics did not depend on a specific type or quality of performance for their appreciation or consumption. As recorded music and radio broadcasts became more widespread and available, emphasis shifted to the specific character and quality of musical performance and to the greater use of popular music in social dancing, which had previously been relegated to the elite realm of ballroom dancing or the folk realm of square dancing and other folk dancing forms.

At the same time that the central characteristic of popular music shifted from composition to performance, African American music gained in exposure and influence on popular music. The first adaptations of black music to European instrumentation and form occurred in New Orleans as black musicians began playing a version of spirituals and field hollers on European band instruments such as trumpets and clarinets. Integrating marches into black music, and emphasizing improvisation over arrangement, jazz music developed into three distinct forms, the blues (the form most closely aligned with traditional African American music), dixieland (marching band instruments performing polyphonic, improvisational music), and ragtime (a more structured version of dixieland for piano). Each of these musical styles did enjoy a measure of popularity, but mainly in watered-down form such as the Tin Pan Alley practice of "ragging" a song, best exemplified by Irving Berlin's "Alexander's Ragtime Band" (1911).

With World War I, and the military's forced closure of Storyville, the official red light district of New Orleans where many jazz musicians found employment, jazz music moved to other urban areas such as Kansas City, Chicago, New York, and Los Angeles. As jazz music spread, the audience for jazz increased, encompassing a young white audience searching for music more dynamic than theatrical music, in addition to a larger black audience. This younger audience also favored music for dancing over home performances or staged performances and therefore appreciated the largely instrumental and rhythmic nature of jazz. With this growing audience, bands grew to include sections of instruments instead of the traditional dixieland arrangement of four or five soloists. Louis Armstrong and Fletcher Henderson pioneered the larger band format by creating multiple trumpet and trombone parts, as well as multiple reeds (clarinet, alto, and tenor saxophones) and rhythm parts. In 1924, Henderson's pathbreaking Roseland Ballroom Orchestra consisted of eleven players, including Coleman Hawkins, Don Redman, and Louis Armstrong. In 1927, the upscale Harlem nightclub, the Cotton Club, hired Duke Ellington and his band; Ellington created an orchestra and jazz style with his own compositions, arrangements, and direction. Ellington's Cotton Club Orchestra reached an avant-garde white audience and sparked the careers of other black bands as well as the creation of white bands playing jazz music, such as Benny Goodman's.

In August of 1935, Benny Goodman ushered in the "Swing Era" when he ended a national tour with his band at the Palomar Ballroom in Los Angeles. After receiving only lukewarm responses from audiences across the country, Goodman filled the final show of the tour with "hot" arrangements by Fletcher Henderson, as opposed to the more "acceptable" dance tunes of other orchestras. The young L.A. audience went crazy over the music and by the time Goodman returned to New York in 1936 he had been named "The King of Swing." The early 1930s had been hard times for jazz musicians since many civic leaders, music critics, and clergy cited the "primitive" nature of jazz music as part of the cultural decline responsible for the Great Depression. Selective use of jazz idioms, such as George Gershwin's symphonic piece "Rhapsody in Blue" (1924) and opera "Porgy and Bess" (1935), did gain respectability and praise for creating a uniquely American musical language, but "pure" jazz, even played by white musicians, was unacceptable. This thinking changed with the success of Benny Goodman and several other newly formed bands such as the Dorsey Brothers (with Glenn Miller as trombonist and arranger), Charlie Barnet, Jimmy Lunceford, Chick Webb, and Bob Crosby.

While live performances were the mainstay of big bands, many were able to increase their audiences through radio shows sponsored by companies eager to tap the youth market. Camel Cigarettes sponsored Benny Goodman and Bob Crosby; Chesterfield sponsored Hal Kemp, Glenn Miller, and Harry James. Philip Morris sponsored Horace Heidt; Raleigh sponsored Tommy Dorsey; Wildroot Cream Oil presented Woody Herman; and Coca-Cola sponsored a spotlight show featuring a variety of bands. Juke boxes also provided a way for

young people to access the music of the big bands, in many cases outside of parental control. Even movie theaters, searching for ways to increase declining depression audiences, booked bands which usually played after several "B" movies. In both dance halls and auditoriums, big bands attracted screaming, writhing crowds, who not only danced differently than their parents, but started dressing differently, most notably with the emergence of the Zoot suit. As big band music became more popular and lucrative, organized resistance to it declined, although it never disappeared. Respectability came in 1938 with the first appearance of a swing band at Carnegie Hall in New York, the bastion of respectable classical music. Benny Goodman and orchestra appeared in tuxedos and performed, among other songs, the lengthy and elaborate, "Sing, Sing, Sing," which included drum solos by Gene Krupa.

The success of these bands, which usually featured about a dozen or more players along with vocalists, allowed band leaders to experiment with more jazz-influenced arrangements and longer sections of improvised solos between the highly arranged "riffs" and melodies. The music was still primarily for dancing, and the youthful audience demanded a more upbeat music to accompany its newer, more athletic style of jitterbug dancing, like the "Lindy Hop," named for record-breaking pilot Charles Lindbergh. The *New York Times,* in 1939, recognized this new music as a form of music specifically representative of a youth culture. "Swing is the voice of youth striving to be heard in this fast-moving world of ours. Swing is the tempo of our time. Swing is real. Swing is alive." Lewis A. Erenberg in *Swingin' the Dream: Big Band Jazz and the Rebirth of American Culture,* sees swing music as an expression of youth culture which connects the youth culture of the 1920s to that of the 1950s. Not only did swing music and the big bands reinforce a new expressiveness among American youth, but big bands also crossed the color line by bringing black and white audiences together and through integrating the bands themselves, as Benny Goodman did in 1936 when he hired Teddy Wilson as his pianist. Even though most sponsored radio was segregated, audiences listening to Goodman's broadcast would often hear black musicians such as Lionel Hampton, Ella Fitzgerald, Count Basie, and Billie Holiday. In addition, remote broadcasts from Harlem's Cotton Club, Savoy Ballroom, and the Apollo Theater, while not national, found syndication to a primarily young, white, late-night audience. Big band swing music was, according to historian David W. Stowe in *Swing Changes: Big-Band Jazz in New Deal America,* "the preeminent musical expression of the New Deal: a cultural form of 'the people,' accessible, inclusive, distinctly democratic, and thus distinctly American." He further states that "swing served to bridge polarities of race, of ideology, and of high and low culture." As the most popular form of music during the Depression and World War II, swing music took advantage of newly developed and fast-spreading technologies such as radio, records, and film (many bands filmed performances which were shown, along with newsreels and serials, as part of a motion picture bill). Much of its appeal to young people was its newness—new arrangements of instruments, new musical elements, new rhythm and tempo, all using the newest media.

The big bands consisted of four sections: saxophones, trumpets, trombones, and rhythm section, in addition to vocalists (soloists, groups, or both). The saxophone section usually consisted of three to five players on soprano, alto, tenor, and baritone saxophones and doubling on clarinet and flute. The trumpet and trombones sections each consisted of three or four members, and the rhythm section consisted of piano, string bass, drums, and sometimes guitar. In most big band arrangements, sections played rhythmically unified and harmonically diverse parts. While one section played the melody, other sections would provide accented "riffs," short musical motifs repeated by one section. Arrangements often introduced riffs, highlighting one after another, culminating in all the riffs being played simultaneously in a polyphonic climax. These arrangements mimic the form of dixieland jazz, but since sections instead of soloists were involved, the music had to be highly arranged and written and not improvised. White bands, such as Goodman, Miller, and Herman's, became known for their elaborate arrangements in songs like "Sing, Sing, Sing," "In The Mood," and "Woodchoppers Ball." Black Bands, such as Ellington, Cab Calloway, and Count Basie, became known for a more driving beat and greater use of improvisation in songs like, "Take the 'A' Train," "Minnie the Moocher," and "Taxi War Dance."

In addition to bringing more jazz influences into mainstream American music, the big bands also developed some new techniques. Duke Ellington trumpeter Bubber Miley was the first horn player to place the working end of a plumber's helper over his trumpet's bell to create a "wah-wah" effect. Swing music also favored a "four-beat" style in which emphasis was placed on all four beats per bar, while older styles of jazz favored a "two-beat" style. By combining elements of theatrical Tin Pan Alley style music, dance music, and jazz, the big bands developed a music which was acceptable to a widespread audience, while integrating elements of African American culture into the American mainstream. Many jazz purists see the big band era as a time of jazzmen "selling out" to commercialism and a period of creative stagnation, especially in light of the development of bebop, cool jazz, and fusion music in the late 1940s, 1950s, and 1960s.

The swing era ended as a result of the effects of World War II on American society. The human toll of war dwindled the ranks of the big bands, with notable losses like the death of Glenn Miller during a concert tour for the troops. The end of wartime restrictions on recorded music, and new developments in recording technology, electric guitars, and radio led to the development of smaller groups and a greater emphasis on singers over musicians. The growth of the postwar baby boom generation created a market for music which, like the swing music of their parents, was reinvigorated with elements of African American music. Swing music, with the use of electric guitars and infused with a blues tonality, became rock and roll music.

Big band music has continued to attract an audience, not only in the United States, but around the world. Throughout the 1960s and 1970s, bands such as the Toshiko Akihoshi-Lew Tabackin continued to further the big band sound, while Stan Kenton integrated third-stream influences into his arrangements by adding strings, french horns, and various percussion instruments, and Maynard Ferguson incorporated jazz/rock fusion elements into his compositions. Big band swing music has enjoyed its greatest resurgence in the late 1990s with the newer, and mainly smaller, bands such as Big Bad VooDoo Daddy, Royal Crown Revue ("Hey Pachuco"), Cherry Poppin' Daddies ("Zoot Suit Riot"), and Squirrel Nut Zippers. Former rockabilly guitarist Brian Setzer, of the Stray Cats, formed his own big band using the same instrumentation as the most popular big bands of the swing era, and scored a hit with Louis Prima's "Jump, Jive, and Wail."

—Charles J. Shindo

FURTHER READING:

Berendt, Joachim E. *The Jazz Book: From Ragtime to Fusion and Beyond.* Westport, Connecticut, Lawrence Hill & Company, 1982.

Erenberg, Lewis A. *Swingin' the Dream: Big Band Jazz and the Rebirth of American Culture.* Chicago, University of Chicago Press, 1998.

Megill, Donald D., and Richard S. Demory. *Introduction to Jazz History.* Englewood Cliffs, New Jersey, Prentice-Hall, 1984.

Stowe, David W. *Swing Changes: Big-Band Jazz in New Deal America.* Cambridge, Harvard University Press, 1994.

Big Bopper (1930-1959)

Moderately famous during his lifetime, recording artist J. P. (Jiles Perry) Richardson, better known as the Big Bopper, gained lasting notoriety through his death in the airplane crash that killed Buddy Holly and Ritchie Valens near Mason City, Iowa.

Richardson was a successful disc jockey in Beaumont, Texas, and a locally known songwriter and performer when he was discovered by a Mercury Records producer. Half-spoken, half-sung recordings of "Chantilly Lace" and "The Big Bopper's Wedding" made it to the Top 40 during 1958 (the former to the Top Ten), while other songs written by Richardson were recorded by more established artists.

He became a familiar fixture on rock and roll tours. It was during a midwestern tour that a chartered airplane carrying three of the headliners crashed shortly after takeoff on February 3, 1959, subsequently called "the day the music died" in Don McLean's song "American Pie."

—David Lonergan

FURTHER READING:

Nite, Norm N. *Rock On Almanac.* 2nd edition. New York, HarperPerennial, 1992.

Stambler, Irwin. *The Encyclopedia of Pop, Rock and Soul,* revised edition. New York, St. Martin's Press, 1989.

Big Little Books

The 1932 debut of Big Little Books was an important harbinger of the direction marketing to children would take in the future. The first inexpensive books available for children, Big Little Books were a precursor to the comics and such series as the Golden Books. The books were sold in dimestores such as Kresge and Woolworth where children could purchase them with their own spending money.

The Whitman Company, a subsidiary of the Western Publishing Company of Racine, Wisconsin, published the books. The first of the Big Little Books was *The Adventures of Dick Tracy Detective,* which was published in 1932. Mickey Mouse, Donald Duck, Orphan Annie, Popeye, Buck Rogers, Don Winslow, and Tarzan were among the many additional heroes. The popularity of the books had other publishers, such as Saalfield Publishing, Engel Van Wiseman, and

Lynn Publishing, soon producing their own similar series. Approximately 508 Big Little Books were published between 1932 and 1949, but in the late 1930s the name changed to Better Little Books.

In pre-television days, Big Little Books provided the popular ''action hero'' and ''girl'' stories for school age children. Eventually the line was expanded to include retellings of classical literature such as *Little Women* and *The Three Musketeers,* cartoon characters from the popular funny papers, and even heroes and heroines taken from radio and movies, such as two books about Mickey Rooney. The books continued to be published into the 1970s, but, once comic books and other children's book series had come onto the market, were never as popular as they had been in the 1930s and 1940s.

In the 1990s Big Little Books were considered a collector's item. Because the printing sizes varied with individual titles, some are scarcer than others and therefore, more valuable. Another factor affecting their value is their condition. Among the most sought after are *The Big Little Mother Goose* and the Whitman-produced premiums from cereal boxes and other products.

—Robin Lent

FURTHER READING:

Jacobs, Larry. *Big Little Books: A Collector's Reference & Value Guide.* Padukah, Kentucky, Collector Books, 1996.

L-W Books, *Price Guide to Big Little Books & Better Little, Jumbo, Tiny Tales, A Fast-Action Story, etc.* Gas City, Indiana, L-W Book Sales, 1995.

Tefertillar, Robert L. ''From Betty Boop to Alley Oop: A Big Bonanza of Big Little Books.'' *Antiques & Collecting.* Vol. 99, No. 5, 1994, 47-49.

The Big Sleep

In *The Simple Act of Murder* (1935) Raymond Chandler (1888-1959), one of America's premier hard-boiled novelists, wrote of his detective hero, Philip Marlowe, '' . . . down these mean streets a man must go who is not himself mean, who is neither tarnished nor afraid. The detective in this kind of story must be such a man. He is the hero; he is everything.'' Unlike James M. Cain and other hard-boiled novelists of his time, Chandler was a romantic whose famous detective was a knight in slightly battered armor. Marlowe appears in Chandler's four most famous novels, *The Big Sleep* (1939), *Farewell My Lovely* (1940), *The Lady in the Lake* (1943), and *The Long Goodbye* (1953) as well as several lesser known works. Philip Marlowe was a character made for Hollywood: street smart, wise cracking but ultimately an honorable man—a prototype for the American detective hero ever since. Several of Chandler's stories, including *The Big Sleep*, were made into Hollywood movies, some more than once.

In *The Big Sleep* Marlowe is hired by wealthy General Sternwood to track down a blackmailer who is trying to extort money out of him with nude pictures of his daughter Carmen. From this rather simple beginning, Marlowe is led into a tangled world of sexual perversion, drug addiction, murder, and deceit. The plot of *The Big Sleep* is complex, leading Howard Hawks, the first and most successful of the filmmakers to adapt it for the movies, to say that he never did

understand who killed one of the characters—and when he telegraphed Chandler for clarification, Chandler himself was unable to provide a definitive answer.

The world of *The Big Sleep* has much in common with the world in other hard-boiled novels and films noir. It is a dark world full of violent and twisted men and women—often the most beautiful and charming are the most savage of all. Chandler's description of Carmen Sternwood is instructive: ''She came over near me and smiled with her mouth and she had little sharp predatory teeth.'' Even Carmen's father describes her as ''a child who likes to pull the wings off flies.''

What sets Chandler apart from other hard-boiled writers is that his work has a moral center in the honorable Marlowe who always prevails in the end—beaten up, disappointed, and cynical, but at the heart of a universe which has a moral standard no matter how threatened it is. Other novels in this genre, like *Double Indemnity,* are less reassuring on this score.

Howard Hawks cast Humphrey Bogart, one of Hollywood's most famous tough guys, as Marlowe. No one has played Marlowe as successfully as Bogart, who had a world weary face and a suitably sarcastic delivery on such classic Chandler lines as ''I'm thirty-three years old, went to college once, and can still speak English if there's any demand for it. There isn't much in my trade.''

Hawks' *The Big Sleep* (1946) is better realized than the Michael Winner version in 1978 which starred Robert Mitchum and is set not in California (where many hard-boiled novels and films are set, and from which they take their flavor), but in London of the 1970s. However, the main problem with Hawks' version, which has generated a good deal of critical interest on its own, is that it ends with Marlowe and Vivian Sternwood falling in love; in the novel Marlowe is the archetypal loner—he must stand apart from the world and its corruption. In true Hollywood fashion this change was made to capitalize on the real world relationship between Bogart and Lauren Bacall, who was cast as Vivian (Bogart left his wife for the very young Bacall during this time, causing a mild Hollywood scandal). This fiscally motivated plot change, however, weakens the noir aspect of the film, and along with the changes which the censorship laws of the era demanded, makes it a far less disturbing experience than the novel.

In some ways *The Big Sleep* seems to be unpromising material for Hawks, who tended to make either action films or comedies. Unlike Fritz Lang and Billy Wilder, who came to film noir from the downbeat German Expressionist cinema of the 1920s, Hawks' cinema is an optimistic one, filled with action, charm, sly humor, and characters who value professionalism and who are ''good enough'' to get a job done. Analyses of the adaptation of novels to films, however, often founder on arguments about the faithfulness of the adaptation. The film is a new work with virtues of its own and as David Thomson writes, Hawks' version is vastly different than Chandler's original in that it ''inaugurates a post-modern, camp, satirical view of movies being about other movies that extends to the New Wave and *Pulp Fiction.*''

—Jeannette Sloniowski

FURTHER READING:

Chandler, Raymond. *The Big Sleep.* New York, Vintage Books, 1976.

———. *The Simple Art of Murder.* New York, Pocket Books, 1964.

Lauren Bacall and Humphrey Bogart in a scene from the film *The Big Sleep*.

Kuhn, Annette. "The Big Sleep: Censorship, Film Text, and Sexuality." *The Power of the Image: Essays on Representation and Sexuality.* London, Routledge & Kegan Paul, 1985.

Mast, Gerald. *Howard Hawks, Storyteller.* New York, Oxford University Press, 1982.

Speir, Jerry. *Raymond Chandler.* New York, Frederick Ungar Publishing Co., 1981.

Thompson, David. *The Big Sleep.* London, British Film Institute Press, 1997.

Walker, Michael. "The Big Sleep: Howard Hawks and Film Noir." *The Book of Film Noir.* Edited by Ian Cameron. New York, Continuum, 1993.

Bigfoot

The North American equivalent of the legendary "Abominable Snowman" or Yeti of the Himalayas, "Bigfoot," whether he exists or not, has been a part of American popular culture since the late 1950s, with isolated reports stretching back even earlier. Bigfoot, also known as "Sasquatch" in Canada, is the generic name for an unknown species of giant, hair-covered hominids that may or may not roam the forests and mountains of the American Northwest and the Alberta and British Columbia regions of Canada. According to a synthesis of hundreds of eyewitness sightings over the years, the creatures are bipedal, anywhere between seven to nine feet tall (with a few specimens reportedly even taller), and completely covered in black or reddish hair. They appear to be a hybrid of human and ape characteristics. Also, they are omnivorous and usually solitary. On occasion, they leave behind enormous footprints (hence the name "Bigfoot"), measuring roughly between 16 and 20 inches. Cryptozoologists (those who study animals still unknown to science) hold out at least some hope that Bigfoot, hidden away in the last really undeveloped wilderness areas of North America, may yet prove to be a reality and not merely a folk legend.

Hairy hominids have been reported in nearly every state in the nation. However, classic American Bigfoot sightings are typically confined to northern California, Oregon, Washington, and Idaho. Additionally, sightings outside of this region often involve some paranormal or supernatural overtones; by contrast, the Pacific Northwest Bigfoot seems decidedly flesh and blood, if elusive. Advocates of Bigfoot's existence often begin by pointing back to Native American legends of human-like giants, such as the Wendigo of the Algonkians, in the forests of these regions. The alleged capture of a

Footage of an alleged Bigfoot sighting taken by Roger Patterson.

small Sasquatch (or escaped chimpanzee) named "Jacko" as reported in the British Columbia newspaper the *Daily British Colonist* in 1884 marks the introduction of Bigfoot to the modern mass media age. In the first few years of the 1900s, a spate of published eyewitness reports of Sasquatches in Canada grabbed attention throughout the Northwest. During the 1930s, the popular British Columbian writer J.W. Burns wrote about a Sasquatch who was a giant, atavistic Indian. However, it was not until 1958 that newspaper accounts of large, human-like footprints discovered by a bulldozer operator named Jerry Crew near a construction site in Willow Creek, California, popularized the term "Bigfoot" for the rest of America. At approximately the same time, a man from British Columbia named Albert Ostman made public his story of being kidnapped and held captive for six days by a group of Sasquatches back in 1924. Ostman only managed to escape, he claimed, when the Sasquatches became sick on his chewing tobacco. Over the years, in spite of skeptical questioning by a number of renowned cryptozoologists, Ostman stuck to his seemingly incredible story.

With the explosion of Bigfoot into public awareness, a number of investigators took to the American northwest to find anecdotal or physical evidence of the existence of the unknown hominid species. Some of the most famous of these investigators were Rene Dahinden, John Green, and Ivan T. Sanderson. The decade of the 1960s was somewhat of a "golden era" in the hunt for Bigfoot, when the mystery was new enough to most Americans to capture widespread interest and just plausible enough for many minds to remain open on the subject. Literally hundreds of eyewitness reports were collected and published in the many popular books written by these investigators. One of the most dramatic of the reports described a terrifying nocturnal attack by "apemen" upon miners in a remote cabin near Mt. St. Helens back in 1924. (The story has since been discredited.)

But by far the most sensational—and hotly disputed—physical evidence of that period is the 28-second, 16-millimeter film taken in 1967 by Roger Patterson in the Bluff Creek area of the Six Rivers

National Forest in California. The film shows what appears to be a female Bigfoot striding away from Patterson's camera. Patterson, accompanied by Bob Gimlin, had taken to the woods in a specific attempt to find and photograph the elusive Bigfoot—a fact which was not lost upon the film's numerous skeptics. However, if the film is a hoax, no one has ever confessed or turned up with a female Bigfoot suit. Frame-by-frame analysis and extensive investigation of the site and the backgrounds of the men involved has so far failed to provide conclusive evidence of deception. Patterson died in 1972, still insisting that he had filmed the real thing. Other Bigfoot films have surfaced from time to time, but unlike Patterson's, most of them have been clearly bogus.

In the early 1970s, a series of popular books and documentaries about Bigfoot appeared and further ensured the cultural longevity of the phenomenon. Inevitably, Bigfoot became a tourist draw for some areas in the Pacific Northwest, and towns and businesses were quick to capitalize upon the name. A few highly publicized expeditions to find and/or capture Bigfoot met with no success. Since that time, the media furor over Bigfoot has subsided, but occasional reports still gain widespread publicity. For example, a sighting in the Umatilla National Forest in Washington in 1982 led to the collection of numerous plaster casts of alleged Bigfoot tracks. A respected anthropologist from Washington State University named Grover Krantz argued for the tracks' authenticity, although other scientists remained unconvinced. The skepticism of the scientific community notwithstanding, Krantz and primatologist John Napier still remain open to the possibility that Bigfoot is more than a legend and mass delusion. For the most part, however, the case for Bigfoot's existence has departed from the front pages and now remains in the keeping of a small number of dedicated investigators prowling through the Northwest woods with plaster and cameras and in some cases tranquilizer darts, ready to make cryptozoological history by presenting the scientific and journalistic world with irrefutable proof of America's mysterious apeman.

—Philip L. Simpson

FURTHER READING:

Coleman, Loren. *The Field Guide to Bigfoot, Yeti, and other Mystery Primates Worldwide*. New York, Avon, 1999.

Green, John. *Encounters with Bigfoot*. Surrey, British Columbia, Hancock House, 1994.

Hunter, Don. *Sasquatch/Bigfoot: The Search for North America's Incredible Creature*. Buffalo, New York, Firefly Books, 1993.

Napier, John. *Bigfoot*. New York, Berkley, 1974.

Sanderson, Ivan T. *Abominable Snowmen: Legend Come to Life*. Philadelphia, Chilton, 1961.

Sprague, Roderick, and Grover S. Krantz, editors. *The Scientist Looks at the Sasquatch*. Moscow, Idaho, University Press of Idaho, 1979.

Bilingual Education

Bilingual education developed into a particularly contentious topic for defining American identity in the twentieth century. While federal legislation since the 1960s has recognized the United States as a multilingual nation, the professed long-range goal of institutionalized bilingual education was not that students should achieve bilingualism but proficiency in English. The vast majority of bilingual education programs were considered "transitional," functioning to introduce younger students with limited English-speaking ability into the general education curriculum where English served historically as the language of instruction. Many bilingual programs were taught principally either in English or in the primary language of the student. However, by the end of the twentieth century, federally funded programs had begun to favor instruction in both English and the primary language, an apparent departure from the goal of achieving proficiency in a single language.

The country's continued difficulty through the late twentieth century in educating immigrant children, mostly from Spanish-speaking countries, forced the federal legislature to institutionalize bilingual education. Following the passage of the Civil Rights Act (1964), Congress passed the Bilingual Education Act (1968), providing the first federal funds for bilingual education. The federal government elaborated its guidelines in the amended Bilingual Education Act of 1974, the same year the Supreme Court rendered its landmark *Lau vs. Nichols* decision, ruling that instructing students in a language they do not understand violates the Fourteenth Amendment of the Constitution.

"Bilingual" was often interpreted as "bicultural," suggesting that the question of bilingual education belonged to a broader debate over the efficacy of a polyglot society. The discussion in the United States focused on the progress of social mobility and the development of a unique American culture. For many, proficiency in English appeared to facilitate social advancement and incorporation into a mainstream culture despite that culture's multifaceted character. The letters of J. Hector St. Jean de Crèvecoeur in the late eighteenth century and Alexis de Tocqueville's published travels *Democracy in America* in 1835 contributed to an understanding of American culture as a "melting pot" of ethnicity. This identity became increasingly complex with the country's continued expansion through the nineteenth century and increasingly vexed with the rise of nationalism in the post bellum era. The nationalist urgency to homogenize the nation after the Civil War, accompanied by notions of Anglo-Saxon supremacy and the advent of eugenics, forced further eruptions of nationalist sentiment, including loud, jingoist cries for a single national language after the first World War. However, by the middle of the twentieth century, efforts to empower underrepresented communities contributed to an increased public interest in multiculturalism and ethnocentric agendas. A dramatic increase in immigration from Spanish-speaking countries during the second half of the twentieth century finally motivated the United States to institutionalize bilingual education.

But the strong opposition to the bilingual education legislation of the early 1970s, expressed in the influential editorial pages of the *Washington Post* and the *New York Times* between 1975 and 1976, suggested that bilingual programs never enjoyed overwhelming public support. The articulate arguments of Richard Rodriguez, an editor at the Pacific News Service and author of *Hunger for Memory* (1982), contributed to this opposition by distinguishing between private (primary language) and public (English) language while influential figures like Pulitzer Prize-winning historian Arthur M. Schlesinger, Jr., author of *The Disuniting of America* (1992), documented an increased national disenchantment with multiculturalism and bilingual education.

Discussions of bilingual education more often centered on Latino communities in metropolitan areas such as Miami, Los Angeles, and New York. But the debate was not exclusively Latino. The *Lau vs. Nichols* verdict, which involved a Chinese-speaking student, along with the advent of post-Vietnam War Asian immigration, suggested that the debate was relevant to other communities in the country. Similar interests were present in localized but nationally observed efforts to incorporate the language of a surrounding community into a school's curriculum. A particularly contentious and widely publicized debate arose over "Ebonics" in Oakland, California, in the early 1990s. Due in part to increasing black nationalism among African American intellectuals, prominent national political figures such as Reverend Jesse Jackson endorsed the incorporation of the local dialect and vernacular variations of language into the curriculum, while figures such as Harvard sociologist Cornel West and Harvard literary and social critic Henry Louis Gates, Jr., suggested that such programs lead to black ghettoization.

California showcased a national concern about bilingual education at the end of the twentieth century. Bilingual education became increasingly contentious in the state in the late 1990s with the passage of a proposition eliminating bilingual instruction. Approval of the initiative occurred in the shadow of two earlier state propositions and a vote by the regents of University of California to effectively terminate Affirmative Action, acts widely perceived in some underrepresented communities as attacks directed at Latino and immigrant communities. Bilingual programs enjoyed public support in cities with wide and long established minority political bases, such as Miami, where they where viewed as beneficial to developing international economies, but California continued to focus the debate primarily on social and cultural concerns.

—Roberto Alvarez

FURTHER READING:

Lau vs. Nichols. United States Supreme Court, 1974.

Porter, Rosalie Pedalino. *Forked Tongue: The Politics of Bilingual Education.* New York, Basic, 1990.

Rodriguez, Richard. *Hunger of Memory: The Education of Richard Rodriguez.* Boston, David R. Godine, 1982.

Schlesinger, Arthur, Jr. *The Disuniting of America.* New York, Norton, 1992.

Tocqueville, Alexis de. *Democracy in America.* 1835.

Billboards

From simple barnside advertisements and other billboarding techniques of the early 1900s, to today's huge high-tech creations on Los Angeles' Sunset Strip, billboards and outdoor advertising have been an integral part of both the landscape and the consciousness of America since the evolution of the American car culture of the early twentieth century.

Like many twentieth-century phenomena, the modern advertising spectacle, which the French have termed *gigantisme,* actually dates back to ancient times and the great obelisks of Egypt. By the late 1400s billboarding, or the mounting of promotional posters in conspicuous public places, had become an accepted practice in Europe. Wide-scale visual advertising came into its own with the invention of lithography in 1796, and by 1870 was further advanced by the technological progress of the Industrial Revolution.

A billboard in Birmingham, Alabama, 1937.

In America early advertising techniques were relatively naive, involving melodramatic situations, body ills, hygiene, and testimonials. Even so, the impact of subliminal suggestion was not unknown, and merchandising through association, with glamour, prestige, sex, and celebrities being the most popular ploys, was discovered early on. Thus, with few variations, the tenets of modern advertising were firmly in place by the twentieth century.

Predecessors of the modern billboard were posters for medicine shows, theatrical troupes, and spots events, and especially famous were those showing exaggerated versions of Barnum and Bailey's circus and Wild West acts. Initially no legal restrictions were placed on the posting of signs, and billboarding became part of the early entertainment world, with representatives traveling ahead of companies and competitively selecting choice locations which were then rented or leased. Thus these poster salesmen became the first pioneers of the outdoor advertising industry.

By the turn of the twentieth century, economic growth peaked in both Europe and America, creating new markets for both products and information. With the development of the automobile in the early 1900s, the stage was set for the rise of the roadside billboard. Sally Henderson notes: "An intense connection between the automobile, auto travel, and the outdoor poster (or billboard) was the natural outcome of a society in which individuals were becoming increasingly mobile. The outdoor ad had been waiting all along for the one product to come along that would change the world's habits, styles of living, and advertising modes: the automobile."

Early billboards were fairly austere, really posters with some kind of framing effect, but with the 1920s both design and the billboard setting (or frame) developed along more aesthetic lines. The focus of a deluxe 1920s billboard was colorful and ornate illustration, in a stylized but usually realistic (if idealized) mode. Product names were emphasized; and messages, if any, were understated and concise. Frames were wooden, mostly painted white, and often mounted on a base of lattice-work panels. Elaborate set-ups included end supports in the form of female figures. These were similar to the caryatid figures found in Greek architecture and were called lizzies. Billboards in the 1920s might also be highly accessorized, including shaded electric light fixtures and illuminated globes, picket fences, and a plot of flowers.

While the first fully electrical billboards appeared in New York in 1891, standard billboard style did not really change a great deal until the 1950s, though with World War II advertisers promoted war bonds along with products, not only out of patriotism, but because they were also given tax breaks to do so. Propagandistic visions of battleships, explosive war scenes, along with promises for a brighter, better tomorrow (to be provided, of course, by the products of the companies sponsoring the billboards) shared space with familiar commercial trademarks during World War II.

In the affluent post war 1950s, an age of cultural paradox when social values were being both embraced and questioned, outdoor advertising finally entered the modern age. A burgeoning youth market also first emerged during this decade, and all these mixed trends were reflected in mass advertising that was both more innovative and less realistic. The 1950s were the "Golden Age of Paint." Painting made possible bigger, glossier presentations, enabling billboards (like the 3-D movies of the early 1950s) to transcend their flat surfaces, as TWA (Trans World Airlines) planes and Greyhound buses suddenly seemed to emerge from the previously circumscribed space of the traditional billboard.

Youth culture in the 1950s exploded into the mid-1960s psychedelic era, and was reflected in the color-drenched surrealism and Op Art effects of billboards now aimed at the under 30 generation, whose ruling passions were fashion, sexuality, and entertainment. Billboards increasingly suggested gigantic recreations of rock LP jackets, and (like certain album covers) sometimes did not even mention the name of the group or product. The Pop Art movement, an ironic, but wry comment on an increasingly materialistic society, blurred the distinction between the fine and commercial arts, and billboards, along with Campbell's soup cans, were considered worthy of critical appraisal. Evolving out of the youth mania was the young adult singles market, and images of the wholesome American family gave way to solo visions of the ruggedly independent Marlboro man and the sexy Black Velvet woman.

As 1970s consumerism replaced 1960s idealism another art movement, Photorealism, became an important element of outdoor advertising, as billboards came to resemble huge, meticulously detailed Photorealist paintings. In the 1980s and 1990s, the failure of any influential art movement to emerge after Photorealism, or indeed the absence of any discernible cultural movements comparable to those of the 1950s or 1960s, contributed to the increasingly generic, if admittedly grandiose high-tech quality of much mainstream advertising. Cued by rapid changes in signage laws and property ownership, a movable billboard was developed in the 1980s. Inflatables, both attached to signs (such as a killer whale crashing through a Marineland billboard) and free-standing like huge Claes Oldenburg soft sculptures, have heightened the surreality of modern life with advertising in three-dimensions.

While some critics view billboards as outdoor art and socio/cultural barometers, concern over the environment and anti-billboard lobbying commenced in the late 1950s, and a 1963 study drew the first connection between the prominent placement of billboards along the New York State Thruway and traffic accidents. Certain minimal standards were established, and today's most grandiose billboards are confined to urban districts such as New York's Times Square, and the Las Vegas and Los Angeles strips, modern meccas whose identities have been virtually defined by the blatant flaunting of their flashy commercial accouterments. But Sally Henderson has also called Los Angeles' famed Sunset Strip "a drive-through gallery, a lesson in contemporary art . . . a twentieth-century art experience, quick and to the point." In the entertainment capital of the world, however, a billboard on the Strip remains as much a gigantic status symbol as an advertising tool or Pop Art artifact.

Pop Art or visual pollution, the outcry against billboards of previous decades has subsided into stoic acceptance of an inescapable tool of capitalism, and one which relentlessly both tells and shows the public that the best things in life are emphatically not free (though actual prices remain conspicuously absent from most billboards). In a unique instance of one pervasive visual medium being used as an effective signifying device within another, however, critical comment on billboards has been immortalized in the movies. Billboards in films are often seen as characteristic signifiers of the ills and ironies of both the American landscape, and the American Dream itself.

In a more optimistic mode, older film musicals used electrical billboards to symbolize the glamour of the big city and stardom. *Singin' in the Rain* (1952) climaxes with a ballet in which a vast set composed of towering Broadway electric signs suddenly blazes to life to illuminate Gene Kelly, who had previously been isolated in darkness. While a visually spectacular moment, the shot also signifies that aspiring dancer Kelly has finally "arrived" at the apex of his dreams. The same message is reenforced at the film's end when Kelly and Debbie Reynolds are seen standing in front of a billboard that mirrors the couple in an advertisement for their first starring roles in a big movie musical. In a more satirical vein, *It Should Happen To You*'s (1954) Judy Holliday makes a name for herself by plastering her moniker on a Columbus Circle billboard. The concept of the film was allegedly based on a real publicity stunt by Mamie Van Doren's agent, and similar billboards promoting Angelyne, a "personality" with no discernible talent or occupation, are still fixtures of modern day Los Angeles.

In later films, billboards were employed as an instantly recognizable symbol of a materialistic culture that constantly dangles visions of affluence in front of characters (and thus a public) who are then programmed for a struggle to achieve it. *No Down Payment* (1957), an exposé of suburban life, opens with shots of billboards hawking real Los Angeles housing developments, while glamorous but Musak-like music plays on the soundtrack. *No Down Payment* was among the first spate of 1950s films shot in CinemaScope, and the opening images of huge California billboards draw a perhaps unintentional parallel between the shape and scale of the American billboard, and the huge new wide-screen projection process that Hollywood hoped would lure patrons away from their new television sets and back into movie theaters.

Billboards are used to even more cynical effect in *Midnight Cowboy* (1969). With an outsider's sharp eye for the visual clutter of the American landscape, British director John Schlesinger (who had already shown keen awareness of the ironies of modern advertising in *Darling*, 1965) uses American billboards throughout the film as an ironic counterpoint to a depressing saga of a naive Texan who aspires to make it as a hustler in the big city. Billboards cue flashbacks to Joe Buck's troubled past life on his bus journey to New York, taunt him with images of affluence as he later wanders destitute through the mean streets of the city, and finally, on their bus journey south at the end of the film, cruelly tantalize both Joe and his ailing companion, Ratso Rizzo, with glossy images of a paradisal Florida which one of them will not live to see.

One of the more bizarre uses of billboard *gigantisme* in modern cinema is *Boccaccio '70* (1962), which also offers a wickedly sly comment on the obsessive use of larger-than-life sexual symbolism in modern outdoor advertising. In the Fellini "Temptation of Dr. Antonio" episode a gigantic figure of Anita Ekberg comes to life and steps down from a billboard on which the puritanical doctor has been obsessing to erotically torment him to the strains of an inane jingle imploring the public to "drink more milk!"

—Ross Care

FURTHER READING:

Blake, Peter. *God's Own Junkyard The Planned Deterioration of America's Landscape.* New York/Chicago/San Francisco, Holt, Rinehart, and Winston. 1964.

Fraser, James Howard. *The American Billboard: 100 Years.* New York, Harry Abrams, 1991.

Henderson, Sally, and Robert Landau. *Billboard Art.* San Francisco, Chronicle Books, 1980.

The Bionic Woman

One of the first female superheroes on prime-time television, the Bionic Woman originated as a character on the popular show *The Six Million Dollar Man*. The Bionic Woman was created on that show when Steve Austin's fiancée suffered a near-fatal parachute accident and was rebuilt with a bionic arm, legs, and ear. Her nuclear-powered prostheses gave her super strength, speed, and hearing, which complimented Steve Austin's bionic powers as they solved crimes and wrongdoings together. Lindsey Wagner starred as the bionic Jamie Sommers and parlayed the Bionic Woman's guest spots on *The Six Million Dollar Man* into a two-year run in her own series, which ran from 1976 to 1978, and later, years of syndication. *The Bionic Woman* could be seen on cable television in the late 1990s.

—P. Andrew Miller

FURTHER READING:

Douglas, Susan J., *Where the Girls Are: Growing Up Female with the Mass Media.* New York, Times Books, 1994.

Bird, Larry (1956—)

Born in 1956 and raised in rural Indiana—a place where basketball has been popular as a spectator sport since the 1910s and 1920s, well before the establishment of successful professional leagues in the 1940s—Larry Bird emerged as one of the premiere sports superstars

Lindsey Wagner in a scene from *The Bionic Woman.*

of the 1980s, as well as one of the most marketable athletes in the National Basketball Association (NBA). Often credited with helping to revive a then-troubled league—along with Earvin "Magic" Johnson—Bird's discipline, unselfish playing style, and enthusiasm for the game made him a hero to basketball fans around the world and a driving force in the NBA's growth.

Bird attained celebrity early in his career; four thousand people, twice the population of his hometown of French Lick, Indiana, attended his final high school game there in 1974. After a short stint at Indiana University, Bird left to play for the Indiana State Sycamores in 1975. During his college career, season ticket sales for the formerly-lagging Sycamores tripled. His college years culminated in a host of honors for Bird, who finished college as the fifth highest scorer in college basketball history. He was named the College Player of the Year (1978-1979), and led his team to a number one ranking and the national championship game. This game, which the Sycamores lost to Earvin "Magic" Johnson's Michigan State team, marked the beginning of the Bird-Johnson rivalry that would electrify professional basketball for the next 12 years.

Originally drafted by the Boston Celtics while he was still in college, Bird joined the team in the 1979-1980 season and proceeded to lead it to one of the most dramatic single-season turnarounds in league history. The year before his NBA debut, the Celtics had won only 29 games and did not qualify for the league playoffs; the 1979-1980 team won 61 games and finished at the top of the Atlantic Division. Bird's accomplishments as a player are remarkable: he was named the NBA's Most Valuable Player in 1984, 1985, and 1986; he played on the Eastern Conference All-Star team for 12 of his 13 pro seasons; he led his team to NBA Championships in 1981, 1984, and 1986; and he won a gold medal in the 1992 Barcelona Olympics as a member of the "Dream Team" (an elite group that also featured his rival, Johnson, as well as Michael Jordan and other superstar players). Hobbled by back injuries and absent from many games in his last two seasons, Bird retired from basketball in 1992. He was inducted into the NBA Hall of Fame on October 2, 1998.

Contributing to the growing prosperity of the NBA in the 1980s and to its emergence as a popular and profitable segment of the entertainment industry were several factors, not least of which were the marketing efforts of league commissioner David Stern. The league used the appeal of its top stars—especially Bird, Johnson, and Jordan—to market itself to fans. Another factor in the league's growth was the fan interest triggered by the intense rivalry between the league's top two teams, the Celtics and the Los Angeles Lakers, which happened to be led by the league's top two players, Bird and Johnson. The Celtics and Lakers met in the NBA Finals three times in the mid-1980s, the excitement of their rivalry being amplified by the charisma of Bird and Johnson; the historic competition between the two teams in the 1960s; and the contrast between their two fundamentally different styles of basketball—East Coast fundamentals vs. West Coast razzle-dazzle.

As Bird and Johnson became the league's brightest stars and as their teams won championships, they helped the NBA to embark on a new era of soaring attendance, sold-out games, escalating salaries, and lucrative television and sponsorship deals in which the players themselves became heavily marketed international celebrities. Increasing both his own income and his stake with fans, Bird appeared in television commercials for several companies, most prominently McDonalds and Converse Shoes.

In order to allow the Celtics and Lakers to keep Bird and Johnson on their teams, the NBA restructured itself economically in 1984, passing an exception to its salary-cap rules that would become known as the "Larry Bird Exception." This move allowed teams to re-sign their star players at exorbitant costs, regardless of the team's salary limit, and led to skyrocketing player salaries in the late 1980s and 1990s.

In 1997, Bird was hired as head coach of the Indiana Pacers. In his first year of coaching, Bird had an effect on his team that recalled his impact as a player nearly two decades earlier. Whereas in 1996 the Pacers had won only 39 games, in 1997 they won 58 and competed in the Eastern Conference championship series against Michael Jordan's Chicago Bulls. At the season's conclusion, Bird was named NBA Coach of the Year.

In the sometimes racially-charged world of professional athletics, Bird's position as a prominent white player garnered much commentary. "[Bird is] a white superstar," Johnson said of his rival in a 1979 interview in *Sports Illustrated.* "Basketball sure needs him." Early in its history, professional basketball had attracted few African American players (due both to societal racism and the success

Birkenstocks

Birkenstocks—the name commonly used for sandals made by the Birkenstock Company—are the parent of "comfort shoes" in the United States. Called hari krishna shoes, monk shoes, Jesus sandals, and nicknamed granolas, Jerusalem cruisers, tree huggers, Flintstone feet, hippie shoes, and beatniks, they have carried numerous social connotations. Nevertheless, the influence that Birkenstocks have had on what Americans wear on their feet goes beyond alternative trappings. Not only have they become a household word in the 1980s, but they have also joined the likes of Nikes in gaining name-brand recognition.

Birkenstocks were created by a family of German shoemakers. Emphasizing comfort rather than fashion, the original Birkenstocks were open-toed, leather-strapped, flat-heeled, slip-ons. In 1964, Karl Birkenstock combined a flexible arch support and a contoured sole—inventions his grandfather Konrad had engineered at the turn of the twentieth century—into an orthopedic shoe. The ergonomically designed sole is shaped like a footprint in wet sand, with cupped heel and raised bar where the toes meet the ball of the foot. The pliable insole is a cork/latex matrix sandwiched between layers of jute and covered in suede leather.

Margot Fraser introduced Birkenstocks to the United States in 1966. While visiting her native Germany she bought a pair to alleviate her foot pain. Back in northern California, she sold a few pairs to friends, never intending to start a business. Quickly convinced that everyone would benefit from such comfortable shoes, she began importing them. Retail shoe store owners, however, balked at selling an unconventional "ugly" shoe. Undaunted, Fraser took Birkenstocks to health fairs and found buyers among owners of health food stores and alternative shops. Having carved out a niche by 1971, she convinced the German parent company to give her sole United States distribution rights and she incorporated the company. The most recognizable and popular Birkenstock style, the Arizona, developed for the American market, was introduced the same year.

By the late 1970s the shoes had become a favorite of hippies, the back-to-the-earth crowd, and the health-conscious, especially women looking for alternatives to the popular narrow-toed, high-heels generally available. Still, the shoes were anti-fashion—they were cited as a fashion "don't" in a women's magazine in 1976. In 1979, the Boston, a closed toe style, was introduced.

The company grew gradually until the late 1980s when it finally got a foothold in the athletic/comfort shoe market. Americans' desire for more comfortable clothing and a nostalgia for the trappings of the 1970s, coupled with Birkenstock's aggressive marketing, set off the shoe's phenomenal rise in popularity and sales in the 1990s. Countering a perceived association with Dead Heads, hippies, and grunge rockers, Birkenstock catalogs featured hip young urbans. Between 1989 and 1992 the company expanded 500 percent and, according to the *New York Times,* between 1992 and 1994 sold more shoes than it had in the previous 20 years. The popularity bred knock-offs by high-end shoemakers such as Rockport, Scholl, Ralph Lauren, and Reebok, and discount copies appeared in stores such as Fayva and Kmart in the 1990s. In 1992, shoemakers Susan Bennis and Warren Edwards created a formal imitation with rhinestone buckles for Marc Jacobs' runway show. Competition from other "comfort shoe" companies such as Teva and Naot began. Birkenstock eventually opened its own stores and the shoes were made available in shops geared toward comfortable footwear and through mail order giants such as L.L.

Larry Bird (right)

of the all-black Harlem Globetrotters), but by 1980, 75 percent of NBA players were African American. Thus, Bird entered a scene in which white stars were indeed rare. Critics labeled his Celtics a "white boy's team," and sportswriters still debated whether African Americans might be somehow inherently more adept at sports than whites. Bird himself referred to this stereotype when he said that he had "proven that a white boy who can't run and jump can play this game."

Bird's impact—both as a player and as a coach—is unparalleled; he helped to change losing teams into champions and a declining professional league into a vibrant and profitable sports and entertainment giant. From a humble high school gymnasium in rural Indiana, Bird came to international attention as one of the best known and most successful athletes in the history of professional sports.

—Rebecca Blustein

FURTHER READING:

Bird, Larry, with Bob Ryan. *Drive: The Story of My Life.* New York, Bantam, 1990.

George, Nelson. *Elevating the Game: Black Men and Basketball.* New York, Harper Collins, 1992.

Hoose, Phillip M. *Hoosiers: The Fabulous Basketball Life of Indiana.* New York, Vintage Books, 1986.

Rader, Benjamin G. *American Sports: From the Age of Folk Games to the Age of Spectators.* Englewood Cliffs, New Jersey, Prentice Hall, 1983.

Bean; mainstream retailers like Macy's and Nordstrom also began to carry Birkenstocks.

Originally Fraser sold four styles, but by the early 1980s the company offered over 20 different models with an expanded color selection. The company also introduced a completely non-leather shoe, the Alternative, for ethical vegetarians. Smaller sizes of the classic styles, made to fit children, were offered around the same time. In the late 1980s and early 1990s, the color selection moved out from neutral and earthy tones like tan, black, white, brown, crimson, and gold to include bright and neon colors like orange and turquoise. During the same time, closed shoes made specifically for professionals who spend most of their workday on their feet, such as restaurant and health care workers, showed up in shops and catalogs.

Birkenstocks, once the ugly duckling, moved to the center of fashion. *Vogue, GQ, Sassy,* and *Details* magazines all featured sandal and clog styles in fashion layouts throughout the 1990s. Birkenstocks were seen on the feet of stars such as Madonna, Tanya Tucker, Harrison Ford, Wesley Snipes, and Yvette Freeman; politicos Norman Schwarzkopf, Donna Shalala, and John F. Kennedy Jr.; sports greats Shaquille O'Neal, Dennis Rodman, and Dan O'Brien and the maven of taste, Martha Stewart, among others. Menswear designer John Scher had custom Birkenstocks made in gold leather, gray corduroy, and wine pinstripe for his fall 1998 collection. Perry Ellis, Sportmax, and Narciso Rodriguez have also featured Birkenstocks in their runway shows.

By the late 1990s Birkenstock had over 50 styles including rubber clogs, trekking shoes, women's wedge heels, multi-colored sandals, anti-static models, as well as mainstays like the Zurich, a style similar to the shoes Margot Fraser brought from Germany in 1966. Fraser is chief executive officer and 60 percent owner of the Novato, California, based company, called Birkenstock Footprint Sandals, Inc., with employees owning the balance. Fraser's corporation has over 3,600 retail accounts, 125 licensed shops, and four company-owned stores in the United States, including the San Francisco flagship store opened in 1997. Birkenstock's sales for fiscal 1997 were an estimated $82 million.

—ViBrina Coronado

FURTHER READING:

"Birkenstock Braces to Fight the Competition." *Personnel Journal.* August 1994, 68.

Brokaw, Leslie. "Feet Don't Fail Me Now." *Inc.* May 1994, 70.

McGarvey, Robert. "Q & A: Margot Fraser." *Entrepreneur.* February 1995.

O'Keefe, Linda. *Shoes: A Celebration of Pumps, Sandals, Slippers and More.* New York, Workman Publishing, 1996.

Patterson, Cecily. "From Woodstock to Wall Street." *Forbes.* November 11, 1991, 214.

The Birth of a Nation

D. W. Griffith's 1915 silent-film epic *The Birth of a Nation* remained as controversial at the end of the twentieth century as at the beginning, largely because of its sympathetic portrayal of the Ku Klux Klan and of white ascendancy in the defeated South during the Reconstruction period following the American Civil War. Galvanized by the film's depiction of the newly freed slaves as brutal and ignorant, civil-rights groups like the National Association for the Advancement of Colored People (NAACP) picketed the film in many cities when it was released and protested again when the Library of Congress added the classic to the National Film Registry in 1992 (though a year later the Library excluded the film from an exhibit of 54 early film works). Still, *The Birth of a Nation* is highly regarded as a cinematographic triumph, a benchmark that helped define film syntax for future directors in a newly emerging genre. The ambiguous legacy of this film was capsulized by a *New York Times* reporter who wrote (Apr. 27, 1994): "Like an orator who says all the wrong things brilliantly . . . [it] manages to thrill and appall at the same time." Few of its most ardent critics deny credit to Griffith for having achieved a work of technical brilliance. Film historian Lewis Jacobs argued in *The Rise of the American Film: A Critical History,* that *The Birth of a Nation* and *Intolerance,* a sequel, released by Griffith in 1916, are "high points in the history of the American movie" that "far surpassed other native films in structure, imaginative power, and depth of content . . . They foreshadowed the best that was to come in cinema technique, earned for the screen its right to the status of an art, and demonstrated with finality that the movie was one of the most potent social agencies in America."

The iconic status of *The Birth of a Nation* is based on several factors. It was heavily promoted and advertised nationwide, making it the prototype of the modern "blockbuster." In a nickelodeon era, it was the first to break the $2-per-ticket barrier, proving that mass audiences could be attracted to serious films that were more than novelty entertainments or melodramas. It was the first film shown in the White House, after which President Woodrow Wilson reputedly said, "It is like writing history with lightning." In addition to establishing D. W. Griffith as America's most important filmmaker, *The Birth of a Nation* also helped to propel the career of Lillian Gish, a 21-year-old actress who, with her sister Dorothy, had appeared in some of Griffith's earlier films. Most importantly, it was a groundbreaking production that set the standard for cinematography and the basic syntax of feature films. Although, in the 1960s, revisionist critics like Andrew Sarris speculated that Griffith's technical sophistication had been overrated, *The Birth of a Nation* is still revered for its pioneering use of creative camera angles and movement to create a sense of dramatic intensity, and the innovative use of closeups, transitions, and panoramic shots, "all fused by brilliant cutting," in the words of Lewis Jacobs. Even the protests engendered by the film helped Americans find their bearings in the first significant cultural wars involving artistic creativity, censorship, and identity politics in the age of the new mass media.

The Birth of a Nation was based on Thomas Dixon, Jr.,'s 1905 drama *The Clansman,* which had already been adapted into a popular play that had toured American theaters. Screenwriter Frank Woods, who had prepared the scenario for Kinemacolor's earlier, abortive attempt to bring Dixon's work to the screen, convinced Griffith to take on the project. "I hoped at once it could be done," Griffith said, "for the story of the South had been absorbed into the very fiber of my being." Griffith also added material from *The Leopard's Spots,* another of Dixon's books that painted a negative picture of Southern blacks during the Reconstruction era. In a 1969 memoir, Lillian Gish recalled that Griffith had optioned *The Clansman* for $2500 and offered the author a 25 percent interest in the picture, which made Dixon a multimillionaire. She quoted Griffith as telling the cast that "I'm going to use [*The Clansman*] to tell the truth about the War

Scene from the film *The Birth of a Nation*.

between the States. It hasn't been told accurately in history books.'' When the film was being shot at a lot on Sunset Boulevard in Los Angeles, the first-time-ever use of artificial lighting to illuminate battle scenes shot at night led to public fears that southern California was under enemy attack from the sea.

Although some scenes depicted the early arrival of slaves in America, the decades of the 1860s and 1870s—Civil War and Reconstruction—constitute the historical timeframe of *The Birth of a Nation*. The film includes enactments of several historical scenes, such as Sherman's march to the sea, the surrender at Appomattox, and the assassination of Lincoln, but the narrative focuses almost exclusively on the saga of two white dynasties, the Stonemans from the North and the Camerons from the South, interlinked by romantic attachments between the younger generations of the two families. An early scene depicts the Cameron plantation in South Carolina as an idyllic estate with benevolent white masters and happy slaves coexisting in mutual harmony until undermined by abolitionists, Union troops, and Yankee carpetbaggers. After the war, Austin Stoneman, the family patriarch, dispatches a friend of mixed-race, Silas Lynch, to abet the empowerment of ex-slaves by encouraging them to vote and run for public office in the former Confederacy. A horrified Ben

Cameron organizes the Ku Klux Klan as an engine of white resistance. The film's unflattering depiction of uncouth African American legislators and of Lynch's attempt to coax Elsie Stoneman into a mixed-race marriage fueled much controversy over the years for reinforcing stereotypes about Negro men vis-à-vis the ''flower of Southern womanhood.'' To create dramatic tension, Griffith juxtaposed images of domestic bliss with unruly black mobs and used alternating close-up and panoramic scenes to give a sense of movement and to facilitate the emotional unfolding of the narrative. During a climactic scene in which the Ku Klux Klan rides to the rescue of the Cameron patriarch from his militant black captors, a title reads: ''The former enemies of North and South are united again in common defense of their Aryan birthright.'' Bowing to protests, Griffith excised some of the more graphic scenes of anti-white violence before the film's premiere, and also added an epilogue, now lost, favorably portraying the Hampton Institute, a prominent black school in Virginia. Interviewed by his biographer, Barnet Bravermann in 1941, D. W. Griffith thought that *The Birth of a Nation* should, ''in its present form be withheld from public exhibition'' and shown only to film professionals and students. Griffith said ''If *The Birth of a Nation* were done again, it would have to be made much clearer.''

The title of the film remained *The Clansman* until a month before its premiere, and was altered to its familiar title upon Dixon's own enthusiastic recommendation. Both Griffith and Dixon defended their work against an avalanche of censorship threats, as in a letter by Dixon to the *Boston Journal* (April 26, 1915), in which he wrote "This play was not written to stir race hatred. It is the faithful record of the life of fifty years ago. It is no reflection on the cultured, decent negro of today. In it are sketched good negroes and bad negroes, good whites and bad whites." Griffith also ardently defended his viewpoint, as in a letter to the *New York Globe* (April 10, 1915) in which he criticized "pro-intermarriage" groups like the NAACP for trying "to suppress a production which was brought forth to reveal the beautiful possibilities of the art of motion pictures and to tell a story which is based upon truth in every vital detail."

The Birth of a Nation had its premiere at New York City's Liberty Theater on March 3, 1915, to critical and popular acclaim, though the NAACP and other groups organized major protests and violence broke out in Boston and other cities. Booker T. Washington refused to let Griffith make a film about his Tuskegee Institute because he did not want to be associated with the makers of a "hurtful, vicious play." W. E. B. Du Bois adopted a more proactive stance, urging members of his race to create films and works of art that would depict its own history in a positive light. But response in the mainstream press was generally favorable. Critic Mark Vance boasted in the March 12 issue of *Variety* how a film "laid, played, and made in America" marked "a great epoch in picturemaking" that would have universal appeal. Reviews in the southern papers were predictably partisan. A critic for the *Atlanta Journal,* Ward Greene, obviously inspired by scenes of triumphant Klan riders, crowed that Griffith's film "is the awakener of every feeling ... Loathing, disgust, hate envelope you, hot blood cries for vengeance ... [you are] mellowed into a deeper and purer understanding of the fires through which your forefathers battled to make this South of yours a nation reborn!" Over the years, *The Birth of a Nation* was used as a propaganda film both by the film's supporters and detractors. Film historian John Hope Franklin remarked to a 1994 Library of Congress panel discussion that the film was used by a resurgent Ku Klux Klan as a recruiting device from the 1920s onward, a point supported by other historians, though disputed by Thomas Cripps, author of several scholarly works on black cinema.

Despite the continuing controversy over the depiction of interracial conflict, *The Birth of a Nation* remains a landmark film in the history of world cinema and its director an important pioneer in the film medium. Writer James Agee, in a rhapsodic defense of Griffith, wrote of him in a 1971 essay: "He achieved what no other known man has ever achieved. To watch his work is like being witness to the beginning of melody, or the first conscious use of the lever or the wheel. ..." *The Birth of a Nation*, continued Agee, was a collection of "tremendous magical images" that equaled "Brady's photographs, Lincoln's speeches, and Whitman's war poems" in evoking a true and dramatic representation of the Civil War era.

—Edward Moran

FURTHER READING:

Barry, Iris. *D.W. Griffith: American Film Master.* New York, Museum of Modern Art, 1965.

Gish, Lillian, with Ann Pinchot. *The Movies, Mr. Griffith, and Me.* Englewood Cliffs, New Jersey, Prentice Hall, 1969.

Grimes, William. "An Effort to Classify a Racist Classic." *New York Times.* April 27, 1994.

Phillips, Mike. "White Lies." *Sight & Sound.* June 1994.

Silva, Fred, editor. *Focus on "The Birth of a Nation."* Englewood Cliffs, Prentice Hall, 1971.

Sarris, Andrew. "*Birth of a Nation* or White Power Back When." *Village Voice.* July 17 and July 24, 1969.

Stanhope, Selwyn. "The World's Master Picture Producer." *The Photoplay Magazine.* January 1915, 57-62.

Birthing Practices

Historically speaking, an overview of changing practices of childbirth offers an overview of the changing dynamics of gender and the increasing authority of professional medicine, particularly in the United States and Western Europe. As midwives began to be "phased out" in the late eighteenth century, they were replaced by male doctors, and birthing practices changed as a result. Increasing medical knowledge and experience reinforced this shift, eventually pathologizing pregnancy and childbirth and tying childbirth to a hospital environment. In the late twentieth century, however, many women began calling for a return to the earlier, less medicalized, models of childbirth, and the debate about the costs and benefits of various birthing practices continues to develop today.

In colonial America, deliveries were attended by midwives as a matter of course. These women drew upon years of experience, often passing their knowledge from one generation to the next, and generally attending hundreds of childbirths during their careers. In some cases, a midwife might call a "barber-surgeon" to assist with a particularly difficult case (though often the surgeon's skills were no better than the midwife's, and the patient and child were lost), but for the most part women (mothers and midwives) controlled the birthing process. With the rise in medical schools, however, and the teaching of obstetrics as the first specialty in eighteenth-century American medical schools, medical doctors began to assume control over childbirth.

Beginning in the 1830s, having a medical doctor in attendance at a birth became a sign of social prestige—middle- and upper-class women could afford to call in a doctor and did so more out of a desire to display their economic and political clout than out of medical necessity. Class pressures ensured that women would choose childbirth assistance from someone of their own class (that is, a medical doctor for the middle and upper classes, a midwife for working classes). These pressures also meant that crusades to persuade middle- and upper-class women that they "deserved" physicians, that no precaution was too great, and so on, were enormously effective in shifting public opinion toward the presumed superiority of medical doctors. As this kind of social pressure continued to spread throughout the Victorian era, lay practitioners lost more and more status, and medical doctors gained more and more control. Furthermore, the systematic exclusion of women from the medical profession, particularly during the nineteenth century, ensured that women themselves began losing control of childbirth, giving it up to the increasing authority of the male medical community.

Throughout the 1800s, doctors employed medical privilege to protect their professional status from the economic and social threat of midwives who lacked formal training. The Boston Women's Health Collective asserts that nineteenth-century physicians "waged a virulent campaign against midwives, stereotyping them as ignorant, dirty, and irresponsible. Physicians deliberately lied about midwifery outcomes to convince legislators that states should outlaw it." These strategies, coupled with the significant risks of childbirth (infant and maternal mortality rates remained high throughout the nineteenth century), helped to create a climate of fear surrounding pregnancy and birth. Rather than seeing childbirth as a natural practice, people began to see it as a medical emergency, one that should be relinquished to a physician's control.

Once childbirth had been pathologized, the door was opened to begin moving women in labor out of their homes and into hospitals where, according to the medical community, the "disease of childbirth" could best be battled. Until the beginning of the twentieth century, it was actually a stigma to have to give birth in a maternity ward, which had generally been reserved for the poor, immigrants, and unmarried girls. As better strategies were developed to prevent disease (especially deadly outbreaks of puerperal fever that had flourished in hospitals throughout the nineteenth century), the hospital birth, with its concomitant costs, was recast as a status symbol. Eventually, however, having babies in hospitals became a matter of course. According to Jessica Mitford, while only 5 percent of babies were born in hospitals in 1900, 75 percent were born in hospitals in 1935, and by the late 1960s, 95 percent of babies were born in hospitals. Eakins' *American Way of Birth* notes, "the relocation of obstetric care to the hospital provided the degree of control over both reproduction and women that would-be obstetricians needed in their ascent to professionalized power." This power was consolidated through non-medical channels, with advice columns, media attention, popular books, and community pressure working to reinforce the primacy of the professional medical community in managing women's childbirth experiences.

In the twentieth century, giving birth in a hospital environment has meant a loss of control for the mother as she becomes subject to numerous, standardized medical protocols; throughout her pregnancy, in fact, she will have been measured against statistics and fit into frameworks (low-risk vs. high-risk pregnancy; normal vs. abnormal pregnancy, and so on). As a result, the modern childbirth experience seems to depersonalize the mother, fitting her instead into a set of patient "guidelines." Women in labor enter alongside the ill, the injured, and the dying. Throughout most of the twentieth century, women were anesthetized as well, essentially being absent from their own birthing experience; fathers were forced to be absent as well, waiting for the announcement of his child's arrival in a hospital waiting room. If a woman's labor is judged to be progressing "too slowly" (a decision the doctor, rather than the mother, usually makes), she will find herself under the influence of artificial practices designed to speed up the process. More often than not, her pubic area will be shaved (a procedure that is essentially pointless) and sometimes cut (in an episiotomy) by medical personnel anxious to control the labor process. Further advances in medical technology, including usage of various technological devices and the rise in caesarian sections (Mitford cites rates as high as 30 percent in some hospitals), have also contributed to a climate of medicalization and fear for many women giving birth. This is not to say, of course, that many of these medical changes, including improved anesthetics (such as epidurals) and improved strategies for difficult birthing situations (breech births, fetal distress, etc.) have not been significant advances for women and their babies. But others argue that many of these changes have been

for the doctors' convenience: delivering a baby while lying on one's back with one's feet in stirrups is surely designed for the obstetrician's convenience, and the rise in caesarian sections has often been linked to doctors' preferences rather than the mothers'.

In the 1960s and 1970s, as a result of their dissatisfaction with the medical establishment and with the rising cost of medical care, various groups began encouraging a return to older attitudes toward childbirth, a renewal of approaches that treat birthing as a natural process requiring minimal (if any) medical intervention. One of the first steps toward shifting the birthing experience away from the control of the medical establishment involved the introduction of childbirth classes for expectant parents. These courses often stress strategies for dealing with the medical community, for taking control of the birthing process, and for maintaining a "natural childbirth" experience through education; the most famous methods of natural childbirth are based on work by Grantly Dick-Read (*Childbirth Without Fear*), Fernand Lamaze, and Robert Bradley.

Also significant were various feminist critiques of the standard birth practices. The publication of the Boston Women's Health Collective's *Our Bodies, Ourselves* in 1984 offered a resource to women who wanted to investigate what had been essentially "underground" alternatives to the medicalized childbirth experience. Through this work (and others), women learned how to question their doctors more assertively about the doctors' practices, to file "birth plans" (which set out the mother's wishes for the birth), and to find networks of like-minded parents, midwives, and doctors who can assist in homebirths, underwater births, and other childbirth techniques. In some states, midwives not attached to hospitals are still outlaws, and groups continue to campaign to change that fact.

Finally, many hospitals are recognizing women's desire to move away from the dehumanizing and pathological approaches to childbirth associated with the professional medical community. In deference to these desires (or, more cynically, in deference to their financial bottom lines), some hospitals have built "Birthing Centers," semi-detached facilities dedicated specifically to treating childbirth as a natural process. Women enter the Birthing Center, rather than the hospital. There they are encouraged to remain mobile, to have family and friends in attendance, and to maintain some measure of control over their bodies. Often patient rooms are designed to look "homey," and women (without complications) give birth in their own room, rather than in an operating theater. Many of these facilities employ Nurse Midwives, women and men who have been trained as nurses in the traditional medical establishment but who are dedicated to demedicalizing the childbirth practice while still offering the security of a hospital environment.

As women and men continue to demand that childbirth be recognized as a natural, rather than unnatural, process, the dominant birthing practices will continue to shift. Additionally, rising pressures from the insurance industry to decrease costs are also likely to contribute to a decrease in the medical surveillance of childbirth— already new mothers' hospital stays have been drastically reduced in length as a cost-cutting measure. Clearly the move in recent years has meant a gradual return to earlier models of childbirth with a return of control to the mother and child at the center of the process.

—Deborah M. Mix

FURTHER READING:

Boston Women's Health Collective. *The New Our Bodies, Ourselves, Updated for the 90s.* New York, Simon and Schuster, 1992.

Eakins, Pamela S., editor. *The American Way of Birth*. Philadelphia, Temple University Press, 1986.

Mitford, Jessica. *The American Way of Birth*. New York, Dutton, 1992.

Black, Clint (1962—)

Since the release of his first album in 1989, Clint Black has become one of country music's biggest stars. He is also one of the most prominent symbols of country's revival in the 1980s and 1990s. It was in the mid-1980s that country music had been written off as dead. In 1985, *The New York Times* reported that this once mighty genre had fallen off the edge of the American entertainment table and it would never regain such stature with its audience. A year later, the same newspaper reversed itself in an article hailing the new creative and commercial vitality of country music, as traditionalists like Randy Travis and young iconoclasts like Steve Earle brought new life into old forms. That, however, was nothing compared to what was just around the corner. Country was about to be taken over by a new

Clint Black

generation of heartthrobs in cowboy hats who were going to capture the imagination of the American public to a degree hitherto unimagined.

Part of country music's revival was due to the creative groundwork that was laid for newcomers in the adventurous creativity of the mid-1980s. Angry song-writing geniuses like Earle, quirky originals like Lyle Lovett, and musical innovators like the O'Kanes all played a part in paving the way for young new artists. Interestingly, the aggressive urban anger of black music in the 1980s also influenced the country scene. Rap drove a lot of middle class whites to a music they could understand, and country radio was playing it. The audience for pop music was also growing older and, in the 1980s, for the first time, a generation over thirty-five continued to buy pop music. Although the children of these suburban middle-class consumers were buying rap, their parents were looking for the singer-songwriters of their youth—the new Dan Fogelbergs and James Taylors—and they found them wearing cowboy hats.

The country superheroes of the 1980s and 1990s were a new breed indeed. They did not have the down-home background of Lefty Frizzell, Porter Wagoner, or Johnny Cash, but they did have their own skills that would help them succeed in the music industry. Garth Brooks was a marketing major in college, and he knew how to market himself; Dwight Yoakam was a theater major, and he knew how to invent himself onstage; and Lyle Lovett's day job at the time he signed his first recording contract was helping his mother run high-level business management training seminars.

Clint Black, who arrived on the scene in 1989, was a "folkie" from the suburbs of Houston. His father advised him against going into country music precisely because he did not think he was country enough. "Stick to doing other folks' songs," he advised. "Real country songwriters, like Harlan Howard. Don't try to write your own. You haven't done enough living—shooting pool, drinking beer, getting into fights—to write a real country song." Black's "Nothing's News," which graced his first album, was an answer to his father and to all those other good old boys who "Spent a lifetime . . . Down at Ernie's icehouse liftin' longnecks to that good old country sound," only to discover ultimately that they had "worn out the same old lines, and now it seems that nothin's news . . . ."

The 1980s were a time when the rock influence hit country with a vengeance. Rock acts like Exile and Sawyer Brown became country acts. Country radio adopted the tight playlists of pop radio. Record company executives from Los Angeles and New York started moving into the little frame houses that served as office buildings on Nashville's Music Row. And even among the neo-traditional acts, rock music management techniques became the norm. Clint Black's career blossomed under the managerial guidance of Bill Ham, who had made his reputation guiding ZZ Top's fortunes. Black's first album, *Killin' Time,* became the first debut album ever, in any genre, to place five singles at number one on the charts.

For many country artists, country superstardom seems to almost automatically raise the question, "Now what?" For Black, marriage was the answer to that question. He married Hollywood television star Lisa Hartman (*Knots Landing*) in 1991 and their marriage has lasted. It has also garnered him a certain amount of gossip column celebrity beyond the country circuit. Although Black also has a movie role in *Maverick* to his credit, his reputation rests solidly on what he does best: writing and singing country songs. Black seems to have settled in for the long haul.

—Tad Richards

FURTHER READING:

Brown, C. D. *Clint Black: A Better Man.* New York, Simon & Schuster, 1993.

Black Mask

One of the most important detective fiction magazines of the twentieth century, *Black Mask* began early in 1920 and introduced and developed the concept of the tough private eye. It also promoted, and in some cases introduced, the work of such writers as Dashiell Hammett, Raymond Chandler, Erle Stanley Gardner, and John D. MacDonald. Hammett's *The Dain Curse, Red Harvest, The Glass Key,* and *The Maltese Falcon* all appeared originally as serials in the magazine and Chandler sold his first detective story to *Black Mask.* In its over 300 issues the pulp showcased the work of dozens of other writers. Though many are forgotten today, such contributors as Frederick Nebel, Norbert Davis, W.T. Ballard, John K. Butler, Raoul Whitfield, Carroll John Daly, Horace McCoy, Lester Dent, and William Campbell Gault all helped shape and define the hardboiled school of mystery writing.

Early in 1919, H. L. Mencken, literary man and dedicated iconoclast, wrote a letter to a friend. ''I am thinking of venturing into a new cheap magazine,'' he explained. ''The opportunity is good and I need the money.'' Mencken and his partner, theater critic George Jean Nathan, required funds to keep their magazine *The Smart Set* afloat. He considered that a quality publication, but in his view the new one that he and Nathan launched early in 1920 was ''a lousy magazine'' that would cause them nothing but ''disagreeable work.'' Their new publication was christened *The Black Mask* and featured mystery stories. Pretty much in the vein of Street & Smith's pioneering *Detective Story* pulp, the early issues offered very sedate, and often British, detective yarns. Nathan and Mencken soon sold out, leaving the magazine in other hands.

Then in 1923 two beginning writers started submitting stories about a new kind of detective. Carroll John Daly, a onetime motion picture projectionist and theater manager from New Jersey, introduced a series about a tough, gun-toting private investigator named Race Williams. Written in a clumsy, slangy first person, they recounted Williams' adventures in a nightmare urban world full of gangsters, crooked cops, and dames you could not trust. Williams explained himself and his mission this way—''The papers are either roasting me for shooting down some minor criminals or praising me for gunning out the big shots. But when you're hunting the top guy, you have to kick aside—or shoot aside—the gunmen he hires. You can't make hamburger without grinding up a little meat.'' This tough, humorless metropolitan cowboy became extremely popular with the magazine's readers, who were obviously tired of the cozy crime stories that the early *Black Mask* had depended on. For all his flaws, Race Williams is acknowledged by most critics and historians to be the first hardboiled detective, and the prototype for others to follow.

Unlike Daly, Dashiell Hammett knew what he was talking about. He had been a private investigator himself, having put in several years with the Pinkerton Agency. Exactly four months after the advent of Race Williams, Hammett sold his first story about the ''Continental Op(erative)'' to the magazine. Titled ''Arson Plus,'' it introduced the plump middle-aged operative who worked out of the San Francisco office of the Continental Detective Agency. Although also in the first person, the Op stories were written in a terse and

Various covers of *Black Mask*.

believable vernacular style that made them sound real. Hammett's private detective never had to brag about being tough and good with a gun; readers could see that he was. His nameless operative soon became Race Williams' chief rival and after he had written nearly two dozen stories and novellas about him, Hammett put him into a novel. The first installment of *Red Harvest* appeared in the November 1927 issue of *Black Mask.* In November of the next year came the second Op serial, *The Dain Curse.* Then in 1929 Hammett introduced a new San Francisco private eye, a pragmatic tough guy he described as resembling a blond Satan. *The Maltese Falcon,* told in the third person, introduced Sam Spade and the quest for the jewel-encrusted bird. The story quickly moved into hardcovers, movies, and international renown. Hammett's *The Glass Key* ran in the magazine in 1930 and his final Op story in the November issue of that year. With the exception of *The Thin Man,* written initially for *Redbook* in the early 1930s, everything that Hammett is remembered for was published in *Black Mask* over a period of less than ten years.

Joseph Shaw was usually called Cap Shaw, because of his Army rank during World War I. Not at all familiar with pulp fiction or *Black Mask* when he took over as editor in 1926, he soon educated himself on the field. Shaw never much liked Daly's work, but kept him in the magazine because of his appeal to readers. Hammett, however, was an exceptional writer and Shaw used him to build the magazine into an important and influential one. ''Hammett was the leader in the thought that finally brought the magazine its distinctive form,'' Shaw explained some years later. ''Without that it was and would still have been just another magazine. Hammett began to set character before situation, and led some others along that path.'' In addition to concentrating on character, one of the goals of the best *Black Mask* authors was to develop prose that sounded the way people talked and not the way writers wrote. In addition to Hammett, Cap Shaw encouraged other writers who had already been contributors when he joined as editor. Among them were Erle Stanley Gardner, Raoul Whitfield, and Frederick Nebel. He asked Nebel to create a new hardboiled private eye and the result was, as a blurb called him, "an iron-nerved private dick" named Donahue. One of the things he got from Whitfield was a serial titled "Death in a Bowl," which introduced Ben Jardinn, the very first Hollywood private eye. In 1933, Shaw bought "Blackmailers Don't Shoot" from Raymond Chandler, a failed middle-aged business man who was hoping he could add to his income by writing pulpwood fiction. The tough and articulate private eye Chandler wrote about for *Black Mask,* and later for its rival *Dime Detective,* was called Mallory and then John Dalmas. When he finally showed up in the novel *The Big Sleep* in 1939, he had changed his name to Philip Marlowe. Among the many other writers Shaw introduced to *Black Mask* were Horace McCoy, Paul Cain, Lester Dent, and George Harmon Coxe.

After Shaw quit the magazine in 1936 over a salary dispute, it changed somewhat. Chandler moved over to *Dime Detective,* where Nebel had already been lured, and the stories were not quite as "hardboiled" anymore. New writers were recruited by a succession of editors. Max Brand, Steve Fisher, Cornell Woolrich, and Frank Gruber became cover names in the later 1930s. *Black Mask* was bought out by Popular Publications in 1940 and started looking exactly like Popular's *Dime Detective.* Kenneth S. White became the editor of both and put even more emphasis on series characters. Oldtime contributors such as H.H. Stinson and Norbert Davis provide recurring detectives, as did newcomers like Merle Constiner, D.L. Champion, and Robert Reeves. Later on John D. MacDonald, Richard Demming, and William Campbell Gault made frequent appearances.

The decade of the 1950s saw the decline and fall of all the pulp fiction magazines. *Black Mask* ceased to be after its July 1951 issue. By then, it was a smaller-sized magazine that included reprints from earlier years with few new detective tales. Attempts to revive it in the 1970s and the 1980s were unsuccessful.

—Ron Goulart

FURTHER READING:

Cook, Michael L., editor. *Mystery, Detective, and Espionage Magazines.* Westport, Greenwood Press, 1983.

Goulart, Ron. *The Dime Detective.* New York, Mysterious Press, 1988.

Sampson, Robert. *Yesterday's Faces.* Bowling Green, Ohio, Bowling Green State University Popular Press, 1987.

Black Panthers

The Black Panther Party (BPP) came to represent the West Coast manifestation of Black Power as well as the angry mood within urban African American communities in the 1960s. The groups main influences were Malcolm X, especially after his 1964 break from the Nation of Islam, and Robert F. Williams, the then Cuban-based civil rights leader and advocate of armed self-defense. Philosophically, the

Black Panthers (from left): 2nd Lt. James Pelser, Capt. Jerry James, 1st Lt. Greg Criner and 1st Lt. Robert Reynolds.

organization was rooted in an eclectic blend of Marxist-Leninism, black nationalism, and in the revolutionary movements of Africa and Asia.

The BPP was founded in October 1966 by Huey Newton and Bobby Seale, two young black college students in Oakland, California. The name of the organization was taken from the Lowndes County Freedom Organization, which had used the symbol and name for organizing in the rural black belt of Alabama in 1965. The BPP was initially created to expand Newton and Seale's political activity, particularly "patrolling the pigs"—that is, monitoring police activities in black communities to ensure that civil rights were respected.

Tactically, the BPP advocated "picking up the gun" as a means to achieve liberation for African Americans. Early on, Newton and Seale earned money to purchase guns by selling copies of Mao Tsetung's "Little Red Book" to white radicals on the University of California-Berkeley campus. The group's "Ten Point Program" demanded self-determination for black communities, full employment, decent housing, better education, and an end to police brutality. In addition, the program included more radical goals: exemption from military service for black men, all-black juries for African Americans on trial and "an end to the robbery by the capitalists of our Black Community." Newton, the intellectual leader of the group, was appointed its first Minister of Defense and Eldridge Cleaver, a prison activist and writer for the New Left journal *Ramparts,* became Minister of Information. Sporting paramilitary uniforms of black leather jackets, black berets, dark sunglasses, and conspicuously displayed firearms, the Panthers quickly won local celebrity.

A series of dramatic events earned the Black Panthers national notoriety in 1967. That spring, as a result of the Panthers' initial police surveillance efforts, members of the California state legislature introduced a bill banning the carrying of loaded guns in public. In response, a group of Black Panthers marched into the capitol building in Sacramento toting loaded weapons. Then, on October 28 of the same year, Newton was arrested on murder charges following an altercation with Oakland police which left one officer dead and Newton and another patrolman wounded. The arrest prompted the BPP to start a "Free Huey!" campaign which attracted national attention through the support of Hollywood celebrities and noted writers and spurred the formation of Black Panther chapters in major cities across the nation. In addition, Newton's arrest forced Seale and Cleaver into greater leadership roles in the organization. Cleaver, in particular, with his inflammatory rhetoric and powerful speaking skills, increasingly shaped public perceptions of the Panthers with incendiary calls for black retribution and scathing verbal attacks against African American "counter-revolutionaries." He claimed the choice before the United States was "total liberty for black people or total destruction for America."

In February 1968, former Student Non-Violent Coordinating Committee (SNCC) leader, Stokely Carmichael, who had been invited by Cleaver and Seale to speak at "Free Huey!" rallies, challenged Cleaver as the primary spokesman for the party. Carmichael's Pan-Africanism, emphasizing racial unity, contrasted sharply with other Panther leaders' emphasis on class struggle and their desire to attract white leftist support in the campaign to free Newton. The ideological tension underlying this conflict resulted in Carmichael's resignation as Prime Minister of the BPP in the summer of 1969 and signaled the beginning of a period of vicious infighting within the black militant community. In one incident, after the Panthers branded head of the Los Angeles-based black nationalist group US, Ron Karenga, a "pork chop nationalist," an escalating series of disputes between the groups culminated in the death of two Panthers during a shoot-out on the UCLA campus in January 1969.

At the same time, the federal government stepped up its efforts to infiltrate and undermine the BPP. In August 1967, the FBI targeted the Panthers and other radical groups in a covert counter-intelligence program, COINTELPRO, designed to prevent "a coalition of militant black nationalist groups" and the emergence of a "black messiah" who might "unify and electrify these violence-prone elements." FBI misinformation, infiltration by informers, wiretapping, harassment, and numerous police assaults contributed to the growing tendency among BPP leaders to suspect the motives of black militants who disagreed with the party's program. On April 6, 1968, police descended on a house containing several Panthers, killing the party's 17-year-old treasurer, Bobby Hutton, and wounding Cleaver, who was then returned to prison for a parole violation. In September, authorities convicted Newton of voluntary manslaughter. In December, two Chicago party leaders, Fred Hampton and Mark Clark, were killed in a police raid. By the end of the decade, 27 members of the BPP had been killed, Newton was in jail (although he was released after a successful appeal in 1970), Cleaver had fled to Algeria to avoid prison, and many other Panthers faced lengthy prison terms or continued repression. In 1970, the state of Connecticut unsuccessfully tried to convict Seale of murder in the death of another Panther in that state.

By the early 1970s, the BPP was severely weakened by external attack, internal division, and legal problems and declined rapidly. After his release from prison in 1970, Newton attempted to wrest

control of the party away from Cleaver and to revive the organization's popular base. In place of Cleaver's fiery rhetoric and support for immediate armed struggle, Newton stressed community organizing, set up free-breakfast programs for children and, ultimately, supported participation in electoral politics. These efforts, though, were undermined by widely published reports that the Panthers engaged in extortion and assault against other African Americans. By the mid-1970s, most veteran leaders, including Seale and Cleaver, had deserted the party and Newton, faced with a variety of criminal charges, fled to Cuba. After his return from exile, Newton earned a doctorate, but was also involved with the drug trade. In 1989, he was shot to death in a drug-related incident in Oakland. Eldridge Cleaver drifted rightward in the 1980s, supporting conservative political candidates in several races. He died on May 1, 1998, as a result of injuries he received in a mysterious mugging. Bobby Seale continued to do local organizing in California. In 1995, Mario Van Pebbles directed the feature film, *Panther,* which attempted to bring the story of the BPP to another generation. The Panthers are remembered today as much for their cultural style and racial posturing as for their political program or ideology.

—Patrick D. Jones

FURTHER READING:

Brown, Elaine. *A Taste of Power: A Black Woman's Story.* New York, Pantheon, 1992.

Chruchill, Ward. *Agents of Repression: The FBI's Secret Wars Against the Black Panther Party and the American Indian Movement.* Boston, South End, 1988.

Cleaver, Eldridge. *Soul On Ice.* New York, Laurel/Dell, 1992.

Hilliard, David. *This Side of Glory: The Autobiography of David Hilliard and the Story of the Black Panther Party.* Boston, Little Brown, 1993.

Keating, Edward. *Free Huey!* Berkeley, California, Ramparts, 1970.

Moore, Gilbert. *Rage.* New York, Carroll & Graf, 1971.

Newton, Huey. *To Die for the People: The Writings of Huey P. Newton.* New York, Random House, 1972.

Pearson, Hugh. *The Shadow of the Panther: Huey Newton and the Price of Black Power In America.* Reading, Massachusetts, Addison-Wesley, 1994.

Seale, Bobby. *Seize the Time: The Story of the Black Panther Party and Huey P. Newton.* New York, Random House, 1970.

Black Sabbath

Formed in Birmingham, England in 1968, Black Sabbath was one of the most important influences on hard rock and grunge music. While the term "heavy metal" was taken from a Steppenwolf lyric and had already been applied to bands such as Cream and Led Zeppelin, in many ways Black Sabbath invented the genre. They were perhaps the first band to include occult references in their music, and they began to distance themselves from the blues-based music which was the norm, although they had started their career as a blues band.

Originally calling themselves Earth, they discovered another band with the same name. After renaming themselves Black Sabbath

Black Sabbath in 1998: Ozzy Osbourne (seated), (standing from left) Bill Ward, Tony Iommi, and Geezer Butler.

the group released their self-titled first album in 1970. *Black Sabbath* was recorded both quickly and inexpensively—it took only two days and cost six hundred pounds. In spite of that, the album reached number 23 on the American charts and would eventually sell over a million copies. *Paranoid* was released later the same year and cracked the top ten in the United States while topping the charts in Britain. Their third album, *Master of Reality,* was equally successful and remained on the Billboard charts in America for almost a year.

Those releases introduced themes which would become staples for future metal bands: madness, death, and the supernatural. Although some considered the band's lyrics satanic, there was often an element of camp present. The group got its name from the title of a Boris Karloff film, and songs such as "Fairies Wear Boots" are at least partly tongue-in-cheek. But vocalist John "Ozzy" Osbourne's haunting falsetto and Tony Iommi's simultaneously spare and thundering guitar work would become touchstones for scores of hard rock bands.

Sabbath released three more albums as well as a greatest hits collection before Osbourne left the group in 1977, reportedly because of drug and alcohol problems. He returned in 1978, then left permanently the following year to start his own solo career. Initially, both Osbourne and the new version of Black Sabbath enjoyed some degree of commercial success, although many of the Sabbath faithful insisted the whole greatly exceeded the sum of its parts. During the 1980s the band would go through an astonishing array of lineup changes and their popularity plummeted.

In the late 1980s and early 1990s, Soundgarden, Helmet, Nirvana, and others in the grunge and resurgent hard rock movements demonstrated that they had been heavily influenced by the early Black Sabbath, and this effectively rehabilitated the band's reputation. While Sabbath had often been viewed as a dated version of the arena rock of the 1970s, grunge indicated not only that their music remained vibrant, but also that it bore many surprising similarities to the Sex Pistols, Stooges, and other punk and proto-punk bands. Sabbath became heroes to a new generation of independent and alternative bands, and the group's first albums enjoyed an enormous resurgence in popularity. Their music returned to many radio stations and was even featured in television commercials. Osbourne organized Ozzfest, an annual and very successful tour which featured many of the most prominent heavy metal and hard rock acts, as well as his own band. Iommi continued to record and tour with Black Sabbath into the late 1990s, although he was the only original member, and listeners and audiences remained largely unimpressed.

—Bill Freind

FURTHER READING:

Bashe, Philip. *Heavy Metal Thunder: The Music, Its History, Its Heroes.* Garden City, New York, Doubleday, 1985.

Walser, Robert. *Running with the Devil: Power, Gender, and Madness in Heavy Metal Music.* Hanover, New Hampshire, University Press of New England, 1993.

Black, Shirley Temple
See Temple, Shirley

Black Sox Scandal

Although gambling scandals have been a part of professional baseball since the sport's beginning, no scandal threatened the game's stature as "the national pastime" more than the revelations that eight members of the Chicago White Sox had conspired to throw the 1919 World Series. Termed the "Black Sox Scandal," the event will go down in history as one of the twentieth century's most notorious sports debacles.

The Chicago White Sox of the World War I period were one of the most popular teams in the major leagues. They were led on the field by "Shoeless" Joe Jackson, an illiterate South Carolinian whose .356 career batting average is the third highest ever, and pitchers Eddie Cicotte and Lefty Williams. The Sox were owned by Charles A. Comiskey, a nineteenth-century ballplayer notorious for paying his star players as little as possible; Cicotte, who led the American League with 29 wins in 1919, earned just $5,500 that season. Comiskey's stinginess included not paying for the team's laundry in 1918—the team continued to play in their dirty uniforms, which is when the sobriquet "Black Sox" originated.

During the 1919 season, the White Sox dominated the American League standings. Several players on the team demanded that Comiskey

The 1919 Chicago White Sox.

give them raises. He refused. First baseman Chick Gandil began discussing throwing the World Series with his fellow players. The eight Sox players who attended meetings on throwing the Series were Cicotte, Gandil, Williams, Jackson, shortstop Swede Risberg, third basemen Fred McMullin and Buck Weaver, and outfielder Happy Felsch. In mid-September, Gandil met with small-time Boston gambler "Sport" Sullivan in New York, telling him his teammates were interested in throwing the upcoming World Series if Sullivan could deliver them $80,000. Two more gamblers, ex-major league pitcher Bill Burns and former boxer Billy Maharg, agreed to contribute money. These three gamblers contacted New York kingpin Arnold Rothstein, who agreed to put up the full $80,000.

Cicotte pitched the Series opener against the Reds. As a sign to the gamblers that the fix was on, he hit the first batter with a pitch. Almost instantly, the gambling odds across the country shifted from the White Sox to the Reds. The Sox fumbled their way to a 9-1 loss in Game One.

Throughout the Series, the White Sox made glaring mistakes on the field—fielders threw to the wrong cutoff men, baserunners were thrown out trying to get an extra base, reliable bunters could not make sacrifices, and control pitchers such as Williams began walking batters. Most contemporary sportswriters were convinced something was corrupt. Chicago sportswriter Hugh Fullerton marked dubious plays on his scorecard and later discussed them with Hall of Fame pitcher Christy Mathewson.

The 1919 Series was a best-of-nine affair, and the underdog Reds led four games to one after five games. When the gamblers' money had not yet arrived, the frustrated Sox began playing to win, beating Cincinnati in the sixth and seventh games. Before Williams started in the eighth game, gamblers approached him and warned him his wife would be harmed if he made it through the first inning.

Williams was knocked out of the box after allowing three runs in the first inning. The Cincinnati Reds won the Series with a commanding 10-5 win.

After the Series, Gandil, who had pocketed $35,000 of the $80,000, retired to California. Fullerton wrote columns during the following year, insisting that gamblers had reached the White Sox; he was roundly criticized by the baseball establishment and branded a malcontent.

The fixing of the 1919 Series became public in September 1920, when Billy Maharg announced that several of the World Series games had been thrown. Eddie Cicotte broke down and confessed his involvement in the fixing; he claimed he took part in taking money "for the wife and kiddies." Joe Jackson, who during the Series batted a robust .375, signed a confession acknowledging wrongdoing. Upon leaving the courthouse, legend has it that a tearful boy looked up to him and pleaded, "Say it ain't so, Joe." "I'm afraid it is," Jackson allegedly replied.

On September 28, 1920 a Chicago grand jury indicted the eight players. They were arraigned in early 1921. That summer they were tried on charges of defrauding the public. The accused were represented by a team of expensive lawyers paid for by Comiskey. At the trial it was revealed that the signed confessions of Jackson, Cicotte, and Williams had been stolen. The defense lawyers maintained that there were no laws on the books against fixing sporting events.

Following a brief deliberation, the eight were found not guilty on August 2, 1921. The impact of the allegation, however, was undeniable. Kennesaw Mountain Landis, a former Federal judge elected as organized baseball's first commissioner in November 1920, declared, "No player who throws a ball game, no player who undertakes or promises to throw a ball game, no player who sits in a conference with a bunch of crooked players and gamblers, where the ways and means of throwing a ball game are planned and discussed and does not promptly tell his club about it, will ever play professional baseball.''

The eight Black Sox players spent the rest of their lives in exile. Jackson played semi-pro baseball under assumed names. Several appealed to be reinstated, but Landis and his successors invariably rejected them. Perhaps the saddest story of all was Buck Weaver's. While he had attended meetings to fix the Series, he had never accepted money from the gamblers and had never been accused of fixing games by the prosecution (in fact, Weaver batted .324 during the Series). But for not having told Comiskey or baseball officials about the fix, he was tried with his seven teammates and thrown out of baseball with them. The last surviving member of the Black Sox, Swede Risberg, died in October 1975.

Most historians credit baseball's subsequent survival to two figures. From on high, Landis ruled major league baseball with an iron fist until his death in 1944 and gambling scandals decreased substantially throughout organized baseball. On the field of play, Babe Ruth's mythic personality and home run hitting ability brought back fans disillusioned by the 1919 scandal, while winning the game millions of new fans.

—Andrew Milner

FURTHER READING:

Asinof, Eliot. *Eight Men Out.* New York, Holt, 1963.

Light, Jonathan Frase. *The Cultural Encyclopedia of Baseball.* Jefferson, North Carolina, McFarland, 1997.

Wallop, Douglass. *Baseball: An Informal History.* New York, W.W. Norton, 1969.

The Blackboard Jungle

Ten years after the end of World War II, writer-director Richard Brooks' film, *The Blackboard Jungle* (1955) was released. The film remains as a moody, entertaining potboiler and an early formula for treating a theme—the rehabilitating education of delinquents and the inner-city underprivileged—that was still being explored in the cinema of the 1980s and 1990s. Films as diverse as the serious and specific *Stand and Deliver* (1988, Edward James Olmos played the beleaguered teacher), the comedic *Renaissance Man* (1994, Danny de Vito), and the sentimental *Dangerous Minds* (1995, Michelle Pfeiffer), can all find their origins in *The Blackboard Jungle,* which, although not a particularly masterful film, was unique in its time, and became a cultural marker in a number of respects. It is popularly remembered as the first movie ever to feature a rock 'n' roll song (Bill Haley and the Comets, ''Rock around the Clock''), and critically respected for its then frank treatment of juvenile delinquency and a powerful performance by actor Glenn Ford. It is notable, too, for establishing the hero image of African American Sidney Poitier, making him Hollywood's first black box-office star, and for its polyglot cast that accurately reflected the social nature of inner-city ghetto communities.

The Blackboard Jungle, however, accrues greater significance when set against the cultural climate that produced it. Despite the post war position of the United States as the world's leading superpower, the country still believed itself under the threat of hostile forces. Public debate was couched exclusively in adversarial terms; under the constant onslaught, the nation succumbed to the general paranoia that detected menace in all things from music to motorcyclists, from people of color and the poor to intellectuals and poets. Even the young were a menace, a pernicious presence to be controlled, and protected from the rock 'n' roll music they listened and danced to, which was rumored as part of a Communist plot designed to corrupt their morals.

From the mid-1940s on, a stream of novels, articles, sociological studies and, finally, movies, sought to explain, sensationalize, vilify, or idealize juvenile delinquency. It was precisely for the dual purpose of informing and sensationalizing that *The Blackboard Jungle* was made, but, like Marlon Brando's *The Wild One* (1954), it served to inflame youthful sentiment, adding tinder to a fire that was already burning strong.

Adapted from a 1954 novel by Evan Hunter, Brooks' film tells the story of Richard Dadier (Ford), a war veteran facing his first teaching assignment at a tough inner-city high school in an unspecified northern city. ''This is the garbage can of the educational system,'' a veteran teacher tells Dadier. ''Don't be a hero and never turn your back on the class.'' Dadier's class is the melting pot incarnate, a mixture of Puerto Ricans, Blacks, Irish, and Italians controlled by two students—Miller (Poitier) and West (Vic Morrow), an Irish youth. West is portrayed as an embryo criminal, beyond redemption, but Miller provides the emotional focus for the movie. He is intelligent, honest, and diligent, and it becomes Dadier's mission to encourage him and develop his potential. However, in its antagonism to Dadier, the class presents a unified front. They are hostile to education in general and the teacher's overtures in particular, and when he rescues a female teacher from a sexual attack by a student the hostility becomes a vendetta to force him into quitting. However, despite being physically attacked, witnessing the victimization of his colleagues, and withstanding wrongful accusations of bigotry while worrying about his wife's difficult pregnancy, Dadier triumphs over the rebellious students and, by extension, the educational system. He retains his idealism, and in winning over his students overcomes his own prejudices.

In setting the film against the background of Dadier's middle-class life and its attendant domestic dramas, it was assumed that audiences would identify with him, the embattled hero, rather than with the delinquent ghetto kids, but the film's essentially moral tone is subverted by the style, the inflections, and exuberance of those kids. Following an assault by West and his cohorts, Dadier's faith begins to waver. He visits a principal at a suburban high school. Over a soundtrack of students singing the ''Star Spangled Banner'' Dadier tours the classrooms filled with clean-cut white students, tractable and eager to learn. He may yearn for this safe environment, but to the teenage audiences that flocked to *The Blackboard Jungle,* it is Dadier's inner city charges that seem vital and alive, while the suburban high school appears as lively as a morgue. The teen response to *The Blackboard Jungle* was overwhelming. ''Suddenly, the festering connections between rock and roll, teenage rebellion, juvenile delinquency, and other assorted horrors were made explicit,'' writes Greil Marcus. ''Kids poured into the theaters, slashed the seats, rocked the balcony; they *liked it.*''

The instigation of teen rebellion was precisely the opposite reaction to what the filmmakers had intended. From the opening title

Sidney Poitier (far right) and Glenn Ford in a scene from the film *The Blackboard Jungle*.

sequence, with "Rock Around the Clock" blaring from the sound track as Glenn Ford makes his way through the school yard crowded with boys dancing, sullenly shaking their heads in time to the music, the tone was set. This massed gathering appeared at once threatening and appealing, something with which teenagers could identify, and the image of exuberant, youthful rebellion stayed with teen audiences.

The film's moral, somewhat hectoring message, was more calculated to appeal to parents, while Brooks himself veiled his own sympathies in subtlety. "These kids were five and six years old in the last war," a cynical police detective tells Dadier. "Father in the army, mother in the defense plant; no home life, no church life. Gang leaders have taken the place of parents." Indeed, the specter of war pervades the film. In one scene, Dadier derides a fellow teacher for using his war injuries to gain the sympathy of his class; in another, he counsels the recalcitrant West, who responds that if his crime lands him in jail for a year, it will at least keep him out of the army, and hence, from becoming another nameless casualty on foreign soil.

One cannot say, however, that Richard Brooks offers a profound critique, or even a very good film. ("[It] it will be remembered for its timely production and release," wrote film critic G.N. Fenin in

summation.) It was not so much the message or the quality of filmmaking that was of import, but the indelible image it left behind of the greasy-haired delinquent snapping his fingers to the beat of Bill Haley and the Comets. This is the nature, the calculus if you will, of exploitation films; that under the rubric of inoculation, they spread the very contagion they are ostensibly striving to contain.

—Michael Baers

FURTHER READING:

Cowie, Peter, editor. *Aspects of American Cinema*. Paris, Edition le Terrain Vague, 1964.

Hunter, Evan. *The Blackboard Jungle*. London, Constable, 1955.

Lewis, Jon. *The Road to Romance and Ruin: Teen Films and Youth Culture*. New York, Routledge, 1992.

Marill, Alvin H. *The Films of Sidney Poitier*. Secaucus, Citadel Press, 1978.

Miller, Jim, editor. *The Rolling Stone Illustrated History of Rock & Roll*. New York, Rolling Stone Press, 1980.

Pettigrew, Terence. *Raising Hell: The Rebel in the Movies*. New York, St. Martin's Press, 1986.

Raffman, Peter, and Jim Purdy. *The Hollywood Social Problem Film: Madness, Despair, and Politics from the Depression to the Fifties*. Bloomington, Indiana University Press, 1981.

Blackface Minstrelsy

Taboo since the early 1950s, blackface minstrelsy developed in the late 1820s just as the young United States was attempting to assert a national identity distinct from Britain's. Many scholars have identified it as the first uniquely American form of popular entertainment. Blackface minstrelsy was a performance style that usually consisted of several white male performers parodying the songs, dances, and speech patterns of Southern blacks. Performers blackened their faces with burnt cork and dressed in rags as they played the banjo, the bone castanets, the fiddle, and the tambourine. They sang, danced, told malapropistic jokes, cross-dressed for "wench" routines, and gave comical stump speeches. From the late 1820s on, blackface minstrelsy dominated American popular entertainment. Americans saw it on the stages of theaters and circuses, read about it in the popular novels of the nineteenth century, heard it over the radio, and viewed it on film and television. Blackface minstrelsy can certainly be viewed as the commodification of racist stereotypes, but it can also be seen as the white fascination with and appropriation of African American cultural traditions that culminated in the popularization of jazz, the blues, rock 'n' roll, and rap music.

While there are accounts of blackface minstrel performances before the American Revolution, the performance style gained widespread appeal in the 1820s with the "Jump Jim Crow" routine of Thomas Dartmouth Rice. Rice is frequently referred to as "the father of blackface minstrelsy." In 1828 Rice, a white man, watched a black Louisville man with a deformed right shoulder and an arthritic left knee as he performed a song and dance called "Jump Jim Crow." Rice taught himself the foot-dragging dance steps, mimicked the

An example of blackface minstrelsy.

disfigurement of the old man, copied his motley dress, and trained himself to imitate his diction. When Rice first performed ''Jump Jim Crow'' in blackface during an 1828 performance of *The Rifle* in Louisville, Kentucky, the audience roared with delight. White audience members stopped the performance and demanded that Rice repeat the routine over 20 times. It is impossible to overstate the sensational popularity which Rice's routine enjoyed throughout the 1830s and 1840s. Gary D. Engle has aptly described Rice as ''America's first entertainment superstar.'' When Rice brought his routine to New York City's Bowery Theater in 1832, the audience again stopped the show and called him back on stage to repeat the routine multiple times. He took his routine to England in 1836 where it was enthusiastically received, and he spawned a bevy of imitators who styled themselves ''Ethiopian Delineators.''

In 1843 four of these ''Ethiopian Delineators'' decided to create a blackface minstrel troupe. They were the first group to call themselves ''Minstrels'' instead of ''Delineators,'' and their group *The Virginia Minstrels* made entertainment history when it served as the main attraction for an evening's performance. Previous blackface shows had been performed in circuses or between the acts of plays. The troupe advertised its Boston debut as a ''Negro Concert'' in which it would exhibit the ''Oddities, peculiarities, eccentricities, and comicalities of that Sable Genus of Humanity.'' Dan Emmett played the violin, Frank Brower clacked the ''bones'' (a percussion instrument similar to castanets), Billy Whitlock strummed the banjo, and Dick Pelham beat the tambourine. Their show consisted of comedy skits and musical numbers, and it enjoyed a six week run in Boston before traveling to England. Dozens of imitators attempted to trade on its success. One of the most famous was *Christy's Minstrels,* which opened in New York City in 1846 and enjoyed an unprecedented seven year run. During the 1840s blackface minstrelsy became the most popular form of entertainment in the nation. Americans who saw performances were captivated by them. ''Everywhere it played,'' writes Robert Toll, ''minstrelsy seemed to have a magnetic, almost hypnotic impact on its audiences.''

Harriet Beecher Stowe's novel *Uncle Tom's Cabin*, published serially between 1851 and 1852, sold over 300,000 copies in its first year in part because it traded on the popularity of blackface minstrelsy. The book opens with a ''Jump Jim Crow'' routine, incorporates blackface malapropistic humor, gives its readers a blackface minstrel dancer in Topsy, and its hero Uncle Tom sings doleful hymns drawn from the blackface minstrel tradition. Indeed, Stowe's entire novel can be read as a blackface minstrel performance in which a white New England woman ''blacks up'' to impersonate Southern slaves.

Uncle Tom's Cabin was immediately adapted for the stage. It not only became the greatest dramatic success in the history of American theater, but it also quickly became what Harry Birdoff called ''The World's Greatest Hit.'' ''Tom shows'' were traveling musical revues of *Uncle Tom's Cabin* that continued the traditions of blackface minstrelsy. One historian has described them as ''part circus and part minstrel show.'' They featured bloodhounds chasing Eliza across the ice (a stage addition not present in Stowe's novel), trick alligators, performing donkeys, and even live snakes. One 1880 performance included 50 actors, 12 dogs, a mule, and an elephant. The ''Tom shows'' competed directly with the traveling circuses of Barnum and Bailey.

After Thomas Edison's invention of moving picture technology in 1889, film versions of *Uncle Tom's Cabin* with whites in blackface were some of the very first films ever made. In 1903 Sigmund Lubin produced a film version of the play, and on July 30 of that same year

Edison himself released a 1-reel version directed by Edwin S. Porter. Edison's film included 14 scenes and a closing tableaux with Abraham Lincoln promising to free the slaves. In 1914 Sam Lucas was the first black man to play Uncle Tom on screen.

Blackface minstrelsy remained on the leading edge of film technology with the advent of ''talkies.'' The first ''talkie'' ever made was *The Jazz Singer* in 1927, starring Al Jolson as a blackface ''Mammy'' singer. The movie's debut marked the beginning of Jolson's successful film career. A list of other film stars of the 1930s and 1940s who sang and danced in blackface is a Who's Who of the period. Fred Astaire played a blackface minstrel man in RKO's movie *Swing Time* (1936). Martha Raye put on blackface for Paramount Pictures' *Artists and Models* (1937). Metro Goldwyn Mayer's 1939 movie *Babes in Arms* closed with a minstrel jubilee in which Mickey Rooney blacked up to sing ''My Daddy was a Minstrel Man,'' and Judy Garland of *Wizard of Oz* fame blacked up with Rooney in the 1941 sequel *Babes on Broadway.* Bing Crosby blacked up to play Uncle Tom in Irving Berlin's film *Holiday Inn* (1942), and Betty Grable, June Haver Leonard, and George M. Cohan were just a few of the other distinguished actors of the period who sang and danced in blackface.

The most successful blackface minstrel show of the twentieth century was not on the silver screen but over the radio waves. *The Amos 'n Andy Show* began as a vaudeville blackface act called *Sam 'n Henry,* performed by Freeman Fisher Gosden and Charles James Correll. In 1925 the *Sam 'n Henry* radio show was first broadcast over Chicago radio. In 1928 the duo signed with Chicago radio station WMAQ and in March of that year they introduced the characters Amos and Andy. The show quickly became the most popular radio show in the country. In 1930 Gosden and Correll made the film *Check and Double Check,* in which they appeared in blackface, and in 1936 they returned to the silver screen for an encore.

The 15 minute version of *The Amos 'n' Andy Show* ran from 1928 until 1943, and it was by far the most listened to show during the Great Depression. Historian William Leonard writes that ''America came virtually to a standstill six nights a week (reduced to five nights weekly in 1931) at 7:00 pm as fans listened to the 15-minute broadcast.'' In 1943 the radio show became a 30 minute program, and in 1948 Gosden and Correll received $2.5 million to take the show from NBC to CBS. In the late 1940s popular opinion began to shift against blackface performances, and Gosden and Correll bristled under criticism that they were propagating negative stereotypes of African Americans.

In 1951 *The Amos and Andy Show* first appeared on television, but with an all-black cast—it made television history as the first drama to have an all-black cast. The NAACP (National Association for the Advancement of Colored People) opposed the show, however, claiming that it demeaned blacks and hindered the Civil Rights Movement. It was canceled on June 11, 1953, but it remained in syndication until 1966.

African Americans have long objected to the stereotypes of the ''plantation darky'' presented in blackface minstrel routines. Frederick Douglass expressed African American frustration with the phenomenon as early as 1848 when he wrote in the *North Star* that whites who put on blackface to perform in minstrel shows were ''the filthy scum of white society, who have stolen from us a complexion denied to them by nature, in which to make money, and pander to the corrupt taste of their white fellow citizens.'' Douglass was incensed that whites enslaved blacks in the South, discriminated against them in the North, and then had the temerity to pirate African American culture for commercial purposes. While blackface minstrelsy has long been condemned as racist, it is historically significant as an early example of the ways in which whites appropriated and manipulated black cultural traditions.

—Adam Max Cohen

FURTHER READING:

Engle, Gary D. *This Grotesque Essence: Plays from the American Minstrel Stage.* Baton Rouge, Louisiana State University Press, 1978.

Leonard, William Torbert. *Masquerade in Black.* Metuchen, New Jersey, Scarecrow Press, 1986.

Lott, Eric. *Love and Theft: Blackface Minstrelsy and the American Working Class.* New York, Oxford University Press, 1993.

Nathan, Hans. *Dan Emmet and the Rise of Early Negro Minstrelsy.* Norman, University of Oklahoma Press, 1962.

Toll, Robert C. *Blacking Up: The Minstrel Show in Nineteenth-Century America.* London, Oxford University Press, 1974.

Wittke, Carl. *Tambo and Bones: A History of the American Minstrel Stage.* Durham, North Carolina, Duke University Press, 1930.

Blacklisting

In 1947, the House Committee on Un-American Activities (HUAC), chaired by J. Parnell Thomas, held a series of hearings on alleged communist infiltration into the Hollywood motion picture industry. Twenty-four "friendly" witnesses—including Gary Cooper, Ronald Reagan, and Walt Disney—testified that Hollywood was infiltrated with communists, and identified a number of supposed subversives by name. Ten "unfriendly" witnesses—including Dalton Trumbo, Lester Cole, and Ring Lardner, Jr.—refused to cooperate with the Committee, contending that the investigations themselves were unconstitutional. The "Hollywood Ten," as they came to be known, were convicted of contempt of Congress and eventually served sentences of six months to one year in jail.

Shortly after the hearings, more than 50 studio executives met secretly at the Waldorf-Astoria Hotel in New York. They emerged with the now infamous "Waldorf Statement," with which they agreed to suspend the Hollywood Ten without pay, deny employment to anyone who did not cooperate with the HUAC investigations, and refuse to hire communists. When a second round of hearings convened in 1951, the Committee's first witness, actor Larry Parks, pleaded: "Don't present me with the choice of either being in contempt of this Committee and going to jail or forcing me to really crawl through the mud to be an informer." But the choice was presented, the witness opted for the latter, and the ground rules for the decade were set.

From that day forward, it was not enough to answer the question "Are you now or have you ever been a member of the Communist Party?" Rather, those called to testify were advised by their attorneys that they had three choices: to invoke the First Amendment, with its guarantee of free speech and association, and risk going to prison like the Hollywood Ten; to invoke the Fifth Amendment, with its privilege against self-incrimination, and lose their jobs; or to cooperate with the Committee—to "purge" themselves of guilt by providing the names of others thought to be communists—in the hope of

continuing to work in the industry. By the mid-1950s, more than 200 suspected communists had been blacklisted by the major studios.

The Hollywood blacklist quickly spread to the entertainment industries on both coasts, and took on a new scope with the formation of free enterprise blacklisters such as American Business Consultants and Aware, Inc., which went into the business of peddling accusations and clearances; and the publication of the manual *Red Channels* and newsletter *Counterattack*, which listed entertainment workers with allegedly subversive associations. Senator Joseph McCarthy (R-Wisconsin), who built his political career on red-baiting and finally lent his name to the movement, was censured by the U.S. Senate in 1954. But the blacklist went virtually unchallenged until 1960, when screenwriter Dalton Trumbo worked openly for the first time since 1947. And it affected others, like actor Lionel Stander, well into the 1960s. The House Committee on Un-American Activities remained in existence until 1975.

That the HUAC investigations were meant to be punitive and threatening rather than fact-finding is evidenced by the Committee's own eventual admission that it already had the information it was allegedly seeking. According to Victor Navasky, witnesses such as Larry Parks were called upon not to provide information that would lead to any conviction or acquittal, but rather to play a symbolic role in a surrealistic morality play. "The Committee was in essence serving as a kind of national parole board, whose job was to determine whether the "criminals" had truly repented of their evil ways. Only by a witness's naming names and giving details, it was said, could the Committee be certain that his break with the past was genuine. The demand for names was not a quest for evidence; it was a test of character. The naming of names had shifted from a means to an end."

The effects of the blacklist on the Hollywood community were devastating. In addition to shattered careers, there were broken marriages, exiles, and suicides. According to Navasky, Larry Parks' tortured testimony and consequent controversiality resulted in the end of a career that had been on the brink of superstardom: "His memorable line, 'Do not make me crawl through the mud like an informer,' was remembered, and the names he named were forgotten by those in the blacklisting business." Actress Dorothy Comingore, upon hearing her husband on the radio testifying before the Committee, was so ashamed that she had her head shaved. She lost a bitter custody battle over their child and never worked again. Director Joseph Losey's last memory was of hiding in a darkened home to avoid service of a subpoena. He fled to England. Philip Loeb, who played Papa on *The Goldbergs,* checked into a room at the Hotel Taft and swallowed a fatal dose of sleeping pills.

There was also resilience, courage, and humor. Blacklisted writers hired "fronts" to pose as the authors of their scripts, and occasionally won Academy Awards under assumed names. Sam Ornitz urged his comrades in the Hollywood Ten to be "at least be as brave as the people we write about" as they faced prison. Dalton Trumbo sardonically proclaimed his conviction a "completely just verdict" in that "I did have contempt for that Congress, and have had contempt for several since." Ring Lardner, Jr., recalled becoming "reacquainted" with J. Parnell Thomas at the Federal Correctional Institution in Danbury, Connecticut, where Thomas was already an inmate, having been convicted of misappropriating government funds while Lardner exhausted his appeals.

Many years later, in an acceptance speech for the highest honor bestowed by the Screenwriters Guild, the Laurel Award, Dalton Trumbo tried to bring the bitterness surrounding the blacklist to an end. "When you [. . .] look back with curiosity on that dark time, as I think occasionally you should, it will do no good to search for villains or heroes or saints or devils because there were none,'' he said, ''there were only victims. Some suffered less than others, some grew and some diminished, but in the final tally we were all victims because almost without exception each of us felt compelled to say things he did not want to say, to do things he did not want to do, to deliver and receive wounds he truly did not want to exchange. That is why none of us—right, left, or center—emerged from that long nightmare without sin. None without sin.''

Trumbo's ''Only Victims'' speech, delivered in 1970, was clearly meant to be healing. Instead, it rekindled a controversy that smoldered for years, with other members of the Hollywood Ten bristling at his sweeping conviction and implied pardon of everyone involved. The social, psychological, legal, and moral ramifications of the Hollywood blacklist have haunted American popular memory for more than half a century. The blacklist has been the subject of numerous books, plays, documentaries, and feature films, the titles of which speak for themselves: *Thirty Years of Treason, Scoundrel Time, Hollywood on Trial, Fear on Trial, Are You Now Or Have You Ever Been, Hollywood's Darkest Days, Naming Names, Tender Comrades, Fellow Traveler,* and *Guilty By Suspicion,* to name a few.

In 1997, the *New York Times* reported that ''The blacklist still torments Hollywood.'' On the 50th anniversary of the 1947 hearings, the Writers Guild of America, one of several Hollywood unions that failed to support members blacklisted in the 1950s, announced that it was restoring the credits on nearly 50 films written by blacklisted screenwriters. There was talk of ''putting closure to all of this'' and feeling ''forgiveness in the air.'' At the same time, however, a debate raged in the arts and editorial pages of the nation's newspapers over whether the Los Angeles Film Critics Association and the American Film Institute were guilty of ''blacklisting'' director Elia Kazan. Kazan appeared before the Committee in 1952 and informed on eight friends who had been fellow members of the Communist Party. His *On the Waterfront* is widely seen as a defense of those who named names. As Peter Biskind remarks, the film ''presents a situation in which informing on criminal associates is the only honorable course of action for a just man.''

Variety advocated a lifetime achievement award for Kazan, describing him as ''an artist without honor in his own country, a celebrated filmmaker whose name cannot be mentioned for fear of knee-jerk reactions of scorn and disgust, a two-time Oscar winner not only politically incorrect but also politically unacceptable according to fashion and the dominant liberal-left Hollywood establishment.'' But as the *New York Times* pointed out, ''Not only did [Kazan] name names, causing lasting damage to individual careers, but he lent his prestige and moral authority to what was essentially an immoral process, a brief but nevertheless damaging period of officially sponsored hysteria that exacted a huge toll on individual lives, on free speech, and on democracy.'' Kazan accepted his lifetime achievement award at the Academy Awards in 1999.

—Jeanne Hall

FURTHER READING:

Benson, Thomas. ''Thinking through Film: Hollywood Remembers the Blacklist.'' In *Rhetoric and Community: Studies in Unity and Fragmentation,* edited by J. Michael Hogan. Columbia, University of South Carolina Press, 1998.

Bernstein, Walter. *Inside Out: A Memoir of the Blacklist.* New York, Alfred A. Knopf, 1996.

Biskind, Peter. ''The Politics of Power in *On The Waterfront.''* In *American Media and Mass Culture: Left Perspectives,* edited by Donald Lezere. Berkeley, University of California Press, 1985.

Ceplair, Larry, and Steven Englund. *The Inquisition in Hollywood: Politics in the Film Community 1930-1960.* Garden City, Anchor Press/Doubleday, 1980.

McGilligan, Patrick, and Paul Buhle. *Tender Comrades: A Backstory of the Blacklist.* New York, St. Martin's Press, 1997.

Navasky, Victor S. *Naming Names.* New York, Viking Press, 1980.

Blade Runner

Ridley Scott's 1982 film adaptation of Philip K. Dick's science fiction novel *Do Androids Dream of Electric Sheep?* (1968) received poor reviews when it opened. It did not take long, however, for *Blade Runner* to become known as one of the greatest science fiction films ever made. The film's depiction of Los Angeles in the year 2019 combines extrapolated social trends with technology and the darkness of film noir to create the movie that gave Cyberpunk literature its visual representation.

In true film noir style, the story follows Rick Deckard (Harrison Ford), who is a ''Blade Runner,'' a hired gun whose job is to retire (kill) renegade ''replicants'' (androids who are genetically designed as slaves for off-world work). The story revolves around a group of replicants who escape from an off-world colony and come to earth to try to override their built in four-year life span. Deckard hunts the replicants, but he falls in love with Rachael (Sean Young)—an experimental replicant. Deckard finally faces the lead replicant (Rutger Hauer) in a struggle that ends with him questioning his own humanity and the ethics of his blade running.

The production of *Blade Runner* was not without problems. Hampton Fancher had written the screenplay that offered a much darker vision than Dick's novel and only drew on its basic concepts. After the success of *Alien* (1979), Ridley Scott showed interest in directing the film. Scott replaced Fancher with David Peoples after eight drafts of the script. Scott's goal was to rework the script to be less action-oriented with a plot involving ''clues'' and more human-like adversaries. He worked closely with Douglas Trumbull—*2001: A Space Odyssey*—to design an original visual concept. Although some of the actors flourished under Scott's directing style, many were frustrated with his excessive attention to the set design and lighting. Eventually, the production company that was supporting the film pulled out after spending two million dollars. New funding was provided by three interests—a subsidiary of Warner Brothers, Run Run Shaw, and Tandem Productions (which gained rights to control the final version).

Preview audiences were befuddled by the film's ambiguous resolution and frustrated by the lack of light-hearted action they expected from Harrison Ford. The response was so weak that Tandem Productions decided to change the film. Scott was forced to include voice-overs, and to add a ''feel good'' ending in which Deckard and Rachael drive off into Blade Runner's equivalent of a sunset.

The film opened strong at the box office, but critics railed against the voice-overs and the happy ending. The release of Steven Spielberg's *E.T.: The Extra Terrestrial,* within two weeks of *Blade Runner,* eclipsed the film and ended its theater run. *Blade Runner* has,

Harrison Ford in a scene from the film *Blade Runner*.

however, endured. In 1993, the National Film Preservation Board selected to preserve *Blade Runner* as one of its annual 25 films deemed ''culturally, historically, or aesthetically important.'' The British Film Institute also included *Blade Runner* in its Modern Classics series.

Part of *Blade Runner's* success is due to its serious treatment of important philosophical and ethical questions. Some look at *Blade Runner* as a rehashing of *Frankenstein*. In true Cyberpunk style, though, the monsters have already escaped and there is an explicit question about whether humans are the real monsters. *Blade Runner* goes beyond that, asking hard questions about religion, the ethics of genetic manipulation, racism and sexism, and human interaction with technology. The film also presents two other major questions: ''What is it to be human?''; and ''How should our society handle its 'kipple?'''—the accumulating garbage (especially human ''kipple''). These issues are so thought provoking that *Blade Runner* has become one of the most examined films in academic circles.

Blade Runner is often touted as the primary visual manifestation of the Cyberpunk movement and the first Cyberpunk film. The film

predated the beginning of the Cyberpunk movement (William Gibson's *Neuromancer*), however, by two years. Hallmark themes of Cyberpunk fiction are the merging of man with machine and a dark, morbid view of the near future mixed with the delight of new technology. With dark and bleak imagery and androids that are ''more human than human,'' it is not surprising that *Blade Runner* became a Cyberpunk watershed, offering a hopeful vision of what technology can do and be.

In 1989, Warner Brothers uncovered a 70mm print of *Blade Runner* and showed it to an eager audience at a film festival. The studio showed this version in two theaters in 1991, setting house attendance records and quickly making them two of the top-grossing theaters in the country. Warner Brothers agreed to fund Scott's creation of a ''director's cut'' of the film. Scott reworked the film and re-released it in 1992 as *Blade Runner: The Director's Cut*. The voice-overs were taken out, the happy ending was cut, and Scott's ''unicorn'' scene was reintegrated.

Because this film was initially so poorly received, no film or television sequels resulted. *Blade Runner* did, however, vault Dick's books past their previous recognition. It also spawned two book sequels by K.W. Jeter both of which received marginal reviews. In 1997, Westwood Studios released the long-awaited CD-ROM game. The Internet bustles with dozens of pages dedicated to the film and discussion groups, which never tire of examining the movie.

Blade Runner's most important contribution has been to the film and television industries, creating a vision of the future that has continued to resonate in the media. Scott's dystopian images are reflected in films and television shows such as *Robocop, Brazil, Total Recall, Max Headroom, Strange Days,* and *Dark City. Blade Runner* has become one of the standards for science fiction imagery, standing right beside *Star Wars* and *2001: A Space Odyssey.* Many reviewers still use *Blade Runner* as the visual standard for science fiction comparisons. It has survived as a modern cult classic and it will certainly impact our culture for a long time to come.

—Adam Wathen

FURTHER READING:

Albrecht, Donald. "'Blade Runner' Cuts Deep into American Culture." *The New York Times.* September 20, 1992, sec. 2, p. 19.

"'Blade Runner' and Cyberpunk Visions of Humanity." *Film Criticism.* Vol. 21, No. 1, 1996, pp. 1-12.

Bukatman, Scott. *Blade Runner.* London, British Film Institute, 1997.

Clute, John, and Peter Nicholls, editors. "Blade Runner." *The Encyclopedia of Science Fiction.* New York, St. Martin's Press, 1993.

Kerman, Judith B., editor. *Retrofitting Blade Runner: Issues in Ridley Scott's Blade Runner and Philip K. Dick's Do Androids Dream of Electric Sheep?* Bowling Green, Ohio, Bowling Green State University Popular Press, 1991.

McCarty, John. "Blade Runner." *International Dictionary of Films and Filmmakers.* Vol. 1, Detroit, St. James Press, 1997.

Romney, Jonathan. "Replicants Reshaped." *New Statesman & Society.* Vol. 5, No. 230, 1992, pp. 33-34.

Sammon, Paul M. *Future Noir: The Making of Blade Runner.* New York, HarperPrism, 1996.

Turan, Kenneth. "Blade Runner 2." *Los Angeles Times Magazine.* September 13, 1992, 19.

Blades, Ruben (1948—)

Musician, actor, and social activist Ruben Blades grew up in Panama and grew to international fame in the United States, becoming in the process a perfect example of the multiculturalism of the Americas. Accepting as correct both the Spanish and English pronunciations of his last name, Blades likewise accepts the different facets of himself and demands no less of the greater culture that surrounds him. Overcoming enormous odds, Blades managed to juggle simultaneous careers as a lawyer, a salsa musician, a Hollywood actor, and finally a presidential candidate while maintaining his principles of social justice and pan-culturalism.

Blades was born in Panama City into a musical family; his father, a police detective, played bongos, and his Cuban-born mother sang and played piano. Along with the Afro-Cuban rhythms he grew up with, Blades was heavily influenced by the rock music of the Beatles, Frankie Lyman, and others. After studying law at the University of Panama ("to please my parents"), he began playing music with a band. In 1974, disenchanted with the political oppression of the military dictatorship in Panama and seeking new horizons in his music career, Blades left his native land and went to New York City.

He arrived in New York with only one hundred dollars in his pocket, but it wasn't long before he had found a job in a band playing salsa music. Salsa, a pan-American music which had been formed when the music of Cuban immigrants married American jazz, was just the kind of flexible Latin sound to absorb the rock and rhythm and blues influences that Blades loved. By the late 1970s, he was recording with salsa musician Willie Colon, and together they produced an album appropriately named *Siembre* (Seed), which became one of the seminal works of salsa music.

Blades also comes by his political activism naturally; his grandmother worked for women's rights in Panama in the 1940s and 1950s. Though Blades loved music, he never let it become an escape; rather he used it in his attempt to change the world, writing more than one hundred fifty songs, most of them political. He became one of the leading creators of the Nuova Cancion (New Song) movement , a Latin music movement that combined political message with poetic imagery and Latin rhythms. His songs, while embraced by those on the left, were often controversial in more conservative circles. His 1980 song "Tiberon" (Shark) about the intervention and imperialism of the superpowers, was banned on radio stations in Miami, and Blades received death threats when he performed there.

After taking a year off to earn a master's degree in international law from Harvard Law School, Blades moved from New York to Los Angeles in 1986. He starred in the low budget film *Crossover Dreams* (1985) about a young Latin American man trying to succeed as a musician in the United States. Blades proved to be a talented actor and continues to appear in major films, some, like Robert Redford's *The Milagro Beanfield War* (1988), with social significance and some, like *Fatal Beauty* (1987) with Whoopi Goldberg, pure Hollywood.

Perhaps Blades's most surprising role began when he returned to Panama in 1992. As the country was struggling to recover from the repressive politics of Manuel Noriega and invasion by the United States, Blades helped in the formation of a new populist political party to combat the dominant corporation-driven politics of Panama. The party, Papa Egoro (Mother Earth in the indigenous language), eventually asked Blades to be its candidate for president. Blades accepted reluctantly but ran enthusiastically, writing his own campaign song and encouraging his constituents to believe that change was possible. "I'm going to walk with the people who are the subjects of my songs," he said, "And I'm going to try to change their lives." One significant change he suggested was a requirement that a percentage of the corporate money that passed through Panama be invested back into the infrastructure of the country to benefit ordinary citizens. Blades lost his bid for the presidency, partly because of lack of campaign funds and a political machine, and partly because he had not lived in Panama for many years and was not taken seriously as a candidate by some voters. However, he came in third out of seven

Ruben Blades

candidates, which many saw as a hopeful sign of a growing populist movement.

Ruben Blades's life and career is an eclectic jumble of impossible feats and improbable juxtapositions. In the superficial world of commercial music and Hollywood film he has succeeded without neutralizing his politics. In the endless freeway that is Los Angeles he has never learned to drive or owned a car ("If I need something, it's only an hour-and-a-half walk to town"). His many releases include an album with Anglo singers singing with him in Spanish, an English album with rock rebels Lou Reed and Elvis Costello, and an album of contemporary Panamanian singers. Blades is proudly pan-American and wants to inspire all Americans to explore our connections. "I will always be viewed with suspicion by some, though not by all," he admits, "because I move against the current."

—Tina Gianoulis

FURTHER READING:

Batstone, David. "Panama's Big Chance to Escape the Past: Politics, Promises Take Center Stage as Election Draws Near." *National Catholic Reporter.* Vol. 30, No. 27, May 6, 1994, 8.

Blades, Ruben. *Yo, Ruben Blades: Confesiones de un Relator de Barrio.* Panama City, Medellin, Ediciones Salsa y Cultura, 1997.

Cruz, Barbara. *Ruben Blades: Salsa Singer and Social Activist.* Springfield, New Jersey, Enslow Publishing, 1997.

Marton, Betty A. *Ruben Blades.* New York, Chelsea House, 1992.

Blanc, Mel (1908-1989)

Mel Blanc, the "Man of a thousand voices," helped to develop animated cartoons into a new comedic art form by creating and performing the voices of hundreds of characters for cartoons, radio, and television.

Melvin Jerome Blanc was born on May 30, 1908 in San Francisco, California, to Frederick and Eva Blank, managers of a women's retail clothing business. A poor student and class cut-up, Blanc was popular with his peers but often annoyed his teachers and principals. At age 16, goaded by an insult from a teacher, Blanc changed the spelling of his last name from "Blank" to "Blanc." Blanc had made his class laugh by giving a response in four different voices, and the incensed teacher said, "You'll never amount to anything. You're just like your last name: blank." Nonetheless, high school gave Blanc some opportunity to practice future material. For example, he took advantage of the great acoustics of the school's cavernous hallways to develop the raucous laugh that eventually became Woody Woodpecker's signature.

After graduating from high school in 1927, Blanc started working part-time in radio, on a Friday evening program called *The Hoot Owls,* and playing tuba with two orchestras. He then went on to play in the NBC Trocaderans radio orchestra. By age 22 he was the youngest musical director in the country, working as the pit conductor for Oregon's Orpheum Theatre. In 1931, Blanc returned to San Francisco to emcee a Tuesday night radio variety show called "The Road Show." The next year, he set out for Hollywood, hoping to make it big. Although his first foray into Tinseltown did not bring him much professional success, it did wonders for his personal life. In 1933, Blanc eloped with Estelle Rosenbaum, whom he had met while swing-dancing at the Ocean Park Ballroom in Santa Monica. The couple moved to Portland, Oregon, where Blanc (with help from Estelle) wrote, produced, and acted in a live, hour-long radio show, *Cobwebs and Nuts.*

In 1935, Blanc and his wife returned to Hollywood to try again. By 1941, Blanc's career as a voice actor had sky-rocketed. In 1936, he joined Warner Brothers, brought on to create a voice for an animated drunken bull for an upcoming production called *Picador Porky,* and starring Porky Pig. But soon afterward, Blanc was asked to replace the actor who provided Porky Pig's voice. In his first demonstration of his new creation, Blanc ad-libbed the famous "Th-uh-th-uh-th-that's all, folks!" Released in 1937, *Picador Porky* was Blanc's first cartoon for Warner Brothers. That same year, Blanc created his second lead character for Warner, Daffy Duck. Around this time, he also changed the way cartoons were recorded by suggesting that each character's lines be recorded separately and then reassembled in sequence. In 1940, Blanc helped create the character with whom he is most closely associated, Bugs Bunny. Bugs had been around in different forms for several years as "Happy Rabbit," but Blanc re-christened him after his animator, Ben "Bugs" Hardaway, and gave him a tough-edged Brooklyn accent. Bugs also provided the inspiration for the most famous ad-lib of his career, "Eh, what's up Doc?" Blanc completed the character by chewing on raw carrots, a vegetable which he detested. Unfortunately, other fruits and vegetables did not produce the right sound. In addition, Blanc found it impossible to chew, swallow, and say his next line. The solution? They stopped recording so that Blanc could spit the carrot into the wastebasket before continuing with the script.

Mel Blanc

In 1945, the studio introduced a romantic lead for Blanc, the skunk Pepe Le Pew. Blanc modeled the character on French matinee idol Charles Boyer, and received amorous fan mail from women who loved the character's accent. The final leading character that Blanc created for Warner Brothers was Speedy Gonzales, the Mexican mouse, the studio's most prolific character in its final years. Of the Warner Brothers characters, Blanc has described the voice of Yosemite Sam as the most difficult to perform, saying that it was like "screaming at the top of your lungs for an hour and a half." Another voice that required a lot of volume was Foghorn Leghorn. His easiest character, and one of his favorites, was Sylvester the Cat. According to Blanc, this voice is closest to his natural speaking voice, but "without the thspray." In his autobiography, Blanc revealed one of the little known tricks used by engineers to manipulate the voices for characters such as Daffy Duck, Henery Hawk, Speedy Gonzales, and Tweety. Using a variable-speed oscillator, lines were recorded below normal speed and then played back conventionally, which raised the pitch of the voices while retaining their clarity.

While at Warner Brothers Blanc worked with a talented group of animators, producers, and directors that included Friz Freleng, Milt Avery, Chuck Jones, and Leon Schlessinger. The studio's work earned five Oscars for cartoons. The first award came in 1947 for *Tweety Pie,* starring Sylvester and Tweety. Blanc calls the 1957 Oscar winner *Birds Anonymous* his all-time favorite cartoon, and producer Eddie Selzer bequeathed its Oscar to Blanc upon his death (cartoon Oscars are only awarded to producers). By the time Warner Brothers closed its animation shop in 1969, Blanc had performed around 700 human and animal characters, and created voices for 848 of the studio's 1,003 cartoons. He also negotiated an unprecedented screen credit that enabled him to get freelance work with other studios and programs. In addition, Blanc occasionally acted as a dialect coach to film stars such as Clark Gable.

During World War II, Blanc appeared on several Armed Forces Radio Service programs, such as *G.I. Journal,* featuring his popular character Private Sad Sack. Hollywood legends who appeared on the show with Blanc included Lucille Ball, Groucho Marx, Frank Sinatra, and Orson Welles. Warner Brothers also produced several war-related cartoons such as *Wacky Blackouts* and *Tokyo Jokio.* In 1946, CBS and Colgate-Palmolive offered Blanc his own show, but it lasted only one season, due, in Blanc's opinion, to "lackluster scripts."

After leaving Warner Brothers, Blanc returned to broadcast full-time. One of his most well-known roles was a dour, forlorn character comically misnamed "The Happy Postman" who appeared on *The George Burns and Gracie Allen Show.* In 1939, Blanc joined the cast of Jack Benny's popular radio show on NBC. Blanc came to regard Benny as his "closest friend in all of Hollywood." On *The Jack Benny Program* many jokes featured Blanc's Union Depot train caller who would call, "Train leaving on track five for Anaheim, Azusa, and Cuc-amonga!" In one series of skits the pause between "Cuc" and "amonga" kept getting longer and longer until in one show a completely different skit was inserted between the first and second part of the phrase. In 1950, *The Jack Benny Program* made a successful transition to television, ranking in the top 20 shows for ten of the fifteen years it was on the air. Television provided even more voice work for Blanc, who began to perform characters for cartoons specifically produced for television. In 1960, Blanc received an offer from the Hanna-Barbera studio to play the voice role of Barney Rubble on a new animated series for adults called *The Flintstones.*

In 1961, Blanc and former Warner Brothers executive producer John Burton started a commercial production company called Mel Blanc Associates. Three days later, while driving to a radio taping, Blanc was hit head-on by a car that lost control on the S-shaped bend of Sunset Boulevard known as "Dead Man's Curve." Although the other driver sustained only minor injuries, Blanc broke nearly every bone in his body, lost nine pints of blood, and was in a coma for three weeks. After regaining consciousness, he stayed an additional two months in a full body cast. While in the hospital, he recorded several tracks for Warner Brothers, and then had a mini-studio installed in his home so that he could continue working while convalescing.

The Blanc's only child, a son Noel was born in 1938. Blanc has joked that he and his wife later realized that in French their son's name translated into "white Christmas," which Blanc noted was "a hell of a name for a Jewish boy." At age 22, Blanc's son Noel joined Mel Blanc Associates, eventually becoming company president. Later, Blanc taught his son the voices of the Warner Brothers characters, so that he could carry on his legacy.

Mel Blanc Associates quickly became known for its humorous commercials. Its client roster included Kool-Aid, Volkswagen, Ford, and Avis Rent-a-car. They also began producing syndicated radio programs. In conjunction with the company's thirtieth anniversary, the renamed Blanc Communications Corporation became a full-service advertising agency. In 1972, Blanc established the Mel Blanc School of Commercials, which offered six courses such as radio and television voiceovers and commercial acting principles. Proving too costly, however, the school only existed for two years. Meanwhile Blanc continued to do voice-work for commercials and programs. In 1988, he had a bit part as Daffy Duck in the film *Who Framed Roger Rabbit.*

Both Blanc and Bugs Bunny have their own stars on the Hollywood Walk of Fame (Blanc's resides at 6385 Hollywood Boulevard). Blanc has said that the honor of which he is most proud is his inclusion in the United States entertainment history collection of the Smithsonian Institution's National Museum of American History. Active in many philanthropic organizations, Blanc received a plethora of civic awards, including the United Jewish Welfare Fund Man of the Year and the First Show Business Shrine Club's Life Achievement Award.

Although Blanc was a pack-a-day smoker, who started when he was eight, a doctor who x-rayed Blanc's throat compared it to the musculature of Italian tenor Enrico Caruso. Blanc quit smoking later in life when he developed severe emphysema and required portable oxygen to breathe. In 1989, Blanc died at the age of 81 from heart disease. The epitaph on his headstone in Hollywood Memorial Park Cemetery reads, "That's All Folks."

—Courtney Bennett

FURTHER READING:

Blanc, M., and P. Bashe. *That's Not All Folks!* New York, Warner Books, Inc., 1988.

Feldman, P. "Mel Blanc Dies; Gave Voice to Cartoon World." *Los Angeles Times.* July 11, 1989, 1.

Bland, Bobby Blue (1930—)

Bobby Blue Bland played a significant role in the development of the blues ballad. Generally ranked by blues fans in the highest echelon of the genre, he specializes in slower, prettier tunes, while remaining within the blues tradition. Bland, along with B. B. King, emerged from the Memphis blues scene. Born in Rosemark, Tennessee, he moved to Memphis at seventeen, and began recording shortly thereafter. During the 1950s, he developed his unique blues ballad sound: in his performances, he walks a thin line between self-control and ecstasy. In the 1960s, he had twelve major hits, including "I Pity the Fool," and the now standard "Turn on Your Love Light." Overall, he has had 51 top ten singles. Bland has never become a major crossover star, but still draws solid audiences on the blues concert circuit.

—Frank A. Salamone

Blass, Bill (1922—)

Bill Blass was the first American designer to emerge from the shadow of manufacturers and establish his name with authority. From a base in womenswear design, Blass achieved a collateral success in menswear with "Bill Blass for PBM" in 1968, another first for an American. Blass then used licensing to expand his brand name globally in a range of products from menswear to automobiles and even to chocolates at one point. A shrewd observer of European style, Blass used his talent to define American fashion, creating separates for day and evening; sportswear with active sports as inspiration; and the mix and match that allows customers to compose an individual and chic style on their own. Blass was one of the first designers to

come out of the backroom of design, mingle with clients, and become famous in his own right. To many, Blass is known as the "dean of American fashion."

—Richard Martin

FURTHER READING:

Daria, Irene. *The Fashion Cycle.* New York, Simon & Schuster, 1990.

Milbank, Caroline Rennolds. *New York Fashion: The Evolution of American Style.* New York, Abrams, 1989.

Morris, Bernadine, and Barbara Walz. *The Fashion Makers.* New York, Random House, 1978.

Blaxploitation Films

Blaxploitation films were a phenomenon of the 1970s. Low-budget action movies aimed at African American audiences, blaxploitation films enjoyed great financial success for several years. Some blaxploitation pictures, such as *Shaft* and *Superfly* launched music and fashion trends as well. Eventually the controversy surrounding these movies brought an end to the genre, but not before nearly one hundred blaxploitation films had been released.

Even during the silent movie period, producers had been making films with all-black casts. An African American entrepreneur named

Pam Grier in a scene from *Foxy Brown*.

William Foster released a series of all-black comedy films beginning in 1910. Oscar Micheaux produced, wrote, and directed nearly forty films between 1919 and 1948. Hundreds of "black only" theaters existed in the United States from the 1920s to the 1950s, and there were low-budget African American films of all genres: musicals, westerns, comedies, horror films, and so forth. The market for these black films started to disappear in the 1950s, when integration brought an end to the "blacks only" theaters and Hollywood began using African American performers more prominently in mainstream studio productions.

By the end of the 1960s, it was common to see films starring African American performers. When Sidney Poitier won the Academy Award in 1964 for his role in *Lilies of the Field*, his victory was seen as a sign of great progress for African American actors. However, a more important role for Poitier was that of police detective Virgil Tibbs in the film *In the Heat of the Night*. He played Tibbs in two more films, *They Call Me MISTER Tibbs* and *The Organization*. Both those movies were released at the beginning of the blaxploitation cycle and clearly influenced many blaxploitation pictures: the forceful, articulate, handsome, and well-educated Virgil Tibbs appears to have been the model for the protagonists of many blaxploitation pictures. The success of *In the Heat of the Night*—it won the Oscar as best picture of 1967—and the ongoing civil rights movement in America led to more films that dealt with racial tensions, particularly in small Southern towns, including *If He Hollers, Let Him Go; tick . . . tick . . . tick . . . ;* and *The Liberation of L.B. Jones*. But all of these movies were mainstream productions from major Hollywood studios; none could be considered a blaxploitation picture.

The Red, White and Black, a low-budget, extremely violent western with a predominantly African American cast can be called the first blaxploitation film. Directed by John Bud Carlos and released in 1969, the movie was the first black western since the 1930s, addressing the discrimination faced by African Americans in post-Civil War America. The most influential movie of this period, however, was *Sweet Sweetback's Baaadasss Song,* which was written, produced, and directed by Melvin van Peebles, who also starred. The protagonist, Sweetback, is a pimp who kills a police officer to save an innocent black man and then has to flee the country. The film became one of the most financially successful independent films in history, and its explicit sex, extreme violence, criticism of white society, and powerful antihero protagonist became standards of the genre.

Shaft further solidified the conventions of the blaxploitation genre. John Shaft is a private detective who is hired to find the daughter of an African American mobster; the daughter has been kidnapped by the Mafia. Shaft, portrayed by Richard Roundtree, is similar to Virgil Tibbs character (both Shaft and Tibbs first appeared in novels by author Ernest Tidyman) and many suave private detectives from film and television. *Shaft* was extremely popular with African American audiences and was widely imitated by other blaxploitation filmmakers: the cool and aloof hero, white villains, sex with both black and white women, heavy emphasis on action and gunplay, and the depiction of the problems of lower income African Americans all became staples of the blaxploitation movie. Isaac Hayes' Academy Award winning "Theme from Shaft" was frequently imitated. Two sequels were made to *Shaft*: *Shaft's Big Score* and *Shaft in Africa*. Roundtree also starred in a brief *Shaft* television series in 1973.

The peak period for blaxploitation films was 1972-74, during which seventy-six blaxploitation films were released, an average of more than two per month. It was in 1972 that *Variety* and other publications began using the term blaxploitation to describe these new action pictures, creating the term by combining "black" with "exploitation." That same year two former football players, Jim Brown and Fred Williamson, both began what would be long-running blaxploitation film careers. Brown starred in *Slaughter,* about a ghetto resident who seeks revenge on the Mafia after hoodlums murder his parents, and in *Black Gunn,* in which he seeks revenge on the Mafia after hoodlums murder his brother. Williamson starred in *Hammer* (Williamson's nickname while playing football), in which he portrayed a boxer who has conflicts with the Mafia. While former athletes Brown and Williamson might have dominated the genre, more accomplished African American actors were also willing to perform in the lucrative blaxploitation market: Robert Hooks starred in *Trouble Man,* William Marshall in *Blacula,* Hari Rhodes in *Detroit 9000,* and Calvin Lockhart in *Melinda.*

The blaxploitation films of this period were extremely popular with audiences and successful financially as well, but they also were the subject of much criticism from community leaders and the black press. These movies were being made by major Hollywood studios but on lower budgets than most of their other pictures, and many critics of blaxploitation films felt that the studios were cynically producing violent junk for the African American audience rather than making uplifting films with better production values, such as the 1972 release *Sounder*. Blaxploitation films were also dismissed as simply black variations on hackneyed material; *Jet* magazine once called blaxploitation films "James Bond in black face." Criticism grew with a second wave of blaxploitation films whose characters were less socially acceptable to segments of the public. The 1973 release *Superfly* is the best known among these films and was the subject of the intense protest at the time of its release. The film is about a cocaine dealer, Priest, who plans to retire after making one last, very large deal. Priest was never explicitly condemned in the movie, and, as portrayed by the charismatic Ron O'Neal, actually became something of a hero to some viewers, who responded by imitating Priest's wardrobe and haircut. Other blaxploitation films of the period that featured criminal protagonists were *Black Caesar* (Fred Williamson as a gangster); *Willie Dynamite* (a pimp); *Sweet Jesus, Preacher Man* (a hitman); and *The Mack* (another pimp).

As the controversy around blaxploitation films grew, producers moved away from crime films for black audiences and attempted making black versions of familiar film genres. Particularly popular were black horror movies, including *Blacula* and its sequel *Scream, Blacula, Scream; Blackenstein; Alabama's Ghost;* and *Abby,* which so resembled *The Exorcist* that its producers were sued for plagiarism. Black westerns, such as *Adios, Amigo,* were also popular, and there were a few black martial arts films, like *Black Belt Jones.* Many producers simply added the word "black" to the title of a previously existing picture, so that audiences were treated to *Black Lolita, Black Shampoo,* and *The Black Godfather.* Comedian Rudy Ray Moore had a brief film career with *Dolemite* and *The Human Tornado.*

The greatest success of the second wave of blaxploitation pictures came from American International Pictures and its series of movies featuring sexy female characters. After appearing in some prison movies for the studio, Pam Grier starred in *Coffy* in 1973, playing a nurse who tries to avenge the death of her sister, a drug addict. Grier subsequently starred in *Foxy Brown, Sheba Baby,* and *Friday Foster* for American International. AIP also made a few "sexy women" blaxploitation films with other actresses: Tamara Dobson starred in *Cleopatra Jones* and *Cleopatra Jones and the Casino of Gold,* and Jeanne Bell played the title role in *TNT Jackson.*

By the late 1970s, the blaxploitation film had run its course. From a high of two dozen blaxploitation films released in 1973, studios moved to four blaxploitation films in 1977 and none at all in 1978. Major studios were now making mainstream black films with performers like Richard Pryor. With the exception of Fred Williamson, who moved to Europe where he continued to produce and appear in low-budget movies, no one was making blaxploitation films by the end of the 1970s. There have been a few attempts to revive the format. Brown, Williamson, O'Neal, and martial artist Jim Kelly appeared in *One Down, Three to Go* in 1982, and *The Return of Superfly* was released in 1990 with a new actor in the lead. Keenen Ivory Wayans parodied blaxploitation films in *I'm Gonna Get You, Sucka.*

Like many movie trends, the blaxploitation film genre enjoyed a rapid success and an almost equally rapid demise, probably hastened by the highly repetitive content of most of the movies. Blaxploitation films were undeniably influential and remained so into the 1990s. Filmmakers such as John Singleton or the Hughes brothers frequently spoke with admiration of the blaxploitation pictures they enjoyed growing up, and Spike Lee frequently asserted that without *Sweet Sweetback's Baaaadasss Song* there would be no black cinema today. Despite their frequent excesses, blaxploitation films were an important part of American motion pictures in the 1970s.

—Randall Clark

FURTHER READING:

James, Darius. *That's Blaxploitation.* New York, St. Martin's, 1995.

Martinez, Gerald, Diana Martinez, and Andres Chavez. *What It Is . . . What It Was!* New York, Hyperion, 1998.

Parrish, James Robert, and George H. Hill. *Black Action Films.* Jefferson, North Carolina, McFarland, 1989.

The Blob

The Blob (1958) is one of a long string of largely forgettable 1950s teenage horror films. The film's action revolves around a purple blob from outer space that has the nasty habit of eating people. At the time, the title was what drew audiences to watch this otherwise ordinary film. It has since achieved notoriety as both a sublimely bad film and the film in which Steve McQueen had his first starring role.

—Robert C. Sickels

FURTHER READING:

Biskind, Peter. *Seeing is Believing: How Hollywood Taught Us To Stop Worrying and Love the Fifties.* New York, Pantheon, 1983.

Warren, Bill. *Keep Watching the Skies: American Science Fiction Movies of the Fifties, Volume II.* Jefferson, North Carolina, McFarland, 1986.

Blockbusters

The term blockbuster was originally coined during World War II to describe an eight-ton American aerial bomb which contained enough explosive to level an entire city block. After the war, the term quickly caught the public's attention and became part of the American vernacular to describe any occurrence that was considered to be epic in scale. However, there was no universal agreement as to what events actually qualified as blockbusters so the post war world was inundated with colossal art exhibitions, epic athletic events, and even "larger than life" department store sales all lumped under the heading of blockbuster.

By the mid-1950s, though, the term began to be increasingly applied to the motion picture screen as a catch-all term for the wide-screen cinemascope epics that Hollywood created to fend off the threat of television, which was taking over the nation's living rooms. Such films as Cecil B. DeMille's *The Ten Commandments*, a remake of his earlier silent film, Michael Anderson's *Around the World in 80 Days*, and King Vidor's *War and Peace*, all released in 1956, established the standards for the blockbuster motion picture. Every effort was made to create sheer visual magnitude in wide film (usually 70mm) processes, full stereophonic sound, and lavish stunts and special effects.

These films were also characterized by higher than average production budgets (between $6,000,000 and $15,000,000), longer running times (more than 3 hours), and the need to achieve extremely high box office grosses to break even, let alone make a profit. Subject matter was generally drawn from history or the Bible and occasionally from an epic novel which provide a seemingly inexhaustible supply of colorful characters, broad vistas, and gripping stories.

By this definition, the blockbuster has a history as old as Hollywood itself. As early as 1898, a version of the passion play was filmed on the roof of a New York high-rise and a one reel version of Ben Hur was filmed in 1907. Yet, by 1912, it was Italy that was establishing the conventions of large scale spectaculars through such lavish productions as Enrico Guazzoni's *Quo Vadis?* (1912) and Giovanni Pastrone's *Cabiria* (1914). Indeed, it was the latter film— with its enormous (for the time) production budget of $100,000 and its world-wide following—that played a major role in taking the motion picture out of the Nickelodeons into modern theaters and in establishing the viability of the feature film as a profitable entertainment medium.

According to some sources, American film pioneer D.W. Griffith was so impressed by *Cabiria* that he owned his own personal copy of the film and studied its spectacular sets, its lighting, and its camera movement as a source of inspiration for his own epics *The Birth of a Nation* (1915) and *Intolerance* (1916). Indeed, *The Birth of a Nation* was not only the first important product of the American cinema, it set the standard for the films to follow. Its budget has been placed at $110,000, which translates into millions of dollars by today's standards. Its gross, however, was much higher approaching 100 million dollars. In fact, a number of historians attest that it may have been seen by more people than any film in history—a fact that might be disputed by proponents of *Gone with the Wind* (1939) and *Titanic* (1997).

The Birth of a Nation did, however, change forever the demographics of the motion picture audience. Prior to its release, films were considered to be primarily for the working classes, mostly immigrants who viewed them in small storefront theaters. Griffith's film, which treated the U.S. Civil War and related it as an epic human drama, captured an audience that had previously only attended the legitimate theater. Through the use of sophisticated camera work, editing, and storytelling, Griffith created a masterpiece that has been re-released many times and still maintains the power to shock and move an audience.

INDESCRIBABLE... INDESTRUCTIBLE! NOTHING CAN STOP IT!

THE BLOB

STEVEN McQUEEN

ANETA CORSEAUT · EARL ROWE

PRODUCED BY JACK H. HARRIS · DIRECTED BY IRVIN S. YEAWORTH, JR. · SCREENPLAY BY THEODORE SIMONSON AND KATE PHILLIPS · FROM AN IDEA BY IRVINE H. MILLGATE A TONYLYN PRODUCTION · COLOR BY DE LUXE

The theatrical poster for the film *The Blob*.

Griffith's second attempt at a blockbuster one year later exposed the inherent risks of big-budget filmmaking. Though *Intolerance* is generally considered as an artistic milestone and is generally credited with influencing the fledgling Soviet film industry in the 1920s, it was a financial disaster for its director. Made on a budget of $500,000 (several million in today's dollars), it never found its audience. Its pacifist tone was out of step with a public gearing itself for America's entry into World War I. Also, instead of one straight forward narrative, it shifted back and forth between a modern story, sixteenth-century France, ancient Babylon, and the life of Christ; the stories were all linked by the common theme of intolerance. The human drama was played out against giant sets and spectacular pageantry. Yet, audiences appeared to balk at the four storylines and stayed away from the theater, making it arguably the first big budget disaster in the history of film.

Although film budgets grew considerably during the next two decades, leading to some notable blockbusters as *Ben-Hur* (1926) and *San Francisco* (1936), it was not until 1939 with the release of *Gone with the Wind* that the form reasserted itself as a major force on the

level of contemporary "event pictures." The film, which was based on a nation-wide best-selling novel by Margaret Mitchell, was produced by David O. Selznick and returned to the theme of the U.S. Civil War covered by Griffith. Although box office star Clark Gable was the popular choice for the role of Rhett Butler, Selznick was able to milk maximum publicity value by conducting a high profile public search for an actress to play the role of Scarlett O'Hara. Fan magazines polled their readers for suggestions but the producer ultimately selected British actress Vivian Leigh, a virtual unknown in the United States. Another publicity stunt was the "burning of Atlanta" on a Culver City backlot consisting of old sets and other debris as the official first scene to be filmed. By the time that the film had its official premiere in Atlanta in 1939, the entire world was ready to experience the "big screen," Technicolor experience that was *Gone with the Wind*.

The film was a monumental success during its initial run and continued to pack audiences in during subsequent reissues in 1947, 1954, 1961, 1967, and 1998. In the 1967 run, the film was blown up to 70mm to effectively compete with the large screen blockbusters of the

1960s such as *Lawrence of Arabia* (1962) and *The Sound of Music* (1965). Thus removed from its natural aspect ratio, it did not fare particularly well against its modern competition. A decade later, when restored to its normal screen size, it made its debut on NBC and drew the largest audience in television history. In terms of sheer hype, marketing, and production values, *Gone with the Wind* constituted the prototype for what the blockbuster would come to be. From the time of its release until 1980, it became, in terms of un-inflated dollar value, the most profitable film ever made.

The blockbuster phenomenon died down until the mid-1950s when the emergence of new wide-screen technologies and the on-slaught of television prompted Hollywood to give its viewers a spectacle that could not be duplicated on the much smaller screen in the living room. Although first dismissed as novelties, these films built on the precedents established by *Gone with the Wind* and built their success on lavish production budgets, biblical and literary source material, and sheer big screen spectacle. The first major success was King Vidor's *War and Peace* in 1956. With a running time of nearly three and one half hours, it was a true visual epic. It was quickly followed by Cecil B. DeMille's remake of his silent epic *The Ten Commandments,* and Michael Anderson's *Around the World in 80 Days.*

Yet, within the very success of these blockbusters were the ingredients that would bring them to a halt in the 1960s. In order to create the large screen spectacles that were the trademark of the wide-screen 1950s films, the producers had to allocate larger production budgets than were the average for their standard releases. This meant that the studio had to drastically decrease the number of films that it made during a given year. Also, the longer running time of the blockbusters reduced the number of showings that a film would receive in the neighborhood theater.

To get around this situation, distributors created the road show exhibition scheme. A large budget film such as *West Side Story* (1961) would open only at large theaters in major metropolitan areas for, in some cases, as long as a year. The film would become an event much like a Broadway play and could command top dollar at the box-office. Both sound and projection systems would feature the latest technology to captivate the audience and make the evening a true theatrical experience. Once this market began to diminish, the film would be released to neighborhood theaters with considerably inferi-or exhibition facilities. Still, the public flocked to these motion pictures to see what all of the shouting was about.

This production and distribution strategy was based on the film being a hit. Unfortunately, most of the films that followed the widescreen extravaganzas of the mid-1950s failed to make their money back. The most notable example was Joseph L. Mankiewicz's 1963 *Cleopatra*, which cost Twentieth Century-Fox more than 40 million dollars to produce over a four year period. Although it had a number of theoretically "sure fire" ingredients—the pairing of Elizabeth Taylor and her then-lover Richard Burton (who were at the center of a highly publicized Hollywood divorce case) and every element of big screen spectacle that its producers could muster—it bombed at the box-office and never made its money back. This debacle almost brought Fox to its knees and illustrated the damage that an ill conceived blockbuster could do to a studio.

Thus although several films, such as *The Sound of Music*, which cost only $8 million to make and which returned $72 million in the domestic market alone, continued to show the profit potential of the blockbuster concept, the practice temporarily died out simply because

studios could not afford to put all of their financial eggs in one cinematic basket.

During the 1970s, production costs for all films began to rise substantially, causing the studios to produce fewer and fewer films and to place a significantly larger share of the budget into advertising and promotion in an attempt to pre-sell their films. This idea was enhanced through a variety of market and audience research to determine the viability of specific subjects, stories, and actors. Such practices led to the production of films carefully tailored to fit the audience's built-in expectations and reduced the number of edgy, experimental projects that studios would be willing to invest in.

The financial success of several conventionally-themed big-budget films at the beginning of the decade, including *Love Story* (1970), *Airport* (1970), and *The Godfather* (1972), proved that the theory indeed worked and proved that the right amount of research, glitz, and hype would pay huge dividends at the box-office. By the end of the decade two other films—*Star Wars* (1977) and *Jaws* (1975)—demonstrated that the equation could even be stretched to generate grosses in the hundreds of millions of dollars if the formula was on target. The latter two films demonstrated that the success of even one blockbuster could effect the financial position of a studio. In 1997, for example, the six top grossing films in the U.S. market accounted for more than one-third of the total revenues of distributors.

Despite the failure of the $40 million *Heaven's Gate* in 1980 and the increasingly high stakes faced by studios in order to compete, the trend toward blockbusters continued unabated into the 1980s. A major factor in this development, however, was the fact that most of the major studios were being acquired by large conglomerates with financial interests in a variety of media types. These companies viewed the motion picture as simply the first stage in the marketing of a product that would have blockbuster potential in a variety of interlocking media including books, toys, games, clothing, and per-sonal products. In the case of a successful film, *Star Wars* or *Batman,* for example, the earnings for these items would far exceed the box office revenues and at the same time create an appetite for a sequel.

This situation often affected the subject matter dealt with by the film. The question thus became "How well can the film stimulate the after-markets." Established products such as sequels and remakes of popular films were deemed to be the most commercial vehicles for developing related lines of merchandise. Original screenplays—unless they were based on successful "crossover" products from best-selling novels, comic books, or stage plays with built-in audi-ences—were deemed to be the least commercial subjects.

At the same time, studios were re-thinking their distribution strategy. Whereas the road show method had worked during the 1960s the merchandising needs of linked media conglomerates re-quired a new concept of saturation booking. According to this strategy, a film would be released simultaneously in more than 2000 theaters all over the United States to create the largest opening weekend possible and generate enough strong "word of mouth" recommendations to create a chain reaction that would open up all of the additional markets world wide and trigger additional markets in video sales, pay TV, and network TV as well as toys and other merchandise.

The primary criteria for creating films that lend themselves to multi-media marketing was to choose subjects which were appealing to the prime 14- to 25-year-old age group but which also had attractions for a family audience. Thus, event films were usually pegged to the two heaviest theater going periods of the year, summer and Christmas. This insures that if the film is targeted at a younger audience, it will still attract the parents of children or teenagers who might accompany them to the theater.

Additionally, the video and television markets also assisted in creating the reception for theatrical projects. The highly successful *Rambo* series of the 1980s began with a moderately successful medium-budget theatrical film, *First Blood* (1982), which might never have generated a sequel had it not been a runaway video hit. The success of the video created a built-in audience for the much higher budgeted *Rambo: First Blood, Part Two* (1985), which in turn generated toys, action figures, video games, and an animated TV series.

In the 1990s, the stakes rose even higher, with higher budgeted films requiring correspondingly higher grosses. Such large budgeted films as *Batman and Robin* (1997) and *Waterworld* (1995) were deemed "failures" because their fairly respectable grosses still did not allow the film to break even due to the scale of their production costs. The ultimate plateau may have been reached with James Cameron's *Titanic*, with a production budget so large—over $200 million—that it took two studios (Twentieth Century-Fox and Paramount) to pay for it.

Titanic became the biggest moneymaking film in the history of motion pictures, with a gross approaching $1 billion worldwide. Such success is largely due to the fact that writer/director James Cameron created a film that appealed to every major audience demographic possible. For the young girls, there was its star Leonardo Di Caprio, the 1990s heartthrob, and a love story; for young men there was the action of the sinking ship; for the adults, there was the historical epic and the love story.

As for the future, the success of *Titanic* will undoubtedly tempt producers to create even larger budgeted films crammed with ever more expensive special effects. Some of these productions will be so large that they will have to be funded by increasingly intricate financial partnerships between two or more production entities simply to get the film off the ground. The stakes will, of course, be enormous, with the fate of an entire studio or production company riding on the outcome of a single feature. Yet, despite the high risk factor, the blockbuster trend will continue to exert a siren-like allure for those at the controls of Hollywood's destiny. Unlike the days of Griffith and Selznick, it is no longer enough to simply tell a good story in a cinematic way. If a film cannot sell toys and software, it may not even get made.

—Steve Hanson and Sandra Garcia-Myers

FURTHER READING:

Aufderheide, Pat. "Blockbuster." In *Seeing Through Movies,* edited by Mark Crispin Miller. New York, Pantheon, 1990.

Cook, David. *A History of Narrative Film.* 3rd ed. New York, W.W. Norton & Company, 1996.

Edgerton, Gary R. *American Film Exhibition and an Analysis of the Motion Picture Industry's Market Structure, 1963-1980.* New York, Garland, 1983.

Gomery, Douglas. *Shared Pleasures: A History of Movie Presentation in the United States.* Madison, University of Wisconsin Press, 1992.

Maltby, Richard, and Ian Craven. *Hollywood Cinema: An Introduction.* New York, Oxford University Press, 1995

Parkinson, David. *The Young Oxford Book of the Movies.* New York, Oxford University Press, 1995.

Wyatt, Justin. *High Concept: Movies and Marketing in Hollywood.* Austin, University of Texas Press, 1994.

Blondie (comic strip)

One of the longest-running marriages in the funnies is that of Blondie Boopadoop and Dagwood Bumstead. The couple first met in 1930, when Blondie was a flighty flapper and Dagwood was a somewhat dense rich boy, and they were married in 1933. They're still living a happy, though joke-ridden life, in close to 2000 newspapers around the world. The *Blondie* strip was created by Murat "Chic" Young, who'd begun drawing comics about pretty young women in 1921.

After several false starts—including such strips as *Beautiful Bab* and *Dumb Dora*—Young came up with *Blondie* and King Features began syndicating it in September of 1930. Initially *Blondie* read like Young's other strips. But after the couple married and the disinherited Dagwood took a sort of generic office job with Mr. Dithers, the feature changed and became domesticated. Blondie turned out to be far from flighty and proved to be a model housewife, gently manipulating her sometimes befuddled husband. The gags, and the short continuities, centered increasingly around the home and the office, frequently concentrating on basics like sleeping, eating, and working.

A four-frame strip from the comic *Blondie*.

The birth of their first child, Baby Dumpling, in the spring of 1934 provided a new source of gags and helped win the strip an even larger audience. Young perfected running gags built around such props and situations as Dagwood's naps on the sofa, his monumental sandwiches, his conflicts with door-to-door salesmen, Blondie's new hats, and his wild rushes to catch the bus to work. Other regular characters were neighbors Herb and Tootsie Woodley, Daisy the Bumstead dog and, eventually, her pups, and Mr. Beasley the postman, with whom Dagwood frequently collided in his headlong rushes to the bus stop. The Bumstead's second child, daughter Cookie, was born in 1941.

King effectively merchandised the strip in a variety of mediums. There were reprints in comic books and Big Little Books and, because of Dagwood's affinity for food, there were also occasional cookbooks. More importantly, Young's characters were brought to the screen by Columbia Pictures in 1938. Arthur Lake, who looked born for the part, played Dagwood and Penny Singleton, her hair freshly bleached, was Blondie. Immediately successful, the series of "B" movies lasted until 1950 and ran to over two dozen titles. The radio version of *Blondie* took to the air on CBS in the summer of 1939, also starring Singleton and Lake. Like the movies, it was more specific about Dagwood's office job and had him working for the J.C. Dithers Construction Company. The final broadcast was in 1950 and by that time Ann Rutherford was Blondie. For the first television version on NBC in 1957 Lake was once again Dagwood, but Pamela Briton portrayed Blondie. The show survived for only eight months and a 1968 attempt on CBS with Will Hutchins and Patricia Harty lasted for just four. Despite occasional rumors about a musical, the Bumsteads have thus far failed to trod the boards on Broadway.

A journeyman cartoonist at best, Young early on hired assistants to help him with the drawing of *Blondie*. Among them were Alex Raymond (in the days before he graduated to *Flash Gordon*), Ray McGill and Jim Raymond, Alex' brother. It was the latter Raymond who eventually did most of the drawing Young signed his name to. When Young died in 1973, Jim Raymond was given a credit. Dean Young, Chic's son, managed the strip and got a credit, too. After Raymond's death, Stan Drake became the artist. Currently Denis Lebrun draws the still popular strip.

—Ron Goulart

FURTHER READING:

Blackbeard, Bill and Dale Crain. *The Comic Strip Century.* Northampton, Kitchen Sink Press, 1995.

Waugh, Coulton. *The Comics.* New York, The Macmillan Company, 1947.

Blondie (rock band)

The 1970s were a transitional period in popular music. Emerging from the new wave and punk rock scene, the band Blondie, featuring Deborah Harry, achieved both critical and commercial success. Blondie transcended mere popularity by moving away from blues-based rock and capitalizing on the personality and musical ingenuity of its lead singer. Blondie successfully incorporated elements from a number of different musical forms into its music, including rap, reggae, disco, pop, punk, and rock.

After a number of early failures, Deborah Harry and Chris Stein formed Blondie in 1973. The name for the band came from the cat calls truck drivers used to taunt Deborah Harry, "Come on Blondie, give us a screw!" Harry parodied the dumb blonde stereotype into platinum. She appeared on stage in torn swimsuit and high heels, vacantly staring into space. In 1977 the act and the talent paid off in the band's hit "Denis," and was soon followed by "Heart of Glass."

The strength of Blondie, Deborah Harry, also proved its weakness. Jealousy led to the dissolution of the group in 1984. Harry went on her own, achieving some success—her tours continually sold-out whether she was alone or with the Jazz Passengers. But her solo success has never reached that of the group Blondie.

By 1997, Blondie had reunited for a tour, completed an album in 1998, and had begun touring once again. The band members claimed not to remember why they split and seemed eager to reunite. Their fans also eagerly anticipated a more permanent reunion. Blondie has greatly influenced the bands that have come after it, and Deborah Harry has continued to explore new genres with success.

—Frank A. Salamone, Ph.D.

Bloom County

A popular daily comic strip of the 1980s, *Bloom County* was written and drawn by Berkeley Breathed. During its run, the comic strip reveled in political, cultural, and social satire. Capturing popular attention with witty comment, the strip also offered a new perspective in the comics.

Bloom County began in 1980 with the setting of the Bloom Boarding House in the mythical Bloom County. Both boarding house and county appeared to be named for a local family, originally represented in the comic strip by the eccentric Major Bloom, retired, and his grandson Milo. Other original residents included Mike Binkley, a neurotic friend of Milo; Binkley's father; Bobbi Harlow, a progressive feminist school teacher; Steve Dallas, a macho despicable lawyer; and Cutter John, a paralyzed Vietnam vet. Over the years, the boarding house residents changed; the Major and Bobbi Harlow vanished and the human inhabitants were joined by a host of animals including Portnoy, a hedgehog, and Hodge Podge, a rabbit. But two other animals became the most famous characters of the strip. One, a parody of Garfield, was Bill the Cat, a disgusting feline that usually just said "aack." The other was the big-nosed penguin named Opus, who first appeared with a much more diminutive honker as Binkley's pet, a sorry substitute for a dog. Opus eventually became the star of the strip and when Breathed ended the comic, he was the last character to appear.

Breathed used his comic menagerie to ridicule American society, culture, and politics. Reading through the strip is like reading through a who's who of 1980s references: Caspar Weinberger, Oliver North, Sean Penn and Madonna, Gary Hart. Breathed made fun of them all. In the later years of the strip, Donald Trump and his outrageous wealth became a chief focus of Breathed's satire. In the world of *Bloom County,* Donald Trump's brain was put in the body of Bill the Cat. The strip supposedly ended because Trump the Cat bought the comic and fired all of the "actors."

Breathed didn't restrain himself to ridiculing individuals. He also attacked American fads, institutions, and corporations. Opus had a nose job and constantly bought stupid gadgets advertised on TV.

Milo and Opus both worked for *the Bloom Picayune,* the local newspaper, and Breathed used them to launch many attacks on the media. He lampooned the American military through the creation of Rosebud, a basselope (part basset hound, part antelope) that the military wanted to use to smuggle bombs into Russia. Corporations such as McDonalds and Crayola felt the barb of Breathed's wit, though not as much as Mary Kay Cosmetics. Breathed had Opus's mother being held in a Mary Kay testing lab. Breathed used this to point out the cruelties of animal testing as well as the extremism of the animal rights terrorists. The terrorists faced off against the Mary Kay Commandos, complete with pink uzis.

Breathed was adept at political satire as well. Whenever the country faced a presidential election, The Meadow Party would emerge with its candidates: Bill the Cat for President and an often reluctant Opus for V.P. Breathed used the two to ridicule not only politicians but the election process and the American public's willingness to believe the media campaigns. Breathed had a definite political slant to his comic, but he made fun of the follies of both conservatives and liberals.

Bloom County was a unique creation not only because of its humor, but because of the unusual perspectives Breathed used. Unlike other comics, *Bloom County*'s animal and human characters interacted as equals and spoke to each other. Breathed also made the strip self-reflexive, often breaking from the comic to give comments from the "management" or from the characters themselves. One sequence featured Opus confused because he hadn't read the script. Setting the comic up as a job for the characters to act in, Breathed was able to acknowledge the existence of other strips, making jokes about them and featuring guest appearances by characters from other comic strips. As *Bloom County* came to an end, Breathed had the characters go off in search of jobs in the other comics strips, such as Family Circle and Marmaduke. While some other comics have used this technique as well, notably *Doonesbury,* it remains rare in comics, and *Bloom County* was most often compared to *Doonesbury* for content and attitude. Also like *Doonesbury,* in 1987 *Bloom County* won the Pulitzer Prize for editorial cartooning.

The strip was not without its flaws, the chief one being a lack of strong female characters, a lack Breathed was well aware of (and commented on in the strip). While the male characters stayed strong, the female characters dropped out. When the strip ended, the only female characters were Ronald-Ann, a poverty stricken African American girl and Rosebud the Basselope who earlier in the comic's run turned out to be female. Besides a lack of women characters, many readers felt that the comic was offensive and not funny and often lodged complaints with Breathed.

Breathed ended the strip in 1989 when he felt he had reached the end of what he could do with these characters. He followed *Bloom County* with a Sunday-only strip called *Outland.* The strip at first featured Opus and Ronald-Ann though most of *Bloom County*'s cast eventually showed up. It never gained the popularity of its predecessor, and Breathed stopped writing comics and turned to the writing of children's books.

—P. Andrew Miller

FURTHER READING:

Astor, David. "Breathed Giving Up Newspaper Comics." *Editor and Publisher.* January 21, 1995.

Breathed, Berkeley. *Bloom County Babylon.* Boston, Little Brown, 1986.

———. *Classics of Western Literature: Bloom County 1986-1989.* Boston, Little Brown, 1990.

Buchalter, Gail. "Cartoonist Berke Breathed Feathers His Nest by Populating Bloom County with Rare Birds." *People Weekly.* August 6, 1984.

Blount, Roy, Jr. (1941—)

An heir to the Southern humor writing tradition of Mark Twain and *Pogo,* Roy Blount, Jr. has covered a wide array of subjects—from a season with an NFL team to the Jimmy Carter presidency—with equal parts incisiveness and whimsy.

Roy Blount, Jr. was born in Indianapolis on October 5, 1941. As an infant, he moved with his parents to their native Georgia, where his father became a civic leader in Decatur, and his family lived a comfortably middle-class life during the 1950s. He attended Vanderbilt University in Nashville on a Grantland Rice scholarship, and much of his early journalism work was, like Rice's, in sportswriting. In 1968, Blount began writing for *Sports Illustrated,* where he quickly became known for his offbeat subjects.

In 1973 Blount decided to follow a professional football team around for one year—from the offseason through a bruising NFL campaign—in order to get a more nuanced look at players and the game. He chose the Pittsburgh Steelers, a historically inept franchise on the verge of four Super Bowl victories. His 1973-1974 season with the Steelers became *About Three Bricks Shy of a Load.* Blount studied each element of the team, from its working-class fans to its front office to its coaches and players, with lively digressions on the city of Pittsburgh, country-western music (Blount once penned a country ballad entitled, "I'm Just a Bug on the Windshield of Life"), and sports nicknames.

With the success of *About Three Bricks Shy of a Load,* Blount became a full-time free-lance humor writer, with contributions in dozens of magazines including *Playboy, Organic Gardening, The New Yorker,* and *Rolling Stone.* In the late 1980s he even contributed a regular "un-British cryptic crossword puzzle" to *Spy* Magazine.

The administration of fellow Southerner Jimmy Carter led to Blount's 1980 book *Crackers,* which featured fictional Carter cousins ("Dr. J.E.M. McMethane Carter, 45, Rolla, Missouri, interdisciplinary professor at the Hugh B. Ferguson University of Plain Sense and Mysterophysics"; "Martha Carter Kelvinator, 48, Bullard Dam, Georgia, who is married to a top-loading automatic washer") and angst-ridden verses about the 39th President:

> I've got the redneck White House blues.
> The man just makes me more and more confused.
> He's in all the right churches,
> and all the wrong pews,
> I've got the redneck White House blues.

Blount's most significant chapter focused on Billy Carter, who frequently embarrassed his brother's White House with impolitic comments and behavior. Blount came to like the younger Carter, and found that his fallibility made the Carters more likable: "I don't want people to be *right* all the time."

Throughout the 1980s Blount continued free-lancing articles and publishing books, with such offbeat titles as *What Men Don't Tell*

Women, One Fell Soup, and *Not Exactly What I Had in Mind.* Blount's subject matter included orgasms, waffles (he wrote a poem to them), baseball batting practice, and the federal budget deficit (Blount suggested that every American buy and throw away $1,000 worth of stamps each, to fill the Treasury's coffers). He eulogized Elvis Presley (titled ''He Took the Guilt out of the Blues'') and profiled ''Saturday Night Live'' cast members Bill Murray and Gilda Radner. And the former sportswriter delivered essays on Joe DiMaggio and Roberto Clemente to baseball anthologies, while also attending a Chicago Cubs fantasy camp under the direction of Hall of Fame manager Leo Durocher.

Blount's first novel was the best-selling *First Hubby,* a comic account of the bemused husband of America's first woman president. His writing attracted the attention of film critic and producer Pauline Kael, who encouraged him to develop screenplays. His first produced effort was the 1996 major motion picture comedy *Larger than Life,* starring Bill Murray, Janeane Garafolo, and a giant elephant.

Blount became one of the most visible humorists in America as a frequent guest on *The Tonight Show with Johnny Carson,* and he often appeared on the long-running *A Prairie Home Companion* radio series, hosted by close friend Garrison Keillor. Despite possessing what he acknowledged as a weak singing voice, Blount triumphantly joined the chorus of the Rock Bottom Remainders, a 1990s novelty rock band composed of such best-selling authors as Dave Barry, Stephen King, and Amy Tan.

Divorced twice, Blount has two children. In 1998 he wrote a best-selling memoir, *Be Sweet,* where he acknowledged his ambivalent feelings towards his parents (at one point actually writing, ''I hated my mother.''). Later that year he also contributed text to a picture book on one of his favorite subjects, dogs, with a truly Blount-esque title: *If Only You Knew How Much I Smell You.*

—Andrew Milner

FURTHER READING:

Blount, Roy, Jr. *Be Sweet.* New York, Knopf, 1998.

———. *Crackers.* New York, Knopf, 1980.

Gale, Stephen H., editor. *Encyclopedia of American Humorists.* New York, Garland Press, 1988.

Blue Jeans

See Jeans; Levi's; Wrangler Jeans

Blue Velvet

Among the most critically acclaimed movies of 1986, *Blue Velvet* was director David Lynch's commentary on small-town America, showing the sordid backside of the sunny facade. That said, the film is not strictly a condemnation of the American small-town so much as it is a kind of coming-of-age story. Lynch described the film as ''a story of love and mystery.'' This statement may ostensibly refer to the relationship between the film's protagonist Jeffrey Beaumont (Kyle MacLachlan) and the police detective's daughter Sandy Williams

Isabella Rossellini in a scene from the film *Blue Velvet*.

(Laura Dern) and the mystery they attempt to solve in plucky Nancy Drew style, but it might also be seen as a statement about the mingling of affection and fear that arises in the movie's examination of the fictional but truthful setting, Lumbertown. One can see *Blue Velvet* as a coming-of-age story, not only for Jeffrey, but for the idea of the idyllic American small town. The loss of innocence may be regrettable, but is ultimately necessary.

The opening scene summarily characterizes *Blue Velvet* in theme and plot. Following the lush, fifties-style opening credits, the screen shows a blue sky, flowers, the local firefighters riding through town waving, and Jeffrey's father watering the lawn, all in brilliant, almost surreal color. Then the scene, which might have come from a generation earlier, is interrupted by a massive stroke that drops Mr. Beaumont to his back. The camera pans deeply into the well groomed lawn and uncovers combating insects. Likewise, the camera plunges unflinchingly into the unseen, discomforting side of Lumbertown.

The story really begins when Jeffrey, walking back from visiting his father in the hospital, discovers a severed ear in the grass by a lake. After turning the ear over to the police, Jeffrey decides to find out the story for himself, and with the help of Sandy, gets enough information to start his own investigation. The trail leads to Dorothy Vallens (Isabella Rossellini) a nightclub singer whose husband and son have been kidnapped. Thus, the story begins as a rather traditional mystery, but the tradition drops away as Jeffrey comes face to face with the most disturbing of people, particularly the demonic kidnapper, Frank Booth (Dennis Hopper). Frank is a killer and drug dealer of almost inhuman proportions and perversions. He alternately calls himself ''daddy'' and ''baby'' as he beats and rapes Dorothy.

That the story has a reasonably happy ending, with villains vanquished and Jeffrey united with Sandy, is not altogether comforting. The film may return to the bright colors and idyllic lifestyle presented in the opening scene, but the audience now knows that something else goes on below the surface. Jeffrey and Sandy tell each other that it's a strange world, but they say it whimsically, the facade restored for the characters, if not for the audience. Perhaps the most significant scene of the film is when, in his own sexual encounter with Dorothy, Jeffrey strikes her on her command. With the blow Jeffrey crosses over from an innocent trapped in a situation beyond his control to a part of the things that go on behind the closed doors of Lumbertown.

The film was a risky one. David Lynch, though recognized for work on films like *The Elephant Man* and *Eraserhead,* was coming off the financial failure of *Dune.* Moreover, this was the first film that was entirely his. He had written the script and insisted on full artistic freedom on what was to clearly be a rather disturbing film, with a violent sexual content unlike any that had previously been seen on screen. He was granted such freedom after agreeing to a minute budget of five million dollars, and half salary for himself. The other half would be paid if the film was a success. It was. The film garnered Lynch an Academy Award nomination for his direction. Despite such accolades, the film was not embraced whole-heartedly by all. The Venice Film Festival, for instance, rejected it as pornography.

The stunning direction of the film combines bald faced directness in presenting repelling scenes of sex and violence with subtle examinations of the mundane. By slowing the film, for instance, the pleasantness of Lumbertown in the open air seems dreamlike and unreal. While shots like these establish an expressionistic, symbolic screen world, others realistically place us in a situation where we see what the characters see, hear what they hear, and these perceptions form an incomplete picture of the action. Similar techniques crop up in earlier Lynch films, but it is here, in what many consider the director's masterpiece, that they come to full fruition. The direction of *Blue Velvet* paved the road for the similar world of *Twin Peaks,* Lynch's foray into television, which itself widened the possibilities of TV drama.

Stylistically, Lynch's body of work, and particularly *Blue Velvet* has greatly influenced filmmakers, especially those working independently from the major Hollywood studios, and even television. Moreover, *Blue Velvet* strongly affected many of its viewers. The large cult following of the movie suggests that it perhaps opened many eyes to the different facets of life, not only in small towns, but in all of idealized America. Or more likely, the film articulated what many already saw. Frank may rage like a demon on screen, like a creature from our darkest nightmares, but the discomfort with the pleasant simplicity of Americana, the knowledge that things are rarely what they seem, is quite real. *Blue Velvet* reminds us of that, even as it looks back longingly, if now soberly, at the false but comforting memory of a romance with the American ideal.

—Marc Oxoby

FURTHER READING:

Chion, Michel. *David Lynch.* London, British Film Institute, 1995.

Kaleta, Kenneth C. *David Lynch.* New York, Twayne, 1993.

Nochimson, Martha P. *The Passion of David Lynch: Wild at Heart in Hollywood.* Austin, University of Texas Press, 1997.

Blueboy

From its first issue in 1975, *Blueboy* was a pioneer in gay monthly magazines. Its focus was on an upscale, urban gay market. While containing slick, full frontal male nude photography, the publication also strove to include contemporary gay authors. Writings by Patricia Nell Warren, Christopher Isherwood, Truman Capote, John Rechy, Randy Shilts, and many others graced the pages. Led by former *TV Guide* ad manager Donald Embinder, the magazine quickly went from a bimonthly to monthly publication in a year and a half. By the late 1970s *Blueboy* was cited in the press as a publishing empire, producing the monthly magazine and a small paperback press collection, and trading on Wall Street. *Blueboy's* style was soon mimicked by other publications. Due to changes in style, content, and format *Blueboy* lost its appeal during the 1980s and 1990s. At the same time, an ever increasing range of competing glossy male magazines, modeled upon *Blueboy* principles, diminished its readership.

—Michael A. Lutes

FURTHER READING:

"A Gay Businessman: Out of the Closet . . . And onto Wall Street." *Esquire.* March 13, 1979, 11.

Kleinfield, N.R. "Homosexual Periodicals Are Proliferating." *New York Times.* August 1, 1978, Sec IV, 4-5.

Bluegrass

Since its development in the mid-1940s, bluegrass music has become one of the most distinctive American musical forms, attracting an intense audience of supporters who collectively form one of popular music's most vibrant subcultures. A close cousin of country music, bluegrass music is an acoustic musical style that features at its core banjo, mandolin, guitar, double bass, and fiddle along with close vocal harmonies, especially high-tenor harmony singing called the "high lonesome sound." Because of its largely acoustic nature, bluegrass is a term often used to describe all kinds of acoustic, noncommercial, "old-timey" music popular among rural people in the United States in the decades prior to World War II. That characterization, however, is incorrect. Bluegrass was developed, and has continued ever since, as a commercial musical form by professional recording and touring musicians. Often seen as being a throwback to this pre-World War II era, bluegrass is instead a constantly evolving musical style that maintains its connections to the past while reaching out to incorporate influences from other musical styles such as jazz and rock music. As such, it remains a vibrant musical form in touch with the past and constantly looking toward the future.

Although bluegrass has connections to old-timey rural music from the American south, as a complete and distinct musical form, bluegrass is largely the creation of one man—Bill Monroe. Born near Rosine, Kentucky on September 13, 1911, Monroe grew up in a musical family. His mother was a talented amateur musician who imparted a strong love of music in all of her eight children, several of whom became musicians. As a child, Bill Monroe learned to play guitar with a local black musician, Arnold Schultz (often accompanying Schultz at local dances), and received additional training from his

IIIrd Tyme Out vocal group, on stage at the IBMA Bluegrass Fan Fest in Kentucky.

uncle, Pendelton Vandiver, a fiddle player who bequeathed to Monroe a vast storehouse of old tunes in addition to lessons about such important musical concepts as timing. Although his early training was on the guitar, Monroe switched to the mandolin in the late 1920s in order to play along with his older brothers Birch and Charlie, who already played fiddle and guitar, respectively. In 1934, Charlie and Bill formed a professional duet team, the Monroe Brothers, and set out on a career in music. They became very popular, particularly in the Carolinas, and recorded a number of records, including *My Long Journey Home* and *What Would You Give in Exchange for Your Soul.* Their partnership was a brief one, however, as their personal differences, often expressed in physical and verbal fighting, sent them in separate directions in 1938.

On his own, and out from under his older brother's shadow, Bill Monroe began to develop his own style of playing that would evolve into bluegrass. He organized a short-lived band called the Kentuckians in 1938. Moving to Atlanta that same year, he formed a new band which he named the Blue Grass Boys in honor of his native Kentucky. The group, consisting of Monroe on mandolin, Cleo Davis on guitar, and Art Wooten on fiddle, proved popular with audiences, and in October 1939 Monroe and the Blue Grass Boys earned a spot on Nashville radio station WSM's popular *Grand Ole Opry* program. The group's appearances on the *Opry* brought Monroe national recognition.

Throughout the war years, Monroe began to put together the major musical elements of bluegrass, including his trademark high-tenor singing, the distinctive rhythm provided by his "chopping" mandolin chords, and a repertoire of old-timey and original tunes.

But it was not until Monroe formed a new version of the Blue Grass Boys at the end of World War II that the classic bluegrass sound finally emerged. In 1945, he added guitarist Lester Flatt, fiddler Chubby Wise, bass player Cedric Rainwater (Howard Watts), and banjoist Earl Scruggs. Of these, the most important was Scruggs, who at the age of 20 had already developed one of the most distinctive banjo styles ever created, the Scruggs "three-finger" style. This playing style, accomplished by using the thumb, forefinger, and index fingers to pick the strings, allowed Scruggs to play in a "rolling" style that permitted a torrent of notes to fly out of his banjo at amazingly fast speeds. This style has since become the standard banjo playing style, and despite many imitators, Scruggs's playing has never quite been equaled. Scruggs, more than anyone else, was responsible for making the banjo the signature instrument in bluegrass, and it is the Scruggs banjo sound that most people think of when bluegrass is mentioned. According to country music historian Bill Malone, with this new band Monroe's bluegrass style fully matured and became "an ensemble style of music, much like jazz in the improvised solo work of the individual instruments."

Like jazz, the bluegrass songs created by Bill Monroe and the Blue Grass Boys began with an instrumental introduction, then a statement of the song's melody and lyric lines, followed by successive instrumental breaks, with the mandolin, banjo, and fiddle all taking solos. Behind them, the guitar and bass kept a steady rhythm, and the mandolin and banjo would add to that rhythm when not soloing. To many bluegrass admirers, this version of the Blue Grass Boys, which lasted from 1945 to 1948, represents the pinnacle of bluegrass music. During their short existence, just over three years, this version of the Blue Grass Boys recorded a number of songs that have since become bluegrass classics, including "Blue Moon of Kentucky," "Will You Be Loving Another Man?," "Wicked Path of Sin," "I'm Going Back to Old Kentucky," "Bluegrass Breakdown," "Little Cabin Home on the Hill," and "Molly and Tenbrooks." Throughout this period as well, Monroe and his group toured relentlessly. They were so popular that many towns did not have an auditorium large enough to accommodate all those wishing to hear the band. To accommodate them, Monroe traveled with a large circus tent and chairs. Arriving in a town, they would also frequently challenge local townspeople to a baseball game. This provided not only much-needed stress relief from the grueling travel schedule, but also helped advertise their shows.

The success of Bill Monroe and his Blue Grass Boys was so great by the later 1940s that the music began to spawn imitators and followers in other musicians, broadening bluegrass' appeal. It should be noted that the name "bluegrass" was not Monroe's invention, and the term did not come about until at least the mid-1950s, when people began referring to bands following in Monroe's footsteps as playing in the "blue grass" style, after the name of the Blue Grass Boys. The first "new" band in the bluegrass style was that formed by two of Monroe's greatest sidemen, Lester Flatt and Earl Scruggs, who left Monroe in 1948 to form their own band, the Foggy Mountain Boys. Flatt and Scruggs deemphasized the role of the mandolin in their new band, preferring to put the banjo talents of Scruggs front and center. They toured constantly in the late 1940s and throughout the 1950s, building a strong and loyal following among listeners hungry for the bluegrass sound. Their popularity also resulted in a recording contract with Mercury Records. There, they laid down their own body of classic bluegrass material, much of it penned by Flatt. There were blisteringly fast instrumental numbers such as "Pike County Breakdown" and "Foggy Mountain Breakdown," and vocal numbers such as "My Little Girl in Tennessee," "Roll in My Sweet Baby's Arms," "My Cabin in Caroline," and "Old Salty Dog Blues," all of which have become standards in the bluegrass repertoire. These songs, much like Monroe's as well, often invoked themes of longing, loneliness, and loss, and were almost always rooted in rural images of mother, home, and country life. During their 20-year collaboration, Flatt and Scruggs became not only important innovators in bluegrass, extending its stylistic capacities, but they helped broaden the appeal of bluegrass, both with their relentless touring and also by producing bluegrass music such as the theme to the early 1960s television show *The Beverly Hillbillies* ("The Ballad of Jed Clampett"), and the aforementioned "Foggy Mountain Breakdown," used as the title song to the 1967 film *Bonnie and Clyde*.

As successful as Flatt and Scruggs were, they were not the only followers of the Monroe style. As historian Bill Malone noted, "the bluegrass 'sound' did not become a 'style' until other musical organizations began copying the instrumental and vocal traits first featured in Bill Monroe's performances." In fact, many later bluegrass greats got their starts as Blue Grass Boys, including, in addition

to Flatt and Scruggs, Mac Wiseman, Carter Stanley, Don Reno, Jimmy Martin, Vassar Clements, Sonny Osborne, Del McCoury, and many others. Under Monroe's tutelage, they learned the essential elements of bluegrass which they later took to their own groups. Among the other important early followers of Monroe was the brother duo of Ralph and Carter Stanley, the Stanley Brothers. They followed very closely on Monroe's heels, imitating his style almost note-for-note. But they were more than simply imitators; they continued and extended the bluegrass tradition with their playing and singing and through Carter Stanley's often bittersweet songs such as "I Long to See the Old Folks" and "Our Last Goodbye."

Along with the Stanley Brothers, other Monroe-inspired bluegrass bands came to prominence in the 1950s, including Mac Wiseman, Don Reno and Red Smiley, Jimmy Martin, the Osborne Brothers, and Jim and Jesse McReynolds. Each brought their own distinctive styles to the emerging bluegrass genre. Don Reno, in addition to his stellar banjo playing, brought the guitar to greater prominence in bluegrass, using it to play lead lines in addition to its usual role as a rhythm instrument. Reno and Smiley also brought bluegrass closer to country music, playing songs in the honky-tonk style that dominated country music in the early 1950s. Guitarist and singer Mac Wiseman was also instrumental in maintaining the strong connections between bluegrass and country, always willing to incorporate country songs and styles into his bluegrass repertoire. In addition, he often revived older songs from the pre-World War II era and brought them into the bluegrass tradition. Also rising to popularity during the 1950s were the Osborne Brothers, Bobby and Sonny. Their country-tinged bluegrass style, which they developed with singer Red Allen, made them one of the most successful bluegrass acts of the 1950s, 1960s, and beyond.

Despite the innovations and success of Monroe, Flatt, and Scruggs, the Osborne Brothers, the Stanley Brothers, and others, the market for bluegrass suffered heavily in the late 1950s as both electrified country and rock 'n' roll took listeners' attention away from bluegrass. While there was still a niche market for bluegrass, its growth and overall popularity fell as a result of this competition. The folk revival of the early 1960s, however, centered in northern cities and on college campuses, brought renewed interest in bluegrass. The folk revival was largely a generational phenomenon as younger musicians and listeners began rediscovering the older folk and old-timey music styles. To many of these young people, these earlier styles were refreshing in their authenticity, their close connection to the folk a welcome relief from commercial America. And, while old blues musicians from the 1920s and 1930s were brought back to stages of the many folk festivals alongside such newcomers as Bob Dylan, the acoustic sounds of bluegrass were also featured. Although it had never dipped that much, Bill Monroe in particular saw his career revive, and he was particularly pleased that the music he created was reaching a new, younger audience.

While bluegrass was reaching new audiences through the folk revival festivals, bluegrass made new inroads and attracted both old and new listeners through the many bluegrass festivals that began in the 1960s. Musician Bill Clifton organized an early one-day festival in 1961 in Luray, Virginia. In 1965, promoter Carlton Haney began the annual Roanoke Bluegrass Festival, a three-day affair that focused solely on bluegrass, where the faithful could see such greats as Bill Monroe, the Stanley Brothers, Don Reno, and others. The success of the Roanoke festival sparked others across the South and Midwest. In 1967, Bill Monroe himself began the Bean Blossom Festival on his property in Brown County, Indiana. More than simply performance spaces, these festivals have become meeting grounds for bluegrass enthusiasts to share their passion for the music in addition to seeing some of the greats of the genre. Many guests camp nearby or often on the festival grounds themselves, and the campsites become the sites of endless after-hours jam sessions where amateur musicians can trade songs and instrumental licks. The festivals are also very informal affairs, and bluegrass fans can often meet and talk with the performers in ways that rarely occur at jazz or rock concerts. These festivals were instrumental in the 1960s and beyond in both expanding the reach of the music while simultaneously providing a form of community for bluegrass fans and musicians.

In the late 1960s and into the 1970s, bluegrass began to move in new directions as younger practitioners of the style brought new rock and jazz elements into the music, including the use of electric basses. This trend, which continued through the 1990s, was not always welcomed by the bluegrass faithful. Many accepted and welcomed it, but others looked at bluegrass as a last bastion of acoustic music, and any fooling around with the classic bluegrass style seemed heresy indeed. Many of those who resisted change were older and often more politically conservative, disliking the long hair and liberal politics of many of the younger bluegrass musicians as much as the new sounds these musicians were introducing. This conflict even prompted the breakup of Flatt and Scruggs's musical partnership as Earl Scruggs formed a new band, the Earl Scruggs Revue, with his sons playing electric instruments and incorporating rock elements into their sound. Lester Flatt preferred the old style and continued to play it with his band the Nashville Grass until his death in 1979.

Among the practitioners of the new "newgrass" or "progressive" bluegrass style, as it was called, were such younger artists and groups as The Country Gentlemen, the Dillards, the New Grass Revival, the Seldom Scene, David Grisman, and J.D. Crowe and the New South. The Country Gentlemen had mixed rock songs and electric instruments into their sound as early as the mid-1960s, and they were a formative influence on later progressive bluegrass artists. A California band, the Dillards, combined traditional bluegrass styles with Ozark humor and songs from the folk revival. They also enjoyed popularity for their appearances on *The Andy Griffith Show* in the early 1960s. By the early 1970s, the progressive bluegrass sound reached a creative peak with the New Grass Revival, formed in 1972 by mandolinist-fiddler Sam Bush. The New Grass Revival brought new jazz elements into bluegrass, including extended improvisations, and also experimented with a wide variety of musical styles. Mandolinist David Grisman began by studying the great masters of his instrument, but he eventually developed a unique hybrid of bluegrass and jazz styles that he later labeled "Dawg" music, performing with other progressive bluegrass artists such as guitarist Tony Rice and fiddler Mark O'Connor, and such jazz greats as Stephane Grappelli. Banjoist Bela Fleck, himself an early member of the New Grass Revival, extended his instrument's reach from bluegrass into jazz and world music styles with his group Bela Fleck and the Flecktones.

As important as progressive bluegrass was in moving the genre in new directions, the break it represented from the traditional style did not signal an end to the classic sound pioneered by Bill Monroe and Flatt and Scruggs. Instead, both styles continued to have ardent practitioners that kept both forms of bluegrass alive. Northern musicians such as Larry Sparks and Del McCoury continued to play traditional bluegrass, bringing it new audiences. And the grand master himself, Bill Monroe, continued to play his original brand of bluegrass with an ever-changing arrangement of younger Blue Grass Boys until his death in 1996 at the age of 85. Other musicians crossed the boundaries between the two bluegrass styles. Most notably among

these was mandolinist-fiddler Ricky Skaggs. Skaggs had apprenticed with traditionalists such as Ralph Stanley's Clinch Mountain Boys, but was just as much at home with newer bands such as J.D. Crowe and the New South and with country artists such as Emmylou Harris.

By the 1990s, bluegrass was not as popular as it had been in the early 1960s, but it continued to draw a devoted following among a small segment of the listening audience. Few bluegrass artists had major-label recording contracts, but many prospered on small labels that served this niche market, selling records via mail order or at concerts. Bluegrass festivals continued to serve the faithful, drawing spirited crowds, many eager to hear both traditional and progressive bluegrass. The 1990s also saw the emergence of a new bluegrass star—fiddler, singer, and bandleader Alison Krauss—one of the few major female stars the genre has ever seen. Her popularity, based on her unique cross of bluegrass, pop, and country elements, retained enough of the classic bluegrass sound to please purists while feeling fresh and contemporary enough to draw new listeners. Her success, and the continuing, if limited, popularity of bluegrass in the 1990s was a strong indication that the genre was alive and well, a healthy mix of tradition and innovation that made it one of the United States' most unique musical traditions.

—Timothy Berg

FURTHER READING:

The Country Music Foundation, editors. *Country: The Music and the Musicians.* New York, Abbeville Press, 1994.

Flatt, Lester, Earl Scruggs, and the Foggy Mountain Boys. *The Complete Mercury Sessions.* Mercury Records, 1992.

Malone, Bill C. *Country Music U.S.A.: A Fifty Year History.* Austin, American Folklore Society, University of Texas Press, 1968.

Monroe, Bill. *The Music of Bill Monroe—from 1936-1994.* MCA Records, 1994.

Rosenberg, Neil V. *Bluegrass: A History.* Urbana, University of Illinois Press, 1985.

Smith, Richard D. *Bluegrass: An Informal Guide.* A Cappella Books, 1995.

The Stanley Brothers. *The Complete Columbia Stanley Brothers.* Sony Music, 1996.

Various Artists. *The Best of Bluegrass, Vol. I.* Mercury Records, 1991.

Willis, Barry R., et al., editors. *America's Music—Bluegrass: A History of Bluegrass Music in the Words of Its Pioneers.* Pine Valley Music, 1997.

Wright, John. *Traveling the High Way Home: Ralph Stanley and the World of Traditional Bluegrass Music.* Urbana, University of Illinois Press, 1995.

Blues

Blues music emerged in the early twentieth century in the United States as one of the most distinctive and original of American musical forms. It is an African American creation and, like its distant relative jazz, blues music is one of the great contributions to American popular culture. Blues music encompasses a wide variety of styles, including unique regional and stylistic variations, and it lends itself

Blues musician Muddy Waters (left) and his band.

well to both individual and group performance. As a cultural expression, blues music is often thought of as being sad music, a form to express the hardships endured by African Americans. And, while it certainly can be that, the blues is also a way to deal with that hardship and celebrate good times as well as bad. Thus, in its long history throughout the twentieth century, blues music has found resonance with a wide variety of people. Although it is still largely an African American art form, the style has had a good number of white performers as well. The audience for blues has also been wide, indicating the essential truths that often lie at the heart of this musical form.

The origins of blues music are not easily traced due to its largely aural tradition, which often lacks written sources, and because there are no blues recordings prior to about 1920. Thus, tracing its evolution out of the distant past is difficult. Still, some of the influences that make up blues music are known. Blues music originated within the African American community in the deep South. Elements of the blues singing style, and the use of primitive stringed instruments, can be traced to the griot singers of West Africa. Griot singers acted as storytellers for their communities, expressing the hopes and feelings of its members through song. African musical traditions undoubtedly came with the large numbers of African slaves brought to the United States in the eighteenth and nineteenth centuries. The mixture of

African peoples who made up the slave population in the South allowed for a mixture of African song and musical styles as well. Those styles would eventually evolve into the blues as the hardships endured by the freed slaves and their descendants continued well into the twentieth century.

The style of music now known as the blues emerged in its mature form after the turn of the twentieth century. No one knows who the first singers or musicians were that put this style together into its now familiar form, as the music evolved before the invention of recording technology. As a musical style, the blues is centered around a 12-bar form with three lines of four bars each. And, while it does use standard chords and instrumentation, it is an innovative music known for the off-pitch ''blue notes'' which give the music its deeper feeling. These blue notes are produced by bending tones, and the need to produce these tones made certain instruments key to playing blues music: the guitar, the harmonica, and the human voice. It is a rather informal music, with plenty of room for singers and musicians to express themselves in unique ways. Thus, the music has given the world a wide variety of unique blues artists whose styles are not easily replicated.

Among the earliest blues recordings were those by black female singers in the 1920s. In fact, the entire decade of the 1920s, the first in which blues music was recorded for a commercial market, was dominated by women. Among the most significant were Bessie

Smith, Ma Rainey, Lucille Bogan, Sippie Wallace, Alberta Hunter, Victoria Spivey, and Mamie Smith. Mamie Smith's "Crazy Blues," recorded in 1920, is largely acknowledged as the first blues recording. These singers incorporated a more urban, jazz style into their singing, and they were often backed by some of the great early jazz musicians, including trumpeter Louis Armstrong. The greatest of these early female blues singers were Ma Rainey and Bessie Smith. Smith's version of W. C. Handy's "St. Louis Blues" and Ma Rainey's version of "See See Rider" are among the classics of blues music. Their styles were earthier than many of their contemporaries, and they sang songs about love, loss, and heartbreak, as well as strong statements about female sexuality and power the likes of which have not been seen since in the blues field. The era of the great female blues singers ended with the coming of the Depression in 1929, as record companies made fewer recordings, preferring to focus their attention on white popular singers. Bessie Smith and Ma Rainey were both dead by 1940, and most of the other popular female singers of the decade drifted off into obscurity, although some had brief revivals in the 1960s.

Other blues styles rose to prominence during the 1930s. The dominant form was Mississippi delta blues, a rural form that originated in the delta of northwest Mississippi. The style was dominated by male singers who accompanied themselves on acoustic guitars that could be carried easily from place to place, allowing these musicians to play for the many poor black farming communities in the area. A number of important bluesmen made their living, at least in part, following an itinerant lifestyle playing blues throughout the delta region. Among the most important innovators in the delta blues style were Tommy Johnson, Bukka White, Charley Patton, Son House, and Robert Johnson. All of these musicians made important recordings during the 1930s that have proven highly influential. Some, such as Robert Johnson, achieved almost mythic status. Johnson recorded only several dozen songs before his death in 1938. His apocryphal story of selling his soul to the devil in order to be the best blues musician (related in his song "Cross Road Blues") drew from an image with a long history in African American culture. Although details about Johnson's life are sketchy, stories of his being a poor guitar player, then disappearing for several months and reappearing as one of the best guitarists around, gave credence to the story of his deal with the devil; his murder in 1938 only added to his legend. The delta blues style practiced by Johnson and others became one of the most important blues forms, and one that proved highly adaptable to electric instruments and to blues-rock forms in later years.

While delta blues may have been a dominant style, it was by no means the only blues style around. In the 1930s and early 1940s, a number of important regional styles also evolved out of the early blues forms. Among these were Piedmont style blues and Texas blues. The Piedmont style was also an acoustic guitar-based form practiced on the east coast, from Richmond, Virginia to Atlanta, Georgia. It featured more syncopated finger-picking with the bass strings providing rhythmic accompaniment to the melody which was played on the upper strings. It was often a more up-tempo style, particularly in the hands of such Atlanta-based musicians as Blind Willie McTell and Barbecue Bob. Both incorporated ragtime elements into their playing, making music that was much more light-hearted than the delta blues style. The Texas blues style, played by musicians such as Blind Lemon Jefferson, Huddie Leadbetter ("Leadbelly"), and Alger "Texas" Alexander in the 1920s and 1930s, was closely connected with the delta style. In the 1940s, the

music took on a more up-tempo, often swinging style in the hands of musicians such as T-Bone Walker. In addition to these two styles, other areas such as Memphis, Tennessee, and the west coast, gave rise to their own distinct regional variations on the classic blues format.

With the migration of a large number of African Americans to northern cities during and after World War II, blues music evolved into new forms that reflected the quicker pace of life in these new environments. The formation of new communities in the north led to new innovations in blues music. Two distinct styles emerged, urban blues and electric, or Chicago blues. Urban blues was a more upscale blues style that featured smooth-voiced singers and horn sections that had more in common with jazz and the emerging rhythm and blues style than it did with rural Mississippi delta blues. The urban blues was epitomized by such artists as Dinah Washington, Eddie Vinson, Jimmy Witherspoon, Charles Brown, and even early recordings by Ray Charles.

More influential was the electric, or Chicago blues style, a more direct descendant of the Mississippi delta blues. Although many musicians contributed to its development, none was more important than McKinley Morganfield, known as Muddy Waters. Waters came of age in the Mississippi delta itself, and learned to play in the local acoustic delta blues style. Moving to Chicago in the mid-1940s, Waters played in local clubs at first, but he had a hard time being heard over the din of tavern conversation. To overcome that obstacle, he switched to an electric guitar and amplifier to play his delta blues. His earliest recordings, on Chess Records in 1948, were "I Can't Be Satisfied" and "I Feel Like Going Home," both of which featured Waters on solo electric guitar playing in the delta blues style. Soon, however, Waters began to add more instruments to his sound, including piano, harmonica, drums, bass, and occasionally a second guitar. This arrangement was to become the classic Chicago blues sound. Instead of the plaintive singing of the delta, Muddy Waters and his band transformed the blues into a hard-edged, driving sound, with a strong beat punctuated by boogie-woogie piano stylings, electric lead guitar solos, and over-amplified harmonicas, all of which created a literally electrifying sound. Throughout the 1950s, Muddy Waters recorded a string of great blues songs that have remained among the finest expressions of the blues, including "Hoochie Coochie Man," "I Just Want to Make Love to You," "Mannish Boy," "I'm Ready," and many, many others. Waters's innovations were highly influential, spawning hundreds of imitators, and were so influential in fact that the Chicago blues style he helped pioneer still dominates the blues sound.

Muddy Waters was not alone, however, in creating the great Chicago blues style. A number of great artists coalesced under the direction of Leonard and Phil Chess, two Polish immigrant brothers who started Chess Records in the late 1940s. Operating a nightclub on Chicago's south side, in the heart of the African American community, the Chess brothers saw the popularity of the emerging electric blues sound. They moved into record production shortly thereafter to take advantage of this new market and new sound. Their roster of blues artists reads like a who's who of blues greats. In addition to Muddy Waters, Chess recorded Howlin' Wolf, Lowell Fulson, Sonny Boy Williamson, Little Walter, John Lee Hooker, Sunnyland Slim, Memphis Minnie, and Koko Taylor, as well as a host of lesser names. While each of these performers brought their unique approach to the blues to Chess Records, the label managed to produce a rather coherent sound. The Chess brothers hired blues songwriter and bassist Willie Dixon as their in-house producer, and Dixon supplied many of the songs and supervised the supporting musicians behind each of the Chess blues artists, creating a unique blues sound.

In the 1960s, blues music experienced a wider popularity than ever before. This was due to a number of factors. First, Chicago continued to be an important center for blues music, and the city was host to important performers such as harmonica player Junior Wells, guitarist Buddy Guy, singer Hound Dog Taylor, and Magic Sam. These performers were often seen at blues and folk festivals across the country, bringing the music to new listeners. Secondly, other blues artists rose to national prominence during the decade, spreading the blues sound even further. Most important was Memphis bluesman B.B. King, whose rich voice and stinging guitar sound proved immensely important and influential. Third, the folk revival that occurred among white college students during the early 1960s throughout the North and West revived an interest in all forms of blues, and many of the acoustic bluesmen who first recorded in the 1920s and 1930s were rediscovered and brought back to perform for these new audiences. Notable among these were such performers as Mississippi John Hurt, Mississippi Fred McDowell, and Bukka White. This revival was a conscious attempt on the part of this younger generation to recover authentic folk music as an antidote to the increasing commercialism of American life in the 1950s and 1960s. All of these factors both revived blues music's popularity and influence and greatly extended its audience.

While many of the great blues performers such as Muddy Waters and Howlin' Wolf continued to perform throughout the 1960s and 1970s, the blues and folk revival of the early 1960s spawned a new crop of white blues performers in both the United States and Great Britain. Some performers, such as Paul Butterfield and John Mayall, played in a straightforward blues style taken from the great Chicago blues masters. But the blues also infected its close cousin, rock 'n' roll. English musicians such as the Rolling Stones covered blues classics on their early albums, influencing the development of rock music during the 1960s. In the later years of the decade new bands incorporated the blues into their overall sound, with British bands such as Cream (with guitarist Eric Clapton) and Led Zeppelin foremost among them. Many of these groups not only played Chicago blues classics, but they reached even further back to rework Robert Johnson's delta blues style in such songs as "Stop Breaking Down" (The Rolling Stones), "Crossroads" (Cream), and "Travelling Riverside Blues" (Led Zeppelin). These developments, both in playing in the blues style and in extending its range into rock music, were important innovations in the history of blues music, and popular music more generally, in the 1960s and early 1970s.

After the blues revival of the 1960s, blues music seemed to settle into a holding pattern. While many of the great bluesmen continued to record and perform in the 1970s, 1980s, and beyond, and while there were new performers such as Robert Cray and Stevie Ray Vaughn who found great success in the blues field during the 1980s, many people bemoan the fact that blues has not seen any major developments that have extended the music in new directions. Instead, the Chicago blues sound continues to dominate the blues scene, attracting new performers to the genre, but they seemed to many people to be more like classical musicians, acting as artisans keeping an older form of music alive rather than making new innovations themselves. Despite, or because of, that fact, blues music in the 1990s continued to draw a devoted group of listeners; most major cities have nightclubs devoted to blues music. Buddy Guy, for example, has had great success with his Legends club in Chicago, not far from the old Chess

studios. More corporate enterprises like the chain of blues clubs called "The House of Blues" have also entered the scene to great success. Blues music at the end of the twentieth century may be a largely static musical form, more devoted to the past than the future, but it remains an immensely important cultural form, with its own rich tradition and an influential legacy that has reached well beyond its original core audience.

—Timothy Berg

FURTHER READING:

Charters, Samuel. *The Country Blues.* New York, Da Capo Press, 1988.

Cohn, Lawrence. *Nothing But the Blues: The Music and the Musicians.* New York, Abbeville Press, 1993.

Guralnick, Peter. *Searching for Robert Johnson.* New York, E.P. Dutton, 1989.

Harrison, Daphne Duval. *Black Pearls: Blues Queens of the 1920s.* New Brunswick, New Jersey, Rutgers University Press, 1990.

Jones, Leroy. *Blues People.* New York, Morrow Quill Paperbacks, 1963.

Palmer, Robert. *Deep Blues.* New York, Viking Press, 1995.

Rowe, Mike. *Chicago Blues: The City and the Music.* New York, Da Capo Press, 1988.

Various Artists. *Chess Blues.* MCA Records, 1992.

The Blues Brothers

Jake and Elwood Blues' "mission from God" was to find $5,000 to rescue a Catholic orphanage from closure. Instead, they set a new standard for movie excess and reinvented the careers of many Blues and Soul Music stars, including Aretha Franklin, Cab Calloway, and Ray Charles. In light of the roots of the Blues Brothers Band, this was the true mission of a movie that critics reviled as excessive but has since become a bona fide cult classic.

The Blues Brothers Band was born during a road trip from New York to Los Angeles. *Saturday Night Live* stars Dan Aykroyd and John Belushi discovered a common love for Blues music. They were already cooperating on writing sketches for *Saturday Night Live,* and they took this love of Blues music and developed a warm-up act for the television show. The popularity of The Blues Brothers in the studio gave them the ammunition they needed to convince the producers to put The Blues Brothers on the telecast, and the reaction was phenomenal.

The Blues Brothers soon followed up their television success with a best-selling album (*Briefcase Full of Blues*), a hit single ("Soul Man"), and a promotional tour. Aykroyd, meanwhile, was working with John Landis (director of *National Lampoon's Animal House*) to bring the band to the big screen. The script they came up with began with Jake Blues being released from Joliet State Penitentiary and returning with his brother to the orphanage where they were raised. Learning it is to close unless they can get the $5,000, the brothers decide to put their band back together. Most of the remainder of the first part of the movie focuses on their attempts to find the rest of the band, while the second half's focus is on the band's fundraising efforts.

Throughout the movie the brothers get involved in many car chases, destroying a mall in one scene, and most of the Chicago Police

Dan Aykroyd and John Belushi as *The Blues Brothers*.

Department's cars in another. The film has been universally criticized for the excessive car chases, but this is a part of the cult status *The Blues Brothers* has since earned. Another part of this cult status is influenced by the performers the brothers encounter on their "Mission from God." In cameos, Blues and Soul performers such as James Brown (a gospel preacher), Cab Calloway (the caretaker at the orphanage), Aretha Franklin (wife of a band member), and Ray Charles (a music storekeeper), appear and steal scenes from the Blues Brothers. Audiences especially remember Aretha Franklin's thundering rendition of "Think."

The Blues Brothers opened in 1980 to a mixed reception. The *Animal House* audience loved it, seeing the return of the Belushi they had missed in his other movies. While his character was not Bluto, it was the familiar back-flipping, blues-howling Joliet Jake Blues from *Saturday Night Live*. Critics, however, thought it was terrible, and one went as far as to criticize Landis for keeping Belushi's eyes covered for most of the movie with Jake's trademark Ray Bans. Yet, one of the most lasting impressions of the movie is the "cool look" of the brothers in their black suits, shades, and hats.

We best remember the movie for its music. The band has released albums, both before and after the movie, that cover some of the best of rhythm and blues music. Since Belushi's death, the band has gone on, at times bringing in his younger brother James Belushi in his place. Aykroyd, too, has continued to develop the Blues legacy, with his House of Blues restaurant and nightclub chain, and, with Landis, a sequel movie, *Blues Brothers 2000* (1998). The latter has Elwood Blues (Aykroyd) coming out of prison to learn that Jake is dead. Rehashing part of the plot of the first movie, Elwood puts the

band back together, with John Goodman standing in for Belushi (and Jake Blues) as Mighty Mack. Besides the obligatory car chases, the sequel is much more of a musical, with many of the same Blues stars returning. Aretha Franklin steals the show again, belting out a new version of her signature song, "Respect." The Blues Brothers, as the title of the new movie implies, are alive and well, and ready for the next millennium.

—John J. Doherty

FURTHER READING:

Ansen, David. "Up From Hunger." *Newsweek*. June 30, 1980, 62.

Hasted, Nick. *"Blues Brothers 2000." New Statesman*. May 22, 1998, 47.

Maslin, Jane. "A Musical Tour." *The New York Times*. June 20, 1980, C16.

Blume, Judy (1938—)

Before Judy Blume's adolescent novels appeared, no author had ever realistically addressed the fears and concerns of kids, especially in regard to puberty and interest in the opposite sex. Beginning in 1970 with the perennially popular *Are You There God? It's Me, Margaret*, Blume's fiction honestly depicted the insecurities of changing bodies, peer-group conflicts, and family dynamics. Often Blume has been faulted for constraining her characters to a white, middle-class suburban milieu, but has received far more criticism from the educational establishment for her deadpan prose, and even worse vilification from religious conservatives for what is construed as the titillating nature of her work. Many of the 21 titles she has written consistently appear on the American Library Association's list of "most-challenged" books across the country, but have sold a record 65 million copies in the three decades of her career.

Born in 1938, Blume grew up in a Jewish household in New Jersey that was partly the inspiration for her 1977 book *Starring Sally J. Freedman as Herself*. A New York University graduate, Blume was married to an attorney and had two children when she took a writing course in which an assignment became her first book, *Iggie's House*. Published by Bradbury Press in 1970, the young-adult story dealt with a black family moving into an all-white neighborhood, a timely topic at the time when civil rights laws had eliminated many of the legal barriers segregating communities in America, yet ingrained prejudices remained.

But it was another book of Blume's published that same year, *Are You There God? It's Me, Margaret*, that caused a greater stir. It begins with 11 year-old Margaret's recent move from Manhattan to New Jersey—perhaps her parents' strategy to woo her from her doting grandmother, Sylvia, who is appalled that her son and daughter-in-law, an interfaith marriage, are "allowing" Margaret to choose her own religion. Margaret immediately makes a group of sixth-grade girlfriends at her new school, suffers embarrassment because she has no religious affiliation, buys her first bra and worries when her friends begin menstruating before she does, and prays to God to help her deal with all of this. Only a 1965 novel by Louise Fitzhugh, *The Long Secret*, had dared broach this last concern, and had been met with

Judy Blume

criticism by the literary establishment for what was termed "unsuitable" subject matter for juvenile fiction. Feminist historian Joan Jacobs Brumberg wrote in her 1997 treatise, *The Body Project: An Intimate History of American Girls,* that as a professor she discovered Blume's book was cited as the favorite novel from their adolescence by young women who had come of age in the 1980s. "My students realized that this was not sophisticated literature," Brumberg wrote, "but they were more than willing to suspend that kind of aesthetic judgment because the subject—how a girl adjusts to her sexually maturing body—was treated so realistically and hit so close to home."

Other works with similar themes followed. *Then Again, Maybe I Won't* followed the various life crises of Tony, who feels out of sorts when his Italian-American family moves to a ritzier New Jersey suburb. He fantasizes about the older teen girl next door, is shocked and fearful when he experiences his first nocturnal emission, and makes his way through the social rituals of the new community. Tony discovers that class differences do not always place the more affluent on a higher moral ground. Blume's third young-adult work, *It's Not the End of the World,* opens with the kind of dinner-table debacle that convinces most older children that their parents are headed for divorce court. In sixth-grader Karen's case, her worst fears come true, and the 1972 novel does not flinch from portraying the nasty side of adult breakups. As in many of Blume's other works, parents—even the caring, educated ones of *Are You There God?, Forever,* and *Blubber*—are a source of continual embarrassment.

Blume's 1973 novel *Deenie* is a recommended book for discussion groups about disabilities and diversity. The attractive, slightly egotistical seventh-grader of the title learns she has scoliosis, or curvature of the spine, and overnight becomes almost a disabled person when she is fitted with a drastic, cage-like brace to correct it. Like all of Blume's young-adult works, it also deals with emerging feelings for the opposite sex and tentative explorations into physical pleasure, both solo and participatory. But Blume's 1975 novel *Forever,* written for older teenagers, gave every maturing Blume fan

what they had longed for: a work that wrote honestly about losing one's virginity. *Forever,* Blume admitted, was written after a suggestion from her 14 year-old daughter, Randy. There was a great deal of teen fiction, beginning in the late 1960s, that discussed premarital sex and pregnancy, but the boy was usually depicted as irresponsible, and the female character had made her choices for all the wrong reasons—everything but love—then was punished for it in the end.

In *Forever,* high-schooler Katherine meets Michael at a party, and their dating leads to heavy petting and eventually Katherine's decision to "go all the way." She assumes responsibility for birth control by visiting a doctor and getting a prescription for birth-control pills. *Forever* became the most controversial of all Blume's books, the target of numerous challenges to have it removed from school and public libraries by parents and religious groups, according to the American Library Association, which tracks such attempts to censor reading materials. In some cases the threats have led to free speech protests by students. Blume noted in a 1998 interview on the *Cable News Network* that controversy surrounding her books has intensified rather than abated over the years.

Aside from her racy themes, as an author Blume has been criticized for her matter-of-fact prose, written in the first person and infused with the sardonic wit of the jaded adolescent. Yet Blume felt that it was important that her writing ring true to actual teen speech; anything less would be utterly unconvincing to her readers. Because her works seem to touch such a nerve among kids, many have written to her over the years, at one point to the tune of 2,000 letters per month. The painful confessions, and admissions that Blume's characters and their dilemmas had made such an impact upon their lives, led to the publication of her 1986 non-fiction book, *Letters to Judy: What Your Kids Wish They Could Tell You.* Blume has also written novels for adults—*Wifey* (1978) and *Summer Sisters* (1998).

Though her books have been updated for the 1990s, the dilemmas of her characters are timeless. Ellen Barry, writing in the *Boston Phoenix,* termed *Forever* "the book that made high school sex seem normal." A later edition of the novel, published in the 1990s, included a foreword by the author that urged readers to practice safe sex. Two academics at Cambridge University collected female rite-of-passage stories for their 1997 book *Sweet Secrets: Stories of Menstruation,* and as Kathleen O'Grady told Barry, she and co-author Paula Wansbrough found that women who came of age after 1970 had a much less traumatic menarcheal experience. Naomi Decter, in a 1980 essay for *Commentary,* theorized that "there is, indeed, scarcely a literate girl of novel-reading age who has not read one or more Blume books."

The *Boston Phoenix's* Barry deemed Blume's books "fourth-grade samizdat: the homes were suburban, the moms swore, kids were sometimes mean, there was frequently no moral to the story, and sex was something that people talked about all the time." Barry noted, "Much of that information has seen us safely into adulthood. We all have different parents, and we all had different social-studies teachers, but there was only one sex-ed teacher, and that was Judy Blume." Postmodern feminist magazines such as *Bust, Ben Is Dead* have run articles on the impact of Blume and her books on a generation of women. Chicago's Annoyance Theater, which gained fame with its re-creations of *Brady Bunch* episodes in the early 1990s, staged *What Every Girl Should Know . . . An Ode to Judy Blume* in its 1998 season. Mark Oppenheimer, writing in the *New York Times Book Review* in 1997, noted that though the academic establishment has largely ignored the impact of Blume's books, "when I got to college, there was no author, except Shakespeare, whom more of my peers had read.'' Oppenheimer concluded his essay by reflecting upon the immense social changes that have taken place since Blume's books first attracted notoriety in the 1970s, and that ''in this age of 'Heather Has Two Mommies,' we clearly live after the flood ... We might pause to thank the author who opened the gates.''

—Carol Brennan

FURTHER READING:

Barry, Ellen. ''Judy Blume for President.'' *Boston Phoenix.* May 26, 1998.

Brumberg, Joan Jacobs. *The Body Project: An Intimate History of American Girls.* New York, Random House, 1997.

Decter, Naomi. ''Judy Blume's Children.'' *Commentary.* March, 1980, pp. 65-67.

''Judy Blume.'' *Contemporary Literary Criticism.* Vol. 30. Detroit, Gale Research, 1984.

Oppenheimer, Mark. ''Why Judy Blume Endures.'' *New York Times Book Review.* November 16, 1997, p. 44.

Weidt, Maryann N. ''Judy Blume.'' *Writers for Young Adults,* edited by Ted Hipple. Vol. 1. New York, Scribner's, 1997, pp. 121-131.

Bly, Robert (1926—)

In the early 1990s, mention of the name ''Robert Bly'' conjured up primordial images of half-naked men gathered in forest settings to drum and chant in a mythic quest both for their absent fathers and their submerged assets of boldness and audacity. It was Bly and his best-selling book *Iron John* that catalyzed a new masculinized movement urging males (especially white, middle-class American baby-boomer ones) to rediscover their traditional powers by casting off the expectations of aggressive behavior. Although this search for the inner Wild Man sometimes approached caricature and cliché, satirized in the popular television sitcom *Home Improvement,* the avuncular Bly is universally acknowledged as an avatar of the modern ''male movement'' who draws on mythology and fairy tales to help men heal their wounds by getting in touch with fundamental emotions. *Iron John* had such a powerful impact on American popular culture that it has all but overshadowed Bly's other significant achievements as a poet, translator, and social critic.

Robert Bly was born in Madison, Minnesota on December 23, 1926, the son of Jacob Thomas Bly, a farmer and Alice (Aws) Bly, a courthouse employee. After Navy service in World War II, he spent a year in the premedical program at St. Olaf College in Northfield, Minnesota, before transferring to Harvard University where he graduated with a bachelor's degree in English literature, magna cum laude, in 1950. He later wrote that at Harvard, ''I learned to trust my obsessions,'' so it was natural for him to choose a vocation as a poet after studying a poem by Yeats one day. After a half-year period of solitude in a Minnesota cabin, he moved to New York City, where he eked out a modest existence on the fringes of the Beat movement. He married short-story writer Carol McLean in 1955 and moved back to a Madison farm a year later, after receiving his M.A. from the University of Iowa Writing Workshop. With a Fulbright grant, he spent a year translating Scandinavian poetry in Norway, his ancestral homeland.

Back in Minnesota, far from the centers of the American literary establishment, Bly founded a journal of literature that turned away from the prevailing New Criticism of T. S. Eliot in favor of contemporary poetry that used surreal imagery. The journal, originally named *The Fifties,* underwent a name change with the beginning of each new decade; it has been known as *The Nineties* since 1990, the year Bly published *Iron John.* In 1962, Bly published his first poetry collection, *Silence in the Snowy Fields,* whose images were deeply informed by the rural landscapes of his native Minnesota. Over the years, Bly has also published dozens of translations of works by such luminaries as Knut Hamsun, Federico García Lorca, Pablo Neruda, Rainier Maria Rilke, St. John of the Cross, and Georg Trakl, among others.

As one of the organizers of American Writers Against the Vietnam War, Bly was one of the first writers to mount a strong vocal protest against that conflict. He toured college campuses around the country delivering sharply polemical speeches and poetry that condemned American policy. When his second collection, *The Light Around the Body,* won a National Book Award for poetry in 1968, he used the occasion to deliver an assault against the awards committee and his own publisher, Harper & Row, for contributing taxes to the war effort, and donated his $1000 prize to a draft-resistance organization. His 1973 poetry collection, *Sleepers Joining Hands,* carried forth his anti war stance. During the 1970s, Bly published more than two dozen poetry collections, mostly with small presses, though Harper & Row published three more volumes, *The Morning Glory* (1975), *This Body is Made of Camphor and Gopherwood* (1979), and *This Tree Will Be Here For a Thousand Years* (1979). In 1981, Dial Press published his *The Man in the Black Coat Turns.* Over the years, Bly has continued to publish small collections of poetry; he has long made it a discipline of writing a new poem every morning.

Influenced by the work of Robert Graves, Bly was already demonstrating interest in mythology and pre-Christian religion and wrote in a book review of Graves's work how matriarchal religion had been submerged by the patriarchs, much to the detriment of Western culture. After his divorce in 1979, he underwent a soul-searching identity crisis and began leading men's seminars at a commune in New Mexico. It was during this period that he adopted the Iron John character from a Brothers Grimm fairy tale as an archetype to help men get in touch with their inner powers. Bly recognized that contemporary men were being spiritually damaged by the absence of intergenerational male role models and initiation rituals as found in premodern cultures. As he wrote in his 1990 preface to his best-known work, *Iron John,* ''The grief in men has been increasing steadily since the start of the Industrial Revolution and the grief has reached a depth now that cannot be ignored.'' To critics who responded that Bly was leading an anti-feminist crusade, the author replied by acknowledging and denouncing the dark side of male domination and exploitation. Still, some feminists argued that Bly was advocating a return to traditional gender roles for both men and women, and other critics assailed what they saw as Bly's indiscriminate New Agey salad of tidbits from many traditions. Still, the book was at the top of the *New York Times* best-seller list for ten weeks and stayed on the list for more than a year.

In 1996, Vintage Books published Bly's *The Sibling Society,* in which Bly warns that our dismantling of patriarchies and matriarchies has led to a society of confused, impulsive siblings. ''People don't bother to grow up, and we are all fish swimming in a tank of half-adults,'' he wrote in the book's preface, calling for a reinvention of shared community. Bly's collaboration with psychologist Marion Woodman on workshops integrating women's issues into the *Iron John* paradigm led to the publication of a jointly written book, *The Maiden King: The Reunion of Masculine and Feminine* (1998).

—Edward Moran

FURTHER READING:

Bly, Robert. *Iron John.* New York, Vintage Books, 1990.

———. *The Light Around the Body,* New York, Harper & Row, 1968.

———. *The Man in the Black Coat Turns.* New York, Dial, 1981.

———. *The Morning Glory.* New York, Harper & Row, 1975.

———. *The Sibling Society.* New York, Vintage Books, 1996.

———. *Silence in the Snowy Fields.* New York, Harper & Row, 1962.

———. *Sleepers Joining Hands.* New York, Harper & Row, 1973.

———. *This Body is Made of Camphor and Gopherwood.* New York, Harper & Row, 1979.

———. *This Tree Will Be Here For a Thousand Years.* New York, Harper & Row, 1979.

Bly, Robert and Marion Woodman. *The Maiden King: The Reunion of Masculine and Feminine.* New York, Holt, 1998.

Jones, Richard, and Kate Daniels, editors. *Of Solitude and Silence: Writings on Robert Bly.* Boston, Beacon Press, 1981.

Nelson, Howard. *Robert Bly: An Introduction to the Poetry.* New York, Columbia University Press, 1984.

Board Games

Board games have been around for thousands of years. Some of the oldest games are some of the most popular, including chess and checkers. Backgammon dates back at least to the first century C.E. when the Roman Emperor Claudius played it. Chess probably had its origin in Persia or India, over 4,000 years ago. Checkers was played as early as 1400 B.C.E. in Egypt. In the United States, board games have become deeply embedded in popular culture, and their myriad forms and examples in this country serve as a reflection of American tastes and attitudes. Major producers such as Parker Brothers and Milton Bradley have made fortunes by developing hundreds of games promising entertainment for players of all ages.

Success at many games is for the most part a matter of luck; the spin of the wheel determines the winner in The Game of Life. In fact, everything in life, from the career one chooses to the number of children one has, is reduced to spins on a wheel. Most games, though, involve a combination of problem solving and luck. In the game of Risk, opponents attempt to conquer the world. Although the final outcome is closely tied to the throw of dice, the players must use strategy and wisdom to know when to attack an opponent. In the popular game of Clue, a player's goal is to be the first to solve a murder by figuring out the murderer, the weapon, and the room where the crime took place. But the dice also have a bearing on how quickly players can position themselves to solve the crime. Scrabble tests the ability of competitors to make words out of wooden tiles containing

A family plays the board game Sorry.

the letters of the alphabet. Although luck plays a role, since players must select their tiles without knowing what letter they bear, the challenge of building words from random letters has made this challenging game a favorite of many over the years.

One of the most enduring board games of this century is Monopoly, the invention of which is usually attributed to Charles Darrow in 1933, although that claim has been challenged by some who contend that the game existed before Darrow developed it. The strategy of the game is to amass money to buy property, build houses and hotels, and ultimately bankrupt other players. One charming feature of the game is its distinctive metal game pieces, which include a dog, a top hat, an iron, and a wheelbarrow. Darrow named the streets in his game after streets in Atlantic City, New Jersey, where he vacationed. Initially, he sold handmade sets to make money for himself while he was unemployed during the Great Depression. In 1935, Parker Brothers purchased the rights to the game. From this small beginning, the game soon achieved national even international fame. Monopoly continues to be one of the most popular board games, and a World Championship attracts participants from all parts of the globe each year.

Most board games are designed for small groups, usually two to four players. But some games are popular at parties. Twister is unusual because the game board is placed on the floor. Players step on colored spots. As the game progresses, competitors must step over and twist around other players in order to step from one colored spot to another on the game board. Trivial Pursuit, a popular game of the 1980s, pits players or groups of players against each other as they answer trivia questions under certain categories such as geography, sports, and literature. The game was so popular that it resulted in various "spin-offs," such as a version designed especially for baby boomers.

Television and the movies have done more to spawn new board games than probably anything else. When children flocked to see Flash Gordon serials at local Saturday matinees in the 1930s people saw the market for Flash Gordon merchandise including a Flash Gordon board game.

Television became the main source of inspiration for board games beginning in the 1950s. A TV series might only last a year or two, but if it was popular with children, related games would inevitably be developed. Cowboy shows produced games about Roy Rogers, the Lone Ranger and Tonto, the Rifleman, and Hopalong Cassidy.

Astronauts replaced cowboys as heroes during the space race of the 1960s. Even before the space race, children played with the game based on the *Tom Corbett* TV show. *Men into Space* was a TV series known for its realistic attempt to picture what initial space travel would be like. A game with rocket ships and cards containing space missions and space dangers allowed the players to "travel into space" as they watched the TV show. As space travel progressed, so did TV shows. *Star Trek, Buck Rogers, Battlestar Galactica,* and *Space 1999* all resulted in games that children put on their Christmas lists or asked for on their birthdays.

Games did not have to involve heroes. Every popular TV show seemed to produce a new game that was actually designed to keep people watching the shows and, of course, the commercials. *The Beverly Hillbillies, Seahunt, Mork and Mindy, Gilligan's Island, The Honeymooners, The Six Million Dollar Man, Charlie's Angels, The Partridge Family,* and *Happy Days* are only a few of literally dozens of shows that inspired board games. Many games were based on TV game shows such as *The Price Is Right* or *The Wheel of Fortune,* replicating the game show experience in the home. While the popularity of some of these games quickly waned as audience interest in the particular show declined, they were wildly popular for short periods of time.

Movies inspired the creation of board games in much the same way as television shows. The *Star Wars* trilogy has produced numerous games. One combined Monopoly with Star Wars characters and themes. The movie *Titanic* generated its own game, marketed in 1998 after the success of the motion picture. The duration of these games' popularity also rested on the popularity of the corresponding movies.

Comic strips also provided material for new board games. A very popular comic strip for many years, *Little Orphan Annie* came alive to children in the Little Orphan Annie's Treasure board game, which was produced in 1933. Children could also play with Batman, Winnie the Pooh, and Charlie Brown and Snoopy through board games.

Many aspects of life have been crafted into board games. Careers, Payday, The Game of Life, and Dream Date were designed to help children think about things they would do as they grew up. But the most enduring life-based games are war games, such as Battleship, Risk, and Stratego, which have been popular from one generation to the next. In the 1960s Milton Bradley produced the American Heritage series, a set of four games based on American wars. This was done during the Civil War centennial celebrations that drew people to battlefield sights. Civil War was a unique game that feaured movers shaped like infantry, cavalry, and artillery. Children moved troops by

rail and fought battles in reenacting this war. Broadsides was based on the War of 1812. Ships were strategically positioned for battle on the high seas and in harbors. Dog Fight involved World War I bi-planes that were maneuvered into battle. Players flew their planes in barrel rolls and loops to shoot down the enemy squadrons. Hit the Beach was based on World War II.

While entertainment remained the goal of most games, some were meant to educate as well. Meet the Presidents was an attractive game in the 1960s. The game pieces looked like silver coins. Even when the game was not being played, the coins served as showpieces. Each coin portrayed a president of the United States on one side and information about him on the other side. Players had to answer questions about the presidents, based on the information on the coins. The Game of the States taught geography and other subjects. As players moved trucks from state to state, they learned the products of each state and how to get from one state to another.

Board games have continued to have a place in popular culture, even in an electronic age. Though computer versions of many popular board games, including Monopoly, offer special effects and graphics that traditional board games cannot, people continue to enjoy sitting around a table playing board games. Seemingly, they never tire of the entertaining, friendly banter that accompanies playing board games with friends and family.

—James H. Lloyd

FURTHER READING:

Bell, Robert Charles. *Board and Table Games from Many Civilizations,* rev. ed. New York, Dover Publications, 1979.

Costello, Matthew J. *The Greatest Games of All Time.* New York, John Wiley, 1991.

The History Channel. *History of Toys and Games.* Videocassette set. 100 minutes.

Polizzi, Rick, and Fred Schaefer. *Spin Again: Board Games from the Fifties and Sixties.* San Francisco, Chronicle Books, 1991.

Provenzo, Asterie Baker, and Eugene F. Provenzo, Jr. *Favorite Board Games that You Can Make and Play.* New York, Dover, 1990.

Sackson, Sid. *The Book of Classic Board Games.* Palo Alto, Klutz Press, 1991.

University of Waterloo, Ontario, Canada. "Museum and Archive of Games." http://www.ahs.uwaterloo.ca/~museum/index.html#samples. February 1999.

Whitehill, Bruce. *Games: American Boxed Games and Their Makers, 1822-1992: With Values.* Radnor, Penn, Wallace-Homestead Book Co., 1992.

Boat People

With the images of Vietnam still fresh on their minds, Americans in the mid-1970s were confronted with horrifying news footage of half-starved Vietnamese refugees reaching the shores of Hong Kong, Malaysia, Thailand, Indonesia, and the Philippines on small, makeshift boats. Many of the men, women, and children who survived the perilous journey across the South China Sea were rescued by passing ships. Over one million boat people from Cambodia, Laos, and Vietnam were eventually granted asylum in the United States and several other countries. Most were lost at sea, thousands of others perished of disease, starvation, and dehydration, or were murdered by pirates. This final chapter in the history of the Vietnam War would live in the collective memory of an entire generation. Personal accounts of the refugees' hardships and courage would inspire countless books, movies, websites, documentaries, magazine articles, and television news reports in the United States. For years to come, the boat people would serve as an enduring testimony to the tragic aftermath of America's defeat in Vietnam.

The Vietnamese exodus began after the fall of Saigon in 1975. Many of the survivors would languish for almost twenty years in refugee camps throughout Asia, awaiting asylum, exile, or forced repatriation. Those boat people who escaped Vietnam in the late 1980s were labeled ''economic migrants'' and not granted refugee status. Finally in 1989, an agreement between the United Nations and the Vietnamese government resulted in the ''orderly departure program,'' which forcibly returned over 100,000 Vietnamese boat people to their homeland. The agreement in Geneva stipulated that the boat people were not to be punished for attempting to escape. By the late 1990s, another 1.6 million boat people had been resettled in various countries around the world.

The term ''boat people'' acquired special significance in the U.S. context during the 1980s and 1990s, when hundreds of thousands of Cubans and Haitians journeyed across the Caribbean Sea in homemade rafts and unseaworthy boats seeking political asylum in the United States. In the years following the 1959 Revolution, the number of Cubans attempting the perilous journey to freedom across the Florida straits on boats and rafts remained relatively small. But in 1980, after several thousand Cubans stormed the Peruvian Embassy in Havana seeking asylum, Castro temporarily eased restrictions on emigration and prompted a flotilla of refugees headed towards Florida's shores. The Mariel boat lift resulted in the mass exodus of an estimated 125,000 Cuban refugees. For the first time in history, Americans experienced a flood of boat people first-hand, watching the events unfold on national television. As thousands of arriving Cubans were greeted by relatives living in exile, the American public responded with increasing fear to the sensational media accounts of prison and insane asylum inmates deported along with the refugees. Later studies would show that the image of the ''Marielitos'' popularized by the press was inaccurate, as only about 1 percent of the Mariel refugees had criminal pasts. But President Jimmy Carter, who had initially welcomed the immigrants, responded by imposing stiff penalties on any vessels returning to U.S. waters carrying Cuban refugees. Boats were impounded and their owners fined or imprisoned. In 1984, Cuba and the United States reached an agreement that capped the flow of boat people.

The agreement was short-lived, however, as economic conditions worsened in Cuba and another wave of about 35,000 Cuban boat people, or ''rafters,'' hit Florida's shores in the 1990s. The U.S. government, in a precedent-breaking decision, refused to grant the Cuban rafters entry. Instead, they set up a tent city in the military base at Guantanamo Bay, Cuba, where thousands of rafters awaited their fate. Those who could prove that they were political refugees fearing death or persecution by the Cuban government were eventually granted asylum and relocated in the United States. Most were absorbed into the Cuban exile community in Miami. Others were sent back to Cuba, where they faced an uncertain future.

Between the late 1970s and mid-1990s, over 100,000 Haitian boat people also sought asylum in the United States. In 1981, President Reagan issued an Executive Order directing the U.S. Coast Guard to intercept Haitian boat people at sea. The majority were labeled economic migrants and repatriated. When President Aristide was ousted in the 1991 coup, political repression and economic hardships increased in Haiti, prompting another exodus. The U.S. Naval Base in Guantanamo Bay again served as a screening facility for boat people seeking refuge in the United States. Most of the 34,000 Haitians interdicted at sea between 1991 and 1992 were taken to Guantanamo and repatriated. Many of those who were granted permission to stay settled in a section of Miami, Florida, that came to be known as ''Little Haiti.''

As late twentieth-century Americans (particularly in Florida) witnessed the first large-scale migration into the United States to occur via make-shift boats, rafts, and inner tubes, they greeted the boat people from neighboring Caribbean countries with both hostility and pity. In Miami, particularly, newspapers carried almost daily reports of bodies washed ashore or emaciated Cubans and Haitians picked up at sea by the U.S. Coast Guard or by volunteer pilots with the Cuban-American organization, Brothers to the Rescue. Popular reaction to the U.S. government's policies towards boat people was also mixed: public outcries alternately charged U.S. government officials with racism, cruelty, or laxity. But one thing was certain: the phenomenon had altered America's—particularly Miami's—demographics forever. It had also added new ingredients to the American cultural stew, as Cuban and Haitian cuisine, art, literature, and music would continue to gain popularity around the country.

—Myra Mendible

FURTHER READING:

Freeman, James M. *Changing Identities: Vietnamese Americans 1975-1995*. Boston, Allyn & Bacon, 1995.

Gardner, Mary. *Boat People: A Novel*. Athens, U of Georgia P, 1997.

Leyva, Josefina. *Freedom Rafters*. Trans. by Dorothy J. Smith. Coral Gables, Florida, Editorial Ponce de Leon, 1993.

Stepick, Alex, and Nancy Foner. *Pride Against Prejudice: Haitians in the United States*. Boston, Allyn & Bacon, 1998.

''Vietnamese Boatpeople Connection.'' http://www.boatpeople.com. December 1998.

Bob and Ray

Bob Elliott (1923—) and Ray Goulding (1922-1990) brought a new kind of low-key satire to radio in the late 1940s. They developed such memorable characters as the drawling cowboy Tex and Wally Ballou, ''radio's highly regarded and totally inept'' remote broadcast reporter who invariably began his reports in mid-sentence, having forgotten to turn on his microphone. Wally often spoke of his wife ''Hulla Ballou'' and son ''Little Boy Ballou.'' Another popular

Bob Elliot (left) and Ray Goulding

creation was Mary McGoon, a quirky talk show hostess who was a combination of Mary Margaret McBride (the First Lady of radio talk shows from 1934 to 1954) and Julia Childs, the radio and television chef.

The creative pair also set their satiric stun guns on popular long-running radio shows of their day, running their version, *One Feller's Family,* as a parody of the popular program *One Man's Family.* Also popular was their *Mary Backstayge, Noble Wife,* a soap opera sketch that spoofed the daytime radio series *Mary Noble, Backstage Wife.* Other vehicles for their offbeat wit included such pseudo programs as *The Transatlantic Bridge, Robin Hood of Sherman Forest, Mr. District Defender,* and *Tales Well Calculated to Keep You in Anxiety. Widen Your Horizons* was a ''self-help'' program on which experts would explain how to look up names in a telephone directory or how to put salt in salt shakers.

Bob and Ray began their professional career at Boston radio station WHDH on an early morning talk and music program. Bob was the show's host and Ray the announcer, with each playing a variety of characters in different voices. All of the shows ended with their trademark salutations, ''Write if you get work'' and ''Hang by your thumbs.'' They added more fans with the show *Matinee with Bob and Ray,* which preceded the Red Sox baseball games and filled the afternoon with their improvised comedy on rain-out days.

After their on-air shenanigans became the talk of Boston, NBC executives offered them a network radio show of their own in 1953. After two years in the Saturday at 8:00 p.m. time slot, during the 1955-1956 season they moved to the Mutual network for a Monday to Friday program at 5:00 p.m. When television took its toll on network

radio, Bob and Ray appeared frequently on local stations in Boston and New York as well as on National Public Radio.

They were also guest stars on a number of television variety shows, including *The Colgate Comedy Hour* (1952) and *The Ed Sullivan Show* (1955). In the fall of 1951, the pair began performing on their own NBC television show in a 15 minute format, Monday through Friday at 7:15 p.m. The show also featured comic actress Audrey Meadows, who played the part of Linda Lovely in their ongoing spoof of soap operas. They hosted a half-hour NBC show featuring Cloris Leachman, playing the part of Mary Backstayge, during the summer of 1952 and returned to the quarter-hour format in the fall in a show known as *Club Embassy* or *Club Time,* again featuring Audrey Meadows. Critics were almost unanimous in the opinion that the satirists' unique brand of wit played better on radio than television.

In 1970 Bob and Ray wrote and performed a two-man stage production, *The Two of Us,* which had a long run on Broadway as well as at various regional theaters and colleges throughout the United States. In the 1970s the pair worked at radio station WOR, along with their television guest and stage appearances. Their voices became known to millions as Burt and Ernie Piel on Piel's beer commercials.

Bob and Ray were forced to retire in the late 1980s due to the illness of Ray, who died of a heart attack in 1990. Bob continues to make television talk show appearances and is a frequent guest speaker at college seminars and at conferences about the ''Golden Age of Radio.''

—Benjamin Griffith

FURTHER READING:

Brooks, Tim, and Earl Marsh. *The Complete Directory to Prime Time TV Shows, 1946 to Present.* New York, Ballantine, 1981.

Buxton, Frank, and Bill Owen. *The Big Broadcast: 1920-1950.* New York, Viking, 1972.

Lackmann, Ron. *Same Time . . . Same Station: An A-Z Guide to Radio from Jack Benny to Howard Stern.* New York, Facts on File, 1996.

The Bobbsey Twins

The very term ''Bobbsey Twins'' has become a kind of slang abbreviation for earnest wholesomeness and do-gooder duos. Generations of American children have grown up with the fictional family of Nan, Bert, Flossie, and Freddie, but the 115 books, dating back to 1904, have always reflected societal changes over the decades. Still, even the modern *Bobbsey Twins* books showcase a perfect world of doting parents, unlimited access to material goods, and just enough adventure and drama to refresh appreciation for the comfort and safety of home and hearth. The books sold millions of copies and were still found on library shelves in America almost a century after their initial debut.

The Bobbsey Twins series was just one of several extremely successful works for children written by the Stratemeyer Syndicate. Founder Edward Stratemeyer had once ghostwritten some of the popular "Horatio Alger" stories that fictionalized the myth of the American dream for millions of nineteenth-century young-adult readers, tales in which a poor boy prospers fantastically through hard work, honesty, and the American free-enterprise system. The Stratemeyer Syndicate's first series was launched in 1899 with *The Rover Boys,* and would later include *The Hardy Boys* and *Nancy Drew* books. All were penned in accordance with a strict plot formula by writers-for-hire contracted to the Syndicate, most of whom earned about $125 per book. The Southern-sounding Laura Lee Hope was the collective pen name for *The Bobbsey Twins* series, which began in 1904 with *The Bobbsey Twins: Or, Merry Days Indoors and Out* (The work was revised in 1961 and retitled *The Bobbsey Twins of Lakeport*).

The Bobbsey plots revolved around away-from-home adventures, the purchase of a miniature railroad or Shetland pony, the mysterious disappearance of a toy, or other mishaps or acquisitions. The twins of the title were the two sets of Bobbsey offspring: older twins Nan and Bert and their juniors Flossie and Freddie. The older duo are dark-haired and serious, while their siblings are mischievous and blonde; the genetic discrepancy is, of course, never explained in the plot. The family lives in Lakeport, perhaps somewhere in the East or Upper Midwest, since it snows in the winter and Mr. Bobbsey owns a lumber business on the shore of Lake Metoka. Mrs. Bobbsey is homemaker, and is assisted in her duties around "their large, rambling house" by an African-American servant, Dinah; Dinah's husband Sam is first a handyman there and later an employee of the lumber business. Though the books always start off in Lakeport, often the family travels to visit relatives in different locales—sometimes a farm, in other instances the seashore. Mr. Bobbsey is usually available to travel with them, despite the demands of his business, and Mrs. Bobbsey exemplifies the patient, cool-headed, but warm-hearted American middle-class mom. Academics have explained the appeal of *The Bobbsey Twins* by citing how the books tap into Sigmund Freud's theory of "family romance," in which an imaginative child creates a substitute family, replete with a more loving set of parents and an elevated economic status.

Like the other so-called "tots" series from the Stratemeyer Syndicate, in *The Bobbsey Twins* books "the predominant image is of cheerful, contented families leading lives bounded on all sides by security and abundance," wrote Deidre Johnson in *Edward Stratemeyer and the Stratemeyer Syndicate.* The Bobbsey Twins are characters that "seem surrounded by a special radiance, blessed by fortune . . . They are born into lives that guarantee them three things: emotional security, or being loved by family; material bounty, or having and perpetually receiving good things; and continual activity, or doing interesting things and visiting different places," noted Johnson.

What is lacking in *The Bobbsey Twins* series is any form of strife or misfortune. Nan and Bert eagerly take daily responsibility for the younger twins, and never inflict cruelty upon them. This seems to be their only real duty; the vast amount of leisure time for the children is never constricted by piano lessons, dance classes, or onerous household chores. The Great Depression did not occur in the series, nor do either World War. Even when typical juvenile carelessness gets a Bobbsey child into trouble, he or she is only mildly reprimanded and never punished. Predominant in the pages of all the books is wholesome food, warm clothing, wonderful toys, and—every child's dream—surprise presents for no reason at all. There are detailed descriptions of celebratory meals, such as Flossie and Freddie's birthday soiree,

complete with creamed chicken, mashed potatoes, and dual cakes. "A more than adequate income makes their lifestyles and vacations possible and shelters them from the type of misfortune others face," wrote Johnson about the Bobbseys in her book. Sometimes they meet children who live in far less fortunate circumstances—orphans, or children who have to work and are treated severely—but always inflict their own charity and ingenuous solutions upon them.

Up until the 1930s, *The Bobbsey Twins* plots were simple adventure stories, mostly concerned with vacations, but the family began becoming embroiled in more complex plots in the 1930s with *The Bobbsey Twins Solve a Mystery* and *The Bobbsey Twins at Mystery Mansion,* among others. By 1937, the series had sold over five million copies, and their popularity continued unabated in the postwar baby boom of the 1950s. The Stratemeyer Syndicate saw fit to revise the older works in the 1950s, books whose text and tone "contributed to sustaining racial and ethnic prejudice in their stock presentations of blacks, Jews, Italians, Irish, and other non-WASP groups," explained Carol Billman in her 1986 book *The Secret of the Stratemeyer Syndicate: Nancy Drew, The Hardy Boys, and the Million Dollar Fiction Factory.*

When Edward Stratemeyer died in 1930, his daughter Harriet Stratemeyer Adams took over the Syndicate. *The Bobbsey Twins* books were published by Grosset & Dunlap after 1912, and early manuscripts and related materials from this era were donated to the New York Public Library for its Rare Books and Manuscripts Division in 1993.

—Carol Brennan

FURTHER READING:

Billman, Carol. *The Secret of the Stratemeyer Syndicate: Nancy Drew, The Hardy Boys, and the Million Dollar Fiction Factory.* New York, Ungar, 1986.

Century, Douglas. "Herman Melville . . . T.S. Eliot . . . Franklin W. Dixon?" *New York.* September 6, 1993, 23.

Johnson, Deidre. *Edward Stratemeyer and the Stratemeyer Syndicate.* New York, Twayne, 1993.

Bobby Socks

Bobby socks (or bobby sox) are ankle-length socks, usually cotton, worn since the 1930s by children, teens, and adult women. By 1935, many teenage girls wore them to school with saddle shoes (two-tones) or loafers, and stores marketed them as campus fashion. They gained widespread fame in 1943 when national media equated them with teenage girls, especially screaming fans of Frank Sinatra, and claimed that ordinary ankle socks instantly became bobby sox when teenagers bought them. *Newsweek* initially defined "bobby soxers" as female juvenile delinquents with loose morals, but the prevailing stereotype declared them silly, uncontrolled swooners who loved to gab on the phone and buy the latest records and fashions. Teenage girls continued to wear the socks, but did not define themselves as "bobby soxers."

—Kelly Schrum

FURTHER READING:

"Combating the Victory Girl." *Newsweek.* March 6, 1944, 88, 91.

Kahn, E. J., Jr. "Profiles Phenomenon: II. The Fave, the Fans, and the Fiends." *The New Yorker.* November 2, 1946, 35-48.

Palladino, Grace. *Teenagers: An American History.* New York, Basic, 1996.

"What Is a Bobby Sock?" *New York Times Magazine.* March 5, 1944, 23.

Bochco, Steven (1943—)

Although he wrote feature film screenplays early in his career, Steven Bochco has made his mark as the creator and producer of successful television series, thus having an impact upon a larger audience than most filmmakers can claim. With such groundbreaking series as *Hill Street Blues, L.A. Law,* and *N.Y.P.D. Blue,* Bochco has managed to up the ante on televised social realism and, at the same time, he has pushed the envelope on the broadcast treatment of sexuality. Bochco's series are noted for well-written scripts featuring a variety of characters portrayed by an expert ensemble cast. The storylines and subplots, overlapping many individual episodes, feature sharp twists and quirky mood swings, from gritty confrontation and sexual banter to unexpected acts of violence. A moment of macabre humor may be juxtaposed with a tender exchange between two characters, followed by the sudden demise of another character. In a medium rife with programming of a bland, repetitious, and formulaic nature, Bochco has distinguished himself by experimenting with fresh concepts. Although, inevitably, some of these ventures— *Cop Rock,* for example—have not proven as successful as others, Bochco's successes have put him at the top of his field. Clear-eyed about the reality that television is a medium whose primary purpose is to advertise, Bochco has nonetheless done work of considerable sophistication which, in turn, has helped pave the way for other producers of adventuresome programming.

Born Steven Ronald Bochco in New York City on December 16, 1943, he was the son of a Russian immigrant who had been a child prodigy on the violin. Growing up with his sister in a tough West Side neighborhood left its mark on young Bochco. In a sense, the violence around him both provided Bochco with a drive to succeed and, ultimately, provided him with the inspiration for the art and craft with which he would do so. An indifferent student, he nevertheless obtained a scholarship at New York University. Within a year, however, he had transferred to the distinguished theater department at Carnegie Institute of Technology (now Carnegie-Mellon University). The winner of an MCA writing fellowship, Bochco eventually secured a summer job at Universal Studios, where he was in charge of other budding screenwriters. This led, following his 1966 graduation from college, to a job assisting the head of Universal's story department. Although Bochco's name would eventually appear in the credits of a respected science fiction film, *Silent Running* (1972), he has focused most of his energies, and earned his greatest rewards, toiling in the vineyards of television. After a variegated apprenticeship, Bochco began writing scripts for the NBC series *The Name of*

the Game in 1968. Within a few years, he was made story editor on the highly popular Peter Falk series *Columbo.*

After *Columbo* Bochco was associated with a number of series and projects which were nowhere near as successful as the Falk mysteries had been. But on one of these shows—*Vampire* (1979)— Bochco served as executive producer and co-writer with Michael Kozoll, who would soon prove to be a most significant collaborator. The following year, the two men were invited by Fred Silverman, president of NBC, to create a police show. The pair accepted the challenge, provided they would be allowed to devise something other than just another run-of-the-mill cop program. Taking as their inspiration a piece of public television cinema verité called *The Police Tapes,* Bochco and Kozoll came up with *Hill Street Blues,* one of the most groundbreaking and successful shows in television history. The main concept, as Bochco later explained to one reporter, was for *Hill Street Blues* "to be a show about people who happen to be cops, as opposed to cops who, in some small corner of their lives, happen to be people." Furthermore, the co-creators saw their show as an expression of their "strong belief in the cop as hero . . . in the sense of an individual performing a thankless task under extreme physical and emotional stress, with no reward to speak of—social, psychological, or financial. . . ."

In casting the new series, Bochco called upon talented troupers he had known in his days at college, such as Charles Haid, Bruce Weitz, and Barbara Bosson (then Mrs. Bochco). Although the show would make stars out of some of its leading players, such as Daniel J. Travanti, *Hill Street Blues* was an ensemble piece roaming from character to character and from plot to plot—most of them overlapping several episodes. In addition to this sense of a free-floating slice of life, what distinguished *Hill Street Blues* from other cop shows— and set the mold for future Bochco enterprises—was an edgy, off-beat tone, a mixture of quirky characters, raw social realism, gallows humor, and frank sexuality (at least, the verbal expression thereof). At the climax of the opening episode, a moment of comedy is followed immediately by the shocking and vicious gunning-down of two of the leading characters.

Hill Street Blues, an MTM production, soared in the ratings and cleaned up at the Emmys for years. It set a high standard for television series drama, and developed a gritty, quirky tone which is still in evidence not only on the tube but in the big-screen projects of Quentin Tarantino and other filmmakers. In 1985, Bochco left MTM under a cloud, though it was not clear whether his differences with the production company had been budgetary—as MTM claimed—or personal, as Bochco asserted. In any event, Bochco re-emerged at Twentieth-Century Fox with a new collaborator, Terry Louise Fisher, a former deputy district attorney and a writer-producer for *Cagney and Lacey.* The result of their creativity was *L.A. Law,* which debuted on NBC in 1986. Although a series about a law firm was by its nature less prone to portray violence than one about a police precinct, *L.A. Law* displayed all the Bochco hallmarks, from an ensemble cast (including Michael Tucker, another old college buddy) and sophisticated dialogue, to high drama and low black comedy. In the opening moments of the premiere episode, a recently deceased lawyer lies face down in his take-out dinner, while the surviving attorneys argue over who shall inherit his office. Once again, a controversial but highly successful, award-winning series was born.

Whatever one's assessment of his products, credit must be given to Bochco for following up *Hill Street Blues* and *L.A. Law* with series concepts that could not be accused of being just more doctor or cop shows. *Doogie Howser, M.D.* (1989), about a teenage surgeon, was inspired by Bochco's father's early years as a child prodigy. *Doogie* ran successfully for several seasons, but the fate of *Cop Rock,* a serious police show with musical numbers, was another story. This 1990s drama was short-lived and, for once, it seemed that Bochco had finally gone too far . . . out. Nevertheless, he has continued to stretch himself and experiment with the conventions of television. Much controversy was aroused when it was announced that Bochco's newest series, *N.Y.P.D. Blue*—created with David Milch—would attempt to reclaim for network television some of the large audience lost to cable by purposefully pushing the envelope of language, sex (i.e., partial nudity), and violence past the commonly accepted broadcast norms and closer to the look and feel of R-rated movies. When it finally debuted on ABC, *N.Y.P.D. Blue* proved to be exactly as advertised, and it has weathered the initial storm of protests to prove itself another durable Bochco success.

—Preston Neal Jones

FURTHER READING:

Moritz, Charles. *Current Biography Yearbook, 1991.* New York, H.W. Wilson Co., 1991.

Body Decoration

Body Decoration is an ancient form of self-expression, which experienced a twentieth-century revival in a variety of forms. The broad category of body decoration, so thoroughly studied by anthropologist Robert Brain and others, includes everything from styles of dress, to cosmetics, to jewelry, to hair dye, to war paint. More specifically, in an American sense, the term refers to the patterned arts of body decoration, such as tattoos or piercing (or even mehndi or branding).

In a number of traditional cultures, body painting exists for an assortment of purposes, from the purely decorative to the ceremonial. Typically, the designs are in a symbolic form that is based on specific cultural or spiritual beliefs. In their American manifestations, however, these designs ordinarily lack a deeply rooted cultural basis. Rather, the symbols are reappropriated by different groups and imbued with new meanings.

Tattoos are one such example, a permanent form of body decoration. For most of the twentieth century, tattooing was a predominately male phenomenon, often accompanying activities considered traditionally male, such as military outings or gang events. Although there were tattoo-devotee subcultures, such as motorcycle gangs, it was not considered an "acceptable" form of adornment by the mainstream American population.

At the end of the 1980s and early 1990s, tattooing experienced a resurgence as a part of the "Generation X" look. American youth, from the working and middle classes, appropriated tattoo markings to symbolize their youth culture. Arm-band and ankle tattoos replaced the older designs usually sported by military men, such as sailors, whose tattoos of mermaids and anchors were well-known during the earlier part of the century.

This subculture, not unlike others, utilized fashion as an outward manifestation or symbol of their identity. In 1991, the term "Generation X" was used by Douglas Copeland to describe "Forty-six million Americans between 18 and 29 [who are] generally blase and bitter over problems created or made worse by their parents, some seventy-two million baby-boomers." Although Copeland's classification was disputed by some, the 1990s was seen by others as "the age of diminished expectations," with a social climate of racism, skyrocketing divorce rates, increased acceptance of social and sexual deviance (as seen on talk shows) and higher rates of unemployment for the college educated. Many of these social factors are similar to the environment in London which spawned the punk movement in the 1970s, when body piercing became a significant fashion symbol.

The American "Gen X" aesthetic of the 1990s was derived from a variety of sources. In addition to the aforementioned social climate, music and fashion media replicated nihilistic images. "Grunge" bands such as Nirvana, Pearl Jam, and Alice in Chains created music which reflected the despair of the Gen Xers. The fashion industry encouraged the grunge image, which progressed to "waif," then to "heroin-chic." Perhaps the most visible designer who embraced and promoted the movement was Calvin Klein with his waifish star model, Kate Moss.

The grunge look was marked by dark and loose clothing, and the conscious attempt to appear disinterested in personal grooming, often expressed by unwashed hair and thrift-shop attire. The "waif" look captured a self-starvation appearance—hollowed-out, sad eyes, and a gray complexion. An interesting paradox ensued in marketing to the Gen-X population: the very styles which attempted to reject commercialism by this anti-establishment youth culture could soon be achieved through commercial outlets. In other words, "vintage," or "retro" clothes were created by designers and marketed in mainstream department stores. Clothing production modeled that which could be found in thrift stores or garage sales.

For Generation Xers, nihilism was brought to the forefront when rock icon Kurt Cobain committed suicide, and his heroin-chic widow Courtney Love rose to fame. (Later in the 1990s, artists such as Marilyn Manson reinforced Cobain-esque nihilism, while Courtney Love traded in her heroin-chic style to model for Versace).

Body piercing also became a popular form of self-expression among Gen Xers, early on as third-hole ear-piercings and eventually as a pierce-anything phenomenon—noses, eyebrows, tongues, lips, nipples, navels, etc. Beyond simple earrings or hoops, other "piercings" surfaced, such as rods, tusks, and bolts, adornments which became increasingly available at specialty stores. Some cultural historians argued that the nationwide body piercing trend originated in California, where navel piercing was popular on the beach. Here, however, it was relatively isolated from the larger Gen X aesthetic, in which it was later nearly essential.

Whether fad or fashion, trend or movement, body piercing became widespread and extreme in the 1990s. Once such example was revealed on a November 21, 1995 broadcast of the Dr. Judy Love Phones show, a syndicated nightly radio call-in show on WHTZ in New York, when a male caller expressed concern over the fact that his girlfriend had recently pierced her clitoris. Body piercing even invaded interior decors: Club USA, and now defunct Manhattan nightclub in Times Square, was decorated with large, theater-sized photographs and props of sexual, sadomasochistic images. One bar

Nineteen-year-old Rainy Blue Cloud Greensfelder displays twenty-one body piercings and flowing purple hair.

doubled as a glass display case, and contained close-up photographs of various clitoral rings and pierced penises. The display was completed by photos of the piercer at work, suggesting that at least in Manhattan, there is someone available to pierce any part of the body.

Another extreme, or even masochistic, form of body decoration is branding or scarring, which became mildly popular among 1990s American youth, but never to the extent of either piercing or tattooing. Branding, the melting of a symbol into human flesh, was offered at some New York City shops.

Significant to most American youth trends is the conspicuous disregard for or rebellion against cultural tradition. Unlike the ornaments worn by Papuan natives, for example, to signify as a religious tradition, American body piercing and tattoos were not connected to any form of formal ceremony. And whereas branding first appeared in the Unites States with slavery, it reemerged as a trend among mostly white, middle class young persons. This paradox was further complicated by the nature of Gen Xers in general, often despairing individuals searching for identity amidst a pervasive consumer environment in which everything seemed to be commodified, including identity.

Whether rock stars or images, most everything was neatly packaged and depicted in the mass media. Cultural expression among American youth is important to their attempt to self-define. As one Los Angeles teenager said in reference to body piercing, ''You feel a common bond when you see others.''

Incidentally, in the mid-1990s, researchers noticed an elevated incidence of a clinical condition known as self-mutilation, wherein teenagers injure themselves as a way of easing emotional distress. It is believed that there were over two million sufferers in the United States in 1997. That year, an article entitled ''The Thin Red Line'' appeared in the *New York Times* magazine, which examined the causes of the behavior and its treatment by researchers. Although experts disagreed about the connection of the behavior to other forms of body modification, they were all keenly aware of the simultaneous rise in both.

After these forms of body decoration became more widely accepted, other forms of body decoration also debuted. One extreme manifestation of the appropriation of other cultural symbols was the sudden interest in 1998 in mehndi, or the Indian art of henna painting.

This was largely made popular by the release of Madonna's *Ray of Light* album and a corresponding music video, in which she is adorned in exotic fabrics and wears mehndi. Here, it is totally decontextualized from its ritual use for Indian brides. After the video, prefabricated mehndi kits were available in a variety of gift and fashion stores.

—Julie Scelfo

FURTHER READING:

Brain, Robert. *The Decorated Body.* New York, Harper & Row, 1979.

Hebdige, Dick. *Subculture: The Meaning of Style.* London, Methuen, 1979.

Polhemus, Ted. *Body Styles.* Luton, Lennard Publishing, 1998.

Rubenstein, Ruth. *Dress Codes: Meanings and Messages in American.* San Francisco, Westview Press, 1995.

Bodybuilding

The term "bodybuilding" has taken on several meanings in popular discourse. The most common usage refers to the organized sport in which men and women compete by posing to display the physiques they have created through weight training, careful dieting, and, in some cases, ergogenic drugs such as anabolic steroids. The term is also used generically to describe the lifestyle followed by many men and women who simply train for greater muscle mass and leanness even though they never compete. These non-competitors train for the "look"—a physical ideal featuring large rounded muscles and minimal body fat. Although the "look" requires enormous dedication and personal sacrifice—and, frequently, drugs—to achieve, it has become pervasive in Western culture. Films, television, comic books, and magazine advertising had all fallen under its sway by the end of the twentieth century.

Although surviving sculpture from Ancient Greece and Rome suggests that both cultures were deeply interested in physical training and body symmetry, there is no evidence to suggest that physique contests were held during these eras. However, the heroic proportions of these early Hellenic and Roman statues are important, for they served as the impetus for the birth of the bodybuilding movement of the nineteenth century. With the importation of the Elgin Marbles to Britain in 1806, a widespread interest in Greek Revivalism spread across Europe, Great Britain, and the United States. This interest in resurrecting the art, architecture, literature and educational systems of Ancient Greece fostered the development of a number of systems of physical training during the nineteenth century and helped create the new science of physical anthropometry—the study of human measurements. Full-sized plaster cast replicas were installed in many colleges, smaller likenesses of ancient statues were manufactured as household ornaments, and advances in printing technology disseminated illustrations and engravings, giving men models of physical perfection against which they could compare themselves. And, as one might expect, sedentary city dwellers discovered that they did not measure up to the ideals presented by the ancient classical civilizations.

Greek Revivalism hit its apex on the shores of Lake Michigan, just outside Chicago, at the 1893 World's Columbian Exhibition. The managers of the World's Fair designed an entire city in the mode of Ancient Greece, and throughout this plaster-of-Paris city they placed

Lou Ferrigno (left) and Arnold Schwarzenegger flex their muscles.

large copies of ancient statuary. Reports from the 1893 Chicago World's Fair nearly all remark on the symbolic importance of these statues, which forced fairgoers to take stock of their own physical condition. Many of the reports also commented on the "living embodiment" of Ancient Greece, strongman Eugen Sandow, who performed in Chicago on a daily basis, and is rightfully recognized as the first major "bodybuilder." Author David Chapman argues that Sandow is the transitional figure from the large and often graceless strongmen, who were ubiquitous in the circuses of the mid- to late-nineteenth century, to the physique stars of the twentieth century. Florenz Ziegfeld (who would later produce the *Ziegfeld Follies*) became Sandow's manager in 1893 and convinced him to alter his act to capitalize on his unique muscularity and physical beauty. Thus, in addition to weightlifting, Sandow added a series of poses at the end of his act. To replicate the classical ideal, he covered himself with white powder and stood against a black velvet backdrop, simulating the poses of classical statuary.

Sandow's appearances at the Chicago World's Fair and his subsequent tours of the United States made him an international celebrity and set off a mania for physical training in the United States and abroad. Back in England in the late 1890s, he began *Sandow's Magazine,* published books, opened a physical training institute, and became the darling of the English upper classes. In 1898, a group of

British aristocrats inspired by Sandow's example joined forces with a local physician, Professor John Atkinson, and held a "Best Developed Man Contest" in conjunction with a weightlifting championships. The winner of that first bodybuilding prize was 1896 Olympic Games heavyweight champion Launceston Elliott (1874-1930), who soon went on the stage and imitated Sandow, both in his grooming and by including poses in his strength act.

The first successful bodybuilding promoter was Sandow himself. In 1898, the year he began his magazine, Sandow announced an ambitious plan to sponsor physique contests in every county in England and then bring the winners together in a magnificent final competition in London. That contest, with 15,000 people in the audience, was held on 14 September 1901 at the Albert Hall, and was won by the 189-pound W.L. Murray of Nottingham, perhaps the least known champion in the history of bodybuilding. Following his victory, Murray, too, became a professional showman, billing himself as "The Most Perfectly Developed Athlete of Modern Times."

The first physique contests in the United states were organized by the eccentric and controversial magazine publisher and health fanatic, Bernarr Macfadden, who was inspired by Sandow's act at the Chicago World's Fair. A gifted promoter, Macfadden began publishing *Physical Culture* magazine in 1898 and by 1900 had reportedly attracted 100,000 subscribers. Quick to understand the value of photography and personal success stories to the magazine's growth, Macfadden announced a world-wide contest for the "Best and Most Perfectly Developed Man and Woman." Contestants submitted photos and measurements that Macfadden then used in his magazine. The most suitable candidates then competed in 13 regional competitions in the United States and England for the privilege of entering the finals. Macfadden's first "Physical Culture Extravaganza" began on December 28, 1903 in Madison Square Garden. With representatives from England competing in both the men's and women's divisions, it was the first international bodybuilding contest and was won by Albert Toof Jennings (1873-1960) and Emma Newkirk. Jennings, a professional strongman known professionally as Al Treloar, was hired as the physical director of the Los Angeles Athletic Club in 1907, a position he held for the next 42 years. Emma Newkirk, from Santa Monica, California, appears to have had no subsequent involvement with women's bodybuilding.

Macfadden held a second competition for men and women in October of 1905, and over the next several decades he sponsored a variety of other physique contests. Some were simply postal meets in which physiques were judged on the strength of photographs and measurements. Others, however, were real competitions, such as the 1921 "America's Most Perfectly Developed Man Contest" won by artist's model Angelo Siciliano (1892-1972), who would go on to revolutionize the mail order training business under the world renowned name of Charles Atlas. The problem with Macfadden's contests, however, was that the judging criteria varied considerably from event to event. The early shows were largely judged by artists and physicians or by prominent people from other walks of life. There were no written rules, no set poses, and no clearly stated aesthetics. Also, with no regular schedule of bodybuilding competitions, the men who entered the early shows rarely worked solely on their physiques. Most were weightlifters, artists' models, or professional strongmen who entered physique contests as a sideline. But that would soon change.

In the 1930s, the British magazine *Health and Strength* began sponsoring a bodybuilding contest as part of its annual physical culture extravaganza. Interest in physique competitions also blossomed in France, where a national championship was held for the first time in 1934. Across the Atlantic, 28-year-old Johnny Hordines sponsored the "Finest Physique Contest" on December 1, 1938 in Schenectady, New York. No overall winner was named in the contest although prizes were given for best body parts and in three height divisions. The following year, on June 10, 1939, Hordines organized a much larger and more elaborate show in which the 30 bodybuilders posed to music on a revolving dais. Although this contest, won by Bert Goodrich, is frequently referred to as the first "Mr. America" contest, Hordines did not advertise it as such. He called it "America's Finest Physique Contest."

The first contest to be held on a regular basis in the United States was the Amateur Athletic Union (AAU) Mr. America contest. The first meet took place on July 4, 1939 in conjunction with the AAU National Weightlifting Championships. As would be the case for many years in the AAU, the physique show was held after the weightlifting, almost as an afterthought. At the 1939 show, no contestant could enter the physique contest who had not competed in the weightlifting event. Ronald Essmaker won the tall class in that first AAU contest, and is thus regarded as the first Mr. America. On May 25, 1940 a Mr. America contest was again held following the National Weightlifting Championships. John Grimek won the overall title for that year and the next, thus becoming the only champion to win two Mr. America titles. In fact, Grimek's physique was so far ahead of his competitors in the early 1940s that the AAU passed a rule forbidding winners from competing in subsequent Mr. America contests.

The establishment of the Mr. America contest validated bodybuilding as a sport. However, for a number of years, nearly all American bodybuilding competitions continued to be held after weightlifting events. The bodybuilding shows often ended well beyond midnight, and thus attracted small audiences and little publicity. Furthermore, in order to fight the notion that large muscles made a person muscle-bound and unathletic, the AAU established an athleticism requirement for all competitors. Men who wanted to be in the physique shows had either to compete in the weightlifting event or prove that they were athletes involved in such things as team sports or track and field. The guiding force behind these regulations was Robert (Bob) Hoffman (1898-1984), owner of the York Barbell Company. Hoffman was a staunch supporter of the Olympic sport of weightlifting, and a strong presence in the AAU. He didn't dislike bodybuilders, and was Grimek's employer, but he worried that the new sport would take young men away from weightlifting. In his magazine, *Strength & Health*, which by the mid-1940s was the most widely circulated muscle magazine in the world, Hoffman gave less space to physique men than he did to weightlifters. These attitudes, coupled with the AAU's continued presentation of bodybuilding as a second class sport, opened the door for the young Weider brothers of Montreal, Canada, and allowed them to take control of the sport.

Joe Weider (1923—) was only 17 years old when he published his first issue of *Your Physique* magazine in 1940. From that inauspicious, mimeographed beginning, *Your Physique*'s circulation grew almost geometrically. By 1943, his readership had spread across Canada, and he began selling exercise equipment as well. In 1946, with his younger brother Ben (1925—) home from the war, Joe organized the first Mr. Canada contest, but after experiencing problems, the ambitious entrepreneurs decided to form their own bodybuilding federation. Ben Weider explained their decision in a 1998 magazine article: "At that time the AAU controlled bodybuilding, not only in America but in Canada as well, through the Weight Lifting

Federation. Although we had asked for and received a permit from the AAU to organize the [1946 Mr. Canada] contest, on the night of the contest, their Canadian representatives . . . arrived and threatened the bodybuilders that they would be expelled from the AAU if they participated. The reaction of Bob Hoffman and the International Weightlifting Federation was aggressive and mean. They did everything to try to destroy and humiliate us. That's when Joe and I decided to organize our own federation and not be under the control of the AAU.''

Over the next several years, Joe and Ben Weider sponsored dozens of contests and traveled throughout the world to enlist member nations for their new International Federation of Bodybuilders (IFBB). During the 1950s and 1960s the IFBB grew steadily in membership and in stature. At the same time, the Weiders' magazine, equipment, and food supplement businesses turned into an empire. By the early 1970s, when the International Weightlifting Federation finally decided to give up what little control they had of bodybuilding, the IFBB was able to assume total control of international bodybuilding. Ben Weider also stepped up his campaign for the acceptance of bodybuilding as an Olympic sport. Although it took another quarter century to see it finally happen, Ben Weider's tireless crusade finally resulted in the International Olympic Committee admitting the IFBB as a ''recognized Olympic sport'' on January 30, 1998. By that time, the IFBB was one of the most international bodies in sport, with well over 100 member nations.

It was clear, however, that before the IFBB would be able to send athletes to the Olympics, it would have to deal more effectively with the drug use that pervaded the sport. The International Olympic Committee has had many drug scandals in other sports, and it would be unlikely fully to embrace a sport that has been dominated by drug use since the 1960s. Because ergogenic drugs such as anabolic steroids and Human Growth Hormone build muscle and reduce body fat, they provide virtually unbeatable advantages to those who use them. The IFBB has attempted, with varying degrees of rigor and with very limited success, to curtail their use by the top competitors, but because the drugs are easy to obtain and, in most cases, relatively inexpensive, and because most drug testing programs have been either half-hearted or short-lived, bodybuilders are drawn to their use. The irony of unhealthy men and women winning competitions that have traditionally symbolized health must be resolved before bodybuilding can become a full-fledged Olympic sport.

Although there were women's beauty contests at Muscle Beach in the 1940s and 1950s, and although some men's contests during the 1950s and 1960s also contained a bikini or beauty contest for women, the first competition at which women were judged on muscularity and symmetry was a 1978 meet promoted by Henry McGhee, a Canton, Ohio, YMCA director. One of the competitors in that contest was a 46-year-old Florida grandmother, Doris Barrilleaux, who decided to form a bodybuilding association for women. The Superior Physique Association sponsored several contests in the southeastern United States but, ultimately, could not compete with the National Physique Committee—the American arm of the IFBB. The first NPC show, The World Pro Championships, was held in 1979. Lisa Lyon, who won that first contest, was heavily promoted by Joe Weider in *Muscle and Fitness* magazine and, seemingly overnight, women's bodybuilding took off. Within two years, the NPC had state, regional, and national meets in place, and in 1980 the IFBB sanctioned the first Ms. Olympia contest, which was won by Rachel McLish of Harlingen, Texas.

Throughout the early and mid-1980s, women's bodybuilding seemed to be on a steady growth curve. However, as women bodybuilders trained harder, and as drug use became more commonplace, concerns began to be raised about the aesthetic direction of the sport. Charles Gaines and George Butler gave voice to some of these concerns in both the film and book *Pumping Iron II: The Unprecedented Woman*. Both were released in 1983 and both juxtaposed the elegant McLish with the larger and more heavily muscled Australian power-lifter, Beverly Francis, who was then making a move into bodybuilding. Since 1983, as the level of muscularity in women's bodybuilding gradually increased, women's bodybuilding seems to have taken a path that fewer and fewer women have cared to follow. As bodybuilding has continued to reward size and muscularity, women bodybuilders have gotten bigger and still bigger; by the mid-1990s they had lost much of the mainstream appeal they enjoyed in the 1980s.

While bodybuilding continued to struggle with its aesthetic direction, another type of contest emerged in reaction to the hyper-muscular bodybuilders. Generically referred to as ''Ms. Fitness'' competitions, the new contests combine elements of bodybuilding, aerobic dance, and gymnastics. By the end of the 1990s, these contests had far surpassed women's bodybuilding in popularity both on television and in the muscle magazines. Apparently, this occurred because of the more traditionally feminine physiques of the competitors. A 1998 study of the covers of *Flex, Muscle and Fitness, Iron Man* and *Muscle Mag International*—the four leading muscle magazines—found that these publications were far more likely to feature fitness competitors than they were women bodybuilders, both inside the magazine and on the cover. In fact, by that time women bodybuilders were almost never featured on the covers of such magazines.

Since its inception in the nineteenth century, bodybuilding has been linked to the entertainment industry. Although most people are aware that there were circus and vaudeville strongmen, some bodybuilder/strongmen also played an important role in the early cinema. For example, Thomas Edison asked Eugen Sandow to pose for his new Kinetoscope in 1894. The brief film clip shows Sandow posing, lifting a barbell, and performing a back flip. It played in Kinetoscopic ''parlors'' where patrons paid only a penny or so to peep through a small hole in a large box-like machine. Sandow also appeared in four brief films for the Biograph company, which he showed as the finale of his act in the mid-1890s.

Over the past century, a number of bodybuilders and strongmen have worked in the film industry largely because their physiques. Josef Grafl, the world heavyweight lifting champion from 1908-1911 played Ursus, the bodyguard of the heroine in the 1913 version of *Quo Vadis*; and Bartolomeo Pagano, under the stage name of Maciste, appeared in a number of films between 1914 and the early 1920s in which his strength and muscularity advanced the script. Joe Bonomo, the training partner of Charles Atlas and a winner of an early physique contest in his own right, worked throughout the 1920s as a Hollywood stunt man and character actor, while Elmo Lincoln found fame as the first screen Tarzan in that same decade.

In the 1950s, a number of largely Italian-made costume epics employed bodybuilders as gladiators and mythic heroes. Mickey Hargitay, who had been part of Mae West's bodybuilder revue, married actress Jayne Mansfield and played in a couple of these, such as *Revenge of the Gladiators* (1968). South African bodybuilding star Reg Park made five Hercules pictures between 1961 and 1965, while former Tarzan Gordon Scott starred in *Goliath and the Vampires* (1961). Until the advent of Arnold Schwarzenegger, the brightest star in this genre was Steve Reeves, whose series of film roles in the 1950s and 1960s made him the number one box-office draw in the world for a brief time.

Many other film stars also have connections to the world of bodybuilding. Oscar winner Sean Connery was a serious bodybuilder in his early adulthood and entered the Mr. Universe contest in 1953. David Prowse, who played Darth Vader in *Star Wars*, looked so large and menacing because he was in reality a 6'7,'' 280-pound former Mr. Universe competitor. And, finally, Schwarzenegger's participation in such early films as *Pumping Iron* (1977) and *Stay Hungry* (1976) helped to popularize the bodybuilding aesthetic and lifestyle to the general public. What's more, many leading actors in the last decades of the twentieth century undertook serious bodybuilding training in order to portray "action characters" to audiences grown used to seeing bodybuilders in magazines and heroically built comic-book characters. Stars such as Clint Walker, Harrison Ford, Clint Eastwood, Mel Gibson, Sylvester Stallone, Jean Claude Van Damme, Robert DeNiro, Christopher Reeves, Nicholas Cage, Carl Weathers, Brendan Frasier, and Ving Rhames realized how much more believable they are when their muscular bodies match their masculine roles. And women such as Linda Hamilton, Jane Fonda, and Sigourney Weaver have also trained and dieted to prepare for roles in which the condition of their bodies was critical.

Other media, too, have been influenced by bodybuilding. Comic books, for instance, have considerably altered the proportions of their superheroes as the years have passed. When Superman, Captain Marvel, and Batman first appeared in the 1930s, they were shown to have athletic but relatively non-muscular physiques. However, as the bodies of the top physique men have become increasingly exaggerated, so have the drawings of the superheroes in comic books, on television cartoons, and in films. Some scholars believe that the depiction of these ultra-hypertrophied superheroes has been a factor in the growing public acceptance of bodybuilding. Television, of course, has also played a major role. Beginning in 1951 with Jack LaLanne's show, bodybuilders have preached the gospel of fitness over the airwaves. In the 1990s, the proliferation of cable television resulted in much more on-air coverage of bodybuilding competitions and many more instructional shows. By far the biggest bodybuilding star on television, however, was Lou Ferrigno, who was very convincing as the Incredible Hulk from 1977 to 1982.

—Jan Todd

FURTHER READING:

Chapman, David L. *Sandow the Magnificent: Eugen Sandow and the Beginnings of Bodybuilding.* Urbana, University of Illinois Press, 1994.

Fair, John. *Muscletown USA: Bob Hoffman and the Manly Culture of York Barbell.* State College, Pennsylvania, Pennsylvania State University Press, 1999.

Gaines, Charles, and George Butler. *Pumping Iron: The Art and Sport of Bodybuilding.* New York, Simon and Schuster, 1977.

———. *Pumping Iron II: The Unprecedented Woman.* New York, Simon and Schuster, 1983.

Roark, Joe. "The Mr. America Contest: A Brief History." *Iron Game History.* Vol. 2, November 1992, 19-20.

Todd, Jan. "Bernarr Macfadden: Reformer of Feminine Form." *Iron Game History.* Vol. 1, March 1991, 3-8.

Webster, David P. *Barbells and Beefcake: An Illustrated History of Bodybuilding.* Irvine, Scotland, self-published, 1979.

Bogart, Humphrey (1899-1957)

The man who would tell Ingrid Bergman, "Here's Looking at You, Kid," at the conclusion of *Casablanca* (1942) was born Humphrey DeForest Bogart in 1899. He would become one of the twentieth century's greatest icons of tough masculinity, a complex blend of "good guy" and "bad guy" at a time when World War II had many Americans re-examining their personal codes of loyalty, honor, and character. Underneath his coarse exterior, Bogart, or simply "Bogie," betrayed an underdog vulnerability and a genuine desire to find the "right" answer in a world that was increasingly chaotic and off-kilter. The star was also well known for his celebrated marriage to co-star Lauren Bacall, whose sultry wit reflected his cynicism but who always drew out his romantic, heroic side.

Although Bogart became known for playing brutish characters from the wrong side of town, he was raised in the world of upper-middle-class New York City. He was eventually expelled from the Phillips Academy in Andover, Massachusetts, and joined the Navy for service during World War I. It was in the war that he suffered an injury which left his lip slightly paralyzed, resulting in the stiff and affected facial gestures which became one of the actor's trademarks.

Bogart began his career on stage in the 1920s and entered Hollywood by playing minor roles a decade later. But when Leslie Howard lobbied for him to co-star in *The Petrified Forest* (1935), he proved that he was well-suited for gangster or villain characters. He generally played this type until *High Sierra* (1941) in which he (with the film's screenwriter John Huston) developed a trope of masculinity which was complicated by ambivalence, pragmatism, and complex moral fortitude. Here, Bogart starred as Mad Dog Earle, an ex-convict on the run and destined for his own demise, who lays bare a particular emotional sensitivity through his sympathy for a simpler, gentler Joan Leslie. He continued to develop his star persona through this kind of role in *The Maltese Falcon* (1941) and *Casablanca* (1941), both of which are considered his watershed films. Though he maintained a turbulent relationship with Warner Brothers, the studio which helped forge his image, Bogart made a comfortable fit with its house style which relied on the gangster genre and films which drew on the topical social problems of the day.

In 1943, the star met his match in Lauren Bacall on the set of *To Have and Have Not* (1944). Twenty-five years his junior, Bacall was a fashion model who had recently been discovered by director Howard Hawks' wife. She was precocious and demure and with, Hawks' help, the two stars launched a chemistry that would be re-lived in *The Big Sleep* (1945, also directed by Hawks) and result in a famous and closely-watched marriage that lasted until Bogart's death. He had been married three times with little success—when he encountered Bacall he was husband to former actress Mayo Methot and their violent feuding had earned them the title "the Battling Bogarts." It took over a year for him to extricate himself from this marriage and fans initially viewed the Bogie/Bacall union with skepticism.

The verbal sparring between Bogart and Bacall in *To Have and Have Not*—in which the latter utters the notorious "put your lips

Humphrey Bogart in a scene from the film *The Maltese Falcon*.

together and blow'' phrase—became a signature of their interpersonal dynamic off-screen as well. Film critic Molly Haskell celebrates them as one of ''the best of the classical couples'' because they brought to the screen ''the kind of morally and socially beneficial 'pedagogic' relationship that Lionel Trilling finds in Jane Austen's characters, the 'intelligent love' in which two partners instruct, inform, educate, and influence each other in the continuous college of love.'' Bogart, who was known for his misogyny and violent temper, had found a woman who knew how to put him in his place with an economical glance or a spontaneous retort. It was common for his ''rat pack'' of male friends to populate the house but Bacall was perceived as a wife who rarely relinquished the upper hand. Their marriage produced two children, Stephen (after Bogart's character in *To Have and Have Not*) and Leslie (after Leslie Howard).

A noticeable shift occurred in the kinds of characters Bogart played in the 1940s. The tough guy attempting to be moral in an immoral world became less socially acceptable as many American husbands and wives tried to settle into a home life that would help anesthetize them from the trauma of war. The complicated and reactive principles associated with the star's persona suddenly seemed more troublesome and less containable. His film *Treasure of the*

Sierra Madre (1948), in which Bogart plays a greedy, conniving prospector, marks this trend but *In a Lonely Place* (1948) is a lesser known and equally remarkable film, partly because his role is that of a screenwriter disenchanted with Hollywood. It was at this time that he also formed his Santana production company which granted him more autonomy in his choice and development of projects.

In the early 1950s, Bogart became one of the key figures to speak out against the House Un-American Activities Committee which gave him an opportunity to voice his ideals of democracy and free speech. He also revived his career with *The African Queen* (1951), for which he won an Academy Award. Later, he experimented with more comedic roles in films such as Billy Wilder's *Sabrina* (1954) and *We're No Angels* (1955). In 1956, the long-time smoker underwent surgery for cancer of the esophagus and he died of emphysema in early 1957.

Bogart's status as a cultural icon was renewed in the 1960s when counter-culture audiences were introduced to his films through film festivals in Boston and New York which then spread to small college towns. The Bogart ''cult'' offered a retreat into macho, rugged individualism at a time when burgeoning social movements contributed to increased anxiety over masculine norms. This cult saw a resurgence in the 1990s with a spate of biographies about the star and the issuance of a commemorative postage stamp.

—Christina Lane

FURTHER READING:

Bacall, Lauren. *Lauren Bacall by Myself.* New York, Ballantine, 1978.

Bogart, Stephen Humphrey, with Gary Provost. *Bogart: In Search of My Father.* New York, Dutton, 1995.

Cohen, Steven. *Masked Men: Masculinity and the Movies of the Fifties.* Bloomington, Indiana University Press, 1997.

Haskell, Molly. *From Reverence to Rape: The Treatment of Women in the Movies.* New York, Penguin Books, 1974.

Huston, John. *An Open Book.* New York, Alfred A. Knopf, 1980.

Hyams, Joe. *Bogart and Bacall: A Love Story.* New York, David McKay Company, 1975.

Meyers, Jeffrey. *Bogart: A Life in Hollywood.* Boston and New York, Houghton Mifflin Company, 1997.

Sklar, Robert. *City Boys: Cagney, Bogart, Garfield.* Princeton, Princeton University Press, 1992.

Sperber, A.M., and Eric Lax. *Bogart.* New York, William Morrow and Company, 1997.

Bok, Edward (1863-1930)

An immigrant from the Netherlands, journalist and social reformer Edward Bok emphasized the virtues of hard work and assimilation in his 1920 autobiography, *The Americanization of Edward Bok,* which won the Pulitzer Prize for biography and was reprinted in 60 editions over the next two decades. As one of America's most prominent magazine editors around the turn of the twentieth century, Bok originated the concept of the modern mass-circulation women's magazine during his 30-year tenure (1889-1919) as editor of the *Ladies' Home Journal.* His editorship coincided with a period of profound change, as the United States shifted from an agrarian to an urban society, and his was a prominent voice in defining and explaining these changes to a newly emergent middle class often unsure of its role in the new order of things. ''He outdid his readers in his faith in the myths and hopes of his adopted country,'' wrote Salme Harju Steinberg in her 1979 study, *Reformer in the Marketplace.* ''His sentiments were all the more compelling because they reflected not so much what his readers did believe as what they thought they should believe.'' Under his guidance, the *Ladies' Home Journal* was the first magazine to reach a circulation of one million readers, which then doubled to two million as it became an advocate of many progressive causes of its era, such as conservation, public health, birth control, sanitation, and educational reform. Paradoxically, the magazine remained neutral on the issue of women's suffrage until Bok finally expressed opposition to it in a March 1912 editorial, claiming that women were not yet ready for the vote.

Edward Bok was born to a politically prominent family in Den Helder, the Netherlands, on October 9, 1863, the younger son of William John Hidde Bok and Sieke Gertrude van Herwerden Bok. After suffering financial reverses, the family emigrated to the United States and settled in Brooklyn, New York, where from the age of ten,

young Edward began working in a variety of jobs, including window washer, office boy, and stringer for the *Brooklyn Daily Eagle.* His first publishing jobs were as a stenographer with Henry Holt & Company and Charles Scribner's Sons. In the 1880s, Bok became editor of the *Brooklyn Magazine,* which had evolved from a publication he edited for Henry Ward Beecher's Plymouth Church. In 1886 he and Frederic L. Colver launched Bok Syndicate Press, the first to widely employ women as contributors. The following year, *Scribner's Magazine* hired Bok as advertising manager.

In 1889, shortly after his 26th birthday, Bok became editor-in-chief of the *Ladies' Home Journal,* which had been founded six years earlier by Cyrus H. K. Curtis, whose only daughter, Mary Louise, became Bok's wife in 1896. Although Bok made the *Ladies' Home Journal* a vehicle for social change, he avoided taking sides in the controversial labor vs. capital political issues of the day. With a solid appeal to the emerging middle classes, Bok's editorials preached a Protestant work ethic couched in an Emersonian language of individual betterment. By employing contributing writers such as Jane Addams, Edward Bellamy, and Helen Keller, Bok helped create a national climate of opinion that dovetailed with the growing progressive movement. While advocacy of ''do-good'' projects put the *Journal* at odds with more radical muckraking periodicals of the period, Bok can still be credited with raising popular consciousness about the ills of unbridled industrialism. His ''Beautiful America'' campaign, for example, raised public ire against the erection of mammoth billboards on the rim of the Grand Canyon, and against the further despoiling of Niagara Falls by electric-power plants. Riding the crest of the ''City Beautiful'' movement that followed the 1892 Chicago World's Fair, Bok opened the pages of the *Journal* to architects, who offered building plans and specifications for attractive, low-cost homes, thousands of which were built in the newer suburban developments. Praising this initiative, President Theodore Roosevelt said ''Bok is the only man I ever heard of who changed, for the better, the architecture of an entire nation, and he did it so quickly and yet so effectively that we didn't know it was begun before it was finished.''

The *Ladies' Home Journal* became the first magazine to ban advertising of patent medicines, and Bok campaigned strenuously against alcohol-based nostrums, a catalyst for the landmark Food and Drug Act in 1906. The magazine was also ahead of its time in advocating sex education, though its editorials were hardly explicit by late-twentieth-century standards. Even before the United States had entered World War I, Bok, who was vice president of the Belgian Relief Fund and an advisor to President Woodrow Wilson, editorialized that American women could contribute to peace and democracy through preparedness, food conservation, and support of the Red Cross and other relief efforts.

After his forced retirement in 1919, Bok published his autobiography and devoted himself to humanitarian causes. Swimming against the tide of isolationism after World War I, Bok tried to get Americans interested in the League of Nations and the World Court. In 1923, he established the American Peace Award, a prize of $100,000 to be awarded for plans for international cooperation. He also endowed the Woodrow Wilson Chair of Government at Williams College, named for the beleaguered president who failed to convince his fellow citizens to join the League of Nations. Bok died on January 9, 1930 and was buried at the foot of the Singing Tower, a carillon he built in a bird preserve in Lake Wales, Florida.

—Edward Moran

FURTHER READING:

Bok, Edward. *America, Give Me a Chance.* New York, Charles Scribner's Sons, 1926.

———. *The Americanization of Edward Bok.* New York, Charles Scribner's Sons, 1920.

Peterson, Theodore. *Magazines in the Twentieth Century.* Urbana, University of Illinois Press, 1964.

Steinberg, Salme Harju. *Reformer in the Marketplace: Edward W. Bok and The Ladies' Home Journal.* Baton Rouge and London, Louisiana State University Press, 1979.

Bolton, Judy

See Judy Bolton

The Bomb

For many observers, "Living with the Bomb" has become the evocative phrase to describe life in twentieth-century America. The cultural fallout from this technological innovation has influenced economics, politics, and social policy and life long after its first testing in the New Mexican desert in 1945. Americans have taken fear of attack so seriously that school policies include provisions for nuclear attack. Global politics became "polarized" by the two nations in possession of nuclear technology. In the 1990s, global relations remained extremely influenced by proliferation and the threat of hostile nations acquiring nuclear capabilities. Clearly, "the

bomb" and all of atomic technology has carved a deep crater of influence.

The technology to manage atomic reactions did not long remain the sole domain of the military. The influence of nuclear weapons and power generation has defined a great deal of domestic politics since the 1960s. In recent years, such attention has come because of nuclear technology's environmental impact. If one considers these broader implications and the related technologies, twentieth-century life has been significantly influenced by "the bomb," even though it has been used sparingly—nearly not at all. The broader legacy of the bomb can be seen on the landscape, from Chernobyl to the Bikini Atoll or from Hiroshima to Hanford, Washington. Hanford's legacy with the bomb spans more time than possibly any other site. In fact, it frames consideration of this issue by serving as site for the creation of the raw material to construct the first nuclear weapons and consequently as the "single most infected" site in the United States, now awaiting Superfund cleanup. The site is a symbol of technological accomplishment but also of ethical lessons learned.

In February 1943, the U.S. military through General Leslie Groves acquired 500,000 acres of land near Hanford. This would be the third location in the triad that would produce the atomic technology. The coordinated activity of these three sites under the auspices of the U.S. military became a path-breaking illustration of the planning and strategy that would define many modern corporations. Hanford used water power to separate plutonium and produce the grade necessary for weapons use. Oak Ridge in Tennessee coordinated the production of uranium. These production facilities then fueled the heart of the undertaking, contained in Los Alamos, New Mexico, under the direction of J. Robert Oppenheimer.

Oppenheimer, a physicist, supervised the team of nuclear theoreticians who would devise the formulas making such atomic reactions possible and manageable. Scientists from a variety of fields were

An atomic bomb mushroom cloud.

involved in this highly complex theoretical mission. Once theories were in place and materials delivered, the project became assembling and testing the technology in the form of a bomb. All of this needed to take place on the vast Los Alamos, New Mexico, compound under complete secrecy. However, the urgency of war revealed that this well-orchestrated, corporate-like enterprise remained the best bet to save thousands of American lives.

By 1944, World War II had wrought a terrible price on the world. The European theater would soon close with Germany's surrender. While Germany's pursuit of atomic weapons technology had fueled the efforts of American scientists, the surrender did not end the project. The Pacific front remained active, and Japan did not accept offers to surrender. "Project Trinity" moved forward, and it would involve Japanese cities, Hiroshima and Nagasaki, as the test laboratories of initial atomic bomb explosions. *Enola Gay* released a uranium bomb on the city of Hiroshima on August 6 and *Bock's Car* released a plutonium bomb on Nagasaki on August 9. Death tolls vary between 300-500,000, and most were Japanese civilians. The atomic age, and life with the bomb, had begun.

Bomb tests in an effort to perfect the technology as well as to design other types of weapons, including Hydrogen bombs, would continue throughout the 1950s, particularly following the Soviet Union's successful detonation in 1949. Many of these tests became publicity opportunities. For instance, the 1946 Pacific tests on the Bikini Atoll were viewed on television and through print media by millions worldwide. The technology became so awe-inspiring and ubiquitous that a french designer named his new, two-piece women's bathing suit after the test. The bikini, linked with terms such as "bombshell," became an enduring representation of the significant impression of this new technology on the world's psyche.

For Oppenheimer and many of the other scientists, the experience of working for the military had brought increasing alarm about what the impact of their theoretical accomplishments would be. Many watched in horror as the weapons were used on Japanese civilians. Oppenheimer eventually felt that the public had changed attitudes toward scientific exploration due to the bomb. "We have made a thing," he said in a 1946 speech, "a most terrible weapon, that has altered abruptly and profoundly the nature of the world . . . a thing that by all the standards of the world we grew up in is an evil thing." It brings up the question of whether or not, he went on, this technology as well as all of science should be controlled or limited.

Many of the scientists involved believed that atomic technology required controls unlike any previous innovation. Shortly after the bombings, a movement began to establish a global board of scientists who would administer the technology with no political affiliation. While there were many problems with such a plan in the 1940s, it proved impossible to wrest this new tool for global influence from the American military and political leaders. The Atomic Energy Commission (AEC), formed in 1946, would place the U.S. military and governmental authority in control of the weapons technology and other uses to which it might be put. With the "nuclear trump card," the United States catapulted to the top of global leadership.

Such technological supremacy only enhanced Americans' post war expansion and optimism. The bomb became an important plank to re-stoking American confidence in the security of its borders and its place in the world. In addition to alcoholic drinks and cereal-box prizes, atomic technology would creep into many facets of American life. Polls show that few Americans considered moral implications to the bombs' use in 1945; instead, 85 percent approved, citing the need to end the war and save American lives that might have been lost in a

Japanese invasion. Soon, the AEC seized this sensibility and began plans for "domesticating the atom." These ideas led to a barrage of popular articles concerning a future in which roads were created through the use of atomic bombs and radiation employed to cure cancer.

Atomic dreaming took many additional forms as well, particularly when the AEC began speculating about power generation. Initially, images of atomic-powered agriculture and automobiles were sketched and speculated about in many popular periodicals. In one book published during this wave of technological optimism, the writer speculates that, "No baseball game will be called off on account of rain in the Era of Atomic Energy." After continuing this litany of activities no longer to be influenced by climate or nature, the author sums up the argument: "For the first time in the history of the world man will have at his disposal energy in amounts sufficient to cope with the forces of Mother Nature." For many Americans, this new technology meant control of everyday life. For the Eisenhower Administration, the technology meant expansion of our economic and commercial capabilities.

The Eisenhower Administration repeatedly sought ways of "domesticating" the atom. Primarily, this effort grew out of a desire to educate the public without creating fear of possible attack. However, educating the public on actual facts clearly took a subsidiary position to instilling confidence. Most famously, "Project Plowshares" grew out of the Administration's effort to take the destructive weapon and make it a domestic power producer. The list was awe-inspiring: laser-cut highways passing through mountains, nuclear-powered greenhouses built by federal funds in the Midwest to routinize crop production, and irradiating soils to simplify weed and pest management. While domestic power production, with massive federal subsidies, would be the long-term product of these actions, the atom could never fully escape its military capabilities.

Americans of the 1950s could not at once stake military dominance on a technology's horrific power while also accepting it into their everyday life. The leap was simply too great. This became particularly difficult in 1949 when the Soviet Union tested its own atomic weapon. The arms race had officially begun; a technology that brought comfort following the "war to end all wars" now forced an entire culture to realize its volatility—to live in fear of nuclear annihilation.

Eisenhower's efforts sought to manage the fear of nuclear attack, and wound up creating a unique atomic culture. Civil defense efforts constructed bomb shelters in public buildings and enforced school children to practice "duck and cover" drills, just as students today have fire drills. Many families purchased plans for personal bomb shelters to be constructed in their backyards. Some followed through with construction and outfitting the shelter for months of survival should the United States experience a nuclear attack. Social controls also limited the availability of the film *On the Beach*, which depicted the effects of a nuclear attack, and David Bradley's book *No Place to Hide*. It was the censorship of Bradley, a scientist and physician working for the Navy at the Bikini tests, that was the most troubling oversight. Bradley's account of his work after the tests presented the public with its first knowledge of radiation—the realization that there was more to the bomb than its immediate blast. The culture of control was orchestrated informally, but Eisenhower also took strong political action internationally. "Atoms for Peace" composed an international series of policies during the 1950s that sought to have the Soviets and Americans each offer the United Nations fissionable material to be applied to peaceful uses. While the Cold War still had many chapters through which to pass, Eisenhower stimulated discourse on the topic of nuclear weapons from the outset.

Eisenhower's ''Atoms for Peace'' speech, given at the United Nations in 1953, clearly instructed the world on the technological stand-off that confronted it. The ''two atomic colossi,'' he forecasted, could continue to ''eye each other indefinitely across a trembling world.'' But eventually their failure to find peace would result in war and ''the probability of civilization destroyed,'' forcing ''mankind to begin all over again the age-old struggle upward from savagery toward decency and right, and justice.'' To Eisenhower, ''no sane member of the human race'' could want this. In his estimation, the only way out was discourse and understanding. With exactly these battle lines, a war—referred to as cold, because it never escalates (heats) to direct conflict—unfolded over the coming decades. With ideology—communism versus capitalism—as its point of difference, the conflict was fought through economics, diplomacy, and the stockpiling of a military arsenal. With each side possessing a weapon that could annihilate not just the opponent but the entire world, the bomb defined a new philosophy of warfare.

The Cold War, lasting from 1949-1990, then may best be viewed as an ongoing chess game, involving diplomats and physicists, while the entire world prayed that neither player made the incorrect move. Redefining ideas of attack and confrontation, the Cold War's nuclear arsenal required that each side live on the brink of war—referred to as brinksmanship by American policy makers. Each ''super power,'' or nuclear weapons nation, sought to remain militarily on the brink while diplomatically dueling over economic and political influence throughout the globe. Each nation sought to increase its ''sphere of influence'' (or nations signed-on as like minded) and to limit the others. Diplomats began to view the entire globe in such terms, leading to wars in Korea and Vietnam over the ''domino'' assumption that there were certain key nations that, if allowed to ally with a superpower, could take an entire region with them. These two conflicts defined the term ''limited'' warfare, which meant that nuclear weapons were not used. However, in each conflict the use of such weapons was hotly debated.

Finally, as the potential impact of the use of the bomb became more clearly understood, the technological side of the Cold War escalated into an ''arms race'' meant to stockpile resources more quickly and in greater numbers than the other superpower. Historians will remember this effort as possibly the most ridiculous outlet of Cold War anxiety, because by 1990 the Soviets and Americans each possessed the capability to destroy the earth hundreds of times. The arms race grew out of one of the most disturbing aspects of the Cold War, which was described by policy-makers as ''MAD: mutually assured destruction.'' By 1960, each nation had adopted the philosophy that any launch of a nuclear warhead would initiate massive retaliation of its entire arsenal. Even a mistaken launch, of course, could result in retaliatory action to destroy all life.

On an individual basis, humans had lived before in a tenuous balance with survival as they struggled for food supplies with little technology; however, never before had such a tenuous balance derived only from man's own technological innovation. Everyday human life changed significantly with the realization that extinction could arrive at any moment. Some Americans applied the lesson by striving to live within limits of technology and resource use. Anti-nuclear activists composed some of the earliest portions of the 1960s counter culture and the modern environmental movement, including Sea Shepherds and Greenpeace which grew out of protesting nuclear testing. Other Americans were moved to live with fewer constraints

than every before: for instance, some historians have traced the culture of excessive consumption to the realization that an attack was imminent. Regardless of the exact reaction, American everyday life had been significantly altered.

If Americans had managed to remain naive to the atomic possibilities, the crisis of 1962 made the reality perfectly obvious. U.S. intelligence sources located Soviet missiles in Cuba, 90 miles from the American coast. Many options were entertained, including bombing the missile sights; President John F. Kennedy, though, elected to push ''brinksmanship'' further than it had ever before gone. He stated that the missiles pressed the nuclear balance to the Soviet's advantage and that they must be removed. Kennedy squared off against Soviet Premier Nikita Kruschev in a direct confrontation with the use of nuclear weapons as the only subsequent possibility for escalation. Thirteen Days later, the Soviet Premier backed down and removed the missiles. The world breathed a sigh of relief, realizing it had come closer to destruction than ever before. For many observers, there was also an unstated vow that the Cuban Missile Crisis must be the last such threat.

The period of crisis created a new level of anxiety, however, that revealed itself in a number of arenas. The well-known ''atomic clock,'' calculated by a group of physicists, alerted the public to how great the danger of nuclear war had become. The anxiety caused by such potentialities, however, played out in a fascinating array of popular films. An entire genre of science fiction films focused around the unknown effects of radiation on subjects ranging from a beautiful woman, to grasshoppers, to plants. Most impressively, the *Godzilla* films dealt with Japanese feelings toward the effects of nuclear technology. All of these films found a terrific following in the United States. Over-sized lizards aside, another genre of film dealt with the possibilities of nuclear war. *On the Beach* blazed the trail for many films, including the well-known *The Day After* television mini-series. Finally, the cult-classic of this genre, *Dr. Strangelove* starred Peter Sellers in multiple performances as it posed the possibility of a deranged individual initiating a worldwide nuclear holocaust. The appeal of such films reveals the construction of what historian Paul Boyer dubs an American ''nuclear consciousness.''

Such faith in nationalism, technological supremacy, and authority helped make Americans comfortable to watch above-ground testing in the American West through the late 1950s. Since the danger of radiation was not discussed, Americans often sat in cars or on lawn chairs to witness the mushroom clouds from a ''safe'' distance. Documentary films such as *Atomic Cafe* chronicle the effort to delude or at least not fully inform the American public about dangers. Since the testing, ''down-winders'' in Utah and elsewhere have reported significant rises in leukemia rates as well as that of other types of cancer. Maps of air patterns show that actually much of the nation experienced some fall-out from these tests. The Cold War forced the U.S. military to operate as if it were a period of war and certain types of risks were necessary on the ''home front.'' At the time, a population of Americans who were familiar with World War II proved to be willing to make whatever sacrifices were necessary; later generations would be less accepting.

Ironically, the first emphasis of this shift in public opinion would not be nuclear arms, but its relative, nuclear power. While groups argued for a freeze in the construction of nuclear arms and forced the government to discontinue atomic weapons tests, Americans grew increasingly comfortable with nuclear reactors in their neighborhoods. The ''Atoms for Peace'' program of the 1950s aided in the development of domestic energy production based on the nuclear reaction. The exuberance for such power production became the complete lack of immediate waste. There were other potential problems, but those were not yet clearly known to the American public. In 1979, a nuclear reactor at Three Mile Island, Pennsylvania, which is located within a working-class neighborhood outside of a major population center, nearly experienced a nuclear melt down. As pregnant women and children were evacuated from Pennsylvania's nearby capital, Harrisburg, the American public learned through the media about the dangers of this technology. Most important, they learned the vast amount that was not clearly understood about this power source. As much of the nation waited for the cooling tower to erupt in the mushroom cloud of an atomic blast, a clear connection was finally made between the power source and the weapon. While the danger passed quickly from Three Mile Island, nuclear power would never recover from this momentary connection to potential destruction; films such as *China Syndrome* (1979) and others made certain.

When Ronald Reagan took office in 1980, he clearly perceived the Cold War as an ongoing military confrontation with the bomb and its production as its main battlefield. While presidents since Richard Nixon had begun to negotiate with the Soviets for arms control agreements, Reagan escalated production of weapons in an effort to ''win'' the Cold War without a shot ever being fired. While it resulted in mammoth debt, Reagan's strategy pressed the Soviets to keep pace, which ultimately exacerbated weaknesses within the Soviet economy. By 1990, the leaders of the two super powers agreed that the Cold War was finished. While the Soviet Union crumbled, the nuclear arsenal became a concern of a new type. Negotiations immediately began to initiate dismantling much of the arsenal. However, the control provided by bipolarity was shattered, and the disintegration of the Soviet Union allowed for their nuclear weapons and knowledge to become available to other countries for a cost. Nuclear proliferation had become a reality.

In the 1990s, the domestic story of the bomb took dramatic turns as the blind faith of patriotism broke and Americans began to confront the nation's atomic legacy. Vast sections of infected lands were identified and lawsuits were brought by many ''down-winders.'' Under the administration of President Bill Clinton, the Department of Energy released classified information that documented the government's knowledge of radiation and its effects on humans. Some of this information had been gathered through tests conducted on military and civilian personnel. Leading the list of fall-out from the age of the bomb, Hanford, Washington, has been identified as one of the nation's most infected sites. Buried waste products have left the area uninhabitable.

The panacea of nuclear safety has, ultimately, been completely abandoned. Massive vaults, such as that in Yucca Mountain, Nevada, have been constructed for the storage of spent fuel from nuclear power plants and nuclear warheads. The Cold War lasted thirty to forty years; the toxicity of much of the radioactive material will last for nearly 50,000 years. The massive over-production of such material has created an enormous management burden for contemporary Americans. This has become the next chapter in the story of the bomb and its influence on American life.

—Brian Black

FURTHER READING:

Boyer, Paul. *By The Bomb's Early Light.* Chapel Hill, University of North Carolina Press, 1994.

Chafe, William H. *The Unfinished Journey.* New York, Oxford University Press, 1995.

Hughes, Thomas P. *American Genesis.* New York, Penguin Books, 1989.

May, Elaine Tyler. *Homeward Bound.* New York, Basic Books, 1988.

May, Ernest R. *American Cold War Strategy.* Boston, Bedford Books, 1993.

Bombeck, Erma (1927-1996)

Erma Bombeck, writer, humorist, and television personality, was primarily identified as a housewife and mother. Because she knew it so well, she was able to offer the housewife's-eye-view of the world in her writing. And it is because she took those roles so seriously that she was able to show the humorous side of the life of homemaker and mother so effectively.

She was born Erma Louise Fiste in Dayton, Ohio. Bombeck's mother, who worked in a factory, was only sixteen when Bombeck was born, and her father was a crane operator who died when she was nine years old. When little Erma showed talent for dancing and singing, her mother hoped to make her into a child star—the next Shirley Temple. But her daughter had other ideas. Drawn to writing very early, Bombeck wrote her first humor column for her school newspaper at age 13. By high school, she had started another paper at school, and begun to work at the Dayton Herald as a copy girl and reporter.

It was while working for the Herald that she met Bill Bombeck and set her cap for him. They married in 1949. Bombeck continued to write for the newspaper until 1953, when she and Bill adopted a child. She stopped working to stay home with the baby and gave birth to two more children over the next five years. Until 1965, Bombeck lived the life of the suburban housewife, using humor to get her through the everyday stress.

When her youngest child entered school, Bombeck wrote a column and offered it to the Dayton newspaper, which bought it for three dollars. Within a year ''At Wit's End'' had been syndicated across the country, and it would eventually be published by 600 papers. Bombeck also published collections of her columns, in books with names like *The Grass is Always Greener Over the Septic Tank* (1976) and *Family: The Ties that Bind . . . and Gag* (1987). Out of twelve collections, eleven were bestsellers, and from 1975 to 1981, she gained popularity on television with a regular spot on *Good Morning America.*

Beginning in the 1960s when most media tried hard to glorify the role of the homemaker with the likes of June Cleaver, Bombeck approached the daily dilemmas of real life at home with the kids with irreverence and affection. Because she was one of them, housewives loved her gentle skewering of housework, kids, and husbands. Even in the 1970s, with the rise of women's liberation, Bombeck's columns retained their popularity. Because she treated her subject with respect—she never made fun of housewives themselves, but of the many obstacles they face—feminists could appreciate her humor. Both mothers with careers and stay-at-home moms could find themselves in Bombeck's columns—and laugh at the little absurdities of life she was so skilled at pointing out.

Though Bombeck never called herself a feminist, she supported women's rights and actively worked in the 1970s for passage of the

Equal Rights Amendment. She also worked for various humanitarian causes, such as cancer research. One of her books, *I Want to Grow Hair, I Want to Grow Up, I Want to Go to Boise,* describes her interactions with children with cancer, something Bombeck herself faced in 1992 when she was diagnosed with breast cancer and had a mastectomy. She managed to find humor to share in writing about even that experience. Shortly after her mastectomy, her kidneys failed, due to a hereditary disease. Refusing to use her celebrity to facilitate a transplant, she underwent daily dialysis for four years before a kidney was available. She died at age 69 from complications from the transplant.

In spite of her fame and success, Bombeck remained unpretentious. She was able to write about American life from the point of view of one of its most invisible participants, the housewife. From that perspective, she discussed many social issues and united diverse women by pointing out commonalities and finding humor in the problems in their lives. Her tone was never condescending, but was always lighthearted and conspiratorial. Fellow columnist Art Buchwald said of Bombeck's writing, ''That stuff wouldn't work if it was jokes. What it was, was the truth.''

—Tina Gianoulis

FURTHER READING:

Bombeck, Erma. *Erma Bombeck: Giant Economy Size.* Garden City, New York, Doubleday, 1983.

Colwell, Lynn Hutner. *Erma Bombeck: Writer and Humorist.* Hillside, New Jersey, Enslow Publishers, 1992.

Edwards, Susan. *Erma Bombeck: A Life in Humor.* New York, Avon Books, 1998.

Jon Bon Jovi

Bon Jovi

Slippery When Wet, Bon Jovi's 1986 break-out album, brought ''metal'' inspired pop music to the forefront of American popular culture. The album was Bon Jovi's third effort for Mercury Records, which had gone through a bidding war to get the group in 1984. *Slippery When Wet* was different from Bon Jovi's earlier albums, the self-titled *Bon Jovi* and *7800 Fahrenheit,* because the group hired a professional songwriter to work on the project. Mercury Records also invested an unprecedented amount of marketing research into the album. The group recorded about 30 songs, which were played for focus groups of teenagers, and the resulting album spawned two number one singles, sold more than 10 million copies, and established Bon Jovi as the premier ''hair metal'' band of the 1980s.

The band had humble beginnings. New Jersey rocker Jon Bongiovi had recorded a single called ''Runaway'' with a group of local notables, and when the single received good radio play he decided to get a more permanent group together for local performances. Along with Bongiovi, who changed his last name to Bon Jovi, guitarist Richie Sambora, bassist Alec John Such, keyboardist David Rashbaum (changed to Bryan), and drummer Tico Torres were the members of a the new group Bon Jovi. Alec John Such eventually left the group in the early 1990s, and after that time no other members have officially been added to Bon Jovi.

After the success of *Slippery When Wet,* the group came back with *New Jersey* in 1988. The album was a big commercial success, selling 8 million copies, but after the *New Jersey* tour the group took some time apart for solo projects. Jon Bon Jovi found success working on the soundtrack to *Young Guns II* in 1990, and guitarist Sambora released *Stranger in this Town* in 1991.

Bon Jovi reunited to release *Keep the Faith* in the midst of the Seattle-based grunge rock movement. Its sales were lower than previous Bon Jovi efforts, but their tenth anniversary hits collection, *Crossroads,* went multi-platinum. The release of *These Days* in 1994 was a departure from their rock-pop roots and had a more contemporary sound. In the late 1990s, Jon Bon Jovi worked on solo projects and an acting career. His first solo album, *Destination Anywhere,* was released in 1997. It was accompanied by a mini-movie that got exposure on MTV.

—Margaret E. Burns

FURTHER READING:

Jeffries, Neil. *Bon Jovi: A Biography.* Philadelphia, Trans-Atlantic Publications, Inc., 1997.

Bonanza

The television series *Bonanza* was more than just another western in an age that had an abundance of them; it was also a clever marketing idea. First aired in 1959, it was especially developed to be filmed for color viewing, in order to compel Americans to buy color televisions. The series' appeal derived from *Bonanza*'s gentle, family orientation, which, of course, differed from *Gunsmoke* and most other westerns. In most westerns, writes literary scholar Jane Tompkins, the west "functions as a symbol of freedom, and of the . . . escape from conditions of life in modern industrial society." *Bonanza* met this basic criteria, but it also contained more fistfights than gunfights and centered around the occurrences of the Cartwrights, a loving, loyal family. Many episodes dealt with important issues like prejudice at a time when such themes were not common on television. In sum, *Bonanza* used the touchstones of the western genre to package a family drama that ran for fourteen years, until 1973.

Typical of westerns, *Bonanza* sought to detail the male world of ranching. Untypical of the genre, *Bonanza* had a softer side to most of its plots that combined with attractive actors to allow the show transgender appeal. The Cartwrights, of course, began with Ben, played by Canadian Lorne Greene. Generally serious and reasonable, Ben kept the ranch running. Thrice widowed, he raised three boys on his own with a little help from the cook, Hop Sing. There were no women on the Ponderosa. *Bonanza*, like *My Three Sons* and *Family Affair*, created a stable family without the traditional gender roles so palpable in 1950s and 1960s America. Part of the popularity of such series derives from the family's success despite its lack of conformity.

Each Cartwright brother served a different constituency of viewers. Adam, the eldest son, was played by Pernell Roberts. More intense than his brothers, Adam had attended college and was less likely to be involved in wild antics or love affairs. Dan Blocker played Hoss Cartwright, gullible and not terribly bright yet as sweet and gentle as he was huge. When not providing the might to defeat a situation or individual, Hoss faced a series of hilarious situations, often created by his younger brother, Little Joe. Michael Landon, who played Little Joe, proved to be the most enduring of these 1960s-style "hunks." The youngest member of the family, he was fun loving, lighthearted, and often in love. The care-free son, Little Joe brought levity to the family and the program. He was looked on by his father and older brothers with affection, and was usually at the center of the most humorous episodes. Landon came to *Bonanza* having starred in feature films, including *I Was A Teenage Werewolf*, and he wrote and directed many of the later episodes of *Bonanza* (though the series was primarily directed by Lewis Allen and Robert Altman).

The West, of course, would always be more than backdrop to the program. The general activities of the Cartwrights dealt with maintaining control and influence over the Ponderosa, their vast ranch. "Conquest," writes historian Patricia Nelson Limerick, "was a literal, territorial form of economic growth. Westward expansion was the most concrete, down-to-earth demonstration of the economic habit on which the entire nation became dependent." The West, and at least partly the genre of westerns, become a fascinating representation for assessing America's faith in this vision of progress. The success of the Cartwrights was never in doubt; yet the exotic frontier life consistently made viewers uncertain. The greatest appeal of *Bonanza* was also what attracted many settlers westward: the Cartwrights controlled their own fate. However, though plots involved them in maintaining or controlling problems on the Ponderosa,

the family's existence was not in the balance. The series succeeded by taking necessary elements from the western and the family drama in order to make *Bonanza* different from other programs in each genre. This balance allowed *Bonanza* to appeal across gender lines and age groups.

—Brian Black

FURTHER READING:

Brauer, Ralph, with Donna Brauer. *The Horse, the Gun, and the Piece of Property: Changing Images of the TV Western*. Bowling Green, Ohio, Popular Press, 1975.

Limerick, Patricia Nelson. *The Legacy of Conquest: The Unbroken Past of the American West*. New York, W.W. Norton, 1988.

MacDonald, J. Fred. *Who Shot the Sheriff?: The Rise and Fall of the Television Western*. New York, Praeger, 1987.

Tompkins, Jane. *West of Everything: The Inner Life of Westerns*. New York, Oxford University Press, 1992.

West, Richard. *Television Westerns: Major and Minor Series, 1946-1978*. Jefferson, North Carolina, McFarland & Co., 1987.

Yoggy, Gary A. *Riding the Video Range: The Rise and Fall of the Western on Television*. Jefferson, North Carolina, McFarland & Co., 1995.

Bonnie and Clyde

Despite their lowly deaths at the hands of Texas Rangers in 1934, Bonnie Parker and Clyde Barrow have enjoyed second lives within America's popular imagination. Gunned down by Texas authorities after a murderous bank-robbing spree, Parker and Barrow occupied a dusty backroom of the national memory until 1967, when a Warner Brothers feature film brought their tale of love, crime, and violence back to the nation's attention. Written by David Newman and Robert Benton and directed by Arthur Penn, *Bonnie and Clyde* tells a historically based yet heavily stylized story of romance and escalating violence that announced the arrival of a "New American Cinema" obsessed with picaresque crime stories and realistic violence. A major box-office hit, the film and its sympathetic depiction of its outlaw protagonists struck a nerve on both sides of the "generation gap" of the late 1960s, moving some with its portrayal of strong, independent cultural rebels while infuriating others by romanticizing uncommonly vicious criminals.

Inspired by the success of John Toland's book *The Dillinger Days* (1963), writers Newman and Benton distilled their screenplay from real-life events. In 1930, Bonnie Parker, a twenty-year-old unemployed waitress whose first husband had been jailed, fell in love with Clyde Barrow, a twenty-one-year-old, down-on-his-heels petty thief. In 1934, following Barrow's parole from the Texas state penitentiary, Barrow and Parker and a growing number of accomplices set off on a peripatetic crime spree. Travelling around the countryside in a Ford V-8, the Barrow gang held up filling stations, dry-cleaners, grocery stores, and even banks in ten states in the

Clyde Barrow and Bonnie Parker.

Southwest and Midwest. In the process, they murdered—in a particularly wanton manner—between twelve and fifteen innocent people. Bonnie and Clyde's bankrobbing binge came to a violent end in May 1934, when a former Texas Ranger named Frank Hamer, along with three deputies, tricked the outlaws into a fatal ambush along a highway outside Arcadia, Louisiana.

The Warner Brothers' cinematic retelling of these events creates the appearance of historical accuracy but makes a few revealing additions and embellishments. The film opens when Bonnie Parker (Faye Dunaway), first seen through the bars of her cage-like bed, restlessly peers out of her window, catching Clyde Barrow (Warren Beatty) attempting to steal her mother's car. Young and bored, Bonnie falls for the excitement that Clyde seems to represent. She taunts the insecure Clyde, whose gun and suggestive toothpick hint at a deep insecurity, into robbing the store across the street. Bonnie's quest for adventure and Clyde's masculine overcompensation drive the film, leading the two into an initially fun-filled and adventurous life of petty larceny. Having exchanged poverty and ennui for the excitement of the highway, the criminal couple soon attract accomplices: Clyde's brother Buck (Gene Hackman), his sister-in-law Blanche (Estelle Parsons), and C.W. (Michael J. Pollard), a mechanically adept small-time thief. In a scene modelled after John Dillinger's life, the film makes Bonnie and Clyde into modern-day Robin

Hoods. While hiding out in an abandoned farmhouse, Bonnie and Clyde meet its former owner, a farmer who lost it to a bank. They show sympathy for him and even claim to rob banks, as if some kind of social agenda motivated their crimes.

Careening around country roads to lively banjo tunes (performed by Lester Flatt and Earl Scruggs), the gang's encounters with the authorities soon escalate, abruptly turning their light-hearted romp into a growing nightmare. Playful scenes of mad-capped fun segue into brutal, bloody shootouts. One police raid ends with Buck's death, Blanche's capture, and a hair-raising getaway by Bonnie, Clyde, and C.W. At this point, apparently tiring of their rootless escapades, Bonnie and Clyde pine for a more traditional family life, but, tragically, find themselves trapped in a cycle of violent confrontations. Their escape comes when C.W's father agrees to lure Bonnie and Clyde into a trap in return for immunity for his son. To the tune of joyful bluegrass, the colorful outlaws drive blithely into the ambush, innocently unaware of the gory slow-motion deaths that await them.

The incongruous brutality of this dark ending left audiences speechless and set off a national debate on film, violence, and individual responsibility. Magazines such as *Newsweek* featured *Bonnie and Clyde* on their covers. Many of the film's themes, it appeared—economic inequality, a younger generation's search for meaning, changing women's roles, celebrity-making, escalation and confrontation, violence—resonated with American audiences struggling to make sense of JFK's assassination, the Vietnam War, the counterculture, student protests, and a mid-1960s explosion of violent crime. Precisely because of Bonnie and Clyde's contemporary relevance, critics such as Bosley Crowther of the *New York Times* decried its claims to historical authenticity. Clearly they had a point: by transforming homely and heartless desperadoes into glamorous folk heroes and by degrading and demonizing the authorities, especially former Texas Ranger Hamer, whom many considered the real hero of the story, the film did distort the historical record.

But glamorizing rebellion and violence, other critics such as Pauline Kael contended, was not the point of the film, which instead aimed to explore how ordinary people come to embrace reckless attitudes toward violence. The film, they point out, punishes Bonnie and Clyde—and by extension the audience—for their insouciant acceptance of lawbreaking. Interestingly, the popular and critical reception of *Bonnie and Clyde* appeared to recreate many of the divides it sought to discuss.

—Thomas Robertson

FURTHER READING:

Cott, Nancy F. "Bonnie and Clyde." *Past Imperfect: History According to the Movies.* Edited by Mark Carnes. New York, Henry Holt and Company, 1995.

Toplin, Robert Brent. "Bonnie and Clyde." *History by Hollywood: The Use and Abuse of the American Past.* Chicago, University of Illinois Press, 1996.

Trehern, John. *The Strange History of Bonnie and Clyde.* Jonathan Cape, 1984.

Bono, Sonny
See Sonny and Cher

Booker T. and the MG's

The longtime Stax Records house band achieved fame not only due to their musical abilities, but as an integrated band (two blacks and two whites) working at a time of significant racial tension in the United States. Though their most significant contribution was as a backup band for Stax artists including Wilson Pickett, Otis Redding, and Albert King, they also produced a number of their own Top 40 instrumentals, including "Green Onions," which reached number three in 1962. Through 1969, they produced five more Top 40 singles.

Though the group officially disbanded in 1971, they were working on a reunion album in 1975 when drummer Al Jackson, Jr. was killed tragically. Since then, the remaining members have continued to record both together and separately. Steve Cropper and Donald "Duck" Dunn, the group's guitarist and bass player respectively, also joined the Blues Brothers Band and appeared in both of their major motion pictures.

—Marc R. Sykes

FURTHER READING:

Bowman, Rob, and Robert M.J. Bowman. *Soulsville, U.S.A.: The Story of Stax Records.* New York, Macmillan, 1997.

Book-of-the-Month Club

When advertising copywriter Harry Scherman founded the Book-of-the-Month Club in 1926, he could hardly have predicted the lasting impact his company would have on the literary and cultural tastes of future generations. The Book-of-the-Month Club (BOMC) developed over time into a cultural artifact of the twentieth century, considered by many to be a formative element of "middlebrow" culture. With the monthly arrival of a book endorsed by a panel of experts, aspirants to middle-class learnedness could be kept abreast of literary trends through the convenience of mail order. The success of this unique approach to book marketing is evidenced by the fact that membership had grown to over one million by the end of the twentieth century.

Born in Montreal, Canada, in 1887, Harry Scherman was a highly resourceful marketer and a devout reader. He believed that the love of reading and of owning books could be effectively marketed to the "general reader," an audience often neglected in the book publishing industry of that period. Scherman's first book marketing scheme involved a partnership with Whitman Candy, in which a box of candy and a small leatherbound book were wedded into one package. These classic works, which he called the Little Leather Library, eventually sold over thirty million copies.

Scherman's ultimate goal was to create an effective means of large-scale book distribution through mail order. The success of direct-mail marketing had already been proven in other industries by the 1920s, but no one had figured out how to successfully market books in this fashion. The difficulty was in applying a blanket marketing approach to a group of unique titles with different topics and different audiences. Scherman's solution was to promote the idea of the "new book" as a commodity that was worthy of ownership solely because of its newness. His approach focused attention on consumers owning and benefiting from these new objects, rather than on the unique qualities of the objects themselves. In 1926, Scherman's idea came to fruition, and with an initial investment of forty thousand dollars by Scherman and his two partners, the Book-of-the-Month Club was born.

Two elements in his design of the early Book-of-the-Month Club were key to its lasting success. First, an editorial panel would carefully select each new book that would be presented to the club's members. Scherman selected five editors to serve on the first panel: Dorothy Canfield Fisher, Harry Canby (editor of *The Saturday Review*), William Allen White, Heywood Broun, and Christopher Morley. Each was known and respected as a writer or journalist, which helped reinforce the recognition of BOMC as a brand name. These literary authorities would save the reader time by recommending which new book to buy. Readers were assured that their selections were "the best new books published each month" and that they would stand the test of time and eventually become classics.

The second vital element to the success of BOMC was the institution of the subscription model, by which subscribers would commit to purchasing a number of books over a period of time. Each month, subscribers to the club would receive BOMC's newest selection in the mail. Later, BOMC modified this approach so that subscribers could exercise their "negative option" and decline the selection of the month in favor of a title from a list of alternates. The automatic approach to purchasing new books allowed BOMC to rely on future book sales before the titles themselves were even announced. Scherman targeted the desire of the club's middle-class subscribers to stay current and was able to successfully convince the public that owning the newest and best objects of cultural production was the most expedient way to accomplish this goal.

BOMC posed an immediate challenge to the insularity of bourgeois culture by presenting a shortcut method for achieving literary knowledge. Janice Radway remarked that the club's critics "traditionally suggested that it either inspired consumers to purchase the mere signs of taste or prompted them to buy a specious imitation of true culture." Skeptics were wary of the transformation of books into a commodity that would be purchased for the sake of its novelty. They were not wrongly suspicious; as Radway explained, BOMC "promised not simply to treat cultural objects as commodities, but even more significantly, it promised to foster a more widespread ability among the population to treat culture itself as a recognizable, highly liquid currency." The market forces that drive the publishing world were laid bare in the direct mail model, and it posed a clear threat to the idea that literature should be published because it is good, not because it appeals to the tastes of the "general public."

Behind that very real concern, however, was a discomfort with the populist approach taken by BOMC. The company's mission was to popularize and sell the book, an object which had previously been considered the domain of society's elite. Middlebrow culture, as it came to be known, developed in opposition to the exclusive academic realm of literary criticism, and it threatened the dominant cultural position of that group. At the other end of the spectrum, middlebrow taste also excluded anything avant-garde or experimental. This centrist orientation continued to make producers of culture uneasy throughout the twentieth century, because it reinforced the exclusion of alternative movements from the mainstream. This mainstream readership, however timid and predictable its taste might be, was a formidable economic group with great influence in the book marketplace.

The club's membership continued to grow past the one million mark by the end of the twentieth century as BOMC's strength in the book marketplace endured. BOMC selection has the power to sky-rocket little-known authors to instant fame and lucrative book deals, so the competition for a spot in the catalog has been fierce. Books are carefully chosen based on criteria that weigh a book's literary merit as well as its likelihood of appealing to a cross-section of the member-ship. For example, even books successful in the traditional market-place might not succeed with BOMC if their content cannot be clearly conveyed in the tight space of a catalog description. BOMC's selection process embodies the larger conflict in the publishing world between quality and marketability. The club's focus on the desires of its subscribers forces an exclusion of both overly commercial titles and the specialized, academic or literary material that would not appeal to the general reader. This customer-focused approach has also fueled a move at BOMC toward the industrywide trend of niche marketing. By the late 1990s, there were ten specialty book clubs that fell under the larger BOMC umbrella, in interest areas including spirituality, cooking, money, and history.

Time, Inc. purchased BOMC in 1977, and as the era of mergers and acquisitions in the 1980s and 1990s progressed, it brought major changes to Harry Scherman's original conception of a book distribu-tion service featuring books selected by an elite group of literary professionals. In 1994, under the ownership of media conglomerate Time-Warner, the BOMC's editorial board was dismantled altogether in favor of a more market-driven approach to acquiring new titles. This decision reflected the trend in the 1990s toward a "bestseller mentality" in the publishing industry, under which editorial judi-ciousness appeared to be almost a luxury.

With so much attention focused on the bottom line, it is not surprising that the company ventured onto the internet to increase sales, an unusual and risky move for a direct-mail marketer. Custom-ers could begin going to the company's website (*www.bomc.com*) to decline the month's selection online, and, the company presumed, order additional titles at the same time. While the paper catalogs mailed 17 times per year contain only about 200 selections each, on the website customers may choose from over 3,200 selections.

The proliferation of online marketing, including many book-sellers that offer discounted books via the internet, is certain to have an impact on BOMC's trademark approach to book distribution. In the end, the internet may be the final step in the process begun by Harry Scherman to promote widespread book distribution; customers can choose from thousands of books from dozens of companies at the click of a mouse. Regardless of the direction that the Book-of-the-Month Club takes in the future, it will always be known as a significant architect of twentieth-century literary taste.

—Caitlin L. Gannon

FURTHER READING:

Lee, Charles. *The Hidden Public: The Story of the Book-of-the-Month Club.* Garden City, New York, Doubleday, 1958.

Machlis, Sharon. "Web Page Beats Paper for Book Club." *Computerworld.* February 23, 1998, 41-44.

Radway, Janice A. *A Feeling for Books: The Book-of-the-Month Club, Literary Taste, and Middle-Class Desire.* Chapel Hill, University of North Carolina Press, 1997.

Rubin, Joan. *The Making of Middlebrow Culture.* Chapel Hill, University of North Carolina Press, 1992.

Boone, Pat (1934—)

With his boyish charm, unfailingly cordial manners, and firm beliefs in religion and the family, singer Pat Boone became the parentally approved antidote to the sexually charged rock 'n' roll acts of the 1950s. The precursor to the "safe" teen idols of the late 1950s and early 1960s, Boone has long been lampooned by critics and historians for his squeaky-clean image, and because he rose to fame by singing cover versions of tunes initially performed by black artists. But by no means was Boone an untalented nor an irrelevant musical force.

At the time that he was delivering renditions of Little Richard's "Tutti Frutti" and Fats Domino's "Blueberry Hill," many main-stream radio stations did not play so-called "race" artists. Certainly, Boone's versions were tame compared to the raw delivery of the original artists, but they also allowed the music to be introduced to audiences who otherwise wouldn't have heard it. Moreover, once Boone moved into pop ballads, with songs such as "April Love" and "Moody River," he became a respected artist in his own right. The mellow-voiced singer was unquestionably popular: following the volatile Elvis Presley, Boone was the second top-selling artist of the era. Since both Boone and Presley hailed from the South, and because they appeared to be polar opposites, they were frequently pitted against one another in the press. In truth, the men were friends; each respected the other's work. But where Presley was single and on the prowl, Boone was a devoted family man who advised young women of the day to refrain from premarital sex. In many ways they represented the duality of the decade.

The great-great-great-great grandson of frontiersman Daniel Boone was born Charles Eugene Pat Boone in Jacksonville, Florida. Raised in Nashville, he grew up singing at picnics, ladies' club meetings, fraternal organizations, and prayer meetings. A high school overachiever, he was captain of the baseball team, president of the student body, and voted most popular in his class. At seventeen he was singing on his own Nashville radio show. At eighteen he won a talent contest which took him to New York, where he appeared on a trio of *Ted Mack's Amateur Hour* television shows. He was nineteen when he married high school sweetheart Shirley Foley, daughter of country star Red Foley. At twenty, following an appearance on TV's *Arthur Godfrey's Talent Scouts,* he was contracted by Dot Records.

Boone enjoyed his first hit with a cover of Fats Domino's "Ain't That a Shame," which went gold. Ensuing tunes climbed the charts. By 1956, Boone had signed a seven-year contract, worth one million dollars, with Twentieth Century-Fox. He also had one million dollar contract with ABC for his own weekly television series, *The Pat Boone Chevy Showroom,* which premiered in October 1957, airing in prime time for three years. Ever pragmatic, Boone also continued his studies. Majoring in speech and English at Columbia University in New York, he was graduated magna cum laude in 1958. By this time he was the father of three daughters. There would later be a fourth.

Boone's movie career began with the back-to-back 1957 teen-oriented musical romances *Bernardine* and *April Love.* Both films generated number one singles, "Love Letters in the Sand" and "April Love," respectively. With the latter, Boone made headlines with his refusal to kiss leading lady Shirley Jones on the lips. In later years, in more adult roles, he did kiss his female costars; but as an actor, he was never able to transcend his image.

Known for the white buck shoes, which inadvertently became a trademark, Boone never made any attempt to downplay his God-fearing beliefs. For instance, the Pat Boone charm bracelet included charms of a 45 rpm record, shoes, a TV set, and a tiny Bible. Nor did Boone hesitate to moralize when he authored *Twixt Twelve and Twenty*, the 1959 teenage advice book. The year's number two nonfiction best-seller, it sold an amazing 207,000 copies during its first eight weeks. In discussing the subject of kissing, Boone wrote, "Kissing for fun is like playing with a beautiful candle in a roomful of dynamite! And it's like any other beautiful thing—when it ceases to be rare it loses its value . . . I really think it's better to amuse ourselves in some other way . . . I say go bowling, or to a basketball game." The man who had married at nineteen also said he did not approve of teenage marriages, "unless your maturity check sheet is literally covered with gold stars."

Like many of his contemporaries, Boone saw his career go stagnant in the midsixties, but he proved resilient, even taking his wholesome singing act to Las Vegas showrooms. In the seventies, he became heavily aligned with Christian ventures, including Jim and Tammy Bakker's PTL Club. He also poked fun at his goody-two-shoes image by doing TV commercials for milk. Following the success of daughter Debby Boone's 1977 single "You Light Up My Life," father and daughter sometimes performed together.

The 1980s found the healthy-looking Boone delivering workout tips to the over-forty crowd via the video *Take Time with Pat Boone*, and he was a pervasive presence on Christian broadcasting venues. In the nineties, he found eager audiences in the resort town of Branson, Missouri, marketed an extensive line of Christian publications and videos, and briefly reinvented himself with a turn as a heavy-metal performer. In the 1997 album *In a Metal Mood: No More Mr. Nice Guy*, Boone delivered versions of Ozzy Osbourne's "Crazy Train" and Mettalica's "Enter Sandman" with big band arrangements and guest musicians including Alice Cooper, Eddie Van Halen, and Slash. To promote the venture, Boone appeared on TV in black leather and wearing an earring. Not surprisingly, the novelty was off-putting to some of his older fans, but the younger generation accepted it for what it was: a grand put-on. The music world's biggest square had pulled off a hip act.

—Pat H. Broeske

FURTHER READING:

Anderson, John. "Rock 'N' Roll's Great White Buck." *Rolling Stone*. January 29, 1976, 27-31.

Boone, Pat. *Twixt Twelve and Twenty*. New York, Prentice-Hall, 1959.

Bronson, Fred. *The Billboard Book of Number One Hits*. New York, Billboard Publications, 1988.

"Pat Boone Boom: He Sets a New Style in U.S. Teen-Age Idols." *Life*. February 2, 1959, 75-81.

Torgerson, Ellen. "Pat Boone's Cup Runneth Over—With Milk." *TV Guide*. April 1, 1978, 32-34.

Whitcomb, Jon. "An Interview with Pat Boone." *Cosmopolitan*. November 1957, 66-71.

Borge, Victor (1909—)

Funny man of the piano, Victor Borge has enjoyed a seven-decade-long international career as a witty pianist-raconteur and popular radio, film, and television personality. His spontaneous comic talents, slapstick comedy routines, and satirical spoofs of classical music mannerisms made him one of the most popular and highest paid entertainers during the early 1940s. His 1950s Broadway show still holds a place in *The Guiness Book of World Records* as the longest running one-man show in theater history. Borge's ability to make light-hearted fun out of "serious" concert music has endeared him to audiences who might otherwise feel intimidated or bored by the traditional decorum of classical music repertoire and presentation.

Børge Rosenbaum (his name before emigrating to the United States) was born on January 3, 1909, in Copenhagen, Denmark. His mother was a pianist, and his father was a violinist with the Royal Danish Philharmonic and Opera orchestras for 35 years ("When he finally came home, my mother hardly recognized him!"). A child prodigy, Rosenbaum studied piano at the Royal Danish Music Conservatory, and later studied with Frederic Lamond and Egon Petri in Berlin. Following his 1926 recital debut in Copenhagen, he became one of Denmark's most popular concert pianists during the 1930s.

Victor Borge

Partly to circumvent his recurring stage fright, Borge developed a performance style combining classical music and quirky comedy. This appealing ''cross-over'' combination established him as a leading nightclub, stage, and film personality in Scandinavia. He had his revue debut in 1933, and in 1937 made the first of his six pre-World War II Danish films. Because of his Jewish background and his pointed satirical critiques of the Nazi regime, Borge was blacklisted and forced to flee Europe when the Germans invaded Denmark in 1940. He traveled to New York with his first wife, Elsie Shilton, an American citizen, and became a United States citizen himself in 1948. This first marriage ended in divorce in 1951, and Borge married again in 1953; he has five children and numerous grandchildren.

After an unsuccessful first appearance in a 1941 Broadway revue, Borge's comic talents were recognized on bandleader Rudy Vallee's radio show the same year. One of Borge's earliest successes was his trademark ''phonetic pronunciation'' act, in which non-verbal sounds indicate punctuation marks in a recited text. This act led to a regular slot on Bing Crosby's *Kraft Music Hall* radio show during the next two years (totaling 54 appearances). In 1943, Borge spoofed himself in a Hollywood film, playing con man ''Sir Victor Fitzroy Victor, K.B.O.B.E.'' in RKO's *Higher and Higher,* which also featured Frank Sinatra in his first starring role. Borge had his own NBC radio show in 1946, and his one-man *Comedy in Music* show enjoyed a phenomenal run at the Golden Theatre in New York from 1953 to 1956, running a record-setting 849 performances.

Borge's hilarious comedy routines include his demonstration of how modern composers write song hits (by cutting and pasting music from the old masters), his insertion of ''Happy Birthday'' into serious classical piano works, his falls off the piano bench at the start of the Tchaikovsky concerto, or his constant admonition to singers not to lean on his instrument (which causes the grand piano's curved indentation). Raising the piano lid to begin a performance, he mutters, ''Maybe we should get some fresh air in here.''

Also known for saying that ''the smile is the shortest distance between people,'' Borge has been called ''The Great Dane'' for his charitable contributions and international goodwill efforts. To acknowledge the heroism of Scandinavians who sheltered persecuted Jews during the Holocaust, he founded the Thanks to Scandinavia Foundation in 1963. Borge has been honored by the United States Congress and the United Nations, and knighted by the five Scandinavian nations.

—Ivan Raykoff

FURTHER READING:

Borge, Victor. *Victor Borge: An Autobiography* (forthcoming English translation).

Borge, Victor, and Robert Sherman. *My Favorite Comedies in Music.* New York, Franklin Watts, 1981.

———. *My Favorite Intermissions.* Garden City New York, Doubleday, 1971.

Borscht Belt

The area of the New York Catskills called the Borscht Belt came into being at the turn of the twentieth century and grew in popularity through the 1970s. During summers and holidays, Jews—primarily of Eastern European descent, from working to upper-middle class, and frequently first generation Americans—flocked to the Borscht Belt, where they enjoyed mainstream American leisure activities and entertainment in a place where they knew they'd be welcomed as Jews. Many people also came to the Borscht Belt to work—as waiters, owners, chefs, musicians, comics, and busboys. Not only did many students earn money for college by working summers in the Borscht Belt resorts, but many nationally known entertainers, especially comedians, got their start there. The Jewish culture that flourished in the Borscht Belt gradually overflowed into the mainstream, where it significantly influenced American popular culture.

The Borscht Belt was about 100 miles northwest of New York City in Sullivan and Ulster counties in the foothills of the Catskill Mountains. Sometimes known as the ''Jewish Alps,'' it covered an area of about 250 square miles. Jewish farmers, encouraged by the Jewish Agricultural Society, started settling this rural area beginning in the 1820s. Prefiguring the ''back-to-the-earth communes'' of the 1960s, some Jewish settlers founded socialist agricultural communities, and some of the bungalow colonies fomented much left-wing activity. In the Mirth Bungalow Colony, for example, ''entertainment'' included political discussions and poetry readings.

As early as the 1870s, middle- and upper-class Jews began to spend summers in this region, but as their numbers increased they were excluded from many resorts due to anti-Semitism. By the late 1890s and early 1900s, farmers started to offer their places as Jewish boarding houses and hotels that served kosher food. One of the largest resorts, The Nevele, continued to be a working farm until 1938. Eventually, most of the farmers realized it was more profitable to rent to visitors than to farm and they completely gave up farming. In the early 1900s, the Workmen's Circle, a left-leaning Jewish group, opened a sanitarium in the Catskills, providing ''fresh air'' for Jewish tuberculosis patients excluded from other sanitariums because of anti-Semitism. Unions such as the ILGWU opened up resorts where workers could recuperate. And perhaps most significantly, Yiddish actor Boris Thomaschevsky opened a resort with large indoor and outdoor theaters, thus beginning the Borscht Belt's influential entertainment tradition.

The postwar boom of the 1950s greatly helped the growth of the Borscht Belt. Not only did more people have disposable income, but also many owned cars, and the government built more highways on which to drive them. By 1952, there were 509 hotels and boarding houses in Sullivan County. During this period of popularity, more than a million people came to the Borscht Belt in the summers. The general trend was for ''stay-at home'' mothers, grandparents, and children to live in these rustic to resort dwellings all summer, while ''working'' fathers came for weekends. The larger resorts became known for their grand (kosher) all-you-can-eat feasts and higher caliber entertainers. However, whether small or large, all the establishments tried to feed the ''American Dream'' of leisure time and excess: advertising exaggerated the caliber of entertainers, the quality of food, and the size of basketball courts and other recreational facilities. Conversely, Jewish guests who were trying to assimilate into mainstream American culture sensationalized, to themselves and others, what was really available to them.

Despite exaggeration, the Borscht Belt birthed innumerable nationally known figures, especially in the entertainment world. Many Jewish entertainers started in the Borscht Belt because of anti-Semitism that excluded them from working in other venues. Additionally, their work included Jewish cultural references, not understood outside the Jewish world. However, as these entertainers became nationally popular, the Jewish content of their work became more familiar and understood in the mainstream *and* their work became more mainstream—with less specific Jewish content. Jewish life became known and integrated into American life and vice versa, often because of Borscht Belt entertainers.

A plethora of well-known comedians got their start in the Borscht Belt, including Henny Youngman, Milton Berle, Rodney Dangerfield, Danny Kaye, Buddy Hackett, Lenny Bruce, and Sid Ceasar. Five-year-old Jerry Lewis debuted at a Borscht Belt hotel singing "Brother Can You Spare A Dime." Others started out as comedians but moved to other areas of the entertainment world, especially TV. Jack Barry, for instance, was a standup comedian who met and teamed up with Dan Enright in Borscht Belt clubs. They started *Winky Dink and You,* a children's show known for the special transparent covers children had to put over the TV screen so they could draw the "hidden pictures" during Winky's adventures. Barry and Enright were also instrumental in producing and hosting early game shows, such as *Concentration* and *Tic Tac Dough.*

Cultural changes beginning in the late 1970s brought on the downfall of the Borscht Belt. As airplane transportation became more affordable, it was both easier and more enticing to travel to places further than the Catskills. Women, especially middle-class women, again entered the work force en masse, which prevented them from spending entire summers in the resorts. Many Jews became more assimilated and felt less of a need to be in separate establishments. Anti-Semitism lessened and many Jewish entertainers did not need to start in Jewish-only establishments.

By the 1980s and 1990s, only a few of the large hotels remained, and their cultural influence was virtually non-existent. Some smaller establishments were burned for insurance and some were sold as meditation centers, ashrams, or drug rehabilitation centers. Bungalow colonies were bought and occupied by Orthodox and Hassidic Jews, whose lifestyle necessitated separate communities. Some Yiddish culture, however, periodically still came alive in the Catskills through the 1990s. For example, *Klezkamp* is a weeklong annual event held in the Catskills at the end of December. Although primarily billed for Klezmer musicians, *Klezkamp* is attended by many families of all ages who go to Yiddish classes, lectures, cooking classes, dances, concerts and more, to experience and preserve rich Yiddish culture.

While some are critical of the term Borscht Belt—believing it to be pejorative—whatever the name, clearly the specific Jewish culture born there affected popular culture for many decades.

—tova gd stabin

Further Reading:

Adams, Joey. *The Borscht Belt.* New York, Bentley Publishing, 1973.

Brown, Phil. *Catskill Culture: A Mountain Rat's Memories of the Great Jewish Resort Area.* Philadelphia, Temple University Press, 1998.

Evers, Alf, and Elizabeth Cromley, Betsy Blackmar, Neil Harris, editors. *Resorts of the Catskills.* New York, St. Martin's Press, 1979.

Frommer, Myrna Katz, and Harvey Frommer. *It Happened in the Catskills: An Oral History in the Words of Busboys, Bellhops, Guests, Proprietors, Comedians, Agents, and Others Who Lived It.* New York, Harcourt Brace, 1996.

Gold, David M., editor. *The River and the Mountains: Readings in Sullivan County History.* South Fallsburg, Marielle Press, 1994.

Kanfer, Stefan. *A Summer World: The Attempt to Build a Jewish Eden in the Catskills from the Days of the Ghetto to the Rise and Decline of the Borscht Belt.* New York, Farrar, Straus & Giroux, 1989.

Lavender, Abraham D., and Clarence B. Steinberg. *Jewish Farmers of the Catskills: A Century of Survival.* Gainesville, University Press of Florida, 1995.

Richman, Irwin. *Borscht Belt Bungalows: Memories of Catskill Summers.* Philadelphia, Temple University Press, 1998.

The Boston Celtics

Perhaps no other team in professional sports is as respected, revered, and successful as the Boston Celtics. The Celtics controlled the ranks of professional basketball in the late 1950s and during the 1960s, overshadowing the entire league. Not until the Chicago Bulls of the 1990s has a team even come close to the heights the Boston Celtics reached at the peak of their success. The team produced some of the most memorable moments in sports history on its way to a record 16 NBA World Championships.

Created as one of the original members of the Basketball Association of America (BAA) on June 6, 1946, the Celtics found hard times in their initial years because Bostonians were much more interested in baseball and hockey in the early years of the franchise. However, their opening home game on November 5, 1946, proved exciting. Future actor and star of *The Rifleman* Chuck Connors broke a backboard with a slam-dunk, delaying the game. The BAA became the National Basketball Association (NBA) after the 1949/50 season, and with the hiring of coach Arnold "Red" Auerbach in 1950, the Celtics started on their road to sports history at the dawn of a new and consolidated league.

The Auerbach years of the Celtics were some of the most magical in all of sports. He revolutionized the way basketball was played by emphasizing the concept of the fast break and the sixth man. In the process, he built one of the most dominant teams in the history of professional sports. The Celtics also made history in the 1950s by drafting the first black player in the NBA, Charles Cooper. In 1956, big man Bill Russell joined the Celtics, thus giving them the most amazing player of the times. Russell also contributed to change in the way basketball was played, doing things on the court that no other player of his size had ever done. Combined with star guard Bob Cousy, Russell led a strong supporting cast of players to the 1957 NBA Championship, the franchise's first, but far from last, victory.

Starting in 1959, the Celtics won the next eight NBA titles in a row, and a total of 11 in a 13-year span. During this stretch, they at one time had three future basketball Hall of Fame members who didn't even start. The Celtics finished off the decade with victories in 1968 and 1969 after which, by their high standards, the team declined somewhat. Nonetheless, they won another pair of NBA titles in 1974 and 1976. Larry Bird, one of the next generation's dominant players, joined the Celtics for the 1979/80 season and, along with teammates Robert Parrish and Kevin McHale, returned the Celtics to their former glory and dominance by leading them to championship seasons in 1981, 1984, and 1986. Some of the greatest players basketball has known wore the Celtic green, among them John Havlicek, K.C. Jones, Dave Cowens, Don Nelson, Tom Heinsohn, and Frank Ramsey.

The Boston Celtics defined what it means to be a dynasty in sports. Their appeal as a hard-working, blue-collar team under Red Auerbach appealed to the city of Boston and gained widespread support, giving definition to the term "Celtic Pride." The familiar parquet floor, the leprechaun mascot, and Celtic green have become familiar images to all followers of basketball, as well as sports fans in general.

—Jay Parrent

FURTHER READING:

Fitzgerald, Joe. *That Championship Feeling: The Story of the Boston Celtics.* New York, Scribner Publishing, 1975.

Heinsohn, Tommy H. and Leonard Lewin. *Tommy, Don't You Ever Smile? The Life and Times of Tommy Heinsohn and the Boston Celtics.* Garden City, New York, Doubleday, 1976.

Henshaw, Tom. *The Boston Celtics: A Championship Tradition.* Englewood Cliffs, New Jersey, Prentice-Hall, 1974.

Boston Garden

One of the most beloved landmarks in New England, the Boston Garden opened in 1928. It was best known as the home court of the Boston Celtics, who won 16 titles while playing there. When the Garden closed in 1995, its bricks and seats were sold as mementos. The arena's parquet basketball floor was its most famous feature. Because of post-World War II lumber shortages, the floor had to be made of small squares of wood which were then pieced together. The floor was notorious for dead spots and warped boards which the Celtics used as an advantage over visiting teams.

—Austin Booth

Boston Marathon

The Boston Marathon is one of the greatest racing events in the world. The idea for the Marathon began in the late nineteenth century when United States Olympic team manager, John Graham, wanted to establish a counterpart to the Olympic Marathon held in Greece in 1896. He wanted to do this in his adopted city of Boston, Massachusetts. Graham drove his horse carriage outside of Boston to try to find a place that resembled the Grecian terrain. He found it in Ashland and began making plans for laying out the course that would stretch to Boston. The Boston Athletic Association (B.A.A.) was the official organizer of the event. The running of the inaugural Boston Marathon occurred on April 19, 1897, Patriot's Day in Massachusetts. There were only eighteen competitors. The Boston Marathon helped bring distance running to the forefront of the American sports world. Equally important, the race has grown into a legitimate event that tests the waters of Olympic and international competition. Even though women were initially banned from the event the Marathon paved the way for the impressive expansion of women's distance running, as well as wheelchair racing, beginning in the 1970s.

In the 1920s the official start of the Marathon would be moved to Hopkington. That town and the surrounding area became quickly absorbed into the marathon world and residents became captivated by the popularity of the event. One negative trait during the first seven decades of the Boston Marathon was that women were not allowed to compete. There were "reports," however, over the years about women running incognito. The Boston Marathon would ultimately have its share of winners, losers, legends, and notorious individuals. Americans like champion-runner Clarence DeMar dominated the Marathon during the race's early period in the 1910s and 1920s. Americans made their mark as sufficient competitors in the world's athletic stage. Yet, some people criticized the Marathon for the lack of foreigners participating in it. But even as early as 1900 the Boston Marathon had an international flavor to it as Canadians competed along with Americans and did extremely well, winning the event.

The 1920s were significant years for the Boston Marathon. The race, for example, witnessed its first European-born winner as Greek national Peter Trivouldas crossed the finish line ahead of everyone else. In 1920 a radio station began broadcasting live coverage of the Marathon. People could now tune-in and receive up to the minute reports and results of the race. It was also announced in that decade that the Boston Marathon would be accepted as the American Olympic Trials to see which American distance runner earned the right to compete in the Olympic Marathon. The "foreign invasion" really began in earnest during the post-World War II era. In fact, from 1946 to 1957 Americans would not win the Marathon. Over the next several decades Boston Marathon winners would include Asians, Europeans, Africans, and Latin Americans making it a true international competitive race.

The groundbreaking years for the Boston Marathon were the 1970s. In 1972, the 76th running of the Boston Marathon, women were officially allowed to compete. Women ran the Boston Marathon during the previous decade but they were not officially acknowledged as entrants or competitors. In 1966, for instance, 23 year-old Roberta Gibb became the first woman to complete the distance. She had applied for entry during that year but was denied so she decided to take matters into her own hands. Before the race she stood on the curb with her hood over her head and patiently waited for the start. When the race started she began running with the hood still over her head. Several miles into the race she took the hood off and felt more comfortable as the crowds acknowledged her and even cheered her on. She finished in under three and a half hours. The Marathon reached another milestone in the 1970s. In 1975, it became the first significant marathon in the country to allow wheelchair athletes to compete. As the number of wheelchair entrants increased in the succeeding years so did the quality of competition and the equipment which the wheelchair racers used. During these years the Marathon became home to the National Wheelchair Marathon Championships and, soon after, wheelchair athletes achieved a tremendous feat by breaking the two-hour barrier. Ever since the 1970s both women and wheelchair racing at the Boston Marathon has grown in popularity and have received tremendous support.

Yet, the Boston Marathon is also filled with controversy. Take, for instance, the infamous Rosie Ruiz episode in 1980. Ruiz is considered a villain of the Marathon. She jumped into the race with about a mile to go and claimed victory despite the fact that no one had seen her at the mile markers and the water stations, nor had the cameras picked her up as well. Ruiz was ultimately stripped of her title a week after she "won" the event because of cheating. She was disqualified from the B.A.A. Her case though was not an isolated one in the history of the race. Cheating had been attempted twice before during the early twentieth century and, in both instances, the men were promptly caught and suspended or disqualified by the B.A.A.

In the late twentieth century the Boston Marathon opened the door for many foreign athletes to display their athletic talents in front of America and the world. It has become common for foreigners to do well at Boston. This trend can be seen in other American marathons such as the New York City, Chicago, and Los Angeles Marathons. The Marathon has become a major trendsetter in American society, helping advance distance running in the wake of the physical fitness craze.

To understand the growth of American road racing over the years one only has to look at the gradual but sure emergence of the popularity of the Boston Marathon in the United States. The two run parallel to each other and, naturally, complement one another. The Boston Marathon itself is an institutional icon in the sports world. No other race is representative of the overall trends, both positive and negative, that have occurred in American society. The Marathon shaped women's running allowing them to compete in a distance event that draws females from around the world in what one hopes to be "friendly," yet very intense, competition. Similarly, wheelchair athletes also enjoy the spotlight that is cast upon the people who run in the Marathon. Both women and wheelchair racing, as a consequence, have grown into legitimate forms of racing divisions that have Olympic ramifications. With regard to the men, the Marathon showcases the best the world has to offer in the sport of running and racing. Winning times seem to get lower which each passing year. The greatest influence the Marathon has on American society is that it inspires many individuals, both young and old, to enter the race. It has become a personal challenge to Americans to enter and finish the event, with a little hard work along the way of course, not necessarily to win it. The identity and lure of the Marathon, then, permeates throughout society and satisfies America's free-spirited fascination with self-gratification.

—David Treviño

FURTHER READING:

Connelly, Michael. *26 Miles to Boston: The Boston Marathon Experience from Hopkington to Copley Square.* Hyannis, Massachusetts, Parnassus Imprints, 1998.

Derderian, Tom. *Boston Marathon: The First Century of the World's Premier Running Event.* Champaign, Illinois, Human Kinetics, 1996.

Falls, Joe. *The Boston Marathon.* New York, Macmillan, 1977.

Higdon, Hal. *Boston: A Century of Running: Celebrating the 100th Anniversary of the Boston Athletic Association Marathon.* New York, St. Martin's Press, 1995.

Hosler, Ray, ed. *Boston, America's Oldest Marathon.* Mountain View, California, Anderson World, 1980.

Krise, Raymond, and Bill Squires. *Fast Tracks: The History of Distance Running since 884 B.C.* Brattleboro, Vermont, The Stephen Greene Press, 1982.

Boston Strangler

The term "Boston Strangler" refers to the person or persons who committed a series of thirteen brutal murders of women in

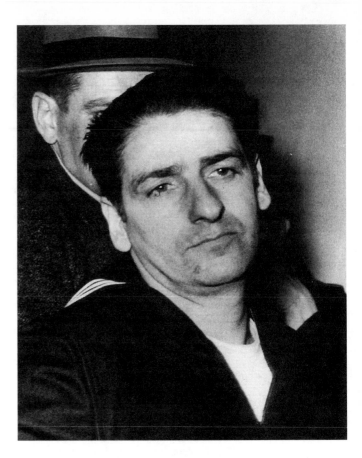

Albert DeSalvo (aka The Boston Strangler).

Boston and the surrounding area in the early 1960s. Although Albert DeSalvo did eventually confess to the killings, neither he nor anyone else ever went to trial for them.

The murderous activities of the Boston Strangler began in June of 1962 and lasted until January of 1964. In twelve of the thirteen murders, the victim was strangled, and some of the victims were also struck violently on the head and/or stabbed. One victim was stabbed repeatedly in the throat and breast in lieu of strangulation. The victims were usually attacked sexually, and the bodies were generally left in degrading positions. The first six murder victims were between 55 and 85 years of age, as were two of the later ones. Five victims were between the ages of 19 and 23.

The serial killings greatly frightened the community. Responding to public concern, Edward Brooke, the Attorney General of Massachusetts, created what was popularly called a "Strangler Bureau" whose mission was to hunt down the murderer(s). A Medical-Psychiatric Committee was constituted in order to develop a profile of the criminal(s). The Committee came up with a multiple-strangler theory, positing one man ("Mr. S") as the killer of the older victims and another man or men as the killer of the younger women. The profile described Mr. S to be a man suffering from impotence and an oedipal complex, both of which supposedly drove him to murderous rages against his victims. This profile did not match DeSalvo, causing the science of profiling to lose esteem in criminal justice circles, although more sophisticated profiling techniques would subsequently be developed.

The Strangler Bureau even called in a Dutch psychic who claimed to be able to learn about people from being in their presence or touching items associated with them. The psychic gave a description of the killer, allegedly based on the auras given off by items associated with the murders. Again, the killer described by the psychic did not match DeSalvo's characteristics.

Neither psychological nor psychic investigation was able to solve the case. Then Albert DeSalvo, a man with a long criminal history, confessed to being the Strangler. After serving time in a juvenile home, he committed a string of burglaries until he joined the Army at 17. While serving in the American forces in Germany, he met and married a German woman, and also became the Army's middleweight boxing champion. He was also accused of molesting a nine-year-old girl, but he was not convicted because the child's parents did not want to pursue the matter. DeSalvo was awarded an honorable discharge in 1956, and brought his wife back with him to the United States.

Convinced that his wife could not satisfy his sexual needs, DeSalvo started visiting the apartments of young women, gaining entrance by pretending to be from a modeling agency. Using this ruse, he tried to fondle the women. Police knew DeSalvo as the "Measuring Man" because he pretended to take the measurements of the women he was molesting. He served a few months in prison for breaking and entering, and soon after his release his activities escalated from molestation to rape. This time, he was known as the "Green Man" on account of the color of the clothes he wore while seeking victims. It was as the Green Man, not as the Boston Strangler, that DeSalvo was finally arrested in 1964.

DeSalvo confessed to being the Strangler while awaiting trial in a psychiatric facility at Bridgewater. The confession was quite detailed, displaying a knowledge of details about the murders that were not available to the public. Either DeSalvo had been fed the information by police, or else he was describing crimes he had actually committed. In 1967, DeSalvo went on trial for the Green Man sexual assaults. He was represented at trial by the nationally famous Boston attorney F. Lee Bailey. The jury convicted DeSalvo on a range of charges, and he was sentenced to life in prison for the Green Man crimes. He was never charged with the Strangler killings, however. In 1973, DeSalvo was killed by a fellow-inmate.

In addition to the obligatory true-crime book, the murders inspired a 1968 movie entitled *The Boston Strangler,* with a cast that included Tony Curtis as Albert DeSalvo, and Henry Fonda. In 1971, the Texas House passed a resolution that commended Albert DeSalvo for his work in the area of population control. The resolution was a practical joke by a legislator who wanted to demonstrate how little attention his colleagues paid to the bills they passed.

—Eric Longley

FURTHER READING:

"Boston Strangler" (video). *Great Crimes and Trials of the Twentieth Century.* Arts and Entertainment Network, 19992.

DeSalvo, Albert. *Confessions of the Boston Strangler.* New York, Pyramid Books, 1967.

Frank, Gerold. *The Boston Strangler.* New York, New American Library, 1966.

Kelly, Susan. *The Boston Stranglers: The Wrongful Conviction of Albert DeSalvo and the True Story of Eleven Shocking Murders.* Secaucus, New Jersey, Carol Publishing Group, 1995.

The Boston Symphony Orchestra

At the beginning of the 1880s, America had no symphony orchestra to equal the great European ensembles. Major Henry Lee Higginson would permanently change that situation by creating the Boston Symphony Orchestra (BSO), which not only set musical standards and became a model for other American orchestras but demonstrated that large audiences could be attracted to what was considered "elitist" culture.

The New York Philharmonic, the nation's oldest orchestra in 1880, had been organized some 40 years earlier. It offered only six concerts and six public rehearsals a season. Players elected conductors and sent last minute substitutes for concerts if more lucrative engagements became available. In fairness to the players, membership dues and fines levied on absentees at concerts served as the orchestra's financial mainstays. Earnings from ticket sales were appallingly low. In 1878, each musician earned only $17.50; in 1886, a relatively good year, each earned just $225.

Audiences responded to the haphazard nature of the enterprise by becoming boisterous, especially if players were openly contemptuous of the conductor. Newspaper accounts discouragingly noted an "ebulliency of animal spirits [that] sometimes overcame . . . [any] sense of decorum."

Except possibly for the behavior of audiences, symphony orchestras fared no better in Boston. Which was why a March 1881 notice in local newspapers, placed by Higginson, generated immediate interest. He called for: "The Boston Symphony Orchestra in the Interest of Good Music." Higginson emphasized that "Notwithstanding the development of musical taste in Boston, we have never yet possessed a full and permanent orchestra, offering the best music at low prices, such as may be found in all the large European cities, or even in the smaller musical centres of Germany."

The real problem was how to finance such an ensemble. Higginson advised that during the course of a season he would present "sixty selected musicians" in 20 concerts and sell subscriptions for "either $10 or $5, according to position," and single tickets at 75¢ or 25¢ each. In addition, tickets would be available for a public rehearsal during "one afternoon of every week."

Higginson understood that ticket sales alone could not finance the orchestra. He was personally worth $750,000 and forthrightly declared that he would provide up to $50,000 of an estimated annual $100,000 budget. The rest of the operational budget would come from ticket sales and from selling the orchestra's services to opera companies—in the summer of 1885, Higginson announced a series of concerts of "lighter music," which became famous as the Boston Pops. Economically inclined, he decided against a pension plan for musicians and would not even entertain the idea of a musicians' union.

As for repertory, Higginson thought "anything worthy could be put on programs, which were to be relatively brief, an hour and three quarters being the upper limit." He defined "unworthy" as the "trash . . . heard in the theatres, sentimental or sensational nonsense." Wagner could be performed, but the composer was not among the Major's favorites. Late Beethoven, possibly "the work of a lunatic," could also be played, since as a fair-minded person, the Major could not see barring "serious music."

Higginson's first choice for conductor turned out to be a mistake. Georg Henschel, a young local musician, allowed regional loyalties to figure in his recruitment of players, so it was an easygoing band of Bostonians who performed in the city's Music Hall on Saturday nights for the relatively high fees of $6 per concert and $3 per rehearsal. Henschel departed Boston in 1884. Higginson's later choices won the approval of critics but were not without controversy. Thus, Arthur Nikisch was described in the local press as having an ''undue passion in comparatively passionless melody.''

What could not be questioned was that the quality Higginson demanded of his musicians had an enormous impact on audiences. From the very first concert, BSO subscribers clamored for tickets. More than 83,000 people attended the first season, and as early as 1886, the orchestra earned $100,000 in five days of advance sales for 24 concerts and 24 public rehearsals of the ''severest classical music.''

By October 1900, just 19 years after its founding, the orchestra had inspired such confidence in its stability that donors gladly made possible a permanent home after Higginson threatened that if a hall was not built, he would disband the ensemble. In 1903, a pension fund was established by and for the musicians, for the benefit of which Higginson permitted a special concert annually.

By the time the BSO was 25 years old, in 1906, it had served as a model for orchestras in Chicago, Cincinnati, and Pittsburgh. Higginson was constantly sought out for advice and solicited for donations to various enterprises. As he lengthened the BSO season, he tried to keep ticket prices as low as possible to attract audiences of all classes. As late as the 1907-08 season, subscriptions were still only $18 and $10.

Higginson himself paid the highest price of all for attendance; up to June 1893, he is known to have contributed $250,000. His players appreciated his generosity. The orchestra's fourth conductor, Emil Paur, declared, ''The reason why the Boston Orchestra plays better than all other existing orchestras is—besides the excellent quality of the men—the comfortable living the men are able to enjoy.''

After Higginson's retirement at the age of 82, the only major change in the BSO's operations occurred in the early 1940s, when the American Federation of Musicians threatened to boycott the orchestra's broadcasts and recordings, prevent guest conductors and soloists from appearing with it, and blacklist concert halls in which it appeared while on tour, unless it unionized. This time forces arrayed against management were too strong. In 1942, the BSO, the only non-unionized ensemble in the nation, came to terms with the union and joined.

—Milton Goldin

FURTHER READING:

Goldin, Milton. *The Music Merchants.* New York, Macmillan, 1969.

Johnson, H. Earle. *Symphony Hall, Boston.* Boston, Little, Brown, 1950.

Shanet, Howard. *Philharmonic: A History of New York's Orchestra.* New York, Doubleday, 1975.

Bouton, Jim (1939—)

Right-handed pitcher Jim Bouton concluded his unspectacular major league career in 1978 with a record of 62-63. But it was the impact he made off the field, with his bestselling clubhouse memoir *Ball Four,* that earned him a place in baseball history. As a New York Yankee between 1962 and 1968, the urbane Bouton was an uneasy presence on one of the hardest-living 25-man squads in the majors. Apparently he was taking notes. *Ball Four,* published in 1970, pulled no punches in describing the drinking and carousing of some of the game's most idealized figures, including Mickey Mantle. The tight-knit ballplayer's fraternity, enraged over Bouton's betrayal of confidence, ostracized the pitcher for decades. Scandalous at the time, *Ball Four* is considered tame in comparison to subsequent tell-all accounts. Nevertheless, the book was selected by the New York Public Library as one of the ''Books of the Century.''

—Robert E. Schnakenberg

FURTHER READING:

Bouton, Jim. *Ball Four (20th Anniversary Edition).* New York, Macmillan, 1990.

Bow, Clara (1905-1965)

With her performance in the 1927 silent movie, *It,* rising film star Clara Bow transformed herself almost overnight into the Jazz Age icon called ''the 'It' Girl.'' The movie's record-breaking popularity turned the single word ''It'' into a national euphemism for sex appeal, and helped make Bow, two years later, the highest paid female actor in Hollywood. Writer and Hollywood trendsetter, Elinor Glyn, first coined the expression in her novella, *It,* then selected Bow as its embodiment in the role of Betty Lou Spence. As ''the 'It' Girl,'' Bow became the dominant sex symbol of the 1920s and 1930s, and a singular identity within Hollywood history as the first wholly American vision of erotic appeal. Before Bow, depictions of bold female sexuality were associated with foreignness, as in the career of the 1910s' star, Theda Bara, whose studio-manufactured image feigned Arabic heritage. Bow's portrayals expressed unabashed attraction to men in ways that American-identified female stars, such as ''virginal'' Lillian Gish, eschewed. Bow's spontaneous style of acting exasperated camera crews of the day, but her abandonment and intuitive skill were the qualities that translated as 'It' to spectators, and to directors like *It*'s Clarence Badger, who learned to ''explain the scene to her and just let her go.''

With her natural red hair, cupid bow lips and hourglass figure, Clara Bow's persona mirrored the liberated decade itself. Onscreen and off, she epitomized the high living, carefree and carnally-emancipated ''flapper.'' Sporting bobbed hair, glittery dresses falling above the knee, and headbands, ''flappers'' were 1920s good-time girls who smoked, drank, frequented jazz clubs and reveled in the nation's prosperity by flouting turn-of-the-century rules for feminine behavior. F. Scott Fitzgerald, the writer who dubbed the decade ''the Jazz Age,'' observed, ''Clara Bow is the quintessence of what the term 'flapper' signifies as a definite description: pretty, impudent, superbly assured, as worldly-wise, briefly-clad, and 'hard-berled' as possible. . . . there are thousands more patterning themselves after her girls, all sorts of girls, their one common trait being that they are

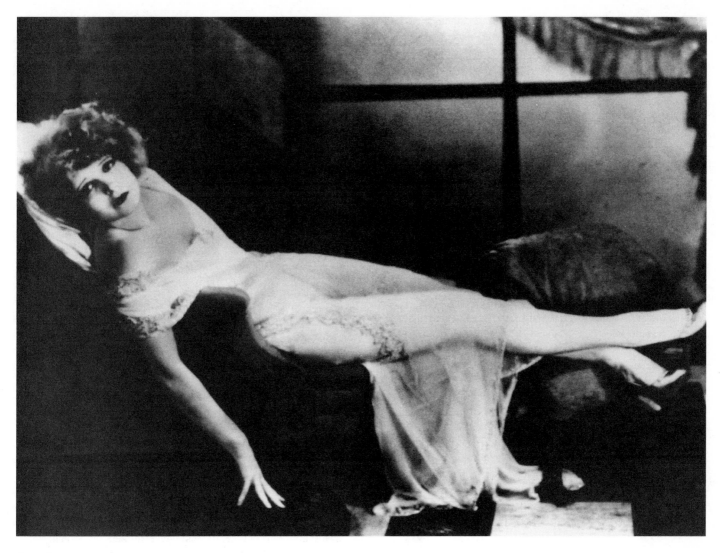

Clara Bow

young things with a splendid talent for living.'' Many novice actresses, including Joan Crawford, also viewed Bow as a role model and imitated her screen type.

Bow's acting ability was innate, but her "talent for living" was acquired. Born July 29, 1905 to impoverished parents eking out an abject existence in the tenement slums of Brooklyn, Bow's childhood was marked by brutal neglect. Her mother, Sarah Bow, née Gordon, struggled with severe mental illness and despised her primarily absent husband, Robert Bow. Oppressive emotional and economic conditions affected Bow the way many a movie star's bleak background did: she sought escape in movie houses and moving picture fan magazines like *Motion Picture Classic* and *Photoplay*. Poring over stories of "America's Sweetheart," Mary Pickford, and the swashbuckling Douglas Fairbanks, Bow vowed to join their ranks. When she confided her dreams of stardom to her mother, Sarah castigated her desires as a prostitute's. Bow's conflict with her mother was not unique. As Nickelodeons across the country gave way to theatrical movie houses in the 1910s and 1920s, movie-going united cross-segments of the culture. But this new entertainment activity also provoked 1920s sensibilities concerned with religious virtue and

threatened by perceptions of movies' degenerate influence on youths. This gap between the public's values and Hollywood's profligate spending, depictions of moral laxity, and offscreen scandals like the rape trial of Fatty Arbuckle, features as a constant in the history of American movie culture. For example, a related outrage over movie violence spurred 1996 Republican presidential candidate Robert Dole to attack the industry as part of his campaign. To impugn his opponent, President Clinton, Dole accused him of being a "Hollywood insider." Had she lived to witness it, Bow's mother would have been horrified by "the 'It' Girl's" appearance in movies titled *Wild Party*, *Daughters of Pleasure*, *Dangerous Curves*, *Kiss Me Again* and *Call Her Savage*.

Bow established a professional Hollywood reputation as hard-working, kind-hearted and unpretentious. She also developed a notoriety that blurred with her fun-loving screen personality and shaded into promiscuity. Her lovers included co-stars Gary Cooper, Gilbert Roland, Frederic March, and director Victor Fleming. Her stardom occurred simultaneously with the increasing popularity of scandal sheets, and the press tracked her every dalliance. What Americans loved onscreen, appalled them in tabloid reports of Bow's refusal to marry. Involved in several financial scandals, she diminished further in the Depression-era public's esteem when details of her spending were publicized during a trial involving a personal secretary, who had attempted to blackmail Bow based on records she secretly kept of Bow's bedroom visitors.

Bow ended her film career in 1933, in response to her loss of fans' affections and a career sagging under the weight of stock roles in uninspired films. Having discovered the Clara Bow formula, Paramount studio exploited it and her unequalled popularity by sticking her in a series of low budget, predictable vehicles co-starring unknowns. Despite reviewers' praise for 1933's *Hoopla,* constant typecasting as the seductive girl with endless self-confidence—dimensions lacking in her own increasingly fragile identity—disgusted Bow. Her retirement also coincided with the emergence of the "talkies." Though she completed several successful movies requiring dialogue, and her voice did not doom her as it did other stars attempting the silent-to-talkie transition (e.g. Pola Negri and John Gilbert), the strain of controlling her Brooklyn accent and memorizing lines took its toll. She abandoned her film career for marriage and motherhood. As other seminal Hollywood personalities like Greta Garbo would, Bow fled Hollywood and entered into seclusion. Despite her escape from the fishbowl pressures of fading stardom, she experienced severe breakdowns requiring hospitalization.

Bow disappeared from the public eye, but "The 'It' Girl's" legend resurfaced in various cultural expressions. In the 1950s, *Life* magazine featured a photo spread of Marilyn Monroe made up as Bow. In the 1980s, entertainer Madonna billed herself as the new "'It' Girl," and musician Prince featured Bow's picture on the cover of an album. In 1998, a cover of Vanity Fair posed the question of whether Hollywood newcomer, Gretchen Mol, might not be the next "'It' Girl." Bow herself identified with Marilyn Monroe, saying of her death, "A sex symbol is a heavy load to carry when one is tired, hurt, and bewildered."

—Elizabeth Haas

FURTHER READING:

MacCann, Richard Dyer. *The Stars Appear.* Metuchen, Scarecrow Press, 1992.

Morella, Joseph, and Edward Z. Epstein. *The "It" Girl.* New York, Delacorte, 1976.

Stenn, David. *Runnin' Wild.* New York, Doubleday, 1988.

Bowie, David (1947—)

David Bowie is a performer on the cutting edge of music culture, whose glamour, fluid sexual identity, and mystery influenced musicians such as Michael Jackson and Culture Club. Bowie shifted like a chameleon over a career spanning seedy British club performances in the 1960s to successful and extravagant world tours in the 1980s. His incarnations include androgynous space messiah Ziggy Stardust, film roles in art house movies, music videos with Mick Jagger and collaborations with electronic music pioneer Brian Eno. He incited

David Bowie

outrage with frank interviews about his bisexuality and his appearance in a dress on the LP cover of the hard rock album *The Man Who Sold the World* (1970). In the 1990s, the artist invented himself anew as a suave, elegant eccentric and faded from the music mainstream, but he continues to be a style icon and reference point.

—Petra Kuppers

Bowling

Bowling, the sport of throwing a heavy ball down a lane and knocking over pins, has been around for centuries, and has become one of America's most democratic pastimes. Often referred to as the "great cultural leveler," bowling is affordable, allows for the participation of both genders, all ages, skill levels, and classes, and encourages a social camaraderie rare in other competitive sports. In fact, an instructional book written in 1987 said that "one of the greatest benefits of bowling is the development of friendships."

Bowling became widely popular almost as soon as it reached the shores of America, in the early 1800s. The Dutch, Germans, and English helped establish the sport in American colonies. English bowls, or lawn bowling, a sport for blue-bloods, was played outdoors on a bowling green. But the modern form of American bowling derives mainly from the German game of *Kegelspiel,* or kegeling, which used nine pins set in a diamond formation. By the 1800s, kegeling Germans established New York as the country's "bowling capital." Kegeling, unlike lawn bowling, was enjoyed by German peasants; this reputation as a common-man's sport has characterized bowling throughout its American history. The first indoor alley, Knickerbocker's in New York City, was built in 1840; soon after this, various establishments attracted the lower classes and genteel alike. By the mid-1800s nine-pins became a widely played sport, and even reached the midwest.

After the Civil War, more Germans began their own clubs with bowling lanes, and tried to establish these as clean and family-oriented places. Their efforts at constructing wholesome reputations for their alleys were largely in vain, as most remained dark places located in saloon basements alongside alcohol consumption, gambling, and prostitution. Reformers' attempts to outlaw nine-pins at the end of the nineteenth century, it is fabled, caused alley owners to add an extra pin.

John Brunswick founded the Brunswick Corporation in 1845, which manufactured billiard tables and fine bar fixtures. In 1884 Brunswick added bowling equipment to his line, becoming the first manufacturer of his kind in America. In 1914, he introduced the Mineralite ball made of hard rubber and organized a world tour with which to promote it; considered so revolutionary, the ball was put on display at the Century of Progress Exposition in 1934.

At the turn of the century most bowling alleys were small establishments that provided the working classes with much needed, if less than wholesome, recreation. The cultural impetus toward rationalization and organization at the end of the nineteenth century also influenced bowling. By the 1880s and 1890s people attempted to standardize the rules and the play, and to improve the reputation of individual alleys and of the sport as a whole. Bowling associations were formed in order to attract more female bowlers. In 1887 A.G. Spalding, who was instrumental in forming baseball's National League, wrote *Standard Rules for Bowling in the United States.*

It was Joe Thum, however, who created what most resembled twentieth-century lanes, and therefore became known as the "father of bowling." In 1886 he opened his first successful alley in the basement of his Bavarian restaurant in New York City. In 1891 he built six lanes in Germania Hall, and in 1901 he opened the world's most elegant alley, "The White Elephant," which featured state-of-the-art lanes, electric lighting, and extravagant interior design in order to redefine bowling as a genteel sport, and to compete with other upper-class recreational areas of the time, like theaters and opera houses.

Thum also encouraged other smaller alley owners to adopt standard rules. By the mid-1890s the United Bowling Clubs (UBC) was organized and had 120 members. The American Bowling Congress (ABC), bowling's official governing body, was established in 1895, and held its first tournament in 1901. Women's bowling evolved alongside men's, with the first women's leagues appearing in 1907, and the Women's International Bowling Congress (WIBC) instituted in the 1910s. These bodies continued to push for standardized rules and regulations for the sport, and also maintained the quest to improve the image of the sport, which was still considered a dirty and tawdry pastime chiefly for lower-class gamblers and drinkers.

The various bowling organizations were successful in determining standards for bowling play and the alleys themselves, which have remained constant throughout the twentieth century. Each lane consists of a pin area, the lane itself, and the approach. Ten pins, each 15 inches high and 5 inches at their widest point and made of wood covered with hard plastic, are arranged twelve inches apart in an equilateral triangle at the far end of the lane. Each lane is 41 1/2 inches wide, 62 5/6 feet long, made of maple and pine, and bordered by two gutters. The balls themselves, which are rolled at the pins, are of hard rubber or plastic, at most 27 inches in circumference, and between eight and sixteen pounds. Each player's turn consists of a "frame"— two chances to knock down all of the pins. Knocking down all ten pins on the first try is a strike, while succeeding with two balls is a spare. Because the scores for strikes and spares are compounded, a perfect game in bowling is 300 points.

By 1920 there were about 450 ABC-sanctioned alleys, a number which grew to about 2,000 by 1929. Prohibition led to the trend of "dry" alleys, and once again helped define the sport as one fit for the entire family. The repeal of Prohibition in 1933 caused an almost immediate push by the breweries for sponsorship. Anxious to get their company names in newspaper sports pages by subsidizing local bowling leagues, beer makers such as Pabst, Schlitz, Blatz, Stroh's, and Budweiser attached their names to teams and individual bowlers, forever cementing bowling's reputation as a working-class sport. Beer-drinking has remained an activity stereotypically associated with bowling; among some players, the fifth frame has been dubbed the "beer frame" and requires the lowest scorer in that frame to buy a round of drinks for the other players.

Also after Prohibition, bowling lanes shifted in style from the fancy Victorian venues and the seedier saloon locales to more independent establishments that embraced the modern Art Deco style. As bowling chronicler Howard Stallings has noted, "The imagery and implements of bowling—the glossy, hard ball speeding down a super-slick blonde, wooden surface, smashing into mathematically arranged, streamlined pins—meshed perfectly with the era's 'need for speed,' the aerodynamic zeitgeist, if you will."

Throughout its history, bowling has remained an affordable sport for the common person. Alleys were located close by, the special shoes needed could be rented, balls were provided by the alley, and the fee for the games themselves was very affordable. It is no surprise, then, that the sport prospered during the Depression and war years, remaining a viable respite for people taxed by financial and emotional burdens. At this time larger institutions also noticed the potential healthful benefits of bowling, causing many alleys to be built in church basements, lodge halls, student unions, industrial plants, and even private homes.

The late 1940s through the 1960s proved to be the golden age of bowling. In 1947 Harry Truman installed lanes in the White House, helping bowling's continual legitimating process among the various classes even more, and defining it as a true national pastime. The same year also saw the first bowling telecast, which helped popularize the sport even more—ABC membership for that year was 1,105,000 (a figure which would grow to 4,575,000 in 1963), and sanctioned individual lanes numbered 44,500 (up to 159,000 by 1963). By 1949, there were over 6,000 bowling centers nationwide. Television proved the perfect medium for bowling because games were easy to shoot and inexpensive to produce. They also fostered the careers of famous bowlers like Don Carter, Earl Anthony, and Dick and Pete Weber. Described as a "quiz show with muscle," the televised bowling program was ubiquitous in the 1950s, and included such telecasts as *Celebrity Bowling, Make That Spare, Bowling for Dollars, ABC's Pro Bowler's Tour,* and *Jackpot Bowling,* hosted by Milton Berle. By 1958 bowling had become a $350,000,000 industry.

Other factors also contributed to bowling's wide-scale success in the 1950s. The automatic pinsetter patented by Gottfried Schmidt and purchased by AMF (American Machine and Foundry) in 1945, was

An example of bowling.

camaraderie, could not compete with larger and more exciting spectator sports. This era also marked the decline of serious league play as dedicated bowlers were growing older and younger potential bowlers were opting for other recreational activities that took them out of doors, like jogging and tennis. In spite of this decline, about 79 million people went bowling in 1993, and it was still the most popular participatory sport in the United States, confirming its overwhelming popularity only a few decades before.

As a sport with an indelible blue-collar image, bowling has achieved the status of being an "everyman's" sport, more synonymous with the American individual character than baseball. It is a uniquely non-competitive sport in which people try to better their own games more than beating others, who are usually friends or family members. In the 1990s it experienced a resurgence in popularity due to its "retro" image, and was a key element in the comedy movies *Kingpin* and *The Big Lebowski*.

—Wendy Woloson

FURTHER READING:

Harrison, Joyce M., and Ron Maxey. *Bowling*. Glenview, Illinois, Scott, Foresman and Company, 1987.

Luby, Mort. *The History of Bowling*. Chicago, Luby Publishing, 1983.

Schunk, Carol. *Bowling*. Philadelphia, W.B. Saunders Company, 1976.

Stallings, Howard. *The Big Book of Bowling*. Salt Lake City, Gibbs Smith, 1995.

Steele, H. Thomas. *Bowl-O-Rama*. New York, Abbeville Press, 1986.

Boxing

From John L. Sullivan, the last of the bare-knuckle champions and the first of the gloved, to "Iron Mike" Tyson, the world's youngest heavyweight champion, the sport of boxing has been consistently dominated by American fighters since the beginning of the twentieth century. No other sport arouses the degree of fascination and distaste as the "Noble Art," nor has any sport been so consistently vilified. The "Sweet Science" is a world unto itself, rich in tradition, ritual, and argot. Boxing generated a genre of Hollywood film all its own and its implicit drama has been assayed in loving detail by some of America's greatest writers. While nowhere near as popular now as they were before World War II, championship fights still draw celebrities in droves to Las Vegas and Atlantic City for often disappointing matches. Although a prize fight can still muster some of the frisson of boxing's heyday, by late in the century the sport was in a period of decline, its status angrily contested.

Boxing traces its roots back to ancient Egypt, where hieroglyphics dating to 4000 B.C. show Egyptian soldiers engaging in a primitive form of the sport, their hands protected by leather straps. From the Nile Delta, boxing spread along the trade routes, south to Ethiopia and along the Aegean coast up to Cyprus, Crete, and the Greek mainland. The Greeks took readily to boxing, including it in their olympic contests, refining the leather coverings for the fist, the cestus, and later, adding a spiked metal attachment to it—the murmex, or limb piercer—that could inflict terrible, often fatal damage. Indeed, bouts went on until one opponent died or was no longer able to stand. Boxers figure heavily in Greek mythology. Theseus, who killed the Minotaur, was a boxing champion as was Odysseus, hero of the

first put into use in 1952, when the first fully operational system was installed. This marked a revolution in alley technology, because owners and players were no longer reliant on the "pin boys" to reset the pins manually. These young workers, who had the dangerous job of standing at the end of the alley dodging balls and careening pins, were often ill-behaved delinquents and troublemakers. The automatic pinsetter made pin resetting and ball retrieval safer, faster, and reliable, making the game itself more fluid. Brunswick produced their first pinsetter in 1955, and also added air conditioning to their new alleys.

In the late 1950s the alleys themselves became more luxurious, incorporating the latest design trends and materials, with tables and seats made of brightly-colored Formica and looking like something from outer space. A 1959 issue of *Life* magazine described the modern bowling alley as an "all-purpose pleasure palace." Indeed, much like drive-in theaters, they tried to be all things for all family members, offering services like child care and beauty parlors, and containing carpeted lobbies, restaurants, cocktail lounges, and billiard tables. League play at this time was also at its peak, affording regular and organized opportunities for various groups to form teams and bowl in "friendly competition."

As the 1960s came to an end, bowling alleys experienced the end of their golden age. Bowling, still rooted in working-class ethics and

A heavyweight fight between champion Mike Tyson (center) and challenger Frank Bruno (right), 1989.

Trojan Wars and Homer's Odyssey, and said to be undefeated in the ring.

The Greek, Aeneas, brought the sport to Rome where it grew in popularity and brutality until with the decline of the Roman Empire, the decadent sport waned in popularity, and then disappeared for a little over a millennium, resurfacing finally in seventeenth century England. Its resurrection has been attributed to the England's republican form of government as well as the English people's affection for the backsword contest. For whatever reason, even before 1650 the blind poet Milton, author of *Paradise Lost*, was advocating the practice of boxing as indispensable to the education of the young gentleman in his *Treatise on Education*. It was the eighteenth century champion, Jack Broughton, who refined boxing into roughly the form of the modern fight. In 1742, Broughton erected an amphitheater for the promotion of bare-knuckle contests and to instruct contenders. The following year he published a rule-book which explicated the proper conduct of fighters and their seconds. Broughton also invented the boxing glove, which he patterned after the Roman cestus, filling a leather glove with soft batting. The glove was only used in training;

bouts were still fought with bare knuckles, and would continue to be until the end of the nineteenth century.

Boxing first came to America by way of the aristocratic Old South, as a result of that cultural fealty wealthy families paid to England. According to John V. Grombach, author of *Saga of Sock,* ''No family who took itself seriously, and these all did, considered its children had acquired the proper polish unless they were educated in England. . . . These youngsters went to prizefights and were taught boxing in the fast and fashionable company of which they were part. . . . Naturally, when these young dandies returned home they had to show off all they had learned abroad, so they boxed against each other. However, since distances between plantations were great . . . they turned to their personal young slaves.'' In fact, many of the early professional boxers in America were slaves freed by their masters after the latter had made a considerable fortune off their chattel. In the early nineteenth century, for instance, Tom Molyneux, the son and grandson of boxing slaves, was defeated by the British champion Tom Cribb. Molyneux can be thought of as an anomaly of boxing history, however, for it would be nearly a century before a black fighter, the heavyweight Jack Johnson, was allowed a shot at a title fight.

Although Grombach assigns the beginning of modern boxing to 1700 A.D., the American era begins with John L. Sullivan, the last of the bare-knuckle fighters. His reign as champion, from 1881 to 1892, saw the introduction of the Marquis of Queensbury rules, which called for gloves, weight classes, and three-minute rounds with one minute intervals of rest in between. His losing bout to "Gentleman Jim" Corbett was held under these new provisions. A flamboyant personality, Sullivan was the first boxer to promote himself as such, touring in theatrical productions between matches. Consequently, his fights drew tremendous crowds; seemingly no one was immune from the desire to witness a loudmouth's disgrace. Typical of his time, he was violently racist and refused to fight a black man, thus depriving the worthy Peter Jackson, the Australian heavyweight champion, of a chance at the title.

It would take Jack Johnson's 1908 capture of the heavyweight title from Tommy Burns to overcome the color barrier. After his 1910 defeat of James J. Jeffries, a white heavyweight champion who came out of retirement to vanquish the Negro upstart, the novelist Jack London publicly sought "a great white hope" to challenge Johnson. Johnson's victory was greeted with public outrage, inflamed by the new champion's profligate lifestyle. The moral character of a fighter has always been a part of his draw. Johnson drank, caroused, and lived openly with a white women, inflaming public sentiment already predisposed against him. He was finally indicted on a morals charge, and fled the country to avoid prosecution.

"To see race as a predominant factor in American boxing is inevitable," writes Joyce Carol Oates in her thoughtful book *On Boxing,* "but the moral issues, as always in this paradoxical sport, are ambiguous. Is there a moral distinction between the spectacle of black slaves in the Old South being forced by their white owners to fight to the death, for purposes of gambling, and the spectacle of contemporary blacks fighting for multi-million-dollar paydays, for TV coverage from Las Vegas and Atlantic City?" Over time, the parameters of the racial subtext have shifted, but in 1937 when Joe Louis, a former garage mechanic, won the heavyweight title from James J. Braddock, his managers, leery perhaps of the furor Jack Johnson had caused, carefully vetted their fighter's public persona, making sure Louis was always sober, polite, and far away from any white women when in the public eye. The colorful "Sugar Ray" Robinson was a showman in the Johnson tradition, but he, too, was careful not to overstep the invisible line of decency.

Black boxers up to the present have been made to play symbolic roles in and outside of the ring. Floyd Patterson, the integrationist civil-rights Negro (who was, incidentally, forced to move from his new house in New Jersey by the hostility of his white neighbors) played the "great white hope" role against Sonny Liston, an unrepentant ex-con street-fighter controlled by the mob. Muhammad Ali, who refused to play the good Negro/bad Negro game, was vilified in the press throughout the 1960s, unpopular among reporters as much for his cocky behavior as for his religious and political militancy. Perhaps race was never quite as crucial an issue in boxing following his reign, but as recently as Mike Tyson's bouts with Evander Holyfield in the 1990s, racial constructs were still very much a part of the attraction, with Holyfield's prominently displayed Christianity facing off in a symbolic battle against the converted Muslim and convicted rapist Tyson.

Class is as much a construct in modern boxing as race. Since before the turn of the century, boxing has offered a way out of poverty for young toughs. For 30 years after Jack Johnson's reign, boxing champions were uniformly white and were often immigrants or sons of immigrants, Irish, Italian, or Eastern European. Boxing's audience was similarly comprised. The wealthy might flock to a championship match at Madison Square Garden, but the garden variety bouts were held in small, smoky fight clubs and appealed to either aficionados, gamblers, or the working class. This provided up-and-coming fighters with the chance to practice their skills on a regular basis, and more importantly, made it possible for fighters, trainers, and managers to make a marginal living off the fight game. As entertainment whose appeal marginally crossed class lines, boxing's status was always contested, and the repeal of prohibition would only exacerbate matters. Organized crime, looking for new sources of income to replace their profits from bootleg liquor, took to fixing fights or controlling the fighters outright (Sonny Liston's mob affiliations were out in the open, adding to his suspect moral rectitude). In the 1940s and 1950s, Jake LaMotta, for example, a contender from the Bronx, was denied a chance at a championship bout until he knuckled under to the demands of the local Mafia patriarch.

Nourished by the many boxing clubs in the New York area—the undisputed capitol of boxing (to fighters and managers, out-of-town meant anywhere not within the five boroughs of New York)—controlled by the mob, the city was the center of a vital boxing culture. Legendary gyms like Stillman's Gym on Eighth Avenue were home to a colorful array of boxers and managers. Fighters like Sugar Ray Robinson, Jake "The Bronx Bull" LaMotta, and "Jersey Joe" Walcott were the heroes of the sport. Trainer Cus D'Amato, the Aristotle of boxing, became a legend for discovering new talent among the city's underclass and resisting all incursions from the mob. D'Amato specialized in saving up-and-coming delinquents from the vagaries of the streets. He would discover heavyweight champion Floyd Patterson and, towards the end of his life, Michael Tyson. Legend has it he slept at his gym with a gun under his pillow. *New Yorker* scribe A. J. Liebling covered the fights and the fighters, leaving an especially vivid portrait of the boxing culture from this time. In his portrait of Manhattan's boxing milieu, he chronicled not only the fights but the bars, the gyms, and the personalities that made boxing such a colorful sport. Stillman's (dubbed by Liebling the University of Eighth Avenue), The Neutral Corner, and Robinson's Harlem Club, Sugar Ray's, its walls festooned with collaged photos of the flamboyant middleweight, all appear in Liebling's many boxing pieces. With his characteristic savoir-faire, he chronicled the last great era of live boxing, or as some would say, the beginning of its decline. Television had killed the small boxing clubs. Fighters who showed promise were pushed up through the ranks too quickly, and without the clubs, their inexperience was sadly apparent on the small screen. Championship bouts still drew large crowds, but for the small time managers, let alone boxers, television could not sustain the vibrant culture so characteristic of boxing up to World War II.

Perhaps to fill this void, a string of boxing pictures started to issue from Hollywood starting in the 1940s. Because of boxing's physicality, moral and psychological truths can be presented in stark contrast. The drama is enacted on the boxer's body, the repository of truth and deception, and the fighter's failure/success is inscribed upon it. Aside from the standard boxing biopic (*Golden Boy,* 1939; *Body and Soul,* 1947; *Champion,* 1949; *Somebody Up There Likes Me,* 1956; *Raging Bull,* 1980), two myths predominate: the triumph of the underdog through perseverance, and the set-up, in which the boxer (the innocent) is undone by the system. The *Rocky* films are perhaps the best known of the former category, recasting the myth in an unabashedly sentimental light. Among the latter, Elia Kazan's *On The Waterfront* (1954), while not technically about boxing, manages to depict the frustrating position of the boxer, dependent on the vagaries of luck and the cooperation of organized crime for a successful career. (Marlon Brando's "I shoulda been a contender" speech immediately entered the popular lexicon, as has his portrait of the paradox of the gentle boxer, murderous in the ring, good-natured outside it). Other films in the latter category include *Requiem for a Heavyweight* (1962), *The Harder They Fall* (1956; based on the preposterous career of Italian circus strong-man, the giant Primo Carnera), and *The Set-Up* (1949), as is Martin Scorcese's triumphant *Raging Bull,* perhaps the most psychologically penetrating of any boxing film.

Boxing has also inspired some great writing. From the chronicler of the English Prize Ring, Pierce Egan, author of *Boxiana* (frequently quoted by Liebling) to Norman Mailer's celebrated book of essays on Muhammad Ali, boxing, being a wordless sport, invites others to define it, to complete it. Hemingway, Ring Lardner, Budd Schulberg, Nelson Algren, Jack London, and many others have written stories on boxing, and some of the best American journalists, not necessarily sports writers, have devoted considerable cogitation to the sport. The locus of modern boxing writing is Muhammad Ali, who was as much a cultural phenomenon as a sports figure, but this does not begin to describe the reason why an anthology of essays was published chronicling his career, nor that writers of the stature of a Tom Wolfe or Hunter S. Thompson have felt it incumbent to weigh in on the subject.

Perhaps it is because boxing is such a personal endeavor, so lacking in artifice, that one cannot hide, neither from one's opponent or from oneself. "Each boxing match is a story—a unique and highly condensed drama without words," writes Joyce Carol Oates. "In the boxing ring there are two principal players, overseen by a shadowy third. The ceremonial ringing of the bell is a summoning to full wakefulness. . . . It sets in motion, too, the authority of Time." This then, is boxing's allure: In the unadorned ring under the harsh, blazing lights, as if in an unconscious distillation of the blinding light of tragedy, the boxer is stripped down to his essence. In other words, boxing "celebrates the physicality of men even as it dramatizes the limitations," in the words of Oates, "sometimes tragic, more often poignant, of the physical."

There can be no secrets in the ring, and sometimes painful truths the boxer is unaware of are revealed before the assembled audience and spectral television viewer. In the three bouts that destroyed Floyd Patterson's career—two against Sonny Liston, and one against Muhammad Ali—Patterson was so demoralized, his faults and emotional weaknesses set in such high relief, that it is a wonder he didn't retire immediately following the 1965 Ali bout (he was already known for packing a fake beard in his luggage, the better to flee the arena). More vividly, Mike Tyson's frustrated mastication of champion Evander Holyfield's ear during their 1997 rematch revealed not only Tyson's physical vulnerability but confirmed an emotional instability first hinted at after his 1993 rape conviction.

Boxing, it would seem, is a sport that runs through periodic cycles. Recently, it has been taken up by women—who have begun to fight professionally—and affluent professionals who have taken up the sport not so much to compete as to train, a boxer's regimen being perhaps the most arduous of any sport. New gyms have sprung up to accommodate this new-found popularity, but they are more often franchises than owner-run establishments. Already a new generation, nourished on *Rocky* pictures, seems to have taken to the arenas to enjoy the live spectacle of two men—or women—slugging it out. But in essential ways, boxing has changed. There are now four different federations—the WBC, the IBF, the WBA, and the WBO—and 68 World Champions, as compared to eight in "the old days." The cynic would attribute this fragmentation to economics: the more championship bouts, the more pay-per-view cable TV profits (the money from box-office revenues comprises only a small fraction of the net profit). Consequently, championship bouts have lost much of their inherent drama inherent in a unified championship match, and the quality of the matches have also decreased, since fighters have so few chances to practice their craft.

Regardless of the devitalizing effects of cable television and multiple boxing federations, boxing still retains a powerful attraction. No sport is so fraught with metaphorical implications, nor has any sport endured for quite so long. Boxing, as Oates points out, aside from going through periods of "crisis" is a sport of crisis. Its very nature speaks to someplace deep in our collective psyche that recognizes the paradoxical nature of violence. Managers and promoters may cheat and steal, matches may be fixed, but when that rare bout occurs where the fighters demonstrate their courage, skill, and intelligence, the sport is redeemed. Boxing is a cyclical sport, rooted ultimately in the vagaries of chance. When will a new crop of talented contenders emerge? That is something no one can predict. The public awaits the rising of new champion worthy of the name, and the promoters await him just as eagerly.

—Michael Baers

FURTHER READING:

Brenner, Teddy, as told to Barney Nagler. *Only the Ring Was Square.* Englewood Cliffs, New Jersey, Prentice-Hall, 1981.

Delcourt, Christian. *Boxing.* New York, Universe, 1996.

Grombach, John V. *The Saga of Sock: A Complete Story of Boxing.* New York, A.S. Barnes and Company, 1949.

Isenberg, Michael T. *John L. Sullivan and His America.* Urbana, University of Illinois Press, 1988.

Liebling, A. J. *A Neutral Corner.* San Francisco, North Point Press, 1990.

———. *The Sweet Science.* New York, Penguin Books, 1982.

Lloyd, Alan. *The Great Prize Fight.* New York, Coward, McCann & Geoghegan, 1977.

Oates, Joyce Carol. *On Boxing.* Hopewell, The Ecco Press, 1994.

Schulberg, Budd. *Sparring with Hemingway: And Other Legends of the Fight Game.* Chicago, I.R. Dee, 1995.

Weston, Stanley, editor. *The Best of ''The Ring: The Bible of Boxing.''* Revised edition. Chicago, Bonus Books, 1996.

Boy Scouts of America

The young people, dressed in uniform, seem part of a tradition from a bygone era. Some cheer as the small, homemade go-carts spin down the track; others struggle to make the perfect knot or pitch in to help clean up the local park. They serve as a emblem of the conformity of the 1950s and the desire to connect our children with

A group of Boy Scouts with their Scout Master.

"rustic" ways of life. In the final judgment, though, these contemporary kids are simply having fun while learning valuable lessons. In an era when scouting has needed to redefine its mission, many of its basic initiatives still possess great worth to society.

Even though contemporary organizations have appealed to boys and girls, scouting began as a gendered organization. At the dawn of the twentieth century, an American boy's life was often either idyllic or full of drudgery, depending on his family's circumstances. During the decade before the Boy Scouts of America (BSA) were founded in 1910, the families of a handful of industrialists lived sumptuously while the vast majority of the population lived much more simply. The Gilded Age of the nineteenth century had brought wealthy Americans a genuine interest in rustic living and the outdoors. Many wealthy urbanites began sending children to summer camps that could provide their children with a connection to the culture of outdoors. Theodore Roosevelt and others began organizations such as the Boone and Crockett Club or the Izaak Walton League. Each group had an offspring for younger male members, with Sons of Daniel Boone proving the most popular. Neither, however, truly sought to reach young men of all economic classes. Ernest Thompson Seton, artist and wildlife expert, founded the Woodcraft Indians in 1902.

Interestingly, he chose to unveil the group through articles in the *Ladies Home Journal*. Shortly afterwards, Seton became the first Chief Scout of BSA when it was established by Robert Stephenson Smyth Baden-Powell.

Early scouting undoubtedly fostered male aggression; however, such feelings were meant to be channeled and applied to "wilderness" activities. Many scholars see such an impulse as a reaction to the 1893 speech by historian Frederick Jackson Turner when he pronounced the frontier "closed." Turner and many Americans wondered how the nation could continue to foster the aggressive, expansionist perspective that had contributed so much to its identity and success. The first BSA handbook explained that a century prior, all boys lived "close to nature." But since then country had undergone an "unfortunate change" marked by industrialization and the "growth of immense cities." The resulting "degeneracy" could be altered by BSA leading boys back to nature.

Roosevelt's personality guided many Americans to seek adventure in the outdoors and the military. BSA sought to acculturate young men into this culture with an unabashed connection to the military. Weapons and their careful use, as well as survival skills, constructed the basis for a great deal of the activities and exercises conducted by

Baden-Powell, a major-general in the British Army. The original Boy Scout guidebook was partly based on the Army manual that Baden-Powell had written for young recruits. World War I would only intensify youth involvement in scouting. The perpetuation of scouting during the post-1950 Cold War era, however, is more attributable to a national interest in conformity and not in militancy. It was only during the early years that such associations with the military were openly fostered.

Seton visited Baden-Powell in London in 1906, where he learned about the Boy Scouts organization. Upon returning to the United States, Seton began gathering support for an organization that would "offer instruction in the many valuable qualities which go to make a good Citizen equally with a good Scout." The first Boy Scout manual, *Scouting for Boys,* contained chapters titled Scoutcraft, Campaigning, Camp Life, Tracking, Woodcraft, Endurance for Scouts, Chivalry, Saving Lives, and Our Duties as Citizens. In 30 years the handbook sold an alleged seven million copies in the United States, second only to the Bible.

Working in cooperation with YMCA (Young Men's Christian Association), the BSA was popular from its outset in 1908. This coordination was particularly orchestrated by William D. Boyce, who guided the official formation of BSA in 1910. The BSA network spread throughout the nation, and in 1912 included *Boys' Life,* which would grow into the nation's largest youth magazine. Most educators and parents welcomed scouting as a wholesome influence on youth. Scores of articles proclaimed such status in periodicals such as *Harper's Weekly, Outlook, Good Housekeeping,* and *Century.*

Within the attributes derived from scouting were embedded stereotypes that contributed to gender roles throughout the twentieth century. Girl scout activities followed scouting for males, yet possessed a dramatically different agenda. Instruction in domestic skills made up the core activities of early scouting for females. Maintaining a connection with nature or providing an outlet for aggressions did not cohere with the ideals associated with the female gender in the early twentieth century. Such shifts would only begin after 1950; however, even today, scouting for girls is most associated with bake sales and the famous girl scout cookies. Still, scouting for both genders has become similar, particularly emphasizing outdoor experiences

Contemporary scouting has changed somewhat, but it also maintains the basic initiatives of early scouting. Most attractive to many parents, scouting involves young people in community outreach activities. In an era when many families find themselves in suburban developments away from community centers or frequently moving, scouting offers basic values including service to others in the community. The proverbial scout aiding an older woman across a street may be a thing of the past, but scouts still work in a variety of community service tasks. These values also continue to include patriotism under the rubric "service to God and country." The inclusion of God, however, has not held as firmly in contemporary scouting. Some parents have refused to let their children participate in any of the quasi-religious portions of scouting, which has led to a few scouts being released. Over BSA's century of life, though, the basic values of scouting have remained strong, while activities have been somewhat modified. Though well known activities such as the "pinewood derby" and "jamborees" continue, the culture of scouting has begun to reflect a changing generation. While its popularity does not near that of the earlier era, the culture of scouting continues to help young Americans grow and mature into solid citizens.

—Brian Black

FURTHER READING:

Nash, Roderick. *Wilderness and the American Mind.* New Haven, Yale University Press, 1982.

Peterson, Robert W. *Boy Scouts: An American Adventure.* New York, American Heritage, 1985.

75 Years of Girl Scouting. New York, Girl Scouts of the U.S.A., 1986.

Bra

The brassiere, more commonly referred to as "the bra," was one of the most influential pieces of women's apparel in the twentieth century. As an item of underwear that was never intended to be seen in public, it shaped women's breasts and presented them to the public in ways that responded to and reflected ideas about women's bodies and their roles in American culture. That the bra went through so many radical changes in design shows how important breasts themselves were in a culture that eroticized, idolized, and objectified them.

Until the first decade of the twentieth century, women relied on the corset as their main undergarment. Rigid, tightly laced to form a "wasp waist," and covering the area from the crotch to the shoulders, the corset was an oppressive article that made it difficult for women to breathe, bend over, or even sit down. In the first decade of the twentieth century, however, breasts were liberated from the corset through the invention of a separate garment which would provide them shape and support. The brassiere, first sold in France in 1907, allowed women to be more comfortable but also meant that society began considering breasts more as objects—almost as separate entities from women's bodies themselves. The "ideal" breast shape changed with developing technologies, fashions, and perceived roles of women.

New York debutante Mary Phelps Jacobs patented the first bra in the United States in 1914, a device which supported the breasts from shoulder straps above rather than pressure from below, as the corset had done. Jacobs eventually sold the rights to her "Backless Brassiere" to the Warner Brothers Corset Company. In 1926, Ida Rosenthal and Enid Bissett, partners in a New York dress firm who did not like the 1920s flapper look that preferred flat chests and boyish figures, sewed more shapely forms right into the dresses they made, and eventually patented a separate bra "to support the bust in a natural position"; they went on to found the successful Maiden Form Brassiere Company.

By the 1930s the separate bra and underpants had become the staples of women's undergarments. In this same decade the Warner Company popularized Lastex, a stretchable fabric that allowed women even more freedom from their formerly constrictive underclothing. In 1935 Warner's introduced the cup sizing system (A through D), which was very quickly adopted by all companies, and assumed that women's bodies could easily fit into distinct and standard categories of size.

Rationing during World War II meant that women had to forego fancy bras of the latest materials, but after the war they reaped the benefits of wartime technology. Bras appeared in nylon, rayon, and parachute silk. In addition, they incorporated "whirlpool" stitching

A woman displays her divested bra during Anti-Bra Day in San Francisco, 1969.

which formed the individual cups into aggressive cones. Maiden Form's 1949 Chansonette, more popularly known as the "bullet bra," became its most popular model, and was a clear example of how women's bodies were shaped by the aesthetics and mindset of the time. After the war, jutting breasts recalled the designs of weaponry like rockets used in the conflict, and also symbolized society's desire for women to forego their wartime jobs and retreat back into the homes to become capable wives and mothers. As if to circumscribe their roles even more, in 1949 Maiden Form also inaugurated its long-lasting "Dream" advertising series, which showed women in numerous situations "dreaming" of various accomplishments, clad only in their Maidenform bras. In the 1950s Playtex began the first bra and girdle advertising on television, but the bras were modeled on plastic bust forms. It was not until the 1990s that television allowed bras to be shown on live models.

While the shape and relative status given to women's breasts in the 1950s reflected women's domestication, their liberation in the 1960s equally expressed women's newly perceived freedom. More and more women saw their breasts as items packaged to suit men's tastes. Acting against this, many went braless and preferred the androgynous appearance of their flapper grandmothers celebrated in the waif-like look of models like Twiggy. Brassiere companies made consolations to accommodate this new sensibility as well. Their

designs became relaxed, giving breasts a more "natural" shape than their pointed precursors. Rudi Gernreich, most famously known for his topless bathing suit, designed the "no-bra bra" in 1965, which was meant to support the breasts but to be invisible. In 1969 Warner's finally caught up with this trend, designing and producing their own Invisible Bra.

By the late 1960s the bra itself became an important political symbol. The first "bra burning" demonstration happened at the 1968 Miss America Pageant, when poet Robin Morgan and members of the Women's Liberation Party picketed the event and threw their bras in a trash can as a gesture against women's objectification. That they actually burned their bras at this demonstration was a myth started by a reporter who likened the event to flag-burning and other incendiary activities of popular protest. After that, bra burning became an overt statement of feminism and women's liberation, and "bra burners" a derisive label for activist women involved in the struggle for equal rights.

By the 1980s and 1990s, America saw a return to more delicate lingerie, hastened by the opening and rapid franchising of Victoria's Secret lingerie stores beginning in 1982. As in the 1950s, breasts were seen as something to display—status symbols for the women who possessed them and the men who possessed the women. In 1988 the push-up bra returned as a less-than-permanent alternative to breast enhancement surgery, which was just becoming popular. The value of large breasts during the late 1980s and through the 1990s was seen alternatively as a positive embodiment of women's new power and assertiveness in the business world and a backlash against feminism that continued to objectify women and their body parts.

Madonna encapsulated these tensions in her 1991 *Truth or Dare* film, a documentary showing a behind-the-scenes glimpse of her performances. In it, she sported a pin-striped business suit whose slits opened to reveal the cups of a large, cone-shaped pink bra designed by Jean-Paul Gaultier. The juxtaposition of the oversized bra cups, dangling garter belts, and business suit presented a parody of traditional gender roles. Her use of these symbols best expressed the power of clothing—layers which could be seen and those which could not, equally—and the power of women to present their bodies in ways that either acquiesced to or subverted the current power dynamics between the genders.

—Wendy Woloson

FURTHER READING:

Ewing, Elizabeth. *Dress and Undress, A History of Women's Underwear.* New York, Drama Book Specialists, 1978.

Fontanel, Beatrice. *Support and Seduction: The History of Corsets and Bras.* New York, Harry N. Abrams, 1997.

Yalom, Marilyn. *A History of the Breast.* New York, Alfred A. Knopf, 1997.

Bradbury, Ray (1920—)

Although well-known to and beloved by many as a leading writer of science fiction, Ray Bradbury is a far more complicated subject than most may realize. In the world of science fiction, he is an object of admiration and dismay, while outside the genre, he is an enigmatic figure who blends a lyricism, nostalgia, and scientific possibility in ways that surprise and delight.

Ray Bradbury was born on August 22, 1920 in Waukegan, Illinois, the third son of Spaulding Bradbury and Esther Marie Moberg Bradbury. By age eight, Bradbury had discovered pulps like *Amazing Stories,* which he began to read voraciously. His father suffered the trials of most Depression-era Americans, moving his family from and back to Waukegan three times, before finally settling in Los Angeles in 1934. That year, Bradbury began to write in earnest, publishing in an amateur fan magazine in 1938 his first story, "Hollerbochen's Dilemma." In 1939 Bradbury started publishing his own fan magazine, *Futuria Fantasia*; in 1941 he began attending a weekly writing class taught by science fiction master Robert Heinlein.

In 1941, Bradbury, with coauthor Henry Hasse, published his first paid short story, "Pendulum," in *Super Science Stories.* Up until this time, Bradbury had been selling papers, a job he gave up in 1942 in order to write full-time. That year he wrote "The Lake," the first story written in the true "Bradbury style." Three years later, he began to publish in the better magazines, at which point various short stories started to receive national recognition: "The Big Black and White Game" was selected for the *Best American Short Stories 1945;*

Ray Bradbury

"Homecoming" for the O. Henry Awards *Prize Stories of 1947;* "Powerhouse" for an O. Henry Award in 1948; and "I See You Never" for *Best American Short Stories 1948.* In 1949, Bradbury was selected by the National Fantasy Fan Federation as best author in 1949. Meanwhile, as he collected more accolades, his personal life also took a fateful swing. In 1947 he married Marguerite McClure, by whom he had four daughters.

Bradbury's major breakthrough came in 1950 with *The Martian Chronicles,* his story cycle of Earth's colonization and eventual destruction of its Martian neighbor. Although the quality of work could easily have stood on its own merits, the strong praise it received from Christopher Isherwood, Orville Prescott, Angus Wilson, and Gilbert Highet established Bradbury as a writer of national merit. Bradbury capitalized on the confidence expressed in his capacity to imagine and write boldly with such seminal works as *The Illustrated Man* (1951), *Fahrenheit 451* (1953), *Dandelion Wine* (1957), *Something Wicked This Way Comes* (1962), and his many excellent short-story collections.

Despite his apparent dominance of the science fiction field, a number of science fiction writers thought the prominence given him by literati unfamiliar with the genre was both unfair and uninformed. Mutterings against Bradbury's qualifications as a writer of "true" science fiction surfaced in 1951 with Edward Wood's "The Case Against Ray Bradbury," in the *Journal of Science Fiction.* This was followed by more substantive criticisms in James Blish's *The Issue at Hand* (1964) and Damon Knight's *In Search of Wonder* (1967). In general Blish and Knight, as well as Thomas M. Disch, Anthony Boucher, and L. Sprague de Camp, would argue that Bradbury's lyrical approach to his topic emanated from a boyish nostalgia that was, at heart, anti-scientific. Yet despite this vigorous criticism, Bradbury fans have remained legion, while more than enough critics have pointed out in return that such criticisms of Bradbury's brand of science fiction offer counter definitions of the genre so narrow they denied it the very richness Bradbury's own fictional style imparted to it.

Whatever the case may be, there is no sidestepping Bradbury's achievement as a writer. What he brings to science fiction is a vision that transformed the steady-state prose of science—applied with so much rigor to fiction by such writers as Isaac Asimov and Arthur C. Clarke—into the lyricism of poetry. Kingsley Amis latches on to this very quality in Bradbury's prose when he writes in *The Maps of Hell*, "Another much more unlikely reason for Bradbury's fame is that, despite his tendency to dime-a-dozen sensitivity, he is a good writer, wider in range than any of his colleagues, capable of seeing life on another planet as something extraordinary instead of just challenging or horrific." By way of example consider the lyricality of the first sentence in Bradbury's description of the colonization of Mars in *The Martian Chronicles:* "Mars was a distant shore, and the men spread upon it in waves." The artfulness of this one sentence, in which "shore" functions as a metaphor that resonates with "waves," is a small illustration of the poetic sensibility so often absent from the common-sense anti-lyricism of postwar science fiction prose. In short, Bradbury's achievement was not to write science fiction in a prose that was anti-scientific in spirit, but to create a subgenre of science fiction that no longer treated poetry as a form of anti-science. In short, Bradbury restored wonder to a genre that, without him, might have proven dull, indeed.

Despite Bradbury's association in the public mind with science fiction, he has shown himself far too ambitious to be limited to a single genre. Bradbury has successfully published in other genres. A closer reading of much of his fiction will reveal tales that, despite their lyrical and overimaginative tone, are, for all intents and purpose, exemplars of light realist fiction, from his autobiographical novel *Dandelion Wine* to the amusing "Have I Got a Candy Bar for You!" Bradbury also has taken stabs at writing drama, poetry, screenplays, detective fiction, and even musical compositions. Although he has never achieved the fame in these genres that he has in his science fiction, there is little doubt the extension of his horizons as a writer into these genres is the direct result of his continuing interest in challenging his limits as a writer, just as he once challenged the limits of science fiction itself.

—Bennett Lovett-Graff

FURTHER READING:

Greenberg, Martin, and Joseph D. Olander, editors. *Ray Bradbury. New York, Taplinger, 1980.*

Johnson, Wayne L. *Ray Bradbury. New York, Frederick Ungar, 1980.*

Mogen, David. *Ray Bradbury.* Boston, G. K. Hall, 1986.

Slusser, George Edgar. *The Bradbury Chronicles.* San Bernardino, California, Borgo Press, 1977.

Toupence, William F. *Ray Bradbury and the Poetics of Reverie: Fantasy, Science Fiction, and the Reader.* Ann Arbor, Michigan, UMI Research Press, 1984.

Bradley, Bill (1943—)

A man of many talents, former New Jersey Senator Bill Bradley perhaps best embodies the modern idea of a Renaissance man. Bradley was an All-American basketball player at Princeton University, then went on to star with the New York Knicks after a stint in Oxford, England as a Rhodes Scholar. Public service beckoned Bradley and he won his first political office in 1978. Despite his wealthy upbringing, Bradley has had to work hard for every success in his life.

Born July 28, 1943, William Warren Bradley led a very organized and orderly childhood. He used to set aside four hours per day for basketball practice. At the time of his high school graduation in 1961, Bradley had scored 3,066 points and had been named to *Scholastic* magazine's All-American team twice. This success on the court earned the attention of many prominent college coaches. Despite offers from better known basketball powerhouses, Bradley chose to attend Princeton University for its prestigious academic environment.

While starring at Princeton, Bradley made All-American three times and was named National Association of Basketball Coaches Player of the Year in 1965. One of Bradley's highlights as an amateur athlete was being a member of the gold medal winning American Olympic team in 1964. After his career, several professional basketball teams courted him for his services. Undeterred, Bradley chose instead to pursue further study at Oxford University as a Rhodes Scholar. While overseas, Bradley picked up the game again and saw that he missed the athletic competition. After playing some for an Italian professional team, he decided to join the New York Knicks in 1967.

Professional basketball in the 1970s was not the kind of place one would expect to find the intellectual Bradley. Teammates once cool toward Bradley warmed to this Ivy League golden boy after they realized his tremendous heart and work ethic. The Knicks went on to win two NBA championships with Bradley playing integral roles in both. He retired from the game in 1977 and was named to the Basketball Hall of Fame in 1982.

With one career complete, Bradley turned down several business offers and decided to pursue public service. The popular ex-Knick won his first office in 1978, as he defeated Republican nominee Jeffrey K. Bell for the New Jersey senatorial race, a seat he would hold for three terms. Senator Bradley would champion issues like the environment, education, and natural resources. He is perhaps best known for the Tax Reform Act of 1986, which followed many of the ideas on tax reform he laid out in his book, *The Fair Tax.* He was briefly mentioned as a candidate for the presidency in 1988, then again in 1992. A moderate Democrat, Bradley became respected and revered throughout the senate and the nation. After his retirement from the Senate, Bradley wrote *Values of the Game* in 1998, about the life lessons he learned from basketball. Its publication again brought Bradley to the media forefront and sparked rumors about his candidacy for the Democratic presidential nomination in 2000.

—Jay Parrent

FURTHER READING:

Bradley, Bill. *Time Present, Time Past—A Memoir.* New York, Alfred A. Knopf, 1996.

———. *Values of the Game.* New York, Artisan Press, 1998.

Jaspersohn, William. *Senator: A Profile of Bill Bradley in the U.S. Senate.* San Diego, Harcourt, Brace, Jovanovich, 1992.

Bradshaw, Terry (1948—)

A country-bred, southern farm boy with a strong passing arm, Terry Bradshaw used the principles of discipline and hard work that he learned as a child to become one of the greatest quarterbacks the game of football has ever seen. His career statistics still stand as a substantial lifetime achievement for any player: two Super Bowl MVPs, 27,989 yards gained, 212 touchdowns passed, and 32 touchdowns rushed in his fourteen-year National Football League career. Though his football fame ensured him a shot at a career as a sports commentator, it is Bradshaw's down-to-earth, unpretentious style that continues to endear him to his audience.

Bradshaw was born in Shreveport, Louisiana, and raised in a farming family. "I was born to work, taught to work, love to work," he said. Even on the football field, he performed his job faultlessly, developing the pinpoint accurate passing that would become his trademark. He attended college at Louisiana Technical University, where he made All-American, an unusual honor since Louisiana Tech was not a Division I team. In 1970, quarterback Bradshaw was the first player selected in the professional football draft.

For the next twelve years the Louisiana boy with the perfect spiral pass led the Pittsburgh Steelers to victory after victory, including four Super Bowl championships. The Steelers were the first team

Terry Bradshaw

to win four Super Bowls, and, in 1979 and 1980, Bradshaw was only the second player ever to win recognition as Most Valuable Player in two back-to-back Super Bowls. Bradshaw was the unanimous choice for the MVP honor in Super Bowls XIII and XIV, a phenomenon that had not occurred since Bart Starr won back-to-back MVP honors in Super Bowls I and II.

By 1982, Bradshaw's amazing passing arm was beginning to show signs of damage. He toughed it out, playing in pain through much of the 1982 season, but the doctors' diagnosis was chronic muscle deterioration, and the prescription was surgery. In March of 1983, Bradshaw underwent the surgery, but he could not withstand pressure from Steelers coach Chuck Noll to return to the game. He resumed playing too soon, causing permanent damage to his elbow. Bradshaw played only a few games in the 1983 season, then was forced to retire.

Though regretting that his retirement from the playing field had not been on his own terms, Bradshaw continued to make football his career. In 1989, he was inducted into the Football Hall of Fame, and the next year he went to work for CBS as co-anchor of *NFL Today.* He worked for CBS for four years, then the FOX network doubled his salary and hired him as a game-day commentator and host of *FOX NFL.* FOX also made surprising use of Bradshaw's homespun talents by giving him a daytime talk show. *Home Team with Terry Bradshaw* was described by one executive as "Martha Stewart meets Monday Night Football." Pundits wondered how the rugged football veteran would handle the traditionally female forum of daytime talk, but Bradshaw's easygoing style seemed to take it all in stride. In fact, it is Bradshaw's unapologetic country-boy persona that seems to appeal to fans. Though critics have called his commentary incompetent and even buffoonish, Bradshaw's "just folks" approach continues to make him popular. His response to critics has been typically disarming, "I stutter, I stammer, I scratch, and I do it all on live television . . . I can't help it. It's me. What are you going to do about it? You can't change who you are."

Bradshaw has appeared in many movies, often alongside fellow ex-football star Burt Reynolds, and has ambitions to have his own television situation comedy. A Christian who found his religion while watching Monday Night Football, he has released two successful gospel albums. However, he has never become part of the entertainment establishment, and he is happiest at home on his Texas cattle ranch, working hard.

—Tina Gianoulis

FURTHER READING:

Benagh, Jim. *Terry Bradshaw: Superarm of Pro Football.* New York, Putnam, 1976.

Bradshaw, Terry. *Looking Deep.* Chicago, Contemporary Books, 1989.

Frankl, Ron. *Terry Bradshaw.* New York, Chelsea House, 1995.

The Brady Bunch

The Brady Bunch was one of the last domestic situation comedies which populated television during the 1950s and 1960s. While it flew below Nielsen radar in its original run, its popularity in syndication led to frequent reincarnations through the 1990s. Generation X viewers treated the series with a combination of irony and reverence.

The cast of *The Brady Bunch*.

In 1966, *Gilligan's Island* executive producer Sherwood Schwartz read a newspaper item stating that 30 percent of American families were stepfamilies—where one or both parents were bringing into a second marriage children from a first marriage ended by death or divorce. Schwartz quickly realized that while TV sitcoms either featured traditional, two-parent families (*Make Room for Daddy, Leave it to Beaver*) or families headed by a widow or widower (*The Ghost and Mrs. Muir, My Three Sons*), no comedy had yet focused on a merging of two families. He spent the next three years developing a series based on this premise. By the time *The Brady Bunch* debuted in the fall of 1969, Hollywood had explored the subject with two box-office hits, *With Six You Get Eggroll* and *Yours, Mine, and Ours* (Schwartz planned to call his sitcom *Yours and Mine*).

The simple theme song laid out the storyline: Mike Brady (played by Robert Reed), a widower architect with three sons—Greg, Peter, and Bobby—met and wed Carol (Florence Henderson), a single mother with three blonde daughters—Marcia, Jan, and Cindy. The series never explained what happened to Carol's first husband; Schwartz intended Carol to be TV's first divorcee with children. The blended family moved into a giant house designed by Mike in the Los Angeles suburbs, complete with a practical and seemingly tireless maid, Alice (Ann B. Davis).

Most of the plots dealt with the six Brady children and the travails of growing up. Schwartz has said the series "dealt with real emotional problems—the difficulty of being the middle girl, a boy being too short when he wants to be taller, going to the prom with zits on your face." Frequently the storylines centered around one of the children developing an inflated ego after receiving a compliment or award; Greg becoming a baseball maven after being coached by Hall of Fame pitcher Don Drysdale, or Cindy turning into an arrogant snob upon being chosen for a TV quiz show. Invariably public or private humiliation followed and, with the loving support of parents and siblings, the prodigal child was inevitably welcomed back into the Brady fold. In contrast to the "real" problems dealt with on the show, *The Brady Bunch* explored more fantastic stories on location several times, including vacations to the Grand Canyon (where the family was taken prisoner by a demented prospector) and, more famously, to Hawaii (where the Brady sons were taken prisoner by a demented archaeologist).

The series never cracked the Top 25 ratings during its initial run, but was enormously popular with the 17-and-under age group. The child actors were prominently featured in teen magazines of the early 1970s, and even formed a pop music group in the style of such TV-inspired groups as *The Monkees* and *The Partridge Family.* Barry Williams, who played eldest son Greg, received upwards of 6,500 fan letters a week. There was also a Saturday morning cartoon spun off from the show, *The Brady Kids.*

The show was cancelled in 1974, and that fall entered syndication, generally airing during the late afternoons. In this child-friendly time period, *The Brady Bunch* became a runaway syndicated hit. In 1977, the cast (minus Eve Plumb, the original Jan) reunited on ABC for *The Brady Bunch Variety Hour,* a bizarre hour-long series featuring inane skits and production numbers; most of the cast could not even dance in step. It was cancelled after several months and is often considered the worst variety show in television history.

The original series' popularity in reruns spurred more reunions, however. *The Brady Girls Get Married* was a 1980 NBC special where Marcia and Jan find husbands. The special led to another short-lived sitcom, *The Brady Brides,* with the two newlywed couples sharing living quarters (in typical sitcom fashion, one husband was an uptight academic, while the other was a laid-back toy salesman).

The biggest Brady-related TV event came in December 1988, with the broadcast of the TV movie *A Very Brady Christmas.* The six children (most with spouses, significant others and children in tow) congregated at the Brady manse to celebrate the holidays. While working at a construction site, Mike was trapped under debris after an accident. Carol and the extended family sang Christmas carols as he was rescued; ironically enough, the location of this Christmas miracle was on 34th Street. It was the highest rated TV movie of the 1988-1989 season, and launched yet another Brady series. *The Bradys* (CBS, 1990) was an hour-long drama attempting to bring serious problems to the Brady landscape. In the series debut, Bobby, now a racecar driver, was paralyzed in a NASCAR accident. Jan and her husband tried in vain to conceive a child. Mike ran for Los Angeles City Council, and stood accused of taking bribes. Marcia became an alcoholic. The series lasted only half a season.

But the original series continues to fascinate. During the early 1990s, theater groups in New York and Chicago staged *The Real Life Brady Bunch,* reenacting complete episodes of the series, on occasion using actual *Brady Bunch* actors in cameo roles.

The series was something of a touchstone to people born during the 1960s and 1970s, many of whom grew up in single-family households or who, like the children in the series, became part of a stepfamily. "*The Brady Bunch,* the way I look at it," Schwartz said in 1993, "became an extended family to those kids." *Brady Bunch* fans developed the singular ability to identify a given episode after only the first line of that episode's dialogue. The 1970s dialogue ("Groovy!" "Far out!") and outrageously colored polyester clothes inspired laughs from 1980s and 1990s audiences. Many of the curious production elements (Why would an accomplished architect such as Mike Brady build a home for six teenagers with only one bathroom? And why didn't that bathroom have a toilet? Why was the backyard lawn merely carpeting? Why didn't any of the windows in the house have panes?) were cause for late-night debate in college dorms and coffee shops. *Letter to the Next Generation,* Jim Klein's 1990 documentary on apathetic college students, had a montage of disparate cliques of Kent State University students singing the complete *Brady Bunch* theme song.

In the spring of 1992 Barry Williams's *Growing Up Brady* was published, a hilarious bestseller recounting the history of the series

and reflecting on what being a "Brady" meant. Williams shared inside gossip:

> Reed, a classically-trained actor and veteran of the acclaimed TV drama *The Defenders* (1961-1965), regularly sent sarcastic notes to Schwartz and the production staff attacking the simplistic storylines and character development. Had the series continued for a sixth season, Schwartz was willing to kill off Mike Brady and have the series revolve around the six kids fixing up the newly single Carol.
>
> The 15-year-old Williams went on a chaste date with the married Henderson. Williams also stated that he dated "Marcia," and that "Peter" and "Jan," and "Bobby" and "Cindy" had similar relationships during the show's run.
>
> Williams admitted that he filmed part of one 1972 episode ("Law and Disorder") while under the influence of marijuana.

Shortly after Williams's book was published, Robert Reed died of colon cancer at age 59. It was subsequently announced that Reed's cancer was caused due to the AIDS virus. The revelation that Reed, the head of TV's most self-consciously wholesome family, had a hidden homosexual life was as stunning to Generation X viewers as news of Rock Hudson's homosexuality had been to many of their parents.

In the tradition of *Star Trek* and *The Beverly Hillbillies, The Brady Bunch* became fodder for a full-length motion picture. To the surprise of many, *The Brady Bunch Movie* (1995) was a critical and box-office smash. The film wisely took a tongue-in-cheek approach to the material, planting the defiantly-1970s Brady family smack dab in the middle of 1990s urban Los Angeles. "Hey there, groovy chicks!" the fringe-wearing Greg courted grunge classmates. There were numerous references to *Brady Bunch* episodes, and cameos from Williams, Henderson, and Ann B. Davis. *A Very Brady Sequel* (1996) continued the approach to equal acclaim.

Schwartz came to comedy writing after receiving an master's degree in biochemistry, and began as a writer for Bob Hope prior to World War II. He won an Emmy as a writer for *The Red Skelton Show* in 1961. The knack for creating popular entertainment clearly runs in the family—brother Elroy wrote for The *Addams Family* and *My Three Sons,* son Lloyd co-produced *The Brady Bunch,* and two of his nephews created the international hit TV series *Baywatch.*

—Andrew Milner

FURTHER READING:

Bellafante, Ginia. "The Inventor of Bad TV," *Time,* March 13, 1995, 111.

Hillard, Gloria, "Brady Bunch Still Draws Crowds," segment on CNN's "Showbiz Today" series, April 20, 1993.

Moran, Elizabeth. *Bradymania! Everything You Always Wanted to Know—And a Few Things You Probably Didn't* (25th Anniversary Edition). New York, Adams, 1994.

Owen, Rob. *Gen X TV: The Brady Bunch to Melrose Place.* Syracuse, Syracuse University Press, 1997.

Williams, Barry. *Growing Up Brady: I Was A Teenage Greg.* New York, Harper Perennial. 1992.

Branch Davidians, The

See Koresh, David, and the Branch Davidians

Brand, Max (1892-1944)

Pulp novelist Max Brand earned millions of dollars from his writing. Like many pulp writers, however, he did not feel that his work was worth very much. Brand wrote over 300 novels in genres such as detective fiction, spy stories, medicine, and fantasy. But he is primarily known for westerns such as *The Bells of San Carlos, The Bells of San Filipo, Bull Hunter,* and *Donnegan.* Clearly able to diversify his talents, Brand also achieved great fame and fortune through his Hollywood film writing. His *Destry Rides Again* inspired numerous imitators, including television's *Maverick.*

Brand, born Frederick Faust, was orphaned at an early age and raised in poverty, but grew up with high literary ambitions. Despite being known as a great western writer, Brand preferred to live in an Italian villa. He spent his time there writing pulp fiction in the morning and serious poetry in the afternoon. He was well read in the classics and often used themes from them in his western tales, for example he used the Iliad in *Hired Gun.* Without question the King of the Pulps, Brand averaged about one million words a year. Outside of his westerns, Dr. Kildare was his most famous creation. His readers were intensely loyal and reached into the millions. Although he preferred that his personal life remain mysterious, he did occasionally offer fans glimpses of himself in autobiographical short stories. In *A Special Occasion,* for example, one of the main characters shares many similarities with Brand—his marriage is on the rocks, he has a mistress who is a clinging vine, he longs for a better profession, and sometimes drinks to excess.

—Frank A. Salamone, Ph.D.

FURTHER READING:

"The Ghost Wagon and Other Great Western Adventures." *Publishers Weekly.* February 12, 1996, 60.

Lukowsky, Wes. "The Collected Stories of Max Brand." *Booklist.* August 1994, 2020-2021.

Nolan, William F., editor. *Western Giant: The Life and Times of Frederick Schiller Faust.* 1985.

Brando, Marlon (1924—)

Marlon Brando remains unchallenged as the most important actor in modern American Cinema, if not the greatest of all time. Though a number of mainstream critics were initially put off by his slouching, brooding "method" style, he was nominated for an Academy Award in only his second film, *A Streetcar Named Desire* (1951), and went on to repeat the accomplishment with each of his next three performances: *Viva Zapata* (1952), *Julius Caesar* (1953), and *On The Waterfront* (1954), with the latter performance finally resulting in the Oscar for best actor.

Handsome enough to be a leading man and gifted enough to lose himself in his characters, Brando brought an animalistic sensuality and rebelliousness to his portrayals unseen in Hollywood before. Not

Marlon Brando

content with simply learning his lines and playing the character as written or directed, the actor became the author of his portrayals. He maintained the view throughout his life that actors cannot achieve greatness without holding a point of view about society, politics, and personal ethics. This has been reflected both in the characters that he has chosen to play (rebels on the fringes of society) and in the shadings that he has brought to them (ethical conflicts about living within or outside the law).

This philosophy was initially ingrained in Brando through his stint at New York's Actor's Studio where he studied with Elia Kazan and Stella Adler, who taught him "The Stanislavsky Method," a style of acting in which the performer internalizes the character he is playing to literally become one with his subject. This was considered a major revision of classic acting styles during the 1950s. Before The Actor's Studio, performers externalized their characters, merely adopting the physical features and gestures conducive to portraying them. Up-and-coming actors including Brando, Paul Newman, and James Dean shocked traditional actors and theater critics with the new style, but there was no argument that it was effective, as Brando was selected Broadway's most promising actor for his role in *Truckline Café* (1946).

As early as his first motion picture acting stint in Fred Zinneman's war film *The Men* (1950), Brando prepared for his part as a wheel chair-bound veteran by spending a month in a hospital viewing first hand the treatment and experiences of paraplegics. Based on his observations, he played his character as an embittered social reject straining against the restraints of his daily existence. From this point on, his performances came to symbolize the frustrations of a post war generation of Americans trying to come to terms with a society that had forgotten them.

His subsequent characters, including Stanley Kowalski in *Streetcar* and Terry Molloy in *On the Waterfront,* to cite two, were literally drawn from the ash heap of society. Brando's interpretation of the two men's speech patterns—though decried by critics as mumbling—actually conveyed a hint of innate if not animalistic intelligence as well as a suppressed power which threatened to erupt in violence. The force of this power is best seen in *The Wild One,* in which Brando plays Johnny, the rebellious leader of an outlaw motorcycle gang that takes over a small town in Northern California. Based on an actual 1947 incident in which a gang vandalized the town of Hollister, California, over the Fourth of July weekend, the story was the perfect vehicle for Brando to display his menacing, barely-controlled rage. When Brando is asked what he is rebelling against, he responds with the now famous, ''What have you got?''

His rage seems more compelling when played against the overt violence of the other bikers because he appears to be so angry that he can't find the words. The audience dreads what will happen when he finally lets go. The interesting thing about the characterization is the fine line that Brando is walking. He is at once the protagonist of the film and, at the same time, potentially the villain, reminiscent of Humphrey Bogart's ambivalent Duke Mantee in *The Petrified Forest* (1936). As long as the violence bubbles beneath the surface, it is possible for the Brando character to be both sympathetic and menacing at the same time, as was Stanley Kowalski in *Streetcar* and the young Nazi officer in *The Young Lions* (1958).

Brando's interpretation marked a turning point in American films and effectively launched the era of the ''rebel.'' Following the film's 1954 release, a succession of young outlaws appeared on the screen: James Dean in *Rebel Without a Cause* (1955); Elvis Presley in *Jailhouse Rock* (1957) and a string of low budget biker films. Even Peter Fonda's hippie rebel character in 1969's *Easy Rider* and Charlie Sheen's rebel pitcher in 1989's *Major League* can trace their roots back to Brando's performance.

In his more finely modulated performances, the violence is translated into a brooding passion that is inner directed and reflects his characters' disillusionment with having whatever idealism and ideological purity they began with tempered by a reality that they are powerless to control. This is the Brando of *Viva Zapata, The Godfather* (1972), *Last Tango in Paris* (1972), and *Quemada!* (1969). In the first three, he is a man living outside the system who is battling in his own way to preserve his manhood and to keep from being ground beneath mainstream society's rules. In the final film, he is a man who has lost whatever idealism and freedom he once maintained and has learned that in order to survive he must not only play by but enforce the rules even though he is unhappy doing so.

In *Zapata,* Brando confronts the dilemma of an individual torn between spontaneous rebellion against injustice versus a full scale revolution to promulgate an abstract ideal. His Zapata is a contradictory character; on one hand full of zeal to right the wrongs that the government has done to the people and fighting for agrarian land reform; on the other, ill at ease with the larger issues of social reform and the institution of a new system of government. The character's inner naiveté is revealed in one particularly sensitive scene preceding Zapata's meeting with President Madero in which he confides to his new bride that he is ill at ease because he does not know how to read. The two sit on the edge of the bed and she begins to teach him in one of the most emotional moments in the film. This scene is reminiscent of Johnny's attempt at making love to Kathie in *The Wild One* in which

he displays a conflicted vulnerability and allows the woman to take charge.

This fundamental contradiction in Brando's characters is evident in his depiction of Don Corleone in *The Godfather,* in which he presents a Mafia chieftain who is comfortable killing men who oppose him and yet can express the deepest tenderness toward the downtrodden and those that he loves. Corleone is no less of a rebel than Zapata. Living on the outskirts of a system that he routinely circumvents for profit and, in a strange way, to achieve justice for the lower echelons of society, he is still, at heart, a rebel. Brando carries this portrayal a step farther in *Last Tango in Paris* when his depiction of Paul not only reveals a man's internal conflicts but actually questions the idea of animal masculinity that typified his characters in the 1950s.

Yet, between his dominant performances in the 1950s and what many consider to be his re-emergence in 1972, his career was sidetracked, in the opinion of many critics, by some dubious roles during the 1960's. Such films as *One Eyed Jacks* (1961), *Mutiny on the Bounty* (1962), *The Ugly American* (1962), *The Chase* (1966), *Reflections in a Golden Eye* (1967), and *A Countess from Hong Kong* (1967), however, still indicate his concern for social injustice and display his characteristic shaping of his characters to reveal the basic conflicts inside all men.

In what a number of film scholars consider to be Brando's real renaissance, 1969's *Quemada!* (*Burn*), directed by Italy's revolutionary filmmaker Gilo Pontecorvo, he gave what may arguably be his finest performance as a conflicted anti-revolutionary. In his previous film, *Battle of Algiers* (1965), Pontecorvo established a film tantamount to a textbook both for initiating and defeating terrorism. But in *Burn,* through the character of British Governor Sir William, Pontecorvo establishes the premise and the practice for effecting a revolution and at the same time shows why it could never succeed. Brando's performance as a man who, as a youth, shared the idealism and concepts of social freedom promulgated by the revolutionaries, but who now knows why such movements must necessarily fail, is a tour de force. He comes across as a man who is still a rebel but who is also aware of the path of military history. Emotionally he is storming the barricades but intellectually he knows what the inevitable outcome will be. On the latter level, his manner reflects the attitude of his earlier character, Major Penderton (in *Reflections*), but on the former level he is the emotional voice crying out to the deaf ears of imperialists as in 1963's *The Ugly American.*

Brando's social sympathies can be seen in his own life as well. For example he had an American Indian woman pick up his second Oscar for the *Godfather* and make some remarks about the treatment of native Americans in the United States. He lives outside of the Hollywood milieu, sometimes in the South Pacific working on environmental concerns, other times in the San Fernando Valley. He works only infrequently and expresses a disdain for the type of material currently being produced in Hollywood, although he does emerge every so often for outrageous sums of money if a role that interests him presents itself. He usually imbues these characters with qualities and social concerns that were not in the original scripts and tends to play them a bit ''over the top'' (see *Superman* [1978] and *Apocalypse Now* [1979]). Yet, he is also not above poking fun at himself as he did in 1990's *The Freshman,* in which he reprised his Don Corleone role, albeit in a satirical manner.

Marlon Brando is one of the few actors of his generation whose entire body of work—both good performances and those of lesser impact—reflect his social concerns, his celebration of the downtrodden, and his examination of the nature of man and the exercise of power. In this respect, he is a true auteur in every sense of the word, shading all of his portrayals with the contradictions inherent in the individual and in society itself. As Mark Kram stated in a November, 1989, *Esquire* article: ''there are people who, when they cease to shock us, cease to interest us. Brando no longer shocks, yet, he continues to be of perennial interest, some of it because of what he did on film, some of it because he resists definition, and maybe mostly because he rejects, by his style of living and his attitudes, much of what we are about as a nation and people. He seems to have glided into the realm of folk mystery, the kind that fires attempts at solution.''

—Steve Hanson

FURTHER READING:

Braithwaite, Bruce. *The Films of Marlon Brando.* St. Paul, Minnesota, Greenhaven Press, 1978.

Brando, Anna Kashfi. *Brando for Breakfast.* New York, Crown, 1979.

Brando, Marlon. *Songs My Mother Taught Me.* New York, Random House, 1994.

Carey, Gary. *Marlon Brando: The Only Contender.* New York, St. Martin's Press, 1986.

Frank, Alan G. *Marlon Brando.* New York, Exeter Books, 1982.

Grobel, Lawrence. *Conversations with Brando.* New York, Hyperion, 1991.

Higham, Charles. *Brando: The Unauthorized Biography.* New York, New American Library, 1987.

Kram, Mark. ''American Originals: Brando.'' *Esquire.* November 1989, 157-160.

McCann, Graham. *Rebel Males: Clift, Brando, and Dean.* New Brunswick, New Jersey, Rutgers University Press, 1993.

Schickel, Richard. *Brando: A Life in Our Times.* New York, Atheneum, 1991.

Schirmer, Lothar. *Marlon Brando: Portraits and Stills 1946-1995 with an Essay by Truman Capote.* New York, Stewart, Tabori and Chang, 1996.

Shipman, David. *Brando.* London, Macmillan, 1974.

Webster, Andy. ''Marlon Brando.'' *Premiere.* October 1994, 140.

Brat Pack

A term that describes a bunch of young upstarts in any industry, the Brat Pack was first used in the 1980s to refer to a group of actors that included Molly Ringwald, Judd Nelson, Ally Sheedy, Andrew McCarthy, Emilio Estevez, Anthony Michael Hall, and Rob Lowe. Honorary Brat Pack members were Demi Moore, Kiefer Sutherland, Mare Winningham, Charlie Sheen, John Cryer, Christian Slater, Robert Downey, Jr., James Spader, John Cusack, Eric Stoltz, Matt Dillon, C. Thomas Howell, and Matthew Broderick. The name is a play on the Rat Pack, a term used for the 1960s Vegas clique of Frank Sinatra, Dean Martin, Sammy Davis, Jr., Peter Lawford, and Joey Bishop.

The den mother of the Brat Pack was writer/director John Hughes, who changed the teen film genre forever. Not content to

leave the celluloid teenage experience at lookin'-to-get-laid comedies, Hughes explored the premise that high school life could be serious and harrowing, and that teenagers were not just a bundle of walking hormones. It was no accident that this became his oeuvre in the 1980s, a decade classified by obsession with money and status. Parents in Hughes' films were often portrayed as well-off but absent, too busy working to notice what was really going on with their kids, who had to learn the important lessons on their own. In Hughes's films, as in Steven Spielberg's, adults were almost always the bad guys. White, middle-class teenage angst, set mostly in the suburbs surrounding Chicago, became the vehicle through which Hughes chastised the confusing values of this superficial decade. And he used a company of young actors, most notably the crimson-tressed Ringwald, to explore this angst.

Sixteen Candles, The Breakfast Club, and *Pretty in Pink* was Hughes' Ringwald trilogy. In *Sixteen Candles* (1984), Samantha (Ringwald) is pursued by a geek (Hall), lusts after a hunk (Dillon), and worst of all, her whole family forgets her sixteenth birthday. The slightly heavier *Pretty in Pink* is about Andie (Ringwald), a girl from the wrong side of the tracks who falls for ''richie'' Blane (McCarthy). Blane's snotty friend Stef (Spader) tells him to stay away from Andie, whom he calls a mutant. The rich and the poor are mutually prejudiced against each other, and the poor are portrayed as the better people. Andie's oddball friend Duckie (Cryer), doesn't want Andie with Blane either, but that's mostly because he's in love with her. Blane finally takes the risk and goes for Andie, after listening to his snobby friends and their values for too long. The original script called for Andie to end up with Duckie, but Hughes thought that such an ending would send the message that the rich and the poor really don't belong together.

The Breakfast Club (1985) was the definitive Brat Pack movie; it focused on the interactions of five high-school students who are stuck in all-day Saturday detention. Each of the students represents a different high school clique. The popular, stuck-up Claire (Ringwald), the princess, and Andy (Estevez), the athlete, might hang out together, but normally they wouldn't associate with smart, nerdy Brian (Hall), the brain, compulsive liar and weirdo Allison (Sheedy), the basket case, and violent, sarcastic Bender (Nelson), the criminal. As the movie unfolds, the students fight and they bond, leaving their stereotypes behind and growing closer together. Face-value judgments are rejected for truer understanding because the students take the time to know each other, something they wouldn't do in the high school hallways. Hughes uses their interactions to explore the universal teen anthem ''I'm not gonna be anything like my parents when I grow up!'' and to reject the superficial classifications that adults put on teens.

What kind of adults will these angst-ridden teenagers grow into? The answer could be found in a film that wasn't from Hughes (the director was Joel Schumacher), but could have been, *St. Elmo's Fire*, the story of an ensemble of overprivileged recent Georgetown University grads trying to adjust to life and disillusionment in the real world. *St. Elmo's Fire* featured Nelson, Sheedy, and Estevez (probably relieved to be playing closer to their ages) as well as McCarthy, Moore, and Lowe.

For a while, Hollywood was on the lookout for any film featuring an ensemble cast of pretty young men and women. Thus moviegoers were treated to *Three Musketeers,* with Sutherland and Sheen, and *Young Guns,* a western with Sutherland, Sheen, and Estevez, among others. But real Brat Pack movies had to include that honorary Brat Pack member, angst. When these actors approached the

The Brat Pack as they appeared in the film *St. Elmo's Fire*: (from left) Ally Sheedy, Judd Nelson, Emilio Estevez, Demi Moore, Rob Lowe, Mare Winningham, and Andrew McCarthy.

age of thirty (in the early 1990s), the Brat Pack wore thin. None of the principal Brats have been able to score as well separately as they did as a youthful, angst-ridden ensemble.

—Karen Lurie

FURTHER READING:

Brode, Douglas. *The Films of the Eighties.* New York, Carol Publishing Group, 1990.

O'Toole, Lawrence. "Laugh Lines after School: The Breakfast Club." *Maclean's.* February 18, 1985, 58.

Palmer, William. *The Films of the Eighties: A Social History.* Carbondale, Southern Illinois University Press, 1993.

Brautigan, Richard (1935-1984)

Author of the widely popular novel *Trout Fishing in America*, Richard Brautigan was a countercultural hero in the United States in the 1960s. Although he never aligned himself with any group, Brautigan, with his long hair, broad-brimmed hat, wire-rim glasses, and hobnail boots, became a hippie icon comparable during his generation to Jack Kerouac and John Lennon.

Brautigan was born on January 30, 1935, in Tacoma, Washington. He moved to San Francisco in the mid-1950s where he met Allen Ginsberg and Lawrence Ferlinghetti and became loosely associated with the Beat poetry movement. In the 1960s, he wrote and published his first three novels, which would be his most popular: *A Confederate General from Big Sur, Trout Fishingin America,* and *In Watermelon Sugar.*

Trout Fishing in America was by far the most enduring and important of these. Published in 1967, it went through four printings before being reissued as mass paperback by Dell and selling two million copies. It was a favorite with college students, and Brautigan developed a cult following. Written in short, self-contained chapters, the book had almost nothing to do with trout fishing and was deceptively easy to read. It was structured such that the reader could open to any page and still enjoy and understand the diary-like ruminations. Some said that Brautigan was to literature what the Grateful Dead was to music—enjoyable while on dope.

Because of the youth of his fans and his status among the counterculture, some critics suggested that Brautigan was a passing fad. Like Kurt Vonnegut and Tom Robbins (who alludes to *Trout*

Fishing in his first novel, *Another Roadside Attraction*), Brautigan was a writer of his time, sometimes even a writer of his "instant." He was the quintessential 1960s writer, sometimes dismissed as dated and insubstantial. To one reviewer, he was "the last gasp of the Beat Generation," but others believed him to be an authentic American literary voice.

Between the 1960s and the early 1980s Brautigan produced ten novels, eleven books of poetry, a book of short stories, and *Please Plant This Book,* a set of poems sold with seed packets. Many of his books played with and parodied mainstream genres, with jokey titles including *The Abortion: An Historical Romance, The Hawkline Monster: A Gothic Western,* and *Dreaming of Babylon: A Private Eye Novel.* In his prose, his humor and childlike philosophies often masked deeper themes of solitude and despair, and his poetry was characterized by offbeat metaphors—comparisons of snow to washing machines, or sex to fried potatoes.

Brautigan was poet-in-residence at California Institute of Technology from 1966-67, but in the early 1970s, he left California for Montana. There he led a hermit-like existence, refusing to give interviews and generally avoiding the public for a decade. His later novels were financial and critical failures, and he had a history of drinking problems and depressions. In 1982, his last book, *So the Wind Won't Blow It All Away,* was published. Two years later, at the age of forty-nine, Brautigan apparently committed suicide—he was found in October of 1984 with a gunshot wound to the head.

His casual, innovative style was widely influential, prompting one critic to say that in the future, authors would write "Brautigans" the way they currently wrote novels. Critics waited for the Brautigan cult to fade, but it was still present at the end of the twentieth century. A folk-rock band called Trout Fishing in America formed in 1979 and was still active after twenty years, and a Brautigan-esque literary journal, *Kumquat Meringue,* was founded in 1990 in Illinois and dedicated to his memory.

—Jessy Randall

FURTHER READING:

Boyer, Jay. *Richard Brautigan.* Boise, Idaho, Boise State University, 1987.

Chénetier, Marc. *Richard Brautigan.* New York, Methuen, 1983.

Foster, Edward Halsey. *Richard Brautigan.* Boston, Twayne Publishers, 1983.

Breakfast at Tiffany's

Paramount Pictures' release of *Breakfast at Tiffany's* in 1961 solidified the cosmopolitan image of Audrey Hepburn and solidified one of the most enduring fashion trends: the little black dress. The movie was based closely on Truman Capote's 1959 short novel by the same name, which most critics called Capote's best work.

The story adeptly portrays the glamorous romantic illusions of Holly Golightly, a young woman travelling in search of a perfect home. She is so driven by her quest that she refuses to name her cat until she finds a home. But her inability to resolve the lingering issues of her past keeps her from finding peace. Only while looking through the window of Tiffany's jewelry store does Holly feel a sense of calm.

Audrey Hepburn as she appeared in the film *Breakfast at Tiffany's*.

Most films about young women, in the early 1960s, portrayed them as living under parental influences until they were married. *Breakfast at Tiffany's* broke that mold and showed Holly as a young woman living on her own the best way she could, as an escort to men she referred to as "rats." While Capote imagined Marilyn Monroe as the perfect actress for the part of Holly because her troubled past closely reflected the turmoil in the life of his character, Paramount Pictures instead cast Audrey Hepburn for the part and downplayed the dark past of the character. In doing so, the film heightened the dramatic importance of Holly's past and allowed Hepburn to bring a sense of mystery to her seemingly flighty character.

Audrey Hepburn's acting was not alone in effecting the romantic qualities of this film. Dressing Holly Golightly in sleeveless black shifts, big black hats, and large black sunglasses, fashion designer Givenchy made the little black dress—a standard cocktail dress since the 1920s—an essential component of stylish women's wardrobes. And Audrey Hepburn inspired Henry Mancini to write the score to "Moon River," the movie's sentimental theme song. Johnny Mercer wrote the lyrics, and the song won two Academy Awards. By the 1990s, *Breakfast at Tiffany's* had long since been considered a classic film and remained the film most associated with Audrey Hepburn's portrayal of a cosmopolitan and youthful romantic sensibility.

—Lisa Bergeron Duncan

FURTHER READING:

Capote, Truman. *Breakfast at Tiffany's*. New York, Vintage Books 1986 ed.

Garson, Helen S. *Truman Capote*. New York, Fredrick Ungar Publishing, 1980.

The Breakfast Club

The Breakfast Club, director/script writer John Hughes' 1985 film about five teenagers coping with the difficulty of crossing boundaries and connecting in high school, set the tone for coming of age films in the 1980s, and catapulted Hughes into the major filmmaker chronicling the problems of a young America in the Reagan years. While lacking in racial and sexual diversity, *The Breakfast Club* tackled issues of self-image, drug use, sex, and social acceptance, as well as the stratification between rich and poor. *The Breakfast Club* also launched the 1980's "brat pack" of marketable actors, Emilio Estevez, Ally Sheedy, Molly Ringwald, Judd Nelson, and Anthony Michael Hall.

—Andrew Spieldenner

Breast Implants

Between one and two million women have breast implants. Before 1992—when the controversy over possible side effects made world headlines—about 150,000 women received implants annually, and since 1994 about 70,000 women a year undergo implantation. About one-fifth of all implant operations are performed for reconstructive purposes following mastectomies, with the remaining 80 percent for cosmetic purposes. The two most common types of implants are silicone and saline, silicone being associated with the greater number of health risks. Few objects are more emblematic of the male obsession with the female breast and the sacrifices women are willing to make in order to live up to the male ideal, with thousands of women now suffering ill effects from having undergone the operation. Some blame the mass media—and even the Barbie doll, which if life-size would measure 40-18-32—for giving women a false self-image. The popularity of implants has alternatively been reviled for and praised for such phenomena as "Penthouse" magazine, the Hooters restaurant chain, and the television show *Baywatch*, and has spawned such backlash products as "Perfect 10" magazine (advertised as bringing you "The world's most naturally beautiful women, NO IMPLANTS!") and the "Playboy" version, "Natural Beauties" (advertised as "a silicone-free zone!").

Derived from sand and quartz, silicone was developed in the early 1940s, and its applications ranged from sealant and lubricant to infant pacifiers and Silly Putty. Immediately after World War II, Japanese cosmetologists began experimenting with ways to enlarge the breasts of Japanese women, mainly prostitutes, because it was known that the U.S. soldiers who were occupying the country preferred women with breasts larger than those of most Japanese

women. The practice of injecting breasts with silicone was soon exported to the United States and, by 1965, more than 75 plastic surgeons in Los Angeles alone were injecting silicone. Topless dancer Carol Doda placed the procedure in the national psyche when she went from an average 36-inch-bust go-go dancer to a 44-inch-bust superstar. But many of the 50,000 American women receiving these injections were soon experiencing health problems, including at least four deaths. In the mid-1960s, the Food and Drug Administration (FDA) defined silicone as a "drug," so they could begin regulating its use. But at the time, medical devices were not regulated by the FDA, and Drs. Frank Gerow and Thomas Cronin came up with the idea of encasing saline inside a silicone shell, with a Dow Corning public relations representative convincing them that filling the bag with silicone gel would more closely duplicate the feel of the female breast. The doctors designed their first breast implant in 1961, they surgically implanted it in 1962, and in 1963 Cronin introduced the implant to the International Society of Plastic and Reconstructive Surgeons (ISPRS), claiming that silicone was a totally inert substance. Cronin patented the device and assigned the rights to Dow Corning, which launched its breast implant business that same year, offering eight sizes, ranging from mini to large extra-fill. Over time, improvements in breast implants evolved, along with psychological justifications for their use; study after study claimed that breast enhancement improved everything from self-esteem to marital bliss. At one point, ISPRS proclaimed small breasts to be deformities that are really a disease—'micromastia'—"which in most patients result in feelings of inadequacy, lack of self-confidence, distortion of body image and a total lack of well-being due to a lack of self-perceived femininity." By proclaiming small breasts to be a disease, there was always the outside chance that insurers would start covering the operation.

In the late 1970s, the medical literature started reporting serious health complications from leaking and ruptured implants. In 1988, the FDA reclassified implants as medical devices requiring the strictest scrutiny, giving implant manufacturers 30 months to provide safety data. Document discovery in a 1991 jury trial, *Hopkins v. Dow Corning Corp.*, produced reams of internal documents—including some "smoking guns" implying that the manufacturers knew of and concealed the health risks associated with their product. When the private watchdog organization Public Citizen won a suit against Dow Corning and the FDA for these and other documents, they became available to plaintiffs' attorneys across the country, and the litigious floodgates opened, with thousands of suits being filed, including several class action suits. In January 1992, FDA Chairman David Kessler declared a moratorium on silicone-gel breast implants. By the end of 1993, more than 12,000 women had filed suit, and by mid-1998, about 136,000 claims had been filed in the United States against Dow Corning alone. As the 1990s ended, breast implants remained symbolic of male fantasies and distorted female self-image, but also had come to symbolize the bias of supposedly objective scientific results, with several manufacturer-financed scientific studies concluding that silicone breast implants have no harmful effects.

—Bob Sullivan

FURTHER READING:

Byrne, John A. *Informed Consent*. New York, McGraw-Hill, 1996.

Hopkins v. Dow Corning Corp., ND IL, No. 90-3240.

Sullivan, Bob. ''FDA Advisory Panel Recommends Limited Access to Implants.'' *Breast Implant Litigation Reporter.* Vol. 1, No. 1, March 1992.

Vasey, Frank B., and Josh Feldstein. *The Silicone Breast Implant Controversy.* Freedom, California, The Crossing Press, 1993.

Zimmermann, Susan M. *Silicone Survivors.* Philadelphia, Temple University Press, 1998.

Brenda Starr

Sixty years a journalist, red-haired Brenda Starr began her career as a funny paper version of the pretty girl daredevil reporter who was a staple of movies and radio over a half century ago. Created by a woman named Dale Messick, *Brenda Starr, Reporter* made its first appearance in 1940. It was a combination of newspaper melodrama and frilly romance. There had been female reporters in the comic sections before her, notably Jane Arden, but Brenda seemed to epitomize the type and she managed to outlast all the competition.

The strip owes its existence in part to the *Chicago Tribune*'s uneasiness about the phenomenal success of comic books. The advent of Superman, Batman and then a host of other costumed heroes had caused hundreds of adventure-based comic books to hit the newsstands and, in many cases, to thrive. To offer its younger readers something similar that would hopefully boost sales, the *Trib* created a *Chicago Tribune Comic Book* that was tucked in with the Sunday funnies as of the spring of 1940. On June 30, 1940 Messick's strip was added to the uncertain mix of reprints and new material. The only feature to become a palpable success, it was eventually transferred to the regular *Trib* lineup. Captain Joseph Medill Patterson, who headed up the Chicago Tribune-New York News Syndicate and was the publisher of the *News,* disliked women cartoonists in general and *Brenda Starr* in particular and the strip never ran in his paper until after his death. He was not opposed, however, to his syndicate selling to as many other newspapers as possible.

Feisty and pretty, Brenda covered all sorts of stories for her paper and that put her in frequent danger from crooks, killers, and conmen. But her job also introduced her to a succession of handsome, attractive, though not always suitable, men. Most notable among them was the mysterious Basil St. John, who wore an eye patch, raised black orchids, and appeared frequently over the years until he and Brenda finally were wed.

Brenda's managing editor was a fellow named Livewright and her closest friend on the paper was a somewhat masculine lady reporter named Hank O'Hair. For her feminine readers Messick included frequent paper dolls in the Sunday page. Messick apparently also drew all the fashionable clothes her characters wore, but for the action stuff and such props as guns, fast cars, and shadowy locales she relied on assistants. John J. Olson worked with her for several decades.

Brenda had a limited merchandising life. The strip was reprinted in Big Little Books as well as comic books, but there was little other activity. She was first seen on the screen by the Saturday matinee crowd. Columbia Pictures released a 13-chapter serial in 1945, starring B-movie veteran Joan Woodbury as the daring reporter. Roughly four decades later a movie was made with Brook Shields as Brenda. The film, which Leonard Maltin has dubbed ''a fiasco,'' was kept on the shelf for three years before being released. When Messick

was retired from the strip, Ramona Fradden, who'd drawn such comic book heroes as Aquaman, took over as artist. More recently June Brigman assumed the drawing.

—Ron Goulart

FURTHER READING:

Goulart, Ron, editor. *Encyclopedia of American Comics.* New York, Facts on File, 1990.

Brice, Fanny (1891-1951)

One of the funniest women of her (or any other) day, singer and comedienne Fanny Brice starred in the *Ziegfeld Follies* for thirteen years becoming, in the process, one of America's most famous women. Combining innate comic talent with a great singing voice, Fanny was a vaudeville star when still a teenager. After signing with Florenz Ziegfeld at nineteen, Brice performed in all but two of the *Ziegfeld Follies* from 1910 to 1923. With her signature song, *My Man,* Brice went on to star on Broadway; she also appeared in eight films. But she was best known around the world as radio's *Baby Snooks.* Married to gambler Nick Arnstein and producer Billy Rose, Brice's life became the subject of the Broadway musical and 1968 film, *Funny Girl,* and its 1975 sequel, *Funny Lady,* starring Barbra Streisand. Her comic legacy—always a lady, Brice nonetheless shocked her audiences with her raunchy humor—is carried on by such contemporary comediennes as Joan Rivers and Bette Midler.

—Victoria Price

FURTHER READING:

Grossman, Barbara W. *Funny Woman: The Life and Times of Fanny Brice.* Indianapolis, Indiana University Press, 1992.

Katkov, Norman. *The Fabulous Fanny: The Story of Fanny Brice.* New York, Alfred A. Knopf, 1953.

Brideshead Revisited

The lavish adaptation of Evelyn Waugh's novel *Brideshead Revisited* was fashioned by Granada Television and first aired on the British channel, ITV, in 1981. Comprising 11 episodes of some 50 minutes each, it chronicles the relationship of a young man with the aristocratic, English Marchmain family between the World Wars. The adaptation proved popular on both sides of the Atlantic; it appeared in the United States under the auspices of PBS in 1982 to great acclaim. Praised for its production values and aura of quality, the series is credited with ushering in a number of heritage England screen representations that appeared during the 1980s. These heritage representations include *The Jewel in the Crown* and *A Room with a View.* Like *Brideshead,* they are distinguished by a nostalgic tone, elegant costumes, and stately locations depicted via lush photography. Brideshead and other heritage representations were challenged by cultural critics in the 1990s as being conservative and retrograde.

—Neal Baker

FURTHER READING:

Brundson, Charlotte. "Problems with Quality." *Screen.* Vol. 31, No. 1, 1990, 67-90.

Golub, Spencer. "Spies in the House of Quality: The American Reception of Brideshead Revisited." In *Novel Images: Literature in Performance,* edited by Peter Reynolds. London, Routledge, 1993.

Bridge

Bridge, a competitive four-person card game, began in the late nineteenth century as a version of partnership whist which incorporated bidding and suit hierarchy. First called bridge-whist, by the turn of the twentieth century its name had been shortened to simply bridge, and was a popular American high-class club game.

Contract bridge, the most commonly played version, was invented by millionaire Harold S. Vanderbilt in 1925—he made technical improvements over a French variety of the game. Soon after this and into the 1930s, bridge became a faddish leisure activity of the upper class in Newport and Southampton.

By the 1950s card games of all kinds were popular forms of leisure that required thinking skills, incorporated competition, encouraged sociability, and demanded little financial outlay. Bridge was no exception and the game became a popular pastime for the upper and upper middle classes. Although daily bridge columns appeared as syndicated features in hundreds of newspapers, most contract bridge players, in fact, tended to be older, better educated, and from higher income brackets than the general population. Through the decades the game continued to be popular and according to the American Contract Bridge League, about 11 million people played bridge in the United States and Canada in 1986.

The game itself was played with two sets of partners who were each dealt 13 cards from a regular deck. The cards ranked from ace high to two low, and the suits were also ranked in the following way, from lowest to highest: clubs, diamonds, hearts, spades, and no trump. The bidding, or "auction" before the actual play of the cards determined the "contract"—optimally, the highest possible tricks that could be won by the most deserving hand, and the designated trump suit. This pre-play succession of bids among the players was as important as the play itself, and served also as an opportunity for players to signal to their partners the general makeup of their hands. The play itself required people to be alert, to keep track of cards played, and to continually refine their strategies as tricks were taken, making it an intellectual activity regardless of whether it was "social" or "duplicate" bridge.

Social, or party bridge, was a casual version of the game that allowed people to converse during play, and had more relaxed rules about proper play and etiquette. Very often people would throw bridge parties, popular especially from the 1950s to the 1970s, as a way to show their hospitality but with little obligation to bear the burden of socializing for an entire evening: playing bridge enabled people to engage in small talk while the intellectual requirements of the game gave people an excuse not to converse if they were not so inclined. Other forms of social bridge were practiced by local bridge clubs, informal groups that met once or twice a week and played for small stakes—usually between $1.50 and $3.00 per session. It was common for members of these bridge groups and those who engaged in regular games of party bridge, usually husbands and wives (who often chose not to play as a team in order to avoid marital tension), to alternate their hosting obligations, establishing reciprocal social relations while setting up informal games of competition. People enjoyed this form of entertainment because it was relaxing, enjoyable, somewhat refined, and inexpensive.

While this form of bridge largely had the reputation of being high-class and a bit priggish, with people believing that only rich white older women played the game as they sat around nibbling crustless sandwiches in the shapes of hearts, spades, clubs, and diamonds, bridge actually had a large influence on the general population. College students took to playing less exacting forms of the game that also employed bidding systems and suit hierarchies, including hearts, spades, euchre, and pinochle.

In contrast, competitive bridge was more combative. People earning "master points" (basic units by which skill was measured according to the American Contract Bridge League—300 points gained one "Life Master" status) would join tournaments with similarly-minded serious bridge players. The most common form of competitive bridge was "duplicate," a game in which competing players at different tables would play the same hand. In this game it was not enough to just win a hand against one's immediate opponents, but it was also necessary to have played the same hand better than rivals at other tables. Competitive bridge players commonly scoffed at social bridge, deeming it too casual a game that allowed for too much luck and chance.

As with many other forms of leisure activities and hobbies, bridge allowed a vast number of Americans to engage in an enjoyable activity on their own terms. While there were basic rules to bridge that defined it as an identifiable game, people incorporated it into their lives in radically different ways. Social players used the game as an excuse to gather among friends and relatives, making games regular (weekly or monthly) occurrences that encouraged group camaraderie. In contrast, duplicate bridge players who sought out more competitive games, often in the form of tournaments, took the game much more seriously and thought of it as a test of their intellect rather than an innocuous pastime.

—Wendy Woloson

FURTHER READING:

Costello, John. "Bridge: Recreation Via Concentration." *Nation's Business.* Vol. 69, January 1981, 77-79.

Parlett, David. *A Dictionary of Card Games.* Oxford, Oxford University Press, 1992.

The Bridge on the River Kwai

As Colonel Nicholson's captured British troops march into the Japanese P.O.W. camp on the River Kwai, they whistle the jaunty "Colonel Bogey March." Nicholson (Alec Guinness) soon enters into a battle of wills with the camp commandant, Colonel Saito (Sessue Hayakawa). Nicholson wins that battle and assumes command of Saito's chief project, the construction of a railroad bridge over the river. Meanwhile, a cynical American sailor, Shears (William Holden), escapes from the camp but is forced to return with a

Jack Hawkins (left) and William Holden (center) in a scene from the film *The Bridge on the River Kwai*.

commando unit on a mission to blow up the bridge. *The Bridge on the River Kwai* (1957) critiques notions of pride, honor, and courage with penetrating character studies of Nicholson, Saito, and Shears. In the end, Doctor Clipton (James Donald) looks on the devastation and offers the final assessment: ''Madness!''

—Christian L. Pyle

FURTHER READING:

Boulle, Pierre. *The Bridge Over the River Kwai.* New York, Vanguard, 1954.

Joyaux, Georges. ''*The Bridge Over the River Kwai*: From the Novel to the Movie.'' *Literature/Film Quarterly,* Vol. 2, 1974, pp. 174-82.

Watt, Ian. ''Bridges Over the Kwai.'' *Partisan Review,* Vol. 26, 1959, pp. 83-94.

The Bridges of Madison County

The Bridges of Madison County, first a book and then a film, remains controversial in popular culture, with people divided into vehement fans and foes of the sentimental love story. Written in 1992 by novice Midwestern writer Robert James Waller, the plot revolves around two lonely, middle-aged people—an Iowan housewife and a worldly photographer—whose paths cross, resulting in a brief but unforgettable love affair. A subplot opens the story, with the grown children of the female character, upon her death, finding a diary recounting the affair; thus, they get a chance to learn more about who their mother really was and her secret life. The book, residing somewhere between romance, literature, and adult fairy tale, holds a fascination for people because of the popular themes it explores: love, passion, opportunity, regret, loyalty, and consequence. As a result, the book has been translated into 25 languages; it topped *Gone with the Wind* as the best-selling hardcover fiction book of all time, and made its author, previously an unknown writer, into an overnight success. Finally, in 1995, it was made into a film (scripted by Richard LaGravenese) directed by Clint Eastwood, who temporarily shed his ''Dirty Harry'' persona to play the sensitive loner who woos a small-town housewife, played by Meryl Streep.

Other factors have contributed to the worldwide dissemination of *The Bridges of Madison County.* The simplistic prose and maudlin story have sparked a debate in and out of writer's circles as to whether the book should be characterized as ''literature'' or ''romance.'' Some say, in the book's defense, that the prose style should not be judged harshly because the book is really story-driven and its themes, although trite, are universal. Yet others say that it is romance fiction disguised and wrongly praised as literature. The author says he prefers ''ordinary people, the kind you meet in a checkout line at the hardware store.'' He chooses moments in which ''the ordinary can take on rather extraordinary qualities.'' Peculiarly, the prose, when combined with the story, does seem to blend the ordinary with the extraordinary. Because of its enormous popularity, more people have read the book than if it had simply been categorized as a ''romance,'' and that has helped to incite an ongoing and larger critique about how the book and its author should be perceived. The film also generated a similar, divided response in people: just as many seem to cry as well as laugh at its sad ending.

No one can deny that Robert James Waller has managed to present a story that deals with engrossing themes. People grow up with ideas of romantic love, nourished—especially in the United States—by the media and visions of celebrities engaged in storybook romances. Due to the uncanny nature of love, there is much room for people to fantasize, and fantasies are not usually practical. Because it is questionable just how much control individuals have over their lives, fate and destiny are appealing and common musings. Romantic love has dominated the subject matter of songs and stories for millennia, and continues to do so. What makes a story like the one in *The Bridges of Madison County* resonate is its attempt to portray the choices that people must make regarding their happiness, and the idea that fate can bring two unlikely people together.

One of the main characters—the woman—commits adultery, which is always a complicated and dramatically satisfying issue. In her case, she is an Italian immigrant who married an American and ended up in a small town in Iowa. She has kept her disappointment to herself because she loves her family, but she feels compromised, being more sophisticated than she lets on. For her, meeting Clint Eastwood's character and hearing stories of his travels reawakens her yearning for a more worldly life. Temporarily alone while her family is away, she is able to succumb to emotions that have been dormant in her. Both experience a passion requited on all levels—emotional and sexual—and end up falling powerfully in love. In the end, she chooses to stay with her husband (mainly because of her children), but does not feel guilty about having had the experience of the affair. He, in turn, walks away as well, respecting her choice and although they separate, their bond is present throughout their lives. The tragedy is complicated but satisfying (for dramatic purposes) in that although the reader wants the two to be together, people tend to be more attracted to yearning and regret (most everyone has an episode of lost love in their history) versus a happier ending; when people get what they want, it is often not as interesting.

—Sharon Yablon

FURTHER READING:

Waller, Robert James. *Border Music.* New York, Warner Books, 1998.

———. *The Bridges of Madison County.* New York, Warner Books, 1992.

———. *Slow Waltz in Cedar Bend.* New York, Warner Books, 1993.

Walsh, Michael. *As Time Goes By: A Novel of Casablanca.* New York, Warner Books, 1998.

Brill Building

The Brill Building, located at 1619 Broadway in New York City, was the center of Tin Pan Alley, New York's songwriting and music publishing industry during the 1920s and 1930s. Although changes in the music industry ended the Tin Pan Alley era by 1945, in the late 1950s the Brill Building again emerged as the center of professional songwriting and music publishing when a number of companies gathered there to cater to the new rock and roll market. In the process, they created what has become known as the ''Brill Building Sound,'' a marriage of finely crafted, professional songwriting in the best Tin Pan Alley tradition with the youthful urgency and drive of rock and roll.

The most important and influential of these companies was Aldon Music, founded by Al Nevins and Don Kirschner in 1958 and located across the street from the Brill Building. Nevins and Kirschner sought to meet two crucial market demands that emerged in the late 1950s. First, the established music industry, represented by such record labels as Columbia, RCA, Capitol, and others, were surprised by the rapid rise of rock and roll, and by the late 1950s they were attempting to find a way to make rock music fit into the long-established Tin Pan Alley mode of music-selling, where professional songwriters wrote music for a variety of artists and groups. Secondly, these record companies, and even prominent upstarts such as Atlantic Records, had an acute need for quality songs that could become hits for their many recording stars. To meet these needs, Nevins and Kirschner established a stable of great young songwriters including Gerry Goffin, Carole King, Barry Mann, Cynthia Weil, Neil Sedaka, and Howard Greenfield, among many others. Often working in teams (Goffin-King, Mann-Weil, Sedaka-Greenfield), they churned out one hit after another for such groups as the Shangri-Las, the Shirelles, the Ronettes, the Righteous Brothers, and the Chiffons. Usually accomplished singers as well as writers, a few had hits of their own as performers, like Neil Sedaka with ''Calendar Girl'' and Barry Mann with ''Who Put the Bomp.''

Working in close proximity on a day-to-day basis, these songwriters developed a common style that became the ''Brill Building Sound.'' Songs such as ''Will You Love Me Tomorrow?'' ''Happy Birthday Sweet Sixteen,'' ''Then He Kissed Me,'' and ''You've Lost That Lovin' Feeling,'' and hundreds of others, spoke directly to teenagers, expressing their thoughts, dreams, and feelings in a simple and straightforward language that made many of these songs huge hits between 1958 and 1965. By assembling a team of gifted songwriters, Nevins and Kirschner brought the standards of professional songwriting to rock and roll music.

Aldon Music's success prompted other companies and songwriters to follow. Among these other songwriters, the most prominent were Doc Pomus and Mort Schuman, who crafted such pop gems as ''This Magic Moment,'' ''Save the Last Dance for Me'' (both huge hits for the Drifters on Atlantic Records), and ''Teenager in Love'' (recorded by Dion and the Belmonts); and Jeff Barry and Ellie Greenwich, whose hits include ''Da Doo Ron Ron'' (a success for the Crystals) and ''Baby I Love You'' (a hit for the Ronettes), all on the Philles Label led by legendary producer Phil Spector.

The most successful challenge to the dominance of Aldon Music's stable of writers came from Jerry Leiber and Mike Stoller.

Leiber and Stoller were actually precursors to Aldon Music, for they began writing hit songs in the rhythm and blues vein beginning in 1950. Although white, they had a true feeling for black rhythm and blues music, and they were responsible for a number of hits on Atlantic Records, one of the pioneer rhythm and blues labels. They later wrote a string of hits for Atlantic with the Coasters such as "Charlie Brown," "Young Blood," "Searchin'," and "Poison Ivy." They were also crucial in the creation of rock and roll, using their rhythm and blues sensibilities to write some of Elvis Presley's biggest hits in the 1950s, including "Hound Dog," "Jailhouse Rock," and "Treat Me Nice." They continued their success into the 1960s, adding to the larger world of Brill Building pop.

The "Brill Building Sound" was essentially over by 1965. With the arrival of the Beatles in 1964, the music industry underwent an important shift. Groups such as the Beatles were not simply great performers; they were great songwriters as well. As rock and roll matured as a musical style, its sound diversified as a wide variety of artists and groups began writing and performing their own music. As a result, the need for professional songwriting lessened, although it did continue in the hands of songwriters such as Burt Bacharach and Hal David, who became producers as well as songwriters in the later 1960s. The great songwriting teams also began to feel the constraints of what has been called "assembly-line" songwriting, and most eventually went their separate ways. Some had solo careers as performers, most notably Carole King, whose *Tapestry* album was a milestone in the singer-songwriter genre of the 1970s and one of the best selling albums of that decade.

The legacy of the "Brill Building Sound" transcends anything resembling an assembly-line. Despite the constraints of pumping out songs on a daily basis, these songwriters produced some of the most enduring rock and pop tunes that defined popular music in the early 1960s. Those songs are among the gems not only of popular music, but of American culture as well.

—Timothy Berg

FURTHER READING:

Cuellar, Carol, editor. *Phil Spector: Back to Mono.* New York, Warner Books, 1993.

Miller, Jim, editor. *Rolling Stone Illustrated History of Rock & Roll.* New York, Rolling Stone Press, 1980.

Various artists. *Phil Spector: Back to Mono (1958-1969).* Phil Spector Records/Abkco Records, 1991.

Bringing Up Baby

Though *Bringing Up Baby* was not a box-office success when released in 1938, it has since become a favorite of film critics and audiences. Directed by Howard Hawks, the film is an example of screwball comedy, a genre which emerged in the early 1930s. Known as a genre depicting "a battle of the sexes," the films present independent women, fast paced dialogue, and moments of slapstick in absurd storylines that eventually lead to romance between the male and female leads, in this case played by Katherine Hepburn and Cary Grant. Like most comedies, the film serves to critique society, particularly masculinity and class.

—Frances Gateward

FURTHER READING:

Gehring, Wes K. *Screwball Comedy: A Genre of Madcap Romance.* New York, Greenwood, 1986.

Shumway, David. "Screwball Comedies: Constructing Romance, Mystifying Marriage." *Cinema Journal,* No. 30, 1991, pp. 7-23.

Brinkley, David (1920—)

As co-anchor of the landmark *Huntley-Brinkley Report* on NBC from 1956 to 1970, as well as a veteran reporter and news show host known for his low-key and witty style, David Brinkley is regarded as one of the most influential journalists in the history of broadcast news. When media historians name the pioneers of television journalism, Brinkley regularly joins the ranks of such notables as Edward R. Murrow and Walter Cronkite.

Brinkley was born on July 10, 1920, in Wilmington, North Carolina. The youngest of five children, Brinkley has described his relatives as a Southern family representing generations of physicians and Presbyterian ministers. His father was a railroad employee who died when Brinkley was eight. Because his siblings were older than him, the younger Brinkley was a loner who occupied himself with the prolific reading of books. At New Hanover High School, Brinkley joined the school newspaper staff, and seemed to apply himself academically only in English classes. After being encouraged by one of his teachers to go into journalism, Brinkley served as an intern at a local newspaper while he was in high school. He dropped out of high school in his senior year to take a job as a full-time reporter for the Wilmington paper.

Between 1940 and 1943, Brinkley tried his hand at a variety of jobs and activities, including serving in the United States Army as a supply sergeant in Fort Jackson, South Carolina; working as a Southern stringer for the United Press International; and being a part-time English student at Emory and Vanderbilt universities. Because of his strong writing ability, Brinkley wrote for UP's radio wire. NBC was so impressed with his talent that the network hired him away from UP. His initial duties in Washington, D.C., were to write news scripts for staff radio announcers, but then expanded to doing journalistic legwork at the White House and on Capitol Hill.

Brinkley broke into the new medium of television in the 1940s, broadcasting reports at a time when radio was still the influential medium. As Brinkley once remarked, "I had a chance to learn while nobody was watching." By the early 1950s, television had established itself as the prominent medium, with Brinkley providing reports on John Cameron Swayze's *Camel News Caravan* from 1951 to 1956. Brinkley also gained notoriety for being among the NBC television reporters who discussed topical issues on the network series *Comment* during the summer of 1954. Critics lauded Brinkley for his pungent and economical prose style, his engaging demeanor, and his dry, sardonic tone of voice.

Cary Grant and Katharine Hepburn in a scene from the film *Bringing Up Baby*.

By the mid-1950s, television's popularity was spreading rapidly. A major point in Brinkley's career came in 1956 when NBC teamed him with Chet Huntley for political convention coverage that did surprisingly well in the ratings. This led to the development of the *Huntley-Brinkley Report,* placing the team at the forefront when television news changed from simply newsreading to information gathering. NBC took full advantage of the differences between the two anchormen, cross-cutting between Brinkley in Washington, D.C., and Huntley in New York City. While Brinkley's approach was often light-hearted and his delivery style was lively, Huntley's style was solemn and very deliberate. Ending each broadcast with "Goodnight, Chet . . . Good night, David . . . and Goodnight for NBC News," the program became a ratings leader. Brinkley received the prestigious Dupont Award in 1958 for his "inquiring mind sensitive to both the elusive fact and the background that illuminates its meaning." In addition, the *Huntley-Brinkley Report* won Emmys in 1959 and 1960, and in 1960 the team's political convention coverage captured 51 percent of the viewing audience. NBC also aired *David Brinkley's Journal* from 1961 to 1963, which earned the host a George Foster Peabody Award and an Emmy.

When Huntley retired in 1970 (he died four years later), NBC slipped in the ratings when it experimented with rotating between Brinkley and two other anchors in the renamed *NBC Nightly News.* In August of 1971, John Chancellor became sole anchor, with Brinkley for the following five years providing commentary for the news show. In June of 1976, Brinkley returned as a co-anchor of the *NBC Nightly News,* where he remained until October of 1979. In the fall of 1980, the network launched the weekly show *NBC Magazine with David Brinkley,* which failed to survive. On September 4, 1981, Brinkley announced he was leaving NBC in order to engage in more extensive political coverage, and two weeks later he was signed by ABC for assignments that included a weekly news and discussion show, political coverage for *World News Tonight,* and coverage of the 1982 and 1984 elections. The hour-long show, *This Week with David Brinkley*, debuted on Sunday morning November 15, 1981. Its format was a departure from typical Sunday fare, beginning with a short newscast by Brinkley, followed by a background report on the program's main topic, a panel interview with invited guests, and a roundtable discussion with correspondents and news analysts. Within less than a year, Brinkley's program overtook *Meet the Press* (NBC) and *Face the Nation* (CBS) in the Sunday morning ratings.

David Brinkley (left) with Chet Huntley in front of the Capitol Building.

Brinkley remained at ABC until his retirement in 1998, with television journalists Sam Donaldson and Cokie Roberts named to host the Sunday morning program. Since retiring, Brinkley has published several nonfiction books and has appeared in commercial endorsements. Brinkley's impact on television journalism was far-reaching, spanning the dawn of TV news to the high-technology reporting of the late 1990s. Author Barbara Matusow summed up Brinkley's legacy by observing, ''Brinkley mastered the art of writing for the air in a way that no one had ever done before. He had a knack for reducing the most complex stories to their barest essentials, writing with a clarity that may be unequaled to this day. In part, he wrote clearly because he thought clearly; he is one of the most brilliant and original people ever to have worked in broadcast news.''

—Dennis Russell

FURTHER READING:

Brinkley, David. *Eleven Presidents, Four Wars, Twenty-two Political Conventions, One Moon Landing, Three Assassinations, Two Thousand Weeks of News and Other Stuff on Television, and Eighteen Years of Growing Up in North Carolina.* New York, Alfred A. Knopf, 1995.

———. *Everyone Is Entitled to My Opinion.* New York, Ballantine Books, 1996.

Frank, Reuven. *Out of Thin Air: The Brief Wonderful Life of Network News.* New York, Simon and Schuster, 1991.

Matusow, Barbara. *The Evening Stars: The Making of the Network News Anchor.* Boston, Houghton Mifflin, 1983.

British Invasion

The British Invasion refers to the fleet of British bands that floated in the wake of the Beatles' hysterical success when they burst upon America in January 1964. It is commonly acknowledged that Beatlemania was generated not only by their fresh new sound but also by certain historical factors which had nothing to do with the Beatles. The first great pop revolution, rock 'n' roll, had begun around 1954 with Bill Haley and the Comets' ''Rock Around the Clock'' and a string of hits by Elvis, but had died out quickly for a number of reasons: in 1957 Little Richard withdrew from rock to pursue religion; in March 1958, Elvis was drafted into the army; later that year, Jerry Lee Lewis's brief success came to a halt when it was discovered that he had married his 14-year-old cousin; on February 3, 1959, Buddy Holly, Ritchie Valens, and the Big Bopper died in a plane crash; and Chuck Berry was arrested in 1959 and imprisoned from 1962 to 1964. Thus rock was decimated. College students were getting interested in folk music, and a folk/pop hybrid spread to the mainstream through Peter, Paul and Mary and countless other folksinging trios. But there was nothing as visceral and exciting to appeal to youth as rock 'n' roll. The Beatles had been introduced to the American market through ''Please, Please Me'' in February 1963, and the album *Introducing the Beatles* in July on the Vee-Jay label. Neither made much impression upon youths. Things were good; America was on top of the world; and we did not need British pop. But this optimism, spearheaded by the young and promising President Kennedy, was shattered with his assassination in November 1963, leaving Americans in a state of shock and depression.

The Beatles burst upon this scene with the buoyant, exuberant sound of ''I Want to Hold Your Hand,'' followed by an appearance on the ''Ed Sullivan Show'' on February 7, 1964. They followed up with a bewildering string of hits which chased away the clouds, and made Americans forget their troubles. It was partly their charming British accents, their quick, sharp wit, and group charisma which charmed Americans during interviews. The matching lounge suits and moptop haircuts were also new and exciting. Superficial as these factors seem, they must have contributed to the overall effect of Beatlemania, considering the poor reception of the Vee-Jay offerings the previous year, when no television publicity had been provided to promote the Beatles' humor. But this time, their new American label, Capitol, dumped $50,000 on a publicity campaign to push the Beatles.

Such an investment could only be made possible by their incredible success in England. Part of the reason Beatlemania and the attendant British Invasion were so successful is because the brew had been boiling in England for several years. But American record labels, confident of their own creations, ignored British pop, disdaining it as an inferior imitation of their own. They felt that England did not have the right social dynamics: they lacked the spirit of rebellion and the ethnic/cultural diversity which spawned American rock 'n' roll.

British youth partly shared this view of their own culture. They had an inferiority complex towards American rock 'n' roll and

American youth, which they perceived as more wild and carefree. This image was conveyed to them through such cult films as *The Wild One* and *Rebel without a Cause*. But the British also responded to the music of black Americans, and embraced the blues more readily than most Americans, who were often ignorant of the blues and still called it "race music." Among British youth, particularly the art school crowd, it became fashionable to study the blues devotedly, form bands, and strive for the "purity" of their black idols (this "purist" attitude was analogous to the "authenticity" fetish of folk music around the same period). Hundreds of blues bands sprouted up in London. Most significant were John Mayall's Bluesbreakers, Cyril Davies' Allstars, and Alexis Korner's Blues Incorporated. Each of these seminal bands produced musicians who would move on to make original contributions to rock. Bluesbreakers provided a training ground for Eric Clapton and Jack Bruce, who went on to form Cream; Peter Green, John McVie, and Mick Fleetwood, who later formed Fleetwood Mac; and Mick Taylor, who eventually replaced Brian Jones in the Rolling Stones. The All-Stars boasted Eric Clapton, Jimmy Page, and Jeff Beck, who all passed through the loose-knit band before, during, or after their stints with the Yardbirds. Blues Incorporated hosted Mick Jagger, Keith Richards, Brian Jones, and Charlie Watts, all of whom eventually formed the Rolling Stones.

In the early 1960s the Rolling Stones and the Animals clung to the purist image common among white blues bands, although they didn't really play pure, authentic blues. The Stones resisted the commercialism of the Beatles, until Lennon and McCartney wrote "I Wanna Be Your Man" for them, and showed them how easy it was to score a hit record. The rest of the British Blues scene took notes from the Beatles' success. Unlike the early Stones, the Kinks and the Who were open to pop influences, and attracted the Mods as their followers. The Kinks and the Who were very similar in spirit. Both were searching for the same sound—something new, subversive, and edgy—but the Kinks beat the Who to it with the spastic simplicity of "You Really Got Me," the hardest, most intense rock ever heard at that time. The Who rose to the challenge with "My Generation." The Kinks broke into the American top ten long before the Who did, though the Who eventually surpassed them in popularity and artistry. However, the two bands displayed a remarkably parallel development throughout their careers.

The Yardbirds had started out as blues players, but Clapton was the only purist in the group. After he left in protest of their pop hit, "For Your Love," the new guitarist, Jeff Beck, combined the guitar virtuosity of whiteboy blues with the avant-gardism of Swinging London, and transformed the Yardbirds into sonic pioneers. After an amazing but all too brief series of recordings which were way ahead of what anyone else was doing, the band mutated into Led Zeppelin, who carried the torch of innovation into the 1970s.

But most bands were less successful at merging their developing blues style with the pop appeal of American radio. Since the establishment held a firm hand over the BBC, most bands at the time (and there were thousands) developed in a club environment, with few aspirations of a pop career. They developed an essentially "live" style, designed to excite a crowd but not always suited for close, repeated listening on vinyl. Manfred Mann tried to maintain a dual identity by delivering pop fluff like "Doo Wah Diddy Diddy" to finance their more earnest pursuit of blues and jazz. Most British bands of the time attempted this double agenda of commercial success and artistic

integrity, with only the commercial side making it across the Atlantic. For Americans, the British Blues scene remained the "secret history" of the British Invasion for several years. The Beatles introduced this developing artform to a vast market of babyboomers who had not seen the movement growing, and they were flooded with a backlog of talent. The Beatles already had two albums and five singles in England when Capitol released "I Want to Hold Your Hand" in America. By April 1964, the Beatles filled the top five positions in the Billboard charts. It was this surplus that made the British Invasion seem so exciting, in spite of the fact that Americans were generally only exposed to the more commercial side of the movement, based on the record companies' guesswork of what would sell in the States.

Thus the Beatles had both a short-term and long-term influence. They inspired countless imitators who cashed in on their success, and most of these turned out to be the one-hit wonders who comprised the bulk of the British Invasion. But they also proved to the more serious musicians that one could still be relevant and innovative in a pop format. They broke down the prudish "purity" of the British blues players and (with Dylan's help) the insular "authenticity" of the American folkies. The British Invasion would have been a flash-in-the-pan phenomenon if it had not beckoned the blues and folk artists to come out and play.

But Americans couldn't always tell the difference between the mere imitators and the artful emulators. The Zombies looked very promising with the haunting vocals and keyboard solos of "She's Not There," "Tell Her No," and "Time of the Season," but they were never heard from again after their first album flopped. On the other hand, neither the Spencer Davis Group nor Them produced an impressive body of memorable recordings, but they became famous for their alumni, Steve Winwood and Van Morrison respectively. The Hollies started out with Beatlesque buoyancy in "Bus Stop" (1966) and then proceeded to snatch up any fad that came along, sounding suspiciously like Credence Clearwater Revival on "Long Cool Woman in a Black Dress." Several tiers below them were Gerry and the Pacemakers, the Dave Clark Five, Herman's Hermits, and the Searchers. The Searchers are sometimes credited for introducing the jangly, 12-string-guitar sound later associated with folk rock (though they didn't actually play 12-string guitars!). Many of these bands didn't even produce enough highlights to yield a decent Greatest Hits collection.

The British Invasion ended when the Americans who were influenced by the Beatles—Dylan, the Byrds, and the Beach Boys—began to exert an influence on the Beatles, around late 1965 when the Beatles released *Rubber Soul*. This inaugurated the great age of innovation and eclecticism in rock which yielded 1966 masterpieces: the Beatles' *Revolver*, the Stones' *Aftermath*, the Yardbirds' *Roger the Engineer*, and the Byrds' *Fifth Dimension*. Henceforth the Beatles' influence was less monopolizing, and British and American rock became mutually influential. The so-called Second British Invasion—led by newcomers Cream, Led Zeppelin, Jethro Tull, and the redoubled efforts of the Beatles, the Stones, and the Who—is a misnomer, since it ignores the burgeoning American scene led by the Velvet Underground, Frank Zappa, the Doors, the Grateful Dead, and so many others. The first British Invasion constituted an unprecedented influx of new music crashing upon a relatively stable musical continuum in America. The next wave of British rock, impressive as it was, mingled with an American scene that was equally variegated and inspired.

—Douglas Cooke

FURTHER READING:

Palmer, Robert. *Rock & Roll: An Unruly History.* New York, Harmony Books, 1995.

Santelli, Robert. *Sixties Rock: A Listener's Guide.* Chicago, Contemporary Books, 1985.

Broadway

If Hollywood is synonymous with the cinema, Broadway has come to signify the American theater. From its humble beginnings in downtown New York City in the early nineteenth century, to its heyday as the Great White Way in the mid-twentieth century, to its status as one of America's chief tourist attractions at the end of the twentieth century, Broadway has lured both aspiring actors and starstruck theatergoers for well over a century, becoming, in the process, one of America's chief contributions to global culture. As the home of the American musical theater and the breeding ground for both popular and cutting-edge drama, Broadway has helped to nurture America's performing arts, even as it has enticed the greatest stars of England and Europe to its stages. In a nation that struggled long and hard to define itself and its artistic community as separate from yet equal to Europe, Broadway stands as one of America's greatest success stories.

As early as 1826, New York City had begun making a name for itself as the hub of the nascent American theater. That year, the Park Theatre featured the debut of the first two American-born actors who would go on to achieve fame and fortune in the theater—Edwin Forrest and James H. Hackett. Later that same year, the 3,000-seat Bowery Theatre opened; it was the first playhouse to have both a press agent and glass-shaded gas-jet lighting. The grand new venue would soon become legendary for the frequently rowdy working-class theatergoers it would attract. Over the next 20 years, Americans flocked to the New York theater district in increasing numbers, and in 1849, when the celebrated British actor William Macready brought

An enormous billboard overlooking Broadway in New York City, 1944.

his *Macbeth* to the Astor Place Opera House, Edwin Forrest supporters turned out en masse to protest the British star. On May 10th, a riot of over 1,000 resulted in the death of 22 people.

During the mid-nineteenth century, the biggest stars of the American theater were Fanny Kemble and Edwin Booth. Booth's 100 performances of *Hamlet* at the Winter Garden would stand as a record for the Shakespearean tragedy until John Barrymore's 1923 production. In addition to European classics, among the most popular of American plays was *Uncle Tom's Cabin*, which, in its first production, ran for 325 performances. But while both dramas and melodramas drew steady audiences, a new kind of revue called vaudeville, featuring burlesques and other musical entertainment, was beginning to come into fashion at the Olympic Theatre.

By 1880, Broadway had become the generic term for American theater. Shows would premiere in the New York theater district, which was then centered downtown at Union Square and 14th Street. From New York, road companies would then travel to other cities and towns with Broadway's hit shows. That year, the world's most famous actress, France's Sarah Bernhardt, would make her American debut at the Booth Theatre. Over the remaining 20 years of the nineteenth century, many of the great English and European actors and actresses such as Lillie Langtree, Henry Irving, and Eleanora Duse, would come to Broadway before making triumphal national tours. Among the most popular American stars of this period were Edwin Booth and his acting partner, Lawrence Barrett; James O'Neill, father of playwright Eugene O'Neill; and Richard Mansfield.

One of Broadway's most successful playwright-cum-impresarios of the late nineteenth and early twentieth century was David Belasco, who made his Broadway debut in 1880 with *Hearts of Oak,* a play that touted stage realism to the degree that the audience could smell the food being served in a dinner scene. European realists such as Henrik Ibsen were also well received in America. But Broadway devoted equal, if not more time, to the growing desire for ''family entertainment,'' and vaudeville became all the rage.

In 1893, the American Theatre opened on 42nd Street, an area that had previously been residential. In ensuing years, the theater district would gradually inch its way uptown to Times Square. By the end of the century, most theaters were located between 20th and 40th Streets, and vaudeville had firmly established itself as the most popular form of family entertainment in America. In just 75 years, the American theater had set down such deep roots that acting schools had begun to open around the country; organizations for the welfare of aging theatrical professionals were formed; and the first periodical devoted exclusively to the stage, *Theatre Magazine,* was founded.

With the start of the twentieth century came the beginnings of the modern American theater. In 1900, three brothers from Syracuse, New York—Sam, Lee, and J.J. Shubert—arrived in New York City, where they quickly made their presence felt. They not only leased the Herald Square Theatre, but they put Broadway star Richard Mansfield under contract and hired booking agent Abe Erlanger. The Shuberts were following the lead of other producers and booking agents, such as the Theatre Syndicate and the United Booking Office, who had begun the theatrical monopolies that soon came to rule Broadway—and the nation. When the Shuberts brought Sarah Bernhardt to the United States for her farewell tour in 1905, the Syndicate blocked her appearance in legitimate theaters throughout the United States. As a publicity ploy, the Shuberts erected a circus tent in New York City, in

which the great star was forced to appear, garnering nationwide publicity, and $1 million in profits. It was during this contentious period that actors began to realize that they needed to form an organization that would guarantee their rights, and in 1912, Actors Equity was founded.

Throughout the beginning of the century, feuds between competing producers, impresarios, theater circuits, and booking companies dominated Broadway, with such famous names as William Morris, Martin Beck, William Hammerstein, and the Orpheum Circuit all getting into the fray. But amidst all the chaos, the American theater continued to grow in both quality and popularity, as new stars seemed to be born almost every day. One of the most distinguished names on turn-of-the-century Broadway was that of the Barrymore family. The three children of actor Maurice Barrymore—sons Lionel and John and daughter Ethel—took their first Broadway bows during this period, rising to dazzling heights during their heyday.

Florenz Ziegfeld, another of the leading lights of Broadway, had made his debut as a producer in 1896. His *Follies of 1907* was the first of the annual music, dance, and comic extravaganzas that would come to bear his name after 1911. Other producers soon followed suit with similar revues featuring comic sketches and songs. Among the most popular of these were the Shuberts' *Passing Shows, George White's Scandals,* and *Irving Berlin's Music Box Revues.* Many composers who would go on to great heights found their starts with these revues, including Irving Berlin, Jerome Kern, and George Gershwin. But even more significantly, these revues catapulted singers and comedians to a new kind of national stardom. Among the household names featured in these reviews were Fanny Brice, Lillian Lorraine, Marilyn Miller, Bert Williams, Ed Wynn, Will Rogers, and Al Jolson.

By the 1910s, music had become an increasingly significant force on Broadway, and a slew of new young composers had begun to make their marks—including Cole Porter and George M. Cohan. By 1917, the United States had entered World War I, and Broadway embraced the war effort, with tunes such as Cohan's ''Over There'' and ''You're a Grand Old Flag'' becoming part of the national consciousness. But as Broadway began to hold increasing sway over popular taste, experimental theater groups such as the Provincetown Players began to crop up downtown near Greenwich Village, where brash young playwrights such as Eugene O'Neill and Edna St. Vincent Millay penned work that veered radically from Broadway melodrama and mainstream musical entertainment. These off-Broadway playhouses emphasized realism in their plays, and soon their experimentation began to filter onto Broadway.

In 1918, the first Pulitzer Prize for drama was awarded ''for the original American play, performed in New York, which shall best represent the educational value and power of the stage in raising the standards of good morals, good taste, and good manners.'' And by 1920, Eugene O'Neill had his first Broadway hit when the Neighborhood Playhouse production of *The Emperor Jones* moved to the Selwyn Theatre. In 1921, he would win his first Pulitzer Prize for drama for *Anna Christie.* He would win a second Pulitzer in the 1920s—the 1927 prize for *Strange Interlude.* The new realism soon came to peacefully coexist with melodrama and the classics, as the acting careers of such leading ladies as Laurette Taylor, Katherine Cornell, and Eva Le Gallienne, and husband-and-wife acting sensations Lynn Fontanne and Alfred Lunt flourished.

Eugene O'Neill's 1921 ''Negro drama,'' *The Emperor Jones,* also heralded a remarkable era of the American theater. Inspired by the burgeoning theatrical movement of Ireland, a powerful African-American theater movement had begun to develop during the late 1910s and the 1920s. Plays about the ''Negro condition'' soon found their way to Broadway and a number of significant African-American stars were born during this era. Chief among these were the incomparable Paul Robeson and Ethel Waters. But with the onslaught of the Great Depression, American concerns turned financial, and African-American actors soon found that mainstream (white) Americans were more focused on their own problems, and many of these actors soon found they were out of work.

But despite the proliferation of superb drama on Broadway, musical theater remained the most popular form of entertainment during the 1910s, and by the 1920s a powerful American musical theater movement was growing in strength and influence under the guidance of Cohan, Kern, Gershwin, Porter, and the team of Richard Rodgers and Lorenz Hart. Songs from such 1920s musical comedies as Gershwin's *Girl Crazy,* Porter's *Anything Goes,* Rogers and Hart's *A Connecticut Yankee* soon became popular hits, and performers such as Ethel Merman, Fred Astaire, and Gertrude Lawrence achieved stardom in this increasingly popular new genre.

In 1927, a new show opened on Broadway—one that would revolutionize the American musical theater. *Showboat,* written by Jerome Kern and Oscar Hammerstein II, , was the first musical in which character development and dramatic plot assumed equal—if not greater—importance than the music and the performers. In this groundbreaking musical, serious dramatic issues were addressed, accompanied by such memorable songs as ''Ol' Man River'' and ''Can't Help Lovin' Dat Man.'' Music, lyrics, and plot thus became equal partners in creating a uniquely American contribution to the musical theater. Over the next 40 years, Broadway witnessed a golden age in which the modern musical comedy became one of America's unique contributions to the world theater. Richard Rodgers teamed up with Oscar Hammerstein II on such classic productions as *Oklahoma!, Carousel, South Pacific, The King and I,* and *The Sound of Music.* Another successful duo, Alan Jay Lerner and Frederick Loewe contributed *Brigadoon, My Fair Lady,* and *Camelot.* Other classic musicals of this era included Frank Loesser's *Guys and Dolls;* Burton Lane and E.Y. Harburg's *Finian's Rainbow;* Cole Porter's *Kiss Me, Kate;* Jule Styne's *Gypsy;* and Leonard Bernstein and Stephen Sondheim's *West Side Story.* This wealth of material naturally produced a proliferation of musical stars, including Mary Martin, Carol Channing, Chita Rivera, Gwen Verdon, Alfred Drake, Zero Mostel, Rex Harrison, Richard Kiley, Robert Preston, John Raitt, and Julie Andrews.

Although the American musical theater was flourishing, drama also continued to thrive on Broadway. Following the Crash of 1929, however, Broadway momentarily floundered, as Americans no longer had the extra money to spend on entertainment. And when they did, they tended to spend the nickel it cost to go to the movies. And, in fact, many of Broadway's biggest stars were being lured to Hollywood by large movie contracts and the prospect of film careers. But by 1936, the lights were once again burning brightly on the Great White Way—with playwrights such as Lillian Hellman, Maxwell Anderson, John Steinbeck, Noel Coward, Thornton Wilder, Clifford Odets, and William Saroyan churning out critically-acclaimed hits, and American and European actors such as Helen Hayes, Sir John Gielguld, Jose Ferrer, Ruth Gordon, Tallulah Bankhead, and Burgess Meredith

drawing-in enthusiastic audiences. A new generation of brash young performers such as Orson Welles, whose Mercury Theater took Broadway by storm during the 1937-38 season, also began to make their mark, as Broadway raised its sights—attempting to rival the well-established theatrical traditions of England and the Continent.

By the start of World War II, Broadway was booming, and stars, producers, and theatergoers alike threw themselves into the war effort. The American Theatre Wing helped to organize the Stage Door Canteen, where servicemen not only were entertained, but also could dance with Broadway stars and starlets. Throughout the war, Broadway stars entertained troops overseas, even as hit shows such as *Oklahoma!, This is the Army, The Skin of Our Teeth, Life with Father,* and *Harvey* entertained theatergoers. But change was afoot on the Great White Way. After the war, New York City was flooded with GIs attending school on the U.S. government's dime. Young men and women flocked to the city as the new mecca of the modern world. And amidst the thriving art and theater scenes, a new breed of actor began to emerge during the late 1940s and throughout the 1950s, trained in the Stanislavski-inspired method by such eminent teachers as Lee Strasberg and Stella Adler. Among these young Turks were future film and theater stars Marlon Brando, Montgomery Clift, James Dean, Paul Newman, Joanne Woodward, and Kim Stanley. Soon a whole new kind of theater took form under the guiding hand of hard-hitting directors such as Elia Kazan and through the pen of such playwrights as Tennessee Williams, whose passionate realism in hit plays such as *Cat on a Hot Tin Roof, The Glass Menagerie,* and *A Streetcar Named Desire* changed the face of the American theater.

In 1947, the American Theatre Wing created the first Tony awards—named after Antoinette Perry—to honor the best work on Broadway. But by the 1950s, the burgeoning television industry had come to rival Broadway and Hollywood in influence and popularity—and soon had superseded both. Statistics revealed that less than two percent of the American public attended legitimate theater performances. But Broadway continued to churn out hit musicals at the same time that it remained a breeding ground for cutting-edge new American drama—such as that being written by Arthur Miller (*Death of a Salesman* and *The Crucible*). And, for the first time in almost thirty years, African Americans were finding work on the Great White Way; in 1958 playwright Lorraine Hansberry won the Pulitzer Prize for drama for *Raisin in the Sun,* while director Lloyd Richards made his Broadway debut.

On August 23, 1960, Broadway blacked out all its lights for one minute—it was the first time since World War II that all the lights had been dimmed. Oscar Hammerstein II had died; an era had ended. During the 1960s, Broadway continued both to expand its horizons as well as to consolidate its successes by churning out popular hits. After a rocky start, *Camelot,* starring Richard Burton and Julie Andrews, became a huge hit in 1960—the same year that a controversial production of Eugene Ionesco's *Rhinoceros* opened on Broadway. Throughout the decade, mainstream entertainment—plays by the most successful of mainstream playwrights, Neil Simon, and musicals such as *A Funny Thing Happened on the Way to the Forum, Funny Girl,* and *Man of La Mancha* occupied equal time with radical new work by playwrights such as Edward Albee (*Who's Afraid of Virginia Woolf*) and LeRoi Jones. By late in the decade, the new mores of the 1960s had found their way to Broadway. Nudity, profanity, and homosexuality were increasingly commonplace on stage, following the success of such hit shows as *Hair* and *The Boys in the Band.* A slew of musicals aimed at the younger generation, incorporating new sounds of soft rock, followed with Stephen Schwartz's *Godspell*; Andrew Lloyd Webber and Tim Rice's *Jesus Christ, Superstar*; and the Who's *Tommy.*

Meanwhile, avant-garde English and European dramatists such as Harold Pinter, Tom Stoppard, and Samuel Beckett brought their radical new work to Broadway, even as a new kind of musical—the concept musical, created by Stephen Sondheim in such hits as *Company* and *Follies*—took the American musical theater in a whole new direction. In this new form of a now time-honored American tradition, narrative plot was superseded by songs, which furthered serial plot developments. Other successful musicals of the type were Kander and Ebb's *Cabaret* and *Chicago,* and Michael Bennett's immensely popular *A Chorus Line.* During the 1970s, two producer-directors who had begun working in the mid-1950s rose to increasing prominence—Hal Prince, who was the guiding hand behind most of Sondheim's hit musicals; and Joseph Papp, whose Public Theatre became the purveyor of New York's high brow and experimental theater.

With the election of President Ronald Reagan in 1980 came an era of conservatism in which Broadway became the virtual domain of two men—composer Andrew Lloyd Webber and producer Cameron Macintosh. *Les Miserables, Cats, Evita, Phantom of the Opera, Sunset Boulevard,* and *Miss Saigon* were among the most successful of the mega-musicals that took over Broadway for more than decade-long runs. At the same time, however, Broadway was hit by the AIDS epidemic, which from 1982 on began to decimate its ranks. Called to activism by the apathy of the Reagan administration, the Broadway community began to rally behind the gay community. In plays from this period such as *Torch Song Trilogy, Bent, M. Butterfly,* and *La Cage aux Folles,* homosexuality came out of Broadway's closet for good. And during the decade, increasing numbers of African-American actors, playwrights, and plays found a permanent home on the Great White Way—from the South African-themed plays of Athol Fugard, to the Pulitzer Prize-winning work of August Wilson, to musicals about the lives of such musicians as Fats Waller and Jelly Roll Morton. Broadway also became increasingly enamored with all things English during the 1980s—from the epic production of *Nicholas Nickleby,* to the increasing presence of top English stars such as Ian McKellen, to the increasing infatuation with the mega-musicals of Andrew Lloyd Webber. But homegrown playwrights such as David Mamet, Neil Simon, John Guare, and August Wilson nonetheless continued to reap the lion's share of the critic's awards, including Pulitzers, New York Drama Critic's Circle, and Tonys.

In the late 1980s, a new phenomenon hit Broadway when Madonna starred in *Speed the Plow.* In her critically acclaimed performance, the pop and film star boosted Broadway box office sales to such a degree that producers soon began clamoring to find Hollywood stars to headline their plays. Throughout the 1990s, as the mega-musicals of Andrew Lloyd Webber, and popular revivals such as *Damn Yankees, Guys and Dolls,* and *Showboat* dominated the box office, Broadway producers sought to make profits by bringing in big names to bolster sales. Over the course of the decade, Hollywood stars such as Kathleen Turner, Robert De Niro, Nicole Kidman, and Glenn Close opened plays and musicals on the Great White Way. But the district received a multi-billion dollar facelift when Disney came into the picture, creating a showcase for its hugely successful musical ventures such as *Beauty and the Beast* and *The Lion King.* But despite what many critics saw as the increasingly commercialization and suburbanization (playing to the tourists) of Broadway, powerful new voices continued to emerge in the plays of Wendy Wasserstein (*The Heidi Chronicles*), Tony Kushner (*Angels in America*), and Jonathan Larson (*Rent*).

At the millennium, Broadway remains one of America's singular contributions to both high and popular culture. Despite the puissance of the film and television industries, the lure of the legitimate theater remains a strong one. Broadway is at once a popular tourist attraction and the purveyor of the tour de force that is the theater. With its luminous 175-year history sparkling in America's memory, Broadway can look forward to a new century filled with change, innovation, extravaganza, and excess—as the continuing mecca of the American theater.

—Victoria Price

FURTHER READING:

Atkinson, Brooks. *Broadway.* New York, Macmillan, 1970.

Baral, Robert. *Revue: A Nostalgic Reprise of the Great Broadway Period.* New York, Fleet, 1962.

Blum, Daniel. *A Pictorial History of the American Theatre, 1860-1970.* New York, Crown, 1969.

Brown, Gene. *Show Time: A Chronology of Broadway and the Theatre from Its Beginnings to the Present.* New York, Macmillan, 1997.

Churchill, Allen. *The Great White Way: A Recreation of Broadway's Golden Era of Theatrical Entertainment.* New York, E.P. Dutton, 1962.

Dunlap, David W. *On Broadway: A Journey Uptown over Time.* New York, Rizzoli, 1990.

Ewen, David. *The New Complete Book of the American Musical Theater.* New York, Holt, Rinehart, and Winston, 1970.

Frommer, Myrna Katz, and Harvey Frommer. *It Happened on Broadway: An Oral History of the Great White Way.* New York, Harcourt, 1998.

Goldman, William. *The Season: A Candid Look at Broadway.* 1969. Reprint, New York, Limelight Editions, 1984.

Brokaw, Tom (1940—)

As the anchor on *NBC Nightly News,* Tom Brokaw has a history of getting there first in the competitive world of network newscasting. He won the Alfred I. Dupont Award for the first exclusive one-on-one interview with Mikhail Gorbachev in 1982, and was the only anchor on the scene the night the Berlin Wall collapsed. He was also first to report on human rights abuses in Tibet and he conducted an exclusive interview with the Dalai Lama. From the White House to the Kremlin, Brokaw has witnessed and reported on many of the twentieth century's biggest events.

Tom Brokaw

Born in Bristol, South Dakota, in 1940, the son of Anthony (Red) and Jean Brokaw, he moved often as the family followed his father, a construction worker, who built army bases and dams during the 1940s. His high school years were spent in Yankton, South Dakota, where he first faced television cameras, appearing with a team of students on *Two for the Money,* a network game show. While a student he began his broadcasting career as a disc jockey on a Yankton radio station and experienced one of his most embarrassing moments. He was asked to interview a fellow student, Meredith Auld, the new Miss South Dakota, whom he been dating. Tom was so excited that he forgot to turn off the mike when the interview was over, and all the Yankton listeners heard his sweet nothings broadcast over the air.

He spent his freshman year at the University of Iowa, where he says he "majored in beer and coeds." He transferred to the University of South Dakota and in his senior year began working at KTIV-TV in Sioux City. After graduation, Tom married Meredith and applied for a job at KMTV in Omaha. They offered him $90 a week, but Tom held out for $100. Explaining why he needed the extra ten dollars, Tom said, "I was the first college graduate in my family, just married, and with a doctor father-in-law a bit unsure about his new son-in-law's future." The station finally agreed to his terms on the condition that he would never be given a raise. "And they never did," he added.

In 1976 Tom moved into the big time in the Big Apple, replacing Barbara Walters as the host of NBC's *Today Show.* As he tells it, he "made a lot of friends" on the program, but he always knew that his "real interest was in doing day-to-day news exclusively." After six

successful years on the morning show, he got his wish. He and Roger Mudd began co-anchoring the *NBC Nightly News* after John Chancellor retired in 1981. Within a year Mudd left the show, leaving Brokaw as the sole anchor, and in 1982 his reputation rose in the wake of his much publicized interview with Gorbachev.

Television critics have complimented Brokaw's low key, easygoing manner, comparing it with Dan Rather's rapid-fire delivery and Peter Jenning's penchant for showmanship. He is particularly noted for his political reporting, having covered every presidential election since 1968 and having served as his network's White House correspondent during the Watergate era. He has also shown versatility in other network assignments, heading a series of prime-time specials examining some of the nation's most crucial problems and acting as co-anchor on *Now with Tom Brokaw and Katie Couric.*

Brokaw is also author of *The Greatest Generation,* a book published in 1998 about his personal memories of that generation of Americans who were born in the 1920s, came of age during the Great Depression, and fought in World War II. He also has written for the *New York Times* and the *Washington Post,* as well as *Life* Magazine. He is best known, however, as the anchor who reported news from the White House lawn, the Great Wall of China, the streets of Kuwait during Operation Desert Storm, the rooftops of Beirut, the shores of Somalia as the American troops landed, and, most famous of all, the Berlin Wall the night it collapsed.

—Benjamin Griffith

FURTHER READING:

Brokaw, Tom. *The Greatest Generation.* New York, Random House, 1998.

Goldberg, Robert, and Gerald Jay Goldberg. *Brokaw, Jennings, Rather, and the Evening News.* Secaucus, New Jersey, Carol Pub. Group, 1990.

Jordan, Larry. "Tom Brokaw: A Heavyweight in a World of Lightweights." *Midwest Today.* February, 1995.

Bronson, Charles (1921—)

Charles Bronson is an American original. He is one of the earliest and most popular tough guys. His lengthy career and dozens of film credits make him a critical figure in the development of the action-adventure film. His steely-eyed stare and his signature moustache are themselves cultural icons. Although Bronson's career began on the stage and he once had his own television series, Bronson is probably best known for his role as Paul Kersey in the *Death Wish* series of films.

Born into grinding poverty as Charles Buchinski, the eleventh of fourteen children, Bronson spent many of his formative years in the coal mining town of Ehrenfield, Pennsylvania. After working to help support his family in the mines and after serving his country as a tail gunner on a B-9 bomber in World War II, Bronson moved to Atlantic City. It was on the Jersey Shore that Bronson developed a taste for acting while he roomed with fellow star-to-be Jack Klugman. Dreams

Charles Bronson (left) and Henry Fonda in a scene from the film *Once Upon a Time in the West*.

of a career on the stage took Bronson to New York, Philadelphia, and then to Pasadena, where he was spotted in 1950 playing the lead in the play *Command Decision*.

From early on, Bronson was regularly cast in roles that fit his arduous background. The post war American penchant for war films and westerns was well suited for an actor with Bronson's history and image. Often times he was cast in the role of a gritty gunslinger or rugged military man. Chief among such roles were his performances in *Machine Gun Kelly, The Dirty Dozen, The Magnificent Seven,* and as Natalie Wood's punch-happy boyfriend in *This Property is Condemned.*

Like many other American cultural phenomena, Bronson's career did not hit the big time until he won over European audiences. Though he had been working steadily stateside, Bronson's film career got its biggest boost in the late 1960s, when he began working in Europe. It was on the continent that his particular brand of American charisma gained its first massive audience. His triumphs in Europe rejuvenated Hollywood's interest in Bronson and movie offers began rolling in. His return to Hollywood was sealed with his role in the

thriller *Rider on the Rain,* which helped him win a Golden Globe award for most popular actor.

Bronson's film career culminated in 1974 with the release of *Death Wish,* a movie about a mild mannered architect out to avenge the murder of his wife. The movie has been credited with spawning an entire genre of vigilante action films that draw on the frustrations of the white middle class over urban crime and violence. Four sequels would follow, each filmed in the first half of the 1980s when middle class paranoia about drugs and crime was perhaps at an all-time peak. Hollywood has often sought to replicate the sort of success Paramount Pictures had with *Death Wish*. Dozens of films featuring ordinary-man-turned-vigilante were churned out in the wake of this film. Key among the early entrants into this subgenre was the *Walking Tall* series of films. Perhaps the last and culminating film among these angry-white-male films was the Michael Douglas flick, *Falling Down,* which caused a great deal of controversy over its racially charged depiction of whites, blacks, and Asians.

Charles Bronson is one of the few Hollywood actors who can legitimately claim success in five decades. The evolution of his characters in the 1970s mark Bronson as one of the few actors to successfully make the leap from westerns and war movies, into the modern, urban-oriented action-adventure era. Though he is largely considered a tough guy, he has played many other roles. Frequently lost in popular memory was Bronson's television series *Man With A Camera,* which ran for two years in the late 1950s. Bronson has also starred in several comedies, a musical, and some children's fare. In the 1990s Bronson has returned to the small screen and has had co-starring roles opposite Christopher Reeves, Daniel Baldwin, and Dana Delany in several made-for-TV productions, including *Family of Cops.*

—Steve Graves

FURTHER READING:

Downing, David. *Charles Bronson.* New York, St. Martin's Press, 1983.

Vermilye, Jerry. *The Films of Charles Bronson.* Secaucus, New Jersey, Citadel Press, 1980.

The Brooklyn Dodgers

As the first team to break baseball's color barrier with the signing of Jackie Robinson in 1947, the Brooklyn Dodgers captured America's imagination during the 1950s, when they fielded a brilliant team of men with nicknames like Duke, The Preacher, PeeWee, and Skoonj. Unable to beat their cross-town rivals, the New York Yankees, in World Series after World Series, the Dodgers became media darlings—a team of talented, loveable, but unlucky underdogs. Cheered on by their legendary loyal fans, the Dodgers finally beat the Yankees in 1955, only to break Brooklyn's heart by leaving for Los Angeles two years later.

The borough of Brooklyn first fielded a baseball team in 1849, as members of the Interstate League and then the American Association. When Brooklyn joined the National League in 1890, the team was nicknamed the Bridegrooms. The club won the pennant that year, but by the end of the decade they had gone through six different managers and had not won another championship. They had, however, acquired a new nickname which finally stuck. As Roger Kahn notes in *The Boys of Summer,* "Brooklyn, being flat, extensive and populous, was an early stronghold of the trolley car. Enter absurdity. To survive in Brooklyn one had to be a dodger of trolleys." Thus, the team became the Trolley Dodgers, which was later shortened to the Dodgers.

The Dodgers reclaimed the National League pennant in 1900, only to see their championship team disperse when many of their players joined the newly formed American League the following year. The team's ownership was also in a state of flux. But a young employee of the team, Charles Ebbets, managed to purchase a small amount of stock and gradually work his way up the ladder. Ebbets eventually took over the team and secretly began buying up land in Flatbush. In 1912, he built Ebbets Field, a gem of a ballpark, which would provide baseball with its most intimate setting for over 40 years.

At first it seemed as if the new field would only bring the team good luck. In 1916, the Dodgers won the pennant and then played in its first World Series. Managed by the dynamic Wilbert "Uncle Robbie" Robinson and led by the incredible hitting of Casey Stengel, the Dodgers nonetheless lost the series to the Boston Red Sox that year, whose team featured a young pitcher named Babe Ruth.

In 1920, the Dodgers took the pennant again, only to lose the series to the Cleveland Indians. Then, for the next two decades, the team fell into a miserable slump, despite being managed by such baseball legends as Casey Stengel and Leo "the Lip" Durocher. But the Dodgers never lost their loyal fans, for, as Ken Burns notes in *Baseball: An Illustrated History,* "No fans were more noisily critical of their own players than Brooklyn's—and none were more fiercely loyal once play began." The team's misfortunes were widely chronicled in the press, who dubbed the team the "Daffiness Dodgers." But sportswriters were oddly drawn to the team, despite its losing ways, and they portrayed the team as an endearingly bad bunch of misfits. The team soon became known as "Dem Bums" and their dismal record the subject of jokes in cartoons, newspaper columns, and even Hollywood movies.

In 1939, Hall of Fame broadcaster Red Barber became the distinctive voice of the Dodgers. He announced the first baseball game ever televised in August 1939. Two years later, president Larry McPhail and coach Leo Durocher had put together a great team, described by Ken Burns as "noisy, hard-drinking, beanballing, and brilliant on the basepaths." They finally won another pennant, and faced the Yankees in a World Series that would lay the groundwork for one of baseball's best rivalries. The Bronx Bombers, led by the bat of Joltin' Joe Dimaggio, won in five games. And, as Burns has written, "The Brooklyn *Eagle* ran a headline that would become a sort of Dodger litany in coming seasons: WAIT TILL NEXT YEAR."

Following the loss, the Dodgers brought in Branch Rickey from St. Louis to be their new general manger. One of baseball's greatest minds, Rickey, a devout, teetotalling Methodist, had revolutionized the game of baseball by developing the farm system. Rickey had long sympathized with the plight of African Americans, who were barred from major league baseball and played in their own Negro Leagues. He believed that "The greatest untapped reservoir of raw material in the history of the game is the black race. The Negroes will make us winners for years to come, and for that I will happily bear being called a bleeding heart and a do-gooder and all that humanitarian rot." But Rickey would be called a lot worse when he decided to break baseball's color barrier following World War II.

Rickey set out to find a great African American player "with guts enough not to fight back" against the abuse he would be bound to endure. He found Jackie Robinson, a brilliant young athlete from Southern California. In 1947, Robinson became the first African American to play major league baseball, when he broke in with the Brooklyn Dodgers. His presence on the field unleashed a torrent of racial hatred, but both Robinson and Rickey stuck to their guns. Baseball would never be the same.

In Robinson's first year in the big leagues, the Dodgers won the National League pennant and Robinson was voted baseball's first Rookie of the Year. On a multi-talented team that featured Duke Snider, Roy Campanella, Pee Wee Reese and Gil Hodges, Robinson's athleticism and competitiveness brought the Dodgers to new heights. Nonetheless, they lost the Series once again to the Yankees. And Brooklyn fans were forced once again to "Wait Till Next Year."

During the early 1950s, Walter O'Malley became president of the organization, Red Barber was joined in the booth by another future Hall of Famer broadcaster, Vin Scully, and the Dodgers fielded teams of such talent that they continued to win every season. The

Several members of the Brooklyn Dodgers after winning the first game of the 1952 World Series: (from left) Joe Black, Duke Snider, Chuck Dressen, Pee Wee Reese, and Jackie Robinson.

1953 team, dubbed the "Boys of Summer," won a record 105 games. But they still could not win the World Series. As Roger Kahn has written, "You may glory in a team triumphant, but you fall in love with a team in defeat . . . A whole country was stirred by the high deeds and thwarted longings of The Duke, Preacher, Pee Wee, Skoonj, and the rest. The team was awesomely good and yet defeated. Their skills lifted everyman's spirit and their defeat joined them with everyman's existence, a national team, with a country in thrall, irresistible and unable to beat the Yankees."

Finally, in 1955, the Dodgers did the unthinkable. They beat the Yankees in the World Series. Two years later, something even more unthinkable occurred. In what historian and lifelong Brooklyn Dodgers fan Doris Kearns Goodwin calls an "invidious act of betrayal," team president Walter O'Malley moved the Dodgers to Los Angeles and an unforgettable era of baseball history came to a close.

—Victoria Price

FURTHER READING:

Burns, Ken, and Geoffrey C. Ward. *Baseball: An Illustrated History.* New York, Alfred A. Knopf, 1994.

Goodwin, Doris Kearns. *Wait Till Next Year: A Memoir.* New York, Simon & Schuster, 1997.

Kahn, Roger. *The Boys of Summer.* New York, HarperPerennial, 1998.

Prince, Carl E. *Brooklyn's Dodgers: The Bums, The Borough, and the Best of Baseball 1947-1957.* New York, Oxford University Press, 1996.

Rampersand, Arnold. *Jackie Robinson: A Biography.* New York, Alfred A. Knopf, 1997.

Brooks, Garth (1962—)

Garth Brooks, the best-selling recording artist of all time, symbolizes the evolution of "new wave" country music in the late twentieth century. Brooks was popular in the late 1980s and throughout the 1990s with a blend of country, honky-tonk, and rock that signaled country's move into the mainstream of popular music. From his first self-titled album in 1989, the Oklahoma singer achieved fame

Garth Brooks

beyond the traditional country listener base to achieve acceptance by a mass audience. Between 1989 and 1996 he sold more than sixty million albums. Prior to Brooks's third album, *Ropin' the Wind,* it was nearly impossible for a country artist to sell a million copies, and no country recording had ever premiered at the top of the pop charts. His stage performances, which were filled with many special effects such as fantastic lighting displays, explosions, and even a harness that allowed him to sing while swinging over his enthusiastic crowds, resembled the stadium rock extravaganzas of the 1970s. Brooks combined his onstage identity as the modern country superstar with an offstage persona emphasizing country music's traditional values of family, patriotism, and devotion to one's fans.

Troyal Garth Brooks, born on February 7, 1962, in Tulsa, Oklahoma, had a strong interest in country music from childhood. His mother, Colleen Carroll Brooks, had been a minor country singer in the 1950s who had recorded several unsuccessful albums for Capitol. After earning an athletic scholarship to Oklahoma State University for his ability with the javelin, Brooks began singing in Stillwater clubs where he had worked as a bouncer. In 1986, he married Sandy Mahl, a woman he had once thrown out of a bar after a restroom altercation. The couple moved to Nashville in 1985 after Brooks's graduation with an advertising degree. The young singer's initial attempt to find fame in the world of country music was a complete failure, and the pair returned to Oklahoma after a mere twenty-three hours in Nashville. Two years later, a more mature Brooks returned to the country music capital and began his career by singing on new songwriter's demo tapes. By 1988, he had been signed by Capitol Records and his first single "Much Too Young (To Feel This Damn Old)" earned much popular acclaim. His subsequent singles— "If Tomorrow Never Comes," "Not Counting You," and "The Dance"—each became number-one hits and marked Brooks's rising crossover appeal.

By 1992, Garth Brooks was a true popular culture phenomenon. He had a string of hit songs and a critically praised network television special (*This Is Garth Brooks*), and he had sold millions of dollars worth of licensed merchandise. *Forbes* magazine listed him as the thirteenth-highest-paid entertainer in the United States, the only country music performer to have made the ranking. Unlike previous country stars, such as Johnny Cash, Kenny Rogers, and Dolly Parton, Brooks made country music fashionable to those beyond its core constituency, a circumstance he credits to the diversity of his early musical influences. Among those whom Brooks cites as having affected his style are such diverse artists as James Taylor, Cat Stevens, John Denver, the Bee Gees, and even some heavy-metal bands. His expanded appeal also stems from his choice not to limit his songs to the traditional country music themes. Brooks's "We Shall Be Free" is an anthem for the oppressed for its advocacy of environmental protection, interracial harmony, and the acceptance of same-sex relationships. His most controversial work of the period, "The Thunder Rolls," dealt with the issues of adultery, wife beating, and revenge. Brooks's desire to expand country presentation and subject matter attracted a sizable audience unknown to earlier country performers. Brooks is considered the leader of a new wave of country vocalists including Travis Tritt, Clint Black, and Alan Jackson.

While Brooks expanded country's scope, he carefully worked to maintain his image as a humble country performer, endorsing various charities and repeatedly professing his overwhelming devotion to his family. In 1991, he considered forsaking his career to become a full-time father. Brooks's most popular offstage act, however, was his devotion to his fans: he signed hundreds of autographs after each show and, most importantly, demanded that his ticket prices remain affordable to the average person.

Few performers in any genre can claim the crossover success exhibited by Garth Brooks in the 1990s. His domination of the country and pop charts proved that ''country'' was no longer a niche format but one acceptable to mainstream audiences. His achievements were recognized in March, 1992, when he was featured on the cover of *Time,* which credited him for creating ''Country's Big Boom.'' His ability to meld traditional country music sounds and sensibilities with pop themes allowed country to advance to new heights of popularity.

—Charles Coletta

FURTHER READING:

Morris, Edward. *Garth Brooks: Platinum Cowboy.* New York, St. Martin's Press, 1993.

O'Meila, Matt. *Garth Brooks.* Norman, University of Oklahoma Press, 1997.

Brooks, Gwendolyn (1917—)

Poet Gwendolyn Brooks's writings explore the discrepancies between appearance and morality, between good and evil. Her images are often ironic and coy; her work is distinctly African American. She won the Pulitzer Prize in 1950, the first time an African American writer received the award. Born in Topeka, Kansas, Gwendolyn Brooks published her first poem at age 13. By 1941 she had moved to Chicago and began studying at the South Side Community Art Center. In the 1960s she turned to teaching until 1971. More recently, she became Illinois Poet Laureate and an honorary consultant in American literature to the Library of Congress. Her publications include *Street in Bronzeville* (1945), *Annie Allen* (1950), *Maud Martha* (1953), *In the Mecca* (1968), and *Report from Part One* (1971).

—Beatriz Badikian

FURTHER READING:

Brooks, Gwendolyn. *Report from Part Two.* Chicago, Third World Press, 1990.

Kent, George E. *A Life of Gwendolyn Brooks.* Lexington, Kentucky, University Press of Kentucky, 1990.

Brooks, James L. (1940—)

Emmy Award-winning television writer-producer, James L. Brooks made an extraordinary feature film debut in 1983 with *Terms of Endearment,* winning five Academy Awards, including Best Screenplay, Director, and Picture. Three further films (including the Oscar-nominated *Broadcast News,* 1987) followed at wide intervals, while Brooks confined himself to wielding his considerable influence

on popular movie and television culture behind the scenes. As a producer of such hits as *Big* (1988), *The War of the Roses* (1989), and *Jerry Maguire* (1996), he confirmed his acute instinct for material with strongly defined characters and popular appeal. Born in New Jersey and educated at New York University, the former television newswriter made his major breakthrough with the creation of *The Mary Tyler Moore Show* before producing such high-rating series as *Taxi, Cheers, Lou Grant,* and *Rhoda.* In 1997, he returned to filmmaking, writing, producing, and directing the Oscar-nominated *As Good as it Gets.*

—Robyn Karney

FURTHER READING:

Willsmer, Trevor. ''James L. Brooks.'' *Who's Who in Hollywood,* edited by Robyn Karney. New York, Continuum, 1993.

Brooks, Louise (1906-1985)

Louise Brooks, American silent film actress and author, achieved only moderate fame in her film career, but emerged as the focus of a still-growing cult of admirers in the 1970s, sparked by the renewed critical interest in her performance as the doomed hedonist Lulu in G. W. Pabst's *Pandora's Box* (1929). The publication of critic Kenneth Tynan's *New Yorker* article ''The Girl in the Black Helmet'' captured the imagination of readers who appreciated her caustic wit and her tales of Hollywood, and also romanticized her hermit-like retreat in Rochester, New York, after a life of alcoholism and excess. Her sleek dancer's body and trademark black bob remain an icon of high style and eroticism. She inspired two comic strips as well as numerous film and literary tributes. Brooks became a bestselling author in the 1980s with her memoir *Lulu in Hollywood.*

—Mary Hess

FURTHER READING:

Brooks, Louise. *Lulu in Hollywood.* New York, Alfred A. Knopf, 1982.

Paris, Barry. *Louise Brooks.* New York, Alfred A. Knopf, 1989.

Tynan, Kenneth. ''The Girl in the Black Helmet.'' *New Yorker.* June 11, 1979.

Brooks, Mel (1926—)

A woman once accosted filmmaker Mel Brooks and angrily told him that his 1968 comedy *The Producers* was ''vulgar.'' ''Madame,'' he said with an air of pride, ''it rises below vulgarity.'' Mel Brooks spent a career as a comedy writer, director, and actor offending vast segments of his audience, while simultaneously making them laugh uproariously. His series of genre spoofs meticulously recreated the feel and look of westerns, horror films, and sci-fi classics, only to upend cliches with an assortment of double-entendres, anachronisms, musical production numbers, Jewish American references, and jokes

Mel Brooks

about bodily functions. The creators of such 1990s phenomena as *South Park* and *There's Something About Mary* are direct descendants of Brooks' comic sensibility.

Brooks was born Melvin Kaminsky on June 28, 1926 in Brooklyn, New York. A boyhood friend was drumming legend Buddy Rich, who taught Brooks how to play. Brooks performed at parties and, during the summers, at largely Jewish resorts in the Catskills in upstate New York. After World War II, Brooks started performing comedy while social director of Grossinger's, the most prestigious Catskills resort, where he became friends with comedian Sid Caesar.

In 1950 Brooks joined the writing staff of NBC television's variety series *Your Show of Shows,* starring Caesar and Imogene Coca. The anarchy of these writing sessions was immortalized in Carl Reiner's 1960s sitcom *The Dick Van Dyke Show* and Neil Simon's 1994 play *Laughter on the 23rd Floor.* Nobody, Caesar's colleagues agreed, was more anarchic than Brooks. When *Your Show of Shows* lost an Emmy for best writing, Brooks stood up from his seat in the auditorium and yelled, "Nietschke was right—there is no God!"

Reiner and Brooks would often improvise comedic characters during the manic writer's meetings. One morning, Reiner introduced Brooks as the only living witness to Christ's Crucifixion. The persona of the "2000 Year Old Man" was born. What began as a private joke eventually became the subject of five comedy albums over a 35 year span. Brooks' character had seen it all and done it all over two millenia, yet his needs and demands were small. "I have over 42,000 children," he once proclaimed, "and not one comes to visit." The Stone Age survivor claimed that the world's first national anthem began, "Let 'em all go to hell, except Cave Seventy Six!"

With Buck Henry, Brooks created the television sitcom *Get Smart!,* a savage sendup of the James Bond films, in 1965. Maxwell Smart (Don Adams) was a thorough incompetent who could not master his collection of Bond-like gadgets, such as a shoe-phone. The bad guys were usually caught with the aid of Smart's truly smart assistant, Agent 99. The series lasted five seasons.

During the 1950s and 1960s Brooks worked on several unsuccessful Broadway shows, and he began wondering what would happen if two guys deliberately decided to produce the worst musical ever. The result was the 1968 classic *The Producers,* Brooks's directoral debut. Zero Mostel and Gene Wilder played the title characters who decide to stage "Springtime for Hitler," a lighthearted toe-tapper about the Nazi leader (complete with dancing SS troopers). Mostel and Wilder collect 100 times more capital than needed. To their dismay, "Springtime for Hitler" becomes a smash hit and the pair, unable to pay their many backers, wind up in jail. The film became a cult hit, and Brooks won an Oscar for Best Screenplay.

Blazing Saddles (1973) inverted virtually every Western movie cliche. Black chain gang workers are ordered to sing a work song— and quickly harmonize on Cole Porter's "I Get a Kick Out of You." Cowboys eating endless amounts of beans by the campfire begin loudly breaking wind. The plot had black sheriff (Cleavon Little) unite with an alcoholic sharpshooter (Wilder) to clean up a corrupt Old West town. Brooks himself appeared in two roles, a Yiddish Indian chief and a corrupt governor. The film offended many (some thought the village idiot, played by Alex Karras, insulted the mentally retarded) but became the highest grossing movie comedy of all time.

Brooks followed with what most consider his masterpiece, *Young Frankenstein* (1974). Gene Wilder starred as the grandson of the famous doctor, who himself attempts to bring a dead man (Peter Boyle) to life. Once resurrected, Boyle ravishes Wilder's virginal fiancee (Madeline Kahn), to her ultimate pleasure. Wilder devises a brain transplant with Boyle; Wilder gives Boyle some of his intellect, while Boyle gives Wilder some of his raging libido. The film was beautifully shot and acted, and the image of Peter Boyle as the Frankenstein monster in top hat and tails singing "Putting on the Ritz" to an audience of scientists ranks as one of the most inspired in cinematic history.

Silent Movie (1976) was the first Hollywood silent movie in four decades. Brooks, Marty Feldman, and Dom Deluise played film producers trying to sign film stars (including Paul Newman, Burt Reynolds, Liza Minelli, and, Brooks' real-life wife, Anne Bancroft) to appear in their silent comedy. *High Anxiety* (1978) satirized Hitchcock films, starring Brooks as a paranoid psychiatrist. *History of the World, Part One* (1981) sent up historical epics; the most memorable scene was a musical comedy number set during the Inquisition, ending in Busby Berkeley style with nuns rising from Torquemada's torture tank atop a giant menorah. Brooks continued his series of movie satires during the 1980s and 1990s. *Spaceballs* (1987) sent up *Star Wars,* while his other films included *Robin Hood: Men in Tights* and *Dracula: Dead and Loving It.*

Upon being introduced to his future second wife (since 1964), the glamorous stage and film actress Anne Bancroft, he told her, "I would KILL for you!" He occasionally did cameo roles in film and television, winning an Emmy as Paul Reiser's uncle on the situation comedy *Mad About You.* In inimitable fashion, Brooks once defined comedy and tragedy: "Tragedy is when I cut my finger on a can opener, and it bleeds. Comedy is when *you* walk into an open sewer and die."

—Andrew Milner

FURTHER READING:

Adler, Bill. *Mel Brooks: The Irreverent Funnyman.* Chicago, Playboy Press, 1976.

Manchel, Frank. *The Box-office Clowns: Bob Hope, Jerry Lewis, Mel Brooks, Woody Allen.* New York, F. Watts, 1979.

Tynan, Kenneth. *Show People.* New York, Simon and Schuster, 1979.

Yacowar, Maurice. *Method in Madness: The Art of Mel Brooks.* New York, St. Martin's, 1981.

Brothers, Dr. Joyce (1928—)

Dr. Joyce Brothers, a psychologist who earned her Ph.D. from Columbia University in 1957, has been a media personality since the late 1950s. She was among the first television celebrities to combine academic credentials with broadcasting savvy and, in many ways, Dr. Brothers pioneered the expert culture on which television talk shows and news magazines now rely for commentary and analysis. In December 1955, Dr. Brothers became the second contestant to win a grand prize on the *$64,000 Question,* the television game show that would later be mired in scandal. The publicity that followed led her to choose a career in broadcasting. In addition to her television and radio

Dr. Joyce Brothers

appearances, Dr. Joyce Brothers has authored several books and writes a syndicated newspaper column.

—Michele S. Shauf

FURTHER READING:

Brothers, Dr. Joyce. *Dr. Brothers' Guide to Your Emotions.* Paramus, New Jersey, Prentice Hall, 1997.

———. *How to Get Whatever You Want Out of Life.* New York, Ballantine Books, 1987.

Brown, Helen Gurley

See Cosmopolitan; *Sex and the Single Girl*

Brown, James (1933—)

Known as the ''Godfather of Soul,'' this influential African-American singer was, in the 1950s and 1960s, one of the seminal figures in the transformation of gospel music and blues to soul. Also known as ''Soul Brother Number 1'' and ''The Hardest Working Man in Show Business,'' Brown amassed a record-setting total of 98 entries on *Billboard*'s top-40 R&B singles chart while influencing scores of performers such as Sly and the Family Stone, Kool and the Gang, and Prince, as well as contemporary rap and hip-hop performers. Brown is also a charter member of the Rock and Roll Hall of Fame and has won numerous awards for his recordings. Despite these professional successes, Brown is notorious for his ''bad-boy'' reputation stemming from several run-ins with the law over the years; he served prison time as a youth for theft and later for resisting arrest and traffic violations. He also experienced serious personal and business troubles in the 1970s, complicated by a longstanding dispute with the IRS over millions of dollars in back taxes that were resolved in part by his hiring of the radical attorney William Kunstler.

Born James Joe Brown, Jr. on May 3, 1933 in Barnwell, South Carolina, Brown early on became accustomed to grinding poverty and the struggle for survival. The family lived in a shack in the woods without plumbing or electricity. His father, Joe Garner Brown, made a living by selling tree tar to a turpentine company. Brown's parents separated when he was four and he continued to live with his father. The family moved to Augusta, Georgia, where his father left him under the guardianship of an aunt who ran a whorehouse. Brown earned money for rent and clothing by buck dancing for soldiers and by shining shoes.

Young James Brown's musical talent emerged at an early age. His father gave him a harmonica that he taught himself to play, and Brown sang gospel with friends, emulating the Golden Gate Quartet. Other members of the Augusta community guided his musical development: the famous Tampa Red taught him some guitar, and Leon Austin and a Mr. Dink taught him piano and drums respectively. Brown listened to gospel, popular music, blues, and jazz. His exposure to Louis Jordan and His Tympany Five's short film *Caldonia* convinced him that he should be an entertainer. At the age of 11, Brown won an amateur-night contest at the Lenox Theater for singing

James Brown

"So Long" and started a trio called Cremona in which he played piano, drums, and sang.

Mired in poverty, Brown began resorting to petty theft for his personal wardrobe, then began stealing automobile parts, for which he was arrested and sentenced to 8-to-18 years in the penitentiary, and later transferred to the Georgia Juvenile Training Institute. While in prison, he formed a gospel quartet, earning the name "Music Box" from his fellow inmates and insisting that gospel music helped him keep his sanity. While incarcerated, he met Bobby Byrd, a musician with whom he would later have a long-lasting professional relationship. After securing an early release based good behavior and a promise to his parole board to develop his creative talents, Brown settled in Toccoa, Georgia, where he lived with Bobby Byrd's family and worked at a car dealership while immersing himself in gospel music after hours. Brown formed a group called the Gospel Starlighters, which eventually evolved into the Famous Flames, an R&B group that consisted of Bobby Byrd, Sylvester Keels, Doyle Oglesby, Fred Pullman, Nash Knox, Baby Roy Scott, and Brown. Later, Nafloyd Scott would join the group as a guitarist.

In 1955, a studio recording of "Please, Please, Please" became the group's first hit, which became a regional favorite. Ralph Bass, a talent scout signed the group for the King/Federal record label. In 1958, the group recorded "Try Me," which rose to the number one spot on the R&B chart. Based on this recording, the group solidified and began to fill major auditoriums with its strong black following. Several hits ensued, but it was the 1963 release of the album *Live at the Apollo* that catapulted Brown into national recognition when it rose to the number two spot on *Billboard*'s album chart. Radio stations played the album as if it were a single and attendance at Brown's concerts increased dramatically.

Throughout most of his career Brown has been sensitive to political and social issues. Though he never graduated from high school, his 1966 recording "Don't Be a Drop Out" posted at number four on the R&B chart, and he approached Vice President Hubert Humphrey with the idea of using the song as the theme for a stay-in-school campaign aimed at inner-city youth. His prominence in this effort encouraged activist H. Rap Brown to urge the singer to be more vocal in the black-power movement, which James Brown often found too extreme for his tastes. Still, during the civil-rights activism of the 1960s, he purchased radio stations in Knoxville, Baltimore, and Atlanta as a way of giving greater clout to blacks in the media, and his recording "Say It Loud—I'm Black and I'm Proud" became one of the unofficial theme songs of the new black consciousness. During those years, Brown wielded political clout and garnered respect and attention in the black community, though he endured criticism in some circles for his association with Humphrey and his later friendship with President Richard Nixon—the singer endorsed Humphrey for President in 1968 and Nixon in 1972, and performed at Duke Ellington's inaugural gala for Nixon in January of 1969. Earlier, in the wake of the urban unrest following the April 1968 assassination of Dr. Martin Luther King, Jr., Brown interrupted his stations' programming with live broadcasts in which he urged nonviolence. In Boston the following day, he acceded to a request by Mayor Kevin White to appear on a live television program advocating a similar response.

While Brown and the Famous Flames secured a number of top ten hits on the R&B charts, "Papa's Got A Brand New Bag" earned Brown his first top ten single on the pop side. Hit after hit followed on both the top ten R&B and pop charts, including "I Got You (I Feel Good)" in 1965, "It's a Man's Man's Man's World" in 1966, "Cold Sweat (Part I)" in 1967, and "I Got the Feelin'" in 1968. Having made his political statement in "Say It Loud—I'm Black and I'm Proud," Brown dropped the Flames and began refining his group, with drummer Clyde Stubblefield providing increasing rhythmic complexity. "Mother Popcorn' in 1969, and "Get Up (I Feel Like Being a) Sex Machine" in 1970 signaled changes in his style.

In 1971, Brown formed a new group, the JBs, and signed with Polydor Records, which soon released two hits, "Hot Pants," and "Make It Funky." In 1973, he suffered three serious setbacks: the tragic death of his son, Teddy, in an automobile accident, the withdrawal from his group of his old friend, keyboardist Bobby Byrd, and an IRS demand for payment of $4.5 million in back taxes. He later blamed Polydor for some of his troubles, writing in his 1990 autobiography *James Brown: The Godfather of Soul*: "The government hurt my business a lot, a whole lot. But they didn't destroy me. Polydor did that. It was basically a German company, and they didn't understand the American market. They weren't flexible; they couldn't respond to what was happening the way King [Records] could. They had no respect for the artist . . . . " Troubles continued to mount for Brown during the 1970s: The popularity of disco diminished interest in his kind of music; he was implicated in a payola scandal; his second wife, Deirdre Jenkins, left him; and he was arrested during a 1978 performance at New York's Apollo Theater because he had left the country in defiance of a court order restricting his travel while the financial affairs of his radio stations were under investigation.

The evolution of Brown's musical style can be divided into three stylistic periods. The first period, in the mid-1950s, consists of ballads ("Please, Please, Please," "Try Me," and "Bewildered") based on popular song forms in a gospel style that are delivered, for that time, in a raw supplicating manner. The second period, in the early to mid-1960s, consists of songs based on a modification of the twelve-bar blues form with gospel vocal styles and increasingly tight and moderately complex horn arrangements used in a responsorial fashion. Compositions from this period include "Night Train" (not an original composition), "I Feel Good," "Papa's Got a Brand New Bag," and "I Got You." The third period, from the late 1960s and beyond, finds Brown as an innovator breaking away from standard forms and a standard singing approach to embark on extensive vamps in which the voice is used as a percussive instrument with frequent rhythmic grunts, and with rhythm-section patterns that resemble West African polyrhythms. Across these three periods, Brown moves on a continuum from blues and gospel-based forms and styles to a profoundly Africanized approach to music making. Most significantly, Brown's frenzied and rhythmically percussive vocal style, based on black folk preaching and hollering, combine with his polyrhythmic approach to generate movement and to recreate in a secular context the ecstatic ambience of the black church. Brown's innovations, especially in his latter period, have reverberated throughout the world, even influencing African pop. From the mid-1980s, as found in his composition "The Funky Drummer," Brown's rhythms, hollers, whoops, screams, and vocal grunts have informed and supplied the core of the new hip-hop music. His influence on artists such as Public Enemy and Candy Flip is evident.

In the midst of his travails during the 1970s, Brown turned to religion and also sought the legal help of William Kunstler. He broke with Polydor Records and began to play in rock clubs in New York. He appeared in several films, including the role of a gospel-singing preacher in *The Blues Brothers* (1980), a part in *Dr. Detroit* (1983), and a cameo appearance in *Rocky IV* (1985), in which he sang "Living in America." It reached number four on the pop charts, his first hit in more than a decade.

Even after these triumphs, Brown again began encountering trouble with the law. In December, 1988 he was dealt two concurrent six-year prison sentences for resisting arrest and traffic violations during an incident in Atlanta in September of that year, when he had brandished a shotgun in a dispute over the use of his private bathroom in his office. After a high-speed police chase and charges of driving under the influence of drugs, he was arrested and convicted only aggravated assault and failing to stop for a police car. As he explained to Jesse Jackson, "I aggravated them and they assaulted me." He was paroled in 1991, after appeals by Jackson, Little Richard, Rev. Al Sharpton, and others. Brown continued to tour and record in the 1990s. He appeared at New York's Paramount Theater in March, 1992, with his new band, the Soul Generals and his female backup group, the Bittersweets. In 1994, his name again appeared on the crime-blotter pages in an incident involving the assault of his wife, Adrienne. Four years later, in 1998, he was charged with possession of marijuana and unlawful use of a firearm.

In the 1990s, Brown became a vocal supporter of the campaign to suppress X-rated lyrics in rap songs by asking rap artists not to include samples of his songs in such works. It was estimated by one critic that 3,000 house and hip-hop records have made use of his original music since the 1980s. In 1987, Brown was one of the first ten charter members elected to the Rock and Roll Hall of Fame, and in 1992, he was honored at the American Music Awards ceremonies with an Award of Merit for his lifetime contribution to the genre.

—Willie Collins

FURTHER READING:

Brown, James, with Bruce Tucker. *The Godfather of Soul: James Brown*. New York, Macmillan, 1986.

Brown, Jim (1936—)

Jim Brown was simply one of the best football players ever. In just nine seasons in the National Football League, Brown collected eight rushing titles en route to setting new records for most yards in a season and most career rushing yards. A three-time MVP, Brown was inducted into the Pro Football Hall of Fame in 1971.

Born on the coastline of Georgia, Brown moved to Long Island, New York, and attended Manhasset High School where he earned all-state honors in basketball, track, and football. After high school Brown declined a minor league contract with the New York Yankees, opting to play football at Syracuse University instead. While playing for the Orangemen he earned All-American honors in both football and lacrosse.

In 1957 he was drafted by the Cleveland Browns of the National Football League, and in his first season he led the Browns to the Championship game. That year Brown also won the league rushing title, which earned him the Rookie of the Year Award. But in his opinion his freshman campaign was not "spectacular." In spite of Brown's modesty, fans thought otherwise as he quickly became a

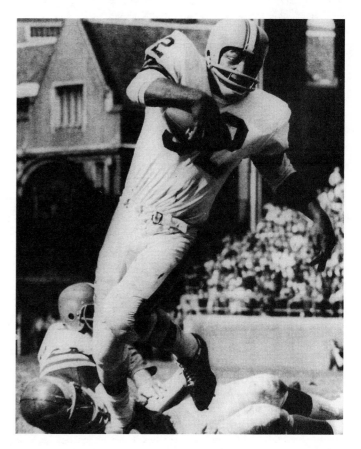

Jim Brown

crowd favorite because of his seemingly fearless and tireless running style.

In 1963 Brown made history when he rushed for a league record 1883 yards. That season he had games of 162 (yards), 232, 175, 123, 144, 225, 154, 179, and 125. "I was twenty-seven years old. I never ran better in my life," said Brown. The following year Brown led his team to the NFL Championship, but in 1965 he shocked football fans by announcing his retirement in the prime of his career.

The popular Brown did not slip quietly into retirement however; he capitalized on his fame by becoming Hollywood's "first black man of action" by starring in several movies such as *Rio Conchos* (1964), the box office hit *The Dirty Dozen* (1967), and other films including *The Grasshopper* (1970), *Black Gunn* (1972), and *Tick. . . Tick. . . Tick. . .* (1970). In 1972 he starred in the world's first authentic blaxploitation movie, *Slaughter,* which was filmed in Mexico on a $75,000 budget. This placed him into competition with other black stars of that genre including Fred Williamson, Jim Kelly, and Pam Grier. Brown's most popular film and to some extent his most controversial was *One Hundred Rifles* (1969), in which Raquel Welch was his love interest. This was one of the first films involving a love scene between a black man and a white woman. "We took a publicity shot of me, with no shirt on, and Raquel, behind me, her arms seductively across my chest. For American film it was revolutionary stuff," said Brown.

In addition to football and acting Brown also was devoted to improving the conditions of the black community. In the late 1960s he formed the Black Economic Union to assist black-owned business and after leaving the silver screen he became a community activist.

In his day, Brown was one of the few athletes who could transcend the playing field and become part of the broader American culture. Even today, he is the standard by which all other NFL runners are measured.

—Leonard N. Moore

FURTHER READING:

Brown, Jim. *Out of Bounds.* New York, Zebra Books, 1989.

James, Darius. *That's Blaxploitation!* New York, St. Martin's Griffin, 1995.

Toback, James. *Jim: The Author's Self-centered Memoir on the Great Jim Brown.* Garden City, New York, Doubleday, 1971.

Brown, Les (1912—)

A band leader for nearly 60 years, Les Brown and his "Band of Renown" were best known as a first-class swing band operating primarily in the pop-music field. Brown was a student at Duke University from 1932-35, where he formed his first dance band, the Duke Blue Devils. After that band folded in September, 1937, Brown worked as a freelance arranger for Larry Clinton and Isham Jones. He formed a new band in 1938, and throughout the 1940s became increasingly well-known, featured on television touring with Bob Hope to entertain service men at Christmas. The band reached its peak when Doris Day was featured as vocalist in 1940 and again from

1943-46. The orchestra's best-remembered arrangements were written by Ben Homer, who also composed the band's theme song, "Sentimental Journey."

—Benjamin Griffith

FURTHER READING:

Balliett, Whitney. *American Musicians.* New York, Oxford, 1986.

Simon, George T. *The Big Bands.* New York, MacMillan, 1974.

Brown, Paul (1908-1991)

Paul Brown, founder and first head coach of both the Cleveland Browns and Cincinnati Bengals, played a major role in the evolution of football. He was the first coach to use detailed game plans, playbooks, and classroom learning techniques. He hired the first full-time coaching staff. He also initiated the use of intelligence tests to measure learning potential and film replays and physical tests such as the 40-yard dash to evaluate players. Brown was also the first coach to send plays in from the bench and to use facemasks on helmets. As a professional coach with the Browns (1946-62) and Bengals (1968-75), he compiled a 222-112-9 record including four AAFC (All-American Football Conference) and three NFL titles. His coaching proteges include Don Shula and Bill Walsh, coaches who led their

Coach Paul Brown and the Cleveland Browns.

respective clubs to Super Bowl championships. Brown was inducted into the Professional Football Hall of Fame in 1967.

—G. Allen Finchum

FURTHER READING:

Brown, Paul and Jack T. Clary. *PB: The Paul Brown Story.* New York, Atheneum, 1979.

Long, Tim. *Browns Memories: The 338 Most Memorable Heroes, Heartaches and Highlights from 50 Seasons of Cleveland Browns Football.* Cleveland, Ohio, Gray and Company, 1996.

Browne, Jackson (1948—)

Romantic balladeer turned political activist, Jackson Browne is one of America's most enduring singer-songwriters. Raised in Southern California, Browne joined the Nitty Gritty Dirt Band while in high school, but quit to pursue a solo career in New York, where he hung out at Andy Warhol's Factory and fell in love with singer Nico. After signing with David Geffen, Browne came home and became part of the L.A. music scene that included Joni Mitchell, the Eagles, and Crosby, Stills and Nash. Browne's first album was released to strong reviews in 1972 and his first single, "Doctor My Eyes," climbed to number eight on Billboard's Top 100. With his poetic songwriting and boyish good looks, Browne's next four albums won both critical

Jackson Browne

Man holding Kodak Brownie camera, 1900.

acclaim and commercial success. In the 1980s, Browne became an outspoken liberal activist and his songwriting began to take on a strongly political cast. After a very public split with actress Darryl Hannah in 1991, Browne's songs once again turned confessional. Long regarded as one of the most important artists to come out of Southern California, Jackson Browne remains one of the music industry's most complex and fascinating figures.

—Victoria Price

FURTHER READING:

DeCurtis, Anthony. "Jackson Browne." *Rolling Stone.* October 15, 1992. 138-139.

Santoro, Gene. "Jackson Browne." *Nation.* Vol. 262, No. 19, May 13, 1996, 32-36.

Brownie Cameras

The Brownie Camera revolutionized popular photography worldwide by bringing it within the reach of all amateurs, including children. Commissioned by George Eastman and manufactured by the Eastman Kodak Company, it was launched in February, 1900. A small box camera that utilized removable roll-film and a simple rotary shutter, the new Brownie sold for just one dollar, plus fifteen cents extra for film. Its name was derived from Palmer Cox's familiar and beloved pixies, whose image Kodak incorporated into its brilliant and concentrated advertising campaign; even the box in which the cameras were packaged featured Cox's colorful characters. The Brownie was an immediate success: 100,000 sold within a single year. Various features were added over the next few decades, including color on the Beau Brownie of the early 1930s, and flash contacts on the Brownie

Reflex introduced in 1946. Many special Brownies were also made, such as the Boy Scout Brownie (1932, 1933-34) and the New York World's Fair Baby Brownie (1939). The last Brownie model, the Brownie Fiesta, was discontinued in 1970.

—Barbara Tepa Lupack

FURTHER READING:

Coe, Brian. *Cameras: From Daguerreotypes to Instant Pictures.* N.p.: Crown Publishers, 1978.

Kodak Homepage. http:\www.kodak.com.

Lothrop, Eaton S., Jr. *A Century of Cameras: From The Collection of the International Museum of Photography at George Eastman House.* Dobbs Ferry, Morgan & Morgan, 1973.

Brubeck, Dave (1920—)

Jazz legend Dave Brubeck is famous both as a composer and pianist. As the leader of the Dave Brubeck Quartet with alto saxophonist Paul Desmond, he achieved overwhelming popular success in the 1950s and 1960s. The Quartet's experimentation with unusual time signatures produced works like "Blue Rondo a la Turk" and "Take Five" among others, and Brubeck introduced millions of enthusiastic young listeners to jazz. In less than a decade, the Dave Brubeck Quartet became one of the most commercially successful jazz groups of all time.

Although some jazz traditionalists felt that Brubeck was playing "watered-down" bebop to sell records, his music brought jazz back into the mainstream of popular music. "Take Five" became Brubeck's signature tune, and it remains one of the most widely recognized jazz compositions in the world.

—Geoff Peterson

FURTHER READING:

Hall, F.M. *It's about Time: The Dave Brubeck Story.* Fayetteville, University of Arkansas Press, 1996.

Bruce, Lenny (1925-1966)

From the late 1940s until his death in the 1960s, Lenny Bruce's unique comedy included social commentary, "lewd" material, and pointed personal monologues. He addressed issues of sex, race, and religion, and often did so using profanity. Many of his era called his humor "sick," and Journalist Walter Mitchell referred to him as "America's #1 Vomic." Police arrested Bruce numerous times for obscenities, which helped him to become a champion of First Amendment rights and of freedom of speech in general. His work on and off stage permanently changed the face of comedy, particularly stand-up comedy, and pushed the limits of what was considered "socially acceptable" in many mediums. By 1990s standards his material was quite tame and is commonly found on television or even in "PG" rated films, but during his time his work was radical. Many well-known comedians, including Joan Rivers, Jonathan Winters, and

Lenny Bruce

Richard Pryor, have attested to Bruce's profound influence on their work.

From approximately the 1920s to the early 1950s, most comedians came out of vaudeville. Comedy, or more precisely jokes, were interspersed in people's vaudeville acts. Jack Benny, for instance, was a vaudeville star who originally did jokes between his violin playing; he eventually played some violin between his jokes or comedy routines. Comedians did a series of "classic" joke-book type jokes, or occasionally a variation on these. In the late 1940s and into the 1950s, comedy began to change with the cultural changes of the times. The United States was experiencing a push towards conservatism; middle-class mores were pervasive and commonly exemplified in such light "comedy" shows as *Father Knows Best* and *Donna Reed*. Additionally, McCarthyism had people fearful of anything "different" they said being held against them. There was, however, also a strong backlash against this conservatism typified in the "Beatnik" movement, including artists such as Allen Ginsburg and Lawrence Ferlinghetti. Bruce was part of this counterculture movement.

Bruce was born Leonard Alfred Schneider on October 13, 1925 in Mineola, New York. His father, Mickey, was a podiatrist and his mother, Sadie, played bit parts as an actor and did routines in small comedy clubs under the names of Sally Marr and Boots Mallow. From a very young age, Bruce's mother took him to burlesque and nightclubs. Her willingness to expose him to this style of "open sexuality" influenced most of his career. Bruce's very early career was doing conventional comedy routines in the "Borscht Belt"—the Jewish area of the Catskills where many (Jewish) comedians, such as

Danny Kaye and Jerry Lewis, got their start; he also did comedy routines in strip clubs. In 1942, Bruce enlisted in the Navy, serving until 1945, when he was dishonorably discharged for claiming to be obsessed with homosexual ideas.

Bruce started developing his own notable style, which not only included the "obscenities" he is often remembered for, but also a running social commentary told in fast-paced, personally-based monologues that used various accents and voices to emphasize his pointed style. He received his first national recognition when he was on the *Arthur Godfrey Talent Show* in 1948. Soon after, his career was furthered when his act at a San Francisco nightclub, Anne's 440, was reviewed by influential cutting-edge columnists Herb Caen and Ralph Gleason (who later wrote many of Bruce's liner notes for his recordings). Some of his early recordings, all under the Fantasy record label, include *Interviews of Our Times, American,* and *The Sick Humor of Lenny Bruce.*

Two quintessential personal events also happened during these "earlier" years—Bruce met stripper Honey Harlow in 1951, whom he married that year in June, and he was introduced to heroin, which became a life-long habit and another reason for his many arrests. Harlow had six abortions, some say at the insistence of Bruce, and later gave birth to a daughter, Brandie Kathleen "Kitty," in 1955. When Bruce and Harlow divorced in 1957, Bruce was awarded custody of Kitty.

In the early 1960s Bruce's career skyrocketed, and by February 1961 he performed to a full house at Carnegie Hall. While he was popular with people immersed in the counter-culture movement, he also attracted many mainstream and even conservative people. Mainstream comedians, such as Steve Allen, understood, appreciated, and supported his comedy; Bruce appeared on Allen's television show three times. Others were highly insulted, not just by his "obscene language," but, for instance, by what they considered his blasphemous attitudes towards organized religion. His act "Religions, Incorporated," in which he compared religious leaders to con artists and crooks, infuriated some and made others praise the raw intelligence and honesty of his comedy. Other people were critical, but titillated by his humor. Bruce often told the story about how people said they were horrified by his common "threat" to urinate on his audience, but when he would not do it people would complain and ask for their money back.

The 1960s brought Bruce's long series of arrests for narcotics and obscenities, as well as his being banned from performing. In September 1961, he was arrested for possession of narcotics, though the charges were dropped because he had authorized prescriptions—but in October 1962 he was once again arrested for possession of narcotics in Los Angeles. With his January 1, 1963 arrest for narcotics possession, however, some began to question whether the circumstances surrounding his arrests were, at the very least, "suspicious"; his convictions were based on testimony by an officer who was at the time suspected of smuggling drugs. Conversely, though, Bruce himself once turned in a small-time drug dealer in exchange for his own freedom from a drug charge.

Bruce's first and probably best known arrest for obscenity was in October 1961. He used the word "cocksucker" in his act at the San Francisco Jazz Workshop; the word violated the California Obscenity Code. (A number of reviewers have pointed out that in the 1980s Meryl Streep won an Academy Award for the movie *Sophie's Choice,* where she also used the term "cocksucker.") With lawyer Albert Bendich—who represented Allen Ginsberg when he was charged

with obscenity for his book *Howl*—Bruce eventually emerged victorious and the event was seen as a landmark win for First Amendment rights.

In October 1962, Bruce was arrested for being obscene during his act at Hollywood's Troubador Theater. In the same year, after two Australian appearances, he was kicked out of Australia and banned from Australian television; he was also deported from England twice. In April 1963, on arriving in England, he was classified as an "undesirable alien" and sent back to the United States within two hours. Upon arrival in the United States, customs agents stripped and internally searched Bruce. Soon after, he was arrested for obscenity in both Chicago and Miami. In 1963, Bruce also published his autobiography, *How To Talk Dirty and Influence People,* and it was eventually serialized in *Playboy* magazine. Despite—or perhaps because of—these events, Bruce continued to make recordings throughout the early 1960s, including *To Is a Preposition, Come is a Verb, The Berkeley Concert,* and *Live at the Curran Theatre.*

Another of Bruce's pivotal and very influential obscenity arrests occurred in April 1964 at New York's Cafe A Go-Go, where Tiny Tim was his warm-up act. Over 100 well-known "alternative" artists and activists, including Dick Gregory, Bob Dylan, Joseph Heller, James Baldwin, and Gore Vidal, signed a petition which Allen Ginsberg helped write. The petition protested New York using obscenity laws to harass Bruce, whom they called a social-satirist on par with Jonathan Swift and Mark Twain. Bruce himself said he did not believe his arrest was about obscenity, but rather his views against the system. New York's District Attorney of that time, Richard Kuh, felt Bruce should not be shown mercy because he lacked remorse; Bruce openly stated he had no remorse and was only seeking justice. On November 4, 1964, his work was deemed illegal for violating "contemporary community standards" and for being offensive to the "average person." This was a severe blow to Bruce, as clubs were afraid to hire him: if New York City responded in such a way, other clubs around the United States would surely be shut down if he were to perform in them. In October 1965, Bruce went to the San Francisco office of the Federal Bureau of Investigation (FBI), complaining that California and New York were conspiring against his rights. Not surprisingly, the FBI took no action.

Between difficulty being hired, his drug addiction, and his financial concerns, Bruce found himself in an extremely difficult predicament. A few days after complaining to the FBI he filed bankruptcy in Federal Court. A few months later, under the influence of drugs, he fell 25 feet out a window, resulting in multiple fractures in both his legs and ankles. His last performance was at the Fillmore West in San Francisco in June 1966, where he played with Frank Zappa and The Mothers of Invention. Two months later, on August 3, 1966, Bruce was dead from a so-called accidental overdose of morphine. Some say the police staged photographs of the scene to make it look as if he accidentally overdosed. Regardless of the circumstances, conspiracy and harassment were on Bruce's mind when he died—at the time of his death he was in the midst of writing about the Fourth Amendment, which guarantees people protection against "unreasonable search and seizure."

Sadly, Bruce neither lived to see his New York obscenity conviction overruled in 1966, nor the dramatic changes that much of his pioneering work helped catalyze. Ironically, by the 1970s, many plays, books, and movies, were produced about Bruce that romanticized and glorified his work. In death, he became part of the mainstream entertainment world that often shunned him. The most well-known and mainstream of these productions was the 1974 film

Lenny, based on the play by Julian Barry and starring Dustin Hoffman as Bruce. Indeed, despite his incredible influence, many born after his time thought of Bruce only as Hoffman's portrayal in this stylized film. Paradoxically, only eight years after his death, the film *Lenny* was only given an ''R'' rating for routines that got Bruce arrested time and time again. That his own work was considered so ''tame'' just a short time after his death is perhaps a testimony to the degree of change Lenny Bruce really initiated.

—tova gd stabin

FURTHER READING:

Barry, Julian. *Lenny: A Play, Based On the Life and Words of Lenny Bruce.* New York, Grove Press, 1971.

Bruce, Lenny. *The Almost Unpublished Lenny Bruce: From the Private Collection of Kitty Bruce.* Philadelphia, Running Press, 1984.

———. *The Essential Lenny Bruce,* edited by John Cohen. New York, Douglas Books, 1970.

———. *How To Talk Dirty and Influence People: An Autobiography.* Chicago, Playboy Press, 1973.

Goldman, Albert Harry. *Ladies and gentlemen—Lenny Bruce!!* New York, Random House, 1974.

Kofsky, Frank. *Lenny Bruce: The Comedian as Social Critic and Secular Moralist.* New York, Monad Press, 1974.

Saporta, Sol. ''Lenny Bruce on Police Brutality.'' *Humor.* Vol. 7, No. 2, 1994, 175.

———. ''The Politics of Dirty Jokes: Woody Allen, Lenny Bruce, Andrew Dice Clay, Groucho Marx, and Clarence Thomas.'' *Humor.* Vol. 7, No. 2, 1994, 173.

Thomas, William Karl. *Lenny Bruce: The Making of a Prophet.* Hamden, Connecticut, Archon Books, 1989.

Bryant, Paul "Bear" (1913-1983)

Legend, hero, homespun philosopher, not to mention fashion statement in his houndstooth check hat, Paul "Bear" Bryant has been called a combination of "ham and humble pie." A museum and a football stadium in Tuscaloosa, Alabama, bear his name, and a movie, released in August 1984, called, simply, *The Bear,* recounts his life. His wife, however, didn't like the film; she couldn't imagine actor Gary Busey playing her husband. "Papa was *handsome*," she said, and it was not only she who thought this. Men as well as women agreed that Bear Bryant was a good-looking man. Morris Franks, a writer for the *Houston Chronicle,* averred, "No Hollywood star ever made a more dramatic entrance. He would jut that granite-like jaw out, turn his camel's hair topcoat collar up and be puffing on a cigarette." The coach evinced a wide-ranging appeal; even his life was a sort of romance. He married his college sweetheart, Mary Harmon, a University of Alabama beauty queen, and for 48 years she remained by his side as best friend, alter ego, and helpmate to the man who had once wrestled a bear in his home state of Arkansas for five bucks and won.

Paul Bryant satisfied America's craving for rags-to-riches and larger-than-life stories. As the eleventh of twelve children, young

Paul grew up dirt poor in rural Arkansas, in a place called Morro Bottom that consisted of six houses on Morro Creek. The Bryant home was made up of four small rooms, a big dining room, and a little upstairs area; but Paul thought of it as a plantation, and in the mornings and evenings before and after school, he worked behind the plow. He didn't own a pair of shoes until age 13, but as he affirmed to the boys who played on his teams, "If you believe in yourself and have pride and never quit, you'll be a winner. The price of victory is high but so are the rewards."

Bryant played college football at the University of Alabama on the same team as Don Hudson, who was thought to be the greatest pass-catching end in football in 1934. Nicknamed "Old 43" or "the Other End," Paul may not have been *The* End, but he became a hero after playing a game against rival Tennessee with a broken leg. When the team doctor removed his cast, Bryant was asked if he thought he could play, and the rest is legend. Number 43 caught an early pass and went for a touchdown. Later in the game, he threw a lateral to a player who scored another. Examining the X-rays of the broken bone, Atlanta sportswriter Ralph McGill, who had initially been doubtful about the injury, acclaimed Bryant's courage, but Bear, in typical big-play fashion, replied, "It was just one little bone."

Bryant went on to head coaching jobs at Maryland, Kentucky, and Texas A & M, before returning to the University of Alabama. When asked to come back to his alma mater, Bryant gave his famous "Mama Called" speech to the fans and players at A & M. He said, "When you were out playing as a kid, say you heard your mother call you. If you thought she just wanted you to do some chores, or come in for supper, you might not answer her. But if you thought she *needed*

Paul "Bear" Bryant

you, you'd be there in a hurry." Bryant served as head coach at the University of Alabama from 1958 to 1982, where he led the Crimson Tide to 323 victories and six national championships. He was named the National Coach of the Year in 1961, 1971, and 1973, and SEC Coach of the Year ten times.

Although he guided the Crimson Tide to thirteen SEC titles, Coach Bryant stood for more than winning; he was a role model. His players maintain that he taught them about life. The coach liked to say that life was God's gift, and a commitment should be made to put something into it.

Paul Bear Bryant never failed in his dedication to the sport he loved. After his death, Bryant's heartfelt eulogies describing what the Bear meant to Alabama, to coaching, and to the players who had been molded by him, led author Mickey Herkowitz to conclude that college football without Bryant would be like New Year's Eve without a clock. It was estimated that some 100,000 mourners lined the interstate from Tuscaloosa to Birmingham, Alabama, to pay their last respects to a small town boy known as Bear. "Thanks for the Memories, Bear," their signs read, "We Love You," and "We'll Miss You." A hero had fallen, but he is remembered. Many feel he can never be replaced.

—Sue Walker

FURTHER READING:

Herskowitz, Mickey. *The Legend of Bear Bryant.* Austin, Texas, Eakin Press, 1993.

Stoddard, Tom. *Turnaround: The Untold Story of Bear Bryant's First Year As Head Coach at Alabama.* Montgomery, Alabama, Black Belt Press, 1996.

Brynner, Yul (1915-1985)

In 1951 Yul Brynner, a Russian-born Mongolian, made a multi-award-winning Broadway debut in *The King and I,* and in 1956 he won the Best Actor Oscar for the screen version. He shaved his head for the role, and it is to this image of baldness as a badge of virile exoticism that he owed his subsequent prolific and highly paid film career during the 1960s and 1970s, as well as his continuing status as a twentieth-century icon. Seemingly ageless, he continued to star in revivals of the show until shortly before his much-publicized death from lung cancer. Much of his early life is shrouded in self-created myth, but he arrived in the United States in 1941, having worked as a trapeze artist with the Cirque d'Hiver in Paris until injury intervened. A largely mediocre actor, who appeared in increasingly mediocre films, relying on his mysterious, brooding personality, he is also remembered for his roles as the pharaoh in *The Ten Commandments* (1956) and the black-clad leader of *The Magnificent Seven* (1960).

—Robyn Karney

FURTHER READING:

Katz, Ephraim. *The International Film Encyclopedia.* New York, HarperCollins, 1994.

Thomson, David. *A Biographical Dictionary of Film.* New York, Alfred A. Knopf, 1994.

Bubblegum Rock

Bubblegum rock emerged in the late 1960s as a commercial response to demographic changes in the rock music industry. With major rock artists such as the Beatles and the Rolling Stones maturing after 1967 toward more adult styles, both musically and lyrically, as they and their audiences grew up, they left behind a major segment of the rock music marketplace: the pre-teen crowd. The music industry rushed to capitalize on this younger market by assembling studio musicians to record novelty songs with catchy hooks and sing-along lyrics and packaging them as real "bands." The approach worked, resulting in a string of hits including, among many others, "Yummy Yummy Yummy" by Ohio Express, "Simon Says" by 1910 Fruitgum Company, and "Sugar Sugar" by the Archies. The genre peaked in 1969, but the tradition continued into the 1990s with such groups as Hanson that appealed to the pre-teen market.

—Timothy Berg

FURTHER READING:

Miller, Jim, editor. *The Rolling Stone Illustrated History of Rock & Roll.* New York, Rolling Stone Press, 1980.

Various Artists. *Bubblegum Classics, Vol. 1-5.* Varese Sarabande, 1995.

Buck, Pearl S. (1892-1973)

Author and humanitarian activist Pearl S. Buck almost single-handedly created the prism through which an entire generation of Americans formed its opinion about China and its people. Her work and personality first came to the attention of a wide audience in 1931, with the publication of her signature novel *The Good Earth,* based on her experiences growing up in China with a missionary family during the convulsive period from the Boxer Rebellion to the civil wars of the 1920s and 1930s. She wrote more than seventy other books—many of which were best-sellers and Book-of-the-Month Club selections—and hundreds of pieces in many genres, including short stories, plays, poetry, essays, and children's literature, making her one of the century's most popular writers. As a contributing writer to *Asia* magazine (later *Asia and the Americas*), published by her second husband, Richard Walsh, she brought a precocious "Third-World" consciousness to Americans by advocating an end to colonialism while advancing the causes of the peasantry, especially women.

In 1938, Buck became the first of only two American women to win the Nobel Prize for literature, though her books have fallen out of favor with critics and academicians and she is rarely anthologized today or studied in college literature courses. Her work has remained a sentimental favorite of millions of readers around the world. Contemporary Chinese-American writer Maxine Hong Kingston has credited Buck with acknowledging Asian voices, especially those of women, for the first time in Western literature. Biographer Peter Conn declared in his 1996 study *Pearl S. Buck: A Cultural Biography* that "never before or since has one writer so personally shaped the imaginative terms in which America addresses a foreign culture. For two generations of Americans, Buck invented China." He quoted historian James Thomson's belief that Buck was "the most influential Westerner to write about China since thirteenth-century Marco Polo." Living in the United States during the second half of her life,

Pearl S. Buck

Buck was prominent in many progressive social movements, lending her support to causes on behalf of disarmament, immigrants, women, and racial minorities. Her outspoken activism, especially during and after World War II, earned her an FBI dossier and the ire of McCarthyists in the 1950s.

Pearl Buck was born Pearl Sydenstricker in Hillsboro, West Virginia, on June 26, 1892, the daughter of Presbyterian missionaries Absalom and Carie (Stulting) Sydenstricker, who were then on leave from their post in China, to which they returned when Pearl was three months old. Except for a brief foray in the States around the time of the Boxer Rebellion, Pearl stayed in China until 1910, when she enrolled in Randolph-Macon Woman's College in Virginia, graduating as president of the class of 1913 and remaining as a teaching assistant in psychology. She returned to China soon afterwards to care for her ailing mother and remained there for most of the next twenty years, during which time she took an avid interest in the daily lives of Chinese peasants as well as the intellectuals' movements for reforms in literature and society that, in 1919, coalesced in the May 4 movement. Since she was fluent in Chinese language and culture, Buck came to support the new wave in Chinese literature, a dissident movement that called for a complete reconstruction of literature as a

way of promoting political and social change. In 1917, she had married John Lossing Buck, an agricultural missionary, and moved with him to Nanhsuchou, where she experienced firsthand the backwardness and poverty that would later find its way into the pages of her fiction and nonfiction.

During the 1920s, Buck began interpreting China to American readers through articles she wrote for the *Atlantic,* the *Nation,* and other magazines. In 1924 she and her husband returned briefly to the United States, both to pursue masters degrees at Cornell University, hers in English and his in agricultural economics. Using a masculine pen name, she won a prestigious campus literary prize for her essay "China and the West," which criticized China's traditional treatment of women and girls while praising the achievements of Chinese art and philosophy. The couple returned to Nanjing but were forced to flee in 1927 during the Chinese civil war, taking refuge in Japan for a while before returning to Shanghai. They were soon alienated by the corruption and elitism of Chiang Kai-shek's Kuomintang and by the violence of Mao Zedong's Communists. Motivated by a need to find a suitable school for their mentally retarded daughter, Carol, the Bucks returned to the United States in 1929 thanks to a Rockefeller Foundation grant for John's agricultural survey work. Pearl had already begun to write novels about her experiences in China; the first of them, *East Wind, West Wind,* was published by John Day in 1930. It was among the first serious novels to interpret to American readers the upheavals in traditional Chinese society, particularly in terms of the changing role of women. On March 2, 1931, John Day published Buck's second novel, *The Good Earth.* The book became an overnight sensation after Will Rogers lauded it on the front page of the *New York Times* as "not only the greatest book about a people ever written but the best book of our generation." *The Good Earth* won Buck a Pulitzer Prize in 1932, was translated into some thirty languages, and was made into a popular motion picture. MGM's offer of $50,000 for the film rights was at the time the most lucrative deal between an author and a Hollywood studio. Buck's always precarious financial situation improved considerably, and she found herself much in demand as a lecturer and writer. She moved to the United States permanently in 1932, the year John Day published her third novel, *Sons.*

Like a prophet without honor in her own country, however, Buck soon found herself the target of criticism from church leaders who objected to the absence of a positive Christian message in *The Good Earth,* as when a Presbyterian bureaucrat complained to Buck that "the artist in you has apparently deposed the missionary." A year later, in the presence of church officials at a Presbyterian women's luncheon in New York, she courageously denounced typical missionaries as "narrow, uncharitable, unappreciative, ignorant" in their zeal for conversion, which put her at the center of an already gathering storm critical of the missionary endeavor. Her break with denominational orthodoxy was sealed in an article she wrote for *Cosmopolitan,* "Easter, 1933," in which she repudiated dogmatism and found humanitarian parallels between the teachings of Christ and the Buddha; shortly after its publication, she resigned as a Presbyterian missionary.

Buck continued writing fiction about China, and John Day published her fourth novel, *The Mother,* in 1934, about the tribulations of an unnamed Chinese peasant widow abandoned by her husband and condemned by custom to a life of loneliness and sexual frustration. In June of 1935, she got a Reno divorce from her husband and, that same day, married Richard Walsh, her editor/publisher at John Day. Buck had already begun to assume a significant role in the company's affairs, especially in the editorial direction of *Asia* magazine, which he had just taken over. With Walsh and Buck at its helm, the periodical quickly changed from being a travel-oriented publication to a serious journal of ideas, with contributions by Lin Yutang, Bertrand Russell, Rabindranath Tagore, Margaret Mead, Agnes Smedley, and other noted writers and intellectuals. As a contributor, Pearl Buck expressed her growing dissatisfaction with Chiang Kaishek's policies while remaining anti-Communist herself.

During this period, the Walshes adopted four children, and in 1936 John Day published Buck's memoir of her mother, *The Exile.* A commercial as well as critical success, it was soon followed with *Fighting Angel*, a memoir of her father. As a boxed set, the two were offered as a joint Book-of-the-Month Club selection, *The Flesh and the Spirit.* It was during this period that Buck began to ally herself with American pacifist and disarmament groups, such as the Women's International League for Peace and Freedom, as well as with the Urban League and other groups advocating racial desegregation. She also became increasingly concerned about the rise of Nazism and the plight of Jews in Europe. The couple founded the China Emergency Relief Committee, with Eleanor Roosevelt as its honorary chair, to give humanitarian aid to victims of Japanese aggression in East Asia.

In 1938, Pearl Buck became the fourth woman and the first American woman to be awarded the Nobel Prize for literature, a decision that was greeted with derision in some American literary circles, who felt Buck was too much of a "popular" writer to deserve such an honor. When told of the award, she remarked in Chinese "I don't believe it," adding in English, "It should have gone to [Theodore] Dreiser." While the prize was given for the entire body of her work, the twin biographies of her parents were specifically cited as her finest works. In her Nobel lecture, she argued that the great Chinese novels should be regarded as highly in the West as the works of Dickens or Tolstoy.

Just before the United States became involved in World War II, Walsh and Buck founded the East and West Association "to help ordinary people on one side of the world to know and understand ordinary people on the other side." This group, and the other nongovernmental organizations in which they were involved, helped solidify a network of American business people and intellectuals that was instrumental in developing American attitudes toward Asia in the postwar period. Also during the 1940s, Buck became more deeply interested in women's issues at home. In 1941 she published *Of Men and Women*, a collection of nine essays on gender politics that challenged the patriarchal hegemony in American society. A *New York Times* critic even argued that Buck's view of gender resembled that of Virginia Woolf's. Resisting the "official" stance of mainstream women's organizations, Buck became a fervid supporter of more radical women's-rights groups that first proposed the Equal Rights Amendment to the U.S. Constitution, though Buck still hesitated to call herself "a feminist or active in women's suffrage."

Buck's novel *Dragon Seed* was published in 1942, after the United States had entered the Pacific War. The book, which called particular attention to war as an example of savagery against women, drew much of its narrative from actual events, such as the Japanese rape of Nanjing, and it also urged its Chinese protagonists to endure privation and create a new, more humanitarian society. At home, she was among the most vociferous critics of segregation and racial discrimination, which she thought unworthy of the noble cause for which American sacrifices were being made. She supported the growing claims of African Americans for equality, and emerged as a strong proponent of the repeal of exclusion laws directed against

Chinese immigration. Buck had been under FBI surveillance since her pacifist activities in the 1930s, and her appearance at rallies with such leftist activists as Paul Robeson and Lillian Hellman earned her a 300-page dossier, one of the longest of any prominent writer. During the postwar era, Buck was accused of membership in several "Communist Front Organizations."

Although she continued to write, little of her later fiction achieved the literary stature of her earlier work, with the possible exception of *Imperial Woman* (1956), a fictionalized account of the last Empress Dowager Tz'u-hsi, who had ruled China during Buck's childhood there. Her autobiography, *My Several Worlds,* was published in 1954; a sequel, *A Bridge to Passing,* appeared in 1962. Her activism continued unabated, however, and she founded Welcome House, an adoption agency for interracial children, especially for Amerasians, which placed children with adoptive parents regardless of race. During the 1960s, her reputation escaped untarnished when her companion, Ted Harris—her husband, Richard Walsh, had died in 1953—was vilified in the press for alleged irregularities and personal wrongdoing in connection with the Welcome House organization.

In the early 1970s, when relations with Communist China began to thaw, Buck hoped to visit China with the Nixon entourage, but her request for a visa was turned down by the Chinese government who accused her works of displaying "an attitude of distortion, smear and vilification towards the people of new China and its leaders." It was obvious that her record of leftist activism did not engender support within the Nixon administration. She became ill soon afterwards, and after a bout with gall bladder complications, she died on March 6, 1973.

—Edward Moran

FURTHER READING:

Conn, Peter. *Pearl S. Buck: A Cultural Biography.* New York, Cambridge University Press, 1996.

Stirling, Nora. *Pearl Buck.* Piscataway, New Century Publishers, 1983.

Buck Rogers

Long before *Star Trek* and *Star Wars,* there was *Buck Rogers,* the first comic strip devoted to science fiction. Debuting early in 1929, it introduced readers to most of its stock features, including rocket ships, space travel, robots, and ray guns, concepts considered by most to be wildly improbable, if not downright impossible. A graduate of a pulp fiction magazine, Anthony "Buck" Rogers served as a sort of ambassador for the science fiction genre, presenting many of its premises, plots, and props to a mass audience. Indeed, it was *Buck Rogers* that inspired a wide range of people, from creators of comic book superheroes and future astronauts to scientists and Ray Bradbury. *Buck Rogers in the 25th Century,* as the strip was initially titled, helped introduce the United States to the possibilities of the future, such as space travel and the atomic bomb, while simultaneously offering quite a few wild and exciting adventures.

Buck Rogers was the creation of Philadelphia newspaperman Philip Francis Nowlan, who was forty when he sold his first science fiction story to *Amazing Stories.* Titled "Armageddon—2419 A.D.," it appeared in the August 1928, issue, and featured twenty-nine-year-old Anthony Rogers, who got himself trapped in a cave-in at an abandoned Pennsylvania coal mine. Knocked out by an accumulation of radioactive gases, Rogers slept for five centuries and awakened to a world greatly changed. America was no longer the dominant power in the world. In fact, the nation was a "total wreck—Americans a hunted race in their own land, hiding in dense forests that covered the shattered and leveled ruins of their once-magnificent cities." The world was ruled by Mongolians, and China was the locus of power. Finding that the Han Airlords ruled North America, Rogers joined the local guerilla movement in its fight against the conquerors, and took advantage of 25th century anti-gravity flying belts and rocket guns, as well as his own knowlege, to concoct winning strategies against them.

His partner was Wilma Deering, destined to be *the* woman in his life, who he met soon after emerging from the mine. A dedicated freedom fighter, Wilma was considerably more competent and active than most comparable female science fiction characters of the time. Rogers and Wilma, along with their other new comrades, saved America in Nowlan's sequel, "The Airlords of Han," which appeared in *Amazing Stories* the following year. By that time, Anthony Rogers, newly-named Buck, was the hero of his own comic strip.

John F. Dille, who ran his own newspaper feature syndicate in Chicago, noticed Nowlan's initial story in *Amazing Stories,* and encouraged him to turn it into a comic strip, "a strip which would present imaginary adventures several centuries in the future—a strip in which the theories in the test tubes and laboratories of the scientists could be garnished up with a bit of imagination and treated as realities." Dille picked artist Dick Calkins to work with Nowlan, who was already on the syndicate staff and had been trying to interest his boss in a strip about cavemen and dinosaurs. Apparently assuming that someone who could depict the dim past ought to be able to do the same for the far future, Dille put Calkins on the team. *Buck Rogers in the 25th Century,* a daily strip at first, began on Monday, January 7, 1929, the same day, coincidentally, that the *Tarzan* comic strip was launched.

Readers responded favorably to *Buck Rogers,* and it began picking up papers across the country. One early fan was a young fellow in the Midwest by the name of Ray Bradbury. Many years later, he recalled the impact that the early strips had on him: "What, specifically, did Buck Rogers have to offer that instantly 'zapped' us into blind gibbers of love? Well, to start out with mere trifles—rocket guns that shoot explosive bullets; people who fly through the air with 'jumping belts'; 'hovercrafts' skimming over the surface of the earth; disintegrators which destroyed, down to the meanest atom, anything they touched; radar-equipped robot armies; television-controlled rockets and rocket bombs; invasions from Mars; the first landing on the Moon."

Among the regular characters, in addition to Buck and Wilma, were Dr. Huer, scientific genius, inventor, and mentor to Buck; Black Barney, a reformed air pirate; Killer Kane, slick-haired traitor and recurrent villain; and Buddy Deering, teenage brother of Wilma. When a Sunday page was added early in 1930, it was devoted chiefly to Buddy's adventures. It was intended to appeal to youthful readers who supposedly made up the majority audience for Sunday funnies. Buddy spent much of his time on Mars, where he was often involved with young Princess Aura of the Golden People. In separate daily sequences, Buck also journeyed to the Red Planet, but concentrated on battling the evil Tiger Men. The Martian equivalent of the Mongols, the Tiger Men had come to earth in their flying saucers to kidnap human specimens. When they grabbed Wilma for one of their experiments, Buck designed and built the world's first interplanetary rocket ship so that he could rescue the victims who had been taken to Mars. "Roaring rockets!" he vowed. "We'll show these Martians who's who in the solar system!"

Astute readers in the 1930s may have noticed that the Sunday pages were considerably better looking than the daily strips. That was because a talented young artist named Russell Keaton was ghosting them. He remained with the feature for several years. When he left to do a strip of his own, he was replaced by another young ghost artist, Rick Yager. *Buck Rogers,* especially on Sundays, was plotted along the lines of a nineteenth-century Victorian picaresque novel. There was a good deal of wandering by flying belt, rocket ship, and on foot. Characters drifted in and out, appeared to be killed, but showed up again later on after having assumed new identities. Reunions and separations were frequent. The strip's trappings, however, were far from Dickensian, offering readers the latest in weapons, modes of transportation, and lifestyles of the future. By 1939, the atomic bomb was appearing in the strip. With the advent of World War II, most of the villains were again portrayed as Asians.

Buck Rogers also played an important role in the development of the comic book. A reprint of a *Buck Rogers* comic book was used as a premium by Kellogg's in 1933, which was before modern format comic books had ever appeared on the newsstands. In 1934, *Famous Funnies,* the first regularly-issued monthly comic, established the format and price for all comic books to follow. The *Buck Rogers* Sunday pages, usually four per issue, began in the third issue. It also seems likely that Buck Rogers and his associates, who were among the first flying people to be seen in comic books, had an influence on the flying superheroes who came along in the original material funny books of the later 1930s.

Almost as impressive as Buck's daring exploits 500 years in the future, was his career as a merchandising star during the grim Depression era. In 1932, a *Buck Rogers* radio show began airing, heard every day in fifteen-minute segments and sponsored by Kellogg's. The serial was heard in various forms throughout most of the decade and into the next. In 1933, the first Big Little Book devoted to the futuristic hero was printed. Buck Rogers was marketed most successfully in the area of toys. Commencing in 1934, Daisy began manufacturing Buck Rogers rocket pistols; that same year the Louis Marx company introduced a toy rocket ship. The zap guns were especially popular, so much so that Daisy began producing them at night and on Saturdays to meet the demand.

Buck Rogers conquered the silver screen in the 1930s. Universal released a twelve-chapter serial in 1939, with Buster Crabbe as Buck, and Constance Moore as Wilma. Anthony Warde, who made a career of playing serial heavies, was Killer Kane. Not exactly a gem in the chapter play genre, *Buck Rogers* took place on Earth and Saturn. The serial was later condensed into a 101-minute feature film. Under the title *Destination Saturn,* it occasionally shows up on late-night television.

Nowlan was removed from the strip shortly before his death in 1940, and Calkins left in 1947. Rick Yager carried on with the Sunday pages and the dailies before Murphy Anderson took over. By the late 1950s, George Tuska, also a graduate of the comic books, was drawing both the Sunday and the daily strips. Science fiction writers such as Fritz Leiber and Judith Merril provided scripts. The Sunday strip ended in 1965, and the daily two years later. But Buck Rogers was not dead.

He returned, along with Wilma and Doc Huer, in a 1979 feature film that starred Gil Gerard. That production led to a television series and another comic strip, written by Jim Lawrence, drawn by Gray

Morrow, and syndicated by the *New York Times*. None of these latter ventures was particularly successful, and more recent attempts to revive Buck Rogers have been even less so.

—Ron Goulart

FURTHER READING:

Dille, Robert C., editor. *The Collected Works of Buck Rogers in the 25th Century.* New York, Chelsea House, 1969.

Goulart, Ron. *The Adventurous Decade.* New Rochelle, Arlington House, 1975.

Sheridan, Martin. *Comics and Their Creators.* Boston, Hale, Cushman and Flint, 1942.

Buckley, William F., Jr. (1925—)

William F. Buckley Jr. found fame as the voice of conservatism. Founder of the *National Review,* the conservative journal of opinion of which he was editor-in-chief until 1990, Buckley also worked as an influential political advisor and popular novelist. Buckley aptly described the effect of his *National Review* through his character Boris Bolgin in his spy novel *Who's on First.* "'Do you ever read the *National Review, Jozsef?',* asks Boris Bolgin, the chief of KGB counter intelligence for Western Europe, 'It is edited by this young bourgeois fanatic. Oh, how they cried about the repression of the counter-revolutionaries in Budapest! But the *National Review* it is also angry with the CIA for—I don't know; not starting up a Third World War, maybe? Last week—I always read the *National Review,* it makes me so funny mad—last week an editorial said'—he raised his head and appeared to quote from memory—'The attempted assassination of Sukarno last week had all the earmarks of a CIA operation. Everybody in the room was killed except Sukarno.'"

William Frank Buckley, Jr. was born in New York City in 1925 into a wealthy Connecticut family of Irish decent. He grew up in a devout Christian Catholic atmosphere surrounded by nine brothers and sisters. He attended Millbrook Academy in New York and then served as a second lieutenant in World War II. After his discharge in 1946 he went to Yale bringing with him, as he wrote, "a firm belief in Christianity and a profound respect for American institutions and traditions, including free enterprise and limited government." He found out that Yale believed otherwise. After graduating with honors in 1950, he published the public challenge to his alma mater *God and Man at Yale* in 1951. It brought him instant fame. He claimed that Yale's "thoroughly collectivist" economics and condescending views towards religion could only lead towards a dangerous relativism, a pragmatic liberalism without a moral heart. What America required and conservatism must supply was a fighting faith, noted David Hoeveler in *Watch on the Right,* and William 'Bill' Buckley, Jr. was just the man for the job.

In 1955 he founded the *National Review,* creating one of the most influential political journals in the country. His syndicated column, *On the Right,* which he started to write in 1962, has made its weekly appearance in more than 300 newspapers. Not only in print has he been America's prime conservative voice, Buckley also hosts the Emmy award-winning show *Firing Line*—Public Broadcasting Service's longest-running show—which he started in 1966. The

Young Americans for Freedom Movement (1960) which aimed at conservative control of the Republican Party was Buckley's brainchild. He has written and edited over 40 books which include political analyses, sailing books and the Blackford Oakes spy novels and has been awarded more than 35 honorary degrees. In 1991 he received the Presidential Medal of Freedom. As a member of the secretive Bilderberg Group and the Council on Foreign Relations—founded in 1921 as an advisory group to the President—he also plays an important political advisory role. His spy novels, however, show most clearly how much he perceived the Cold War to be essentially a spiritual struggle.

Remarking to his editor at Doubleday, Samuel Vaughan, that he wanted to write something like 'Forsyth,' Vaughan expected a Buckley family saga in Galsworthy's *Forsythe Saga* tradition. But Buckley was referring to Frederick Forsyth's *The Day of the Jackal* and produced *Saving the Queen,* which made the best-seller lists a week before its official publication date. After watching the anti-CIA movie *Three Days of the Condor,* Buckley—who himself worked briefly (nine months) as a CIA covert agent—set out to write a book in which "the good guys and the bad guys were actually distinguishable." That history is the "final" fiction is one of the themes of his Blackford Oakes novels that always take as their starting point an historical "fact." But his main interest lay in countering the charges that there was no moral difference between Western intelligence and its Soviet counterpart. In his *Craft of Intelligence,* former CIA Director Allen Dulles, who figures frequently in Buckley's novels, claimed that "Our intelligence has a major share of the task of neutralizing hostile activities. Our side chooses the objective. The opponent has set up the obstacles." Buckley frames it differently in his novel *Stained Glass:* "Our organization is defensive in nature. Its aim is to defeat your aggressive intentions. You begin by the dissimilarities between Churchill and Hitler. That factor wrecks all derivative analogies."

Buckley's conservatism is deeply spiritual but never orthodox. In a direct contradiction of conservative and Republican politics, he claimed in a 1996 cover story of the *National Review* "The War on Drugs Is Lost," that "the cost of the drug war is many times more painful, in all its manifestations, than would be the licensing of drugs combined with an intensive education of non-users and intensive education designed to warn those who experiment with drugs." In his syndicated column he wrote of his sister's cancer chemotherapy and her need for medical marijuana. Buckley's public stand and personal drama are closely related. In *Watch on the Right,* David Hoeveler sees this communal and familial conservative pathos as a defining quality of Buckley's character: "The conservative movement for Buckley was a family affair, it flourished with friendships within and struck forcefully at the enemy without." Nine of the ten Buckley children at one time contributed to the *National Review.*

Being Catholic always mattered more to him than being conservative, Gary Willis noted in his *Confessions of a Conservative.* When asked in an *Online Newshour* interview about his book *Nearer, My God: An Autobiography of Faith,* how his Christian belief influenced his views on conservatism, he laughed his reply: "Well, it's made me right all the time."

—Rob van Kranenburg

FURTHER READING:

Buckley, William F., Jr. *God and Man at Yale: The Superstitions of Academic Freedom.* Chicago, Regnery, 1951.

————. *Nearer, My God: An Autobiography of Faith.* New York, Doubleday, 1997.

————. *Saving The Queen.* New York, Doubleday, 1976.

————. *Stained Glass.* New York, Doubleday, 1978.

————. *Who's on First.* New York, Doubleday, 1980.

Dulles, Allen. *The Craft of Intelligence.* New York, Harper and Row, 1963.

Hoeveler. J. David, Jr. *Watch on the Right: Conservative Intellectuals in the Reagan Era.* Madison, The University of Wisconsin Press, 1991.

Willis, Gary. *Confessions of a Conservative.* New York, Simon and Schuster, 1979.

Buckwheat Zydeco (1947—)

Stanley ''Buckwheat'' Dural, Jr. is one of the premier performers and representatives of the black Creole dance music of southwest Louisiana known as zydeco. In 1979, after playing for nearly three years in Clifton Chenier's band, he added Zydeco to his nickname and formed the Ils Sont Partis Band, which takes its title from the announcer's call at the start of each horse race at Lafayette's Evangeline Downs, in the heart of French-speaking Louisiana. An accomplished accordionist, Buckwheat has perhaps done more than anyone else to popularize zydeco and increase its appeal within a wider popular culture. He played for President Clinton's inaugural parties and for the closing ceremonies of the 1996 Summer Olympics in Atlanta. His tunes now find their way on to television commercials and movie soundtracks, but even multiple Grammy Award nominations have not diminished his allegiance to what he calls his ''roots music.''

—Robert Kuhlken

FURTHER READING:

Nyhan, Patricia, Brian Rollins, David Babb, and Michael Doucet. *Let the Good Times Roll! A Guide to Cajun & Zydeco Music.* Portland, Maine, Upbeat Books, 1997.

Tisserand, Michael. *The Kingdom of Zydeco.* New York, Arcade Publishing, 1998.

Budweiser

Along with Coca-Cola, Budweiser beer is America's drink. One out of five alcoholic drinks sold in America is a Bud, and, now that the King of Beers is being sold in more than 60 countries worldwide, Budweiser is the world's most popular beer. This lightly-hopped, smooth lager has a long history in the United States, but it was beginning in the 1970s that Budweiser became a true icon of American culture, thanks to a model of commercial development that is the envy of the world. Faced with increasing competition from the Miller Brewing Company, Budweiser parent Anheuser-Busch began putting the Budweiser name everywhere: on coolers, blimps, and boxer shorts; on football games, car races, and other sports. The company's carefully crafted advertising campaigns were equally ubiquitous: ''This Bud's for you''; ''Budweiser . . . The King of

A large, inflatable Budweiser beer can on Cocoa beach in Florida.

Beers''; the Bud Bowl; the Budweiser frogs and lizards; and, of course, the Budweiser Clydesdales all kept the Budweiser brands alive in the consumers' mind. The brewery bought the St. Louis Cardinals baseball team and opened theme parks in Florida and Virginia; these were family entertainments, but the ties to the beer brands were always evident. Such marketing tactics were backed by the most efficient beer production and distribution systems in the world.

The Anheuser-Busch brewing company traced its history back to St. Louis breweries in the mid-1800s. In 1865, the brewery produced 8,000 barrels; these numbers grew quickly when Budweiser Lager Beer was introduced in 1876. The brewing company expanded horizontally, purchasing bottlers and glass companies. Soon it controlled all the means for producing its beer and in 1901 Anheuser-Busch was well on its way to being America's brewery, breaking the million-barrel mark for the first time with 1,006,494 barrels. With the nation under the grips of National Prohibition in 1920, the brewery unveiled Budweiser near-beer (selling 5 million cases) and began manufacturing ice cream. With the retraction of Prohibition in 1933 the company introduced the Budweiser Clydesdales, which have remained an icon of the company's commitment to tradition. In the 1950s, the company implemented plans to open Busch drinking gardens in various cities, in an attempt to tap into a European tradition. In addition, advertising gimmicks became a significant part of Bud's appeal. From the Clydesdales of the 1930s, advertisers welcomed ''Bud Man'' in 1969, a campaign which sought to tie the beer to gender roles and expectations of masculinity. Today, Budweiser still uses the saying ''This Bud's for you,'' but it most often aims toward a broader, un-gendered public with advertising gimmicks such as the ''Bud Bowl'' and talking frogs. Budweiser was also one of the first beers to incorporate requests for responsible-drinking in its advertisements in the late 1980s.

In 1980 Budweiser made history by expanding into the global marketplace with agreements to brew and sell in Canada, Japan, and elsewhere. This corporate development fueled Anheuser-Busch's staggering rise in production, which exceeded 100 million barrels per year in the late 1990s and gave the company nearly half of all beer sales worldwide and around 40 percent of beer sales in the United States. Budweiser—along with the brand extensions Bud Light, Bud Dry, and Bud Ice—is thus poised to become to the rest of the world what it already is to the United States: a mass-produced, drinkable beer that symbolizes the ''good life'' made possible by corporate capitalist enterprise. Beer purists and fans of locally-produced microbrews may decry the bland flavor and lack of body of the world's best-selling beer, but millions of beer drinkers continue to put their money down on the bar and ask for a Bud.

—Brian Black

FURTHER READING:

''Budweiser.com.'' http://www.budweiser.com. April 1999.

Hernon, Peter, and Terry Ganey. *Under the Influence: The Unauthorized Story of the Anheuser-Busch Dynasty.* New York, Simon & Schuster, 1991.

Plavchan, Ronald Jan. *A History of Anheuser-Busch, 1852-1933.* New York, Arno Press, 1976.

Price, Steven D. *All the King's Horses: The Story of the Budweiser Clydesdales.* New York, Viking Penguin, 1983.

Rhodes, Christine P., editor. *The Encyclopedia of Beer.* New York, Henry Holt & Co., 1997.

Yenne, Bill. *Beers of North America.* New York, Gallery Books, 1986.

Buffalo Springfield

Despite releasing three accomplished albums which were innovative and influential exemplars of the ''West Coast sound'' of the mid- to late 1960s, Buffalo Springfield only had a limited impact on the public consciousness during its brief and tempestuous heyday. However, the continued cultural resonance of their solitary hit single, ''For What It's Worth,'' combined with the subsequent critical acclaim and commercial success of its alumni, has ensured Buffalo Springfield of a somewhat mythical status in popular music history.

The genesis of Buffalo Springfield proceeded slowly through various musical styles and right across the North American continent. Stephen Stills and Richie Furay met in folk music mecca Greenwich Village, and first played together in an eccentric nine-man vocal ensemble called the Au Go Go singers, which released an obscure album in 1964. Fellow singer-songwriter Neil Young encountered Stills in Ontario, and Furay in New York, before befriending bassist Bruce Palmer on the Toronto coffee-house music scene. Young and Palmer joined a blues-rock group, The Mynah Birds, which was

Members of the group Buffalo Springfield c. 1967, featuring Stephen Stills (top) and Neil Young (right).

briefly signed to Motown in 1965. The four young musicians finally came together as a group when Stills and Furay spotted the two Canadians in a Los Angeles traffic jam in early 1966. Supplemented by another Canadian, experienced session drummer Dewey Martin, the fledgling Buffalo Springfield were, in the words of Johnny Rogan, ''potentially the most eclectic unit to appear on the West Coast scene since the formation of the Byrds.''

Byrds' bassist Chris Hillman arranged for Buffalo Springfield to play at the prestigious Los Angeles club Whisky A Go Go, and the gigs immediately attracted such local luminaries as David Crosby, the Mamas and Papas, and Sonny and Cher. Furay, Stills and Young would later assert that Buffalo Springfield peaked during these early live appearances, and that by comparison, in Young's words, ''All the records were great failures.'' The band released the first of those records in July 1966, Young's precocious ''Nowadays Clancy Can't Even Sing'' backed with Stills' ''Go and Say Goodbye.'' The single was not a commercial success, but it provides a suitable example of the contrast at this time between Stills' stylish but typical ''teenybop'' narratives of young love, and Young's more lyrically obtuse repertoire. As Stills later noted, ''He [Young] wanted to be Bob Dylan and I wanted to be The Beatles.''

Buffalo Springfield's eponymous debut album was released in February 1967. The lyrics to Young's ''Burned,'' ''Out of My Mind'' and ''Flying on the Ground Is Wrong'' all alluded to the effects of fashionable psychedelic drugs. Buffalo Springfield achieved commercial success with their next single, ''For What It's Worth,'' which reached number 7 on the national chart. An artistic leap for Stills, the song was a coolly sardonic study of the violent action of police against hippy protesters on Sunset Strip in late 1966. Though ''For What It's Worth'' captured the significance of the conflict between the authorities and the emerging ''counterculture,'' the single's sales were concentrated in California, suggesting that middle America had little empathy with such provocative lines as ''What a field day for the heat [police]/A thousand people in the street.''

By early 1967, Buffalo Springfield was riven with problems. Palmer had been charged with possession of drugs and deported back to Canada, and Young began to work with former Phil Spector associate Jack Nietzsche. The group played an acclaimed concert with Palmer and without Young at the Monterey Pop Festival in June 1967. Renegade Byrd David Crosby substituted for Young at this legendary zenith of the hippy era. Young returned to Buffalo Springfield in September 1967 and the band released their second long-player. Though *Rolling Stone* pertinently observed that ''This album sounds as if every member of the group is satisfying his own musical needs,'' the diverse and ambitious *Buffalo Springfield Again* is an acknowledged classic. The album included Young's impressionistic six-minute collage ''Broken Arrow,'' Stills' guitar and banjo epic ''Bluebird,'' and ''Rock 'n' Roll Woman,'' an ode to Jefferson Airplane singer Grace Slick co-written by Stills and Crosby.

Buffalo Springfield unravelled in early 1968: Palmer was busted and deported again in January, and in March, Young, Furay and the latest bassist, Jim Messina, were arrested on a drugs charge with Cream member Eric Clapton. When Buffalo Springfield finally disbanded in May, *Rolling Stone* cited ''internal hassle, extreme fatigue coupled with absence of national success and run-ins with the fuzz.'' The hippy argot rather disguised the extent to which the internecine egotism of Stills and Young, even more than the drug busts, had dissolved Buffalo Springfield. It was left to Furay and Messina to organise tracks recorded at the end of 1967 for the inevitably inconsistent *Last Time Around,* released in August 1968 after Buffalo Springfield had disbanded.

Stills joined Crosby in the prototypical ''supergroup'' Crosby, Stills and Nash; Young became a significant solo artist and occasionally augmented CSN; and Furay and Messina formed the country-rock outfit Poco. A reunion of the original members occurred in 1982, but it never advanced beyond rehearsals. Despite being inducted into the Rock 'n' Roll Hall of Fame in 1997, Buffalo Springfield remains disproportionately represented in popular culture by ''For What It's Worth,'' a standard of the soundtracks to many documentaries and movies (*Good Morning Vietnam, Forrest Gump*) about the cultural conflicts of the 1960s. In 1998, the song was more imaginatively utilised by rap group Public Enemy in the title song for the film *He Got Game.* Stills' famous riff and lyrics were combined with the rhymes of Public Enemy's frontman, Chuck D, in an inspired meeting of two radically different forms and eras of political popular music.

—Martyn Bone

FURTHER READING:

Einarson, John, with Richie Furay. *For What It's Worth: The Story of Buffalo Springfield.* Toronto, Quarry Press, 1997.

Jenkins, Alan, editor. *Neil Young and Broken Arrow: On a Journey Through the Past.* Bridgend, Neil Young Appreciation Society, 1994.

Rogan, Johnny. *Neil Young: The Definitive Story of His Musical Career.* London, Proteus, 1982.

Buffett, Jimmy (1946—)

Devoted fans—affectionately dubbed Parrot Heads—find escapism in Jimmy Buffett's ballads, vicariously experiencing through his strongly autobiographical songs Buffett's life of beaches, bars, and boats. Yet Buffett's life has been far more than rum-soaked nights and afternoon naps in beachside hammocks. Even though Buffett relishes his image of ''the professional misfit,'' this millionaire ''beach bum'' is actually an ambitious and clever entrepreneur.

Born on Christmas Day, 1946 in Pascagoula, Mississippi, Jimmy Buffett spent most of his youth in the Catholic school system in Mobile, Alabama. During college he learned to play the guitar and started singing in clubs. While attending the University of Southern Mississippi, about 80 miles from New Orleans, Buffett played regularly at the Bayou Room on Bourbon Street. Once he had a taste of performing, his life course was set. Even though he married and took a job at the Mobile shipyards after college, Buffett continued to spend his nights playing at hotel cocktail lounges.

Lacking the money to move to Los Angeles, where Jimmy had a job offer at a club, the Buffetts moved instead to Nashville. Buffett made a living by writing for *Billboard* magazine, but he also continued to write new songs. The first of these songs to get recorded was ''The Christian?'' on Columbia Records' Barnaby Label. In 1970, Buffett recorded an album, *Down to Earth,* for the Barnaby label. Sales were so disappointing that Barnaby did not release Buffett's next album, *High Cumberland Jubilee,* recorded in 1971, until 1977. Buffett hired a band and toured in an attempt to promote his first

Jimmy Buffett

album, but within a few months he ran out of money. Career frustrations took a toll on his marriage.

In his mid-twenties, Buffett found himself broke, divorced, and hating Nashville. Then in 1971, Jimmy Buffett took a trip that changed his life and his music. Fellow struggling singer Jerry Jeff Walker invited Buffett down to his home in Summerland Key, just 25 miles from Key West. It was the beginning of Key West's "decade of decadence," and Buffett quickly immersed himself in the Conch subculture's nonstop party that they referred to as the "full-tilt boogie." To maintain the freedom of his new lifestyle Buffett ran up bar tabs, literally played for his supper, and got involved in the local cottage industry—drug smuggling.

The lifestyle and the local characters became the substance of Buffett's songs. The first of the Key West-inspired songs appeared in 1973 when he landed a record deal with ABC/Dunhill and recorded *A White Sport Coat and a Pink Crustacean.* The tongue-in-cheek "The Great Filling Station Holdup" made it to number 58 on Billboard's country charts. The most infamous song from the album, "Why Don't We Get Drunk (and Screw)," became a popular jukebox selection and the favorite Buffett concert sing-along song.

ABC's rising star, Jim Croce, died in 1973, and the record company looked to Jimmy Buffett to fill his shoes. They even promoted Buffett's next album, 1974's *Living and Dying in 3/4 Time,* with a fifteen-minute promotional film that showed in ABC-owned theaters. "Come Monday" made it all the way to number 30 on the billboard pop charts. For years, Buffett had been making reference to, even introducing, his mythical Coral Reefer Band. In the summer of 1975 he put together an actual Coral Reefer Band to tour and promote his third ABC/Dunhill album, *A1A.* The album contains "A Pirate Looks at Forty," which became a central tale in the mythos Buffett was spinning, and a virtual theme song for every Buffett fan as they neared middle age. 1976's *Havana Daydreamin'* got good reviews and fed the frenzy of his growing cult following; but it was 1977's *Changes in Latitude, Changes in Attitude* that was the defining moment of his career. The album's hit single, "Margaritaville," stayed in the Billboard Top 40 charts for fifteen weeks, peaking at number eight. That summer "Margaritaville" permeated the radio and Buffett opened for the Eagles tour. The exposure helped *Changes in Latitude, Changes in Attitude* go platinum.

The song "Margaritaville" gave a name to the place fans escaped when they listened to Jimmy Buffett's music. And Margaritaville was wherever Jimmy Buffett was playing his music, be that Key West, Atlanta, or Cincinnati. Supposedly it was at a concert in Cincinnati in the early 1980s that Eagles bassist Timothy B. Schmidt looked out at the fans in wild Hawaiian shirts and shark fin hats and dubbed them Parrot Heads. By the late 1980s the Parrot Head subculture had grown to the point that Buffett had become one of the top summer concert draws. The concerts were giant parties with colorful costumes, plentiful beer, and almost everyone singing along out of key with the songs they knew by heart. The concerts were more about the experience than about hearing Jimmy Buffett sing.

Buffett soon found ways to extend the experience beyond the concerts. Although he continued to average an album a year, he also began to develop diverse outlets for his creativity, and aggressively marketed the Margaritaville mythos. The Caribbean Soul line of clothing appeared in 1984, and in 1985 he opened Jimmy Buffett's Margaritaville store in Key West. A few months after opening the store, he sent out a 650 copy initial mailing of *Coconut Telegraph,* a combination fan newsletter and advertising flyer for Buffett parapher-nalia. It was in the April 1985 issue that the term Parrot Head was first

officially used to refer to Buffett's fans. By the end of the decade, the newsletter had 20,000 subscribers.

Buffet reasoned that anyone who wanted to read his newsletter would buy a book with his name on it. His first literary effort, in 1988, was *Jolly Mon,* a children's book he co-wrote with his daughter Savannah Jane. The following year, Buffett's collection of short stories, *Tales from Margaritaville,* became a bestseller. His first novel, *Where is Joe Merchant?,* warranted a six figure advance and became a bestseller in 1992. By this time Buffett had opened a Margaritaville cafe next to the store in Key West. Eventually, he opened Margaritaville clubs and gift shops in New Orleans, Charleston, and Universal Studios in Florida.

More than anything else, Jimmy Buffett is a lifestyle artist. Whether it be a Caribbean meal, a brightly colored shirt, a CD, or a live performance, Buffett transports his fans to the state of mind that is Margaritaville.

—Randy Duncan

FURTHER READING:

Eng, Steve. *Jimmy Buffett: The Man from Margaritaville Revealed.* New York, St. Martin's Press, 1996.

Humphrey, Mark, and Harris Lewine. *The Jimmy Buffett Scrapbook.* New York, Citadel Press, 1995.

Ryan, Thomas. *The Parrot Head Companion: An Insider's Guide to Jimmy Buffett.* Secaucus, New Jersey, Carol Publishing, 1998.

Bugs Bunny

One of the most beloved animated characters of all time, Bugs Bunny proved the likable combination of casual and wise guy who speaks insouciantly with a Brooklyn accent (voiced by Mel Blanc). Bugs has been both comic aggressor and straight man, but his essence is that he is always sympathetic, responding only to provocation (a character wants to eat him, wants him as a trophy, as a good luck piece, as an unwilling participant in an experiment, etc.). Bugs never engages an opponent without a reason, but once he is engaged, it's a fight to the finish with Bugs the comic winner. He can be mischie-vous, cunning, impudent, a rascally heckler, a trickster, saucy, and very quick with words, but he is never belligerent and prefers to use his wits rather than resort to physical violence.

An embryonic version of Bugs first appeared in Ben Hardaway's 1938 cartoon "Porky's Hare Hunt," in which the rabbit is a screwy tough guy in the wacky and wild tradition of early Daffy Duck. The character is given a screwball, Woody Woodpecker kind of laugh, hops about wildly, and even flies, using his ears as propellers. He has Bugs' penchant for wisecracks ("Here I am, fatboy!"), as well as Bugs' occasional appeals to sympathy ("Don't shoot!"). He also expresses Bugs' later catchphrase (borrowed from Groucho Marx in Duck Soup), "Of course you realize, this means war!" However, the white hare is also more aggressively wacky than the later character and would torment his opponents mercilessly.

The character was designed by former Disney animator Charlies Thorsen, and although unnamed in the cartoon itself, was christened Bugs Bunny because the design sheet for director Ben "Bugs"

Hardaway was designated ''Bugs' Bunny.'' Hardaway also guided the hare through his second outing (and his first in color) in ''Hare-um Scare-um.'' Director Frank Tashlin alleged that ''Bugs Bunny is nothing but Max Hare, the Disney character in 'The Tortoise and the Hare.' We took it—Schlesinger took it, whoever—and used it a thousand times.'' While both are brash and cocky characters, Bugs was both wilder and funnier, eventually developing into a very distinctive character. Animator and later director Robert McKimson redesigned Bugs Bunny into the modern figure seen in the 1990s.

Bugs faced a number of antagonists over the years, the most famous being Elmer Fudd (voiced by Arthur Q. Bryan), a large-headed hunter with a speech impediment. The pair were first teamed by Charles ''Chuck'' Jones in ''Elmer's Candid Camera,'' with Elmer stalking the ''wascally wabbit'' with a camera instead of his usual gun. The team was then appropriated by Fred ''Tex'' Avery for ''A Wild Hare,'' in which some of Bugs' rougher edges were softened to make him less loony and annoying. Avery also coined Bugs' signature opening line, ''Eh, what's up, Doc?'' as a memorably incongruous response to a hunter preparing to pepper him with bullets.

Bugs really hit his stride under the direction of Bob Clampett in such cartoons as ''Wabbit Trouble,'' ''Tortoise Wins by a Hare,'' ''What's Cooking, Doc?,'' ''Falling Hare,'' and ''The Old Grey Hare.'' Clampett's Bugs was one of the funniest and wildest incarnations of the character and is much more physical than he later became. These cartoons were later compiled into a feature, *Bugs Bunny Superstar,* where Clampett took sole credit for inventing Bugs Bunny. This did not set well with Jones, who when it came time to assemble *The Bugs Bunny/Road Runner Movie* credited every Bugs Bunny director except Clampett.

Director Friz Freleng specialized in pitting Bugs against Yosemite Sam, a runt-sized alter ego of Freleng himself equipped with an oversized hat, eyebrows, and mustache. Freleng found that Elmer Fudd was too sympathetic and wanted to create an outright villain in Sam. Sam's attempts to get the better of Bugs, the varmint, were eternally and comically frustrated. Sam made his first appearance in ''Hare Trigger,'' and Freleng's Bugs and Sam won an Academy Award for their teaming in ''Knighty Knight Bugs.''

However, Bugs' finest interpreter was Chuck Jones, who always felt that the rabbit should be motivated to wreak his mischief by an antagonist who tries to push the supposedly timid woodland creature around. Jones found his conception of Bugs materializing in ''Case of the Missing Hare,'' ''Super-Rabbit,'' and ''Hare Conditioned.'' Jones and gag man Michael Maltese created terrific comic sparks by allowing Bugs to play straightman to the forever frustrated Daffy Duck whose plans to get Bugs shot instead of himself constantly go awry. Three titles stand out: ''Rabbit Fire,'' ''Rabbit Seasoning,'' and ''Duck! Rabbit! Duck!''

Jones also created the musically based classic Bugs cartoons ''Long-Haired Hare,'' ''Rabbit of Seviolle,'' ''Baton Bunny'' and ''What's Opera, Doc?'' as well as using the character to parody the conventions of fairy tales, science fiction, and other genres in ''Haredevil Hare,'' ''Frigid Hare,'' ''Bully for Bugs,'' ''Beanstalk Bunny,'' and ''Ali Baba Bunny.'' These are among the funniest cartoons ever created and ample reason for Bugs' enduring popularity.

—Dennis Fischer

FURTHER READING:

Beck, Jerry, and Will Friedwald. *Looney Tunes and Merrie Melodies.* New York, Henry Holt, 1989.

Jones, Chuck. *Chuck Amuck: The Life and Times of an Animated Cartoonist.* New York, Farrar Straus Giroux, 1989.

———. *Chuck Reducks.* New York, Warner Books, 1996.

Lenburg, Jeff. *The Great Cartoon Directors.* New York, De Capo Press, 1993.

Maltin, Leonard. *Of Mice and Magic.* New York, New American Library, 1980.

Bumper Stickers

The bumper sticker was first used after World War II when new developments in plastic materials led to the production of paper strips with adhesive on the back which allowed them to be fastened onto car bumpers. The first bumper stickers were used almost exclusively during political campaigns to promote candidates and parties. This continued until the mid-1960s when personal statements such as ''Make Love, Not War'' or ''America—Love It Or Leave It'' began to appear. The bumper sticker has become a form of folk broadcasting, allowing anyone who owns a car to send out a slogan or message to anyone who happens to read it. Ranging from the serious to the satirical, many of the popular messages which appear on bumper stickers can offer valuable information about Americans' attitudes and concerns over religion, politics, regionalism, abortion, the environment, or any other debatable issue.

—Richard Levine

FURTHER READING:

Gardner, Carol W. *Bumper Sticker Wisdom: America's Pulpit Above the Tailpipe.* Oregon, Beyond Words Publishing, 1995.

Harper, Jennifer. ''Honk if You Love Bumper Stickers.'' *Washington Times.* July 26, 1988, p. E1.

Bundy, Ted (1946-1989)

Ted Bundy, perhaps the most notorious serial killer in American history, was executed amidst much media attention in Florida on the morning of January 24, 1989, for the murder of a 12 year-old girl. At the time of his execution, Bundy had also been convicted for the murders of two Florida State University students and was confessing to the murders of more than 20 other women across the length of the United States. Investigators, however, suspect Bundy actually committed anywhere between 36 to 100 murders in a killing spree that may have begun when he was a teenager in the Pacific Northwest and ended in north Florida. The media spectacle and public celebration outside the walls of the Florida death-house where Bundy was executed climaxed a long-term public fascination with one of the country's most photogenic, charismatic, and seemingly intelligent multiple murderers. Details of Bundy's gruesome murders, his remarkable escapes from police custody, and his ''fatal attraction'' for women have all managed to circulate throughout American popular mythology.

Ted Bundy's early history is at once ordinary and portentous. Bundy was born Theodore Robert Cowell on November 24, 1946, to Eleanor Louise Cowell in a home for unwed mothers in Burlington,

A car encrusted with bumper stickers.

Vermont. Ostracized by community and family after her pregnancy became an open secret, Louise traveled from her parents in Philadelphia to give birth to Ted, left him at the home in Burlington for a few months to discuss Ted's future with her family, and then finally brought Ted back to the Cowell house. Three years after that, Louise moved with Ted to Tacoma, Washington, to stay with his uncle Jack, a man whose education and intelligence Bundy much admired as he grew up. In Tacoma, Louise met and married a quiet man named Johnnie Bundy, and Ted's last name became Bundy. Much of the literature on Bundy, both popular and academic, focuses on the fact that his mother Louise was unwed and that the father's identity to this day remains a matter of conjecture. Bundy himself frequently downplayed the significance of his illegitimacy to his chroniclers, but he also on occasion implied how his youthful discovery that he was a ''bastard'' forever changed him.

Also debated in the extensive Bundy literature is the extent to which emotional and/or physical abuse distorted his development. All through the years of Bundy's public notoriety, he and some of his immediate family members insisted that, for the most part, his childhood was a loving, harmonious time. Since a series of psychiatric examinations of Bundy in the 1980s, however, doctors such as Dorothy Lewis have brought to light more of Bundy's early domestic traumas and many have come to believe that Bundy was emotionally damaged by witnessing his grandfather's alleged verbal and sometimes physical rages against family members. In any event, it seems clear that Bundy developed a fascination for knives and stories of murder quite early in his life—as early as three years of age. During his adolescence, Bundy became secretly obsessed with pornography, voyeurism, and sexually violent detective magazines.

As Bundy matured into a young man, he consciously cultivated an image or public face not dissimilar to how he perceived his uncle Jack: refined, educated, witty, public spirited, and stylish. Early on, he became active in community church events and the Boy Scouts. He later achieved modest academic success in high school and college, eventually attaining admission to law school. He became a worker for the Washington State Republican Party, strongly impressing then Governor Dan Evans. He manned the phone lines at a suicide crisis center and (ironically) studied sexual assault for a Seattle investigatory commission.

Much of Bundy's image making seemed designed to manipulate women in particular. Though the level of Bundy's sex appeal has been exaggerated and romanticized by the media, particularly in the highly rated 1986 NBC television movie *The Deliberate Stranger* (where he was played by handsome actor Mark Harmon), Bundy did engage in a number of romantic relationships during his life. Again, it has become standard in Bundy lore to focus on his relationship with a beautiful,

Ted Bundy (center) at his trial, 1979.

wealthy student when he was a junior in college. When the woman jilted Bundy, he vowed to become the kind of sophisticated man who could win her back. When they subsequently became engaged, Bundy coldly rejected her. According to writers such as Ann Rule, this woman is the physical and cultural prototype of Bundy's victims, who tended to be pretty, longhaired, and privileged co-eds. Another of Bundy's long-term lovers, a woman who wrote about her life with Bundy under the penname of Liz Kendall, has become publicly emblematic of the female intimates in Bundy's life who were so damaged by the revelation that he had killed dozens of women and yet remain strangely compelled by the memory of his personality. Even after his 1976 conviction for kidnapping a Utah woman brought Bundy to the national spotlight as a suspected serial killer, he continued to attract favorable female attention, eventually marrying a woman named Carole Boone in a bizarre courtroom ceremony during his second murder trial in 1980.

Bundy's criminal career stretched from coast to coast. He began murdering young college women in Washington State in 1974, either by sneaking into their homes in the middle of the night to abduct and kill them or by luring them with feigned helplessness and/or easy charm from the safety of a crowd into his private killing zone. He next moved on to Utah, where he attended law school by day and killed women by night. He also committed murders in Colorado and Idaho

during this time. In August of 1975, Bundy was arrested for a traffic violation and while he was in custody, police investigators from Utah and Washington compared notes and realized that Bundy was a viable suspect in the multi-state series of murders and kidnappings. Bundy was convicted in the kidnapping and assault of a young Utah woman, sent to prison, and later extradited to Colorado to stand trial for murder. During a lull in the legal proceedings at a courthouse in Aspen in 1977, Bundy escaped from an open window and remained free for five days. Recaptured, Bundy again escaped six months later, this time from a county jail. The second escape was not discovered for hours—time enough for Bundy to be well on his way to his eventual destination at Florida State University (FSU) in Tallahassee. At FSU, Bundy killed two sorority women in the Chi Omega House and shortly thereafter killed a 12 year-old girl in Lake City. These were the last of Bundy's murders.

Bundy's arrest and conviction for the Florida murders twice earned him the death penalty: in 1979 and 1980. His appeals lasted for years, but it became apparent in late 1988 that Bundy would be executed in January of 1989. In a desperate ploy to buy more time, Bundy began confessing details of select murders to investigators from across the country, including Robert Keppel, one of the original detectives assigned to Bundy's murders in the Pacific Northwest. Bundy also granted a widely publicized videotaped interview to evangelist James Dobson, during which Bundy blamed the pernicious influence of pornography for the murders. In spite of the last-minute confessions, however, Bundy was executed in "Old Sparky," Florida's electric chair, as a mob of spectators outside Raiford Prison waved signs with such slogans as "Burn Bundy Burn" and "Chi-O, Chi-O, It's Off to Hell I Go."

—Philip Simpson

FURTHER READING:

Kendall, Elizabeth. *The Phantom Prince: My Life with Ted Bundy.* Seattle, Madrona, 1981.

Keppel, Robert D., and William J. Birnes. *The Riverman: Ted Bundy and I Hunt for the Green River Killer.* New York, Pocket Books, 1995.

Larsen, Richard W. *Bundy: The Deliberate Stranger.* New York, Pocket Books, 1986.

Michaud, Stephen G., and Hugh Aynesworth. *The Only Living Witness: A True Account of Homicidal Insanity.* New York, Signet, 1984.

———. *Ted Bundy: Conversations with a Killer.* New York, Signet, 1989.

Rule, Ann. *The Stranger Beside Me.* New York, Signet, 1981.

Winn, Steven, and David Merrill. *Ted Bundy: The Killer Next Door.* New York, Bantam, 1980.

Bungalow

Though we may say so of the American ranch house, the bungalow serves as the archetypal style of American housing. As ideas of homemaking and house planning took shape around the turn of the twentieth century, designers sought a single style that embodied the evolving American ideals in a form that could be dispersed widely. While the sensibility of home design may have seemed modern, it in fact grew out of a regressive tradition known as the Arts and Crafts movement. The bungalow—meaning "in the Bengali style"—with its simplicity of design and functionality of layout, proved to be the enduring product of modernist thought combined with traditional application.

In the late nineteenth century, massive industrial growth centered Americans in cities and often in less than desirable abodes. The arts and crafts movement argued for society to change its priorities and put control back in human hands. One of the most prominent popularizers of the Arts and Crafts movement in the United States was Gustav Stickley. Inspired by William Morris and others, Stickley began publishing *The Craftsman* in 1901 in hopes of initiating a social and artistic revolution. Reacting against industrialization and all of its trappings (from tenement squalor to the dehumanization of labor), Stickley offered readers designs for his well-known furniture and other materials—all handmade. The plans in *The Craftsman* led naturally to model houses, featuring both interior and exterior plans. The Stickley home, wrote the designer-writer, was a "result not of elaborating, but of elimination." Striking a Jeffersonian chord, Stickley sought a design that would fulfill what he called "democratic architecture": a way of living for all people. The design for this unpretentious, small house—usually one-storied with a sloping roof—became known as bungalow and would make it possible for the vast majority of Americans to own their own home.

The homes of such designs played directly into a growing interest in home management, often referred to as home economics. At the turn of the twentieth century, American women began to perceive of the home as a laboratory in which one could promote better health, families, and more satisfied individuals with better management and design. The leaders of the domestic science movement endorsed simplifying the dwelling in both its structure and its amenities. Criticizing Victorian ornamentation, they sought something clean, new, and sensible. The bungalow fulfilled many of these needs perfectly.

While popular literature disseminated such ideals, great American architects also attached the term to the greatest designs of the early 1900s. Specifically, brothers Charles and Henry Green of California and the incomparable Frank Lloyd Wright each designed palatial homes called bungalows. Often, this terminology derived from shared traits with Stickley's simple homes: accentuated horizontality, natural materials, and restraint of the influence of technological innovation. Such homes, though, were not "democratic" in their intent.

The most familiar use of "bungalow" arrived as city and village centers sprawled into the first suburbs for middle-class Americans, who elected to leave urban centers yet lacked the means to reside in country estates. Their singular homes were often modeled after the original Stickley homes or similar designs from *Ladies' Home Journal.* Housing the masses would evolve into the suburban revolution on the landscape; however, the change in the vision of the home can be traced to a specific type: the unassuming bungalow.

—Brian Black

FURTHER READING:

Clark, Clifford Edward, Jr. *The American Family Home.* Chapel Hill, University of North Carolina Press, 1986.

Wright, Gwendolyn. *Building the Dream.* Cambridge, MIT Press, 1992.

Burger King

Burger King is a fast-food restaurant franchise that, along with McDonald's, has come to typify the U.S. "hamburger chain" concept that saw thousands of identical outlets spring up along the nation's highways after World War II and, later, in cities and towns from coast to coast and around the world. With its orange-and-white signs, Burger King, the "Home of the Whopper," was founded in Miami in 1954 by James McLamore and David Edgerton. Its first hamburgers were sold for 18 cents, and its flagship burger, the Whopper, was introduced in 1957 for 37 cents. Opened a year before rival McDonald's was franchised, Burger King was the first among the fast food drive-ins to offer indoor dining. By 1967, when the Pillsbury Corporation bought the company, there were 274 Burger King restaurants nationwide, employing more than 8,000 people. As of the end of 1998, there were 7,872 restaurants in the United States and 2,316 in more than 60 countries selling 1.6 billion Whopper sandwiches each year. Despite complaints from nutritionists about the fatty content of fast-food meals, many time-pressed consumers prefer them for their convenience and economy.

Burger King carved out its own niche in fast-food merchandising by means of several factors: its distinctive Whopper product, a cooking method that relies on flame-broiling instead of frying, and the company's aggressive and creative advertising campaigns. Even so, Burger King remains a distant second to its chief competitor, holding only 19 percent of the market compared to McDonald's 42 percent. The two fast-food giants have long had an ongoing rivalry, each claiming superior products, and even marketing competitive versions of each others' sandwiches. One of Burger King's most successful advertising campaigns in the 1970s mocked the uniformity and inflexibility of its rival's fast-food production with the slogan, "Have it Your Way," implying that customized orders were more easily available at Burger King than at McDonald's.

In 1989, Pillsbury was bought by a British firm, Grand Metropolitan (now Diagio), which acquired Burger King in the bargain. Knowing little about the American tradition of fast food, the British corporation tried to "improve" on the burger/fries menu by offering sit-down dinners with waiters and "dinner baskets" offering a variety of choices. This well-intentioned idea sent profits plummeting, and Burger King did not truly recover for nearly a decade. Also in the late 1990s, Burger King, in cooperation with government attempts at welfare reform, joined an effort to offer employment to former welfare clients. Critics pointed out that fast-food restaurant jobs in general are so low-paid and offer such little chance of advancement that their usefulness to individual workers is limited. Occasionally the defendant in racial discrimination suits, the corporation that owns Burger King was taken to task in 1997 by the Congressional Black Caucus for discriminatory practices against minority franchise owners. The company has increased its investments in African-American banks and its support for efforts of the fledgling Diversity Foods in Virginia in its efforts to become one of the largest black-owned businesses in the United States.

Despite Burger King's second position after McDonald's, the market for fast food is large. Perhaps one of Burger King's own past slogans sums up the outlook of the franchise best, "America loves burgers, and we're America's Burger King."

—Tina Gianoulis

FURTHER READING:

McLamore, James W. *The Burger King: Jim McLamore and the Building of an Empire*. New York, McGraw-Hill, 1998.

Burlesque

The word "burlesque" can refer either to a type of parody or to a theatrical performance whose cast includes scantily-clad women. The second art form grew out of the first: "burla" is Italian for "trick, waggery," and the adjective "burlesca" may be translated as "ludicrous." Borrowed into French, "burlesque" came to mean a takeoff on an existing work, without any particular moral agenda (as opposed to satire). The genre enjoyed a robust life on the French stage throughout the nineteenth century, and found ready audiences in British theaters as well.

The first American burlesques were imports from England, and chorus lines of attractive women were part of the show almost from the start. In 1866, Niblo's Garden in New York presented *The Black Crook*, its forgettable plot enlivened, as an afterthought, by some imported dances from a French opera, *La Biche au bois*. Public reception was warm, according to burlesque historian Irving Zeidman: "The reformers shrieked, the 'best people' boycotted it," but the bottom line was "box receipts of sin aggregating over $1,000,000 for a profit of $650,000." The show promptly spawned a host of imitations—*The Black Crook Junior, The White Crook, The Red Crook, The Golden Crook*—capitalizing shamelessly, and profitably, on Niblo's success.

Two years later an English troupe, Lydia Thompson and Her Blondes, made their New York debut at Woods' Museum and Menagerie on 34th St., "sharing the stage," writes Zeidman, "with exhibitions of a live baby hippopotamus." The play this time was F.C. Burnand's classical travesty *Ixion*, in which the chorus, costumed as meteors, eclipses, and goddesses, thrilled the audience by flashing their ruffled underpants in the Parisian can-can style.

The Thompson company was soon hired away to play at Niblo's in an arabesque comedy called *The 40 Thieves*. The orientalist turn soon worked its way into other shows, including those of Madame Celeste's Female Minstrel Company, which included numbers such as "The Turkish Bathers" and "The Turkish Harem." (Even as late as 1909, Millie De Leon was being billed as "The Odalisque of the East," i.e., the East Coast.) Orientalism was just one avenue down which American burlesque in the last three decades of the nineteenth century went in search of its identity in a tireless quest for plausible excuses to put lots of pretty women on stage while still managing to distinguish itself from what were already being called "leg shows." Minstrelsy and vaudeville were fair game; so were "living pictures," in which members of the troupe would assume the postures and props of famous paintings, preferably with as little clothing as could be gotten away with. (This method of art-history pedagogy was still being presented, with a straight face, half a century later as one of the attractions at the 1939 New York World's Fair.)

By the turn of the century, burlesque shows could be seen on a regular schedule at Manhattan's London Theatre and Miner House and across the East River in Brooklyn at Hyde and Behman's, the Star, and the Empire Theatres. Philadelphia offered burlesque at the Trocadero, 14th Street Opera House, and the Arch, Kensington, and Lyceum Theatres. Even staid Boston had burlesque at the Lyceum, Palace, and Grand Theatres as well as the Howard Atheneum, where young men who considered themselves lucky to catch a glimpse of an ankle if they stood on street corners on rainy days (according to Florence Paine, then a young businesswoman in the Boston shoe trade), "could go to see women who wore dresses *up to their knees*." (And wearing tights; bare legs would not come until later, even in New York.)

A "reputable" burlesque show of the Gay Nineties, according to Zeidman, might have a program such as was offered by Mabel Snow's Spectacular Burlesque Company: "New wardrobes, bright, catchy music and pictures, Amazon marches, pretty girls and novelty specialty acts." By 1917, according to Morton Minsky (proprietor, as were several of his brothers, of a famous chain of New York burlesque houses) the basic ingredients of burlesque were "girls, gags, and music." Minsky describes in detail the first time he saw one of his brothers' burlesque shows at the Winter Garden that year, the first half of which included a choral number (with much kicking of legs in unison, Minsky notes), a comedy skit, a rendition of Puccini's "Un bel di," a turn by a "cooch dancer" (or hootchy-kootch, vaguely derived from Near Eastern belly dancing and the prototype of what would later be called "exotic dancing"), a serious dramatic sketch about a lad gone wrong who commits suicide, a second chorus,

A view from the wings of a typical burlesque show.

an appearance by the company soubrette (originally the saucy maid-servant in French comedy, the term later came to mean a woman who sang such parts), another comedy skit, a third chorus, some vaudeville acrobats, and a choral finale with the entire company, reprising the earlier numbers. A similar but shorter mix followed the intermission. This would remain the structure of Minsky shows for the next two decades.

Nor was such entertainment limited to the East Coast. Burlesque prospered at such houses as the Mutual Theater in Indianapolis, the Star and Garter in Chicago, and the Burbank Theatre in Los Angeles. The Columbia Amusement Company, under the leadership of medicine-show veteran Sam Scribner, operated a circuit called the Eastern Wheel whose chief rival, the Empire Circuit or Western Wheel, it absorbed in 1913. Scribner managed to balance business instinct and a personal goal of creating a cleaner act, and for a time the Columbia Wheel offered what it called "approved" burlesque while competing with upstart organizations (such as the short-lived Progressive Wheel) with its own subsidiary circuit called the American Wheel, whose "standard" burlesque featured cooch dancers, comic patter laced

with double-entendre, and runways for the chorus line extending from the stage out into the audience (an innovation first imported to the Winter Garden by Abe Minsky, who had seen it in Paris at the Folies Bergère). The American Wheel offered 73 acts a year, playing to a total audience of about 700,000 in 81 theaters from New York to Omaha.

Though Scribner's quest for clean burlesque ultimately proved quixotic, he was neither hypocritical nor alone. The founding editor of *Variety,* Sime Silverman, took burlesque shows seriously as an art form, though he too recognized that this was an uphill fight at best, writing in a 1909 editorial that "Were there no women in burlesque, how many men would attend? The answer is the basic principle of the burlesque business." (*Billboard*'s Sidney Wire concurred, flatly asserting in 1913 that "Ninety percent of the burlesque audiences go to burlesque to see the girls.") This fact was not lost on the Mutual Circuit, which arose to put Columbia Entertainment out of business in the 1920s, nor on the Minskys, whose theaters flourished until the final crackdown on New York burlesque under Mayor Fiorello LaGuardia and License Commissioner Paul Moss in 1937.

Although the leggy chorus line was an indispensable element of burlesque shows from the start (and would survive them by a half-century with the perennial Rockettes at Radio City Music Hall) the cooch dance became a burlesque standard only after promoter Abe Fish brought Little Egypt and Her Dancers, a troupe of Syrians specializing in the sexually suggestive ''awalem'' dances performed at Syrian weddings, to the World's Columbian Exposition at Chicago in 1893. The transition from cooch dancer to striptease was gradual. Soubrettes in the earliest days of burlesque often showed off their youthful bodies even as they sang and danced in solo numbers, but some, like Rose Sydell of the Columbia Wheel, were star clotheshorses instead, displaying breathtakingly elaborate costumes on stage.

Still, as the public responded favorably to more flesh and less clothing as the years wore on, the soubrette's song-and-dance role came to be supplanted by the striptease artist. By 1932, according to Zeidman, there were ''at least 150 strip principals, of whom about 75 percent were new to the industry.'' The sudden rise in demand for strippers was partly a corollary of rising hemlines on the street, so that, as one writer for *Billboard* pointed out, ''leg shows lost their sex appeal and, in self-defense, the operators of burlesque shows introduced the strutting strips . . . as far as the police permitted.'' (Ironically it was one police raid in 1934, at the Irving Palace Theatre, that eliminated runways in New York, somewhat to the relief of theater owners, for whom they were ill suited to the innuendo and soft lighting effects that were part and parcel of an effective strip act.)

Star strippers included Sally Rand, whose two-fan dance got a nod in the popular song ''I'm Like a Fish Out of Water,'' and Gypsy Rose Lee, who solved the jammed-zipper menace by holding her costume together with pins which she would remove one by one and throw to the audience. (Lee would go on to write a mystery novel, *The G-String Murders,* and an autobiography, *Gypsy,* also made into a movie). Other celebrated strippers included Anna Smith (said to have been the first to cross the line between above-the-waist nudity and baring her bottom), Carrie Finnell, Margie Hart, Evelyn Meyers, and Ann Corio.

By the late 1930s many burlesque shows had ceased to be much more than showcases for strippers. A burlesque troupe which would have had one soubrette and a half-dozen comics at the time of the World War I now often had at least five or six strippers and as few as two comics and a straight man. In New York, burlesque was effectively put out of business by LaGuardia and Moss by the end of 1937, although it survived in New Jersey for a few more years in theaters served by shuttle buses running from Times Square until its mostly-male audience was called off to war.

Though many performers from the burlesque circuits toured with the USO during World War II and the Korean conflict, burlesque itself barely survived into the postwar world, and most houses were closed for good by the mid-1950s. (Boston's Old Howard, vacant for several years, burned beyond repair in 1961.) In 1968 Ann Corio's book *This Was Burlesque* and Norman Lear's film *The Night They Raided Minsky's* were released, both nostalgic retrospectives on a vanished era.

Nevertheless, ''legitimate'' American entertainment, especially comedy, owed a lasting debt to burlesque throughout most of the twentieth century, for many of the nation's stars had either gotten their start or worked for some time in the genre, including Fannie Brice, Eddie Cantor, Lou Costello, Joey Faye, W. C. Fields, Jackie Gleason, Al Jolson, Bert Lahr, Pinky Lee, Phil Silvers, Red Skelton, and Sophie Tucker. Burlesque enriched America's vocabulary as

well, with such terms as bump and grind, flash, milking the audience, shimmy, and yock.

—Nick Humez

FURTHER READING:

Alexander, H. M. *Strip Tease: The Vanished Art of Burlesque.* New York, Knight Publishers, 1938.

Allen, Ralph G. *Best Burlesque Sketches.* New York, Applause Theatre Books, 1995.

Allen, Robert C. *Horrible Prettyness: Burlesque and American Culture.* Chapel Hill, University of North Carolina Press, 1991.

Corio, Ann. *This Was Burlesque.* New York, Grosset and Dunlap, 1968.

Lear, Norman, producer. *The Night They Raided Minsky's.* Culver City, MGM-UA Home Video, 1990.

Lee, Gypsy Rose. *The G-String Murders.* New York, Simon and Schuster, 1941.

———. *Gypsy/Gypsy Rose Lee.* London, Futura, 1988.

Minsky, Morton. *Minsky's Burlesque.* New York, Arbor House, 1986.

Scott, David Alexander. *Behind the G-String: An Exploration of the Stripper's Image, Her Person, and Her Meaning.* Jefferson, McFarland and Company, 1996.

Smith, H. Allen. *Low Man on a Totem Pole.* Garden City, Doubleday, Doran & Company, 1941.

Sobel, Bernard. *Burleycue: An Underground History.* New York, Farrar & Rinehart, 1931.

Zeidman, Irving. *The American Burlesque Show.* New York, Hawthorn Books, 1967.

Burma-Shave

From 1925 to 1963, a brushless shaving cream called Burma-Shave became a ubiquitous and much-loved part of the American scene—not because of the product itself, but because of the roadside signs that advertised it in the form of humorous poems. Motorists in 43 states enjoyed slowing down to read six signs spelling out the latest jingle, always culminating in the Burma-Shave trademark. A typical example might be ''PITY ALL / THE MIGHTY CAESARS / THEY PULLED / EACH WHISKER OUT / WITH TWEEZERS / BURMA SHAVE.'' The inspiration of Burma-Vita, a family-owned business in Minneapolis, the signs caught the public fancy with their refreshing ''soft sell'' approach. The uniqueness of the venue was another plus, and in time the Burma company took to offering jingles that promoted highway safety and similar public services—still finishing off, however, with that sixth Burma-Shave sign. Even the public itself was eventually invited to help create the jingles. The Burma-Shave phenomenon was a public relations technique without precedent, and its popularity was reflected in everything from radio comedy sketches to greeting cards. Though long gone, the Burma-Shave signs remain a fondly recalled memory of American life in the mid-twentieth century.

In the early 1920s, the Odell family of Minneapolis, Minnesota, marketed, albeit without much success, a salve which, because key ingredients came from Burma, they called Burma-Vita. The next product that they developed was a refinement of brushless shaving cream, which they naturally dubbed Burma-Shave. The Shave wasn't selling much better than the Vita when family member Allan Odell happened to notice a series of roadside signs advertising a gas station—''GAS,'' ''OIL,'' ''RESTROOMS,'' etc.—and he had a brainstorm. ''Every time I see one of these setups,'' he thought, ''I read every one of the signs. So why can't you sell a product that way?'' In the autumn of 1925, the Odells drove their first experimental signposts into the soon-to-be-freezing soil along the side of two roads outside Minneapolis. These first serial messages were neither humorous nor poetic—but they worked. For the first time, the Odells started receiving repeat orders from druggists whose customers traveled those two highways.

As their business started thriving, the Odells began to develop the pithy, light-hearted, rhyming jingles for which Burma-Shave quickly became famous. Hitherto, advertising orthodoxy had stipulated that most ad-copy should be verbose and serious. Obviously, verbosity was out of the question when the medium was a series of roadside signs instead of a magazine page. And the Odells preferred not to browbeat their potential customers while they were enjoying a drive in the country. The result was such refreshingly unpretentious verse as the following: ''DOES YOUR HUSBAND / MISBEHAVE / GRUNT AND GRUMBLE / RANT AND RAVE / SHOOT THE BRUTE SOME / BURMA-SHAVE.'' Or: ''THE ANSWER TO / A MAIDEN'S / PRAYER / IS NOT A CHIN / OF STUBBY HAIR / BURMA-SHAVE.'' It was discovered that the time it took a driver to go from one sign to the next afforded him more seconds to absorb the message than if he were reading an ad in a newspaper. What's more, as Alexander Woollcott pointed out, it was as difficult to read just one Burma-Shave sign as it was to eat one salted peanut. And the humorous content, so unlike the common run of dreary ad copy, further served to endear the signs to the driving public. Families would read them aloud, either in unison or with individual members taking turns.

Eventually the Burma-Shave jingles were as universally recognized as any facet of contemporary Americana. A rustic comedian could joke about his hometown being so small that it was located between two Burma-Shave signs. The signs themselves often figured in the radio sketches of such notable funnymen as Amos n' Andy, Fred Allen, Jimmy Durante, and Bob Hope. The popularity of the signs encouraged the Odells to devote a certain portion of their jingles each year to such public service causes as fire prevention and highway safety, as in: ''TRAIN APPROACHING / WHISTLE SQUEALING / PAUSE! / AVOID THAT / RUN-DOWN FEELING!'' Eventually, the public was brought into the act via heavily promoted contests that invited people to come up with their own jingles, many of which were bought and used. Often, the attention given the signs in the media amounted to free public relations and goodwill for the Burma-Shave company.

Ironically, one of the greatest instigators for free publicity was the company's announcement in 1963 that they would be phasing out the signs. Although this news was greeted by a wave of national nostalgia, the fact was that the Burma-Vita company—one of the last holdouts against corporate takeovers—had finally allowed itself to be absorbed into the Phillip Morris conglomerate, and they could no longer justify the expense of the signs in light of the decreasing return on its advertising investment. It was simply a different world than the one in which the Burma-Shave signs had been born, and it was time to retire them gracefully. While it lasted, their fame had seemed all pervasive. As one 1942 jingle put it: ''IF YOU / DON'T KNOW / WHOSE SIGNS / THESE ARE / YOU CAN'T HAVE / DRIVEN VERY FAR / BURMA-SHAVE.'' That the mythos of Burma-Shave

has outlasted the physical reality of the signs is evidenced in the fact that they are still being parodied and imitated to this day—and, whenever this is done, people still get the joke.

—Preston Neal Jones

FURTHER READING:

Rowsome, Frank. *The Verse by the Side of the Road: The Story of the Burma-Shave Signs and Jingles.* New York and Brattleboro, Vermont, Stephen Greene Press, 1965.

Vossler, Bill. *Burma-Shave: The Rhymes, The Signs, The Times.* St. Cloud, Minnesota, North Star Press, 1997.

Burnett, Carol (1933—)

One of the best-loved comedians of the twentieth century, Carol Burnett set the standard for the variety shows of the 1960s and 1970s. *The Carol Burnett Show* (1967-1979) offered a blend of music and comedy and showcased the popular stars of the period. The highlight of the show for many, however, was the opening when Burnett

A scene from *The Carol Burnett Show.*

answered questions from her audience. A number of her characters have become legend, including the char lady, Eunice, Norma Desmond, and the gum-chewing, wise-cracking secretary. Perhaps the most memorable skit of the series took place when Burnett played Scarlet O'Hara to Harvey Korman's Rhett Butler. Decked out in her green velvet curtains, complete with rods, Carol Burnett demonstrated why she is the queen of comedy. The Eunice skits may have been closer to Burnett's own roots than any of the others, allowing her to laugh at the painful memory of growing up with alcoholic parents and being constantly torn by the constant bickering of her mother and the beloved grandmother who raised her. The role of Mama in the Eunice skits was played by Vicki Lawrence, who won her place on the Burnett show because of her resemblance to Burnett. After the show went off the air, Lawrence continued the role in *Mama's Family* (1983-90) and was occasionally visited by Burnett.

Carol Burnett was born on April 26, 1933, in San Antonio, Texas. Her parents left her with Nanny, her maternal grandmother, and moved to Hollywood, seeking success, which proved to be elusive. In her autobiography, *One More Time: A Memoir by Carol Burnett,* Burnett traces a history of poverty, disillusionment, and enduring love growing up in a family that could never seem to deal with reality. She talks of ''Murphy,'' a folding bed that was never folded, as if it were a player in the drama that made up her family life. Perhaps it was. It represented stability for her, since the bed frequently contained her grandmother, the most significant influence on her life. Upon graduating from high school, Burnett had few hopes of realizing her dream of attending UCLA to pursue an acting career, when an envelope containing $50 mysteriously showed up in her mail box. Years later when she wanted to move to New York to pursue a Broadway career, another benefactor loaned her $1000 with the stipulations that she pay it back in five years and that she help others who needed it. The move to New York was fortuitous for Burnett, allowing her to move both herself and her younger sister toward a more stable, affluent lifestyle.

Burnett married Don Soroyan, her college boyfriend, in 1955 while striving for success in New York. As her career blossomed, his did not, and they divorced in 1962. Burnett had achieved her dream of playing Broadway in 1959 with *Once Upon A Mattress,* but it was television that would prove to be her destiny. She began by winning guest shots on variety shows, such as *The Steve Allen Show* and *The Garry Moore Show.* Her big break came when she was invited to sing her comedic rendition of ''I Made A Fool of Myself Over John Foster Dulles'' on *The Ed Sullivan Show.* Dulles, of course was the sedate, acerbic Secretary of State at the time. When Garry Moore won a spot on the prime time roster, he invited Burnett to come along; she appeared regularly on his show from 1959 to 1962. She won an Emmy in 1962, and after that there was no stopping her. In 1963 she married producer Joe Hamilton, with whom she had three daughters: Carrie, an actress, Jodie, a businesswoman, and Erin, a homemaker and mom. Even though Burnett and Hamilton divorced, they remained close until his death.

Carol Burnett was never afraid to fight for what was important to her. As a young actress told to call agents and producers after she was ''in something,'' she put on her own show. As an established actress, she successfully sued the tabloid, *The National Enquirer,* for claiming she was drunk in public. As a mother, she publicly fought to rescue one of her daughters from drug addiction, and she generously shared her pain and frustration with others, trying to help those in similar situations or who were likely to be so. Burnett continues to battle for a number of charitable causes, including AIDS.

Despite her assured place in the field of comedy, Carol Burnett broke new ground with such dramatic roles as the mother of a slain soldier in television's *Friendly Fire* (1979). She won critical acclaim for her hilarious turn as Mrs. Hannigan in the movie version of *Annie* (1982). Thirty-five years after winning her first Emmy on *The Garry Moore Show,* Burnett won an Emmy for her portrayal of Jamie Buchman's mother in the popular television series, *Mad About You.* In 1998 Burnett returned to television playing opposite Walter Matthau in *The Marrying Fool.* After almost four decades in televison, Carol Burnett remains an integral part of the American psyche and an enduring memorial to television's ''Golden Years.''

—Elizabeth Purdy

FURTHER READING:

Burnett, Carol. *One More Time: A Memoir by Carol Burnett.* Thorndike, Maine, Thorndike Press, 1986.

Carpozi, George. *The Carol Burnett Story.* New York, Warner Books, 1975.

Burnett, Chester

See Howlin' Wolf

Burns, George (1896-1996), and Gracie Allen (1895-1964)

George Burns and Gracie Allen formed one of the most renowned husband and wife comedy teams in broadcasting throughout the 1930s, 1940s, and 1950s. The cigar-chomping Burns played straight man to Allen's linguistically subversive and enchantingly ditzy housewife in a variety of entertainment media for thirty-five years. After meeting in 1923 and performing their comedy routine on the vaudeville circuit and in a few movies, the team reached its professional peak in broadcasting, first on radio and then on television. Their *Burns and Allen Show* on CBS television from 1950 to 1958 proved particularly innovative as it contained sitcom plots that were bracketed by Burns's vaudeville-inspired omniscient narration and monologues. Their act seemed to be a caricature of their offstage marriage and working relationship, and the duo openly courted the conflation. After Allen died in 1964, Burns eventually continued his career on his own in films and on television specials, but he never quite got over losing Gracie. He lovingly incorporated his late wife in his performances and best-selling memoirs, as if encouraging Allen to remain his lifelong partner from beyond the grave.

Allen was, quite literally, born into show business. Her father, George Allen, was a song-and-dance man on the West Coast who, upon retirement, taught dance and gymnastics in a homemade gym in his backyard. The youngest daughter in the San Francisco-based Scottish/Irish family of six, Allen first appeared on stage at the age of three singing an Irish song for a benefit. Her older sisters became accomplished dancers and while on the vaudeville circuit would occasionally include Gracie in their act. Gracie's true gift however, lay not in song and dance, but in comedy. Recognizing this, she began to play the fool for her sisters and then as a ''Colleen'' in an Irish act.

George Burns and Gracie Allen.

Burns also started his career as a child performer. Following a fairly typical rags-to-riches story of a vaudevillian headliner, Burns (born Nathan Birnbaum) was the son of a poor Austrian Jewish family in New York's Lower East Side. As a small child he performed for pocket change on street corners and saloons in the neighborhood, eventually forming a child act, the Pee Wee Quartet, when he was seven years old. Working in small-time vaudeville by the time he was a teenager, the aspiring vaudevillian joined a number of comedy teams under various names including Harry Pierce, Willie Delight, Nat Burns, and finally, George Burns.

In 1923, Allen and Burns met in Union Hill, New Jersey, while both were looking for new partners. At the time, Allen was rooming with Mary Kelly (later to be known as Mary Livingstone), Jack Benny's girlfriend. Kelly introduced Allen to Burns, who had just split with his partner Billy Lorraine. Originally interested in becoming Lorraine's partner, Allen eventually agreed to try working with Burns. At first Allen played the straight part, but they quickly discovered that the audience laughed at Allen much more than Burns. "I knew right away there was a feeling of something between the audience and Gracie," said Burns in a 1968 interview. "They loved her, and so, not being a fool and wanting to smoke cigars for the rest of my life, I gave her the jokes." Working for many years as what was known in the business as a disappointment act—an on-call position for cancellations—they transformed a traditional "dumb Dora act" into something far more complicated.

After traveling around the country on the Keith-Orpheum circuit playing onstage lovers, Allen and Burns initiated their offstage relationship in 1925. Following a somewhat whirlwind courtship, the pair were married on January 7, 1926. Just as their romance had solidified into marriage, their act started to crystallize into two very distinct characters—one frustratingly obtuse and the other patently down-to-earth. Yet, there was an obvious intelligence behind the pair's verbal sparring. Burns, who wrote the majority of their material, called it "illogical logic"—an alternative linguistic universe in which the character of Gracie was the sole inhabitant. Their act went on to be highlighted in such films as *Fit to Be Tied* (1931) and *The Big Broadcast of 1932*. But, it was their variety-format radio program *The Adventures of Gracie* (later known as *Burns and Allen,* 1932-1950) that really won the hearts and minds of American audiences. Playing a young boyfriend and girlfriend for the program's first eight years, they eventually chose to place their characters within the domestic setting of a Beverly Hills home. This allowed them to introduce new material and base their characters on their own lives as a middle-aged married couple raising children in suburbia.

During their years on radio the press focused intently on their private lives, often trying to answer the question of whether or not Allen was as daffy as her onstage character. Articles in fan and women's magazines covered every detail of the entertainers' domestic life, including their friendship with fellow luminaries and neighbors the Bennys, as well as their adoption of two children, Sandra and Ronnie. Burns and Allen were exceptionally adept at using the media attention they received to extend the narrative of their program into the realm of "reality." Not only did they purposely muddy the distinction between their lives and that of their characters, but they also played on-air stunts to their maximum effect. For example, in 1933, Gracie began a protracted hunt for her "missing brother," a stunt concocted by a CBS executive to raise their ratings. This enabled her to acquire extra air by guest starring on Jack Benny's and Eddie Cantor's programs under the guise of continuing her search, and to attract attention from other media outlets. The press played right along, photographing her looking for her brother at New York landmarks and printing letters from fans claiming to have had sightings of him. George Allen, Gracie's real brother, was forced into hiding because of the incredible attention and pressure he felt from radio listeners and the press. In 1940 Allen topped her missing brother gag by announcing that she would run for president. Campaigning under the slogan "Down with common sense, vote for Gracie," the stunt, which was originally planned as a two-week, on-air gag, snowballed. The mayor of Omaha offered to host a national "surprise ticket party" convention for Allen, and the president of the Union Pacific Railroad gave her a presidential train to travel from Los Angeles to Omaha in a traditional "whistle stop" campaign.

By the time television became an option for the comedy duo in the late 1940s, Burns and Allen were among the most well-known and beloved comedians of their generation. Like most radio stars, they were initially reluctant to test the new medium. So, in an effort to avoid television's taxing weekly production schedule and propensity to devour material, they scheduled their live program *The Burns and Allen Show* to appear only every other Thursday. Although it contained many of the basic elements of their radio show, their television program's narrative structure and characterizations became more nuanced. Besides the few minutes of vaudeville routine that would end the show (including the now famous lines "Say goodnight, Gracie!"), Gracie and their neighbors would exist solely within the narrative world of their sitcom. Burns, however, crossed back and forth between the sitcom set and the edges of the stage from which it was broadcast. Talking directly to the camera and the studio audience,

Burns would comment on the plot or Gracie's wacky antics, introduce a song or dance act, or tell some jokes. He would then jump across the stage and enter into the plot in progress. Burns came up with this strategy as a way to link the show together—blending elements of the variety format with the domestic sitcom. Burns's technique was incredibly effective and helped the program last through television's tumultuous transition in the mid-1950s from the variety show to the sitcom, which killed off other once-popular variety programs such as *Texaco Star Theatre.*

In 1958, Allen said "Goodnight, Gracie" for the last time. By retiring from show business because of chronic heart problems, Allen forced the couple's run on television to a close. Burns tried to continue on television playing a television producer in *The George Burns Show,* but the program was canceled after only one season. He attempted to revive his television career after Allen's death in 1964 of a heart attack, but almost every program he starred in was short-lived. It wasn't until 1975, when Burns was given the co-starring role in *The Sunshine Boys* with Walter Matthau, that his career recuperated. He went on to make a few more films (including the *Oh God!* films), star in some television specials, and write several books. He never remarried and, despite the occasional jokes of his sexual prowess, remained in love with Gracie. Burns opened his 1988 memoir *Gracie: A Love Story* by saying, "For forty years my act consisted of one joke. And then she died." Burns passed away in 1996 at the age of one hundred, famous for his longevity and endless dedication to his wife, his friends, and his fans.

—Sue Murray

FURTHER READING:

Allen, Gracie, as told to Jane Kesner Morris. "Gracie Allen's Own Story: Inside Me." *Woman's Home Companion.* March 1953, 122.

Blythe, Cheryl, and Susan Sackett. *Say Goodnight Gracie! The Story of Burns and Allen.* New York, Dutton, 1986.

Burns, George. *Gracie: A Love Story.* New York, Putnam, 1988.

Burns, George, with Cynthia Hobart Lindsay. *I Love Her, That's Why!* New York, Simon and Schuster, 1955.

Burns, George, with David Fisher. *All My Best Friends.* New York, Putnam, 1989.

Wilde, Larry. *The Great Comedians Talk about Comedy.* New York, Citadel Press, 1968.

Burns, Ken (1953—)

Documentary filmmaker Ken Burns received Oscar nominations for two early works, *Brooklyn Bridge* (1981) and *The Statue of Liberty* (1986). But it was his miniseries *The Civil War* (1990) that brought new viewers to public television and to documentaries and made Burns the most recognizable documentary filmmaker of all time. The style of *The Civil War* merged period images with the voices of celebrities reading the diaries and letters of Civil War participants. Burns followed *The Civil War* with *Baseball* (1994) and *Lewis & Clark: The Journey of the Corps of Discovery* (1997).

—Christian L. Pyle

Burr, Raymond (1917-1993)

Like so many actors before and after him, Raymond Burr found one of those roles that he did so much to define, but which, at the same time, virtually defined him. His portrayal of a lawyer in the mystery television series *Perry Mason,* which ran from 1957 to 1966, and in 26 made-for-television movies, set firmly in the minds of the viewing public what a defense lawyer should look like, how he should behave, and how trials should transpire. Realistic or not, his success, his interaction with clients, suspects, the police, and the district attorney, established in people's imaginations a kind of folk hero. For many, "Perry Mason" became shorthand for lawyer, as Einstein means genius or Sherlock Holmes means detective. This compelling image held sway for years before the profession was subjected to so much negative scrutiny in real life and in the media. Yet, Burr, again like so many others, did not achieve overnight fame. His role as Perry Mason overshadowed decades of hard work in radio, the theater, and films, as well as his business and philanthropic successes and personal tragedies.

Raymond William Stacy Burr was born on May 21, 1917 in New Westminster, British Columbia, Canada. When he was six years old, his parents separated, and his mother took him and his siblings to Vallejo, California. His earliest taste of acting came in junior high school drama classes, followed by a theatrical tour in Canada in the summer of his twelfth year. As he grew up, he held a variety of jobs: in the Forestry Service, and as a store manager, traveling salesman, and teacher. He furthered his education in places as diverse as Chungking, China, Stanford, and the University of California, where he obtained degrees in English and Psychology. He also worked in radio, on and off the air, wrote plays for YMCA productions, and did more stagework in the United States, Canada, and Europe. While he was working as a singer in a small Parisian nightclub called Le Ruban Bleu, Burr had to return to the United States when Hitler invaded France.

In the early 1940s, he initiated a long association with the Pasadena Playhouse, to which he returned many times to oversee and participate in productions. After years of trying, he landed a few small roles in several Republic Studios movies, but returned to Europe in 1942. He married actress Annette Sutherland and had a son, Michael, in 1943. Leaving his son with his grandparents outside London while Annette fulfilled her contract with a touring company, Burr came back to the United States. In June 1943, Annette was killed while flying to England to pick up Michael and join her husband in America when her plane was shot down.

Burr remained in the United States, working in the theater, receiving good notices for his role in *Duke of Darkness,* and signing a contract with RKO Pictures in 1944. Weighing over 300 pounds, a problem he struggled with all his life, Burr was usually given roles as a vicious gangster or menacing villain. Late in the decade he was in various radio programs, including *Pat Novak for Hire* and *Dragnet* with Jack Webb. A brief marriage that ended in separation after six months in 1948, and divorce in 1952, was followed by the tragic death of his son from leukemia in 1953. His third wife died of cancer two years later. Despite the misfortunes in his personal life, the roles he was getting in radio, such as *Fort Laramie* in 1956, and in films, continued to improve. By the time *Perry Mason* appeared, he had been in *A Place in the Sun* (1951), as the district attorney, which played a part in his getting the role of Mason, Hitchcock's *Rear Window* (1954), and the cult classic *Godzilla* (1954). After years of being killed off in movies, dozens of times, according to biographer Ona L. Hill, he was about to experience a complete role reversal.

Ken Burns (right) at hearing on Capitol Hill.

The first of over eighty Perry Mason novels by Erle Stanley Gardner had been published in 1933. Ill served, Gardner felt, by earlier movie versions of his hero, and dissatisfied with a radio program which ran for twelve years, he was determined to have a strong hand in the television series. Burr auditioned for the part of the district attorney on the condition that he be allowed to try out for the lawyer as well. Reportedly, Gardner spotted him and declared that he was Perry Mason. The rest of the cast, Barbara Hale as his secretary Della Street, William Hopper as private eye Paul Drake, William Talman as the district attorney, and Ray Collins as Lt. Tragg, melded, with the crew, into a kind of family that Burr worked hard to maintain. In retrospect, it is difficult to imagine the program taking any other form: from its striking theme music to the core ensemble of actors to the courtroom dramatics. He also gave substance to the vaguely described character from the books, fighting unrelentingly for his clients, doing everything from his own investigating to bending the law and playing tricks in court to clear them and finger the guilty. In the words of Kelleher and Merrill in the *Perry Mason TV Show Book,* he was "part wizard, part snakeoil salesman."

One of the pieces of the formula was that Mason would never lose a case. One of the shows in which he temporarily "lost" generated thousands of letters of protest. When asked about his unblemished record, Burr told a fan, "But madam, you only see the cases I try on Saturday." Despite many ups and downs, including hassles between Gardner and the producer and scripts of varying quality, the show ran for 271 episodes. Though his acting received some early criticism, Burr eventually won Best Actor Emmys in 1959 and 1961. The program was criticized for casting the prosecutor as the villain, the police as inept, and the lawyer as a trickster, but most lawyers, along with Burr, felt that the shows like *Perry Mason* "opened people's eyes to the justice system," according to Collins' the *Best of Crime and Detective TV.* Burr developed an interest in law that resulted in his speaking before many legal groups and a long association with the McGeorge School of Law.

In March 1967, Burr reappeared on television as wheelchair-bound policeman Ironside in a pilot that led to a series the following September. Assembling a crime-solving team played by Don Galloway, Barbara Anderson, and Don Mitchell, Burr, gruff and irascible, led them until early 1975 and in 1993's *The Return of Ironside* movie. In 1976-77 he starred as an investigative reporter in *Kingston Confidential.* Major activities in the early 1980s included a featured role in five hours of the multipart *Centennial* and in *Godzilla '85.* He was associated with the Theater Department at Sonoma State University in 1982 and some programs at California Polytechnic State University. In December 1985, he reprised his most famous role in *Perry Mason Returns,* which led to a string of 25 more TV movies.

In spite of his busy career and many personal and medical problems, Burr still found time to become involved in various business projects and charitable works. In 1965, he purchased an island in Fuji, where he contributed substantially to improving living conditions and the local economy. He also grew and sold orchids there and in other places around the world, and had ventures in Portugal, the Azores, and Puerto Rico. He collected art, and for several years helped operate a number of art galleries. During the Korean War he visited the troops twelve times, and made ten "quiet" trips to Vietnam, usually choosing to stop at far-flung outposts. Though the latter were controversial, he insisted, according to Hill in *Raymond Burr*: "I supported the *men in Vietnam, not* the war." Besides financially supporting many relatives and friends over the years, he had over 25 foster and adopted children from all over the world, in many cases providing them with medical care and educational expenses. He was involved in numerous charitable organizations, including the Cerebral Palsy Association, B'nai B'rith, and CARE, and created his own foundation for philanthropic, educational, and literary causes.

Burr was a complex man. Kelleher and Merrill describe him this way: "Approachable to a point, yet almost regally formal. Quiet, but occasionally preachy. Irreverent yet a student of [religions]. Intensely serious, yet a notorious prankster . . . [and] generous to a fault." Unquestionably, he worked incessantly, often to the detriment of his health, seldom resting for long from a myriad of acting, business, and philanthropic projects. His diligence seems to have been as much a part of his personality as his generosity. It was in many ways emblematic of his life and character that, despite advanced cancer, he finished the last Perry Mason movie in the summer before he died on September 12, 1993.

—Stephen L. Thompson

FURTHER READING:

Bounds, J. Dennis. *Perry Mason: The Authorship and Reproduction of a Popular Hero.* Westport, Greenwood Press, 1993.

Collins, Max Allan, and John Javna. *The Best of Crime and Detective TV: Perry Mason to Hill Street Blues, The Rockford Files to Murder, She Wrote.* New York, Harmony Books, 1988.

Hill, Ona L. *Raymond Burr: A Film, Radio and Television Biography.* Jefferson, North Carolina, McFarland & Company, Inc., 1994.

Kelleher, Brian, and Diana Merrill. *Perry Mason TV Show Book.* New York, St. Martin's Press, 1987.

Riggs, Karen E. "The Case of the Mysterious Ritual: Murder Dramas and Older Women Viewers." *Critical Studies in Mass Communication.* Vol. 13, No. 4, 1996, 309-323.

Burroughs, Edgar Rice (1875-1950)

Perhaps best known as the creator of Tarzan the Apeman, Edgar Rice Burroughs did much to popularize science fiction and adventure fantasy during the first half of the twentieth century. When he turned to writing in his mid-thirties after a mediocre and varied business life, Burroughs met with quick success when his first publication, *Under the Moons of Mars,* was serialized in *All-Story* magazine in 1912.

Edgar Rice Burroughs

Noted for his fertile imagination, Burroughs created several imaginary societies for his popular adventure series: one set on Mars, one in the primitive world called Pellucidar located inside the earth, and another on Venus. His Tarzan series (started in 1918) was also set in an imaginary Africa, much to the dismay of some readers. The constant theme running through Burroughs' stories was a detailing of how alien or primitive societies inspired heroic qualities in characters. Typically Burroughs' stories depicted powerful men saving beautiful women from terrible villains. Besides Tarzan, Burroughs' most famous character was Virginian gentleman John Carter of his Mars series, who became the "greatest swordsman of two worlds." Though his plots were often predictable and his characters lacked depth, Burroughs successfully captured readers' interest in life-and-death struggles brought on by environmental impediments. His slapdash depictions of how primitive environments catalyze greatness in humans have continued to entertain readers and inspire more intricate science fiction writing.

—Sara Pendergast

FURTHER READING:

Holtsmark, Erling B. *Edgar Rice Burroughs.* Boston, Twayne Publishers, 1986.

Zeuschner, Robert B. *Edgar Rice Burroughs: The Exhaustive Scholar's and Collector's Descriptive Bibliography of American Periodical, Hardcover, Paperback, and Reprint Editions.* Jefferson, North Carolina, McFarland, 1996.

Burroughs, William S. (1914-1997)

During the 1950s, William S. Burroughs blazed many trails to and from the elucidation of human suffering, and his obsession with the means to this end became an enduring facet of popular culture. He exuded the heavy aura of a misogynistic, homosexual, drug-addicted gun nut, both in life and in print. Yet he inspired a generation of aimless youths to lift their heads out of the sands of academe, to question authority, to travel, and, most importantly, to intellectualize their personal experiences.

Born William Seward Burroughs February 5, 1914 in St. Louis, Missouri, he was the son of a wealthy family (his grandfather invented the Burroughs adding machine) and lived a quiet mid-Western childhood. He graduated from Harvard, but became fascinated with the criminal underworld of the 1930s and sought to emulate the gangster lifestyle, dealing in stolen goods and eventually morphine, to which he became addicted. He moved to Chicago for a time to support his habit, then to New York City where, in 1943, he met Jack Kerouac and Allen Ginsberg at Columbia University. He encouraged these younger hipster prodigies to write, and they were impressed by his dark wit and genteel poise wizened through years of hard living, though they rarely joined him in his escapades.

In 1947 Burroughs entered into a common law marriage to Joan Vollmer, a Benzedrine addict whom he had also met at Columbia. They moved to New Orleans where drugs were more easily obtainable, and later to Texas where they grew oranges and marijuana, raised two children (one was Bill's), and lived in drug-addled poverty. On the advice of a friend, Burroughs began work on a "memory exercise" which would become his first book—*Junky: Confessions of an Unredeemed Drug Addict*—published in 1953 under the pseudonym William Lee.

Then, on September 6, 1951, while in Mexico City on the run from the law, Bill shot and killed Joan, allegedly during their "William Tell routine." After a night of heavy drinking, Bill suggested she place a glass on her head, and he would shoot at it from across the room. "Why I did it, I do not know," he later claimed. "Something took over." His son went to live with his parents, but Burroughs was never prosecuted. Instead, he embarked upon a quest to exorcize what he called "The Ugly Spirit" which had compelled his lifestyle choices and now convinced him he "had no choice but to write my way out."

Burroughs fled to South America in search of the mystical drug *yage*, and wrote *The Yage Letters* (1963) to Allen Ginsberg. Soon Bill was back in New York City, still addicted and on the run, and eventually ended up in The International Zone of Tangier, Morocco. He, however, hallucinated "Interzone," an allegorical city in which "Bill Lee" was the victim, observer, and primary instigator of heinous crimes against all humanity. He began "reporting" from this Interzone—a psychotic battleground of political, paranoid intrigue whose denizens purveyed deceit and humiliation, controlling addicts of sex, drugs, and power in a crumbling society spiritually malnourished and bloated on excess.

When Kerouac and Ginsberg came to Tangier in 1957, they found Burroughs coming in and out of the throes of withdrawal. He had been sending them "reports," reams of hand-written notes which they helped to compile into Burroughs' jarring magnum opus *Naked Lunch* (1959), a work he "scarcely remembers writing." This novel's blistering satire of post-World War II, pre-television consumer culture, and its stark presentation of tormented lost souls, were the talk of

William S. Burroughs

the burgeoning beatnik scene in the States, as were its obscene caricatures and "routines" that bled from a stream of junk-sick consciousness.

Burroughs was soon regarded as the Godfather of the Beat Generation, a demographic that came of age during World War II while Bill was out looking for dope, and which aimed to plumb the depths of existence in post-modern America. Mainstream appeal would prove elusive to these writers, though, until *Naked Lunch* became the focus of a censorship trial in 1965. The proceedings drew attention—and testimony—from such literati as Norman Mailer, John Ciardi, and Allen Ginsberg, whose reputation had grown as well. After the furor died down, *Naked Lunch* remained largely an underground hit. Burroughs also stayed out of sight, though he published *The Soft Machine* (1961), *The Ticket That Exploded* (1962), and *Nova Express* (1964) using an editing technique with which he had been experimenting in Tangier and called "cut-ups": the random physical manipulation of preconceived words and phrases into coherent juxtapositions.

In the 1970s, Burroughs holed up in his New York City "bunker" as his writing became the subtext for his gnarled old junky image. Though he had been an inspiration to authors, he found himself rubbing elbows with post-literate celebrity artistes yearning for the Ugly Spirit. Later, Burroughs enjoyed a spate of speaking tours and cameos in films. He also published books revisiting the themes of his early routines, and in 1983 was inducted into the American Academy and Institute of Arts and Letters. He later recorded and performed with John Giorno Poetry Systems, Laurie Anderson, Material, the Disposable Heroes of Hiphoprisy, and Kurt Cobain of Nirvana, among others. In the 1990s his face and silhouette, as well as his unmistakable thin, rattling voice quoting himself out of context, were used to promote everything from running shoes to personal computers. He spent most of his last years in seclusion in Lawrence, Kansas, where he died August 2, 1997.

Burroughs' influence on popular culture is evident in every medium, though he is more often referred to than read. From subversive comedic diatribes on oppressive government to the gritty realism of crime drama, from the drug chic youth culture enjoys (and has enjoyed since the early 1960s) to paranoia over past, present, and future drug wars, Burroughs made hip, literate cynicism both popular and culpable.

—Tony Brewer

FURTHER READING:

Caveney, Graham. *Gentleman Junkie: The Life and Legacy of William S. Burroughs*. Canada, Little Brown, 1998

Miles, Barry. *William Burroughs: El Hombrè Invisible: A Portrait.* New York, Hyperion, 1993.

Morgan, Ted. *Literary Outlaw: A Life of William S. Burroughs*. New York, Holt, 1988.

Buster Brown

Buster Brown first appeared in the *New York Herald* on May 4, 1902. Accompanied by his dog Tige, Buster Brown was a mischievous young boy given to playing practical jokes. He resolved weekly to improve his ways, but always strayed. The strip was the second major success for Richard Outcault (1863-1928) who had earlier created the Yellow Kid. Outcault licensed the image and the name of his character to a wide variety of manufactures and the name Buster Brown is probably more familiar to Americans as a brand of shoes or children's clothing than as the title of a comic strip. Unlike Outcault's early work *Buster Brown* was distinctly a comic strip appearing weekly in twelve panel full page stories. Once again William Randolph Hearst lured Outcault to his newspapers and *Buster Brown* commencing there January 21, 1906. The resulting court cases over copyright determined that Outcault owned all subsidiary rights to the Buster Brown name having purchased them for $2 when he signed with the *Herald* to produce the strip. Outcault derived considerable income from his licensing efforts and his advertising agency, which produced over 10,000 advertisements for Buster Brown related products. The last original episode of the strip was published December 11, 1921.

—Ian Gordon

FURTHER READING:

Gordon, Ian. *Comic Strips and Consumer Culture, 1890-1945*. Washington, D.C., Smithsonian Institution Press, 1998.

Butch Cassidy and the Sundance Kid

This 1969 film, the first deconstructionist Western, set the tone for future buddy comedies, helped revive the Western film genre, and made a superstar out of Robert Redford, whose Sundance Institute has become the major supporter of independent films. Also starring Paul Newman as Butch and Katherine Ross as Etta Place, and directed by George Roy Hill, this lighthearted, ''contemporary'' Western paved the way for modern Westerns such as *Young Guns* and *The Long Riders.*

Butch Cassidy and the Sundance Kid was based on the lives of two actual Old West outlaws—Robert Leroy Parker (Butch) and Harry Longabaugh (Sundance). By the 1890s, Butch was the head of the largest and most successful outlaw gang in the West, known as both the Wild Bunch and the Hole-in-the-Wall Gang. Butch was chosen leader based solely on his personality; he was a poor shot who never killed anyone until later in life. Sundance, who got his nickname from spending eighteen months in jail in Sundance, Wyoming, was a gang member and a phenomenal gunman who, incidentally, did not know how to swim (a fact yielding the film's best joke). Based at their hideout at Hole-in-the-Wall near Kaycee, Wyoming, the gang members robbed banks and trains throughout the West. When the railroads hired the Pinkerton Agency to catch the gang and the agency formed a relentless superposse, Butch, Sundance, and female companion Etta Place moved to South America and bought a ranch in Argentina. They tried to make an honest living but eventually began robbing banks in several South American countries. It is believed they were killed after being trapped by troops in Bolivia—although some maintain that Butch and Sundance spread the story after another pair of outlaws was gunned down by Bolivian troops.

Screenwriter William Goldman first came across the Butch Cassidy story in the late 1950s, and he researched it on and off for the next eight years. An established novelist, Goldman decided to turn the story into a screenplay for the simple reason ''I don't like horses.'' He didn't like anything dealing with the realities of the Old West. A screenplay would be simpler to write and wouldn't involve all the research necessary to write a believable Western novel. From the outset, this screenplay established itself as more contemporary than the typical Western or buddy film. In the film, Butch and Sundance do what typical Western movie heroes never do, such as run away halfway through the story or kick a rival gang member in the groin rather than fight with knives or guns. While there had been buddy films in the past, including those starring Abbott and Costello, and Bob Hope and Bing Crosby, those films were joke factories, variations on old vaudeville routines. Part of the challenge for Goldman was to write dialogue that was funny without being too funny; nonstop jokes abruptly interrupted by a hail of gunfire would be too great a transition to expect an audience to make. Goldman found the right tone, a kind of glib professionalism emphasizing chemistry over jokes, and it is the chemistry between Newman and Redford that made the film such a success.

This glib professional tone since has been put to good use in a number of other films and television shows, as in the *48 Hours* and *Lethal Weapon* films. *Butch Cassidy and the Sundance Kid* also led to the sequel, *Wanted: The Sundance Woman,* and the prequel, *Butch and Sundance—The Early Years;* and Newman and Redford successfully teamed up again for *The Sting* (1973).

—Bob Sullivan

Robert Redford (left) and Paul Newman in a scene from the film *Butch Cassidy and the Sundance Kid.*

FURTHER READING:

Goldman, William. *Adventures in the Screen Trade.* New York, Warner Books, 1983.

———. *Four Screenplays with Essays.* New York, Applause Books, 1995.

Wukovits, John. *Butch Cassidy.* New York, Chelsea House Publishing, 1997.

Butkus, Dick (1942—)

If a Hollywood scriptwriter were authoring a football movie and needed to conjure up an ideal name for a hard-nosed middle linebacker who breakfasted on nails and quarterbacks, he could do no better than Dick Butkus. Not only was Butkus, who played in the National Football League between 1965 and 1972, the dominant middle linebacker of his era, but he singlehandedly redefined the position. What made him extra-special was his well-earned reputation for being one of the toughest and most feared and revered players ever to play the game. Butkus also brought a high level of intelligence and emotion to the playing field, which only embellished his physical talents.

If the stereotypical quarterback is a pretty boy who comes of age in a sun-drenched Southern California suburb, Butkus' background fits that of the archetypal dirt-in-your-fingernails linebacker or tackle: he grew up on Chicago's South Side, as the ninth child in a blue-collar Lithuanian family. He attended the University of Illinois, where he won All-America honors in 1963 and 1964; in the latter year, he was a Heisman Trophy runner-up. In 1965, the 6'3", 245-pounder was a first-round draft pick of the Chicago Bears. During his nine-year career with the Bears, which ended prematurely in 1973 due to a serious knee injury, Butkus had 22 interceptions, was All-NFL for seven years, and played in eight Pro Bowls.

On the football field he was all seriousness, and a picture of non-stop energy and intensity. Butkus would do whatever was necessary to not just tackle an opponent but earn and maintain everlasting respect. He was noted for his ability to bottle up his anger between Sundays, and free that pent-up fury on the playing field. Occasionally, however, he was not completely successful in this endeavor, resulting in some legendary alcohol-soaked escapades involving his pals and teammates along with tiffs with sportswriters and in-the-trenches

Dick Butkus

haggling with Bears owner-coach George Halas. Of special note is his long-standing feud with Dan Jenkins of *Sports Illustrated,* who wrote a piece in which he labeled Butkus "A Special Kind of Brute with a Love of Violence."

After retiring from the Bears, Butkus became a football analyst on CBS's *NFL Today* and went on to a career as a television and film actor. He would win no Oscar nominations for his performances in *Hamburger. . . The Motion Picture, Necessary Roughness* and *Gremlins 2: The New Batch,* and no Emmy citations for *My Two Dads, The Stepford Children, Superdome* and *Half Nelson.* But his grid credentials remain impeccable. Butkus entered the Football Hall of Fame in 1979, and is described in his biographical data as an "exceptional defensive star with speed, quickness, instinct, strength . . . great leader, tremendous competitor, adept at forcing fumbles. . . . People [still] should be talking about the way Dick Butkus played the game," noted broadcaster and ex-NFL kicker Pat Summerall, over a quarter century after Butkus' retirement. Along with fellow linebackers Ted Hendricks, Willie Lanier, Ray Nitschke, Jack Hamm, Jack Lambert, and Lawrence Taylor, he was named to NFL's 75th Anniversary Team.

Ever since 1985, the Dick Butkus Award has been presented to the top collegiate linebacker. Herein lies Butkus' gridiron legacy. To the generations of football players in the know who have come in his wake—and, in particular, to all rough-and-tumble wannabe defensive

standouts—Dick Butkus is a role model, an icon, and a prototypical gridiron jock.

—Rob Edelman

FURTHER READING:

Butkus, Dick, and Pat Smith. *Butkus; Flesh and Blood: How I Played the Game,* New York, Doubleday, 1997.

Butkus, Dick, and Robert W. Billings. *Stop-Action.* New York, Dutton, 1972.

Butler, Octavia E. (1947—)

As the premier black female science fiction writer, Octavia E. Butler has received both critical and popular acclaim. She describes herself as "a pessimist if I'm not careful, a feminist, a Black, a former Baptist, an oil-and-water combination of ambition, laziness, insecurity, certainty and drive." Butler's stories cross the breadth of human experience, taking readers through time, space, and the inner workings of the body and mind. She frequently disrupts accepted notions of race, gender, sex, and power by rearranging the operations of the human body, mind, or senses. Ironically, her significance has been largely ignored by academics. Her notable books include *Kindred, Wild Seed, Mind of My Mind, Dawn* and *Parable of the Sower.* She has won the coveted Hugo and Nebula awards for "Speech Sounds" and "Bloodchild," and in 1995 was awarded a MacArthur "Genius" grant for pushing the boundaries of science fiction.

—Andrew Spieldenner

FURTHER READING:

Salvaggio, Ruth. *Octavia Butler.* Mercer Island, Washington, Starmont House, 1986.

Butterbeans and Susie

The married couple Jodie (1895-1967) and Susie Edwards (1896-1963), performing as Butterbeans and Susie, were among the most popular African American musical comedy acts of the mid-twentieth century. From 1917 until Susie's death in 1963, they toured regularly. Their act featured double entendre songs, ludicrous costuming, domestic comedy sketches, and Butterbeans' famous "Heebie Jeebie" dance. Racial segregation shaped their career in important ways—their recordings were marketed as "Race" records, and at their peak they played primarily in segregated venues. Their broad humor exploited racial stereotypes in a manner reminiscent of minstrel shows. Yet within the world of African American show business such strategies were common, and clearly Butterbeans and Susie's antics delighted African American audiences. Butterbeans and Susie achieved success by working with dominant racial images within the discriminatory racial structures of America.

—Thomas J. Mertz

FURTHER READING:

Sampson, Henry T. *Blacks in Blackface: A Source Book on Early Black Musical Shows.* Metuchen, New Jersey, The Scarecrow Press Inc., 1980.

Buttons, Red (1919—)

In 1952, *The Red Buttons Show* was widely acclaimed as the most promising new show on television, and its star was featured on the cover of *Time* Magazine. Millions of children did their versions of Buttons's theme song, hopping and singing ''Ho! Ho!, He! He!, Ha! Ha! . . . Strange things are happening.'' Indeed, strange things did happen. By the end of the second season the show's popularity had declined and CBS dropped it. It did no better when NBC briefly picked up the show the following season. Buttons was out of work in 1957 when he was selected to play the role of Sergeant Joe Kelly in the film *Sayonara*. He won an Academy Award as best supporting actor for this tragic portrayal and went on to appear in 24 other movies.

Born Aaron Chwatt in the Bronx borough of New York City in 1919 and raised on the Lower East Side of Manhattan, he was the son of an immigrant milliner. He contracted the show business bug when he won first place in an amateur-night contest at age 12. By age 16 he was entertaining in a Bronx tavern as the bellboy-singer, and the manager, noting his bright-colored uniform, gave him the stage name

Red Buttons

of Red Buttons. Adding stand-up comedy to his talents, Buttons worked in Catskill Mountain resorts and later joined a burlesque troupe as a baggy-pants comic.

Buttons made his Broadway debut in 1942, playing a supporting role in a show called *Vickie*. When he was drafted for World War II service in the army, he was assigned to special services as an entertainer. He appeared in the stage and film productions of *Winged Victory,* a patriotic show designed to encourage the purchase of war bonds.

When CBS offered a contract in 1952 for *The Red Buttons Show,* a broad experience in show business had prepared Buttons well. He had already developed some of his most popular characters—a punchy boxer named Rocky Buttons, a lovable little boy named the Kupke Kid, a hapless, bungling German named Keeglefarven, and the jinxed, luckless Sad Sack. He also did husband-and-wife sketches with Dorothy Joiliffe (later with Beverly Dennis and Betty Ann Grove) in a style to be emulated by George Gobel in the late 1950s.

When the show moved to NBC, it started as a variety show, but the format was soon changed to a situation comedy. Buttons played himself as a television comic who was prone to get into all kinds of trouble. Phyllis Kirk, later to become a star in Broadway musicals, played his wife; Bobby Sherwood was his pal and television director, and newcomer Paul Lynde played a young network vice president who had continual disputes with the star. Dozens of writers worked on the show at various times, but nothing seemed to click, and it was scratched after one season.

After his Tony Award success with the movie *Sayonara,* Buttons's Hollywood career took off. Appearing in *Imitation General, The Big Circus,* and *One Two Three* led in 1961 to a role in that year's Hollywood blockbuster, the film portrayal of the World War II invasion of Normandy, *The Longest Day.* Buttons is remembered for his portrayal of a lovable, sad sack paratrooper whose parachute is impaled on a church steeple in a small French town, leaving him hanging while the camera recorded his animated facial expressions.

He is also remembered for his comic role in the 1966 remake of *Stagecoach,* starring Bing Crosby and Ann Margaret. He received an Academy Award nomination for best supporting actor in 1969 for *They Shoot Horses, Don't They?* This was a grim tale about a marathon dance contest during the Great Depression. He was also featured in the 1972 underwater disaster saga, *The Poseidon Adventure.*

Frequent guest spots on television talk shows and the continuation of his film career as a both a comic and serious character actor until 1990 kept Buttons before the public. He had an extended and important career in show business, but some remember that on the networks he was never able to fulfill the exalted promise of his first show in its first season.

—Benjamin Griffith

FURTHER READING:

Brooks, Tim, and Earle Marsh. *The Complete Directory to Prime Time Network TV Shows: 1946 to Present.* New York, Ballantine, 1981.

Inman, David. *The TV Encyclopedia.* New York, Perigee, 1991.

McNeil, Alex. *Total Television: A Comprehensive Guide to Programming from 1948 to the Present.* New York, Penguin, 1991.

The Byrds

The Byrds began as a folk-rock band in 1965 led by Jim McGuinn (later renamed Roger following his conversion to Subud). The harmonies arranged by David Crosby and McGuinn's electric twelve-string guitar gave them a rich, fresh sound. Often described as the American Beatles, The Byrds were nevertheless distinctly original. On their first two albums, *Mr. Tambourine Man* and *Turn! Turn! Turn!* (1965), they covered Bob Dylan and traditional folk songs, and wrote their own material. On "Eight Miles High" (1966) McGuinn exhibited the influence of Indian ragas and the improvisational style of John Coltrane. The Byrds explored a psychedelic sound on *Fifth Dimension* (1966) and *Younger than Yesterday* (1967). They continued in the folk/psychedelic style on *The Notorious Byrd Brothers* (1968), but Crosby left halfway through the recording of this album, later forming Crosby, Stills, and Nash. The Byrds' next album,

Sweetheart of the Rodeo (1968), detoured into country-western. Throughout the next five albums, the band suffered numerous personnel changes. McGuinn remained the only original member, but somehow the newcomers persuaded him to continue recording country music and The Byrds abandoned their exploratory spirit. They disbanded in 1973. Today The Byrds are remembered for the classics of their folk and psychedelic period, some of which were immortalized in the film *Easy Rider* (1969).

—Douglas Cooke

FURTHER READING:

Fricke, David. Liner notes for *The Byrds*. New York, Columbia Records, 1990.

Rogan, Johnny. *Timeless Flight: The Definitive Biography of the Byrds*. London, Scorpion Publications, 1981.

C

Cabbage Patch Kids

The Cabbage Patch Kids doll-craze was an unprecedented phenomenon among children and their parents that swept America during the 1980s, reflecting, perhaps, the cultural leanings of an era intent on expressing family values. By comparison with the Cabbage Patch collecting mania, later collectors of the mass-marketed Beanie Babies, Tamogotchis, and Tickle Me Elmos in the 1990s had it easy.

The 16-inch, soft-bodied Cabbage Patch dolls, the ultimate "must have" toy, were in such high demand during the 1983 Christmas season that the $25 retail Kids were "adopted" on the black market for fees as high as $2,000. Toy manufacturer Coleco Industries never expected that their homely, one-of-a-kind Kids—complete with birth certificates and adoption papers—would be the impetus behind department-store stampedes across the country, resulting in sales of over six million dolls during their first nine months on the market.

Xavier Roberts, a dollmaker in Columbus, Georgia, began "adopting" his Little People—soft-sculpture, handmade Cabbage Patch prototypes—out of Babyland General Hospital in 1979. Roberts' gimmicks—from adoption papers and pledges, to hiring "doctors" and "nurses" to deliver dolls from Babyland's indoor Cabbage Patch every few minutes to the delight of visitors—won his company,

A Cabbage Patch Kid complete with birth certificate.

Original Appalachian Artworks, a licensing deal with Coleco in late 1982. By the late 1980s, Roberts' hand-signed Little People were worth up to 60 times their original $75-200 cost. When Coleco filed for bankruptcy in May 1988, Mattel (one of the manufacturers who had passed on licensing rights to the dolls in 1982) took over the Cabbage Patch license.

The mythos that Roberts created for his Cabbage Patch Kids—born from a cabbage patch, stork-delivered, and happy to be placed with whatever family would take them—encouraged the active participation of parents and children alike, and fostered strong faith in the power of fantasy, but the American public's reaction to the dolls was anything but imaginary. By virtue of their homely, one-of-a-kind identities, and the solemnity with which buyers were swearing to adoption pledges (due in no small part to the dolls' scarcity), Cabbage Patch Kids became arguably the most humanized playthings in toy history: some "parents" brought their dolls to restaurants, high chair and all, or paid babysitters to watch them, just as they would have done for real children.

The psychological and social effects of the Kids of the Cabbage Patch world were mixed. Adoption agencies and support groups were divided over the advantages and disadvantages that the dolls offered their "parents." On one hand, they complained that the yarn-haired dolls both desensitized the agony that parents feel in giving children up for adoption, and objectified adoptees as commodities acquired as easily as one purchases a cabbage. On the other hand, psychologists such as Joyce Brothers argued that the dolls helped children and adults alike to understand that we do not have to be attractive in order to be loved. The dolls, proponents argued, helped erase the stigma that many adopted children were feeling before the Kids came along.

When before Cabbage Patch Kids did American mass-market toy consumers demand one-of-a-kind, personalized playthings? Who since Xavier Roberts has been at once father, creator, publicist, and CEO of his own Little "Family"? Cabbage Patch Kids' popularity hinged on a few fundamental characteristics: a supercomputer that ensured that no two Kids had the same hair/eye/freckle/name combination, Roberts' autograph of authenticity stamped on each Cabbage tush, an extended universe of over 200 Cabbage-licensed products, and the sad truth that there were never enough of them to go around.

—Daryna M. McKeand

FURTHER READING:

Hoffman, William. *Fantasy: The Incredible Cabbage Patch Phenomenon.* Dallas, Taylor Publishing, 1984.

Sheets, Kenneth R., and Pamela Sherrid. "From Cabbage to Briar Patch." *U.S. News and World Report.* July 25, 1988, 48.

Cable TV

Considering the fact that in the late 1990s many experts view existing television cables as the technological groundwork for what may be the most important and far reaching media innovations since the printing press, the origins of cable television are quite humble. In the early 1950s millions of Americans were beginning to regularly tune in their television sets. However, a large number of Americans in rural areas were not able to get any reception. Just as these folks wanted TV, so too did television companies want them, for the more people that watched, the more money the networks (ABC, CBS, and NBC) and their advertisers made. Hence, the advent of community antennae television (CATV), commonly known as ''cable TV,'' a system in which television station signals are picked up by elevated antennas and delivered by cables to home receivers. By the late 1990s the majority of American households were cable subscribers. Because of cable's rise to prominence, the ways in which Americans are entertained have been irrevocably transformed. Furthermore, many people think that in the twenty-first century new innovations utilizing cable technology will lead to revolutionary changes in the ways in which Americans live their daily lives.

In the early years of cable many saw it as an additional venue through which to offer more viewing choices to consumers. But for the most part, in the 1950s and 1960s the Federal Communications Commission (FCC) was reluctant to grant licenses to cable operators, ostensibly due to fear of putting the mostly local UHF stations out of business. It is likely, however, that pressure on the FCC from the networks, who didn't want additional competition, also played a role in the FCC's reluctance to grant licenses to cable operators. While there was some optimism about the possibilities for cable TV in the early 1950s, in the early 1960s the progress of cable television was slowed to a near standstill by a series of court cases. At issue was whether or not the FCC had control over cable broadcasts, which were transmitted through cables rather than airwaves. Cable companies were literally pirating the broadcasts of local stations, which legitimately threatened their existence. Although the cable industry won some early cases, heavy pressure from the networks resulted in the FCC declaring itself as having jurisdiction over cable broadcasts. Cable companies fought the ruling, but the courts upheld it. The FCC established prohibitive regulations that severely limited cable TV's growth potential, thus protecting the financial interests of local stations and, more importantly, the networks.

However, in 1972 the FCC finally began allowing satellite transmissions to be used by cable TV operators, which resulted in the beginning of the cable revolution when a small Time Warner subsidiary named Home Box Office (HBO) transmitted the motion picture *Sometimes a Great Notion* over a cable system in Wilkes-Barre, Pennsylvania. Although it would be three years before HBO became a national presence, that first transmission altered forever the shape of American television by paving the way for commercial cable service, which first became widely available to consumers in 1976. Early cable customers generally had to have a satellite dish in order to pick up the signals. The dish provided a better picture than traditional TV, as well as a greater number of stations, but it proved to be cost prohibitive to too many customers for it to be financially successful. Cable providers quickly adapted and created a system in which a cable could be attached to just about anyone's TV, provided one lived in an area where cable TV was available. Providers soon realized that most people would willingly pay a monthly fee for better reception and more channels. Public demand for cable TV grew so fast that companies could barely keep up with demand. In 1972 there were only 2,841 cable systems nationwide. By 1995 that number had grown to 11,215. Concurrently, the percentage of households subscribing to cable service jumped from 16.6 percent in 1977 to nearly 70 percent in 1998.

By the mid-1970s the commercial possibilities of cable became apparent. The problem for cable operators was how to attract an audience to their channels when the networks were already free and in nearly every home in America. Conversely, the networks could see that cable would only become more prevalent. The question for them was how could they get in on the cable bonanza. The solution was both ingeniously simple and immensely profitable. The networks agreed to sell their old shows to the cable networks, who would in turn run them endlessly; thus was born the concept of ''syndication.'' For a while this arrangement worked quite well. The networks, on the basis of their original programming, continued to dominate the market, especially during the lucrative 8 PM to 11 PM time slot known as ''Prime Time'' because of the amount of people (consumers) that watch during those hours. The cable networks were able to enjoy profitability because even though they paid exorbitant franchise fees for the rights to broadcast the networks' old shows, they didn't have to invest in costly production facilities.

As a result of this arrangement between networks and cable operators, an interesting thing happened among the American populace. Whereas previous generations of TV viewers were generally only aware of the TV shows that originated during the lifetime, beginning in the late 1970s Americans became TV literate in a way they had never been before. Americans who came of age after the rise of cable soon became generally conversant in all eras of television programming. Fifteen year olds became just as capable of discussing the nuances of *The Honeymooners, I Love Lucy,* and *Star Trek* as they were the shows of their own era. Partly because of cable, television trivia has become shared intelligence in America; however, this shared cultural knowledge is not necessarily a good thing, for it has, for many, been learned in lieu of a more traditional and useful humanistic and/or scientific education. Accordingly, in the late 1990s Americans are collectively more uninformed about the world in which they live than at any other time in the twentieth century, which can be attributed at least in part to the fact that most Americans spend much more time watching TV than they do reading all forms of printed media combined. Cable was originally thought to have great potential as an educational tool. But even though there are a few cable networks that educate as well as entertain, for the most part cable stations are just as subservient to advertising dollars as their network counterparts. As a result, advertising dollars play a large role in dictating the direction of cable programming, just as they do on network television.

For a number of years cable networks were content to run a combination of old network programming, a mix of relatively new and old Hollywood movies, and occasional pay-per-view events such as concerts and sporting events. The first cable network to gain a national foothold was Ted Turner's TBS ''Superstation,'' which ran a format similar to that of the networks, sans original programming. But by the early 1980s it became clear to most cable operators that in order to achieve the financial success they desired cable channels were going to have to come up with their own programming. Thus was born the greatest period of television programming innovation seen to that point. Since their ascent to television dominance in the early 1950s, the networks attempted to appeal to as a wide a general audience as possible. The cable networks correctly assumed that they couldn't compete with the networks by going after the same type of broad audience. Instead, they followed the example set by radio after the rise of television in the early 1950s: they developed specific subject formats that mixed syndicated and original programming and attracted demographically particular target audiences for their advertisers.

Americans quickly had access to an unprecedented quantity of television stations; unfortunately, in most cases television's quality did not rise concurrently.

Nevertheless, many of the resulting stations have contributed significantly to the direction of American popular culture. The herald of cable TV's importance to popular culture was a channel known as Music Television, or MTV. Started in 1981, its rise to success was as meteoric as it was astonishing. For American youth MTV became their network, the network that provided the soundtrack for the trials and tribulations of youths everywhere. Michael Jackson and Madonna's status as cultural icons would not be so entrenched were it not for their deft use of MTV as a medium for their videos. Beavis and Butthead would have never caused such a ruckus among concerned parents were it not for MTV. And the music industry, which was flagging in the early 1980s, might not have survived were it not for MTV, which was a virtual non-stop advertisement for recording artists. Neither the ''grunge'' revolution started in the early 1990s by the incessant playing of Nirvana's ''Smells Like Teen Spirit'' video nor the ensuing gangster rap, hip hop, and swing movements would have occurred were it not for MTV. The trademark jump cutting found in MTV videos has crossed over to become common place in network television and Hollywood movies. But perhaps the most important realization was for advertisers, who suddenly had unlimited access to a youthful audience never before thought to be a viable consumer market. MTV's audience specific success opened the floodgates for the cable channels that followed.

Among the many cable channels that have made their mark on American culture are the themed channels such as ESPN and ESPN 2, Court TV, C-SPAN, The Weather Channel, Comedy Central, Black Entertainment Television, The Animal Channel, Lifetime, Arts & Entertainment, and the Food Channel. In addition, seemingly countless news channels have followed on the heels of Ted Turner's Cable News Network (CNN), which made its debut in 1980. There are also a number of shopping channels, on which companies can not only hawk their products, but sell them directly to the people as well. For advertisers, cable has greatly increased access to the American buying public, which has resulted in immense profits.

And yet, despite its inarguably providing countless and diverse contributions to popular culture, ranging from the wall to wall televising of O.J. Simpson's murder trial and President Clinton's impeachment to a mainstream venue for *South Park, The Simpsons,* and endless wrestling events, many find it difficult to characterize cable's overall contribution to American culture as positive. Clearly television is an incredible medium for entertainment and advertising, but as William F. Baker and George Dessart argue in *Down the Tube: An Inside Account of the Failure of American Television,* that it should be used almost exclusively for such purposes is a tragedy. Regrettably, television's potential as an educational tool has never been realized. For every Ken Burns documentary there are a hundred episodes of *The Jerry Springer Show.* As a result, the rise of cable has only increased the size of the vast wasteland that is television.

After the success of so many cable stations, the networks realized they were missing out on the financial gold mine. They profited from the sale of their shows to cable networks, but the real money came from ownership. However, it was illegal for a network to own a cable system. But in 1992 the FCC dropped this regulation; the networks could now own cable systems. What followed was literally a feeding frenzy, as the networks both battled with each other to buy existing cable networks and scrambled to start their own. What resulted was the illusion of even greater choice for the American

viewing public. Although there were way more channels, there weren't appreciably more owners due to the fact that the networks quickly owned many of the cable systems. Despite their claims to the contrary, in actuality, in the late 1990s the networks controlled television almost as much as they always had.

In 1992 Vice President Al Gore began singing the praises of ''the information superhighway,'' a synthesis of education, goods, and services to be delivered through American televisions via existing cable systems. Cable has always offered the possibility of two-way communications. With the proper devices, Americans could send out information through their cables as well as receive it. The technology was not new, but its implementation was. Although at the time Gore was considered by many to be a futuristic dreamer, industry insiders quickly saw that two-way, or ''interactive,'' TV could be the wave of the future. By incorporating interactive technology, cable TV could transform American TVs into incredible machines capable of being a TV, a computer, a superstore, a stereo, a library, a school, a telephone, a post office, a burglar alarm, and a fire alarm all at once. However, a relatively obscure computer network known as the ''internet'' already utilized two way phone lines to provide its users with interactive ability. The phone companies saw the internet's potential and beat cable TV to the punch. By the late 1990s the internet was in as many as half of all American homes and businesses. But phone lines aren't as effective at transferring information as cables. Fortunately for the phone companies, FCC deregulation in the early 1990s made it possible for them to own cable networks as well. Whether we want it or not, it is just a matter of time before interactivity comes to American televisions. But, judging by how fast and pervasively the once free form internet became commercialized, it is hard to say whether interactive TVs will change lives for the better or just intensify the already oppressive amount of advertising to which Americans are constantly subjected.

In addition to the networks and phone companies buying cable networks, in the early 1990s other corporations began purchasing the networks and phone companies. The reign of independent cable mavericks such as Ted Turner gave way to a new age of corporate cable barons. By the late 1990s cable and network television was largely controlled by a half dozen massive media conglomerates, one of which is Rupert Murdoch's News Corp., which owns countless companies, including Twentieth Century Fox studios, the Los Angeles Dodgers, and Fox Television. The money making possibilities for corporations like Murdoch's are virtually endless. For example, Fox TV not only features new episodes of its own original shows, such as *The X Files* and *The Simpsons,* it also runs them endlessly once they're syndicated. The L.A. Dodgers frequently appear on Fox's Major League Baseball broadcasts. And Twentieth Century Fox feature films routinely make their television debuts on Fox TV. All of these activities result in profits for the parent company, Fox News Corp. Furthermore, corporate ownership can threaten what integrity TV has, as evidenced in the summer of 1998 when Disney, which owns ABC, reportedly killed a negative ABC Nightly News story about how Disney World's lack of background checks resulted in their hiring criminals. Although the ownership of television was largely in the hands of relatively few monopolies, in the late 1990s there was growing public and government rumblings about the increasing ''conglomeratization'' of America, which led to the backlash and subsequent anti-trust case against Bill Gates's Microsoft

Corporation. But as of 1999 cable television's many channels are in the hands of a few and, despite appearances, Americans' TV options remain quite limited.

As James Roman writes in *Love, Light, and a Dream: Television's Past, Present, and Future,* the pioneers of cable television "could never have realized the implications their actions would come to have on the regulatory, economic, and technological aspects of modern communications in the United States." In 1999 cable television is America's dominant entertainment and information medium, and, due to the fact that 70 percent of Americans subscribe to some form of cable TV, will remain so for the foreseeable future. For cable subscribers, the future is approaching at breakneck speed. Without consulting the public, the conglomerates have already made their decisions concerning the direction of cable TV; in only a few short years fully interactive television will almost certainly become a reality and American life, for better or worse, will likely experience changes in ways not yet imagined. And what about the 30 percent of those for whom cable, either for financial or geographical reasons, is not an option? Will they be able to compete in an increasingly interactive world or will they be permanently left behind? Will the advent of interactive TV create yet another social group, the technologically disadvantaged, for whom a piece of the pie is not a realistic aspiration? Is it at all possible that the people who have cable will defy all prognostications and not embrace the new technologies that will purportedly change their lives for the better? As of 1999 these remain unanswerable questions but it is likely that the direction of American popular culture in the early twenty-first century will be dictated by their outcome.

—Robert C. Sickels

FURTHER READING:

Baker, William F., and George Dessart. *Down the Tube: An Inside Account of the Failure of American Television.* New York, Basic Books, 1998.

Baldwin, Thomas F., D. Stevens McVoy, and Charles Steinfield. *Convergence: Integrating Media, Information & Communication.* Thousand Oaks, California, Sage Publications, 1996.

Baughman, James L. *The Republic of Mass Culture: Journalism, Filmmaking, and Broadcasting in America since 1941.* Baltimore, The Johns Hopkins University Press, 1992.

Bray, John. *The Communications Miracle: The Telecommunication Pioneers from Morse to the Information Superhighway.* New York, Plenum Press, 1995.

Davis, L. J. *The Billionaire Shell Game: How Cable Baron John Malone and Assorted Corporate Titans Invented a Future Nobody Wanted.* New York, Doubleday, 1998.

Dizard, Wilson, Jr. *Old Media New Media: Mass Communications in the Information Age.* White Plains, New York, Longman Press, 1994.

Frantzich, Stephen, and John Sullivan. *The C-Span Revolution.* Norman, University of Oklahoma Press, 1996.

Roman, James. *Love, Light, and a Dream: Television's Past, Present, and Future.* Westport, Connecticut, Praeger Publishers, 1996.

Whittemore, Hank. *CNN: The Inside Story.* Boston, Little, Brown, 1990.

Cadillac

For several decades of the twentieth century, the Cadillac, a car made by General Motors' luxury automobile division, was the most enduring symbol of middle-class achievement for status-conscious Americans. Nowhere is the past and somewhat faded glory of the Cadillac sedan more visible than in the affluent suburbs of Detroit, where silver-haired retired automotive-industry executives and their elegantly-coiffed wives, each stylized living relics of another era, can still be seen tooling around in dark-hued Sevilles, while in other such enclaves of prosperity across America, luxury cars from Germany and Japan have long dominated this demographic.

The most popular luxury carmaker in the United States began its history in 1902 in Detroit as one of the many new, independent automobile companies in town. Founded by Henry Leland, who gave it the name of the seventeenth-century French explorer who had founded Detroit, Cadillac earned a devoted following with a reputable and technologically innovative engine. Absorbed into the General Motors family in 1909, the carmaker enhanced its reputation over the years by numerous engineering achievements. For instance, Cadillac was the first car company to successfully use interchangeable parts that fit into the same model and did not require costly hand-tooling. In 1912, a new Cadillac was introduced with the Delco electric ignition and lighting system. The powerful V-8 engine was also a Cadillac first, and its in-house advertising director (the man who later founded the D'Arcy MacManus agency), began using the advertising slogan "Standard of the World." Another print ad, titled "The Penalty of Leadership," made advertising history by never once mentioning Cadillac by name, a master stroke of subtlety.

Harley Earl, the legendary automotive designer, began giving Cadillacs their elegant, kinetic look in the 1920s. He is credited with introducing the first tailfin on the new designs in the late 1940s, inspired in part by the fighter planes of World War II. A decade later, nearly all American cars sported them, but Cadillac's fins were always the grandest. Purists despised them as style gimmicks, but the public adored them. In the postwar economic boom of the 1950s the Cadillac came to be viewed as the ultimate symbol of success in America. They were among some of the most costly and weightiest cars ever made for the consumer market: some models weighed in at over 5,000 pounds and boasted such deluxe accoutrements as imported leather seats, state-of-the-art climate and stereo systems, and consumer-pleasing gadgets like power windows. The brand also began to take hold in popular culture: Chuck Berry sang of besting one in a race in his 1955 hit "Maybellene," and Elvis Presley began driving a pink Caddy not long after his first few chart successes.

Cadillac's hold on the status-car market began to wane in the 1960s when both Lincoln and Chrysler began making inroads with their models. Mismanagement by GM engendered further decline. Cadillac production reached 266,000 cars in 1969, one of its peak years. That model year's popular Coupe DeVille (with a wheelbase of over ten feet) sold for $5,721; by contrast the best-selling Chevrolet, the Impala, had a sticker price of $3,465. There were media-generated rumors that people sometimes pooled their funds in order to buy a Cadillac to share. In the 1970s, the brand became indelibly linked with the urban American criminal element, the ride of choice for pimps and mob bosses alike. Furthermore, more affluent American car buyers began preferring Mercedes-Benz imports, and sales of

The 1931 Cadillac

such German sedans (BMW and Audi also grew in popularity) began to eclipse Cadillac. The car itself "became the costume of the *nouveau-riche*—or the *arrivistes,* rather than those who enjoyed established positions of wealth," wrote Peter Marsh and Peter Collett in *Driving Passion: The Psychology of the Car.* "People who are busy clambering up the social ladder still imagine that those at the top share their reverence for Cadillacs."

Combined with the spiraling away of the brand's cachet, the periodic Middle East oil crises of the decade made "gas guzzlers" such as the heavy V-8 Cadillacs both expensive and unfashionable. Furthermore, mired in posh executive comfort and unable to respond to the market, Detroit auto executives failed to direct the company toward designing and making smaller, more fuel-efficient luxury cars. Engineering flaws often plagued the few such models that were introduced by Cadillac—the Seville, Cimarron, and Allante—and gradually the brand itself began to be perceived as a lemon. GM allowed Cadillac to reorganize in the early 1980s, and the company somewhat successfully returned to the big-car market by the mid-1980s, but by then had met with a new host of competition in the field—the new luxury nameplates from the Japanese automakers, Acura, Lexus, and Infinity.

Still, the Caddy remains a symbol of a particularly American style and era, now vanished. When U.S. President Richard Nixon visited the Soviet Union in May of 1972, he presented Premier Leonid Brezhnev with a Cadillac Eldorado, which the Communist leader reportedly very much enjoyed driving around Moscow by himself. The Cadillac Ranch, outside of Amarillo, Texas, is a peculiarly American art-installation testament to the make: it consists of vintage Caddies partially buried in the Texas earth, front-end down.

—Carol Brennan

FURTHER READING:

Editors of *Automobile Quarterly* Magazine. *General Motors: The First 75 Years of Transportation Products.* Princeton, New Jersey, Automobile Quarterly Magazine and Detroit, General Motors Corporation, 1983.

Esquire's American Autos and Their Makers. New York, Esquire, 1963.

Jorgensen, Janice, editor. *Encyclopedia of Consumer Brands, Volume 3: Durable Goods.* Detroit, St. James Press, 1994.

Langworth, Richard M., and the editors of *Consumer Guide. Encyclopedia of American Cars, 1940-1970.* Skokie, Illinois, Publications International, 1980.

Marsh, Peter, and Peter Collett. *Driving Passion: The Psychology of the Car.* Boston, Faber, 1986.

Caesar, Sid (1922—)

Sid Caesar was one of the most familiar and talented television performers of the 1950s. His skills as a dialectician, pantomime, and monologist made him a favorite of the critics and a fixture on Saturday night television from 1950 to 1954. Along with co-star Imogene Coca and a writing staff that included Carl Reiner, Mel Brooks, Larry Gelbart, and a young Woody Allen, Caesar captivated the new television audience with film parodies, characterizations, and sitcom-style sketches on NBC's *Your Show of Shows*. Caesar was also infamous for his dark side, an apparent byproduct of his comedic brilliance. A large man, carrying up to 240 pounds on his six-foot-one-inch frame, articles in the popular press described his eating and drinking habits as excessive and his mood as mercurial. In an age when many top comedy television performers suffered physical and mental breakdowns from the exacting demands of live television production, Caesar stood out as a damaged man prone to self-destruction and addiction. He was one of the first broadcast stars to talk openly about his experiences in psychotherapy.

Surprisingly, Caesar did not begin his career in entertainment as a comedian, but rather as a saxophonist. Brought up in Yonkers, New York, by European Jewish immigrant parents, as a child Caesar

Sid Caesar and Imogene Coca

developed his abilities as a dialectician by mimicking the voices of the Italian, Russian, and Polish émigrés who patronized his parents' restaurant. But it was the customer who left behind an old saxophone in the restaurant who had the most direct impact on Caesar's career as an entertainer. The young Caesar picked up the instrument and over the years became an accomplished musician. After graduating from high school, Caesar moved to Manhattan, played in various orchestras, and took summer work at Jewish hotels in the Catskills (commonly known as the "borscht belt"). Although contracted as a musician, he began to appear in the hotel program's comedy acts as a straight man and was so successful that he eventually decided to emphasize his comedic skills over his musical talent.

Theatrical producer Max Liebman, who worked with Caesar on revues in the Catskills and Florida, was central to Caesar's entry into the nascent medium of television. After years performing on stage, in nightclubs, and in the Coast Guard recruiting show "Tars and Spars" (later made into a Hollywood film), the budding comedian was paired with Imogene Coca in Liebman's production "Admiral Broadway Revue." At Liebman's prodding, NBC President Pat Weaver saw the show, and he signed the entire cast and staff to do a television version of their production under the same title. But the program's sponsor, Admiral, a major manufacturer of television sets, found the program too expensive for its limited advertising budget. Weaver encouraged Liebman to give television another try, using most of his original cast and staff for a ninety-minute Saturday night program eventually titled *Your Show of Shows*. Premiering in February of 1950 and following on the heels of shows such as *Texaco Star Theatre, Your Show of Shows* was conceived as a fairly straightforward vaudeville-style variety program. However, with its talented cast and writing staff, the show developed into more than just slapstick routines, acrobatic acts, and musical numbers. Although ethnic jokes, borscht-belt-style monologues, and sight gags were considered central to the success of early variety programs, Caesar proved that these basics could be incorporated into a highly nuanced and culturally rich program that would appeal to popular and high culture tastes simultaneously. His film parodies and array of characters such as jazz musician Progress Hornsby, the German Professor, and storyteller Somerset Winterset became the most popular and memorable aspects of the show.

As a result of his unique talents, critics began to call Caesar television's Charlie Chaplin, and one usually tough critic, John Crosby of the *New York Herald Tribune,* considered the comedian "one of the wonders of the modern electronic age." Yet, despite such ardent admiration, Caesar could not quiet the insecurities that had plagued him since childhood. Known for his overindulgence of both food and alcohol, it was said that Caesar would finish off a fifth or more of Scotch daily. In an attempt to control his addiction, doctors prescribed sedatives. However, the "cure" fueled the drinking habit as Caesar took his medication with his daily dose of alcohol. This combination intensified his bouts with depression and worsened the quick temper that often revealed itself on the set or in writing meetings.

The season after *Your Show of Shows* ended its run in 1954, Caesar immediately returned to television with *Caesar's Hour* on Monday nights on NBC. Although many of his problems were well-known in the industry and by his fans, in 1956 he spoke on the record about his emotional issues and subsequent entry into psychoanalysis in an article in *Look* magazine. Claiming that analysis had cured him of his depression and addiction, Caesar blamed his psychological state on the emotional neglect of his parents during childhood. He revealed that "On stage, I could hide behind the characters and inanimate objects I created. Off stage, with my real personality for all to see, I was a mess . . . I couldn't believe that anyone could like me for myself."

Despite his public proclamation of being cured, Caesar continued to suffer. After his second television program was taken off the air in 1957 because it no longer could compete against ABC's *The Lawrence Welk Show,* the comedian's mental and physical health declined even further. Although he returned to television a few more times during his career, he was never quite the same. During the 1960s and 1970s he appeared in bit roles in movies such as *Grease, History of the World, Part I,* and *It's a Mad, Mad, Mad, Mad World,* but he spent most of his time in isolation grappling with his problems. It wasn't until 1978 that he had completed his recovery. In his seventies he continued to nurture a small but respectable movie career in *The Great Man Swap* and *Vegas Vacation,* but he remained best known as one of the most intelligent and provocative innovators of television comedy.

—Susan Murray

FURTHER READING:

Adair, Karen. *The Great Clowns of American Television.* New York, McFarland, 1988.

Caesar, Sid. *Where Have I Been? An Autobiography.* New York, Crown Publishers, 1982.

Caesar, Sid, as told to Richard Gehman. "What Psychoanalysis Did for Me." *Look.* October 2, 1956, pp. 49, 51-52.

Davidson, Bill. "Hail Sid Caesar!" *Colliers.* November 11, 1950, pp. 25, 50.

Cagney and Lacey

The arrival of *Cagney and Lacey* in 1982 broke new and significant ground in television's ever-increasing proliferation of popular cop series in that the stars were women—a pair of undercover detectives out there with New York's finest, unafraid to walk into the threat of violence, or to use a gun when necessary. Effectively, writers Barney Rosenzweig, Barbara Avedon and Barbara Corday offered audiences a female *Starsky and Hutch,* cleverly adapting the nuances of male partner-and-buddy bonding to suit their heroines. Although jam-packed with precinct life and crime action, the series was character driven, with careful attention given to the private lives of the two detectives, sharply contrasted for maximum interest in both the writing and the casting. Mary Beth Lacey, dark-haired, New York Italian working-class, combined her career with married life and the struggle to raise her children; Christine Cagney, more sophisticated, more ambitious, single, blonde, and very attractive, struggled with a drinking problem. The relationships between them and their male colleagues were beautifully and realistically brought to life by Tyne Daly and Sharon Gless, respectively. Gless was a late addition, brought in to counter criticisms that the show was too harsh and

Sharon Gless (left) and Tyne Daly in a scene from the television movie *Cagney and Lacey: The Return.*

unfeminine: Loretta Swit had played Cagney in the pilot, followed by Meg Foster in the short first series, which failed to find favor in its depiction of women in so unglamorous a context. However, with Gless in tow, the show's treatment of female solidarity and hard-hitting issues won the CBS show a huge popular following, and lasted for seven seasons until 1988.

—Nickianne Moody

FURTHER READING:

Fiske, John. "*Cagney and Lacey*: Reading Character Structurally and Politically." *Communication.* Vol. 9, No. 3/4, 1987, 399-426.

Cagney, James (1899-1986)

One of the greatest tough-guy personas of twentieth-century film, James Cagney worked hard to refine his image to meet his responsible Catholic background. The result was a complex set of characters who ranged from the hard-working immigrant striving to make his way in America, to the American hero of Cold War times who fought to preserve our way of life against Communist infiltrators. Cagney's various personas culminated in one as different from the others as can be imagined—he began to play characters on the edge of (in)sanity. It is his image as a tough guy, however, that is most enduring.

In 1933, during the filming of *Lady-Killer,* Darryl F. Zanuck sent a memo to his crew of writers in which he detailed the studio's requirements for the Cagney persona: "He has got to be tough, fresh, hard-boiled, bragging—he knows everything, everybody is wrong but him—everything is easy to him—he can do everything and yet it

James Cagney in a scene from the film *White Heat*.

is a likeable trait in his personality.'' During the 1930s, Cagney's uptempo acting style—the rat-a-tat-tat of his reedy voice—and his distinctly Irish-puck appearance, created a decidedly lower-East side aura. He was a city boy.

Cagney was born in New York City on July 17, 1899. Although studio publicity promoted stories about a tough east-side upbringing and life above a saloon, Cagney was, in fact, raised in the modest middle-class neighborhood of Yorkville. Two of his brothers became doctors. On screen, however, Cagney played tough guys—characters who were immigrants fighting to fit in identified.

Public Enemy, Cagney's first starring role, remains famous for an enduring still of Cagney, with lips pursed, hair awry, and eyes enraged, smashing a grapefruit in Mae Clarke's face. But it was Tom Powers' contempt for assimilation that alarmed educators and reformers. In 1932, armed with the Payne Fund Studies, a group of reformers feared that immigrant youths over identified with certain screen stars and surrendered their parents' values for falsely ''Americanized'' ones. In his popularization of the Payne report, Henry James Forman echoed these fears when he identified one second-generation

Italian youth's praise for Cagney: ''I eat it. You get some ideas from his acting. You learn how to pull off a job, how he bumps off a guy and a lot of things.''

Because of the uproar from reformers and the ascendancy of President Roosevelt and his accompanying call for collective action, Warner Brothers shifted their image of Cagney. He no longer embodied lost world losers but common men fighting to make it in America. And Cagney's image of fighting to make it spoke to New York's immigrants (Italians, Jews, Poles, Slavs), who in 1930 comprised 54.1 percent of New York City's households. From 1932-39 (a period in which he made 25 films), Cagney represented an ethnic in-between. As an Irish-American, he was an icon for immigrants because he represented a complex simultaneity—he was both a part of and apart from Anglo-Saxon society. In a series of vehicles, Cagney was the outlaw figure, a character who did not want to conform to the dictates of the collective, and yet, through the love of a WASPish woman or the demands of the authoritative Pat O'Brien (the Irish cop figure in *Here Comes the Navy* [1934] and *Devil Dogs of the Air* [1935]) Cagney harnessed his energies to communal good.

Regardless of how Cagney's image was read by immigrants, sociologists, and reformers, he was not happy with how he perceived Zanuck and the Warner Brothers' script writers had structured his persona. A devout Catholic and a shy, soft-spoken man off-screen, he was tired of roughing up women and playing street punks on screen. Three times (1932, 1934, 1936) he walked off the studio lot to protest his typecasting. In March 1936, Cagney won a breech of contract suit against Warner Brothers, and later that year signed with Grand National where he filmed *Great Guy* (1936) and *Something to Sing About* (1937). Unfortunately, neither effort changed his persona, and with Grand National falling into receivership, Cagney returned to Warner Brothers.

To enhance Cagney's return, Warner Brothers immediately teamed him with old pal and co-star Pat O'Brien in *Angels With Dirty Faces* (1938). As Rocky Sullivan, Cagney received an Academy Award nomination and the New York Critics Award for best actor. The film's most memorable scene features Cagney's death-row walk in which his ''performance'' switches the Dead End Kids' allegiances from one father figure (Cagney) to another (O'Brien). It is an explosive moment of ambiguity in which a character destroys his reputation for the audience in the film (the Kids) but gains, through his sacrifice, saintliness from the audience in the theater (largely immigrant).

By the 1940s, Cagney's image had radically changed under the pressures of the Martin Dies' ''Communist'' innuendoes. With war raging in Europe the competing images in Cagney's persona (the anarchic individual at odds with the collective; the Irish-American trying to make it in WASP—White Anglo-Saxon Protestant—society) were transformed into a homogenized pro-United States figure. The plight of the immigrant was replaced by Warner Brothers' all-American front to the Axis. *Yankee Doodle Dandy* (1942) culminated the change as Cagney was galvanized into a singing, dancing super-patriot. Cagney won an Academy Award for this dynamic performance.

Following a second try at independence (United Artists, 1943-48), the post-World War II Cagney struggled to maintain a contemporary persona. Much of his New York City audience had grown up and moved to the suburbs. Too old and lace-curtain Irish to remain an ethnic in-between, the post-war Cagney bifurcated into two types: a strong-willed patriarch or a completely insane figure who needed to be destroyed. *White Heat* mirrored the switch in emphasis. No longer was Cody Jarret fighting to realize the immigrant dream; instead he fought a mother complex.

On March 18, 1974 more than 50 million Americans watched Cagney accept the American Film Institute's second annual life-time achievement award. Although he had fought Zanuck, Wallis, and the studio's construction of his ''tough, fresh, hard-boiled'' image, he embraced it during the tribute. In his acceptance speech Cagney thanked the tough city boys of his past: ''they were all part of a very stimulating early environment, which produced that unmistakable touch of the gutter without which this evening might never have happened.'' James Cagney died on Easter Sunday, 1986.

—Grant Tracey

FURTHER READING:

Forman, Henry James. *Our Movie Made Children.* New York, MacMillan, 1933.

Kirstein, Lincoln (as Forrest Clark). ''James Cagney.'' *New Theater.* December, 1935, 15-16, 34.

McGilligan, Patrick. *Cagney: The Actor as Auteur.* San Diego, A.S. Barnes, 1982.

Naremore, James. *Acting for the Cinema.* Berkeley, University of California Press, 1988.

Sklar, Robert. *City Boys: Cagney, Bogart, Garfield.* New Jersey, Princeton University Press, 1992.

Tynan, Ken. ''Cagney and the Mob.'' *Sight and Sound.* May, 1951, 12-16.

Cahan, Abraham (1860-1951)

The flowering of Jewish-American fiction in the 1950s and 1960s had its origin in the pioneering work of Abraham Cahan: immigrant, socialist, journalist, and fiction writer. With William Dean Howells' assistance, Cahan published *Yekl: A Tale of the New York Ghetto* (1896) and *The Imported Bridegroom* (1898). But it is *The Rise of David Levinsky* (1917) that is his masterwork. Using Howells's *Rise of Silas Lapham* as his model, Cahan explores an entire industry (ready-made clothing) and immigrant experience (Eastern European Jews) by focusing on a single character and his bittersweet ascent from Russian rags to Manhattan riches. A major work of American literary realism, *The Rise of David Levinsky* is also an example of reform-minded Progessivism and began as a series of sketches in *McClure's Magazine* alongside the work of muckrakers Upton Sinclair and Ida Tarbell. Although he is best remembered for this one novel (rediscovered in 1960 thanks to the popularity of a later generation of postwar Jewish-American writers), Cahan's most influential act was the founding of the world's leading Yiddish newspaper, the *Jewish Daily Forward,* in 1902.

—Robert A. Morace

FURTHER READING:

Chametsky, Jules. *From the Ghetto: The Fiction of Abraham Cahan.* Amherst, University of Massachusetts Press, 1977.

Marowitz, Sanford E. *Abraham Cahan.* New York, Twayne, 1996.

Cakewalks

An elegant and stately dance created by African slaves on Caribbean and North American plantations, the cakewalk enjoyed a long history. During slavery, plantation owners judged the dance and the finest dancer was rewarded with a cake. It became the first African-American dance to become popular among whites. The cakewalk was features in several contexts including the minstrel show finale, early black musicals including *Clorindy, or The Origin of the Cakewalk* in 1898 and *The Creole Show* in 1899, and on ballroom floors thereafter. The cakewalk embodied an erect body with a quasi-shuffling movement that developed into a smooth walking step.

—Willie Collins

FURTHER READING:

Cohen, Selma Jeanne, ed. *International Encyclopedia of Dance.* New York, Oxford University Press, 1998.

Emery, Lynne Fauley. *Black Dance in the United States from 1619 to 1970*. Palo Alto, California, 1972.

Caldwell, Erskine (1903-1987)

Although Erskine Caldwell gradually descended into obscurity, during his heyday in the 1930s and 1940s his books were perennial best-sellers. Notorious for the explicit sexuality in his novels about Southern poor whites, Caldwell withstood several obscenity trials and saw his work banned on a regular basis. Caldwell's trademark mixture of sex, violence, and black humor garnered various reactions. Southerners in particular felt that Caldwell pandered to stereotypes of the South as a land of ignorance, sloth, and depravity, but many respected literary critics saw burlesque humor, leftist political activism, or uncompromising realism in Caldwell's writing. Caldwell's major fiction included *Tobacco Road* (1932), *God's Little Acre* (1933), *Kneel to the Rising Sun and Other Stories* (1935), *Trouble in July* (1940), and *Georgia Boy* (1943). In addition to novels and short stories, Caldwell coauthored a number of photograph-and-text books with his second wife, photographer Margaret Bourke-White, the most popular of which were *You Have Seen Their Faces* (1937) and *Say, Is This the U.S.A.?* (1941).

Caldwell was born in rural White Oak, Georgia. He inherited his social conscience from his father, a minister in the rigorous Associated Reformed Presbyterian Church. Because of his father's ministry, Caldwell's family moved frequently, and their financial situation was often strained. Caldwell had little formal education. His mother taught him at home during his early childhood, and he never formally graduated from high school. He later spent brief periods at three different colleges but never obtained a degree. After a long series of odd jobs and some newspaper work for the *Atlanta Journal,* Caldwell moved to Maine in 1927 to concentrate on writing fiction. He would never again live in the South, though he made occasional visits for documentary projects or creative inspiration.

Caldwell's early years in Maine were spent in utter poverty. His first three books attracted little attention, but his fourth, *Tobacco Road,* defined his career and made him rich. Published in 1932, *Tobacco Road* featured Jeeter Lester and family, a brood of destitute sharecroppers in rural Georgia. The dysfunctional Lester clan starved and stole and cussed and copulated throughout the book, which initially received mixed reviews and posted lackluster sales. Jack Kirkland changed all that when he translated *Tobacco Road* into a phenomenally successful Broadway play. The play ran from December of 1933 through March of 1941, an unprecedented seven-year stretch that was a Broadway record at the time. Touring versions of the play traveled the nation for nearly two decades, playing to packed houses throughout the country. Caldwell's book sales skyrocketed.

Through the 1940s Caldwell's books continued to sell well in dime-store paperback versions with lurid covers, but reviews of his new books were increasingly harsh. Though he continued writing at a prolific pace, Caldwell was never able to repeat the critical success of his earlier work. The quality of his work plummeted, and his relationships with publishers and editors, often strained in the past, deteriorated further.

Despite Caldwell's waning literary reputation, he had a lasting impact on American popular culture. A pioneer in the paperback book trade, he was one of the first critically acclaimed writers to aggressively market his work in paperback editions, which were considered undignified at the time. Most of Caldwell's astonishing sales figures came from paperback editions of books that were first published in hardback years earlier. These cheap editions were sold not in bookstores, but in drug stores and magazine stands; consequently they reached a new audience that many publishers previously had ignored. Sexually suggestive covers aided Caldwell's sales and forever changed the marketing practices for fiction. His censorship battles made Caldwell a pivotal figure in writers' battles for First Amendment rights. Without question, however, Caldwell's greatest legacy has been his depiction of Southern poor whites. The Lesters have been reincarnated in *The Beverly Hillbillies, Snuffy Smith, L'il Abner, The Dukes of Hazzard,* and countless other poor white icons. Though its origin seems largely forgotten, the term ''Jeeter'' survives as a slang expression for ''poor white trash.''

—Margaret Litton

FURTHER READING:

Cook, Sylvia Jenkins. *Erskine Caldwell and the Fiction of Poverty.* Baton Rouge, Louisiana State University, 1991.

MacDonald, Scott, editor. *Critical Essays on Erskine Caldwell.* Boston, G. K. Hall, 1981.

Miller, Dan B. *Erskine Caldwell: The Journey from Tobacco Road.* New York, Knopf, 1995.

Mixon, Wayne. *Erskine Caldwell: The People's Writer.* Charlottesville, University of Virginia Press, 1995.

Silver, Andrew. ''Laughing over Lost Causes: Erskine Caldwell's Quarrel with Southern Humor.'' *Mississippi Quarterly.* Vol. 50, No. 1, 1996-97, 51-68.

Calloway, Cab (1907-1994)

Known as ''The Hi-De-Ho Man,'' jazz singer, dancer, and bandleader Cab Calloway was one of the best-known entertainers in the United States from the early 1930s until his death in 1994. Calloway's musical talents, however, were only part of the story. His live performances at Harlem's Cotton Club became legendary because of Calloway's wild gyrations, facial expressions, and entertaining patter.

Born Cabell Calloway on Christmas Day, 1907, in Rochester, New York, Calloway spent most of his childhood years in Baltimore. The younger brother of singer Blanche Calloway, who made several popular records in the early 1930s before retiring, Cab discovered show business during his teen years, frequenting Chicago clubs while attending that city's Crane School. When Calloway encountered financial difficulties, he naturally turned to moonlighting in the same clubs, first as an emcee and later as a singer, dancer, and bandleader.

Although Calloway was attending law school and his hopes for a career in that field looked promising, he elected to drop out and try to make it as a singer and dancer. He led a successful Chicago group, the Alabamians, who migrated to New York but found the competition

Cab Calloway

too harsh to survive. Calloway had better luck with his next group, the Missourians, appearing in the Broadway revue *Connie's Hot Chocolates* in 1929.

Soon after, Calloway was offered a position as the headline act at the Cotton Club, and he readily accepted. He also had begun recording, and in 1931 produced his best-known single, "Minnie the Moocher." Minnie and her companion, Smokey Joe, were the first of many fictional characters Calloway invented to entertain his audiences. He continued Minnie's saga with such "answer" records as "Minnie the Moocher's Wedding Day" and "Mister Paganini, Swing for Minnie," which took a satirical look at classical music. He continued to develop his talents as a jazz singer and was one of the first "scat" singers, improvising melodies while singing nonsense lyrics. Blessed with a wide vocal range, Calloway employed it to his fullest advantage, especially on his famous "hi-de-ho" songs, which included "You Gotta Hi-De-Ho" and the "Hi-De-Ho Miracle Man."

Calloway's orchestra was a showcase and proving ground for some of the most prominent musicians in the history of jazz. Walter "Foots" Thomas, Doc Cheatham, Danny Barker, Dizzy Gillespie, and Ike Quebec, among many others, gained notoriety by appearing with Calloway, who paid higher salaries—and demanded better work—than any other bandleader.

Calloway had so much visual appeal that he was cast in several movies, including *Stormy Weather* (1943). More recently, Calloway played a thinly veiled version of himself in the 1980 blockbuster *The Blues Brothers*, dispensing fatherly advice to protagonists Jake and Elwood Blues (John Belushi and Dan Aykroyd) as well as turning in a spectacular performance of "Minnie the Moocher" at the film's climax.

Although the single "Blues in the Night" was a major hit in 1942, Calloway found little commercial success after the Depression years. With the end of the big-band era after World War II, Calloway reluctantly disbanded his orchestra in 1948 and thereafter performed solo or as a featured guest in other groups. His love of entertaining led him to continue performing for fans until his death in 1994.

—Marc R. Sykes

FURTHER READING:

Calloway, Cab, and Bryant Rollins. *Of Minnie the Moocher and Me.* New York, Crowell, 1976.

Calvin and Hobbes

Imaginative, hilariously drawn, at times philosophical—all the while retaining a child's perspective— this daily and Sunday comic strip has been compared to the best of the classic comics. Written and drawn by Bill Watterson, *Calvin and Hobbes* debuted in 1985 and featured the adventures of Calvin, a hyperactive, overly imaginative, bratty six-year-old, and his best friend, the stuffed tiger Hobbes. Other regularly appearing characters included Calvin's stressed out parents; Susie Derkins, the neighborhood girl; Miss Wormwood, the much put-upon school teacher; Mo, the school bully; and Rosalyn, the only baby-sitter willing to watch Calvin.

Part of the charm of the strip was the fact that Watterson often blurred the distinction between what was imaginary and what was "real." Calvin saw his tiger as real. When Calvin and Hobbes were by themselves, Watterson drew Hobbes as a walking tiger with fuzzy cheeks and an engaging grin. When another character appeared with Calvin and Hobbes, Hobbes was drawn simply as an expressionless stuffed tiger. The "real" Hobbes was more intellectual than Calvin and also liked to get "smooches" from girls, unlike the girl-hating Calvin (though both were founding members of G.R.O.S.S.—Get Rid of Slimy girlS).

Unlike Dennis the Menace, *Calvin and Hobbes* went beyond the hijinks of a holy terror. It explored childhood imagination and the possibilities of that imagination. For instance, one of Calvin's chief toys besides Hobbes was a large cardboard box. When it was right side up, the box was a time machine that transported Calvin and Hobbes back to the Jurassic. When Calvin turned it over, the box became the transmogrifier, which could transmogrify, or transform, Calvin into anything he wished. The transmogrifier was later converted into a duplicator, producing lots of Calvins. Imagination sequences such as these have been imitated by other comic strips such as Jim Borgman and Jerry Scott's *Zits*.

Calvin's imaginary world contained other memorable characters and devices. Calvin became the fearless Spaceman Spiff whenever he needed to escape the doldrums of school or the rebuke of his parents, who clearly loved but did not always like Calvin, a view of the family different from many others seen on the comics page. Calvin would don a cape and cowl and become Stupendous Man. His repertoire also included a tyrannosaur, or Calvinosaur, a robot, and a werewolf. Calvin also liked to sit in front of the television set, a behavior Watterson satirized, evidencing his contempt of television as opposed to personal imagination.

Most of the strips featured Calvin's antics, such as hitting Susie with a snowball or running away from his mother at bath time. Other common gags included his reluctance to eat dinner, his hatred of school and homework, and his antagonism toward Rosalyn. Calvin also enjoyed building deformed or dismembered snowmen on the front lawn. Besides these gags, though, the strip would at times deal with the philosophical nature of humanity as seen by a child and a tiger. Given the names of the characters, this was only to be expected. The comic strip's title characters are named after John Calvin and Thomas Hobbes. Calvin was a Protestant reformer famous for his ideas on predestination and the sovereignty of God. Calvin believed men, and children, to be sinners. Hobbes, author of the *Leviathan,* believed in submission to the sovereign of the state, since he too believed men were evil. Watterson occasionally commented on such issues between his two characters, usually as they headed down a hill in either a wagon or a sled.

Watterson ended *Calvin and Hobbes* in 1995. Watterson was known to dislike the deadlines, commercialization, and restraints of syndicated comics, which most likely motivated his retirement. While Watterson never permitted merchandising of his Calvin and Hobbes characters, *Calvin and Hobbes* reprints remained in stores, and Calvin images, though most likely unlicensed, continued to be displayed in cars and trucks. *Calvin and Hobbes* collections include *Something under the Bed Is Drooling* (1988), *Yukon Ho!* (1989), and *The Calvin and Hobbes Lazy Sunday Book* (1989).

Like Gary Larson of *The Far Side,* Watterson had a unique honor bestowed on him by the scientific community. On one adventure, Calvin and Hobbes explored Mars. When the Mars Explorer sent back pictures of Mars, NASA scientists named two of the Mars rocks Calvin and Hobbes.

—P. Andrew Miller

FURTHER READING:

Holmen, Linda, and Mary Santella-Johnson. *Teaching with Calvin and Hobbes.* Fargo, North Dakota, Playground Publishing, 1993.

Kuznets, Lois Rostow. *When Toys Come Alive.* New Haven, Connecticut, Yale University Press, 1994.

Watterson, Bill. *Calvin and Hobbes.* New York, Andrews and McMeel, 1987.

Camacho, Héctor "Macho" (1962—)

In 1985, boxer Héctor Camacho, known for his flashy style and flamboyant costuming as a "Macho Man" and "Puerto Rican Superman," became the first Puerto Rican to have won the World Boxing Championship (WBC) and World Boxing Organization (WBO) championships in the lightweight division. Born in Bayamón, Puerto Rico, in 1962, Camacho won 40 of his first 41 fights culminating with his victory over José Luis Ramos for the WBC lightweight championship. In 1987, Camacho moved up to the super lightweight division, in which he fought only seven sluggish battles before retiring in 1994. The two highlights of this latter career were his victory over World Boxing Association (WBA) lightweight champion Ray "Boom Boom" Mancini in 1989 and his 1992 fight with Julio César Chávez for a $3 million payoff.

—Nicolás Kanellos

Héctor "Macho" Comacho

FURTHER READING:

Tardiff, Joseph T., and L. Mpho Mabunda, editors. *Dictionary of Hispanic Biography.* Detroit, Gale, 1996.

Camelot

Camelot, a musical by Alan Jay Lerner and Frederick Loewe based on T.H. White's version of the Arthurian romance *The Once and Future King*, was one of the most successful Broadway musicals of the 1960s. The original production starred Julie Andrews, Richard Burton, and Robert Goulet. Songs included "I Wonder What the King Is Doing Tonight," "Camelot," "How to Handle a Woman," "C'est Moi," and "If Ever I Would Leave You." The 1967 film version featured Richard Harris, Vanessa Redgrave, and Franco Nero. Camelot contemporized the era of King Arthur and made the legend accessible and appealing to 20th-century audiences through the use of 1960s popular music styles, a skillful libretto, and well-known performers. The influence of *Camelot* extended well beyond the musical theater. It became a symbol of the administration of President John F. Kennedy, an era—like that of King Arthur—whose days were cut tragically short. The *Oxford History of the American*

People (1965) even ends with a quote from the show: ''Don't let it be forgot that once there was a spot, for one brief shining moment that was known as Camelot.''

—William A. Everett

FURTHER READING:

Citron, Stephen. *The Wordsmiths: Oscar Hammerstein 2nd & Alan Jay Lerner.* New York, Oxford University Press, 1995.

Everett, William A. ''Images of Arthurian Britain in the American Musical Theater: *A Connecticut Yankee* and *Camelot.*'' *Sonneck Society Bulletin.* Vol. 23, No. 3, 1997, 65, 70-72.

Lerner, Alan Jay. *The Street Where I Live.* New York, W.W. Norton, 1970.

Camp

''Camp asserts that good taste is not simply good taste; that there exists, indeed, a good taste of bad taste.'' In her well known 1964 piece, *Notes on Camp,* Susan Sontag summarized the fundamental paradox that occupies the heart of ''camp,'' a parodic attitude toward taste and beauty which was at that time emerging as an increasingly common feature of American popular culture. Avoiding the drawn-out commentary and coherence of a serious essay format, *Notes on Camp* dashes off a stream of anecdotal postures, each adding its own touches to an outline of camp sensibility. ''It's embarrassing to be solemn and treatise-like about Camp,'' Sontag writes. ''One runs the risk of having produced a very inferior piece of Camp.'' And she was right. To take camp seriously is to miss the point. Camp, a taste of bad taste which languishes between parody and self parody, doesn't try to succeed as a serious statement of taste, but stages its own failure as taste by doing and overdoing itself. In this way, failure is camp's greatest triumph and to take it away through a serious analysis would, for Sontag, be tantamount to an annihilation of the subject. In fact, since camp's self-parody leaves no durable statement of taste, it should only be spoken of as a verb: ''camping,'' the act of subverting a taste by exaggerating its pomp and artifice to the point of absurdity.

Writing in 1964, Sontag already had a short history of popular camp to reflect upon. From the mid 1950s, a peculiar sense of the beauty of bad taste had crept into American culture thorough the pages of *MAD* magazine and the writings of Norman Mailer—a parodic smirk that would creep across the face of counter culture of the 1960s and ultimately etch itself deeply into the American cultural outlook. By the mid 1960s, camp's triumphs were many: the glib, colorful, and disposable styles of Pop gave way to the non-conformity of hippie camp, which in turn inspired 1970s glam-rock camp, the biting camp of punk and the irony and retro of the 1980s and 1990s camp, while throughout the inflections of gay and drag camp were never far away. In each case, camp's pattern is clear: camp camps taste. Less a taste in itself, more an attitude toward taste in general, camp's failed seriousness exaggerates to absurdity the whole posture of serious taste, it ''dethrones seriousness,'' and reveals the vanity and folly that underlies every expression of taste. And camp's failure is contagious. By affirming style over substance, the artifice of taste over the content of art, and by undermining one's own posture of good taste by exaggerating its vanity and affect, camp exposes the lie of

taste in general—without confronting it with a superior standard. Sontag writes: ''Camp taste turns its back on the good-bad axis of ordinary aesthetic judgment. Camp doesn't reverse things. It doesn't argue that the good is bad or the bad is good. What it does is to offer for art (and life) a different—a supplementary—set of standards.'' Free from seriousness, camp can be cruel or kind: at moments camp offers a boundless carnival of generosity to anyone willing to don a disguise and share in the pomp and pretense that is taste, while at other moments camp's grotesque vanity might fly into jealous rage at the competitor, the campier than thou, that threatens to rain on the charade.

Sontag traces camp to its origins as a gay sensibility in the writings of Oscar Wilde and Jean Genet, who sought to dethrone the seriousness of Victorian literary convention and the tastes of the French bourgeoisie. In America, camp largely emerged from the need to dethrone the conformity and banality of the consumer culture of the 1950s. ''Pop'' styles sprang out of a reaction to the conformity imposed by the mass-produced culture provided by a ''society of abundance,'' which unconvincingly advocated the virtues and pleasures of life in a world of consumer goods. By the 1960s, that promise was less and less convincing, and the adornments of the suburban home seemed sadly inadequate as stand-ins for human satisfaction. The colorful, flamboyant and garish styles of ''Pop'' provided some relief for an American middle class increasingly inundated with ''serious'' consumer tastes in which it had no trust. In Britain a group of painters calling themselves The International Group (whose members included Richard Hamilton, John McHale, and Magda Cordell) set out to sing the praises of the new culture of plenty in a slightly off-key refrain: Hamilton's famous 1956 collage of a suburban living room asks with a conspicuous sincerity, ''Just What Is It That Makes Today's Homes So Different, So Appealing?'' The piece lampoons the optimism and complacency of the new domestic bliss, while celebrating its artifice. Camping the Americanization of the 1950s, British Pop spread quickly to the garrets of New York where Roy Lichtenstein, Jasper Johns, and Andy Warhol quickly picked up the trick of praising the land of opulence with the tongue squarely in the cheek.

''Pop'' resonated in the mainstream of American cultural life with the first of what would be many terrifically successful British Invasions. Dethroning the ''good taste'' of mass culture with stylish overkill, pop clothing, decoration, and graphics were exaggerated, colorful and garish, silly and trite. The fashions of Mary Quant, the photography of David Bailey, and ultimately the music of the Rolling Stones and the Beatles offered stylistic excess as the antidote to the ''square'' tastes of the older generation. The pop-psychedelic expressions of later years would confirm the superiority of mockery over taste. The fad *Vogue* dubbed ''Youthquake'' trumpeted the shallow excessiveness of a youthful taste as an endorsement of style over substance—a camping of mass culture. Commercial imagery, camped in this way, shaped the counter culture of the 1960s, from the Beatles' *Sergeant Pepper* album cover to Warhol's soup cans to the garish colors of psychedelic attire to the magazine clipping collages that covered many a teenager's bedroom walls: camping was at once subversive, clever, and affirming of one's taste for bad taste. One image in particular expresses this camping of mass culture that was the achievement of Pop: Twiggy, the slim and youthful British model who took Madison Avenue by storm in 1967, was pictured in a *New Yorker* article posing in Central Park, surrounded by children, all of whom wore Twiggy masks, photographic representations of the face of the model. Camping the artifice of mass stardom had become part of stardom itself.

It was, however, the camp of the drag queen that would ultimately triumph in the counter culture, and claim the camp legacy for the next decade. As early as Warhol's Factory days, where Manhattan drag queens like Candy Darling and Holly Woodlawn were featured prominently in such films as *Chelsea Girls* (1966), drag had always had a cozy relationship with the counter culture. The relationship became closer after the Stonewall riots of 1969, when drag style emerged as the motif that gave rock a disturbing and intriguing gender ambiguity. By the early 1970s, rock became increasingly open to camp inflections of drag: Mick Jagger developed a strutting, effeminate stage presence; David Bowie, Elton John, and Alice Cooper brought excess and artifice together with gender ambiguity that was taken directly from lively drag scenes and the queens who populated the 1970s gay scene. The raucous screenings of Jim Sharman's 1974 *Rocky Horror Picture Show* and John Waters' 1973 *Pink Flamingos* remain an enduring rite of college frat life.

As the 1970s wore on, New Wave and Punk movements drew on camp's preoccupation with dethroning the seriousness of taste. Such early punk acts as the New York Dolls sharpened the whimsy of Sharman's Dr. Frankenfurter character into a jarring sarcasm, less playful and flamboyant, more the instrument of an outraged youth, cornered by the boredom and banality of a co-opted counter-culture, a valueless society and the diminished hopes of a job market plagued by economic recession. Unlike the witticisms of Wilde and the flourish of Marc Boland and other dandies of glam rock, Punk's version of camp was meant to sting the opponent with a hideous mockery of consumer pleasure. The Sex Pistols' *Holiday in the Sun* album begins with a droning comment on low budget tourism: "cheap holiday in other people's misery," while the B-52s' manic celebration of the faux leisure of consumerism chided the ear with shrill praises of "Rock Lobster" and "Girls of the U.S.A." Punk camp, however, would have to be de-clawed before it could achieve mainstream influence, which ultimately happened in the early 1980s with the invasion (again from Britain) of such campy "haircut" acts as Duran Duran and Boy George's Culture Club. The effect of punk camp on American popular culture has yet to be fully understood, though it seems clear that ironic distance (cleansed of punk's snarl) became a staple of the culture of the 1980s and 1990s. Retro (a preferred terrain of camp, which finds easy pickings in tastes already rendered "bad" by the relentless march of consumer obsolescence) preoccupied the 1980s, where the awkward styles of the 1950s could be resurrected in such films as *Back to the Future*, and every aging rock star from Paul McCartney to Neil Young could cop a 50s greaser look in an effort to appear somehow up to date, if only by appealing to the going mode of obsolescence.

If irony and detachment had by the 1990s become defining features of the new consumer attitude, the camping of America is partly to blame, or credit. However, the 1990s also witnessed an unprecedented mainstreaming of drag in a manner quite different from that of the 1970s. In the 1990s, figures like Ru Paul and films like *Wigstock* signaled the visibility of drag styles worn by the drag queens themselves, not by straight rockstars taking a walk on the wild side. That drag could metamorphose over twenty years from a psychological aberration and criminal act to a haute media commodity testifies to the capacity of American culture to adjust to and absorb precisely those things it fears most. In the camping of America, where the abhorrent is redeemed, the drag queen fares well.

—Sam Binkley

FURTHER READING:

Roen, Paul. *High Camp: A Gay Guide to Camp and Cult Films.* San Francisco, Leyland Publications, 1994.

Ross, Andrew. "Uses of Camp." In *No Respect: Intellectuals and Popular Culture.* New York, Routledge, 1989.

Sontag, Susan. "Notes on Camp." In *Against Interpretation.* New York, Laurel, 1966.

Campbell, Glen (1936—)

After establishing himself as a reputable session guitarist for acts including the Monkees and Elvis Presley in the early 1960s, Glen Campbell came into his own as a country vocalist with a decided pop twist. Delivering pieces by ace songwriters like Jimmy Webb, Campbell's hit singles of the mid-1960s—most notably "Witchita Lineman" and "By the Time I Get To Phoenix"—fused the steel guitar sound of country with lilting string arrangements. By the early 1970s, Campbell had placed a number of singles in the upper tiers of both pop and country charts, and was even given the helm of his own popular variety show, *The Glen Campbell Good Time Hour,* but after "Southern Nights," his final number one hit, Campbell kept a relatively low profile.

—Shaun Frentner

FURTHER READING:

Campbell, Glen, with Tom Carter. *Rhinestone Cowboy: An Autobiography.* New York, Villard, 1994.

Campbell, Naomi (1971—)

Discovered while shopping in 1985, British model Naomi Campbell became an instant success in the United States, where she metamorphosed from a sweet schoolgirl into a polished—and, many would say, primadonna—professional. Her long dark hair, fey eyes, and feline figure established her as the first and for a long time the only black supermodel; her looks were distinctively African in origin but appealed to conservative Caucasian consumers as well. Her 1994 novel about the fashion business, *Swan,* focused primarily on white characters but made an impassioned argument in favor of widening modeling's ethnic base; she also recorded an album and starred in other artists' music videos. Guarding her stardom jealously, Campbell sometimes refused to appear in fashion shows alongside other black models, and she was known for making outrageous demands for hotel rooms and entertainment. Campbell eventually had to face accusations of abuse from modeling agencies and a former assistant.

—Susann Cokal

FURTHER READING:

Campbell, Naomi. *Swan.* London, Heinemann, 1994.

Gross, Michael. *Model: The Ugly Business of Beautiful Women.* New York, William Morrow & Company, 1995.

Tresniowski, Alex. "Out of Fashion." *People.* November 23, 1998, 132-40.

Camping

Humans tamed the first campfires over 500,000 years ago, and the word "camp" itself comes from the Latin *campus,* or "level field," but recreational camping as a popular cultural practice did not emerge in the United States until the end of the nineteenth century, when large numbers of urban residents went "back to nature," fleeing the pressures of industrialization and increased immigration for the temporary pleasures of a primitive existence in the woods.

The camping movement began in earnest in the mid-nineteenth century, when upper-class men from New York, Boston, and other northeastern cities traveled to the Catskills, the Adirondacks, and the White Mountains to hunt, fish, and find solace in the beauty and sublimity of untrammeled nature. Encouraged by such books as William H. H. Murray's *Adventures in the Wilderness; or, Camp-life in the Adirondacks* (1869), these men sought to improve their moral and physical health and test their masculinity against the wilderness, much as their working-class brethren had tested it on the battlefields of the Civil War. They also set the tone of nostalgic nationalism that would characterize camping throughout the twentieth century, identifying themselves with idealized images of the pioneer frontiersmen as rugged individualist and the American Indian as Noble Savage.

By the end of the nineteenth century, and especially after the "closing of the frontier" in 1890, camping had developed into an established middle-class activity, one that relied as much on cities and industries as it sought to flee them. Its increasing popularity could be seen in the formation of outdoor clubs, such as the Boone and Crockett Club (1887) and the Sierra Club (1892); the publication of camp manuals, such as George W. Sears's *Woodcraft* (1884) and Horace Kephart's *Camping and Woodcraft* (1906); and the appearance of related periodicals, such as *Forest and Stream* (1873), *Outing* (1882), and *Recreation* (1894). Easy access to remote areas was made possible by the railroads, and the growth of the consumer culture—as evidenced by the development of department stores, such as Montgomery Ward (1872), and the mail-order business of Sears, Roebuck (1895)—provided campers with the proper gear for their wilderness voyages. At the same time, however, many campers supported the

A group of boys at camp toasting marshmallows over an open fire.

conservation and preservation movements, which helped to establish the first national parks and forests.

The same forces of urbanization and industrialization that influenced the popularity of recreational camping among adults also affected the development of organized camping for children and young people. Although a long summer vacation made sense for a rural, agricultural population, technological advancements, and the expansion of the cities made this seasonal break from compulsory education increasingly obsolete in the late nineteenth century. Nevertheless, many schools continued to close for the months of June, July, and August, and parents, educators, and church leaders were forced to look elsewhere for ways to keep children occupied during the hot summer months. Camp provided the perfect solution.

The first organized camping trip in the United States is said to have occurred in 1861, when Frederick William Gunn and his wife supervised a two-week outing of the Gunnery School for Boys in Washington, Connecticut, but the first privately operated camp did not appear until 1876, when Joseph Trimble Rothrock opened a camp to improve the health of young boys at North Mountain in Luzerne County, Pennsylvania. The oldest continuously operating summer camp in the United States—"Camp Dudley," located on Lake Champlain—was founded in 1886 by Sumner F. Dudley, who had originally established his camp on Orange Lake, near Newburgh, New York. By 1910, the organized camping movement had grown extensive enough to justify the founding of the American Camping Association, which by the 1950s boasted more than five thousand members.

Classifiable as either day camps or residential camps, summer camps have generally provided a mixture of education and recreation in a group-living environment in the out-of-doors, and their proponents have claimed that the camps build character, encourage health and physical fitness, enhance social, psychological, and spiritual growth, and foster an appreciation for the natural world. The majority of camps have been run by nonprofit organizations, such as the Boy and Girl Scouts, Camp Fire Girls, Boys' and Girls' Clubs, 4-H Clubs, Salvation Army, YMCA, YWCA, YM-YWHA, and churches, synagogues, and other religious groups. Others have been private camps run by individuals and corporations, or public camps run by schools, municipal park and recreation departments, and state and federal agencies. Especially notable in the twentieth century has been the advent of innumerable special-interest camps, such as Christian and Jewish camps, sports camps, computer camps, language camps, space camps, weight-loss camps, and camps for outdoor and arts education.

Recreational camping developed in parallel with organized camping in the early twentieth century, influenced in part by the popularity of such nature writers as Henry David Thoreau, John Muir, and John Burroughs. Equally influential was the mass-production of the automobile and the creation of the modern highway system, which led to the development of motor camping and the formation of such organizations as the American Automobile Association, the Recreational Vehicle Association, and the Tin Can Tourists of America. The growth of camping reached a milestone in the 1920s, with camping stories being written by Ernest Hemingway and Sinclair Lewis; new products being developed by L. L. Bean and Sheldon Coleman (whose portable gas stove appeared in 1923), and the first National Conference on Outdoor Recreation being held in 1924.

The postwar suburbanization of the United States, combined with advances in materials technology and packaging, helped to turn camping into a mass cultural activity in the late twentieth century, one whose popularity not only affected the management of natural areas

but also called into question its own reason for being. Nearly ten million recreational vehicles, or RVs, were on the road in the late 1990s, forcing national parks to install more water, sewer, and power lines and close less desirable tent-camping sites. Meanwhile, the introduction of aluminum-frame tents in the 1950s, synthetic fabrics in the 1960s, freeze-dried foods in the 1970s, chemical insect repellents in the 1980s, and ultra-light camp stoves in the 1990s allowed campers to penetrate further into the backcountry, where they often risked disturbing ecologically sensitive areas. With the invention of cellular telephones and global positioning satellites, however, many campers have begun to wonder whether their days as primitive recreators may in fact be numbered, and whether it will ever again be possible to leave technology and civilization behind for the light of an evening campfire and the silence of a beeperless world.

—Daniel J. Philippon

FURTHER READING:

Belasco, Warren James. *Americans on the Road: From Autocamp to Motel, 1910-1945.* 1979. Baltimore, Johns Hopkins University Press, 1997.

Eells, Eleanor. *History of Organized Camping: The First 100 Years.* Martinsville, Indiana, American Camping Association, 1986.

Joselit, Jenna Weissman, ed. *A Worthy Use of Summer: Jewish Summer Camping in America.* With Karen S. Mittelman. Intro. Chaim Potok. Philadelphia, National Museum of American Jewish History, 1993.

Kephart, Horace. *Camping and Woodcraft: A Handbook for Vacation Campers and Travelers in the Wilderness.* Rev. ed. Intro. Jim Casada. 1917. Knoxville, University of Tennessee Press, 1988.

Kraus, Richard G., and Margaret M. Scanlin. *Introduction to Camp Counseling.* Englewood Cliffs, New Jersey, Prentice-Hall, 1983.

Schmitt, Peter J. *Back to Nature: The Arcadian Myth in Urban America.* Foreword by John R. Stilgoe. 1969. Baltimore, Johns Hopkins University Press, 1990.

Cancer

Cancer is not a single disease, but rather a monster with many faces. Doctors and scientists have listed more than 200 varieties of cancer, each having different degrees of mortality, different means of prevention, different hopes for a cure. Carcinomas hit mucous membranes or the skin, sarcomas attack the tissues under the skin, and leukemia strikes at the marrow—and these are just a few varieties of cancer. Cancers are all characterized by an uncontrolled proliferation of cells under pre-existing tissues, producing abnormal growths. Yet popular attitudes toward cancer have been less bothered with medical distinctions than with providing a single characterization of the disease, evoking a slow and painful process of decay that comes as a sort of punishment for the patient. "Cancerphobia" is, as Susan Sontag and James T. Patterson have shown, deeply rooted in American culture.

Cancer is a very ancient disease, dating back to pre-historic times. Archeological studies have allowed scientists to detect breast cancer in an Egyptian mummy, while precise descriptions of different cases of cancer started in the eighteenth century. The word cancer comes from the Latin ''cancer-cancri'' and the Greek karkinos (used by Hippocrates in the fifth century B.C.), meaning both cancer and crab. The two words are linked via images of creeping, voracity, and obliqueness. Just like crabs, cancers creep inside the organism and eat away at it. The association of cancers and crabs has lasted throughout the centuries: Rudyard Kipling used the expression ''Cancer the Crab,'' and an American cartoon booklet from the 1950s shows a giant crab crushing its victims with its huge pincers, the words ''Cancer the killer'' appearing above the scene. Adopting a typically apocalyptic mood, Michael Shimkin claimed that American citizens had defeated the ''pale rider of pestilence'' and the ''cadaverous rider of hunger,'' but that they now had to face two different riders—''one in shape of a mushroom cloud and one in the shape of a crab''.

In the United States, cancer made its first big public appearance with the illness and death in 1884-1885 of the national hero who had led the Union troops to victory in the Civil War: Ulysses S. Grant. Public use of the word cancer, as James Patterson has pointed out, had been uncommon until then. Grant's cancer received exceptional newspaper coverage and the readers of the age were fascinated by it. Unofficial remedies and healers came to the forefront, positing for the first time what would be a recurrent dichotomy in the history of cancer research: the orthodox medicine of the ''cancer establishment'' versus the unorthodox medicine of the ''cancer counter-culture.'' Cancer, with its slow but unrelenting progression, seemed the very denial of several developments taking place during the late nineteenth century (such as higher life expectancy and economic growth) which contributed to the people's perception of the United States as the land of progress and opportunity for a well-to-do life. The denial of death played an important part in this quest for a well-to-do life, and James Patterson explains that this particular attitude ''account[s] for many responses to cancer in the United States during the twentieth century, including a readiness to entertain promises of 'magic bullets.' In no other nation have cancerphobia and 'wars' against cancer been more pronounced than in the United States.'' Since the late 1970s, the war on cancer has been coupled with a fierce battle against smoking (which medical specialists have singled out as the main cause of lung cancer), a battle featuring scientific researchers pitted against tobacco lobbies and their powerful advertising experts.

Military metaphors have been widely used in the battle against cancer. One of the posters of the American Society for Control of Cancer from the 1930s urges us to ''fight cancer with knowledge''; the message appears below a long sword, the symbol of the Society. As part of the growing pressure for a national war on the disease during the 1960s, cancer activists asked for more money to be devoted to research and prevention by claiming that cancer was worse than the Vietnam War; the latter had killed 41,000 Americans in four years, while the former had killed 320,000 in a single year. Nixon was the first president of the United States to declare war on cancer. In January 1971, he declared in his State of the Union message that ''the time has come when the same kind of concentrated effort that split the atom and took the man on the moon should be turned toward conquering this dread disease.'' Later in the same year, two days before Christmas, Nixon signed the National Cancer Act (which greatly increased the funds of the National Cancer Institute, or NCI) and called for a national crusade to be carried out by 1976, the two hundredth anniversary of the birth of the United States. And yet this program revealed itself to be too optimistic and the association of cancer and Vietnam reappeared. People started to compare the inability of the NCI to deliver a cure to the disastrous outcome of the

Vietnam War. Dr. Greenberg, a cancer researcher, declared in 1975 that the war on cancer was like the Vietnam War: ''Only when the public realized that things were going badly did pressure build to get out.'' Gerald Markle and James Petersen, comparing the situation to the fight against polio, concluded that ''the war on cancer is a medical Vietnam.''

The military rhetoric of wars and crusades has also been applied to drugs, poverty, and other diseases in our society. Susan Sontag has claimed that military metaphors applied to illnesses function to represent them as ''alien.'' Yet the stigmatization of cancer leads inevitably to the stigmatization of the patients as well. Many scientific attempts to explain the causes of cancer implicitly blame patients. As late as the 1970s, Lawrence LeShan and Carl and Stephanie Simonton claimed that stress, emotional weakness, self-alienation, depression, and consequent defeatism were the distinctive features of a ''cancer personality'' and could all be causes of cancer. Sontag maintained that the theory that there was ''a forlorn, self-hating, emotionally inert creature'' only helped to blame the patient. This particular focus on stress was also based on a traditionally American distrust of modern industrialized civilization and urban life, which were to be blamed for the intensification of the pace of living and the consequent rise in anxiety for human beings. The wide circulation of these ideas pointed to popular dissatisfaction with most official medical explanations of cancer. Not surprisingly, cancer itself has become a powerful metaphor for all that is wrong in our society. Commentators often talk about the cancer of corruption effecting politics or about the spreading cancer of red ink in the federal budget. No other disease has provided metaphors for such a wide range of social and economic issues.

''Cancerphobia'' has been a constant source of inspiration for popular literature, cinema, and television. While cancer was mainly a disease for supporting actors (Paul Newman's father in Cat on a Hot Tin Roof, 1958) in the 1950s and 1960s, since the 1970s cancer movies have often served as vehicles for stars such as Ali McGraw and Ryan O'Neal in Love Story (1970), James Caan in Brian's Song (1972), Debra Winger in Terms of Endearment (1983), Julia Roberts in Dying Young (1991), Jack Lemmon in Dad (1989), Tom Hanks and Meg Ryan in Joe Versus the Volcano (1990), Michael Keaton in My Life (1993), and Susan Sarandon and Julia Roberts in Stepmom (1998). Most of these few-days-to-live-stories are melodramatic, tear-jerking accounts of cancer which rely on the popular perception of the illness as mysterious and deceiving. In Terms of Endearment, Debra Winger discovers she has cancer almost by chance and dies shortly after having declared that she feels fine. In Dad, Jack Lemmon's cancer disappears, giving everyone false hopes, only to reappear fatally after a short while. These stories are often told with a moralizing intent: cancer is perceived as providing opportunities for the redemption of the characters involved in the drama—in Terms of Endearment, Winger and her husband Jeff Daniels, who have both been unfaithful, reconcile at her deathbed; in Dad, cancer brings Jack Lemmon and his son Ted Danson closer together after years of estrangement; and in Stepmom the disease rekindles female bonds that had been obscured by misunderstandings and rivalries over men. And in Love Story and Dying Young, cancer serves as the medium through which two young people from different economic backgrounds are brought together despite their parents' opposition.

The (melo)drama of cancer in American culture is characterized by an enduring dichotomy of hope and fear. The official optimism for a cure, such as that placed in the 1980s on interferon, a protein able to stop the reproduction of cancerous cells, has always been countered by obstinate popular skepticism. Medical progress has been unable to discourage popular faith in unorthodox approaches to the disease. On the contrary, as James Patterson has argued, popular skepticism has often been fostered by "the exaggerated claims for science and technological medicine" and still makes cancer retain its malignant grip on the American popular imagination as "an alien, surreptitious, and voracious invader."

—Luca Prono

FURTHER READING:

LeShan, Lawrence. *You Can Fight For Your Life: Emotional Factors in the Causation of Cancer.* New York, M. Evans & Co., 1977.

Markle, Gerald, and James Petersen, editors. *Politics, Science and Cancer.* New York, AAAS, 1980.

Patterson, James T. *The Dread Disease: Cancer and Modern American Culture.* Cambridge, Harvard University Press, 1987.

Shimkin, Michael. *Science and Cancer.* Bethesda, Maryland, National Institute of Health, 1980.

Simonton, Carl and Stephanie. *Getting Well Again.* Los Angeles, J.P. Tarcher, 1978.

Sontag, Susan. *Illness as Metaphor.* New York, Farrar, Strauss, and Giroux, 1978.

Candid Camera

As a television show, *Candid Camera* enjoyed immense popularity with American viewers at mid-twentieth century even as it fundamentally changed the way in which Americans perceived behavior on the television screen and their own vulnerability to being observed. The catch phrase "candid camera" had been current in American English by the 1930s, thanks to the development of fine-grained, high-speed films which made spontaneous picture-taking of unselfconscious subjects a staple of news and backyard photographers alike, freeing them from the constraints of long exposures and conspicuously large apparatus. But it was Allen Funt's brash sequences of ordinary people caught unawares on film that made "candid camera" synonymous with uninhibited surveillance of our unguarded moments, whether for the amusement of the studio audience or the more sinister purposes of commercial and state-sponsored snooping.

Funt was a former research assistant at Cornell University. His prior broadcast experience included gag-writing for the radio version of *Truth or Consequences,* serving as a consultant to Franklin D. Roosevelt's wife, Eleanor, for her radio broadcasts during her husband's presidency, and independent radio production for such programs as *Ladies Be Seated.* During the Second World War he served in an Army Signal Corps unit in Oklahoma, where, using equipment assigned to him for recording soldiers' letters home, he began hidden-microphone taping of gripes by his fellow servicemen for broadcast on Armed Forces Radio. Funt's *Candid Microphone,* a postwar civilian version of the same idea, was first broadcast in 1947. A year later, he took the show to television, and ABC carried it—still as *Candid Microphone*—from August through December of 1948. The program, now renamed *Candid Camera,* shuffled among the three networks for the next five years, ending with NBC in the summer of 1953.

Allen Funt of *Candid Camera.*

After a seven year hiatus, *Candid Camera* was revived on CBS, where it ran from October of 1960 through September of 1967. Co-hosting the show in its first season was Arthur Godfrey, followed by Durward Kirby for the next five years, and Bess Myerson (ironically destined to become New York City's consumer-affairs director) in 1966-1967. As its fame spread, *Candid Camera* was imitated even overseas: in Italy, a program called *Lo Specchio Segreto* ("I See It in Secret"), emceed by Nanni Loy, first aired in 1964 on the RAI network; it too spawned numerous imitations. Funt, meanwhile, returned to America's airwaves with a syndicated version of the program, *The New Candid Camera,* which was broadcast on various networks from 1974 to 1978. Moviegoers were also exposed to *Candid Camera,* both in Funt's 1970 film *What Do You Say to a Naked Lady?* and in a generous handful of 1980s home-video reprints of episodes from the shows as well.

Some of Funt's stunts have become classics in the manipulation of frame and the reactions of the unsuspecting victims (almost always punchlined by Funt or one of his accomplices saying "You're on *Candid Camera.*") In one sequence, a roadblock was stationed at a border-crossing from Pennsylvania into Delaware to turn motorists back with the explanation, "The state is full today." Taste was a timeless source of merriment: an airport water cooler was filled with lemonade; and customers in a supermarket were asked to sample and comment on a new candy bar made with ingredients in a combination designed to be revolting.

The relationship between the television studio and the psychology laboratory was not lost on Funt, who told readers of *Psychology Today* that he had switched from sound recording to television because he "wanted to go beyond what people merely said, to record what they did—their gestures, facial expressions, confusions and delights." By comparison with later (and sassier) imitators such as *America's Funniest Home Videos* and *Totally Hidden Video,* both of which premiered in the late 1980s, Funt was scrupulous about declining to air, and actually destroying, off-color or overly intrusive footage. *Candid Camera* aspired to be humor but also art: "We used the medium of TV well," Funt would write proudly. "The audience saw ordinary people like themselves and the reality of events as they were unfolding. Each piece was brief, self-contained and the simple humor of the situation could be quickly understood by virtually anyone in our audience."

The New Candid Camera returned to television in the 1990s, now touted as "the granddaddy of all 'gotcha' shows" and co-hosted by Funt's son Peter, who as a child had made his debut on the show posing as a shoeshine boy charging $10 a shoe. Although the revival was not renewed by King Productions for the 1992-1993 season, specials continued to be made throughout the decade, mixing contemporary situations (a petition drive in Toronto advocating joint United States-Canada holidays, a fake sales rep selling a fictitious and overpriced line of business equipment to unsuspecting office managers) with classic sequences from the old shows. By this time Allen Funt, now in his eighties, was living comfortably in retirement.

—Nick Humez

FURTHER READING:

Dunning, John. *Tune In Yesterday.* Englewood Cliffs, New Jersey, Prentice Hall, 1976.

Funt, Allen. *Eavesdropping at Large: Adventures in Human Nature with Candid Mike and Candid Camera.* New York, Vanguard Press, 1952.

Loomis, Amy. "Candid Camera." *Museum of Broadcast Communications Encyclopedia of Television.* Ed. Horace Newcomb. Chicago, Fitzroy Dearborn Publishers, 1997, 305-307.

McNeil, Alex. *Total Television.* New York, Penguin Books, 1991.

West, Levon (writing as "Ivan Dmitri"). *How to Use Your Candid Camera.* New York, Studio Publications, 1932.

Zimbardo, P. "Laugh Where We Must, Be Candid Where We Can." *Psychology Today.* June 1985, 42-47.

Caniff, Milton (1907-1988)

A popular and innovative adventure-strip artist, and one who was much imitated, Milton Caniff began drawing newspaper features in the early 1930s and kept at it for the rest of his life. He was born in Hillsboro, Ohio, in 1907 and raised in Dayton. Interested in drawing from childhood, in his early teens he got a job in the art department of the local paper. By the time he was in college at Ohio State, Caniff was working part-time for the *Columbus Dispatch.* It was there that he met and became friends with Noel Sickles, the cartoonist-illustrator who was to have such a profound effect on his approach to drawing. Caniff created three continuity strips: *Dickie Dare, Terry and the Pirates,* and *Steve Canyon.* From almost the beginning, his story lines

Milton Caniff

and dialogue were relatively sophisticated, influenced by the movies, as was his drawing style, which used cinematic shots and impressionistic inking.

—Ron Goulart

FURTHER READING:

Goulart, Ron. *The Funnies.* Holbrook, Adams Publishing, 1995.

Harvey, Robert C. *The Art of the Funnies.* Jackson, University Press of Mississippi, 1994.

Cannabis
See Marijuana

Canova, Judy (1916-1983)

Comedienne Judy Canova was one of the hidden gems American popular culture, ignored by critics and overlooked by ratings systems that valued big city audiences yet beloved by audiences in smaller markets. As a musical comedienne whose lifelong comic persona was that of a yodeling country bumpkin, Judy Canova was famous on stage, screen, and radio throughout the 1930s, 1940s and 1950s, but largely because of the perceived low status of her audience, her popularity has often been overlooked.

Judy Canova was born Juliette Canova on November 20, 1916, in Starke, Florida. Her career in show business began while she was still a teenager when she joined with her older brother and sister in a musical trio which played the club circuit in New York. In addition to belting out many of the same country songs she would perform for the rest of her life, Canova also developed her comic persona during this period as well—that of a good-natured, horse-faced, broadly grinning hillbilly whose lack of education and etiquette was transcended by boisterous good spirits, an apparent absence of pretense, and a naive humor with which her audience could both identify and feel superior to simultaneously. "I knew I would never be Clara Bow," she later recalled. "So I got smart and not only accepted my lack of glamour, but made the most of it." She usually wore her hair in pigtails, and soon began wearing the checkered blouses and loosely falling white socks which helped emphasize her almost cartoonlike appeal. The comic portrait was soon completed with the development of a repeated catchphrase ("You're telling I") and her use of what film historian Leonard Maltin has referred to as "an earsplitting yodel." With her character firmly in place by the early 1930s, it remained only for Canova to find the appropriate outlet for its display.

Canova's film career reached its high point in 1935 with her brief appearance in the Busby Berkeley-directed *In Caliente*, in which she performed what biographer James Robert Parish refers to as "her most memorable screen moment." In the middle of leading lady Winifred Shaw's serious performance of the soon-to-be popular "Lady in Red," Canova appeared in hillbilly garb and belted out a comic parody of the song in a performance singled out by audiences and reviewers alike as the highlight of the movie. This success fueled her stage career, leading to a notable appearance in the *Ziegfeld Follies of 1936,* but Paramount's attempt to make her a major film star the following year (in *Thrill of a Lifetime*) didn't pan out, and Canova's movie career was shifted to the lower budget projects of Republic Studios. Here she starred in a series of consistently popular musical comedies (*Scatterbrain* (1940), *Sis Hopkins* (1941), and *Joan of Ozark* (1942) being among the most successful) in which she played her well-established "brassy country bumpkin with a heart of gold" in stories which enabled her to deliver a lot of bad puns and yodel songs while demonstrating both the comic naiveté and moral superiority of "the common people." Behind the scenes, however, Canova was anything but the untutored innocent she played onscreen, and she is important as one of the first female stars to demand and receive both a share of her film's profits and, later, producing rights through her own company.

While she was a minor star in the world of film, Canova was a major success in radio. Earlier performances on the Edgar Bergen-Charlie McCarthy *Chase and Sanborn Hour* (including a highly publicized "feud" in which Canova claimed that the dummy had broken up her "engagement" to Edgar) garnered such response that *The Judy Canova Show* was all but inevitable. Even in her own time, however, much of Canova's popularity was "hidden" by conventional standards, and it was not until 1945 when the new Hooper ratings system (which measured the listening habits of small-town and rural audiences for the first time) revealed that Canova's program was one of the top ten radio shows on the air. *The Judy Canova Show* remained popular until its demise in 1953, a casualty of the declining era of old-time radio. Radio allowed Judy to give full vent to the characteristics which had endeared her to her audience, playing a country bumpkin (with her own name) hailing from Unadella, Georgia, but making constant visits to the big city to visit her rich aunt, and

passing a fastpaced series of corny jokes and songs with a series of stock characters. A typical episode would be certain to have Pedro the gardener (Mel Blanc) apologize to Judy "for talking in your face, senorita," Judy telling her aunt that she would be happy to sing "Faust" at the aunt's reception since she could sing "Faust or slow," and close with Judy's trademark farewell song, "Goodnight, Sweetheart."

After the end of her radio show, Canova continued her stage career (including a primary role in 1971's notable revival of the musical *No, No Nanette*), made a few forays into early television, and even attempted a more serious dramatic role in 1960's *The Adventures of Hucklberry Finn.* For the most part, however, she lived comfortably in retirement, often accompanied by her actress daughter Diana, product of her fourth marriage. The comic persona she created, and the ethic it expressed, remain popular today in sources as diverse as *The Beverly Hillbillies* and many of the characters played by the hugely successful Adam Sandler, both of whom owe a large if "hidden" debt to a horsefaced yodeler with falling socks who never let the city folk destroy her spirit.

—Kevin Lause

FURTHER READING:

Maltin, Leonard, editor. *Leonard Maltin's Movie Encyclopedia.* New York, Dutton, 1996.

Parish, James Robert. *The Slapstick Queens.* New York, A.S. Barnes and Company, 1973.

Parish, James Robert, and William T. Leonard. *The Funsters.* New Rochelle, Arlington House, 1979.

Canseco, Jose (1964—)

Baseball's Rookie of the Year in 1986, slugging outfielder Jose Canseco helped the Oakland Athletics to World Series appearances from 1988 to 1990, while becoming the first ballplayer ever to hit over 40 homers and steal 40 bases in a season (1988). Auspicious beginnings, teen-idol looks, and Canseco was suddenly the sport's top celebrity. As big money, 1-900 hotlines, and dates with Madonna ensued, Canseco's on-field and off-field behavior became erratic. Headlines detailed a weapons arrest, reckless driving, and an acrimonious public divorce. Traded away from Oakland in 1992, he blew out his arm in a vanity pitching appearance and topped blooper reels when a fly ball bounced off his head for a home run. Having dropped out of both the limelight and the lineup, he eventually recovered to hit 46 homers for Toronto in 1998 (the same year his former Oakland "Bash Brother" Mark McGwire hit a record 70).

—C. Kenyon Silvey

FURTHER READING:

Aaseng, Nathan. *Jose Canseco: Baseball's 40-40 Man.* Minneapolis, Lerner Publications, 1989.

Scheinin, Richard. *Field of Screams: The Dark Side of America's National Pastime.* New York, W. W. Norton & Company, 1994.

Cantor, Eddie (1882-1964)

Dubbed "Banjo Eyes" for his expressive saucer-like orbs, and "The Apostle of Pep" for his frantically energized physical style, comic song-and-dance man Eddie Cantor came from the vaudeville tradition of the 1920s, and is remembered as a prime exponent of the now discredited blackface minstrel tradition, his brief but historic movie association with the uniquely gifted choreographic innovator Busby Berkeley, and for turning the Walter MacDonald-Gus Kahn song "Making Whoopee" into a massive hit and an enduring standard. In a career that spanned almost 40 years, Cantor achieved stardom on stage, screen, and, above all, radio, while on television he was one of the rotating stars who helped launch the *Colgate Comedy Hour.*

Cantor's is a prototypical show business rags-to-riches story. As Isadore Itzkowitz, born into poverty in a Manhattan ghetto district and orphaned young, he was already supporting himself in his early teens as a Coney Island singing waiter with a piano player named Jimmy Durante before breaking into burlesque and vaudeville (where he sang songs by his friend Irving Berlin), and made it to Broadway in 1916. The small, dapper Jewish lad became a Ziegfeld star, appearing in the Follies of 1917 (with Will Rogers, W.C. Fields, and Fanny Brice), 1918, and 1919. In the first, he sang a number in blackface,

Eddie Cantor and Dinah Shore

and also applied the burnt cork to team in a skit with black comedian Bert Williams, with whom he would work several times over the years. Irving Berlin wrote the 1919 songs and Cantor introduced "You'd be Surprised." A bouncy, hyperactive performer, he rarely kept still and would skip and jump round the stage, clapping his white-gloved hands while performing a song. He also rolled his prominent eyes a lot and a Ziegfeld publicity hack came up with the Banjo Eyes sobriquet.

After a falling out with Flo Ziegfeld, Cantor starred in other people's revues for a few years. Reconciled with Ziegfeld, he starred in the musicals *Kid Boots* and *Whoopee!* The first became the silent screen vehicle for his Hollywood debut in 1926; the second, based on a play *The Nervous Wreck,* cast Cantor as a hypochondriac stranded on a ranch out West, introduced the song "Making Whoopee," and brought him movie stardom when Samuel Goldwyn filmed it in 1930. *Whoopee!* was not only one of the most successful early musicals to employ two-tone Technicolor, but marked the film debut of Busby Berkeley, who launched his kaleidoscopic patterns composed of beautiful girls (Betty Grable was one) to create a new art form. The winning formula of Berkeley's flamboyance and Cantor's insane comedic theatrics combined in three more immensely profitable box-office hits: *Palmy Days* (1931), which Cantor co-wrote; *The Kid from Spain* (1932), in which Berkeley's chorus included Grable and Paulette Goddard; and, most famously, the lavish, and for its day outrageous, *Roman Scandals* (1933), in which the young Lucille Ball made a fleeting appearance. A dream fantasy, in which Cantor is transported back to ancient Rome, the star nonetheless managed to incorporate his blackface routine, while the "decadent" production numbers utilized black chorines in a manner considered demeaning by modern critics.

Meanwhile, the ever-shrewd Cantor was establishing himself on radio ahead of most of his comedian colleagues. In 1931 he began doing a show for Chase and Sanborn Coffee. By its second year, according to radio historian John Dunning, it was the highest rated show in the country. The star gathered a couple of eccentric comedians around him, beginning with Harry "Parkyakarkus" Einstein, who impersonated a Greek, and Bert Gordon, who used a thick accent to portray The Mad Russian, while, over the years, the show also featured young singers such as Deanna Durbin, Bobby Breen, and Dinah Shore. Cantor remained on the air in various formats until the early 1950s, backed by such sponsors as Texaco, Camel cigarettes, toothpaste and laxative manufacturers Bristol Myers, and Pabst Blue Ribbon beer. His theme song, with which he closed each broadcast, was a specially arranged version of "One Hour with You."

After his flurry of screen hits during the 1930s, Cantor's movie career waned somewhat, but he enjoyed success again with *Show Business* (1944) and *If You Knew Susie* (1948), both of which he produced. A cameo appearance in *The Story of Will Rogers* (1952) marked the end of his 26-year, 16-film career, but in 1950 he had begun working on television, alternating with comedians such as Bob Hope, Martin and Lewis, and his old buddy Durante, as the star of Colgate's *Comedy Hour.* In the autumn of 1952 Cantor had a serious heart attack right after a broadcast and left the air for several months. He returned in 1953, but began gradually withdrawing from the entertainment world.

Eddie Cantor wrote four autobiographical books, and in 1953, Keefe Brasselle played the comedian in a monumentally unsuccessful biopic, *The Eddie Cantor Story*. In 1956 the Academy honored him with a special Oscar for "distinguished service to the film industry." In 1962, the year he published the last of four autobiographical books, he was predeceased by his wife, Ida, immortalized in the song, "Ida, Sweet as Apple Cider," to whom he was married for 48 years. Eddie Cantor died two years later. His screen persona was not, and is not, to everyone's taste, and in life, some found him egocentric and difficult. He remains, however, inimitable.

—Ron Goulart

FURTHER READING:

Barrios, Richard. *A Song in the Dark*. New York, Oxford University Press, 1995.

Bordman, Gerald. *American Musical Theatre*. New York, Oxford University Press, 1978.

Dunning, John. *On The Air*. New York, Oxford University Press, 1998.

Goldman, Herbert G. *Banjo Eyes: Eddie Cantor and the Birth of Modern Stardom*. New York, Oxford University Press, 1997.

Fisher, James. *Eddie Cantor: A Bio-Bibliography*. Westport, Connecticut, Greenwood Press, 1997.

Koseluk, Gregory. *Eddie Cantor: A Life in Show Business*. Jefferson, North Carolina, McFarland, 1995.

Capital Punishment

Throughout the twentieth century, America remained one of the few industrialized countries which carried out executions of criminals. Most trace this attitude to the Biblical roots of the country and the dictum of "eye for an eye" justice. Those who wished to abolish the death penalty saw the practice as bloodlust, a cruel and unusual punishment anachronistic in modern times. In the late 1990s, the issue remains a controversial one, with many states opting for the death penalty. In response and with an ironic twist, America has searched for ways to carry out executions as quickly and painlessly for the condemned as possible.

At the turn of the twentieth century, America was trying to shake a lingering sense of Old West vigilante justice. Thomas Edison, among others, had campaigned for the relatively humane death offered by electrocution. By the 1900s the electric chair had already become the most popular form of execution, supplanting hanging. In 1924 Nevada instituted and performed the first gas chamber execution, which many believed again was the most humane method of execution to date.

Spearheading the movement against the death penalty was attorney Clarence Darrow, best known as defense counsel in the Scopes Trial. Few were surprised when in 1924 Darrow, a champion of lost causes, represented 18-year-old Richard Loeb and 19-year-old Nathan Leopold, notorious friends and lovers who kidnapped and murdered a 14-year-old boy. Darrow advised the two to plead guilty in an attempt to avoid the death penalty. In what has been characterized as the most moving court summation in history, lasting over 12 hours, Darrow succeeded in convincing the judge to sentence the boys to life in prison. Darrow commented, "If the state in which I live is not kinder, more human, and more considerate than the mad act of these two boys, I am sorry I have lived so long." In spite of his eloquent pleas, support for the death penalty remained high, with the highest number of executions of the century occurring in the 1930s.

In one of the most notorious cases of the twentieth century, the Italian immigrant workers Nicola Sacco and Bartolomeo Vanzetti were convicted of murder and sentenced to death in 1920. Worldwide response to their sentencing was overwhelming. The case against them was not airtight—many believe later evidence suggested their innocence. But their status as communists spelled their doom. According to the editors of *Capital Punishment in the United States,* "Many people believed that they were innocent victims of the frenzied 'Red Scare' that followed World War I, making every foreigner suspect—especially those who maintained unpopular political views." Celebrities such as George Bernard Shaw, H.G. Wells, Albert Einstein, and Sinclair Lewis protested the verdicts, to no avail as the two were executed in the Massachusetts electric chair in 1927.

The so-called "Trial of the century," the case of the kidnapping and murder of the Lindbergh baby in 1935, also involved an immigrant: German-born defendant Bruno Hauptmann, convicted in 1935 and executed for the crimes in 1936. The trial defined the term "media circus," with columnist Walter Winchell at the forefront calling for swift punishment of Hauptmann. In spite of compelling circumstantial evidence linking Hauptmann to the crime, his proclamation of his innocence to the end—even after being offered commutation of his sentence in return for his confession—made many uncomfortable because the case still seemed to lack closure.

Fear of communism ran at a fever pitch in the 1950s, contributing to the execution of Julius and Ethel Rosenberg for treason in 1953. Convicted of passing information about the atomic bomb to the Soviet Union, the Rosenbergs were blamed by the trial judge for communist aggression in Korea and the deaths of over 50,000 people. Polls at the time showed enormous support for the death penalty in cases of treason, largely due to the media notoriety of the Rosenberg case. Still, a groundswell of reaction against the sentencing occurred, forcing President Eisenhower himself to uphold the decision. While the case against Julius Rosenberg was strong, the case against Ethel was not, and many attribute her death as a casualty of the Cold War communist scare.

After the Rosenbergs, the majority of executions in the United States involved murderers. The Charles Starkweather case in the 1950s helped shape public perception of serial killers. After kidnapping 14-year-old Caril Ann Fugate as a companion, Starkweather went on a killing spree from Nebraska through Montana, murdering 11 people. When captured, Starkweather relished the media attention as if he were a Hollywood star; he fancied himself a James Dean type, heroically rebelling against society. Later, Bruce Springsteen's song "Nebraska," along with the 1973 movie *Badlands,* would immortalize the Starkweather persona—both also helped form the basis of the killers in the movies *Wild at Heart, True Romance,* and *Natural Born Killers.*

No one, however, defined the image of the serial killer more completely than Charles Manson. He also linked himself to the popular media; his obsession with the Beatles' *White Album,* in particular the song "Helter Skelter," became the impetus for the savage murders he orchestrated through his ''family'' of followers. During his trial he alternately declared himself Christ and Satan, at one point shaving his head and tattooing an ''X'' (later modified to a swastika) between his eyes. Though Manson did not personally commit murder, he was convicted in 1971 and sentenced to die. While he waited on death row, the Supreme Court ruled in 1972 that the death penalty was not applied equally and was therefore unconstitutional. As a result, over 600 prisoners on death row, including Manson, had their sentences commuted to life. In the years that followed, Manson regularly came up for parole. Throughout the 1980s and 1990s, Manson resurfaced on television interview shows, still seeming out of his mind. The specter of such a criminal possibly being released always spurred a fresh outpouring of public outrage. Very likely as a direct result of the Manson case, support for the death penalty continued to rise, reaching a record high of 80 percent in 1994.

Once the states rewrote uniform death penalty laws that satisfied the Supreme Court, executions resumed when Utah put Gary Gilmore to death in 1977. A circus atmosphere surrounded this case, as both supporters and opponents of the death penalty crowded outside the prison. Gilmore's face appeared on T-shirts as he too became a national celebrity. Gilmore himself, however, actually welcomed the death penalty; he refused all appeals and led the campaign for his right to die. Later, Norman Mailer wrote a bestselling book entitled *The Executioner's Song,* which was subsequently made into a popular film.

When Ted Bundy was convicted as a serial killer in 1980, he put a vastly different face on the image of murderer. Bundy was handsome and personable, traits which enabled him over two decades to lure at least 30 women to their deaths. During his numerous appeals of his death sentence Bundy claimed that consumption of pornography had molded his behavior, warping his sense of sexual pleasure to include violence against women. While his pleas helped raise debate over the issues of pornography, they failed to save his life and Bundy was executed in 1989.

The drifter Henry Lee Lucas, whose confessions to over 600 murders would make him the most prolific murderer of the century, was sentenced to death in 1984. His exploits were fictionalized in the cult movie *Henry: Portrait of a Serial Killer* (1990). Later, however, Lucas recanted all of his confessions and his sentence was commuted to life in prison in 1998.

Television talk show host Phil Donahue, a death penalty opponent, campaigned vigorously in the 1980s to televise a live execution. Some thought the idea merely a macabre publicity stunt while others thought the public should be made to witness its sanctioned form of punishment. Although Donahue was unsuccessful in his attempts, in 1995 the academy award winning movie *Dead Man Walking* intimately depicted the last days of convicted murderer Patrick Sonnier. The movie's portrayal of the incident suggested that even death by lethal injection—first used in Texas in 1982 in an effort to achieve a more humane ending—was neither antiseptic nor instantaneous.

In 1997 the case of Karla Faye Tucker was brought to the attention of the national media in an effort led by television evangelist Pat Robertson. Tucker, a convicted double murderer, reportedly had experienced a religious conversion while on death row. Based on this and a profession of remorse for the crimes she committed, Robertson argued for mercy. Tucker's image captured the imagination of many Americans: she was a young, attractive woman with a mild demeanor, not at all the serial killer image America had come to expect from its

death-row inmates. While Tucker was not granted a new hearing and was executed by lethal injection in 1998, her case influenced the staunchest traditional supporters of the death penalty. For many religious conservatives, the Tucker case reminded them that any search for a truly humane punishment must eventually confront the entire spectrum of emotions ... not only revenge, but also the qualities of mercy.

—Chris Haven

FURTHER READING:

Currie, Elliott. *Crime and Punishment in America.* New York, Holt, 1998.

Darrow, Clarence. *Clarence Darrow on Capital Punishment.* Chicago, Chicago Historical Bookworks, 1991.

Kronenwetter, Michael. *Capital Punishment: A Reference Handbook.* New York, ABC-Clio, 1993.

Lester, David. *Serial Killers: The Insatiable Passion.* Philadelphia, Charles Press, 1995.

Prejean, Helen. *Dead Man Walking: An Eyewitness Account of the Death Penalty in the United States.* New York, Vintage, 1996.

Vila, Brian, and Cynthia Morris, editors. *Capital Punishment in the United States: A Documentary History.* Westport, Greenwood Press, 1997.

Capone, Al (1899-1947)

Perhaps the most recognizable figure in the history of organized crime in the United States, Al Capone gained international notoriety during the heady days of Prohibition when his gang dominated the trade in bootleg alcohol in Chicago. Known as ''Scarface'' for the disfiguring scars that marked the left side of his face, Capone fascinated Chicago and the nation with his combination of street brutality, stylish living, and ability to elude justice during the 1920s. Even after his conviction on charges of tax evasion in 1931, Capone remained a dominant figure in the national culture, with the story of his rise and fall—which author Jay Robert Nash has succinctly described as being from ''rags to riches to jail''—serving as the archetype of gangster life in film and television portrayals of American organized crime.

Capone was born to Italian immigrant parents on January 17, 1899, in the teeming Williamsburg section of Brooklyn, New York. By age eleven he had become involved with gang activities in the neighborhood; he left school in the sixth grade following a violent incident in which he assaulted a female teacher. Developing expert street-fighting skills, Capone was welcomed into New York's notorious Five Points Gang, a vast organization that participated in burglary, prostitution, loan-sharking, and extortion, among its myriad criminal activities. He came under the influence of Johnny Torrio, an underboss who controlled gambling, prostitution, and influence peddling in Williamsburg. Under Torrio, Capone worked as an enforcer and later got a job as a bouncer and bartender at the gang-controlled

Al Capone (left)

suburban Cicero by the O'Bannions in 1926. In the most notorious event of the period, which became known as the St. Valentine's Day Massacre, Capone hired a crew to kill rival Bugs Moran on February 14, 1929. Capone's operatives, posing as police officers, executed all seven men they found in Moran's headquarters. Moran, however, was not among the victims, and the public expressed outrage at the brutal mass murder. By 1930 Capone had effectively eliminated his criminal competitors, but he faced a new adversary in federal authorities. When it was discovered that he had failed to pay income taxes for the years 1924 to 1929, the Internal Revenue Service made its case, and Capone was convicted of tax evasion in October 1931. He was sentenced to eleven years in federal custody but was released because of illness in 1939. He had developed paresis of the brain, a condition brought on by syphilis, which he likely had contracted from a prostitute during the 1920s. Suffering diminished mental capacity, Capone lived the remainder of his life in seclusion at his Palm Island, Florida, estate. He died in 1947.

—Laurie DiMauro

FURTHER READING:

Dorigo, Joe. *Mafia.* Seacaucus, New Jersey, Chartwell Books, 1992.

Nash, Jay Robert. *Encyclopedia of World Crime.* Vol. I. Wilmette, Illinois, CrimeBooks, 1990.

———. *World Encyclopedia of Organized Crime.* New York, De Capo Press, 1993.

Sifakis, Carl. *The Encyclopedia of American Crime.* New York, Smithmark, 1992.

Harvard Inn. During this time an altercation with a knife-wielding bar patron resulted in the famous scars that came to symbolize Capone's violent persona. He was arrested for suspicion of murder in 1919 in New York City, but the charges were dismissed when witnesses refused to testify against him. He followed Torrio to Chicago later in the same year after killing another man in a fight.

Posing as a used furniture dealer, Capone quickly became a significant force in the underworld of Chicago, where the number of corrupt law enforcement and government officials helped to create an atmosphere of lawlessness. When the Volstead Act outlawed the manufacture and distribution of liquor in 1920, Capone and Torrio entered into a bootlegging partnership, and Capone assassinated the reigning syndicate boss, ''Big Jim'' Colosimo, to clear the way for their profiteering. The combined operations of prostitution and bootleg liquor were generating millions of dollars in profits in the mid-1920s, but the Torrio-Capone organization repeatedly battled violently with rival gangs in the city, most notably with the operations headed by Dion O'Bannion on Chicago's north side. Following O'Bannion's murder in November 1924, Torrio was convicted of bootlegging and several days later was wounded in a retaliatory attack by O'Bannion's men. He subsequently left the city, and Capone gained full control of the multimillion dollar criminal activities in gambling, prostitution, and liquor.

The late 1920s saw increasingly reckless violence in the streets of Chicago among the warring criminal factions. Several attempts were made on Capone's life by his enemies, including an attempted poisoning and a machine-gun attack on Capone's headquarters in

Capote, Truman (1924-1984)

Truman Capote is one of the more fascinating figures on the American literary landscape, being one of the country's few writers to cross the border between celebrity and literary acclaim. His wit and media presence made for a colorful melange that evoked criticism and praise within the same breath. For many, what drew them to him was, for lack of a better word, his ''attitude.'' Capote relished deflating fellow writers in public fora. In a televised appearance with Norman Mailer, he said of Jack Kerouac's work, ''That's not writing. That's typewriting.'' In his unpublished exposé, *Answered Prayers,* his description of Jean-Paul Sartre and Simone de Beauvoir at the Pony Royal Bar in Paris could hardly have been less flattering: ''Walleyed, pipe-sucking, pasty-hued Sartre and his spinsterish moll, de Beauvoir, were usually propped in a corner like an abandoned pair of ventriloquist's dolls.'' And when wit had been set aside, he could be just downright abusive, as when he described Robert Frost as an ''evil, selfish bastard, an egomaniacal, double-crossing sadist.'' Capote's place in the twentieth century American literary landscape, however, is clear. He contributed both to fiction and nonfiction literary genres and redefined what it meant to join the otherwise separate realms of reporting and literature.

The streak of sadism that characterized Capote's wit stemmed largely from his troubled childhood. Capote was born Truman Streckfus

Truman Capote

Persons on September 30, 1924 in New Orleans, the son of Archuylus (Archie) Persons and Lillie May Persons Capote. At the age of four, his parents divorced, and Truman became the itinerant ward of various relatives in Alabama, several of whom would serve as inspiration for his fictional creations in such works as his classic short tale ''A Christmas Memory'' and first novel, *Other Voices, Other Rooms*. When he was ten years old, he won a children's writing contest sponsored by the *Mobile Press Register* with his submission of ''Old Mr. Busybody.'' Apropos of his later claim to fame as literary gossip par excellence, the story itself, according to Capote, was based on a local scandal that ended his brief writing career in Monroeville, Alabama, for the next half-decade. At age 15, Capote rejoined his mother and her second husband, Joseph Capote, in New York, where he attended several local boarding schools. At age 17, Capote decided to leave school for good, taking work as a copyboy at *The New Yorker*.

From *The New Yorker*, Capote soaked up much of the literary atmosphere. He also spent his leisure hours reading in the New York Society Library, where, he claimed, he met one of his literary heroines, Willa Cather. Capote's career at *The New Yorker* ended after two years when he supposedly fell asleep during a reading by Robert Frost, who promptly showed his ire by throwing what he was reading at the young reporter's head. A letter to Harold Ross from the fiery Frost resulted in Capote's dismissal, and with that change in circumstances, Capote returned to Alabama to labor three years over his first major work, *Other Voices, Other Rooms* (1948). Between 1943-46, as Capote worked on his novel, a steady stream of short stories flowed from his pen, such as ''Miriam,'' ''The Walls Are Cold,'' ''A Mink of One's Own,'' ''My Side of the Matter,'' ''Preacher's Legend,'' and ''Shut a Final Door.'' The response to the *Other Voices, Other Rooms* was immediate and intense. The lush writing and homosexual theme came in for much criticism, while the famous publicity shot of Capote supine on a couch, languidly staring into the camera's eye invited an equal mix of commentary and scorn.

Capote was only 23 years of age when he became a literary star to be lionized and chastened by the critical establishment. Hurt and surprised by the novel's reception, although pleased by its sales, Capote left to tour Haiti and France. While traveling, Capote served as a critic and correspondent for various publications, even as he continued to publish annually over the next three years *Tree of Night and Other Stories* (1949), *Local Color* (1950), and *The Grass Harp* (1951). By 1952, Capote had decided to try his hand at writing for stage and screen. In 1952, Capote rewrote *The Grass Harp* for Broadway and later in 1954 a musical called *House of Flowers*. During this period, he also wrote the screenplay *Beat the Devil* for John Huston. None fared particularly well, and Capote decided to avoid theater and movie houses by resuming his activities as a correspondent for *The New Yorker*. Joining a traveling performance of *Porgy and Bess* through the Soviet Union, he produced a series of articles that formed the basis for his first book-length work of nonfiction, *The Muses Are Heard*.

Capote continued to write nonfiction, sporadically veering aside to write such classics as *Breakfast at Tiffany's* and his famous short tale, ''A Christmas Memory.'' The former actually surprised Capote by the unanimously positive reception it received from the literary establishment (including such curmudgeonly contemporaries as Norman Mailer). In late 1959, however, Capote stumbled across the story that would become the basis for his most famous work, *In Cold Blood*. Despite the remarkable difference in content, *The Muses Are Heard* trained Capote for this difficult and trying work that helped establish ''The New Journalism,'' a school of writing that used the literary devices of fiction to tell a story of fact. The murder of the Clutter family in Kansas by Perry Smith and Dick Hickok was to consume Capote's life for the next six years. Although many quarreled with Capote's self-aggrandizing claim that he had invented a new genre that merged literature with reportage, none denied the power and quality of what he had written. Whatever failures Capote may have experienced in the past were more than made up for by the commercial and critical success of *In Cold Blood*.

Capote would never write a work as great as *In Cold Blood*, and with good reason, for the six years of research had taken a terrible toll. He did, however, continue to write short stories, novellas, interviews, and autobiographical anecdotes, all of which were collected in such works as *A Christmas Memory, The Thanksgiving Visitor, House of Flowers, The Dog's Bark*, and *Music for Chameleons*. On August 25, 1984, Truman Capote died before completing his next supposedly major work, *Answered Prayers*, a series of profiles so devastating to their subjects that Capote underwent a rather humiliating ostracism from the social circles in which he had so radiantly moved. Still, no one disputes Capote's contribution to literature as a writer who taught reporters how to rethink what they do when they ostensibly record ''just the facts.''

—Bennett Lovett-Graff

FURTHER READING:

Clarke, Gerald. *Capote*. New York, Simon & Schuster, 1988.

Garson, Helen S. *Truman Capote: A Study of the Short Fiction*. Boston, Twayne, 1992.

Grobel, Lawrence. *Conversations with Capote*. New York, New American Library, 1985.

Plimpton, George. *Truman Capote: In Which Various Friends, Enemies, Acquaintances, and Detractors Recall His Turbulent Career.* Garden City, New Jersey, Doubleday, 1997.

Capp, Al

See Li'l Abner

Capra, Frank (1897-1991)

Although he is one of the most successful and popular directors of all time, Frank Capra is seldom mentioned as one of Hollywood's great film auteurs. During his peak, as well as in the years that followed, critics referred to his work as simplistic or overly idealistic, and labeled his unique handling of complex social issues as "Capricorn." The public on the other hand loved his films and came back again and again to witness a triumph of the individual (predicated on the inherent qualities of kindness and caring for others) over corrupt leaders who were dominating an ambivalent society.

The Italian-born Capra moved to the United States at age six, where he lived the "American Dream" he would later romanticize in his films. Living in Los Angeles and working to support himself through school, he sold newspapers, and worked as a janitor before graduating with a degree in Chemical Engineering from Caltech (then called Throop Polytechnic Institute) in 1918. After serving in the military Capra stumbled onto an opportunity in San Francisco when he talked his way into directing the one-reel drama *Ballad of Fultah Fisher's Boarding House* in 1922. The experience was significant in that it convinced the young engineer to move back to Los Angeles and pursue a film, rather than an engineering, career. Upon returning to Los Angeles, Capra began the process of learning the film business from the ground up. Starting as a propman and later becoming a "gag writer," Capra worked with directors Hal Roach and Mack Sennett before hooking up as a director with silent comedian Harry Langdon.

Capra directed parts of three films produced during the peak of Langdon's career, including *The Strong Man* (1926), before the two went their separate ways. Langdon is rumored to have tarnished the young Capra's name, which, despite his success, made it impossible for him to find work in Hollywood. Unwilling to give up, Capra went to New York for an opportunity to make a film with a new actress, Claudette Colbert, titled *For The Love of Mike* (1927). Although the film was Capra's first flop, he signed a contract with studio head Harry Cohn and began his relationship with Columbia Pictures. Capra remained at Columbia for 11 years, and during this time he made at least 25 films. All but two of them made money for the studio and Capra is credited by many as being the key to Columbia's rise to the status of "major" Hollywood studio.

During his early years with Columbia some of Capra's most memorable works were the "service films" including: *Submarine* (1928), *Flight* (1929), and *Dirigible* (1931). While producing profitable films at a fast pace for the studio, Capra decided in 1931 that he wanted to tackle tougher social issues. While the country was in the throes of the Depression, Capra hooked up with writer/collaborator

Robert Riskin, with whom he worked off and on for almost 20 years. Together, Capra and Riskin produced a string of five Oscar-nominated films between 1933 and 1938. Included in this group were: *Lady for a Day* (1933, nominated for Best Picture and Best Director); *It Happened One Night* (1934, winner Best Director); *Mr. Deeds Goes to Town* (1936, nominated Best Picture, winner Best Director); *Lost Horizon* (1937, nominated Best Picture); and *You Can't Take it With You* (1938, winner Best Picture and Best Director). Although Capra continued to collaborate with Riskin on two of his most memorable works, *Mr. Smith Goes to Washington*, (1939) and *It's a Wonderful Life* (1946) were penned in collaboration with others. It is, of course, impossible to gauge how much credit Riskin deserves for Capra's meteoric rise in Hollywood. Some observers have suggested that even though Riskin wasn't involved in films like *Mr. Smith Goes To Washington,* the form and structure clearly follow the pattern the two successfully developed during their years of collaboration. Others, like Capra himself, would point to the successful films without Riskin as proof that the common denominator was the individual who insisted his name come before the title of the film. Capra even called his autobiography *The Name Above the Title,* and claims that he was the first to be granted this status. Whether or not Capra's claim has validity, there is no doubt that people all over the country flocked to the theaters during the 1930s and 1940s to see films directed by Frank Capra.

Capra's films regularly engaged political and social issues, and in his professional life he was equally active. Capra served as the President of the Academy of Motion Pictures Arts and Sciences during a crucial period of its development. During his tenure Capra oversaw a strengthening of the Academy and their annual Oscar banquet. In 1936 he worked with the Screenwriters Guild to avoid a boycott of the awards banquet, and in 1939 while serving as head of the Directors Guild, Capra resigned his post with the Academy to lead a director's boycott of the Oscars which was instrumental in gaining key concessions from the Academy. Never afraid to tackle tough political issues in his films, Capra was no stranger to controversy or difficult decisions in his professional career either.

While most of us today know Capra best from the perennial holiday favorite *It's A Wonderful Life,* the Capra myth is most solidly grounded in *Mr. Smith Goes To Washington.* After the film was previewed in Washington, D.C., it is rumored that Columbia was offered $2 million (twice the cost of the film) not to release the film. The alleged leader of this movement to shelve the film was Joseph P. Kennedy, who was then Ambassador to Great Britain. Kennedy was not alone in his concern over the film's impact. In response to *Mr. Smith Goes To Washington,* Pat Harrison, the respected publisher of the Harrison Reports, asked exhibitors to appeal to Congress for the right to refuse films that were "not in the interests of our country." Ironically, this film was perhaps Capra's most patriotic moment— presenting the individual working within the democratic system to overcome rampant political corruption. Needless to say, Capra and Columbia refused to have the film shelved. The status of *Mr. Smith Goes to Washington* was further established several years later when the French were asked what films they wanted to see prior to the occupation, and the overwhelming choice was none other than Capra's testimony for the perseverance of democracy and the American way, *Mr. Smith Goes To Washington.*

Following *Mr. Smith,* Capra demonstrated his patriotic duty by enlisting in the United States Signal Corps during World War II.

Although he had served in the military before, and was old enough to sit this one out, Capra had an intense desire to prove his patriotism to his adopted land. While a member of the Armed Forces, Capra oversaw the production of 11 documentaries under the series title *Why We Fight*. The series was originally intended to indoctrinate American troops and explain why it was necessary for them to fight the Second World War. When the first documentaries were completed Army and government officials found them so powerful that they felt the films should also be released to theaters so that everyone in America could see them. Considered by many to be some of the best propaganda films ever made, the *Why We Fight* series is still broadcast and used as a teaching tool today.

Following the war, Capra found success with *It's A Wonderful Life* and *State of the Union,* but he increasingly came to feel out of step with a changing film industry. While his themes had struck a chord with the Depression era society, his films seemed saccharin and out of touch in prospering post-war America. Moving to Paramount in 1950, Capra claimed that he became so disillusioned with the studio that he quit making films by 1952. In his autobiography he blames his retirement on the rising power of film stars (compromising the ability to realize his artistic vision), and the increasing budgetary and scheduling demands that studios placed upon him. Joseph McBride, in *The Catastrophe of Success,* however, points out that Capra's disillusionment coincided with the questions and difficulties surrounding the House Committee on Un-American Activities (HUAC) communist witch-hunt, which ended many Hollywood careers.

During a regrettable period of postwar hysteria Capra, despite his military service and decorations, was a prime-target for Senator Joseph McCarthy's Red-baiting committee. Although Capra was never called to testify, his past associations with blacklisted screenwriters such as Sydney Buchman, Albert Hackett, Ian McLelan Hunter, Calrton Moss, and Dalton Trumbo (to name a few) led to his being "greylisted" (but employable). Determined to demonstrate his loyalty he attempted to rejoin the military for the Korean War, but was refused. When invited as a civilian to participate in the Defense Department's Think Tank project, VISTA, he jumped at the opportunity, but was later denied necessary clearance. These two rejections were devastating to the man who had made a career of demonstrating American ideals in film. Capra later learned that his application to the VISTA was denied because he was part of a picket-line in the 1930s, sponsored Russian War Relief, was active in the National Federation for Constitutional Liberties (which defended communists), contributed to the Joint Anti-Fascist Refugee Committee in the 1940s, and had a number of associates who were linked to the Communist Party.

Significantly, Capra made few films once the blacklisting began, and none of them approached his previous critical and box office success. By 1952, at the age of 55, Capra effectively retired from feature filmmaking to work with Caltech and produce educational programs on science. Once one of the most popular and powerful storytellers in the world, Capra's disenchantment with the business and political climate of filmmaking left him disconnected from a culture that was rapidly changing. Although he did make two more major motion pictures *A Hole in the Head* (1959) and *Pocketful of Miracles* (1961), Capra would never again return to the perch he occupied so long atop the filmmaking world. In 1971 he penned his autobiography *The Name Above the Title,* which served to revive interest in his work and cement his idea of "one man, one film." And

since his death in 1991, Frank Capra has been honored as one of the seminal figures in the American century of the cinema.

—James Friedman

FURTHER READING:

American Film Institute. *Frank Capra: Study Guide.* Washington D.C., The Institute, 1979.

Capra, Frank. *The Name Above the Title: An Autobiography.* New York, Macmillan 1971.

Carney, Raymond. *American Vision: The Films of Frank Capra.* Cambridge, Cambridge University Press, 1986.

Maland, Charles J. *Frank Capra.* New York, Twayne Publishers, 1995.

McBride, Joseph. *Frank Capra: The Catastrophe of Success.* New York, Simon & Schuster, 1992.

Sklar, Robert and Vito Zagarrio, editors. *Frank Capra: Authorship and the Studio System.* Philadelphia, Temple University Press, 1998.

Captain America

Captain America is one of the oldest and most recognizable superhero characters in American comic books. A flagship property of Marvel Comics, Captain America has entertained generations of young people since the 1940s. Perhaps no other costumed hero has stood as a bolder symbol of patriotic American ideals and values. Indeed, the history of Captain America can not be understood without attention to the history of America itself.

Captain America sprang forth from the political culture of World War II. In early 1941, Joe Simon and Jack Kirby created the character for Marvel Comics, which was struggling to increase its share of the comic-book market. As early as 1939, comic books had periodically featured stories that drew attention to the menace of Nazi Germany. Simon and Kirby, who were both Jewish, felt very strongly about what was happening in Europe under the Nazis and were emboldened to defy the still powerful mood of isolationism in America. Captain America would make the not-very-subtle case for American intervention against the Axis powers.

The cover of the first issue of *Captain America Comics* portrayed the superhero in his red-white-and-blue costume, punching Adolf Hitler in the mouth. That brash image set the aggressive tone for the entire series. In the first issue, readers were introduced to Steve Rogers, a fiercely patriotic young American. Physically inadequate for military service, Rogers volunteers for a secret government experiment to create an army of super soldiers. After drinking a serum developed by Dr. Reinstein, Rogers is transformed into a physically perfect human fighting machine. Immediately thereafter, a Nazi spy assassinates Dr. Reinstein, whose secret formula dies with him, thus insuring that Rogers will be the only super soldier. Donning a mask and costume derived from the American flag and wielding a striped shield, Rogers adopts the identity of Captain America and pledges to wage war against the enemies of liberty at home and abroad.

Assisted by his teenage sidekick Bucky, Captain America spent the war years safeguarding American interests against conniving German and Japanese agents. Simon and Kirby dreamed up some of the most delightfully grotesque Axis caricatures to pit against the heroes. Foremost among these was the Red Skull, a sinister Nazi mastermind who became Captain America's perennial archenemy. Jack Kirby's artwork for the series was among the most exuberant, energetic, and imaginative in the field and helped to establish him as one of the most influential superhero comic-book artists.

Captain America quickly became Marvel's most popular attraction and one of the most successful superheroes of the World War II years. Despite some early hate mail from isolationists who did not appreciate the Captain America's politics, the character found an avid readership among young people receptive to the simple and aggressive Americanism that he embodied. More than any other superhero, Captain America epitomized the comic-book industry's unrestrained assault on the hated "Japanazis." Indeed, the star-spangled superhero owed so much to the wartime popular culture that he seemed to drift when the war ended. During the postwar years, Captain America's sales declined along with those of most other costumed superheroes. Even the replacement of Bucky with a shapely blond heroine named Golden Girl failed to rejuvenate interest in the title. In 1949 Marvel cancelled Captain America.

Marvel revived the hero in 1954 and recast him for the Cold War era. Now billed as "Captain America—Commie Smasher," the hero embarked on a crusade to purge America of Reds and traitors. Reentering the glutted comic-book market at a time when horror comics predominated and McCarthyism was going into decline, it was little wonder that this second incarnation of Captain America became a short-lived failure.

The Captain's third resurrection proved far more successful. In 1964, at the height of Marvel's superhero renaissance, Stan Lee and Jack Kirby revived the hero in issue number four of *The Avengers.* The story explained that Captain America's absence over the years was due to the hero having literally been frozen in suspended animation since the end of World War II. In keeping with Marvel's formula of neurotic superheroes, the revived Captain America struggled with an identity crisis: Was he simply a naive relic of a nostalgic past? Could he remain relevant in an era when unquestioning patriotism was challenged by the turmoil of the Civil Rights movement, the Vietnam War, and youth revolts?

By the early 1970s, Captain America symbolized an America confused over the meaning of patriotism and disillusioned with the national mission. The hero himself confessed that "in a world rife with injustice, greed, and endless war . . . who's to say the rebels are wrong? I've spent a lifetime defending the flag and the law. Perhaps I should have battled less and questioned more." Accordingly, Captain America loosened his longtime affiliation with the U.S. government and devoted himself to tackling domestic ills like poverty, pollution, and social injustice. He even took on a new partner called the Falcon, one of the first African-American superheroes.

In a memorable multi-part series unfolding during the Watergate scandal, Captain America uncovered a conspiracy of high-ranking U.S. officials to establish a right-wing dictatorship from the White House. This story line, written by a young Vietnam veteran named Steve Englehart, left Captain America deeply disillusioned about American political leadership—so much so that for a time he actually discarded his stars and stripes in favor of a new costume and identity of "Nomad—the Man Without a Country." But Captain America returned shortly thereafter, having concluded that even in this new age of cynicism, the spirit of America was still alive and worth defending.

Captain America has remained a popular superhero in the last decades of the twentieth century. The character may never be as popular as he was during World War II, but as long as creators can continue to keep him relevant for future generations, Captain America's survival seems assured. Although his patriotic idealism stands in stark contrast to the prevailing trend of cynical outsider superheroes like the X-Men, the Punisher, and Spawn, Captain America's continued success in the comic-book market attests to the timelessness and adaptability of the American dream.

—Bradford Wright

FURTHER READING:

Captain America: The Classic Years. New York, Marvel Comics, 1998.

Daniels, Les. *Marvel: Five Fabulous Decades of the World's Greatest Comics.* New York, Harry N. Abrams, 1991.

Simon, Joe, with Jim Simon. *The Comic Book Makers.* New York, Crestwood/II Publications, 1990.

Captain Kangaroo

For those who were either children or parents from 1955 through 1991, the perky theme music of *Captain Kangaroo,* accompanied by the jingling of the Captain's keys as he unlocked the door to the Treasure House, arouses immediate feelings of nostalgia. The longest running children's television show in history, *Captain Kangaroo* dominated the early morning airwaves for over 30 years, offering a simple and gently educational format for very young children.

The central focus of the show was always the Captain himself, a plump, teddy bear-like figure with Buster Brown bangs and a mustache to match. Much like another children's television icon, Mister Rogers, the Captain welcomed children to the show with a soft-voiced sweetness that was never condescending, and guided viewers from segment to segment chatting with the other inhabitants of the Treasure House. Bob Keeshan created the comforting role of Captain Kangaroo, so named because of his voluminous pockets. His friends on the show included a lanky farmer, Mr. Greenjeans, played by Hugh Brannum, and Bunny Rabbit and Mr. Moose, animated by puppeteer Gus Allegretti. Zoologist Ruth Mannecke was also a regular, bringing unusual animals to show the young audience.

Captain Kangaroo also had regular animated features such as "Tom Terrific and His Mighty Dog Manfred." One of the most popular segments was "Story Time," where the Captain read a book out loud while the camera simply showed the book's illustrations. It is "Story Time" that perhaps best illustrates Bob Keeshan's unassuming approach to children's entertainment, operating on the theory that children need kind and patient attention from adults more than attention-grabbing special effects.

A typical moment from the *Captain Kangaroo* show.

Keeshan got his start in the world of television early, working as a page at NBC when he was a teenager in Queens, New York. He left New York to perform his military service in the Marines, then returned to NBC where he got a job with the newly-popular *Howdy Doody Show*. He created and played the role of Clarabell the Clown on that show and was so successful that in 1955 CBS offered to give him his own show. Keeshan created *Captain Kangaroo,* and the show ran for 30 years on CBS. In 1984, it moved to PBS (Public Broadcasting System), where it continued to run for another six years.

A father of three, and later a grandfather, Keeshan had always been a supporter of positive, educational entertainment for children. Even after leaving the role of the Captain, he continued to be an advocate for children: as an activist, fighting for quality children's programming; as a performer, planning a cable television show about grandparenting; and as a writer, producing gently moralistic children's books as well as lists for parents of worthwhile books to read to children.

The soft-spoken Keeshan was so identified with the role of Captain Kangaroo that he was horrified when, in 1997, Saban Entertainment— producers of such violence- and special effects-laden shows as *Power Rangers* and *X-Men*—began to search for a new, hip Captain to take the helm of *The All-New Captain Kangaroo.* Saban had offered the role to Keeshan, but withdrew the offer when

he insisted on too much creative control over the show. Keeshan did not want modern special effects and merchandising to interfere with the Captain's gentle message. ''I really think they believe that kids are different today than they were in the 1960s or 1970s,'' he said. ''That's nonsense. They're still the same, still asking the same questions, 'Who am I? Am I loved? What does the future hold for me?''' In the end, however, Saban chose to stay with the proven formula by choosing John McDonough to play the new Captain. Neither hip nor slick, McDonough is a middle-aged, soft-spoken lover of children, not so different from Keeshan's Captain.

In an ironic twist, in 1995, the Motion Picture Association of America, trying to forestall legislation against violence in children's programming, insisted that violence in programming does not lead to violent activity. In fact, they suggested that the opposite might be true and that perhaps *Captain Kangaroo* and other mild programming of the 1950s led directly to the unrest of the 1960s and 1970s. Though Keeshan scoffed at the implication, the tactic seems to have worked and the legislation was defeated.

The media now abounds with choices of children's programming. With dozens of cable channels, children's shows can be found somewhere on television almost 24 hours a day. If that fails, parents can buy videos to pop in whenever some juvenile distraction is needed. In 1955, when the Captain debuted, and for many years afterwards, there were only three television channels that broadcast from around six a.m. until midnight. For children seeking entertainment, for parents seeking amusement for their children, even for adults seeking something to wile away the early morning hours, there was only *Captain Kangaroo*. For these people, the Captain was like an old friend, quietly accepting and unchanged over 30 years on the air.

In the 1960s, country music performers The Statler Brothers had a hit song, "Countin' Flowers on the Wall," where a young man describes his bleak and sleepless nights after being left by his girl. Perhaps no one born after the video-and-cable era will be able to completely grasp the desolate joke in the lines, "Playin' solitaire 'til dawn / With a deck of fifty-one / Smokin' cigarettes and watchin' / *Captain Kangaroo* / Now, don't tell me / I've nothing to do."

—Tina Gianoulis

FURTHER READING:

Bergman, Carl, and Robert Keeshan. *Captain Kangaroo: America's Gentlest Hero.* New York, Doubleday, 1989.

Keeshan, Robert. *Good Morning Captain: Fifty Wonderful Years With Bob Keeshan, TV's Captain Kangaroo.* Minneapolis, Fairview Press, 1996.

Raney, Mardell. "Captain Kangaroo for Children's TV." *Educational Digest.* Vol. 62, No. 9, May 1997, 4.

Captain Marvel

Captain Marvel was among the most popular comic-book superheroes of the 1940s. Created in 1940 by Bill Parker and C.C. Beck for Fawcett Publications, Captain Marvel was an ingeniously simple premise. When teenager Billy Batson speaks the magic word "Shazam," he transforms into a muscular adult superhero. Like DC Comics' Superman, Captain Marvel possessed superhuman strength, invulnerability, and the power of flight.

Captain Marvel enlisted along with most other comic-book superheroes into World War II and did his part to disseminate patriotic propaganda about the virtues of America's war effort. He was the top-selling comic-book character of the war years—even outperforming Superman for a time. By 1954, however, falling sales and a long-standing lawsuit by DC over the character's alleged similarities to Superman forced Captain Marvel into cancellation. DC later purchased the rights to the character and has published comic books featuring him since the 1970s.

—Bradford Wright

FURTHER READING:

Benton, Mike. *Superhero Comics of the Golden Age.* Dallas, Taylor Publishing, 1992.

O'Neil, Dennis. *Secret Origins of the Super DC Heroes.* New York, Warner, 1976.

Captain and the Kids, The

See Katzenjammer Kids, The

Car 54, Where Are You?

The situation comedy *Car 54, Where Are You?*, which ran on NBC from 1961 to 1963, occupies a unique place in television history. While it is a truly humorous look at the shenanigans of the police officers assigned to the fictional 53rd precinct in the Bronx, it is most often remembered as a minor cult classic filled with performers better known from other series and for its catchy opening theme song. The show focused on patrol-car partners Gunther Toody (Joe E. Ross) and Francis Muldoon (Fred Gwynne) as they attempted to serve and protect the citizens of New York. A more unlikely pairing of police officers had never been seen on television. Toody was a short and stocky, often slow-witted, talkative cop, and Muldoon was a tall and gangly, usually laconic, intellectual. Episodes were filled with the usual sitcom fare as the partners' bumbling caused misunderstandings within their squad, such as the time Toody attempted to make a plaster cast of a fellow patrolman's aching feet and chaos ensued. Each week the pair caused their superior, Captain Block, to become infuriated as they made more trouble for the Bronx than they resolved.

In many respects, *Car 54, Where Are You?* can be considered somewhat of a sequel to the popular 1950s sitcom *You'll Never Get Rich*, which is also known as *The Phil Silvers Show*. That series, created by writer-producer-director Nat Hiken and starring comedian Phil Silvers as Sergeant Bilko, focused on the misadventures of an oddball assembly of soldiers at Fort Baxter, a forgotten outpost in Kansas. Hiken was a gifted writer who had worked on Fred Allen's

A publicity shot from the television show *Car 54, Where Are You?*

radio show and later contributed to Milton Berle's *Texaco Star Theater*. The Silvers show had been a great hit as Sgt. Bilko and his motor pool staff schemed, gambled, and tried to avoid all types of work. When that series ended in 1959, Hiken decided to translate some of its comic sensibility to another setting. Like its predecessor, *Car 54* was a series about men who failed to live up to the dignity of their uniform. Unlike the schemers of Fort Baxter, however, the police of the 53rd precinct were trying their best—though often failing. Hiken filled the series with many performers featured on the earlier show. Joe E. Ross had played Mess Sergeant Rupert Ritzik "the Lucretia Borgia of Company B." The character of Gunther Toody was an exact replica of the Ritzik character even down to his trademark expression of "oooh-oooh-oooh." Toody's nagging wife Lucille was played by Beatrice Pons, the actress who had appeared as Mrs. Ritzik. Fred Gwynne, who had been a Harvard educated advertising man, was also a featured player on the Bilko show. Furthermore, many of the other officers had been seen as soldiers at the mythical Fort Baxter.

The core of the series was the great friendship Toody and Muldoon had forged from their many years patrolling the streets in Car 54. Their contrasting natures had meshed perfectly despite the fact they had absolutely nothing in common. Author Rick Mitz best captured their relationship when he described the pair by noting, "Toody was the kind of guy who would say that he thought he should get a police citation for 'having the cleanest locker.' Muldoon was the kind of guy who would say nothing." Many episodes took place away from the police station and explored the partners' home lives. Toody and his frustrated wife often included the shy bachelor into their evening plans. One of the series' best episodes centered on Toody's mistaken idea that Lucille and Muldoon were having an affair. Surrounding them was a cast of top character actors including Paul Reed, Al Lewis, Charlotte Rae, Alice Ghostley, and Nipsey Russell. Many of these performers would later graduate to star in their own TV shows. All the characters on the program depicted an ethnic reality little seen on early television. Toody's Jewishness and Muldoon's Irish-Catholic background were more realistic than the bland characters, with no discernable heritage, seen on other programs. The series was also distinguished by Hiken's decision to film on the streets of New York. Sets were constructed on the old Biograph Studio in the Bronx. For street scenes, Toody and Muldoon's patrol car was painted red and white to indicate to New Yorkers that it was not actually a police vehicle. In black-and-white film, Car 54's unique colors looked identical to the genuine New York police vehicles.

When it premiered in 1961, the series caused some controversy after several police associations claimed it presented a demeaning picture of police officers. The police department in Dayton, Ohio dropped their own Car # 54 from the fleet after constant teasing from the public. However, most viewers understood the series was intended as a satire that bore little relation to the lives of actual police officers. Viewers' affection for the show was evident in Nyack, New York where a patrol car stolen from the police station parking lot was nicknamed "Car 54." The series ended in 1963 after failing to match the success of Hiken's earlier Phil Silvers program. Neither Nat Hiken, who died in 1968, nor Joe E. Ross, who passed away in 1982, ever again achieved the limited success they found with *Car 54*. Following the show's cancellation, Fred Gwynne and Al Lewis (who played Sgt. Schnauzer) achieved TV immortality playing "Herman"

and "Grandpa" on the monster sitcom *The Munsters*. Gwynne died in 1993.

The sitcom *Car 54, Where Are You?* is an energetic series that never really attained a mass audience. Its presentation of the misadventures of Officers Toody and Muldoon gained a small cult audience that only expanded after the series began to be replayed on cable's Nick at Night network. An awful 1994 movie version update of the show (which was filmed in 1991) starred David Johansen and John C. McGinley as Toody and Muldoon. It also featured rising stars Rosie O'Donnell and Fran Drescher. Viewers of the original sitcom can ignore the film and enjoy a quirky short-lived series that offers an amusing update of the Keystone Kops. Furthermore, after one viewing it's almost impossible to forget that opening theme, which began: "There's a holdup in the Bronx / Brooklyn's broken out in fights / There's a traffic jam in Harlem that's backed up to Jackson Heights. . . ."

—Charles Coletta

FURTHER READING:

Brooks, Tim. *The Complete Directory to Prime Time TV Stars.* New York, Ballatine Books, 1987.

Castleman, Harry, and Walter Podrazik. *Harry and Wally's Favorite TV Shows.* New York, Prentice Hall Press, 1989.

Mitz, Rick. *The Great TV Sitcom Book.* New York, Perigee, 1983.

Car Coats

Car coats originated in the United States in the 1950s with the American migration to suburbia. Popular through the 1960s, they were designed to be convenient for driving, at hip to three-quarter length. Car coats were regulation outerwear: woollen, semi-fitted, frequently double-breasted, with various design features such as back-belts and toggles. The same coat is known to 1990s consumers as the stadium, toggle, or mackinaw coat.

—Karen Hovde

Caray, Harry (1919-1998)

In his 53 years as a Major League Baseball broadcaster, Harry Caray's boisterous, informal style, passionate support for the home team, and willingness to criticize players and management made him a controversial fan favorite; and towards the end of his career, something of an anachronism. During his first 25 seasons (1945-69) with the St. Louis Cardinals, KMOX's 50,000 watt clear channel signal and an affiliated network of small stations in the South, Southwest, and Midwest gave Caray regional exposure. He is perhaps best known for his catch phrase "Holy Cow," and the sing-along-with-Harry rendition of "Take Me Out to the Ballgame." Caray achieved national prominence when he moved to WGN and the

Harry Caray

Chicago Cubs in 1983. Cable television was then in its infancy, and largely on the strength of its sports programming, WGN became one of the first national superstations.

—Thomas J. Mertz

FURTHER READING:

Caray, Harry, with Bob Verdi. *Holy Cow.* New York, Villard Books, 1988.

Smith, Curt. *Voices of the Game: The First Full-Scale Overview of Baseball Broadcasting, 1921 to the Present.* South Bend, Indiana, Diamond Publishing, Inc., 1987.

Carey, Mariah (1970—)

An uproar of praise accompanied Mariah Carey's 1990 musical debut. Her first single, "Vision of Love," immediately established her as a major talent and showcased her trademark vocal sound: a masterful, multi-octave range, acrobatic phrasing, ornamented vocal trills, and uncanny, piercing notes in her upper vocal register. It was a sound that was clearly influenced by soul music tradition, yet one that Carey made uniquely her own. Unlike many popular singers, she wrote or co-wrote much of her music. Because of her beautiful and visually striking appearance, she gained additional popularity as a sex

symbol, appearing continually—often seductively or even scantily dressed—in national magazines. She found great success year after year, following her debut, and was, for nearly a decade, America's most popular musician.

—Brian Granger

FURTHER READING:

Whitburn, Joel. *The Billboard Book of Top 40 Hits.* New York, Billboard Publications, 1996.

Carlin, George (1938—)

During the 1960s, George Carlin revolutionized the art of stand-up comedy. He employed observational humor, adding a comic twist to everyday occurrences in order to comment on language, society, sports, and many mundane aspects of American daily life. His captivating stage presence and seemingly endless supply of material enabled him to succeed in giving comedy concerts. Rarely before had a comedian drawn such large crowds to a theater just to hear jokes.

George Carlin was born on May 12, 1938, in the Bronx, New York City. With one older brother, Pat, George grew up in Morningside Heights, which he calls "White Harlem," and took the title of his album *Class Clown* from his role in school as a child. He dropped out of high school and enlisted in the Air Force. He ended up in Shreveport, Louisiana, where he became a newscaster and DJ at radio

George Carlin

station KJOE, while still serving in the Air Force, and after his discharge continued worked in radio, moving to Boston in 1957 where he joined radio station WEZE.

Over the next few years, Carlin had many radio jobs, and in 1959 he met newsman Jack Burns at KXOL in Fort Worth, Texas. Teaming with Burns in the early 1960s, he moved to Hollywood where he came to the attention of Lenny Bruce. Burns and Carlin secured spots in mainstream comedy clubs and made an appearance on *The Tonight Show* with Jack Paar. When Jack Burns left the team to work with Avery Shrieber, George Carlin began to make a name for himself as a stand-up comedian, and during the decade became a fixture on television, appearing on the Johnny Carson, Mike Douglas, and Merv Griffin shows, and writing for Flip Wilson. His first comedy album, *Take-Offs and Put-Ons,* came out in 1972.

Also in 1972, he was arrested after doing his "Seven Words You Can Never Use on Television" routine at a Milwaukee concert. The charges were thrown out by the judge, but George Carlin will forever be associated with an important test of the First Amendment as applied to broadcasting—the routine was later the crux of a Supreme Court case, FCC v. Pacifica Radio, whose station WBAI in New York City broadcast the offending album. The case helped launched the FCC's "safe harbor" policy, allowing profanity on the air only after 10 PM (later changed to midnight and then extended to a 24-hour ban on indecent material).

Carlin continued releasing albums, *Occupation: Foole, FM/AM,* and *Toledo Window Box,* among others, and earning Grammy awards. Throughout the 1970s, 1980s, and 1990s, Carlin kept a public career in comedy going through television and movie appearances, recordings and live concerts, frequently performing at colleges and music festivals. He has continued developing his particular brand of humor, with its combination of satire, wordplay, and social commentary.

—Jeff Ritter

FURTHER READING:

Carlin, George. *Brain Droppings.* New York, Hyperion, 1997.

———. *Sometimes a Little Brain Damage Can Help.* Philadelphia, Pennsylvania, Running Press, 1984.

Carlton, Steve (1944—)

During the second half of his major league pitching career, Steve Carlton did not speak to reporters, preferring to let his left arm do the talking for him. Out of such determined resolve Carlton fashioned an exceptional career that left him destined for the Baseball Hall of Fame. A multiple Cy Young award winner, second only to Nolan Ryan in career strikeouts, Carlton became the first major leaguer since Robert Grove and Vernon Gomez to be universally known as "Lefty."

A Miami native, Carlton signed with the St. Louis Cardinals franchise and entered the major leagues in 1965. He became the team's number two starter, behind the fierce right-hander Bob Gibson, and helped the Cardinals to two pennants and the 1967 World Series. Yet Carlton never seemed to get respect; even the 1969 game when he struck out a then record nineteen New York Mets came during a defeat. After a salary dispute with Cardinals management in late 1971, he was traded to the woebegone Philadelphia Phillies for

Steve Carlton

pitcher Rick Wise. Wise was the only star on the perennial also-rans, as well as the Phillies' most popular player. Carlton responded to his uncomfortable new surroundings with one of the most dominant seasons in baseball history. While the 1972 Phillies won only 59 games, Carlton won 27, or nearly half his team's total, all by himself. During one stretch he won 15 games in a row. Combined with a 1.97 earned run average and 310 strikeouts, Carlton won his first National League Cy Young Award.

As Carlton developed, gradually so did the Phillies, as Carlton was joined by third baseman Mike Schmidt and, eventually, Tug McGraw, and Pete Rose. Carlton led the team to six division titles and two pennants between 1976 and 1983. And in 1980 his two victories in the World Series gave the Phillies their first world championship.

Carlton was an efficient left-hander who routinely led the major leagues by pitching nine-inning games in less than two hours and twenty minutes. Hitting him, slugger Willie Stargell once lamented, was like drinking coffee with a fork. Under the tutelage of Phillies trainer Gus Hoefling, Carlton embarked on a rigorous physical regimen, including karate, meditation, and stretching his left arm in a bag of rice. He also stopped talking to the media in 1979, following a feud with a Philadelphia columnist. While Carlton was loquacious with teammates on many subjects (in particular his hobby, wine collecting), he was mute to the press.

In 1983 and 1984, Carlton competed with the ageless Nolan Ryan for bragging rights to the all-time career strikeout record. Carlton held the top spot intermittently before Ryan pulled away in 1984. Carlton's total of 4,136 strikeouts is still the second highest of all time, and over 600 more than Walter Johnson's previous record.

In 1982, the 37-year-old Carlton won 23 games and a record fourth Cy Young Award. The next season, he won his 300th career game and again led the league in strikeouts. With his sophisticated training and focus, Carlton seemed capable of pitching in the major leagues until he was 50. Unfortunately, his pitching ability faded with age. He won only 16 games after his 40th birthday, and poignantly moved from team to team in the last two seasons of his career before retiring in 1988 with a won-loss record of 329-244.

Carlton's election to the Baseball Hall of Fame in 1994 (in his first year of eligibility) was marred by an incident weeks later. Ending his silence with the press, Carlton gave a rambling interview in *Philadelphia Magazine* from his mountainside compound in Colorado, where he claimed that AIDS was concocted by government scientists, that teacher's unions were part of an organized conspiracy to indoctrinate students, and that world affairs were controlled by twelve Jewish bankers in Switzerland. Most Phillies fans ignored his idiosyncratic political commentary, however, and attended his Cooperstown induction that summer.

—Andrew Milner

FURTHER READING:

Aaseng, Nathan. *Steve Carlton: Baseball's Silent Strongman.* Minneapolis, Lerner Publishing, 1984.

James, Bill. *The Bill James 1982 Baseball Abstract.* New York, Ballantine, 1982

———. *The Bill James Historical Baseball Abstract.* New York, Villard, 1988.

Westcott, Rich. *The New Phillies Encyclopedia.* Philadelphia, Temple University Press, 1993.

Carmichael, Hoagy (1899-1981)

Children who play the perennial "Heart and Soul" duet on the family piano might not realize that the tune was written in 1938 by one of America's most prolific popular song composers, Hoagy Carmichael. Carmichael also became one of the century's most iconic pianists, as his distinctive appearance—gaunt and glum, hunched over the upright piano in a smoky nightclub—endures through numerous Hollywood films from the 1940s and 1950s, including classics such as *To Have and Have Not* and *The Best Years of Our Lives* (in *Night Song* he even shares billing with classical concert pianist Arthur Rubinstein). Carmichael's music lives on, too, having thoroughly entered the American musical canon. Of his 250 published songs, "Stardust" (1927) is probably one of the most frequently recorded of all popular songs (with renditions by artists ranging from Bing Crosby and Nat King Cole to Willie Nelson and Carly Simon); "The Lamplighter's Serenade" (1942) proved to be Frank Sinatra's solo recording debut; and "Georgia on My Mind" (1931) has become that state's official song.

Hoagy Carmichael

Carmichael's roots were in the 1920s Midwest, where traditional Americana intersected with the exciting developments of jazz. Hoagland Howard Carmichael was born on November 22, 1899, in Bloomington, Indiana. His father was an itinerant laborer; his mother, an amateur pianist, played accompaniment for silent films. In 1916, his family moved to Indianapolis, where Carmichael met ragtime pianist Reggie DuValle, who taught him piano and stimulated his interest in jazz. In 1919 Carmichael heard Louis Jordan's band in Indianapolis; as Carmichael relates in his autobiography *Sometimes I Wonder,* the experience turned him into a "jazz maniac." While studying law at Indiana University, Carmichael formed his own small jazz band, and also met 19-year-old legendary cornetist Leon "Bix" Beiderbecke, who became a close friend as well as a strong musical inspiration. Carmichael's earliest surviving composition, the honky-tonk "Riverboat Shuffle," was written in 1924 and recorded by the Wolverines, Beiderbecke's jazz band (Carmichael, incidentally, wrote the soundtrack music and played a supporting role in Hollywood's 1950 fictionalized version of Beiderbecke's life, *Young Man with a Horn,* starring Kirk Douglas, Lauren Bacall, and Doris Day).

After receiving his degree, Carmichael practiced law in Palm Beach, Florida, hoping to capture part of the real estate boom market there. Soon deciding to devote his efforts to music, Carmichael moved to New York, but met with little success on Tin Pan Alley. It was not until Isham Jones's orchestra made a recording of "Stardust" in 1930 that Carmichael had his big break. Within a year Louis Armstrong, Duke Ellington, and the Dorsey brothers had recorded their own versions of other Carmichael songs (including "Georgia

On My Mind,'' ''Rockin' Chair,'' and ''Lazy River'') for the burgeoning radio audience.

During the next decade, Carmichael worked with lyricists Johnny Mercer, Frank Loesser, and Mitchell Parish, among others. In the late 1930s he joined Paramount Pictures as staff songwriter (his first film song was ''Moonburn,'' introduced in the 1936 Bing Crosby film *Anything Goes),* and also began appearing in films himself (the first film he sang in was *Topper,* performing his own ''Old Man Moon''). In 1944, ''Hong Kong Blues'' and ''How Little We Know'' were featured in the Warner Brothers film *To Have and Have Not,* starring Humphrey Bogart and Lauren Bacall, which also marked Carmichael's debut as an actor. In one year (1946) Carmichael had three of the top four songs on the Hit Parade, and in 1947 his rendition of his own song ''Old Buttermilk Sky'' (featured in the film *Canyon Passage,* and nominated for an Academy Award) held first place on the Hit Parade for six consecutive weeks. Carmichael described his own singing as a ''native wood-note and flatsy-through-the-nose voice.'' It was not until 1952, however, that Carmichael and lyricist Mercer won an Academy Award for Best Song with ''In the Cool, Cool, Cool of the Evening,'' performed by Bing Crosby in Paramount's *Here Comes the Groom).* Carmichael also made appearances on television during the 1950s, hosting his own variety program, *The Saturday Night Revue* (a summer replacement for Sid Caesar's *Your Show of Shows),* in 1953. In 1959 he took on a straight dramatic role as hired ranch hand Jonesy on the television Western series *Laramie.*

Carmichael continued composing into the 1960s, but his two orchestral works—''Brown County in Autumn''—and his 20-minute tribute to the Midwest—''Johnny Appleseed''—were not as successful as his song compositions. In 1971, Carmichael's contributions to American popular music were recognized by his election to the Songwriters Hall of Fame as one of the ten initial inductees. He retired to Palm Springs, California, where he died of a heart attack on December 27, 1981.

—Ivan Raykoff

FURTHER READING:

Carmichael, Hoagy. *The Stardust Road.* New York, Rinehart, 1946.

Carmichael, Hoagy, with Stephen Longstreet. *Sometimes I Wonder: The Story of Hoagy Carmichael.* New York, Farrar, Staus, and Giroux, 1965.

Carnegie, Dale (1888-1955)

Aphorisms, home-spun wisdom, and an unflagging belief in the public and private benefits of positive thinking turned Dale Carnegie's name into a household phrase that, since the 1930s, has been uttered with both gratitude and derision. Applying the lessons that he learned from what he perceived to be his failures early in life, Carnegie began to teach a course in 1912. Ostensibly a nonacademic, public-speaking course, Carnegie's class was really about coming to terms with fears and other problems that prevented people from reaching their full potential. Through word of mouth the course became hugely popular, yet Carnegie never stopped tinkering with the curriculum, excising portions that no longer worked and adding new material based on his own ongoing life experience. In 1936, he increased his profile exponentially by publishing *How to Win Friends and Influence People,* which ranks as one of the most purchased

books of the twentieth century. Although Carnegie died in 1955, his course has continued to be taught worldwide, in virtually unchanged form, into the late 1990s.

Carnegie (the family surname was Carnagey, with an accent on the second syllable; Carnegie changed it when he moved to New York, partly because of his father's claim that they were distant relatives of Andrew Carnegie and partly because the name had a cachet of wealth and prestige) grew up on a farm in Missouri; his family was, according to his own accounts, poverty-stricken. His mother, a strict and devout Methodist, harbored not-so-secret hopes that her son might become a missionary; some missionary zeal can be seen in Carnegie's marketing of his course. At the age of eighteen, Carnegie left home to attend Warrensburg State Teacher's College. There, he made a name for himself as a riveting and effective public speaker. Just short of graduating, he decided to quit and start a career as a salesman in the Midwest. Despite his knack for expressing himself, his heart was never in sales, and he was less than successful. In 1910, Carnegie headed for New York City and successfully auditioned for admission into the prestigious American Academy of Dramatic Arts. The new style of acting taught at the school, radical for its time, stressed sincerity in words and gestures. Students were encouraged to emulate the speech and movement of ''real people'' and to move away from posturing and artificiality. Carnegie spent even less time as a professional actor than he did as a salesman, but this new method of acting would become a vital part of his course.

In 1912 Carnegie was back in sales, working for the Packard car and truck company, after a disillusioning tour with a road company that was staging performances of Molly Mayo's *Polly of the Circus.* Living in squalor and unable to make ends meet, Carnegie nonetheless walked away from his Packard sales job and began doing the one thing he felt qualified to do: teach public speaking to businessmen. The director of a YMCA on 125th Street in Harlem agreed to let Carnegie teach classes on commission. (At that time most continuing adult education took place at the YMCA or YWCA.) Carnegie's breakthrough came when he ran out of things to say and got the class members to talk about their own experiences. No class like this had ever been offered, and businessmen, salesmen, and, to a lesser extent, other professionals praised the course that gave them the opportunity to voice their hopes and fears, and the means to articulate them. Both academic and vocational business courses were in short supply during this time, and most professionals had little understanding of communications or human relations principles. Carnegie anticipated this need and geared his course toward the needs of the business professional.

From 1912 until his death in 1955, Carnegie's chief concern was the fine-tuning and execution of his course, formally titled The Dale Carnegie Course in Public Speaking and Human Relations, but fondly known to millions of graduates as the ''Dale Course.'' Carnegie also attempted to publish a novel, *The Blizzard,* which was ill-received by publishers. His publishing luck changed in 1936, when Leon Shimkin of Simon & Schuster persuaded him to write a book based on lectures he gave in various sessions of the course. *How to Win Friends and Influence People* was published in November of that year and became an instant best-seller. Following this accomplishment, Carnegie published a few similar works that also became bestsellers, most notably *How to Stop Worrying and Start Living.* None of his subsequent literary endeavors, however, matched the success of *How to Win Friends,* although they are all used, to some extent, in his course.

With the huge sales of the book, Carnegie faced a new challenge: meeting the growing public demand for the course. In 1939, he agreed to begin licensing the course to other instructors throughout the

Dale Carnegie

country. By now divorced from his first wife (the marriage ended unhappily in 1931—Carnegie's *Lincoln the Unknown,* with its unflattering portrayal of Mary Todd Lincoln, was later revealed by the author to be "largely autobiographical"), he met Dorothy Vanderpool, whom he would marry in 1941. Dorothy, a graduate of the Dale Course, became an ardent supporter of her husband's work and was responsible for making the business a successful enterprise long after her husband's death. When she died, on August 6, 1998, the Dale Carnegie Course, mostly unchanged in form and content, was still going strong.

The Great Depression transformed Carnegie's program from a relatively successful endeavor into a cultural monument. His low-key optimism and no-nonsense approach to human relations proved irresistible to the massive number of Americans who were unemployed. The publication of his book meant that his message, and his appeal, could spread much further and faster than it had through the auspices of the course. A year after its publication, the book's title was a permanent part of the language; the phrase "How to Win Friends and Influence People" quickly overshadowed Dale Carnegie and his course, and became a catch-phrase for enthusiasm borne of naiveté, as well as a euphemism for manipulative styles of dealing with others.

Carnegie's appeal was always complex and convoluted. His book spoke to the hopes and fears of an entire nation beset by serious economic difficulties, and yet many people thought his ideas were too simplistic and out of tune with the times to take without a heavy dose of irony. He had his share of famous critics as well, such as James Thurber and Sinclair Lewis, who reviled *How to Win Friends* in their writings. Apart from the high-minded criticism of these and other intellectuals, the main obstacle that kept people from signing up for Carnegie's course was the same thing that won over many other graduates: enthusiasm. The unbridled enthusiasm that was such a part of the course, and that students demonstrated during open-house sessions, could be off-putting as well as inspiring; people were unsure whether it was contrived or real. There was a surge of renewed public interest in the late 1980s, when Lee Iacocca revealed in his autobiography the extent to which Carnegie's course had influenced him and his willingness to pay for his employees to take the course. In the end, Carnegie's sustained popularity was due as much to the controversy caused by the public's inability to take him completely seriously as to the man's teachings and writings.

—Dan Coffey

FURTHER READING:

Carnegie, Dale. *How to Stop Worrying and Start Living.* New York, Simon & Schuster, 1984.

———. *How to Win Friends and Influence People.* New York, Simon & Schuster, 1981.

Conniff, Richard. "The So-So Salesman Who Told Millions How to Make It Big." *Smithsonian.* Vol. 18, October 1987, 82-93.

Kemp, Giles, and Edward Claflin. *Dale Carnegie: The Man Who Influenced Millions.* New York, St. Martin's Press, 1989.

Longgood, William. *Talking Your Way to Success: The Story of the Dale Carnegie Course.* New York, Association Press, 1962.

Carnegie Hall

The world's most famous concert hall, New York City's Carnegie Hall, opened in 1891, proved important as an institution and, by setting a critical precedent for financing in the 1950s, for the future of the performing arts in America.

Designed by William Burnet Tuthill, an architect with a musical ear, the hall was praised for both its architecture and its acoustics following the opening performances by Tchaikovsky. Carnegie Hall's prestigious reputation was established by the quality of the performers who appeared there, and the way to get there was to "practice, practice, practice," the success or failure of a Carnegie Hall debut often determining whether or not a performer established a successful career.

Olin Downes, a music critic at the *New York Times,* wrote, "In the first quarter of this century [the city] became the musical center of the world. Nowhere else was to be met in the course of a season so many commanding personalities, interpretive and creative, of the period. New York was transformed from a cultural colony into a cultural capital." During that Golden Age and particularly between 1910-30, every one of the world's greatest instrumentalists appeared at least once every season in Carnegie Hall. Among conductors and orchestras, Arturo Toscanini conducted the New York Philharmonic there and Leopold Stokowski brought the Philadelphia Orchestra for regular annual series, as did the various conductors of the Boston

Carnegie Hall

Symphony. Jascha Heifetz, Fritz Kreisler, Joseph Szigeti, Vladimir Horowitz, Sergey Rachmaninoff, and Artur Rubinstein appeared for annual recitals or with the orchestras.

Although he provided two million dollars to build it, linking steel magnate Andrew Carnegie's name to the hall is among the great ironies of American cultural life. Carnegie's musical interests centered on bagpipe melodies and Scottish folk tunes and hymns played on an organ that awakened him each morning. The best statement of purpose he could offer the public when the cornerstone was laid in 1890 was the hope that the structure would "intertwine itself with the history of our country." On opening night, May 5, 1891, Morris Reno, president of the stock company that Carnegie had set up to manage the enterprise (for a profit), would advise that the hall had been "founded with the loftiest purposes, free from all disturbing private interests, devoted solely to the highest ideals of art. . . ."

In fact, Carnegie had no such ideals. Nor was he motivated by needs for publicity or acclaim common to tycoons of the Gilded Age. Finally, his unspeakable treatment of workers at his Homestead, Pennsylvania, plant does not suggest sympathy for the common man who, hopefully, would attend performances. The best that can be said about Carnegie's plan for the hall was that, like his plan for the libraries he later founded, it was not an end in itself. For the libraries, he would make a grant for construction, and then it was up to the local community to raise operating funds. But it immediately became clear that such a pattern would not fit the Music (later, Carnegie) Hall. There simply was not enough rental business, and Carnegie had to underwrite operating deficits, which he did with frequent complaints.

New York's highly competitive social and musical establishments were unenthused by his generosity to begin with. In advance of opening night, the *New York Times* hoped that Music Hall presentations would educate rather than "merely entertain." William Steinway, a piano manufacturer who had a concert hall of his own, scoffed that "Mr. Carnegie's hall will never pay. Take our present Philharmonic concerts, for instance . . . increase the number of these high-class concerts to twelve, and financial disaster would be certain. The public can only stand a certain amount of this sort of music. . . ."

A constant pressing need for cash inspired Carnegie's company to encourage not only musical but other types of renters. In December 1915, a large audience witnessed the launching of the first mass fundraising campaign in American Jewish history for the relief of overseas brethren. Fresh from the Versailles Peace Conference in July 1919, President Woodrow Wilson disembarked in Hoboken, New Jersey, and proceeded immediately to the hall, where he made the first speech in his unsuccessful campaign for congressional approval of United States membership in the League of Nations. Tenants such as the American Academy of Dramatic Arts, whose graduates included Cecil B. De Mille, Agnes Moorehead, Rosalind Russell, and Spencer Tracy, contributed to the hall's international fame.

Carnegie Hall opened its 1925-26 season under new management. Carnegie had died in 1919, and although his board of directors continued to run the hall together with the Carnegie estate, it had remained unprofitable. Robert E. Simon, a prosperous realtor, then bought the building and kept his promise not to tear it down, although there were hints that he and his son wavered during the years of Simon family ownership.

Finally, when plans for Lincoln Center for the Performing Arts were announced in 1959, Robert Simon Jr. announced that the hall would be razed in favor of a skyscraper. Music lovers were outraged, but New York was constantly tearing itself down and rebuilding, and there was no march by the masses to the hall in protest.

A volunteer Citizens' Committee for Carnegie Hall decided on behalf of all city residents (without any referendum) that the hall should be saved—and not with private funds. The committee favored the idea that the city should issue bonds to pay for the hall's purchase and renovation, with the bonded indebtedness to be paid off by a Carnegie Hall Corporation. Once the bonds were retired, the hall would become the property of the corporation, which could, if it wished, apply to the city for additional operating funds.

Thus was realized the concept that although cultural interests could not be legislated into existence, the financing for them could be, a precedent critical for future financing of the performing arts.

—Milton Goldin

FURTHER READING:

Damrosch, Walter. *My Musical Life*. New York, Charles Scribner's Sons, 1924.

Schickel, Richard. *The World of Carnegie Hall*. New York, Messner, 1960.

The Carpenters

Between 1970 and 1975, The Carpenters, a brother-sister musical act, were one of the most popular and recognized pop groups.

Karen and Richard Carpenter

Because they emerged following a decade (the 1960s) in which the most influential performers were those who pushed the bounds of pop music, they were often criticized for their wholesome, straightforward style. However, Karen Carpenter, with her extraordinary voice and girl-next-door good looks, and Richard Carpenter, with his world-class composing abilities, overcame the criticism to produce 19 top-10 singles during the 1970s.

Karen (1950-1983), who was both a singer and a drummer, and Richard (1946—), who was the group's arranger, producer, and keyboardist, were born in New Haven, Connecticut, to Harold Bertram Carpenter and Agnes Tatum. While children, they developed an enthusiasm for popular music. While Richard pursued music avidly, Karen played the flute briefly, but was more interested in sports. The family moved to Downey, California, in 1963. In 1966, Karen and Richard teamed up with bassist Wes Jacobs to form the Richard Carpenter Trio, an instrumental band. Karen also signed a solo singing contract with the Magic Lamp record label, and recorded "Looking for Love" and "I'll Be Yours," released as singles. Shortly after, the Richard Carpenter Trio won "The Battle of the Bands" at the Hollywood Bowl.

It wasn't until 1969, however, that the band, refashioned as the Carpenters and with Karen singing as well as playing drums, was "discovered" by world-famous trumpeter Herb Alpert, leader of the Tijuana Brass, and co-founder of the A&M record label. Upon hearing a demo tape of the Carpenters, he immediately recognized the extraordinary quality of Karen Carpenter's voice. "It was full and round, and it was . . . amazing. This voice was buzzing into my body, and it was the way they presented it." Their first album, *Offering*, was released on the A&M record label in 1969. It did not sell well, although their cover of the Beatles' "Ticket to Ride" reached number 54 on the U.S. singles charts. In 1970, their album *Close to You*, included their first number one single of the same name (which sold more than 300,000 copies), and the duo began international tours that would include up to 200 concerts in a year. That year they also released the hit singles "We've Only Just Begun," and "For All We Know." They won Grammy Awards in 1970 for best contemporary vocal performance by a group for "Close to You," and also for best new artist. In 1970, "For All We Know," featured in the film "Lovers and Other Strangers," captured an Academy Award.

Between 1970 and 1975, the Carpenters were one of the hardest working bands in pop music. Richard was the guiding force behind the duo's production and arrangements, and also wrote songs with Richard Bettis. But material supplied by songwriters Burt Bacharach, Paul Williams, and Roger Nichols helped the Carpenters gain astounding success with 17 million-selling albums between 1970 and 1981. Other well-known standards released by the duo during this period were "Rainy Days and Mondays," "Superstar," "Sing," "Yesterday Once More," and "Top of the World." Their compilation album, *The Singles 1969-1973,* was on the U.S. album charts for 115 weeks. By the late 1990s, the Carpenters had demonstrated that their success was more than fleeting, with worldwide sales topping 100 million units.

The Carpenters bucked 1970s pop music trends by conveying a wholesome, middle-class image, and were even mocked by the pop music establishment, who viewed their songs as insipid and their popularity as fleeting. Music critic Rob Hoerburger (*New York Times,* Nov. 3, 1991) wrote "They always dressed as if they were going to church, and they sang sticky songs about love (but never sex). Worst of all, parents loved their music." During their heyday, rock critics described their music as "treacle," "drippy easy listening," "schlock music," and their personalities as "squeaky," "smiley," and "saccharine." Fortunately for their record company, A&M, and their in-house mentor, Herb Alpert, the listening public purchased their records by the millions and their concerts sold out consistently. Their popularity was not confined to the United States. They also had strong fan bases in Great Britain and Japan, and they were also popular in many other European and Asian countries. In 1973, they were honored by then-President Richard Nixon by being asked to perform at a state visit by West German Chancellor Willy Brandt.

The Carpenters enjoyed their greatest success between 1970 and 1975. After that time, the duo was beset by serious health problems. Richard spent several years addicted to the sedative Quaalude, and recovery took another several years. Karen, meanwhile, battled anorexia nervosa, a psychophysiological disorder whose cluster of symptoms begins usually with a fear of being overweight and continues with severe weight loss due to self-starvation. She fought this disease for years, with her "normal" weight of 120 pounds (she was 5'4" tall) dropping to 79 pounds several times between 1975 (when she collapsed onstage in Las Vegas while singing "Top of the World"), and her death in 1983. Though few were aware of anorexia nervosa as a disease during the 1970s, Carpenter's death from the disorder drew a great deal of attention to the disease. Indeed, she may be as important a figure in American popular culture because of the way she died as because of the way she achieved fame. After her death anorexia nervosa became well-known to the American public, and many sought help for themselves or their (often) teenage daughters after reading or hearing media accounts of her symptoms and the cause of her death.

The Carpenters experienced a new surge of popularity in the late 1980s and 1990s as their catalog was re-released on compact disk, most notably the four-disk set *From the Top*. In 1994, a compilation of their songs entitled *If I Were a Carpenter*, performed by some of the most popular "alternative" music groups, became a top-selling record. Many of these rock stars, including Sonic Youth, Cracker, and the Cranberries, said that they had been strongly influenced by the Carpenters' sound. Jeff McDonald of Redd Kross, one of the bands featured on the CD, echoed the beliefs of many musicians and critics who had reassessed their music almost twenty years after their peak popularity. "I'd always been a huge fan of the Carpenters, and an admirer of their songs. The quality of their songs was so wonderful, they were lyrically very sophisticated, not this teenybop fare . . . Most bands just want to write perfect pop songs. And these are perfect pop songs."

Richard Carpenter's music career continued on a considerably reduced basis after his sister's death, although he continues to tour and produce. Most notably, he produced his sister's last solo album, *Karen Carpenter*, released in 1996, and his own album, *Pianist—Arranger—Composer—Conductor,* came out in 1998.

—Jeff Merron

FURTHER READING:

Coleman, Ray. *The Carpenters: The Untold Story: An Authorized Biography*. New York, HarperCollins, 1994.

Carr, John Dickson (1906-1977)

Considered one of the twentieth century's grand masters of the detective story for his innovative use of subtlety, ingenuity, and atmosphere, John Dickson Carr, alias Carter Dickson and Carr Dickson, produced numerous short stories, non-fiction works, and over 70 neo-gothic and historical mystery novels during his lifetime. His best known tales, commonly referred to as locked room mysteries, feature horrific crimes committed seemingly without human agents; subsequently, his sleuths must exercise pure reason to solve them. Amidst an atmosphere of suspense, a small dose of the supernatural, and sometimes high comedy, Carr cleverly presents clues, suspects, and motives such that few readers are able to predict the solutions. His characters Henri Bencolin, Dr. Gideon Fell, Sir Henry Merrivale, and Colonel March rank high among the most memorable detectives within the genre, and Carr's skill in detailing their exploits continues to influence contemporary mystery novelists in the 1990s.

Born in Uniontown, Pennsylvania, on November 30, 1906, Carr first gained his lifelong interest in crime and detection from his father, Wooda Nicholas Carr, a politician and lawyer. From an early age, he enjoyed reading authors L. Frank Baum, Alexandre Dumas, and Robert Louis Stevenson, though he later preferred the works of Sir Arthur Conan Doyle and G. K. Chesterton. In his early teens, he began writing for a local newspaper and developed a keen interest in detective stories that featured solutions to impossible crimes. He attended the Hill, a preparatory school, and entered Haverford College in 1925. At Haverford, Carr's writing career blossomed. After becoming editor of *The Haverfordian,* a monthly literary magazine, he began to write not only short historical romances, but also a series of detective stories about impossible crimes solved by Paris policeman Henri Bercolin.

Circa 1928, Carr's parents sent him to Paris to study at the Sorbonne; however, Carr never attended the school and seriously pursued writing instead. Determined to hone his craft in Paris, he wrote but later destroyed an historical novel, then wrote another Henri Bencolin story entitled ''Grand Guignol.'' Upon his return to America, he submitted this manuscript to *The Haverfordian,* which published it as a short novel in early 1929. Carr later revised the story, expanded its length, and submitted the manuscript to Harper & Bros. Published in 1930, *It Walks by Night* marked the beginning of Carr's successful career as a detective novelist. In 1932, he married Clarice Cleaves, an Englishwoman, and the following year, moved to England. During the remainder of the 1930s, he produced three to five novels a year, adding Dr. Gideon Fell and Sir Henry Merrivale to his repertoire of impossible crime solvers. He also began to write short stories for popular magazines. In 1935, he published ''Terror's Dark Tower,'' one of his best short stories about murder in a sealed room, and by the end of the decade, his works were regularly featured in major magazines such as *The Illustrated London News* and *The Strand.*

During the 1940s, Carr produced fewer mystery novels; his talents were needed elsewhere. Supporting the war effort, he wrote and narrated propaganda broadcasts for the British Broadcasting Corporation. Concurrently, he also wrote mystery dramas for the BBC and CBS network in America and was instrumental in creating the style of the great radio plays. At the end of World War II, he began

a definitive biography of Sir Arthur Conan Doyle that was eventually published in 1949.

Dissatisfied with the rise of socialism in England, Carr returned to America with his family in 1948 and was elected President of the Mystery Writers of America in 1949. During this period, he embarked on a new phase in his writing career. A lifelong admirer of the past, he decided to write mysteries situated in specific historical time frames and that sometimes involved time travel. This innovative decision proved fortuitous; his meticulously researched historical novels received both critical and popular acclaim. In 1950, he published *The Bride of Newgate,* a high adventure set in 1815 England. The following year, he published *The Devil in Velvet,* in which a modern professor bargains with Satan for a transfer back to eighth-century England. Considered by Carr to be his best work, *The Devil in Velvet* was the most successful of his novels.

Between 1951 and 1965, Carr moved back and forth between England and America before finally settling in Greenville, South Carolina. Due to increasing ill health, he wrote no more fiction after 1972, but contributed to a review column in *Ellery Queen's Mystery Magazine* and began a series about seventeenth- and eighteenth-century criminals which was never completed. He died March 1, 1977, at age 70.

During his lifetime, Carr was the recipient of the Mystery Writers of America's highest honor, the Grand Master Award, and was the first American ever admitted into the almost exclusively British Detection Club. Indeed, his stories reflect the qualities that he felt should always be present in the detective novel at its best: fair play, sound plot construction, and ingenuity.

—Marlena E. Bremseth

FURTHER READING:

Greene, Douglas G. *John Dickson Carr: The Man Who Explained Miracles.* New York, Otto Penzler Books, 1995.

———, editor. *The Door to Doom and Other Detections.* New York, Harper & Row, 1980.

Panck, Leroy. *Watteau's Shepherds: The Detective Novel in Britain, 1914-1940.* Bowling Green, Ohio, Popular Press, 1979.

The Cars

With their campy groundbreaking videos and catchy songs, The Cars emerged from the late-1970s/early-1980s New Wave movement to become one of America's best selling musical acts. This Boston band led by Ric Ocasek scored thirteen *Billboard* Top 40 hits from 1978 to 1987 with thinly-veiled sexual innuendo songs like ''Shake It Up,'' ''You Might Think,'' ''Drive,'' and ''Tonight She Comes.''

Formed in 1976 out of the ashes of various local Boston bands, including the Jonathan Richman-fronted Modern Lovers, The Cars landed a major label deal with Elektra after a demo of ''Just What I Needed'' became a hit on local Boston radio stations. The group consisted of Ric Ocasek on vocals and guitar, Ben Orr handling vocals and bass duties, Elliot Easton on guitar, Greg Hawkes playing

The Cars

keyboards and former Modern Lovers drummer David Robinson behind the drum kit. The Cars' aesthetic jumping-off point fell somewhere between AM radio bubblegum pop, new wave quirkiness, Brian Ferry-esque art-pop, and the bombast of Album Oriented Radio: a combination that appealed to a wide variety of consumers.

Early on, The Cars established themselves as one of the best-selling new wave bands in America. Their self-titled debut album was released in 1978, spawning a number of hit singles, going platinum, and staying in the album charts for two and a half years. They released a string of hit albums, including *Candy-O, Panorama, Shake It Up,* and *Heartbeat City,* before they took a two year break starting in 1985 so that Ocasek, Orr, and Easton could record solo albums and pursue other projects (such as Ocasek's appearance in the John Waters film, *Hairspray*). By the time The Cars regrouped to release 1987's *Door to Door,* the band had run its course, creatively and commercially. After a tour supporting *Door to Door,* The Cars broke up in 1988.

Although their pop radio-friendly songs were a major reason for their popularity, The Cars also gained attention with their music videos—something that distinguished the post-MTV era from other periods of popular music. Their most acclaimed video was the Andy Warhol directed ''You Might Think,'' which sported groundbreaking (for the time) computer animation. The success The Cars had with their videos, along with a few other artists that were regularly played on MTV, demonstrated the burgeoning music channel's power as a marketing device.

In addition to his work as the frontman of The Cars, Ric Ocasek produced a number of important underground, avant-garde, and punk bands that didn't sell a lot of records, but which proved extremely influential. Among the most significant Ocasek-produced bands were the Washington D.C. hardcore punk group Bad Brains and the New York City duo, Suicide. Ocasek also produced albums by the commercially successful Romeo Void in the early 1980s and, in 1994, he produced the platinum debut by Weezer. Because of his role as a major contributor to American underground and commercial music, Ric Ocasek had a large number of high-profile fans like Billy Corgan, the leader of 1990s alternative rock icons, Smashing Pumpkins. Corgan paid homage to Ocasek by producing Ocasek's 1997 solo album, *Troublizing.*

—Kembrew McLeod

FURTHER READING:

The Trouser Press Guide to New Wave. Ed. Ira A. Robbins. New York, Scribners, 1983.

Heylin, Clinton. *From the Velvets to the Voidoids: A Pre-Punk History for a Post-Punk World.* New York, Penguin, 1993.

Carson, Johnny (1925—)

In January 1965, Johnny Carson appeared at Lyndon Baines Johnson's presidential inauguration gala. Carson took the stage directly opposite the president and bragged "I've done more for birth control than Enovid." The claim is questionable, but it is vintage Johnny Carson. Like most Carson jokes, it looks neither particularly funny nor particularly racy on paper. In its delivery, however, Carson won much of the audience over, created a flurry of scandal, and effectively situated himself in American cultural history. Carson made one of television's greatest careers by playing his impish wit off his Midwestern charm, bringing the sexual revolution to middle America, middle America to the world, and establishing the form for television variety and humor that continues to dominate.

Carson was born on October 23, 1925 in Corning, Iowa, and spent the first eight years of his life moving throughout Iowa as his father established a management career in the Iowa-Nebraska Electric Light and Power Company. In 1933, the Carson family settled in Norfolk, Nebraska, population 10,000. Carson came of age in Norfolk, premiering his magic act, "The Great Carsoni," there. Carson, along with his magician alter-ego, enlisted in the Navy in 1943, hoping to be a fighter pilot in the Second World War. His military career, however, was more notable for its hilarity than its heroics.

In the fall of 1946, Carson left the Navy and enrolled in the University of Nebraska. As a student he initiated his broadcast career, appearing in a western comedy on KFAB, a Lincoln, Nebraska, radio station. Also at the University of Nebraska, Carson met the first of his

Johnny Carson

many loves—Jodi Wolcott, "The Great Carsoni's" magician's assistant and a native of Western Nebraska.

Wolcott and Carson married in 1949, just after they moved to Omaha where Johnny had taken a broadcasting position at NBC's Nebraska affiliate, WOW. It was the dawn of television, and WOW had just branched out of the radio market to broadcast the region's first television signals. Carson got in early, with an afternoon program called *Squirrel's Nest*. The Carsons had their first child in 1950, but Carson was unwilling to settle down. In 1951, he set out, alone, in the family Oldsmobile, determined to make it big in California.

The journey was a success, and soon the whole clan made the trek, Jodi pregnant for the second time. In Los Angeles, Carson rose rapidly from late night announcer to host of the prime-time *Johnny Carson Show*. That first show was a flop, but it led to another, and by 1962, when Carson took over *The Tonight Show* from Jack Paar, he had already hosted three incarnations of *The Johnny Carson Show,* two game shows, and several short-run broadcasts.

Even as Carson's corn-fed persona gained prominence in national television, his family was disintegrating. He divorced Jodi Wolcott in 1965, endured hostile publication over his reluctance to pay child support for his three boys, and read his mother's dismissive comments about his show business career in *Time* magazine. In the years to come, Carson would have two more divorces and three more wives, but somehow, the image of Johnny Carson, the good Midwestern boy with a mean streak survived, and *The Tonight Show* was a hit.

In 1968, Carson discovered Tiny Tim, a Greenwich Village performer with a ukulele, a falsetto voice, and an odd blend of hippie-left appearance and Barry Goldwater conservatism. Tim and Carson spoke about premarital sex and birth control (Carson was an advocate and Tim an opponent). Tim plugged his album, *God Bless Tiny Tim,* a collection of obscure American pop tunes, and it became one of the year's best sellers. Before long, Tim was a regular on the show. On December 17, 1969, Tiny Tim married Miss Vicky live on *The Tonight Show.* Carson biographer Laurence Leamer called the wedding "the most-watched even in late-night television history."

Meanwhile, Carson perfected his trademark animal skits, bantered in his calculated casual manner with such luminaries as Muhammed Ali, Richard Nixon, Luciano Pavarotti, and Ronald Reagan, and became a fixture in American popular culture. In 1972, *The Tonight Show* moved to beautiful downtown Burbank, California where it was to play for another 20 years; its spartan set of office furniture and indoor plants becoming instantly recognizable to millions of American television viewers. *The Tonight Show* routine, from Ed McMahon's "Here's Johnny!" through Carson's free-wheeling monologue and its selection of short skits and guests became the model for late-night television. *Tonight Show* producers Rudy Tellez described the program's formula as "the bland leading the bland." But, combined with Carson's mildly risque sense of humor, it consistently worked, facing and defeating competing shows from Dick Cavett, Joey Bishop, Merv Griffin, Alan Thicke, David Brenner, and Joan Rivers.

Johnny Carson became famous as the man who lulled America to sleep at night. When he left the air in May 1992, his reign was undiminished, his persona was untarnished, and as the *Washington Post* put it, "he was late night TV."

—Thurston Domina

FURTHER READING:

Haley, Alex. *The Playboy Interviews*. New York, Ballantine, 1993.

Leamer, Laurence. *The King of the Night: The Life of Johnny Carson*. New York, Morrow, 1989.

Smith, Ronald L. *Johnny Carson: An Unauthorized Biography*. New York, St. Martin's Press, 1987.

The Carter Family

One of the founding acts of modern country music, the Carter Family began recording in the late 1920s and developed a national following that lasted throughout the 1930s and into the 1940s. Among the first stars of hillbilly music, as country was labeled during that era, they created popular versions of traditional folk songs, influencing countless future country and folk artists. Their material included classic songs such as ''Wabash Cannonball,'' and the melodies of their songs were borrowed by other composers—among them Woody Guthrie, who used one of their tunes as the musical basis for ''This Land Is Your Land.'' The group was known for their vocal harmonies, in addition to Maybelle Carter's (1909-1978) innovative guitar technique, in which she used her thumb to pluck out a melody on the bass strings while using her fingers to strum a rhythm accompaniment on the treble strings. Referred to as the ''Carter scratch,'' this unique style of playing transformed the role of the guitar in traditional music ensembles by making it the lead instrument. While the original Carter

The Carter Family, from left: Maybelle, A.P., and Sara.

Family ceased performing and recording in 1943, Maybelle continued her career for several decades, first in a group with her daughters, and later as a solo artist.

Alvin Pleasant (A.P.) Delaney Carter (1891-1960) was a carpenter in his early twenties when he married sixteen-year-old Sara Dougherty (1899-1979) in 1915. The couple lived near Clinch Mountain, in the tiny community of Maces Spring, Virginia, where they provided musical entertainment at a variety of local social gatherings. Sara led the singing with her resonant alto and strummed an autoharp or guitar, while A.P. sang bass. They were occasionally joined in these performances by some of their relatives, including Sara's cousin Maybelle Addington, a talented teenage guitarist and singer who married A.P.'s brother Ezra in 1926. The following year, this trio traveled to Bristol, Tennessee, where a New York talent scout for the RCA Victor label named Ralph Peer was auditioning and recording new artists. On August 1 and 2, the Carters recorded six songs, and a few days later an unknown singer named Jimmie Rodgers also made his first recordings. The Bristol sessions were later recognized as the beginning of the modern country music industry, which grew as the result of the commercial success of these two hillbilly acts and the tremendous effect they had on the artists who followed them.

As sales of the Carters' first recordings increased, Peer made arrangements for a second session that took place in Camden, New Jersey, in the spring of 1928. There the group recorded several songs that became country music standards, such as ''Keep on the Sunny Side,'' which later became their theme, and ''Wildwood Flower.'' As their popularity increased, the Carter Family began touring regularly and continued recording. To sustain their popularity, A.P. sought to supplement their repertoire of rural folk songs with material he gathered on song-hunting trips. On some of these journeys, he was joined by Lesley Riddle, an African-American blues guitarist who may have also influenced Maybelle's innovative guitar style. When the Carter Family recorded songs discovered by A.P., he usually received credit for the arrangement, a common practice that allowed performers to receive publishing royalties for songs they did not actually write. By the time they disbanded in 1943, the Carters had recorded over 300 songs. While some were original compositions, many recordings were derived from the songbooks and sheet music A.P. collected, or traditional oral sources, or in some instances a combination of both. Since many of these folk songs had never been recorded, the versions popularized by the Carter Family served as invaluable documents for music historians and hillbilly enthusiasts alike.

Sara and A.P. were separated in 1933 and divorced six years later, although they maintained a professional relationship for ten years after the separation. Toward the end of the 1930s, she married A.P.'s first cousin, Coy Bayes, and they moved to California. While performing on Texas border radio stations during this period, the Carter Family sometimes included Maybelle's three daughters, Helen, June, and Anita, as well as Sara and A.P.'s children, Gladys, Jeanette, and Joe. After the breakup of the original Carter Family, Sara and A.P. retired from music, while Maybelle started a new group with her daughters. Calling themselves the Carter Sisters and Mother Maybelle, they performed during the 1940s and joined the *Grand Ole Opry* in 1950. Within a few years, the sisters parted ways to pursue different interests. June married country artist Carl Smith in 1952, and a few years later gave birth to Rebecca Carlene Smith (who began performing in the late 1970s as Carlene Carter and was married to British rocker Nick Lowe). In 1961, the year after A.P. Carter's death,

June began singing with Johnny Cash, and the two were married in 1968, after she helped him overcome his drug addiction.

Anita Carter also achieved success as a performer in the 1960s, as did Mother Maybelle, who developed a new following as the result of the folk music revival that began on college campuses toward the end of the 1950s. The autoharp became her primary instrument, and she impressed audiences with her ability to pick out melodies on the strings rather than simply strumming chords. Maybelle performed at the 1963 Newport Folk Festival, and she and Sara reunited a few years later to record an album. In the late 1960s, Maybelle toured with Johnny and June Carter Cash, and she was one of several influential older country and bluegrass artists featured on the Nitty Gritty Dirt Band's 1972 double album *Will the Circle Be Unbroken*. Two years after failing health caused her to stop performing, Maybelle died in October of 1978, three months before Sara's death. The original Carter Family was inducted into the Country Music Hall of Fame in 1970, and they are often called "The First Family of Country Music." In the mid-1990s, Rounder Records released eight compact discs containing all of their RCA Victor recordings. Seventy years after the Carter Family first began recording, their timeless music continued to interest and influence listeners.

—Anna Hunt Graves

FURTHER READING:

Bufwack, Mary A., and Robert Oermann. *Finding Her Voice: The Saga of Women in Country Music*. New York, Crown, 1993.

Carter, Janette. *Living with Memories*. Hiltons, Virginia, Carter Family Memorial Music Center, 1983.

Dawidoff, Nicholas. *In the Country of Country: People and Places in American Music*. New York, Pantheon, 1997.

Dew, Joan. *Singers and Sweethearts: The Women of Country Music*. Garden City, New York, Doubleday and Company, 1977.

Malone, Bill C. *Country Music, U.S.A.* Austin, University of Texas Press, 1985.

Caruso, Enrico (1873-1921)

Enrico Caruso, the quintessential Italian tenor, was the most beloved singer of his day. Critics agreed that he was also probably the best. Known throughout the Western world for his interpretations of operatic roles, he also captured the popular imagination with Neapolitan songs, sentimental period ballads, and that patriotic favorite of World War I, *Over There*, rendered in his unique variant of the English language. The emergence of the phonograph made Caruso an entertainer as well as an artist, and he, perhaps more than anyone else, demonstrated its potential as a creative medium.

Born in Naples near the end of Europe's most placid century, Caruso was one of 18 children of working class parents. At considerable financial sacrifice, he studied voice with Vergine, a noted Neapolitan teacher, who, nevertheless, envisioned for him only a modest future. Singing first in provincial theaters and later with touring companies, Caruso gradually made his way to important opera houses in Monte Carlo, Milan, and London. Though his initial reviews were not always good, audiences responded to him. Despite his increasing girth and a slightly comical stage appearance, his exuberance and dramatic sense well complemented a voice that was

Enrico Caruso

soon being described as "golden." With little formal education, Caruso was a dedicated artist, who continued to refine his theatrical skills and musicianship throughout his life.

By the beginning of the twentieth century, Caruso had developed from a lyric into a dramatic tenor. Brazil, Argentina, Mexico, and Russia, along with Western Europe, clamored for his appearances, but it was the United States that made him a true national hero. First engaged by New York's Metropolitan Opera in 1903, he made this house his home base for the rest of his life. Together with his fellow countryman Arturo Toscanini, he established "the Met" as America's premier company and one of the great opera houses of the world. He performed the full Italian repertoire, distinguishing himself as Canio in *Pagliacci*, the Duke in *Rigoletto*, Radames in *Aida*, and Samson in *Samson et Delila*. He visited synagogues and studied Jewish life in preparation for his role as Eleazar in *La Juive*. But his special love for things American was evident in his odd interpretation of Dick Johnson in Puccini's *La Fanciulla del West*. The composer himself attended the Met opening. With his broad Mediterranean gestures and throaty sobs, Caruso was not entirely convincing as a Wild West outlaw hanged for his crimes, but audiences applauded nevertheless.

Like other Italians successful in the New World, Caruso suffered brushes with New York's Black Hand, which attempted to extort money from him. Rather than comply with their demands, Caruso cooperated with authorities and two gangsters were apprehended. A more embarrassing episode occurred in 1906 when the singer was visiting the Central Park Zoo. A mysterious woman, who later disappeared, accused him of molesting her in the monkey house.

Caruso denied the charge; at the most he was probably demonstrating a Southern Italian mode of admiration for an attractive woman. Despite extensive newspaper coverage, the public soon chose to forget the incident.

Two sons were born from Caruso's long liaison with Ada Giacchetti, an Italian soprano whose earlier marriage prevented a regularization of their union. After deserting him in favor of her chauffeur, Ada caused Caruso further suffering by publicly announcing that she had never loved him. Near the end of his life, the singer finally found domestic happiness in his marriage to Dorothy Park Benjamin, a shy woman 20 years his junior. Formerly relegated to the role of housekeeper and recluse by her wealthy and overbearing father, Dorothy Caruso blossomed as the cherished wife of this demonstrative man. The birth of a daughter, the only thing Dorothy said she could give her husband that he had never had or could not buy, brought further happiness to the last two years of his life.

Caruso's generosity was legendary; he once hired a valet for his own valet. Even rival singers invariably warmed to his personality. They treasured the friendly caricatures he drew of them during rehearsals. John McCormick, the Irish tenor of almost equal acclaim, said: "I never loved any other man so much as Caruso." America and the world richly rewarded its favorite Italian with wealth and affection. But his obsession with honoring his commitments and fear of disappointing his fans probably led to his premature death. Worn out by exhaustion and lung ailments, he died at the age of 48, still in his vocal glory. Headlines in American newspapers sadly announced "The Golden Voice Is Stilled."

When asked what makes a superb singer, Caruso liked to answer: "A big chest, a big mouth, ninety percent memory, ten percent intelligence, lots of hard work and something in the heart." Clearly, he had these requisites in the proper amounts. Henry Pleasants observed that in this singer a beautiful voice and a beautiful nature seemed perfectly united, that his radiance did not originate merely in his throat but in the man himself. Decades after his death, the highest compliment that could be given a tenor was to suggest he might be "the New Caruso." His Victor recordings, available in remastered compact disk format, endure. Finally, the mega-concerts of leading tenors of the 1990s, which blended classical and popular songs, continued to perpetuate the legacy of Caruso in bringing the highest musical artistry to the masses.

—Allene Phy-Olsen

FURTHER READING:

Caruso, Dorothy. *Enrico Caruso, His Life and Death.* New York, Simon and Schuster, 1945.

Greenfeld, Howard. *Caruso.* New York, G.P. Putnam's Sons, 1983.

Pleasants, Henry. *The Great Singers.* New York, Simon and Schuster, 1966.

Robinson, Francis. *Caruso, His Life in Pictures.* New York, Bramwell House, 1957.

Carver, Raymond (1938-1988)

Raymond Carver's success derived as much from the renewed interest in the short story brought about by the publication of *The Stories of John Cheever* in 1978 and the backlash against 1960s

metafiction as it did from Carver's own genius. Although considered one of the most recognizable and imitated stylists of his time, Carver was in fact one of a growing number of minimalists whose "dirty realism" came to be associated with (and for some demonstrated the shortcomings of) university writing workshops. What chiefly distinguished Carver's stories from the similarly laconic, uninflected, disquietingly detached, and paratactic work of others was his focusing on the marginal lives of generally working-class characters trying, and often failing, to make do. Carver's semi-autobiographical fiction offered an alternative not only to earlier reports of the deaths of author and character alike but to the pursuit of affluence and the extolling of the entrepreneurial spirit during the Reagan years. The triumph achieved in a number of Carver's later stories was more spiritual than material and even then carefully qualified.

—Robert A. Morace

FURTHER READING:

Meyer, Adam. *Raymond Carver.* New York, Twayne, 1994.

Salzman, Arthur M. *Understanding Raymond Carver.* Columbia, University of South Carolina Press, 1988.

Casablanca

The script for *Casablanca* (1942), one of the most successful films of all time, arrived at the Warner Brothers Studio the day after the Japanese attack on Pearl Harbor, December 8, 1941. Timing is just one of the many reasons why this legendary film about patriotism, love, exile, and sabotage is often referred to as the happy result of a series of accidents. If the studio had carried out its original plans to cast Ronald Reagan as Rick Blaine or Ella Fitzgerald as Sam, now

Ingrid Bergman and Humphrey Bogart in a scene from the film *Casablanca.*

infamous lines and lyrics like "Here's lookin' at you, kid" and "As Time Goes By" may never have attained the same powerful significance they have had for generations of movie fans. Set in French Morocco during WWII, *Casablanca* was directed by Michael Curtiz and starred Humphrey Bogart, Ingrid Bergman, Paul Henreid, Peter Lorre, Claude Rains, Sydney Greenstreet, and Conrad Veidt. Based loosely on a play entitled *Everybody Comes to Rick's*, *Casablanca* profiles the life of Rick Blaine (Bogart), an embittered nightclub owner with a broken heart and a checkered past. Blaine is exiled in Casablanca as a result of the Nazi invasion in Europe. His elegant casino/bar, Café Americain, is the unofficial meeting point for war refugees attempting to purchase exit visas on the black market to reach the United States. Rick's life comes to a halt when when his long lost love, Ilsa (Bergman) comes into town in search of exit papers for herself and her husband, famed resistance fighter Victor Laszlo (Henreid).

This comparatively low-budget, romance/adventure film was recognized as a masterpiece from the beginning. *Casablanca* won several Oscars at the 1943 Academy Awards, including Best Picture, Best Director, and Best Writing. The film also received nominations for Best Actor, Best Cinematography, Best Editing, and Best Music of a Dramatic or Comedy Picture. Some critics attribute the timeless freshness of the movie's dialogue to the fact that nobody working on the film, including the scriptwriters, knew how the film would turn out until the last minute. In spite of the relatively low-budget of the film, playwrights Murray Burnett and Joan Alison were offered the highest fee ever paid for an unproduced play—$20,000—for *Everybody Comes to Rick's*.

Filmed almost entirely in the Warner Brothers soundstage in Burbank, *Casablanca* is one of the most popular films of all time. In 1973, a *Los Angeles Times* headline announced that *Casablanca* was ranked as Warner Brothers' most popular film in fifty years. The runners-up in this public poll were *The Maltese Falcon* (1941), *Who's Afraid of Virginia Woolf* (1966), *A Streetcar Named Desire* (1951) and *The Treasure of Sierra Madre* (1948). In 1977, the American Film Institute disclosed its list of the best American films of all time before President Carter and a television audience at the John F. Kennedy Center for the Performing Arts. *Casablanca* came in third place, behind *Gone With the Wind* (1939) and *Citizen Kane* (1941).

The film's director, Michael Curtiz, was born Mihaly Kertesz in Hungary. Curtiz came to Warner Brothers from Austria in 1926, having already made 62 silent pictures, and went on to become one of the studio's top money-earners. Between the period of 1930 and 1940 alone, he directed 45 talking films ranging in genre from horror to westerns to gangster films. Curtiz's *Mission to Moscow* (1943) was listed in the FBI's "Communist Infiltration of the Motion Picture Industry" file as a source of Communistic propaganda. Though Jack Warner defended the film while it was in production in a letter to Ambassador Davies, his later humiliation and fear as a result of making the movie have been attributed to his readiness to turn dozens of employees over to the House Committee on Un-American Activites (HUAC) in 1947.

Given the fact that most Americans resisted the idea of U.S. involvement in the war in Europe at the time during which *Casablanca* was set, Jack Warner has been viewed as having declared war on Germany early, not only with *Casablanca*, but with earlier films like *Confessions of a Nazi Spy* (1939) and *Underground* (1941). Of all the Hollywood moguls at the beginning of the war, Harry and Jack Warner were anti-Nazi at a time when opposition to Hitler was far from common. In July 1934, Warner Brothers became the first studio

to close down operations and leave Germany. MGM, Fox, and Paramount, by contrast, continued to operate in Germany up to 1939. Between the period of 1942 and 1945, Hollywood produced 500 features films which dealt with war subjects directly and were designed to foster the nation's support for the Allied war effort.

One of the more popular interpretations of *Casablanca*'s success posits that it is a political movie centered around resistance to fascism. A 1942 *Motion Picture Herald* article portrayed the film as a tribute to the occupied people of France. Its opening night performance in New York was sponsored by the organizations "France Forever" and "Free French War Relief." A French delegation of Foreign Legionnaires, recently returned from battle, as well as leaders from the DeGaulle movement, marched in a parade from Fifth Avenue to the opening of the film at the Hollywood Theater. The political film interpretation focuses on the anti-fascist aspects of *Casablanca* and places importance on Ingrid Bergman's character and her relationship to fascism.

According to critic Umberto Eco, writing in "*Casablanca*: Cult Movies and Intertextual Collage," *Casablanca* can also be seen as a cult object. As such, it possesses the following qualities: it provides its audience with a completed vision of the world which fans can incorporate into their own world; using quotes and trivia from the film as a form of shared expertise, the narrative can be dislocated so that one need only remember a part of it, regardless of its original relationship to the whole film; and the film displays a variety of ideas and does not contain a central philosophy of composition. The cult paradigm revolves around near worship of Bogart's masculinity and patriarchal discourse and the repitition of key moments in the film's narrative. *Casablanca* diehards, for example, have elevated the status of the song "As Time Goes By," a song which references the romantic relationship between Rick and Ilsa, at the expense of other important songs, like "La Marseillais." What *Casablanca* possesses, Eco argues, is a heavy amount of archetypal appeal which creates a feeling of déjà vu, drawing audiences to the film again and again.

Regardless of how the movie is interpreted, stories of the movie's making continue to enthrall fans. According to Ingrid Bergman, for example, the movie's narrative was invented at the same time the movie was shot. Not even Curtiz knew whether Ilsa would end up with Rick or with Victor until far into the shoot. Because of this continual state of improvisation on the set, the scriptwriters conjured up any number of archetypal tropes and threw them into the plot. Some claim that this almost baroque overabundance of stock formulas is the secret to *Casablanca*'s timeless success. Ingrid Bergman, known for her cleanly appearance and objection to wearing makeup, was universally liked on the set of *Casablanca*, by hairdressers and wardrobe people alike. She was patient, easy to work with, and did not demand privileges, though she was not given to forming lasting friendships with any of the people on the set. By contrast, Humphrey Bogart is said to have been obsessive about everything from his love scenes, to the script, to his own personal life. He has been called every name in the book, from "troublemaker" to a "real guy"; Warner Brothers publicist Ezra Goodman once called him "sadistic." Bogart is said to have been good friends with Claude Rains and Peter Lorre. Lorre and Bogart lived a few blocks from each other in the Hollywood Hills and worked together on two other Bogart movies, *The Maltese Falcon* (1941) and *All Through the Night* (1942).

Popular for nearly six decades, *Casablanca* has reverberated throughout American culture. Aside from numerous songs, book titles, comedy routines, commercials, and magazine advertisements that have made reference to the film over the years, in 1972, Woody

Allen made his own tribute to *Casablanca,* entitled *Play it Again Sam,* in which he wore a trenchcoat like Rick Blaine and repeated the famous "Here's looking at you, kid" speech in the context of a narrative about sexual difficulties and masculinity. In this scenario, *Casablanca* was recreated as a cult object which references Bogart and his style of masculinity. Bogart's character is said to have sparked an onslaught on trench coat sales, and the image of him in the coat in the original Warner Brothers poster purportedly launched the movie poster business. In the late 1940s and 1950s, *Casablanca* was an important film on college campuses as cinema began to be viewed as a serious art form. In the 1970s, a string of Rick Blaine-styled bars and cafes began to appear in a variety of cities in the United States with names like Play It Again Sam (Las Vegas), Rick's Café Americain (Chicago), and Rick's Place (Cambridge, Massachusetts).

—Kristi M. Wilson

FURTHER READING:

Eco, Umberto. "*Casablanca*: Cult Movies and Intertextual Collage." In *Modern Criticism and Theory: A Reader,* edited by David Lodge. London and New York, Longman, 1988.

Francisco, Charles. *You Must Remember This. . . : The Filming of Casablanca.* Englewood Cliffs, New Jersey, Prentice-Hall, 1980.

Harmetz, Aljean. *Round Up the Usual Suspects: The Making of Casablanca: Bogart, Bergman, and World War II.* New York, Hyperion, 1992.

Koch, Howard. *Casablanca.* New York, The Overlook Press, 1973.

Lebo, Harlan. *Casablanca: Behind the Scenes.* New York, Simon & Schuster, 1992.

McArthur, Colin. *The Casablanca File.* London, Half Brick Images, 1992.

Miller, Frank. *Casablanca, As Time Goes By. . . : 50th Anniversary Commemorative.* Atlanta, Turner Publishing, 1992.

Siegel, Jeff. *The Casablanca Companion: The Movie and More.* Dallas, Texas, Taylor Publishing, 1992.

Cash, Johnny (1932—)

Significantly, country music star Johnny Cash's career coincided with the birth of rock 'n' roll. Cash's music reflected the rebellious outlaw spirit of early rock, despite the fact that it did not sound much like the new genre or, for that matter, even like traditional country music. Something that perhaps best sums up his image is a famous picture of Cash, with a guitar slung around his neck and an indignant look on his face giving the middle finger to the camera. As the self-dubbed "Man in Black," Johnny Cash has evolved from a Nashville outsider into an American icon who did not have to trade his mass popularity for a more mainstream, non-country sound. Despite a number of setbacks, the most prominent of which was a debilitating addiction to pills and numerous visits to jail, Cash has maintained his popularity since releasing his first single in 1955.

Cash was born in Kingsland, Arkansas on February 26, 1932. He grew up in the small Arkansas town of Dyess, a bible-belt town that published Sunday school attendance figures in the weekly newspaper. Cash hated working on the family farm, preferring instead to escape into his own world listening to the Grand 'Ol Opry or its smaller

Johnny Cash

cousin, The Louisiana Hayride. By the age of 12 he was writing his own songs and he also experienced what many claim to be his first setback, perhaps fueling much of his reckless behavior—his brother Jack was killed in a farming accident. In 1950, Cash enlisted in the Air Force during the Korean War. It was during this time that he bought his first guitar, taught himself how to play, and started writing prolifically—one of the songs written during this period was the Johnny Cash standard, "Folsom Prison Blues." After his time in the Air Force he married Vivian Leberto, moved to Memphis in 1954, and began playing in a trio with guitarist Luther Perkins and bassist Marshall Grant.

Johnny Cash's first singles were released on Sam Phillips' legendary Sun Records, the Memphis-based 1950s independent label that also launched the careers of Roy Orbison, Jerry Lee Lewis, Carl Perkins, and Elvis Presley. It was this maverick environment that fostered Cash's original sound, which was characterized by his primitive rhythm guitar playing and the simple guitar picking of Cash's early lead guitarist, Luther Perkins. His lyrics overwhelmingly dealt with the darker side of life and were delivered by Cash's trademark deep baritone voice that sounded like the aural equivalent of the parched, devastated ground of the depression-era mid-west dust bowl. "Folsom Prison Blues" was sung from the perspective of an unrepentant killer and contained the infamous line, "I shot a man in

Reno just to watch him die.'' Another prison song, ''Give My Love to Rose,'' was a heartbreaking love letter to a wife that was left behind when the song's character was sent to jail. Other early songs like ''Rock Island Line,'' ''Hey Porter,'' ''Get Rhythm,'' and ''Luther Played the Boogie'' could certainly be characterized as raucous and upbeat, but Cash also had a tendency to write or cover weepers like Jack Clement's ''I Guess Things Happen That Way,'' the tragic classic country ballad ''Long Black Veil,'' or his own ''I Still Miss Someone.''

It was not long before Cash cultivated an outsider, outlaw image that was exacerbated by his relatively frequent visits to jail— if only for a day or two—for fighting, drinking, or possessing illegal amphetamines. The frequent concerts he played for prisoners inside jails created an empathy between Cash and those at the margins of society. The fact that he never shed his rural, working-class roots also created a connection with everyday folks. His simple, dark songs influenced a generation of country singer-songwriters that emerged in the early 1960s. They include Willie Nelson, Waylon Jennings, and Merle Haggard. In fact, Haggard became inspired to continue playing music after Cash gave a prison concert where Haggard was serving a two year sentence for armed robbery.

Cash is a heap of contradictions: a devout Christian who is given to serious bouts with drugs and alcohol; a family man who, well into his sixties, spends the majority of the year on the road; and a loving, kindhearted man who has been known to engage in violent and mean-spirited behavior. His life has combined the tragic with the comic as illustrated by a bizarre incident in 1983. During one of his violent spells, he swung a large piece of wood at his eight-foot-tall pet ostrich, which promptly kicked Cash in the chest, breaking three ribs. To ease the pain he had to take painkillers. Cash had already spent time at the Betty Ford clinic to end addiction to painkillers.

Cash's career has gone through ups and downs. After an initial burst of popularity during the Sun years, which fueled his rise to country music superstardom on Columbia Records, his sales began to decline in the mid-1960s, due partially to the debilitating effects of drugs. During this period, Cash experienced a creative slump he has not quite recovered from. For the most part he stopped writing his own songs and instead began to cover the songs of others. After his Sun period and the early Columbia years, original compositions became more and more infrequent as he focused more on being a performer and an interpreter rather than an originator. Although the stellar music became increasingly infrequent, he still created great music in songs like ''Ring of Fire,'' ''Jackson,'' and ''Highway Patrolman.'' Despite countless albums of filler and trivial theme albums— ''Americana,'' ''Train,'' ''Gunfighter,'' ''Indian,'' and ''True West''—there are still enough nuggets to justify his continued recording career. This is true even in consideration of his lackluster mid-1980s to the early 1990s Mercury Records years. In 1994, however, Cash's career was reignited again with the release of his critically praised all-acoustic *American Recordings,* produced by Rick Rubin. Rubin's experience with Tom Petty, RUN-DMC, Red Hot Chili Peppers, The Beastie Boys, and The Cult certainly prepared him for a hit with Cash.

Meaning many things to many people, Cash has been able to maintain a curiously eclectic audience throughout his career. For instance, Johnny Cash was a hero to the southern white working class—what some might call ''rednecks''—and college educated northerners alike. He has cultivated an audience of criminals and fundamentalist Christians—working closely, at times, with conservatives like Billy Graham—and has campaigned for the civil rights of

Native Americans. During the late 1960s, he was embraced by the counterculture and played with Bob Dylan on his *Nashville Skyline* album, while at the same time performing for Richard Nixon at the White House—Nixon was not the only president who admired him . . . Cash even received fan mail from then president Jimmy Carter. He has also been celebrated by the middle-American mainstream as a great entertainer, and had a popular network television variety show during the late 1960s and early 1970s called *The Johnny Cash Show.*

During the 1990s, Cash has played both ''oldies'' concerts for baby boomers and down home family revue-type acts, cracking Southern flavored jokes between songs. During this time, Cash was dismissed as a relic of a long-forgotten age by Nashville insiders who profited from the likes of country music superstars Garth Brooks and Shania Twain. After the release in 1994 of his *American Recordings* album, however, he has been celebrated by a young hip audience as an alternative rock icon and an original punk rocker.

—Kembrew McLeod

FURTHER READING:

Dawidoff, Nicholas. *In the Country of Country: A Journey to the Roots of American Music.* New York, Vintage, 1997

Dolan, Sean. *Johnny Cash.* New York, Chelsea House, 1995.

Hartley, Allan. *Hello, I'm Johnny Cash.* New York, Revell, 1982.

Loewen, Nancy. *Johnny Cash.* New York, Rourke Entertainment, 1989.

Wren, Christopher S. *Winner Got Scars Too: The Life and Legends of Johnny Cash.* New York, Ballantine, 1974.

Casinos
See Gambling

Caspar Milquetoast

Caspar Milquetoast was a comic strip character created by the cartoonist Harold Tucker Webster (1885-1952) for the New York *Herald Tribune* and other newspapers in the late 1920s. The central figure in many of Webster's witty, urbane, and mildly satirical cartoons during the interwar years was frequently a middle-class professional man who was rather mild-mannered and retiring. The most notable and best known of these was Caspar Milquetoast, self-effacing, obedient to a fault, and, quite literally, scared of his own shadow—the personification of timidity. This character's manner and richly imagistic surname yielded the epithet ''a milquetoast,'' still part of the American vernacular although it is unlikely that very many of those who currently use the epithet have any knowledge of its origin.

—John R. Deitrick

FURTHER READING:

Webster, H.T. *Best of H.T. Webster.* New York, Simon and Schuster, 1953.

Cassette Tape

Compact, convenient, and easy to operate, the audio cassette became the most widely used format for magnetic tape and dominated the field for prerecorded and home-recorded music during the 1970s and 1980s. Although superseded by digital players and recorders in the 1990s, the cassette tape remains the dominant form of sound recording worldwide.

Introduced in the 1940s, magnetic tape recording offered important advantages over revolving discs—longer playback time and more durable materials—but its commercial appeal suffered from the difficulties that users experienced in threading the tape through reel-to-reel tape recorders. One solution to this problem was the tape cartridge, which came in either the continuous loop format or the two-spooled cassette, which made it possible to rewind and fast forward with ease. By the 1960s there were several tape cartridge systems under development, including the four-track, continuous-loop cartridge devised by the Lear Company, the Fidelipac system used by radio broadcasters, and the "Casino" cartridge introduced by the RCA company for use in its home audio units. Tape cartridges also were developed for the dictating machines used in business.

In 1962 the Philips Company developed a cassette using tape half as wide as the standard 1/4-inch tape which ran between two reels in a small plastic case. The tape moved half the speed of eight-track tapes, getting a longer playing time but paying the price in terms of its limited fidelity. The Philips compact cassette was introduced in 1963. During the first year on the market, only nine thousand units were sold. Philips did not protect its cassette as a proprietary technology but encouraged other companies to license its use. The company did require all of its users to adhere to its standards, which guaranteed that all cassettes would be compatible. An alliance with several Japanese

manufacturers ensured that there were several cassette players available when the format was introduced for home use in the mid-1960s. The first sold in the United States were made by Panasonic and Norelco. The Norelco Carry-Corder of 1964 was powered by flashlight batteries and weighed in at three pounds. It could record and play back, and came complete with built-in microphone and speaker.

Public response to the compact cassette was very favorable, encouraging more companies to make cassette players. By 1968 about eighty-five different manufacturers had sold more than 2.4 million cassette players worldwide. In that year the cassette business was worth about $150 million. Because of worldwide adherence to the standards established by the Philips company, the compact cassette was the most widely used format for tape recording by the end of the decade.

The fidelity of the cassette's playback was inferior compared to phonograph discs and the slower-moving reel-to-reel tape, consequently the serious audiophile could not be persuaded to accept it. The cassette had been conceived as a means of bringing portable sound to the less discriminating user—a tape version of the transistor radio. It was in this role that the cassette made possible two of the most important postwar innovations in talking machines: the portable cassette player or "boombox" and the personal stereo system with headphones, introduced by Sony as the Walkman.

These highly influential machines were based on technological advances in three fields: magnetic tape, batteries, and transistorized circuits. For the first time, high-fidelity stereo sound and high levels of transistorized amplification—capable of pouring out sound at ear-deafening levels, hence the "boombox" name—could be purchased in a compact unit and at a reasonable price. The portable cassette player became one of the great consumer products of the 1970s and 1980s, establishing itself in all corners of the globe. Players were incorporated into radios, alarm clocks, automobile stereos, and even

A cassette tape.

shower units. The ubiquitous cassette made it possible to hear music anywhere.

The personal stereo was developed around the cassette and was intended to be the ultimate in portable sound—so small it could fit into a pocket. The stereo's headphones surrounded the listener in a cocoon of sound, eliminating much of the annoying noise found in urban life but often at the price of damaging the hearing of the listener. Since its introduction in 1979, Sony's Walkman has been copied by countless other manufacturers and can now be found in cassette and digital formats, including compact disc and digital tape.

In the 1990s several digital tape formats were introduced to compete with the audio cassette tape, and the manufacturers and record companies did their best to phase out the elderly technology by ceasing to manufacture both players and prerecorded tapes. Cassette tape was "hisstory" said one advertisement for noise-free digital recording, but consumers were unwilling to desert it. Although no longer a viable format for prerecorded popular music (with the exception of rap and hip-hop), cassette tapes live on in home recording and in automobile use.

—Andre Millard

FURTHER READING:

Kusisto, Oscar P. "Magnetic Tape Recording: Reels, Cassettes, or Cartridges?" *Journal of the Audio Engineering Society.* Vol. 24, 1977, 827-31.

Millard, Andre. *America on Record: A History of Recorded Sound.* Cambridge University Press, 1995.

Morita, Akio, E. Reingold, and M. Shimomura. *Made in Japan: Akio Morita and Sony.* New York, Dutton, 1980.

Cassidy, David (1950—)

David Cassidy may not have been the first teenage idol, but he was the first to demand control of his life, walking away from the entertainment industry's star-machinery even as it went into over-drive. And when that industry discarded him, Cassidy's resolve to return was more self-fulfilling than the first time around.

Cassidy was born on April 12, 1950, the son of actors Jack Cassidy and Evelyn Ward. His parents divorced when he was three, and David lived with his mother in West Orange, New Jersey. At 11, Cassidy and his mother moved to Los Angeles, and David spent his teen years hanging out in San Francisco's Haight-Ashbury scene, graduating from a private school and pursuing small acting jobs. He moved to New York City in his late teens, working in a textile factory by day and taking acting classes by night, before starring in the 1969 Broadway play, *Fig Leaves Are Falling.* With a stint on Broadway to his name, Cassidy returned to Los Angeles and landed bit parts on popular television shows.

The turning point came in 1969, when the ABC network was casting for the musical comedy series, *The Partridge Family,* which was based loosely upon the late 1960s folk-music family, the Cowsills. David's stepmother, actress Shirley Jones, was cast as the lead. Unbeknownst to Jones, the producers had 19-year-old David read for the part of the good-looking pop-music prodigy Keith Partridge.

Cassidy once claimed that when he was a child, his life was changed forever upon seeing the Beatles on the Ed Sullivan show. But

David Cassidy

that could never have prepared him for the tsunami of publicity generated by the success of *The Partridge Family.* The show was a runaway hit, and Cassidy's visage was pinned up on teenage girls' bedroom walls all over the country. The merchandising of Cassidy remains a blueprint for the careers of all of the teen heartthrobs who followed him. Posters, pins, t-shirts, lunchboxes, and magazine covers proclaimed Cassidy-mania. He used the success of the show to further his rock and roll career, playing to overflowing arena crowds of teenage girls that were so hungry for a piece of their idol that Cassidy had to be smuggled in and out of venues by hiding in laundry trucks or the trunks of sedans.

After years of seven-day weeks running from television tapings to recording studios to tour buses, the 23-year-old singer was starting to feel the burn-out inevitably linked with fame. In a May, 1972, cover story in *Rolling Stone,* Cassidy spoke candidly about his success, bragging about taking drugs and having sex with groupies and—in a moment of career suicide—railing against the pressures of his chosen field.

During a 1974 concert in London, England, a 14-year-old girl died of a heart attack. The rude awakening forced Cassidy to take a long hard look at himself. His response was to retire from live performances and the television show in order to make a conscious break from teeny-bopper fantasy to serious actor. Not long afterward, *The Partridge Family* slipped in its ratings and was canceled; record contracts were no longer forthcoming, and the window of opportunities available to Cassidy was closing quickly. He was free of the rigors of show business, but industry professionals looked askance at his quick rise-and-fall career.

The actor's personal life was chaotic as well; his father, from whom he had been estranged for nine months, died in a fire in his penthouse apartment. Cassidy was drinking heavily at the time, and found out that he was bankrupt. A 1977 marriage to actress Kay Lenz lasted for four years; a second marriage to horse-breeder Meryl Tanz in 1984 lasted just a year. He entered psychoanalysis soon after his second divorce.

In 1978, Cassidy appeared in a made-for-TV movie, *A Chance to Live.* The success of the movie prompted producers to create a spin-off series titled *David Cassidy: Man Undercover,* which was poorly received. In the late 1970s, he took the lead in a Broadway production of *Joseph and the Amazing Technicolor Dreamcoat* (ironically replacing drug-damaged teen idol Andy Gibb), and later ended up in London's West End theater district as the star of Dave Clarke's play, *Time.* While living in London, Cassidy recorded an album for the Ariola label.

In the 1990s Cassidy devoted his time entirely to acting. In 1993, he appeared with his half-brother Shaun Cassidy (himself a former teen idol turned actor and producer) and British singer Petula Clark in the stage drama *Blood Brothers.* In 1994, he wrote a tell-all memoir about his television exploits entitled *C'mon Get Happy: Fear and Loathing on the Partridge Family Bus.* In 1996, he helped relaunch the MGM Grand Hotel in Las Vegas, appearing in the science-fiction musical variety show *FX.* While most teen idols stay forever trapped in the history books, David Cassidy worked hard to make sure he wasn't trapped by a "sell-by" date like most entertainment commodities.

—Emily Pettigrew

FURTHER READING:

Allis, Tim. "The Boys Are Back." *People.* November 1, 1993, 66.

Behind the Music: David Cassidy. VH-1. November 29, 1998.

Cassidy, David. *C'mon, Get Happy: Fear and Loathing on the Partridge Family Bus.* New York, Warner Books, 1994.

"Elvis! David!" *New Yorker.* June 24, 1972, 28-29.

Graves, R. "D-day Sound Was a High-C Shriek." *Life.* March 24, 1972, 72-73.

Thomas, Dana. "Teen Heartthrobs: The Beat Goes On." *Washington Post.* October 3, 1991, C1.

Vespa, Mary. "Now Back Onstage, David Cassidy Has a New Fiancee and a Confession: His Rock days Were No Picnic." *People.* May 16, 1983, 75.

Castaneda, Carlos (1925-1998)

Little consensus has been reached about Carlos Castaneda, whose books detailing his apprenticeship to the Yaqui Indian shaman Don Juan Matus have sold over eight million copies in 17 languages and contributed to defining the psychedelic counterculture of the 1960s as well as the New Age movement. Castaneda's anthropological and ethnographic credibility together with his intellectual biography and personal life have been a constant source of puzzlement for critics and colleagues. Castaneda himself contributed to complicate the mystery surrounding his identity by supplying false data about his birth and childhood and by refusing to be photographed, tape recorded, and, until a few years before his death (which was kept secret for more than two months), even interviewed. In spite of (or perhaps thanks to) Castaneda's obsession with anonymity and several blunt critical attacks on his works by anthropologists his international fame has been long-lasting.

Born in Cajamarca, Perù (not in São Paulo, Brazil, as he maintained), Castaneda became a celebrity almost overnight thanks to the publication of *The Teachings of Don Juan: A Yaqui Way of Knowledge* in 1968, when he was still a graduate student at the University of California. In *The Teachings of Don Juan* as well as in nine other books, Castaneda described the spiritual and drug-induced adventures he had with the Yaqui Indian Don Juan, whom he maintained to have met in 1960 while doing research on medicinal plants used by Indians. During the course of the books, the author himself becomes an apprentice shaman, sees giant insects, and learns to fly as part of a spiritual practice that tends to break the hold of ordinary Western perception. Castaneda defined his method of research as "emic," a term that was used in the 1960s to distinguish ethnography that attempted to adopt the native conception of reality from ethnography that relied on the ethnographer's conception of reality ("etic"). Because of several chronological and factual inconsistencies among the books and because Don Juan himself was never found, many scholars agreed that Castaneda's books were not based on ethnographic research and fieldwork, but are works of fiction—products of Castaneda's imagination.

Jay Courtney Fikes pointed out that Castaneda's books "are best interpreted as a manifestation of the American popular culture of the 1960s." The works of Aldous Huxley, Timothy Leary, and Gordon Wasson stirred interest in chemical psychedelics such as LSD and some of the psychedelic plants that Don Juan gave his apprentice Castaneda, such as peyote and psilocybin mushrooms. These psychedelics played an important part of the counterculture of the 1960s as a political symbol of defection from the Establishment. Castaneda's books contained exactly the message that the members of the counterculture wanted to hear: taking drugs was a non-Western form of spirituality. Several episodes in *The Teachings of Don Juan* link taking psychedelic plants to reaching a higher spiritual realm: Don Juan teaches Castaneda to fly under the influence of jimsonweed and to attain magical powers by smoking a blend of psilocybin mushrooms and other plants. Castaneda's books met the demands of a vast audience that was equally disappointed by anthropology as well as by traditional religion.

In the early 1990s, Castaneda decided to become more visible to the public in order to "disseminate Don Juan's ideas." He organized New Age seminars to promote the teaching of Tensegrity, which he described as "the modernized version of some movements called magical passes developed by Indian shamans who lived in Mexico in times prior to the Spanish conquest." Castaneda, who at the time of the seminars was dying of cancer, claimed that "practicing Tensegrity . . . promotes health, vitality, youth and general sense of well-being, [it] helps accumulate the energy necessary to increase awareness and to expand the parameters of perception," in order to go beyond the limitations of ordinary consciousness.

Carlos Castaneda's death was just as mysterious as his life. His adopted son claimed that he died while a virtual prisoner of the cult-like followers of Cleargreen Inc., the group that marketed his works in his late years. Castaneda was described by George Marcus and Michael Fisher in *Anthropology as Cultural Critique: An Experimental Moment in the Human Sciences* as an innovative anthropologist whose books "have served as one of several stimuli for thinking about alternative textual strategies within the tradition of ethnography." However, Jay Courtney Fikes, in *Carlos Castaneda: Academic Opportunism and the Psychedelic Sixties,* called him a careless ethnographer who "didn't try diligently enough to distinguish between what was true and what was false." Others condemned him as a fraud and religious mythmaker for our post-modern era. Definitions are difficult to apply to such an elusive personality. Paradoxically, the best representation of Castaneda can be viewed in the portrait that Richard Oden drew in 1972 and that Castaneda himself half-erased.

—Luca Prono

FURTHER READING:

"Carlos Castaneda's Tensegrity, Presented by Cleargeen Incorporated." http://www.castaneda.org. May 1999.

DeMille, Richard. *Castaneda's Journey: The Power and the Allegory.* Santa Barbara, Capra Press, 1976.

Fikes, Jay Courtney. *Carlos Castaneda, Academic Opportunism and the Psychedelic Sixties.* Victoria, Millennia Press, 1993.

Marcus, George, and Michael Fisher. *Anthropology as Cultural Critique: An Experimental Moment in the Human Sciences.* Chicago, University of Chicago Press, 1986.

Castle, Vernon (1887-1918), and Irene (1893-1969)

Widely admired for their graceful dance routines and smart fashion sensibilities, ballroom dancers Vernon and Irene Castle spurred the national craze for new, jazz-oriented dance styles in the years before World War I. In an age of widespread racism, the Castles helped popularize African-American and Latin-American dances, including the foxtrot and tango, previously considered too sensual for white audiences. With the opening of their own dance school and rooftop night club, the Castles became the darlings of New York City café society. National dancing tours, movie appearances, and a steady stream of magazine and newspaper articles swelled the couple's celebrity status to include increasing numbers of middle class men and women. Often depicted as the most modern of married couples, it was the Castles' successful use of shared leisure activities to strengthen their marriage, as much as their superior dance talents, that made them the most popular dancers of their time.

—Scott A. Newman

FURTHER READING:

Castle, Irene. *Castles in the Air.* Garden City, New York, Doubleday, 1958.

Erenberg, Lewis A. *Steppin' Out: New York Nightlife and the Transformation of American Culture, 1890-1930.* Chicago, University of Chicago Press, 1981.

The Castro

Though the Castro district has been a distinctly defined neighborhood of San Francisco since the 1880s, the district did not gain worldwide fame until the 1970s when it became a mecca for a newly liberated gay community—in effect a west coast equivalent to New York's Christopher Street. It has been said that if San Francisco is America's gay capital, Castro Street is its gay Main Street.

The Castro district had a rebellious reputation from its beginnings: the street was named in 1840 for General Juan Castro, who led the Mexican resistance to white incursions into Northern California. By the 1880s, Eureka Valley, as it was then called, was a bustling working-class neighborhood, populated largely by Irish, German, and Scandinavian immigrants. After World War II, many of the area's residents joined the widespread exodus to the suburbs, leaving empty houses behind them. Coincidentally, post-World War II anti-gay witch hunts resulted in the discharge of hundreds of gay military personnel. Many were discharged in the port of San Francisco, and others were drawn there by the comparatively open and tolerant attitudes to be found there. Low housing prices in the unassuming district around Castro Street attracted many of these migrants, and gay bars began opening quietly in the 1950s. In 1960, the "gayola" scandal erupted in San Francisco when it was discovered that a state alcohol-board official had taken bribes from a gay bar. The scandal resulted in increased police harassment of gay bars but also sparked pleas for tolerance from religious and city officials. It was this reputation for tolerance that drew counterculture youth to San Francisco, culminating in the "Summer of Love" in 1967. Soon, thousands of gay men and lesbians were finding the Castro district an attractive place to live and open businesses, and during the 1970s the Castro thrived as a gay civic center.

The 1970s were heady years for the gay and lesbian community. Tired of the oppressive days of secrecy and silence, gay men created the disco scene where they could gather to the beat of loud music, with bright lights flashing. The new bars in the Castro, with names like Toad Hall and the Elephant Walk, had big glass windows facing the street, a reaction against the shuttered back-street bars of the 1950s. Since the 1960s, more than seventy gay bars have opened in the Castro. Many lesbians disavow the male-dominated Castro, however, with its 70:30 male-to-female population ratio; they claim nearby Valencia Street as the heart of the lesbian community.

Harvey Milk, a grassroots politician who would become the first openly gay man elected to public office in a major city, played a large part in creating the Castro phenomenon. Known as the "Mayor of Castro Street," Milk ran for the San Francisco Board of Supervisors (city council) until he finally won in 1977. With an exceptional gift for coalition politics, Milk forged alliances between gay residents and the local Chinese community as well as with unions such as the Teamsters, building bridges where divisions had existed, and mobilizing the political influence of the thousands of gay men and lesbians in the city. In November of 1978, Milk and San Francisco mayor Dave Moscone were assassinated by a former city employee, Dan White. When the gay community heard the news, a spontaneous outpouring of Milk's supporters took to the streets of the Castro, and thousands marched there in a silent candlelight procession. Some weeks later, when Dan White was sentenced to only seven years in prison, it was not grief but anger that sent protesters into the streets for the "White Night Riots." Cars were torched and windows were smashed by rioters; when they dispersed, the police followed them back to the Castro in a rampage of violence that left sixty-one police and 100 protesters hospitalized.

Though the energetic early days of gay liberation are over, and notwithstanding the heavy toll taken by the AIDS epidemic of the 1980s, the Castro is still a center of gay life in San Francisco, and famous the world over. The district is renowned for its street festivals, such as Gay Pride and the Castro Street Fair. The best-known party, the Halloween bash, was moved in 1996 to the civic center at the request of Castro merchants, who complained of rowdiness and vandalism. The district has only half as many people of color as the city at large, and the median age of residents is around thirty.

A walk down Castro Street in the 1990s still shows it to be very gay identified, with gay symbols, such as the pink triangle and the rainbow flag, adorning many stores and houses. Shops containing everything from men's haute couture fashions to leather-fetish dog collars and leashes attract both residents and tourists. Whether it is called a gay ghetto or a gay capitol, the Castro is clearly a political entity to the city of San Francisco and a symbol of liberation for the world.

—Tina Gianoulis

FURTHER READING:

Diaman, N.A. *Castro Street Memories*. San Francisco, Persona Productions, 1988.

Shilts, Randy. *The Mayor of Castro Street: The Life and Times of Harvey Milk.* New York, St. Martin's Press, 1982.

Stryker, Susan, and Jim Van Buskirk. *Gay by the Bay: A History of Queer Culture in the San Francisco Bay Area.* San Francisco, Chronicle Books, 1996.

"Uncle Donald's Castro." http://www.backdoor.com/CASTRO/welcome.html. April 1999.

Vojir, Dan. *The Sunny Side of Castro Street.* San Francisco, Strawberry Hill Press, 1982.

Casual Friday

Casual Friday, also called Dress Down Day, Casual Dress Day, and Business Casual Day, is a loosening of the business world's unwritten dress codes on designated days. Employees trade suits, ties, high heels, silk shirts, scarves, and other formal business attire for slacks, sports coats, polo shirts, pressed jeans, loafers, knit tunics, and flat-heeled shoes. Casual days arose in the mid-1980s influenced by the jeans-T-shirt-sneakers uniform of the computer industry, as well as increased numbers of women in the workplace and work-at-home employees. The concept caught on in the early 1990s and, fueled partly by Levi Strauss's marketing, by the mid-1990s had become a corporate institution. By the late 1990s, employees below middle management in one third of U.S companies had gone casual five days a week, according to an Evans Research Associates survey.

—ViBrina Coronado

FURTHER READING:

Bureau of National Affairs. *Dress Policies and Casual Dress Days.* PPF Survey no. 155. Washington, D.C., Bureau of National Affairs, 1998.

Gross, Kim Johnson, and Jeff Stone and Robert Tardio. *Work Clothes—Casual Dress for Serious Work.* Photographs by J. Scott Omelianuk. New York, Knopf, 1996.

Himelstein, Linda, and Nancy Walser. "Levi's vs. The Dress Code." *Business Week.* April 1, 1996, 57-58.

Levi-Strauss & Company. *How to Put Casual Businesswear to Work.* Version four. San Francisco, California, Levi-Strauss & Co. Consumer Affairs, 1998.

Molloy, John T. "Casual Business Dress." *New Women's Dress for Success.* New York, Warner Books, 1996, 209-249.

Savan, Leslie. "The Sell." *The Village Voice.* April 16, 1996, 16-17.

Weber, Mark. *Dress Casual for Success . . . for Men.* New York, McGraw-Hill, 1997.

Catalog Houses

Beginning with the first mail order catalog in the 1890s, people have turned pages to weave together images of the perfect home or the ideal wardrobe. From about 1900 through 1940, hundreds of thousands of customers also selected their most important purchase, a house, from a catalog. Catalog houses were essentially do-it-yourself homebuilding kits. When a customer ordered a house through a catalog, he or she received all of the parts, usually cut to length and numbered for proper assembly, to build the selected home. In the first half of the twentieth century, catalog houses helped meet a demand for well-built, reasonably priced houses in America's expanding cities and suburbs.

Although pattern books and house plans had been widely available throughout the mid-nineteenth century, catalog housing did not begin in earnest until the early twentieth century with the founding of the Aladdin Company in 1907. One of the longest-lived catalog housing companies, Aladdin remained in business through 1983. Robert Schweitzer and Michael W. R. Davis in *America's Favorite Houses*, a survey of catalog house companies, estimated that the Aladdin Company sold 50,000 houses during its 76-year history.

Aladdin was soon joined by a number of national and regional companies, including Gordon Van-Tine, Lewis Manufacturing Company, Sterling Homes, and Montgomery Ward. Probably the best known producer of mail order and catalog homes was Sears, Roebuck & Company, which sold homes through its Modern Homes catalog from 1908 until 1940. In addition to these national companies, a variety of regional and local companies also sold catalog houses.

A variety of factors contributed to the success of the companies that sold houses through the mail. In the early decades of the twentieth century, American cities were growing rapidly, due both to increased foreign immigration and to migration from rural areas. According to Schweitzer and Davis, the population of the United States increased by 50 percent from 1890 to 1910. Much of this growth was in American cities. As a result, there was a great demand for affordable, well built houses. Catalog housing helped to meet this need.

In addition to the growth of urban areas, technological advances made catalog houses possible. Steam-powered lumber mills made lumber available year round, and the national railroad system enabled building parts to be readily transported. This allowed the catalog house companies both to create a nationwide system of suppliers and made it possible to easily ship house components and other goods. Sears owned lumber mills in Illinois and Louisiana, and a millwork plant in Norwood, Ohio.

The catalog house companies did their utmost to insure that their houses were ready to assemble. One of the innovations introduced by Aladdin in 1911 and quickly adopted by other manufacturers were parts that were ''Readi-cut.'' More than an advertising slogan, the concept of lumber that was, as Sears called it, ''already cut and fitted,'' meant that the structural components were precut to exact lengths and ready for assembly. The benefits of this were many: The do-it-yourselfer or contractor building the house did not have to spend time on the job cutting the lumber to fit; it reduced wasted materials and construction mistakes; and, in an age before power tools, it simplified house building.

Part of the fascination with catalog houses in the late twentieth century is how inexpensive they seem. In 1926 it was possible to buy a six-room house from Sears for as little as $2,232. This price included all of the lumber needed to construct the house, together with the shingles, millwork, flooring, plaster, windows, doors, hardware (including nails), the siding and enough paint for three coats. It did not include the cost of the lot nor the labor required to build the house, nor did it include any masonry such as concrete for the foundation. If the house came from Sears, plumbing, heating, wiring, and storm and screen doors and windows were not part of the original package, but could, of course, be purchased from Sears at extra cost. The buyer of a catalog house also received a full set of blue prints and a complete construction manual.

One of the common elements of catalog houses was their design. Catalogs from Sears, Roebuck & Co., Ray H. Bennett Lumber Company, the Radford Architectural Company, and Gordon Van-Tine show houses that seem nearly interchangeable. Bungalows, American Four-Squares, and Colonial Revival designs dominate. Sears regularly reviewed the design of its houses and introduced new models and updated the more popular designs. A small four-room cottage, the Rodessa, was available in 11 catalogs, between 1919 an 1933. The floor plan remained basically the same over the years although details changed.

Sears had several sources for its house designs. The company often bought designs for houses that had already been built and were well received by the public. Sears also purchased designs from popular magazines and reproduced those houses exactly. Beginning in 1919, the company created its own in-house architectural division that developed original house designs and adapted other contemporary designs for sale by Sears. The Architects' Council, as it was called, became a selling point for Sears, which promoted the ''free'' architectural service provided to buyers of Sears' houses.

Apart from reflecting the growth of city and suburb and the growth of a mass market for housing, catalog houses were designed to meet changing concepts of house and home. New materials, such as linoleum, and laborsaving devices such as vacuum cleaners and electric irons, made houses easier to manage. This reduced the need for servants, which meant that houses could be smaller. At the same time, lifestyles became less formal. The catalog house plans reflected these changes, often eliminating entry vestibules and formal parlors. The catalogs helped to reinforce and promote the interest in smaller houses and less formal living spaces through their pages. Similar ideas were promoted by popular magazines, such as *Ladies' Home Journal*, which sold house plans designed by Frank Lloyd Wright and others, and organizations such as the American Institute of Architects, which created the Small House Service Bureau, known as the ASHB in 1919.

Advertising played an important role in the success of mail order housing companies. The most effective tool used was annual catalogs. The catalogs not only advertised the range of models available but promoted the value of home ownership over paying rent, and provided the potential customer with testimonials and guarantees promoting the quality of houses offered by each manufacturer.

The guarantees provided by the catalog firms were one of the most effective tools used to promote their products. Sears provided a written ''Certificate of Guarantee'' with each house; the guarantee promised that sufficient materials of good quality would be received to complete the house. Other companies offered similar guarantees of quality and satisfaction; Aladdin, for example, promoted its lumber to be ''knot-free'' by offering consumers a ''Dollar-a-knot'' guarantee. Liberty offered its customers an ''iron-clad guarantee,'' while Lewis had a seven-point protection plan.

In addition to their catalogs, the mail-order house companies advertised in popular magazines, including the *Saturday Evening Post*, *Collier's*, and *House Beautiful*. Early in their history, the ads were small and placed in the back pages of magazines; the emphasis was to promote confidence in the products in order to develop a market. The ads emphasized the cost savings, sound quality, and fast delivery. Later ads were much larger and often consisted of a one- or two-page spread emphasizing that the homes sold were both stylish and well built.

Each of the catalog housing companies had their own philosophy about providing financing. Sears first provided financing for its houses in 1911. At first loans were for the house only; by 1918, however, Sears began advancing capital for the labor required to build the house. Eventually, Sears also loaned buyers the money to pay for the lot and additional material. Other companies selling houses through the mail were more conservative. Aladdin never provided financing and required a 25 percent deposit at the time the order was placed, with the balance due upon delivery. Sterling offered a 2 percent discount for customers paying in cash, as did Gordon-Van Tine.

Sears vigorously promoted its easy payment plan throughout its catalogs. The 1926 catalog includes an advertisement that assures the reader that ''a home of your own does not cost you any more than your present mode of living. Instead of paying monthly rental, by our Easy Payment Plan you may have . . . a beautiful home instead of worthless rent receipts.'' And, in the event that the reader missed the two-page layout promoting Sears' financing plan, each catalog page illustrating a house plan included a reminder of the availability of the ''easy payment plan.''

Just as a combination of conditions led to the initial success of catalog houses, a number of factors contributed to their demise. The company's liberal financing policies are often cited as a contributing factor in the death of Sears' Modern Homes program. During the depression of the 1930s, the company was forced to foreclose on thousands of mortgages worth more than $11 million, and lost additional money by reselling the houses below cost.

After World War II, social policy and technology passed by catalog housing. There was no longer a niche for people who wanted to build their own houses. The returning veterans and their brides were anxious to return to normal lives, and they no longer had the time or inclination to build their own houses. However, they did have the wherewithal to buy houses built by others. Subdivisions of builder-constructed housing, beginning with Levittown, sprang up across the country to meet this need. The builders of postwar housing capitalized on the great demand by adapting Henry Ford's assembly line principles to home construction. The desire for houses that were well built disappeared in the need for houses that were quickly built.

—Leah Konicki

FURTHER READING:

Gowans, Alan. *The Comfortable House: North American Suburban Architecture 1890-1930.* Cambridge, Massachusetts, M.I.T. Press, 1986.

Schweitzer, Robert, and Michael W. R. Davis. *America's Favorite Homes: Mail Order Catalogues as a Guide to Popular Early 20th Century Houses.* Detroit, Wayne State University Press, 1990.

Sears, Roebuck and Co. *Sears, Roebuck Catalog of Houses, 1926: An Unabridged Reprint.* New York, Dover Publications, Inc. and Athenaeum of Philadelphia, 1991.

Stevenson, Katherine C., and H. Ward Jandl. *Houses by Mail: A Guide to Houses from Sears, Roebuck and Company.* Washington, D.C., Preservation Press, 1986.

Catch-22

Hailed as "a classic of our era," "an apocalyptic masterpiece," and the best war story ever told, Joseph Heller's blockbuster first novel, *Catch-22* (1961), not only exposed the hypocrisy of the military, but it also introduced a catchphrase to describe the illogic inherent in all bureaucracies, from education to religion, into the popular lexicon. The "Catch-22" of the novel's title is a perverse, protean principle that covers any absurd situation; it is the unwritten loophole in every written law, a frustratingly elliptical paradox that defies solution. As Heller demonstrates in his novel, Catch-22 has many clauses, the most memorable of which allows only crazy men to be excused from flying the life-threatening missions ordered by their military superiors. To be excused from flying, a man needs only to ask for release; but by asking, he proves that he is sane and therefore he must continue flying. "That's some catch," observes one of the flyers. "It's the best there is," concurs Doc Daneeka.

Heller drew deeply on his personal experiences in the writing of his novel, especially in his depiction of the central character, Yossarian, a flyer who refuses any longer to be part of a system so utterly hostile to his own values. Like Yossarian, Heller served in the Mediterranean during the later years of World War II, was part of a squadron that lost a plane over Ferrara, enjoyed the varied pleasures that Rome had to offer, and was decorated for his wartime service. And like Yossarian, Heller passionately strove to become an *ex*-flyer. (After one of his missions, in fact, Heller's fear of flight became so intense that, when the war ended, he took a ship home and refused to fly again for 15 years afterward.)

Although critics usually refer to *Catch-22* as a war novel, the war itself—apart from creating the community within which Yossarian operates—plays a relatively small part in the book. While the military establishment comprises an entire society, self-contained and absolute, against which Yossarian rebels, it is merely a microcosm of the

Martin Balsam in a scene from the film *Catch-22*.

larger American society and a symbol for all other repressive organizations. In the novel, there is little ideological debate about the conflict between Germany and the United States or about definitions of patriotism. Heller, in fact, deliberately sets *Catch-22* in the final months of the war, during which Hitler is no longer a significant threat and the action is winding down. The missions required of the flyers have no military or strategic importance except among the administrators, each of whom wants to come out of the war ahead. Inversely, however, the danger to Yossarian from his superiors intensifies as the war draws to a close. Yossarian wisely realizes that the enemy is "anybody who's going to get you killed, no matter *which* side he's on." And Heller surrounds Yossarian with many such enemies—from generals Dreedle and Peckem, who wage war on each other and neglect the men under their command; to Colonel Scheisskopf—literally the Shithead in charge—who is so fanatic about military precision that he considers implanting metal alloys in his men's thighbones to force them to march straighter; to Colonel Cathcart, obsessed with getting good aerial photos and with making the cover of the *Saturday Evening Post,* who keeps raising the number of requisite flights; and Colonel Korn, who is so concerned that men might actually learn something at their educational sessions that he implements a new rule: only those who never ask questions will be allowed to do so. Entrepreneur extraordinaire and legendary double-dealer Milo Minderbinder is a new age prophet of profit: he steals and resells the morphine from flight packs and leaves instead notes for the wounded soldiers that what is good for business is actually good for them as well. (To prove his point, he notes that even the dead men have a share in his "syndicate.") Captain Black insists that everyone "voluntarily" sign his Glorious Loyalty Oath, except his nemesis, who will not be allowed to sign "even if he wants to." And Nately's whore, out to avenge her lover's death, persists in trying to kill the innocent Yossarian. (In Heller's logically illogical world, the whore is symbolic of the universal principle that Yossarian will always be unjustly beset upon—and will probably always deserve it.)

Yossarian's increasingly dramatic acts of insubordination against such an irrational system begin with his self-hospitalizations, where he meets the ultimate symbol of the bureaucracy's indifference to the individual: the soldier in white, a faceless, nameless symbol of imminent death. After his friend Snowden's death, Yossarian's insubordination escalates to his refusal to fly or wear a uniform again, and it ends with his decision not to compromise but instead to emulate his comrade Orr's impossible achievement and to affirm life by rowing a small boat to Sweden.

In the film adaptation of *Catch-22* (1970), by focusing incrementally—as Heller did—on the Avignon incident during which Snowden literally loses his guts and Yossarian metaphorically loses his, director Mike Nichols succeeds in recreating the novel's circularity and its deliberately repetitive structure. By downplaying much of the novel's truculent satire of American capitalism, however, Nichols is able to concentrate on the traumatizing fear of death, a reality Yossarian (Alan Arkin) cannot face until he re-imagines it through the death of Snowden (Jon Korkes). Nichols also reformulates the well-intentioned capitalistic Milo Minderbinder; played by baby-faced Jon Voight, the film's Milo is a callous and sinister destroyer of youth, every bit as corrupt as his superior officers, the colonels Korn (Buck Henry) and Cathcart (Martin Balsam). Balancing the cynicism of the selfish officers is the affecting naïveté of their victims, including the earnest Chaplain Tappman (Anthony Perkins), the innocent Nately (Art Garfunkel), and the perpetually bewildered Major Major (Bob Newhart).

An even more effective balance is the one Nichols strikes between noise and silence: in sharp contrast to the busy confusion of some of the film's episodes, which aptly reflect the noisy chatter of the novel and the jumble of word games Heller plays, there are subtle moments of silence. The opening scene, for instance, begins in blackness, without words or music; then there appears a tranquil image of approaching dawn, replaced suddenly with the loud roar of plane engines being engaged. It is as if the viewer is seeing the scene through Yossarian's eyes, moving with him from a dream state to the waking nightmare (one of the film's recurring motifs) of his reality. Replete with inside jokes linking it to the Vietnam War (Cathcart's defecating in front of Chaplain Tappman, for instance, recalls LBJ's habit of talking to his aides while sitting on the toilet), Nichols' film adaptation of *Catch-22* is thus an interesting and original work as well as a noteworthy reinterpretation of Heller's classic novel.

—Barbara Tepa Lupack

FURTHER READING:

Heller, Joseph. *Catch-22.* New York, Simon & Schuster, 1961.

Kiley, Frederick, and Walter McDonald, editors. *A Catch-22 Casebook.* New York, Thomas Y. Crowell, 1973.

Lupack, Barbara Tepa. "Seeking a Sane Asylum: *Catch-22.*" In *Insanity as Redemption in Contemporary American Fiction.* Gainesville, University Press of Florida, 1995.

————, editor. *Take Two: Adapting the Contemporary American Novel to Film.* Bowling Green, Popular Press, 1994.

Merrill, Robert. *Joseph Heller.* Boston: Twayne, 1987.

Merrill, Robert and John L. Simons. "The Waking Nightmare of Mike Nichols' Catch-22." In *Catch-22: Antiheroic Antinovel,* edited by Stephen W. Potts. New York, Twayne, 1989.

The Catcher in the Rye

The Catcher in the Rye, the only novel of the reclusive J. D. Salinger, is the story of Holden Caulfield, a sixteen-year-old boy who has been dismissed from Pencey Prep, the third time he has failed to meet the standards of a private school. He delays the inevitable confrontation with his parents by running away for a forty-eight hour "vacation" in New York City. A series of encounters with places and people in the city serves to further disillusion Holden and reinforce his conviction that the world is full of phonies. He plans to escape by going West and living alone, but even his little sister Phoebe, the only person with whom Holden can communicate, realizes that her brother is incapable of taking care of himself. When Phoebe reveals her plan to go with him, Holden accepts the futility of his escape plan and goes home.

A focus of controversy since its publication in 1951, *The Catcher in the Rye* has consistently appeared on lists of banned books. The American Library Association's survey of books censored from 1986 to 1995 found that Salinger's novel frequently topped the list. Just as consistently, however, the novel has appeared on required reading lists for high school and college students. Critical views of *The Catcher in the Rye* show the same polarization. Some critics have praised its honesty and idiomatic language; others have faulted its self-absorbed hero and unbalanced view of society. Holden Caulfield has been called a twentieth-century Huck Finn, an autobiographical neurotic, an American classic, and a self-destructive nut.

Through the decades, as the controversy has ebbed and flowed, *The Catcher in the Rye* has remained a favorite with adolescent readers who see their own experience reflected in Holden Caulfield's contempt for the "phoniness" of adult life. The very qualities that lead some parents and other authorities to condemn Salinger's novel—the profanity, the cynicism, the preoccupation with sex—predispose youthful readers to champion it. In Holden, adolescents see the eternal outsider, sickened by the world around him, unable to communicate the emotions that consume him, and aware that his innocence has been irretrievably lost. It is a familiar image to many adolescents. Arthur Heiserman and James E. Miller, Jr., in an early essay on *The Catcher in the Rye* observed that Holden Caulfield is unique among American literary heroes because he both needs to return home and needs to leave home. But these conflicting needs, while they may be unique in an American hero, are typical of adolescents struggling to achieve a separate identity. Holden may be faulted for his self-absorption, but in his consciousness of self, as in his angst, the character is true to adolescent experience.

Even the obscenities and profanities that Holden speaks, a major cause of official objections to the novel, affirm his status as quintessential adolescent. He sees obscene speech as the only valid response to the obscene hypocrisies of the profane adult world. The irony, of course, is that Holden himself has already been contaminated by the world he despises. The child of affluent parents, he clearly enjoys the benefits their "phony" world affords him. He spends money on taxi rides and nightclub visits, and even as he condemns lies and fakery, he himself lies and participates in the fakery. He is acquiring the survival skills that will allow him to operate in the fallen adult world, a fact he himself acknowledges: "If you want to stay alive, you have to say that stuff."

Critics often classify *The Catcher in the Rye* as a quest story, but Holden's quest, if such it be, is aimless and incomplete. Holden's New York misadventures occur during the Christmas season, a time when Christendom celebrates the birth of a child who became a savior. But the Holy Child has no place in this world where the cross that symbolizes his sacrifice has become merely a prop carried by actors on a Radio City stage. A self-proclaimed atheist, Holden inhabits a world where true transcendence can never be achieved. Yet longing for a heroic role, he dreams of being the "catcher in the rye," of saving "thousands of little kids" from plunging over the cliff into the abyss of adulthood. Ultimately, however, as he comes to realize while watching his little sister Phoebe circling on the carousel in Central Park, children cannot be saved from adulthood. Only the dead like his younger brother Allie are safe. Heroes belong in coherent worlds of shared values and meaningful connections; Holden's world is the waste land, all fragments and dead ends. Would-be heroes like Holden are "crazy mixed-up kids" who end up in California institutions.

The Catcher in the Rye is most frequently compared to Mark Twain's *The Adventures of Huckleberry Finn*, another account of an adolescent male's escape from the confinement of education and civilization. The similarities between the two novels are obvious. The narrator/protagonist in each is a teenage boy who repudiates adult hypocrisies and runs away in search of a less flawed world; both youthful protagonists speak in richly idiomatic language, and both are comic figures whose humor sometimes offers grim truths. But Huck's longing for freedom is undiluted by dreams of saving others, and Huck's world has a duality that Holden's slick society lacks. For Huck, the corruptions on land are balanced by the "free and easy" life on the raft. Huck has the Mississippi; Holden has a duck pond. Huck's abusive father is balanced by the tenderness and concern of Jim; Holden's father is irrelevant, a disembodied payer of bills. Other adult figures who have the potential to nurture Holden through his crisis are mere passing images like the nuns to whom he gives money or phony betrayers like Mr. Antolini who seems to offer Holden compassion and understanding only to make sexual advances to him later. His peers offer Holden no more than do the adults. They too are phonies, like the pseudo-sophisticated Carl Luce and Sally Hayes, or absent, idealized objects like Jane Gallagher.

Nowhere is Holden more clearly a creature of his time than in his inability to connect, to communicate. *The Catcher in the Rye* is filled with aborted acts of communication—truncated conversations, failed telephone calls, an unconsummated sexual encounter. Most of the things which awaken a sense of connection in Holden are no longer part of the actual world. The precocious Allie who copies Emily Dickinson poems on his baseball glove, the museum mummy, even Ring Lardner and Thomas Hardy, the writers Holden admires and imagines that he would like to call up and talk to—all are dead. In a particularly revealing moment Holden fantasizes life as a deaf-mute,

a life that would free him from "useless conversation with any body" and force everyone to leave him alone. Yet this fantasy indicates Holden's lack of self-knowledge, for his isolation would be an act, his deaf-muteness a pretense. He defines alienation as a job in a service station and a beautiful, deaf-mute wife to share his life. Therein lies the pathos of Holden Caulfield. He can neither commit to the inner world and its truths nor celebrate the genuine that exists amid the phoniness of the public world. *The Catcher in the Rye,* for all its strength, fails as a coming of age story precisely because its protagonist, who is terrified of change, never changes. Mark Twain's Huck Finn sets out for the territory and freedom, James Joyce's Stephen Dedalus experiences his epiphany, T. S. Eliot's Fisher King hears the message of the thunder. J. D. Salinger's Holden Caulfield can only, as he himself says at the novel's end, "miss everybody."

—Wylene Rholetter

FURTHER READING:

Bloom, Harold, ed. *Holden Caulfield.* New York, Chelsea House, 1990.

Engel, Stephen, ed. *Readings on the Catcher in the Rye.* San Diego, Greenhaven, 1998.

Pinsker, Sanford. *The Catcher in the Rye: Innocence Under Pressure.* New York, Twayne, 1993.

Salinger, J. D. *The Catcher in the Rye.* Little Brown, 1951.

———. *Franny and Zooey.* Little Brown, 1961.

———. *Nine Stories.* Little Brown, 1953.

———. *Raise High the Roof Beam, Carpenter and Seymour: An Introduction.* Little Brown, 1963.

Salzberg, Joel, ed. *Critical Essays on Salinger's Catcher in the Rye.* New York, Macmillan, 1989.

Salzman, Jack, ed. *New Essays on the Catcher in the Rye.* Cambridge and New York, Cambridge University Press, 1992.

Cather, Willa (1873-1947)

Willa Cather, variously perceived by critics as realistic, regionalist, or sentimental, as well as an unusual literary stylist of unhurried elegance, memorably exploited themes long regarded as part of the American mythos. She wrote 12 novels and over 60 short stories, contrasting nature's wilderness with the social veneer of her characters, and achieved critical and popular acclaim for works such as *O Pioneers!* (1913) and *My Antonia* (1918), which depict the Nebraska frontier, and, most famously and enduringly perhaps, her "Santa Fe" novel, *Death Comes for the Archbishop* (1927), which treats the history of the Southwest after the Mexican War. According to Susan Rosowski, Cather "saw herself as the first of a new literary tradition, yet one which evolved out of the past and from native traditions rather than in revolt against them." Novels like *O Pioneers!*, *The Song of the Lark* (1915), and *My Antonia* favor cultural diversity as embodied in the experiences of immigrant settlers, and showcase the strength of their heroic female characters Alexandra Bergson, Antonia Shimerda, and Thea Kronborg, respectively. Cather's work also affirms appreciation for a simpler era when America espoused spiritual ideals. In the 1920s, in novels such as *One of Ours* (1922), *A Lost Lady* (1923), and *The Professor's House* (1925), she indicted a society that had rejected revered traditional values to embrace materialism. Her last novels—*Shadows on the Rock* (1931) and *Sapphira and the Slave Girl* (1940)—reflect the writer's retreat to a past further removed from her own time, when order, stability, and noble principles governed human life. Born in Virginia and educated at the University of Nebraska, Cather wrote poetry, and spent six years as a journalist with *McClure's* magazine before devoting her life full-time to fiction. She spent 40 years until her death living in New York with her devoted companion Edith Lewis.

—Ed Piacentino

FURTHER READING:

O'Brien, Sharon. *Willa Cather: The Emerging Voice.* New York, Oxford University Press, 1987.

Rosowki, Susan J. *The Voyage Perilous: Willa Cather's Romanticism.* Lincoln, University of Nebraska Press, 1986.

Woodress, James. *Willa Cather: A Literary Life.* Lincoln, University of Nebraska Press, 1987.

Cathy

The comic strip *Cathy,* by American artist and writer Cathy Guisewite, addresses the insecurities and desires of a new generation of women trying to balance traditional pressures with the responsibility of careers and other personal freedoms. Premiering in November of 1976, *Cathy* introduced a character struggling with a mother urging marriage and children, a demanding boss, a noncommittal boyfriend, and a loathing for her figure. Although Guisewite was instrumental in bringing women's issues to the daily comics, *Cathy* also has its detractors who long for a less scattered, more self-confident female character. Nevertheless, *Cathy* has grown to syndication in more than 1,400 newspapers and has spawned books, television specials, and a line of merchandise.

—Geri Speace

FURTHER READING:

Friendly, Jonathan. "Women's New Roles in Comics." *New York Times.* February 28, 1983, p. B5.

Moritz, Charles, editor. *Current Biography.* New York, H.W. Wilson, 1989.

Sjoerdsma, Ann G. "Guisewite Could Be a Stronger, More Profound Voice for Single Women." *Knight-Ridder/Tribune News Service.* August 15, 1997.

Cats

By the end of the twentieth century, *Cats* had lived up to its billing of "Now and Forever," as it became the longest-running

Andrew Lloyd Webber musical in both London and New York. The tuneful score, inspired by T.S. Eliot's *Old Possum's Book of Practical Cats,* includes songs in a wide variety of styles. John Napier's elaborate set transforms the entire theater into a garbage dump upon which the feline cast learn which one of them will gain an extra life at the Jellicle Ball. Various cats tell their tales through song, but the winner is Grizabella, the glamour cat who became an outcast. Grizabella's number, "Memory," is one of Lloyd Webber's most famous songs; by 1992, it had been recorded in no fewer than 150 different versions. *Cats* opened in London in 1981 and in New York the following year. The innovative costumes and choreography coupled with the eclectic musical score which culminates in "Memory" account for its continued popularity. A video version of *Cats,* filmed during a London performance, was released in 1998.

—William A. Everett

FURTHER READING:

Lloyd Webber, Andrew. *Cats: The Book of the Musical.* London, Faber & Faber, 1981; San Diego, Harcourt, Brace, and Jovanovich, 1983.

Richmond, Keith. *The Musicals of Andrew Lloyd Webber.* London, Virgin, 1995.

Cavett, Dick (1936—)

"Sophisticated," "witty," "urbane," "intelligent," and "literate" are among the adjectives commonly used to describe Dick Cavett, the Nebraska-born talk show host who experienced fame during a relatively brief period of his early career and professional struggle thereafter. *The Dick Cavett Show* was seen five nights a week for seven years on ABC-TV from 1968 until 1975 and then once weekly on Public Television until 1982. Cavett won three Emmy awards during these years. His interviews with such individuals as Lawrence Olivier, Katharine Hepburn, Noel Coward, Orson Welles, Groucho Marx, and Alfred Hitchcock are classics in the field, as Cavett's lively mind allowed a degree of candor and spontaneity generally lacking in the attempts of less gifted colleagues. For many viewers, his show was the saving grace of commercial television and a good reason to stay up late.

A Yale graduate, Cavett began his career as an actor and standup comic without great success. While working as a copy boy for *Time* magazine in 1960, he decided to try his hand at comedy writing. Since Jack Paar was one of his early idols as a performer, he wrote a series of jokes designed for Paar's opening monologue on the *Tonight Show* and finagled a plan to deliver the jokes directly to Paar. The plan succeeded, Paar liked the jokes, and Cavett landed a job writing for the show. From the Paar show, he got his first chance as a talk-show host on morning television and soon moved on to his spot opposite Johnny Carson (Paar's successor) on ABC.

After the Cavett show's demise, its host found various other venues but never again reached the same level of visibility. An attempted variety show series predictably fell flat, as scripted sketches were not Cavett's metier. Through the years since 1982, he has

The cast of _Cats_.

hosted numerous talk shows on cable stations including Showtime and CNBC, taken cameo roles in the theater, and narrated a PBS series on Japan. His gift for conversation keeps him popular on the lecture circuit, and his clear, uninflected Midwestern diction makes him an ideal candidate for commercial voice-overs. In short, Cavett has kept relatively busy, but his varied activities go mostly unnoticed by the general public.

Cavett's name came into the news in 1997 when he was sued for breach of contract over a syndicated radio talk show he was scheduled to host. He left the show after two weeks, and word went out through his lawyer that Cavett's premature departure was due to a manic-depressive episode. The civil suit was eventually dismissed.

Prior to this turn of events, Cavett had been relatively open about his chronic suffering with depression, even going on record about his successful treatment with controversial electroconvulsive (otherwise known as ''shock'')therapy. As a spokesperson on psychiatric illness, Cavett, like William Styron, Art Buchwald, and others, has put his verbal skills to use in articulating his experiences with the disease that has plagued him intermittently throughout his career. He recalls, for instance, in an interview for _People_ magazine, a time before his ''big break'' when he was living alone in New York City, and ''I did nothing but watch Jack Paar on _The Tonight Show_. I lived for the Paar show. I watched it from my bed on my little black-and-white set on my dresser, and I'd think, 'I'll brush my teeth in a minute,' and then I'd go to sleep and wake up at three the following afternoon.'' It is ironic that this brilliant conversationalist, the life of a sophisticated nightly party, would once again enter the public eye by virtue of his melancholia.

—Sue Russell

FURTHER READING:

Cavett, Dick, and Christopher Porterfield. _Cavett_. New York, Harcourt Brace, 1974.

———. _Eye on Cavett_. New York, Arbor House, 1983.

Cavett, Dick, and Veronica Burns. ''Goodbye, Darkness.'' _People_, August 3, 1992, p. 88.

Dick Cavett (center) with Muhammad Ali and Juergen Blin on *The Dick Cavett Show*.

CB Radio

The Citizens Band Radio, familiarly known as the CB, was a device that enabled free mobile communication up to a ten mile radius for those who owned the requisite microphone, speaker, and control box. Although the Federal Communications Commission (FCC) first introduced it in 1947, the CB did not experience its heyday until 30 years later, when hundreds of thousands of automobile and tractor trailer drivers installed them in their vehicles.

In order to popularize the device among individuals for their personal use, the FCC, in 1958, opened up part of the broadcasting spectrum originally reserved for ham radio operators. This Class D band enabled the manufacture of higher quality, less expensive CB sets that were useful and affordable to ordinary people. By 1959 the average set cost between $150 and $200, but there were only 49,000 users licensed with the FCC. From 1967 to 1973, the FCC registered about 800,000 licensees. Although one did not need to obtain a license to operate a CB radio, the number of licensees shot up dramatically from 1973 to the end of the decade, when more than 500,000 people were applying for licenses each month in direct response to cultural shifts at the time. The Vietnam War had ended with America less than victorious; the Watergate scandal rocked the Nixon White House; and

the oil crisis from 1973 to 1974 led to a capping of national speed limits at 55 miles per hour. The CB afforded people—many of whom were distressed by recent governmental decisions—an opportunity to create their own communities over the airwaves.

The CB, as a "voice of the people" and the fastest growing communications medium since the telephone, rekindled a sense of camaraderie during an era when people felt oppressed by a seemingly monolithic federal government and looming corporate control. Although manufacturers encouraged people to use CBs for emergency purposes (broadcasting on channel 9) or to relieve the stress and boredom of long automobile trips, the CB transcended these practical functions and became a tool of empowerment, enabling each person to be his or her own broadcaster on the 40 channels of airwaves.

Like all small communities, CB culture developed its own language and sensibility. People liked these devices because they could use them to evade the law by communicating with drivers up ahead to find out the location of speed traps and police. They also liked the CB because it allowed for mobility, anonymity, and a chance to invent oneself. For example, instead of using proper names, CBers (or "ratchet-jaws," as users called themselves) had "handles"— nicknames they would use while on air. They also utilized a very colorful vocabulary, which included words like "Smokey" for police (so named because of their Smokey Bear-type hats), "Kodiaks with

Kodaks'' for police using radar, ''negatory'' for ''no,'' ''10-4'' for message received, and ''let the hammer down'' for speeding. Broadcast sign-offs were equally baroque: people would not just say goodbye, but rather phrases such as, ''Keep your nose between the ditches and the Smokeys off your britches.''

An essential component of the growing CB popularity was the acknowledgment and celebration of a ''trucker culture,'' summed up by the ubiquitous phrase of the time, ''Keep on Truckin'.'' Tractor trailer drivers had been using these radios to communicate among themselves over the long haul for decades, and in 1973, the CB was an integral device that enabled truckers to organize strike activities. Soon after, ordinary people began to identify with the trucker, who represented a freedom, heroism, and rugged individualism on the open road. But this trucker culture was not just confined to the roadways and airwaves. It also appeared as a recurring theme in the popular media. ''Convoy,'' by C.W. McCall, was a novelty song about a trucker named ''Rubber Duck'' who leads a speeding pack of trucks across the country, avoiding police along the way; it hit number one on the Billboard chart in 1976. ''Six Days on the Road'' was another trucker-inspired song. The film industry also became enamored of truckers and their CBs: *Smokey and the Bandit,* a film directed by Hal Needham and starring Burt Reynolds and Sally Field, came out in 1977, and in that same year Jonathan Demme directed *Handle with Care,* another trucker film. In 1978 the song ''Convoy'' was made into a film with the same title, directed by Sam Peckinpah and starring Kris Kristofferson and Ali McGraw. And television enjoyed *BJ and the Bear* during this same period.

While the American public's love affair with the CB radio and truckers did not last long—the glamour and glitz of the 1980s made truckers seem backward and unhip—it did have lasting repercussions that made people more accepting of new communications technology. Cellular phones and the Internet were just two examples of the continuation of the CB sensibility. Cellular phones offered a portable means of communication that people could use in their cars for ordinary needs and for emergencies. Internet chatrooms, while not offering mobility, did offer a sense of anonymity and group camaraderie and membership. The CB was the first technology that truly offered Americans their contradictory wishes of being part of a solidified group while their personae remained wholly anonymous if not entirely fabricated.

—Wendy Woloson

FURTHER READING:

Hershey, Cary, et.al. ''Personal Uses of Mobile Communications: Citizens Band Radio and the Local Community.'' *Communications for a Mobile Society: An Assessment of New Technology.* Ed. Raymond Bowers. Beverly Hills, Sage, 1978, 233-255.

Stern, Jane, and Michael Stern. *Jane and Michael Stern's Encyclopedia of Popular Culture.* New York, HarperPerennial, 1992.

The CBS Radio Mystery Theater

Premiering on January 6, 1974, the *CBS Radio Mystery Theater* was a notable attempt to revive the tradition of radio thrillers like *Suspense* (1942-1962) and *Inner Sanctum Mysteries* (1941-52). Created by *Inner Sanctum* producer Himan Brown, the *CBS Radio*

Mystery Theater featured many voices from the golden age of radio, including Agnes Moorehead, Les Tremayne, Santos Ortega, Bret Morrison, and Mercedes McCambridge. E. G. Marshall was its first host. The series ended on December 31, 1982.

—Christian L. Pyle

Celebrity

Celebrity is the defining issue of late twentieth-century America. In recent years, much has been made and written of the rise of contemporary celebrity culture in the United States. Writers, thinkers, and pundits alike warn us of the danger of our societal obsession with celebrity, even as more and more Americans tune into *Hard Copy* and buy *People* magazine. Andy Warhol's cynical prediction that everyone will be famous for fifteen minutes has virtually become a national rallying cry as television airwaves overflow with venues for everyone's opportunity to appear in the spotlight. The more that is written about fame, the less shocked we become. That's the way things are, we seem to say, so why not grab our moment in the sun?

Fame, of course, is nothing new. In his comprehensive volume *The Frenzy of Renown: Fame and Its History,* Leo Braudy has traced man's desire for recognition and need for immortality back to Alexander the Great, noting: ''In great part the history of fame is the history of the changing ways by which individuals have sought to bring themselves to the attention of others and, not incidentally, have thereby gained power over them.'' The desire to achieve recognition is both timeless and universal. What is particular to late twentieth-century America, however, is the democratization of fame and the resultant ubiquity of the celebrity—a person, as Daniel Boorstin so famously noted, ''who is known for his well-knownness.''

The origin of the unique phenomenon of twentieth-century celebrity may be found in the words of one of America's Founding Fathers, John Adams, who wrote, ''The rewards . . . in this life are esteem and admiration of others—the punishments are neglect and contempt. . . . The desire of the esteem of others is as real a want of nature as hunger—and the neglect and contempt of the world as severe as a pain. . . . It is the principal end of the government to regulate this passion, which in its turn becomes the principal means of order and subordination in society, and alone commands effectual obedience to laws, since without it neither human reason, nor standing armies, would ever produce that great effect.'' Indeed, the evolution of celebrity as the Zeitgeist of the twentieth century is a direct result of democracy.

As Alexis De Tocqueville noted in the early 1830s, the equality implied by a democracy creates the need for new kinds of distinction. But there are problems inherent in this new social order, as Tocqueville wrote: ''I confess that I believe democratic society to have much less to fear from boldness than from paltriness of aim. What frightens me most is the danger that . . . ambition may lose both its force and its greatness, that human passions may grow gentler and at the same time baser, with the result that the progress of the body social may become daily quieter and less aspiring.'' A prescription, it would seem, for twentieth-century celebrity. Indeed, some 150 years later, Daniel Boorstin would describe a celebrity thus: ''His qualities—or rather his lack of qualities—illustrate our peculiar problems. He is neither good nor bad, great nor petty. . . . He has been fabricated on purpose to satisfy our exaggerated expectations of human greatness. He is morally neutral. The product of no conspiracy, of no group promoting vice or emptiness, he is made by honest, industrious men of high professional ethics doing their job, 'informing' us and educating us. He is made by all of us who willingly read about him, who like to see him on television, who buy recordings of his voice, and talk about him to our friends. His relation to morality and even to reality is highly ambiguous.''

What Tocqueville foresaw and Boorstin confirmed in his empty definition of celebrity seems, however, to belie the fact that, as a nation, we have come to define success by celebrity. It is the singular goal to which our country aspires. But how and why has this hollow incarnation of fame become our benchmark of achievement?

The great experiment inaugurated by the signing of the Declaration of Independence proposed a classless society in which the only prerequisite for success was the desire and the will to succeed. In fact, however, though founded on a noble premise, America was and is a stratified society. Yet the myth of classlessness, of limitless opportunity open to anyone with ambition and desire, has been so pervasive that it has remained the unifying philosophy that drives society as a whole. In a world where dream and reality do not always mesh, a third entity must necessarily evolve, one which somehow links the two. That link—the nexus between a deeply stratified society and the myth of classlessness—is celebrity.

According to Braudy: ''From the beginning, fame has required publicity.'' The evolution (or perhaps devolution) of fame into celebrity in the twentieth century was the direct result of inventions such as photography and telegraphy, which made it possible for words and images to be conveyed across a vast nation. Abraham Lincoln went so far as to credit his election to a photograph taken by Matthew Brady and widely dispersed throughout his campaign. Before the invention of photography, most Americans could have passed a president on the street and not known it. A mania for photography ensued and, during the nineteenth century, photograph galleries sprang up throughout the country to satisfy the public's increasing hunger for and fascination with these images. The ideal vehicle for the promulgation of democracy, photography was accessible to anyone, and thus it soon contributed to the erosion of visible boundaries of class, even as it proclaimed a new ideal for success—visual fame.

The late nineteenth and early twentieth centuries witnessed an avalanche of inventions that would transform America from a rural country of provincial enclaves to a more unified nation of urban centers. The rapid growth of mass media technologies spawned increasing numbers of national publications eager to make news. And make it they did—searching out stories that might not have been recognized as newsworthy a decade before. As Richard Schickel writes in *Intimate Strangers: The Culture of Celebrity*: ''The pace of life was quickening, the flow of information beginning to speed up while mobility both geographic and social was stepping up as well. People began to need familiar figures they could carry about as they moved out and moved up, a sort of portable community as it were, containing representations of good values, interesting traits, a certain amount of within-bounds attractiveness, glamour, even deviltry.'' Thus the stage was set for the invention of the motion picture.

The birth of celebrity is, of course, most closely tied to the motion picture industry, and its embrace by a public eager to be entertained. Paying a penny, or later a nickel, audiences from cities to small towns could gather in a darkened movie theatre, an intimate setting in which they could escape the reality of their daily lives and become part of a fantasy. But how was this different from live theatre?

In part, movie houses existed all over America, and so hundreds of thousands of people had the opportunity to see the same actor or actress perform. Furthermore, films were churned out at a phenomenal rate, thus moviegoers could enjoy a particular performer in a dozen or more pictures a year. This engendered a new kind of identification with performers—a sense of knowing them. Additionally, Schickel cites the influence of a cinematic innovation by director D. W. Griffith: the close-up, which had ''the effect of isolating the actor in the sequence, separating him or her from the rest of the ensemble for close individual scrutiny by the audience. To some immeasurable degree, attention is directed away from the role being played, the overall story being told. It is focused instead on the reality of the individual playing the part.'' The intimacy, immediacy, and constancy of movies all fostered an environment ripe for celebrity.

Audiences clamored to know more about their favorite actors and actresses, and a new kind of public personality was born—one whose success was not measured by birth, wealth, heroism, intelligence, or achievement. The fledgling movie studios quickly grasped the power of these audiences to make or break them, and they responded by putting together a publicity machine that would keep the public inundated with information about their favorite performers. From studio publicists to gossip columnists, the movie industry was unafraid to promote itself and its product, even if it meant making private lives totally public. But the effect was electrifying. Almost overnight, fame had ceased to be sole property of the moneyed elite. Movie stars, America believed, might be young, beautiful, even rich, but otherwise they were no different from you or me. In Hollywood, where most of the movie studios were run by Jewish immigrants, where new stars were discovered at soda fountains, where it didn't matter where you came from or what your father did, anyone could become rich or famous. This new fame carried with it the most basic American promise of life, liberty, and the pursuit of happiness. It proved the system worked. Whatever the reality might be of the daily lives of Americans, Hollywood celebrities proved that, with a little luck, good timing, and a modicum of talent, anyone could become somebody.

The Hollywood celebrity factory churned out stars from the very beginning. In silent pictures, Gloria Swanson, Rudolph Valentino, and Greta Garbo captured America's imagination. But when sound came to pictures, many silent stars faded into obscurity, betrayed by squeaky voices, stutters, or Brooklyn accents. In their place were new stars, and more of them, now that they could talk. During the Golden Age of Hollywood, the most famous were the handsome leading men such as Robert Taylor, Gary Cooper, and Cary Grant, and beautiful leading ladies such as Vivien Leigh, Ava Gardner, and Elizabeth Taylor. But Hollywood had room for more than beauty—there were dancers such as Fred Astaire and Gene Kelly, singers such as Judy Garland and Bing Crosby, funny men such as Bob Hope and Danny Kaye, villains such as Edward G. Robinson, horror stars such as Boris Karloff, starlets such as Betty Grable, cowboys such as Gene Autry. The beauty of celebrity was that it seemed to have no boundaries. You could create your own niche. As Braudy wrote: ''Fame had ceased to be the possession of particular individuals or classes and had become instead a potential attribute of every human being that needed only to be brought out in the open for all to applaud its presence.''

With the invention of television, the pervasiveness and power of celebrity grew. By bringing billions of images into America's homes, thousands of new faces to be ''known,'' celebrity achieved a new intimacy. And with the decline of the studio system, movie stars began to seem more and more like ''regular people.'' If the stars of the

Golden Age of Hollywood had been America's ''royalty,'' now no such pretensions existed. From the mumbling Marlon Brando to the toothy Tom Cruise, the stars of the new Hollywood seemed to expand the promise of celebrity to include everyone.

Celebrity, of course, did not remain the sole property of Hollywood. During the Roaring Twenties, Americans experienced a period of prosperity unlike any that had existed in the nation's 150-year history. With new wealth and new leisure time, Americans not only flocked to the movies, they went to baseball games and boxing matches, and there they found new heroes. Babe Ruth became an icon whose extraordinary popularity would pave the way for such future superstars as Joe DiMaggio and Michael Jordan. During the 1920s, however, Ruth's popularity would be rivaled by only one other man, a hero from a new field—aviation. When Charles Lindbergh became the first person to fly solo across the Atlantic Ocean, he was hailed as a national savior. America's hunger for celebrity seemed unquenchable as each new star seemed a new fulfillment of a country's promise, of the American Dream.

The history of the twentieth century is the history of the growing influence of celebrity. No area of American society has remained untouched. The entertainment industry is no longer confined to Hollywood. Sports, music, art, literature, and even politics have embraced the celebrity ethos in order to succeed. It has been said that if Franklin Delano Roosevelt—a man in a wheelchair—were to run for president today, he would not be elected. We live in a society bounded and defined by the power of images, by the rules of celebrity. Dwight D. Eisenhower hired former matinee idol Robert Montgomery to be his consultant on television and media presentations. John F. Kennedy, an Irish Catholic, won the presidency because he looked like a movie star and he knew how to use the media, unlike Richard Nixon, who dripped with sweat and seemed uncomfortable on camera. Ronald Reagan, a former actor with little political ability, used his extensive media savvy to become a two-term president. Today, a politician cannot even be considered a presidential hopeful unless he has what it takes to be a celebrity. Visual appearance and the ability to manipulate the press are essential to becoming our chief of state, political knowledge and leadership come second.

Yet the more pervasive celebrity has become, the more it is decried, particularly by celebrities themselves, who claim that they have been stripped of their privacy. As Braudy describes this paradox: ''Fame is desired because it is the ultimate justification, yet it is hated because it brings with it unwanted focus as well, depersonalizing as much as individualizing.'' The greater the need for audience approval, the more powerful the audience—and thus the media—has become. With the death of Princess Diana, an outcry for privacy was heard from the celebrity community and blame was cast on the media, even as hundreds of thousands of people poured into London to pay tribute to the ''People's Princess'' and millions mourned her death on television around the globe. Celebrity's snare is subtle—even as the public itself vilifies the press, it craves more. And even as celebrities seek to put limits on their responsibilities to their audience, they are, in fact, public servants.

By the late twentieth century, celebrity has become so ubiquitous that visibility has become a goal in itself. Tocqueville's prediction has come true. Americans no longer seem to aspire to greatness. They aspire to be seen. John Lahr wrote: ''The famous, who make a myth of accomplishment, become pseudo-events, turning the public gaze from the real to the ideal. . . . Fame is America's Faustian bargain: a passport to the good life which trivializes human endeavor.'' But despite the deleterious effects of celebrity, it continues to

define the American social order. After all, as Mae West once said, ''It is better to be looked over than overlooked.''

—Victoria Price

FURTHER READING:

Boorstin, Daniel. *The Image: A Guide to Pseudo-Events in America.* New York, Vantage Books, 1987.

Braudy, Leo. *The Frenzy of Renown: Fame and Its History.* New York and Oxford, Oxford University Press, 1986.

Brownstein, Ronald. *The Power and the Glitter: The Hollywood-Washington Connection.* New York, Pantheon Books, 1990.

De Tocqueville, Alexis. *Democracy in America.* J. P. Mayer, editor. New York, Harper Perennial, 1988.

Gabler, Neal. *Walter Winchell: Gossip, Power, and the Culture of Celebrity.* New York, Alfred A. Knopf, 1994.

Gamson, Joshua. *Claims to Fame: Celebrity in Contemporary America.* Berkeley, University of California Press, 1994.

Lahr, John. ''Notes on Fame.'' *Harper's.* January 1978, 77-80.

Schickel, Richard. *Intimate Strangers: The Culture of Celebrity.* Garden City, Doubleday, 1985.

Celebrity Caricature

Celebrity caricature in America has become a popular twentieth-century permutation of the longstanding art of caricature—the distortion of the face or figure for satiric purposes—which claims an extensive tradition in Western art. For centuries, comically exaggerated portrayals have served the purpose of ridicule and protest, probing beneath outward appearances to expose hidden, disreputable character traits. In the early twentieth century, however, American caricaturists based in New York City deployed a fresh approach, inventing a new form of popular portraiture. They chose for their subjects the colorful rather than the corrupt personalities of the day, reflecting the preoccupation with mass media-generated fame. During the height of its vogue between the two World Wars, celebrity caricature permeated the press, leaving the confines of the editorial cartoon to flourish on the newspaper's entertainment pages, at the head of a syndicated column, on a magazine cover, or color frontispiece. Distorted faces appeared on café walls, silk dresses, and cigarette cases; Ralph Barton's caricature theater curtain depicting a first-night audience caused a sensation in 1922. Caricaturists did not attempt to editorialize or criticize in such images. ''It is not the caricaturist's business to be penetrating,'' Barton insisted, ''it is his job to put down the figure a man cuts before his fellows in his attempt to conceal the writhings of his soul.'' These artists highlighted the public persona rather than probing beneath it, reconstructing its exaggerated components with a heightened sense of style and wit. Mocking the celebrity system, caricature provided a counterbalance to unrestrained publicity.

American caricaturists sought a modern look, derived from European art, to express a contemporary urbanity. They departed from comic conventions, selectively borrowing from the radical art movements of the day. Like advertisers, they began to simplify, elongate, geometricize, and fragment their figural forms. Eventually,

Alfred Hitchcock in profile.

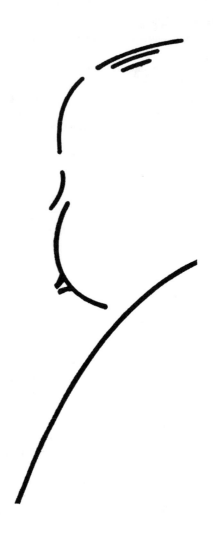

A caricature of Alfred Hitchcock in profile.

their stylish mockery would be fueled by the abstractions, collage techniques, color dissonances, and unexpected conflations of Cubism, Fauvism, and Surrealism. Humor and a recognizable face made modernist stylization palatable. Artist and critic Carlo de Fornaro, arriving in New York around 1898, was the first to advocate a Parisian style of caricature that was closely related to French poster art. His india ink newspaper caricatures combined an art nouveau elongation of the figure with a bold simplification of form. Caricaturist Al Frueh abbreviated images of theatrical figures into quintessential summaries of their characteristics. Critics marveled at Frueh's ability to evoke a personality with a minimum of lines, and Alfred Stieglitz, the acknowledged ringleader of the New York avant-garde before World War I, exhibited his drawings in 1912.

Mexican-born artist Marius de Zayas's approach to caricature especially intrigued Stieglitz, who mounted three exhibitions of his work. De Zayas drew dark, atmospheric charcoal portraits suggestive of pictorialist photographs and enigmatic symbolist drawings. Influenced by Picasso, he even experimented with "abstract caricature," a radical departure from visual realism. Many critics admired the aesthetic sophistication of this updated art form. "Between modern caricature and modern 'straight' portraiture," the *New York*

World's Henry Tyrrell wrote, "there is only a thin and vague line of demarcation."

Ties to the avant-garde raised the prestige of caricature and encouraged its use in such "smart" magazines of the post war era as *Life, Judge, Vanity Fair,* and the *New Yorker.* Caricature reflected a new strain of light, irreverent parody that pervaded the Broadway stage, the vaudeville circuit, Tin Pan Alley, magazine verses, newspaper columns, and the writings of the Algonquin Round Table wits. In the early 1920s, *Vanity Fair,* a leading proponent of this art, recruited the young Mexican artist Miguel Covarrubias to draw portraits of café society luminaries. His powerful ink line lent an iconic, monumental quality to his figures. "They are bald and crude and devoid of nonsense," Ralph Barton wrote, "like a mountain or a baby." Advances in color printing gave caricature an additional appeal in the 1930s. Will Cotton provided portraits in bright pastels, employing color as a comic weapon. Artist Paolo Garretto used collage, airbrushed gouache, and a crisp Art Deco stylization to create vivid visual effects.

The best artists in the increasingly crowded field honed their clever deformations with a distinctive style. William Auerbach-Levy eliminated details and distilled shapes into logo-like faces that were printed on stationery and book jackets. Covarrubias, working in watercolor, lampooned the leveling nature of celebrity. Visual contrasts of such opposite personalities as Martha Graham and fan dancer Sally Rand, in his famous "Impossible Interviews" series, were undermined by the commonality of fame. Few could evoke the dynamic movement of performance as well as Al Hirschfeld, whose swooping curves and sharp angles captured in mid-step the familiar look of a dancer or actor.

Caricature exploited the appetite for modern celebrity whetted by the developing mass media. The nature of fame had changed, and notability was no longer tied to traditional areas of accomplishment. As *Vanity Fair* explained, caricature subjects were selected "because of their great interest as personalities." Information about the famous became increasingly standardized: publicity photographs, syndicated stories, records, films, and news clips consolidated the celebrity image. Caricature consistently reflected the narrow, shallow exaggerations that the mass media dispensed. The famous learned to appreciate the compliment. H.L. Mencken wrote to one artist that he liked his caricature: "It is grotesque and yet it does justice to my underlying beauty." Emily Post, unflatteringly portrayed in a magazine, thanked the editor for the "delicious publicity."

The celebrity caricature fad peaked in the 1920s and 1930s. The trend even inspired star-studded animated cartoons, and collectible dolls, masks, and puppets of film idols. By mid-century, it was on the wane. The Depression years and advent of World War II demanded sharper satiric voices. And, although magazines of the 1940s still published caricature, editors turned increasingly to photography. Influenced by changes in art, humor, literature, and fame in an age of television, caricature evolved into new forms and specialized niches. In its heyday, caricature helped people adapt to change, alleviating the shock of modern art, leveling high and low cultural disparities, and mocking the new celebrity industry. Furthermore, in the celebrity-crazed press of the late twentieth century, witty, personality-based celebrity caricature seemed to be making a come-back.

—Wendy Wick Reaves

FURTHER READING:

Auerbach-Levy, William. *Is That Me? A Book about Caricature.* New York, Watson-Guptill, 1947.

Barton, Ralph. "It Is to Laugh." *New York Herald Tribune.* October 25, 1925.

Bruhn, Thomas P. *The Art of Al Frueh.* Storrs, Connecticut, William Benton Museum of Art, 1983.

Hirschfeld, Al. *The World of Hirschfeld.* New York, Harry Abrams, 1970.

Hyland, Douglas. *Marius de Zayas: Conjuror of Souls.* Lawrence, Spencer Museum of Art, University of Kansas, 1981.

Kellner, Bruce. *The Last Dandy: Ralph Barton, American Artist, 1891-1931.* Columbia, University of Missouri Press, 1991.

Reaves, Wendy Wick. *Celebrity Caricature in America.* New Haven, Yale University Press, 1998.

Reilly, Bernard F., Jr. "Miguel Covarrubias: An Introduction to His Caricatures." In *Miguel Covarrubias Caricatures.* Washington, D.C., Smithsonian Institution Press, 1985, 23-38.

Updike, John. "A Critic at Large: A Case of Melancholia." *New Yorker.* February 20, 1989, 112-120.

Williams, Adriana. *Covarrubias.* Austin, University of Texas Press, 1994.

Wright, Willard Huntington. "America and Caricature." *Vanity Fair.* July 1922, 54-55.

Cemeteries

Cemeteries reflect society's interpretation of the continuing personhood of the dead. Colonial America's small rural family graveyards and churchyard burial grounds were an integral part of the community of the living, crowded with tombstones bearing the picturesque iconography of winged skulls, hourglasses, and soul-effigies, and inscriptions ranging from the taciturn to the talkative—some with scant facts of name, age, and date of death, others offering thumbnail biographies, unusual circumstances of decease ("They froze to death returning from a visit"), homilies in verse ("As I am now, so you shall be, / Remember death and follow me"), and even the occasional dry one-liner ("I expected this, but not so soon").

In the nineteenth century, alarmed by public health problems associated with increasing industrial urbanization, the rising medical profession pressed for new cemeteries on the outskirts of towns, where the buried bodies could not pollute nearby wells and where any "noxious exhalations" thought to cause disease would be dissipated in the fresh suburban air. These new "garden cemeteries" would also function as places to which the inhabitants of the teeming cities could go for recreation and the inspiration of the beauty of nature.

First of the new genre was Mount Auburn Cemetery, picturesquely sited on a bend in the Charles River between the cities of Boston and Cambridge. Three years in the making, with carriage paths and artful landscaping (thanks to the collaboration of the Massachusetts Horticultural Society), it opened in 1831 to enthusiastic reviews and was soon followed by Mount Hope in Bangor, Maine; Laurel Hill in Philadelphia; Spring Grove in Cincinnati; Graceland in Chicago; Allegheny County Cemetery in Pittsburgh; and the battlefield burial ground at Gettysburg. By the end of the 1800s there were nearly two hundred garden cemeteries in America.

The boom in street-railway construction in the 1870s made the outlying cemeteries readily accessible to the public for day-trips and picnics. In several cities the departed could ride the rails to the cemetery, too. (The United Railways and Electric Company of Baltimore owned the "Dolores," a funeral car with seats for thirty-two plus a compartment for the casket. Philadelphia had a streetcar hearse as well, the "Hillside.") But the streetcar revolution also fueled suburban development of the open spaces surrounding the cities of the dead, even as parks for the living began to compete for the shrinking acreage of undeveloped land. (Frederick Law Olmsted, while designing New York's Central Park, completed just after the Civil War, is reported to have said: "They're not going to bury anyone in this one.")

With the passing of the Victorian age and the splitting off of parks from cemeteries, cemetery management began to stress efficiency and profitability. A pioneer of this new approach was Dr. Hubert Eaton, a former mine owner who bought a down-at-heels graveyard called Forest Lawn in Glendale, California, in 1917, and over the next four decades metamorphosed it into a flagship of twentieth-century cemetery design and culture with hundreds of miles of underground piping for sprinklers and flat bronze markers in place of headstones (allowing the trimming of vast areas by rotary-blade machines and of maintenance costs by as much as 75 percent). Area themes included ''Babyland'' and ''Wee Kirk o' the Heather,'' accented by sculptures such as *Duck Frog* and the occasional classical reproduction.

While not every memorial park could aspire to be a Forest Lawn, by the end of World War II, private cemetery management had become a thriving industry with its own trade journals—such as *American Cemetery, Cemeterian,* and *Concept: The Journal of Creative Ideas for Cemeteries*—and a ready target for both the biting satire of Evelyn Waugh's 1948 novel *The Loved One* and the merciless investigative reporting of Jessica Mitford's 1963 exposé, *The American Way of Death.*

Attitudes toward death itself were changing as well. The medicalization of dying, with its removal from home to hospital, helped to transform the awe-inspiring last event of the human life cycle into a brutal, even trivial fact. Whether from denial or mere pragmatism, two-thirds of the students polled at three universities said they would favor cremation, while a rise in the number of anatomical donors prompted medical schools in the greater Boston area to begin sharing excess cadavers with one another whenever one school had a surplus.

Public policy also took an increasingly utilitarian tack. In 1972, ninety years after the U.S. Supreme Court upheld the nonprofit status of cemeteries owing to their ''pious and public purpose,'' the Department of Housing and Urban Development declared that burial was a marginal land use and proposed establishing cemeteries under elevated highways, in former city-dump landfills, or on acreage subject to airport runway noise.

''After thirty years a grave gets cold,'' one mausoleum builder ruefully told cemetery historian Kenneth T. Jackson, who noted the high mobility of Americans near the end of the twentieth century and the fact that older cemeteries ''run out of space, and few people still alive remember anyone buried there.'' As individual markers and statuary fell into disrepair or were vandalized, indifferently maintained graveyards became less and less attractive places—ironically turning again into recreational areas, but now for persons and activities unwelcome in the public parks.

Notable exceptions to this trend are sites where the famous are buried, such as the Tomb of the Unknown Soldier and of President Kennedy in Arlington National Cemetery, or Elvis Presley's grave site at his Graceland mansion in Memphis, which continue to draw thousands of pilgrims every year.

—Nick Humez

FURTHER READING:

Allen, Francis D., compiler. *Documents and Facts, Showing the Fatal Effects of Interment in Populous Cities.* New York, F. D. Allen, 1822.

Drewes, Donald W. *Cemetery Land Planning.* Pittsburgh, Matthews Memorial Bronze, 1964.

Jackson, Kenneth T. *Silent Cities: The Evolution of the American Cemetery.* New York, Princeton Architectural Press, 1989.

Klupar, G. J. *Modern Cemetery Management.* Hillside, Catholic Cemeteries of the Archdiocese of Chicago, 1962.

Linden-Ward, Blanche. *Silent City on a Hill: Landscapes of Memory and Boston's Mount Auburn Cemetery.* Columbus, Ohio State University Press, 1989.

Miller, John Anderson. *Fares, Please! A Popular History of Trolleys, Horsecars, Streetcars, Buses, Elevateds, and Subways.* New York, Dover, 1960.

Mitford, Jessica. *The American Way of Death.* New York, Simon and Schuster, 1963.

Shomon, Joseph James. *Crosses in the Wind.* New York, Stratford House, 1947.

Waugh, Evelyn. *The Loved One.* Boston, Little, Brown and Company, 1948.

Weed, Howard Evarts. *Modern Park Cemeteries.* Chicago, R. J. Haight, 1912.

Central Park

The first major public example of landscape architecture, Manhattan's Central Park remains the greatest illustration of the American park, a tradition that would become part of nearly every community following the 1860s. This grand park offers a facility for recreation and peaceful contemplation, a solution to the enduring American search for a ''happy medium'' between the natural environment and human civilization.

Initially, the construction of parks responded to utilitarian impulses: feelings began to develop in the early 1800s that some urban areas were becoming difficult places in which to reside. Disease and grime were common attributes attached to large towns and cities. Of particular concern, many population centers possessed insufficient interment facilities within churchyards. The first drive for parks began with this need for new cemeteries. The ''rural cemetery'' movement began in 1831 with the construction of Mount Auburn outside of Boston. Soon, many communities possessed their own sprawling, green burial areas on the outskirts of town.

From this point, a new breed of American landscape architect beat the path toward Central Park. Andrew Jackson Downing designed many rural cemeteries, but more importantly, he popularized and disseminated a new American ''taste'' that placed manicured landscapes around the finest homes. Based out of the Hudson River region and operating among its affluent landowners, Downing designed landscapes that brought the aesthetic of the rural cemetery to the wealthy home. His designs inspired the suburban revolution in American living. Downing became a public figure prior to his untimely death in 1852 through the publication of *Horticulturalist* magazine as well as various books, the initial designs for the Mall in Washington, D.C., and, finally, his call for a central area of repose in the growing city on Manhattan Island.

Wealthy New Yorkers soon seized Downing's call for a ''central park.'' This landscaped, public park would offer their own families an attractive setting for carriage rides and provide working-class New Yorkers with a healthy alternative to the saloon. After three years of debate over the park site and cost, the state legislature authorized the city to acquire land for a park in 1853. Swamps and bluffs punctuated by rocky outcroppings made the land between 5th and 8th avenues and 59th and 106th streets undesirable for private development. The extension of the boundaries to 110th Street in 1863 brought the park to its current 843 acres. However, the selected area was not empty: 1,600 poor residents, including Irish pig farmers and German gardeners, lived in shanties on the site; Seneca Village, at 8th Avenue and 82nd

A view of New York's Central Park.

Street, was one of the city's most stable African-American settlements, with three churches and a school.

In 1857, the Central Park Commission held the country's first landscape design contest and selected the "Greensward Plan," submitted by Frederick Law Olmsted, the park's superintendent at the time, and Calvert Vaux, an English-born architect and former partner of Downing. The designers sought to create a pastoral landscape in the English romantic style. In order to maintain a feeling of uninterrupted expanse, Olmsted and Vaux sank four transverse roads eight feet below the park's surface to carry cross-town traffic. From its inception, the site was intended as a middle ground that would allow the city's life to continue uninterrupted without infringing on the experience of park goers.

The park quickly became a national phenomenon. First opened for public use in the winter of 1859 when thousands of New Yorkers skated on lakes constructed on the site of former swamps, Central Park opened officially in 1863. By 1865, the park received more than seven million visitors a year. The city's wealthiest citizens turned out daily for elaborate late-afternoon carriage parades. Indeed, in the park's first decade more than half of its visitors arrived in carriages, costly vehicles that fewer than five percent of the city's residents could afford. Olmsted had stated his intention as "democratic recreation," a park accessible to everyone. There would be no gates or

physical barriers; however, there would be other methods of enforcing class selectivity. Stringent rules governed early use of the "democratic" park, including a ban on group picnics—which discouraged many German and Irish New Yorkers; a ban on small tradesmen using their commercial wagons for family drives in the park; and restricting ball playing in the meadows to school boys with a note from their principal. New Yorkers repeatedly contested these rules, however, and in the last third of the nineteenth century the park opened up to more democratic use.

Central Park's success fueled other communities to action. Olmsted became the park movement's leader as he tied such facilities to Americans' "psychological and physical health." Through Olmsted's influence and published writing, parks such as Central Park were seen to possess more than aesthetic value. The idea of determining the "health" of the community through its physical design was an early example of modernist impulses. However, the park movement's attachment to traditions such as romanticism gave parks a classical ornamentation. Olmsted's park planning would lead to the "City Beautiful" movement in the early 1900s and to the establishment of the National Park system.

As the uses of Central Park have varied, its popularity has only increased. In the 1960s, Mayor John Lindsay's commissioners welcomed "happenings," rock concerts, and be-ins to the park, making it a symbol of both urban revival and the counterculture. A decline in the park's upkeep during the 1970s stimulated the establishment of the Central Park Conservancy in 1980. This private fund-raising body took charge of restoring features of the Greensward Plan. By 1990, the Central Park Conservancy had contributed more than half the public park's budget and exercised substantial influence on decisions about its future. Central Park, however, continues to be shaped by the public that uses it: joggers, disco roller skaters, softball leagues, bird watchers, nature lovers, middle-class professionals pushing a baby's stroller, impoverished individuals searching for an open place to sleep.

—Brian Black

FURTHER READING:

Blackmar, Elizabeth, and Roy Rosenzweig. *The Park and the People.* New York, Henry Holt, 1992.

Schuyler, David. *Apostle of Taste.* Baltimore, The Johns Hopkins University Press, 1996.

Century 21 Exposition (Seattle, 1962)

The world's fair that opened in Seattle on April 21, 1962, better known as the Century 21 Exposition, was one of the most successful world's fairs in history. Originally intended to commemorate the 50th

The dramatic symbol of the Century 21 Exposition, a 600 foot Space Needle in Seattle, Washington.

anniversary of the Alaska-Yukon-Pacific Exposition held in Seattle in 1909, Century 21, although opening three years late, was still a boon to the city itself and to the entire Northwest region of the United States.

Joseph Gandy and Ewen Dingwall started organizing the fair in 1955, but their efforts were thwarted by both potential investors and citizens of Seattle, who worried about the profitability of a fair held in such a far-away location and the effects it would have on the local area. Compared to other fairs, the Century 21 project seemed dubious at best. The 1958 Brussels Fair covered 550 acres, while the Century 21 was only 74 acres: boosters called it the "jewel box fair," while critics dubbed it the "postage stamp fair." Others worried that Seattle would not draw masses of tourists to its relatively remote region, especially since New York was hosting its own world's fair only a year later.

Ultimately, however, Century 21 proved to be financially and culturally successful. While the New York World's Fair of 1963-1964 lost $18 million, Century 21 actually turned a profit of $1 million after all expenses were paid—an almost unheard of feat when it came to such endeavors. During its six month run, the fair hosted over 10 million visitors from the United States and overseas. News of the fair appeared in the popular press, including newspapers like the *New York Times* and magazines like *Newsweek, Time, Popular Mechanics,* and *Architectural Review.* This mass of publicity and the increase in tourism transformed Seattle from a minor, provincial city into an energetic metropolis that garnered respect even among its east coast rivals.

In addition to improving its reputation, Century 21 also changed the physical space of Seattle. The fair was held just north of the center of the city, creating an entirely new complex, Seattle Center, that remained long after the fair had closed. The physical structures of the fair also changed Seattle's skyline with the addition of the Monorail and the Space Needle.

The theme of Century 21 was "life in the twenty-first century," which meant that the fair itself, at which 49 countries participated, celebrated scientific developments, technology, and visions of projected life in the next century. For example, the United States Science Pavilion, designed by Seattle-born architect Minoru Yamasaki, covered seven acres, consisted of six buildings which incorporated courtyards and pools, and featured five tall white slender aluminum gothic arches that signified the future more than recalling the past. This building became the Pacific Science Center after the fair.

The Monorail was an even more successful representation of the future, and was an important component of the fair both in presence and function. An elevated version of a subway employed to alleviate parking problems, the Monorail demonstrated a futuristic mode of urban transportation at work that took people from downtown Seattle into the middle of the fair. Designed by the Swedish firm Alweg and built in West Germany, the Monorail was capable of going 70 miles per hour, although it never reached this speed while in use at the fair.

The most visible symbol of the fair and of the future, however, was the Space Needle—a 600 feet high spire of steel topped with what resembled a flying saucer; during the fair, the Space Needle netted $15,000 a day from visitors who paid to ride its elevators up to the top to view the greater Seattle area and to eat in its revolving restaurant. Influenced by the design of a television tower in Stuttgart, but also incorporating the decade's aesthetic of the future—flattened disks juxtaposed with pointed shapes—the Space Needle became the Exposition's main icon, signifying "soaring and aspiration and progress" according to one of its proponents. It remained an integral part of Seattle's identity, permanently affixed to its skyline, and represented both the city itself and the subsequently outdated 1960s vision and version of the future.

—Wendy Woloson

FURTHER READING:

Allwood, John. *The Great Exhibitions.* London, Studio Vista, 1977.

Berklow, Gary M. "Seattle's Century 21, 1962." *Pacific Northwest Forum.* Vol. 7, No. 1, 1994, 68-80.

Morgan, Murray. *The Story of the Seattle World's Fair, 1962.* Seattle, Acme Press, 1963.

Century of Progress (Chicago, 1933)

Taking place during a "golden age" of world's fairs, Chicago's 1933-34 Century of Progress International Exposition marked the prevalence of modern architecture and was notable for its colorful nighttime lighting. Century of Progress commemorated the one

The Hall of Science at the 1933 Chicago World's Fair.

hundredth anniversary of the incorporation of the City of Chicago with exhibits highlighting scientific discoveries and the changes these discoveries made in industry and everyday life.

The fair opened on May 27, 1933, when the lights were turned on with energy from the rays of the star Arcturus. The rays were focused on photoelectric cells in a series of astronomical observatories and then transformed into electrical energy which was transmitted to Chicago. Under the direction of general manager Lenox R. Lohr and president of the Board of Trustees Rufus C. Dawes, the fair covered 427 acres (much of it landfill) on Lake Michigan immediately south of Chicago's downtown area, from 12th Street to 39th Street (now Pershing Road). Today, Meigs Field and McCormick Place occupy this site. Originally planned to close in November 1933, the fair was extended through 1934 because of its popularity and to earn enough money to cover its debts. Century of Progress was the first international fair in American history to pay for itself. The grand total of attendance was 48,769,227.

The fair's most recognizable buildings, the Hall of Science and the Transportation Building typified the linear, geometric Art Deco style which was the trademark of this world's fair. The outstanding feature of the Transportation Building was its domed roof, suspended on cables attached to twelve steel towers around the exterior. Also notable were the pavilions of General Motors, Chrysler, and, added in 1934, the Ford Motor Company. The House of Tomorrow was designed using technologically advanced concepts like electrically controlled doors and air that recirculated every ten minutes. The controversial "Rainbow City" color scheme of Century of Progress dictated that buildings be painted in four hues from a total of twenty-three colors. Although the colors were restricted to ten in 1934, this still was quite a contrast from the World's Columbian Exposition held in Chicago in 1893 when all the buildings were white. At night, the Century of Progress buildings were illuminated with white and colored lights which made the effect even more vibrant. In 1934, the coordination of color schemes throughout the fairground helped people make their way through the grounds.

The Midway, with its rides and attractions, was one of the most popular places at the fair, as was Enchanted Island, an area set aside for children. Youngsters could slide down Magic Mountain, view a fairy castle, or see a play staged by the Junior League of Chicago. The Belgian Village, which many exhibiting countries imitated during the second year of the fair, was a copy of a sixteenth-century village complete with homes, shops, church, and town hall. The Paris exhibition included French restaurants, strolling artists, and an "English Village." The Sky Ride, a major landmark of Century of Progress, transported visitors 218 feet above the North Lagoon in enclosed cars supported between two 628-foot steel towers. Recreations of the cabin of Jean Baptiste Point du Sable, the first permanent settler of Chicago, and Fort Dearborn, built in 1803, depicted Chicago-area history where Michigan Avenue crosses the Chicago River in present-day downtown Chicago.

Although three buildings (the Administration Building, the Fort Dearborn replica, and the golden Temple of Jehol) were temporarily left intact after the fair's demolition, today only Balbo's Column remains on its original site east of Lake Shore Drive at 1600 South (opposite Soldier Field). A gift of the Italian government, this column was removed from the ruins of a Roman temple in Ostia. It commemorates General Balbo's trans-Atlantic flight to Chicago in 1933.

—Anna Notaro

FURTHER READING:

A Century of Progress Exposition Chicago 1933. B. Klein Publications, 1993.

Findling, John E. and Kohn E. Findling. *Chicago's Great World's Fairs (Studies in Design and Material Culture).* Manchester, Manchester University Press, 1995.

Linn, James Weber. *The Official Pictures of a Century of Progress Exposition Chicago 1933.* B. Klein Publications, 1993.

Rossen, Howard M. *World's Fair Collectibles: Chicago, 1933 and New York, 1939.* Schiffer Publishing, 1998.

Challenger Disaster

The explosion of NASA space shuttle *Challenger* shortly after liftoff on January 28, 1986, shocked the nation. The twenty-fifth shuttle flight had been dubbed the "Teacher in Space" mission; the plan was to excite children about the possiblity of space travel by having a teacher deliver televised lectures from the orbiting shuttle. Christa McAuliffe, a high-school social studies teacher, was chosen for the expedition after a highly publicized nationwide search. Other crew members included Michael Smith (pilot), Dick Scobee (commander), Judith Resnik (mission specialist), Ronald McNair (mission specialist), Ellison Onizuka (mission specialist), and Gregory Jarvis (payload specialist). None survived the disaster. The cause of the explosion was eventually traced to faulty gaskets known as O-rings. Coming at a time when the United States space program had seemingly regained its footing after two decades of decline, it forced many to grapple with the risks associated with pioneering technologies. Nowhere was the need for explanation more pressing than in the nation's classrooms, where children had gathered to witness the wonders of space travel.

—Daniel Bernardi

FURTHER READING:

Coote, Rodgers. *Air Disasters.* New York, Thomson Learning, 1993.

Penley, Constance. *NASA/Trek: Popular Science and Sex in America.* New York, Verso, 1997.

"51-L (25)." http://www.ksc.nasa.gov/shuttle/missions/51-l/mission-51-l.html. January 1999.

Chamberlain, Wilt (1936—)

On the basketball court, Wilt Chamberlain was one of the most dominating players of his day. His intimidating stature (7' 1'' and 265 pounds) and his ability to score at will made him one of professional basketball's most popular players. In his third season he led the league with a remarkable 50.4 scoring average, a record that still stands after nearly forty years. By dominating both ends of the court Chamberlain single-handedly revolutionized professional basketball.

Born on August 21, 1936, in Philadelphia, Pennsylvania, Chamberlain attended Overbrook high school, where he led his team to a

Los Angeles Laker center Wilt Chamberlain is defended by Bill Russell of the Boston Celtics.

58-3 record and three All-Public school titles. His dominating athleticism at Overbrook drew the attention of nearly every college basketball program in the country, and after a hectic recruiting period Chamberlain decided to attend Kansas University. Upon hearing the news, legendary KU basketball coach Phog Allen remarked: "Wilt Chamberlain's the greatest basketball player I ever saw. With him, we'll never lose a game; we could win the national championship with Wilt, two sorority girls and two Phi Beta Kappas." In spite of Allen's predictions, Kansas failed to win a NCAA championship during Chamberlain's two-year stint. But nonetheless, as a college player he was as a man among boys. During his short stay at Kansas the *Saturday Evening Post* ran a story titled, "Can Basketball Survive Chamberlain," leading the NCAA to make several rule changes to curtail his dominance, and later Look magazine published an article titled, "Why I Am Quitting College," which was an exclusive piece on his decision to leave Kansas. This media coverage was virtually unprecedented for an African-American college athlete.

After leaving Kansas, Chamberlain had a brief one-year tour with the Harlem Globetrotters before joining the Philadelphia Warriors in 1959. In his first game with the Warriors, Chamberlain had 43 points and 28 rebounds. This was just a glimpse of what was to come. Throughout his rookie year he scored fifty points or more five times, en route to earning league Rookie of the Year and MVP honors, marking the first time that anyone had ever won both awards the same year. Throughout the next couple of years Chamberlain continued to pick up individual honors. In his third year with the Warriors Chamberlain continued his dominance and did the unthinkable, scoring 100 points in a single game, after which the minuscule 4,124 fans in attendance "came pouring out of the stands and mobbed me." As a result of his prowess on the court the NBA followed the NCAA's lead and made several rule changes of their own, simply because of Chamberlain's dominance.

Although Chamberlain continued to be a leader in scoring and rebounding throughout his career (which included stints in San Francisco and then later in Los Angeles), he was often maligned in the national media. He was frequently labeled a "loser" because of his team's inability to beat Bill Russell and the Boston Celtics (although he did win championships in 1967 and 1972), and he was often viewed as a troublemaker because of his candid personality. In the mid-1960s he was roundly criticized in the media for a story *Sports Illustrated* published concerning his attitude with the NBA. Under the headline: "My life in a Bush League," Chamberlain criticized the administrators, coaches, and players of the NBA. "For a sports superstar who was supposed to be bubbling over with gratitude for every second he got to play, those were some pretty harsh words. I could understand why some people got upset," Chamberlain remarked in his biography. But Chamberlain was never one to champion black causes. In the late 1960s he drew the ire of the black community when he denounced the Black Power movement while supporting Richard Nixon's presidential campaign, and he likewise drew criticism from both blacks and whites alike when he expressed a preference for white women. He was truly a colorful figure.

In 1978 Chamberlain was inducted into the NBA Hall of Fame in his first year of eligibility and in 1996-1997 he was selected to the NBA 50th Anniversary All-Star Team.

As the NBA's first $100,000 man, Chamberlain had an enormous impact on the rise of the NBA. His dominating play sparked the interest of the country into a league that was forced to compete with the more popular pastimes of baseball and football. He was personally responsible for filling up arenas throughout the country as Americans paid top dollar to see "Wilt the Stilt." He was without question a one-man show.

—Leonard N. Moore

FURTHER READING:

Chamberlain, Wilt. *View From Above: Sports, Sex, and Controversy.* New York, Dutton Books, 1992.

————. *Wilt: Just Like Any Other 7-Foot Black Millionaire Who Lives Next Door.* New York, Macmillan, 1973.

Frankl, Ron. *Wilt Chamberlain.* New York, Chelsea House, 1995.

Libby, Bill. *Goliath: The Wilt Chamberlain Story.* New York, Dodd, Mead, 1977.

Chan, Charlie

See Charlie Chan

Chandler, Raymond (1888-1959)

Raymond Thornton Chandler started writing fiction in middle-age, out of economic necessity, after being fired from his job. Despite his late start and relatively brief career, Chandler's influence on detective fiction was seminal. He and fellow writer Dashiell Hammett generally are seen as the Romulus and Remus of the hard-boiled detective subgenre. Hammett's experience as a Pinkerton detective provided him with material very different from that of the genteel murder mystery imported from England. Chandler, who cut his teeth on the *Black Mask* school of "tough-guy" fiction, from the outset shunned the classical mystery for a type of story truer to the violent realities of twentieth-century American life. As he said, his interest was in getting "murder away from the upper classes, the weekend house party and the vicar's rose garden, and back to the people who are really good at it."

Chandler's education and upbringing both hindered and spurred his writing, for he came to the American language and culture as a stranger. Although born in Chicago in 1888, at the age of seven he was taken to London by his Anglo-Irish mother and raised there. After a classical education in a public school, Chandler worked as a civil servant and as a literary journalist, finding no real success in either field. In 1912, on money borrowed from an uncle, he returned to the United States, eventually reaching California with no prospects but, in his words, "with a beautiful wardrobe and a public school accent."

Robert Mitchum as Philip Marlowe on the cover of *The Big Sleep.*

For several years he worked at menial jobs, then became a bookkeeper. In 1917, he joined the Canadian Army and served as a platoon commander in France. After the war, he began to work in the oil business and rapidly rose to top-level management positions. In the 1920s, his drinking and womanizing grew steadily worse, until his immoderation, along with the Great Depression, finally cost him his job in 1932.

As a young man in London, Chandler had spent three years working as a literary journalist and publishing romantic, Victorian-style poetry on the side. Now, with only enough savings to last a year or two, he turned back to writing in an attempt to provide a living for his wife and himself. Initially, his literary sophistication inhibited his attempts to write pulp fiction; however, he persevered through an arduous apprenticeship and ultimately succeeded not only in writing critically acclaimed commercial fiction but also in transcending the genre. By the time of his death, Chandler had become a prominent American novelist.

Chandler published his first story, ''Blackmailers Don't Shoot,'' in the December 1933 issue of *Black Mask*. Under the editorship of Joseph Shaw, it had emerged as the predominant pulp magazine. Shaw promoted ''hard-boiled'' fiction in the Hammett mode, and Chandler quickly became one of Shaw's favorite contributors, publishing nearly two dozen stories in *Black Mask* between 1933 and 1941. Chandler's first novel, *The Big Sleep,* was immediately compared to the work of Dashiell Hammett and James Cain by critics, who hailed Chandler as an exciting new presence in detective fiction. His second novel, *Farewell, My Lovely,* appeared in 1940, followed by novels *The High Window* (1942), *The Lady in the Lake* (1943), *The Little Sister* (1949), *The Long Good-bye* (1954), and *Playback* (1958). Chandler's collection of short stories, *The Simple Art of Murder,* contains, in addition to twelve pulp stories, an important and oft-quoted essay on detective fiction.

Like his contemporary, Ernest Hemingway, Chandler's impact on American literature was fueled by his interest in style. His English upbringing caused him to experience American English as a half-foreign, fascinating language; and few American writers, with the possible exceptions of Gertrude Stein and Hemingway, ever thought more carefully about or cared more for the American language. Chandler originated a terse, objective, colloquial style which has had a vital influence on succeeding mystery writers, as well as on mainstream literary writers, and even on Latin American authors such as Hiber Conteris and Manuel Puig. Chandler skillfully cultivated a subtle prose style that is actually literary while appearing to be plain and colloquial. The hallmark of this style is the witty, exaggerated simile. These similes often appear in the wise-cracks of Chandler's hero, Philip Marlowe; the effect being to add color to the dialogue and to emphasize Marlowe's rugged individualism. Chandler's irreverent, wise-cracking private detective set the tone for many of the hard-boiled heroes who followed, such as Jim Rockford of television's *The Rockford Files* and Spenser, the protagonist of Robert B. Parker's novels.

Just as Chandler's style is only superficially objective, becoming subjective in its impressionistic realization of Marlowe's mind and emotions, Chandler's fiction is hard-boiled only on the surface. Marlowe never becomes as violent or as tough-minded as did some of his predecessors, such as Hammett's Continental Op. In fact, Marlowe is sometimes, in the words of James Sandoe, ''soft-boiled.'' Lonely, disillusioned, depressive, Marlowe is yet somehow optimistic and willing to fight injustice at substantial personal cost. Chandler

saw his hero as a crusading, but rather cynical, working-class knight who struggles against overwhelming odds to help the powerless and downtrodden. Marlowe maintains his chivalrous code in the face of constant temptation and intimidation; his integrity is absolute, his honesty paramount. Thus he manages to achieve some justice in a corrupt, unjust world.

This archetypal theme places Chandler in the mainstream of American fiction. The courageous man of action, the rugged individualist who performs heroic deeds out of a sense of duty, has been a staple of American literature since the early days of the nation. This quintessential American hero originated in regional fiction, such as James Fennimore Cooper's *Leather-Stocking Tales,* and moved westward with the frontier, appearing in many guises. The tough hero was further developed by the dime novelists of the nineteenth century and by early-twentieth-century progenitors of the Western genre. American detective story writers found a distinctly American hero waiting for them to adapt to the hard-boiled sub-genre.

Another theme prevalent in Chandler's work is the failure of the American Dream. For Chandler, the crime and violence rampant in newspaper headlines was rooted in the materialism of American life. In their desperate grasping, Americans often stooped to extreme and even unlawful measures. Chandler himself was not immune to the lure of the greenback. He became an established Hollywood screenwriter, though temperamentally unsuited to the collaborative work. Notable among his film work is his and Billy Wilder's 1943 adaptation for the screen of James M. Cain's novel *Double Indemnity*. Filmed by Paramount, the movie received an Academy Award nomination for best script. The voice-over narration Chandler devised for *Double Indemnity* became a convention of *film noir*. For Chandler, the voice-over narration, so like the cynical, ironical voice of his Marlowe, must have seemed natural.

After the death of Chandler's beloved wife Cissy in 1954, he entered a period of alcoholic and professional decline that continued until his death in 1959. Like his hero, Philip Marlowe, Raymond Chandler lived and died a lonely and sad man. But his contribution to literature is significant, and his work continues to give pleasure to his many readers.

—Rick Lott

FURTHER READING:

Bruccoli, Matthew J. *Raymond Chandler: A Descriptive Bibliography.* Pittsburgh, University of Pittsburgh Press, 1979.

Durham, Philip. *Down These Mean Streets a Man Must Go: Raymond Chandler's Knight.* Chapel Hill, University of North Carolina Press, 1963.

Gardiner, Dorothy, and Katherine Sorley Walker, editors. *Raymond Chandler Speaking.* Boston, Houghton Mifflin, 1962.

MacShane, Frank. *The Life of Raymond Chandler.* New York, Dutton, 1976.

Marling, William. *The American Roman Noir: Hammett, Cain, and Chandler.* Athens, University of Georgia Press, 1995.

———. *Raymond Chandler.* Boston, Twayne, 1986.

Speir, Jerry. *Raymond Chandler.* New York, Ungar, 1981.

Van Dover, J.K. *The Critical Response to Raymond Chandler.* Westport, Connecticut, Greenwood Press, 1995.

Wolfe, Peter. *Something More Than Night: The Case of Raymond Chandler.* Bowling Green, Ohio, Bowling Green State University Popular Press, 1985.

Chandu the Magician

This atmospheric radio adventure series first sounded its trademark opening gong in 1932, appearing at the forefront of a popular interest in magic and the occult which also produced Chandu's more famous fellow heroic students of the black arts, *The Shadow* and *Mandrake the Magician.* Like any talented prestidigitator, Chandu was able to appear in several different places simultaneously, and thus managed to frustrate the world-dominating ambitions of his arch-enemy Roxor in a feature film (1932) and a movie serial (1934) while also holding down his day job in radio. Chandu disappeared in 1935 when the initial series of 15-minute adventures came to a close, but the master magician had one more trick up his dapper sleeves, reappearing out of the ether to a delighted public in 1948 in a new production of the original scripts before vanishing for good in 1950. Thus, in the words of radio historian John Dunning, *Chandu The Magician* "... became one of the last, as well as one of the first, juvenile adventure shows of its kind."

—Kevin Lause

FURTHER READING:

Dunning, John. *On the Air: The Encyclopedia of Old-Time Radio.* New York, Oxford University Press, 1998.

Harmon, Jim, and Donald F. Glut. *The Great Movie Serials.* New York, Doubleday, 1972.

Lackmann, Ron. *Same Time, Same Station: An A-Z Guide to Radio from Jack Benny to Howard Stern.* New York, Facts On File, 1996.

Chanel, Coco (1883-1971)

Modern fashion has no legend greater than Gabrielle "Coco" Chanel. A strong woman, her life has inspired biographies, aphorisms, and even a Broadway musical entitled "Coco." She was one of the most powerful designers of the 1920s, using knit, wool jersey, and fabrics and styles associated with menswear to remake the modern woman's wardrobe with soft, practical clothing. She invented the little black dress in the 1920s, and in the 1920s and 1930s, she made the Chanel suit—a soft, cardigan-like jacket often in robust materials with a skirt sufficiently slack to imply concavity between the legs—a modern staple. Indomitable in life, Chanel enjoyed many affairs with important men. One affair with a German officer prompted Chanel's eight year exile in Switzerland before reopening in 1954. She died in 1971 before one of her new collections was completed. The fragrance Chanel No. 5, created in 1922, has driven the company with its reputation and profit. As the chief designer since 1983, Karl Lagerfeld has combined a loyalty to Chanel's style signatures with an unmistakably modern taste.

—Richard Martin

FURTHER READING:

Baudot, Francois. *Chanel.* New York, Universe, 1996.

Leymarie, Jean. *Chanel.* New York, Skira/Rizzoli, 1987.

Chaplin, Charlie (1889-1977)

Comedian, actor, writer, producer, and director Charlie Chaplin, through the universal language of silent comedy, imprinted one of the twentieth century's most distinctive and lasting cultural images on the collective consciousness of the entire civilized world. In his self-created guise the Tramp, an accident-prone do-gooder, at once innocent and devious, he sported a toothbrush mustache, baggy pants, and tattered tails, tilting his trademark bowler hat and jauntily swinging his trademark cane as he defied the auguries of a hostile world. The Little Tramp made his first brief appearance in *Kid Auto Races at Venice* for Mack Sennett's Keystone company in 1914, and bowed out 22 years later in the feature-length *Modern Times* (United Artists, 1936). In between the Tramp films, Chaplin made countless other short-reel silent comedies, which combined a mixture of Victorian melodrama, sentiment, and slapstick, enchanted audiences worldwide, and made him an international celebrity and the world's highest

Charlie Chaplin

paid performer. At the dawn of the twenty-first century, 86 years after he first appeared on the flickering silent screen, Chaplin was still regarded as one of the most important entertainers of the twentieth century. He was (and arguably still is) certainly the most universally famous. On screen, he was a beloved figure of fun; off-screen, however, his liberal political views brought accusations of Communism and close official scrutiny, while his notorious private life heaped opprobrium on his head. Despite his personal failings, however, Chaplin's Tramp and astonishing achievements made him, in the words of actor Charles Laughton, "not only the greatest theatrical genius of our time, but one of the greatest in history."

Born Charles Spencer Chaplin in London on April 16, 1889, the man who would become one of the world's wealthiest and most instantly recognizable individuals was raised in circumstances of appalling deprivation, best described as "Dickensian." The son of music hall entertainers who separated shortly after his birth, Chaplin first took the stage spontaneously at age five when his mentally unstable mother, Hannah Chaplin, lost her voice in the midst of a performance. He sang a song and was showered with pennies by the appreciative audience. Hannah's health and career spiraled into decline soon after, and she was committed to a state mental institution. She was in and out of various such places until 1921, when Charlie brought her to live in California until her death in 1928. Meanwhile, the boy and his elder half-brother, Sydney, found themselves in and out of state orphanages or living on the streets, where they danced for pennies. Forced to leave school at age ten, Charlie found work with various touring theatrical companies and on the British vaudeville circuit as a mime and roustabout. In 1908 he was hired as a company member by the famous vaudeville producer Fred Karno, and it was with Karno's company that he learned the craft of physical comedy, developed his unique imagination and honed his skills while touring throughout Britain. He became a leading Karno star, and twice toured the United States with the troupe. While performing in Boston during the second of these tours in 1912, he was seen on stage by the great pioneering filmmaker of the early silent period Mack Sennett, who specialized in comedy. Sennett offered the diminutive English cockney a film contract, Chaplin accepted, and joined Sennett's Keystone outfit in Hollywood in January 1914.

Chaplin, soon known to the world simply as "Charlie" (and to the French as "Charlot"), made his film debut as a villain in the 1914 comedy *Making a Living*. In a very short time, he was writing and directing, as well as acting, and made numerous movies with Sennett's famous female star, Mabel Normand. His career thrived, and he was lured away by the Essanay company, who offered him a contract at $1,250 a week to make 14 films during 1915. They billed Chaplin as "the world's greatest comedian" and allowed him to control all aspects of his work including production, direction, writing, casting, and editing. At Essanay Chaplin made a film actually called *The Tramp*, and, in the course of the year, refined and perfected the character into, as film historian Ephraim Katz wrote, "the invincible vagabond, the resilient little fellow with an eye for beauty and a pretense of elegance who stood up heroically and pathetically against overwhelming odds and somehow triumphed."

In February 1916, however, Chaplin left Essanay for Mutual and a stratospheric weekly salary of $10,000 plus a $150,000 bonus, sums that were an eloquent testimony to his immense popularity and commercial worth. Among his best films of the Mutual period are *The Rink* (1916), *Easy Street,* and *The Immigrant* (both 1917) and during this period he consolidated his friendship and frequent co-starring partnership with Edna Purviance. By mid-1917, he had moved on to a

million-dollar contract with First National, for whom his films included *Shoulder Arms* (1918) and, famously, *The Kid* (1921). This last, in which comedy was overlaid with sentiment and pathos, unfolded the tale of the Tramp caring for an abandoned child, unveiled a sensational and irresistible performance from child actor Jackie Coogan, and marked Chaplin's first feature-length film. Meanwhile, in 1919, by which time he had built his own film studio, Chaplin had joined Mary Pickford, Douglas Fairbanks, and D. W. Griffith to form the original United Artists, designed to allow artistic freedom free of the conventional restraints of studio executives, a venture of which it was famously said that it was a case of "the lunatics taking over the asylum." As he moved from shorts to longer features, Chaplin increasingly injected his comedy with pathos.

In 1918, Chaplin had a liaison with an unsuitable 16-year-old named Mildred Harris. He married her when she claimed pregnancy, and she did, in fact, bear him a malformed son in 1919, who lived only a couple of days. The ill-starred marriage was over months later, and divorce proceedings were complete by November of 1920. In 1924, shortly before location shooting began in the snowy wastes of the Sierra Nevada for one of Chaplin's great feature-length masterpieces, *The Gold Rush* (1925), he found a new leading lady named Lillita Murray, who had appeared in *The Kid*. She was now aged 15 years and 10 months. He changed her name to Lita Grey, became involved with her and, once again called to account for causing pregnancy, married her in November of 1924. By the beginning of 1927, Lita had left Charlie, taking their two sons, Charles Spencer Jr. and Sidney, with her. Their divorce was one of the most public displays of acrimony that Hollywood had witnessed. Lita had been replaced by Georgia Hale in *The Gold Rush,* a film whose meticulous preparation had taken a couple of years, and whose finished version was bursting with inspirational and now classic set pieces, such as the starving Tramp making a dinner of his boots.

In 1923, Chaplin had departed from his natural *oeuvre* to direct a "serious" film, in which he did not appear himself. Starring Edna Purviance and Adolphe Menjou, *A Woman of Paris* was, in fact, a melodrama, ill received at the time, but rediscovered and appreciated many decades later. By the end of the 1920s, the sound revolution had come to the cinema and the silents were a thing of the past. Chaplin, however, stood alone in famously resisting the innovation, maintaining that pantomime was essential to his craft, until 1936 when he produced his final silent masterpiece *Modern Times*. Encompassing all his comic genius, the film, about a demoralized factory worker, is also a piece of stringent social criticism. It co-starred Paulette Goddard, whom he had secretly married in the Far East (they divorced in 1942), and ends happily with an eloquent and archetypal image of the Tramp waddling, hand-in-hand, with his girl, down a long road and disappearing into the distance. With World War II under way, Chaplin made his entry into sound cinema with *The Great Dictator* (1940). Again co-starring with Goddard, he essayed the dual role of a humble barber and a lookalike dictator named Adenoid Hynkel. A scathing satire on Adolf Hitler, the film is an undisputed masterpiece that, however, caused much controversy at the time and brought Chaplin into disfavor in several quarters—not least in Germany. It garnered five Oscar nominations and grossed a massive five million dollars, the most of any Chaplin film, for United Artists.

The Great Dictator marked the last Chaplin masterpiece. *Monsieur Verdoux* (1947) featured Chaplin as a Bluebeard-type murderer, fastidiously disposing of wealthy women, but it manifested a dark political message, ran foul of the censors, and was generally badly received. He himself regarded it as "the cleverest and most brilliant film I have yet made,'' and certain students of his work have come to regard it as the most fascinating of the Chaplin films, redolent with his underlying misogyny and rich in savage satire. By 1947 he had been the victim of a damaging paternity suit brought by starlet Joan Barry. In a bizarre judgment, based on forensic evidence, the court found in his favor but nonetheless ordered him to pay child support, and that year he received a subpoena from the HUAC, beginning the political victimization that finally drove him from America. He had, however, finally found what would be lifelong personal happiness with Oona O'Neill, daughter of playwright Eugene. The couple married in 1943, when she was 18 and he 54 and had eight children, one of whom became actress Geraldine Chaplin, who played Charlie's mother Hannah in Richard Attenborough's film, *Chaplin* (1992).

October 1952 saw the premiere of what is perhaps Charlie Chaplin's most personal film, *Limelight*. It is a collector's piece insofar as it features Chaplin and Buster Keaton together for the first and only time. It also marked the debut of the then teenaged British actress Claire Bloom but, most significantly, this tale of a broken-down comedian is redolent of his own childhood background in its return to the long gone era of music hall, and the slum streets of Victorian London. Remarkable for its atmosphere, it is, however, mawkish and clumsily shot. After this, there were only two more features to come, neither of which were, or are, considered successful. *A King in New York* (1957) is an attack on Mccarthyism; *A Countess from Hong Kong* (1967), starring Marlon Brando and Sophia Loren, is a lightweight comedy that misfired disastrously to become the great filmmaker's biggest single disaster and an unworthy swan song.

By the time *Limelight* was released, Chaplin had been accused of Communist affiliations. It was the culmination of many years of resentment that he had not adopted American citizenship, and had further outraged the host country where he found fame by his outspoken criticisms and his unsuitable string of liaisons with teenage girls. He did not return from his trip to London, but settled with his family at Corsier sur Vevey in Switzerland, where, by then Sir Charles Chaplin, he died in his sleep on December 25, 1977. On March 1, 1978, his body was stolen from its grave, but was recovered within a couple of weeks, and the perpetrators were found and tried for the theft.

By the time of his death, America had "forgiven" Chaplin his sins. On April 16, 1972, in what writer Robin Cross called "a triumph of Tinseltown's limited capacity for cosmic humbug" Chaplin, old, overweight, frail, and visibly overcome with emotion, returned to Hollywood to receive a special Oscar in recognition of his genius. That year, too, his name was added to the "Walk of Fame" in Los Angeles, and a string of further awards and honors followed, culminating in his knighthood from Queen Elizabeth in London in March, 1975. Charlie Chaplin, who published *My Autobiography* in 1964, and *My Life in Pictures* in 1974, once said, "All I need to make a comedy is a park, a policeman, and a pretty girl." His simple, silent comedies have grown more profound as the world has grown increasingly chaotic, noisy, and troubled.

—Charles Coletta

FURTHER READING:

Robinson, David. *Chaplin: His Life and Art.* London, William Collins Sons & Co., 1985.

Douglas, Ann. "Charlie Chaplin." *Time.* June 8, 1998, 118-121.

Katz, Ephraim. *The Film Encyclopedia.* New York, HarperCollins, 1994.

Karney, Robyn, and Robin Cross. *The Life and Times of Charlie Chaplin.* London, Green Wood Publishing, 1992.

Kerr, Walter. *The Silent Clowns.* New York, Plenum Press, 1975.

Shipman, David. *The Great Movie Stars.* New York, Hill & Wang, 1979.

Charles, Ray (1930—)

Musician Ray Charles is generally considered a musical genius, and is so in many fields. He has had enormous success in jazz, blues, soul music, country and western, and crossover pop. Acknowledged as an expert vocalist, pianist, saxophonist, and all-around entertainer, Charles first burst into popular attention in the 1950s as the virtual inventor of soul music.

Charles was born Ray Charles Robinson in Albany, Georgia, on September 23, 1930, and raised in Greenville, Florida. A neighbor gave Charles piano lessons after Charles had taught himself how to play at the age of three. This neighbor owned a small store that served as a juke joint as well. Charles not only took piano lessons in the juke joint, he also absorbed the blues, jazz, and gospel music on the jukebox.

When he was six, Charles lost his sight to glaucoma. He continued his music studies at the St. Augustine School for the Deaf and Blind, where he studied for nine years, learning composition and a number of instruments. Upon leaving the school, he worked in a

Ray Charles

number of settings with many different groups in the Florida area. Eventually, he moved to California and recorded with a trio very much in the style of Nat King Cole.

In 1952, Charles signed with Atlantic Records in a move that greatly aided both parties: Atlantic gave him free artistic reign, and Charles responded with a string of hits. These included songs that have become classic rhythm and blues features: "I Got a Woman," "Hallelujah I Love Her So," "Drown in My Own Tears," and "What'd I Say." Charles described his music at the time as "a crossover between gospel music and the rhythm patterns of the blues." This combination violated a long-standing taboo separating sacred and secular music, but the general public did not mind, and soul music, a new musical genre, was born. Many of his fans consider this Atlantic period as his greatest.

Charles once stated that he became actively involved in the Civil Rights movement when a promoter wanted to segregate his audience. Charles, an African American, said that it was all right with him if all the blacks sat downstairs and all the whites in the balcony. The promoter said that Charles had it backwards; his refusal to perform the concert eventually cost him a lawsuit, but he was determined to support Martin Luther King openly and donated large sums of money to his cause.

Charles later moved to ABC/Paramount and branched out into country and western music. In 1962, his country and western album was number one on the Billboard list for fourteen weeks.

Charles's mastery of a number of musical genres and ranking among the very best of America's vocalists (such as Frank Sinatra, Billie Holiday, Ella Fitzgerald, and Nat King Cole) is amply demonstrated by the fiftieth-anniversary collection. Although containing songs even his strongest fans will not like, there are great moments on every tune no matter what the genre. Ray Charles became more than just another singer; he became a representative of his times.

—Frank A. Salamone, Ph.D.

FURTHER READING:

Alkyer, Frank. "Genius and Soul: The 50th Anniversary Collection." *Down Beat*. Vol. 65, No. 1, January 1998, 54.

Genius & Soul: The 50th Anniversary Collection (sound recording). Rhino.

Sanjek, David. "One Size Does Not Fit All: The Precarious Position of the African American Entrepreneur in Post-World War II American Popular Music." *American Music*. Vol. 15, No. 4, Winter 1997, 535.

Silver, Marc. "Still Soulful after All These Years." *U.S. News & World Report*. Vol. 123, No. 11, September 22, 1997, 76.

Charlie Chan

The Chinese detective Charlie Chan remains author Earl Derr Biggers' (1884-1933) greatest legacy. Biggers based his fictional Asian sleuth on Chang Apana, a Chinese American police detective who lived in Honolulu. Biggers' introduced Chan in *The House without a Key* in 1925, the first of six Chan novels. Beginning in 1926, the Chan character hit the silver screen and was eventually featured in more than thirty films. Three different actors portrayed Chan in films:

Warner Oland, Sidney Toler, and Roland Winters. While Chan's character was based on an Asian person, his resemblance to Chinese Americans was remote. White actors played Chan as a rotund, slow-moving detective who spoke pithy sentences made to sound like Confucian proverbs. In contrast to the evil Fu Manchu (another film character), Chan was a hero. But ultimately, his depiction created a new stereotype of Asian Americans as smart, yet inscrutable and inassimilable.

—Midori Takagi

FURTHER READING:

Busch, Frederick. "The World Began with Charlie Chan." *The Georgia Review*. Vol. 43, Spring 1989, 11-12.

Henderson, Lesley, editor. *Twentieth-Century Crime and Mystery Writers*. London, St. James Press, 1991.

Charlie McCarthy

The wooden puppet known as Charlie McCarthy was a precocious adolescent sporting a monocle and top hat, loved by the public for being a flirt and a wise-guy, and a raffish brat who continually got the better of his "guardian," mild-mannered ventriloquist Edgar Bergen (1903-1978). The comedy duo got their start in vaudeville and gave their last performance on television, but—amazingly—they found their greatest fame and success in the most unlikely venue for any ventriloquist: radio. Since the need for illusion was completely obviated by radio, whose audiences wouldn't be able to tell whether or not Bergen's lips were moving, the strength of Bergen and McCarthy as a comedy team was the same as it was for Laurel and Hardy or Abbott and Costello: they were funny. Bergen created and maintained in Charlie a comic persona so strong that audiences almost came to think of him as a real person. Eventually, "the woodpecker's pin-up boy" was joined by two other Bergen creations, hayseed Mortimer Snerd and spinster Effie Klinker, but neither surpassed Charlie in popularity. A broadcast sensation, Bergen and McCarthy also guest-starred in several films, including a couple that gave Charlie the chance to continue his radio rivalry with W. C. Fields. Not until the advent of television would such puppets as Howdy Doody and Kukla and Ollie gain such universal renown. But unlike these latter-day characters, Charlie was designed to appeal equally to adults as to children.

As a child growing up in Chicago, Edgar Bergen discovered that he had the talent to "throw his voice," and he put this gift to mischievous purposes, playing such pranks on his parents as making them think that an old man was at the door. When he reached high school age, young Edgar studied ventriloquism seriously and then commissioned the carving of his first puppet to his exacting specifications: thus was Charlie McCarthy born, full-grown from the head—and larynx—of Bergen. Although he began pre-med studies, Bergen quickly abandoned education for vaudeville. Before long, Bergen and McCarthy were a success, touring internationally. When vaudeville began to fade in the 1930s, Edgar and Charlie switched to posh nightclubs, which eventually led to a star-making appearance on Rudy Vallee's radio show. By 1937, Bergen and McCarthy had their own show, and its phenomenal success lasted for two decades.

Charlie's Angels: (from left) Farrah Fawcett-Majors, Kate Jackson, and Jaclyn Smith.

As Jim Harmon has pointed out in *The Great Radio Comedians,* "The humor (of Bergen and McCarthy) sprang from (an) inevitable misunderstanding between a rather scholarly man and a high-school near-dropout with native wit and precocious romantic interests. What resulted was wildly comic verbal fencing, perfect for the sound-oriented medium. . . . Exasperating to some adults, but we who were children at the time loved it." Not unlike Groucho Marx, Charlie appealed to listeners of all ages because he could get away with saying something naughty or insulting to parental and authority figures. With such catch phrases as "Blow me down!," Charlie endeared himself to generations of listeners and viewers, and paved the way for many successful ventriloquism acts that followed. Bergen's skill as a comedy writer was such that he purposefully let Charlie have all the laughs. When asked once whether he ever felt any hostility toward Charlie, Bergen replied, "Only when he says something I don't expect him to say."

In 1978, ten days after announcing his retirement, Edgar Bergen died. In his will, the ventriloquist had donated Charlie to the Smithsonian. In addition to the memory of decades of laughter, Bergen also bequeathed to the world of show business his daughter, actress/writer/photographer Candice Bergen.

—Preston Neal Jones

FURTHER READING:

Bergen, Candice. *Knock Wood.* Boston, G. K. Hall, 1984.

Bergen, Edgar. *How to Become a Ventriloquist.* New York, Grosset & Dunlap, 1938.

Harmon, Jim. *The Great Radio Comedians.* Garden City, N.Y., Doubleday, 1970.

Charlie's Angels

Despite its pretensions as a prime-time detective show featuring three women as "private eyes," *Charlie's Angels* was primarily about glamour and bare skin. This proved to be a winning combination for the ABC network from 1976 to 1981 when the show broke into the top ten of the Nielson ratings in its first week and improved its position with each subsequent airing. While this success was due, in no small part, to the machinations of ABC's programming genius Fred Silverman, who put it up against two short-lived, male dominated adventure shows—*Blue Knight* and *Quest*—one cannot discount the appeal of three pretty women to viewers of both sexes.

Yet, the program's concessions to its female audience were slim. Beyond the symbolic breakthrough of having three women performing in roles normally reserved for men, while paying attention to fashions and hairstyles, most of the show was dedicated to keeping male viewers in a state of titillation and expectation. While likening Charlie to little more than a glorified ''pimp,'' feminist journalist Judith Coburn commented in a 1976 article that Charlie's Angels was one of the most ''misogynist'' shows that the networks had ever produced. ''Supposedly about strong women, it perpetuates the myth most damaging to women's struggle to gain professional equality: that women always use sex to get what they want, even on the job.''

Generally, the plots revolved around the three sexy female detectives who have left the police department to work for an unseen boss named Charlie (John Forsythe) who conveyed his assignments by telephone and through an assistant named John Bosley (David Doyle). Each weekly episode usually called for one of the three women to appear in a bikini or shorts within the first few minutes of the show to hook the male viewers. After that, most of the stories would be set in exotic locations such as Las Vegas, Palm Springs, or other areas within easy reach of Los Angeles to provide ample opportunities for the ''Angels'' to strip down to bare essentials while ostensibly staying within the confines of the shows' minimal plots.

Yet, ironically, all of the sex was in the dialogue. While viewers reveled in the sight of three gorgeous women in a variety of scanty attire, they never saw them in bed. This might detract from their status as consummate professionals in the detective business. According to the show's publicity, the angels were more than simply pretty faces, sexy tummies, and cascading hair, they were martial arts experts, race car drivers, and shrewd poker players. Of the initial cast, Sabrina (Kate Jackson), was the multilingual, intellectual type; Jill Munroe (Farrah Fawcett-Majors) the physical, action-oriented member, and Kelly Garrett (Jaclyn Smith), the former showgirl, was the cool experienced ''been around'' member of the team who provided calm leadership under pressure.

The idea for the show originated with producers Aaron Spelling and Leonard Goldberg, who had previously specialized in action adventure shows normally dominated by the gritty realism of the inner city. But these were dominated by male policemen and private detectives. In an effort to compete with an upsurge of female dominated action series such as *Police Woman, The Bionic Woman,* and *Wonder Woman,* Spelling and Goldberg decided to inject the traditional private detective genre with a dose of feminine pulchritude with three gorgeous women who not only solved crimes but looked great doing it.

Although the show was initially intended to feature Kate Jackson, then the best known actress of the three, it was Farrah Fawcett-Majors who became the most recognizable icon. Due to some ''cheesecake'' publicity photos, including a swimsuit poster that quickly appeared on the bedroom walls of every thirteen-year-old boy in America, and a mane of cascading blonde hair, Farrah quickly became a fad, appearing on T-shirts and on toy shelves as Farrah dolls swept the nation. She became caught up in the publicity and left the show after the first season in hopes of capitalizing on her fame and becoming a movie star. Spelling and Goldberg replaced her in 1977 with Cheryl Ladd as her younger sister Kris Munroe and the show continued unimpeded.

—Sandra Garcia-Myers

FURTHER READING:

Hano, Arnold. ''They're Not Always Perfect Angels.'' *TV Guide.* December 29, 1979, 19-23.

O'Hallaren, Bill. ''Stop the Chase—It's Time for My Comb-Out.'' *TV Guide.* September 25, 1976, 25-30.

''TV's Superwomen.'' *Time.* November 22, 1976, 67-71.

Charm Bracelets

While charms and amulets, trinkets and tokens to ward off evil, were worn on the body in ancient Egyptian civilization and virtually every other early culture, the twentieth-century charm is far removed from such apotropaic forms. Rather, modern charms are often signs of travel, place, and popular culture, suggesting sentiment and affinity more than prophylaxis. Their peak came in the 1930s when silver or base-metal charms could be accumulated over time and in hard times constituted affordable jewelry. Bakelite and other new materials could also make charms even less expensively. By the 1950s, charm bracelets were chiefly associated with high-school girls and the prospect of being able in high-school's four years to fill all the links of a bracelet with personal mementos. A 1985 fad for the plastic charm bracelets of babies—letter blocks and toys—worn by adults for infantilizing effect lasted less than a year.

—Richard Martin

FURTHER READING:

Congram, Marjorie. *Charms to Collect,* Martinsville, New Jersey, Dockwra Press, 1988.

Chase, Chevy (1943—)

Comedian, writer, and actor Chevy Chase met instant critical success and stardom on *Saturday Night Live*(SNL), first coming to public attention as the anchor of the show's ''Weekend Update'' news spoof with his resounding ''Good evening. I'm Chevy Chase, and you're not!'' His mastery of the pratfall, deadpan outrage, and upper-class demeanor made him a standout from the rest of the SNL cast, and only a year later, Chase was Hollywood-bound and starring in movies that capitalized on his SNL persona. Chase appeared as a guest host of SNL in February 1978, and the show received the highest ratings in its history.

Born Cornelius Crane Chase (his paternal grandmother gave him the nickname Chevy) on October 8, 1943, in New York City, Chase earned a bachelor's degree from Bard College in 1967. He worked on a series of low-level projects, developing his talents as a comedy performer and writer. In 1973 he appeared in the off-Broadway *National Lampoon's Lemmings,* a satire of the Woodstock festival, in which he portrayed a rabid motorcycle gang member and a John Denver type singing about a family freezing to death in the Rockies. In 1974 he wrote and performed for *National Lampoon's White House Tapes* and the *National Lampoon Radio Hour.* Chase went to Hollywood in 1975, where he wrote for Alan King (receiving the Writers Guild of America Award for a network special) and *The Smothers Brothers* television series.

Chevy Chase on *Saturday Night Live*.

negative comments about their artistic quality. In 1983, returning to his comedy roots, Chase starred as Clark Griswold, a role perfectly suited to his deadpan humor, in *National Lampoon's Vacation*. The movie was a great success and has since been followed by three sequels.

About this time, the actor also was coping with substance-abuse problems. Like many other early alumni of SNL, he was exposed to drugs early in his career, but he also had become addicted to painkillers for a degenerative-disk disease that had been triggered by his comic falls. He was able to wean himself from drugs through the Betty Ford clinic in the late 1980s. In the meantime, he continued to star in movies such as *Fletch* (1985).

His career began to flag at the start of the 1990s. Chase was heard to remark that he missed the danger of live television, so it came as no surprise to those that knew him that he took a major risk in launching *The Chevy Chase Show*, a late-night talk show which was one of several efforts by comedians in 1993 to fill the void left by the retirement of Johnny Carson. Like many of the others, it was soon canceled. Since then, Chase has made a number of attempts to revive his movie career. He made the fourth *Vacation* movie (*Vegas Vacation*) in 1997 and began work on a new *Fletch* movie in 1999. Many critics, however, see him as just going through the motions, cashing in on his name and characters before it is too late. The public, however, still thinks of him as Chevy Chase, man of many falls and few competitors.

—John J. Doherty

FURTHER READING:

"Chase, Chevy." *Current Biography Yearbook.* Edited by Charles Moritz. New York, H. W. Wilson Co., 1979.

Hill, Doug, and Jeff Weingrad. *Saturday Night: A Backstage History of Saturday Night Live.* New York, Beech Tree, 1986.

Murphy, Mary. "He's Chevy Chase and They're Not." *TV Guide.* August 28-September 3, 1993, 14-17.

The Chautauqua Institution

During its first eighty years, more famous men and women, including American presidents, appeared under the auspices of the Chautauqua Institution, located on the shore of Lake Chautauqua in an obscure part of northwestern New York, than at any other place in the country. Built in 1874, Chautauqua was headquarters for a phenomenally successful late nineteenth-century religious and mass education movement that satisfied a deep hunger throughout America for culture and "innocent entertainment" at reduced prices.

Philosopher William James visited the site in 1899 and was astonished by the degree to which its small-town values informed nationwide programs. The institution reflected the inexhaustible energies and interests of two founders, Lewis Miller, a wealthy Akron, Ohio, manufacturer of farm machinery (and Thomas A. Edison's future father-in-law), and John Heyl Vincent, who at eighteen had been licensed in Pennsylvania as a Methodist "exhorter and preacher." Both had grown up in rural America, and both were especially knowledgeable about the tastes and yearnings of their fellow citizens.

Long before James's visit, Miller had helped finance revival meetings in a hamlet near Lake Chautauqua, but attendance had

While in a line for movie tickets, Chase met future SNL producer Lorne Michaels, who was so entertained by Chase's humor that he offered him a job writing for the new show, which debuted October 18, 1975. In addition to writing, however, Chase moved in front of the camera, sometimes with material he had written for "Weekend Update" just minutes before. Besides this role, he most famously appeared as President Gerald Ford. His impersonation focused on pratfalls, and served to create an image of a clumsy Ford, which the president himself enjoyed: Ford appeared in taped segments of one episode of SNL declaring "I'm Gerald Ford, and you're not." Chase won two Emmys—one for writing and one for performing—for his SNL work, but his standout success on a show that was supposed to rely on a repertory of actors led to strained relations with the equally popular John Belushi, Michaels, and other colleagues, especially since Chase was not being paid as a performer but as a writer. Chase left SNL in October 1976 and, tempted by movie offers, moved back to California.

In 1978, Chase's first major movie, *Foul Play*, received mixed reviews, but his name was enough to ensure that it was profitable. The movies that followed, including *Caddyshack* and *Oh Heavenly Dog* (both in 1980) also made some money, but Chase himself made declined. While searching for a way to continue his vision of the Lord's work, Miller read some of Vincent's writings, came to the belief that financial salvation was attainable if some new purpose for the site could be found, and contacted Vincent. Vincent disliked razzle-dazzle evangelism but agreed that training young men and women as Sunday school teachers could be the worthy purpose that Miller sought.

A Sunday School Assembly was formed and enjoyed immediate success. However, a looming problem was that as the school's enrollment steadily increased, so did concerns about chaperoning students. Miller and Vincent feared possible scandals in sylvan glades, unless idle time could be filled with regular and wholesome educational and entertainment programs. To direct such activities, they engaged William Rainey Harper, an Ohio-born educator, who would later be John D. Rockefeller's choice to serve as president of the University of Chicago.

Like Miller and Vincent, Harper never opposed an idea because it was new or unproven. Four years after the Sunday School Assembly began operations the Chautauqua Literary Scientific Circle came into being. One measure of its success was that within twenty years, ten thousand reading circles, all of which took their lead from the institution's example, were operating throughout America. One fourth were in villages of fewer than five hundred people, and Chautauqua served them diligently, providing reading lists and other materials.

But innovations at Chautauqua did not stop with the training of Sunday school teachers and reading circles. As early as 1883, it chartered itself as a university and would remain one for twelve years, until established universities began to offer summer courses. Some three hundred "independent" or loosely affiliated similar institutions used Chautauqua as a model without charge by the institution. As early as 1885, a Chautauqua Assembly was held in Long Beach, California, where rollers breaking on wide stretches of white sand and bracing sea air further encouraged those who sought spiritual and intellectual enlightenment during summer months.

For the benefit of those who could not afford travel to New York, California, or independent Chautauquas, "tent chautauquas" came into being. A tent would be pitched in a meadow and lecturers engaged to inform locals on history, politics, and other subjects of general as well as religious interest. Among the speakers, William Jennings Bryan is said to have given fifty lectures in twenty-eight days. The average price for admission was fifty cents, and no drinking or smoking was allowed. A Methodist Dining Tent or Christian Endeavor Ice Cream Tent supplied all refreshments.

Just after the turn of the century, Chautauqua was a "cultural phenomenon with some of the sweep and force of a tidal wave," wrote historian Russell Lynes. Women, who heretofore had little chance to attend college, for the first time had an organization aware of their educational needs that sought to begin opening up opportunities for them. By 1918, more than a million Americans would take correspondence courses sponsored by the institution. A symphony orchestra was created there, and in 1925 George Gershwin composed his Concerto in F in a cabin near the Lake.

In the late 1920s, however, the advent of the automobile and the mobility it offered the masses seemed to signal Chautauqua's end. Not only were untold millions abandoning stultifying small towns for the temptations of metropolises, but those who stayed put had easy access to cities for year-round education and entertainment.

In 1933 the institution went into receivership. Somehow it refused to die. By the early 1970s, with buildings in disrepair and attendance lagging, it appeared finally to be in its death throes—at

which point it renewed its existence. Richard Miller, a Milwaukee resident and great-grandson of founder Lewis Miller, became chairman of the Chautauqua board. He began an aggressive fund-raising campaign and built up financial resources until at the end of the twentieth century the institution had $40 million and held pledges of another $50 million from wealthy members.

More importantly, the Chautauqua Institution reached out for new publics even as it preserved its willingness to continue a tradition of serving people with insatiable curiosity about the world in which they lived and a never-ending need for information. Although the tone of its evangelical heritage remained, Catholics were welcome, about 20 percent of Chautauquans were Jews, and members of the rapidly expanding black middle class were encouraged to join.

"This is a time of growth," declared eighty-five-year-old Alfreda L. Irwin, the institution's official historian, whose family had been members for six generations, in 1998. "Chautauqua is very open and would like to have all sorts of people come here and participate. I think it will happen, just naturally."

—Milton Goldin

FURTHER READING:

Harrison, Harry P. (as told to Karl Detzer). *Culture under Canvas: The Story of Tent Chautauqua.* New York, Hastings House, 1958.

Lynes, Russell. *The Taste-Makers.* New York, Harper, 1954.

Smith, Dinitia. "A Utopia Awakens and Shakes Itself." *New York Times.* August 17, 1998, E1.

Chavez, Cesar (1927-1993)

Rising from the status of a migrant worker toiling in the agricultural fields of Yuma, Arizona, to the leader of America's first successful farm worker's union, Cesar Chavez was once described by Robert F. Kennedy as "one of the heroic figures of our time." Although by nature a meek and humble man known more for his leadership abilities than his public speaking talents, Chavez appealed to the conscience of America in the 1970s by convincing seventeen million people to boycott the sale of table grapes for five consecutive years. Chavez's United Farm Workers Organizing Committee (UFWOC) spearheaded the drive for economic and social justice for Mexican and Mexican American farm workers. Lending their support for this cause was a wide cross section of Americans, including college students, politicians, priests, nuns, rabbis, protestant ministers, unionists, and writers. By forming one of the first unions to fight for the rights of Mexican Americans, Chavez became an important symbol of the Chicano movement.

It would be a vast understatement to say that Chavez rose from humble beginnings. Born in 1927, Chavez spent his early years on his family's small farm near Yuma. When his parents lost their land during the Great Depression, they moved to California to work in the fields as migrant workers. Young Chavez joined his parents to help harvest carrots, cotton, and grapes under the searing California sun. The Chavez family led a nomadic life, moving so often in search of migrant work that Cesar attended more than thirty elementary schools, many of which were segregated. By seventh grade, Cesar dropped out of school to work in the fields full time.

Following service in the U.S. Navy during World War II, Chavez moved to Delano, California, with his wife Helen Fabela. It was in Delano that Chavez made the decision to take an active role in improving the dire working conditions of migrant workers. In 1952, Chavez became a member of the Community Service Organization, which at the time was organizing Mexican Americans into a coalition designed to confront discrimination in American society. Chavez's job was to register Mexican Americans in San Jose to vote, as well as serve as their liaison to immigration officials, welfare boards, and the police.

It was in the early 1960s, however, that Chavez began working exclusively to ameliorate the economic and labor exploitation of Mexican American farm workers. He formed the Farm Workers Association in 1962, which later became the National Farm Workers Association (NFWA). By 1965, 1,700 families had joined the NFWA, and during that same year the organization had convinced two major California growers to raise the wages of migrant workers. After the NFWA merged with an organization of Filipino workers to form the United Farm Workers Organizing Committee (UFWOC), the UFWOC in 1966 launched a campaign picketing grape growers in Delano who paid low wages. This campaign, which nationally became known as *La Huelga* (The Strike), proved to be the defining moment in Chavez's work as a labor activist. The highly publicized five-year strike against grape growers in the San Joaquin, Imperial, and Coachella valleys raised America's consciousness about the conditions of migrant workers and transformed Chavez into a national symbol of civil disobedience. By holding hunger strikes, marches, and sit-ins, as well as having himself arrested in order to gain attention to his cause, Chavez led a boycott that cost California grape growers millions of dollars. In 1970, the growers agreed to grant rights to migrant workers and raised their minimum wage.

La Huelga was the first of many successful boycotts that Chavez organized on behalf of grape and lettuce pickers, and he also fought for the civil rights of African Americans, women, gays, and lesbians. Although membership in the UFWOC eventually waned, Chavez remained a beloved figure in the Mexican American community and nationally represented the quest for fairness and equality for all people. When Chavez died on April 23, 1993, at the age of sixty-six, expressions of bereavement were received from a host of national and international leaders, and a front-page obituary was published in the *New York Times*.

—Dennis Russell

FURTHER READING:

Dunne, John Gregory. *Delano: The Story of the California Grape Strike*. New York, Farrar, Straus & Giroux, 1967.

Ferriss, Susan, and Ricardo Sandoval. *The Fight in the Fields: Cesar Chavez and the Farmworkers Movement*. New York, Harcourt Brace, 1997.

Levy, Jacques. *Cesar Chavez: Autobiography of La Causa*. New York, W. W. Norton, 1975.

London, Joan, and Henry Anderson. *So Shall Ye Reap: The Story of Cesar Chavez and the Farm Workers' Movement*. New York, Thomas Y. Crowell Co., 1970.

Matthiessen, Peter. *Sal Si Puedes: Cesar Chavez and the New American Revolution*. New York, Dell Publishing Co., 1969.

Taylor, Ronald B. *Chavez and the Farm Workers*. Boston, Beacon Press, 1975.

Chavis, Boozoo (1930—)

As the leading exponent of a unique musical tradition known as zydeco, Boozoo Chavis is a genuine artist who is inextricably enveloped within the regional landscapes of his culture. Lake Charles, Louisiana, sits at the western apex of a roughly triangular area of south Louisiana that is home to the black French-speaking population known as Creoles. Here, among the horse pastures and the patchwork fields of rice and sweet potatoes, Boozoo Chavis learned to play "la-la music" on the accordion for the rural house dances that formed the centerpiece of Creole social life. When the urbanized sounds of rhythm and blues caught on among local blacks, it was Chavis who first successfully blended traditional la-la songs with a more contemporary bluesy sound and with lyrics sung in English. In 1954 he recorded the now classic "Paper in My Shoe," which told of poverty but with a beat that let you deal with it. Along with Clifton Chenier who recorded "Ay Tete Fee" the following year, Boozoo Chavis is a true pioneer of zydeco music.

In an unfortunate turn of events, Chavis felt he did not receive what was his due from making that early record, and left off pursuing music as an avocation, turning instead to raising race horses at "Dog Hill," his farm just outside Lake Charles. Though he continued to play for local parties and traditional Creole gatherings such as Trail Rides, he did not begin playing commercially again until 1984. Since coming out of semi-retirement he has not wasted any time, however, and has recorded some seven albums loaded with pure gems. *Hey Do Right!* is titled after the nickname for his daughter Margaret.

Wilson Anthony Chavis was born October 23, 1930 some 60 miles east of the Lake Charles area where he would grow up. He does not recall where his peculiar nickname came from, but it is a moniker widely recognized among legions of zydeco fans today—caps and t-shirts in south Louisiana proclaim in bright letters: "Boozoo, that's who!" Even as he approaches his seventieth birthday, Chavis still knows how to work a crowd. Whether it is in the cavernous recesses of a legendary local club like Richard's in Lawtell or Slim's Y-Ki-Ki in Opelousas, or commanding an outdoor stage at the congested New Orleans Jazz and Heritage Festival, Boozoo performs like the seasoned professional he has become, with great vigor and joie de vivre. He characteristically runs through a long sequence of tunes one after another, without even taking a break. His trademark clear plastic apron keeps the sweat from damaging the bellows of his diatonic button accordion, which he still prefers over the piano key instrument that is more common among zydeco artists of his generation. Every Labor Day, Boozoo hosts a picnic at Dog Hill which is open to the public, thereby continuing the tradition of rural house dances where zydeco began. Numerous bands contribute to the day's entertainment, and Boozoo always plays last, making the final definitive statement of what this music is all about.

Afraid of flying, he mainly limits touring to places within easy driving distance of Lake Charles, to all points between New Orleans and Houston, the extremities of zydeco's heartland. But with increasing recognition of his talent and position as leading exponent of zydeco, Chavis has begun to travel more widely, heading for locations like New York, Washington, D.C., San Francisco, or Seattle. No matter where he plays, Boozoo has never strayed from the recognition that zydeco is first and foremost dance music. His songs include many of the old French waltzes and two-steps from earlier times, but are always spiced up a bit in his inimitable fashion. In a recently published book, zydeco observer Michael Tisserand characterized Boozoo's playing as a "punchier, more percussive style." Thematically, Chavis stays close to home, writing songs about his family, friends, farm, and beloved race horses that sport names such as "Camel" and "Motor Dude."

In the face of ever more urban and homogenizing influences on zydeco, Boozoo Chavis remains rooted in the music's rural traditions. He is just as likely to be fixing up the barn or working with his horses as playing at a dance or a concert. While a half-serious, half in jest controversy has simmered over the years regarding who should follow the reign of Clifton Chenier as the King of Zydeco, most cognoscenti agree that of all the leading contenders for the crown, Boozoo Chavis is most deserving of the accolade. He is the perennial favorite at the Zydeco Festival in Plaisance, Louisiana, where he often waits in the shade of the towering live oaks to greet his many fans and sign autographs. His music, like the person that he is, is the real article.

—Robert Kuhlken

FURTHER READING:

Broven, John. *South to Louisiana: The Music of the Cajun Bayous.* Gretna, Louisiana, Pelican Publishing, 1983.

Nyhan, Patricia, et al. *Let the Good Times Roll! A Guide to Cajun & Zydeco Music.* Portland, Maine, Upbeat Books, 1997.

Tisserand, Michael. *The Kingdom of Zydeco.* New York, Arcade Publishing, 1998.

Chayefsky, Paddy (1923-1981)

Distinguished playwright, novelist, and screenwriter Paddy (born Sidney) Chayefsky was a major force in the flowering of post-World War II television drama, sympathetically chronicling the lives and problems of ordinary people. His most famous piece of this period is *Marty,* about the love affair between two homely people, which became an Oscar-winning film in 1955. Bronx-born and college educated, he attempted a career as a stand-up comic before military service, and began writing when wounded out of the army. The most acclaimed of his Broadway plays is *The Tenth Man* (1959), drawing on Jewish mythology, but he found his wider audience through Hollywood, notably with original screenplays for *The Hospital* (1971) and *Network* (1976), both of which won him Academy Awards and revealed that he had broadened his scope into angry satire. He controversially withdrew his name from the 1980 film of his novel *Altered States* (1978), which he had adapted himself, and died a year later.

—Robyn Karney

FURTHER READING:

Considine, Shaun. *Mad as Hell: The Life and Work of Paddy Chayefsky.* New York, Random House, 1994.

Checker, Chubby (1941—)

One of several popular male vocalists to emerge from the Philadelphia rock 'n' roll scene in the late 1950s and early 1960s, Chubby Checker was the chief beneficiary of the fervor created by the dance known as the Twist.

Checker was born Ernest Evans on October 3, 1941 in Spring Gully, South Carolina, the child of poor tobacco farmers. At the age of nine he moved to Philadelphia and eventually began working at a neighborhood produce market where he acquired his famous nickname "Chubby" from his employer. Evans' big break, however, came at age 16 while working at a local poultry market. Proprietor Henry Colt overheard Evans singing a familiar tune as he went about his work. Colt was impressed with Evans' talent and referred him to a songwriter friend named Cal Mann who was, at that time, working with Dick Clark.

Dick Clark and his *American Bandstand* had a lot to do with the popularity of many Philadelphian singers who frequently appeared on the program. Frankie Avalon, Bobby Rydell, Fabian, and Checker were among the teen idols who careers took off after they gained exposure to millions of American teenagers via television. Checker was one of very few black teen idols of that period, however. In his case, even his stage name derived from contact with Dick Clark. Clark and his wife were looking for someone to impersonate Fats Domino for an upcoming album. Hoping to give Evans' career a boost, Clark's wife is said to have dubbed the young performer "Chubby Checker" because the name sounded like Fats Domino.

Chubby Checker

The song entitled "The Twist" was originally released as the flip side of a 45 rpm single by Hank Ballard and the Midnighters, a popular R&B singing group. Checker released "The Twist" as an A-side on the Parkway label in August 1960, aggressively promoting the record and the dance in personal appearances and on television. Numerous Chubby Checker performances on programs like the Philadelphia-based *American Bandstand* helped fuel both the Twist Craze and Checker's career.

Chubby Checker's recording of "The Twist" went to #1 on the *Billboard* Top 40 charts in mid-September, 1960. Eager to capitalize on the success of that record, Checker released several other Twist-related singles such as "Let's Twist Again," "Twist It Up," and "Slow Twistin'." In fact, almost all of his records were dance tunes, such as the #1 hit "Pony Time," "The Hucklebuck," "The Fly," and the #2 hit "Limbo Rock."

Several films were produced in an attempt to cash in on the popularity of the Twist, and Chubby Checker was the star of two of them. Alan Freed's *Rock around the Clock* and *Don't Knock the Rock* were the first rock 'n' roll exploitation films ever made, back in 1956; in 1961 Chubby Checker starred in *Twist around the Clock* and *Don't Knock the Twist,* remakes of the Freed films made after only five years had passed. Checker also went on to appear in other movies such as *Teenage Millionaire.*

Perhaps as a result of the Twist movies being released in the second half of 1961, the Twist craze resurfaced and Checker's version of "The Twist" was re-released by Parkway. The record was even more successful the second time around, and "The Twist" was the first #1 record of 1962. This is the only case during the rock 'n' roll era of the same record earning #1 on the Top 40 on two different occasions.

Four months later, in May 1962, Chubby Checker was awarded a Grammy for best rock and roll recording of 1961, ostensibly for "Let's Twist Again." The latter was a moderate (#8) hit in 1961, but in no sense the best rock 'n' roll song of the year. Checker's triumphant re-release of "The Twist" did set a new record, but that achievement took place in 1962, and technically the song was not eligible for a 1961 Grammy.

Chubby Checker continued to release singles and albums of rock and roll, primarily dance music. Although he had a few more hits, such as "Limbo Rock" in 1962, no subsequent dances were ever as good to Checker as the Twist had been. By the end of 1965 he had placed 22 songs on the Top 40, including seven Top Ten hits, but his best period was over by the end of 1962.

Since the mid-1970s Checker has benefitted from another trend, oldies nostalgia. Along with many other former teen idols, Checker has seen a resurgence of his career at state fairs and on oldies tours, playing the old songs again for a multi-generational audience.

—David Lonergan

FURTHER READING:

"Australian Fan Site of Chubby Checker." http://www.ozemail. com.au/~facerg/chubby.htm. February 1999.

Morrison, Tonya Parker. "Chubby Checker: 'The Wheel that Rock Rolls On,'" American Press, 30 October 1998.

Nite, Norm N. *Rock On Almanac.* 2nd edition. New York, HarperPerennial, 1992.

Stambler, Irwin. *The Encyclopedia of Pop, Rock and Soul.* Revised edition. New York, St. Martin's Press, 1989.

Whitburn, Joel. *The Billboard Book of Top 40 Hits.* 6th edition. New York, Billboard Books, 1996.

Cheech and Chong

Cheech and Chong were a comedy team of the early 1970s that opened for rock bands, recorded a series of popular comedy albums, performed on the college circuit, and appeared in their own movies. Their comedy routines consisted largely of "doper jokes," reflecting the drug culture and scatological humor of the 1960s. Richard "Cheech" Marin (1946—) and Tommy Chong (1938—) met in 1968 in Vancouver, British Columbia, where Cheech had fled to avoid the U.S. draft during the Vietnam War. Together they co-founded an improv group called City Works, and performed in a nightclub owned by Chong's brother. By 1970 they were known as Cheech and Chong, and were performing in nightclubs in Toronto and Los Angeles.

Canadian-born Tommy Chong, half Chinese and half Scottish-Irish, was playing the guitar in a band called Bobby Taylor and the Vancouvers when he met Cheech, who started out singing with the band. Cheech, born of Mexican parents in South Central Los Angeles, grew up in Granada Hills, near the San Fernando Valley. The duo recorded several successful comedy albums in the early 1970s. In 1971, *Cheech and Chong* was nominated for a Grammy for Best Comedy Recording, and their 1972 album *Big Bambu* retained the record of being the largest-selling comedy recording for many years. *Los Cochinos* won the Grammy for Best Comedy Recording in 1973.

Cheech Marin (left) and Tommy Chong

Their humor, although very vulgar at times, was entertaining, with Cheech playing a jaunty marijuana smoking dopehead, and Chong playing a burned out, laid back musician.

Their successful movies of the late 1970s and early 1980s became doper cult classics. *Up in Smoke* was released in 1978, *Cheech & Chong's Next Movie* in 1980, and *Cheech & Chong's Nice Dreams* in 1981. In these three movies they play simple-minded pot heads, or left over hippies, but their comic teamwork has been compared to Laurel and Hardy. The screenplays were written by both Cheech and Chong, with the directing done primarily by Chong. Their last films together were *Things Are Tough All Over* (1982), in which they both play dual roles; *Still Smokin'* (1983); *The Corsican Brothers* (1984), in which they go "straight"; and *Cheech and Chong Get Out of My Room,* directed by Cheech in 1985 for the cable channel Showtime.

The pair split up in 1985, and from there Tommy Chong's career fizzled. He starred in the 1990 film *Far Out Man,* which bombed, and he tried stand-up comedy in 1991 without much success. Cheech Marin, on the other hand, went on to a successful career as a director and actor in several films and television shows. His film *Born in East L.A.* (1987) has become a classic among Mexican Americans and is often included in academic classes of Chicano Studies. In the 1990s he received small supporting roles in several films, including a well-received part in the hit *Tin Cup,* starring Kevin Costner, and played the television role of Joe Dominquez in *Nash Bridges.*

—Rafaela Castro

FURTHER READING:

Chong, Thomas, and Cheech Marin. *Cheech and Chong's Next Movie.* New York, Jove Publicatons, 1980.

Goldberg, Robert. "From Drugs to Duels: Cheech and Chong Go Straight". *Wall Street Journal.* July 24, 1984.

Menard, Valerie. "Cheech Enjoys Second Career in TV." *Hispanic.* Vol. 9, No. 9, 1998, 12-14.

Mills, David. "Tommy Chong: Reefer Sadness." *Washington Post.* June 15, 1991, C1.

Cheerleading

Few archetypes so exemplify every stereotype of women in modern culture as that of the cheerleader. An uneasy juxtaposition of clean-cut athlete, ultra-feminine bubble-headed socialite, skilled dancer, and buxom slut, the cheerleader is at the same time admired and ridiculed, lusted after and legitimized by everyone from junior high school girls to male sports fans. Though cheerleading began as an all-male domain, and there are still male cheerleaders, it is for girls that the role of cheerleader is a rite of passage, whether to be coveted or scorned. Public figures as widely diverse as Gloria Steinem, John Connally, and Paula Abdul spent part of their early years urging the crowd to cheer for their athletic team.

Cheerleading as we know it began in November 1898 at a University of Minnesota football game, when an enthusiastic student named Johnny Campbell jumped up to yell:

Rah, Rah, Rah

Sku-u-mah
Hoorah, hoorah
Varsity, varsity
Minn-e-so-ta!

The idea caught on, and in the early 1900s at Texas A&M, freshmen, who were not allowed to bring dates to athletic events, styled themselves as yell leaders, with special sweaters and megaphones. They became so popular, especially with women, that soon the juniors and seniors took the role away from the freshmen.

Only men took on the highly visible role of cheerleading until after World War II, when women began to form cheerleading squads, wearing demure uniforms with skirts that fell well below the knee. In the late 1940s, the president of Kilgore College in Texas had the idea of creating an attractive female dancing and cheering squad as a tactic to keep students from going to the parking lot to drink during half time. He hired a choreographer, commissioned flashy costumes, and the idea of cheerleading as a sort of sexy show-biz entertainment took off. By the 1990s, there were over three million cheerleaders nationwide, almost all of them female.

Cheerleading means different things on the different levels it is practiced. In junior high, high school, and college, cheerleading is very much a social construct. Cheerleading tryouts appeal to girls for many reasons. Some seek the prestige and social status afforded those who make the cut. These chosen few are admired by the boys and envied by the girls as they represent their school at games and hobnob with the boys' elite—the athletic teams. Those who are rejected after tryouts often experience deep humiliation. Of course there are many who reject the school status hierarchies and who view the cheerleaders as shallow snobs rather than social successes. Another way to view cheerleaders is as strong athletes who seek recognition in one of the only areas acceptable for females. In fact, in many schools, prior to the Title IX laws of the 1970s, there were no athletic teams for girls, and cheerleading was the only outlet where girls could demonstrate athletic skill.

Many supporters of cheerleading stress the athletic side of cheerleading and the strength required to perform the jumps and gymnastic feats that accompany cheers. There are local and national cheerleading competitions, where squads compete and are judged on creativity, execution, degree of difficulty, and overall performance. Over the years, cheerleading has developed from simple gestures and jumps to difficult gymnastic stunts and complex dance routines. As the athletic skill required to become a cheerleader has increased, so has the number of cheerleading-related injuries. In 1986, the reputation of cheerleading suffered when two cheerleaders in different schools were involved in major accidents within a week. A young woman was killed and a young man paralyzed while practicing their cheerleading stunts. A Consumer Product Safety Commission study in 1990 found 12,405 emergency room injuries that year were related to cheerleading, prompting parental demands for greater safety precautions.

Another sort of cheerleading is found in professional sports. While fitting a standard mold of attractiveness is one of the primary requisites of any sort of cheerleading, the professional squads have taken it to extremes. Tryouts for squads like the Dallas Cowboy Cheerleaders, the New Orleans Saints' Saintsations, and the Buffalo Bills' Buffalo Jills, seem almost like auditions for a Broadway play, with hundreds of flamboyantly made-up dancers and performers competing for a few openings. The cheerleaders perform for exposure and love of their team rather than money. In an industry where the

A group of cheerleaders from Mississippi State University.

athletes might earn millions, most cheerleaders are paid only ten to twenty-five dollars a game. Some are able to acquire contracts for local advertising to supplement their income, and some hope to go on to show business careers, but for many, just as in high school, it is the admiration of the crowd and the identification with the team that is the payoff.

It is in the professional arena that the risqué side of cheerleading has received the most publicity. Because cheerleaders are almost always chosen for standard good looks and shapely bodies in addition to whatever skills may be required, even in high schools, rumors of immorality circulate. In the professional squads, where outfits are often skimpy and the routines flirtatious, the rumors are even more graphic. Though most squads advertise a high moral standard, the stereotype of the sexpot cheerleader has been hard to defeat. Movies such as the XXX rated *Debbie Does Dallas* contribute to this, as did the 1979 *Playboy Magazine* spread featuring nude photos of a fictional cheerleading squad called the Texas Cowgirls.

Cheerleading has also grown into a big business. In the 1950s, a former Texas high school cheerleader named James Herkimer (he developed a cheerleading jump called the "herkie") founded the National Cheerleader Association. The NCA is a for-profit enterprise based in Dallas that runs hundreds of cheerleading camps nationwide, teaching young aspiring cheerleaders jumping and cheering skills at a reasonable rate. The cost of the camps is kept low, but the cheerleading squads who attend the camps usually purchase their uniforms and other accoutrements from the NCA-affiliated National Spirit group. Since it costs about $200 to outfit the average cheerleader, 3 million cheerleaders represent a sizable market, and by the 1990s, the NCA was grossing over 60 million dollars a year.

The huge profits have attracted competition. In the 1970s, Jeff Webb, a former protégé of James Herkimer, began his own company in Memphis, the Universal Cheerleading Association, and its parent

company, the Varsity Spirit Corporation. While Herkimer has clung to the classic cheerleading style, with athletic jumps and rhythmic arm motions, Webb opted for a more modern approach; his camps teach elaborate gymnastic stunts and dance routines, and his supply company markets flashier uniforms and specialty items. Varsity Spirit Corp. has even expanded abroad, signing a deal in Japan, where cheerleading is very popular. Though NCA and UCA are the largest, the expanding "school spirit industry" has prompted the creation of many other cheerleading camp/supplier companies.

Because cheerleaders play such an important role in many schools, cheerleading has become a battleground for social issues. In 1969 over half of the public school students in Crystal City, Texas, staged a walkout for twenty-eight days in protest of their school's racist policies concerning cheerleader selection. In a district where 85 percent of the students were Chicano, it was not unusual for only one Chicana cheerleader to be selected. The students' action was successful and it was the root of the Chicano movement organization, Raza Unida. In 1993, four cheerleaders on a high school squad in Hempstead, Texas, found they were pregnant. Only one was allowed to return to cheering; she had an abortion, and she was white. The other students, who were African American, fought the decision with the support of the National Organization for Women and the American Civil Liberties Union. They were finally reinstated. In 1991, another student charged the University of Connecticut with discrimination when they dropped her from the cheering squad for being, at 130 pounds, over the weight limit. Her suit resulted not only in her reinstatement but in the abolition of the weight requirement.

The fierce competition surrounding cheerleading has been documented in a cable-TV movie starring Holly Hunter in the title role of *The Positively True Adventures of the Alleged Texas Cheerleader-Murdering Mom.* The movie takes playful liberties with the true story of Wanda Holloway, who plotted to have the mother of her daughter's cheerleading rival killed. Journalists in Texas, where cheerleading is taken seriously, were surprised only by the fact that Holloway presumed that the murder would prevent the rival from trying out for the squad. The media is full of other such stories: the New Jersey cheerleaders who in 1998 fed the opposing squad cupcakes filled with laxatives, and the South Carolina cheerleaders who spiced up a 1995 Florida competition by holding their own private contest—in shoplifting.

Cheerleaders are easy targets for satire, their *raison d'être* construed as boosterism, and they are often stereotyped as being stupid and superficial. In 1990, the University of Illinois was prompted to take the soft-core sexual image of cheerleaders seriously. Noting the high rate of sexual assault on campus, a university task force recommended banning the cheerleaders, the Illinettes, because the all-female squad maintained a high-profile image as sexual objects. In this light, it is easy to see that male cheerleading is a distinctly different phenomenon; men in letter sweaters with megaphones yelling and doing acrobatics clearly fill a different role than scantily-clad women doing the same yells and acrobatics.

Debate continues over whether cheerleaders are athletes or bimbos; whether cheerleading is, in itself, a sport, or an adjunct to the *real* (mostly male) sports. Some women devote their lives to cheerleading, for themselves or their daughters; some women condemn it because it turns women into boosters at best and sex objects at worst. Some men delight in watching the dances of the flamboyant squads at half-time; some men see them as a distraction to the game and belive they should be abolished. And in junior high and high schools across the country, girls, even many who profess not to care, still train to perform difficult routines for tryouts and anxiously watch bulletin boards to see if they made the squad.

—Tina Gianoulis

FURTHER READING:

Hanson, Mary Ellen. *Go! Fight! Win!: Cheerleading in American Culture.* Bowling Green, Ohio, Bowling Green State University Popular Press, 1995.

Ralston, Jeannie. "Rah! Power." *Texas Monthly.* Vol. 22, No. 10, October, 1994, 150.

Scholz, Suzette, Stephanie Scholz, and Sheri Scholz. *Deep in the Heart of Texas: Reflections of Former Dallas Cowboy Cheerleaders.* New York, St. Martin's Press, 1991.

Cheers

Cheers was the longest-running and most critically acclaimed situation comedy on 1980s television. Combining physical and verbal gags with equal dexterity, *Cheers* turned the denizens of a small Boston bar into full-fledged American archetypes. By the end of the show's run, author Kurt Vonnegut, Jr., was moved to call *Cheers* the "one comic masterpiece" in TV history. The author of many comic fiction classics added, "I wish I'd written [*Cheers*] instead of everything I *had* written. Every time anybody opens his or her mouth on that show, it's significant. It's *funny*."

Cheers was set at a Boston bar of the same name owned by Sam Malone (Ted Danson), a good-looking former relief pitcher for the woebegone Boston Red Sox whose career was cut short by a drinking problem. His alcoholism under control, he reveled in his semi-celebrity and status as a ladies' man. Tending bar was Sam's old Red Sox coach, the befuddled Ernie Pantuso (Nicholas Colasanto), a character obviously modeled on baseball great Yogi Berra. In early 1985, Colasanto suddenly died. He was replaced behind the bar by an ignorant Indiana farm boy, Woody Boyd (Woody Harrelson). Carla Tortelli (Rhea Perlman) was the foul-mouthed waitress; a single mother, she bore several children out of wedlock during the show's eleven-year run. To one woman she threatened, "You sound like a lady who's getting tired of her teeth." The bar's regulars were the pathetic Norm Peterson (George Wendt), a perpetually unemployed accountant trapped in a loveless marriage to the unseen Vera; and the equally pathetic Cliff Clavin (John Ratzenberger), the resident trivia expert and career postal worker, who still lived with his domineering mother.

In the series' first episode Diane Chambers (Shelley Long), a pretentious, well-to-do graduate student, was abandoned at the bar by her fiancé en route to their wedding. Sam offered her a job waitressing, thus beginning one of the most complex romances in prime time TV history. Sam and Diane swapped insults for most of the first season, and a volley of insults on the season's last episode culminated in their first kiss. They consummated their relationship in the first episode of the second season:

SAM: You've made my life a living hell.
DIANE: I didn't want you to think I was easy.

Yet Sam and Diane never tied the knot. Diane left Sam and received psychiatric help from Dr. Frasier Crane (Kelsey Grammer), with whom she promptly fell in love. Diane and Frasier planned a European wedding, but she left him at the altar. By the 1986-87 season Sam and Diane were engaged when, on the eve of their wedding, Diane won a sizable deal to write her first novel. Sam allowed her to leave for six months to write, knowing it would be forever.

Sam sold the bar to go on a round-the-world trip. He humbly returned to become the bartender for the bar's new manager, Rebecca Howe (Kirstie Alley), a cold corporate type. The bar was now owned by a slick British yuppie, Robin Colcord, who had designs on Rebecca. When Robin was arrested for insider trading, Sam was able to buy back the bar for a dollar.

Life went on for the Cheers regulars. Dumped by Diane, the cerebral Frasier grew darker and more sarcastic, barely surviving a marriage to an anal-retentive, humorless colleague, Lilith (Bebe Neuwirth). Sam and Rebecca enjoyed a whirlwind romance and contemplated having a baby together out of wedlock. Carla married a professional hockey player, who was killed when a Zamboni ran over him. Woody fell in love with a naive heiress, and by the final season won a seat on the Boston City Council. Norm and Cliff remained loyal customers, serving as Greek chorus to the increasingly bizarre happenings.

Despite the wistful theme song ("Sometimes you want to go / Where everybody knows your name"), the characters were frequently cruel to one another. Norm once stood up for the unpopular Cliff this way: "In his defense, he'll probably never reproduce." During one exchange Carla asked Diane, "Did your Living Bra die of boredom?" They also engaged in elaborate practical jokes; Sam

Ted Danson (second from right) and Shelley Long (right) with the rest of the cast in a scene from the sitcom *Cheers*.

devised one prank which ended with Cliff, Carla, Norm, and Woody on an endless cross-country bus trek. The sadism reached its zenith during a petty rivalry throughout the run of the series with a competing bar, Gary's Olde Time Tavern. The feud culminated during the final season, when the Cheers gang convinced the smug Gary that an investor would pay him $1 million for his land. Gary gleefully took a wrecking ball to his establishment.

Cheers ended in 1993 after 11 seasons and 269 episodes. Series co-creators Glen and Les Charles had once confessed their ideal *Cheers* ending: Sam and Diane admit they can't live with or without each other and take each other's life in a murder-suicide. In the actual finale, Diane did return to the bar, contemplating a reconciliation with Sam, but the two finally realized they were no longer suitable for each other. In other developments, upwardly mobile Rebecca impulsively married a plumber, Cliff won a promotion at the post office, and— miracle of miracles—Norm finally got a steady job. In the last moments of the series, the regulars sat around the bar to discuss the important things in life. As the show faded out one final time, Sam walked through the empty bar, obviously the most important thing to him, at closing time.

There has been no consensus as to the best single episode of *Cheers*. Some prefer the Thanksgiving episode at Carla's apartment, ending in a massive food fight with turkey and all the trimmings in

play. Others recall Cliff's embarrassing appearance on the *Jeopardy!* game show, with a cameo from host Alex Trebek. There was also the penultimate episode, where the vain Sam revealed to Carla that his prized hair was, in fact, a toupee. Perhaps the finest *Cheers* was the 1992 hour-long episode devoted to Woody's wedding day, a classic, one-set farce complete with a Miles Gloriosus-like soldier, horny young lovers, and a corpse that wouldn't stay put.

Cheers was inspired by the BBC situation comedy *Fawlty Towers* (1975, 1979), set at a British seaside hotel run by an incompetent staff. That show's creator/star, John Cleese, appeared on *Cheers* in an Emmy-winning 1987 cameo as a marriage therapist who went to great lengths to convince Sam and Diane that they were thoroughly incompatible. Co-creator James Burrows was the son of comedy writing great Abe Burrows, responsible for the long-running 1940s radio comedy *Duffy's Tavern* (''where the elite meet to eat''), a program set in a bar which was also noted for its eccentric characters and top-notch writing.

Grammer reprised his role of Frasier Crane in the spin-off series *Frasier*, which debuted in the fall of 1993 to high ratings and critical acclaim. The series won Best Comedy Emmy awards during each of its first five seasons.

—Andrew Milner

FURTHER READING:

Bianculli, David. *Teleliteracy.* New York, Ungar, 1993.

Javna, John. *The Best of TV Sitcoms: The Critics' Choice: Burns and Allen to the Cosby Show, the Munsters to Mary Tyler Moore.* New York, Harmony Books, 1988.

Chemise

Fashion designer Cristobal Balenciaga's "chemise" dramatically altered womenswear in 1957. Since Christian Dior's New Look in 1947, women wore extremely narrow waists, full wide skirts, and fortified busts. The supple shaping of Balenciaga's chemise, which draped in a long unbroken line from shoulder to hem, replaced the hard armature of the New Look. The chemise was a hit not only in couture fashion, where Yves Saint Laurent showed an A-line silhouette in his first collection for Dior, but also in Middle America, where Americans copied the simple shape which required far less construction and was therefore cheaper to make. Uncomfortable in the body conformity of the New Look, women rejoiced in a forgiving shape and the chemise, or sack dress, became a craze. The craze was parodied in an *I Love Lucy* episode in which Lucy and Ethel pine for sack dresses but end up wearing feed sacks.

—Richard Martin

FURTHER READING:

Chappell, R. "The Chemise—Joke or No Joke . . . " *Newsweek.* May 5, 1959.

Chenier, Clifton (1925-1987)

Although he passed away in the late 1980s, Clifton Chenier remains the undisputed King of Zydeco. It was Clifton Chenier who took the old dance music of the rural Louisiana Creoles and added blues, soul, and country and stirred it all up until it became what we now call zydeco. His name was virtually synonymous with this type of music, and he became the most respected and influential zydeco artist in the world. Chenier popularized the use of the big piano key accordion, which allowed him to play a diversity of styles within the expanding zydeco genre. He pushed the envelope with energetic renditions of French dance standards or newer tunes transformed through zydeco's characteristic syncopated rhythms and breathy accordion pulses. Chenier assembled a band of musicians who were not just good but were the best in the business; they were a close-knit group that became legendary for high intensity concerts lasting four hours straight without a break. And there at the helm was Chenier, gold tooth flashing like the chrome of his accordion, having the time of his life.

Clifton Chenier was born on June 25, 1925 into a sharecropping family near Opelousas, Louisiana. He became dissatisfied early on with the farming life, and headed west with his brother Cleveland to work in the oil refineries around Port Arthur, Texas. Having learned from his father how to play the accordion, Chenier decided to attempt a transition toward performing as a professional. Driving a truck during the day and playing music at night, Chenier, along with his

Clifton Chenier

brother on rubboard, soon became a popular attraction in local roadhouses. Often the pair comprised the entire band, and this was zydeco in its purest form, an extension of the earlier French "la-la" music played at Creole gatherings throughout southwest Louisiana, now taken to new heights and amplitude for a wider audience. Chenier credits Rhythm and Blues (R & B) artist Lowell Fulson with showing him how to be a good performer, always mixing it up and pleasing the crowd—these lessons stayed with him for the rest of his career. One of his earliest recordings, "Ay-Tete-Fee" became a hit record in 1955.

During the early 1960s, Chenier began recording albums for Chris Strachwitz's west coast Arhoolie Records, where he eventually became that label's biggest seller. His first Arhoolie album, *Louisiana Blues and Zydeco,* was a hard-fought compromise between the producer's desire for traditional zydeco, and Chenier's wish to cross over into soul and the potentially even more lucrative R & B. The final version of the album represented a mixture of these two directions and included for the first time on record a blues number sung in French. Following that release, Chenier's popularity soared, and a frenetic schedule of touring ensued. Over the next few years, Clifton Chenier would realize the wisdom of Strachwitz's insistence on sticking close to unadulterated zydeco, which was already a musical gumbo of various ingredients, and he became more of a traditionalist himself, championing Creole culture and the French language wherever he played.

All through the 1970s Chenier and his Red Hot Louisiana Band traveled the "crawfish circuit" between New Orleans and Houston, playing in parking lots, in clubs and bars, and in Catholic church halls where zydeco dances were sponsored with increasing frequency. This kept the music rooted in its place of origin, and served to accentuate the rising awareness of Creole ethnic identity. When touring further afield, he became a regular attraction at blues festivals around the country and even made a successful sweep through Europe. It was about this time that he began wearing a crown on stage, dubbing himself the "King of Zydeco." His musical performances were featured in several documentary films, including *Hot Pepper* and *J'ai Ete au Bal*. In 1984, Chenier won a Grammy Award for the album *I'm Here,* and was now a nationally, and even internationally recognized musician. But his health had gone downhill. Plagued by poor circulation, he was diagnosed with diabetes and had portions of both legs amputated. After a final, tearful performance at the 1987 Zydeco Festival in Plaisance, Louisiana, he canceled a scheduled tour due to illness, and on December 12, 1987, at the age of 62, Clifton died in a Lafayette hospital. His legacy lives on, as does his fabled Red Hot Louisiana Band, now led by son C.J. Chenier, an emerging zydeco artist in his own right.

There has never been anyone, before or since, who could play the accordion like Clifton Chenier. While his vocal renditions of songs were truly inspired, his voice always served as accompaniment to the accordion, rather than the other way around. Besides having talent and the gift of making music, he was able to establish a warm and unaffected rapport with his audience. He knew who he was, he loved what he was doing, and he genuinely enjoyed people. Fans and critics alike are unreserved in their emphatic assessment of Clifton Chenier's artistry and his place in the annals of popular music. And musicians in the Red Hot Louisiana Band fondly recall the feeling of playing with this soulful master who had so much energy and who injected such pure feeling into his music. As former member Buckwheat Zydeco put it, "Clifton Chenier was the man who put this music on the map."

—Robert Kuhlken

FURTHER READING:

Broven, John. *South to Louisiana: The Music of the Cajun Bayous.* Gretna, Louisiana, Pelican Publishing, 1983.

Tisserand, Michael. *The Kingdom of Zydeco.* New York, Arcade Publishing, 1998.

Cher

See Sonny and Cher

Cherry Ames

Packed with wholesome values and cheerfulness, the Cherry Ames nursing mystery series was popular with girls in the mid-twentieth century. Cherry, a dark-haired, rosy-cheeked midwestern girl, was always perky and helpful, ready to lend a hand in a medical emergency and solve any mysteries that might spring up along the way. The books never claimed to have literary quality. Their creator, Helen Wells, admitted they were formulaic—not great literature, but great entertainment.

The series consisted of 27 books published by Grosset and Dunlap between 1943 and 1968, authored by Helen Wells and Julie Tatham. Aggressively marketed to girls, the books contained all sorts of consumer perks: the second book in the series was offered free with the first, and each book showed a banner on the last page advertising the next exciting adventure. The first 21 volumes were issued in colorful dust jackets showing Cherry in her uniform, proclaiming "It is every girl's ambition at one time or another to wear the crisp uniform of a nurse." (Indeed, this uniform was described over and over, along with Cherry's off-duty snappy outfits.) Early copies in the series had yellow spines, but the format was quickly changed to green spines, probably to avoid confusion with the ubiquitous Nancy Drew books. There was also a companion volume written by Wells in 1959, entitled *Cherry Ames' Book of First Aid and Home Nursing.*

In the early years, the novels were patriotic, pro-nursing tales in which Cherry called for other girls to join her and help win World War II. The later books were mysteries, with Cherry as a girl sleuth. Titles followed the format of *Cherry Ames, Student Nurse* and included *Cherry Ames, Cruise Nurse, Cherry Ames, Chief Nurse, Cherry Ames, Mountaineer Nurse,* among many others. Cherry's nursing duties brought her to such exotic locales as a boarding school, a department store, and even a dude ranch.

Wells (1910-1986), the creator of the series and author of most of the books, was no stranger to girls' series—she was also the author of the Vicki Barr flight attendant series and other books for girls. Tatham (1908—), wrote a few books in the middle of the series. Under the pseudonym Julie Campbell she also authored both the Trixie Belden and Ginny Gordon series.

The Cherry Ames series became internationally popular, with editions published in England, France, Italy, the Netherlands, and Japan. In England, books spawned a set of Cherry Ames Girls' Annuals. There was a Parker Brothers board game produced in 1959, "Cherry Ames' Nursing Game," in which players vie to be the first to complete nursing school.

By the 1970s, the Cherry Ames books were out of print and were being phased out of libraries. The character had a rebirth in the 1990s, however, when author and artist Mabel Maney created a series of wickedly funny gay parodies of the girl-sleuth series books, bringing out their (almost certainly unintentional) lesbian subtext. In her first book, *The Case of the Not-So-Nice Nurse,* the "gosh-golly" 1950s meet the "oh-so-queer" 1990s when lesbian detectives "Cherry Aimless" and "Nancy Clue" discover more than just the answer to the mystery.

—Jessy Randall

FURTHER READING:

Mason, Bobbie Ann. *The Girl Sleuth: A Feminist Guide.* New York, Feminist Press, 1975.

Parry, Sally E. "'You Are Needed, Desperately Needed': Cherry Ames in World War II." *Nancy Drew and Company: Culture, Gender, and Girls' Series.* Edited by Sherrie A. Inness. Bowling Green, Ohio, Popular Press, 1997.

Chessman, Caryl (1921-1960)

In 1948, a career criminal named Caryl Chessman was charged with being a "red light bandit" who raped and robbed couples in lovers' lanes near Los Angeles. Chessman was sentenced to death for kidnapping two of the victims. His 12-year effort to save himself from California's gas chamber intensified the debate over capital punishment. Chessman was successful in persuading various judges to postpone his execution. This gave him time to make legal arguments against his conviction and death sentence and to write *Cell 2455 Death Row,* an eloquent, bestselling book which purportedly described the author's life and criminal career.

The courts ultimately ruled against Chessman's legal claims. Many celebrities opposed his execution, including the Pope and Eleanor Roosevelt. In February 1960, Chessman was granted a stay of execution while the state legislature considered California Governor Edmund Brown's plea to abolish the death penalty. The Governor's effort, however, failed and Chessman was executed on May 2, 1960.

—Eric Longley

FURTHER READING:

Brown, Edmund G., and Dick Adler. *Public Justice, Private Mercy: A Governor's Education on Death Row.* New York, Weidenfeld and Nicolson, 1989.

Chessman, Caryl. *Cell 2455 Death Row.* New York, Prentice-Hall, 1954.

Kunstler, William M. *Beyond a Reasonable Doubt? The Original Trial of Caryl Chessman.* New York, William Morrow and Company, 1961.

Largo, Andrew O. *Caryl Whittier Chessman, 1921-1960: Essay and Critical Bibliography.* San Jose, California, Bibliographic Information Center for the Study of Political Science, 1971.

The Chicago Bears

Like their home city, the Chicago Bears are a legendary team of "broad shoulders" and boundless stamina. One of the original members of the National Football League (NFL), the Bears have captured the attention of football fans since the heyday of radio. An organization built on innovation and achievement both on and off the field, the Bears' remarkable victories earned them the nickname "Monsters of the Midway." Bears players from Red Grange to Walter Payton swell the ranks of the famous in football. By the 1990s the Bears had achieved more victories than any other team in the NFL, and have 26 members in the Pro Football Hall of Fame.

In 1920, A.E. Staley, owner of the Staley Starch Works in Decatur, Illinois, hired 25-year-old George Halas to organize a professional football team. It was a daunting task. Halas approached his former boss, Ralph Hay of the Canton Bulldogs, with the idea of forming a professional football league. On September 17, 1920, Halas met with 12 other team officials in Ralph Hay's Humpmobile dealership in Canton, Ohio, where they created the American Professional Football Association, the predecessor of the modern National Football League. Of the 13 teams in the original league, only the Bears and Cardinals remain in existence.

The Decatur Staleys—as the Bears were first called—played their first game on October 3, 1920 at Staley Field. The Decatur team was one of only a few to show a profit in the first year of operation. Due to a recession in 1921, Staley was forced to withdraw support for the team; but Halas assumed ownership and transferred the franchise to Chicago. The team selected Wrigley Field as its home. Halas compared the rough and tumble stature of his players to the baseball stars of the Chicago Cubs, and renamed the team the Chicago Bears in January 1922. The team colors, blue and orange, were derived from Halas's alma mater, the University of Illinois.

The first major signing for the team occurred in 1925, when University of Illinois star Red Grange was hired by Halas. Grange proved to be a strong gate attraction for the early NFL organization. Although he only played in several games due to injury, he nonetheless managed to draw a game crowd of 75,000 in Los Angeles. During the 1920s the team was a success on the field and at the gate, posting a winning season every year except one.

The Bears quickly established a reputation as a tough, brawling team capturing many hard-fought victories. New and exciting players typified the team over succeeding seasons. Bronko Nagurski, a tenacious runner requiring several players to take him down, joined the illustrious 1930 lineup. An opposing coach was rumored to have said the only way to stop Nagurshi was to shoot him before he went on the field. Nagurski's two-yard touchdown pass to Red Grange beat Portsmouth in the 1932 championship game, the first football game played indoors at Chicago Stadium. Sidney Luckman was recruited as the premiere T-formation quarterback in 1939. With Luckman at passer, the reinvigorated T-formation decimated the Washington Redskins in a 73-0 title game rout. The Bears became the "Monsters of the Midway," and Luckman the most famous Jewish sports legend. The fighting power of the Bears was strengthened by the addition of unstoppable George "One Play" McAfee at halfback. He could score running, passing, kicking, or receiving. Clyde "Bulldog" Turner was selected as center and linebacker to assist McAfee. Turner proved to be one of the fastest centers in NFL history.

Following up-and-down seasons during the 1950s, the Bears regained notoriety by capturing another NFL title in 1963. This was the first game broadcast on closed circuit television. The recruitment of running back Gale Sayers in 1965 revitalized the Bears' fighting spirit. Sayers was an immediate sensation, setting an NFL scoring record in his rookie year, and rushing records in subsequent years. Sportswriters honored Sayers as the greatest running back in pro football's first half century. Standing in the shadow of Gale Sayers was halfback Brian Piccolo. The two men were the first interracial roommates in the NFL. Piccolo seldom played until Sayers's knee injury in 1968. When Sayers was awarded the George Halas Award for pro football's most courageous player in 1970, he dedicated the award to Piccolo, who was dying of cancer. The bond between Piccolo and Sayers was the subject of the television movie, *Brian's Song,* as well as several books. The Bears were bolstered by the daunting presence of premiere middle linebacker Dick Butkus, who became the heart and soul of the crushing Bears defense. George Halas announced his retirement in 1968, after 40 seasons, with 324 wins, 15 loses, and 31 one ties. Halas remained influential in the operation of the Chicago Bears and the NFL until his death in 1983.

The Bears played their final season game at Wrigley Field in 1970, and then moved to Soldier Field. Successive coaches Abe Gibron, Jack Pardee, and Neil Armstrong produced mediocre seasons with the Bears during the 1970s. The one bright spot during this period was the recruitment of Walter Payton. Called "Sweetness" because of his gentle manner, Payton led the NFL in rushing for five successive years (1976-1980). After four coaching seasons Armstrong was replaced by former Bears tight end Mike Ditka. Under Ditka's command the Bears began winning again. In 1984, Walter Payton broke Jim Brown's career rushing record, and at the end of 1985 the team posted a 15-1 regular season mark, tying an NFL record. On January 26, 1986, in their first Super Bowl appearance, the Bears trounced New England 46-10, setting seven Super Bowl records, including the largest victory margin and most points scored.

The 1990s were a milestone decade for the NFL Chicago franchise: The team played its 1,000th game in 1993, and was the first team to accumulate 600 victories. Mike Ditka was replaced as head coach by Dave Wannstedt in 1993. Following the 1998 season Wannstedt's contract was terminated, and Jacksonville Jaguars defensive coordinator Dick Jauron was named head coach. For almost 80 years, the Chicago Bears have been one of the powerhouse teams in American football. Through all their ups and downs, they have remained true to the city that has been their home—as a tough, proud, all-American sports franchise, whose influence continues to be felt throughout popular culture.

—Michael A. Lutes

FURTHER READING:

Chicago Bears 1998 Media Guide. Chicago, Chicago Bears Public Relations Department, 1998.

Mausser, Wayne. *Chicago Bears, Facts and Trivia.* Wautoma, Wisconsin, E. B. Houchin, 1995.

Roberts, Howard. *The Chicago Bears.* New York, G.P. Putnam's Sons. 1947.

Vass, George. *George Halas and the Chicago Bears.* Chicago, Regnery Press. 1971.

Whittingham, Richard. *Bears: A Seventy-Five-Year Celebration.* Rochester, Minnesota, Taylor Publishing, 1994.

————. *The Bears in Their Own Words: Chicago Bear Greats Talk About the Team, the Game, the Coaches, and the Times of Their Lives.* Chicago, Contemporary Books. 1991.

————. *The Chicago Bears: An Illustrated History.* Chicago, Rand McNally. 1979.

The Chicago Bulls

One of professional basketball's dynasty teams, the Chicago Bulls were led by perhaps the best basketball player ever, Michael Jordan, from 1984-1993 and 1995-1998. When they began their first season in 1966, the Bulls were a second-rate team, and continued to be so, even posting a dismal 27-win record in 1984. That finish gave them the opportunity to draft the North Carolina shooting guard, and from then on, with his presence, the Bulls never failed to make the playoffs. Jordan led the Chicago team to six National Basketball Association championships, from 1991 to 1993 and again from 1996 to 1998. In the process, the team's bull emblem and distinctive red and black colors became as recognizable on the streets of Peking as they were in the gang neighborhoods of Chicago's South Side. Jordan became a worldwide celebrity, better known than President Bill

Clinton. When he retired from basketball on January 13, 1999, his Chicago news conference was broadcast and netcast live worldwide. Fellow players Dennis Rodman and Scottie Pippen and team coach Phil Jackson never became as well known as the legendary Jordan, but were nonetheless important contributors during the Bulls' championship years.

—Richard Digby-Junger

FURTHER READING:

Bjarkman, Peter C. *The Encyclopedia of Pro Basketball Team Histories.* New York, Carroll & Graf Publishers, 1994, 98-114.

Broussard, Mark, and Craig Carter, editors. *The Sporting News Official NBA Guide, 1996-97 Edition.* St. Louis, The Sporting News Publishing Co., 1996.

Sachare, Alex, editor. *The Official NBA Basketball Encyclopedia.* New York, Villard Books, 1994.

The Chicago Cubs

Secure in their roles as major-league baseball's "lovable losers," the National League's Chicago Cubs have not appeared in a World Series since 1945 and have not won a World Series title since 1907. Despite a legacy of superstar players including 1990s home-run hero Sammy Sosa, 1980s MVP Ryne Sandberg, and the legendary Ernie "Mr. Cub" Banks engaged in the most dramatic home-run race in the history of baseball. He and St. Louis Cardinals slugger Mark McGwire battled each other shot for shot throughout the season, with the Cardinal first-baseman finally slamming 70 home runs to Sosa's 66. Both players shattered Roger Maris's long-standing single-season home run record of 61 while helping to revive the popularity of baseball, whose status had suffered following the 1994 strike.

—Jason McEntee

FURTHER READING:

Bjarkman, Peter C., editor. *Encyclopedia of Major League Baseball Team Histories.* Westport, Connecticut, Meckler, 1991.

The Chicago Cubs Media Guide. Chicago, Chicago National League Ball Club, 1991.

Golenbock, Peter. *Wrigleyville: A Magical History Tour of the Chicago Cubs.* New York, St. Martin's Press, 1996.

"The Official Web Site of the Chicago Cubs." http:www.cubs.com. May 1999.

Chicago Jazz

Although New Orleans is the acknowledged birthplace of jazz, Chicago is regarded as the first place outside of the South where jazz

Chicago Bulls' captain Michael Jordan holding his series MVP trophy and head coach Phil Jackson holding the Bulls' sixth NBA Championship Trophy.

was heard, and New Orleans-style jazz was first recorded in Chicago. Popular in the 1920s, ''Chicago Jazz'' refers to a white style of music, closely related to New Orleans Jazz, in which soloists were more prominent than the ensemble. The music is also tighter or less rhythmically realized than the New Orleans style.

When World War I increased employment opportunities for African Americans outside the South, Chicago became a center of the black community. Jazz moved to Chicago to fill the need for familiar entertainment. From the black neighborhoods, jazz moved into the white areas of Chicago, where young Chicago kids were fascinated with the new sounds.

The Original Dixieland Jazz Band, a group of white New Orleans musicians who were the first band to record jazz, included Chicago musicians for their famous appearance at the Friar's Inn. That appearance and their 1917 jazz recording increased its visibility and attracted a large following for the new music. The New Orleans Rhythm Kings, an influence on the great Bix Beiderbecke, followed in 1922 but were no match for King Oliver's Creole Jazz Band, which Oliver had formed in New Orleans and taken to Chicago in 1918, where Louis Armstrong joined in 1922. The Creole Jazz Band recorded the most significant examples of New Orleans-style jazz.

King Oliver's band brought African-American jazz to Chicago and soon attracted a following comparable to that of rock stars today.

Armstrong often played at more than one club in a night. Other New Orleans greats who came to Chicago in the 1920s included Sidney Bechet, both Johnny and Baby Dodds, Jimmy Noone, and Freddie Keppard.

Banjoist Eddie Condon (1905-1973) is considered the leader of the Chicago School, carrying on battles against the boppers, whom he considered to have spoiled jazz. His musicians included cornetist Jimmy McPartland (1907-1991), Bud Freeman, Frankie Teschemacher, and Red McKenzie. This was the core of the Austin High Gang, the core of the Chicago Jazz movement. The first recording of the Chicago style was on December 10, 1927. But Condon says that they were just a bunch of guys who happened to be from Chicago. Condon pioneered multi-racial recordings, getting many of the New Orleans musicians together with white musicians.

Jimmy McPartland (1907-1991), the other link in the Chicago Jazz School, was the center of the Austin High Gang. He learned the solos note for note of the New Orleans Rhythm Kings and then copied Bix Beiderbecke's work. He even replaced Bix in the Wolverines. McPartland carried the message of classic Dixieland cornet around the world and remained associated with the Chicago Jazz style until his death.

—Frank A. Salamone

FURTHER READING:

Ian Carr, et al. *Jazz: The Rough Guide*. London, Rough Guides, 1995.

The Chicago Seven

It was violent clashes between anti-war protesters and police during the Chicago Democratic Convention of 1968 that created the Chicago Seven's place in political and cultural history. The seven political radicals were indicted for the so-called ''Rap Brown'' law, which made it illegal to cross state lines and make speeches with the intent to ''incite, organize, promote, and encourage'' riots, conspiracy, and the like. There were originally eight defendants: David Dellinger, a pacifist and chairman of the National Mobilization against the Vietnam War; Tom Hayden and Rennie Davis, leaders of the Students for a Democratic Society (SDS); Abbie Hoffman and Jerry Rubin, leaders of the Youth International Party—or ''Yippies;'' John Froines and Lee Weiner, protest organizers; and Bobby Seale, co-founder of the Black Panther Party. The riots and subsequent trial triggered more massive and violent anti-war demonstrations around the country. The conflict in Chicago, however, was not simply about America's involvement in Vietnam. The conflict was also about the political system, and to those millions who watched the confrontations between police and demonstrators on television, it marked a crisis in the nation's social and cultural order.

The demonstrators, many of whom had been involved with civil rights battles in the South, saw their protests at the convention as an opportunity to draw media attention to their cause. Following the murders of Martin Luther King Jr. and Robert Kennedy, many protesters were anxious to become more confrontational and militant with political and police forces. The Yippies, led by Hoffman and Rubin, looked to harness the energy of America's rebellious youth culture, with its rock music and drugs, to bring about social and political change. The Yippies were formed solely for the purpose of confronting those involved with the Democratic Convention. They believed that the mass media and music could lead young people to resist injustices in the political system. Hoffman and Rubin, the most flamboyant and disruptive participants in the court trial—after Seale was removed—did not believe that the ''New Left'' would be able to bring about change through rational discourse with existing powers. Hence, they led a movement which relied upon guerrilla theater, rock music, drug experiences, and the mass media to broadcast their agenda of social revolution to a generation of alienated young people brought up on television and advertising. Influencing policies or candidates was not the aim behind the radicalism of the Chicago Seven. Rather, they worked to reveal the ugliness of a country full of poverty, racism, violence, and war through a confrontation with the armed State. The fact that their actions took place in America's second largest city, during a nationally televised political convention, only intensified their message of resistance and rejection.

Chicago mayor Richard Daley and his police force characterized the demonstrations as attacks upon their city and the law. They viewed the Chicago Seven and the national media as outside agitators who trampled on their turf. The Walker Report, however, which was later commissioned to investigate the events of the convention week, concluded that the police were responsible for much of the violence during the confrontations. Perhaps the most memorable statement about the events surrounding the rebellion were uttered by Mayor Daley at a press conference during the convention: ''The policeman isn't there to create disorder. The policeman is there to preserve disorder.''

Members of the Chicago Seven: (back row from left) Lee Weiner, Bob Lamb, Tom Hayden, (front row from left) Rennie Davis, Jerry Rubin, and Abbie Hoffman.

The trial of the eight defendants began in September of 1969 and lasted for five months. Judge Julius Hoffman inflexibility and obvious bias against the defendants provoked righteous anger, revolutionary posturing, guerrilla theater, and other forms of defiant behavior from the defendants. Bobby Seale's defiant manner of conducting his own defense—his attorney was in California recuperating from surgery—resulted in his spending three days in court bound and gagged. Judge Hoffman then declared his case a mistrial and sentenced him to four years in prison for contempt of court. Hence, the Chicago Eight became the Chicago Seven. William Kunstler and Leonard Weinglass were the defense attorneys. Judge Hoffman and prosecutor Thomas Foran constantly clashed with the defendants who used the court as a setting to continue to express their disdain for the political and judicial system. In February, all of the defendants were acquitted of conspiracy but five were found guilty of crossing state lines to riot. Froines and Weiner were found innocent of teaching and demonstrating the use of incendiary devices. An appeals court overturned the convictions in 1972, citing procedural errors and Judge Hoffman's obvious hostility to the defendants.

—Ken Kempcke

FURTHER READING:

Epstein, Jason. *The Great Conspiracy Trial: An Essay on Law, Liberty, and the Constitution.* New York, Vintage Books, 1971.

Farber, David. *Chicago '68.* Chicago, University of Chicago Press, 1988.

Hayden, Tom. *Trial.* New York, Holt, Rinehart, and Winston, 1970.

Schultz, John. *The Chicago Conspiracy Trial.* New York, Da Capo, 1993.

Child, Julia (1912—)

Julia Child made cooking entertainment. A well-bred, tall, ebullient woman who came to cooking in the middle of her life, Julia Child appeared on television for the first time in the early 1960s and inaugurated a new culinary age in America. Blessed with an ever-present sense of humor, a magnetic presence in front of the camera, and the ability to convey information in a thoroughly engaging manner, Julia Child spirited Americans away from their frozen foods and TV dinners and back into the kitchen, by showing them that cooking could be fun.

For someone who would become one of the most recognizable and influential women in the world, it took Julia Child a long time to find her true calling. She spent the first 40 years of her life in search of her passion—cooking—and when she found it, she was unrelenting in promoting it. But like so many privileged women of her generation, Julia Child was not brought up to have a career. Born on August 15, 1912 into the conservative affluence of Pasadena, California, Julia McWilliams was the daughter of an aristocratic, fun-loving mother and a well-off, community-minded businessman father. Raised in a close family, who provided for her every need, Julia was a tree-climbing tomboy who roamed the streets of Pasadena with her passel of friends. Her childhood was full of mischievous fun, and food formed only the most basic part of her youth. Her family enjoyed hearty, traditional fare supplemented by fresh fruits and vegetables from nearby farms.

Julia Child

By her early teenage years, Julia was head and shoulders taller than her friends, on her way to becoming a gigantic, rail thin 6 feet 2 inches. Lithe and limber, the athletic teenager enjoyed tennis, skiing, and other sports, and was the most active girl in her junior high school. When she graduated from ninth grade, however, her parents decided it was time for Julia to get a solid education, and so they sent her to boarding school in Northern California. At the Katherine Branson School for Girls, Julia quickly became a school leader, known, as her biographer Noël Riley Fitch has written, for "her commanding physical presence, her verbal openness, and her physical pranks and adventure." As "head girl," Julia stood out among her classmates socially, if not intellectually. She was an average student, whose interests chiefly lay in dramatics and sports and whose greatest culinary delight was jelly doughnuts. But her education was solid enough to earn her, as the daughter of an alumna, a place at prestigious Smith College in Massachusetts.

In her four years at Smith, Julia continued in much the same vein as in high school. She was noted for her leadership abilities, her sense of adventure, and, as always, her height. At 6 feet 2 inches, she was once again the tallest girl in her class. At Smith, she received a solid education. But, as Julia would later remark, "Middle-class women did not have careers. You were to marry and have children and be a nice mother. You didn't go out and do anything." And so after graduation, Julia returned home to Pasadena. After a year, however, she grew restless and returned to the East Coast, hoping to find a job in New York City. Sharing an apartment with friends from Smith and supported mostly by her parents, Julia found a job at Sloane's, a prestigious home-furnishing company. She worked for the advertising manager, learning how to write press releases, work with photographers, and handle public relations. She loved having something to do and reveled in the job. Having always been interested in writing, Julia also began submitting short pieces to magazines such as the *Saturday Review of Literature.* Her life now had some larger purpose.

But Julia's stay in New York would only last a few years. Unhappy over the breakup of a relationship and worried about her mother's health, Julia returned home to Pasadena, where her mother died two months later. As the oldest child, Julia decided to stay in California to take care of her father and soon found work writing for a new fashion magazine and later heading up the advertising department for the West Coast branch of Sloane's. But by the early 1940s, with America at war, Julia had grown impatient with her leisurely California life. A staunch Rooseveltian Democrat, Julia wanted to be a part of the war effort and so applied to the WAVES and the WACS. But when her height disqualified her from active service, Julia moved to Washington, D.C., where she began work in the Office of Strategic Services, the American branch of secret intelligence.

With her gift for leadership, Julia quickly rose in the ranks, working six days a week, supervising an office of 40 people. She still dreamed of active service, and when the opportunity arose to serve overseas, she jumped at the chance. In early 1944, 31-year-old Julia McWilliams sailed for India. In April, she arrived in Ceylon, where she went to work at the OSS headquarters for South East Asia. Although she considered the work drudgery, she loved being in a foreign country, as well as the urgency of the work at hand. She met many interesting people, men and women, not the least of whom was a man ten years older than she, an urbane officer named Paul Child.

Stationed in Ceylon and later in China, Julia and Paul became good friends long before they fell in love. She was fascinated by his background—a multilingual artist, he had lived in Paris during the 1920s and was a true man of the world. One of his great passions was food, and he gradually introduced Julia to the joys of cuisine. In China, the two friends would eat out at local restaurants every chance they could. She would later write: "The Chinese food was wonderful and we ate out as often as we could. That is when I became interested in food. There were sophisticated people there who knew a lot about food . . . I just loved Chinese food."

Julia recognized it first—she had fallen in love. It took Paul a little longer to realize that he was head-over-heels for this tall, energetic, enthusiastic Californian. In fact, after the war, the two went their separate ways, only coming together later in California. In their time apart, Julia had begun perfunctory cooking lessons, hoping to show off her newfound skills to Paul. By the time they decided to drive across country together, they knew they would be married. Julia and Paul Child set up house together in Washington, D.C., awaiting Paul's next assignment. When they were sent to Paris, both were ecstatic.

Julia's first meal upon landing in France was an epiphany. She later reflected, "The whole experience was an opening up of the soul and spirit for me . . . I was hooked, and for life, as it turned out." While settling in Paris, Julia and Paul ate out at every meal, and Julia was overwhelmed by the many flavors, textures, and sheer scope of French cuisine. She loved everything about it and wanted to learn more. In late October 1949, Julia took advantage of the GI Bill and enrolled at the Cordon Bleu cooking school. It was the first step in a long journey that would transform both her life and American culinary culture.

The only woman in her class, Julia threw herself into cooking, spending every morning and afternoon at the school and coming home to cook lunch and dinner for Paul. On the side, she supplemented her schooling with private lessons from well-known French chefs, and she attended the Cercle des Gourmettes, a club for French women dedicated to gastronomy. There she met Simone Beck and Louisette Bertholle. The three soon became fast friends and, after Julia graduated from Cordon Bleu, they decided to form their own cooking school geared at teaching Americans in Paris. L'Ecole des Trois Gourmands was formed in 1952 and was an instant success. Out of this triumvirate came the idea for a cookbook that would introduce Americans to French cuisine.

With the help of an American friend, the idea was sold to Houghton Mifflin. The most popular American cookbooks, *The Joy of Cooking* and *Fanny Farmer,* were old classics geared toward traditional American fare. Julia envisioned a cookbook that would capture the American feel of *The Joy of Cooking* in teaching Americans about French cuisine. For the next ten years, Julia and her companions labored tirelessly over their cookbook. Even when Paul and Julia were transferred, first to Marseille then to Bonn, Washington, and Oslo, the Trois Gourmands remained hard at work. Julia was meticulous and scientific, testing and re-testing each recipe, comparing French food products to American, keeping up with American food trends, and polishing her writing and presentation style. Less than a year from the finish, however, Houghton Mifflin suddenly pulled out and it seemed that the project would never come to fruition.

Then Knopf stepped in and in 1961, shortly after Julia and Paul returned to the United States for good, *Mastering the Art of French Cooking* was released. An immediate success, the cookbook, with its superb quality, clear and precise recipes, and unique pedagogical approach to cooking, became the standard against which all other cookbooks would come to be judged. At 49 years old, Julia Child was hailed as a great new American culinary voice. In a country where most people's meals consisted of canned items, frozen foods, and TV dinners, the food community hailed her classical training. As Karen Lehrman wrote in "What Julia Started," "In the 1950s, America was a meat-and-potatoes kind of country. Women did all of the cooking and got their recipes from ladies' magazine articles with titles like 'The 10-Minute Meal and How to Make It.' Meatloaf, liver and onions, corned beef hash—all were considered hearty and therefore healthy and therefore delicious. For many women, preparing meals was not a joy but a requirement." Julia Child would change all that.

Julia and Paul settled in Cambridge, Massachusetts, a decision that would ultimately make Julia Child a household name. As the home of many of the country's finest institutions of higher learning, Cambridge boasted the best-funded educational television station, WGBH. Early in 1962, WGBH approached Julia about putting together a cooking show. Filmed in black and white in rudimentary surroundings, the show was a success from the very start. Julia Child was a natural for television. Although each show was carefully planned and the meals meticulously prepared, on-air Julia's easy going manner, sense of humor, and joie de vivre shone through, making her an instant hit.

Within a year, Julia Child's *The French Chef* was carried on public television stations around the country and Julia Child was a household name with a huge following. As Karen Lehrman describes, "Julia may or may not have been a natural cook, but she certainly was a natural teacher and comedian. Part of the entertainment came from her voice alone, which can start a sentence on a bass note and end of falsetto, and elongate in different keys several seemingly random words in between. But she also had an exceptional presence, a keen sense of timing and drama, and a superb instinct for what's funny. Most important, she completely lacked pretension: She played herself. She made noises (errgh, oomph, pong), called things weird or silly, clashed pot lids like cymbals, knocked things over, and in general made quite a mess. 'When, at the end of the program, she at last brings the finished dish to the table,' Lewis Lapham wrote in 1964, 'she does so with an air of delighted surprise, pleased to announce that once again the forces of art and reason have triumphed over primeval chaos.'''

For the next 30 years, Julia Child would appear on television, but because she viewed herself as a teacher, only on public television. Supported by Paul every step of the way, Julia would transform cooking from a housewife's drudgery to a joyous event for both men and women. In doing so, she changed the culinary face of America. She became a universally recognizable and much loved pop culture icon. Her shows became the object of kindhearted spoof and satire—the best of which was done by Dan Ackroyd on *Saturday Night Live*—and her image appeared in cartoons. But mostly it was Julia herself who continued to attract devoted viewers of both sexes, all ages, and many classes. As Noël Riley Fitch wrote, ''The great American fear of being outré and gauche was diminished by this patrician lady who was not afraid of mistakes and did not talk down to her audience.'' Julia-isms were repeated with glee around the country, such as the time she flipped an omelet all over the stove and said, ''Well, that didn't go very well,'' and then proceeded to scrape up the eggs and put them back in the pan, remarking, ''But you can always pick it up if you're alone. Who's going to see?'' Her ability to improvise and to have fun in the kitchen made her someone with whom the average American could identify. As Julia herself said, ''People look at me and say, 'Well, if she can do it, I can do it.'''

As America got turned on to food, be it quiche in the 1970s, nouvelle cuisine in the 1980s, or organic food in the 1990s, Julia stayed on top of every trend, producing many more exceptional cookbooks. The Grande Dame of American cuisine, Julia Child remains the last word on food in America. Founder of the American Institute of Wine and Food, Julia Child continues to bring together American chefs and vintners in an effort to promote continued awareness of culinary issues and ideas both within the profession—which, thanks to Julia, is now among the fastest growing in America—and among the public. Popular women chefs, such as Too Hot Tamales, Susan Feniger and Mary Sue Miliken, abound on television, thanks to Julia who, though she did not think of herself as a feminist, certainly liberated many women through her independence and passionate commitment to her career. Karen Lehrman has written, ''Julia Child made America mad for food and changed its notions of class and gender.'' A uniquely American icon, Julia Child not only transformed the culinary landscape of this country, but she became a role model for men and women of all ages and classes.

—Victoria Price

FURTHER READING:

Child, Julia. *Mastering the Art of French Cooking.* New York, Alfred A. Knopf, 1961.

Fitch, Noël Riley. *Appetite for Life: The Biography of Julia Child.* New York, Doubleday, 1997.

Lehrman, Karen. ''What Julia Started.'' *U.S. News and World Report.* Vol. 123, No. 11, September 22, 1997, 56-65.

Reardon, Joan. *M.F.K Fisher, Julia Child, and Alice Waters: Celebrating the Pleasures of the Table.* New York, Harmony Books, 1994.

Villas, James. ''The Queen of Cuisine.'' *Town and Country.* Vol. 148, No. 5175, December 1994, 188-193.

Child Stars

In Hollywood, it has been said that beauty is more important than talent, but youth is most important of all. The image of America conveyed by the motion picture industry is one of beautiful, young people in the prime of life. The most youthful of all are the children—fresh-faced innocents in the bloom of youth transformed into Hollywood stars who represent the dreams of a nation. Certainly this was the case during the Depression, when child stars such as Shirley Temple, Freddie Bartholomew, and Deanna Durbin were the motion picture industry's top box office draws, inspiring a global mania for child actors. In what has come to be known as the Child Star Era, these juvenile audience favorites often single-handedly supported their studios, becoming more famous than their adult counterparts. When the Golden Age of Hollywood came to an end after World War II, so did the Child Star Era. But the appeal of child stars remains strong in

Shirley Temple and Bill ''Bojangles'' Robinson.

film, television, and music. Popular culture will ever worship at the Fountain of Youth.

From the early days of vaudeville in the nineteenth century, child actors have held their own against adult stars. Adored by fans, many became household names across America. In the first decade of the twentieth century, during the infancy of motion pictures, film directors hoped to lure the top tykes from the stage onto the screen, but most stage parents refused, feeling that movies were beneath them and their talented children. Everything changed when a curly haired, sweet-faced sixteen-year-old, who had been a big Broadway star as Baby Gladys, fell on hard times and reluctantly auditioned for movie director D. W. Griffith. Griffith hired the former Baby Gladys on the spot, renamed her Mary Pickford, and made her into "America's Sweetheart." She became America's first movie star. As noted in *Baseline*'s *Encyclopedia of Film,* Mary Pickford was, "if popularity were all, the greatest star there has ever been. . . . Little Mary became the industry's chief focus and biggest asset, as well as the draw of draws—bigger, even, than Chaplin."

The success of Mary Pickford in many ways paralleled the ascendancy of movies themselves. As audiences embraced the young star, they embraced the medium, and movies grew into a national obsession. Along with Pickford, Charlie Chaplin, himself a former child star in British vaudeville, became one of the motion picture industry's success stories. A huge star by the late teens, Chaplin made the films that America wanted to see. When he discovered a young boy performing in vaudeville who reminded him of himself as a child, Chaplin created a film for them both to star in. Little Jackie Coogan's endearing performance in *The Kid* made the six-year-old a household name and launched Hollywood's Child Star Era.

During the 1920s, studios churned out silent films at an amazing rate. Westerns, action pictures, murder mysteries, and romances all drew audiences to the theatres. After *The Kid,* so did movies starring children, including the immensely popular Our Gang series. Movie studios sent out continual casting calls in search of clever and cute kids, and parents from all over America began to flock to Hollywood in search of fame and fortune for their offspring. When Jackie Coogan was awarded a million-dollar movie contract in 1923, the race to find the next child star was on. As Diana Serra Carey, a former child star who became very famous during the 1920s and 1930s as Baby Peggy, has written: "Although the child star business was a very new line to be in, it opened up a wide choice of jobs for many otherwise unskilled workers, and it grew with remarkable speed. Speed was, in fact, the name of the game. Parents, agents, producers, business managers, and a host of lesser hangers-on were all engaged in a desperate race to keep ahead of their meal ticket's inexorable march from cuddly infant to graceless adolescent." Soon Hollywood was filled with a plethora of people pushing their youthful products.

In 1929, when the stock market crashed and America fell into the Great Depression, the movie industry faced a crisis: in a time of severe economic hardship, would Americans part with their hard-earned money to go to the movies? But sound had just come in, and America was hooked. For a nickel, audiences could escape the harsh reality of their daily lives and enter a Hollywood fantasy. Movies boomed during the Depression, and child stars were a big part of that boom.

By the early 1930s, children had come to mean big business for Hollywood. The precocious and versatile Mickey Rooney had been a consistent money earner since the mid-1920s, as were new stars such as *The Champ*'s Jackie Cooper. But nothing would prepare Hollywood, or the world, for the success of a curly haired six-year-old sensation named Shirley Temple.

The daughter of a Santa Monica banker and his star-struck wife, Shirley Temple was a born performer. At three, the blond-haired, dimpled cherub was dancing and singing in two-reelers. By six, when she starred in *Stand Up and Cheer,* she had become a bona fide movie star. *Baseline*'s *Encyclopedia of Film* notes: "Her bouncing blond curls, effervescence and impeccable charm were the basis for a Depression-era phenomenon. Portraying a doll-like model daughter, she helped ease the pain of audiences the world over." In 1934, she received a special Academy Award. A year later, she was earning one hundred thousand dollars a year. For most of the 1930s, Shirley Temple was the number one box office star. Twentieth-Century Fox earned six million dollars a year on her pictures alone.

During the height of the Child Star Era, the major studios all boasted stables of child actors and schoolrooms in which to teach them. Among the top stars of the decade were the British Freddie Bartholomew, number two to Shirley Temple for many years; Deanna Durbin, the singing star who single-handedly kept Universal Studios afloat; and the incredibly gifted Judy Garland. But for every juvenile star, there were hundreds of children playing supporting and extra roles, hoping to become the next Shirley Temple.

As America emerged from the Depression and faced another World War, the child stars of the 1930s faced adolescence. Shirley Temple, Freddie Bartholomew, and Jackie Cooper had become teenagers, and Hollywood didn't seem to know what to do with them. Audiences were not interested in watching their idols grow up on screen, and most child stars were not re-signed by their studios. Shirley Temple was literally thrown off the lot that she had grown up on. But there were always new kids to take the place of the old, and in the 1940s, Hollywood's top stars included Roddy McDowall, Margaret O'Brien, Natalie Wood, and Elizabeth Taylor. As their predecessors had done, these child stars buoyed American audiences through difficult times. And again, when their own difficult times came with adolescence, American audiences abandoned them. Fortunately, for many of the child stars of the 1940s, times were changing, and so was Hollywood. As the studio system and Child Star Era began to crumble in the late 1940s, these youthful actors and actresses found work in independent films and in television.

By the early 1950s, audiences were calling for a different kind of film, and Hollywood was complying. Television became the new breeding ground for child stars, as youthful actors were called upon to appear in such popular sitcoms as *Leave It to Beaver* in the 1950s, *My Three Sons* in the 1960s, *The Brady Bunch* in the 1970s, *Diff'rent Strokes* in the 1980s, and *Home Improvement* in the 1990s. Although TV audiences were interested in watching the children on their favorite shows grow up on the air, making the transition from child to teenager more easily accomplished, because the life of a series was generally short, youthful TV stars faced the same trouble as their child movie star predecessors once the show went off the air. They found it difficult to be taken seriously as adult actors. They also found it difficult to adjust to a life out of the limelight. As Jackie Cooper once said: "One thing I was never prepared for was to be lonely and frightened in my twenties."

The music industry, too, has always had its fair share of child prodigies. From Mozart to Michael Jackson, audiences have always been drawn to youthful genius. But while some young stars such as Little Stevie Wonder managed to make the transition to adult stardom, there are equally as many children who have not made it. And when the music industry began creating child acts to promote, it soon found itself facing the same problems as had movies and television. Would audiences who found child singers cute still buy their records when they were less-than-talented adults? In too many cases, the answer was no.

When little Ronnie Howard of *The Andy Griffith Show* was cast as a teenager on *Happy Days,* it was a big step for a child star. When he became a successful movie director, he was lauded as having dodged the stigma of child stardom. Others have followed in his footsteps, most notably Jodie Foster, a two-time Academy Award winner who is one of Hollywood's most respected actresses and directors. And, of course, Shirley Temple went on to have a distinguished political career, serving as a United States ambassador. But for every Ron Howard, Jodie Foster, Roddy McDowall, or Shirley Temple, there are hundreds of former child stars who have had to face falling out of the spotlight. For all the former child stars who have managed to create for themselves a normal adult life, there are far too many who have fallen into a life of dysfunction or drug use. For others, such as Rusty Hamer, a child star for nine years on *Make Room for Daddy,* or Trent Lehman, who played Butch on *Nanny and the Professor,* the transition from child star to adulthood ended in suicide.

In 1938, twenty-four-year-old Jackie Coogan went to court to sue his mother for his childhood earnings, which were between two and four million dollars. Married to a rising young starlet named Betty Grable, Coogan was broke and sought to get what was legally his. By the end of the trial, his millions were found to be almost all gone, and the strain of the trial destroyed his marriage. But out of Coogan's tragedy came the Coogan Act, a bill which forced the parents of child actors to put aside at least half of their earnings. That still hasn't prevented child stars such as Gary Coleman from having to go to court to fight for their hard-earned millions, however.

During the 1980s and 1990s, the motion picture industry has witnessed a resurgence of interest in child stars. River Phoenix and Ethan Hawke, both teenage actors, managed to make the difficult transition to adult roles. But Phoenix, although a seemingly mature young man praised for his formidable talents, found the pressures of a Hollywood lifestyle too much and died of an accidental drug overdose in 1993. In the early 1990s, Macaulay Culkin was perhaps the biggest child star since Shirley Temple. But when audiences lost interest in the teenager, he stopped working altogether. Soon his parents were engaged in a battle over custody and money, while the tabloids ran articles about Culkin's troubled life.

Despite the object lessons drawn from the lives of so many child stars, audiences will continue to pay to see juvenile performers even as the television, movie, and music industries will continue to promote them. Child stars represent the duel-edged sword that is American popular culture. Epitomizing the youthful glamour by which Americans are taught to be seduced, children have entranced audiences throughout the twentieth century. But on the other side of glamour and fame are the bitter emptiness of rejection and the harsh reality of life out of the spotlight. Perhaps former child star Paul Petersen said it best: "Fame is a dangerous drug and should be kept out of the reach of children—and their parents as well."

—Victoria Price

FURTHER READING:

Cary, Diana Serra. *Hollywood's Children: An Inside Account of the Child Star Era.* Dallas, Southern Methodist University, 1997.

Monaco, James, and the editors of *Baseline. The Encyclopedia of Film.* New York, Perigee, 1991.

Moore, Dick. *Twinkle, Twinkle Little Star: And Don't Have Sex or Take the Car.* New York, Harper and Row, 1984.

Zierold, Norman J. *The Child Stars.* New York, Coward-McCann, 1965.

The China Syndrome

Possibly more than any other film, *The China Syndrome*'s popularity benefited from a chance occurrence. *The China Syndrome* showed many Americans their worst vision of technology gone wrong, but it proved entirely too close to reality when its release coincided with a near meltdown at Three Mile Island, Pennsylvania. In the film, Jane Fonda and Michael Douglas play the television news team who, while researching the newly perfected nuclear technology, capture on film an accident resulting in a near meltdown of the power plant. Fonda and Douglas's characters find themselves trapped between the public's right to know and the industry's desire to bury the incident. The nuclear accident depicted by the film became the platform for "NIMBY" culture, in which expectations of comfort and a high standard of safety compelled middle-class Americans to proclaim "Not in my backyard!" Together, these incidents—one fictional and another all too real—aroused enough concern among Americans to prohibit nuclear energy from ever becoming a considerable source of power for the nation.

—Brian Black

Chinatown

Roman Polanski directed this 1974 classic film portraying the mystery and intrigue of Raymond Chandler's fascinating novel. Jack Nicholson played Jake Gittes, a private detective trapped in the odd Asian-immigrant culture of the desert West. Hired to investigate the murder of the chief engineer for the Los Angeles Power and Water Authority in 1930s California, Gittes finds himself pulled into the unique political and economic power structure of the arid region: water politics with all its deceits and double dealings dominates planning and development.

The film acquired a cult following because of its dark, intriguing story—seemingly based in another world and era—and the enduring popularity of Jack Nicholson. *Chinatown*'s film noir setting places it in a long line of fine films deriving from the 1940s mysteries of Alfred Hitchcock. The defining characteristic of such films is uncertainty—of character and plot. Gittes repeatedly appears as the trapped character searching in vain for truth; indeed, the viewer searches with him. In the end, the evil is nearly always exposed. However, typical to film noir, *Chinatown*'s conclusion leaves the viewer strangely unsure if truth actually has emerged victorious.

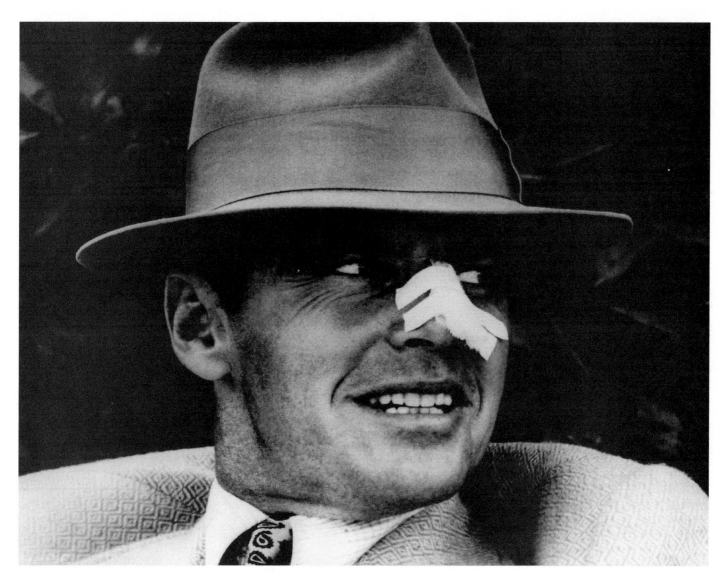

Jack Nicholson in a scene from the film *Chinatown*.

In 1990, Nicholson starred in and directed *Chinatown*'s sequel, *The Two Jakes,* set in 1948 California. Oil has replaced water as the power source for regional wealth, creating a fine backdrop for another dark mystery based on adultery and intrigue.

—Brian Black

The Chipmunks

The Chipmunks—Alvin, Simon, and Theodore—were the only cartoon rodents to sell millions of records and star in their own television series. The voices of all three chipmunks, as well as the part of David Seville, were performed by actor/musician Ross Bagdasarian (1919-1972). As Seville, Bagdasarian had enjoyed a #1 hit with ''Witch Doctor'' in early 1958; later that year he released ''The Chipmunk Song'' (''Christmas Don't Be Late'') in time for the

Christmas season, and sold over four million singles in two months. The Chipmunks, with their high warbling harmonies, churned out a half dozen records in the late 1950s and early 1960s. All of Bagdasarian's records were on the Liberty label, and the chipmunks were named for three of Liberty's production executives.

The Chipmunks' popularity led to a primetime cartoon series (*The Alvin Show*) on CBS television during the 1961-62 season. In 1983, Ross Bagdasarian, Jr., revived the act with a second successful cartoon series, *Alvin and the Chipmunks,* which aired on NBC from 1983 to 1990, and a new album, *Chipmunk Punk.*

—David Lonergan

FURTHER READING:

Brooks, Tim, and Earle Marsh. *The Complete Directory to Prime Time Network TV Shows.* 5th edition. New York, Ballantine Books, 1992.

''Cartoon-O-Rama Presents: The Alvin Show.'' http://members.aol.com/PaulEC1/alvin.html. February 1999.

Whitburn, Joel. *The Billboard Book of Top 40 Hits.* 6th edition. New York, Billboard Books, 1996.

Chong, Tommy

See Cheech and Chong

Choose-Your-Own-Ending Books

Thanks to the interactive capabilities of the computer, traditional styles of linear narrative in storytelling can be altered by means of hypertext links that allow readers the ability to alter the direction of a story by making certain decisions at various points, in effect choosing their own endings. This interactive style was presaged in the 1970s when several children's publishers began offering books that invited readers to custom-design the flow of a story by offering a choice of different pages to which they could turn. Strictly speaking, "Choose-Your-Own-Ending Books" refer to several series of children's books published by Bantam Books since 1979. Originated by author Edward Packard, Bantam's "Choose-Your-Own-Adventure" series numbered about 200 titles in the first 20 years of publication, with spinoffs such as "Choose Your Own Star Wars Adventure" and "Choose Your Own Nightmare."

The "Choose Your Own Adventure" series has proven to be immensely popular among its young readers, who unwittingly gave their blessing to the concept of interactive fiction even before it became commonplace on computer terminals or CD-ROMs. A 1997 profile of Packard in *Contemporary Authors* quoted an article he wrote for *School Library Journal* in which he stated that "multiple plots afford the author the opportunity to depict alternative consequences and realities. Complexity may inhere in breadth rather than in length." The technique appealed to young readers for whom active participation in the direction of a narrative was a sign of maturity and ownership of the text.

The first book Packard wrote in this style, *Sugarcane Island,* a story about a trip to the Galapagos Islands, did not excite interest among publishers so he put it aside for five years. It finally found a home with Vermont Crossroads Press, an innovative children's book publisher, which brought out the book in 1976. The fledgling series gained national attention when the *New York Times Book Review* (April 30, 1978) devoted half a page to a Pocket Books/Archway edition of *Sugarcane Island* and to a Lippincott edition of Packard's *Deadwood City.* Reviewer Rex Benedict wrote: "Dead or alive, you keep turning pages. You become addicted."

Other reviewers, especially in the school library press, felt that the books were gimmicky and that they prevented children from developing an appreciation for plot and character development. An article in the journal *Voice for Youth Advocates* endorsed the books for their participatory format, however, noting that "readers' choices and the resulting consequences are fertile ground for developing students' ability to predict outcomes or for group work on values clarification."

Writers who have contributed to the series and its various spinoffs have included Richard Brightfield, Christopher Golden, Laban Carrick Hill, Robert Hirschfeld, Janet Hubbard-Brown, Vince Lahey, Jay Leibold, Anson Montgomery, R. A. Montgomery, and Andrea Packard.

—Edward Moran

FURTHER READING:

Contemporary Authors, New Revision Series, vol. 59. Detroit, Gale Research, 1998.

Packard, Edward. *Cyberspace Warrior.* New York, Bantam, 1994.

———. *Deadwood City.* Philadelphia and New York, J. B. Lippincott, 1978.

———. *Fire on Ice.* New York, Bantam, 1998.

———. *Sugarcane Island.* Vermont Crossroads Press, 1976.

Christie, Agatha (1890-1979)

Deemed the creator of the modern detective fiction novel and nicknamed the Duchess of Death, Agatha Christie continues to be one of the most popularly read authors since the publication of her first book, *The Mysterious Affair at Styles,* in 1920. Since then, more than 100 million copies of her books and stories have been sold.

Born Agatha Miller on September 15, 1890, in Torquay, located in Devonshire, England, Christie enjoyed a Victorian childhood where her parents' dinner parties introduced her to Henry James and Rudyard Kipling. Formally educated in France and debuting in Cairo,

Agatha Christie

Agatha began writing seriously after she married Archibald Christie in 1914. She wrote her first novel in 1916 in just two weeks. Several publishers rejected the manuscript. Almost two years later, John Lane accepted the book and offered her a contract for five more.

While her creative interests increased, Christie's relationship with her husband steadily declined until he left her in 1926 for his mistress, Nancy Neele. On December 6 of the same year, Christie disappeared for eleven days. Her car was found abandoned at Newlands Corner in Yorkshire. Later, employees at the Hydro Hotel in Harrogate recognized Christie as a guest at the spa resort, where Christie had identified herself to hotel employees and guests as Teresa Neele from South Africa. Christie later claimed to have been suffering from selective amnesia; she never wrote about her disappearance.

Divorcing her first husband in 1928, Christie married Max Mallowan in 1930 after meeting him during an excursion to Baghdad in 1929. Accompanying him on archeological excavations, Christie traveled extensively in the Middle East and also to the United States in 1966 for his lecture series at the Smithsonian Institute. While stateside, Christie began to write a three-part script based on Dickens's *Bleak House.* She only completed two parts of the project before withdrawing herself from the script. While she enjoyed novel and short story writing, Christie cared little for scriptwriting and even less for the film adaptations made from her novels, even though critics praised Charles Laughton's and Marlene Dietrich's performances in *Witness for the Prosecution* (1955).

Several national honors arose in accordance with Christie's popular fame as a novelist. In 1956, she was named Dame Commander of the Order of the British Empire, and in 1971, Christie was appointed Dame of the British Empire. Despite these accolades, Christie continued to lead a quiet private life, writing steadily until her death in 1979.

Though mystery novels as a genre became fashionable in the nineteenth century, Christie popularized the format so successfully that mystery writers continue to follow her example. Christie built on an early modern theme of comedies: a misunderstanding, crime, or murder occurs in the first act, an investigation follows with an interpolation of clue detection and character analysis, and the story concludes with a revelation, usually of mistaken identities, leading to the capture of the murderer.

During her life, Christie wrote sixty-six novels, more than one hundred short stories, twenty plays, an autobiography, and other various books of poetry and nonfiction. Though her play *The Mouse-trap* (1952) is the longest running play in London's West End, Christie's most enduring work incorporates the two now-famous fictional detectives Hercule Poirot and Jane Marple.

A Belgian immigrant living in London, Hercule Poirot embodies the ideal elements of a modern detective, though Christie clearly fashioned him after Sir Arthur Conan Doyle's Sherlock Holmes. Like Holmes, Poirot studies not only the clues of the crime but also the characters of the suspects. What distinguishes him from Holmes is Poirot's attention to personal appearance. Even while traveling by train in *Murder on the Orient Express,* Poirot finds time to set and style his moustache. Because of his attention to detail, Poirot, in a time before fingerprint matches and DNA testing, solves mysteries by using what he terms "the little gray cells."

Miss Marple, an elderly spinster, acts as Poirot's antithesis except for her ability to solve mysteries. Marple is a successful detective because of her unobtrusive and innocuous presence. Few suspects assume an older woman with a knitting bag can deduce a motive behind murder. Marple, like Poirot, however, does embody a particularly memorable trait: she doesn't trust anyone. In Christie's autobiography, the author describes Miss Marple: "Though a cheerful person she always expected the worst of everyone and everything and was, with almost frightening accuracy, usually proved right."

Both detectives have been made famous in the United States by the critically acclaimed television series *Poirot* and *Agatha Christie's Miss Marple,* produced by and aired on the Arts and Entertainment network, and beginning in 1989, and on the PBS weekly program *Mystery!* Although more than sixty-five film and made-for-television adaptations have been produced from Christie's novels, none claims the following these series command. Immortalizing the roles of Hercule Poirot and Miss Marple, David Suchet and Joan Hickson have indelibly imprinted images of the detectives in the minds of fans. Though Agatha Christie died long before the creation of the series, her legacy of detective fiction will be remembered in the United States not only in print but on the small screen as well.

—Bethany Blankenship

FURTHER READING:

Bargainnier, Earl F. *The Gentle Art of Murder: The Detective Fiction of Agatha Christie.* Bowling Green, Ohio, Bowling Green University Popular Press, 1980.

Christie, Agatha. *An Autobiography.* London, William Collins Sons & Co, 1977.

Gerald, Michael C. *The Poisonous Pen of Agatha Christie.* Austin, University of Texas Press, 1993.

Keating, H. R. F. *Agatha Christie: First Lady of Crime.* London, Weidenfeld & Nicolson, 1977.

Osborne, Charles. *The Life and Crimes of Agatha Christie.* London, Michael O'Mara Books Limited, 1982.

Wagoner, Mary S. *Agatha Christie.* Boston, Twayne Publishers, 1986.

Christmas

For Americans, the celebration of Christmas is often considered one of the most important holidays of the year. Because of the diverse heritages and customs, in addition to Kwanzaa, a tradition begun in the later part of the twentieth century, the American Christmas consists of traditions from not only the German, but English, Dutch, and other Eastern European countries as well. Having religious significance, Christmas also celebrates the child found in each individual and the desire for peace. Falling during the same month as the Jewish observance of Chanukah or Hanukkah (the Feast of Lights) and the African-American celebration of Kwanzaa, the season of Christmas serves as a time of celebration, feasting, and a search for miracles.

While Christmas generally is considered the celebration of Jesus's birth, the early Puritans, who settled the New England region, refused to celebrate the occasion. Disagreeing with the early church fathers who established the holiday around a pagan celebration for easy remembrance by the poor, the Puritans considered the observance secular in nature. Set during the winter solstice when days grow dark early, Christmas coincides with the Roman holiday of Saturnalia; the date, December 25, marks the celebration of Dies Natalis Invicti Solis, or the birth day of the Unconquered Sun by the Romans.

An early Coca-Cola advertising poster featuring the company's famed Santa Claus.

Puritans believed that these pagan customs, which included no work, feasting, and gift giving, were inappropriate for the celebration of the Lord's birth. While the northern colonists did not observe the day, the southern colonists celebrated in much the same style as their British counterparts—with banquets and family visits. Firecrackers or guns were used to welcome the Christ Child at midnight on Christmas. The residents of New York (New Amsterdam) celebrated the season in a similar fashion as their Dutch ancestors had with St. Nicholas Day (December 6), established to honor the patron saint of children. Gradually, all observances became centered around the date December 25, with traditions becoming mixed and accepted between different ethnic backgrounds.

With these strong ties to religion, Christmas serves an important role for the Christian faith. The four Sundays before Christmas, or the season of Advent, prepares the congregation for the arrival of the Messiah. With wreathes consisting of greenery, four small purple candles, and one large white candle, church members are reminded of the four elements of Christianity: peace, hope, joy, and love. This season of the church year ends with the lighting of the Christ candle on Christmas morning, signalling the two week period of Christmastide.

Nativity scenes, or creches, adorn altars as a visual reminder of the true meaning of Christmas.

While attendance at church services and midnight masses seems commonplace, the first visible sign of the Christmas season appears in the decoration of the home. Some families decorate the outside of their home with multi-strings of colored lights, while others focus their decorations around an evergreen tree of spruce, fir, or cedar. In the 1960s, a new type of Christmas tree appeared on the market which allows families to prepare for the season early and leave their decorations up well into the New Year. Artificial trees have ranged in style from the silver aluminum trees (1960s) to the imitation spruce and snow-covered fir. A custom attributed to Martin Luther, the Christmas tree often appears decorated with lights and ornaments consisting of family heirlooms—a central theme which had meaning to the family—or religious symbols. Christmas trees became widely used after 1841 when Prince Albert placed one for his family's use at Windsor Castle. Originally, the Christmas tree was decorated with candles. With the introduction of electricity, however, strings of small and large bulbs ranging in color from white to multi-color illumine the tree. The lighting of the tree dates back to the days when light was used to dispel the evil found in darkness. Around the base of the tree, gifts, creches, or large scale displays of Christmas villages represent some important memory or tradition in the family's heritage or life.

The Christmas tree is not the only greenery used during the holiday season. Wreaths of holly, fir, and pine appear on doors and in windows of homes. Each represents a part of the mystical past or ancestors' beliefs. The holly, which the ancients used to protect their home from witches, also represents the crown of thorns worn by Jesus at His crucifixion. The evergreen fir and pine represent everlasting life. Mistletoe, a Druid tradition and hung in sprigs or as a Kissing Ball, brings the hope of a kiss to the one standing beneath the spray. The red and white flowering poinsettia, native to Central American countries and brought to the United States by Dr. Joel Poinsett, represents the gift of a young Mexican peasant girl to the Christ Child.

Christmas serves as a time when gifts are exchanged between family and friends. This custom, while attributed to the gifts brought by the Magi to the Christ Child, can be traced to the earlier celebration of Saturnalia by the Romans. While the name varies with the country of origin, the bearer of gifts to children holds a special place in people's hearts and comes during the month of December. The most recognized gift-giver is based on Saint Nicholas, a bishop of Myra in 300 to 400 A. D., and the tradition was brought to America by the Dutch of New York. Saint Nicholas' appearance went undefined until the early 1800s when he appeared in the stories of Washington Irving.

While Irving's stories would include general references to Saint Nicholas, Clement Clark Moore would give Americans the image most commonly accepted. A professor of Divinity, in 1822 Moore wrote "A Visit from Saint Nicholas," also known as "The Night Before Christmas," as a special gift for his children. A friend, hearing the poem, had it published anonymously the following year in a local newspaper. Telling the story of the visit of Saint Nicholas, the poem centers around a father's experience on Christmas Eve; the poem reveals and establishes a new vision of St. Nicholas. St. Nicholas drives a miniature sleigh pulled by eight reindeer named Dasher, Dancer, Prancer, Vixen, Comet, Cupid, Donner, and Blitzen. Moore's description of Saint Nicholas describes the clothing worn by the man. "He was dressed all in fur, from his head to his foot, / And his clothes were all tarnished with ashes and soot; / A bundle of toys he had flung on his back, / And he looked like a peddler just opening his sack.'' For the nineteenth century reader, the image of someone dressed like a peddler with a bag of toys on his back could be easily visualized.

Moore did not end his description here, but gave a physical description of the man as well. With twinkling eyes and dimples, Saint Nicholas has a white beard which gives him a grandfatherly appearance. In addition, Moore added: ''He had a broad face and a little round belly, / That shook, when he laughed, like a bowlful of jelly.'' The jolly gentleman of childhood Christmas fantasy has become a reality. The description is so vivid that artists began to feature this portrait of Saint Nicholas in their seasonal drawings. In 1881 Thomas Nast, a cartoonist in New York, would define the gentleman and give him the characteristics for which he has become known. Saint Nicholas's name has changed to the simplified Santa Claus and has become a lasting part of the Christmas tradition.

Santa Claus and his miraculous gifts have played such a part of the Christmas celebration that many articles, movies, and songs have been written about the character. The most famous editorial ''Yes, Virginia, There Is a Santa Claus,'' appeared in *The Sun* in 1897 after a child wrote asking about Santa's existence. The response to the child's letter is considered a Christmas classic, with many newspapers repeating the editorial on Christmas Day. This same questioning regarding Santa Claus' existence is portrayed in the film *Miracle on 34th Street* (1947), where a young girl learns not only to believe in what can be seen but also in the unseen. Johnny Marks adds to the legend of Santa Claus and his reindeer with the song ''Rudolph the Red-nosed Reindeer'' (1949), which is performed most notably by Gene Autry. This song, while using Moore's names for the reindeer, adds a new one, Rudolph, to the lexicon of Santa Claus.

The spirit of Santa Claus has not only given the season a defining symbol, but has also created a season with an emphasis on commercialization. Santa's bag of toys means money for the merchants. Christmas items and the mention of shopping for Christmas may begin as early as the summer, with Christmas tree displays appearing in retail stores in September and October. Christmas has become so important to the business world that some specialty stores dedicate their merchandise to promoting the business of Christmas year-round. Shopping days are counted, reminders are flashed across the evening news, and advertisements are placed in newspapers. The images of Christmas not only bring joy, but also anxiety as people are urged to shop for the perfect gift and to spend more money.

While the season of Christmas symbolizes various things to different people, the Christ Child and Santa Claus represent two differing views of the celebration. The traditions and customs of the immigrant background have merged and provide the season with something for everyone. Adding to the celebration the Jewish festival Chanukah, and the African-American celebration Kwanzaa, the season of Christmas seems to run throughout the month of December. With the merging of the sacred and the pagan, magic is revisited and dreams are fulfilled while money is spent in the never-ending cycle of giving.

—Linda Ann Martindale

FURTHER READING:

Barnett, James H. *The American Christmas: A Study in National Culture.* New York, Macmillan Company, 1954.

Barth, Edna. *Holly, Reindeer and Colored Lights: The Story of the Christmas Symbols.* New York, Seabury Press, 1971.

Moore, Clement C. *The Night Before Christmas.* New York, Harcourt Brace and Company, 1999.

Nissenbaum, Stephen. *The Battle for Christmas.* New York, Alfred A. Knopf, 1997.

Weinecke, Herbert H. *Christmas Customs Around the World.* Philadelphia, Westminster Press, 1959.

Christo (1935—)

The most well-known environmental artist of this half century, Christo first captured the public's attention in the 1960s by wrapping large-scale structures such as bridges and buildings. In the following three decades his artworks became lavish spectacles involving millions of dollars, acres of materials, and hundreds of square miles of land. His projects are so vast and require so much sophisticated administration, bureaucracy, and construction, that he is best thought of as an artist whose true medium is the real world.

Christo Vladimiorov Javacheff was born in Gabrovo, Bulgaria, into an intellectually enlightened family. After study in the art academy in Bulgaria, his work for the avant-garde Burian Theatre in 1956 proved decisive. Christo began wrapping and packaging objects—a technique called ''empaquetage''—a year after his move to Paris in 1957. Empaquetage was a reaction to the dominance of tachiste painting, the European version of American abstract expressionism. Conceptual in nature, wrapping isolates commonplace objects and imbues them with a sense of mystery. Christo often used transparent plastic and rope to wrap cars, furniture, bicycles, signs and, for brief periods, female models.

In Paris, Christo became acquainted with the Nouveau Réalistes group, which was interested in using junk materials and with the incorporation of life into art. Soon his artworks utilized tin cans, oil drums, boxes, and bottles. He married Jeanne-Claude de Guillebon, who became his inseparable companion, secretary, treasurer, and collaborator. So close is their partnership that Christo's works often bear Jeanne-Claude's name as well as his own.

The early sixties witnessed Christo's first large-scale projects. Several of these involved barrels, the most famous of which was *Iron Curtain—Wall of Oil Drums* (1962). A response to the then-new Berlin wall, it consisted of more than two hundred barrels stacked twelve feet high. It effectively shut down traffic for a night on a Paris street. As the sixties wore on, and particularly after Christo moved to New York, his works became larger and even more conceptual. He created *Air Packages* (large sacs of air that sometimes hovered over museums), wrapped trees, and even packaged a medieval tower. In 1968 Christo wrapped two museum buildings, the Künsthalle Museum in Bern, Switzerland, and the Museum of Contemporary Art in Chicago. The latter required sixty-two pieces of brown tarpaulin and two miles of brown rope.

About this time, Christo's attention turned to the vast spaces of landscape. For *Wrapped Coast—One Million Square Feet, Little Bay, Australia* (1969) he covered a rocky, mile-long stretch of coastline with a million square feet of polythene sheeting and thirty-six miles of

The ''Wrapped Trees'' project by Christo and his wife Jeanne-Claude in the park of the Foundation Beyeler in Riehen, Switzerland, 1998.

rope. The work was the first of his projects in which Christo had to solve problems connected to government agencies and public institutions. Controversy erupted when nurses on the privately owned land protested because they thought that hospital money was being diverted and that a recreational beach would be shut down. Actually, Christo paid for the project himself and allowed for the beach to remain open.

While teaching in Colorado, Christo became intrigued by the Rocky Mountain landscape. *Valley Curtain* (1971-72, Rifle Gap, Colorado) was composed of two hundred thousand square feet of nylon hung from a cable between two cliffs. The bright orange nylon curtain weighed four tons. Organizational, economic, and public relations problems delayed construction for a time, but these were exactly the challenges Christo and Jeanne-Claude had become so adept in solving. To raise the $850,000 needed, the couple created the Valley Curtain Corporation. As would become customary, Christo's drawings, plans, models, and photographs of *Valley Curtain* were sold as art objects to raise money for building the massive artwork. The first curtain was almost instantly ripped to pieces by high winds; a union boss had told his workers to quit for the day before it was properly secured. The second curtain was ruined by a sandstorm the day after it was hung, but not before it was unfurled to the cheers of media, news crews, and onlookers. A half-hour documentary was

made to register the course of the work's construction. In all of Christo's projects, photography and documentary film are used extensively to record the activities surrounding what are essentially temporary structures.

For his next project, *Running Fence* (1976), Christo raised two million dollars through the sale of book and film rights and from works of art associated with the project. Christo obtained the permission of fifty-nine private ranchers and fifteen government organizations. Ironically, the strongest opposition came from local artists who regarded the project as a mere publicity stunt. Christo then became a passionate lobbyist for his project, appearing at local meetings and agency hearings. Winding through Marin and Sonoma counties, the eighteen-foot-high fence traversed twenty-four miles over private ranches, roads, small towns, and subdivisions on its way to a gentle descent into the Pacific Ocean. Open-minded viewers found it lyrically beautiful; indeed, beauty is one of Christo's unabashed aims.

Surrounded Islands, Biscayne Bay, Greater Miami, Florida, 1980-83 was Christo's major work of the eighties and involved floating rafts of shocking pink polypropane entirely enclosing eleven small islands. It required more than four hundred assistants and $3.5 million to complete. Sensitive to the environment, Christo decided not to surround three islands because they were home to endangered manatees, birds, and plants. Even so, Christo and Jeanne-Claude still had to contend with lawsuits, lawyers, and public groups. Though *Surrounded Islands* extended for eleven miles and traversed a major city, it was strikingly lovely. Like *Running Fence, Surrounding Islands* existed for only two weeks.

Christo staged *The Umbrellas, Japan—U.S.A. 1984-91* simultaneously in the landscapes north of Tokyo and of Los Angeles. Roughly fifteen hundred specially designed umbrellas (yellow ones in California, blue ones in Japan) dotted the respective countrysides over areas of several miles. Only twenty-six landowners had to be won over in California; in Japan, where land is even more precious, the number was 459. The umbrellas were nearly twenty feet high and weighed over five hundred pounds each. Having cost the artist $26 million to produce, the umbrellas stood for only three weeks beginning on October 9, 1991. Christo ended the project after a woman in California was killed when high winds uprooted an umbrella. During the dismantling of the umbrellas in Japan, a crane operator was electrocuted.

Altogether, Christo's art involves manipulating public social systems. As the artist has said, ''We live in an essentially economic, social, and political world. . . . I think that any art that is less political, less economical, less social today, is simply less contemporary.''

—Mark B. Pohlad

Further Reading:

Baal-Teshuva, Jacob. *Christo and Jeanne-Claude.* Cologne, Benedikt Taschen, 1995.

Christo: The Reichstag and Urban Projects. Munich, Prestel, 1993.

Laporte, Dominique G. *Christo.* Translated from the French by Abby Pollak. New York, Pantheon Books, 1986.

Spies, Werner. Introduction to *Christo, Surrounded Islands, Biscayne Bay, Greater Miami, Florida, 1980-83,* by Christo. New York, Abrams, 1985.

Vaizey, Marina. *Christo.* New York, Rizzoli, 1990.

Chrysler Building

A monument to the glitzy Jazz Age of the 1920s, the Chrysler Building in New York City is America's most prominent example of Art Deco architecture and the epitome of the urban corporate headquarters. This unabashedly theatrical building, which was briefly the world's tallest after its completion in 1930, makes an entirely different statement than its nearby competitor, the Empire State Building. The Chrysler Building's appeal was summarized by architectural critic Paul Goldberger, who wrote, ''There, in one building, is all of New York's height and fantasy in a single gesture.''

The Chrysler Building was originally designed for real estate speculator William H. Reynolds by architect William Van Alen. In 1928, Walter Percy Chrysler, head of the Chrysler Motor Corporation, purchased the site on the corner of Lexington Avenue and 42nd Street in midtown Manhattan, as well as Van Alen's plans. But those plans were changed as the design began to reflect Chrysler's dynamic personality. The project soon became caught up in the obsessive quest for height that swept through the city's commercial architecture in the 1920s and 1930s. Buildings rose taller and taller as owners sought both to maximize office space as well as to increase consumer visibility. Van Alen's initial design projected a 925-foot building with

The Chrysler Building (foreground)

a rounded, Byzantine or Moorish top. At the same time, however, Van Alen's former partner, H. Craig Severance, was building the 927-foot Bank of the Manhattan Company on Wall Street. Not to be outdone, Van Alen revised his plans, with Chrysler's blessing, to include a new tapering top that culminated in a spire, bringing the total height to 1,046 feet and establishing the Chrysler Building as the world's tallest. The plans were kept secret, and near the end of construction the spire was clandestinely assembled inside the building, then hoisted to the top. The entire episode defined the extent to which the competition for height dominated architectural design at the time. The Chrysler Building's reign was brief, however; even before it was finished, construction had begun on the Empire State Building, which would surpass the Chrysler by just over two-hundred feet.

The finished building is a dazzling display of panache and corporate power. The most famous and notable aspect of the Chrysler Building is its Art Deco decoration. With its polychromy, zigzag ornamentation, shining curvilinear surfaces, and evocation of machines and movement, the Art Deco style—named after the 1925 Exposition Internationale des Arts Decoratifs et Industriels Modernes in Paris—provided Van Alen with a means to express the exuberance and vitality of 1920s New York, as well as the unique personality of the building's benefactor. The interior of the Chrysler Building reflects the company's wealth. In the unique triangular lobby, reminiscent of a 1930s movie set, the lavish decorative scheme combines natural materials like various marbles, onyx, and imported woods with appropriate machine-age materials like nickel, chrome, and steel. Outside, a white brick skin accentuated by gray brick trim was laid over the building's steel frame in a pattern that emphasized the building's verticality. Steel gargoyles in the form of glaring eagles—representing both America and hood ornaments from Chrysler Company automobiles—were placed at the corners of the building's highest setback. (These gargoyles became famous after a photo of photographer Margaret Bourke-White standing atop one of them was widely circulated). The crowning achievement of the building, both literally and figuratively, is the spire. A series of tapering radial arches, punctuated by triangular windows, rise to a single point at the top. The spire's stainless steel gleams in the sun. The arches at the spire's base were based on automobile hubcaps. In fact, the entire building was planned with an elaborate iconographic program, including radiator cap gargoyles at the fourth setback, brick designs taken from Chrysler automobile hubcaps, and a band of abstracted autos wrapping around the building. The use of such company-specific imagery incorporated into the building's design anticipated the postmodern architecture of the 1980s.

The Chrysler Building was not the first corporate headquarters specifically designed to convey a company's image, but it may have been the most successful. The unique building was a more effective advertising tool for the Chrysler Company than any billboard, newspaper, or magazine ad. The Chrysler Building, with its shining telescoped top, stood out from the rather sedate Manhattan skyscrapers. While some observers see the building as kitsch or, in the words of critic Lewis Mumford, "inane romanticism," most appreciate its vitality. Now one of the world's favorite buildings, the Chrysler Building has become an American icon, symbolizing the pre-Depression glamour and the exuberant optimism of the Jazz Age.

—Dale Allen Gyure

FURTHER READING:

The Chrysler Building. New York, Chrysler Tower Corporation, 1930.

Douglas, George H. *Skyscrapers: A Social History of the Very Tall Building in America.* Jefferson, North Carolina, McFarland & Company, 1996.

Goldberger, Paul. *The Skyscraper.* New York, Alfred A. Knopf, 1992.

Reynolds, Donald Martin. *The Architecture of New York City.* New York, Macmillan Publishing Company, 1984.

Chuck D (1960—)

The primary rapper in one of the most significant hip-hop groups in the genre's history, Chuck D founded the New York City-based Public Enemy in order to use hip-hop music as an outlet to disseminate his pro-Black revolutionary messages. Because of the millions of albums Public Enemy sold and the way the group changed the landscape of hip-hop and popular music during the late-1980s, Public

Enemy's influence on popular music specifically, and American culture in general, is incalculable.

Chuck D (born Carlton Ridenhour August 1, 1960) formed Public Enemy in 1982 with fellow Long Island friends Hank Shocklee and Bill Stepheny, both of whom shared Chuck D's love of politics and hip-hop music. In 1985, a Public Enemy demo caught the attention Def Jam label co-founder Rick Rubin, and by 1986 Chuck D had revamped Public Enemy to include Bill Stepheny as their publicist, Hank Shocklee as a producer, Flavor Flav as a second MC, Terminator X as the group's DJ and Professor Griff as the head of Public Enemy's crew of onstage dancers. Public Enemy burst upon the scene in 1987 with their debut album *Yo! Bum Rush the Show,* and soon turned the hip-hop world on its head at a time when hip-hop music was radically changing American popular music. Chuck D's early vision to make Public Enemy a hotbed of extreme dissonant musical productions and revolutionary politics came into fruition with the release of 1988's *It Takes a Nation of Millions to Hold Us Back.* Recognized by critics at *Rolling Stone, SPIN, The Source* and the *Village Voice* as one of most significant works of popular music of the twentieth century, *It Takes a Nation. . .* took music to new extremes. That album combined furiously fast rhythms, cacophonous collages of shrieks and sirens, and Chuck D's booming baritone delivery that took White America to task for the sins of racism and imperialism.

Chuck D once remarked that hip-hop music was Black America's CNN, in that hip-hop was the only forum in which a Black point of view could be heard without being filtered or censored. As the leader of Public Enemy, a group that sold millions of albums (many to White suburban teens) Chuck D was one of the only oppositional voices heard on a widespread scale during the politically conservative 1980s.

Public Enemy's commercial and creative high point came during the late 1980s and early 1990s. The group recorded their song "Fight the Power" for Spike Lee's widely acclaimed and successful 1989 film *Do the Right Thing,* increasing Public Enemy's visibility even more. After the much-publicized inner group turmoil that resulted from anti-Semitic remarks publicly made by a group member, Chuck D kicked that member out, reorganized the group and went to work on the biggest selling album of Public Enemy's career, *Fear of a Black Planet.*

By then, Chuck D had perfected the "Public Enemy concept" to a finely-tuned art. He used Public Enemy's pro-Black messages to rally and organize African Americans, the group's aggressive and propulsive sonic attack to capture the attention of young White America, and their high visibility to edge Chuck D's viewpoints into mainstream discourse. Throughout the 1990s, Chuck D appeared on numerous talk shows and other widely broadcast events.

Taking advantage of his notoriety, Chuck D often lectured at college campuses during the late 1980s and throughout the 1990s. He became a political election correspondent for music video network MTV and, in 1997, he published a book on race and politics in America titled *Fight the Power.*

In a musical genre driven by novelty and innovation, Public Enemy's—and Chuck D's—influence and commercial success began to wane by the mid-1990s. In 1996 he released the commercially unsuccessful solo album, *Autobiography of Mista Chuck.* But unlike many artists who change their formula when sales decline, Chuck D

Chuck D speaks to Columbia University students in 1998.

never changed Public Enemy's course, and in 1998 the group released a highly political and sonically dense soundtrack album for Spike Lee's film *He Got Game.*

—Kembrew McLeod

FURTHER READING:

Chuck D. *Fight the power: Rap, Race, and Reality.* New York, Delacorte Press, 1997.

Fernando, S.H., Jr. *The New Beats: Exploring the Music, Culture, and Attitudes of Hip-Hop.* New York, Anchor Books, 1994.

Chun King

Chun King was one of the earliest brands of mass-marketed Chinese food in the United States, offering convenient "exotic" dinners in a can. Beginning with chicken chow mein in 1947, Chun King later expanded its menu to include eggrolls and chop suey. Although chow mein was Chinese-American, the maker of Chun King foods was not. The founder and president of Chun King was Jeno F. Paulucci, the son of Italian immigrants. Paulucci began his career in the food industry working in a grocery, and later sold fruits and vegetables from a car. Paulucci saw an opportunity in Chinese food and began canning and selling chow mein. The business grew into a multi-million dollar industry, and in the late 1960s Paulucci sold the company for $63 million. In the 1990s ConAgra and Hunt-Wesson marketed Chun King chow mein, beansprouts, eggrolls, and sauces.

—Midori Takagi

FURTHER READING:

Cao, Lan, and Himilce Novas. *Everything You Need to Know About Asian-American History.* New York, Penguin, 1996.

Church Socials

A gathering of church members for celebratory, social, or charitable purposes, church socials in America have remained popular—while becoming more varied and elaborate—throughout the past two centuries.

Church socials in America are rooted in ancient Jewish festivals. Jews traveled to Jerusalem to participate in public worship activities that commemorated important events or celebrated the harvest. Because the tribes of Israel were separated geographically, these festivals served the additional purpose of providing the cement needed for national unity. Old prejudices and misunderstandings were often swept away by these major events.

With the birth of the church, Christians shared common meals designed to enhance relationships within the church. The Bible says in Acts 2:46, ''. . . They broke bread in their homes and ate together with glad and sincere hearts.'' Eventually, the Agape meal or ''love feast'' became popular. It provided fellowship and opportunity to help the poor and widows. It was later practiced in the Moravian and Methodist churches.

Socials enhance church celebrations of Easter, Christmas, and other holidays. Because the Bible says that Jesus' resurrection took place at dawn, Christians often meet together early on Easter morning for a ''Sunrise Service'' followed by a breakfast. An Easter egg hunt is often included, though some frown on this as a secular activity. Churches plan various Christmas socials such as caroling, exchanging gifts, and serving special dinners. Opinions vary on whether to include Christmas trees and Santa Claus. Some avoid them as secular symbols while others include them because they believe these traditions have Christian origins. As American society embraced other holidays such as Mother's Day, Father's Day, Valentine's Day, the Fourth of July, and Thanksgiving, churches discovered fresh opportunities for social activities including mother-daughter, father-son, sweetheart, and Thanksgiving banquets. Churches in communities sometimes join together for patriotic celebrations on the Fourth of July.

Socials get people together in informal settings so that they will become better acquainted and work together more effectively in the church. Congregations in rural and small town America enjoy popular social activities involving food and games. Ham, bean, and cornbread dinners, chili suppers, ''pot luck'' meals, homemade ice cream socials, wiener roasts, picnics, hayrides, softball games, watermelon eating contests, and all-day singing events are only a few examples. In fact, for these rural congregations, church socials have often been the only source of social activities in a community. In some cases, homes were so far apart, separated by acres of farmland, that churches were the only places where people could go to meet others. Many people went to church socials on dates, and was a place where they often met their future spouses. Some churches included dancing and alcoholic beverages, but others believed those activities were inappropriate for churches to sponsor. Churches in both rural and urban areas often have family nights designed especially for busy families. A family comes to church on a weeknight and shares a meal with other families before Bible study or other small group activities.

In the latter half of the twentieth century, churches began planning more elaborate socials. Churches in or near urban areas attend professional sports. This is so widespread that most professional stadiums offer discount rates for church groups. Churches join together to sponsor basketball, softball, and volleyball leagues. While most churches rent community facilities, some have built their own gymnasiums and recreation halls. Other social activities involve trips to major recreation areas such as amusement parks. Swimming, picnicking, camping, and enjoying amusement rides are a few of the activities that round out these outings that last whole days or even entire weekends. Some church groups in recent years have provided cruises, trips to major recreational sites such as Branson, Missouri, and even vacations to other countries. While more elaborate, a cruise

for Christian singles, for example, serves the same purpose as the traditional hayride and wiener roast.

As the early church was concerned for widows, orphans, the sick and the poor, and gave generously to meet those needs, so modern church socials may be founded on the desire to assist the needy or fund church programs. As a result, activities such as homemade-ice-cream socials, sausage-and-pancake suppers, and craft bazaars are opened to the public. Some Catholic churches sponsor festivals that take on the flavor of county fairs. Amusement rides, carnival games, and food booths draw thousands of people. Money is used to pay for parochial schools or some other church project. (Some Catholic and many non-Catholic churches believe that these activities are too secular. Card playing, gambling, and the drinking of alcoholic beverages included in some of these events have also been quite controversial.) Some churches use their profits to support Christian retirement homes and hospitals. Some believe churches should not sell food or merchandise, but they give free meals away to the poor in the community. Other groups such as the Amish still have barn raising and quilting socials to help others in their community.

—James H. Lloyd

FURTHER READING:

Clemens, Frances, Robert Tully, and Edward Crill. *Recreation in the Local Church.* Elgin, Ill., Brethren Press, 1961.

Conner, Ray. *A Guide to Church Recreation.* Nashville, Convention Press, 1977.

Roadcup, David, ed. *Methods for Youth Ministry: Leadership Development, Camp, VBS, Bible Study, Small Groups, Discipline, Fine Arts, Film, Mission Trips, Recreation, Retreats.* Cincinnati, Standard Publishing, 1986.

Smith, Frank Hart. *Social Recreation and the Church.* Nashville, Convention Press, 1983.

Cigarettes

It is highly unlikely that in 1881, when James A. Bonsack invented a cigarette-making machine, that he or anybody else could have predicted the mélange of future symbolism contained in each conveniently packaged stick of tobacco. The cigarette has come to stand for more than just the unhealthy habit of millions in American popular culture. It represents politics, money, image, sex, and freedom.

The tobacco plant held residence in the New World long before Columbus even set sail. American Indians offered Columbus dried tobacco leaves as a gift and, it is rumored, he threw them away because of the fowl smell. Later on, however, sailors brought tobacco back to Europe where it gained a reputation as a medical cure-all. Tobacco was believed to be so valuable that during the 1600s, it was frequently used as money. In 1619, Jamestown colonists paid for their future wives' passage from England with 120 pounds of tobacco. In 1621, the price went up to 150 pounds per mate. Tobacco later helped finance the American Revolution, also known as ''The Tobacco War,'' by serving as collateral for loans from France.

Tobacco consumption took many forms before reaching the cigarette of the modern day. Spanish colonists in the New World smoked tobacco as a *cigarito*: shredded cigar remnants rolled in plant husks, then later in crude paper. In France, the cigarito form was also

James Thurber enjoying a cigarette.

popular, especially during the French Revolution. As aristocrats commonly consumed the snuff version of tobacco, the masses chose an opposing form. A moderate improvement to the Spanish cigarito, the French *cigarette* was rolled in rice straw. In 1832, an Egyptian artilleryman in the Turkish/Egyptian War created the paperbound version of today whose popularity spread to the British through veterans of the Crimean War. In England, a tobacconist named Philip Morris greatly improved the quality of the Turkish cigarette but still maintained only a cottage industry, despite the cigarette's growing popularity.

By the 1900s cigarettes rose to the highest selling form of tobacco on the market. Mass urbanization picked up the pace of daily life and popularized factory-made products such as soap, canned goods, gum, and the cigarette. James A. Bonsack's newly invented cigarette machine could turn out approximately 200 cigarettes per minute, output equal to that of forty or fifty workers. Cigarettes were now a more convenient form of tobacco consumption—cleaner than snuff or chew, more portable than cigars or pipes—and also were increasingly more available. England's Philip Morris set up shop in America as did several other tobacco manufacturers: R.J. Reynolds (1875), J.E. Liggett (1849), Duke (1881, later, the American Tobacco Company), and the oldest tobacco company in the United States, P. Lorillard (1760). The cigarette quickly became enmeshed in American popular culture. In 1913, R.J. Reynolds launched its Camel brand whose instant appeal, notes Richard Kluger in *Ashes to Ashes*, helped inspire this famous poem from a Penn State publication: "Tobacco is a dirty weed. I like it. / It satisfies no moral need. I like it. / It makes you thin, it makes you lean / It takes the hair right off your bean / It's

the worst darn stuff I've ever seen. / I like it." Since their introduction, cigarettes have maintained a status as one of the best-selling consumer products in the country. In 1990, 4.4 billion cigarettes were sold in America. That same year, several states restricted their sale.

The greatest propagator of what King James I of England referred to as "the stinking weed," has been war: the American Revolution, the French Revolution, the Mexican and Crimean Wars, the U.S. Civil War, and the greatest boost to U.S. cigarette consumption—World War I. During the first World War, cigarettes were included in soldiers' rations and as Kluger suggests, "quickly became the universal emblem of the camaraderie of mortal combat, that consummate male activity." Providing the troops with their daily intake of cigarettes, a very convenient method of consumption during combat, was viewed as morale enhancing if not downright patriotic. Regardless of intention, the tobacco manufacturers ensured themselves of a future market for their product.

At the same time, women became more involved in public life, earning the right to vote in 1920, and entering the work force during the absence of the fighting men. Eager to display their new sense of worth and fortitude, women smoked cigarettes, some even publicly. The tobacco industry responded with brands and advertisements aimed especially at women. While war may have brought the cigarette to America, marketing has kept it here. Since the introduction of the cigarette to America, the tobacco industry has spent untold billions of dollars on insuring its complete assimilation into U.S. popular culture. Despite the 1971 ban of radio and television advertisements for cigarettes, the industry has successfully inducted characters such as Old Joe Camel, The Marlboro Man, and the Kool Penguin into the popular iconography. A 1991 study published by the *Journal of the American Medical Association* revealed that 91 percent of six year olds could identify Joe Camel as the character representing Camel cigarettes and that Joe Camel is recognized by preschoolers as often as Mickey Mouse. Aside from advertising, cigarettes have been marketed, most notably to the youth market, through a myriad of other promotional activities from industry-sponsored sporting and entertainment events to product placement in movies. In 1993 alone, the tobacco industry spent $6 billion keeping their cigarettes fresh in the minds of Americans.

While Hollywood has inadvertently, and sometimes quite intentionally, made the cigarette a symbol of glamour and sexuality—the smoke gingerly billowing as an afterglow of, or substitute for, the act itself—anti-tobacco activists have equally pursued an agenda of disclosure, regulation, and often, prohibition. A war has been waged on the cigarette in America and everyone, smoker or not, was engaged by the end of the 1990s. The health hazards of smoking have been debated since at least the 1600s, but litigation in the twentieth century revealed what the tobacco industry had known but denied for years: that nicotine, the active substance in cigarettes, is an addictive drug, and that cigarette smoking is the cause of numerous diseases and conditions which claim the lives of nearly half a million Americans each year. The cigarette has thus become for many an emblem of deception and death for the sake of profit, or even, with the discovery of second-hand smoke as a carcinogen, a catalyst for social review. For others, it remains a symbol of money and power and politics or the Constitutional First Amendment invoked by so many smokers in their time of need. The cigarette is indeed a dynamic symbol in American society—habit, hazard, inalienable right.

—Nadine-Rae Leavell

FURTHER READING:

Glantz, Stanton A., and John Slade, Lisa A. Bero, Peter Hanauer, Deborah E. Barnes. *The Cigarette Papers.* Berkeley, University of California Press, 1996.

Kluger, Richard. *Ashes to Ashes: America's Hundred-Year Cigarette War, the Public Health, and the Unabashed Triumph of Philip Morris.* New York, Vintage Books, 1996.

McGowen, Richard. *Business, Politics, and Cigarettes: Multiple Levels, Multiple Agendas.* San Rafael, California, Quantum Books, 1995.

Smith, Jane Webb. *Smoke Signals: Cigarettes, Advertising, and the American Way of Life: An Exhibition at the Valentine Museum, Richmond, Virginia, April 5-October 9, 1990.* Chapel Hill, North Carolina Press, 1990.

Circus

Long before the advent of film, television, or the Internet, the circus delivered the world to people's doorsteps across America. Arriving in the United States shortly after the birth of the American republic, the growth of the circus chronicled the expansion of the new nation, from an agrarian backwater to an industrial and overseas empire. The number of circuses in America peaked at the turn of the twentieth century, but the circus has cast a long shadow on twentieth century American popular culture. The circus served as subject matter for other popular forms like motion pictures and television, and its celebration of American military might and racial hierarchy percolated into these new forms. From its zenith around 1900, to its decline and subsequent rebirth during the late twentieth century, the circus has been inextricably tied to larger social issues in American culture concerning race, physical disability, and animal rights.

In 1793, English horseman John Bill Ricketts established the first circus in the United States. He brought together a host of familiar European circus elements into a circular arena in Philadelphia: acrobats, clowns, jugglers, trick riders, rope walkers, and horses. By the turn of the twentieth century, the circus had become a huge, tented amusement that traveled across the country by railroad. In an age of monopoly capitalism, American circuses merged together to form giant shows; for example, the Ringling Brothers circus bought Barnum and Bailey's Greatest Show on Earth in 1907. The biggest shows employed over 1,000 people and animals from around the world. These circuses contained a free morning parade, a menagerie and a sideshow. Their canvas big tops could seat 10,000 spectators and treated audiences to three rings and two stages of constant entertainment. Contemporary critics claimed that the circus was "too big to see all at once." In the early 1900s, nearly 100 circuses, the biggest number in American history, rambled across the country.

In 1900, "circus day" was a community celebration. Before dawn, hundreds of spectators from throughout a county gathered to watch the circus train rumble into town. The early morning crowd witnessed scores of disciplined muscular men, horses, and elephants transform an empty field into a temporary tented city. In mid-morning, thousands more lined the streets to experience, up close, the circus parade of marching bands, calliopes, gilded wagons, exotic animals, and people winding noisily through the center of town. In the

United States, the circus reached its apex during the rise of American expansion overseas. Circus proprietors successfully marketed their exotic performances (even those featuring seminude women) as "respectable" and "educational," because they showcased people and animals from countries where the United States was consolidating its political and economic authority. With its displays of exotic animals, pageants of racial hierarchy (from least to most "evolved"), and dramatizations of American combat overseas, the circus gave its isolated, small-town audiences an immediate look at faraway cultures. This vision of the world celebrated American military might and white racial supremacy. The tightly-knit community of circus employees, however, also provided a safe haven for people ostracized from society on the basis of race, gender, or physical disability.

In the early twentieth century, the circus overlapped considerably with other popular amusements. Many circus performers worked in vaudeville or at amusement parks during the winter once the circus finished its show season. Vaudeville companies also incorporated circus acts such as juggling, wire-walking, and animal stunts into their programs. In addition, the Wild West Show was closely tied to the circus. Many circuses contained Wild West acts, and several Wild West Shows had circus sideshows. Both also shared the same investors. Circuses occasionally borrowed their subject matter from other contemporary amusements. At the dawning of the American empire, international expositions like the Columbia Exposition in Chicago (1893) profitably displayed ethnological villages; thus, circuses were quick to hire "strange and savage tribes" for sprawling new ethnological congresses of their own. The new film industry also used circus subjects. Thomas Edison's Manufacturing Company produced many circus motion pictures of human acrobatics, trick elephants, and dancing horses, among others. Circuses such as the Ringling Brothers Circus featured early film as part of their novel displays. During the early twentieth century, the circus remained a popular film subject in movies like Charlie Chaplin's *Circus* (1928) and Tod Browning's *Freaks* (1932). Several film stars, such as Burt Lancaster, began their show business careers with the circus. Cecil B. DeMille's *The Greatest Show on Earth* won an Oscar for Best Picture in 1952. These popular forms capitalized on the circus' celebration of bodily feats and exotic racial differences.

The American circus began to scale back its sprawling features in the 1920s, owing to the rise of the automobile and the movies. Most circuses stopped holding a parade because streets became too congested with cars. As motion pictures became increasingly sophisticated—and thus a more realistic mirror of the world than the circus—circuses also stopped producing enormous spectacles of contemporary foreign relations. Yet, despite its diminishing physical presence, the circus was still popular. On September 13, 1924, 16,702 people, the largest tented audience in American history, gathered at Concordia, Kansas, for the Ringling Brothers Barnum and Bailey circus. In the milieu of the rising movie star culture of the 1920s, the circus had its share of "stars," from bareback rider May Wirth to aerialist Lillian Leitzel and her dashing trapeze artist husband, Alfredo Codona. Like their movie star counterparts in the burgeoning consumer culture, circus stars began to advertise a wealth of products in the 1920s—from soap to sheet music. Leitzel became so famous that newspapers around the world mourned her death in 1931, after she fell when a piece of faulty equipment snapped during a performance in Copenhagen, Denmark.

During the Great Depression, the colorful traveling circus provided a respite from bleak times. When nearly a quarter of the United

States workforce was periodically unemployed, clown Emmett Kelly became a national star as ''Willie,'' a tramp character dressed in rags, a disheveled wig, hat, and smudged face, who pined for lost love and better circumstances. The circus continued to profit during World War II, when railroad shows traveled under the auspices of the Office of the Defense Transportation. Circuses exhorted Americans to support the war effort. Yet Ringling Brothers and Barnum and Bailey's ''Greatest Show On Earth'' nearly disintegrated after 168 audience members died in a big top fire (sparked by a spectator who dropped a lit cigarette) during a performance in Hartford, Connecticut, on July 6, 1944.

By the early 1950s, circus audience numbers were in decline, in part because the circus no longer had a monopoly on novelty or current events. Television, like movies and radio, provided audiences with compelling and immediate images that displaced the circus as an important source of information about the world. Yet, as a way to link itself to familiar, well-established popular forms, early television often featured live circus and vaudeville acts; circus performers were also featured on *Howdy Doody* as well as game shows like *What's My Line?* Ultimately, however, television offered Americans complete entertainment in the privacy of the home—which dovetailed nicely with the sheltered, domestic ethos of suburban America during the early Cold War. In this milieu, public amusements like movies and the circus attracted fewer customers. In 1956, just 13 circuses existed in America. As audiences shrank, showmen scaled back even further on their labor-intensive operations. Moreover, the rise of a unionized workforce (during the industrial union movement during the 1930s) meant that circus owners could no longer depend on a vast, cheap labor pool. Thus, John Ringling North cut his workforce drastically in 1956 when he abandoned the canvas tent for indoor arenas and stadiums. Circus employees and fans alike mourned the ''death'' of the familiar tented circus—a fixture of the circus business since 1825.

American social movements also transformed the circus. Circus performances of racial difference became increasingly controversial during the 1950s. Civil rights leaders had long objected to racist performances in American popular entertainment, but in the context of the Cold War between the United States and the Soviet Union, officials in the United States also protested because they feared that racist performances would legitimize Soviet claims that American racism was a product of American capitalism. Consequently, officials no longer aided circus agents' efforts to hire foreign performers slated to work as ''missing links,'' ''savages,'' or ''vanishing tribes,'' and performances of ''exotic'' racial difference, particularly at the sideshow, slowly disappeared from the 1950s onward. In addition, disabled rights activists effectively shut down the circus sideshow and its spectacles of human abnormality by the early 1980s.

Lastly, the spread of the animal rights movement in the 1970s transformed the circus. Fearful of picketers and ensuing bad publicity, several circuses in the 1990s arrive silently at each destination and stop at night to avoid protesters. Cirque du Soleil, an extraordinarily successful French Canadian circus from Montreal (with a permanent show in Las Vegas), uses no animals in its performances. Instead, troupe members wear tight lycra body suits, wigs, and face paint to imitate animals as they perform incredible aerial acrobatics to the beat of a slick, synthesized pop musical score and pulsating laser lights. Yet, arguably, Cirque du Soleil (among others) is actually not a circus because of its absence of animals: throughout its long history, the circus has been defined by its interplay of humans and animals in a circular arena.

Despite the transformation of its content, the American circus endures at the turn of the twenty first century. Certainly, towns no longer shut down on ''circus day,'' yet a growing number of small one-ring circuses have proliferated across America. Shows like the Big Apple Circus, Circus Flora, and Ringling Brothers Barnum and Bailey's show, ''Barnum's Kaleidoscope,'' have successfully recreated the intimate, community atmosphere of the nineteenth century one-ring circus, without the exploitation of physical and racial difference that characterized the older shows. Ultimately, in the 1990s, a decade of increasingly distant, fragmented, mass-mediated, ''virtual'' entertainment, the circus thrives because it represents one of the few intimate, live (and hence unpredictable) community experiences left in American popular culture.

—Janet Davis

FURTHER READING:

Albrecht, Ernest. *The New American Circus.* Gainesville, University Press of Florida, 1995.

Bogdan, Robert. *Freak Show: Presenting Human Oddities for Amusement and Profit.* Chicago, University of Chicago Press, 1988.

Cooper, Diana Starr. *Night After Night.* Washington, D.C., Island Press, 1994.

Hammarstrom, David Lewis. *Big Top Boss: John Ringling North and the Circus.* Urbana and Chicago, University of Illinois Press, 1992.

Speaight, George. *A History of the Circus.* London, Tantivy Press, 1980.

Taylor, Robert Lewis. *Center Ring: The People of the Circus.* Garden City, New York, Doubleday and Co., 1956.

Cisneros, Sandra (1954—)

Born and raised in Chicago, Chicana writer and poet Sandra Cisneros is best known for *The House on Mango Street* (1983), a series of interconnected prose poems. She is one of a handful of Latina writers to make it big in the American literary scene and the first Chicana to sign with a large publishing firm. Cisneros graduated from Loyola University in Chicago and went on to the prestigious Iowa Writers Workshop at the University of Iowa where she earned an MFA. Her poetry collections include *My Wicked, Wicked Ways* (1987) and *Loose Woman* (1994). She also has authored a collection of essays and short stories, *Woman Hollering Creek* (1991). Her poems and stories offer a conversational style, chatty and rambling. Her writing is lean and crisp, peppered with Spanish words.

—Beatriz Badikian

FURTHER READING:

Doyle, Jacqueline. ''More Room of Her Own: Sandra Cisneros's *The House on Mango Street.*'' *The Journal of the Society for the Study of the Multi-Ethnic Literature of the United States.* Vol. 19, No. 4, Winter 1995, 5-35.

Kanoza, Theresa. ''Esperanza's Mango Street: Home for Keeps.'' *Notes on Contemporary Literature.* Vol. 25, No. 3, May 1995, 9.

Citizen Kane

Orson Welles' film *Citizen Kane* has been consistently ranked as one of the best films ever made. A masterpiece of technique and storytelling, the film helped to change Hollywood film-making and still exerts considerable influence today. However, at the time of its premiere in 1941, it was a commercial failure that spelled disaster for Welles' Hollywood career.

Citizen Kane tells the story of millionaire press magnate Charles Foster Kane (played by Welles). The film opens with Kane on his death bed in his magnificent Florida castle, Xanadu, murmuring the word "Rosebud." A newsreel reporter (William Alland) searches for clues to the meaning of the word and to the meaning of Kane himself. Interviewing many people intimately connected with Kane, the reporter learns that the millionaire was not so much a public-minded statesman as he was a tyrannical, lonely man. The reporter never learns the secret of Kane's last word. In the film's final moments, we see many of Kane's possessions being thrown into a blazing furnace. Among them is his beloved childhood sled, the name "Rosebud" emblazoned across it.

Citizen Kane encountered difficulties early on. Welles fought constantly with RKO over his budget and against limits on his control of the production. Furthermore, because the film was based in part on the life of publisher William Randolph Hearst, Hearst's papers actively campaigned against it, demanding that *Citizen Kane* be banned and then later refusing to mention or advertise it altogether. Although the scheme backfired, generating enormous publicity for the movie, a frightened RKO released the film only after Welles threatened the studio with a lawsuit.

Critics reacted positively, but were also puzzled. They enthusiastically applauded *Citizen Kane*'s many technical innovations. Throughout the film, Welles and his crew employed depth of field (a method in which action in both the foreground and background clearly are in focus, and used to great effect by cinematographer Gregg Toland), inventive editing, sets with ceilings, chiaroscuro lighting, and multilayered sound. Although sometimes used in foreign film, many of these techniques were new to Hollywood. They have since, however, become standard for the industry.

Critics also were impressed by *Citizen Kane*'s many virtuoso sequences: a "March of Time"-type newsreel recounting the bare facts of Kane's life; the breakfast table scene, where in a few minutes his first marriage deteriorates to the strains of a waltz and variations (by noted screen composer Bernard Herrmann, in his first film assignment); a tracking shot through the roof of a nightclub; and a faux Franco-Oriental opera. None of these sequences, however, are showstoppers; each propels the narrative forward.

Orson Welles (center) in a scene from the film *Citizen Kane*.

That narrative proved puzzling both to critics and to audiences at large. Written by Herman J. Mankiewicz and Welles (although there is considerable controversy over how much Welles contributed), the narrative employs a series of flashbacks that tell different pieces of Kane's life story and reveal the witnesses' various perceptions of him. By arranging these pieces out of order, the script opened the door for later screenwriters to avoid the demands of strict chronology. At the time, however, this innovation confused most audiences.

While *Citizen Kane* did well in New York, the film did poor business in small-town America. The film was a commercial failure, allowing RKO's officials to eventually let go of Welles. Thereafter, he found it increasingly difficult to make movies in Hollywood. Shunned by the studio system, he was forced to spend much of his time simply trying to raise money for his various projects.

For a while, *Citizen Kane* itself seemed to suffer a similar fate. Although the film was nominated for a host of Oscars, Academy members took RKO's side in the studio's battle with Welles, awarding the movie only one Oscar for best original screenplay. The film lost to *How Green Was My Valley* for best picture. *Citizen Kane* soon sank into obscurity, rarely discussed, except when described as the beginning of the end of Welles' film career.

After World War II, RKO, seeking to recoup its losses, released *Citizen Kane* in European theaters hungry for American films and also made it available for American television. Exposed to a new generation of moviegoers, the film received new critical and popular acclaim. Riding the wave of *Citizen Kane*'s new-found popularity, Welles was able to return to Hollywood, directing *Touch of Evil* in 1958.

Consistently ranked number one on *Sight and Sound's* top ten films list since the mid-1950s, *Citizen Kane* continues to attract, inspire, and entertain new audiences. In 1998, it was voted the best American film of the twentieth century by the American Film Institute.

—Scott W. Hoffman

FURTHER READING:

Carringer, Robert L. *The Making of Citizen Kane*. Berkeley, University of California Press, 1996.

Higham, Charles. *The Films of Orson Welles*. Berkeley, University of California Press, 1970.

Kael, Pauline. *The Citizen Kane Book*. Boston, Little, Brown and Company, 1971.

McBride, Joseph. *Orson Welles*. New York, Viking Press, 1972.

Naremore, James. *The Magic World of Orson Welles*. New York, Oxford University Press, 1978.

City Lights

A silent film at the dawn of the talking picture technological revolution, *City Lights* appeared to popular acclaim and remains, for many, Charlie Chaplin's finest achievement. When Chaplin, known the world over for his "Little Tramp" character, began filming *City Lights* in 1928, talking pictures had become the rage in the movie industry, and most filmmakers who had originally conceived of their works as silent films were now adapting them into partial talkies or junking them altogether. Chaplin halted production on *City Lights* to weigh his options, and, when he resumed work several months later, he stunned his Hollywood peers by deciding to keep the film in a

Charlie Chaplin in a scene from the film *City Lights*.

silent form. "My screen character remains speechless from choice," he declared in a *New York Times* essay. "*City Lights* is synchronized [to a musical score] and certain sound effects are part of the comedy, but it is a non-dialogue picture because I preferred that it be that." For many, the film that resulted is a finely wrought balance of pathos and comedy, the very quintessence of Chaplin. The movie debuted in 1931.

Chaplin, who not only produced, directed, and starred in *City Lights* but also wrote and edited it and composed its musical score, centered his film on the Little Tramp and his relationship with a young, blind flower vendor who has mistaken him for a rich man. The smitten Tramp, not about to shatter her fantasy, undergoes a series of comic misadventures while trying to raise money for an operation that would restore her vision. He interrupts the suicide attempt of a drunken man who turns out to be a millionaire. The two become friends, but unfortunately the millionaire only recognizes the Tramp when drunk. Determined to help the young woman, the Tramp takes on such unlikely occupations as street sweeping and prize fighting (both of which go comically awry) before the millionaire finally offers him one thousand dollars for the operation. Robbers attack at just that moment, knocking the millionaire in the head. Police arrive and assume the Tramp is the thief (the millionaire, sobered by the blow, does not recognize him), but the Tramp manages to give the money to the woman before they catch him and haul him off to jail. After his release, he discovers that the young woman, now sighted, runs her own florist shop. She doesn't recognize the shabbily dressed Tramp at first and playfully offers him a flower. When she at last realizes who he is, the film concludes with the most poignant exchange of glances in the history of world cinema.

Chaplin found the casting of the nameless young blind woman to be particularly difficult. According to his autobiography, one of his biggest challenges "was to find a girl who could look blind without detracting from her beauty. So many applicants looked upward, showing the whites of their eyes, which was too distressing." The filmmaker eventually settled on Virginia Cherrill, a twenty-year-old Chicagoan with little acting experience. "To my surprise she had the faculty of looking blind," Chaplin wrote. "I instructed her to look at me but to look inwardly and not to see me, and she could do it." He later found the neophyte troublesome to work with, however, and fired her about a year into production. He recruited Georgia Hale, who had co-starred with him in *The Gold Rush* in 1925, to replace her but eventually re-hired Cherrill after realizing how much of the film he would have to re-shoot.

Chaplin's problems extended to other aspects of the movie. He filmed countless retakes and occasionally stopped shooting for days on end to mull things over. Most famously, he struggled for eighty-three days (sixty-two of which involved no filming whatsoever) on the initial encounter of the Tramp and the young woman, unable to find a way of having the woman conclude that the Tramp is wealthy. Inspiration finally struck, and Chaplin filmed a brief scene in which a limousine door slammed shut a moment before the Tramp met her.

Chaplin's difficulties on the set mattered little to audiences. They loved his melancholy yet comic tale of two hard-luck people and made it an unqualified hit (the movie earned a profit of five million dollars during its initial release alone). A few reviewers criticized the film's old-fashioned, heavily sentimental quality, but the majority praised Chaplin's work. Its regressive form and content notwithstanding, *City Lights* appealed strongly to audiences and critics alike.

—Martin F. Norden

FURTHER READING:

Chaplin, Charles. *My Autobiography.* New York, Simon and Schuster, 1964.

———. "Pantomime and Comedy." *New York Times.* January 25, 1931, H6.

Maland, Charles J. *Chaplin and American Culture: The Evolution of a Star Image.* Princeton, Princeton University Press, 1989.

Molyneaux, Gerard. *Charlie Chaplin's City Lights.* New York, Garland, 1983.

The City of Angels

The official slogan for the city of Los Angeles (L.A.) is "Los Angeles brings it all together." Its unofficial name is "The City of Angels." In the first instance, reality belies the motto in that Los Angeles' most salient feature is its diffuse layout. In the second, it is difficult to think of someone saying "The City of Angels" without a Raymond Chandler-esque sneer. But that, too, is L.A.; duplicitous, narcissistic, and paradoxical. Perhaps no city has been loved or abhorred with such equal vigor, or typified by so many contradictions. For postmodern philosophers (especially Europeans) who study the city as they would a text, the city fascinates with its sheer modernity—a tabula rasa over which the thick impasto of America's aspirations and proclivities has been smeared. Viewed from the air, the city

terrifies with its enormity, but one can discern a map of sorts, a guidepost pointing towards the future.

From its very beginning Los Angeles has existed more as a sales pitch than a city; a marketing campaign selling fresh air, citrus fruits, and the picturesque to the elderly and tubercular. In the 1880s, when Los Angeles was little more than a dusty border town of Spanish Colonial vintage, attractively packaged paeans to sun-kissed good-living were flooding the Midwest. Pasadena was already a well-known summer destination for East Coast millionaires, and the campaign sought to capitalize on a keeping-up-with-the-Jones sentiment calculated to attract prosperous and status conscious farmers. Behind the well-heeled came the inevitable array of servants, lackeys, and opportunists. The farm boom dried-up, and the transplanted, oftentimes marooned mid-westerners sat on their dusty front porches wondering where they went wrong—a dominant leit motif of L.A. literature along with conflagrations, earthquakes, floods, crowd violence, and abject chicanery.

Until the film industry invaded in the early 1910s, Los Angeles could offer few incentives to attract industry, lacking a port or even ready access to coal. The only way civic leaders could entice businessmen was by offering the most fervently anti-labor municipal government in the country, and Los Angeles developed a reputation for quelling its labor unrest with great dispatch. L.A.'s leading lights were as canny at pitching their real estate holdings as they were ruthless in ensuring the city's future prosperity. To insure adequate water to nourish the growing metropolis, founding father William Mulholland bamboozled the residents of Owens Valley, some 250 miles to the northeast, into selling their water rights under false pretenses and building an enormous aqueduct into the San Fernando Valley. In 1927 the embittered farmers, having witnessed their fertile land return to desert, purchased an advertisement in the *Los Angeles Times* which read: "We, the farming communities of the Owens Valley, being about to die, salute you." The publisher of the newspaper, General Harrison Gray Otis, was a major investor in Mulholland's scheme. Even back then, irony was a way of life in Southern California.

Fate was kind to Los Angeles. With the film industry came prosperity, and a spur to real estate growth. But beneath the outward prosperity, signs of the frivolity and moral disintegration L.A. was famous for provoking were apparent to those with an eye for details. Thus, Nathaniel West, author of the quintessential Los Angeles novel, *Day of the Locust,* could write of a woman in man's clothing preaching the "crusade against salt" or the Temple Moderne, where the acolytes taught "brain-breathing, secret of the Aztecs," while up on Bunker Hill, a young John Fante would chronicle the lives of the hopelessly displaced Midwest pensioners and the sullen ghetto underclass from his cheap hotel room overlooking downtown. Across town, European luminaries such as Arnold Schoenberg, Thomas Mann, and Bertolt Brecht found the leap from Hitler's Germany to palm trees and pristine beaches a difficult transition to make. The contrast between the European exiles and their American counterparts was as plain as day, and illustrates the contradictory schools of thought about the City of Angels. The Europeans regarded the city as a curiosity to be tolerated, or wondered at, while West, Fante, and their better known brethren were almost uniform in their strident denunciations of what they perceived as overt Philistinism. British novelist Aldous Huxley oscillated between condemnation and approval. These foreigners perceived the myriad contradictions of Los Angeles: The beauty of its locale and the crassness of its people; the film industries' pollyanna-like flights of fancy and the bitter labor struggles that accompanied their creation; the beauty of the art deco style that Los Angeles adopted as its own, and the eyesores (building shaped like hot-dogs, space ships, ginger-bread houses) constructed alongside them.

For obvious reasons, L.A. became a center for the defense industry during World War II, and the factories springing up like mushrooms on the table-flat farmland attracted the rootless detritus of the Depression, who only a few years back were regularly turned back at the Nevada border by the California Highway Patrol. The great influx of transplants flourished in their well-paid aerospace assembly line jobs, enjoying a semblance of middle class living. It became the clarion call of a new sales pitch—the suburban myth. The suburbs marketed a dream, that of single family homes, nuclear families, and healthful environment. Within a few years, pollution from the legions of commuters who clogged L.A.'s roadways dispelled the illusion of country living. Another recent innovation, the shopping mall, while invented in Seattle, was quickly adopted as a native institution, to the further degradation of downtown Los Angeles.

The veterans had children, who, nourished on their parent's prosperity, became a sizeable marketing demographic. The children took to such esoteric sports as surfing, hot rodding, and skateboarding, fostering a nationwide craze for surf music and the stylistic excesses of hot-rod artists such as Big Daddy Roth. For a time, Los Angeles persevered under this placid illusion, abruptly collapsed by the 1965 Watts riots and the Vietnam war. In a city without discernible boundaries, the idea of a city center is an oxymoron. Downtown Los Angeles, the nexus of old money Los Angeles, slowly withered, crippled further by urban renewal projects that made the downtown ghost town something of a self-fulfilling prophecy.

This, then, is L.A., a heady mixture of status and sleaze, weirdness and conformity, natural beauty and choking pollution. Los Angeles is indeed the most postmodern of cities, a city with more of a reflection than an image, and where the only safe stance is the ironic one. In the early 1990s, L.A. was hit by earthquakes, fires, and another riot of its black populace, this time provoked by the acquittal of policeman accused of beating a black motorist more briskly than usual. Los Angeles once again managed to recover, refusing once again to be crippled by its inner contradictions. With its limited array of tropes, the city trots out its endgame against any natural limitations to its growth. As the city evolves, postmodern theoreticians stand by rubbing their palms together, predicting the city's inevitable denouement while the sun shines mercilessly overhead.

—Michael Baers

FURTHER READING:

Davis, Mike. *City of Quartz*. New York, Verso, 1990.

———. *Ecology of Fear*. New York, Metropolitan Books, 1998.

Didion, Joan. *Slouching Towards Bethlehem*. New York, Washington Square Press, 1981.

Fante, John. *Ask the Dust*. Santa Barbara, Black Sparrow Press, 1980.

Klein, Norman. *The History of Forgetting*. New York, Verso, 1997.

Lovett, Anthony R., and Matt Maranian. *L.A. Bizarro*. Los Angeles, Buzz, 1997.

Pynchon, Thomas. *The Crying of Lot 49*. New York, Lippincott, 1963.

West, Nathanael. *Day of the Locust*. New York, Random House, 1939.

Civil Disobedience

Civil disobedience is a nonviolent, deliberate, and conspicuous violation of a law or social norm, or a violation of the orders of civil authorities, in order to generate publicity and public awareness of an issue. Protesters directly confront the rule and confront authorities who would enforce it, and demand a change in the rule. Civil disobedience communicates the protesters' unity and strength of interest in an issue and provides evidence of their commitment and willingness to sacrifice for the cause. It also presents a latent threat of more overt action if the regime fails to act on the issue.

Civil disobedience is a form of political participation available to citizens without the money, media support, lobbying resources, voting strength, political skills, or political access necessary to influence decision-makers through more traditional means. The tactic was used by Mahatma Gandhi in the 1940s to secure the end of British colonial rule in India; by Martin Luther King, Jr. and other American civil rights leaders in the 1960s to end legal racial segregation and to secure voting rights for African Americans; and by non-voting age college students during the 1960s to protest America's war in Vietnam. Civil disobedience brings people into the political system who were previously outside the system and is one of the few tactics available to empower concerned citizens who lack any other means to press their demands for change. Social minorities and deviant subcultures use civil disobedience to challenge and change the norms of society or to demand their independence from the rules of society.

Civil disobedience usually takes one of three forms. First, civil disobedience may take the form of deliberate and purposeful violation of a specific targeted statute or social norm in order to focus popular and media attention on the rule, to encourage others to resist the rule, and to encourage authorities to change the rule. Examples include 1960s American civil rights sit-ins and demands for service at segregated lunch counters, anti-war protesters refusing to submit to selective service calls, and feminists publicly removing restrictive brassieres in protest of clothing norms. In the 1970s, trucker convoys deliberately exceeded the 55-mile-per-hour federal highway speed limit to protest the limit. According to Saul Alinsky in *Rules for Radicals*, this tactic is effective only in non-authoritarian and non-totalitarian regimes with a free press to publicize the violation of the law and basic civil rights to prevent civil authorities and social majorities from overreacting to the violation.

Second, civil disobedience may take the form of passive resistance in which protesters refuse to respond to the orders of authorities but are otherwise in full compliance with the law. Examples have included civil rights protesters and anti-war activists who ignore police orders to disperse and force police to physically carry them from a public protest site. Feminists have resisted social norms by refusing to shave their legs. The organization Civilian Based Defense promoted passive resistance as a national defense strategy and suggested that the threat of withholding cooperation and engaging in active non-cooperation with the enemy may be as effective a deterrent to an invader's aggression as the use of military force.

Third, civil disobedience may take the form of non-violent illegal activity in which protesters disrupt activities they oppose and seek to be arrested, punished, and even martyred to gain publicity and to influence public opinion. Examples have included anti-war protesters who trespass on military installations and illegally seize military property by chaining themselves to it, radical environmentalists who

Student protesters at Woolworth's lunch counter, Atlanta, Georgia, 1960.

"spike" trees with nails to disrupt logging activities, and animal rights activists who throw blood on persons wearing animal fur coats.

Civil disobedience is distinctly different from nonconformity, social pathology, eccentricity, or social disorganization. Nonconformity is willful violation of a rule because the values established in the rule are contrary to the social, cultural, or moral values and norms of a subgroup of the civil society—but the violation is not intended to encourage a change in the rule. For example, a fundamentalist Mormon practices polygamy because he believes religious proscriptions require him to do so, not because he seeks to change or protest the marriage laws of the state. Social pathology is the failure to conform to civil law because failures in the individual's socialization and education processes leave the individual normless and, therefore, free to pursue his personal self-interest and selfish desires without concern for law. Eccentricity is socially encouraged nonconformance in which a cultural hero, genius, intellectual, or artist is granted cultural license to violate the law based on the person's unique status or contributions to society. Finally, social disorganization is the failure of the political or social system to enforce its rules because authority has become ineffective or has been destroyed in war or revolution, leaving individuals in a state of anarchy and licensed to make their own rules.

Civil disobedience as a political tactic and social process increases in popularity and use as society decreases its reliance on violence and force to achieve political goals or to gain the advantage in social conflict or competition. It also increases in popularity when political outsiders seek to assert themselves in the political process and find all other avenues of political participation beyond their abilities and resources or find all other avenues prohibited to them by political insiders or by civil authorities.

—Gordon Neal Diem

FURTHER READING:

Alinsky, Saul. *Rules for Radicals.* New York, Random House, 1971.

Ball, Terence. *Civil Disobedience and Civil Deviance.* Beverly Hills, California, Sage Publications, 1973.

Bay, Christian, and Charles Walker. *Civil Disobedience: Theory and Practice.* Saint Paul, Minnesota, Black Rose Books, 1975.

Bedau, Hugo. *Civil Disobedience: Theory and Practice.* New York, Pegasus, 1969.

King, Jr., Martin Luther. *Letter from the Birmingham Jail.* San Francisco, Harper San Francisco, 1994.

Thoreau, Henry David. *Civil Disobedience.* 1866. Boston, D. R. Godine, 1969.

van den Haag, Ernest. *Political Violence and Civil Disobedience.* New York, Harper & Row, 1972.

Zashin, Elliot M. *Civil Disobedience and Democracy.* New York, Free Press, 1972.

Civil Rights Movement

The African-American struggle for civil rights marks a turning point in American history because it represents the period when African Americans made their entry into the American mainstream. Although the focus of the long persistent drive for civil rights was centered around political issues such as voting, integration, educational opportunities, better housing, increased employment opportunities, and fair police protection, other facets of American life and culture were affected as well. Most noticeably, African Americans came out of the civil rights movement determined to define their own distinct culture. New styles of politics, music, clothing, folktales, hairstyles, cuisine, literature, theology, and the arts were all evident at the end of the civil rights movement.

Although African Americans have a long tradition of protest dating back to the seventeenth century, the mid-1950s represented a turning point in the black struggle for equal rights. With the historic *Brown v. Board of Education* Supreme Court decision that outlawed the 1896 *Plessy v. Ferguson* doctrine of "Separate But Equal," African Americans realized that the time was right to end all vestiges of Jim Crow and discrimination. On the heels of *Brown*, black Southerners undertook battles to achieve voting rights and integration, under the broad leadership of Martin Luther King, Jr. Through marches, rallies, sit-ins, and boycotts, they were able to accomplish their goals by the late 1960s. With voting rights and integration won in the South, African Americans next shifted their attention to the structural problems of northern urban blacks. However, non-violent direct-action was not the preferred tool of protest in the North where the self-defense message of Malcolm X was popular. Rather, the method of protest was urban unrest, which produced very few meaningful gains for African Americans other than the symbolic election of black mayors to large urban centers.

Immediately, the civil rights movement ushered in a new black political culture. With the right to vote won in 1965 with the passage of the Voting Rights Act, African Americans now began to place a

A protest for Civil Rights.

tremendous emphasis on political participation. Throughout the South African Americans went to the polls in large numbers seeking to elect representatives that would best represent their interests. In the North where the right to vote had been in existence since the mid-nineteenth century, a different type of political culture emerged. As a result of the civil rights movement black voters in the North began to move away from the idea of coalition building with white liberals, preferring instead to establish all-black political organizations. These clubs would not only attack the conservativeness of the Republican Party but they would also begin to reassess their commitment to the democratic party at the local, state, and national level. In essence, the race was moving toward political maturity; no longer would their votes be taken for granted.

Another aspect of the nascent black political culture was a re-emergence of black nationalism which was re-introduced into American society by Malcolm X. While a spokesman for the Nation of Islam, Malcolm X made African Americans feel good about themselves. He told them to embrace their culture and their heritage, and he also spoke out openly against white America. Via his autobiography and lectures, Malcolm X quickly emerged as the instrumental figure in this renewed black consciousness. Shortly after his assassination in 1965, the proprietors of black culture immediately gave Malcolm deity status. His name and portrait began to appear everywhere: bumper stickers, flags, T-shirts, hats, and posters. Although Malcolm popularized this new revolutionary frame of mind, by no means did he have a monopoly on it. Throughout the 1960s African Americans spoke of black nationalism in three main forms: territorial, revolutionary, and cultural. Territorial nationalists such as the Republic of New Afrika and the Nation of Islam, called for a portion of the United States to be partitioned off for African Americans as payment for years of slavery, Jim Crow, and discrimination. But they insisted that by no means would this settle the issue. Instead, this would just be partial compensation for years of mistreatment. Revolutionary nationalists such as the Black Panther Party sought to overthrow the capitalist American government and replace it with a socialist utopia. They argued that the problems faced by African Americans were rooted in the capitalist control of international economic affairs. Thus, the Black Panthers viewed the black nationalist struggle as one of both race and class. Lastly, the cultural nationalism espoused by groups such as Ron Karenga's US organization sought to spark a revolution through a black cultural renaissance. In the eyes of his supporters, the key to black self-empowerement lay in a distinct black culture. They replaced European cultural forms with a distinct Afro-centric culture. One of Karenga's chief achievements was the development of the African-American holiday "Kwanzaa." Kwanzaa was part of a broader theory of black cultural nationalism which suggested that African Americans needed to carry out a cultural revolution before they could achieve power.

One of the most visible effects of the civil rights movement on American popular culture was the introduction of the concept of "Soul." For African Americans of the 1960s, Soul was the common denominator of all black folks. It was simply the collective thread of black identity. All blacks had it. In essence, soul was black culture, something separate and distinct from white America. No longer would they attempt to deny nor be ashamed of their cultural heritage; rather they would express it freely, irrespective of how whites perceived it. Soul manifested itself in a number of ways: through greetings, "what's up brother," through handshakes, "give me some skin," and even through the style of walk. It was no longer acceptable to just walk, one who had soul had to "strut" or "bop." This was all a part of the attitude that illustrated they would no longer look for white acceptance.

One of the most fascinating cultural changes ushered in by the civil rights movement was the popularity of freedom songs, which at times were organized or started spontaneously during the midst of demonstrations, marches, and church meetings. These songs were unique in that although they were in the same tradition as other protest music, this was something different. These were either new songs for a new situation, or old songs adapted to the times. Songs such as "I'm Gonna Sit at the Welcome Table," "Everybody Says Freedom," "Which Side Are You On," "If You Miss Me at the Back of the Bus," "Keep Your Eyes on the Prize," and "Ain't Scared of Your Jails," all express the feelings of those fighting for black civil rights. While these songs were popularized in the South, other tunes such as "Burn, Baby, Burn," and the "Movement's Moving On," signaled the movements shift from non-violence to Black Power. Along with freedom songs blacks also expressed themselves through "Soul music," which they said "served as a repository of racial consciousness." Hits such as "I'm Black and I'm Proud," by James Brown, "Message from a Black Man," by the Temptations, Edwin Starrs's "Ain't It Hell Up in Harlem," and "Is It Because I'm Black" by Syl Johnson, all testified to the black community's move toward a cultural self-definition.

African Americans also redefined themselves in the area of literary expression. Black artists of the civil rights period attempted to counter the racist and stereotyped images of black folk by expressing the collective voice of the black community, as opposed to centering their work to gain white acceptance. Instrumental in this new "black arts movement," were works such as Amiri Baraka's *Blues People*, *Preface to a Twenty-Volume Suicide Note*, and *Dutchman*. These works illustrate the distinctiveness of black culture, while simultaneously promoting race pride and unity.

The black revolution was principally the catalyst for a new appreciation of black history as well. Prior to the civil rights movement, the importance of Africa in the world and the role of African Americans in the development of America was virtually ignored at all levels of education, particularly at the college and university level. Whenever people of African descent were mentioned in an educational setting they were generally introduced as objects and not subjects. However, the civil rights movement encouraged black students to demand that their history and culture receive equal billing in academia. Students demanded black studies courses taught by black professors. White university administrators reluctantly established these courses, which instantly became popular. Predominantly white universities and colleges now offered classes in Swahili, Yoruba, black history, and black psychology to satisfy the demand. Due to the heightened awareness, all black students were expected to enroll in black studies courses, and when they didn't, they generally had to provide an explanation to the more militant factions on campus. Students not only demanded black studies courses but they also expressed a desire for colleges and universities that would be held accountable to the black community. Traditional black colleges and universities such as Howard, Spelman, and Fisk, were now viewed with suspicion since they served the racial status quo. Instead, schools such as Malcolm X College of Chicago and Medgar Evers College of CUNY became the schools of choice since they were completely dedicated to the black community.

The 1960s generation of African Americans also redefined themselves in the area of clothing. Again, they were seeking to create something unique and distinct from the white mainstream. The new attire consisted of wide-brimmed hats, long full-cut jackets, platform shoes, bell-bottoms, leather vests, and wide-collar shirts. These outfits were complimented by African-like beads, earrings, belts, medallions, and bracelets. However, the more culturally conscious rejected all types of western culture in favor of dashikis, robes, and sandals. In response to these new cultural tastes clothing companies began specifically targeting the black consumer by stating that their items were designed to meet the body style of blacks. To complement the new clothing look African Americans also began to reject the European standard of beauty. Whereas African Americans were once ashamed of their full lips, broad nose, high cheekbones, and coarse hair, they now embraced them. Black women took hair straighteners and hot combs out of their bathrooms and began to wear ''naturals,'' cornrows, and beads, which many considered to be the most visible sign of black self-expression.

Interestingly enough, black Americans also experienced a slight shift in eating tastes. Although collard greens, ''chitlins,'' catfish, pigs feet, and fried-chicken had been a staple in the black diet for years, it was now labeled ''soul food,'' because it provided a cultural link to the African ancestral homeland.

African-American folktales took on a whole new importance during the civil rights movement as the famed ''trickster tales'' became more contemporary. Folklorists made the black hero superior to that of other culture's, by stressing its mental agility, brute physical strength, and sexual prowess. These heroes also reversed the traditional socio-economic arrangements of America as well. Characters such as Long-Shoe Sam, Hophead Willie, Shine, and Dolemite, all used wit and deceit to get what they wanted from white America. In the eyes of black America, traditional heroes such as Paul Bunyan and Davy Crockett were no match for this new generation of black adventurers.

The civil rights movement also encouraged blacks to see God, Jesus, and Mary as black. As their African ancestors, these deities would assist African Americans in their quest for physical, mental, and spiritual liberation. By stressing that a belief in a white God or Jesus fostered self-hatred, clergyman such as Rev. Albert Cleague of Detroit sought to replace the traditional depiction of God and Jesus with a black image. Throughout the country black churches followed Cleague's lead as they removed all vestiges of a white Christ in favor of a savior they could identify with. Followers of this new Black Christian Nationalism also formulated a distinct theology, in which Jesus was viewed as a black revolutionary who would deliver African American people from their white oppressors.

As with other facets of black popular culture, television also witnessed a change as a result of the black revolution. With the renewed black consciousness clearly evident, the entertainment industry sought to capitalize by increasing the visibility of black actors and actresses. Whereas in 1962 blacks on TV were only seen in the traditional stereotyped roles as singers, dancers, and musicians, by 1968 black actors were being cast in more positive roles, such as Greg Morris in *Mission Impossible*, Diahann Carroll in *Julia*, Clarence Williams III in the *Mod Squad*, and Nichelle Nichols, who starred as Uhura in *Star Trek*. While these shows did illustrate progress, other shows such as *Sanford and Son* and *Flip Wilson's Show* all reinforced the traditional black stereotype. In the film industry, Hollywood would not capitalize on the renewed black consciousness until the early 1970s with blaxploitation films. In the mid-1960s however, African Americans were continually portrayed as uncivilized, barbaric, and savage, in movies such as *The Naked Prey*, *Dark of the Sun*, and *Mandingo*.

The principal effect of the civil rights movement on American popular culture was a renewed racial consciousness not witnessed since the Harlem Renaissance. This cultural revolution inspired African Americans to reject the white aesthetic in favor of their own. Although they had fought and struggled for full inclusion into American society, the civil rights drive also instilled into African Americans a strong appreciation of their unique cultural heritage. Through new styles of music, clothing, literature, theology, cuisine, and entertainment, African Americans introduced a completely new cultural form that is still evident today.

—Leonard N. Moore

FURTHER READING:

Anderson, Terry. *The Movement and the Sixties: Protest in America from Greensboro to Wounded Knee.* Oxford, Oxford University Press, 1995.

Dickstein, Morris. *Gates of Eden: American Culture in the Sixties.* New York, Basic Books, 1977.

Seeger, Pete, and Bob Reiser. *Everybody Says Freedom.* New York, W.W. Norton and Company.

Van Deburg, William. *Black Camelot: African-American Culture Heroes in Their Times, 1960-1980.* Chicago: University of Chicago Press, 1997.

———. *New Day in Babylon.* Chicago, University of Chicago Press, 1992.

Civil War Reenactors

Reenactors are those people whose hobby involves dressing in the manner of soldiers from a particular period of time in order to recreate battles from a famous war. Those individuals who choose to restage Civil War battles form the largest contingent of reenactors. They are part of a larger group of Civil War buffs who actively participate in genealogy research, discussion groups, and roundtables. The American Civil War divided the country in bitter warfare from 1861 to 1865 but its legacy has endured long since the fighting ceased. The war wrought extensive changes which shaped United States society and its inhabitants. Historian Shelby Foote, renowned for his participation in Ken Burns' popular PBS series *The Civil War,* observes that ''any understanding of this nation has to be based, and I mean really based, on an understanding of the Civil War. I believe that firmly. It defined us.'' The importance of the Civil War in American culture and memory makes it significant in popular culture. The Civil War has a long history of serving ''as a vehicle for embodying sentiments and politics in our day.'' The Civil War has therefore been entwined with popular culture before, during, and since its actual battles occurred as popular cultural producers fought to determine how its meaning would apply to postwar society.

Civil War reenactments range in size from small one-day skirmishes to large encampments like the 125th Anniversary of Gettysburg that attracted 12,000 soldiers and 100,000 audience members. The larger events are great tourist attractions that feature concerts, lectures, exhibitions, encampments, and demonstrations of camp life, hospitals, Civil War fashions, and other topics. These large reenactments are often cosponsored by the National Park Service and local museums as they involve numerous volunteers and intensive

A reenactment of the battle at Andersonville, Georgia.

preparations. The battles themselves are choreographed events where the soldiers shoot blanks and show a great concern for the safety of all involved. The reenactors who stage these events are part of the amateur and living history movement that encourages direct audience interaction and has enjoyed increasing popularity in the late twentieth century. Living history museums rose in popularity in the United States in the 1920s with the founding of automobile giant Henry Ford's Greenfield Village in Michigan and John D. Rockefeller's Colonial Williamsburg village in Virginia. The majority of the people in the United States learn their history from popular culture rather than academic books and classes. Popular cultural forms of history provide their audiences with forms, images, and interpretations of people and events from America's past. Their popularity makes their views on history widely influential. Civil War reenactors understand that popular history is a valuable form of communication. They view living history as a valuable education tool, viewing their participation as a learning experience both for them and for their audience.

The first group to reenact the Civil War consisted of actual veterans belonging to a society known as the Grand Army of the Republic. These late-nineteenth-century encampments were places where these ex-soldiers could affirm the passion and the sense of community to fellow soldiers that their wartime experiences engendered. Veterans also showed their respect for the former enemies who

had endured the same indescribable battle-time conditions. Community sponsored historical pageants replaced the early reenactments as the veterans largely died off, until the fragmentation of society after World War II broke apart any strong sense of community. Reenacting emerged in its late-twentieth-century form during the 1960s Civil War centennial commemorations. The battles staged during this period found a receptive audience. Public enthusiasm for reenactments faded in the late 1960s and 1970s as the result of a national mood of questioning blind patriotism and American values. The phenomenal popularity of the living history movement in the 1980s, however, quickly led to a resurgence of Civil War reenacting.

Twentieth-century Civil War reenactors have found themselves involved in the controversies between amateur and professional historians. Academics have accused the reenactors of engaging in cheap theatrics to capture their audience's interest and questioned the morality of the use of actual battlefields as reenactment sites. They have also been criticized for their sentimentalized historical portraits.

Civil War reenactors have a highly developed sense of culture among themselves. Most are generally white males in their thirties and are very passionate about the endeavor. There are a few women and African-Americans who participate, but they often meet with hostility. Reenactors are mostly not academic historians but are usually quite knowledgeable, conducting considerable research to create their historical characters and outfit themselves in meticulous detail. They categorize their fellow reenactors by a tiered system that demonstrates their amount of dedication to the activity and to the goal of complete authenticity. ''Farbs'' are those reenactors who lack seriousness and attention to detail and are usually more interested in the social and alcoholic aspects of the encampments. ''Authentic'' reenactors concern themselves with detail but are willing to allow some twentieth-century comforts whereas ''hard core'' reenactors share a precise and uncompromising commitment to accuracy. ''Hard core'' reenactors are also those who wish to ban women from participation despite the fact that many women disguised as men actually fought in the Civil War. Reenacting involves a great deal of preparation time as participants must obtain proper clothing and hardware and memorize complicated drills for public exhibition. Magazines such as the *North-South Trader's Civil War, Civil War Book Exchange and Collector's Newspaper, Blue and Gray, America's Civil War, Civil War News, Civil War Times,* and the *Camp Chase Gazette* cater to the large market of Civil War buffs and reenactors looking for necessary clothing and equipment. The reenactor must also make every effort to stay in character at all times, especially when members of the public are present.

The reenactors are largely unpaid amateur history fans who often travel great distances to participate in what can prove to be a very expensive hobby. Many participants welcome the chance to escape everyday life and its worries through complete absorption in the action of staged battles, the quiet of camp life, and the portrayal of their chosen historical character. Many also seek a vivid personal experience of what the Civil War must have been like for its actual participants. They are quite intense in their attempt to capture some sense of the fear and awe that must have overwhelmed their counterparts in reality. They find that experiential learning provides a much better understanding of the past than that provided by reading dry academic works. Jim Cullen observes in that by ''sleeping on the ground, eating bad food, and feeling something of the crushing fatigue that Civil War soldiers did, they hope to recapture, in the most direct sensory way, an experience that fascinates yet eludes them.'' The immediacy of the battles and surrounding camp life is part of the hobby's appeal. Cullen also suggests one of reenacting's more negative aspects in observing that certain participants seek a ritual reaffirmation of their own past which may hide a thinly veiled racism in the face of a growing emphasis on new multicultural pasts.

—Marcella Bush Treviño

FURTHER READING:

Bodner, John E. *Remaking America: Public Memory, Commemoration, and Patriotism in the Twentieth Century.* Princeton, Princeton University Press, 1992.

Catton, Bruce. *America Goes to War: The Civil War and Its Meaning in American Culture.* Lincoln, University Press of Nebraska, 1985.

Cullen, Jim. *The Civil War in Popular Culture: A Reusable Past.* Washington, D.C., Smithsonian Institution Press, 1995.

Hadden, R. Lee. *Reliving the Civil War: A Reenactor's Handbook.* Mechanicsburg, Pennsylvania, Stackpole Press, 1996.

———. *Returning to the Civil War: Grand Reenactments of an Anguished Time.* Gibbs Smit, 1997.

Claiborne, Liz (1929—)

After spending 25 years in the fashion business, Liz Claiborne became an overnight success when she opened her own dress company in 1976. By the time she and husband Arthur Ortenberg retired in 1989, their dress company had grown into a fashion colossus that included clothing for men and children as well as accessories, shoes, fragrances, and retail stores. Claiborne successfully combined an emphasis on sensible dresses with a keen intuition for the professional woman's desire to appear sophisticated and dressed up at the office. Her sensibility to what people want in fashion carried over into a successful sportswear line. Her genius as a fashion designer was highlighted by the fact that Claiborne was one of most stable fashion companies on the New York Stock Exchange, serving as a model for publicly-owned fashion companies until it faltered in the 1990s.

—Richard Martin

FURTHER READING:

Klensch, Elsa. ''Dressing America: The Success of Liz Claiborne.'' *Vogue.* August, 1986.

''Liz Claiborne.'' *Current Biography.* June, 1989.

Clairol Hair Coloring

In 1931, Lawrence M. Gelb, a chemical broker, discovered and bought ''Clairol'' hair color in Europe to market in the United States. From the start, he promoted Clairol with the idea that beautiful hair was every woman's right, and that hair color, then considered risqué, was no different from other cosmetics. With the 1956 introduction of ''Miss Clairol,'' the first at-home hair coloring formula, Clairol hair color and care products revolutionized the world of hair color. The do-it-yourself hair color ''was to the world of hair color what computers were to the world of adding machines,'' Bruce Gelb, who worked with his father and brother at Clairol, told *New Yorker* contributor Malcolm Gladwell.

The firm's 1956 marketing campaign for a new, Miss Clairol product ended the social stigma against hair coloring and contributed to America's lexicon. Shirley Polykoff's ad copy—which read ''Does she or doesn't she? Hair color so natural only her hairdresser knows for sure!''—accompanied television shots and print photos of wholesome-looking young women, not glamorous beauties associated with professional hair color but attractive homemakers with children. With ads that showed mothers and children with matching hair color, Miss Clairol successfully divorced hair coloring from its sexy image. Moreover, women could use the evasive ''only my hairdresser knows for sure'' to avoid divulging the tricks they used to craft an appealing public self. For women in the 1950s, hair color was a ''useful fiction—a way of bridging the contradiction between the kind of woman you were and the woman you were supposed to be,'' wrote Gladwell.

Hair color soon became an acceptable image-enhancing cosmetic. In 1959 Gelb's company was purchased by Bristol Meyers, which has continued to expand the line into the 1990s. From the decade Miss Clairol was introduced to the 1970s, the number of American women coloring their hair increased dramatically, from 7 to 40 percent. By the 1990s, store shelves were crowded with many brands of at-home hair colorings and the image of hair coloring had changed as the brands proliferated. Hair color was no longer something women hid. Instead women celebrated their ability to change their look on a whim. Supermodel Linda Evangelista would appear as a platinum blonde one day, a redhead the next, and a brunette the next. The brand Féria advertised hair color that didn't pretend to be natural. Clairol's ads accommodated this change as well. While keeping with the image of the-girl-next-door, Clairol's shampoo-in color Nice 'n Easy ads featured Julia Louis-Dreyfus, well-known as Elaine on the popular sitcom *Seinfeld,* spotting women on the street and giving them public hair colorings. Clairol had initiated an appealing formula that gave women new freedom to shape their image as they pleased.

—Joan Leotta

FURTHER READING:

"Clairol's Influence on American Beauty and Marketing." *Drug & Cosmetic Industry.* New York, August, 1996.

Gladwell, Malcolm. "True Colors." *New Yorker.* New York, March 22, 1999, 70-81.

Clancy, Tom (1947—)

Known for his potboiling thrillers with political, military, and espionage themes, author Tom Clancy's influence on American popular culture has been incalculable. Within the high-tech action adventure that has proved so beguiling to the movie industry and its audiences, as well as to a vast number of people who buy books of escapist fiction, Clancy evokes a disturbing picture of the world we live in, and has come to be regarded as the spokesman for the American nation's growing mistrust of those who govern them. If his name is instantly identified with the best-selling *The Hunt for Red October* (1984) and the creation of his Cold Warrior hero Jack Ryan (incarnated on screen by Harrison Ford) in a series beginning with *Patriot Games* (1992), his work is considered to have a serious significance that transcends the merely entertaining.

On February 28, 1983, the Naval Institute Press (NIP) received a manuscript from a Maryland insurance broker, whose only previous writings consisted of a letter to the editor and a three-page article on MX missiles in the NIP's monthly magazine, *Proceedings of the U.S. Naval Institute.* The arrival of the manuscript confounded the recipients. As the publishing arm of the U.S. Naval Institute, NIP is an academic institution responsible for *The Bluejackets' Manual* which, according to them, has served as "a primer for newly enlisted sailors and as a basic reference for all naval personnel from seaman to admiral" for almost a century. NIP created an astonishing precedent by publishing the manuscript, and the obscure insurance broker became a world-famous best-selling author of popular genre fiction.

Clancy's manuscript was based on the fruitless attempt of the Soviet missile frigate *Storozhedoy* to defect from Latvia to the Swedish island of Gotland on November 8,1975. The mutiny had been led by the ship's political officer Valeri Sablin, who was captured, court-marshaled, and executed. In Clancy's tale, Captain First Rank Marko Ramius successfully defects to the United States, not in a frigate, but in a submarine, the *Red October.* The Naval Institute Press published *The Hunt for Red October* in October 1984, its first venture into fiction in its long academic history. It skyrocketed onto *The New York Times* best-seller list when President Reagan

pronounced it "the perfect yarn." In March 1985, author and president met in the Oval office, where the former told the latter about his new book on World War II. According to Peter Masley in *The Washington Post,* Reagan asked, "Who wins?" to which Clancy replied, "The good guys."

Born on April 12, 1947 in Baltimore, Thomas L. Clancy, Jr. grew up with a fondness for military history in general and naval history in particular. In June 1969, he graduated from Baltimore's Loyola College, majoring in English, and married Wanda Thomas in August. A severe eye weakness kept him from serving in the Vietnam War, and he worked in insurance for 15 years until the colossal success of his first novel. The book was a bestseller in both hard cover and paperback, and was successfully filmed—although not until 1990—with an all-star cast headed by Sean Connery. Meanwhile, he was free to continue writing, building an impressive *oeuvre* of both fiction and non-fiction. In a 1988 *Playboy* interview, Marc Cooper claimed that Clancy had become "a popular authority on what the U.S. and the Soviets really have in their military arsenals and on how war may be fought today." Indeed, his novels have been brought into use as case studies in military colleges.

In April 1989, Clancy was invited to serve as an unpaid consultant to the National Space Council, and has lectured for the CIA, DIA, and NSA. A 1989 *Time* magazine review added a moral dimension to his growing public authority: "Clancy has performed a national service of some sorts: he has sought to explain the military and its moral code to civilians. Such a voice was needed, for Vietnam had created a barrier of estrangement between America's warrior class and the nation it serves. Tom Clancy's novels have helped bring down this wall." It is the dawning of the idea that the novel as a textual form is slowly attempting to replace that which we conventionally labeled "history" that has been an important factor in the growing critical interest in Clancy's thrillers, dealing as they do with the politics of our times. Whereas the "literary" aspect of a text is traditionally located in its ability to deal with the ontological and existential problems of man and being, we now find "literary" values in those texts that deal with pragmatic problems: man and being in the here and now. Read from this standpoint, Clancy's thrillers can be seen not as an escape from reality, but as presenting real, and relevant, issues and experiences, drawing on society's loss of trust in the great myths of existence: truth, and the questionable value of official and governmental assurances.

Although Clancy claims, in *The Clancy Companion,* that he writes fiction "pure and simple . . . projecting ideas generally into the future, rather than the past," critics have labeled him the father of the techno-thriller. In his novels *Red Storm Rising* (a Soviet attack on NATO; 1986), *Cardinal of the Kremlin* (spies and Star Wars missile defense; 1988), *Clear and Present Danger* (the highest selling book of the 1980s, dealing with a real war on drugs; 1989), *Debt of Honor* (Japanese-American economic competition and the frailty of America's financial system; 1994) and *Executive Orders,* (rebuilding a destroyed U.S. government; 1996), the machine is hero and technology is as dominant as the human characters. In both his fiction and nonfiction the scenarios predominantly reflect the quality of war games. "Who the hell cleared it?" the former Secretary of the Navy, John Lehman, remarked after reading *The Hunt for Red October.* Clancy, whose work includes his "Guided Tour" series (*Marine, Fighter Wing*) and the "Op-Center" series (created by Clancy and Steve Pieczenik, but written by other authors), has always insisted that he finds his information in the public domain, basing his Naval technology and Naval tactics mostly on the $9.95 war game *Harpoon.*

In November 1996 Tom Clancy and Virtus Corporation founded Red Storm Entertainment to create and market multiple-media entertainment products. It released its first game, *Politika,* in November 1997, the first online game ever packaged with a mass-market paperback, introducing "conversational gaming" in a net based environment. Clancy has called it "interactive history." The huge success of his books, multimedia products, and movies that are based on his novels allowed him to make a successful $200 million bid for the Minnesota Vikings football team in March 1998.

—Rob van Kranenburg

FURTHER READING:

Greenberg, Martin H. *The Tom Clancy Companion.* New York, Berkley Pub Group, 1992.

Clapton, Eric (1945—)

Eric Clapton, a lifelong student of the blues, has been in more bands that he himself formed than any other guitarist in rock music. He first distinguished himself with the group, the Yardbirds, where he earned the ironic nickname, "Slowhand," for his nimble leads. When the Yardbirds went commercial, Clapton left them to pursue pure blues with John Mayall, a singer, guitarist, and keyboard player who was regarded as the Father of British Blues for his discovery and promotion of luminary musicians in the field. Clapton proved to be Mayall's greatest discovery. On *John Mayall's Blues Breakers, Featuring Eric Clapton* (1966) Clapton displayed an unprecedented fusion of technical virtuosity and emotional expressiveness, giving rise to graffiti scribbled on walls in London saying, "Clapton is God."

When jazz-trained bassist Jack Bruce joined the Blues Breakers, Clapton grew intrigued by his improvisational style. He recruited Bruce and drummer Ginger Baker to form the psychedelic blues-rock power-trio Cream. They became famous for long, bombastic solos in concert, and established the "power trio" (guitarist-bassist-drummer) as the definitive lineup of the late 1960s, a form also assumed by Blue Cheer, the Jimi Hendrix Experience, and Rory Gallagher's band, Taste. Cream disbanded after four excellent studio albums, having set a new standard for rock musicianship and Clapton, bored with the improvisational style, became interested in composing songs.

Blind Faith, a band comprised of established musicians from other famous bands and often called the first "supergroup," was formed by Clapton in 1969. He retained Ginger Baker, and recruited guitarist/pianist Steve Winwood (from the recently disbanded Traffic) and bassist Rick Grech. They produced only one album (*Blind Faith,* 1969), for Clapton soon transferred his interest to the laid-back, good-vibes style of Delaney and Bonnie, who had opened for Blind Faith on tour. Delaney and Bonnie encouraged him to develop his singing and composing skills, and joined him in the studio to record *Eric Clapton* (1970). Clapton then formed Derek and the Dominos with slide guitarist Duane Allman in 1970 and released *Layla and Other Assorted Love Songs,* one of the finest blues-rock albums ever made. Unfortunately, the band, beset with intense personal conflicts and drug problems, was dissolved and Clapton, increasingly reliant on heroin, became a recluse.

In 1973 Pete Townsend organized the Rainbow Concert with Steve Winwood and other stars to bring Clapton back to his music.

Clapton kicked the heroin habit, and in 1974 resumed his solo career with the classic *461 Ocean Boulevard.* Although *Layla* could never be surpassed on its own terms, *461* was a worthy follow-up, mature and mellow, and set the tone for the remainder of Clapton's career. He had become attracted to minimalism, in search of the simplest way to convey the greatest amount of emotion. Developments in the 1980s included work on film soundtracks and a regrettable tilt toward pop under producer Phil Collins, but the 1990s found him once again drawn to the blues, while still recording some beautiful compositions in the soft-rock vein.

The subtleties of the mature Clapton are not as readily appreciated as the confetti-like maestro guitar work of Cream or Derek and the Dominos. Once regarded as rock's most restlessly exploring musician, too complex to be contained by any one band, by the 1990s Clapton had become the "Steady Rollin' Man," the self-assured journeyman of soft rock. A younger generation, unaware of his earlier work, was often puzzled by the awards and adulation heaped upon this singer of mainstream hits like "Tulsa Time," but a concert or live album showed Clapton displaying the legendary flash of old. Except for a few low points (*No Reason to Cry,* 1976), and the Phil Collins-produced albums *Behind the Sun* (1985) and *August* (1986), Eric Clapton aged better than many of his contemporaries, finding a comfortable niche without pandering to every new trend.

—Douglas Cooke

FURTHER READING:

DeCurtis, Anthony, "Eric Clapton: A Life at the Crossroads." Included in the CD boxed set *Eric Clapton: Crossroads.* Polydor, 1988.

Headlam, Dave. "Blues Transformations in the Music of Cream." In *Understanding Rock: Essays in Musical Analysis,* edited by John Covach and Graeme M. Boone. New York, Oxford University Press, 1997.

Roberty, Marc. *The Complete Guide to the Music of Eric Clapton.* London, Omnibus, 1995

Schumacher, Michael. *Crossroads: the Life and Music of Eric Clapton.* London, Little, Brown and Company, 1995.

Shapiro, Harry. *Eric Clapton: Lost in the Blues.* New York, Da Capo Press, 1992.

Clark, Dick (1929—)

As host of *American Bandstand* for more than 30 years, Dick Clark introduced rock 'n' roll music via television to a whole generation of teenaged Americans while reassuring their parents that the music would not lead their children to perdition. With his eternally youthful countenance, collegiate boy-next-door personality, and trademark "salute" at the close of each telecast, Clark is one of the few veterans of the early days of television who remains active after nearly half a century in broadcasting.

Richard Wagstaff Clark was born in 1929 in Mount Vernon, New York. His father owned radio stations across upstate New York, and his only sibling, older brother Bradley, was killed in World War II. Clark grew up enamored of such radio personalities as Arthur Godfrey and Garry Moore, and instantly understood the effectiveness and appeal of their informal on-air approach. Clark studied speech at

Dick Clark

Syracuse University, supplementing his studies with work at campus radio station WAER. After graduating in 1951, he worked for several radio and television stations in central New York radio and television, and even briefly adopted the on-air name "Dick Clay," to his later embarrassment.

In 1953 Clark moved to Philadelphia to host an afternoon radio show, playing popular vocalists for local teenagers. Three years later, he was chosen as the new host of a local-TV dance show, *Bandstand*, which featured the then-new sounds of rock 'n' roll music. The show's previous host, Bob Horn, had been arrested on a morals charge.

Clark was an instant hit with his viewers. By the fall of 1957, *Bandstand* was picked up nationally by the ABC network. *American Bandstand* quickly became a national phenomenon, the first popular television series to prominently feature teenagers. Clark demanded that the teens who appeared on the program observe strict disciplinary and dress-code regulations. Boys were expected to wear jackets and ties, and girls, modest skirts and not-too-tight sweaters. Many of the teens who danced on the show, from Italian-American neighborhoods in south and west Philadelphia, became national celebrities themselves. One of the most popular segments of *American Bandstand* was one in which members of the studio audience were asked to rate

new songs, a poll whose results were taken seriously by record executives. New styles of rock music rose or fell on the whims of the teenagers, who would explain their decisions by such statements as "I'd give it an 87. . . it's got a good beat, and you can dance to it." Interestingly, Clark's audience panned "She Loves You," the Beatles' first hit. The *Bandstand* audiences introduced a national audience to such dance moves as the Pony, the Stroll and, most famously, the Twist, by Philadelphia native Chubby Checker.

As Clark was becoming a millionaire, his career was threatened by the payola scandals of the 1950s, when it was learned that record companies illegally paid disc jockeys to play their rock and roll records. Clark admitted that he partially owned several music publishers and record labels that provided some of the music on *American Bandstand,* and he immediately sold his interests in these companies as the scandal broke, while insisting, however, that songs from these companies did not get preferential treatment on his show. Clark made such a convincing case before a House committee studying payola in 1959 that Representative Owen Harris called him "a fine young man" and exonerated him. Clark thus provided rock music with a clean-cut image when it needed it the most.

Clark produced and hosted a series of *Bandstand*-related concert acts that toured the United States in the 1950s and 1960s. During their tours in the South, these were among the first venues where blacks and whites performed on the same stage. Eventually, even the seating in these arenas became desegregrated. In 1964, *Bandstand* moved from Philadelphia to Los Angeles, coinciding with the popularity of Southern California "surf" music by The Beach Boys and Jan and Dean. From that point, the show began relying less on playing records and more on live performers. Many of the top acts of the rock era made their national television debut on *Bandstand,* such as Buddy Holly and the Crickets, Ike and Tina Turner, Smokey Robinson and the Miracles, Stevie Wonder and the Talking Heads, and the teenaged Simon and Garfunkel, known then as Tom and Jerry.

During the 1970s and 1980s, Clark expanded his television presence beyond *Bandstand* with Dick Clark Productions, which generated between 150 and 170 hours of programming annually at its peak. During these years, Clark hosted the long-running *$10,000 Pyramid* game show from 1973 through the late 1980s; in subsequent versions, the word association-based *Pyramid* expanded with inflation, eventually offering $100,000, and featured numerous celebrity guests. In 1974 ABC lost the broadcast rights to the Grammy Awards, and asked Clark to create an alternative music awards show. The American Music Awards quickly became a significant rival to the Grammys, popular among artists and audiences alike. In the 1980s, Clark also produced and hosted a long-running NBC series of highly-rated "blooper" scenes composed of outtake reels from popular TV series. His co-host was Ed McMahon of the *Tonight Show,* who had been friends with Clark since they were next-door neighbors in Philadelphia during the 1950s. Clark also replaced Guy Lombardo as America's New Year's Eve host, emceeing the televised descent of the giant ball in New York's Times Square on ABC beginning in 1972.

The seemingly ageless Clark, dubbed "America's oldest living teenager" by *TV Guide,* ushered his series with aplomb through the turbulent 1970s. It was on *Bandstand* where an audience first body-spelled "Y.M.C.A." to The Village People's number-one hit. With changes in musical tastes and practices, the popularity of *Bandstand* began to wane. What had begun as a local two-and-a-half hour daily show in the mid-1950s had gradually been whittled down to a weekly, hour-long show by the 1980s. There were several culprits: competing network music programs, including *The Midnight Special, Solid*

Gold, and even *Saturday Night Live* were competing with *Bandstand* to get the hottest acts of the day. The advent of MTV in 1981, with round-the-clock music videos, further cut into the series' influence. As the years passed, new rock groups devoted more time to video production and promotion, and less to appearing live on shows. Clark retired from *Bandstand* in the spring of 1989; with a new host, a syndicated version of the long-running show called it quits later that year, only weeks shy of making it into the 1990s.

Ironically enough, however, MTV's sister station had a hand in reviving interest in *American Bandstand.* In 1997, VH-1 ran a weekly retrospective, hosted by Clark, of highlights from the 1970s and 1980s version of *Bandstand.* The success of the reruns coincided with the fortieth anniversary of the show's national debut, and Clark returned to Philadelphia to unveil a plaque on the site of the original *American Bandstand* television studio. That same year, Clark published a comprehensive anniversary volume, and he also announced the founding of an American Bandstand Diner restaurant chain. Modeled after the Hard Rock Café and Planet Hollywood chains, each diner was designed in 1950s style, with photos and music of the greats Clark helped make famous.

—Andrew Milner

FURTHER READING:

Clark, Dick and Bronson, Fred. *Dick Clark's American Bandstand.* New York, Harper Collins, 1997.

Jackson, John A. *American Bandstand: Dick Clark and the Making of a Rock and Roll Empire.* New York, Oxford University, 1997.

The Rolling Stone Illustrated History of Rock and Roll. New York, Random House, 1992.

Clarke, Arthur C. (1917—)

British writer Arthur Charles Clarke's long and successful career has made him perhaps the best-known science fiction writer in the world and arguably the most popular foreign-born science fiction writer in the United States. Clarke is best known for *2001: A Space Odyssey* (1968), the film script he wrote with noted director Stanley Kubrick.

Clarke's writings are in genre of "hard" science fiction—stories in which science is the backbone and where technical and scientific discovery are emphasized. He is considered one of the main forces for placing "real" science in science fiction; science fiction scholar Eric Rabkin has described Clarke as perhaps the most important science-oriented science fiction writer since H. G. Wells. His love and understanding of science coupled with his popularity made him a central figure in the development of post-World War II science fiction. Clarke's success did much to increase the popularity of science and create support for NASA and the U.S. space program.

For Clarke, technological advancement and scientific discovery have been generally positive developments. While he was cognizant of the dangers that technology can bring, his liberal and optimistic view of the possible benefits of technology made him one of the small number of voices introducing mass culture to the possibilities of the future. His notoriety was further enhanced domestically and globally when he served as commentator for CBS television during the Apollo 11, 12, and 15 Moon missions.

A second theme found in Clarke's work which resonates in popular culture suggests that no matter how technologically advanced humans become, they will always be infants in comparison to the ancient, mysterious wisdom of alien races. Humanity is depicted as the ever-curious child reaching out into the universe trying to learn and grow, only to discover that the universe may not even be concerned with our existence. Such a theme is evident in the short story "The Sentinel" (1951), which describes the discovery of an alien artifact created by an advanced race, millions of years earlier, sitting atop a mountain on the moon. This short story provided the foundation for *2001* (1968). One of Clarke's most famous books, *Childhood's End* (1950), envisions a world where a portion of earth's children are reaching transcendence under the watchful eyes of alien tutors who resemble satanic creatures. The satanic looking aliens have come to earth to assist in a process where select children change into a new species and leave earth to fuse with a cosmic overmind—a transformation not possible for those humans left behind or for their satanistic alien tutors.

Clarke's achieved his greatest influence with *2001,* which was nominated for four Academy Awards, including best picture, and ranked by the American Film Institute as the 22nd most influential American movie in the last 100 years. Clarke's novelization of the movie script, published under the same title in 1968, had sold more that 3 million copies by 1998 and was followed by *2010: Odyssey Two* (1982). The sequel was made into a film directed by Peter Hyams, *2010: The Year We Make Contact* (1984, starring Roy Scheider). Clarke has followed up the first two books in the Odyssey series with *2061: Odyssey Three* (1988) and *3001: The Final Odyssey* (1997).

The impact of *2001* is seen throughout American popular culture. The movie itself took audiences on a cinematic and cerebral voyage like never before. As Clarke said early in 1965, "MGM doesn't know it yet, but they've footed the bill for the first six-million-dollar religious film." The film gave the public an idea of the wonder, beauty, and promise open to humanity at the dawn of the new age of space exploration, while simultaneously showing the darker side of man's evolution: tools for progress are also tools for killing. Nowhere is this more apparent than in HAL, the ship's onboard computer. Although Clarke possesses a liberal optimism for the possibilities found in the future, HAL poignantly demonstrates the potential dangers of advanced technology. The name HAL, the computer's voice, and the vision of HAL's eye-like optical sensors have since become synonymous with the danger of over reliance on computers. This is a theme seen in other films ranging from *Wargames* (1983) to the *Terminator* (1984, 1991) series. The killings initiated by HAL and HAL's subsequent death allow the surviving astronaut to pilot the ship to the end of its voyage. Here the next step of man takes place as the sole survivor of this odyssey devolves into an infant. The Star Child is born; Man evolves into an entity of pure thought. The evolution/devolution of the astronaut completes the metaphor that humanity does not need tools to achieve its journey's end, our final fulfillment, but only ourselves.

The message of *2001* is powerfully reinforced by the music of Richard Strauss. Strauss' dramatic "Also Sprach Zarathustra," composed in 1896, was used several times during the movie but never with more impact than in the "Dawn of Man" segment. As the movie progressed, this music (as well as music composed by Johan Strauss) came to carry the narrative nearly as effectively as the dialogue.

Some have even suggested that the film influenced the language of the astronauts aboard the Apollo 13 mission. When HAL reports the "failure" of the AE 35 Unit, he says "Sorry to interrupt the festivities, but we have a problem." On the Apollo 13 command module, named Odyssey, the crew had just concluded a TV broadcast which utilized the famous "Zarathustra" theme when an oxygen tank exploded. The first words sent to Earth were "Houston, we've had a problem."

—Craig T. Cobane

FURTHER READING:

Boyd, David. "Mode and Meaning in *2001*." *Journal of Popular Film.* Vol. VI, No. 3, 1978, 202-15.

Clarke, Arthur C. *Astounding Days: A Science Fictional Autobiography.* New York, Bantam Books, 1989.

McAleer, Neil. *Odyssey: The Authorised Biography of Arthur C. Clarke.* London, Victor Gollancz, 1992.

Clemente, Roberto (1934-1972)

Longtime Pittsburgh Pirates rightfielder Roberto Clemente is much more than one of the premier major leaguers of his generation. While his statistics and on-field accomplishments earned him election

Roberto Clemente

to the Baseball Hall of Fame, equally awe-inspiring are his sense of professionalism and pride in his athleticism, his self-respecting view of his ethnicity, and his humanism. Clemente, who first came to the Pirates in 1955, died at age 38, on New Year's Eve 1972, while attempting to airlift relief supplies from his native Puerto Rico to Nicaraguan earthquake victims. He insisted on making the effort despite bad weather and admonitions that the ancient DC-7 in which he was flying was perilously overloaded. This act of self-sacrifice, which came scant months after Clemente smacked major-league hit number 3,000, attests to his caliber as a human being and transformed him into an instant legend.

Roberto Walker Clemente was born in Barrio San Anton in Carolina, Puerto Rico. While excelling in track and field as a youngster, his real passion was baseball—and he was just 20 years old when he came to the major leagues to stay. On the ballfield, the muscular yet sleek and compact Clemente dazzled as he bashed extra-base hits, made nifty running catches, and fired perfect strikes from deep in the outfield to throw out runners. He was particularly noted for his rifle arm. As Brooklyn/Los Angeles Dodgers announcer Vin Scully once observed, "Clemente could field a ball in New York and throw out a guy in Pennsylvania."

Clemente's on-field record is exemplary. In his 18 seasons with the Pirates, he posted a .317 batting average. He won four National League batting crowns, and earned 12 consecutive Gold Gloves for his fielding. On five occasions, he led National League outfielders in assists. He played in 12 all-star games. He was his league's Most Valuable Player (MVP) in 1966, and was the World Series MVP in 1971. When he doubled against Jon Matlack of the New York Mets on September 30, 1972, in what was to be his final major league game, he became just the eleventh ballplayer to belt 3,000 hits.

Yet despite these statistics and the consistency he exhibited throughout his career, true fame came to Clemente late in life. In the 1960 World Series, the first of two fall classics in which he appeared, he hit safely in all seven games. He was overshadowed, however, by his imposing opponents, the Mickey Mantle-led New York Yankees, and by teammate Bill Mazeroski's dramatic series-winning home run in game 7. Clemente really did not earn national acclaim until 1971, when he awed the baseball world while starring in the World Series, hitting .414, and leading his team to a come-from-behind championship over the favored Baltimore Orioles. According to sportswriter Roger Angell, it was in this series that Clemente's play was "something close to the level of absolute perfection."

Clemente was fiercely proud of his physical skills. Upon completing his first season with the Pirates, his athletic ability was likened to that of Willie Mays, one of his star contemporaries. The ballplayer's response: "Nonetheless, I play like Roberto Clemente." During the filming of the 1968 Neil Simon comedy *The Odd Couple*, a sequence, shot on location at Shea Stadium, called for a Pittsburgh Pirate to hit into a triple play. In the film, Bill Mazeroski is the hitter. Supposedly, Clemente was set to be at bat during the gag, but pulled out because of the indignity.

In the decade-and-a-half before his 1971 World Series heroics, Clemente yearned for the kind of acknowledgment won by a Mays or a Mantle. Certainly, he was deserving of such acclaim. Had he been playing in New York, Los Angeles, or Chicago, rather than in a city far removed from the national spotlight, he might have been a high profile player earlier in his career. Compounding the problem was Clemente's ethnic background. Furthermore, Clemente was keenly aware of his roots, and his ethnicity; he even insisted that his three sons (who were two, five, and six when he died) be born in Puerto Rico. Unfortunately, this pride often was misconstrued—and arguably, one reason why he was not beloved earlier on was racism. The expectation that he blend in rather than exude ethnicity is epitomized by the fact that on all of Clemente's Topps baseball cards issued between 1958 and 1969, his name is Americanized as "Bob" Clemente.

Adding to the affront was that whenever Clemente would comment that other ballplayers of equal accomplishment were luxuriating in the limelight, he would be labeled a complainer and hypochondriac. "As a teammate," fellow Pittsburgh Pirate Willie Stargell observed, "we had a chance to marvel at talents a lot of people didn't understand." So it was no surprise that after the 1971 World Series, upon being handed the MVP trophy, Clemente pointedly declared, "I want everybody in the world to know that this is the way I play all the time. All season. Every season." Then, ever so typically, he spoke in Spanish, asking for his father's blessing.

The rule requiring a ballplayer to be retired for five years prior to earning Hall of Fame eligibility was waived for Clemente. He was inducted a year after his death, becoming the first Hispanic to be so honored. Since then, he has inspired thousands of Latino ballplayers. "Growing up in Puerto Rico, we got to learn a lot about his character," observed Bernie Williams, one of the major league stars of the 1990s. "Clemente is a great hero for all Latin players," added Juan Gonzalez, a Williams peer and fellow Puerto Rican. "Not only was he one of the best baseball players ever, but he was a great human being as well." Clemente also has been cherished by his teammates. After pinch-hitting a game-winning ninth inning single in Game 2 of 1979 World Series, Pirate catcher Manny Sanguillen declared that he wished his feat to be dedicated to the memory of Clemente. "He helped us in a lot of ways," summed up Willie Stargell, "to be the players we were."

Clemente was the second ballplayer (after Jackie Robinson) to be featured on a United States postage stamp. In 1973, the government of the Commonwealth of Puerto Rico granted acreage for the development of Roberto Clemente Sports City, which allows Puerto Ricans to participate in a wide range of athletic pastimes. In 1993, his eldest son, Roberto, Jr., established the Roberto Clemente Foundation, which offers recreational and educational activities for Pittsburgh-area children while stressing the relevance of community involvement. In 1994, the Pirates unveiled a statue of Clemente outside Three Rivers Stadium. Throughout 1998—the twenty-fifth anniversary of his death—the Baseball Hall of Fame issued a special Roberto Clemente commemorative admission ticket. Each year, one major leaguer receives the True Value/Roberto Clemente Man of the Year Award for combining on-field heroics with community responsibility.

Roberto Clemente merits every honor he has received. In an era of pampered, egocentric athletes who charge big bucks to little kids for autographs, the manner in which Clemente lived and died is all the more poignant and praiseworthy. As he once observed, "Any time you have an opportunity to make things better and you don't, then you are wasting your time on this earth."

—Rob Edelman

FURTHER READING:

Markusen, Bruce. *Roberto Clemente: The Great One*. Champaign, Illinois, Sports Publishing, Inc., 1998.

Miller, Ira. *Roberto Clemente*. New York, Tempo Books, 1973.

Musick, Phil. *Who Was Roberto? A Biography of Roberto Clemente*. Garden City, New York, Doubleday, 1974.

Wagenheim, Kal. *Clemente!* New York, Praeger Publishers, 1973.

Walker, Paul Robert. *Pride of Puerto Rico: The Life of Roberto Clemente*. New York, Harcourt Brace Jovanovich, 1988.

Cleopatra

The story of Cleopatra has been a perennial favorite for the Hollywood cinema. The most notorious version remains the 1963 epic starring Elizabeth Taylor and Richard Burton—a film whose box office failure is credited with helping to destroy the Hollywood studio system. Made for a then staggering 44 million dollars, the production was fraught with setbacks and scandals, and film historian David Cook noted that the "disastrous" four-hour film had not broken even, some thirty-six years later. Received badly by both audiences and critics, *Cleopatra* paled in comparison to the off-screen antics of its stars. The cast's real-life adultery, life-threatening illness, and the grand passion between Taylor and Burton provoked the first major paparazzi feeding frenzy of the 1960s.

—Jeannette Sloniowski

FURTHER READING:

Brodsky, Jack, and Nathan Weiss. *The Cleopatra Papers: A Private Correspondence*. New York, Simon and Schuster, 1963.

Cook, David. *A History of Narrative Film*. 2nd ed. New York, W.W. Norton and Company, 1990.

Clift, Montgomery (1920-1966)

Four years older than Brando, eleven years senior to James Dean, but finding stardom only just ahead of both, Montgomery Clift is invariably bracketed with them—the leader of the great trio of the beautiful and doomed who emerged from the Actors Studio in New York City to transform the postwar face of screen acting with their individual and collective intensity. He died too soon to recover from his failures and too late to become a mythic icon like Dean or Marilyn Monroe, but to examine his all-too-short filmography is to be reminded of his achievements that have been all too often buried beneath the rubble of his ruined life.

Only cast in serious dramas, the fragile and gifted Clift, frequently quivering with painful introspection, was the screen's great outsider, misfit, or victim during the 1950s—the ultimately rejected fortune hunter of *The Heiress* (1949); driven by despair to murder and by murder to guilt in *A Place in the Sun* (1951), his first film with Elizabeth Taylor; beaten and humiliated for his refusal to fight in the boxing ring as Prewitt in *From Here to Eternity* (1953); a priest tormented by the secrets of the confessional in Hitchcock's *I Confess* (1953); the columnist unable to cope with the pain of the lovelorn in *Lonelyhearts* (1959); a victim of the Nazi concentration camps in *Judgment at Nuremberg* (1961); and last, but far from least, one of John Huston's *Misfits* (1961), corralling wild horses with Clark Gable and Marilyn Monroe.

Montgomery Clift

Born Edward Montgomery Clift in Omaha, Nebraska, the twin brother of a sister and the son of a neurotic, social-climbing and dangerously possessive mother, Clift was taken traveling in Europe from an early age. He acquired polish, manners, and the right acquaintance with art and literature. Precocious and sophisticated, he began acting at age fourteen and was on Broadway a year later. His rise was rapid, his connections influential, and by the time he appeared in two Thornton Wilder plays, *The Skin of Our Teeth* and *Our Town,* he was destined for theater stardom. Encouraged by Elia Kazan, he became a founding student of the Actors Studio in 1947 but soon succumbed to Hollywood, which had been courting him for some time.

Clift's first film was Howard Hawks's *Red River* (1948), which cast him as a cowboy, pitting his almost girlish persona against John Wayne, whose adopted son he played. The film was, however, not released until after Clift's next, *The Search* (1948) for Fred Zinnemann, which gained him the first of his four Oscar nominations for his sensitive performance as a soldier helping a stateless orphan in war-torn Germany find his missing mother. When *Red River* came out Clift became a star, the darling of the fan magazines and the adoring young girls of America.

But Clift, anguished by his homosexuality and increasingly addicted to drugs and alcohol, was an unhappy man with a disastrous private life that he strove to keep secret. In 1956, after a party given by his most devoted friend, Elizabeth Taylor, the actor was involved in a car crash. His severe injuries included the severing of nerves that rendered the left side of his face immobile, effectively destroying the perfection of his fine beauty. He was filming *Raintree County* (1957)

with Taylor at the time and, despite director Edward Dmytryk's efforts to photograph him in such a way as to avoid exposing the extent of the damage, both Clift and the film remained inert.

Driven ever further into self-destruction and loss of control, the actor did well to emerge with credit from *Judgment at Nuremberg* and *The Misfits,* but he was disastrously cast as *Freud* (1962), John Huston's altogether misguided biopic about the analyst, during the making of which Clift, whose staring eyes had become a too-prominent feature of his on-screen face, underwent a double cataract operation. After *Freud,* Clift's mainstream career was over. He had been overshadowed by his nemesis, Brando, in *The Young Lions* (1958) and was of little account in the overwrought *Suddenly Last Summer* (1959) with Taylor and Katharine Hepburn. He dragged himself out of the murky private world into which he had descended to play one last loner in a French film, *L'Espion* (*The Defector*) in 1966, before dying of a heart attack at the age of forty-five.

—Robyn Karney

FURTHER READING:

Bosworth, Patricia. *Montgomery Clift: A Biography.* New York, Harcourt, Brace, Jovanovich, 1978.

Hoskyns, Barney. *Montgomery Clift, Beautiful Loser.* London, Bloomsbury Publishing, 1991.

Kalfatovic, Mary C. *Montgomery Clift: A Bio-Bibliography.* Connecticut, Greenwood Publishing, 1994.

Thomson, David. *A Biographical Dictionary of Film.* New York, Alfred A. Knopf, 1994.

Cline, Patsy (1932-1963)

Known for her smooth, powerful delivery, Patsy Cline became the first successful crossover female country vocalist with hits in the pop market during the early 1960s. Cline was an aggressive artist who fought against efforts to mold her into a pop sensation. She initially disliked many of the songs that became her biggest hits, preferring up-tempo country tunes to the more accessible ballads that made her famous. As her relatively brief career came to an end in 1963 when she died in a plane crash, the slick recording style known as the "Nashville sound" was taking over the industry. In *Country Music, U.S.A.,* historian Bill C. Malone notes that Cline "moved female country singing closer to the pop mainstream and light years away from the sound" of artists with a more traditional, rural style such as Kitty Wells. Despite her resistance to being typecast as a pop artist, Cline played a major role in Nashville's transformation from hillbilly to "countrypolitan."

Born Virginia Patterson Hensley on September 8, 1932, in Gore, Virginia, Cline began performing at an early age. She won a dancing contest at the age of four, and a few years later she was playing the piano by ear. By the time her family moved to the larger town of Winchester, the teenage Cline was interested in singing professionally. She began appearing regularly on a local radio show after approaching the announcer, who recalls being impressed by her nerve and her voice. In 1948, she traveled to Nashville to audition for the Grand Ol' Opry, and appeared on Roy Acuff's radio program on WSM. Without an immediate offer, however, she could not afford to stay in town for long and returned home after a few days. Winchester

Patsy Cline

band leader Bill Peer hired Cline to be the lead singer of his act, the Melody Boys and Girls, in 1952. Peer became her manager, and proposed that she use the stage name Patsy; shortly thereafter, she met and married Gerald Cline.

In 1954, Cline signed a recording contract with Four Star Records that would prove to be a major stumbling block in her career. The contract paid her only small royalties and included a stipulation that her material had to be approved by the label. As a result, almost all of Cline's pre-1960 recordings were songs chosen by the label's owner, Bill McCall, and published by Four Star, enabling the label to profit from the publishing royalties. Four Star made a deal that allowed major label Decca Records to lease Cline's music, giving her the opportunity to work with top Nashville session musicians and a gifted producer, Owen Bradley. Although Cline's talent was apparent to those who heard her sing, the recordings she made in the mid-1950s were largely ignored. A fan of pop singer Kay Starr, she was capable of styles other than country, and Bradley quickly recognized this. Though Cline preferred country material, the songs from her early recordings ran the gamut.

At the end of 1956, at McCall's insistence, Cline recorded ''Walkin' After Midnight,'' a tune she reportedly described as

''nothin' but a little ol' pop song,'' according to biographer Ellis Nassour. Before the record's release she made her national television debut on *Arthur Godfrey's Talent Scouts* in January of 1957. Cline favored the western outfits commonly worn by country singers of that era, but for this performance she was told to wear a cocktail dress. Godfrey's staff also encouraged her to abandon country music and move to New York. She was not persuaded, however, and continued to promote the record with appearances on the Opry and a rock 'n' roll show in New York hosted by Alan Freed. The song became a Top Ten hit on the country charts and went to number 17 on the pop charts.

That same year, Patsy and Gerald Cline were divorced, and in the fall she married Charlie Dick. Over the next two years, she released several singles and gave birth to her first child. During the summer of 1959, she hired Ramsey ''Randy'' Hughes as her manager. As the result of Cline's failure to record any major hits after ''Walkin' After Midnight,'' McCall chose not to renew her Four Star contract. At the beginning of 1960, she began performing regularly on the Opry, fulfilling a childhood dream. Decca signed her later that year, and Bradley found the perfect song for her first session. In 1961, ''I Fall to Pieces,'' featuring the background vocals of the Jordanaires, became her first number one country hit, reaching number 12 on the pop charts. The success of this record confirmed Bradley's belief that Cline could capture a much larger audience by focusing her efforts on pop ballads. Later hits such as ''Crazy'' and ''She's Got You'' established her as a torch singer, and Bradley began using string accompaniments on a semi-regular basis. These lush arrangements typified the Nashville sound, and Bradley became a proponent for this new style. By late 1962, she was headlining a month long engagement in Las Vegas, wearing evening gowns. On March 5, 1963, a plane crash outside Camden, Tennessee, killed Cline, along with Cowboy Copas, Hawkshaw Hawkins, and Randy Hughes.

Throughout her career, Cline had a reputation for being outspoken and opinionated. Those who knew her described her as a ''brassy'' woman who drank and cursed along with her male counterparts. She was also noted for being kindhearted and generous, particularly toward other female country artists struggling for success. The male-dominated recording industry of the 1950s was unaccustomed to self-confident women, and Cline's headstrong temperament led to arguments with Bradley over her material. The contradictions between her professional image and her personal background reflect the conflicting forces that were shaping country music in the early 1960s. Despite changes in country and pop styles, the legendary voice of Patsy Cline remains timeless. She gained a new following in 1985, when Jessica Lange starred in the film biography *Sweet Dreams*. Over three decades after her death her recordings continued to appear on the charts.

—Anna Hunt Graves

FURTHER READING:

Jones, Margaret. *Patsy: The Life and Times of Patsy Cline.* New York, HarperCollins, 1994.

Kingsbury, Paul. *The Patsy Cline Collection.* Nashville, MCA Records/Country Music Foundation, 1991.

Lewis, George H., editor. *All That Glitters: Country Music in America.* Bowling Green, Bowling Green State University Popular Press, 1993.

Malone, Bill C. *Country Music, U.S.A.* Austin, University of Texas Press, 1985.

Nassour, Ellis. *Patsy Cline.* New York, Dorchester, 1985.

Clinton, George (1940—)

George Clinton was a doo-wop singer until he discovered acid rock and protest music in the late 1960s, a combination to which he added cosmological rants and booming bass lines to create a new style of socially conscious, Afrocentric funk. His bands Parliament and Funkadelic reached black and white audiences alike in the 1970s with their psychedelic live shows and infectious, tongue-in-cheek concept albums *(Mothership Connection,* 1976; *One Nation Under a Groove,* 1978). Clinton disappeared amid drug and financial entanglements, but reemerged in 1983 as rappers and hip-hop artists began sampling his music and borrowing his aesthetics. In response, he formed the P-Funk All-Stars (a permutation of his many splinter groups) to support new albums and reissues of classic works, reinforcing the vitality of his universal—yet pointedly black—music.

—Tony Brewer

FURTHER READING:

Marsh, David. *George Clinton and P-Funk: An Oral History (For the Record).* New York, Avon, 1998.

Vincent, Rickey, and George Clinton. *Funk: The Music, the People, and the Rhythm of the One.* New York, St. Martin's Press, 1996.

A Clockwork Orange

A Clockwork Orange is one of the finest sociological and science fiction films ever made. With its highly stylized and often comic violence, its over-the-top set decoration, and its unlikeable protagonist, the film has exerted a wide-ranging influence on popular culture. Opening in New York on December 20, 1971, to mostly ecstatic praise, *A Clockwork Orange* immediately revolutionized the science fiction film by opening the way for more elaborate dystopian narratives and intelligent cinematic analyses of social dilemmas.

Based on Anthony Burgess's 1966 novel of the same name, *A Clockwork Orange* tells the story of Alex (Malcolm McDowell), a brilliant young thug whose thirst for violence, rape, and aggression lands him in prison. To free himself from prison, he must submit to a perverse behavior modification technique that strips him of his free will. Director Stanley Kubrick's portrayal of conditioned-reflex therapy, behavioral psychology, and systematized and bureaucratic cruelty placed audiences in the uncomfortable position of feeling sympathy for a brutal and seemingly immoral character.

Kubrick counters Alex's brutality with that of the State police. Alex's earlier crimes pale in comparison to his torture by his old gang buddies-cum-cops. His medical rehabilitation by the Ludovico technique, which includes viewing endless scenes of rape, murder,

lynching, and violence while listening to the music of Alex's beloved "Ludwig Van" (Beethoven), seems more egregious than any injury Alex inflicted. These juxtapositions force the audience to make an uncomfortable moral choice between the virtue of free will with all its perversions and the appeal of legislative/social control with its tendency toward totalitarianism. Though Kubrick had touched on these themes in his earlier films—including, *Paths of Glory* (1957), *Dr. Strangelove, Or, How I Stopped Worrying and Learned to Love the Bomb* (1964), and even *Spartacus* (1960) and *2001: A Space Odyssey* (1968)—none illustrated his message as well as *A Clockwork Orange.*

Kubrick accentuates the moral choices in the film with brilliant cinematic couplings. He sets a murder/rape scene to "Singin in the Rain," a song celebrating the optimism and bliss of life. He pairs Alex's desire for pain and violence with his love and devotion to Beethoven, which is highlighted by Kubrick's use of both classical and electronic music throughout the film. His elaborate set designs contrast the blue- and white-collar worlds with the State. The Cat Lady's enormous penis sculpture and the submissive, objectified naked female sculptures at the Korova Milkbar are strikingly different from the "flatblock" State architecture of the prison and Alex's parents' home, which is an eerie twin of the Housing Authority projects littering the inner cities of the world. Kubrick also highlights the differences between the flatness of the "official" language and the vitality of the teenage argot, Nasdat: a home is called "HOME," but in Nasdat "horrorshow" means awe and pleasure and "in-out-in-out" is a evocative term for sex.

These cinematic exercises are reflected by innovations in technique specific to Kubrick's filmmaking. His hallmarks include chilling natural lighting, extreme close-ups, interminable tracking or panning shots, jump-cut sequencing, extreme wide-angle lenses, and low-angle and slow motion shots. Kubrick's technical precision is matched only by his deeply intellectual consideration of timeless issues of freedom, pleasure, law, and punishment. Though *New York Times* film critic Pauline Kael criticized the lack of "motivating emotion" in the protagonist and comic violence, many film directors found much worth borrowing from it. Films using similar techniques include *THX-118, Westworld,* and *A Boy and His Dog.* Reflections of the movie's highly complex and ambiguous antihero can be seen in films by Martin Scorsese, David Lynch, and Quentin Tarantino. In addition, the midnight movie crowd adopted the film's unique language called Nasdat and would shout along with the movie on college campuses across the country. Kubrick's daring vision for *A Clockwork Orange* was rewarded with the New York Film Critics Award for Best Picture as well as four Academy Award nominations. The film placed its director in the company of the most influential and creative artists of the twentieth century.

—Scott Thill

FURTHER READING:

Kagan, Norman. *The Cinema of Stanley Kubrick, New Expanded Edition.* New York, Continuum Publishers, 1995.

Nelson, Thomas Allen. *Kubrick: Inside a Film Artist's Maze.* Bloomington, Indiana University Press, 1982.

Walker, Alexander. *Stanley Kubrick Directs, Expanded Edition.* New York, Harcourt, Brace and Jovanovich, 1972.

A scene from the film *A Clockwork Orange*.

Clooney, Rosemary (1928—)

No one more epitomized female vocalists of the 1950s, a time when America was hooked on novelty songs, than Rosemary Clooney. With her strong, belting, melodious style and novelty hits "Come on a My House," "Mambo Italiano," and "This Old House," Rosemary Clooney swiftly achieved stardom in the early 1950s. She also joined the ranks of the era's top female vocalists, including such stars as Jo Stafford, Peggy Lee, and Patty Page. Her career transcended the concert circuit, including television and film appearances; she proved a perfect match for the rapidly developing television industry. During the later years of Clooney's career, with a more smoky, rich voice, critics compared her with top performers such as Ella Fitzgerald, Mel Torme, and Frank Sinatra.

Born in Maysville, Kentucky, on May 28, 1928, Rosemary and her sister Betty often performed at political rallies for their paternal grandfather. When Rosemary was 13, the family moved to Cincinnati, Ohio. During her high-school years Rosemary and sister Betty performed with a local band until, at the age of 16, the two were hired by Cincinnati radio station WLW to perform on a nightly music program. Performing under the name "The Clooney Sisters," the duo continued to work at the station for two years. By 1945, however, the Clooney Sisters had joined the Tony Pastor band and were performing one-night stands across the country in theaters, hotel ballrooms, and at high school proms. Due to her better mid-range voice, Rosemary sang solos for the sister team. The Clooney Sisters performed with Tony Pastor for two years until, suddenly, during a performance in Elkhart, Indiana in 1949, Betty quit during the intermission. Soon after, Rosemary embarked on a solo career.

Following her departure from the Tony Pastor Band, Clooney signed a modest recording contract with Columbia Records. She had a modicum of success at Columbia with the children's songs "Me and My Teddy Bear" and "Little Johnny Chickadee." Mixed in with recording dates were appearances at night clubs, on radio stations, and on television. It was, however, her performance on *Arthur Godfrey's Talent Scouts* in 1950 that led to her run on *Songs for Sale,* premiering July 7, 1950. Simulcast on radio and television, the program showcased the talents of aspiring songwriters, with Rosemary Clooney and Tony Bennett as vocalists for the program. It was also during this period in her life that, under the influence of Columbia's artist and repertoire man Mitch Miller, Rosemary Clooney produced her first big hit "Come on a My House," which sold over a million copies. This was followed by pop hits "Botcha Me" and "Suzy Snowflake." Countless other chart busters followed including her ballad "Tenderly," "This Old House," and "Hey There."

Rosemary Clooney

Bing Crosby, a big fan of Clooney's music, recommended her for a screen test at Paramount Studios. Cast as a New York vaudevillian who attempts to hide an illegal alien, she made her premiere in the 1953 film *The Stars Are Singing.* Later that year she appeared with Bob Hope in the comedy *Here Come the Girls,* but her most notable achievement in motion pictures occurred in 1954 when she appeared with Bing Crosby in the hit film *White Christmas.* During this period she also began a CBS radio program called *The Rosemary Clooney Show,* which lasted for one season, and made the television variety show circuit as a guest on the *Ed Sullivan Show, Perry Como Show,* and *Steve Allen Show.*

In 1957, the Music Corporation of America (MCA) contracted Clooney to produce the syndicated half-hour television program *The Rosemary Clooney Show.* The program was well received by the general public and critics alike, and included notable musical talents the Nelson Riddle Orchestra and the Hi-Los. Seemingly never without energy or creativity, she then began a NBC variety series titled *The Lux Show Starring Rosemary Clooney* in the fall of 1957. Because of personal conflicts between her husband, Jose Ferrer, and Mitch Miller, her career was at an end with Columbia Records and she joined the RCA label.

During the 1960s Clooney's life was in turmoil. Her marriage to Jose Ferrer was on-again-off-again, finally ending in divorce. Clooney was left with five children to rear. She appeared on a number of variety shows and specials on network television, and also performed on the cabaret circuit. By 1968, Clooney was heavily dependent on drugs and had just ended a two-year relationship with a drummer. After working with the Robert Kennedy presidential campaign in

1968, she was devastated by his assassination and suffered a severe nervous breakdown during a performance at Harold's Club in Reno Nevada. She underwent extensive psychotherapy for eight years following the breakdown. She chronicled her psychiatric problems in her autobiography *This for Remembrance,* which was dramatized on television as *Escape From Madness.*

During the 1980s, a much happier and heavier Rosemary Clooney emerged with an assured straightforward belting style all her own. She performed on the Las Vegas nightclub circuit, toured with theatrical revues, appeared on network television programs, and assisted in the television production of her life story *Rosie: The Rosemary Clooney Story,* providing the soundtrack singing voices.

An emblematic figure, at the close of the twentieth century she finds herself revisiting many of her classics from the 1940s and 1950s at concerts and on recordings. Like the changing times in which she lived, Clooney proved that a woman could have a successful career, a family, and survive many setbacks. Her work in the music industry, like many post-World War II female singers, helped pave the way for future generations of women artists.

—Michael A. Lutes

FURTHER READING:

Clooney, Rosemary. *This for Remembrance: The Autobiography of Rosemary Clooney, an Irish-American Singer.* New York, Playboy Press, 1977.

Close Encounters of the Third Kind

With its elaborate, unprecedented use of special effects and novel portrayal of extraterrestrials, *Close Encounters of the Third Kind* opened to popular acclaim in November 1977, eventually earning $240 million in worldwide release and significantly contributing to director Steven Spielberg's status as the most commercially profitable filmmaker in the new Hollywood. *Close Encounters* depicts an escalation in the number of UFO sightings worldwide and climaxes in the first "diplomatic" contact between mankind and extraterrestrials at a remote military/scientific base in the Wyoming wilderness. In stark contrast to numerous earlier cinematic portrayals of alien visitors as hostile fiends intent on world domination, Spielberg's utopian film presented the extraterrestrials as childishly mischievous but benign: wondrous new friends from the stars. Spielberg would return to some of *Close Encounters*'s themes again in 1982's *E.T.: The Extra-Terrestrial,* another worldwide blockbuster and for a time the most lucrative motion picture ever.

Two parallel stories are developed in *Close Encounters.* The first focuses on a scientific team, led by a Frenchman named Lacombe (famous French film director Francois Truffaut), that tracks global UFO activity. The second centers around a midwestern everyman named Roy Neary (Richard Dreyfuss), who is destined to be humanity's emissary to the stars. The film opens in the windswept Mexican desert, where the airplanes (minus their pilots) of a long-lost military training flight have mysteriously appeared. Lacombe's team discovers that the antique airplanes are in perfect working order. Meanwhile, the skies over the American Midwest are abuzz with strange objects and lights. A power company lineman, Neary sees a group of UFOs flying down lonely back roads near Muncie, Indiana, and becomes

A UFO makes contact, in a scene from the film *Close Encounters of the Third Kind*.

obsessed with encountering the aliens again. Unhappy with the demands of adult married life, Neary shares his obsession with a local woman named Jillian (Melinda Dillon), who is in search of her young son, Barry, following his abduction by a UFO.

As the international scientific team moves closer to setting up a secret landing site at the base of Devil's Tower in Wyoming to beckon the visitors, Neary becomes more fixated on a mental image—that of an oddly shaped mountain—implanted in his head during his UFO encounter. Eventually, his tortured attempts to re-create the image in reality lead him to build a mountain of mud and garbage in his living room and thus drive his family away for good. When he sees Devil's Tower on television during coverage of a supposed nerve-gas spill in the area (actually a hoax concocted by the military to give the UFO team the required secrecy for first contact), Neary finally knows where he has to go and takes Jillian with him. After a hazardous cross-country trek, Neary and Jillian reach the secret landing site and witness mankind's first attempts to communicate with the swarms of beautifully illuminated extraterrestrial craft through a five-note musical tone keyed to a light board. A gigantic mothership—a literal city of light in the night sky—arrives to release numerous abductees, including Jillian's son. Different types of aliens also disembark and mingle with the delighted scientists. Meanwhile, Neary, with Lacombe's blessing, suits up for a long journey aboard the mothership. As soon as

the ecstatic Neary and his alien escort disappear inside it, the mothership soars majestically back into the night.

The film originated in Spielberg's memories of his formative years in Arizona, where as a teenager he had made an 8mm sound film on the subject of UFOs entitled *Firelight*. Throughout the beginning of his career as a professional filmmaker, Spielberg intended to remake his amateur film and call it *Watch the Skies*. During production of *Jaws* (1975), Spielberg often entertained his crew with tales about UFOs and his plans to make a film about them; with the critical and financial success of *Jaws*, Spielberg had the clout to do so. He and other writers, including Paul Schrader, worked on various screenplay drafts, although it was Spielberg who received sole credit. He also re-titled the film *Close Encounters of the Third Kind*—a puzzling title to all except UFO buffs, who would recognize the phrase as UFO expert and Northwestern University professor Dr. J. Allen Hynek's terminology for physical contact with extraterrestrials.

Columbia Studios agreed to finance the project at an initial cost of $16 million. Pre-production scouting settled on the Devil's Tower location as a suitably mysterious backdrop for the film's climax. The film quickly went over budget, finally costing approximately $20 million because of a host of factors, including the logistical demands of location shooting in Wyoming and India (for a brief sequence involving thousands of extras pointing to the sky); the lengthy climactic scene, which required an enormous and problem-plagued set in a hangar in Alabama; and the special effects, supervised by Douglas Trumbull, which involved months of planning and consumed millions of extra dollars. Spielberg's fanatic attention to detail and demands for secrecy on the set added to the studio headaches and delayed the film's release date. Producer Julia Phillips did not approve of some key figures associated with the production, including Truffaut, and was eventually fired by the studio head, David Begelman. Columbia itself was suffering from major financial problems and scandals, and a negative early review of the film did nothing to improve frazzled nerves in the production offices. However, once the film opened, the reviews were much more positive, and the film began to make enough money to be considered another huge success for Spielberg.

There are several different versions of the film in existence. A few years after its initial run, Spielberg returned to the film, re-titling it *Close Encounters of the Third Kind: The Special Edition.* At a cost of $2 million and a seven-week shoot, he filmed new scenes, the most notable of which is a rather disappointing look inside the mothership, and removed some of the lengthy middle portion of the film detailing Neary's breakdown. He also added a brief rendition of ''When You Wish upon a Star'' to the musical score accompanying the mothership's ascent to the heavens. The new version, actually a few minutes shorter than the original, was released in 1980. A later television version combined elements of both films. The special edition was the version most widely available on videostore shelves until a 1998 video release, subtitled *The Collector's Edition,* a re-edited mix of the original version plus five short sequences from the 1980 special edition.

—Philip L. Simpson

FURTHER READING:

Balaban, Bob. *Close Encounters of the Third Kind Diary.* New York, Paradise Press, 1978.

Brode, Douglas. *The Films of Steven Spielberg.* New York, Citadel Press, 1995.

Mott, Donald R., and Cheryl McAllister Saunders. *Steven Spielberg.* Boston, Twayne, 1986.

Perry, George. *Steven Spielberg Close Up: The Making of His Movies.* New York, Thunder's Mouth Press, 1998.

Taylor, Philip M. *Steven Spielberg: The Man, His Movies, and Their Meaning.* New York, Continuum, 1992.

The Closet

Since the 1950s, ''coming out of the closet'' has been the commonly accepted expression for a gay or lesbian person revealing their sexual orientation since the 1950s. Though many advances in gay rights and gay pride have been realized since then, coming out of the closet remained a major milestone in any gay person's life into the late 1990s.

The expression ''coming out'' originated in the early twentieth century when stylish drag ''debutante'' balls were popular society events. Especially in African American communities, the drag queen in-the-know aspired to be presented at these balls, just as young heterosexual women ''came out'' to society at their debutante balls. It was only later, in the 1950s atmosphere of hiding the abnormal, that

the connotation came to be that of coming out of a dark closet. Perhaps playing on the expression ''skeleton in the closet,'' meaning a guilty secret, homosexuals themselves were the sinister skeletons lurking behind the closet door. In the decades since gay liberation began, the expression has slipped into popular usage, and ''coming out of the closet'' is used in a lighthearted way for any admission of a slightly guilty secret.

The closet remains a metaphor for the shame and oppression that forces many gays to hide their identities. ''Closeted'' or ''closet-y'' are also used as adjectives, sometimes derisively, to describe gays who pretend to be heterosexual. ''Closet case'' refers to someone suspected of being gay but unaware of it or hiding it. ''Coming out'' is used among gays to signify the first time they acted on their sexuality (as in, ''I came out when I was fifteen with my best friend'') as well as the traditional means of announcing their sexuality ''to the world.'' ''Outing'' has gained usage as a verb meaning the exposure of someone else's gayness, particularly someone who is well-known and closeted.

Because of the widespread assumption of heterosexuality in American society, coming out of the closet is a lifelong endeavor for gays. Gay men and lesbians must decide whether to come out to friends, to immediate family, to extended family, at work, and so on, and each decision involves a new set of worries and consequences. Even relatively well-known gays must continually assert their identity in new situations or remain in the closet by default.

Gay activists have long touted the importance of coming out of the closet, insisting that much of the oppression gays experience would be diffused if their true numbers were known. In this spirit, the first National Coming Out Day was declared on October 11, 1988, the first anniversary of the second gay and lesbian March on Washington, D.C. The idea behind National Coming Out Day is to encourage gays to come out of the closet to at least one person on that day. Some organizations have even distributed printed cards for gays to give to bank tellers and store clerks announcing that they have just served a gay client.

Though in the days of gay sitcom characters, noted gays on magazine covers, and many openly gay organizations, the closet may seem like a quaint remnant of a former time. Yet gays who do not live in urban areas, do not have protected jobs, or do not have understanding families still fear the repercussions of coming out. It may be true that tolerance will come only when the public realizes how many gay people there are, even among their friends, family, and most respected public figures. However, to gays who have been harassed or beaten, or gays who have lost or had to fight court battles to keep their children, gays who have lost their jobs, coming out of the closet may seem a luxury they can ill afford.

—Tina Gianoulis

FURTHER READING:

Bono, Chastity, and Billie Fitzpatrick. *Family Outing.* New York, Little, Brown and Company, 1998.

Day, Nancy E., and Patricia Schoenrade, ''Staying in the Closet Versus Coming Out: Relationships between Communication about Sexual Orientation and Work Attitudes.'' *Personnel Psychology.* Vol. 50, No. 1, Spring 1997, 147.

Harbeck, Karen M., editor. *Coming Out of the Classroom Closet: Gay and Lesbian Students, Teachers, and Curricula.* New York, Haworth Press, 1992.

CNN

CNN (Cable News Network) was rated "the most believable" of television news sources in a 1990 *Times Mirror* poll. By the end of the twentieth century it had established itself as the leading news-gathering organization, not only in the United States, but in the world. Although in its early days CNN was a little-respected, self-described "rough around the edges" long-shot, by the 1990s other television news departments feared its domination so much that NBC and Fox decided to compete directly, on cable. Early CNN critics doubted that television could host a 24 hour news channel, but executives soon agreed that there was enough of a market for a number of them. By the end of the twentieth century, CNN's growth into a family of networks—CNN Headline News, CNN International, CNN en Espanōl, CNNfn (financial news), CNN-SI (sports), CNN Airport Network, CNN Radio, and CNN Interactive (Internet)—has positioned it as the first in a now long line of network news shows which feed America's hunger for critical analysis of daily events.

When Peter Arnett appeared live on CNN from Bagdad while the city was under attack by American bombers, the network's reputation as the source of first resort for major international news was cemented. Founder Ted Turner had called it "the world's most important network" from the beginning, but now many others commented on

The CNN newsroom.

the "CNN effect"; how all participants in the war monitored the network for primary information and often seemed to design military movements and press briefings with particular concern for how they would appear on CNN. World leaders now routinely mention the Cable News Network and its programming. Its influence is such that it is referred to as "the sixteenth member of the U.N. Security Council." At the end of 1980, after half a year of broadcasting, CNN reached 4.3 million subscribers; by 1998 it claimed 184 million households worldwide.

Ted Turner's 1979 announcement about forming a 24 hour cable news network elicited scoffs and scorn from the mainstream media. The idea that such an enterprise could be profitable, let alone become a dominant world-wide news source, seemed ridiculous. Several major news organizations had looked into forming just such a service, but had determined that it would be far too expensive. The three networks each spent over one hundred million dollars a year on their news divisions, the result of which was the material for a half-hour broadcast each evening. Turner proposed running 24-hour-a-day programming on a budget of less than half that amount.

The America's cup, WTCG, and the Braves had already made Ted Turner well-known. He had won the Cup in 1977 and was featured on the cover of *Sports Illustrated*. After inheriting a modest billboard business in 1963, Turner built a media company by buying struggling UHF stations in Atlanta and Charlotte, North Carolina. He surprised the established media in 1972 when his channel 17, WTCG (later WTBS), beat out WSB, the largest television station in the south, for the rights to broadcast Atlanta Braves baseball games. In 1976 Turner bought the Braves, the Hawks of the NBA (National Basketball Association), and the Chiefs of professional soccer, largely to assure that they would remain in Atlanta where he could continue to broadcast their games. WTCG's signal was made available via satellite in December 1976. During the 1970s, cable television was still in its infancy—Home Box Office, one of the first cable channels, was launched in 1975—with only about 14 percent of American households subscribed to cable.

Turner recruited a team of committed news people and for the most part left the planning of the new network to them. They were excited by his vision of a channel dedicated entirely to reporting the news and decided that the emphasis should be on live coverage. Operating out of a former country club, CNN went on the air on June 1, 1980. It started out with a staff of 300 and seven bureaus: Atlanta, New York, Chicago, Los Angeles, Detroit, London, and Rome. Disparagingly referred to as the "Chicken Noodle Network," the disparity between its budget and those of the broadcast network news programs sometimes showed in production quality in its first few years. Gaffes and mixed signals seemed endemic at times. More often, CNN claimed, the "raggedness" was unavoidable with uncompromising, unfiltered breaking news coverage to which the network was dedicated. Ignoring the naysayers, producers pushed for close monitoring of potentially developing situations so that when something happened, they could cut to it immediately. Producer Ted Kavanau became known for calling out, "take it!" when he wanted a switch made at once.

It was not until 1985, as it worked to increase viewership and fend off rivals, that Cable News Network was profitable. In 1981, Westinghouse, which owned major cable-provider Group W, announced a partnership with ABC News to take on CNN; they named the venture SNC (Satellite NewsChannel). In direct response, CNN launched Headline News on December 31, 1981, almost six months before SNC was introduced on June 21, 1982. Still, the direct competition proved to be the greatest challenge to CNN's survival. Ted Turner spent millions of dollars competing with SNC, and finally defeated the network by buying it for 25 million dollars. It ceased programming on October 27, 1983.

For the 1980 major-party political conventions, CNN did not even have floor credentials, but by the 1992 conventions the traditional broadcast networks cited CNN's in-depth, gavel-to-gavel coverage as a primary reason for their limited coverage. Originally CNN had to fight for equal access to the White House, but by October 1987 the White House invited anchors from "all four networks" for a "chat." Respect was acquired gradually. CNN gave the first American report of the Pope's shooting in May 1981 and extensive coverage to the Falkland War in April 1982. The network was providing the only live coverage of the Space Shuttle Challenger launch on January 28, 1986, when it tragically exploded 96 seconds after take-off.

Despite great logistical problems and restrictions by governments, 1989 provided CNN with many riveting images: the Tiananmen Square massacre in May, the failed Russian coup in August (with Boris Yeltsin rallying the throngs from atop a tank), the November fall of the Berlin Wall, and the invasion of Panama in December. These milestones bolstered the network's reputation little by little, but it was the Gulf War that elevated CNN's status to that of undisputed authority for major, breaking news. President George Bush told diplomats, "I learn more from CNN than I do from the CIA."

Time-Warner bought CNN from Ted Turner in 1996 for three billion dollars. Turner also stayed on as an executive vice president. CNN's credibility, however, was damaged in 1998 after an investigative report on the new program *Newsstand*, alleging that American forces used nerve gas in Laos in 1970. Attacks on the credibility of the story led the network to retract the story and fire the producers of the piece.

Despite CNN's undeniable influence, all of the networks again considered starting their own cable news channels in the early 1990s; NBC and Fox went ahead with theirs. Rupert Murdoch, media magnate owner of Fox, said that he wanted to counter what he called CNN's "liberal bias." Ted Turner cast CNN as an agent of global understanding and peace. From the dedicatory ceremony in front of the original CNN headquarters, where a United Nations flag flew alongside those of the United States and the State of Georgia, he has insisted that CNN is a world network, not American. The word "international" is preferred to "foreign," correspondents from all over the world are employed, and CNN's tolerant reporting on many totalitarian governments has provoked withering attacks from some American conservatives. Turner also saw the network as a key element in the "Third Wave" of futurist Alvin Toffler. Toffler predicts that the information age will lead to a global age. Marshal McLuhan also influenced Turner; writer Joshua Hammer writes, "If Marshal McLuhan's global village exists, its capital is the CNN headquarters in Atlanta." CNN International was launched in 1985 and in 1987 CNN introduced a new show called *World Report*, a two hour program featuring unedited three minute segments from local television journalists world-wide.

CNN claims to be different from older network television news because it is an all-news network and it is on cable. Its cable home means that CNN receives approximately half of its income from fees, making it is less dependent on ratings than free broadcast channels are. Therefore, CNN officials argue, the network can cover news more objectively, with less concern for what may titillate viewers. Its news-only format means that it feels no influence from larger entertainment division. In the 1990s CNN was watched by an average half

million households in prime time, while the big three broadcast evening news programs were seen by around 25 million viewers. CNN executives routinely refer to the large broadcast networks as "the entertainment networks." Largely due to its commitment to world-wide, unfiltered coverage, as *Time* magazine wrote on January 6, 1992, "It has become the common frame of reference for the world's power elite." A 1992 poll found CNN the fourth most respected brand name in the United States, surpassed only by Mercedes-Benz, Kodak, and Disney. Despite its relatively low ratings (except during moments of crisis), CNN can legitimately call itself the world's premier television news service, essentially the network of record, equivalent to the *New York Times* in print journalism.

—Paul Gaffney

FURTHER READING:

Diamond, Edwin. *The Media Show: The Changing Face of the News, 1985-1990.* Cambridge, MIT Press, 1991.

Flournoy, Don M., and Robert K. Stewart. *CNN: Making News in the Global Market.* Luton, United Kingdom, University of Luton Press, 1997.

Kerbel, Matthew Robert. *Edited for Television: CNN, ABC, and American Presidential Elections.* 2nd edition. Boulder, Colorado, Westview Press, 1998.

Whittemore, Hank. *CNN: The Inside Story.* Boston, Little, Brown and Co., 1990.

Cobb, Ty (1886-1961)

The most fear-inspiring presence in baseball history, Ty Cobb was unmatched as a performer during his 24-year career in the major leagues. Cobb set statistical marks that, on the eve of the twenty first century, no major-leaguer has equaled. His .367 lifetime batting average is 23 points higher than Ted Williams' second best mark. Cobb's 2,244 runs scored put him well ahead of Babe Ruth. His feat of leading his league in batting average 12 times easily tops Honus Wagner's eight, and his 37 steals of home plate may never be broken. But Cobb is equally well known for his violent style of play and his ferocious temper. Lou Gehrig, angered one day when Cobb brutally spiked a Yankee pitcher on a play at first base, complained that "Cobb is about as welcome to American League parks as a rattlesnake." He was so hated by his teammates that for much of his career he carried a gun in a shoulder strap just in case a group of them jumped him. Cobb's career began at a time when baseball's rules were still in flux, and spanned the "dead-ball" and "rabbit-ball" eras of the first two decades of the twentieth century.

Tyrus Raymond Cobb was born on December 18, 1886 in an area of Georgia known as the Narrows, near Banks County. His mother, Amanda Chitwood, had been a child bride of only 12 years of age in 1883 when she married William Herschel Cobb, then a 20-year-old schoolteacher. Despite these modest beginnings in poor rural Georgia, Ty Cobb was the latest in a long roster of prominent ancestors. The Cobb tribe dated back to Joseph Cobb, who emigrated from England in 1611 and who eventually became a Virginia tobacco tycoon. Thomas Willis Cobb was a colonel in the Revolutionary War and an aide to General Washington. Thomas Reade Rootes Cobb died as a Confederate brigadier general at Fredericksburg and Howell

Ty Cobb

Cobb, who served as Georgia's Governor in 1851, was captured by the Federals at Macon in 1865.

Cobb's father impressed upon him the need to uphold the family tradition by either entering a profession, such as medicine or the law, or by attending West Point. Cobb, however, showed little interest in these potential futures. In 1901, at the age of 15, Cobb became aware of major league baseball. He learned, to his astonishment, that in the game he and his friends played with a flat board and a homemade twine ball major league celebrities could earn up to $8,000 per season.

In 1902, against his father's wishes, Cobb joined the Royston Reds, a semi-pro team that toured Northeastern Georgia. Semi-pro "town-ball" was tough stuff. At this time one of the rules held over from the game's pioneer forms was "soaking," in which base runners could be put out not only by throws to a bag and by hand, but by throwing to hit them anywhere on the body. Hitting the runner in the skull was preferable, because it might take a star opponent out of the lineup. On more than one occasion Cobb was put out by a "soaker" to the ear, which did little to endear baseball to his father.

In 1904 Cobb succeeded in making the roster of the class "C" Augusta Tourists, a league that drew scouts from the major leagues. At Augusta Cobb began to develop his distinctive playing style.

Rather than pull pitches to his natural direction of right field, the left-handed Cobb stood deep in the batter's box, choked up on his 38 ounce bat with a split hands grip, and opened his stance as the pitcher fired the ball. His trademark was to chop grounders and slice line-drives through third-base gaps and into an often unguarded left-field. The Cobb-style bunt, destined to become one of the most deadly weapons since Willie Keeler's "Baltimore Chop," took shape when Cobb retracted his bat and punched the ball to a selected spot between the third baseman and the pitcher, just out of reach. He also began to pull bunts for base hits and once on base he ran with wild abandon, stealing when he wished and running through the stop signs of base coaches, always using his great speed to wreak havoc with opposing defenses. Included in his techniques was a kick slide, in which he would kick his lead leg at the last minute in an effort to dislodge the ball, the glove, and perhaps even the hand of a middle infielder waiting to tag him out. This would, at the major league level, develop into the dreaded "Cobb Kiss," in which Cobb would slide, or often leap, feet first into infielders and catchers with sharpened spikes slashing and cutting. Unique among players of his era, Cobb kept notebooks filled with intelligence on opposing pitchers and defenses. He studied the geometry and angles of the baseball field, and through his hitting and base running strategies engaged in what he called "scientific baseball," a style that would revolutionize the game in the so-called "dead-ball" era before Babe Ruth.

But although he could outrun everybody, had a rifle arm in center field, and hit sizzling singles and doubles to all fields, already at Augusta Cobb was hated by his teammates. He was a loner who early in his career did not drink or chase women, and preferred to read histories and biographies in his room. He constantly fought with his manager, whose signs he regularly ignored. Eventually, none of his teammates would room with him, especially after he severely beat pitcher George Napoleon "Nap" Rucker, a roommate of Cobb's for a short time. Rucker's "crime" had been taking the first hot bath in their room after a game. Cobb's explanation to a bloodied Rucker was "I've got to be first at everything—all the time!" Rucker and the other Tourists considered Cobb mentally unbalanced and dangerous if provoked.

On August 8, 1905 William Cobb was killed by a shotgun blast, fired by his young wife Amanda. Although eventually cleared of charges of voluntary manslaughter, rumors of marital infidelity and premeditated murder continued to swirl around Cobb's mother. The violent death of his father, who had never seen Cobb play but who had softened toward his son's career choice shortly before his death, made Cobb's volatile nature even worse. As Cobb later observed of himself during this period, "I was like a steel spring with a growing and dangerous flaw in it. If it is wound too tight or has the slightest weak point, the spring will fly apart and then is done for."

Late in the 1905 season, a Detroit Tiger team weakened by injuries needed cheap replacements and purchased Cobb's contract. Cobb joined major league baseball during a period in which the game was reshaping itself. In 1901 the foul-strike rule had been adopted, whereby the first and second foul balls off the bat counted as strikes. But of greater importance were the actions of Byron "Ban" Johnson, who changed the name of his minor Western League to the American League and began signing major league players in direct competition with the National League. By 1903 bifurcated baseball and the modern World Series were born, leading to a boom in baseball's popularity as Cobb joined the Tigers.

Cobb impressed from his first at bat, when he clubbed a double off of "Happy" Jack Chesbro, a 41 game winner in 1904. His aggressive style won over the fans immediately, but from the beginning his Tiger teammates despised Cobb. Most of the Tigers were northerners and mid-westerners, and Cobb, with his pronounced southern drawl and stiff, formal way of addressing people stood out. But more importantly, his sometimes spectacular play as a rookie indicated that he might be a threat to the established outfield corps, and in the hardscrabble game of the turn of the twentieth century such rookies faced intense hazing. Cobb fought back against the veterans and took to carrying a snub-nosed Frontier Colt pistol on his person for protection. The tension led to a mental breakdown for Cobb in mid-summer 1906, leading to a 44 day stay in a sanatorium. Upon his release, Cobb returned to the Tigers with an even greater determination to succeed. ''When I got back I was going to show them some ballplaying like the fans hadn't seen in some time,'' Cobb later recalled.

Cobb fulfilled his promise. He lead Detroit to the World Series in 1907, 1908, and 1909, hitting a combined .361 in those seasons with a remarkable 164 stolen bases. Although Detroit faded as a contender after that, Cobb's star status continued to rise. In 1911 he hit .420 with 83 stolen bases and 144 RBIs (runs batted in). In 1912 he hit .410 with 61 steals and 90 RBIs. He batted over .300, the traditional benchmark for batting excellence, in 23 consecutive seasons, including a .323 mark in 1928, his final season, at the age of 42. But while Cobb remained remarkably consistent, the game of baseball changed around him. In 1919 the Boston Red Sox sold their star player, Babe Ruth, to the New York Yankees. In 1920 Ruth hit 54 Home Runs, and in 1921 he hit 59. The ''dead-ball'' era and scientific baseball was replaced by the ''rabbit-ball'' era and big bang baseball. Cobb felt that Ruth was ''unfinished'' and that major league pitchers would soon adjust to his style; they did not. Cobb never adjusted or changed his style. ''The home run could wreck baseball,'' he warned. ''It throws out a lot of strategy and makes it fence-ball.'' As player-manager late in his career, Cobb tried to match the Yankee's ''fence-ball'' with his own ''scientific ball''—and he failed miserably.

Along the way, Cobb initiated a move toward player emancipation by agitating in Congress for an investigation of baseball's reserve clause that tied a player to one team for life. He took the lead in forming the Ball Players Fraternity, a nascent player's union. In retirement he spent some of his estimated $12 million fortune, compiled mainly through shrewd stock market investments, in supporting destitute ex-ballplayers and their families. But he also burned all fan mail that reached him and ended long-term relationships with friends such as Ted Williams over minor disputes. When he died in 1961, just three men from major league baseball attended his funeral, one of which was old ''Nap'' Rucker from his Augusta days. Not a single official representative of major league baseball attended the funeral of the most inventive, detested, and talented player in baseball history.

—Todd Anthony Rosa

FURTHER READING:

Alexander, Charles. *Ty Cobb.* New York, Oxford University Press, 1984.

Astor, Gerald, and Joe Falls. *The Detroit Tigers.* New York, Walker & Company, 1989.

Cobb, Ty, with Al Stump. *My Life in Baseball: The True Record.* Garden City, New York, Doubleday, 1961.

Seymour, Harold. *Baseball: The Early Years.* New York, Oxford University Press, 1960.

———. *Baseball: The Golden Age.* New York, Oxford University Press, 1971.

Stump, Al. *Cobb: A Biography.* Chapel Hill, North Carolina, Algonquin Books, 1994.

Ward, Geoffrey C. *Baseball: An Illustrated History.* New York, A.A. Knopf, 1994.

Coca, Imogene (1908—)

Imogene Coca is best remembered as one of the driving forces behind the popular variety show *Your Show of Shows* (1950-54), in which she starred with Sid Caesar. Her physical, non-verbal comedy perfectly offset Caesar's bizarre characterizations and antics. Coca won an Emmy for Best Actress in 1951 for her work on the series. After *Your Show of Shows* was canceled, however, neither Coca nor Caesar were ever able to attain a similar level of popularity and all of Coca's sitcom attempts were soon canceled. Even a series that reunited the two in 1958 was unsuccessful, proving that television popularity is more a function of viewer mood than an actor's talent.

—Denise Lowe

FURTHER READING:

Brooks, Tim, and Earle Marsh. *The Complete Directory to Prime Time Network and Cable TV Shows, 1946-Present.* New York, Ballentine Books, 1995.

Martin, Jean. *Who's Who of Women in the Twentieth Century.* New York, Crescent Books, 1995.

Coca-Cola

Coca-Cola, also known as Coke, began in the chaos of the post-Reconstruction South. In May 1886, Georgia pharmacist John Styth Pemberton succeeded in creating what he intended, a temperance drink. With cries against alcohol reaching a fever pitch in the region Pemberton worked to create a drink that could satisfy the anti-alcohol crowd as well as his need to turn a profit. In the ensuing mixing and re-mixing he came up with the syrup base for Coca-Cola. The reddish brown color and ''spicy'' flavor of the drink helped mask the illegal alcohol that some of his early customers added to the beverage. Little did he know that this new drink, made largely of sugar and water, would quickly become the most popular soft drink in the United States and, eventually, the entire world.

Although John Pemberton created the formula for Coca-Cola it fell to others to turn the product into a profitable enterprise. Fellow pharmacist Asa Candler bought the rights to Coke in 1888, and he would begin to push the drink to successful heights. Through a variety of marketing tools Candler put Coca-Cola onto the long road to prosperity. Calendars, pens, metal trays, posters, and a variety of other items were emblazoned with the Coke image and helped breed familiarity with the drink. Additionally, although the beverage included negligible amounts of cocaine, Candler gave in to the sentiment of the Progressive Era and removed all traces of cocaine from Coca-Cola in 1903. Candler followed the slight formula switch with an advertising campaign emphasizing the purity of the drink. The ad

1894   1899–1902   1900 ----- 1916   1915   1923   1937   1957   1961   1975

Nov. 16

Dec. 25

Aug. 3
(D-105529)

Applied Color
Label (ACL)

One-Way Bottle
(OWB)

One-Way Bottle
(Plastic)

Assorted bottle styles of Coke.

campaign was enhanced by the development of the unique Coca-Cola bottle in 1913. The new Coke bottle, with its wide middle and ribbed sides, made the Coca-Cola bottle, and by relation its contents, instantly identifiable.

For all of the success that he had engineered at Coca-Cola, Asa Candler lost interest in the soft drink business. Candler turned the company over to his sons who would in turn eventually sell it to Ernest Woodruff. It was Woodruff, and eventually his son, Robert, who guided the company to its position of leadership in the soda-pop industry. As one company employee remarked ''Asa Candler gave us feet, but Woodruff gave us wings.'' The Woodruffs expanded company operations, initiated the vending-machine process, changed fountain distribution to ensure product uniformity and quality, and presided over the emergence of the six-pack. It was also the Woodruffs who recognized that Coke's greatest asset was not what it did, but what it could potentially represent; accordingly, they expanded upon company advertising in order to have Coke identified as the pre-eminent soft drink and, ultimately, a part of Americana.

Coca-Cola advertising was some of the most memorable in the history of American business. Through the work of artists such as Norman Rockwell and Haddon Sundblom, images of Coca-Cola were united with other aspects of American life. In fact, it was not until Sundblom, through a Coke advertisement, provided the nation with a depiction of the red-suited, rotund Santa Claus, that such an image (and by relation Coca-Cola) was identified with the American version of Christmas. Coke's strategic marketing efforts, through magazines, billboards, calendars, and various other product giveaways emblazoned with the name Coca-Cola, made the product a part of American culture. The success of Coke advertising gave the product an appeal that stretched far beyond its simple function as a beverage to quench the thirst. Coke became identified with things that were American, as much an icon as the Statue of Liberty or Mount Rushmore. This shift

to icon status was catalyzed by the company's actions during World War II.

At the outset of the war Coke found its business potentially limited by wartime production statutes. Sugar, a major ingredient in the drink, was to be rationed in order to ensure its availability to the nation's military forces. The company, though not necessarily facing a loss of market share, faced the serious possibility of zero growth during the conflict. Therefore, Robert Woodruff announced that the company would work to ensure that Coke was available to every American serviceman overseas. Through this bold maneuver Coca-Cola was eventually placed on the list of military necessities and allowed to circumvent limits on its sugar supply. Also, thanks in part to Chief of Staff George C. Marshall, the company was able to avoid the massive expense of ensuring Coke's delivery. Marshall believed that troop morale would be improved by the availability of Coca-Cola, and that it was a good alternative to alcohol. Therefore, he allowed for entire bottling plants to be transported overseas at government expense. Thanks to Marshall and others Coca-Cola was able to expand its presence overseas at a faster rate and at less expense than other beverages.

Thousands of American servicemen, from Dwight Eisenhower to the common soldier, preferred Coke to any other soft drink. The availability of the beverage in every theater of the war helped Coke to be elevated in the minds of GI's as a slice of America. In many of their letters home, soldiers identified the drink as one of the things they were fighting for, in addition to families and sweethearts. Bottles of Coke were auctioned off when supplies became limited, were flown along with bombing sorties, and found their way onto submarines. One GI went so far as to call the liquid ''nectar of the Gods.'' Thanks to its presence in the war effort, the affinity which GI's held for the beverage, and the establishment of a presence overseas, Coke became identified by Americans and citizens of foreign countries with the

American Way. After World War II, Coca-Cola was on its way to becoming one of a handful of brands recognized around the world.

However, the presence of Coca-Cola was not always welcomed overseas. During the political and ideological battles of the Cold War, Coke was targeted by European communists as a symbol of the creeping hegemony of the United States. The drink found itself under attack in many European countries and in some quarters its existence was denounced as ''Coca-Colonialism.'' In addition, the drink often found its presence opposed by local soft drink and beverage manufacturers. A variety of beverage manufacturers in Germany, Italy, and France actively opposed the spread of Coca-Cola in their countries. Despite the opposition, however, the spread of Coca-Cola continued throughout the Cold War. In some cases the sale of the soft drink preceded or immediately followed the establishment of relations between the United States and another country. By the 1970s, the worldwide presence of Coke was such that company officials could (and did) claim that, ''When you don't see a Coca-Cola sign, you have passed the borders of civilization.''

Beginning in the 1970s, Coca-Cola found its greatest challenges in the domestic rather than international arena. Facing the growth of its rival, Pepsi-Cola, Coke found itself increasingly losing its market share. Coke executives were even more worried when the Pepsi Challenge convincingly argued that even among Coke loyalists the taste of Pepsi was preferred to that of Coke. The results of the challenge led Coke officials to conclude that the taste of the drink was inferior to that of Pepsi and that a change in the formula was necessary. The result of this line of thinking was the marketing debacle surrounding New Coke.

In the history of corporate marketing blunders the 1983 introduction of New Coke quickly took its place alongside the Edsel. After New Coke was introduced company telephone operators found themselves besieged by irate consumers disgusted with the product change. Coke's error was that blind taste tests like the Pepsi Challenge prevented the consumer from associating the thoughts and traditions with a particular soda. Caught up in ideas of product inferiority the company seemingly forgot its greatest asset—the association that it had with the life experiences of millions of consumers. Many Americans associated memories of first dates, battlefield success, sporting events, and other occasions with the consumption of Coca-Cola. Those associations were something that could not be ignored or rejected simply because when blindfolded customers preferred the taste of one beverage over another. In many cases the choice of a particular soft drink was something passed down from parents to children. Consequently, the taste tests would not make lifelong Coke drinkers switch to a new beverage; the tradition and association with Coca-Cola were too powerful for such a thing to occur.

After introducing New Coke the company found itself assaulted not for changing the formula of a simple soft drink, but for tampering with a piece of Americana. Columnists editorialized that the next step would be changing the flag or tearing down the Statue of Liberty. Many Americans rejected New Coke not for its taste but for its mere existence. Tradition, as the Coca-Cola company was forced to admit, took precedence over taste. Four months after it was taken off of the shelves, the traditionally formulated Coke was returned to the marketplace under the name Coca-Cola Classic. Company president Don Keough summed up the episode by saying ''Some critics will say Coca-Cola made a marketing mistake. Some critics will say that we planned the whole thing. The truth is we are not that dumb and not that

smart.'' What the company was smart enough to do was to recognize that they were more than a soft drink to those who consumed the beverage as well as to those who did not. What they were to seemingly the entire nation, regardless of individual beverage preference, was a piece of America as genuine and identifiable with the country as the game of baseball.

As a beverage the consumption of Coca-Cola has a rather limited physical impact. The drink was able to quench the thirst and to provide a small lift due to its caffeine and sugar content. Beyond its use, however, Coca-Cola was, as Pulitzer Prize-winning newspaper editor William Allen White once remarked, the ''sublimated essence of all that America stands for. . . .'' Though the formula underwent changes and the company developed diet, caffeine free, and cherry-flavored versions, what Coca-Cola represents has not changed. Coca-Cola, a beverage consumed by presidents, monarchs, and consumers the world over has remained above all else a symbol of America and its way of life.

—Jason Chambers

FURTHER READING:

Allen, Frederick. *Secret Formula: How Brilliant Marketing and Relentless Salesmanship Made Coca-Cola the Best-Know Product in the World.* New York, HarperCollins, 1994.

Dietz, Lawrence. *Soda Pop: The History, Advertising, Art, and Memorabilia of Soft Drinks in America.* New York, Simon and Schuster, 1973.

Hoy, Anne. *Coca-Cola: The First Hundred Years.* Atlanta, The Coca-Cola Company, 1986

Kahn, Jr. E.J. *The Big Drink: The Story of Coca-Cola.* New York, Random House, 1960.

Louis, J.C., and Yazijian, Harvey Z. *The Cola Wars.* New York, Everest House, Publishers, 1980.

Thomas, Oliver. *The Real Coke, The Real Story.* New York, Penguin Books, 1986

Watters, Pat. *Coca-Cola: An Illustrated History.* Garden City, Doubleday, 1978.

Cocaine/Crack

Erythroxlon coca, a shrub indigenous to the upper jungles of the Andes mountains in South America, has been consumed for millennia by the various Indian tribes that have inhabited the region. The primary alkaloid of this plant, cocaine (first called erythroxyline), earned a reputation throughout the twentieth century as the quintessential American drug. Psychologist Ronald Siegel noted that ''its stimulating and pleasure-causing properties reinforce the American character with its initiative, its energy, its restless activity and its boundless optimism.'' Cocaine—which one scholar called ''probably the least understood and most consistently misrepresented drug in the pharmacopoeia''—symbolizes more than any other illicit drug the twin extremes of decadent indulgence and dire poverty that characterize the excesses of American capitalism. The drug has provoked both wondrous praise and intense moral condemnation for centuries.

For the Yunga and Aymara Indians of South America, the practice of chewing coca was most likely a matter of survival. The coca leaf, rich in vitamins and proteins as well as in its popular mood-altering alkaloid, was an essential source of nourishment and strength in the Andes, where food and oxygen were scarce. The word "coca" probably simply meant "plant," suggesting the pervasiveness of the shrub in ancient life. The leaf also had both medical and religious applications throughout the pre-Inca period, and the Inca empire made coca central to religious cosmology.

Almost immediately upon its entrance into the Western frame of reference, the coca leaf was inextricable from the drama and violence of imperial expansion. In the sixteenth century the Spaniards first discounted Indian claims that coca made them more energetic, and outlawed the leaf, believing it to be the work of the Devil. After seeing that the Indians were indeed more productive laborers under the leaf's influence, they legalized and taxed the custom. These taxes became the chief support for the Catholic church in the region. An awareness of the political significance of coca quickly developed among the Indians of the Andean region, and for centuries the leaf has been a powerful symbol of the strength and resilience of Andean culture in the face of genocidal European domination.

In the mid-nineteenth century, when the cocaine alkaloid was isolated and extracted, cocaine began its rise to popularity in Europe and North America. The drug is widely praised during this period for its stimulating effects on the central nervous system, with many physicians and scientists, including Sigmund Freud, extolling its virtues as a cure for alcohol and morphine addiction. Others praised its appetite-reduction properties, while still others hailed it as an aphrodisiac. In 1859 Dr. Paolo Mantegazza, a prominent Italian neurologist, wrote, "I prefer a life of ten years with coca to one of a hundred thousand without it." Americans beamed with pride at the wonder drug that had been discovered on their continent; one American company advertised at least 15 different cocaine products and promised that the drug would "supply the place of food, make the coward brave, the silent eloquent and render the sufferer indifferent to pain."

Angelo Mariana manufactured coca-based wine products, boasting having collected 13 volumes of praise from satisfied customers, who included well-known political leaders, artists, and an alarming number of doctors, "including physicians to all the royal households of Europe." Ulysses S. Grant, according to Mariana, took the coca-wine elixir daily while composing his memoirs. In 1885 John S. Pemberton, an Atlanta pharmacist, also started selling cocaine-based wine, but removed the alcohol in response to prohibitionist sentiment and began marketing a soft drink with cocaine and gotu kola as an "intellectual beverage and temperance drink" which he called Coca-Cola.

It was not until the late 1880s and 1890s that cocaine's addictive properties begin to capture public attention in the United States. While cocaine has no physically addictive properties, the psychological dependence associated with its frequent use can be just as debilitating as any physical addiction. By the turn of the twentieth century the potential dangers of such dependence had become clear to many, and reports of abuse began to spread.

By 1900 the drug was at the center of a full-scale moral panic. Scholars have noted the race and class overtones of this early cocaine panic. In spite of little actual evidence to substantiate such claims, the *American Journal of Pharmacy* reported in 1903 that most cocaine users were "bohemians, gamblers, high- and low-class prostitutes,

night porters, bell boys, burglars, racketeers, pimps, and casual laborers." The moral panic directly targeted blacks, and the fear of cocaine fit perfectly into the dominant racial discourses of the day. In 1914 Dr. Christopher Koch of Pennsylvania's State Pharmacy Board declared that "Most of the attacks upon the white women of the South are the direct result of a cocaine-crazed Negro brain." David Musto characterized the period in this way: "So far, evidence does not suggest that cocaine caused a crime wave but rather that anticipation of black rebellion inspired white alarm. Anecdotes often told of superhuman strength, cunning, and efficiency resulting from cocaine. These fantasies characterized white fear, not the reality of cocaine's effects, and gave one more reason for the repression of blacks."

Cocaine was heavily restricted by the Harrison Narcotics Act in 1914 and was officially identified as a "narcotic" and outlawed by the United States government in 1922, after which time its use went largely underground until the late 1960s and early 1970s, when it spread first in the rock 'n' roll subculture and then through the more affluent sectors of American society. It became identified again with American wealth and power, and its dangers were downplayed or ignored. As late as 1980 the use of powder cocaine was recognized even by some medical authorities as "very safe."

During the early 1970s, however, a coca epidemic began quietly spreading throughout South America. While the centuries-old practice of chewing fresh coca leaves by coqueros had never been observed to cause abuse or mania, in the 1970s a new practice developed of smoking a paste, called basuco or basé, that was a byproduct of the cocaine manufacturing process. Peruvian physicians began publicly warning of a paste-smoking epidemic. The reports, largely ignored at the time in the United States, told of basuco-smoking pastaleros being driven crazy by the drug, smoking enormous quantities chronically, in many cases until death.

In early 1974, a misinterpretation of the term basé led some San Francisco chemists to reverse engineer cocaine "base" from pure powder cocaine, creating a smokable mixture of cocaine alkaloid. The first "freebasers" thought they were smoking basuco like the pastaleros, but in reality they were smoking "something that nobody else on the planet had ever smoked before." The costly and inefficient procedure of manufacturing freebase from powder cocaine ensured that the drug remained a celebrity thrill. This was dramatized in comedian Richard Pryor's near-death experience with freebase in 1980.

Crack cocaine was most likely developed in the Bahamas in the late 1970s or early 1980s when it was recognized that the expensive and dangerous procedures required to manufacture freebase were unnecessary. A smokable cocaine paste, it was discovered, could be cheaply and easily manufactured by mixing even low quality cocaine with common substances such as baking soda. This moment coincided with a massive glut of cheap Colombian cocaine in the international market. The supply of cocaine coming into the United States more than doubled between 1976 and 1980. The price of cocaine again dropped after 1980, thanks at least partly to a CIA (Central Intelligence Agency)-supported coup in Bolivia.

Throughout the 1980s, cocaine again became the subject of an intense moral panic in the United States. In October of 1982, only seven months after retracting his endorsement for stronger warnings on cigarette packs, President Reagan declared his "unshakable" commitment "to do whatever is necessary to end the drug menace." The Department of Defense and the CIA were officially enlisted in support of the drug war, and military activity was aimed both at Latin American smugglers and at American citizens. While the United

States Administration frequently raised the specter of ''narcoterrorism'' associated with Latin American rebels, most analysts agree that United States economic and military policy has consistently benefitted the powerful aristocracies who manage the cocaine trade.

In the mid-1980s, in the heat of the Iran-Contra scandal, evidence that members of the CIA's contra army in Nicaragua were heavily involved in the cocaine trade began to surface in the American press. This evidence was downplayed and denied by government officials, and generally ignored by the public until 1996, when an explosive newspaper series by Gary Webb brought the issue to public attention. While Webb's award-winning series was widely discredited by the major media, most of his claims have been confirmed by other researchers, and in some cases even admitted by the CIA in its self-review. The Webb series contributed to perceptions in African-American communities that cocaine was part of a government plot to destroy them.

As was the case at the turn of the twentieth century, the moral outrage at cocaine turned on race and class themes. Cocaine was suddenly seen as threatening when it became widely and inexpensively available to the nation's black and inner-city poor; its widespread use by the urban upper class was never viewed as an epidemic. The unequal racial lines drawn in the drug war were recognized by the United States Sentencing Commission, which in 1995 recommended a reduction in the sentencing disparities between crack and powder cocaine. Powder cocaine, the preferred drug of white upper class users, carries about 1/100th the legal penalties of equivalent amounts of crack.

The vilified figure of the inner-city crack dealer, however, may represent the ironic underbelly to the American character and spirit that has been associated with cocaine's stimulant effects. Phillippe Bourgois noted that ''ambitious, energetic, inner-city youths are attracted to the underground economy precisely because they believe in Horatio Alger's version of the American dream. They are the ultimate rugged individualists.''

—Bernardo Alexander Attias

FURTHER READING:

Ashley, Richard. *Cocaine: Its History, Uses, and Effects.* New York, Warner Books, 1975.

Belenko, Steven R. *Crack and the Evolution of Anti-Drug Policy.* Westport, Connecticut, Greenwood Press, 1993.

Bernfeld, Siegfried. ''Freud's Studies on Cocaine, 1884-1887.'' *Yearbook of Psychoanalysis.* Vol. 10, 1954-1955, 9-38.

Eddy, Paul, Hugo Sabogal, and Sara Walden. *The Cocaine Wars.* New York, W. W. Norton, 1988.

Grinspoon, Lester, and James B. Bakalar. *Cocaine: A Drug and its Social Evolution.* New York, Basic Books, 1976.

Morales, Edmundo. *Cocaine: White Gold Rush in Peru.* Tuscon, University of Arizona Press, 1989.

Mortimer, W. G. *Peru History of Coca, ''The Divine Plant'' of the Incas.* New York, J. H. Vail and Company, 1901.

Musto, David F. ''America's First Cocaine Epidemic.'' *Washington Quarterly.* Summer 1989, 59-64.

————. *The American Disease: Origins of Narcotic Control.* New Haven, Connecticut, Yale, 1973.

Reeves, Jimmie L., and Richard Campbell. *Cracked Coverage: Television News, the Anti-Cocaine Crusade, and the Reagan Legacy.* Durham, North Carolina, Duke University Press, 1994.

Webb, Gary. *Dark Alliance: The CIA, the Contras, and the Crack Cocaine Explosion.* New York, Seven Stories Press, 1998.

Cocktail Parties

Noted essayist and tippler H. L. Mencken once wrote that the cocktail was ''the greatest of all the contributions of the American way of life to the salvation of humanity.'' While Mencken's effusive evaluation of the cocktail might be challenged today, the cocktail and the cocktail party remain a distinctively American contribution to the social landscape of the twentieth century.

Although the cocktail party is most closely associated with the Cold War era, Americans were toasting with mixed drinks well before the 1950s. The origin of the word cocktail remains the subject of some debate, with a few bold scholars giving the honors to the troops of George Washington, who raised a toast to the ''cock tail'' that adorned the General's hat. Whatever its origins, by the 1880s the cocktail had become an American institution, and by the turn of the century women's magazines included recipes for cocktails to be made by hostesses, to insure the success of their parties.

The enactment of the 18th Amendment in 1920 made Prohibition a reality, and cocktails went underground to speakeasies. These illegal night clubs caused a small social revolution in the United States, as they allowed men and women to drink together in public for the first time. But it was not until after World War II that the cocktail-party culture became completely mainstream. As young people flocked to the new suburbs in the 1950s, they bought homes that were far removed from the bars and lounges of the city. Cocktail parties became a key form of socializing, and the market for lounge music records, cocktail glasses, and shakers exploded. By 1955 even the U.S. government had realized the importance of these alcohol-oriented gatherings, as the National Institute of Mental Health of the U.S. Public Health Service launched a four-year sociological study of cocktail parties, with six lucky agents pressed into duty attending and reporting back on high-ball-induced behavior. The testing of atomic bombs during the early 1950s in the deserts of Nevada sparked a short-lived fad for atomic-themed cocktails.

The most emblematic drink of cocktail culture remains the martini. The outline of the distinctively shaped glass has become a universal symbol for bars and lounges. As with many aspects of cocktail culture, the origins of the martini remain hazy. One history suggests that the first martini was mixed by noted bartender ''Professor'' Jerry Thomas at the bar of the Occidental Hotel in San Francisco in the early 1860s for a miner on his way to the town of Martinez. The martini was insured lasting fame by being the favored libation of the popular movie spy James Bond, whose strict allegiance to a martini that was ''shaken, not stirred'' so that the gin not be ''bruised,'' encouraged a generation of movie-goers to abandon their swizzle sticks in favor of a cocktail shaker.

In the mid-1990s, cocktail culture experienced a revival through the efforts of a few well-publicized bands interested in reviving the cocktail party lounge sound. The press dubbed the movement, sparked by the 1994 release of Combustible Edison's album *I, Swinger,* ''Cocktail Nation,'' and young people appropriated the sleek suits, snazzy shakers and swinging sounds made popular by their parents' generation. Cocktail nostalgia reached its peak with the 1996 release of Jon Favreau's *Swingers,* a movie about cocktail culture in contemporary Los Angeles.

—Deborah Broderson

FURTHER READING:

Edmunds, Lowell. *Martini Straight Up: The Classic American Cocktail.* Baltimore, Johns Hopkins University Press, 1998.

Lanza, Joseph. *The Cocktail: The Influence of Spirits on the American Psyche.* New York, St. Martin's Press, 1995.

Murdock, Catherine. *Domesticating Drink: Women, Men and Alcohol in America 1870-1940.* Baltimore, Johns Hopkins University Press, 1998.

Cody, Buffalo Bill, and his Wild West Show

Buffalo Bill was not the originator of the Wild West Show or, indeed, the only person to stage one. Frontier extravaganzas had

William Cody

existed in one form or another from as early as 1843. Yet Buffalo Bill Cody is largely responsible for creating our romantic view of the Old West that continues largely unabated to this day. This is due to a combination of factors, not the least of which was Cody's own flair for dramatizing his own real life experiences as a scout, buffalo hunter, and Indian fighter.

The legend of William F. Cody began in 1867 when, as a 21-year-old young man who had already lived a full life as a Pony Express rider, gold miner, and ox team driver, he contracted to supply buffalo meat for construction workers on the Union Pacific railroad. Although he did not kill the number of huge beasts attributed to him (that was accomplished by the "hide hunters" who followed and nearly decimated the breed), he was dubbed Buffalo Bill. He followed this experience with a four-year stint as Chief of Scouts for the Fifth United States Cavalry under the leadership of former Civil War hero Lieutenant General Philip Sheridan. During this service, Cody participated in 16 Indian skirmishes including the defeat of the Cheyenne at Summit Springs in 1869. After this, Cody earned a living as a hunting guide for parties of celebrities, who included politicians and European royalty. On one of these, he encountered the author Ned Buntline who made him the hero of a best-selling series of stories in *The New York Weekly,* flamboyantly titled "The Greatest Romance of the Age." These stories spread the buffalo hunter's fame around the world.

After witnessing a Nebraska Independence Day celebration in 1883, Cody seized upon the idea of a celebration of the West, and played upon his newfound fame to create Buffalo Bill's Wild West, an outdoor extravaganza that depicted life on the frontier from his unique perspective. The show (although he steadfastly avoided the use of the word) was composed of a demonstration of Pony Express riding, an attack on the Deadwood Stage (which was the actual Cheyenne and Black Hills Stage line coach used on the Deadwood run), and a number of rodeo events including riding wild steers, bucking broncos, calf roping, horse races, and shooting. Whenever he could, Cody also employed authentic Western personages such as scout John Nelson; Chief Gall, who participated in the defeat of Custer at Little Big Horn; and later Sitting Bull, to make personal appearances in the show. The grand finale usually consisted of a spectacle incorporating buffalo, elk, deer, wild horses, and steers stampeding with cowboys and Indians.

In 1884, the show played the Cotton Exposition in New Orleans, where Cody acquired his greatest drawing card—sharpshooter Annie Oakley, who was billed as "Little Sure Shot." The following year, Sitting Bull, the most famous chief of the Indian Wars, joined the show. Ironically, Cody's use of Sitting Bull and other Indians as entertainers remains controversial to this day. To his critics, the depictions of Indians attacking stagecoaches and settlers in a vast arena served to perpetuate the image of the Indian as a dangerous savage. On the other hand, he was one of the few whites willing to employ Native Americans at the time, and he did play a role in taking many of them off the reservation and providing them with a view of the wider world beyond the American frontier.

Yet even as many Indians were touring the country with Buffalo Bill's Wild West Show, the Indian Wars were still continuing on the frontier. Some of Cody's Indians returned to help in the Army's peacemaking efforts, and Cody himself volunteered his services in the last major Sioux uprising of 1890-91 as an ambassador to Sitting Bull, who had returned from Canada to lend his presence as a spiritual leader to his countrymen. This effort was personally called off by President Benjamin Harrison, and Sitting Bull was shot by Indian police the next day while astride a show horse given to him by Cody. According to historian Kevin Brownlow, the horse, trained to kneel at the sound of gunfire while appearing in the Wild West Show, proceeded to bow down while its famous rider was being shot. When the Indians were ultimately defeated, Cody was able to free a number of the prisoners to appear in his show the following season—a dubious achievement, perhaps, but one that allowed them a measure of freedom in comparison to confinement on a reservation.

Buffalo Bill's Wild West Show reached the peak of its popularity in 1887 when Cody took his extravaganza to London to celebrate Queen Victoria's Golden Jubilee. According to sources, one performance featured an attack on a Deadwood Stage driven by Buffalo Bill himself with the Prince of Wales and other royal personages on board. This performance was followed in 1889 with a full European tour, beginning with a gala opening in Paris. It is perhaps this tour, along with Ned Buntline's Wild West novels, that have formed the basis for European idealization of the romance of the Old West.

Returning to the United States in 1893, Buffalo Bill's Wild West Show logged the most successful season in the history of outdoor stadium shows. After that high water mark, however, the show began to decline. Other competitors had entered the field as early as 1887 and Wild West shows began to proliferate by the 1890s. In 1902, Cody's partner, Ante Salisbury, died and the management of the show was temporarily turned over to James Bailey of the Barnum and Bailey Circus, who booked it for a European tour that lasted from 1902 to 1906. After Bailey's death, the show was merged with rival Pawnee Bill's Far East and went on the road from 1909 to 1913, before failing due to financial difficulties. Buffalo Bill kept the show going with several other partners until his death in 1917, and the show ended a year later.

Buffalo Bill's Wild West Show remains important today because it was perhaps the single most significant historical factor in the creation of the romantic notion of the West that has formed the basis for the countless books, dramatizations, and motion pictures that have become part of the American fabric. Though the authenticity of Cody's depictions was somewhat debatable, they were nonetheless based on his personal experiences on the frontier and were staged in dramatic enough fashion to create an impact upon his audiences. The show was additionally responsible for bringing Native Americans, frontier animals, and Western cultural traditions to a world that had never seen them close-up. Whether his show was truly responsible for creating an awareness of the endangered frontier among its spectators cannot be measured with accuracy, but it undoubtedly had some impact. And certainly the romantic West that we still glorify today remains the West of Buffalo Bill.

—Steve Hanson

FURTHER READING:

Brownlow, Kevin. *The War, The West, and the Wilderness.* New York, Alfred A. Knopf, 1979.

Cody, William F. *An Autobiography of Buffalo Bill (Colonel W.F. Cody).* New York, Cosmopolitan Book Corporation, 1923.

———. *The Business of Being Buffalo Bill: Selected Letters of William F. Cody, 1879-1917.* New York, Praeger, 1988.

Lamar, Howard R., editor. *The Readers Encyclopedia of the American West.* New York, Harper & Row, 1977.

Leonard, Elizabeth Jane. *Buffalo Bill, King of the Old West.* New York, Library Publishers, 1955.

Cody, William F.

See Cody, Buffalo Bill, and his
Wild West Show

Coffee

A strong, stimulating beverage with a distinctive aroma and complex flavor, coffee has been a popular drink for centuries. Brewed by the infusion of hot water and ground, roast coffee beans, coffee is enjoyed at any time of the day and night, though it is most associated with a morning pick-me-up. Coffee's primary active ingredient, the stimulant caffeine, is mildly addictive but to date no serious medical complications have been associated with its use. Local establishments such as cafés, coffee houses, coffee bars, and diners attract millions of customers worldwide. Specialty coffee shops serve dozens of varieties, each identified by the geographic growing region and degree of roast. Methods of preparation also vary widely, but in general coffee is served hot, with or without the addition of milk or cream, and sugar or other sweetener. Though coffee has always been popular, it wasn't until the 1980s that a number of specialty coffee retailers enhanced the cachet of coffee by raising its price, differentiating varieties, and associating the drink with a connoisseur's lifestyle.

Coffee houses have been regarded as cultural meeting places since the 17th century in western civilization, when artists, writers, and political activists first started to meet and discuss topics of social interest over a cup of this stimulating drink. The poet Baudelaire, in

A coffee shop sign in Seattle, Washington.

Paris in the 1840s, described coffee as best served "black as night, hot as hell, and sweet as love." Coffee seems always to have been part of the American landscape, as it was a common feature on the chuckwagons of the prairie pioneers and cattle ranchers, and in the break-rooms of companies and board rooms. Coffee is so popular in diners and roadside eateries that it is served almost as often as water. But for most of its history, coffee was just coffee, a commodity that was not associated with brand name or image. All that changed beginning in the 1980s, as the result of a convergence of two trends. Americans looking for a socially-acceptable alternative to drug and alcohol intake were well-served by a proliferation of retailers eager to provide high-priced "gourmet" coffee to discriminating drinkers. Specialty shops such as Starbucks in Seattle and Peet's Coffee in Berkeley have expanded to national chains whose popularity has eclipsed that of national brands such as Maxwell House and Folgers, which spread across America in the fifties. In addition, hundreds of independent cafés and coffee houses were founded in every major American city throughout the 1990s. In the Pacific Northwest—the capital of coffee consumption in America—drive-up espresso shacks line the roadsides, providing a variety of coffee drinks to commuters willing to pay $3.50 for a 20-ounce Café Mocha with a double shot of espresso. Even a small town like Snohomish, Washington, with a population of only 8,000, boasts a dozen espresso shacks.

Percolated coffee, made by a process where coffee is boiled and spilled over coffee grounds repeatedly, was very popular in the 1950s but made coffee which tasted sour, bitter, and washed-out. It has virtually been replaced by filtered or automatic drip coffee and the more exotic "cafe espresso," an Italian invention whereby hot water is forced through densely packed coffee grounds resulting in very dark, highly-concentrated coffee. Espresso is a popular favorite in specialty coffee shops and in European cafes. These coffee houses offer a more healthful daytime solution to social interaction than the local bar, which centered around the drinking of alcoholic beverages. The stimulating effects of coffee quite naturally encourage conversation and social discourse. Many coffee houses show artwork and host local musicians; some feature newsstands or shelves of books encouraging patrons to browse at their leisure. Coffee shops are also found around most college and university campuses.

The earliest recorded instances of coffee drinking and cultivation date back at least to the sixth century in Yemen, and coffee houses were popular establishments throughout Arabia for centuries before Europeans caught on, since it was forbidden to transport the fertile seed of the coffee plant. There is botanical evidence that the coffee plant actually originated in Africa, most likely in Kenya. Centuries later, coffee plants were imported by French colonists to the Caribbean and eventually to Latin America, and by the Dutch to Java in Indonesia. Today coffee production is centered in tropical regions throughout the world, with each region boasting distinctive kinds of coffee.

There are two distinct varieties of the coffee plant: caffea arabica, which comprises the majority of global production and grows best at high elevations in equatorial regions; and caffea robusta, discovered comparatively recently in Africa, which grows at somewhat lower elevations. The robusta bean is grown and harvested more cheaply than arabica. It is used as a base for many commercial blends even though the taste is reported to be poorer by connoisseurs. The coffee bean, which is the seed of the coffee plant, varies widely in flavor dependent on the region, soil and climactic conditions in which it is grown. These flavors are locked inside, for the most part, and must be developed by a roasting process during which the woody

structure of the bean is broken down and the aromatic oils are released. The degree of roasting produces a large degree of variation in how the final coffee beverage looks and tastes.

The principal active ingredient in coffee is caffeine, an alkaloid compound which produces mildly addictive stimulation to the central nervous system, and stimulation to a lesser degree of the digestive system. The medical effects of drinking coffee vary depending on the amount of caffeine in each serving, the tolerance which has been built up from repeated use, and the form in which it is being ingested. Coffee is often served in restaurants as a digestive stimulant, either enhancing the appetite when served before a meal, such as at breakfast, or as an aid to digestion when served, for example, as a "demi-tasse" (French for "half-a-cup") in restaurants after a fine meal. Although American medical literature reports that up to three cups of coffee may be drunk daily without any serious medical effects, individual limits of consumption vary widely. Many people drink five or six cups or more per day, while coffee consumption has been restricted in cases where gastrointestinal complications and other diagnoses may be aggravated by overstimulation. Though not medically significant, many coffee users experience rapid heartbeat, jumpiness, and irritation of the stomach due to excessive coffee consumption. All of these side effects may seem worth it to a coffee drinker who relies on the certain stimulating effects of multiple cups of coffee. Withdrawal symptoms such as headaches occur when coffee is taken out of the diet due to caffeine deprivation, but these effects usually subside after a few days.

With all the concern about caffeine in coffee, it was a matter of time before scientists found ways to remove caffeine while maintaining coffee's other more pleasurable characteristics such as taste and aroma. The first successful attempt to remove the kick out of coffee came at the end of the nineteenth century. Distillation and dehydration/reconstitution resulted in a coffee beverage with less than two percent caffeine content. The caffeine-free powder was marketed successfully as Sanka (from the French "sans caffeine" meaning "without caffeine"). Since then, other processes of refinement have succeeded in removing caffeine from coffee while preserving greater and greater integrity of the coffee flavor complex. Most of these decaffeination processes involve rinsing and treating coffee while still in the bean stage. One process, which uses the chemical solvent methylene chloride, has been judged by coffee experts to produce the best tasting decaffeinated coffee since the chemical specifically adheres to and dissolves the caffeine molecule while reacting with little else. Popular outcry arose concerning the use of methylene chloride in the late 1980s when a report was released indicating that it could cause cancer in laboratory animals, but the claim was soundly refuted when it was explained that virtually no trace of the element ever remained in coffee after having been roasted and brewed. Use of methlyne chloride was curtailed in the mid-1990s nonetheless, due to a discovery that its production could have an adverse impact on the earth's ozone layer. Several other methods of decaffeination are currently used, such as the Swiss water method and the supercritical carbon dioxide process, to meet the growing consumer demand. The vast majority of coffee drinkers, however, still prefer their coffee to deliver a caffeine kick.

—Ethan Hay

FURTHER READING:

Braun, Stephen. *Buzz: The Science and Lore of Alcohol and Caffeine.* New York, Oxford University Press, 1996.

Castle, Timothy James. *The Perfect Cup: A Coffee Lover's Guide to Buying, Brewing, and Tasting.* Reading, Massachusetts, Anis Books, 1991.

Cherniske, Stephen. *Caffeine Blues: Wake Up to the Hidden Dangers of America's #1 Drug.* New York, Warner Books, 1998.

"Coffee Madness." *Utne Reader.* #66, November/December, 1994.

Davids, Kenneth. *Coffee: A Guide to Buying, Brewing, and Enjoying.* Santa Rosa, California, Cole Group, 1991.

Kummer, Corby. *The Joy of Coffee: The Essential Guide to Buying, Brewing, and Enjoying.* Boston, Houghton Mifflin, 1997.

Nile, Bo, and Veronica McNiff. *The Big Cup: A Guide to New York's Coffee Culture.* New York, City & Co., 1997.

Sewell, Ernestine P. *How the Cimarron River Got Its Name and Other Stories about Coffee.* Plano, Texas, Republic of Texas Press, 1995.

Shapiro, Joel. *The Book of Coffee and Tea: A Guide to the Appreciation of Fine Coffees, Teas, and Herbal Beverages.* New York, St. Martin's Press, 1975.

Cohan, George M. (1878-1942)

The musical comedy stage of New York was home to George M. Cohan, vaudeville song-and-dance man, playwright, manager, director, producer, comic actor, and popular songwriter. During the first two decades of the twentieth century, Cohan's style of light comedic drama dominated American theatre, and the lyrics he composed are still remembered at the end of the twentieth century for their flag-waving patriotism and exuberance. His hit song "Over There" embodied the wartime spirit of World War I, and "I'm a Yankee Doodle Dandy" and "Grand Old Flag," have been passed from generation to generation as popular tunes celebrating the American spirit.

Born on July 3 in Providence, Rhode Island, Cohan spent his childhood as part of a vaudevillian family. Living the typical vaudeville life, Cohan and his sister traveled a circuit of stages, slept in boarding houses and backstage while their parents performed, and only occasionally attended school. At nine years old, Cohan became a member of his parents' act, reciting sentimental verse and performing a "buck and wing dance." By the age of eleven, he was writing comedy material, and by thirteen he was writing songs and lyrics for the act, which was now billed as The Four Cohans. In 1894, at the age of sixteen, Cohan sold his first song, "Why Did Nellie Leave Home?" to a sheet music publisher for twenty-five dollars.

In his late teens, Cohan began directing The Four Cohans, which became a major attraction, earning up to a thousand dollars for a week's booking. Cohan wrote the songs and sketches that his family performed, and had the starring roles. At twenty years of age, managing the family's business affairs, he was becoming a brazen, young man, proud of his achievements. When he was twenty-one, he married his first wife, Ethel Levey, a popular singing comedienne, who then became the fifth Cohan in the act.

Within two years, seeking the fame, high salaries, and excitement that life in New York theatre offered, Cohan centered his career on the Broadway stage. His first Broadway production, *The Governor's Son,* was a musical comedy that he wrote and in which he performed in 1901. It was not the hit he hoped for, but after two more

attempts, Cohan enjoyed his first Broadway success with *Little Johnny Jones* in 1904. In this musical, Cohan played the role of a jockey and sang the lyrics that would live through the century: "I'm a Yankee Doodle Dandy, / A Yankee Doodle, do or die; / A real live nephew of my Uncle Sam's / Born on the Fourth of July." Among the other hit songs from the play was "Give My Regards to Broadway." In Cohan's 1906 hit *George Washington, Jr.,* he acted in a scene with which he would be identified for life: he marched up and down the stage carrying the American flag and singing "You're a Grand Old Flag," the song that would become one of the most popular American marching-band pieces of all time. Other of Cohan's most famous plays are *Forty-Five Minutes from Broadway* (1906), *The Talk of New York* (1907), *The Little Millionaire* (1911), *The Song and Dance Man* (1923), and *Little Nelly Kelly* (1923).

In 1917, when America entered World War I, Cohan was inspired to compose "Over There," the song that would become his greatest hit. Americans coast to coast listened to the recording made by popular singer Nora Bayes. Twenty-five years later, President Franklin Delano Roosevelt awarded Cohan the Congressional Medal of Honor for the patriotic spirit expressed in this war song.

Cohan achieved immortality through his songs and performances, and the 1942 film *Yankee Doodle Dandy* perpetuated his image. In it, James Cagney portrayed Cohan with all of Cohan's own enthusiasm and brilliance. The film told the story of Cohan's life and included the hit songs that made him an American legend. The film was playing in American theatres when Cohan died in 1942. President Roosevelt wired his family that "a beloved figure is lost to our national life."

—Sharon Brown

FURTHER READING:

Buckner, Robert, and Patrick McGilligan. *Yankee Doodle Dandy.* Madison, University of Wisconsin Press, 1981.

Cohan, George Michael. *Twenty Years on Broadway, and the Years It Took to Get There: The True Story of a Trouper's Life from the Cradle to the "Closed Shop."* Westport, Connecticut, Greenwood Press, 1971.

McCabe, John. *George M. Cohan: The Man Who Owned Broadway.* Garden City, New York, Doubleday, 1973.

Morehouse, Ward. *George M. Cohan, Prince of the American Theater.* Westport, Connecticut, Greenwood Press, 1972.

Colbert, Claudette (1903-1996)

The vivacious, Parisian-born Claudette Colbert was one of America's highest-paid and most popular actresses during her sixty-year career on stage, films, and television. Her popular "screwball comedies" enchanted movie audiences, and her classic performance as the fleeing heiress in *It Happened One Night* (1934) earned her an Academy Award. Although she continued to star in comedies, she was also an Oscar-nominee for the dramatic film *Since You Went Away* (1944). Her most talked-about scene was the milk bath in *The Sign of the Cross.* In the 1950s she returned to Broadway, and, still active in her eighties, starred in a television miniseries in 1987. She was honored with an award for lifetime achievement at Kennedy Center in 1989.

—Benjamin Griffith

FURTHER READING:

Everson, William K. *Claudette Colbert.* New York, Pyramid Publications, 1976.

Parish, James Robert. *The Paramount Pretties.* New Rochelle, New York, Arlington House, 1972.

Quinlan, David. *The Illustrated Directory of Film Stars.* New York, Hippocrene, 1982.

Quirk, Lawrence J. *Claudette Colbert: An Illustrated Biography.* New York, Crown, 1985.

Shipman, David. *The Great Movie Stars: The Golden Years.* New York, Crown, 1970.

Cold War

Struggle between the Western democracies and the Eastern Communist nations was probably inevitable from the first shot fired in the Russian Revolution of 1917. Guided by one of the essential tenets of Karl Marx and Friedrich Engels' Communist doctrine—"Capitalism contains within itself the seeds of its own destruction"—Eastern nations believed in the eventual worldwide triumph of Communism and were motivated to help speed the day. The nations of the West, on the other hand, long regarded Communism (and those governments espousing it) as a threat striking at the very heart of the capitalist economies that formed the basis of many Western democracies. The differences between these two ideological standpoints produced a state of disharmony that broke into open, if limited, warfare twice (in Korea and Vietnam), but remained for the most part a muted conflict—a "cold" war.

Historians disagree about the exact point at which the Cold War began. Some date it from Winston Churchill's 1946 speech, given in Fulton, Missouri, in which he declared that an "iron curtain" had come down in Europe, dividing the Soviet-occupied countries from those allied with the West. Others argue that the "long twilight struggle," as President Kennedy described it, began in 1947 with the Truman Doctrine—a declaration that the United States would act decisively to prevent the further spread of Communism in Europe. There are even those scholars who believe that the Cold War began when the ink dried on the documents containing the Japanese surrender to the Allies in 1945.

If there is a lack of consensus regarding the cold war's beginning, virtual unanimity exists about its end. In 1991, the Soviet Communist Party was dissolved, and the Union of Soviet Socialist Republics reverted to what it had once been—a collection of separate slavic nations, the largest being Russia. Although China, the world's most populous country, remained a Communist state, as did North Korea, Cuba, and Vietnam, it is generally believed that when Soviet Communism died, so did the Cold War.

During the approximately 45 year struggle, the opposing nations battled on many levels: economic, political, scientific, diplomatic—and through popular culture. Indeed, there is not an aspect of American popular culture that was unaffected by the Cold War. The principal media involved included film, both commercial and governmental, television, fiction, and to a lesser extent, theater.

While the government eventually found more subtle ways to communicate anti-Communist messages to the American public, in the early years of the Cold War the U.S. government contributed directly to popular culture by producing a number of "documentaries." These documentaries, produced mostly during the 1950s, alerted citizens to the dangers of Communism. Some, like *The Bell* (1950), took a positive, pro-American outlook, using the Liberty Bell as a symbol behind which people from all walks of American life could rally. Most of these films—such as *Communist Blueprint for Conquest* (1955), *The Communist Weapon of Allure* (1956), and *Communist Target: Youth* (1962), which included an introduction by then-Attorney General Robert Kennedy—were strongly negative in tone and made Communism the object of their censure. The most memorable of these propaganda films, however, was not made in the traditional documentary mode, but rather like an episode of *The Twilight Zone,* a television program that would not appear for another four years. In *Red Nightmare* (1955), narrator Jack Webb (of *Dragnet* fame) presents a typical small-town American family, then shows what their lives would be like if the Communists took over America. Religion is forbidden, education becomes indoctrination, and love of family is made subordinate to party loyalty. When the head of the household (played by Jack Kelly) protests, he is sentenced to be shot. Just as the firing squad is taking aim, he wakes up, back in his beloved America, free from his horrible "red nightmare." As the movie ends, the narrator reminds us that it could happen in America, if citizens ever relaxed their vigilance. Distributed free of charge to civic groups, Scout troops, churches, and schools, the films were even broadcast by local television stations.

The government also distributed films on a related subject: civil defense. Although the United States had never experienced aerial attack, serious discussions of the possibility started early in the Cold War, especially in 1949 when the Soviet Union exploded its first atomic bomb. In response to the perceived military threat, America's leaders greatly increased military budgets, and designed a civil defense program to reassure average citizens that nuclear war could be survived. While most government experts privately shared the view that no man-made structure could withstand a nuclear blast, and that an all-out nuclear exchange with the Soviet Union would produce American casualties numbering in the tens of millions, they also agreed that if the public knew the actual dangers, a panic, or worse, an outbreak of "Better Red than dead" defeatism would threaten the country. Thus, to preserve public morale, the underlying theme of the civil defense program became the illusion of safety. The program conveyed its messages of optimism through pamphlets, posters, and films with titles like *Survival under Atomic Attack, Operation Cue, The Atom Strikes,* and *You Can Beat the A-Bomb.* At least one civil defense film was intended primarily for schools. Entitled *Duck and Cover,* it featured an animated character named Bert the Turtle. Bert taught children that, in case of atomic attack, all they had to do to protect themselves was crouch down and cover their heads. The patent absurdity of this "defense" against a nuclear blast would be illustrated decades later, in the 1982 satirical documentary *The Atomic Cafe,* and in a 1997 episode of the "adult" television cartoon show *South Park.*

Hollywood films also reflected, and helped to create, the culture of the Cold War. Studios eagerly produced anti-Communist films in the 1950s—partly as a reflection of the temper of the times, but also

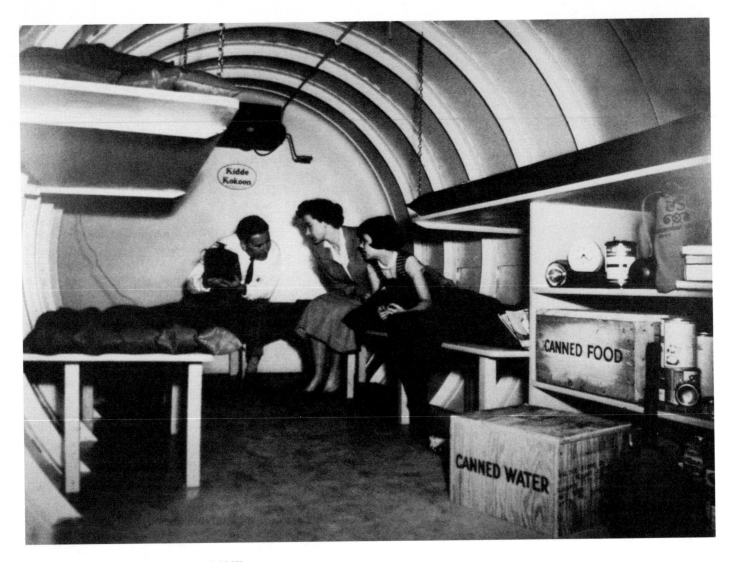

A typical bomb shelter built during the Cold War.

because filmmakers themselves had come under investigation by Washington's Red-raiders. During World War II, several Hollywood studios had made pro-Soviet films, such as *Mission to Moscow* (1943) and *Song of Russia* (1944), and these films had been made with both the permission and encouragement of the U.S. government, which wanted to maintain good relations with its Soviet ally. By the 1950s however, the House Un-American Activities Committee (known as the HUAC) came to regard the studios with suspicion. Mindful of the influence that motion pictures can have upon the citizenry, and fearful that the persuasive powers of film might be used to advance the cause of Communism, the HUAC and Senator Joseph McCarthy put the film industry in the thick of the anti-Communist investigations. The atmosphere produced in the industry by these investigations may explain the production of such blatantly anti-Red films as *I Married a Communist* (1950), *I Was a Communist for the FBI* (1951), *My Son John* (1952), *Big Jim McLain* (1952), and *Invasion U.S.A.* (1952).

But by the 1960s, Hollywood's way of dealing with the "Red Menace" changed. Because the heat from Washington had largely abated, and because the propaganda films had not been profitable ventures, Hollywood's depictions of the Cold War began to diversify. Some of the 1960s films dealt with nuclear brinkmanship between the United States and the Soviet Union. *Fail-Safe* (1964), based on a popular novel, posits a technical glitch that accidentally sends a flight of American nuclear bombers on its way to a pre-assigned target: Moscow. The computer has sent its "war" message to the bombers, and they cannot be recalled. The basic premise of *Fail-Safe* was brilliantly but viciously satirized by Stanley Kubrick in his 1964 film *Dr. Strangelove: Or How I Learned To Stop Worrying and Love the Bomb*. It is a thoroughly "black" comedy, as any film that attempts to find humor in nuclear war must be. Another "cold war" film released the same year was *Seven Days in May*, which involves a plot by the U.S. military to take over the government after the President negotiates an unpopular arms-reduction treaty with the Soviets.

A separate course for cold war cinema was charted in 1962, with the release of the first James Bond movie, *Dr. No*. The success of the film, along with the even larger grosses earned by its successors *From Russia with Love* (1963) and *Goldfinger* (1964)—with many others to follow—created a "spy craze" in American popular culture that lasted into the next decade. The "Bond" influence was seen in other films, both serious (*The Spy Who Came in from the Cold*; *The Quiller Memorandum*; *The Ipcress File*) and satirical (*Our Man Flint*; *The Silencers*; *Murderer's Row*), as well as television programs (*I Spy*;

Secret Agent; *The Man from U.N.C.L.E.*) and even men's toiletries (''007'' brand cologne; ''Hai Karate'' aftershave).

As U.S.-Soviet relations improved, the Cold War gradually thawed during the 1970s. The temperature dropped again in 1980, however, with the election of conservative Ronald Reagan to the White House. In his first term, at least, Reagan was frequently given to tough talk about the Communists. In one speech, he referred to the Soviet Union as an ''evil empire.'' On another occasion, just prior to a radio address, Reagan obliged a request for a sound check by saying, ''This is the President speaking. I have just outlawed Russia. Bombing begins in five minutes.''

In accordance with the Reagan Administration's bellicose attitude toward the Communist world, a new wave of anti-Communist cinema came in the 1980s. *Red Dawn* (1984) portrayed a Soviet occupation of the United States and focused on the activities of a band of American teenagers waging guerrilla warfare against the invaders. *Rocky IV* (1985) pitted Sylvester Stallone's gutsy pugilist against the seemingly unbeatable Drago, the best fighting machine that the Soviet state could produce. *Rambo: First Blood Part II* (1985) sent another popular Stallone character to rescue American POWs still held in Vietnam (and also to kill Communists by the score). The 1984 film *Missing in Action* (along with two sequels) returned Chuck Norris to Vietnam on a series of missions similar to Rambo's. *Invasion U.S.A.* (1985) featured Norris against a small army of Soviet infiltrators sent to disrupt American society. *Rambo III* (1988) saw Stallone's character battling the evil Russians in Afghanistan. *Top Gun* (1986) starred Tom Cruise and extolled the skill and bravery of the Navy's fighter pilots (who even got to shoot down a few Russians in a skirmish near the film's end).

Throughout the Cold War, other forms of entertainment also showed an awareness of some of the issues involved in the East-West struggle. Theater was not one of the hotbeds of social activism during the Cold War, at least until the Vietnam War became a burning issue. But one notable exception to this observation is Arthur Miller's 1953 play *The Crucible*. Nominally concerned with the Salem witch trials of 1692, the play is based on events and characters from the actual trials, but few watching the performance at the time could have any doubt that the play was a commentary on the anti-Communist hysteria gripping the nation. Miller has since been very clear that he intended *The Crucible* as a condemnation of the McCarthy ''witch hunts'' in which so many reputations, careers, and even lives were destroyed, often without any evidence to support the accusations made.

Miller did face some hostility from the Right over this play, as he had for some of his earlier dramas. Political tensions in the United States affected many Left-wing writers in the 1950s. Once a writer had been branded ''subversive'' by the HUAC, Senator McCarthy, or some other ''authority,'' many bookstores would not put his or her books on the shelves. Blacklisting limited the works of writers like Dalton Trumbo, Ring Lardner, Jr., Howard Fast, and Dashiell Hammett to a few bookstores dedicated to the writings of the Left.

This did not mean that the Cold War could not be portrayed in novels. Many books were written about the era while it happened, and they were often very successful—as long as they had the ''right'' viewpoint. *The Ugly American* (1958) by William Lederer and Eugene Burdick critiqued American diplomacy in Asia, and is believed to have given John F. Kennedy the idea for what would become the Peace Corps. Richard Condon's novel *The Manchurian Candidate* (1958) posited that U.S. soldiers captured during the Korean War could be so thoroughly ''brainwashed'' by the Chinese as to become human robots upon their return home, awaiting only the

right signal to carry out the nefarious missions for which they had been programmed. This novel of political paranoia was later made into a successful film by director John Frankenheimer.

As with film, cold war fiction changed as America entered the 1960s. The early part of the decade featured a number of novels about nuclear brinkmanship. *Fail-Safe* (1962) and *Seven Days in May* (1962) were both written in this period and were soon made into films. Other novels dealing with the possibilities of nuclear war included Pat Frank's *Alas, Babylon* (1959) and William Miller's *A Canticle for Liebowitz* (1959). The novels *The 480* by Eugene Burdick (1964), *Advise and Consent* by Allen Drury (1959), *Night of Camp David* by Fletcher Knebel (1965), and *The Man* by Irving Wallace (1964) explored similar kinds of domestic cold war political tensions found at the heart of *Seven Days in May*.

Although these kinds of political novels continued to appear in the second half of the 1960s, they were far outnumbered by the same genre that had come to dominate the movie screens by that time: the spy story. Although Ian Fleming, the creator of James Bond, died in 1964, the literary trend he started continued long after his passing. Several of Fleming's countrymen wrote spy fiction that was popular in the United States, including John Le Carré, who wrote the bestseller, *The Spy Who Came in From the Cold* (1963). Another British writer, Elleston Trevor, used the pen name Adam Hall to write a series of suspenseful cold war novels featuring a secret agent known only as Quiller, including *The Ninth Directive* (1966) and *The Striker Portfolio* (1969). Many American authors also used the Cold War as a background for tales of suspense and adventure, including Donald Hamilton, who wrote a series of paperback novels featuring ''the American James Bond,'' a U.S. government assassin named Matt Helm. Some of the many titles in this well-written series include *The Ambushers* (1963) and *The Menacers* (1968). Former CIA man David Atlee Phillips wrote a number of novels under the pseudonym Philip Atlee, all of them featuring secret agent Joe Gall, who saved the nation from the Reds in such titles as *The Green Wound Contract* (1963) and *The Trembling Earth Contract* (1969). Even Mickey Spillane, best known for his ''tough guy'' private eye novels featuring Mike Hammer, began to write spy novels with *Day of the Guns* (1964), which introduced secret agent Tiger Mann.

Television also played its role in the Cold War, through both entertainment programming and news specials. In the 1950s, a number of suspense shows with anti-Communist themes debuted, including *Foreign Intrigue, Passport to Danger, I Led Three Lives, The Man Called X, Soldiers of Fortune,* and *Behind Closed Doors,* but few of these shows captured audience interest. In the 1960s, television also participated in the ''spy craze.'' In addition to ''serious'' espionage shows, 1960s television offered spoofs of the genre, including *Get Smart* (with Don Adams as an inept secret agent) and *The Wild, Wild West* (a Bondian satire set in the Old West).

While local television stations made good use of government-produced short films, both those with anti-Communist themes and those concerned with civil defense, national television stations produced their own documentaries about the dangers posed by world Communism. *Call to Freedom* focused on the history of Austria, to show how that country was able to free itself from partial Soviet occupation following World War II. *Nightmare in Red* was a history of the Soviet Union that suggested that Czarist rule was better than the oppression, tyranny, and drudgery of life in the modern Soviet state. Television also showed the cartoon series *The Adventures of Rocky and Bullwinkle,* with its ''villains'' the bumbling spies Boris Badinov and Natasha Fatale.

Television provided the American public with one of the clearest views into the HUAC's investigations. Many of Senator Joseph McCarthy's committee's hearings were televised live. At first, the coverage proved to be excellent publicity for McCarthy and his Red-baiting activities. But eventually McCarthy's bullying, demagoguery, and carelessness with facts caught up with him. When attorney Joseph Welch asked McCarthy, live on camera, ''Have you no decency, sir? Have you no decency at all?'' millions of Americans found themselves pondering the same question about the Senator from Wisconsin—and television made it possible.

—Justin Gustainis

FURTHER READING:

Barson, Michael. *''Better Dead Than Red'': A Nostalgic Look at the Golden Years of Russiaphobia, Red-baiting, and Other Commie Madness.* New York, Hyperion, 1992.

Henriksen, Margot A. *Dr. Strangelove's America: Society and Culture in the Atomic Age.* Berkeley, University of California Press, 1997.

MacDonald, J. Fred. *Television and the Red Menace: The Video Road to Vietnam.* New York, Praeger, 1985.

Whitfield, Stephen J. *The Culture of the Cold War.* Baltimore, Johns Hopkins University Press, 1991.

Nat ''King'' Cole

Cole, Nat ''King'' (1916?-1965)

Nat ''King'' Cole, pianist, songwriter, vocalist, and actor was one of the most influential African American performers from the early 1940s until his untimely death in 1965. Cole's warm, open, liquid, smooth voice was blessed with perfect intonation and diction, and appealed to a crossover audience, garnering not only acceptance in America but also worldwide. As a personality, Cole epitomized the suave sophistication that urban blacks were beginning to aspire to in the 1940s.

Cole's date of birth is in question. For his two marriages in 1937 and in 1948, Cole gave birthdates of 1915 and 1919, respectively. For the selective service he gave the year 1916. James Haskins and Leslie Gourse, two Cole biographers, accepted 1916 since it was his draft registration. Born Nathaniel Adams Coles in Montgomery, Alabama on March 17, Cole was exposed to many types of black music. At the age of four, the family moved to Chicago where jazz and gospel were evolving. Cole's father, Edward James Coles, Sr., was a Baptist minister. His mother, Perlina Adames Coles, a pianist and choir director, taught him to play the piano by ear. At 12, Cole played organ, sang in his father's church, and studied classical piano. In high school, his mentors were N. Clark Smith, bandmaster, and Walter Dyett. His family was indeed musical. His three brothers Eddie, Fred, and Isaac were jazz musicians.

In Chicago, Cole led the Rogues of Rhythm and the Twelve Royal Dukes that often played Earl Hines arrangements. In 1936, Cole left Chicago to lead a band in a revival of the 1921 all black musical comedy *Shuffle Along,* with music by Eubie Blake and lyrics by Noble Sissle. When the show folded in Los Angeles, Cole landed a job as a pianist at the Century Club in Santa Monica. Cole's playing was impressive and thereafter, he began a stint at the Swanee Inn in Hollywood. Bob Lewis, the booking agent is said to have mused ''Old King Cole'' and billed Cole as ''King'' Cole. The name stuck with him throughout his career.

While Cole was best known as a vocalist and occasional pianist, his most musically enduring work can be heard in the trio format. Cole's piano stylings and compositions draw from be-bop, among other influences. The trio won the coveted Downbeat small combo award from 1944-1947, and the Metronome Apollo award in 1945-1948. Initially called King Cole and His Swingsters and later known as the King Cole Trio, the group was the first African American jazz combo to have its own sponsored radio series, from 1948-1949.

In the trio format, Cole dipped into the wellsprings of black music. The element of play and rhythmic vocal nuances can be heard in ''Gone with the Draft.'' The influence of jive, folk narratives appear in the lyric ''cool papa, don't you blow your top,'' from ''Straighten Up and Fly Right.'' In ''Are You Fer It,'' and ''This Side Up,'' Cole delves into the early California blues tradition with riffs (repetitive phrases) in harmony with Moore's guitar. The new emerging style of be-bop is shown to good advantage in ''Babs,'' while scatting (the interpolation of non-sense syllables) can be heard in ''I Like to Riff.''

Fats Waller, Count Basie, and principally Earl Hines influenced Cole's piano playing and, in turn, Cole's trio format and piano and vocal stylings influenced a number of subsequent musicians. Notable jazz trios that adopted Cole's instrumental format were the Oscar Peterson Trio, Art Tatum's Trio, and Johnny Moore's Three Blazers, among others. Cole also recorded with Lester Young in a session in Los Angeles in 1942.

The Nat King Cole Trio captured the attention of the popular market and paved the way for Cole to crossover from the rhythm and blues market to the pop charts, and to launch his successful solo career. From 1943 on, many of Cole's songs appealed to popular taste, beginning with "All For You" (1943), "Straighten Up and Fly Right" (1944), "Gee Baby, Ain't I Good to You?" (1944), and "Get Your Kicks on Route 66" (1946). It was "The Christmas Song" (1946), however, that squarely validated his crossover appeal. These standards, with string accompaniment led by arrangers such as Nelson Riddle, would help to build Capital records, Cole's principal recording label. From 1946, Cole became hugely successful as a popular vocalist and by 1951 had abandoned the trio format. Selected songs in this format include "I Love You for Sentimental Reasons" (1946), "Nature Boy" (1948), another recording of "The Christmas Song" (1949), "Mona Lisa" (1950), "Too Young" (1951), "Pretend" (1953), the rhythm and blues flavored "Send for Me" (1957), "Looking Back" (1958), and the country and western tinged "Ramblin' Rose" (1962). Throughout the 1950s, Cole continued to perform in clubs while putting on concerts abroad in Cuba, Australia, and Latin America. Cole also took singing and acting roles in a number of movies such as *Small Town Girl, The Blue Gardenia,* and *Haija Baba,* with his most effective role in *St Louis Blues,* where he played W. C. Handy.

Despite Cole's enormous appeal he could not escape the racism rampant in America. When he purchased a house in Los Angeles's fashionable Hancock Park, some white neighbors protested. He had to abandon his series on network television because of the lack of a national sponsor. Cole compromised by playing to segregated audiences, which drew impassioned criticism from the National Association for the Advancement of Colored People (NAACP). Thurgood Marshall, chief counsel for the NAACP, commented that all Cole needed to complete his role as Uncle Tom was a banjo. In the 1960s, with the emergence of the civil rights movement, neither Cole's image as a popular vocalist nor his actions adopted the cause of black pride and consciousness. In spite of these setbacks, Cole's music penetrated many boundaries. In his time, Cole was a seminal figure in jazz and popular music, and leaves a legacy of enduring music—both as a vocalist and pianist—that continues to enrich us. Cole, a heavy chain smoker, succumbed to lung cancer and died on February 15, 1965.

—Willie Collins

FURTHER READING:

Cole, Maria, with Louie Robinson. *Nat King Cole, An Intimate Biography.* London, W. H. Allen, 1972.

Gourse, Leslie. *Unforgettable: The Life and Mystique of Nat King Cole.* New York, St. Martin's Press, 1991.

Haskins, James, with Kathleen Benson. *Nat King Cole: A Personal and Professional Biography.* Chelsea, Scarborough House, 1980.

Whitburn, Joel. *Top R & B Singles 1942-1988.* Menomonee Falls, Record Research Inc., 1988.

College Fads

Over the course of the twentieth century, each generation of college students seems to have been identified in the public mind with mindless, often madcap fads, perhaps adopted as a silly counterpoint to the demands of intellectual life. Some of these phenomena have become iconic markers of their decades: the raccoon-coat craze of the 1920s, goldfish swallowing in the 1930s, panty raids and telephone-booth stuffing in the 1950s, piano smashing in the 1960s, and streaking in the 1970s.

The goldfish-swallowing era of campus lunacy peaked in the spring of 1939. Although there were political events unfolding in Europe that would lead to World War II, newspapers devoted much space to this college fad. It all began when Harvard freshman Lothrop Withington, Jr. told friends that he had observed goldfish being swallowed on a Honolulu beach, and that he had done it himself. Someone challenged Lothrop, and a $10 bet was made, leading to a demonstration in the freshman dining hall on March 3, 1939. While cameras recorded a bit of history, Lothrop picked up a three-inch goldfish by the tail, dropped the little wiggler into his mouth, chewed, and swallowed. Whipping out a toothbrush, he ceremoniously cleaned his teeth. Before sitting down to a dinner of fried sole, he remarked that the "scales caught a bit in my throat."

During the economic depression of the 1930s, there was no large annual college-student migration to Florida, and the less expensive fad of fish-swallowing sufficed for springtime excitement, becoming at once a kind of intercollegiate sport. Frank Hope of Franklin and Marshall College topped Withington by salting and peppering three goldfish and putting them away without chewing. The following day, a classmate named George Raab swallowed six fish. Harvard's Irving Clark vaulted far ahead by force-feeding himself two dozen of the little creatures, also announcing his willingness to eat beetles, spiders, and worms. Subsequent records were soon posted and quickly bested on campuses nationwide: University of Michigan (28), Boston College (29), Albright College (33), and MIT (42). When a student at Kutztown State in Pennsylvania broke the record by swallowing 43, he was suspended for "conduct unbecoming to a student."

After a professor of anatomy at UCLA concluded that an average-size male could safely down 150 live goldfish, the all-time record is reported to have zoomed to 210 fish at one sitting, swallowed by an anonymous BMOC (big man on campus) at St. Mary's University. Within a month, students were looking for variations on the theme, but the munching of 78-rpm phonograph records at the University of Chicago or the masticating of magazines at Lafayette College never captured the public imagination as did the swallowing of little live fish. In the late 1960s goldfish swallowers reappeared briefly on college campuses, but during that hectic era of student protests, such meaningless pranks were generally ignored by the press.

In the spring of 1952, an outbreak of panty raids began at the University of Michigan. When 600 students gathered outside a dorm to listen to music on the first evening of spring, someone shouted, "To the women's dorms!" Suddenly the mob of male students forced their way into a dormitory and began dashing into rooms to steal lingerie. Copycat raids quickly followed at colleges and universities from coast to coast. To a writer in *U.S. News & World Report* the fad seemed inappropriate for a nation at war in Korea, and he asked why the panty-raiders were not "in the army if they have so much energy and so little to do?" Some university officials tried to resist, but at the University of Miami panty-obsessed males tore down a heavy wire fence to get to the girls' dorms. A wily director of women's residences at the University of Indiana took the opposite approach and left a barrel of women's underwear in plain view, ready to be confiscated by the fistful. That same spring at Ann Arbor, where the madness had begun, 500 coeds broke into the men's dorm in search of Jockey

An example of the college fad of car stuffing.

shorts and other male underwear. Panty raids have not been revived later, as many fads have been, and one writer suggested a reason: ''Probably because the age of sexual permissiveness has rendered such symbolic action as this meaningless.''

Telephone-booth stuffing began on American campuses in the spring of 1959, spreading out from California. At UCLA seventeen men squeezed like sardines into a conventional seven-foot high booth, followed quickly by an eighteen-man stuffing at California's St. Mary's University. With all their planning and knowledge of physics, students at MIT could only break that record by one. When students at Modesto Junior College in California reported thirty-four men in one booth, the record was investigated and then thrown out because the booth had been laid on its side, permitting considerably more horizontal stuffers to be accommodated. The most aesthetic booth-stuffing occurred in Fresno, where coeds in one-piece bathing suits gracefully wedged themselves into a booth submerged in a swimming pool. The fad began and ended in the spring of 1959, and was copied several years later by a brief fad involving students stuffing themselves into Volkswagens.

In 1963 a jangling, cacophonous din rose on college campuses as students used sledgehammers and axes to shatter full-size pianos. Students at California Tech did the job in 10 minutes, 44 seconds, but a Wayne State crew set the ultimate record: 4 minutes, 51 seconds. A *Life* Magazine writer called the piano hacking ''Andante on a Choppin' Theme,'' noting that the grand finale was ''Chopsticks.'' Since it was a time of student protest, one of the Caltech choppers called the act a comment on the ''obsolescence of society.'' One group of dismemberers called its members by the academic-sounding name, The Piano Reduction Society.

From late January to mid-March, 1974, when the nation was suffering through a grim economic recession as well as the pains of the Nixon impeachment inquiry, there suddenly appeared the most merrily scandalous of all the college fads: streaking. Beginning in the warmer climates of California and Florida, nude students began to leap from behind bushes and dash across campus, parachute to earth in their birthday suits, and bike through the town *en masse* and unclad. Soon the fad spread throughout the country, even to the University of Alaska, where streakers dashed out in sub-zero weather. The new craze was difficult for student governments and town fathers to combat. The mayor of Dover Township, New Jersey, threatened to fine streakers one dollar for every pound of flesh they exposed. In Honolulu a male student streaked through an official governmental assembly, declaring himself loudly, "the Streaker of the House." Spring graduations at many colleges and universities were marked by the shedding of caps and gowns for a short streak. *Newsweek* magazine called the fad "the sort of totally absurd phenomenon the nation needed after a winter of lousy news."

For the most part it was a male phenomena, but Laura Barton, a freshman at Carleton College, was widely recognized as the first female streaker when she appeared *au naturel* for a curtain call following the college production of *Measure for Measure*. The record for the largest crowd of streakers is claimed by the University of Georgia, which mustered 1,543 nude students for a race through campus. They had been preceded in fame by students at the universities of South Carolina, Maryland, and Colorado.

The commercial value of the fad soon became recognized, and a Connecticut jewelry company sold medallions plated with silver and gold, inscribed for the "free spirit shedding his inhibitions." Psychological theorists explained the phenomenon as "the peaking of the sexual revolution, which made public nudity, long a taboo, an annoyance for some and an amusement for others."

—Benjamin Griffith

FURTHER READING:

Marum, Andrew, and Frank Parise. *Follies and Foibles: A View of 20th Century Fads.* New York, Facts on File, 1984.

Panati, Charles. *Panati's Parade of Fads, Follies, and Manias.* New York, HarperCollins, 1991.

Skolnik, Peter L., with Laura Torbet and Nikki Smith. *FADS: America's Crazes, Fevers, and Fancies: From the 1890's to the 1970's.* New York, Crowell, 1972.

College Football

Until the advent of television, college football was far more popular than its professional counterpart. From the late nineteenth century onward, many of the games greatest moments occurred on the collegiate gridiron. Well before the epochal feats of Jim Brown, Gale Sayers, Joe Willie Namath, and Joe Montana were being relayed by television transmission, sport-writers and radio broadcasters had immortalized Jim Thorpe, Knute Rockne, Red Grange.

Employed as initiation rites beginning in the early nineteenth century, the first college games proved disorderly and were outlawed by university officialdom. After the Civil War, two versions of football appeared at northeastern schools, one resembling soccer, with the picking up of the ball prohibited. On November 6, 1869, approximately 200 spectators watched Princeton and Rutgers battle in New Brunswick, New Jersey. With 25 players on each side, kicking prevailed as Rutgers triumphed 6-4. Another brand of football, similar to rugby, which allowed for the touching of the ball, cropped up at Harvard. In 1876, the Intercollegiate Football Association was formed, with representatives from Princeton, Columbia, Yale, and

Harvard. A touchdown counted for only one point, while a kicked goal was worth four.

Not surprisingly, Ivy League schools dominated college football's early days. Yale's Walter Camp, deemed "the Father of Football," devised many of the initial rules, thereby ensuring its unique American quality. By 1880, thanks to Camp's input, "American football began," according to football historian Tom Perrin. As befitting broader changes in American life, it also acquired a more professional cast. The game now featured 11-man lineups, scrimmage lines separating offensive and defensive teams, and the quarterback at the center of the offensive action. Soon, Camp had a hand in reducing the playing field in half, allowing the offense to obtain a first down after amassing five yards in three attempts, devising yard lines, and initiating a modern scoring schema. The offensive line and backs lined up apart from one another, and rules prohibited passes beyond the line of scrimmage. Soon, offensive players were allowed to block for ball carriers. In 1888, Camp called for tackling below the waist. In this same period, graduate coaches—who were generally former players—were often hired; at Yale, Camp served as the adviser to Yale captains and graduate coaches.

Yale was the greatest team of the era, compiling a 324-17-18 record from 1872-1909 and winning 11 national championships, three coached by Camp. At the outset, college football's big games pitted Yale against Princeton or Harvard. In 1889, Camp began announcing his All-American teams, which were dominated by college football's Big Three for the next decade; Yale's greatest star was 5'9'', 150 pound Frank Hinkey, a four-time All American end who was proclaimed the top player of his generation. Camp also wrote a series of sports books, advised other coaches, and watched Yale alumni teach his methods across the land.

Football served as a unifying force for the increasingly larger and more diverse pool of college students who almost religiously identified with their teams. Pleased university administrators viewed football as a means to acquire a still larger student body. The Big Game, greater pageantry, mascots, nicknames, songs, and contests attracting 40,000 fans to the Polo Grounds or Manhattan Field, all demonstrated football's increased popularity. So too write-ups in newspapers, which increasingly devoted a full-page or more to sports coverage. Piquing public controversy, however, were injuries and fatalities that led President Theodore Roosevelt to invite representatives from Harvard, Yale, and Princeton "to come to a gentlemen's agreement not to have mucker play." Led by Camp, promises were made to avoid excessive "roughness, holding, and foul play." In late 1905, delegates from 62 universities established the Intercollegiate Athletic Association, which in 1910 became the National Collegiate Athletic Association. Rule changes allowing for the forward pass and requiring ten yards to be gained within a four down set eventually resulted in a more wide-open game. In 1912, the value of touchdowns was increased to six points.

Equally important for the sports's increased popularity were mythical tales spun about legendary teams, coaches, and players. The 1901 Michigan Wolverines, spearheaded by newly arrived head coach Fielding H. "Hurry Up" Yost, began a five-year run marred only by one tie in fifty-seven games. Scoring 2821 points, Michigan allowed a mere 40 and shut-out Stanford 49-0 in the first Rose Bowl. In 1905, Michigan's winning streak was ended by Amos Alonzo Stagg's University of Chicago squad, which featured its 5'7'', 145 pound quarterback, Walter Eckersall. Following his arrival at Harvard in 1908, Percy Haughton turned the Fighting Crimson into college football's premier team, winning three national championships in a four-year span, beginning in 1910. Glenn ''Pop'' Warner's 1912 Carlisle Indians employed the single-wing formation to display the versatility of tailback Jim Thorpe, whose 25 touchdowns and 198 points established a new collegiate scoring record. In 1913, Notre Dame stunned heavily favored Army, 35-13, relying on the passing combination of quarterback Gus Dorias and end Knute Rockne; the previous year's reduction of the ball's circumference helped the aerial game.

In 1918, Rockne became head coach at Notre Dame, which he guided to five perfect seasons and a 105-12-5 record over the next thirteen years. Competing against teams from throughout the land, Rockne helped to popularize college football nationwide. Notre Dame's victory march became the best known, while Rockne ushered in a wide-open brand of football. Attendance at college games soared, and universities built great concrete and steel stadiums that could seat 70,000 or more fans. Notre Dame under Rockne featured stars like All-American fullback George Gipp and the so-called Four Horsemen, the famed 1924 backfield. On his deathbed in 1920, Gipp reportedly told his coach, ''Sometime, Rock, when the team is up against it, when things are wrong and the breaks are beating the boys, ask them to win one for the Gipper.'' After watching the 1924 Notre Dame-Army contest, Grantland Rice waxed eloquently: ''Outlined against the blue-gray October sky, the Four Horsemen rode again. In dramatic lore they were known as famine, pestilence, destruction, and death. These are only aliases. Their real names are Stuhldreher, Miller, Crowley, and Layden.'' Playing in its lone bowl game until 1970, national champion Notre Dame defeated Pop Warner's Stanford team, headed by its great fullback Ernie Nevers, 27-10. The 1929 and 1930 seasons also concluded with Notre Dame as the best team in the nation, but a plane crash near Bazaar, Kansas, in March 1931 took Rockne's life. Rockne left an unsurpassed winning percentage of .881, the use of shock troops that set the stage for platooning, the positioning of an end apart from other offensive linemen, and a more exciting brand of football. Under Rockne, moreover, Notre Dame acquired a national following, particularly among Catholics and ethnics in a period that witnessed the resurgence of the Ku Klux Klan.

The greatest individual player during college football's so-called golden era was halfback Harold ''Red'' Grange of Bob Zuppke's Fighting Illini. From 1923-1925, the Galloping Ghost used his blinding speed to top the nation's rushing charts, lead Illinois to a national championship, and perform epochal feats on the gridiron. In the initial twelve minutes of the 1924 contest against Michigan, Grange scored four out of the first eight times he touched the ball, on a 95 yard kickoff return, and on runs from scrimmage of 67, 56, and 44 yards. He later added a 15 yard touchdown and tossed an 18 yard touchdown pass, leading Illinois to a 39-14 victory. Playing against Penn in Philadelphia in 1925, Grange, disregarding a sloppy field, scored three times, while gaining 363 yards on 36 carries.

By the mid-1930s, the balance of power in the league was shifting, and new football powerhouses were emerging. From 1934-1936, Bernie Bierman's Minnesota Gophers were considered as fine as any team in the country; 1936 witnessed the introduction of the weekly press poll by Alan Gould, Associated Press sports editor. Overland attacks were prominently featured during the depression decade, with Alabama, featuring its ends, Don Hutson and Paul Bryant, beating Stanford 29-13 in the 1935 Rose Bowl. That year, Chicago's halfback Jay Berwanger was named recipient of the first Heisman Award handed out by New York's Downtown Athletic

Club. Jimmy Crowley of Four Horsemen fame constructed a potent unit at Fordham, relying on the ''Seven Blocks of Granite,'' a line that included guard Vince Lombardi, who would later go on to become the legendary coach of professional football's Green Bay Packers. In 1938, 5'7', 150 pound quarterback and Heisman trophy winner Davey O'Brien took TCU to a national title. In 1939—the year USC's Howard Jones won his fifth national championship—Michigan's Tom Harmon led the nation in rushing; the following year, he scored 16 touchdowns and won the Heisman.

While Bierman once again won national championships with Minnesota in 1940 and 1941, followed by Paul Brown's 1942 Ohio State Buckeyes, college football, not surprisingly, was soon dominated by Notre Dame and Army. Frank Leahy, while compiling a record just short of Rockne's—107-13-9—won national crowns with quarterbacks like Angelo Bertelli and John Lujack, and battled Army in a series of monumental games. By 1944, Army coach Earl ''Red'' Blaik boasted an incredibly deep roster, which included halfback Glenn Davis and fullback Felix ''Doc'' Blanchard. Eventually, both Mr. Outside and Mr. Inside won Heismans, while Davis twice finished second in the balloting. In 1944, Army, which scored 504 points in nine games, crushed defending national champion Notre Dame 59-0. In 1945, Army won 48-0, while again leading the nation in scoring with a 45.8 point average. Blanchard scored 18 touchdowns, Davis tallied 19 and chalked up an 11.74 yards per carry rushing average. Leahy's team, loaded with All-Americans like guard Bill Fischer, end Leon Hart, and tackle George Connor, rebounded in 1946, battling Army to a 0-0 tie. The Southwest Conference again offered an exciting brand of football, and terrific performers like SMU's Doak Walker, the 1948 Heisman recipient, and Kyle Rote and Texas's Bobby Layne. SMU finished unbeaten in 1947, its record marred only by ties with TCU—a 19-19 game in which Walker was responsible for 471 yards in total offense—and Penn State, in the Cotton Bowl.

In the American heartland, Bud Wilkinson, a guard-turned-quarterback on Bernie Bierman's 1935 and 1936 championship teams, continued crafting a stellar record at Oklahoma, which eventually left him with a 145-29-4 record. He also won three national championships and compiled an unbeaten streak of 47 games. Back-to-back undefeated regular seasons in 1949 and 1950 led to Wilkinson's first national title team, as determined by both the AP and the new United Press International polls, although that squad, which had won 31 straight games, lost in the Sugar Bowl to Paul ''Bear'' Bryant's Kentucky Wildcats, 13-7. Wilkinson's stars included stellar halfbacks Billie Vessels (the 1952 Heisman Award winner), Tommie McDonald, and Joe Don Looney. Oklahoma took the 1955 and 1956 national titles, before finally losing to Notre Dame 7-0 in 1957, ending college football's longest winning streak. While remaining a Big 8 Conference heavyweight, Wilkinson's Sooners increasingly had a tough time defeating Darrell Royal's Texas Longhorns at their annual game in Dallas.

The Wilkinson era ushered in a period of top-notch coaches at many universities. The University of Texas, during Royal's 19 year reign, repeatedly vied for national supremacy, ending up with three national crowns and victories over Roger Staubach and the Naval Academy in the 1964 Cotton Bowl; Joe Namath and Bryant's Alabama Crimson Tide in the 1965 Orange Bowl, and Ara Parseghian's Notre Dame squad in the 1970 Cotton Bowl. UT's triple-option led to 30 consecutive wins before Notre Dame and quarterback Joe Theisman defeated the Longhorns 24-11 in the 1971 Cotton Bowl. That enabled

Nebraska's Bob Devaney to claim share of the first of two successive national titles. Out west, John McKay grabbed four national championships, featuring Heisman trophy tailbacks Mike Garrett and O. J. Simpson. Ohio State's Woody Hayes, relying on a ground game, took hold of three national titles, while Bryant guided Alabama to an unprecedented six national championships. Beginning in 1964, Parseghian revitalized the then dormant program at college football's most historic campus, Notre Dame. After the 1966 and 1973 seasons, his Fighting Irish ended up at the top of the polls, as they would following the 1977 and 1988 campaigns, under coaches Dan Devine and Lou Holtz, respectively. In 1968, Penn State's Joe Paterno had his first of five undefeated seasons, although only one concluded with a national title; on another occasion, his once-beaten Nittany Lions were ranked number one. During the 1980s, Miami won four national titles, twice under coach Dennis Erickson. Devaney's successor at Nebraska, Tom Osborne, did him one better, ending his career with three national championships in his last four years. With crowns in 1974, 1975, and 1985, Oklahoma's Barry Switzer equalled Wilkinson's championship record. Florida State's Bobby Bowden took one lone national title, but his Seminoles were ranked in the top four at the close of twelve consecutive seasons. Following the 1996 season, Grambling's Eddie Robinson retired with a record 402 victories; Bryant's 323 wins topped the charts for Division 1-A coaches.

From the 1960s onward, college football's appeal was heightened by the impact of television. Two-platoon systems and clock-stopping rule changes that ushered in many more plays made for an open-ended game, featuring passes and wishbone offenses. Seeking improved television packages, schools withdrew from traditional conferences and joined reconfigured ones. Penn State, for example, entered the Big Ten, while Miami joined the Big East. The historic Southwest Conference collapsed, with Texas, Texas A & M, Baylor, and Texas Tech linking up with the former Big Eight schools to establish the Big Twelve. Professionalization of the sport continued, with elaborate athletic facilities created, nationwide recruiting undertaken, and large bureaucratic apparatuses appearing. Unfortunately, scandals also brewed, with SMU's highly-ranked football program receiving the so-called "death penalty" in February 1987.

—Robert C. Cottrell

FURTHER READING:

Baker, William J. *Sports in the Western World*. Totowa, New Jersey, Rowman and Littlefield, 1982.

Gorn, Elliot J., and Warren Goldstein. *A Brief History of American Sports*. New York, Hill and Wang, 1993.

Nelson, David M. *Anatomy of a Game: Football, the Rules, and the Men Who Made the Game*. Newark, University of Delaware Press, 1994.

Newcombe, Jack, editor. *The Fireside Book of Football*. New York, Simon and Schuster, 1964.

Oriard, Michael. *Reading Football: Sport, Popular Journalism, and American Culture, 1876-1913*. Chapel Hill, University of North Carolina Press, 1993.

Perrin, Tom. *Football: A College History*. Jefferson, North Carolina, McFarland & Company, 1987.

Rader, Benjamin G. *American Sports: From the Age of Folk Games to the Age of Televised Sports*. Englewood Cliffs, New Jersey, Prentice Hall, 1996.

Riess, Steven A. *Sport in Industrial America, 1850-1920*. Wheeling, Illinois, Harlan Davidson, 1975.

Roberts, Randy, and James Olson. *Winning Is the Only Thing: Sports in America Since 1945*. Baltimore, Johns Hopkins University Press, 1989.

Smith, Ronald A. *Sports & Freedom: The Rise of Big-Time College Athletics*. New York, Oxford University Press, 1990.

Sperber, Murray. *Shake Down the Thunder: The Creation of Notre Dame Football*. New York, Henry Holt, 1995.

Collins, Albert (1932-1993)

Guitarist Albert Collins helped modernize blues and bring it to a new audience, blending classic traditions with rock and funk into his high-energy delivery. Born in Leona, Texas, Collins's early influences included T-Bone Walker, John Lee Hooker, and family friend Lightnin' Hopkins. He was also influenced by jazz organists Jimmy Smith and Jimmy McGriff, and saxophone players Arnett Cobb and Illinois Jacquet. Collins's first recording success was the instrumental single "Frosty" recorded in 1962. He signed with Imperial Records in 1968 and moved to the West Coast, where he inspired Robert Cray, Johnny Winter, and Janis Joplin. Collins reached the height of his powers with Chicago's Alligator Records in the 1980s, recording the Grammy Award-winning *Showdown* album with Cray and fellow Texan Johnny Copeland in 1985. He signed with Virgin Records in 1990 and recorded three more albums before his death from lung cancer.

—Jon Klinkowitz

FURTHER READING:

Milkowski, Bill. "Mr. Freeze." *Guitar World*. September 1990, 74-80, 99.

Obrecht, Jas, editor. *Blues Guitar: The Men Who Made the Music*. San Francisco, GPI Books, 1990.

Whiteis, David. "Albert Collins: Ice on the Telecaster, Fire on the Belly." *Down Beat*. May 1991, 24.

Coltrane, John (1926-1967)

Saxophonist John Coltrane exerted a huge influence on the generation of jazz musicians that followed him. In fact, many view Trane, as he was known, as a kind of sacred leader. It is certain that he fostered trends in jazz, while developing those already present. While taking bop trends in harmonization to their ultimate logical conclusion with his stream-of-sound style in the 1950s, Coltrane also explored the simpler modal style as well as Free Jazz, which emphasized melodic development free from the confines of chordal progression. In common with other innovators, he never entirely abandoned the use of one style while moving toward another.

Coltrane was born in Hamlet, North Carolina, in 1926 and grew up in High Point, North Carolina, where his maternal grandfather was a preacher. His father was an established tailor and, thus, in common

John Coltrane

with many jazz musicians, Coltrane came from the black middle class. Both his parents were musical and he grew up in a musical environment. He was only 12 when his father died, but his mother kept the family together and provided him with economic and emotional stability. She moved to Philadelphia where jobs were more plentiful in the World War II economy but sent money home for his support. After graduating from high school in 1943, Coltrane joined his mother in Philadelphia, where he studied alto saxophone at the Orenstein School and made an impression with his seriousness, discipline, and eagerness. Drafted into the navy, he spent his service time playing in the navy band in Hawaii, and after his discharge he resumed his saxophone studies. Soon after, he played in a number of rhythm and blues bands, most notably that of Eddie "Cleanhead" Vinson. The spectacle of the serious Coltrane tossing horns to Vinson in a vaudeville setting is hard to imagine but that is what he did, and did well, according to contemporary accounts. Certainly, that rhythm and blues influence was always discernible in his playing and added depth to his ballad performances.

By the mid-1940s Trane was playing tenor saxophone, a switch originally made so as not to compete with Vinson. He listed Dexter Gordon as a major influence but also absorbed the work of many other musicians. Indeed, Coltrane listened to everyone and adapted elements from many that accorded with his own developing style. Unfortunately, Coltrane's various addictions began to catch up with him at this time. He was an alcoholic, a heroin user, a heavy smoker, and was addicted to sweets—habits that caused the disruption of his personal and professional relationships and damaged his reputation. Eventually, he managed to kick all his habits except his sugar

addiction, which cost him his teeth. Having refused dental care, all his teeth ultimately decayed and had to be removed.

From 1949 to 1951 Coltrane played with Dizzy Gillespie's band, and it is with them that he recorded his first solo. In 1951, he moved back to Philadelphia with his mother and resumed formal musical studies at the Graniff School of Music. In addition to studying saxophone, he studied theory with Dennis Sandole. Some critics have traced Coltrane's fascination with bi-tonality and the use of scalar composition to this period in his career. In 1952 he resumed work with a rhythm and blues band, that of Earl Bostic who, interestingly, like Vinson, was primarily noted for his work on alto saxophone. Bostic's R&B style was enormously popular in the early 1950s and Coltrane was once again exposed to large dance audiences and their emotional reactions to the music. Coltrane soon left Bostic to work with his early idol, Johnny Hodges. Hodges had left Duke Ellington's band for a brief time to head his own band, one that has been underrated or forgotten over the years. In 1954 Hodges fired Trane because his heroin addiction had made him erratic and undependable.

Once more he returned to Philadelphia where he suffered from physical and emotional problems. In this period, he met Juanita Grubbs, known as Naima, and married her in 1955. He sorted out his problems to the extent that he was able to resume playing, and joined Miles Davis's classic 1955 quintet. By this time, his style had incorporated elements of Charlie Parker and Coleman Hawkins. While Trane could play gorgeous melodic lines like Parker, in the 1950s he generally preferred to construct arpeggio-like vertical runs at breakneck speed. Alcohol and drug abuse, however, cost him his job with Miles Davis in 1957. Again, he returned to Philadelphia and his mother, but this time he determined to conquer his multiple addictions, locked himself in his room, and subsisted on water for some days. When he emerged he was ready to resume his life and work.

From this time on, he became fascinated by Eastern religions. Although he never practiced an Eastern faith, he studied the teachings and incorporated elements into his music as well as his personal philosophy. Open use of these elements, however, awaited the 1960s and its ethos. Meanwhile, later in 1957, Trane picked up his career with a stunning engagement with Thelonius Monk at the Five Spot in Manhattan. Working with Monk was worth more than all the theory courses combined. Coltrane perfected his sheets-of-sound style with Monk, while absorbing Monk's unique approach to harmonic conception. Unfortunately, only one record of this fertile period has emerged, but it demonstrates just how vital the partnership was in Coltrane's development.

When Sonny Rollins left Miles Davis, Coltrane returned. Davis showed some courage in bringing him back against the advice of many friends who considered Trane as too erratic and a man who should have left much of his performance in the practice room. His tone and style were not yet the models they soon became, but Coltrane played well on what is now regarded as one of the classic jazz albums of all time, 1959's *Kind of Blue*. Record contracts soon followed, and Trane became the darling of the Hard Boppers, his sheets-of-sound period seeming a logical extension of the bop movement.

In 1960 Coltrane struck out on his own and explored different styles of playing. In his 1959 *Giant Steps* album he showed his ability to develop an older style while moving into a newer one. He developed his hard-bop soloing on some cuts while moving into polytonality and modal areas on others. His album *My Favorite Things* (1960) marked the return of the soprano saxophone to jazz. Although many, notably Johnny Hodges, had used it over the years since Sidney Bechet had mastered it, no other major jazz exponent had really turned it into a popular jazz instrument on a regular basis. Trane openly acknowledged Bechet's influence on his soprano work. The instrument, he said, allowed him to play in the higher registers in which he heard music in his head. It also made his modal playing accessible to a larger audience. *My Favorite Things* made the top 40 charts and began Coltrane's career as a show business figure, commanding healthy fees and continuing to release soprano hits such as ''Greensleeves.''

Meanwhile he grew interested in Ornette Coleman's Free Jazz movement and released ''The Invisible'' with Don Cherry and Billy Higgins and ''India'' in 1961. This movement into free jazz, predictably, did not entail an abandonment of earlier styles. *A Love Supreme* (1964) is a modal album and sold 250,000 copies. Such sales resulted from the popular upsurge of interest in Eastern religions and mysticism during the 1960s, and the album was bought by many who had no idea of jazz but were attracted by the music's connections with mysticism. Even in the midst of his freest experiments, ''Ascension'' and ''Expressions,'' when he recorded with Freddie Hubbard, Archie Shepp, Eric Dolphy, Pharoah Sanders, and Rashid Ali, Coltrane never totally abandoned his love of harmony and melody. He once performed with Thelonious Monk near the end of his life. When it was over, Monk asked Trane when he was going to come back to playing real music such as he had performed that day. Reputedly, Trane responded that he had gone about as far as he could with experimental music and missed harmonic jazz. He promised Monk that he would return to the mainstream.

Whether he was comforting an old friend or speaking his heart, nobody knows, but *Expressions* (1967) was his last recording and included elements from all his periods. Coltrane died at the top of his form when he passed away in 1967 at the age of 40. Though doctors said he died of liver cancer, his friends claimed that he had simply worn himself out. His creative flow had not dried up and it is reasonable to assume that, had he lived, he would have continued to explore new styles and techniques. As it was, he left a body of music that defined and shaped the shifting jazz styles of the period, as well as a reputation for difficult music and a dissipated lifestyle that confirmed the non-jazz lover's worst—and inaccurate—fears about the music and its decadent influence on American culture.

—Frank A. Salamone

FURTHER READING:

Cole, Bill. *John Coltrane.* New York, Da Capo, 1993.

Kofsky, Frank. *John Coltrane and the Jazz Revolution of the 1960s.* New York, Pathfinder Press, 1998.

Nisenson, Eric. *Ascension: John Coltrane and His Quest.* New York, St. Martin's Press, 1993.

Porter, Lewis. *John Coltrane: His Life and Music.* Ann Arbor, University of Michigan Press, 1998.

Simpkins, Cuthbert Ormond. *Coltrane: A Biography.* New York, Black Classic Press, 1988.

Strickland, Edward. ''What Coltrane Wanted.'' *Atlantic Monthly.* December 1987, 100-102.

Thomas, J. C. *Chasin' the Train: The Music and Mystique of John Coltrane.* New York, Da Capo Press, 1988.

Woodleck, Carl, editor. *The John Coltrane Companion: Four Decades of Commentary.* New York, Schrimmer Books, 1998.

Columbo

Lieutenant Columbo, played by Peter Falk, remains the most original, best-written detective in television history. Other shows featuring private detectives (*The Rockford Files*) or policemen (*Hill Street Blues*) may contain more tongue-in-cheek humor or exciting action sequences, but when it comes to pure detection, brilliant plotting, and intricate clues, *Columbo* remains unsurpassed. Its uniqueness stems from the fact that it is one of the few ''inverted'' mysteries in television history. While other mysteries like *Murder, She Wrote* were whodunits, *Columbo* was a ''how's-he-gonna-get-caught?'' Whodunit was obvious because the audience witnessed the murder firsthand at the start of each episode—also making the show unique in that the star, Falk, was completely missing for the first quarter hour of most episodes. This inversion produced a more morally balanced universe; while the murderer in another show might spend 90 percent of its running time enjoying his freedom, only to be nabbed in the last few scenes, in *Columbo* the murderer's carefree lifestyle was short-lived, being replaced by a sick, sweaty angst as the rumpled detective moved closer and closer to the truth. The climatic twist at the end was merely the final nail in the coffin. The show was consistently riveting with no gunplay, no chase sequences, and virtually all dialogue. The inverted mystery is not new, having been devised by R. Austin Freeman for such books as *The Singing Bone,* but never has the form been better utilized.

Columbo sprang from the fertile minds of Richard Levinson and William Link, who met in junior high school and began writing mysteries together. They finally sold some to magazines, then to television, adapting one story they'd sold to *Alfred Hitchcock's Mystery Magazine* for television's *The Chevy Mystery Show.* When Bert Freed was selected to play the part of the detective in this mystery, called ''Enough Rope,'' he became the first actor to play Lieutenant Columbo. Levinson later said the detective's fawning manner came from Petrovich in Dostoyevsky's *Crime and Punishment,* and his humbleness came from G. K. Chesterton's Father Brown. Deciding to dabble in theater, Levinson and Link adapted this story into the play *Prescription: Murder,* which opened in San Francisco starring Joseph Cotton, Agnes Moorehead, and Thomas Mitchell as Columbo. When made-for-TV movies became a popular form, the writers opened up their stagebound story to make it more cinematic, but they needed to cast a new actor as the detective because Mitchell had died since the play's closing. The authors wanted an older actor, suggesting Lee J. Cobb and Bing Crosby, but they were happy with Falk as the final choice once they saw his performance. The film aired in 1968 with Gene Barry as the murderer, and the show received excellent ratings and reviews. Three years later, when NBC was developing the *NBC Mystery Movie,* which was designed to have such series as *McCloud* and *McMillan and Wife* in rotation, the network asked Levinson and Link for a *Columbo* pilot. The writers thought that *Prescription: Murder* made a fine pilot, but the network wanted another—perhaps to make sure this ''inverted'' form was repeatable and sustainable—so ''Ransom for a Dead Man'' with Lee Grant as the murderer became the official pilot for the series. These two made-for-TV movies do not appear in syndication with the series' other forty-three episodes, though they frequently appear on local stations.

NBC Mystery Movie premiered in September 1971, and the talent the show attracted was phenomenal. That very first episode, "Murder by the Book," was written by Steven Bochco (*Hill Street Blues, NYPD Blue*) and was directed by Steven Spielberg. The series also employed the directorial talents of Jonathan Demme, Ben Gazzara, Norman Lloyd, Hy Averback, Boris Sagal, and Falk himself, among others. Acting talents such as Ray Milland, Patrick McGoohan, John Cassavetes, Roddy McDowell, Laurence Harvey, Martin Landau, Ida Lupino, Martin Sheen, and Janet Leigh contributed greatly to the series, though what made it a true classic was Falk's Emmy-winning portrayal of the rumpled detective. The raincoat, the unseen wife, the dog named Dog, the ragtop Peugeot, the forgetfulness—much of this was in the writing, but Falk added a great deal and made it all distinctly his own. Levinson said, "We put in a servile quality, but Peter added the enormous politeness. He stuck in sirs and ma'ams all over the place." He said another of the lieutenant's quirks evolved from laziness on the writers' part. When writing the play *Prescription: Murder,* there was a scene that was too short, and Columbo had already made his exit. "We were too lazy to retype the scene, so we had him come back and say, "Oh, just one more thing." On the show, the disheveled, disorganized quality invariably put the murderers off their guard, and once their defenses were lowered, Columbo moved in for the kill. Much of the fun came from the show's subtle subversive attack on the American class system, with a working-class hero, totally out of his element, triumphing over the conceited, effete, wealthy murderer finally done in by his or her own hubris.

The final NBC episode aired in May 1978, when Falk tired of the series. Ten years later, Falk returned to the role when ABC revived *Columbo,* first in rotation and then as a series of specials, with at least twenty new episodes airing throughout the 1990s. Levinson and Link wrote other projects, and Falk played other roles, but as Levinson once said, referring to himself and Link, "If we're remembered for anything, it may say *Columbo* on our gravestones."

—Bob Sullivan

FURTHER READING:

Conquest, John. *Trouble Is Their Business: Private Eyes in Fiction, Film, and Television, 1927-1988.* New York, Garland Publishing, 1990.

Dawidziak, Mark. *The Columbo Phile: A Casebook.* New York, The Mysterious Press, 1989.

De Andrea, William L. *Encyclopedia Mysteriosa.* New York, Prentice Hall General Reference, 1994.

Levinson, Richard, and William Link. *Stay Tuned: An Inside Look at the Making of Prime-Time Television.* New York, St. Martin's Press, 1981.

Columbo, Russ (1908-1934)

Russ Columbo was a popular romantic crooner of the 1920s and early 1930s. Often referred to as "Radio's Valentino," Columbo was so popular he was immortalized in a song of the day, "Crosby, Columbo, and Vallee." Born Ruggerio de Rudolpho Columbo, he

became a concert violinist, vocalist, songwriter, and bandleader. He wrote many popular songs, mainly with partner Con Conrad. One of his biggest hits also became his theme song, "You Call It Madness (But I Call it Love)."

Columbo appeared in a few films and had just signed with Universal Pictures for a series of musicals when he was tragically killed. While looking at the gun collection of friend Lansing Brown, one of the guns discharged, hitting Columbo in the eye. He died a short time later.

—Jill Gregg

FURTHER READING:

Hemming, Roy, and David Hajdu. *Discovering Great Singers of Classic Pop.* New York, Newmarket Press, 1991.

Parish, James Robert, and Michael R. Pitts. *Hollywood Songsters: A Biographical Dictionary.* New York, Garland Publishing, 1991.

Comic Books

Comic books are an essential representation of twentieth-century American popular culture. They have entertained readers since the time of the Great Depression, indulging their audience in imaginary worlds born of childhood fantasies. Their function within American culture has been therapeutic, explanatory, and commercial. By appealing to the tastes of adolescents and incorporating real-world concerns into fantasy narratives, comic books have offered their impressionable readers a means for developing self-identification within the context of American popular culture. In the process, they have worked ultimately to integrate young people into an expanding consumer society, wherein fantasy and reality seem increasingly linked.

With their consistent presence on the fringes of the immense American entertainment industry, comic books have historically been a filter and repository for values communicated to and from below. Fashioned for a mostly adolescent audience by individuals often little older than their readers, comic books have not been obliged to meet the critical and aesthetic criteria of respectability reserved for works aimed at older consumers (including newspaper comic strips). Neither have comic books generally been subject to the sort of intrinsic censorship affecting the production of expensive advertising and investment-driven entertainment projects. Consequently, comic books have often indulged in outrageous situations and images more fantastic, grotesque, and absurd than those found elsewhere in American mass culture. These delightfully twisted qualities have always been central to the comic book's appeal.

Comic books first emerged as a discrete entertainment medium in 1933, when two sales employees at the Eastern Color Printing Company, Max C. Gaines and Harry I. Wildenberg, launched an entrepreneurial venture whereby they packaged, reduced and reprinted newspaper comic strips into tabloid-sized magazines to be sold to manufacturers who could use them as advertising premiums and giveaways. These proved so successful that Gaines decided to put a ten-cent price tag on the comic magazines and distribute them directly to newsstands. The first of these was *Famous Funnies,* printed by Eastern Color and distributed by Dell Publications. Other publishers soon entered the emerging comic-book field with similar products. In 1935 a pulp-magazine writer named Malcolm Wheeler-Nicholson began publishing the first comic books to feature original material. A few years later, his company was bought out by executives of the Independent News Company who expanded the operation's line and circulation. In 1937 they launched *Detective Comics*, the first comic book to feature adventure stories derived more from pulp magazines and ''B'' movies than from newspaper ''funnies.'' The company later became known by the logo DC—the initials of its flagship title.

By 1938 an embryonic comic-book industry existed, comprising a half-dozen or so publishers supplied by several comic-art studios all based in the New York City area. That same year, the industry found its first original comic-book ''star'' in Superman. The creation of two teenagers named Jerry Siegel and Joe Shuster, Superman's adventures pointed to the fantastic potential of comic books. Because their content was limited only by the imagination and skill of the writers and artists who crafted them, comic books could deal in flights of fantasy unworkable in other visual entertainment media. As an instant commercial success, Superman prompted a succession of costumed superhero competitors who vied for the nickels and dimes of not-too-discerning young consumers. Comic-book characters like DC's Batman, Wonder Woman, and Green Lantern; Marvel Comics' Captain America, and Fawcett Publications' Captain Marvel all defined what comic-book historians and collectors term the ''Golden Age'' of comic books. Although comic books would later embrace a variety of genres, including war, western, romance, crime, horror, and humor, they have always been most closely identified with the costumed superheroes who made the medium a viable entertainment industry.

Creating most of these early comic books was a coterie that was overwhelmingly urban, under-thirty, lower middle class, and male. They initially conceived Depression-era stories that aligned superheroes on the side of the poor and the powerless against a conspiracy of corrupt political bosses, greedy stockbrokers, and foreign tyrants. As the nation drifted towards World War II, comic books became increasingly preoccupied with the threat posed by the Axis powers. Some pointed to the danger as early as 1939—well ahead of the rest of the nation. Throughout the war, comic books generally urged a united national front and endorsed patriotic slogans derived from official U.S. war objectives. Many eviscerated the enemy in malicious and often, in the case of the Japanese, racist stereotypes that played to the emotions and fears of their wartime audience, which included servicemen as well as children. At least a few publishers, most notably DC Comics, also used the occasion of the war against fascism to call for racial and ethnic tolerance on the American home front.

The war years were a boom time for the comic-book industry. It was not uncommon for a single monthly issue to sell in excess of 500,000 copies. The most popular comic books featuring Superman, Batman, Captain Marvel, and the Walt Disney cartoon characters often sold over one million copies per issue. When the war ended, however, sales of most superhero comic books plummeted and the industry lost its unity of purpose. Some publishers, like Archie Comics, carved out a niche for themselves with innocuous humor titles that enjoyed a certain timeless appeal for young children. But as other publishers scrambled for new ways to recapture the interest of adolescent and adult readers, some turned to formulas of an increasingly controversial nature. Many began to indulge their audience in a seedy underworld of sex, crime, and violence of a sort rarely seen in other visual entertainment. These comic books earned the industry legions of new readers and critics alike. Young consumers seemed to have a disturbing taste for comic books like *Crime Does Not Pay* that dramatized—or, as many would charge, glorified—in graphic detail the violent lives of criminals and the degradation of the American dream. Parents, educators, professionals, and politicians reacted to

these comic books with remarkable outrage. Police organizations, civic groups, and women's clubs launched a grassroots campaign at the local and state levels to curb or ban the sale and distribution of objectionable comic books. Only a few years after the end of its participation in a world war, the comic-book industry found itself engaged in a new conflict—a cultural war for the hearts and minds of the postwar generation.

As the Cold War intensified, comic-book makers responded by addressing national concerns at home and abroad, while hoping to improve their public image in the process. Romance comic books instructed young females on the vital qualities of domesticity and became, for a time in the late 1940s and early 1950s, the industry's top-selling genre. War comic books produced during the Korean War underscored the domestic and global threat of Communism. But, as part of the industry's trend toward more realistic stories, many of these also illustrated the ambivalence and frustration of confronting an elusive enemy in a war waged for lofty ideals with limited means.

Neither the subject matter of romance nor war could, in any case, deflect the mounting public criticism directed at comic books. Throughout the postwar decade comic-book makers found themselves confronted by a curious alliance of liberals and conservatives who feared that forms of mass culture were undermining—even replacing—parents, teachers, and religious leaders as the source of moral authority in children's lives. As young people acquired an unprecedented degree of purchasing power in the booming economy, they had more money to spend on comic books. This in turn led to more comic book publishers trying to attract young consumers with increasingly sensational material. Thus, in an irony of postwar culture, the national affluence so celebrated by the defenders of American ideals became perhaps the most important factor accounting for the existence and character of the most controversial comic books.

The most outrageous consequence of the keen competition among publishers was the proliferation of horror comic books. Popular and widely imitated titles like EC Comics' *Tales From the Crypt* celebrated murder, gore, and the disintegration of the American family with a willful abandon that raised serious questions about the increasing freedom and power of mass culture. At the vanguard of the rejuvenated forces aligned against comic books was a psychiatrist and self-proclaimed expert on child behavior named Dr. Fredric Wertham. His 1954 book *Seduction of the Innocent* set forth a litany of charges against comic books, the most shocking and controversial being that they contributed to juvenile delinquency. Such allegations led to a 1954 U.S. Senate investigation into the comic-book industry. Comic-book publishers surrendered to the criticism by publicly adopting an extremely restrictive self-censoring code of standards enforced by an office called the Comics Code Authority. By forbidding much of what had made comic books appealing to adolescents and young adults, the Comics Code effectively placed comic books on a childlike level. At a time when publishers faced stiff competition from television, and rock'n'roll emerged as the new preeminent expression of rebellious youth culture, the Code-approved comic books lost readers by the score.

By the start of the 1960s the industry showed signs of recovery. DC Comics led the resurgence by reviving and revamping some of its popular superheroes from the 1940s including the Flash, the Green Lantern, and the Justice League of America. These characters marked the industry's return to the superhero characters that had made it so successful in the beginning. But the pristine, controlled, and rather stiff DC superheroes proved vulnerable to the challenge posed by Marvel Comics. Under the editorial direction of Stan Lee, in collaboration with artists Jack Kirby and Steve Ditko, Marvel launched a series of new titles featuring superheroes "flawed" with undesirable but endearing human foibles like confusion, insecurity, and alienation. Marvel superheroes like the Fantastic Four, the Incredible Hulk, Spider-Man, the Silver Surfer, and the X-Men found a large and loyal audience among children, adolescents, and even adults drawn to the anti-establishment and clever mythical qualities of the Marvel comic books.

During the late 1960s a new wave of "underground" comic books, sometimes called "comix," emerged as an alternative to the mainstream epitomized by DC and Marvel. These underground comics flourished despite severely limited exposure, and were usually confined to counterculture audiences. With unrestrained subject matter that celebrated drugs, violence, and especially sex, these publications shared more in common with the avant-garde movement and adult magazines than they did with most people's conception of comic books. Artists like Robert Crumb, Rick Griffin, and Art Spiegelman later found some mainstream success and fame (with *Fritz the Cat, Zippy the Pinhead*, and *Maus*, respectively) after getting their start in underground comix. And independent comic books inspired by the underground comix movement continue to enjoy some popularity and sales through comic-book stores throughout the 1980s and 1990s.

Since the 1960s, however, the comic-book industry has been dominated by the superheroes of publishing giants Marvel and DC. Successive generations of comic-book creators have come to the industry as fans, evincing a genuine affection and respect for comic books that was uncommon among their predecessors, most of whom aspired to write or illustrate for other media. During the late 1960s and early 1970s these creators used comic books to comment upon the most pressing concerns of their generation. Consequently, a number of comic books like *The Amazing Spider-Man, The Green Lantern,* and *Captain America* posed a moderate challenge to the "Establishment" and took up such liberal political causes as the civil rights movement, feminism, and opposition to the Vietnam War.

Aware of the country's changing political mood, publishers in 1971 liberalized the Comics Code, making it easier for comic books to reflect contemporary society. Comic-book makers initially took advantage of this new creative latitude to launch a number of ambitious and often self-indulgent efforts to advance mainstream comic books as a literary art form. While many of these new 1970s comic books were quite innovative, nearly all of them failed commercially. Nevertheless, they indicated the increasing willingness of the major publishers to encourage writers and artists to experiment with new ideas and concepts.

As the 1970s drew to a close, the comic-book industry faced some serious distribution problems. Traditional retail outlets like newsstands and "mom-and-pop" stores either disappeared or refused to stock comic books because of their low profit potential. Since the early 1980s, however, comic books have been distributed and sold increasingly through specialty comic-book stores. Publishers earned greater profits than ever before by raising the cost of their comic books, distributing them to these outlets on a non-returnable basis, and targeting the loyal fan audience over casual mainstream readers.

The most popular comic books of the past few decades indicate the extent to which alienation has become the preeminent theme in this medium of youth culture. In the early 1980s, a young writer-artist named Frank Miller brought his highly individualistic style to Marvel's *Daredevil, the Man without Fear* and converted it from a second-tier title to one of the most innovative and popular in the field. Miller's explorations of the darker qualities that make a superhero

inspired others to delve into the disturbing psychological motivations of the costumed vigilantes who had populated comic books since the beginning. Miller's most celebrated revisionism in this vein came in the 1986 "graphic novel" *Batman: The Dark Knight Returns.* Such revisionism in fact became the most common formula of recent comic books. Besides such stalwarts as Spider-Man and Batman, the best-selling superheroes of the 1980s and 1990s included the X-Men, the Punisher, the Ghost Rider, and Spawn. All featured brooding, obsessive, alienated antiheroes prone to outbursts of terrifying violence. This blurring of the lines between what makes a hero and a villain in comic books testifies to the cynicism about heroes generally in contemporary popular culture and to the eagerness of comic-book publishers to tap into the adolescent disorientation and anxieties that have, to some degree, always determined the appeal of comic-book fantasies.

Although comic books remained popular and profitable throughout the 1990s, the major publishers faced some formidable crises. The most obvious of these was the shrinking audience for their product. Comic-book sales peaked in the early 1990s before falling sharply in the middle years of the decade. Declining fan interest was, in part, a backlash against the major publishers' increasing tendency to issue drawn-out "cross-over" series that compelled readers to buy multiple issues of different titles in order to make sense of convoluted plots. Many other jaded buyers were undoubtedly priced out of the comic-book market by cover prices commonly over \$2.50. Special "collector's editions" and graphic novels frequently sold at prices over \$5.00. Most troubling for comic-book makers, however, is the threat that their product may become irrelevant in an increasingly crowded entertainment industry encompassing cable TV, video games, and internet pastimes aimed directly at the youth market. Retaining and building their audience in this context is a serious challenge that will preoccupy creators and publishers as the comic-book industry enters the twenty-first century.

—Bradford W. Wright

FURTHER READING:

Benton, Mike. *The Comic Book in America: An Illustrated History.* Dallas, Taylor Publishing, 1993.

Daniels, Les. *DC Comics: Sixty Years of the World's Favorite Comic Book Heroes.* Boston, Little, Brown, 1995.

———. *Marvel: Five Fabulous Decades of the World's Greatest Comics.* New York, Harry N. Abrams, 1991.

Goulart, Ron. *Over Fifty Years of American Comic Books.* Lincolnwood, Illinois, Mallard Press, 1991.

Harvey, Robert C. *The Art of the Comic Book: An Aesthetic History.* Jackson, University Press of Mississippi, 1996.

Jacobs, Will, and Gerard Jones. *The Comic Book Heroes.* Rocklin, California, Prima Publishing, 1998.

Savage, William W., Jr. *Comic Books and America, 1945-1954.* Norman, University of Oklahoma Press, 1990.

Comics

Comic strips and comic books have been two mainstays of American culture during the entire twentieth century. Comic strips rapidly became a defining feature of modern American culture after their introduction to newspapers across the nation in the first ten years of the twentieth century. Likewise comic books captured the imagination of many Americans in the late 1930s and early 1940s, particularly after the appearance of costumed heroes such as Superman, Batman, and Captain Marvel. From the beginning, comics produced distinct, easily recognized characters whose images could be licensed for other uses. Comic characters united entertainment and commerce in ways that became ubiquitous in American culture.

Although the origin of comic strips is generally traced to the first appearance of the Yellow Kid—so named because the printers chose his nightshirt to experiment with yellow ink—in the *New York World* in 1895, the antecedents of comics are somewhat more complex. When the *World* began a Sunday humor supplement in 1889, it did so to attract the audience of American illustrated humor magazines such as *Puck, Judge,* and *Life.* These magazines had drawn on European traditions of broadsheets, satirical prints, comic albums, and journals such as *Fliegende Blätter, Charivari,* and *Punch* to create a sharp-edged American style of satirical visual humor. The appearance of the Yellow Kid—in the *Hogan's Alley* series—was not a particularly startling moment but rather grew out of an international and local tradition of illustrated humor. What set the Yellow Kid apart from previous versions of the city urchin genre of illustrated humor were his distinct features and regular appearance in large-scale comic panels.

In October 1896 William Randolph Hearst launched a humor supplement to the Sunday edition of his *New York Journal* and contracted the services of Richard Outcault, the Yellow Kid's creator. In addition, the *Journal* employed Rudolph Dirks and Frederick Opper. Although the Yellow Kid established the importance in comic art of a regularly appearing, distinctive character, Outcault did not use with any regularity two other important features of modern comics—sequential panels and word balloons, both of which had been used for centuries in European and American graphic art. Dirks and Opper introduced and developed these features in the pages of the *Journal.* Between December 1897 and March 1901 Dirks's *Katzenjammer Kids* and Opper's *Happy Hooligan* brought together the essential features of modern comics: a regular, distinctive character or cast of characters appearing in a mass medium, the use of sequential panels to establish narrative, and the use of word balloons to convey dialogue. More often than not Dirks's and Opper's strips used twelve panels on a broadsheet page to deliver a gag.

Between 1900-03 newspaper owners and syndicates licensed comic strips and supplements to newspapers across the country. This expansion was tied to broader developments in American culture including the establishment of national markets and ongoing developments in communication and transportation. Comic supplements were circulation builders for newspapers, and by 1908 some 75 percent of newspapers with Sunday editions had a comics supplement. For most newspapers the introduction of a comic supplement saw a rise in sales. The development of daily comic strips, which started with Bud Fischer's *Mutt and Jeff,* first published in November 1907 in the *San Francisco Chronicle,* added another dimension to the medium. In 1908 only five papers ran daily comic strips; five years later at least ninety-four papers across the country ran daily strips. By 1913 newspapers had also begun to group their daily strips on a single page. In a relatively short space of time comic strips moved from being something new to being a cultural artifact. *Comic Strips and Consumer Culture, 1890-1945* quotes surveys showing that by 1924 at least 55 percent and as high as 82 percent of all children regularly read comic strips. Likewise it showed that surveys by George Gallup

and others in the 1930s revealed that the mean average adult readership of comic strips was 75 percent.

The daily comic strip's four or five panels and black-and-white format as opposed to the Sunday comics' twelve color panels was the first of many thematic and aesthetic innovations that fed the popularity of strips. An important development in this process was the blossoming of the continuity strip. Comics historian Robert Harvey has argued that Joseph Patterson, the proprietor of the *Chicago Tribune* and the *New York Daily News,* was instrumental in establishing continuing story lines in comic strips through his development and promotion of Sidney Smith's *The Gumps,* a comic strip equivalent of a soap opera with more than a hint of satire. The continuity strip gave rise to adventure strips such as *Wash Tubbs* and *Little Orphan Annie,* which in turn led to the emergence of science fiction strips like *Buck Rogers* and *Flash Gordon.* Even gag strips such as the working girl strip *Winnie Winkle* adopted continuous story lines for extended periods. The continuity strips led to comic art styles less caricatured in appearance, which for want of a better expression might be dubbed realistic strips, although the story content remained fanciful. No one style of strip ever came to dominate the comics pages, where gags strips, adventure strips, and realistic strips still appear side by side.

From the start, the existence of distinctive characters in comics had offered commercial possibilities beyond the pages of newspapers. The image of the Yellow Kid was used to sell cigars, crackers, and ladies' fans, to name but a few of his appearances. Theater producer Gus Hill staged a musical around the Kid in 1898 and continued to produce comic-strip-themed musicals into the 1920s. Doll manufacturers likewise produced comic strip character dolls. Buster Brown gave his name to shoes, clothing, and a host of other products including pianos and bread. The Yellow Kid's adventures had been reprinted in book form as early as 1897, and throughout the first two decades of the twentieth century publishers such as Cupples and Leon, and F. A. Stokes issued book compilations of popular comic strips. In the early 1930s the commercial dimensions of comic strips were expanded further when advertising executives realized that the mass readership of strips meant that the art form could be used in advertising to draw consumers to a product through entertainment. In 1933, following this strategy, the Eastern Color Printing Company sold a number of companies on the idea of reprinting comic strips in "books" and giving them away as advertising premiums.

After producing several of these advertising premium comic books, Eastern published *Famous Funnies* in 1934, a sixty-four-page comic book of reprinted strips priced at ten cents. Although the company lost money on the first issue, it soon showed a profit by selling advertising space in the comic book. Pulp writer Major Malcolm Wheeler-Nicholson saw an opportunity and joined the fledgling industry with his all-original *New Fun* comic book in February 1935. Wheeler-Nicholson's limited financial resources necessitated a partnership with his distributor, the Independent News Company, run by Harry Donenfeld and Jack Liebowitz, and the three formed a partnership to launch *Detective Comics* in 1937. By 1938 Donenfeld and Liebowitz had eased Wheeler-Nicholson out of the company. Shortly thereafter the two decided to publish a new title, *Action Comics,* and obtained a strip for the first issue that M. C. Gaines at the McClure Syndicate had rejected. Superman by Jerry Siegel and Joe Shuster appeared on the cover of the first issue dated June 1938. The initial print run was two hundred thousand copies. By 1941, *Action Comics* sold on average nine hundred thousand copies.

The company followed this success with the first appearance of Batman in *Detective Comics* in May 1939.

The success of Superman and DC Comics, as the company was now known, led other comic book companies to introduce costumed heroes in the late 1930s and early 1940s including All American's (DC's sister company) Wonder Woman and The Flash; Timely's (later Marvel) Captain America, the Human Torch, and the Submariner; and Fawcett's Captain Marvel. Comic book sales increased dramatically and, according to Coulton Waugh, by 1942 12.5 million were sold monthly. Historians such as Ron Goulart have attributed the boom in superhero comic books to Depression-era searches for strong leadership and quick solutions, and the cultural and social disruption brought on by World War II. Moreover, comic books often served as a symbol of America for servicemen overseas who read and amassed them in large numbers.

America's entry into the war also derailed a campaign against comics begun by Sterling North, the literary editor of the *Chicago Daily News*. In 1947 the sales of comic books reached sixty million a month, and they seemed beyond attempts at censorship and curtailing their spread. But in 1948 a New York psychiatrist, Fredric Wertham, began a campaign that led eventually to a Senate investigation on the nature of comic books and the industry's establishing a Comics Code in a successful attempt to avoid formal regulation through self-censorship. Wertham's 1954 book *Seduction of the Innocent* was the culmination of his attempts to mobilize public sentiment against the danger that he believed comic books posed to children's mental health. Wertham's ideas were picked up by the Senate Subcommittee on Juvenile Delinquency and its prime mover Senator Estes Kefauver. A prime target of the subcommittee's hearings was William M. Gaines, the publisher of EC Comics, which had begun a line of horror comics in 1950. Wertham's attack and the introduction of the Comics Code are often blamed for the demise of a "Golden Age" of comics, but historian Amy Nyberg argues that only EC suffered directly, and other factors such as changes in distribution and the impact of television account for the downturn in comic book publishing.

Whatever the impact of Wertham, the comic book industry shrugged it off relatively quickly. In 1956 DC relaunched its character The Flash, which began a resurrection of superhero comic books. In 1960 DC published the *Justice League of America,* featuring a team of superheroes. According to Les Daniels, the good sales of this book prompted DC's competitor to develop its own team of heroes, and in 1961 Stan Lee and Jack Kirby's *Fantastic Four* appeared under the Marvel imprint. The resulting boom in superhero comics, which saw the debut of Spiderman and the Uncanny X-Men, is referred to by fans as the Silver Age of comics. In the late 1950s and 1960s these fans were particularly important in shaping the direction of comic books and comics history. These fans were interested in comic art and story construction rather than simply the entertainment value of the comic books. That many of these fans were young adults had important ramifications for the future direction of comic books. Likewise, their focus on superheroes meant that these comic books have been accorded the most attention, and books from publishers such as Harvey, Dell, and Archie Comics figure little in many discussions of comic book history because their content is held to be insignificant, at least to young adults.

Perhaps the first publisher to recognize that comic books directed specifically at an older audience would sell was William M. Gaines. When Wertham's campaign put an end to his horror line of comics, Gaines focused his attention on converting the satirical comic book *Mad* into a magazine. *Mad*'s parodies of American culture influenced many young would-be artists. In the late 1960s a number of these artists, including Robert Crumb, S. Clay Wilson, and Gilbert Shelton, began publishing underground comics, or comix, which, as the x designated, transgressed every notion of social normality. Nonetheless, the artists demonstrated a close familiarity with the graphic and narrative conventions of comic art. Discussing these comix, Joseph Witek has suggested that they should be seen as part of the mainstream of American comic history not least of all because comix helped transform comic book content and the structure of the industry.

A major shift in the industry occurred in the late 1970s and early 1980s when entrepreneurs following the example of the undergrounds set up specialist comic shops, comic book distribution companies, and their own comic book publishing companies in which artists retained ownership of their characters. These changes led to more adult-oriented comics at the smaller companies and at the two industry giants, DC and Marvel, which between them accounted for about 75 percent of the market in 1993. DC and Marvel also responded to changes in the industry by giving their artists more leeway on certain projects and a share in profits from characters they created. These changes took place during a boom time for the industry with the trade paper Comic Buyer's Guide estimating increases in comic book sales from approximately $125 million in 1986 to $400 million in 1992.

This comic book boom was related to the synergies created by the media corporations that owned the major comic book companies. DC had been acquired by Warner in the 1960s for its licensing potential. In 1989 Warner's Batman movie heated up the market for comic books and comic-book-related merchandise. DC, Marvel, the comic book stores, and distributors promoted comics as collectibles, and many people bought comics as an investment. When the collectibility bubble burst in the mid 1990s the industry encountered a downturn in which Marvel wound up bankrupt. Marvel's difficulties point to the necessity of large comic book companies diversifying their characters appearances along the lines of the DC-Warner endeavor. On August 29, 1998, the *Los Angeles Times* reported in some detail the frustrations Marvel had experienced over thirteen years in trying to bring Spiderman to the screen.

As the century draws to a close the art form remains strong in both its comic strip and comic book incarnations. The development of the Internet-based World Wide Web has seen the art delivered in a new fashion where strips can be read and related merchandise ordered on-line. At the close of the twentieth century, then, the essential feature of comics remains its distinctive characters who unite entertainment and commerce.

—Ian Gordon

FURTHER READING:

Barrier, Michael, and Martin Williams. *A Smithsonian Book of Comic-Book Comics*. Washington, D.C., Smithsonian Institution Press, 1981.

Blackbeard, Bill, and Martin Williams. *The Smithsonian Collection of Newspaper Comics*. Washington, D.C., Smithsonian Institution Press, 1977.

Daniels, Les. *Comix: A History of Comic Books in America*. New York, Outerbridge & Dienstfrey, 1971.

———. *DC Comics: Sixty Years of the World's Favorite Comic Book Heroes*. Boston, Bulfinch Press, 1995.

———. *Marvel: Five Fabulous Decades of the World's Greatest Comics*. New York, Abrams, 1991.

Gordon, Ian. *Comic Strips and Consumer Culture, 1890-1945*. Washington, D.C., Smithsonian Institution Press, 1998.

Goulart, Ron. *Over 50 Years of American Comic Books*. Chicago, Publications International Limited, 1991.

Harvey, Robert. *The Art of the Funnies: An Aesthetic History*. Jackson, Mississippi, University Press of Mississippi, 1994.

Krause Publications. *Comic Buyer's Guide 1993 Annual*. Iola, Wisconsin, Krause Publications, 1993.

Marschall, Richard. *America's Great Comic Strip Artists*. New York, Abbeville Press, 1989.

McAllister, Matthew Paul. "Cultural Argument and Organizational Constraint in the Comic Book Industry." *Journal of Communication*. Vol. 40, 1990, 55-71.

Nyberg, Amy Kiste. *Seal of Approval: The History of the Comics Code*. Jackson, Mississippi, University Press of Mississippi, 1998.

Sabin, Roger. *Adult Comics: An Introduction*. New York, Routledge, 1993.

Waugh, Coulton. *The Comics*. Jackson, Mississippi, University Press of Mississippi, 1990, [1947].

Wertham, Fredric. *Seduction of the Innocent*. New York, Holt, Rinehart and Winston, 1954.

Witek, Joseph. *Comic Books as History: The Narrative Art of Jack Jackson, Art Spiegelman, and Harvey Pekar*. Jackson, Mississippi, University Press of Mississippi, 1989.

Comics Code Authority

When the Comics Code was drafted in 1954, it was touted by its creators as "the most stringent code in existence for any communications media." It certainly created a fervor, and sparked heated debate about the role of comic books and what they could and should do. The Comics Code Authority, however, was quick to diminish as a censoring body, challenge after challenge reducing it to relative powerlessness. Still, the Code, along with the events leading up to it, had made its impact, not only changing the direction and aesthetics of American comic books, but also affecting this artistic form internationally. Conventions were shaped, as artists endeavored to tell their stories within the Code's restrictions. Meanwhile, working outside of the Code, some artists took special care to flout such circumscription.

Although many factors may be considered in the establishment of the Code, the most widely discussed has been psychiatrist Frederic Wertham's book, *Seduction of the Innocent*, which, in a scathing attack on comic books, claimed that reading comics could lead to juvenile delinquency. The book reproduced isolated panels from several comics and argued that such scenes had a negative impact on the psychology of children. Although some psychologists argued against Wertham's claims, the book was generally well received, becoming a best-seller and creating a furor over the supposed insidiousness of the comic book industry. The release of the book was followed by hearings—commonly referred to as the Kefauver Hearings after presiding senator Estes Kefauver—before the Senate subcommittee on delinquency. Called to testify, Wertham continued his attack on comic books, concluding "I think Hitler was a beginner

compared to the comic book industry." William Gaines, publisher of the much-maligned EC line of comics, argued that these comics were not intended for young children and should not be subjected to protective censorship. Still he found himself forced into a defense not of comics as an expressive art form, but of what constituted "good taste" in a horror comic.

After all was said and done, however, it was not from the outside that the code was imposed, but rather from within the industry itself. The Comic Magazine Association of America(CMAA) was formed on October 26, 1954 by a majority of publishers, in an effort to head off more controversy and to resuscitate declining sales figures. The CMAA served as a self-censoring body, creating a restrictive code forbidding much violence and sexual content as well as anti-authoritarian sentiment, and even limiting the use of specific words like "crime," "terror," or "horror" on comic book covers. Publishers were now obliged to submit their comics for review by the Comics Code Authority (CCA). Approved magazines were granted the cover seal stating, "Approved by the Comics Code Authority." Publishers that failed to meet Code restrictions or that declined to have their books reviewed by the CCA found their distribution cut off as retailers declined to carry unapproved books. Such publishers eventually either submitted to the Code or went out of business. Notably, Wertham had been in favor of restrictions that would keep certain comics out of the hands of children, but he was troubled by what he saw in Code-approved books, which he often found no less harmful than the pre-Code comics.

Two companies, Dell and Gilberton, already regarded as publishers of wholesome comics such as the Disney and Classics Illustrated titles, remained exempt from the Code. Other publishers worked around the Code. Some resorted to publishing comics in magazine format to avoid restrictions. Given the virtual elimination of crime and horror comics, several publishers began to place more emphasis on their superhero books, in which the violence was bigger than life and far from the graphically realistic portrayals in crime and horror comics. It was during these ensuing years that superheroes came to dominate the form and that DC and Marvel Comics came to command the marketplace.

In the 1960s a very different response to the Code manifested itself in the form of underground comics. These independently-produced comic books included graphic depictions of sex, violence, drug use—in short, anything that the code prohibited. Moreover, these comics often paid tribute to pre-Code books and raged against the very censoring agents that had led to their demise.

The first overt challenge to the Code came from Marvel Comics in 1971. Although the Code explicitly prohibited mention of drugs, writer/editor-in-chief Stan Lee, at the request of the Department of Health Education and Welfare, produced a three-issue anti-drug story line in Amazing Spider-Man. Despite being released without the code, these comics were distributed and sold wonderfully, aided by national press. It was with this publication that the Code finally changed, loosening up slightly on its restrictions regarding drugs and clothing to reflect a change in times. Still, most of the restrictions remained largely intact.

The power of the CCA was still further reduced with the rise of direct distribution. Shops devoted to selling only comic books, which received their comics directly from publishers or, later, comic distributors, rather than general news distributors began to spring up during the 1970s. With this new system, the vigilance against non-Code books was bypassed. The new marketplace allowed major publishers to experiment with comics geared towards an adult readership, and allowed more adventurous small publishers to distribute their wares. The way was paved for major "independent" publishers, like Image and Dark Horse, who refused to submit to the CCA's restrictions.

Although the CCA has but a shadow of its former power over the industry, and although the Code itself has been criticized—even from within the CMAA—as an ineffectual dinosaur, there can be no question of its impact. The comics industry, both economically and aesthetically, owes a great deal to the Comics Code Authority, having been shaped variously by accommodation and antagonism.

—Marc Oxoby

FURTHER READING:

Daniels, Les. *Comix: A History of Comic Books in America.* New York, Bonanza, 1971.

Nyberg, Amy Kiste. *Seal of Approval: The History of the Comics Code.* Jackson, University Press of Mississippi, 1998.

Sabin, Roger. *Adult Comics: An Introduction.* London, Routledge, 1993.

Coming Out

Since the 1960s, the expression "coming out"—once reserved for young debutantes making their entrée into society—has been subverted to mean "coming out of the closet," announcing publicly that one is gay or lesbian. The phrase is ordinarily used in proclaiming one's identity to a broader public, though it can also mean acknowledging one's sexual orientation to oneself, or even refer to the first time one acts on that knowledge.

Coming out as a subverted assertion originated in the early twentieth century among the drag "debutante" balls, which were popular social events in the American Southeast, especially among African Americans. Drag queens were presented at these balls, just as young heterosexual women came out at their own events. It was only later, in the 1950s ambiance that placed a premium on hiding the abnormal and atypical, that the connotation of coming out of a dark closet was added, perhaps because of the expression "skeleton in the closet," i.e., a guilty secret.

In the post-Stonewall days of gay liberation, many younger gay men and lesbians believed that repressing their sexual identities was unhealthy, a stance supported by a growing body of psychological evidence and that reflected the loosening of strict gender demarcations in American society. From the 1970s, aspects of gay culture that had once been secret became widely known for the first time: Straight culture picked up the term "coming out" and began to broaden its meaning. In the tell-all society that emerged in the U.S. after the 1970s, people came out on talk shows and in tabloid confessions as manic-depressives, as neatniks, as witches, and other unexpected forms of identification, some lighthearted, some deeply serious. Even within the gay and lesbian community, the usage has expanded as people came out as everything from bisexuals and transgendered folk to sado-masochists and born-again Christians.

Another related term, "outing," emerged in the late 1980s as the opposite of the voluntary confession that had by then achieved generally favorable connotations. Some gay activists, angered when some public and successful gay person insisted on remaining in the closet, deemed it a political necessity to reveal that closeted figure's

identity, especially when his or her public pronouncements were at odds with private behavior. The practice divided the gay and lesbian community, with more radical voices arguing that outing was mere justice, while others holding it to be the ultimate violation of privacy. Outing has also been practiced by vindictive or well-meaning straight people, or by the media, as was the case with lesbian activist Chastity Bono.

Activists have long insisted that much of the oppression gays experience would be diffused if all homosexual people came out publicly. The first National Coming Out Day was declared on October 11, 1988, the first anniversary of the second gay and lesbian March on Washington, D.C. Hoping to maintain some of the spirit of hope and power engendered by the march, organizers encouraged gays to come out of the closet to at least one person on that day. Some organizations have even distributed printed cards for gays to give to bank tellers and store clerks announcing that they have just served a gay client.

Perhaps it is because American society has grown so fond of intimate revelation that the term "coming out" has gained such popularity. Once it was an "in-crowd" phrase among lesbians and gays, who chortled knowingly when the good witch in *The Wizard of Oz* sang, "Come out, come out, wherever you are." With book titles like Lynn Robinson's *Coming Out of the Psychic Closet,* and Martin Liberman's *Coming Out Conservative,* coming out has gone beyond sexual identity to include any form of self-revelation.

—Tina Gianoulis

FURTHER READING:

Bono, Chastity, and Billie Fitzpatrick. *Family Outing.* New York, Little, Brown and Company, 1998.

Bosanquet, Camilla. *Growing Up and Coming Out.* New York, State Mutual Book & Periodical Service, 1985.

Vargo, Marc E. *Acts of Disclosure: The Coming-Out Process of Contemporary Gay Men.* Binghamton, New York, Haworth Press, 1998.

The Commodores

The Lionel Richie-led soul band the Commodores, whose career peaked in the late 1970s before Richie left for solo fame, is a prime example of an R & B crossover success. Beginning as an opening act during the early 1970s for The Jackson Five, the southern-based Commodores released a handful of gritty funk albums before slowly phasing into ballad-oriented material, which gained them the most commercial success. As their audience transformed from being largely black to largely white, the Commodores' sound changed as well, moving toward the smooth lightness of songs like "Still," "Three Times a Lady," and "Easy."

Formed in 1968 in Tuskegee, Alabama, the group—Lionel Richie on vocals and piano, Walter "Clyde" Orange on drums, Milan Williams on keyboards and guitar, Ronald LaPread on bass and trumpet, Thomas McClary on guitar, and William King Jr. playing a variety of brass instruments—was signed to Motown in the early 1970s. Avoiding Motown's assembly-line mode of music production—which included in-house songwriters, musicians, and producers to help create "the Motown sound"—this self-contained group of

The Commodores

talented musicians and songwriters remained relatively autonomous. They maintained their gritty southern-fried funk sound over the course of three albums: their 1974 debut, *Machine Gun;* 1975's *Caught in the Act;* and 1975's *Movin' On.* These three albums built the group a strong base of R & B fans with their consistently good up-tempo funk jams such as "Machine Gun" and "The Zoo (Human Zoo)," but they had not yet made the crossover move. *Hot on the Tracks* (1976) showed signs of this move with its slower cuts ("Just to Be Close to You" and "Sweet Love" are notable examples). Their big crossover move came with 1977's self-titled breakthrough album, which contained such party favorites as "Brick House" and "Slippery When Wet," as well as the adult- and urban-contemporary radio staple "Easy."

It was the massive success of "Easy" that signaled a new direction for the group and prompted a solo attempt by Richie (who, nonetheless, remained in the band for another four years). Next came the Top 40 hit "Three Times a Lady" from the 1978 album *Natural High* and the Billboard number one single, "Still," from 1979's *Midnight Magic* album—both of which continued the Commodores' transformation from a chitlin' circuit southern funk party band to background music for board meetings, housecleaning, and candle-lit dinners. *In the Pocket,* from 1981, was Richie's last album with the Commodores, and within a year he left to pursue a solo career.

Without Richie's songwriting (his songs would always be the Commodores' strength) and charisma, the group floundered through most of the 1980s, with the sole exception of their 1985 Top 40 hit single "Nightshift," for which album J. D. Nicholas assumed lead singing duties. The Commodores suffered another blow when producer/arranger James Anthony Carmichael, the man responsible for shaping the majority of the group's hits, followed Richie's departure in the early 1980s.

Richie went on to have a hugely successful solo career before virtually disappearing from the commercial landscape in the 1990s. Between 1981-87, he had thirteen Top Ten hits, which included a staggering five number one singles—"Endless Love," "Truly," "All Night Long," "Hello," and "Say You, Say Me."

—Kembrew McLeod

FURTHER READING:

Koenig, Teresa. *Lionel Richie.* Mankato, Crestwood House, 1986.

Nathan, David. *Lionel Richie: An Illustrated Biography.* New York, McGraw-Hill, 1985.

Plutzik, Roberta. *Lionel Richie.* New York, Dell, 1985.

Communes

Close, interdependent communities not based on family relationships, communes have a long history in the United States and continue to represent a strand of American culture and ideology that sanctions the search for a utopia of peace, love, and equality. Researcher Benjamin Zablocki defines a commune as a group of unrelated people who voluntarily elect to live together for an indefinite time period in order to achieve a sense of community that they feel is missing from mainstream American society. Most commonly associated with the hippie and flower child members of the 1960s and 1970s counterculture, communes have professed a variety of reasons for existence and can be politically, religiously, or socially based and exist in both rural and urban environments. Keith Melville has observed that commune members are linked by ''a refusal to share the dominant assumptions that are the ideological underpinnings of Western society.'' They are extremely critical of the status quo of the American consumer society in which they live, and they promote a new value system centered on peace and love, personal and sexual freedom, tolerance, and honesty. Members wish to begin living their vision of a better society away from mainstream society and enjoy the support of their fellow believers.

Communes have existed throughout world history and in the United States since its founding in the seventeenth century. Famous nineteenth-century communes such as the Oneida and Shaker settlements consisted of mostly older, middle-class idealists who strongly believed in the possibility of creating their vision of the ideal society. They shared strong religious or political convictions and were more structured than their twentieth-century counterparts. Many of the later communes would carry on their utopian mission.

The immediate predecessors of the twentieth-century communal movement were the beatniks and African-American activists who fought for social changes that the communalists would later adopt in their created society in a desire to create a new ethics for a new age. While communes promoted rural, community, and natural values in an urban, individualistic, and artificial society, popular cultural images of communes depict isolated, run-down rural farms where barely clothed hippies enjoyed economic sharing and free love while spending most of their days in a drug-induced haze. The high visibility of the countercultural movement with which communes were associated made them a large component in the national debate

A commune in Lawrence, Kansas in 1972.

over the societal effects of the growth of ''sex, drugs, and rock 'n' roll. Commune members were predominantly young, white, middle-class males; and the communes tended to be smaller, unstructured, anarchistic, and more democratically governed than their predecessors. Most twentieth-century communes were not political in nature even though they were generally sympathetic to the left and politically oriented groups such as Students for a Democratic Society and the militant poor.

Famous twentieth-century communes ranged in location from the Farm in Tennessee to Drop City in Colorado and ranged in ideology from the secular Morning Star Ranch to the religious Hare Krishna communal farm. There were also a number of short-lived communal arrangements at the many rock festivals of the period, including the famous Hog Farm at Woodstock. Communes required a strong commitment to the group and a willingness to sacrifice some individual freedom for the group's welfare. Twentieth-century communes proved to be very fragile, and most existed for only a year or two before internal disputes attributed to male chauvinism, lack of direction, and weak structure broke them apart. The communal movement has continued in relative obscurity since the 1960s and 1970s, and will thus continue to be associated with that time period and the countercultural movement.

Communes have had both positive and negative images in United States society and in popular culture. On the positive side, the nation has always professed to value the new and different, and in the late twentieth century has placed increasing emphasis on the toleration of dissent and diversity exemplified by the multicultural movement. The twentieth-century mass media favored communes as they sought the new and eccentric, good drama, and escapist entertainment. The popular media thus focused on the colorful and controversial aspects of the communal movement including its association with widespread drug use, free love, wild clothing and hair styles, and rock 'n' roll music. Communes have also met with the strong negative attitudes of many members of mainstream society who favor the status quo and disagree with the communalists' values or lifestyles. These people comprise the so-called ''Establishment'' from which the hippies wished to break away. Communal members have been harassed with zoning suits, refused admittance to businesses, spat at, threatened with violence, and attacked. The communal movement also experienced a backlash in the late twentieth century as many people lamented the disrespect and defiance of youth to their elders. The reactionary right wing of American politics used hippies and communalists as conveniently visible scapegoats for all the evils of modern American society. There are also communal links to certain late twentieth-century cults that have generated extremely negative publicity. These included Jim Jones's followers, who committed mass suicide at Jonestown in the 1970s; Charles Manson's murderous followers of the 1960s; the Branch Davidians led by David Koresh, who battled the FBI at Waco in the 1990s; and the Heaven's Gate cult, whose mass suicide also received widespread coverage in the 1990s. Negative associations portray commune members as social deviants who threaten established society.

While communes face the problems of decreasing population and visibility in the late twentieth-century United States, they have not disappeared from the American scene. Communes remain prevalent in the smaller cities and college towns where a hip subculture flourishes. The value system of the hippie communes that slowly faded away in the late 1970s has had a large impact on twentieth-century society. Their legacy is evident in such American cultural phenomena as an increasing awareness of environmental issues, an emphasis on the importance of health and nutrition, a rise in New Age spiritualism, and a rise in socially conscious businesses such as Ben and Jerry's Ice Cream.

—Marcella Bush Treviño

FURTHER READING:

Hedgepeth, William. *The Alternative: Communal Life in New America.* New York, Macmillan, 1970.

Melville, Keith. *Communes in the Counter Culture: Origins, Theories, Styles of Life.* New York, Morrow, 1972.

Miller, Timothy. *The Hippies and American Values.* Knoxville, University of Tennessee Press, 1991.

Robert, Ron E. *The New Communes: Coming Together in America.* Englewood Cliffs, N.J., Prentice-Hall, 1971.

Veysey, Laurence. *The Communal Experience: Anarchist and Mystical Counter-Culture in America.* New York, Harper and Row, 1973.

Zablocki, Benjamin. *Alienation and Charisma: A Study of Contemporary American Communes.* New York, Free Press, 1980.

Zicklin, Gilbert. *Countercultural Communes: A Sociological Perspective.* Westport, Conn., Greenwood Press, 1983.

Communism

Originally outlined by Karl Marx and Friedrich Engels in *The Communist Manifesto* (1848), Communism is a social and political system in which all property is owned communally and all wealth distributed among citizens according to need. Although it was a product of large-scale industrialization in the nineteenth century, Communism has had a profound influence on the global politics and economics of the twentieth century. In the United States, Communism became popular among American industrial workers during the Depression, and played a more public role in politics during the 1930s. In the 1940s and during the Cold War, the treatment of Communist groups and individuals within the United States sometimes raised questions about the fairness not only of the American justice system, but of the Constitution itself.

Communism is most often associated with the revolution which took place in Russia in November 1917, and the establishment of the federalist Soviet Union (USSR) in 1922. Its first leader was Vladimir Ilich Lenin, whose version of Marxism, known as Marxism-Leninism, became the dominant political and economic theory for communist groups the world over. Under Joseph Stalin after World War II, the USSR succeeded in gaining military and political control over much of Eastern Europe, placing it in direct opposition to the capitalist economies of the United States and Western Europe. When Stalin died in 1953, many of his more brutal policies were renounced by the new regime; but Communism had become a byword for threats to personal freedom and for imperialist aggression. A climate of distrust between the USSR and Western governments, backed by the threat of global nuclear war, prevailed until the late 1980s.

The history of Communism in the United States begins long before the Cold War, however. Left-wing activists and socialist parties had been at work from before the beginning of the century, but communist parties first appeared in the United States in 1919, partly in response to the political developments in Russia. Communism has unsettled American governments from the beginning, and after a series of raids sanctioned by the Attorney General in 1919, left-wing organizations were forced to become more secretive. It was another ten years before the parties merged to form the Communist Party of the United States of America (CPUSA). The CPUSA's goal of regaining support from union members was certainly helped by the onset of the Depression, and Communism was popular among those who suffered most, such as African American workers and Eastern European immigrants.

Despite dire warnings from the political right, and although large crowds turned out for rallies against unemployment, communists remained a small faction within the trade union movement, and thus were isolated in politics. Only in the 1930s, bravely fielding a black vice-presidential candidate in 1932, opposing fascism in Europe, and openly supporting Roosevelt in some of his New Deal policies, did the CPUSA gain credibility with significant numbers of American voters. Besides industrial workers and the unemployed, communist or socialist principles also proved attractive to America's intelligentsia. Writers such as Theodore Dreiser, Sherwood Anderson, and John Dos Passos all declared themselves as Communist Party voters in 1932, while the radical playwrights Clifford Odets and Lillian Hellman were among many left-wing intellectuals to emerge from 1920s literary New York to work in Hollywood.

In 1940, the Smith Act made membership in revolutionary parties and organizations whose aim was to overthrow the U.S. government illegal, and in 1950, under the McCarran Act, communists had to register with the U.S. Department of Justice. In the same period, Senator Joseph McCarthy began Senate investigations into communists in government, and the House Un-American Activities Committee (HUAC) challenged the political views of individuals in other areas. Many prominent people in government, the arts, and science were denounced to HUAC as dangerous revolutionaries. Because of the moral tone of the investigations and the presentation of Communism as "Un-American," many promising careers ended through mere association with individuals called to explain themselves to the committee. One widely held myth was that the CPUSA was spying for the Soviet government, a fear that, among other things, resulted in the execution of Ethel and Julius Rosenberg in 1953. In most cases there was no evidence for McCarthy's accusations of "un-American activity," and his own career was to end abruptly when he was censured by the Senate in 1954.

Perhaps because of the USSR's imperialist ambitions after World War II, Communism has frequently been presented to the American people since then as a moral threat to "American" values such as individualism and enterprise. U.S. involvement in wars in Korea (1950-53) and Vietnam (1964-72), and military and political actions elsewhere, such as South America and Cuba, have been justified as attempts to prevent the spread of Communism, with anti-war protesters often being branded as "Reds." The Cold War continued until the late 1980s, when Ronald Reagan, who had previously referred to the Soviet Union as the "Evil Empire," began talks with Mikhail Gorbachev over arms reduction and greater political cooperation. In the late 1990s, following the collapse of the USSR in 1991, few communist regimes remained in place, and although Communism remains popular in Eastern Europe, communists in the West form a tiny minority of voters. Their continuing optimism is fuelled by Lenin's claim that true Communism will only become possible after the collapse of a global form of Capitalism.

—Chris Routledge

FURTHER READING:

Fried, Richard M. *Nightmare in Red: The McCarthy Era in Perspective.* New York, Oxford University Press, 1990.

Klehr, Harvey. *The Heyday of American Communism: The Depression Decade.* New York, Basic Books, 1984.

Marx, Karl and Friedrich Engels. *The Communist Manifesto.* 1848. New York, Oxford University Press, 1998.

Ottanelli, Fraser M. *The Communist Party of the United States from the Depression to World War II.* New Brunswick, Rutgers University Press, 1991.

Shindler, Colin. *Hollywood in Crisis: Cinema and American Society, 1929-1939.* New York, Routledge, 1996.

Community Media

Between 1906 and 1922 radio amateurs—who referred to themselves as "distance fiends"—ruled the airwaves. In their enthusiasm to share common concerns, forge friendships with distant strangers, and explore the expressive potential of the new medium, the radio enthusiasts championed democratic communication through electronic media. By the mid-1920s, however, commercial sponsorship of radio programming and corporate control of the newly developed broadcasting industry stifled the participatory potential of the "wireless." At the end of the twentieth century, the rapid commercialization of the internet poses yet another threat to the democratic possibilities of a new communication medium. Although the distance fiends are largely forgotten, their passionate embrace of the communitarian potential of electronic communication lives on through the work of community media organizations around the world.

Community media play a significant, but largely unacknowledged, role in popular culture. Unlike their commercial and public service counterparts, community media give "everyday people" access to the instruments of radio, television, and computer-mediated communication. Through outreach, training, and production support services, community media enhance the democratic potential of electronic communication. Community media also encourage and promote the expression of different social, political, and cultural beliefs and practices. In this way, community media celebrate diversity amid the homogeneity of commercial media and the elitism of public service broadcasting. Most important, perhaps, worldwide interest in community media suggests an implicit, cross-cultural, and timeless understanding of the profound relationship between community cohesion, social integration, and the forms and practices of communication. Despite their growing numbers, however, community media organizations remain relatively unknown in most societies. This obscurity is less a measure of community media's cultural significance, than an indication of its marginalized status in the communications landscape.

In the United States, the origins of the community radio movement can be traced to efforts of Lew Hill, founder of KPFA: the flagship station of the Pacifica radio network. A journalist and conscientious objector during World War II, Hill was disillusioned with the state of American broadcasting. At the heart of Hill's disdain for commercial radio was an astute recognition of the economic realities of radio broadcasting. Hill understood the pressures associated with commercial broadcasting and the constraints commercial sponsorship places on a station's resources, and, ultimately, its programming. Hill and his colleagues reasoned that noncommercial, listener supported radio could provide a level of insulation from commercial interests that would ensure challenging, innovative, and engaging radio. Overcoming a number of legal, technical, and economic obstacles, KPFA-Berkeley signed on the air in 1949. At a time of anti-Communist hysteria and other threats to the democratic ideal of freedom of speech, KPFA and the Pacifica stations represented an indispensable alternative to mainstream news, public affairs, and cultural programming.

Although listener-supported radio went a long way toward securing local enthusiasm and financial support for creative and provocative programming, this model presented some problems. During the early 1970s demands for popular participation in and access to the Pacifica network created enormous rifts between local community members, Pacifica staff, and station management. Conflicts over Pacifica's direction and struggles over the network's resources continue to contribute to the divisiveness that remains somewhat synonymous with Pacifica at the end of the twentieth century. Still, KPFA and its sister stations consistently broadcast programs dealing with issues considered taboo by commercial and public service broadcasters alike.

Equally important, the Pacifica experience generated remarkable enthusiasm for alternative radio across the country. For instance, in 1962 one of Lew Hill's protégés, Lorenzo Milam, founded KRAB, a listener-supported community radio station in Seattle, Washington. Throughout the 1960s, Milam traveled the country, providing technical and logistical support to a number of community radio outlets: a loose consortium of community stations that came to be known as the KRAB Nebula. By 1975, the National Alternative Radio Konference (NARK) brought together artists, musicians, journalists, and political activists with an interest in participatory, locally-oriented radio. Within a few months the National Federation of Community Broadcasters (NFCB) was established to represent the interests of the nascent community radio movement. Committed to providing ''nonprofessional'' individuals and marginalized groups with access to the airwaves, the NFCB played a pivotal role in the rise of community radio in the United States. Still active, the NFCB continues to promote noncommercial, community-based radio. Organizations such as the World Association for Community Broadcasters (AMARC) provide similar support services for the community radio movement worldwide.

While Americans were exploring the possibilities of participatory radio, Canadians turned their attention to television. In 1967, the Canadian National Film Board undertook one of the earliest and best known attempts to democratize television production. As part of the experimental broadcast television series *Challenge for Change,* The Fogo Island project brought the subjects of a television documentary into a new, collaborative relationship with filmmakers. Embracing and elaborating upon the tradition of the social documentary championed by Robert Flaherty and John Grierson, *Challenge for Change* undertook the ambitious and iconoclastic task of systematically involving the subjects of their films in the production process. Senior producer Colin Low and his crew invited island residents to contribute story ideas, screen and comment on rushes, and collaborate on editorial decisions. By involving island residents throughout the filmmaking process, producers sought to ''open up'' television production to groups and individuals with no formal training in program production. Initially conceived as a traditional, broadcast

documentary, the Fogo Island project evolved into the production of 28 short films that focused on discrete events, specific issues, and particular members of the Fogo Island community. The Fogo Island experience stands as a precursor to the community television movement. Not only did the project influence a generation of independent filmmakers and community television producers, the use of participatory media practices to enhance community communication, to spur and support local economic initiatives, and to promote a sense of common purpose and identity has become the hallmark of community media organizations around the world.

The dominance of commercial media in the United States made democratizing television production in this country far more challenging. In response to criticisms that American television was a ''vast wasteland'' the US Congress passed the Public Broadcasting Act of 1967 which sought to bring the high quality entertainment and educational programming associated with public service broadcasting in Canada and the United Kingdom to American audiences. Throughout its troubled history—marked by incessant political pressure and chronic funding problems—the Public Broadcasting Service (PBS) has provided American television audiences with engaging, informative, and provocative programming unlike anything found on commercial television. However, rather than decentralize television production and make television public in any substantive fashion, PBS quickly evolved into a fourth national television network. Although PBS remains an important outlet for independent film and video producers, the level of local community access and participation in public television production is minimal at best.

Significantly, the early days of public television in the United States provided the early community television movement with some important precedents and helped set the stage for public access television as we know it today. Throughout the mid-1960s, the development of portable video equipment coupled with an urgent need for programming prompted a unique, if sporadic, community-based use of public television. Media historian Ralph Engelman notes, ''Early experimentation in the use of new equipment and in outreach to citizens took place on the margins of public television in the TV laboratories housed at WGBH-TV in Boston, KQED-TV in San Francisco, and WNET-TV in New York.'' These innovations, most notably, WGBH's *Catch 44* gave local individuals and groups an opportunity to reach a sizable, prime time, broadcast audience with whatever message they desired. These unprecedented efforts were short-lived, however, as public television quickly adopted programming strategies and practices associated with the commercial networks.

Recognizing public television's deficiencies, an assortment of media activists turned their attention away from broadcasting to the new technology of cable television. These media access advocates hoped to leverage the democratizing potential of portable video recording equipment with cable's ''channels of abundance'' to make television production available to the general public. In the late 1960s, New York City was the site of intense, often contentious, efforts to ensure local participation in cable television production and distribution. George Stoney—often described as the father of public access television in the United States—was a leading spokesperson for participatory, community oriented television in Manhattan.

Stoney began his career in the mid-1930s working in the rural South as part of the New Deal. Through his training as a journalist and educational filmmaker, Stoney understood the value of letting people speak for themselves through the media. The use of media to address local issues and concerns and to promote the exchange of perspectives and ideas pervades Stoney's work as filmmaker and access television advocate. Following a successful term as executive producer for *Challenge for Change,* Stoney returned to the United States in 1970 and, with the his colleague, Canadian documentary filmmaker Red Burns, established the Alternative Media Center (AMC).

The AMC's legacy rests on its successful adaptation of the *Challenge for Change* model of participatory media production. Like the Canadian project, the AMC gave people the equipment and the skills to produce their own videotapes. Through the AMC, individual citizens and local nonprofit groups became active participants in the production of television programming by, for, and about their local communities. In addition, the Center provided the technical resources and logistical support for producing and distributing community oriented programming on local, regional, and national levels. One of the AMC's primary strategies was to train facilitators who would then fan out across the country and help organize community access centers. Over the next five years, the Alternative Media Center played a crucial role in shaping a new means of public communication: community television. Organizations such as the U.S.-based Alliance for Community Media and international groups like Open Channel, were created to promote community television through local outreach programs, regulatory reform measures, and media literacy efforts.

Like previous technological developments, computers and related technologies have been hailed as a great democratizing force. Much has been made of computer-mediated communication's (CMC) ability to enhance social interaction, bolster economic redevelopment, and improve civic participation in local communities. However, for those without access to computers—or the skills to make efficient and productive use of these tools—the Information Age may intensify social and political inequities. Community networking, like community radio and television, provides disenfranchised individuals and groups with access to communication technologies.

Early experiments in community networking date back to the mid-1970s. In Berkeley, California, the Community Memory project was established specifically to promote community cohesion and encourage community-wide dialogue on important issues of the day. Project administrators installed and maintained terminals in public spaces, such as libraries and laundromats, to encourage widespread use of these new technologies. Somewhat akin to public telephones, these computer terminals were coin operated. Although users could read messages free of charge, if users wanted to post a message, they were charged a nominal fee.

By the mid-1980s computer bulletin boards of this sort were becoming more common place. In 1984, Tom Grundner of Case Western University in Cleveland, Ohio created St. Silicon's Hospital: a bulletin board devoted to medical issues. Using the system, patients could ask for and receive advice from doctors and other health professionals. The bulletin board was an unprecedented success and quickly evolved into a city-wide information resource. After securing financial and technical support from AT&T, Grundner and his associates provided public access terminals throughout the city of Cleveland and dial up access for users with personal computers. The first of its kind, the Cleveland Free-Net uses a city metaphor to represent various types of information. For example, government information is available at the Courthouse & Government Center, cultural information is found in the Arts Building, and area economic resources are located in the Business and Industrial Park section. In addition to database access, the Cleveland Free-Net supports electronic mail and newsgroups. By the mid-1990s, most community

networks typically offered a variety of services including computer training, free or inexpensive e-mail accounts, and internet access.

Through the work of the now-defunct National Public Telecomputing Network (NPTN) Grundner's Free-Net model has been adopted by big cities and rural communities throughout the world. In countries with a strong public service broadcasting tradition like Australia and Canada, federal, state, and local governments have played a significant role in promoting community networking initiatives. In other instances, community networks develop through public-private partnerships. For instance, the Blacksburg Electronic Village (BEV) was established through the efforts of Virginia Tech, the city of Blacksburg, Virginia, and Bell Atlantic. A number of organizations such as the U.S.-based Association for Community Networking (AFCN), Telecommunities Canada, the European Alliance for Community Networking (EACN), and the Australian Public Access Network Association (APANA) promote community networking initiatives on local, regional, and national levels.

Like other forms of community media, community networks develop through strategic alliances between individuals, non-profit groups, businesses, government, social service agencies, and educational institutions; it is the spirit of collaboration between these parties that is central to efficacy of these systems. The relationships forged through these community-wide efforts and the social interaction these systems facilitate help create what community networking advocate Steve Cisler refers to as "electronic greenbelts": localities and regions whose economic, civic, social, and cultural environment is enhanced by communication and information technologies (CIT).

Due in part to their adversarial relationship, mainstream media tend to overshadow, and more often than not denigrate, the efforts of community media initiatives. The majority of popular press accounts depict community media organizations as repositories for depraved, alienated, racist, or anarchist slackers with too much time on their hands, and precious little on their minds. Writing in *Time Out New York,* a weekly entertainment guide in New York City, one critic likens community access television to Theater of the Absurd and feigns praise for access's ability to bring "Nose whistlers, dancing monkeys and hairy biker-chefs—right in your own living room!" Likewise, entertainment programs routinely dismiss community television out of hand. For example in their enormously popular *Saturday Night Live* skit—and subsequent blockbuster feature films—*Wayne's World*'s Dana Carvey and Mike Meyers ridicule the crass content, technical inferiority, and self-indulgent style of community access television.

Although few community media advocates would deny the validity of such criticisms, the truly engaging, enlightening, and provocative output of community media organizations goes largely ignored. Yet, the sheer volume of community radio, television, and computer-generated material attests to the efficacy of grassroots efforts in promoting public access and participation in media production and distribution. Furthermore, this considerable output highlights the unwillingness, if not the inability, of commercial and public service media to serve the distinct and diverse needs of local populations. Most important, however, the wealth of innovative, locally-produced programming indicates that "non-professionals" can make creative, substantive, and productive use of electronic media.

Community media serve and reflect the interests of local communities in a number of unique and important ways. First, community media play a vital role in sustaining and preserving indigenous cultures. For instance, in Porcupine, South Dakota community radio

KILI produces programming for local Native Americans in the Lakota language. Similarly, in the Australian outback, Aboriginal peoples use community television to preserve their ancient cultural traditions and maintain their linguistic autonomy. Second, community media reflect the rich cultural diversity of local communities. For example, some of the most interesting sites on Victoria Australia's community network (VICNET) are the pages celebrating Victoria's multicultural heritage (www.vicnet.net.au). These sites contain information of interest to Victorian's Irish, Polish, Hungarian, Vietnamese, and Filipino populations. Likewise, Manhattan Neighborhood Network (MNN) features a variety of programs that showcase Manhattan's eclecticism. On any given day, audiences can tune in to a serial titled *Glennda and Friends* about "two socially-conscious drag queens," unpublished poetry and fiction by an expatriate Russian writer, a municipal affairs report, or *Each One Teach One* a program dedicated to African-American culture. Finally, community media play a decisive role in diversifying local cultures. Aside from celebrating the region's rich musical heritage, WFHB, community radio in Bloomington, Indiana, exposes local audiences to world music with programs like *Hora Latina* (Latin music), *The Old Changing Way* (Celtic music), and *Scenes from the Northern Lights* (music from Finland, Norway, and Sweden). What's more, WFHB brings local radio from America's heartland to the world via the internet (www.wfhb.org). As corporate controlled media consolidate their domination of the communication industries and public service broadcasters succumb to mounting economic and political pressures, the prospects for more democratic forms of communication diminish. Community media give local populations a modest, but vitally important, degree of social, cultural, and political autonomy in an increasingly privatized, global communication environment.

—Kevin Howley

FURTHER READING:

Barlow, William. "Community Radio in the U.S.: The Struggle for a Democratic Medium." *Media, Culture and Society.* Vol. 10, 1988, 81.

Cisler, Steve. *Community Computer Networks: Building Electronic Greenbelts.* http://cpsr.org/dox/program/community-nets/building₉lectronic₉reenbelts.html, November 11, 1998.

Engelman, Ralph. *Public Radio and Television in America: A Political History.* Thousand Oaks, California, Sage, 1996.

Lewis, Peter. *Media for People in Cities: A Study of Community Media in the Urban Context.* Paris, UNESCO, 1984.

Milam, Lorenzo. *Sex and Broadcasting: A Handbook on Starting a Radio Station for the Community.* San Diego, MHO & MHO, 1988.

Schuler, Doug. *New Community Networks: Wired for Change.* New York, ACM, 1996.

Community Theatre

Community theatre represents the majority of theatres in the United States, including community playhouses and university and college programs. Although the term "community theatre" has

disparate meanings the term can be applied generally to theatres—whether professional or not—that draw from their communities. The history of community theatre offers a unique perspective on the struggles between artistic endeavors and commercial profit in theatrical productions. While once a product of a movement to improve the artistic quality of theatrical productions, by the end of the twentieth century community theatre had become a venue more for community participation in the arts than a fertile source of avant-garde theatrical productions.

The roots of community theatre can be traced to the "Little Theatre" movement that started in the 1910s. The movement came as a reaction to the monopolistic "Syndicate" theatre system as well as an attempt to join the growing discourse about non-commercial theatre. According to Mary C. Henderson in her book, *Theater in America,* "The 'little-theater' movement, launched so spectacularly in Europe in the 1880s, finally reached America and stimulated the formation of groups whose posture was anti-Broadway and noisily experimental."

By 1895, touring companies became the primary source for theatrical entertainment in the United States. Theatrical producers Sam Nixon, Fred Zimmerman, Charles Frohman, Al Hayman, Marc Klaw, and Abraham Erlanger saw the opportunity to gain control of the American theatre and formed what came to be called "The Syndicate." The Syndicate purchased theatres across the country and blacklisted ones that refused to cooperate with its business practices. By 1900, the Syndicate monopolized the American theatre scene, and between 1900 and 1915, theatre became a mainly conservative and commercial venture. Due to public dissatisfaction, Frohman's death, and an anti-trust suit, the Syndicate system became largely ineffective by 1916.

During this period many of Europe's finest independent theatres began touring the United States; these included the Abbey Theatre (1911), the Ballets Russes (1916), and Théâtre du Vieux Colombier (1917-1919). Robert E. Gard and Gertrude S. Burley noted in *Community Theatre* that "Their tour aroused the antagonism of American citizens against the feeble productions of the commercial theatre, and seemed to be the catalyst that caused countless dramatic groups to germinate all over America, as a protest against commercial drama." In addition, the end of World War I led to a greater awareness of the European theatrical practices of France's Andre Antoine, Switzerland's Adolphe Appia, England's Gordon Craig, and Russia's Vsevelod Meyerhold and Konstantine Stanislavsky.

The publication of Sheldon Cheney's *Theatre Arts Magazine* (1916) helped to broaden audiences for non-commercial theatre and influenced its readers' thoughts surrounding commercial theatre. In 1917 Louise Burleigh wrote *The Community Theatre in Theory and Practice* in which she coined the phrase "Community Theatre" and defined it as "any organization not primarily educational in its purpose, which regularly produces drama on a noncommercial basis and in which participation is open to the community at large." Other publications such as Percy MacKaye's *The Playhouse and the Play* (1909) extolled the merits of "a theatre wholly divorced from commercialism."

During this time several little theatres established themselves. These included the Toy Theatre in Boston (1912); the Chicago Little Theatre (1912); the Neighborhood Playhouse in New York (1915); the Provincetown Players in Massachusetts (1915); the Detroit Arts and Crafts Theatre (1916); and the Washington Square Players (1918). By 1917 there were 50 little theatres, most of which had less than 100 seats and depended upon volunteers for labor and subscribers for financial support. By 1925 almost 2,000 community or little theatres were registered with the Drama League of America. In her essay *"Theatre Arts Monthly" and the Construction of the Modern American Theatre Audience,* Dorothy Chansky observed that "The common goals of all these projects were to get Americans to see American theatre as art and not as mere frivolity."

Eventually, drama programs were introduced into colleges and universities. In 1903 George Pierce Baker taught the first course for playwrights at Radcliffe College and by 1925 he had established the Yale School of Drama, which provided professional theatre training. Graduates of Baker's program included such noted theatre artists as playwright Eugene O'Neill and designer Robert Edmund Jones. In 1914, Thomas Wood Stevens instituted the country's first degree-granting program in theatre at the Carnegie Institute of Technology. And by 1940, theatre education was widely accepted at many universities in the United States.

Community theatre was also aided by government support. As part of F. D. Roosevelt's Works Progress Administration (WPA), The Federal Theatre Project was established in 1935. Headed by Hallie Flanagan Davis, the project employed 10,000 persons in 40 states. During this time 1,000 productions were staged and more than half were free to the public. Despite its mandate to provide "free, adult, uncensored theatre," the political tone of some productions eventually alienated members of Congress and funding was discontinued in 1939. In 1965, however, the federal government established the National Endowment for the Arts (NEA) and also facilitated states in establishing individual arts councils. This, coupled with the inclusion of theatres as non-profit institutions, helped many community theatres remain operational. By 1990, the NEA's budget was cut drastically, but community theatres continued to thrive at the end of the twentieth century despite economic hardships.

Although the artistic ideals of the "Little Theatre" movement have been assumed by larger, professional regional theaters, the drive to produce theatre as a voluntary community activity remains solely in the realm of the community theatre. Though most community theatres no longer feature daring experimental works—offering instead local productions of popular plays and musicals—community theatres remain the most common source for community involvement in the theatrical arts.

—Michael Najjar

FURTHER READING:

Brockett, Oscar G. *History of the Theatre.* 7th ed. New York, Allyn and Bacon, 1995.

Burleigh, Louise. *The Community Theatre.* Boston, Little Brown, 1917.

Chansky, Dorothy. "Theatre Arts Monthly and the Construction of the Modern American Audience." *Journal of American Drama and Theatre.* Vol. 10, Winter 1998, 51-75.

Gard, Robert E., and Gertrude S. Burley. *Community Theatre: Idea and Achievement.* Westport, Connecticut, Greenwood Press, 1975.

Henderson, Mary C. *Theater in America: 250 Years of Plays, Players, and Productions.* New York, Harry N. Abrams, 1996.

Macgowan, Kenneth. *Footlights Across America: Towards a National Theater.* New York, Harcourt, Brace, 1929.

MacKaye, Percy. *The Playhouse and the Play: Essays.* New York, Mitchell Kennerley, 1909.

Young, John Wray. *Community Theatre: A Manual for Success.* New York, Samuel French, 1971.

Como, Perry (1912—)

Crooner Perry Como rose to become one of the dominant American male vocalists of the 1940s and 1950s, and retained a rare degree of popularity over the decades that followed. He achieved his particular fame for the uniquely relaxed quality of his delivery that few have managed to emulate—indeed, so relaxed was he that his detractors considered the effect of his smooth, creamy baritone soporific rather than soothing, and a television comedian once parodied him as singing from his bed.

Born Pierino Como in Canonsburg, Pennsylvania, the seventh of 13 children of Italian immigrants, Como began learning the barber trade as a child, with the intention of buying his own shop as early as his teens. Forced by his mill-worker father to finish high school, he finally set up his own barber shop in 1929. In 1934 he auditioned as a vocalist with a minor orchestra, and sang throughout the Midwest for the next three years, before joining the Ted Weems Orchestra. The orchestra thrived until Weems disbanded it in 1943 when he joined the army, but by then Como had developed quite a following through the years of touring and performing on radio, and his effortless baritone was a popular feature of Ted Weems's 78 rpm records. CBSrecruited Como to radio, thus starting him on what proved to be one of the most successful and long-running solo vocal careers of the

Perry Como

century. He also became a highly popular nightclub performer, and signed a recording contract with RCA Victor. Several of his singles sold over two million copies, one over three million, and he had many Top Ten and several number one hits over the years.

By late 1944 Perry Como had his own thrice-weekly radio show, *Supper Club,* on CBS, which from 1948 on was renamed *The Perry Como Show* and broadcast simultaneously on radio and television. He became one of the most popular of TV stars, keeping that show until 1963, and then hosting *The Kraft Music Hall* every few weeks until 1967. One of his noteworthy contributions to music as a radio showman was to invite Nat "King" Cole, R&B group The Ravens, and other black entertainers to guest on his program when most shows were still segregated, or featured blacks only in subservient roles.

In 1943 Como was signed to a motion picture contract by Twentieth Century-Fox. He appeared in *Something For The Boys* (1944), *Doll Face* (1945), *If I'm Lucky* (1946), and, at MGM, one of a huge all-star musical line-up in the Rodgers and Hart biopic, *Words and Music* (1948), but did not pursue a film career further, preferring to remain entirely himself, singing and playing host to musical shows. Como's best-selling singles included "If I Loved You," "Till the End of Time," "Don't Let the Stars Get In Your Eyes," "If," "No Other Love," "Wanted," "Papa Loves Mambo," Hot Diggity," "Round and Round," and "Catch a Falling Star"—for which he won a Grammy Award in 1958 for best male vocal performance. As well as his numerous chart-topping successes, he earned many gold discs, and recorded dozens of albums over the years, which continued to sell very well when the market for his singles tailed off towards the end of the 1950s. In 1968, however, he was approached to sing the theme song from *Here Come the Brides,* a popular ABC program. The resulting "Seattle" was only a minor hit, but it got Perry Como back on the pop charts after a four-year absence, and his singles career further revived in 1970 with "It's Impossible," which reached number ten on the general charts and number one on the Adult Contemporary charts.

After the 1960s, Como chose to ease himself away from television to spend his later years in his Florida home. Nevertheless, he continued to tour the United States twice a year well into the 1990s, enjoying popularity with an older audience. In 1987 he was a Kennedy Center honoree, and was among the inductees into the Television Academy Hall of Fame a few years later. Few performers have enjoyed such lasting success.

—David Lonergan

FURTHER READING:

Brooks, Tim, and Earle Marsh. *The Complete Directory to Prime Time Network TV Shows.* 5th Ed. New York, Ballantine Books, 1992.

Nite, Norm N. *Rock On Almanac.* 2nd Ed. New York, Harper Collins, 1992.

Whitburn, Joel. *The Billboard Book of Top 40 Hits.* 6th Ed. New York, Billboard Books, 1996.

Compact Discs

With the 1983 mass market introduction of CDs (compact discs), the face of the music recording and retail industry changed dramatically. As the price of compact disc players tumbled from $1,500 to $500 and below, CDs were quickly adopted by music consumers and pushed the long-playing vinyl record virtually off the market.

CDs offered extremely high sound quality, free from the scratches or needle dust "noise" found on vinyl records. Compact discs were the first introduction of digital technology to the general public. Records and tapes had been recorded using analog technology. Digital recording samples sounds and represents them as a series of numbers encoded in binary form and stored on the disc's data surface. The CD player's laser light reads this data and when it is converted back into an electric signal, it is then amplified and played through headphones or loudspeakers. On a CD nothing except light touches the disc with no wear to the recording. In addition to the superior sound of CDs, the new technology also allowed any song, or any part of a song, to be accessed quickly. Most CD players could be programmed to play specific songs, omit songs, or reorder them, providing a "customization" previously unavailable with cassette tapes or records.

While the portability of cassette tapes—with hand-held cassette players like the Sony Walkman and the ubiquity of cassette players in automobiles—slowed the domination of CDs in the market, manufacturers quickly produced products to offer the superior sound quality, flexibility, and longevity of CDs in automobiles and for personal use. By the end of the century, CD players that could hold several CDs at a time were installed in automobiles and people could carry personal CD players to listen to their favorite music with headphones while exercising. Although manufacturers and record companies had for the most part stopped manufacturing both cassette players and prerecorded tapes, cassette tapes continued to be used in home recording and in automobiles. By the late 1990s, cassettes were no longer a viable format for prerecorded popular music in the United States although they remained the most used format for sound recording worldwide.

The physical size of CDs altered the nature of liner notes and album covers. The large size of LP covers had long offered a setting for contemporary graphic design and artwork, but the smaller size of the CD package, or "jewel box," made CD "cover art" an oxymoron. Liner notes and song lyrics became minuscule as producers tried to fit their material into 5-by-5 inch booklets. The "boxed set," a collection of two or more CDs in a longer cardboard box, became popular as retrospectives for musicians and groups, collecting all of a musician or groups' output including rare and unreleased material with a booklet of extensive notes and photographs. Ironically, the average playing time of a CD was more than 70 minutes but most albums continued to hold about 40 minutes of music, the amount available on LPs.

Though the long-playing records were technologically obsolete and no longer stocked on the shelves of major music retailers, they were still found in stores specializing in older recordings and used by rap and hip-hop performers who scratched and mixed records to make their music. LPs also experienced a minor resurgence in 1998 from sales to young people interested in the "original" sound of vinyl. Nevertheless, the CD had become the dominant medium for new music by the end of the century.

—Jeff Ritter

FURTHER READING:

Millard, Andre. *America on Record: A History of Recorded Sound.* Cambridge University Press, 1995.

Concept Album

The concept album, initially defined as an LP (long-playing record) recording wherein the songs were unified by a dramatic idea instead of being disparate entities with no common theme, became a form of expression in popular music in the mid-1960s, thanks to The Beatles. Their 1967 release of *Sergeant Pepper's Lonely Hearts Club Band* is generally recognized as the first concept album, although ex-Beatle Paul McCartney has cited *Freak Out!*, an album released in 1966 by Frank Zappa and the Mothers of Invention, as a major influence on the conceptual nature of *Sergeant Pepper*. During the rest of the decade, the concept album remained the province of British artists. The Rolling Stones made an attempt—half-hearted, according to many critics—at aping the Beatles' artistic achievement with *Their Satanic Majesties Request* (1967). Other British rock bands, notably The Kinks and The Who, were able to bring new insights into the possible roles of the concept album in popular music, and it is at this point that the hard and fast definition of the concept album came to be slightly more subjective.

The Kinks, in a series of albums released in the late 1960s, mythologized the perceived decline of British working class values. The songs on these albums told the stories of representative characters and gave the albums on which they appeared conceptual continuity. If the lyrics were conceptually driven, the music was still straightforward rock 'n' roll. The Who, however, experimented with the form of the music as well as the lyrics, creating a conceptual structure unlike anything that had come before in rock music. Songwriter Pete Townshend was largely responsible for the band's best known work, *Tommy* (1969), also popularly known as the first "rock opera." This allegorical story of the title character, a "deaf, dumb and blind kid" who finds spiritual salvation in rock music and leads others towards the same end, was communicated as much through the lyrics as by the complex and classically-derived musical themes and motifs that appeared throughout the album's four sides.

Tommy was The Who's most ambitious and successful conceptual effort, but it was not the last. *Quadrophenia*, recorded in 1973, used the same style of recurring themes and motifs, but the characterization and storytelling in the lyrics was considerably more opaque than its predecessor. Both these works were adapted into films, and *Tommy* became a musical stage production in the early 1990s. Largely due to *Tommy*'s popularity, the concept album became synonymous with rock operas and rock and roll musical productions. The recordings of late 1960s and early 1970s works such as *Hair, Godspell,* and *Jesus Christ Superstar* are commonly referred to as concept albums, further broadening the scope of their definition.

The burgeoning faction of popular music known as progressive rock, which gained momentum in the late 1960s and early 1970s, embraced the form of the concept album and used it as a means to explore ever more high-flown and ambitious topics. Although the classical portion of the album did not necessarily tie into the concept, The Moody Blues nevertheless used the London Symphony Orchestra to aid in the recording of *Days of Future Passed* (1967), an album consisting entirely of songs that dealt with the philosophical nature of time. This work marked the concept album's transition from simply telling a story to actually being able to examine topics that were heretofore considered too lofty to be approached through the medium of rock music. The excesses to which critics accused progressive rock groups of going also tainted the image of the concept album, making it synonymous with pretentiousness in the minds of most contemporary

music fans. With such records as Jethro Tull's send-up of organized religion in *Aqualung* (1971) and *A Passion Play* (1973), Genesis' *The Lamb Lies Down on Broadway* (1974), an allegory of existential alienation, and Yes' *Tales from Topographic Oceans* (1974), a sprawling, overblown musical rendering of *Autobiography of a Yogi*, the concept album reached an absurd level of pomposity. When progressive rock became déclassé in the punk era of the late 1970s, the concept album was recognized as the symbol of its cultural and artistic excesses.

The concept album did not die out completely with the demise of progressive rock, just as it never was solely the province of that genre despite common misconceptions. Ambitious and brave, singer-songwriters periodically returned to this form throughout the late 1970s and the following decades. Notable among post-progressive rock concept albums were Dan Fogelberg's *The Innocent Age* (1981), Kate Bush's *Hounds of Love* (1985), Elvis Costello's *The Juliet Letters* (1993), and Liz Phair's *Exile in Guyville* (1993), a song-by-song response to the Rolling Stones' *Exile on Main Street*. A curious attribute of these latter day concept albums were their ability to produce popular songs that could be enjoyed on their own terms, apart from the overall conceptual nature of the albums to which they belonged.

Concept albums can be seen to embody two similar but separate camps: the epic, grandiose albums conceived by progressive rock groups, and the more subtle conceptually-based albums created by singer-songwriters who tended to veer away from what was considered to be the mainstream. These singer-songwriters took the baton proffered by The Beatles and The Who in a slightly different direction. Albums like Laura Nyro's *Christmas and the Beads of Sweat* (1970), Van Dyke Parks' *Song Cycle* (1968), and Lou Reed's *Berlin* (1973) directly influenced most of the post-progressive rock albums that were produced from the mid-1970s on.

Other genres of popular music were also infiltrated by the concept album phenomenon. Soul music in the 1970s was one example, evidenced by works such as Marvin Gaye's *What's Going On* (1971) and *Here, My Dear* (1978), Sly and the Family Stone's *There's a Riot Goin' On* (1971), and the outrageous science fiction storylines of several Funkadelic albums. Curtis Mayfield's soundtrack to the movie *Superfly* (1972) also deserves mention, having achieved an artistic success far beyond that of the film. Country and Western was another genre of popular music with its share of concept albums. It could be argued, according to author Robert W. Butts, that some Country and Western artists were attempting to make concept albums long before The Beatles came along; these artists displayed a desire to make their albums more meaningful than "a simple collection of tunes which would hopefully provide a hit or two." It was in the 1970s, however, with "the conscious and successful exploitation of the concept of a concept," according to Butts, that artists like Willie Nelson, Emmylou Harris, and Johnny Cash fully realized the potential of the concept album within the Country and Western genre.

While the concept album in all these genres may have served to raise the level of the respective art forms, the concept album in the cultural consciousness of the late twentieth century exists mainly as a symbol of excess and pseudo-intellectualism in popular music, forever branded by its association with progressive rock. The concept album did not cease to exist as a form of musical expression, but never again did it enjoy the hold it had on the imagination of record buyers, who viewed the phenomenon in the late 1960s and 1970s with excitement, and who eventually became disenchanted with its further developments.

—Dan Coffey

FURTHER READING:

Butts, Robert W. ''More than a Collection of Songs: The Concept Album in Country Music.'' *Mid-America Folklore.* Vol. 16, No. 2, 1988, 90-99.

Covach, John, and Graeme M. Boone, editors. *Understanding Rock: Essays in Musical Analysis.* New York, Oxford University Press, 1997.

Schafer, William J. *Rock Music: Where it's Been, What it Means, Where it's Going.* Minneapolis, Augsburg Publishing House, 1972.

Stump, Paul. *The Music's All That Matters: A History of Progressive Rock.* London, Quartet Books, 1997.

Whiteley, Sheila. *The Space Between the Notes.* New York, Routledge, 1992.

Conceptual Art

Conceptual art transformed the art world beginning in the 1960s by shifting the focus of the work from the art object itself to the ideas and concepts that went into its creation. Such works rose to prominence as a reaction to Western formalist art and to the art writings of Clement Greenberg, Roger Fry, and Clive Bell, theorists who championed the significance of form and modernism. Not far removed from the ideas of the Dadist movement of the early twentieth century and artist Marcel Duchamp's ready-mades, conceptualism insists that ideas, and the implementations of them, become the art itself; often there is an absence of an actual object. Conceptual art worked in the spirit of postmodernism that pervaded post-1960s American culture.

Joseph Kosuth, one of the primary participants and founders of the conceptual art movement, first formulated the ideas of the movement in his writings of 1969, ''Art After Philosophy, I and II''. Along with Sol Lewitt's 1967 treatise ''Paragraphs on Conceptual Art'' (which coined the term ''conceptual art''), this article defined the basic ideas of the movement. In general, conceptual art has a basis in political, social, and cultural issues; conceptual art reacts to the moment. Many conceptual art pieces have addressed the commercialization of the art world; rebelling against the commodification of art, artists employed temporary installations or ephemeral ideas that were not saleable. As a result, all art, not just conceptual pieces, has since moved outside of traditional exhibition spaces such as galleries and museums and into the public sphere, broadening the audience. The expansion of viable art venues allowed for a widening scope of consideration of worthy artworks. With the prompting of conceptual artists, photography, bookworks, performance, and installation art all were validated as important art endeavors.

Conceptual artists such as Sol LeWitt, Joseph Kosuth, John Baldassari, and the British group Art and Language created works that were self-referential; the work became less about the artist and the creative process and more about the concepts behind the work. Contemporary artists like Barbara Kruger and Jenny Holzer adapted such tenets from earlier works, and used them in a more pointed way

in the 1980s and 1990s. Their work, along with many other contemporary artists' work, addresses specific political and social issues such as race, gender, and class. Such works attempt to reach beyond an educated art audience to a general population, challenging all who encounter it to reevaluate commonly held stereotypes.

—Jennifer Jankauskas

FURTHER READING:

Colpitt, France, and Phyllis Plous. *Knowledge: Aspects of Conceptual Art.* Seattle, University of Washington Press, 1992.

Kosuth, Joseph. ''Art After Philosophy, I and II.'' *Studio International.* October 1969.

LeWitt, Sol. ''Paragraphs on Conceptual Art,'' *Artforum.* Summer 1967.

Meyer, Ursula. *Conceptual Art.* New York, E.P. Dutton, 1972.

Morgan, Robert C. *Conceptual Art: An American Perspective.* Jefferson, North Carolina, McFarland & Company, 1994.

Condé Nast

Condé Nast is the name for both a worldwide publishing company and the man who founded it. Condé Nast (1873-1942), the man, was noted for his innovative publishing theories and flair for nurturing readers and advertisers. With the purchase and upgrading of *Vogue* in 1909, he established the concept of specialized or class publications, magazines that direct their circulation to a particular group or class of people with common interests. By 1998, Condé Nast Publications, Inc. (CNP) held 17 such titles, many of which are the largest in their respective markets. Like its founder, the magazine empire is one of the most powerful purveyors of popular culture, with an average circulation of over 13 million readers a month and an actual readership of more than five times that. The company, now owned by illustrious billionaire S.I. Newhouse, continues to be the authority for many aspects of popular culture.

After purchasing *Vogue* in 1909, Condé Nast transformed its original format as a weekly society journal for New York City elites (established in 1892) to a monthly magazine devoted to fashion and beauty. Over the century, and with a series of renowned editors, *Vogue* became a preeminent fashion authority in the United States and abroad. Its dominance and innovation spanned the course of the century, from its transition to a preeminent fashion authority (under the first appointed editor, Edna Woolman Chase); to the middle of the century when *Vogue* published innovative art and experimented with modernistic formats; and during the end of the century, when editor Anna Wintour (appointed in 1988) redirected the focus of the magazine to attract a younger audience.

Condé Nast bought an interest in *House & Garden* in 1911, and four years later took it over completely. Nast transformed the magazine from an architectural journal into an authority on interior design, thereby establishing another example of a specialized publication. Around this time, Condé Nast refined his ideas about this approach to magazine publishing. In 1913 Nast told a group of merchants: ''Time and again the question of putting up fiction in *Vogue* has been brought up; those who advocated it urging with a good show of reason that the addition of stories and verse would make it easy to maintain a much larger circulation. That it would increase the *quantity* of our circulation we granted, but we were fearful of its effect on the 'class' value.''

In 1914, Nast introduced *Vanity Fair,* a magazine that became an entertaining chronicle of arts, politics, sports, and society. Over a period of 22 years, *Vanity Fair* was a Jazz Age compendium of wit and style but attracted fewer than 100,000 readers a month. Perhaps because it was too eclectic for its time, the original *Vanity Fair* eventually failed altogether (and merged with *Vogue* in 1936). After a 46-year absence, however, CNP revived the magazine in 1983, with a thick, glossy, and ''self-consciously literate'' format. After nearly a year of stumbling through an identity crisis, Newhouse brought in the 30-year-old British editor Tina Brown (who later served as editor of *The New Yorker*), who remade *Vanity Fair* into a successful guide to high-rent popular culture, featuring celebrity worship, careerism, and a glossy peek inside the upper class.

In general, Condé Nast magazines were innovative not only for their content but also for their format. In order to have the preeminent printing available at the time, Condé Nast decided to be his own printer in 1921, through the purchase of a small interest in the now defunct Greenwich, Connecticut, Arbor Press. Despite the hard times that followed the 1929 stock market crash, Condé Nast kept his magazines going in the style to which his readers were accustomed. Innovative typography and designs were introduced, and within the pages of *Vogue, Vanity Fair,* and *House & Garden,* color photographs appeared. In 1932, the first color photograph appeared on the cover of *Vogue.*

Glamour was the last magazine Condé Nast personally introduced to his publishing empire (1939), but the growth did not end there. In 1959, a controlling interest in what was now Condé Nast Publications Inc. was purchased by S.I. Newhouse. Later that same year, *Brides* became wholly owned by CNP, and CNP acquired Street & Smith Publications, Inc., which included titles such as *Mademoiselle* and the *Street & Smith's* sports annuals (*College Football, Pro Football, Baseball,* and *Basketball*). Twenty years later, *Gentleman's Quarterly* (popularly known as *GQ*) was purchased from Esquire, Inc., and *Self* was introduced. *Gourmet* was acquired in 1983, the same year that saw the revival of *Vanity Fair.* Rounding out the collection, CNP added *Condé Nast Traveler* in 1987, *Details* in 1988, *Allure* in 1991, *Architectural Digest* and *Bon Appetit* in 1993, *Womens' Sports and Fitness* (originally *Condé Nast Sports for Women*) in 1997, and *Wired* magazine in 1998. Advance Publications (the holding company that owns CNP) acquired sole ownership of *The New Yorker* in 1985, but it did not become a member of the CNP clan until 1999. In 1999, CNP moved into its international headquarters in the Condé Nast Building, located in the heart of Manhattan's Times Square. Additionally, there are number of branch offices throughout the United States for the more than 2,400 employed in CNP domestic operations.

Condé Nast's influence on American magazine publishing has been considerable, for he introduced the specialized publications that have since come to dominate the American magazine market. And CNP, with its family of popular publications claiming a total readership of over 66 million, and exposure even beyond that, has exerted a lasting influence of American culture. With such a large reach, CNP publications are a favorite of advertisers, who use the magazines pages to reach vast numbers of consumers. As a source of culture, CNP covers a variety of subjects, although none more heavily than the beauty and lifestyle industries.

—Julie Scelfo

FURTHER READING:

Fraser, Kennedy. ''Introduction.'' In *On the Edge: Images from 100 Years of Vogue.* New York, Random House, 1992.

Nast, Condé. *The Merchants' and Manufacturers' Journal of Baltimore.* June, 1913.

Nourie, Alan and Barbara Nourie. *American Mass-Market Magazines.* New York, Greenwood Press, 1990.

Peterson, Theodore. *Magazines in the Twentieth Century.* Urbana, University of Illinois Press, 1964.

Seebohm, Caroline. *The Man Who Was Vogue: The Life and Times of Condé Nast.* New York, Viking, 1982.

Tebbel, John. *The American Magazine: A Compact History.* New York, Hawthorn Books, 1969.

Tebbel, John and Mary Ellen Zuckerman. *The Magazine in America, 1741-1990.* New York, Oxford University Press, 1991.

Condoms

Once kept in the back of pharmacies, condoms have become common and familiar items in the 1980s and 1990s because of the AIDS crisis. Apart from sexual abstinence, condoms represent the safest method of preventing the transmission of the HIV virus through sexual intercourse, and, consequently, condoms figure prominently in safer-sex campaigns. The increase in demand has led to a diversified production to suit all tastes, so that condoms have been marketed not only as protective items but also as toys that can improve sex. Condoms are so ubiquitous that conservative writer Richard Panzer has despaired that we all live in a Condom Nation and a world of latex.

Condoms are as old as history: a type of modern-day condom may have been used by the Egyptians as far back as 1000 B.C. History blends with myth, and several legends record the use of primitive condoms: Minos, the king of Crete who defeated the Minotaur, is said to have had snakes and scorpions in his seed which killed all his lovers. He was told to put a sheep's bladder in their vaginas, but he opted instead to wear small bandages soaked with alum on his penis. Condoms have been discussed by writers as diverse as, to name but a few, William Shakespeare (who called it ''the Venus glove''), Madame de Sévigné, Flaubert, and the legendary lover Giacomo Casanova.

If it is difficult to come up with a date of birth for condoms, it is even more complicated, perhaps quite appropriately, to establish who fathered (or mothered) them. Popular belief attributes the invention of condoms and their name to a certain Dr. Condom, who served at the court of the British King Charles II. According to a more scientific etymology, the name derives from the Latin ''condere'' (to hide) or ''condus'' (receptacle).

Early condoms were expensive and made of natural elements such as lengths of sheep intestine sewn closed at one end and tied with a ribbon around the testicles. Modern rubber condoms were created immediately after the creation of vulcanized rubber by Charles Goodyear in the 1840s and have been manufactured with latex since the 1930s. Also called ''sheath,'' ''comebag,'' ''scumbag,'' ''cap,'' ''capote,'' ''French letter,'' or ''Port Said garter,'' a condom is a tube of thin latex rubber with one end closed or extended into a reservoir tip. In the 1980s and 1990s condoms have appeared on the market in

Workers of the Gay Men's Health Crisis hand out free Valentine's condoms and AIDS information.

different shapes, colors, flavors, lubrications, and sizes. Some are equipped with ribs, bumps, dots, or raised spirals to enhance stimulation. The safe-sex message originally associated with condoms is now being complemented by the marketing strategy claiming that using condoms is fun, and some are even intended to be used for entertainment only (and not for protection from disease or pregnancy).

Once seen as a great turn off, the condom has appeared with increasing frequency in (mainly) gay porno movies, especially, although not exclusively, in the educational safer-sex shorts produced by AIDS charities and groups of activists. As Jean Carlomusto and Gregg Bordowitz have summarized, the aim of these safer-sex shorts is to make people understand that "you can have hot sex without placing yourself at risk for AIDS." This has raised important questions about the possibility of using pornography as pedagogy. This new use of pornography as a vehicle for safer-sex involves, as safer-sex short director Richard Fung has pointed out, a "dialogue with the commercial porn industry, about the representation of both safer-sex, and racial and ethnic difference."

Looking at the dissemination of "condom discourse" one might be tempted to conclude that society has finally become more liberated. There are condom shops, condom ads, condom jokes, condom gadgets such as key-rings, condom shirts, condom pouches, condom web-sites with international condom clubs from where chocolate lovers can top off their evening with the perfect no-calorie dessert: the hot fudge condom. Yet how effective really is this "commodification of prophylaxis" (to use Gregory Woods's words) in terms of prevention and saving of human lives? Is it, in the end, just another stratagem to speak about everything else but health care and human rights?

—Luca Prono

FURTHER READING:

Carlomusto, Jean, and Bordowitz, Gregg. "Do It! Safer Sex Porn for Girls and Boys Comes of Age." *A Leap in the Dark.* Edited by Allan Klusacek and Ken Morrison. Montréal, Vehicule Press, 1992.

Chevalier, Eric. *The Condom: Three Thousand Years of Safer Sex.* Puffin, 1995.

Fung, Richard. "Shortcomings: Questions about Pornography as Pedagogy." *Queer Looks—Perspectives on Lesbian and Gay Film and Video.* Edited by Martha Gever, John Greyson, and Pratibha Parmar. New York, Routledge, 1993.

Panzer, Richard A. *Condom Nation—Blind Faith, Bad Science.* Westwood, Center for Educational Media, 1997.

Woods, Gregory. "We're Here, We're Queer and We're Not Going Catalogue Shopping." *A Queer Romance—Lesbians, Gay Men and Popular Culture.* Edited by Paul Burston and Colin Richardson. New York, Routledge, 1995.

Coney Island

Coney Island, with its beach, amusement parks, and numerous other attractions, became emblematic of nineteenth- and early- twentieth-century urban condition while at the same time providing relief from the enormous risks of living in a huge metropolis. On Coney Island, both morals and taste could be transgressed. This was the place where the debate between official and popular culture was first rehearsed, a debate which would characterize the twentieth century in America.

Discovered just one day before Manhattan in 1609 by explorer Henry Hudson, Coney Island is a strip of sand at the mouth of New York's natural harbor. The Canarsie Indians, its original inhabitants, had named it "Place without Shadows." In 1654 the Indian Guilaouch, who claimed to be the owner of the peninsula, traded it for guns, gunpowder, and beads, similar to the more famous sale of Manhattan. The peninsula was known under many names, but none stuck until people called it Coney Island because of the presence of an extraordinary number of coneys, or rabbits.

Coney Island, 1952.

In 1823 the first bridge which would connect Manhattan to the island was built, and Coney Island, with its natural attractions, immediately became the ideal beach resort for the ever-growing urban population of Manhattan. By the mid-nineteenth century large resort hotels had been built. Corrupt political boss John Y. McKane ruled the island, turning a blind eye to the gangsters, con men, gamblers, and prostitutes who congregated on the west end of the island. In 1865 the railroad finally allowed the metropolitan masses their weekend escape to Coney Island, and the number of visitors grew enormously, creating a great demand for entertainment and food. The hot dog was invented on Coney Island in the 1870s. In 1883 the Brooklyn Bridge made the island even more accessible to the Manhattan masses, who flocked to the island's beach, making it the most densely occupied place in the world. The urban masses demanded to be entertained, however, thus the need for pleasure became paramount in the island's development. Typical of the time, what happened on Coney Island was the attempt to conjugate the quest for pleasure and the obsession with progress.

The result was the first American "roller coaster," the Switchback Railway, built by LaMarcus Adna Thompson in 1884. In 1888, the short-lived Flip-Flap coaster, predecessor of the 1901 Loop-the-Loop, used centrifugal force to keep riders in their seats, and an amazed public paid admission to watch. By 1890 the use of electricity made it possible to create a false daytime, thus prolonging entertainment to a full twenty-four hours a day.

The nucleus of Coney Island was Captain Billy Boyton's Sea Lion Park, opened in 1895, and made popular by the first large Shoot-the-Chutes ride in America. In competition with Boyton, George C. Tilyou opened Steeplechase Park in 1897, where science and technology came together for pleasure and Victorian inhibitions were lifted. The park was centered around one of the most popular rides on Coney Island, the Steeplechase Race Course, in which four couples "raced" each other atop wheeled, wooden horses. Steeplechase Park burned in 1907, but Tilyou rebuilt and reopened it the following year, and it remained in operation until 1964.

When Boyton went broke, Frederic Thompson and Elmer Dundy took over Sea Lion Park, remodeled it and opened it as Luna Park in 1903. Luna was a thematic park where visitors could even board a huge airship and experience an imaginative journey to the moon from one hundred feet in the air. Coney Island was the testing ground for revolutionary architectural designs, and Luna Park was an architectural spectacle, a modern yet imaginary city built on thirty-eight acres and employing seventeen hundred people during the summer season, with its own telegraph office, cable office, wireless office, and telephone service. For Thompson, Luna Park was an architectural training ground before he moved to Manhattan to apply his talent to a real city. Luna Park eventually fell into neglect and burned in 1944. The land became a parking lot in 1949.

In the meantime, Senator William H. Reynolds was planning a third park on Coney Island, "the park to end all parks." The new park was aptly called Dreamland. In Reynolds's words, this was "the first time in the History of Coney Island Amusement that an effort has been made to provide a place of Amusement that appeals to all classes." Ideology had got hold of entertainment. Opening in 1904, Dreamland was located by the sea and was noticeable for its lack of color—everything was snow white. The general metaphor was that Dreamland represented a sort of underwater Atlantis. There were detailed reconstructions of various natural disasters—the eruption of Vesuvius at Pompeii, the San Francisco earthquake, the burning of

Rome—as well as a simulated ride in a submarine, two Shoot-the-Chute rides, and, interestingly, the Incubator Hospital, where premature babies were nursed. Other Dreamland attractions were the Blue Dome of Creation, the "Largest Dome in the World," representing the universe; the "End of the World according to the Dream of Dante"; three theaters; a simulated flight over Manhattan—before the first airplane had flown; a huge model of Venice; a complete replica of Switzerland; and the Japanese Teahouse. One of the most important structures of Dreamland was the Beacon Tower, 375 feet high and illuminated by one hundred thousand electric lights, visible from a distance of more than thirty miles. Dreamland was a success insofar as it reproduced almost any kind of experience and human sensation. In May 1911, just before a more efficient fire-fighting apparatus was due to be installed, a huge fire broke out fanned by a strong sea wind. In only three hours Dreamland was completely destroyed. It was Coney's last spectacle. Manhattan took over as the place of architectural invention.

In 1919, Coney Island seemed to regain a sparkle of its old glory when the idea circulated of building a gigantic Palace of Joy—a sort of American Versailles for the people—which would be a pier containing five hundred private rooms, two thousand private bath houses, an enclosed swimming pool, a dance hall, and a skating rink. Sadly, the Palace of Joy was never built. Soon, the main attraction of Coney Island became again its beach, an overcrowded strip of land. In the hand of Commissioner Robert Moses, the island fell under the jurisdiction of the Parks Department. In 1957, the New York Aquarium was established on the island, a modernist building which had nothing of the revolutionary, dreamlike structure of the buildings of Reynolds's era. By now 50 percent of Coney Island's surface had become parks again. Nature's sweet revenge.

—Anna Notaro

FURTHER READING:

Creedmor, Walter. "The Real Coney Island." *Munsey's Magazine.* August 1899.

Denison, Lindsay. "The Biggest Playground in the World." *Munsey's Magazine.* August 1905.

Griffin, Al. *"Step Right Up, Folks!"* Chicago, Henry Regnery, 1974.

History of Coney Island. New York, Burroughs & Co., 1904.

Huneker, James. *The New Cosmopolis.* New York, 1915.

Long Island Historical Society Library. *Guide to Coney Island.* Long Island Historical Society Library, n.d.

McCullough, Edo. *Good Old Coney Island.* New York, Charles Scribner's Sons, 1957.

Pilat, Oliver, and Jo Ransom. *Sodom by the Sea.* New York, Doubleday, 1941.

Confession Magazines

During their first 175 years of existence, American magazines preached long and occasionally in loud tone on personal morality, but rare was the published foray into the real lives of lower-class Americans. That oversight ended in 1919 with the introduction of *True Stories*, the first of what came to be known as confession magazines. Founded by health and physical fitness zealot Bernarr

Macfadden, *True Stories* "had the conscious ring of public confession, such as is heard in a Salvation Army gathering, or in an old-fashioned testimony meeting of Southern camp religionists," according to Macfadden's first biographer Fulton Oursler.

It and other confession magazines were "a medium for publishing the autobiographies of the unknown," as one editor explained, a substitute among the poor for lawyers, doctors, and educators. Although *True Stories* eventually reached a circulation of 2.5 million during the 1930s, it cost less to produce than most other magazines, and therefore earned as much as $10,000 a day for its founder. *True Stories* and other confession magazines also provided a valuable outlet for otherwise disconnected people to learn appropriate private and public social behavior. During times of rapid change, these magazines helped women to re-establish their identities through the experiences of other women like themselves. Most importantly, in an era when sex was rarely mentioned in public, the confession magazines taught both women and men that sex was natural, healthy, and enjoyable under appropriate circumstances.

The first American magazines were written for upper-class men. Beginning in the 1820s, sections and eventually titles were aimed at upper-class women, but they were written in a highly moralistic tone because women were considered to be the cultural custodians and moral regulators of society. Belles lettres, popular moralistic fiction, became the staple of mid-nineteenth century women's magazines such as *Godey's Ladies Book* and *Peterson's.* Writers sentimentalized about courtship and marriage but offered little practical information on sex to readers. Another generation of women's magazines appeared after the Civil War, including *McCall's, Ladies Home Journal,* and *Good Housekeeping.* These magazines attracted massive circulations, but were focused on the rapidly changing domestic duties of women, still carried a highly moralistic tone, and had little to say about sex. Even into the twentieth century, the advertising and editorial content of women's magazines reflected prosperity, social status, and consumerism; hardly the core problems of everyday existence for the lower classes.

The first confession magazine publisher was born August 16, 1868, in Mill Springs, Missouri. Before Bernarr Macfadden was ten, his father had died of an alcohol-related disease and his mother from tuberculosis. Relatives predicted the sickly, weak boy would die young as well. Shifted from relative to relative, the young Macfadden dropped out of school and worked at an assortment of laborer jobs, learning how to set newspaper type in 1885. But he was drawn into the world of physical culture as a teen. He studied gymnastics and physical fitness in St. Louis and developed his body and health as he coached and taught others. To raise money to promote his ideas on exercise and diet, he wrestled professionally and promoted touring wrestling matches. In 1899 he founded *Physical Culture*, a magazine that was devoted to "health, strength, vitality, muscular development, and the general care of the body." It was the forerunner of contemporary health and fitness publications. Macfadden argued that "weakness is a crime" and offered instruction on physical development. Macfadden's diets were opposed by medical authorities and the nude or nearly nude photographs in his magazine and advertising circulars came under the scrutiny of obscenity crusader Anthony Comstock and his followers. Macfadden was fined $2,000 for a *Physical Culture* article in 1907 and the magazine is considered to be the start of the nude magazine industry.

Physical Culture was immensely popular, climbing to a circulation of 340,000 by the early 1930s. Macfadden made large profits with it and other publishing ventures including books such as *What a*

Young Husband Ought to Know and *What a Young Woman Ought to Know*. His wife Mary later claimed that she suggested he expand his publishing horizons beyond physical fitness around the time of World War I. She had read the thousands of letters to the editor that poured into *Physical Culture* detailing why punching bags, lifting dumbbells, and doing deep knee bends did not always change an individual's love life. Other letters revealed how so-called fallen women who had discovered physical culture had found new lives for themselves as wives and mothers. "The folly of transgression, the terrible effects of ignorance, the girls who had not been warned by wise parents—a whole series of tragedies out of the American soil were falling, day after day, on the desk of [*Physical Culture*'s] editor," Macfadden's biographer Fulton Oursler explained.

In May 1919, the first issue of *True Story* appeared with the motto "Truth is stranger than fiction." For 20 cents a copy, twice the price of most other magazines, readers received 12 stories with titles such as "A Wife Who Awoke in Time" and "My Battle with John Barleycorn." Most of the protagonists were sympathetic characters, innocent, lower-class women who appealed to a feminine readership. Instead of drawings, live models were photographed in a clinch of love or clad in pajamas while a man brandished a pistol, adding more realism to the confessions. The first cover featured a man and woman looking longingly at each other with the caption, "And their love turned to hated!" The magazine also offered "$1,000.00 for your life romance," a cheap price compared to what many magazines paid for professional contributions. The result was an immediate success, selling 60,000 issues, and the circulation quickly climbed into the millions.

Between 1922 and 1926, Macfadden capitalized on *True Stories* by producing a host of related titles, including *True Romances*, *True Love and Romances*, and *True Experiences*. Young Hollywood hopefuls such as Norma Shearer, Jean Arthur, and Frederic March were used in *True Story* photographs. Movie shorts featuring dramatizations of the magazine's stories were shown in theaters simultaneously with publication. A weekly "True Story Hour" started on network radio in 1928, and editions were published in England, Holland, France, Germany, and the Scandinavian countries. Imitators quickly appeared, each using some combination of the words true, story, romance, confessions, and love. The most successful was *True Confessions*, founded by Wilford H. Fawcettin 1922, who was a one-time police reporter for the *Minneapolis Journal*. Fawcett's first publication, *Captain Billy's Whiz Bang*, started as a mimeographed naughty joke and pun sheet in 1919, and went on to become the male magazine metaphor for the 1920s decline of morality and flaunting of sexual immodesty. *Captain Billy's Whiz Bang* was memorialized in fellow Minnesotan Meredith Willson's 1962 Broadway musical *Music Man* in a recitation attached to the song "Trouble." *True Confessions* attracted a circulation in the millions and became the cornerstone of Fawcett Publications, which eventually included titles such as *Mechanix Illustrated* and comic books like *Captain America*.

By its own 1941 account, *True Story* and its imitators were magazines for the lower classes, readers too unsophisticated, uneducated, and poor to be of interest to other magazines or advertisers. They "made readers of the semi-literate" as the wife of one editor said. Still, a rise in the standard of living during the 1920s meant that lower-class readers finally had enough income to buy magazines. The confession magazines gave them a forum to air their concerns and share solutions in ways not possible in any other publications. Magazine historian Theodore Peterson maintained that confession

magazines were not a new innovation, just another spin on the old rule that sex and crime sell. Before confession magazines there was sob sister journalism, the sentimentalized reporting of crimes of passion and other moral tales in newspapers. Before newspapers, there were fictionalized first-person narratives detailing the temptations of young women such as *Moll Flanders*. And before novels there were seventeenth-century broadsides, written in the first person with a strong moralizing tone, describing the seductions and murders of scullery maids and mistresses. Bernarr Macfadden and his wife Mary simply rediscovered an old formula and applied it the magazine industry.

The mainstream press was predictably critical of confession magazines. At their best, they were considered mindless entertainment for the masses. At their worst, confession magazines parlayed to the worst common denominator of the lower classes; sex and reproduction. *Time* maintained that *True Story* set "the fashion in sex yarns." A writer in *Harper's* complained that "to pound into empty heads month after month the doctrine of comparative immunity cannot be particularly healthy" and that "it is impossible to believe that the chronic reader of 'confessions' has much traffic with good books." Interestingly, a 1936 survey of *True Story* readers showed that a majority believed in birth control, thought wives shouldn't work, opposed divorce, and were religious yet tolerant of other faiths. A study of *True Story* between 1920 and 1985 revealed that the magazine reinforced traditional notions of motherhood and femininity, and challenged rather than supported patriarchal class relations.

Macfadden continued to champion genuine reader confessionals in his publications during the 1920s and ordered that manuscripts should be edited for grammatical mistakes only. Subsequent editors established more control over their productions, beginning with *True Stories*' William Jordan Rapp in 1926. Professionals were hired to rewrite and create stories, especially after Macfadden was successfully sued for libel in 1927. Still, a survey of 41 *True Story* contributors in 1983 revealed that 16 had written of personal experiences, had never published a story before, and did not consider themselves to be professional writers. Macfadden lost interest in his confession magazines, becoming involved in the founding of the *New York Daily Graphic* newspaper in 1924, "the *True Confessions* of the newspaper world." The newspaper failed in 1932, losing millions of dollars but it created a sensation among lower-class newspaper readers.

By 1935, the combined circulation of Macfadden's magazines was 7.3 million, more than any other magazine publisher, but he was forced to sell his holdings in 1941 following accusations that he had used company funds to finance unsuccessful political campaigns, including a bid for the Republican presidential nomination in 1936. Macfadden died a pauper in 1955, succumbing to jaundice aggravated by fasting, failing to live 150 years as he had predicted. *True Stories* took a more service-oriented path after World War II, offering food, fashion, beauty, and even children's features. The major confession magazines had an aggregate circulation of more than 8.5 million in 1963. The successors of Macfadden Publications acquired the major contenders to *True Stories; True Confessions* in 1963 and *Modern Romances* in 1978, and continue to publish confessional magazines, but circulation and advertising revenues have dropped. Soap operas, made-for-television movies, and cable channels such as Lifetime and the Romance Channel compete for potential readers along with supermarket tabloids such as the *National Enquirer*. As well, lower-class readers are better educated and have more options for guidance or help in their personal lives. In the end, the ultimate legacy of the confession magazines, beyond giving readers information on sex and appropriate social behavior, will be that they truly put the word mass in mass media.

—Richard Digby-Junger

FURTHER READING:

Cantor, Muriel G., and Elizabeth Jones. "Creating Fiction for Women." *Communication Research.* January 1983, 111-37.

Emery, Michael, and Edwin Emery. *The Press and America: An Interpretive History of the Mass Media.* 7th ed. Englewood Cliffs, N.J., Prentice-Hall, 1992, 283-86.

Fabian, Ann. "Making a Commodity of Truth: Speculations on the Career of Bernarr Macfadden." *American Literary History.* Summer 1993, 51-76.

History and Magazines. New York, True Story Magazine, 1941, 42.

Hunt, William R. *Body Love: The Amazing Career of Bernarr Macfadden.* Bowling Green, Ohio, Bowling Green University Popular Press, 1989.

Hutto, Dena. *"True Story."* In *American Mass-Market Magazines,* edited by Alan Nourie and Barbara Nourie. New York, Greenwood Press, 1990, 510-19.

Macfadden, Mary Williamson, and Emile Gauvreau. *Dumbbells and Carrot Strips: The Story of Bernarr Macfadden.* New York, Henry Holt and Co., 1953.

Oursler, Fulton. *The True Story of Bernarr Macfadden.* New York, Lewis Copeland, 1929, 213-14.

Peterson, Theodore. *Magazines in the Twentieth Century.* Urbana, University of Illinois Press, 294-303.

Simonds, Wendy. "Confessions of Loss: Maternal Grief in *True Story,* 1920-1985." *Gender and Society.* Spring 1988, 149-71.

Sonenschein, David. "Love and Sex in Romance Magazines." *Journal of Popular Culture.* Spring 1970, 398-409.

Taft, William H. "Bernarr Macfadden: One of a Kind." *Journalism Quarterly.* Winter 1968, 627-33.

Wilkinson, Joseph F. "Look at Me." *Smithsonian Magazine.* December, 1997, 136-44.

Yagoda, Ben. "The True Story of Bernarr Macfadden." *American Heritage.* December, 1981, 22-9.

Coniff, Ray (1916—)

Through a unique combination of genuine musical talent fused with a keen sense of both commercial trends and evolving recording technologies of the 1950s, arranger/conductor/instrumentalist Ray Coniff emerged as one of the most popular and commercially successful musicians during the dawn of the stereo age in the late 1950s. Coniff carried on the big band sound long beyond the music's original heyday in the 1940s, and charted 53 albums between 1957 and 1974, including two million-sellers, and 13 other LPs that reached the Top Ten and/or went gold.

Coniff was born into a musical family in Attleboro, Massachusetts, on November 6, 1916, and followed in his father's musical footsteps when he became the lead trombonist of the Attleboro High School dance band (in which he also gained his first arranging experience). After graduating in 1934 he pursued a musical career in Boston, and in 1936 moved to New York where he became involved with the emerging swing movement of the late 1930s and early 1940s, playing, arranging, and recording for such top names as Bunny Berigan, Bob Crosby, Glen Gray, and Artie Shaw. With the advent of World War II, Coniff spent two years in the army arranging for the Armed Forces Radio Service, and upon his discharge in 1946 continued arranging for Shaw, Harry James, and Frank DeVol.

But by the late 1940s the Big Band swing era in which Coniff had made his first mark was coming to an end, and, as one source put it, "Unable to accept the innovations of bop, he left music briefly around 1950." While freelancing at various nonmusical jobs to support his wife and three children, Coniff also made a personal study of the most popular and commercially successful recordings of the day in an effort to develop what he hoped might prove a new and viable pop sound. His efforts paid off in 1955 when Coniff was hired by Columbia Records. At Columbia he was soon providing instrumental backup for chart-toppers by the label's best artists, among them Don Cherry's "Band of Gold," which hit the Top Ten in January 1956, Guy Mitchell's "Singing the Blues," Marty Robbins's "A White Sport Coat," and two million-sellers by Johnny Mathis.

His singles arrangements led to Coniff's first album under his own name: *S'Wonderful!* (1956) sold half a million copies, stayed in the Top 20 for nine months, and garnered Coniff the Cash Box vote for "Most promising up-and-coming band leader of 1957." Coniff's unique yet highly commercial sound proved irresistible to both listeners and dancers (and stereophiles) and *S'Wonderful!* launched a long series of LPs, the appeal of which has endured into the digital age.

The classic sound of the Ray Coniff Orchestra and Singers was a simple, but unique, and instantly recognizable blend of instrumentals and choral voices doubling the various orchestral choirs with "oooos," "ahs," and Coniff's patented "da-da-das." His imaginative arrangements were grounded in the solid 1940s big band sound of his early years, while now placing a greater emphasis on recognizable melody lines only slightly embellished by improvisation. Touches of exotic instrumentation such as harp and clavinet sometimes also found their way into the orchestrations. This jazz-tinged but accessibly commercial sound was backed up by danceable, sometimes electrified modern beats derived in equal parts from the classic shuffle rhythms which Coniff made his own, and more contemporary Latin and rock-derived rhythms. Coniff's initially wordless backup chorus soon graduated to actual song lyrics and, as the Ray Coniff Singers, recorded many successful albums on their own.

The emergence of commercial stereo in the late 1950s emphatically influenced the new Coniff sound, and his Columbia albums brilliantly utilized the new stereophonic, multitrack techniques. Even today they remain showcases of precise, highly defined, and processed stereo sound. Coniff's popularity on records during this period led to live performances, and with his popular "Concert in Stereo" tours the maestro was among the first artists to accurately duplicate the electronically enhanced studio sound of his recordings in a live concert hall setting.

Coniff's best and most enduringly listenable albums date from the period of his initial popularity on Columbia Records in the late 1950s and early 1960s: among them, *Say It with Music* (1960), probably his best and glossiest instrumental album, and *It's the Talk of the Town* (1959) and *So Much in Love* (1961), both with the Ray Coniff Singers. These albums and much of Coniff's original Columbia repertory were drawn mostly from the popular, Broadway, and movie song standards that also had been favored in the big band era.

Coniff also recorded two *Concert in Rhythm* albums showcasing rhythmic pop adaptations of melodies by Tchaikovsky, Chopin, Puccini, and other classical composers. But as his popularity and repertory grew, an increasing emphasis was placed on the contemporary Hit Parade. "*Memories Are Made of This*" (1963), with its calculated awareness of "Top 40" teen hits, was a prophetic album in this respect. By the late 1960s Coniff exclusively recorded contemporary songs, and two vocal albums, *It Must Be Him,* and *Honey,* both went gold.

Coniff's sales fell off after 1962 but were revived in 1966 by the release of *Somewhere My Love.* The album's title tune was a vocal adaptation of French composer Maurice Jarre's orchestral "Lara's Theme" from the popular 1965 film version of the Boris Pasternak novel *Doctor Zhivago,* and the LP won Coniff a Grammy, hitting No. 1 on both the pop and easy listening charts. While *Somewhere* put Coniff back on the charts, it also ensconced his sound in the "easy listening" mode which would more or less persist throughout the rest of his prolific recording career. (It also might be noted that in 1966 Coniff shared the million-seller charts with the Beatles, the Monkees, and the Mindbenders.)

Coniff continued recording and performing his popular international tours and Sahara Hotel engagements at Lake Tahoe and Las Vegas through the 1980s and 1990s. In March of 1997, at age 80 and after a 40-year collaboration with Columbia/CBS Records/Sony Music that resulted in more than 90 albums selling over 65 million copies, Coniff signed a new recording contract with Polygram Records which released his one hundredth album, *I Love Movies. My Way,* an album of songs associated with Frank Sinatra, was released in 1998.

—Ross Care

FURTHER READING:

Kernfeld, Barry, editor. *New Grove Dictionary of Jazz.* London, Macmillan Press Limited, New York, Grove's Dictionaries of Music Inc., 1988.

Murrells, Joseph, editor. *Million Selling Records from the 1900s to the 1980s: An Illustrated History.* New York, Arco Publishing, Inc., 1985.

Connors, Jimmy (1952—)

Born September 2, 1952 in East St. Louis, Illinois, James Scott (Jimmy) Connors started playing tennis at the age of two, and grew up to become one of the most recognizable and successful pros in the history of the sport. His rise to the top of the game helped spark the tennis boom that took place in America in the mid-1970s, bringing unprecedented numbers of spectators out to the stands. Like his equally competitive (and even more temperamental) compatriot John McEnroe, tennis fans either loved Connors or hated him. His determination, intensity, and will to win could be denied by no one, and his penchant for becoming embroiled in controversial disputes over tour policy was legendary.

As was the case with his one-time fiance, American tennis legend Chris Evert, Connors was raised to play the game by a determined parent who also happened to be a teaching pro. Gloria Thompson Connors had her son swinging at tennis balls even before he could lift his racket off the ground; this early training, combined

Jimmy Connors

with Connors' natural ability and never-say-die attitude, paved the way for his later success. At the 1970 United States Open in Forest Hills, an 18-year-old and still unknown Connors teamed with his much older mentor Pancho Gonzalez to reach the quarterfinals in doubles. A year later, while attending the University of California at Los Angeles, Connors would become the first freshman ever to win the National Intercollegiate Singles title. But neither that honor, nor his All-American status, was enough to prevent him from dropping out of school in 1972 to become a full-time participant on the men's pro circuit.

Connors finished 1973 sharing the number one ranking in the United States with Stan Smith. The next year he reigned supreme, not just in the States but around the world. Winner of an unbelievable 99 out of 103 matches, and 14 of the 20 tournaments he entered (including the Australian Open, Wimbledon, the United States Open, and the United States Clay Court Championships), Connors totally dominated the competition in a sport that was exhibiting spectacular growth. Two surveys taken in 1974 showed an eye-popping 68 percent hike in the number of Americans claiming to play tennis recreationally, and a 26 percent jump in the number of those saying they were fans of the pro circuit. As a result, tournament prize money increased dramatically. In 1978, Connors became the first player to exceed $2 million in career earnings.

Although many potential fans refused to jump on the Connors bandwagon—his behavior towards umpires, linesmen, and opposing players was often reprehensible, and he repeatedly refused to participate in the international Davis Cup team tournament—few tennis lovers could resist watching him perform. Bill Riordan, Connors' shrewd manager, capitalized on his client's charismatic persona by arranging a pair of made-for-television exhibition singles matches dubbed the "Heavyweight Championship of Tennis." Connors, never one to shy away from the spotlight, won them both (years later, he would defeat Martina Navratilova in a gimmicky "Battle of the Sexes" handicap match). The unprecedented media coverage of these much-hyped events landed Connors a *Time* magazine cover photo in 1975. Riordan was also behind the highly publicized $40 million antitrust suit Connors brought against the Association of Tennis Professionals and Commercial Union Assurance (sponsor of the ILTF Grand Prix) a year earlier. It was alleged that these organizations were conspiring to monopolize professional tennis by barring any player who had signed up to play in the newly formed World Tennis League from competing in the 1974 French Open. Thus, Connors was denied his shot at the elusive Grand Slam that year. By the end of 1975, Connors split with Riordan and dropped the hotly contested lawsuit; only then did his relations with fellow tour players begin to improve.

None of Connors' off-court battles had an adverse effect on his game in the 1970s. Though he lacked overpowering strokes, Connors was a dynamic shotmaker with the mentality of a prizefighter. His trademark two-fisted backhand, along with an outstanding return of serve, surprising touch, and the ability to work a point, all contributed to his success. Number one in the world five times (1974-78), Connors won a total of eight Grand Slam singles championships, including five United States Opens. He is also the only player to have won that title on three different surfaces (grass, clay, and hard courts).

In 1979, Connors disclosed that he and former *Playboy* Playmate-of-the-Year Patti McGuire had gotten married in Japan the previous year. Around this time his game suffered something of a decline. He failed to reach the final round of the United States Open for the first time in six years, and his once-fierce rivalry with Bjorn Borg lost its drama as he got crushed by the Swede four times. But predictably for someone of his competitive spirit, Connors recommitted himself, and won two more United States Open titles in the 1980s.

For a long time, it seemed certain that Connors' biggest contribution to American culture would be the sense of mischief and passion he brought to the once aristocratic game of tennis. But his determination to postpone retirement and continue fighting on court in the latter stages of a storied 23-year career gave him a new claim to fame, as he endeared himself to older spectators and even non-tennis fans. At age 39, Connors rose from number 936 in the world at the close of the previous year to make it all the way to the semifinals of the United States Open in 1991. En route, he came from way behind to defeat a much younger Aaron Krickstein in dramatic fashion. Ironically, it is likely that the match people will remember most is the one that came in a tournament he did not win. Considering that Connors holds 109 singles titles—tops in the Open era—along with 21 doubles titles, this is nothing for him to lose any sleep over. In 1998, Connors was inducted into the International Tennis Hall of Fame.

—Steven Schneider

FURTHER READING:

Burchard, Marshall. *Jimmy Connors*. New York, G.P. Putnams, 1976.

Collins, Bud, and Zander Hollander, editors. *Bud Collins' Modern Encyclopedia of Tennis*. New York, Doubleday, 1980.

Consciousness Raising Groups

A tactic usually associated with the U.S. Women's Liberation Movement (WLM) and other feminist-activist groupings born in the late 1960s, consciousness raising involved a range of practices that stressed the primacy of gender discrimination over issues of race and class. Grounded in practical action rather than theory, consciousness raising aimed to promote awareness of the repressed and marginal status of women. As proclaimed in one of the more enduring activist slogans of the 1960s—"The personal is political"—consciousness raising took several forms, including the formation of devolved and non-hierarchical discussion groups, in which women shared their personal (and otherwise unheard) experiences of everyday lives lived within a patriarchal society. Accordingly, the agenda of consciousness raising in the early days very often focused on issues such as abortion, housework, the family, or discrimination in the workplace, issues whose political dimension had been taken for granted or ignored by the dominant New Left groupings of the 1960s.

As a political tactic in its own right, consciousness raising received an early definition in Kathie Sarachild's "Program for Feminist Consciousness Raising," a paper given at the First National Convention of the Women's Liberation Movement in Chicago, in November 1968. Many of those involved in the early days of WLM had been politicized in the Civil Rights struggle and the protests against the Vietnam War. But they had become disenchanted with the tendency of nominally egalitarian New Left organizations, such as the Student Nonviolent Coordinating Committee (SNCC) and Students for a Democratic Society (SDS), to downplay or omit altogether the concerns of women, and had struck out on their own. When challenged on the position of women within his organization in 1964, SNCC leader Stokely Carmichael had replied that "The only position for women in SNCC is prone." As late as 1969 SDS produced a pamphlet that observed that "the system is like a woman; you've got to fuck it to make it change." The frustration of feminist activists in the 1960s produced a new women's movement, which stressed the patriarchal content of New Left dissent, almost as much as it raised awareness about gender and power in the everyday arenas of home and work.

As a political strategy, consciousness raising placed a high value on direct, practical action, and like much political activism of the 1960s and early 1970s, it produced inventive outlets for conducting and publicizing political activity. In 1968 the WLM took consciousness raising to the very heart of New Left concerns by conducting a symbolic "burial" of traditional femininity at Arlington Cemetery—the site of many protests at the ongoing conflict in Vietnam. As an exercise in consciousness raising, the mock funeral aimed to publicize the patriarchal tendency to define grieving mothers and bereaved widows in terms of their relationships with men. Similar guerilla style demonstrations marked the high point of consciousness raising as a form of direct action during the late 1960s. The New York Radical Women (NYRW) disrupted the Miss America pageant at Atlantic City in September 1968; the WITCH group protested the New York Bridal Fair at Madison Square Garden on St. Valentines Day 1969.

Other groups who employed similar tactics during this period included the Manhattan-based Redstockings, the Feminists, and the New York Radical Feminists.

The emphasis which early WLM consciousness raising placed upon small groups of unaffiliated women shows its roots in the anti-organizational politics of the New Left against which it reacted. The WLM may have reacted sharply against what it saw to be the patriarchal politics of SDS, but it shared with the New Left an emphasis on localized political activity exercised through small devolved "cells," which valorized the resistance of the individual to institutional oppression. In common with certain tendencies of the New Left, the premium placed upon an overtly personal politics has at times served to obscure the original commitment of consciousness raising to a more collective revolution in social definitions of gender and gender roles. One of the more visible legacies of consciousness raising can be seen in the proliferation of Women's Studies courses and departments at universities and colleges during the closing decades of the twentieth century.

—David Holloway

FURTHER READING:

Buechler, Steven M. *Women's Movements in the United States: Woman Suffrage, Equal Rights, and Beyond.* New Brunswick, Rutgers University Press, 1990.

Castro, Ginette. *American Feminism: A Contemporary History.* New York, New York University Press, 1990.

Whelehan, Imelda. *Modern Feminist Thought: From the Second Wave to Post-Feminism.* Edinburgh, Edinburgh University Press, 1995.

Conspiracy Theories

Once the province of the far right, conspiracy theories have gained a wider cultural currency in the last quarter of the twentieth century, and have become widely disseminated in our popular culture through diverse sources. Spanning every topic from UFOs to ancient secret societies to scientific and medical research, conspiracy theories are frequently disparaged as the hobby of "kooks" and "nuts" by the mainstream. In fact, many theories are well substantiated, but the belief in a "smoke-filled room" is a patently uncomfortable thought for most. Although the populace has generally shown a preference for dismissing conspiracy theories en masse, nevertheless it is now a common belief that a disconnect exists between the official line and reality. Crisis and scandal have left their mark on the American psyche, and popular culture—especially film and television—have readily capitalized on public suspicions, becoming an armature of the culture of paranoia.

What exactly is a conspiracy theory? Under its broadest definition, a conspiracy theory is a belief in the planned execution of an event—or events—in order to achieve a desired end. "At the center [of a conspiracy] there is always a tiny group in complete control, with one man as the undisputed leader," writes G. Edward Griffin, author of *The Creature from Jekyll Island,* a work on the Federal Reserve Board which, in passing, touches on many conspiracy theories of this century. "Next is a circle of secondary leadership that, for the most part, is unaware of an inner core. They are led to believe

that they are the inner-most ring. In time, as these conspiracies are built from the center out, they form additional rings of organization. Those in the outer echelons usually are idealists with an honest desire to improve the world. They never suspect an inner control for other purposes." This serves as an able definition of conspiracy, but for a conspiracy to be properly considered as conspiracy theory, there must be a level of supposition in the author's analysis beyond the established facts. Case in point: the ne plus ultra of conspiracy theories, the assassination of John F. Kennedy. Regardless of who was responsible for his murder, what is germane is the vast labyrinthian web of suspects that writers and researchers have uncovered. It is these shadowy allegations that comprise a conspiracy theory. The validity of different arguments aside, in the case of JFK, it is the speculative nature of these allegations which has left the greatest impression on popular culture.

Conspiracy theories tend, in the words of James Ridgeway, author of *Blood in the Face,* "to provide what seems to be a simple, surefire interpretation of events by which often chaotic and perplexing change can be explained." While it would be comforting to be so blandly dismissive, in the end, a conspiracy theory can only be as sophisticated as its proponent. Naturally, in the hands of a racist ideologue, a theory such as a belief in the omnipotence of Jewish bankers is a justification for hatred. Furthermore, as conspiracy theorists are wont to chase their quarry across the aeons in a quest for first causes, their assertions are often lost in the muddle, further exacerbated by the fact that more often than not, conspiracy theorists are far from able wordsmiths. Yet, as the saying goes, where there's smoke there's fire, and it would be injudicious to lump all conspiracy theories together as equally without merit.

A brief exegesis of one of the most pervasive conspiracy theories might well illustrate how conspiracy theories circulate and, like the game of telephone—in which a sentence is passed from one listener to the other until it becomes totally garbled—are embellished and elaborated upon. At the close of the eighteenth century, the pervasive unrest was adjudged to be the work of Freemasons and the Illuminati, two semi-secret orders whose eighteenth-century Enlightenment theories of individual liberty made them most unpopular to the aristocracy. These groups were widely persecuted and then driven into hiding. But waiting in the wings, was that most convenient of scapegoats, the Jews.

The Jews had long been viewed with distrust by their Christian neighbors. Already viewed as deicides, in the Middle Ages it was also commonly believed that Jews used the blood of Christian children in their Sabbath rituals. Communities of Jews were often wiped out as a result. Association, as it had so often been for the Jews, was sufficient to establish guilt. Early in the nineteenth century, a theory developed propounding an international Jewish conspiracy, a cabal of Jewish financiers intent on ensnaring the world under the dominion of a world government. The Jews were soon facing accusations of being the eminence grise behind the Illuminati, the Freemasons, and with complete disdain for the facts, the French Revolution.

Stories of an international Jewish cabal percolated until, in 1881, *Biarritz,* a novel by an official in the Prussian postal service, gave dramatic form to them. In a chapter entitled "In the Jewish Cemetery in Prague," a centennial congregation of Jewish leaders was depicted as they gathered to review their nefarious efforts to enslave the Gentile masses. The chapter was widely circulated in pamphlet form and later expanded into a book, *The Protocols of Zion,* used as inflammatory propaganda and distributed by supporters of the Czar. Distributed widely throughout Europe and America, Hitler would later cite *The Protocols* as a cardinal influence in his mature political beliefs.

The Jewish conspiracy made its way to America in the 1920s, where the idea was taken up by a rural, white, nativist populace already convinced the pope was an anti-Christ, Jews had horns, and all non-Anglo foreigners were agents of Communism. The industrialist Henry Ford fanned the flames by demonizing Jews in his newspaper, the *Dearborn Independent,* in which he published sections of *The Protocols.* Whether directly associated with Jews or not, the theory that American sovereignty was being slowly undermined became an enduring feature of the nativist right wing. It would be used to explain everything from the two world wars to the Bolshevik Revolution to the establishment of the IRS. Unfortunately, alongside the most rabid anti-Semitic screed there sits many an assertion, both accurate and well documented, and it is this indiscriminate combination of fact and fantasy that makes the allegations so disturbing.

For mainstream America, one could properly say that the age of the conspiracy theory began in the 1950s. More than any obscurantist's diatribe, movies gave life and breath to the conviction that civilization was governed from behind the scenes. Movies were a release valve in which the fears of that era—fears of Communist invasion, nuclear annihilation, UFOs—found release, sublimated into science fiction or crime dramas. The 1950s gave us films with a newfound predilection for ambiguity and hidden agendas—film noir. Films like *Kiss Me Deadly, The Shack out on 101, North by Northwest,* and *The Manchurian Candidate* explicate a worldview that is patently conspiratorial. They are a far cry from anything produced in the previous decades. The angst and nuances of film noir carried over to the science fiction genre. No longer content with fantasy, the frivolousness of early science fiction was replaced by a dread-laden weltanschauung, a world of purposeful or malevolent visitors from another planet: visitors with an agenda. *The Day the Earth Stood Still, Invasion of the Body-Snatchers,* and *Them* are standouts of the era, but for each film that became a classic, a legion of knockoffs stood arrayed behind.

By the time of Kennedy's assassination, Americans were looking at world events with a more jaundiced eye. The movement from Kennedy to Watergate, from suspicion to outright guilt, was accompanied by a corollary shift in media perception. The United States government was directly portrayed as *the* enemy—no longer intuited as it had been in the oblique, coded films of the 1950s. Robert Redford and Warren Beatty made films—*All the President's Men, Three Days of the Condor,* and *The Parallax View*—that capitalized on the suspicion of government that Watergate fostered in the public.

It wasn't until the release of Oliver Stone's *JFK* that conspiracy theories made a reentry into the mainstream. Shortly thereafter, the phenomenally popular TV series *The X-Files,* a compendium of all things conspiratorial—properly sanitized for middle-class sensibilities—made its auspicious debut in 1992. For a generation to whom the likelihood of UFOs outweighed their belief in the continuance of social security into their dotage; for whom the McCarthy Era was history, Watergate but a distant, childhood memory, and JFK's murder the watershed in their parents' history, conspiracy theories received a fresh airing, albeit heavy on the exotic and entirely free of racism, xenophobia, and government malfeasance. The show's success triggered a national obsession for all things conspiratorial, and a slew of books, films, and real-life TV programming made the rounds. There was even a film titled *Conspiracy Theory* starring the popular actor Mel Gibson as a paranoid cabby whose suspicions turn out to be utterly justified.

By their very nature conspiracy theories are difficult to prove, and this fact in and of itself largely explains their popularity. They inhabit a netherworld where truth and fiction mingle together in an endless dance of fact and supposition. They tantalize, for within this symbiosis explanations are set forth. After all, it is easier to acknowledge a villain than to accept a meaningless absurdity. Therefore, as the world grows increasingly complex, it is likely that conspiracy theories will continue, like the game of telephone mentioned earlier, to mutate and multiply—serving a variety of agendas. Their presence in the cultural zeitgeist, however, is no longer assailable: paranoia is the mainstream.

—Michael J. Baers

FURTHER READING:

Allen, Gary. *None Dare Call It Conspiracy.* Seal Beach, Concord Press, 1971.

Bramley, William. *Gods of Eden.* New York, Avon Books, 1989.

Epperson, A. Ralph. *The Unseen Hand: An Introduction to the Conspiratorial View of History.* Tucson, Publius Press, 1985.

Griffin, G. Edward. *The Creature from Jekyll Island.* Appleton, American Opinion, 1994.

Moench, Doug. *The Big Book of Conspiracies.* New York, Paradox Press, 1995.

Mullins, Eustace. *The World Order: A Study in the Hegemony of Parasitism.* Staunton, Ezra Pound Institute of Civilization, 1985.

Quigley, Carrol. *Tragedy and Hope.* New York, MacMillan, 1966.

Ravenscraft, Trevor. *The Spear of Destiny.* New York, G. P. Putnam's Sons, 1973.

Ridgeway, James. *Blood in the Face.* New York, Thunder's Mouth Press, 1990.

Still, William. *New World Order: The Ancient Plan of Secret Societies.* Lafayette, Huntington House Publishers, 1990.

Consumer Reports

Published since 1936, *Consumer Reports* has established a reputation as a leading source of unbiased reporting about products and services likely to be used by the typical American. It counts itself among the ten most widely disseminated periodicals in the United States, with a circulation in 1998 of 4.6 million. In all of its more than sixty years of production, the journal has never accepted free samples, advertisements, or grants from any industry, business, or agency. Maintaining this strict independence from interest groups has helped make *Consumer Reports* a trusted source of information.

Consumer Reports is published by Consumers Union, a not-for-profit organization based in Yonkers, New York. Along with the print monthly, Consumers Union also creates and distributes many guide books for consumers, such as the *Supermarket Buying Guide* and the *Auto Insurance Handbook,* as well as newsletters about travel and health issues, and a children's magazine called *Zillions.* There are *Consumer Reports* syndicated radio and television shows, and a popular and successful web page with millions of subscribers. Stating its mission as to ''test products, inform the public and protect consumers," Consumers Union has more than 450 persons on its staff and operates fifty test labs in nine departments: appliances, automobiles, chemicals, electronics, foods, home environment, public service, recreation and home improvement. The Union operates three advocacy offices, in Washington, D.C., Austin, Texas, and San Francisco, that help citizens with questions, complaints, and legal action about products and services. Consumers Union was also instrumental in the formation of the Consumer Policy Institute in Yonkers, which does research in such areas as biotechnology and pollution; and Consumer International, founded in 1960, which seeks to unite worldwide consumer interests. All together, the organizations that comprise Consumers Union have been pivotal in the creation of a consumer movement and have been responsible for many defective product recalls, fines on offending industries, and much consumer-protection legislation.

The history of the founding of *Consumer Reports* gives a condensed picture of the consumer movement in the United States. In 1926, Frederick Schlink, an engineer in White Plains, New York, founded a "consumer club," with the goal of better informing citizens about the choices of products and services facing them. With the industrial revolution not far behind them, consumers in the 1920s were faced with both the luxury and the dilemma of being able to purchase many manufactured items that had formerly had to be custom made. Schlink's club distributed mimeographed lists of warnings and recommendations about products. By 1928, the little club had expanded into a staffed organization called Consumers' Research, whose journal, *Consumers' Research Bulletin,* accepted no advertising. That same year Schlink and another Consumers' Research director, engineer Arthur Kallet, published a book about consumer concerns called *100,000,000 Guinea Pigs: Dangers in Everyday Foods, Drugs, and Cosmetics.*

In 1933, when Schlink moved his organization to the small town of Washington, New Jersey, he was confronted with his own ethical dilemmas. When some of his own employees formed a union, Schlink fired them, prompting a strike by forty other workers demanding a minimum-wage guarantee and reinstatement of their fired colleagues. Schlink responded by accusing the strikers of being communists and by hiring scabs. In 1936, the Consumers' Research strikers formed their own organization with Arthur Kallet at its head. They called it Consumers Union. Their original charter promised to "test and give information to the public on products and services" in the hopes of "maintaining decent living standards for ultimate consumers."

Early Consumers Union product research was limited because of lack of funds to buy expensive products to test, but they did research on items of everyday concern to Depression-era consumers, such as soaps and credit unions. Within three months of its formation, Consumers Union published the first issue of *Consumers Union Reports,* continuing the tradition of refusing commercial support. Along with information on product safety and reliability, the new journal maintained a leftist slant by reporting on social issues such as business labor practices. Its first editorial stated, "All the technical information in the world will not give enough food or enough clothes to the textile worker's family living on $11 a week." Threatened by this new progressive consumer movement, business began to fight back. Red-baiting articles appeared in such mainstream journals as *Reader's Digest* and *Good Housekeeping.* Between 1940 and 1950, the union appeared on government lists of subversive organizations.

By 1942, *Consumers Union Reports* had become simply *Consumer Reports* to broaden its public appeal. Both consumption and the purchase of consumer research had been slowed by the Depression

and World War II, but with the return of consumer spending after 1945, the demand for *Consumer Reports* subscriptions shot up. In the postwar economic boom, businesses had very consciously and successfully urged citizens to become consumers. Having learned to want more than food and shelter, people also learned to want more in less material arenas. They wanted something called "quality of life." They wanted clean air and water, they wanted to be able to trust the goods and services they purchased, and they wanted their government to protect their safety in these areas.

In the boom economy of the 1950s and 1960s, business felt it had little to fear from organized consumers and did little to fight back. This, combined with the rise of socially conscious progressive movements, gave a boost of power and visibility to the consumer movement. In 1962, liberal president John F. Kennedy introduced the "consumer bill of rights," delineating for the first time that citizens had a right to quality goods. The same year, Congress overcame the protests of the garment industry to pass laws requiring that children's clothing be made from flame-resistant fabric. In 1964, the Department of Labor hired lawyer Ralph Nader to investigate automobile safety, resulting in landmark vehicle-safety legislation. A committed consumer activist, Nader joined the Consumers Union board of directors from 1967 through 1975.

In 1962, Rachael Carson sparked a new view of the environment with her ecological manifesto, *Silent Spring,* a work so clearly connected to the consumer movement that Consumers Union published a special edition. The new environmentalists did research that resulted in the passage in 1963 of the first Clean Air Act and in 1965 of the Clean Water Act.

The consumer movement and the movement to clean up the environment attracted much popular support. By 1967, the Consumer Federation of America had been formed, a coalition of 140 smaller local groups. The long-established Consumers Union opened its office in Washington, D.C. to better focus on its lobbying work. Working together, these groups and other activists were responsible for the formation of the Environmental Protection Agency, the Consumer Product Safety Commission, and countless laws instituting safety standards, setting up fair business practices, and regulating pollution.

The thriving consumer movement is one of the most significant legacies of the turbulent period of social change that spanned the period from the 1950s through the 1970s. As more and more products and services have been introduced, activists have continued to instigate legislation and create organizations and networks to help consumers cope with the flood of options. From its roots as a club for consumer advice, Consumers Union has grown into a notable force for consumer and environmental protection, offering research and advice on every imaginable topic of interest to consumers from automobiles and appliances to classical music recordings, legal services, and funerals. It has retained a high standard of ethics and value pertaining to the rights of the common citizen. For most of them, thoughts of a large purchase almost inevitably lead to the question, "Have you checked *Consumer Reports*?" The organization has clung to its progressive politics while weathering the distrust of big business about its motivations and effectiveness.

—Tina Gianoulis

FURTHER READING:

"Consumer Reports." http://www.consumerreports.org. May 1999.

Gelston, Steven W. *A Guide to Documents of the Consumer Movement: A National Catalog of Source Material.* Mount Vernon,
New York, Consumers' Union Foundation, 1980.

Silber, Norman Isaac. *Test and Protest: The Influence of Consumers
Union.* New York, Holmes and Meier, 1983.

Warne, Colston E. *The Consumer Movement: Lectures.* Manhattan,
Kansas, Family Economics Trust Press, 1993.

Consumerism

Consumerism is central to any study of the twentieth century. In
its simplest form, it characterizes the process of purchasing goods
such as food, clothing, shelter, electricity, gas, water, or anything else,
and then consuming or using those goods. The meaning of consumerism, however, goes well beyond that definition, and has undergone a
striking shift from the way it was first used in the 1930s to describe a
new consumer movement founded in opposition to the increased
prevalence of advertising. It is with much irony that by the end of the
twentieth century, consumerism came to mean a cultural ethos
marked by a dependence on commerce and incessant shopping and
buying. This shift in meaning reflects the shift in how commercial
values transformed American culture over the century.

In the early decades of the twentieth century, social life became
increasingly commercialized. According to the famous *Middletown*
studies, automobiles conferred mobility on millions, and amusement
parks, movie theaters, and department stores had become serious
competitors to leisure pursuits that traditionally had been provided by
church, home, and family centered activities. By 1924, commercial
values had significantly changed home and leisure life as compared to
1890; even school curriculums were being altered in order to accommodate an increasingly commercialized world.

As a response to these changes, a consumer movement emerged,
and in the 1920s was focused on sanitary food production and
workers' conditions. But by the 1930s, the rapid commercialization
taking place shifted the consumer movement's attention to advertising. This reform movement was predicated on the idea that the
modern consumer often has insufficient information to choose effectively among competing products, and that in this new era of
increased commercialization, advertisements should provide potential consumers with more information about the various products.
They also objected to advertising which was misleading, such as the
image-based advertising which often played on people's fears and
insecurities (such as suggesting that bad breath or old-fashioned
furnishings prevented professional and social success).

Accordingly, the consumer movement sought policies and laws
which regulated methods and standards of manufacturers, sellers, and
advertisers. Although the preexisting 1906 Food and Drug Act had
made the misbranding of food and drugs illegal, the law only applied
to labeling and not to general advertising. With the support of a New
York senator and assistant Secretary of Agriculture Rexford G.
Tugwell, a bill was introduced in the U.S. Senate in 1933 which
would prohibit "false advertising" of any food, drug, or cosmetic,
defining any advertisement false if it created a misleading impression
by "ambiguity or inference." Ultimately, a significantly less strict
form of the bill was passed, called the Wheeler-Lea Amendment,
which is still the primary law governing advertising today.

In the 1930s, the consumer movement—which was first to use
the term consumerism—sought assurances about the quality of goods
sold to the public. For most people, shopping in the early part of the
century was still a novelty, and certainly wasn't central to daily life.
This was due, in part, to the (relatively) modest amount of goods
available, and to the nature of the shopping environment, which was
typically an unembellished storefront. Often, the shopkeeper was an
acquaintance of the buyer, and frequently the act of buying was
dependent upon an active exchange of bargaining. This changed,
however, with the expansion of fixed-priced and display-laden department stores which flourished after World War II (though they had
been in existence since just after the Civil War).

The end of World War II marked a significant point in the
development of consumer culture in its second meaning, which
strongly contrasts with the perspective of the consumer movement. At
the end of World War II, the return of soldiers, a burgeoning
economy, and a boom in marriage rates and child-birth created a new
and unique set of circumstances for the American economy. Unprecedented prosperity in the 1950s led people to leave the cities and move
to the suburbs; the increased manufacturing capabilities meant a rapid
rise in the quantity and variety of available goods; and the rise and
popularity of television and television advertising profoundly altered
the significance of consumerism in daily life.

The heretofore unprecedented growth in inventions and gadgets
inspired an article which appeared in *The New Yorker* on May 15,
1948 claiming "Every day, there arrive new household devices,
cunningly contrived to do things you don't particularly want done."
The author described Snap-a-cross curtains, the Mouli grater, and the
Tater-Baker as examples of the inventive mood of the era. Prepared
cake mixes were introduced in 1949; Minute Rice in 1950; and
Pampers disposable diapers in 1956. The variety of goods was
staggering: Panty Hose debuted in 1959, along with Barbie (the most
successful doll in history); and in 1960, beverages began to be stored
in aluminum cans. Due to their increased prevalence and an increase
in advertising, these items went from novelties to an everyday part of
American life. By the end of the century, many of these items were no
longer viewed as luxuries but as necessities.

During this time, the government responded by encouraging
behavior which favored economic growth. For example, the American government supported ads which addressed everything from
hygiene to the "proper" American meal and, ultimately, the media
campaign was a crucial element in the development of consumerism,
or what had become a consumer culture. In *Mad Scientist,* media critic
Mark Crispin Miller argues that American corporate advertising was
the most successful propaganda campaign of the twentieth century.

Because most of the consumption was geared towards the
household, many television advertisements were geared towards the
housewife, the primary consumer in American households. In addition to advertisements, other factors specifically attracted women to
shopping, such as the development of commodities which (supposedly) reduced household chores, an activity for which women were
primarily responsible. Ironically (but quite intentionally), "new"
products often created chores which were previously unknown, such
as replacing vacuum bag filters or using baking soda to "keep
the refrigerator smelling fresh." In 1963, Betty Friedan published
The Feminine Mystique which derided suburbia as "a bedroom
and kitchen sexual ghetto," a critique partially based on what
many experienced as the cultural entrapment of women into the
role of homemaker, an identity that was endlessly repeated in
advertising images.

The mass migration to the suburbs also resulted in the construction of new places to shop. The absence of traditional downtown areas

along with the popularity of automobiles gave rise to the suburban shopping mall, where typically, one or two large department stores anchor a variety of other stores, all under one roof. The by-now prevalent television advertising was another significant factor contributing to the spread of shopping malls, by further creating demand for material goods. Unlike older downtown centers, the new mall was a physical environment devoted solely to the act of shopping.

The abundance of goods and ease with which to buy them led to a change in the American attitude towards shopping. Visits to shopping locations became more frequent, and were no longer viewed as entirely a chore. Although it remained "work" for some, shopping also became a form of entertainment and a leisure-time activity.

Like the world's fairs before them, suburban shopping malls displayed the wonders of modern manufacturing and reflected a transition from store as merchant to store as showroom. In what was now a crowded marketplace, imagery became increasingly critical as a way of facilitating acts of consumption. According to Margaret Crawford in her essay "The World in a Shopping Mall": "The spread of malls around the world has accustomed large numbers of people to behavior patterns that inextricably link shopping with diversion and pleasure." Although this phenomenon originated outside the United States and predated the twentieth century, American developers—with their "bigger is better" attitude—perfected shopping as a recreational event.

As a result, malls eventually became a central fixture of American social life, especially in the 1980s. Increasingly bigger malls were built to accommodate the rapid proliferation of chain stores and in order to provide the "consummate" shopping experience (and, conveniently, to eliminate the need to leave the mall), additional attractions and services were added. By the 1980s, food courts, movie theaters, and entertainment venues enticed shoppers. These centers became such popular gathering places that they functioned as a substitute for other community centers such as parks or the YMCA. Teenagers embraced malls as a place to "hang-out" and in response, many shops catered specifically to them, which aided advertising in cultivating consumer habits at an early age. Some chain stores, such as Barnes and Noble, offer lectures and book readings for the public. Some shopping malls offered other community activities, such as permitting their walkways to be used by walkers or joggers before business hours. The largest mall in the United States was the gigantic Mall of America, located in Bloomington, Minnesota, which covered 4.2 million square feet (390,000 square meters) or 78 acres. (The largest mall in North America is actually a million square feet larger—the West Edmonton Mall, located in Canada).

Increasingly, many elements of American social life were intermixed with commercial activity, creating what has become known as a consumer culture. Its growth was engineered in part by "Madison Avenue," the New York City street where many advertising agencies are headquartered. As advertising critics note, early advertising at beginning of the century was information based, and described the value and appeal of the product through text. Advertisers quickly learned, however, that images were infinitely more powerful than words, and they soon altered their methods to fit. The image-based approach works by linking the product with a desirable image, often through directly juxtaposing an image with the product (women and cars, clean floors and beautiful homes, slim physiques and brand-names). Although such efforts to promote "image identity" were already sophisticated in the 1920s and 1930s, the proliferation of television significantly elevated its influence.

The marriage of image advertising and television allowed advertising to achieve some of its greatest influences. First, ads of the 1950s and early 1960s were successful in cultivating the ideal of the American housewife as shopper. Advertisements depicted well-scrubbed, shiny nuclear families who were usually pictured adjacent to a "new" appliance in an industrialized home. Second, advertising promoted the idea of obsolescence, which means that styles eventually fall out of fashion, requiring anyone who wishes to be stylish to discard the old version and make additional purchases. Planned obsolescence was essential to the success of the automotive and fashion industries, two of the heaviest advertisers.

A third accomplishment of image-based advertising was creating the belief, both unconscious and conscious, that non-tangible values, such as popularity and attractiveness, could be acquired by consumption. This produced an environment in which commodification and materialism was normalized, meaning that people view their natural role in the environment as related to the act of consumption. Accordingly, consumerism or "excess materialism," (another definition of the term) proliferated.

Advertising, and therefore television, was essential to the growth of consumerism, and paved the way for the rampant commercialism of the 1980s and 1990s. Concurrently, there was a tremendous increase in the number of American shopping malls: to around 28,500 by the mid-1980s. The explosion of such commercialism was most evident in the sheer variety of goods created for purely entertainment purposes, such as Cabbage Patch Kids, VCR tapes, Rubik's cubes, and pet rocks. So much "stuff" was available from so many different stores that new stores were even introduced which sold products to contain all of the stuff. By the mid-1980s, several 24-hour shopping channels were available on cable television and, according to some sources, more than three-fourths of the population visited a mall at least once a month, evidence of the extent to which shopping was part of daily life.

It is important to note that with the development of consumer culture, consumerism in its earlier sense was still being practiced. Ralph Nader (1934—) is credited with much of the movement's momentum in the late 1960s. In 1965, Nader, a Harvard lawyer, published a book about auto-safety called *Unsafe at Any Speed: The Designed-in Dangers of the American Automobile*. This and the revelation that General Motors Corporation had been spying on him and otherwise harassing him led to passage of the National Traffic and Motor Vehicle Safety Act in 1966. Nader went on to author other books on consumer issues, and established several nonprofit research agencies, including Public Citizen, Inc. and the Center for Study of Responsive Law. Other organizations also arose to protect consumer interests such as the Federal Trade Commission (FTC), the Food and Drug Administration (FDA), and the Better Business Bureau (BBB). The Consumers Union, which was founded in 1936, continues to be the most well-known consumer organization because of its monthly magazine *Consumer Reports*, which evaluates competing products and services.

Aside from the efforts of such consumerist groups, the forces of consumer culture were unstoppable. By the late 1980s and 1990s, the proliferation of commercial space reached every imaginable venue, from the exponential creation of shopping malls and "outlet stores"; to the availability of shopping in every location (QVC; Internet; mid-flight shopping); to the use of practically all public space for advertising, (including airborne banners, subway walls, labels adhered to fruit, and restroom doors). This omnipresent visual environment reinforced what was by now an indoctrinated part of American life: consumerism.

The ubiquitousness of consumer culture was so prevalent that a number of artists throughout the century made it their subject matter. Andy Warhol, along with Roy Lichtenstein and others, won worldwide celebrity with endlessly repeated portraits of commodities (Coke bottles, Campbell's soup cans) and of celebrities, which seemed to be wrapped and packaged along with all of the other products. Holidays were created based on buying gifts (Secretary's Day, Halloween), and malls and stores which are sometimes viewed as community space replaced other venues which used to be popular public spaces (bowling alleys, YMCAs, community centers, town halls).

Consumerism became so critical to Americans that millions of people went significantly into debt to acquire goods. Credit, which permits the purchase of goods and services with little or no cash, was essential for average people to be able to buy more and more. Credit cards functioned like cash and, in 1990, the credit card debt of Americans reached a staggering $243 billion. By 1997, that number more than doubled, reaching $560 billion, according to the Bureau of the Census. This dramatic increase in credit card spending was undertaken, in part, because of the seemingly constant need to acquire newer or better goods. Oprah Winfrey even held segments on her talk show about how people were dealing with debt, and how to cut up your credit cards.

The relentless consumption over the century has had the inevitable result of producing tons—actually millions of tons—of consumer waste. According to a report produced by Franklin Associates, Ltd. for the Environmental Protection Agency, approximately 88 million tons of municipal solid waste was generated in 1960. By 1995, the figure had almost tripled, to approximately 208 million tons. This means each person generated an average of 4.3 pounds of solid waste per day. For example, Americans throw away 570 diapers per second—or 49 million diapers a year. This astonishing level of waste production has had the effect of rendering the United States a world leader in the generation of waste and pollutants. In 1998, it was projected that annual generation of municipal solid waste will increase to 222 million tons by the year 2000 and 253 million tons in 2010. A full one-third of all garbage discarded by Americans is packaging—an awesome amount of mostly non-decomposable material for the planet to reckon with.

Further, as a variety of social critics such as Sut Jhally have pointed out, consumerism is popular because advertisements sell more than products: they sell human hopes and dreams, such as the need for love, the desire to be attractive, etc. It is inevitable that the hopes and dreams can never be reached through the acquisition of a product, which, in turn, has lead to a profound sense of disillusionment and alienation, a problem noted by public thinkers throughout the century, from John Kenneth Galbraith to Noam Chomsky.

Sports Utility Vehicles promise security through domination, Oil of Olay promises beauty in aging, and DeBeers promises eternal love with diamonds. Since these empty solutions run counter to the inevitability of the human condition, no product can ever meet its promise. But in the meantime, people keep on consuming. . . .

—Julie Scelfo

FURTHER READING:

Barber, Benjamin. *Jihad vs. McWorld: How Globalism and Tribalism are Reshaping the World.* New York, Ballantine Books, 1995.

Bentley, Amy. *Eating for Victory: Food Rationing and the Politics of Domesticity.* Chicago, University of Illinois Press, 1998.

Brobeck, Stephen, editor. *Encyclopedia of the Consumer Movement.* Santa Barbara, California, ABC-CLIO, 1997.

Cox, Reavis. *Consumers' Credit and Wealth: A Study in Consumer Credit.* Washington, National Foundation for Consumer Credit, 1965.

Crawford, Margaret. ''The World in a Shopping Mall.'' In *Variations on a Theme Park: The New American City and the End of Public Space,* edited by Michael Sorkin. New York, Noonday Press, 1992.

Ewen, Stuart. *All Consuming Images: The Politics of Style in Contemporary Culture.* New York, Basic Books, 1988.

Fox, Richard Wightman, and T. J. Jackson Lears, editors. *The Culture of Consumption: Critical Essays in American History, 1880-1990.* New York, Pantheon, 1983.

Hebdige, Dick. *Subculture: The Meaning of Style.* London, Methuen, 1979.

Jhally, Sut. *Codes of Advertising.* New York, St. Martin's Press, 1987.

Kallen, Horace. *The Decline and Rise of the Consumer.* New York, D. Appleton-Century Company, 1936.

Leach, William. *The Land of Desire: Merchants, Power, and the Rise of a New American Culture.* New York, Pantheon, 1993.

Lears, Jackson. *Fables of Abundance: A Cultural History of Advertising in America.* New York, Basic Books, 1994.

Lynd, Robert, and Helen Lynd. *Middletown.* New York, Harcourt Brace, 1929.

Marchand, Roland. *Advertising the American Dream: Making Way for Modernity 1920-1940.* Berkeley, University of California Press, 1985.

Miller, Mark Crispin. *Mad Scientist.* Forthcoming.

Miller, Michael. *The Bon Marché: Bourgeois Culture and the Department Store, 1869-1920.* Princeton, Princeton University Press, 1981.

Veblen, Thorstein. *The Theory of the Leisure Class.* New York, Macmillan, 1899.

Consumers Union

See Consumer Reports

Contemporary Christian Music

In the late 1990s a genre of music, unknown to most of America, began push its way onto the popular American music scene. Contemporary Christian Music or CCM traced its roots to Southern Gospel and Gospel music, but only began to be noticed by a larger audience when the music industry changed the way it tracked record sales in the mid-1990s.

In the late 1960s, Capitol Records hassled a blond hippie named Larry Norman for wanting to call his record *We Need a Whole Lot*

More of Jesus and a Lot Less Rock and Roll. In response, Norman decided to make and distribute his own records. Norman's records shocked the religious and irreligious alike. He mixed his strict adherence to orthodox Christianity with honest cultural observations in songs like "Why Don't You Look into Jesus," which included the lines "Gonorrhea on Valentines Day, You're still looking for the perfect lay, you think rock and roll will set you free but honey you'll be dead before you're 33."

Before long Norman's dreams of artistic freedom had become a nightmare when executives took over and created CCM the genre which, unlike the artists who dreamed of singing songs about Jesus for non-Christians, quickly focused on marketing the records to true believers. CCM had become a large industry, signing and promoting artists who were encouraged to make strictly religious records that were heavy on theology but lacking in real world relevance. CCM also began to cater to best-selling "secular" artists who experienced Christian conversions, helping them to craft religious records which both alienated longtime fans and couldn't be distributed through ordinary music channels. Among these were once popular performers like Mark Farner of Grand Funk Railroad, Dan Peek of America, B.J. Thomas, Richie Furay of Poco and Buffalo Springfield, Al Green, Dion, Joe English of Wings, Rick Cua of the Outlaws, and many others.

By the 1980s, other studios became receptive to Christian music, and allowed artists more flexibility with song lyrics. In 1983 a heavy metal band named Stryper comprised of born again Christians emerged from the L.A. metal scene and signed a record deal with a "secular" label Enigma which had produced many of the early metal artists. In 1985 Amy Grant signed her own direct deal with A&M that got her a top 40 single "Find A Way," and led to two number one singles "The Next Time I Fall," in 1987 and "Baby, Baby," in 1991. Leslie Phillips dropped out of CCM in 1987, changed her name to Sam, and signed with Virgin, a company with whom she recorded several critically lauded albums. Michael W. Smith signed with Geffen in 1990 and produced a number six hit "Place In This World."

With the commercial success of Grant and others, many CCM artists no longer wanted to be identified as such, preferring to be known simply as artists. In their view, being identified by their spiritual and religious beliefs limited the music industry's willingness to widely disseminate their music and alienated some consumers. Many of these artists left their CCM labels and signed with "secular" record labels or arranged for their records to be distributed in both the "Christian" and "secular" music markets. By the mid-1990s artists like dc Talk, Jars of Clay, Bob Carlisle, Kirk Franklin, Fleming and John, Julie Miller, BeBe and CeCe Winans, punk band MxPx, Jon Gibson, and others once mainstays of CCM, had signed with "secular" labels.

Christian artists' attractiveness to "secular" record labels increased with the introduction of a new mode of calculating record sales. The introduction of SoundScan, a new tracking system, brought attention to CCM in the mid-1990s. SoundScan replaced historically unreliable telephone reports from record store employees with electronic point-of-purchase sales tracking. SoundScan also began to tabulate sales in Christian bookstores. The result suddenly gave CCM increased visibility in popular culture as many artists who had heretofore been unknown outside the Christian community began to find themselves with hit records.

Jars of Clay, a rookie band which formed at college in Greenville, Illinois, was among the first of these success stories. Signed with a tiny CCM label called Essential Records, their debut record was selling briskly in the Christian world when one single, "Flood," came to the attention of radio programmers who liked it, and unaware that it was a song from a "Christian" band, began to give it significant airplay in several different formats. Before long "Flood" was a smash hit played in heavy rotation on VH-1 and numerous other music video outlets. Mainstream label Zomba, which had recently purchased Jars' label, re-released the record into the mainstream market and the Jars Boys—as they were affectionately known—began to tour with artists like Sting, Jewel, and the Cowboy Junkies. Their second release "Much Afraid," benefitted from the SoundScan arrangement by debuting at number eight on the Billboard Album chart.

Another band which benefitted from the increased attention that the SoundScan arrangement brought to CCM was a band which formed at Jerry Falwell's Liberty University in the late 1980s and consisted of three young men, one black and two white, who hailed from the Washington D.C. area. dc Talk, as they were known, began as a rap band but evolved over the years into a grunge-pop sound which culminated in their 1995 release "Jesus Freak." Soundscan recorded the strong debut of "Jesus Freak" on the Billboard charts and had many industry executives inquiring about dc Talk. Kaz Utsunomiya, an executive at Virgin Records dispatched one of his assistants to Tower Records to fetch a copy of the album and liked what he heard. Virgin soon signed dc Talk to a unique deal that made them Virgin artists but allowed dc Talk's CCM market label Forefront to continue to distribute to the world of Bible bookstores. Virgin also released a single "Just Between You And Me," which cracked the top 40 list. And dc Talk's follow up album, *Supernatural,* showed the band's power, debuting at number four. Sandwiched between Marilyn Manson and Kiss on the music charts, the debut was rife with symbolism, for Manson was an unabashed Satanist and Kiss, had been labeled—probably unfairly—as Satanists for years by Christians who were convinced that its initials stood for something sinister like "Kings In Satan's Service."

But the greatest triumph belonged to a most unlikely artist named Bob Carlisle who would see his record *Butterfly Kisses,* displace the Spice Girls at the top of the charts. Carlisle was unlikely because he was a veteran of the CCM market who had recently been dropped by the major CCM label Sparrow and picked up by the small independent label Diadem. Carlisle had long played in CCM bands beginning in the 1970s and in the early 1990s had gone solo. Trained to write cheerful, upbeat numbers which the CCM world preferred, Carlisle prepared songs for his record with Diadem, and strongly considered not including "Butterfly Kisses," a song he had written with longtime writing partner Randy Thomas, because it was a melancholy song that was personal to Carlisle and his daughter and one which he wasn't sure the religious marketplace would appreciate. Carlisle's wife's opinion prevailed and he included it. When a radio programmer's daughter in Florida heard the track at church, she told her father who played it on the radio and received an overwhelmingly positive response. Soon word of the song reached Clive Calder, the president of Zomba Music which had recently engineered the purchase of Carlisle's label, Diadem.

In a brilliant series of moves, Calder repackaged and re-released Carlisle's album, replacing Carlisle's too sincere cover pose with an artists rendering of a butterfly and changing the serious title of the record *Shades Of Grace* to *Butterfly Kisses.* Fueled as well by a tear-inspiring performance on Oprah Winfrey's daytime talk show, a feature in the *Wall Street Journal* and airplay on Rush Limbaugh's radio show, "Butterfly Kisses" headed for the top of the album charts and became both a country and pop radio smash hit. Though success proved elusive for Carlisle—his next record quickly dropped off of the charts—the larger point had been made that large audiences could be interested in CCM if the music was packaged in ways that would appeal to people who didn't necessarily share the artists' deep Christian convictions.

Tens of other artists who considered themselves serious Christians wanted to avoid the restrictive CCM market. But just as they had once been told to stay out of politics by their more conservative brethren, Christians had long been told to stay out of rock music. Christians feared the world associated with rock 'n' roll and many described it as a dirty place, but others couldn't deny the impact that rock music had on American culture. Some Christians wanted the impact of rock 'n' roll to carry their messages, and wanted to avoid the stigma attached to religious music. Some of these artists included King's X, The Tories, Hanson, Gary Cherone of Extreme, and Van Halen, Lenny Kravitz, Moby, Full On The Mouth, Judson Spence, Collective Soul, and Burlap To Cashmere.

Even with so many crossover artists, some artists continued to struggle with labels that kept their music from the general record buying public. Artists like dc Talk and Jars of Clay asked to be treated "normally" and not as religious artists, but they continued to receive Grammy awards in the "Gospel" category and record stores continued to stock their music in the "Inspirational" or "Christian" bins. Nevertheless, by the end of the twentieth century, CCM had evolved to the extent that Christian music could be found not only in the traditional religious categories, but also throughout the many genres of popular music.

—Mark Joseph

FURTHER READING:

Baker, Paul. *Why Should The Devil Have All The Good Music?* Waco, Word Books, 1979.

Fischer, John. *What On Earth Are We Doing?* Michigan, Servant Publications, 1997.

Peacock, Charlie. *At The Crossroads.* Nashville, Broadman & Holman, 1999.

Rabey, Steve. *The Heart Of Rock And Roll.* New Jersey, Revell, 1985.

Turner, Steve. *Hungry For Heaven.* Illinois, Intervarsity Press, 1996.

Convertible

Glamorous automobiles with enormous emotional appeal—conjuring up romantic images of youthful couples speeding across wide-open spaces, sun shining on their tanned faces, wind rushing through their hair as rock music blasts from the radio—convertibles have survived to the end of the century as a symbol of the good life in America.

The term "convertible" refers to a standard automobile body-style designation adopted by the Society of Automotive Engineers in 1928. Short for "convertible coupe," a convertible typically describes a two-door car with four seats, a folding fabric roof (hence the convertible synonym "ragtop") that is permanently attached to the frame and may be lifted and lowered at the driver's discretion, a fixed-position windshield, and roll-up side windows. In the early days,

when automobiles were still built in backyards and small blacksmith shops, they resembled the familiar horse-drawn carriages of the day. Open body vehicles, some came with optional folding tops similar to those on wagons. By the teen years, manufacturers had begun to design automobiles that no longer resembled carriages and to offer various body styles to the driving public. By the late 1920s, practicality pushed closed cars to the forefront, and, ever since, convertibles have been manufactured in smaller numbers than closed cars.

The first true convertibles, an improvement on the earlier roadsters and touring sedans, appeared in 1927 from eight manufacturers. During the 1930s, the convertible acquired its image as a sporty, limited-market auto, surviving the Depression because of its sales appeal—it was the best, most luxurious, and most costly of a manufacturer's lineup, a sign that better days were ahead. 1957-67 was the golden age of convertibles, with the sixties the best years: convertibles held 6 percent of the market share from 1962-66. By the 1970s, however, market share had dropped to less than 1 percent.

Their decline came about because of their relative impracticality (deteriorating fabric tops, lack of luggage space and headroom, and poor fuel economy because of heavier curb weight); the introduction of air-conditioning as an option on most automobiles, which made closed cars quieter and more comfortable; the introduction of the more convenient sunroofs and moonroofs; decline in wide-open spaces; availability of cheaper, reliable imports; the impact of the Vietnam War on a generation of car buyers; and changes in safety standards—due to the efforts of Ralph Nader and insurance companies alarmed by the enormous power of many cars during the 1960s, Washington mandated higher standards of automotive safety and required manufacturers to include lap and shoulder belts, collapsible steering columns, side impact reinforcement, chassis reinforcement, energy-absorbing front ends, and five mph crash bumpers; the threat to pass Federal Motor Vehicle Safety Standard No. 216 (roof crush standard) caused manufacturers to lose their enthusiasm for convertibles. Furthermore, the adage in the automotive industry, "When the market goes down, the top goes up," may have been proven true again as the recession of the 1970s drove a stake through the convertible's heart during that decade. In fact, according to Lesley Hazelton in "Return of the Convertible," no mass-market convertibles were available from the early seventies through the early eighties, though a driver could purchase a convertible "for a price: the Rolls-Royce Corniche; the Alfa Romeo Spider; the Mercedes-Benz 450SL, 380SL, or 560SL."

In 1982, Lee Iacocca, chairman of Chrysler, brought back the convertible after a six-year absence. Buick introduced a new convertible that year, and Chevrolet, Ford, Pontiac, and Cadillac soon followed. With only seven American convertibles and a handful of European and Japanese convertibles being manufactured in the mid-1990s, some question whether the convertible will remain after the turn of the century. Others believe that convertibles will remain an automotive option so long as there are romantic drivers who wish to feel the wind in their hair.

—Carol A. Senf

FURTHER READING:

Gunnell, John "Gunner." *Convertibles: The Complete Story.* Blue Ridge Summit, Penn., Tab Books, 1984.

Hazleton, Lesley. "Return of the Convertible." *The Connoisseuer.* Vol. 22, May 1991, 82-87.

A 1950s Ford T-Bird Convertible.

Langworth, Richard M., and the auto editors of *Consumer Guide. The Great American Convertible.* New York, Beekman House, 1988.

Newbery, J. G. *Classic Convertibles.* New York, Brompton Books, 1994.

Wright, Nicky. *Classic Convertibles.* New York, Metro Books, 1997.

Conway, Tim (1933—)

As the perennial comedy sidekick, Tim Conway was a television comedy mainstay for four decades. He debuted as a repertory player on Steve Allen's 1950s variety show, and co-starred as the nebbishy Ensign Parker on the popular *McHale's Navy* situation comedy during the 1960s. He then became a reliable second banana on *The Carol Burnett Show*, which ran from 1967 until 1978, where he was often paired with the lanky Harvey Korman. Conway's characters included the laconic boss to Burnett's dimwitted secretary, Mrs. Wiggins. He was also a regular performer in children's movies for Walt Disney during the 1970s. In the late 1980s, Conway created his best-known comedy persona by standing on his knees and becoming Dorf, a klutzy sportsman. As Dorf, Conway produced and starred in several popular TV specials and videos. Conway starred in a succession of short-lived TV series in his attempts to be a leading man; he good-naturedly acquired a vanity license plate reading ''13 WKS,'' the usual duration of his starring vehicles.

—Andrew Milner

FURTHER READING:

Allen, Steve. *More Funny People.* New York, Stein and Day, 1982.

Brooks, Tim, and Earle Marsh. *The Complete Directory to Prime Time Network and Cable TV Shows 1946-Present.* 6th ed. New York, Ballantine, 1995.

Cooke, Sam (1935-1964)

During the late 1950s and early 1960s, Soul music star Sam Cooke laid the blueprint for many of the Soul and R&B artists who followed him. One of the first major Gospel stars to cross over into secular music, Cooke was also among the first Soul or R&B artists to found his own music publishing company. During a time when many black artists lost financial and artistic control of their music to greedy independent and major record labels, Cooke started his own record company, leading the way for other artists such as Curtis Mayfield to do the same. But it was Cooke's vocal delivery, which mixed a sweet smoothness and the passion of Gospel music, that proved the greatest influence on a number of major Soul stars, most significantly Curtis Mayfield, Bobby Womack, Al Green, and Marvin Gaye. Because Sam Cooke was one of Gaye's musical idols, the man born Marvin Pentz Gay, Jr. went so far as to add an ''e'' to the end of his name when he began singing professionally, just as Sam Cooke did.

Sam Cooke was born into a family of eight sons in Clarkesdale, Mississippi, and began singing at an early age in church, where his father was a Baptist minister. He and his family later moved to Chicago, Illinois, where Cooke began singing in a Gospel trio called the Soul Children, which consisted of Cooke and two of his brothers. As a teenager, Cooke joined the Highway QCs, and by the time he was in his early twenties, Cooke became a member of one of the most important longstanding Gospel groups, the Soul Stirrers. While he was with the Soul Stirrers, Cooke recorded a number of Gospel classics for Specialty Records, such as the Cooke-penned "Touch the Hem of His Garment," "Just Another Day," and "Nearer to Thee."

In a controversial move, Cooke crossed over into the secular market with the single "Lovable" while he was still singing with the Soul Stirrers. So contentious was this move that the single was released under the pseudonym "Dale Cook." More importantly, Specialty Records owner Art Rupe distanced the label from Cooke by releasing him from his contract for fear of losing Specialty's Gospel fan base. Cooke's breakthrough Pop hit was 1957's "You Send Me," essentially a rewrite of a well-known Gospel tune of the time, but with lyrics about the love of another person rather than God. With its Gospel influenced vocal delivery, "You Send Me" provided the foundation for Soul music for forty years to come—a foundation that never strayed very far away from Gospel, no matter how profane the subject matter became.

"You Send Me" went to number one on the *Billboard* charts, beginning a string of thirty-one Pop hits for Cooke from 1957 to 1965 that included "I'll Come Running Back To You," "Chain Gang," "You Were Made for Me," "Shake," and "Wonderful World." While some of his Pop material was frivolous ("Everybody Likes to Cha Cha Cha," "Twistin' the Night Away," and "Another Saturday Night"), Cooke's ardent support of the 1960s Civil Rights struggle was evident during interviews at the time. His music also reflected his commitment to the struggle in songs such as "A Change is Gonna Come," a response to Bob Dylan's "Blowin' in the Wind." Then, at the height of his career, Sam Cooke was killed on December 11,

1964—shot three times in the Los Angeles Hacienda Motel by a manager who claimed to be acting in self-defense after she asserted Cooke raped a 22-year-old woman and then turned on her. Although the shooting was ruled justifiable homicide, there were a number of details about that night that remained hazy and unanswered, and there has never been a sufficient investigation of his death. For years after his death Cooke has remained a significant presence within Soul music, and in 1986 he was inducted into the Rock & Roll Hall of Fame.

—Kembrew McLeod

FURTHER READING:

McEwen, Joe. *Sam Cooke: A Biography in Words and Pictures*. New York, Sire Books, 1977.

Wolff, Daniel. *You Send Me: The Life and Times of Sam Cooke*. London, Virgin, 1996.

Cooper, Alice (1948—)

Rock stars come and go, but Alice Cooper's contributions to the canon of rock 'n' roll showmanship have been remarkably lasting. In a career spanning three decades, Cooper has elevated the live presentation of rock music with bizarre theatrics, taboo subjects, and an uncompromising hard-rock sound.

Alice Cooper was born Vincent Furnier in Detroit, Michigan, on February 4, 1948, the son of Ether (an ordained minister) and Ella Furnier. The family moved quite frequently. Living in Phoenix, Arizona, Vincent was a high-school jock who was on the track team, and reported for the school newspaper. During his time in school, he met Glen Buxton, a tough kid with an unsavory reputation as a juvenile delinquent who was a photographer for the newspaper. Buxton played guitar; the young Furnier wrote poetry. It wasn't too long after school that the duo moved to Los Angeles in search of rock 'n' roll dreams.

While in L.A., Furnier and Buxton enlisted Michael Bruce, Neal Smith, and Dennis Dunnway and began calling themselves the Earwigs. In 1968, the band changed their name to Alice Cooper, noting that it sounded like a country and western singer's stage name. (Another legend about the name's origin included a drunken session with an Ouija Board in tow.) In 1974, Furnier legally changed his name to Alice Cooper. Iconoclastic musician Frank Zappa went to one of the group's Los Angeles club shows. Impressed with their ability to clear a room, Zappa offered the band a recording contract with his label Straight, a subsidiary of Warner Bros. The band recorded two records for Straight, *Pretties For You* and *Easy Action*, before signing with Warner Bros. in 1970.

The band's first album for Warner Bros., 1971's *Love It To Death,* featured the underground FM radio hit, "I'm Eighteen," a paean to youth apathy that predated the nihilistic misanthropy of the punk scene by five years. Later that year, the band recorded *Killer,* which featured some of their most celebrated songs such as "Under My Wheels," "Be My Lover," and "Dead Babies."

The tour in support of *Killer* elevated the band's reputation in the rock world. Cooper—with his eyes circled in dark black make-up—pulled theatrical stunts such as wielding a sword with an impaled baby

Sam Cooke

Alice Cooper

doll on the end or singing with his pet boa constrictor coiled around him. For the grand finale, Alice was sentenced to ''die'' by hanging on a gallows set up on stage. The crowds adored him, the critics took note of the band's energy, and soon Alice Cooper and his band were poised to bid farewell to underground obscurity.

The band followed *Killer* with their breakthrough album, 1972's *School's Out.* The title song was an anti-authority rant that became a hit single. The subsequent tour that followed was no less controversial, for the singer was placed in an onstage guillotine (operated by master illusionist James Randi) and decapitated. Later Cooper returned in top hat and tails singing ''Elected.'' With each year, the presentations became increasingly absurd—with Alice fighting off oversized dancing teeth with an enormous toothbrush during the tour supporting their 1973 album, *Billion Dollar Babies*—and both fans and critics thought the music was beginning to suffer.

The final album by the original Alice Cooper band, 1974's *Muscle Of Love,* was a financial and artistic failure. The band split up, and Alice pursued a solo career. His 1975 album, *Welcome to My Nightmare,* spawned a hit single (the controversial ballad ''Only Women Bleed''), a theatrically-released film of the same name, and

widespread mainstream fame. Cooper became one of the first rockers to perform at Lake Tahoe, play Pro-Am golf tourneys, and appear in films and mainstream shows like *Hollywood Squares* and *The Tonight Show with Johnny Carson.*

Cooper's post-band work was informed by then-current trends in music and his personal life. He went public with his battle with alcoholism, an experience chronicled on his 1978 album, *From the Inside.* He used synthesizers and rhythm machines on such new-wave tinged records as *Flush the Fashion* (1980) and *DaDa* (1983), and enlisted the services of the late Waitresses singer Patty Donahue for his 1982 *Zipper Catches Skin* album. None of these records catapulted his name back up the charts, and Warner Bros. chose not to pick up an option on his contract.

Cooper returned to the rock marketplace in 1986 with a new album *Constrictor,* on a new label, MCA. He was aping the overproduced metal scene, and the record was a flop. Critics blasted Cooper for staying in the rock game well past his shelf life. But it wasn't until 1990, when Cooper signed with Epic Records, and made several rock hard albums, *Trash* (1989) and *Hey Stoopid* (1991), that exposed the singer to a new generation of metalheads. In May 1994,

Cooper released *The Last Temptation,* a concept album based on the characters created by respected graphic novelist Neil Gaiman.

Alice Cooper's career is marked by dizzying highs of grandeur and influence, and miserable lows of bargain-bin indifference. The shock-rockers of the 1990s such as Marilyn Manson and Nine Inch Nails are merely driving down the same roads that were originally paved by Alice Cooper's wild imagination.

—Emily Pettigrew

FURTHER READING:

''Alice Cooper Presents.'' http://www.alicecoopershow.com. March 1999.

Cooper, Alice, with Steven Gaines. *Me, Alice: The Autobiography of Alice Cooper.* New York, Putnam, 1976.

Henssler, Barry. ''Alice Cooper.'' *Contemporary Musicians.* Vol. 8. Detroit, Gale Research, 1992.

Koen, D. ''Alice Cooper: Healthy, Wealthy and Dry.'' *Rolling Stone.* July 13-27, 1989, 49.

''Mr. America.'' *Newsweek.* May 28, 1973, 65.

''Schlock Rock's Godzilla.'' *Time.* May 28, 1978, 80-83.

Cooper, Gary (1901-1961)

In American cinema history, Gary Cooper reigned almost un-challenged as the embodiment of male beauty—''swooningly beautiful'' as Robin Cross defined it in his essay in *The Movie Stars Story*—and an enduring emblem of innocent ideals and heroic virtues. Lanky and laconic, his screen persona often shy and hesitant, there was about him the aura of a solitary man, his clear compelling eyes seemingly focused on a distant and private horizon. Cooper contributed comprehensively to every genre of Hollywood film, working with an unparalleled range of directors and leading ladies. His career spanned 35 years, shorter than that of several of his contemporaries, yet he made an astonishing number of films by any standard—92 in all—which carried him through as a leading man from the silent era to the commencement of the 1960s.

Irrespective of the material, Cooper's casual, laconic delivery remained unmodified by any change of pace or nuance, yet his very simplicity lent truth to his performances. In the public mind, Cooper remains an archetypal Man of the West, most movingly defined by his Sheriff Will Kane in *High Noon* (1952). What he never played, however, was a man of villainy or deceit.

Christened Frank Cooper, he was born on May 7, 1901 to British immigrant parents in Helena, Montana, where his father was a justice of the Supreme Court. He was educated in England from 1910-17, returning to attend agricultural college in Montana, work on a ranch, and study at Grinnell College in Iowa. There, he began drawing political cartoons. He was determined to become an illustrator and eventually went to Los Angeles in 1924 to pursue this goal. Unable to find a job, he fell into work as a film extra and occasional bit player, mainly in silent Westerns, and made some 30 appearances before

Gary Cooper

being picked up by director Henry King as a last-minute substitute for the second lead in *The Winning of Barbara Worth* (1926).

The camera loved Cooper as it did Garbo, and his instant screen charisma attracted attention and a long tenure at Paramount, who built him into a star. He made a brief appearance in *It* (1927) with Clara Bow and became the superstar's leading man in *Children of Divorce* the same year, a film whose box-office was helped considerably by their famous off-screen affair. It was the first of many such liaisons between Cooper and his leading ladies who, almost without exception, found his virile magnetism and legendary sexual prowess irresistible. He finally settled into marriage with socialite Veronica Balfe, a relationship that survived a much-publicized affair with Patricia Neal, Cooper's co-star in the screen version of Ayn Rand's *The Fountainhead* (1949). These exploits did nothing to dent his image as a gentle ''Mr. Nice Guy'' replete with quiet manly strength or his growing popularity with men and women alike, and by the mid-1930s his star status was fully established and remained largely unshakable for the rest of his life.

Cooper made his all-talkie debut in *The Virginian* (1929), the first of his many Westerns, uttering the immortal line, ''When you call me that, smile!'' In 1930, for Von Sternberg, he was the Foreign Legionnaire in *Morocco* with Dietrich and emerged a fully established star. He was reunited with her in Frank Borzage's *Desire* in

1936, by which time he had successfully entered the arenas of romantic comedy and melodrama, played the soldier hero of *A Farewell to Arms* (1932), and survived a few near-misses to embark on his best period of work.

From 1936-57 Cooper featured on the Exhibitors' Top Ten List in every year but three, and ranked first in 1953. His run of hits in the 1930s, which began with *The Lives of a Bengal Lancer* (1935), brought one of his most famous roles in 1936, that of Longfellow Deeds, the simple country boy who inherits a fortune and wishes to give it away to the Depression-hit farmers of America. The film, *Mr. Deeds Goes to Town*, directed by Frank Capra, earned Cooper the first of his five Oscar nominations, while another country boy-turned-patriotic hero, Howard Hawks' *Sergeant York* (1941) marked his first Oscar win.

The 1940s brought two films with Barbara Stanwyck, the quintessentially Capra-esque drama, *Meet John Doe* (1941), then Hawks' comedy *Ball of Fire* (1942), in which he was a memorable absent-minded professor. His sober portrayal of baseball hero Lou Gehrig in *The Pride of the Yankees* (1942) won another Academy nomination, as did *For Whom the Bell Tolls* (1943) with Ingrid Bergman. The 1950s brought mixed fortunes. In 1957 Billy Wilder cast the 56 year-old Cooper opposite 28 year-old gamin Audrey Hepburn in the sophisticated comedy romance *Love in the Afternoon*. Cooper, suffering from hernias and a duodenal ulcer, precursors of the cancer that would kill him, looked drawn and older than his years, and the May-December partnership was ill received.

The decade did, however, cast him in some notable Westerns. He was a striking foil to Burt Lancaster's wild man in *Vera Cruz* (1954) and was impressive as a reformed outlaw forced into eliminating his former partners in Anthony Mann's *Man of the West* (1958), his last masterpiece in which the ravages of age and illness were now unmistakably apparent. But it was his awesomely contained, determined, and troubled sheriff, going out to face the forces of evil alone in *High Noon* that won him another Oscar and cemented the Cooper image for future generations.

At the 1960 Academy Awards ceremony in April 1961, Gary Cooper was the recipient of a special award for his many memorable performances and the distinction that he had conferred on the motion picture industry. He was too ill to attend and his close friend James Stewart accepted on his behalf. A month later, on May 13, 1961, Gary Cooper died, leaving one last film—the British-made and sadly undistinguished *The Naked Edge* (1961)—to be released posthumously. Idolized by the public, he was loved and respected by his peers who, as historian David Thomson has written, "marveled at the astonishingly uncluttered submission of himself to the camera."

—Robyn Karney

FURTHER READING:

Cross, Robin. "Gary Cooper." *The Movie Stars Story.* New York, Crescent Books, 1986.

Meyers, Jeff. *Gary Cooper: American Hero.* New York, Morrow, 1998.

Shipman, David. *The Great Movie Stars: The Golden Years.* London, Angus & Robertson, 1979.

Thomson, David. *A Biographical Dictionary of Film.* New York, Knopf, 1994.

Cooperstown, New York

Home to the National Baseball Museum and Hall of Fame, Cooperstown, a restored nineteenth-century frontier town and country village of about 2,300 inhabitants at the close of the twentieth century, is visited annually by up to 400,000 tourists. Baseball has been described as America's national pastime, and it is fair to say that Cooperstown, in central New York State, draws to its village thousands of American tourists in search of their country's national identity.

When the National Baseball Hall of Fame opened in 1939, Americans from coast to coast read about it and heard radio broadcasts of the opening induction ceremonies. Cy Young, Babe Ruth, Ty Cobb, Grover Alexander, and Walter Johnson were among those inducted as the hall's first members. Every year on the day after the annual inductions, a Major League game is played at nearby Doubleday Field, seating approximately ten thousand, on the spot where many believe baseball to have originated. A legend of the origin of baseball claims that the game was developed in Cooperstown in 1839. According to a three-year investigation of the Mills Commission in the early 1900s, Abner Doubleday and his young friends played a game of "Town Ball" with a hand-stitched ball and a four-inch flat bat. Doubleday is said to have introduced bases, created the positions of pitcher and catcher, and established the rules that defined the game of baseball. Though this legend is disputed by some, even those who disagree accept the village as a symbolic home for the game's creation.

Philanthropist and Cooperstown native Stephen C. Clark founded the Baseball Hall of Fame. Clark inherited his fortune from his grandfather, Edward Clark, who earned his wealth as a partner to Isaac Merrit Singer, inventor of the Singer sewing machine. Through the generosity of the Clark family toward their birthplace, Cooperstown gained not only the baseball museum, but also a variety of other attractions. In the nineteenth century, when Cooperstown was becoming a summer retreat, Edward Clark built Kingfisher Tower, a sixty-foot-high tower that overlooks the natural beauty of Otsego Lake, which spans nine miles north from its shore at Cooperstown. Stephen Clark and his brother, Edward S. Clark, built the Bassett Hospital to honor Dr. Mary Imogene Bassett, a general practitioner of Cooperstown and one of the first female physicians in America. Stephen Clark also brought the New York State Historical Association to Cooperstown in 1939; the village has since been the annual summer site of the association's seminars on American culture and folk art. In 1942, Stephen Clark established the Farmer's Museum, a cultural attraction that displays the customs of pre-industrial America. The museum continued to grow with the 1995 addition of an American Indian Wing containing more than six hundred artifacts that reflect the cultural diversity and creativity of Native Americans.

The exhibits of Native American culture are well suited to Cooperstown since it was a traditional fishing area of the Susquehannock and the Iroquois Indians until Dutch fur traders occupied it in the seventeenth century. It was also the birthplace of James Fenimore Cooper (1789-1851), the early nineteenth-century writer whose novels romantically depict Native Americans and the frontier life of early America. *The Pioneers* (1823), the first of Cooper's Leatherstocking Tales, is a novel set in the blossoming village of Cooperstown, and one of its main characters is based on James Fenimore Cooper's father, Judge William Cooper, the founder of the village in 1786. Another of Cooper's works, *The Chronicles of Cooperstown* (1838), provides a history of the village. The novel *The Deerslayer* (1841) takes place at Otsego Lake during the beginning of the French and Indian War.

An additional Cooperstown attraction, the Glimmerglass Opera opened in 1975 with performances in the auditorium of the Cooperstown High School. In 1987, the Alice Busch Opera Theater was completed to permanently host the Glimmerglass, which has become an internationally recognized organization, producing performances for thirty-six thousand opera fans during the summer festival seasons.

Overall, Cooperstown provides many opportunities to enjoy American culture. Appreciating the music, viewing the scenery, experiencing the American past in this historic village with its cultural museums and the National Baseball Hall of Fame appeals to many as an enjoyable diversion.

—Sharon Brown

FURTHER READING:

Birdsall, Ralph. *The Story of Cooperstown.* Cooperstown, A. H. Christ Co., 1920.

Cooperstown Chamber of Commerce. *Visitor's Guide.* Cooperstown Chamber of Commerce, Cooperstown, 1998.

Jones, Louis Clark. *Cooperstown.* Cooperstown, New York State Historical Association, 1982.

New York State Historical Association, *Main Street, Cooperstown: A Mile of Memories.* Cooperstown, New York State Historical Association, 1992.

Smith, Ken. *Baseball's Hall of Fame.* New York, Grosset and Dunlap, 1958.

Taylor, Alan. *William Cooper's Town: Power and Persuasion on the Frontier of the Early American Republic.* New York, Alfred A. Knopf, 1995.

Coors

"Pure Rocky Mountain Spring Water" isn't just a marketer's phrase; it is the ingredient that fueled Adolph Coors' dream of owning his own brewery in the 1870s, and then went on to make Coors the third largest brewing company in the United States. It might seem easy to dismiss Coors as just another brewery, but Coors has achieved what many other companies—beer or otherwise—would cherish: a mystique that reaches out to more than just beer drinkers.

Adolph Coors (1847-1929) was born in Barmen, Prussia, and worked as an apprentice at the Henry Wenker Brewery in Dortmund, Germany. In 1868, he fled a war-ravaged Germany to the United States as a stowaway on a ship, and in 1872 he arrived in Denver, Colorado, anxious to pursue his dream of owning a brewery. In Golden, Colorado, along the banks of Clear Creek, he found the water that he believed would make the finest tasting beer. Establishing his brewery on the site it still inhabits today, Adolph Coors soon began supplying beer to miners. During Prohibition, which began in Colorado in 1916, Coors kept the business alive by selling malted milk, a near-beer called Mannah, and the porcelain products that Coors still produces.

With the death of Adolph Coors in 1929, Coor's son Adolph Jr. took over operations and, after Prohibition was repealed, he expanded the market to ten Western states. In 1941, Coors introduced Coors Light, but government restrictions due to World War II forced Coors to limit product offerings. In 1959, Coors introduced the country's first all-aluminum can and got a jump on the ecologists by offering a penny for each can returned for recycling. The mid-1970s brought unrest and decline for the Coors company when Local Union #366 demanded a boycott of Coors beer. Sales dropped and, for the first time in its history, employees were laid off. Although contract negotiations revolved around wages and benefits, the company was affected by bad press about Coors' policy of making potential employees submit to polygraph testing. Workers went on strike on April 5, 1977. The strike officially lasted a little over a year; unofficially it lasted much longer as the company continued to suffer from bad press regarding its treatment of minorities and women, as well as the breakup of the union. These allegations ultimately proved untrue, and Coors was vindicated in 1982 when *60 Minutes* interviewed Coors executives and employees. Coors received a rare favorable report from *60 Minutes* and the judgment that it had been the victim of a smear campaign by the AFL-CIO. An agreement between Coors and the AFL-CIO finally was reached in 1987.

By the late 1970s, consumers were clamoring for a product with fewer calories. In 1978, Coors reintroduced Coors Light, the beer destined to become their number one product and one of the best-selling beers in the country, creating a larger demand for Coors in every state. In 1981, Coors expanded across the Mississippi and by 1991 had reached all 50 states. Operations were expanded to include two new breweries—one in Virginia's Shenandoah Valley, the other in Memphis, Tennessee—both acclaimed for the high-quality water that the Coors family would not compromise.

Coors achieved legendary, even cult, status in the 1960s and 1970s. This "mystique madness" may have started during World War II. Believing that beer would help the morale of the troops, the U.S. government subsidized breweries' materials and costs. Coors allocated half of its production to go overseas. When the war ended and soldiers returned, the Coors beer they had become accustomed to drinking was found in only the Western states, leaving soldiers to pine over what they had left behind. A visit to Colorado eventually became a way to smuggle the Rocky Mountain brew home. Former U.S. President Gerald Ford was known to return to the White House with several cases of Coors aboard Air Force One, as would his Secretary of State, Henry Kissinger. Actor Paul Newman was often seen at functions with a Coors in hand. The mystique of Coors beer was featured in the movie *Smokey and the Bandit*, starring Burt Reynolds. In the story line, Reynolds is challenged to smuggle a truckload of Coors beer from Texarkana to Atlanta in 28 hours for a reward of $80,000.

What began as a German immigrant's dream in 1873 is now one of the largest and most ethical corporations in America. Its philanthropic endeavors include environmental activities, start-up businesses run by minorities, literacy programs, and veteran affairs. Not content to limit these endeavors to outside interests, Coors also supports better environments for its employees, such as its parental leave policy, its Wellness Center, and its health benefits to partners of

A truck carries three enormous Coors beer cans (each complete with its own tap).

gay and lesbian employees. But even though it is one of the largest corporations in the country, the employees at Coors still talk about its "family feel." The mystique lives on.

—Cheryl A. Smith

FURTHER READING:

Banham, Russ. *Coors: A Rocky Mountain Legend.* Lyme, Connecticut, Greenwich Publishing Group, Inc., 1998.

Van Munching, Philip. *Beer Blast: The Inside Story of the Brewing Industry's Bizarre Battles for Your Money.* New York, Random House, 1997.

Yenne, Bill. *Beers of North America.* New York, Gallery Books, 1986.

Copland, Aaron (1900-1990)

One of the greatest American composers of the twentieth century, Aaron Copland wrote music for American audiences with genuine American themes. He changed the face of a composer's lifestyle by being involved in activities outside of the concert hall, and he wrote music according to the popular trends of his time. This ability to tap into the pulse of American popular culture elevated Copland to the status of musical icon, although Copland was a humble man who did not have the same ambition to acquire the huge audiences and fame that other musicians sought out. Copland's range of musical styles was diverse, including jazz, opera, and American folk styles. He also taught, lectured, and wrote books on musical topics. To him, music was the ultimate symbol of passion and vigor in a personality.

Copland's family came from Poland and Lithuania to the United States in the 1870s. Aaron was born on November 14, 1900, the youngest of five children. Harris and Sarah Copland, whose department store earned the label "Macy's of Brooklyn," gave their children a strong work ethic and a sense of orderliness and self-determination that one can see in Copland over the course of his musical career. As a youngster, he quickly realized his love for music as he studied the works of Tchaikovsky, Debussy, and Ravel, among others. He played the piano, and an older sister served as a tutor, but he soon realized that he needed a professional musician if he was going to make a career out of it.

Despite his father's disappointment with his career choice, Copland went to Paris in 1921 to study at the new music school for Americans at Fontainebleau and take in the city's rich, vibrant culture. He studied harmony under a superb music instructor, Nadia Boulanger. He toured other European cities such as Berlin and Vienna, two world-famous musical centers, to take in as many musical influences as he could. But Copland soon longed for New York, and he returned to the United States in 1924.

During his years in Europe, Copland had formulated a better contemporary understanding of music. He discovered that there were vast differences in musical tastes between Americans and Europeans—the music scene was much more energetic and accomplished in Paris than in New York. Copland's experiences enabled him to write his first major piece, *Symphony for Organ and Orchestra*, in 1924, which premiered with the New York Symphony Orchestra at Carnegie Hall in early 1925. Copland worked with jazz styles and rhythms in his *Music for the Theater* (1925) and *Piano Concerto* (1926). He showed a more abstract style in *Short Symphony* (1933) and *Statements for Orchestra* (1933-35). He changed his style in the following decades and concentrated more on producing works with American folkloric themes, which gained him a wider audience. His most important works during these years included *Billy the Kid* (1938), *Rodeo* (1942), and *Appalachian Spring* (1944). Copland also experimented with opera: *The Second Hurricane* (a ''play opera'' for high school students in 1937) and *The Tender Land* (1954). His most famous orchestral scores include *El Salón México* (1936) and *A Lincoln Portrait* (1942) with spoken excerpts from Abraham Lincoln's famous speeches. Copland also composed music for films such as *Of Mice and Men* (1939), *Our Town* (1940), *The Red Pony* (1949), and *The Heiress* (1949, for which his score won an Oscar), and he became known as one of the leading composers of movie scores.

Aaron Copland

Copland was the recipient of many distinguished commissions, awards, and prizes, such as the Medal of Freedom in 1964 awarded by the United States Government. Copland's books include *What to Listen for in Music* (1939), *Copland on Music* (1960), and a two-volume autobiography with Vivian Perlis. Copland ceased composing after 1970 but continued to conduct, write, and lecture. He died in Tarrytown, New York, on December 2, 1990.

—David Treviño

FURTHER READING:

Berger, Arthur. *Aaron Copland*. New York, De Capo Press, 1990.

Butterworth, Neil. *The Music of Aaron Copland*. New York, Universe Books, 1986.

Copland, Aaron, and Vivian Perlis. *Copland: 1900 through 1942*. Boston, Faber and Faber, 1984.

———. *Copland: Since 1943*. New York, St. Martin's Press, 1989.

Dobrin, Arnold. *Aaron Copland: His Life and Times*. New York, Thomas Y. Crowell Company, 1967.

Corbett, James J. (1866-1933)

Professional prizefighting in the nineteenth century was a semi-legal, bare-fisted fight to the finish, often featuring more wrestling than punching. As the twentieth century approached, changes were made, ostensibly to legitimize ''boxing'' as credible athletic competition. On September 7, 1892, in New Orleans, the first Heavyweight championship match contested under the relatively new Marquess of Queensberry rules took place. These new rules stipulated three minute rounds with one minute rest periods and the use of five-ounce gloves, worn to protect the combatant's hands. A relic from the bare-knuckle age by the name of John L. Sullivan—''The Boston Strongboy''—was the reigning champion. Sullivan personified nineteenth-century America: rugged, racist individualism. He triumphed in brutal contests of stamina and strength despite his heavy drinking; he sauntered into saloons boasting ''I can lick any man in the house!'' and he drew the color line, refusing to fight leading black contender Peter Jackson. Sullivan's challenger, a fellow Irish-American pugilist named James J. Corbett, seemed to personify the direction in which boxing was moving, perhaps as a reflection of American society. ''Gentleman Jim,'' as Corbett would come to be known, both for his style of dress outside the ring and his fighting style inside it, was born on September 1, 1866 in San Francisco, California. The son of a livery stable owner, he graduated high school but always found himself fighting, first in the streets and then eventually at the San Francisco Olympic Club. Where Sullivan was an east coast, blue-collar roughneck, Corbett was a west coast, white-collar scientific boxer, who was employed as a bank teller when he began his professional prizefighting career.

Corbett had earned his title shot with a win against an old bareknuckle nemesis of Sullivan's, Jake Kilrain—with two wins against contender Joe Choynski (who would go on to defeat the great Jack Johnson); and with a 61 round draw with the same Peter Jackson whom Sullivan refused to fight. Gentleman Jim toured the country, fighting from San Francisco to Brooklyn, all the while clamoring for a

A reproduction of a fight between James J. Corbett (left) and John L. Sullivan.

match with the feared and beloved reigning champ. He got his chance in New Orleans, where after 21 rounds Jim Corbett's new-age science prevailed over John L. Sullivan's old-world machismo. In what boxing historian Bert Randolph Sugar nearly a century later called "the most important round in boxing history," the smaller, faster, fitter Corbett claimed the heavyweight throne with a shattering knockout. Modern boxing was born with this fight, as speed, conditioning, and technique triumphed over brute force. Corbett, and especially the Corbett-Sullivan fight, epitomized the evolution of the fight game from a foul-plagued virtual free-for-all to a more organized contest of fists and wit. In a Darwinian twist, after the rules were changed, Corbett-like fighters, who previously had not been as successful as their larger and more powerful Sullivan-like counterparts, were now better adapted for success in boxing.

After his title winning effort, Corbett followed a path similar to John L. Sullivan's. Cashing in on his newfound fame, Corbett toured in theater and vaudeville. By the time he defended his title against Bob Fitzsimmons, Corbett had fought only once in the five years since the Sullivan bout. Gentleman Jim lost his title to Fitzsimmons,

suffering a 14th round knockout. He made two attempts to regain the crown, both against the big and powerful James J. Jeffries. In both fights, Corbett's "science" seemed at first to be carrying the day, but the younger, fresher, Jeffries eventually caught up with the old boxing master, winning with knockout's in the twenty-third round of their first fight and the tenth round of the rematch. With all of the changes in boxing epitomized by Corbett's defeat of Sullivan, there was one aspect of the sport that no rule change could alter, one that remains constant to this day: father time beats all comers.

—Max Kellerman

FURTHER READING:

Corbett, James J. *My Life and Fights.* London, John Ousley, 1910.

———. *The Roar of the Crowd.* London and New York, Knickerbocker Press, 1925.

Heyn, Ernest V., ed. *Twelve More Sport Immortals.* New York, Bartholomew House, 1951.

Corman, Roger (1926—)

The king of "B" movies, Roger Corman has produced and/or directed more than two hundred films, half of which have made a profit. After graduating from Stanford with an engineering degree, Corman went into the movie business, working his way up from messenger boy to screenwriter. After a studio tampered with his first screenplay, he decided to produce his own films. *The Monster from the Ocean Floor* (1954) established the Corman formula, as noted in *Baseline's Encyclopedia of Film*: "Quirky characters; offbeat plots laced with social commentary, clever use of special effects, sets, and cinematography; employment of fresh talent; and above all, minuscule budgets (under $100,000) and breakneck shooting schedules (5-10 days)." Corman's movies, such as *The Little Shop of Horrors, Machine Gun Kelly,* and the six Edgar Allan Poe pictures starring Vincent Price, became instant cult classics in the 1950s and 1960s. Always quick to spot and sponsor talent, Corman formed his own production company, which became a training ground for such A-list directors and actors as Francis Ford Coppola, Martin Scorsese, Jonathan Demme, Jack Nicholson, Robert De Niro, and Dennis Hopper. With his eye for talent, knack for business, and willingness to take risks, Roger Corman made low-budget movies a staple of American popular culture.

—Victoria Price

FURTHER READING:

Arkoff, Samuel Z., and Richard Trubo. *Flying through Hollywood by the Seat of My Pants.* New York, Birch Lane Press, 1992.

Corman, Roger, and Jim Jerome. *How I Made a Hundred Movies in Hollywood and Never Lost a Dime.* New York, DaCapo Press, 1998.

Monaco, James, and the editors of *Baseline. Encyclopedia of Film.* New York, Perigee, 1991.

Corvette

In 1953 General Motors introduced the Chevrolet Corvette sports car, America's first mass-produced automobile with a fiberglass body. With its sleek design and Americanized European styling, it quickly became the "dream car" of thousands of auto enthusiasts. Though the economy was experiencing a postwar boom in automobile sales, the base price of $3,498 was prohibitive for many, and only 300 Corvettes were produced the first year. In 1960, its popularity was enhanced by a television series called *Route 66* (1960-1964), which featured two adventurous guys—actors Martin Milner and George Maharis—tooling around the country in a Corvette.

The car was the brainchild of Harley Earl, an auto designer who had made his name turning out one-of-a-kind car bodies for movie stars. Earl's first design after joining General Motors was the spectacular 1927 Cadillac LaSalle, which was to help convince the automobile industry of the importance of styling. He scored another design coup by putting tail fins on the 1948 Cadillacs, making him the top man in GM styling and giving him the clout to persuade the company to build an entirely new car. Earl noticed that GIs had brought back a distinctive kind of automobile from Europe, a sports car that was fun to drive and had become a kind of cult object to the owners who gathered to race them on dirt tracks. Detroit made no

vehicle to compete with the popular two-seat sports cars such as the MG and Jaguar until Earl convinced his bosses to let him build an American sports car to present at the 1953 Motorama, GM's traveling show. GM executives agreed after insisting that standard GM parts be used under its proposed fiberglass body. Legend has it that the designers cleared away a ping-pong table and in one night "laid out the whole skin for the first Corvette." After discarding almost three hundred suggestions for a name, they selected Corvette, the name of a swift fighting ship in the old British navy.

Despite the secrecy surrounding the new Corvette, word leaked out to sports car enthusiasts, and in January, 1953, long lines of curious car buffs waited outside the Waldorf-Astoria Hotel in New York City for the Motorama to open. The 300 original models were polo white convertibles with red interiors, and all handmade body panels. The critics pronounced them beautiful, but not very satisfactory as sports cars due to an inadequate, rough-riding suspension system. They proved, however, to be superb investments, and those still owned by collectors are said to be worth more than $100,000 each. The number of original 1953 cars still existing is variously estimated at 120 to 290.

The engineering problems persisted, and in 1954, only half of the output of 3600 Corvettes were sold. A former racer on the European circuit, Zora Arkus-Duntov, came to GM's rescue by writing a memo to GM executives outlining the Corvette's shortcomings and urging the company to create a separate department within Chevrolet to oversee the Corvette's development. After GM hired Duntov for its Corvette project, his first step was to put a V-8 engine in the 1955 model, and that year GM sold all 700 of the Corvettes that were built.

Duntov went on to become Corvette's first chief engineer. In 1956 he replaced the automatic transmission with a three-speed manual, and the car became one of GM's hottest sellers. Corvette owners raced and defeated Jaguars and other European cars, and a modified 240 hp 1956 Corvette—with Duntov driving—set a record-breaking average of 150.583 mph at the Daytona Beach raceway. John Fitch drove a standard Corvette to a new production-car record of 145 mph during Daytona Speed Week in 1956. Later that year, in the 12 Hours of Sebring race, a Corvette showed its durability by winning first in its class. In 1960 three white Corvettes competed in the 24 Hours of LeMans race in France, finishing eighth overall. A 1968 Corvette reached a speed of 210.762 mph in the 1979 Bonneville Speed Week at the Utah Salt Flats, becoming the fastest carbureted car in the world.

The 250,000th Corvette, a gold convertible, rolled off the assembly line in 1969. Although Harley Earl had retired in 1958, being replaced as chief stylist by Bill Mitchell, the car underwent redesigns in 1963, 1968, and 1984. It was Mitchell who got the idea for the body shape of the XP-775, the Corvette Shark, after landing such a fish in deep sea off the Bahamas. The 500,000th Corvette was built in 1977, and the following year a Corvette was used as the pace car for the 62nd Indianapolis 500. In June of 1978 a movie, *Corvette Summer,* premiered in Maumee, Ohio, attracting a parade of Corvette owners that made the *Guinness Book of World Records,* the number estimated at between five and seven thousand cars. That October, another movie, *High Rolling in a Hot Corvette,* was released.

Into the 1980s the Corvette turned a profit for GM of about $100 million with a small production of around 25,000 cars annually. The Corvettes continued to act as a proving ground for new suspensions, new electronics, new chassis fabrication techniques, and new fiberglass or plastic materials for body parts. The Corvette sold out nearly every year, and Corvette clubs worldwide were filled with proud

The 1953 Corvette

owners who esteemed the cars and hailed the arrival of each new model, despite nagging problems such as rattles in the removable hardtop and the resistance of the fiberglass body to durable paint.

In the early months of 1989 was begun the long process of developing a new Corvette from scratch. The dream of developing the C5, the fifth-generation Corvette, coincided with a time of financial disaster at General Motors, which reported a $2 billion loss in 1990 and predicted even worse results in 1991. Despite this fiscal situation, new competitions were launched to design a C5 Corvette. The next five years proved to be a roller-coaster ride for the prototype due to internal rivalry at GM and budget cutbacks. Problems emerged involving the lubrication of the all-new aluminum engine, the electronic throttle control, and a new fiberglass side structure that failed to pass early tests in the crash laboratory. By 1996 the problems were solved, and C5s were being tested in long-distance drives throughout the United States. In Australia the new model Corvettes were set on cruise control in 110-degree heat and run on the outback roads for 90 to 120 minutes straight, with no problems.

When the new fifth-generation, cherry-red Corvette was unveiled at the Motorama Show the following January, fans were ecstatic about the car's new silhouette and its all-new 5.7-liter V8 345-hp engine, capable of moving from zero to sixty miles per hour in five seconds and delivering a top speed of 172 mph. Though it was still unmistakably a Vette, the wheelbase was longer, and the nose had been lowered for greater aerodynamics and road visibility. The new design reflected the sleekness of the '83 Corvette and the muscle of the '68 model. Other links to past Corvette generations included the air scoop on the front quarter panel, the familiar quad taillamps, and the concealed headlamps. The new version has one-third fewer parts despite the addition of a four-channel anti-lock braking system and complex traction control. Automobile writers raved about this sports car that was ''as comfortable as a limousine.'' GM boasted that with

all the improvements, the $44,990 sticker price was $635 less than the 1996 Corvette.

—Benjamin Griffith

FURTHER READING:

Adler, Dennis. *Corvettes, 1953-1995.* New York, Krause, 1996.

Schefter, James. *All Corvettes Are Red: The Rebirth of an American Legend.* New York, Simon & Schuster, 1996.

Zeichner, Walter. *Chevrolet Corvette, 1953-1986.* New York, Schiffer, 1990.

Corwin, Norman (1910—)

Throughout the 1940s, Norman Corwin elevated the fledgling medium of live broadcast radio theatre to its artistic zenith in America. Regarded as radio's poet laureate by fans and contemporaries, Corwin's earnest prosody adapted naturally and easily to radio broadcast, and he wielded the medium to its utmost, celebrating the American citizen during World War II, elucidating the dread of war with a journalist's precision, impugning despotism, or merely lending credence to the vox populi with his intellectual, imaginative use of words, music, and dramatic interplay. Corwin's dramatic use of radio defined an era and an art form. Though Corwin was revered and admired during radio's Golden Age, his popularity ultimately paralleled that of network radio.

Born May 3, 1910, in Boston, Massachusetts, Norman Lewis Corwin was the third of four children in a Jewish Russian-Hungarian family. He was a prankster and a storyteller, and his grades in school were uneven, though teachers discovered early his talent for writing and appreciation for poetry. Upon graduating from high school, Norman wrote for the *Springfield Republican* covering human-interest stories. When infant station WBZA requested that the newspaper provide a radio news reader, Corwin was assigned, and soon he was producing a poetry program—*Rhymes and Cadences*—while writing newspaper articles and radio copy as well as his first (failed) attempt at a novel. But at twenty-one, Corwin was restless and traveled to Europe with his brother and a friend.

In Germany, in the shadow of World War I, Corwin reflected on the senselessness of war, the ethnic hatred growing in the Weimar Republic, and the political pessimism spreading into adjacent nations. When Corwin returned to the States, his idealism resolved into a sense of purpose, a defiance of inevitability. In 1935 he began reading news on WLW in Cincinnati, Ohio. Less than three weeks later, though, he was fired for challenging a managerial memo forbidding the announcement of a local labor strike. He returned to the *Republican,* but not for long.

Arts, education, and social service organizations were accusing commercial radio stations of polluting the airwaves with a huckstering orgy, serving their own financial interests, and neglecting the quality of their programming. Faced with losing their licenses in a proposed decentralization of frequencies, many stations began hiring writers and directors to expand the formulaic format of commercial broadcasting with ''sustaining programs'' for discerning audiences.

After a brief stint as a publicity writer for Twentieth Century-Fox, Corwin was hired by the Columbia Broadcast System in 1938 and immediately proved himself a considerable talent, writing (in verse) and directing a fanciful play called *The Plot to Overthrow*

Norman Corwin

Christmas on his new program *Words without Music.* Later he impressed even the venerable CBS newsman Edward R. Murrow with *They Fly through the Air with the Greatest of Ease,* a sharp response to the indifference of Italian bombardiers. Corwin went on to produce and direct the *Columbia Workshop,* showcasing some of the finest writers, actors, and musicians available.

In 1941, Corwin wrote, directed, and produced a live broadcast each week for the eponymous *26 by Corwin* series. With unprecedented autonomy—network censors literally had no time to review his scripts prior to broadcast—Corwin spun each whimsical, fantastic, or dramatic tale, often reminding listeners of the war a horizon away. Later, Corwin produced a celebration piece for the 150th anniversary of the Bill of Rights (''We Hold These Truths'') to be aired on all four networks simultaneously and starring Hollywood luminaries James Stewart, Edward G. Robinson, Marjorie Main, Orson Welles, and many others, as well as president Franklin D. Roosevelt. On December 7, 1941, however, the Japanese attack on Pearl Harbor caught the nation by surprise, and Corwin retooled the program into a galvanizing documentation of American political determination. Eight days later, more than sixty million people heard ''We Hold These Truths'' as America's position on the war became clear: we would fight.

Throughout World War II, Corwin churned out poignant dramatizations of patriotism and thrilled audiences with his candor and eloquence. His series *This Is War!* (1942) was considered radio's first all-out effort at wartime domestic propaganda, and his series *An American in England,* coproduced on location by Edward R. Murrow, brought the human faces of shell-shocked Britain into American homes. In 1944, CBS broadcast *Columbia Presents Corwin,* a collection of war-inflected plays similar to the *26* series.

When the war in Europe ended, Corwin had prepared a special broadcast for V-E Day, May 8, 1945. Refraining from wild celebration, as the war was still alive in the Pacific Theatre, ''On a Note of Triumph'' asked tough moral questions of both citizen and government in a relentless prose poem equally evaluating America's losses and victories punctuated by sound effects and a powerful score by Bernard Hermann. For V-J Day, after the first atomic bombs were dropped on the cities of Hiroshima and Nagasaki, and Japan subsequently surrendered, Corwin created a solemn closure piece called simply ''14 August'' (1945), ''a fistful of lines'' delivered by Orson Welles.

After the war, Corwin received the first Wendell Wilkie One World award and traveled the war-torn globe recording his impressions, producing from these tapes the series *One World Flight* (1947). Corwin's association with CBS ended in 1948 when the network began to compromise his artistic integrity. He joined United Nations Radio in 1949 amid a national obsession with Communism in which Corwin himself ironically was suspect and created *Pursuit of Peace* (1950), a series which espoused the unity of the world's nations.

As radio became less lucrative and as the medium of television captured America's imagination, Corwin faded from public view. Though he authored more than seventeen books and wrote numerous screenplays, he could never recapture the immediate glory of radio's Golden Age. His programs have long been in circulation among old-time radio enthusiasts, however, and in the 1990s National Public Radio rebroadcast many of his works to commemorate the fiftieth anniversary of World War II and even commissioned new plays created by this bard of the airwaves.

—Tony Brewer

FURTHER READING:

Bannerman, R. LeRoy. *Norman Corwin and Radio: The Golden Years.* Alabama, University of Alabama Press, 1986.

Dunning, John. *On the Air: Encyclopedia of Old-Time Radio.* New York, Oxford University Press, 1998.

Maltin, Leonard. *The Great American Broadcast: A Celebration of Radio's Golden Age.* New York, Dutton, 1997.

Stuart, Lyle. *13 for Corwin: A Paean of Praise for Norman Corwin, the #1 Writer-Director-Producer during Radio's Golden Age.* New Jersey, Barricade Books, 1985.

Cosby, Bill (1937—)

As one of the most influential and gifted comics of his time, Bill Cosby dissolved racial barriers on television from the 1960s to the 1980s, created the epochal situation comedy *The Cosby Show,* produced memorable educational programs for children, and made a series of much adored advertisements. Cosby's enormously influential style as an on-stage comic influenced a generation. On the 1968 album *To Russell, My Brother, Whom I Slept With,* Cosby's comedy brings everyday experience away from any broader historical meaning to the level of the mundane and thus, the "universal." This quality of universality helps to account for his ability to traverse ordinarily sensitive racial, gender, and age divides with ease and grace.

Bill Cosby

In the style developed during his early years performing at nightclubs and recording a number of successful comedy albums, Cosby *became* his audience in their most ordinary, everyday aspects. Aware that while there were others who could tell "jokes" as well as or better than he, Cosby's inimitable signature was the domestic anecdote—a charming and instantly recognizable little tale of everyday family experience. Cosby remembers experience to such a degree that he revitalizes it.

Cosby deliberately eliminated anything in his comic presentation that might have divided his audience. According to biographer Caroline Latham, Cosby explained during an interview in the 1960s why he does not do "racially oriented material": "When I told racial jokes, the Negroes looked at the whites, the whites looked at the Negroes, and no one laughed—until I brought them together again, and then I had to tell the jokes over again. . . I try to find a common identity with an audience. I create a situation and say, 'Hey, this happened to me and you're laughing with me about it, so can we really be that different?'"

Born William Henry Cosby, Jr. on July 12, 1937, Cosby grew up in a rough part of Philadelphia essentially a fatherless child. When Cosby was eight years old his six-year-old brother died. Bill's father retreated from this unbearable reality and joined the Navy, leaving his family in dire financial straits. Whatever money he sent home was woefully inadequate to the family's needs and they slid quickly down the economic ladder, occasionally landing on the welfare rolls. Not long after what must be considered a desertion, Cosby's mother obtained a divorce.

"My father left home many times," Cosby has said. "He would leave home when the rent was due, or come home penniless on payday, swearing to my mother that he'd been robbed and leave again. Once he vanished just before Christmas and we didn't have a cent." Cosby's mother Anna assumed the role of family breadwinner and Bill, as the oldest child, was left to "mother" his younger siblings. He cooked, cleaned, and kept order among the kids. Latham quotes Cosby's brother Russell: "He kept us in line and whipped us when we got out of line." His boyhood responsibilities as a caretaker were not something he could either take or leave. It was his responsibility to keep everyday domestic life going. The small joys and pains of this life were as much his experience as they are for any "mother." The structure of Cosby's comedy is rooted in his communication of this experience.

In the routines he would later fashion for the stage, his albums, and for the 1984-1992 sit-com *The Cosby Show,* his portrayals of family life are always idyllic. Annoyance is most often involved but never despair or genuine frustration. The one word observers use to describe the experience of Cosby's comedy more than any other is "reassurance." In Cosby's comedy there is always a sort of small internal war waged between his desire to relate the feel of his actual experience and his apparent need to suppress that experience with a fantasy of patriarchal authority that clearly did not exist for him when he was a child.

Initially a high school dropout, Cosby signed up for a four year Navy hitch when he got his equivalency diploma. . . and did not stop there. While most celebrities settle for honorary degrees, Cosby later returned to college and got his bachelors, masters, and Ed.D. Education became a dragon Cosby would be forever trying to slay; during his career, he always maintained his interest in creating educational programming such as the beloved cartoon *Fat Albert and The Cosby Kids.*

After two years on a track scholarship at Temple University, Cosby started telling jokes professionally, and within a short time became television's Jackie Robinson in his role as Alexander Scott in the NBC series *I Spy* (1965-68). It was the first time an African American character had so significant a role on a television series. While appreciative of the opportunity, Cosby had some reservations about how the character was written: "If Alexander Scott doesn't get to go out with a girl once in a while," Cosby complained at one point, "people are going to wonder about me." According to Latham, Producer Sheldon Leonard (the Branch Rickey of television) responded: "I am not going to feed the concept that says a Negro only responds to the sex drive. We want him to have girls, but there has to be sweetness and dignity to it."

During the 1970s, while Cosby worked toward his doctorate at the University of Massachusetts at Amherst, he fashioned a new comedy routine apparently based on his domestic experiences as a father of four daughters and one son. He used the substance of the routine as the foundation for his enormously popular and structurally groundbreaking television series, *The Cosby Show*. The show focused almost entirely on the often-overlooked yet familiar everyday activities of an ordinary, intact upper-middle-class African American family. No such family had ever before been depicted on American television and the show became a landmark success. Cosby finally had a fitting vehicle to fully realize his comic potential and appeal to virtually all segments of American society.

After the show finished its run in the early 1990s, Cosby soon had another sitcom—named simply *Cosby*—that became a moderate success. Then, on the morning of January 15, 1997, Cosby's only son Ennis—the model for the fictional "Theo" of *The Cosby Show*—was shot to death by a man who tried to rob him. Bill Cosby took virtually no time to mourn in private; neither his on-stage nor off-stage attitude could help him confront an experience so far outside of the familiar everyday world he created in his work.

—Robin Markowitz

FURTHER READING:

Adler, Bill. *The Cosby Wit: His Life and Humor*. New York, Carroll and Graf, 1986.

Cosby, Bill. *Time Flies*. New York, Doubleday, 1987.

Fuller, Linda K. *The Cosby Show: Audiences, Impact, and Implications*. Westport, Connecticut, Greenwood Press, 1992.

Latham, Caroline. *Bill Cosby—For Real*. New York, Tom Doherty Associates, 1985.

Smith, Ronald L. *Cosby*. New York, St. Martin's Press, 1986; revised edition, Amherst, New York, Prometheus Books, 1997.

The Cosby Show

The Cosby Show, a situation comedy that ran for eight seasons on NBC Television, was one of the most intensely and immediately popular shows ever broadcast in America. The show, which began in the fall of 1984, featured comedian Bill Cosby in the role of obstetrician-father Cliff Huxtable and his family: attorney-wife Claire, daughters Sondra (18), Denise (15), Vanessa (11), Rudy (5), and son Theo (13). According to the December 5, 1985 issue of *USA Today,* the program premiered at the number one spot on the Nielson ratings,

reached that spot ten times during the first season, and was number one in every age group. An estimated 62 million people tuned in every Thursday night during the early years of the show's run. More significantly, *The Cosby Show* was the first American television show to feature the daily adventures of a prosperous, intact upper-middle class family of African descent.

The source of the show's popularity and significance in television history stemmed not from Bill Cosby's own intentional presentation of the ideology of African-American upward mobility and the restoration of traditional family values to popular culture, but in the sheer pleasure of the nearly plotless structure of the show. On *The Cosby Show,* the focus on the seemingly "insignificant" bits of business of everyday life became the show's main attraction. It was truly the first "show about nothing" that *Seinfeld* later claimed to be. The first several episodes were drawn almost without alteration from Cosby's early 1980s stand-up routines and it is primarily from his comic vision that the show emerged whole. The show created a safe, crisis-free world that viewers had a chance to enter for a half-hour every week. Regardless of their ethnicity, gender, or age, many viewers immediately recognized themselves in the show: the Huxtable characters enacted the strikingly real ordinary domestic activities of the viewing audience. In its mid-1980s heyday, Thursday night became "Cosby night," a time anticipated with relish.

Only one family comedy before *The Cosby Show* came close to this structural breakthrough. *The Adventures of Ozzie and Harriet* (1951-1966) portrayed a "real" family who "played themselves," as it were. These shows were relaxed in the extreme and the Nelsons themselves seemed to exist in a state of grace; Ozzie, the "head of the household," never seemed to have an occupation and simply sauntered around the house all day. He lived the domestic life of a retired man with a servant (Harriet). There was, more importantly, some slight shift of focus to the everyday "doings" of life rather than on a very tight plotline. We see here only a glimmer of what *The Cosby Show* would bring to fruition and *Seinfeld* would later be so widely noted for.

One early episode of *The Cosby Show,* which concerned Cliff's looking after a slumber party of five-year-olds, disposed of some five to ten minutes of Cliff playing "bucking bronco" with the children: that is, bouncing some ten of them, one at a time, upon his knee. Someone connected with the show told *T.V. Guide* in 1985 that it was "one long Jello commercial." The episode was perhaps the most loosely scripted sitcom episode ever produced: the audience simply delighted in watching Bill Cosby make real children laugh. At this point, it was clear that the show's meandering tone was no mistake, no bug that needed to be worked out (as one might have originally suspected), but in fact, the very secret of show's success. Watching *The Cosby Show,* it appeared as though the cameras were simply stuck in a window, left on, and the finished product assembled at random. Viewers of the show luxuriated in a sort of celebration of banal, ordinary existence and thus participated in a validation of their own, often-overlooked daily life.

The most fascinating aspect of this is that the show's creators seemed utterly unaware of the reasons why people were glued to their show. Bill Cosby, for his part, told Larry King in 1989 that the show was successful because now the parents always get to "win." He reported his distress at programs such as *Silver Spoons* that depicted weak, incompetent parents led around by clever children. Cosby saw himself as the avenging parental Rambo of domestic comedy. The world the show created stands however, quite apart from (and indeed, opposed to) the ideological message Cosby sought to deliver.

What distinguished the Cosby show from virtually all others in the family comedy genre was the almost total absence of struggle or conflict. There is a sense that some measure of real suffering and discord occurred in the past, in previous generations, but not anymore. The grandparents' function in the show is to give some hint of this, as is the display of various icons scattered about the Huxtable home. A picture of Martin Luther King, Jr. reposed on the wall of eldest daughter Sondra's room and in another episode all of the trivial action stopped dead in its tracks when King's 1963 ''I Have A Dream'' speech appeared unexpectedly on the living room TV screen. It was as if the savior himself had appeared in an apparition. The message was clear: without that struggle, the Huxtables idyllic existence would not be. Now, of course, all struggle is ended. If ever there were an ideal representation of Reagan-era complacency, this was it.

''Significant'' things seem to actually go on beyond the door of the Huxtable household, but almost never within its borders. The Huxtables experienced only the banal, uninterrupted hubbub of the everyday, only those aspects of life to which real people rarely give much thought and attention. Every Thursday night during the show's run we watched the children's endless squabbles, activities useful mainly in their ability to allay boredom (playing chess, shooting baskets), recreational cooking (Cliff's Special Secret Spaghetti Sauce), and the annoyances—but never the life-altering burdens of working parents caring for a young child. In a memorable vignette, Cliff asks five-year-old Rudy if she needs to use the bathroom before he puts her into her elaborate snowsuit and, of course once she's zipped into it, she exclaims, giggling, ''I have to go to the bathroom!'' An exasperated Cliff sent her to her mother.

Observers eventually tried explaining the unprecedented success of the show by suggesting that its success reflected ''the love in the house.'' In fact, a record album released during the show's heyday of theme music connected with the program is called *A House Full of Love*. The reason for this is not the adequacy of the explanation, but Cliff's use of the language of ''love'' to diffuse any potential conflict. We love each other; therefore we cannot *have* a problem.

In the alternative universe of the Huxtables, it is clear, problems are only apparent: they can't *really* exist. In one episode, Claire knocks 14-year-old son Theo's notebook off the kitchen table. A marijuana joint falls out of the book. The parents look at each as if the sky has fallen. This cannot be happening in our house! Our house full of love! Theo is summoned to make some explanation of the event. He tells them it is not his and they believe him. (Huxtables, like George Washington, cannot tell lies.) This does not thoroughly satisfy Theo, who fears the loss of his parents' trust, so he drags the culprit who hid the joint in his book home with him to explain the situation to his parents. Cliff tells the boy from the errant outside world to see some adult about his problem—perhaps even the good doctor himself. It was not possible for Theo to have been the affected youth. Things like that did not happen to Huxtables.

In an episode from the 1885-86 season, one of the girls tells Cliff that a friend needs a medical appointment with him and that he not contact the girl's parents. Cliff sees her and although it turns out to be a simple problem of no moral consequence, he becomes troubled (a strange state for Cliff). He is worried that his own children will not come to him if they have a problem. He gathers the children around to tell them that they must talk to him if they're ever in trouble; the kids let slip that may have already happened. When the tension increases, they indicate that they were, of course, only kidding. The episode

ends on this note with nary a suspicion that they may have been telling the truth. Cliff had no reason to worry in the first place.

What we saw on *The Cosby Show* is what happens in that part of a fairy tale *after it ends*. The Huxtables were an upwardly-mobile black American family living happily ever after. It was a life devoid of crisis and conflict, a fantasy of upward mobility with no costs: a real American dream. What viewers wanted from the show was a chance to sink into this vision of utopia, this perfect world in which to spend their half-hour. Viewers responded to a utopian vision rooted in real aspects of the lives they actually lived, not Cosby's own ideological utopia of restored traditional family values. Cosby said he wanted his show to serve as both a teaching tool and a means to counter the prevailing trend of ''weak parents'' in both television and popular culture in general; he made the perhaps incorrect assumption that this message was what viewers most appreciated.

Near the end of the show's run, Cosby's own overt ideological intentions came to overcome the structure of the show. Cliff's funny faces that repress all tension were now backed up by overtly intimidating displays of parental might and even instances of outright emotional cruelty directed toward even the youngest Huxtable. At that point, ratings began to dip and other shows with characteristics similar to the earlier episodes of *The Cosby Show* soon appeared.

There was a time when Cosby himself saw the response to his show perhaps clearer than most observers. ''I hardly ever watch my work, but with this show it's different,'' he says. ''I watch every week. And at the end of every segment, I find myself with a smile on my face, because I really like that family and the feeling they give me.''

—Robin Markowitz

FURTHER READING:

Brooks, T. and Marsh, E. *The Complete Directory to Prime Time Network TV Shows: 1946 to Present.* New York, Ballentine Books, 1985.

Ginzberg, E. *The Middle-Class Negro in the White Man's World.* New York, Columbia University Press, 1967.

Kronus, S. *The Black Middle Class.* Columbus, Ohio, Charles E. Merrill Publishing Company, 1971.

Latham, Caroline. *Bill Cosby: For Real.* New York, Tom Doherty Associates, 1985.

Smith, R. *Cosby.* New York, St. Martin's Press, 1986.

Cosell, Howard (1918-1995)

Identified as the foremost sports television journalist of the 1970s, Howard Cosell consistently distinguished himself from the field by his presentation and content. He was, as a *TV Guide* poll in the 1970s revealed, both the most popular and the least popular sportscaster of his day. Though Cosell proclaimed that he was ''just telling it like it is,'' his careful manipulation of his image helped to make him a celebrity in his own right.

Born Howard William Cohen on March 25, 1918, Cosell grew up in Brooklyn, New York, attended law school, and opened his own Manhattan firm. His clientele included several actors and athletes, the most famous being Willie Mays. Cosell also represented the Little

Howard Cosell (left) with Muhammad Ali

League of New York, a connection that soon landed him his first broadcasting job. In 1953, Cosell began hosting a Saturday morning program for ABC in which kids asked sports questions of professional athletes.

Cosell cut his teeth as a boxing commentator for ABC in the 1960s. Cosell critiqued everything in sight that would provide him with fan appeal and approval, yet his career was most clearly tied to the emergence of Muhammad Ali. For many viewers, Cosell's voice provided the soundtrack as The Greatest ''floated like a butterfly and stung like a bee.'' The sportscaster served as one of Ali's chief defenders when he was stripped of his title after refusing to join the military due to religious beliefs. Cosell's public support was direct: ''What the government did to this man was inhuman and illegal under the Fifth and Fourteenth amendments. Nobody says a damned word about the professional football players who dodged the draft. But Muhammad was different; he was black and he was boastful.'' Cosell covered the sport of boxing until 1982. After a particularly brutal heavyweight bout, Cosell walked away from the sport, saying: ''Boxing is the only sport in the world where the clear intention is for

one person to inflict bodily harm upon the other person. . . .'' Evidently, the smooth moves of Ali had prohibited Cosell from realizing this basic reality earlier.

In the late 1960s, ABC President Roone Arledge, who was well known for his innovative ideas in sports broadcasting, approached Cosell with what many observers considered a ridiculous idea: would he like to host an evening sporting event that competed for prime-time viewers? Cosell teamed with Don Meridith and Frank Gifford to introduce Monday Night Football in 1970. Led by Cosell, the program became a kind of traveling road show as fans flocked around the broadcast booth, either to praise Cosell or damn him. Cosell's witty and sometimes caustic exchanges with his fellow broadcasters often drew more attention than the games themselves. Monday Night Football became—improbably—one of the most talked about programs of the 1970s.

Though he had a long record of support for civil rights and had offered prominent support to the protests of black runners Tommie Smith and John Carlos at the 1968 Summer Olympics, Cosell drew the wrath of viewers when, while watching Washington Redskin's receiver Alvin Garrett carry the ball during one Monday Night Football broadcast, he said "Look at that little monkey run." Hounded by critics, Cosell eventually left the broadcast booth in 1984, claiming that pro football had become a "stagnant bore." Cosell briefly hosted a program called *Sportsbeat* (1985), but the publication of his autobiography *I Never Played the Game*—which contained scathing criticisms of many ABC personnel—soon led to the program's cancellation. Cosell broadcast intermittently on radio thereafter and retired in 1992, reportedly bitter about his exclusion from a profession he helped to create. He died on April 23, 1995.

No matter the sport he covered, Cosell's trademark was a steady flow of language unmatched in the trade. He refused to simplify his terminology, often using his nasal voice to introduce polysyllabic words into the foreign area of the boxing ring. He left the game description for his ex-jock colleagues, and he blazed the trail of the commentator role that has become standard in modern broadcasting. Arledge discussed Cosell in 1995: "He became a giant by the simple act of telling the truth in an industry that was not used to hearing it and considered it revolutionary." This knack grew directly from what others called an "over-blown ego." When Cosell misspoke about the game, his colleagues would call him to task. The irrepressible Cosell would typically respond with his well-known "heh, heh, heh" admission.

—Brian Black

FURTHER READING:

Barber, Red. *The Broadcasters.* New York, DaCapo Press, 1986.

Cosell, Howard, with Peter Bonventre. *I Never Played the Game.* New York, Morrow, 1985.

Sinks, Charles. *Up Close.* Tarpon Springs, Artist Resource Group, 1993.

Cosmopolitan

Cosmopolitan magazine holds a spot as one of the most successful women's magazines of all time. In the late 1990s it boasted a circulation of 2.4 million readers in the United States, and an impressive 29 editions in other languages. Its distinctive, come-hither covers seem designed more to catch a man's eye than any potential female newsstand browser, and inside its pages features give women very specific advice on how to lure—and keep—a man. Yet the *Cosmopolitan* ideology—revolutionary in the 1960s, fitting in perfectly with the liberated-women zeitgeist of the 1970s, and setting the big-haired tone of the 1980s—was the creation of one very female mind: Helen Gurley Brown. The author of the bestselling *Sex and the Single Girl* (1962), as *Cosmopolitan* editor, Brown deployed her array of self-improvement strategies into a monthly format that made her name synonymous with the magazine and enshrined *Cosmo,* as it came to be called, in popular print journalism's hall of fame.

By tying the consciousness of the sexual revolution of the 1960s—brought about in part by the launch of the oral contraceptive pill on the United States market in 1960—with an accessible, affordable magazine format, *Cosmopolitan* succeeded beyond anyone's vision. The periodical had actually been in existence since 1886 as a

An American tourist reads *Cosmopolitan* while sunbathing.

general-interest literary magazine; it was a Hearst Corporation holding after 1905, and for years found success with a high-caliber output of fiction. The "Cosmopolitan Girl" originally referred to the illustrated covers of the pre-World War II era; the term would take on an entirely different meaning a few decades later. In the 1950s *Cosmopolitan* began to focus more on attracting female readers with less fiction and more editorial features on women's problems. Circulation, however, continued to plummet.

Helen Gurley Brown had already attained a certain level of notoriety in the United States with her 1962 book *Sex and the Single Girl.* The onetime advertising copywriter had penned a chatty but frank little how-to guide for young single women aspiring to be glamorous urban sophisticates; *Sex and the Single Girl* dovetailed perfectly with the trend of a greater number of female college graduates in the postwar boom years, a lessening of stigmas attached to unmarried women living on their own, and a delay in the average age of marriage. Brown posited that it was not only okay to be single, but a happy and emotionally healthy way to live—a revolutionary idea at the time, to say the least. The book's tacit acknowledgment that sex occurred regularly between single, consenting adults outside of the bonds of matrimony was even more radical. Brown tried to find a backer for a magazine of her own after the runaway success of *Sex*; she planned to name it *Femme* and aim it at new young working women. Instead Hearst hired her to revamp the moribund *Cosmopolitan,* which was near death at the time. With almost no journalism experience Brown became its first female editor.

The first revamped *Cosmo* in July of 1965 launched a new era in women's magazines. It addressed sex in frank terms and gave readers a barrage of upbeat self-improvement tips for sex, work, and the physical self. Naomi Wolf, author of *The Beauty Myth,* termed *Cosmopolitan* the first of ''the new wave of post-women's movement magazines'' that depicted women as sexual beings. Compared to its predecessors among women's service magazines, *Cosmopolitan,* wrote Wolf, set forth ''an aspiration, individualist, can-do tone that says that you should be your best and nothing should get in your way.... But the formula must also include an element that contradicts and then undermines the overall prowoman fare'' with anxiety-proving articles about cellulite, breast size, and wrinkles.

Brown always focused her magazine's editorial slant on the reader she termed ''the mouseburger.'' Clearly a self-referential term, Brown defined it for Glenn Collins of the *New York Times* in 1982: ''A mouseburger is a young woman who is not very prepossessing,'' Brown said. ''She is not beautiful. She is poor, has no family connections, and she is not a razzle-dazzle ball of charm and fire. She is a kind of waif.'' With a heavy editorial emphasis on sex and dating features, tell-all stories, and beauty and diet tips, *Cosmopolitan* had become an American institution by the 1970s, and the term ''Cosmo Girl'' seemed synonymous with the ultra-liberated woman in her twenties who had several ''beaus,'' a well-paying job, and a hedonistic lifestyle. The magazine also introduced the male centerfold with a much-publicized spread of actor Burt Reynolds in its April 1972 issue.

Yet the reality was somewhat different: *Cosmopolitan's* demographics were rooted in the lower income brackets, attracting readers with little college education who held low-paying, usually clerical jobs. The ''Cosmo Girl'' on the cover and the few vampy fashion pages inside reflected this—the *Cosmo* style was far different from the more restrained, elegant, or avant-garde look of its journalistic sisters like *Vogue* or even *Mademoiselle,* which focused on a more middle class readership. Though often a top model or celebrity, the women on *Cosmo's* covers were usually shown in half-or three-quarter-length body shots, often by Francesco Scavullo for several years, to show off the low-cut evening wear. The hair was far more overdone—read ''big''—than usual for women's magazines, and skimpy beaded gowns alternated with lamé and halter tops, a distinctly downmarket style. The requisite ''bedroom eyes'' and pouty mouth completed the ''Cosmo Girl'' cover shot.

Framing the cover model were teasing blurbs written by Brown's husband, a film producer, such as ''You've Cheated. Do You Ever Tell?'' Blurbs also trumpeted the pull-out ''Bedside Astrology Guide,'' an annual feature, and articles like ''How to Close the Deal''—how to get your boyfriend to agree to marriage. ''Irma Kurtz's Agony Column'' placated readers with true-life write-in questions and answers from readers with often outrageous personal problems borne of their own bad decisions. ''The magazine allows women the impression of a pseudo-sexual liberation and a vicarious participation in the life of an imaginary 'swinging single' woman,'' wrote Ellen McCracken in her book *Decoding Women's Magazines.* ''Although most readers will never dress or behave as the magazine urges, *Cosmopolitan* offers them momentary opportunity to transgress the predominant sexual mores in the privacy of their homes.''

By 1981 *Cosmopolitan's* circulation had quadruped its 1965 figures. Brown never seemed surprised that her magazine had succeeded so well. As she told Roxanne Roberts in the *Washington Post,*

''Cosmo really is this basic message: Just do what's there every day, and one thing will finally lead to another and you'll get to be somebody.... I believe most 20-year-old women think they're not pretty enough, smart enough, they don't have enough sex appeal, they don't have the job they want, they've still got some problems with their family,'' Brown told Roberts. ''All that raw material is there to be turned into something wonderful. I just think of my life. If I can do it, anybody can.''

For 16 years the magazine, under Brown's editorship, was one of the Hearst chain's top performers. At one point in the 1980s it had the highest number of advertising pages of all women's magazines in the United States. Most of the copies—about 2.5 million—were purchased at the newsstand, an impulse buy and thus more profitable for Hearst than the discounted subscription price, and its ''pass-around'' rate was also much higher than its competition.

Not surprisingly, *Cosmopolitan* has always been a particular target of feminist ire. As early as 1970 it appeared in the Appendix of the classic tome *Sisterhood Is Powerful: An Anthology of Writings from the Women's Liberation Movement* on the ''Drop Dead List.'' But Brown defended her magazine in the 1982 interview with Collins of the *New York Times.* ''Cosmo predated the women's movement, and I have always said my message is for the woman who loves men but who doesn't want to live through them.... I sometimes think feminists don't read what I write. I am for total equality. My relevance is that I deal with reality.'' The reality was that sometimes women did sleep with their bosses, or date married men, or use psychological ruses to maintain a relationship or force a marriage, and *Cosmopolitan* was one of the few women's magazines to write about such issues in non-judgmental terms. It was criticized, however, for failing to address safe-sex issues after the advent of AIDS (Acquired Immune Deficiency Syndrome) in the 1980s.

Helen Gurley Brown retired in 1997 after an interim joint-editorship with the launch editor of *Marie Claire,* Bonnie Fuller. A *Cosmopolitan*-ized version of the French original, *Marie Claire* is the closest American offering on the newsstands to *Cosmopolitan,* but features a more sophisticated, *Elle*-type fashion slant. ''The Hearst move was about acknowledging change,'' noted *Mediaweek's* Barbara Lippert, describing Brown as almost a relic from a quainter, more innocent age. ''These days, however, everybody's negotiating a new, much more complicated set of questions than how to land a man ... the whole Little Miss Secretary Achiever thing is anathema to some twentysomethings, who are more interested in cybersex and the single girl,'' Lippert wrote. Both the age and the income level of *Cosmopolitan's* average American reader had climbed somewhat, and a higher percentage of married women now read it. By the time of Brown's retirement, *Cosmopolitan* was an international phenomenon, with 29 editions in several different languages. The 1960s-era themes of sexual liberation seemed to catch on most successfully in the newly ''de-Communized'' countries of the Eastern Bloc, where equal rights for women had once been a hallmark of their legal, social, and economic systems. ''Think of it,'' wrote the *Washington Post's* Roberts. ''Cosmo girls everywhere. Like McDonald's with cleavage.''

—Carol Brennan

FURTHER READING:

Collins, Glenn. ''At 60, Helen Gurley Brown Talks about Life and Love.'' *New York Times.* September 19, 1982, 68.

"Cosmopolitan." In *American Mass-Market Magazines,* edited by Alan Nourie and Barbara Nourie. Westport, Connecticut, Greenwood Press, 1990.

"Cosmopolitan." In *Women's Periodicals in the United States: Consumer Magazines,* edited by Kathleen T. Endress and Therese L. Lueck. Westport, Connecticut, Greenwood Press, 311-317.

Ferguson, Marjorie. "Cosmopolitan: The Cross-Cultural Cult Message." *Forever Feminine.* London, Heinemann, 1982.

Lippert, Barbara. "Gurley Show." *Mediaweek.* March 4, 1996, MR40.

McCracken, Ellen. "Cosmopolitan: Pseudo-liberation, Vicarious Eroticism, and Traditional Moral Values." In *Decoding Women's Magazines: From Mademoiselle to Ms.* New York, St. Martin's Press, 1993.

Roberts, Roxanne. "The Oldest Living Cosmo Girl." *Washington Post.* January 31, 1996, D1.

Costas, Bob (1952—)

Preeminent broadcast journalist and sportscaster Bob Costas began announcing basketball games for a St. Louis radio station at the age of twenty-two. He joined NBC in 1980, quickly becoming one of the network's most valuable assets through his work covering major league baseball, football, basketball, and college events, and hosting various shows including *NBA Showtime, NFL Live,* and *Costas Coast to Coast.* In 1992, a high-profile stint as the network's prime-time anchor at the XXV Olympics in Barcelona, Spain, earned him nationwide name recognition. A three-time Emmy winner for his sports announcing and hosting, his colleagues have also named him outstanding sportscaster of the year four times. Moving beyond sports in 1988, he launched a late-night interview television program, *Later with Bob Costas,* that won him another Emmy. When the series ended in 1994, Costas expanded his duties at NBC, contributing to *Dateline, Today, NBC News,* and anchoring MSNBC's *Internight.*

—Courtney Bennett

FURTHER READING:

Costas, Bob. *Bob Costas: Costas on Sports.* New York, Bantam Doubleday Dell, 1997.

Smith, Curt. *The Story Tellers: From Mel Allen to Bob Costas, Sixty Years of Baseball Tales from the Broadcast Booth.* New York, Macmillan, 1995.

Costello, Elvis (1955—)

Born Declan Patrick Aloysius McManus, British singer, guitarist, and composer Elvis Costello has been a mainstay of the popular music scene since his 1977 debut disc, *My Aim Is True.* The son of a jazz bandleader, Costello rode to prominence on the initial wave of British punk—and thanks in part to a stage persona that made obvious reference to Buddy Holly. A gifted lyricist with a flair for wordplay, he did his best work in collaboration with the Attractions, a virtuoso backing band anchored by Bruce Thomas (bass), Pete Thomas

(drums), and Steve Nieve (keyboards). The band's early records, polished to a metallic sheen by producer Nick Lowe, combined Beatlesque pop smarts with an appreciation for American soul. The best of these are *This Year's Model, Armed Forces,* and *Trust.* Costello escaped from Lowe's clutches to record what is considered his masterwork, 1982's lyrically bruising, intricately textured *Imperial Bedroom.*

—Robert E. Schnakenberg

FURTHER READING:

Hinton, Brian. *Elvis Costello: Let Them All Talk.* London, Sanctuary Publishing, 1998.

Thomas, Bruce. *The Big Wheel.* New York, Faber & Faber, 1991.

Costner, Kevin (1955—)

Kevin Costner has as many fans as detractors; he is a steadfast box-office attraction but must strive for artistic respectability with each new film. Seen as the sexy embodiment of a healthy, positive image of American masculinity at the peak of his career in the early 1990s, Costner's public persona has suffered since then from his failure to live up to the standards set by his predecessors, the male stars of Hollywood's glamorous past. Because of his role as the dreamer who, guided by a mysterious voice, builds a baseball field in

Kevin Costner in a scene from the film *Dances with Wolves.*

the middle of his cornfield in *Field of Dreams* (1989), Costner was compared, above all, to the Jimmy Stewart of Frank Capra's films. This and other allusions to Gary Cooper, prompted by Costner's similar handsome looks, possibly traced a path for him in the audience's and the critics' imagination very unlike the one Costner actually would follow. This divergence may explain why he is not unanimously greeted as one of the greatest Hollywood stars of the 1990s.

Three main aspects contribute to shaping Costner's uneven career. First, his rather unwise choice of roles, alternating between less popular high quality products like *JFK* (1991) or *A Perfect World* (1993)—in which he plays demanding roles—with impossible block-busters like *The Bodyguard* (1992). Second, his irregular work as director, which includes a hit like *Dances with Wolves* (1990) and a flop like *The Postman* (1997). And third, the loss of his reputation as the long-married perfect husband in favor of a less popular reputation as a womanizer developed shortly after reaching stardom, which clearly affected his star image. The man destined to represent America's most cherished virtues on the screen has turned out to be a star with little sense of his own limitations as an actor, director, or public figure and with, arguably, an excessive sense of his own value as an artist.

Costner became a rising star with *Silverado* (1985) and *The Untouchables* (1987). Stardom definitively came thanks to two baseball films, *Bull Durham* (1988) and *Field of Dreams*. Games are indeed a leit-motif in Costner's career, which includes two more sports-related films, *Tin Cup* (1996) and *For the Love of the Game* (1999). The success of his excellent performance in *Field of Dreams* prompted Costner to fulfill a long-cherished ambition: directing a film, the low-budget Western epic *Dances with Wolves* based on the novel by Michael Blake. Despite the misgivings of many who thought (even wished) that Costner's film would be an utter failure, this long film well deserves the awards (Oscars for Best Picture, Best Director and Best Adapted Screenplay) and the popular esteem it reaped, for it is a courageous attempt to instill new life into the dying western genre. Unlike typical westerns, Costner's film deals with the confrontation between the white man and the native American from a distinctly antiracist perspective, allowing the language of the native tribes to be heard as was never heard before in cinema. Nonetheless, the film still fails to shift the focus away from the white man—Costner himself plays the main role—and onto the native American.

The paradox is that instead of consolidating Costner's career, the Oscar seems rather to have disrupted it. His role in his friend Kevin Reynold's *Robin Hood, Prince of Thieves* (1991) earned him little sympathy, while his decision to play the pathetic killer in Clint Eastwood's *A Perfect World*—possibly his best performance to date—was ill-timed, following hot on the heels of his very popular but insubstantial role as Whitney Houston's bodyguard. *The Bodyguard* has, though, the redeeming merit of depicting an interracial romantic relationship under a positive light, which might explain its popularity.

But the two films that have clearly become a sign of Costner's rising megalomania and self-indulgence—at least for his detractors—are *Waterworld* (1995) and *The Postman*. The former, which he co-directed with Kevin Reynolds, was in its time the most expensive film ever made but it failed to generate enough box-office receipts to recoup the impressive investment. Those who ridiculed Costner's wish to film *Dances with Wolves* but were silenced by the Oscars the film won seemingly came back with a vengeance to prey on *Waterworld*. The film broke records eliciting the highest number of negative comment even before actual shooting began. Although it did not

become the success Costner expected, *Waterworld* nonetheless attracted a much larger audience than the critics foretold. Yet, far from learning a lesson from this expensive experiment, Costner plunged next into depths he had not known for years. *The Postman*, Costner's second film as director, simply flopped, despite the good reputation of the novel by David Brin from which it was adapted.

Costner's case is, arguably, paradigmatic of the advantages and the disadvantages that the current system of Hollywood film production offers to today's stars. In the past, Costner's good looks and acting talent would have guaranteed for him a stable place in the sun of any of the main studios. He would have had to sacrifice personal choice to stardom, with all the loss of artistic freedom that this entails. But, in his case, the freedom of choice enjoyed by today's stars seems to be working against him. Other male stars like Arnold Schwarzenegger or Mel Gibson, clearly (and paradoxically) enjoy a steady popularity despite their occasional mistakes. Costner does not. The key to the different treatment Costner meets might well have to do with his reluctance to distance himself from his own star image—in short, to his inability to laugh at his mistakes. The integrity that he exuded in *Field of Dreams* or *The Untouchables* has been subtly transformed into self-centeredness and this is a fault on which his detractors thrive. Fortunately for him, his achievement in *Dances with Wolves* shows that this perceived shortcoming could be forgiven in an artist.

—Sara Martin

FURTHER READING:

Brown, C. "'Water' Torture." *Premiere*. August 1995, 66-71.

Caddies, Kelvin. *Kevin Costner: Prince of Hollywood.* London, Plexus, 1995.

Costner, Kevin, et al. *Dances with Wolves: The Illustrated Screenplay and Story Behind the Film.* New York, Newmarket Press, 1991.

Davis, S. O. "Kevin Costner: Myth or Man?" *Ladies' Home Journal.* April 1991, 138-139.

Klein, E. "Costner in Control." *Vanity Fair.* January 1992, 72-77.

Vollers, M. "Costner's Last Stand." *Squire.* June 1996, 100-107.

Cotten, Joseph (1905-1994)

One of Hollywood's most versatile actors, Joseph Cotten is chiefly associated with the films of Orson Welles. Cotten was a latecomer to Hollywood, arriving at age thirty-six after acting on Broadway in Welles's Mercury Theatre. In 1940, Cotten made his first film—Welles's *Citizen Kane*—a film that would come to be regarded as the greatest film ever made. For the remainder of the decade, it seemed as if the talented actor could not turn in a bad performance. Although Cotten continued to work with Welles—starring in *Journey into Fear* and *The Magnificent Ambersons*—many A-list directors clamored to work with the versatile star. Cotten appeared in such classics as George Cukor's *Gaslight,* Carol Reed's *The Third Man,* and Alfred Hitchcock's *Shadow of a Doubt.* With his offbeat good looks and exceptional acting ability, Cotten soon evolved into one of Hollywood's most sought-after leading men, appearing opposite such top stars as Ingrid Bergman, Jennifer Jones, Loretta Young, and Joan Fontaine. Although his career continued well into the 1980s, the good parts were fewer and farther between. Through his association with Welles, however, his movie immortality remains assured.

—Victoria Price

FURTHER READING:

Callow, Simon. *Orson Welles: The Road to Xanadu.* New York, Viking, 1995.

Cotten, Joseph. *Joseph Cotten: An Autobiography.* New York, Avon Books, 1987.

Leaming, Barbara. *Orson Welles: A Biography.* New York, Viking Press, 1985.

The Cotton Club

Founded by the British-born gangster Owney Madden, the Cotton Club nightclub opened its doors on December 4, 1923, at a time when the black cultural revival known as the Harlem Renaissance was going into full swing. The club provided entertainment for white New Yorkers who wanted to go to Harlem but were afraid of its more dangerous aspects. The Cotton Club has never been surpassed as Harlem's most outrageous club and its lavish entertainment is still a matter of awe even in this day of Las Vegas excess. The Cotton Club presented the best in black entertainment to an exclusively white audience and became famous for its use of light skinned, or ''cotton colored,'' black women in its chorus line.

Madden opened the club to provide an outlet for his bootleg beer. The club floor was in a horseshoe shape, designed by Joseph Urban. It was decorated with palm trees and other jungle elements. There were two tiers of tables and a ring of banquettes. The menu offered not only Southern food but also elaborate European specialties. Prices were the highest in Harlem but the food was not particularly memorable. The entertainment, however, was spectacular. Black waiters provided an elegant setting with their sophisticated demeanor, a contrast to the whirling servers in neighboring clubs. These waiters also informed patrons that it was not fashionable to put their bottles of beer on the floor. Rather they were instructed to place them in their pockets. Failure to comply led to ejection.

Cotton Club entertainment, or floor shows, lasted as long as two hours. There was a featured act and the gorgeous Cotton Club chorus line. The girls were beautiful and uniformly light skinned; they were also young—under 21—and tall—five-foot six inches or more. Cab Calloway's songs ''She's Tall, She's Tan and She's Terrific'' and ''Cotton Colored Gal of Mine'' are apt reflections of the girls in the

The Cotton Club

line. The shows were fast-paced and featured the greatest black entertainment possible. Ethel Waters, Adelaide Hall, Duke Ellington, Cab Calloway, and others performed there.

The Cotton Club was part of the area of Harlem known as ''Jungle Alley.'' This strip, located on 133rd Street between Lenox and Seventh Avenues, was densely packed with clubs. The Cotton Club was one of eleven clubs in the area, most of which served a white trade. The Cotton Club, Connie's Inn, and Small's Paradise were the most renowned.

The color line was strictly enforced at the Cotton Club, and performers and audience were kept separate. White mobsters owned the club, its shows were written by whites (Dorothy Fields was a major contributor), and the audience was all white. Black performers often went next door to drink or smoke marijuana. The only African Americans officially allowed in the Cotton Club were its outstanding performers. On December 4, 1927, Duke Ellington began his run at the Cotton Club, one of the more important engagements in jazz history. The run lasted into 1932, with breaks for movies and tours allowed. In addition to playing his music regularly, writing for the shows, and providing a basic income to keep his men together, the gig provided Ellington with a large radio audience who came to know his music. At this time, Ellington developed what he termed his ''jungle sound,'' a use of various tonal colors that he associated with Africa, a constant theme in his ever-evolving music. He debuted ''It Don't Mean a Thing (If It Ain't Got That Swing)'' and ''Mood Indigo'' to Cotton Club audiences.

The Cotton Club of the late 1920s and 1930s helped to define the emergence of African-American culture in the period, coinciding as it did with the Marcus Garvey movement, W. E. B. DuBois's Pan African Movement, and the flowering of African American literature known as the Harlem Renaissance. The Cotton Club of this era has since been memorialized in E. L. Doctorow's historical novel *Billy Bathgate* (1989) and in the Francis Ford Coppola movie *The Cotton Club* (1984).

—Frank A. Salamone

FURTHER READING:

Haskins, Jim. *The Cotton Club.* New York, New American Library, 1977.

Kennedy, William, and Francis Ford Coppola. *The Cotton Club* (screenplay). New York, St. Martins's Press, 1986.

Mayer, Clarence. *The Cotton Club: New Poems.* Detroit, Broadside Press, 1972.

Coué, Emile (1857-1926)

A French provincial pharmacist, Emile Coué was responsible for a therapeutic mind-over-matter system of ''autosuggestion'' known as Couéism that influenced the popular culture of the United States when, as in England, it became something of a national craze during the early 1920s. By daily repetition of its still familiar mantra, ''Day by day, in every way, I am getting better and better,'' Couéism's adherents hoped to achieve health and success by positive thinking and the expectation of beneficial results. The most succinct definition of Couéism was perhaps Coué's own: ''Couéism is an especial

Emile Coué

technique . . . for the teaching and application of auto- and other methodical suggestion. It is more: it is an attitude of mind directed toward progressive improvement.''

Coué was born of old noble Breton stock in Troyes, France, and attended pharmacy school in Paris before establishing an apothecary in his home town. Observing that he could effect positive results in his clients by encouragement as well as medication, he developed an informal counseling service that became the foundation of his later work. Moving to Nancy in 1896, he came across an advertisement touting hypnotism as a tool for business success. His investigations in this field led him to develop his own system, though he always insisted that positive thinking—not hypnotic trance—was the basis of Couéism, and that he was merely harnessing imagination in the service of will. In 1913 he founded the Lorraine Society of Applied Psychology and, in 1922, the Coué Institute for Psychical Education at Paris. During World War I, he lectured in Paris and Switzerland, with proceeds used for the relief of war victims.

His book *Self-Mastery Through Conscious Autosuggestion* caused a sensation when it was published in England and the United States, in 1920 and 1922, respectively. A steady stream of British pilgrims to Nancy turned Coué's facilities into a kind of secular Lourdes, especially after such luminaries as Julian Huxley and Sir Alfred Downing Fripp, the King's physician, endorsed the method. *Emile Coué: The Man and His Work,* a 1935 book by J. Louis Orton, a disaffected ex-associate, quotes Huxley: ''He [Coué] goes further than any of the orthodox medical men in his claims for the power of mind over body; he effects remarkable cures, and finally he sums up his ideas in one or two simple generalizations.''

Coué was invited to lecture in England regularly after 1921, where his reputed cure of Lord Curzon's insomnia only added to his reputation. On January 4, 1923 he arrived in the United States for a tumultuous lecture tour that was given substantial coverage in the popular press, especially by the New York *World*. Over the next several weeks, he gave 81 "séances" in major eastern cities, where his treatment of prominent socialites such as Mrs. W. K. Vanderbilt further served to advance his cause. His appeal to American optimism and efficiency was undoubtedly the source of much of his popularity; industrialist Henry Ford was reported to have said, "I have read Coué's philosophy: *he has the right idea.*" And Coué himself was described as the "Henry Ford of psychology" by Gertrude Mayo in her 1923 book, *Coué for Children.* She wrote, "Just as M. Coué had first started the engine of the subconscious mind with hypnotic hetero-suggestion and later had substituted the self-starter of conscious auto-suggestion . . . thanks to him people . . . who had never known before they possessed unconscious minds, were finding not only that they had but that they could command them to their great personal advantage and convenience."

A National Coué Institute was founded in New York to train instructors to teach the method, and the American Library Service began publishing his books from New York. Despite Coué's decidedly secular point of view, his lectures evoked comparisons with the faith-healing revivals that were popular at the time, attracting, in the words of J. Louis Orton, "paralytics, asthmatics, and stammerers" seeking respite from their ills. Couéism came under fire from orthodox religious leaders and even Christian Science—which it somewhat resembled—for its secular viewpoint and its purported Freudianism, which it resembled not at all. Coué returned to the United States in 1924 for an extensive lecture tour of the western states, but took ill in England the following year after complaining his nose had been improperly cauterized to cure his recurring nosebleeds during a British lecture tour. He died in his homeland on July 2, 1926, and a huge crowd attended his funeral at a Roman Catholic church. Although his Institutes continued his work in Europe and the United States, the movement quickly declined and was soon all but forgotten.

Thus the Coué craze, especially in America, ended almost as soon as it had begun, leaving the Freudians and fundamentalists to battle it out for the ownership of the "mind-over-matter" question. The popularity of Couéism can be seen as representing a response by mass consumer culture to the spiritual devastation of World War I, which had spawned nihilism, Dada, socialism, and fascism in other contexts. Its pseudoscientific, quasi-religious trappings appealed to a disillusioned public hungry for non-material fulfillment during the 1920s, a decade that embodied the triumph of a modernistic, mechanistic culture. And as an early example of how publicity, hype, and celebrity endorsement were enlisted on behalf of non-material fulfillment, Couéism presaged the work of other self-help gurus and systems during the twentieth century, with voices as diverse as Norman Vincent Peale, L. Ron Hubbard, Maharishi Mahesh Yogi, and Werner Erhard perpetuating their own versions of Coué's self-help message.

—Edward Moran

FURTHER READING:

Coué, Emile. *My Method: Including American Impressions.* Garden City, New York, Doubleday, 1923.

———. *Self-Mastery Through Conscious Autosuggestion.* New York, American Library Service, 1922.

Mayo, Gertrude. *Coué for Children.* New York, 1923.

Orton, J. Louis. *Emile Coué: The Man and His Work.* London, Francis Mott, 1935.

Coughlin, Father Charles E. (1891-1979)

Long before the emergence of present-day radio "shock-jocks," Father Charles E. Coughlin, the "radio priest" of the 1930s, realized the power of using the airwaves as a political pulpit and means to achieve celebrity status. Along with Huey Long, the controversial senator from Louisiana who advocated a massive wealth-redistribution program, Coughlin reflected the frustrations of Americans mired in a seemingly endless Great Depression. Beginning his career as a talented parish priest who used radio broadcasts as a means to raise funds for his church, he became perhaps the most popular voice of protest of his day, reaching millions of listeners each week with a populist message that pitted the common man against the forces of the "establishment." Over time his message developed from one of protest to demagoguery; his career perhaps illustrates both the potentialities and dangers of political uses of mass media.

Born in 1891 in Hamilton, Ontario, Coughlin grew up in a devout Catholic family. There was never doubt that he would enter the priesthood, and at the age of twelve Charles enrolled at St.

Father Charles E. Coughlin

Michael's College in Toronto. He matriculated to a seminary in 1911. After taking the vows of priesthood, he was assigned as parish priest in Royal Oak, Michigan, a suburban community just north of Detroit. Although the parish was tiny and operated on a shoestring budget, Coughlin had grandiose plans for the church—which seemed futile considering the modest number of Catholics in Royal Oak. Two weeks after a new church was built, local members of the Ku Klux Klan burned a cross on the church lawn. Coughlin, known for having a streak of militancy, vowed to overcome local resistance and transform the struggling church into a vibrant, flourishing parish.

His plans for bolstering the church were innovative and wildly successful. He renamed the church the Shrine of the Little Flower and became an indefatigable fund-raiser. He invited members of the Detroit Tigers baseball team to the church as a way to attract attention—Babe Ruth even attended the church once while playing the Tigers and held a basket for donations at the church door. Yet Coughlin's most lucrative idea was to turn to the airwaves. He contacted the manager at local radio station WJR about broadcasting a weekly radio sermon that would confront local issues and raise awareness of the church. The medium was perfect for Coughlin, whose warm, mellow voice attracted listeners throughout Detroit. His sermons offered a variety of religious themes, such as discussions of Christ's teachings and Biblical parables. Soon mail was pouring into the station, hundreds and sometimes thousands of letters each week, most with financial contributions from listeners. Coughlin's plans for the Shrine of the Little Flower were soon realized: a new church was built, with a seating capacity of more than twenty-six hundred, complemented by a tall, granite tower. Attendance boomed as people throughout the region came to catch a glimpse of the ''radio priest.''

Coughlin's radio talents soon were noticed by executives outside of Detroit. Columbia Broadcasting Service, based in New York, offered Coughlin a deal in 1930 that gave him a national audience, and soon he was reaching as many as forty million listeners each week. Yet as his popularity increased, the tone and content of his broadcasts began to change. Sermons on religious themes gave way to discourses on politics and economics. The Great Depression, he declared, demanded a fundamental restructuring of society in order to overcome the evils of greed and corruption, much of which was intrinsic to ''predatory capitalism.'' Boldly confronting his critics on the air, Coughlin's political speeches generated controversy, so much so that CBS decided to cancel his show despite his growing listener base.

Undaunted, Father Coughlin signed contracts with independent radio stations and continued to reach millions of listeners weekly. His political messages, although impassioned, were rather vague. He supported Franklin Roosevelt in the 1932 presidential election, hailing the New Deal as ''Christ's Deal.'' His greatest complaint was with wealthy financiers and bankers, most of them on the East Coast, who were bilking the ''common man.'' With time, however, he moved away from Roosevelt, believing that New Deal reforms were too mild for a society that required radical change. In 1934, Coughlin founded the National Union for Social Justice, an organization designed to promote his political ideas, which included nationalization of American banks and currency inflation through the coinage of silver. Over the next two years, the organization developed into a third party, the Union Party, and offered William Lemke, a congressman from North Dakota, as a presidential candidate to oppose the reelection of Roosevelt.

After the failure of the Union Party to either capture or significantly influence the 1936 presidential election, Coughlin's popularity began to wane. His weekly radio broadcasts continued to attract a national audience, but he never recaptured his earlier fame. By the late

1930s, his speeches were increasingly shrill. Listeners detected anti-Semitism and demagoguery in his broadcasts—elements that had appeared occasionally before, yet now were becoming more vocal and more frequent. What had in the past, for example, been occasional references to ''Shylocks'' and international financial conspirators undermining the country became an outright assault against ''Communist Jews''; Coughlin also borrowed from the speeches of German Nazi propagandist Joseph Goebbels. He opposed American entry into World War II vehemently, arguing that Jews had been responsible for bringing the nation into the conflict. Such extreme positions lost for Coughlin any significant audience that had remained with him, and he retired from public life during the war and returned to the Shrine of the Little Flower. He died in 1979, at the age of eighty-eight.

—Jeffrey W. Coker

FURTHER READING:

Brinkley, Alan. *Voices of Protest: Huey Long, Father Coughlin and the Great Depression.* New York, Alfred A. Knopf, 1982.

Marcus, Sheldon. *Father Coughlin: The Tumultuous Life of the Priest of the Little Flower.* New York, Little Brown, 1973.

Schlesinger, Arthur M., Jr. *The Politics of Upheaval.* New York, Houghton Mifflin, 1960.

Tull, Charles J. *Father Coughlin and the New Deal.* Syracuse, University of Syracuse Press, 1965.

Country Gentlemen

Founded in 1957, the Country Gentlemen were the first bluegrass act to bridge the gap between the music's country origins and an urban audience. Combining singer Charlie Waller's Louisiana roots and mandolinist John Duffey's urbane tastes with inspired musicianship, the Gentlemen rode the 1960s folk revival to prominence with a repertoire ranging from ancient ballads to Bob Dylan songs, culminating in the 1971 release of ''Fox On The Run.'' Their version of the number—originally a failed rock 'n' roll single—became one of the few bluegrass songs to achieve popular culture immortality.

—Jon Weisberger

Country Music

Country music has a history that is deeply rooted in traditional white Southern working-class values, patriotism, conservative politics, and lyrics that tell the unblinking truth about life. An old joke asks, ''What do you get when you play a country record backwards?'' The answer: ''You get your wife back, your truck back, and your dog back.'' However, country music is much more than songs of hard luck in love and life. Those lyrics that face ''the cold hard facts of life,'' in the words of a Porter Wagoner song of the 1970s, are more than a series of laments. They look at both success and failure, joy and despair with sentiment and realism. And though most country music and country music fans might advocate a straight and narrow conservative path, the lyrics of country songs deal with the dilemmas of life with a complexity not found in any other popular music.

Ricky Skaggs (middle) on stage with members of Bill Monroe's Bluegrass Boys at the Chicago Country Music Festival.

Country music's earliest roots are found in the ballads of the Appalachian Mountains, songs that stemmed from a tradition brought to America by the English, Scots, and Irish who settled that territory. Their religion was a strict Calvinism, and many of their songs were dark cautionary tales of sexuality and retribution. Playwright Tennessee Williams, who came from that Southern Gothic tradition, put these words in the mouth of Blanche Dubois, his most famous heroine: "They told me to take a streetcar named Desire, then transfer to one called Cemeteries." Williams had learned the message of those old songs: "A false-hearted lover will lead you to your grave" ("On Top of Old Smoky"). One song after another told the story of seduction followed by murder. Pretty Polly's false lover tells her, "I dug on your grave the best part of last night." The false lover on the banks of the Ohio admits that "I held my knife against her breast/As into my arms she pressed." In perhaps the most famous of these songs, Tom Dooley meets his lover on the mountain and stabs her with his knife. These dark songs were not the only part of the Southern mountain tradition, however. There were children's play-party songs, danceable tunes, and upbeat, optimistic songs. But the murder songs were so striking, coming as they did out of a tradition of sexual repression combined with stark realism, that they are the most memorable.

The music of the Southern mountains became something more in 1927, when Ralph Peer, a recording engineer for the Victor Talking Machine Co. (later RCA Victor), went to Bristol, Tennessee, to make some regional recordings of what was then called "hillbilly music." He sent out word that he would pay $50 for every song he recorded, and came away with the first recorded country music.

Peer recorded two memorable acts. The first was the Carter Family (A. P., Sara, and Maybelle Carter), whose songs included both the anthems of optimism ("Keep on the Sunny Side") and the ballads of sex and death ("Bury Me beneath the Willow"). In those recordings, still in print and still considered classics of American

music, the Carter Family created an archetype of country music. From their harmonies to their guitar styles to their plain-spoken emotional directness, they created a template for the music that followed them.

Second, and even more important, was Jimmie Rodgers, a one-time railroad man (on his records he was known as "the Singing Brakeman") who had taken to playing music after ill health had forced him off the railroad. When Rodgers showed up for his first session with Peer, he sang popular songs of the day, which earned him no more than a rebuke. Peer was interested in recording folk singers, singing their indigenous music, and he told Rodgers to come back with some traditional folk songs. Rodgers did not know any traditional music, but he needed the few dollars that Peer was offering for the session. With the help of his sister, Elsie McWilliams, Rogers wrote his own "traditional" tunes, hoping that Peer wouldn't notice the difference. The songs they created made music history.

Rodgers' songs struck a chord with rural America. He glorified and romanticized the day-to-day issues of small-town working people—family, sweetheart, the struggles of the hoboes and the working class—and he placed these issues forever in the lexicon of country music. More importantly, Rodgers introduced the blues to country music. His first big hit, "T For Texas (The Blue Yodel)," created the Jimmie Rodgers sound—a traditional twelve bar blues, ending in a yodel. Rodgers was so steeped in the blues that Louis Armstrong played on one of his blue yodels, and his blues-based style was one of the first important melds of black and white styles in American popular music.

The blues had taken the country by storm in the 1920s, first in the urban, jazz-inflected recordings of artists like Bessie Smith, and then in the rural, country blues recordings of Charley Patton, Blind Lemon Jefferson, and others. The surprise commercial success of phonograph records aimed at a rural black audience encouraged companies like Victor to make a similar pitch to rural whites. The same success followed. Jimmie Rodgers sold between 6 and 20 million records (by various estimates) before his death in 1933. The blues were hit hard as a commercial medium by the depression, but country music did well in the 1930s. Radio, a more viable medium for white music, kept country music in the public ear with various local "barn dance" programs, including the phenomenally successful *Grand Ole Opry*, which started in 1925.

One singer who emerged from regional radio in the 1930s to reshape country music was Gene Autry. Autry, who had scored a hit record in 1931 with "That Silver-Haired Daddy of Mine," a sentimental song in the Jimmie Rodgers mode, was summoned to Hollywood in 1934, as the answer to a Republic Studios mogul's brainstorm: The hottest new trend in movies was the musical talkie, like *The Jazz Singer,* and perennial cinema moneymaker was the Western. With Autry's enormous success as a singing cowboy in films, "country" became "country and western." Gene Autry became the first country star to gain an audience beyond the rural South and West, even drawing a million fans at a 1939 performance in Dublin, Ireland. Rather than authentic western songs, Autry sang music composed by Hollywood songwriters, calculated to appeal to audiences that listened to Cole Porter and Irving Berlin as well as Jimmie Rodgers and the Carter Family. The new songs succeeded so well that Berlin would ultimately write his own cowboy song, "Don't Fence Me In."

This was country's first flirtation with the mainstream of American music. Roy Rogers followed Autry's path to success, and soon they were imitated by a multitude of lesser singing cowboys. There was no country music industry as such in the 1930s, but this outsider/mainstream dichotomy would remain an issue throughout country's history. The other significant innovation in the country music of the 1930s also came from the West, and was another unlikely fusion. In Texas, Bob Wills and his Texas Playboys blended jazz and country to create a new and infectious dance music.

In the 1940s, country music had its own hit parade, as *Billboard* magazine created its first country chart in 1944. First called the "folk music" chart, it became the "country and western" chart in 1949, and its first number one hit was Al Dexter's "Pistol Packin' Mama." "Folk music" being loosely defined, the early charts included artists like Louis Jordan, Nat "King" Cole, and Bing Crosby. But country was starting to amass its first generation of major stars—singers like Ernest Tubb, Hank Snow, Red Foley—and the new sound of bluegrass music, which had been popularized by Bill Monroe in the 1930s, but gained its full maturity when Lester Flatt and Earl Scruggs joined Monroe's Bluegrass Boys in the mid-1940s.

In an important sense, country's key figure in the 1940s was Roy Acuff. Acuff joined the *Grand Ole Opry* in 1938, and not long after became the *Opry*'s host, presiding over its period of greatest popularity. In 1942, Acuff and songwriter Fred Rose started a music publishing company, Acuff-Rose, which signed country songwriters, and created a new standard of professionalism in the field. The *Opry* and Acuff-Rose were, together, the most significant factors in solidifying the place of Nashville as the country music capital of America. World War II brought a lot of young GIs from the north down to army bases in the South, where they heard Acuff's music and broadened country's listening base even further.

In 1946, Acuff-Rose signed Hank Williams to a writing contract, and in 1947 Williams had his first chart hit, "Move It on Over." He joined the *Louisiana Hayride,* the second most influential of the country radio shows (Elvis Presley also began his career on the *Hayride*), in 1948, and came to the *Opry* in 1949. With Hank Williams, country had a star who outshone all who came before, and

who set the standard for all who came after. His songs (like Rodgers' were deeply blues-influenced) were as simple as conversation, but unforgettable. "Your Cheatin' Heart," "Hey, Good Lookin'," "Cold, Cold Heart," and "I Can't Help It if I'm Still in Love with You" are just a few Williams' tunes that are still classics. Williams, like his contemporaries, jazzman Charlie Parker and poet Dylan Thomas, lived out the myth of the self-destructive, tormented artist and died too young in the back seat of his limosine on the way to a concert on New Year's Day in 1953; he was 29 years old.

As the 1950s began, mainstream American popular music was becoming moribund. The creative energy of the "Tin Pan Alley" songwriters, the New York-centered, Broadway-oriented popular song crafters, seemed to be flagging. Singers like Tony Martin, Perry Como, Teresa Brewer, and the Ames brothers were only marginally connected to the pulse of the new generation. Country music and rhythm and blues both began to make inroads into that mainstream, but at first it was only the songs, not the singers, that gained popularity. Red Foley had a number one pop hit with "Chattanoogie Shoe Shine Boy" in 1950, but for the most part it was pop singers like Tony Bennett and Jo Stafford, the McGuire Sisters and Pat Boone who took their versions of country and R&B songs up the pop charts.

At the same time, country and R&B music were making an alliance of their own. Nashville was now entrenched as the capital of the country music establishment, but the new music came from Sun Records in Memphis, where Sam Phillips recorded Elvis Presley, Carl Perkins, Jerry Lee Lewis, and Johnny Cash. It was called rock 'n' roll, and the country music establishment did not like it. Elvis began his career as "The Hillbilly Cat," and was featured on *Louisiana Hayride,* but he never sang on the *Opry,* and rock 'n' roll, denounced by Roy Acuff, never made an impact there. Racism certainly played a part in the country establishment's rejection of rock 'n' roll. The new music was widely denounced throughout the South by organizations like the White Citizen's Council. At the same time, however, country music was beginning to outgrow its raffish, working-class roots. Eddie Arnold, the biggest star of the late 1940s and early 1950s, called himself "The Tennessee Plowboy," a nickname he had acquired early in his career, but he was no plowboy. He wore a tuxedo on stage, and had only the barest trace of hillbilly nasality in his voice.

Perhaps the city of Nashville exerted an influence, too. Although Acuff-Rose and other music companies had made Music Row the symbol of Nashville everywhere else in the country, it was an embarrassment to Nashville society. When a Tennessee governor in the mid-1940s was quoted as saying, "hillbilly music is disgraceful," Roy Acuff responded by announcing his candidacy for governor (he never followed through), but there was a growing feeling that country's image should not be too raw or "low-class." So while rhythm and blues performers responded to rock 'n' roll by joining it, the country establishment rejected it. This was the first of a series of decisions that had the effect of marginalizing what might have become America's dominant musical style. The country establishment has always sought status and recognition, but until the 1990s, it consistently made the wrong choices in following that ambition. As rock 'n' roll's hard edge took over not only the United States but the world, country music became softer and smoother. Brilliant musicians and producers, such as guitar virtuoso Chet Atkins, pooled their considerable talents and came up with The Nashville Sound, a string-sweetened Muzak that was suited to the stylings of Arnold, Jim Reeves, and Patsy Cline, but not to the grittiness of Presley, Perkins, Lewis, and Cash.

Contrary to the popular stereotype, country music has not always been associated with political conservatism. One of the *Opry's* first stars, Uncle Dave Macon, was a fiery radical leftist. Even Gene Autry, early in his career, recorded "The Death of Mother Jones," a tribute to the legendary left-wing labor organizer. But New Deal populism was replaced, over the years, by entrenched racism, Cold War patriotism, and the growing generation gap. By the 1960s, youth, rebellion, and rock 'n' roll were on one side of a great divide, and country music was on the other.

The anthems of 1960s country conservatism were Merle Haggard's anti-hippie "Okie From Muskogee" and chip-on-the-shoulder patriotic "Fightin' Side of Me." But Haggard, an ex-convict who had been in the audience when Johnny Cash recorded his historic live album at Folsom Prison, represented his own kind of rebellion. Along with Buck Owens, Haggard had turned his back on not only the Nashville Sound but Nashville itself, setting up their own production center in the dusty working-class town of Bakersfield, California, and making music that recaptured the grittier sound of an earlier era. Haggard and Owens, for all their right-wing posturing, were adopted by the rockers. The Grateful Dead recorded Haggard's "Mama Tried," and Creedence Clearwater Revival sang about "listenin' to Buck Owens."

The conservative cause stood in staunch opposition to the women's movement, but in the 1960s women gained their first major foothold in country music. There had been girl singers before, even great ones like Patsy Cline, but now Loretta Lynn, Tammy Wynette, and especially Dolly Parton established themselves as important figures. Lynn and Parton wrote their own songs, often with incisive lyrics about the female experience, and Parton handled much of her own production. Country music has been described as "the voice of the inarticulate," and these singers gave a powerful voice to a segment of the population that had never had their dreams and struggles articulated in this way.

The Nashville establishment was still hitching its wagon to a star that shone most brightly over Las Vegas. Still distrustful of rebellion and rough edges, they looked to Vegas pop stars for their salvation. In 1974 and 1975, John Denver and Olivia Newton-John swept the Country Music Association Awards (Denver was Entertainer of the Year in 1975). Country's creative edge moved away from Nashville to Bakersfield and elsewhere. Singer-songwriters Willie Nelson and Waylon Jennings grew their hair long and hung out with hippies and rockers at the Armadillo World Headquarters in Austin, Texas. They made the country establishment nervous, but it did eventually accept the so-called Outlaw Movement, and by 1979, Nelson was Entertainer of the Year. The real working-class music of the new generation of Southern whites never got that acceptance. Although the 1950s rockabilly rebels like Cash, Lewis, and the Everly Brothers now played country venues, the young rockers still scared Nashville. There was too much Jimi Hendrix in their music, too much hippie attitude in their clothes and their hair. The Allman Brothers, Lynyrd Skynyrd, and others played something called Southern Rock that could have been called country, but wasn't. Nevertheless, the kid at the gas station in North Carolina was listening to them, not to John Denver or Barbara Mandrell. By cutting them out (along with white Midwestern working-class rockers like Bob Seger), country music lost a large portion of its new generation of potential listeners.

The country establishment still sought the Vegas crossover secret, and they seemed to find it in 1980, when the movie *Urban Cowboy* created a craze for yoked shirts and fringed cowboy boots. Records by artists like Mickey Gilley, Johnny Lee, and Alabama shot up the pop charts for a short time, but the "urban cowboy" sound was passing fad, and country music seemed to disintegrate with it. In 1985, *The New York Times* solemnly declared that country music was finished as a genre, and would never be revived.

However, it was already being revived, by going back to its roots. Inspired by the example of George Jones, a country legend since the late 1950s, who is widely considered to possess the greatest voice in the history of country music, country's new generation came to be known as the New Traditionalists. Some of its most important figures were Ricky Skaggs, a brilliant instrumentalist who brought the bluegrass tradition back into the mainstream, Randy Travis, a balladeer in the style of Jones, the Judds, who revived country harmony and the family group, and Reba McEntire, who modernized the tradition of Parton, Wynette, and Lynn, while keeping a pure country sound. The late 1980s brought a new generation of outlaws, too, singer-songwriters who respected tradition, but had a younger, quirkier approach. They included Lyle Lovett, Nanci Griffith, and Steve Earle. These musicians gained a following (Earle, who self-destructed on drugs, but gradually rebuilt a career in the 1990s, remains the most influential songwriter of the era). However, country radio, the center of the country establishment, gave them little air time, and they moved on to careers in other genres.

There had always been country performers on television, Tennessee Ernie Ford in the 1950s, Glen Campbell and Johnny Cash in the 1960s, and Barbara Mandrell in the "urban cowboy" days of the early 1980s. The 1980s also brought cable television, and in 1983, The Nashville Network went on the air with an all-country format of videos, live music, and interview shows. In 1985, TNN broadcast country music's Woodstock—Farm Aid, a massive benefit organized by Willie Nelson for America's farm families. TNN broadcast the entire 12 hours of Farm Aid live, and audiences who tuned in to see the rock stars like Neil Young and John Mellencamp who headlined the bill, also saw new country stars like Dwight Yoakam.

The creative energy that drove country music in the 1980s, had settled into a formula by the 1990s, and it was the most successful formula the genre had ever seen. In 1989, Clint Black, became the first performer to combine the traditionalism of Travis and George Strait, the innovation of Lovett and Earle, and MTV/TNN-era good looks and video presence. Close behind Black came Garth Brooks. With Brooks, the resistance to rock which had limited country's potential for growth for four decades finally crumbled completely.

Brooks modeled himself after 1970s arena rockers like Journey and Kiss, and after his idol, Billy Joel. Rock itself was floundering in divisiveness, and audiences were excited by the new face of country. In a 1991 interview, Rodney Crowell said, "I play country music because I love rock 'n' roll, and country is the only genre where you can still play it." Brooks' second album, *Ropin' The Wind*, debuted at number one on the pop charts, swamping a heavily hyped album by Guns 'n Roses, rock's biggest name at that time. Pop music observers compared the new country popularity to the "urban cowboy" craze, and many predicted it would fizzle again. However, with country finally catching up to rock 'n' roll, 40 years late. Country music had taken on a lot of the trappings that had been associated with rock—sexy young singing idols, arena tours, and major promotions. Country music's audience had also broadened; the kid at the gas station joined the country traditionalists and country's new suburban audience. Country music has as many faces as American society itself, and no doubt will keep re-inventing itself with each generation.

—Tad Richards

FURTHER READING:

The Country Music Foundation, editors. *Country—The Music and the Musicians.* New York, Abbeville Press, 1994.

Hemphill, Paul. *The Nashville Sound: Bright Lights and Country Music.* New York, Simon and Schuster, 1970.

Horstman, Dorothy. *Sing Your Heart Out, Country Boy.* Nashville, Country Music Foundation Press, 1985.

Leamer, Laurence. *Three Chords and the Truth.* New York, HarperCollins, 1997.

Malone, Bill C. *Country Music USA, Revised Edition.* Austin, University of Texas Press, 1985.

Mansfield, Brian, and Gary Graff, editors. *Music Hound Country: The Essential Album Guide.* Detroit, Visible Ink, 1997.

Nash, Alana. *Behind Closed Doors: Talking With the Legends of Country Music.* New York, Knopf, 1988.

Richards, Tad, and Melvin B. Shestack. *The New Country Music Encyclopedia.* New York, Simon and Schuster, 1993.

Cousteau, Jacques (1910-1997)

Jacques Cousteau is the world's most acclaimed producer of underwater film documentaries. His adventurous spirit and undersea explorations, documented in over forty books, four feature films, and more than one hundred television programs, popularized the study of marine environments, and made him a household name in many parts of the world. As principal developer of the world's first aqualung diving apparatus and underwater film cameras, he opened up the world's waters to millions of scuba divers, film makers, and television viewers. A pioneering environmentalist, Cousteau brought home to the public mind the importance of the world's oceans and inspired generations of young scientists to become ecologists and oceanographers.

Jacques-Yves Cousteau was born on June 11, 1910, in the market town of St.-Andre-de-Cubzac, France. Following service in the French Navy, he became commander of the research vessel Calypso in 1950. The Calypso, where most of his subsequent films were produced, served as his base of operations. His first book, *The Silent World,* sold more than five million copies in 22 languages. A film of the same name won both the Palme d'Or at the 1956 Cannes International Film Festival and an Academy Award for best documentary in 1957. Television programs bearing the Cousteau name earned 10 Emmys and numerous other awards. In the 1950s and 1960s, Cousteau established a series of corporations and nonprofit organizations through which he financed his explorations, promoted his environmental opinions, and championed his reputation as the world's foremost underwater researcher and adventurer. He died in Paris on June 25, 1997.

—Ken Kempcke

FURTHER READING:

Madsen, Axel. *Cousteau: An Unauthorized Biography.* New York, Beaufort, 1986.

Munson, Richard. *Cousteau: The Captain and His World.* New York, Morrow, 1989.

Covey, Stephen (1932—)

Stephen Covey, one of America's most prominent self-help gurus, owes much to Dale Carnegie, whose best-selling book, *How To Win Friends and Influence People,* and its corresponding public speaking course are models upon which Covey built his success. The first of numerous books written by Covey, *The 7 Habits of Highly Effective People,* was published in 1989 and helped his rise to the position of unofficial consultant to the leaders of corporate America, and guru to those in the lower levels of corporate management. His company, the Covey Leadership Center, founded in 1983, subsequently capitalized on the success of *7 Habits,* which became a catch phrase for any number of simplistic and appealing ideas dealing with personal happiness and efficiency in the workplace.

Covey was born into a Mormon family in Provo, Utah. During the 1950s he completed a bachelor's degree in business administration at the University of Utah and an M.B.A. at Cambridge. In between his academic studies, he served as a missionary in Nottingham, England, training the leaders of recently formed Mormon congregations, and thus became aware of what it meant to train and motivate leaders. As a result of the particular nature of his training experience, a combination of religious and family values formed the core of his programs and writings. Covey taught at Brigham Young University where, in 1976, he earned a Ph.D. in business and education, but left that institution in 1983 to start the Covey Leadership Center.

The Center had an immediate, and almost exclusive appeal to the corporate culture, partly due to its marketing strategies, but also because of the timbre of the times. Corporate America was in a state of unease and flux, and workers and managers were ripe for guidance in their search for a sense of stability in their jobs and careers. The Covey Leadership Center promised solutions to their problems, and both managers and employees were as eager to attend Covey's programs as the corporate leaders—hoping for improved efficiency and morale of their personnel—were to send them. When *The 7 Habits of Highly Effective People* was published, six years after the inception of the Center, it became hugely popular, appearing on the *New York Times* bestseller list for well over five years. The book stood out from the vast quantity of positive-thinking books available in the late 1980s, partially because of Covey's already established credibility, and partly because, as with the courses and programs, there was a real need for his particular take on self-help literature. The sales of the book increased the already sizable interest and enrollment in his leadership programs. Throughout the 1990s, according to *Current Biography,* ''hundreds of corporations, government agencies, and universities invited Covey to conduct seminars with, or present talks to, their employees.''

While many people attended these seminars and workshops, it is the *7 Habits* book that defines Stephen Covey's identity as a self-help guru. Initially an integral part of corporate management literature, the appeal of Covey's message, as transmitted in his book, spread to people in all walks of life. Its popularity was such that magazine and newspaper editors, in their bids to increase circulation, would play on the ''Seven Habits'' theme in headlines and articles in much the same way that the title of Robert Pirsig's novel *Zen and the Art of Motorcycle Maintenance* spawned countless sophomoric imitations in the print media.

Stephen Covey was the first to admit that there is nothing new in his writing; indeed the very simplicity of his philosophy has accounted both for its popular acclaim, and for the not insubstantial negative criticism it has attracted in certain quarters. Each "habit" presented in the book ("Be proactive," "Begin with the end in mind," "Put first things first") draws on time-tested truisms and age-old common-sense principles. Covey's fans applauded him for putting these adages into print, in a useful modern context; detractors blasted him for repackaging well-worn and well-known information. Covey himself claimed that his book is based on common sense ideas, but that they needed to be restated, because, as he said in an interview in the *Orange County Register*, ". . . [W]hat is common sense isn't common practice." Another criticism frequently leveled at Covey is that, in his effort to show that each person is responsible for his or her own success, he trivializes the effects that flaws in the larger corporate system may have on performance. Thus, any failure is blamed only on the individual.

The 7 Habits of Highly Effective People has transcended the corporate world and entered into the American collective psyche. The Covey Leadership Center, which merged with the Franklin Quest Company in 1997 to form the Franklin Covey Co., has turned itself into a cottage industry, supplying customers with all manner of related merchandise: magazines, audiotapes, videos, and, perhaps most pervasively, "day-planners". Once the chief product of the Franklin Quest company, these trendy signs-of-the-times began, after the merger, to include quotes from Covey's books. In addition to the *7 Habits* book, Covey wrote a number of other books on related topics, including *First Things First*, and *Principle-Centered Leadership*. In 1997, he published a "follow-up" to his popular book, entitled *The 7 Habits of Highly Effective Families*, which promptly landed on the *New York Times* best-seller list. Redirecting the thrust of his wisdom towards problems between family members, Covey seemed to anticipate the changing mood and tone of America, which, in the wake of contradictory political messages, had become, by the late 1990s, more concerned with "family values."

Stephen Covey is, perhaps, not quite a household name, but the "7 Habits" phrase, and the concept and book from which it originates, has become an emblem of the American people's desire for stability and self-improvement, in their careers and in their personal lives. It represents the people's search for an antidote to the confusing, contradictory and often disturbing events in the corporate and political worlds during the 1990s. The extent to which "7 Habits" has permeated the culture shows a desire, in the face of growing and changing technology, for simple truths, and for courses of action that can be easily understood and executed.

—Dan Coffey

FURTHER READING:

Covey, Stephen R. *The 7 Habits of Highly Effective Families: Building a Beautiful Family Culture in a Turbulent World.* New York, Golden Books, 1997.

———. *The 7 Habits of Highly Effective People.* New York, Simon & Schuster, 1992.

Current Biography. New York, H.W. Wilson. January, 1998, 19-21.

Smith, Timothy K. "What's So Effective About Stephen Covey?" *Fortune.* December 12, 1994, 116-22.

Walker, Theresa. "Stephen Covey." *The Orange County Register.* March 3, 1998.

Wolfe, Alan. "Capitalism, Mormonism, and the Doctrine of Stephen Covey." *The New Republic.* February 23, 1998, 26-35.

The Cowboy Look

The cowboy look is a fanciful construction of an ideal cowboy image. Originally, cowboy clothing provided primarily function over fashion, but through America's century-long fascination with this romantic Great Plains laborer, image has surpassed reality in what a cowboy ought to look like. With the supposed closing of the frontier at the end of the nineteenth century, the ascendancy of the Cowboy President, Theodore Roosevelt, and the growing popularity of artists such as Frederick Remington and Charley Russell, who reveled in a nostalgia for cowboy life, wearing cowboy clothes became akin to a "wearing of history" as twentieth-century Americans tried to hold onto ideals of individualism, opportunity, and adventure supposedly tied to the clothes' frontier heritage.

Of primary importance in the construction of cowboy fashion are the highly stylized cowboy boots. A mass-produced and mail-order footwear near the turn of the century, these boots protected against rough vegetation with their durable cowhide uppers and provided ease of movement in and out of stirrups with their flat soles and high wooden heels. As cowboys became heroes through the massive popularity of Buffalo Bill's Wild West Show during the late nineteenth and early twentieth century and later through Hollywood films, cowboy clothing came into vogue in popular culture. Boots in particular started to assume a sense of personalized fashion as specialized bootmakers cropped up in the West, especially in Texas. These bootmakers produced boots from hides as far-ranging as ostrich, elephant, eel, or stingray. The fancy stitching, colored leather, and occasional inlaid precious stone lent these custom boots an air of fashionable individuality. Custom cowboy boots, among those wealthy enough to afford them, became a distinctive mark of an individual's flair combined with a sense of Western spirit.

But cowboy boots were only a single part of Western fashion popular throughout most of the twentieth century. Necessary fashion accouterments included denim jeans, a Western shirt (usually with designs on the shoulders), large belt buckles, and a broad-brimmed cowboy hat. This fashion remained essentially the same, barring various preferences for shirt designs and boot styles, throughout the twentieth century. Early Western film stars like William S. Hart and Tom Mix popularized the cowboy look, perpetuating the myth of the cowboy hero (always clad in a white hat) over the image of the ranch hand laborer. From the 1930s to the mid-1950s, the cowboy look found immense popularity among children. This trend coincided with the popularity of cowboy movie stars and singers Gene Autry and Roy Rogers who, according to Lonn Taylor and Ingrid Maar in *The American Cowboy,* acted as surrogate fathers for children whose fathers were away fighting in World War II. As television Westerns became more popular in America in the 1950s, the image of a noble and righteous cowboy fighting for justice and ideological harmony on the American frontier found a resurgence once again as America turned its attention to the Cold War.

Along with the popularity of the cowboy look from 1950s television, country music's presence in popular culture became notable; though most country music from this era sprang from the South, the fashion of the time was essentially Western and demanded cowboy boots and hats. But with the popularity of rock 'n' roll during the late 1950s and 1960s, cowboy fashion faded from the mainstream of popular culture. By the early 1970s, however, the boots, hats, tight jeans, and plaid work shirts of cowboy fashion started to appear in more urban settings. Growing from the seemingly timeless myth of

John Travolta and Madolyn Smith in a scene from the film *Urban Cowboy* that illustrates the cowboy look.

the cowboy loner—epitomized in 1902 by Owen Wister's *The Virginian*—, the cowboy look now hit city streets less as a costume and more as a fashion statement. This look culminated with the 1980 release of *Urban Cowboy*, starring John Travolta as an unlikely cowboy figure who finds romance and country dancing in late 1970s Texas honky tonks.

The cowboy look also benefitted from the resurgence in the popularity of country music music between the mid-1980s and the mid-1990s. Without any major changes in the foundations, the cowboy look became the Western look, incorporating into the basic clothes some Hollywood glitz and rhinestones, Southwestern Hispanic and Native American styles such as silver and turquoise, and a new kind of homegrown, rural sensibility. The jeans became tighter, the shirts louder, and hats took on the personalized importance of boots. As country music became more popular, huge Western clothing super-stores opened throughout America dedicated solely to supplying the fashion needs of country music's (and country dancing's) new devotees.

The icon of Western fashion could no longer be found in movies. Instead, country music stars such as George Strait or Reba McEntire presented the measure for the new cowboy look. The new cowboy look did not focus on the Western hero, the knight in the white hat so popular in the early part of the century, but rather was aimed at the American worker who gets duded-up to play on the weekend. This new cowboy look was used to sell fishing equipment and especially pick-up trucks to people aspiring toward country or Western lifestyles. Though this country look still appeared as a "wearing of history," its devotees found in this new fashion a distillation of the American work ethic (that allowed for outlets on Friday and Saturday nights) that had supposedly grown from a country ranching and farming lifestyle. The cowboy look no longer represented the hero, but the American rural laborer, albeit in an overly sanitized fashion. Like the popular country music that spurred this fashion trend, the cowboy look now affected rural authenticity over urban pretensions, valued family and the honor of wage labor, and, like its earlier permutations, elevated American history and culture over any other traditions.

—Dan Moos

FURTHER READING:

Beard, Tyler. *The Cowboy Boot Book.* Layton, Utah, Gibbs Smith, 1992.

Savage, William W., Jr., *The Cowboy Hero: His Image in American History and Culture.* Norman, University of Oklahoma Press, 1979.

Taylor, Lonn, and Ingrid Maar. *The American Cowboy.* New York, Harper and Row, 1983.

Cox, Ida (1896-1967)

Billed as the "Uncrowned Queen of the Blues," Ida Cox (born Ida Prather) never achieved the fame of her contemporaries Bessie Smith and Gertrude "Ma" Rainey. Though she spent most of the 1920s and 1930s touring the United States with various minstrel troupes, including her own "Raisin' Cain Revue," she also found time to record seventy-eight sides for Paramount Records between 1923 and 1929. Among these was her best known song, "Wild Women Don't Have the Blues," which was identified by Angela Y. Davis as "the most famous portrait of the nonconforming, independent woman."

Noted record producer John Hammond revitalized Cox's career by highlighting her in the legendary "Spirituals to Swing" concert at Carnegie Hall in 1939. Cox continued her recording career until she suffered a stroke in 1944. Six years after a 1961 comeback attempt that produced the album *Blues for Rampart Street,* Ida Cox died of cancer.

—Marc R. Sykes

FURTHER READING:

Davis, Angela Y. *Blues Legacies and Black Feminism: Gertrude "Ma" Rainey, Bessie Smith, and Billie Holiday.* New York, Pantheon, 1998.

Harrison, Daphne Duval. *Black Pearls: Blues Queens of the 1920s.* New Brunswick, Rutgers University Press, 1988.

Cranston, Lamont
See Shadow, The

Crawford, Cindy (1966—)

Beginning in the 1980s and continuing through the 1990s, Cindy Crawford was America's most celebrated fashion model and one of the most famous in the world, embodying the rise of the "super model" as a late twentieth century cultural phenomenon. Although there had been star models in previous decades—Twiggy in the 1960s, for example, or Lauren Hutton and Cheryl Tiegs in the 1970s—they did not sustain prolonged mainstream recognition. Cindy Crawford and her contemporaries (Kate Moss and Naomi Campbell among them) no longer merely posed as nameless faces on magazine covers, calendars, and fashion runways but, rather, became celebrities whose fame rivaled that of movie stars and rock musicians. Cindy Crawford stood at the forefront of this insurgence.

Although she found fame through her physical appearance, the brown-haired, brown-eyed Crawford first distinguished herself through her intellectual attributes. A native of DeKalb, Illinois, who was born Cynthia Ann Crawford on February 20, 1966, she was a fine student and class valedictorian at her high school graduation. She enrolled in Chicago's Northwestern University to take a degree in chemical engineering, but her academic career proved short-lived when, during her freshman year, she left college to pursue a modeling career. Her entrance into the tough, competitive world of high fashion was eased by her winning the "Look of the Year" contest held by the Elite

Cindy Crawford

Modeling Agency in 1982. Within months the statuesque (five-foot-nine-and-a-half inches), 130-lb model was featured on the cover of *Vogue.*

The widespread appeal of Cindy Crawford lay in looks that appealed to both men and women. Her superb body, with its classic 34B-24-35 measurements, attracted men, while her all-American looks and trademark facial mole stopped her short of seeming an unattainable ideal of perfect beauty, and thus she was not threatening to women. Furthermore, her athletic physique was in distinct contrast to many of the overly thin and waif-like models, such as Kate Moss, who were prevalent during the 1990s.

Cindy Crawford stepped off the remote pedestal of a celebrity mannequin or a glamorous cover girl when she began to assert her personality before the public. She gave interviews in which she discussed her middle-class childhood, her parents' divorce, and the trauma of her brother's death from leukemia. These confessions humanized her image and made her approachable, and she went on to host MTV's *House of Style,* a talk show that stressed fashion and allowed her to conduct interviews that connected with a younger market. The Cindy Crawford phenomenon continued with her involvement in fitness videos, TV specials, commercial endorsements, and film (*Fair Game,* 1995, was dismissed both by audiences and critics, but did little to diminish her popularity.) Meanwhile, her already high profile increased with her brief 1991 marriage to actor Richard Gere. The couple was hounded by rumors of homosexuality, fuelled after Crawford appeared on a controversial *Vanity Fair* cover with the openly lesbian singer k.d. lang. She later wed entrepreneur Rande Gerber.

After the arrival of Cindy Crawford, it was not uncommon to see models promoting a vast array of products beyond fashion and cosmetics. Crawford herself signed a multi-million dollar deal to promote Pepsi, as well as her more conventional role with Revlon. Her status was so high that ABC invited her to host a special on teen sex issues with the provocative title of *Sex with Cindy Crawford*. The opening of the Fashion Café theme restaurant in the mid-1990s marked the height of the super model sensation sparked by Crawford. The café's association with Crawford and other high profile models revealed the extent to which the "super model" had become a major figure in American culture. By the end of the twentieth century, Cindy Crawford was still the best known of these celebrities due to the combination of her wholesomely erotic image and her professional diversification through the many available media outlets.

—Charles Coletta

FURTHER READING:

"Cindy.com." http://www.cindy.com. April 1999.

Crawford, Cindy. *Cindy Crawford's Basic Face.* New York, Broadway Books, 1996.

Italia, Bob. *Cindy Crawford.* Edina, Minnesota, Abdo and Daughters, 1992.

Crawford, Joan (1904?-1977)

From her 1930s heyday as a leading MGM box-office draw, to her 1962 performance in the horror classic and cult favorite *Whatever Happened to Baby Jane?,* Joan Crawford incarnated, in the words of Henry Fonda, "a star in every sense of the word." The MGM style of star packaging emphasized glamour, and Crawford achieved her luminous appearance through an extensive wardrobe and fastidious presentations of her gleaming, trademark lips, arched eyebrows, sculpted cheek and jaw bones, and perfectly coiffured hair. Crawford herself famously said, "I never go out unless I look like Joan Crawford the movie star. If you want to see the girl next door, go next door."

Born Lucille LeSueur in San Antonio, Texas, on March 23, 1904, Crawford embarked on a dancing career when only a teenager. She worked cabarets and travelling musical shows until her discovery in the Broadway revue *The Passing Show of 1924*. It would not be long before an MGM executive noted her exuberant energy and athletic skill. Exported to Hollywood on a $75.00/week contract, Lucille changed her name as part of a movie magazine promotion that urged fans to "Name Her and Win $1,000." This early link between her professional life and fan magazines presaged a union that would repeatedly shape her long movie star tenure. Throughout five decades, she appeared in magazine advertisements endorsing cosmetics, food products, and cigarettes. She dutifully answered fan letters and once fired a publicity manager who turned away admirers at her dressing room door. Her first marriage to Douglas Fairbanks, Jr., turned into a publicity spectacle. It was a reported feud between Crawford and co-star Bette Davis that was used to generate interest in *Whatever Happened to Baby Jane?* A conflation of Crawford's roles and fan magazine publicity with her personal life formed both the public view of her and her own sense of identity.

Joan Crawford

Crawford garnered her first film role in 1925 and made over 20 silent pictures before 1929, the year of her first hit *Untamed*. Her early career coincided with Hollywood's investment in the production and cultivation of stars as bankable assets. One of the industry's earliest successes, Crawford mutated her star persona over the decades to retain currency. Her first image was as a "flapper," a 1920s free-spirited woman who danced all night in speakeasies and jazz clubs. In the 1928 movie *Our Dancing Daughters,* Crawford's quintessential flapper whips off her party dress and dances the Charleston in her slip. Her date asks, "You want to take all of life, don't you?" Crawford's character replies, "Yes—all! I want to hold out my hands and catch at it." Crawford's own dance-till-dawn escapades frequently provided fodder for the gossip columns.

In the wake of the Depression Crawford transformed into a 1930s "shopgirl"—a willful, hard-working woman determined to overcome adversity, usually on the arm of a wealthy, handsome man played by the likes of Clark Gable or second husband, Franchot Tone. With this new character type, song-and-dance movies gave way to melodramatic fare, in which she uttered lines like this one from the 1930s movie *Paid:* "You're going to pay for everything I'm losing in life." To encourage fan identification with Crawford's "shopgirl" image, MGM promoted Crawford's own hard-luck background, highlighting her travails as a clerk at a department store in Kansas City, Missouri. In 1930, she was voted most popular at the box office. Inherent to this genre was a literal rags-to-riches metamorphosis. *Possessed,* produced in 1931, begins with Crawford working a factory floor in worn clothing and charts her rise in status through increasingly extravagant costume changes. This particular formula teamed her with *haute couture* designer Adrian, and together they sparked fashion trends. In *Paid,* Crawford dons a huge, black fur-collared coat that, by virtue of her appearance in it, turned into a best-selling item in clothing stores along fifth Avenue in New York. The most famous instance occurred in 1932 with the Letty Lynton dress, reportedly the most frequently copied film-gown in American movies. Featuring enormous, ruffled sleeves and layers of white organdy, the Letty Lynton dress-craze confirmed Hollywood's place as showcase for fashion. The Letty Lynton phenomenon also marked the debut of Crawford's clothes-horse image. The importance of how Crawford looked in a movie soon eclipsed the significance of how she acted.

Crawford's popularity diminished in the 1940s as younger actresses claimed the best MGM parts. She responded by retooling herself into a matriarchal, self-sacrificing businesswoman, her strength symbolized by shoulder pads and dramatically tailored suits. To brook this transition, Crawford departed glamour-factory MGM in 1943 and signed with the crime picture studio, Warner Brothers. The role of the driven self-made restaurateur in the 1945 film noir, *Mildred Pierce,* earned her an Academy Award for Best Actress. At the end of this period, she began portraying desperate, emotionally disturbed women like the lover-turned-stalker *Possessed* (1947), and the neat-freak homemaker whose obsession turns to madness in the title role of *Harriet Craig* (1950). Movie culture in the 1950s expressed anxiety over dominant, self-sufficient female roles, popular in World War II and immediate post-War America, by straight-jacketing Crawford—literally—in *Straight Jacket,* produced by "B" horror film king William Castle in 1964. The 1960s limited her to cheap horror films—*I Saw What You Did, Beserk, Trog*—and traded on her now severe, lined face and its striking contrast with her trim, dancer's figure. Crawford's late career also ushered in the Hollywood use of product placement. As an official representative of Pepsi-Cola—her fourth and last husband, Howard Steele, was a Pepsi executive—Crawford featured displays of Pepsi-Cola signs and merchandise in several of her last films. For example, while probing a series of ghoulish murders at a circus owned by Crawford in a scene from *Beserk* (1968), investigators pause under a "Come Alive! With Pepsi" banner.

In *Mommie Dearest,* a movie based on an expose written by Crawford's adopted daughter and featuring Faye Dunaway, Crawford is depicted as a bizarrely cruel disciplinarian. The movie not only made a horrific joke of Crawford, but it also maligned Dunaway's acting ability. Portions of the movie became staple skits on late-night television shows like the satiric *Saturday Night Live.* The 1980s and 1990s, however, turned her into a favorite icon of gays and lesbians with Internet websites celebrating her masculine performances in, for example, *Johnny Guitar* (1954). In this movie she plays a gun-belted, top-booted saloon keep whose show-down is against another mannish-looking woman.

—Elizabeth Haas

FURTHER READING:

Considine, Shaun. *Bette & Joan: The Divine Feud.* New York, E.P. Dutton, 1989.

Gledhill, Christine, editor. *Stardom: Industry of Desire.* New York, Routledge, 1991.

Thomas, Bob. *Joan Crawford: A Biography.* New York, Simon & Schuster, 1978.

Walker, Alexander. *Joan Crawford: The Ultimate Star.* London, Weidenfeld & Nicholson Ltd., 1983.

Cray, Robert (1953—)

Robert Cray's fusion of blues, R & B, jazz, pop, and soul music earned him critical acclaim and widespread recognition as a critical figure in the "blues boom" of the 1980s and 1990s. Indeed, his original approach to the genre brought an entirely new audience to what had been considered a dying art form. Though blues purists dismissed him as a "tin-eared yuppie blues wannabe," Cray nonetheless enjoyed success unmatched by any other blues artist.

Born into an army family in 1953, Cray had the opportunity to live in many different regions of the United States before his family settled in Tacoma, Washington, when Cray was fifteen years old. Already a devotee of soul and rock music, Cray became interested in blues after legendary Texas guitarist Albert Collins played at his high school graduation dance. Cray formed his first band in 1974, and this group eventually became Collins's backing band, touring the country with him before striking out on its own.

After a series of moves—to Portland, Seattle, and finally to San Francisco—the Robert Cray Band signed a record deal with Tomato Records and released its first album, *Who's Been Talking?* (later re-released as *Too Many Cooks*), in 1980. Though the album featured convincing performances of classic blues songs, it generated little excitement. Cray and his band subsequently toured with Chicago

Robert Cray

legend Muddy Waters and were featured on the Kings of the Boogie world tour with John Lee Hooker and Willie Dixon.

In 1983, Cray tried a different approach with the funky, original *Bad Influence,* released on the HighTone label. His follow-up effort, *False Accusations,* proved to be the breakthrough. The album made *Newsweek*'s list of top ten LPs and shot up to number one on the Billboard pop music charts. That same year, Alligator Records released the Grammy Award-winning *Showdown!,* which featured Cray collaborating with now-deceased blues guitarists Collins and Johnny Copeland.

Success earned Cray the support of a major label, Mercury, and his debut effort for the company is widely believed to be the best work of his career. Released in 1986, *Strong Persuader* was certified platinum (sales of more than one million copies) and put Cray's picture on the cover of *Rolling Stone.* The success of the album also ensured more high-profile collaborations, such as an appearance in the concert and film tribute to Chuck Berry, *"Hail! Hail! Rock 'n' Roll!"* produced by Keith Richards. After covering Cray's "Bad Influence" on his *August* album, Eric Clapton invited Cray to appear on his *Journeyman* and *24 Nights* albums. Cray also appeared in the Tina Turner video "Break Every Rule," becoming a familiar face on the MTV network.

Cray continued to experiment with soul music on 1990's *Midnight Stroll,* which featured the legendary Memphis Horns, and showed a jazzier side on *I Was Warned,* released two years later. Albert Collins joined Cray and his band on the 1993 album *Shame + a Sin,* the most traditional of Cray's later works. Cray continued to be in demand as a guest performer, appearing on three John Lee Hooker albums including the Grammy-winning *The Healer,* as well as B. B. King's *Blues Summit.* Cray's 1997 release *Sweet Potato Pie* featured a return to the Memphis soul that had characterized his sound from the early 1980s. Despite being panned by the "bluenatics," as Cray labelled the blues purists, the album achieved significant sales, confirming Cray's continuing commercial viability.

—Marc R. Sykes

FURTHER READING:

Davis, Francis. *The History of the Blues.* New York, Hyperion, 1995.

Russell, Tony, ed. *The Blues: From Robert Johnson to Robert Cray.* New York, Schirmer, 1997.

Creationism

Creationism is a Christian doctrine holding that the world and the living things in it—human beings in particular—were created by God. There have been a variety of creationist viewpoints, and some of these viewpoints are in conflict with mainstream scientific theories, especially the theory of evolution.

After Charles Darwin published his *Origin of Species* (1859), which not only defended the pre-existing theory of evolution but also maintained that evolution took place through natural selection, many fundamentalist Christians reacted with horror. Then as now, anti-evolutionists maintained that evolution was contrary to the Bible, that it was atheistic pseudo-science, and that, by proposing that man descended from lower animals, it denied man's spiritual nature. Evolutionists denounced creationists for allegedly misinterpreting both the Bible and the scientific evidence.

In the 1920s, William Jennings Bryan, a former Nebraska Senator, Presidential candidate, and U.S. Secretary of State, joined the movement to prevent the teaching of evolution. In response to lobbyists like Bryan, the state of Tennessee passed a law making it a crime for a public-school teacher or state college professor to teach the allegedly un-Scriptural doctrine that man evolved from a lower order of animals. However, under the Butler Act (and similar laws in other states), it remained permissible to teach the theory of evolution as applied to species other than humans.

A test case of the Tennessee law was arranged in Dayton, Tennessee, in 1925. A teacher named John Thomas Scopes was charged with violating the law. Bryan was brought in to help the prosecution, and an all-star legal defense team, including famed attorney Clarence Darrow, was brought in to defend the young teacher. Scopes was convicted after a highly-publicized trial, but his conviction was overturned on a technicality by the Tennessee Supreme Court. A play based on the Scopes Monkey trial, *Inherit the Wind,* was turned into a movie in 1960. Spencer Tracy, Gene Kelly, and Frederic March were among the cast of this popular and anti-creationist rendering of the trial. The movie altered some of the historical details, but the movie version of the trial was probably better-known than the actual trial.

Arkansas had also passed a "monkey law" similar to Tennessee's Butler Act. In 1968, the United States Supreme Court ruled that the Arkansas law was designed to promote religious doctrine, and that therefore it was an unconstitutional establishment of religion which violated the First Amendment. The *Epperson* decision had no effect on the Tennessee Butler law, since that law had been repealed in 1967.

Since the Scopes trial, the views of some creationists have been getting closer to secular scientific position. Scientists who were evangelical Christians formed an organization called the American Scientific Affiliation (ASA) during World War II. ASA members pledged support for Biblical inerrancy and declared that the Christian scriptures were in harmony with the evidence of nature. Within this framework, however, the ASA began to lean toward the "progressive creation" viewpoint—the idea that God's creation of life was accomplished over several geological epochs, that the six "days" of creation mentioned in Genesis were epochs rather than literal days, and that much or all of mainstream science's interpretation of the origins of life could be reconciled with the Bible. These "progressive creation" tendencies were articulated in *Evolution and Christian Thought Today,* published in 1959. Some of the contributors to this volume seemed to be flirting with evolution, with two such scientists indicating that Christian doctrine could be reconciled with something resembling evolution.

Other creationists moved in another direction entirely—towards "flood geology." This is the idea that God had created the world in six 24-hour days, that all species, including man, had been specially created, and that the fossil record was a result, not of evolution over time but of a single catastrophic flood in the days of Noah. George McCready Price, a Canadian-born creationist, had outlined these ideas in a 1923 book called *The New Geology.* At the time, Price's ideas had not been widely accepted by creationists outside his own Seventh Day Adventist denomination, but in 1961 Price's ideas got a boost. Teacher John C. Whitcomb, Jr. and engineer Henry M. Morris issued *The Genesis Flood,* which, like *The New Geology,* tried to reconcile the geological evidence with a strong creationist viewpoint.

In 1963, the Creation Research Society (CRS) was formed. The founders were creationist scientists (many of them from the fundamentalist Lutheran Church-Missouri Synod), and voting membership was limited to scientists. The CRS was committed to Biblical inerrancy and a creationist interpretation of the Bible, an interpretation which in practice coincided with the doctrine of flood geology.

The CRS and others began lobbying for the inclusion of creationist ideas in school curricula. This was a delicate task, on account of the *Epperson* decision of the Supreme Court, which prohibited the introduction of religious doctrines into the curriculum of the public schools. Creationists campaign all over the country, trying to get creationism (now often dubbed ''creation science'') into textbooks on an equal basis with evolution. Some states allowed the use of creationist texts like Henry M. Morris' *Scientific Creationism.* The Texas Board of Education required that textbooks used by the state must emphasize that evolution was merely a theory, and that other explanations of the origins of life existed. On the other hand, California—which together with Texas exerted a great influence over educational publishers due to its mass purchasing of textbooks— rejected attempts to include creationism in school texts.

Laws were passed in Arkansas and Louisiana requiring that creation science get discussed whenever evolution was discussed. However, the federal courts struck down these laws. The U.S. Supreme Court struck down the Louisiana law in 1987, on the grounds that creation science was a religious doctrine that could not constitutionally be taught in public schools.

In Tennessee, home of the Scopes trial, the legislature passed a law in 1973 which required that various ideas of life's origin— including creationism—be included in textbooks. A federal circuit court struck down this law. An 1996 bill in the Tennessee legislature, authorizing school authorities to fire any teacher who taught evolution as fact rather than as theory, was also unsuccessful. But in Tennessee and other states, the campaign for teaching creationism continues.

—Eric Longley

FURTHER READING:

de Camp, L. Sprague. *The Great Monkey Trial.* Garden City, New York, Doubleday, 1968.

Edwards v. Aguilland, 482 U.S. 578 (1987).

Epperson v. Arkansas, 393 U.S. 97 (1968).

Harrold, Francis B., and Raymond A. Eve, editors. *Cult Archeology & Creationism.* Iowa City, University of Iowa Press, 1995.

Irons, Peter. *The Courage of Their Convictions.* New York, Free Press, 1988.

Johnson, Robert C. ''70 Years After Scopes, Evolution Hot Topic Again.'' *Education Week.* March 13, 1996.

———. ''Tenn. Senate to Get New Chance to Vote on Evolution Measure.'' *Education Week.* March 27, 1996.

Kramer, Stanley, producer and director. *Inherit the Wind,* motion picture (original, 1960). Culver City, California, MGM/UA Home Video, 1991.

Lawrence, Jerome, and Robert E. Lee. *Inherit the Wind.* New York, Random House, 1955.

Mitchell, Colin. *The Case for Creationism.* Grantham, United Kingdom, Autumn House, 1995.

Numbers, Ronald L. *The Creationists.* New York, Borzoi, 1992.

Sommerfeld, Meg. ''Lawmakers Put Theory of Evolution on Trial.'' *Education Week.* June 5, 1996.

Webb, George E. *The Evolution Controversy in America.* Lexington, University Press of Kentucky, 1994.

Credit Cards

The small molded piece of polyvinyl chloride known as the credit card has transformed the American and the world economy and promises to be at the heart of the future economic system of the world. Social scientists have long recognized that the things people buy profoundly affect the way they live. Microwave ovens, refrigerators, air conditioners, televisions, computers, the birth control pill, antibiotics—all have affected peoples' lives in profound ways. The credit card has changed peoples' lives as well, for it allows unprecedented access to a world of goods. The emergence of credit cards as a dominant mode of economic transaction has changed the way people live, the way they do things, the way they think, their sense of well being, and their values. When credit cards entered American life, ordinary people could only dream of an affluent life style. Credit cards changed all that.

Credit cards were born in the embarrassment of Francis X. McNamara in 1950. Entertaining clients in a New York City restaurant, Mr. McNamara reached for his wallet only to find he had not brought money. Though his wife drove into town with the money, McNamara went home vowing never to experience such disgrace again. To guarantee it, he created the Diners Club Card, a simple plastic card that would serve in place of cash at any establishment that agreed to accept it. It was a revolutionary concept.

Of course, credit had long been extended to American consumers. Neighborhood merchants offered credit to neighborhood customers long before McNamara's embarrassing moment. In the 1930s oil companies promoted ''courtesy cards'' to induce travelers to buy gas at their stations across the country; department stores extended revolving credit to their prime customers. McNamara's innovation was to create a multipurpose (shopping, travel, and entertainment) and multi-location card that was issued by a third party independent of the merchant. He took to the road and signed up merchants across the country to save others from his fate.

McNamara's success led to a host of imitators. Alfred Bloomingdale of Bloomingdale's department store fame introduced Dine and Sign in California. Duncan Hines created the Signet Club. *Gourmet* and *Esquire* magazines began credit card programs for their readers. But all of McNamara's early imitators failed. Bankers, however, saw an opportunity. Savvy as they are about giving out money for profit, bankers were more successful in offering their own versions of national cards. Success came to Bank of America and Master Charge, who came to dominate the credit card business in the 1960s. In the late 1970s Bank Americard became VISA and Master Charge became MasterCard. In 1958, American Express introduced its card. Their success the first year was so great—more than 500,000 people signed up—that American Express turned to computer giant IBM for help. Advanced technology was the only way for companies to manage the vast numbers of merchants and consumers who linked themselves via their credit cards, and in the process created a mountain of debt. Technology made managing the credit card business profitable.

To make their system work, credit card companies needed to get as many merchants to accept their cards and as many consumers to use them as they possibly could. They were aided by the sustained economic growth of the post-World War II era, which saw the United States realize the potential for becoming a true consumption-based society. Credit card companies competed with each other to get their cards in the hands of consumers. With direct mail solicitations, televisions advertisements, and the ubiquitous placement of credit applications, these companies reached out to every segment of the consumer market. Affluent Americans were flooded with credit card offers at low interest rates, but poorer Americans were also offered credit, albeit with high interest rates, low credit lines, and annual fees. As the cards filled the wallets and purses of more and more consumers, the credit card became the essential tool of the consumer society. At the same time the competition for the consumer heated up at the retail end. First to differentiate themselves from and then to keep up with competitors, more and more retailers, businesses, and services began accepting the cards.

By the 1990s, just 50 years after the birth of the modern credit card, there were more than 450 million credit cards in the United States—about 1.7 cards for each woman, man, and child. Moreover, more than 3 billion offers of credit cards are made annually. VISA administered about 50 percent of the credit cards in circulation. MasterCard had 35 percent, the Discover Card 10 percent, and American Express 5 percent.

The amount of money channeled through credit cards is staggering. By the late 1990s, about 820 billion dollars were charged annually—approximately $11,000 per family—and credit cards accounted for $444 billion of debt. About 17 percent of disposable income was spent making installment payments on credit card balances; the average cardholder owed approximately $150 per month. Eight billion transactions per year involve credit cards. Simply put, credit cards have a profound effect on the economy. To put the force of credit cards into some perspective, in 1998 the Federal Reserve put 20 billion dollars of new money into the economy, while U.S. banks unleashed the equivalent of 20-30 billion dollars of new money into the same economy via new credit cards and increased spending limits.

Given the strong tie between credit card spending and the economy, the fact that consumers have freely used credit cards to fuel their lifestyles has been good for the country, for the stock market, and for retirement plans. But spending is more than simply an economic issue. Spending reflects deeper and broader social and psychological processes. These processes may underlie the true meaning of credit cards in American culture.

Spending money to reflect or announce one's success is certainly not a new phenomenon. Anthropologists have long reflected upon tribal uses of possessions as symbols of prestige. In the past the winners were the elites of the social groups from which they came. But credit cards have leveled the playing field, affording the "common folk" entry into the game of conspicuous consumption. Indeed, the use of credit cards allows people with limited incomes to convince others that they are in the group of winners. Credit cards have thus broken the link that once existed between the possession of goods and success.

Money does buy wonderful things, and many derive satisfaction from knowing that they can buy many things. Credit cards allow consumption to happen more easily, more frequently, and more quickly. The satisfactions achieved through consumption are not illusory. Goods can be authentic sources of meaning for consumers. Indeed, goods are democratic. The Mercedes the rich person drives is the same Mercedes that the middle class person drives. Acquiring possessions brings enjoyment, symbolizes achievement, and creates

identity. Because credit cards make all this possible, they have become a symbolic representation of that achievement. Having a Gold card is prestigious and means you have achieved more in life than those with a regular card. (A Platinum card is, of course, even better.) Credit cards are more than modes of transaction—they are designer labels of life, and thus impart to their user a sense of status and power. People know what these symbols mean and desire them.

The ways that people pay for their goods differ in important social, economic, and psychological ways. Unlike cash, credit cards promote feelings of membership and belongingness. Having and using a credit card is a rite of passage, creating the illusion that the credit card holder has made it as an adult and a success. Unique designs, newsletters, rewards for use, and special deals for holders make owners of cards feel that they are part of a unique group. Prestige cards such as the American Express Gold Card attempt to impress others with how much the user seems to be worth. Finally, credit cards are promoted as being essential for self-actualization. You have made it, card promoters announce, you deserve it, and you shouldn't leave home without it; luckily, it's everywhere you want to be, according to VISA's advertising slogan. Self-actualized individuals with credit cards have the ability to express their individuality as fully as possible.

There are, however, costly, dangerous, and frightening problems associated with credit card use and abuse. First, credit cards act to elevate the price of goods. Merchants who accept credit cards must pay anywhere from 0.3 to 3 percent of the value of the transaction to the credit card company or bank. Such costs are not absorbed by merchants but are passed on to all other consumers (who may not own or use credit cards) in the price of products and services. Second, credit cards create trails of information in credit reports that reveal much about the lives of users, from the doctors they visit to their choice of underwear. Not only do such reports reveal to anyone reading them information that the credit card user might not want made available, but confusion between users can result in embarassing and costly mistakes. Third, credit card fraud creates billions of dollars in costs which are paid for in high fees and interest rates and, eventually, in the price of goods. VISA estimated that these costs amount to between 43 and 100 dollars per thousand dollars charged. In 1997 credit card companies charged off 22 billion dollars in unpaid bills, 60 million a day. Finally, consumers pay in direct and indirect ways for the personal bankruptcies that credit card abuse contributes too. In 1997 the 1.6 million families who sought counseling with debt counselors claimed 35 billion in debt they could not pay, much of it credit card debt. The result of these problems is the same: consumers pay more for goods.

One of the untold stories in the history of credit cards is the manner in which the poorer credit card holders subsidize the richer. Payments on credit card balances (with interest rates that normally range from 8 to 21 percent) subsidize those who use the credit card as a convenience and pay no interest by paying their charges within the grace period. The 50 to 60 percent of consumers who pay their balances within the grace period have free use of this money, but they could not do so unless others were paying the credit card companies for their use of the money. The people who pay the highest interest rates are, of course, the people with the lowest incomes.

In an obvious way, the convenience of using credit cards increases the probability that consumers will spend more than they might have otherwise. But using credit cards is also a bit like the arms race: the more the neighbors spend, the more consumers spend to stay even. Such competitive spending, while a source of sport for the wealthy, can be potentially devastating to those on more limited incomes.

Interestingly, credit card spending may facilitate spending in a more insidious manner. Research has shown that the facilitation effect of credit cards is both a conscious/rational and unconscious process. At the rational end credit cards allow easy access to money that may only exist in the future. People spend with credit cards as a convenience and as a means to purchase something that they do not have the money for now but will in the near future. However, as an unconscious determinant of spending, credit cards can irrationally and unconsciously urge consumers to spend more, to spend more frequently, and make spending more likely.

Credit card spending has become an essential contributor—some would argue a causal determinant—of a good economy. Spending encourages the manufacture of more goods and the commitment of capital, and creates tax revenues. By facilitating spending, credit cards are thus good for the economy. Credit cards are tools of economic expansion, even if they do bring associated costs.

In 50 years, credit cards have gone from being a mere convenience to being crucial facilitators of economic transacations. Some would have them do even more. Credit card backers promote a vision of a cashless economy in which a single credit card consolidates all of a person's financial and personal information needs. And every day consumers vote for the evolution to a cashless electronic economic and information system by using their credit cards. Americans are willing prisoners of and purveyors of credit cards, spending with credit cards because of what they get them, what they symbolize, and what they allow them to achieve, experience, and feel. In many ways credit cards are the fulfillment of the ultimate dream of this country's founders—they offer life, liberty, and the pursuit of happiness.

—Richard A. Feinberg and Cindy Evans

FURTHER READING:

Buchan, James. *Frozen Desire: The Meaning of Money.* New York, Farrar Straus Giroux, 1997.

Dietz, Robert. *Expressing America: A Critique of the Global Credit Card Society.* Thousand Oaks, California, The Pine Forge Press Social Science Library, 1995.

Evans, David S., and Richard Schmalensee. *Paying with Plastic: The Digital Revolution in Buying and Borrowing.* Cambridge, Massachusetts, MIT Press, 1999.

Galanoy, Terry. *Charge It: Inside the Credit Card Conspiracy.* New York, G.T. Putnam and Sons, 1981.

Hendrickson, Robert A. *The Cashless Society.* New York, Dodd Mead, 1972.

Klein, Lloyd. *It's in the Cards: Consumer Credit and the American Experience.* Westport, Connecticut, Praeger, 1997.

Mandell, Lewis. *Credit Card Use in the United States.* Ann Arbor, Michigan, The University of Michigan, 1972.

Ritzer, George. *Expressing America: A Critique of the Global Credit Card Economy.* Thousand Oaks, California, Pine Forge Press, 1995.

Simmons, Matty. *The Credit Card Catastrophe: The 20th Century Phenomenon That Changed the World.* New York, Barricade Books, 1995.

Creedence Clearwater Revival

By the late 1960s, when Creedence Clearwater Revival (CCR) released its first album, rock 'n' roll was transforming into rock, the more "advanced" and "sophisticated" cousin of the teenaged riot whipped up by Elvis Presley and Little Richard. While their contemporaries (Moody Blues, Pink Floyd, King Crimson, etc.) were expanding the sonic and lyrical boundaries of Rock 'n' Roll, CCR bucked the trend by returning to the music's roots. On their first album and their six subsequent releases, this Bay Area group led by John Fogerty fused primal rockabilly, swamp-boogie, country, r&b and great pop songwriting, and—in doing so—became one of the biggest selling rock bands of the late 1960s and early 1970s.

Most of the members of CCR played in what were essentially bar bands around San Francisco and its suburbs. Along with El Cerrito junior high school friends Stu Cook and Doug "Cosmo" Clifford, Tom and John Fogerty formed the Blue Velvets in the late 1950s. The group eventually transformed into the Golliwogs, recording a number of singles for the Berkeley-based label, Fantasy, and then changed its name to Creedence Clearwater Revival in 1967. If the Blue Velvets and the Golliwogs were dominated by Tom Fogerty, then Creedence Clearwater Revival was John Fogerty's vehicle, with John writing and singing the vast majority of CCR's songs. It was clear that John Fogerty's influence was what made the group popular, because under Tom's control, the Golliwogs essentially went nowhere. Further, when John let other members gain artistic control on CCR's *Pendulum,* that album became the first CCR album not to go platinum.

Like Bruce Springsteen, John Fogerty's songs tackle subjects that cut deep into America's core; and like any great artist, Fogerty was able to transcend his own experience and write realistic and believable songs (for instance, the man who wrote "Born on the Bayou" had never even been to Louisiana's bayous until decades later). Despite Fogerty's talents as a songwriter, CCR's first hits from its debut album were covers—Dale Hawkins' "Suzie Q" and Screamin' Jay Hawkins' "I Put a Spell on You." But with the release of "Proud Mary" backed with "Born on the Bayou" from CCR's second album, the group released a series of original compositions that dominated the U.S. *Billboard* charts for three years.

Despite its great Top Forty success and its legacy as the preeminent American singles band of the late 1960s, CCR was able to cultivate a counter-cultural and even anti-commercial audience with its protest songs and no-frills rock 'n' roll. Despite the fact that they were products of their time, "Run Through the Jungle," "Fortunate Son," "Who'll Stop the Rain," and CCR's other protest songs remain timeless classics because of John's penchant for evoking nearly-universal icons (for North American's, at least) rather than specific cultural references.

John's dominance proved to be the key to the band's success and the seeds of its dissolution, with Tom leaving the group in 1971 and John handing over the reigns to be split equally with Stu Cook and Doug Clifford, who equally contributed to the group's last album, *Mardi Gras,* which flopped. Tom released a few solo albums, and so did John, who refused to perform his CCR songs well until the early 1990s as the result of a bitter legal dispute that left control of the CCR catalog in the hands of Fantasy Records. One of the most bizarre copyright infringement lawsuits took place when Fantasy sued Fogerty for writing a song from his 1984 *Centerfield* album that sounded too much like an old CCR song. After spending $300,000 in legal fees and

Creedence Clearwater Revival

having to testify on the stand with his guitar to demonstrate how he wrote songs, Fogerty won the case.

—Kembrew McLeod

FURTHER READING:

Bordowitz, Hank. *Bad Moon Rising: The Unauthorized History of Creedence Clearwater Revival.* New York, Schirmer Books, 1998.

Hallowell, John. *Inside Creedence.* New York, London, 1971.

Crichton, Michael (1942—)

Published in 1969, *The Andromeda Strain* established Michael Crichton as a major best-selling novelist whose popularity was due as much to the timing and significance of his subject matter as to the quality of his writing and the accuracy of his research. As Crichton had correctly judged, America was ready for a tale that treated both the rationalism and the paranoia of the Cold War scientists' response to a biological threat. From that first success onwards, Crichton continued to embrace disagreeable or disturbing topical trends as a basis for exciting, thriller-related fiction. That several have been

made into highly commercial movies, and that he himself expanded his career into film and television, has made him a cultural fixture in late twentieth-century America. If this was in doubt, his position was cemented by *ER,* the monumentally successful television series, which he devised.

Born on October 23, 1942 in Chicago, Illinois, by the time *The Andromeda Strain* appeared, Crichton had received his A.B. degree *summa cum laude* from Harvard, completed his M.D. at Harvard Medical School, and begun working as a post-doctoral fellow at the Salk Institute for Biological Studies. Most impressively, he had already published six novels (under various pseudonyms), written largely during weekends and vacations, while still at medical school. As an undergraduate, he had intended to major in English, but poor grades convinced him that no amount of creative talent would deter Harvard's faculty from altering its absurdly high expectations. Incipient scientist that he was, Crichton tested this theory by submitting an essay by George Orwell under his own name, and received a B-minus.

This tale, recounted in Crichton's spiritual autobiography, *Travels,* perhaps explains his own lack of interest in producing anything other than commercial fiction. As a result, his journey through medical school seems, in retrospect, more of a detour than a career path, for, by the end of his schooling, he had decided once and for all to become a writer. During his final rotation Crichton concentrated

Michael Crichton

more on the emotional than the physical condition of his patients, research that formed the basis of his non-fiction work, *Five Patients: A Hospital Explained.*

But it was *The Andromeda Strain* that permanently changed the trajectory of his future. His previous novels have all fallen out of print, with the exception of *A Case of Need,* published under the pseudonym Jeffrey Hudson and winner of the 1968 Edgar Award from the Mystery Writers of America. While the success of *The Andromeda Strain* lifted Crichton's career to new heights, it did not prevent him from completing other less successful works already in progress. In 1970 and 1971, using the name John Lange, he finished three more novels (*Drug of Choice, Grave Descend,* and *Binary*), and with his brother Douglas, co-wrote *Dealing,* under the prescient name Michael Douglas. (The actor would star in the film versions of several of Crichton novels). With three of his novels already filmed—*The Andromeda Strain* (1970), *Dealing* (1972), and *A Case of Need* (retitled *The Carey Treatment,* 1972)—Crichton, who had directed the made-for-TV film *Pursuit* (1972) made his feature film directing debut in 1973 with *Westworld.* Starring Yul Brynner, the film was adapted from his futuristic thriller *Binary* (1971). Crichton now pursued a dual career as moviemaker and writer, having published the second novel to appear under his own name, *The Terminal Man,* in 1972. Dealing with a Frankenstein-type experiment gone haywire, it confirmed its author's storytelling powers, sold in the millions, and was filmed in 1974.

Through the rest of the 1970s and into the 1980s Crichton the author continued to turn out such bestsellers as *The Great Train Robbery* (1975), *Congo* (1980), and *Sphere* (1987), but Crichton the

director fared less well. His successes with *Coma* (1977), a terrific nailbiter based on Robin Cook's hospital novel and starring the real Michael Douglas, and *The Great Train Robbery* (1978), were offset by such mediocrities as *Looker* (1981), *Runaway* (1984), and *Physical Evidence* (1989). A major turnaround came when he stopped directing and concentrated on fiction once again. The fruits of his labors produced *Jurassic Park* (1990), *Rising Sun* (1992), *Disclosure* (1994), and *Lost World* (1995). All were bestsellers, with *Rising Sun* and *Disclosure* leaving a fair share of controversy in their wake—the last particularly so after the film, starring Michael Douglas and Demi Moore, was released. In the meantime, Crichton shifted from director to producer, convincing NBC to launch *ER,* which he created and which had been his dream for 20 years. By the end of the 1990s, he was an established and important presence in Hollywood as well as in publishing, enjoying a professional longevity given only to a handful of popular novelists and screenwriters.

Not unlike Tom Clancy, whose success came in the 1980s, Crichton is a masterful storyteller who has been credited with the invention of the modern "techno-thriller." His prose is clear and concise; his plotting strong; his research accurate and, at times, eerily prescient. On the other hand, in common with many fiction writers who depend heavily on premises drawn largely from the science fiction genre, his character development is weak. Despite his protests to the contrary, his penchant for using speculative science as the basis for much of his fiction has landed him willy-nilly within the gothic and science fiction traditions. In *Michael Crichton: A Critical Companion,* Elizabeth Trembley details the extent to which Crichton's work revisits earlier gothic or science fiction classics, from H. Rider Haggard's *King Solomon's Mines,* for example, to *Jurassic Park,* a modern retelling of H. G. Wells' *The Island of Doctor Moreau.*

Michael Crichton's popularity is perhaps best explained by his intuition for presenting through the medium of fiction our own anxieties in consumable form. Often fiction relieves anxieties by reconfiguring them as fantasy. Crichton senses that we worry about biological weapons (*The Andromeda Strain*), mind control technology (*The Terminal Man*), human aggression (*Sphere*), genetic engineering (*Jurassic Park*), and competitive corporate greed (*Rising Sun* and *Disclosure*). His gift is the ability to turn these fears into a form that lets us deal with them from the safety of the reading experience.

—Bennett Lovett-Graff

FURTHER READING:

Crichton, Michael. *Travels.* New York, Ballantine Books, 1988.

Heller, Zoe. "The Admirable Crichton." *Vanity Fair,* January, 1994, 32-49.

Trembley, Elizabeth. *Michael Crichton: A Critical Companion.* Westport, Connecticut, Greenwood, 1996.

Crime Does Not Pay

Crime Does Not Pay was a comic book published from 1942-1955 by the Lev Gleason company. Inspired by the MGM documentary series of the same name, *Crime* featured material based loosely on true criminal cases. The stories indulged in graphic violence, sadism, and brutality of a sort that was previously unheard of in children's entertainment. Bullet-ridden corpses, burning bodies, and horrific gangland tortures were among the more predictable themes found in these comic books.

An unusual comic book when it first appeared amidst the superheroes of the World War II era, *Crime* found a huge audience after the war. Arguably the first "adult" comic book, *Crime* also became one of the most popular titles ever, selling in excess of one million copies monthly. When *Crime*'s formula became widely imitated throughout the industry, it attracted the wrath of critics who charged that crime comic books caused juvenile delinquency.

—Bradford Wright

FURTHER READING:

Benton, Mike. *Crime Comics*. Dallas, Taylor Publishing, 1993.

Goulart, Ron. *Over Fifty Years of American Comic Books*. Lincolnwood, Illinois, Mallard Press, 1991.

Crinolines

In 1859, French writer Baudelaire wrote that "the principal mark of civilization . . . for a woman, is invariably the crinoline." The crinoline, or horsehair ("crin") hoop, allowed women of the 1850s and 1860s to emulate Empress Eugénie in ballooning skirts supported by these Crystal Palaces of lingerie. From Paris to Scarlett O'Hara, women moved rhythmically and monumentally during "crinolineomania" (1856-68), assuming some power if only by taking up vast space. A culture of boulevards and specatorship prized the volume of crinolines. In the 1950s, crinolineomania recurred: prompted by Christian Dior's New Look, any poodle skirt or prom dress could be inflated by nylon crinolines as if to become the female version of mammoth 1950s cars and automobile fins. A culture of big cars valued the crinoline as well.

—Richard Martin

FURTHER READING:

Calzaretta, Bridget. *Crinolineomania: Modern Women in Art, 1856-68* (exhibition catalogue). Purchase, New York, Neuberger Museum, 1991.

The Crisis

Founded as the monthly magazine of the National Association for the Advancement of Colored People in 1910, the *Crisis* has played an important role in the formation and development of African-American public opinion since its inception. As the official voice of America's leading civil rights organization, the *Crisis* gained entry into a variety of African-American and progressive white homes, from the working class and rural poor to the black middle class. Through the mid-1930s, the *Crisis* was dominated by the character, personality, and opinions of its first editor and NAACP board member, W. E. B. Du Bois. Because of his broad stature within black communities, Du Bois and the NAACP were synonymous for many African Americans. One of his editorials or essays could literally sway the opinions of thousands of black Americans.

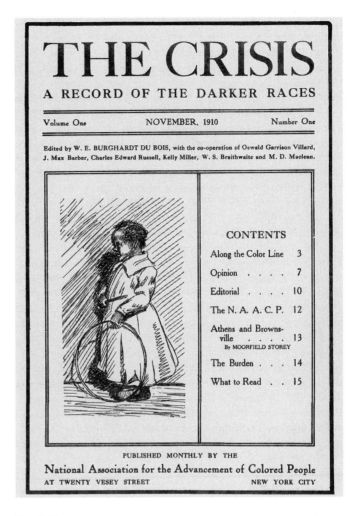

The Crisis

The teens were a time of dynamic change within black communities as the Great Migration began to speed demographic shifts and African-American institutions grew and expanded. As black newspapers and periodicals gained prominence within these rapidly developing communities, the New York-based magazine the *Crisis* emerged as one of the most eloquent defenders of black civil rights and racial justice in the United States. During this era, the magazine led the pursuit of a federal anti-lynching law, equality at the ballot box, and an end to legal segregation. As war approached, the *Crisis* ran vigorous denunciations of racial violence in its columns. Following a bloody riot in east St. Louis in 1917, Du Bois editorialized with melancholy, "No land that loves to lynch 'niggers' can lead the hosts of the Almighty." In the same year, after black servicemen rampaged through the streets of Houston, killing seventeen whites and resulting in the execution of thirteen African Americans, the *Crisis* bitterly lamented, "Here at last, white folks died. Innocent, adventitious strangers, perhaps, as innocent as the thousands of Negroes done to death in the last two centuries. Our hands tremble to rise and exult, our lips strive to cry. And yet our hands are not raised in exultation; and yet our lips are silent, as we face another great human wrong."

After the initial success of black troops stationed in France during the summer of 1918, Du Bois penned the controversial editorial "Close Ranks." In it, he wrote, "Let us, while this war lasts, forget our special grievances and close our ranks shoulder to shoulder with our own white fellow citizens and the allied nations that are fighting for democracy. We make no ordinary sacrifice, but we make it gladly and willingly with our eyes lifted to the hills.'' Appealing to the ideals of patriotism, citizenship, and sacrifice connected to military service, the *Crisis* editors believed that by fighting a war ''to make the world safe for democracy,'' African Americans would be in a better position to expect a new era of opportunity and equality after the war's end. As the war drew to a close and black soldiers returned home, the *Crisis* continued its determined efforts to secure a larger share of democracy for African Americans. In ''Returning Soldier,'' the magazine captured the fighting spirit of the moment: ''*We return. / We return from fighting. / We return fighting.* Make way for democracy! We saved it in France, and by the Great Jehovah, we will save it in the United States of America, or know the reason why.''

The next two decades, though, did not bear out the optimism of *Crisis* editors. During the 1920s, as racial conservatism set in nationwide and the hopes of returning black soldiers dimmed, the *Crisis* shifted its focus to the development of the cultural politics of the ''New Negro'' movement in Harlem. With the addition of celebrated author Jessie Fauset to the editorial board, the *Crisis* printed essays from Harlem Renaissance architect Alain Locke, as well as early works of fiction and poetry by Fauset, Langston Hughes, and Zora Neale Hurston, among others. The 1930s proved contentious years for the *Crisis* as it went to battle with the Communist Party over the fate of nine African Americans in the Scottsboro case. In addition, the Depression put the magazine in financial peril. As Du Bois struggled to find solutions to the dire circumstances facing most black Americans, he published a series of essays advocating the creation of ''urban black self-determination'' through the creation of race-based economic cooperatives. This stance irked many NAACP leaders who saw the remarks as a repudiation of the organization's integrationist goals. The clash precipitated a split within the group which resulted in the resignation of Du Bois from both the magazine and the NAACP board in 1934.

What the *Crisis* lost in the departure of Du Bois, it regained with the rapidly increasing membership of the NAACP during the Second World War and the rising tide of civil rights protest throughout the nation. While the magazine no longer had the stature, intellectual respect, or skillful writing associated with Du Bois, it remained an important public African-American voice. In particular, as the NAACP legal attack on segregation crescendoed in 1954 with the *Brown* v. *Board of Education* decision, the *Crisis* ran a special issue dedicated solely to the NAACP victory, featuring the full text of the decision, historical overviews, and analysis. One editorial gloated, ''The 'separate but equal' fiction as legal doctrine now joins the horsecar, the bustle, and the five-cent cigar.'' While the *Crisis* trumpeted the victory, it also kept a pragmatic eye on the unfinished business of racial justice in America, stating, ''We are at that point in our fight against segregation where unintelligent optimism and childish faith in a court decision can blind us to the fact that legal abolition of segregation is not the final solution for the social cancer of racism.''

Over the next decade, as the NAACP struggled to find its place in the post-*Brown* movement, the *Crisis* maintained its support of nonviolent civil rights activity, although it no longer set the agenda. Thurgood Marshall, in an article on the student sit-in wave sweeping the South in 1960, compared Mississippi and Alabama to South Africa and argued, ''Young people, in the true tradition of our democratic principles, are fighting the matter for all of us and they are

doing it in the most effective way. Protest—the right to protest—is basic to a democratic form of government.'' Of the 1963 ''Jobs and Freedom'' march on Washington, D.C., the *Crisis* beamed, ''Never had such a cross section of the American people been united in such a vast outpouring of humanity.'' Similarly, in 1964, with the passage of the historic Civil Rights Act, the *Crisis* editorialized, ''[the Act] is both an end and a beginning: an end to the Federal Government's hands-off policy; a beginning of an era of Federally-protected rights for all citizens.''

As the movement spun off after 1965 toward Black Power, increasing radicalization and, in some cases, violence, the NAACP and the *Crisis* began to lose their prominent position in shaping African-American attitudes and opinions. Against these new politics, the *Crisis* appeared more and more conservative. Continuing to oppose violent self-defense and separatism, the *Crisis* also came out against radical economic redistribution as well as the Black Studies movement of the late sixties and early seventies. Over the next two decades, the *Crisis* evolved into a more mainstream popular magazine, upgrading its pages to a glossy stock and including more advertisements, society articles, and human interest stories. Unable to recapture the clear programmatic focus that had driven its contents during the previous fifty years, the *Crisis* articles tended to be more retrospective and self-congratulatory than progressive. In the late 1980s, the *Crisis* took a brief hiatus but reappeared in the 1990s in a revised form, focusing primarily on national politics, cultural issues, and African-American history.

—Patrick D. Jones

FURTHER READING:

Ellis, Mark. '''Closing Ranks' and 'Seeking Honors': W. E. B. Du Bois in WWI.'' *Journal of American History*. Vol. 79, No. 1, 1992.

Hughes, Langston. *Fight for Freedom: The Story of the NAACP*. New York, Berkeley Publishing, 1962.

Lewis, David Levering. *W. E. B. Du Bois: Biography of a Race*. New York, Holt Publishing Company, 1994.

———. *The Writings of W. E. B. Du Bois*.

Waldon, Daniel, ed. *W. E. B. Du Bois: The Crisis Writings*. Greenwich, Connecticut, Fawcett Publishing, 1997.

Croce, Jim (1943-1973)

Singer and songwriter Jim Croce is remembered for beautiful guitar ballads like ''Time In a Bottle'' and, in contrast, his upbeat character-driven narratives like ''Bad, Bad Leroy Brown'' that deftly combined folk, blues, and pop influences. Croce's brief but brilliant musical career was tragically cut short by his death in a plane accident in 1973.

Born to James Alford and Flora Croce in Philadelphia, Pennsylvania, Croce's interest in music got off to a slow start. He learned to play ''Lady of Spain'' on the accordion at the age of five, but didn't really take music seriously until his college years. He attended Villanova College in the early 1960s, where he formed various bands and played parties. One such band had the opportunity to do an Embassy tour of the Middle East and Africa on a foreign exchange

Jim Croce

program, which encouraged Croce to focus on his music. He earned a degree in psychology from Villanova in 1965.

The music career came slowly, though, interrupted by the other odd jobs he took to make a living. Croce worked in construction, welded, and even joined the army. He spun records as a university disc jockey on a folk and blues show in Philadelphia and wrote ads for a local R&B station. He married Ingrid in 1966, and the two spent the summer teaching at a children's camp in Pine Grove, Pennsylvania. He taught guitar, and she taught ceramics and leather crafts. The following autumn he served as a teacher for problem students at a Philadelphia High School.

Finally becoming truly serious about a career in music, Croce moved to New York in 1967 where he and his wife Ingrid played folk clubs and coffee houses. By 1969, the pair were signed to Capital Records where they released an album called *Approaching Day.* The album's lack of success led the couple to give up New York and return to Pennsylvania. Jim started selling off guitars, took another job in construction, and later worked as a truck driver. Ingrid learned how to can foods and bake bread to help stretch the budget. On September 28, 1971, they had a son, Adrian James Croce.

But Croce never lost his love of music, and he played and sang on some commercials for a studio in New York. His break came when Croce sent a demo tape to Tommy West, a Villanova college pal who had found success as a New York record producer. West and his friend Terry Cashman helped Croce land a contract with ABC records. He also had a fortuitous meeting with guitarist Maury Muehleisen while working as a studio freelancer. Croce had played backup guitar on Muehleisen's record, *Gingerbread.* The album

flopped, but Croce remembered the young guitarist and called him in to work with him. The two worked closely in the studio, trading rhythm and lead parts. The first album, *You Don't Mess Around with Jim,* was a huge success, giving Croce two top ten hits with the title track and ''Operator (That's Not The Way It Feels).'' Before long Croce was a top-billing concert performer, known as much for his friendly and charming personality as for his songs.

His second album, *Life and Times,* had a hit with the July, 1973, chart topper ''Bad, Bad Leroy Brown.'' This first blush of success turned bittersweet for his family and friends, however. Leaving a concert venue at Northwestern State University in Natchitoches, Louisiana on September 20, 1973, Croce's plane snagged the top of a pecan tree just past the runway, and he and Maury Muehleisen, as well as four others, were killed. Croce is buried at Haym Salomon Memorial Park in Frazer, Pennsylvania. The third album, *I've Got a Name,* was released posthumously, and the hits kept coming. The next chart hit was the title track, and ''Time In a Bottle'' was the number one hit of the year in 1973. The following year, ''I'll Have to Say I Love You in a Song'' and ''Workin' at the Car Wash Blues'' hit the charts. The ongoing string of hits only highlighted the tragic loss of a performer who was just coming into his own.

Jim's widow Ingrid opened Croce's Restaurant and Jazz Bar 1985 in San Diego's Gaslamp Quarter in Jim's memory. The restaurant features musical acts nightly and is decorated with Jim Croce memorabilia. Ingrid Croce also wrote a book of recipes and memories called *Thyme in A Bottle.* Son A. J. Croce started his own musical career in the 1990s. He released his eponymous first album in 1993, a 1995 follow-up, *That's Me in the Bar,* and 1997's *Fit to Serve.* He said of his father, ''I think the most powerful lesson I learned from him was the fact there is no reason to write a song unless there is a good story there. He was a great storyteller and, for me, if there is any way that we are similar, it's that we both tell stories.''

—Emily Pettigrew

FURTHER READING:

Crockett, Jim. ''Talking Guitar.'' *Guitar Player.* April, 1973, 18.

Dougherty, S. ''Don't Mess Around with A.J.'' *People.* August 17, 1992, 105-06.

''Epitaph for Jim.'' *Time.* February 11, 1974, 56.

''Jim Croce.'' http://www.hotshotdigital.com/WellAlwaysRemember.3/JimCroceBio.html. February 1999.

''Jim Croce: The Tribute Page.'' http://www.timeinabottle.com. February, 1999.

Makarushka, Mary. ''At Last, He Got a Name.'' *Entertainment Weekly.* September 15, 1995, 124.

Nelton, S. ''A Legend in Her Own Right.'' *Nation's Business.* December, 1992, 14.

Cronkite, Walter (1916—)

Walter Cronkite's 19-year tenure as anchorman of the *CBS Evening News* was an uncanny match of man and era. Two generations of Americans came to rely upon his presence in the CBS

Walter Cronkite

television anchor chair in times of war and crisis, scandal and celebration. His was a forthright, solemn presence in a time when each new dawn brought with it the prospect of nuclear annihilation or a second American civil war. Yet the master journalist was also a master performer—Cronkite was able and quite willing to display a flash of emotion or anger on the air when it suited him; this combination of stoic professionalism and emotional instinct earned the broadcaster two enduring nicknames: the man known familiarly as "Uncle Walter" was also called "The Most Trusted Man in America." When Cronkite closed the *Evening News* each night with his famous sign-off "And that's the way it is," few doubted he was telling them the truth.

Cronkite's broadcasting career had a unique prologue; the young war correspondent did what few others dared: he turned down a job offer from Edward R. Murrow. The CBS European chief was already a legend; the radio correspondents known as "Murrow's Boys" were the darlings of the American press, even as they defined the traditions and standards of broadcast journalism. Cronkite, however, preferred covering the Second World War for the United Press. It was an early display of his preference for the wire-service style and attitude; the preference would mark Cronkite's reporting for the rest of his career.

When Cronkite accepted a second CBS offer several years later, the budding broadcaster found himself assigned—perhaps relegated—to airtime in the new medium that seemed little more than a journalistic backwater: television.

He anchored the local news at Columbia's Washington, D.C., affiliate starting soon after the Korean War began in 1950, his broadcast a combination of journalism and experimental theater. There were no rules for television news, and Cronkite had come in on the ground floor. He had little competition; few of the old guard showed much interest in the new medium. Cronkite was pressed into service to anchor the 1952 political conventions and election for CBS television, his presence soon taken for granted in the network anchor chair. Walter Cronkite had established himself firmly as the network's "face" in the medium which was, by now, quite obviously the wave of the future.

He continued to anchor much of CBS's special events coverage, including the 1956 and 1960 political conventions. In 1962, he succeeded Doug Edwards as anchor of the *CBS Evening News,* in those days a fifteen-minute nightly roundup that found itself regularly beaten in the ratings by the runaway success of NBC's anchor team of Chet Huntley and David Brinkley.

Ratings aside, however, television news was finally coming of age; CBS news was expanding staff, adding bureaus and airtime. That TV news veered away from the staged, hackneyed style of its most obvious model, the movie newsreels—and instead became a straightforward, serious purveyor of hard news—is thanks in no small part to the efforts and sensibilities of Cronkite and his colleagues. His *Evening News* expanded to thirty minutes in September, 1963, premiering with an exclusive interview of President John F. Kennedy.

Yet Cronkite, like Doug Edwards before him, regularly spoke to an audience much smaller than that of Huntley and Brinkley. And while it is Cronkite's shirtsleeves pronouncement of the Kennedy assassination that is usually excerpted on retrospective programs and documentaries (''From Dallas, Texas, the flash, apparently official. . . President Kennedy. . . died. . . this afternoon. . . ''), the simple fact is that NBC was the clear audience choice for much of the early and mid-1960s.

Cronkite's ratings dropped so low during the 1964 Republican convention, the behind-the-scenes turmoil growing so intense, that he was removed from his anchor chair, replaced for the Democratic convention by Robert Trout and Roger Mudd, two fine veteran broadcasters whose selection nonetheless was a thinly veiled effort to capture some of the Huntley-Brinkley magic. It didn't work; a viewer uprising and a well-timed prank (a walk through a crowded hotel lobby with a high NBC executive) quickly led to Cronkite's re-instatement.

Meanwhile, Cronkite threw himself into coverage of the American space program. He displayed obvious passion and an infectious, even boyish enthusiasm. His cries of ''Go, baby, go!'' became familiar accompaniment to the roar of rockets lifting off from Cape Canaveral. Cronkite anchored CBS's coverage of every blast-off and splashdown; arguably the single most memorable quote of his career came as astronauts Neil Armstrong and Buzz Aldrin touched down on the moon the afternoon of July 20, 1969. ''The Eagle has landed,'' Armstrong radioed, and Cronkite added his benediction: ''Gosh! Oh, boy!'' He later recalled it as the only time he'd come up speechless on the air. That afternoon, Cronkite's audience was more than that of NBC and ABC combined. Huntley-Brinkley fever had cooled. Walter Cronkite had become ''the most trusted man in America,'' and his stature in American living rooms resounded throughout the television industry.

This was the age in which local television news departments strove to emulate the networks—not the other way around—and the success of Cronkite's dead-earnest *Evening News* led many local TV newscasts soon to adapt a distinctly Cronkite-ish feel. Likewise, there's no official count of how many anchormen around the world, subconsciously or not, had adapted that distinctive Cronkite cadence and style. Politicians and partisans on all sides complained bitterly that Cronkite and CBS were biased against them; this was perhaps the ultimate tribute to the anchorman's perceived influence on American life in the late 1960s.

In truth, Cronkite had grown decidedly unenthusiastic about the Vietnam War. A trip to Vietnam in the midst of the Tet offensive led to arguably the most courageous broadcast of the anchorman's career . . . Cronkite returned home, deeply troubled, and soon used the last few moments of a CBS documentary to call for an end to the war. It was a shocking departure from objectivity, easily the most brazen editorial stand since Ed Murrow criticized Senator Joe McCarthy nearly a decade-and-a-half earlier. At the White House, President Lyndon Johnson is said to have remarked ''If I've lost Cronkite, I've

lost middle America.'' Whether the anecdote is apocryphal is irrelevant; that it is widely accepted as fact is the real testament to Cronkite's influence as the 1960s drew to a close.

Cronkite rode his *Evening News* to ratings victory after victory through the 1970s, the whole of CBS news now at the pinnacle of its ability and influence. Cronkite cut short his summer vacation to preside over the August 8, 1974 resignation of President Nixon; he anchored an all-day-and-all-night television bicentennial party on July 4, 1976; later he stubbornly closed every nightly newscast by counting the number of days the American hostages had been held captive in Iran. The Carter administration likely was not amused. When the hostages' release on January 20, 1981 coincided with the inauguration of President Ronald Reagan, Cronkite held forth over his last great news spectacular, calling the historic convergence of events ''one of the great dramatic days in our history.''

By then, Cronkite was on his way out, giving up the anchor chair to Dan Rather, narrowly forestalling Rather's defection to ABC. Cynics have long speculated Cronkite was, in fact, pushed aside to make way for Rather, but everyone involved—including Cronkite—has clung to the story that the veteran anchorman was genuinely tired of the grind and had repeatedly asked to be replaced. His final *Evening News* came March 6, 1981, his final utterance of ''And that's the way it is'' preceded by a brief goodbye speech . . . ''Old anchormen don't go away, they keep coming back for more.'' He couldn't have been more wrong.

Cronkite had not intended to retire completely upon stepping down from the anchor chair, but to his utter astonishment, he found the new CBS news management literally would not let him on the air. An exclusive report from strife-torn Poland was given short shrift; later, his already limited participation in the network's 1982 Election Night coverage was reportedly reduced even further when anchorman Rather simply refused to cede the air to Cronkite. The new brass feared reminding either viewers or a jittery, ratings-challenged Rather of Cronkite's towering presence; Rather himself was apparently enjoying a little revenge. ''Uncle Walter'' had for years been known behind-the-scenes as a notorious air-hog, filling airtime with his own face and voice even as waiting correspondents cooled their heels. Now, suddenly, the original ''800-pound gorilla'' was getting a taste of his own medicine.

It only got worse. Cronkite's fellow CBS board members roundly ignored the elder statesman's heated protests of mid-1980s news budget cuts, even as it appeared the staid, substance-over-style approach of Cronkite's broadcasts was falling by the CBS wayside. His legacy was fading before his very eyes. That he never pulled up stakes and left the network (as a disgruntled David Brinkley had recently bolted from NBC) is a testament either to true professional loyalty . . . or an iron-clad contract.

In the 1990s, however, Cronkite made a broadcasting comeback. He produced and narrated a series of cable documentaries, including a multi-part retrospective of his own career; his 1996 autobiography was a major bestseller. In late 1998, Cronkite accepted CNN's offer to co-anchor the network's coverage of astronaut John Glenn's return to space. On that October day, Cronkite returned to the subject of one of his great career triumphs: enthusiastic, knowledgeable coverage of a manned spaceflight. It was thrilling for both audience and anchor; yet it was also clear Cronkite's day had come and gone. He was frankly a bit deaf; and he thoroughly lacked the preening, all-smiles, shallow aura of hype that seems to be a primary qualification for today's news anchors. His presence that day was, however, undoubtedly a glorious reminder of what Cronkite had been to the nation for so long: the very manifestation of serious, hard news in the most powerful communications medium of the twentieth century. He was a rock, truly an anchor in some of the stormiest seas our nation has ever navigated.

—Chris Chandler

FURTHER READING:

Boyer, Peter. *Who Killed CBS?* New York, Random House, 1988.

Cronkite, Walter. *A Reporter's Life.* New York, Alfred A. Knopf, 1996.

Joyce, Ed. *Prime Times, Bad Times.* New York, Doubleday, 1988.

Leonard, Bill. *In the Storm of the Eye.* New York, G.P. Putnam's Sons, 1987.

Slater, Robert. *This ... Is CBS.* Englewood Cliffs, New Jersey, Prentice Hall, 1988.

Crosby, Bing (1903-1977)

Bing Crosby is widely recognized as one of the most influential entertainers of all time. He first came to popularity as America's most popular crooner during the 1930s, with his much-copied low-key manner, and during his long career he recorded more than sixteen hundred songs. He also starred in a long string of highly successful movies, including the classic *Going My Way* (1944), and, having amassed a huge fortune, eventually became a major presence behind the scenes in Hollywood.

Bing Crosby

Born Harry Lillis Crosby into a large family in Tacoma, Washington, Crosby grew up to study law at Gonzaga University in Spokane but soon became more interested in playing drums and singing with a local band. It was then that he adopted his professional name, reportedly borrowing the "Bing" from his favorite comic strip, *The Bingville Bugle*. In the early 1930s Crosby's brother Everett sent a record of Bing singing "I Surrender, Dear" to the president of CBS. Crosby's live performances from New York ended up being carried over the national radio network for twenty consecutive weeks in 1932. Crosby recorded more than sixteen hundred songs for commercial release beginning in 1926 and ending in 1977. With his relaxed, low-key manner and spontaneous delivery, Crosby set a crooning style that was widely imitated for decades. At the time of his death, he was considered the world's best-selling singer. Crosby's records have sold in the hundreds of millions worldwide, perhaps more than a billion, and some of his recordings have not been out of print in more than sixty years. He received twenty-two gold records, signifying sales of at least a million copies per record, and was awarded platinum discs for his two biggest selling singles, "White Christmas" (1960) and "Silent Night" (1970).

Crosby's radio success led Paramount Pictures to contract him as an actor. He starred in more than fifty full-length motion pictures, beginning with *The Big Broadcast of 1932* (1932) and ending with the television movie *Dr. Cook's Garden* (1971). His large ears were pinned back during his early films, until partway through *She Loves Me Not* (1934). His career as a movie star reached its zenith during his association with Bob Hope. Crosby and Hope met for the first time in the summer of 1932 on the streets of New York and in December performed together at the Capitol Theater, doing an old vaudeville routine that included two farmers meeting on the street. They did not work together again until the late 1930s, when Crosby invited Hope to appear with him at the opening of the Del Mar race track north of San Diego. The boys reprised some old vaudeville routines that delighted the celebrity audience. One of the attendees was the production chief of Paramount Pictures, who then began searching for a movie vehicle for Crosby and Hope and ended up finding an old script intended originally for Burns and Allen, then later Jack Oakie and Fred MacMurray. The tentative title was *The Road to Mandalay,* but the destination was eventually changed to Singapore. To add a love interest to the movie, the exotically beautiful Dorothy Lamour was added to the main cast. Although *The Road to Singapore* was not considered as funny as the subsequent "Road" pictures, the chemistry among the three actors came through easily and the film was a hit nevertheless.

At least twenty-three of Crosby's movies were among the top ten box office hits during the year of their release. He was among the top ten box office stars in at least fifteen years (1934, 1937, 1940, 1943-54), and for five consecutive years (1944-48) he was the top box office draw in America. But real recognition of his talent as an actor came with *Going My Way*: his performance as an easygoing priest guaranteed him the best actor Oscar. His work in *The Country Girl* (1954)—in which Crosby played an alcoholic down on his luck opposite Grace Kelly—also received excellent critiques.

Crosby married singer Dixie Lee in 1930, and the couple had four sons—Garry, Dennis and Phillip (twins), and Lindsay—all of whom unsuccessfully attempted careers as actors. Widowed in 1952, Crosby married movie star Kathryn Grant (thirty years his junior) in 1957. She bore him two more sons—Harry and Nathaniel—and a girl, Mary , a TV and film actress famed for her role as the girl who shot J. R. Ewing in the television series *Dallas*.

During his four decades as an entertainer, Crosby gathered a fortune from radio, records, films, and TV and invested wisely in a broad array of business ventures. Second in wealth only to Bob Hope among showbiz people, Crosby's fortune was at one time estimated at anywhere between 200 and 400 million dollars, including holdings in real estate, banking, oil and gas wells, broadcasting, and holdings in the Coca-Cola Company. From the 1940s to the 1960s, Crosby owned 15 percent of the Pittsburgh Pirates baseball team, but playing golf was what he liked the most. He died playing at a course outside Madrid—after completing a tour of England that had included a sold-out engagement at the London Palladium.

After his death, Crosby's Hollywood persona—established largely by his role as the warm-hearted, easygoing priest in *Going My Way*—underwent much reassessment. Donald Shepherd and W. H. Allen composed an unflattering portrait of Crosby as an egotistic and heartless manipulator in their biography, *Bing Crosby—The Hollow Man* (1981). In *Going My Own Way* (1983), Garry Crosby, his eldest son, told of his experiences as a physically and mentally abused child. When Bing's youngest son by Dixie Lee, Lindsay Crosby, committed suicide in 1989 after finding himself unable to provide for his family, it was revealed that Crosby had stipulated in his will that none of his sons could access a trust fund he had left them before reaching age sixty-five.

—Bianca Freire-Medeiros

FURTHER READING:

Crosby, Bing. *Call Me Lucky.* New York, Da Capo Press, 1993.

MacFarlane, Malcolm. *Bing Crosby: A Diary of a Lifetime.* Leeds, International Crosby Circle, 1997.

Mielke, Randall G. *Road to Box Office: The Seven Film Comedies of Bing Crosby, Bob Hope, and Dorothy Lamour, 1940-1962.* Jefferson, N.C., McFarland & Co., 1997.

Osterholm, J. Roger. *Bing Crosby: A Bio-Bibliography.* Westport, Conn., Greenwood Press, 1994.

Shepherd, Donald, and Robert Slatzer. *Road to Hollywood (The Bing Crosby Film Book).* England, 1986.

Shepherd, Donald, and W. H. Allen. *Bing Crosby: The Hollow Man.* London, 1981.

Crosby, Stills, and Nash

David Crosby, Stephen Stills, and Graham Nash came together in the late 1960s as idiosyncratic individual talents in flight from famous groups. Their 1969 debut album arguably initiated the dominance of singer-songwriters in popular music until the mid-1970s. After appearing at the Woodstock festival, augmented by Neil Young, they achieved a wider public role as the artistic apotheosis of the hippie ideals of "music, peace, and love." As the 1970s progressed, however, CSN(&Y) became infamous for an inability to show enough peace and love to one another to continue playing and recording music together.

David Crosby had been an integral member of folk-rock pioneers The Byrds until he left the group amidst acrimony in 1967. Crosby had first encountered Stephen Stills when the latter's band, Buffalo Springfield, supported The Byrds in concert in early 1966. In May 1968, just after the demise of Buffalo Springfield, Crosby and

Stills met disillusioned Hollies frontman Graham Nash. As suggested by the unassuming name, Crosby, Stills, and Nash was conceived as a loose collective in order to foster creative freedom and forestall the internal strife which each individual had experienced in his previous band. Yet, with the release of *Crosby, Stills and Nash,* CSN was hailed as a "supergroup," and not just because of their prestigious genealogy. Lyrics which concurred with the ideals of the "counterculture" were immersed in acoustic guitars and immaculate vocal harmonies. Crosby and Stills' "Wooden Ships" envisioned a new Eden in the aftermath of nuclear apocalypse, while Nash's "Marrakesh Express" less grandly located utopia on the Moroccan hippie trail.

Stills' Buffalo Springfield colleague and rival Neil Young was recruited in June 1969 in order to bolster their imminent live shows. Ominously, there were squabbles over whether Young should get equal billing. With only one recently released record to their name, and in only their second ever concert performance, CSN&Y wowed the Woodstock festival in July 1969. There was a certain amount of manipulation involved in the rapid mythologization of CSN&Y as the epitome of the "Woodstock nation." Their manager, David Geffen, who also represented many of the other acts which appeared, threatened to withdraw his cooperation from the film of the festival unless CSN&Y's cover of Joni Mitchell's Woodstock was used over the opening credits. Their record label, Atlantic, disproportionately featured CSN&Y on two very successful soundtrack album sets. In contrast, CSN&Y's appearance at The Rolling Stones' disastrous free festival at Altamont in December 1969 was, as Johnny Rogan has observed, "effectively written out of rock history" by journalists sympathetic to the CSN&Y-Woodstock cause.

There were unprecedented pre-release orders worth over $2 million for *Deja Vu,* released in March 1970. Though it was somewhat more abrasive than the debut album, due to the arrival of Young and his electric guitar, *Deja Vu* was suffused with hippie vibes. These were amusingly conveyed on Crosby's "Almost Cut My Hair," but Nash's "Teach Your Children" sounded self-righteous. In May 1970, CSN&Y rush-released the single "Ohio," Young's stinging indictment of President Nixon's culpability for the killing of four student protesters by the National Guard at Kent State University. After completing a highly successful tour in 1970 (documented on the double-album *Four-Way Street*), CSN&Y were lauded by the media as the latest American answer to the Beatles, a dubious honor first bestowed on The Byrds in 1965, but which CSN&Y seemed capable of justifying.

Instead, the foursome diverged into various solo ventures. While this was informed by their insistence that, in Crosby's words, "We're not a group, just one aggregate of friends," individual rivalries and the tantalizing example of Young's flourishing solo career were also determining factors. The flurry of excellent solo albums in the early 1970s, invariably featuring the "friends" as guests, only increased interest in the enigma of the "aggregate." When CSN&Y finally regrouped in 1974, popular demand was met by a mammoth worldwide tour of sport stadia which redefined the presentation, scale, and economics of the rock'n'roll spectacle. But CSN&Y failed to complete an album after this tour, and they never again attained such artistic or cultural importance. After further attempts at a recorded reunion failed, Crosby, Stills, and Nash eventually reconvened without Young for *CSN* (1977). The album was another huge seller and spawned CSN's first top 10 single, Nash's "Just a Song Before I

(From left) David Crosby, Stephen Stills, Graham Nash, and Neil Young, 1988.

Go.'' Nevertheless, each member was past his peak in songwriting terms, and their musical style and political views were being vociferously challenged by punk rock and its maxim, ''Never trust a hippie.''

Crosby was becoming ever more mired in cocaine and heroin addiction. A farcical series of drug-related arrests culminated in his incarceration in 1986. In that year's ''Hippie Dream,'' Neil Young transformed Crosby's personal fate into a fable of the descent of countercultural idealism into rock 'n' roll hedonism (''the wooden ships / were just a hippie dream / capsized in excess''). Crosby's physical recovery resulted in a much-publicized first CSN&Y album in 18 years, *American Dream* (1988). The artistic irrelevance of Crosby, Stills, and Nash, however, was highlighted not only by comparisons between the new CSN&Y record and *Deja Vu,* but also by *Freedom* (1989), the opening salvo of Neil Young's renaissance as a solo artist. In the early 1990s, while Young was being lauded as the ''Godfather of Grunge,'' Crosby, Stills, and Nash operated, as Johnny Rogan observed, ''largely on the level of nostalgia. This was typified by their appearance at ''Woodstock II'' in August 1994. Young refused to appear with CSN, and instead designed a range of hats

depicting a vulture perched on a guitar, a parody of the famous Woodstock logo featuring a dove of peace. It was Young's pithy comment on the commodification of a (counter) cultural memory with which his erstwhile colleagues were, even 25 years later, inextricably associated.

—Martyn Bone

FURTHER READING:

Crosby, David. *Long Time Gone.* London, Heinemann, 1989.

Rogan, Johnny. *Crosby, Stills, Nash and Young: The Visual Documentary.* London, Omnibus Press, 1996.

———. *Neil Young: The Definitive Story of His Musical Career.* London, Proteus, 1982.

Cross-Dressing
See Drag

Crossword Puzzles

Once a peripheral form of entertainment, crossword puzzles have become a popular national institution. They appear in almost every newspaper, have become the focus of people's daily and weekend rituals, are published in their own books and magazines, appear in foreign languages—including Chinese—and have inspired other gridded word games like acrostic, cryptic, and diagramless puzzles.

Arthur Wynne constructed the first crossword, which appeared in 1913 in the *New York World.* His word puzzle consisted of an empty grid dotted with black squares. Solvers entered letters of intersecting words into this diagram; when correctly filled in, the answers to the "across" and "down" numbered definitions would complete, and hence solve, the puzzle. The layout and concept of the crossword has not changed since its inception.

Although crossword puzzles appeared in newspapers after Wynne's debut, the *New York Times* legitimized and popularized the pastime. The *Times*'s first Sunday puzzle appeared in the *New York Times Magazine* in 1942, and daily puzzles began in 1950.

—Wendy Woloson

FURTHER READING:

Shepard, Richard F. "Bambi Is a Stag and Tubas Don't Go Pah-Pah." *New York Times Magazine.* February 18, 1992, 31-9.

Cruise, Tom (1962—)

Tom Cruise is perhaps the most charismatic actor of the 1980s and 1990s. Although initially dismissed as little more than a pretty face with a million dollar smile when he made his screen debut as a member of Hollywood's "Brat Pack" generation of youthful leading men in the early 1980s, he has demonstrated considerable staying power and fan appeal. At one point between 1987 and 1989, four of his films combined to post more than one billion dollars in box office receipts. Yet, at the same time, he has proven to be a very serious actor earning Academy Award nominations for "Best Actor" in 1989 in *Born on the Fourth of July,* in which he portrayed disabled Vietnam Vet Ron Kovic, and again in 1996 for a high energy performance in *Jerry Maguire.* The latter film, in fact, served as an extremely insightful commentary on many of the cocky, swaggering characters he had portrayed in such exuberant films as *Top Gun* (1986), *The Color of Money* (1986), *Cocktail* (1988), and *Days of Thunder* (1990).

Cruise made the jump to producer in 1996 with the blockbuster *Mission Impossible,* a big screen remake of the popular 1960s television series. In 1999, he took on his most challenging leading role in Stanley Kubrick's sexual thriller *Eyes Wide Shut,* teaming with his wife, Nicole Kidman.

—Sandra Garcia-Myers

FURTHER READING:

Broeske, Pat H. "Cruising in the Media Stratosphere." *Los Angeles Times Calendar.* May 25, 1986, 19-20.

Corliss, Richard. "Tom Terrific." *Time.* December 25, 1989, 74-9.

Greene, Ray. "Man with a Mission." *Boxoffice.* April, 1996, 12-16.

Tom Cruise in a scene from the film *Mission: Impossible.*

Crumb, Robert (1943—)

Robert Crumb is the most famous and well respected of all underground comic artists, and the first underground artist to be accepted into the mainstream of popular American culture. His comics are notable for explicit, detailed, and unflattering self-confessions, in which strange sexual fantasies abound. When not writing about himself, he has targeted the American consumer-culture establishment, but also anti-establishment hippies and dropouts as subjects for his satire. Crumb's art veers from gritty, grubby realism to extremes of Expressionism and psychedelia. As both an artist and a writer, Crumb is a true original. Relentlessly unrestrained and impulsive, his work reflects few influences other than the funny animal comics of Carl Barks and Walt Kelley, and the twisted, deformed monster-people of *Mad* artist Basil Wolverton.

The Philadelphia-born Crumb lived his childhood in many different places, including Iowa and California. Seeking refuge from an alienated childhood and adolescence, he began drawing comics with his brothers Charles and Max. As a young adult he lived in Cleveland, Chicago, and New York before moving to San Francisco in 1967, the year he began his rise to prominence. He had worked for a greeting card company until he was able to produce comic books full time, and his first strips appeared in underground newspapers such as

Robert Crumb

New York's *East Village Other* before the first issues of his *Zap* comic book were published in 1967. *Zap* introduced many of Crumb's most popular characters, as well as the unforgettable "Keep On Truckin'" logo, and made a tremendous impact on the underground comics scene. In 1970, particularly dazzling examples of his bizarre and imaginative art appeared—with little in the way of story—in the excellent *XYZ Comics* (1970).

Among Crumb's most notable characters are Mr. Natural, a sort of sham guru who lives like a hedonist and prefers to tease, and occasionally exploit, his devotees rather than enlighten them, and his occasional disciple, Flakey Foont, emblematic of the suburban nebbish fraught with doubts and hang-ups. Others include Angelfood McSpade, a simple African girl exploited by greedy and lecherous white Americans, diminutive sex-fiend Mister Snoid, and Whiteman (a big-city businessman, proudly patriotic and moralistic yet inwardly repressed and obsessed with sex). But Crumb's most famous character is Fritz the Cat, who first appeared in *R. Crumb's Comics and Stories* (1969). Fritz, a disillusioned college student looking for freedom, knowledge, and counterculture kicks, became popular enough to star in the 1972 animated movie *Fritz The Cat*, directed by Ralph Bakshi, which became the first cartoon ever to require an X-rating. While the movie proved a huge success with the youth audience, Crumb hated the film and retaliated in his next comic book by killing Fritz with an ice pick through the forehead.

By the late 1990s, Crumb's comic-book work had been seen in a host of publications over the course of three decades. In the early days he was featured in, among other publications, *Yellow Dog, Home*

Grown Funnies, Mr. Natural, Uneeda Comix, and *Big Ass.* In the 1980s, he was published in *Weirdo* and *Hup.* In addition to his comic-book work, he became well known for his bright, intense cover for the *Cheap Thrills* album issued by Janis Joplin's Big Brother and the Holding Company in 1968. Though much of Robert Crumb's best-loved work was produced in the late 1960s and early 1970s, he reached a peak of widespread fame in the mid-1990s with the successful release of filmmaker Terry Zwigoff's mesmerizing documentary, *Crumb* (1995), which interspersed shots of Crumb's works between frank interviews with the artist and his family, and comments from media and culture critics. *Crumb* won the Grand Jury prize at the Sundance Film Festival and was widely praised by critics. The film's impact is twofold: viewers are stunned by Crumb's genius, while being both moved and disturbed by the images of an unfortunate and dysfunctional family. The film is honest in acknowledging controversial aspects of the artist's work, with critics on-camera pointing out the racist caricatures, perverse lust, and, above all, the overt misogyny that runs through much of Crumb's *oeuvre.* Some of those images have depicted scantily clad buxom women with bird heads, animal heads, or no heads at all.

Despite the controversy, however, the 1980s and 1990s brought a multitude of high quality Crumb compilations and reprints, including coffee-table books, sketchbooks, and complete comics and stories from the 1960s to the present. Meanwhile, his continuing output has included the illustration of short stories by Kafka and a book on early blues music. Profiles of Crumb have appeared in *Newsweek* and *People* magazines, and on BBC-TV, while his art has been featured at New York's Whitney Museum and Museum of Modern Art, as well as in numerous gallery shows in the United States, Europe, and Japan. His comic characters have appeared on mugs, T-shirts, patches, stickers, and home paraphernalia.

A fan of 1920s blues and string band music, Crumb started the Cheap Suit Serenaders band in the 1970s, with himself playing banjo, and recorded three albums. Remarkable in his personality as well as his work, the shy Crumb prefers to dress, not like a bearded longhair in the style of most male underground artists, but like a man-on-the-street from the 1950s, complete with suit, necktie, and short-brimmed hat. In 1993, he left California to settle in southern France with his wife and daughter.

—Dave Goldweber

FURTHER READING:

Beauchamp, Monte. *The Life and Times of R. Crumb: Comments from Contemporaries.* New York, St. Martin's Griffin, 1998.

Crumb, Robert. *Carload O' Comics.* New York, Belier, 1976.

————, compiled by Carl Richter. *Crumb-ology: The Works of R. Crumb, 1981-1994.* Sudbury, Massachusetts, Water Row Press, 1995.

————. *The Complete Crumb.* Westlake, Fantagraphics, 1987-98.

Estren, Mark James. *A History of Underground Comics.* Berkeley, Ronin, 1974; reissued, 1993.

Fiene, Donald M. *R. Crumb Checklist of Work and Criticism: With a Biographical Supplement and a Full Set of Indexes.* Cambridge, Massachusetts, Boatner Norton Press, 1981.

Crystal, Billy (1947—)

Billy Crystal went from stand-up comedy to playing Jodie Dallas, American TV's first major gay character, on the sitcom *Soap* (1977-81). As a cast member on *Saturday Night Live* (1984-85), Crystal was known for the catch-phrases ''you look mahvelous'' and ''I hate it when that happens.'' After he moved from the small screen to films, Crystal's endearing sensitivity and gentle wit brought him success in movies such as *Throw Momma from the Train* (1987), *When Harry Met Sally* (1989), and *City Slickers* (1991). He made his directorial debut with *Mr. Saturday Night* (1992), the life story of Buddy Young, Jr., a fictional Catskills comedian Crystal created on *Saturday Night Live*.

—Christian L. Pyle

FURTHER READING:

Crystal, Billy, with Dick Schaap. *Absolutely Mahvelous.* New York, G. P. Putnam's Sons, 1986.

Cukor, George (1899-1983)

An American film director whose career spanned over fifty years, Cukor was particularly adept at female-centered melodrama (*Little Women,* 1933; *The Women,* 1939), romantic comedy (*The Philadelphia Story,* 1940; *Adam's Rib,* 1949), and musicals (*A Star Is Born,* 1954; *My Fair Lady*, 1964, for which he received a Best Director Oscar). Often derided as a workman-like technician, revelations about Cukor's homosexuality led to reappraisals of his work by, in particular, queer academics, who focused on his predilection for more 'feminine' genres and gender-bending narratives, as seen in *Sylvia Scarlett* (1935), for example. Cukor has thus, like fellow director Dorothy Arzner, come to be perceived as an auteur, whose sexual identity influenced the final form taken by the Hollywood material he handled.

—Glyn Davis

FURTHER READING:

McGilligan, Patrick. *George Cukor: A Double Life.* London, Faber and Faber, 1991.

Cullen, Countee (1903-1946)

Among the most conservative of the Harlem Renaissance poets, Harvard educated Countee Cullen exploded onto the New York literary scene with the publication of *Color* (1925) and solidified his reputation with *Copper Sun* (1927) and *The Black Christ and Other Poems* (1929). His verse defied the expectations of white audiences. Where earlier black poets like Paul Laurence Dunbar had written in dialect, Cullen's tributes to black life echoed the classical forms of Keats and Shelley. The young poet was the leading light of the African-American literary community during the 1920s. Although his reputation waned after 1930 as he was increasingly attacked for ignoring the rhythms and idioms of Black culture, Cullen's ability to

present black themes in traditional European forms made him one of the seminal figures in modern African-American poetry.

—Jacob M. Appel

FURTHER READING:

Baker, Houston A. *Afro-American Poetics: Revisions of Harlem and the Black Aesthetic.* Madison, University of Wisconsin Press, 1988.

Ferguson, Blanche E. *Countee Cullen and the Negro Renaissance.* New York, Dodd Mead, 1966.

Harris, Trudier, editor. *Afro-American Writers from the Harlem Renaissance to 1940.* Detroit, Gale Research Co., 1987.

Turner, Darwin T. *In a Minor Chord: Three Afro-American Writers and Their Search for Identity.* Carbondale, Southern Illinois University Press, 1971.

Cult Films

Cult films are motion pictures that are favored by individual groups of self-appointed connoisseurs who establish special meanings for the films of a particular director or star or those which deal with a particular theme. In practical terms, however, cult status can be conferred on almost any film. In fact, such an occurrence is particularly sought after by filmmakers to maintain interest in the film once its initial theatrical run has been completed. Thus cult films might be more accurately defined as those special films which, for one reason or another, ''connect'' with a hard-core group of fans who never tire of viewing them or discussing them.

Cult films, by their very nature, deal with extremes, eschewing, for the most part, middle of the road storylines and character stereotypes commonly seen in Hollywood studio products. These normally small movies present unusual if not totally outrageous protagonists involved in bizarre storylines that resolve themselves in totally unpredictable ways. According to Daniel Lopez's *Films by Genre,* cult films may be divided into three basic categories: popular cult, clique movies, and subculture films.

A prime example of the first type is George Lucas's 1977 *Star Wars,* which began as an evocation of the Saturday matinee serials of the 1940s and 1950s. Using a basic cowboys vs. Indians theme borrowed from the westerns of his childhood, Lucas updated the frontier theme by adding technology and relocating the drama to outer space. His effort, while failing to do much for the Western, created a resurgence of interest in the science fiction and ''cliffhanger'' serial genres. In the years that followed, Hollywood was inundated with sci-fi thrillers, of which the most popular were the *Star Trek* sagas. At the same time, another Lucas creation, the Indiana Jones films, showed that there was still some interest in action adventure serials, a fact that was further illustrated by Warner Bros. resurrection of the Batman character, who had first come to the screen in the multi-episode adventure short subjects of the 1940s. *Star Wars* elevation to cult status was re-affirmed when it was re-released in theaters in 1997 and broke all existing box-office records as its fans rushed to view it over and over.

Yet widespread popularity and big box office receipts are usually the antithesis of what most cult films are about, a fact illustrated by the so called ''clique'' films that appeal to a select few. These are films that tend to be favored by special interest groups such as film societies, cinefiles, and certain academics. Generally speaking the films that appeal to cliques are either foreign, experimental, or representative of a neglected genre. In the latter case, in particular, proponents of a specific film usually believe that it has either been overlooked or misinterpreted by filmgoers at large. They rediscover the works of ''B'' movie directors such as Douglas Sirk or Sam Fuller and, through retrospective screenings and articles in film journals, attempt to make the case for their status as auteurs whose body of works yield a special message heard only by them. In many cases, the cult status awarded these directors has led to a re-evaluation of their contributions to film by historians and scholars and to the distribution of new prints of their works.

This process also works with individual films made by established directors that somehow made only a slight impact during their initial theatrical runs. The major example is Frank Capra's *It's a Wonderful Life* (1946). Originally dismissed as a sentimental bit of fluff, the film was seen primarily at Christmas Eve midnight screenings for its faithful band of adherents until the 1980s, when it was rediscovered by television and designated a classic. Similar transformations have occurred for John Ford's *The Searchers* (1956) and, surprisingly, Victor Fleming's *The Wizard of Oz*, which was first released in 1939 to a lackluster reception and did not make money until its second and third re-releases in the late 1940s.

The third type of cult film and, perhaps, the first one that comes to mind for the average person is the ''subculture cult film.'' These are small films created in a cauldron of controversy, experimentation, and contention in every aspect of their production ranging from story themes to casting. They are often cheaply made and usually don't last long at the box-office. Yet, to their fans, these films contain special messages sent by the filmmakers and by the stars. Through word-of-mouth contacts and, increasingly, by a variety of new media including video and the Internet, cultists recruit new fans for the film, thus serving to keep it alive well beyond its maker's original intentions. What is particularly fascinating, however, is the fact that all over the world, a certain segment of filmgoers will react to these exact films in the same way without word-of-mouth or advance indoctrination as to its special status. This is the true measure of a film's cult potential.

The fanatical appeal of these subculture favorites has also altered the traditional patterns of movie going and the unique role of the audience. In traditional viewing, the audiences are essentially passive, reacting to onscreen cues about when to laugh or cry and whom to root for. The subculture film audience, however, takes on an auteurial role on a performance-by-performance basis. This is due to the fact that the viewers have seen the film so many times that they know all of the lines and the characters by heart. Thus, they attend the screening in the attire of their favorite characters and, once that character appears on the screen, begin to shout out new dialogue that they have constructed in their minds. The new script, more often than not, alludes to the actor's physical characteristics or foreshadows future dialogue or warnings about plot twists. In many cases, audience members will yell out stage directions to the actor, telling him that he should come back and turn out a light or close a door.

Perhaps the most notable example of this auteuristic phenomenon is the undisputed queen of cult films, the British production *The Rocky Horror Picture Show* (1975), which treats the plight of two newlyweds, Brad (Barry Bostwick) and his virgin bride Janet (Susan Sarandon), who become trapped in a spooky house on a rainy night in Ohio. They are met by a group of fun loving aliens from the planet Transylvania who are being entertained by Dr. Frankenfurter (Tim Curry), who struts around in sexy female underwear and fishnet stockings belting out gender bending tunes such as ''I'm a Sweet Transvestite From Transsexual Transylvania.'' He is in the process of creating a Frankenstein type monster, Rocky Horror (Peter Hinwood), to be employed strictly for sexual purposes. During the course of the evening, however, he manages to seduce both of the newlyweds and also causes a suddenly liberated Janet to pursue a fling with Rocky Horror, as well.

The film proved to be a box-office disaster when it was released in 1975 but it did develop an underground ''word-of-mouth'' reputation, causing its American producer, Lou Adler, to convince Twentieth-Century Fox to search for alternative ways to publicize it in order to prevent a total disaster. The film was re-released at the Waverly Theater in Greenwich Village and soon after at theaters throughout the country for midnight performances. Its first audiences consisted primarily of those groups represented in the film—transvestites, gays, science fiction fans, punk rockers, and college psychology majors (who presumably attended to study the rest of the audience).

For its avid viewers, attendance at a midnight screening began to take on the form of a ritual. In addition to wearing costumes, members of the audience would talk to the screen, create new dialogue, dance in the aisles, and shower their fellow viewers with rice during the wedding scene and water during the rainy ones. Experienced fans, of course, attended with umbrellas but virgins (those new to the film) generally went home bathed in rice and water. In the years since its first screenings, the film has become a staple at midnight screenings around the country and has achieved its status as the most significant cult film of all time.

Performers in subculture films have acquired cult followings as well. Many hard-core fans, in fact, view their favorite performers as only revealing their real personalities in their ''special'' film. In attempting to interpret the actor's performance in this context, the fans will also bring into play all of the performer's previous characterizations in the belief that they have some bearing on this particular role. To such fans, the actor's whole career has built toward this performance. Although this perception has had little effect on the careers of major stars, at least during their lifetimes, it has enhanced the careers of such ''B'' movie icons as Divine and horror film actor Bruce Campbell, making them the darlings of the midnight theatrical circuit and major draws at fan conventions. Even deceased performers have been claimed by cult film devotees. The screen biography of Joan Crawford, *Mommie Dearest* (1981), elevated—or lowered—her from stardom to cult status, and Bela Lugosi attracted posthumous fame with fans who revisited his old horror films with an eye to the campy elements of his performances.

While not everyone agrees on which films are destined to achieve special status with subcultures, a great many of them fall into the horror and science fiction genres. The horror films that appeal to this audience share most of the characteristics of cult films in general. They are only rarely major studio productions but they frequently ''rip off'' such larger budgeted mainstream productions as *The Exorcist* (1973), *The Omen* (1976), or the various manifestations of Bram Stoker's *Dracula*. Cult horror films inhabit the margins of the cinema in pursuit of off-beat themes, controversial subject matter, and shocking scenes of mayhem. They are either so startlingly original as to be too ''far out'' for most viewers or they are such blatant derivations of existing films that they are passed over by general audiences and critics alike.

Horror films take on a special status with cultists for a number of reasons. First and foremost is the authorial role certain films allow the audience to play. Most horror film directors do not intend to send out a specific message with their work. They simply want to make some money. For this reason, most plots involve a demonic disruption in the normal order of things which must be righted by each film's protagonist before the status quo can be restored. This fundamentally safe view of the world allows the audience to write its own text with any number of subjective meanings regardless of what happens in the story as a whole. The conservative stance of the filmmakers leaves plenty of room for re-readings of the text to allow issues incorporating a questioning of authority, a rejection of government and the military-industrial complex, sexism, and a host of environmental concerns that inevitably arise when horror films deal with the impact of man upon nature. Perhaps the first cult horror film to raise such issues was Tod Browning's *Freaks* (1932), which was banned for 30 years following its initial release. The film basically dealt with the simple message that beauty is more than skin deep. When the protagonist, a circus trapeze star, attempts to toy with the affections of a side show midget, she is set upon by the side show "freaks," who transform her physical beauty into a misshapen form to reflect the ugliness within her. While Browning was clearly attempting an entertaining horror film which stretched the boundaries of the genre, there is no evidence that he intended the many metaphysical meanings regarding the relationship of good and evil and body and soul that audiences have brought to the film in the 60 years since its initial release.

Another film, 1956's *Invasion of the Body Snatchers*, has been celebrated by scholars as a tract against the McCarthyism of the 1950s, though it is probably more rightly read as a more general statement against conformity and repression of individual thought that transcends its period. Similarly, George Romero's legendary *Night of the Living Dead* (1968) was not only the goriest movie of its time but it also worked on our basic fears. Like its inspiration, Alfred Hitchcock's *The Birds* (1963), it deals with a group of people confined to a certain geographic area while nature runs amok because man has transgressed against the natural law. The film is particularly effective because it deals with gradations of insanity, beginning with stark fear and escalating to show that man is totally powerless to deal with the things that he fears most. Audiences sat riveted to their seats, convinced that there was no way out except death. The film began as the second feature on drive-in movie double bills and, through strong word-of-mouth and gradual acceptance from critics, took on a second life in college retrospectives and museum screenings (where it was declared a masterpiece) before winding up on the midnight movie circuit.

Another reason for the cult appeal of low budget horror films is the fact that they often push the limits of what is traditionally thought to be acceptable. For example, the legendary *Blood Feast* (1976) became the first film to go beyond mere blood to the actual showing of human entrails, a technique that was later picked up by Hollywood for much larger special effects laden films. Another low budget film, *Evil Dead II* (1987), directed by Sam Raimi, surpassed its bloody predecessor presenting extreme violence at such a fast pace that the human eye could barely register the images flashing by.

A final appeal of low budget horror films is the fact that a number of major actors and directors—including Jack Nicholson, Tom Hanks, Francis Ford Coppola, and Roger Corman—got their start in them. Corman once referred to these pictures as a film school where he learned everything he would ever need to become successful in motion pictures. But it worked the other way as well. Many stars on the downslope of their careers appeared in grade "B" horror films to keep their fading careers alive, hoping that they might accidentally appear in a breakthrough film. Former box-office stars—including Boris Karloff (*The Terror*), Bela Lugosi (*Plan Nine From Outer Space*), Yvonne DeCarlo (*Satan's Cheerleaders*), and Richard Basehart (*Mansion of the Doomed*)—who had been forgotten by Hollywood received a new type of stardom in these grade "B" films, and often spent the last years of their careers appearing at comic book and horror film conventions for adoring fans.

Science fiction films are very similar to horror movies in that they push the cinematic envelope by their very identification with their genre. They are futuristic, technologically-driven films that employ astonishing special effects to create a world that does not yet exist but might in the future. Sci-fi movies can also be horror films as well. It took technology to create the Frankenstein monster and it took technology to encounter and destroy the creature in *Alien* (1979). But, like horror films, they also question the impact of man and his technology on the world that he lives in. They make political statements through their futuristic storylines, saying, in effect, that 20 or more years in the future, this will be mankind's fate if we do not stop doing certain things.

Science fiction films that achieve cult status do so because, even within this already fantastic genre, they are so innovative and experimental that they take on a life of their own. With the exceptions of the *Star Wars, Star Trek,* and *Planet of the Apes* series and a number of individual efforts such as *2001* (1968), the films that attract the long term adulation of fans are generally not large studio products. They are normally small films such as the Japanese Godzilla pictures; minor films from the 1950s with their dual themes of McCarthyism and nuclear monsters; and low budget favorites from the 1970s and 1980s.

Again, as in horror, the pictures seem to fall into three categories of fan fascination. These include films such as *Brain Eaters* (1958), *Lifeforce* (1985), and *The Incredible Two-Headed Transplant* (1971) that feature major stars such as Leonard Nimoy, Patrick Stewart, and Bruce Dern on the way up. Conversely, a number of major stars ranging from Richard Burton and Henry Fonda appeared in some otherwise forgettable science fiction films during the twilight of their careers which have made their performances memorable to aficionados of embarrassing moments on film. Still other stars, however, are able to turn almost any film that they are in into a sci-fi cult film. The list is headed by Zsa Zsa Gabor, Vincent Price, Bela Lugosi, and John Agar.

In the final analysis, cult films say more about the people who love them than about themselves. To maintain a passion for a film that would compel one to drive to the very worst parts of town dressed in outlandish costumes to take part in a communal viewing experience sets the viewer apart as a special person. He or she is one of a select few that has the ability to interpret a powerful message from a work of art that has somehow escaped the population at large. In pursuing the films that they love, cultists are making a statement that they are not afraid to set themselves apart and to take on the role of tastemakers for the moviegoers of the future. In many cases, the films that they celebrate influence filmmakers to employ new subjects, performers, or technology in more mainstream films. In other instances, their special films will never be discovered by the mainstream world. But that is part of the appeal: to be different, to be "out there," is to be like the cult films themselves.

—Steve Hanson

FURTHER READING:

Everman, Welch. *Cult Horror Films: From ''Attack of the 50-Foot Woman'' to ''Zombies of Mora Tau.''* Secaucus, New Jersey, Carol Publishing Group, 1993.

———. *Cult Science Fiction Films*. New York, Carol Publishing Group, 1995.

Henttzi, Gary. ''Little Cinema of Horrors.'' *Film Quarterly*. Spring 1993, 22-27.

Lopez, Daniel. *Films by Genre*. Jefferson, North Carolina, McFarland & Co., 1993.

Margules, Edward, and Stephen Rebello. *Bad Movies We Love*. New York, Plume, 1993.

Peary, Danny. *Cult Movies: The Classics, the Sleepers, the Weird, and the Wonderful*. New York, Gramercy Books, 1998.

———. *Cult Movie Stars*. New York, Simon & Schuster, 1991.

Cults

The 1978 Jonestown Massacre, where 913 of the Reverend Jim Jones' followers were forced to commit suicide, marked the high point in America's condemnation of cults. Spread across newspaper front pages and national magazines from coast to coast, the slaughter gave focus to an alarm that had grown throughout the decade. Were cults spreading like wildfire? Were Rasputin-like religious leaders luring the nation's youth into oblivion like modern-day Pied Pipers? The Jonestown coverage reinforced the common perception that, in cults, America harbored some alien menace. The perception could not be further from the truth. In a sense, America was founded by cults, and throughout the nation's history, cults and splinter groups from established religions have found in America a fertile cultural terrain. That modern-day Americans find cults alarming is yet another example of America's paradoxical culture.

Webster's Collegiate Dictionary defines a cult as ''a religion regarded as unorthodox and spurious; also: its body of adherents.'' Cults as they are understood in the popular imagination have some additional characteristics, and can include: any religious organization that spends an inordinate amount of time raising money; any religion that relies on a virulent us-vs.-them dogmatism, thereby alienating its members further from mainstream society; and any religion where the temporal leader holds such sway as to be regarded as a deity, a deity capable of treating cult members as financial, sexual, or missionary chattel to be exploited to the limits of their endurance. In this expanded definition, a Pentecostal such as Aimee Semple McPherson, the Los Angeles preacher, and not technically a cult leader, fits adequately into the definition, as does Jim Jones, Charles Manson, or Sun Myung Moon.

Originally, America was a land of pilgrims, and the Plymouth colonists were not the last to view the New World as a holy land. And as in all times and all religions, religious charlatans were a constant. By the close of the nineteenth century, Americans had founded some peculiar interpretations of Christianity. The Mormons, Seventh Day Adventists, Christian Scientists, and Jehovah's Witnesses all had their origins in the nineteenth century, and by dint of accretion, they had developed from dubious, persecuted faiths into respectable institutions. In the history of Mormonism one can discover much that is pertinent to understanding modern-day cults; elements of this tale

are reminiscent of the histories of Scientology, The Unification Church, and People's Temple, among others. A charismatic leader, claiming divine inspiration and not above resorting to trickery, amasses a following, who are viewed with derision by the general populace. The faith aggressively recruits new members and later attempts to gloss over its dubious origins, building enormous and impressive edifices and going out of its way to convey an image of solidity.

From time to time, waves of religious fervor have swept across America—the Shakers and Pentecostals early in the nineteenth century, for instance, or the Spiritualist and Theosophy movements at century's end. In western New York state, where the Church of Latter Day Saints originated, so many evangelical movements caught fire in the 1820s that it was nick-named the ''Burned-over District.'' The church's founder, Joseph Smith, claimed to have received revelation directly from an angel who left Smith with several golden tablets on which were inscribed the story of Hebraic settlers to the New World. Smith and his band of youthful comrades ''was regarded as wilder, crazier, more obscene, more of a threat'' writes Tom Wolfe, ''than the entire lot of hippie communes put together.'' Smith's contemporaries called him ''a notorious liar,'' and, ''utterly destitute of conscience'' and cited his 1826 arrest for fortune-telling as evidence of his dishonesty. But by the time Smith fled New York in 1839, he was accompanied by 10,000 loyal converts who followed him to Nauvoo, Illinois, with an additional 5,000 converts from England swelling their numbers. After Smith began a systematic power-grab, using the Mormon voting block in gaining several elected positions, he was lynched by the locals, and (shades of Jim Jones' flight to Guyana) the Mormons continued westward to Utah, where the only threat was the Native Americans.

An earnest desire to bring people into the fold has often devolved into hucksterism in the hands of some religious leaders. Throughout the twentieth century, Elmer Gantry-esque religious leaders, from the lowly revivalist preacher to the television ministries of a Jimmy Swaggart or Oral Roberts, have shown as much concern with fleecing their followers as with saving their souls. When the founder of the Church of Christ, Scientist, Mary Baker Eddy, died in 1910, she left a fortune of three million dollars. George Orwell once mused that the best way to make a lot of money is to start one's own religion, and L. Ron Hubbard, founder of Scientology, took Orwell's maxim to heart.

A pulp fiction writer by trade, Hubbard originally published his ''new science of Dianetics,'' a treatise on the workings of the mind, in the April, 1950 issue of *Astounding Science Fiction*. Dianetics was a technique for self-actualization and understanding, and Hubbard couched his theories in scientific rhetoric and obscure phraseology to appeal to a well-educated, affluent constituency. Published in book form, *Dianetics* became an overnight success, and Hubbard quickly set up a ''research institute'' and began attracting adherents. Dianetics, as practiced by Hubbard, straddled the gap between the self-actualization movements typical of later religious cults, and religion (though Scientology's mythos was not set down until shortly before Hubbard's death). In Dianetics, an auditor ran a potential follower through a list of questions and their emotional response was measured with an e-meter, a simple galvanic register held in both hands. This meter revealed the negative experiences imprinted in one's unconscious in an almost pictorial form called an engram, and Dianetics promised to sever the unconscious connection to negative experiences and allow the follower to attain a state of ''clear,'' an exalted state similar to enlightenment. Hubbard's idea appeared scientific, and like psychotherapy, it was an inherently expensive, time-consuming process.

From the beginning, Hubbard ran into all manner of legal troubles. He squabbled with the I.R.S. over the church's tax-exempt status, and the F.D.A. over the use of the e-meter. Scientology met stiff government opposition in every country in which it operated. An Australian Board of Inquiry, convened in 1965, called Scientology ''evil, its techniques evil, its practice a serious threat to the community, medically, morally, and socially. . . . Scientology is a delusional belief system, based on fictions and fallacies and propagated by falsehoods and deception''; it was banned from Australia until 1983. The British government banned foreign Scientologists in 1968, and Hubbard was convicted on fraud charges, *in absentia,* by a Paris court in 1978. The Church lost its tax-exempt status in France and Denmark in the mid-1980s, and has had to seriously curtail its operations in Germany. More than most cults, Scientology's travails appeared to be symptomatic of its founder's mental instability. As an institution, Scientology was marked by an extreme fractiousness and a pronounced penchant for litigation. Ruling in a 1984 lawsuit brought by the church, a Los Angeles judge stated, ''The organization clearly is schizophrenic and paranoid, and this bizarre combination seems to be a reflection if its founder.''

In many ways Scientology anticipated the tactics of the wave of cult groups that would sweep America in the 1960s and 1970s. There numbers are almost innumerable, therefore, a look at two of the most infamous—the Unification Church and the Hare Krishnas—must suffice to explain this religious revival, what Tom Wolfe termed ''the Third Wave.'' Better known by the pejorative term, Moonies, in 1959, the Unification Church, a radical offshoot of Presbyterianism, founded its first American church in Berkeley. Its founder, the Reverend Sun Myung Moon, converted from his native Confucianism as a child, receiving a messianic revelation while in his teens. Moon was expelled from his church for this claim, as well as his unorthodox interpretation of Christianity, but by the late-1950s he had established a large congregation and the finances necessary to begin missionary work abroad. Like many cults, the church's teachings were culturally conservative and spiritually radical. Initially, it appealed to those confused by the rapid changes in social mores then prevalent, offering a simple theology and rigid moral teachings.

The Unification Church was aggressive in its proselytizing. Critics decried its recruitment methods as being callous, manipulative, and deceitful; the charge of brainwashing was frequently leveled against the church. Adherents preyed on college students, targeting the most vulnerable among them—the lonely, the disenfranchised, and the confused. The unsuspecting recruit was typically invited over to a group house for dinner. Upon arrival, he or she was showered with attention (called ''love-bombing'' in church parlance), and told only in the most general terms the nature of the church. The potential member was then invited to visit a church-owned ranch or farm for the weekend, where they were continually supervised from early morning until late at night.

Once absorbed, the new member was destined to take his/her place in the church's vast fund-raising machine, selling trinkets, candy, flowers, or other cheap goods, and ''witnessing'' on behalf of the church. Often groups of adherents traveled cross country, sleeping in their vehicles, renting a motel room once a week to maintain personal hygiene, in short, living lives of privation while funneling profits to the church. Moonie proselytizers were known for their stridency and their evasions, typically failing to identify their church affiliation should they be asked. On an institutional level, the church resorted to this same type of subterfuge, setting up dozens of front

groups, and buying newspapers and magazines—usually with a right-wing bias (Moon was an avowed anti-Communist, a result of his spending time in a North Korean POW camp). The Unification Church also developed an elaborate lobbying engine; it was among the few groups that actually supported Richard Nixon, organizing pro-Nixon demonstrations up until the last days of his administration. Allusive, shadowy connections to Korean intelligence agencies were also alleged. The church, with its curious theology coupled with a rabid right-wing agenda, was and is a curious institution. Like Hubbard, many Christian evangelists, and other cult leaders, Moon taught his followers to be selfless while he himself enjoyed a life of luxury. But the depth and scope of his political influence is profound, and among cults, his has achieved an unprecedented level of political power.

Like the Unification Church, the International Society for Krishna Consciousness (ISKCON), better known as the Hare Krishna movement, has drawn widespread criticism. Unlike the Unification Church, the Hare Krishnas evince little concern for political exigencies, but their appearance—clean-shaven heads and pink sari—make the Hare Krishnas a very visible target for anti-cult sentiments, and for many years, the stridency of their beliefs exacerbated matters. A devout Hindu devotee of Krishna, A.C. Bhaktivedanta Swami Prabhupada, was charged by his guru with bringing Hinduism to the west. Arriving in America in 1965, Prabhupada's teachings became popular with members of the emerging hippie populace, who adopted the movement's distinctive uniform, forswearing sex and drugs for non-chemical bliss. Hare Krishnas lived in communes, practicing a life of extreme asceticism and forsaking ties with family and friends. Complete immersion in the group was de rigueur. The movement spread rapidly, becoming infamous for its incessant street proselytizing, in which lines of devotees would play percussion instruments while chanting for hours. The sect's frequenting of airports and train stations, importuning travelers with flowers or Prabhupada's translation of the classic Indian text, the Bhagavad-Gita, also drew public scorn. Like the Moonies, the Hare Krishna's fundraising efforts helped turn public opinion against the cult.

In the 1970s, as more and more American joined such groups as the Unification Church, the Hare Krishnas, or the ''Jesus People'' (an eclectic group of hippies who turned to primitive charismatic Christianity while retaining their dissolute fashions and lifestyle), parental concern intensified. An unsubstantiated but widely disseminated statistic held that a quarter of all cult recruits were Jewish, provoking alarm among Jewish congregations. To combat the threat, self-proclaimed cult experts offered to abduct and ''deprogram'' cult members for a fee, and in the best of American traditions, deprogramming itself became a lucrative trade full of self-aggrandizing pseudo-psychologists. The deprogrammers did have some valid points. Many cults used sleep deprivation, low-protein diets, and constant supervision to mold members into firmly committed zealots. By stressing an us-vs.-them view of society, cults worked on their young charges' feelings of alienation from society, creating virtual slaves who would happily sign over their worldly possessions, or, as was the case with a group called the Children of God, literally give their bodies to Christ as prostitutes.

For those who had lost a child to a cult, the necessity of deprogramming was readily apparent. But in time, the logic of the many cult-watch dog groups grew a bit slim. If anything, the proliferation of anti-cult groups spoke to the unsettling aftershocks of the 1960s counterculture as much as any threat presented by new religions. Were all religious groups outside the provenance of an established church to be equally condemned? Were all religious beliefs that weren't intrinsically exoteric to be rejected out of hand? By stressing conformity, many watch-dog groups diluted their moral authority.

Ironically, while cult watchdog groups focused public outrage on the large, readily identifiable cults—Scientology, ISKCON, the Unification Church—it was usually the smaller, homegrown varieties that proved the most unstable. Religions are concerned with self-perpetuation. When a charismatic leader dies, stable religious groups often grow more stable and moderate and perpetuate themselves (as has the now respectable Church of Latter Day Saints). But smaller cults, if they do not dissolve and scatter, have often exploded in self-destruction. The People's Temple, the Branch Davidians (actually a sect of Presbyterianism), and the Manson Family were such groups. In 1997, Heaven's Gate, a cult with pronounced science fiction beliefs based in California, committed mass suicide in accordance with the passing of the Hale-Bopp comet.

The Jonestown massacre in the Guyanese jungle in 1978 marks the period when cult awareness was at its height, although incidents like the Heaven's Gate mass suicide have kept cults in the headlines. Such is the degree of public suspicion of cults that, when necessary, government agencies could tap into this distrust and steer blame away from their own wrongdoing, as was the case when the Bureau of Alcohol, Tobacco, and Firearms and the F.B.I. burned the Branch Davidian compound in Waco, Texas, to the ground in 1993 after followers of cult leader David Koresh refused to surrender themselves to authorities. At the time of the massacre, media reportage was uniform in its condemnation of Koresh, and vociferous in its approval of the F.B.I.; it was only with the release of *Waco: The Rules of Engagement,* a 1997 documentary on the FBI's mishandling of the situation, that a dissenting note was finally heard.

America is not unique in its war between the "positive," socializing aspects of religion, and the esoteric, ecstatic spiritualism running in counterpoint beside it. "As Max Weber and Joachim Wach have illustrated in detail," writes Tom Wolfe, "every major modern religion, as well as countless long-gone minor ones, has originated not with a theology or set of values or a social goal or even a vague hope of a life hereafter. They have all originated, instead, with a small circle of people who have shared some overwhelming ecstasy or seizure, a 'vision,' a 'trance,' an hallucination; in short, an actual neurological event." This often-overlooked fact explains the suspicion with which mainstream religions view the plethora of cults that rolled over America since its founding, as well as the aversion cult members show to society at large once they have bonded with their fellows in spiritual ecstasy. It is precisely these feelings of uniqueness, of privileged insight, that fraudulent cult leaders work on in their efforts to mold cult members into spiritual slaves. The problem is this: not all cults are the creation of charlatans, but the opprobrium of society towards cults is by now so ingrained that on the matter of cults, there is no longer any question of reconciling the historical precedent with the contemporary manifestation.

But one salient fact can still be gleaned from the history of cults in modern America: to quote H.L. Mencken, "nobody ever went broke underestimating the intelligence of the American people." Americans are and will continue to be endlessly susceptible to simple, all-encompassing explanations, and what most cults share is a rigid dogmatism that brooks no argument, a hermetically sealed belief-system, eternally vulnerable to exposure from the world-at-large. The rage of a Jim Jones or Charles Manson springs from not only their personal manias, but in their impotence in controlling the world to suit their teachings. When cults turn ugly and self-destructive, it is often in reaction to this paradox. Like a light wind blowing on a house of cards, cults are fragile structures—it does not take much to set them tumbling down. Still, given mankind's pressing spiritual needs, and despite society's abhorrence, it seems likely that cult groups will continue to emerge in disturbing and occasionally frightening ways.

—Michael Baers

FURTHER READING:

Barrett, David V. *Sects, "Cults," and Alternative Religions: A World Survey and Sourcebook.* London, Blandford, 1996.

Christie-Murray, David. *A History of Heresy.* London, Oxford University Press, 1976.

Collins, John J. *The Cult Experience: An Overview of Cults, their Traditions, and Why People Join Them.* Springfield, Illinois, C. C. Thomas, 1991.

Jenkins, Philip. *Stoning the Prophets: Cults and Cult Scares in Modern America.* Oxford and New York, Oxford University Press, 2000.

Lane, Brian. *Killer Cults: Murderous Messiahs and their Fanatical Followers.* London, Headline, 1996.

Robbins, Thomas. *Cults, Converts & Charisma.* London, Sage Publications, 1988.

Stoner, Carroll, and Jo Anne Parke. *All God's Children.* Radnor, Pennsylvania, Chilton, 1977.

Wolfe, Tom. *Mauve Gloves and Madmen, Clutter and Vine: The Me Decade and the Third Great Awakening.* Toronto, Collins Publishers, 1976.

Yanoff, Morris. *Where Is Joey?: Lost Among the Hare Krishnas.* Athens, Ohio University Press, 1981.

Zellner, William W., and Marc Petrowsky, editors. *Sects, Cults, and Spiritual Communities: A Sociological Analysis.* Westport, Connecticut, Praeger, 1998.

Cunningham, Merce (1919—)

The dancer and choreographer Merce Cunningham influenced 20th century art with his postmodern dance and his collaborations with other important figures of the American art scene such as John Cage, Robert Rauschenberg, and Andy Warhol. With his own dance company, founded in 1953, Cunningham challenged traditional ideas of dance and the expectations of audiences. Cunningham declared all elements of a performance—music, dancing bodies, set, and costumes—to be of equal importance, and dispensed with conventional plots. His pioneering video work further questioned the use of the stage. Cunningham and his collaborators incorporated chance into the elaborate systems of their performances, creating abstract and haunting dances.

—Petra Kuppers

FURTHER READING:

Harris, Melissa, editor. *Merce Cunningham: Fifty Years.* New York, Aperture, 1997.

Kostelanetz, Richard, editor. *Merce Cunningham: Dancing in Space and Time.* New York, Da Capo Press, 1998.

Curious George

Since 1941, when Curious George was first introduced in an eponymous children's book, the mischievous monkey has been embraced by children and adults alike and has become a cultural icon. The hero of seven books for children co-created by H. A. and Margaret Rey, Curious George retains his appeal because he is like a universal child who often does what his readers are too afraid to do. As well-known author Madeleine L'Engle writes in the introduction to *The Complete Adventures of Curious George,* "George, like most true heroes, is a creature of action; he acts, rather than being acted upon."

Often referred to as the "father" of Curious George, Hans Augusto Rey (1898-1977) began drawing at the age of two. He had a passion for animals, which could be seen in his initial drawings and the menagerie of animals he kept as pets over the years. In his native Hamburg, Germany, H. A. often visited the nearby Hagenbeck Zoo, where he perfected his animal imitations. A love of languages helped H. A. to master four different tongues and encouraged a lifelong fascination with the study of linguistics. As a soldier fighting in World War I, H. A. would pass the time by studying the constellations in the evening sky. His interest in astronomy would later lead to two books on the subject, one written for a younger audience and the other for a more advanced reader.

Prior to leaving Germany in 1923 for Rio de Janeiro, H. A. met Margaret (1906-1996) through mutual friends. While H. A. was selling bathtubs in Brazil for a relative's firm, Margaret was studying art at the Bauhaus in Dessau, the Academy of Art in Dusseldorf, and attending art school in Berlin. She worked as a newspaper reporter and a copywriter for an advertising agency. In her memoir, included in *The Complete Adventures of Curious George,* Margaret explains how writing a jingle for a margarine campaign inspired a lifelong distaste for commercials.

In 1935 Margaret left Germany for Rio, where she and H. A. became collaborators in business as well as in life. According to Margaret, they formed "a sort of two-person advertising agency, doing a little of everything..." to make ends meet. After their marriage in 1936, the Reys traveled to Paris, planning to spend only a few weeks. Instead, their visit lasted four years. It was here in Paris that the little monkey first appeared on paper. H. A. had drawn funny illustrations of a giraffe for a Parisian magazine, which caught the attention of French publishing house Gallimard, who approached the illustrator about writing a children's story using the drawings. The result was *Cecily G. and the Nine Monkeys.* This book, which featured a monkey named George, led to other children's books, and if not for the start of World War II, the Reys might have remained in Paris.

In a tale that has become as legendary as their fictional creation, the Reys escaped Paris on bicycles one rainy morning in June of 1940. Strapped to their bike racks were their manuscripts, which included a draft of their first book, *Curious George.* Abandoning their bikes at the French-Spanish border, the Reys hopped a train to Lisbon. By October of that same year, they arrived in New York intent on selling their stories. Shortly after their arrival, they sold *Curious George* to publishers Houghton Mifflin, who released the book in 1941. For the next 20 years, the Reys lived and worked in New York, turning out six more Houghton Mifflin books about the curious monkey and his trusted companion, the man with the yellow hat.

According to Margaret, the Reys did not want to write another book about Curious George, and they took nearly six years to do other things before they published *Curious George Takes a Job* in 1947. Despite their apparent simplicity, the Curious George books took nearly a year to write and were often quite challenging for the couple. "Sometimes, it became more like mathematics than writing a book," Margaret once told an interviewer. Inspiration came from many places: friends, newspaper stories, even chance conversations with strangers. Generally, H. A. presided over the illustrations and Margaret wrote the stories, but the books more often were a complicated merger of the couple's various talents. As Margaret writes in her memoir, "at times it confused even us."

Many have pondered the appeal of Curious George since the first book appeared in 1941. Children like how the pictures tell the story, which liberates non-readers from their literate older brothers, sisters, or parents, and allows them to tell themselves the stories again and again. H. A.'s illustrations deftly capture a sense of George's mischievousness. In *Curious George,* the little monkey takes an unexpected swim in the ocean on his voyage from Africa to the United States, and the illustration of George coughing up sea water and swimming fish delightfully conveys the results of his curiosity. Children also can

An illustration depicting Curious George.

relate to George's curiosity and the trouble this frequently inspires. When the Reys wrote, ''George promised to be good, but sometimes little monkeys forget. . . ,'' they could have been writing about any little girl or boy. While George's adventures are thrilling, they also can be scary, and the man with the yellow hat adds a soothing quality to the stories since he often helps George out of his scrapes. George also shows readers that it is okay to be afraid and to cry, but his quick mind demonstrates the benefits of becoming self-reliant, too. Above all, Curious George entertains and delights readers of all ages.

In the 1960s, after writing nearly all of the seven *Curious George* books, the Reys moved from New York to Massachusetts. After a long illness, H. A. died in 1977. In the 1980s, Margaret and collaborator Alan J. Shelleck worked together on a second series of Curious George stories. Through various licensing agreements carefully selected by Margaret and secured through a series of legal battles in the 1990s, the instantly recognizable image of the curious little monkey began appearing on greeting cards, children's toys, clothing, and even CD-ROMs. Since 1941 when the first book appeared, the *Curious George* stories have sold more than 20 million copies and continue to have solid sales each year. *Curious George* sales received a boost in 1994 when the movie *Forrest Gump* featured a scene with Forrest's mother (played by Sally Field) reading a *Curious George* book to her son (played as an adult by Tom Hanks).

Poet W. H. Auden once wrote that a good children's book also should interest a clever adult. If this is true, then the *Curious George* series certainly qualify as good children's books. The stories have been translated into many languages, which further demonstrates their wide appeal. ''It does not matter much that there are some I cannot read,'' wrote Margaret about the different language versions of her books. ''It so happens that I know the story.''

—Alison Macor

FURTHER READING:

Rey, Margaret and H. A. Rey. *The Complete Adventures of Curious George.* Boston, Houghton Mifflin Company, 1994.

Williams, Karen. ''She Wrote From the Heart and Touched the Child in All of Us.'' *The Christian Science Monitor.* May 23, 1996, B3.

Currier and Ives

The decorative and hugely popular colored lithographs mass produced by Currier and Ives in the nineteenth century and familiar to subsequent generations through Christmas cards and calendars illustrate sporting scenes and sailing ships, noteworthy triumphs and disasters, Indian uprisings and comic vignettes, rustic beauty and domestic bliss, and, in general, evoke an idealized and sentimental view of life in nineteenth-century America. Typically, a well-known artist's work would be reproduced as a black-and-white lithograph, hand colored by a team of women, and distributed by the thousands at costs ranging from a few cents to a few dollars, depending on size. The firm was founded in New York City in 1834 by Nathaniel Currier, employed James Merritt Ives in 1852, and became Currier and Ives in 1857; the two were succeeded by their sons, who managed the company until its closing in 1907, by which time more than seven thousand different prints had been produced.

—Craig Bunch

FURTHER READING:

Baragwanath, Albert K. *Currier and Ives.* New York, Abbeville Press, 1980.

Currier and Ives: A Catalogue Raisonné. Detroit, Gale Research, 1984.

D

Dahmer, Jeffrey (1960-1994)

At his 1992 trial, Jeffrey Dahmer, an alcoholic worker in a chocolate factory, admitted to the murder of seventeen young men during a thirteen-year killing spree. His gruesome full disclosure, including accounts of cannibalism, fired the popular imagination and helped spawn a virtual cottage industry of books, trading cards, movies, and other products. But behind the monstrous ghoul of popular imagination, there lurked a desperately lonely young man whose killings were the result of years of progressive mental illness.

While pregnant with Dahmer, his mother, Joyce, endured a particularly trying pregnancy, suffering extended bouts of nausea and nervousness and strange fits of rigidity. Doctors prescribed morphine and phenobarbital, among other medications. At one point Joyce was taking twenty-six pills a day, immersing her fetus in a soup of powerful depressants. Joyce Dahmer also found nursing to be acutely unpleasant and within a week of Dahmer's birth was nursing him from a bottle. Nevertheless, Dahmer grew into a happy, normal child, although displaying an aversion to the roughhousing of most boys and a predilection for nonconfrontational games based on themes of stalking and concealment, such as hide-and-seek or kick the can. But after a hernia operation, six-year-old Dahmer's behavior changed profoundly. He became remote, fearful, and distant—sitting for hours

Jeffrey Dahmer

in front of the television without moving. Even his body language changed. His movements grew stiff and labored, like those of an old man.

By the time he began grade school, Dahmer had become so shy and reclusive that a teacher felt compelled to bring his behavior to his parents' attention. Nothing was done, and young Dahmer grew increasingly remote, submerged in a realm of unpleasant fantasies and, in increasing degrees, alcohol. In early adolescence, he often occupied himself by collecting road kills, stripping the flesh and assembling the bones in a nearby wood—once mounting a dog's head on a stick as a bizarre totem. In his late teens, Dahmer's obsessions had begun to overwhelm him. So fearful was he of others that he could only relate to them as inert objects. In 1978 he committed his first murder, picking up a hitchhiker and bringing him back to his parents' house where he plied him with beer and marijuana. As the hitchhiker prepared to depart, Dahmer killed the boy with a piece of gym equipment.

Unaware of Dahmer's blossoming psychosis, his father, Lionel—divorced and remarried—continued to counsel the apathetic boy to the best of his ability, insisting on his enrollment at Ohio State University. At the end of Dahmer's first quarter, he had earned a cumulative GPA of .45. He was returned home, and Lionel drove to the university to pick up his possessions, where he was further dismayed to learn that his son had done little else than drink, selling his plasma to secure the necessary funds. In frustration, his father insisted Dahmer join the military. Packed off to boot camp, Dahmer seemed to blossom under the rigid discipline, but the improvement was short-lived. Stationed for active duty in Germany, his behavior quickly lapsed into a nonstop debauch. He received an early discharge for drunkenness.

Now at his wits' end, the elder Dahmer packed his son off to live with his aging grandmother in a suburb outside Milwaukee. There, Dahmer's behavior became increasingly bizarre. Once, his grandmother found a fully clothed male mannequin in his closet; another time, a .357 under his bed. At times the house would be suffused with unpleasant odors. As he had in the past, Dahmer lamely explained away his activities, though he now convinced no one. Finally, he moved out of his grandmother's house. On the first day at his new apartment, he was arrested for drugging and molesting a thirteen-year-old Laotian boy. Dahmer served a year in a Milwaukee work-release program, during which time his father lobbied aggressively for additional treatment for his alcoholism. It was to no avail. In March of 1990, Dahmer was released on probation.

In the year and a half before his arrest, Dahmer, now living on his own, was able to indulge his tastes fully, killing thirteen men in the ensuing months. His modus operandi consisted of haunting the bars and street corners, trolling for a likely victim from amongst the hustlers who worked his neighborhood, many of them black, a fact that would later lead to charges that the murders were racially motivated when, in fact, the race of his victims was merely a consequence of proximity. To conceal his activities, Dahmer bought a freezer, installed an elaborate security system, and separated his bedroom from the rest of the apartment with a heavy metal door. Once secure within apartment 213, Dahmer would drug, then strangle his victim, molest the corpse, and finally eat or preserve parts of his victim as he saw fit, disposing of the remains with quicklime and an enormous plastic bucket. He was finally apprehended when a victim escaped his clutches, returning accompanied by police officers, who discovered polaroids of dead and dismembered men strewn about Dahmer's bedroom.

Hoping an insanity defense might lead to institutionalization rather than imprisonment, Dahmer chose a jury trial—during which he was protected from would-be assailants with the aid of a bullet-proof glass booth. Dahmer had said he wanted to find out why he did such things, but the only elucidation to come was to the ravenous public, who ate up the details of Dahmer's crimes. The jury, unmoved by his plea of insanity, sentenced him to nine consecutive life terms.

In prison, Dahmer found Jesus as well as the death he had long desired. He was fatally bludgeoned in 1994 while mopping a bathroom facility. (Dahmer's assailant, himself a convicted killer of questionable mental health, claimed he had acted under God's direction.) A figure at once pathetic and monstrous, Dahmer was generally reviled, although there was still something in his deflated appearance that generated sympathy. The wounded little boy had not been vanquished by the man's acts. And the enormous volume of letters Dahmer received after his incarceration, more often sympathetic than threatening, would seem to bear this out: he was not alone in his alienation. Ultimately, Dahmer killed not out of hatred, but out of loneliness.

In a final footnote to Dahmer's story, in 1996 a Milwaukee civic group bought his belongings for $407,000 to prevent their public auction on behalf of the victims' families. Instead of the auction block, Dahmer's possessions were incinerated, and the money was distributed to the families without fanfare.

—Michael J. Baers

FURTHER READING:

Baumann, Ed. *Step into My Parlour*. Chicago, Bonus Books, 1991.

Dahmer, Lionel. *A Father's Story*. New York, William Morrow and Company, 1994.

Dvochak, Robert, and Lisa Holewa. *Milwaukee Massacre: Jeffrey Dahmer and the Milwaukee Murders*. New York, Dell Paperbacks, 1991.

Masters, Brian. *Killing for Company: The Case of Dennis Nilsen*. New York, Stein and Day, 1985.

Ressler, Robert K., and Tom Shachtman. *I Have Lived in the Monster*. New York, St. Martin's Press, 1997.

Schwartz, Ann E. *The Man Who Could Not Kill Enough: The Secret Murders of Jeffrey Dahmer*. New York, Carol Publishing Group, 1992.

Tithecot, Richard. *Of Men and Monsters: Jeffrey Dahmer and the Construction of the Serial Killer*. Madison, University of Wisconsin Press, 1997.

Dallas

With the 1980 episode that answered the question "Who Shot J.R.?," *Dallas* became the most-watched program in the history of television. The originator of the prime-time soap opera, *Dallas'* serial

Larry Hagman (seated) with Steve Kanaly and Linda Gray as they appeared on *Dallas*.

stories about the exploits of a Texas oil family provided fodder for water-cooler gossip as well as real bookie-joint wagering. The program enjoyed a 13 year run, making superstars of Larry Hagman, Victoria Principal, Patrick Duffy, and others. The program foundered in the early 1990s and is remembered more than any other program as the epitome of the unabashedly capitalistic Reagan era.

Premiering April 2, 1978 on CBS, the series revolved around the relationships and tribulations of patriarch Jock Ewing and wife "Miss Ellie" (played by Jim Davis and Barbara Bel Geddes) and their three sons: J.R. (Hagman), the deceitful, conniving businessman who with his father ran the family oil company; Bobby (Duffy) a freewheeling playboy as the series began; and Gary (first David Ackroyd, then Ted Shackelford), a weak-willed alcoholic who long ago had fled the family's Southfork Ranch. J.R.'s wife was boozy Sue Ellen (Linda Gray). Bobby, in the series' first episode, eloped with Pamela (Victoria Principal), the sexy daughter of family arch-enemy Digger Barnes. Their marriage set the stage for years of conflict, especially with Pamela's brother Cliff (Ken Kercheval).

In early episodes, the series was structured as a traditional weekly drama; each episode presented a stand-alone story, with Pamela ostensibly the focal point of the narrative. It quickly became clear, however, that wily J.R. was the real favorite of both the series' writers and the audience. By 1979, the series threaded continuing stories through several stand-alone episodes. Alcoholic Sue Ellen turned up pregnant: was the baby J.R.'s or Cliff's? J.R.'s turncoat secretary Julie (Tina Louise) was murdered: would J.R. succeed in framing Cliff for the killing?

The series settled into a Friday at 10:00 p.m time-slot, growing in popularity until the final episode of the 1979-1980 season, when J.R. was shot by an unknown assailant. There was no shortage of suspects: he had spent the season acquiring, then unloading what proved to be worthless Asian oil leases, swindling everyone from the family banker to his own mother in the process; he had driven Bobby and Pam off Southfork; and he had shipped wife Sue Ellen off to a sanitarium, even as he bedded her younger sister.

During that summer of 1980, *Dallas* fever exploded. "Who Shot J.R.?" was a sensation, the subject of everything from fan speculation to Las Vegas betting. The press scrambled in vain to uncover details of the fall scripts; elaborate security precautions were put into effect at the studio. Producers took no chances; each actor was brought in to film scenes of his or her character "shooting" J.R.

A lingering actors' strike—and Larry Hagman's demand for a raise—threatened the solution to the mystery, but the public finally learned the answer on November 21, 1980. Sue Ellen's sister Kristin, J.R.'s former mistress, had pulled the trigger, infuriated by J.R.'s attempts to run her out of town. Sue Ellen herself solved the mystery, realizing her sister was plotting to frame her for the crime. Unfortunately, Kristin revealed she was pregnant with J.R.'s baby; instead of sending her to prison, J.R. shipped his assailant off to California, where she would have her illegitimate child in secret. The episode set an all-time ratings record: an unprecedented 53.3 Nielsen mark, meaning more than half of America's television households were tuned in—the highest rating in history, a figure exceeded only once in later years.

Dallas was now the most popular series on American television. Actor Jim Davis passed away in early 1981 and Jock was eventually written out of the series. His will set up a power struggle at Ewing Oil that unfolded over most of the 1982-1983 season, arguably the series' creative peak. Barbara Bel Geddes (Miss Ellie) departed for health reasons in 1984; she was replaced by Donna Reed. Barely a year later, Reed was reportedly livid to discover she had been fired to make way for Bel Geddes' return. She sued the series' producers.

Meanwhile, J.R. and Sue Ellen divorced, remarried, then divorced again; Bobby and Pam had also divorced by 1984. The characters were moving toward reconciliation when actor Patrick Duffy announced he was leaving the show. In the final episode of the 1984-1985 season, Bobby was killed—murdered by his deranged former sister-in-law, even as he had just professed his undying love for Pam.

Yet even as the series spun its larger-than-life stories, it also managed to capture the real-life flavor of a turbulent decade: the 1982-1983 recession figured prominently in the story; later, the mid-decade mania of big-business mergers and take-overs was reflected on-screen. The fictional Ewing Oil was now worth two billion dollars, but the *Dallas* franchise itself was priceless to CBS and its affiliates.

The series had begotten one spin-off (brother Gary and wife Val set up housekeeping in *Knots Landing* in 1979) and a host of imitators, from *Falcon Crest* to *Flamingo Road* to *Dynasty*. *Dynasty*, in particular, caught the public's fancy. Where *Dallas'* stories had at least some grounding in real life, *Dynasty* was simply glamorous, over-the-top high camp. By the end of the 1984-1985 season, *Dynasty* ran neck-and-neck with *Dallas* for the number one position in the ratings.

A behind-the-scenes shakeup followed; that *Dallas* suddenly looked a lot more like *Dynasty*—soapier plots, more elaborate costumes—was apparently no coincidence. When a *Cosby*-led sitcom resurgence pushed all the evening soaps down the ratings chart by 1986, the production staff was overhauled again: much of the old guard returned, and Larry Hagman began assuming some creative control over the series. Hagman himself reportedly engineered one of the biggest television coups of 1986 when he personally convinced Patrick Duffy to return to the series. In the final 1985-1986 episode, Pamela awoke from a night's sleep, only to find the long-dead Bobby lathering up in her shower. The audience was left to wonder all summer: Who was that? How did he get there? The cliffhanger was nearly as big a sensation as "Who Shot J.R." had been six years earlier, and the producers hyped it expertly—going so far as to film fake footage, then allowing it to find its way into the tabloids.

"Bobby in the Shower" was an inspired stunt; the resolution was a disaster. In the opening moments of the fall season, it was revealed that Bobby had never died; instead, Pamela had simply dreamt the entire 1985-1986 season. An entire year's worth of narrative and character development were simply wiped out. Fans howled in protest; the move was a critical and creative debacle.

The episode also turned out to be the last great moment of the "prime-time soap" craze. *Dynasty*'s ratings had collapsed; *Dallas,* while strong, was losing ground. Victoria Principal departed in 1987; several supporting characters were written out about the same time. Everyone from Priscilla Presley to a young Brad Pitt had passed through Southfork by this time, but the characters' antics were becoming sillier. A stranger claimed to be the presumed-dead Jock; he was revealed as an impostor. J.R's dirty dealings finally cost him Ewing Oil; he went into business for himself. In 1988, J.R. was held captive by some good ol' boys in Arkansas; he later married their virgin young sister. The character's 1990 stay in a mental institution (he had infiltrated it to meet a business contact, only to find himself committed by his disgruntled illegitimate son) was a low point.

Yet even in its dotage, the series made waves. Location filming in Europe and the Soviet Union in 1989 drew considerable press; later that year, CBS switchboards lit up when Linda Gray's final appearance as Sue Ellen was interrupted for news bulletins (the network repented by showing the "missing minutes" in late-night several weeks later). An experimental return to single-story episodes in 1988 drew little attention; a try-out of several-episode "story arcs" in 1990 featured a guest appearances by Susan Lucci and a reunion with Hagman's *I Dream of Jeannie* co-star Barbara Eden. The venerable series ended its run in May, 1991, with a take-off of *It's A Wonderful Life* where J.R. was visited not by an angel, but by a messenger of Satan (Joel Grey) who, along with favorite characters from the past, presented a series of vignettes demonstrating what life would have been had J.R. never been born. In the series' final scene, the mysterious visitor goaded the character into an apparent suicide attempt.

A pair of mid-1990s reunion movies (J.R. of course had not killed himself, but merely shot a mirror!) failed utterly to capture the spirit of the series in its best day. Inevitably, *Dallas*'s day had come and gone. The free-wheeling, politically incorrect, every-man-for-himself age of the 1980s had long since passed; indeed, *Dallas* was as much period piece as soap, a true historical artifact that both reflects and explains the culture that elevated it to its legendary status.

—Chris Chandler

FURTHER READING:

Brooks, Tim, and Earle Marsh. *The Complete Directory To Prime Time Network And Cable TV Shows.* New York, Ballantine Books, 1995.

The Dallas Cowboys

The NFL's Dallas Cowboys have been characterized as America's team, thanks to their winning ways and their once squeaky clean image. Their immense popularity comes largely from their success, for the team has won five Super Bowls. The stability of the organization has also been unique. The team has had only three owners and four head coaches, Tom Landry, Jimmy Johnson, Barry Switzer, and Chan Gailey. The first three men led the Cowboys to Super Bowl wins. Landry established himself as one of the greatest coaches in the history of the National Football League. Star players also established the Cowboy's legacy. A brief list of some of the Cowboys reads like a Who's Who of the football world; Bob Lilly, Mel Renfro, Roger Staubach, Randy White, Tony Dorsett, Michael Irvin, Emmitt Smith, and Troy Aikman are just a few of the names associated with the

success of the Dallas Cowboys. The Cowboys are also well known for the prominence of their cheerleading squad, named simply the Dallas Cowboy Cheerleaders. Emerging in the mid-1970s as beguiling half-time entertainment, the cheerleading squad has thousands of fans of its own, as evidenced by the sales of calendars and the turnout at promotional events.

Dallas was awarded a National Football League expansion franchise in 1960. The Cowboys lost their inaugural game 35-28 to Pittsburgh on September 24, 1960. The Cowboys got their first win in 1961 with a 27-24 victory over the Pittsburgh Steelers in the Cotton Bowl in Dallas. In 1966, the Cowboys won their first Eastern Conference championship but lost the NFL Championship to the Green Bay Packers 34-27. Throughout the 1960s the Cowboys were prime competitors for the NFL championship. In 1967, the Cowboys fell to Green Bay 21-17 in the NFL Championship. The game, generally regarded as one of the greatest games in the history of professional football, has become known as the Ice Bowl because it was played in Green Bay in temperatures dropping as low as 13 degrees below zero. In 1969, Cowboy quarterback Don Meredith, who went on to further fame announcing Monday Night Football with Howard Cosell and Frank Gifford, retired. As an announcer Meredith was best known for singing the phrase, ''Turn out the lights. The party's over,'' once the outcome of a game was no longer in doubt.

The Dallas Cowboy Cheerleaders

In 1970, the Cowboys once again won the Eastern Division championship, but lost in their first Super Bowl appearance to the Baltimore Colts, 16-13. In 1971, the Cowboys moved from the Cotton Bowl in Dallas to Texas Stadium in suburban Irving, a facility known for a large hole in the roof, left to preserve the atmosphere of an outdoor stadium, but providing fans with protection from the rain. That year the Cowboys marched through the playoffs and won their first NFL Championship by beating the Miami Dolphins 24-3 in Super Bowl VI in New Orleans. Dallas quarterback Roger Staubach passed for two touchdowns and was named the Most Valuable Player.

The Cowboys missed the playoffs for the first time in eight years when they stumbled to an 8-6 record in 1974. In 1975, the Cowboy's returned to the playoffs as a wild card team. In the opening round, they shocked Minnesota on a last second 50-yard touchdown completion from Roger Staubach to Drew Pearson. One of the most famous plays in NFL history, the pass became known as the Hail Mary. Despite contending for the championship for the next several years, the Cowboys would not win the title again until 1977, when Dallas defeated the Denver Broncos 27-10. Defensive linemen Harvey Martin and Randy White were named co-Most Valuable Players.

On March 31, 1980, legendary quarterback Roger Staubach retired, and on August 2, 1980, Bob Lilly became the first Cowboy to enter the Professional Football Hall of Fame. Behind new quarterback Danny White, the Cowboys made the playoffs as a wild card team and beat Los Angeles 34-13 and Atlanta 30-27 to advance to the NFC Championship, where they lost 20-7 to Philadelphia. In May of 1984 Clint Murchison sold the Cowboys to H.R. ''Bum'' Bright. The Cowboys then went on to post a 9-7 record and miss the playoffs for the first time in 10 years.

In 1986, the Cowboys streak of 20 consecutive winning seasons was broken when the club finished 7-9. Jerry Jones purchased the Cowboys from Bright in 1989 and shocked the city of Dallas, the state of Texas, and Cowboy fans everywhere when he unceremoniously replaced Tom Landry, the Cowboy's only coach for 29 seasons, with University of Miami head coach Jimmy Johnson. Landry was inducted into the Pro Football Hall of Fame on August 4, 1990.

In 1991, for the first time since 1985, Dallas was back in the playoffs as a wild card. Dallas defeated the Chicago Bears 17-13 in the opening round of the playoffs but then lost 38-6 to the Detroit Lions. The Cowboys claimed the Eastern Division Championship in 1992. They then advanced to the NFC Championship, where they beat the San Francisco 49ers 30-20 and then defeated the Buffalo Bills 52-17 in Super Bowl XXVII in Pasadena. The Cowboys repeated as Super Bowl champions the following year, when they again defeated Buffalo by the score of 30-13.

Due to difficulties with owner Jerry Jones, Jimmy Johnson resigned as the Cowboys head coach, and Barry Switzer became the third head coach in team history on March 30, 1994. Tony Dorsett and Randy White were inducted into the Pro Football Hall of Fame on July 30, 1994. Later that year the Cowboys went on to capture the Eastern Division Championship. However, the Cowboys lost the NFC Championship game to San Francisco 38-28.

In 1995, the Cowboys were again Eastern Division Champions. Dallas beat Green Bay 38-27 to advance to Super Bowl XXX, where the Cowboys knocked off Pittsburgh 27-17. Mel Renfro was inducted into the Pro Football Hall of Fame in 1996; but the Cowboys did not continue to enjoy success under Switzer, and he was replaced by Chan Gailey after the 1997 season. In Gailey's first season as the Cowboys head coach, Dallas won the NFC Eastern Division, but lost in the first round of the playoffs to Arizona 20-7. Few teams in NFL history can

claim the consistent record of success associated with the Dallas Cowboys. They remain one of the preeminent franchises in football history.

—Kerry Owens

FURTHER READING:

''Cowboys.'' http://www.dallascowboys.com. April 1999.

Donovan, Jim, Ken Sins, and Frank Coffey. *The Dallas Cowboys Encyclopedia: The Ultimate Guide to America's Team.* Revised edition. Secaucus, New Jersey, Carol Publishing Group, 1999.

Golenbock, Peter. *Cowboys Have Always Been My Heroes: The Definitive Oral History of America's Team.* New York, Warner Books, 1997.

Johnson, Jimmy, and Ed Hinton. *Turning the Thing Around: Pulling America's Team Out of the Dumps.* New York, Heperton Press, 1993.

Landry, Tom, and Greg Lewis. *Tom Landry: An Autobiography.* Grand Rapids, Michigan, Zondervan Publishing House, 1990.

St. John, Bob. *Tex! The Man Who Built the Dallas Cowboys.* Englewood Hills, New Jersey, Prentice Hall, 1988.

Stowers, Carlton. *Dallas Cowboys: The First Twenty-Five Years.* Dallas, Taylor Publishing, 1984.

Sugar, Bert Randolph. *I Hate the Dallas Cowboys: And Who Elected Them America's Team Anyway?* New York, St. Martin's Griffin, 1997.

Wolfe, Jane. *The Murchisons: The Rise and Fall of a Texas Dynasty.* New York, St. Martin's Press, 1989.

Daly, Tyne (1946—)

Actress Tyne Daly earned her high profile through her three-dimensional portrayal of Mary Beth Lacey, the dark-haired, well-grounded foil and partner to Sharon Gless's blonde, less stable Christine Cagney in television's pioneering female cop series in the 1980s. She went on to demonstrate her versatility with a stunning, Tony Award-winning performance as Mama Rose in the Broadway revival of the musical *Gypsy* in 1989.

Born Ellen Tyne Daly in Madison, Wisconsin, one of four children of actors James Daly and Hope Newell, she drifted into acting over her parents' objections. Ironically, she audition for the role of young Louise (Gypsy Rose Lee) to Ethel Merman's Mama Rose in the original *Gypsy* in 1959, but failed to get the part. Her first television appearance was in *The Virginian,* followed by a brief run with the soap opera *General Hospital* and guest appearances on several other shows. Daly made a handful of films, including *The Enforcer* (1976) opposite Clint Eastwood, before earning her first Emmy Award nomination for the television movie *Intimate Strangers* (1977), and made a number of other TV films before beginning her run in *Cagney and Lacey* in 1982. In real life a divorced mother of three children, Daly brought sympathy and conviction to her role as an undercover detective, coping with the pressures of New York police work while dealing with husband, home, children, and even pregnancy. Her consistently appealing performance over the show's seven seasons earned her six Emmy nominations and four best actress awards.

—James R. Belpedio

FURTHER READING:

Brooks, Tim and Earle Marsh. *The Complete Directory to Prime Time Network and Cable TV Shows 1946-Present.* 6th edition. New York, Ballantine Books, 1995.

Dana, Bill (1924—)

In the heyday of the network era of broadcasting, writer, actor, and producer Bill Dana created a nationally recognized comic character who endured in the American consciousness for over a decade. When that character first uttered his signature phrase, "My name . . . Jose Jimenez," on *The Steve Allen Show* in 1959, he became one of the clearest representatives of a familiar American type. Portraying a Mexican immigrant on the bottom half of the social ladder, Dana's Jimenez worked at various times as an elevator operator and a bellboy. By today's standards, that portrayal, which included Jimenez's broken English and naive innocence, appears to many condescending at best. However, Jimenez was a singularly noble character, possessing goodness, wisdom, and sincerity, traits comparatively unusual in the history of American TV characters. Although he exhibited

Bill Dana

stereotypical racial characteristics common to the period, at the same time Jimenez displayed more positive tendencies. He was confused and clueless, but also resourceful and crafty; he had a stereotypically huge family back home, but he supported them faithfully through the sweat of his own brow; he worked as a salaried servant of the wealthier residents of the hotel, but he often proved kinder and smarter than his social superiors.

Like many film and television actors, the public identity of Bill Dana became inseparable from the celebrated persona he portrayed. What was unusual about Dana/Jimenez, however, was that he was able to escape the show on which he first appeared and to move fluidly, and often simultaneously, to an assortment of other venues. After Dana introduced Jimenez on *The Steve Allen Show,* the character resurfaced regularly over the next five years on *The Spike Jones Show, The Danny Thomas Show,* and *The New Steve Allen Show,* as well as becoming the principal character of *The Bill Dana Show* (NBC, 1963-1965). Through the 1960s, Dana also made guest appearances as Jimenez on a wide variety of contemporary TV series and featured the character in several comedy record albums. Dana (as Jimenez) even showed up briefly in the 1983 feature film, *The Right Stuff.*

By 1970, the ethnic humor and dialect comedy upon which Jose Jimenez depended was growing increasingly less fashionable. The fact that Dana was not himself Hispanic intensified developing claims that the character was a racist representation. As American television moved into the more politically conscious "relevance" era of the 1970s with shows like *All in the Family, M*A*S*H,* and *The Mary Tyler Moore Show,* Jimenez became a vestige of a bygone time and all but disappeared. Released from his signature creation, however, Dana would reemerge in other roles.

Born William Szathmary in Quincy, Massachusetts, on October 5, 1924, Dana entered the television industry in 1950 as a page at NBC in New York City. Through the 1950s he performed in nightclubs and played bit parts on television shows. He worked as a production assistant on *The Phil Silvers Show,* wrote for *The Milton Berle Show,* and got his big break when he was hired as a writer on *The Steve Allen Show* in 1956. He moved up to head writer, earning an Emmy nomination for his work, and became a performer on the show in 1959.

Though his other achievements were eclipsed by the popularity of his Jose Jimenez, Dana also wrote and produced for the several shows in which Jimenez was featured, and, as a character actor of some note, he played guest roles on a number of series, including *Get Smart, The Man from U.N.C.L.E.,* and *Batman.* Dana's presence on American TV waned after the retirement of the Jose Jimenez character, though he did continue to play occasional parts in TV series into the 1970s. One of the brightest spots in his career came in 1972 when he wrote the classic episode of *All in the Family* in which Sammy Davis, Jr. visits the Bunker household.

In the 1980s, when Jose Jimenez had become a distant memory, Bill Dana moved into a new period of activity. Having appeared in *Get Smart,* he co-wrote and acted in *The Nude Bomb* (1980), a feature film based upon the TV comedy. He was in the principal cast of two network comedy series, *No Soap, Radio* (ABC, 1982) and *Zorro and Son* (CBS, 1983), but neither of these lasted longer than a few months. In 1988 and 1989, he also wrote for and appeared on a series of specials featuring the Smothers Brothers, who had appeared regularly on *Steve Allen* in 1961. During this decade, Dana was also reunited with many other of his co-stars from *The Steve Allen Show,* including Allen himself, Jayne Meadows, Louis Nye, and Tom Poston, all of whom played recurring guest roles with Dana on the hit medical drama *St. Elsewhere* (NBC, 1982-1988).

—Robert Thompson

Dance Halls

Dancing has been regarded as a social institution in America for over a century. Many famous dance venues, from the Cotton Club and Roseland in New York, the Avalon Ballroom on Catalina Island, Aly Baba in Oakland, to the Old Roosevelt Hotel in New Orleans, attest to the tremendous influence which dancing has had on American culture. These are just a few of the popular meeting spots where people interact socially and can be seen publicly, dancing to the popular music of the day. Local community dance halls thrive in recreation centers, churches, and high school gymnasia as well as commercial night clubs. The primary requirement in any dance hall is to provide ample music and the room for people to dance. Food and beverages are often served as light refreshments, and seating arrangements allow people to meet, to comment, and to view others who are out on the dance floor. An important concept of the dance hall is ''to see and be seen,'' and rites of passage into society including coming-of-age events, proms and pageants, ceremonies such as weddings, and musical debuts have centered around dance events and subsequently are popular uses for dance halls.

The forum of entertainment generally known as the dance hall evolved over the course of several centuries, taking on a distinctive function and purpose in each succeeding generation. The notion of halls as social meeting places may have its origins in northern Europe during the middle ages, when one large, central room with an elevated ceiling was used for dining, reveling, convening, and even sleeping by large groups of tenants and visitors of no particular relation. The British connotation of the word ''hall'' more often refers to a large common room used as a meeting place for particular events. By contrast, the American sense of the word, as a central space or passageway usually into which the front door opens, is related in the sense that the hall is a room common to all people who enter a particular building.

As feudal houses grew in stature and European nobility became more pronounced, ''great halls'' were designed as distinct chambers for meeting and gathering. Great halls were featured in many palaces and country manors of the 14th through 18th century, used as places of social gathering for important events, coronations, festivals, and celebrations. Court dancing evolved in these great halls throughout Europe, developing intricate codes of conduct and ritual which persisted through the turn of the 20th century. Grand balls were an important social component of the 17th through the 19th centuries, and dancing was regarded as a prime element of display, courtship, and social manners. Dance balls of the Victorian era usually lasted entire evenings, where the hosts served multi-coursed suppers and attendees literally danced ''until they dropped,'' finding back rooms and quiet corners to sleep when they could dance no longer. It is notable that most dance events of the western hemisphere are for the celebration of social occasions. In the east, dancing is more often reserved strictly for religious ceremonies, with elaborate costumes and traditions which have remained intact for centuries.

The modern dance hall has a more obscure origin. Dance halls in America seem to have grown out of refugee immigration from eastern and southern Europe during the mid-1900s. Folk dancing, most particularly the polka, has enjoyed a rich tradition in the immigrant working-class, who find dancing to be an essential element of recreation after long hours in labor-intensive jobs. Dance halls naturally grew up around this need to socialize. Many dance hall regulars attribute the Polish immigration of the 1940s and 1950s with the establishment of the American dance hall. The Nazi and Soviet occupations, leading up to the outbreak of World War II, forced thousands of working-class and minority Poles and Slavs to come to the United States. Once arrived, Polish immigrants succeeded in venerating traditional customs including social folk dancing. Primary among these was the polka. Polka parties, international polka associations, and dance competitions continue to thrive in the late 20th century in the United States, while in eastern Europe this dance form has virtually died out, mostly likely due to the influence of foreign political regimes.

In rural areas, dance halls are generally known for their live bands, and it is not unusual for attendees to drive in from 50 to 100 miles away. Dance halls in rural areas tend to feature food and beverages more prominently, whereas the urban disco will emphasize dance floor decorations, settings, and acoustics. The dance hall's modern cousin, the discotheque or night club, has distinctly urban origins. Discotheques, or discos, began in Paris with the advent of the phonograph album in the late 1950s and early 1960s. Discos tend to feature more modern forms of popular music, and many new dances have been invented in reaction to new music. Whether the music is being played live or in recordings, the important feature of all dance halls, night clubs, and discos is the emphasis on dancing and socializing.

A resurgence in vintage dancing, most notably 1930s-1940s era swing parties and 19th century Victorian dance balls, has flowered in the United States during the 1980s and 1990s. Vintage dance balls tend to emphasize social entertainment through historic recreation. These recreations can be very elaborate, and authentic period attire or costume recreations, selected beverages and foods of the era, and the teaching and calling of traditional dance forms are key elements of vintage dance events. Attendees are often educated professionals or middle-class descendants of European immigrants. Music is most often supplied by live musicians, although recorded music may be featured in regular clubs.

Dance halls in the 1990s have often featured a wide variety of dance events on their calendars. Many dance halls are rented out for rehearsals, parties, social occasions and receptions, or are otherwise used for public recreational evenings which may or may not feature noted bands. Attendees tend to favor one form or series of forms over others based on cultural bias, perceived social stature, or personal tastes. Fans of noted bands will anticipate scheduled appearances and may prepare for occasions for months in advance. In general, attendees may gather for celebration of a particular event such as a wedding reception, or as a regular social activity with their friends.

—Ethan Hay

FURTHER READING:

Blank, Les. *In Heaven There Is No Beer?* (video). El Cerrito, California, Flower Films, 1984.

Croce, Arlene. *Going to the Dance*. New York, Knopf, 1982.

Jonas, Gerald. *Dancing: The Pleasure, Power, and Art of Movement*. New York, Harry N. Abrams, 1992.

Keller, Kate Van Winkle. *The Playford Ball.* Remington, New Jersey, A Capella Books, 1990.

McDonagh, Don. *Dance Fever.* New York, Random House, 1979.

Saltie, Randolph. *Putting On Perfect Proms, Programs and Pageants.* New York, F. Watts, 1991.

Dandridge, Dorothy (1924-1965)

Born in Cleveland, Ohio, actor-singer-entertainer Dorothy Dandridge was smart, immensely talented, and alluringly beautiful. In her three-decade career in Hollywood she endured the bittersweet distinction of being the first sexy black woman film artist of the postwar period. Dandridge attempted to forge a career in Hollywood when the only roles for black women were as servants, or in brief, non-speaking cameo roles. Dandridge claimed a number of "firsts": she was the first African American woman to grace the covers of *Life* magazine; the first black woman to showcase the posh, all-white Waldorf-Astoria; and the first black woman to receive an Oscar nomination for a leading role. Dandridge's film credits include *Bright Road* (1953), *Carmen Jones* (1954), *Tamango* (1957), *Island in the Sun* (1957), *The Decks Ran Red* (1958), *Porgy and Bess* (1959) and *Malanga* (1959). Dandridge's tragedy-filled life and her mysterious death on September 8, 1965, resulted in exposés, film biographies, and a major biography.

—Pamala S. Deane

Charlie Daniels

FURTHER READING:

Bogle, Donald. *Blacks in American Films and Television.* New York: Garland, 1988.

———. *Dorothy Dandridge: A Biography,* New York, Amistad, 1997.

Dandridge, Dorothy, and Earl Conrad. *Everything and Nothing: The Dorothy Dandridge Tragedy.* New York, Abelard-Schuman, 1970.

"Dorothy Dandridge, 41, Found Dead in Home." *Washington Evening Star.* September 9, 1965.

"Dorothy Dandridge, Victim of Freak Fall." *The Afro American* (Baltimore, Maryland). September 18, 1965.

"Dorothy Dandridge's Greatest Triumph." *Ebony.* July, 1954.

"Hollywood's New Glamour Queen." *Ebony.* April, 1951.

"Island In the Sun: Dandridge, Belafonte Star in Romantic Interracial Film." *Ebony.* July, 1957.

Johnson, Albert. "Beige, Brown, or Black." *Film Quarterly.* Fall, 1959.

"The Private World of Dorothy Dandridge." *Ebony.* June, 1962.

Robinson, Louie. "Dorothy Dandridge: Hollywood's Tragic Enigma." *Ebony.* March, 1966.

Daniels, Charlie (1936—)

Charlie Daniels came to prominence during the early 1970s, at a time when country music was caught up in Vietnam patriotism and anti-hippie sentiment. Rock was the music of the counterculture, which saw the South through newsreels of civil rights battles and movies like *Easy Rider.* A white southern band had to choose one or

the other, and many followed the lead of the likes of the Allman Brothers to create the sound known as Southern Rock. The Charlie Daniels Band began as Southern Rockers with an anti-redneck anthem, "Uneasy Rider" (1973), a song about a longhaired guy going into a bar full of good old boys. One of the few musicians to fit into both rock and country genres, Daniels' manipulated his image and music brilliantly in an attempt to capture his place in twentieth-century popular culture.

Most of the Southern Rockers separated themselves totally from country music . . . and they remained separate. Even in the 1980s and 1990s, when rock had become a staple of the new country sound, groups like the Allman Brothers, Little Feat, and the Marshall Tucker Band never showed up at country concerts or on the country charts. Daniels was an exception. Right from the start he managed to keep a presence in both worlds, working as a studio fiddle player on Nashville sessions. When pop came to Nashville, Daniels was there, playing hot fiddle parts on Bob Dylan's album *Nashville Skyline.* Even "Uneasy Rider" made the lower rungs of the country charts (it was in the top ten on the pop charts).

Southern Rock faded as a chart phenomenon with the end of the 1970s; it did, however, retain a core audience. Daniels then made his move toward country. In 1980, country music was in the grip of the Urban Cowboy phenomenon, and there was a lot of country overlap on the pop charts. Daniels was no Urban Cowboy, but he was an artist with the capacity to play to both audiences, and he made the most of it with his biggest hit "The Devil Went Down to Georgia," which hit number one on the country charts and was number three as a pop hit. It won him a Grammy for best country music performance by a group, and the Country Music Association award for Single of the Year. The single was Daniels' high water mark as his career was middling through the 1980s. He continued to have a mystique of sorts, remaining signed to the same label (Epic), releasing one record after another, and never cracking the top ten—mostly, in fact, languishing near the bottom of the charts.

Then, in 1989, Daniels had another career breakthrough. His hit album, *A Simple Man,* aggressively advocated the lynching of bad guys and hopped onto the anti-communist bandwagon (a little late) by suggesting that it would not be such a bad idea to assassinate Gorbachev. And, as a final rejection of his youthful fling with the counterculture, he recorded a new version of ''Uneasy Rider'' in which the hero is himself—one of the good old boys from whom the original uneasy rider had his narrow escape. This time, he accidentally wanders into a gay bar. Daniels had made himself over completely, from protest-era rebel to Reagan-era conservative.

—Tad Richards

Dannay, Frederic

See Queen, Ellery

Daredevil, the Man Without Fear

Daredevil, the Man Without Fear is a superhero comic book published by Marvel Comics since 1965. Blinded by a childhood accident involving radioactivity that has also mysteriously enhanced his remaining senses to superhuman levels, defense attorney Matt Murdock trains himself to physical perfection, and crusades for justice as the costumed Daredevil.

Daredevil remained a consistently popular but decidedly second-tier Marvel superhero until the late 1970s when writer/artist Frank Miller assumed the creative direction of the series. By emphasizing the disturbing obsessive and fascistic qualities of the superhero as a modern vigilante, Miller transformed *Daredevil* into one of the most graphic, sophisticated, and best written comic books of its time. His work on the series became a standard for a new generation of comic-book creators and fans who came to expect more violence and thematic maturity from their superheroes.

—Bradford Wright

FURTHER READING:

Daniels, Les. *Marvel: Five Fabulous Decades of the World's Greatest Comics.* New York, Harry N. Abrams, 1991.

Lee, Stan. *Origins of Marvel Comics.* New York, Simon & Schuster, 1974.

Dark Shadows

In the world of continuing daytime drama, or ''the soaps,'' *Dark Shadows* remains an anomaly. Unlike any other day or evening

television show, *Dark Shadows'* increasing popularity over the course of its five year run from 1966 to 1971 led to the creation of two feature films entitled *House of Dark Shadows* and *Night of Dark Shadows,* a hit record album of themes from the show, and a series of 30 novels, comic books, and other paraphernalia—a development unheard of in the world of daytime television. *Dark Shadows* had unexpectedly evolved from another afternoon soap into a cultural phenomenon and franchise. Indeed, *Dark Shadows* was in a genre all to itself during this period of twentieth-century television history.

Like other soaps, *Dark Shadows* dealt with forbidden love and exotic medical conditions. Unlike any other, however, its conflicts tended to extend beyond the everyday material most soaps cover into more ''otherworldly'' phenomena. Nestled in the fog-enshrouded coastal town of Collinsport, Maine, the Collins family was repeatedly plagued by family curses which involved ghosts, vampires, werewolves, and ''phoenixes''—mothers who come back from the dead to claim and then kill their children. In fact, there were as many curses as there were locked rooms and secret passageways in the seemingly endless family estate known as Collinwood. Characters had to travel back and forth in time, as well as ''parallel time'' dimensions, in order to unravel and solve the mysteries that would prevent future suffering.

Amazingly, despite its cancellation some 30 years ago and the fact that during its time on the air it was constantly threatened with cancellation by the management of ABC, *Dark Shadows* is fondly remembered by many baby-boomers as ''the show you ran home after school to watch'' in those pre-VCR days. It is the subject of dozens of fan websites and chatrooms, an online college course, and even a site where fans have endeavored to continue writing episodes speculating what might have transpired after the last episode was broadcast in 1971. There are even yearly conventions held by the International Dark Shadows Society celebrating the show and featuring former cast members who are asked to share their memories.

The concept for *Dark Shadows* originated in the mind of Emmy-winning sports producer Dan Curtis, who wanted to branch out into drama. His dream of a mysterious young woman journeying to an old dark house—which would hold the keys to her past and future—became the starting point, establishing the gothic tone which combined elements of Jane Eyre with *The Turn of the Screw*—the latter of which would figure repeatedly in later plotlines.

The young woman was known as Victoria Winters (Alexandra Moltke). She accepted a post as a governess of ten-year-old David Collins (David Henesy), heir to the family fortune and companion to Collinwood's stern and secretive mistress, Elizabeth Collins (Joan Bennett). Believing herself to be an orphan (she is in fact the illegitimate daughter of Elizabeth Collins), Victoria senses that the keys to her past and future lie with the Collins family.

While plot complications in the first few months of the show concerned mysterious threats on Victoria's life, there was little in the turgid conflicts between the Collins family and a vengeful local businessman to attract viewers, and ratings were declining rapidly. This is when Curtis decided to jazz things up by introducing the first of the series' many ghosts. While exploring in an obscure part of the rambling Collins estate, young David encounters the ghost of a young woman, Josette DuPres. As ratings began to rise, Josette becomes integral in helping to protect David from Curtis' next supernatural phenomenon—the arrival of Laura Collins (Diana Millea), David's deceased mother who has risen from the dead as a phoenix to claim him.

While this influx of the supernatural buoyed up the flailing ratings, it was the introduction of Jonathan Frid as vampire Barnabas

Collins—originally intended to be yet another short term monster to be dealt with and destroyed—that established the tone for the show and caused its popularity to steadily rise. Cleverly, Barnabas was not depicted as a mere monster, but as a man tortured by his conscience. Barnabas had once been in love with Josette DuPres and, upon encountering local waitress Maggie Evans (Kathryn Leigh Scott), he attempts to hypnotize her into becoming Josette, hoping to then drink her blood and transform her into his eternal vampire bride. His efforts, however, are thwarted by the intervention of yet another benevolent ghost.

The increasing popularity of the tortured Barnabas and his sufferings in love led the writers to attempt yet another first—in a seance Victoria Winters is instantaneously transported to 1795, and there, along with the audience, witnesses the events surrounding the original Barnabas/Josette love story. This extended flashback—with the cast of actors playing the ancestors of their present characters—ran for months to high ratings as young uncursed Barnabas goes to Martinique on business, and there meets and prepares to marry young Josette DuPres, the daughter of a plantation owner. Simultaneously, he initiates an affair with her maid Angelique Bouchard (Lara Parker), who is herself in love with Barnabas and attempts to use witchcraft to possess him. When he attempts to spurn her, Angelique places an irreversible curse on him and, suddenly, a vampire bat appears and bites him. Though he manages to kill Angelique before he can transform Josette into his vampire bride, the spirit of Angelique appears to her, shows her the hideousness of her future, and in response the traumatized girl runs from Barnabas and throws herself off the edge of Widow's Hill, to be dashed on the rocks below. The fateful lovers' triangle of Barnabas, Josette, and Angelique was repeated in various forms throughout the life of the show.

Always searching for a novel twist, the writers then toyed with the concept of "parallel time." Barnabas discovers a room on the estate in which he witnesses events transpiring in the present, but the characters are all in different roles—the result of different choices they made earlier. This is essentially a parallel dimension, and he enters it, hoping to learn that there he is not a vampire. Kathryn Leigh Scott suggested that this innovation proved to be so complex that it hastened the demise of the show, for both the writers and audience were having trouble keeping track of the various characters in "real" time versus the variations they played in alternate "parallel times." But as Victoria Winters had suggested in her opening voice-over, essentially the past and present were "one" at Collinwood.

Over the course of its approximately 1,200 episodes, *Dark Shadows'* ratings ebbed and peaked, drawing an extremely diverse audience. By May of 1969, the show was at its peak of popularity as ABC's number one daytime drama which boasted a daily viewership of some 20 million. It was this status that led producer/creator Dan Curtis to envision a *Dark Shadows* feature film—yet another first for a daytime drama. Despite the show's success, however, most studios laughed off the idea until Metro-Goldwyn-Meyer (MGM) green-lighted it and *House of Dark Shadows* became the first of the show's movie adaptations. For this big screen incarnation, Curtis decided to go back to the central and most popular plotline involving Barnabas' awakening/arrival at Collinwood, his meeting Maggie Evans, and his subsequent effort to remake her into his lost love Josette. Curtis did attempt to change the tone of the film version of the story—instead of being the vampire with a conscience, Barnabas would be what Curtis originally envisioned him to be; a monster that would motivate the greater gore ratio Curtis intended for the film audiences.

Released in 1971, *House of Dark Shadows* was such a success that some claim it helped to save a failing MGM, and Curtis was commissioned by the studio to create another film. Its successor, *Night of Dark Shadows* was a smaller scale effort. Adapting one of the parallel time plotlines, Quentin Collins (David Selby) inherits the Collins' estate and brings his young wife (played by Kate Jackson, later of *Charlie's Angels* and *Scarecrow and Mrs. King)* there to live. There he begins painting the image of Angelique, whose ghost appears to seduce and take possession of him. Less successful than its predecessor, but still a moneymaker, there were plans to make a third film when *Dark Shadows* was canceled and Curtis decided to move on to other projects.

Some 20 years later, in 1991, Curtis joined forces with NBC to recreate *Dark Shadows* as a prime-time soap opera. In this incarnation, Curtis attempted to initiate things with the arrival of Barnabas Collins (played by *Chariots of Fire* Oscar nominee Ben Cross) and the subsequent recounting of his history via the 1795 flashback. As he did with Joan Bennett before her, veteran actress (and fan of the original show) Jean Simmons took over the role of Elizabeth Collins Stoddard, and British scream queen Barbara Shelley was cast as Dr. Julia Hoffman. This casting also included Lysette Anthony as Angelique, and Adrian Paul—future star of *Highlander: The Series*—as Barnabas' younger brother Jeremiah Collins. Despite much anticipation by fans, the show debuted as a mid-season replacement just as the Gulf War began. It was both pre-empted and shifted around in its time slot due to low ratings until the producers finally chose to cancel it after 12 episodes.

—Rick Moody

FURTHER READING:

Scott, Kathryn Leigh. *Dark Shadows: The 25th Anniversary Collection.* Los Angeles, Pomegranate Press, 1991.

———. *My Scrapbook Memories of Dark Shadows.* Los Angeles, Pomegranate Press, 1986.

Scott, Kathryn Leigh, and Jim Pierson. *The Dark Shadows Almanac.* Los Angeles, Pomegranate Press, 1995.

Scott, Kathryn Leigh, and Kate Jackson. *The Dark Shadows Movie Book.* Los Angeles, Pomegranate Art Books, 1998.

Darrow, Clarence (1857-1938)

Sometimes reviled for his defense of unpopular people and causes, Clarence Darrow was the most widely known attorney in the United States at the time of his death in 1938. He practiced law in the Midwest, eventually becoming chief attorney for the Chicago and North Western Railways. By 1900 he had left this lucrative position to defend Socialist leader Eugene Debs, who had organized striking American Railway Union workers. Involved in several other labor-related cases and an advocate of integration, he also worked as a defense attorney, saving murderers Nathan Leopold and Richard Loeb from the electric chair in 1924. His 1925 courtroom battle against bible-thumping politician William Jennings Bryant in the Scopes trial—called the "Monkey Trial" due to its focus on teaching Darwin's theory of evolution in schools—was immortalized in the play and film *Inherit the Wind*. Darrow wrote several books, including *Crime: Its Cause and Treatment* (1922).

—Pamela L. Shelton

FURTHER READING:

Kurland, Gerald. *Clarence Darrow: "Attorney for the Damned."* Charlottesville, Virginia, SamHar Press, 1992.

Stone, Irving. *Clarence Darrow for the Defense.* Garden City, New York, Doubleday, 1941.

Tierney, Kevin. *Darrow: A Biography.* New York, Crowell, 1979.

Weinberg, Arthur, and Lila Weinberg. *Clarence Darrow, a Sentimental Rebel.* New York, Putnam, 1980.

Davis, Bette (1908-1989)

Born Ruth Elizabeth Davis in 1908, Bette Davis was one of the biggest stars of the Hollywood Studio Era. During her illustrious career, which spanned six decades, she appeared in over 100 films and made numerous television appearances. Her talents were recognized with 11 Academy Award nominations and two awards (1935 and 1938); three Emmy nominations and one award (1979); and she won a Life Achievement Award from the American Film Institute in 1997. In films such as *Marked Woman* (1937), *Jezebel* (1938), and *All About Eve* (1950) she played women who were intelligent, independent, and defiant, often challenging the social order. It is perhaps for these reasons that she became an icon of urban gay culture, for more often than not, her characters refused to succumb to the strict restraints placed on them by society.

—Frances Gateward

FURTHER READING:

Davis, Bette. *The Lonely Life: An Autobiography.* New York, Lancer Books, 1963.

Higham, Charles. *The Life of Bette Davis.* New York, MacMillan, 1981.

Ringgold, Gene. *The Complete Films of Bette Davis.* Secaucus, New Jersey, Citadel, 1990.

Davis, Miles (1926-1992)

Trumpet player Miles Davis became famous among both jazz buffs and people who know very little about the art form. He did so through a combination of intelligence, charisma, awareness of his own abilities, and a feel for the music scene rarely equaled in jazz. Some critics note that he did so with less natural technical ability than most jazz stars.

In spite of attempts to portray himself otherwise, Davis was not a street kid. Rather, he came from comfortable, upper-middle-class surroundings. His father was a dentist in East St. Louis, and his

Miles Davis

mother was a trained pianist who taught school. Miles grew up listening to classical and popular music. In common with many teens of his day, he played in the school band and worked in a jazz combo around town. Davis learned quickly from older musicians, and many took a liking to a young man they all described as "shy" and "withdrawn." Shy and withdrawn as he may have been, young Davis found the audacity to ask Billy Eckstine to sit in with his band. By all accounts, Davis was "awful," but the musicians saw something special beneath the apparently shy exterior and limited technical ability.

In 1945 Davis went to New York to study at the Juilliard School of Music. In a typical move, he tracked down Charlie "Bird" Parker and moved in with him. Bird sponsored Davis's career and used him on recordings and with his working band from time to time. Certainly, this work aided Davis in getting jobs with Benny Carter's band and then taking Fats Navarro's chair in the Eckstine band. In 1947 Davis was back with Bird and stayed with him for a year and a half. Although he still was not the most proficient trumpet player on the scene, Davis was attracting his own following and learning with each experience. It was, however, becoming obvious that his future fame would not be based on playing in the Dizzy Gillespie style so many other young trumpeters were imitating and developing.

In 1949 Davis provided a clear indication of his future distinctive style and pattern. He emerged as the leader of a group of Claude Thornhill's musicians, and from that collaboration sprang *Birth of the Cool* and the style of jazz named after it. That Davis, still in his early twenties, would assume leadership of the group that boasted Lee Konitz, Gerry Mulligan, Gil Evans, and others was in itself remarkable, but that he had successfully switched styles and assumed leadership of the style that he did much to shape was a pattern he repeated throughout his life.

Unfortunately, Davis's heroin addiction became the predominant force in his life, and for the next few years he did little artistically. Stories about his wrecked life circulated in the jazz world, which Davis confronted in his 1990 autobiography. Whether Clifford Brown actually did blow Miles off the stage and scare him straight, which Davis denied, depends upon whose version one believes. The fact is that the challenge of young giants like Brownie, who was Davis's opposite in so many ways, did stir up Davis's pride and led to his kicking his habit.

By 1954 Miles was back and heading toward the most artistically successful years of his life. The Davis style was fully matured; that style of the 1950s and early 1960s was marked by use of the Harmon mute, half valves, soft and fully rounded tones, reliance on the middle register, snatches of exquisite melodic composition, and general absence of rapid-fire runs. Davis attributed his sound to Freddie Webster, a St. Louis trumpet master, and his use of space to Ahmad Jamal, a pianist of great genius.

In the mid-1950s Davis pioneered the funk movement with songs like ''Walkin'.'' He kept his own rather cool approach, accentuated by unparaled use of the Harmon mute while typically surrounding himself with ''hotter'' players, such as Jackie McClean or Sonny Rollins. In 1955 the style came together with his ''classic'' quintet at the Newport Jazz Festival, where the quintet's enormous success led to a lucrative contract with Columbia Records, reputedly making Davis the highest paid jazz artist in history. The Miles Davis Quintet, consisting of John Coltrane on tenor sax, Paul Chambers on bass, Philly Joe Jones on Drums, and Red Garland on piano, was a band of all-stars and the stuff of which jazz legends are made. With the addition of Cannonball Adderly on alto sax, the sextet was able to use combinations and colorations that shaped the course of modern jazz. Above it all was the ultimate personification of cool, *Milestones* and *Bye, Bye, Blackbird* pointing the way to Miles's next experiments.

Davis's 1958 Paris recording of the music for *The Elevator to the Gallows* was a high point in his career. His use of unexpected note placement leading to suspended rhythms and simple harmonic structures led logically into the use of modes or scalar improvisation. (In modal improvisation the improviser uses one or two modes as the basis for improvisation rather than changing chord/scales each measure or even more frequently.) John Coltrane had taken that style to its logical conclusion, developing the work of Gillespie at a frantic pace. Davis had never been comfortable with playing at frantic speeds.

Kind of Blue, which featured Bill Evans on a number of cuts, fueled the modal explosion in jazz. Considered one of the finest jazz albums ever made, it was a commercial success, and Davis continued to use compositions from the album over a long period of his career. He did not, however, exclusively feature modal tunes in his repertoire. In fact, it should be noted that Davis never totally dropped one style as he moved on to another one. And the challenge of Free Jazz was about to launch him into another phase of his career, a series of records with his friend Gil Evans featuring a big band. The first album, which some consider the best, was *Sketches of Spain,* featuring ''Concierto.'' Davis did not abandon his small group career, although he did frequently perform with a big band and recorded more albums in that format, including *Porgy and Bess,* featuring the marvelous ''Summertime.''

By 1964 Davis was ready to change again. His albums were not selling as they once had. They were receiving excellent reviews, but they were not reaching the pop audience. Davis still refused to try the Free Jazz route of Don Cherry and Ornette Coleman or even of his former colleague, John Coltrane. Davis was more inclined to reach out for the audience his friend Sly Stone had cultivated—the huge rock audience, including young blacks. It was at this point that Davis, already possessing something of a reputation as a ''bad dude,'' truly developed his image of a nasty street tough. He had always turned his back on audiences and refused to announce compositions or performers, but now he exaggerated that image and turned to fusion.

Beginning in 1967 with *Nefertiti* and following in 1968 with *Filles de Kilimanjaro,* Davis began incorporating rock elements into his work. He used Chick Corea on electric piano and replaced his veterans with other younger men, including Tony Williams on drums, Ron Carter on bass, and Wayne Shorter on tenor sax. The success of these records, although somewhat short of his expectations, forced Miles to explore the genre further. That led to his use of John McLaughlin on *In a Silent Way* in 1969 and the all-out fusion album, *Bitches Brew,* the same year. *Bitches Brew,* which introduced rock listeners to jazz, marked a point of no return for Davis. The 1970s were a period that led to great popular success for his group. Davis changed his clothing and performing styles. He affected the attire of the pop music star, appeared at Fillmore East and West, attracted young audiences, attached an electric amp mike to his horn, and strode the stage restlessly.

For a period of years, he stopped performing, and rumors once again surfaced regarding his condition. In the early 1980s Davis made a successful comeback with a funk-oriented group. This was a different sort of funk, however, from ''Walkin''' and his other 1950s successes. He was still able to recruit fine talent from among young musicians, as saxophonist Kenny Garett attests. As the 1980s came to an end, however, Davis's loyal jazz followers saw only a few sparks of the Miles Davis whom they revered. There were, however, enough of these sparks to fuel the hope that Davis might just once more play in his old style.

Finally, at the Montreux Festival of 1992, Quincey Jones convinced Davis to relive the work he had done with Gil Evans. Davis had some fears about performing his old hits, but as he rehearsed those fears subsided, and the documentary based on that performance, as well as the video and CD made of it, demonstrate that he gained in confidence as he performed. While not quite the Davis of the 1950s and 1960s, he was ''close enough for jazz.'' These performances as well as the soundtrack of *Dingo* have gone far to fuel the jazz fans' lament for what might have been. They display a Davis filled with intelligence, wit, and emotion who responds to the love of his audience and who is for once at ease with his own inner demons.

The rest of the Montreux performance featured Miles Davis with members from his various groups over the years. The range of the groups offered proof of Davis's versatility and his self-knowledge of his strengths and weaknesses. After the festival, Davis performed in a group with his old friend Jackie McClean. Rumors persist of tapes they made in Europe which have not yet surfaced commercially. In December 1992, Davis died of pneumonia, leaving a rich legacy of music and enough fuel for controversy to satisfy jazz fans for many years.

—Frank A. Salamone

FURTHER READING:

Carner, Gary, ed. *The Miles Davis Companion: Four Decades of Commentary.* New York, Schimer Books, 1994.

Chamber, Jack. *Milestones: The Music and Times of Miles Davis.* New York, Da Capo, 1996.

Cole, Bill. *Miles Davis: The Early Years.* New York, Da Capo, 1994.

Davis, Miles, and Quincey Troupe. *Miles: The Autobiography.* New York, Touchstone Books, 1990.

Kirchner, Bill, ed. *A Miles Davis Reader: Smithsonian Readers in American Music.* Washington, Smithsonian Institution Press, 1996.

Nisenson, Eric. *Around about Midnight: A Portrait of Miles Davis.* New York, Da Capo, 1996.

Davy Crockett

Walt Disney's 1950s television adaptation of the Davy Crockett legend catapulted the coonskin-capped frontiersman into a national role model who has had an enduring appeal for both academic historians and popular culture producers and their audiences through the end of the twentieth century. The marketing frenzy surrounding the Crockett fad represented the first real mass-marketing campaign in American history, promoting a new way of marketing films and television shows. Many baby boomers can still recite the lyrics to "The Ballad of Davy Crockett" and have passed down their treasured items, such as Crockett lunch boxes, to their children.

One of the legendary American heroes whose stories dramatize American cultural values for a wide popular audience, the historical David Crockett was born on August 17, 1786, near Limestone, Tennessee. He went from a local folk hero to national media hero during his lifetime when the Whig party adopted him as a political party symbol in the early nineteenth century. He served as commander of a battalion in the Creek Indian War from 1813 to 1814, was a member of the Tennessee state legislature from 1821 to 1824, and was a member of the United States Congress from 1827 to 1831 and again from 1833 to 1835. He was renowned for his motto "be always sure you are right, then go ahead."

The myths surrounding Crockett began as the Whig party created his election image through deliberate fabrication so that they could capitalize on his favorable political leanings. His penchant for tall tales also made him a folk legend rumored to be capable of killing bears with his bare hands and of performing similar feats of strength. Even his trusty rifle, "Betsy," achieved fame and name recognition. Crockett was one of the several hundred men who died defending the Alamo from Mexican attack in March of 1836 as Texas fought for independence from Mexico with the aid of the United States. His legend quickly emerged as a widespread public phenomenon after his heroic, patriotic death at the Alamo. His tombstone reads "Davy Crockett, Pioneer, Patriot, Soldier, Trapper, Explorer, State Legislator, Congressman, Martyred at The Alamo. 1786-1836." His symbolic heroism and larger-than-life figure soon found its way into such popular cultural media as tall tales, folklore, journalism, fiction, dime novels, plays, television, movies, and music. Historian Margaret J. King has called him "as fine a figure of popular culture as can be imagined."

Disney understood the ability of popular culture to manipulate popular historical images and the power of the entertainer to educate. Disney took the Crockett legend and remade it to suit his 1950s audience. Disney planned a three-part series (December 15, 1954's

"Davy Crockett Indian Fighter," January 26, 1955's "Davy Crockett Goes to Congress," and February 23, 1955's "Davy Crockett at the Alamo") to represent the Frontierland section of his Disneyland theme park. Aired on the ABC television network, the series helped ABC become a serious contender among the television networks and catapulted Disney's Davy Crockett, little-known actor Fess Parker, to stardom. The American frontier spirit that formerly had been embodied by Daniel Boone now immediately became associated with Davy Crockett. Walt Disney himself was surprised by the size and intensity of the overnight craze: King quotes him as having said, "It became one of the biggest overnight hits in television history and there we were with just three films and a dead hero." Disney quickly rereleased the series as feature film *Davy Crockett, King of the Wild Frontier* (1955) in order to cash in on the Crockett craze. The weekly television show, which aired on Wednesday nights, also spawned *Davy Crockett and the River Pirates* (1956), which was made from two of the television shows, including the Mike Fink keelboat race story.

Disney's interpretation of the Crockett legend arrived soon after television enjoyed widespread ownership for the first time and leisure activities began to center around the television. Disney proved the powerful ability of television to capture and influence wide audiences. Television programmers and mass advertisers discovered sizable new markets in the children and baby boom audience who quickly became infatuated with all things Crockett. The promotional tie-in has enjoyed widespread success ever since the first young child placed Davy's coonskin cap on his head so that he could feel like Davy Crockett as he hunted "b'ars" in the backyard. Raccoon skin prices dramatically jumped practically overnight. Hundreds of products by various producers quickly saturated the market as Disney was unable to copyright the public Crockett name. Guitars, underwear, clothes, toothbrushes, moccasins, bedspreads, lunch boxes, toys, books, comics, and many other items found their way into many American homes. Many producers simply pasted Crockett labels over existing western-themed merchandise so as not to miss out on the phenomenon. Various artists recorded sixteen versions of the catchy theme song "The Ballad of Davy Crockett," which was originally created as filler. It went on to sell more than four million copies.

The legendary Davy Crockett was born of a long tradition of creating national heroes as embodiments of the national character, most in the historical tradition of the great white male. Disney's Davy Crockett was a 1950s ideal, a dignified common man who was known for his congeniality, neighborliness, and civic-mindedness. He was also an upwardly mobile, modest, and courageous man. He showed that God's laws existed in nature and came from a long line of American heroes who represented the national ideal of the noble, self-reliant frontiersman. It was men such as the legendary Davy Crockett that led the American people on their divinely appointed mission into the wilderness and set the cultural standard for the settlements that would follow. Some detractors, however, felt that some of Crockett's less refined qualities were not the American ideals that should be passed on to their children. This led to a debate over the Disney Crockett's effectiveness and suitability as a national hero. King terms such controversy as exemplary of the volatile encounter among mass media, national history, and the popular consciousness. Disney's Davy Crockett, and the many popular Crocketts that went before, are central figures in the search for how American historical legends have affected what Americans understand about their history and how this understanding continues to change over time.

—Marcella Bush Treviño

FURTHER READING:

Cummings, Joe, and Michael A. Lofaro, eds. *Crockett at Two Hundred: New Perspectives on the Man and the Myth.* Knoxville, University of Tennessee Press, 1989.

Hauck, Richard Boyd. *Davy Crockett: A Handbook.* Lincoln, University of Nebraska Press, 1982.

King, Margaret J. ''The Recycled Hero: Walt Disney's Davy Crockett.'' In *Davy Crockett: The Man, the Legend, the Legacy, 1786-1986,* edited by Michael A. Lofaro. Knoxville, University of Tennessee Press, 1985.

Lofaro, Michael A., ed. *Davy Crockett: The Man, the Legend, the Legacy, 1786-1986.* Knoxville, University of Tennessee Press, 1985.

Day, Doris (1924—)

Vocalist and screen actress Doris Day, a freckle-faced buttercup blonde with a sunny smile that radiated wholesome good cheer,

Doris Day

embodied the healthy girl-next-door *zeitgeist* of 1950s Hollywood. The decade marked the fall of the Hollywood musical and Day, with her pleasing personality and distinctive voice, huskily emotive yet pure and on-note, helped to prolong the genre's demise. Thanks largely to her infectious presence, a series of mostly anodyne musical films attracted bobby-soxers and their parents alike during the otherwise somber era of the Cold War and McCarthyism.

Behind the smile, however, Doris Day's life was marked by much unhappiness endured, remarkably, away from the glare of publicity. She was born Doris von Kappelhoff in Cincinnati, Ohio on April 3, 1924, the daughter of German parents who divorced when she was eight. She pursued a dancing career from an early age, but her ambitions were cut short by a serious automobile accident in her mid-teens, and she turned to singing as an alternative. She had two disastrous early marriages, the first, at the age of 17, to musician Al Jorden, by whom she had a son. She divorced him because of his violence, and later married George Weidler, a liaison that lasted eight months. By the age of 24, she had worked her way up from appearing on local radio stations to becoming a popular band singer with Bob Crosby and Les Brown, and had begun to making records.

In 1948, Warner Brothers needed an emergency replacement for a pregnant Betty Hutton in *Romance on the High Seas.* Day was suggested, got the part and, true to the cliché, became a star overnight. The movie yielded a huge recording hit in ''It's Magic,'' establishing a pattern which held for most of her films and secured her place as a best-selling recording artist in tandem with her screen career. The songs as sung by Day threaded themselves into a tapestry of cultural consciousness that has remained familiar across generations. Notable among her many hits are the wistfully romantic and Oscar-winning ''Secret Love'' from *Calamity Jane* (1953) and the insidious ''Que Sera Sera'' from Hitchcock's *The Man Who Knew Too Much* (1956), which sold over a million at the time and earned her a Gold Disc.

No matter what the role or the plot of a movie, Day retained an essentially ''virginal'' persona about which it was once fashionable to make jokes. She confounded derision, however, with sheer energy and professionalism, revealing a range that allowed her to broaden her scope and prolong her career in non-musicals—an achievement that had eluded her few rivals.

Early on, her string of Warner musicals, which paired her with Jack Carson, then Gordon MacRae, or Gene Nelson, were interrupted by a couple of straight roles (opposite Kirk Douglas' Bix Beiderbecke in *Young Man With a Horn* and murdered by the Klan in *Storm Warning,* both 1950), but it was for Metro-Goldwyn-Meyer (M-G-M), in the biopic *Love Me or Leave Me* (1955), that Day won her colors as an actress of some accomplishment and grit. As Ruth Etting, the famed nightclub singer of the 1920s who suffered at the hands of her crippled hoodlum husband (played by James Cagney), she was able to meet the acting challenge while given ample opportunity to display her vocal expertise. She had, however, no further opportunity to develop the dramatic promise she displayed in this film.

The most effervescent and enduring of Day's musicals, the screen version of the Broadway hit *The Pajama Game* (1957), marked the end of her Warner Brothers tenure, after which she studio-hopped for three undistinguished comedies, *Tunnel of Love* (M-G-M 1958, with Richard Widmark), *Teacher's Pet* (Paramount 1958, with Clark Gable), and *It Happened to Jane* (Columbia, 1959, with Jack Lemmon). A star of lesser universal appeal might have sunk with these leaden enterprises, but her popularity emerged unscathed—indeed, in 1958 the Hollywood Foreign Press Association voted her the World's

Favorite Actress, the first of several similar accolades that included a Golden Globe in 1962.

In 1959, any threat to Day's star status was removed by a series of monumentally profitable comedies in which oh-so-mild risqué innuendo stood in for sex, and the generally farcical plots were made to work through the light touch and attractive personalities of Day and her coterie of leading men. The first of these, *Pillow Talk* (1959), teamed her with Rock Hudson, grossed a massive $7.5 million and won her an Oscar nomination for her masquerade as a buttoned-up interior designer. The Day-Hudson formula was repeated twice more with *Lover Come Back* (1962) and *Send Me No Flowers* (1964). In between, *That Touch of Mink* (1962) co-starred her with Cary Grant, while *The Thrill of it All* and *Move Over Darling* (both 1963) added James Garner to her long list of leading men. The last years of the 1960s saw a decline in both the number and the quality of her films, and she made her last, *With Six You Get Eggroll,* in 1968, exactly 20 years after the release of her first film.

Her third husband Martin Melcher, who administered her financial affairs and who forced the pace of her career in defiance of her wishes, produced most of Doris Day's comedies. After his death in 1968, nervous exhaustion, coupled with the discovery that he had divested her of her earnings of some $20 million, leaving her penniless, led to a breakdown. She recovered and starred for five years in her own television show to which Melcher had committed her without her knowledge, and in 1974 was awarded damages (reputed to be $22 million) against her former lawyer who had been a party to Melcher's embezzlement of her fortune.

Other than making a series of margarine commercials and hosting a television cable show *Doris Day and Friends* (1985-1986), she retired from the entertainment profession in 1975 to devote herself to the cause of animal rights. She married Barry Comden in 1976, but they divorced four years later. From her ranch estate in Carmel, she now administers the Doris Day Animal League, working tirelessly to lobby for legislative protection against all forms of cruelty. Her recordings still sell and her films are continually shown on television. To some, Doris Day is a hopeless eccentric, to many a saint, but she continues to enjoy a high profile and the loyalty of her many fans—her celluloid image of goodness lent veracity by her actions.

—Robyn Karney

FURTHER READING:

Braun, Eric. *Doris Day.* London, Orion, 1992.

Hirschhorn, Clive. *The Hollywood Musical.* New York, Crown, 1981.

Hotchner, A.E. *Doris Day: Her Own Story.* New York, Morrow, 1975.

Shipman, David. *The Great Movie Stars: The International Years.* London, Angus and Robertson, 1980.

The Day the Earth Stood Still

The Day the Earth Stood Still (1951), still playing in cinema revivals in the 1990s, at outdoor summer festivals, and regularly on cable channels, was at the forefront of the science fiction film explosion of the 1950s. A number of its basic elements, from its moralizing to its music, from its fear of apocalypse to its menacing

A scene from the film *The Day the Earth Stood Still.*

robot, are aspects of the genre which remain today. Though the film did not bring all these elements to science fiction for the first time, the film's strong and sophisticated visual and aural style was to have a lasting impact on how the scenario of alien visitation has subsequently been presented. *The Day the Earth Stood Still* outlined creatively, some might even say factually, the images of alien visitation that have fascinated increasing numbers of people in the second half of the twentieth century.

Between 1950 and 1957, 133 science fiction movies were released. *The Day the Earth Stood Still* was one of the earliest, most influential, and most successful. Its story was relatively simple: the alien Klaatu (with his robot, Gort) arrives on this planet and attempts to warn Earthlings, in the face of increasing fear and misunderstanding, that their escalating conflicts endanger the rest of the universe. The film was unusual as a science fiction film in this period in that it was produced by a major production company (Twentieth Century-Fox) on a large budget, and this is reflected in the pool of talent the film was able to call upon, in terms of scripting, casting, direction, special effects, and music. The commentator Bruce Fox has even claimed, in *Hollywood Vs. the Aliens,* that the film's resonance in the depiction of alien visitation reflected testimony and information withheld by the government from the public concerning sightings and contact with "real" UFOs at the time.

Director Robert Wise had worked as an editor for Orson Welles (1915-1985) and directed a number of Val Lewton (1904-1951) horror films. In *The Day the Earth Stood Still,* Wise is restrained in the use of special effects (though Klaatu's flying saucer cost more than one hundred thousand dollars), maintaining their effectiveness by contrasting them with scenes showing a claustrophobic and suspicious Washington in a light we might usually associate with film noir. Edmund North's script, based on the story "Farewell to the Master" by the famous science fiction magazine editor Harry Bates (1900-1981), emphasizes distinct religious parallels while balancing the allegory with Klaatu's direct experience with individual humans' hopes and fears. The film's mood of anxiety is underlined by the score of Bernard Herrmann (1911-75), who was to do the music for a clutch of Hitchcock films and Martin Scorsese's *Taxi Driver* (1976). Herrmann's use of the precursor of electronic instruments, the theremin, as well as the more usual piano, percussion, and brass helped create a disturbing background. It is not until towards the end of the film that the art direction and special effects take over. More than the spaceship, however, the film's biggest selling point was the eight-foot Gort. Though clumsy and simplistic by today's standards, his huge stature and featureless face give a real sense of presence and menace. The talismanic phrase that had to be said to Gort to save the world, "Klaatu, Barada, Nikto," was on the lips of many a schoolchild of the period.

In many ways *The Day the Earth Stood Still* is far from being the most representative or the most original science fiction film of this period. There were many more thematically interesting films that appeared risible because they lacked the budget of Wise's film. The film's liberal credentials seem rather compromised by its lack of belief in the ordinary individual to avoid panic and suspicion in the face of anything different, while there is something rather patrician in the idea that, because Earth cannot be trusted to guard its own weapons of mass destruction, it must be put in the charge of a larger, wiser, scientifically more advanced intergalactic power. This faith in the rationality of the scientist to overcome all the fears and anxieties of the period was far from a unanimously held view.

Despite these drawbacks, *The Day the Earth Stood Still* is a successful film in popular terms for other reasons. Its influence is obvious: its opening scenes of the flying saucer coming in over the symbols of American democracy in Washington, D.C., resonate all the way down to similar scenes in *Independence Day* (1996); the alien craft and the tense scenes when figures descend from the craft to face a watching crowd create an archetypal image repeated again and again in science fiction films, most potently in *Close Encounters of the Third Kind* (1977); finally, Gort is the prototype for the robot in the American science fiction film, a figure both menacing and protective, a precursor to every man-made humanoid machine from Robbie the Robot to the Terminator, one of the most original and beguiling figures the science fiction genre has offered the cinemagoer.

—Kyle Smith

FURTHER READING:

Biskind, Peter. *Seeing Is Believing: How Hollywood Taught Us to Stop Worrying and Love the Fifties.* London, Pluto, 1983.

Fox, Bruce. *Hollywood Vs. the Aliens: The Motion Picture Industry's Participation in UFO Disinformation.* California, Frog Ltd, 1997.

Hardy, P. *The Encyclopaedia of Science Fiction Movies.* London, Octopus, 1986.

Jancovich, Mark. *Rational Fears: American Horror in the 1950s.* Manchester, Manchester University Press, 1996.

Pringle, David, editor. *The Ultimate Encyclopaedia of Science Fiction.* London, Carlton, 1996.

Days of Our Lives

Developed by Ted Corday, Irna Phillips, and Alan Chase, the daytime drama *Days of Our Lives* premiered on NBC in 1965. With Phillips' creation for Procter & Gamble, *As the World Turns* serving as a model, *Days* proceeded to put increasingly outrageous twists on established formulae for the next three decades. By the mid-1990s, its flights into the postmodern and the macabre had themselves become models for a struggling genre.

"Like sands through the hourglass, so are the days of our lives," proclaims the show's opening narration, voiced by former film actor MacDonald Carey over the appropriate image. Carey portrayed patriarch Tom Horton, all-purpose physician in *Days'* midwestern hamlet of Salem, from the program's inception until the passing of both actor and character in 1994. Accompanied by dutiful wife Alice (Frances Reid), the elder Hortons are two of a handful of veterans who evolved over the years as virtual figureheads on a conspicuously youth-oriented program.

After Ted Corday's passing in 1966, and under the stewardship of his widow, Betty, and headwriter Bill Bell, *Days* began, in the words of author Gerard Waggett, "playing around with the incest taboo." Young Marie Horton (Marie Cheatham) first married and divorced the father of her ex-fiance and then fell for a man later discovered to be her prodigal brother. Marie was off to a nunnery, and the "incest scare" was to pop up on other soaps, including *Young and the Restless,* Bell's future creation for CBS.

The incest theme carried the show into the early 1970s with the triangle of Mickey Horton (John Clarke), wife Laura Spencer (Susan Flannery), and her true desire, Mickey's brother Bill (Edward Mallory)—a story which inspired imitation on *Guiding Light.* Bill's rape of Laura, whom he would later wed, muddied the issue of whether "no" always means "no." Co-writer Pat Falken Smith later penned the similarly controversial "rape seduction" of *General Hospital's* Laura by her eventual husband, Luke. *Days* soon featured another familial entanglement in which saloon singer Doug Williams (Bill Hayes) romanced young Julie Olson (Susan Seaforth), only to marry and father a child by her mother before being, predictably, widowed and returning to Julie's side.

Bell's departure in 1973 provided Smith with interrupted stints as headwriter, as the show's flirtations with lesbian and interracial couplings were short-circuited due to network fears of a viewer backlash. The introduction of popular heroine Dr. Marlena Evans (Deidre Hall) late in the decade was a highlight, but the "Salem Strangler" serial killer storyline spelled the end for many cast members by the early 1980s. Marlena's romance with cop Roman Brady (Wayne Northrop) created a new "super couple" and established the Bradys as a working-class family playing off the bourgeois Hortons.

General Hospital's Luke and Laura, along with their fantasy storylines—which were attractive to younger viewers in the early 1980s—were emulated, and thensome, by *Days.* Marlena and Roman were followed by Bo and Hope (Peter Reckell and Kristian Alfonso), Kimberly and Shane (Patsy Pease and Charles Shaughnessy), and Kayla and Steve (Mary Beth Evans and Stephen Nichols), who anchored Salem's supercouple era, and whose tragic heroines are profiled in Martha Nochimson's book, *No End to Her.* Their Gothic adventures involved nefarious supervillains such as Victor Kiriakis (John Aniston) and, later, Stefano DiMera (Joseph Mascolo), whose

The cast of *Days of Our Lives*.

multiple resurrections defied any remaining logic. Kayla and Steve's saga revived the program's sibling triangle and rape redemption scenarios. Identities also became tangled, with Roman returning as the enigmatic John Black, portrayed by another actor (Drake Hogestyn), and brainwashed to temporarily forget his ''true'' identity. When Wayne Northrop was available to reclaim the role, however, Black's identity became a mystery once again.

In the 1990s, with the next generation, Ken Corday was at the producer's helm, and with innovative new headwriter James Reilly, *Days* crossed a horizon into pure fantasy. Vivian Alamain (Louise Sorel) had one rival buried prematurely and purloined another's embryo. Marlena, possessed by demons, morphed into animals and levitated. Later, she was exorcised by John Black, now found to have been a priest, and imprisoned in a cage by Stefano. Super triangles supplanted supercouples, as insecure and typically female third parties schemed to keep lovers apart. The most notorious of these was teen Sami Brady (Alison Sweeney), whose obsession with Austin Reed (Patrick Muldoon, later Austin Peck), produced machinations plaguing his romance with Sami's sister, Carrie (Christie Clark), and led Internet fans to nickname her ''Scami.'' While many longtime fans lamented the program's new tone, younger viewers adored it. By 1996, the program had risen to second in ratings and first in all-important demographics.

To the chagrin of their fans, other soaps soon found themselves subject to various degrees of ''daysification,'' even as *General Hospital* was devoting itself to sober, socially relevant topics. But overall viewership of the genre had diminished, and when *Days'* ratings dipped in the late 1990s, its creators seemed not to consider that postmodern escapism might work to lure very young fans but not to hold them. NBC hired Reilly to develop a new soap and threatened its other soaps with cancellation if they did not get up to pace. Its stories were risky, but in eschewing the socially relevant and truly

bold, *Days of Our Lives* might have succeeded in further narrowing the genre's purview and, with it, its pool of potential viewers for the new millennium.

—Christine Scodari

FURTHER READING:

Nochimson, Martha. *No End to Her: Soap Opera and the Female Subject.* Berkeley, University of California Press, 1992.

Russell, Maureen. *Days of Our Lives: A Complete History of the Long-Running Soap Opera.* New York, McFarland Publishing, 1996.

Scodari, Christine. '''No Politics Here': Age and Gender in Soap Opera 'Cyberfandom.''' *Women's Studies in Communication.* Fall 1998, 168-87.

Waggett, Gerard. *Soap Opera Encyclopedia.* New York, Harper Paperbacks, 1997.

Zenka, Lorraine. *Days of Our Lives: The Complete Family Album.* New York, Harper Collins, 1996.

Daytime Talk Shows

The daytime television talk show is a uniquely modern phenomenon, but one with roots stretching back to the beginning of broadcasting. Daytime talk programs are popular with audiences for their democratic, unpredictable nature, with producers for their low cost, and with stations for their high ratings. They have been called everything from the voice of the common people to a harbinger of the end of civilization. Successful hosts become stars in their own right, while guests play out the national drama in a steady stream of confession, confrontation, and self-promotion.

Daytime talk shows can be classified into two basic formats. Celebrity-oriented talkers have much in common with their nighttime counterparts. The host performs an opening monologue or number, and a series of celebrity guests promote their latest films, TV shows, books, or other product. The host's personality dominates the interaction. These shows have their roots in both talk programs and comedy-variety series. The basic formula was designed by NBC's Sylvester ''Pat'' Weaver, creator of both *Today* and *The Tonight Show.* Musical guests and comic monologues are frequently featured along with discussion. Merv Griffin, Mike Douglas, Dinah Shore, and Rosie O'Donnell have all hosted this type of show.

The more common and successful category of talk shows is the issue-oriented talker. Hosts lead the discussion, but the guests' tales of personal tragedy, triumph, and nonconformity are at the center. Phil Donahue was the first, beginning in 1979, to achieve national prominence with this style of talk show. Oprah Winfrey was transformed from local Chicago television personality to national media magnate largely on the strength of her talk program. In the 1990s, these shows grew to depend more and more on confession and confrontation. The trend has reached its apparent apotheosis with *The Jerry Springer Show*, on which conflicts between guests frequently turn physical, with fistfights erupting on stage.

With the tremendous success in the 1980s of *Donahue,* hosted by Phil Donahue (most daytime talk programs are named for the host or hosts) and *The Oprah Winfrey Show,* the form has proliferated. Other popular and influential hosts of the 1980s and 1990s include Maury Povich, Jenny Jones, Sally Jesse Raphael, former United States Marine Montel Williams, journalist Geraldo Rivera, actress Ricki Lake, and Jerry Springer, who had previously been Mayor of Cincinnati. On the celebrity-variety side, actress-comedienne Rosie O'Donnell and the duo of Regis Philbin and Kathie Lee Gifford have consistently drawn large audiences.

The list of those who tried and failed at the daytime talk format includes a wide assortment of rising, falling, and never-really-were stars. Among those who flopped with issue-oriented talk shows were former *Beverly Hills, 90210* actress Gabrielle Carteris, actor Danny Bonaduce of *The Partridge Family,* ex-*Cosby Show* kid Tempestt Bledsoe, Mark Walberg, Rolanda Watts, Gordon Elliott, Oprah's pal Gayle King, Charles Perez, pop group Wilson Phillips' Carnie Wilson, retired Pittsburgh Steelers quarterback Terry Bradshaw, and the teams of gay actor Jim J. Bullock and former televangelist Tammy Faye Baker Messner and ex-spouses George Hamilton and Alana Stewart. Others have tried the celebrity-variety approach of Mike Douglas and Merv Griffin; singer-actress Vicki Lawrence and *Night Court*'s Marsha Warfield both failed to find enough of an audience to last for long.

Issue talk shows like *Sally Jesse Raphael* and *The Jerry Springer Show* rely on ''ordinary'' people who are, in some way, extraordinary (or at least deviant.) Though celebrities do occasionally appear, the great majority of guests are drawn from the general population. They are not celebrities as traditionally defined. Though the talk show provides a flash of fleeting notoriety, they have no connection with established media, political, or social elites. They become briefly famous for the contradictory qualities of ordinariness and difference. Show employees called ''bookers'' work the telephones and read the great volume of viewer mail in search of the next hot topic, the next

great guest. Those chosen tend to either lead non-traditional lifestyles—such as gays, lesbians, bisexuals, prostitutes, transvestites, and people with highly unorthodox political or religious views—or have something to confess to a close confederate, usually adultery or some other sexual transgression. If the two can be combined, e.g., confessing a lesbian affair, which *The Jerry Springer Show* has featured, then so much the better. The common people gain a voice, but only if they use it to confess their sins.

Like all talk shows, daytime talkers rely on the element of unpredictability. There is a sense that virtually anything can happen. Few shows are broadcast live, they are taped in a studio with a ''cast'' of nonprofessional, unrehearsed audience members. The emotional reaction of the audience to the guest's revelations becomes an integral part of the show. The trend in the late 1990s was deliberately to promote the unexpected. The shows trade heavily on the reactions of individuals who have just been informed, on national television, that a friend/lover/relative has been keeping a secret from them. Their shock, outrage, and devastation becomes mass entertainment. The host becomes the ringmaster (a term Springer freely applies to himself) in an electronic circus of pain and humiliation.

Sometimes the shock has implications well beyond the episode's taping. In March of 1996, *The Jenny Jones Show* invited Jonathan Schmitz onto a program about secret admirers, where someone would be confessing to a crush on him. Though he was told that his admirer could be either male or female, the single, heterosexual Schmitz assumed he would be meeting a woman. During the taping, a male acquaintance, Scott Amedure, who was gay, confessed that he was Schmitz's admirer. Schmitz felt humiliated and betrayed by the show, and later, enraged by the incident, he went to Amedure's home with a gun and shot him to death. Schmitz was convicted of murder, but was granted a new trial in 1998. In a 1999 civil suit, the *Jenny Jones Show* was found negligent in Amedure's death and the victim's family was awarded $25 million. The ruling forced many talk shows to consider how far they might go with future on-air confrontations.

Talk, as the content of a broadcasting media, is nothing new. The world's first commercial radio broadcast, by KDKA Pittsburgh on November 2, 1920, featured an announcer giving the results of the Presidential election. Early visions of the future of radio and TV pictured the new media as instruments of democracy which could foster participation in public debate. Broadcasters were, and still are, licensed to operate in ''the public interest, convenience and necessity,'' in the words of the communications Act of 1934. Opposing views on controversial contemporary issues could be aired, giving listeners the opportunity to weigh the evidence and make informed choices. Radio talk shows went out over the airwaves as early as 1929, though debate-oriented programs took nearly another decade to come to prominence. Commercial network television broadcasts were underway by the fall of 1946, and talk, like many other radio genres, found a place on the new medium.

Television talk shows of all types owe much to the amateur variety series of the 1940s and 1950s. Popular CBS radio personality Arthur Godfrey hosted *Arthur Godfrey's Talent Scouts* on TV in prime time from 1948 to 1958. *The Original Amateur Hour,* hosted by Ted Mack, ran from 1948 to 1960 (at various times appearing on ABC, CBS, NBC, and Dumont.) These amateur showcases were genuinely democratic; they offered an opportunity for ordinary people to participate in the new public forums. Talent alone gave these guests a brief taste of the kind of recognition usually reserved for celebrities. Audiences saw themselves in these hopeful amateurs looking for their big break. Winners were a source of inspiration; losers provided a laugh. Godfrey added another element to this mix: unconventionality. He was unashamedly emotional and unafraid to push the envelope of acceptable (for the era) host behavior. Breaking the rules became part of his persona, and that persona made him a star. Talk show hosts from Jack Paar to David Letterman to Jerry Springer would put Godfrey's lesson to productive use.

One of the earliest daytime talkers was *Art Linkletter's House Party*. Many of the elements of the successful, modern talk show were in place: Linkletter was a genial host who interacted with a live audience. They participated in the program by confessing their minor transgressions and foibles. Linkletter responded with calm platitudes, copies of his book (*The Confessions of a Happy Man*), and pitches for Geritol and Sominex. No matter what the trouble, Linkletter could soothe his audience members' guilt with reassurances that they were after all perfectly normal, and that "people are funny" (an early title for the series.) Sin (albeit venial) was his subject, but salvation was his game. Each show concluded with his "Kids Say the Darnedest Things" segment, wherein Linkletter milked laughs from children's responses to questions about grown-up subjects. This bit proved both endearing and enduring; in 1998 it was revived in prime time by CBS as a vehicle for another genial comedian, Bill Cosby.

Linkletter gave the modern talk show confession, but Joe Pyne gave it anger. *The Joe Pyne Show,* syndicated from 1965 to 1967, offered viewers a host as controversial as his guests. Twenty years before belligerent nighttime host Morton Downey, Jr., Pyne smoked on the set and berated his guests and audience. The show was produced at Los Angeles' KTTV. At the height of the Watts riots of 1965, Pyne featured a militant black leader; both men revealed, on the air, that they were armed with pistols. Other guests included the leader of the American Nazi Party and Lee Harvey Oswald's mother. Pyne, like Downey, lasted only a short time but made a major impression.

In the 1960s and 1970s, the celebrity-variety talk show flourished. This was the era of Mike Douglas, Merv Griffin, and Dinah Shore. Douglas was a former big-band vocalist who occasionally sang on his show. *The Mike Douglas Show* ran in syndication from 1961 to 1982. His variation on the daytime talk formula was to have a different celebrity co-host from Monday to Friday each week. For one memorable week in the early 1970s he was joined by rock superstars John Lennon and Yoko Ono. His guests ran the gamut from child actor Mason Reese to pioneering heavy metal rock band KISS. In 1980 his production company replaced him with singer-actor John Davidson, in an unsuccessful attempt to appeal to a more youthful audience. Douglas stayed on the air for two more years, then faded from public view. His impact on daytime talk shows was underappreciated by many until 1996, when *The Rosie O'Donnell Show* premiered to immediate acclaim and ratings success. Multiple-Emmy winner O'Donnell frequently cited both Douglas and Merv Griffin as major inspirations.

The modern issue-oriented daytime talk show began with *Donahue*. From the beginning, Phil Donahue knew he was doing something different, neither purely journalism nor purely entertainment. It was not news, but it was always new. The issues were real, the guests were real, but the whole package was ultimately as constructed a piece of entertainment as any of its predecessors. By making television spectacle out of giving voice to the voiceless, Donahue found an audience, thus meeting commercial broadcasting's ultimate imperative: bringing viewers to the set. Though the market has since become saturated with the confessional show, Phil Donahue's concept was as radical as it was engaging. For the first time, the

marginalized and the invisible were given a forum, and mainstream America was fascinated.

A true heir to Donahue's throne did not appear until 1986, with the premiere of *The Oprah Winfrey Show*. Winfrey was a Chicago TV personality who burst onto the national scene with her Academy Award-nominated performance in Steven Spielberg's *The Color Purple* (1985). She took Donahue's participatory approach and added her own sensibility. Winfrey, an African-American and sexual abuse survivor, worked her way out of poverty onto the national stage. When her guests poured out their stories, she understood their pain. Unlike many who followed, Winfrey tried to uplift viewers rather than offer them a wallow in the gutter. She started "Oprah's Book Club" to encourage viewers to read contemporary works she believed important. She sought to avoid the confrontations so popular on later series. After one guest surprised his wife on the air with the news that he was still involved with his mistress, and had, in fact, impregnated her, Winfrey vowed such an episode would never occur again. In 1998, in response to the popularity of *The Jerry Springer Show,* Oprah Winfrey introduced a segment called "Change Your Life Television," featuring life-affirming advice from noted self-help authors. *The Oprah Winfrey Show* has received numerous accolades, including Peabody Awards and Daytime Emmys. Winfrey may well be the most powerful woman in show business, as strong an influence on popular culture as any male Hollywood mogul.

The next big daytime talk success was *Geraldo*. Host Geraldo Rivera made his reputation as an investigative journalist on ABC's newsmagazine series *20/20*. After leaving that show, his first venture as the star of his own show was a syndicated special in 1986. The premise was that Rivera and a camera crew would enter Chicago mobster Al Capone's long-lost locked vault. The program was aired live. All through the show Rivera speculated on the fantastic discoveries they would make once the vault was open. When it finally was opened, they found nothing. What he did find was an audience for the daytime talk series that premiered soon after. He also found controversy, most notably when, during a 1988 episode featuring Neo-Nazis, a fight broke out and one "skinhead" youth hit Rivera with a chair, breaking his nose. In 1996, Rivera ended *Geraldo* and signed with cable network CNBC for a nighttime news-talk hour. Though often accused of sensationalism, even he had become disgusted with the state of talk TV, especially the growing popularity of *The Jerry Springer Show.*

A new era of daytime talk began with Jerry Springer. His is the most popular daytime talk show of the late 1990s, often beating *The Oprah Winfrey Show* in the ratings. Springer's talker began its life as another undistinguished member of a growing pack. Viewership picked up when the subject matter became more controversial and the discussion more volatile. Confrontation over personal, often sexual, matters is Springer's stock in trade. Guests frequently face lovers, friends, and family members with disapproval over their choice of lifestyle or romantic partner. Taking the drama a step beyond other daytime talkers, these arguments have frequently come to physical blows. The fights have become a characteristic, almost expected part of the show, which, indeed, is sometimes accused of choreographing them. The content of the series has inspired some stations to banish it from daytime to early morning or late night hours when children are less likely to be watching. Springer's production company sells several volumes of *Too Hot For TV* videos, featuring nudity, profanity, and violence edited from the broadcasts. Critics declaim the show as a further symptom of the moral decline of America, especially

American television. Some bemoan the ''Springerization'' of the nation. Springer defends his show as reflecting the lives of his guests, and giving his audience what they want to see. The series' consistently high ratings, at least, seem to bear out his claim. Springer saw less success when the show became the first daytime talk program to inspire a feature film version, *Ringmaster* (1999). It was a failure at the box office.

With Springer and Winfrey still drawing large audiences, and Rosie O'Donnell's show a breakout hit, daytime talk shows faced the end of the 1990s more popular than ever. New contenders like former sitcom star Roseanne, comedian Howie Mandel, and singing siblings Donny and Marie Osmond have joined the veteran hosts in the battle for a share of the large talk audience, and new talk programs premiere every season. Many people say that they turn on the television for ''company,'' and talk shows bring a wide variety of acquaintances into American living rooms, kitchens, and bedrooms. Their revelations, whether it is an unguarded moment with a celebrity or a painful confession from an unknown, give audiences a taste of intimacy from a safe distance. In a world many Americans perceive as more and more dangerous, this is the ultimate paradox of television, the safe invitation of strangers into the house. Whether they inspire sympathy or judgement, talk shows have become a permanent part of the television landscape.

—David L. Hixson

FURTHER READING:

Burns, Gary, and Robert J. Thompson. *Television Studies: Textual Analysis.* New York, Praeger, 1989.

Carbaugh, Donal. *Talking American: Culture Discourses on ''Donahue.''* Norwood, New Jersey, Ablex, 1988.

Fiske, John. *Television Culture.* New York, Metheun, 1987.

Mincer, Deanne, and Richard Mincer. *The Talkshow Book: An Engaging Primer on How to Talk Your Way to Success.* New York, Facts On File Publications, 1982.

Munson, Wayne. *All Talk: The Talk Show in Media Culture.* Philadelphia, Temple University Press, 1993.

Newcomb, Horace, editor. *Television: The Critical View, Fourth Edition.* New York, Oxford University Press, 1987.

Postman, Neil. *Amusing Ourselves to Death: Public Discourse in the Age of Show Business.* New York, Viking Press, 1985.

Slide, Anthony, editor. *Selected Radio and Television Criticism.* Metuchen, New Jersey, Scarecrow Press, 1987.

Daytona 500

The five-hundred-mile, National Association for Stock Car Auto Racing (NASCAR) Daytona 500 is commonly referred to as ''the Great American Race.'' Its reputation for exciting finishes, horrendous crashes, Florida-in-February weather, and bumper-to-bumper and door-handle-to-door-handle racing along the Daytona International Speedway's two-and-a-half-mile, tri-oval, high-banked track with the long back-straight thrills the fans and challenges the drivers and mechanics. Stock car legends are born here.

The first race of the NASCAR season, the Daytona 500 is the final, paramount event of a spring speedweek featuring three weeks of racing starting with the world-famous 24 Hours of Daytona and two qualifying races. Thanks to television and professional marketing, the Daytona 500 is the premier stock car race of the year, bringing the thrills and violence of racing into the homes of millions. Sponsors of the top cars are afforded a three-and-a-half-hour commercial. Although the Indianapolis 500 has a larger viewing audience, in-car cameras at the Daytona 500 allow the viewer to watch the driver, the cars in front, and the cars behind from the safety of the roll cage. A roof-mounted camera shows the hood buckle in the wind. Another allows the viewer to ride out a spin at two hundred miles per hour. Another planted under the rear bumper allows the viewer to read bumper stickers on the car behind.

The winner of the race is awarded the Harley J. Earl Daytona 500 trophy and a quarter million dollars in prize money. (Earl, 1839-1969, was responsible for the design of the modern American car while at General Motors in the 1930s, 1940s, and 1950s when the ''stock car'' was born.)

The track was started in 1957 by Bill France to take his fledgling NASCAR franchise off the beach of Daytona and bring it into a legitimate race facility. The first Daytona 500 was run in 1959 and won by Lee Petty. Since that time, the number of fans as well as the speed of the cars have increased. The cost of racing has also gone up, and NASCAR and the Daytona track owners have continued to enlarge their entertainment empire. The corporation that owns Daytona also owns Darlington (South Carolina), Talladega (Alabama), and Watkins Glen (New York) race tracks.

The track design and the speeds require an appreciation, if not a dread, on the part of the mechanics and drivers of the modern high-speed professional racing leagues that use the track. The turns—wide U-shaped continuous corners—are banked at thirty-one degrees, and because there are no short chutes between them, they are called one-two and three-four, too steep to walk up let alone drive on. The tri-oval (sort of a turn five) is relatively flat at eighteen degrees but is connected by short, flat straights from the exit of turn four to the entrance of turn one. Flipped up on their sides by the banking, the drivers look ''up'' to see ahead in the turns, and have to deal with a downforce caused by the car wanting to sink down into the pavement. Drivers actually steer fairly straight to accomplish a 120-degree change in direction (one thousand foot radius for three thousand feet of turn). Drivers must do all that and keeping his 3,400-pound car out of the front seat of the one next to him.

The road abruptly flattens after three thousand feet of turns one-two where the equally long straight that is the signature of Daytona now requires the driver to draft within a yard of the car in front, race three wide, keep his foot to the floor, and relax—for a moment—until the car upends again in turns three-four. The driver and car suffer gravitational forces that push down and out in the high banks, immediately followed by a tremendous downward slam at the start of the back-straight, and then in the tri-oval the g-forces are more outward than down. The suspension has to keep the wheels evenly on the surface, and the aerodynamics have to keep the car in a line with itself. Two hundred laps, six hundred left turns, three or four stops for gasoline, all lead to one winner.

Daytona is the track where ''Awesome Bill from Dawsonville'' Elliott acheived fame and fortune, and Lee Petty began the Petty dynasty. It is the race Dale Earnhardt took twenty-one years to win after winning NASCAR races everywhere else. It is the race Mario

Stock cars racing around a curve at the Daytona International Speedway during the Daytona 500, February 18, 1996.

Andretti won once in 1967, but, like Indy (1969), never repeated. Two lasting images from the race are Donnie Allison and Cale Yarborough (1968, 1977, and 1983 winner) duking it out in the back-stretch grass, and Richard Petty and David Pearson colliding with each other after coming out of turns three-four on the last lap—Petty spinning off the track with a dead motor and Pearson sliding along the track killing his engine, too. As Petty, farther downtrack than Pearson, frantically tried to restart, Pearson ground the starter with his Mercury in gear to creep across the finish line and win the race.

—Charles F. Moore

DC Comics

As the leading publisher during the first three decades of the comic book industry, DC Comics was largely responsible for the look and content of mainstream American comic books. By the end of the twentieth century, DC had become not only the longest established purveyor of comic books in the United States, but arguably the most important and influential in the history of comic book publishing. Home to some of the genre's most popular characters, including Superman, Batman, and Wonder Woman, DC's initial innovations in the field were quickly and widely imitated by its competitors, but few achieved the consistent quality and class of DC's comic books in their heyday.

In 1935, a 45-year-old former U.S. Army major and pulp magazine writer named Malcolm Wheeler-Nicholson started up a small operation called National Allied Publishing. From a tiny office in New York City, Wheeler-Nicholson launched *New Fun* and *New Comics.* Although modeled after the new comics magazines like

Famous Funnies, Wheeler-Nicholson's titles were the first to feature original material instead of reprinted newspaper funnies. The Major, remembered by his associates as both an eccentric and something of a charlatan, started his publishing venture with insufficient capital and little business acumen. He met with resistance from distributors still reluctant to handle the new comic books, fell hopelessly into debt to his creditors and employers, and sold his struggling company to the owners of his distributor, the Independent News Company. The new owners, Harry Donenfeld and Jack Liebowitz, would eventually build the Major's tiny operation into a multi-million dollar company.

In 1937 Donenfeld and Liebowitz put out a third comic book title, *Detective Comics.* Featuring a collection of original comic strips based on detective-adventure themes, *Detective Comics* adapted those genres most associated with "B" movies and pulp magazines into a comics format, setting a precedent for all adventure comic books to come. With their own distribution company as a starting point, Donenfeld and Liebowitz developed important contacts with other national distributors to give their comic books the best circulation network in the business. Their publishing arm was officially called National Periodical Publications, but it became better known by the trademark—DC— printed on its comic books and taken from the initials of its flagship title.

What truly put DC on top, however, was the acquisition of Superman. In 1938 Jerry Siegel and Joe Shuster reluctantly sold the rights to their costumed superhero to DC for $130. When Superman debuted in the first issue of DC's *Action Comics,* the impact on the market was immediate. Sales of the title jumped to half-a-million per issue by year's end, and DC had the industry's first original comic book star. In 1939 Bob Kane and Bill Finger created Batman for DC as a follow-up to Superman, and this strange new superhero quickly became nearly as popular as his predecessor. DC's competitors took note of the winning new formula and promptly flooded the market with costumed imitators. DC immediately served notice that it would protect its creative property and its domination of the market by suing the Fox Syndicate for copyright infringement over "Wonderman," a flagrant imitation of Superman. It would later do the same to Fawcett Publications over Captain Marvel, in a lawsuit of dubious merit that dragged on for over a decade.

DC made it a policy to elevate the standards of its material over that of the increasing competition. In 1941 the company publicized the names of its Editorial Advisory Board, which was made up of prominent educators and child-study experts, and it assured parents that all of DC's comic books were screened for appropriate moral content. The strategy worked to deflect from DC much of the public criticism being directed at comic books in general, but it also deprived their publications of the edgy qualities that had made the early Superman and Batman stories so compelling. DC stayed with this conservative editorial policy for the next several decades.

The World War II years were a boom time for DC (as for most other comic book publishers). They added to their stable of stars such popular characters as Wonder Woman, the Green Lantern, the Flash, and the Justice Society of America. More so than any other publisher, DC worked to educate readers on the issues at stake in the war. Rather than simply bombard young people with malicious stereotypes of the enemy as most of the competition did (although there was plenty of that to be found in DC's comics as well), DC's comic books stressed the principles of national unity across ethnic, class, and racial lines, and repeatedly stated a simplified forecast of the postwar vision proclaimed by the Roosevelt administration. The company was also consistent enough to continue its celebration of a liberal postwar order well into the postwar era itself, although it generally did so in dry educational features rather than within the context of its leading adventure stories.

During the 1940s and 1950s DC strengthened and consolidated its leading position in the industry. The publisher remained aloof when its competitors turned increasingly toward violent crime and horror subjects and, although it made tentative nods to these genres with a few mystery and cops-and-robber titles, DC was rarely a target of the criticism directed at the comic book industry during the late 1940s and early 1950s. When the industry adopted the Comics Code in 1954, DC's own comic books were already so innocuous as to be scarcely affected. Indeed, spokesmen for DC took the lead in extolling the virtues of the Code-approved comics. With its less scrupulous competitors fatally tarnished by the controversy over crime and horror, DC was able to dominate the market as never before, even though the market itself shrank in the post-Code era. By 1962, DC's comic books accounted for over 30 percent of all comic books sold.

The company published comics in a variety of genres, including sci-fi, humor, romance, western, war, mystery, and even adaptations of popular television sitcoms and movie star-comics featuring the likes of Jerry Lewis and Bob Hope. But DC's market strength continued to rest upon the popularity of its superheroes, especially Superman and Batman. While the rise of television hurt comic book sales throughout the industry, DC enjoyed the cross-promotional benefits of the popular *Adventures of Superman* TV series (1953-1957). Beginning in 1956, DC revised and revamped a number of its 1940s superheroes, and the new-look Flash, Green Lantern, Hawkman, and Justice League of America comprised the vanguard of what comic book historians have termed the "Silver Age" of superhero comics (as opposed to the "Golden Age" of the 1930s-1940s).

DC's comic books were grounded firmly in the culture of consensus and conformity. In accordance with the Comics Code and

DC's long-standing editorial policies, the superheroes championed high-minded and progressive American values. There was nothing ambiguous about the character, cause, or inevitable triumph of these heroes, and DC took pains to avoid the implication that they were glorified vigilantes and thus harmful role models for children. All of the superheroes held respected positions in society. When they were not in costume, most of them were members of either the police force or the scientific community: Hawkman was a policeman from another planet; the Green Lantern served in an intergalactic police force; the Atom was a respected scientist; the Flash was a police scientist; and Batman and his sidekick, Robin, were deputized members of the Gotham City police force. Superman, of course, was a citizen of the world. These characters all underscored the importance of the individual's obligation to the community, and did so to an extent that, in fact, minimized the virtues of individualism. All of the DC heroes spoke and behaved the same way. Always in control of their emotions and their environment, they exhibited no failings common to the human condition. Residing in clean green suburbs, modern cities with shining glass skyscrapers, and futuristic unblemished worlds, the superheroes exuded American affluence and confidence.

The pristine comic books promoted by DC were, however, highly vulnerable to the challenge posed by the new "flawed" superheroes of Marvel Comics. Throughout the 1960s, figures such as Spider-Man, the Incredible Hulk, and the Fantastic Four garnered Marvel an anti-establishment image that was consciously in synch with trends in contemporary youth culture. DC's star performers, on the other hand, epitomized the "Establishment," seeming like costumed Boy Scout Troop leaders by comparison. By the late 1960s, DC recognized their dilemma and clumsily introduced some obvious ambiguity and angst into their superhero stories, but the move came too late to reverse the company's fall from the top. By the mid-1970s Marvel had surpassed DC as the industry's leading publisher.

In spite of falling sales, DC's characters remained the most popular and the most lucrative comic book properties. In 1968 DC was purchased by the powerful Warner Brothers conglomerate, which would later produce a series of blockbuster movies featuring Superman and Batman. Throughout the 1970s DC enjoyed far greater success with licensing its characters for TV series and toy products than it did selling the actual comics. In 1976 Jeanette Kahn became the new DC publisher charged with the task of revitalizing the comic books. In the early 1980s Kahn helped to institute new financial and creative incentives at the company. This attracted some of the top writers and artists in the field to DC and set a precedent for further industry-wide creator's benefits.

From the late 1980s DC found success in the direct-sales market to comic book stores with a number of titles labeled "For Mature Readers Only," and also took the lead in the growing market for sophisticated and pricey "graphic novels." Established superheroes such as Batman and Green Arrow gained new life as violent vigilante characters and were soon joined by a new generation of surreal postmodern superheroes like the Sandman and Animal Man. Such innovative and ambitious titles helped DC to reclaim much of the creative cutting edge from Marvel. Although DC's sales lagged behind Marvel's throughout the 1990s, the company retained a loyal following among discerning fans as well as longtime collectors, remaining highly respected among those who appreciate the company's historical significance as the prime founder of the American comic book industry.

—Bradford W. Wright

FURTHER READING:

Daniels, Les. *DC Comics: Sixty Years of the World's Favorite Comic Book Heroes.* Boston, Little, Brown, and Co., 1995.

The Greatest 1950s Stories Ever Told. New York, DC Comics, 1991.

The Greatest Golden Age Stories Ever Told. New York, DC Comics, 1990.

Jacobs, Will, and Gerard Jones. *The Comic Book Heroes.* Rocklin, California, Prima Publishing, 1998.

O'Neil, Dennis, editor. *Secret Origins of the Super DC Heroes.* New York, Warner Books, 1976.

De La Hoya, Oscar (1972—)

Nicknamed ''The Golden Boy'' for his Olympic boxing achievement during the 1992 Summer Games, Oscar De La Hoya promised his dying mother that he would win the gold medal for her and did just that. He then turned pro and cashed in on his amateur fistic glory. The only fighter campaigning below heavyweight to command eight-figure purses since Sugar Ray Leonard, De La Hoya's appeal crossed over from mostly male boxing fans to women attracted by his charm and good looks. Guided with savvy by promoter Bob Arum, De La Hoya became one of America's richest and best-known athletes even before taking on any of the world's best young fighters. In addition to exploiting the markets that Leonard did before him, De La Hoya also has a huge Latin American fan base as a result of his Mexican American heritage. His willingness to engage opponents in exciting fights makes him a television favorite as well.

—Max Kellerman

De Niro, Robert (1943—)

For approximately a decade from the mid-1970s, screen actor Robert De Niro came to embody the ethos of urban America—most particularly New York City, where he was born, raised, and educated—in a series of performances that demonstrated a profound and introspective intelligence, great power, and the paradigm skills of the acting technique known as the Method at its best.

In his gallery of violent or otherwise troubled men and social misfits, it is in his portrayal of Travis Bickle in Martin Scorsese's *Taxi Driver* (1976) that his image is likely to remain forever enshrined. As the disturbed, nervy, under-educated Vietnam vet who, through the skewed vision of his isolation and ignorance, sets out on a bloody crusade to cleanse society's ills, De Niro displayed an armory of personal gifts unmatched by any actor of his generation. The film itself was a seminal development in late-twentieth-century cinema, and it is not too fanciful to suggest that, without its influence, certain films in which De Niro excelled for other directors, notably Michael Cimino's *The Deer Hunter* (1978), might not have existed—at least not in as uncompromising a form. It is impossible to catalogue or categorize De Niro's work without examining his significant actor-director relationship with Martin Scorsese, for, while the actor's substantial skills and the concentrated intensity of his persona were very much his own, it is to that symbiotic collaboration that much of his success could be credited. Scorsese explored, interpreted, and recorded the underbelly of Manhattan as no director before him—not even Francis Coppola—had done.

It was *Mean Streets* (1973), Scorsese's picture of small-time gangster life in New York's Little Italy, that focused major attention on De Niro, albeit his role as Johnny Boy, a brash, none-too-bright and volatile hustler, was secondary to that played by Harvey Keitel. De Niro had already appeared in Roger Corman's *Bloody Mama* (1970) and the unfunny Mafia comedy *The Gang That Couldn't Shoot Straight* (1971) at the time of *Mean Streets,* and he soon became stamped as American cinema's most authoritative and interesting purveyor of criminals, large and small.

The son of an artist-poet father and an artist mother, Robert De Niro decided in his teens to become an actor and studied at several institutions, including the Stella Adler Studio and with Strasberg at the Actors Studio in New York City. He worked in obscurity off-Broadway and in touring theater companies before Brian De Palma discovered him and used him in his first three little-seen films—*The Wedding Party* (1963, released 1969), *Greetings* (1968), and *Hi Mom!* (1969). In these, the young De Niro revealed an affinity with the anarchic, and, indeed, De Palma perhaps came closest to Scorsese in being, at that time, a natural director for De Niro. They worked together again almost twenty years later when De Niro, honed in cold villainy, enhanced *The Untouchables* (1989) as a mesmerizing Al Capone. It was his supporting role in *Bloody Mama* that brought De Niro meaningful attention, and several minor movies followed before *Mean Streets* and his first real mainstream appearance as the baseball player in *Bang the Drum Slowly* (1973), which earned him the New York Critics Circle best actor award.

His rising reputation and compelling presence survived his somewhat uncomfortable inclusion in Bertolucci's Italian political epic *1900* and his blank, if elegant, performance in Elia Kazan's disastrous *The Last Tycoon* (both 1976). His Oscar-nominated Travis Bickle, followed by his Jimmy Doyle in Scorsese's *New York, New York* (1977) fortunately superseded both. The director's dark take on a musical genre of the 1940s was badly cut before its release and suffered accordingly. Underrated at the time and a commercial failure, it nonetheless brought plaudits for De Niro, essaying a saxophonist whose humor and vitality masks arrogance, egotism, and an inability to sustain his love affair with, and marriage to, Liza Minnelli's singer.

Next came *The Deer Hunter,* giving the actor a role unlike anything he had done before, albeit as essentially another loner. A somber treatment of male relationships, war, and heroism in which a bearded De Niro, voice and accent adjusted to the character, was as tough and tensile as the steel he forged in a small, bleak Pennsylvania town. His Michael is the authoritative leader of his pack of hunting and drinking buddies, a fearless survivor—and yet locked into a profound and unexpressed interior self, permitted only one immensely effective outbreak of overt emotion when confronted by the death wish of his buddy (Christopher Walken), which his own heroics are finally powerless to conquer.

De Niro began the 1980s with a triumphant achievement, shared with Scorsese. *Raging Bull* (1980), filmed in black-and-white, dealt with the rise, fall, and domestic crises of middleweight boxing champ Jake LaMotta, an Italian American who copes with his personal insecurities with braggadocio and bullying. It was known that De

Niro went to lengths in preparing his roles, keeping faith with the letter and spirit of the Method in his search for authenticity. In preparing to play LaMotta, he trained in the ring, entering some amateur contests, and famously put on sixty pounds for the later-life sequences. It was a bravura performance in one of the best fight films ever made. The actor was garlanded with praise and awards, including the Best Actor Oscar, and nine years later the film was voted the best of the decade. It was a faultless achievement for both star and director.

Inexplicably, although widely acknowledged and admired as a great *actor,* De Niro, for all his achievements, was not proving a great *movie star*—a label that refers to marquee value and box office clout. It was to the Stallones and the Schwarzeneggers that producers looked for big financial returns, which might account for some of De Niro's erratic choices during the 1980s. He was brilliant on familiar ground, aging thirty years as a gangster in Sergio Leone's epic *Once upon a Time in America* in 1983, the year of *The King of Comedy* for Scorsese. This superb collector's piece for the cognoscenti failed disastrously at the box office, despite De Niro's deathless portrayal of would-be comedian Rupert Pupkin, a pathetically disturbed misfit whose obsessional desire for public glory through television leads him to kidnap TV star Jerry Lewis and demand an appearance on his show as ransom. The film is cynical, its title ironic: tragedy lies at its heart. It lost a fortune, and director and star went their separate ways for seven years.

Until then, and for much of the 1990s, De Niro's career had no discernible pattern. Desirous of expanding his repertoire on the one hand, and seeming bored with the ease of his own facility on the other, he appeared in numerous middle-of-the-road entertainments which had little need of him, nor he of them. After *King of Comedy,* he went into *Falling in Love* (1984) with Meryl Streep, about an abortive affair between two married commuters, largely perceived as a contemporary American reworking of *Brief Encounter.* The result was a disappointment and a box-office failure. *Variety* accurately noted that ''The effect of this talented pair acting in such a lightweight vehicle is akin to having Horowitz and Rubinstein improvise a duet on the theme of 'Chopsticks.'''

Other attempts to break the mold between 1985 and 1999 included a Jesuit priest in *The Mission* (1986), worthy but desperately dull; his good-natured bounty hunter in *Midnight Run* (1988), entertaining but unimportant; an illiterate cook in *Stanley and Iris* (1990), a film version of the novel *Union Street* that verged on the embarrassingly sentimental; *Guilty by Suspicion* (1991) an earnest but uncompelling attempt to revisit the McCarthy era in which De Niro played a film director investigated by the HUAC—the list is endless.

On the credit side, among the plethora of undistinguished or otherwise unworthy vehicles and performances delivered on automatic pilot, De Niro met a major challenge in Penny Marshall's *Awakenings* (1990), earning an Academy Award nomination for his moving portrayal of a patient awakened from a twenty-year sleep by the drug L-dopa; he did all that could have been expected of him in the political satire *Wag the Dog* (1997); and he gave an accomplished character performance in Quentin Tarantino's *Jackie Brown* (1997). Almost unrecognizable as a shambling wreck of an ex-con, he seemed initially disconcertingly blank, but this proved deceptive as, in one of the film's best moments, he revealed the chilling hole where a man's heart would normally reside.

It was, however, three more films with Scorsese that made public noise. Their long separation was broken by *GoodFellas* (1990), a brilliant and violent evocation of the Mafia hierarchy, but while De Niro shared in the accolades and acquitted himself with the expertise that was only to be expected, he was in a sense retreading familiar ground. The same was true of the over-long and less successful *Casino* (1995). In between, he scored his biggest success as Max Cady, the vengeful psychopath in Scorsese's remake of *Cape Fear* (1991). Threateningly tattooed, the actor broke the bounds of any conventional villainy to come up with a character so evilly repellent as almost, but not quite, to flirt with parody. The film, and his uncompromising performance, raised up his star profile once more, only for it to dissipate in the run of largely unmemorable films.

An intensely private man, Robert De Niro has eschewed publicity over the years and been notoriously uncooperative with journalists. His unconventional private life has been noted but caused barely a ripple of gossip. Married from 1975 to 1978 to Diahnne Abbott, by whom he had a son, he fathered twins by a surrogate mother for his former girlfriend Toukie Smith, and he married Grace Hightower in 1997. He seemed to grow restless during these years of often passionless performances, seeking somehow to reinvent himself and broaden the horizons of his ambition. In 1988 he bought an eight-story building in downtown Manhattan and set up his TriBeCa Film Center. Aside from postproduction facilities and offices, it housed De Niro's Tribeca restaurant, the sought-after and exclusive haunt of New York's media glitterati.

It was from there that De Niro launched himself as a player on the other side of the camera, producing some dozen films between 1992 and 1999. One of these, *A Bronx Tale* (1993), marked his directing debut. Choosing a familiar milieu, he cast himself as the good guy, a bus driver attempting to keep his young son free of the seemingly glamorous influence of the local Mafia as embodied by Chazz Palminteri—a role that he once would have played himself.

After attempting to regain the acting high ground as a tough loner in John Frankenheimer's ambiguous thriller *Ronin* (1998)—material inadequate to the purpose—De Niro began displaying a new willingness to talk about himself. What emerged was a restated ambition to turn his energy to directing because, as he told the respectable British broadsheet *The Guardian* in a long interview during the fall of 1998, ''directing makes one think a lot more and I have to involve myself—make my own decisions, my own mistakes. It's more consuming. The actor is the one who has to grovel in the mud and jump through hoops.''

His words had the ring of a man who had exhausted his own possibilities and was searching for a new commitment, but whatever the outcome, Robert De Niro's achievements had long assured his place in twentieth-century American cultural history.

—Robyn Karney

FURTHER READING:

Dougan, Andy. *Untouchable—A Biography of Robert De Niro.* New York, Thunder's Mouth Press, 1997.

Friedman, Lawrence S. *The Cinema of Martin Scorsese.* New York, Continuum, 1997.

Le Fanu, Mark. ''Robert De Niro.'' *The Movie Stars Story.* Edited by Robyn Karney. New York, Crescent Books, 1986.

———. ''Robert De Niro.'' *Who's Who in Hollywood.* Edited by Robyn Karney. New York, Continuum, 1994.

Thomson, David. *A Biographical Dictionary of Film.* New York, Alfred A. Knopf, 1994.

The Dead Kennedys

Singer Jello Biafra's politically confrontational lyrics lived up to the provocative billing of his group's name: the Dead Kennedys. Biafra's equal-opportunity outrage reproached a wide collection of targets: callow corporations, the Reagan Administration, the Moral Majority, then-California Governor Jerry Brown, feeble liberals, punk rockers with fascist leanings, and MTV. When asked if playing a concert on the anniversary of John F. Kennedy's assassination wasn't distasteful, guitarist East Bay Ray responded that the assassination wasn't in particularly good taste either. Generally acknowledged as pioneers in the American hardcore scene, which was centered in Washington, D.C., and Los Angeles in the early 1980s, the Dead Kennedys' faster variant of punk never fully matched the fury in Biafra's lyrics. By the mid-1980s, in the midst of a political backlash against rock music, Biafra, the group, and its record label became the targets of a misguided obscenity trial. The Dead Kennedys' case was a forewarning of future prosecutions against musicians and record retailers.

The Dead Kennedys' 1981 debut, *Fresh Fruit for Rotting Vegetables,* was released on the group's own label, Alternative Tentacles, and featured the political sarcasm that became the group's strength. The album's opening track, "Kill the Poor," is a Swiftian

The Dead Kennedys with singer Jello Biafra.

proposal about the neutron bomb. "California Uber Alles" imagines Jerry Brown's "Zen Fascist" state: "Your kids will meditate in school . . . You will jog for the master race . . . Mellow out or you will pay." During the same year, the Dead Kennedys' released *In God We Trust, Inc.,* which attacked corporate religion's self-righteousness in the age of televangelism. *Plastic Surgery Disasters* (1982) ridiculed personal identifications such as the preppy, the car enthusiast, and the RV tourist. *Frankenchrist,* the group's first release after a three-year break, was an uneven mixture of scathing commentary and didacticism.

However one felt about his vitriol, Biafra's political carpings often included some sort of constructive solution. For Biafra, merely pointing out the shortcomings in American society was not an answer: "You fear freedom / 'Cos you hate responsibility," he sang in 1985's "Stars and Stripes of Corruption." Even Michael Guarino, the Los Angeles deputy city attorney who unsuccessfully prosecuted the band, was forced to acknowledge the band's social commitment, commenting in the *Washington Post* that, "midway through the trial we realized that the lyrics . . . were in many ways socially responsible, very anti-drug and pro-individual." Biafra's fourth-place run for mayor of San Francisco in 1979 showed that 6600 people had been equally discontented with the establishment and that Biafra's level of political involvement ran deeper than mere complaint. Although his campaign was farcical at times—Biafra's platform suggested that all downtown businessmen wear clown suits—there were serious proposals from the candidate whose slogan was, "There's always room for Jello." For example, Biafra's platform called for neighborhood elections of police officers long before the Rodney King beating compelled urban leaders to demand that local police departments hold themselves more accountable.

Ultimately, the Dead Kennedys' attacks on the status quo didn't provoke authorities so much as the H. R. Giger "Landscape #20" poster in *Frankenchrist* did. Commonly referred to as "Penis Landscape," the poster's artwork depicted an endless series of alternating rows of copulating penises and anuses. Biafra decided that the poster merited inclusion for its depiction of everyone getting screwed by everyone else. A Los Angeles parent filed a complaint in 1986, and police raided Biafra's San Francisco apartment, Alternative Tentacles' headquarters, and the label's distributor. Police confiscated copies of *Frankenchrist* and the Giger poster, charging the Dead Kennedys with "distribution of harmful matter to minors."

The year 1985 had marked the beginning of a national backlash against rock music that had lasting effects. The Parents Music Resource Center, a political action group cofounded by Tipper Gore, held congressional hearings on rock music lyrics. The hearings focused on rap and heavy metal music, but the ensuing publicity questioned rock lyrics in monolithic terms. In 1986, the PMRC succeeded in pressuring the Recording Industry Association of America to voluntarily include warning stickers ("Parental Advisory: Explicit Lyrics") on albums. A series of First Amendment disputes was under way as rock and rap artists faced obscenity charges, and retailers who sold stickered albums to minors faced fines and imprisonment.

Biafra soundly contended that the group's political views, and the limited resources of their independent record company, made them an expedient target. The band found support from other underground musicians who performed benefit concerts to augment the band's defense fund. Pre-trial wrangling pushed the trial's length to a year and a half, and with that, the Dead Kennedys were effectively finished. In 1987, the case was dismissed, due to a hung jury that leaned toward acquittal. His band finished, Biafra became a spoken word performer, recording *No More Cocoons* (1987), a collection of political satire in the tradition of Lenny Bruce. Biafra recounted the trial in 1989's *High Priest of Harmful Matter—Tales from the Trial*.

The history of censorship in rock and roll reverts back to Elvis Presley's first television appearance, when cameras cut off his performance at the waist. New to this history are politically organized forces of censorship. Large superstores, like Wal-Mart, by threatening not to sell albums that have warning labels, have compelled artists to change lyrics or artwork. These gains by the anti-rock forces made the Dead Kennedys' legal victory a crucial one; the case was an invaluable blueprint for rap groups with incendiary lyrics or sexually explicit lyrics, like 2 Live Crew, who faced prosecution in the late 1980s.

—Daryl Umberger

FURTHER READING:

Kester, Marian. *Dead Kennedys: The Unauthorized Version.* San Francisco, Last Gasp of San Francisco, 1983.

Segal, David. "Jello Biafra: The Surreal Deal. The Life and Times of an Artist Provocateur; Or, How a Dead Kennedy Got $2.2 Million in Debt." *Washington Post.* May 4, 1997, G01.

Dean, James (1931-1955)

Perhaps no film actor is as emblematic of his own era as is James Dean of his. Certainly, no screen-idol image has been as widely disseminated—his brooding, enigmatic, and beautiful face has sold everything from blue jeans to personal computers, and 45 years after his death, his poster-size image was still gracing the bedroom walls of millions of teenage girls and beaming down on the customers in coffee bars throughout America and Europe.

Whether or not he intended to take it to its logical and tragic conclusion, James Dean's credo was to live fast, die young, and leave a good-looking corpse. Thus, his legendary legacy is comprised of only three major motion pictures (though he had small roles in three others prior to this), a handful of seldom-seen television dramas, and an admired Broadway stage performance seen only by a relative handful of people. But Dean, like Brando whom he idolized, was able to blend his life and his art so seamlessly that each seemed an extension of the other. And he harbored a long-festering psychic wound, a vulnerability that begged for redemption. It was the omnipresent wounded child in Dean's persona that made him so appealing, and gave his acting such visceral impact.

Born in Marion, Indiana, James Dean spent his early childhood in Los Angeles where his father worked as a dental technician for the Veterans Administration. His mother, Mildred, overly protective of her son and with a preternatural concern for his health, died of cancer when he was nine, and he was sent to live with his father's sister in Fairmount, Indiana. There, he developed the hallmark traits of an orphan: depression, an inexplicable feeling of loneliness, and antisocial behavior. But Dean's childhood was bucolic as well as tormented. His aunt and uncle doted on him, and nurtured his natural talents. Good at sports, particularly basketball (despite his short stature), and theater, the bespectacled teenager nevertheless required a reputation for rebelliousness that made him *persona non grata* with

James Dean

the parents of his classmates—particularly those of female students who, even then, were fascinated by this mysterious, faintly melancholy youth. Dean was also attractive to older men, and it was a local preacher in Fairmount who first sensed the boy's emotional vulnerability, grew fond of him, and showered him with favors and attention. This quality in the young Dean was a dubious asset that he would exploit to his advantage frequently over the course of his brief career.

Dean never entertained the idea of any career but acting. Upon graduating, he rejoined his father in Los Angeles and attended Santa Monica City College and UCLA before dropping out to pursue acting full-time. According to his fellow drama students at the latter institution, he showed little talent. After quitting UCLA, he lived hand to mouth, picking up bit parts on television and film. His acting may have been lackluster, but he had a pronounced gift for evoking sympathy, and it was during a lean stretch that he acquired his first patron. Dean had taken a job parking cars at a lot across from CBS and it was there that he met the director Rogers Brackett, who took a paternal, as well as a sexual, interest in the young man. Eventually Dean moved in with Brackett and was introduced to a sophisticated homosexual milieu. When Brackett was transferred to Chicago in 1951, he supplied Dean with the necessary money and connections to take a stab at New York.

There was nothing predestined about James Dean's eventual success. He went about just as any other young actor, struggling to eat, relying on the kindness of others, and changing addresses like he changed his clothes. At first he was timid; legend has it that he spent his first week either in his hotel room or at the movies, but just as he had a flair for cultivating older men, he had an impeccable ear for self-promotion and slanting his stories for maximum advantage. Fortunately, his relationship with Brackett gave him entrée to an elegant theater crowd that gathered at the Algonquin and, helped by Brackett's influential contacts, Dean found television work and an agent. In the summer of 1952, he auditioned for, and was accepted into, the prestigious Actors Studio. Once again, the Dean mystique has distorted the facts to fit the legend: he never appeared in a studio production and his fellow members remembered him only as a vague presence, uncommunicative and sullen.

From a purely practical point of view, Dean's casual morals gave him one advantage over his struggling contemporaries. He was not averse to peddling his sexual favors to further his career, and his first real break came from his seduction of Lemuel Ayers, a successful businessman who invested money in the theater, and helped secure the aspiring actor a role in a forthcoming Broadway play called *See the Jaguar*. The play folded after four performances, but 1954 brought him *The Immoralist*, adapted from André Gide's novel, in which he played the North African street Arab whose sexual charisma torments a male married writer struggling with homosexual tendencies. Dean's own sexual charisma was potent, and his performance attracted notice, praise, and Hollywood. By the end of the following year, 1955, he had starred in *East of Eden* for Elia Kazan—mentor to Montgomery Clift and Brando—and, under Nicholas Ray's direction, became the idolized voice of a generation as the *Rebel Without a Cause*.

Many writers have attributed James Dean's winning combination of vulnerability and bravado to his mother's early death; certainly, he seemed aware of this psychic wound without being able rectify it. "Must I always be miserable?" he wrote to a girlfriend. "I try so hard to make people reject me. Why?" Following his Broadway success, he abandoned his gay friends, as if in revenge for all the kindness they had proffered, and when he was cast in *East of Eden*, he broke away from his loyal patron, Rogers Brackett, then fallen on hard times. When a mutual friend upbraided him for his callousness, his response was, "I though it was the john who paid, not the whore." But to others, Dean seemed unaffected by success. He was chimerical, yet remarkably astute in judging how far (and with whom) he could take his misbehavior. This trait fostered his Jekyll-and-Hyde image—sweet and sensitive on the one hand, callous, sadistic, and rude on the other.

The actor's arrival in Hollywood presented a problem for studio publicists unsure how to market this unknown, uncooperative commodity. They chose to focus on inflating Dean's sparse Broadway credentials, presenting him as the New York theater actor making good in Hollywood. In New York, Dean had been notorious for skulking sullenly in a corner at parties and throwing tantrums and, although he could be perfectly delightful given sufficient motivation, he was not motivated to appease the publicists. What were taken for Dean's Actors Studio affectations—his ill-kempt appearance, slouching, and mumbling—was actually his deliberate attempt to deflate Hollywood bombast and pretension. The reigning queens of Hollywood gossip, Louella Parsons and Hedda Hopper, both took umbrage at Dean's behavior. His disdain for Hollywood was so overt that, before *East of Eden* was even complete, he had managed to set much of the entertainment press squarely against him. *East of Eden*, however, made a huge impact, won Dean an Academy Award nomination and launched him into the stratospheric stardom that was confirmed later the same year with the success of *Rebel Without a Cause*. In both films, the young actor played complex adolescents, alienated from the

values of the adult world around them—tormented, haunted by an extraordinarily mature recognition of pain that comes from being misunderstood and needing to be loved. The animal quality he brought to conveying anguish and frustration struck a chord in the collective psyche of 1950s American youth, and his almost immediate iconic status softened the scorn of journalists. His on-screen charisma brought forgiveness for his off-screen contemptuousness, and his uncouth mannerisms were suddenly accorded the indulgence shown a naughty and precocious child.

Stardom only exacerbated Dean's schizoid nature, which, paradoxically, he knew to be central to his appeal. When a young Dennis Hopper quizzed him about his persona, he replied, ". . . in this hand I'm holding Marlon Brando, saying, 'Fuck you!' and in the other hand, saying, 'Please forgive me,' is Montgomery Clift. 'Please forgive me.' 'Fuck you!' And somewhere in between is James Dean." But while playing the *enfant terrible* for the press, he reacted to his overnight fame with naïve wonder, standing in front of the theater unnoticed in his glasses and watching the long queues forming for *East of Eden* with delight. That was Dean's sweet side. He exorcised his demons through speed, buying first a horse, then a Triumph motorcycle, an MG, and a Porsche in short order. He delighted in scaring his friends with his reckless driving. Stories of Dean playing daredevil on his motorcycle (which he called his "murdercycle") are legion. Racing became his passion, and he managed to place in several events. His antics so alarmed the studios that a "no-ride" clause was written into his contract for fear that he would be killed or disfigured in the middle of shooting.

With the shooting of *Rebel* completed, he made his third film, co-starring with Rock Hudson and Elizabeth Taylor in *Giant*. As Jet Rink, the graceless farm laborer who strikes oil and becomes a millionaire, Dean was able to play to type for the first half of the film, but was seriously too young to meet the challenge of the second half in which Rink has become a dissipated, middle-aged tycoon. Nonetheless, he collected a second Oscar nomination—but was no longer alive to hear the announcement. On September 30, 1955, almost immediately after the completion of filming, James Dean and a mechanic embarked for a race in Salinas in the actor's new Porsche Spyder. Fate, in the form of a Ford, struck the tiny car head-on, breaking Dean's neck. He was dead at 24 years old.

Part of James Dean's enduring allure rests in the fact that he was dead before his two biggest films were complete. His legacy as an artist and a man is continually debated. Was he gay or straight? Self-destructive or merely reckless? Perhaps he didn't know himself, but doom hung about him like a shroud, and it came as no surprise to many of his colleagues when they learned of his fatal accident. Elia Kazan, upon hearing the news, sighed "That figures." After his death, his friend Leonard Rosenman commented, "Jimmy's main attraction was his almost pathological vulnerability to hurt and rejection. This required enormous defenses on his part to cover it up, even on the most superficial level. Hence the leather-garbed motorcycle rider, the tough kid having to reassure himself at every turn of the way by subjecting himself to superhuman tests of survival, the last of which he failed." Whether Dean had a death wish or simply met with an unfortunate accident will continue to be batted around for eternity; there are as many who will attest to his self-destructiveness as to his hope for the future. So, was it mere bravado or a sense of fatalism that made him remark to his friend and future biographer John Gilmore: "You remember the movie Bogie made—*Knock on Any Door*—and the line, 'Live fast, die young, have a good-looking corpse?' Shit, man, I'm going to be so good-looking they're going to have to cement me in the coffin.''

—Michael Baers

FURTHER READING:

Alexander, Paul. *Boulevard of Broken Dreams: The Life, Times, and Legend of James Dean.* New York, Plume, 1994.

Gilmore, John. *Live Fast—Die Young: Remembering the Short Life of James Dean.* New York, Thunder's Mouth Press, 1997.

Holley, Val. *James Dean, The Biography.* New York, Saint Martin's Press, 1995.

Howlett, John. *James Dean: A Biography.* London, Plexus, 1975.

McCann, Graham. *Rebel Males: Clift, Brando, & Dean.* New Brunswick, Rutgers University Press, 1993.

Riese, Randall. *The Unabridged James Dean: His Life and Legacy from A to Z.* Chicago, Contemporary, 1991.

Death of a Salesman

In all of twentieth-century American drama, it is Arthur Miller's 1949 masterpiece *Death of a Salesman* that has been lauded as the greatest American play. The play deals with both the filial and social realms of American life, exploring and exploding the concept of the American dream. From its debut in New York in 1949 to its many international stagings since, *Death of a Salesman* has spoken to the concerns of middle-class workers worldwide and their struggle for existence in capitalist society. The play and its initial production set the tone for American drama for the rest of the century through its sociopolitical themes, its poetic realism, and its focus on the common man. Brenda Murphy observes, ''Since its premier, there has never been a time when *Death of a Salesman* was not being performed somewhere in the world.''

The play revolves around the story of the aging salesman Willy Loman, his wife, Linda, and their sons, Biff and Happy. Willy has reached a critical point whereby he cannot work as a traveling salesman and is disappointed in Biff's unwillingness to fulfill his father's dreams. When Willy finally summons the courage to ask his employer to be transferred to New York, he is fired. Linda informs Biff that Willy has secretly attempted suicide, and through a series of flashbacks it is revealed that Biff had found his father with a mistress, which led to Biff's decline. Two other subplots—involving Willy's neighbors, Charley and Bernard, and the appearance of Willy's dead brother Ben—interweave the story. Charley becomes Willy's creditor, and Bernard is the successful son Willy never had. Ben is the pioneering capitalist Willy could never be. Because he has a life insurance policy, Willy decides he is worth more dead, and he commits suicide. Linda is left at his grave uttering the famous lines ''We're free and clear . . . We're free . . . And there'll be nobody home.''

The play's subtitle is ''Certain Private Conversations in Two Acts and a Requiem.'' Miller's first concept of the play was vastly different from its current form. ''The first image that occurred to me which was to result in *Death of a Salesman* was of an enormous face

the height of the proscenium arch which would appear and then open up, and we would see the inside of a man's head. In fact, *The Inside of His Head* was the first title.'' Instead, Miller gives us a cross-section of the Loman household, simultaneously providing a realistic setting and maintaining the expressionistic elements of the play.

Miller also employs the use of realism for scenes of the present and a series of expressionistic flashbacks for scenes from the past. In his essay ''*Death of a Salesman* and the Poetics of Arthur Miller,'' Matthew C. Roudanè writes, ''Miller wanted to formulate a dramatic structure that would allow the play textually and theatrically to capture the simultaneity of the human mind as that mind registers outer experience through its own inner subjectivity.'' Hence, the play flashes back to visits from Ben and scenes from Willy's affair. Miller's juxtaposition of time and place give the play added dimension; Miller never acknowledges from whose point of view the story is told and whether the episodes are factual or recreations based on Willy's imagination. Miller also uses flute, cello, and other music to punctuate and underscore the action of the play.

Many critics have attempted to make connections between the name Loman and the position of the character in society, but Miller refuted this theory in his 1987 autobiography *Timebends: A Life*. He explained that the origin of the name Loman was derived from a character called ''Lohmann'' in the Fritz Lang film *The Testament of Dr. Mabuse*. ''In later years I found it discouraging to observe the confidence with which some commentators on *Death of a Salesman* smirked at the heavy-handed symbolism of 'Low-man,''' Miller wrote. ''What the name really meant to me was a terror-stricken man calling into the void for help that will never come.'' Miller describes the play simply: ''What it 'means' depends on where on the face of the earth you are and what year it is.''

Death of a Salesman originates from two genres: the refutation of the ''rags-to-riches'' theory first set forth by Horatio Alger, and the form of Miller's self-proclaimed ''Tragedy and the Common Man.'' In stories such as *Ragged Dick,* Alger put forth the theory that even the poorest, through hard work and determination, could eventually work their way to the upper class. Willy Loman seems the antithesis of this ideal, as the more he works toward security the further he is away from it. Thomas E. Porter observes, ''Willy's whole life has been shaped by his commitment to the success ideology, his dream based on the Alger myth; his present plight is shown to be the inevitable consequence of this commitment.''

Miller attempted to define Willy Loman as an Aristotelian tragic figure in his 1949 essay ''Tragedy and the Common Man.'' Miller stated that he believed ''the common man is as apt a subject for tragedy in its highest sense as kings were.'' He went on to parallel Willy's fall with that of Oedipus and Orestes, claiming that tragedy was ''the consequence of a man's total compulsion to evaluate himself justly.'' Despite Miller's claims, he has been attacked for his views by literary critic Harold Bloom. ''All that Loman shares with Lear or Oedipus is agony; there is no other likeness whatsoever. Miller has little understanding of Classical or Shakespearean tragedy,'' Bloom wrote in *Willy Loman*. ''He stems entirely from Ibsen.''

The play's placement in the history of American drama is critical, as it bridged the gap between the melodramatic works of Eugene O'Neill and the Theatre of the Absurd of the 1960s. The original production was directed by Elia Kazan and designed by Jo Mielziner, the same team that made Tennessee Williams's *The Glass Menagerie* a Broadway success. Along with the works of Tennessee Williams, Arthur Miller's plays of this period defined ''serious''

John Malkovich (left) and Dustin Hoffman in a scene from the television production of Arthur Miller's *Death of a Salesman*.

Broadway theatre. In the 1950s and 1960s, Miller's refusal to submit to the House Committee on Un-American Activities and the on-slaught of the avant-garde in the theatre both served to squelch his dramatic voice.

Several productions of *Death of a Salesman* have been per-formed to great acclaim, including the 1975 George C. Scott produc-tion and the 1984 Michael Rudman production starring Dustin Hoffman, John Malkovich, and Kate Reid, which was later filmed for television. Other notable productions include the 1983 production at the Beijing People's Art Theatre and the 1997 Diana LeBlanc production at Canada's Stratford Festival.

—Michael Najjar

FURTHER READING:

Bloom, Harold, editor. *Willy Lowman*. New York, Chelsea House Publishers, 1991.

Klaus, Carl H., Miriam Gilbert, and Bradford S. Field, Jr. *Stages of Drama: Classical to Contemporary Masterpieces of the Theater.* 2nd ed. New York, St. Martin's Press, 1991.

Martine, James J. *Critical Essays on Arthur Miller.* Boston, G. K. Hall & Co, 1979.

Miller, Arthur. *Timebends: A Life.* New York, Grove Press, 1987.

Roudané, Matthew C. "*Death of a Salesman* and the Poetics of Arthur Miller." *Cambridge Companion to Arthur Miller.* Edit-ed by Christopher Bigsby. Cambridge, Cambridge University Press, 1997.

Debs, Eugene V. (1855-1926)

Eugene Victor Debs, labor leader and five-time Socialist candi-date for President, was born in Terre Haute, Indiana, on November 5, 1855. Working on the railroads since he was 14, Debs founded the American Railway Union in 1893. The following year, the union was destroyed and Debs served six months in jail after a failed strike against the Pullman company in Chicago. Subsequently, Debs joined the Socialist Party of America and was their presidential candidate in 1900, 1904, 1908, and in 1912 when he received about 6 percent of votes cast. Opposing United States entry into World War I, Debs was sentenced to 10 years in prison for sedition in 1918. In 1920, from his prison cell in Atlanta, Georgia, Debs ran for the presidency again gaining about 3.5 percent of the vote. A year later President Warren G. Harding commuted his sentence and Debs spent his last years in relative obscurity until his death on October 20, 1926. Debs is remembered as the most viable Socialist candidate for the nation's highest office and as a champion of workers' rights.

—John F. Lyons

FURTHER READING:

Ginger, Ray. *The Bending Cross: A Biography of Eugene Victor Debs.* New Brunswick, Canada, Rutgers University Press, 1949.

Salvatore, Nick. *Eugene V. Debs: Citizen and Socialist.* Urbana, University of Illinois, 1982.

Debutantes

The debutante (from the French *débuter,* to begin) is a young woman, usually of age 17 or 18, who is formally introduced to affluent society at a ball or "coming out" party. The original purpose of the "debut" was to announce that young women of prominent social standing were available for courtship by eligible young men. This social ritual was necessitated by the traditional upper-class

The Seattle Rhinestone debutantes of 1956.

practice of sending girls away to boarding school where they were virtually hidden from view—prohibited from dating, attending parties of mixed company, or socializing with adults. A formal announcement thus introduced the debutante to her social peers and potential suitors. The custom had been long established among the aristocracy and the upper classes in England, where debutantes were, until the mid-twentieth century, presented at Court. In America, the debutante ball derived from the formal etiquette of the nineteenth century, but the ritual has been transformed by each generation's evolving notions about the proprieties of class, sexual freedom, and the role of women.

According to the 1883 etiquette reference, *The Manners That Win,* a debutante should have graduated school, sing or play an instrument gracefully, dance with elegance, and know the rules governing polite society. Having mastered these essential skills, she was presumed ready for courtship, leading, of course, to marriage—at the time the single vocational avenue open to the well-to-do woman. A second purpose was, however, implicit in debut parties of the Gilded Age. Since debutante balls were private affairs, held at the family's residential estate or at a fashionable hotel until the early twentieth century, they also pointed to a given family's wealth, prestige, and style.

By the 1920s, some latitude had relaxed the rules of the debut. In her seminal *Etiquette: The Blue Book of Social Usage* (1922), Emily Post described several ways that a young woman might be introduced to society. These included a formal ball, an afternoon tea with dancing, a small dance, or a small tea without music. In addition, Post listed a fifth and more modest way for a family to announce that a daughter had reached the age of majority: mother and daughter might simply have joint calling cards engraved. For the most part, private debuts had become a thing of the past, replaced by public cotillions or assemblies that invited prominent young women to make their debuts collectively. These long established debutante balls include the Passavant Cotillion in Chicago; Boston's Cotillion; the Junior Assemblies in New York; and the Harvest Ball at the Piedmont Driving Club in Atlanta.

After World War II, the debutante ball spread to almost every city in America and enjoyed a heyday during the conservative Eisenhower years. Yet a decade later, anti-establishment sentiment led many young women of even the most affluent status to abandon the event, dismissing it as anachronistic snobbery. In addition, sexual liberation and the feminist movement challenged the very basis of the century-old convention, as women began to seek both sexual and professional fulfillment outside of marriage. In the exuberantly prosperous 1980s, the debutante ball witnessed a popular resurgence and, by the century's end, cotillions were frequently being sponsored by charitable organizations that extended invitations exclusively to philanthropically active women.

If there is one rule that has not changed over the years, though, it is the debutante's dress. She is to wear a white gown, though a pastel shade may be considered acceptable. Loud colors or black have remained always inappropriate.

—Michele S. Shauf

FURTHER READING:

Post, Peggy. *Emily Post's Etiquette.* New York, Harper Collins, 1997.

Roosevelt, Eleanor. *Eleanor Roosevelt's Book of Common Sense Etiquette.* New York, Macmillan., 1962.

Schlesinger, Arthur M. *Learning How to Behave.* New York, Macmillan, 1947.

Tuckerman, Nancy, and Nancy Dunnan. *The Amy Vanderbilt Complete Book of Etiquette.* New York, Doubleday, 1985.

The Deer Hunter

Before Director Michael Cimino's 1978 film *The Deer Hunter,* the only cinematic treatment of the Vietnam War most Americans had seen was John Wayne's *The Green Berets* a decade earlier. By 1978, however, American audiences were finally ready to deal with the war on-screen. *The Deer Hunter* was popular with audiences and critics alike, nominated for nine Academy Awards and winning five, including Best Picture, Best Director, and Best Supporting Actor (Christopher Walken). *The Deer Hunter* broke the ground in the cinematic treatment of Vietnam, opening the door for films like *Apocalypse Now* a year later, *Platoon* (1986), and *Full Metal Jacket* (1987). All of these ''Vietnam'' films shared the same shattering emotional impact on audiences, but none was as moving as *The Deer Hunter.*

The Deer Hunter deals not only with Vietnam, but also foregrounds the contrast between the soldier's comparatively gentle life at home with the brutal trauma of war. The film opens in the Clairton, Pennsylvania steel mill where Michael (Robert DeNiro), Nick (Christopher Walken), and Steve (John Savage) are working their last shift before shipping out to Vietnam. The quotidian details of their working-class lives revolve around work, hunting, drinking, and playing pool. But Steve, like so many soldiers before him, is getting married before he leaves for the war. Cinematographer Vilmos Zsigmond beautifully photographs the Russian Orthodox wedding ceremony, but portents of the war intrude upon the revelry. A Green Beret mysteriously appears at the wedding like Coleridge's Ancient Mariner, foreshadowing the death and destruction that await in Vietnam.

The brutal rituals of war replace the rituals back in Pennsylvania; however, Cimino and co-writer Deric Washburn use Russian roulette in a North Vietnamese prison camp as their metaphor for combat. The Russian roulette game is an ironic, terrifying counterpoint to the trios hunting and pool playing stateside, and the prison camp scenes are a chilling condensation of the Vietnam war itself— bamboo, rain, and death. The end of the film leaves us with three characters that represent the spectrum of the Vietnam veterans' experience. Nick

A scene from *The Deer Hunter* featuring (from left) John Cazale, Chuck Aspegren, Christopher Walken, Robert De Niro, and John Savage.

dies, Steve returns home in a wheelchair, and Michael returns emotionally crippled.

Besides the emotional impact of the story and the photography, the film benefits from its excellent ensemble cast. In addition to Oscar winner Christopher Walken, Oscar nominee Robert DeNiro (Best Actor), and John Savage, the film stars Meryl Streep (nominee for Best Supporting Actress), George Dzundza, and John Cazale in his last film (Cazale died of cancer right after filming was completed). Stanley Myers' powerful, melancholy musical score, mostly consisting of a solitary, plaintive guitar, adds to the film's heartbreaking effect.

The Deer Hunter, according to literary critic Leslie Fiedler, is "the reenactment of a fable, a legend as old as America itself: a post-Vietnam version of the myth classically formulated in James Fenimore Cooper's *The Deerslayer* and *Last of the Mohicans.*" The myth that is played out in *The Deer Hunter* is an ancient one: The transition from innocence to experience. War films, according to author John Newsinger, "are tales of masculinity. They are stories of boys becoming men, of comradeship and loyalty, of bravery and endurance, of pain and suffering, and the horror and the excitement of battle. Violence—the ability both to inflict it and to take it—is portrayed as an essential part of what being a man involves." No film before *The Deer Hunter* and few since have so brutally captures war as an initiation rite.

—Tim Arnold

FURTHER READING:

Dittmar, Linda, and Gene Michaud, editors. *From Hanoi to Hollywood: The Vietnam War in American Film.* New Brunswick, New Jersey, Rutgers University Press, 1990.

Eberwein, Robert T. "Ceremonies of Survival: The Structure of *The Deer Hunter.*" *The Journal of Popular Film and Television.* Vol. 7, 1979, 352-64.

Fiedler, Leslie. "Mythicizing the Unspeakable." *Journal of American Folklore.* Vol. 103, 1990, 390-99.

Hellman, John. *American Myth and the Legacy of Vietnam.* New York, Columbia University Press, 1986.

Newsinger, John. "'Do You Walk the Walk?': Aspects of Masculinity in Some Vietnam War Films." *You Tarzan: Masculinity, Movies and Men.* Ed. Pat Kirkham and Janet Thurmim. New York, St. Martin's Press, 1993.

DeGeneres, Ellen (1958—)

Ellen DeGeneres attracted massive media attention when she came out as a lesbian on her television show in 1997. Known as "the puppy episode," the program stirred controversy and drew criticism from conservative sectors. DeGeneres and her partner, actress Anne Heche, came out at the same time, DeGeneres appearing on the covers of national magazines. The caption accompanying her photograph on the cover of *Time* read, "Yep, I'm Gay." Her place in history as TV's first gay lead character was thus secured.

Born in New Orleans in 1958, DeGeneres' sometimes difficult life inspired her to use humor as a coping device. After her parents' divorce when she was 13, she and her mother, Betty, moved to Texas.

Ellen DeGeneres

It was a hard time, and DeGeneres used humor to buoy her mother's spirits. "My mother was going through some really hard times and I could see when she was really getting down, and I would start to make fun of her dancing," DeGeneres has said. "Then she'd start to laugh and I'd make fun of her laughing. And she'd laugh so hard she'd start to cry, and then I'd make fun of that. So I would totally bring her from where I'd seen her start going into depression to all the way out of it."

After graduating from high school in 1976, DeGeneres moved back to New Orleans where she worked a series of dead-end jobs: house painter, secretary, oyster shucker, sales clerk, waitress, bartender, and vacuum salesperson. At the encouragement of friends, she tried out her comedy on an amateur-hour audience, in 1981. Her act went over well, and her niche had been found. Only a year later, she entered and won Showtime's "Funniest Person in America" contest. The title, which brought both criticism and high expectations, was her springboard to stardom.

One of her better-known stand-up routines, "A Phone Call to God," came from one of her own darkest moments of despair, when a close friend and roommate had been killed in a car accident while out on a date. The girl was only 23, and it seemed very unfair to DeGeneres. She wanted to question God about a lot of things that seemed unnecessary, and again she turned to humor. She sat down one night and considered what it would be like if she could call God on the phone and ask him about some of the things that troubled her. As if it was meant to be, the monologue poured from her pen to paper, and it was funny, focusing on topics such as fleas and what their purpose might be. DeGeneres performed "A Phone Call to God" on the Johnny Carson show six years later. Everything clicked that night, and Carson signaled her over to sit on the couch after her perform-ance. She was the only female comedian Carson ever called to come over and talk to him on a first appearance on the *Tonight Show.*

DeGeneres continued on the comedy circuit and started acting; one memorable performance was with dancing fruit in Very Fine juice commercials. She eventually landed small roles in several short-lived television series: *Duet, Open House,* and *Laurie Hill.* Her feature acting debut was in the 1993 movie *Coneheads.*

By 1994 she was starring in a series called *These Friends of Mine* on ABC. The first season was aided by a prime slot, following Tim Allen's *Home Improvement.* The network had such confidence in her that they announced that she would be the ABC spokesperson for radio ads and on-air promos, allowing her to introduce the debut of every show in the fall lineup. She also co-hosted the 1994 Emmy Awards ceremony.

Despite DeGeneres' fervent backing by ABC, the show had a number of problems, not the least of which were critical comparisons to *Seinfeld,* and a number of personnel changes on both sides of the camera. The show's name was changed to *Ellen* for its second season, its concept was changed, and Ellen was given more creative input.

By the third season, *Ellen* had failed to find an audience, however, and the show needed a boost. DeGeneres and her producers decided to announce the character's homosexuality to give the show a new edge—and to tell the truth. As DeGeneres told *Time:* ''I never wanted to be the lesbian actress. I never wanted to be the spokesperson for the gay community. Ever. I did it for my own truth.'' After months of hinting around on the show, Ellen came out in an hour-long episode featuring guest stars Laura Dern, Melissa Etheridge, k.d. lang, Demi Moore, Billy Bob Thornton, and Oprah Winfrey. The result was a clamor among conservatives and the religious right; evangelist Jerry Falwell called DeGeneres a ''degenerate.'' The show won an Emmy for best writing in a comedy series, and a Peabody award for the episode. *Entertainment Weekly* named DeGeneres the Entertainer of the Year in 1997. In 1998, the Gay and Lesbian Alliance against Defamation (GLAAD) awarded DeGeneres the Stephen F. Kolzak Award for being an openly gay celebrity who has battled homophobia. The series itself was given the award for Outstanding TV Comedy. The show was even praised by vice president Al Gore for forcing Americans ''to look at sexual orientation in a more open light.''

In the following season the show continued to focus mainly on gay issues, despite declining ratings, and ABC decided not to renew the show for a sixth season. Critics noted that the show had become one-dimensional, with Ellen's homosexuality overshadowing all oth-er topics. As the show declined, however, DeGeneres began branch-ing out, writing a book, *My Point . . . And I Do Have One,* in 1996 and releasing an album collection of stand-up material called *Taste This.* She also had her first leading role in a film, a romantic comedy with actor Bill Pullman called *Mr. Wrong.* Meanwhile, her series was picked up in syndication by the Lifetime channel in 1998.

—Emily Pettigrew

FURTHER READING:

Carter, Bill. ''At Lunch with Ellen DeGeneres.'' *New York Times.* April 13, 1994, C1.

DeGeneres, Ellen. *My Point . . . And I Do Have One.* New York, Bantam, 1995.

———. ''Roll Over, Ward Cleaver.'' *Time.* April 14, 1997.

Handy, Bruce. ''He Called Me Ellen Degenerate?'' *Time.* April 14, 1997.

Hooper, J. ''The Dirty Mind of Ellen DeGeneres.'' *Esquire.* May 1994, 29.

Kronke, David. ''True Tales of TV Trauma: 3 Comics Chase Roseanne-dom.'' *Los Angeles Times.* September 4, 1994.

Tracy, Kathleen. *Ellen DeGeneres Up Close: The Unauthorized Biography of the Hot New Star of ABC's Ellen.* New York, Pocket Books, 1994.

———. *Ellen: The Real Story of Ellen DeGeneres.* Secaucus, New Jersey, Carol Publishing Group, 1999.

Del Río, Dolores (1905-1983)

Acclaimed as the female Rudolph Valentino, Dolores del Río starred in more than 50 full-length motion pictures including *Flying Down to Rio* (1933), *Journey Into Fear* (1942), *Las Abandonadas* (1944), *Doña Perfecta* (1950), and *El Niño y la Niebla* (1953). With her first husband, millionaire Jaime Martínez del Río, she traveled around the world, learned several languages and moved to Holly-wood. She had an intense love life, marrying three times and having affairs with Gilbert Roland and Orson Welles, among others. In 1942, when her career started to decline, she returned to Mexico City. Del Rio dropped her ''femme fatale'' image and through Gabriel Figueroa's camera and Emilio Fernández's direction she helped create the so-called Mexican Cinema Golden Era, winning the Ariel (the Mexican equivalent of the Academy Award) three times, in 1946, 1952, and 1954. In her later years, her work with orphan children was highly praised.

—Bianca Freire-Medeiros

FURTHER READING:

Gonsior, Marian C. ''Dolores Del Rio.'' In *Latinas! Women of Achievement,* edited by Diane Telgen and Jim Kamp. Detroit, Visible Ink Press, 1996.

Ramon, David. *Dolores del Rio.* Mexico, Clio, 1997.

Reyes, Aurelio de los. *Dolores Del Rio.* Ciudad de Mexico, Grupo Condumex, Fernandez Cueto Editores, 1996.

DeMille, Cecil B. (1881-1959)

Director Cecil B. DeMille epitomized the film epic and Holly-wood's ''Golden Age.'' From the 1910s through the 1950s, he was able to anticipate public taste and gauge America's changing moods. He is best known for his spectacularly ambitious historical and biblical epics, including *The Sign of the Cross, The Crusades, King of Kings, The Ten Commandments, Cleopatra, Unconquered,* and *The Greatest Show on Earth,* but he also made domestic comedies such as *The Affairs of Anatol.* Originating the over-the-top reputation of

Cecil B. DeMille

Hollywood filmmakers, DeMille is famous for his huge crowd scenes, yet his films also clearly demonstrate his mastery as a storyteller. He avoided camera trickery and developed plots in a traditional manner that film audiences appreciated. In narrative skill and action, DeMille had few competitors.

Cecil Blount DeMille was born in Ashfield, Massachusetts, on August 12, 1881. His father was of Dutch descent and an Episcopalian lay preacher, Columbia professor, and playwright. His mother, Beatrice Samuel, also occasionally wrote plays and ran a girls' school. DeMille attended the Pennsylvania Military Academy from 1896 to 1898 and the American Academy of Dramatic Arts in New York from 1898 to 1900. He had his Broadway acting debut in 1900 and struggled to make his living as an actor for the next decade.

Abandoning his acting career in 1913, DeMille went into partnership with vaudeville musician Jesse L. Lasky and glove salesman Samuel Goldfish (later changed to Goldwyn) to form the motion-picture production company that would eventually become Paramount Studios. It was then that DeMille directed his first film, *The Squaw Man,* shot on location in the Los Angeles area, bringing

DeMille to the southern California locale he would help develop into the enclave of Hollywood. The film's success and popularity established DeMille in the nascent motion-picture industry; he was understood to be the creative force at Paramount, not only directing many films but also overseeing the scripts and shooting of Paramount's entire output.

DeMille capitalized on the same themes throughout his lengthy career. He often used a failing upper-class marriage, an exoticized Far East, and obsessive, hypnotic sexual control between men and women. At the same time, he emphasized Christian virtues alongside heathenism and debauchery. He repeatedly mixed Victorian morality with sex and violence. DeMille's popularity can largely be attributed to his dexterity with these seemingly contradictory positions and their appeal to audiences.

Instead of focusing on big-name stars, DeMille tended to develop his own roster of players. With the money he saved, he centered his energies on higher production values and luxurious settings. The players he developed include soprano Geraldine Ferrar in *Carmen, Joan the Woman, The Woman God Forgot, The Devil Stone,* and

Gloria Swanson in *Male and Female, Why Change Your Wife?, Something to Think About,* and *The Affairs of Anatol.*

DeMille produced and directed 70 films and participated in many more. He co-founded the Screen Directors Guild in 1931, and from 1936 to 1945, he was a producer for Lux Radio Theater of the Air, a position that consisted of adapting famous films and plays to be read by noted actors and actresses. He was awarded the Outstanding Service Award from the War Agencies of the United States government and he also received a Special Oscar for lifetime achievement in 1949. His long list of awards continues with the Irving Thalberg Award from the Academy of Motion Pictures in 1952, the Milestone Award by the Screen Producers' Guild in 1956, and an honorary doctorate from the University of Southern California.

—Liza Black

FURTHER READING:

DeMille, Cecil B. *The Autobiography of Cecil B. DeMille.* New Jersey, Prentice-Hall, 1959.

Higashi, Sumiko. *Cecil B. DeMille: A Guide to References and Resources.* Boston, G. K. Hall, 1985.

———. *Cecil B. DeMille and American Culture: The Silent Era.* Berkeley, University of California Press, 1994.

Higham, Charles. *Cecil B. DeMille.* New York, Charles Scribner's Sons, 1973.

Democratic Convention of 1968

See Chicago Seven, The

Dempsey, Jack (1895-1983)

Boxer Jack Dempsey heralded the Golden Age of Sports. Like Babe Ruth, Red Grange, Bill Tilden, and Bobby Jones, Dempsey was the face of his sport. "In the ring, he was a tiger without mercy who shuffled forward in a bobbing crouch, humming a barely audible tune and punching to the rhythm of the song," wrote Red Smith in the *Washington Post,* adding, "he was 187 pounds of unbridled violence." Jack Dempsey was a box-office magnet, attracting not only the first $1 million but also the first $2 million gate. He held the world heavyweight boxing title from July 4, 1919, when he knocked out Jesse Willard—who retired at the end of the third round with a broken jaw, two broken ribs, and four teeth missing—until September 23, 1926, when he lost it to Gene "The Fighting Marine" Tunney on points after ten rounds. Of a total of 80 recorded bouts he won 60, lost 6, drew 8, and fought 6 "No Decisions." He knocked out 50 opponents, 25 in the first round; his fastest KO came in just 14 seconds.

Born William Harrison Dempsey in Manassa, Colorado, on June 24, 1895, into a Mormon family of thirteen, young Jack started doing odd jobs early on but eventually finished eighth grade. At fifteen his brother Bernie (a prizefighter with a glass chin) started training William Harry. Dempsey chewed pine gum to strengthen his jaw, "bathing his face in beef brine to toughen the skin," as he wrote in his *Autobiography.* A year later he got his first serious mining job, earning three dollars a day. When William Harry wasn't mining, he was fighting. By 1916 he had already fought dozens of amateur fights.

Jack Dempsey

As "Kid Blackie" he hopped freight trains and rode the rails from town to town, announcing his arrival in the nearest gym and boasting that he would take on anyone.

"Kid Blackie" became "Jack" Dempsey on November 19, 1915, when he TKOed George Copelin in the seventh round. Dempsey was actually substituting for his brother Bernie, who had until then fought under the name of Jack Dempsey, in honor of the great Irish middleweight Jack Dempsey the Nonpareil, who died in 1895, the year in which William Harrison was born. The newly named Jack Dempsey flooded New York sports editors with clippings of his 26 KOs, though no one noticed him but journalist Damon Runyon, who nicknamed him the "Manassa Mauler." Late in 1917 Dempsey caught the attention of canny fight manager Jack "Doc" Kearns, who recruited him. Under Kearns, the ballyhoo began: Dempsey KOed his way through the top contenders and within 18 months he took the heavyweight title from Jesse Willard. Dempsey's glory was short-lived, however, for the very next day writer Grantland Rice labelled Dempsey a "slacker" in his *New York Tribune* column, referring to his alleged draft evasion. Though a jury found him not guilty of the charge in 1920, it took Dempsey six years to overcome the stigma associated with the label and become a popular champion.

Dempsey soon found himself in a peculiarly modern position: he became a sports hero—or anti-hero—whose image took on extraordinary significance in the climate of publicity and marketing that was coming to dominate sports promotion. Pre-television marketing techniques which stressed his rogue style of fighting and his alleged draft evasion turned his title fight against the decorated French combat pilot George Carpentier into a titanic clash between "Good" and "Evil." The July 2, 1921, match was a fight of firsts: it was the first fight ever to be broadcast on radio, the first fight to gross over a million dollars, and it was fought before the largest crowd ever to witness a sporting event up to that time. Amid a chorus of cheers and jeers of "Slacker!," Dempsey dispatched Carpentier in round three and somehow won over the 90,000 member crowd. Dempsey defended his crown several more times, most notably against Argentinian Luis Angel "The Bull of the Pampas" Firpo. Dempsey sent Firpo to the floor seven times before Firpo knocked the champ clear out of the ring to close the first round. Dempsey made it back into the ring and ended the fight 57 seconds into the second round with a knockout.

Dempsey lost his title on points to Gene Tunney. The resulting rematch would become one of the most contested fights in boxing history. Chicago's Soldier Field was swollen with the 104,943 fans who packed the stadium for the September 23, 1927, fight and provided boxing's first two-million dollar gate. Referee Dave Barry made the terms of the fight clear: "In the event of a knockdown, the man scoring the knockdown will go to the farthest neutral corner. Is that clear?" Both men nodded. Tunney outboxed Dempsey in the first six rounds, but in the seventh Dempsey unloaded his lethal left hook and sent Tunney to the floor. Barry shouted, "Get to a neutral corner!" but Dempsey stood still. At the count of three he moved to the corner; at five he was in the neutral zone. In one of the most momentous decisions in boxing history, referee Barry restarted the count at "One." Tunney got up on "Nine"—which would have been "Fourteen" but for Barry's restart. Tunney stayed out of Dempsey's reach for the rest of the round, floored Dempsey briefly in the eighth, and won a 10-round decision. The bout, immortalized as "The Battle of the Long Count," has been described in an *HBO* sports documentary as "purely and simply the greatest fistic box-office attraction of all time." Despite the fact that Dempsey lost, the fight allowed him to reinvent himself, according to Steven Farhood, editor-in-chief of *Ring* magazine: "He was viewed as a villain, not a hero, but after losing to Tunney, he was a hero and he remained such until his death."

Dempsey retired after this match, although he still boxed exhibitions. A large amount of the $3.5 million that he earned in purses was lost in the Wall Street Crash, but Dempsey was a shrewd businessman who had invested well in real estate. In 1936 he opened Jack Dempsey's Restaurant in New York City and hosted it for more than thirty years. During World War II, he served as a physical education instructor in the Coast Guard, thus wiping his alleged "slacker" slate clean. Jack Dempsey, "the first universally accepted American sports superstar," according to Farhood, died on May 31, 1983, at the age of 87 in New York City.

—Rob van Kranenburg

FURTHER READING:

Dempsey, Jack, with Barbara Piatelli Dempsey. *Dempsey.* New York, Harper & Row, 1977.

Evensen, Bruce J. *When Dempsey Fought Tunney: Heroes, Hokum, and Storytelling in the Jazz Age.* Knoxville, University of Tennessee Press, 1996.

Roberts, Randy. *Jack Dempsey: The Manassa Mauler.* Baton Rouge, Louisiana State University Press, 1979.

Smith, Toby. *Kid Blackie: Jack Dempsey's Colorado Days.* Ouray, Colorado, Wayfinder Press, 1987.

Denishawn

In 1915, dancers Ruth St. Denis and Ted Shawn founded a pioneering company and training school in Los Angeles that became known as Denishawn. The training they provided for their students—who also served as company members—was highly disciplined and extremely diverse in its cultural and stylistic range. Denishawn toured worldwide and was the first dance company to tour extensively in America, bringing the concept of serious dance and an appreciation of unknown cultures to American audiences. Denishawn students Martha Graham, Doris Humphrey, and Charles Weidman went on to become legendary dancer-choreographers. Musical director Louis Horst led the way in the composition of music for dance, while Pauline Lawrence became a legendary accompanist, costume designer, and dance administrator. These students instructed and inspired succeeding generations, and in this way, the "family tree" of Denishawn influenced virtually every American dancer and choreographer in the twentieth century.

—Brian Granger

FURTHER READING:

The Drama of Denishawn Dance. Middletown, Connecticut, Wesleyan University Press, 1979.

Sherman, Jane. *Denishawn, The Enduring Influence.* Boston, Massachusetts, Twayne Publishers, 1983.

Denver, John (1943-1997)

John Denver, so much a part of 1970s music, always marched to the beat of his own drummer. At a time when the simplicity of rock 'n' roll was fading to be replaced with the cynicism of punk rock, Denver carved out his own niche and became the voice of the recently disenfranchised folk-singer/idealist who believed in love and hope and fresh air. With his fly-away blond hair and his signature granny glasses, Denver had a cross-generational appeal, presenting a nonthreatening, earnest message of gentle social protest.

John Denver was born Henry John Deutschendorf on December 31, 1943, in Roswell, New Mexico. His entire life was shaped by trying to measure up to his father, who was a flight instructor for the Air Force. In his autobiography *Take Me Home, Country Roads,* Denver described his life as the eldest son of a family shaped by a stern father who could never show his love for his children. Denver's mother's family was Scotch-Irish and German Catholic, and it was they who imbued Denver with a love of music. His maternal grandmother gave him his first guitar at the age of seven.

Since Denver's father was in the military, the family moved often, making it hard for young John to make friends and fit in with people his own age. Constantly being the new kid was agony for the introverted youngster, and he grew up always feeling as if he should

John Denver

be somewhere else but never knowing where that "right" place was. Denver was happier in Tucson, Arizona, than anywhere else; but his father was transferred to Montgomery, Alabama, in the midst of the Montgomery boycotts. John Denver saw Alabama as a place of hatred and mistrust, and he wanted no part of it. It was in Montgomery, however, that he discovered that music was a way to make friends. When he sang and played his guitar, others paid attention to him. Nonetheless, he continued to feel alienated and once refused to speak for several months when he was severely bruised by a broken romance.

Attending high school in Fort Worth, Texas, was a distressing experience for the alienated Denver. Once he gave a party to which no one came. In his third year of high school, he took his father's car and ran away to California to visit family friends and pursue a musical career. However, he returned obediently enough when his father flew to California to retrieve him, and he finished high school.

While studying architecture at Texas Tech, Denver became disillusioned and dropped out in his third year to follow his dreams. He managed to get a job at Ledbetter's, a night club that was a mecca for folk singers, as an opening act for the Backporch Majority. Destiny had placed John Denver in the ideal spot for an aspiring young singer because he found himself living and working with more established artists who taught the idealistic young entertainer how to survive in his new world. It was then that he was encouraged to change his name. He chose Denver to pay homage to the mountains that he loved so dearly.

John Denver's big break came when he met Milt Okum, who represented the folk group Peter, Paul, and Mary. Okum was looking for a replacement singer for another group, the Chad Mitchell Trio,

and Denver perfectly fit the requirements. Although the group disbanded not long after Denver joined, his experience with them taught him much about the world of professional musicians. When the group disbanded because of huge debts, Denver felt a personal obligation to pay them off.

In 1967, while laying over in a Washington airport, John Denver wrote "Oh, Babe, I Hate to Go," or as it became known, "Leaving on a Jet Plane" out of his sense of loneliness and the desire for someone to ease that desolation. Both the Mitchell Trio and Spanky and Our Gang recorded the song, but it was Peter, Paul, and Mary who turned it into a number one hit in 1969. After being turned down by 16 record companies, Okum negotiated a recording contract for Denver with RCA Records.

Denver met his first wife Annie in 1966 while touring, and they were married in June 1967. In 1970 the couple moved to Aspen, Colorado. They could not afford to build a house on the land they bought, so they rented and saved. No matter, John Denver had come home. He had discovered the place he had been seeking his entire life. Unable to have children, John and Annie adopted Zachery and Anna Kate. Unfortunately, nothing could hold the marriage together, and it ended it bitter divorce. A subsequent marriage also ended unhappily, leaving him with daughter Jessie Bell.

Denver admitted in his autobiography that he had less trouble talking to large groups of people than to those whom he loved. This ability that caused him so much damage in his personal life gave him the uncanny ability to connect with the audience that set his music apart. His purpose was always greater than simple entertainment. He clothed his messages in everyday scenes to which everyone could relate, whether it be the airport of "Leaving on a Jet Plane" or the forests of "Annie's Song" or the mountains of "Rocky Mountain High" or the homecoming of "Back Home Again" or the country roads of "Take Me Home, Country Roads" or the feather bed of "Thank, God, I'm a Country Boy" or the bad days of "Some Days Are Diamonds (Some Days Are Stone)." People related to John Denver as if he were a friend who shared their personal history. His message behind the simple pleasures of life was always to protect the world that provides so much beauty and to enjoy life to the fullest every day because life is a gift.

John Denver's success would have been impressive at any time, but it was particularly impressive in the changing environment that made up the 1970s music scene. He had 13 top ASCAP hits, 9 platinum albums, one platinum single ("Take Me Home, Country Roads"), 13 gold albums, and six gold singles. He also had gold records in Canada, Australia, and Germany. In 1975 he was named CMA's Entertainer of the Year and "Take Me Home, Country Roads" won the best song of the year. He won a People's Choice Award, a Carl Sandburg People's Poet Award, and was named the Poet Laureate of Colorado. He made 21 television specials, 8 of which won awards. He was also a successful actor, starring in *Oh, God* and *Walking Thunder*. Denver had come a long way from the young boy whose friends had ignored his party.

Once his consciousness was raised in the early 1970s, Denver became an activist for the causes he loved, including campaigning against nuclear arms and nuclear energy. In 1976, when he was the country's biggest recording star, Denver established the Windstar Foundation on 1000 acres in Snowmass, Colorado, to fight world hunger. He was deeply hurt when he was not invited to join in the noted album, "We Are the World," dedicated to that same cause. Denver was also the moving force behind Plant-It 2000, a group that promoted the planting of as many trees as possible by the year 2000.

Denver made his first trip to Africa when he was appointed to President Jimmy Carter's Commission on World Hunger. Always fascinated by space exploration he unsuccessfully sought to be included in a space mission. Upon his first visit to Alaska, Denver was captivated by its beauty and worked hard for its preservation. He became the first American musician to perform in the Soviet Union and mainland China and even collaborated with Russian musicians on a project. He often said that he considered himself a "global citizen" because he believed so strongly in an interconnected world.

After the 1970s, Denver's career declined in the United States and he was arrested for drugs and driving while intoxicated. He was involved in a plane crash from which he walked away. Devastated by his two unsuccessful marriages, Denver remained close to his children. He also continued to be a strong presence on the international music scene. Before his death he had begun to reclaim his domestic audience. With his "Wildlife Concert" in 1995, it was plain to see that he had matured. The glasses were gone, as was the innocence. His hair was shorter and neater. His face was lined and often sad. Yet, his voice was stronger, more sure and arresting. He was still John Denver, and he still knew how to connect with the audience. Denver followed the success of the "Wildlife Concert" with a hit album, *Best of John Denver* in 1997. Tragically, his comeback was cut short on October 12, 1997, when his experimental aircraft crashed into Monterey Bay.

—Elizabeth Purdy

FURTHER READING:

Denver, John. *Take Me Home, Country Roads: An Autobiography.* New York, Harmony Books, 1994.

Flippo, Chet. "Artist, Activist Denver Lost to Crash," *Billboard,* October 25, 1997, 1.

"John Denver—Poet for the Planet." *Earth Island Journal,* Winter 1997-98, 43.

Kemp, Mark. "Country-pop Star Dies in Plane Crash." *Rolling Stone,* November 27, 1997, 24.

Department Stores

With the creation of the first department stores at the end of the nineteenth century, came the inception of that most American of diversions—shopping. Though people had always purchased necessities, it was the development of the emporium that turned the perusal of a wide variety of goods, both the necessary and the frivolous, the affordable and the completely out of reach, into a leisure pastime. Between the late 1800s and the 1970s, department stores continued to grow and evolve as the quintessential modern market-place, both elite and accessible. Huge department stores, named for the families who founded them, dominated urban centers, and store and city became identified with each other. Filene's of Boston, Macy's and Bloomingdale's of New York, Marshall Field of Chicago, and Rich's of Atlanta are only a few of the stores recognized nationwide as belonging to their city. The era of the department store is rapidly fading, replaced by consumer choices that are more consistent with modern economics, just as the department stores themselves once replaced their predecessors.

As the nineteenth century drew to a close, citizens began to enjoy the benefits of a new cash economy. Improved postal service and a

Macy's, New York City.

new nationwide rail network allowed for an unprecedented flow of goods. Previously, consumers had been dependent on traveling peddlers, who carried such stock as sewing needles, thread, and fabrics from town to town in bulky packs on their backs or in horse-drawn carts. As these peddlers grew more prosperous, they began to settle in small storefronts. As economic times improved with the modernizations of the late 1800s, savvy shopkeepers began to expand, offering not only a wider variety of goods, but also an air of refinement and personal service that had previously been available only to the very rich. An example of this was Marble Dry Goods, opened by A. T. Stewart in Manhattan in 1846. Stewart set up posh parlors for his female customers with attentive sales clerks and the first Parisian style full-length mirrors in the United States. Thus, department stores drew all classes of customers by making them feel as if they were part of society's elite while shopping there.

Owners of the new department stores were able to undercut the prices of their competitors in the specialty shops by going directly to the manufacturers to purchase goods, bypassing the wholesalers' mark-up. Some even manufactured their own products. Where once stores had been slow, sedate places where goods had to be requested from behind the counter, the lively new department store displayed products prominently within reach and encouraged browsing. To keep customers from leaving, stores expanded to sell anything they could possibly need. Smaller stores responded with outraged protests that the larger stores were employing unfair practices and running them out of business, but they had little success in slowing the growth of the giant emporiums.

As the cities grew, so did the stores, becoming multi-floor edifices that were the primary generators of retail traffic in newly burgeoning downtown areas. Women, who were enjoying some new rights due to the wave of feminism in the late 1800s and early 1900s, began to have more control over the shopping dollar. By 1915, women did 90 percent of consumer spending in the United States, and the department stores catered to women and began to hire them to work as salesclerks.

Stores competed with each other to have the most refined atmosphere, the cheapest bargain basement, the most fashionable tea room, the fastest delivery, and, most of all, the most attentive service—the most important product offered in the grand emporiums.

In 1911, Sears and Roebuck offered credit to their customers for large mail order purchases, and by the 1920s the practice had spread to most of the large department stores. Customers carried an imprinted metal "charge plate," particular to each store. Because they were the only form of credit available at the time, department store charge accounts inspired loyalty, and increased their store's customer base.

In 1946, writer Julian Clare described Canada's famous department store, Eaton's, in *MacClean's* magazine: "You can have a meal or send a telegram; get your shoes half-soled or buy a canoe. You can have your other suit dry cleaned and plan for a wedding right down to such details as a woman at the church to fix the bride's train. You can look up addresses in any Canadian city. You can buy stamps or have your picture taken." Department stores also developed distinctive departments, with features designed to attract trade. Filene's in Boston made the bargain basement famous, with drastically reduced prices on premium goods piled on tables, where economically-minded customers fought, sometimes physically, over them, and even undressed on the floor to try on contested items. Department store toy departments competed to offer elaborate displays to entertain children, who were often sent there to wait for parents busy shopping. Marshall Field's toy department introduced the famous puppet act "Kukla, Fran, and Ollie" to the Chicago public before they found their way onto television screens, while Bullocks in Los Angeles had a long wooden slide from the toy department to the hair salon on the floor below, where children might find their mothers. Department store window displays were also highly competitive, fabulous artistic tableaux that drew "window shoppers" just to admire them.

Department stores even had an effect on the nation's calendar. Ohio department store magnate Fred Lazarus convinced President Franklin Roosevelt to fix Thanksgiving on the fourth Thursday of November, rather than the last Thursday that had been traditional. The extra week of Christmas shopping afforded by the switch benefitted the department stores and, Lazarus assured the president, the nation. John Wanamaker of the famous Philadelphia store created Mother's Day, turning a little-known Catholic religious holiday into another national day of spending. Christmas itself became strongly identified with the stores as thousands of department store Santas were photographed holding future customers on their laps.

In the 1950s, middle class families began to abandon the cities for the suburbs. More and more, only less affluent people were left in the urban centers, and as a result, the great flagship downtown department stores began to lose money. Suburban shopping malls began to spring up, and most department stores opened branches

there. For over 20 years it was considered necessary to have a large department store as an "anchor" for a mall, and customers continued to patronize the department stores as their main retail sources. Beginning in 1973, however, the oil crisis, inflation, and other economic problems began to cause a slowing of growth in the department stores. The arrival of bank credit cards such as Visa and MasterCard put an end to customer dependence on department store credit. Discount stores, large stores that offered a wide inventory like the department stores, but without the grand style and attentive service, often had lower prices. In an economy more and more focused on lower prices and fewer amenities, department stores waned and discount stores grew.

Gradually, many of the once-famous department stores went out of business. Gimbals', B. Altman's, and Ohrbach's in New York, Garfinckel's in Washington, D. C., Frederick and Nelson's in Seattle, and Hutzler's in Baltimore are just a few of the venerable emporiums that have closed their doors or limited their operations. They have been replaced by discount stores, specialty chains, fast-growing mail order businesses, and cable television shopping channels like QVC. Huge discount chains like Wal-Mart inspire the same protests that the department stores drew from their competition at the early part of the twentieth century: they are too big and too cheap, and they run the competition out of business, including the department stores. Chains of specialty shops fill the malls, having national name recognition and offering customers the same illusion of being part of the elite that the department stores once did. Mail order houses flood potential customers with catalogs and advertisements—over fourteen billion pieces a year—and QVC reached five billion dollars in sales within five years of its inception, a goal department stores took decades to achieve.

Besides bringing together an enormous inventory under one roof and customers from a wide range of classes to shop together, department stores helped define the city centers where they were placed. The failure of the department stores and the rise of the suburban shopping mall and super-store likewise define the trends of late twentieth century society away from the city and into the suburb. Though acknowledgment of class difference is far less overt than it was at the beginning of the century, actual class segregation is much greater. As the cities have been relegated to the poor, except for those who commute there to work during the day, public transportation (except for commuter rush hours) and other public services have also decreased in the city centers. Rather than big stores that invite everyone to shop together, there are run-down markets that sell necessities to the poor at inflated prices and specialty shops that cater to middle class workers on their lunch hour. There are few poor people in the suburbs, where car ownership is a must and house ownership a given. There too, shopping is more segregated, with the working and lower middle class shopping at the discount houses and the upper middle class and wealthy frequenting the smaller, service-oriented specialty stores. The department stores that remain have been forced to reduce their inventory. Priced out of the market by discount stores in appliances, electronics, sewing machines, fabrics, books, sporting goods, and toys, department stores are now mainly clothing stores with housewares departments.

—Tina Gianoulis

FURTHER READING:

Benson, Susan Porter. *Counter Cultures: Saleswomen, Managers, and Customers in American Department Stores, 1890-1940.* Urbana, University of Illinois Press, 1986.

Cohen, Daniel. "Grand Emporiums Peddle Their Wares in a New Market." *Smithsonian*. Vol. 23, No. 12, March 1993, 22.

Harris, Leon A. *Merchant Princes: An Intimate History of Jewish Families Who Built Great Department Stores*. New York, Kodansha International, 1994.

Leach, William. *Land of Desire: Merchants, Power, and the New American Culture*. New York, Pantheon, 1994.

Schwartz, Joe. "Will Baby Boomers Dump Department Stores?" *American Demographics*. Vol. 12, No. 12, December 1990, 42.

Depression

One of the most common modern emotional complaints, depression is sometimes referred to as "the common cold of psychiatric illness." In its everyday usage, the word "depression" describes a feeling of sadness and hopelessness, a down-in-the-dumps mood that may or may not be directly attributed to an external cause and usually lasts for weeks or months. Sometimes it is used casually ("That was a depressing movie") and sometimes it is far more serious ("I was depressed for six months after I got fired"). Though depression has been recognized as an ailment for hundreds of years, the numbers of people experiencing symptoms of depression has been steadily on the rise since the beginning of the twentieth century.

The cause of depression is a controversial topic. Current psychiatric thinking treats depression as an organic disease caused by chemical imbalance in the brain, while many social analysts argue that the roots of depression can be found in psychosocial stress. They blame the increasing incidence of depression on an industrial and technological society that has become more and more isolating and alienating as support systems in communities and extended families break down. Though some depression seems to descend with no explanation, more often depression is triggered by trauma, stress, or a major loss, such as a relationship, job or home. Many famous artists, writers, composers, and historical figures have reportedly suffered from depressive disorders, and images and descriptions of depression abound in literature and art.

In its clinical usage, "depression" refers to several distinct but related mental conditions that psychiatrists and psychologists classify as mood disorders. Although the stresses of modern life may leave a great many people with feelings of sadness and hopelessness, psychiatrists and psychologists make careful distinctions between episodes of "feeling blue" and "clinical depression." According to the *Diagnostic and Statistical Manual of Mental Disorders (DSM-IV)*, an episode of depression is not a "disorder" in itself, but rather a "building block" clinicians use in making a diagnosis. For example, psychiatrists might diagnose a person suffering from a depressive episode with substance-induced depression, a general medical condition, a major depression, chronic mild depression (dysthymia), or a bipolar disorder (formerly called manic depression).

Psychiatrists attribute specific symptoms to "major depression," which is diagnosed if a client experiences at least five of them for at least two weeks. In addition to the familiar sad feeling, the symptoms of major depression include: diminished interest and pleasure in sex and other formerly enjoyable activities; significant changes in appetite and weight; sleep disturbances; agitation or lethargy; fatigue; feelings of worthlessness and guilt; difficulty concentrating; and thoughts of death and/or suicide.

Although people of all ages and backgrounds are diagnosed with major depression, age and culture can affect the way they experience and express their symptoms. Children who suffer from depression often display physical complaints, irritability, and social withdrawal, rather than expressing sadness, a depressed mood, or tearfulness. While they may not complain of difficulty concentrating, such difficulties may be inferred from their school performance. Depressed children may not lose weight but may fail to make expected weight gains, and they are more likely to exhibit mental and physical agitation than lethargy.

Members of different ethnic groups may also describe their depressions differently: complaints of "nerves" and headaches are common in Latino and Mediterranean cultures; weakness, tiredness, or "imbalance" are more prevalent among Asians; and Middle Easterners may express problems of the "heart." Many non-western cultures are likely to manifest depression with physical rather than emotional symptoms. However, certain commonalities prevail, such as a fundamental change of mood and a lack of enjoyment of life. Many studies have shown that cross-national prevalence rates of depression seem to be at least partially the result of differing levels of stress. For example, in Beirut, where a state of war has existed since the 1980s, nineteen out of one hundred citizens complained of depression, as compared to five out of one hundred in the United States.

One thing that does appear to be true across lines of culture and nationality is that women are much more likely than men to experience depression. The DSM-IV reports that women have a 10-25 percent lifetime risk for major depression, whereas men's lifetime risk is 5-12 percent. Some theorists argue that this difference may represent an increased organic propensity for depressive disorders, or may be due to gender differences in help-seeking behaviors, as well as clinicians' biases in diagnosis. Feminists, however, have long linked women's depression to social causes. Poverty, violence against women, and lifelong discrimination, they contend, offer ample triggers for depression, especially when coupled with women's socialized tendency to internalize the pain of difficult situations. Whereas men are socialized to express their anger outwardly and are more likely to be diagnosed with antisocial personality disorder, women are far more likely to entertain feelings of guilt and thoughts of suicide. Interestingly, there is evidence that in matriarchal societies, such as Papua New Guinea, the statistics of male and female depression are reversed.

Manic depression or bipolar disorder is the type of depression which has received the most publicity. The theatrical juxtaposition of the flamboyant manic state and incapacitating depression has captured the public imagination and been the inspiration for colorful characters in print and film from Sherlock Holmes to Holly Golightly. Clinicians diagnose a bipolar disorder when a person experiences a manic episode, whether or not there is any history of depression. The DSM-IV defines a manic episode as "a distinct period of abnormally and persistently elevated, expansive or irritable mood that lasts at least one week," and is characterized by: inflated self-esteem or grandiosity; decreased need for sleep; excessive speech; racing thoughts; distractibility; increased goal-directed activity and/or agitation; and excessive pleasure-seeking and risk-taking behaviors (the perfect personality for a dramatic hero). Bipolar disorders are categorized according to the type and severity of the manic episodes, and the pattern of alteration between mania and depression.

Depression is not only an unpleasant experience to live through, it is often fatal. Up to 15 percent of those with severe depression commit suicide, and many more are at risk for substance abuse and other self-destructive behavior. It is no wonder that doctors have tried for centuries to treat those who suffer from depression. Aaron Beck, author of *Depression: Clinical, Experimental, and Theoretical Aspects,* credits Hippocrates with the first clinical description of melancholia in the fourth century B.C.E. and notes that Aretaeus and Plutarch—both physicians in the second century C.E.—described conditions that would today be called manic-depressive or bipolar disorders. Beginning in antiquity, melancholia was attributed to the influence of the planet Saturn, and until the end of the seventeenth century, depression was believed to be caused by an accumulation of black bile, resulting in an imbalance in the four fluid components of the body. Doctors of the time used purgatives and blood-letting to treat depression. Despite changes in the nomenclature and the attribution of causes for melancholia, contemporary psychiatric criteria for major depression and the bipolar disorders are strikingly consistent with the ancient accounts of melancholia.

In the nineteenth century, melancholia was similarly described by such clinicians as Pinel, Charcot, and Freud. In his essay ''Mourning and Melancholia,'' written in the 1930s, Sigmund Freud distinguished melancholia from mourning—the suffering engendered by the loss of a loved one. In melancholia, Freud argued, the sufferer is experiencing a perceived loss of (a part of) the self—a narcissistic injury that results in heightened self-criticism, self-reproach, and guilt, as well as a withdrawal from the world, and an inability to find comfort or pleasure. Freud's psychoanalytic interpretation of melancholia reflected a shift from away from biological explanations.

Following Freud, clinicians ascribed primarily psychological causes—such as unresolved mourning, inadequate parenting, or other losses—to the development of depression, and prescribed psychotherapy to seek out and resolve these causes. Today, the pendulum has swung back to include the biological in the understanding of depressive disorders. While most contemporary clinicians consider psychological causes to be significant in triggering the onset of depressive episodes, research has indicated that genetics play a significant role in the propensity toward clinical depression. In the 1960s and 1970s radical therapy movements, along with feminism and other social movements, began to question the entirely personal interpretation placed on depression by many psychiatrists and psychologists. These activists began to look to society for both the cause and the cure of depression and to question therapy itself as merely teaching patients to cope with unacceptable societal situations.

Along with ''talking therapy,'' science continues to search for a medical cure. In the 1930s, Italian psychiatrists Ugo Cerletti and Lucio Bini began to experiment with electricity to treat their patients. Electroconvulsive shock therapy (ECT) became a standard treatment for schizophrenia and depression. ECT lost favor in the 1960s when many doctors and anti-psychiatry activists, who considered it as barbaric and dangerous as leeches, lobbied against its use. Shock therapy was often a painful and frightening experience, sometimes used as a punishment for recalcitrant patients. Public feeling against it was aroused with the help of books such as Ken Kesey's *One Flew Over the Cuckoo's Nest* in 1963, actress Frances Farmer's 1972 autobiography *Will There Really be a Morning?,* and Janet Frame's *Angel at My Table* in 1984. Perhaps as a testimony to the inherent drama of depression and its treatment by ECT, each of these books were made into films: *One Flew Over a Cuckoo's Nest* (1975), *Frances* (1982), and *Angel at My Table* (1990). ECT made a comeback in the 1990s, when proponents claimed that improved techniques made it a safe, effective therapy for the severely depressed patient. Side effects of ECT still include loss of memory and other

brain functions, however, and in 1999, Italy, its birthplace, severely restricted the use of ECT.

Many medications have been developed in the fight against depression. The tricyclics—which include imipramine, desipramine, amitriptyline, nortriptyline, and doxepin—have been found to be effective in controlling classic, melancholic depression, but are known for triggering side effects associated with the ''flight or fight'' response: rapid heart rate, sweating, dry mouth, constipation, and urinary retention. Another class of antidepressant medication, the monoamine oxidase inhibitors (MAOIs) have been more effective in alleviating the ''non-classical'' depressions that aren't helped by tricyclics. Although the MAOIs—phenelzine, isocarboxazid, nialamide, and tranylcypromine—are more specific in their action, they are also more problematic, due to their potentially fatal interactions with some other drugs, alcohol, tricyclic antidepressants, anesthetics, and foods containing tyramine. The most dramatic and widely publicized development in the psychopharmacological treatment of both major depression and chronic mild depression has been the availability of a new class of antidepressant medication, the selective serotonin reuptake inhibitors (SSRIs). SSRIs increase brain levels of serotonin, a neurotransmitter linked to mood. These medications—which include Prozac, Paxil, and Zoloft—are highly effective for many people in alleviating the symptoms of major depression, and have had a surprising success in lifting chronic depressions as well. They are touted as having far fewer adverse effects than drugs previously used to treat depression, which has contributed to their enormous popularity. However, they do have some serious side effects. These include reduced sexual drive or difficulty in having orgasms, panic attacks, aggressive behavior, and potentially dangerous allergic reactions. Prozac, probably one the most widely advertised medicinal brand names in history, has also had considerable exposure on television talk shows and other popular media, and has become the antidepressant of the masses. By 1997, just ten years after it was placed on the market, twenty-four million people were taking Prozac in almost one hundred countries. While most of these were grasping at the appealing notion of a pill to make them feel happier, Prozac is also prescribed in a wide variety of other cases, from aiding in weight loss to controlling adolescent hyperactivity.

In general, psychiatrists do not prescribe antidepressant medications in the treatment of bipolar disorders, because of the likelihood of triggering a manic episode. Rather, extreme bipolar disorders are treated with a mood stabilizer, such as Lithium. Lithium is a mineral, which is found naturally in the body in trace amounts. In larger amounts it can be toxic, so dosages must be closely monitored so that patients do not develop lithium toxicity. Lithium has received much popular publicity as a dramatic ''cure'' for manic-depression, notably in television and film star Patty Duke's autobiography, *Call Me Anna* (1987), where Duke recounts her own struggles with violent mood swings. Other, more extreme, drugs also continue to be prescribed to fight depression. These are the anti-psychotics, also called neuroleptics or even neurotoxins. These drugs, such as Thorazine, Mellaril, or Haldol—may be used to alleviate the psychotic symptoms during a major depressive episode. The neuroleptics can have extremely harsh adverse effects, from Parkinson's disease to general immobility, and are sometimes referred to as ''pharmacological lobotomy.'' The stereotypical movie mental patient with glazed eyes and shuffling gait is derived from the effects of drugs like Thorazine, which are often used to subdue active patients.

In 1997, antidepressants represented an almost $7 billion a year industry. Though safer and more widely available antidepressant medication has clearly been a breakthrough for many of those who suffer from debilitating depression, three out of ten depression sufferers don't respond at all to a given antidepressant, and of the seven who respond, many do so only partially or find that the benefits "wear out." Some therapists and other activists worry about the implications of the "chemical solution," claiming that antidepressants are over-prescribed. For one thing, all of the drugs have worrisome adverse effects, which are often downplayed in manufacturers' enthusiastic advertisements. For another, there has been successful research into using antidepressants to help victims of rape, war, and other traumatic stress. In a study at Atlanta's Emory University, four out of five rape victims became less depressed after a twelve-week program of the SSRI Zoloft. While some greet this as a positive development, others are chilled at the prospect of giving victims pills to combat their natural reactions to such an obvious social ill. Most responsible psychologists continue to see the solution to depression as a combination of drug therapy with "talking therapy" to explore a client's emotional reactions.

Many famous artists and historical figures have reportedly suffered from depression (melancholia) or bipolar disorder (manic depression). Aristotle wrote that many great thinkers of antiquity were afflicted by "melancholia," including Plato and Socrates, and cultural historians have included such names as Michaelangelo, Danté, Mary Wollstonecraft, John Donne, Charles Baudelaire, Samuel Coleridge, Vincent Van Gogh, Robert Schumann, Hector Berlioz, Virginia Woolf, Sylvia Plath, and Anne Sexton among their lists of melancholic artists, writers and composers.

Depression has also been described in literary texts throughout history. In his seminal essay "Mourning and Melancholia," Freud referred to Shakespeare's Hamlet as the archetype of the melancholic sufferer, and Moliere's "Misanthrope" was "atrabilious," a term denoting the "black bile" that medieval medicine considered to be the cause of melancholia. Descriptions of characters suffering from depression can also be found in Flaubert's *Madame Bovary* and Kafka's *Metamorphosis*. The poetry of Edna St. Vincent Millay presents a depressed cynicism that is the result perhaps of both personal loss and the wider cultural loss of disillusion and war. And of course, Sylvia Plath's *The Bell Jar* (1963) is one of the most finely crafted modern portraits of the depressed heroine, "the perfect set-up for a neurotic. . . wanting two mutually exclusive things at the same time." In recent years, perhaps in response to the increasing discussion of depression, a new genre has appeared, the memoir of depression. *Darkness Visible* (1990) by William Styron, *Prozac Nation: Young and Depressed in America* (1995) by Elizabeth Wurtzel, and *An Unquiet Mind* by Kay R. Jamison (1995) are examples of this genre, where the author explores her/his own bleak moods, their causes, their effects on living life, and—hopefully—their remedy.

Whether one defines depression as a biological tendency that is activated by personal experience or as a personal experience that is activated by socio-political realities, it is clear that depression has long been a significant part of human experience. Coping with the complexities and contradictions of life has always been an overwhelming prospect; as society becomes more complex, the job of living becomes even more staggering. In words that still ring true, Virginia Woolf, who ended her own recurrent depressions with suicide at age 59, described this feeling:

Why is life so tragic; so like a little strip of pavement over an abyss. I look down; I feel giddy; I wonder how I am ever to walk to the end.

—Tina Gianoulis and Ava Rose

FURTHER READING:

Diagnostic and Statistical Manual of Mental Disorders: DSM-IV. Washington, D.C., American Psychological Association, 1994.

Freud, Sigmund. "Mourning and Melancholia." In *Collected Papers, Vol. 4.* London, Hogarth Press, 1950, 152.

Jackson, Stanley. *Melancholia and Depression: From Hippocratic Times to Modern Times.* New York, Yale University Press, 1986.

Miletich, John J. *Depression: A Multimedia Handbook.* Westport, Connecticut, Greenwood Press, 1995.

Oddenini, Kathy. *Depression: Our Normal Transitional Emotions.* Annapolis, Maryland, Joy Publications, 1995.

Schwartz, Arthur. *Depression: Theories and Treatments: Psychological, Biological, and Social.* New York, Columbia University Press, 1993.

Derleth, August (1909-1971)

A better description of August Derleth's massive output could not be found than in Alison M. Wilson's *August Derleth: A Bibliography.* Born February 24, 1909, "August Derleth . . . one of the most versatile and prolific American authors of the twentieth century is certainly one of its most neglected. In a career that spanned over 40 years, he produced a steady stream of novels, short stories, poems, and essays about his native Wisconsin; mystery and horror tales; and biographies, histories, and children's books, while simultaneously writing articles and reviewing books for countless magazines and newspapers, and running his own publishing house." Despite the flood that streamed from his pen, none of Derleth's critically acclaimed regional novels ever sold over 5,000 copies, while his fantasy, children's, and mystery fiction fared only marginally better. Since his death in 1971, he is best remembered for his Solar Pons stories, modeled closely on Doyle's Sherlock Holmes tales, and for his founding with Donald Wandrei in 1939 of Arkham House, a publishing concern that specialized in macabre fiction. Arkham House was notable for publishing the work of neglected pulp fiction horror and fantasy writers of the 1930s like H. P. Lovecraft, as well as European weird fiction writers such as Arthur Machen and Lord Dunsany.

—Bennett Lovett-Graff

FURTHER READING:

Derleth, August. *Arkham House: The First Twenty Years: 1939-1959.* Sauk City, Wisconsin, Arkham House, 1959.

———. *August Derleth: Thirty Years of Writing, 1926-1956.* Sauk City, Wisconsin, Arkham House, 1956.

———. *Thirty Years of Arkham House, 1939-1969.* Sauk City, Wisconsin, Arkham House, 1970.

Wilson, Alison M. *August Derleth: A Bibliography.* Metuchen, New Jersey, Scarecrow Press, 1983.

Detective Fiction

Mysteries and their solutions have always been used in fiction, but detective fiction as a recognisable genre first appeared in the mid-nineteenth century. Despite detective fiction becoming one of the most popular of literary genres of the twentieth century, disputes over the point at which a story containing detection becomes a detective fiction story continued. In its most obvious incarnation detective fiction is to be found under the heading "Crime" in the local bookstore; it includes tales of great detectives like Holmes and Dupin, of police investigators, of private eyes, and little old ladies with a forensic sixth sense. But detective fiction can also be found disguised in respectable jackets, in the "Classic Literature" section under the names Dickens and Voltaire. Within detective fiction itself, there are many varieties of detectives and methods of detection; in its short history, the genre has shown itself to be a useful barometer of cultural conditions.

Defining detective fiction, then, is fraught with problems. Even its history is in dispute, with critics claiming elements of detective fiction in Ancient Greek tragedies, and in Chaucer. Part of the problem is that while the category "Crime Fiction" includes all fiction involving crime, and, very often, detective work as well, "Detective Fiction" must be restricted only to those works that include, and depend upon, detection. Such a restrictive definition leads inevitably to arguments about what exactly constitutes "detective work," and whether works that include some element of detection, but are not dependent on it, should be included. Howard Haycraft is quite clear on this in his book *Murder for Pleasure* (1941), when he says, "the crime in a mystery story is only the means to an end which is—detection."

Perhaps the first work in English to have its entire plot based around the solution to a crime is a play, sometimes attributed to Shakespeare, called *Arden of Faversham.* The play was first published in 1592, and is based on the true story of the murder of a wealthy, and much disliked landowner, Thomas Arden, which took place in 1551. Arden's body is discovered on his land, not far from his house. The fact that the body is outside points to his having been murdered by neighbouring farmers and labourers, jealous at Arden's acquisition of nearby land. What the detective figure, Franklin, sets out to prove is that Arden was murdered in his house, by his adulterous wife, Alice, and her lover. He manages to achieve this by revealing a clue, a piece of rush matting lodged in the corpse's shoe, which could only have found its way there when the body was dragged across the floor of the house.

Although the plot of *Arden of Faversham* revolves around the murder of Thomas Arden and the detection of its perpetrators, Julian Symons suggests that the purpose of the play itself lies elsewhere, in characterization, and, among other things, the moral issues surrounding the allocation of land following the dissolution of the monasteries. Because the element of crime and detection is merely a vehicle for other concerns, the place of *Arden of Faversham* in the canon of detective fiction remains marginal. But this is a debatable point. As Symons says, the exact position of the line that separates detective from other fiction is a matter of opinion. Nevertheless, early detective stories such as this play, and others, by writers such as Voltaire, certainly prefigure the techniques of detectives like Sherlock Holmes and Philo Vance.

What critical consensus there is on this topic suggests that the earliest writer of modern popular detective fiction is Edgar Allan Poe.

In three short stories or "tales," "The Murders in the Rue Morgue" (1841), "The Mystery of Marie Rogêt" (1843), and "The Purloined Letter" (1845), Poe established many of the conventions that became central to what is known as classical detective fiction. Perhaps reacting to the eighteenth-century idea that the universe is a mechanical system, and as such can be explained by reason, Poe devised a deductive method, which, as he shows in the stories, can produce seemingly miraculous insights and explanations. This deductive method, sometimes known as "ratiocination," goes some way in defining the character of the first "great detective," C. Auguste Dupin, whose ability to solve mysteries borders on the supernatural, but is, as he insists to the narrator sidekick, entirely rational in its origins. The third important convention Poe established is that of the "locked room," in which the solution to the mystery lies in the detective's working out how the criminal could have left the room unnoticed, and leaving it locked from the inside.

Other writers, such as Wilkie Collins and Emile Gaboriau, began writing detective stories after Poe in the mid-nineteenth century, but rather than making their detectives aristocratic amateurs like Dupin, Inspectors Cuff and Lecoq are professionals, standing out in their brilliance from the majority of policemen. Gaboriau's creation, Lecoq, is credited with being the first fictional detective to make a plaster cast of footprints in his search for a criminal. Perhaps the most famous of the "great detectives," however, is Sir Arthur Conan Doyle's creation Sherlock Holmes, whose method of detection, bohemian lifestyle, and faithful friend and narrator, Watson, all suggest his ancestry in Poe's creation, Dupin, but also look forward to the future of the genre. Although Conan Doyle wrote four short novels involving Holmes, he is best remembered for the short stories, published as "casebooks," in which Holmes's troubled superiority is described by Watson with a sense of awe that the reader comes to share. Outwitting criminals, and showing the police to be plodding and bureaucratic, what the "great detective" offers to readers is both a sense that the world is understandable, and that they themselves are unique, important individuals. If all people are alike, Holmes could not deduce the intimate details of a person's life from their appearance alone, and yet his remarkable powers also offer reassurance that, where state agents of law and order fail, a balancing force against evil will always emerge.

While Holmes is a master of the deductive method, he also anticipates detectives like Sam Spade and Philip Marlowe by his willingness to become physically involved in solving the crime. Where Dupin's solutions come through contemplation and rationality alone, Holmes is both an intellectual and a man of action, and Doyle's stories are stories of adventure as well as detection. Holmes is a master of disguise, changing his appearance and shape, and sometimes engaging physically with his criminal adversaries, famously with Moriarty at the Reichenbach Falls.

The Poe-Gaboriau-Doyle school of detective fiction remained the dominant form of the genre until the late 1920s in America, and almost until World War II in England, although the influence of the short story gradually gave way to the novel during that time. Many variations on the "great detective" appeared, from G. K. Chesterton's priest-detective, Father Brown, solving crime by intuition as much as deduction, through Dorothy L. Sayers's return to the amateur aristocrat in Lord Peter Wimsey, Agatha Christie's unlikely detective Miss Marple, and her eccentric version of the type, Hercule Poirot. In Christie's work in particular, the "locked room" device that appeared in Poe occurs both in the form of the room in which the crime is committed, and at the level of the general setting of the story; a country house, an isolated English village, a long-distance train, or a Nile riverboat, for example. This variation of the detective story became so dominant in England that classical detective fiction is often known as the "English" or "Country House" type.

However, detective fiction of the classical type was very popular on both sides of the Atlantic and the period from around 1900 to 1940 has become known as the "Golden Age" of the form. In America, writers like R. Austin Freeman, with his detective Dr. Thorndike, brought a new emphasis on forensic science in the early part of the twentieth century. Both Freeman and Willard Huntingdon Wright (also known as S. S. Van Dine), who created the detective Philo Vance, wrote in the 1920s that detective fiction was interesting for its puzzles rather than action. Van Dine in particular was attacked by critics for the dullness of his stories and the unrealistic way in which Philo Vance could unravel a case from the most trivial of clues. Nevertheless, huge numbers of classical detective stories were published throughout the 1920s and 1930s, including, in the United States, work by well-known figures like Ellery Queen (the pseudonym for cousins Frederic Dannay and Manfred B. Lee), John Dickson Carr (Carter Dickson), and Erle Stanley Gardner, whose series detective, Perry Mason, has remained popular in print and on screen since he first appeared in 1934. Elsewhere, the classical detective story developed in the work of writers such as Georges Simenon, Margery Allingham, and Ngaio Marsh. While all of these writers have their own particular styles and obsessions—Carr is particularly taken by the locked room device, for example—they all conform to the basic principles of the classical form. Whatever the details of particular cases, the mysteries in works by these writers are solved by the collection and decoding of clues by an unusually clever detective (amateur or professional) in a setting that is more or less closed to influences from outside.

Just as the classical form of the detective story emerged in response to late eighteenth and early nineteenth-century beliefs in the universe as rationally explicable, so hard-boiled detective fiction appeared in the United States in the 1920s perhaps in response to doubts about that view. Significantly, just as the influence of the short story was declining in the classical form, early hard-boiled detective fiction appeared in the form of short stories or novellas in "pulp magazines" like *Dime Detective* and *Black Mask*. These magazines were sold at newspaper stalls and station bookstores, and the stories they published took a radical turn away from the sedate tone of classical detective fiction.

Hard-boiled detective stories, as they became known, for their clipped, unembroidered language, focus not on the detective's intellectual skill at interpreting clues, but on his—and, since the 1980s, her—experiences. This type of detective fiction encourages the reader to identify with the detective, rather than look upon him/her as a protective authority; it champions the ability of "ordinary" people to resist and combat the influences of crime and corruption on their lives. As part of their rejection of the puzzle as a center for their narratives, hard-boiled detective stories are also concerned with the excitement generated by action, violence, and sex. So graphic did their description of these things seem in the 1920s that some stories were considered to border on the pornographic. The effect of this on detective fiction as a genre, however, was profound for other reasons. Hard-boiled detective stories described crimes taking place in settings that readers could recognize. No longer was murder presented as a remote interruption to genteel village life, but something that happened to real people. Crime was no longer the subject of an interesting

and challenging puzzle, but something with real human consequences, not only for the victim, but for the detective, and society at large. This new subject matter had limited impact within the restricted space of the short story, but came to the fore in the hard-boiled detective novels that gained popularity from the late 1920s onwards.

Carroll John Daly is usually credited with the invention of the hard-boiled detective, in his series character Race Williams, who first appeared in *Black Mask* in 1922. But Dashiell Hammett, another *Black Mask* writer, did the most to translate the hard-boiled detective to the novel form, publishing his first, *Red Harvest,* in 1929. The longer format, and the hard-boiled form's emphasis on the detective's actions, meant that Hammett's detectives, who include the famous Sam Spade, could confront, more directly than classical detectives, complex moral decisions and emotional difficulties. Raymond Chandler, who also began his career writing for *Black Mask* in the 1930s, took this further, creating in his series detective, Philip Marlowe, a sophisticated literary persona, and moving the focus still further away from plot and puzzle and on to the detective's inner life. Chandler is also well known for his realistic descriptions of southern California, and his view of American business and politics as underpinned by corruption and immorality.

Other writers picked up where Hammett and Chandler left off; some began using their work to explore particular issues, such as race or gender. Ross MacDonald, whose "Lew Archer" novels are generally considered to follow on from Chandler in the 1950s and 1960s, addresses environmental concerns. Mickey Spillane, who began publishing in the late 1940s, and has continued into the 1990s, took the sub-genre further by having his detective, Mike Hammer, not only confront moral dilemmas but take the law into his own hands. Sara Paretsky, writing in the 1980s and 1990s, reinvents the masculine hard-boiled private eye in V.I. Warshawski, a female detective whose place in a masculine environment enables her to explore feminist issues, while Walter Mosley uses a black detective to explore problems of race. While hard-boiled detective fiction shifts the focus from the solution of the problem to the search for that solution, and in doing so is able to address other topics, it remains centred on the idea of the detective restoring order in one way or another. Hard-boiled detectives do, in most cases, solve mysteries, even if their methods are more pragmatic than methodical.

In the 1920s, hard-boiled detective fiction was considered a more realistic approach to crime and detection than the clue-puzzles of the classical form. Since the early 1970s, however, the idea that a single detective of any kind is capable of solving crimes has seemed more wishful than realistic. In the three decades since then, the police-procedural has become the dominant form of detective fiction, overturning the classical depiction of the police as incompetent, and the "hard-boiled" view of them as self-interested and distanced from the concerns of real people. Police-procedurals adapt readily for TV and film, and come in many forms, adopting elements of the classical and hard-boiled forms in the police setting. They range from the tough "precinct" novels of Ed McBain, to the understated insight of Colin Dexter's "Inspector Morse" series, or P. D. James's "Dalglish" stories. The type of detection ranges from the violent, chaotic, and personal approach of the detectives in James Ellroy's L.A. series, to the forensic pathology of Kay Scarpetta in Patricia Cornwell's work. What all of these variations have in common, however, is that the detectives are backed up by state organization and power; they are clever, unusual, inspiring characters, but they cannot operate as detectives alone in the way that Sherlock Holmes and Philip Marlowe can.

This suspicion that detectives are not the reassuring figures they once seemed is explored in a variation of the classical form known as "anti-detective" fiction. In the 1940s, Jorge Luis Borges produced clue-puzzle detective stories whose puzzles are impossible to fathom, even by the detective involved. At the time, the hard-boiled novels of Dashiell Hammett and Raymond Chandler were also challenging the idea that the detective could know or fathom everything, but Borges's work undermines even the very idea of finding truth through deductive reasoning. In one well-known story, "Death and the Compass" (1942), Borges's detective unwittingly deduces the time and place of his own murder. In the 1980s, Paul Auster's *New York Trilogy* (1988) explored contemporary theories about language and identity to produce detective stories with no solution, no crime, and no detective. Anti-detective fiction provides an interesting view of detection, and a comment on the futility of trying to understand the universe, but it is of limited scope and popular appeal.

Detective fiction in the 1990s remains highly popular in all its forms. It has also begun to be appreciated in literary terms; it appears as a matter of course on college literature syllabuses, is reviewed in literary journals, and individual writers, like Conan Doyle and Chandler, are published in "literary" editions. Much of that academic attention might seem to go against the popular, commercial, origins of the form. But whatever its appeal, detective fiction seems to reflect society's attitudes to problems of particular times. That was as true for Poe in the 1840s, exploiting his culture's fascination with rationality and science, as it is for the police-procedural and our worries about state power, violence, and justice at the end of the twentieth century.

—Chris Routledge

FURTHER READING:

Haycraft, Howard. *Murder for Pleasure: The Life and Times of the Mystery Story.* New York, Appleton-Century, 1941.

Klein, Kathleen Gregory. *The Woman Detective: Gender and Genre.* Urbana and Chicago, Illinois, University of Illinois Press, 1988.

Knight, Stephen. *Form and Ideology in Crime Fiction.* London, Macmillan, 1980.

Messent, Peter, editor. *Criminal Proceedings: The Contemporary American Crime Novel.* Chicago, Illinois, Pluto Press, 1997.

Symons, Julian. *Bloody Murder: From the Detective Story to the Crime Novel.* London, Faber and Faber, 1972; revised, 1995.

Winks, Robin W., editor. *Detective Fiction: A Collection of Critical Essays.* Woodstock, Vermont, Foul Play Press, 1988.

The Detroit Tigers

Baseball—with its cheap bleacher seats, Sunday doubleheaders, and working-class heroes—is the most blue-collar of all sports. It is therefore no surprise that one of the most famous, durable, and successful baseball teams should be from the bluest of blue-collar cities, Detroit, Michigan. With a professional club dating back to 1881, Detroit was one of the charter members of the American League in 1901. While never as successful as the New York Yankees, the Tigers have a rich history and tradition. Like the city's dominant economic force, General Motors, the Tigers have been a conservative force, resisting change to the game. When free-agent frenzy hit in the

1970s, the Tigers reacted to the new high salaries, according to baseball writer Bill James, "like a schoolmarm on a date with a sailor."

While the Tigers have not always had the best teams, many times they have had the brightest star on the field. Ty Cobb was baseball's first superstar: he *was* Tiger baseball from 1905 to 1928, their top player and, in his later years, the team's manager. He played hero for hometown fans, but acted as villain on road trips when his intensity led to many violent confrontations, some with fans. Cobb was suspended in 1912 for punching a fan, but the team backed him and went on strike, forcing management to put together a team of sandlot players for a game against Philadelphia.

The year 1912 also moved the Tigers into Navin Field on the corner of Michigan and Trumbull. Named after team owner Frank Navin, the ballpark would remain in use for the rest of the century. Although led by Cobb, as well as stars like Sam Crawford, the team competed for some years without capturing a pennant. In the 1930s, three future Hall of Fame icons—Charlie Gehringer, Hank Greenberg, and Mickey Cochrane—wore Tiger uniforms. The decade also gave birth to another Detroit tradition: when spectators hurled garbage onto the field during the 1934 World Series, they initiated a tradition of hooliganism among Tiger fans which persisted for years afterward.

After a World Series victory in 1935, the Tigers ownership changed hands when Walter Briggs, an auto parts manufacturer, purchased the team. His family owned not only the team but also its playing field, which was renamed Briggs Stadium. Although they enjoyed a World Series win in 1945, the Tigers—like the rest of the American league—were overshadowed by the dominance of the Yankees from 1949 to 1964. Only the development of outfielder Al Kaline, who played his entire Hall of Fame career with the Tigers, highlighted this period of Tiger history. The Briggs family sold the team in 1952 to a group of 11 radio and television executives led by John Fetzer, an event that foreshadowed the marriage of media and sports that became a trend in the next decades. Thus, for once, the Tigers were ahead of the curve. With Detroit's WJR station broadcasting games across the entire Midwest, the team's following spread beyond Michigan to Ohio, Wisconsin, Indiana, and across the river to Ontario, Canada. Later, its TV broadcasting team, with former Tiger George Kell on play-by-play, created even more fans.

With the Tigers' conservative tradition and the arguably racist nature of both its management and its blue-collar fans, Detroit was slow to integrate black players into the team. Despite the steady increase in Detroit's black population, throughout the 1960s the team rarely included more than a small handful of black players, among them the city's already established sandlot star Willie Horton. The contradictions of racial politics in Detroit exploded, literally, in the 1967 riots that changed the history of the city. The violence resulted in unprecedented white flight that left parts of the city, including the neighborhoods around Tiger Stadium, devastated. Ravaged and divided, the city came together as the Tigers won the 1968 World Series. Although the factual basis for the team's role in uniting Detroit communities has remained debatable, sports historian Patrick Harrington noted that "the myth of unity is important, illustrating the impact many Detroiters give baseball as a bonding element."

The key to the 1968 team was Denny McLain, an immature wonderkid with a great arm, who won 31 games that year, but whose career then self-destructed. McLain was baseball's equivalent to football's Joe Namath—brash, cocky, quotable, and unconventional. The 1968 Tigers team held together for a few more years and, managed by Billy Martin, another brash, cocky and quotable figure, won the Eastern division crown on the last day of the 1972 season. While the team attempted to rebuild its strengths over the next decade, it endured many setbacks. Racial tensions and economic conditions in the city worsened, spectator attendances declined, and the Tigers lost 100 games in the 1975 season. Yet, from the mire emerged one more bright shining star: Mark ''the Bird '' Fidrych. Nicknamed after the *Sesame Street* character Big Bird because of his lanky appearance and curly blond mane, Fidrych was a right-handed pitcher with the eccentric on-field habit of talking to the baseball. Already a local hero, he burst into the national spotlight with a masterfully pitched victory over the Yankees on ABC's *Monday Night Baseball* in 1976. He was quickly on the cover of *Sports Illustrated* and his games, both at home and on the road, were sellouts. Yet, like McLain before him, Fidrych's immaturity (he injured his knee horsing around in the outfield) led to his rapid decline.

The franchise, however, was improving. The devastation of the economy in Detroit in the late 1970s led to the dispersal of Tiger fans across the country, but the team's popularity in the 1980s was acknowledged when Tom Selleck's *Magnum PI* character donned the navy blue Tigers cap with the Old English ''d'' on it. The Tigers were a hot item. After hiring manager Sparky Anderson and developing a stable of great young players, the Tigers went 35-5 to start the 1984 season. This was the first year of new ownership under Tom Monaghan, a lifelong Tiger fan who made his fortune with the Domino's Pizza franchise. The 1984 World Series win by the Tigers was the ''fast food series''—the Kroc family of McDonald's fame owned the opposing Padres. The 1984 season was also marked by two significant spectator developments. Fans at Tiger Stadium popularized ''the wave,'' a coordinated mass cheer from fans who jumped from their seats with their hands in the air in succession around a stadium. Less happily for the game, they also popularized the ritual of turning victory celebrations into all-night melees, with some becoming near riots as Detroit fans gave the city another black eye. Coupled with the annual ''Devil's Night'' fires and Detroit's dubious position as leader of the nation's crime rate, even the frenzy over the Tigers' triumph couldn't mask the problems in the Motor City.

Monaghan ran into financial problems and sold the team to his business rival, Mike Illitch, owner of the Little Caesar's pizza chain, in 1992. The franchise had been in trouble for many reasons, among them ''a series of public relations disasters, including the botched dismissal of popular announcer Ernie Harwell that alienated its most loyal followers,'' according to Harrington. At the same time, the city was harming rather than helping as ''a bellicose mayor alienated the suburbanites and outsiders. A few highly publicized incidents in the downtown area magnified fear of coming to the Stadium. . . . The club became separate from the city, and the wider community divorced itself from the city.'' Despite having Cecil Fielder, a home-run hero and the team's first black superstar in over 20 years, the main interest in the Tigers concerned the team's future. By the late 1990s, following years of bitter debate, lawsuits, and public hearings, the building of a new stadium was begun in downtown Detroit to keep the team in town. Although the 1994 baseball strike, and poor teams devastated Tiger attendance in the late 1990s, the new century held promise with a new ballpark. The move marked a break with the past as baseball prepared to leave the corner of Michigan and Trumbull, accompanied by the hopes of owners and city leaders, that the tradition of blue-collar support for the Tigers would continue in the new millennium.

—Patrick Jones

FURTHER READING:

Anderson, William M. *The Detroit Tigers: A Pictorial Celebration of the Great Players and Moments in Tigers' History.* South Bend, Indiana, Diamond Communications, 1992.

Falls, Joe. *The Detroit Tigers: An Illustrated History.* New York, Walker and Company, 1989.

Harrington, Patrick. *The Detroit Tigers: Club and Community, 1945-1995.* Toronto, University of Toronto Press, 1997.

James, Bill. *This Time Let's Not Eat the Bones.* New York, Villard Books, 1989.

Devers, Gail (1966—)

Labeled ''the world's fastest woman'' after she won the 100-meter dash and a gold medal in the summer Olympics at Barcelona in 1992, Gail Devers has become exemplary of excellence, grace, and courage, and has served as an inspiration to other athletes, especially women, throughout the world. In 1988, she set an American record in the 100-meter hurdles (12:61). What happened to Devers between 1988 and 1992, however, created a story, notes Walter Leavy in *Ebony,* ''that exemplifies the triumph of the human spirit over physical adversity,'' for Devers was sidelined with Graves disease, a debilitating thyroid disorder. After nearly having to undergo the amputation of both feet in March 1991, Devers not only recovered to run triumphantly in 1992 but went on to win her second gold in the 100 meters at the Atlanta Olympics in 1996, becoming only the second woman to win back-to-back gold medals in this competition.

—John R. Deitrick

FURTHER READING:

Gutman, Bill. *Gail Devers.* Austin, Texas, Raintree Steck-Vaughn, 1996.

Leavy, Walter. ''The Many Splendored Faces of Today's Black Woman.'' *Ebony.* March, 1997, 90.

Devo

Proving that America's most engaging and original artists do not have to come from culture industry hubs like New York and Los Angeles, Ohio's Devo crawled out of the Midwest industrial city of Akron to become one of the most well-known conceptual-art-rock outfits of the late twentieth century. Formed in 1972 by a pair of offbeat art student brothers and their drummer friend, Devo began making soundtracks for short films such as *The Truth About De-evolution.* Over the course of the 1970s, the group went from being an obscure Midwest oddity to, for a brief moment, one of New Wave's most popular exports. While Devo did adopt a more accessible sound at their commercial peak, they never toned down the ''weirdness factor,'' something that may have alienated mainstream audiences once they ran out of ultra-catchy songs.

Devo was formed by brothers Jerry and Bob Casale (bass and guitar, respectively) and Mark, Jim, and Bob Mothersbaugh (vocals,

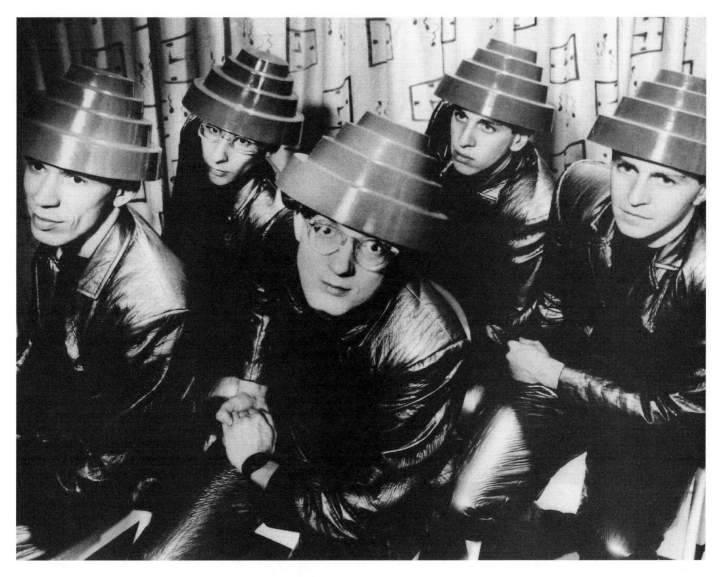

Devo

drums, and lead guitar, respectively—Alan Myers replaced Jim Mothersbaugh early in Devo's career). The name Devo is derived from their guiding conceptual principle, ''de-evolution.'' As a concept, ''de-evolution'' is based on the notion that, rather than evolving, human beings are actually de-volving—and the proof is manifested in the myriad of social problems of the late twentieth century that, from Devo's point of view, are the result of a conformist American ideology that renders its population mindless clones. ''De-evolution'' was derived from a crackpot text the brothers found entitled *The Beginning Was the End: Knowledge Can Be Eaten,* which maintained that humans are the evolutionary result of a race of mutant brain-eating apes.

Part joke, part art project, part serious social commentary, Devo went on to make the short film, *The Truth About De-evolution,* which won a prize at the Ann Arbor Film Festival in 1976, garnering them significant—though small scale—attention. This helped push the band to move to Los Angeles, where Devo gained even more attention as a bizarre live act which, in turn, led to a hit British single on the Stiff label and, soon after, an American contract with Warner Brothers

Records. Between the band's formation and its Brian Eno-produced debut album in 1978, the band recorded a number of tracks on a basement four track recording studio; many of these songs were documented on Rykodisc's two volume *Hardcore Devo* series. These unearthed songs showcase a band that, with the exception of the arty-weirdos the Residents, created music without precedent. At a time dominated by prog-rock bands, disco acts, and straightforward pop/rock, Devo was crafting brief, intense bursts of proto-punk noise that fused electronic instruments, rock 'n' roll fervor, and ironic detachment.

The Brian Eno-produced *Q: Are We Not Men? A: We Are Devo!* announced to the world their de-evolution philosophy, and sold respectfully, though not spectacularly. Sonically speaking, the group's second album, *Duty Now for the Future,* matched Devo's conceptual weirdness to the point that it was their most challenging album. Their breakthrough came with the ironically titled *Freedom of Choice,* where the group adopted a more New Wave synth-pop sound that did not reduce Devo's musical punch, it just made them more accessible to a wider audience. The success of ''Whip It,'' the group's sole Top 40 hit, was in part due to their edgy video, making them one of the few

American groups to embrace music videos during the early stages of MTV (Music Television).

Devo's popularity and artistic quality steadily dropped off with their release of *New Traditionalists, Oh, No! It's Devo,* and *Shout,* all of which replace the playful quirkiness of their earlier albums with a more heavy-handed rendering of their philosophy (which may have been a reaction to their brief popularity). During the mid-1980s when Devo was largely inactive, Mark Mothersbaugh made a name for himself as a soundtrack producer on the demented Pee-Wee Herman Saturday morning live action vehicle *Pee-Wee's Playhouse,* which led to numerous other scoring jobs. In 1988 Devo returned with *Total Devo* on the indie label Enigma, which did not restore anyone's faith in this band's relevance. They followed that album with an even less worthwhile effort, the live *Now it Can Be Told.* Still, they were able to produce a few decent songs, such as "Post-Post-Modern Man" from their 1990 album *Smooth Noodle Maps.* In 1996, Devo released a CD-Rom and soundtrack album, *Adventures of the Smart Patrol,* and played a few dates for the Alternative music festival, Lollapalooza.

—Kembrew McLeod

FURTHER READING:

Contemporary Musicians: Profiles of the People in Music, Vol. 13. Detroit, Gale, 1995.

Heylin, Clinton. *From the Velvets to the Voidoids: A Pre-Punk History for a Post-Punk World.* New York, Penguin, 1993.

Diamond, Neil (1941—)

In a career spanning four decades, Neil Leslie Diamond offered his listeners a collection of songs that were sometimes schmaltzy, sometimes openly patriotic, but always melodic and well-sung. Beginning his career while a student at New York University, Diamond worked as a Tin Pan Alley writer before starting his solo career. His songs, ranging from "Solitary Man" (1966) to "Headed to the Future" (1986), reflected the condition of the era in which they were written and performed, while songs like "Heartlight" (1982) reflected a nation's consciousness. Known for his pop hits, Diamond also tried his hand at country music and traditional Christmas songs. Diamond's ventures into films include *Jonathan Livingston Seagull* (1973) and *The Jazz Singer* (1980), in which he starred. Diamond's works have been performed by such diverse groups as the Monkees and UB40.

—Linda Ann Martindale

FURTHER READING:

Grossman, Alan. *Diamond: A Biography.* Chicago, Contemporary Books, 1987.

Harvey, Diana Karanikas, and Jackson Harvey. *Neil Diamond.* New York, Metro Books, 1996.

Miller, Jim, editor. *The Rolling Stone Illustrated History of Rock & Roll.* New York, Random House/Rolling Stone Press, 1980.

Wiseman, Rich. *Neil Diamond: Solitary Star.* New York, Dodd, Mead, 1987.

Diana, Princess of Wales (1961-1997)

The most charismatic and publicly adored member of the British royal family, Diana, Princess of Wales not only imposed her own distinctly modern style and attitudes on Great Britain's traditionalist monarchy, but served to plunge that institution into its lowest level of public unpopularity, fueling support for Republicanism and, after her death, forcing the Royal family to moderate its aloof image. However, as a glamorous and sympathetic icon of an image-driven and media-fueled culture, Diana's celebrity status and considerable influence traveled across continents. Her fame, matched by only a handful of women during the twentieth century, notably Jacqueline Kennedy Onassis and Princess Grace of Monaco (Grace Kelly), made her a significant popular figure in the United States, where her visits were welcomed with the fervor once reserved for the most famous stars of the Golden Age of Hollywood. Diana was the most photographed woman in the world, and from the time of her marriage to her premature and appalling death in 1997, she forged a public persona that blended her various roles as princess, wife, mother, goodwill ambassador for England, and international humanitarian. Diana's fortuitous combination of beauty and glamour, her accessible, sympathetic, and vulnerable personality, and an ability to convey genuine concern for the affairs of ordinary people and the world's poor and downtrodden, set her apart decisively from the distant formality of the British monarchy. She became an object of near-worship, and her lasting fame was ensured. Ironically, the intense media attention and public adulation that came to define her life were widely blamed for

Diana, Princess of Wales

the circumstances of her death. Her untimely demise, however, served only to amplify the public's romantic perception of her as a modern goddess cruelly destroyed by a faithless husband, unsympathetic in-laws, and prying *paparazzi*. The life and death of the Princess of Wales, is, indeed, a monument to sad contradictions and ironies.

Lady Diana Spencer was born into aristocratic privilege, the daughter of Viscount Althorp, on July 1, 1961 at the remote and spacious family estate near Sandringham in Norfolk. Her parents divorced when she was still a child, leaving Diana and her siblings in the care of her father and his second wife. She was a shy child, unhappy about the absence of her mother, and early on developed a passion for children, which led her to become a nursery school teacher in London. At 18, she re-met Prince Charles, 13 years her senior and heir to the British throne, whom she had known slightly in childhood. Their courtship became public, and she had the first taste of the media circus that was to dog her every move for the rest of her life. On July 29, 1981, three weeks before her twentieth birthday, Diana married her prince—the first English woman in 300 years to become the wife of a future English king—in a wedding aptly described by the Archbishop of Canterbury as ''the stuff of which fairy tales are made.'' The ceremony took place before an overflowing congregation of some 2,500 in London's St. Paul's Cathedral and drew a record-breaking global radio and television audience of nearly one billion. A worldwide media event, the wedding affirmed Diana's value as an internationally marketable personality whose image soon appeared not only in magazines, newspapers, and television programs across the globe, but also adorned an unending stream of merchandise ranging from postage stamps to coffee mugs.

Diana's married life revolved around her official Court duties and, increasingly, her own public causes. Ten days after her twenty-first birthday, the princess gave birth to the next heir apparent, Prince William, and, two years later, to Prince Henry (known as Harry). She insisted on taking her young sons on ''normal'' outings to cinemas and theme parks and on informal holidays abroad, and she bestowed lavish affection on them in public. Her conduct represented a sharp break from the stiff conventions of royalty and contributed to her position as the media's darling and to the discomfiture of her less demonstrative mother-in-law. On the one hand, Diana seemed determined to protect her sons from the harsh glare of public scrutiny; on the other, she kept the people abreast of the family's life by granting interviews and making numerous public appearances. She fed the media's hunger even while expressing despair at its persistence.

By the mid-1980s, rumors of a rift between Charles and Diana were growing, accompanied by whispers of infidelity and reports that the princess was far from well or happy. By the end of the decade, it was public knowledge that Diana was suffering from bulimia, a fact that she courageously admitted in public in hopes of helping other sufferers; that Charles had resumed his long-standing love affair with Mrs. Camilla Parker-Bowles early in his marriage; and that Diana had sought solace in an affair with an army officer named James Hewitt, who co-operated in a scandalous tell-all book about their relationship.

For a time, Diana was cruelly treated by the media and criticized by the public, who simultaneously relished and disapproved of a spate of further revelations. When, however, Charles consented to an in-depth television interview with his biographer Jonathan Dimbleby, and confessed to the Parker-Bowles affair, Diana retaliated with her

own interview that effectively put the knife into the royal family and re-established her position in the public affection. To the evident distress of the queen, the couple announced a separation in 1992, the year in which Britain and America were agog at the publication of Andrew Morton's book, *Diana, Her True Story.* The royal divorce followed four years later.

Her marital woes and personal troubles only served to raise Diana's public profile even higher, and she took advantage of the media's relentless coverage of her every move by redirecting their attention from her private life to her charity work. Though stripped of her full title—no more Her Royal Highness—she continued to upstage her beleaguered husband and his family in the public eye. She ruffled the feathers of politicians with her international campaign for the banning of land mines, visited lepers, and indicated her sympathy and support for AIDS sufferers by embracing one such for the television cameras.

But even as Diana worked to focus the world's attention on her pet causes, the public remained most keenly interested in her post-divorce love life. The public's seemingly insatiable appetite for detail was both whetted and offended by Diana's sudden whirlwind romance with Egyptian playboy Dodi Al-Fayed, which hit the headlines in 1997. Her new lover was the son of Mohammed Al-Fayed—the owner of Harrod's department store and the Ritz Hotel in Paris, from where the couple left on their last fateful car journey—and had long been a figure of ugly controversy in Britain. When the Mercedes in which Diana and Al-Fayed were traveling crashed at high speed in a Paris tunnel on the night of August 30, 1997, immediate blame was laid at the door of the press photographers who were giving chase to the car, and gave rise to protracted legal hearings in Paris in a futile attempt to charge somebody with the couple's senseless deaths.

The news of Princess Diana's death sent shock waves around the world and plunged millions into a near-hysterical frenzy of grief. The profound sense of loss that was experienced, particularly in Britain, elevated Diana's mythic-martyr status to unprecedented levels. In the aftermath of Diana's death, her brother, Earl Spencer, remembered his sister as ''the very essence of compassion, of duty, of style, and of beauty.'' Indeed, when, in the eyes of the public, the queen failed to show the requisite level of emotion at the news of Diana's death, she endured outraged criticism for ''not responding to the pain of Britons.'' To quell the anger, she spoke publicly about Diana's death on television, and agreed to lower the Union Jack atop Buckingham palace to half-mast—an honor that had, for nearly a thousand years, been reserved solely for reigning monarchs. As further evidence of Diana's impact on staid British institutions, although a divorcee, she was given a state funeral on September 5, 1997. Her coffin was borne, in a simple but ceremonial procession, from her home at Kensington Palace to Westminster Abbey, where the service was conducted in the presence of television cameras. The cameras then followed the cortege to her final resting-place at Althorp, and two-and-a-half billion television viewers in 210 countries worldwide watched the hours of filmed coverage. In Britain, sporting events were postponed, bells chimed every minute, and a moment of silence was observed before the take-off of each British airline flight in memory of the princess.

In death, Diana hardly eluded the international cult of celebrity that had haunted her during her life. Thriving on the controversy over who was to blame for her death, the international media sold more magazines and newspapers worldwide than they had at any time during her life. Even the charities to which she had been patron were complicit in exploiting her valuable name and image. The Diana, Princess of Wales Memorial Fund, established to endow a suitable memorial, was still riven by indecision, controversy and exploitation by the end of the 1990s, while her name and likeness was continually exploited by the souvenir market. While Diana's status as an exemplary mother and world-class humanitarian became cemented in the popular imagination, she left behind a darker legacy, that of a public figure who became a past master at manipulating the media and the celebrity culture that had both exploited and promoted her. As the object of the world's infatuation, Diana was, in the words of her brother, ''the most hunted person of the modern age.'' The British Prime Minister, Tony Blair, however, addressing the nation on the Sunday morning following the accident, dubbed her ''The People's Princess.'' So she was, and so she is remembered.

—Lauren Supance

FURTHER READING:

Battiscombe, Georgina. *The Spencers of Althorp.* London, Constable, 1984.

Campbell, Lady Colin. *Diana in Private: The Princess Nobody Knows.* New York, St. Martin's Press, 1992.

Davies, Nicholas. *Diana: A Princess and Her Troubled Marriage.* Secaucus, New Jersey, Carol Publishing Group, 1992.

Holden, Anthony. *The Tarnished Crown: Princess Diana and the House of Windsor.* New York, Random House, 1993.

Martin, Ralph G. *Charles and Diana.* New York, Putnam, 1985.

Morton, Andrew. *Diana: Her True Story.* New York, Simon & Schuster, 1992.

DiCaprio, Leonardo (1974—)

After his critically-acclaimed performances in *This Boy's Life* (1993) and *What's Eating Gilbert Grape* (1993), Leonardo DiCaprio quickly gained a reputation for playing tormented young men in such films as *The Basketball Diaries* (1995), *Total Eclipse* (1995), and *William Shakespeare's Romeo and Juliet* (1996). His boyish good looks and sensitive, troubled persona made DiCaprio a favorite of young women. Starring in the romantic tragedy *Titanic* (1997), which grossed more money than any film ever had before, broadened DiCaprio's popularity even further.

—Christian L. Pyle

FURTHER READING:

Bego, Mark. *Leonardo DiCaprio: Romantic Hero.* Kansas City, Andrews & McMeel, 1998.

Catalano, Grace. *Leonardo: A Scrapbook in Words and Pictures.* New York, Dell, 1998.

———. *Leonardo DiCaprio: Modern-Day Romeo.* New York, Bantam Books, 1997.

Krulik, Nancy. *Leonardo DiCaprio: A Biography.* New York, Archway/Pocket Books, 1998.

Looseleaf, Victoria. *Leonardo: Up Close and Personal.* New York, Ballantine, 1998.

Dick and Jane Readers

For nearly 40 years, from 1930 through about 1970, more than 85 million American schoolchildren learned to read using the *Dick and Jane* readers that were part of a series published by the Scott Foresman Company. The books took their name from the series' lead characters who, with a dog named Spot and a kitten named Puff, inhabited a nostalgic, innocent American landscape of white picket fences and neighborliness. So deeply have the *Dick and Jane* stories been etched into the minds of the Baby Boomer generation and their immediate predecessors that the repetitive phrase ''See Spot run! Run, Spot, run!'' is today remembered by millions as the very first sentences they could read on their own. It has been estimated that four-fifths of the nation's schools were using *Dick and Jane* readers, ranking the books with the venerable *McGuffey Readers* of the nineteenth century as a tool of universal literacy.

With an emphasis on methodology over content, the *Dick and Jane* series was conceived in part as a rebellion against then in-vogue didactic traditions that relied heavily on moralistic and patriotic texts drawn from the Bible, Shakespeare, and American historical legends. The *Dick and Jane* readers emphasized non-phonic sight reading and repetitive, limited vocabulary, a formula that became a parody of itself by the time their approach was jettisoned in the tumultuous 1960s, to be replaced by phonics and books with more diverse characters and situations. The fact that method trumped content in the choice of storylines for the Dick and Jane readers provoked frequent criticism, such as this acerbic remark from educational critic Arther S. Trace: ''Students could learn a great deal indeed from early American readers, but the only possible answer to what children can learn from the *Dick-and-Jane* type reader is, 'Nothing of any consequence.'''

The *Dick and Jane* program was developed by three people— Dr. William S. Gray, an authority on pedagogy, and by Zerna Sharp and Harry B. Johnston. Working with teachers and school psychologists, the three worked as a team to develop the Scott Foresman series, using the limited vocabulary technique advocated by Dr. Gray. Thus, the first grade *Dick and Jane* readers had only about 300 words, the third grade reader about 1,000, and the sixth grade reader about 4,000. Writers for the series had to adhere to strict guidelines about using limited words, and were required to introduce only a few of them on each page, then repeat them frequently in forthcoming pages. Poetry and imaginative literature were nonexistent. All this led to criticism that the books were uninteresting and unnatural.

Dick and Jane first made their appearance in 1930, in a pre-primer of the *Elson-Gray* basic reader series, with stories in large type under vividly colored heavy-line illustrations set in boxes according to 1920s graphics conventions. It was not until 1941, when Eleanor Campbell began illustrating the series, that the Dick and Jane characters, in pastel, took on the rounder, ''cuter'' form known to most Baby Boomers, inviting comparisons with Norman Rockwell for their evocation of idyllic small-town life and situations. Within a short time, other books were added to the series, including *More Dick and*

Jane Stories and *Dick and Jane.* In 1937, a pre-primer *Before We Read* was introduced. The concept caught on, and by the end of the 1930s half of America's schoolchildren were learning to read with Dick and Jane.

The *Dick and Jane* series was completely revised in 1940, introducing Campbell's illustrations and three paper-bound pre-primers—*We Look and See, We Work and Play,* and *We Come and Go,* which prepared students for the 160 page primer *Fun With Dick and Jane.* It was in this edition that "Baby" became known as "Sally," that Spot became a long-haired spaniel, and in which the kitten previously known as "Little Mew" was renamed "Puff." In 1950 another revision introduced *The New Basic Readers,* with updating of storylines and illustrations to reflect a more suburban postwar lifestyle.

In 1941, a special edition of the *Dick and Jane* readers was developed for Roman Catholic schools, the nation's largest non-public school system. Called the *Cathedral* series, this version featured Catholic situations and even changed the names of the characters to children with more "Catholic" names—John, Jean, and Judy.

The universe of the *Dick and Jane* readers was one of optimism and innocence, inviting criticism that the situations were unreal and stereotypical. As Sara Goodman Zimet writes in *What Children Read in School:* "Dick and Jane's world is a friendly one, populated by good, smiling people who are ready and eager to help children whenever necessary . . . There are no evil impulses to be controlled. Instead, free rein and encouragement is given for seeking more and more fun and play." Arther S. Trace, Jr. complained that the *Dick and Jane* readers ironically painted authority figures in an unfavorable light, noting that "Father behaves like a candidate for the all-American clown. He acts, in fact, like an utter ass, and Mother is almost as good a representative of the female of the species . . . These stories do, of course, help adjust students to life if their fathers and mothers are fools . . . The Dick and Jane readers for the early grades are comic books in hard covers." City life is generally ignored in the *Dick and Jane* readers, leading other critics to implicate the books as partially responsible for low reading scores in inner-city schools. The series was not adapted for racial diversity until shortly before its demise; it was not until 1965 that African American characters were introduced in the form of Dick and Jane's neighbors, Mike, Pam, and Penny. The *Dick and Jane* readers fell into general disfavor around this time, partly due to changes in reading pedagogy that advanced more realistic and relevant storylines, and partly because of complaints of the book's racial and sex-role stereotyping. Still, the books retain a sentimental hold over the millions of Americans who learned their first words within their covers, and the *Dick and Jane* readers have become both collectors' items and cultural icons.

—Edward Moran

FURTHER READING:

Kismaric, Carole, and Marvin Heiferman. *Growing Up with Dick and Jane.* San Francisco, Collins, 1996.

Trace, Arther S., Jr. *Reading without Dick & Jane.* Chicago, Henry Regnery Company, 1965.

Zimet, Sara Goodman, editor. *What Children Read in School: Critical Analysis of Primary Reading Textbooks.* New York, Grune & Stratton, 1972.

Dick, Philip K. (1928-1982)

Author of 26 novels and 112 short stories, Philip K. Dick started his career as a science fiction writer in 1952. He was awarded the Hugo Award, a presentation made by fans, for his novel *The Man in the High Castle* in 1962, but he had to wait until the late 1970s to receive critical acclaim rivalling his popular reputation. His novels are uneven in quality, most containing powerful social satire. Dick has been immensely influential in contemporary science fiction writing, identifying many of the prominent concerns of cyberpunk, particularly consumerism, the cyborg, issues surrounding memory, surveillance, and mediated or artificial reality. *Bladerunner* (1982), the film version of his novel *Do Androids Dream of Electric Sheep?* (1968), has become a central reference point for critical discussions of both science fiction and modern technologically driven society.

Dick's career can be roughly divided into three main stages. In the 1950s, after he had been expelled from the University of California at Berkley, he produced fiction for magazines and Ace books. Writing against a backdrop of McCarthyism, the first novels Dick produced present satirical dystopias, exaggerating aspects of contemporary social experience. *Solar Lottery* (1955) presents an economic

The cover illustration of Philip K. Dick's *Time Out of Joint.*

dystopia, *The World Jones Made* (1956) concerns the power of the police, *Vulcan's Hammer* (1956) the rise of a computer technocracy, and *The Man Who Japed* (1956) examines the totalitarianism inherent in democracy. These novels also established his interest in themes of political power and messianic figures.

It is, however, the consideration of different levels of reality and the world of appearances imposed upon ordinary characters which marks out Dick's work as radically creative and culturally astute. *The Eye in the Sky* (1957), *The Cosmic Puppets* (1956), and *Time Out of Joint* (1959), which all have structural inconsistencies in the worlds they portray, each deal with shifting realities and characters who defy illusion. These convoluted plots circle the issue of defining the real from the ersatz, which is a predominant theme throughout Dick's work.

The Man in the High Castle (1962), which earned Dick his Hugo Award, also debates the same theme. It is an alternate history, where the Allies have lost World War II. The novel stands out from his earlier work because it is less allegorical; its length allows Dick the space for deeper characterization and to dwell on ambiguity and irony. From this point Dick writes about existence within depleted environments and derelict worlds, particularly the harshness visualized in the Martian colonies. In *The Three Stigmata of Palmer Eldritch* (1964) Dick concentrates on the use of drugs which allow Martian colonists to escape the severity of their lives. Dick's fiction often explores the social use of drugs, including their economic and psychological effects. This interest culminates in *A Scanner Darkly* (1977), where drugs promote such powerful illusions that they pre-empt reality.

Flow My Tears the Policeman Said (1974) was nominated for both the Nebula (writers) and the Hugo (fan) awards and it won the John W. Campbell Award, which is presented by academic writers for the best science fiction novel of the year. The book marked a stage in which Dick was ready to cast aside the more traditional conventions of science fiction, e.g., time travel, space colonies, technology, aliens, and telepathy, in order to focus on the more philosophical concerns of mainstream writing. He wrote a series of non-generic novels during the 1950s, but only one—*Confessions of a Crap Artist* (1975)—was published in his lifetime. His last novels, *VALIS* (1981), *The Divine Invasion* (1982), and *The Transmigration of Timothy Archer* (1982) combine autobiography and realism with the metaphysical search for God.

Dick will be most remembered for *Do Android's Dream of Electric Sheep?*, which best exemplifies his preoccupation with the nature of humanity, realized in the dystopia of a society that has wiped out animal life and supplanted it with androids. It is a novel of deep existential insight which expands its hardboiled genre for the popular market. Dick died of a stroke just before the completion of *Blade Runner*. In acknowledgement of his achievements, the Philip K. Dick award was established after his death to recognize the best novel of the year published originally in paperback.

—Nickianne Moody

FURTHER READING:

Gillespie, Bruce, editor. *Philip K. Dick: Electric Shepherd.* Melbourne, Norstrilia Press, 1975.

Olander, J. D., and M. H. Greenberg, editors. *Philip K. Dick.* New York, Taplinger, 1983.

Robinson, K. S. *The Novels of Philip K. Dick.* Michigan, UMI Research Press, 1984.

Dick Tracy

Dick Tracy has been called America's most famous detective, but his fame does not stop in this country. With his chiseled countenance and tough-guy morality, Tracy has become recognizable throughout the world. When Chester ''Chet'' Gould created the character—the first *Dick Tracy* comic strip ran on October 4, 1931—he could not have foreseen the influence of his tough but honest police detective. In fact, the influence extends well beyond the comics, into film, radio, and television. The timing of the comic strip's release was perfect. The Depression paved the way for a character who upheld traditional values even as he fell hard on the sordid underworld—he was just a regular guy fighting to make the world a better place. Moreover, prohibition, though nearing its demise, had established heretofore unknown levels of underground criminal activity. The strip also suggested better times with its presentation of new inventions, tools to continue the war against crime, and more importantly, inspiring signs of progress to come. *Dick Tracy* was created as a reflection of his times, and Gould's genius is reflected in the fact that the comic strip has survived for so long.

Gould always regarded himself as a cartoonist and he had done quite a number of odd illustration jobs before showing a strip called *Plainclothes Tracy* to Captain Joseph Medill Patterson, co-founder and director of the New York Daily News. Patterson was himself something of a powerhouse in the world of comics. He was the editorial force behind the development of such strips as *Little Orphan Annie, Moon Mullins,* and *Gasoline Alley.* Patterson saw promise in ''Plainclothes Tracy'' and set up a meeting with Gould. It was Patterson who was responsible for the name change. The name ''Dick'' was slang for a detective, and complemented ''Tracy,'' Gould's play on the word ''tracing.'' Patterson also suggested a basic outline for the first story, in which the father of Tess Trueheart, Tracy's sweetheart, was robbed and murdered and, consequently, Tracy went into the crime fighting business. Dick Tracy made his premier in the Detroit *Sunday Mirror* and about a week later, on October 12, 1931, began as a daily.

Dick Tracy quickly became not only Gould's claim to fame, but also Patterson's greatest success in the field. For readers, *Dick Tracy* was something completely different. Moral tales in the comics, nearly half of which at the time were serial strips like *Dick Tracy,* were not uncommon. But *Dick Tracy* presented a rough kind of morality. Tracy was always good, the villains always evil, and the confrontations always flamboyant. The level of violence was new to the comics, and Gould was not above bringing his villains to the cruelest of all possible ends. Audiences were also fascinated by the details of police procedure. Fisticuffs and gunfire were there, but Gould always remembered that Dick Tracy was first and foremost a detective.

The strip also gained notoriety for its take on technology and its pageant of some of the most bizarre villains to appear anywhere. Of the inventions, the most famous was the two-way wrist radio which later became a television and, finally, a computer. Gould believed that technology was the key to the future. Because of this, he was always experimenting with new fictional inventions that would range from items that would eventually find equivalents in the real world, like the Voice-O-Graph voice print recorder, to the absurd. His placement of an antennaed race of humanoids and giant snails on the moon is, however, regarded by many as the low point of the strip. At any rate, Gould lent the strip a gruesome edge with the villains whose corrupted morals were reflected by their physical deformities. The names of the criminals are evocative in and of themselves: The Blank, Flyface, The Mole, Pruneface, and B-B Eyes.

When Chester Gould retired from *Dick Tracy* in December of 1977, its artistic responsibilities were taken over by Gould's longtime assistant Rick Fletcher while the writing became the responsibility of Max Allan Collins. Collins was a young mystery novelist who would also go on to script comic books like *Batman* along with his own detective creation, Ms. Tree. Fletcher was eventually replaced by Pulitzer Prize winning political cartoonist Dick Locher in 1983 and Collins was later replaced by Mike Killian.

Although Gould himself did not give it much consideration, Dick Tracy refused to be simply confined to the comics page. He would appear on radio and television, in books and movies—serial and feature—and in animated cartoons. He has been personified by the likes of Ralph Byrd, Morgan Conway, Ray MacDonnell, and, in a 1990 motion picture, Warren Beatty. In addition, Dick Tracy has been the basis for a great multitude of licensed products, from toys to clothing, and, of course, watches.

Clearly, the influence of *Dick Tracy* can be seen across a spectrum of media. Although the serial strip has lost much of its foothold in American newspaper comics, comic books owe much to *Dick Tracy*. Though perhaps not the greatest draftsman to work in comics, Gould was, without a doubt, original. His use of shadows opened doors for comics to explore darker visuals. One might even see Gould's work as a precursor of sorts to the techniques of *film noir*, and the police procedure of Dick Tracy became a staple of detective stories in virtually all narrative media. Dick Tracy also served as the model for yet another icon of American culture. Bob Kane credited Dick Tracy as the inspiration for his own creation, the Batman, and Gould's menagerie of grotesque villains found reflection in the likes of the Joker and Two-Face, a virtual duplicate of Gould's Haf-and-Haf. It could be argued that *Dick Tracy* invented the look that would come to be associated with both an era and a type of character. When we hear the words "hard-boiled" we can't help but think of the trenchcoat and fedora pioneered by the famed Dick Tracy.

—Marc Oxoby

FURTHER READING:

Crouch, Bill Jr. *Dick Tracy: America's Most Famous Detective.* New York, Citadel Press, 1987.

Roberts, Garyn G. *Dick Tracy and American Culture: Morality and Mythology, Text and Context.* Jefferson, McFarland, 1993.

Dickinson, Angie (1931—)

An attractive and talented film actress of the 1960s and 1970s, and star of the popular television show *Police Woman,* Angie Dickinson's lasting image was thrust upon her by Brian De Palma in 1980. By then an elegant and sophisticated presence, she was cast in De Palma's *Dressed to Kill* as a woman who is brutally and shockingly slashed to death in an elevator. Competing with the shower scene in *Psycho* as one of the most uncomfortably enduring celluloid murders of modern times, Dickinson's bloody demise guaranteed her immortality. Earlier in her career, Dickinson (born Angeline Brown in North

Dakota), exuded a unique blend of up-front acting, all-American girl charm, sympathetic femininity, and good-natured sex appeal. She was perfect as both foil and comfort to the men in her several male-oriented films, beginning with *Rio Bravo* (1959). Although she played many sympathetic characters, a tougher quality was exploited in *The Killers* (1964) and *Point Blank* (1967). She was married for a time to Burt Bacharach.

—Robyn Karney

FURTHER READING:

Cross, Robin. "Angie Dickinson." In *Who's Who in Hollywood,* edited by Robyn Karney. New York, Continuum, 1993.

Diddley, Bo (1928—)

Best known for the "shave-and-a-haircut" beat that bears his name, Bo Diddley helped build the rhythmic foundations of rock and roll with a string of hits during the mid-1950s. Diddley came out of the Chicago blues scene, but also brought the African American traditions of child game songs, tall-tale telling, and ritualized rounds

Bo Diddley

of bragging and insults into popular music, making him an early practitioner of rap. Diddley's chunky riffs and early use of distortion and tremolo effects on his unique square guitar were later used in 1960s funk and 1970s heavy metal.

The history of Diddley's beat has been traced to African Yoruba and Kongo cultures in Nigeria, and from there to Cuba, where the clave pattern was the basis for nineteenth century dance hall music. Early New Orleans jazz composer Jelly Roll Morton employed it in "Black Bottom Stomp" in the early twentieth century, and it was a common rhythm played by children on diddley bows—homemade single-stringed instruments—in rural Mississippi. The rhythm is also commonly referred to as "hambone," a method of slapping and stomping often used by shoeshine boys.

Diddley was born Ellas McDaniel in McComb, Mississippi, and moved to Chicago at the age of eight where he was undoubtedly exposed to these traditions. "Truthfully, I don't know where it came from exactly. I just started playing it one day," Diddley said in George R. White's biography *Bo Diddley: Living Legend*. "I figured there must be another way of playing, and so I worked on this rhythm of mine. I'd say it was 'mixed-up' rhythm: blues, and Latin American, and some hillbilly, a little spiritual, a little African and a little West Indian calypso . . . I like gumbo, you dig? Hot sauces, too. That's where my music come from: all the mixture."

Young Ellas was entranced one day shortly after moving to Chicago by a man playing a violin. He signed up for classical lessons from Professor O.W. Frederick at the Ebenezer Baptist Church, where he studied for 14 years. After hearing John Lee Hooker on the radio, however, he decided to play guitar. His sister, Lucille, bought Diddley his first guitar when he was 13. According to Diddley, " . . . the violin was the railroad track, or lifeline, to me playing a guitar . . . I used the bow licks with the guitar pick, and that's the reason for the weird sounds. That was my way of imitating with the bow on the violin strings, and that was the closest I could get to it."

Diddley attended Foster Vocational High School, where he learned to build violins and guitars, but quit school to work manual labor jobs and play on street corners. He formed a small group and played in neighborhood taverns, recording a demo that got the attention of Chess Records. Diddley, along with maracas player Jerome Green, joined Otis Spann on piano, Lester Davenport on harmonica, and Frank Kirkland on drums to record "Bo Diddley" and "I'm a Man" in 1955.

Chess was prepared to issue the single under McDaniel's real name, but harmonica player Billy Boy Arnold suggested Bo Diddley, a slang term for a comical-looking, bow-legged, short guy. The name and the single caught on, reaching number two on Billboard's rhythm and blues singles chart. He charted six more singles through 1960 on Checker, a Chess subsidiary, and recorded 22 albums for Chess/Checker through 1974.

Countless artists have had hits using Diddley's rhythm, including Buddy Holly ("Not Fade Away") and Johnny Otis ("Willie and the Hand Jive"). Many more, including the Rolling Stones and Eric Clapton, have had hits covering these tunes. The Who, the Yardbirds, Ronnie Hawkins, and the Doors all employed Diddley's beat at one time or another. Unfortunately for Diddley, American copyright law does not cover a beat or rhythm—only lyrics or a melody—and he therefore never received royalties from these songs.

Diddley released a few albums in the 1980s and 1990s with his own company, BoKay Productions, and other small labels, but he found it difficult to fit in with the new style of popular music. Diddley returned to form with the release of *A Man Amongst Men* on Atlantic

Records in 1996. Featuring guest musicians Jimmie Vaughan, Ron Wood, Richie Sambora, Billy Boy Arnold, Johnnie Johnson, and Johnny "Guitar" Watson, the album was nominated for a Grammy Award as Best Traditional Blues Album.

—Jon Klinkowitz

FURTHER READING:

DeCurtis, Anthony. "Living Legends." *Rolling Stone*. September 21, 1989, 89-99.

Kiersh, Edwards. *Where Are You Now, Bo Diddley?: The Stars Who Made Us Rock and Where Are They Now?* Garden City, New York, Doubleday, 1986.

Lydon, Michael. *Boogie Lightning*. New York, Dial, 1974.

White, George R. *Bo Diddley: Living Legend*. Chessington, Great Britain, Castle Communications, 1995.

Didion, Joan (1934—)

Joan Didion has proven herself one of the most acute observers of and commentators on American life in the latter half of the twentieth century. Her widely anthologized essays have been required reading for two generations of college students. Combining old-fashioned investigative reporting and New Journalistic subjectivity, she has brought her trademark style and deeply skeptical intelligence to bear on a variety of cultural phenomena, from her own marriage and the rock group the Doors, to the terror in El Salvador, Cuban exiles in Miami, and the Central Park jogger case. Her highly cinematic novels are stylistically and tonally of a piece with her nonfiction and have become increasingly journalistic and more political over the years. Focusing on women who are affluent but adrift, Didion's decidedly pessimistic novels expose not just her characters' self-delusions, but the political and psychological shortcomings of an American Dream gone sour. As such, the novels, along with the essays, give laconic voice to the disillusionment and pessimism that is the other face of the radicalism of the 1960s.

—Robert A. Morace

FURTHER READING:

Felton, Sharon, editor. *The Critical Response to Joan Didion*. Westport, Connecticut, Greenwood, 1994.

Winchell, Mark Roydon. *Joan Didion*. Boston, Twayne, 1989.

Didrikson, Babe (1911-1956)

More than a hero to feminists and young women who aspire to athletic achievement, athlete Babe Didrikson was a sports hero in the finest American tradition, larger than life, with super-sized faults to match her virtues. Carrying a chip on her shoulder from her rough and tumble upbringing, Didrikson approached life with a swagger and a wisecrack. She brought controversy and excitement to the refined world of women's golf, and challenged assumptions everywhere she went. She broke world records regularly and broke barriers set up

Babe Didrikson

against women. Her statistics are an inspiration to women athletes everywhere. But it is the flesh and blood Didrikson, angry, cocky, competitive, and irrepressible, that forged her place in history's sports hall of fame.

"Before I was even into my teens I knew exactly what I wanted to be when I grew up," Didrikson wrote, "My goal was to be the greatest athlete who ever lived." Didrikson achieved her goal. The Associated Press named her Female Athlete of the Year six times between 1932 and 1954, and in 1950, they gave her the title Female Athlete of the Half Century. She was an All-American basketball player, an Olympic gold medal winner in track and field, a record-breaking golf champion, and a proficient dabbler in other sports from swimming to shooting pool. Didrikson's athletic achievements clearly transcend the footnote usually allowed for women in sports.

Mildred Didrikson was born in the south Texas town of Beaumont. The sixth of seven children in a working-class family, she learned early the value of toughness and self-reliance. Roaming the streets of Beaumont, she taught herself to run by racing the streetcars and learned hurdles from leaping over hedges. It was the boys in her hometown who gave her the name "Babe" because she hit so many home runs in their sandlot games.

Didrikson dropped out of high school and was playing semi-professional basketball when she was made an All-American in 1932. That year she participated in an Amateur Athletic Union track-and-field championship as a one-woman team. She entered eight events and won six, and the championship. A team of twenty-two women came in second, eight points behind Didrikson. That day on the field, the smart-aleck kid from south Texas set world records for the high jump, the eighty-meter hurdles, the javelin, and the baseball throw. A few weeks later, competing in the Olympics in Los Angeles, she won gold medals for the javelin and the eighty-meter hurdles and a silver for the high jump. She would have won the gold for the high jump, but her best jump was disqualified on a technicality because her head went over the bar before her feet.

In 1935, Didrikson took the golf world by storm. Before her career was over she had won fifty-five professional and amateur tournaments and set a record with seventeen wins in a row. Staid golfing audiences were put off by Didrikson's irreverent, wisecracking style, but her drives were regularly fifty to one hundred yards longer than her opponents', and it was not uncommon for her to come in well under the men's par, so she was hard to dismiss. The upper-class golfing establishment tried to exclude her because she played professionally and most women's golf consisted of amateur events, but Didrikson got around them in typical aggressive style. In 1949, she helped found the Ladies Professional Golfers Association to put women's golf on more even footing with men's by giving professional women golfers a venue.

Didrikson remained the cocky, streetwise, tough kid from south Texas. Her style was both confrontational and comic, sometimes charming her audiences with silly trick golf shots, sometimes shocking them with her directness. Many of her opponents hated her, perhaps because she was an egotistical and graceless winner. The press nicknamed her "muscle moll," and college physical education departments warned women against emulating her. Didrikson was unabashed. She continued to start her golf matches with a grin and the quip, "Well, I'm just gonna have to loosen my girdle and let 'er fly!" She also continued to play almost every sport available. She played exhibition games in baseball and football, shot exhibition pool, and even sang and played harmonica on the vaudeville stage. When asked if there was anything she didn't play, Didrikson answered dryly, "Yeah. Dolls."

Didrikson married professional wrestler George Zaharias in 1938. They had met when they were partnered in the Los Angeles Open golf tourney. In 1941, Didrikson underwent surgery for colon cancer, and doctors told her that her athletic career was over. With typical unconcern for the opinions of naysayers, she continued to play, and in 1954, she won five golf tournaments, playing with pain, fatigue, and a colostomy bag. Two years later, she died. The epitaph on her tombstone in Galveston, Texas, reads "Babe Didrikson Zaharias—1911-1956—World's Greatest Woman Athlete."

—Tina Gianoulis

FURTHER READING:

Cayleff, Susan E. *Babe: The Life and Legend of Babe Didrikson Zaharias.* Urbana, Illinois, University of Illinois Press, 1995.

Knudson, R. Rozanne. *Babe Didrikson: Athlete of the Century.* New York, Viking Kestrel, 1985.

Lynn, Elizabeth A. *Babe Didrikson Zaharias.* New York, Chelsea House, 1989.

Dieting

It would be hard to find anyone in the United States, or in any other part of the Western world, who has not at one time gone on a weight-loss diet. Perhaps the most long-lived fad of our society, the diet craze has grown and expanded its influence until almost every issue of every popular publication contains at least one diet article and television talk shows regularly feature diet gurus and those offering weight loss testimonials. With little evidence that such diets work, and with quite a bit of evidence to the contrary, a multi-billion dollar industry has grown up around the modern obsession with thinness. Women are the vast majority of consumers in the diet industry, and, though men do diet, it is almost exclusively women who focus a significant portion of their time and energy on the effort to become thin.

Though Americans are constantly bombarded with the concept of thinness as an ideal of health and beauty, it is a relatively new concept that would have seemed laughable just one hundred years ago. Though standards of beauty have varied from culture to culture and from century to century, plumpness has widely been viewed as signaling health, success, and sensuality. Many modern cultures do not place the same value on thinness as much of western society. Some, such as those in Polynesia and east and central Africa, value fat women to the extent of fattening up daughters to make them more marriageable.

Human bodies evolved in response to a struggle to survive with an uncertain food supply. The ability to store fat was a valued genetic trait. As long ago as 30,000 to 10,000 B.C.E., statues like the so-called Venus of Willendorf show an ideal of feminine beauty that includes large thighs, broad buttocks and pendulous breasts. The Biblical book of Proverbs says, "He that putteth his trust in the Lord shall be made fat." Even in Medieval Europe, when the religious art showed lank, acetic Marys and Eves, the secular art pictured round, fleshy women, brimming with laughter and sexuality. A fat, dimpled buttock or thigh was a universal symbol of sex appeal.

On the contrary, thinness was viewed as a sign of weakness, disease, and poverty. Eighteenth-century diet specialist Jean-Anthelme Brillat-Savarin called thinness "a terrible misfortune" for a woman. "Every thin woman wishes to put on weight," he said, "This is an ambition that has been confided to us a thousand times." He obliged them by prescribing fattening diets. By the end of the nineteenth century, women had begun to slim their waists through the use of tightly laced corsets, but ample cleavage and voluminous hips were still very much the style, helped along by contrivances called farthingales, panniers, and bustles. These were wire frames worn under the clothes to add desirable inches (or feet) to hips and buttocks. Indeed, most changes deemed necessary in the body were effected by additions to the costume. Only later would women begin to consider the idea of altering the body itself.

As the 1900s began, the country was in an era of tremendous growth and change. The industrial revolution was bringing science into the day-to-day lives of common citizens. A feminist age was beginning as women entered the work force in unprecedented numbers and began to demand more rights. Along with these changes came a new look in women's fashions. The corsets and cumbersome contraptions were gone and so was the abundant flesh. By the 1920s women were supposed to be slim, straight, and boyish. Hair was bobbed, breasts and hips were bound, and women began to try to lose weight. Along with such extreme treatments as electrotherapy, tapeworm pills, and hot baths to melt fat off, miracle diets promised to fatten the scrawny as well as slim the stout.

Around the same time, the newly burgeoning insurance industry began to study the effects of weight and other features on longevity. Inspired perhaps by the fashion of thinness, researchers tended to ignore the evidence that the underweight and the tall had higher death rates too, and they only focused on the overweight. Even though their research methods were questionable and their samples included only the upper classes who had the money and inclination to purchase life insurance, the insurance tables were popularly accepted as fact in terms of optimum height-weight ratios. These tables have remained a standard by which modern people measure themselves, even though their recommendations have varied widely over the decades.

It was also around the 1920s that doctors began to abandon their condemnation of thinness as a sign of the common disorder "neurasthenia" and to attack excess weight as the cause of many health problems. Even then, there was not widespread belief that people could control their body size, and doctors worried that dieting, especially the dieting of young women, was dangerous to health.

The Roaring Twenties' dieting craze, which never penetrated much beyond the upper classes, waned during the late 1930s and early 1940s, as the poverty of the depression years deepened. But by the 1950s, the preference for thinness and disgust with fat was on its way to becoming a national obsession. This obsession was perhaps useful to a society which was trying to distract women from the increased responsibility they had been given during the war and refocus them on home, family, and fashion. The number of magazine articles about weight and diet skyrocketed, and fatness, which once had been viewed as a physical characteristic like any other, had become a vice and a moral failing. Weight loss products and diet foods began to appear on grocery shelves, and dieters bought them in huge quantities. Pharmaceuticals firm Mead and Johnson created an all-liquid diet food called Metrecal that boosted their earnings over 300 percent in the years between 1958 and 1960. Just as quickly, however, profits dropped again, as unsuccessful dieters moved on to try other products. Amphetamines, a fairly new drug about which little was known, were prescribed freely to women as a weight loss aid.

Diet books also began to appear, some with a health food bent, others purely fashionable. Exercise had long been seen as having a negative effect on weight loss because it stimulated the appetite, but modern experts made the case for exercise as an adjunct to a weight-loss diet. Fad and novelty diets began to pop up, often having nothing more to recommend them than sheer weirdness, but promising "miracle" results. The Drinking Man's Diet, offered permission to imbibe; the grapefruit diet ascribed extraordinary fat burning qualities to the acidic yellow fruit which was to be eaten several times a day. One diet prescribed only steak, another suggested eating foods high in fat. Americans were willing to try anything that promised results.

Medical opinions about the effects of obesity continued to follow closely the guidelines and research done by the insurance industry, even though that research was proved flawed and limited on many occasions. Since the major factor in body size seemed to be genetic, doctors began to prescribe weight-loss diets even for pregnant women and young children. As fat was seen as the result of moral flaws such as lack of willpower, it was also seen as a psychological problem, and fat people were sent to psychiatrists to seek the deep root causes of their body size.

The 1960s and 1970s saw the continued increase of the thinness obsession, perhaps more than coincidentally with the rise of a second wave of women's liberation. Some feminists speculate that each time women gained power and pushed for more rights, they were purposely distracted by a cultural insistence on an unattainable female body ideal. Women, though genetically predisposed to be fatter than men, have always borne the brunt of the weight-loss fad. Though some dieting occurs among men, it is far more common that even men who do not fit the media mold of beauty have little shame over exposing bellies and bare chests in public, while women, even admired models and actresses, experience shame and self-loathing about their bodies. Perhaps because men have had more economic and political power, it has been necessary for women to fit the mold most pleasing to men. If the eating disorders and obsession with dieting that women exhibit are reflected anywhere among men, it is among gay men, who have the same need that heterosexual women have to fit the male standard of beauty. Nowhere has that standard been challenged more strongly than within the lesbian community. Though not immune to cultural beauty standards, lesbians' relative independence from men has given them both room and incentive to question those standards. That questioning has led to pioneering work in the fat acceptance movement, which challenges the diet industry and medical establishment's demonization of fatness.

By the 1990s the diet fad has become so widespread that most Americans are continually on one sort of weight-loss plan or another, and most women consider themselves fat, no matter what their actual size. Studies have been done that show a high percentage of girls as young as eight years old have begun to diet. Fashion models appear acutely undernourished and even they must have their pictures airbrushed to remove offending flesh. Eating disorders such as anorexia (the rejection of food to achieve ever-increasing thinness) and bulimia (binge eating followed by forced vomiting or laxative-induced diarrhea) which once were rare, have become epidemic. Surgical procedures such as stomach-stapling and liposuction are in demand even though they are known to have dangerous or even deadly effects.

The media abounds with new "miracle" diets, and the diet business has grown from a few companies with names like Weight Watchers and Slenderella to a 50 billion dollar-a-year industry. With ads offering such perplexing promises as "Lose ten pounds for only ten dollars," these diet companies have perhaps finally achieved the perfect American solution to excess weight. If willpower, therapy, and even prayer don't work, one can *buy* weight loss.

The success of products like Metrecal in the 1950s has led to a boom in diet products and organizations. While some products like SlimFast and Lean Cuisine specialize in diet food, others have jumped on the bandwagon by offering "lite" or "lo-fat" versions of their products. Soft drink companies were among the first to offer profitable diet alternatives. These are guzzled in astounding quantities by Americans of all sizes, even though their artificial sweeteners, first saccharin, then cyclamates, and most recently aspartame, have in some cases been found to have damaging effects on the body. Often, as in Metrecal's case, when a new product is introduced, there is a rush to try it. When it proves to be less than miraculous, sales may drop as consumers move on to the next new promise.

Another form of diet business is the dieter's organization or "club." Affluent dieters often pay high prices to attend spas and "fat farms" to help them lose weight. For middle and working class dieters there are more affordable alternatives. Organizations like Weight Watchers and Jenny Craig offer counseling and group support for a price, plus a line of food products that are required or strongly suggested to go with the program. The twelve-step approach of Alcoholics Anonymous is emulated by groups like Take Off Pounds Sensibly (TOPS) and Overeaters Anonymous, which tend to view fatness as a sign of addictive attitudes towards food and offer free support groups to combat the addiction.

Over the years, many weight-loss "gurus" have risen to media prominence, producing books or videos to promote their personal recommendation for weight loss. As early as 1956, Roy de Groot published his low-protein "Revolutionary Rockefeller Diet" in *Look* magazine, leading the way for Robert Atkins' *Dr. Atkins' Diet Revolution* in 1972, Herbert Tarnower's "Scarsdale" diet in 1979, and Jane Fonda's books and videos in the 1980s and 1990s. Trading on medical credentials or celebrity, these diet "experts" often become corporations in themselves, profiting handsomely from sales and public appearances.

Yet many Americans are still overweight. In fact, diets have never been successful at making fat people thin. Only about ten percent of dieters lose anything close to their goals, and only about half of those keep the weight off for an extended period of time. The body is an efficient processing machine for food and its response to the starvation message sent by dieting is to become even more efficient, thereby needing less food to maintain the same weight. The World Health Organization's definition of starvation is 1200 calories per day, the same intake as an average weight-loss diet. Even when caloric reduction causes the body to use stored resources, there is no guarantee that unwanted fat will be used. The body might as easily draw from muscle tissue, even from the brain or heart, with life-threatening results.

Some researchers claim that the rising numbers of fat people are caused by the incessant dieting practiced by most Americans. Each bit of weight loss causes the body to respond as it would to recurring famine, by storing food, and fat, more efficiently. Even aside from overtly dangerous diets, such as liquid protein diets or extreme 400 to 500 calorie diets, any sort of weight-loss diet can have seriously negative effects. Depression, irritability, and fatigue are frequent side effects, along with amenorrhea for women, muscle damage, and stress on liver, kidneys, and the cardiovascular system. In the long run, medical studies on the negative effects of being fat become useless, for, in a society where everyone diets, fat people, persecuted for being fat, often spend a large part of their lives dieting. It is difficult to separate the effect of weight on health from the effects of long-term dieting and from the stress of being fat in a culture that demeans fat people.

Though dieting has become so entrenched in American culture, some voices are being raised in protest. The fat-positive movement (also called the size-acceptance or size-diversity movement) is growing, energized by people who are no longer willing to devote their lives to fitting an impossible ideal. An anti-diet movement has arisen, drawing attention to the dangers of dieting with an annual International No-Diet Day. Concerned by the rising numbers (over 11 million in the 1990s) of young girls afflicted with anorexia and bulimia, some parents and educators are calling for more focus on raising the self-esteem of adolescent girls. However, surveys still report that a large percentage of women would prefer being run over by a truck or killed by a terrorist to being fat, and American culture has a long way to go to leave superficial values behind. Perhaps as long as there is still so much money to be made off of Americans' preoccupation with thinness, dieting will remain a lifestyle and an obsession.

—Tina Gianoulis

FURTHER READING:

Atrens, Dale. *Don't Diet.* New York, William Morrow and Company, 1988.

Bennett, William, and Joel Gurin. *The Dieter's Dilemma: Eating Less and Weighing More.* New York, Basic Books, 1982.

Chernin, Kim. *The Obsession: Reflections on the Tyranny of Slenderness.* New York, Harper and Row, 1981.

Seid, Roberta Pollack. *Never Too Thin: Why Women Are Obsessed with Their Bodies.* New York, Prentice Hall, 1989.

Dietrich, Marlene (1901-1992)

Marlene Dietrich is a mythical woman and actress who worked actively on the creation of her myth. Her ability to create and manipulate a recognizable and durable star image influenced modern popular icons such as Madonna. The German Marlene Dietrich emerged onto the world stage as a screen idol taking Hollywood by storm in the 1930s, moved on to become a troop entertainer during the Second World War, and ended her career as an age-defying concert singer in the 1950s and 1960s. Gender-bending Marlene enjoyed many decades of a stardom that was predicated on one core attribute—her ability to remain ambivalent and mysterious.

Maria Magdalene Dietrich was born a policeman's daughter in Berlin, although her father died when she was young. She was a schoolgirl during the upheavals of World War I, during which her step-father, a colonel, died of war wounds. Although Marlene—a contraction of her first two names—played the violin and the piano, she was not accepted at the Weimar music school. Thus, after the depression following the war and with Weimar cultural life blooming around her, Marlene forsook her middle-class background and embarked on a more dangerous and decadent path: the stage. She found

Marlene Dietrich

entry into the Max Rheinhardt School, a renowned theater school with very good stage connections. By 1922, Marlene Dietrich was on the stage. With ceaseless energy, Dietrich worked her way through small supporting roles and, like many stage actors of the time, appeared in many silent films. By 1927, Dietrich had made it. Her sensuous appearance had won her the Berlin audience. Two years later, a big Hollywood director decided to come to Berlin to look for his latest star for the film *The Blue Angel* (1930), and a Hollywood legend began: the collaboration of Marlene Dietrich and Joseph von Sternberg. Dietrich was already well aware of her ability to embody ambivalent sex. Her risque performances with well-known lesbian Maro Lion in their duet "It's in the air" had been deliciously scandalous. Under the guidance of her "Svengali" von Sternberg, this ability became the core of her star persona. Together, they fashioned the myth of Dietrich, a myth of sex, sadomasochism, cool poise, and darkness, which transplanted surprisingly well from permissive Weimar Berlin to a more strict Hollywood. In *The Blue Angel,* Dietrich played Lola Lola, the ruin of a professor who falls desperately in love with her and is treated cruelly and dismissively by his love object. In this film, Dietrich established her gender-bending image for the American audience by donning tails and a top hat. Another trademark which was to become mythical was displayed in detail to U.S. audiences—the long, sensual Dietrich legs.

The legs and trousers became fetishes of a woman surrounded by mystery. Dietrich wore her slacks outside the studio and, as a result, was called "the best dressed man in Hollywood." In a time when studios had a morality clause in their contracts allowing them to dispense with any star overstepping the rules, Dietrich's open bisexual affairs were indulged. Her foreign, ambivalent, dangerously sexual image, portrayed by an equally mysterious foreigner with strange tastes, was recognized as the main box-office draw. Films such as *Morocco* (1930) and *Blonde Venus* (1932) consolidated Dietrich as the cool, poised femme fatale in feathers and fur: an image of an erotic and sophisticated dominatrix made immortal in Sacher-Masoch's novel *Venus in Furs.* After the end of her relationship with von Sternberg, Dietrich continued to be a successful and (in)famous star, even if occasionally touted as "box office poison." Dietrich's desire to broaden her appeal and develop her image led to leads in productions by Ernst Lubitsch—*Desire* (1936) and *Angel* (1937)—which allowed her to display humor as well as sex. Other ventures into different genres include a western parody, *Destry Rides Again,* directed by George Marshall and released in 1939.

During the war-years, however, a new side was added to Marlene Dietrich's image. Her foreign origin, accent, and the decadent sexual persona of continental European ancestry were a recognized part of her image, but now a vehemently anti-Nazi stance and a belief in the American way of life led Dietrich to help the war effort. She worked for the United States Entertainment Organization, appeared at fund-raising events, and entertained the troops on the frontlines in Europe. Her most famous song, "Lili Marleen", stems from this period. The head of the German Nazi Ministry of Culture had earlier asked her to return, to be a great Nazi star, even after some of her films were banned in Germany. As an answer, Dietrich became a United States citizen in 1939. In 1945, she was back in Germany, to bury her mother, and, according to her daughter Maria Riva, to bury the Germany she once knew and loved.

After the war, Dietrich's film roles were sporadic. Films such as *Rancho Notorious* (1952) and *A Touch of Evil* (1958) are tongue-in-cheek takes on her own carefully nurtured star persona. Dietrich's main activity was now the stage: she had recaptured her original calling from the years in Weimar, and embarked on a new, successful career as an international cabaret star. Although her singing voice was criticized, Dietrich's delivery was a full-blown stage cabaret show. Her repertoire embraced sexy songs, often originally written for male singers, allowing her worldly charm and eroticism full range. Numbers recorded by Dietrich include "One for My Baby," "One More for the Road," and "Makin' Whoopee." The older image of Dietrich as femme fatale was soon supplemented by a newer strand of anti-war songs including *"Sag mir wo die Blumen sind"* (Where Have All the Flowers Gone), as well as other Pete Seeger and Bob Dylan songs. During her concert in Israel she broke the taboo against the German language by singing her cry against wars in her mother tongue. She also went back to Germany, despite the fact that the voices calling her a traitor had not stopped. The concert was a success.

Dietrich paid a price for her decades of working and the self-fashioned myths around her. More and more scotch accompanied her touring. Finally, she ended her stage career when she broke a leg on stage in 1975. With many of her old friends dead, including her husband from her Weimar years, Dietrich led a lonely existence in Paris.

For decades, she had been a focal point for the famous. Her rumored lovers included Ernest Hemingway, Greta Garbo, and Jean Gabin. At the end of her career, she claimed that it was not vanity that made her camera-shy, but her need to sustain and nurture the myth of what she had become—an icon of glamour, ambivalent sexuality, erotic sophistication, and unknowable mystery. Her skill was well rewarded. Later generations of artists have plundered and recycled the rich image of Dietrich. Her most well-known "interpreter" has become Madonna—another star of ambivalence and mystery.

In her book *ABC,* Dietrich writes: "Dietrich—In the German language the name for a key that opens all locks. Not a magic key. A very real object, necessitating great skill in the making." Even her death did not erase this fascinating object.

—Petra Kuppers

FURTHER READING:

Bach, Steven. *Marlene Dietrich—Life and Legend.* New York, William Morrow, 1992.

Riva, Maria. *Marlene Dietrich.* New York, Alfred A. Knopf, 1992.

Spoto, Donald. *Marlene Dietrich.* New York, Doubleday, 1992.

Diff'rent Strokes

For eight seasons and 189 episodes, Americans tuned in to *Diff'rent Strokes,* a sitcom chronicling the family life of a wealthy white industrialist who adopts two African American children. The tepid comedy's lengthy television run made many cultural observers wonder if its creators had made a deal with the devil. Certainly the show's trinity of child stars seems to have spent the ensuing years in show business purgatory.

Developed by Norman Lear, the brains behind *All in the Family, Diff'rent Strokes* began as a well-meaning, if patronizing, look at America's racial and economic divides. Conrad Bain, a veteran of Lear's *Maude,* was cast as Philip Drummond, the white Daddy Warbucks to black ragamuffins Arnold and Willis Jackson, played by

(From left) Gary Coleman, Dody Goodman, and Conrad Bain in a scene from *Diff'rent Strokes.*

Gary Coleman and Todd Bridges. Stringy Dana Plato rounded out the main cast as Drummond's natural daughter, Kimberly. A succession of brassy housekeepers, vanguarded by Charlotte Rae, commented mordantly on the goings-on.

Conceived as an ensemble, *Diff'rent Strokes* quickly became a star vehicle for the adorable Coleman, a natural comedic talent relegated to Lilliputian stature by a congenital kidney condition. "What you talkin' 'bout, Willis?," Coleman's Arnold would bellow repeatedly at his older, worldlier sibling. Eventually this interrogative came to be something of a catch phrase, flung promiscuously by Coleman at any of the show's characters and accompanied by a mugging double take. As the years went by, however, Coleman's stunted growth began to take on an eerie, side show quality. Only at the very end of the eight-year run was his character allowed to grow up, "dramatically speaking," date girls, and behave like something other than a mischievous eight-year-old. Coleman was 17 at the time.

Medical oddities aside, *Diff'rent Strokes* was little more than light entertainment for the home-on-Saturday-night crowd. It did, however, occasionally tackle meaningful subject matter. In one memorable episode, Arnold converted to Judaism after attending a friend's bar mitzvah. Likening the solemn ceremony to a "Jewish Academy Awards," and pleased with his complimentary "yamaha," the diminutive adoptee was dissuaded from his change of faith only after Drummond engineered a visit from Milton Berle as a wisecracking rabbi. Terrified by the prospect of Hebrew School and Jewish dietary obligations, the impressionable tyke opted to forego his opportunity to celebrate "Harmonica."

Not all series installments, however, addressed weighty issues with such rampant insensitivity. Rotund *WKRP* fixture Gordon Jump played a child molester (all too believably) in one topical episode, while First Lady Nancy Reagan herself dropped by for a memorable 1983 show about drug abuse. The jaded Coleman was non-plussed by the visit from the power-suited astrology enthusiast, who stiffly hugged a group of child actors for the cameras and accepted a pair of *Diff'rent Strokes* tee-shirts from Conrad Bain before departing in a four-car motorcade. "It was just another show," Coleman shrugged after Reagan's visit. "We didn't talk about much. She came in, did her job, and left."

When the program's three young stars made their exits following *Diff'rent Strokes'* 1986 cancellation by ABC, they had no way of knowing that a living tabloid hell awaited them. Dana Plato posed nude for *Playboy* in 1989 to pay off her mounting personal debt, then robbed a Las Vegas video store at gunpoint in 1991 after being turned down for a job cleaning toilets. Her career reached a nadir in 1997 with an appearance in a porno film entitled *Different Strokes: The Story of Jack and Jill . . . and Jill.* (Plato died of an accidental drug overdose in 1999.) Todd Bridges was arrested for cocaine possession and later for shooting an accused drug dealer in a crack house. (He was subsequently acquitted of the latter crime.) He later blamed his problems on a cocaine habit dating back to 1982.

Even Gary Coleman, the little pixie with the atrophied kidney, could not escape controversy. In 1989 he sued his real-life adoptive parents and his former business manager, claiming they had stolen more than $1 million from him. Tabloid rumors began to circulate reporting that Coleman had legally changed his name to Andy Shane and asked a female housemate if he could suck her toes. In 1998, the tubby actor, now working as a mall security guard, was himself sued by a Los Angeles bus driver who alleged that he had assaulted her after she asked him for an autograph.

"The world don't move to the beat of just one drum," went the theme to *Diff'rent Strokes,* the television show. "What might be right for you, may not be right for some." The program's troubled stars seem to have been following a rhythm all their own in their personal lives as well.

—Robert E. Schnakenberg

FURTHER READING:

Armstrong, Lois. "For Gary Coleman, Acting with the First Lady Is No Big Deal." *People Weekly,* March 28, 1983.

Sporkin, Elizabeth. "Diff'rent Strokes, Fallen Stars." *People Weekly,* March 25, 1991.

Dilbert

Dilbert's subject matter "strikes a nerve," as *Newsweek*'s cover story shouted in August of 1996, because it "portrays the bedrock truth of the American workplace, at least in the white-collar caverns where clerks, engineers, marketers, and salespeople dwell." This comic strip presents aspects of the corporate culture that veterans of the cubicle easily identify with: company monitoring of employee e-mail; management double talk; carpal tunnel syndrome; endless and pointless meetings; inane team-building exercises; and lower back pains resulting from excessive hours in front of the computer screen. Since his initial appearance in the early 1990s as the brain-child of

MBA-trained former Pacific Bell software engineer Scott Adams, Dilbert, a nerdy engineer and the strip's main character, has become a sort of corporate everyman.

The strip centers around an anonymous company where Dilbert is employed in an unnamed department. With co-workers, he struggles to meet deadlines, withstand management trends, and endure other indignities. Each of the strip's main characters is described in Adams' 1997 retrospective *Seven Years of Highly Defective People,* and was inspired and shaped by bits and pieces of Adams's own experience at Pacific Bell. Much of the subject matter is supplemented by "war stories" taken directly from reader e-mail and visitors to the "Dilbert Zone," Adams' web site. Each character, therefore, embodies some facet of actual corporate reality, which is probably why readers familiar with the environment identify with the strip's material so readily.

The more significant of Dilbert's co-workers are Wally, a fellow engineer and "thoroughly cynical employee who has no sense of company loyalty and feels no need to mask his poor performance or his total lack of respect," and Alice, a no-nonsense go-getter known for her "pink suit, her fluffy hair, her coffee obsession, her technical proficiency, and her take-no-crap attitude." Other characters include the "generic guy" Ted, whose manic work habits go unnoticed by the company bigwigs, and Tina, the technical writer who resents the engineers for their failure to appreciate her talents.

This motley cast struggles to withstand the whimsical machinations and inane directives of Dilbert's dog, the annoying know-it-all Dogbert; his cat, the head of the Evil Human Resources, Catbert; the troglodytes of the Accounting Department; the Teflon-coated PR types in marketing who have no clue about what engineers do; and ultimately, the "Pointy-Haired Boss," whose coif reflects his ultimately demonic stature as a figure of management inanity and cluelessness. Together, these characters represent the worst face of corporate culture, and are frequently seen drafting dehumanizing policies, issuing obscure directives, arbitrarily demonstrating their authority, and generally making miserable the lives of the employees who nonetheless "see through" their motives.

The reality of Dilbert's world isn't too different from that of his audience of real-life counterparts who identify with his struggle to maintain his sanity. In the mid 1990s, *Dilbert* became a hot topic for discussion among management strategists and human resource officers, and a voice of late-capitalist corporate worker cynicism. Management Consultant Tom Brown notes that Adams' strip "take(s) virtually every HR issue of the past 20 years and catapults it to the top of many management agendas via trenchant cartoons and scathing essays in books. . . . *Dilbert* is about human rights, human purpose, and human potential. It's what the human resources profession is about, or ought to be, as well." Indeed, recent years have seen Adams' comic lampoons of corporate America achieve their status as mandatory reading for those in the management and human resource professions.

Along with his stature as an embodiment of worker frustration, Dilbert has also become a prosperous commodity as a merchandising icon. In the late 1990s, the nerdy engineer's visage could be found on everything from ties to mouse pads to coffee mugs, and his website was both the bane and the boon to other corporations, some of whom advertised on it while others blocked employee access to it. An *Economist* article from April 1997 observed that "There are Dilbert Dolls, Dilbert calendars and ties, a $20m contract for another five Dilbert books, plus plans for Dilbert-based television programmes and computer software. There is even talk of a Dilbertland theme park, complete with boss-shooting galleries. Mr. Adams only real worry is over-exposure—and, as he happily points out, 'you can't get to over-exposure without going through filthy rich first.''' The prediction of a television show came true in 1999, when the pilot for *Dilbert* was aired on the Fox network.

Given its run of success, the strip has inevitably prompted criticism from those who see it as yet another management tool. Its critics argue that it nothing less than a statement that champions the virtues of efficacy, good sense, and common sense by assailing foolish bureaucracy, reductive company policy, and faddish but ineffective management schemes. In his 1997 critique *The Trouble with Dilbert: How Corporate Culture Gets the Last Laugh,* author Norman Solomon contends that with *Dilbert,* ''corporate America is not selling us the rope to hang it with; corporate America is selling us the illusions to exculpate it with. To mistake pop-culture naughtiness for opposition to the corporate system is an exercise in projection—and delusion.'' Others have also found it easy to point to the strip's popularity and overexposure as signs that it represents not a paean to disenfranchised workers, but just another capitalist success story.

Within its series of strategies for avoiding work while still looking busy, *Dilbert*'s ultimate message is that the greater the technological and organizational sophistication in the workplace, the more opportunities exist to create the false image of actual productivity, as well as the documentation to validate it as production. Whether it be regarded as a subversive attack on the corporation or merely as a ''steam valve'' to give release to the corporate worker's frustrations, *Dilbert* continues to provide an important voice in the dialogue between the corporation and those at the lower levels who make it run.

—Warren Tormey

FURTHER READING:

Adams, Scott. *The Dilbert Principle: A Cubicle's-Eye View of Bosses, Meetings, Management Fads, and Other Workplace Afflictions.* New York, HarperBusiness, 1996.

———. *Seven Years of Highly Defective People: Scott Adams' Guided Tour of the Evolution of Dilbert.* Kansas City, Missouri, Andrews McMeel, 1997.

''The Anti-Management Guru: Scott Adams Has Made a Business of Bashing Business. Why Does the Hand He Bites Love to Feed Him?'' *The Economist.* April 5, 1997, 64.

Brown, Tom. ''What Does Dilbert Mean to HR?'' *HRFocus.* February, 1997, 12-13.

''The Dilbert Zone.'' http:\www.dilbertzone.comcomicsdilbert. June 1999.

Levy, Steven. ''Working in Dilbert's World.'' *Newsweek.* August 12, 1996, 52-57.

Solomon, Norman. *The Trouble with Dilbert: How Corporate Culture Gets the Last Laugh.* Monroe, Maine, Common Courage Press, 1997.

Dillard, Annie (1945—)

One of the best-known writers of the twentieth century and winner of the 1975 Pulitzer Prize for general nonfiction, Annie

Dillard developed a following unique among writers. Her readers embrace her mixture of literary, philosophical, theological, and scientific themes regardless of the genre in which they appear, from the essays of *Pilgrim at Tinker Creek, Holy the Firm,* and *Teaching a Stone to Talk,* to the poetry of *Tickets for a Prayer Wheel* and *Mornings Like This,* and from the autobiographical prose of *Encounters with Chinese Writers, An American Childhood,* and *The Writing Life* to the literary criticism of *Living by Fiction* and the fiction of *The Living.* In part, Dillard achieved her popularity because of her ongoing interest in spiritual experience, interdisciplinary knowledge, and aesthetic creation, all topics that mirror the concerns of a growing segment of the reading public.

Born Meta Ann Doak in Pittsburgh, Pennsylvania, on April 30, 1945, Dillard was the oldest of Frank and Pam Doak's three daughters. She spent her youth reading books, studying the natural world, and ''getting religion,'' experiences she recounts in detail in *An American Childhood.* After graduating from the Ellis School in Pittsburgh, she attended Hollins College in Roanoke, Virginia, where she received her B.A. (1967) and M.A. (1968) in English literature. While there, she met her first husband—her writing teacher, Richard Dillard—whom she married in 1965 and whose name she retained after the marriage ended.

Her first book, the slim volume of poetry titled *Tickets for a Prayer Wheel* (1974), was well received, but its publication was overshadowed by *Pilgrim at Tinker Creek* (1974), released only a few months later. Described by Dillard, quoting Thoreau, as "a meteorological journal of the mind," the book recounts the year (1972) she spent walking, reading, and journal-keeping while living on Tinker Creek in the Blue Ridge Mountains of Virginia. After advance chapters were published in *Harper's* and the *Atlantic,* the book was widely and enthusiastically reviewed, launching its 29-year-old author into instant literary celebrity.

Disturbed by the attention she was receiving, especially after winning the Pulitzer Prize, Dillard accepted a position as scholar-in-residence at Western Washington University in 1975 and moved to an isolated island in Puget Sound. There she wrote *Holy the Firm* (1977), a short but powerful prose narrative about the relationship between beauty and violence, a topic she had previously begun to explore in *Pilgrim.* Inspired by a plane crash in which a neighbor's child was badly burned, the book relates Dillard's process of coming to terms with the seeming contradiction between the existence of human suffering and the idea of a loving and all-powerful God.

In 1979, Dillard took up a new post as visiting professor of creative writing at Wesleyan University in Middletown, Connecticut, where she subsequently remained as writer-in-residence. Having divorced her first husband in 1975, Dillard married anthropologist Gary Clevidence in 1980. In 1982 she published two books, *Teaching a Stone to Talk: Expeditions and Encounters* and *Living by Fiction.* The first, a collection of essays, received excellent reviews; the second, a work of literary criticism, garnered more muted praise. She followed these two works in 1984 with *Encounters with Chinese Writers,* an account based in part on her visit to China in 1982 as a member of a cultural delegation.

In 1988, having published *An American Childhood* (1987), Dillard divorced Gary Clevidence and married Robert D. Richardson, Jr., whom she had met after reading his biography, *Henry Thoreau: A Life of the Mind* (1986). At this time she also worked on *The Writing Life* (1989), a description of the writing process and the creative energies it entails.

Dillard published her first novel, *The Living,* in 1992. Expanding a short story of the same name that she had written for *Harper's* in 1978, the story spans 42 years, from 1855 to 1897, and explores the frontier history of Whatcom, a town on Bellingham Bay in Washington State. Although the tale is related by an omniscient narrator, *The Living* nonetheless reflects Dillard's continuing concerns throughout her books with the arbitrariness of death, the insignificance of individuals in an indifferent universe, and the necessity of faith despite the knowledge of these uncomfortable truths.

The popularity of Dillard's writing during the late 1980s and 1990s can be judged by the frequency with which her work was reprinted during these decades. As well as excerpts included in multi-author collections, the four-volume *Annie Dillard Library* appeared in 1989, followed by *Three by Annie Dillard* (1990), and *The Annie Dillard Reader* (1994). During these years, she also served as the co-editor of two volumes of prose—*The Best American Essays* (1988), with Robert Atwan, and *Modern American Memoirs* (1995), with Cort Conley—and crafted *Mornings Like This: Found Poems* (1995), a collection of excerpts from other writers' prose, which she reformatted into verse.

Though a minor work, *Mornings Like This* could be said to encapsulate all of the qualities that have made Dillard's work consistently popular among readers: clever and playful, it displays her wide learning and eclectic tastes, her interest in the intersection of nature and science with history and art, and her desire to create beauty and unity out of the lost and neglected fragments of human experience.

—Daniel J. Philippon

FURTHER READING:

Dillard, Annie. *An American Childhood.* New York, Harper and Row, 1987.

———. *The Annie Dillard Reader.* New York, HarperCollins, 1994.

———. *Pilgrim at Tinker Creek.* New York: Harper's Magazine Press, 1974.

Johnson, Sandra Humble. *The Space Between: Literary Epiphany in the Work of Annie Dillard.* Kent, Ohio, Kent State University Press, 1992

Parrish, Nancy C. *Lee Smith, Annie Dillard, and the Hollins Group: A Genesis of Writers.* Baton Rouge, Louisiana State University Press, 1998.

Smith, Linda L. *Annie Dillard.* Boston, Twayne, 1991.

Diller, Phyllis (1917—)

Comedienne Phyllis Diller occupies a unique position in the annals of American stand-up comedy as the first woman to make her name in that previously all-male preserve. Remarkably, her show business career began in 1955 when she was 37 years old. In four decades, Diller progressed from being the only touring female comedienne within the United States to one of the world's most successful and best-loved comics, and the acknowledged forerunner to the many female comics who have followed her.

Diller was born Phyllis Ada Driver in Lima, Ohio. She studied classical piano at the Sherwood Conservatory of Music and received a music education degree from Bufferton College, but shelved her music career to marry Sherwood Diller and start a family. It wasn't until almost fifteen years and five children later, in California, when desperation rather than dormant ambition drove her to reconsider a stage career.

As a housewife and mother, Diller's life began to fall apart in 1953. Her husband had lost his job, bills were past due, and it began to look as if the family would lose their house. Gathering her courage, Diller found herself a job writing for a local radio station; two years later, turning courage into chutzpah, she quit that job to pursue a career as a stand-up comic. She auditioned at San Francisco's Purple Onion, and, though female comedians were extremely rare, she was engaged for a two-week stint. Her instant popularity with audiences turned the two weeks into an 87-week run. In 1959 she appeared before the nation on Jack Paar's *Tonight Show,* and in 1960 she performed at Carnegie Hall, not at the piano, but on it—vamping and slithering, and singing satirical songs interspersed with rapid-fire comic patter.

Calling her comedy "tragedy revisited," Diller based her act on her experiences as a housewife. Dressed in outrageous costumes, with wildly disheveled bleached-blonde hair and a raucous maniacal laugh, she lampooned housework, her neighbors, a fictitious husband she called "Fang," and, most of all, herself. She has always written her own material, and the jokes come fast and furious, sometimes as many as twelve punch lines a minute. She takes pride in the fact that her jokes are "clean," though she has been criticized by feminists for her self-deprecating put-downs of her own looks and abilities. Though "Fang" is a creation of her act and, she claims, not based on either of her two husbands, the family of her first husband once brought an unsuccessful lawsuit against her for denigrating him in her routine.

Diller continued to perform her comedy act in arenas as diverse as Las Vegas supper clubs and Madison Square Garden. She did, however, return to her classical music roots from 1971 to 1982, when she played as a soloist with over a hundred different symphony orchestras around the country, using the "virtuoso" name, Illya Dillya. She has also performed in stage shows and many films. Her one dramatic role was a surprising tour de force as the wife of Zero in the film version of Elmer Rice's expressionistic play, *The Adding Machine* (1969); while a high point of her stage career was on Broadway in 1970 where, for several months, she played Dolly Levi in *Hello Dolly!*

Though it was the comedic projection of herself as a frumpy grotesque that won Diller her fame and fortune, her image covered an intense insecurity about her looks. Determined to change the things she did not like about her face and body, she became notorious for her relationship with cosmetic surgery. Blatantly outspoken, she has always admitted to having herself "fixed," saying, "I used to be young and ugly. Now I'm old and gorgeous." Her very public admission of her many procedures—facelifts, nose job, tummy tuck, cheek implants, and straightened teeth among them—have caused plastic surgeons to hail her as a boon to their business. She has written humor books, and made many best-selling comedy albums. A gourmet chef, she turned entrepreneur to market her own chili and has sold her own lines of cosmetics and jewelry. There is, however, another side to Phyllis Diller. Like many celebrities, she has used her fame and wealth to support humanitarian causes and has been honored accordingly.

—Tina Gianoulis

FURTHER READING:

Borns, Betsy. "Phyllis Diller." *Interview*. Vol. 16, September, 1986, 25.

Smith, Ronald L. "Diller's Choice." *Writer's Digest*. Vol. 62, November, 1982, 20.

Dillinger, John (1903-1934)

During the Great Depression, many Americans, nearly helpless against forces they didn't understand, made heroes of outlaws who took what they wanted at gunpoint and stole from the institutions that they felt were oppressing them. Of all these lurid desperadoes, John Dillinger came to evoke this Gangster Era, and stirred mass emotion to a degree rarely seen in this country.

In truth, Dillinger was not the leader of a crime syndicate but was merely a brutal thief and a cold-blooded murderer. From September, 1933, until July, 1934, he and his violent gang terrorized the Midwest, killing 10 men, wounding seven others, robbing banks and police arsenals, and staging three memorable jail breaks, killing a sheriff

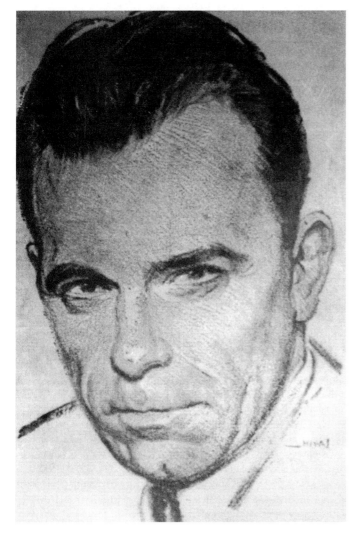

John Dillinger

during one and wounding two guards in another. He became something of a folk hero for successfully thwarting his pursuers for a time.

John Herbert Dillinger was born on June 22, 1903, in the middle-class Oak Hill section of Indianapolis. His father, a hardworking grocer, raised him in an atmosphere of disciplinary extremes, harsh and repressive on some occasions, but generous and permissive on others. John's mother died when he was three, and when his father remarried six years later, John resented his stepmother.

In adolescence, Dillinger was frequently in trouble. Finally, he quit school and got a job in a machine shop in Indianapolis. Although intelligent and a good worker, he soon became bored and often stayed out all night. His father, worried that the temptations of the city were corrupting his teenaged son, sold his property in Indianapolis and moved his family to a farm near Mooresville, Indiana. However, John reacted no better to rural life than he had to that in the city and soon began to run wild again.

After being arrested for auto theft, Dillinger was given the opportunity to enlist in the Navy. There he soon got into more trouble and deserted his ship when it docked in Boston. Returning to Mooresville, he married 16-year-old Beryl Hovius in 1924 and moved to Indianapolis. Dillinger, finding no work in the city, joined the town pool shark, Ed Singleton, in his quest for easy money. They tried to rob a Mooresville grocer, but were quickly apprehended. Singleton pleaded not guilty, stood trial, and was sentenced to two years. Dillinger, following his father's advice, confessed, was convicted of assault and battery with intent to rob and conspiracy to commit a felony, and received joint sentences of 2-to-14 years and 10-to-20 years in the Indiana State Prison. Stunned by the harsh sentence, Dillinger became a tortured, bitter man in prison.

Dillinger's notoriety grew when he made a successful prison break. On May 10, 1933, he was paroled from prison after serving 8-1/2 years of his sentence, and almost immediately Dillinger robbed a bank in Bluffton, Ohio. Dayton police arrested him on September 22, and he was lodged in the county jail in Lima, Ohio, to await trial. In frisking Dillinger, the Lima police found a document outlining a plan for a prison break, but the prisoner denied knowledge of any plan. Four days later, using the same plans, eight of Dillinger's friends escaped from the Indiana State Prison, using shotguns and rifles that had been smuggled into their cells and shooting two guards.

On October 12, three of the escaped prisoners and a parolee from the same prison, Harry Pierpont, Russell Clark, Charles Makley, and Harry Copeland, showed up at the Lima jail where Dillinger was incarcerated. They told the sheriff that they had come to return Dillinger to the Indiana State Prison for violation of his parole. When the sheriff asked to see their credentials, one of the men pulled a gun, shot the sheriff, and beat him into unconsciousness. Then, taking the keys to the jail, the bandits freed Dillinger, locked the sheriff's wife and a deputy in a cell, and, leaving the sheriff to die on the floor, made their getaway.

Dillinger and his gang pulled several bank robberies and also plundered the police arsenals at Auburn, Indiana, and Peru, Indiana, stealing several machine guns, rifles, and revolvers, a quantity of ammunition, and several bulletproof vests. On December 14, John Hamilton, a Dillinger gang member, shot and killed a police detective in Chicago. A month later, the Dillinger gang killed a police officer during the robbery of the First National Bank of East Chicago, Indiana. Then they made their way to Florida and, subsequently, to Tucson, Arizona. There on January 23, 1934, a fire broke out in the hotel where Clark and Makley were hiding under assumed names. Firemen recognized the men from their photographs, and local police arrested them, as well as Dillinger and Harry Pierpont. They also seized three Thompson submachine guns, two Winchester rifles mounted as machine guns, five bulletproof vests, and more than $25,000 in cash, part of it from the East Chicago robbery.

Dillinger was sequestered at the county jail in Crown Point, Indiana, to await trial for the murder of the East Chicago police officer. Authorities boasted that the jail was "escape proof," but on March 3, 1934, Dillinger cowed the guards with what he claimed later was a wooden gun he had whittled. He forced them to open the door to his cell, then grabbed two machine guns, locked up the guards and several trustees, and fled in the sheriff's car, hightailing it to nearby Illinois. The stunt earned headlines around the world and put Dillinger as a top priority on FBI director J. Edgar Hoover's hit list.

By stealing the sheriff's car and driving it across a state line, Dillinger had violated the National Motor Vehicle Theft Act, which made it a Federal offense to transport a stolen motor vehicle across a state line. A Federal complaint was sworn charging Dillinger with the theft and interstate transportation of the sheriff's car, which actively involved the FBI in the nationwide search for Dillinger.

Meanwhile, Pierpont, Makley, and Clark were returned to Ohio, convicted of the murder of the Lima sheriff, with Pierpont and Makley being sentenced to death, and Clark to life imprisonment. But in an escape attempt, Makley was killed and Pierpont was wounded. A month later, Pierpont had recovered sufficiently to be executed.

Hoover protégé Melvin Purvis was put in charge of capturing Dillinger, and in late April, "Nervous" Purvis received a tip-off that the bandit was holed up at Little Bohemia, a lakeside resort in Wisconsin. Purvis and his team blundered onto the resort grounds and blazed away indiscriminately at what proved to be innocent customers leaving a restaurant.

While an agent was telephoning about the debacle, the operator broke in to tell him there was trouble at another cottage about two miles away. FBI Special Agent W. Carter Baum, another FBI agent, and a constable went there and found a parked car which the constable recognized as belonging to a local resident. They pulled up and identified themselves. Inside the other car, "Baby Face" Nelson, a member of Dillinger's gang, was holding three local residents at gunpoint. He turned, leveled a revolver at the lawmen's car, and ordered them to step out. But without waiting for them to comply, Nelson opened fire. Baum was killed, and the constable and the other agent were severely wounded. Nelson jumped into the Ford they had been using and fled.

For the second time in three weeks, Dillinger had made the Feds look like fools. Hoover appointed a trusted Washington inspector, Sam Cowley, to take thirty handpicked men and form a special Dillinger squad in Chicago, though Purvis remained Agent in Charge. Dillinger was rated Public Enemy Number One and was featured on Wanted posters all over the United States. Eliminating him had become a public relations imperative, despite the lack of proof that he personally had ever killed anyone.

Late in the afternoon of Saturday, July 21, 1934, the madam of a brothel in Gary, Indiana, contacted one of the police officers with information. This woman called herself Anna Sage; however, her real name was Ana Cumpanas, and she had entered the United States from her native Rumania in 1914. Because of the nature of her profession, she was considered an undesirable alien by the Immigration and Naturalization Service, and deportation proceedings had started. Anna was willing to sell the FBI some information about Dillinger for a cash reward, plus the FBI's help in preventing her deportation.

At a meeting with Anna, Cowley and Purvis were cautious. They promised her the reward if her information led to Dillinger's capture, but said all they could do was call her cooperation to the attention of the Department of Labor, which at that time handled deportation matters. Satisfied, Anna told the agents that a girl friend of hers, Polly Hamilton, had visited her establishment with Dillinger. Anna had recognized Dillinger from a newspaper photograph.

Anna told the agents that she, Polly Hamilton, and Dillinger probably would be going to the movies the following evening at either the Biograph or the Marbro Theaters. She said that she would notify them when the theater was chosen. She also said that she would wear a red dress so that they could identify her.

On Sunday, July 22, Anna Sage called to confirm the plans, but she still did not know which theater they would attend. Therefore, agents and policemen were sent to both theaters. At 8:30 p.m., Anna Sage, John Dillinger, and Polly Hamilton strolled into the Biograph Theater to see Clark Gable in *Manhattan Melodrama*. Purvis phoned Cowley, who shifted the other men from the Marbro to the Biograph.

Cowley also phoned Hoover for instructions, who cautioned them to wait outside rather than risk a shooting match inside the crowded theater. Each man was instructed not to unnecessarily endanger himself and was told that if Dillinger offered any resistance, it would be each man for himself.

At 10:30 p.m., Dillinger, with his two female companions on either side, walked out of the theater and turned to his left. As they walked past the doorway in which Purvis was standing, Purvis lit a cigar as a signal for the other men to close in. Dillinger quickly realized what was happening and acted by instinct. He grabbed a pistol from his right trouser pocket as he ran toward the alley. Five shots were fired from the guns of three FBI agents. Three of the shots hit Dillinger and he fell face down on the pavement. At 10:50 p.m. on July 22, 1934, John Dillinger was pronounced dead in a little room in the Alexian Brothers Hospital.

The agents who fired at Dillinger were Charles B. Winstead, Clarence O. Hurt, and Herman E. Hollis. Each man was commended by J. Edgar Hoover for fearlessness and courageous action. None of them ever said who actually killed Dillinger. The events of that sultry July night in Chicago marked the beginning of the end of the Gangster Era. Eventually, 27 persons were convicted in Federal courts on charges of harboring and aiding and abetting John Dillinger and his cronies during their reign of terror. "Baby Face" Nelson was fatally wounded on November 27, 1934, in a gun battle with FBI agents in which Special Agents Cowley and Hollis also were killed.

Dillinger was buried in Crown Point Cemetery in Indianapolis, Indiana. It has long been rumored that his supposedly generously endowed member was kept in storage at the Smithsonian. In his 1970 book *The Dillinger Dossier,* Jay Robert Nash, citing flaws in the autopsy evidence and detailed testimony, even offers the thesis that Dillinger did not die in Chicago at all, but rather an underworld fall guy sent to take his place.

In 1945, former bootleggers turned filmmakers, the King Brothers, Frank and Maurice, produced a low budget, largely non-factual biography of Dillinger called *Dillinger,* which starred Lawrence Tierney and was scripted by famous front Philip Yordan. It surprised the film industry by turning a tidy profit. A third of the film consisted of stock footage lifted from other classic gangster films, from Howard Hawks' *Scarface* to Fritz Lang's *You Only Live Once.* The film's non-stop action set a pattern for future gangster epics from the 1960s onward, but was unique for its time.

Writer-director John Milius made his film debut with another biography of Dillinger called simply *Dillinger* (1973) and starring Warren Oates, though it too owes little to the actual facts of Dillinger's life. Dillinger's noted demise also inspired Lewis Teague's film *The Lady in Red* (1979; also known as *Guns, Sin and Bathtub Gin*), scripted by John Sayles with Robert Conrad playing the famed bank robber. Other treatments of Dillinger on film include *Young Dillinger* (1965), *Dillinger and Capone* (1995), and a documentary, *Appointment with Death: The Last Days of John Dillinger* (1971).

Dillinger's legacy continued to be enshrined in song and story. Hoover put a plaster cast of the gangster's face on display at FBI headquarters and for years Hoover's reception room contained a .38 automatic that was purported to be Dillinger's gun, even though the particular make of Colt did not leave the factory until December 1934, five months after the Dillinger shooting. Dillinger had been inflated from a simple bank robber into a legend, and remains one to this day.

—Dennis Fischer

FURTHER READING:

Cromie, Robert, and Joseph Pinkston. *Dillinger: A Short and Violent Life.* New York, McGraw-Hill, 1962.

Girardin, G. Russell. *Dillinger: The Untold Story.* Bloomington, Indiana University Press, 1994.

Nash, Jay Robert. *The Dillinger Dossier.* Highland Park, Illinois, December Press, 1983

Nash, Jay Robert, and Ron Offen. *Dillinger: Dead or Alive?* Henry Regnery, 1970.

Summers, Anthony. *Official and Confidential: The Secret Life of J. Edgar Hoover.* New York, G.P. Putnam's Sons, 1993.

Toland, John. *The Dillinger Days.* New York, Random House, 1963.

DiMaggio, Joe (1914-1999)

Joe DiMaggio is one of the few athletes who truly transcend their sport. His Hall of Fame career, leading the Yankees to nine World Series in 13 years, bridged two great eras of baseball—the post-war days of Babe Ruth and the post-integration days of Jackie Robinson. But he will always be best known as "Joltin' Joe," whose record-breaking 56 game hitting streak in 1941 captivated the country. DiMaggio's fame only grew after retirement, with his brief, but highly publicized marriage to movie star Marilyn Monroe, and frequent public appearances. The cool, classy ballplayer was immortalized in music and literature, as an enduring symbol of decency and order during a confusing era. In the words of the *New York Times* on the day of his retirement, DiMaggio had "something that no baseball averages can measure."

He was born Joseph Paul DiMaggio in San Francisco in 1914, one of nine children; his parents were part of a wave of Sicilian immigrants to emigrate to the United States at the turn of the twentieth century. The shy, unsociable DiMaggio was expected to get an education, but his only true interest was baseball, so he dropped out of school at age 16 . . . a decision he would later regret. The story of DiMaggio's discovery has become baseball legend; a member of the San Francisco Seals organization spotted the thin 17 year old peaking through a hole in the outfield fence, hoping to find his brother Vince, a Seals player. The Seals offered the talented sand-lot player an

opportunity to play, and he stayed for four years, becoming a hero in the Italian community in San Francisco. The year 1933 proved to be a harbinger of things to come; DiMaggio chalked up a minor league record with his 61 game hitting streak.

At the end of the 1935 season, the New York Yankees signed DiMaggio, hoping he would lead the team into the post-Ruth era. Despite the pressures of following Ruth, DiMaggio had a fabulous rookie season in 1936, hitting .323 with 29 home runs, 125 RBIs, and a league leading 15 triples. Writers across the country marvelled at his exceptional clutch hitting, skilled base running, and graceful defensive play. The shy, conservative DiMaggio, a sharp contrast from the wild gregarious Ruth, became an instant celebrity. He led the Yankees to four straight World Series titles from 1936 to 1939 and constantly appeared among the leaders in batting, home runs, and RBIs. He became the most popular player in baseball, although he angered fans in 1938, sitting out the beginning of the season due to a contract dispute, a theme prevalent throughout his career. Despite the new celebrity status, DiMaggio continued to live a very normal life, returning to San Francisco to live with his family during the winter. At the end of the 1939 season, DiMaggio married Dorothy Arnold, and two years later, they had a son, Joe Jr.

All of the fanfare could not prepare DiMaggio for the 1941 season. DiMaggio collected a hit in every game from May 15th to July 14th, an astonishing stretch of 56 games. Never before did an individual sports record receive so much public attention; radio stations across the country regularly interrupted broadcasts to give updates on "the streak." It seemed to come at a perfect time for a nation on the brink of war. Songwriter Alan Courtney wrote "Joe, Joe, DiMaggio, we want you on our side," as if his hitting streak could protect America from the turmoil overseas. DiMaggio himself joined the Air Force at the end of the 1942 season, while in the prime of his baseball career. Like many ballplayers, he saw no combat, spending the majority of his service time entertaining the troops in exhibition games. But the distance from his family was frustrating, and in 1944 Dorothy DiMaggio filed for divorce.

When DiMaggio returned to baseball in 1946, his finest years were clearly in the past. He did, however, add to his fame by constantly playing though injury. In 1949, he made a remarkable comeback from a leg injury and "took his place in that select circle of athletes, like Babe Ruth and Jack Dempsey, who are no only adored but beloved," according to *Life Magazine*. DiMaggio continued to show flashes of his former brilliance, but lost consistency and fought with Yankee manager Casey Stengal. At the end of the 1951 season, DiMaggio retired having amassed a .325 lifetime average and 361 career home runs in 13 seasons. That same year, he was immortalized in the Ernest Hemingway classic *The Old Man and the Sea,* the tale of an tired, aging fisherman, stuck at seas for days, and turning to "the Great DiMaggio" for solace.

Unlike many former players, DiMaggio had little trouble adjusting to life without baseball. He spent his first year of retirement working as a broadcaster for the Yankees, and went on to work in public relations with a variety of companies and charitable foundations. DiMaggio reentered the public consciousness in 1952 when he met a young Marilyn Monroe. The relationship between these two very different celebrities—the quiet, conservative former ballplayer and the beautiful but troubled movie star—was instant front page news. They married on January 14, 1954, but constantly fought over DiMaggio's traditional views of marriage and views of the Hollywood life, and divorced just nine months later. DiMaggio remained a close, dependable friend to Monroe, right until her death in 1962. He

Joe DiMaggio

made all the funeral arrangements, excluding the Hollywood crowd in the hope it would restore some dignity to her tragically short life.

In 1967, DiMaggio was introduced to a new generation of Americans by Paul Simon and Art Garfunkel's ''Mrs. Robinson,'' a sad lament to lost innocence from the film *The Graduate*. Simon and Garfunkel asked ''Where have you gone, Joe DiMaggio?,'' looking for a hero to guide them through troubled times. More than 25 years after the magical summer of 1941, Joltin' Joe became a symbol of fundamental good to a confused generation. His image continued to grow through the 1970s and 1980s, through his charitable work and public appearances. DiMaggio died on March 8, 1999, after a bout with cancer.

—Simon Donner

FURTHER READING:

Allen, Meary. *Where Have You Gone Joe DiMaggio: The Story of America's Last Hero.* New York, E. P. Dutton and Company, 1975.

Moore, Jack B. *Joe DiMaggio: A Bio-bibliography.* Westport, Connecticut, Greeenwood Press, 1986.

Schoor, Gene. *Joe DiMaggio: A Biography.* New York, Doubleday, 1980.

Seidel, Michael. *Streak: Joe DiMaggio and the Summer of '41.* New York, McGraw-Hill, 1988.

Whittingham, Richard, editor. *The DiMaggio Albums: Selections from Public and Private Collections Celebrating the Baseball Career of Joe DiMaggio.* New York, G.P. Putnam and Son, 1989.

Dime Novels

A popular form of literary entertainment in the late nineteenth and early twentieth centuries, dime novels were works of sensational fiction published in paper-covered booklets, issued at regular intervals, and priced at five to ten cents. Profitable mainstays of the

American publishing industry for many years, dime novels gradually waned as pulp magazine consumption increased, and by 1915, motion pictures had replaced dime novels as inexpensive forms of entertainment. Since that time, dime novels have become significant resources for examining the development of American popular culture in that they exemplify early printing methods, serve as rudimentary forms of genre fiction, and reflect aspects of the social history of the United States.

Published in four basic formats between 1860 and 1915, dime novels usually possessed pictorial covers with black-and-white or colored illustrations, ranged in size from four by six inches to eight by 12 inches, and varied in length from 32 to 250 pages. Initially produced for an adult market, early versions detailed life on the American frontier. Later publications, however, featured detective mysteries, adventure stories, and science fiction tales and were primarily read by juveniles.

The idea of producing cheap paper-covered novels in a continuous series was conceived by Irwin P. Beadle. In 1860, Beadle, along with his older brother, Erastus, and Robert Adams, established the publishing firm of Beadle & Adams in New York City and launched *Malaeska, the Indian Wife of the White Hunter* by Mrs. Ann S. Stephens, as the first entry in a series entitled *Beadle's Dime Novels.* Achieving success with the publication of this story and others, Beadle & Adams were for a time the principal publishers of dime novels until competitors George P. Munro, his brother Norman L. Munro, Frank Tousey, and Street & Smith began to publish dime novels as well.

Dime novel authors had strict guidelines to follow—stories had to be exciting, entertaining, and moral. Each of the major publishers employed regulars who wrote for a particular series. In some instances, authors published stories for several firms. Prolific contributors to *Beadle's Dime Novels* (1860-1874) included Mrs. Ann S. Stephens, Mrs. Metta Victor, Edward S. Ellis, Edward L. Wheeler, Philip S. Warne, and Ned Buntline. George P. Munro's *Old Sleuth Library* (1885-1905) highlighted the detective adventures of Old Sleuth, a pseudonym for Harlan Page Halsey, and other authors. His brother, Norman, published works by W. I. James in the *Old Cap Collier Library* (1883-1899), another dime-novel detective series. Frank Tousey's small group of authors wrote under so many pseudonyms that the amount of contributors to the *Wide Awake Library* (1878-1898) appeared greater than it actually was. Street & Smith, as the last major publishing firm to produce dime novels, featured authors Horatio Alger, Jr., Ned Buntline, Gilbert Patten, and Colonel Prentiss Ingraham, among others, in several series between 1883 and 1899. When dime-novel production ceased, most of the once prolific authors faded into obscurity.

Often, characters appearing in dime-novel series were better known than their authors were. Ned Buntline's famous western hero, Buffalo Bill, based on United States scout and performer William Frederick Cody, appeared in numerous publications by Beadle & Adams, Street & Smith, and Frank Tousey. Amateur detective Nick Carter proved to be so popular after his first appearance in *The Old Detective's Pupil* (1886), that Street & Smith featured his adventures in three different series between 1891 and 1915, *The Nick Carter Library, The New Nick Carter Weekly,* and *Nick Carter Stories.* Similarly, the exploits of Deadwood Dick, Kit Carson, Jr., Jesse James, Old Sleuth, Young Wild West, Frank Reade, Jr., Tiger Dick, and Frank Merriwell appeared in more than one dime novel.

Covering a wide variety of subjects, dime novels promoted traditional American values of patriotism, rugged individualism, and moral behavior. Many of the early dime novel stories focused on historical events such as the Revolutionary War, the War of 1812, and conflicts with Native Americans. Others were set in gold mining camps or towns within the expanding western frontier, and featured gunfighters, villains, and damsels in distress. Reflecting the urbanization of cities, the industrial revolution, and increased transportation modes, subsequent dime novel subjects included circuses, railroad workers, firefighters, sports, science fiction, fantasy, sea or polar explorations, and mysteries with detectives from every walk of life. Moving beyond the borders of America, a few detail adventures in distant places.

In the 1990s, few original dime novels exist outside of libraries and personal collections. Moreover, owing largely to their sheer numbers and past popular appeal, dime novels are seldom considered by literary scholars to be good examples of American literature. Their value as historical artifacts, however, is considerable.

—Marlena E. Bremseth

FURTHER READING:

Denning, Michael. *Mechanic Accents: Dime Novels and Working Class Culture in America.* London, Verso, 1987.

Johannsen, Albert, *The House of Beadle & Adams and Its Nickel and Dime Novels: The Story of a Vanished Literature.* Vol. 1. Norman, University of Oklahoma Press, 1950.

Sullivan, Larry E., and Lydia C. Schurman. *Pioneers, Passionate Ladies, and Private Eyes: Dime Novels, Series Books, and Paperbacks.* New York, The Haworth Press, Inc., 1996.

Dime Stores/Woolworth's

Dime Stores, or five-and-dimes, maintained a central place in American life from before 1900 until after World War II. Woolworth's was the original and dominant dime-store chain. In the first half of the twentieth century, the main street of virtually every town and city in the United States featured a Woolworth's; it was the first place many people went to look for basic merchandise of all sorts. Woolworth's offered its customers a wide assortment of very affordable household items and the working class appreciated finding basic things at basic prices. The dime store's lunch counter was a common meeting place, its toys made it a favorite destination of children, and its endless locations meant it served as the neighborhood store for many. Although part of Woolworth's appeal was in its ubiquitous presence, local stores were also encouraged to remain local institutions. They varied widely from region to region and from city to town. Each filled a particular role and developed its own character.

In 1919, when F. W. Woolworth died, his chain of five-and-dimes consisted of 1,081 stores in the United States and Canada. At that time, department stores were all regional; Woolworth's was one of a very few nationwide chains. Department stores were also notably more lavish and expensive than dime stores. Millions of working people depended on Woolworth's and other five-and-dimes for many basic needs. As the nation's largest food-service retailer by the 1940s, Woolworth's maintained nearly a thousand inexpensive lunch counters across the United States before the first McDonald's opened.

Before Woolworth, shopping meant bartering. Merchandise was kept behind counters or on inaccessible shelves and customers had to ask clerks to show them an item. Fixed pricing had begun appearing in

An F. W. Woolworth Co. five and dime store.

a few places, notably Michigan, in the 1870s, but was sporadic and unorganized. Other merchants had set up five-cent counters from time to time for limited runs, but no one had worked hard to make it consistently profitable, and certainly no one had devoted an entire variety store to the same fixed price. Frank Woolworth was not a natural salesman or bargainer, but he held a strong Yankee work ethic and recognized and exploited a good idea. He assiduously sharpened his bargaining skills until he became known for them. They helped him negotiate endless deals with wholesalers which allowed Woolworth's to make a profit on items under 10¢.

He had opened his first "5¢ store" in Utica, New York, on February 22, 1879, with $350 loaned him by his former employer. That first store barely turned a profit, but it spawned twenty more over the next ten years, twelve of which were partnerships and five of which failed within a few months. His fourth store, opened in Scranton, Pennsylvania, on November 6, 1880, was the first "5-&-10¢ store." Frank Woolworth never stopped opening or buying new stores: he ran twelve in 1890, fifty-four in 1900, two hundred thirty-eight in 1910, and three hundred nineteen by the December 1911 merger that created F. W. Woolworth & Co. Combined with his brother Charles's fifteen stores, his cousin Seymour Knox's ninety-eight, Fred Kirby's ninety-six, Earle Charlton's thirty-five, and William Moore's two, Woolworth became the first retail company to operate stores in all forty-eight states. As he planned for the merger that created F. W. Woolworth & Co., Frank Woolworth also oversaw the construction of the Woolworth Building in Manhattan. The tallest building in the world at the time of its completion in 1913, Woolworth insisted that it surpass the Metropolitan Life Building, which company had refused him a policy when he was laying the foundation for his empire.

Frank Woolworth said that he aimed "to open a store in every civilized town throughout the world." He expanded into England in 1909, then Germany, Canada, South Africa, and elsewhere. Woolworth's critics complained that Woolworth's was creating a monopoly and Congressman John J. Cochran championed legislation that would have taxed Woolworth's into collapse. Many people were dismayed by "the chain store menace" of Woolworth's in the 1930s, just as many recoiled when Wal-Mart built stores in their communities in the 1980s and 1990s. In 1935 Representative Cochran led a congressional investigation into the "super-lobby" of chain store interests. Woolworth's and drug-store chain A&P were the primary targets. Fortunately for the chains, a 1939 bill that would have broken them up died in committee. Woolworth's did indeed try to drive out or buy out much of its competition. The company knew that many of the towns and districts where they opened could not support more than one dime store.

Woolworth's remained literally a dime store for over fifty years, until 1932, when the top price was raised to 20¢. In 1935 the limited price policy ended as the company expanded into higher-priced merchandise such as furniture and appliances. Despite fixed, low prices, Woolworth paid better wages than most of his competitors. He introduced minimum wages for all positions, paid vacations, and Christmas bonuses. These things were far from standard early in the twentieth century. Woolworth's was also a major employer of women, although by the 1950s many were protesting their lack of promotion in the company.

Woolworth's lunch counters will be long remembered as the site of civil-rights sit-ins in 1960. The first one began at the Woolworth's in Greenville, North Carolina, on February 1, 1960. Soon protesters throughout the South were occupying lunch counters and calling for a nationwide boycott against Woolworth's. The company's earnings dropped 8.9 percent in March. Many cities integrated their restaurants after a few weeks, but Greenville endured sit-ins and demonstrations until July 25.

Woolworth's perfectly filled a key place in American culture in the first half of the twentieth century, but as the culture changed after World War II, Woolworth's importance waned. As other chains emulated Woolworth's low-cost approach, it became little more than another department store. The 2,850 Woolworth's stores of the early 1960s sold enormous quantities of merchandise, but held onto a very thin profit margin.

In the postwar era, Woolworth's seemed stale and staid; its workforce aged with its clientele as it failed to change with the times. A succession of company-trained presidents found it impossible to halt the gradual decline. The last 400 Woolworth's in North America were closed in 1997 and 1998. Woolworth's survives in the United States as Venator, a corporation consisting primarily of Footlocker athletic shoe stores. In Great Britain and Australia Woolworth's remains a major variety and, in Australia, grocery chain.

Yet the legacy of the dime store thrives in the myriad discount department stores throughout the world, in the many "dollar stores" now occupying the neighborhood malls that have taken the place of downtown shopping districts, and in the merchandise purchasing, display, and pricing policies that have become standards of modern commerce.

—Paul Gaffney

FURTHER READING:

Brough, James. *The Woolworths*. New York, McGraw-Hill, 1982.

Raucher, Alan R. "Dime Store Chains: The Making of Organization Men, 1880-1940." *Business History Review*. 1991, volume 65:1.

Winkler, John K. *Five and Ten*. New York, Robert McBride & Co, 1940.

Wolff, Miles. *Lunch at the 5 & 10*. Revised and expanded edition. Chicago, Ivan R. Dee, 1990.

Diners

Restaurants commonly referred to as "diners" have held a special place in American popular culture since the 1930s. Once sleek, futuristic icons of post-war optimism, they now capture our attention as objects of nostalgia. As the precursor to fast-food restaurants, diners were one of the unique building types spawned by the burgeoning automobile society. Their very appearance—with streamlined, movement-implying shapes and bright neon lights—captured the spirit of the new mobile culture.

The diner evolved from horse-drawn night lunch wagons of the late nineteenth century. These convenient wagons served walk-up customers in downtown areas after restaurants had closed for the evening. The next generation of wagons featured indoor seating; by the turn of the century, many lunch wagons had become stationary. The early diners' forte was the quick, inexpensive meal—atmosphere was not important. The clientele consisted of night workers and late revelers. Sandwiches, hamburgers, pies, hot dogs, and breakfast fare were standard items. By the 1890s, Thomas H. Buckley was mass-producing lunch wagons and had placed them in at least 275 cities across the country. Early diners were also converted from railroad or trolley cars.

The diner that has become the object of popular affection dates to the 1930s and 1940s. The machine-influenced, Art Deco or Moderne design style that emphasized smooth curves, simplicity, and shiny surfaces was inherent in much product design of the time, but in the diner it was integrated into a total environment. Diners from the Golden Age were long and low in shape, with streamlined effects and clean surfaces, evoking a feeling of both futurism and movement. Formica, stainless steel, and Naugahyde were the most popular interior materials. Diners contained booths, but the highlight of the interior was a long, shiny counter. Meals were simple and inexpensive. The imagery of speed and progress fit perfectly with the rapidly developing mobile society, in which the automobile was reshaping the landscape and creating opportunities for new building.

In the 1950s, as more families began to eat outside the home, and the diner became more "respectable," diners expanded in size and menu. The 1960s marked a turning point for the diner, as the fast-food restaurant industry proliferated. Fast-food represented standardization, as opposed to the uniqueness of diners. You knew beforehand what was on the McDonald's menu, while every diner had a specialty and a different atmosphere. In response, many diners tried to emphasize their individuality by expanding their menus and adopting more conservative imagery. Apart from their smaller size and the word "diner," many of these diners became difficult to distinguish from standard restaurants. Booth and table service came to predominate over the traditional counter. Colonial and Mediterranean architectural styles often replaced the Art Deco model familiar from past decades.

Beginning in the 1970s, diners began to make a comeback as nostalgic reminders of a more innocent time. They also became legitimate subjects of study by architectural and popular culture scholars. In 1978 the Cooper-Hewitt branch of the Smithsonian held an exhibit on architectural packaging which looked at four popular American building types: fast-food restaurants, diners, gasoline stations, and museum-village restorations. An article by Richard Oliver and Nancy Ferguson, the curators of the exhibit, appeared in *Architectural Record* for February 1978 and also as a reprint catalog. Also, Barry Levinson's 1982 movie *Diner* helped introduce the phenomenon to a new audience. In the late 1990s, diners were still being manufactured and patronized. Many older models have been restored. Diners are the subject of books and museum exhibitions. The Henry Ford Museum in Dearborn, Michigan, now includes a 1946 diner as part of its collection of twentieth-century cultural artifacts, in an exhibition entitled, "The Automobile in American Life." Diners have thus been recognized as unique cultural inventions which, like

An example of the diner, 1952.

the gas station and fast-food restaurant, were byproducts of the automobile revolution of the twentieth century.

—Dale Allen Gyure

FURTHER READING:

Baeder, John. *Diners.* New York, Harry N. Abrams, 1978.

Gutman, Richard J. S. *American Diner Then and Now.* New York, HarperCollins, 1993.

Gutman, Richard J. S., and Elliott Kaufman. *American Diner.* New York, Harper and Row, 1979.

Oliver, Richard, and Nancy Ferguson. "Place, Product, Packaging." *Architectural Record.* Vol. 163, February 1978, 116-20.

Yorke, Douglas, Jr. "Stopping at Stars: The Architecture of the American Diner." *Architectural Association Quarterly.* Vol. 8, No. 2, 1976, 45-54.

Dionne Quintuplets (1934—)

Yvonne, Annette, Cécile, Émilie, and Marie Dionne are the first monozygotic—all from one fertilized ovum—quintuplets known to have survived to adulthood. They were nearly sextuplets, but the sixth fetus miscarried in the third month of pregnancy. Born to Oliva and Elzire Dionne, French-Canadian peasants, in their seven-room farmhouse near Callander, Ontario, the premature babies weighed a total of 13 pounds, 6 ounces. They owe their survival to the quick and intelligent care of the local general practitioner, Dr. Allan Roy Dafoe, who collected virtually every incubator in the province and kept the tiny girls alive through his excellent scientific care. Nevertheless, the significance of the Dionne Quintuplets rests not in their place in medical history, but as examples of exploitation and publicity. Their birth and survival created a worldwide sensation, and their father collected a fortune by serving as their "manager," selling the right to photograph them, to have them appear in motion pictures, and to secure their "endorsement" of various products. They were made wards of the Canadian government in 1935, and for their first ten years were raised in a special nursery built for them out of public funds. After a protracted lawsuit, their parents recovered custody in 1944.

The birth of multiple children in the United States never garnered as much interest as that of the Dionne quintuplets. However, the subsequent birth of the Thompson sextuplets and the McCaughey septuplets in 1997 brought to light racial tensions in the United States. Unlike the worldwide attention given to the Dionne family, the birth of the first African-American sextuplets on May 8, 1997 came with little fanfare. Living in a two-bedroom apartment, the Thompson family struggled to make ends meet with the money Linden Thompson could make from his two jobs. Only after the much-publicized birth of the white McCaughey septuplets, seven months later that year, did corporations extend the same free products and aid to the Thompson sextuplets as well. Although not the riches given to the Dionne family, the lifetime of free diapers, college scholarships, and use of a mini-van relieved some of the stresses on the newly enlarged families.

—Gerald Carpenter

FURTHER READING:

Barker, Lillian. *The Dionne Legend: Quintuplets in Captivity.* Garden City, New York, Doubleday, 1951.

Berton, Pierre. *The Dionne Years: A Thirties Melodrama.* Toronto, McClelland and Stewart, 1977.

Blatz, W. E., et al. *Collected Studies on the Dionne Quintuplets.* Toronto, University of Toronto Press, 1937.

Braudy, Leo. *The Frenzy of Renown: Fame and Its History.* New York, Random House, 1986.

Nihmey, John, and Stuart Foxman. *Time of Their Lives: The Dionne Tragedy, a True-Life Fairy Tale.* Ottawa, Canada, NIVA, 1986.

Roberts, Penni. ''Thompson Sextuplets Offered Four-Year Scholarships.'' *Philadelphia Tribune,* December 26, 1997.

The Dirty Dozen

Directed by Robert Aldrich, *The Dirty Dozen* tells the story of Major Reisman (Lee Marvin) and the twelve hardened convicts he selects to join him on a suicide mission behind German lines in 1944. *The Dirty Dozen* remains an interesting and popular film, as it is meticulously crafted, deftly edited, and features several future stars at the beginning of their careers (including Donald Sutherland, Charles Bronson, and Telly Savalas). Although released in 1967 at the height of the anti-Vietnam war movement, *The Dirty Dozen* was nevertheless a success, becoming one of the biggest box-office hits in MGM's history. War protesters readily accepted the film's depiction of officers as indiscriminate killers, while more militaristic moviegoers approved of the film's brutal combat scenes.

—Robert C. Sickels

FURTHER READING:

Basinger, Jeanine. *The World War II Combat Film: Anatomy of a Genre.* New York, Columbia University Press, 1986.

Manuell, Roger. *Films and the Second World War.* New Jersey, A.S. Barnes and Co., 1974.

Disability

The presence of disability in popular culture has taken many forms; indeed, people with disabilities (PWDs) have appeared frequently across the pop-culture spectrum: movies, television, print media, dance, theater, music, and sports. Disability representations have never been in short supply, though many produced by the mainstream cultural industries remain questionable at best, hurtful and divisive at worst.

Images of disability have perhaps found their most frequent expression in movies, with the vast majority created from the perspective of able-bodied filmmakers and intended primarily for able-bodied audiences. The earliest silent movies, each only a few minutes long, tended to portray PWDs as comic figures given to pursuing others or being pursued themselves, as in *The Legless Runner* (1907), *The Invalid's Adventure* (1907), and *Don't Pull My Leg* (1908). As the medium matured, moviemakers borrowed heavily from such nineteenth-century literary fare as *Moby Dick, A Christmas Carol, Notre Dame de Paris (The Hunchback of Notre Dame), Treasure Island,* and *The Two Orphans,* to create more intricate narratives that

portrayed disabled people either as innocent victims or incarnations of evil. The films in this tradition included *Orphans of the Storm* (1921), *The Hunchback of Notre Dame* (1923, but many versions made since), *The Sea Beast* (1926), and numerous adaptations of *A Christmas Carol.* The 1930s saw a continuing interest in such stereotypical extremes—most notably in *Moby Dick* (1930), Charlie Chaplin's *City Lights* (1931), Todd Browning's famous gallery of grotesques, *Freaks* (1932), and a 1939 remake of *Hunchback.* Such images began fading during the World War II era in favor of relatively realistic and sensitive portraits of disabled veterans. *Pride of the Marines* (1945) and *Bright Victory* (1951) both dealt with blinded ex-servicemen; real-life veteran Harold Russell, whose service legacy was to lose his hands (replaced by metal hooks), played himself in *The Best Years of Our Lives* (1946), and Fred Zinnemann's *The Men* (1951), Marlon Brando's first film, dealt with paraplegics. These images, in turn, began giving way to famously larger-than-life civilians who ''triumphed'' over their disabilities: opera singer Marjorie Lawrence and Franklin D. Roosevelt, both polio victims, in *Interrupted Melody* (1955) and *Sunrise at Campobello* (1960) respectively, Helen Keller, deaf, dumb, and blind, in *The Miracle Worker* (1962). Stanley Kubrick's *Dr. Strangelove* (1964), however, mocked these latter types with its title character, and signaled their temporary demise.

With alarming regularity, Hollywood has continued churning out regressive disability movies such as *Hook* (1991), *The Fugitive* (1993), *Speed* (1994), and *Forrest Gump* (1994), reflecting the age-old practice of linking evil or innocence with disability, but an increasing number of films since the 1960s have offered positive images. Hollywood has often reserved the most resonant and poignant portrayals for disabled Vietnam veterans, as in *Coming Home* (1978), *Cutter's Way* (1981), and *Born on the Fourth of July* (1989). Other memorable, if not entirely progressive, films since the 1960s include *The Other Side of the Mountain* (1975), *The Elephant Man* (1980), *Children of a Lesser God* (1986), *Rain Man* (1988), and *Scent of a Woman* (1992), which range over a variety of afflictions and film styles.

Despite its relatively short history, the television industry has also demonstrated an interest in portraying the disabled experience, with a number of series presenting disabled characters in continuing roles. *Gunsmoke*'s mobility-impaired sidekick Chester Goode, played by Dennis Weaver for nine seasons (1955-1964) during the program's 20-year run, competes with Raymond Burr's wheelchair-dependent police detective on *Ironside* (1967-1975), as television's most popular disabled character, while James Franciscus played a blind insurance investigator on *Longstreet* (1971-1972). Taking a different approach, nuclear-powered prostheses and implants turned disabled figures Steve Austin (Lee Majors) and Jaime Sommers (Lindsay Wagner) into the title characters of *The Six Million Dollar Man* (1974-1978) and *The Bionic Woman* (1976-1978), respectively. Later, LeVar Burton played the blind chief engineer Lt. Geordi LaForge in *Star Trek: The Next Generation* (1987-1994) and a string of follow-up movies.

Most of these films and TV programs featured able-bodied actors playing the disabled characters, a situation that some disability activists have likened to the now discontinued practice of white actors masquerading in blackface as African Americans or Shakespeare's Othello. Actors with actual disabilities have been employed only sporadically in the film and television industries, but their influence continues to rise. Some old-line actors, such as Sarah Bernhardt, Harold Lloyd, Herbert Marshall, and Lionel Barrymore, tended to mask their disabilities before the cameras (Barrymore's performance in the 1946 film *It's a Wonderful Life* is a notable exception), but for more recent actors, their disabilities became part of the characters they played. Harold Russell, whose hands were blown off in a demolition exercise, won two Oscars for his work in *The Best Years of Our Lives,* and Marlee Matlin, a hearing-impaired performer, won an Oscar for her role in *Children of a Lesser God* (1986) and went on to play bank-robber-turned-mayor Laurie Bey in the final years of the acclaimed TV series *Picket Fences.* Chris Burke, a developmentally disabled actor, co-starred as Corky Thatcher on the popular drama *Life Goes On* during its 1989-1993 run, and wheelchair-user Nancy Becker Kennedy played a sharp-tongued secretary on *The Louie Show* in 1996. Mitch Longley, a wheelchair-using heartthrob who once modeled shirts for Ralph Lauren, appeared as Byron Pierce on the soap opera *Another World* during the 1991/92 season and, beginning in 1997, played the double role of Dr. Matt Harmon and Eric Mancusi on the long-running soap opera, *General Hospital,* and its spin-off, *Port Charles.*

Longley is only one of several PWDs who have also made inroads into the modeling field. One of the most famous, wheelchair-user Ellen Stohl, posed nude for the July 1987 issue of *Playboy,* making her that magazine's first disabled centerfold, while runway models now have PWDs among their ranks, including Kitty Lunn and Kim Barreda. A number of American corporations, such as McDonald's and K-Mart, have begun using disabled performers in their commercials. A prime example is The Home Depot, which has featured disabled employees Henry Gibson and Dan Brady in its ads.

Since the latter decades of the twentieth century, PWDs have taken a more direct role in the creation of a pop-culture presence. Ron Kovic, a disabled Vietnam veteran who wrote the searing autobiography, *Born on the Fourth of July,* in 1976, also co-wrote the screenplay, in which he was played by Tom Cruise, for the like-titled movie in 1989. Three years later, Neil Jimenez wrote and co-directed *The Waterdance,* a film modeled largely on his own experiences as a newly disabled person. Billy Golfus, who suffered brain damage during a 1984 vehicular accident, eventually secured funding through the Independent Television Service to produce *When Billy Broke His Head . . . and Other Tales of Wonder* in 1995. This documentary film told not only his story but also the "tales" of other PWDs and their struggles for civil rights. Disabled journalist and poet Mark O'Brien collaborated with Jessica Yu on *Breathing Lessons: The Life and Work of Mark O'Brien* (1996), an Oscar-winning film for best short-subject documentary and a recipient of a special National Educational Media Network award. In 1992, Greg Smith founded *On a Roll,* a nationally syndicated radio talk show dedicated to disability issues, while John Hockenberry, a two-time Peabody Award-winning TV network correspondent, shared his perspectives about life as a disabled person in a 1995 memoir, *Moving Violations,* and in his one-man show, *Spokesman,* produced off-Broadway in 1996. Christopher Reeve, whose spinal cord was severed in a 1995 horseback-riding accident, directed a one-hour AIDS drama in 1997 titled *In the Gloaming,* and served as an executive producer for the 1998 TV remake of Hitchcock's *Rear Window,* in which he played the James Stewart role of a wheelchair-bound man who witnesses a murder across the courtyard of his apartment building.

Many other PWDs have contributed to the performing arts. Among the more notable are three singers who happen to be blind: Ray Charles and Stevie Wonder, who have enjoyed long careers as popular musicians; and Andrea Bocelli, who crossed over from opera to become something of a pop sensation. The National Theater of the Deaf, a mixed troupe of hearing and deaf actors founded in 1965, has performed across the country and on national TV. Mary Verdi-Fletcher, a wheelchair-user born with spina bifida, founded the Cleveland Ballet Dancing Wheels, a group of dancers with differing degrees of mobility that has given hundreds of performances on several continents.

PWDs have had their greatest successes in the literary field, with memoirs and poetry volumes. Nancy Mairs' *Waist-High in the World* (1996) and Kenny Fries' anthology *Staring Back* (1997) are prominent among the countless examples. The influence of the disability press has also grown appreciably, with *New Mobility, The Ragged Edge* (formerly *The Disability Rag*), and *Mouth* playing crucial roles.

In the world of sports, the Paralympic Games typically attracts thousands of amateur athletes and delegates from more than a hundred countries and are by far the most famous of competitions for PWDs. Among professional athletes, Monty Stratton pitched professional baseball for a few seasons in the 1940s despite having lost a leg in a 1938 hunting accident. He went on to supervise *The Stratton Story* (1949), a movie based on his life, which starred James Stewart. Despite a congenitally deformed hand, Jim Abbott enjoyed several seasons as a Major League pitcher and threw a no-hitter for the New York Yankees in 1993. In the National Football League, New Orleans Saints place kicker Tom Dempsey, born without a right hand and only half a right foot, used that foot to kick a 63-yard field goal against the Detroit Lions in 1970, a NFL record that stood unmatched for 28 years. Casey Martin, a professional golfer with a rare and painful birth defect in his right leg, made headlines in early 1998 by suing the PGA Tour and winning the right to ride in a cart while participating in the pro golf tour.

Of all pop-culture arenas, comic-strip art is decidedly the most problematic as regards the treatment of disability. Berke Breathed's syndicated cartoon strip *Bloom County* and its wheelchair-using Vietnam vet, Cutter John, are among the high points, but the field has generally been dominated by cartoonists such as Charles Addams and Gahan Wilson, long known for their "sick-humor" takes on such topics as blindness, deformity, and dismemberment. Their work arguably paved the way for John Callahan's repellent *Hustler* cartoon images and Gary Larson's skewed view of disabling conditions in his near-legendary strip, *The Far Side.*

Despite the excesses of comic-strip art and certain other media, however, the pop-culture representation of disability is constantly advancing. As more and more PWDs get involved in the creation of popular culture, the images can only improve.

—Martin F. Norden

FURTHER READING:

Cumberbatch, Guy, and Ralph Negrine. *Images of Disability on Television.* New York, Routledge, 1992.

Fries, Kenny, editor. *Staring Back: The Disability Experience from the Inside Out.* New York, Plume, 1997.

Gartner, Alan, and Tom Joe, editors. *Images of the Disabled, Disabling Images.* New York, Praeger, 1987.

Hockenberry, John. *Moving Violations: War Zones, Wheelchairs, and Declarations of Independence.* New York, Hyperion, 1995.

Klobas, Lauri E. *Disability Drama in Television and Film.* Jefferson, McFarland, 1988.

Mairs, Nancy. *Waist-High in the World: A Life Among the Nondisabled.* Boston, Beacon Press, 1996.

Norden, Martin F. *The Cinema of Isolation: A History of Physical Disability in the Movies.* New Brunswick, Rutgers University Press, 1994.

Disaster Movies

In disaster movies, natural disasters, accidents, and terrorist actions provide the setting for daring escapes and incredible heroism. The films rely heavily on special effects to recreate on screen the violent consequences of earthquakes, plane crashes, and meteorite storms; the category also includes monster-disaster movies in which an enraged, oversized creature destroys buildings and other large objects. It is an important part of disaster movies that in them heroic acts are performed by unlikely heroes—by people with psychological wounds, with limited experience of the things they are asked to do, and in situations where the odds against success seem impossibly high. Because these films are about averting and surviving disaster, it may be significant that disaster movies began to be produced in large numbers in the years after the horrors of World War II. If the twentieth century has seen great advances in technology, disaster movies reflect a fear that technology alone will not save us. Although their plots are often unrealistic and the acting and special effects unconvincing, they offer the message that, through self-belief and the right moral choices, people just like us have the ability to save themselves.

Disasters featured in disaster movies can be divided into three main types: natural disasters, disasters caused by technology failing or being accidentally damaged, and disasters caused by terrorism or by the recklessness of an individual or agency. The most successful disaster movies are usually the simplest, but popular disaster-based films can contain elements of one, two, or even all of these scenarios. The actual type of disaster involved is only one of many reasons for a particular film's popularity. Among other things, audiences want to know how the characters will escape with their lives, they watch for the special effects, and also for sentimental reasons; popular disaster movies almost always include a love affair developing alongside the disaster plot. When the type of disaster is significant, it is often because it reflects current or local concerns. In the 1990s, for example, perhaps cashing in on pre-millennium fears, a rash of films such as *Independence Day* (1996) and *Deep Impact* (1998) appeared, with plot lines based around threats to life on earth posed by attacks from extraterrestrials or from asteroids. Similarly, in the 1980s films such as *Testament* (1983) and *The Day After* (1983) appeared in response to the threat posed by the nuclear arms race. Because most disaster movies are made in Hollywood and Japan, it is probably no

Passengers struggle for survival during a scene from the disaster film *The Poseidon Adventure*.

coincidence that a large number of them feature earthquakes, tidal waves, and volcanic eruptions.

The history of disaster movies is a relatively short one. Although disasters have featured in movies from the beginning of the twentieth century, films in which the disaster is the reason for making and watching the film did not become common until the 1950s when alien invasion and monster movies were popular. Before then, disasters of various kinds had appeared in adventure films and films about war, but true disaster movies were rare. One precursor to modern monster-disaster movies such as *Jurassic Park* (1993) is Cooper and Schoedsack's *King Kong* (1933), but the film is really an exotic adventure thriller with only a small element of disaster movie action. Such extravagant special effects as were needed to make the famous scene on the Empire State Building are remarkable for their time, but it was not until the 1950s that such effects could be achieved with much regularity.

In the 1950s, advances were made in film technology that allowed filmmakers to make better use of special effects techniques pioneered in the 1930s. Many of the resulting films were a combination of science fiction and horror, but disaster was often at their heart, as titles such as *When Worlds Collide* (1951) and *War of the Worlds* (1954) suggest. It has been suggested that the new threat of nuclear destruction meant that filmmakers and audiences became concerned with global, rather than local, conflicts and many of the monster-based disaster movies of the 1950s involve mutant creatures terrorizing and destroying cities. New film techniques such as "3-D," made possible by improvements in color film, made monster movies still more thrilling as giant creatures appeared to step off the screen and into the audience. Perhaps because of the Japan's own experience of nuclear destruction the Japanese film industry has been prolific in the field of atomic monsters, its most famous being Inoshiro Honda's *Godzilla, King of Monsters* (1954).

In the 1960s, science fiction disaster movies and nuclear accident films remained popular in Japan, where Honda's *Godzilla* and other monster series continued until late in the decade. Although extra footage of well-known American actors was added to Honda's films for American distribution, disaster movies in the United States generally did less well in this period. American disaster movies in the 1950s had mostly upheld Hollywood's conservative values and, in the 1960s, the genre perhaps seemed less suitable for exploring the new moral climate than, for example, the westerns of Sam Peckinpah or the thoughtful science fiction of Stanley Kubrick's *2001: A Space Odyssey*. It was not until 1970, with the release of *Airport*, that disaster movies became popular again.

The Golden Age for American disaster movies was the 1970s. As Hollywood re-embraced the idea of making popular, big budget features, the disaster movie became an important format for demonstrating spectacular special effects and for drawing in audiences to watch destruction on a large scale. Exactly what appeals to audiences in watching planes crash, ships sink, trains collide, and tall buildings burn will probably never be known for sure, but films like *The Poseidon Adventure* (1972), *The Towering Inferno* (1974), and the *Airport* series gave Hollywood some of its most lucrative successes. Unlike the futuristic films of the 1950s, disaster movies in the 1970s often dealt with familiar events and situations, ones that already caused anxiety for many people. For example, the number of miles Americans travelled by air doubled between 1965 and 1970, and air travel is one of the most common themes for disaster movies of the 1970s. Similarly, at a time when many new highrise blocks were being built and planned, Paul Newman and Steve McQueen braved flames and smoke to rescue people from a party on the top floor of "the tallest building in the world" in John Guillermin's *The Towering Inferno*.

While the special effects in films like *The Towering Inferno* are impressive for their time, as with many disaster movies the biggest challenge its makers faced was to prevent the record-breaking skyscraper—the "Tower of Glass"—from looking like a model. In the 1990s the situation has been helped by improvements in digital technology and, in particular since the late 1980s, the ability to mix live action with what are known as Computer Generated Images (CGI). CGI has become widely used in the production of many kinds of films, but it is used most spectacularly in disaster movies which, in the 1990s, have become much more realistic in terms of sound and vision. The turning point in the relationship between conventional filmmaking and CGI was James Cameron's deep-sea disaster movie *The Abyss* (1989). The plot of Cameron's film peripherally involves a research team working on the edge of a deep ocean trench, whose seabed living quarters seem certain to be dragged down into the abyss. The discovery of friendly aliens living at the bottom of the trench allows the opportunity for some impressive effects, such as a suspended column of seawater known as a "pseudopod," exploring the corridors of the deep-sea craft. Cameron used CGI and improved digital sound technology to excellent effect in his 1997 disaster film *Titanic,* creating convincing footage of the great ship's final hours. Director Steven Spielberg used similar techniques to bring dinosaurs back to life in *Jurassic Park* (1993) and the more overtly disaster-based *The Lost World* (1997).

Disaster movies have a tendency to take themselves too seriously and if improvements in special effects mean that comical visual effects are rarer in the 1990s, disaster movie plots have improved very little. Emotions are still crudely acted and contrived situations—such as the appearance of a dinosaur in San Diego in Spielberg's *The Lost World*—still challenge audiences to believe. Because of these weaknesses and responding to the popularity of disaster movies in the 1970s, parodies of disaster movies have also proved popular. In particular, the *Airport* series of films, the last of which appeared in 1979, was parodied in 1980 by *Airplane!,* a film advertised with the tag-line "What's slower than a speeding bullet, and able to hit tall buildings in a single bound?" The film spoofs the typical disaster movie plot when a pilot who is afraid of flying becomes the only person capable of flying the plane, while the score by Elmer Bernstein parodies the melodramatic music that accompanies all popular disaster movies.

While disaster movies have tended to be made as fictional entertainment, other categories of disaster movie have taken a more serious approach. There are films based on the Exxon Valdez oil spill and the Mount St. Helens volcanic eruptions, while others, such as the many Titanic disaster films, add a fictional or semi-fictional dramatic element to the real-life story. Still others, such as the British-made semi-documentary *Threads* (1985), mix documentary reporting with dramatization to make a serious point, in this case about the threat of nuclear war and its long-term effects. Whatever the reason for their appeal, in the 1990s disaster movies continue to be produced in large numbers and with great commercial success. Hard-core disaster movie fans will argue that they watch for the scenes of destruction and to revel in the special effects, but the importance of even a basic human story unfolding alongside the disaster suggests that their popularity has as much to do with sentiment as with spectacle.

—Chris Routledge

FURTHER READING:

Annan, David. *Catastrophe: The End of the Cinema?* New York, Bounty Books, 1975.

Broderick, Mick. *Nuclear Movies: A Critical Analysis and Filmography of International Feature Length Films Dealing with Experimentation, Aliens, Terrorism, Holocaust and Other Disaster Scenarios, 1914-1989.* Jefferson, North Carolina, McFarland and Co., 1991.

Cook, David A. *A History of Narrative Film.* New York, W.W. Norton and Company, 1996.

Keyser, Les. *Hollywood in the Seventies.* San Diego, A.S. Barnes, 1981.

Disc Jockeys

Since the early days of radio broadcasting, the disc jockey or DJ has been an essential part of radio, not just playing records but serving as an intermediary between the listening audience and the stars of popular music. Disc jockeys enjoyed the most influence on their listeners in the 1950s and 1960s, when they introduced new music to Americans and made rock and roll the dominant force in youth culture.

In the first two decades of radio in the United States, the person who introduced records and made station announcements was usually a technician who worked the broadcast equipment. It was a policy of the large radio networks to avoid recorded sound as much as possible and rely on live programming. Thus there was little call for disc jockeys in the 1920s and 1930s. The radio networks were forced to drop their opposition to canned music as their studio musicians were called up to join the armed forces in the 1940s. Thus began the rise of the radio announcer who played recordings on the air, the so-called disc jockey.

The most popular was Martin Block, whose ''Make Believe Ballroom'' invited listeners to a pretend concert and entertained them with humor and records. His program was networked in the 1940s and reached a national audience. The monopoly of the three national radio networks—NBC, CBS and ABC—was broken in the 1950s and this allowed many small independent stations to go on the air. Lacking the programming resources of the great networks, the independent stations relied on recorded music. The man spinning the records also made commercial announcements and read the news. At this time an estimated 75 percent of all programming on American radio came from records, providing many job opportunities for young men with ambitions in the music industry. Many important entertainers, record producers, and entrepreneurs of the 1950s got their start on local radio

Famed disc jockey Wolfman Jack.

stations playing records, including Bill Haley, Norman Petty, and Sam Phillips.

African Americans in southern cities and urban ghettos in the Northeast were an important new market for independent radio and many urban stations began to realign their programs to suit a predominately African American audience. Ownership of black radio remained in the hands of whites, but gradually black disc jockeys were allowed to broadcast. It was this group that began to play rhythm and blues records and create a new kind of radio personality who was to inaugurate the era of rock and roll.

Most radio announcers maintained a dignified demeanor and spoke in clear, correct English, but some African American disc jockeys broke all the rules of on-air behavior and invented outrageous alter egos for themselves. Their antics were rapidly copied by their white counterparts, who also stole the most commercial songs from their playlists and introduced them to the great white teenaged audience.

It is significant that the term ''rock and roll'' was coined by a white disc jockey from Cleveland, who played rhythm and blues records and created an entertaining on-air personality for himself. Alert to telephone requests and the sales of records in local stores, Alan Freed responded quickly to the growing appeal of R&B and turned his show into a showcase for the music. In 1951 he started to call it rock and roll. Such was the success of his ''Moondog's Rock and Roll Party'' that he moved to New York in 1954 and a much larger audience. The program climbed to the top of the ratings chart as rock music became more and more popular. Freed was America's most influential disc jockey, a conduit through which the ''race'' music of the 1940s became the rock and roll music of the 1950s.

The disc jockey of the late 1950s and early 1960s was an extremely important figure in the business of popular music. Radio play constituted the main form of promoting a record and many stations allowed the disc jockey to choose what records were to be broadcast. He decided which up-and-coming bands would get the radio play essential to selling records and moving up to bigger audiences and better paying shows. Disc jockeys found that repeated play of a record could make it a hit and the mythology of rock and roll is full of stories of unknown performers becoming stars overnight because of a radio personality who ''broke'' the record to his listening audience. Disc jockeys did a lot more than play records—they managed bands, promoted tours and public appearances, acted as master of ceremonies in rock shows, and became friends and advisors to the stars. Their name would share equal billing on the billboard of a typical rock and roll performance of the 1950s and early 1960s, as announcer and promoter. They became active intermediaries between rock and roll musicians and their audiences. Several of them, such as Alan Freed and ''Murray the K'' Kaufman, became stars of popular culture in their own right. Murray the K of station WINS of New York played an important part in introducing American youth to the Beatles during their first tour of the United States in 1964. Kaufman certainly promoted the Beatles but his position on the Beatles' bandwagon also helped his own career and his station.

The great power enjoyed by disc jockeys in the marketing of recordings encouraged corruption. The practice of ''payola'' (a contraction of ''pay'' and ''Victrola'') in which the disc jockey was bribed with money or a share of the publishing rights of the song was widely used to get airplay. The smaller record companies commonly paid disc jockeys and juke box operators to use their recordings. This practice came under scrutiny of the U.S. House of Representatives at the end of the 1950s and the ensuing Payola scandal ended the careers of several influential disc jockeys, including that of Alan Freed. The

payola scandal was only one of the factors reducing the power of disc jockeys in the 1960s. The move to the Top 40 format—in which the playlist was based on the Billboard charts—narrowed down the choice of records to be played, and the gradual consolidation of the radio industry—with one business organization controlling several stations—often took the decision about what records were to be played out of the hands of the on-air staff.

The great technological watershed of the late 1960s and 1970s was the migration from AM to FM broadcast bands, which brought a significant increase in sound quality and encouraged stations to use high fidelity long playing records rather than the 45 rpm singles that had been the staple of commercial radio for two decades. The typical disc jockey of the FM album-oriented station was much quieter and unobtrusive compared with the radio personalities of the 1950s and 1960s. The person playing the records was expected to have more knowledge of the music and indulge in less histrionics. Women were now finding it easier to get jobs in radio stations as the archetype of the disc jockey was recast.

Although disc jockeys were still instrumental in finding new music and introducing new performers, their power in popular music was in constant decline in the 1970s and 1980s. Commercial radio relied less on the individual in front of the microphone and more on the programming director and market analyst to chose the records to be played. The flamboyant radio personality survived only on the morning show; the rest of the days broadcast was handled by anonymous interchangeable voices. Disc jockeys did find opportunities to set themselves up as independent businessmen who played parties and clubs. The creation of rap and hip-hop came out of the activities of disc jockeys in the New York area, who kept the records playing while ''toasters'' or master of ceremonies spoke over and in between the music. The introduction of music television in the 1980s raised expectations that the presenter would wield some influence but the ''vee jay'' proved as disposable and ephemeral as his or her counterpart on the radio. The continuing pattern of consolidation in the American radio industry in the 1990s ensured that the disc jockey would be the person playing the records not the unique performer influencing musical trends and making the stars of popular culture.

—Andre Millard

FURTHER READING:

Chapple, Steve, and Rebe Garofalo. *Rock'n'Roll Is Here to Pay.* Chicago, Nelson Hall, 1977.

Gillett, Charlie. *The Sound of the City: The Rise of Rock and Roll.* New York, Pantheon, 1984.

Passman, Arnold. *The Deejays.* New York, MacMillan, 1971.

Sterling, Christopher, and John M. Kittross. *Stayed Tuned: A Concise History of American Broadcasting.* Belmont, California, Wadsworth, 1990.

Williams, Gilbert. *The Legendary Pioneers of Black Radio.* Westport, Connecticut, Praeger, 1998.

Disco

Derived from the French discotheque, disco refers not only to a musical style but to a unique brand of dance-club decor, a sexy-synthetic manner of dress, a style of dance, and an attitude toward sexual promiscuity and night life, all of which came together during the 1970s as "disco," one of the most glitzy and celebrated fads in American popular cultural history. Between 1975 and 1979, the established sensibilities of rock and pop, which emphasized sincerity, emotion, and rebellion, gave way to the enchantment of dance floor rhythms, which colonized popular imagination as an alluring dreamscape of pleasure and sexual utopia. In disco, the boundary between commercial fabrication and real experience became blurred. Disco ushered in a new post-1960s concept of hedonistic weekends, holidays, and exciting after-hours activity that was open to anyone with a reasonable income, a basic sense of rhythm and a good body. However, for all its fashionable accouterments, what lay at the essential heart of the disco craze was the music. Characterized by an insistently repetitive base and a hypnotic beat, overlaid with teasing, sexy vocals, it captivated and mesmerized its adherents.

Though psychedelic dance bars had experimented with combinations of dance, music, and lighting since the 1960s ("oil wheels" and "sound-to-light" systems), it was during the 1970s that the technological, musical, and fashion elements that define the culture of the dance club were refined and popularized. In the early 1970s discos began expanding their equipment to include a wider array of musical and visual props. The "mirror ball," which could fragment a white spotlight into a million rotating dots, became the symbol of the new disco, along with synchronized lights that were matched to the bass track of a record. Later, with the appearance of the smoke machine and dry ice, came the "pin spot" light, which could stab through a cloud of smoke to cast an illuminated shaft across a darkened room. Throughout the 1970s, commercial dance clubs sprang up across the country, ranging from fashionable and exclusive big city venues like New York's Studio 54, to more modest hotel discos and revamped bars and clubs. The larger venues included advanced lighting and music systems controlled by a disc jockey, or DJ, who lorded over the collective euphoria from an elevated booth, cajoling the crowd to "get down and boogie." Disco fashions highlighted the tight fit, high heels, platforms, and the funky "gentleman's" three-piece suits, and displayed an unabashed preference for polyester.

Pop music had always been danceable and flamboyant, but what set disco apart was that it was not only music *for* dancing, but also music *about* dancing. The disco beat was the anthem of the dancers, the disco floor a wonderland of sexual promise where anything might happen, providing the perfect environment to indulge the pursuit of one's fantasy. Unlike the "be-ins," the pot parties, and other escapades favored by hippies, disco promised an experience of the exotic that could be easily slotted into a well ordered working week and coordinated with a regular pattern of one night stands. Film titles such as *Thank God It's Friday* and *Saturday Night Fever* reflected the compartmentalized nature of this package-tour utopia. Though disco's dreamland of sexual fulfillment is often remembered as the longing of the heterosexual male libido, the real origins of disco's sexual imagery lie in the gay club scene of New York and San Francisco, where its camp atmosphere of sexual reverie was first born. This fact was largely obscured from disco's audiences at the time. With hindsight, it is astonishing that middle-class, heterosexual listeners were oblivious to the homo-erotic suggestions that permeate the songs of such widely accepted groups as The Village People—songs such as "Macho Man," "In the Navy," and "YMCA." As it matured, disco sanitized and commercialized itself and, at its peak, it was targeted at an age group too young to be admitted to a real dance club, let alone have any clue as to what separated gay from straight dance culture.

Disco's real ground zero, however, was not the concert hall or even the dance floor, but the AM radio dial. Mainstream radio started playing disco music in the mid-1970s, and by December 1978, 200 disco-only formats aired across the country. Six months later, the number had increased by a further 50. In 1974 and 1975 respectively, George McCrae's "Rock Your Baby" and Van McCoy's "The Hustle" introduced the sounds of disco to AM radio, though it was a few years before artists such as Kool & The Gang, Gloria Gaynor, Donna Summer, the Bee Gees, KC and The Sunshine Band, Sister Sledge, Diana Ross, and the Village People rode the wave of disco enthusiasm. By the time disco dominated the airwaves in 1979, even Rod Stewart and the Rolling Stones were among those who had hopped onto the bandwagon.

No group stands out as more emblematic of the period than the Bee Gees, who began the 1970s as a British-Australian pop phenomenon with moderate sales, and made a sensational break through on the soundtrack of *Saturday Night Fever*. The film, which made a star of John Travolta, focused on a working-class youth who escapes the mundane reality of life by becoming a demi-god of the local disco scene. The soundtrack was originally released as a double LP in 1977, becoming the industry's biggest selling soundtrack album and producing ten singles hits from its 17 tracks, of which "How Deep Is Your Love," "Stayin' Alive," and "Night Fever" dominated the pop charts in 1977 and 1978. The famous image of Travolta, wearing a white polyester suit, his pelvis thrust forward and his finger raised skyward against a background of disco lights, came to define the decade, an emblem of disco's garish eroticism. The Bee Gees, whose thumping, squealing ballads of sexual enterprise saturated the film, typified disco music for the remainder of the decade. Ironically, both Travolta and the Bee Gees later fell victim to the fickleness of fads and fashion, and became easy objects of ridicule for some years to come.

By the end of 1979, disco's celebration of the fanciful and the fake was beginning to wear thin. After a stream of "one-hit wonders," disco seemed to be more the product of producers and promoters than of the artists themselves. One of the problems was that disco music seemed to lack talented performing musicians: electronically manipulated sounds replaced the bass, drums and guitar that had typified rock, and in live performances disco stars came to rely increasingly on recorded tracks and off-stage musical support. The Village People, largely a stage act, kept back-up singers entirely out of view of the audience. More than this, disco proved notoriously adaptable to a variety of commercial marketing devices. A record called *Hooked on Classics,* whose cover featured a Mozart-like character mimicking Travolta's famous pose from *Saturday Night Fever,* mixed well-known classical music hits to a disco beat. Novelty songs like "disco duck" climbed the AM charts, and even the theme from the film *2001: A Space Odyssey,* was re-recorded as a disco hit.

Perhaps the most interesting thing about disco was its strange demise and long disgrace. Its commercialism, its ersatz sexuality and its reliance on radio to reach an average music consumer—rather than record sales to reach a "fan" market of countercultural listeners—seemed to violate everything rock stood for, and provoked a powerful backlash from fans of "real" rock. Hostility came to a head in 1979 when a "Disco Demolition Derby" was organized by radio DJ Steve Dahl at a baseball game at Detroit's Tiger Stadium. Anti-disco fans burned more than 100,000 albums, hoisted "disco sucks" banners, and rioted, forcing the cancellation of the game. The precise nature of this backlash remains unclear: Dahl's event, which has since been compared to fascist book burnings, may have been homophobic, sexist or racist, or it may have expressed a widespread disappointment with the increasing commercialism of a supposedly rebellious musical form. It was most likely a combination of these factors, but, whatever the case, not since John Lennon's fateful remark about the Beatles being more famous than Christ had there been such a widespread consumer revolt against the music industry. The reaction against disco's commercialism, cheap sentiment, and *faux* sexuality fueled the emergence of other more ''authentic'' expressions of youth culture, punk and heavy metal. By 1981 the disco boom was bust.

—Sam Binkley

FURTHER READING:

Haden-Guest, Anthony. *The Last Party: Studio 54, Disco, and the Culture of the Night.* New York, William Morrow, 1997.

Disney (Walt Disney Company)

When it was founded in 1923, Walt Disney Productions consisted of a small cracker-box studio in Hollywood housing a small group

Mickey and Minnie Mouse in Disneyland.

of creative artists headed by a young visionary who had recently arrived from the Midwest to produce cartoons for the movies. Beyond that, there was little more than a paper menagerie of barnyard animals and a mouse nicknamed ''Mickey'' who emerged at night to seek crumbs left behind by the artists. Five years later, that mouse had made the jump to the silver screen starring in *Plane Crazy* (1928) with the assistance of artist Ub Iwerks who supplied the artwork and Walt Disney, himself who came up with the trademark squeaky voice. The company was on its way.

At the end of the twentieth century, The Walt Disney Co. was considered by many to be the most influential company in the world surpassing even its founder's vision as it has established footholds not only in motion pictures but in such diverse industries as television, electronic media, book publishing, hotels, transportation, tourism, amusement parks, real estate, sports, and communications. In an industry where ''vertical integration'' had become increasingly important, Disney and its chief rival Time Warner have their corporate fingers in more pies than any other entertainment entities. Yet, the mouse continued to lead the way.

Perhaps, the most recognizable logo in the history of the world, Mickey Mouse has left his footprints on every country and culture in the world but the road to success has not been entirely without its share of ups and downs. Walt Disney was born in Chicago in 1901, the son of a ne'er-do-well father who drifted from one job to another. He learned to work hard early in life and had very little escape from the drudgery of his life except for the drawings he would create when no one was looking. This early experience instilled two traits in Disney that would follow him for all of his life. One was that he learned the value of hard work and became a compulsive ''workaholic.'' The other was a firm belief that the public thirsted for escapism and ''happy endings.''

In 1919, Disney went to work for the Kansas City Film Ad Company where he put his drawing talents to use working on short animated commercials for local merchants. He also met another young artist named Ub Iwerks. Together the two learned the fundamentals of animation and decided to strike out on their own producing a series of ads and comic shorts called Newman's Laugh-O-Grams for the local Newman's Theater. In 1922, Disney took the Newman's concept further by creating pure entertainment oriented theatrical cartoons satirizing popular fairy tales. Unfortunately, he had the habit of spending more money on the production and technical aspects of each film than they brought in. The result was that, artistically, the films were quite polished for their time with full background detail and a full spectrum of wash tones that served to establish the basic Disney style. Financially, however, the company was forced to go out of business because it's production costs were simply too high.

In 1923, Disney moved to Hollywood with his brother Roy and formed the Disney Brothers studio to produce short subjects which combined both live action and animation. The impetus for the move was based on an experimental short subject based on *Alice in Wonderland* which was a reversal of rival animator Max Fleischer's *Out of the Inkwell* series which featured a cartoon clown having adventures against a live background. Disney's version featured a live Alice character juxtaposed with cartoon backgrounds and animated characters. The series, which was dubbed *Alice in Cartoonland* was picked up by a Los Angeles distributor named M.J. Winkler. Yet, with the formation of the company, both Disney brothers realized that animation was not a one or two man job. Additionally, Walt realized that he was not the animator that his friend Ub Iwerks was so he hired a small staff including Iwerks and an up and coming animator named

Hugh Harmon. Some of the titles in the "Alice Series" included *Alice's Wild West Show* (1924), *Alice's Egg Plant* (1925), and *Alice Chops the Suey (1925).* These shorts were innovative in that they integrated the real and animated action, showing a live girl jumping out of an animated ink well or blowing animated smoke rings or being splattered with cartoon eggs. Yet, at the speed that the small studio was required to turn them out (approximately one every two weeks), they couldn't experiment with too many ideas and the novelty began to wear off.

Disney quickly introduced a new character and series—"Oswald the Lucky Rabbit." These cartoons reflected a higher quality of animation and experimented with a variety of visual effects, particularly the manipulation of light and shadow, not seen in the Alice series. In addition, the use of an animated central character as opposed to a live figure made a certain reality defying flexibility possible. In one adventure, Oswald attempts to kiss a medieval maiden's hand and arm and keeps pulling more and more arm out of her sleeve until he has a seemingly endless expanse of arm to kiss. In another cartoon, his car expands and contracts to fit a variety of continuously changing road conditions.

Like the cartoons themselves, the planning sessions for them were equally flexible. Instead of formal scripts, the stories were conceived at what amounted to corporate bull sessions consisting of Disney and four other animators. Ideas were tossed into the ring until a basic plot evolved. Disney would then divide the elements into four sequences with each animator responsible for his own area of the cartoon's action. Each animator could then freely improvise within his own area subject to Disney's approval.

The Oswald series was so fresh and innovative that it made Disney's company a modest success. Yet, when he approached his current distributor Charles Mintz who had taken over the Winkler Company for larger production budgets, Mintz refused and took both Oswald and all of the key animators who participated in the project away from Disney. Only Iwerks remained. The experience made the Disney brothers determined to own all of their own films and copyrights in the future.

In 1928, Disney and Iwerks fashioned another animal character to replace Oswald. However, Mickey Mouse who made his debut in *Plane Crazy* followed by *Galloping Gaucho* was not an immediate success. Although the animation and story ideas were good, the character itself looked like Oswald with shorter ears and a longer nose. There was nothing intrinsically interesting about the character to separate it from the multitudes of other animals cavorting on the screen. It took the invention of sound in 1928 to make Mickey Mouse a superstar. While the first live action sound films such as *The Jazz Singer* (1928) put the sound in somewhat gratuitously counting on the technology to thrill the audience, Disney created an integrated film in which sound and images worked together. When *Steamboat Willie* was released at the end of the year, audiences were captivated by the idea that a character plainly drawn with pen and ink could actually sing and dance in rhythm. The secret was that Disney began with song and music first and then drew the characters and backgrounds to reflect the sounds.

Disney built on the success of *Steamboat Willie* by working with his musical director Carl Stallings to create animated cartoons based on specific musical pieces. The first of these was *Skeleton Dance* (1928), a non-character cartoon that demonstrated animation's ability to evoke mood and atmosphere. Suddenly cartoons were no longer the poor relative of live action feature films but works of art in themselves. In the years that followed, Disney created the *Silly Symphonies*

series of music-based animation and introduced new characters including Pluto (1930), Minnie Mouse (1933), and Donald Duck (1934). In 1932, he switched to the new medium of Technicolor for *Flowers and Trees* and won the Academy Award for "Best Short Subject." After that, the young company maintained an exclusive agreement with Technicolor for all of their animated productions.

But, cartoon shorts could only evolve so far. Disney became determined to create a feature length animated film. Although conventional Hollywood wisdom dictated that an animated cartoon could not hold audience interest beyond seven minutes, Disney envisioned a fairly simple structure, which would allow one sequence to flow into another and in which musical numbers would evolve from and add to character development, as a viable formula for such a film. In *Snow White and the Seven Dwarfs* (1938), he created seven distinctly individual personalities in addition to his main characters, a feat which never before had been accomplished in animation. To accomplish such distinction, Disney crafted the characters, particularly Snow White, in such a degree of detail that they could convey human emotions in a believable manner. Audiences reacted to *Snow White* as if the characters were real, showing a variety of emotions ranging from horror at the sight of the queen's transformation into a witch to happiness as Snow White frolics with the dwarves and charms the woodland animals.

Following *Snow White* came a steady flow of animated features, each one expanding the techniques of animation. By the beginning of the 1940s, the company geared up to produce a steady stream of animated features and literally become an animation factory employing hundreds of artists and technical personnel even though the studio had not gained "major" status as a full production/distribution entity on a par with Warner Brothers or Columbia. *Pinocchio* and *Fantasia* appeared in 1940, blazing a trail for such other notable productions as *Dumbo* (1941), *Bambi* (1942), *Cinderella* (1950), *Sleeping Beauty* (1959), and *101 Dalmations* (1961). Interspersed with these animated features were documentary and live action productions, including *The Living Desert* (1953), *20,000 Leagues Under the Sea* (1954), and *Mary Poppins* (1964). During the early 1950s, Disney founded his own distribution company, Buena Vista, to release these films thus freeing him from his reliance on RKO and other larger companies to determine the venues for his products.

But Disney did not confine himself to one medium. In 1954, he made the jump to the new medium of television with a weekly series called *Disneyland* which would be followed by an afternoon children's series the *Mickey Mouse Club*. In 1955, he fulfilled his personal vision by creating an escapist world in Anaheim, California, in which reality dare not intrude. The Disneyland theme park featured a nostalgic Main Street USA and four thematically constructed "lands": Adventureland, Fantasyland, Frontierland, and Tomorrowland. Each of these lands reflected motifs first delineated in Disney films or television programs. It was a "first" for the entertainment industry in that for the first time, viewers could actually enter the world of their favorite Disney films and interact with fictional characters. The company also led the way in creating spin-off products from the films and theme parks with lines of toys, clothing, records, and similar merchandise. By the end of the 1950s, Walt Disney was America's undisputed king of family entertainment.

After its founder's death in 1966, the company coasted along for a number of years turning out acceptable products and fulfilling several of Disney's unrealized dreams, notably an updated East Coast version of Disneyland, Walt Disney World in Orlando, Florida, in 1971, and the futuristic Epcot Center several years later. Under the management of Disney's successor E. Cardon Walker, the company was faced by a defection of a number of its leading animators led by Don Bluth, who felt that the company's standards had deteriorated after Walt's death. Yet, after venturing out on their own, they quickly discovered that while they could duplicate the legendary Disney animation, they could not capture the elusive Disney touch which transformed drawings into real characters capable of expressing human emotions within innovative storylines.

Walker's successor Ron Miller, faced with declining film revenues created a new division called Touchstone in 1984 to turn out more adult products than the Disney image would allow. This prompted Roy Disney, still a major shareholder in the company to resign from the board of directors, initiating a management struggle for control of the company which by the mid-1980s was producing only four films a year and was reliant on the theme parks for the bulk of its revenue (nearly 83 percent in 1983 alone).

Miller resigned under pressure in September 1984 just as Touchstone's first release, *Splash,* boosted the film division's earnings to record highs, and became the highest grossing film in Disney history while making a star of Tom Hanks. His successor, Michael Eisner, lured from Paramount Pictures, appeared cut from the Disney mold. He followed up on the success of *Splash* with two more nontraditional features *Down and Out in Beverly Hills* (1985) and *Three Men and a Baby* (1987). These would be followed by the worldwide mega-hit *Pretty Woman* (1990), a story of a romance between a prostitute and a millionaire which took the old Cinderella story in a modern direction that Walt probably would not have approved of. With chairman Jeffrey Katzenberg, Eisner effected a renaissance of the animated feature at a time when conventional wisdom had declared it moribund. Beginning with the critically acclaimed *The Black Cauldron* in 1985, Eisner started a new golden age of animation which surpassed the box-office successes of the 1930s and 1940s. Yet, the formula was very much the same: realistic characters that tugged at the viewers emotions, superb animation, and memorable music. Such films as *The Little Mermaid* (1989), *Beauty and the Beast* (1991), *Aladdin* (1992), and *The Lion King* (1994) generated grosses in the hundreds of millions prompting many of Hollywood's major studios to jump into animation in order to compete. *Beauty and the Beast* became the first animated feature to be nominated for an Academy Award.

By the mid-1990s, production at Disney had risen from the four films per year of a decade earlier to more than 20 per anum. Eisner's strategy of producing tightly budgeted films pairing "low cost name talent" such as Richard Dryfuss and Bette Midler who were in temporary career lulls with widely appealing stories paid major dividends. Films such as the aforementioned *Pretty Woman, Sister Act, Stakeout,* and *Honey I Shrunk the Kids* achieved grosses that greatly exceeded their small (by Hollywood standards) production budgets. The success of these features prompted the studio to open a third production entity, Hollywood Pictures, in 1990.

Disney had at last acquired major studio status by the 1990s. It's distribution company Buena Vista was regularly in the top one or two in film grosses and it was out-producing all of the studios in Hollywood in sheer number of films. With its ownership of a cable TV channel, a successful video distribution empire, and the ability to distribute its product worldwide via satellite, Disney became one of the earliest studios to realize the financial value of a large library. In 1996, the company purchased the ABC television network for $19 billion, giving it a national outlet for its product as well as an all encompassing venue for plugging its upcoming films. While the network has not regained the top spot it held in the 1970s, it nonetheless presents some of the more innovative new shows on television and is a leader in sports and news programming.

Eisner also took major steps to revitalize the theme park side of the ledger by creating EuroDisney outside of Paris in 1992, a wild animal theme park in Florida in 1997 and by starting a project to expand the original Disneyland in Anaheim, California. The ancillary markets for Disney product were expanded as well. The company refurbished the El Capitan Theater in Hollywood as a showcase for its new releases and added promotional stage acts as well as a place to buy the company's products in the lobby.

On the opposite coast, Disney refurbished a Broadway theater and began to turn its film hits, including *Beauty and the Beast* and *The Lion King,* into musical plays with new numbers and scenes added to make them successful on the stage. Similarly, several of the animated productions were turned into ice extravaganzas which toured the country blending the traditional stories and songs with fancy skating numbers arranged specifically for the frozen medium.

Yet, the ultimate spin-off of a motion picture concept occurred in the early 1990s when Eisner bought an Anaheim NHL hockey franchise and named it after a moderately successful live action feature *The Mighty Ducks.* The company purchased the Anaheim Angels baseball team and the highly popular cable TV station Entertainment and Sports Network (ESPN). After these purchases, Disney had only two rivals in the sports arena: Rupert Murdoch with his Fox Sports Cable Channel on the Fox Network; and the ownership of the Los Angeles Dodgers, the Angels' chief rival for the L.A. sports dollar.

By the end of the twentieth century, The Walt Disney Company had grown from the small Hollywood studio of 1923 to a recreational empire. With holdings so expansive, the nostalgic Disney vision has been applied beyond mere entertainment. The company's theme-oriented steamship line (floating Disneylands), Disney Stores, innovative theme parks, music, video and television endeavors, have allowed the company unprecedented power to shape the perceptions of consumers, offering people the chance to see, experience, and purchase Disney-styled versions of Americana.

—Steve Hanson

FURTHER READING:

Bailey, Adrian. *Walt Disney's World of Fantasy.* New York, Everest House, 1982.

Coleman, Todd. "Mouse Trap." *The Hollywood Reporter.* November 25, 1996, 29+.

Hanson, Steve. "The Mouse That Roared." *Stills,* October 1984, 24-27.

Koepp, Stephen, "Do You Believe in Magic? Starring in its own Cinderella Story, Disney Transforms Itself." *Time.* April 25, 1988, 66-75.

Maltin, Leonard. *Of Mice and Magic: A History of American Animated Cartoons.* New York, The New American Library, 1980.

Schickel, Richard. *The Disney Version.* New York, Simon and Schuster, 1968.

Smith, Dave. *Disney A to Z: The Official Encyclopedia.* New York, Hyperion, 1996.

Solomon, Charles. *The Disney That Never Was: The Stories and Art From Five Decades of Unproduced Animation.* New York, Hyperion, 1995.

Taylor, John. *Storming the Magic Kingdom: Wall Street, the Raiders and the Battle for Disney.* New York, Alfred A. Knopf, 1987.

West, John G., Jr. *The Disney Live Action Productions.* Milton, Washington, Hawthorne & Peabody, 1994.

Ditka, Mike (1939—)

Football player-turned-football coach "Iron" Mike Ditka is described in his Football Hall of Fame enshrinee data as a "fast, rugged, outstanding blocker [and a] great competitor." In 1960, he was a consensus All-American at the University of Pittsburgh, and became the Chicago Bears' number one draft pick the following year. From 1961 through 1972, Ditka was a hard-nosed tight end for the Bears, Philadelphia Eagles, and Dallas Cowboys. He was the NFL rookie of the year in 1961, starred on the Bears' 1963 NFL title squad, and scored the final touchdown for the Cowboys in Super Bowl VI. During his career, he caught 427 passes for 5,812 yards and 43 touchdowns. He made all-NFL four times, played in five straight Pro Bowls, was named to the NFL 75th Anniversary Team, and in 1988 became the first tight end to enter the Hall of Fame.

Despite Ditka's eminence as a player, he is best known today as an NFL head coach. He worked as an assistant under Tom Landry in Dallas from 1973 through 1981, and was hired to lead the Bears in 1982. While Ditka has willingly parodied his in-your-face, bullying, drill-instructor coaching style on television shows and particularly in TV commercials, he is all business when it comes to winning football games. During eleven seasons coaching the Bears, he led the team to six NFC Central crowns, three trips to the NFC Championship game, and a 46-10 whipping of the New England Patriots in Super Bowl XX. After retiring from the Bears in 1992 and working as an NBC sports broadcaster, he was lured back onto the field in 1997 as coach of the New Orleans Saints.

—Rob Edelman

FURTHER READING:

Ditka, Mike, and Jim Stamborski. *Don't Get Me Wrong: Mike Ditka's Insights, Outbursts, Kudos and Comebacks.* Chicago, Chicago Review Press, 1988.

Ditka, Mike, with Don Pierson. *Ditka: An Autobiography.* Chicago, Bonus Books, 1986.

Keteyian, Armen. *Ditka: Monster of the Midway.* New York, Pocket Books, 1992.

Divine (1945-1988)

The obese transvestite character-actor Divine personified self-consciously campy underground films and ushered in a new threshold of bad taste in cinema. Starring mainly in the films of offbeat director John Waters, Divine cultivated an outrageous drag queen image, with gaudy makeup, a blonde mane the texture of cotton candy, and tight dresses on his more-than-300-pound frame. In the majority of his films, he played female characters and dressed in women's garb during his short-lived career as a singer. Though Divine was poised to break through into mainstream film and television at the end of his

Divine (right) with Grace Jones.

life, most of his appearances were in films with shocking subject matter. He will likely remain famous for his role as the Filthiest Person Alive" in the 1972 Waters film *Pink Flamingos,* especially due to the notorious scene at the end in which he consumes freshly excreted poodle dung."

Divine was born Harris Glenn Milstead on October 19, 1945, and raised in an upper-middle-class home in a suburb of Baltimore, Maryland, the city that provided the backdrop for the bulk of his films. His parents ran a successful nursery and regularly attended a local Baptist church. As a teen, Divine was active in school plays, and began associating with Waters, who lived nearby. They were both outcasts, and Divine noted in Waters' book *Shock Value* that he required a daily police escort to and from school to avoid constant beatings by other students. After high school, Divine graduated from beauty school and became known as an excellent stylist. His parents even bought him his own salon, but he became bored with it. He later opened a fashion boutique in Provincetown, Massachusetts. Meanwhile, he also began acting in Waters' independent movies. His first role was in *Roman Candles* (1966), a home movie of Waters' friends stealing and then modeling dresses. It was at this time that Waters recognized the actor's potential and renamed his friend "Divine."

After that unceremonious induction into film, Divine starred in *Eat Your Makeup* (1968), in which he played the part of Jacqueline

Kennedy in the movie's central scene re-enacting President John Kennedy's assassination. Subsequently, Waters made another film of questionable taste that is rarely noted in official sources, *The Diane Linkletter Story,* named after Art Linkletter's daughter, who committed suicide allegedly after taking large amounts of hallucinogenic drugs. In 1969, Waters and his troupe, known as the Dreamlanders, made *Mondo Trasho,* which established Divine's bizarre look. In *Not Simply Divine,* Bernard Jay quoted Divine as saying that his new image was based on Waters' concept of a blend of "the wicked stepmother in *Cinderella,* the evil queen of *Snow White,* and the bad witch in *The Wizard of Oz,*" combined with a touch of Jayne Mansfield. Continuing down a slippery slope of poor taste, *Mondo Trasho* was followed by *Multiple Maniacs* in 1970, which professed that Divine was the actual killer in what were later dubbed the Manson Family murders. It also featured Divine being raped by a 15-foot-tall lobster.

After *Multiple Maniacs,* Divine and Waters garnered a good deal of attention from underground publications. Their next collaboration, though, dwarfed their previous efforts. *Pink Flamingos* was the tale of a battle for the title of "Filthiest Person Alive," and featured a couple who kidnaps women, impregnates them, and sells the babies to lesbians on the black market in order to raise money for their elementary school heroin ring. They want to take the distinction away from Divine, an incestuous, trailer-dwelling matriarch who firmly maintains her disgusting reputation with the dog excrement scene. *Pink Flamingos* generated a flurry of attention and became one of the premier cult films of all time.

Divine had acted in stage plays in San Francisco in the early 1970s, and after *Pink Flamingos,* began appearing off-Broadway in productions such as *Women Behind Bars* (1976) and *The Neon Woman* (1978). He also launched a disco singing career. In fact, he often attended the legendary Studio 54 disco in full drag and mingled with other icons of the day. Divine made a number of other films with Waters throughout the years, including *Female Trouble* (1975), *Polyester* (1981), and *Lust in the Dust* (1985), as well as a few on his own. Though Divine made his mark as the garish caricature of himself that people usually saw, he grew weary of dressing in drag and yearned to be accepted as a talented character actor. Finally, in 1988 he was noticed for his dual role in Waters' *Hairspray* as both proud stage mother Edna Turnblad and bigoted television executive Arvin Hodgepile. After that, he was slated to appear on the popular television program *Married . . . With Children,* and was eager to line up other work as well. Just as he seemed on the verge of making an entrance into the mainstream, however, Divine died of a heart attack in a hotel room in Los Angeles on March 7, 1988. Almost a decade after his death, *Pink Flamingos* stirred a new wave of publicity with its 25 year anniversary release, padded with new footage and commentary by Waters.

—Geri Speace

FURTHER READING:

Clark, John. "Ready for the Return of 'Flamingos'?" *Los Angeles Times,* April 10, 1997, 8.

Jay, Bernard. *Not Simply Divine.* New York, Simon & Schuster, 1993.

Waters, John K. *Shock Value: A Tasteful Book about Bad Taste.* New York, Dell Publishing, 1981.

Divine

Marriage, the legally sanctioned and structured pairing of heterosexual couples, has long been an established practice in human civilization all over the world. Divorce, the dissolution of a marriage agreement, is as old as marriage itself. Since the 1960s, rapidly rising divorce rates have placed the ending of marriage among the most common rituals of modern society. In the late 1990s, almost half of all marriages ended in divorce, and the prevalence of divorce has changed not only the nature of marriage, but the definition of family as well.

Early cultures often permitted divorce with relative ease. Roman law allowed couples to divorce simply by mutual consent, while Jewish Talmudic law granted divorce on a variety of grounds, including adultery and desertion. Greek, Germanic, and Frankish law also recognized couples' right to divorce, as did Islam and the Orthodox Church. The Roman Catholic Church became one of the first institutions to outlaw divorce, claiming marriage as a sacrament of the church. Dissolution of marriage could only be granted by the church under special circumstances, such as an annulment if one's spouse was a close relative, or a "judicial separation," where husband and wife were permitted to live apart without remarrying. Repercussions of the attitudes of the Catholic church about divorce were felt into future centuries and in lands as far apart as Ireland, Latin America, and parts of the American South.

The Protestant Reformation brought with it new perspectives on marriage. While Catholics had viewed it as a sacred sacrament, taken for life, Protestants saw marriage as a contract, changeable if it no longer met the needs of the contracted parties. Likewise, while Catholics had primarily defined the purpose of marriage as procreation, Protestants included in it such functions as companionship, support, and sexual pleasure, inspiring radical Protestants, such as poet John Milton, to argue that divorce should be allowed for simple incompatibility.

In the United States, from colonial times to the present, divorce was widely permitted but frowned upon socially. By the time of the Civil War, divorces were granted in most parts of the country on grounds of cruelty, abandonment, drunkenness, nonsupport, or verbal threats or insults. As legal divorces became easier to obtain, the divorce rate began to climb steadily. By the early 1900s the United States was granting the most divorces of any Western country, six times as many as France, in second place. The number had risen dramatically, from 7,380 divorces nationwide in 1860 to 83,045 in 1910.

In the 1950s, divorce dropped somewhat with that decade's glorification of the nuclear family. Women who worked as homemakers, supported by their husbands, found themselves unprepared to support themselves and their children should they divorce. In contrast, the 1960s and 1970s saw more women graduating from college with career aspirations and the skills to achieve them. The divorce rate shot up, as these women no longer felt forced to remain in unhappy marriages.

Though more and more marriages ended in divorce each decade, divorce was still largely stigmatized by society and pathologized by experts who defined divorced people as neurotic and sought cures for their ills. This perception finally began to change in the 1970s when feminism and the sexual revolution combined to give divorce a positive new image of liberation and independence. In the 1980s, rates dipped once again as the threat of AIDS encouraged monogamy. In addition, married baby boomers of the 1980s began to find financial reasons to stay together, since two incomes were needed to support their lifestyles. These factors, coupled with the 1980s political conservatism and backlash against feminism, caused more couples to seek counseling to save their marriages. The divorce lull did not last, however. Rates continue to climb as, approaching the twenty-first century, generation Xers, many the children of divorce themselves, attempt to determine the boundaries of commitment. Divorce is such a commonplace that while many couples still use lawyers to work out their disputes, others now go to mediators and many more execute their own divorces quite amicably. Along with divorcing couples, there are now numerous cases of children divorcing their parents and vice versa.

Until fairly recently, wives were considered little more than the property of their husbands, and the treatment of women in the divorce process has reflected this attitude. Though many women have been unhappy in the marital roles assigned them, women have always had more to lose financially from divorce. Less valued in the marketplace than men, women often lose further ground by removing themselves from the work force while working as mothers and homemakers. When a woman divorces, the standard of living for her and her children falls an average of 73 percent, often placing them below poverty level. Men, by contrast, released from familial obligations, are free to put more energy into their existing jobs. After divorce, a man's average standard of living rises 42 percent. The devaluing of women's role in the home has also contributed to unfair distribution of assets after divorce. Except in "community property" states, where any property acquired by either partner during the marriage is divided equally, a woman may receive little or none of the family resources, which may be in the husband's name.

Beginning with the so-called "tender years" legislation of the nineteenth century, custody of young children has traditionally been awarded to the mother in divorce settlements. Courts may also choose to award child support and alimony, or spousal support payments, which also traditionally were paid by the husband as the primary earner. In recent years, courts have begun to change assumptions about gender roles, sometimes awarding custody and even spousal support to the husband if he is judged to be the better parent or the wife has greater earning power. "No-fault" divorce, a concept developed in the 1980s, has further eroded the system of spousal support by removing the factor of blame and responsibility for the end of the marriage. While many applaud these changes, they often have resulted in even worse conditions for women following divorce.

Another product of the rising divorce rate has been the pre-nuptial agreement, wherein couples plan for the possibility of divorce before they are married and agree upon future division of property. Originated by the lawyers of wealthy people who felt they had lost an unfair amount in a divorce, the "pre-nup" is now as much a part of an upper-class wedding as the wedding cake.

Social attitudes toward men and women surrounding divorce have tended to be quite different, especially prior to the 1970s. Divorced men have often been viewed as roguish or even slightly dangerous, not undesirable qualities in a male. Also, the addition of another available man to the social pool is generally looked upon as a good thing. Divorced women, on the other hand, have been seen traditionally as promiscuous, and the addition of an unattached woman to society is usually viewed as threatening to other women.

Images of divorce in the media have contributed to these perceptions. Entertainers have always lived by their own rules, and even in decades when divorce was most stigmatized in ordinary society, the public avidly followed the marital adventures of the movie stars. Even in the repressive 1950s, actors such as Elizabeth Taylor and Mickey Rooney set records for numbers of marriages that are still impressive today. Fascinated fans reacted with outrage when divorcee Taylor broke up the "idyllic" marriage of Eddie Fisher and Debbie Reynolds. In the mid-1970s they formed strong opinions about the so-called "palimony" suit following the breakup of long-term unmarried lovers Lee Marvin and Michelle Triola when Triola insisted that she was entitled to spousal support after their six-year relationship ended.

Films tended to both reflect and mold social attitudes. In 1934, Fred Astaire and Ginger Rogers danced their way through lighthearted marital misunderstandings in *The Gay Divorcee.* In the early 1960s, anti-divorce attitudes won out in *The Parent Trap,* when twin daughters (played by Hayley Mills) of a divorced couple managed to reunite their parents, whose breakup was clearly ill-advised. The 1980s backlash was represented nowhere better than in the Oscar winner for best picture *Kramer vs. Kramer,* in which Dustin Hoffman and Meryl Streep played divorcing parents. Both were motivated by their own selfishness, but in the end it was the husband who was redeemed by learning the joys of familyhood and was rewarded with custody of the couple's son.

By the 1990s, divorce was so common that it had lost much of its social stigma and much of its value as scandal. Fans still followed the love lives of the stars, but it took an exceptionally short marriage or brutal breakup to arouse much public interest. Celebrity-watchers felt vindicated when superstar Julia Roberts walked away from unlikely spouse Lyle Lovett after only a few months, and they cheered for beloved icon Carol Channing when she left her forty-one-year marriage at age seventy-seven, citing lack of sex as one of the reasons. Film portrayals tended to show divorce as a positive solution to a bad situation. The 1989 film *The War of the Roses* was a disturbing comedy about violent breakup where neither partner was presented in a positive light, while *The First Wives Club* (1996) was a sort of revenge comedy where the mistreated wives took action against their boorish ex-husbands.

In past centuries, marriage was a pragmatic agreement and the family an economic unit, whether industrial or agricultural. Members each had a unique function and derived stability and protection from their place in the unit, which was most often an extended family comprising elders, adults, and children. Marriage and the creation of a family was part of survival. As American society evolved, the nuclear family replaced the extended family as the major social unit, and its function has more and more become that of emotional support and physical caretaking rather than working together. As partners enter marriage, they have higher expectations of happiness and satisfaction. Some sociologists cite these rising expectations as the reason for rising rates of divorce, while others contend that since marriage and family are no longer a necessity of physical survival, it is natural that couples tend to drift apart.

As divorce becomes more prevalent, the image of the family continues to change. Though political and religious conservatives have tried to restore a more traditional concept of the nuclear family, they have not been able to stop these changes. While many bemoan the ill-effects of divorce on children, most modern studies show that children do not benefit from growing up in a traditional nuclear family where the parents are unhappy together. The definition of family is now broadening to include not only nuclear families, but also unmarried heterosexuals and gays living together, single-parent families, stepfamilies, foster and adoptive families, childlessness, nonmonogamous relationships, and multiple-adult households. Family is not only biological, but also chosen, a complex network of economic support and affection that is no longer easily catalogued. Even Madison Avenue has begun to understand and speak to these changes, as companies such as Hallmark Greeting Cards and John Hancock Insurance develop advertising campaigns directed at the families of divorce and other nontraditional units. A Rite-Aid Drug ad, first screened in 1998, shows two girls helping their mother get ready for her first (postdivorce) date, while a 1991 MCI Communications ad shows a workaholic father sadly explaining how his personal toll-free number helps him keep in touch with the son who now lives with his mother far away. These images show how the reality of divorce has been incorporated into American culture, and, indeed, culture worldwide.

—Tina Gianoulis

FURTHER READING:

Basch, Norma. *Framing American Divorce: From the Revoltionary Generation to the Victorians.* Berkeley, University of California Press, 1999.

Chused, Richard H. *Private Acts in Public Places: A Social History of Divorce in the Formative Era of American Family Law.* Philadelphia, University of Pennsylvania Press, 1994.

DiFonzo, J. Herbie. *Beneath the Fault Line: The Popular and Legal Culture of Divorce in Twentieth-Century America.* Charlottesville, University Press of Virginia, 1997.

Ganong, Lawrence H. *Changing Families, Changing Responsibilities: Family Obligations following Divorce and Remarriage.* Mahwah, New Jersey, Lawrence Erlbaum Associates, 1999.

May, Elaine Tyler. *Great Expectations: Marriage and Divorce in Post-Victorian America.* Chicago, University of Chicago Press, 1980.

Phillips, Roderick. *Putting Asunder: A History of Divorce in Western Society.* Cambridge, Cambridge University Press, 1988.

Riley, Glenda. *Divorce: An American Tradition.* New York, Oxford University Press, 1991.

Talbot, Margaret. ''Love, American Style: What the Alarmists about Divorce Don't Get about Idealism in America.'' *The New Republic.* April 14, 1997, 30.

Dixieland

Dixieland jazz is a style that blends New Orleans jazz and classic jazz—also called ''Chicago jazz''—of the 1920s. The music is generally thought of as a collective improvisation during the choruses, with individual solos that include riffing by the horns, and a two- to four-bar call and response tag game between the drummer and the full group at the closing of the song. While almost any song can be played in the dixieland style, the music is most often associated with about forty songs, including ''That's a Plenty'' and ''Tin Roof Blues.'' Most dixieland bands are comprised of a trumpet or cornet, a harmonizing trombone, a clarinet, and a piano, string bass, or tuba. Occasionally a guitar or banjo is also included. The style has enjoyed many revivals throughout the years and ''dixieland'' has become a blanket term for the earliest blending of New Orleans and Chicago jazz between 1917 and 1923, as well as the many revivals of the style.

Despite the wide use of the term, some confine the definition of dixieland jazz to New Orleans music played by white New Orleans performers or in their style. Others limit the definition to the earliest white players in Chicago. Some of the most important albums of the dixieland style include Louis Armstrong's 1927 *Hot Fives and Sevens, Vol. 3,* Eddie Condon's 1939 *Dixieland All-Stars,* Kid Ory's Creole Jazz Band's 1955 *Legendary Kid,* and Pete Fountain's 1965 *Standing Room Only.*

Despite the controversy surrounding how the term should be used, many musicians have been labeled and identified as playing dixieland music. The white Chicago musicians usually included as dixieland musicians are Jimmy McPartland, Bud Freeman, and Frank Teschemacher. These musicians first heard the white New Orleans bands of the 1920s associated with Nick LaRocca in the Original Dixieland Jass (later Jazz) Band which began recording in 1917, and with Paul Mares in the New Orleans Rhythm Kings (originally the Friar's Society Orchestra), which recorded between 1922 and 1923. This ''white'' style had a great influence on the development of jazz and was not too far removed from the style of the great black pioneers. White New Orleans bands and their dixieland followers drew less on ragtime and ethnic African sources than did the black pioneers. They also drew quite heavily on European sources. One of the most inspirational musicians of the dixieland sound of the 1920s was Louis Armstrong, who noted opera as a strong influence on his style.

The popularization of jazz beyond the New Orleans area and the development of dixieland can be traced to the U.S. Navy's 1917 closure of the Storyville base near New Orleans' red light district. The closure put many musicians out of work. Seeking work, musicians relocated to Chicago, Illinois. Joe ''King'' Oliver was the hottest cornetist in New Orleans in 1917 and by 1918 he had moved to Chicago. Jelly Roll Morton, jazz's first noted composer and innovative pianist, had moved to Chicago at the turn of the century. Many of New Orleans' best musicians followed and played for a time in Chicago. Others moved elsewhere: from 1919-1924 Kid Ory worked in Los Angeles and Sidney Bechet, the fine clarinetist and soprano saxophonist, played in London. As the musicians moved, the music they played changed and dixieland became a discernable style.

The carefree style of dixieland music soon lost favor to swing, especially after the stock market crash in 1929, but it did not disappear. From 1945 through 1960 dixieland actually became one of the more popular forms of jazz. The revival of dixieland in the 1940s can be traced to Lu Watters' Yerba Buena Jazz Band out of San Francisco. Much of the music was based on King Oliver's Creole Jazz Band, but Watters' developed his own style, sometimes called San Francisco Jazz. Eddie Condon was also influential in the revival of dixieland; he featured a dixieland band on his weekly half-hour radio broadcast *Town Hall Concerts* from 1944 to 1945 and led a band at his Chicago nightclub for a few decades. And though there were many styles of jazz at the time, Louis Armstrong disbanded his big band in 1947 and led his All-Stars as a dixieland style sextet for the rest of his career. Despite the overwhelming popularity of rock 'n' roll after the 1950s, Armstrong proved dixieland's lasting appeal in 1964 with the success of his ''Hello Dolly.''

The success of the dixieland style in the mid-1940s ignited the release of a flurry of hasty and uninspired imitations of the music. By the 1950s dixieland was often associated with the embarrassingly garish groups who played amateurishly and donned straw hats and wore vintage clothing. Nevertheless, serious and competent musicians still played dixieland music. In 1974 the first Sacramento Dixieland Jubilee was held, the success of which inspired other such events. By the end of the twentieth century, jazz festivals that feature dixieland along with other styles could be found throughout the year and many record labels such as Stomp Off, GHB, and Jazzology continued to release dixieland music. Many of the greatest players and innovators of dixieland are dead, but younger musicians like Winston Marsalis and Jim Cullum continue to incorporate the dixieland style into their music.

—Frank A. Salamone

FURTHER READING:

Condon, Eddie, and Thomas Sugrue. *We Called It Music.* New York, Da Capo Press, 1947.

Deffaa, Chip. *Voices of the Jazz Age: Profiles of Eight Vintage Jazzmen.* Urbana, University of Illinois Press, 1990.

Gottlieb, Bill. "Dixieland Nowhere, Says Dave Tough." *Down Beat.* September 23, 1946.

Griffiths, David. *Hot Jazz: From Harlem to Storyville.* Lanham, Maryland, Scarecrow Press, 1998.

Hadlock, Richard. *Jazz Masters of the Twenties.* 1965. Reprint, with new introduction by author, New York, Da Capo, 1988.

Hennessey, Thomas J. *From Jazz to Swing: Afro-American Jazz Musicians and Their Music, 1890-1935.* Detroit, Wayne State University Press, 1994.

Schuller, Gunther. *Early Jazz: Its Roots and Musical Development.* 1968. Reprint, New York, Oxford University Press, 1986.

Wilber, Bob, and Derek Webster. *Music Was Not Enough.* New York, Oxford University Press, 1987.

Do the Right Thing

As many film scholars have noted, the Hollywood film industry's construction of race has been problematic, reflecting the racial divisions of the wider culture. While whites have been considered as representing the "norm," people of color have been rendered invisible, stereotyped, and denigrated in every decade and in every genre. A major shift occurred in the 1980s, when an unprecedented number of studio-backed films written and directed by African-American filmmakers were released. This movement was led by Spike Lee, whose arthouse success, *She's Gotta Have It,* opened doors previously closed to black filmmakers. Able to control the images presented, Lee and the African-American directors who followed brought to the screen issues and concerns so often ignored by Hollywood. One such film, *Do the Right Thing,* written and directed by Lee and released in 1989, is a postmodern masterpiece and a controversial film about issues of race, gender, class, and politics.

The film is set in the predominantly African-American neighborhood of Bedford Stuyvesant, located in Brooklyn, New York. It covers twenty-four hours of the hottest day of the year, which is communicated well by the award winning cinematography of Ernest Dickerson, with its use of highly saturated reds and orange. Featuring an ensemble cast—Ossie Davis, Ruby Dee, Giancarlo Esposito, Rosie Perez, Danny Aiello, John Turturro, Bill Nunn, Robin Harris, Roger Guenveur Smith, and Lee himself—the film presents a tense atmosphere of varied characters with differing political outlooks. Full of numerous confrontations, the main conflict concerns the decor of

the local pizzeria, Sal's, owned by an Italian American. Buggin Out, who wants the "wall of fame" to display pictures of African Americans rather than Italian Americans, tries to organize the community in a boycott. Incensed, he enters the pizzeria with Radio Raheem, who carries with him a portable stereo blaring the anthem "Fight the Power" by hip hop artists Public Enemy. Radio Raheem engages in a physical dispute with Sal and, in the midst of the struggle, is killed by a policeman's stranglehold. A riot ensues and Sal's Pizzeria is burned to the ground.

As noted above, the film created a controversy in both critical and popular circles. What is the right thing? Does the film advocate violence? Some panned the film because it did not make use of well-rounded, complex characters, did not support productive collective action, and presented less-than-positive images of women. Yet the film brought forth a dialogue about one of the most ingrained aspects of American culture—racism. It presents the issue as complex and multi-faceted, while at the same time questioning the ideologies represented by the numerous characters.

—Frances Gateward

FURTHER READING:

Lee, Spike, Lisa Jones, and David Lee. *Do the Right Thing: The New Spike Lee Joint.* New York, Simon & Schuster, 1989.

Reid, Mark, editor. *Spike Lee's "Do the Right Thing."* Cambridge, Cambridge University Press, 1997.

Dobie Gillis

The Many Loves of Dobie Gillis is a classic sitcom of the late 1950s. If on the surface the show seems unassuming and standard early sitcom fare, just below the surface is a show that breaks new ground in television. Two significant aspects set it apart from the other shows of that era and make it watchable and influential well into the 1990s. First is the show's focus on teenagers. Second is the addition of a new type of character in the form of Maynard G. Krebs, the outsider.

Dobie Gillis is a teenager in small-town America; the plot revolves around Dobie's life and thoughts. In the course of the show Dobie graduates from high school, briefly joins the army, and returns to the same town to attend college. The show was adapted from Max Shulman's short stories of the 1930s and was updated for the teenagers of the 1950s. It premiered in September of 1959 and ran until 1963. The main characters were Dobie Gillis (Dwayne Hickman), the forever-girl-chasing and money-short lead; his best friend and side-kick Maynard (Bob Denver) the cool jazz beatnik; Dobie's hard-working father Herbert T. Gillis (Frank Faylen); and Zelda Gilroy (Sheila James), who was determined to marry Dobie one day.

Before Dobie there had been teenagers in television shows but always in secondary roles and usually within the confines of a very structured family—e.g., *The Adventures of Ozzie and Harriet* and *Father Knows Best.* While there were occasional episodes dealing with teenage issues, they were usually reserved for comic relief or family homilies. *Dobie Gillis* offered an entirely different way of viewing the subject. Although most of the stories deal with the basic trials and tribulations of teenage life—getting a date, getting money, and getting out of work—they are taken seriously; each show starts and ends with Dobie speaking to us from a pose near a replica of the

A publicity shot for *The Many Loves of Dobie Gillis*.

Rodin sculpture known as "The Thinker." In this way, we are told that the problems of money, girls, and work are important to the youth.

Dobie's world includes several recurring characters who provide the basic themes for the show. His father runs the Gillis Grocery Store and cannot understand his son (he continually tries to instill in him the need for hard work), while his mother (Florida Friebus) attempts to mediate between father and son. In the beginning of the series Tuesday Weld plays Thalia Meninger, Dobie's dream girl whom he hesitates to pursue because he does not have money. As one might expect, there are several rivals who do have money—Milton Armitage (Warren Beatty), followed by Chatsworth Osborne Jr. (Stephen Franken). It is their presence that generates many of the show's conflicts.

As the series unfolds a more striking character also takes form, that of Maynard. Maynard is the classical beatnik: he has the goatee, the ripped sweatshirt, the love of jazz, and the "like" vocabulary. He seems out of place in this little town, and that is the point. Maynard (played by Bob Denver, later of *Gilligan's Island*) is Dobie's "good buddy" and he is loyal to him to the end. While Dobie dreams of money so that he can get the girls, Maynard has no need for either. His mannerisms and clothes make him stand out from everyone, and his simple ways and shuddering at the thought of work seem to hold him apart from the suburban dream. Maynard sets a standard for every other outsider with a message in shows to come.

Despite the concentration on themes of money and dating, or perhaps because of it, the show occasionally slides into uncharted areas. Dobie tends to think and speak about life in terms of big questions or, more accurately, he tends to make whatever he is thinking about seem big. Dobie, like many teenagers, is in search of many things, including an understanding of himself and the world in which he lives.

The impact of this show extends far beyond the 1950s. Shows that centered on teens and tried to gather the baby-boomer-market would be a staple from the 1960s on. The outsider beatnik character could easily metamorphose into to the hippie of the 1960s or even to "The Fonz" of *Happy Days*. Dobie has since resurfaced in two sequels; a 30-minute pilot for a revival of the show in 1977 named *What Ever happened to Dobie Gillis?,* and a reunion movie in 1988 called *Bring Me the Head of Dobie Gillis.*

—Frank E. Clark

FURTHER READING:

Denver, Bob. *Gilligan, Maynard & Me.* New York, Citadel Press, 1993.

Hickman, Dwayne, and Joan Roberts Hickman. *Forever Dobie: The Many Lives of Dwayne Hickman.* New York, Birch Lane Press, 1994.

Marschall, Rick. *The Golden Age of Television.* New York, Bison Books, 1987.

McNeil, Alex. *Total Television: A Comprehensive Guide to Programming from 1948 to the Present.* New York, Penguin Books, 1991.

Putterman, Barry. *On Television and Comedy: Essays on Style, Theme, Performer and Writer.* Jefferson, North Carolina, McFarland, 1995.

Doby, Larry (1923—)

African-American baseball player Larry Doby was an unlikely Civil Rights pioneer. Unlike Major League Baseball's first Black player, Jackie Robinson, Doby was "shy, quiet, and unassuming"; he'd grown up in integrated Patterson, New Jersey, attended predominantly white Long Island University and lived a life far more sheltered from the stings and arrows of racial prejudice than the vast majority of African Americans. Yet it was Doby, even more than Jackie Robinson, whose courage and determination helped transform Major League Baseball into a national pastime for people of all races. In 1947, Doby became the first African-American player in the American League; he was also the first player to jump straight from the Negro Leagues to the majors. He later integrated Japanese baseball in 1962 and went on to become the sport's second Black manager and one of its first African-American executives. However it was in his role as the second Black player in baseball that Doby had his most significant impact on professional athletics. His Major League debut demonstrated to the American public that Jackie Robinson's entrance into white baseball was not a publicity stunt and that Black players were destined to become permanent fixtures in Major League Baseball.

When integration-minded Cleveland Indians owner Bill Veeck sought to sign a Black player in 1947, the Newark Eagle's Doby appeared to be the obvious choice. The twenty-two year old Doby, a former high school football and basketball star, led the Negro National League with a batting average of .458 and thirteen home

Larry Doby

runs. He was the top Black prospect who had not already signed a contract with the Brooklyn Dodgers (After Jackie Robinson's successful debut, the Dodgers had acquired several other talented African Americans for their minor league clubs). Veeck, unlike the Dodgers' general manager Branch Rickey, was determined to integrate his organization from the top down. On July 5, 1947, he purchased Doby's contract from the Eagles for $10,000. Three hours later, he sent the surprised young athlete onto the field as a pinch hitter against the Chicago White Sox. This courageous decision, coming without warning, drew 20,000 letters of protest from irate fans.

Doby's sudden entrance into the majors relieved much of the pressure on the Dodgers' Robinson. Both men faced extraordinary pressures that first season, including open hostility from teammates and opposition players, and they formed a close relationship that endured through their lifetimes. Upon Doby signing, Robinson stated, ''I no longer have the feeling that if I don't make good, it will kill the chances of other Negro players.'' Doby's debut opened the way for three more Blacks to enter the majors within a month and made it clear that baseball was on a permanent course toward integration. His presence on the Indians also contributed to the more general cause of Civil Rights for African Americans when Washington's exclusive

Hotel Statler, formerly whites-only, permitted Doby to room with his team.

After a rough first season in which he batted only .156 in a limited thirty at-bats, Doby found his stride and became one of the game's marquee figures. In 1948, he batted an impressive .301 with 14 homeruns and 65 runs batted in. He led the Indians to a victory over the Boston Braves in the World Series, becoming the first African American to play on a World Series Champion team. He later led the American league in home runs in 1952 and again in 1954. When he retired after thirteen seasons with the Indians, White Sox, and Detroit Tigers, he had a formidable career batting average of .283 and 253 lifetime homeruns. For these achievements, he was elected to Baseball's Hall of Fame in 1998.

Long after Major League baseball had fully integrated, Doby continued to be a pioneer among Black athletes. In 1962, he became one of the first Blacks to play professional baseball in Japan. He returned to the United States and served in several administrative jobs with the Montreal Expos, Indians, and White Sox. He became the Indians' manager in 1978—after Frank Robinson, the second African American ever to manager a Major League club. He later returned to executive duties as a special assistant to Dr. Gene Budig, the President of the America League. Throughout the 1960s and 1970s—when Blacks were welcome on the baseball field and in the stands but not in the front office—Doby continued to push for expanded opportunities for African Americans.

After Jackie Robinson's death, the ''Silk City Slugger'' became a living symbol of the early Civil Rights movement. He is indisputably the most popular player in the history of the Cleveland Indians and, along with later Black stars Willie Mays and Hank Aaron, continues to be one of baseball's chief attractions at special events and Old Timers' games.

—Jacob M. Appel

FURTHER READING:

Boundreau, Lou, with Ed Fitzgerald. *Player-Manager*. Boston, Little Brown, 1952.

Frommer, Harvey. *Rickey and Robinson: The Men Who Broke Baseball's Color Barrier*. New York, Macmillan, 1960.

Moore, Joseph Thomas. *Pride Against Prejudice: The Biography of Larry Doby*. New York, Greenwood Press, 1988.

Tygiel, Jules. *Baseball's Great Experiment*. New York, Oxford, 1997.

Veeck, Bill. *Veeck—As in Wreck: The Autobiography of Bill Veeck*. New York, G. P. Putnam's Sons, 1962

Young, Andrew ''Doc.'' *Great Negro Baseball Stars and How They Made The Major Leagues*. New York, A. S. Barnes, 1953.

Doc Martens

More than just functional footwear, Doc Martens shoes and boots have become a staple among decades of style-conscious subcultures and eventually emerged as a fashion phenomenon. Once synonymous with angry British youth, Doc Martens, like their sturdy leather uppers, have mellowed with age. Bavarian physician Claus Maerten designed the clunky, cushiony, thick-soled boot out of old tires in 1945 after a skiing accident necessitated more comfortable footgear. Bunion-plagued customers became converts until the 1960s, when fascist skinheads appropriated the boots. Rock stars soon followed the trend, and after punk rockers in the 1970s began painting on their own designs, the company came out with wildly colored and patterned models. The brand was a must-have for the young and hip throughout the 1980s, from hip-hop to grunge fans. By the late 1990s, women accounted for seventy percent of the fast-growing market, picking up the pairs at upscale department stores.

—Geri Speace

FURTHER READING:

Morais, Richard C. "What's Up, Doc?" *Forbes.* January 16, 1995, p. 42.

Doc Savage

During the 16-year run of *Doc Savage Magazine,* Clark Savage, Jr. (better known as Doc) was one of the most exciting and popular pulp magazine characters. The appeal of Doc Savage is succinctly stated in the promotional blurb that appears on the back of the Bantam paperback editions that reprint his pulp adventures: "To his fans he is the greatest adventure hero of all time, whose fantastic exploits are unequaled for hair-raising thrills, breathtaking escapes, and bloodcurdling excitement." Doc is a transitional hero who unites the intellect

Ron Ely stands beside a painting of the pulp fiction character Doc Savage, who he played on screen in 1975.

of Sherlock Holmes and the physical prowess of Tarzan with the best gadgets imagined by the new genre of science fiction. In bringing together all of these elements, Doc Savage served as a model for the superheroes that followed.

Doc Savage was the creation of Street and Smith business manager Henry Ralston and editor John Nanovic, who hoped to duplicate the success of the company's first single-character pulp magazine, *The Shadow.* While Ralston and Nanovic created the concept, the characters, and even many of the colorful details, it was a young writer named Lester Dent who brought Doc Savage to life. The house byline used was Kenneth Robeson, and there were six different authors who contributed Doc Savage stories under that byline. Lester Dent, however, wrote the vast majority of the Doc tales and edited, or at least approved, the work of the writers who ghosted for him. It was also Lester Dent, following his "master plot" outline and hammering out his pithy prose, who established the distinctive style of the Doc Savage adventures.

Doc Savage appeared in 181 fantastic pulp magazine adventures from 1933 to 1949. In October of 1964, Bantam Books began paperback reprints of every one of the pulp stories, plus one previously unpublished Doc manuscript by Lester Dent *(The Red Spider).* In 1991 Bantam began publishing original Doc Savage material. *Escape from Loki* was written by long-time Doc aficionado Philip Jose Farmer. Doc Savage fan and scholar Will Murray wrote seven books based on Lester Dent story fragments and outlines. There was a Doc Savage radio show in the 1930s, a Doc Savage movie in the 1970s, another radio show in the 1980s, and Doc Savage comic books from at least six different publishers, but the true Doc Savage adventures are the 182 stories written for the pulps.

Doc Savage is a hero of mythic proportions. Clark Savage, Jr., was born one stormy night aboard a tiny schooner anchored off Andros island in the infamous Bermuda Triangle. Doc dwells far above ordinary humans on the eighty-sixth floor of the Empire State Building. Both his strength and intellect are herculean. At the age of 14 months he began his strenuous and life-long training. Even after Doc reaches adulthood and begins traveling the globe to right wrongs and help the oppressed, he adheres faithfully to a two-hour routine of intensive exercises for his muscles, senses, and mind. Though he excels in virtually every endeavor, Doc displays his most prodigious talent in the practice of medicine. By the time he was 30, Doc Savage was the world's most brilliant surgeon. In fact, he "rehabilitates" criminals using an intricate brain surgery procedure only he has the skill to perform.

When Doc first appears in 1933 he is six feet tall and weighs 200 pounds. In later tales Doc is usually described as somewhat larger— around six feet eight inches and weighing 270 pounds. Yet, his build has such symmetry and proportion that he does not look big unless he is standing next to someone. Beneath his sun-bronzed skin, his muscles are "like cables" or "bundles of piano wire." When he flexes those great muscles he often rips his shirt and coat. His hair is combed straight back and resembles a metal skullcap. Doc's most riveting characteristic is the gently swirling flakes of gold in his eyes. Thanks to the dynamic covers painted by James Bama for the Bantam reprints, a virtual costume was established for Doc. On most paperback covers Doc wore boots, aviator pants, and a very precisely ripped shirt.

The first Doc Savage story, *The Man of Bronze,* establishes that the men who compose Doc's amazing crew are "the five greatest brains to ever assemble in one group." They include: "Long Tom," the frail-looking wizard of electricity who is a wildcat in a fight;

"Renny," a grim-faced giant of a man who likes to smash his huge fists through solid panel doors and is the greatest engineering expert of his time; the tall, gaunt, bespectacled Johnny, with his bulging forehead and big words, who is one of the world's foremost experts on geology and archaeology; "Ham," who is a dapper clothes horse and possibly the greatest lawyer Harvard has ever produced; and the most remarkable of Doc's companions "Monk," a short, barrel-chested man whose knuckles nearly drag the ground. Although he looks like a red-haired ape pretending to be a man, he is one of the world's top chemists. Monk, however, would much rather work with his fists than with test tubes. The frontispiece of the Bantam paperbacks gives this characterization of the men who joined Doc Savage in his work: "Together with their leader, they would go anywhere, fight anyone, dare everything—seeking excitement and perilous adventure."

Although Doc Savage is a relatively minor fictional character, he has influenced some major popular culture icons. Superman is the most obvious "descendent" of Doc. In fact, in the stories themselves and in the advertisements for the magazine, Doc was often referred to as a "superman." In addition to sharing the first name Clark, both heroes have a Fortress of Solitude somewhere in the arctic. Both also have female cousins that look like them, have their powers, and want to horn in on their adventures. Doc was known as the Man of Bronze, and Superman is known as the Man of Steel. Doc's connection to Batman is less obvious, but more fundamental. Both heroes are "self-made supermen" who, beginning in childhood, devoted themselves to intense training. Both have considerable scientific know-how, as evidenced by Doc's utility vest and Batman's very similar utility belt. It is even possible that the batmobile is patterned after Doc's bulletproof and gadget-filled sedan.

—Randy Duncan

FURTHER READING:

Cannaday, Marilyn. *Bigger Than Life: The Creator of Doc Savage.* Bowling Green, Ohio, Bowling Green State University Popular Press, 1990.

Farmer, Philip Jose. *Doc Savage: His Apocalyptic Life.* New York, Playboy Paperbacks, 1973.

Murray, Will. *Secrets of Doc Savage.* Odyssey Publications, 1981.

Doctor Who

Doctor Who is the world's longest continually produced science fiction serial. It aired on the British BBC network from 1963 until 1989, and was revived briefly as a television movie in 1996. In the United States, *Doctor Who* first began broadcasts on independent channels in 1972, and was still broadcasting on some local PBS affiliates in the late 1990s. It has, like *Star Trek*, engendered movies, radio dramas, lucrative novel series, non-fiction, comic books, and an extensive home video market.

Doctor Who revolves around the adventures of the mysterious time-traveling title character, simply known throughout as The Doctor. The Doctor, as first seen in the 1963 pilot episode, broadcast in the midst of the BBC's coverage of the Kennedy Assassination, is outwardly human. William Hartnell, the actor to first portray the Doctor (1963-1966), presented audiences with a cranky old man who

had a gross lack of basic human kindness. Initially, the Doctor was accompanied on his travels through time and space by his grand-daughter and her human school teachers. In the serial's second episode, he seemed to encourage his companion to kill an incapacitated caveman. Later, his selfish, obsessive desire to learn placed him and his companions in danger when they met the alien Daleks. The character began to soften his edges as he was exposed to the ideals and attitudes of his human companions. His scientific curiosity and towering ego remain, but his ego became tempered with an increasing respect for his companions and the races that he encountered.

When Hartnell became too ill to continue the role, the producers came up with the ingenious idea of having the character "regenerate" into a new body with a new personality. Since 1966, the Doctor has been played by seven more actors: Patrick Troughton (1966-1970), Jon Pertwee (1970-1974), Tom Baker (1974-1981), Peter Davison (1981-1983), Colin Baker (1983-1986), Sylvester McCoy (1986-1989), and Paul McGann (1996). Richard Hurndall also played the role of the First Doctor in place of the late William Hartnell in the 1983 anniversary serial "The Five Doctors." This change in the lead actor (and usually in the rest of the cast and the production teams) allowed the show to adapt to and change with the times. Hartnell's serials began originally as a children's program, but by the late 1970s Tom Baker's serials were also targeted towards the science fiction aficionado. Low ratings and lack of support from the BBC (it went on an 18 month hiatus in the middle of Colin Baker's tenure) soon saw the serial descending into self-parody. Towards the end it began to recover some of its ground, but in 1989 it was taken off the air, though never officially canceled. The 1996 television movie was co-produced by the BBC and the FOX Network in the United States at a sum of $5 million (an unusual amount for such a production), but it did not achieve great ratings. There are constant rumors among fans of another revival; meanwhile the serial continues in original novels published first by Virgin Books and later by BBC Books.

Two theatrical movies were made in the 1960s, based on the scripts of two of the television serials, *Doctor Who and the Daleks* (1965) and *Daleks—Invasion Earth, 2150 A.D.* (1966), starring Peter Cushing as the Doctor. In the television serial, it was the popularity of the Daleks, created by writer Terry Nation and a BBC special effects wizard, that propelled the Doctor to instant stardom in the United Kingdom. It was not until the first Tom Baker serials began broadcasting in the United States, however, that the show earned anything more than an American cult audience. The Doctor has since earned cameos in episodes of *The Simpsons,* and cancellation of the serial usually results in a PBS station being inundated with masses of fan mail.

Like *Star Trek,* the fans of *Doctor Who* run major conventions every year which are attended in the thousands by fans sporting scarves and cricket jackets. Instantly recognizable at these conventions is the Doctor's unique TARDIS—an acronym for Time and Relative Dimension in Space. On the outside it resembles a battered London police call box. Inside, however, it is, in reality, a large ship, its cavernous interior seemingly endless. The Doctor and his fans also have a strong presence on the Internet, where hints of new television projects compete for attention with spoilers of the novel plots.

Icons of the show include the pepperpot shaped Daleks, and the silver enshrouded Cybermen. Also earning a place in history was the show's electronic theme music, which evolved over the years but still retained an eerie hint of the otherworldly. On the whole, the show was a hodge-podge of what is good and bad about long-running serial television: devoted audiences, a long history, and very bad continuity.

The video market ensures that the show is introduced to new audiences and that it has a life beyond its original television run.

—John J. Doherty

FURTHER READING:

Howe, David J., and Stephen James Walker. *Doctor Who: The Television Companion.* London, BBC Books, 1998.

Tulloch, John, and Manuel Alvarado. *Doctor Who: The Unfolding Text.* New York, St. Martin's, 1983.

Doctor Zhivago

This only novel by the famed Russian poet Boris Pasternak received the 1958 Nobel Prize for literature. The story traces the experiences of a Moscow doctor, Yuri Zhivago, during the Russian Revolution of 1917 and the ensuing civil war from 1918 to 1921. Zhivago's independence, religious convictions, and conflict with the Soviet regime were considered too controversial for publication by the editors of the leading Soviet literary journal, *Novy Mir,* to which Pasternak had submitted his work, despite the fact that the Soviet Union was experiencing greater openness following the death of dictator Joseph Stalin in 1953. Pasternak had the manuscript smuggled out of the Soviet Union in late 1956, and it was first published in Italy in November 1957. The book was translated into more than twenty languages in the next two years and became an international best-seller. A 1965 film adaptation of the book, directed by David Lean, received five Academy Award nominations.

—Jason George

FURTHER READING:

Fleishman, Lazar. *Boris Pasternak: The Poet and His Politics.* Cambridge, Harvard University Press, 1990.

Hingley, Ronald. *Pasternak: A Biography.* New York, Alfred A. Knopf, 1983.

Pasternak, Boris. *Doctor Zhivago.* New York, Pantheon Books, 1991.

Doctorow, E. L. (1931—)

As Matthew Henry noted in *Critique,* "E.L. Doctorow has made a career out of historical fiction, and he is renowned for both examining and rewriting the American past . . . because for Doctorow there is no fact or fiction, only narrative." In his attempt to examine the cultural myths of America and their impact on society, E.L. Doctorow created some of the most noted works of postmodern historical fiction of the late twentieth century through his unique ability to weave documented historical facts and figures with invented ones. As Henry noted, this brand of historical fiction allowed Doctorow to present different histories, not only those accepted by consensus. Doctorow's approach to history and his style of writing mark him as one of the significant contributors to the postmodern literary movement.

Edgar Laurence Doctorow was born in 1931 in New York City, the setting of many of his novels. Doctorow began his writing career

E. L. Doctorow

within a decade after graduating from Kenyon College in 1952. His first three novels were experiments with different fiction genres. The first novel, *Welcome to Hard Times,* was a western and focused on the common theme of man's relationship to evil. *Big as Life,* Doctorow's second novel, was a science fiction work about two giants materializing in New York City. Yet, it was not until Doctorow experimented with the historical form in his third novel, *The Book of Daniel,* that he achieved commercial and critical success. It was here, in Doctorow's account of Julius and Ethel Rosenberg and their children, where he first experimented with what would later be called postmodern historical fiction—historical facts blended with contemporary fiction styles and elements.

Doctorow's postmodern historical fiction approached the writing of history as a reconstitution of history. Unlike the many historical fiction writers before him, he did not attempt to present history as fact. As he did with the Rosenbergs in *The Book of Daniel,* Doctorow's interweaving of historical facts and figures with fictional ones was best done in his fourth novel, *Ragtime.* This novel intertwined the lives of many famous historical figures, such as Harry Houdini, Henry Ford, and Emma Goldman, with three fictional families—an upper class white family, a poor immigrant family, and a ragtime black musician's family. By mixing history with fiction, Doctorow confused and, to a degree, falsified history as he investigated the myths and realities of the American dream in *Ragtime,* a theme that reappears in his next novel, *Loon Lake.*

It is Doctorow's approach to history and writing style that make his novels postmodern. Just as Toni Morrison did in her novel *Jazz,* Doctorow used the combination of the repetition and improvisation in music to create a relentless narrative prose style in *Ragtime,* a style that would continue in his following novels. What at first may look like out of control prose became finely crafted prose that worked on multiple levels of meaning and interpretation, what Andrew Delbanco called more associative than sequential and what Michelle Tokarczyk called "accessible experimentation." Doctorow experimented with syntactical structures as well as point of view and voice, so there were many instances in his novels where it was difficult to ascertain who was saying what to whom, where the narrative did not instantly reveal itself. This postmodern language play added to the historical reconstructions, sometimes labeled allegorical romances, of twentieth-century American life as it occurred in Doctorow's novels.

In addition to writing novels, in the 1990s Doctorow has used his position in American society to take on many social issues. Citing what he called a "gangsterdom of the spirit," Doctorow believed American life near the end of the twentieth century was suffering from a loss of cohesion and morality. Some of his social projects of the 1990s include the saving of Walden Woods in Massachusetts, developing a cable television channel dedicated to books, peacefully settling the American conflict with Iraq, and analyzing the presidencies of Ronald Reagan and Bill Clinton.

—Randall McClure

FURTHER READING:

Delbanco, Andrew. "Necropolis News—The Waterworks by E.L. Doctorow." *The New Republic.* July 18, 1994, 44.

Doctorow, E. L. *Big as Life.* New York, Simon and Schuster, 1966.

———. *The Book of Daniel.* New York, Random House, 1971.

———. "A Gangstersterdom of the Spirit." *The Nation.* October 2, 1989, 348-354.

———. *Loon Lake.* New York, Random House, 1980.

———. *Ragtime.* New York, Random House, 1975.

———. *The Waterworks.* New York, Random House, 1994.

———. *Welcome to Hard Times.* New York, Simon and Schuster, 1960.

Fowler, Douglas. *Understanding E.L. Doctorow.* Columbia, University of South Carolina Press, 1992.

Henry, Matthew A. "Problematized Narratives: History as Fiction in E.L. Doctorow's Billy Bathgate." *Critique.* Fall 1997, 32-40.

Tokarczyk, Michelle. *E.L. Doctorow: An Annotated Bibliography.* New York, Garland Publishing, 1988.

———. "The Waterworks." *Literary Review.* Spring 1996, 435.

Docudrama

Docudrama is a film genre which is found primarily, but not exclusively, on television. *Brian's Song* (1970)—the story of the tragic death of football player Brian Piccolo—was the first notable U.S. example. The success of *Brian's Song* proved to the television networks that the made-for-television, reality-based telefilm could be both a critical and popular success. However, the docudrama has been a controversial form in North America because of its apparently cavalier mixture of truth and fiction, drama and documentary—a case of blurred boundaries which unsettles some viewers and critics. The genre has had at least a dozen names and several uncomplimentary epithets applied to it: drama-documentary, dramatized documentary, dramadoc, faction, infotainment, reconstruction, historical drama, biographical drama, historical romance, thesis drama, problem play, and "based-on-fact."

For many of those who do not like the form, the television docudrama is a cheap replacement for the more distinguished Hollywood social-issue picture. But docudramas have been extremely popular with audiences (and hence advertisers), and cheaper to make than theatrical feature films. Because the majority of them are based on some well-known recent event, they require much less in the way of promotion since the audience already knows at least part of the story. The turnaround time (the time between a public event and the film based on it) for such films has become incredibly brief; the most infamous example was the filming of the story about the violent deaths of several FBI agents and members of a religious cult in Waco, Texas, while those tragic events were still unfolding (*In the Line of Duty: Ambush in Waco,* 1993).

Until very recently, the docudrama has generally been considered a hybrid form, caught somewhere between documentary and drama, often doing justice to neither. Film and television critics have tried to define its conventions with mixed success since the seventies. Andrew Goodwin and Paul Kerr, authors of the *BFI Drama-Documentary Dossier,* even claim that it is impossible to define the genre, arguing that such failure is a result of "the break up of consensual views of social reality" in a postmodern world. For these critics and others the mixture of fact and fiction leads to the creation of a "hyperreality" where audiences can no longer make the distinction between truth and fiction—with the result that history, as told by the media, tends to become reality itself. Steven Spielberg's *Schindler's List* (1993) is often cited as a prime example since the only information that many people around the world have about the Holocaust comes from the film, known for its fictionalizing of "the truth."

Critic Derek Paget has argued that the docudrama has been around long enough to be considered a genre in itself with well established conventions. He traces the U.S. history of the form from early documentary-like television anthology programs like *Armstrong Circle Theatre* or *Kraft Television Theatre,* through a second phase of made-for-TV movies like *Brian's Song* or *Roots* (1977), and finally to a more controversial type of "trauma drama" which has been largely influenced by tabloid television with stories based upon well-known scandals such as the Amy Fischer "Long Island Lolita" attempted murder, *Amy Fisher: My Story* (1992) and *The Amy Fisher Story* (1993), or the O.J. Simpson murder trial, *The O.J. Simpson Story* and *The Trial of O.J. Simpson* (both 1995).

Critical quibbling aside, the docudrama is one of the most popular and lucrative genres in North America, perhaps because it blurs the boundaries between reality and fiction and in the process draws attention to the media's manipulation of "fact." One need only think of the battles fought in the United States over docudramas like Oliver Stone's *JFK* (1991) or *Nixon* (1995) to see the heat which docudrama has generated. The docudrama has become a culturally important form which is the site of political battles over the nature of "truth," "reality," and the tabloidization of everyday life.

—Jeannette Sloniowski

FURTHER READING:

Breitbart, Eric. "From the Panorama to the Docudrama: Notes on the Visualization of History." *Radical History Review.* Vol. 25, 1981, 115-25.

Brode, Douglas. "Video Verite: Defining the Docudrama." *Television Quarterly.* Vol. 20, No. 4, 1984, 7-21.

Carveth, Rod. "Amy Fisher and the Ethics of 'Headline'; Docudramas." *Journal of Popular Film and Television.* Vol. 21, No. 3, 1993.

Corner, John. *The Art of Record: A Critical Introduction to Documentary.* Manchester, Manchester University Press, 1996.

Edgerton, Gary. "High Concept Small Screen: Reperceiving the Industrial and Stylistic Origins of the American Made-for-TV Movie." *Journal of Popular Film and Television.* Vol. 19, No. 3, 1991, 114-27.

Gomery, Douglas. "Brian's Song: Television, Hollywood, and the Evolution of the Movie Made for Television." In *American History, American Television: Interpreting the Video Past,* edited by John O'Connor. New York, Ungar, 1983.

Goodwin, Andrew, Paul Kerr, and Ian Macdonald, editors. *BFI Dossier #19: Drama-Documentary.* London, BFI, 1983.

Hartley, John. *Tele-ology: Studies in Television.* London, Routledge, 1992.

Hoffer, Thomas, and Richard Alan Nelson. "The Evolution of Docudrama on American Television Networks: A Content Analysis, 1966-1978." *Southern Speech Communication Journal.* Vol. 45, Winter 1980, 149-63.

Kerr, Paul. "F for Fake? Friction over Faction." In *Understanding Television,* edited by Andrew Goodwin and Gary Whannel. London, Routledge, 1990.

Margulies, Lee. "Academy of Television Arts & Sciences Docu-Drama Symposium." *Emmy: The Magazine of the American Academy of Arts & Sciences.* Summer 1979, D2-D40.

Paget, Derek. *No Other Way to Tell It: Dramadoc/Documentary Drama on Television.* Manchester, Manchester University Press, 1998.

Petley, Julian. "Fact Plus Fiction Equals Friction." *Media, Culture and Society.* Vol. 18, No. 1, 1996, 11-25.

Rapping, Elaine. *The Movie of the Week: Private Stories, Public Events.* Minneapolis, University of Minnesota Press, 1992.

Rosenthal, Allen, editor. *Why Docudrama? Fact-Fiction on Film and TV.* Carbondale, Southern Illinois University Press, 1998.

Do-It-Yourself Improvement

The term "do-it-yourself" applies in its broadest sense to a range of tasks, usually domestic projects of repair or improvement, completed by individuals who are amateurs in the field. Instead of hiring professional contractors, many homeowners enjoy the challenge of learning new skills, adapting individual styles, and incorporating materials and techniques from local sources to beautify and improve their homes. The high degree of personal satisfaction, not to mention cost-of-labor savings, provide substantial incentives to many do-it-yourselfers. Many view the work they do on their homes as a hobby, and do-it-yourselfers can now learn and master home improvement methods and techniques from an enormous variety of books, television shows, and mulitimedia computer programs.

Though people had relied on manual skills before industrialization, personal skills and expertise gave way to organized labor and specialized craftsmanship by the early nineteenth century when early industrialization and the infusion of power-driven machinery created a revolution in manufacture. Items which had been hand-crafted and individually created could now be produced by machine automation. The novelty of mass production generated a craze in the purchase of prefabricated goods. By the 1950s in America, mass production had spread to home building, as evidenced by the first neighborhood tract homes.

People have turned to hand-crafting in times of hardship such as the Great Depression and World War II when there were shortages of building materials and sundry items. Shortages fostered the development of independent home improvement solutions ranging from construction using found materials to the brewing of homemade beer. Propaganda during war time also encouraged individual thrift and problem-solving as important contributions to the war effort. In addition, following the Allied victory, many people returned home with new skills gained through military service and focussed on rebuilding their homes and families. Do-it-yourself home building kits were available in America as early as the late 1940s.

But during the prosperity of the 1950s, home improvement was enjoyed as a family hobby and social activity among neighbors. By the 1960s, young homeowners began home-crafting and personalized home improvement less as a hobby and more as a statement of individuality. While rebelling against what was generally called "the establishment," young people saw opportunities in home industry which provided an avenue of freedom from commercial and industrial ventures. Homemade items from clothing to bread to wall-hangings and interior decorations enjoyed popularity throughout the 1960s and 1970s.

Interest in homemade items waned in the 1980s as Americans returned to more conservative politics, but the spirit of being able to "do-it-yourself" continued not only among first-time home-buyers, who were principally interested in savings (not to mention putting a personal "stamp" on their new homes), but also among the wealthy who continued the trend in home improvement as a personal hobby. Many chose to develop home improvement projects themselves not because politics or economics dictated that they do so, but out of the personal satisfaction derived from individual achievement. A weekend painting project, for example, provided the opportunity to enhance one's self-esteem as well as reduce stress. People who do-it-themselves tend to see themselves as competent, capable, and goal-oriented.

In this light many women increased their involvement in home improvement activities throughout the 1990s, taking on plumbing, minor carpentry, and mechanical repair jobs which were previously considered to be a man's job. In this way women have been able to express their self-confidence and ability in ways which had previously been discouraged.

By the end of the twentieth century, do-it-yourself projects were supported by a growing network of home improvement stores. With vast inventories and knowledgeable salespeople providing instruction, stores like the Home Depot, HomeBase, and Lowe's Improvement Warehouse helped people finish their own projects.

—Ethan Hay

FURTHER READING:

Consumer's Guide, editors. *Do-It-Yourself and Save Money!* New York, Harper & Rowe, 1980.

Family Handyman Magazine, editors. *The Family Handyman Home Improvement Book.* New York, Scribner, 1973.

Gladstone, Bernard. *The Simon and Schuster Complete Guide to Home Repair and Maintenance.* New York, Simon and Schuster, 1984.

Price, Bernard. *Do-It-Yourself Projects from Attic to Basement.* New York, Rodale Press/Popular Science Books, 1986.

Reader's Digest, editors. *New Fix-It-Yourself Manual.* Pleasantville, New York, Reader's Digest Association, 1996.

Roberts, Jason, editor. *The Learn 2 Guide: How to Do Almost Anything.* New York, Villard, 1998.

Schultz, Morton. *Fix It Yourself for Less.* Yonkers, New York, Consumer Reports Books, 1992.

Tompkins, Susie. *I Can Fix That: A Guide for Women Who Want to Do It Themselves.* Toronto/New York, Harlequin Books, 1996.

Vivian, John, editor. *Living On Less.* Arden, North Carolina, Mother Earth News, 1997.

Domino, Fats (1928—)

The music of Fats Domino embodies the spirit of early rock and roll. His work reveals the links between rock and roll, rhythm and blues, and the black Southern singers of the early twentieth century. His music was recorded by most of the rock artists of the 1950s, who recognized his significant contribution to establishing the rock and roll sound, and he is acknowledged as a pioneer in leading the way across the racial barriers of the music industry. With more than 65 million record sales, Domino was second only to Elvis Presley in popularity during the 1950s, and is credited with bringing mass attention to the New Orleans sound, inspiring many other Southern black singers to record for white audiences.

Domino's New Orleans style of piano playing is a combination of traditional jazz, Latin rhythms, blues, Cajun, and boogie woogie that reflects that city's rich heritage of cultural amalgamation. From the mid-1940s through the early 1950s he was an established rhythm and blues recording artist who had successfully toured the nation, but his pounding playing style made him well suited to crossover into the emerging rock format. Domino's greatest popularity arrived in 1955 with the release of "Ain't That a Shame," which became an early rock hit, and although his career began to fade somewhat in the 1960s, he continued to tour and record into the 1990s.

The man considered the most famous New Orleans-born musician since Louis Armstrong was born Antoine Domino, one of a large family, on February 26, 1928. He developed an early interest in music, began playing the piano at age nine, and was performing publicly at local honky-tonks a year later. He quit school at 14 and took a job at a bedspring factory so that his nights would be free to play the area bars and clubs. A large young man, at this time he acquired the nickname "Fats" from bandleader Bill Diamond. The entertainer was spotted in 1949 by trumpeter Dave Bartholomew and Lew Chudd of Imperial Records, who soon signed him to a recording contract. His first hit song, "The Fat Man," sold more than a million

Fats Domino

copies. Domino formed an especially close professional relationship with Bartholomew, and the pair co-wrote, arranged, and produced most of the singer's material for the next two decades. Among his hits of this period are "Goin' Home," "Goin' to the River," and "Every Night about This Time."

Domino's rollicking piano playing allowed him to cross onto the pop charts in the mid-1950s, the time when young white audiences were discovering rock and roll. However, white artists were also covering his initial pop records—Teresa Brewer recorded "Bo Weevil" and Pat Boone's mild version of "Ain't That a Shame" sold even more copies than Domino's own—but he broke into the pop Top Ten himself with the release of "I'm in Love Again." Fats Domino became a national sensation and was one of the first black recording stars to prove that he could appeal to white listeners. He proceeded to enjoy a string of major hits from 1955 to 1960, of which the most instantly recognizable are "Blueberry Hill," "Blue Monday," "I'm Walkin'," "My Blue Heaven," "Whole Lotta Loving," and "Walking to New Orleans."

The second half of Fats Domino's career lacked the continuous commercial success of the first half. Although he continued to tour and did occasionally produce some notable recordings, more magnetic (and frenetic) performers such as Little Richard, Chuck Berry, and Jerry Lee Lewis eclipsed his gentle, laid-back stage persona. In the 1970s, he released a New Orleans-style version of the Beatles' "Lady Madonna" that gained some attention, and in 1993 he returned to the recording studio for the first time in nearly 25 years to produce his *Christmas Is a Special Day* set. The results received much critical acclaim. In his later years Domino was much honored for his achievements: in 1986 he was in the inaugural group of artists inducted into the Rock and Roll Hall of Fame, and in 1998 President Clinton awarded him the National Medal of Arts. By the late 1990s, though entering his seventies, Fats Domino was still touring in between enjoying life in his palatial New Orleans home.

—Charles Coletta

FURTHER READING:

Aquila, Richard. *That Old Time Rock & Roll: A Chronicle of an Era, 1954-1963.* New York, Schirmer Books, 1989.

Donahue, Phil (1935—)

Talk show host Phil Donahue is credited with pioneering the daytime television talk show format. His programs introduced viewers to sensitive and intelligent discussions of topics and issues that had never before been seen on the small screen. From the debut of *The Phil Donahue Show* in 1969, which originated out of Dayton, Ohio, Donahue challenged, informed, and entertained daytime audiences and helped establish the talk show as one of television's most prolific

and profitable formats. Beginning in the 1970s, his promotion of feminism, and the frequent airing of women's health issues on his program identified him as the embodiment of the "sensitive man." As daytime TV shows became raunchier in the 1990s, Donahue came to be viewed as the patriarch of the genre. While he did present programs with outrageous content—senior citizen strippers, for example—he continued to offer sober conversations about politics and social concerns and a mix of celebrity interviews. Phil Donahue's decision to treat the female television viewer as an intelligent, active, and aware participant in society challenged those programmers wedded to the conviction that women would only watch soap operas and cookery demonstrations.

For a man who later symbolized the modern era's willingness to talk openly about the most personal issues, Donahue's beginnings were very traditional. He was born Phillip John Donahue, the son of a furniture salesman in Cleveland, Ohio, on December 21, 1935. He was an altar boy and, after graduating high school, studied for a B.A. in theology at the University of Notre Dame. After completing his degree, he found work as a radio announcer in Cleveland and, later, Dayton. (One of his first professional positions involved delivering the five a.m. hog report.) His first talk show was a Dayton radio program titled *Conversation Piece*, which aired from 1963 to 1967. He later accepted a position with Dayton's WLWD television station

Phil Donahue (right) and guests on *The Phil Donahue Show*.

to host a local call-in talk show but, unable to attract top guests, he and his producers focused each episode on relevant issues of the day.

The Phil Donahue Show premiered in November 1967 with an appearance by celebrated atheist Madalyn Murray O'Hair, who was considered by some most hated woman in America for her anti-religion stance. That first week also included film of a woman giving birth and a discussion on the appropriateness of anatomically correct male dolls. Donahue's likable personality and his ease in addressing often uncomfortable issues tempered the daring subject matter. A further innovation was his solicitation of questions and comments from the studio audience, previously regarded as little more than background for hosts and their guests. Donahue's charm, coupled with his bold choice of topics, attracted national attention when he moved his show, renamed simply *Donahue*, to Chicago in 1974. The program was soon syndicated nationwide and boasted millions of viewers, of whom 85 percent were women.

In a career that spanned more than 6000 hours of programming, there was no subject that Phil Donahue was unwilling to confront and present to mainstream America. Some complained that his choices were often inappropriate or too outlandish. TV host Merv Griffin expressed the opinion of many when he complained that Donahue and his imitators were most interested in controversy and titillation. Griffin stated, ''What they have to resort to in subject matter is sometimes a pain in the neck. You know, the sex lives of Lithuanian doctors and dentists is not all that interesting.'' Donahue did, indeed, parade bizarre guests at times and was not above risking offense to capture high ratings. He interviewed nudists, drag queens, neo-Nazis, and strippers of all sorts. The episode that caused the most controversy and hysteria was titled ''Transvestite Fashion Show'' and featured Donahue wearing a dress.

However, complaints that daytime talk shows peddled only salacious material ignored Donahue's many episodes that focused on serious issues such as race relations, class differences, and feminist causes. In 1982, he presented the first national program devoted to the AIDS crisis, and a high point of his series was a 1988 discussion of the disease in children, led by the HIV-positive boy Ryan White. Over the years the series also welcomed politicians and advocates from across the political spectrum to express their views. In the late 1980s, Donahue initiated a series of ''space bridge'' shows with Russian TV host Vladimir Pozner, designed to promote understanding between the peoples of the United States and the Soviet Union. The host's own stand on abortion rights, the Equal Rights Amendment, and other feminist causes, identified him as one of TV's outstanding liberal voices.

Donahue's success continued into the 1980s and 1990s. In 1980, the divorced father of five married actress Marlo Thomas, best known for TV's *That Girl*. The couple had met several years earlier when Thomas was a guest on Donahue's program. The series relocated to New York in 1985, but the following year saw the first real challenge to Donahue's ratings dominance with the arrival of Oprah Winfrey. The pair battled for the position of TV's top daytime talk show host for a decade until Donahue announced his retirement in 1996. The final episode of his show was a national event.

After his departure, daytime TV sank into a mire of freak shows, fights, and shocking behavior. The intelligence, curiosity, and humane probing that characterized Donahue's approach were sadly absent in an era filled with hosts such as Geraldo Rivera, Jenny Jones, and Jerry Springer. Where Donahue had sought to inform and entertain, others set out to demean, to provoke and to shock—an unworthy tribute to Phil Donahue's ability to present often controversial subjects to the mass American audience which had once appeared

to mark the nation's growing willingness to confront previously taboo topics.

—Charles Coletta

FURTHER READING:

Anderson, Christopher. *The New Book of People*. New York, G.P. Putnam's Sons, 1986.

Donahue, Phil. *My Own Story*. New York, Simon & Schuster, 1980.

Winship, Michael. *Television*. New York, Random House, 1988.

Donovan (1946—)

The rise and fall of British singer Donovan's career and popularity paralleled that of the 1960s counterculture. In the dreamy world of the late 1960s, the exotic and popular performer personified the earthly flower child. Appearing simultaneously wide-eyed and cynical, a little silly yet nobody's fool, and an intensely commercial hippie, he seemed to embrace antithetical categories in popular

Donovan (right) with his musical director, David John Mills.

culture. For five years between 1965 and 1970, he lived so close to the cutting edge of each new trend that it almost seemed as if he had initiated them. Then, with shocking rapidity, he became irrelevant, discarded—like the counterculture—by critics and audiences alike as passé and/or uncool. Yet, for a singer so identified with that specific time and world view, his best songs never lost either their catchiness or their ability to charm.

Donovan Leitch was born in an old section of Glasgow, Scotland, but his family moved to the outskirts of London in 1955. He learned the rudiments of music at folk enclaves in St. Albans, north of London and in the coastal artists' colony of St. Ives in Cornwall. At age 18 he began recording demo discs which were heard by talent scouts from the British rock television show *Ready Steady Go,* and he began appearing regularly on the program in 1965. Initially, Donovan's music was entirely acoustic and, while noting his English accent and more romantic attitude, critics labeled him "Britain's answer to Bob Dylan." In 1965, thousands of youngsters learned to play the guitar using the chords to his first hit, "Catch the Wind." Follow-up singles included the folksy "Colours," Buffy St. Marie's "Universal Soldier" (a standard of the anti-war movement), and a jazzy drug-tour of "Sunny Goodge Street," with one of the first explicit references to hashish in rock music. Donovan made his American debut at the Newport Folk Festival in 1965, the same year the crowd booed Bob Dylan for performing with electric accompaniment.

By 1966, the 20-year-old Donovan had shed his anti-bomb rhetoric and completely reinvented himself as a psychedelic troubadour of "flower power," the epitome of 1960s mysticism. With Mickie Most, his new producer at Epic Records (with whom he worked until 1969), Donovan kept the folk-like refrains of his songs, but added quirky pop instrumentation (sitars, flutes, cellos, and harps). His work in this period often exhibited wonderful musical inventiveness and a fine ear for a lyrical phrase, although he occasionally crossed the line into pomposity and pretension. His biggest hit, "Sunshine Superman," reached number one in July 1966 in both Britain and the United States, and remains one of the most engaging and innovative singles of the 1960s. The album of the same name also included drug favorites, "The Trip," and the ominous "Season of the Witch." Later that year, Donovan released "Mellow Yellow" (which reached the number two spot with lines whispered by Paul McCartney). Baby boomers everywhere debated whether the lyrics advocated smoking banana peels, although Donovan later claimed the song concerned an electric dildo. His subtle drug references endeared him to the hippie movement, though some complained that his songs were mawkish, the lyrics overloaded with images of trees, sunny days, and laughing children.

Donovan seemed omnipresent in the late 1960s, hanging out with the Byrds, the Rolling Stones, and Dylan, and parodied in Peter, Paul and Mary's "I Dig Rock 'n' Roll Music." The hits kept coming, including the druggie "Epistle to Dippy," and "Young Girl Blues," with its perfectly captured sense of rock ennui set off by the shocking-for-the-times sexual imagery. He was a "must" to headline the Monterey Pop Festival in 1967, but his visa was revoked due to a drug charge. He then traveled to India at the same time as the Beatles to study with the Maharishi Mahesh Yogi. Shortly thereafter, he publicly renounced drug use and requested that his followers substitute meditation for getting stoned. Donovan now appeared on stage in flowing robes with love beads; one album cover depicted him, scepter in hand, in a ceremonial barge at England's romantic Bodiam Castle, a leaf-strewn lake in the foreground.

Nowhere was Donovan's versatility better displayed than in the hit singles he penned in rapid succession in 1968. His acoustic skill was featured in the sweet hymn to childhood, "Jennifer Juniper"; in "Wear Your Love Like Heaven," the soft, layered harmonies consisted of little more than the names of exotic colors, and the song later gained wide circulation as the ubiquitous advertising jingle for Love cosmetics. At the other end of the popular music spectrum, the drug/fairy tale imagery of the Top Ten hit "Hurdy Gurdy Man," featured Donovan's distinctive, tremulous intonation against layers of Jimmy Page's wailing guitars. Three-quarters of the future Led Zeppelin group played on the single, and they later used the same contrast between acoustic and electric sound to great effect.

Donovan's work continually displayed an original bent and a desire to move beyond traditional popular forms while retaining commercial appeal. "There is a Mountain," a hypnotic calypso-based song with lyrics inspired by Japanese haiku, reached the top fifteen in 1967, and he also borrowed successfully from West Indian traditions in "Rikki-Tikki-Tavi" (1970). In 1969, the unique, albeit bizarre story-song "Atlantis" was the last of his efforts to make the top ten. He also experimented with jazz-based sound, most noticeably in "Goo Goo Barabajagal (Love is Hot)," a searing collaboration with the Jeff Beck Group that marked the end of his string of popular hits.

Ironically, just as the singer-songwriter movement seemed to peak in the early 1970s, Donovan completely fell from commercial grace. A critical backlash intensified after he released a double album of children's songs, and the underrated album *Open Road* in 1970 failed to stem the decline. After his sparsely attended 1971 American tour, he became involved with movies, and wrote scores for, among others, Franco Zeffirelli's *Brother Sun, Sister Moon* (1973). His early 1970s albums met with mixed critical acclaim and declining sales. Among these was *7-Tease* (1974), a conceptual album about a young hippie and his search for inner peace, which also toured as a stage revue with some collaboration from David Bowie. By 1980 Donovan had ceased to be a concert attraction and lacked any major record company affiliation. He recorded only sporadically in the next decade.

After several inactive years, the musician enjoyed a minor renaissance in the 1990s. The spacey British dance band Happy Mondays brought Donovan back into favor by praising his work and touring with him. In 1991, they included an irreverent tribute to Donovan on *Pills 'n' Thrills and Bellyaches*; the hit album precipitated a flood of Donovan reissues. There was considerable interest in *Sutras,* Donovan's "comeback" effort in 1996, but the purely acoustic work, filled with cosmically sincere and occasionally cloying material, found no audience.

Donovan will undoubtedly be forever associated with naive psychedelia. This is unfortunate, because he was a consistently imaginative lyricist who pioneered novel sounds such as Caribbean forms long before such work became fashionable. His popular music career may have fit the typical rock star paradigm, but the best of his work remains uniquely original.

—Jon Sterngass

FURTHER READING:

Donovan. *Troubadour: The Definitive Collection, 1964-1976,* compact disc. Epic/Legacy E2K 46986, 1992.

Friedenberg, Edgar. "Current Patterns of a Generational Conflict." *Journal of Social Issues.* 25, 1969, 21-38.

Leitch, Donovan. *Dry Songs and Scribbles.* Garden City, New York, Doubleday, 1971.

The Doobie Brothers

The Doobie Brothers, or "Doobies," are a California-based rock band, formed in 1970, whose most popular singles stand among the definitive songs in 1970s rock and roll. Their hits "Listen to the Music," "Long Train Running," "China Grove," and "Takin' It to the Streets" all possess the trademark upbeat, easygoing, Doobie Brothers sound, influenced by R&B and soul. Their two number one hits, "Black Water" (1975) and "What a Fool Believes" (1979) have become soft-rock classics. Not quite as original or as influential as the Eagles, the Allman Brothers, or Steely Dan, the Doobie Brothers must yet be counted among the best of the American light rock and country rock groups of the 1970s. Successful on stage as well as over the airwaves, they continued to tour after the peak of their popularity had passed, and still released occasional albums throughout the 1980s and 1990s.

—Dave Goldweber

FURTHER READING:

Bego, Mark. *The Doobie Brothers.* New York, Fawcett, 1980.

Christgau, Robert. *Rock Albums of the '70s.* New York, Da Capo, 1981.

Edwards, John W. *Rock 'n' Roll, 1970-1979.* Jefferson, McFarland, 1993.

Doonesbury

On October 26, 1970, Garry Trudeau's comic strip *Doonesbury* debuted in 28 newspapers around the United States, revolutionizing the language and cultural significance of cartoon art forever with its depth of focus, breadth of satirical targets, and richness of character development. From its roots as a *Yale Daily News* strip satirizing college life, *Doonesbury* expanded the horizons of its content and its popularity until, almost 30 years after its first national appearance, it was a feature in over 1,350 newspapers across the country.

Following on ground broken by Walt Kelly's *Pogo*, Trudeau challenged the definition of the comic page as escape and silliness by bringing sharp satire, social commentary, and adult issues into his strip. His heroes, and their quirky responses to the ups and downs of life in the late twentieth century, have stood the test of time, chronicling the changing priorities and dilemmas of the baby-boom generation from college into middle age. His style of cartooning, with its panels of complex artwork and extensive bubble-free dialogue, has been much imitated.

In the 1970s, the initial *Doonesbury* focus was on the inhabitants of an anonymous eastern college campus and its nearby Walden commune. Conservative, gung-ho football star B.D. (a tribute to a real Yale athlete, Brian Dowling) and his loopy, girl-crazy roommate Mike Doonesbury formed the initial core of the strip. Soon they were joined by "Megaphone Mark" Slackmeyer, a campus radical, Calvin, a revolutionary Black Panther, and Zonker, a stoned, irreverent hippie. B.D.'s cheerleader girlfriend Boopsie, and her intellectual roommate Nicole have perpetual disagreements about women's liberation, while the clueless college president constantly tries to sidestep controversy. As time passes, Mike learns about economics, racism, and class when he tutors a savvy inner-city black kid, while B.D. takes his raging drive to win from the football field to Vietnam, where he is captured by Phred, a charming Viet Cong terrorist who teaches him something about the history of Vietnam and the absurdities of war. Those still left at school move to a communal house on idyllic Walden Puddle, where they are joined by still more refugees of the turbulent 1970. One such is Joanie Caucus, an older housewife who has left her stifling life and her husband behind to return to college, and becomes the spokesperson for women's liberation while she tries to get into law school.

Across the decades, these core characters, and many others, tracked the trends and current events of their time and place in history, graduating from college, surviving the yuppie years, and experiencing marriage, divorce, and parenthood. Through many thousands of ingeniously created panels, Doonesbury has offered complex insights into personal relationships together with incisive social commentary. Joanie Caucus, remarried to Washington, D.C. columnist Rick Redfern, bemoans the difficulty of non-sexist child rearing as her young son, holding the doll she gave him for Christmas as if it were the rifle she would never buy him, aims it straight at her. Radio talk-show host Mark Slackmeyer, still the leftist radical, comes out as gay late in the 1980s, but his boyfriend is a dyed-in-the-wool conservative who gets along with Mark's right wing father better than Mark ever did. The quandaries of everyday modern life ring true, as does Trudeau's ironic, wish-I'd-said-that dialogue.

Interspersed with the "personal" stories of the characters are direct visitations from public figures. A favorite *Doonesbury* scenario is a four-panel strip with the White House in each panel, unchanged except for dialogue. In these, presidents from Nixon to Clinton are effectively skewered by the words Trudeau puts in their mouths. In later years, with a technique possibly inspired by the icons of modern computer jargon, presidents and others have been represented only by meaningful icons—a floating feather for vice-president Dan Quayle, for example, or a buttery waffle for Bill Clinton, proving perhaps that a symbol may be worth a thousand caricatures.

One of the most powerful symbols Trudeau created is that of Mr. Butts, the talking spokes-cigarette for the tobacco lobby. Mr. Butts originally appeared in a troubled Mike Doonesbury's nightmares when Mike, by then an advertising agent, is asked to design a campaign to improve tobacco's image. The cynical Mr. Butts has reappeared frequently thereafter to lampoon the tobacco lobby, becoming a powerful image in the anti-smoking campaign. Indeed, *Doonesbury* has frequently been a catalyst for change as well as presaging events. Senator Bob Dole once called the strip the "best source for what's going on in Washington." In 1971, well before the conservative Reagan years, a forward-looking B.D. called Ronald Reagan his "hero." In 1984, almost 10 years before Congressman Gingrich became Speaker of the House, another character worried that he would "wake up someday in a country run by Newt Gingrich." Repressive laws in the wealthy town of Palm Beach, Florida, allowed people of color to be stopped regularly by police, and required domestic servants to register with local authorities. After the bright light of *Doonesbury*'s satire was focused on the town's policies for a time, the laws were repealed.

Because of its mission to attack difficult issues and mock public figures, *Doonesbury* has always roused controversy. Many newspapers place the strip on their editorial page, considering it inappropriate for the comics, while others regularly pull individual strips when the content is judged too extreme. In the 1990s, when *Doonesbury* came out with a series of strips in support of legalization of marijuana for medical use, the attorney general of California railed against the strip and tried unsuccessfully to have it pulled from papers in the state. It is this hard-hitting political satire that earned Garry Trudeau the Pulitzer Prize for political cartoon commentary in 1975, the first time that honor had ever been conferred on a comic strip.

Trudeau, born into a family of physicians in New York City in 1948, came honestly by his gift for trouble-causing satire—his great-great-grandfather was driven out of New York because of the caricatured sculptures he made of his colleagues. Known for his avoidance of the press, Trudeau, an avid student and researcher of the U.S. political scene, also writes editorials and draws editorial cartoons for the *New York Times*. He has written film scripts, and the book for a Broadway musical of *Doonesbury* in 1983, though many critics did not think the cartoon translated well to the stage. He has also created *Doonesbury* television specials and a musical revue called *Rap Master Ronnie*, spoofing the Reagan years. For decades, he refused to compromise the principles of his creation by allowing merchandising, but he finally succumbed in 1998, when he permitted *Doonesbury* products to be sold, with all proceeds going to the campaign for literacy.

In 1988, when president George Bush said of Trudeau, "He speaks for a bunch of Brie-tasting, Chardonnay-sipping elitists," he was simply referring to the most negative baby boomer stereotype of the 1980s, the pampered yuppie. But Trudeau's strip speaks for more than the elite, clearly addressing a far wider audience than liberal Americans of a certain generation. *Doonesbury* fills a need in the American press for progressive readers who appreciate the demystification of complex issues through no-nonsense, direct language and humor. Though, by the late 1990s, many other comics had appeared that attempted to fill this need (even one especially for conservative readers), *Doonesbury* paved the way for these, and for a comics page that explores adult issues through humor. The characters who inhabit the panels of Doonesbury are old friends to its readers, and one of Trudeau's great talents is his ability to make these characters—with the possible exception of faceless politicos—lovable to his readers. They keep reading to enjoy a cynical and satirical take on current events. And they keep reading to see how life is turning out for the old gang.

—Tina Gianoulis

FURTHER READING:

Satin, Allan D. *A Doonesbury Index: 1970-1983*. Metuchen, New Jersey, Scarecrow Press, 1985.

Trudeau, G. B. *Flashbacks: Twenty-Five Years of Doonesbury*. Kansas City, Andrews and McMeel, 1995.

The Doors

With their mix of music, poetry, theater, and daring, the Doors emerged as America's most darkly innovative, eerily mesmerizing musical group of the 1960s. Founded concurrently with the English invasion, the college-educated, Los Angeles-based group stood apart from the folk-rock movement of Southern California and the peace and flower power bands of San Francisco. In exploring death, doom, fear, and sex, their music reflected the hedonistic side of the era. Writing for the *Saturday Evening Post* in 1967, Joan Didion called them "the Norman Mailers of the Top 40, missionaries of apocalyptic sex." The group's flamboyant lead singer, Jim Morrison, said, "Think of us as erotic politicians." A seminal rock figure, Morrison's dark good looks and overt sexuality catapulted him to sex symbol status, akin to that of Elvis Presley.

Morrison's provocative stage presence, combined with the group's mournfully textured, blues-rooted music, suggested the musical theater of Kurt Weill and Bertolt Brecht, and the edginess of the avant-garde troupe, The Living Theater. But the complicated, clearly troubled Morrison could not overcome personal demons, which he sated with drugs and alcohol. By late 1968, his frequently "stoned" demeanor became off-putting, his on-stage rants pretentious. His behavior at a Miami concert in March 1969, and his resulting arrest on charges including indecent exposure, represented not only his downfall but also the Doors' looming disintegration. But if the group's rise and fall was fast and furious, encompassing just four years, their anarchist influence is undeniable. Their hard-driving music bridged the heavy-metal 1970s; their murky, cerebral lyrics spanned the new wave 1980s, and the alternative 1990s, and Jim Morrison remains the undisputed forerunner of the sexy, leather-clad, on-the-edge rock martyr.

The Doors' saga began in the summer of 1965 on the beach at Venice, California, where singer-musician Ray Manzarek ran into his former UCLA classmate, Jim Morrison. After listening to Morrison sing the haunting lyrics to a song he had written called "Moonlight Drive," Manzarek proposed they start a band, and "make a million dollars." Manzarek then approached two other musicians who were studying with him at a Maharishi meditation center. Thus, with Manzarek on piano and organ, songwriter Robbie Krieger on guitar, John Densmore on drums, and Morrison before the microphone, the group was in place. It was Morrison who came up with their moniker, derived from a William Blake passage, which had inspired the title of Aldous Huxley's book about his mescaline experiences, *The Doors of Perception*. As paraphrased by Morrison: "There are things that are known and things that are unknown, in between [are] the doors."

Working their way through the Los Angeles club scene, the Doors initially performed blues and rock 'n' roll standards, in addition to material written by Morrison. They were playing the London Fog on the Sunset Strip, making five dollars apiece on weeknights, ten dollars apiece weekends, when they were spotted by a female talent booker who was especially struck by the star quality of the lead singer. Hired to work the Strip's popular Whiskey a Go Go, the Doors became the club's unofficial house band, second-billed to groups including the Turtles, Them, and Love. During sets, the group was an anomaly; the four members appeared disparate, as if each were on a plane all his own, but their sound had a synchronicity. And there was no denying the allure of the group's pretty-boy singer.

The Doors: (from left) John Densmore, Robbie Krieger, Ray Manzarek, and Jim Morrison.

In his earliest performances, Morrison was so introverted that he performed with his back to the audience. Some nights, his baritone was barely audible. However, his confidence grew with the group's reputation and, certainly, his stage presence was unique. He had languid body movements, tended to throttle the microphone, and often emoted with closed eyes as if in a spectral trance. Also, he could be counted on to be unpredictable. Sometimes he dropped to the floor to sob out his lyrics; other times he danced with abandon as if possessed. One night at the Whiskey in late 1966, he delivered an improvised rendition of his oedipal song, "The End." The eleven-and-a-half minute song climaxed with a young man's screaming threat to kill his father and rape his mother, but Morrison used a word other than "rape," bringing the entire club, including the go-go girls in hanging cages, to a stunned silence. That very night the Doors were fired. They would, however, ultimately have left on their own accord, for they already had a contract with Elektra Records.

Released in January 1967, their debut album *The Doors* included "Light My Fire," which, at six minutes and 50 seconds, was considered too long for Top 40 airplay. As the group toured nationally, a shorter version began climbing the AM charts; meanwhile, the full-length version became a favorite of FM. Eschewing the matching costumes that were then in vogue among music groups, the Doors also had no official leader, but in interviews, as well as on the stage, it was invariably Morrison who took the spotlight. Shrewdly, the photogenic singer-songwriter exploited his rapport with the camera, as well as his appeal to journalists, who found him sensual, mystical, and eminently quotable. For the erudite rock star was also a poet, who read and quoted the nineteenth-century French poets Arthur Rimbaud and Charles Baudelaire, and German philosopher Friedrich Nietzsche. Moreover, when not waxing metaphysical or apocalyptic, Morrison could be surprisingly playful. When asked how he had prepared for stardom, he once quipped, "I stopped getting haircuts."

In his Elektra Records publicity biography, he claimed to have no family; in fact, he was the son of a Navy rear admiral, and from a family of career militarists. As a performer, Morrison assumed various alter egos. For a while, he called himself the "King of Orgasmic Rock," and as the "Lizard King" he donned tight-fitting snakeskin pants. He also claimed to be possessed by the spirit of a dead Indian, the result of a childhood trip across the desert. He and his family had once passed an overturned truck, which had resulted in fatalities, and Morrison claimed that the spirit of one of the dead Indians somehow entered him. He accessorized that persona by donning a concho belt, leather pants, and dancing in a ritualistic style.

But the role he played to the hilt was that of the rebel. When the Doors appeared on *The Ed Sullivan Show* in September 1967, Morrison defied the famed host's request that a particular line, with possible drug connotations, be deleted from ''Light My Fire.'' Three months later, the singer made headlines when he was arrested on stage in New Haven, Connecticut, on charges including ''breach of the peace'' and indecent and immoral exhibition. In August 1968 he was again arrested, this time for disorderly conduct on board a flight to Phoenix.

Increasingly, Doors concerts became known for their dangerous atmosphere, as an incorrigible and no-longer-slender Morrison staggered across the stage, taunting the audience, inciting them to riot, screaming at them to ''Wake up!'' He also clutched at his crotch and tugged threateningly at his pants. The Doors were in a slump when they embarked on a 21-city tour in March 1969 and, following the arrest of the bloated, bearded Morrison in Miami, the rest of the tour was canceled. The group's symbiosis was on the wane when they recorded their blues-oriented collection, *L.A. Woman.* Afterward, it was a burned-out Morrison who headed for Paris to concentrate on his poetry. He was just 27 when he died on July 3, 1971, reportedly of a heart attack suffered while in the bathtub. Because of Morrison's penchant for substance abuse, and the curious handling of his death and burial by several close friends, questions persist over how he actually died. Since his body was found by his common-law wife, who died in 1974 of a heroin overdose, there have long been allegations that drugs were a factor. Whatever the cause, his death was yet another reminder of the perils of the dark side of rock 'n' roll. It was also the third untimely passing of a rock star in less than a year, following those of heavy metal guitarist Jimi Hendrix and rock-blues queen Janis Joplin, both of whom died of overdoses.

Following Morrison's death, the surviving Doors recorded two additional albums. Manzarek also sought to reinvent the group, with Iggy Pop as lead singer, but it was clear that the magic had died with Morrison. It was Morrison's mystique that led to a Doors rediscovery that has enshrined the rock star as a modern-day Dionysus, the Greek god of revelry and wine who was dismembered, and later resurrected. The 1980 rock biography, *No One Here Gets Out Alive,* by rock journalist Jerry Hopkins and Doors associate Danny Sugerman, spurred on the revival, and sent other biographers in search of similarly debauched rock subjects. And the 1980 reissue of the Doors' *Greatest Hits* album, which entered *Billboard's* Top 10 Chart, proved that defunct groups can sell as well as those still active. *Rolling Stone* acknowledged the power of dead celebrity with its September 1981 Morrison cover story, proclaiming ''He's hot, he's sexy and he's dead.'' Hollywood heralded Morrison in 1990 when a decade-long quest to make a feature film was realized by controversial filmmaker Oliver Stone, with the movie *The Doors,* starring Val Kilmer.

In the era of incarnations that dawned in the 1990s, Morrison was depicted as a poet trapped in a self-created rock star image. He is, after all, buried in Pere La Chaise Cemetery, the famous final resting-place in Paris of such notables as Edith Piaf, Oscar Wilde, Honoré de Balzac, and Frédéric Chopin. Moreover, the poetry he self-published in 1970 was republished in the late 1980s and during the 1990s. His writings have also been the subject of scholarly studies, including one in which he is compared to his idol, the French symbolist, Rimbaud.

Yet if the Doors' spotlight remains on Morrison, his musical legacy came from his collaborative work with Manzarek, Krieger, and Densmore. Benchmarks of the 1960s Doors songs—among them ''Light My Fire,'' ''Hello, I Love You,'' ''Touch Me,'' ''Love Her Madly,'' ''People Are Strange,'' and ''Riders on the Storm''—have

remained accessible. Staples of the airwaves, they attest to the power of provocative music, and to the seemingly-enduring interest wrought by the potent combination of sex, drugs, and rock 'n' roll.

—Pat H. Broeske

FURTHER READING:

Breslin, Rosemary. ''Jim Morrison, 1981: Renew My Subscription to the Resurrection.'' *Rolling Stone,* September 17, 1981, 31-34.

Broeske, Pat H. ''Jim Morrison: Back to the Sixties, Darkly.'' *Los Angeles Times.* January 7, 1990, 6-7, 19-24.

Didion, Joan. ''Waiting for Morrison.'' *Saturday Evening Post.* March 9, 1968, 16.

Hopkins, Jerry, and Daniel Sugerman. *No One Here Gets Out Alive.* New York, Warner, 1980.

Rocco, John M., editor. *The Doors Companion: Four Decades of Commentary.* New York, Schirmer, 1997.

Sugerman, Danny. *The Doors: The Illustrated History.* New York, William Morrow, 1983.

Doo-wop Music

''Doo-wop'' is a form of close-harmony singing, based in rhythm-and-blues. The style became popular in the 1950s, originating among African-American vocal groups in urban centers. One of the most common rhythm phrases used by 1950s groups in performance and on their recordings, ''doo-wop'' came to name the musical style. To sing in the doo-wop style, phonetic or nonsense words are used as rhythmic parts in harmonic arrangements. Usually this is done by a trio or quartet of vocalists, over which a soloist sings a melody. The melody is expressed through understandable words, often accented by the nonsense words of the vocal accompaniment. By the end of the 1960s, doo-wop groups were losing popularity. Yet rock 'n' roll musicians would often use doo-wop for their background vocal arrangements, and in this way the style continued to develop beyond the 1950s and to exert its influence on popular music.

—Brian Granger

FURTHER READING:

Gribin, Dr. Anthony J., and Dr. Matthew M. Schiff. *Doo-wop: The Forgotten Third of Rock 'n' Roll.* Iola, Wisconsin, Krause Publications, 1992.

Pruter, Robert. *Doowop: The Chicago Scene.* Urbana and Chicago, University of Illinois Press, 1996.

Dorsey, Jimmy (1904-1957)

In the 1920s, Jimmy Dorsey toured with the Paul Whiteman and Red Nichols bands, and was considered an excellent clarinet performer and the leading jazz performer on alto saxophone, influencing such

Tommy (left) and Jimmy Dorsey

jazz greats as Charlie Parker and Lester Young. He and his brother, Tommy, founded the Dorsey Brothers Orchestra 1933, starring Glenn Miller on trombone and Ray McKinley on drums. After Tommy left to form his own orchestra in 1935, Jimmy Dorsey led the band to national stardom in the 1940s, featuring the popular singing duo of Helen O'Connell and Bob Eberly. The song "Green Eyes," as sung by O'Connell, was the band's most requested number. In 1953, the brothers reunited.

—Benjamin Griffith

FURTHER READING:

Atkins, Ronald, editor. *All That Jazz.* New York, Carlton, 1996.

Balliett, Whitney. *American Musicians.* New York, Oxford Press, 1986.

Simon, George T. *The Big Bands.* New York, MacMillan, 1974.

Dorsey, Tommy (1905-1956)

A trombone-player known for his warm, silken tone on ballads as well as upbeat improvisations, Tommy Dorsey, "The Sentimental Gentleman of Swing," led one of the most versatile orchestras of the big band era. With its premier jazz stars, the band could swing with the best, and none equaled its style on slow ballads, as sung by Frank Sinatra and Jo Stafford.

By age 25, Tommy had become a successful free-lance radio and recording star, and in 1933 he and his brother Jimmy formed the Dorsey Brothers Orchestra. Within two years Tommy left to start his own orchestra. His band's best-selling record was the swinging *Boogie-Woogie,* selling over four million copies, but the most requested number was the poignant "I'll Never Smile Again." The brothers reunited in 1953.

—Benjamin Griffith

FURTHER READING:

Atkins, Ronald, editor. *All That Jazz.* New York, Carlton, 1996.

Balliett, Whitney. *American Musicians.* New York, Oxford Press, 1986.

Simon, George T. *The Big Bands.* New York, MacMillan, 1974.

Double Indemnity

Double Indemnity (1935) is one of the classic, tough-talking murder stories of the late 1930s. Written by controversial mystery novelist James M. Cain (1892-1977), *Double Indemnity* is based upon a true story about a weak-willed insurance agent, Walter Huff, who falls for sultry blond, Phyllis Nirdlinger. Nirdlinger's inconvenient husband has to be eliminated so that his wife and her lover can collect on his life insurance, a policy which doubles in value if the holder dies by accident.

Like *The Postman Always Rings Twice,* upon which it is modeled, l'amour fou, or sexually charged obsessive love, is at the heart of this psychologically realistic novel. Cain, along with, for example, Raymond Chandler and Dashiell Hammett have been called, perhaps unjustly in Cain's case, members of the hard-boiled school of detective novelists. Edmund Wilson has referred to them as "the poets of the tabloid murder" because of their interest in the low life aspects of American culture, and the often sordid stories of murder, eroticism, and adultery that fascinated them.

Unlike Chandler, with whom he has been compared (and who wrote the screenplay for the film version of *Double Indemnity),* Cain's writing is deeply pessimistic and far less romantic. His characters are terribly flawed yet very human in their failings, and the eroticism of many of his novels made them controversial in their day. Cain's interests and lean writing style also made him stand apart from much of the popular writing of his time. His gritty, downbeat, stories, like *The Postman Always Rings Twice, Mildred Pierce,* and *Double Indemnity* had a pictorial quality which made them attractive for adaptation to the movies. All, however, underwent considerable sanitation before the more censorship-plagued Hollywood studios could make them into films.

In the case of *Double Indemnity,* the novel ends with Huff and Phyllis on a freighter going nowhere in particular, unable to return to the United States because of their murderous pasts, and contemplating suicide by jumping off the boat into shark infested waters. As Phyllis says, "There's nothing ahead of us, is there Walter." And Walter replies, "No, nothing." This existential gloom did not survive in the film version where Walter, after narrating his sordid tale of adultery and betrayal, lies dying from a gunshot wound inflicted by, perhaps, Phyllis, who he has murdered a few hours before.

Billy Wilder turned the novel into a convention-setting film noir in 1944, starring Fred MacMurray, Barbara Stanwyck, and Edward G.

Barbara Stanwyck and Fred MacMurray in a scene from *Double Indemnity*.

Robinson. Told in a confessional flashback by the dying insurance agent, Wilder's more cynical, but less gloomy version, helped establish flashback—first person narration as a convention in film noir. The unconventional casting of Fred MacMurray, who was noted for his roles in comedy, helped the audience identify with the amoral, but ruthless Huff, who is now called Walter Neff.

In the film version, the first person narration helps to draw the audience into a morally complex position where they viscerally experience the amoral world in which Neff and Phyllis operate—we see the events unfold through his eyes. To put the spectator on edge, Wilder sets the rigid and righteous Barton Keyes (Edward G. Robinson), an insurance investigator and Neff's boss and friend, up against the Neff character, giving the audience a choice between identifying with a slippery, ruthless, and greasily charming insurance salesman or his cold and obsessive nemesis. As in Alfred Hitchcock films, the audience becomes ethically involved with the criminals hoping that they will elude the ever present, relentless Keyes. With its raw, more naturalist flavor, and serious, unsentimental prose the novel makes identification with the characters more difficult. Thus in the film

when Neff sets out to kill Phyllis, the audience is uncomfortably aware that they have identified with a hero who is a callous and brutal loner.

—Jeannette Sloniowski

FURTHER READING:

Cain, James M. *Double Indemnity.* New York, Random House, 1978.

Evans, Peter William. "Double Indemnity (or Bringing up Baby)." In *The Book of Film Noir,* edited by Ian Cameron. New York, Continuum, 1993, 165-73.

Johnston, Claire. "Double Indemnity." In *Women in Film Noir,* edited by E. Ann Kaplan. London, The British Film Institute Press, 1980, 100-11.

Palmer, R. Barton. *Hollywood's Dark Cinema.* New York, Twayne Publishers, 1994.

Schickel, Richard. *Double Indemnity.* London, British Film Institute, 1992.

Silver, Alain, and Elizabeth Ward, editors. *Film Noir: An Encyclopedic Reference to the American Style.* Woodstock, New York, Overlook Press, 1992.

Douglas, Lloyd C. (1878-1951)

With the publication of *The Robe* in 1942, Lloyd C. Douglas became the most influential religious novelist in the world. Following in the tradition of Lew Wallace's *Ben Hur* (1880), Douglas' novels satisfied a reading public's demands for rollicking adventure and historical romance, combined with piety. *The Robe* purports to tell what happened to the Roman soldier who acquired Jesus' garment at the Crucifixion. After many adventures, this soldier meets St. Peter and accepts Christianity, later to die a happy martyr's death. Douglas, who retired from the Congregational ministry to write, never pretended his novels were refined works of literature. He graciously suffered the attacks of reviewers, who found him loquacious and sentimental. Yet he proved incapable of writing a book that did not become a best seller; the public loved his vintage narratives of decent characters who worked through problems to happy resolutions. In 1953, Henry Koster directed a major Hollywood film adaptation of *The Robe* which is still highly regarded. Douglas' continuing though diluted influence may be seen in books by Fulton Oursler, Taylor Caldwell, and Frank G. Slaughter.

—Allene Phy-Olsen

FURTHER READING:

Douglas, Lloyd C. *Time to Remember.* Boston, Houghton Mifflin, 1951.

Hackett, Alice P. *60 Years of Best Sellers, 1895-1955.* New York, R.R. Bowker, 1956.

Schneider, Louis, and Sanford M. Dornbusch. *Popular Religion: Inspirational Books in America.* Chicago, University of Chicago Press, 1958.

Douglas, Melvyn (1901-1981)

Although he acted in motion pictures from the early 1930s to the late 1970s, Melvyn Douglas was never especially fond of most of the more than three score and ten movies in which he starred. He much preferred the theater and returned to the stage whenever he got the chance. A versatile actor, he excelled in both dramatic and comedy roles. He appeared in horror films, mysteries, and melodramas, but is best remembered for playing opposite Greta Garbo in the comedy *Ninotchka* (1939). Later in his screen career, when he'd ceased doing dapper leading man roles and was showing up in character parts, Douglas earned two supporting actor Oscars. A dedicated liberal, he was active in politics and his wife, Helen Gahagan Douglas, ran against Richard Nixon for the United States Senate but was defeated.

Born Melvyn Hesselberg in Macon, Georgia, he grew up in the Midwest. He served in the Army during World War I, but never went overseas—"The closest I personally came to death was in the kitchen, narrowly avoiding a meat cleaver thrown at me by a furious cook," he remembered in *See You at the Movies.* After the war, he joined his family—his father was a modestly successful concert pianist—in Chicago. Douglas hadn't yet picked a career and had "no idea what to do with my life." By the early 1920s he'd decided on the theater and was touring the Midwest. After several years of this, with an assortment of companies, he reached Broadway in 1928 in *A Free Soul.* He played the gangster, a role that made Clark Gable a star when he appeared later in the movie version.

Melvyn Douglas's work in the 1930 Broadway comedy *Tonight or Never* changed his life in two important ways. It was in the play that he first met Helen Gahagan, his costar, and fell in love with her. And when the play was filmed, Douglas repeated his role in Hollywood. He went on to make several films in the early 1930s, including *The Vampire Bat* (1933), *The Old Dark House* (1932), and *As You Desire Me* (1932), in which he first starred opposite Garbo. Unimpressed with the movie business, the actor left Hollywood for a time to return to the New York stage. "I had gotten disgusted with being photographed at close range," he later explained, "with a microphone down my throat."

He soon was lured back to Hollywood and began working again in a wide variety of films. He played such reformed rogues as the Lone Wolf and Arsene Lupin and a range of sleuths in mystery movies such as *Fast Company* (1938), *Tell No Tales* (1939), and *There's That Woman Again* (1939). He also began to shine in a successful string of screwball comedies. He worked opposite Irene Dunne in *Theodora Goes Wild* (1936), with Marlene Dietrich in *Angel* (1937), and with Myrna Loy in *Third Finger Left Hand* (1940). In 1939 he made Garbo laugh in Ernst Lubitsch's *Ninotchka.*

Douglas said that he didn't become politically active until "just before Roosevelt's reelection in 1936." His wife was a singer as well as an actress and he'd accompanied her on a tour that took her to Germany. Once they saw Hitler's campaign against the Jews firsthand, Helen Douglas cancelled her tour and they returned home. Melvyn Douglas joined the Hollywood Anti-Nazi League, worked for the rights of migrant workers, campaigned for the Democratic candidate for governor, and in June of 1938 he organized the Motion Picture Democratic Committee, the earliest group of movie people to campaign for a specific political party. Never a Communist, Douglas found himself attacked by the local members of the party when he called Russia as big a totalitarian threat as Germany and Italy. And for his criticisms of Nazi Germany he was labeled a "premature anti-Fascist." When Helen Gahagan Douglas ran against fledgling politician Richard Nixon for the U.S. Senate in 1950, some of Nixon's campaigners introduced a strong note of anti-Semitism. And in speaking of his opponent, the future President of the United States would often refer to her as Mrs. Hesselberg. One of Nixon's more extreme supporters, the racist Gerald L. K. Smith, told his followers that they must "*not* send to the Senate the wife of a Jew."

During World War II Douglas enlisted in the Army and was eventually stationed in the China-Burma-India war area. He returned to the movies after the war—notably in *Mr. Blandings Builds His Dream House* (1948) with Cary Grant and Myrna Loy. But after 1951, he concentrated on the stage again, winning a Tony for his performance in Gore Vidal's political drama, *The Best Man.* Older, and letting his age show, Douglas reentered motion pictures once again in the early 1960s. He made over a dozen films in his last years, including *Hud* (1963) for which he won his first Oscar, and *Being There* (1979) for which he won his second.

—Ron Goulart

FURTHER READING:

Douglas, Melvyn and Arthur, Tom. *See You at the Movies.* Lanham, University Press of America, 1986.

Mitchell, Greg. *Tricky Dick and the Pink Lady.* New York, Random House, 1998.

Douglas, Mike (1925—)

Daytime television talk show host Mike Douglas personified mainstream popular entertainment during the 21-year run of *The Mike Douglas Show* from 1961 to 1982. The show, which initially originated from Cleveland, Ohio, and later moved to Philadelphia, Pennsylvania, was a 90-minute syndicated program that dominated the ratings during the important weekday afternoon/early evening time slots. Douglas served as an affable Midwestern everyman who welcomed guests from show business, politics, and current events. Unlike many daytime shows of the 1990s, which focused primarily on confrontations between outrageous and often vulgar guests, *The Mike Douglas Show* offered viewers a mixture of thoughtful conversation and wholesome entertainment. Douglas once described his personality and appeal to the mass audience by stating, "I'd have to say I'm square and I'm happy that I am." His charming "Mr. Nice Guy" image made him the quintessential TV host and encouraged such personalities as Marlon Brando, John Lennon, Barbra Streisand, Rose Kennedy, and Princess Grace of Monaco to choose his program for their rare talk show appearances.

Born Michael Dowd on August 11, 1925, in Chicago, Illinois, Mike Douglas served in the Navy during World War II and first attracted attention with an impromptu singing performance while visiting the famous Hollywood Canteen. His rendition of "When Irish Eyes Are Smiling" so impressed nightclub manager Earl Carroll that the young sailor was given a standing offer of a job as a singer as soon as he was free to take it. However, upon leaving the service in 1945, Dowd turned down Carroll's offer and a Hollywood film contract to join Kay Kayser's big band as a featured male singer. For five years Douglas, whose professional name was bestowed upon him during a performance by Kayser, sang on both the radio and television versions of *Kay Kayser's Kollege of Musical Knowledge.* Among his most popular songs with Kayser and his own spin-off group Michael Douglas & The Campus Kids were "Ole Buttermilk Sky" (1946) and "The Old Lamplighter" (1947). Upon Kayser's retirement in 1950, Douglas began a solo singing career. His most noteworthy performance of this period occurred when he provided the singing voice for Prince Charming in Walt Disney's animated fairytale classic *Cinderella* (1950).

Douglas moved into television in the early 1950s and appeared on numerous programs originating from Chicago. In 1961, he arrived in Cleveland to launch his own talk show. Westinghouse, which syndicated the Douglas show, owned KYW-TV in Cleveland and believed it would be most cost-effective to originate the program from those facilities. Later, an FCC ruling on a legal technicality forced Westinghouse and NBC to swap their stations in Cleveland and Philadelphia. In 1965, Douglas and his successful program relocated to Philadelphia's Independence Mall. Each episode of *The Mike Douglas Show* began with Douglas singing an opening number (most often "On a Wonderful Day Like Today") and then commenting on his personal life with his wife Genevieve and their three daughters.

He then welcomed various guests and participated in comedy-variety segments.

One of the most noteworthy elements of the *Douglas Show* was the inclusion of a celebrity guest co-host each week. Performers such as Rosemary Clooney, Jim Nabors, Fred Astaire, Gene Kelly, and Gloria Swanson would join Mike in this role for five days. Perhaps Douglas's most unconventional co-hosts were John Lennon and Yoko Ono, who appeared for a week in February 1972. The couple introduced Douglas and his Middle American audience to such counterculture figures as Jerry Rubin, Black Panther Bobby Seale, and several segments of performance art. Highlights of the unusual week included Lennon playing with his rock idol Chuck Berry and Douglas joining the couple in an unrehearsed segment where they phoned strangers to say they loved them.

Mike Douglas symbolized family entertainment during the turbulent 1960s and 1970s. He was extremely popular and prominent on the American scene. Beyond his own afternoon program, he often substituted for Johnny Carson on *The Tonight Show.* Douglas even produced a hit record, "The Men in My Little Girl's Life," a song about fatherhood that reached number three on the *Billboard* charts. He was even seen on the big screen when he made a cameo appearance as a southern governor in the Burt Reynolds film *Gator* (1976). After *The Mike Douglas Show* ceased production in 1982, the host moved to the fledgling CNN cable network to briefly host an interview show. Douglas remained out of the spotlight until 1996 when he made a special guest appearance during the premiere week of *The Rosie O'Donnell Show.* Rosie O'Donnell credited Douglas as the inspiration for the positive, entertainment-based, and family-friendly show she hoped to create. Her great success in the late 1990s proved the daytime talk show format pioneered by Mike Douglas still resonated with many Americans.

—Charles Coletta

FURTHER READING:

Douglas, Mike. *Mike Douglas: My Story.* New York, Putnam, 1978.

White, Mel. *Mike Douglas: When the Going Gets Tough.* Waco, Texas, Word Books, 1982.

Downs, Hugh (1921—)

Throughout his more than sixty years in broadcasting, Hugh Downs has been the embodiment of reassurance and congeniality. Learning his craft as a radio announcer in the late 1930s and 1940s, Downs became the master host of television. After serving as announcer on *Caesar's Hour* and *The Tonight Show,* Downs simultaneously hosted an early morning series, *Today,* and a daily game show, *Concentration.* Always curious about health and science, Downs oversaw the first successful series on aging, *Over Easy,* for PBS. When the magazine series, *20/20,* was floundering, ABC lured the affable Downs out of semi-retirement to anchor the show in 1978. He reported on many of his special interests, including sailing, psychology, and astronomy, for *20/20,* helping to make it the network's signature primetime newsmagazine for over two decades. Because of his decency and trustworthiness, Downs is one of the most familiar and reassuring figures in the history of television, clocking more hours on the air than any other network personality according to *The Guinness Book of World Records.*

—Ron Simon

FURTHER READING:

Downs, Hugh. *On Camera: My Ten Thousand Hours on Television.* New York, Putnam, 1986.

Doyle, Arthur Conan (1859-1930)

So great is the influence of Sherlock Holmes, that only the truest of the great detective's fans know that his creator, Arthur Conan Doyle, thought far less of Holmes than he did of his other creative efforts. For Doyle was not a stock-in-trade mystery writer, a genre that was still finding its legs. He certainly had not "invented" the genre of detective fiction, a privilege that belonged to Edgar Allan Poe and his own creation, master detective August Dupin. Although Doyle claimed that Holmes had been modeled on his medical school teacher, Dr. Joseph Bell, the writings of Edgar Allan Poe, as well as Emile Gaboriau, Charles Dickens, Eugene Vidocq, and Wilkie Collins, were what provided Doyle with the basic elements for building his mythic detective.

Arthur Conan Doyle was born on May 22, 1859 in Edinburgh, the eldest son of Charles Altimont Doyle and his wife, Mary Foley. Doyle's father, a builder and designer in the Edinburgh Public Works

Arthur Conan Doyle

Office, was from a staunchly Catholic family. In 1869, Doyle was enrolled in Hodder Preparatory, a Jesuit school in Lancashire. Two years later he attended the Jesuit college, Stonyhurst School, also in Lancashire. Upon graduating, he traveled to Austria, where he spent a year studying German in Feldkirch School before entering Edinburgh University in 1876 to study medicine. Despite his Jesuit education, Doyle's year in Austria proved a major turning point, as a crisis of faith led him to abandon his Catholic upbringing for a studied agnosticism. This change in religious perspective, based on his own faith in scientific reasoning, prepared Doyle for the rigors of medical school.

Interestingly, it was Doyle's avowed agnosticism and unwavering commitment to honest dealing that led to his becoming a writer. After he informed his father's well-to-do family of his religious disillusionment, all social and financial help was withdrawn. Barely able to support himself, Doyle turned in his third year in medical school to writing fiction for extra cash, using as material his own adventures serving while in school as a ship's doctor on a whaling vessel to the Antarctic and later on an African freighter. Between the few stories he published, which paid just enough to keep him and his family afloat, Doyle racked up a good number of rejections before achieving steady work as a writer.

In 1882, Doyle established a private practice in Southsea, Portsmouth. Three years later, he married Louise Hawkins, whose own small family income offered him greater freedom to write more. His first novel, *The Firm of Girdlestone,* written in 1886, was soundly rejected by the British publishing industry and did not see publication until 1890. His next work was his first Sherlock Holmes story, the novella *A Study in Scarlet,* which after several initial rejections, was published in the 1887 issue of *Beeton's Christmas Annual.* Despite Doyle's faith in the quality and originality of the story's hero, *A Study in Scarlet* gained little notice among readers. His next novel, however, *Micah Clarke* (1889), caused a great stir after its publication— following the usual round of rejections by British publishers—by Andrew Lang, as chief editor at Longmans Publishing Company. *Micah Clarke,* a story about the dangers of fanaticism, was Doyle's first work of historical fiction and an immediate success, propelling the author into literary stardom in England.

Meanwhile, despite the poor showing Holmes had made in his creator's home country, Doyle's detective fared quite well in the United States, where a request for another story about the master detective was made to Doyle while he was deep in his next historical novel, *The White Company* (1890). As soon as Doyle had completed *The White Company,* which was to be his personal favorite, he dashed off *The Sign of Four* (1890) which was, once again, well received in America. Fortunately for Doyle, Holmes' stock, despite his poor initial showing, was beginning to rise in England by leaps and bounds. In July 1891, Doyle wrote his first of six Sherlock Holmes tales for *The Strand,* making Doyle England's most popular serialized fiction writer. Doyle continued to write Sherlock Holmes stories over the next two years until he decided to have Holmes killed by his arch-nemesis, Dr. Moriarty, in December 1893, with the story "The Final Problem."

Doyle's decision was a momentous one. Holmes' death was met with howls of outrage and large-scale subscription cancellations of the magazine. The pressure on Doyle was enormous to continue the series, but he was adamant about letting Holmes rest in peace. As it was, the production of a Holmes story for serial publication proved to be an enormous strain on Doyle's creative powers, draining precious energy that he thought better spent on his now little known historical novels, such as *Rodney Stone* (1896) and *Uncle Bernac* (1897). In the early 1900s, Doyle added to his output two works of historical nonfiction, *The Great Boer War* (1900) and *The War in South Africa* (1902), which sought not only to document the Boer War but to defend the British role in it.

In 1901, Doyle published *The Hound of the Baskervilles,* in which Holmes was reintroduced to solve one of his older cases. By 1903, Doyle had accepted an American offer of $5,000 per story for a series of new tales about the great detective, regardless of how many Doyle wrote or how often. Doyle continued to write stories of Holmes and his companion Watson over the next 20 years, although they tended to appear in short bursts, when they appeared at all. After Holmes' resurrection, Doyle's early passion for historical fiction sought an outlet in other genres, such as the scientific romance, resulting in the writing of *The Lost World* (1912), *The Poison Belt* (1913), and *The Land of Mist* (1926). Concurrent with these began a spate of Spiritualist works that included *The New Revelation* (1918), *The Vital Message* (1919), *The Wanderings of a Spiritualist* (1921), *The Coming of the Fairies* (1922), and the two-volume *History of Spiritualism* (1926).

Many consider Doyle's turn to spiritualism at the end of his life one of the strangest events to occur in the life of a man whose greatest creation was a detective who drew his conclusions from a hard and cold reality that disavowed all things supernatural. Few, however, recognize the important nuances in Doyle's thoughts about spiritualism, as well as the nuances within the spiritualist movement itself, which sought to treat spirits as a scientific reality, a view that Doyle favored. Doyle, after all, was an agnostic, not an atheist, and there is little doubt that notwithstanding his medical training and belief in scientific method, he remained unable to reconcile the loss of his childhood Catholic faith with his belief in a greater good that directed human conduct and morals. Indeed, Holmes' own work as a detective of "setting the world to rights" suggests a moral imperative that is explained more by Doyle's faith—in goodness, in man, and perhaps even in God—than his reason.

—Bennett Lovett-Graff

FURTHER READING:

Carr, John Dickson. *The Life of Sir Arthur Conan Doyle.* New York, Harper, 1949.

Clausen, Christopher. "Sherlock Holmes, Order, and the Late-Victorian Mind." *Georgia Review.* Vol. 38, No. 1, Spring 1984, 104-123.

Green, R.L. , editor. *A Bibliography of A. Conan Doyle.* London and New York, Oxford University Press, 1983.

Nordon, Pierre. *Conan Doyle: A Biography,* trans. Frances Partridge. London, John Murray, 1966.

Dr. J
See Erving, Julius "Dr. J"

Dr. Jekyll and Mr. Hyde

The phrase "Dr. Jekyll and Mr. Hyde" is a popular metaphor to express the dual nature of human beings, who are capable of such

great goodness and almost unbelievable evil. It is derived from the respectable Victorian doctor with a demonic alter ego who first appeared in the eponymous novella (1886) by Scottish writer Robert Louis Stevenson (1850-94). The tragedy of the scientist who finds the formula to isolate his evil side but fails to control it has been frequently transferred to the screen. The story was first filmed in 1908, and versions range from Robert Mamoulian's 1931 film, with Academy Award-winner Fredric March in the title role, to Stephen Frears' irregular *Mary Reilly* (1995). However, the presence of Jekyll and Hyde can be detected in many other films, novels, and comics of the last one hundred years only remotely inspired by Stevenson. Stories dealing with scientists involved in fatal accidents, tormented serial killers, and even secret superheroes are ultimately indebted to Stevenson's Gothic masterpiece.

—Sara Martin

FURTHER READING:

Frayling, Christopher. *Nightmare: The Birth of Horror.* London, BBC Books, 1996, 114-61.

Geduld, Harry M. *The Definitive Dr. Jekyll and Mr. Hyde Companion.* New York, Garland, 1983.

King, Charles. "Dr. Jekyll and Mr. Hyde: A Filmography." *The Journal of Popular Film and Television.* Vol. 25, No. 1, 1997, 9-20.

Rose, Brian A. *Jekyll and Hyde Adapted: Dramatizations of Cultural Anxiety.* Contributions in Drama and Theatre Studies 66. London, Greenwood, 1996.

Skal, David. *The Monster Show: A Cultural History of Horror.* London, Plexus, 1993.

Veeder, William, and Gordon Hirsch, editors. *Dr. Jekyll and Mr. Hyde after One Hundred Years.* Chicago, University of Chicago Press, 1988.

Dr. Kildare

In 1938 Metro Goldwyn Mayer (MGM) acquired the rights to author Max Brand's creation, *Dr. Kildare,* and began a series of popular films about a young intern in a metropolitan hospital, and his struggle to learn his profession and earn the respect of a crusty senior doctor in his specialty, internal medicine. In 1961 the same characters, with different actors, made a nationwide success of the television adaptation of *Dr. Kildare,* becoming the forerunner of the many medical dramas, like *ER* and *Chicago Hope,* that lit up the small screen in the 1990s.

In the cinema version, Lew Ayres starred in the title role and Lionel Barrymore played the senior doctor, a sharp-tongued old curmudgeon with a heart of gold, which he tried to conceal. The first in the series, *Young Dr. Kildare* (1938), presented a cast of regular characters that included Nat Pendleton as the ambulance driver and featured Laraine Day, who stayed in the troupe for five pictures. MGM released three Kildare pictures in 1940 alone, including *Dr. Kildare Goes Home, Dr. Kildare's Crisis,* and *Dr. Kildare's Strange*

Case. Dr. Kildare's Wedding Day, Laraine Day's last in the series, was one of the most popular and was marked by one of Red Skelton's early screen appearances. Lew Ayres, who had chosen to be a conscientious objector and refuse certain military duties, left the cast in 1941. Van Johnson and Keye Luke vied to become Dr. Gillespie's assistant in two films, *Dr. Gillespie's Criminal Case* and *Dr. Gillespie's New Assistant.*

Finding the right stars to play Kildare and Gillespie on television was a challenge. The first pilot shot for the series had Lew Ayres return to his role as a more mature Kildare, but executive producer Norman Felton said "The result was a clinical sort of film, too much like a documentary." They decided on a second pilot and quickly signed Raymond Massey, a Canadian actor famous for his portrayal of Lincoln, as Dr. Gillespie. More than 35 actors read for the Kildare part, and William Shatner was the leading contender for the role until he canceled out to accept the Captain's chair in a new science fiction series called *Star Trek.* One of the remaining actors was a nervous newcomer named Richard Chamberlain, who had done a few minor television roles and was then collecting $38 a week at the unemployment office. Despite his lack of experience, the producer thought he had just the right physical appearance and decided to let him take the lead in the pilot film.

The show was an overnight success, and Chamberlain found himself the object of mobs of squealing women wherever he went. His boyish blond looks attracted 4,500 fan letters a week. The character of Dr. Kildare, however, a medical crusader and straight-arrow idealist, did not entirely appeal to Chamberlain. He told an interviewer in the *Saturday Evening Post* that Kildare is "nobler than humans prefer other humans to be. If I were to mold Kildare, I would make him more subject to faults and weaknesses—like the rest of us. I might even have him pinch a nurse or two." It was an attitude Dr. Gillespie would not have endorsed.

Despite the development of the show into a world-wide hit, with more than 80 million admirers around the globe, the series ended in 1966 after a five year run. Toward the end, the ratings declined somewhat as the show strayed from the key relationship between Kildare and Gillespie and focused more on the medical problems of its guest star patients. During the final season, some of the episodes were serialized in a 30 minute format rather than continuing in the hour-long version that had been so effective. Following the show's demise, Chamberlain, rather than being forced to return to the unemployment line as he feared, went on to become the "king of the miniseries" in the 1970s and 1980s, starring in such blockbusters as *Shogun, The Thornbirds,* and *Centennial.*

In 1972 MGM tried to revive the series in a new format called *Young Dr. Kildare,* starring Mark Jenkins as Kildare and Gary Merrill as Gillespie, but the series had a brief run, followed by a short after-life in syndication. Many have commented on the coincidence that two of the most successful medical shows ever to air on television arrived in the year 1961, with *Ben Casey* premiering four days after *Dr. Kildare.*

—Benjamin Griffith

FURTHER READING:

Books, Tim, and Earle Marsh. *The Complete Directory of Prime Time Network TV Shows: 1946 to Present.* New York, Ballantine, 1981.

Sackett, Susan. *Prime-Time Hits: Television's Most Popular Network Programs.* New York, Billboard Books, 1993.

Dr. Seuss (1904-1991)

Author, illustrator, editor, and publisher, Dr. Seuss revolutionized materials directed at young readers by introducing humorous, rhymed, and colorful books using limited vocabularies and simple, appealing illustrations. Uniquely inventive in the annals of twentieth-century children's books, Seuss openly acknowledged that helping to kill off the predictable "Dick and Jane" primers of the 1950s was one of his proudest accomplishments. The bizarre creatures of his stories, which contained subtle moral messages that could be read on different levels, often acted with what their author termed "logical insanity." For example, if an animal had two heads, he must also have two toothbrushes.

Twice-married but childless, Seuss had not started out to be a children's book innovator. He was born Theodor Seuss Geisel in Springfield, Massachusetts, the son of a German immigrant who ran a brewery until the arrival of Prohibition. He later commented that his father was on track to become company president until circumstances forced him to switch his careers and become commissioner of parks. This helped instill an early cynicism in the future Dr. Seuss, while his frequent trips to the zoo thereafter helped to stimulate his fertile imagination.

Theodor "Dr. Seuss" Geisel

His mother, Henrietta Seuss Geisel, unwittingly lent him her maiden name, which he first used when writing a humorous scientific piece. While reading for a B.A. in English from Dartmouth, Seuss contributed to the school humor magazine, *Jack O'Lantern,* then studied literature for one year at Oxford. Returning to the United States in 1927, Seuss sold cartoons to the *Saturday Evening Post, Judge,* and *Vanity Fair.* He always considered himself to be an artist first and an author second. This belief received some confirmation in many of his books for which he initially drew sketches, afterwards devising dialogue to accompany them. When he later wrote books without illustrating them himself, Seuss used the pseudonym Theo LeSieg (Geisel spelled backwards.)

Seuss composed advertising illustrations for Standard Oil of New Jersey for 15 years after a company executive saw his cartoon of a knight trying to kill dragons with the insecticide Flit. This led to one of the 1930s most famous ad slogans, "Quick, Henry, the *Flit.*" In 1932, Seuss wrote an ABC book for children but could not find a publisher. In 1936, while crossing the Atlantic by ship, he composed *And to Think That I Saw It On Mulberry Street* in rhyme inspired by the rhythm of the vessel's engines. About a boy whose imagination transformed a horse and wagon into various beasts, the book became his first published monograph, bought by Vanguard Press after some 20 other publishing houses had turned it down.

Vanguard also published his next book, *The 500 Hats of Bartholomew Cubbins,* in 1938. Seuss then moved on to Random House, where he remained for the rest of his life, founding its Beginner Books division in 1958. The year 1939 witnessed both *The King's Stilts* and Seuss's only novel, *The Seven Lady Godivas,* a commercial failure and one of only two books he wrote for adults. From 1940 to 1942, he worked as a political cartoonist for the anti-isolationist *PM* newspaper, revealing both his political concerns and his preference for drawing. The perennial favorite *Horton Hatches the Egg* appeared in 1940. Critics variously regard this first Horton book as a parable about the virtue of intervening in crises, about protecting unborn life, about perseverance and integrity, or as just an amusing story.

During a stint in the army Seuss worked with Warner Brothers cartoonist Chuck Jones (who later brought *How the Grinch Stole Christmas* to television) on training films. He also collaborated on documentaries in the Army Signal Corps with film director Frank Capra, from whom he learned the importance of plot development, and one could argue that the triumph of physically weak protagonists and the essential goodness that Seuss saw in most people reflect a Capraesque sensibility. Seuss garnered three Academy Awards in his lifetime: for two documentaries, *Hitler Lives* (1946) and *Design for Death* (1947, about the Japanese people), and for his animated cartoon *Gerald McBoing-Boing* (1951).

His postwar book production continued with *McElligot's Pool* (1947), *Thidwick the Big-Hearted Moose* (1948), *Bartholomew and the Oobleck* (1949), *If I Ran the Zoo* (1950), *Scrambled Eggs Super!* (1953), *Horton Hears a Who* (1954), *On Beyond Zebra* (1955), *If I Ran the Circus* (1956), and *How the Grinch Stole Christmas* (1957). But the debut of *The Cat in the Hat* in 1957 was the event that established Seuss's reputation. Produced as a supplementary first-grade reader with a controlled vocabulary of 223 words, it was the tale of a mischief-maker who teaches children to misbehave while their mother is away. Its success allowed Seuss to establish Beginner Books.

According to E. J. Kahn, Jr., writing in a December 1960 issue of *The New Yorker,* Geisel was a perfectionist. He often labored more than a year on a book and threw away 99 percent of his material before he was satisfied, afterwards haunting the production department to ensure that it got his material right. Geisel later observed that his favorite book was *The Lorax* (1971), which came almost effortlessly to him, allegedly taking only 45 minutes to compose. This environmentally conscious allegory about trees so loved that they are all cut down and become extinct, was also the only one of his books that anyone ever tried to ban. That effort occurred in 1989 in the northern California logging town of Laytonville. Other direct message books such as *Yertle the Turtle and Other Stories* (1958), about a deceitful leader, and *The Sneetches and Other Stories* (1961), about a hateful competition between two kinds of creatures, had received uniformly welcome responses.

The characters in the Dr. Seuss books often encounter fearful situations, but wit and good luck see them through. Even the baddies are not irredeemably evil. The Grinch, for example, who starts out with a heart two sizes too small, ends up with one three sizes bigger than before. Seuss's trademarks are nonsense, humor, mischief, galloping rhymes, and tongue twisters. Some of his words are his own inventions; others, such as "burp," had never before been used in children's books. His illustrations—gangling cartoon-style figures, generally depicted in simple primary colors—are of ordinary characters with which children readily identify. All of his people look very much alike, which perhaps is part of the message. The lead characters are also invariably male, if they can be identified by gender at all. The novelist Alison Lurie asserted in the *New York Review of Books* in 1990 that there was an inherent sexism in his characters' roles. One book with a female protagonist, however, *Daisy-Head Mayzie* (1995), was published posthumously. Seuss's focus on the issues of aging, tolerance, laziness, individuality, and persistence were usually subtly intertwined in his stories.

In a career that spanned six decades, Dr. Seuss published 48 books, including his second for adults, this time the successful *You're Only Old Once: A Book for Obsolete Children* (1986). They sold 100 million copies in 18 languages. According to *Publishers' Weekly* in 1996, of the top 10 bestselling children's books of all time, Seuss wrote three: *The Cat in The Hat, Green Eggs and Ham* (1960, written in response to a challenge from publisher Bennett Cerf to write a book using 50 words or less), and *One Fish Two Fish Red Fish Blue Fish* (1960). Many others of his works were not far behind in popularity.

The last of Seuss's books to be published in his lifetime, *Oh, the Places You'll Go!* (1990), addressed the highs and lows of human experience—facing fear, loneliness, and confusion—and fittingly appealed to both adults and children. With its presence on the *New York Times* adult best-seller list for two years (1990-92), its author could say: "I no longer write for children, I write for people!" Older readers could appreciate the satire, younger readers the charm. In the end, Seuss's hegemony was challenged by lushly illustrated and more pragmatic books with more direct messages, but his books have retained their popularity.

—Frederick J. Augustyn, Jr.

FURTHER READING:

Fensch, Thomas, editor. *Of Sneetches and Whos and the Good Dr. Seuss: Essays on the Writings and Life of Theodor Geisel.* London, McFarland & Company, 1997.

Lurie, Alison. "The Cabinet of Dr. Seuss." *The New York Review of Books.* December 20, 1990.

Peter Sellers (left) as President Muffley in a scene from Stanley Kubrick's *Dr. Strangelove, or How I Learned to Stop Worrying and Love the Bomb.*

Martin, Patricia Stone. *Dr. Seuss: We Love You.* Vero Beach, Florida, Rourke Enterprises, 1987.

Morgan, Judith, and Neil Morgan. *Dr. Seuss & Mr. Geisel.* New York, Random House, 1995.

Wheeler, Jill C. *Dr. Seuss.* Edina, Minnesota, Abdo & Daughters, 1992.

Dr. Strangelove or: How I Learned to Stop Worrying and Love the Bomb

Produced and directed by Stanley Kubrick, this dark satire on Cold War relations paints a searing portrait of a world accidentally plunged into nuclear warfare. Intermingling sex, love, and war in unexpected ways (for example, its characters' names often suggest "strange loves" of various types), *Dr. Strangelove* (1964) is a rich, provocative film that stands up well to repeat viewings.

Dr. Strangelove tells the story of an insane Air Force general named Jack D. Ripper who orders a bomber wing to drop a nuclear bomb on the Soviet Union. Ripper, who favors rainwater as a drink mixer, believes the Soviets are poisoning "our precious bodily fluids," an allusion to an actual Cold War belief that the fluoridation

of America's water supply was a Communist plot. As the bomber unit headed by Major T. J. "King" Kong relentlessly approaches its primary target—a missile complex called Lapuda, a reference to a place in Jonathan Swift's satiric 1726 novel *Gulliver's Travels*— Soviet Ambassador de Sadesky confronts the president of the United States in the latter's "War Room" and tells him that a nuclear strike will detonate a Doomsday Device that will annihilate all living things on the surface of the planet. The wheelchair-using Dr. Strangelove, a presidential advisor on international political affairs and weapons development, explains the ramifications of the Doomsday Device while attempting to keep his bionic arm under control; during tense moments, the prosthesis has a tendency to choke its owner or give Nazi salutes. While making plans with others in the War Room for living underground in the post-Armageddon world, Strangelove unexpectedly rises out of his wheelchair and takes a few steps. "Mein Führer, I can walk!" he exclaims to the president, but his excitement is short-lived; Major Kong's bomber wing completes its grim mission at that moment, and a series of thermonuclear bomb blasts accompanied by the strains of the schmaltzy Vera Lynn tune "We'll Meet Again" concludes the film.

Kubrick began developing *Dr. Strangelove* in 1961 after reading *Red Alert* (also known as *Two Hours to Doom),* a 1958 Cold War novel written by ex-Royal Air Force officer Peter George. Kubrick purchased the novel's screen rights and began working with George on the script with the hope of maintaining the book's solemn tone. His plans changed, though, as the screenplay took shape. As Kubrick told *New York Times* reporter Eugene Archer, "I was fascinated by the book—*Red Alert,* a serious suspense novel about what happens when one of the great powers pushes the wrong button. The film keeps the same suspense frame. But the more I worked on it, the more I was intrigued by the comic aspects—the facade of conventional reality being pierced." Shortly before filming started in early 1963, Kubrick brought in Terry Southern, a writer known for his sardonic humor, to play up the script's sense of absurdity.

Kubrick assembled an eclectic group of actors for his film, including Sterling Hayden as General Ripper, Slim Pickens as Major Kong, Keenan Wynn as Colonel "Bat" Guano, George C. Scott as General Buck Turgidson, Peter Bull as Ambassador de Sadesky, and James Earl Jones as Lieutenant Lothar Zogg. Heading the cast was Peter Sellers, a highly versatile actor at the peak of his powers. Sellers played three roles: British Col. Lionel Mandrake; American president Merkin Muffley; and Dr. Strangelove, a German presidential advisor—Kubrick wanted him to play a fourth character, Major Kong, but eventually assigned the role to Slim Pickens after Sellers begged off. Kubrick, who shot the movie in Great Britain mainly to accommodate Sellers, allowed the actor to improvise much of the Strangelove character, including the dramatic rise from the wheelchair. Sellers greatly appreciated the artistic license given him. "I especially enjoyed doing the mad scientist in *Dr. Strangelove* because Stanley Kubrick likes free improvisation that can be so stimulating," he told *New York Times* writer Howard Thompson. "Given a free hand, you can build, construct into the characterization. It's all any actor could ask for." His improvisation, in turn, helped Kubrick develop a strong finish for the film (he had originally filmed a monumental pie fight in the War Room but abandoned it, believing its slapstick tone would conflict with the rest of film).

Though its power has diminished somewhat during the post-Cold War era, *Dr. Strangelove* and its nightmarish visions of a world gone mad remains an important milestone in screen satire.

—Martin F. Norden

FURTHER READING:

Archer, Eugene. "How to Learn to Love World Destruction." *New York Times.* January 26, 1964, B-13.

Falsetto, Mario. *Stanley Kubrick: A Narrative and Stylistic Analysis.* Westport, Connecticut, Greenwood Press, 1994.

Kagan, Norman. *The Cinema of Stanley Kubrick.* New York, Holt Rinehart and Winston, 1972.

Nelson, Thomas A. *Kubrick: Inside a Film Artist's Maze.* Bloomington, Indiana University Press, 1982.

Thompson, Howard. "Pause for Reflection with Peter Sellers." *New York Times.* October 25, 1964, B-7.

Dracula

Cursed to an endless life, Count Dracula is eternally resurrected in film and fiction, as well as in the vampire myth. Bela Lugosi's Dracula has become an indelible figure haunting the popular imagination since the release of *Dracula* in 1931. The definitive vampire,

Bela Lugosi as "Dracula."

Lugosi's well-groomed Count has spawned a diverse group of vampires, including Sesame Street's Count, Grandpa Munster, Blackula, Duckula, and Count Chockula. The only vampire most people know by name, Dracula has sold innumerable books, plays, movies, costumes, toys, consumer products, and even tours of Romania.

Tod Browning's 1931 film *Dracula* is probably the most famous version of Bram Stoker's 1897 novel. Often criticized for its over resemblance to the drawing-room melodrama from which it was derived, the film has nevertheless had a tremendous and lasting impact on both film and popular culture. The film follows the journey of Renfield, a British businessman, who is visiting Count Dracula in Transylvania in order to sell the Count some London property. Slowly, Renfield realizes that he is a prisoner and that the Count is a vampire. Once in London, the Count must battle Professor Van Helsing, a doctor who specializes in ferreting out and eradicating the undead. Van Helsing and Count Dracula fight over the soul of the innocent Mina, and finally Van Helsing kills the Count by plunging a wooden stake through the vampire's heart.

Dracula was so successful that, almost single-handedly, it rescued Universal Studios from folding, giving the studio its first profit in two years. More importantly, it established talking horror movies as a popular and profitable genre. Lugosi's quintessential Dracula set the stage for the filmic and fictional vampires that followed. Certainly Lugosi's sartorial elegance has become a trademark of Count Dracula—as George Hamilton complains in *Love at First Bite* (1979), "How would you like to spend 400 years dressed like a head waiter?" From the 1950s forward, Lugosi's image graced a staggering number of incongruous consumer goods, including swizzle sticks, jewelry, card games, decals, transfers, tattoos, cleaning products, Halloween costumes, albums, pencil sharpeners, greeting cards, plastic and wax figurines, clothing, puzzles, wind-up toys, candy, comic books, and bath products. By the 1960s, *Dracula* had become such a marketable image that he could be co-opted to sell just about anything.

The late 1950s and 1960s saw a resurgence of interest in monster culture centered around television showings of classic horror movies by hosts including Vampira and Ghoulardi, the proliferation of magazines like *Famous Monsters of Filmland,* and the development of popular television series like *The Munsters* and *The Addams Family,* which parodied the American nuclear family. Lugosi's disdainful Count (barely even interested in his female victims) was recreated by Christopher Lee in five films, beginning with *Horror of Dracula* (1958); by Jack Palance in a prime-time version of *Dracula* (1973); and by Louis Jordan in a BBC miniseries, *Count Dracula* (1978). While the kitsch market bearing Dracula's image continues to spread seemingly unabated, like vampirism itself, a new vampire has emerged who bears a resemblance to Lugosi's elegant, aristocratic Dracula, and yet who is markedly sympathetic as well as erotic. Beginning with Anne Rice's *Interview with the Vampire,* published in 1976, novels and movies told from the vampire's point of view have become increasingly popular, as have vampire stories and films created by and for women (e.g., the films *Lust for a Vampire* and *The Hunger,* and the novels *The Vampire Tapestry* (1983) and *A Taste of Blood Wine* (1992).

The repeated adaptation of a text can serve as a guide to changes in popular understandings of psychological and social issues. Vampirism has been read as a metaphor for gender and racial "otherness"; for the simultaneous desire and fear of female sexuality, male sexuality, and/or homosexuality; for contagion of all sorts; and for the relationship between the "new" worlds of Western Europe and North America and the "old" world of Eastern Europe. *Dracula* itself has been variously interpreted as a parable of the oppression and resistance of marginalized groups, the power and alienation resulting from technological reproduction, the repression of sexuality and desire, the effects of industrial capitalism on the working class, and the complex interdependencies of colonialism. Of course, on one level, *Dracula's* popularity lies in its face-value: the fear of (and possible desire for belief in) the notion that the dead are not really dead. Like much horror and monster culture, *Dracula* deals in the (linked) questions of sex and death. And like most horror films, *Dracula* tells the story of a contest between good and evil, between the normal and the abnormal or pathological.

Dracula also follows generic conventions by installing normalcy at the end of its story, reinstating and reaffirming the good and the true after an anxious yet enjoyable period of peril. And yet, *Dracula* plays with the boundary between good and evil, between the normal and the pathological, in a way that goes a long way in explaining the story's popularity. *Dracula* blurs and transgresses the distinctions between living and dead, East and West, male and female, heterosexual and homosexual, aristocratic and professional, healthy and diseased, and British and foreign before finally reinstating those terms as pairs of fixed opposites with the (apparent) death of the Count. It is Dracula's ability to appear normal, after all, to pass in the nighttime streets of London, which make him both so dangerous and fascinating. Dracula does not look like a monster—in fact, he looks like an upscale version of his victims. It is, in the end, Dracula's very adaptability, his ability to confuse epistemological and social categories, which ensures his everlasting capacity to both frighten and entertain us.

—Austin Booth

FURTHER READING:

Glut, Donald F. *The Dracula Book.* Metuchen, New Jersey, Scarecrow Press, 1975.

Gordon, Joan, and Veronica Hollinger, editors. *Blood Read: The Vampire as Metaphor in Contemporary Culture.* Philadelphia, University of Pennsylvania Press, 1997.

Skal, David J. *Hollywood Gothic: The Tangled Web of Dracula from Novel to Stage to Screen.* New York, Norton, 1990.

The Draft

From America's founding through the twentieth century, the draft has been a familiar way to ensure the country's safety in terms of the numbers of soldiers it can mobilize to fight in wars. In the twentieth century, the draft has been used—in one way or another—during all of our major wars, from World War I to the Vietnam War. Naturally, then, draft-dodging has also played a part in American war history. From the famous to the infamous, numerous Americans—for one reason or another—have used whatever means they could to change their lot in the military during times of war or to avoid participation in war altogether.

The draft existed before American independence. In the colonies, young and middle aged (white) men were declared by law to constitute the militia of the colony, and such men were subject to compulsory militia training. After the adoption of the federal Constitution, Congress left militia matters largely to the judgment of the states.

In response to the Civil War, a federal draft law was passed in 1863 (and modified in 1864). The Civil War draft was not particularly effective: The draft law brought 46,000 draftees and 118,000 substitutes into the Union Army, which was eight percent of the federal army's total strength.

Congress passed a draft law in May, 1917 which lasted during America's participation in World War I. A majority of American troops who went to France during this war were draftees. The draft was administered by a decentralized civilian agency, the Selective Service System, whose power was largely exercised by local draft boards (the Civil War draft had been administered by the military).

In 1940, Congress again passed a draft law. Except for a draft-free period in 1947 and 1948, this law was renewed at four-year intervals until 1971, when it was renewed for two years. The draft then expired in 1973 when Congress failed to renew it. A Selective Service System, similar to that of World War I, supervised the draft.

During both world wars, the government eventually chose to rely solely on the draft for its military manpower needs, and volunteering for the military was forbidden. After World War II, however, the bans were lifted but by 1953 (the last year of the Korean War), still over half of enlisted men were draftees. After Korea, the military increasingly came to rely on volunteers (some of them motivated by the desire to avoid the draft), and the proportion of draftees in the armed forces was further reduced. There was an upsurge in the use of draftees during the Vietnam period, but the majority of enlisted men remained volunteers.

Some young men were able to find various techniques of dodging the draft. Draft-dodging was a widespread practice whenever the United States had a draft. Draft-dodging means deliberately modifying one's behavior—legally or illegally—for the purpose of avoiding the draft. Draft-dodging is different from draft resistance, which involves the open defiance of the draft law.

One popular method of draft-dodging was to volunteer for military service before the draft caught up with you. To enter military service voluntarily had certain advantages over the draft. A volunteer had some control over which branch of the service he entered, whereas draftees tended to end up in the Army rather than the Navy or Air Force. A volunteer could choose a branch of the armed services, or a specialty, where there was less of a danger of doing infantry combat duty. For those who volunteered for the National Guard, one's tour of duty would be done in the United States. A Vietnam-era study of those who had volunteered for the armed forces found that 40 percent of the respondents indicated that the draft led them to enlist. The number of draft-dodgers in the Vietnam-era National Guard and reserves was even higher—70.7 percent, according to a 1964 Defense Department survey.

Another method of dodging the draft was simply ignoring the law. According to one estimate, 160,000 men on the side of the Union failed to appear when summoned by their draft boards during the Civil War. During the World War I draft, between 2,400,000 and 3,600,000 men failed to register for the draft as required. The federal government held "slacker raids" during World War I in which federal authorities (civil and military), with help from vigilantes, would stop and detain draft-age men and find out if they were properly registered. In other periods, the draft laws were enforced by more conventional law enforcement techniques.

Married men were more likely to get deferments, a fact which did not escape draft-dodgers. The draft law of 1940 seems to have prompted some marriages: While in 1939 there was a total of 1,404,000 marriages, there were over 5,000,000 marriages in 1940 in the 18 to 29-year-old group alone. The Selective Service was aware that some men were using marriage and fatherhood to avoid their military responsibilities, and tightened the regulations in response. By the Vietnam-era, marriage and having children were not particularly effective ways of dodging the draft.

Fleeing abroad was another method of avoiding the draft. Mexico was a destination for some draft-dodgers during World War I, while Canada was a destination during the Civil War and the Vietnam War—Sweden was also a popular destination for some Vietnam-era draft-dodgers.

Under the old militia laws in the various states, a man who had enough money could avoid militia duty by paying someone to go in his place. This method of hiring substitutes was included in the federal draft law in the Civil War. Until June 1864, those who could not afford substitutes could avoid the draft by paying a commutation fee of $300.00. Many local and state governments gave financial assistance so that draftees could hire substitutes.

After World War II, attending a post-secondary school could also be a method of draft-dodging. If a college student satisfied the Selective Service that he had a good academic record, he could stave off the draft at least until graduation (in 1967, Congress made

deferments available to all undergraduates, regardless of their academic standing).

Draft-dodgers (and draft resisters) have sometimes benefitted from Presidential amnesties, including Franklin Roosevelt's limited amnesty for World War I offenders in 1933, Harry Truman's limited amnesty for World War II offenders in 1947, and Jimmy Carter's complete amnesty for non-violent Vietnam-era offenders in 1977.

Eminent draft-dodgers include future President Grover Cleveland, who hired a substitute so as to avoid the Civil War draft, future President William Clinton, who made use of student exemptions and the ROTC program to avoid the Vietnam War, and future Vice-President Dan Quayle, who joined the Indiana National Guard.

—Eric Longley

FURTHER READING:

Chambers, John Whiteclay II. *To Raise an Army: The Draft Comes to Modern America.* New York, Free Press, 1987.

Curry, G. David. *Sunshine Patriots: Punishment and the Vietnam Offender.* Notre Dame, Indiana, University of Notre Dame Press, 1985.

Flynn, George Q. *The Draft, 1940-1973.* Lawrence, Kansas, University Press of Kansas, 1993.

Haig-Brown, Alan. *Hell No, We Won't Go: Vietnam Draft Resisters in Canada.* Vancouver, Raincoast Books, 1996.

Polner, Murray, editor. *When Can I Come Home? A Debate on Amnesty for Exiles, Anti-war Prisoner, and Others.* Garden City, New York, Anchor Books, 1972.

Drag

"Drag" was originally a theatrical term used to describe the women's clothing a man wore on stage. It came into use in the 1870s at the same time that cross-dressing, or dressing as the opposite sex, became popular in vaudeville variety shows. Men would dress in "drag" and women would "wear breeches," each one poking fun at the foibles and anxieties of the opposite sex. By the 1940s, drag had come to describe professional female impersonators and had begun to take on meanings associated with male homosexuality. Gay men who wore women's clothes off-stage started to be characterized as men in "drag" by mid-century.

Since the 1950s, the term "drag" has come to describe a form of cross-dressing for both men and women that intends to expose itself as false. In other words, men and women in drag broadcast the fact that they are *dressed up* as one sex or the other. Unlike some cross-dressers, they are not interested in wearing costumes that disguise who they "really" are underneath. Instead, they make costumes that are clearly costumes, putting on clothes that are stereotypically men's or women's, like floor length evening gowns, high heels, bow ties, or three-piece suits. Men and women in drag work to exaggerate masculine and feminine gestures, facial expressions, tones of voice,

A man in ''drag'' applies lipstick before a photo shoot in Philadelphia, 1995.

and scenarios in order to simultaneously enhance their performance and underline the fact that they are performing. Drag is most commonly associated with ''drag queens,'' or male performers who dress up as women. But, it can still describe women dressed as men, or even women dressed as women or men dressed as men as long as their outfits are designed to produce the sense that the gender they are performing is self-consciously acted out.

Gay male nightclubs often host ''drag shows'' as part of their nightly or weekly ritual, especially in urban areas with large gay populations like San Francisco or New York. These variety shows usually feature a line-up of drag queens who ''lip-sync'' to popular songs by female artists—moving their lips and performing along with previously recorded music. These numbers are often outrageously dramatic, extremely sentimental, or bitingly satirical. Each one is treated as an opportunity to experiment with the meanings of gender on stage. Sometimes performers make fun of mainstream gender relations, while at other times they take the insights of the songs they sing very seriously. Drag shows are usually emceed by a drag performer, who often presents a comedy routine on topics ranging

from gay sex to contemporary politics. Some clubs only hire professional performers, while others are strictly amateur.

There are many fewer drag kings then drag queens and they are far less visible. However, some lesbian clubs do sponsor drag shows that provide a forum for drag king performances. These shows often feature women dressed up in female drag as well as male drag. In other words, women dress in ''campy'' or exaggerated female clothes that draw attention to the ways that they must perform their femininity as they interact with other women who are dressed as men and who are drawing attention to their self-conscious decision to dress as their chosen gender.

Ultimately, drag performers explain, drag exposes the ways that everyone ''performs'' their gender, even when they are ''wearing'' the socially appropriate role. If gender can be successfully understood through sex-role behavior that is outrageous and clearly fake, then logically it follows that those traits and characteristics that we uncritically associate with one sex or the other are being put on or taken off by everyone. Rather than naturally coming out of biological sex, sex-role behavior is learned, performed, and always unreal.

Drag has become more mainstream in the last decade, both within the gay community and in American culture more generally. RuPaul was a crossover sensation in the early 1990s, and was, according to *People* magazine "the first drag queen ever to land on the pop charts." Her album, *Supermodel of the World,* brought her into the limelight in 1993 and her perfectly accessorized seven foot frame has kept her in the public eye. Like other drag performers, RuPaul often openly reflects on the meanings of drag. "Drag queens," she once explained, "are like the shamans of our society, reminding people of what's funny and what's a stereotype."

Wigstock, an annual day-long drag show held on Labor Day in New York City, is another example of the mainstreaming of drag. It has attracted thousands of spectators and hundreds of local and national performers throughout the mid to late 1990s. A number of movies have also caught the national eye. The popularity of the Australian film *The Adventures of Priscilla, Queen of the Desert* in the United States as well as the success of *To Wong Foo, Thanks for Everything, Julie Newmar* attest to the American cultural interest in drag and particularly drag queens in the 1990s. Both of them feature a group of drag queens travelling across their respective countries and ultimately finding themselves stranded in backward small towns. *To Wong Foo,* especially, captures the bland moral most commonly associated with drag queens in popular culture. By first experiencing discrimination and then "educating" the provincial residents with whom they come into contact, the three drag queens represent American cultural fantasies about victimized people. Confronting and overcoming their oppression by drawing on the drag queen "spirit," the queens of *To Wong Foo* tell Americans what they already think they know: that a good attitude on the part of oppressed people is the best way to overcome injustice.

While mainstream movies make these simple connections, drag queens and kings themselves discuss the disruptive potential of drag. Rather then reinforcing American's comfort with oppression and their resolve not to take responsibility for victimization, drag underlines American cultural anxieties about difference and forces men and women to think critically about how cultural ideas structure their identities and their sense of possibility.

—Karen Miller

FURTHER READING:

Brown, Susan, *Persona.* New York, Rizzoli, 1997.

Bullough, Vern L. *Cross Dressing, Sex, and Gender.* Philadelphia, University of Pennsylvania Press, 1993.

Chermayeff, Catherine, Jonathan David, and Nan Richardson. *Drag Diaries.* San Francisco, Chronicle Books, 1995.

Ekins, Richard, and Dave King, eds. *Blending Genders: Social Aspects of Cross-Dressing and Sex-Changing.* New York, Routledge, 1996.

Ferris, Lesley, ed. *Crossing the Stage: Controversies on Cross-Dressing.* New York, Routledge, 1993.

Garber, Marjorie B. *Vested Interests: Cross-Dressing & Cultural Anxiety.* New York, Routledge, 1992.

Pettiway, Leon E. *Honey, Honey, Miss Thang: Being Black, Gay, and on the Streets.* Philadelphia, Temple University Press, 1996.

Drag Racing

Drag racing, an acceleration contest from a standing start between two vehicles covering a measured distance, is probably as old as the automobile itself. As a legal and commercially organized sport, however, it began on Sunday, June 19, 1950. On that day at an airstrip near Santa Ana, California, C. J. Hart, originally of Findlay, Ohio, hosted with two partners the Santa Ana Drags. A year before that, in Goleta, California, a drag race was held on a closed-off section of road with approval of the police, but it was only a one-time event. The surge of returning veterans at the end of World War II, many of whom could afford an automobile and had a sense of adventure as well as a desire to test the performance of their machines, gave rise to street racing or "hot rodding." It was street racing, illegal and dangerous, which led to the need for safely organized events. Today drag meets take place all across the United States with some contests attracting upwards of 50,000 spectators.

Although drag racing has become more professional and commercialized than in the beginning, many hobbyists still have the opportunity to participate. There are a multiplicity of race classes, each held to certain rules regarding the weight of the vehicle, engine size and modification, and body configuration. In any major drag-race event there will be dozens of class winners. Drag meets in the United States are sanctioned by the National Hot Rod Association (NHRA), the American Hot Rod Association (AHRA), or the International Hot Rod Association (IHRA). These associations establish and enforce contest and safety rules. The NHRA, founded in 1951 by Wally Parks, remains the most influential drag-racing entity. The first NHRA national championship meet was held in Great Bend, Kansas, in 1951.

The measured course for most races is a quarter-mile, although some competitions are limited to one-eighth of a mile. The track is a straight strip made of asphalt or concrete. Race events usually begin with each class conducting trials; the 16 drivers with the lowest times are allowed starting positions in the official competition. After the 16 compete, eight winners advance to the semi-finals until the two remaining victors drag for the championship. The format and rituals of the race are generally the same for all race classes. In the "burnout box" behind the starting line, drivers will spin their rear tires to generate heat for better traction. Then on signal by the Christmas tree, the electronic starting pole, they will advance to the staging area and then to the starting line. The race will begin when three amber lights, mounted in a vertical row for each driving lane, flash in quick secession from top to bottom, followed by the green light. Should a racer start too soon, a red light at the very bottom of the Christmas tree will turn on, meaning automatic disqualification for the driver at fault. Most races, which last from five to ten seconds, are won and lost at the starting line for either "red lighting" or for not "attacking the green," respectively.

Broadly, the main professional categories of racers are pro stock, top fuel, and funny cars. The pro stockers consist of production cars in which the engine is made by the same manufacturer as the body with the wheel base remaining unaltered. Otherwise, many performance modifications are allowed, including rebuilt engines, hood scoops, and header exhaust systems. While pro stockers must run only on gasoline, top fuel dragsters burn nitro, an explosive mixture of nitromethane and alcohol, commonly known as rocket fuel. The V-shaped racers—known as dragsters, rails, stilettos, or slingshots—are

Shirley Muldowney during a typical race.

25 feet long, 3 feet wide, and 3 feet high, and can clock speeds in excess of 300 miles per hour. Funny cars, sometimes called floppers, also run on nitro, but they have a body made of one piece of lightweight fiberglass or carbon fiber, not metal, and it is mounted over top of the driver and hooked to the chassis, or frame, of the vehicle. Both top fuelers and funny cars must use parachutes to aid in braking at the end of the race.

Three legendary top-fuel competitors are Don "Big Daddy" Garlits of Tampa, Florida; Don "The Snake" Prudhomme of Southern California; and Shilrey Muldowney of Mount Clemens, Michigan. In 1964 Garlits was the first to break the barrier of 200 miles-per-hour. Later, Prudhomme would clock a speed of 300 miles-per-hour. During the 1980s Muldowney won the top-fueler championship three times. Both Prudhomme and Muldowney had started out racing funny cars. Muldowney's life story was dramatized in the Hollywood movie *Heart Like a Wheel* (1983), starring Bonnie Bedalia. In 1984 Garlits opened his Museum of Drag Racing and International Drag Racing Hall of Fame in Ocala, Florida.

The culture of drag racing has been represented in various media, from a plethora of specialized magazines—including *Hot Rod Magazine*—and novels such as Henry Gregor Felsen's *Street Rod* (1953), to recording group Tommy Dugan and the Hot Rodders. In the early 1960s, Charlie Ryan recorded several songs on car racing,

including the popular "Hot Rod Lincoln." During the 1960s and 1970s, the California rock band the Beach Boys further glamorized hot rodding with the hits "Little Deuce Coup," "409," "Shut Down," and "Fun, Fun, Fun." Mattel, one of the first toy manufacturers to recognize the appeal of drag racing to young people, introduced Hot Wheels, a line of miniature die-cast cars, which included replicas of funny cars raced by Don "The Snake" Prudhomme and Tom "Mongoose" McEwen. In 1992, the NHRA established the Junior Drag Racing League, where drivers between the ages of eight and 17 could race half-sized copies of top fuelers, funny cars, and pro stockers.

—Roger Chapman

FURTHER READING:

Engel, Lyle Kenyon. *The Complete Book of Stock-Bodied Drag Racing*. New York, Four Winds Press, 1970.

Post, Robert C. *High Performance: The Culture and Technology of Drag Racing, 1950-1990*. Baltimore, The Johns Hopkins University Press, 1994.

Redlauer, Edward. *Drag Racing: Quarter Mile Thunder*. New York, Abelard-Schuman, 1966.

Wallace, Dave, Jr. *Petersen's History of Drag Racing.* Los Angeles, Petersen Publishing Company, 1981.

Dragnet

Within two years of its 1952 small-screen debut, the eight-year long (1949-1957) radio series *Dragnet* had become television's number-one rated program. Created by actor Jack Webb, the series broke new ground from the outset, offering radio listeners rare authenticity of experience as they "accompanied" the police in following a case from beginning to final sentencing. Each episode unfolded at a measured pace, as detectives Friday and Smith followed clues, interviewed witnesses both friendly and hostile, and checked with various branches of law enforcement for information. Documentary realism was a key element of the show's appeal, with Jack Webb's own deadpan delivery and opening gambit, "This is the city. Los Angeles, California," making the mundane routine seem hip and cool.

The idea for *Dragnet* came to Webb after he had played a police lab technician in Anthony Mann's *He Walked by Night* (1948). He shared a belief with that film's technical adviser, Sgt. Marty Wynn of the LAPD, that pure investigative procedure was dramatic enough without introducing the traditional melodrama of the fictional hard-boiled private eye. In early 1949, Webb secured the cooperation of the LAPD and Chief William H. Parker. As long as Webb didn't compromise confidentiality, or portray the police in any "unflattering entanglements," Parker granted him access to all actual case files. Early in 1949, thus armed, Webb approached NBC with his radio pilot for *Dragnet.*

Webb's radio style was to underplay. He stood way back from the microphones and potted everything up high so that all of the ambient sounds could be heard. He told *Time* magazine that "underplaying is still acting . . . . We try to make it as real as a guy pouring a cup of coffee." And the series *was* realistic. When Webb and his partner walked up the steps to headquarters, listeners heard the *exact* number of steps it took. With his tremendous success on radio, Webb took *Dragnet* to television.

On television, *Dragnet* was extraordinarily conservative. Webb put the hard-boiled edge of nonconformist heroes like Sam Spade and Philip Marlowe into the conformist mouth of a downtown cop: "My name's Friday. I carry a badge." The character of Friday had no tolerance or sympathy for anyone outside the system. Los Angeles lawbreakers had to be punished, and Friday's investigations were carried out with a terse, no-nonsense approach. "Just the facts, ma'am," he often said to witnesses who digressed from the point. He had no interest in witnesses as personalities, nor did he have any interests in life outside of police work. His whole duty was to "serve and protect." By contrast, his partner Frank Smith, played by former child star Ben Alexander, was much more human, and often fretted over his health or his wife, Fay. Friday's diligence, however, fit well within a 1950s Cold War context of conformity. During a time in which Americans feared the spread of Communism and atomic weaponry, Friday was a figure of dependability and stability. During *Dragnet*'s seven-year run, so pervasive was his image that, despite the rise in the national crime rate, the public came to believe that crime had diminished and that their city streets were safer than ever before.

The conservative tenor adopted by Webb can be detected in several episodes that border on a hysterical and paranoid vision. In "The Big Producer," a bunch of "dirty" joke books and nude photographs make their way into a high school, but Friday and Smith can't bring themselves to label the materials pornography. Instead, a series of ellipses between the two convey their fear over this "filth." In "The Big Seventeen," the duo cracks down on drugs, "H" for heroin, in the schools, but they are too late to save a 17-year old boy from overdosing. The endings of this, and several other episodes, were downbeat, and in a 1950s context, the hysteria and paranoia worked. When *Dragnet* was revived for the "Go-Go" years, 1967-1970, the hysterical mood was far too judgmental for later audiences.

Stylistically, *Dragnet* generated a unique syntax on the American landscape in its use of abbreviations and numerical codes. MO (modus operandi), DMV (Department of Motor Vehicles), and APB (All Points Bulletin) became part of everyday speech, along with 212 (robbery), 459 (burglary), and 311 (lewd conduct). Walter Schumann's four-note theme musical theme, "Dum-de-dum-dum," was a motif evoking justice and retribution, but also a mood of agitation. The motif was taken up in popular culture as a metonym for trouble. In "Better Living Through TV," an episode of *The Honeymooners,* for example, Norton hums Schumann's *Dragnet* motif when Alice catches wind of another one of Ralph's "hare-brained schemes." And in the 1980s, a series of Tums ads that attacked antacid modified Schumann's theme to "Tum-te-tum-tum."

The series was immensely popular. Parodies of it abounded in the 1950s. *Mad Magazine* attacked its conformity and shilling for Chesterfield cigarettes. Radio comedians such as Stan Freberg and Bob and Ray had fun with its narrative excesses while, in a classic Chuck Jones cartoon, *Rocket Squad* (1954), featuring Daffy Duck and Porky Pig in the Friday and Smith parts, the two intrepid heroes become the villains. Moreover, the look of *Dragnet,* its reliance on shot/reverse shots and eyeline matches to connote judgment—a witness says something; Friday shakes his head and looks at an offscreen Smith; Smith shakes his head and looks in return at the offscreen Friday—became an industry standard in shooting such scenes with effective economy of style.

No doubt the success of *Dragnet,* and its chief ratings rival, *I Love Lucy,* in the early 1950s helped shape the direction of television's cop shows and sitcoms for years to come. The series also contributed to the positive portrayal of law enforcement that prevailed until the shocking images of Rodney King's beating in the early 1990s shook enlightened Americans' faith in the police. When loyal cop supporter Jack Webb died of a heart attack on December 23, 1982, the LAPD flew its flags at half-staff.

—Grant Tracey

FURTHER READING:

Dunning, John. *On the Air: An Encyclopedia of Old-Time Radio.* New York, Oxford University Press, 1998.

"Jack, Be Nimble!" *Time.* March 15, 1954, 47-50.

Marc, David. *Demographic Vistas: Television in American Culture.* Philadelphia, University of Pennsylvania Press, 1996.

Stark, Steven D. "Dragnet and the Policeman as Hero." In *Glued to the Set: The 60 Television Shows and Events that Made Us Who We Are Today.* New York, The Free Press, 1997, 31-36.

Dragon Lady

In movies and comic strips, the Dragon Lady epitomized a mythic female legend; the seductive, "exotic," yet deadly Asian black widow. Although there is no evidence that a real Dragon Lady ever existed, her character was treated as real and was embodied by Anna May Wong in the 1931 Fu Manchu thriller, *Daughter of the Dragon*. The Dragon Lady persona gained additional popularity in Milton Caniff's 1930s comic strip *Terry and the Pirates*. In this comic, the Dragon Lady "captivates men with her beauty then tramples them like insects when they cross her." During World War II, the Dragon Lady persona became associated with an English-speaking radio announcer for Radio Tokyo, whose voice was broadcast to American soldiers. The American media dubbed her Tokyo Rose, and portrayed her as an Asian Mata Hari. Rose turned out to be a naive Japanese American girl named Iva Ikuko Toguri.

—Midori Takagi

FURTHER READING:

Cao, Lan, and Himilce Novas. *Everything You Need to Know About Asian American History*. New York, Plume, 1996.

Kutler, Stanley I. "Forging a Legend: The Treason of 'Tokyo Rose.'" *Wisconsin Law Review*. 1980, 1341-1382.

Dream Team

The United States' vaunted Dream Team—unquestionably the greatest collection of basketball talent ever assembled—rolled to a gold medal in the 1992 Olympic Games in Barcelona, Spain. Comprised of eleven National Basketball Association members and one collegian, the Dream Team's very existence was made possible by a 1989 agreement with the International Amateur Basketball Federation to allow professionals to participate in the Olympic Games. While the American team was greatest beneficiary of the rule change, its international organization, USA Basketball, had voted against the inclusion of NBA players. As David Wallechinsky noted, concerns were expressed that financial support for women's and junior basketball programs would diminish and that one-sided games would markedly reduce the television audience.

The American team, averaging 117 ¼ points per game, swept to eight consecutive wins in Barcelona, while holding its opponents to 73 ½ points a game; the actual margin of victory could have been even greater had not various ailments afflicted several of the U.S. players, while others held back through fear of injury. The American roster nevertheless was star-studded. The Dream Team boasted the presence of Michael Jordan, Larry Bird, Magic Johnson, Charles Barkley, Karl Malone, Patrick Ewing, David Robinson, Scottie Pippen, Clyde Drexler, and John Stockton, all to be inducted into the Hall of Fame later. Also on the team were NBA star Christopher Mullin and Duke University's Christian Laettner, while the coaches included Detroit's Chuck Daly, Atlanta's Lenny Wilkens, Portland's P. J. Carlesimo, and Duke's Mike Krzyzewski.

With the United States having lost the 1972 and 1988 Olympic Games, as well as a series of subsequent international events, Chicago Bull Michael Jordan, who had recently led his team to its second consecutive NBA championship, asserted, "We've got to regain our

Dream Team member Magic Johnson (center) watches as Michael Jordan (right) and David Robinson (left) go for a rebound.

sense of pride, our dignity. Some way—even if it's just basketball. We can at least show the world that *we can take control of something*." But it was the possibility of a financial windfall that undoubtedly led the NBA to support the sending of its greatest players to Barcelona, with Commissioner David Stern envisioning the possibility of a transoceanic league. NBA teams had recently added Lithuania's Sarunas Marciulionis, Croatia's Drazen Petrovic, Germany's Detlef Schrempf, and Yugoslavia's Vlade Divac to their rosters, and looked expectantly to the likes of Toni Kukoc, Arvidas Sabonis, and Dino Radja.

With its opponents already thoroughly intimidated before the first jump ball, the Dream Team, whose members received the public adulation generally reserved for pop stars, had to contend with the fact that the competition often seemed thrilled just to occupy the same basketball court. While the U.S. team was crushing defending champions Argentina 128-87 at the Tournament of the Americas, Jordan dunked the ball, resulting in wild cheering from the Argentine bench. Center Hernan Montenegro declared, "I played with great happiness against the monsters." Guard Marcelo Milanesio stated, "When we met at the center of the court, I was very excited that it was Magic Johnson shaking my hand." After a 136-57 shellacking, Cuban coach Miguel Gomez philosophized, "One finger cannot cover the sun." American observers, such as Princeton coach Pete Carril, also waxing eloquent about the American players, said, "This is not a great team. This is the greatest team ever."

During the Barcelona Olympics, the Americans, despite playing under international rules—two 20 minute halves, a shorter three-point line, and zone defenses—scored better than 100 points each time out. The two closest games involved Croatia, featuring Petrovic and Kukoc, but the margins of victory were each better than 30 points. In their meeting, Chicago's Pippen shut down Kukoc, who had been offered more money by Bulls' general manager Jerry Krause than Jordan's teammate had been. The greatest notoriety involved Barkley's elbowing of an Angolan player in the midst of an opening-game rout (116-48). Jordan remarked, "Charles is Charles. He's not crazy. He just likes to push his behavior to the edge." Angolan coach Victorino Cunha dismissed the concerns: "We know Charles Barkley. No problem. He does this ten times a year in the NBA."

Following the Dream Team's gold medal win over Croatia, 117-85, Mullin mused about "everybody willing to throw egos, individual statistics and all that other stuff out the window to prepare to be the best team ever. Nope, it won't happen again." Johnson, speaking rhetorically, asked reporters, "When will there be another Olympic team as good as this one? Well, you guys won't be around, and neither will we." While Barkley led the team in scoring with an 18.0 point average, Jordan contributed 14.9 points per game and provided a tournament-high 37 steals. The most perceptive analyst of the Dream Team, *Sports Illustrated*'s Jack McCallum, insisted that "on the most star-studded team in history, Jordan was, simply, the star stud. When Magic was on the floor finishing the fast break, Jordan was his finisher. When Jordan was called upon to run the offense, he did so with control and a few dazzling no-look passes. When Daly gave the ball to Scottie Pippen, Jordan acted as a decoy. When the [team] needed a defensive stopper, Jordan got the call. And when the team need a scoring jolt, Jordan went out early and kick-started the offense." The Dream Team was, indeed, as Coach Daly described it, "a majestic team."

—Robert C. Cottrell

FURTHER READING:

Bradley, Michael. "It's in the Bag for Now: The Future of American Basketball in Olympic Competition." *Sport*. Vol. 83, August 1992, 56, 58, 60, 62.

Daly, Chuck and Alex Sachare. *America's Dream Team: The 1992 USA Basketball Team*. Atlanta, Turner Publications, 1992.

Deford, Frank. "Team of Dreams." *Newsweek*. Vol. 120, July 6, 1992, 26-8.

McCallum, Jack. "Barcelona Dreamin.'" *Sports Illustrated*. Vol. 77, August 3, 1992, 22.

———. *The Dream Team: The Inside Story of the 1992 U.S. Olympic Basketball Team*. New York, Little, Brown, 1992.

Stauth, Cameron. *The Golden Boys: The Unauthorized Inside Look at the U.S. Olympic*

Basketball Team. New York, Pocket Books, 1992.

Witteman, Paul A. "Are They Kidding?" *Time*. Vol. 140, July 27, 1992, 60-1.

Dreiser, Theodore (1871-1945)

A journalist turned novelist, Dreiser was at the forefront of the battle for social fact and sexual candor in the early twentieth-century novel, treating popular sentimental and realist subjects with a refreshing lack of moralizing. Dreiser produced a number of dense, uneven, and controversial novels about the attempts of men and women to adapt themselves to the new urban, secular order of industrial capitalism. *An American Tragedy* (1925), Dreiser's great public success, is one of the first serious psychological studies of an American murderer.

Dreiser escaped a very poor and deeply religious upbringing through a successful career in journalism in the 1890s, writing his first novel, *Sister Carrie,* in 1900. Though the book had been recommended by rising author Frank Norris, publisher Doubleday's management was unhappy with what it considered the immorality of the story and published it without publicity. This, coupled with reviews uneasy with both its moral tone and scrappy prose, saw the book achieve initial sales of a mere nine hundred. This fiasco and Dreiser's failing marriage brought on a nervous breakdown, and he returned to journalism, not publishing another novel for a decade. His second novel, *Jennie Gerhardt,* (1911), began an increasingly fruitful fictional output (though his sexual frankness and social criticism continued to hamper his success) during the next fourteen years, including *The Financier* (1912), *The Titan* (1914), *The Genius* (1915), and most favorably, *An American Tragedy*. This last was based on a number of real-life murder cases and told the story of Clyde Griffiths: his youth, the murder of his pregnant girlfriend, and the court case that followed. The novel became a play and was filmed twice: in 1931 by Joseph von Sternberg and in 1951 under the title *A Place in the Sun*. Dreiser's output reduced once more as he involved himself with various left-wing causes.

Dreiser grew out of the newspaper and magazine revolution of the 1880s and 1890s, and though his novels reflect many of the themes of the sentimental tradition (marked by the love of the rags-to-riches story), he handles them in a way inflected by issues that came to the fore in the best journalism of his day (crime, disease, prostitution, vagrancy, and the violence and double-dealing behind huge wealth). Dreiser's subject matter also appears journalistic in its use of personal experience (*Sister Carrie* was based on one of his sisters) and real-life stories (*The Financier* is the first of a trilogy of novels based on Chicago financier Charles T. Yerkes, and *An American Tragedy* was based, centrally, on the murder trial of Chester Gillette). Dreiser's books, though berated for their style—their circumlocution, inversion, uncertain vocabulary, and overburdened syntax—are marked by a singular level of excited detail and documented fact. This reliance on facts and details reflects a contemporary scientific methodology pursued eagerly by Dreiser (he read widely on the subjects of biology, psychology, and sociology). Although Balzac, Zola, Tolstoy, and Hardy were all important literary models for him, literary allusions appear much less prevalent than scientific ones: his interest in every minute detail of biological and sociological influences on his characters pushes the literary into the background.

The characterization of his central figures is Dreiser's main achievement. His interest in what drives Carrie Meeber or Clyde Griffiths makes the figures around them appear little more than phenomena affecting them, while these major characters themselves become little more than the drives and desires brought on by economic, genetic, and psychological circumstances. These desires were not necessarily beautiful, imaginative, or morally right, and it was this, coupled with Dreiser's unflinching candor, that made his books so controversial. Dreiser simply ignored genteel aspirations and probity, as he drew characters, logically and objectively, whose aspirations were powerful enough for a poor girl to become a kept woman, for a boy to kill a pregnant lover. Such desires destroy everything in their paths and do not bring happiness, certainly not the familial stability and financial security of the middle classes.

Dreiser was not the first novelist of his generation to write of the squalor, poverty, and violence of the city; both Stephen Crane and Frank Norris had done that before him, but he was singular in his personal experience of poverty. This is undoubtedly a major reason he was able to capture in such detail the desire to escape poverty and the desire to possess wealth in a society that was in a period of transformation. The tide of migration from country to city; the impersonal nature of the urban setting of factories, tenements, and department stores; the contrast of poverty and wealth; the new culture of conspicuous consumption were all at the center of Dreiser's work. Where many of the new journalistic, realist writers around him attempted to represent want, its nature and effects, Dreiser investigated wanting, one of the central mechanisms of the twentieth century. His attempts to delineate desire are what made him interesting and influential to many writers from F. Scott Fitzgerald to Saul Bellow. It is in showing a less intellectualized, aspirational, amorality deep within the American way of life that makes Dreiser the most radical, the most realistic, writer of his generation.

—Kyle Smith

FURTHER READING:

Moers, Ellen. *Two Dreisers.* New York, Viking, 1969.

Pizer, Donald. *The Novels of Theodore Dreiser: A Critical Study.* Minneapolis, University of Minnesota Press, 1976.

Salzman, Jack. *Theodore Dreiser: The Critical Reception.* New York, David Lewis, 1972.

The Drifters

When Clyde McPhatter formed The Drifters in 1953, a new musical voice emerged. Combining doo-wop with gospel stylings, rhythm and blues changed. Songs like "Money Honey" (1953) and "White Christmas" (1954), second only to Bing Crosby's version, increased their popularity. McPhatter left the group in 1954, and a series of lead singers fronted the group until the arrival of Ben E. King in 1959, who changed the Drifters' image and sound. The baion, a Latino rhythm, and the addition of strings made songs like "There Goes My Baby" (1959) a success. From 1953 to 1966, The Drifters proved a driving force for Atlantic Records from which many rising musicians gained inspiration. The Drifters, who were inducted into the Rock 'n' Roll Hall of Fame in 1990, provided the music for a southeastern coastal dance, "the shag."

—Linda Ann Martindale

FURTHER READING:

Barnard, Stephen. *Rock: An Illustrated History.* New York, Schirmer Books, 1986.

Hirshey, Gerri. *Nowhere to Run: The Story of Soul Music.* New York, Da Capo Press, 1994.

Drive-In Theater

As early as 1928, Richard Hollingshead, Jr., owner of an auto products business, was experimenting with screening films outdoors. In the driveway of his New Jersey home he mounted a Kodak projector atop his car and played the image on a nearby screen. In time, Hollingshead refined and expanded his idea, registering his patent for a drive-in theater in 1933. In doing so, he not only recreated an American pastime, but he also contributed to American popular culture for some time to come.

Drive-in theaters, also known as "ozoners," "open-air operators," "fresh-air exhibitors," "outdoorers," "ramp houses," "under-the-stars emporiums," "rampitoriums," and "auto havens," were just that . . . places where people drove their cars to watch movies on a huge outdoor screen. This was a seemingly preposterous idea—one would drive to a gate, pay an admission fee, park their car on a ramp to face the movie screen, and watch the movie from the car, along with hundreds of other people. But the drive-in caught on because it tapped into America's love for both automobiles and movies; going to the drive-in became a wildly popular pastime from its inauguration in the 1930s through the 1950s.

The first drive-in opened on June 6, 1933, just outside of Camden, New Jersey. The feature film was *Wife Beware,* a 1932 release starring Adolph Menjou. This movie was indicative of those commonly shown at drive-ins: the films were always second rate (B movies like *The Blob* or *Beach Blanket Bingo)* or second run. People, however, did not object. Throughout the drive-in's history its films were always incidental to the other forms of attractions it offered its patrons.

Around 1935, Richard Hollingshead sold most of his interest in the drive-in, believing that the poor sound and visuals, the great expense of construction, the limited choice of films, and other factors (like reliance on good weather) were enough to keep investors and customers alike from embracing this new form of entertainment. But people did not mind that viewing movies outdoors was not qualitatively as "good" as their experiences watching movies at indoor theaters. Just a few years after the first New Jersey drive-in opened, there were others in Galveston, Texas, Los Angeles, Cape Cod, Miami, Boston, Cleveland, and Detroit. By 1942 there were 95 drive-ins in over 27 states; Ohio had the most at 11, and the average lot held 400 cars.

Drive-ins peaked in 1958, numbering 4,063. They proved to be popular attractions for many reasons. After World War II, industries turned back to the manufacture of domestic products and America enjoyed a burgeoning "car culture." In addition, the post-War "baby boom" meant that there were more families with more children who needed cheap forms of entertainment. Packing the family into a car and taking them to the drive-in was one way to avoid paying a babysitter, and was also a way that a family could enjoy a collective activity "outdoors." Indeed, in the 1940s and 1950s many owners capitalized on this idea of the drive-in being a place of family entertainment and offered features to attract more customers. Drive-ins had playgrounds, baby bottle warmers, fireworks, laundry services, and concession stands that sold hamburgers, sodas, popcorn, candy, hotdogs, and other refreshments.

A typical drive-in theater.

Although owners emphasized family activities, by the 1940s and 1950s teenagers had taken over rows at the drive-in to engage in more private endeavors. Known as "passion pits," drive-ins became places where kids went to have sex, since they could not go to their parents' houses but did have access to automobiles. Therefore, families parked their cars in the front rows, dating teens sat in the middle rows, and teens having sex occupied the dark back rows. Sneaking into drive-ins was another popular teenage activity, with kids hiding in the trunk until the car was parked well away from the entrance booth. Teenagers from the 1960s on also used drive-ins as places to drink alcohol and smoke marijuana.

In the late 1940s, drive-ins became more popular than indoor theaters. One improvement that led to this was the development of a viable in-car speaker through which to hear a movie's sound. Before the implementation of individualized speakers, drive-in owners used "directional sound," three central speakers that projected the movie's soundtrack over the entire drive-in. The sound was not only distorted, but also was nearly impossible for the cars in the back rows to hear. In addition, it was so loud that owners received complaints from neighbors who were usually unhappy about a drive-in's presence to begin with. The first in-car speakers were put into production by RCA in 1946. In the 1950s people began experimenting with transmitting movie sound over radio waves; this was not feasible until 1982, when 20-30 percent of drive-ins asked viewers to tune in their radios. By 1985, 70 percent of drive-ins were using this sound transmission technique.

The drive-in business started to stagnate in the 1960s and began its decline in the 1970s. Land prices were increasing and drive-ins took up a lot of space that could be made more profitable with other ventures. By this time the original drive-ins were also in need of capital improvements in which many owners chose not to invest. In addition, theaters continued to get only B movies or second or third run pictures, and the industry charged higher rental fees and required longer runs, making it extremely difficult to compete with the multiplex indoor cinemas.

In the 1980s, the drive-ins lost most of their key audiences—by 1983 there were only 2,935 screens. Families could stay home and watch movies on cable television or on their video cassette recorders. When teenagers found other places to have sex, the drive-in was no longer a necessary locale for this activity. Due to gasoline shortages, many people opted for compact cars, which were not comfortable to sit in during double or triple movie features. By the 1990s there were few drive-ins left; those that remained were reminders of an American era that revered cars and freedom, with a little low-budget entertainment thrown in.

—Wendy Woloson

FURTHER READING:

Jonas, Susan, and Marilyn Nissenson. *Going, Going, Gone: Vanishing Americana.* San Francisco, Chronicle Books, 1994.

Sanders, Don. *The American Drive-In Movie Theater.* Osceola, Wisconsin, Motorbooks International, 1997.

Segrave, Kerry. *Drive-In Theaters: A History from Their Inception in 1933.* Jefferson, North Carolina/London, McFarland & Co., 1992.

Drug War

The Drug War has attempted to diminish the flow of drugs into the country, the manufacture of drugs within American borders and the desire to use drugs with supply and demand tactics. On the supply side, legislators have created severe penalties for possession and sale, and toughened border patrols. To reduce the demand for drugs, community programs, television campaigns and crime-watch programs educate citizens on the dangers of drug use and abuse. The Drug War helped create drug-free school zones and increased penalties for drug crimes that involved weapons.

Although the intensity of the drug war escalated in the mid-1980s, legislators first enacted drug laws in 1914 with the Harrison Narcotics Act which taxed narcotics and required licensure for those who dispensed drugs. The Marijuana Tax Act of 1937 categorized marijuana as a narcotic for taxation and legislation purposes. Mandatory prison terms for drug use and sale were first introduced in the 1956 Narcotics Control Act.

Prior to the 1914 Harrison Narcotics Act, highly addictive opiates were the primary ingredient in the widely used elixirs. The users were mostly middle-class women and their addictions were not seen as a societal problem. The Civil War, however, brought the subject of addictions to the forefront. When physicians treated soldiers with morphine, they developed an addiction referred to as "soldier's disease."

When drug abuse was confined to non-threatening social classes, public knowledge and debate were minimal. In 1900, society pitied drug addicts. They were considered unfortunate citizens with medical problems. By 1920, the drug user became known as a drug fiend, an immoral outcast who spread his addictive disease to everyone he touched. Anti-drug campaigns blamed Chinese immigrant laborers who were railroad workers in California for bringing opiates into the country and encouraging Americans to smoke opium. In the South, anti-drug campaigns said blacks developed super-human strength after sniffing cocaine. The Mexicans were blamed for marijuana's popularity.

Legislation and anti-drug campaigns helped contain drug use until it became mainstream in the 1960s. In 1971, President Richard Nixon declare the first a "war on drugs" when he coordinated drug policies and legislation, and provided federal funds for education and prevention. He consolidated federal agencies into the Drug Enforcement Agency.

Cocaine use rose in the 1970s and 1980s. With the media sensationalism of such events as the death of Boston Celtic Len Bias and the arrest and conviction of Manuel Noriega, the drug war grew rapidly. Despite the lack of proof that a national drug use epidemic existed, Americans bought the media portrayal of the "crack baby" and inner city drug busts. In reality, the "crack baby" was the result of poverty and malnutrition and crack the result of prohibition. The television reports of inner-city warfare and drug busts pinpointed young black men as the primary perpetrators.

By the mid-1980s, Congress and most state legislators enacted mandatory prison sentences based on the weight or quantity of a drug. The majority of federal and state drug offenders incarcerated in the 1990s were low-level sellers and dealers. High level traffickers and other dealers with information to share would trade information for lenient sentences. The prison industry grew faster than any other American industry in the 1990s and Americans incarcerated more of its own citizens than any other nation in the world.

The Drug Abuse Act of 1986 and 1988 set draconian penalties for drug possession and sale, including life in prison to property forfeiture. Other measures designed to curtail drug use and sale include denying convicted ex-drug offenders social programs such as government-backed college loans and grants, and welfare assistance. The Omnibus Crime Act of 1984 allowed police to confiscate property without due process. Authorities only needed an accusation or suspicion to enter such private domains as homes and cars, and conduct warrantless searches and seizures. Many critics argue that this practice violates basic personal liberties.

In the 1990, critics of the Drug War stated that American drug policies failed to put a dent in the drug trade. The U.S. government spent billions of dollars each year to improve border interdiction, increase the number of drug arrests and convictions, and build more prisons to house drug offenders.

The Drug War is also known for such issues as medical marijuana availability, legalization and decriminalization. Critics of the drug war argue that prohibition increases crime, deepens social and class conflict and defies basic democratic ideals. It increases health problems by denying treatment to and incarcerating addicts. It tears families apart by incarcerating small-time users and sellers for long prison sentences. It promotes poverty by denying welfare and educational assistance to ex-offenders and their dependents, and increases recidivism. Critics relate issues such as AIDS, IV drug use, street-level dealers, and gang-warfare to drug prohibition, not drug use.

—Debra Lucas Muscoreil

FURTHER READING:

Gray, Mike. *Drug Crazy: How We Got Into This Mess and How We Can Get Out.* New York, Random House, 1998.

Lindesmith, Alfred R. *The Addict and the Law.* Bloomington, Indiana University Press, 1965.

Musto, David F. *The American Disease: Origins of Narcotics Control.* New Haven, Yale University Press, 1973.

Wisotsky, Steven. *Beyond the War on Drugs: Overcoming a Failed Public Policy.* Buffalo, Prometheus Books, 1990.

Du Bois, W. E. B (1868-1963)

William Edward Burghardt Du Bois is remembered as one of twentieth-century America's foremost black leaders, intellectuals, and spokesmen. Multi-talented, in a long life he wrote as a sociologist, historian, poet, short story writer, novelist, autobiographer, and editor—and in all of these roles he was a crusading champion of racial justice. Though his ideological outlook changed many times during

W. E. B. Du Bois

increased popular interest in black vernacular art forms. Graduating from Fisk in 1888, Du Bois took a second undergraduate degree at Harvard in 1890. In 1895 he became the first African American to gain a doctoral degree from Harvard, and publishing his thesis in 1896, *The Suppression of the African Slave Trade to the United States, 1638-1870,* Du Bois launched successful academic and publishing careers.

Accepting an invitation from the University of Pennsylvania to conduct a study examining the condition of the black population in Philadelphia, Du Bois published *The Philadelphia Negro: A Social Study* in 1899—this seminal critical survey cemented his academic reputation, and was cited as an influential model by sociologist Gunnar Myrdal some 45 years later. Between 1897 and 1910, Du Bois taught history and economics at Atlanta University. Here he had one of his most productive spells as a writer, and began to advance a political program that insisted on higher education as the foundation for black racial progress. This emphasis upon the ideals of the academy, together with his political activity in first, the Niagara Movement, then later as one of the founders of the National Association for the Advancement of Colored People (NAACP), placed Du Bois in opposition to the more vocationally oriented and seemingly accommodationist approach of Booker T. Washington. Editing and directing the publication of a multi-volume study of African Americans under segregation known as the Atlanta University Studies series, and a journal *The Horizon* from 1907-1910, Du Bois was gaining prominence as the self-appointed spokesman of what he called the black community's "Talented Tenth"—"developing the Best of this race that they may guide the Mass away from the contamination and death of the Worst, in their own and other races." Du Bois enhanced this position as race leader in his role as the editor of *The Crisis* from 1910 to 1934, the official organ of the NAACP that grew to have over 100,000 subscribers by the end of World War I. In this magazine, Du Bois featured the indignities and atrocities of racism in the United States, including regular reports and investigations into lynching, yet his appeal remained for the most part limited to the privileged literate Northern black middle classes and their white supporters.

As a scholar, propagandist, and organizer of the Pan-Africanist movement, Du Bois sought the means of uniting and making sense of the apparent disparate experiences of diaspora blacks. Unlike another of his African American political rivals of the 1920s, Marcus Garvey, Du Bois did not advocate a return to Africa as the route to black American political liberation. Instead, for Du Bois, Africa was more a source of common identity for blacks, and in the continent's battle against European colonial domination, he found parallels with African Americans struggling for civil rights. Following his decision to leave the NAACP and resign his post at *The Crisis,* Du Bois no longer commanded a popular audience. In this period, however, he returned to Atlanta as Professor of Sociology and produced some of his most significant work, writing a history of *Black Reconstruction* (1935), *Dusk of Dawn* (1940), an autobiography, and founding *Phylon: The Atlanta University Review of Race and Culture* (1940). Although he briefly returned for a second period with the NAACP during World War II, Du Bois' politics of self-segregation and a Marxist interpretation of history soon put him at odds again with the organization's leadership and he was dismissed at the age of 80 in 1948. Du Bois' life ended in intellectual exile from the United States, joining the Communist Party in 1961 and moving to Ghana where he died in 1963, the day before Martin Luther King Jr. led the long planned Civil Rights March on Washington.

his life, through phases of Darwinism, elitism, socialism, Pan-Africanism, voluntary self-segregation, and ultimately official communism, Du Bois consistently reiterated the view that the major problem of the twentieth century was "the problem of the color-line." As historian Eric Sundquist has noted, Du Bois was born in Great Barrington, Massachusetts, 1868, the same year as the Fourteenth Amendment to the Constitution was adopted, and spent his life attempting to make the principles, promises, and protections of this landmark political article a reality for black Americans.

Despite the complex mixture of a racial background he summarized as "a flood of Negro blood, a strain of French, a bit of Dutch, but thank God! no 'Anglo-Saxon,'" the young Du Bois soon learned that his black ancestry assumed the greatest significance in the minds of his white school companions, the fact of his darker skin placing a "vast veil" between their social worlds. An exceptional student, Du Bois won a scholarship to enter Fisk University in 1885. The Nashville black college gave him the experience of extreme Southern racism and a new racial identity fostered by exposure to the region's strong sense of African American culture and community. Moved by the religious faith and "sorrow songs" he came across during his stay in Tennessee, Du Bois later used these distinctive cultural expressions to recover, highlight, and discuss the meaning of the black historical experience in *The Souls of Black Folk*—which in turn inspired an

Perhaps *The Souls of Black Folk* is Du Bois' most valuable literary legacy. Its recovery of the neglected black voices from the days of slavery, potent idea of "double-consciousness," and critique of modernity, continues to influence generations of black novelists (including Jean Toomer, Richard Wright, Ralph Ellison, and Alice Walker), historians, and scholars of culture and civilization in equal numbers.

—Stephen C. Kenny

FURTHER READING:

Du Bois, W.E.B. *The Autobiography of W.E.B. DuBois.* New York, International Publishers, 1968.

———. *The Souls of Black Folk.* New York, Bantam, 1989.

Gilroy, Paul. *The Black Atlantic: Modernity and Double-Consciousness.* Cambridge, Harvard University Press, 1993.

Marable, Manning. *W.E.B. DuBois: Black Radical Democrat.* Boston, G.K. Hall, 1986.

Sundquist, Eric J., editor. *The Oxford W.E.B. DuBois Reader.* New York and Oxford, Oxford University Press, 1996.

Duck Soup

Though it failed at the box office upon its release, The Marx Brothers' 1933 feature *Duck Soup* is widely regarded as the comedy team's masterwork. By turns madcap, scathingly satirical, and genially surreal, the film chronicles the war fever that engulfs the mythical nation of Freedonia when Groucho becomes its dictator. Harpo and Chico play bumbling spies, with Zeppo relegated to the romantic subplot. Some critics found an anti-war subtext in the proceedings, but the brothers always denied any political agenda. Classic scenes abound, including the famous "mirror routine" and a rousing musical finale. Woody Allen paid homage to *Duck Soup*'s enduring comedic power by including scenes from it in the climax of his own classic *Hannah and Her Sisters* in 1986.

—Robert E. Schnakenberg

FURTHER READING:

Adamson, Joe. *Groucho, Harpo, Chico, and Sometimes Zeppo.* New York, Simon & Schuster, 1973.

Seaton, George. *The Marx Brothers: Monkey Business, Duck Soup, and a Day at the Races (Classic Screenplay).* New York, Faber & Faber, 1993.

The Dukes of Hazzard

The *Dukes of Hazzard* television show, airing on CBS from 1979 to 1985, blended down-home charm, handsome men, beautiful women, rip-roaring car chases, and the simple message of good triumphing over evil; this successful combination made the program a ratings success and a longstanding campy cult favorite. The Dukes were country cousins Bo, Luke, and Daisy Duke, who lived in backwoods Hazzard County on their Uncle Jesse's farm. The formula storyline

usually involved the Dukes versus the town's gluttonous bigwig, Boss Hogg, and his lackey, Sheriff Rosco P. Coltrane. Episodes were liberally punctuated with raucous car chases in their orange 1969 Dodge Charger, the "General Lee," and Daisy's trademark short shorts inspired a 1993 hit rap song, "Dazzey Dukes," which led to the term's use as a synonym for such apparel. The cast reunited for a television movie on CBS in 1997.

—Geri Speace

FURTHER READING:

Baldwin, Kristen. "Bringing Up Daisy: Bach Puts Up Her 'Dukes.'" *Entertainment Weekly.* April 25, 1997, p. 54.

Bark, Ed. "'Seinfeld,' 'Dukes,' Yada, Yada, Yada." *The Dallas Morning News,* April 24, 1997, p. 1C.

Graham, Jefferson. "The 'Dukes' Ride High Again in Nashville Network Reruns." *USA Today.* August 14, 1996, p. 3D.

Werts, Diane. "Hazzard-ous Material." *Newsday.* April 20, 1997, p. C24.

Duncan, Isadora (1877-1927)

The great American icon of dance, Isadora Duncan, who rose to prominence early in the twentieth century and met a tragic death at age 50, was ahead of her time in both her artistic ideals, her modes of physical expression, and her controversial private life. Greatly admired by many, she also became an object of scorn and derision, mocked for her uninhibited approach to her work and pilloried for her scandalous love affairs and "bohemian" associations and lifestyle. Ironically, Isadora Duncan's art has always been more highly valued abroad than in her native land, but her cultural influence in America was considerable. The development of the modern dance form as exemplified by Martha Graham and her contemporaries and successors owed much to Duncan's unshakable belief in the power and force of female self-expression.

Angela Isadora Duncan was born in San Francisco, the daughter of poor but liberal, art-loving parents, who gave relatively free rein to their children. Isadora and her siblings became involved with movement and dance early on, and taught the waltz and the mazurka to their friends. Meanwhile, Isadora attended sessions in gymnastics, a vigorous and increasingly fashionable form of exercise, free of the constraints of corsets or heavy clothing. The contrast with the rigidly formal balletic style that she and her family saw on the stages of local theaters was marked, and held more appeal for her. Isadora was still in her teens when she and her sister Elisabeth were listed in the San Francisco directory as teachers of dance, an occupation in which their brothers soon joined them. The Duncans loved to perform, and soon Isadora was part of a small family variety show touring California.

It did not take Duncan long to combine her love of expressive movement with the relative freedom offered to the female body by gymnastics. Delsarte's movement vocabulary, which sought exact expressions of emotions and inner states through physical actions, was much in fashion during the 1880s, and Duncan's later dances showed this influence in her use of a trained body, able to single out and intensify a whole-body expression. Another influence from her early years could be traced to the 1893 World Exhibition in Chicago. There, the Art Nouveau displays made a strong impression on her

Isadora Duncan

imagination, and her dances later reflected the organic lines and swirls that characterized Art Nouveau design.

After two years with a touring company and many excursions into acting, singing, and dancing, Isadora Duncan became bored with a theatrical environment which did not allow for the expression of her individuality. She began to develop her own style and work on a dance repertoire, and on March 14, 1899 she gave a solo performance in New York in which she danced to poetry. Her bare arms and legs caused some ladies to leave the auditorium, but those that remained were entranced by the classical purity of her art. Duncan had found her way out of the "low art" of club and theater dance to a new, high form of dancing, whose form was influenced by Greek statues, classical music, and poetry, and whose physical disciplines had their roots in calisthenics. Her favorite poet, Walt Whitman, inspired her to use her body as the instrument of a new poetry.

Later the same year, declaring the dedication of her life to Art and Beauty, Isadora Duncan embarked on travelling the world, taking her art to the sophisticated centers of 1920s bohemia: London, Paris, Berlin, and Moscow. She caused a sensation wherever she went and became an inspiration to poets, musicians, and painters, taking a succession of lovers from among their ranks. Among her most famous

liaisons was that with the famed English stage designer of the time, Gordon Craig, and she married the Russian poet Essenin.

In performance, Duncan was a euphoric dancer of sensual dreams. A free-thinking woman and an artistic visionary, she focused on the concerns of her time and translated them into movement, deserting the relatively static displays of the period for generous, sensitive dances in which she brought the accompanying music to three-dimensional life. To music that ranged from Schubert through Wagner to Chopin, she would fill the stage, her voluptuous body dressed in a Greek-style tunic, or veils, expressing her feelings and emotions through movement, able to communicate her presence to the audience. The influence of this style, while considerable, was concealed within the images of free, gracious, sensuous, and powerful dancing that mesmerized her audience through its simplicity—the Duncan approach could not be studied through preserved step patterns, finished dances, or her writings.

Parallel with her position as an exponent of a new form of dance, Duncan became an early symbol of personal women's liberation, and of general political freedom. In her writings she attacked the constraints imposed on women, and exercised none in the conduct of her permissive sexual life. She even danced while pregnant. Although Duncan advocated the equality of both men and women in a new morality, she did not perceive her own work as erotic: her freedom was the freedom of the naked Greeks. Her audiences appreciated her in different ways, some for her purity of expression, others undoubtedly with prurient interest as they waited (successfully) for her breasts to fall out of her loose costume. It was not only gender politics that excited her: she saw Communism as a way forward, and offered her services to the Russian republic.

After a wandering life filled with ideas, achievements, personal tragedies such as the death of her children, many men, and few places to call home, Duncan died in a horrible yet appropriately flamboyant way. Her trademark flowing silk scarf became entangled in the wheels of a Bugatti sports car, causing a fatal broken spine.

The schools Duncan founded did not do very well, and few of her adopted daughters took on the mantle of teaching the next generation. Ballet masters dismissed her dances of free expression for their lack of technique, and saw Duncan herself as a mere amateur. Her writings were revived in the back-to-nature days of the 1970s, but had very little sustained influence on the further development of modern dance, but her powerful, free, and beautiful image has stayed with dancers all over the world. Isadora is cemented as one of the great feminine myths of the twentieth century, and was played by Vanessa Redgrave in Karel Reisz's 1969 film, *The Loves of Isadora* (aka *Isadora*).

—Petra Kuppers

FURTHER READING:

Daly, Ann. *Done into Dance. Isadora Duncan in America.* Bloomington, Indiana, Indiana University Press, 1995.

Duncan, Isadora. *The Art of Dance,* edited by Sheldon Cheney. New York, Theatre Arts Books, 1977.

Dungeons and Dragons

Dungeons and Dragons, more commonly and affectionately known by its players as D&D, is the first and most famous of the fantasy role playing games (RPGs). Dungeons and Dragons is based on traditional fantasy literature such as J.R.R. Tolkien's *Lord of the Rings* trilogy. In the game, players cast themselves as imaginary characters and go on imaginary adventures in a fantasy world of their own design. Gaining popularity in the 1980s, D&D perhaps symbolized the existential angst of a youth worried about inheriting a world that was not their own.

In D&D, the Dungeon Master (DM) creates an imaginary world full of monsters, dangers, and magic. Character-players then journey through the DM's world fighting battles, stealing treasures, or outwitting monsters. The game is played verbally with conflicts settled by a role of dice.

The players create characters for themselves based on a variety of traits; strength, intelligence, and endurance are three key qualities. The level of each trait that a character acquires is determined by the roll of a dice before the game starts. Players can choose a variety of roles for their characters such as thief, assassin, fighter, and cleric, among others. Players can also choose the race for each character; choices include humans, elves, and dwarfs. The game can be played with varying degrees of complexity, depending on the experience of the players and the Dungeon Master.

D&D was originally created by Gary Gygax and Dave Arneson. They simplified the game, moving from the action of regiments to the actions of individual fighters to create D&D. The first two print runs of the game sold out. TSR, Inc. produced the Dungeons and Dragons series starting in 1974. When D&D became very popular, especially among the college crowd, a whole industry arose. TSR published supplementary guides, including books of monsters and demigods based on world myths and legends. *Dragon Magazine* and other magazines devoted to gaming campaigns hit the newsstands. TSR also published book lines like *Forgotten Realms* and *Dragonlance* that had their origins in the games. Other fantasy authors incorporated D&D motifs into novels as well.

In addition to being popular, D&D was also very controversial. Campaigns can take hours, days, and sometimes even weeks to finish. Tales arose of promising college students flunking out of school because they spent all their time playing D&D. Other accusations against the game were even harsher. Many people accused it of instilling violence in the minds of the players; others said it produced suicidal tendencies, especially when a player over-identified with a character that had been killed during a game. Organizations and religious groups accused the game of being Satanic since it sometimes dealt with demons and conjuring devils. The campaign against Dungeons and Dragons eventually spawned a group known as BADD, (Bothered About Dungeons and Dragons). The group was founded by a woman who claimed that her child killed himself because of the game. The game took another publicity hit when the television movie *Mazes and Monsters* came out. The movie was based on an account of how D&D players took their role playing too seriously and started acting out the campaigns in the tunnels and sewers of their college.

Proponents of the games fought back, arguing that a game alone could not be the main cause of any psychological problems certain players were exhibiting. Advocates emphasized the notion that the game helped stimulate imagination and problem solving skills. Others claimed it helped vent violent feelings through imaginary play instead of acting such feelings out.

The debates about D&D generated negative publicity for the games and many concerned parents did not want their children playing. TSR continued its own positive publicity, and they began to tone down some of their manuals and game-based fiction, especially the parts that dealt with demons and conjuring. Eventually, new technologies helped D&D and other role playing games recover some popularity. One player made an interactive on-line computer version of the game called a M.U.D., a Multi-User Dungeon. MUDs became the place where computer aficionados went to play.

The greatest blow against TSR and Dungeons and Dragons came in the 1990s, not from concerned parents but from bad business. TSR had its book contracts through Random House, which distributed the books through chain book stores. When the chain book stores stopped carrying the books, they tore off the covers and dumped them. Instead of a check from Random House, TSR received a huge bill they were not prepared to pay. In 1997, Wizards of the Coast, the producers of *Magic: The Gathering Cards,* another type of game playing, bought them out. Wizards of the Coast revived many TSR projects, including *Dragon Magazine* and D&D, in an attempt to keep the game alive. In the year following the buyout, the gaming industry started to swing back to RPGs and away from card games. Indeed, the future of RPGs continues to look promising.

—P. Andrew Miller

FURTHER READING:

Advanced Dungeons and Dragons Players Handbook. 2nd Edition. Lake Geneva, Wisconsin, TSR, Inc. 1989.

Gygax, Gary. *Advanced Dungeons and Dragons Players Handbook.* Lake Geneva, Wisconsin, TSR, Inc. 1978.

Martin, Daniel, and Gary Alan Fine. ''Satanic Cults, Satanic Play: Is 'Dungeons and Dragons' a Breeding Ground for the Devil?'' In *The Satanism Scare,* edited by James T. Richardson, Joel Best, and David G. Bromley. New York, Aldine De Gruyter, 1991.

Dunkin' Donuts

Associated with the working man's coffee break, Dunkin' Donuts catered to Americans' desire for a strong cup of coffee and a sweet treat long before Starbucks' coffee shops first started selling fancy pastries and gourmet coffee. Started in 1950, Dunkin' Donuts was ranked by *Entrepreneur* and *Franchise Times* magazines as one of the top franchises of 1998, when it was operating over 3,700 stores in 21 countries worldwide. In addition to coffee and doughnuts, the retail chain, with its ubiquitous pink and orange signs, sells muffins, bagels, and other bakery products. The world's largest chain of coffee and doughnut shops in the 1990s, founder William Rosenberg developed the chain from a string of canteen trucks after World War II. He bequeathed the business to his son Robert, who had managed doughnut shops during summer breaks from Harvard Business School. In 1989, Allied Domecq PLC, a British-based food and beverage conglomerate, whose portfolio of American quick service restaurants also includes Baskin-Robbins ice cream stores and Togo's sandwich shops, acquired Dunkin' Donuts. Dunkin' Donuts is Allied Domecq's flagship American operation, accounting for 70 percent of its total United States sales of $2.5 billion in 1998.

—Courtney Bennett

FURTHER READING:

Allen, Robin Lee. "It's Time to Leave the Donuts: Dunkin's Rosenberg Retires." *Nation's Restaurant News.* June 2, 1998.

Carrol, F. *Food Business Reference on Donut Shops and Other Pastry Shops.* N.p., Prosperity and Profit Unlimited, 1984.

Dunne, Finley Peter

See Mr. Dooley

Dunne, Irene (1898-1990)

Dubbed "The First Lady of Hollywood" in her day, her persona always charming, sweet, resourceful, and dignified, Irene Dunne evokes nostalgia for an era of romantic escape from harsh reality. Kentucky-born Dunne carved a successful career in musical comedy before entering films in 1930 (she starred as Magnolia in *Show Boat,* 1936), and was in the first rank of sympathetic screen heroines throughout the 1930s. She suffered gracefully through several sentimental, sometimes tragic, love stories, famously including *Back Street* (1932), *Magnificent Obsession* (1935), and *Love Affair* (1939), but also revealed an exceptional aptitude for comedy in such films as *Theodora Goes Wild* (1936) and *The Awful Truth* (1937). She received her fifth Oscar nomination for *I Remember Mama* (1947) which, together with *Life with Father* (1948), marked her last big successes. Dunne retired from the screen to devote herself to civic, philanthropic, and Republican political causes. Also a prolific radio and television performer, in 1985 she was honored at the Kennedy Center for her achievement in the performing arts.

—Robyn Karney

FURTHER READING:

Schultz, Margie. *Irene Dunne: A Bio-Bibliography.* Connecticut, Greenwood Press, 1991.

Thomson, David. *A Biographical Dictionary of Film.* New York, Alfred A. Knopf, 1994.

Dural, Stanley, Jr.

See Buckwheat Zydeco

Durán, Roberto (1951—)

Roberto "Manos de Piedra" (Stone Hands) Durán is one of the few boxers in history to win world boxing titles in four different weight divisions—lightweight, welterweight, junior middleweight, and middleweight. Born in the poverty-stricken barrio of Chorillo, Panama, on June 16, 1951, Durán only received a third-grade education, after which he became a "street kid," making his living selling newspapers, shining shoes, committing petty theft, and doing whatever else he could to earn some money for his mother and eight siblings. Clearly one of the most talented boxers to enter the ring, Durán is also well known for his contributions to the poor and his loyalty to family and friends.

Durán eventually followed an older brother into boxing and turned professional at the age of 16. A wealthy ex-athlete, Carlos Eleta, befriended Durán and arranged for his training with one of the best tacticians in American boxing, Ray Arcel, who taught Durán to become ambidextrous in the ring. Arcel also hired Freddie Brown, a trainer for 12 world champions, to work with Durán.

All of the attention paid off in 1972, when Durán won his first title as a lightweight against Ken Buchanan. Durán defended his title 11 times and won 70 of his first 71 fights. He reigned as a national hero in Panama, where he fed the poor, gave to numerous charitable causes, and was more than generous to his family. He made sure, in addition, to employ residents from his old barrio on his estate and in his various enterprises. In 1975, the most famous (or infamous) promoter in the fight game took on Durán—Don King. Durán's appetite for food forced him to move up in the weight divisions, as did the larger prizes that were offered through the assistance of King. One of the highlights of his career was his victory over one of the greatest boxers of all time, Sugar Ray Leonard in 1980 for the WBC (World Boxing Confederation) welterweight championship.

After this pinnacle of success, Durán gorged himself and could not control his weight before the Leonard rematch; he trained in a rubber corset and took diuretics before the weigh in, but soon stuffed himself with steaks and, by the time of the match, was too bloated and exhausted from the desperate training to put up a credible fight. Durán walked out of the ring in the eighth round, exclaiming a now infamous phrase: "No más . . . no peleo más" (No more . . . I won't fight anymore). Durán explained to the press that he had stomach cramps, but his reputation was sullied in the world sports press and among late-night television hosts, who satirized his surrender mercilessly. Durán, nevertheless, had earned $3 million for the fight, but had lost Brown and Arcel from his team. In Panama, he was shunned and all of his acts of charity and goodwill were quickly forgotten.

In 1983, Durán made a comeback by winning the junior middleweight title from Davey Moore at Madison Square Garden, but soon lost a round of bouts. He came back once again to win the WBC middleweight title in 1989, after 22 years in the ring. Durán continued to fight into his forties, and became known as "the old man of boxing."

—Nicolás Kanellos

FURTHER READING:

Tardiff, Joseph T., and L. Mpho Mabunda, editors. *Dictionary of Hispanic Biography.* Detroit, Gale, 1996.

Durbin, Deanna (1921—)

Deanna Durbin's overnight rise to fame as an adolescent movie star began with *Three Smart Girls* (1936) and *One Hundred Men and a Girl* (1937). Her box office success was widely credited with saving Universal Studios from bankruptcy. Fans and critics alike were taken by her mature soprano voice and her wholesome, yet feisty, characters. Born Edna Mae Durbin in Winnipeg, Canada, she was dubbed "America's Kid Sister" and in 1939 was awarded a miniature Oscar. Although praised for her successful transition to adult roles in the 1940s, her popularity declined. In 1948, she permanently traded her

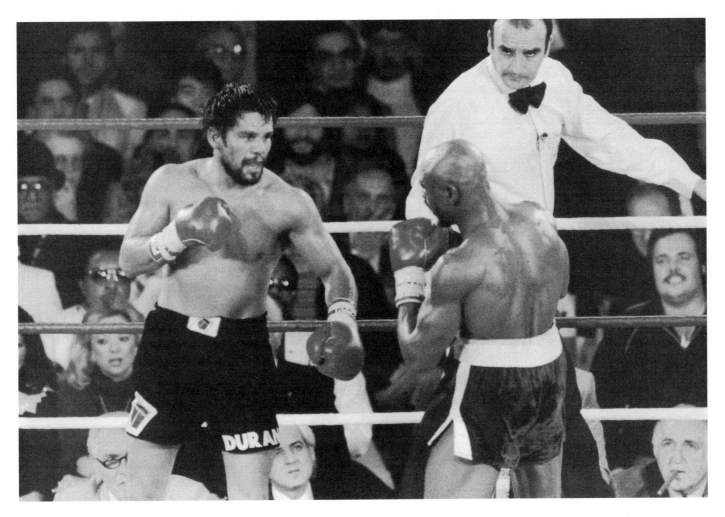

Roberto Durán (left) in a match against Marvelous Marvin Hagler, 1983.

13-year, 21-film career for a private life in France with her third husband, French filmmaker Charles David, and their family.

—Kelly Schrum

FURTHER READING:

"Deanna Durbin." *Current Biography.* New York, H. W. Wilson Co., 1941, 246-248.

Scheiner, Georganne. "The Deanna Durbin Devotees: Fan Clubs and Spectatorship." *Generations of Youth: Youth Cultures and History in Twentieth-Century America,* edited by Joe Austin and Michael Nevin Willard. New York, New York University Press, 1998, 81-94.

Shipman, David. "Nostalgia: Deanna Durbin." *Film and Filming.* December 1983, 24-27.

Zierold, Norman J. *The Child Stars.* London, MacDonald, 1965, 190.

Durocher, Leo (1905-1991)

Leo Durocher, states one baseball publication, "was squarely at the center of some of the most exciting and controversial events in the history of the game." Durocher's colorful and eventful baseball career spanned nearly 50 years as a major league player, manager, coach, and television commentator. But it was his tenure as a manager in New York City from 1941 to 1955 that made him a national sports celebrity and placed him at the heart of so many significant baseball events. Baseball writer Roger Kahn fondly remembered that era "when the Yankees, Giants, and Dodgers ruled the world." On the field, Durocher managed both the Brooklyn Dodgers and the New York Giants; was directly involved in the controversy surrounding the game's first black player, Jackie Robinson; and was a participant in what many sports writers consider the greatest game in baseball history—the 1951 final playoff between the Giants and the Dodgers.

Born in the industrial slums of West Springfield, Massachusetts, the young Durocher worked in factories and hustled pool to make money. He was suspended from high school for slapping a teacher and never returned. He began playing baseball on a railroad company team and made it to the major leagues in 1925. His playing career was mediocre at best, and his hitting was weak, but his flashy and acrobatic fielding was enough to make him an All-Star in 1936, 1938, and 1940. Durocher played for two of the most celebrated teams of the early twentieth century: in 1928 he spent his first full season in the major leagues with the legendary New York Yankees, led by Babe Ruth; and in 1934, he captained the St. Louis Cardinals, a team better

Former Giants manager Leo Durocher with his son.

known as the "Gas House Gang." Those boisterous Cardinals were a hell-raising group that played hard on and off the field. Durocher and the Cardinals won the 1934 World Series.

In 1939, Durocher became player-manager for the Brooklyn Dodgers. He helped the Dodgers to a National League pennant in 1941 and, in what was perhaps his finest moment in baseball, stymied a 1947 rebellion by some Dodgers players protesting the presence of Jackie Robinson on the team. During spring training, Durocher discovered that several Dodgers were circulating a petition vowing they would never play on the same team as Robinson. Durocher called the team together and told them that Robinson was a great player and would help them to victory. He declared that, "He's only the first, boys, only the first! There are many more colored ballplayers coming right behind him and they're hungry, boys. They're scratching and diving. Unless you wake up, these colored ballplayers are going to run you right out of the park. I don't want to see your petition, I don't want to hear anything else. This meeting is over."

But he never had the opportunity to manage Jackie Robinson. A controversial figure, Durocher was suspended by the baseball commissioner for the entire 1947 season on the vague charge of moral turpitude. He had been under suspicion for being too friendly with New York gamblers and other shady characters, such as mobster Bugsy Siegel; and he had married movie actress Laraine Day in Mexico before her California divorce was final. Already a twice-divorced Catholic, Durocher had made enemies of powerful Roman Catholic Church officials and politicians in Brooklyn. Thus, public pressure, and the threat of keeping Catholic youth organizations from the ballpark, forced Durocher's year-long sabbatical.

When he returned in 1948, the Dodgers faltered and he was fired early in the season. To the amazement of New York fans, however, he was immediately hired as manager of the cross-town rival, the New York Giants. He was also managing the Giants at the time of the legendary 1951 playoff game with the Brooklyn Dodgers on 12 August 1951. The Giants, trailing the first-place Dodgers by 13½

games, tied their rivals by season's end and forced a three-game playoff. In game three, the Dodgers were leading 4-1 in the final inning when Bobby Thomson hit a dramatic home run to win the pennant for the Durocher-led Giants. Durocher took the team to two World Series, winning the 1954 contest, but despite these successes, the Giants finished a weak third in 1955 and Durcoher was fired at the end of the season.

After working as a television commentator and coaching for several years with the Los Angeles Dodgers, Durocher returned to manage the Chicago Cubs in 1966. The Cubs had been one of the worst teams in baseball for nearly three decades, but Durocher helped turn them into winners. In 1969, his Cubs held a 9 ½-game lead in early August, but they folded in the last two months of the season and lost the National League pennant to the New York Mets. Durocher was criticized for not resting his players during the humid days of summer. He left the Cubs in 1972 and managed one more season with the Houston Astros before retiring.

Leo Durocher remains among the all-time leaders in games managed (3,740) and games won (2,010). In addition, he is the only baseball player cited in Bartlett's Quotations. His quote, "Nice Guys Finish Last," is also the title of his autobiography, which he wrote after leaving baseball. That renowned quotation was attributed to Durocher in 1947 and referred to his opinion of then Giants manager Mel Ott, whose team had been underachieving during the season. "Leo the Lip," as the irascible Durocher was called, maintained that Ott and most of the Giants players were nice guys, but they would never be winners because nice guys finish last.

—David E. Woodard

FURTHER READING:

Durocher, Leo and Ed Linn. *Nice Guys Finish Last.* New York, Simon & Schuster, 1975.

Hynd, Noel. *The Giants of Polo Grounds: The Glorious Times of Baseball's New York Giants.* New York, Doubleday, 1988.

Kahn, Roger. *The Era, 1947-1957: When the Yankees, the Giants, And the Dodgers Ruled the World.* New York, Ticknor & Fields, 1993.

Neft, David and Richard Cohen, eds. *The Sports Encyclopedia: Baseball.* 16th edition. New York, St. Martin's Griffin, 1996.

Shatzkin, Mike, ed. *The Ballplayers: Baseball's Ultimate Biographical Reference.* New York, Arbor House, William Morrow & Company, 1990.

Thorn, John and Pete Palmer, eds. *Total Baseball.* 2nd edition. New York, Warner Books, 1991.

Duvall, Robert (1931—)

Veteran American actor Robert Duvall has been an integral part of a large portion of Hollywood cinema throughout his lengthy career, thanks to his ability to metamorphose fully into each character he plays. He is also a skilled director, producer, screenwriter, singer, and songwriter. One of his most memorable roles is as Colonel Kilgore in the 1979 Francis Ford Coppola film *Apocalypse Now,* in which he uttered the classic line, "I love the smell of napalm in the morning."

Duvall also won an Academy Award for best actor for his part as a country singer in 1983's *Tender Mercies,* for which he wrote and performed some of the songs. In 1997 Duvall won critical plaudits for *The Apostle,* a pet project that was a long time coming. He wrote, directed, starred in, and funded the picture about a flawed southern minister.

—Geri Speace

FURTHER READING:

Duvall, Robert. "The 'Apostle' Speaks." *Newsweek.* April 13, 1998, 60.

Moritz, Charles, editor. *Current Biography Yearbook 1977.* New York, H.W. Wilson Co., 1977.

Dyer, Wayne (1940—)

Charismatic and camera-friendly, Wayne Dyer became well-known after the phenomenally successful publication of his first best-selling book, *Your Erroneous Zones* in 1976. From that time, he became a constant proponent of such typically "New Age" concepts as "living in the moment" and making "choices that bring us to a higher awareness," as he told a reporter for the *St. Petersburg Times* in 1994. Since *Your Erroneous Zones,* Dyer has used books, tapes, and the broadcast media to his advantage, securing his position as a

Wayne Dyer

late-twentieth-century cultural icon, and a leading light in the areas of motivation and self-awareness.

Wayne W. Dyer was born in Detroit, Michigan, and began his professional career in Detroit as a high-school guidance counselor in 1965. In 1971, after earning a doctorate of education, he was appointed a professor of counselor education at St. John's University in Jamaica, New York, and began contributing articles to professional journals and co-authoring books on counseling with his colleague John Vriend. These established his credentials in academia, while, at the same time, he ran a lucrative private clinical psychology practice. His lectures at St. John's taught exercises in motivational speaking, and his upbeat, positive message was very well-received; students began bringing their friends to Dyer's lectures, and he amassed a small following.

News of these lectures intrigued a literary agent, who approached Dyer about the possibility of writing a book based on their ideas. He agreed, and wrote *Your Erroneous Zones,* sales of which were initially abysmal. Undaunted, its author bought up all the copies and, quitting both his teaching position and his practice, set out on the road with the books to make publishing and self-marketing history. In four months, Dyer covered all of the contiguous United States, making personal appearances at bookstores and giving radio and television interviews. By the end of his journey, he had been a guest on nationally televised talk shows and was interviewed by the likes of Phil Donahue, Johnny Carson, and Merv Griffin.

Wayne Dyer's status as a celebrity allowed him to publish more books on the same theme, and to generate an audience for his informal lecture tours. These tours cemented his following, and became the basis for the many acclaimed, high-selling audiotape sets that he recorded. His message offered something for everyone, since it was not specific to either any religion, or any particular portion of society. This was in contrast to self-help heroes such as Dale Carnegie and Stephen Covey, whose philosophies were somewhat hemmed in by their affiliations and concerns with the business and corporate worlds. Dyer even resisted the New Age tag, warning his audience in one of his tapes that the New Age phenomenon and its proponents were often superficial and could be dangerously misleading.

While his books all offered variations on the same theme, that theme became steadily more convoluted and esoteric as his career continued, accruing a certain degree of mysticism to accompany his pop psychology. In *Real Magic* (1993), for example, he discusses the potential for spiritual experience, while *Your Sacred Self* (1996) further expounds on the benefits of attaining a higher consciousness. Having remarried in 1979, he and his wife were raising a family of eight children throughout the 1980s, and his books largely recounted experiences and anecdotes culled from his family life. In 1998 he published *Wisdom of the Ages,* a collection of essays that reflected on the essence of certain literary quotations.

Dyer often said that his own life was his own best example, and much of his appeal can be attributed to his life experience, which he used consistently as an entry point into his discussions and writings. Many of his pre-teen years were spent in an orphanage, and although he grew up to be successful, he was also profoundly unhappy until he decided to take responsibility for his own life in the mid-1970s. The fact that his ideas were based on the psychological mechanisms that worked so well for him gave him his credibility among the consumers of self-development media.

Although the book sales and attendance numbers at Dyer's lectures were a testament to his following, and his continued appearance on talk shows throughout the 1980s kept him in the wider public eye, he had his share of critics. Interviewing him in a 1983 issue of *Life* magazine, Campbell Geeslin suggests that Dyer's message is "a gospel in praise of the superficial" and that "Dyer is selling simplistic solutions to life's inevitable difficulties." Wayne Dyer, who was his own best advertisement in the late 1970s, turned out to be his own saboteur in the early 1990s. While remaining a hugely successful author, his increasingly mystical approach to his subject matter made him less desirable as a guest on the talk-show circuit and, while still visible, his voice and message no longer saturate the airwaves.

—Dan Coffey

FURTHER READING:

Alim, Fahizah. "Breaking Free." *The Sacramento Bee.* May 16, 1993.

Dyer, Wayne W. *Real Magic.* New York, HarperCollins, 1993.

———. *Your Erroneous Zones.* New York, HarperPerennial, 1991.

———. *Your Sacred Self.* New York, HarperCollins, 1996.

Geeslin, Campbell. "Dr. Wayne Dyer; Pulling Those Same Old Strings With a New Book." *Life.* April, 1983, 19-22.

Reynolds, Cynthia Furlong. "You Can Choose to Become a New Person." *St. Petersburg Times.* October 26, 1994.

Dykes to Watch Out For

In the mid-1980s lesbian cartoonist Alison Bechdel began to create the family of lesbians who comprise her popular comic strip, *Dykes to Watch Out For.* By the mid-1990s, the strip—the first continuing lesbian cartoon—had been syndicated in over 50 lesbian, gay, and alternative periodicals and had been published in more than seven collections. *Dykes to Watch Out For* had become an institution.

The strip is a little like a soap opera, with a developing storyline, and a lot like a peek behind the scenes of any lesbian community. The cast of characters is a group of lesbian friends in a nameless mid-size city in the United States. Just as in any real group of friends, pairings change and priorities evolve, influenced by events both internal and external. Much of the action takes place at Madwimmin Books, a feminist bookstore owned by Jezanna, a no-nonsense lesbian entrepreneur. Among the staff at Madwimmin are Mo, a lovable curmudgeon filled with leftist angst, and Lois, a butch rake with a girl in every port. Their friends include Toni and Clarice, an accountant and lawyer with a baby boy—however uncomfortably, they are upwardly mobile and nuclear-family-bound. Lois lives in a group house with Ginger, an academic, and Sparrow is a pagan spiritualist who works at a battered women's shelter.

These women, and the friends who ebb and flow around them, form a diverse community. Through them, Bechdel pokes gentle fun at the foibles of lesbians, be they politically earnest, promiscuous, or pretentious. She also allows them to change as they experience the events of the real world, mirroring the real changes that occur both among lesbians and in the larger community. Just as traditional media reflects the effects of phenomena on the larger culture, *Dykes to Watch Out For* reflects lesbian culture. Presidential elections, the O.J. Simpson trial, prozac, sado-masochism, transsexuality—all appear in the panels of the comic strip, analyzed and digested by Bechdel's family of lesbians.

Bechdel calls her strip "half op-ed column and half endless Victorian novel." While her primary alter-ego is clearly Mo, the anguished leftist, Bechdel does not take herself or her characters too seriously. She occasionally has her characters break the "fourth wall" and address her readers directly, or interact with each other as if they are quite different characters performing in the strip. One of the strip's calendars shows a large panel of the "green room" where characters display heretofore unseen personality traits as they wait for their "entrance" onto the strip. In another strip, characters of color, a Jewish character, and a disabled character bewail their token status in the storyline.

It is a tribute to Bechdel's skill as an artist and a writer that she can bring her characters enough life to argue with her from the page. Her drawings are clean yet complex, filled with subtle references and in-jokes for her audience, and the dialogue is lively and incisive. In fact, Bechdel's work and the success of *Dykes To Watch Out For* drew the attention of the mainstream press when Universal Press Syndicate approached her with an offer that could have placed her in the daily "funny papers." Though their interest was exciting to Bechdel, it only took a moment's thought to realize that whittling down her work to fit the narrow niche of the mainstream would have changed her work beyond recognition. The title would have to go, "dykes" being far too controversial, and out of six main characters only two would have been allowed to be lesbians. Unwilling to give up her vision of a strip that reflected the realities of lesbian life, Bechdel refused the offer and remained in the alternative press, where her uncensored style was welcome.

Her strips, collections, and calendars have always been eagerly awaited by her fans. In fact, the main dilemma for Bechdel's readers seems to be expressed by an urgent letter she received from a fan. "DO YOU HAVE ANY IDEA," the reader wrote, "WHAT IT'S LIKE TO HAVE A CRUSH ON A CARTOON CHARACTER?!!?"

—Tina Gianoulis

FURTHER READING:

Bechdel, Alison. *The Indelible Alison Bechdel: Confessions, Comix, and Miscellaneous Dykes to Watch Out For.* Ithaca, New York, Firebrand Books, 1998.

Rhoades, Heather. "Cartoonist to Watch Out For." *The Progressive.* Vol. 56, No. 4, April 1992, 13.

Dylan, Bob (1941—)

The most influential musician to emerge out of the social unrest of the early 1960s, Bob Dylan dramatically expanded the aesthetic and political boundaries of popular song. Recognized almost immediately as the voice of his generation, Dylan began his brilliant career by performing blues, folk ballads, and his own topical compositions, many of which addressed issues of racial injustice and protested against the threat of nuclear war. By 1965 he transformed himself into a rock star, the first of many metamorphoses he would undergo over the next three decades. Mercurial, iconoclastic, and enigmatic, Dylan variously presented himself as a poet, gospel singer, bluesman, country musician, and minstrel, recording more than thirty albums that would make him one of the major popular artists of the twentieth century.

"Dylan has invented himself. He's made himself up from scratch," wrote playwright Sam Shepard. The point, Shepard suggested, "isn't to figure [Dylan] out but to take him in," to use him "as

Bob Dylan

a means to adventure.'' Dylan began his extraordinary odyssey as Robert Zimmerman, the son of Jewish merchants from Hibbing, Minnesota, where he enjoyed a comfortable middle-class life. Although he was bar mitzvahed, Dylan listened to prophets who were unfamiliar to his parents. Little Richard, Elvis Presley, and Hank Williams inspired the young guitar player, while the rebels James Dean and Marlon Brando shaped the attitude he carried to the University of Minnesota in 1959.

His days as a student were numbered. Having received an assortment of Huddie ''Leadbelly'' Leadbetter's recordings for graduation gifts, Dylan was more interested in music than his studies and promptly matriculated to Dinkytown, a hip section of Minneapolis renowned for its folk scene. It was here that he obtained a copy of Woody Guthrie's autobiography, *Bound for Glory* (1943), a book that inspired him to learn the Dust Bowl balladeer's compositions and to perform them in local coffeehouses. By 1960, this nineteen-year-old changed his name and adopted Guthrie's nomadic ways, embarking on a cross-country trip that ended in New York City early in 1961.

Dylan immersed himself in the bohemian culture of Greenwich Village, where leftists old and new were participating in the folk music revival. Pete Seeger, Ramblin' Jack Elliot, Ralph Rinzler, and scores of other young people enamored with folk music attended jam sessions in Washington Square Park and gathered regularly to pay

homage to Guthrie, the movement's patron saint. Hospitalized with Huntington's chorea, Guthrie made weekend visits to the East Orange, New Jersey, home of Bob and Sidsell Gleason, where Dylan temporarily resided. The two men established a warm relationship. Disease had nearly destroyed Guthrie's creative and communicative abilities, but he managed to express his enthusiasm for his admirer. When Dylan debuted at Gerde's Folk City in April, 1961, he donned one of his mentor's old suits for the occasion.

A self-described ''Woody Guthrie juke box,'' Dylan recalled that he was ''completely taken over by his spirit,'' a claim to which his self-titled album (1962), attests. Released soon after he was signed to Columbia Records by John Hammond, this collection of folk standards and two originals established Dylan's credentials as an authentic traditional artist, and as a nasal-voiced, road-weary traveler who had hoboed for most of his young life. The album included the poignant ''Song to Woody,'' a ballad written to the tune of Guthrie's ''1913 Massacre'' that musically, stylistically, and lyrically declared Dylan's intent to carry his hero's mantle. Cover versions of songs by bluesmen Blind Lemon Jefferson and Bukka White placed Dylan firmly in the folk tradition as did a 1961 press interview, during which he claimed to have played with Jefferson and the Texas songster Mance Lipscomb.

Bored with the predictability and sheltered nature of his middle-class life, Dylan fabricated a past full of hard traveling and hard living. If, like his fellow baby boomers, his life was smothered by relative affluence and haunted by the specter of nuclear war, his ersatz travels were filled with adventure and possibility. But if Dylan responded to his generation's ennui and malaise, he also began to absorb and shape its politics. ''Whether he liked it or not, Dylan *sang for us*,'' wrote the former president of Students for a Democratic Society, Todd Gitlin. ''We followed his career as if he were singing our song; we got in the habit of asking where he was taking us next.''

The Freewheelin' Bob Dylan (1963) was born out of his emerging political consciousness. Perhaps the most stinging indictment of the United States government ever released by the commercial recording industry, ''Masters of War'' condemned the men who produce weapons of mass destruction and warned them that even the most benevolent God would not absolve their transgressions. The politics of *Freewheelin'* did not stop here. ''Oxford Town'' mocked segregation at the University of Mississippi; ''A Hard Rain's A-Gonna Fall'' imagined a stark and terrifying post-nuclear landscape; and ''Blowin' in the Wind,'' which became a hit for Peter, Paul and Mary, was a simple, though poetic, call for racial harmony. After becoming the star of the 1963 Newport Folk Festival, Dylan actively supported a number of political causes, performing at a voter registration rally in Mississippi and at the March on Washington that summer. Meanwhile, the title track for his third album, *The Times They Are A-Changin'* (1964), furnished the anthem for a generation dedicated to transforming the social order.

Another Side of Bob Dylan (1964) suggested, however, that the artist was moving in new directions. Bitter love songs such as ''It Ain't Me Babe'' replaced the moralism of *Freewheelin'* and *Times,* while ''Chimes of Freedom'' cloaked its social concerns beneath a virtuosic lyricism. Both the album and Dylan's promotion of it at the 1964 Newport Festival were poorly received by members of the folk press, many of whom opined that their hero's preoccupation with aesthetics forsook his political commitment. Their accusations were not unfounded. Unwilling to be shackled with the duties of generational spokesman, Dylan publicly renounced his involvement with the New

Left and, after shedding his denim shirt for black leather and sunglasses, repackaged himself as a poet and rock star.

By the end of 1965, perhaps the most important year in Dylan's career, the transformation was complete. Following the release of *Bringing It All Back Home* that March, Dylan embarked on a tour of England where he was met by transfixed crowds, screaming girls, and adoring musicians. D.A. Pennebaker's documentary film *Don't Look Back* (1967) chronicles the tour, presenting an increasingly arrogant artist who sounded more like an existentialist than a proponent of civil rights. In his interactions with the press, an irreverent Dylan attacked those who tried to categorize and explain his art. In fact, his most recent material seemed to question the ability of language to convey a sense of reality. Rather than writing topical songs, he assailed the social order by intimating that it was unreal, absurd, a mere construction of language. *Home*'s ''Mr. Tambourine Man'' (which the Byrds successfully covered in 1965) suggested that drugs may have been helping Dylan alter his own private reality, but the apocalyptic images encountered by the bizarre characters who traveled *Highway 61 Revisited* (1965)—Napoleon in rags, Einstein disguised as Robin Hood, and Mr. Jones—insinuated that an unjust present could only be transcended by the act of artistic creation itself.

To be sure, Dylan's complex, poetic lyrics altered the face of pop music and legitimated the genre as an art form. When Bruce Springsteen inducted Dylan into the Rock and Roll Hall of Fame in 1988, he recalled that when he first heard ''Like a Rolling Stone,'' it ''sounded like somebody'd kicked open the door to your mind.'' The six-minute single redefined the limits of popular song, declaring, Springsteen later recalled, that ''everything''—aesthetics, politics, power, and perhaps reality itself—''was up for grabs.''

Those who followed Dylan's career closely should not have been surprised when he turned his back on the folk revival at Newport in 1965. The breaking off of his romantic relationship with Joan Baez, his work on a collection of poems entitled *Tarantula* (eventually published in 1971), his arcane lyrics, and his interest in the musical arrangements of the Beatles, whom he had met on his British tour, all pointed to his intention to leave the movement. Nevertheless, his followers were shocked when Dylan appeared with an electric guitar. Among the stalwarts who suggested that rock-and-roll musicians had sold out to commercial interests, Seeger was rumored to have been so outraged that he tried to cut the power supply. The audience nearly booed Dylan from the stage. Although shaken, Dylan remained resolute about his artistic decision. After meeting The Band (then the Hawks) in the summer of 1965, he took his electric show on a tour of England, during which he continued to incur the wrath of folk purists. This reaction—as well as the stunning music that Dylan and The Band produced—is documented on *Live 1966* (released in 1998). Recorded at Manchester's Free Trade Hall, this concert included a riveting acoustic set which ultimately yielded to a full-blown rock show, where Dylan's voice and the masterful playing of his musicians soared above the audience's cries of betrayal.

Exhausted from the tour, Dylan returned to the United States, where, after sustaining serious injury in a motorcycle accident, he repaired to his home in Woodstock, New York. The silence of his convalescence ended in the summer of 1967, when he and the Band initiated a five-month jam session, most of which was released as the critically acclaimed *Basement Tapes* (1975). The search for personal redemption (''I Shall Be Released''), a sense of disillusionment and abandonment (''Tears of Rage''), and a persistent existential angst (''Too Much of Nothing''), remained prominent themes, but if the Dylan of 1966 was trying to inter the musical past, the *Basement*

Dylan exhumed it. Dock Boggs, Clarence Ashley, and Jefferson, traditional musicians whom Dylan encountered on the Folkways *Anthology of American Folk Music,* seemed to have a palpable presence on these recordings.

The Basement Tapes provide a segue between the modernism of *Blonde on Blonde* (1966) and *John Wesley Harding* (1968), the first album to appear after the accident. Replete with Biblical allusions, *Harding* was a largely acoustic collection of parables and allegories, one of which, ''All Along the Watchtower,'' became a standard in Jimi Hendrix's repertoire. But if the children of Woodstock continued to embrace one of upstate New York's most famous residents, the artist himself seemed to be far removed from the Summer of Love. In the same year that flower children frolicked in the rain and mud, Dylan traveled south to record *Nashville Skyline* (1969), a collection of country-tinged love songs that included a duet with Johnny Cash. The man who began his career with protest songs ended the turbulent 1960s by embracing the form that such artists as Merle Haggard used to condemn the anti-war movement.

The albums that carried Dylan into the 1970s showed little of the genius that characterized his earlier work. The soundtrack to *Pat Garrett and Billy the Kid* (1973), a film in which Dylan played a bit part, was notable for the inclusion of ''Knockin' on Heaven's Door,'' a song later covered by Eric Clapton and Guns 'n' Roses. *Before the Flood* (1974), a live album recorded with The Band, suggested that Dylan was perhaps undergoing a creative renaissance, an assessment that *Blood on the Tracks* (1975) confirmed. Here again were songs of love, but crisp acoustic guitar, wailing harmonica, and a voice filled with doubt and disappointment convey the pain, anguish, and longing of ''Tangled Up in Blue'' and ''Shelter from the Storm'' with remarkable weight and precision.

Desire (1976) indicated a renewed interest in politics. ''Hurricane,'' the lengthy centerpiece, was the angriest song Dylan had recorded since ''Masters of War.'' Co-written with Jacques Levy, this fierce narrative impugned the American justice system by considering the murder trial of former professional boxer Rubin ''Hurricane'' Carter. Contending that Carter's trial had been conducted unfairly, Dylan publicized the jailed athlete's case by marshaling the forces of his Rolling Thunder Revue, a melange of some seventy artists—Baez, Shepard, Elliot, and Allen Ginsberg among them—that toured the States under Dylan's direction. Dylan, who performed most of the shows with his face covered in white pancake make up, designated appearances in Madison Square Garden and the Astrodome as benefits for Carter. Although the Revue's efforts may have played a part in convincing a New Jersey court to throw out Carter's first conviction, the boxer was found guilty a second time. *Hard Rain* (1976) provides a sampling of the dramatic ways that Dylan rearranged his music during the tour.

After the unremarkable *Street-Legal* (1978), Dylan chose a path previously untrodden: the artist who spent much of the early 1970s exploring his Jewish roots suddenly became a born again Christian. Fans and critics had little tolerance for the musician's choice, particularly when he proselytized at concerts and refused to play his better-known songs. The dogmatic lyrics may have made audiences uneasy, but the music on *Slow Train Coming* (1979), *Saved* (1980), and *Shot of Love* (1981) was triumphant and exhilarating. Backed by powerful gospel arrangements, Dylan sings with a passion that convinces the congregation that he had finally found his direction home. ''Gotta Serve Somebody,'' the single from *Train*, earned Dylan his first Grammy Award.

Infidels (1983) explored both political and spiritual issues, but perhaps because it eschewed the religious fanaticism of his previous efforts, it received warm praise from critics. Indeed, when such songs as ''Jokerman,'' ''License to Kill,'' and ''I and I,'' are heard alongside ''Blind Willie McTell'' and ''Foot of Pride,'' both of which were released on *The Bootleg Series, Volumes 1-3* (1991), these sessions rate among the most innovative of Dylan's career.

If Dylan's commitment to Christianity had not faded on *Infidels,* it was clear he had change a of heart when, on *Empire Burlesque* (1985), he proclaimed that he ''never could learn to drink that blood and call it wine.'' That same year he released *Biograph,* a retrospective of his career that included much previously unreleased material and initiated the ''boxed-set'' format to the recording industry. With his popularity again peaking, he participated in efforts to alleviate famine in Ethiopia, joining the chorus of U.S.A. for Africa to record ''We Are the World'' and issuing a ragged performance at the Live Aid Concert in Philadelphia. Political commentary extended into the 1990s. When he accepted a Grammy for lifetime achievement during 1991 Gulf War, he performed ''Masters of War.''

Although Dylan released lackluster studio albums in the mid-1980s, he launched separate but noteworthy tours with Tom Petty and the Heartbreakers and the Grateful Dead. Perhaps his most interesting work from this period came as a member of the Traveling Wilburys, a group comprised of Petty, George Harrison, Roy Orbison, and Jeff Lynne. Released in 1988, the first of the Wilburys two albums included the foot-tapping singles ''Handle Me with Care'' and ''End of the Line.'' Dylan capped the 1980s with the critically acclaimed *Oh Mercy* (1989), which included the socially conscious ''Political World'' as well as ''What Was It You Wanted,'' a song that recalled the bitterness of such earlier compositions as ''Don't Think Twice, It's All Right.''

His fourth decade of recording brought accolades and continued success. In October 1992, a panoply of artists including Harrison, Cash, Petty, Lou Reed, and Neil Young assembled at Madison Square Garden to celebrate the thirtieth anniversary of Dylan's first album. When the honoree opened his own set with ''Song for Woody,'' he indicated that his career had come full circle. To be sure, his next two albums returned to his roots: *Good As I Been to You* (1992) and *World Gone Wrong* (1993) were both collections of traditional folk songs. Because these releases contained no new material, critics opined that Dylan's creative powers were again on the wane. Their diagnosis was premature. In 1997, this man who once issued a resonant challenge to the American political system was recognized as one of the nation's most important artists when he was feted at the Kennedy Center Honors. Soon thereafter he experienced a life-threatening illness and responded with the Grammy-winning *Time Out of Mind* (1997). Here the aging Dylan tried to come to terms with the emptiness of love and the limits of his own humanity. ''The shadows are falling and I've been here all day,'' he sings in ''Not Dark Yet.'' ''It's too hot to sleep and time is running away.'' The hobo's travels had not yet ended, but he was now worried about ''Tryin' to get to heaven before they closed the door.''

Dylan's career had not yet ended, but the photograph that appeared on the inside cover of the *Time Out of Mind* compact disc box proclaimed a sense of closure. Shot from the shoulders up, a corpse-like Dylan stares into the camera, the soft focus connoting an elusiveness, his pale, worn face suggesting a weariness, his eyes glistening with the sadness of experience yet not devoid of hope, his riverboat minstrel costume, complete with string tie, underscoring the timelessness so powerfully communicated by the soulful and battered vocal performance rendered on the album. As a new generation embraced him, as his son, Jacob, began his own recording career with the Wallflowers, Dylan had, like the hard-traveling minstrel he emulated, become the progenitor of the cultural and musical traditions he so carefully studied. His remarkable body of work and enigmatic persona had, in effect, delivered him out of time, had elevated him to the status of national myth. Nearly forty years after his first record, Dylan continued to provide audiences with a ''means to adventure.''

—Bryan Garman

FURTHER READING:

Cantwell, Robert. *When We Were Good: The Folk Revival.* Cambridge, Harvard University Press, 1996.

Garman, Bryan. *A Race of Singers: Making an American Working Class Hero.* Forthcoming.

Gitlin, Todd. *The Sixties: Years of Hope, Days of Rage.* New York, Bantam, 1987.

Heylin, Clinton. *Bob Dylan: Behind the Shades: A Biography.* New York, Summit Books, 1991.

Marcus, Greil. *Invisible Republic: Bob Dylan's Basement Tapes.* New York, Henry Holt, 1997.

Shelton, Robert. *No Direction Home: The Life and Music of Bob Dylan.* New York, Beech Tree Books, 1986.

Shepard, Sam. *Rolling Thunder Logbook.* New York, Limelight Editions, 1987.

Thomson, Elizabeth, and David Gutman, editors. *The Dylan Companion.* New York, Delta, 1990.

Dynasty

Produced by Aaron Spelling for the ABC television network, *Dynasty* was introduced to American television as a three-hour movie, and lasted nine seasons in the form of a weekly one-hour drama serial, from 1981-89. Perfect for the decade, which, despite the conservatism and family values of the Reagan years, was characterized by increasing mass consumption, materialism, and the ''me generation,'' *Dynasty* celebrated glamour, wealth, and capitalism. Inspired by the monumentally popular CBS program *Dallas, Dynasty,* along with *Dallas* and *Falcon Crest* (also on CBS) helped to define a new genre—the prime-time soap opera—while reaching unprecedented heights of melodramatic, over-the-top, escapist absurdity. Like their daytime counterparts such as *General Hospital,* the prime-time soaps presented serialized narratives, with each episode ending on a ''cliffhanger,'' or storyline left unresolved at the highest point of tension, to be taken up in the next installment. The technique ensured a captive audience, and *Dynasty* came to be one of the most popular shows of the decade, dominating television screens not only in the United States, but also in more than 70 other countries.

The show centered on the lives of the dynastic Carrington family, headed by the patriarch Blake Carrington (John Forsythe), a Denver oil tycoon. To the traditional story formula of the daytime soaps was added a potent brew of adultery, murder, and deceit, as well as complicated plotlines centered in corporate greed, rivalries, takeovers, and mergers consonant with the patina of outrageous wealth that

Members of the cast of *Dynasty*: (from left) John Forsythe, Linda Evans, Rock Hudson, and Ali MacGraw.

Much of *Dynasty*'s action involved the rivalry between Alexis, as Blake's ex-wife, and Krystle (Linda Evans), his current spouse, as they battled for dominance, both figuratively and literally, in numerous "cat fights." One of the most interesting aspects of their characters lay in presenting them as glamorous and sexy, albeit that they were over 40—a rare departure for American television which, like the movies, has tended to regard such attributes as belonging to the younger generation (of whom *Dynasty* had its fair share of both sexes). Audiences found the character of Alexis so deliciously conniving that she became the center of the weekly spectacle.

Because of their highly stylized representations of domesticity and personal problems, often characterized by excess, soap operas have been much denigrated by the high-minded. However, *Dynasty* was enjoyed by huge numbers of educated and intellectual viewers and, as many scholars have pointed out, it is the soap opera that has brought to American television those inflammatory issues so often ignored by more seriously intentioned programs. Towards the end of its run, it featured the first significant African American character in a prime-time soap, Dominique Deveraux, played by Diahann Carroll. Though the program did not directly confront issues of racism, Deveraux's presence raised the subject of interracial relationships, while in Steven Carrington (played by Al Corley and later, Jack Coleman), it introduced one of popular television's first regular homosexual characters.

—Frances Gateward

FURTHER READING:

Dynasty: The Authorized Biography of the Carringtons. Garden City, New York, Doubleday, 1984.

Geraghty, Christine. *Women and Soap Opera: A Study of Prime Time Soaps.* Cambridge, England, Polity, 1991.

Gripsrud, Jostein. *The Dynasty Years: Hollywood Television and Critical Media Studies.* London and New York, Routledge, 1995.

was evident everywhere. Women were integral to *Dynasty,* no more so than the character of Alexis, who became a byword for female power and high-octane glamour. Ruthless, vengeful and cunning, she was played by Joan Collins and the role made her a major star and a household name in America and many other countries.